COLLINS POCKET DICTIONARY OF THE ENGLISH LANGUAGE

COLLINS POCKET DICTIONARY OF THE ENGLISH LANGUAGE

COLLINS
London and Glasgow

First Edition 1981
New Edition 1989
Latest Reprint 1989
© William Collins Sons & Co. Ltd. 1989
ISBN 0 00 433001 3

British Library Cataloguing in Publication Data
Collins pocket English dictionary
1. English language. Dictionaries
423

NOTE
Entered words that we have reason to believe
constitute trademarks have been designated as such.
However, neither the presence nor absence of
such designation should be regarded as affecting the
legal status of any trademark.

Computer typeset by C R Barber & Partners
Wrotham, England

Printed and bound in Great Britain
by William Collins Sons & Co. Ltd.
P.O. Box, Glasgow G4 0NB

CONTENTS

FOREWORD

The Collins Pocket English Dictionary is a completely new version of this popular and handy dictionary. It is designed to be practical, up to date, easy to use, and easy to understand. Every word defined is given as a main entry in a single alphabetical sequence. Every definition is presented in clear concise straightforward English. Where a word has more than one sense, the one given first is the normal everyday meaning in today's language. Other senses of a word — for example historical and technical senses — are explained after the main present-day meaning. Each sense is separately numbered, so that it is easy to see how many different senses a word has and to find the one required.

The entries contain not only the spelling and meaning of each word, but also a guide to its pronunciation and its grammatical class. Etymologies in the dictionary give information about the origins of words. Guidance is also given on appropriate levels of usage: for example, some uses are appropriate only in informal contexts, others in extremely formal contexts. These are clearly marked as such. Words and meanings that have gone out of use are marked as obsolete or archaic; they are included in the dictionary if they are common in the literature of the past. The introductory pages contain brief notes on all these matters. These introductory notes can be used to help make most effective use of the dictionary, but they are also suitable for study in their own right, as a first introduction to these important aspects of English vocabulary.

Although this is only a small dictionary, the compilers have been able to draw on an unprecedented range of data as raw material. In the first place, the dictionary is based on the Collins English Dictionary databank, which has been painstakingly constructed over the years by Collins lexicographers and their expert advisers in many different fields of knowledge. The work of collecting new words and senses for this databank continues unabated and has provided a number of new words and senses, first recorded here.

Computer technology has, in addition, provided other kinds of evidence, not previously available. The compilers were able to consult the Cobuild corpus of 20 million words of contemporary English, a collection of texts assembled and studied using computers at the English Department of the University of Birmingham. In many cases, the examples of use given in this dictionary are based on an examination of the uses recorded in the Cobuild corpus.

The compilers also had access to a different kind of computerized corpus: a collection of modern school text books used in teaching GCSE subjects, likewise collected at Birmingham University. By checking the vocabulary used in this GCSE corpus, the compilers were able to ensure that the dictionary is particularly useful to pupils studying for GCSE exams, as well as more general users.

The Collins Pocket English Dictionary has thus used the latest techniques to provide in one handy volume a practical and clear guide to today's language for today's users.

PWH

INTRODUCTION: LANGUAGE AND THE DICTIONARY

Different Levels of Language Use

Some words, or particular meanings of words, are not equally appropriate in all contexts of use. The dictionary shows this by the following labels:

Slang   means that the word or sense is informal and restricted, for example, to members of a particular social or cultural group. Slang words are inappropriate in formal speech or writing.

Informal   means that, although the word or sense may be widely used, especially in conversation, it is not suitable in formal contexts. Informal usage differs from slang usage in being more general and not restricted to a particular social or cultural group.

Formal   means that the word or sense is characteristically used in written English rather than in conversation, and typically occurs in an official context.

Offensive   means that the word or sense may be regarded as hurtful or derogatory by the person described or referred to, even if the speaker uses the word without any unkind intention.

Taboo   means that the word or sense is not acceptable in polite use.

Not standard   means that the word or sense, although it is often used, is generally regarded as incorrect.

Not universally accepted   means that the word or sense, although it is often used, is regarded by some people as incorrect. Often, this label indicates a usage that is in the process of changing, and may become generally accepted in the future.

Archaic   means that the word or sense is not used in modern English but may be found in literature of the past or used to give a historical tone in modern writing.

Obs. (Obsolete)   means that the word or sense is no longer in use. In technical subjects, this label often indicates that the term has been superseded.

    In addition to the above, the dictionary uses a wide variety of italic labels that show areas of usage or specialist fields, but which are self-explanatory. Examples of such labels are:
Poetic, Euphemistic, Computers, History.

The Pronunciation of English

There are many accents found throughout the English-speaking world, with which the dictionary user will be familiar. In the USA, Scotland, Ireland, and Devonshire, and elsewhere, for example, the letter 'r' is sounded distinctly in words such as *fern* and *arm*, while in the speech of Southeast England it is not. In many areas of Britain, words like *castle* and *fast* are pronounced with a short 'a' sound (æ) rather than the long 'a' (ɑ:) of Southern England. For speakers with these accents, *aunt*, which in Southern England is (ɑ:nt), may sound exactly like *ant* (ænt). There is nothing incorrect about these accents. But for the sake of simplicity, the accent represented in this dictionary is the one that is still most widely used as an international standard for teaching and for everyday use, namely, the 'Received Pronunciation' of Southeast England. The pronunciations in this dictionary are shown in the symbols of the International Phonetic Alphabet, and the dictionary user will interpret the symbols according to his or her own speech habits. A key to the pronunciation symbols will be found on page xvii.

Derivations of Words

English words derive from a large number of different languages of origin, and in many cases their development is a complex series of stages reflecting our linguistic and cultural heritage. In this dictionary, for those users who are interested in knowing something of this fascinating subject, the origin (etymology) of every main word is shown, in square brackets, after the definitions.

For words derived from Greek, Latin, the Romance languages, and other modern languages, it is usually possible to give the root word in the form in which it is recorded in the source language. In the case of words of Germanic origin, the Old English form is usually given. If there is no Old English form recorded, only the language itself is mentioned in the etymology, since the ancient Germanic language was not recorded in writing, and so it is not possible to show the exact form of the original. The same applies to words derived from Old Norse, where only the Icelandic forms exist in a recorded literature.

The etymologies, in most cases other than the above, show the language of origin, the root word as it is recorded in that language (unless it is the same in form as the modern English word), and the meaning of the root word if it differs from the meaning of the modern English word.

New Words from Existing Elements

New words are being created in English every day. This dictionary lists and explains all the common ones, and these explanations can be used to interpret many of the new coinages. For example, *antinuclear* has been coined from the elements *anti-* and *nuclear*, both of which are included in the dictionary. On this basis, it is easy enough to interpret a coinage such as *antiracist*. Other derived words, such as *slowly* and *quickness*, need no explanation, and are shown in the dictionary as subentries after the main entries *slow* and *quick*.

There are in English many words, formed from existing elements, whose meaning or meanings cannot be deduced from the sum of the two parts of which they are composed. Some examples are: *nonstandard, nonvoting, replace, replay, unfrock, unguarded*. Words of this kind, formed by the addition of a main word to a prefix, but having acquired a distinct or specialist meaning, are included in the main text of the dictionary.

At the other extreme, English includes a substantial and ever-growing class of words that are formed by adding a word to a prefix to produce a self-explanatory compound. Examples of such words are: *nonalcoholic, reapply,* and *unacceptable*. In this dictionary, words such as these are printed, without explanation, in bold type at the foot of the page, and not included in the main text. Prefixed words treated in this way are those beginning with: *non-, over-, re-, self-, semi-, un-,* and *under-*.

Guide to Grammar

It is part of the function of a dictionary to identify the grammatical class (or 'part of speech') to which each word belongs. The following abbreviations are used in this dictionary to identify the grammatical class of each word:

adj.	= *adjective*. Adjectives are words that modify the meaning of a noun. Adjectives are usually placed either in front of a noun, or after one of a small selection of verbs, which include *be, smell,* and *look*. Thus, *tall* is an adjective, as in *a tall man*. *Ill* is an adjective, as in *he is very ill, he looks ill*. There are some adjectives which can only come after a verb e.g. *afloat*.
adv.	= *adverb*. There are several different ways in which adverbs are used. The main types are as follows:

1. Most adverbs can modify the meaning of a verb, e.g. *quickly* in *She was walking quickly; he quickly ran to the corner*.

2.   Some adverbs are used to comment on the meaning of a whole statement, introducing the opinion of the writer or speaker. These are sometimes called *sentence adverbs*. Thus, *unfortunately* is a sentence adverb in *Unfortunately, he had forgotten his notes.*

3.   Some adverbs are used to modify the meaning of an adjective or another adverb. These are sometimes called *adverbs of degree* or *submodifiers. Very* is an adverb of degree, as in *It was very unfortunate.*

conj.   = ***conjunction.*** Conjunctions are words such as *and, or,* and *but,* which are used to join together two sentences, phrases, or words.

Some other words, such as *if, when,* and *how,* are used as conjunctions, joining a subordinate clause to a main clause, as in *If it happens, I shall be very pleased.*

det.   = ***determiner.*** Determiners are words that introduce a noun phrase, saying more about what the noun phrase refers to. The main types of determiner are as follows:

1.   The most common determiners are *the,* sometimes called the *definite article,* and *a* (or *an*), sometimes called the *indefinite article.*

2.   Another group of determiners are the words *this* and *that, these* and *those.* They used to be called *demonstrative adjectives.*

3.   A third group of determiners used to be called *possessive adjectives.* They are the words *his, her, its, my, your, our,* and *their.*

4.   A fourth group of determiners are sometimes called *partitives* or *quantifiers*: they include the words *some, any,* and *enough.*

5.   *Numbers* can be used as determiners too, as in *three girls, four albatrosses.*

interj.   = ***interjection.*** Interjections, also called exclamations, are cries expressing reactions such as alarm, surprise, anger, pleasure, etc., for example *Oh, damn,* and *hurrah.*

n.   = ***noun.*** Nouns are words that refer to people, things, and abstract ideas. *Student, dog, desk, money, health,* and *information* are all nouns. There are three main types of noun:

1.   *Countable nouns* can be used with the determiner *a* (or *an*) or with numbers. They have a plural form, usually ending in *-s.* Thus *student* is a countable noun: you can say *a student, three students.* Nouns that are always or nearly always plural are labelled *pl. n.* or *n.* (*usually pl.*) in this dictionary. Thus, senses 1 and 2 of *rein* are marked (*often pl.*) and (*pl.*). Sense 2 of *hostility,* 'fighting; warfare', is marked (*pl.*); the word only has this meaning when it is used in the plural, *hostilities.*

Sometimes, it is not clear from the form of a word whether it should be used with a singular or plural verb. In this dictionary, the function is explained in such cases. E.g. *economics* is explained as (*functioning as sing*).

2.   *Uncountable nouns* (sometimes called *mass nouns*) cannot be used with *a* or with *numbers,* and do not have a plural form. *Health* and *information* are uncountable nouns. You cannot say 'three informations'.

3.   The third main class of nouns is *proper nouns*: names like *John, London,* and *Baxter.* There are very few proper nouns in this dictionary, since proper nouns refer to individuals, not to general classes of items which can be explained in a dictionary.

It is very common in English to find a noun in front of another noun, modifying its meaning rather like an adjective. These are called *noun modifiers.* Examples are *oil* in *an oil well, production* in *production capacity,* and *capacity* in *a capacity crowd.* Some nouns, such as *dairy,* are most commonly used as modifiers.

prep. — **preposition**. Prepositions are words such as *by, with,* or *from,* used before a noun phrase or a pronoun to express its relation to the rest of the sentence or to some part of the rest of the sentence, for example *by* in *The book is by a well-known author,* and *in* in *the table by the window.*

pron. — **pronoun**. Pronouns are single words used to refer to people or things without naming or describing them. There are five main classes of pronouns:

1. *Personal pronouns* are words like *I, me, you, he, she, it, we,* and *they,* which refer to people or things.

2. *Possessive pronouns* are words such as *mine, yours, ours,* and *theirs,* used to identify ownership.

3. *Relative pronouns* are used to join relative clauses to main clauses. The main relative pronouns are *who* and *which.*

4. *Reflexive pronouns* refer back to a noun or personal pronoun earlier in the same clause. They are formed with *-self* or *-selves.* E.g. *She hurt herself; they did it for themselves.* Reflexive pronouns can also be used for emphasis, as in *The President himself did not know what was going on.*

5. *Indefinite pronouns* are used to avoid referring to a particular individual, e.g. *anyone, somebody, nobody, everything.*

vb. — **verb**. Verbs are words that describe actions and states. There are several different aspects to the classification of verbs. The main ones are as follows:

1. *Types of verb.* There are two different types of English verb: *main verbs* (sometimes called *lexical verbs*) and *auxiliary verbs.* Main verbs, such as *talk, expect, grow,* and *think,* carry the main meaning of the action. All well-formed English sentences have a main verb.

Auxiliary verbs help to refer to such matters as the time, possibility, or necessity of the action.

The form of a verb phrase that refers to the time of the action is called its *tense.* The main auxiliary verbs used in forming tenses are as follows:

be: forms continuous tenses, e.g. *am* in *I am thinking of you; was* in *he was thinking of you; be* in *I shall be thinking of you.*

have: forms perfect tenses, e.g. *have* in *we have finished, had* in *they had already left.*

shall, will: form future tenses, e.g. *shall* in *I shall finish soon.*

Another group of auxiliary verbs are called *modal verbs.* They refer to the possibility or necessity of an action. These are the words *can, could, may, might, must, ought to, should,* and *would.*

The verb *do* is used as an auxiliary verb in forming questions and negatives, as in *Do you know him? I didn't see anything.*

The auxiliary verb *be* is also used to form the *passive voice:* see point 3 below.

2. *Subject and object.* Verbs can be analysed according to the words that occur around them.

In almost every well-formed sentence of English, except commands, the verb has a *subject,* which is either a noun phrase or a pronoun. Normally, the subject comes before the verb. Thus, in the sentence *Peter expected some benefit,* 'Peter' is the subject. In *The whole Smith family expected some benefit,* 'The whole Smith family' is the subject. In *Some benefit was expected,* 'Some benefit' is the subject. In *It was expected,* 'It' is the subject.

Some verbs usually occur only with a particular subject or kind of subject. Where this is so, the subject is indicated in this dictionary in brackets before the definition. Thus, sense 7 of *hold* begins '(of the weather)'. Sense 2 of *rend* begins '(of a noise or cry)'.

Many verbs in English have a noun phrase or pronoun after them as well as before. The noun phrase or pronoun that follows a verb is called its *direct object* and a verb that has a direct object is called a *transitive verb*. Thus, in the sentence *Peter expected some benefit*, 'some benefit' is the direct object of the transitive verb 'expected'. In this dictionary, the type of direct object required is often indicated in brackets in the definition of a verb. Thus, definition 1 of *supply* reads 'to provide (a person or an institution) with something required'.

The words in brackets show what kind of direct object goes with *supply* in this sense.

Intransitive verbs do not have a direct object: *laugh* is an intransitive verb, as in *he laughed,* or *he laughed at her.* An intransitive verb cannot be used in the passive.

Some verbs require more than one object. In the sentence *John gave Peter a dirty look,* 'a dirty look' is the direct object, and 'Peter' is the indirect object.

In many cases, a verb in a particular sense is always or often followed by a particular preposition or other word. Where this is so, it is stated in the dictionary. Thus, *ram* sense 5, 'to force or drive, as by heavy blows' is labelled '(usually foll. by *into*)'.

3. *Active* and *Passive.* Notice the relationship between the following two sentences:

> Peter expected some benefit.
> Some benefit was expected by Peter.

They mean almost the same thing, but in the first one, 'Peter' is the subject, while in the second, 'some benefit' is the subject. The verb in the first sentence is in the *active voice*. In the second sentence, the verb, formed with 'was', is in the *passive voice*. The direct object of an active verb can always be made the subject of a passive verb. In this dictionary, verbs that are always, or nearly always, passive, are labelled (*passive*) or (*usually passive*).

4. *Phrasal verbs.* Some verbs are used with an adverb or preposition to form a special kind of verb, called a *phrasal verb*. Phrasal verbs are expressions like *take in, take off, take over; act up; run down; break in,* and so on. The meaning of a phrasal verb is often very different from the meaning of the verb and the adverb used on their own. Phrasal verbs are given as separate main entries in this dictionary.

Many words can belong to more than one grammatical class. For instance, *fall* can be a verb as in 'all fall down' or a noun as in 'a fall of snow'. In the dictionary the grammatical class is shown at the beginning of the entry and if there is another grammatical class this is shown later in the entry after the sign ∼.

Phrases or *Idioms*
Sometimes a word is so often used in a particular phrase that it has a separate meaning from the ordinary sense of the word. In such cases, the phrase is printed in bold type after the definition number, and explained as a whole. Thus, at *rack* sense 8, the phrase '*rack one's brains*' is treated in this way.

Guide to Spelling Forms

FORMING THE PLURALS OF NOUNS

Plurals are formed by adding -s except in the following cases:

1. When a word ends in -ch, -s, -sh, -x, or -z the plural is formed by adding -es (e.g. *benches, gases, dishes, taxes, buzzes*).

2. When a word ends in -y preceded by a consonant the plural form is -ies (e.g. *parties, bodies, policies*). When a word ends in -y preceded by a vowel the plural is formed by adding -s (e.g. *trays, joys, keys*).

3. When a word ends in -o the more common plural ending is -oes (e.g. *cargoes, potatoes, heroes, goes*). In many less familiar words or when the final -o is preceded by a vowel the plural ending is -os (e.g. *avocados, armadillos, studios, cameos*).

4. When a word ends in -f the plural is formed either by adding -s (e.g. *beliefs, cuffs, whiffs*) or by changing the -f to -v and adding -es (e.g. *thieves, loaves*). Some words may take both forms (e.g. *scarf, hoof, wharf*).

5. When a word ends in -ex or -ix the more formal plural ending is -ices. In more general contexts -es is used (e.g. *appendices, appendixes; indices, indexes*).

6. When a word from Latin ends in -is the plural form is -es (e.g. *crises, analyses*).

With compound words (like *court-martial*) it is usually the most important part which is pluralized (e.g. *courts-martial, lord-justices, mothers-in-law*). In certain cases the plural form of a word is the same as the singular (e.g. *deer, sheep, grouse*) and in some words both forms end in -s (e.g. *measles, corps, mews*).

There are two main types of plural which take either singular or plural verbs.

a. words like *media* and *data*. These are in common use as singular nouns although, strictly, this is incorrect.

b. words ending in -ics. Generally, these are treated as plural when the word relates to an individual person or thing (e.g. *his mathematics are poor; the hall's acoustics are good*) and as singular when it is regarded more strictly as a science (e.g. *mathematics is an important subject*).

VERB FORMS

Most verbs in English have four different forms. Some have five. The forms are:

the base form, e.g. *talk, expect, grow, think, swim*.
the third person present singular, e.g. *talks, expects, grows, thinks, swims*.
the present participle, e.g. *talking, expecting, growing, thinking, swimming*.
the past tense, e.g. *talked, expected, grew, thought, swam*.
the past participle, e.g. *talked, expected, grown, thought, swum*.

Notice that the past tense and the past participle are identical for many verbs, but for a few, e.g. *grew/grown* and *swam/swum*, they are different. The past tense is used as in *he grew some prize vegetables*. The past participle is used for perfect tenses, as in *He has grown some prize vegetables*, and for the passive voice, as in *Some prize vegetables were grown*. See also the section on verbs in the *Guide to Grammar* on pages xi, xii.

1. *Forming the third person singular of verbs.* The third person singular form of English verbs ends in -s (e.g. *expects*), and the rules for forming it are generally the same as for the plural of nouns. An exception is *knife*, where the third person singular is *knifes*, but the plural of the corresponding noun is *knives*.

2. *Forming the present participle.* The present participle is regularly formed by adding -ing to the base form (e.g. *walk, walking; invent, inventing*). Verbs that end in a consonant plus -e regularly drop the final -e before the addition of -ing (e.g. *locate, locating; snare, snaring*).

Verbs that end in a single consonant double that consonant before the addition of -ing (e.g. *pin, pinning; submit, submitting*). Exceptions to this are verbs of more than one syllable with no stress on the last syllable, such as *rivet, gather (rivet, riveting; gather, gathering*) but this does not apply to verbs ending in -l, such as *label, revel*, which double the l (*label, labelling; revel, revelling*).

Irregular forms and other forms that may cause doubt are shown in the dictionary.

3.　*Forming the past tense and past participle of verbs.* Verbs that end in a consonant plus -e regularly drop the final -e before the addition of -ed (e.g. *locate, located; snare, snared*).
Verbs that end in a consonant plus -y regularly change the -y to an -i before the addition of -ed (e.g. *pity, pitied*).
Verbs that end in a single consonant double that consonant before the addition of -ed (e.g. *pin, pinned; submit, submitted*).
Exceptions to this are verbs with two vowels before the final consonant (e.g. *train, trained*) or verbs of more than one syllable with no stress on the last syllable such as *rivet, gather (rivet, riveted; gather, gathered*) but this does not apply to verbs ending in -l such as *label, revel* which double the l (*label, labelled; revel, revelled*).

Irregular forms and other forms that may cause doubt are shown in the dictionary.

FORMS OF ADJECTIVES

Adjectives can be used in three different forms: the basic word (e.g. *strong*), the comparative (e.g. *stronger*), and the superlative (e.g. *strongest*). The comparative is regularly formed by adding -er to the base word, and the superlative by adding -est.

Adjectives that end in a consonant plus -e regularly drop the -e before -er and -est (e.g. *fine, finer, finest*).
Adjectives ending in -y, such as *pretty*, regularly change the -y to -i before adding -er or -est (*prettier, prettiest*).
Adjectives ending in -ey usually change the -ey to -i (e.g. *dicey, dicier, diciest*).
Short adjectives (of one syllable and with a short vowel sound) that end in a consonant, double the consonant before adding -er or -est (e.g. *fat, fatter, fattest; big, bigger, biggest*).

These and any other spelling changes that occur for comparative or superlative forms are shown in the dictionary.

A different way of expressing the comparative and superlative of an adjective is to use *more* for the comparative and *most* for the superlative before the adjective. This is done with longer adjectives, such as some that have two syllables and all that have three or more syllables (e.g. *faithful, more faithful, most faithful* and *beautiful, more beautiful, most beautiful*).

This form is also used with adjectives like *afraid* or *alone* and with those adjectives that come from past participles (e.g. *tired, refined*). Sometimes the sound of an adjective makes this form more suitable (e.g. *eager, bizarre, correct*).

Guide to Punctuation

apostrophe　The sign (') is usually used to indicate possession. In the singular -'s is used (e.g. *Peter's dog*). In the plural the apostrophe is added to the end of the word (e.g. *the neighbours' dog*). Plurals that do not end in -s take -'s (e.g. *children's toys*). Proper names ending in -s either add an apostrophe alone (e.g. *Jesus' life, Keats' poetry*) or add -'s (e.g. *Thomas's house, Mr Jones's garden*).

brackets　These serve to isolate part of a sentence which could be omitted and still leave an intelligible statement. Punctuation of the rest of the sentence should run as if the bracketed portion were not there, e.g. *That house over there (with the blue door) is ours.* Square brackets are used where an editor or writer inserts his own information into a text or quotation, e.g. *He claimed that the honourable member [John Smith] was misleading the House.*

capital letters　These are used at the beginning of a sentence, and for proper names and titles of people and organizations, e.g. *Mr Robertson, Dr Smith, South America, British Rail.*

colons　The function of these is to provide more of a break than a comma, and less than a full stop. The colon is used to introduce a following statement, e.g. *Take it or leave it: the choice is yours.* It is also used to introduce a list, quotation, or summary. See also **semicolons**.

commas　1.　These make divisions between groups of words in a sentence, e.g. *She stormed out, slamming the door behind her.*

2.   Commas are used to divide units in a series of nouns, adjectives, or phrases, e.g. *The cupboard was full of pots, pans, and crockery.* In such a series the last comma (i.e. before 'and' or 'or') is optional. It is not usual to place a comma between the last of a series of adjectives and the noun, e.g. *It was a long, hot, humid day.*

3.   Commas are also used to mark off a word or phrase in a sentence which adds a comment but is not an essential part of the sentence. Dashes and brackets have a similar function. Commas give the lightest degree of separation, dashes produce a jerky effect, and brackets cut off part of a sentence most firmly, e.g.
He hurried home, taking a short cut, but still arrived too late.
It's a long time — over two years — since we last met.
They both went to Athens (unaware of each other's plans) and stayed in the same hotel.

4.   Commas are also used to separate a clause (group of words) that adds some information about a noun, but is not an essential part of the meaning, e.g. *the dodo, which is now extinct, inhabited Mauritius.* Here the clause *which is now extinct* adds a comment on *dodo*. It is an addition, not an essential part, so it is separated off by commas. Compare this with *I like people who make me laugh.* Here the words *people who make me laugh* are to be interpreted as a whole. The clause is therefore not separated off by commas.

5.   When two phrases are linked by a conjunction they do not normally have a comma between them unless there is a contrast, e.g. *People are either dark or fair,* but *She was dark, but her brother was fair.*

6.   When addressing a person, commas are used before and after the person's name or title, e.g. *Well, Mrs Smith, how are you today?*

exclamation marks   These are used after exclamations such as *Oh! Damn!* or *Hurrah!* and not after ordinary statements.

full stops   These mark the end of a complete sentence, e.g. *You may think you can get away with it. Not a chance.* Full stops are also often used after abbreviations and initial letters standing for the whole word (as in *fig., a.m.*). Abbreviations which include the first and last letters of a word are equally acceptable without the stop (*Dr, Mr, ft*) or with the stop (*Dr., Mr., ft.*). It is also usual to write titles like BBC, USA, TUC without stops.

hyphens   Compound words, like *lay-by* or *fire engine*, or words with a prefix, like *antinuclear*, may or may not contain a hyphen. It is generally used when the compound is new and dropped as it becomes familiar, becoming one word unless there is any awkwardness in joining the two words. When a compound adjective comes before a noun it should be hyphenated to stress that the constituent parts are not to be used independently, e.g. *He has a half-Italian wife; this is a user-friendly dictionary.*

inverted commas (quotation marks, quotes)
1.   These are used for direct quotation, not for indirect speech. It is usual to have a comma before and after a quotation if the sentence is resumed, e.g. *He said, "Follow me", and set off down the street.*

2.   Single quotation marks can be used to indicate a title or quotation within a speech, e.g. *"I loved 'War and Peace'," she said, "but it took so long to read."* Where such a distinction is not required, either single or double quotation marks may be used. Nowadays the single style is more often used.

question marks   These are used at the end of direct questions, but not after reported ones.

semicolons   These can be used instead of a full stop or instead of a conjunction between two sentences that are closely related, e.g. *I was late home; the fire was out.*

ABBREVIATIONS AND SYMBOLS USED IN THE DICTIONARY

adj.	adjective	N	North(ern)
adv.	adverb(ial)	n.	noun
Anat.	Anatomy	Naut.	Nautical
Archaeol.	Archaeology	NE	Northeast(ern)
Archit.	Architecture	NW	Northwest(ern)
Astrol.	Astrology	N.Z.	New Zealand
Astron.	Astronomy		
Austral.	Australian		
		Obs.	Obsolete
		orig.	originally
Biol.	Biology		
Bot.	Botany		
Brit.	Britain; British		
		Photog.	Photography
		pl.	plural
°C	degrees Celsius	p.p.	past participle
Canad.	Canadian	prep.	preposition(al)
cap.	capital	pron.	pronoun
Chem.	Chemistry	Psychol.	Psychology
comp.	comparative	p.t.	past tense
conj.	conjunction		
E	east(ern)	S	south(ern)
Econ.	Economics	S. African	South African
esp.	especially	Scot.	Scottish; Scots
		SE	southeast(ern)
		sing.	singular
fem.	feminine	sup.	superlative
foll.	followed	SW	southwest(ern)
Geog.	Geography		
Geol.	Geology	Theol.	Theology
Geom.	Geometry		
		U.S.	United States
imit.	imitative		
interj.	interjection		
		var.	variant
lit.	literally	vb.	verb
masc.	masculine		
Maths.	Mathematics	W	west(ern)
Med.	Medicine		
Mil.	Military		
Myth.	Mythology	Zool.	Zoology

PRONUNCIATION KEY

The following consonant symbols have their usual English values: *b, d, f, h, k, l, m, n, p, r, s, t, v, w, z*. The remaining symbols and their interpretations are listed below.

ɑː	as in *father* ('fɑːðə), *heart* (hɑːt)
æ	as in *act* (ækt)
aɪ	as in *dive* (daɪv)
aɪə	as in *fire* ('faɪə)
aʊ	as in *out* (aʊt)
aʊə	as in *flour* ('flaʊə)
ɛ	as in *bet* (bɛt)
eɪ	as in *paid* (peɪd)
ɛə	as in *bear* (bɛə)
g	as in *get* (gɛt)
ɪ	as in *give* (gɪv)
iː	as in *see* (siː)
ɪə	as in *fear* (fɪə)
j	as in *yes* (jɛs)
ɒ	as in *pot* (pɒt)
əʊ	as in *note* (nəʊt)
ɔː	as in *thaw* (θɔː), *organ* ('ɔːgən)
ɔɪ	as in *void* (vɔɪd)
ʊ	as in *pull* (pʊl)
uː	as in *zoo* (zuː)
ʊə	as in *poor* (pʊə)
ə	as in *potter* ('pɒtə), *alone* (ə'ləʊn)
ɜː	as in *fern* (fɜːn), *burn* (bɜːn)
ʌ	as in *cut* (kʌt)
ʃ	as in *ship* (ʃɪp)
ʒ	as in *treasure* ('trɛʒə)
tʃ	as in *chew* (tʃuː)
dʒ	as in *jaw* (dʒɔː)
θ	as in *thin* (θɪn)
ð	as in *these* (ðiːz)
ŋ	as in *sing* (sɪŋ), *finger* ('fɪŋgə)
̩	as in *bundle* ('bʌndˀl), *button* ('bʌtˀn)
x	as in *loch* (lɒx)

Stress marks are placed immediately *before* the affected syllable. Primary or strong stress is shown by ', while secondary or weak stress is shown by ,. Unstressed syllables are not marked. In *photographic* (ˌfəʊtə'græfɪk), for example, the first syllable carries secondary stress and the third primary stress, while the second and fourth are unstressed.

Length
The symbol : denotes length and is shown together with certain vowel symbols when the vowels are typically long.

A

a or **A** (eɪ) *n., pl.* **a's, A's,** or **As. 1.** the first letter of the English alphabet. **2.** the first in a series. **3. from A to Z.** from start to finish.

a (ə; *emphatic* eɪ) *det.* (*indefinite article*; used before an initial consonant. Compare **an**) **1.** used preceding a singular countable noun that has not been mentioned before: *a dog; a great pity.* **2.** used preceding a noun or determiner of quantity: *a dozen eggs; a great many; to read a lot.* **3.** (preceded by *once, twice, several times,* etc.) each or every; per: *once a day.*

A 1. *Music.* the sixth note of the scale of C major. **2.** ampere(s). **3.** atomic: *an A-bomb.*

Å angstrom unit.

A. answer.

a- or before a vowel **an-** *prefix.* not; without: *atonal; asocial; anaphrodisiac.* [Greek]

A1, A-1, or **A-one** ('eɪ'wʌn) *adj. Informal.* first-class; excellent.

A4 *n.* a standard paper size, 297 × 210 mm.

AA 1. Alcoholics Anonymous. **2.** (in Britain) Automobile Association.

AAA ('θriː'eɪz) *Brit.* Amateur Athletic Association.

A & R artists and repertoire.

aardvark ('ɑːd,vɑːk) *n.* an African mammal which has long ears and snout and which feeds on termites. [obs. Afrikaans: earth pig]

AB able-bodied seaman.

ab- *prefix.* away from; opposite to: *abnormal.* [Latin]

aback (ə'bæk) *adv.* **taken aback.** startled or disconcerted.

abacus ('æbəkəs) *n.* **1.** a counting device consisting of a frame holding rods on which beads are moved backwards and forwards by the person doing the counting. **2.** *Archit.* the flat upper part of the capital of a column. [Greek, from Hebrew]

abaft (ə'bɑːft) *adv., adj. Naut.* closer to the stern of a ship. [Old English *be* by + *æftan* behind]

abalone (,æbə'ləʊnɪ) *n.* an edible sea creature with an ear-shaped shell lined with mother-of-pearl. [American Spanish]

abandon (ə'bændən) *vb.* **1.** to leave (someone or something): *he abandoned his wife.* **2.** to give up completely: *abandon hope.* **3.** to surrender (oneself) to emotion without restraint. ~*n.* **4.** freedom from inhibitions or restraint. [Old French *a bandon* under one's control] —a'**bandon-ment** *n.*

abandoned (ə'bændənd) *adj.* **1.** deserted: *an abandoned windmill.* **2.** uninhibited: *abandoned behaviour.*

abase (ə'beɪs) *vb.* **abase oneself.** to degrade oneself. [Old French *abaissier*] —a'**basement** *n.*

abashed (ə'bæʃt) *adj.* embarrassed and ashamed. [Old French *esbair* to be astonished]

abate (ə'beɪt) *vb.* to make or become less strong: *the storm abated.* [Old French *abatre* to beat down] —a'**batement** *n.*

abattoir ('æbə,twɑː) *n.* a slaughterhouse. [French *abattre* to fell]

abbacy ('æbəsɪ) *n., pl.* **-cies.** the office or jurisdiction of an abbot or abbess. [Church Latin *abbātia*]

abbé ('æbeɪ) *n.* a French abbot or other clergyman.

abbess ('æbɪs) *n.* the female superior of a convent. [Church Latin *abbātissa*]

abbey ('æbɪ) *n.* **1.** a building inhabited by monks or nuns. **2.** a church associated with such a building. **3.** a community of monks or nuns. [Church Latin *abbātia* ABBACY]

abbot ('æbət) *n.* the superior of an abbey of monks. [Aramaic *abbā* father]

abbreviate (ə'briːvɪ,eɪt) *vb.* **1.** to shorten (a word) by omission of some letters **2.** to cut short. [Latin *brevis* brief] —abbrevia-tion (ə,briːvɪ'eɪʃən) *n.*

ABC *n.* **1.** the alphabet. **2.** an alphabetical guide.

abdicate ('æbdɪ,keɪt) *vb.* **1.** to give up the throne formally. **2.** to give up (one's responsibilities). [Latin *abdicāre* to disclaim] —,abdi'**cation** *n.*

abdomen ('æbdəmən) *n.* the part of the body that contains the stomach and intestines; belly. [Latin] —**abdominal** (æb-'dɒmɪn'l) *adj.*

abduct (æb'dʌkt) *vb.* to remove (a person) by force; kidnap. [Latin *abdūcere* to lead away] —ab'**duction** *n.* —ab'**ductor** *n.*

abeam (ə'biːm) *adv., adj.* at right angles to the length of a vessel or aircraft.

Aberdeen Angus (,æbə'diːn 'æŋgəs) *n.* a black hornless breed of beef cattle originating in Scotland.

aberrant (ə'berənt) *adj.* deviating from what is right, true, or normal.

aberration (,æbə'reɪʃən) *n.* **1.** deviation from what is right, true, or normal **2.** a lapse: *a mental aberration.* [Latin *aberrāre* to wander away]

abet (ə'bet) *vb.* **abetting, abetted.** to assist or encourage (someone) in wrongdoing. [Old French *abeter* to lure on]

abeyance (ə'beɪəns) *n.* (usually preceded by *in* or *into*) a state of being put aside temporarily. [Old French *abeance*, lit.: a gaping after]

abhor (əb'hɔː) *vb.* **-horring, -horred.** to detest (something) vehemently. [Latin *abhorrēre*]

abhorrent (əb'hɒrənt) *adj.* hateful; loathsome. —ab'**horrence** *n.*

abide (ə'baɪd) vb. **1.** to tolerate: *I can't abide liars.* **2. abide by. a.** to comply with: *to abide by the decision.* **b.** to remain faithful to: *to abide by your promise.* **3.** *Archaic.* to dwell. [Old English *ābīdan*, from *a-* (intensive) + *bīdan* to wait]

abiding (ə'baɪdɪŋ) adj. permanent; enduring.

ability (ə'bɪlɪtɪ) n., pl. **-ties. 1.** possession of the necessary skill or power to do something. **2.** great skill or competence: *a man of ability.* **3.** (pl.) special talents. [Latin *habilitās*]

abject ('æbdʒɛkt) adj. **1.** utterly miserable: *abject poverty.* **2.** contemptible; servile. [Latin *abjectus* thrown away] —'**abjectly** adv.

abjure (əb'dʒʊə) vb. to renounce or retract (something) under oath. [Latin *abjurāre* to deny on oath] —,**abju'ration** n.

ablation (æb'leɪʃən) n. **1.** the surgical removal of an organ or part. **2.** the melting of a part, such as the heat shield of a space re-entry vehicle. **3.** the wearing away of a rock or glacier. [Latin *auferre* to carry away]

ablative ('æblətɪv) *Grammar.* ~adj. **1.** (in Latin) denoting a case of nouns indicating the agent, instrument, or place of the action. ~n. **2.** the ablative case.

ablaze (ə'bleɪz) adj. **1.** on fire. **2.** brightly illuminated: *ablaze with lights.* **3.** emotionally aroused: *ablaze with anger.*

able ('eɪb²l) adj. **1.** having the necessary power, skill, or opportunity to do something. **2.** capable; talented. [Latin *habilis*]

-able *suffix forming adjectives.* **1.** capable of: *washable.* **2.** inclined to: *variable.* [Latin *-ābilis, -ībilis*] —'**ably** *suffix forming adverbs.* —**ability** *suffix forming nouns.*

able-bodied adj. strong and healthy.

able-bodied seaman *or* **able seaman** n. a seaman who is trained in certain skills.

able rating n. a seaman of the lowest rank in a navy.

ablutions (ə'bluːʃənz) pl. n. **1.** the act of washing: *perform one's ablutions.* **2.** *Mil. informal.* a washing place. [Latin *ablūere* to wash away]

ably ('eɪblɪ) adv. competently or skilfully.

ABM antiballistic missile.

abnegation (,æbnɪ'geɪʃən) n. the act of giving something up. [Latin *abnegāre*]

abnormal (æb'nɔːməl) adj. not normal; deviating from the usual or typical. —**abnormality** (,æbnɔː'mælɪt) n. —**ab'normally** adv.

aboard (ə'bɔːd) adv., adj., prep. on, in, onto, or into (a ship, plane, or train).

abode (ə'bəʊd) n. one's home. [from ABIDE]

abolish (ə'bɒlɪʃ) vb. to do away with (laws, regulations, or customs). [Latin *abolēre* to destroy]

abolition (,æbə'lɪʃən) n. **1.** the act of abolishing or the state of being abolished. **2.** (cap.) the ending of slavery. —,**abo'litionist** n., adj.

A-bomb n. short for **atom bomb**.

abominable (ə'bɒmɪnəb²l) adj. detestable; very bad: *an abominable waste of money.* —a'**bominably** adv.

abominable snowman n. a large man-like or apelike creature alleged to inhabit the Himalayas. [translation of Tibetan *metohkangmi* foul snowman]

abominate (ə'bɒmɪ,neɪt) vb. to dislike intensely; detest. [Latin *abōmināri* to regard as an ill omen] —**abomination** (ə,bɒmɪ'neɪʃən) n.

aboriginal (,æbə'rɪdʒɪn²l) adj. existing in a place from the earliest known period.

Aboriginal (,æbə'rɪdʒɪn²l) adj. **1.** of the Aborigines of Australia. ~n. **2.** an Aborigine.

aborigine (,æbə'rɪdʒɪnɪ) n. an original inhabitant of a country or region. [Latin *ab origine* from the beginning]

Aborigine (,æbə'rɪdʒɪnɪ) n. a member of a dark-skinned people who were already living in Australia when European settlers arrived.

abort (ə'bɔːt) vb. **1.** (of a woman) to end a pregnancy before the fetus is viable; miscarry. **2** to perform an abortion on (a pregnant woman). **3.** to terminate (a mission or project) prematurely or (of a mission or project) to be terminated prematurely. [Latin *abortāre*]

abortion (ə'bɔːʃən) n. **1.** an operation to terminate pregnancy. **2.** the premature termination of pregnancy by expulsion of a nonviable fetus from the womb. **3.** the failure of a mission or project. **4.** *Informal.* something that is grotesque. —a'**bortionist** n.

abortive (ə'bɔːtɪv) adj. failing to achieve a purpose.

abound (ə'baʊnd) vb. **1.** to exist in large numbers. **2. abound in.** to have a large number of. [Latin *abundāre*]

about (ə'baʊt) prep. **1.** relating to; concerning. **2.** near to. **3.** carried on: *I haven't any money about me.* **4.** on every side of. ~adv. **5.** near in number, time, or degree; approximately. **6.** nearby. **7.** here and there: *walk about to keep warm.* **8.** all around; on every side. **9.** in or to the opposite direction. **10.** in rotation: *turn and turn about.* **11.** used to indicate understatement: *it's about time you stopped.* **12. about to.** on the point of; intending to: *she was about to jump.* **13. not about to.** determined not to: *I'm not about to miss the game.* ~adj. **14.** active: *up and about.* [Old English *abūtan, onbūtan*]

about turn *or* *U.S.* **about face** interj. **1.** a military command to reverse the direction in which one is facing. ~n. **about-turn** *or* *U.S.* **about-face.** **2.** reversal of the direction in which one is facing. **3.** a complete change of opinion or direction.

above (ə'bʌv) prep. **1.** higher than; over. **2.** greater than in quantity or degree: *above average.* **3.** superior to or higher than in quality, rank, or ability. **4.** too high-minded for: *above petty gossiping.* **5.** too respected for; beyond: *above suspicion.* **6.** too difficult to be understood by: *the talk* *was above me.* **7.** louder or higher than (other noise). **8.** in preference to. **9. above all.** most of all; especially. ~*adv.* **10.** in or to a higher place: *the sky above.* **11.** in a previous place (in something written or printed). **12.** higher in rank or position. ~*n.* **13. the above.** something previously mentioned. ~*adj.* **14.** appearing in a previous place (in something written or printed). [Old English *abufan*]

above board *adj.* in the open; without dishonesty.

abracadabra (ˌæbrəkəˈdæbrə) *n.* a word used in magic spells, which is supposed to possess magic powers. [magical word used in certain Gnostic writings]

abrasion (əˈbreɪʒən) *n.* **1.** a scraped area on the skin; graze. **2.** *Geog.* the erosion of rock by rock fragments scratching and scraping it. [Latin *abrādere*]

abrasive (əˈbreɪsɪv) *adj.* **1.** irritating in manner. **2.** causing abrasion; rough. ~*n.* **3.** a substance used for cleaning, smoothing, or polishing.

abreast (əˈbrɛst) *adj.* **1.** alongside each other and facing in the same direction: *two abreast.* **2. abreast of.** up to date with.

abridge (əˈbrɪdʒ) *vb.* to reduce the length of (a written work) by condensing it. [Late Latin *abbreviāre*] —a**ˈbridgment** *or* a**ˈbridgement** *n.*

abroad (əˈbrɔːd) *adv.* **1.** to or in a foreign country or countries. **2.** (of rumours) in general circulation.

abrogate (ˈæbrəʊˌɡeɪt) *vb.* to cancel (a law or an agreement) formally. [from Latin *abaway* + *rogāre* to propose a law] —**abroˈgation** *n.*

abrupt (əˈbrʌpt) *adj.* **1.** sudden; unexpected. **2.** rather rude in speech or manner. [Latin *abruptus* broken off] —ab**ˈruptly** *adv.* —ab**ˈruptness** *n.*

abscess (ˈæbsɛs) *n.* **1.** a swelling containing pus as a result of inflammation. ~*vb.* **2.** to form a swelling containing pus. [Latin *abscēdere* to go away] —**ˈabscessed** *adj.*

abscissa (æbˈsɪsə) *n., pl.* **-scissas** *or* **-scissae** (-ˈsɪsiː). *Maths.* (in a two-dimensional system of Cartesian coordinates) the distance from the vertical axis measured parallel to the horizontal axis. [New Latin *linea abscissa* a cut-off line]

abscond (æbˈskɒnd) *vb.* to run away secretly, usually to avoid prosecution. [Latin *abscondere* to conceal]

abseil (ˈæbsaɪl) *Mountaineering.* ~*vb.* **1.** to descend a steep drop by a rope secured from above and coiled around one's body. ~*n.* **2.** an instance of abseiling. [German]

absence (ˈæbsəns) *n.* **1.** the state of being away. **2.** the time during which a person or thing is away. **3.** the fact of being without something; lack.

absent *adj.* (ˈæbsənt). **1.** not present. **2.** lacking. **3.** inattentive. ~*vb.* (æbˈsɛnt). **4. absent oneself.** to stay away. [Latin *abesse* to be away] —**ˈabsently** *adv.*

absentee (ˌæbsənˈtiː) *n.* **a.** a person who is absent. **b.** (*as modifier*): *an absentee landlord.*

absenteeism (ˌæbsənˈtiːɪzəm) *n.* persistent absence from work or school.

absent-minded *adj.* preoccupied; forgetful. —ˌabsent-**ˈmindedly** *adv.*

absinthe *or* **absinth** (ˈæbsɪnθ) *n.* a potent green alcoholic drink, originally containing wormwood. [Greek *apsinthion* wormwood]

absolute (ˈæbsəˌluːt) *adj.* **1.** complete; perfect. **2.** free from restrictions or exceptions: *an absolute ruler.* **3.** undoubted; certain: *the absolute truth.* **4.** not dependent on or relative to anything else. **5.** pure; unmixed: *absolute alcohol.* ~*n.* **6.** something that is absolute. **7. the Absolute.** *Philosophy.* that which is totally unconditioned, perfect, or complete. [Latin *absolūtus*]

absolutely (ˌæbsəˈluːtlɪ) *adv.* **1.** completely or perfectly. ~*interj.* **2.** yes indeed; certainly.

absolute majority *n.* a number of votes totalling over 50 per cent, such as the total number of votes that beats the combined opposition.

absolute pitch *n.* the ability to identify exactly the pitch of a note without comparing it with another.

absolute zero *n. Physics.* the lowest temperature theoretically attainable, at which the particles that make up matter would be at rest: equivalent to $-273.15°C$ or $-459.67°F$.

absolution (ˌæbsəˈluːʃən) *n. Christianity.* a formal forgiveness of sin pronounced by a priest.

absolutism (ˈæbsəluːˌtɪzəm) *n.* the principle of a political system in which a monarch or dictator has unrestricted power.

absolve (əbˈzɒlv) *vb.* to clear (someone) of all blame. [Latin *absolvere* to make loose]

absorb (əbˈsɔːb) *vb.* **1.** to soak up (a liquid). **2.** to engage the interest of (someone). **3.** to receive the force of (an impact). **4.** *Physics.* to take in (radiant energy) and retain it. **5.** to take in; incorporate: *the refugees were absorbed into the community.* [Latin *absorbēre*] —ab**ˈsorbent** *adj.* —ab**ˈsorbing** *adj.*

absorption (əbˈsɔːpʃən) *n.* **1.** the process of absorbing something or the state of being absorbed. **2.** *Physiol.* the process by which nutrients enter the tissues of an animal or a plant. —ab**ˈsorptive** *adj.*

abstain (əbˈsteɪn) *vb.* **1.** to choose to refrain: *he abstained from drinking alcohol.* **2.** to refrain from voting. [Latin *abstinēre*] —ab**ˈstainer** *n.*

abstemious (əbˈstiːmɪəs) *adj.* sparing in the consumption of alcohol or food. [Latin *abstēmius*] —ab**ˈstemiously** *adv.* —ab**ˈstemiousness** *n.*

abstention (əbˈstɛnʃən) *n.* **1.** the act of abstaining from something, such as drinking alcohol. **2.** the act of withholding one's vote.

abstinence (ˈæbstɪnəns) *n.* the act or practice of refraining from some action, such as drinking alcohol. —**ˈabstinent** *adj.*

abstract *adj.* (ˈæbstrækt). **1.** referring to ideas or qualities rather than material objects: *an abstract noun.* **2.** not applied or practical; theoretical: *abstract science*. **3.** denoting art in which the subject is represented by shapes and patterns rather than by a realistic likeness. ~*n*. (ˈæbstrækt). **4.** a summary. **5.** an abstract word or idea. **6.** an abstract painting or sculpture. **7. in the abstract**. without referring to specific circumstances. ~*vb*. (æbˈstrækt). **8.** to remove oneself or an object. **9.** to summarize. [Latin *abstractus* drawn off]

abstracted (æbˈstræktɪd) *adj*. lost in thought; preoccupied. —**abˈstractedly** *adv*.

abstraction (æbˈstrækʃən) *n*. **1.** preoccupation. **2.** a generalized concept formulated by extracting common qualities from specific examples: *good and evil are abstractions*.

abstruse (əbˈstruːs) *adj*. not easy to understand. [Latin *abstrūsus*]

absurd (əbˈsɜːd) *adj*. incongruous; ridiculous. [Latin *absurdus* out of time] —**abˈsurdity** *n*. —**abˈsurdly** *adv*.

abundance (əˈbʌndəns) *n*. **1.** a great amount. **2.** degree of plentifulness. [Latin *abundāre* to abound] —a**ˈbundant** *adj*.

abundantly (əˈbʌndəntlɪ) *adv*. **1.** very: *he made it abundantly plain*. **2.** plentifully; in abundance.

abuse *vb*. (əˈbjuːz). **1.** to use incorrectly: *he abuses his position*. **2.** to mistreat: *the child had been physically abused*. **3.** to speak insultingly or cruelly to. ~*n*. (əˈbjuːs). **4.** improper use. **5.** mistreatment; injury. **6.** insulting comments. [Latin *abūtī*] —a**ˈbuser** *n*.

abusive (əˈbjuːsɪv) *adj*. rude or insulting: *abusive language*. —a**ˈbusively** *adv*.

abut (əˈbʌt) *vb*. **abutting, abutted**. (foll. by *on*) to adjoin, touch, or border on (something) at one end. [Old French *abouter*]

abutment (əˈbʌtmənt) *n*. a construction that supports the end of a bridge.

abysmal (əˈbɪzməl) *adj*. *Informal*. extremely bad. [Medieval Latin *abysmus* abyss] —a**ˈbysmally** *adv*.

abyss (əˈbɪs) *n*. a very deep hole in the ground. [Greek *abussos* bottomless]

Ac *Chem*. actinium.

AC 1. alternating current. **2.** athletic club.

a/c 1. account. **2.** account current.

acacia (əˈkeɪʃə) *n*. a shrub or tree with small yellow or white flowers. [Greek *akakia*]

academic (ˌækəˈdɛmɪk) *adj*. **1.** relating to a college or university. **2.** of theoretical interest only: *the question is academic as a decision has already been reached*. **3.** (of pupils) having an aptitude for study. **4.** relating to studies such as languages and pure science rather than technical or professional studies. ~*n*. **5.** a member of the teaching or research staff of a college or university. —ˌaca**ˈdemically** *adv*.

academy (əˈkædəmɪ) *n*., *pl*. **-mies**. **1.** a society for the advancement of literature, art, or science. **2.** a school for training in a particular skill: *a military academy*. **3.** (in

Scotland) a secondary school. [Greek *akadēmeia* the place where Plato taught] —ˌaca**ˈdemical** *adj*.

acanthus (əˈkænθəs) *n*. **1.** a plant with large spiny leaves and spikes of white or purplish flowers. **2.** a carved ornament based on the leaves of the acanthus plant. [Greek *akantha* thorn]

ACAS (ˈeɪkæs) (in Britain) Advisory Conciliation and Arbitration Service.

acc. *Grammar*. accusative.

accede (ækˈsiːd) *vb*. (foll. by *to*) **1.** to give one's consent to. **2.** to take up (an office or position): *the prince acceded to the throne*. [Latin *accēdere*]

accelerando (ækˌsɛləˈrændəʊ) *adv*. *Music*. with increasing speed. [Italian]

accelerate (ækˈsɛləˌreɪt) *vb*. **1.** to move or cause (something) to move more quickly; speed up. **2.** to cause (something) to happen sooner than expected. [Latin *accelerāre*] —**acceleration** (ækˌsɛləˈreɪʃən) *n*.

accelerator (ækˈsɛləˌreɪtə) *n*. **1.** a pedal in a motor vehicle that is pressed to increase speed. **2.** *Physics*. a machine for increasing the speed and energy of charged particles.

accent *n*. (ˈæksənt). **1.** the distinctive style of pronunciation of a person or group from a particular area, country, or social background. **2.** the relative prominence of a spoken or sung syllable. **3.** a mark used in writing to indicate the prominence of a syllable or the way a vowel is pronounced. **4.** *Music*. stress placed on certain notes. **5.** a distinctive characteristic of anything: *a wine bar with a nautical accent*. **6.** particular emphasis: *an accent on learning*. ~*vb*. (ækˈsɛnt). **7.** to mark with an accent. **8.** to lay particular emphasis on. [Latin *accentus*]

accentuate (ækˈsɛntjʊˌeɪt) *vb*. to stress or emphasize. —acˌcentu**ˈation** *n*.

accept (əkˈsɛpt) *vb*. **1.** to take or receive (something offered). **2.** to agree to. **3.** to take on the responsibilities of: *he accepted office*. **4.** to consider (something) as true. **5.** to receive (someone) into a community or group. **6.** to receive (something) as adequate or valid. [Latin *acceptāre*]

acceptable (əkˈsɛptəbʰl) *adj*. **1.** satisfactory; adequate. **2.** tolerable. —acˌcept**ˈability** *n*. —ac**ˈceptably** *adv*.

acceptance (əkˈsɛptəns) *n*. **1.** the act of accepting something. **2.** favourable reception. **3.** belief or assent.

accepted (əkˈsɛptɪd) *adj*. commonly approved or recognized; established.

access (ˈæksɛs) *n*. **1.** a means of approaching or entering a place. **2.** the condition of allowing entry, for example entry to a building by wheelchairs or prams. **3.** the right to approach, enter, or make use of something. ~*vb*. **4.** to obtain (information) from a computer. [Latin *accēdere* to accede]

accessible (əkˈsɛsəbʰl) *adj*. **1.** easy to approach, enter, or use. **2. accessible to**. **a.** obtainable by; available to. **b.** understandable by. —acˌcessi**ˈbility** *n*.

accession (ək'sɛʃən) *n.* the act of taking up an office or position: *accession to the throne.*

accessory (ək'sɛsərɪ) *n., pl.* **-ries. 1.** a supplementary part or object. **2.** a small accompanying item of dress, such as a belt. **3.** a person involved in a crime although absent during its commission. [Late Latin *accessōrius*]

access road *n.* a road providing a way to a particular place or on to a motorway.

access time *n.* the time required to retrieve a piece of stored information from a computer.

accident ('æksɪdənt) *n.* **1.** a mishap, usually one causing injury or death. **2.** an unforeseen event or one without apparent cause: *I met him by accident.* [Latin *accidere* to happen]

accidental (ˌæksɪ'dɛntˀl) *adj.* **1.** occurring by chance or unintentionally. ~*n.* **2.** *Music.* a symbol denoting that the following note is a sharp, flat, or natural that is not a part of the key signature. —ˌacci'dentally *adv.*

accident-prone *adj.* (of a person) often involved in accidents.

acclaim (ə'kleɪm) *vb.* **1.** to acknowledge publicly the excellence of (a person or act). **2.** to acknowledge publicly: *they acclaimed him king.* ~*n.* **3.** an enthusiastic expression of approval. [Latin *acclāmāre*]

acclamation (ˌæklə'meɪʃən) *n.* **1.** an enthusiastic reception or exhibition of approval. **2.** *Canad.* an instance of being elected without opposition.

acclimatize *or* **-tise** (ə'klaɪmə,taɪz) *vb.* to adapt to a new climate or environment. —ac,climati'zation *or* -ti'sation *n.*

accolade ('ækə,leɪd) *n.* **1.** an award, praise, or honour. **2.** a touch on the shoulder with a sword conferring knighthood. [Latin *ad-* to + *collum* neck]

accommodate (ə'kɒmə,deɪt) *vb.* **1.** to supply or provide (someone) with lodgings. **2.** to oblige or do a favour for (someone). **3.** to adapt. **4.** to have room for (someone or something). [Latin *accommodāre*]

accommodating (ə'kɒmə,deɪtɪŋ) *adj.* willing to help; obliging.

accommodation (ə,kɒmə'deɪʃən) *n.* **1.** lodgings. **2.** willingness to oblige.

accommodation address *n.* an address on letters to a person who cannot or does not wish to receive mail at a permanent address.

accompaniment (ə'kʌmpənɪmənt) *n.* **1.** something that accompanies something else. **2.** *Music.* a supporting part for an instrument, a band, or an orchestra.

accompanist (ə'kʌmpənɪst) *n.* a person who plays a musical accompaniment.

accompany (ə'kʌmpənɪ) *vb.* **-nying, -nied. 1.** to go along with. **2.** to occur or be associated with. **3.** to provide a musical accompaniment for. [Old French *accompaignier*]

accomplice (ə'kʌmplɪs) *n.* a person who helps another commit a crime. [Latin *complicāre* to complicate]

accomplish (ə'kʌmplɪʃ) *vb.* **1.** to manage to do; achieve. **2.** to complete. [Latin *complēre* to fill up]

accomplished (ə'kʌmplɪʃt) *adj.* **1.** expert; proficient. **2.** successfully completed.

accomplishment (ə'kʌmplɪʃmənt) *n.* **1.** the act of successfully completing something. **2.** something successfully completed. **3.** (*pl.*) social or other skills.

accord (ə'kɔːd) *n.* **1.** agreement; accordance. **2.** a settlement, for example between nations. **3. of one's own accord.** voluntarily. **4. with one accord.** unanimously. ~*vb.* **5.** (foll. by *with*) to fit in with or be consistent with. **6.** to grant; give: *he accorded the courtesy accorded him.* [Latin *ad-* to + *cor* heart]

accordance (ə'kɔːdəns) *n.* **in accordance with.** in conformity with.

according (ə'kɔːdɪŋ) *adj.* **1. according to. a.** as stated by. **b.** in conformity with. **2. according as.** depending on whether.

accordingly (ə'kɔːdɪŋlɪ) *adv.* **1.** in an appropriate manner. **2.** consequently.

accordion (ə'kɔːdɪən) *n.* a box-shaped musical instrument consisting of metallic reeds, a set of bellows controlled by the player's hands, and studs or keys by which notes are produced. [German] —ac'cordionist *n.*

accost (ə'kɒst) *vb.* to approach, stop, and speak to (a person), for example to ask a question or solicit sex. [Latin *ad-* to + *costa* side, rib]

account (ə'kaʊnt) *n.* **1.** a report or description. **2.** an explanation of conduct. **3.** importance or value: *it's of no account.* **4.** profit or advantage: *to good account.* **5.** part or behalf: *don't bother on my account.* **6.** *Finance.* a business relationship between a bank or other institution and a customer permitting the latter certain banking or credit services. **7.** a statement of financial transactions with the resulting balance. **8. call someone to account. a.** to insist that someone explains himself. **b.** to reprimand someone. **9. give a good account of oneself.** to perform well. **10. on account. a.** on credit. **b.** as partial payment. **11. on account of.** because of. **12. take account of** *or* **take into account.** to take into consideration; allow for. ~*vb.* **13.** to consider as: *he accounts himself poor.* [Old French *acont*]

accountable (ə'kaʊntəbˀl) *adj.* responsible to someone or for some action. —ac,count-a'bility *n.*

accountant (ə'kaʊntənt) *n.* a person concerned with the maintenance and auditing of business accounts. —ac'countancy *n.*

account for *vb.* **1.** to give reasons for. **2.** to make or provide a reckoning of (expenditure).

accounting (ə'kaʊntɪŋ) *n.* the skill or practice of maintaining and auditing business accounts.

accoutrements (ə'kuːtrəmənts) *or U.S.* **accouterments** (ə'kuːtərmənts) *pl. n.* clothing and equipment for a particular activity. [Old French *accoutrer* to equip]

accredit (əˈkrɛdɪt) vb. **1.** to give official recognition to. **2.** to certify as meeting required standards. **3.** to send (a diplomat) with official credentials to a particular country. **4.** to attribute (a quality or an action) to (a person). **5.** N.Z. to pass (a candidate for university entrance) on school recommendation, without external examination. [French *accréditer*] —**ac-,credi'tation** n.

accretion (əˈkriːʃən) n. **1.** a gradual increase in size, through growth or addition. **2.** something added, such as an extra layer. [Latin *accretiō*]

accrue (əˈkruː) vb. **-cruing, -crued. 1.** (of money or interest) to increase gradually over a period of time. **2.** (foll. by *to*) to fall naturally to. [Latin *accrēscere*]

accumulate (əˈkjuːmjʊˌleɪt) vb. to gather together in an increasing quantity; collect. [Latin *accumulāre* to heap up] —**ac'cumulative** adj.

accumulation (ə,kjuːmjʊˈleɪʃən) n. **1.** the act or process of collecting together or becoming collected. **2.** something that has been collected.

accumulator (əˈkjuːmjʊˌleɪtə) n. **1.** a rechargeable device for storing electrical energy. **2.** Horse racing, Brit. a collective bet on successive races, with both stake and winnings being carried forward to accumulate progressively.

accuracy (ˈækjʊrəsɪ) n. faithful representation of the truth; precision.

accurate (ˈækjʊrɪt) adj. faithfully representing the truth; precise. [Latin *accūrāre* to perform with care] —**'accurately** adv.

accursed (əˈkɜːsɪd) adj. **1.** hateful; detestable. **2.** under a curse.

accusation (,ækjʊˈzeɪʃən) n. **1.** an allegation that a person is guilty of some wrongdoing. **2.** a formal charge brought against a person.

accusative (əˈkjuːzətɪv) Grammar. ~adj. **1.** denoting the object case in some languages. ~n. **2.** the accusative case.

accuse (əˈkjuːz) vb. to charge (a person or persons) with wrongdoing. [Latin *accūsare*] —**ac'cuser** n. —**ac'cusing** adj. —**ac'cusingly** adv.

accused (əˈkjuːzd) n. the. Law. the defendant appearing on a criminal charge.

accustom (əˈkʌstəm) vb. (foll. by *to*) to make (oneself) familiar with or used to. [Old French *acostumer*]

accustomed (əˈkʌstəmd) adj. **1.** usual; customary. **2. accustomed to. a.** used to. **b.** in the habit of.

ace (eɪs) n. **1.** a playing card with one symbol on it. **2.** Tennis. a winning serve that the opponent fails to reach. **3.** a fighter pilot who has destroyed several enemy aircraft. **4.** Informal. an expert. **5. within an ace of.** very close to. ~adj. **6.** Informal. superb; excellent. [Latin *as* a unit]

acerbic (əˈsɜːbɪk) adj. harsh or bitter. [Latin *acerbus* sharp, sour]

acerbity (əˈsɜːbɪtɪ) n., pl. **-ties. 1.** embittered speech or temper. **2.** bitterness of taste.

acetaldehyde (,æsɪˈtældɪ,haɪd) n. Chem. a colourless volatile liquid, used as a solvent.

acetate (ˈæsɪˌteɪt) n. **1.** Chem. any salt or ester of acetic acid. **2.** Also: **acetate rayon.** a synthetic textile fibre made from cellulose acetate. **3.** an audio disc with an acetate lacquer coating.

acetic (əˈsiːtɪk) adj. Chem. of, containing, producing, or from acetic acid or vinegar. [Latin *acētum* vinegar]

acetic acid n. Chem. a strong-smelling colourless liquid used to make vinegar.

acetone (ˈæsɪˌtəʊn) n. Chem. a strong-smelling colourless liquid used as a solvent for paints and lacquers.

acetylene (əˈsɛtɪˌliːn) n. Chem. a colourless soluble flammable gas used in welding metals.

ache (eɪk) vb. **1.** to feel or be the source of a continuous dull pain. **2.** to suffer mental anguish. ~n. **3.** a continuous dull pain. [Old English *acan*]

achieve (əˈtʃiːv) vb. to gain (something) by hard work or effort. [Old French *a chef* to a head] —**a'chiever** n.

achievement (əˈtʃiːvmənt) n. **1.** something that has been accomplished by hard work, ability, or heroism. **2.** the condition of having been accomplished.

Achilles heel (əˈkɪliːz) n. a small but fatal weakness. [*Achilles* in Greek mythology was killed by an arrow in his unprotected heel]

Achilles tendon n. the fibrous cord that connects the muscles of the calf to the heelbone.

achromatic (,eɪkrəˈmætɪk) adj. **1.** without colour. **2.** refracting light without breaking it up into its component colours. **3.** Music. involving no sharps or flats. —,**achro'matically** adv.

acid (ˈæsɪd) n. **1.** any substance that when dissolved in water yields a sour corrosive solution, turning litmus red. **2.** a sour-tasting substance. **3.** Slang. LSD. ~adj. **4.** Chem. of, from, or containing acid. **5.** sharp or sour in taste. **6.** sharp in speech or manner. [Latin *acidus*] —**'acidly** adv.

Acid House or **Acid** n. a type of funk-based, electronically edited disco music of the late 1980s, which has hypnotic sound effects and which is associated with hippie culture and the use of the drug ecstasy. [*acid* (LSD) + *House* music]

acidic (əˈsɪdɪk) adj. containing acid.

acidify (əˈsɪdɪˌfaɪ) vb. **-fying, -fied.** to convert into acid.

acidity (əˈsɪdɪtɪ) n. **1.** the quality of being acid. **2.** the amount of acid in a solution.

acid rain n. rain containing pollutants released into the atmosphere by burning coal or oil.

acid test n. a rigorous and conclusive test of worth or value. [from the testing of gold with nitric acid]

acidulous (əˈsɪdjʊləs) adj. **1.** rather sour. **2.** sharp in speech or manner.

ack-ack (ˈæk,æk) n. Mil. anti-aircraft fire.

[World War I phonetic alphabet for AA, anti-aircraft]

acknowledge (ək'nɒlɪdʒ) *vb.* **1.** to recognize or admit the truth of (a statement). **2.** to indicate recognition of (a person) by a greeting or glance. **3.** to express gratitude for (a favour or compliment). **4.** to make known the receipt of (a letter or message). [Old English *oncnāwan* to understand]

acknowledgment *or* **acknowledgement** (ək'nɒlɪdʒmənt) *n.* **1.** the act of acknowledging something or someone. **2.** something done or given as an expression of gratitude.

acme ('ækmɪ) *n.* the highest point of achievement or excellence. [Greek *akmē*]

acne ('æknɪ) *n.* a skin disease in which pus-filled spots form on the face. [New Latin]

acolyte ('ækə,laɪt) *n.* **1.** a follower or attendant. **2.** *Christianity*. a person who assists a priest. [Greek *akolouthos*]

aconite ('ækə,naɪt) *n.* **1.** a poisonous plant with hoodlike flowers. **2.** dried aconite root, used as a narcotic. [Greek *akoniton*]

acorn ('eɪkɔːn) *n.* the fruit of the oak tree, consisting of a smooth nut in a scaly cuplike base. [Old English *æcern*]

acoustic (ə'kuːstɪk) *adj.* **1.** of sound, hearing, or acoustics. **2.** designed to absorb sound: *an acoustic hood*. **3.** (of a musical instrument) without electronic amplification. [Greek *akouein* to hear] —**a'coustically** *adv.*

acoustics (ə'kuːstɪks) *n.* **1.** (*functioning as sing.*) the scientific study of sound. **2.** (*functioning as pl.*) the characteristics of a room or theatre that determine how well sound can be heard within it.

acquaintance (ə'kweɪntəns) *n.* **1.** a person whom one knows slightly. **2.** slight knowledge of a person or subject. **3. make the acquaintance of.** to come into social contact with. **4.** those persons collectively whom one knows: *a lawyer of my acquaintance*.

acquainted (ə'kweɪntɪd) *adj.* **1.** on terms of familiarity but not intimacy. **2.** (foll. by *with*) familiar with: *acquainted with the facts*. [Latin *accognōscere* to know well]

acquiesce (,ækwɪ'ɛs) *vb.* to assent to someone's wishes without protest. [Latin *acquiēscere*] —,**acqui'escence** *n.* —,**acqui'escent** *adj.*

acquire (ə'kwaɪə) *vb.* to get or develop (something such as an object, trait, or ability). [Latin *acquīrere*] —**ac'quirement** *n.*

acquired taste *n.* **1.** a liking for something at first considered unpleasant. **2.** the thing liked.

acquisition (,ækwɪ'zɪʃən) *n.* **1.** the act of acquiring something. **2.** something acquired, often to add to a collection.

acquisitive (ə'kwɪzɪtɪv) *adj.* eager to acquire material possessions. —**ac'quisitively** *adv.* —**ac'quisitiveness** *n.*

acquit (ə'kwɪt) *vb.* **-quitting, -quitted. 1.** to pronounce (someone) not guilty: *he was acquitted of arson*. **2.** to conduct (oneself):

she acquitted herself well in the exams. [Old French *aquiter*] —**ac'quittal** *n.*

acre ('eɪkə) *n.* **1.** a unit of area equal to 4840 square yards or 4046.86 square metres. **2.** (*pl.*) **a.** a large area of land. **b.** *Informal*. a large amount: *acres of flesh*. [Old English *æcer*]

acreage ('eɪkərɪdʒ) *n.* land area in acres.

acrid ('ækrɪd) *adj.* **1.** unpleasantly strong-smelling. **2.** sharp in speech or manner. [Latin *ācer* sharp, sour] —**acridity** (ə'krɪdɪtɪ) *n.* —**acridly** *adv.*

acrimony ('ækrɪmənɪ) *n.* bitterness or sharpness of speech or manner. [Latin *ācer* sharp, sour] —**acrimonious** (,ækrɪ'məʊnɪəs) *adj.*

acrobat ('ækrə,bæt) *n.* an entertainer who performs acts that require skill, agility, and coordination, such as swinging from a trapeze. [Greek *akrobatēs* one who walks on tiptoe] —,**acro'batic** *adj.* —,**acro'batically** *adv.*

acrobatics (,ækrə'bætɪks) *pl. n.* the skills or feats of an acrobat.

acronym ('ækrənɪm) *n.* a word made from a series of initial letters or parts of words, for example *UNESCO* for the *United Nations Educational, Scientific, and Cultural Organization*. [Greek *akros* outermost + *onoma* name]

acrophobia (,ækrə'fəʊbɪə) *n.* abnormal fear of being at a great height. [Greek *akron* summit + *phobos* fear]

acropolis (ə'krɒpəlɪs) *n.* the citadel of an ancient Greek city. [Greek *akros* highest + *polis* city]

across (ə'krɒs) *prep.* **1.** from one side to the other side of. **2.** on or at the other side of. ~*adv.* **3.** from one side to the other. **4.** on or to the other side. [Old French *a croix* crosswise]

across-the-board *adj.* affecting everyone in a particular group or place equally: *an across-the-board pay rise*.

acrostic (ə'krɒstɪk) *n.* a number of lines of writing, such as a poem, in which the first or last letters form a word or proverb. [Greek *akros* outermost + *stikhos* line of verse]

acrylic (ə'krɪlɪk) *adj.* **1.** made of acrylic fibre or acrylic resin. ~*n.* **2.** short for **acrylic fibre** *or* **acrylic resin.** [Latin *ācer* sharp + *olēre* to smell]

acrylic acid *n. Chem.* a strong-smelling colourless corrosive liquid, used in the manufacture of acrylic resins.

acrylic fibre *n.* a man-made fibre used for clothes and blankets.

acrylic resin *n. Chem.* any of a group of polymers of acrylic acid, used as synthetic rubbers, in paints, and as plastics.

act (ækt) *n.* **1.** something done. **2.** a formal decision reached or law passed by a lawmaking body: *an act of parliament*. **3.** a major division of a play. **4.** a short performance, such as a sketch or dance. **5.** a pretended attitude. **6. get in on the act.** *Informal*. to become involved in something in order to share the benefit. **7. get one's act together.** *Informal*. to organize oneself. ~*vb.* **8.** to do something. **9.** to perform (a part or role) in a play, film, or broadcast. **10.** to present (a play) on stage. **11.** (foll. by *for*) to be a substitute for: *I'm acting for the headmaster.* **12.** (foll. by *as*) to serve the function of. **13.** to conduct oneself: *she acts like a lady.* **14.** to behave in an unnatural way. ~See also **act up.** [Latin *actum* a thing done]

acting ('æktɪŋ) *adj.* **1.** taking on duties temporarily: *the acting headmaster.* ~*n.* **2.** the art of an actor.

actinide series ('æktɪˌnaɪd) *n. Chem.* a series of 15 radioactive elements with increasing atomic numbers from actinium to lawrencium.

actinium (æk'tɪnɪəm) *n. Chem.* a radioactive element of the actinide series, occurring as a decay product of uranium. Symbol: Ac [Greek *aktis* ray]

action ('ækʃən) *n.* **1.** the process of doing something. **2.** something done. **3.** movement during some physical activity. **4.** activity, force, or energy. **5.** (*pl.*) behaviour. **6.** a lawsuit. **7.** the operating mechanism in a gun or machine. **8.** the way in which something operates or works. **9. out of action.** not functioning. **10. the action. a.** the events that form the plot of a story or play. **b.** *Slang.* the main activity in a place. **11.** *Mil.* **a.** a minor engagement. **b.** fighting.

actionable ('ækʃənəb^al) *adj. Law.* giving grounds for legal action.

action painting *n.* an art form in which paint is thrown, smeared, dripped, or spattered on the canvas.

action replay *n.* the rerunning of a small section of a television tape, for example of a sporting event, usually in slow motion.

action stations *pl. n.* the positions taken up by individuals in preparation for battle or for some other activity.

activate ('æktɪˌveɪt) *vb.* **1.** to make (something) active. **2.** *Physics.* to make (something) radioactive. **3.** *Chem.* to increase the rate of (a reaction).

active ('æktɪv) *adj.* **1.** moving, working, or doing something. **2.** busy and energetic. **3.** effective: *an active ingredient.* **4.** *Grammar.* denoting a form of a verb used to indicate that the subject is performing the action, for example *kicked* in *The boy kicked the football.* **5.** fully engaged in military service. **6.** (of a volcano) erupting periodically. ~*n.* **7.** *Grammar.* the active form of a verb. —**'actively** *adv.*

active list *n. Mil.* a list of officers available for full duty.

activism ('æktɪˌvɪzəm) *n.* a policy of taking direct action to achieve a political or social goal. —**'activist** *n.*

activity (æk'tɪvɪtɪ) *n.* **1.** the state of being active. **2.** lively movement. **3.** (*pl.* -**ties**) any specific action or pursuit: *recreational activities.*

act of God *n. Law.* a sudden occurrence caused by natural forces, such as a flood.

actor ('æktə) *or* (*fem.*) **actress** ('æktrɪs) *n.* a person who acts in a play, film, or broadcast.

actual ('æktʃʊəl) *adj.* existing in reality or as a matter of fact. [Latin *āctus* act]

actuality (ˌæktʃʊ'ælɪtɪ) *n., pl.* -**ties.** reality.

actually ('æktʃʊəlɪ) *adv.* as an actual fact; really.

actuary ('æktʃʊərɪ) *n., pl.* -**aries.** a statistician who calculates insurance risks, policy premiums, and dividends. [Latin *āctuārius* one who keeps accounts] —**actuarial** (ˌæktʃʊ'eərɪəl) *adj.*

actuate ('æktʃʊˌeɪt) *vb.* **1.** to start up (a mechanical device). **2.** to motivate (someone). [Medieval Latin *actuāre*]

act up *vb. Informal.* to behave in a troublesome way.

acuity (ə'kjuːɪtɪ) *n.* acuteness of vision or thought. [Latin *acūtus* acute]

acumen ('ækjʊˌmen) *n.* the ability to judge well; insight. [Latin: sharpness]

acupuncture ('ækjʊˌpʌŋktʃə) *n.* the practice of inserting needles into someone's skin at specific points to treat various disorders by stimulating nerve impulses. [Latin *acus* needle + *puncture*] —**'acuˌpuncturist** *n.*

acute (ə'kjuːt) *adj.* **1.** penetrating in perception or insight. **2.** sensitive; keen: *an acute sense of smell.* **3.** of extreme importance; crucial. **4.** severe or intense: *acute embarrassment.* **5.** *Maths.* (of an angle) less than 90°. **6.** (of a disease) sudden and severe. ~*n.* **7.** an acute accent. [Latin *acūtus*] —**a'cutely** *adv.* —**a'cuteness** *n.*

acute accent *n.* the mark (´), used in some languages to indicate that the vowel over which it is placed is pronounced in a certain way.

ad (æd) *n. Informal.* an advertisement.

A.D. *or* **AD** (indicating years numbered from the supposed year of the birth of Christ) in the year of the Lord. [Latin *anno Domini*]

ad- *prefix.* **1.** to; towards: *adverb.* **2.** near; next to: *adrenal.* [Latin. As a prefix in words of Latin origin, ad- became ac-, af-, ag-, al-, an-, acq-, ar-, as-, and at- before c, f, g, l, n, q, r, s, and t, and became a- before gn, sc, sp, and st]

adage ('ædɪdʒ) *n.* a traditional saying that is generally accepted as being true. [Latin *adagium*]

adagio (ə'dɑːdʒɪˌəʊ) *Music.* ~*adv.* **1.** slowly. ~*n., pl.* -**gios.** **2.** a movement or piece to be performed slowly. [Italian]

Adam ('ædəm) *n.* **1.** *Bible.* the first man (Genesis 2–3). **2. not know someone from Adam.** to have no knowledge of someone.

adamant ('ædəmənt) *adj.* unshakable in determination or purpose; inflexible. [Greek *adamas* unconquerable] —**'adamantly** *adv.*

Adam's apple *n.* the lump of thyroid cartilage at the front of a man's neck.

adapt (ə'dæpt) *vb.* **1.** (often foll. by *to*) to adjust (something or oneself) to different conditions. **2.** to modify (something) to suit a new purpose. [Latin *adaptāre*] —**a'daptable** *adj.* —**aˌdapta'bility** *n.*

adaptation (ˌædəp'teɪʃən) *n.* **1.** the act of

adapting. **2.** something that is produced by adapting something else.

adaptor *or* **adapter** ('ædæptə) *n.* **1.** a device used to connect several electrical appliances to a single socket. **2.** any device for connecting two parts of different sizes or types.

add (æd) *vb.* **1.** to combine (numbers or quantities) so as to make a larger number or quantity. **2.** to join (something) to something else so as to increase its size, effect, or scope: *to add insult to injury.* **3.** to say or write (something) further. **4. add in.** to include. ~See also **add up.** [Latin *addere*]

addendum (ə'dɛndəm) *n., pl.* **-da** (-də). **1.** an addition. **2.** an appendix to a book or magazine.

adder ('ædə) *n.* **1.** a common viper, found in Britain, which has a black zigzag pattern along the back. **2.** any of various similar snakes. [Old English *nædre*]

addict ('ædɪkt) *n.* **1.** a person who is addicted to narcotic drugs. **2.** *Informal.* a person who is devoted to something: *a TV addict.* [Latin *addictus* given over] —**ad'dictive** *adj.*

addicted (ə'dɪktɪd) *adj.* **1.** dependent on a narcotic drug. **2.** *Informal.* devoted to something: *addicted to chocolate.* —**ad'diction** *n.*

addition (ə'dɪʃən) *n.* **1.** the act of adding. **2.** a person or thing that is added. **3.** a mathematical operation in which the sum of two or more numbers or quantities is calculated. **4. in addition to.** besides; as well as. —**ad'ditional** *adj.*

additive ('ædɪtɪv) *n.* any substance added to something, such as food, to improve it or prevent deterioration.

addle ('æd°l) *vb.* **1.** to make (someone's mind or brain) confused. **2.** to make rotten: *addled eggs.* ~*adj.* **3.** indicating a confused state: *addle-brained.* [Old English *adela* filth]

address (ə'drɛs) *n.* **1.** the conventional form by which the location of a building is described. **2.** the place at which someone lives. **3.** a formal speech. **4.** *Computers.* a number giving the location of a piece of stored information. ~*vb.* **5.** to mark (a letter or parcel) with an address. **6.** to speak to (someone). **7. address oneself to. a.** to speak or write to. **b.** to apply oneself to: *he addressed himself to the task.* **8.** to direct (a message or warning) to someone. **9.** to direct one's attention to (a problem or an issue). [Latin *ad-* to + *directus* direct]

addressee (,ædrɛ'siː) *n.* a person to whom a letter or parcel is addressed.

adduce (ə'djuːs) *vb.* to cite (something) as evidence. [Latin *addūcere* to lead to]

add up *vb.* **1.** to calculate the sum of (two or more numbers or quantities). **2.** *Informal.* to make sense. **3.** (foll. by *to*) to amount to.

adenoidal (,ædɪ'nɔɪd°l) *adj.* having a nasal voice or impaired breathing because of enlarged adenoids.

adenoids ('ædɪ,nɔɪdz) *pl. n.* a mass of

tissue at the back of the throat. [Greek *adenoeidēs*]

adept *adj.* (ə'dɛpt). **1.** proficient in something requiring skill. ~*n.* ('ædɛpt). **2.** a person skilled in something. [Latin *ad-* to + *apiscī* to attain] —**a'deptness** *n.*

adequate ('ædɪkwɪt) *adj.* sufficient without being abundant or outstanding. [Latin *ad-* to + *aequus* equal] —**adequacy** ('ædɪkwəsɪ) *n.* —**'adequately** *adv.*

à deux ('ɑː 'dɜː) *adj., adv.* of or for two persons. [French]

adhere (əd'hɪə) *vb.* (foll. by *to*) **1.** to stick to. **2.** to be devoted to (a political party or religion). **3.** to follow (a rule) exactly. [Latin *adhaerēre*]

adherent (əd'hɪərənt) *n.* **1.** a supporter or follower. ~*adj.* **2.** sticking or attached. —**ad'herence** *n.*

adhesion (əd'hiːʒən) *n.* **1.** the quality or condition of sticking together. **2.** attachment, for example to a political party or religion. **3.** *Pathol.* the joining together of two structures or parts of the body that are normally separate, for example after surgery.

adhesive (əd'hiːsɪv) *adj.* **1.** able or designed to stick to things. ~*n.* **2.** a substance used for sticking things together.

ad hoc (æd 'hɒk) *adj., adv.* for a particular purpose only. [Latin: to this]

adieu (ə'djuː) *interj., n., pl.* **adieus** *or* **adieux** (ə'djuːz). goodbye. [French]

ad infinitum (æd ,ɪnfɪ'naɪtəm) *adv.* endlessly: *and so on ad infinitum.* [Latin]

adipose ('ædɪ,pəʊs) *adj.* of or containing fat; fatty: *adipose tissue.* [Latin *adeps* fat]

adj. adjective.

adjacent (ə'dʒeɪs°nt) *adj.* next: *the adjacent room; the house adjacent to ours.* [Latin *ad-* near + *jacēre* to lie]

adjective ('ædʒɪktɪv) *n.* a word that describes a noun or pronoun. [Latin *ad-* to + *jacere* to throw] —**adjectival** (,ædʒɪk'taɪv°l) *adj.*

adjoin (ə'dʒɔɪn) *vb.* to be next to and joined onto. —**ad'joining** *adj.*

adjourn (ə'dʒɜːn) *vb.* **1.** (of a court) to close at the end of a session. **2.** to postpone or be postponed. **3.** *Informal.* to go elsewhere: *shall we adjourn to the pub?* [Old French *ajourner* to defer to an arranged day] —**ad'journment** *n.*

adjudge (ə'dʒʌdʒ) *vb.* to declare (someone) to be something specified: *he was adjudged guilty.*

adjudicate (ə'dʒuːdɪ,keɪt) *vb.* **1.** to give a formal decision on (a dispute). **2.** to serve as a judge, for example in a competition. [Latin *adjūdicāre*] —**ad,judi'cation** *n.* —**ad'judi,cator** *n.*

adjunct ('ædʒʌŋkt) *n.* **1.** something added that is not essential. **2.** a person who is subordinate to another. [Latin *adjunctus*]

adjure (ə'dʒʊə) *vb.* **1.** to command (someone) to do something. **2.** to appeal earnestly to (someone). [Latin *adjūrāre*] —**adjuration** (,ædʒʊə'reɪʃən) *n.*

adjust (ə'dʒʌst) *vb.* **1.** to alter (something) slightly, so as to achieve accuracy. **2.** to adapt to a new environment. **3.** to arrange (one's clothing). **4.** *Insurance.* to determine the amount payable in settlement of (a claim). [Old French *adjuster*] —**ad'justable** *adj.* —**ad'juster** *n.*

adjustment (ə'dʒʌstmənt) *n.* **1.** the act of adjusting. **2.** a slight alteration.

adjutant ('ædʒətənt) *n.* an officer in an army who acts as administrative assistant to a superior. [Latin *adjūtāre* to aid]

ad-lib (æd'lɪb) *vb.* **-libbing, -libbed. 1.** to improvise while speaking. ∼*adj.* **2.** improvised: *an ad-lib remark.* ∼*n.* **3.** an improvised remark. ∼*adv.* **ad lib. 4.** spontaneously; freely. [short for Latin *ad libitum*, lit.: according to pleasure]

Adm. Admiral.

adman ('ædˌmæn) *n., pl.* **-men.** *Informal.* a man who works in advertising.

admin ('ædmɪn) *n. Informal.* administration.

administer (əd'mɪnɪstə) *vb.* **1.** to manage (an organization or estate). **2.** to dispense: *administer justice.* **3.** to give (medicine) to someone. **4.** to supervise the taking of (an oath). [Latin *ad-* to + *ministrāre* to minister]

administrate (əd'mɪnɪˌstreɪt) *vb.* to manage (an organization).

administration (ədˌmɪnɪ'streɪʃən) *n.* **1.** management of the affairs of an organization. **2.** the duties of an administrator. **3.** the people who administer an organization. **4.** a government: *the Reagan administration.* **5.** the act of administering something, such as medicine or an oath. —**ad'ministrative** *adj.*

administrator (əd'mɪnɪˌstreɪtə) *n.* a person who administers an organization or estate.

admirable ('ædmərəbᵊl) *adj.* deserving or inspiring admiration; excellent. —**'admirably** *adv.*

admiral ('ædmərəl) *n.* **1.** Also called: **admiral of the fleet.** a naval officer of the highest rank. **2.** any of various brightly coloured butterflies. [Arabic *amīr-al* commander of]

Admiralty ('ædmərəltɪ) *n.* the government department in charge of naval affairs.

admire (əd'maɪə) *vb.* to regard (someone or something) with esteem or approval. [Latin *admīrārī*] —**admiration** (ˌædmə'reɪʃən) *n.* —**ad'mirer** *n.* —**ad'miring** *adj.* —**ad'miringly** *adv.*

admissible (əd'mɪsəbᵊl) *adj. Law.* (of evidence) capable of being admitted in a court of law.

admission (əd'mɪʃən) *n.* **1.** permission or the right to enter. **2.** the price charged for entrance. **3.** acceptance for a position or as a member of an institution. **4.** a confession: *he was, by his own admission, a compulsive gambler.*

admit (əd'mɪt) *vb.* **-mitting, -mitted. 1.** to confess or acknowledge (a crime or mistake). **2.** to concede (the truth of something). **3.** to allow to enter. **4.** (foll. by *to*) to allow (someone) to participate in something. **5. admit of.** to allow for: *his plan does not admit of defeat.* [Latin *admittere*]

admittance (əd'mɪt'ns) *n.* **1.** the right to enter. **2.** the act of giving entrance.

admittedly (əd'mɪtɪdlɪ) *adv.* willingly conceded: *admittedly I am afraid.*

admixture (əd'mɪkstʃə) *n.* **1.** a mixture. **2.** an ingredient.

admonish (əd'mɒnɪʃ) *vb.* to reprove (someone) firmly but not harshly. [Latin *admonēre*] —**admonition** (ˌædmə'nɪʃən) *n.* —**ad'monitory** *adj.*

ad nauseam (æd 'nɔːzɪˌæm) *adv.* to a disgusting extent: *she went on and on ad nauseam about her new job.* [Latin: to (the point of) nausea]

ado (ə'duː) *n.* bustling activity; fuss: *without more ado.* [Middle English *at do* a to-do]

adobe (ə'dəʊbɪ) *n.* **1.** a sun-dried brick. **2.** a building constructed of such bricks. **3.** the clayey material from which such bricks are made. [Spanish]

adolescence (ˌædə'lesəns) *n.* the period between puberty and adulthood. [Latin *adolēscere* to grow up]

adolescent (ˌædə'les'nt) *adj.* **1.** of or relating to adolescence. **2.** *Informal.* (of behaviour) immature. ∼*n.* **3.** an adolescent person.

Adonis (ə'dəʊnɪs) *n.* a handsome young man. [name of a handsome youth in Greek myth]

adopt (ə'dɒpt) *vb.* **1.** *Law.* to take (someone else's child) as one's own. **2.** to choose (a plan or method). **3.** to choose (a country or name) to be one's own. [Latin *adoptāre*] —**a'doption** *n.*

adoptive (ə'dɒptɪv) *adj.* due to adoption: *an adoptive parent.*

adorable (ə'dɔːrəb'l) *adj.* very attractive; lovable.

adore (ə'dɔː) *vb.* **1.** to love (someone) intensely or deeply. **2.** to worship (a god) with religious rites. **3.** *Informal.* to like very much: *I adore chocolate.* [Latin *adōrāre*] —**adoration** (ˌædə'reɪʃən) *n.* —**a'doring** *adj.* —**a'doringly** *adv.*

adorn (ə'dɔːn) *vb.* to decorate; increase the beauty or distinction of. [Latin *adōrnāre*] —**a'dornment** *n.*

ADP automatic data processing.

adrenal (ə'driːn'l) *adj. Anat.* **1.** on or near the kidneys. **2.** of or relating to the adrenal glands. [Latin *ad-* near + *rēnēs* kidneys]

adrenal glands *pl. n. Anat.* two endocrine glands covering the upper surface of the kidneys.

adrenaline or **adrenalin** (ə'drenəlɪn) *n. Biochem.* a hormone secreted by the adrenal gland in response to stress. It increases heart rate, pulse rate, and blood pressure.

adrift (ə'drɪft) *adj., adv.* **1.** drifting. **2.** without purpose. **3.** *Informal.* off course.

adroit (ə'drɔɪt) *adj.* **1.** skilful or dexterous. **2.** quick: *mentally adroit.* [French *à droit* rightly] —**a'droitly** *adv.* —**a'droitness** *n.*

adsorb (əd'sɔːb) *vb.* (of a substance such as a gas) to accumulate on the surface of a solid, forming a thin film. [Latin *ad-* to +

sorbēre to drink in] —**ad'sorbent** *adj.* —**adsorption** (ədˈsɔːpʃən) *n.*

ADT Atlantic Daylight Time.

adulation (ˌædjʊˈleɪʃən) *n.* uncritical admiration. [Latin *adūlāri*]

adult (ˈædʌlt, əˈdʌlt) *n.* **1.** a mature fully grown person, animal, or plant. ~*adj.* **2.** having reached maturity; fully developed. **3.** of or intended for mature people. [Latin *adultus* grown up] —**'adulthood** *n.*

adulterant (əˈdʌltərənt) *n.* **1.** a substance that adulterates. ~*adj.* **2.** adulterating.

adulterate (əˈdʌltəˌreɪt) *vb.* to debase (something) by adding inferior material. [Latin *adulterāre*] —**a,dulter'ation** *n.*

adulterer (əˈdʌltərə) *or (fem.)* **adulteress** *n.* a person who has committed adultery.

adultery (əˈdʌltərɪ) *n., pl.* **-teries.** sexual intercourse between a married person and someone other than his or her spouse. [Latin *adulterium*] —**a'dulterous** *adj.*

adumbrate (ˈædʌmˌbreɪt) *vb.* **1.** to give a faint indication of. **2.** to obscure. [Latin *adumbrāre* to cast a shadow on] —**,adum-'bration** *n.*

adv. adverb.

ad valorem (æd vəˈlɔːrəm) *adj., adv.* (of taxes) in proportion to the estimated value of the goods taxed. [Latin]

advance (ədˈvɑːns) *vb.* **1.** to go or bring forward. **2.** (foll. by *on*) to move towards (someone) in a threatening manner. **3.** to present (an idea) for consideration. **4.** to further (a cause). ~*n.* **5.** to lend (someone a sum of money). ~*n.* **6.** a forward movement. **7.** improvement. **8.** a payment made before it is legally due. **9.** a loan of money. **10.** an increase in price: *any advance on fifty pounds?* **11. in advance. a.** beforehand. **b.** (foll. by *of*) ahead of in time or development. **12.** (*modifier*) previous: *advance booking.* ~See also **advances.** [Latin *ab-* away + *ante* before]

advanced (ədˈvɑːnst) *adj.* **1.** ahead in development, knowledge, or progress. **2.** in a comparatively late stage: *a man of advanced age.*

Advanced level *n.* a formal name for **A level.**

advancement (ədˈvɑːnsmənt) *n.* promotion in rank or status.

advances (ədˈvɑːnsɪz) *pl. n.* overtures made in an attempt to start a romantic or sexual relationship with someone.

advantage (ədˈvɑːntɪdʒ) *n.* **1.** a more favourable position; superiority. **2.** benefit or profit: *to my advantage.* **3.** Tennis. the point scored after deuce. **4. take advantage of. a.** to make good use of. **b.** to impose upon the weakness or good nature of. **c.** to seduce. **5. to advantage.** to good effect. [Latin *abante* from before]

advantaged (ədˈvɑːntɪdʒd) *adj.* in a superior social or financial position.

advantageous (ˌædvənˈteɪdʒəs) *adj.* producing advantage. —**,advan'tageously** *adv.*

advection (ədˈvɛkʃən) *n.* the transference

of heat in a horizontal stream of gas. [Latin *ad-* to + *vehere* to carry]

advent (ˈædvɛnt) *n.* an arrival: *before the advent of television.* [Latin *ad-* to + *venīre* to come]

Advent (ˈædvɛnt) *n.* the season that includes the four Sundays preceding Christmas.

Adventist (ˈædvɛntɪst) *n.* a member of a Christian group that believes that the Second Coming of Christ is imminent.

adventitious (ˌædvɛnˈtɪʃəs) *adj.* added or appearing accidentally. [Latin *adventicius* coming from outside]

adventure (ədˈvɛntʃə) *n.* **1.** a risky undertaking of unknown outcome. **2.** exciting or unexpected events. [Latin *advenīre* to happen to (someone), arrive]

adventure playground *n. Brit.* a playground for children that contains building materials and other equipment to build with or climb on.

adventurer (ədˈvɛntʃərə) *or (fem.)* **adventuress** *n.* **1.** a person who seeks adventure. **2.** a person who seeks money or power by unscrupulous means.

adventurism (ədˈvɛntʃəˌrɪzəm) *n.* recklessness in politics or finance.

adventurous (ədˈvɛntʃərəs) *adj.* daring or enterprising.

adverb (ˈædvɜːb) *n.* a word that modifies a sentence, verb, adverb, or adjective, for example *easily, very,* and *happily* in *They could easily envy the very happily married couple.* [Latin *adverbium,* lit.: added word] —**ad'verbial** *adj.*

adversary (ˈædvəsərɪ) *n., pl.* **-saries.** an opponent in a fight, disagreement, or sporting contest. [Latin *adversus* against]

adverse (ˈædvɜːs) *adj.* **1.** antagonistic; hostile. **2.** unfavourable to one's interests: *adverse circumstances.* [Latin *ad-* towards + *vertere* to turn] —**'adversely** *adv.*

adversity (ədˈvɜːsɪtɪ) *n., pl.* **-ties.** affliction; hardship.

advert (ˈædvɜːt) *n. Informal.* an advertisement.

advertise (ˈædvəˌtaɪz) *vb.* **1.** to present or praise (goods or a service) to the public, in order to encourage sales. **2.** to make (a vacancy, an event, or an article for sale) publicly known. [Latin *advertere* to turn one's attention to] —**'adver,tiser** *n.* —**'adver,tising** *n.*

advertisement (ədˈvɜːtɪsmənt) *n.* any public announcement designed to sell goods or publicize an event.

advice (ədˈvaɪs) *n.* **1.** recommendation as to appropriate choice of action. **2.** formal notification of facts. [Latin *ad* to + *vīsum* view]

advisable (ədˈvaɪzəbˈl) *adj.* worthy of recommendation; prudent. —**ad,visa'bility** *n.*

advise (ədˈvaɪz) *vb.* **1.** to offer advice to (someone). **2.** to inform or notify (someone). [Latin *ad-* to + *vidēre* to see] —**ad-'viser** *or* **ad'visor** *n.*

advisedly (ədˈvaɪzɪdlɪ) *adv.* deliberately; after careful consideration: *I use the word advisedly.*

advisory (əd'vaizəri) adj. empowered to make recommendations.

advocaat ('ædvəʊ,kɑː) n. a liqueur with a raw egg base. [Dutch]

advocacy ('ædvəkəsɪ) n. active support of a cause or course of action.

advocate vb. ('ædvə,keit). 1. to recommend (a course of action) publicly. ~n. ('ædvəkɪt). 2. a person who upholds or defends a cause or course of action. 3. a person who speaks on behalf of another in a court of law. 4. Scots Law. a barrister. [Latin advocāre to call, summon]

adze or U.S. **adz** (ædz) n. a tool with a blade at right angles to the handle, used for shaping timber. [Old English adesa]

AEA Atomic Energy Authority.

AEC U.S. Atomic Energy Commission.

aegis ('iːdʒɪs) n. **under the aegis of.** with the sponsorship or protection of. [Greek aigis shield of Zeus]

aeolian harp (iː'əʊlɪən) n. a musical instrument that produces sounds when the wind passes over its strings. [after Aeolus, god of winds in Greek myth]

aeon or U.S. **eon** ('iːən) n. 1. an immeasurably long period of time. 2. the longest division of geological time; two or more eras. [Greek aiōn]

aerate ('ɛəreɪt) vb. to put gas into (a liquid), for example when making fizzy drinks. —**aer¹ation** n.

aerial ('ɛərɪəl) adj. 1. existing, moving, or operating in the air. 2. extending high into the air. 3. of or relating to aircraft. ~n. 4. the part of a radio or television system which transmits or receives radio waves. [Greek aēr air]

aero ('ɛərəʊ) n. (modifier) of or relating to aircraft or aeronautics.

aero-, **aeri-**, or **aer-** combining form. 1. denoting air, atmosphere, or gas. 2. denoting aircraft. [Greek aēr air]

aerobatics (,ɛərəʊ'bætɪks) n. (functioning as sing. or pl.) spectacular manoeuvres, such as loops or rolls, performed by aircraft. [AERO- + (ACRO)BATICS]

aerobic (ɛə'rəʊbɪk) adj. designed for or relating to aerobics: aerobic shoes; aerobic dances.

aerobics (ɛə'rəʊbɪks) n. (functioning as sing.) exercises to increase the amount of oxygen in the blood and strengthen the heart and lungs.

aerodrome ('ɛərə,drəʊm) n. a small airport.

aerodynamics (,ɛərəʊdaɪ'næmɪks) n. (functioning as sing.) the study of the dynamics of air and gases and of bodies passing through air. —**aerody¹namic** adj.

aero engine n. an engine for an aircraft.

aerofoil ('ɛərəʊ,fɔɪl) n. a cross section of the wing, fin, or rotor blade of an aircraft.

aerogram ('ɛərə,græm) n. an air-mail letter on a single sheet of light paper that folds and is sealed to form an envelope.

aerolite ('ɛərə,laɪt) n. a stony meteorite.

aeronautics (,ɛərə'nɔːtɪks) n. (functioning as sing.) the study or practice of flight through the air. —**aero¹nautical** adj.

aeroplane ('ɛərə,pleɪn) or U.S. & Canad. **airplane** n. a heavier-than-air powered flying vehicle with fixed wings. [French aéroplane, from AERO- + Greek -planos wandering]

aerosol ('ɛərə,sɒl) n. a small metal pressurized container from which a substance can be dispensed in a fine spray. [AERO- + SOL(UTION)]

aerospace ('ɛərə,speɪs) n. 1. the earth's atmosphere and space beyond. 2. (modifier) of rockets or space vehicles: the aerospace industry.

aerostatics (,ɛərə'stætɪks) n. (functioning as sing.) the study of gases in equilibrium and bodies held in equilibrium in gases.

aesthete or U.S. **esthete** ('iːsθiːt) n. a person who has or who affects a highly developed appreciation of beauty.

aesthetic or U.S. **esthetic** (ɪs'θetɪk) adj. relating to the appreciation of art and beauty. [Greek aisthanesthai to perceive, feel] —**aes¹thetically** or U.S. **es¹thetically** adv. —**aestheticism** or U.S. **estheticism** (ɪs'θetɪ,sɪzəm) n.

aesthetics or U.S. **esthetics** (ɪs'θetɪks) n. (functioning as sing.) 1. the branch of philosophy concerned with the study of the concepts of beauty and taste. 2. the study of the rules and principles of art.

aether ('iːθə) n. same as **ether** (senses 2, 3).

a.f. audio frequency.

afar (ə'fɑː) n. **from afar.** from a great distance.

affable ('æfəb²l) adj. showing warmth and friendliness; easy to talk to. [Latin affābilis] —**,affa¹bility** n. —**¹affably** adv.

affair (ə'fɛə) n. 1. a thing to be done or attended to: it's not my affair. 2. an event or happening: the Profumo affair. 3. something previously specified: our house is a tumbledown affair. 4. a sexual relationship outside marriage. [Old French à faire to do]

affairs (ə'fɛəz) pl. n. 1. personal or business interests. 2. matters of public interest: current affairs.

affect¹ (ə'fekt) vb. 1. to influence (someone or something): the postal strike will affect us all. 2. to move (someone) emotionally: I was deeply affected by that film. 3. (of pain or disease) to attack: measles affects mainly children. [Latin afficere]

affect² (ə'fekt) vb. 1. to put on a show of: to affect ignorance. 2. to wear or use by preference: he affects a white straw hat. [Latin affectāre to strive after]

affectation (,æfek'teɪʃən) n. an attitude or manner put on to impress others.

affected (ə'fektɪd) adj. 1. behaving or speaking in a manner put on to impress others. 2. pretended: affected indifference.

affecting (ə'fektɪŋ) adj. arousing feelings of pity; moving.

affection (ə'fekʃən) n. 1. fondness or

tenderness for a person or thing. **2.** (pl.) emotions: *to play on his affections*.

affectionate (ə'fekʃənɪt) *adj.* having or displaying tenderness, affection, or warmth. —**af'fectionately** *adv.*

affianced (ə'faɪənst) *adj. Old-fashioned.* engaged to be married. [Medieval Latin *affidāre* to trust (oneself) to]

affidavit (ˌæfɪ'deɪvɪt) *n. Law.* a declaration in writing made upon oath. [Medieval Latin, lit.: he declares on oath]

affiliate *vb.* (ə'fɪlɪˌeɪt). **1.** (foll. by *to* or *with*) to bring (someone) into close connection or association with a larger body or group. ~*n.* (ə'fɪlɪt). **2.** a person or organization that is affiliated with another. [Medieval Latin *affiliātus* adopted as a son] —**af,fili'ation** *n.*

affiliation order *n. Law.* an order that the father of an illegitimate child shall contribute towards the child's maintenance.

affinity (ə'fɪnɪtɪ) *n., pl.* -**ties.** **1.** a feeling of closeness to and understanding of a person. **2.** a close similarity in appearance, structure, or quality. [Latin *affinis* bordering on, related]

affirm (ə'fɜːm) *vb.* **1.** to declare (something) to be true. **2.** to uphold or confirm (an idea or a belief). [Latin *ad-* to + *firmāre* to make firm] —**affirmation** (ˌæfə'meɪʃən) *n.*

affirmative (ə'fɜːmətɪv) *adj.* **1.** indicating agreement: *an affirmative reply*. ~*n.* **2.** a word or phrase indicating agreement, such as *yes*.

affix *vb.* (ə'fɪks). **1.** to attach or fasten. ~*n.* ('æfɪks). **2.** a word or syllable added to a word to produce a derived or inflected form, as *-ment* in *establishment*. [Medieval Latin *affixāre*]

afflict (ə'flɪkt) *vb.* to cause (someone) suffering or unhappiness. [Latin *afflīgere* to knock against]

affliction (ə'flɪkʃən) *n.* **1.** a condition of great distress or suffering. **2.** something that causes physical or mental suffering.

affluent ('æfluənt) *adj.* rich; wealthy. [Latin *ad-* to + *fluere* to flow] —**'affluence** *n.*

affluent society *n.* a society in which the material benefits of prosperity are widely available.

afford (ə'fɔːd) *vb.* **1.** (preceded by *can* or *could*) to be able to do or spare something without risking financial difficulties or undesirable consequences. **2.** to give or supply: *the union affords us some protection*. [Old English *geforthian* to further, promote] —**af'fordable** *adj.*

afforest (ə'fɒrɪst) *vb.* to plant trees on. [Medieval Latin *afforestāre*] —**af,forest'ation** *n.*

affray (ə'freɪ) *n.* a noisy fight in a public place. [Vulgar Latin *exfridāre* (unattested) to break the peace]

affront (ə'frʌnt) *n.* **1.** a deliberate insult. ~*vb.* **2.** to insult; offend the pride or dignity of. [Old French *afronter* to strike in the face]

Afghan ('æfgæn) *n.* **1.** a person from

Afghanistan. ~*adj.* **2.** of Afghanistan or its people.

Afghan hound *n.* a large slim dog with long silky hair.

aficionado (ə,fɪsjə'nɑːdəʊ) *n., pl.* -**dos.** a devotee of some sport or pastime. [Spanish]

afield (ə'fiːld) *adv.* **far afield.** far away.

aflame (ə'fleɪm) *adj., adv.* **1.** in flames. **2.** deeply aroused: *aflame with desire*.

afloat (ə'fləʊt) *adj., adv.* **1.** floating. **2.** aboard ship; at sea. **3.** free of debt: *to keep the business afloat*.

afoot (ə'fʊt) *adj., adv.* in operation; astir: *there's trouble afoot*.

afore (ə'fɔː) *adv., prep., conj. Archaic or dialect.* before.

aforementioned (ə'fɔːˌmenʃənd) *adj.* mentioned before.

aforesaid (ə'fɔːˌsɛd) *adj.* referred to previously.

aforethought (ə'fɔːˌθɔːt) *adj.* premeditated: *malice aforethought*.

a fortiori (eɪ ˌfɔːtɪ'ɔːraɪ) *adv.* for similar but more convincing reasons. [Latin]

Afr. Africa(n).

afraid (ə'freɪd) *adj.* **1.** feeling fear or apprehension. **2.** regretful: *I'm afraid I can't help you*. [Medieval English *affraied* frightened]

afresh (ə'freʃ) *adv.* once more; anew.

African ('æfrɪkən) *adj.* **1.** of Africa or its peoples or languages. ~*n.* **2.** a person from Africa.

Africana (ˌæfrɪ'kɑːnə) *n.* objects of cultural or historical interest from Africa.

Africander (ˌæfrɪ'kændə) *n.* a breed of humpbacked cattle originally from southern Africa. [Afrikaans]

African lily *n.* a S African plant with blue or white funnel-shaped flowers.

African time *n. S. African slang.* unpunctuality.

African violet *n.* a flowering house plant with hairy leaves.

Afrikaans (ˌæfrɪ'kɑːns, -'kɑːnz) *n.* an official language of South Africa, closely related to Dutch and Flemish. [Dutch]

Afrikaner (ˌæfrɪ'kɑːnə) *n.* a White native of South Africa whose native language is Afrikaans.

Afro ('æfrəʊ) *n., pl.* -**ros.** a wide frizzy bushy hairstyle.

Afro- *combining form.* indicating Africa or African: *Afro-Asiatic*.

Afro-American *n.* **1.** an American Black. ~*adj.* **2.** of American Blacks, their history, or their culture.

aft (ɑːft) *adv., adj. Chiefly naut.* towards or at the rear. [earlier *abaft*]

after ('ɑːftə) *prep.* **1.** following in time or place. **2.** in pursuit of: *he's only after your money*. **3.** concerning: *to inquire after someone's health*. **4.** considering: *after what you have done, you shouldn't complain*. **5.** next in excellence or importance to. **6.** in imitation of; in the manner of. **7.** in accordance with: *a man after my own heart*. **8.** the same name as: *I'm called after my grandmother*. **9.** *U.S.* past (the hour of): *twenty after three.* **10. after all. a.** in spite of everything: *it's only a game after all.* **b.** in spite of expectations or efforts. **11. after you.** please go before me. ~*adv.* **12.** at a later time; afterwards. ~*conj.* **13.** at a time later than the time when: *after they left, the party really livened up.* ~*adj.* **14.** *Naut.* further aft: *the after cabin.* [Old English *æfter*]

afterbirth ('ɑːftə,bɜːθ) *n.* the placenta and fetal membranes expelled from the mother's womb after the birth of a baby or young animal.

aftercare ('ɑːftə,kɛə) *n.* the help and support given to a person discharged from a hospital or prison.

afterdamp ('ɑːftə,dæmp) *n.* a poisonous gas formed after the explosion of firedamp in a coal mine.

aftereffect ('ɑːftər,ɪfɛkt) *n.* any result occurring some time after its cause.

afterglow ('ɑːftə,gləʊ) *n.* **1.** the glow left after the source of a light has disappeared, for example after sunset. **2.** a pleasant feeling remaining after an enjoyable experience.

afterlife ('ɑːftə,laɪf) *n.* life after death or at a later time in a person's lifetime.

aftermath ('ɑːftə,mæθ) *n.* signs or results of an event considered collectively: *the aftermath of war.* [*after* + Old English *mæth* a mowing]

aftermost ('ɑːftə,məʊst) *adj.* closest to the rear; last.

afternoon (,ɑːftə'nuːn) *n.* the period between noon and evening.

afterpains ('ɑːftə,peɪnz) *pl. n.* pains caused by contraction of a woman's womb after childbirth.

afters ('ɑːftəz) *n. Brit. informal.* dessert; sweet.

aftershave ('ɑːftə,ʃeɪv) *n.* a scented lotion applied to a man's face after shaving.

aftershock ('ɑːftə,ʃɒk) *n.* one of a series of minor tremors occurring after the main shock of an earthquake.

aftertaste ('ɑːftə,teɪst) *n.* a taste that lingers on after eating or drinking.

afterthought ('ɑːftə,θɔːt) *n.* **1.** something thought of after the opportunity to use it has passed. **2.** an addition to something already completed.

afterwards ('ɑːftəwədz) *or* **afterward** *adv.* after an earlier event or time. [Old English *æfterweard*]

Ag *Chem.* silver. [Latin *argentum*]

again (ə'gɛn, ə'geɪn) *adv.* **1.** another or a second time: *do it again.* **2.** once more in a previously experienced state or condition: *here we are again.* **3.** in addition to the original amount: *half as much again.* **4.** on the other hand. **5.** moreover; furthermore. **6. again and again.** continually; repeatedly. [Old English *ongegn* opposite to]

against (ə'gɛnst, ə'geɪnst) *prep.* **1.** standing or leaning beside: *a ladder against the wall.* **2.** coming in contact with: *he bumped against me.* **3.** in contrast to: *silhouettes are outlines against a light background.* **4.** opposed to; in disagree-

ment with. **5.** having an unfavourable effect on: *the system works against small companies.* **6.** as a protection from: *a safeguard against contaminated water.* **7.** in exchange for. **8. as against.** as opposed to; as compared with. [Middle English *ageines*]

agape (ə'geɪp) *adj.* **1.** (of the mouth) wide open. **2.** (of a person) very surprised.

agar ('eɪgə) *or* **agar-agar** *n.* a jelly-like substance obtained from certain seaweeds and used as a culture medium for bacteria and for thickening food. [Malay]

agaric ('ægərɪk) *n.* any fungus with gills on the underside of the cap, for example the edible mushroom. [Greek *agarikon*]

agate ('ægɪt) *n.* a hard semiprecious form of quartz with striped colouring. [Greek *akhatēs*]

agave (ə'geɪvɪ) *n.* a tropical Amercian plant with tall flower spikes rising from thick fleshy leaves. [Greek *agauos* illustrious]

age (eɪdʒ) *n.* **1.** the period of time that a person, animal, or plant has lived. **2.** the period of time that something, such as an object or group, has existed. **3.** a period or state of human life. **4.** the latter part of human life. **5.** a period of history marked by some feature. **6.** (*pl.*) *Informal.* a long time. **7. come of age.** to become legally responsible for one's actions (usually at 18 years). ~*vb.* **aging** *or* **ageing, aged.** **8.** to become old. **9.** to begin to seem older or cause (someone) to seem older: *she has aged a lot in the past year; that hairstyle ages her.* [Latin *aetās*]

-age *suffix forming nouns.* indicating: **1.** a collection or set: *baggage.* **2.** an action or its result: *breakage.* **3.** a state or relationship: *bondage.* **4.** a house or place: *orphanage.* **5.** a charge or rate: *postage.* [Late Latin *-āticum* belonging to]

aged *adj.* **1.** ('eɪdʒɪd) advanced in years; old. **2.** (eɪdʒd) having the age of: *a woman aged twenty.*

ageing *or* **aging** ('eɪdʒɪŋ) *n.* **1.** the fact or process of growing old. ~*adj.* **2.** becoming or appearing older.

ageless ('eɪdʒlɪs) *adj.* **1.** apparently never growing old. **2.** timeless; eternal.

agency ('eɪdʒənsɪ) *n., pl.* **-cies. 1.** an organization providing a specific service: *an employment agency.* **2.** the business or functions of an agent. **3.** *Old-fashioned.* action or power: *we met through the agency of fate.* [Latin *agere* to do]

agenda (ə'dʒɛndə) *n.* a schedule or list of items to be attended to, for example at a meeting. [Latin: things to be done]

agent ('eɪdʒənt) *n.* **1.** a person who acts on behalf of another person or organization. **2.** a person or thing that is the means or cause of something happening. **3.** a substance or organism that exerts some force or effect: *a chemical agent.* **4.** a travelling salesman.

agent provocateur ('æʒɒn prə,vɒkə'tɜː) *n., pl* **agents provocateurs** ('æʒɒn prə,vɒkə'tɜː). a secret agent who provokes people to commit illegal acts and so be discredited or liable to punishment. [French]

age-old *adj.* very old; ancient.

agglomerate *vb.* (ə'glɒmə,reɪt). **1.** to form or be formed into a mass. ~*n.* (ə'glɒmərɪt). **2.** a confused mass. **3.** a volcanic rock consisting of fused angular fragments of rock. ~*adj.* (ə'glɒmərɪt). **4.** formed into a mass. [Latin *agglomerāre*] —**ag,glomer'ation** *n.*

agglutinate (ə'gluːtɪ,neɪt) *vb.* to stick with or as if with glue. [Latin *agglūtināre*] —**agglutination** (ə,gluːtɪ'neɪʃən) *n.*

aggrandize *or* **-dise** (ə'grændaɪz) *vb.* to increase the power, wealth, prestige, or scope of. [Old French *aggrandir*] —**aggrandizement** *or* **-disement** (ə'grændɪzmənt) *n.*

aggravate ('ægrə,veɪt) *vb.* **1.** to make (a disease, situation or problem) worse. **2.** *Informal.* to annoy. [Latin *aggravāre* to make heavier] —**aggra,vating** *adj.* —,**aggra'vation** *n.*

aggregate *n.* ('ægrɪgɪt). **1.** an amount or total formed from separate units. **2.** *Geol.* a rock, such as granite, consisting of a mixture of minerals. **3.** the sand and stone mixed with cement and water to make concrete. **4. in the aggregate.** taken as a whole. ~*adj.* ('ægrɪgɪt). **5.** formed of separate units collected into a whole. ~*vb.* ('ægrɪ,geɪt). **6.** to combine or be combined into a whole. **7.** to amount to (a particular number). [Latin *aggregāre* to add to a flock or herd] —,**aggre'gation** *n.*

aggression (ə'greʃən) *n.* a tendency to make unprovoked attacks or an instance of unprovoked attack. [Latin *aggrēdi* to attack] —**ag'gressor** *n.*

aggressive (ə'gresɪv) *adj.* **1.** quarrelsome or belligerent. **2.** assertive; vigorous. —**ag'gressively** *adv.*

aggrieved (ə'griːvd) *adj.* upset and angry. [Latin *aggravāre* to aggravate]

aggro ('ægrəʊ) *n. Brit. slang.* aggressive behaviour. [from *aggravation*]

aghast (ə'gɑːst) *adj.* overcome with amazement or horror. [Old English *gǣstan* to frighten]

agile ('ædʒaɪl) *adj.* **1.** quick in movement; nimble. **2.** mentally quick or acute. [Latin *agilis*] —**agility** (ə'dʒɪlɪtɪ) *n.*

agin (ə'gɪn) *prep. Informal or dialect.* against: *I'm agin capital punishment.* [obs. *again* against]

agitate ('ædʒɪ,teɪt) *vb.* **1.** to excite, disturb, or trouble (someone). **2.** to shake, stir, or disturb (a liquid). **3.** to attempt to stir up public opinion for or against something. [Latin *agitāre*] —**'agi,tated** *adj.* —'**agi,tatedly** *adv.* —,**agi'tation** (,ædʒɪ-'teɪʃən) *n.* —'**agi,tator** *n.*

agitprop ('ædʒɪt,prɒp) *n.* any promotion of political propaganda. [Russian *Agitprop-byuro*]

agley (ə'glaɪ) *adv. Scot.* awry; askew. [from *gley* squint]

aglitter (ə'glɪtə) *adj.* sparkling; glittering.

aglow (ə'gləʊ) *adj.* glowing.

aglu *or* **agloo** ('ægluː) *n. Canad.* a breathing hole made in ice by a seal. [Eskimo]

AGM annual general meeting.

agnostic (æg'nɒstɪk) *n.* **1.** a person who believes that it is impossible to know whether God exists. **2.** a person who claims that the answer to some specific question cannot be known with certainty. ~*adj.* **3.** of or relating to agnostics. [A- + GNOSTIC] —**agnosticism** (æg'nɒstɪ,sɪzəm) *n.*

ago (ə'gəʊ) *adv.* in the past: *years ago.* [Old English *āgān* to pass away]

agog (ə'gɒg) *adj.* eager or curious. [Old French *en gogues* in merriments]

agonize *or* **-nise** ('ægə,naɪz) *vb.* **1.** to suffer or cause (someone) to suffer agony. **2.** to struggle; strive. —'**ago,nizing** *or* -,**nising** *adj.* —'**ago,nizingly** *or* -,**nisingly** *adv.*

agony ('ægənɪ) *n., pl.* **-nies.** acute physical or mental pain. [Greek *agōn* contest]

agony aunt *n.* a person who replies to readers' letters in an agony column.

agony column *n.* a newspaper or magazine feature offering advice on readers' personal problems.

agoraphobia (,ægərə'fəʊbɪə) *n.* an illogical fear of open spaces. [Greek *agora* marketplace + *phobos* fear] —,**agora'phobic** *adj., n.*

AGR advanced gas-cooled reactor.

agrarian (ə'grɛərɪən) *adj.* of or relating to land or agriculture. [Latin *ager* field] —**a'grarianism** *n.*

agree (ə'griː) *vb.* **agreeing, agreed. 1.** (often foll. by *with*) to be of the same opinion (as). **2.** to give assent; consent. **3.** to reach a joint decision: *we agreed on a price for the car.* **4.** (foll. by *with*) to be consistent with. **5.** (foll. by *with*) to be agreeable or suitable to (one's health or appearance): *prawns don't agree with me.* **6.** to concede: *they agreed that the price was too high.* **7.** *Grammar.* to be the same in number, gender, and case as a connected word. [Old French *a gre* at will]

agreeable (ə'griːəb'l) *adj.* **1.** pleasing; pleasant. **2.** prepared to consent: *we would like to move in right away if you are agreeable.* —**a'greeably** *adv.*

agreement (ə'griːmənt) *n.* **1.** the act or state of agreeing. **2.** a settlement, esp. one that is legally enforceable, or the document containing it.

agriculture ('ægrɪ,kʌltʃə) *n.* the rearing of crops and livestock; farming. [Latin *ager* field + *cultūra* cultivation] —,**agri'cultural** *adj.* —,**agri'culturalist** *n.*

agrimony ('ægrɪmənɪ) *n.* a plant with long spikes of small yellow flowers and bristly burlike fruits. [Greek *argemōnē*]

agronomy (ə'grɒnəmɪ) *n.* the science of land cultivation, soil management, and crop production. [Greek *agros* field + *nemein* to manage] —**a'gronomist** *n.*

aground (ə'graʊnd) *adv.* onto the ground: *the ship ran aground.*

ague ('eɪgjuː) *n.* **1.** malarial fever with successive stages of fever and chills. **2.** a fit of shivering. [Old French (*fievre*) *ague* acute fever]

ah (ɑː) *interj.* an exclamation expressing pleasure, pain, sympathy, etc., according to the intonation of the speaker.

aha (ɑːˈhɑː) *interj.* an exclamation expressing triumph, surprise, etc., according to the intonation of the speaker.

ahead (əˈhɛd) *adv.* **1.** at or in the front; before. **2.** forwards: *go straight ahead.* **3. get ahead.** to achieve success. ~*adj.* **4.** in a leading position: *Cram is ahead with one lap to go.*

ahem (əˈhɛm) *interj.* a clearing of the throat, used to attract attention or express doubt.

ahoy (əˈhɔɪ) *interj. Naut.* a hail used to call a ship or to attract attention.

AI 1. artificial insemination. **2.** artificial intelligence.

aid (eɪd) *vb.* **1.** to help financially or in other ways. ~*n.* **2.** assistance; help; support. **3.** a person or device that helps or assists. [Latin *adjūtāre*]

Aid *or* **-aid** *n. combining form.* denoting a charitable organization that raises money for a particular cause: *Band Aid; Ferryaid.*

AID artificial insemination by donor.

aide (eɪd) *n.* an assistant: *the President's aides.*

aide-de-camp (ˈeɪd də ˈkɒŋ) *n., pl.* **aides-de-camp.** a military officer serving as personal assistant to a senior. [French: camp assistant]

AIDS (eɪdz) acquired immunodeficiency syndrome: a viral disease that destroys the body's ability to fight infection.

AIH artificial insemination by husband.

ail (eɪl) *vb. Literary.* **1.** to trouble; afflict. **2.** to feel unwell. [Old English *eglan*]

aileron (ˈeɪlərɒn) *n.* a hinged flap on the back of an aircraft wing which controls rolling. [French *aile* wing]

ailing (ˈeɪlɪŋ) *adj.* unwell over a long period.

ailment (ˈeɪlmənt) *n.* a slight illness.

aim (eɪm) *vb.* **1.** to point (a weapon or missile) or direct (a blow or remark) at a particular person or object. **2.** to propose or intend: *I aim to finish by Friday.* ~*n.* **3.** the action of directing something at an object. **4. take aim.** to point a weapon or missile at a person or object. **5.** intention; purpose. [Latin *aestimāre* to estimate]

aimless (ˈeɪmlɪs) *adj.* having no purpose or direction. —**ˈaimlessly** *adv.*

ain't (eɪnt) *Not standard.* am not, is not, are not, have not, *or* has not: *I ain't seen it.*

air (ɛə) *n.* **1.** the mixture of gases that forms the earth's atmosphere. It consists chiefly of nitrogen, oxygen, argon, and carbon dioxide. **2.** the space above and around the earth; sky. **3.** a breeze; slight wind. **4.** a distinctive quality, appearance, or manner: *an air of authority.* **5.** a simple tune. **6.** transportation in aircraft: *we're going by air.* **7. in the air.** in circulation; current: *there's a rumour in the air.* **8. into thin air.** leaving no trace behind. **9. on the air.** in the act of broadcasting on

radio or television. **10. up in the air.** uncertain. ~*vb.* **11.** to let fresh air into (a room) so as to cool or freshen it. **12.** to expose or be exposed to warm or heated air so as to dry: *to air linen.* **13.** to make known publicly: *to air one's opinions.* ~See also **airs.** [Greek *aēr*]

air base *n.* a centre from which military aircraft operate.

airborne (ˈɛəˌbɔːn) *adj.* **1.** carried by air. **2.** (of aircraft) flying; in the air.

air brake *n.* a brake in heavy vehicles that is operated by compressed air.

airbrick (ˈɛəˌbrɪk) *n. Chiefly Brit.* a brick with holes in it, put into the wall of a building for ventilation.

airbus (ˈɛəˌbʌs) *n.* a short-distance airliner.

air chief marshal *n.* a very senior officer in an air force.

air commodore *n.* a senior officer in an air force.

air conditioning *n.* a system for controlling the temperature and humidity of the air in a building. —**ˈair-conˌditioned** *adj.* —**air conditioner** *n.*

aircraft (ˈɛəˌkrɑːft) *n., pl.* **-craft.** any machine capable of flying, such as a glider or aeroplane.

aircraft carrier *n.* a warship with a long flat deck for the launching and landing of aircraft.

aircraftman (ˈɛəˌkrɑːftmən) *n., pl.* **-men.** a serviceman of the most junior rank in an air force. —**ˈaircraftˌwoman** *fem. n.*

air cushion *n.* **1.** an inflatable cushion. **2.** the pocket of air that supports a hovercraft.

Airedale (ˈɛəˌdeɪl) *n.* a large rough-haired tan-coloured terrier with a black back. [district in Yorkshire]

airfield (ˈɛəˌfiːld) *n.* a landing and taking-off area for aircraft.

air force *n.* the branch of a nation's armed services that is responsible for air warfare.

air gun *n.* a gun fired by means of compressed air.

air hostess *n.* a stewardess on an airliner.

airily (ˈɛərɪlɪ) *adv.* **1.** in a jaunty or high-spirited manner. **2.** in a light or delicate manner.

airing (ˈɛərɪŋ) *n.* **1.** exposure to air or warmth for drying or ventilation. **2.** exposure to public debate: *I shall give my proposal an airing at tomorrow's meeting.*

airing cupboard *n.* a heated cupboard in which laundry is aired and kept dry.

airless (ˈɛəlɪs) *adj.* lacking fresh air; stuffy.

air letter *n.* same as **aerogram.**

airlift (ˈɛəˌlɪft) *n.* **1.** the transportation by air of troops or cargo when other routes are blocked. ~*vb.* **2.** to transport by an airlift.

airline (ˈɛəˌlaɪn) *n.* an organization that provides scheduled flights for passengers or cargo.

airliner ('εə,laɪnə) n. a large passenger aircraft.

airlock ('εə,lɒk) n. 1. a bubble in a pipe causing an obstruction. 2. an airtight chamber used to gain access to a space that has air under pressure in it.

air mail n. 1. the system of conveying mail by aircraft. 2. mail conveyed by aircraft.

airman ('εəmən) n., pl. -**men**. a man serving in an air force.

air marshal n. 1. a senior Royal Air Force officer of equivalent rank to a vice admiral in the Royal Navy. 2. a Royal New Zealand Air Force officer of the highest rank when chief of defence forces.

airplane ('εə,pleɪn) n. U.S. & Canad. an aeroplane.

airplay ('εə,pleɪ) n. (of a gramophone record) the fact of being played on radio.

air pocket n. a small descending air current that causes an aircraft to lose height suddenly.

airport ('εə,pɔːt) n. a landing and taking-off area for civil aircraft, with facilities for aircraft maintenance and passenger arrival and departure.

air pump n. a device for pumping air into or out of something.

air raid n. an attack by enemy aircraft.

air rifle n. a rifle fired by means of compressed air.

airs (εəz) pl. n. manners put on to impress people: to put on airs.

airship ('εə,ʃɪp) n. a lighter-than-air self-propelled aircraft.

airsick ('εə,sɪk) adj. nauseated from travelling in an aircraft.

airspace ('εə,speɪs) n. the atmosphere above a particular country.

airspeed ('εə,spiːd) n. the speed of an aircraft relative to the air in which it moves.

airstrip ('εə,strɪp) n. a cleared area for the landing and taking-off of aircraft.

air terminal n. a building in a city from which air passengers are transported to an airport.

airtight ('εə,taɪt) adj. 1. sealed so that air cannot enter. 2. having no weak points: an airtight argument.

air vice-marshal n. a senior officer in an air force.

airwaves ('εə,weɪvz) pl. n. Informal. radio waves used in radio and television broadcasting.

airy ('εərɪ) adj. **airier, airiest. 1.** (of a room or building) spacious and well ventilated. **2.** jaunty; nonchalant. **3.** fanciful; insubstantial: airy promises.

aisle (aɪl) n. a passageway separating seating areas in a church, theatre, or cinema, or separating rows of shelves in a supermarket. [Latin āla wing]

aitch (eɪtʃ) n. the letter h. [phonetic spelling]

aitchbone ('eɪtʃ,bəʊn) n. a cut of beef from the rump bone. [Latin natis buttock]

ajar (ə'dʒɑː) adj., adv. (of a door) slightly open. [Old English cierran to turn]

AK Alaska.

akimbo (ə'kɪmbəʊ) adv. (**with**) **arms akimbo.** with hands on hips and elbows turned out. [in kenebowe in kene (i.e. sharp) bow]

akin (ə'kɪn) adj. **akin to.** similar to; very close to: that is akin to murder.

Al Chem. aluminium.

AL or **Ala.** Alabama.

à la (ɑː lɑː) prep. 1. in the manner or style of. 2. as prepared in, by, or for. [French]

alabaster ('ælə,bɑːstə) n. a kind of white stone used for making statues and vases. [Greek alabastros]

à la carte (ɑː lɑː 'kɑːt) adj., adv. (of a menu) having dishes individually priced. [French]

alacrity (ə'lækrɪtɪ) n. speed; eagerness: we accepted with alacrity. [Latin alacer lively]

à la mode (ɑː lɑː 'məʊd) adj. fashionable. [French]

alarm (ə'lɑːm) n. 1. fear aroused by awareness of danger. 2. a noise warning of danger: sound the alarm. 3. a device that transmits a warning, such as the bell or buzzer in an alarm clock. 4. short for **alarm clock.** ~vb. 5. to fill (someone) with fear. 6. to warn (someone) about danger. [Old Italian all'arme to arms] —a'larming adj.

alarm clock n. a clock that sounds at a set time to wake a person up.

alarmist (ə'lɑːmɪst) n. 1. a person who alarms others needlessly. ~adj. 2. alarming others needlessly.

alas (ə'læs) adv. 1. unfortunately; regrettably: there were, alas, none left. ~interj. 2. Archaic. an exclamation of grief or alarm. [Old French ha las!]

Alas. Alaska.

alb (ælb) n. a long white linen robe worn by a Christian priest. [Latin albus white]

albacore ('ælbə,kɔː) n. a sea fish with very long pectoral fins that is a valued food fish. [Arabic]

albatross ('ælbə,trɒs) n. a large bird of cool southern oceans that has very long wings. [Portuguese alcatraz pelican]

albeit (ɔːl'biːɪt) conj. even though. [Middle English al be it although it be (that)]

albino (æl'biːnəʊ) n., pl. -**nos.** a person or animal with white or almost white hair and skin and pinkish eyes. [Latin albus white] —**albinism** ('ælbɪ,nɪzəm) n.

Albion ('ælbɪən) n. Archaic or poetic. Britain or England. [Latin]

album ('ælbəm) n. 1. a book with blank pages, for keeping photographs or stamps in. 2. a long-playing record. [Latin: blank tablet]

albumen ('ælbjʊmɪn) n. 1. egg white. 2. Biochem. same as **albumin.** [Latin albus white]

albumin or **albumen** ('ælbjʊmɪn) n. Biochem. a water-soluble protein found in blood plasma, egg white, milk, and muscle.

alchemy ('ælkəmɪ) n. a medieval form of chemistry concerned with trying to change base metals into gold and to find an elixir to prolong life indefinitely. [Arabic *al* the + *kīmiyā* transmutation]—**'alchemist** *n*.

alcohol ('ælkə,hɒl) *n*. **1.** a colourless flammable liquid, the active principle of intoxicating drinks. **2.** intoxicating drinks generally. [Arabic *al-kuhl*]

alcoholic (,ælkə'hɒlɪk) *n*. **1.** a person who is addicted to alcohol. ~*adj*. **2.** of or relating to alcohol.

alcoholism ('ælkəhɒ,lɪzəm) *n*. a condition in which dependence on alcohol harms a person's health and everyday life.

alcove ('ælkəʊv) *n*. a recess in the wall of a room. [Arabic *al-qubbah* the vault]

aldehyde ('ældɪ,haɪd) *n. Chem.* any organic compound containing the group -CHO, derived from alcohol by oxidation. [New Latin *al(cohol) dehyd(rogenātum)* dehydrogenated alcohol]

alder ('ɔːldə) *n*. a tree with toothed leaves and conelike fruits, which grows in damp places. [Old English *alor*]

alderman ('ɔːldəmən) *n., pl.* **-men. 1.** (in England and Wales until 1974) a senior member of a local council, elected by other councillors. **2.** (in the U.S. and Canada) a member of the governing body of a city. [Old English *ealdor* chief + *mann* man]

ale (eɪl) *n*. **1.** an alcoholic drink made by fermenting a cereal such as barley, originally without hops. **2.** *Chiefly Brit.* beer. [Old English *alu, ealu*]

aleatory ('eɪlɪətərɪ) *adj*. dependent on chance. [Latin *ālea* game of chance]

alehouse ('eɪl,haʊs) *n. Archaic.* a public house.

alembic (ə'lɛmbɪk) *n*. **1.** an obsolete type of container used for distillation. **2.** anything that distils or purifies things. [Arabic *al-anbīq* the still]

alert (ə'lɜːt) *adj*. **1.** watchful and attentive. **2. alert to.** aware of. ~*n*. **3.** a warning or the period during which a warning remains in effect. **4. on the alert.** watchful. ~*vb*. **5.** to warn (someone) of danger. **6.** (foll. by *to*) to make (someone) aware of (a fact). [Italian *all'erta* on the watch]

A level *n. Brit.* **1.** the advanced level of a subject taken for the General Certificate of Education. **2.** a pass in a subject at A level.

alfalfa (æl'fælfə) *n*. a plant widely used for feeding farm animals. [Arabic *al-fasfasah*]

alfresco (æl'frɛskəʊ) *adj., adv.* in the open air. [Italian]

algae ('ældʒiː) *pl. n., sing.* **alga** ('ælgə). plants which grow in water or moist ground, and which have no true stems, roots, or leaves. [Latin *alga* seaweed]

algebra ('ældʒɪbrə) *n*. a branch of mathematics in which arithmetical operations are generalized by using symbols to represent numbers. [Arabic *al-jabr* the reunion of broken parts] —**algebraic** (,ældʒɪ'breɪɪk) *adj*.

ALGOL ('ælgɒl) *n*. a computer programming language designed for mathematical and scientific purposes. [*alg(orithmic) o(riented) l(anguage)*]

algorism ('ælgə,rɪzəm) *n*. the Arabic or decimal system of counting. [from *al-Khuwārizmi*, 9th-cent. Persian mathematician]

algorithm ('ælgə,rɪðəm) *n*. a logical arithmetical or computational procedure for solving problems. [changed from *algorism*]

alias ('eɪlɪəs) *adv*. **1.** also known as: *William Bonney, alias Billy the Kid.* ~*n., pl.* **-ases. 2.** a false name. [Latin *alius* other]

alibi ('ælɪ,baɪ) *n., pl.* **-bis. 1.** *Law.* a plea of being elsewhere at the time a crime was committed. **2.** *Informal.* an excuse. ~*vb.* **3.** to provide (someone) with an alibi. [Latin *alibī* elsewhere]

alien ('eɪlɪən) *n*. **1.** a person who is a citizen of a country other than the one in which he lives. **2.** a person who does not seem to fit in with his environment. **3.** a being from another world. ~*adj*. **4.** foreign. **5.** (foll. by *to*) repugnant or opposed to: *deceit is alien to her nature.* **6.** from another world. [Latin *alius* other]

alienable ('eɪlɪənəb'l) *adj. Law.* transferable to another owner.

alienate ('eɪlɪə,neɪt) *vb*. **1.** to cause (a friend) to become unfriendly or hostile. **2.** *Law.* to transfer the ownership of (property) to another person. —,**alien'ation** *n*.

alight¹ (ə'laɪt) *vb*. alighting, alighted *or* **alit. 1.** (foll. by *from*) to step out of (a vehicle). **2.** to land: *birds alighting on the lawn.* [Old English *ālīhtan*]

alight² (ə'laɪt) *adj., adv.* **1.** on fire. **2.** illuminated.

align (ə'laɪn) *vb*. **1.** to place in a line. **2.** to bring (parts) into proper coordination. **3.** to bring (a person or country) into agreement with the policy of another. [Old French *à ligne* into line] —a**'lignment** *n*.

alike (ə'laɪk) *adj*. **1.** similar: *the two brothers are very alike.* ~*adv*. **2.** in a similar manner: *we think alike.* **3.** considered together: *men and women alike.* [Old English *gelīc*]

alimentary (,ælɪ'mɛntrɪ) *adj*. of or relating to nutrition.

alimentary canal *n*. the tubular passage in the body through which food is passed and digested.

alimony ('ælɪmənɪ) *n. Law.* (formerly) an allowance paid under a court order by one spouse to another after separation. [Latin *alere* to nourish]

A-line ('eɪ,laɪn) *adj*. (of a skirt) slightly flared.

aliphatic (,ælɪ'fætɪk) *adj. Chem.* (of an organic compound) having an open chain structure. [Greek *aleiphar* oil]

aliquant ('ælɪkwənt) *adj. Maths.* denoting or belonging to a number that is not an exact divisor of a given number. [Latin *aliquantus* somewhat]

aliquot ('ælɪ,kwɒt) *adj. Maths.* denoting or belonging to an exact divisor of a number. [Latin: several]

alive (ə'laɪv) *adj*. **1.** living; having life. **2.** in existence: *the way to keep your marriage alive.* **3.** lively. **4. alive to.** aware of; sensitive to. **5. alive with.** teeming with. [Old English *on life* in life]

alkali (ˈælkəˌlaɪ) *n*. **1.** *Chem.* a soluble base or a solution of a base. **2.** a soluble mineral salt that occurs in arid soils. [Arabic *al-qili* the ashes (of saltwort)]

alkaline (ˈælkəˌlaɪn) *adj. Chem.* having the properties of or containing an alkali. —**alkalinity** (ˌælkəˈlɪnɪtɪ) *n*.

alkaloid (ˈælkəˌlɔɪd) *n. Chem.* any of a group of nitrogenous compounds found in plants. Many are poisonous and some are used as drugs.

all (ɔːl) *det*. **1.** the whole quantity or number (of): *all the rice; all are welcome*. **2.** every one of a class: *all men are mortal*. **3.** the greatest possible: *in all earnestness*. **4.** any whatever: *beyond all doubt*. **5. all along.** since the beginning. **6. all but.** nearly. **7. all in all.** everything considered. **8. all over. a.** finished. **b.** everywhere in or on: *all over the world*. **c.** *Informal.* typically: *that's him all over*. **9. all the.** so much (more or less) than otherwise: *we must work all the faster now*. **10. at all.** used for emphasis: *nothing at all; I'm surprised you came at all*. **11. be all for.** *Informal.* to be strongly in favour of. **12. for all.** in spite of: *for all my pushing, I still couldn't move it*. **13. in all.** altogether: *there were five in all*. ~*adv*. **14.** (in scores of games) each: *the score was three all*. ~*n*. **15. give one's all.** to make the greatest possible effort. [Old English *eall*]

Allah (ˈælə) *n*. the name of God in Islam.

allay (əˈleɪ) *vb*. to relieve (pain or grief) or reduce (fear or anger). [Old English *ālecgan* to put down]

all clear *n*. a signal indicating that danger is over.

allegation (ˌælɪˈɡeɪʃən) *n*. an unproved assertion or accusation.

allege (əˈlɛdʒ) *vb*. to state (something) without proof. [Latin *allēgāre* to dispatch on a mission]

alleged (əˈlɛdʒd) *adj*. stated to be such: *the alleged rape*. —**allegedly** (əˈlɛdʒɪdlɪ) *adv*.

allegiance (əˈliːdʒəns) *n*. loyalty or dedication to a person, cause, or belief. [Old French *lige* liege]

allegory (ˈælɪɡərɪ) *n., pl*. **-ries.** a poem, play, or story in which the characters and events have a moral or spiritual meaning. [Greek *allēgorein* to speak figuratively] —**alleˈgorical** *adj*. —**ˈallego ˌrize** *or* **-ˌrise** *vb*.

allegretto (ˌælɪˈɡrɛtəʊ) *Music.* ~*adv*. **1.** fairly quickly or briskly. ~*n., pl*. **-tos.** **2.** a piece or passage to be performed fairly quickly or briskly. [Italian]

allegro (əˈlɛɡrəʊ) *Music.* ~*adv*. **1.** in a brisk lively manner. ~*n., pl*. **-gros.** **2.** a piece or passage to be performed in a brisk lively manner. [Italian]

alleluia (ˌælɪˈluːjə) *interj*. praise the Lord! [Hebrew *halleluyah*]

allergen (ˈæləˌdʒɛn) *n*. a substance capable of causing an allergy. —**ˌallerˈgenic** *adj*.

allergic (əˈlɜːdʒɪk) *adj*. **1.** having or caused by an allergy. **2.** (foll. by *to*)

Informal. having an aversion to: *allergic to work*.

allergy (ˈælədʒɪ) *n., pl*. **-gies.** **1.** extreme sensitivity to a substance such as a food or pollen, which causes the body to react to any contact with it. **2.** *Informal.* an aversion. [Greek *allos* other + *ergon* activity]

alleviate (əˈliːvɪˌeɪt) *vb*. to lessen (pain or suffering). [Latin *levis* light] —**alˌleviˈation** *n*.

alley[1] (ˈælɪ) *n*. **1.** a narrow passage between or behind buildings. **2. a.** a building containing lanes for tenpin bowling. **b.** a long narrow wooden lane down which the ball is rolled in tenpin bowling. **3.** a path in a garden, often lined with trees. [Latin *ambulāre* to walk]

alley[2] (ˈælɪ) *n*. a large playing marble. [from *alabaster*]

alleyway (ˈælɪˌweɪ) *n*. a narrow passage; alley.

all found *adj*. (of charges for accommodation) inclusive of meals, heating, and other living expenses.

Allhallows (ˌɔːlˈhæləʊz) *n*. same as **All Saints' Day.**

alliance (əˈlaɪəns) *n*. **1.** the state of being allied. **2.** a formal agreement between two or more countries or political parties to work together. **3.** the countries or parties involved. [Old French *alier* to ally]

allied (ˈælaɪd) *adj*. united by a common aim or common characteristics.

alligator (ˈælɪˌɡeɪtə) *n*. a large reptile of the southern U.S. and China, similar to the crocodile but with a shorter broader snout. [Spanish *el lagarto* the lizard]

all in *adj*. **1.** *Informal.* exhausted. **2.** (of wrestling) freestyle. ~*adv*. **3.** with all expenses included.

alliteration (əˌlɪtəˈreɪʃən) *n*. the use of the same letter at the beginning of each word or each stressed word in a phrase or line of verse, as in *round the rock the ragged rascal ran*. [Latin *litera* letter] —**alˈliterative** *adj*.

allocate (ˈæləˌkeɪt) *vb*. to assign (something) to someone or for a particular purpose. [Latin *locus* a place] —**alloˈcation** *n*.

allopathy (əˈlɒpəθɪ) *n. Med.* a method of treating a disease by using remedies that will produce effects that are opposed to the symptoms of the disease. [Greek *allos* other + *pathos* suffering] —**allopathic** (ˌæləˈpæθɪk) *adj*.

allot (əˈlɒt) *vb*. **-lotting, -lotted.** to assign (something) to someone or for a particular purpose. [Old French *lot* portion]

allotment (əˈlɒtmənt) *n*. **1.** a portion allotted. **2.** *Brit.* a small piece of land rented by a person to grow vegetables on.

allotrope (ˈæləˌtrəʊp) *n. Chem.* any of two or more physical forms in which an element can exist.

allotropy (əˈlɒtrəpɪ) *n. Chem.* the existence of an element in two or more physical forms. [Greek *allos* other + *tropos* manner] —**allotropic** (ˌæləˈtrɒpɪk) *adj*.

all-out adj. Informal. using one's maximum powers.

allow (ə'laʊ) vb. **1.** to permit (someone) to do something. **2.** to set aside: five hours were allowed to do the job. **3.** to acknowledge (a point or claim). **4.** **allow for.** to take into account. [Late Latin allaudāre to extol] —**al'lowable** adj.

allowance (ə'laʊəns) n. **1.** an amount of money or food given at regular intervals. **2.** (in Britain) an amount of a person's income that is not subject to income tax. **3.** **make allowances for.** **a.** to treat or judge (someone) less severely because he has special problems. **b.** to take (something) into account in one's plans.

allowedly (ə'laʊɪdlɪ) adv. by general admission; admittedly.

alloy ('ælɔɪ) n. **1.** a mixture of two or more metals. ~vb. **2.** to mix (metals) in order to obtain a substance with a desired property. [Latin alligāre to bind]

all-purpose adj. useful for many purposes.

all right adj. **1.** adequate; satisfactory. **2.** unharmed; safe. ~interj. **3.** an expression of approval or agreement. ~adv. **4.** satisfactorily. **5.** safely. **6.** without doubt.

all-round adj. **1.** having many skills; versatile: an all-round player. **2.** comprehensive: an all-round education.

all-rounder n. a person with many skills, for example a cricketer who is good at both batting and bowling.

All Saints' Day n. a Christian festival celebrated on Nov. 1 to honour all the saints.

All Souls' Day n. R.C. Church. a day of prayer (Nov. 2) for the dead in purgatory.

allspice ('ɔːl,spaɪs) n. a spice used in cooking, which comes from the berries of a tropical American tree.

all-time adj. Informal. unsurpassed: he's one of the all-time greats.

allude (ə'luːd) vb. (foll. by to) to refer indirectly to. [Latin allūdere to play]

allure (ə'lʊə) vb. **1.** to entice or attract (someone). ~n. **2.** attractiveness; appeal. [Old French alurer] —**al'luring** adj.

allusion (ə'luːʒən) n. an indirect reference.

alluvial (ə'luːvɪəl) adj. **1.** of or relating to alluvium. ~n. **2.** same as **alluvium.**

alluvium (ə'luːvɪəm) n., pl. **-via** (-vɪə). a fertile soil consisting of mud, silt, and sand deposited by flowing water. [Latin]

ally n. ('ælaɪ), pl. **-lies.** **1.** a country, person, or group having an agreement to support another. ~vb. (ə'laɪ), **-lying, -lied.** **2.** **ally oneself with.** to agree to support another country, person, or group. [Latin ligāre to bind]

alma mater ('ælmə 'mɑːtə) n. the school, college, or university that one attended. [Latin: bountiful mother]

almanac ('ɔːlmə,næk) n. a yearly calendar with information about matters such as the phases of the moon and anniversaries. [Late Greek almenikhiaka]

almighty (ɔːl'maɪtɪ) adj. **1.** having power over everything. **2.** Informal. very great: an almighty row. ~n. **3.** **the Almighty.** God.

almond ('ɑːmənd) n. an edible nut with a yellowish-brown shell, which grows on a small tree. [Greek amugdalē]

almoner ('ɑːmənə) n. Brit. a former name for a trained hospital social worker. [Old French almosne alms]

almost ('ɔːlməʊst) adv. very nearly.

alms (ɑːmz) pl. n. Old-fashioned. donations of money or goods to the poor. [Greek eleēmosunē pity]

almshouse ('ɑːmz,haʊs) n. Brit. (formerly) a house, financed by charity, which offered accommodation to the poor.

aloe ('æləʊ) n. **1.** a plant with fleshy spiny-toothed leaves. **2.** (pl.) a bitter drug made from aloe leaves. [Greek]

aloft (ə'lɒft) adv. **1.** in the air. **2.** Naut. in the rigging of a ship. [Old Norse ā lopt]

alone (ə'ləʊn) adj., adv. **1.** without anyone or anything else. **2.** **leave someone or something alone.** to refrain from annoying someone or interfering with something. **3.** **let alone.** not to mention: he can't afford beer, let alone whisky. [Old English al one]

along (ə'lɒŋ) prep. **1.** over part or all of the length of: running along the road. ~adv. **2.** moving in a particular direction: running along. **3.** in company with another or others: come along for the ride. **4.** **along with.** together with: consider the advantages along with the disadvantages. [Old English andlang]

alongside (ə,lɒŋ'saɪd) prep. **1.** close beside. ~adv. **2.** near the side of something.

aloof (ə'luːf) adj. distant or haughty in manner. [obs. a loof to windward]

alopecia (,ælə'piːʃə) n. loss of hair, usually due to illness. [Greek alōpekia mange in foxes]

aloud (ə'laʊd) adv. **1.** in a normal voice. **2.** in a spoken voice; not silently.

alp (ælp) n. **1.** a high mountain. **2.** **the Alps.** a high mountain range in S central Europe. [Latin Alpes]

alpaca (æl'pækə) n. **1.** a South American mammal related to the llama, with dark shaggy hair. **2.** wool or cloth obtained from this hair. [South American Indian allpaca]

alpenstock ('ælpən,stɒk) n. a stout stick with an iron tip used by hikers and mountain climbers. [German]

alpha ('ælfə) n. **1.** the first letter in the Greek alphabet (A, α). **2.** Brit. the highest grade in an examination or for a piece of academic work. **3.** **alpha and omega.** the first and last.

alphabet ('ælfə,bɛt) n. a set of letters in fixed conventional order, used in a writing system. [alpha + beta, the first two letters of the Greek alphabet]

alphabetical (,ælfə'bɛtɪk'l) adj. in the conventional order of the letters of an alphabet. —**alpha'betically** adv.

alphabetize or **-ise** ('ælfəbə,taɪz) vb. to arrange in conventional alphabetical order. —**alphabeti'zation** or **-i'sation** n.

alphanumeric (ˌælfənjuːˈmɛrɪk) adj. consisting of alphabetical and numerical symbols.

alpha particle n. Physics. a positively charged particle, emitted during some radioactive transformations.

alpha ray n. Physics. a stream of alpha particles.

alpine (ˈælpaɪn) adj. 1. of high mountains. 2. (cap.) of the Alps. ~n. 3. a plant grown in or native to high altitudes.

already (ɔːlˈrɛdɪ) adv. before the present time or an implied or expected time.

alright (ɔːlˈraɪt) adj., adv. Not universally accepted. same as **all right.**

Alsatian (ælˈseɪʃən) n. a large wolflike dog.

also (ˈɔːlsəʊ) adv. in addition; too. [Old English alswā]

also-ran n. a loser in a race, competition, or election.

Alta. Alberta.

altar (ˈɔːltə) n. 1. (in Christian churches) the communion table. 2. a raised structure where sacrifices are offered and religious rites performed. [Latin altus high]

altarpiece (ˈɔːltəˌpiːs) n. a work of art set above and behind the altar in a Christian church.

alter (ˈɔːltə) vb. to make or become different; change. [Latin alter other]

alteration (ˌɔːltəˈreɪʃən) n. a change or modification.

altercation (ˌɔːltəˈkeɪʃən) n. a heated argument. [Latin altercārī]

alter ego (ˈɔːltər ˈiːɡəʊ) n. 1. a second self. 2. a very close friend. [Latin: other self]

alternate vb. (ˈɔːltəˌneɪt). 1. to occur or cause to occur by turns. 2. to interchange regularly or in succession. ~adj. (ɔːlˈtɜːnɪt). 3. occurring by turns. 4. every second (one) of a series: alternate Fridays. 5. being a second choice; alternative. [Latin alternāre] —**alternately** adv. —**alternation** (ˌɔːltəˈneɪʃən) n.

alternate angles pl. n. Geom. two angles at opposite ends and on opposite sides of a line intersecting two other lines.

alternating current n. an electric current that reverses direction at frequent regular intervals.

alternative (ɔːlˈtɜːnətɪv) n. 1. a possibility of choice between two or more things. 2. either or any of such choices. ~adj. 3. presenting a choice between two or more possibilities. 4. denoting a lifestyle, culture, etc., that is less conventional, materialistic, or institutionalized than that of contemporary society. —**alternatively** adv.

alternative medicine n. the treatment of disease by osteopathy, homeopathy, or other nonconventional means.

alternator (ˈɔːltəˌneɪtə) n. an electrical machine that generates an alternating current.

although (ɔːlˈðəʊ) conj. in spite of the fact that.

altimeter (ˈæltɪˌmiːtə) n. an instrument that indicates altitude. [Latin altus high + -METER]

altitude (ˈæltɪˌtjuːd) n. height above sea level. [Latin altus high, deep]

alto (ˈæltəʊ) n., pl. **-tos.** 1. short for **contralto.** 2. the highest adult male voice. 3. a singer with an alto voice. 4. a musical instrument that is the second or third highest in its group. ~adj. 5. denoting such an instrument. [Italian]

altogether (ˌɔːltəˈɡɛðə) adv. 1. completely. 2. with everything included. 3. on the whole. ~n. 4. **in the altogether.** Informal. naked.

altruism (ˈæltruːˌɪzəm) n. unselfish concern for the welfare of others. [Italian altrui others] —**altruist** n. —**altruistic** adj.

alum (ˈæləm) n. Chem. a double sulphate of aluminium and potassium, used in manufacturing and in medicine. [Latin alūmen]

aluminium (ˌæljʊˈmɪnɪəm) or U.S. & Canad. **aluminum** (əˈluːmɪnəm) n. Chem. a lightweight malleable silvery-white metallic element that resists corrosion. Symbol: Al

aluminize or **-ise** (əˈluːmɪˌnaɪz) vb. to cover with aluminium.

alumnus (əˈlʌmnəs) or (fem.) **alumna** (əˈlʌmnə) n., pl. **-ni** (-naɪ) or **-nae** (-niː). Chiefly U.S. & Canad. a graduate of a school or college. [Latin: nursling, pupil]

always (ˈɔːlweɪz) adv. 1. without exception: he always arrives on time. 2. continually: he is always moaning. 3. in any case: you could always take a day off work. [Old English ealne weg all the way]

alyssum (ˈælɪsəm) n. a garden plant with clusters of small yellow or white flowers. [Greek alussos curing rabies]

am (æm) vb. (used with I) a form of the present tense of **be.** [Old English eam]

Am Chem. americium.

AM amplitude modulation.

Am. America(n).

a.m. before noon. [Latin ante meridiem]

amadoda (ˌæməˈdɒdə) pl. n. S. African. men. [Bantu]

amah (ˈɑːmə) n. (in the East, formerly) a nurse or maidservant. [Portuguese]

amalgam (əˈmælɡəm) n. 1. a blend or combination. 2. an alloy of mercury with another metal: dental amalgam. [Medieval Latin amalgama]

amalgamate (əˈmælɡəˌmeɪt) vb. 1. to combine or unite. 2. to alloy (a metal) with mercury. —**amalgamation** (əˌmælɡəˈmeɪʃən) n.

amanuensis (əˌmænjʊˈɛnsɪs) n., pl. **-ses** (-siːz). a person employed to take dictation. [Latin servus ā manū slave at hand]

amaranth (ˈæməˌrænθ) n. 1. Poetic. an imaginary flower that never fades. 2. a plant with small green, red, or purple flowers. [Greek a- not + marainein to fade]

amaryllis (ˌæməˈrɪlɪs) n. a plant native to southern Africa with large lily-like reddish or white flowers. [Amaryllis, Greek name for a shepherdess]

amass (əˈmæs) vb. to accumulate or collect

(riches or information). [Latin *ad-* to + *massa*]

amateur ('æmətə) *n.* **1.** a person who engages in a sport or other activity as a pastime rather than for gain. **2.** a person unskilled in a subject or activity. ~*adj.* **3.** not professional. [Latin *amātor* lover] —'**amateurish** *adj.* —'**amateurism** *n.*

amatory ('æmətrɪ) *adj.* of or relating to romantic or sexual love. [Latin *amāre* to love]

amaze (ə'meɪz) *vb.* to fill (someone) with surprise; astonish. [Old English *āmasian*] —a'**mazement** *n.* —a'**mazing** *adj.*

Amazon ('æməz°n) *n.* **1.** *Greek myth.* one of a race of women warriors of Scythia near the Black Sea. **2.** any tall, strong, or aggressive woman. [Greek] —**Amazonian** (,æmə'zəʊnɪən) *adj.*

ambassador (æm'bæsədə) *n.* **1.** a diplomat of the highest rank, sent to another country as permanent representative of his own country. **2.** a representative or messenger. [Old Provençal *ambaisador*] —**ambassadorial** (æm,bæsə'dɔːrɪəl) *adj.*

amber ('æmbə) *n.* **1.** a yellow translucent fossil resin, used in jewellery. ~*adj.* **2.** brownish-yellow. [Arabic *'anbar* ambergris]

ambergris ('æmbə,griːs) *n.* a waxy substance secreted by the intestinal tract of the sperm whale, which is used in the manufacture of perfumes. [Old French *ambre gris* grey amber]

ambidextrous (,æmbɪ'dekstrəs) *adj.* equally expert with each hand. [Latin *ambi-* both + *dexter* right hand]

ambience *or* **ambiance** ('æmbɪəns) *n.* the atmosphere of a place.

ambient ('æmbɪənt) *adj.* surrounding. [Latin *ambi-* round + *īre* to go]

ambiguity (,æmbɪ'gjuːɪtɪ) *n., pl.* -**ties.** the possibility of interpreting an expression in more than one way.

ambiguous (æm'bɪgjʊəs) *adj.* having more than one possible interpretation. [Latin *ambigere* to go around] —**am'biguously** *adv.*

ambit ('æmbɪt) *n.* limits or boundary. [Latin *ambīre* to go round]

ambition (æm'bɪʃən) *n.* **1.** strong desire for success. **2.** something so desired; a goal. [Latin *ambitiō* a going round (of candidates)]

ambitious (æm'bɪʃəs) *adj.* **1.** having a strong desire for success. **2.** requiring great effort or ability: *an ambitious plan.*

ambivalence (æm'bɪvələns) *n.* the state of feeling two conflicting emotions at the same time. —**am'bivalent** *adj.*

amble ('æmb°l) *vb.* **1.** to walk at a leisurely pace. ~*n.* **2.** a leisurely motion in walking. [Latin *ambulāre* to walk]

ambrosia (æm'brəʊzɪə) *n.* **1.** *Classical myth.* the food of the gods, said to bestow immortality. **2.** anything delightful to taste or smell. [Greek: immortality]

ambulance ('æmbjʊləns) *n.* a motor vehicle designed to carry sick or injured people. [Latin *ambulāre* to walk]

ambush ('æmbʊʃ) *n.* **1.** the act of waiting in a concealed position to make a surprise attack. **2.** an attack from such a position. ~*vb.* **3.** to attack (people) suddenly from a concealed position. ~Also: **ambuscade** (,æmbə'skeɪd). [Old French *embuschier*]

ameliorate (ə'miːljə,reɪt) *vb.* to make (something) better. [Latin *melior* better] —a,**melio'ration** *n.*

amen (,eɪ'mɛn, ,ɑː'mɛn) *interj.* so be it: used at the end of a prayer. [Hebrew: certainly]

amenable (ə'miːnəb°l) *adj.* likely or willing to cooperate. [Latin *mināre* to drive (cattle)]

amend (ə'mɛnd) *vb.* to improve or correct (something). [Latin *ēmendāre* to emend]

amendment (ə'mɛndmənt) *n.* an improvement or correction.

amends (ə'mɛndz) *pl. n.* **make amends for.** to compensate for some injury or insult.

amenity (ə'miːnɪtɪ) *n., pl.* -**ties.** a useful or enjoyable facility. [Latin *amoenus* agreeable]

amenorrhoea *or esp. U.S.* **amenorrhea** (eɪ,mɛnə'rɪə) *n.* abnormal absence of menstruation. [Greek *a-* not + *mēn* month + *rhein* to flow]

American (ə'mɛrɪkən) *adj.* **1.** of the United States of America or the American continent. ~*n.* **2.** a person from the United States of America or the American continent.

American Indian *n.* **1.** a member of any of the original peoples of America. ~*adj.* **2.** of any of these peoples, their languages, or their cultures.

Americanism (ə'mɛrɪkə,nɪzəm) *n.* an expression or custom that is peculiar to or characteristic of the people of the United States.

americium (,æmə'rɪsɪəm) *n. Chem.* a white metallic element artificially produced from plutonium. Symbol: Am [from *America* (where it was first produced)]

amethyst ('æmɪθɪst) *n.* **1.** a purple or violet variety of quartz used as a gemstone. ~*adj.* **2.** purple or violet. [Greek *amethustos* not drunken]

Amharic (æm'hærɪk) *n.* the official language of Ethiopia.

amiable ('eɪmɪəb°l) *adj.* having a pleasant nature; friendly. [Latin *amīcus* friend] —,**amia'bility** *n.* —'**amiably** *adv.*

amicable ('æmɪkəb°l) *adj.* characterized by friendliness: *an amicable agreement.* [Latin *amīcus* friend] —,**amica'bility** *n.* —'**amicably** *adv.*

amice ('æmɪs) *n.* a rectangular piece of white linen worn by Christian priests around the neck and shoulders. [Latin *amictus* cloak]

amid (ə'mɪd) *or* **amidst** *prep.* in the middle of; among. [Old English *on middan* in the middle]

amide ('æmaɪd) *n. Chem.* **1.** any organic compound containing the group -CONH₂. **2.** an inorganic compound having the general formula M(NH₂)ₓ, where M is a metal atom. [from *ammonia*]

amidships (ə'mɪdʃɪps) *adv. Naut.* at, near, or towards the centre of a ship.

amine (ə'miːn) *n. Chem.* an organic base formed by replacing one or more of the hydrogen atoms of ammonia by organic groups. [from *ammonium*]

amino acid (ə'miːnəʊ) *n. Chem.* any of a group of organic compounds containing the amino group, -NH₂, and one or more carboxyl groups, -COOH, esp. one that is a component of protein.

amir (ə'mɪə) *n.* same as **emir.** [Arabic]

amiss (ə'mɪs) *adv.* **1.** in an incorrect or defective manner. **2. take something amiss.** to be offended by something. ~*adj.* **3.** wrong or faulty. [Middle English *a mis*, from *mis* wrong]

amity ('æmɪtɪ) *n.* friendship; cordiality. [from Latin *amīcus* friend]

ammeter ('æmɪˌmiːtə) *n.* an instrument for measuring an electric current in amperes. [*am(pere)* + -METER]

ammo ('æməʊ) *n. Informal.* ammunition.

ammonia (ə'məʊnɪə) *n.* a colourless strong-smelling gas used in fertilizers and as a refrigerant and solvent. [ult. from a substance found near the shrine of the Roman-Egyptian god Jupiter *Ammon*]

ammonite ('æməˌnaɪt) *n.* the coil-shaped fossilized shell of an extinct sea creature. [Latin *cornū Ammōnis* horn of Ammon]

ammonium (ə'məʊnɪəm) *n.* (*modifier*) *Chem.* of or containing the chemical group NH₄⁻ or the ion NH₄⁺.

ammunition (ˌæmjʊ'nɪʃən) *n.* **1.** bullets, bombs, and shells that can be fired from or as a weapon. **2.** any means of defence or attack in an argument. [French, by mistaken division of *la munition*]

amnesia (æm'niːzɪə) *n.* a partial or total loss of memory. [Greek: forgetfulness] —**amnesiac** (æm'niːzɪˌæk) *adj., n.*

amnesty ('æmnɪstɪ) *n., pl.* **-ties. 1.** a general pardon for offences against a government. **2.** a period during which a law is suspended, to allow people to confess to crime or give up weapons without fear of prosecution. [Greek *a-* not + *mnasthai* to remember]

amniocentesis (ˌæmnɪəʊsɛn'tiːsɪs) *n., pl.* **-ses** (-siːz). removal of amniotic fluid from the womb of a pregnant woman in order to detect possible abnormalities in the fetus. [*amnion* + Greek *kentēsis* a pricking]

amnion ('æmnɪən) *n., pl.* **-nia** (-nɪə). the innermost of two membranes enclosing an embryo. [Greek: a little lamb] —**amniotic** (ˌæmnɪ'ɒtɪk) *adj.*

amniotic fluid *n.* the fluid surrounding the fetus in the womb.

amoeba or *U.S.* **ameba** (ə'miːbə) *n., pl.* **-bae** (-biː) or **-bas.** a microscopic single-cell creature that lives in fresh water or soil or as a parasite in other animals. [Greek *ameibein* to change]

amok (ə'mʌk, ə'mɒk) or **amuck** *adv.* **run amok.** to run about in a violent frenzy. [Malay *amoq* furious assault]

among (ə'mʌŋ) or **amongst** *prep.* **1.** in the midst of: *he lived among the Indians.* **2.** to each of: *divide it among yourselves.* **3.** in the group, class, or number of: *among the greatest writers.* **4.** with one another within a group: *decide it among yourselves.* [Old English *amang*]

amontillado (əˌmɒntɪ'lɑːdəʊ) *n.* a medium-dry sherry. [Spanish *vino amontillado* wine of Montilla, a town in Spain]

amoral (ˌeɪ'mɒrəl) *adj.* without moral standards or principles. —**amorality** (ˌeɪmɒ'rælɪtɪ) *n.*

amorous ('æmərəs) *adj.* feeling, displaying, or relating to sexual love or desire. [Latin *amor* love]

amorphous (ə'mɔːfəs) *adj.* **1.** lacking a definite shape. **2.** of no recognizable character or type. [Greek *a-* not + *morphē* shape]

amortize or **-tise** (ə'mɔːtaɪz) *vb. Finance.* to liquidate (a debt or mortgage) by payments or by periodic transfers to a sinking fund. [Latin *ad* to + *mors* death]

amount (ə'maʊnt) *n.* **1.** extent; quantity. ~*vb.* **2.** (foll. by *to*) to be equal or add up to. [Old French *amonter* to go up]

amour (ə'mʊə) *n.* a secret love affair. [Latin *amor* love]

amp (æmp) *n.* **1.** an ampere. **2.** *Informal.* an amplifier.

amperage ('æmpərɪdʒ) *n.* the strength of an electric current measured in amperes.

ampere ('æmpeə) *n.* the basic unit of electric current. Symbol: A [after A. M. *Ampère*, French physicist & mathematician]

ampersand ('æmpəˌsænd) *n.* the character &, meaning *and.* [shortened from *and per se and*, that is, the symbol & by itself (represents) *and*]

amphetamine (æm'fɛtəˌmiːn) *n.* a drug used for its stimulant action. [shortened from chemical name]

amphibian (æm'fɪbɪən) *n.* **1.** a vertebrate, such as a newt, frog, or toad, that lives on land but breeds in water. **2.** a vehicle that can travel on both water and land.

amphibious (æm'fɪbɪəs) *adj.* **1.** able to live or operate both on land and in or on water. **2.** relating to military forces launching an attack from the sea against a shore. [Greek *amphibios* having a double life]

amphitheatre or *U.S.* **amphitheater** ('æmfɪˌθɪətə) *n.* a circular or oval building without a roof, in which tiers of seats rise from a central open arena. [Greek *amphi-* around + *theatre*]

amphora ('æmfərə) *n., pl.* **-phorae** (-fəˌriː). a Greek or Roman two-handled narrow-necked jar. [Greek *amphi-* on both sides + *phoreus* bearer]

ample ('æmp'l) *adj.* **1.** more than sufficient: *an ample helping.* **2.** large: *of ample proportions.* [Latin *amplus*]

amplifier ('æmplɪˌfaɪə) *n.* an electronic device used to increase the strength of a current or sound signal.

amplify ('æmplɪˌfaɪ) *vb.* **-fying, -fied. 1.**

Electronics. to increase the strength of (a current or sound signal). **2.** to expand (a speech or story). **3.** to increase the size, extent, or effect of. [Latin *amplificāre*] —**amplification** (ˌæmplɪfɪˈkeɪʃən) *n.*

amplitude (ˈæmplɪˌtjuːd) *n.* **1.** greatness of extent; breadth or scope. **2.** *Physics.* the maximum displacement from the zero or mean position of a wave or oscillation. [Latin *amplus* spacious]

amplitude modulation *n. Electronics.* a method of transmitting information using radio waves in which the amplitude of the carrier wave is varied in accordance with the amplitude of the input signal.

amply (ˈæmplɪ) *adv.* fully; generously.

ampoule (ˈæmpuːl) *or U.S.* **ampule** *n. Med.* a small glass container in which liquids for injection are sealed. [French]

ampulla (æmˈpʊlə) *n., pl.* **-pullae** (-ˈpʊliː). **1.** *Christianity.* a container for the wine and water, or the oil, used in church. **2.** a Roman two-handled bottle for oil, wine, or perfume. [Latin]

amputate (ˈæmpjʊˌteɪt) *vb.* to remove (all or part of a limb). [Latin *am-* around + *putāre* to prune] —**amputation** (ˌæmpjʊˈteɪʃən) *n.*

amuck (əˈmʌk) *adv.* same as **amok.**

amulet (ˈæmjʊlɪt) *n.* a trinket or jewel worn as a protection against evil; charm. [Latin *amulētum*]

amuse (əˈmjuːz) *vb.* **1.** to entertain or divert (someone). **2.** to cause (someone) to laugh or smile. [Old French *amuser* to cause to be idle] —**a'musing** *adj.*

amusement (əˈmjuːzmənt) *n.* **1.** something that amuses someone. **2.** the state of being amused.

an (æn) *det. (indefinite article)* a form of **a,** used before an initial vowel sound: *an old car; an hour.* [Old English *ān* one]

an- *prefix.* See **a-.**

Anabaptist (ˌænəˈbæptɪst) *n.* **1.** a member of a 16th-century Protestant movement that believed in adult baptism. ~*adj.* **2.** of this movement. [Late Greek *anabaptizein* to baptize again]

anabolic steroid (ˌænəˈbɒlɪk) *n.* a synthetic steroid hormone used to stimulate muscle and bone growth.

anabolism (əˈnæbəˌlɪzəm) *n. Biol.* a metabolic process in which body tissues are synthesized from food. [Greek *anabole* a rising up]

anachronism (əˈnækrəˌnɪzəm) *n.* **1.** the representation of something in a historical context in which it could not have occurred or existed. **2.** a person or thing that seems to belong to another time. [Greek *ana* against + *khronos* time] —**a,nachro'nistic** *adj.*

anaconda (ˌænəˈkɒndə) *n.* a very large S American snake. [prob. from Sinhalese *henakandayā* whip snake]

anaemia *or U.S.* **anemia** (əˈniːmɪə) *n.* a deficiency of red blood cells or their haemoglobin content, resulting in paleness and lack of energy. [Greek *an* without + *haima* blood]

anaemic *or U.S.* **anemic** (əˈniːmɪk) *adj.* **1.** having anaemia. **2.** pale and sickly-looking; lacking vitality.

anaerobe (æˈnɛərəʊb) *n. Biol.* an organism that does not require oxygen. [Greek *an* not + *aēr* air + *bios* life] —**,anae'robic** *adj.*

anaesthesia *or U.S.* **anesthesia** (ˌænɪsˈθiːzɪə) *n.* loss of bodily sensation caused by disease or accident or by drugs such as ether: called **general anaesthesia** when consciousness is lost and **local anaesthesia** when only a specific area of the body is involved. [Greek]

anaesthetic *or U.S.* **anesthetic** (ˌænɪsˈθɛtɪk) *n.* **1.** a substance that causes anaesthesia. ~*adj.* **2.** causing anaesthesia.

anaesthetist (əˈniːsθɪtɪst) *n. Brit.* a doctor who administers anaesthetics.

anaesthetize, anaesthetise, *or U.S.* **anesthetize** (əˈniːsθɪˌtaɪz) *vb.* to cause (someone) to feel no pain by administering an anaesthetic.

Anaglypta (ˌænəˈɡlɪptə) *n. Trademark.* a thick embossed wallpaper, designed to be painted.

anagram (ˈænəˌɡræm) *n.* a word or phrase the letters of which can be rearranged into another word or phrase. [Greek *anagrammatizein* to transpose letters]

anal (ˈeɪn²l) *adj.* of or relating to the anus. [New Latin *ānālis*]

analgesic (ˌæn²lˈdʒiːzɪk) *n.* **1.** a drug that relieves pain. ~*adj.* **2.** pain-relieving. [Greek]

analog (ˈæn²ˌlɒɡ) *n. U.S. & computers.* same as **analogue.**

analogize *or* **-gise** (əˈnæləˌdʒaɪz) *vb.* **1.** to use analogy in argument. **2.** to reveal analogy between (one thing and another).

analogous (əˈnæləɡəs) *adj.* similar in some respect. [Greek *analogos* proportionate]

analogue *or U.S.* **analog** (ˈæn²ˌlɒɡ) *n.* **1. a.** a physical object or quantity used to measure or represent another quantity. **b.** *(as modifier): an analogue watch.* **2.** something that is analogous to something else.

analogy (əˈnælədʒɪ) *n., pl.* **-gies. 1.** a similarity, usually in a limited number of features. **2.** a comparison made to show such a similarity. [Greek *analogia*] —**analogical** (ˌænəˈlɒdʒɪk²l) *adj.*

analyse *or U.S.* **-lyze** (ˈæn²ˌlaɪz) *vb.* **1.** to examine (something) in detail in order to discover its meaning or essential features. **2.** to break (something) down into its components. **3.** to psychoanalyse (someone).

analysis (əˈnælɪsɪs) *n., pl.* **-ses** (-ˌsiːz). **1.** the division of a whole into its constituent parts to examine or determine their relationship. **2.** a statement of the results of this. **3.** short for **psychoanalysis.** [Greek *analusis* a dissolving]

analyst (ˈænəlɪst) *n.* **1.** a person who is skilled in analysis. **2.** short for **psychoanalyst.**

analytic (ˌænəˈlɪtɪk) *or* **analytical** *adj.* relating to or using analysis.

anarchism (ˈænəˌkɪzəm) *n.* a doctrine advocating the abolition of government and its replacement by a social system based on voluntary cooperation.

anarchist ('ænəkɪst) *n.* **1.** a person who advocates anarchism. **2.** a person who causes disorder or upheaval. —ˌanar'chistic *adj.*

anarchy ('ænəkɪ) *n.* **1.** general lawlessness and disorder. **2.** the absence of government. [Greek *an* without + *arkh-* leader] —**anarchic** (æn'ɑːkɪk) *adj.*

anathema (ə'næθəmə) *n.* a detested person or thing. [Greek: something accursed]

anathematize *or* **-tise** (ə'næθəməˌtaɪz) *vb.* to curse (someone or something).

anatomy (ə'nætəmɪ) *n., pl.* **-mies. 1.** the science of the physical structure of animals and plants. **2.** the structure of an animal or plant. **3.** *Informal.* a person's body: *a delicate part of his anatomy.* **4.** any detailed analysis: *the anatomy of a murder.* [Greek *ana* up + *temnein* to cut] —**anatomical** (ˌænə'tɒmɪkᵊl) *adj.*

ancestor ('ænsɛstə) *n.* **1.** a person in former times from whom one is descended; forefather. **2.** a forerunner: *the ancestor of the modern camera.* [Latin *antecēdere* to go before]

ancestral (æn'sɛstrəl) *adj.* of or inherited from ancestors.

ancestry ('ænsɛstrɪ) *n., pl.* **-tries. 1.** lineage or descent: *of Italian ancestry.* **2.** forerunners collectively.

anchor ('æŋkə) *n.* **1.** a hooked device attached to a boat by a cable and dropped overboard so as to grip the sea bottom and restrict movement. **~vb. 3.** to use an anchor to hold (a boat) in one place. **4.** to fasten (something) securely. [Greek *ankura*]

anchorage ('æŋkərɪdʒ) *n.* a place to anchor boats.

anchorite ('æŋkəˌraɪt) *n.* a religious recluse. [Greek *anakhōrein* to retire]

anchor man *n.* **1.** a broadcaster in a central studio, who links up and presents items from outside camera units and reporters in other studios. **2.** the last person to compete in a relay team.

anchovy ('æntʃəvɪ) *n., pl.* **-vies.** a small marine food fish with a salty taste. [Spanish *anchova*]

ancien régime ('ɒnsjɑːn reɪ'ʒiːm) *n.* **1.** the political and social system of France before the 1789 Revolution. **2.** a former system. [French: old regime]

ancient ('eɪnʃənt) *adj.* **1.** dating from very long ago. **2.** very old. **3.** of the far past, esp. before the collapse of the Western Roman Empire (476 A.D.). **~n. 4.** (*pl.*) people who lived in the ancient world, esp. Greeks or Romans. [Latin *ante* before]

ancillary (æn'sɪlərɪ) *adj.* **1.** auxiliary; supplementary: *hospital ancillary workers.* **2.** subsidiary. [Latin *ancula* female servant]

and (ænd; *unstressed* ənd) *conj.* **1.** in addition to: *boys and girls.* **2.** as a consequence: *he fell and cut his knee.* **3.** afterwards: *we pay and go in.* **4.** used for emphasis or to indicate repetition or continuity: *it rained and rained.* **5.** used to express a contrast between instances of something: *there are jobs and jobs.* **6.** *Informal.* used in place of *to* in infinitives after verbs such as *try, go,* and *come: try and see it my way.* [Old English]

andante (æn'dæntɪ) *Music.* **~adv. 1.** moderately slowly. **~n. 2.** a passage or piece to be performed in this manner. [Italian *andare* to walk]

andantino (ˌændæn'tiːnəʊ) *Music.* **~adv. 1.** slightly faster than andante. **~n., pl.** **-nos. 2.** a passage or piece to be performed in this manner.

andiron ('ændˌaɪən) *n.* either of a pair of metal stands for supporting logs in a hearth. [Old French *andier*]

and/or *conj.* Not universally accepted. either one or the other or both.

androgynous (æn'drɒdʒɪnəs) *adj.* (of a person, animal, or plant) having both male and female characteristics. [Greek *aner* man + *gune* woman]

android ('ændrɔɪd) *n.* a robot resembling a human being. [Late Greek *androeidēs* manlike]

anecdote ('ænɪkˌdəʊt) *n.* a short amusing account of an incident. [Greek *anekdotos* unpublished] —**anec'dotal** *adj.*

anemia (ə'niːmɪə) *n. U.S.* anaemia.

anemometer (ˌænɪ'mɒmɪtə) *n.* an instrument for recording the speed of wind.

anemone (ə'nɛmənɪ) *n.* a flowering plant related to the buttercup, which has white or coloured flowers. [Greek: windflower]

aneroid barometer ('ænəˌrɔɪd) *n.* a device for measuring atmospheric pressure, consisting of a partially evacuated chamber, in which variations in pressure cause a pointer on the lid to move. [Greek *a* not + *nēros* wet]

anesthesia (ˌænɪs'θiːzɪə) *n. U.S.* anaesthesia.

aneurysm *or* **aneurism** ('ænjəˌrɪzəm) *n. Med.* a permanent swelling of a blood vessel. [Greek *aneurunein* to dilate]

anew (ə'njuː) *adv.* **1.** once more. **2.** in a different way.

angel ('eɪndʒəl) *n.* **1.** a spiritual being believed to be an attendant or messenger of God. **2.** a conventional representation of an angel as a human being with wings. **3.** *Informal.* a person who is kind, pure, or beautiful. **4.** *Informal.* an investor in a theatrical production. [Greek *angelos* messenger]

angel cake *or esp. U.S.* **angel food cake** *n.* a very light sponge cake.

angelfish ('eɪndʒəlˌfɪʃ) *n., pl.* **-fish** *or* **-fishes.** a South American aquarium fish with large fins.

angelic (æn'dʒɛlɪk) *adj.* **1.** very kind, pure, or beautiful. **2.** of or relating to angels. —**an'gelically** *adv.*

angelica (æn'dʒɛlɪkə) *n.* **1.** an aromatic plant used in medicine and cookery. **2.** the candied stems of this plant, used in sweet dishes. [Medieval Latin (*herba*) *angelica* angelic herb]

Angelus ('ændʒɪləs) *n. R.C. Church.* **1.** prayers recited in the morning, at midday, and in the evening. **2.** the bell signalling the times of these prayers. [Latin *Angelus domini nuntiavit Mariae* the angel of the Lord brought tidings to Mary]

anger ('æŋgə) *n.* 1. a feeling of annoyance or antagonism; rage; wrath. ~*vb.* 2. to make (someone) angry; enrage. [Old Norse *angr* grief]

angina (æn'dʒaɪnə) *or* **angina pectoris** ('pɛktɔrɪs) *n.* a sudden intense chest pain caused by momentary lack of adequate blood supply to the heart muscle. [Greek *ankhonē* a strangling]

angle[1] ('æŋg'l) *n.* 1. the space between or shape formed by two straight lines or surfaces that extend from a common point. 2. the divergence between two such lines or surfaces, measured in degrees. 3. a recess; corner. 4. point of view. ~*vb.* 5. to move in or place (something) at an angle. 6. to produce (something, such as an article) from a particular point of view. [Latin *angulus* corner]

angle[2] ('æŋg'l) *vb.* 1. to fish with a hook and line. 2. (foll. by *for*) to attempt to get: *he was angling for a compliment.* [Old English *angul* fish-hook]

angler ('æŋglə) *n.* a person who fishes with a hook and line.

Angles ('æŋg'lz) *pl. n.* a people from N Germany who settled in E and N England in the 5th and 6th centuries A.D. [Latin *Anglus* a person from Angul, Germany]

Anglican ('æŋglɪkən) *adj.* 1. of or relating to the Church of England. ~*n.* 2. a member of the Anglican Church. [Latin *Anglicus* English, of the Angles] —'**Anglican,ism** *n.*

Anglicism ('æŋglɪ,sɪzəm) *n.* an expression or custom that is peculiar to or characteristic of the English.

anglicize *or* **-cise** ('æŋglɪ,saɪz) *vb.* **-cizing, -cized** *or* **-cising, -cised.** to make or become English in outlook, form, etc.

angling ('æŋglɪŋ) *n.* the art or sport of fishing with a hook and line.

Anglo ('æŋgləʊ) *n., pl.* **-glos.** 1. *U.S.* a White inhabitant of the U.S. who is not of Latin extraction. 2. *Canad.* an English-speaking Canadian of Anglo-Celtic origin.

Anglo- *combining form.* denoting English or England: *Anglo-Saxon.* [Medieval Latin *Anglī*]

Anglo-French *adj.* 1. of England and France. 2. of the Anglo-French language. ~*n.* 3. the Norman-French language of medieval England.

Anglo-Indian *adj.* 1. of England and India. 2. denoting or relating to Anglo-Indians. ~*n.* 3. a person of mixed English and Indian descent. 4. an English person who has lived for a long time in India.

Anglo-Norman *adj.* 1. of or relating to the Norman conquerors of England or their language. ~*n.* 2. a Norman inhabitant of England after 1066. 3. the Anglo-French language.

Anglophile ('æŋgləʊfaɪl) *n.* a person who admires England or the English.

Anglo-Saxon *n.* 1. a member of any of the West Germanic tribes that settled in Britain from the 5th century A.D. 2. any White person whose native language is English. 3. same as **Old English.** 4. *Informal.* plain, blunt, and often rude English. ~*adj.* 4. of the Anglo-Saxons or the Old English language. 5. of the White Protestant culture of Britain and the U.S.

angora (æŋ'gɔːrə) *n.* 1. a variety of goat, cat, or rabbit with long silky hair. 2. the hair of the angora goat or rabbit. 3. cloth made from the hair of the angora goat or rabbit. [*Angora*, former name of Ankara, in Turkey]

Angostura Bitters (,æŋgə'stjʊərə) *pl. n. Trademark.* a bitter aromatic tonic, used to flavour alcoholic drinks. [from *Angostura* in Venezuela]

angry ('æŋgrɪ) *adj.* **-grier, -griest.** 1. feeling or expressing annoyance or antagonism. 2. dark and stormy: *angry clouds.* 3. severely inflamed: *an angry wound.* —'**angrily** *adv.*

angst (æŋst) *n.* acute but nonspecific anxiety. [German]

angstrom ('æŋstrəm) *n.* a unit of length equal to 10^{-10} metre, used to measure wavelengths. [after Anders J. *Ångström*, Swedish physicist]

anguish ('æŋgwɪʃ) *n.* extreme pain or misery; agony. [Latin *angustus* narrow]

anguished ('æŋgwɪʃt) *adj.* feeling or showing extreme pain or misery.

angular ('æŋgjʊlə) *adj.* 1. lean and bony. 2. having an angle or angles. 3. measured by an angle: *angular momentum.* —**angularity** (,æŋgjʊ'lærɪtɪ) *n.*

anhydrous (æn'haɪdrəs) *adj. Chem.* containing no water. [Greek *an* without + *hudōr* water]

anil ('ænɪl) *n.* a West Indian shrub which is a source of indigo. [Arabic *an-nīl*, the indigo]

aniline ('ænɪ,liːn) *n. Chem.* a colourless oily poisonous liquid, obtained from coal tar and used for making dyes, plastics, and explosives.

animadversion (,ænɪmæd'vɜːʃən) *n.* criticism or censure. [Latin *animus* mind + *advertere* to turn to]

animal ('ænɪməl) *n.* 1. *Zool.* any living being that is capable of voluntary movement and possesses specialized sense organs. 2. any living being other than a human being. 3. any living being with four legs. 4. a brutish person. 5. *Facetious.* a person or thing: *there is no such animal.* ~*adj.* 6. of or from animals. 7. of or relating to physical needs or desires; carnal. [Latin *animālis* (adj.) living, breathing]

animalcule (,ænɪ'mælkjuːl) *n.* a microscopic animal.

animal husbandry *n.* the science of breeding, rearing, and caring for farm animals.

animalism ('ænɪmə,lɪzəm) *n.* 1. preoccupation with physical matters; sensuality. 2. the doctrine that human beings lack a spiritual nature.

animality (,ænɪ'mælɪtɪ) *n.* 1. the animal side of human beings. 2. the state of being an animal.

animalize or **-ise** ('ænɪmə,laɪz) vb. to make (a person) brutal or sensual.

animal magnetism n. the quality of being sexually attractive.

animal spirits pl. n. boisterous exuberance. [from a vital force once supposed to be dispatched by the brain to all points of the body]

animate vb. ('ænɪ,meɪt). 1. to give life to. 2. to make lively. 3. to produce (a story) as an animated cartoon. ~adj. ('ænɪmɪt). 4. having life. [Latin *anima* breath, spirit] —'**ani,mated** adj. —'**ani,matedly** adv.

animated cartoon n. a film produced by photographing a series of gradually changing drawings, which give the illusion of movement when the series is projected rapidly.

animation (,ænɪ'meɪʃən) n. 1. the techniques used in the production of animated cartoons. 2. vivacity.

animism ('ænɪ,mɪzəm) n. the belief that natural objects possess souls. [Latin *anima* breath, spirit] —'**ani'mistic** adj.

animosity (,ænɪ'mɒsɪtɪ) n., pl. **-ties.** a powerful dislike or hostility. [see ANIMUS]

animus ('ænɪməs) n. intense dislike; hatred; animosity. [Latin: mind, spirit]

anion ('æn,aɪən) n. a negatively charged ion. [Greek *ana-* up + *ienai* to go] —**anionic** (,ænaɪ'ɒnɪk) adj.

anise ('ænɪs) n. a Mediterranean plant with liquorice-flavoured seeds. [Greek *anison*]

aniseed ('ænɪ,siːd) n. the liquorice-flavoured seeds of the anise plant, used for flavouring.

ankh (æŋk) n. a T-shaped cross with a loop on the top, which symbolized eternal life in ancient Egypt. [Egyptian *'nh* life, soul]

ankle ('æŋkªl) n. 1. the joint connecting the leg and the foot. 2. the part of the leg just above the foot. [Old Norse]

anklet ('æŋklɪt) n. an ornamental chain worn around the ankle.

ankylosis (,æŋkɪ'ləʊsɪs) n. abnormal immobility of a joint, caused by a fibrous growth within the joint. [Greek *ankuloun* to crook]

anna ('ænə) n. a former Indian coin. [Hindi *ānā*]

annals ('ænªlz) pl. n. 1. yearly records of events. 2. regular reports of the work of a society or other organization. [Latin (*libri*) *annālēs* yearly (books)] —'**annalist** n.

anneal (ə'niːl) vb. to toughen (glass or metal) by heat treatment. [Old English *onǣlan*]

annelid ('ænəlɪd) n. a worm with a segmented body, for example the earthworm. [Latin *ānulus* ring]

annex vb. (ə'nɛks). 1. to seize (territory) by conquest or occupation. 2. to take (something) without permission. 3. to join or add (something) to something larger. [Latin *annectere* to attach to] —,**annex'a-tion** n.

annexe or esp. U.S. **annex** ('ænɛks) n. a. an extension to a main building. b. a building used as an addition to a main one nearby.

annihilate (ə'naɪə,leɪt) vb. 1. to destroy (a place or a group of people) completely. 2. *Informal.* to defeat (someone) totally in an argument or a contest. [Latin *nihil* nothing] —**annihilation** (ə,naɪə'leɪʃən) n.

anniversary (,ænɪ'vɜːsərɪ) n., pl. **-ries.** 1. the date on which an event, such as a wedding, occurred in some previous year. 2. the celebration of this. [Latin *annus* year + *vertere* to turn]

annotate ('ænə,teɪt) vb. to supply (a written work) with critical or explanatory notes. [Latin *nota* mark] —**annotation** (,ænə'teɪʃən) n.

announce (ə'naʊns) vb. 1. to make (something) known publicly. 2. to declare the arrival of (a person). 3. to be a sign of: *the dark clouds announced rain.* [Latin *annuntiāre*] —**an'nouncement** n.

announcer (ə'naʊnsə) n. a person who introduces programmes on radio or television.

annoy (ə'nɔɪ) vb. 1. to irritate or displease. 2. to harass (someone) sexually. [Latin *in odiō* (*esse*) (to be) hated] —**annoyance** n. —**an'noying** adj.

annual ('ænjʊəl) adj. 1. occurring or done once a year: *my annual holiday.* 2. lasting for a year: *an annual subscription.* ~n. 3. a plant that completes its life cycle in one year. 4. a book published once every year. [Latin *annus* year] —'**annually** adv.

annualize or **-ise** ('ænjʊə,laɪz) vb. to calculate (a rate) for or as if for a year.

annuity (ə'njuːɪtɪ) n., pl. **-ties.** a fixed sum payable at specified intervals over a period. [Latin *annuus* annual]

annul (ə'nʌl) vb. **-nulling, -nulled.** to declare (something, such as a marriage) invalid. [Latin *nullus* not any]

annular ('ænjʊlə) adj. ring-shaped. [Latin *ānulus* ring]

annular eclipse n. an eclipse of the sun in which a ring of sunlight can be seen surrounding the shadow of the moon.

annulate ('ænjʊlɪt) adj. having, composed of, or marked with rings. [Latin *ānulus* ring]

annulment (ə'nʌlmənt) n. the formal invalidation of something such as a marriage.

Annunciation (ə,nʌnsɪ'eɪʃən) n. 1. the. the announcement by the angel Gabriel to the Virgin Mary of her conception of Christ. 2. the festival commemorating this, on March 25 (Lady Day). [Latin *annuntiāre*]

anode ('ænəʊd) n. *Electronics.* the positive electrode in an electrolytic cell or in an electronic valve or tube. [Greek *anodos* a way up]

anodize or **-dise** ('ænə,daɪz) vb. *Chem.* to coat (a metal) with a protective oxide film by electrolysis.

anodyne ('ænə,daɪn) n. 1. something that relieves pain or distress. ~adj. 2. capable of relieving pain or distress. [Greek *an-* without + *odunē* pain]

anoint (ə'nɔɪnt) vb. to apply oil to (someone) as a sign of consecration. [Latin *inunguere*]

anomalous (ə'nɒmələs) adj. deviating from the normal or usual order or type. [Greek *an-* not + *homalos* even]

anomaly (ə'nɒməlɪ) n., pl. **-lies.** something that deviates from the normal; an irregularity.

anomie or **anomy** ('ænəmɪ) n. lack of social or moral standards. [Greek *a-* without + *nomos* law]

anon (ə'nɒn) adv. Archaic or informal. soon: see you _non. [Old English *on āne* in one, that is, immediately]

anon. anonymous.

anonymous (ə'nɒnɪməs) adj. **1.** (of an action or thing) by someone whose name is unknown or withheld: *an anonymous letter.* **2.** having no known name: *an anonymous donor.* **3.** lacking distinguishing characteristics. [Greek *an-* without + *onoma* name] —**anonymity** (,ænə'nɪmɪtɪ) n.

anorak ('ænə,ræk) n. a waterproof hip-length jacket, usually with a hood. [Eskimo *ánorâq*]

anorexia (,ænə'rɛksɪə) or **anorexia nervosa** (nɜː'vəʊsə) n. a disorder characterized by the fear of becoming fat and the consequent refusal of food. [Greek *an-* without + *orexis* appetite] —**ano'rexic** adj., n.

another (ə'nʌðə) det. **1.** one more: *another chance; help yourself to another.* **2.** a different one: *another country; try one, then another.* [orig. *an other*]

anserine ('ænsə,raɪn) adj. of or resembling a goose. [Latin *anser* goose]

answer ('ɑːnsə) n. **1.** a reply to a question, request, letter, or article. **2.** a reaction or response. **3.** a solution to a mathematical problem. ~vb. **4.** to reply or respond (to) by word or act. **5.** to reply correctly to a question. **6.** to respond or react: *the steering answers to the slightest touch.* **7.** to meet the requirements of. **8.** to be responsible (to a person). **9.** to give a defence of (a charge). [Old English *andswaru*]

answerable ('ɑːnsərəbᵊl) adj. (foll. by *for* or *to*) responsible for or accountable to.

answer back vb. to reply rudely to (someone).

ant (ænt) n. a small often wingless insect, typically living in highly organized colonies. [Old English *æmette*]

antacid (ænt'æsɪd) Chem. ~n. **1.** a substance used to treat acidity. ~adj. **2.** having the properties of this substance.

antagonism (æn'tægə,nɪzəm) n. openly expressed opposition.

antagonist (æn'tægənɪst) n. an opponent or adversary. —**an,tago'nistic** adj.

antagonize or **-nise** (æn'tægə,naɪz) vb. to make (someone) hostile; annoy or irritate. [Greek *anti-* against + *agōn* contest]

antalkali (ænt'ælkə,laɪ) n. Chem. a substance that neutralizes alkalis.

Antarctic (ænt'ɑːktɪk) n. **the.** the area around the South Pole. [Greek *antarktikos*]

Antarctic Circle n. the imaginary circle around the earth at latitude 66° 32′ S.

ante ('æntɪ) n. **1.** the stake put up before the deal in poker by the players. **2.** Informal. a sum of money representing a person's share. ~vb. **-teing, -ted** or **-teed. 3.** to place (one's stake) in poker. **4.** (foll. by *up*) Informal. to pay. [Latin: before]

ante- prefix. before in time or position: *antedate; antechamber.* [Latin]

anteater ('ænt,iːtə) n. a mammal with a long snout used for eating termites.

antecedent (,æntɪ'siːdᵊnt) n. **1.** an event or circumstance that happens or exists before another. **2.** Grammar. a word or phrase to which a relative pronoun, such as *who*, refers. **3.** (pl.) a person's ancestors and past history. ~adj. **4.** preceding in time or order; prior. [Latin *antecēdere* to go before]

antechamber ('æntɪ,tʃeɪmbə) n. an anteroom.

antedate (,æntɪ'deɪt) vb **1.** to be or occur at an earlier date than. **2.** to give (something) a date that is earlier than the actual date.

antediluvian (,æntɪdɪ'luːvɪən) adj. **1.** belonging to the ages before the biblical Flood. **2.** old-fashioned. [Latin *ante-* before + *dīluvium* flood]

antelope ('æntɪ,ləʊp) n., pl. **-lopes** or **-lope.** any of a group of graceful deerlike mammals of Africa and Asia, which have long legs and horns. [Late Greek *antholops* a legendary beast]

antenatal (,æntɪ'neɪtᵊl) adj. before birth; during pregnancy.

antenna (æn'tɛnə) n. **1.** (pl. **-nae** (-niː)) one of a pair of mobile feelers on the heads of insects, lobsters, and certain other creatures. **2.** (pl. **-nas**) an aerial. [Latin: sail yard]

antepenult (,æntɪpɪ'nʌlt) n. the third last syllable in a word. [Latin (*syllaba*) *antepaenultima*]

antepenultimate (,æntɪpɪ'nʌltɪmɪt) adj. **1.** third from last. ~n. **2.** anything that is third from last.

anterior (æn'tɪərɪə) adj. **1.** at or towards the front. **2.** earlier. [Latin]

anteroom ('æntɪ,ruːm) n. a small room giving entrance to a larger one, often used as a waiting room.

anthem ('ænθəm) n. **1.** a song of loyalty or devotion: *a national anthem.* **2.** a musical composition for a choir, usually set to words from the Bible. [Late Latin *antiphōna* antiphon]

anther ('ænθə) n. Bot. the part of the stamen of a flower in which the pollen matures. [Greek *anthos* flower]

ant hill n. a mound of soil built by ants around the entrance to their nest.

anthology (æn'θɒlədʒɪ) n., pl. **-gies.** a collection of poems or other literary pieces by various authors. [Greek *anthos* flower + *legein* to collect] —**an'thologist** n.

anthracite ('ænθrə,saɪt) n. a hard coal that

burns slowly with little smoke or flame but intense heat. [Greek *anthrax* coal]

anthrax ('ænθræks) *n.* a dangerous infectious disease of cattle and sheep, which can be transmitted to man. [Greek: carbuncle]

anthropocentric (ˌænθrəpəʊ'sɛntrɪk) *adj.* regarding the human being as the central factor in the universe. [Greek *anthrōpos* human being]

anthropoid ('ænθrəˌpɔɪd) *adj.* **1.** resembling a human being. ~*n.* **2.** an ape, such as the chimpanzee, that resembles a human being.

anthropology (ˌænθrə'pɒlədʒɪ) *n.* the study of human origins, institutions, and beliefs. [Greek *anthrōpos* human being + *logos* word] —**anthropological** (ˌænθrəpə'lɒdʒɪk³l) *adj.* —**anthro'pologist** *n.*

anthropomorphism (ˌænθrəpə'mɔːfɪzəm) *n.* the attribution of human form or behaviour to a god, animal, or object. —**anthropo'morphic** *adj.*

anthropomorphous (ˌænθrəpə'mɔːfəs) *adj.* shaped like a human being. [Greek *anthrōpos* human being + *morphē* form]

anti ('æntɪ) *Informal.* ~*adj.* **1.** opposed to a party, policy, or attitude. ~*n.* **2.** an opponent of a party, policy, or attitude.

anti- *prefix.* **1.** against; opposed to: *antiwar.* **2.** opposite to: *anticlimax.* **3.** counteracting or neutralizing: *antifreeze.* [Greek]

anti-aircraft (ˌæntɪ'ɛəkrɑːft) *n.* (modifier) for defence against aircraft attack.

antiballistic missile (ˌæntɪbə'lɪstɪk) *n.* a missile designed to destroy a ballistic missile in flight.

antibiotic (ˌæntɪbaɪ'ɒtɪk) *n.* **1.** a chemical substance capable of destroying bacteria. ~*adj.* **2.** of or relating to antibiotics.

antibody ('æntɪˌbɒdɪ) *n., pl.* **-bodies.** a protein produced in the blood, which destroys bacteria.

Antichrist ('æntɪˌkraɪst) *n.* **1.** New Testament. the principle antagonist of Christ. **2.** an enemy of Christ or Christianity.

anticipate (æn'tɪsɪˌpeɪt) *vb.* **1.** to foresee and act in advance of: *I had anticipated his question.* **2.** to look forward to (something). **3.** to make use of (something, such as one's salary) before receiving it. **4.** to mention (part of a story) before its proper time. [Latin *ante-* before + *capere* to take] —**an'tici,patory** *adj.*

anticipation (æn,tɪsɪ'peɪʃən) *n.* the act of anticipating; expectation, premonition, or foresight.

anticlerical (ˌæntɪ'klɛrɪk³l) *adj.* opposed to the power and influence of the clergy in politics.

anticlimax (ˌæntɪ'klaɪmæks) *n.* a disappointing conclusion to a series of events. —**anticlimactic** (ˌæntɪklaɪ'mæktɪk) *adj.*

anticline ('æntɪˌklaɪn) *n. Geol.* a fold of rock raised up into a broad arch so that the strata slope down on both sides.

anticlockwise (ˌæntɪ'klɒk,waɪz) *adv., adj.* in the opposite direction to the rotation of the hands of a clock.

anticoagulant (ˌæntɪkəʊ'æɡjʊlənt) *n.* a

substance that prevents the clotting of blood.

antics ('æntɪks) *pl. n.* absurd acts or postures. [Italian *antico* something grotesque (from fantastic carvings found in ruins of ancient Rome)]

anticyclone (ˌæntɪ'saɪkləʊn) *n. Meteorol.* an area of moving air of high pressure in which the winds rotate outwards.

antidepressant (ˌæntɪdɪ'prɛs³nt) *n.* **1.** a drug used to treat depression. ~*adj.* **2.** denoting such a drug.

antidote ('æntɪˌdəʊt) *n.* **1.** Med. a substance that counteracts a poison. **2.** anything that counteracts a harmful condition. [Greek *anti-* against + *didonai* to give]

antifreeze ('æntɪˌfriːz) *n.* a liquid added to water to lower its freezing point, used in the radiator of a motor vehicle to prevent freezing.

antigen ('æntɪdʒən) *n.* a substance, usually a toxin, that causes the body to produce antibodies. [*anti*(body) + *-gen* (suffix) producing]

antihero ('æntɪˌhɪərəʊ) *n., pl.* **-roes.** a central character in a novel, play, or film, who lacks the traditional heroic virtues.

antihistamine (ˌæntɪ'hɪstəˌmiːn) *n.* a drug that neutralizes the effects of histamine, used in the treatment of allergies.

antiknock (ˌæntɪ'nɒk) *n.* a substance added to motor fuel to reduce knocking in the engine caused by too rapid combustion.

antilogarithm (ˌæntɪ'lɒɡəˌrɪðəm) *n. Maths.* a number corresponding to a given logarithm.

antimacassar (ˌæntɪmə'kæsə) *n.* a cloth put over the back of a chair to prevent soiling. [*anti-* + *Macassar* (oil)]

antimatter ('æntɪˌmætə) *n. Physics.* a hypothetical form of matter composed of antiparticles.

antimony ('æntɪmənɪ) *n. Chem.* a silvery-white metallic element that is added to alloys to increase their strength. Symbol: Sb [Medieval Latin *antimōnium*]

antinomian (ˌæntɪ'nəʊmɪən) *adj.* **1.** holding the view that by faith a Christian is released from the obligation of observing moral law. ~*n.* **2.** a member of a Christian sect holding this view.

antinomy (æn'tɪnəmɪ) *n., pl.* **-mies.** contradiction between two laws or principles that are reasonable in themselves. [Greek *anti-* against + *nomos* law]

antinovel ('æntɪˌnɒv³l) *n.* a type of prose fiction in which conventional elements of the novel are rejected.

antinuclear (ˌæntɪ'njuːklɪə) *adj.* opposed to nuclear weapons or nuclear power.

antiparticle ('æntɪˌpɑːtɪk³l) *n. Nuclear physics.* an elementary particle that has the same mass as its corresponding particle, but opposite charge and opposite magnetism.

antipasto (ˌæntɪ'pæstəʊ) *n., pl.* **-tos.** an appetizer in an Italian meal. [Italian: before food]

antipathy (æn'tɪpəθɪ) *n.* a feeling of dislike or hostility. [Greek *anti-* against +

patheia feeling] —**antipathetic** (ˌæntɪpə-ˈθetɪk) *adj.*

antipersonnel (ˌæntɪˌpɜːsəˈnel) *adj.* (of weapons or bombs) designed to be used against people rather than equipment.

antiperspirant (ˌæntɪˈpɜːspərənt) *n.* a substance applied to the skin to reduce or prevent perspiration.

antiphon (ˈæntɪfən) *n.* a hymn sung in alternate parts by two groups of singers. [Greek *anti-* against + *phōnē* sound]

antipodes (ænˈtɪpəˌdiːz) *pl. n.* **1.** any two places that are situated diametrically opposite one another on the earth's surface. **2. the Antipodes.** Australia and New Zealand. [Greek pl. of *antipous* having the feet opposite] —**antipodean** (ænˌtɪpəˈdiːən) *adj.*

antipope (ˈæntɪˌpəʊp) *n.* a pope set up in opposition to the one chosen by church laws.

antipyretic (ˌæntɪpaɪˈretɪk) *adj.* **1.** reducing fever. ~*n.* **2.** a drug that reduces fever.

antiquarian (ˌæntɪˈkwɛərɪən) *adj.* **1.** collecting or dealing with antiquities or rare books. ~*n.* **2.** an antiquary.

antiquary (ˈæntɪkwərɪ) *n., pl.* **-quaries.** a person who collects, deals in, or studies antiques or ancient works of art.

antiquated (ˈæntɪˌkweɪtɪd) *adj.* obsolete or old-fashioned. [Latin *antiquus* ancient]

antique (ænˈtiːk) *n.* **1.** a decorative object or piece of furniture, of an earlier period, that is valued for its beauty, workmanship, and age. ~*adj.* **2.** made in an earlier period. **3.** *Informal.* old-fashioned. [Latin *antiquus* ancient]

antiquity (ænˈtɪkwɪtɪ) *n., pl.* **-ties. 1.** great age. **2.** the far distant past, esp. before the Middle Ages. **3.** (*pl.*) remains that date from ancient times.

antirrhinum (ˌæntɪˈraɪnəm) *n.* a two-lipped flower of various colours. [Greek *anti-* like, imitating + *rhis* nose]

antiscorbutic (ˌæntɪskɔːˈbjuːtɪk) *adj.* preventing or curing scurvy.

anti-Semitic (ˌæntɪsɪˈmɪtɪk) *adj.* discriminating against Jews. —**anti-Semite** (ˌæntɪˈsiːmaɪt) *n.* —**anti-Semitism** (ˌæntɪˈsemɪˌtɪzəm) *n.*

antiseptic (ˌæntɪˈseptɪk) *adj.* **1.** preventing infection by killing germs. ~*n.* **2.** an antiseptic substance.

antiserum (ˈæntɪˌsɪərəm) *n.* blood serum containing antibodies used to treat or provide immunity to a disease.

antisocial (ˌæntɪˈsəʊʃəl) *adj.* **1.** avoiding the company of other people. **2.** (of behaviour) annoying to other people.

antistatic (ˌæntɪˈstætɪk) *adj.* reducing the effects of static electricity.

antitank (ˌæntɪˈtæŋk) *adj.* (of weapons) designed to destroy military tanks.

antithesis (ænˈtɪθɪsɪs) *n., pl.* **-ses** (-ˌsiːz). **1.** the exact opposite. **2.** *Rhetoric.* the placing together of contrasting ideas or words to produce an effect of balance, such as *where gods command, mere mortals*

must obey. [Greek *anti-* against + *tithenai* to place] —**antithetical** (ˌæntɪˈθetɪkˀl) *adj.*

antitoxin (ˌæntɪˈtɒksɪn) *n.* an antibody that acts against a toxin. —**antitoxic** *adj.*

antitrades (ˈæntɪˌtreɪdz) *pl. n.* winds blowing in the opposite direction from and above the trade winds.

antitrust (ˌæntɪˈtrʌst) *adj. Chiefly U.S.* (of laws) opposing business monopolies.

antler (ˈæntlə) *n.* one of a pair of branched horns on the heads of male deer. [Old French *antoillier*]

antonym (ˈæntənɪm) *n.* a word that means the opposite of another. [Greek *anti-* opposite + *onoma* name]

antrum (ˈæntrəm) *n., pl.* **-tra** (-trə). *Anat.* a natural cavity, esp. in a bone. [Greek *antron*]

anus (ˈeɪnəs) *n.* the opening at the end of the alimentary canal, through which faeces are discharged. [Latin]

anvil (ˈænvɪl) *n.* a heavy iron block on which metals are hammered into particular shapes. [Old English *anfealt*]

anxiety (æŋˈzaɪɪtɪ) *n., pl.* **-ties. 1.** a state of uneasiness about what may happen. **2.** eagerness: *her anxiety to please.*

anxious (ˈæŋkʃəs, ˈæŋ fəs) *adj.* **1.** worried and tense. **2.** causing anxiety: *an anxious time.* **3.** intensely desiring: *anxious to succeed.* [Latin *anxius*; rel. to *angere* to torment] —**ˈanxiously** *adv.*

any (ˈenɪ) *det.* **1.** one, some, or several, no matter how much or what kind: *you may take any clothes you like; take any you like.* **2.** (*used with a negative or question*) even the smallest amount or even one: *I can't stand any noise; don't give her any.* **3.** whatever or whichever: *any dictionary will do.* **4.** an indefinite or unlimited: *any number of friends.* ~*adv.* **5.** (*used with a negative or question*) to even the smallest extent: *it isn't any worse.* [Old English *ænig*]

anybody (ˈenɪˌbɒdɪ) *pron.* same as **anyone.**

anyhow (ˈenɪˌhaʊ) *adv.* same as **anyway.**

anyone (ˈenɪˌwʌn) *pron.* **1.** any person; anybody. **2.** (*used with a negative or question*) a person of any importance: *is he anyone?*

anything (ˈenɪˌθɪŋ) *pron.* **1.** any object, event, or action whatever: *anything might happen.* ~*adv.* **2.** in any way: *he wasn't anything like his father.* **3.** *anything but.* not at all: *she was anything but happy.*

anyway (ˈenɪˌweɪ) *adv.* **1.** at any rate; nevertheless. **2.** carelessly. **3.** in any manner.

anywhere (ˈenɪˌwɛə) *adv.* **1.** in, at, or to any place. **2.** *get anywhere.* to be successful: *you'll never get anywhere with that attitude.*

Anzac (ˈænzæk) *n.* (in World War I) a soldier serving with the Australian and New Zealand Army Corps.

AOB (on the agenda for a meeting) any other business.

aorta (eɪˈɔːtə) *n., pl.* **-tas** or **-tae** (-tiː). the main artery of the body, which carries oxygen-rich blood from the heart. [Greek *aortē* something lifted]

apace (ə'peɪs) *adv. Literary.* quickly.

Apache (ə'pætʃɪ) *n., pl.* **Apaches** *or* **Apache.** a North American Indian of the southwestern U.S. and N Mexico. [Mexican Spanish]

apache dance (ə'pæʃ) *n.* a fast violent dance in French vaudeville, supposedly between a Parisian gangster and his girl. [after the *Apaches*, Indian people of the SW U.S.]

apart (ə'pɑːt) *adj., adv.* **1.** to or in pieces: *he took the television apart.* **2.** separate in time, place, or position: *he stood apart from the group.* **3.** not being taken into account: *these difficulties apart, the project ran smoothly.* **4.** individual; distinct: *a race apart.* **5. apart from.** other than: *all sports apart from athletics.* [Old French *a part* at (the) side]

apartheid (ə'pɑːthaɪt) *n.* the official government policy of racial segregation in South Africa. [Afrikaans *apart* apart + *-heid* -hood]

apartment (ə'pɑːtmənt) *n.* **1.** any room in a building, usually one of several forming a suite, used as living accommodation. **2.** Chiefly U.S. & Canad. a flat. [French *appartement*]

apathy ('æpəθɪ) *n.* lack of interest or enthusiasm. [Greek *a-* without + *pathos* feeling] —**apathetic** (,æpə'θɛtɪk) *adj.*

ape (eɪp) *n.* **1.** an animal, such as a chimpanzee or gorilla, which is closely related to human beings and the monkeys, and which has no tail. **2.** a stupid, clumsy, or ugly man. ~*vb.* **3.** to imitate. [Old English *apa*] —**'ape,like** *adj.*

apeman ('eɪp,mæn) *n., pl.* **-men.** an extinct primate thought to have been the forerunner of true humans.

aperient (ə'pɪərɪənt) *Med.* ~*adj.* **1.** having a mild laxative effect. ~*n.* **2.** a mild laxative. [Latin *aperīre* to open]

apéritif (ə,pɛrɪ'tiːf) *n.* an alcoholic drink taken before a meal. [French]

aperture ('æpətʃə) *n.* **1.** a hole or opening. **2.** an opening in a camera or telescope that controls the amount of light entering it. [Latin *aperīre* to open]

apex ('eɪpɛks) *n.* the highest point. [Latin: point]

APEX ('eɪpɛks) Advance Purchase Excursion: a reduced fare for journeys booked a specified period in advance.

aphasia (ə'feɪzɪə) *n.* a disorder of the central nervous system that affects the ability to use and understand words. [Greek *a-* not + *phanai* to speak]

aphelion (æ'fiːlɪən) *n., pl.* **-lia** (-lɪə). *Astron.* the point in the orbit of a planet or comet when it is farthest from the sun. [Greek *apo-* from + *hēlios* sun]

aphid ('eɪfɪd) *or* **aphis** ('eɪfɪs) *n., pl.* **aphids** *or* **aphides** ('eɪfɪ,diːz). a small insect which feeds by sucking the juices from plants. [New Latin]

aphorism ('æfə,rɪzəm) *n.* a short clever saying expressing a general truth. [Greek *aphorizein* to define]

aphrodisiac (,æfrə'dɪzɪæk) *n.* **1.** a substance that arouses sexual desire. ~*adj.* **2.** arousing sexual desire. [Greek *aphrodisios* belonging to *Aphrodite*, goddess of love]

apiary ('eɪpɪərɪ) *n., pl.* **-aries.** a place where bees are kept. [Latin *apis* bee] —**'apiarist** *n.*

apical ('eɪpɪk'l) *adj.* of, at, or being an apex.

apiculture ('eɪpɪ,kʌltʃə) *n.* the breeding and care of bees. [Latin *apis* bee + culture] —**,api'culturist** *n.*

apiece (ə'piːs) *adv.* each: *they were given two apples apiece.*

apish ('eɪpɪʃ) *adj.* **1.** stupid; foolish. **2.** resembling an ape.

aplomb (ə'plɒm) *n.* stylish self-possession. [French: uprightness]

apocalypse (ə'pɒkəlɪps) *n.* the end of the world or some other event of great destructive violence. [Greek *apo-* away + *kaluptein* to hide] —**a,poca'lyptic** *adj.*

Apocalypse (ə'pɒkəlɪps) *n.* **the.** *Bible.* the Book of Revelation.

Apocrypha (ə'pɒkrɪfə) *n.* (functioning as *sing.* or *pl.*) **the.** the 14 books included as an appendix to the Old Testament, which are not in the Hebrew canon. [Late Latin *apocrypha (scripta)* hidden (writings), Greek *apokruptein* to hide away]

apocryphal (ə'pɒkrɪfəl) *adj.* of questionable authenticity.

apogee ('æpə,dʒiː) *n.* **1.** *Astron.* the point in its orbit around the earth when the moon or an artificial satellite is farthest from the earth. **2.** the highest point. [Greek *apogaios* away from the earth]

apolitical (,eɪpə'lɪtɪk'l) *adj.* not concerned with political matters.

apologetic (ə,pɒlə'dʒɛtɪk) *adj.* showing or expressing regret. —**a,polo'getically** *adv.*

apologetics (ə,pɒlə'dʒɛtɪks) *n.* (functioning as *sing.*) the branch of theology concerned with the reasoned defence of Christianity.

apologia (,æpə'ləʊdʒɪə) *n.* a formal written defence of a cause.

apologist (ə'pɒlədʒɪst) *n.* a person who offers a formal defence of a cause.

apologize *or* **-gise** (ə'pɒlə,dʒaɪz) *vb.* to say that one is sorry for some wrongdoing.

apology (ə'pɒlədʒɪ) *n., pl.* **-gies.** **1.** an expression of regret for some wrongdoing. **2.** (foll. by *for*) a poor example of: *an apology for a man.* **3.** same as **apologia.** [Greek *apologia* a verbal defence, speech]

apophthegm ('æpə,θɛm) *n.* a short clever saying expressing a general truth. [Greek *apophthengesthai* to speak frankly]

apoplectic (,æpə'plɛktɪk) *adj.* **1.** of apoplexy. **2.** *Informal.* furious.

apoplexy ('æpə,plɛksɪ) *n. Med.* a stroke. [Greek *apoplēssein* to cripple by a stroke]

apostasy (ə'pɒstəsɪ) *n., pl.* **-sies.** abandonment of one's religious faith, political party, or cause. [Greek *apostasis* desertion]

apostate (ə'pɒstɪt) *n.* **1.** a person who has

abandoned his religion, political party, or cause. ~*adj.* **2.** guilty of apostasy.

a posteriori (eɪ pɒsˌtɛrɪˈɔːtraɪ) *adj. Logic.* involving reasoning from effect to cause. [Latin: from the latter]

apostle (əˈpɒsˀl) *n.* **1.** (*cap.*) one of the 12 disciples chosen by Christ to preach his gospel. **2.** an ardent supporter of a cause or movement. [Greek *apostolos* a messenger]

apostolic (ˌæpəˈstɒlɪk) *adj.* **1.** of or relating to the Apostles or their teachings. **2.** of or relating to the pope.

Apostolic See *n.* the see of the pope, at Rome.

apostrophe[1] (əˈpɒstrəfɪ) *n.* the punctuation mark ' used to indicate the omission of a letter or letters, such as *he's* for *he has* or *he is*, and to form the possessive, as in *John's father*. [Greek *apostrephein* to turn away]

apostrophe[2] (əˈpɒstrəfɪ) *n. Rhetoric.* a digression from a speech to address an imaginary or absent person or thing. [Greek: a turning away]

apostrophize *or* **-phise** (əˈpɒstrəˌfaɪz) *vb. Rhetoric.* to address an apostrophe to.

apothecary (əˈpɒθɪkərɪ) *n., pl.* **-caries.** *Archaic.* a chemist. [Greek *apothēkē* storehouse]

apotheosis (əˌpɒθɪˈəʊsɪs) *n., pl.* **-ses** (-siːz). **1.** elevation to the rank of a god. **2.** a perfect example: *the apotheosis of generosity.* [Greek]

appal *or U.S.* **appall** (əˈpɔːl) *vb.* **-palling,** **-palled.** to fill (someone) with horror. [Old French *appalir* to turn pale]

appalling (əˈpɔːlɪŋ) *adj.* **1.** causing dismay, horror, or revulsion. **2.** very bad. —**ap'pallingly** *adv.*

apparatus (ˌæpəˈreɪtəs, -ˈrɑːtəs) *n.* **1.** a collection of equipment used for a particular purpose. **2.** any complicated device, system, or organization. [Latin *apparāre* to make ready]

apparel (əˈpærəl) *n. Archaic.* clothing. [Latin *parāre* to prepare]

apparent (əˈpærənt) *adj.* **1.** readily seen or understood; obvious. **2.** seeming, as opposed to real: *his apparent innocence.* [Latin *appārēre* to appear] —**ap'parently** *adv.*

apparition (ˌæpəˈrɪʃən) *n.* a ghost or ghostlike figure. [Latin *appārēre* to appear]

appeal (əˈpiːl) *n.* **1.** an earnest request for money or help. **2.** the power to attract, please, or interest people. **3.** an application to a higher authority to change a decision that has been made. **4.** *Law.* a request for a review by a superior court of the decision of a lower tribunal. ~*vb.* **5.** to make an earnest request. **6.** (foll. by *to*) to attract, please, or interest (someone). **7.** to resort to a higher authority to change a decision. **8.** to call on in support of an earnest request: *I appealed to his sense of reason.* **9.** *Law.* to apply to a superior court to review (a case or issue decided by a lower tribunal). **10.** *Cricket.* to request the umpire to declare a batsman out. [Latin *appellāre* to entreat] —**ap'pealing** *adj.*

appear (əˈpɪə) *vb.* **1.** to come into sight. **2.** to seem: *the evidence appears to support you.* **3.** to develop; occur: *faults appeared during testing.* **4.** to be published or become available: *his biography appeared last month.* **5.** to perform: *he has appeared in many London productions.* **6.** to be present in court before a magistrate or judge: *he appeared on two charges of theft.* [Latin *appārēre*]

appearance (əˈpɪərəns) *n.* **1.** the act or an instance of appearing. **2.** the outward aspect of a person or thing. **3. keep up appearances.** to maintain the public impression of wellbeing or normality. **4. put in an appearance.** to attend an event briefly. **5. to all appearances.** apparently.

appease (əˈpiːz) *vb.* **1.** to pacify (someone) by yielding to his demands. **2.** to satisfy or relieve (a feeling). [Old French *apaisier*] —**ap'peasement** *n.*

appellant (əˈpɛlənt) *Law.* ~*n.* **1.** a person who appeals to a higher court to review the decision of a lower tribunal. ~*adj.* **2.** same as **appellate.**

appellate (əˈpɛlɪt) *adj. Law.* **1.** of appeals. **2.** (of a tribunal) having the power to review appeals.

appellation (ˌæpɪˈleɪʃən) *n.* a name or title.

append (əˈpɛnd) *vb.* to add as a supplement: *to append a footnote.* [Latin *pendere* to hang]

appendage (əˈpɛndɪdʒ) *n.* a secondary part attached to a main part.

appendicectomy (əˌpɛndɪˈsɛktəmɪ) *or esp. U.S. & Canad.* **appendectomy** (ˌæpənˈdɛktəmɪ) *n., pl.* **-mies.** surgical removal of the appendix. [*appendix* + Greek *tomē* a cutting]

appendicitis (əˌpɛndɪˈsaɪtɪs) *n.* inflammation of the appendix.

appendix (əˈpɛndɪks) *n., pl.* **-dixes** *or* **-dices** (-dɪˌsiːz). **1.** separate additional material at the end of a book. **2.** *Anat.* a short thin tube, closed at one end and attached to the large intestine at the other end. [Latin]

appertain (ˌæpəˈteɪn) *vb.* (foll. by *to*) to belong to, relate to, or be connected with. [Latin *ad-* to + *pertinēre* to pertain]

appetence (ˈæpɪtəns) *or* **appetency** *n., pl.* **-tences** *or* **-tencies.** a craving or desire. [Latin *appetentia*]

appetite (ˈæpɪˌtaɪt) *n.* **1.** a desire for food or drink. **2.** (foll. by *for*) a liking or willingness: *a great appetite for work.* [Latin *appetere* to desire ardently]

appetizer *or* **-iser** (ˈæpɪˌtaɪzə) *n.* a small amount of food or drink taken at the start of a meal to stimulate the appetite.

appetizing *or* **-ising** (ˈæpɪˌtaɪzɪŋ) *adj.* stimulating the appetite; looking or smelling delicious.

applaud (əˈplɔːd) *vb.* **1.** to show approval of (a performance, an entertainer, or a speaker) by clapping one's hands. **2.** to express approval of: *I applaud your decision.* [Latin *applaudere*]

applause (əˈplɔːz) *n.* appreciation shown by clapping one's hands.

apple ('æp'l) n. **1.** a round firm fruit with red, yellow, or green skin and crisp whitish flesh, that grows on trees. **2. apple of one's eye.** a person that one loves very much. [Old English æppel]

apple-pie bed n. a bed made with the sheets folded so as to prevent the person from entering it.

apple-pie order n. **in apple-pie order.** *Informal.* very tidy.

appliance (ə'plaɪəns) n. a machine or device that has a specific function.

applicable ('æplɪkəb'l) adj. appropriate or relevant.

applicant ('æplɪkənt) n. a person who applies for something, such as a job or grant.

application (,æplɪ'keɪʃən) n. **1.** a formal request, for example for a job. **2.** the act of applying something to a particular use. **3.** diligent effort: *a job requiring application.* **4.** the act of putting something, such as a lotion or paint, on to a surface.

applicator ('æplɪ,keɪtə) n. a device for applying cosmetics, medication, or some other substance.

applied (ə'plaɪd) adj. put to practical use: *applied mathematics.*

appliqué (æ'pliːkeɪ) n. a kind of decoration in which one material is cut out and sewn or fixed onto another. [French: applied]

apply (ə'plaɪ) vb. **-plying, -plied. 1.** (foll. by *for*) to make a formal request for (something, such as a job or grant). **2.** to put (a rule or theory) to practical use. **3.** to be relevant or appropriate. **4.** to put (something, such as a lotion or paint) on to a surface. **5. apply oneself.** to concentrate one's efforts or faculties. [Latin *applicāre* to attach to]

appoint (ə'pɔɪnt) vb. **1.** to assign (someone) officially, to a job or position. **2.** to establish (a time or place for an event). **3.** to equip or furnish: *a well-appointed hotel.* [Old French *apointer* to put into a good state] **—appoin'tee** n.

appointment (ə'pɔɪntmənt) n. **1.** an arrangement to meet a person. **2.** the act of placing someone in a job or position. **3.** the person appointed. **4.** the job or position to which a person is appointed. **5.** (*pl.*) fixtures or fittings.

apportion (ə'pɔːʃən) vb. to divide, distribute, or assign shares of.

apposite ('æpəzɪt) adj. appropriate; apt. [Latin *ad-* near + *pōnere* to put]

apposition (,æpə'zɪʃən) n. a grammatical construction in which a noun or group of words is placed after another to modify its meaning, for example *my friend the mayor.*

appraisal (ə'preɪz'l) n. an assessment of the worth or quality of a person or thing; valuation.

appraise (ə'preɪz) vb. to assess the worth, value, or quality of. [Old French *prisier*]

appreciable (ə'priːʃəb'l) adj. enough to be noticed; significant. **—ap'preciably** adv.

appreciate (ə'priːʃɪ,eɪt) vb. **1.** to feel grateful for: *I appreciate your kindness.* **2.** to be aware of and understand: *I appre-*ciate *your problem.* **3.** to value highly: *he doesn't appreciate good music.* **4.** to increase in value. [Latin *pretium* price]

appreciation (ə,priːʃɪ'eɪʃən) n. **1.** gratitude. **2.** awareness and understanding of a problem or difficulty. **3.** sensitive recognition of good qualities, as in art. **4.** an increase in value.

appreciative (ə'priːʃɪətɪv) or **appreciatory** adj. feeling or expressing appreciation.

apprehend (,æprɪ'hend) vb. **1.** to arrest (someone) and take him into custody. **2.** to grasp (something) mentally; understand. [Latin *apprehendere* to lay hold of]

apprehension (,æprɪ'henʃən) n. **1.** anxiety or dread. **2.** the act of arresting. **3.** understanding.

apprehensive (,æprɪ'hensɪv) adj. fearful or anxious about the future.

apprentice (ə'prentɪs) n. **1.** someone who works for a skilled person for a fixed period in order to learn his trade. ~vb. **2.** to take or place (someone) as an apprentice. [Old French *aprendre* to learn] **—ap'prentice,ship** n.

apprise or **-ize** (ə'praɪz) vb. (foll. by *of*) to make (someone) aware: *let me apprise you of the facts.* [French *apprendre* to teach; learn]

appro ('æprəʊ) n. **on appro.** *Informal.* on approval.

approach (ə'prəʊtʃ) vb. **1.** to come close or closer to (someone or something). **2.** to make a proposal or suggestion to (someone). **3.** to begin to deal with (a matter). ~n. **4.** the act of coming close or closer. **5.** the way or means of reaching a place; access. **6.** a proposal or suggestion made to a person. **7.** a way of dealing with a matter. **8.** the course followed by an aircraft preparing for landing. **9.** an approximation. [Latin *ad-* to + *prope* near] **—ap'proachable** adj.

approbation (,æprə'beɪʃən) n. approval or permission.

appropriate adj. (ə'prəʊprɪt). **1.** right or suitable. ~vb. (ə'prəʊprɪ,eɪt). **2.** to take (something) for one's own use without permission. **3.** to put (money) aside for a particular purpose. [Latin *ad-* to + *proprius* one's own] **—ap'propriately** adv.

appropriation (ə,prəʊprɪ'eɪʃən) n. **1.** the act of putting money aside for a particular purpose. **2.** money put aside for a particular purpose.

approval (ə'pruːv'l) n. **1.** consent. **2.** a favourable opinion. **3. on approval.** (of articles for sale) with an option to return them to the shop if not suitable: *I got this hat on approval.*

approve (ə'pruːv) vb. **1.** (foll. by *of*) to consider fair, good, or right. **2.** to authorize or sanction. [Latin *approbāre*]

approx. approximate.

approximate adj. (ə'prɒksɪmɪt). **1.** almost exact. ~vb. (ə'prɒksɪ,meɪt). **2.** (foll. by *to*) to come close to; be almost the same as. [Latin *ad-* to + *proximus* nearest]

—ap'proximately adv. **—approximation** (ə,prɒksɪ'meɪʃən) n.

appurtenances (ə'pɜːtɪnənsɪz) pl. n. minor or additional features or possessions. [Old French apartenance]

Apr. April.

après-ski (,æpreɪ'skiː) n. social activity following a day's skiing.

apricot ('eɪprɪ,kɒt) n. **1.** a yellowish-orange juicy fruit which resembles a small peach and which grows on a tree. ~adj. **2.** yellowish-orange. [Latin praecox early-ripening]

April ('eɪprəl) n. the fourth month of the year. [Latin Aprīlis]

April fool n. a victim of a practical joke played on the first of April (**April Fools' Day** or **All Fools' Day**).

a priori (eɪ praɪ'ɔːraɪ) adj. Logic. involving reasoning from cause to effect. [Latin: from the previous]

apron ('eɪprən) n. **1.** a garment worn over the front of the body to protect one's clothes. **2.** the part of a stage extending in front of the curtain. **3.** a hard-surfaced area at an airport or hangar for manoeuvring and loading aircraft. **4. tied to one's mother's** or **wife's apron strings.** dominated by one's mother or wife. [Middle English: mistaken division of a napron, from mappa napkin]

apropos (,æprə'pəʊ) adj. **1.** appropriate. ~adv. **2.** by the way; incidentally. **3. apropos of.** with regard to. [French à propos to the purpose]

apse (æps) n. a domed or vaulted semicircular recess at the east end of a church. [Greek apsis a fitting together]

apsis ('æpsɪs) n., pl. **apsides** ('æpsɪˌdiːz). Astron. either of two points lying at the extremities of the elliptical orbit of a planet or satellite. [see APSE]

apt (æpt) adj. **1.** suitable; appropriate. **2.** having a tendency (to behave as specified): I am apt to forget my keys. **3.** quick to learn: an apt pupil. [Latin aptus fitting] **—'aptly** adv. **—'aptness** n.

apteryx ('æptərɪks) n. same as **kiwi.** [Greek a- without + pteron wing]

aptitude ('æptɪˌtjuːd) n. natural tendency or ability.

aqua ('ækwə) adj. bluish-green. [Latin: water]

aqua fortis ('fɔːtɪs) n. Obs. nitric acid. [Latin: strong water]

aqualung ('ækwəˌlʌŋ) n. a self-contained underwater breathing apparatus consisting of a mouthpiece attached to air cylinders strapped to one's back.

aquamarine (,ækwəmə'riːn) n. **1.** a clear greenish-blue stone used in jewellery. ~adj. **2.** greenish-blue. [Latin: sea water]

aquaplane ('ækwəˌpleɪn) n. **1.** a board on which a person stands to be towed by a motorboat for sport. ~vb. **2.** to ride on an aquaplane. **3.** (of a motor vehicle) to skim uncontrollably on a thin film of water.

aqua regia ('riːdʒɪə) n. a mixture of nitric acid and hydrochloric acid. [New Latin:

royal water; referring to its use in dissolving gold, the royal metal]

aquarium (ə'kwɛərɪəm) n., pl. **aquariums** or **aquaria** (ə'kwɛərɪə). **1.** a tank in which fish and other underwater creatures are kept. **2.** a building in a zoo in which fish and other underwater creatures are kept. [Latin aquārius relating to water]

Aquarius (ə'kwɛərɪəs) n. Astrol. the eleventh sign of the zodiac: the water carrier. [Latin]

aquatic (ə'kwætɪk) adj. **1.** growing or living in water. **2.** Sport. performed in or on water. ~n. **3.** an aquatic animal or plant. **4.** (pl.) water sports. [Latin aqua water]

aquatint ('ækwə,tɪnt) n. a print resembling watercolour, produced by etching copper with acid. [Italian acqua tinta dyed water]

aqua vitae ('viːtaɪ) n. Archaic. brandy. [Medieval Latin: water of life]

aqueduct ('ækwɪ,dʌkt) n. a structure, often a bridge, that carries water across a valley or river. [Latin aqua water + dūcere to convey]

aqueous ('eɪkwɪəs) adj. **1.** of, like, or containing water. **2.** produced by the action of water. [Latin aqua water]

aqueous humour n. Physiol. the watery fluid in the eyeball, between the cornea and the lens.

aquifer ('ækwɪfə) n. a deposit of rock, such as sandstone, containing water that can be used to supply wells. [Latin aqua water + ferre to carry]

aquiline ('ækwɪ,laɪn) adj. **1.** (of a nose) curved like an eagle's beak. **2.** of or like an eagle. [Latin aquila eagle]

Ar Chem. argon.

AR Arkansas.

Arab ('ærəb) n. **1.** a member of a Semitic people originally from Arabia. **2.** a small horse, used for riding. ~adj. **3.** of or relating to the Arabs. [Arabic 'Arab]

arabesque (,ærə'bɛsk) n. **1.** a ballet position in which the dancer has one leg raised behind and the arms extended. **2.** an ornate piece of music. **3.** Arts. an elaborate design of intertwined leaves, flowers, and scrolls. [Italian arabesco in the Arabic style]

Arabian (ə'reɪbɪən) adj. **1.** of Arabia or the Arabs. ~n. **2.** same as **Arab.**

Arabic ('ærəbɪk) n. **1.** the language of the Arabs. ~adj. **2.** of this language, the Arabs, or Arabia.

Arabic numeral n. one of the numbers 1,2,3,4,5,6,7,8,9,0.

arable ('ærəb'l) adj. (of land) suitable for growing crops on. [Latin arāre to plough]

arachnid (ə'ræknɪd) n. an eight-legged insect-like creature, such as a spider, scorpion, or tick. [Greek arakhnē spider]

arak ('ærək) n. same as **arrack.**

Aramaic (,ærə'meɪɪk) n. a branch of the Semitic group of languages, spoken in parts of Syria and the Lebanon.

arbiter ('ɑːbɪtə) n. **1.** a person empowered to judge in a dispute; referee. **2.** a person having influence over something: *the arbiter of good taste.*

arbitrary ('ɑːbɪtrərɪ) *adj.* **1.** based on one's personal choice or whims. **2.** dictatorial. —**'arbitrarily** *adv.*

arbitrate ('ɑːbɪ,treɪt) *vb.* to settle (a dispute) by arbitration. [Latin *arbitrāri* to give judgment] —**'arbi,trator** *n.*

arbitration (,ɑːbɪ'treɪʃən) *n.* the hearing and settlement of a dispute by an impartial referee chosen by both sides.

arbor[1] ('ɑːbə) *n.* U.S. same as **arbour.**

arbor[2] ('ɑːbə) *n.* a revolving shaft or axle in a machine. [Latin: tree]

arboreal (ɑː'bɔːrɪəl) *adj.* **1.** of or resembling a tree. **2.** living in or among trees.

arboretum (,ɑːbə'riːtəm) *n., pl.* **-ta** (-tə). a botanical garden where rare trees or shrubs are cultivated. [Latin *arbor* tree]

arboriculture ('ɑːbərɪ,kʌltʃə) *n.* the cultivation of trees or shrubs. [Latin *arbor* tree + *culture*]

arbor vitae ('ɑːbə 'vaɪtaɪ) *n.* an evergreen tree. [New Latin: tree of life]

arbour *or* U.S. **arbor** ('ɑːbə) *n.* a shelter in a garden shaded by trees or climbing plants. [Latin *herba* grass]

arbutus (ɑː'bjuːtəs) *n.* an evergreen shrub with berries like strawberries. [Latin]

arc (ɑːk) *n.* **1.** something curved in shape. **2.** *Maths.* a section of a circle or other curve. **3.** *Electricity.* a stream of very bright light that forms when an electric current flows between two electrodes separated by a small gap. ~*vb.* **4.** to form an arc. [Latin *arcus* bow, arch]

ARC AIDS-related complex: relatively mild symptoms suffered in the early stages of infection with the AIDS virus.

arcade (ɑː'keɪd) *n.* **1.** a covered passageway, usually lined with shops. **2.** a set of arches and their supporting columns. [Latin *arcus* bow, arch]

Arcadian (ɑː'keɪdɪən) *adj.* **1.** ideally rustic. ~*n.* **2.** a person who leads a quiet simple country life. [*Arcadia*, rural district of Ancient Greece]

arcane (ɑː'keɪn) *adj.* very mysterious. [Latin *arcānus* secret]

arch[1] (ɑːtʃ) *n.* **1.** a curved structure that spans an opening or supports a bridge or roof. **2.** something curved like an arch. **3.** the curved lower part of the foot. ~*vb.* **4.** to form an arch or cause (something) to form an arch. [Latin *arcus* bow, arch]

arch[2] (ɑːtʃ) *adj.* knowing or superior; coyly playful: *an arch look.* [independent use of ARCH-] —**'archly** *adv.*

arch- *or* **archi-** *combining form.* chief; principal: *archbishop.* [Greek *arkhein* to rule]

Archaean *or esp.* U.S. **Archean** (ɑː'kiːən) *adj.* of the earliest geological period.

archaeology *or* **archeology** (,ɑːkɪ-'ɒlədʒɪ) *n.* the study of ancient cultures by the scientific analysis of physical remains. [Greek *arkhaiologia* study of what is ancient] —**archaeological** *or* **archeological** (,ɑːkɪə'lɒdʒɪk³l) *adj.* —**,archae'ologist** *or* **,arche'ologist** *n.*

archaeopteryx (,ɑːkɪ'ɒptərɪks) *n.* an extinct primitive bird with teeth, a long tail, and well-developed wings. [Greek *arkhaios* ancient + *pteryx* winged creature]

archaic (ɑː'keɪk) *adj.* **1.** ancient; of a much earlier period. **2.** out of date; old-fashioned. **3.** (of a word or phrase) no longer in everyday use; found only in literature of an earlier period. [Greek *arkhē* beginning] —**ar'chaically** *adv.*

archaism ('ɑːkeɪ,ɪzəm) *n.* **1.** the use or imitation of archaic words or style. **2.** an archaic word or style. —**,archa'istic** *adj.*

archangel ('ɑːk,eɪndʒəl) *n.* an angel of the highest rank.

archbishop ('ɑːtʃ'bɪʃəp) *n.* a bishop of the highest rank.

archbishopric ('ɑːtʃ'bɪʃəprɪk) *n.* the rank, office, or diocese of an archbishop.

archdeacon ('ɑːtʃ'diːkən) *n.* a church official ranking just below a bishop. —**'arch-'deaconry** *n.*

archdiocese (,ɑːtʃ'daɪə,siːs) *n.* the diocese of an archbishop.

archduchess ('ɑːtʃ'dʌtʃɪs) *n.* the wife of an archduke.

archduchy ('ɑːtʃ'dʌtʃɪ) *n., pl.* **-duchies.** the territory ruled by an archduke or archduchess.

archduke ('ɑːtʃ'djuːk) *n.* a chief duke, esp. a prince of the former Austrian imperial dynasty.

Archean (ɑː'kiːən) *adj.* U.S. same as **Archaean.**

archenemy ('ɑːtʃ'enɪmɪ) *n., pl.* **-mies.** a chief enemy.

archeology (,ɑːkɪ'ɒlədʒɪ) *n.* same as **archaeology.**

archer ('ɑːtʃə) *n.* a person who shoots with a bow and arrow. [Latin *arcus* bow]

archery ('ɑːtʃərɪ) *n.* the art or sport of shooting with a bow and arrow.

archetype ('ɑːkɪ,taɪp) *n.* **1.** a perfect or typical specimen. **2.** an original model; prototype. [Greek *arkhetupos* first-moulded] —**,arche'typal** *adj.*

archfiend (,ɑːtʃ'fiːnd) *n.* **the.** the Devil.

archidiaconal (,ɑːkɪdaɪ'ækən³l) *adj.* of an archdeacon or his office.

archiepiscopal (,ɑːkɪɪ'pɪskəp³l) *adj.* of an archbishop or his office.

archipelago (,ɑːkɪ'pelə,gəʊ) *n., pl.* **-gos.** **1.** a group of islands. **2.** a sea studded with islands. [Greek *arkhi-* chief + *pelagos* sea]

architect ('ɑːkɪ,tekt) *n.* **1.** a person qualified to design buildings or other structures and to supervise their construction. **2.** any planner or creator. [Greek *arkhi-* chief + *tektōn* workman]

architecture ('ɑːkɪ,tektʃə) *n.* **1.** the science of designing and superintending the construction of buildings or other structures. **2.** a style of building. **3.** the structure or design of anything. —**,archi'tectural** *adj.*

architrave ('ɑːkɪ,treɪv) *n. Archit.* **1.** a beam that rests on top of columns. **2.** a moulding around a doorway or window opening. [Italian, from *arch-* + *trave* beam]

archive ('ɑːkaɪv) *n.* **1.** a place where records or documents are kept. **2.** (*pl.*) a collection of records or documents.

archivist ('ɑːkɪvɪst) *n.* a person in charge of archives.

archway ('ɑːtʃ,weɪ) *n.* a passageway under an arch.

arctic ('ɑːktɪk) *adj. Informal.* cold; freezing.

Arctic ('ɑːktɪk) *n.* **the.** the area around the North Pole. [Greek *arktikos* northern, lit.: pertaining to (the constellation of) the Bear]

Arctic Circle *n.* the imaginary circle around the earth at latitude 66° 32′ N.

arctic hare *n.* a large hare of the Canadian Arctic whose fur turns white in winter.

arctic willow *n.* a low-growing shrub of the Canadian Arctic.

arc welding *n.* a technique in which metal is welded by heat generated by an electric arc.

ardent ('ɑːdⁿt) *adj.* **1.** passionate. **2.** intensely enthusiastic; eager. [Latin *ārdēre* to burn] —**'ardently** *adv.*

ardour *or U.S.* **ardor** ('ɑːdə) *n.* **1.** emotional warmth; passion. **2.** intense enthusiasm. [Latin *ārdēre* to burn]

arduous ('ɑːdjuəs) *adj.* difficult to accomplish; strenuous. [Latin *arduus* steep, difficult]

are¹ (ɑː) *vb.* the plural form of the present tense of **be** and the singular form used with *you.* [Old English *aron*]

are² (ɑː) *n.* a unit of area equal to 100 square metres. [Latin *ārea* piece of ground]

area ('ɛərɪə) *n.* **1.** a section, part, or region. **2.** a part having a specified function: *reception area.* **3.** any flat, curved, or irregular expanse of a surface. **4.** the size of a two-dimensional surface. **5.** range or scope. **6.** a subject field. **7.** a sunken area giving access to a basement. [Latin: level ground, threshing floor]

arena (ə'riːnə) *n.* **1. a.** an area surrounded by seats, where sports events take place. **b.** a building housing an arena. **2.** the area of an ancient Roman amphitheatre where gladiators fought. **3.** a sphere of intense activity: *the political arena.* [Latin *harēna* sand]

aren't (ɑːnt) are not.

areola (ə'rɪələ) *n., pl.* **-lae** (-,liː) *or* **-las.** a small circular area, such as the coloured ring around the human nipple. [Latin]

arête (ə'reɪt, ə'rɛt) *n.* a sharp ridge separating valleys. [French: fishbone]

argon ('ɑːgon) *n.* an unreactive odourless element of the rare gas series, forming almost 1 per cent of the atmosphere. Symbol: Ar [Greek *argos* inactive]

argosy ('ɑːgəsɪ) *n., pl.* **-sies.** *Archaic or poetic.* a large merchant ship, or a fleet of such ships. [Italian *Ragusea* (nave) (ship) of Ragusa, a former name for Dubrovnik]

argot ('ɑːgəʊ) *n.* slang or jargon peculiar to a particular group. [French]

argue ('ɑːgjuː) *vb.* **-guing, -gued. 1.** to quarrel. **2.** to try to prove by presenting reasons. **3.** to debate. **4.** to persuade: *we argued her out of going.* **5.** to suggest: *her looks argue despair.* [Latin *arguere* to make clear, accuse] —**'arguable** *adj.* —**'arguably** *adv.*

argument ('ɑːgjumənt) *n.* **1.** a quarrel. **2.** a discussion. **3.** a point presented to support or oppose a proposition.

argumentation (,ɑːgjumen'teɪʃən) *n.* the process of reasoning methodically.

argumentative (,ɑːgju'mentətɪv) *adj.* given to arguing.

argy-bargy *or* **argie-bargie** ('ɑːdʒɪ'bɑːdʒɪ) *n., pl.* **-bargies.** *Brit. informal.* a wrangling argument. [Scot.]

aria ('ɑːrɪə) *n.* an elaborate song for solo voice, esp. from an opera. [Italian]

Arianism ('ɛərɪə,nɪzəm) *n.* the doctrine of Arius, 3rd-century A.D. Greek, who asserted that Christ was not of one substance with God. —**'Arian** *adj., n.*

arid ('ærɪd) *adj.* **1.** having little or no rain. **2.** devoid of interest. [Latin *āridus*] —**aridity** (ə'rɪdɪtɪ) *n.*

Aries ('ɛəriːz) *n. Astrol.* the first sign of the zodiac: the Ram. [Latin]

aright (ə'raɪt) *adv.* correctly; properly.

arise (ə'raɪz) *vb.* **arising, arose, arisen** (ə'rɪzⁿn). **1.** to come into being. **2.** to get or stand up. **3.** to come into notice. **arise from.** to proceed as a consequence of. [Old English *ārīsan*]

aristocracy (,ærɪ'stɒkrəsɪ) *n., pl.* **-cies. 1.** a class of people of high social rank. **2.** a group of people considered to be outstanding in a particular sphere of activity. [Greek *aristos* best + *kratein* to rule]

aristocratic (,ærɪstə'krætɪk) *adj.* **1.** of the aristocracy. **2.** grand or elegant. —**'aris-to,crat** *n.*

Aristotelian (,ærɪstə'tiːlɪən) *adj.* of or relating to Aristotle, 4th-century B.C. Greek philosopher, or to his philosophy.

arithmetic *n.* (ə'rɪθmətɪk). **1.** the branch of mathematics concerned with numerical calculations, such as addition, subtraction, multiplication, and division. **2.** calculations involving numerical operations. **3.** knowledge of or skill in arithmetic: *my arithmetic is rotten.* ~*adj.* (,ærɪθ'metɪk), *also* **arithmetical. 4.** of or using arithmetic. [Greek *arithmos* number] —**arith-'metically** *adv.* —**a,rithme'tician** *n.*

arithmetic mean *n.* the average value of a set of terms, expressed as their sum divided by their number: *the arithmetic mean of 3, 4, and 8 is 5.*

arithmetic progression *n.* a sequence, each term of which differs from the preceding term by a constant amount, such as 3,6,9,12.

Ariz. Arizona.

ark (ɑːk) *n. Bible.* the vessel that Noah built, which survived the Flood. [Old English *arca* box, chest]

Ark (ɑːk) *n. Judaism.* **1.** Also called: **Holy Ark.** the cupboard in a synagogue in which the Torah scrolls are kept. **2.** Also called:

Ark of the Covenant. a chest containing the laws of the Jewish religion, regarded as the most sacred symbol of God's presence among the Hebrew people.

Ark. Arkansas.

arm[1] (ɑːm) n. **1.** (in humans, apes and monkeys) either of the upper limbs from the shoulder to the wrist. **2.** an object that covers or supports the arm, such as a sleeve or the side of a chair. **3.** anything resembling an arm in appearance or function: *the arm of a record player.* **4.** an administrative subdivision of an organization: *an arm of the government.* **5.** authority: *the arm of the law.* **6. arm in arm.** with arms linked. **7. at arm's length.** at a distance. **8. with open arms.** with warmth and hospitality. [Old English]

arm[2] (ɑːm) vb. **1.** to equip with weapons. **2.** to provide (a person or thing) with something that strengthens, or protects. **3.** to prepare (an explosive device) for use. ~See also **arms.** [Latin *arma* arms, equipment] —**armed** adj.

armada (ɑːˈmɑːdə) n. **1.** a large number of ships. **2. the Armada.** the great fleet sent by Spain against England in 1588. [Medieval Latin *armāta* fleet, armed forces]

armadillo (ˌɑːməˈdɪləʊ) n., pl. -**los.** a burrowing mammal of Central and South America with a covering of strong horny plates. [Spanish *armado* armed (man)]

Armageddon (ˌɑːməˈgedᵊn) n. **1.** *New Testament.* the final battle between good and evil at the end of the world. **2.** a catastrophic and extremely destructive conflict. [Hebrew *har megiddōn,* mountain district of *Megiddo* (in N Palestine)]

armament (ˈɑːməmənt) n. **1.** the weapon equipment of a military vehicle, ship, or aircraft. **2.** preparation for war. [Latin *armāmenta* equipment]

armature (ˈɑːmətjʊə) n. **1.** a revolving structure in an electric motor or generator, wound with the coils that carry the current. **2.** a soft iron or steel bar placed across the poles of a magnet to close the magnetic circuit. **3.** *Sculpture.* a framework to support the clay or other material used in modelling. [Latin *armātūra* armour, equipment]

armchair (ˈɑːmˌtʃeə) n. **1.** an upholstered chair with side supports for the arms. **2.** (modifier) taking no active part: *an armchair revolutionary.*

armed forces pl. n. all the military forces of a nation or nations.

armhole (ˈɑːmˌhəʊl) n. the opening in an article of clothing through which the arm passes.

armistice (ˈɑːmɪstɪs) n. an agreement between opposing armies to stop fighting. [Latin *arma* arms + *sistere* to stop]

Armistice Day (ˈɑːmɪstɪs) n. the anniversary of the signing of the armistice that ended World War I, on Nov. 11, 1918.

armlet (ˈɑːmlɪt) n. a band or bracelet worn around the arm.

armorial (ɑːˈmɔːrɪəl) adj. of or relating to heraldry or heraldic arms.

armour or *U.S.* **armor** (ˈɑːmə) n. **1.** cloth-ing of plate metal or chain mail worn by medieval warriors for protection in battle. **2.** the protective metal plates on a tank or warship. **3.** *Mil.* armoured fighting vehicles in general. **4.** any protective covering, such as the shell of certain animals. **5.** a quality or attitude that gives protection. ~vb. **6.** to equip or cover with armour. [Latin *armātūra* armour, equipment]

armoured or *U.S.* **armored** (ˈɑːməd) adj. **1.** having a protective covering. **2.** comprising armoured vehicles: *an armoured brigade.*

armourer or *U.S.* **armorer** (ˈɑːmərə) n. **1.** a person who makes or mends arms and armour. **2.** a person in charge of small arms in a military unit.

armour plate n. a tough heavy steel for protecting warships and vehicles. —ˌarmour-ˈplated adj.

armoury or *U.S.* **armory** (ˈɑːmərɪ) n., pl. -**mouries** or -**mories.** **1.** a secure place for the storage of weapons. **2.** military supplies. **3.** resources on which to draw: *a few choice terms from her armoury of invective.*

armpit (ˈɑːmˌpɪt) n. the depression beneath the arm where it joins the shoulder.

armrest (ˈɑːmˌrest) n. the part of a chair or sofa, that supports the arm.

arms (ɑːmz) pl. n. **1.** weapons collectively. **2.** military exploits: *prowess in arms.* **3.** the heraldic symbols of a family, state, etc. **4. take up arms.** to prepare to fight. **5. under arms.** armed and prepared for war. **6. up in arms.** indignant; prepared to protest strongly.

army (ˈɑːmɪ) n., pl. -**mies.** **1.** the military land forces of a nation. **2.** a large number of people or animals. [Medieval Latin *armāta* armed forces]

aroha (ˈɑːrəhə) n. *N.Z.* love, compassion, or affectionate regard. [Maori]

aroma (əˈrəʊmə) n. **1.** a distinctive, usually pleasant smell. **2.** a subtle pervasive quality or atmosphere. [Greek: spice]

aromatherapy (əˌrəʊməˈθerəpɪ) n. massage with fragrant oils to relieve tension.

aromatic (ˌærəˈmætɪk) adj. **1.** having a distinctive, usually fragrant smell. **2.** (of an organic compound) having an unsaturated ring of atoms, usually six carbon atoms. ~n. **3.** something, such as a plant or drug, giving off a fragrant smell.

arose (əˈrəʊz) vb. the past tense of **arise.**

around (əˈraʊnd) prep. **1.** situated at various points in: *a lot of shelves around the house.* **2.** from place to place in: *driving around Ireland.* **3.** somewhere in or near. **4.** approximately in: *around 1957.* ~adv. **5.** in all directions from a point of reference: *he owns the land for ten miles around.* **6.** in the vicinity, esp. restlessly but idly: *to stand around.* **7.** in no particular place or direction: *dotted around.* **8.** *Informal.* present in some unknown or unspecified place. **9.** *Informal.* available: *that type of phone has been around for years.* **10. have been around.** *Informal.* to have gained considerable experience of a worldly or social nature.

arouse (ə'rauz) vb. **1.** to produce (a reaction, emotion, or response). **2.** to awaken from sleep. —**a'rousal** n.

arpeggio (ɑː'pedʒɪəʊ) n., pl. -**gios.** a chord whose notes are played or sung in rapid succession. [Italian]

arquebus ('ɑːkwɪbəs) n. a portable longbarrelled gun dating from the 15th century. [Middle Dutch hakebusse hook gun]

arr. 1. arranged (by). **2.** arrival. **3.** arrive(d).

arrack or **arak** ('ærək) n. a coarse spirit distilled in Eastern countries from grain or rice. [Arabic 'araq sweat, sweet juice]

arraign (ə'reɪn) vb. **1.** to bring (a prisoner) before a court to answer a charge. **2.** to accuse. [Old French] —**ar'raignment** n.

arrange (ə'reɪndʒ) vb. **1.** to put into a proper or systematic order. **2.** to agree. **3.** to plan in advance: we arranged for her to be met. **4.** to adapt (a musical composition) for performance in a different way, esp. on different instruments. [Old French a- to + rangier to put in a row, range]

arrangement (ə'reɪndʒmənt) n. **1.** (often pl.) a preparation. **2.** an understanding. **3.** a thing composed of various ordered parts: a flower arrangement. **4.** the form in which things are arranged. **5.** an adaptation of a piece of music for performance in a different way.

arrant ('ærənt) adj. utter; out-and-out: an arrant fool. [Middle English var. of errant (wandering, vagabond)]

arras ('ærəs) n. a wall hanging, esp. a tapestry. [Arras, a town in N France]

array (ə'reɪ) n. **1.** an impressive display or collection. **2.** an orderly arrangement, as of troops in battle order. **3.** Poetic. rich clothing. **4.** Computers. a data structure in which elements may be located by index numbers. ~vb. **5.** to arrange in order. **6.** to dress in rich attire. [Old French arayer to arrange]

arrears (ə'rɪəz) pl. n. **1.** something outstanding or owed. **2. in arrears.** late in paying a debt or meeting an obligation. [Latin ad to + retrō backwards]

arrest (ə'rest) vb. **1.** to take (a person) into custody. **2.** to slow or stop the development of (a disease or growth). **3.** to catch and hold (one's attention). ~n. **4.** the act of taking a person into custody. **5. under arrest.** being held in custody by the police. **6.** the slowing or stopping of something: a cardiac arrest. [Latin ad at, to + restāre to stand firm, stop]

arresting (ə'restɪŋ) adj. attracting attention; striking.

arrival (ə'raɪv°l) n. **1.** the act of arriving. **2.** a person or thing that has just arrived. **3.** Informal. a recently born baby.

arrive (ə'raɪv) vb. **1.** to reach a place or destination. **2.** to come to a conclusion, idea, or decision. **3.** to occur eventually: the moment arrived when pretence was useless. **4.** Informal. to be born. **5.** Informal. to attain success. [Latin ad to + rīpa river bank]

arrogant ('ærəgənt) adj. having or showing an exaggerated opinion of one's own importance or ability. [Latin arrogāre to claim as one's own] —**'arrogance** n. —**'arrogantly** adv.

arrogate ('ærə,geɪt) vb. to claim, for oneself or another, without justification. [Latin arrogāre] —,**arro'gation** n.

arrow ('ærəʊ) n. **1.** a long slender pointed weapon, usually having feathers at one end, that is shot from a bow. **2.** an arrow-shaped sign or symbol, such as one used to show the direction to a place. [Old English arwe]

arrowhead ('ærəʊ,hed) n. the pointed tip of an arrow.

arrowroot ('ærəʊ,ruːt) n. an easily digestible starch obtained from the rhizomes of a West Indian plant.

arse (ɑːs) or U.S. & Canad. **ass** n. Taboo. the buttocks or anus. [Old English]

arsehole ('ɑːs,həʊl) or U.S. & Canad. **asshole** n. Taboo. **1.** the anus. **2.** a stupid person; fool.

arsenal ('ɑːsən°l) n. **1.** a building for storing and making arms and ammunition. **2.** a store of anything regarded as weapons. [Arabic dār house + siñ'ah manufacture]

arsenic n. ('ɑːsnɪk). **1.** a toxic metalloid element. Symbol: As **2.** a nontechnical name for **arsenic trioxide**, used as rat poison and an insecticide. ~adj. (ɑː'senɪk), also **arsenical. 3.** of or containing arsenic. [Syriac zarnīg]

arson ('ɑːs°n) n. the crime of intentionally setting fire to property. [Latin ārdēre to burn] —**'arsonist** n.

art[1] (ɑːt) n. **1.** the creation of works of beauty or other special significance. **2.** human creativity as distinguished from nature. **3.** works of art collectively. **4.** any branch of the visual arts, esp. painting. **5.** skill: the art of government. **6. get something down to a fine art.** to become proficient at something through practice. [Latin ars craftsmanship]

art[2] (ɑːt) vb. Archaic. (used with thou) a singular form of the present tense of **be.** [Old English eart]

Art Deco ('dekəʊ) n. a style of design, at its height in the 1930s, characterized by geometrical shapes. [French décoratif]

artefact or **artifact** ('ɑːtɪ,fækt) n. something made by man, such as a tool or a work of art. [Latin ars skill + facere to make]

arterial (ɑː'tɪərɪəl) adj. **1.** of or affecting an artery or the blood that circulates in the arteries. **2.** being a major route.

arteriosclerosis (ɑː,tɪərɪəʊsklɪə'rəʊsɪs) n., pl. -**ses** (-siːz). thickening and loss of elasticity of the walls of the arteries. Nontechnical name: **hardening of the arteries.**

artery ('ɑːtərɪ) n., pl. -**teries. 1.** any of the tubular vessels that convey oxygenated blood from the heart to various parts of the body. **2.** a major road or means of communication. [Latin artēria]

artesian well (ɑː'tiːzɪən) n. a well receiving water from a higher altitude, so the water is forced to flow upwards. [from

Old French *Arteis* Artois, old province, where such wells were common]

art form *n.* a recognized mode or medium of artistic expression.

artful ('ɑːtfʊl) *adj.* **1.** cunning. **2.** skilful in achieving a desired end. —'**artfully** *adv.*

arthritis (ɑː'θraɪtɪs) *n.* inflammation of a joint or joints characterized by pain and stiffness. [Greek *arthron* joint] —**arthritic** (ɑː'θrɪtɪk) *adj., n.*

arthropod ('ɑːθrə,pɒd) *n.* a creature, such as an insect or a spider, which has jointed legs and a hard case on its body. [Greek *arthron* joint + *pous* foot]

artic (ɑː'tɪk) *n. Informal.* an articulated lorry.

artichoke ('ɑːtɪ,tʃəʊk) *n.* **1.** Also called: **globe artichoke.** the flower head of a thistle-like plant, edible when cooked. **2.** same as **Jerusalem artichoke.** [Arabic *al-kharshūf*]

article ('ɑːtɪk'l) *n.* **1.** an item or object. **2.** a written composition in a magazine or newspaper. **3.** *Grammar.* any of the words *a*, *an*, or *the*. **4.** a clause in a written document. [Latin *articulus* small joint]

articled ('ɑːtɪk'ld) *adj.* bound by a written contract, such as one that governs a period of training: *an articled clerk.*

articular (ɑː'tɪkjʊlə) *adj.* of or relating to joints. [Latin *articulus* small joint]

articulate *adj.* (ɑː'tɪkjʊlɪt). **1.** able to express oneself fluently and coherently. **2.** distinct, clear, or definite: *an articulate document.* **3.** *Zool.* possessing joints. ~*vb.* (ɑː'tɪkjʊ,leɪt). **4.** to speak clearly and distinctly. **5.** to express coherently in words. [Latin *articulāre* to divide into joints] —**ar'ticulately** *adv.*

articulated lorry *n.* a large lorry in two separate sections connected by a pivoted bar.

articulation (ɑː,tɪkjʊ'leɪʃən) *n.* **1.** the expressing of an idea in words. **2.** the process of articulating a speech sound or the sound so produced. **3.** a being jointed together. **4.** *Zool.* a joint between bones or arthropod segments.

artifact ('ɑːtɪ,fækt) *n.* same as **artefact.**

artifice ('ɑːtɪfɪs) *n.* **1.** a clever expedient. **2.** subtle deception. **3.** skill; cleverness. [Latin *ars* skill + *facere* to make]

artificer (ɑː'tɪfɪsə) *n.* a skilled craftsman.

artificial (,ɑːtɪ'fɪʃəl) *adj.* **1.** produced by man; not occurring naturally. **2.** made in imitation of a natural product: *artificial cream.* **3.** pretended or affected. [Latin *artificiālis* belonging to art] —**artificiality** (,ɑːtɪ,fɪʃɪ'ælɪtɪ) *n.* —,**arti'ficially** *adv.*

artificial insemination *n.* introduction of semen into the womb by means other than sexual union.

artificial respiration *n.* any method of restarting breathing after it has stopped.

artillery (ɑː'tɪlərɪ) *n.* **1.** large-calibre guns. **2.** military units specializing in using such guns. [Old French *artillier* to equip with weapons]

artisan ('ɑːtɪ,zæn, ,ɑːtɪ'zæn) *n.* a skilled workman; craftsman. [French]

artist ('ɑːtɪst) *n.* **1.** a person who practises or is skilled in painting, drawing, or sculpture. **2.** a person skilled in some task or occupation. **3.** same as **artiste.** —**ar'tistic** *adj.* —**ar'tistically** *adv.*

artiste (ɑː'tiːst) *n.* an entertainer, such as a singer or dancer.

artistry ('ɑːtɪstrɪ) *n.* **1.** artistic ability. **2.** great skill.

artless ('ɑːtlɪs) *adj.* **1.** free from deceit; ingenuous: *an artless remark.* **2.** natural; unpretentious. —**artlessly** *adv.*

Art Nouveau (ɑː nuː'vəʊ) *n.* a style of art and architecture of the 1890s, characterized by sinuous outlines and stylized natural forms. [French: new art]

arts (ɑːts) *pl. n.* **1. the.** the nonscientific branches of knowledge. **2.** See **fine art. 3.** cunning schemes.

arty ('ɑːtɪ) *adj.* **artier, artiest.** *Informal.* having an affected interest in art. —**'artiness** *n.*

arum ('ɛərəm) *n.* a plant with arrow-shaped leaves and a white sheath-like leaf surrounding a spike of flowers. [Greek *aron*]

arum lily *n.* a plant with a white funnel-shaped leaf surrounding a yellow spike of flowers.

Aryan ('ɛərɪən) *n.* **1.** (in Nazi ideology) a non-Jewish person of the Nordic type. **2.** a person supposedly descended from the Indo-Europeans. ~*adj.* **3.** of Aryans. [Sanskrit *ārya* of noble birth]

as (æz) *conj.* **1.** (often preceded by *just*) while; when: *he caught me as I was leaving.* **2.** in the way that: *dancing as only she can.* **3.** that which; what: *I did as I was told.* **4.** (of) which fact or event (referring to the previous statement): *to become wise, as we all know, is not easy.* **5. as it were.** in a way; in a manner of speaking: *they are, as it were, being used as human guinea pigs.* **6.** since; seeing that. **7.** for instance. ~*adv., conj.* **8.** used to indicate extent, amount, etc.: *she is as heavy as her sister; the same height as her sister.* ~*prep.* **9.** in the role of; being: *as his friend, my opinions are probably biased.* **10. as for** or **to.** with reference to. **11. as if** or **though.** as it would be if: *he talked as if he knew all about it.* **12. as (it) is.** in the existing state of affairs. [Old English *alswā* likewise]

As *Chem.* arsenic.

ASA Amateur Swimming Association.

asafoetida (,æsə'fɛtɪdə) *n.* a plant resin with an unpleasant smell, formerly used to treat flatulence. [Medieval Latin *asa* gum + Latin *foetidus* evil-smelling]

a.s.a.p. as soon as possible.

asbestos (æs'bɛstɒs) *n.* a fibrous mineral which does not burn, formerly widely used as a heat-resistant material. [Greek *asbestos* inextinguishable]

asbestosis (,æsbɛs'təʊsɪs) *n.* inflammation of the lungs resulting from chronic inhalation of asbestos particles.

ascend (ə'sɛnd) vb. 1. to go or move up (a ladder, hill, or slope). 2. to slope upwards. 3. **ascend the throne.** to become king or queen. [Latin *ascendere*]

ascendancy, ascendency (ə'sɛndənsɪ) or **ascendance, ascendence** n. the condition of being dominant.

ascendant or **ascendent** (ə'sɛndənt) adj. 1. dominant or influential. ~n. 2. *Astrol.* the sign of the zodiac that is rising on the eastern horizon at a particular moment. 3. **in the ascendant.** having or increasing in influence.

ascension (ə'sɛnʃən) n. the act of ascending.

Ascension (ə'sɛnʃən) n. *Christianity.* the passing of Jesus Christ from earth into heaven.

ascent (ə'sɛnt) n. 1. the act of ascending; upward movement. 2. an upward slope.

ascertain (ˌæsə'teɪn) vb. to find out definitely. [Old French *acerteiner* to make certain] —ˌascer'tainment n.

ascetic (ə'sɛtɪk) n. 1. a person who abstains from worldly comforts and pleasures. ~adj. 2. rigidly abstinent and self-denying. [Greek *askētikos*]

ascorbic acid (ə'skɔːbɪk) n. same as **vitamin C.** [A- + SCORBUTIC]

ascribe (ə'skraɪb) vb. 1. to credit or assign, as to a particular origin. 2. to consider that (a particular quality) is possessed by something or someone: *ascribing virtue to hypocrisy.* [Latin *ad* in addition + *scrībere* to write] —**ascription** (ə'skrɪpʃən) n.

aseptic (eɪ'sɛptɪk) adj. free from harmful bacteria. —**a'sepsis** n.

asexual (eɪ'sɛksjʊəl) adj. 1. having no apparent sex or sex organs. 2. (of reproduction) not involving sexual activity. —**a'sexually** adv.

ash[1] (æʃ) n. 1. the powdery substance formed when something is burnt. 2. fine particles of lava thrown out by an erupting volcano. [Old English *æsce*]

ash[2] (æʃ) n. a tree with grey bark and winged seeds. [Old English *æsc*]

ashamed (ə'ʃeɪmd) adj. 1. overcome with shame or remorse. 2. (foll. by *to*) unwilling through fear of humiliation or shame. [Old English *āscamod*]

ash can n. *U.S.* dustbin.

ashen ('æʃən) adj. drained of colour through shock.

ashes ('æʃɪz) pl. n. 1. remains, as after burning. 2. the remains of a human body after cremation.

Ashes ('æʃɪz) pl. n. **the.** a cricket trophy competed for by England and Australia since 1882. [from a mock obituary of English cricket after a great Australian victory]

ashlar or **ashler** ('æʃlə) n. 1. a square block of hewn stone for use in building. 2. a thin dressed stone used to face a wall. [Old French *aisselier* crossbeam]

ashore (ə'ʃɔː) adv. towards or on land.

ashram ('æʃrəm) n. a religious retreat where a Hindu holy man lives. [Sanskrit *āśrama*]

ashtray ('æʃˌtreɪ) n. a receptacle for tobacco ash and cigarette butts.

Ash Wednesday n. the first day of Lent, named from the former Christian custom of sprinkling ashes on penitents' heads.

ashy ('æʃɪ) adj. **ashier, ashiest.** 1. pale greyish. 2. covered with ash.

Asian ('eɪʃən, 'eɪʒən) adj. 1. of or from Asia, the largest of the continents, or any of its peoples or languages. ~n. 2. a person from Asia or a descendant of one.

Asiatic (eɪzɪ'ætɪk) adj. Asian.

aside (ə'saɪd) adv. 1. to one side. 2. out of other people's hearing: *she took me aside to tell me her fears.* 3. out of mind: *he put aside all fears.* 4. into reserve: *to put aside money for one's old age.* ~n. 5. an actor's words supposedly heard only by the audience and not by the other characters. 6. a confidential statement in undertones. 7. an incidental remark.

asinine ('æsɪˌnaɪn) adj. obstinate or stupid. [Latin *asinus* ass]

ask (ɑːsk) vb. 1. to say or write (something) in a form that requires an answer: *she asked me the time; "When is the next bus?" Jim asked.* 2. to inquire about: *she asked the way.* 3. to make a request or demand: *they asked for a deposit.* 4. to expect: *to ask too much of someone.* [Old English *āscian*]

ask after vb. to make polite inquiries about the health of: *he asked after her mother.*

askance (ə'skæns) adv. 1. with an oblique glance. 2. with doubt or mistrust. [origin unknown]

askew (ə'skjuː) adv., adj. towards one side.

ask for vb. 1. to request (of). 2. *Informal.* to behave in a provocative manner that is regarded as inviting (trouble, etc.): *you're asking for it.*

asking price n. the price suggested by a seller.

asleep (ə'sliːp) adj. 1. in or into a state of sleep. 2. *Informal.* not listening or paying attention. 3. (of limbs) numb.

asp (æsp) n. a viper of S Europe, similar to but smaller than the adder. [Greek *aspis*]

asparagus (ə'spærəgəs) n. the young shoots of a plant of the lily family, which can be cooked and eaten. [Greek *asparagos*]

aspartame (ə'spɑːˌteɪm) n. an artificial sweetener.

aspect ('æspɛkt) n. 1. a distinct feature or element in a problem or situation. 2. the way in which a problem or idea may be considered. 3. appearance: *a severe aspect.* 4. a position facing a particular direction: *the southern aspect of a house.* [Latin *ad-* to, at + *specere* to look]

aspen ('æspən) n. a poplar tree whose leaves quiver in the wind. [Old English *æspe*]

asperity (æ'spɛrɪtɪ) n., pl. **-ties.** roughness

or sharpness of temper. [Latin *asper* rough]

aspersion (ə'spɜːʃən) *n.* **cast aspersions on someone.** to make disparaging or malicious remarks about someone. [Latin *aspergere* to sprinkle]

asphalt ('æsfælt) *n.* **1.** a black tarlike substance used in road-surfacing and roofing materials. ~*vb.* **2.** to cover with asphalt. [Greek *asphaltos*, prob. from *a-* not + *sphallein* to cause to fall; referring to its use as a binding agent]

asphyxia (æs'fiksiə) *n.* unconsciousness or death caused by lack of oxygen. [Greek *a-* without + *sphuxis* pulse]

asphyxiate (æs'fiksi,eit) *vb.* to smother or suffocate. —**as,phyxi'ation** *n.*

aspic ('æspik) *n.* a savoury jelly based on meat or fish stock, used as a mould for vegetables. [French]

aspidistra (,æspi'distrə) *n.* a house plant with long tough evergreen leaves. [Greek *aspis* shield]

aspirant ('æspirənt) *n.* a person who aspires, as to a powerful position.

aspirate *Phonetics.* ~*vb.* **1.** ('æspi,reit) to pronounce (a word or syllable) with an initial *h.* ~*n.* ('æspirit) **2.** the sound represented in English and several other languages as *h.*

aspiration (,æspi'reiʃən) *n.* **1.** strong desire to achieve something. **2.** the aim of such desire. **3.** *Phonetics.* the pronunciation of an aspirated consonant. —,**aspi'rational** *adj.*

aspirator ('æspi,reitə) *n.* a device for removing fluids from a body cavity by suction.

aspire (ə'spaiə) *vb.* (usually foll. by *to*) yearn (for), or hope (to do or be): *to aspire to be a great leader.* [Latin *aspīrāre* to breathe upon] —**as'piring** *adj.*

aspirin ('æsprin) *n.*, *pl.* **-rin** *or* **-rins. 1.** a white crystalline compound widely used to relieve pain and fever. **2.** a tablet of aspirin. [German]

ass[1] (æs) *n.* **1.** a mammal resembling the horse but with longer ears. **2.** a foolish person. [Old English]

ass[2] (æs) *n.* *U.S. and Canad.* taboo. same as **arse.** [Old English *ærs*]

assail (ə'seil) *vb.* **1.** to attack violently. **2.** to criticize vehemently. **3.** to disturb: *his mind was assailed by doubts.* [Latin *assilīre*] —**as'sailant** *n.*

assassin (ə'sæsin) *n.* a murderer of a prominent political figure. [Arabic *hashshāshīn*, pl. of *hashshāsh* one who eats hashish]

assassinate (ə'sæsi,neit) *vb.* **1.** to murder (a political figure). **2.** to ruin or harm (a person's reputation or character) by slander. —**as,sassi'nation** *n.*

assault (ə'sɔːlt) *n.* **1.** a violent attack, either physical or verbal. ~*vb.* **2.** to make an assault upon. [Old French *asaut*]

assault and battery *n. Criminal law.* a threat of attack to another person followed by actual attack.

assault course *n.* an obstacle course designed to give soldiers practice in negotiating hazards.

assay *vb.* (ə'sei). **1.** to analyse (a substance, such as gold) to find out how pure it is. ~*n.* (ə'sei, 'æsei). **2.** an analysis of the purity of an ore or precious metal. [Old French *assai*]

assegai *or* **assagai** ('æsə,gai) *n.*, *pl.* **-gais.** a sharp light spear used in southern Africa. [Arabic *az zaghāyah*]

assemblage (ə'semblidʒ) *n.* **1.** a number of things or persons assembled together. **2.** the act of assembling.

assemble (ə'semb°l) *vb.* **1.** to collect or congregate. **2.** to fit together the parts of (something, such as a machine). [Old French *assembler*]

assembler (ə'semblə) *n.* **1.** a person or thing that assembles. **2.** a computer program that converts a set of low-level symbolic data into machine language.

assembly (ə'sembli) *n.*, *pl.* **-blies. 1.** a number of people gathered together, esp. for a formal meeting held at regular intervals. **2.** the act of assembling.

assembly line *n.* a sequence of machines and workers in a factory, arranged so that at each stage a further process is carried out.

assemblyman (ə'semblimən) *n.*, *pl.* **-men.** a member of a legislative assembly, esp. that of Northern Ireland.

assent (ə'sent) *n.* **1.** agreement, consent. ~*vb.* **2.** to agree. [Latin *assentīrī*]

assert (ə'sɜːt) *vb.* **1.** to insist upon (one's rights, etc.). **2.** to state or declare. **3. assert oneself.** to put oneself forward in an insistent manner. [Latin *asserere* to join to oneself]

assertion (ə'sɜːʃən) *n.* **1.** a positive statement, usually made without evidence. **2.** the act of asserting.

assertive (ə'sɜːtiv) *adj.* dogmatic or aggressive. —**as'sertively** *adv.* —**as'sertiveness** *n.*

assess (ə'ses) *vb.* **1.** to judge the worth or importance of. **2.** to estimate the value of (income or property), as for taxation purposes. [Latin *assidēre* to sit beside] —**as'sessment** *n.*

assessor (ə'sesə) *n.* **1.** a person who values property for taxation or insurance purposes. **2.** a person with technical expertise called in to advise a court. **3.** a person who evaluates the merits of something.

asset ('æset) *n.* **1.** a thing or person that is valuable or useful. **2.** (*pl.*) any property owned by a person or firm. [Latin *ad-* to + *satis* enough]

asset-stripping *n. Commerce.* the practice of taking over a failing company at a low price and then selling the assets piecemeal. —**'asset-,stripper** *n.*

asseverate (ə'sevə,reit) *vb.* to declare solemnly. [Latin *assevērāre* to do (something) earnestly] —**as,sever'ation** *n.*

assiduous (ə'sidjuəs) *adj.* **1.** hardworking; persevering. **2.** undertaken with perseverance and care. [Latin *assidēre* to sit beside] —**assiduity** (ˌæsɪ'djuːɪtɪ) n. —**as'siduously** adv.

assign (ə'saɪn) vb. **1.** to select (someone) for a post or task. **2.** to allot (a task). **3.** to set apart (a place or time) for a particular function or event: to assign a day for the meeting. **4.** to attribute to a specified cause. **5.** to transfer (one's right, interest, or title to property) to someone else. [Latin assignāre]

assignation (ˌæsɪg'neɪʃən) n. a secret arrangement to meet, esp. one between lovers. [Latin assignātiō a marking out]

assignment (ə'saɪnmənt) n. **1.** something that has been assigned, such as a task. **2.** the act of assigning. **3.** Law. the transfer to another of a right, interest, or title to property.

assimilate (ə'sɪmɪˌleɪt) vb. **1.** to learn (information) and understand it thoroughly. **2.** to absorb (food). **3.** to become absorbed, incorporated, or learned and understood. **4.** to adjust or become adjusted: the new immigrants assimilated easily. [Latin ad- to + similis like] —**as'similable** adj. —**as,simi'lation** n.

assist (ə'sɪst) vb. to give help or support (to). [Latin assistere to stand by]

assistance (ə'sɪstəns) n. help; support.

assistant (ə'sɪstənt) n. **1.** a helper or subordinate. **2.** same as **shop assistant**. ~adj. **3.** junior or deputy: assistant manager.

assizes (ə'saɪzɪz) pl. n. (formerly in England and Wales) the sessions of the principal court in each county. [Latin assidēre to sit beside]

assoc. **1.** associate(d). **2.** association.

associate vb. (ə'səʊʃɪˌeɪt, -sɪ-). (usually foll. by with) **1.** to connect in the mind. **2.** to mix socially: to associate with writers. **3. be associated** or **associate oneself with.** to be involved with (a group or an organization), esp. because of shared views: she had long been associated with the far right. ~n. (ə'səʊʃɪɪt, -sɪ-). **4.** a person joined with another or others in an enterprise or business. **5.** a companion or friend. ~adj. (ə'səʊʃɪɪt, -sɪ-). **6.** joined with another or others in an enterprise or business: an associate director. **7.** having partial rights or subordinate status: an associate member. [Latin ad- + sociāre to join]

association (əˌsəʊsɪ'eɪʃən, -ʃɪ-) n. **1.** a group of people having a common interest; a society or club. **2.** the act of associating or the state of being associated. **3.** friendship: their association will not last. **4.** a mental connection of ideas or feelings.

association football n. same as **soccer**.

associative (ə'səʊʃɪətɪv, -sɪ-) adj. Maths. (of an operation such as multiplication or addition) producing the same answer regardless of the way the elements are grouped: $(2 \times 3) \times 4 = 2 \times (3 \times 4)$.

assonance ('æsənəns) n. the use of the same vowel sound with different consonants, as in verse, e.g. time and light. [Latin assonāre to sound]

assorted (ə'sɔːtɪd) adj. **1.** consisting of various kinds mixed together. **2.** classified: assorted categories. **3.** matched: an ill-assorted couple. [Old French assorter]

assortment (ə'sɔːtmənt) n. a collection of various things or sorts.

assuage (ə'sweɪdʒ) vb. to relieve (grief, pain, or thirst). [Latin suāvis pleasant]

assume (ə'sjuːm) vb. **1.** to take for granted; suppose. **2.** to undertake or take on or over: to assume office. **3.** to make a pretence of: he assumed indifference. **4.** to take or put on; adopt: the problem assumed gigantic proportions. [Latin ad- to + sūmere to take up]

assuming (ə'sjuːmɪŋ) conj. (often foll. by that) if it is assumed or taken for granted: assuming for the moment that it was Davis.

assumption (ə'sʌmpʃən) n. **1.** the act of taking something for granted or something that is taken for granted. **2.** the act of assuming power or possession. [Latin assūmptiō a taking up]

Assumption (ə'sʌmpʃən) n. Christianity. the taking up of the Virgin Mary into heaven when her earthly life was ended.

assurance (ə'ʃʊərəns) n. **1.** a statement or assertion intended to inspire confidence. **2.** freedom from doubt; certainty. **3.** Chiefly Brit. insurance providing for certainties such as death as contrasted with fire.

assure (ə'ʃʊə) vb. **1.** to convince: he assured her of his love. **2.** to promise; guarantee. **3.** to make (an event) certain. **4.** Chiefly Brit. to insure against loss of life. [Latin ad- to + sēcūrus secure]

assured (ə'ʃʊəd) adj. **1.** sure; guaranteed. **2.** self-assured. **3.** Chiefly Brit. insured. —**assuredly** (ə'ʃʊərɪdlɪ) adv.

Assyrian (ə'sɪrɪən) n. an inhabitant of ancient Assyria, a kingdom of Mesopotamia.

AST Atlantic Standard Time.

astatine ('æstəˌtiːn) n. a radioactive element occurring naturally in minute amounts or artificially produced by bombarding bismuth with alpha particles. Symbol: At [Greek astatos unstable]

aster ('æstə) n. a plant having white, blue, purple, or pink daisy-like flowers. [Greek astēr star]

asterisk ('æstərɪsk) n. **1.** a star-shaped character (*) used in printing or writing to indicate a cross-reference, omission, etc. ~vb. **2.** to mark with an asterisk. [Greek asterískos a small star]

astern (ə'stɜːn) adv., adj. Naut. **1.** at or towards the stern. **2.** backwards. **3.** behind a vessel.

asteroid ('æstəˌrɔɪd) n. any of the small celestial bodies that move around the sun mainly between Mars and Jupiter. [Greek asteroeidēs starlike]

asthma ('æsmə) n. a respiratory disorder characterized by difficulty in breathing. [Greek] —**asth'matic** adj., n.

astigmatic (ˌæstɪg'mætɪk) adj. of, having, or correcting astigmatism. [Greek a- without + stigma spot, focus]

astigmatism (ə'stɪgməˌtɪzəm) n. a defect

of a lens, esp. of the eye, resulting in the formation of distorted images, caused by light rays not meeting at a single focal point.

astir (ə'stɜː) *adj*. 1. out of bed. 2. in motion.

astonish (ə'stɒnɪʃ) *vb*. to surprise greatly. [Latin *ex-* out + *tonāre* to thunder] —**a'stonishing** *adj*. —**a'stonishment** *n*.

astound (ə'staʊnd) *vb*. to overwhelm with amazement. [Old French *estoner*] —**a'stounding** *adj*.

astraddle (ə'stræd²l) *prep*. astride.

astrakhan (,æstrə'kæn) *n*. 1. a fur made of the closely curled dark wool of lambs from Astrakhan in the U.S.S.R. 2. a cloth resembling this.

astral ('æstrəl) *adj*. relating to or resembling the stars. [Greek *astron* star]

astray (ə'streɪ) *adj., adv*. out of the right or expected way. [Old French *estraier* to stray]

astride (ə'straɪd) *adj*. 1. with a leg on either side. 2. with legs far apart. ~*prep*. 3. with a leg on either side of. 4. spanning.

astringent (ə'strɪndʒənt) *adj*. 1. severe; harsh. 2. causing contraction of body tissues, checking blood flow. ~*n*. 3. an astringent drug or lotion. [Latin *astringēns* drawing together] —**as'tringency** *n*.

astro- *combining form*. indicating a star or stars: *astrology*. [Greek]

astrolabe ('æstrə,leɪb) *n*. an instrument formerly used to measure the altitude of stars and planets. [Greek *astron* star + *lambanein* to take]

astrology (ə'strɒlədʒɪ) *n*. the study of the alleged influence of the planets, sun, and moon on human affairs. [Greek *astron* star + *logos* word, account] —**as'trologer** *or* **as'trologist** *n*. —**astrological** (,æstrə-'lɒdʒɪk²l) *adj*.

astronaut ('æstrə,nɔːt) *n*. a person trained for travelling in space. [Greek *astron* star + *nautēs* sailor]

astronautics (,æstrə'nɔːtɪks) *n*. (*functioning as sing.*) the science and technology of space flight. —**astro'nautical** *adj*.

astronomical (,æstrə'nɒmɪk²l) *or* **astronomic** *adj*. 1. enormously large. 2. of astronomy. —**astro'nomically** *adv*.

astronomy (ə'strɒnəmɪ) *n*. the scientific study of celestial bodies. [Greek *astron* star + *nomos* law] —**as'tronomer** *n*.

astrophysics (,æstrəʊ'fɪzɪks) *n*. (*functioning as sing.*) the study of the physical and chemical properties of celestial bodies. —**astro'physical** *adj*. —**astro'physicist** *n*.

astute (ə'stjuːt) *adj*. having insight; shrewd. [Latin *astūtus*] —**as'tutely** *adv*. —**as'tuteness** *n*.

asunder (ə'sʌndə) *adv., adj*. into parts or pieces; apart.

asylum (ə'saɪləm) *n*. 1. shelter; refuge; sanctuary. 2. refuge afforded to a political refugee from a foreign country. 3. (formerly) a mental hospital. [Greek *asulon*]

asymmetry (æ'sɪmɪtrɪ, eɪ-) *n*. lack of symmetry. —**asymmetric** (,æsɪ'mɛtrɪk, eɪ-) *or* **asym'metrical** *adj*.

asymptote ('æsɪm,təʊt) *n*. a straight line that is closely approached but never met by a curve. [Greek *asumptōtos* not falling together] —**asymptotic** (,æsɪm'tɒtɪk) *adj*.

at (æt) *prep*. 1. indicating location or position: *are they at the table?* 2. towards; in the direction of: *looking at television*. 3. indicating position in time: *come at three o'clock*. 4. engaged in: *children at play*. 5. during the passing of: *he used to work at night*. 6. for; in exchange for: *it's selling at four pounds*. 7. indicating the object of an emotion: *shocked at his behaviour*. [Old English *æt*]

At *Chem.* astatine.

at. 1. atmosphere. 2. atomic.

atavism ('ætə,vɪzəm) *n*. 1. the recurrence of primitive characteristics that were present in distant ancestors but not in more recent ones. 2. reversion to a former type. [Latin *atavus* great-grandfather's grandfather, ancestor] —**ata'vistic** *adj*.

ataxia (ə'tæksɪə) *n*. *Pathol*. lack of muscular coordination. [Greek] —**a'taxic** *adj*.

ate (ɛt, eɪt) *vb*. the past tense of **eat**.

atheism ('eɪθɪ,ɪzəm) *n*. the belief that there is no God. [Greek *a-* without + *theos* god] —**'atheist** *n*.

atherosclerosis (,æθərəʊsklɪə'rəʊsɪs) *n., pl.* **-ses** (-siːz). a disease characterized by thickening of the walls of the arteries by deposits of fat. [Greek *athērōma* tumour + SCLEROSIS] —**atherosclerotic** (,æθərəʊsklɪə'rɒtɪk) *adj*.

athirst (ə'θɜːst) *adj*. (often foll. by *for*) longing: *athirst for knowledge*.

athlete ('æθliːt) *n*. 1. a person trained to compete in sports or exercises. 2. *Chiefly Brit.* a competitor in track-and-field events. [Greek *athlos* a contest]

athlete's foot *n*. a fungal infection of the skin of the feet.

athletic (æθ'lɛtɪk) *adj*. 1. physically fit or strong. 2. of or for an athlete or athletics. —**ath'letically** *adv*. —**ath'leticism** *n*.

athletics (æθ'lɛtɪks) *n*. (*functioning as pl. or sing.*) *Chiefly Brit.* track-and-field events.

athwart (ə'θwɔːt) *adv*. transversely; from one side to another.

Atlantic (ət'læntɪk) *n*. **the**. short for the **Atlantic Ocean**, the world's second largest ocean. [Greek (*pelagos*) *Atlantikos* (the sea) of Atlas (so called because it lay beyond the Atlas Mountains)]

Atlantis (ət'læntɪs) *n*. (in ancient legend) a continent said to have sunk beneath the Atlantic west of Gibraltar.

atlas ('ætləs) *n*. a collection of maps, usually in book form. [Greek; first applied to maps because Atlas, a Titan in Greek myth., was shown supporting the heavens in 16th- cent. books of maps]

atmosphere ('ætməs,fɪə) *n*. 1. the gaseous envelope surrounding the earth or any other celestial body. 2. the air in a particular place. 3. a pervasive feeling or mood: *the atmosphere was tense.* **4.** a unit of pressure equal to the normal pressure of the air at sea level. [Greek *atmos* vapour + *sphaira* sphere] —**atmospheric** (ˌætməsˈfɛrɪk) *adj.* —ˌatmosˈpherically *adv.*

atmospherics (ˌætməsˈfɛrɪks) *pl. n.* radio interference; static.

at. no. atomic number.

atoll (ˈætɒl) *n.* a circular coral reef surrounding a lagoon. [*atollon*, native name in the Maldive Islands]

atom (ˈætəm) *n.* **1. a.** the smallest quantity of an element that can take part in a chemical reaction. **b.** this entity as a source of nuclear energy. **2.** a very small amount. [Greek *atomos* that cannot be divided]

atom bomb *or* **atomic bomb** *n.* a type of bomb in which the energy is provided by nuclear fission.

atomic (əˈtɒmɪk) *adj.* **1.** of or using atom bombs or atomic energy. **2.** of atoms. —**aˈtomically** *adv.*

atomic energy *n.* same as **nuclear energy.**

atomic mass unit *n.* a unit of mass that is equal to one twelfth of the mass of an atom of carbon-12.

atomic number *n.* the number of protons in the nucleus of an atom of an element.

atomic theory *n.* any theory in which matter is regarded as consisting of atoms.

atomic weight *n.* the ratio of the average mass per atom of an element to one twelfth of the mass of an atom of carbon-12.

atomize *or* **-ise** (ˈætəˌmaɪz) *vb.* **1.** to separate into free atoms. **2.** to reduce or be reduced to fine particles or spray. **3.** to destroy by nuclear weapons.

atomizer *or* **-iser** (ˈætəˌmaɪzə) *n.* a device for reducing a liquid to a fine spray.

atonality (ˌeɪtəʊˈnælɪtɪ) *n.* absence of an established musical key in a composition. —**aˈtonal** *adj.*

atone (əˈtəʊn) *vb.* to make amends (for sin or wrongdoing).

atonement (əˈtəʊnmənt) *n.* **1.** satisfaction or expiation given for a wrong. **2.** *Christian theol.* the reconciliation of man with God through the sacrificial death of Christ. [Middle English *at onement* in harmony]

atop (əˈtɒp) *prep.* on top of.

atrium (ˈeɪtrɪəm) *n., pl.* **atria** (ˈeɪtrɪə). **1.** the open main court of a Roman house. **2.** a central hall that extends through several storeys in a modern building. **3.** *Anat.* the upper chamber of each half of the heart. [Latin] —**ˈatrial** *adj.*

atrocious (əˈtrəʊʃəs) *adj.* **1.** extremely cruel or wicked. **2.** horrifying or shocking. **3.** *Informal.* very bad. [Latin *ātrōx* dreadful] —**aˈtrociously** *adv.*

atrocity (əˈtrɒsɪtɪ) *n., pl.* **-ties. 1.** behaviour or action that is wicked or cruel. **2.** (*pl.*) acts of extreme cruelty.

atrophy (ˈætrəfɪ) *n., pl.* **-phies. 1.** a wasting away of an organ or part, or a failure to grow. ~*vb.* -**phying, -phied. 2.** to waste away or cause to waste away. [Greek *atrophos* ill-fed]

atropine (ˈætrəˌpiːn) *n.* a poisonous alkaloid obtained from deadly nightshade. [Greek *atropos* (inflexible), the Fate who cut the thread of life]

attach (əˈtætʃ) *vb.* **1.** to join, fasten, or connect. **2. attach oneself** or **be attached to.** to become associated with or join. **3.** (foll. by *to*) to be connected (with): *responsibility attaches to the job.* **4.** to ascribe: *he attaches great importance to the way he looks.* **5.** *Law.* to arrest or take (a person or property) with lawful authority. [Old French *atachier*]

attaché (əˈtæʃeɪ) *n.* a specialist attached to a diplomatic mission. [French]

attaché case *n.* a flat rectangular briefcase for carrying documents and papers.

attached (əˈtætʃt) *adj.* (foll. by *to*) **1.** fond (of). **2.** married, engaged, or in an exclusive sexual relationship.

attachment (əˈtætʃmənt) *n.* **1.** a fastening. **2.** (often foll. by *to*) affection or regard (for). **3.** an accessory that can be fitted to a device to change what it can do. **4.** the lawful seizure of property.

attack (əˈtæk) *vb.* **1.** to launch a physical assault (against). **2.** to take the initiative in a game or sport. **3.** to criticize vehemently. **4.** to turn one's energies to (a job or problem). **5.** to begin to affect adversely: *a car attacked by rust.* ~*n.* **6.** the act of attacking. **7.** any sudden appearance of a disease or symptoms: *a bad attack of mumps.* [Old Italian *attaccare*] —**atˈtacker** *n.*

attain (əˈteɪn) *vb.* **1.** to achieve or accomplish (a task or aim). **2.** to reach. [Latin *attingere*] —**atˈtainable** *adj.*

attainment (əˈteɪnmənt) *n.* an achievement or the act of achieving; accomplishment.

attar (ˈætə) *n.* a perfume made from damask roses. [Persian]

attempt (əˈtɛmpt) *vb.* **1.** to make an effort (to do or achieve something); try. **2.** to try to climb or surmount (an obstacle). ~*n.* **3.** an endeavour to achieve something; effort. **4. attempt on someone's life.** an attack on someone with the intention to kill. [Latin *attemptāre*]

attend (əˈtɛnd) *vb.* **1.** to be present at (an event). **2.** to give care (to); look after. **3.** to pay attention. **4.** to accompany. **5.** (foll. by *on* or *upon*) to follow as a consequence (of). **6.** (foll. by *to*) to apply oneself: *I must attend to the weeding.* [Latin *attendere* to stretch towards]

attendance (əˈtɛndəns) *n.* **1.** the act of attending. **2.** the number of persons present. **3.** regularity in attending.

attendant (əˈtɛndənt) *n.* **1.** a person employed to assist, guide, or provide a service. ~*adj.* **2.** being in attendance. **3.** associated.

attention (əˈtɛnʃən) *n.* **1.** concentrated direction of the mind. **2.** consideration, notice, or observation. **3.** detailed care or treatment. **4.** (*pl.*) an act of courtesy. **5.** the upright motionless position of formal military alertness.

attentive (ə'tɛntɪv) *adj.* **1.** paying attention. **2.** (often foll. by *to*) careful to fulfil the needs (of). —**at'tentively** *adv.* —**at'tentiveness** *n.*

attenuate (ə'tɛnjʊ,eɪt) *vb.* **1.** to weaken. **2.** to make or become thin; extend. [Latin *attenuāre*] —**at,tenu'ation** *n.*

attest (ə'tɛst) *vb.* **1.** to affirm the truth of. **2.** to witness or bear witness to (an act or event). **3.** to provide evidence for something being true. [Latin *testārī* to bear witness] —**attestation** (,ætɛ'steɪʃən) *n.*

attested (ə'tɛstɪd) *adj. Brit.* (of cattle) certified to be free from a disease, such as tuberculosis.

attic ('ætɪk) *n.* **1.** a space or room within the roof of a house. **2.** *Archit.* a storey above the cornice of a classical façade. [from use of Attic-style pilasters on façade of top storey]

Attic ('ætɪk) *adj.* **1.** of or relating to Attica, the area around Athens, or the dialect of Greek spoken there. **2.** (*often not cap.*) classically elegant. —*n.* **3.** the dialect of Ancient Greek in Athens.

attire (ə'taɪə) *n.* fine or formal clothes. [Old French *atirier* to put in order]

attired (ə'taɪəd) *adj.* dressed in a specified way.

attitude ('ætɪ,tjuːd) *n.* **1.** the way a person views something. **2. strike an attitude.** to pose for effect. **3.** a position of the body. **4.** the orientation of an aircraft or spacecraft in relation to some plane or direction. [Latin *aptus* apt]

attitudinize *or* **-nise** (,ætɪ'tjuːdɪ,naɪz) *vb.* to adopt a pose or opinion for effect.

attorney (ə'tɜːnɪ) *n.* **1.** a person legally appointed to act for another. **2.** *U.S.* a lawyer. [Old French *atourner* to direct to]

attorney general *n., pl.* **attorneys general** *or* **attorney generals.** a chief law officer of some governments.

attract (ə'trækt) *vb.* **1.** to exert a pleasing or fascinating influence (upon). **2.** to draw to oneself (esp. in **attract attention**). **3.** to exert a force on (a body) that tends to oppose a separation. [Latin *attrahere* to draw towards]

attraction (ə'trækʃən) *n.* **1.** the act or quality of attracting. **2.** a person or thing that attracts. **3.** a force by which one object attracts another.

attractive (ə'træktɪv) *adj.* appealing to the senses or mind. —**at'tractively** *adv.* —**at'tractiveness** *n.*

attribute *vb.* (ə'trɪbjuːt). **1.** (usually foll. by *to*) to regard as belonging (to): to *attribute a painting to Picasso.* —*n.* ('ætrɪ,bjuːt). **2.** a quality or feature representative of a person or thing. [Latin *attribuere* to associate with] —**at'tributable** *adj.* —**attribution** (,ætrɪ'bjuːʃən) *n.*

attributive (ə'trɪbjʊtɪv) *adj.* **1.** relating to an attribute. **2.** *Grammar.* (of an adjective) preceding the noun modified.

attrition (ə'trɪʃən) *n.* **1.** the act of wearing away, as by friction. **2.** constant wearing

down to weaken or destroy (often in **war of attrition**). [Latin *atterere* to weaken]

attune (ə'tjuːn) *vb.* to adjust or accustom (a person or thing); acclimatize.

atypical (eɪ'tɪpɪk³l) *adj.* not typical. —**a'typically** *adv.*

Au *Chem.* gold. [Latin *aurum*]

aubergine ('əʊbə,ʒiːn) *n.* the dark purple fruit of a tropical plant, cooked and eaten as a vegetable. [French, from Arabic *al-bādindjān*]

aubrietia (ɔː'briːʃə) *n.* a trailing purple-flowered rock plant. [after Claude *Aubriet,* painter of flowers and animals]

auburn ('ɔːb³n) *adj.* (esp. of hair) reddish-brown. [(orig. meaning: blond) Latin *albus* white]

auction ('ɔːkʃən) *n.* **1.** a public sale at which the highest bidder secures each item. ~*vb.* **2.** to sell by auction. [Latin *auctiō* an increasing]

auctioneer (,ɔːkʃə'nɪə) *n.* a person who conducts an auction.

audacious (ɔː'deɪʃəs) *adj.* **1.** recklessly bold or daring. **2.** impudent or presumptuous. [Latin *audāx* bold] —**audacity** (ɔː'dæsɪtɪ) *n.*

audible ('ɔːdɪb³l) *adj.* loud enough to be heard. [Latin *audīre* to hear] —,**audi'bility** *n.* —**'audibly** *adv.*

audience ('ɔːdɪəns) *n.* **1.** a group of spectators or listeners at a concert or play. **2.** the people reached by a book, film, or radio or television programme. **3.** a formal interview. [Latin *audīre* to hear]

audio ('ɔːdɪəʊ) *n. (modifier)* **1.** of or relating to sound or hearing. **2.** of or for the transmission or reproduction of sound. [Latin *audīre* to hear]

audio frequency *n.* a frequency in the range 20 hertz to 20 000 hertz, audible to the human ear.

audiometer (,ɔːdɪ'ɒmɪtə) *n.* an instrument for testing hearing.

audiotypist ('ɔːdɪəʊ,taɪpɪst) *n.* a typist trained to type from a dictating machine. —**'audio,typing** *n.*

audiovisual (,ɔːdɪəʊ'vɪʒʊəl) *adj.* (esp. of teaching aids) involving both hearing and sight.

audit ('ɔːdɪt) *n.* **1.** an inspection and verification of business accounts by a qualified accountant. **2.** any thoroughgoing examination or check. ~*vb.* **3.** to inspect, correct, and certify (accounts). [Latin *audīre* to hear]

audition (ɔː'dɪʃən) *n.* **1.** a test of a performer's or musician's ability for a particular role. ~*vb.* **2.** to judge by or be tested in an audition. [Latin *audīre* to hear]

auditor ('ɔːdɪtə) *n.* a person qualified to audit accounts. [Latin *audītor* a hearer]

auditorium (,ɔːdɪ'tɔːrɪəm) *n., pl.* **-toriums** *or* **-toria** (-'tɔːrɪə). **1.** the area of a concert hall or theatre in which the audience sits. **2.** *U.S. & Canad.* a building for public meetings. [Latin]

auditory ('ɔːdɪtrɪ) *adj.* of or relating to hearing. [Latin *audīre* to hear] *au fait* (ˌəʊ ˈfeɪ) *adj.* fully informed; expert. [French: to the point]

Aug. August.

Augean (ɔːˈdʒiːən) *adj.* extremely dirty or corrupt. [from *Augeas*, in Gk myth., king whose filthy stables Hercules cleaned in one day]

auger (ˈɔːɡə) *n.* a hand tool with a corkscrew-like point for boring holes in wood. [Old English *nafugār* nave, i.e. hub, (of a wheel) spear]

aught (ɔːt) *pron. Archaic or literary.* anything whatever (esp. in **for aught I know**). [Old English *āwiht*]

augment (ɔːɡˈmɛnt) *vb.* to make or become greater in number or strength. [Latin *augēre* to increase] —**ˌaugmenˈtation** *n.*

augmentative (ɔːɡˈmɛntətɪv) *adj.* tending to augment.

au gratin (ˌəʊ ˈɡrætæn) *adj.* covered and cooked with breadcrumbs and sometimes cheese. [French]

augur (ˈɔːɡə) *vb.* to foreshadow future events: *this augurs well for us.* [Latin]

augury (ˈɔːɡjʊrɪ) *n., pl.* **-ries.** an omen.

august (ɔːˈɡʌst) *adj.* dignified or imposing. [Latin *augustus*]

August (ˈɔːɡəst) *n.* the eighth month of the year. [Latin, after the emperor *Augustus*]

Augustan (ɔːˈɡʌstən) *adj.* **1.** of the Roman emperor Augustus Caesar or the poets writing during his reign. **2.** of any literary period noted for refinement and classicism.

auk (ɔːk) *n.* a diving bird of northern oceans with a heavy body, narrow wings, and a black-and-white plumage. [Old Norse *ālka*]

auld lang syne (ˈɔːld læŋ ˈsaɪn) *n.* times past. [Scot., lit.: old long since]

aunt (ɑːnt) *n.* **1.** a sister of one's father or mother. **2.** the wife of one's uncle. **3.** a child's term of address for a female friend of the parents. [Latin *amita* a father's sister]

auntie *or* **aunty** (ˈɑːntɪ) *n., pl.* **-ies.** *Informal.* an aunt.

Aunt Sally (ˈsælɪ) *n., pl.* **-lies.** *Brit.* **1.** a figure used in fairgrounds as a target. **2.** any target for insults or criticism.

au pair (əʊ ˈpɛə) *n.* a young foreign woman who undertakes housework in exchange for board and lodging. [French]

aura (ˈɔːrə) *n., pl.* **auras** *or* **aurae** (ˈɔːriː). **1.** a distinctive air or quality associated with a person or thing. **2.** any invisible emanation. [Greek: breeze]

aural (ˈɔːrəl) *adj.* of or using the ears or hearing. [Latin *auris* ear] —**ˈaurally** *adv.*

aureate (ˈɔːrɪɪt) *adj.* **1.** covered with gold. **2.** excessively elaborate. [Latin *aurum* gold]

aureole (ˈɔːrɪˌəʊl) *or* **aureola** (ɔːˈriːələ) *n.* **1.** a border of light enveloping the head of a figure represented as holy. **2.** the sun's corona, visible as a faint halo during eclipses. [Latin *aurum* gold]

au revoir (ˌəʊ rəˈvwɑː) *interj.* goodbye. [French]

auric (ˈɔːrɪk) *adj.* of or containing gold, esp. in the trivalent state. [Latin *aurum* gold]

auricle (ˈɔːrɪkᵊl) *n.* **1.** the upper chamber of the heart. **2.** the external part of the ear. [Latin *auris* ear]

auricula (ɔːˈrɪkjʊlə) *n., pl.* **-lae** (-ˌliː) *or* **-las.** an alpine primrose with leaves shaped like a bear's ear. [Latin *auris* ear]

auriferous (ɔːˈrɪfərəs) *adj.* containing gold. [Latin *aurum* gold + *ferre* to bear]

aurochs (ˈɔːrɒks) *n., pl.* **-rochs.** a recently extinct European wild ox. [German]

aurora (ɔːˈrɔːrə) *n., pl.* **-ras** *or* **-rae** (-riː). **1.** an atmospheric phenomenon of bands, curtains, or streamers of light, sometimes seen in polar regions. **2.** *Poetic.* the dawn. [Latin: dawn]

aurora australis (ɒˈstreɪlɪs) *n.* the aurora seen around the South Pole. [New Latin: southern aurora]

aurora borealis (ˌbɔːrɪˈeɪlɪs) *n.* the aurora seen around the North Pole. [New Latin: northern aurora]

auscultation (ˌɔːskəlˈteɪʃən) *n.* the listening to of the internal sounds made by the body, usually with a stethoscope, to help with medical diagnosis. [Latin *auscultāre* to listen attentively]

auspices (ˈɔːspɪsɪz) *pl. n.* **under the auspices of.** with the support and approval of. [Latin *auspicium* augury from birds]

auspicious (ɔːˈspɪʃəs) *adj.* favourable or propitious.

Aussie (ˈɒzɪ) *n., adj. Informal.* Australian.

austere (ɒˈstɪə) *adj.* **1.** stern or severe. **2.** self-disciplined or ascetic. **3.** severely simple or plain. [Greek *austēros* astringent]

austerity (ɒˈstɛrɪtɪ) *n., pl.* **-ties.** **1.** the state of being austere. **2.** reduced availability of luxuries and consumer goods.

austral (ˈɒstrəl) *adj.* of or from the south. [Latin *auster* the south wind]

Austral. **1.** Australasia. **2.** Australia(n).

Australasian (ˌɒstrəˈleɪzɪən) *adj.* of or from Australia, New Zealand, and neighbouring islands.

Australian (ɒˈstreɪlɪən) *n.* **1.** a person from Australia. ~*adj.* **2.** of Australia or the Australians.

autarchy (ˈɔːtɑːkɪ) *n., pl.* **-chies.** unlimited authority; autocracy. [Greek *autarkhia*]

autarky (ˈɔːtɑːkɪ) *n., pl.* **-kies.** a policy of economic self-sufficiency. [Greek *autarkeia*]

authentic (ɔːˈθɛntɪk) *adj.* **1.** of undisputed origin or authorship; genuine. **2.** trustworthy; reliable. [Greek *authentikos*] —**auˈthentically** *adv.* —**authenticity** (ˌɔːθɛnˈtɪsɪtɪ) *n.*

authenticate (ɔːˈθɛntɪˌkeɪt) *vb.* to establish as genuine. —**auˌthentiˈcation** *n.*

author (ˈɔːθə) *n.* **1.** a person who writes a book, article, or other written work. **2.** an originator or creator. [Latin *auctor*]

authoritarian (ɔːˌθɒrɪˈtɛərɪən) *adj.* **1.** favouring or characterized by strict obedience to authority. ~*n.* **2.** a person who favours or practises authoritarian policies.

authoritative (ɔːˈθɒrɪtətɪv) *adj.* **1.** recognized as being reliable. **2.** possessing authority; official.

authority (ɔːˈθɒrɪtɪ) *n., pl.* **-ties.** **1.** the

power or ability to influence, control, or judge others. **2.** (*often pl.*) a person or group of people having this power. **3.** a position that commands such a power or right (often in **in authority**). **4.** official permission: *you have no authority to do that.* **5.** an expert or authoritative work in a particular field. **6.** evidence or testimony. **7.** confidence resulting from expertise. [Latin *auctor* author]

authorize *or* **-rise** ('ɔːθəˌraɪz) *vb.* **1.** to confer authority upon (someone to do something). **2.** to give official permission. —ˌauthori'zation *or* -ri'sation *n.*

Authorized Version *n.* **the.** an English translation of the Bible published in 1611.

authorship ('ɔːθəˌʃɪp) *n.* **1.** the origin or originator of a written work or plan. **2.** the profession of writing.

autism ('ɔːtɪzəm) *n. Psychiatry.* abnormal self-absorption, usually affecting children, characterized by lack of response to people and limited ability to communicate. [Greek *autos* self] —**au'tistic** *adj.*

auto ('ɔːtəʊ) *n., pl.* **-tos.** *U.S. & Canad. informal.* short for **automobile.**

auto- *or sometimes before a vowel* **aut-** *combining form.* **1.** self; of or by the same one: *autobiography.* **2.** self-propelling: *automobile.* [Greek *autos* self]

autobahn ('ɔːtəˌbɑːn) *n.* a German or Austrian motorway. [German, from *Auto* car + *Bahn* road]

autobiography (ˌɔːtəʊbaɪ'ɒɡrəfɪ) *n., pl.* **-phies.** an account of a person's life written by that person. —ˌautobi'ographer *n.* —**autobiographical** (ˌɔːtəˌbaɪə'ɡræfɪkəl) *adj.*

autoclave ('ɔːtəˌkleɪv) *n.* an apparatus for sterilizing objects by steam under pressure. [AUTO- + Latin *clāvis* key]

autocracy (ɔː'tɒkrəsɪ) *n., pl.* **-cies.** government by an individual with unrestricted authority.

autocrat ('ɔːtəˌkræt) *n.* **1.** a ruler with absolute authority. **2.** a dictatorial person. [AUTO- + Greek *kratos* power] —ˌauto'cratic *adj.* —ˌauto'cratically *adv.*

autocross ('ɔːtəʊˌkrɒs) *n.* a sport in which cars race over a circuit of rough grass.

Autocue ('ɔːtəʊˌkjuː) *n. Trademark.* an electronic television device displaying a speaker's script, unseen by the audience.

auto-da-fé (ˌɔːtəʊdɑː'feɪ) *n., pl.* **autos-da-fé.** **1.** *History.* the ceremonial passing of sentence on heretics by the Spanish Inquisition. **2.** the burning to death of heretics. [Portuguese, lit.: act of the faith]

autogiro *or* **autogyro** (ˌɔːtəʊ'dʒaɪrəʊ) *n., pl.* **-ros.** a self-propelled aircraft supported mainly by unpowered rotating horizontal blades.

autograph ('ɔːtəˌɡrɑːf) *n.* **1.** a handwritten signature of a famous person. ~*vb.* **2.** to write one's signature on or in. [AUTO- + Greek *graphein* to write]

automat ('ɔːtəˌmæt) *n.* *U.S.* a vending machine.

automate ('ɔːtəˌmeɪt) *vb.* to make (a manufacturing process) automatic.

automatic (ˌɔːtə'mætɪk) *adj.* **1. a.** (of a device or mechanism) able to activate or regulate itself. **b.** (of a process) performed by such automatic equipment. **2.** performed without conscious thought. **3.** occurring as a necessary consequence: *promotion is automatic.* **4.** (of a firearm) utilizing some of the force of each explosion to reload and fire continuously. ~*n.* **5.** an automatic firearm. **6.** a motor vehicle having automatic transmission. [Greek *automatos* acting independently] —ˌauto'matically *adv.*

automatic pilot *n.* **1.** a device that automatically maintains an aircraft on a preset course. **2. on automatic pilot.** repeating an action or process without thought.

automatic transmission *n.* a transmission system in a motor vehicle in which the gears change automatically.

automation (ˌɔːtə'meɪʃən) *n.* the use of automatic, often electronic, methods to control industrial processes.

automaton (ɔː'tɒmətʰn) *n., pl.* **-tons** *or* **-ta.** **1.** a mechanical device operating under its own power. **2.** a person who acts mechanically. [Greek *automatos* spontaneous]

automobile ('ɔːtəməˌbiːl) *n.* *U.S.* a motor-car.

automotive (ˌɔːtə'məʊtɪv) *adj.* **1.** relating to motor vehicles. **2.** self-propelling.

autonomous (ɔː'tɒnəməs) *adj.* **1.** having self-government. **2.** independent of others. [AUTO- + Greek *nomos* law]

autonomy (ɔː'tɒnəmɪ) *n., pl.* **-mies.** **1.** the right or state of self-government. **2.** freedom to determine one's own actions and behaviour. [Greek *automonia*]

autopilot (ˌɔːtə'paɪlət) *n.* an automatic pilot.

autopsy ('ɔːtɒpsɪ, ɔː'tɒp-) *n., pl.* **-sies.** examination of a dead body to determine the cause of death. [Greek *autopsia* seeing with one's own eyes]

autoroute ('ɔːtəʊˌruːt) *n.* a French motorway. [French, from *auto* car + *route* road]

autostrada ('ɔːtəʊˌstrɑːdə) *n.* an Italian motorway. [Italian, from *auto* car + *strada* road]

autosuggestion (ˌɔːtəʊsə'dʒɛstʃən) *n.* a process in which a person unconsciously supplies the means of influencing his own behaviour or beliefs.

autumn ('ɔːtəm) *n.* **1.** the season of the year between summer and winter. **2.** a period of late maturity, esp. followed by a decline. [Latin *autumnus*] —**autumnal** (ɔː'tʌmnʰl) *adj.*

aux. auxiliary.

auxiliaries (ɔːɡ'zɪljərɪz, -'zɪlə-) *pl. n.* foreign troops serving another nation.

auxiliary (ɔːɡ'zɪljərɪ, -'zɪlə-) *adj.* **1.** secondary or supplementary. **2.** supporting. ~*n., pl.* **-ries.** **3.** a person or thing that supports or supplements. [Latin *auxilium* help]

auxiliary verb *n.* a verb used to indicate the tense, voice, or mood of another verb, such as *will* in *he will go.*

AV Authorized Version.

av. 1. average. 2. avoirdupois.

avail (ə'veɪl) vb. 1. to be of use, advantage, or assistance (to). 2. **avail oneself of (something).** to make use of (something) to one's advantage. ~n. 3. use or advantage (esp. in **of no avail**). [Latin valēre to be strong]

available (ə'veɪləb'l) adj. obtainable or accessible; capable of being made use of. —**a,vaila'bility** n. —**a'vailably** adv.

avalanche ('ævə,lɑːntʃ) n. 1. a fall of large masses of snow and ice down a mountain. 2. a sudden or overwhelming appearance of a large quantity of things. [French]

avant-garde (,ævɒŋ'gɑːd) n. 1. those artists, writers or musicians, whose techniques and ideas are in advance of those generally accepted. ~adj. 2. (of a work of art) using ideas or techniques in advance of those generally accepted. [French: vanguard]

avarice ('ævərɪs) n. extreme greed for riches. [Latin avēre to crave] —**avaricious** (,ævə'rɪʃəs) adj.

avast (ə'vɑːst) interj. Naut. stop! cease! [prob. Dutch hou'vast hold fast]

avatar ('ævə,tɑː) n. Hinduism. the manifestation of a god in human or animal form. [Sanskrit avatāra a going down]

avdp. avoirdupois.

Ave ('ɑːvɪ) or **Ave Maria** (mə'riːə) n. same as **Hail Mary.** [Latin: hail, Mary!]

Ave. avenue.

avenge (ə'vɛndʒ) vb. to inflict a punishment in retaliation for (harm done) or on behalf of (the person harmed). [Latin vindicāre] —**a'venger** n.

avenue ('ævɪnjuː) n. 1. a street. 2. an approach road, as to a country house. 3. a road bordered by two rows of trees. 4. a line of approach: try all avenues before giving up. [French, from avenir to come to]

aver (ə'vɜː) vb. **averring, averred.** to state to be true. [Latin vērus true] —**a'verment** n.

average ('ævərɪdʒ, 'ævrɪdʒ) n. 1. the typical or normal amount or quality. 2. the result obtained by adding the numbers or quantities in a set and dividing the total by the number of members in the set. 3. **on (the or an) average.** usually; typically. ~adj. 4. usual or typical. 5. mediocre or inferior. 6. constituting a numerical average. ~vb. 7. to obtain or estimate a numerical average of. 8. to assess the general quality of. 9. to amount to or be on average. [Middle English averay loss arising from damage to ships, ult. from Arabic awār damage]

averse (ə'vɜːs) adj. (usually foll. by to) opposed, disinclined, or loath. [Latin āvertere to turn from]

aversion (ə'vɜːʃən) n. 1. (usually foll. by to or for) extreme dislike or disinclination. 2. a person or thing that arouses this.

avert (ə'vɜːt) vb. 1. to turn away: to avert one's gaze. 2. to ward off: to avert danger. [Latin āvertere to turn from]

Avesta (ə'vɛstə) n. a collection of sacred writings of Zoroastrianism.

avian ('eɪvɪən) adj. of or like a bird. [Latin avis bird]

aviary ('eɪvjərɪ) n., pl. **aviaries.** a large enclosure in which birds are kept. [Latin avis bird]

aviation (,eɪvɪ'eɪʃən) n. the art or science of flying aircraft. [Latin avis bird]

aviator ('eɪvɪ,eɪtə) n. Old-fashioned. the pilot of an aircraft. —**'avi,atrix** fem. n.

avid ('ævɪd) adj. 1. very keen; enthusiastic: an avid reader. 2. (often foll. by for or of) eager: avid for revenge. [Latin avēre to long for] —**avidity** (ə'vɪdɪtɪ) n. —**'avidly** adv.

avocado (,ævə'kɑːdəʊ) n., pl. **-dos.** a pear-shaped fruit with a leathery green skin and greenish-yellow edible pulp. [Spanish aguacate]

avocation (,ævə'keɪʃən) n. Archaic. 1. a minor occupation undertaken as a diversion. 2. a person's regular job. [Latin āvocāre to distract]

avocet ('ævə,sɛt) n. a long-legged shore bird having a long slender upward-curving bill. [Italian avocetta]

avoid (ə'vɔɪd) vb. 1. to keep out of the way of. 2. to refrain from doing. 3. to prevent from happening. [Old French esvuidier] —**a'voidable** adj. —**a'voidably** adv. —**a'voidance** n.

avoirdupois or **avoirdupois weight** (,ævədə'pɔɪz) n. a system of weights based on the pound, which contains 16 ounces or 7000 grains. [Old French aver de peis goods of weight]

avow (ə'vaʊ) vb. 1. to state or affirm. 2. to admit openly. [Latin advocāre to call upon] —**a'vowal** n. —**a'vowed** adj. —**avowedly** (ə'vaʊɪdlɪ) adv.

avuncular (ə'vʌŋkjʊlə) adj. friendly, helpful or caring. [Latin avunculus (maternal) uncle]

await (ə'weɪt) vb. 1. to wait for. 2. to be in store for.

awake (ə'weɪk) vb. **awaking; awoke** or **awaked; awoken** or **awaked.** 1. to emerge or rouse from sleep. 2. to become or cause to become alert. ~adj. 3. not sleeping. 4. (sometimes foll. by to) alert or aware: awake to the danger. [Old English awacan]

award (ə'wɔːd) vb. 1. to give (something, as for merit). 2. Law. to declare to be entitled, as by decision of a court. ~n. 3. something awarded, such as a prize. 4. Law. the decision of an arbitrator or court. [Old French eswarder to decide after investigation]

aware (ə'weə) adj. 1. (foll. by of) having knowledge: aware of his error. 2. informed: politically aware. [Old English gewær] —**a'wareness** n.

awash (ə'wɒʃ) adv., adj. 1. at a level with the surface of the sea. 2. washed over by the waves.

away (ə'weɪ) adv. 1. from a particular

place: *swim away*. **2.** in or to another, a usual, or a proper place: *to put toys away*. **3.** at a distance: *keep away from strangers*. **4.** out of existence: *fade away*. **5.** indicating motion or distance from a normal or proper place: *to turn one's head away*. **6.** continuously: *laughing away*. ~*adj.* **7.** not present: *away from school*. **8.** distant: *a good way away*. **9.** *Sport*. played on an opponent's ground. [Old English *on weg* on way]

awayday (ə'weɪˌdeɪ) *n.* a day trip taken for pleasure. [from *awayday ticket* a special-rate day return by train]

awe (ɔː) *n.* **1.** overwhelming wonder, respect, or dread. ~*vb.* **2.** to inspire with reverence or dread. [Old Norse *agi*]

aweigh (ə'weɪ) *adj. Naut.* (of an anchor) no longer hooked into the bottom.

awesome ('ɔːsəm) *adj.* inspiring or displaying awe.

awful ('ɔːful) *adj.* **1.** very bad; unpleasant. **2.** *Archaic*. inspiring reverence or dread. **3.** *Informal*. large or great: *an awful pity*. ~*adv.* **4.** *Not standard*. very: *an awful cold day*.

awfully ('ɔːfəlɪ) *adv.* **1.** in an unpleasant, bad, or reprehensible manner. **2.** *Informal*. very: *I'm awfully keen to come*.

awhile (ə'waɪl) *adv.* for a brief period.

awkward ('ɔːkwəd) *adj.* **1.** clumsy or ungainly. **2.** unwieldy: *this keyboard is awkward to use*. **3.** embarrassing: *an awkward moment*. **4.** embarrassed: *he felt awkward about leaving*. **5.** difficult to deal with. [Old Norse *ǒfugr* turned the wrong way round] —*'awkwardly adv.* —*'awkwardness n.*

awl (ɔːl) *n.* a pointed hand tool for piercing wood, leather, etc. [Old English *æl*]

awn (ɔːn) *n.* any of the bristles growing from the flowering parts of certain grasses and cereals. [Old English *agen* ear of grain]

awning ('ɔːnɪŋ) *n.* a roof of canvas supported by a frame to provide protection from the weather. [origin unknown]

awoke (ə'wəʊk) *vb.* a past tense and (now rare or dialectal) past participle of **awake**.

AWOL ('eɪwɒl) *Mil.* absent without leave but without intending to desert.

awry (ə'raɪ) *adv., adj.* **1.** with a twist to one side; askew. **2.** amiss. [Middle English *on wry*]

axe or *U.S.* **ax** (æks) *n., pl.* **axes. 1.** a hand tool with one side of its head sharpened to a cutting edge, used for felling trees and splitting timber. **2. an axe to grind.** an ulterior motive. **3.** *Informal*. a severe cut in spending or in the number of staff employed. ~*vb.* **4.** to chop with an axe. **5.** *Informal*. to dismiss (employees), re-

strict (expenditure), or terminate (a project). [Old English *æx*]

axes¹ ('æksiːz) *n.* the plural of **axis**.

axes² ('æksɪz) *n.* the plural of **axe**.

axial ('æksɪəl) *adj.* **1.** forming or of an axis. **2.** in, on, or along an axis. —*'axially adv.*

axil ('æksɪl) *n.* the upper angle between a leafstalk and the stem from which it grows. [Latin *axilla* armpit]

axiom ('æksɪəm) *n.* **1.** a generally accepted proposition or principle. **2.** a self-evident statement. [Greek *axios* worthy]

axiomatic (ˌæksɪə'mætɪk) *adj.* **1.** self-evident. **2.** containing axioms. —*ˌaxio'matically adv.*

axis ('æksɪs) *n., pl.* **axes. 1.** a real or imaginary line about which a body can rotate or about which an object or geometrical construction is symmetrical. **2.** one of two or three reference lines used in coordinate geometry to locate a point in a plane or in space. [Latin]

axle ('æksəl) *n.* a shaft on which a wheel or pair of wheels revolves. [Old Norse *ǒxull*]

axolotl (ˌæksə'lɒt³l) *n.* an aquatic salamander of N America. [Mexican Indian, water doll]

ayah ('aɪə) *n.* (in parts of the former British Empire) a native maidservant or nursemaid. [Hindi *āyā*]

ayatollah (ˌaɪə'tɒlə) *n.* one of a class of Islamic religious leaders in Iran. [Arabic *aya* sign + *allah* God]

aye or **ay** (aɪ) *interj.* **1.** yes. ~*n.* **2.** an affirmative vote or voter. [prob. from *I*, expressing assent]

Ayrshire ('ɛəʃə) *n.* one of a breed of brown-and-white dairy cattle. [*Ayrshire*, former Scot. county]

AZ Arizona.

azalea (ə'zeɪljə) *n.* a shrub allied to the rhododendron cultivated for its showy flowers. [Greek *azaleos* dry]

azimuth ('æzɪməθ) *n.* **1.** *Astron., navigation*. the angle between the north or south point of the horizon and the intersection with the horizon of a vertical circle passing through a celestial body. **2.** *Surveying*. the horizontal angle of a bearing measured clockwise from north. [Arabic *as-samt* the path]

Aztec ('æztɛk) *n.* **1.** a member of a Mexican Indian people who established a great empire, overthrown by the Spanish in the early 16th century. **2.** the language of the Aztecs. ~*adj.* **3.** of the Aztecs or their language. [*Aztlan*, their traditional place of origin, lit.: near the cranes]

azure ('æʒə, 'eɪ-) *n.* **1.** the deep blue colour of a clear blue sky. **2.** *Poetic*. a clear blue sky. [Arabic *lāzaward* lapis lazuli]

B

b *or* **B** (biː) *n., pl.* **b's, B's,** *or* **Bs. 1.** the second letter of the English alphabet. **2.** the second in a series, class, or rank.

B 1. *Music.* the seventh note of the scale of C major. **2.** the less important of two things. **3.** *Chem.* boron. **4.** *Chess.* bishop.

b. 1. born. **2.** *Cricket.* **a.** bowled. **b.** bye.

Ba *Chem.* barium.

BA 1. Bachelor of Arts. **2.** British Airways.

baa (baː) *vb.* **baaing, baaed. 1.** to make the cry of a sheep. ~*n.* **2.** the cry made by a sheep.

baas (baːs) *n. S. African.* a boss. [Afrikaans]

baasskap (ˈbaːsˌkæp) *n.* (in South Africa) control by Whites of non-Whites. [Afrikaans]

babbalas (ˈbæbəˌlæs) *n. S. African.* a hangover. [Zulu *ibhabhalasi*]

babble (ˈbæbᵊl) *vb.* **1.** to utter (words or sounds) in an incoherent jumble. **2.** to talk foolishly or irrelevantly. **3.** to disclose (secrets) carelessly. **4.** (of streams or birds) to make a low murmuring sound. ~*n.* **5.** incoherent or foolish speech. **6.** a murmuring sound. [prob. imit.] —**ˈbabbler** *n.*

babe (beɪb) *n.* **1.** a baby. **2.** *Informal.* a naive or gullible person. **3.** *Slang, chiefly U.S.* a girl.

babel (ˈbeɪbᵊl) *n.* **1.** a confusion of noises or voices. **2.** a scene of noise and confusion. [Hebrew *Bābhél*]

baboon (bəˈbuːn) *n.* a medium-sized monkey with a long face, large teeth, and a fairly long tail. [Middle English *babewyn* gargoyle]

baby (ˈbeɪbɪ) *n., pl.* **-bies. 1.** a newborn child. **2.** the youngest or smallest of a family or group. **3.** a recently born animal. **4.** an immature person. **5.** *Slang.* a sweetheart. **6.** a project of personal concern. **7. be left holding the baby.** to be left with a responsibility. ~*adj.* **8.** comparatively small of its type: *a baby car.* ~*vb.* **-bying, -bied. 9.** to treat (someone) like a baby; pamper. [prob. childish reduplication] —**ˈbabyhood** *n.* —**ˈbabyish** *adj.*

baby bonus *n. Canad. informal.* Family Allowance.

baby-sit *vb.* **-sitting, -sat.** to act or work as a baby-sitter. —**ˈbaby-ˌsitting** *n., adj.*

baby-sitter *n.* a person who takes care of a child while the parents are out.

baccalaureate (ˌbækəˈlɔːrɪɪt) *n.* the university degree of Bachelor of Arts. [Medieval Latin *baccalārius* bachelor]

baccarat (ˈbækəˌrɑː, ˌbækəˈrɑː) *n.* a card game in which the punters gamble against the banker. [French *baccara*]

bacchanal (ˈbækənᵊl) *n.* **1.** a follower of Bacchus, Greek god of wine. **2.** a drunken celebration.

bacchanalia (ˌbækəˈneɪlɪə) *pl. n.* **1.** an ancient Roman festival in honour of Bacchus. **2.** any drunken revelry.

bacchant (ˈbækənt) *or (fem.)* **bacchante** (bəˈkæntɪ) *n., pl.* **bacchants** *or* **bacchantes** (bəˈkæntɪz). **1.** a priest, priestess, or worshipper of Bacchus. **2.** a drunken reveller.

Bacchic (ˈbækɪk) *adj.* of Bacchus.

baccy (ˈbækɪ) *n. Brit. informal.* tobacco.

bachelor (ˈbætʃələ) *n.* **1.** an unmarried man. **2.** a person who holds the lowest university degree. [Old French *bacheler* youth, squire] —**ˈbachelorhood** *n.*

bachelor girl *n.* a young unmarried woman.

Bachelor of Arts *n.* a person with a first degree from a university or college, usually in the arts.

bacillary (bəˈsɪlərɪ) *adj.* of or caused by bacilli.

bacillus (bəˈsɪləs) *n., pl.* **-cilli** (-ˈsɪlaɪ). a rod-shaped bacterium, esp. one causing disease. [Latin *baculum* walking stick]

back (bæk) *n.* **1.** the rear part of the human body, from the neck to the pelvis. **2.** the spinal column. **3.** the part or side of an object opposite the front. **4.** the part of anything less often seen or used. **5.** *Ball games.* a defensive player or position. **6. at the back of one's mind.** not in one's conscious thoughts. **7. behind someone's back.** secretly or deceitfully. **8. put** *or* **get someone's back up.** to annoy someone. **9. turn one's back on someone.** to refuse to help someone. ~*vb.* **10.** to move or cause to move backwards. **11.** to provide money for (a person or enterprise). **12.** to bet on the success of: *to back a horse.* **13.** to provide (a singer) with a musical accompaniment. **14.** (foll. by *on* or *onto*) to have the back facing (towards): *the house backs onto a river.* **15.** (of the wind) to change direction anticlockwise. ~*adj.* **16.** situated behind. **17.** owing from an earlier date: *back rent.* **18.** remote: *a back road.* ~*adv.* **19.** at, to, or towards the rear. **20.** to or towards the original starting point or condition: *I went back home.* **21.** in reply or retaliation: *to hit someone back.* **22.** in concealment or reserve: *to keep something back.* **23. back and forth.** to and fro. **24. back to front. a.** in reverse. **b.** in disorder. ~See also **back down, back out, back up.** [Old English *bæc*]

backbencher (ˈbækˈbentʃə) *n. Brit., Austral., N.Z., etc.* a Member of Parliament who does not hold office in the government or opposition.

backbite (ˈbækˌbaɪt) *vb.* **-biting, -bit; -bitten** *or* **-bit.** to talk spitefully about (an absent person). —**ˈbackˌbiter** *n.*

back boiler *n.* a tank at the back of a fireplace for heating water.

backbone (ˈbækˌbəʊn) *n.* **1.** the spinal column. **2.** strength of character; courage.

backbreaking (ˈbækˌbreɪkɪŋ) *adj.* (of work) exhausting.

backburn (ˈbækˌbɜːn) *Austral. & N.Z.* ~*vb.* **1.** to clear (an area of bush) by creating a new fire that burns in the opposite direction from the line of advancing fire. ~*n.* **2.** the act or result of backburning.

backchat (ˈbækˌtʃæt) *n. Informal.* the act of answering back, esp. impudently.

backcloth (ˈbækˌklɒθ) *n.* a painted curtain at the back of a stage set. Also called: **backdrop.**

backcomb (ˈbækˌkəʊm) *vb.* to comb (the hair) towards the roots to give more bulk to a hairstyle.

back country *n. Austral. & N.Z.* land remote from settled areas.

backdate (ˌbækˈdeɪt) *vb.* to make (a document) effective from an earlier date.

back door *n.* a means of entry to a job or position that is secret or obtained through influence.

back down *vb.* to withdraw an earlier claim.

backer (ˈbækə) *n.* a person who gives financial or other support.

backfire (ˌbækˈfaɪə) *vb.* **1.** (of an internal-combustion engine) to make a loud noise as a result of an explosion of unburnt gases in the exhaust system. **2.** (of a plan or scheme) to fail to have the desired effect.

backgammon (ˈbækˌgæmən) *n.* a game for two people played on a board with pieces moved according to throws of the dice. [*back* + obs. *gammon* game]

background (ˈbækˌgraʊnd) *n.* **1.** the part of a scene furthest from the viewer. **2.** an inconspicuous position: *in the background.* **3.** the space behind the chief figures or objects in a picture. **4.** a person's social class, education, or experience. **5.** the events or circumstances that help to explain something.

backhand (ˈbækˌhænd) *n.* **1.** *Tennis, etc.* a stroke made across the body with the back of the hand facing the direction of the stroke. **2.** the side on which backhand strokes are made.

backhanded (ˌbækˈhændɪd) *adj.* **1.** (of a blow or shot) performed with the arm moving across the body. **2.** ambiguous or sarcastic: *a backhanded compliment.*

backhander (ˈbækˌhændə) *n.* **1.** *Slang.* a bribe. **2.** a backhanded stroke or blow.

backing (ˈbækɪŋ) *n.* **1.** support. **2.** something that forms or strengthens the back of something. **3.** musical accompaniment for a pop singer.

backing dog *n. N.Z.* a dog that moves a flock of sheep by jumping on their backs.

backlash (ˈbækˌlæʃ) *n.* **1.** a sudden and adverse reaction. **2.** a recoil between interacting badly fitting parts in machinery.

backlog (ˈbækˌlɒg) *n.* an accumulation of uncompleted things to be dealt with.

back number *n.* **1.** an old issue of a newspaper or magazine. **2.** *Informal.* a person or thing considered to be old-fashioned.

back out *vb.* (often foll. by *of*) to withdraw (from an agreement).

backpack (ˈbækˌpæk) *n.* **1.** a rucksack. ~*vb.* **2.** to go hiking with a backpack.

back passage *n.* the rectum.

back-pedal *vb.* -pedalling, -pedalled or *U.S.* -pedaling, -pedaled. to retract or modify a previous opinion or principle.

back room *n.* **a.** a place where secret research or planning is done. **b.** (*as modifier*): *back-room boys.*

back seat *n. Informal.* a subordinate or inconspicuous position: *I prefer to take a back seat.*

back-seat driver *n. Informal.* a person, for example a passenger in a car, who offers unwanted advice.

backside (ˌbækˈsaɪd) *n. Informal.* the buttocks.

backslide (ˌbækˈslaɪd) *vb.* -sliding, -slid. to relapse into former bad habits or vices. —ˌback'slider *n.*

backspace (ˌbækˈspeɪs) *vb.* to move a typewriter carriage or computer cursor backwards.

backspin (ˈbækˌspɪn) *n. Sport.* a backward spin imparted to a ball to reduce its speed at impact.

backstage (ˌbækˈsteɪdʒ) *adv.* **1.** behind the stage in a theatre. ~*adj.* **2.** situated backstage.

backstairs (ˌbækˈsteəz) or **backstair** *adj.* underhand: *backstairs gossip.*

backstreet (ˈbækˌstriːt) *n.* **1.** a street in a town remote from the main roads. **2.** (*modifier*) denoting secret or illegal activities: *a backstreet abortion.*

backstroke (ˈbækˌstrəʊk) *n. Swimming.* a stroke performed on the back, using backward circular strokes of each arm.

backtrack (ˈbækˌtræk) *vb.* **1.** to return by the same route by which one has come. **2.** to retract or reverse one's opinion or policy.

back up *vb.* **1.** to support. **2.** *Computers.* to make a copy of (a data file), esp. as a security copy. ~*n.* **backup. 3.** a support or reinforcement. **4. a.** a reserve or substitute. **b.** (*as modifier*): *a backup copy.*

backveld (ˈbækˌfɛlt, -ˌvɛlt) *n. S. African informal.* a remote sparsely populated rural area. [Afrikaans]

backward (ˈbækwəd) *adj.* **1.** directed towards the rear. **2.** retarded in physical, material, or intellectual development. **3.** reluctant or bashful. ~*adv.* **4.** same as **backwards.** —ˈbackwardness *n.*

backwards (ˈbækwədz) or **backward** *adv.* **1.** towards the rear. **2.** with the back foremost. **3.** in the reverse of the usual direction. **4.** into a worse state. **5.** towards the point of origin. **6. bend over backwards.** *Informal.* to make a special effort to please someone.

backwash (ˈbækˌwɒʃ) *n.* **1.** water washed

backwards by the motion of oars or a ship.
2. a repercussion.

backwater ('bæk,wɔːtə) n. **1.** a body of stagnant water connected to a river. **2.** an isolated or backward place or condition.

backwoods ('bæk,wʊdz) pl. n. **1.** partially cleared, sparsely populated forests. **2.** any remote sparsely populated place. —'**back,woodsman** n.

back yard n. **1.** a yard at the back of a house, etc. **2. in one's own back yard. a.** close at hand. **b.** involving or implicating one.

bacon ('beɪkən) n. **1.** meat from the back and sides of a pig, dried, salted, and usually smoked. **2. bring home the bacon.** Informal. **a.** to achieve success. **b.** to provide material support. [Old French]

bacteria (bæk'tɪərɪə) pl. n., sing. -**rium.** a large group of microorganisms, many of which cause disease. [Greek baktron rod] —**bac'terial** adj.

bacteriology (bæk,tɪərɪ'ɒlədʒɪ) n. the study of bacteria. —**bac,teri'ologist** n.

Bactrian camel ('bæktrɪən) n. a two-humped camel. [Bactria, ancient country of Asia]

bad (bæd) adj. **worse, worst. 1.** not good; of poor quality. **2.** lacking skill or talent: bad at maths. **3.** harmful: smoking is bad for you. **4.** immoral; evil. **5.** naughty; mischievous. **6.** rotten; decayed: a bad egg. **7.** severe: a bad headache. **8.** incorrect; faulty: bad grammar. **9.** sorry or upset: I feel bad about saying no. **10.** unfavourable; distressing: bad news. **11.** offensive; unpleasant: bad language. **12.** not valid: a bad cheque. **13.** not recoverable: a bad debt. **14. (badder, baddest)** Slang. good; excellent. **15. not bad** or **not so bad.** Informal. fairly good. **16. too bad.** Informal. (often used dismissively) regrettable. ~n. **17.** unfortunate or unpleasant events: you've got to take the bad with the good. ~adv. **18.** Not standard. badly: to want something bad. [Middle English] —'**badness** n.

bad blood n. a feeling of intense hatred or hostility; enmity.

bade (bæd, beɪd) or **bad** vb. a past tense of **bid.**

badge (bædʒ) n. **1.** a distinguishing emblem or mark worn to signify membership or achievement. **2.** any revealing feature or mark. [Old French bage]

badger ('bædʒə) n. **1.** a stocky burrowing mammal with a thick coat striped black and white on the head. ~vb. **2.** to pester or harass. [origin unknown]

badinage ('bædɪ,nɑːʒ) n. playful and witty conversation. [French]

badly ('bædlɪ) adv. **worse, worst. 1.** poorly; inadequately. **2.** unfavourably: our scheme worked out badly. **3.** severely: badly hurt. **4.** very much: need badly. **5. badly off.** poor.

badminton ('bædmɪntən) n. a game played with rackets and a shuttlecock which is hit back and forth across a high net. [Badminton House, Glos]

baffle ('bæf°l) vb. **1.** to perplex; puzzle.

2. to frustrate (someone's plans or efforts). ~n. **3.** a mechanical device to limit or regulate the flow of fluid, light, or sound. [origin unknown] —'**bafflement** n. —'**baffling** adj.

bag (bæg) n. **1.** a flexible container with an opening at one end. **2.** the contents of such a container. **3.** a piece of luggage. **4.** a handbag. **5.** anything that sags, such as a loose fold of skin under the eyes. **6.** any sac in the body of an animal. **7.** the amount of game taken by a hunter. **8.** Offensive slang. an ugly or bad-tempered woman: an old bag. **9. in the bag.** Slang. almost assured of succeeding. ~vb. **bagging, bagged. 10.** to put into a bag. **11.** to bulge or cause to bulge. **12.** to capture or kill, as in hunting. **13.** Brit. informal. to secure the right to do or to have: he bagged the best chair. ~See also **bags.** [prob. Old Norse baggi]

bagatelle (,bægə'tɛl) n. **1.** something of little value. **2.** a board game in which balls are struck into holes. **3.** a short piece of music. [French]

bagel ('beɪg°l) n. a hard ring-shaped bread roll. [Yiddish beygel]

baggage ('bægɪdʒ) n. **1.** suitcases packed for a journey; luggage. **2.** an army's portable equipment. [Old French bagage]

baggy ('bægɪ) adj. -**gier, -giest.** (of clothes) hanging loosely. —'**bagginess** n.

bag lady n. a homeless woman who wanders the streets with all her possessions in shopping bags.

bagpipes ('bæg,paɪps) pl. n. a musical wind instrument in which sounds are produced in reed pipes by air from an inflated bag.

bags (bægz) pl. n. **1.** Informal. a lot. ~interj. **2.** Also: **bags I.** Children's slang, Brit. an indication of the desire to be, or have something.

bah (bɑː, bæ) interj. an expression of contempt or disgust.

bail¹ (beɪl) Law. ~n. **1.** a sum of money deposited with the court as security for a person's reappearance in court. **2.** the person giving such security. **3. jump bail.** to fail to appear in court to answer to a charge. **4. stand** or **go bail.** to act as surety for someone. ~vb. **5.** (foll. by out) to obtain the release of (a person) from custody, security having been made. [Old French: custody]

bail² or **bale** (beɪl) vb. (foll. by out) to remove (water) from (a boat). See also **bale out.** [Old French baille bucket]

bail³ (beɪl) n. **1.** Cricket. either of two small wooden bars across the tops of the stumps. **2.** a partition between stalls in a stable or barn. **3.** Austral. & N.Z. a framework in a cowshed used to secure the head of a cow during milking. **4.** a movable bar on a typewriter that holds the paper against the platen. [Old French baile stake]

bailey ('beɪlɪ) n. the outermost wall or court of a castle. [Old French baille enclosed court]

Bailey bridge ('beɪlɪ) n. a temporary

bridge that can be rapidly assembled. [after Sir Donald Coleman *Bailey*, its designer]

bailiff ('beɪlɪf) *n.* **1.** *Brit.* the agent of a landlord or landowner. **2.** a sheriff's officer who serves writs and summonses. [Old French *baillif*]

bailiwick ('beɪlɪwɪk) *n.* **1.** *Law.* the area over which a bailiff has jurisdiction. **2.** a person's special field of interest. [*bailie* + obs. *wick* district]

bail up *vb. Austral. & N.Z.* to confine (a cow) or (of a cow) to be confined by the head in a bail.

bain-marie (,bænmæ'riː) *n., pl.* **bains-marie** (,bænmæ'riː). a vessel for holding hot water, in which sauces and other dishes are gently cooked or kept warm. [French: bath of Mary, alleged author of a treatise on alchemy]

bairn (bɛən) *n. Scot. & N English.* a child. [Old English *bearn*]

bait (beɪt) *n.* **1.** something edible fixed to a hook or in a trap to attract fish or animals. **2.** an enticement; temptation. ~*vb.* **3.** to put a piece of food on or in (a hook or trap). **4.** to persecute or tease. **5.** to set dogs upon (a bear or badger). [Old Norse *beita* to hunt]

baize (beɪz) *n.* a woollen fabric resembling felt, used for the tops of billiard or card tables. [Old French *bai* reddish-brown]

bake (beɪk) *vb.* **1.** to cook by dry heat as in an oven. **2.** to cook bread, pastry, or cakes. **3.** to make or become hardened by heat. **4.** *Informal.* to be extremely hot. [Old English *bacan*]

baked beans *pl. n.* haricot beans, baked and tinned in tomato sauce.

baker ('beɪkə) *n.* a person whose business is to make or sell bread, cakes, etc.

baker's dozen *n.* thirteen.

bakery ('beɪkərɪ) *n., pl.* **-eries.** a place where bread, cakes, etc., are baked or sold.

baking powder *n.* a powdered mixture that contains sodium bicarbonate and cream of tartar: used in baking as a substitute for yeast.

baksheesh ('bækʃiːʃ) *n.* (in some Eastern countries) money given as a tip or present. [Persian *bakhshīsh*]

Balaclava (,bælə'klɑːvə) *or* **Balaclava helmet** *n.* a close-fitting woollen hood that covers the ears and neck. [*Balaklava*, Crimea]

balalaika (,bælə'laɪkə) *n.* a Russian musical instrument with a triangular body and three strings. [Russian]

balance ('bæləns) *n.* **1.** a weighing device, with a horizontal beam pivoted at its centre, from the ends of which two pans are suspended. **2.** a state of equilibrium. **3.** stability of mind or body: *lose one's balance.* **4.** harmony in the parts of a whole. **5.** the power to influence or control: *the balance of power.* **6.** something that remains: *the balance of what you owe.* **7.** *Accounting.* **a.** the matching of debit and credit totals in an account. **b.** a difference between such totals. **8. in the balance.** in an undecided condition. **9. on balance.** after weighing up all the factors. ~*vb.*

10. to weigh in or as if in a balance. **11.** to be or come into equilibrium. **12.** to bring into or hold in equilibrium. **13.** to compare the relative weight or importance of. **14.** to arrange so as to create a state of harmony. **15.** *Accounting.* to compare or equalize the credit and debit totals of (an account). [Latin *bilanx* having two scales]

balance of power *n.* the equal distribution of military and economic power among countries.

balance of trade *n.* the difference in value between exports and imports of goods.

balance sheet *n.* a statement that shows the financial position of a business.

balcony ('bælkənɪ) *n., pl.* **-nies. 1.** a platform projecting from a building with a balustrade along its outer edge, often with access from a door. **2.** an upper tier of seats in a theatre or cinema. [Italian *balcone*]

bald (bɔːld) *adj.* **1.** having no hair or fur, esp. (of a man) having no hair on the scalp. **2.** lacking natural covering. **3.** plain or blunt: *a bald statement.* **4.** (of a tyre) having a worn tread. [Middle English *ballede*] —**baldly** *adv.* —**baldness** *n.*

balderdash ('bɔːldə,dæʃ) *n.* stupid or illogical talk. [origin unknown]

balding ('bɔːldɪŋ) *adj.* becoming bald.

bale¹ (beɪl) *n.* **1.** a large bundle of hay or goods bound by ropes or wires for storage or transportation. ~*vb.* **2.** to make (hay) or put (goods) into a bale or bales. [Old High German *balla* ball]

bale² (beɪl) *vb.* same as **bail²**.

baleen (bə'liːn) *n.* whalebone. [Latin *bālaena* whale]

baleen whale *n.* same as **whalebone whale.**

baleful ('beɪlful) *adj.* harmful, menacing, or vindictive. —**balefully** *adv.*

bale out *or* **bail out** *vb.* **1.** to make an emergency parachute jump from an aircraft. **2.** *Informal.* to help (a person or organization) out of a predicament.

balk *or* **baulk** (bɔːk, bɔːlk) *vb.* **1.** to stop short: *the horse balked at the jump.* **2.** to recoil: *he balked at the idea of murder.* **3.** to thwart, check, or foil: *he was balked in his plans.* ~*n.* **4.** a roughly squared timber beam. **5.** an obstacle; hindrance. [Old English *balca*]

Balkan ('bɔːlkən) *adj.* of a peninsula in SE Europe, between the Adriatic and Aegean Seas.

ball¹ (bɔːl) *n.* **1.** a spherical or nearly spherical object. **2.** a round or roundish object of a size suitable for use in various games. **3.** a single delivery of the ball in a game. **4.** a solid nonexplosive projectile for a firearm or cannon. **5.** any more or less rounded part: *the ball of the foot.* **6. have the ball at one's feet.** to have the chance of doing something. **7. on the ball.** *Informal.* alert; informed. **8. play ball.** *Informal.* to cooperate. **9. start** *or* **keep the ball rolling.** to initiate or maintain the progress of an action, discussion, or project. ~*vb.* **10.** to form into a ball. ~See also **balls, balls-up.** [Old Norse *böllr*]

ball² (bɔːl) *n.* **1.** a lavish or formal social function for dancing. **2. have a ball.** *Informal.* to have a very enjoyable time. [Late Latin *ballāre* to dance]

ballad (ˈbæləd) *n.* **1.** a narrative song with a recurrent refrain. **2.** a narrative poem in short stanzas of popular origin. **3.** a slow sentimental song. [Old Provençal *balada* song accompanying a dance]

ballade (bæˈlɑːd) *n.* **1.** *Prosody.* a verse form consisting of three stanzas and an envoy, all ending with the same line. **2.** *Music.* a romantic instrumental composition.

ball-and-socket joint *n. Anat.* a joint in which a rounded head fits into a rounded cavity, allowing a wide range of movement.

ballast (ˈbæləst) *n.* **1.** a substance, such as sand, used to stabilize a ship when it is not carrying cargo. **2.** crushed rock used for the foundation of a road or railway track. ~*vb.* **3.** to give stability or weight to. [prob. Low German]

ball bearing *n.* **1.** a bearing consisting of steel balls placed between moving parts of a machine in order to reduce friction. **2.** a metal ball used in such a bearing.

ball boy or (*fem.*) **ball girl** *n.* (in tennis) a person who retrieves balls that go out of play.

ball cock *n.* a device consisting of a floating ball and valve for regulating the flow of liquid into a tank or cistern.

ballerina (ˌbæləˈriːnə) *n.* a female ballet dancer. [Italian]

ballet (ˈbæleɪ, bæˈleɪ) *n.* **1.** a classical style of expressive dancing based on precise conventional steps. **2.** a theatrical representation of a story performed by ballet dancers. [Italian *balletto* a little dance] —**balletic** (bæˈlɛtɪk) *adj.*

ball game *n.* **1.** *U.S. & Canad.* a game of baseball. **2.** *Informal.* a state of affairs: *a whole new ball game.*

ballista (bəˈlɪstə) *n., pl.* **-tae** (-tiː). an ancient catapult for hurling stones. [Greek *ballein* to throw]

ballistic missile *n.* a missile guided automatically in flight but which falls freely at its target.

ballistics (bəˈlɪstɪks) *n.* (*functioning as sing.*) the study of the flight of projectiles and the effects of firing on firearms. —**ballistic** *adj.*

ballocks (ˈbɒləks) *pl. n., interj.* same as **bollocks.**

balloon (bəˈluːn) *n.* **1.** an inflatable rubber bag used as a plaything or party decoration. **2.** a large bag inflated with a lighter-than-air gas, designed to rise and float in the atmosphere with a basket for carrying passengers. **3.** an outline containing the words or thoughts of a character in a cartoon. ~*vb.* **4.** to fly in a balloon. **5.** to inflate or be inflated. [Italian dialect *ballone* ball] —**balˈloonist** *n.*

ballot (ˈbælət) *n.* **1.** the practice of selecting a representative or course of action by

voting secretly. **2.** the number of votes cast in an election. **3.** the actual vote or paper indicating a person's choice. ~*vb.* **-loting, -loted. 4.** to vote or ask for a vote from: *we balloted the members on this issue.* **5.** to vote for or decide on something by ballot. [Italian *ballotta* a little ball]

ballot box *n.* a box into which ballot papers are dropped after voting.

ballot paper *n.* a paper used for voting.

ballpark (ˈbɔːlˌpɑːk) *n.* **1.** *U.S. & Canad.* a stadium used for baseball games. **2.** *Informal.* approximate range: *in the right ballpark.*

ballpoint or **ballpoint pen** (ˈbɔːlˌpɔɪnt) *n.* a pen having a small ball bearing as a writing point.

ballroom (ˈbɔːlˌruːm, -ˌrʊm) *n.* a large hall for dancing.

ballroom dancing *n.* social dancing in couples to music in conventional rhythms, such as the waltz.

balls (bɔːlz) *pl. n. Taboo slang.* **1.** the testicles. **2.** nonsense.

balls-up *Taboo slang.* ~*n.* **1.** something botched or muddled. ~*vb.* **balls up. 2.** to muddle or botch.

bally (ˈbælɪ) *adj., adv. Brit. slang, euphemistic.* bloody.

ballyhoo (ˌbælɪˈhuː) *n. Informal.* **1.** a noisy or confused situation. **2.** sensational advertising. [origin unknown]

balm (bɑːm) *n.* **1.** an aromatic substance obtained from certain tropical trees and used for healing and soothing. **2.** something comforting or soothing. **3.** an aromatic herb, lemon balm. [Latin *balsamum* balsam]

balmy (ˈbɑːmɪ) *adj.* **balmier, balmiest. 1.** (of weather) mild and pleasant. **2.** same as **barmy.**

baloney or **boloney** (bəˈləʊnɪ) *n. Informal.* nonsense. [*Bologna* (sausage)]

balsa (ˈbɔːlsə) *n.* **1.** a tree of tropical America that yields light wood used for making rafts, models, etc. **2.** a light raft. [Spanish: raft]

balsam (ˈbɔːlsəm) *n.* **1.** an aromatic resin obtained from various trees and shrubs and used in medicines and perfumes. **2.** any plant yielding balsam. **3.** a flowering plant, such as busy lizzie. [Greek *balsamon*]

Baltic (ˈbɔːltɪk) *adj.* denoting or relating to the Baltic Sea in N Europe, or the states bordering it.

baluster (ˈbæləstə) *n.* any of a set of posts supporting a rail. [French *balustre*]

balustrade (ˌbæləˈstreɪd) *n.* an ornamental rail supported by balusters. [French]

bamboo (bæmˈbuː) *n.* a tall treelike tropical grass with hollow stems which are used to make canes, furniture, etc. [prob. from Malay *bambu*]

bamboozle (bæmˈbuːzᵊl) *vb. Informal.* **1.** to cheat; mislead. **2.** to confuse. [origin unknown] —**bamˈboozlement** *n.*

ban (bæn) *vb.* **banning, banned. 1.** to prohibit or forbid, esp. officially. ~*n.* **2.**

an official prohibition. [Old English *bannan* to proclaim]

banal (bə'nɑːl) *adj.* lacking force or originality. [Old French] —**banality** (bə'nælɪtɪ) *n.*

banana (bə'nɑːnə) *n.* a crescent-shaped fruit that grows on a tropical or subtropical treelike plant. [Spanish or Portuguese, of African origin]

banana republic *n. Informal.* a small politically unstable country whose economy is dominated by foreign interests.

band¹ (bænd) *n.* **1.** a group of musicians playing together, esp. on brass or percussion instruments. **2.** a group of people having a common purpose: *a band of revolutionaries.* ~*vb.* **3.** (foll. by *together*) to unite. [Germanic]

band² (bænd) *n.* **1.** a strip of some material, used to hold objects together: *a rubber band.* **2.** a strip of fabric used as an ornament or to reinforce clothing. **3.** a stripe of contrasting colour or texture. **4.** a driving belt in machinery. **5.** *Physics.* a range of frequencies or wavelengths between two limits. **6.** a section of a gramophone record. ~*vb.* **7.** to fasten or mark with a band. [Germanic]

bandage ('bændɪdʒ) *n.* **1.** a piece of material used to dress a wound or bind a broken limb. ~*vb.* **2.** to cover or bind with a bandage. [French *bande* strip]

bandanna *or* **bandana** (bæn'dænə) *n.* a large brightly-coloured handkerchief or neckerchief. [Hindi *bāndhnū* tie-dyeing]

b. and b. *or* **B & B** bed and breakfast.

bandbox ('bænd,bɒks) *n.* a lightweight usually cylindrical box for hats.

bandeau ('bændəʊ) *n., pl.* **-deaux** (-dəʊz). a narrow ribbon worn round the head. [French]

banderole ('bændə,rəʊl) *n.* **1.** a narrow flag usually with forked ends. **2.** a ribbonlike scroll bearing an inscription. [Old French]

bandicoot ('bændɪ,kuːt) *n.* **1.** a ratlike marsupial of Australia with a long pointed muzzle and a long tail. **2. bandicoot rat.** any of three burrowing rats of S and SE Asia. [Telugu (language of SE India) *pandikokku*]

bandit ('bændɪt) *n.* a robber, esp. a member of an armed gang. [Italian *bandito*] —**'banditry** *n.*

bandmaster ('bænd,mɑːstə) *n.* the conductor of a band.

bandoleer *or* **bandolier** (,bændə'lɪə) *n.* a shoulder belt with small pockets for cartridges. [Old French *bandouliere*]

band saw *n.* a power-operated saw consisting of an endless toothed metal band running over two wheels.

bandsman ('bændzmən) *n., pl.* **-men.** a player in a musical band.

bandstand ('bænd,stænd) *n.* a roofed outdoor platform for a band.

bandwagon ('bænd,wægən) *n.* **climb** *or* **jump on the bandwagon.** to join a party or movement that seems assured of success.

bandy ('bændɪ) *adj.* **-dier, -diest. 1.** Also:

bandy-legged. having legs curved outwards at the knees. **2.** (of legs) curved thus. ~*vb.* **-dying, -died. 3.** to exchange (words) in a heated manner. **4.** (foll. by *about*) to circulate (a name, rumour, etc.). [prob. from Old French *bander* to hit back and forth]

bane (beɪn) *n.* **1.** a person or thing that causes misery or distress: *the bane of my life.* **2.** a fatal poison: *ratsbane.* [Old English *bana*] —**'baneful** *adj.*

bang (bæŋ) *n.* **1.** a short loud explosive noise, as of the report of a gun. **2.** a hard blow or loud knock. **3.** *Taboo slang.* an act of sexual intercourse. **4. with a bang.** successfully: *the party went with a bang.* ~*vb.* **5.** to hit or knock, esp. with a loud noise. **6.** to close (a door) noisily; slam. **7.** to make or cause to make a loud noise, as of an explosion. **8.** *Taboo slang.* to have sexual intercourse (with). ~*adv.* **9.** with a sudden impact: *the car drove bang into a lamppost.* **10.** precisely: *bang in the middle.* [Old Norse *bang, banga* hammer]

banger ('bæŋə) *n. Brit.* **1.** *Slang.* a sausage. **2.** *Informal.* an old decrepit car. **3.** a firework that explodes loudly.

bangle ('bæŋg³l) *n.* a bracelet worn round the arm or sometimes round the ankle. [Hindi *bangri*]

banian ('bænjən) *n.* same as **banyan.**

banish ('bænɪʃ) *vb.* **1.** to send (someone) into exile. **2.** to drive away: *to banish gloom.* [Old French *banir*] —**'banishment** *n.*

banisters *or* **bannisters** ('bænɪstəz) *pl. n.* the railing and supporting balusters on a staircase. [altered from *baluster*]

banjo ('bændʒəʊ) *n., pl.* **-jos** *or* **-joes.** a stringed musical instrument with a long neck and a circular drumlike body. [U.S. pronunciation of earlier *bandore,* from Greek *pandora*] —**'banjoist** *n.*

bank¹ (bæŋk) *n.* **1.** an institution offering services, such as the safekeeping of money and lending of money at interest. **2.** the building used by such an institution. **3.** the funds held by a banker or dealer in some gambling games. **4.** any supply, store, or reserve: *a data bank.* ~*vb.* **5.** to deposit (cash or cheques) in a bank. **6.** to transact business with a bank. ~See also **bank on.** [prob. from Italian *banca* bench, moneychanger's table]

bank² (bæŋk) *n.* **1.** a long raised mass, esp. of earth; ridge. **2.** a slope, as of a hill. **3.** the sloping side and ground on either side of a river. ~*vb.* **4.** to form into a bank or mound. **5.** to cover (a fire) with ashes and fuel so that it will burn slowly. **6.** to cause (an aircraft) or (of an aircraft) to tip to one side in turning. [Scandinavian]

bank³ (bæŋk) *n.* **1.** an arrangement of similar objects in a row or in tiers. ~*vb.* **2.** to arrange in a bank. [Old French *banc* bench]

bank account *n.* an account created by the deposit of money at a bank by a customer.

bank *or* **banker's card** *n.* same as **cheque card.**

banker[1] ('bæŋkə) n. **1.** a person who owns or manages a bank. **2.** the keeper of the bank in various gambling games.

banker[2] ('bæŋkə) n. Austral. & N.Z. informal. a stream almost overflowing its banks: the creek was running a banker.

banker's order n. same as **standing order** (sense 1).

bank holiday n. (in Britain) a public holiday when banks are closed by law.

banking ('bæŋkɪŋ) n. the business engaged in by a bank.

banknote ('bæŋk,nəut) n. a promissory note issued by a central bank, serving as money.

bank on vb. to rely on.

bankrupt ('bæŋkrʌpt, -rəpt) n. **1.** a person, declared by a court to be unable to pay his debts, whose property is sold and the proceeds distributed among his creditors. **2.** a person whose resources in a certain field are exhausted: a spiritual bankrupt. ~adj. **3.** declared insolvent. **4.** financially ruined. **5.** depleted in resources: spiritually bankrupt. ~vb. **6.** to make bankrupt. [Old Italian banca BANK[1] + rotta broken] —**'bankruptcy** n.

banner ('bænə) n. **1.** a long strip of material displaying a slogan, advertisement, etc. **2.** a placard carried in a demonstration. **3.** Also called: **banner headline.** a large headline in a newspaper extending across the page. [Old French baniere]

bannock ('bænək) n. a round flat cake made from oatmeal or barley. [Old English bannuc]

banns (bænz) pl. n. the public declaration of an intended marriage. [pl. of obs. bann proclamation]

banquet ('bæŋkwɪt) n. **1.** an elaborate formal dinner often followed by speeches. ~vb. **-queting, -queted. 2.** to hold or take part in a banquet. [Italian banco a table]

banshee ('bænʃiː, bæn'ʃiː) n. (in Irish folklore) a female spirit whose wailing warns of impending death. [Irish Gaelic bean sídhe woman of the fairy mound]

bantam ('bæntəm) n. **1.** a small breed of domestic fowl. **2.** a small but aggressive person. [after Bantam, village in Java, said to be the original home of this fowl]

bantamweight ('bæntəm,weɪt) n. **1.** a professional boxer weighing up to 118 pounds or an amateur weighing up to 54 kg. **2.** an amateur wrestler weighing usually up to 57 kg.

banter ('bæntə) vb. **1.** to tease jokingly. ~n. **2.** teasing or joking conversation. [origin unknown]

Bantu ('bɑːntuː) n. **1.** a group of languages of Africa. **2.** (pl. **-tu** or **-tus**) Offensive. a Black speaker of a Bantu language. ~adj. **3.** of the Bantu languages or the peoples who speak them. [Bantu Ba-ntu people]

Bantustan ('bɑːntu,stɑːn) n. Offensive. an area reserved for occupation by a Black African people. [Bantu + Hindi -stan country of]

banyan or **banian** ('bænjən) n. an Indian tree whose branches grow down into the

soil forming additional trunks. [Hindi baniyā]

baobab ('beɪəu,bæb) n. an African tree that has a very thick trunk, angular branches, and a gourdlike fruit. [prob. from a native African word]

bap (bæp) n. Brit. a large soft bread roll. [origin unknown]

baptism ('bæp,tɪzəm) n. a Christian religious rite in which a person is immersed in or sprinkled with water as a sign of being cleansed from sin and accepted as a member of the Church. —**bap'tismal** adj.

baptism of fire n. **1.** a soldier's first experience of battle. **2.** any initiating ordeal.

Baptist ('bæptɪst) n. **1.** a member of a Protestant denomination that believes in the necessity of baptism by immersion. **2. the Baptist.** John the Baptist.

baptize or **-ise** (bæp'taɪz) vb. **1.** Christianity. to immerse (a person) in water or sprinkle water on (a person) as part of the rite of baptism. **2.** to give a name to; christen. [Greek baptein to bathe, dip]

bar[1] (bɑː) n. **1.** a rigid usually straight length of metal, wood, etc., used as a barrier or structural part. **2.** a solid usually rectangular block of any material: a bar of soap. **3.** anything that obstructs or prevents. **4.** a counter or room where alcoholic drinks are served. **5.** a narrow band or stripe, as of colour or light. **6.** a heating element in an electric fire. **7.** See **Bar. 8.** the place in a court of law where the accused stands during trial. **9.** Music. a group of beats that is repeated with a consistent rhythm throughout a piece of music. **10.** Football, etc. same as **crossbar. 11.** Heraldry. a narrow horizontal line across a shield. **12. behind bars.** in prison. ~vb. **barring, barred. 13.** to secure with a bar: to bar the door. **14.** to obstruct: the fallen tree barred the road. **15.** to exclude: to bar a person from membership. **16.** to mark with a bar or bars. ~prep. **17.** except for. [Old French barre]

bar[2] (bɑː) n. a cgs unit of pressure equal to 10^6 dynes per square centimetre. [Greek baros weight]

Bar (bɑː) n. **1. the.** barristers collectively. **2. be called to the Bar.** Brit. to become a barrister.

barathea (,bærə'θɪə) n. a fabric made of silk and wool. [origin unknown]

barb (bɑːb) n. **1.** a point facing in the opposite direction to the main point of a fish-hook, harpoon, etc. **2.** a cutting remark. **3.** a beardlike growth, hair, or projection. ~vb. **4.** to provide with a barb or barbs. [Latin barba beard] —**barbed** adj.

barbarian (bɑː'bɛərɪən) n. **1.** a member of a primitive or uncivilized people. **2.** a coarse or vicious person. ~adj. **3.** uncivilized. **4.** uncultured or brutal.

barbaric (bɑː'bærɪk) adj. **1.** of barbarians. **2.** primitive; unrestrained. **3.** brutal.

barbarism ('bɑːbə,rɪzəm) n. **1.** a brutal, coarse, or ignorant act. **2.** the condition of being backward, coarse, or ignorant. **3.** a substandard word or expression.

barbarity (bɑːˈbærɪtɪ) n., pl. **-ties.** 1. the state of being barbaric or barbarous. 2. a vicious act.

barbarous (ˈbɑːbərəs) adj. 1. uncivilized. 2. brutal or cruel. 3. lacking refinement. [Greek barbaros barbarian, non-Greek]

barbecue (ˈbɑːbɪˌkjuː) n. 1. a grill on which meat, fish, etc., is cooked over hot charcoal, usually out of doors. 2. the food so cooked. 3. a party or picnic at which barbecued food is served. ~vb. **-cuing,** **-cued.** 4. to cook (meat, fish, etc.) on a grill, usually over charcoal. [American Spanish barbacoa frame made of sticks]

barbed wire n. strong wire with sharply pointed barbs at close intervals.

barbel (ˈbɑːbʔl) n. 1. a long thin growth that hangs from the jaws of certain fishes, such as the carp. 2. a freshwater fish with such a growth. [Latin barba beard]

barbell (ˈbɑːˌbel) n. a metal rod to which heavy discs are attached at each end for weightlifting.

barber (ˈbɑːbə) n. a person whose business is cutting men's hair and shaving beards. [Latin barba beard]

barberry (ˈbɑːbərɪ) n., pl. **-ries.** a shrub with orange or red berries. [Arabic barbāris]

barbershop (ˈbɑːbəˌʃɒp) n. (modifier) denoting a type of close four-part harmony for male voices: a barbershop quartet.

barber's pole n. a barber's sign consisting of a pole painted with red-and-white spiral stripes.

barbican (ˈbɑːbɪkən) n. a walled defence to protect a gate or drawbridge of a fortification. [Old French barbacane]

barbiturate (bɑːˈbɪtjurɪt, -ˌreɪt) n. a derivative of barbituric acid used in medicine as a sedative or hypnotic.

barbituric acid (ˌbɑːbɪˈtjuərɪk) n. a crystalline solid used in the preparation of barbiturate drugs. [German Barbitursäure]

barcarole or **barcarolle** (ˈbɑːkəˌrəul) n. 1. a Venetian boat song. 2. an instrumental composition resembling this. [French]

bar code n. an arrangement of numbers and parallel lines on a package, which can be electronically scanned at a checkout to give the price of the goods.

bard (bɑːd) n. 1. **a.** (formerly) an ancient Celtic poet. **b.** a poet who wins a verse competition at a Welsh eisteddfod. 2. Archaic or literary. any poet. [Scottish Gaelic]

bare (bɛə) adj. 1. unclothed: used esp. of a part of the body. 2. without the natural, conventional, or usual covering. 3. lacking appropriate furnishings, etc. 4. simple: the bare facts. 5. just sufficient: the bare minimum. ~vb. 6. to uncover. [Old English bær] —**'bareness** n.

bareback (ˈbɛəˌbæk) adj., adv. (of horse-riding) without a saddle.

barefaced (ˈbɛəˌfeɪst) adj. obvious or shameless: a barefaced lie.

barefoot (ˈbɛəˌfut) or **barefooted** adj., adv. with the feet uncovered.

bareheaded (ˌbɛəˈhedɪd) adj., adv. with the head uncovered.

barely (ˈbɛəlɪ) adv. 1. only just: barely enough. 2. scantily: barely furnished.

bargain (ˈbɑːgɪn) n. 1. an agreement establishing what each party will give, receive, or perform in a transaction. 2. something acquired or received in such an agreement. 3. something bought or offered at a low price. 4. **into the bargain.** in excess; besides. ~vb. 5. to negotiate the terms of an agreement or transaction. [Old French bargaigne]

bargain for vb. to expect; anticipate.

bargain on vb. to rely or depend on.

barge (bɑːdʒ) n. 1. a flat-bottomed boat, used for transporting freight, esp. on canals. 2. a boat, often decorated, used in pageants, etc. ~vb. Informal. 3. (foll. by into) to bump into. 4. to push (someone or one's way) violently. 5. (foll. by into or in) to interrupt rudely: to barge into a conversation. [Medieval Latin barga]

bargee (bɑːˈdʒiː) n. a person in charge of a barge.

bargepole (ˈbɑːdʒˌpəul) n. 1. a long pole used to propel a barge. 2. **not touch with a bargepole.** Informal. to refuse to have anything to do with.

bar graph n. a graph consisting of vertical or horizontal bars whose lengths are proportional to amounts or quantities.

baritone (ˈbærɪˌtəun) n. 1. the second lowest adult male voice. 2. a singer with such a voice. [Greek barus low + tonos tone]

barium (ˈbɛərɪəm) n. a soft silvery-white metallic chemical element. Symbol: Ba [Greek barus heavy]

barium meal n. a preparation of barium sulphate, which is opaque to x-rays, used in x-ray examination of the alimentary canal.

bark¹ (bɑːk) n. 1. the loud harsh cry of a dog or certain other animals. 2. a similar sound, such as one made by a person or gun. ~vb. 3. (of a dog or other animal) to make its typical cry. 4. to shout in a angry tone: he barked an order. 5. **bark up the wrong tree.** Informal. to misdirect one's attention or efforts. [Old English beorcan]

bark² (bɑːk) n. 1. a protective layer of dead corklike cells on the outside of the stems of woody plants. ~vb. 2. to scrape or rub off skin, as in an injury. 3. to remove the bark from (a tree). [Old Norse börkr]

barker (ˈbɑːkə) n. a person at a fairground who loudly addresses passers-by to attract customers.

barley (ˈbɑːlɪ) n. 1. a tall grasslike plant with dense bristly flower spikes, widely cultivated for grain and forage. 2. the grain of this grass used in making beer and whisky and for soups. [Old English bere]

barleycorn (ˈbɑːlɪˌkɔːn) n. a grain of barley, or barley itself.

barley sugar n. a brittle clear amber-coloured sweet.

barley water *n.* a drink made from an infusion of barley.

barm (bɑːm) *n.* the yeasty froth on fermenting malt liquors. [Old English *bearm*]

barmaid ('bɑː,meɪd) *n.* a woman who serves in a pub.

barman ('bɑːmən) *n., pl.* **-men.** a man who serves in a pub.

bar mitzvah (bɑː 'mɪtsvə) *Judaism. ~adj.* **1.** (of a Jewish boy) having assumed full religious obligations, being at least thirteen years old. *~n.* **2.** the occasion or celebration of this. [Hebrew: son of the law]

barmy ('bɑːmɪ) *adj.* **-mier, -miest.** *Slang.* insane. [orig., full of *barm*, frothing, excited]

barn (bɑːn) *n.* a large farm outbuilding, chiefly for storing grain, but also for livestock. [Old English *bere* barley + *ærn* room]

barnacle ('bɑːnək²l) *n.* **1.** a marine shellfish that lives attached to rocks, ship bottoms, etc. **2.** a person or thing that is difficult to get rid of. [Old French *bernac*] —'**barnacled** *adj.*

barnacle goose *n.* a goose with a black-and-white head and body. [it was formerly believed that the goose developed from a shellfish]

barn dance *n.* **1.** *Brit.* a progressive round country dance. **2.** *U.S. & Canad.* a party with square-dancing.

barney ('bɑːnɪ) *n. Informal.* a noisy fight or argument. [origin unknown]

barn owl *n.* an owl with a pale brown-and-white plumage and a heart-shaped face.

barnstorm ('bɑːn,stɔːm) *vb.* **1.** to tour rural districts putting on shows. **2.** *Chiefly U.S. & Canad.* to tour rural districts making speeches in a political campaign. —'**barn,storming** *n., adj.*

barnyard ('bɑːn,jɑːd) *n.* a yard adjoining a barn.

barograph ('bærə,grɑːf) *n. Meteorol.* a barometer that automatically keeps a record of changes in atmospheric pressure. [Greek *baros* weight + *graphein* to write]

barometer (bə'rɒmɪtə) *n.* an instrument for measuring atmospheric pressure, used to determine altitude or weather changes. [Greek *baros* weight + *metron* measure] —**barometric** (,bærə'mɛtrɪk) *adj.*

baron ('bærən) *n.* **1.** a member of the lowest rank of nobility in the British Isles. **2.** a powerful businessman or financier: *a press baron.* [Old French] —**baronial** (bə'rəʊnɪəl) *adj.*

baroness ('bærənɪs) *n.* **1.** the wife or widow of a baron. **2.** a woman holding the rank of baron.

baronet ('bærənɪt, -,nɛt) *n.* a commoner who holds the lowest hereditary British title. —'**baronetcy** *n.*

baron of beef *n.* a cut of beef consisting of a double sirloin joined at the backbone.

barony ('bærənɪ) *n., pl.* **-nies.** the domain or rank of a baron.

baroque (bə'rɒk, bə'rəʊk) *n.* **1.** a highly ornamented European style of architecture and art from the late 16th to the early 18th century. **2.** a highly ornamented 17th-century style of music. *~adj.* **3.** denoting, in, or relating to the baroque. [Italian *barroco*]

baroscope ('bærə,skəʊp) *n.* any instrument for measuring atmospheric pressure.

barouche (bə'ruːʃ) *n.* a four-wheeled horse-drawn carriage with a retractable hood over the rear half. [German (dialect) *Barutsche*]

barque (bɑːk) *n.* **1.** a sailing ship, esp. with three masts. **2.** *Poetic.* any boat. [Old Provençal *barca*]

barrack¹ ('bærək) *vb.* to house (soldiers) in barracks.

barrack² ('bærək) *vb. Informal.* to criticize loudly or shout against (a team or speaker); jeer. [Irish: to boast]

barracks ('bærəks) *pl. n. (sometimes functioning as sing.)* **1.** a building or group of buildings used to accommodate military personnel. **2.** a large and bleak building. [French *baraque*]

barracuda (,bærə'kjuːdə) *n., pl.* **-da** or **-das.** a predatory marine mostly tropical fish, which attacks man. [American Spanish]

barrage ('bærɑːʒ) *n.* **1.** *Mil.* the firing of artillery continuously over an area. **2.** a continuous delivery of something, as questions. **3.** a construction across a watercourse. [French *barrer* to obstruct]

barrage balloon *n.* a tethered balloon with cables or net suspended from it, used to deter low-flying air attack.

barratry ('bærətrɪ) *n.* a fraudulent act by the master or crew of a ship that causes loss to the owner. [Old French *baraterie* deception]

barre (bɑː) *n.* a rail at hip height used for ballet practice. [French]

barrel ('bærəl) *n.* **1.** a cylindrical container usually bulging outwards in the middle and held together by metal hoops. **2.** a unit of capacity of varying amount in different industries. **3.** the tube through which the projectile of a firearm is discharged. **4. over a barrel.** *Informal.* powerless. *~vb.* **-relling, -relled** or *U.S.* **-reling, -reled.** **5.** to put into a barrel or barrels. [Old French *baril*]

barrel organ *n.* an instrument consisting of a cylinder turned by a handle and having pins on it that interrupt the air flow to certain pipes or pluck strings, thereby playing tunes.

barren ('bærən) *adj.* **1.** incapable of producing offspring; sterile. **2.** unable to support the growth of crops, fruit, etc.: *barren land.* **3.** dull. **4.** unprofitable: *a barren period.* [Old French *brahain*] —'**barren**ness *n.*

barricade (,bærɪ'keɪd, 'bærɪ,keɪd) *n.* **1.** a barrier, esp. one erected hastily for defence. *~vb.* **2.** to erect a barricade across (an entrance). [Old French *barrique* a barrel]

barrier ('bærɪə) *n.* **1.** anything that blocks a way or makes a separation, such as a gate. **2.** anything that prevents progress.

3. anything that separates or hinders union: *a language barrier.* [Old French *barre* bar]

barrier cream *n.* a cream used to protect the skin, esp. of the hands.

barrier reef *n.* a long narrow coral reef near the shore, separated from it by deep water.

barring ('bɑːrɪŋ) *prep.* unless (something) occurs; except for.

barrister ('bærɪstə) *n.* a lawyer who is qualified to plead in the higher courts. [from BAR[1]]

barrow[1] ('bærəʊ) *n.* **1.** same as **wheelbarrow. 2.** a handcart, used esp. by street vendors. [Old English *bearwe*]

barrow[2] ('bærəʊ) *n.* a heap of earth placed over a prehistoric tomb. [Old English *beorg*]

barrow boy *n. Brit.* a man who sells his wares from a barrow.

bar sinister *n.* same as **bend sinister.**

Bart. Baronet.

barter ('bɑːtə) *vb.* **1.** to trade (goods or services) in exchange for other goods or services, rather than for money. ~*n.* **2.** trade by the exchange of goods. [Old French *barater* to cheat]

baryon ('bærɪ,ɒn) *n.* an elementary particle that has a mass greater than or equal to that of the proton. [Greek *barus* heavy]

baryta (bə'raɪtə) *n.* a compound of barium, such as barium oxide. [Greek *barus* heavy]

barytes (bə'raɪtiːz) *n.* a colourless or white mineral: a source of barium. [Greek *barus* heavy]

basal ('beɪs³l) *adj.* **1.** at, of, or constituting a base. **2.** basic; fundamental.

basalt ('bæsɔːlt) *n.* a dark volcanic rock. [Greek *basanitēs* touchstone] —**ba'saltic** *adj.*

bascule ('bæskjuːl) *n.* a drawbridge that operates by a counterbalanced weight. [French]

base[1] (beɪs) *n.* **1.** the bottom or supporting part of anything. **2.** the fundamental principle or part. **3.** a centre of operations, organization, or supply. **4.** a starting point: *the new discovery became the base for further research.* **5.** the main ingredient of a mixture: *to use rice as a base in cookery.* **6.** a chemical compound that combines with an acid to form a salt. **7.** the lower side or face of a geometric construction. **8.** *Maths.* the number of units in a counting system that is equivalent to one in the next higher counting place: *10 is the base of the decimal system.* **9.** a starting or finishing point in any of various games. ~*vb.* **10.** (foll. by *on* or *upon*) to use as a basis for; found on. [Latin *basis* pedestal]

base[2] (beɪs) *adj.* **1.** dishonourable or immoral: *base motives.* **2.** of inferior quality or value: *base metal.* **3.** debased; counterfeit: *base currency.* [Late Latin *bassus* of low height]

baseball ('beɪs,bɔːl) *n.* a team game in which the object is to score runs by batting the ball and running round all four bases.

baseless ('beɪslɪs) *adj.* not based on fact; unfounded.

baseline ('beɪs,laɪn) *n.* **1.** a value or starting point on an imaginary scale with which other things are compared. **2.** a line at each end of a tennis court that marks the limit of play.

basement ('beɪsmənt) *n.* a partly or wholly underground storey of a building.

base metal *n.* a common metal such as copper or lead, as distinct from a precious metal.

bases[1] ('beɪsiːz) *n.* the plural of **basis.**

bases[2] ('beɪsɪz) *n.* the plural of **base.**

bash (bæʃ) *Informal.* ~*vb.* **1.** to strike violently or crushingly. **2.** (foll. by *into*) to crash into. ~*n.* **3.** a heavy blow. **4. have a bash.** *Informal.* to make an attempt. [origin unknown]

bashful ('bæʃful) *adj.* shy or modest. [*bash*, short for *abash*] —**'bashfully** *adv.*

-bashing *n.* and *adj. combining form. Informal or slang.* **a.** indicating a malicious attack on members of a group: *union-bashing.* **b.** indicating various other activities: *Bible-bashing.* —**basher** *n. combining form.*

basic ('beɪsɪk) *adj.* **1.** of or forming a base or basis; fundamental. **2.** elementary or simple. **3.** excluding additions or extras: *basic pay.* **4.** *Chem.* of or containing a base. ~*n.* **5.** (*pl.*) fundamental principles, facts, etc. —**'basically** *adv.*

BASIC ('beɪsɪk) *n.* a computer programming language that uses common English terms. [*b(eginner's) a(ll-purpose) s(ymbolic) i(nstruction) c(ode)*]

basic slag *n.* a slag produced in steelmaking, containing calcium phosphate.

basil ('bæz³l) *n.* an aromatic herb used for seasoning food. [Greek *basilikos* royal]

basilica (bə'zɪlɪkə) *n.* **1.** a Roman building, used for public administration, which had a rectangular nave with an aisle on each side and a rounded end. **2.** a Christian church of similar design. [Greek *basilikē oikia* the king's house]

basilisk ('bæzɪ,lɪsk) *n.* **1.** (in classical legend) a serpent that could kill by its breath or glance. **2.** a lizard of tropical America with an inflatable head crest. [Greek *basiliskos* royal child]

basin ('beɪs³n) *n.* **1.** a round container open and wide at the top. **2.** the amount a basin will hold. **3.** a washbasin or sink. **4.** any partially enclosed area of water where ships or boats may be moored. **5.** the catchment area of a particular river. **6.** a depression in the earth's surface. [Old French *bacin*]

basis ('beɪsɪs) *n., pl.* -ses (-siːz). **1.** something that underlies, supports, or is essential to something else, esp. an idea. **2.** a principle on which something depends. [Greek: step]

bask (bɑːsk) *vb.* (foll. by *in*) **1.** to lie in or be exposed to (pleasant warmth, esp. that of the sun). **2.** to feel secure under (some kindly influence or favourable conditions). [Old Norse *bathask* to bathe]

basket ('bɑːskɪt) n. 1. a container made of interwoven strips of wood or cane. 2. the amount a basket will hold. 3. *Basketball.* **a.** the high fixed hoop through which a player must throw the ball to score points. **b.** a point scored in this way. [Middle English] —**'basketry** n.

basketball ('bɑːskɪt,bɔːl) n. a team game in which points are scored by throwing the ball through a high horizontal hoop.

basket weave n. a weave of yarns, resembling that of a basket.

basketwork ('bɑːskɪt,wɜːk) n. same as **wickerwork.**

basking shark n. a very large plankton-eating shark, often floating at the sea surface.

basque (bæsk) n. a type of tight-fitting bodice for women. [French]

Basque (bæsk, bɑːsk) n. 1. a member of a people living in the W Pyrenees in France and Spain. 2. the unique language of this people. ~*adj.* 3. of this people or their language. [Latin *Vascō*]

bas-relief (,bɑːrɪ'liːf, 'bæsrɪ,liːf) n. sculpture in which the forms project slightly from the background. [Italian *basso rilievo*]

bass[1] (beɪs) n. 1. the lowest adult male voice. 2. a singer with such a voice. 3. *Informal.* same as **bass guitar, double bass.** ~*adj.* 4. relating to or denoting the lowest range of musical notes. [Middle English *bas*]

bass[2] (bæs) n. 1. any of various sea perches. 2. a European spiny-finned freshwater fish. [Middle English]

bass clef (beɪs) n. the clef that establishes F a fifth below middle C on the fourth line of the staff.

bass drum (beɪs) n. a large drum of low pitch.

basset hound ('bæsɪt) n. a smooth-haired hound with short legs and long ears. [French *bas* low]

bass guitar (beɪs) n. an electrically amplified guitar with the same pitch and tuning as a double bass.

bassinet (,bæsɪ'nɛt) n. a wickerwork or wooden cradle or pram, usually hooded. [French: little basin]

basso ('bæsəʊ) n., pl. **-sos** or **-si** (-sɪ). a singer with a bass voice. [Late Latin *bassus* low]

bassoon (bə'suːn) n. a woodwind instrument, the tenor of the oboe family. [Italian *basso* deep] —**bas'soonist** n.

bast (bæst) n. fibrous material obtained from the inner tissue of jute and flax, used for making rope, matting, etc. [Old English *bæst*]

bastard ('bɑːstəd, 'bæs-) n. 1. a person born of parents not married to each other. 2. *Informal, offensive.* an obnoxious or despicable person. 3. *Informal.* something extremely difficult or unpleasant. ~*adj.* 4. illegitimate by birth. 5. counterfeit; spurious. [Old French *bastart*] —**'bastardy** n.

bastardize *or* **-ise** ('bɑːstə,daɪz, 'bæs-)

vb. 1. to debase. 2. to declare illegitimate.

baste[1] (beɪst) *vb.* to sew with loose temporary stitches. [Old French *bastir* to build]

baste[2] (beɪst) *vb.* to moisten (meat) during cooking with hot fat. [origin unknown]

baste[3] (beɪst) *vb.* to beat; thrash. [origin unknown]

bastinado (,bæstɪ'neɪdəʊ) n., pl. **-does.** 1. a beating on the soles of the feet with a stick. ~*vb.* **-doing, -doed.** 2. to beat (a person) thus. [Spanish *baston* stick]

bastion ('bæstɪən) n. 1. a projecting part of a fortification. 2. a thing or person regarded as defending a principle, etc.: *the last bastion of opposition.* [French *bastille* fortress]

bat[1] (bæt) n. 1. any of various types of club used to hit the ball in certain sports, such as cricket. 2. *Cricket.* a batsman. 3. **off one's own bat. a.** of one's own accord. **b.** by one's own unaided efforts. ~*vb.* **batting, batted.** 4. to strike with or as if with a bat. 5. *Cricket, etc.* to take a turn at batting. [Old English *batt* club]

bat[2] (bæt) n. 1. a nocturnal mouselike animal flying with a pair of leathery wings. 2. **blind as a bat.** having extremely poor eyesight. [Scandinavian]

bat[3] (bæt) *vb.* **batting, batted.** 1. to wink or flutter (one's eyelids). 2. **not bat an eyelid.** *Informal.* to show no surprise. [prob. from obs. *bate* flutter, beat]

batch (bætʃ) n. 1. a group of similar objects or people, esp. if sent off, handled, or arriving at the same time. 2. the bread, cakes, etc., produced at one baking. ~*vb.* 3. to group (items) for efficient processing. [Middle English *bache*]

batch processing n. a system by which the computer programs of a number of users are submitted as a single batch.

bated ('beɪtɪd) *adj.* **with bated breath.** in suspense or fear.

bath (bɑːθ) n., pl. **baths** (bɑːðz). 1. a large container in which to wash the body. 2. the act of washing in such a container. 3. the amount of liquid in a bath. 4. (pl.) a public swimming pool. 5. **a.** a liquid solution for maintaining a constant temperature, developing photographs, etc. **b.** the vessel containing such a solution. ~*vb.* 6. *Brit.* to wash in a bath. [Old English *bæth*]

Bath chair n. a wheelchair for invalids.

bath cube n. a cube of soluble scented material for use in a bath.

bathe (beɪð) *vb.* 1. to swim in open water, esp. for pleasure. 2. to apply liquid to (the skin or a wound) in order to cleanse or soothe. 3. to immerse or be immersed in a liquid. 4. *Chiefly U.S. & Canad.* to wash in a bath. 5. to suffuse: *bathed in sunlight.* ~n. 6. *Brit.* a swim in open water. [Old English *bathian*] —**'bather** n.

bathos ('beɪθɒs) n. a sudden ludicrous descent from exalted to ordinary matters or style in speech or writing. [Greek: depth] —**bathetic** (bə'θɛtɪk) *adj.*

bathrobe ('bɑːθ,rəʊb) n. 1. a loose-fitting garment for wear before or after a bath or swimming. **2.** *U.S. & Canad.* a dressing gown.

bathroom ('bɑːθˌruːm, -ˌrʊm) *n.* **1.** a room with a bath or shower, washbasin, and toilet. **2.** *U.S. & Canad.* a toilet.

bathyscaph ('bæθɪˌskæf) *or* **bathyscaphe** ('bæθɪˌskeɪf, -ˌskæf) *n.* a deep-sea diving vessel for observation. [Greek *bathus* deep + *skaphē* light boat]

bathysphere ('bæθɪˌsfɪə) *n.* a strong steel deep-sea diving sphere, lowered by cable. [Greek *bathus* deep + *sphere*]

batik ('bætɪk) *n.* **a.** a process of printing fabric in which parts not to be dyed are covered by wax. **b.** fabric printed in this way. [Javanese: painted]

batiste (bæ'tiːst) *n.* a fine plain-weave cotton. [French]

batman ('bætmən) *n.*, *pl.* **-men.** an officer's servant in the armed forces. [Old French *bat* packsaddle]

baton ('bætən) *n.* **1.** a thin stick used by the conductor of an orchestra or choir. **2.** *Athletics.* a short bar transferred from one runner to another in a relay race. **3.** a police truncheon. [French]

baton round *n.* same as **plastic bullet.**

batrachian (bə'treɪkɪən) *n.* **1.** any amphibian, esp. a frog or toad. ~*adj.* **2.** of or relating to frogs and toads. [Greek *batrakhos* frog]

bats (bæts) *adj. Informal.* mad or eccentric.

batsman ('bætsmən) *n.*, *pl.* **-men.** *Cricket, etc.* a person who bats or specializes in batting.

battalion (bə'tæljən) *n.* a military unit comprised of three or more companies. [French *bataillon*]

batten[1] ('bæt°n) *n.* **1.** a sawn strip of wood used to cover joints, support lathing, etc. **2.** a lath used for holding a tarpaulin along the side of a hatch on a ship. ~*vb.* **3.** to strengthen or fasten with battens. [French *bâton* stick]

batten[2] ('bæt°n) *vb.* (foll. by *on*) to thrive, esp. at the expense of (someone else). [prob. from Old Norse *batna* to improve]

batter[1] ('bætə) *vb.* **1.** to hit (someone or something) repeatedly. **2.** to damage or injure, as by blows, heavy wear, etc. **3.** to subject (a person, esp. a close relative) to repeated physical violence. [Middle English *bateren*] —'**batterer** *n.* —'**battering** *n.*

batter[2] ('bætə) *n.* a mixture of flour, eggs, and milk, used in cooking. [Middle English *bater*]

batter[3] ('bætə) *n. Baseball, etc.* a player who bats.

battering ram *n.* (esp. formerly) a large beam used to break down fortifications.

battery ('bætərɪ) *n.*, *pl.* **-teries.** **1.** two or more primary cells connected, usually in series, to provide a source of electric current. **2.** a number of similar things occurring together: *a battery of questions.* **3.** *Criminal law.* unlawful beating or wounding of a person. **4.** a fortified structure on which artillery is mounted. **5.** *Chiefly Brit.* **a.** a series of cages for intensive

rearing of poultry and other farm animals. **b.** (*as modifier*): *battery hens.* [Latin *battuere* to beat]

battle ('bæt°l) *n.* **1.** a fight between large armed forces. **2.** conflict; struggle. ~*vb.* **3.** to fight in or as if in military combat. **4.** to struggle: *he battled through the crowd.* [Latin *battuere* to beat]

battle-axe *n.* **1.** *Informal.* a domineering woman. **2.** (formerly) a large broadheaded axe.

battle cruiser *n.* a high-speed warship of battleship size but with lighter armour.

battle cry *n.* **1.** a slogan used to rally the supporters of a campaign, movement, etc. **2.** a shout uttered by soldiers going into battle.

battledore ('bæt°lˌdɔː) *n.* **1.** Also called: **battledore and shuttlecock.** an ancient racket game. **2.** a light racket used in this game. [Middle English *batyldoure*]

battledress ('bæt°lˌdres) *n.* the ordinary uniform of a soldier.

battlefield ('bæt°lˌfiːld) *or* **battleground** *n.* the place where a battle is fought.

battlement ('bæt°lmənt) *n.* a wall with indentations, originally for shooting through. [Old French *bataille* battle]

battle royal *n.* **1.** a fight involving many combatants. **2.** a long violent argument.

battleship ('bæt°lˌʃɪp) *n.* a heavily armoured warship of the largest type.

batty ('bætɪ) *adj.* **-tier, -tiest.** *Slang.* **1.** insane; crazy. **2.** odd; eccentric. [from BAT[2]]

bauble ('bɔːb°l) *n.* a trinket of little value. [Old French *baubel* plaything]

baulk (bɔːk, bɔːlk) *vb.*, *n.* same as **balk.**

bauxite ('bɔːksaɪt) *n.* a claylike substance that is the chief source of aluminium. [(*Les*) *Baux* in southern France, where orig. found]

bawdy ('bɔːdɪ) *adj.* **bawdier, bawdiest.** (of language, writing, etc.) containing humorous references to sex. [Old French *baud* merry] —'**bawdily** *adv.* —'**bawdiness** *n.*

bawdyhouse ('bɔːdɪˌhaʊs) *n. Archaic.* a brothel.

bawl (bɔːl) *vb.* **1.** to utter long loud cries, as from pain. **2.** to shout loudly, as in anger. ~*n.* **3.** a loud shout or cry. [imit.] —'**bawling** *n.*

bay[1] (beɪ) *n.* a wide semicircular indentation of a shoreline. [Old French *baie*]

bay[2] (beɪ) *n.* **1.** a recess in a wall. **2.** any partly enclosed compartment. **3.** same as **bay window.** **4.** an area off a road in which vehicles may park or unload. **5.** a compartment in an aircraft: *the bomb bay.* [Old French *baee* gap]

bay[3] (beɪ) *n.* **1.** a deep howl, esp. of a hound on the scent. **2. at bay. a.** forced to turn and face attackers: *the dogs held the deer at bay.* **b.** at a distance: *keeping poverty at bay.* **3. bring to bay.** to force into a position from which retreat is impossible. ~*vb.* **4.** to howl in deep prolonged tones. [Old French, imit.]

bay[4] (beɪ) *n.* **1.** a Mediterranean laurel tree

with glossy aromatic leaves. **2.** (*pl.*) a wreath of bay leaves. [Latin *bāca* berry]

bay[6] (bei) *adj.* **1.** reddish-brown.—*n.* **2.** a reddish-brown horse. [Latin *badius*]

bayberry ('beibəri) *or* **bay** *n., pl.* **-ries.** a tropical American tree that yields an oil used in making bay rum.

bay leaf *n.* the dried leaf of a laurel, used in cooking to flavour soups and stews.

bayonet ('beiənit) *n.* **1.** a blade that can be attached to the muzzle of a firearm and used as a weapon. ~*vb.* **-neting, -neted** *or* **-netting, -netted. 2.** to stab or kill with a bayonet. [*Bayonne*, a port in France, where it originated]

bay rum *n.* an aromatic liquid, used in medicines, etc., and originally obtained by distilling bayberry leaves with rum.

bay window *n.* a window projecting from a wall and forming an alcove of a room.

bazaar (bə'zɑ:) *n.* **1.** (esp. in the Orient) a market area, esp. a street of small stalls. **2.** a sale in aid of charity. [Persian *bāzār*]

bazooka (bə'zu:kə) *n.* an antitank rocket launcher. [after a comic pipe instrument]

BB Boys' Brigade.

BBC British Broadcasting Corporation.

BC 1. (indicating years numbered back from the supposed year of the birth of Christ) before Christ. **2.** British Columbia.

BCG Bacillus Calmette-Guérin (antituberculosis vaccine).

BCNZ Broadcasting Corporation of New Zealand.

B complex *n.* short for **vitamin B complex.**

BD Bachelor of Divinity.

bdellium ('deliəm) *n.* an aromatic gum resin produced by an African or W Asian tree. [Greek *bdellion*]

BDS Bachelor of Dental Surgery.

be (bi:; *unstressed* bi) *vb.* present sing. *1st person am*; *2nd person* **are**; *3rd person* **is.** present pl. **are.** past sing. *1st person* **was**; *2nd person* **were**; *3rd person* **was.** past pl. **were.** present participle **being.** past participle **been. 1.** to have presence in perceived reality; exist; live: *I think, therefore I am.* **2.** to pay a visit; go: *have you been to Spain?* **3.** to take place: *my birthday was last Thursday.* **4.** used as a linking verb between the subject of a sentence and its complement: *John is a musician; honey is sweet; the dance is on Saturday.* **5.** forms the progressive present tense: *the man is running.* **6.** forms the passive voice of all transitive verbs: *a good film is being shown on television tonight.* **7.** expresses intention, expectation, or obligation: *the president is to arrive at 9.30.* [Old English *bēon*]

Be *Chem.* beryllium.

BE Bachelor of Engineering.

be- *prefix forming verbs mainly from nouns.* **1.** to surround or cover: *befog.* **2.** to affect completely: *bedazzle.* **3.** to consider as or cause to be: *befriend.* **4.** to provide or cover with: *bejewel.* **5.** (from

verbs) at, for, against, on, or over: *bewail.* [Old English]

beach (bi:tʃ) *n.* **1.** an area of sand or pebbles, esp. between the high- and low-water marks on a seashore. ~*vb.* **2.** to run or haul (a boat) onto a beach. [origin unknown]

beachcomber ('bi:tʃ,kəumə) *n.* a person who searches shore debris for anything of worth.

beachhead ('bi:tʃ,hed) *n.* *Mil.* a beach captured from the enemy, on which troops and equipment are landed.

beacon ('bi:kən) *n.* **1.** a signal fire or light on a hill or tower, esp. formerly as a warning of invasion. **2.** a lighthouse. **3.** a radio or other signal marking a flight course in air navigation. **4.** same as **Belisha beacon.** [Old English *beacen*]

bead (bi:d) *n.* **1.** a small pierced usually spherical piece of glass, wood, plastic, etc., which may be strung with others to form a necklace, rosary, etc. **2.** a small drop of moisture. **3.** a small metallic knob acting as the sight of a firearm. **4. draw a bead on.** to aim a rifle or pistol at. ~*vb.* **5.** to decorate with beads. [Old English *bed* prayer] —**beaded** *adj.*

beading ('bi:dɪŋ) *n.* a narrow rounded strip of moulding used for edging or ornamentation on furniture.

beadle ('bi:d'l) *n.* **1.** *Brit.* (formerly) a minor parish official who acted as an usher. **2.** *Scot.* a church official who attends the minister. [Old English *bydel*]

beady ('bi:dɪ) *adj.* **beadier, beadiest.** small, round, and glittering: *beady eyes.*

beagle ('bi:g'l) *n.* a small hound with a smooth coat, short legs, and drooping ears. [origin unknown]

beak[1] (bi:k) *n.* **1.** the projecting horny jaws of a bird. **2.** *Slang.* a person's nose. **3.** the pouring lip of a bucket, jug, etc. [Latin *beccus*] —**beaky** *adj.*

beak[2] (bi:k) *n.* *Brit. slang.* a judge, magistrate, or headmaster. [orig. thieves' jargon]

beaker ('bi:kə) *n.* **1.** a tallish drinking cup. **2.** a lipped glass container used in laboratories. [Old Norse *bikarr*]

beam (bi:m) *n.* **1.** a long thick piece of wood, metal, etc., used in building. **2.** the breadth of a ship at its widest part. **3.** a ray of light. **4.** a broad smile. **5.** the central shaft of a plough to which all the main parts are attached. **6.** a narrow flow of electromagnetic radiation or particles: *an electron beam.* **7.** the crossbar of a balance. **8. off (the) beam.** *Informal.* mistaken or irrelevant. **9. on the beam.** *Informal.* correct, relevant, or appropriate. ~*vb.* **10.** to send out or radiate. **11.** to divert or aim (a radio signal, light, etc.) in a certain direction: *to beam a programme to Tokyo.* **12.** to smile broadly. [Old English]

beam-ends *pl. n.* **on one's beam-ends.** out of money.

bean (bi:n) *n.* **1.** the edible seed or pod of various leguminous plants. **2.** any of various beanlike seeds, as coffee. **3. full of**

beans. *Informal.* full of energy and vitality. **4. not have a bean.** *Slang.* to be without money. [Old English]

beanbag ('biːn‚bæg) *n.* **1.** a small cloth bag filled with dried beans and thrown in games. **2.** a very large cushion filled with polystyrene granules and used as a seat.

beanfeast ('biːn‚fiːst) *n. Brit. informal.* **1.** an annual dinner for employees. **2.** any festive or merry occasion.

beano ('biːnəʊ) *n., pl.* **beanos.** *Brit. slang.* a celebration or party.

beanpole ('biːn‚pəʊl) *n.* **1.** a tall stick used to support bean plants. **2.** *Slang.* a tall thin person.

bean sprout *n.* the sprout of a bean seed, eaten esp. in Chinese dishes.

bear[1] (bɛə) *vb.* **bearing, bore, borne.** **1.** to support or hold up. **2.** to bring: *to bear gifts.* **3.** to accept the responsibility of: *to bear an expense.* **4.** (**born** in passive use except when foll. by *by*) to give birth to. **5.** to produce as by natural growth: *to bear fruit.* **6.** to tolerate or endure. **7.** to stand up to; sustain: *his story does not bear scrutiny.* **8.** to hold in the mind: *to bear a grudge.* **9.** to show or be marked with: *he still bears the scars.* **10.** to have, be, or stand in (relation or comparison): *his account bears no relation to the facts.* **11.** to move in a specified direction: *bear left.* **12. bring to bear.** to bring into effect. ~See also **bear down on, bear on,** etc. [Old English *beran*]

bear[2] (bɛə) *n., pl.* **bears** or **bear.** **1.** a large heavily-built mammal with a long shaggy coat. **2.** a bearlike animal, such as the koala. **3.** an ill-mannered person. **4.** *Stock Exchange.* a speculator who sells in anticipation of falling prices to make a profit on repurchase. **5. like a bear with a sore head.** *Informal.* bad-tempered; irritable. [Old English *bera*]

bearable ('bɛərəb'l) *adj.* endurable; tolerable.

bear-baiting *n. Hist.* an entertainment in which dogs attacked a chained bear.

beard (bɪəd) *n.* **1.** the hair growing on the lower parts of a man's face. **2.** any similar growth in animals. ~*vb.* **3.** to oppose boldly. [Old English] —**'bearded** *adj.*

bear down on *vb.* **1.** to press down on (something). **2.** to approach (someone) in a determined manner.

bearer ('bɛərə) *n.* **1.** a person or thing that bears, presents, or upholds. **2.** a person who presents a note or bill for payment.

bear garden *n.* a scene of tumult.

bear hug *n.* a rough tight embrace.

bearing ('bɛərɪŋ) *n.* **1.** a part of a machine that supports another part, esp. one that reduces friction. **2.** (foll. by *on* or *upon*) relevance (to): *it has no bearing on this problem.* **3.** a person's general social conduct. **4.** the act of producing fruit or young. **5.** the angular direction of a point measured from a known position. **6.** the position, as of a ship, fixed with reference to two or more known points. **7.** (*pl.*) a sense of one's relative position: *I lost my*

bearings in the dark. **8.** *Heraldry.* a device on a heraldic shield.

bear on *vb.* to be relevant to.

bear out *vb.* to show to be truthful: *the witness will bear me out.*

bearskin ('bɛə‚skɪn) *n.* **1.** the pelt of a bear, esp. when used as a rug. **2.** a tall fur helmet worn by certain British Army regiments.

bear up *vb.* to endure cheerfully: *is she bearing up under the strain?*

bear with *vb.* to be patient with.

beast (biːst) *n.* **1.** a large wild animal. **2.** savage nature or characteristics: *the beast in man.* **3.** a brutal or uncivilized person. [Latin *bestia*]

beastly ('biːstlɪ) *Informal.* ~*adj.* **-lier, -liest.** **1.** unpleasant; disagreeable. ~*adv.* **2.** extremely: *the weather is so beastly hot.*

beat (biːt) *vb.* **beating, beat; beaten** or **beat.** **1.** to strike with a series of violent blows. **2.** to punish by striking; flog. **3.** to move (wings) up and down. **4.** to throb rhythmically; pulsate. **5.** *Cookery.* to stir or whisk vigorously. **6.** to shape (metal) by repeated blows. **7.** *Music.* to indicate (time) by one's hand or a baton. **8.** to produce (a sound) by striking a drum. **9.** to overcome; defeat. **10.** to form (a path or track) by repeated use. **11.** to arrive, achieve, or finish before (someone or something). **12.** (foll. by *back, down, off,* etc.) to drive, push, or thrust. **13.** to scour (woodlands or undergrowth) so as to rouse game for shooting. **14.** *Slang.* to puzzle or baffle: *it beats me.* ~*n.* **15.** a stroke or blow. **16.** the sound made by a stroke or blow. **17.** a regular throb. **18.** an assigned route, as of a policeman. **19.** the basic rhythmic unit in a piece of music. **20.** pop or rock music characterized by a heavy rhythmic beat. ~*adj.* **21.** *Slang.* totally exhausted. ~See also **beat down, beat up.** [Old English *bēatan*]

beatbox ('biːt‚bɒks) *n.* same as **drum machine.**

beat down *vb.* **1.** *Informal.* to force or persuade (a seller) to accept a lower price. **2.** (of the sun) to shine intensely.

beater ('biːtə) *n.* **1.** a device used for beating: *a carpet beater.* **2.** a person who rouses wild game.

beatific (‚biːə'tɪfɪk) *adj.* **1.** displaying great happiness. **2.** conferring a state of celestial happiness. [Latin *beātus*]

beatify (bɪ'ætɪ‚faɪ) *vb.* **-fying, -fied.** **1.** *R.C. Church.* to declare (a deceased person) to be among the blessed in heaven: the first step towards canonization. **2.** to make extremely happy. —**beatification** (bɪ‚ætɪ-fɪ'keɪʃən) *n.*

beatitude (bɪ'ætɪ‚tjuːd) *n.* supreme blessedness or happiness. [Latin *beātitūdō*]

Beatitude (bɪ'ætɪ‚tjuːd) *n. Christianity.* any of the blessings on the poor, meek, etc., in the Sermon on the Mount.

beatnik ('biːtnɪk) *n.* a type of young person in the late 1950s who rebelled against conventional attitudes, dress, etc. [BEAT (*n.*) + -NIK]

beat up *Informal.* ~*vb.* **1.** to strike or

kick (someone) repeatedly, so as to inflict severe physical damage. ~*adj.* **beat-up. 2.** worn-out; dilapidated.

beau (bəʊ) *n., pl.* **beaus** (bəʊz) *or* **beaux. 1.** a man who is greatly concerned with his appearance. **2.** *Chiefly U.S.* a boyfriend. [French]

Beaufort scale (ˈbəʊfət) *n. Meteorol.* a scale of wind velocities from 0 (calm) to 12 (hurricane). [after Sir Francis *Beaufort*, who devised it]

Beaujolais (ˈbəʊʒəˌleɪ) *n.* a red or white wine from southern Burgundy in France.

beauteous (ˈbjuːtɪəs) *adj. Poetic.* beautiful.

beautician (bjuːˈtɪʃən) *n.* a person who works in a beauty salon.

beautiful (ˈbjuːtɪful) *adj.* **1.** possessing beauty. **2.** highly enjoyable; very pleasant. —**ˈbeautifully** *adv.*

beautify (ˈbjuːtɪˌfaɪ) *vb.* **-fying, -fied.** to make or become beautiful. —**beautification** (ˌbjuːtɪfɪˈkeɪʃən) *n.*

beauty (ˈbjuːtɪ) *n., pl.* **-ties. 1.** the combination of all the qualities of a person or thing that delight the senses and mind. **2.** a very attractive woman. **3.** *Informal.* an outstanding example of its kind. **4.** *Informal.* an advantageous feature: *one beauty of the job is the short hours.* [Latin *bellus* handsome]

beauty queen *n.* a woman who has won a beauty contest.

beauty salon *or* **parlour** *n.* an establishment that provides services such as hairdressing, facial treatment, and massage.

beauty spot *n.* **1.** a place of outstanding beauty. **2.** a small dark-coloured spot formerly worn on a lady's face as an adornment.

beaver[1] (ˈbiːvə) *n.* **1.** a large amphibious rodent with soft brown fur, a broad flat tail, and webbed hind feet. **2.** its fur. **3.** a tall hat made of this fur. ~*vb.* **4. beaver away.** to work industriously or steadily. [Old English *beofor*]

beaver[2] (ˈbiːvə) *n.* a movable piece on a medieval helmet used to protect the lower face. [Old French *baver* to dribble]

bebop (ˈbiːbɒp) *n.* same as **bop.** [imit. of the rhythm]

becalmed (bɪˈkɑːmd) *adj.* (of a sailing ship) motionless through lack of wind.

became (bɪˈkeɪm) *vb.* the past tense of **become.**

because (bɪˈkɒz, -ˈkəz) *conj.* **1.** on account of the fact that; since: *because it's so cold we'll go home.* **2. because of.** on account of: *I lost my job because of her.* [Middle English *bi cause*]

béchamel sauce (ˌbeɪʃəˈmɛl) *n.* a thick white sauce flavoured with onion and seasonings. [after the Marquis of *Béchamel,* its inventor]

beck[1] (bɛk) *n.* **at someone's beck and call.** subject to someone's slightest whim. [Middle English *becnen* to beckon]

beck[2] (bɛk) *n.* (in N England) a stream. [Old English *becc*]

beckon (ˈbɛkən) *vb.* **1.** to summon with a gesture. **2.** to lure: *fame beckoned.* [Old English *biecnan*]

become (bɪˈkʌm) *vb.* **-coming, -came, -come. 1.** to come to be; develop or grow into: *he became a monster.* **2.** (foll. by *of*) to happen to: *what became of him?* **3.** to suit: *that dress becomes you.* [Old English *becuman*]

becoming (bɪˈkʌmɪŋ) *adj.* suitable; appropriate.

becquerel (ˌbɛkəˈrɛl) *n.* the SI unit of activity of a radioactive source. [after A.H. *Becquerel,* physicist]

bed (bɛd) *n.* **1.** a piece of furniture on which to sleep. **2.** *Informal.* sexual intercourse. **3.** a plot of ground in which plants are grown. **4.** the bottom of a river, lake, or sea. **5.** any underlying structure or part. **6.** a layer of rock, esp. sedimentary rock. **7. get out of bed on the wrong side.** *Informal.* to begin the day in a bad mood. **8. go to bed with.** to have sexual intercourse with. ~*vb.* **bedding, bedded. 9.** (foll. by *down*) to go to or put into a place to sleep or rest. **10.** to have sexual intercourse with. **11.** to place firmly into position; embed. **12.** *Geol.* to form or be arranged in a distinct layer. **13.** to plant in a bed of soil. [Old English *bedd*]

BEd Bachelor of Education.

bed and breakfast *n. Chiefly Brit.* overnight accommodation and breakfast.

bedaub (bɪˈdɔːb) *vb.* to smear over with something sticky or dirty.

bedbug (ˈbɛdˌbʌg) *n.* a small bloodsucking wingless insect that infests dirty houses.

bedclothes (ˈbɛdˌkləʊðz) *pl. n.* sheets, blankets, and other coverings for a bed.

bedding (ˈbɛdɪŋ) *n.* **1.** bedclothes, sometimes with a mattress. **2.** litter, such as straw, for animals. **3.** the stratification of rocks.

bedeck (bɪˈdɛk) *vb.* to cover with decorations.

bedevil (bɪˈdɛvˀl) *vb.* **-illing, -illed** *or U.S.* **-iling, -iled. 1.** to harass or torment. **2.** to throw into confusion. —**beˈdevilment** *n.*

bedew (bɪˈdjuː) *vb.* to wet as with dew.

bedfellow (ˈbɛdˌfɛləʊ) *n.* **1.** a person with whom one shares a bed. **2.** a temporary associate.

bedizen (bɪˈdaɪzˀn, -ˈdɪzˀn) *vb. Archaic.* to dress gaudily or tastelessly. [BE- + obs. *dizen* to dress up]

bedlam (ˈbɛdləm) *n.* a noisy confused situation. [from Hospital of St Mary of *Bethlehem,* a former mental hospital in London]

bed linen *n.* sheets and pillowcases for a bed.

Bedouin (ˈbɛduɪn) *n.* **1.** (*pl.* **-ins** *or* **-in**) a nomadic Arab tribesman of the deserts of Arabia, Jordan, and Syria. **2.** a wanderer. [Arabic *badw* desert]

bedpan (ˈbɛdˌpæn) *n.* a shallow vessel used as a toilet by bedridden people.

bedraggled (bɪˈdrægˀld) *adj.* having hair or clothing that is untidy or dirty, as with rain or mud.

bedridden ('bɛd,rɪd²n) *adj.* confined to bed because of illness, esp. for a long period.

bedrock ('bɛd,rɒk) *n.* **1.** the solid rock beneath the surface soil. **2.** basic principles or facts.

bedroom ('bɛd,ruːm, -,rʊm) *n.* **1.** a room used for sleeping. **2.** (*modifier*) containing references to sex: *a bedroom comedy*.

Beds (bɛdz) Bedfordshire.

bedside ('bɛd,saɪd) *n.* the space beside a bed, esp. a sickbed.

bedsitter ('bɛd,sɪtə) *or* **bedsit** *n.* a furnished sitting room with a bed.

bedsore ('bɛd,sɔː) *n.* a chronic ulcer on the skin of a bedridden person, caused by prolonged pressure.

bedspread ('bɛd,sprɛd) *n.* a top cover on a bed.

bedstead ('bɛd,stɛd) *n.* the framework of a bed.

bedstraw ('bɛd,strɔː) *n.* a plant with small white or yellow flowers.

bed-wetting *n.* involuntarily urinating in bed.

bee[1] (biː) *n.* **1.** a four-winged insect that collects nectar and pollen to make honey and wax. **2. have a bee in one's bonnet.** to be obsessed with an idea. [Old English *bīo*]

bee[2] (biː) *n.* Chiefly U.S. a social gathering to carry out a communal task: *quilting bee.* [prob. from Old English *bēn* boon]

Beeb (biːb) *n.* **the.** Informal. the BBC.

beebread ('biː,brɛd) *n.* a mixture of pollen and nectar prepared and eaten by some bees.

beech (biːtʃ) *n.* **1.** a European tree with smooth greyish bark. **2.** the hard wood of this tree. **3.** See **copper beech.** [Old English *bēce*]

beechnut ('biːtʃ,nʌt) *n.* the small brown triangular edible nut of the beech tree.

beef (biːf) *n.* **1.** the flesh of a cow, bull, or ox when killed for eating. **2.** Informal. human flesh, esp. when muscular. **3.** Slang. a complaint. ~*vb.* **4.** Slang. to complain. ~See also **beef up.** [Old French *boef*, from Latin *bōs* ox]

beefburger ('biːf,bɜːgə) *n.* a flat fried cake of minced beef; hamburger.

beefcake ('biːf,keɪk) *n.* Slang. musclemen as photographs.

beefeater ('biːf,iːtə) *n.* a yeoman warder of the Tower of London.

beef tea *n.* a drink made by boiling pieces of lean beef.

beef up *vb.* Informal. to strengthen; reinforce.

beefy ('biːfɪ) *adj.* **beefier, beefiest.** **1.** like beef. **2.** Informal. muscular; brawny. —**beefiness** *n.*

beehive ('biː,haɪv) *n.* **1.** a man-made receptacle used to house bees. **2.** a place where busy people are assembled.

beekeeper ('biː,kiːpə) *n.* a person who keeps bees for their honey. —**beekeeping** *n.*

beeline ('biː,laɪn) *n.* **make a beeline for.** to take the most direct route to.

Beelzebub (bɪˈɛlzɪ,bʌb) *n.* Satan or any devil. [Hebrew *báʿal zebūb*, lit.: lord of flies]

been (biːn, bɪn) *vb.* the past participle of **be.**

beep (biːp) *n.* **1.** a high-pitched sound, as made by a car horn. ~*vb.* **2.** to make or cause to make such a noise. [imit.]

beer (bɪə) *n.* **1.** an alcoholic drink brewed from malt, sugar, hops, and water. **2.** a glass, can, or bottle containing this drink. [Old English *bēor*]

beer and skittles *n.* (*functioning as sing.*) Informal. enjoyment or pleasure.

beer parlour *n.* Canad. a licensed place in which beer is sold and drunk.

beery ('bɪərɪ) *adj.* **beerier, beeriest.** smelling or tasting of beer.

beeswax ('biːz,wæks) *n.* **1.** a wax secreted by honeybees for constructing honeycombs. **2.** this wax after refining, used in polishes, etc.

beeswing ('biːz,wɪŋ) *n.* a filmy crust that forms in some wines after long storage.

beet (biːt) *n.* a plant widely cultivated in such varieties as the sugar beet and beetroot. [Old English *bēte*]

beetle[1] ('biːt²l) *n.* **1.** an insect with a hard wing-case closed over the back for protection. ~*vb.* **2.** (foll. by *along, off,* etc.) Informal. to scuttle or scurry; hurry. [Old English *bitela*]

beetle[2] ('biːt²l) *vb.* **1.** to overhang; jut. ~*adj.* **2.** overhanging; prominent. [origin unknown] —**beetling** *adj.*

beetle-browed *adj.* having bushy or overhanging eyebrows.

beetroot ('biːt,ruːt) *n.* a variety of the beet plant with a dark red root that may be eaten as a vegetable, in salads, or pickled.

beet sugar *n.* the sucrose obtained from sugar beet.

befall (bɪˈfɔːl) *vb.* **-falling, -fell, -fallen.** Archaic or literary. to happen to (someone). [Old English *befeallan*]

befit (bɪˈfɪt) *vb.* **-fitting, -fitted.** to be appropriate to or suitable for. —**be'fitting** *adj.*

before (bɪˈfɔː) *conj.* **1.** earlier than the time when. **2.** rather than: *he'll resign before he agrees to it.* ~*prep.* **3.** preceding in space or time; in front of; ahead of: *standing before the altar.* **4.** in the presence of: *to be brought before a judge.* **5.** in preference to: *to put friendship before money.* ~*adv.* **6.** previously. **7.** in front. [Old English *beforan*]

beforehand (bɪˈfɔː,hænd) *adj., adv.* early; in advance; in anticipation.

befriend (bɪˈfrɛnd) *vb.* to be a friend to; assist.

befuddle (bɪˈfʌd²l) *vb.* to stupefy or confuse, as with alcoholic drink.

beg (bɛg) *vb.* **begging, begged.** **1.** to solicit (for money or food), esp. in the street. **2.** to ask formally, humbly, or earnestly: *I beg forgiveness; I beg to differ.* **3. beg the question.** to assume the thing under examination as proved. **4. go begging.** to be unwanted or unused. [prob. from Old English *bedecian*]

began (bɪˈgæn) *vb.* the past tense of **begin.**

beget (bɪˈgɛt) *vb.* **-getting, -got** *or* **-gat; -gotten** *or* **-got.** **1.** to father. **2.** to cause or create. [Old English *begietan*]

beggar (ˈbɛgə) *n.* **1.** a person who begs, esp. one who lives by begging. **2.** *Chiefly Brit.* a fellow: *lucky beggar!* ~*vb.* **3. beggar description.** to be impossible to describe. —**ˈbeggarly** *adj.*

begin (bɪˈgɪn) *vb.* **-ginning, -gan, -gun.** **1.** to start or cause to start (something or to do something). **2.** to bring or come into being; arise or originate. **3.** to start to say or speak. **4.** to have the least capacity (to do something): *he couldn't begin to compete.* [Old English *beginnan*] —**beˈginner** *n.*

beginner's luck *n.* exceptional luck supposed to attend a beginner.

beginning (bɪˈgɪnɪŋ) *n.* **1.** a start. **2.** (*pl.*) an early part or stage. **3.** the place where or time when something starts. **4.** an origin; source.

begone (bɪˈgɒn) *interj.* go away!

begonia (bɪˈgəʊnjə) *n.* a plant of warm and tropical regions, with ornamental leaves and waxy flowers. [after Michel *Bégon*, patron of science]

begot (bɪˈgɒt) *vb.* a past tense and past participle of **beget.**

begotten (bɪˈgɒtʰn) *vb.* a past participle of **beget.**

begrudge (bɪˈgrʌdʒ) *vb.* **1.** to give, admit, or allow unwillingly. **2.** to envy (someone) the possession of (something).

beguile (bɪˈgaɪl) *vb.* **1.** to charm; fascinate. **2.** to delude, cheat, or mislead. —**beˈguiling** *adj.*

beguine (bɪˈgiːn) *n.* **1.** a dance of South American origin. **2.** music for this dance. [French *béguin* flirtation]

begum (ˈbeɪgəm) *n.* (in certain Muslim countries) a woman of high rank. [Turkish *begim*]

begun (bɪˈgʌn) *vb.* the past participle of **begin.**

behalf (bɪˈhɑːf) *n.* **on** *or U.S. & Canad.* **in behalf of.** in the interest of or for the benefit of. [Old English *be* by + *halfe* side]

behave (bɪˈheɪv) *vb.* **1.** to act or function in a specified or usual way. **2.** to conduct (oneself) in a specified way: *he behaved badly.* **3.** to conduct (oneself) properly. [Middle English: see BE-, HAVE]

behaviour *or U.S.* **behavior** (bɪˈheɪvjə) *n.* **1.** manner of behaving. **2.** *Psychol.* the response of an organism to a stimulus. —**beˈhavioural** *or U.S.* **beˈhavioral** *adj.*

behavioural science *n.* the scientific study of the behaviour of organisms.

behaviourism *or U.S.* **behaviorism** (bɪˈheɪvjəˌrɪzəm) *n.* a school of psychology that regards objective observation of the behaviour of organisms as the only valid subject for study. —**beˈhaviourist** *or U.S.* **beˈhaviorist** *adj., n.*

behead (bɪˈhɛd) *vb.* to remove the head from. [Old English *behēafdian*]

beheld (bɪˈhɛld) *vb.* past of **behold.**

behemoth (bɪˈhiːmɒθ) *n.* **1.** *Bible.* a gigantic beast described in Job 40:15. **2.** a huge person or thing. [Hebrew *bĕhēmāh* beast]

behest (bɪˈhɛst) *n.* an order or earnest request. [Old English *behǣs*]

behind (bɪˈhaɪnd) *prep.* **1.** in or to a position further back than. **2.** in the past in relation to: *I've got the exams behind me now.* **3.** late according to: *running behind schedule.* **4.** concerning the circumstances surrounding: *the reasons behind his departure.* **5.** supporting: *I'm right behind you in your application.* ~*adv.* **6.** in or to a position further back. **7.** remaining after someone's departure: *he left his books behind.* **8.** in arrears: *to fall behind with payments.* ~*adj.* **9.** in a position further back. ~*n.* **10.** *Informal.* the buttocks. [Old English *behindan*]

behindhand (bɪˈhaɪndˌhænd) *adj., adv.* **1.** in arrears. **2.** backward. **3.** late.

behold (bɪˈhəʊld) *vb.* **-holding, -held.** *Archaic or literary.* to look (at); observe. [Old English *bihealdan*] —**beˈholder** *n.*

beholden (bɪˈhəʊldʰn) *adj.* indebted; obliged.

behove (bɪˈhəʊv) *vb.* *Archaic.* to be necessary or fitting for: *it behoves me to warn you.* [Old English *behōfian*]

beige (beɪʒ) *adj.* **1.** very light brown, sometimes with a yellowish tinge. ~*n.* **2.** a fabric made of undyed wool. [Old French]

being (ˈbiːɪŋ) *n.* **1.** the state or fact of existing. **2.** essential nature; self. **3.** something that exists or is thought to exist: *a being from outer space.* **4.** a human being.

bejewelled *or U.S.* **bejeweled** (bɪˈdʒuːəld) *adj.* decorated with jewels.

bel (bɛl) *n.* a measure for comparing two power levels, equal to 10 decibels. [after A. G. *Bell*, scientist]

belabour *or U.S.* **belabor** (bɪˈleɪbə) *vb.* to attack verbally or physically.

belated (bɪˈleɪtɪd) *adj.* late or too late: *belated greetings.* —**beˈlatedly** *adv.*

belay (bɪˈleɪ) *vb.* **-laying, -layed.** **1.** *Naut.* to secure (a line) to a pin or cleat. **2.** *Naut.* to stop. **3.** (ˈbiːˌleɪ). *Mountaineering.* to secure (a climber) by fixing a rope round a rock or piton. [Old English *belecgan*]

belch (bɛltʃ) *vb.* **1.** to expel wind from the stomach noisily through the mouth. **2.** to expel or be expelled forcefully: *smoke belching from factory chimneys.* ~*n.* **3.** an act of belching. [Old English *bialcan*]

beleaguer (bɪˈliːgə) *vb.* **1.** to lay siege to. **2.** to harass. [BE- + obs. *leaguer* a siege]

belfry (ˈbɛlfrɪ) *n., pl.* **-fries.** **1.** the part of a tower or steeple in which bells are hung. **2.** a tower or steeple. [Germanic]

Belial (ˈbiːlɪəl) *n.* the devil or Satan. [Hebrew *balīyya'al* worthless]

belie (bɪˈlaɪ) *vb.* **-lying, -lied.** **1.** to show to be untrue: *the facts belied the theory.* **2.** to misrepresent: *her looks belied her age.*

3. to fail to justify: *the promises were soon belied.* [Old English *beléogan*]

belief (bɪˈliːf) *n.* **1.** a principle, etc., accepted as true, esp. without proof. **2.** opinion; conviction: *it's my firm belief.* **3.** religious faith. **4.** trust or confidence: *belief in progress.*

believe (bɪˈliːv) *vb.* **1.** to accept as true or real: *I believe God exists.* **2.** to accept the statement or opinion of (a person) as true. **3.** (foll. by *in*) to be convinced of the truth or existence of: *to believe in fairies.* **4.** to have religious faith. **5.** to think, assume, or suppose: *I believe you know my mother.* [Old English *beliefan*] —**be'lievable** *adj.* —**be'liever** *n.*

Belisha beacon (bəˈliːʃə) *n. Brit.* a flashing orange globe mounted on a post, indicating a pedestrian crossing. [after L. Hore-*Belisha*, politician]

belittle (bɪˈlɪtᵊl) *vb.* to treat (something or someone) as having little value or importance.

bell¹ (bɛl) *n.* **1.** a hollow, usually metal, cup-shaped instrument that emits a ringing sound when struck. **2.** the sound made by such an instrument. **3.** an electrical device that rings or buzzes as a signal. **4.** something shaped like a bell. **5.** *Brit. slang.* a telephone call. **6. ring a bell.** to sound familiar; recall something previously experienced. [Old English *belle*]

bell² (bɛl) *n.* **1.** a bellowing or baying cry. ~*vb.* **2.** to utter (such a cry). [Old English *bellan*]

belladonna (ˌbɛləˈdɒnə) *n.* **1.** a drug obtained from deadly nightshade. **2.** same as **deadly nightshade.** [Italian, lit.: beautiful lady; supposed to refer to its use as a cosmetic]

bell-bottoms *pl. n.* trousers that flare from the knee. —**'bell-ˌbottomed** *adj.*

belle (bɛl) *n.* a beautiful woman, esp. the most attractive woman at a function: *the belle of the ball.* [French]

belles-lettres (ˌbɛlˈlɛtrə) *n.* (functioning as *sing.*) literary works, esp. essays and poetry. [French]

bellicose (ˈbɛlɪˌkəʊs, -ˌkəʊz) *adj.* warlike; aggressive. [Latin *bellum* war]

belligerence (bɪˈlɪdʒərəns) *n.* the act or quality of being belligerent or warlike.

belligerent (bɪˈlɪdʒərənt) *adj.* **1.** marked by readiness to fight; aggressive. **2.** relating to or engaged in a war. ~*n.* **3.** a person or country engaged in war. [Latin *bellum* war + *gerere* to wage]

bell jar *n.* a bell-shaped glass cover used to protect flower arrangements or cover apparatus to confine gases in experiments.

bellow (ˈbɛləʊ) *vb.* **1.** to make a loud deep cry like that of a bull; roar. **2.** to shout (something), as in anger. ~*n.* **3.** the characteristic noise of a bull. **4.** a loud deep sound, as of pain or anger. [prob. from Old English *bylgan*]

bellows (ˈbɛləʊz) *n.* (functioning as *sing.* or *pl.*) **1.** an instrument consisting of an air chamber with flexible sides that is used to create a stream of air, as for producing a draught for a fire or for sounding organ pipes. **2.** a flexible corrugated part, as that connecting the lens system of some cameras to the body. [pl. of Old English *belig* belly]

bell pull *n.* a handle or cord pulled to operate a bell.

bell push *n.* a button pressed to operate an electric bell.

bell-ringer *n.* a person who rings church bells or musical handbells. —**'bell-ˌringing** *n.*

bellwether (ˈbɛlˌwɛðə) *n.* a sheep that leads the flock, often bearing a bell.

belly (ˈbɛlɪ) *n., pl.* **-lies. 1.** the part of the body of a vertebrate containing the intestines and other organs; abdomen. **2.** the stomach. **3.** the front, lower, or inner part of something. ~*vb.* **-lying, -lied. 4.** to swell out or cause to swell out; bulge. [Old English *belig*]

bellyache (ˈbɛlɪˌeɪk) *n.* **1.** *Informal.* a pain in the abdomen. ~*vb.* **2.** *Slang.* to complain repeatedly.

bellybutton (ˈbɛlɪˌbʌtᵊn) *n. Informal.* the navel.

belly dance *n.* **1.** a sensuous dance performed by women, with undulating movements of the abdomen. ~*vb.* **-dance. 2.** to dance thus. —**belly dancer** *n.*

belly flop *n.* **1.** a dive into water in which the body lands horizontally. ~*vb.* **belly-flop, -flopping, -flopped. 2.** to perform a belly flop.

bellyful (ˈbɛlɪˌfʊl) *n.* **1.** *Slang.* more than one can tolerate. **2.** as much as one wants or can eat.

belly laugh *n.* a loud deep hearty laugh.

belong (bɪˈlɒŋ) *vb.* **1.** (foll. by *to*) to be the property of. **2.** (foll. by *to*) to be bound to by ties of affection, etc. **3.** (foll. by *to, under, with,* etc.) to be classified with: *this plant belongs to the daisy family.* **4.** (foll. by *to*) to be a part of: *this lid belongs to that tin.* **5.** to have a proper or usual place. **6.** *Informal.* to be acceptable, esp. socially. [Middle English *belongen*]

belonging (bɪˈlɒŋɪŋ) *n.* secure relationship: *they have a strong sense of belonging.*

belongings (bɪˈlɒŋɪŋz) *pl. n.* the things that a person owns or has with him.

beloved (bɪˈlʌvɪd, -ˈlʌvd) *adj.* **1.** dearly loved. ~*n.* **2.** a person who is dearly loved.

below (bɪˈləʊ) *prep.* **1.** at or to a position lower than; under. **2.** less than. **3.** unworthy of; beneath. ~*adv.* **4.** at or to a lower position. **5.** at a later place (in something written). **6.** *Archaic.* on earth or in hell. [Middle English *bilooghe*]

belt (bɛlt) *n.* **1.** a band of cloth, leather, etc., worn around the waist. **2.** an area where a specific thing is found; zone: *a belt of high pressure.* **3.** same as **seat belt. 4.** a band of flexible material between rotating shafts or pulleys to transfer motion or transmit goods: *a fan belt; a conveyer belt.* **5.** *Informal.* a sharp blow. **6. below the belt.** *Informal.* unscrupulous or cowardly. **7. tighten one's belt.** to reduce expenditure. **8. under one's belt.** as part of one's experience: *he had a degree under his belt.* ~*vb.* **9.** to fasten with or as if with a belt. **10.** to hit with a belt. **11.** *Slang.* to give (someone) a sharp blow. **12.** (foll. by *along*) *Slang.* to move very fast. [Old English]

belt out *vb. Informal.* to sing (a song) loudly.

belt up *vb.* **1.** *Slang.* to stop talking. **2.** to fasten something with a belt.

beluga (bɪˈluːɡə) *n.* **1.** a large white sturgeon of the Black and Caspian Seas: a source of caviar and isinglass. **2.** same as **white whale.** [Russian *byeluga*]

belvedere (ˈbɛlvɪˌdɪə, ˌbɛlvɪˈdɪə) *n.* a building, such as a summerhouse, sited to command a fine view. [Italian: beautiful sight]

bemoan (bɪˈməʊn) *vb.* to lament: *he's always bemoaning his fate.*

bemused (bɪˈmjuːzd) *adj.* preoccupied; lost in thought.

ben *n. Scot., Irish.* a mountain peak: *Ben Lomond.* [Gaelic *beinn*]

bench (bɛntʃ) *n.* **1.** a long seat for more than one person. **2.** a plain stout worktable. **3. the bench. a.** a judge or magistrate sitting in court. **b.** judges or magistrates collectively. **4.** (in a gymnasium) a low table, which may be inclined, used for various exercises. [Old English *benc*]

bench mark *n.* **1.** a mark on a fixed object, used as a reference point in surveying. **2.** a criterion by which to measure something.

bend[1] (bɛnd) *vb.* **bending, bent. 1.** to form or cause to form a curve. **2.** to turn or cause to turn from a particular direction: *the road bends left.* **3.** (often foll. by *down*, etc.) to incline the body; stoop. **4.** to submit or cause to submit: *to bend before superior force.* **5.** to turn or direct (one's eyes, steps, or attention). **6. bend the rules.** *Informal.* to ignore or change rules to suit oneself. ~*n.* **7.** a curved part. **8.** the act of bending. **9. round the bend.** *Brit. slang.* mad. [Old English *bendan*] —**bendy** *adj.*

bend[2] (bɛnd) *n. Heraldry.* a diagonal line across a shield. [Old English: a band, strip]

bender (ˈbɛndə) *n. Informal.* a drinking bout.

bends (bɛndz) *pl. n.* (*functioning as sing. or pl.*) **the.** *Informal.* decompression sickness.

bend sinister *n. Heraldry.* a diagonal line across a shield, indicating a bastard line.

beneath (bɪˈniːθ) *prep.* **1.** below, esp. if covered or obscured by. **2.** not as good as would be demanded by: *beneath his dignity.* ~*adv.* **3.** below; underneath. [Old English *beneothan*]

Benedictine *n.* **1.** (ˌbɛnɪˈdɪktɪn, -taɪn). a monk or nun of the order of Saint Benedict. **2.** (ˌbɛnɪˈdɪktiːn). a liqueur first made by Benedictine monks. ~*adj.* (ˌbɛnɪˈdɪktɪn, -taɪn). **3.** of Saint Benedict or his order.

benediction (ˌbɛnɪˈdɪkʃən) *n.* **1.** a prayer for divine blessing. **2.** a Roman Catholic

service in which the congregation is blessed with the sacrament. [Latin *benedictio*] —**bene'dictory** *adj.*

benefaction (ˌbɛnɪˈfækʃən) *n.* **1.** the act of doing good, esp. by giving a donation to charity. **2.** the donation or help given. [Latin *bene* well + *facere* to do]

benefactor (ˈbɛnɪˌfæktə, ˌbɛnɪˈfæk-) *n.* a person who supports a person or institution, esp. by giving money. —**'bene,factress** *fem. n.*

benefice (ˈbɛnɪfɪs) *n. Christianity.* an endowed Church office yielding an income to its holder. [Latin *beneficium* benefit]

beneficent (bɪˈnɛfɪsⁿt) *adj.* charitable; generous. [Latin *beneficus*] —**be'neficence** *n.*

beneficial (ˌbɛnɪˈfɪʃəl) *adj.* advantageous. [Latin *beneficium* kindness]

beneficiary (ˌbɛnɪˈfɪʃərɪ) *n., pl.* **-ciaries. 1.** a person who gains or benefits. **2.** *Law.* a person entitled to receive funds or property under a trust, will, etc.

benefit (ˈbɛnɪfɪt) *n.* **1.** something that improves or promotes. **2.** advantage or sake: *I'm doing this for your benefit.* **3.** a payment made by an institution or government to a person who is ill, unemployed, etc. **4.** a theatrical performance or sports event to raise money for a charity. ~*vb.* **-fiting, -fited** *or U.S.* **-fitting, -fitted. 5.** to do or receive good; profit. [Latin *bene facere* to do well]

benefit society *n. U.S.* same as **friendly society.**

benevolence (bɪˈnɛvələns) *n.* **1.** inclination to do good; charity. **2.** an act of kindness. —**be'nevolent** *adj.*

Bengali (bɛnˈɡɔːlɪ, bɛŋ-) *n.* **1.** a member of a people living chiefly in Bangladesh and West Bengal (in NE India). **2.** their language. ~*adj.* **3.** of Bengal, the Bengalis, or their language.

benighted (bɪˈnaɪtɪd) *adj.* lacking cultural, moral, or intellectual enlightenment.

benign (bɪˈnaɪn) *adj.* **1.** showing kindliness. **2.** favourable; propitious. **3.** *Pathol.* (of a tumour, etc.) not malignant. [Latin *benignus*] —**be'nignly** *adv.*

benignant (bɪˈnɪɡnənt) *adj.* **1.** kind; gracious. **2.** same as **benign** (senses 2, 3). —**be'nignancy** *n.*

benignity (bɪˈnɪɡnɪtɪ) *n., pl.* **-ties.** kindliness.

bent[1] (bɛnt) *adj.* **1.** not straight; curved. **2.** *Slang.* **a.** dishonest; corrupt. **b.** sexually deviant. **3. bent on.** determined to pursue (a course of action). ~*n.* **4.** personal inclination or aptitude.

bent[2] (bɛnt) *n.* **1.** a grass with irregularly branched flowers. **2.** *Archaic.* any stiff grass or sedge. [Old English *bionot*]

Benthamism (ˈbɛnθəmɪzəm) *n.* the utilitarian philosophy of Jeremy Bentham, which holds that the ultimate goal of society should be to promote the greatest happiness of the greatest number. —**'Benthamite** *n., adj.*

bentwood (ˈbɛntˌwʊd) *n.* **a.** wood bent in moulds, used mainly for furniture. **b.** (*as modifier*): *a bentwood chair.*

benumb (bɪˈnʌm) vb. **1.** to make numb or powerless. **2.** to stupefy (the mind, senses, will, etc.).

benzene (ˈbɛnziːn) n. a flammable poisonous liquid used as a solvent, insecticide, etc. [from benzoin, a fragrant resin from certain Asiatic trees]

benzine (ˈbɛnziːn, bɛnˈziːn) n. a volatile liquid obtained from coal tar and used as a solvent.

bequeath (bɪˈkwiːð, -ˈkwiːθ) vb. **1.** Law. to dispose of (property) by will. **2.** to hand down. [Old English becwethan]

bequest (bɪˈkwɛst) n. **1.** the act of bequeathing. **2.** something that is bequeathed.

berate (bɪˈreɪt) vb. to scold harshly.

Berber (ˈbɜːbə) n. **1.** a member of a Muslim people of N Africa. **2.** the language of this people. ~adj. **3.** of this people or their language.

berberis (ˈbɜːbərɪs) n. any of a genus of mainly N temperate shrubs. [Medieval Latin]

berceuse (bɛəˈsɜːz) n. **1.** a lullaby. **2.** an instrumental piece suggestive of this. [French]

bereaved (bɪˈriːvd) adj. having recently lost a close relative or friend through death. [Old English bereafian] —be-ˈreavement n.

bereft (bɪˈrɛft) adj. (foll. by of) deprived: bereft of hope.

beret (ˈbɛreɪ) n. a round close-fitting brimless cap. [French béret]

berg (bɜːg) n. short for **iceberg.**

bergamot (ˈbɜːgəˌmɒt) n. **1.** a small Asian tree with sour pear-shaped fruit. **2.** essence of bergamot. a fragrant essential oil from the fruit rind of this plant, used in perfumery. [French bergamote]

beriberi (ˌbɛrɪˈbɛrɪ) n. a disease, endemic in E and S Asia, caused by dietary deficiency of thiamine (vitamin B₁). [Sinhalese]

berk (bɜːk) n. Brit. slang. same as **burk.**

berkelium (bɜːˈkiːlɪəm, ˈbɜːklɪəm) n. a radioactive element produced by bombardment of americium. Symbol: Bk [after Berkeley, California, where it was discovered]

Berks (bɑːks) Berkshire.

Bermuda shorts (bəˈmjuːdə) pl. n. close-fitting shorts that come down to the knees. [after Bermudas, islands in NW Atlantic]

berry (ˈbɛrɪ) n., pl. -ries. **1.** any of various small edible fruit such as the strawberry. **2.** Bot. a fruit with seeds and a fleshy pulp, such as the grape. [Old English berie]

berserk (bəˈzɜːk, -ˈsɜːk) adj. go berserk to become violent or destructive. [Icelandic björn bear + serkr shirt]

berth (bɜːθ) n. **1.** a bunk in a ship or train. **2.** Naut. a place assigned to a ship at a mooring. **3.** Naut. sufficient room for a ship to manoeuvre. **4.** give a wide berth to. to keep clear of. **5.** Informal. a job, esp. as a member of a ship's crew. ~vb. **6.** Naut. to dock (a vessel). **7.** to provide with a sleeping place. **8.** Naut. to pick up a mooring in an anchorage. [prob. from BEAR¹]

beryl (ˈbɛrɪl) n. a green, blue, yellow, pink, or white hard mineral, used as a source of beryllium and as a gemstone. [Greek bērullos]

beryllium (bɛˈrɪlɪəm) n. a toxic silvery-white metallic element. Symbol: Be [Greek bērullos]

beseech (bɪˈsiːtʃ) vb. -seeching, -sought or -seeched. to ask (someone) earnestly (to do something or for something); beg. [Middle English: see BE-, SEEK]

beset (bɪˈsɛt) vb. -setting, -set. **1.** to trouble or harass constantly. **2.** to surround or attack from all sides.

beside (bɪˈsaɪd) prep. **1.** next to; at, by, or to the side of. **2.** as compared with. **3.** away from; wide of: beside the point. **4.** beside oneself. overwhelmed; overwrought: beside oneself with grief. ~adv. **5.** at, by, to, or along the side of something or someone. [Old English be sīdan]

besides (bɪˈsaɪdz) prep. **1.** apart from; even considering. ~adv. **2.** as well. **3.** anyway; moreover.

besiege (bɪˈsiːdʒ) vb. **1.** to surround (a fortified area) with military forces to bring about its surrender. **2.** to hem in. **3.** to overwhelm, as with requests.

besmirch (bɪˈsmɜːtʃ) vb. to sully (someone's name or reputation).

besom (ˈbiːzəm) n. a broom made of a bundle of twigs tied to a handle. [Old English besma]

besotted (bɪˈsɒtɪd) adj. **1.** stupefied with alcohol. **2.** infatuated. **3.** foolish; muddled.

besought (bɪˈsɔːt) vb. past of **beseech.**

bespangle (bɪˈspæŋgᵊl) vb. to cover with or as if with spangles.

bespatter (bɪˈspætə) vb. **1.** to splash, as with dirty water. **2.** to defile; besmirch.

bespeak (bɪˈspiːk) vb. -speaking, -spoke; -spoken or -spoke. **1.** to engage or ask for in advance. **2.** to indicate or suggest.

bespectacled (bɪˈspɛktəkᵊld) adj. wearing spectacles.

bespoke (bɪˈspəʊk) adj. Chiefly Brit. **1.** (esp. of a suit) made to the customer's specifications. **2.** making or selling such suits: a bespoke tailor.

best (bɛst) adj. **1.** the superlative of **good.** **2.** most excellent of a particular group, category, etc. **3.** most suitable, desirable, etc. ~adv. **4.** the superlative of **well.** **5** in a manner surpassing all others; most attractively, etc. ~n. **6.** the best. the most outstanding or excellent person, thing, or group in a category. **7.** the utmost effort: I did my best. **8.** a person's finest clothes. **9.** at best. a. in the most favourable interpretation. b. under the most favourable conditions. **10.** for the best. a. for an ultimately good outcome. b. with good intentions. **11.** get the best of. to defeat or outwit. **12.** make the best of. to cope as well as possible with. ~vb. **13.** to defeat. [Old English betst]

bestial (ˈbɛstɪəl) adj. **1.** brutal or savage.

2. of or relating to a beast. [Latin *bestia* beast]

bestiality (,bɛstɪˈælɪtɪ) n., pl. **-ties. 1.** bestial behaviour, character, or action. **2.** sexual activity between a person and an animal.

bestiary (ˈbɛstɪərɪ) n., pl. **-aries.** a medieval collection of descriptions of animals.

bestir (bɪˈstɜː) vb. **-stirring, -stirred.** to cause (oneself) to become active.

best man n. the male attendant of the bridegroom at a wedding.

bestow (bɪˈstəʊ) vb. to present (a gift) or confer (an honour). —**beˈstowal** n.

bestrew (bɪˈstruː) vb. **-strewing, -strewed; -strewn** or **-strewed.** to scatter or lie scattered over (a surface).

bestride (bɪˈstraɪd) vb. **-striding, -strode.** to have or put a leg on either side of.

best seller n. a book or other product that has sold in great numbers. —**best-ˈselling** adj.

bet (bɛt) n. **1.** an agreement between two people that a sum of money or other stake will be paid by the loser to the one who correctly predicts the outcome of an event. **2.** the stake risked. **3.** a course of action: *your best bet is to go to the local library.* **4.** *Informal.* an opinion: *my bet is that you've been up to no good.* ~vb. **betting, bet** or **betted. 5.** to make or place a bet with (a person or persons). **6.** to stake (money, etc.) in a bet. **7.** *Informal.* to predict (a certain outcome): *I bet he doesn't turn up.* **8. you bet.** *Informal.* of course. [prob. short for *abet*]

beta (ˈbiːtə) n. **1.** the second letter in the Greek alphabet (Β or β). **2.** the second in a group or series.

beta-blocker n. a drug that increases the activity of the heart: used in the treatment of high blood pressure and angina pectoris.

betake (bɪˈteɪk) vb. **-taking, -took, -taken. betake oneself.** to go; move.

beta particle n. a high-speed electron or positron emitted by a nucleus during radioactive decay or nuclear fission.

betatron (ˈbiːtə,trɒn) n. a type of particle accelerator for producing high-energy beams of electrons.

betel (ˈbiːtˀl) n. an Asian climbing plant, the leaves and nuts of which are chewed by some Asians. [Malayalam *vettila*]

bête noire (,beɪt ˈnwɑː) n., pl. **bêtes noires** (,beɪt ˈnwɑː). a person or thing that one particularly dislikes or dreads. [French, lit.: black beast]

betide (bɪˈtaɪd) vb. to happen or happen to: *woe betide us if we're not ready on time.* [BE- + obs. *tide* to happen]

betimes (bɪˈtaɪmz) adv. *Archaic.* in good time; early. [Middle English *bitimes*]

betoken (bɪˈtəʊkən) vb. to indicate; signify.

betray (bɪˈtreɪ) vb. **1.** to hand over or expose (one's nation, friend, etc.) treacherously to an enemy. **2.** to disclose (a secret or confidence) treacherously. **3.** to break (a promise) or be disloyal to (a person's trust). **4.** to reveal unintentionally: *his grin betrayed his satisfaction.* [Latin *trādere* to hand over] —**beˈtrayal** n. —**beˈtrayer** n.

betroth (bɪˈtrəʊð) vb. *Archaic.* to promise to marry or to give in marriage. [Middle English *betreuthen*] —**beˈtrothal** n.

betrothed (bɪˈtrəʊðd) adj. **1.** engaged to be married. ~n. **2.** the person to whom one is engaged.

better (ˈbɛtə) adj. **1.** the comparative of **good. 2.** more excellent than others. **3.** more suitable, attractive, etc. **4.** improved or fully recovered in health. **5. better off.** in more favourable circumstances, esp. financially. **6. the better part of.** a large part of. ~adv. **7.** the comparative of **well. 8.** in a more excellent manner. **9.** in or to a greater degree. **10. had better.** would be sensible, etc., to: *I had better be off.* ~n. **11. the better.** something that is the more excellent, useful, etc., of two such things. **12.** (pl.) people who are one's superiors, esp. in social standing. **13. get the better of.** to defeat or outwit. ~vb. **14.** to improve upon; surpass. [Old English *betera*]

better half n. *Humorous.* one's spouse.

betterment (ˈbɛtəmənt) n. improvement.

better-off adj. comparatively affluent: *suburbs were originally built for the better-off workers who could afford to travel.*

betting shop n. (in Britain) a licensed bookmaker's premises not on a racecourse.

between (bɪˈtwiːn) prep. **1.** at a point intermediate to two other points in space, time, etc. **2.** in combination; together: *between them, they saved enough money to buy a car.* **3.** confined to: *between you and me.* **4.** indicating a linking relation or comparison. **5.** indicating alternatives, strictly only two alternatives. ~adv. also **in between. 6.** between one specified thing and another. [Old English *betwēonum*]

betwixt (bɪˈtwɪkst) prep., adv. **1.** *Archaic.* between. **2. betwixt and between.** in an intermediate or indecisive position.

bevel (ˈbɛvˀl) n. **1.** a surface that meets another at an angle other than a right angle. ~vb. **-elling, -elled** or *U.S.* **-eling, -eled. 2.** to be inclined; slope. **3.** to cut a bevel on (a piece of timber, etc.). [Old French *baer* to gape]

bevel gear n. a toothed gear meshed with another at an angle to it.

beverage (ˈbɛvərɪdʒ, ˈbɛvrɪdʒ) n. any drink other than water. [Old French *bevrage*]

beverage room n. *Canad.* same as **beer parlour.**

bevvy (ˈbɛvɪ) n., pl. **-vies.** *Dialect.* **1.** an alcoholic drink. **2.** a night of drinking. [prob. from Old French *bevee, buvee* drinking]

bevy (ˈbɛvɪ) n., pl. **bevies. 1.** a flock of quails. **2.** a group, esp. of girls. [of unknown origin]

bewail (bɪˈweɪl) vb. to express great sorrow over (a person or thing); lament.

beware (bɪˈwɛə) vb. (often foll. by *of*) to

be wary (of); be on one's guard (against). [*be* (imperative) + obs. *war* wary]

bewilder (bɪ'wɪldə) *vb.* to confuse utterly; puzzle. [BE- + obs. *wilder* to lose one's way] —**be'wildering** *adj.* —**be'wilderment** *n.*

bewitch (bɪ'wɪtʃ) *vb.* **1.** to attract and fascinate. **2.** to cast a spell over. [Middle English *bewicchen*] —**be'witching** *adj.*

bey (beɪ) *n.* **1.** (in modern Turkey) a title of address, corresponding to *Mr.* **2.** (in the Ottoman Empire) a title given to provincial governors. [Turkish: lord]

beyond (bɪ'jɒnd) *prep.* **1.** at or to a point on the other side of; at or to the further side of: *beyond those hills.* **2.** outside the limits or scope of. ~*adv.* **3.** at or to the other or far side of something. **4.** outside the limits of something. ~*n.* **5. the beyond.** the unknown, esp. life after death. [Old English *begeondan*]

bezel ('bɛz'l) *n.* **1.** the sloping edge of a cutting tool. **2.** the slanting face of a cut gem. **3.** a groove holding a gem, watch crystal, etc. [French]

bezique (bɪ'ziːk) *n.* a card game for two or more players. [French *bésigue*]

B/F *or* **b/f** *Book-keeping.* brought forward.

BFPO British Forces Post Office.

bhang (bæŋ) *n.* a preparation of the leaves and flower tops of Indian hemp, which when chewed or smoked acts as a narcotic and intoxicant. [Hindi]

bhangra ('bæŋgrə) *n.* a type of traditional Indian folk music of the Punjab, now sometimes combined with elements of Western pop music. [Hindi]

bhp brake horsepower.

Bi *Chem.* bismuth.

bi- *combining form.* **1.** having two: *bifocal.* **2.** occurring or lasting for two: *biennial.* **3.** on both sides, directions, etc.: *bilateral.* **4.** occurring twice during: *biweekly.* **5.** *Chem.* **a.** denoting a compound containing two identical cyclic hydrocarbon systems: *biphenyl.* **b.** indicating an acid salt of a dibasic acid: *sodium bicarbonate.* [Latin *bis* twice]

biannual (baɪ'ænjʊəl) *adj.* occurring twice a year. —**bi'annually** *adv.*

bias ('baɪəs) *n.* **1.** mental tendency, esp. prejudice. **2.** a diagonal cut across the weave of a fabric. **3.** *Bowls.* a bulge or weight inside one side of a bowl that causes it to roll in a curve. ~*adv.* **4.** diagonally. ~*vb.* **-asing, -ased** *or* **-assing, -assed.** **5.** to cause to have a bias; prejudice. [Old French *biais*] —**'biased** *or* **'biassed** *adj.*

bias binding *n.* a strip of material cut on the bias, used for binding hems.

biaxial (baɪ'æksɪəl) *adj.* (esp. of a crystal) having two axes.

bib (bɪb) *n.* **1.** a piece of cloth or plastic worn to protect a child's clothes while eating. **2.** the upper front part of some aprons, dungarees, etc. [Middle English *bibben* to drink]

bibcock ('bɪb,kɒk) *n.* a tap with a nozzle bent downwards.

bibelot ('bɪbləʊ) *n.* an attractive or curious trinket. [Old French *beubelet*]

bibl. **1.** bibliographical. **2.** bibliography.

Bible ('baɪb'l) *n.* **1. the.** the sacred writings of the Christian religion, comprising the Old and New Testaments. **2.** (*usually not cap.*) a book regarded as authoritative. [Greek *biblos* papyrus] —**biblical** ('bɪblɪk'l) *adj.*

bibliography (,bɪblɪ'ɒgrəfɪ) *n., pl.* **-phies.** **1.** a list of books on a subject or by a particular author. **2.** a list of sources used in a book, etc. **3.** the study of the history, etc., of literary material. [Greek *biblion* book + *graphein* to write] —**,bibli'ographer** *n.*

bibliophile ('bɪblɪə,faɪl) *n.* a person who collects or is fond of books. [Greek *biblion* book + *philos* loving]

bibulous ('bɪbjʊləs) *adj.* addicted to alcohol. [Latin *bibere* to drink]

bicameral (baɪ'kæmərəl) *adj.* (of a legislature) consisting of two chambers. [BI- + Latin *camera* chamber]

bicarb ('baɪkɑːb) *n.* short for **bicarbonate of soda.**

bicarbonate (baɪ'kɑːbənɪt, -,neɪt) *n.* a salt of carbonic acid.

bicarbonate of soda *n.* sodium bicarbonate, esp. as medicine or a raising agent in baking.

bicentenary (,baɪsɛn'tiːnərɪ) *or U.S.* **bicentennial** (,baɪsɛn'tɛnɪəl) *adj.* **1.** marking a 200th anniversary. ~*n., pl.* **-naries.** **2.** a 200th anniversary.

biceps ('baɪsɛps) *n., pl.* **-ceps.** *Anat.* a muscle with two origins, esp. the muscle that flexes the forearm. [BI- + Latin *caput* head]

bicker ('bɪkə) *vb.* to argue over petty matters; squabble. [origin unknown]

bicolour (baɪ'kʌlə), **bicoloured** *or U.S.* **bicolor, bicolored** *adj.* two-coloured.

bicuspid (baɪ'kʌspɪd) *adj.* **1.** having two points. ~*n.* **2.** a bicuspid tooth; premolar.

bicycle ('baɪsɪk'l) *n.* **1.** a vehicle with a metal frame and two wheels, one behind the other. The rider propels the vehicle by means of pedals. ~*vb.* **2.** to ride a bicycle. [BI- + Greek *kuklos* wheel]

bid (bɪd) *vb.* **bidding; bad, bade,** *or* (esp. for senses 1, 3, 4) **bid; bidden** *or* (esp. for senses 1, 3, 4) **bid.** **1.** to offer (an amount) in attempting to buy something. **2.** to say (a greeting, etc.): *to bid farewell.* **3.** to order; command: *do as you are bid!* **4.** *Bridge, etc.* to declare how many tricks one expects to make. ~*n.* **5. a.** an offer of a specified amount. **b.** the price offered. **6. a.** the quoting by a seller of a price. **b.** the price quoted. **7.** an attempt, esp. to attain power. **8.** *Bridge, etc.* the number of tricks a player undertakes to make. [Old English *biddan*] —**'bidder** *n.*

biddable ('bɪdəb'l) *adj.* docile; obedient.

bidding ('bɪdɪŋ) *n.* **1.** an order; command. **2.** an invitation; summons. **3.** the bids in an auction, card game, etc.

biddy ('bɪdɪ) n., pl. **-dies.** Informal. a woman, esp. an old gossipy one. [pet form of Bridget]

bide (baɪd) vb. **biding, bided** or **bode, bided.** **1.** Archaic or dialect. to continue in a certain place or state; stay. **2. bide one's time.** to wait patiently for an opportunity. [Old English bīdan]

bidet ('biːdeɪ) n. a small low basin for washing the genital area. [French: small horse]

biennial (baɪ'ɛnɪəl) adj. **1.** occurring every two years. ∼n. **2.** a plant that completes its life cycle in two years.

bier (bɪə) n. a stand on which a corpse or a coffin rests before burial. [Old English bēr]

biff (bɪf) Slang. ∼n. **1.** a blow with the fist. ∼vb. **2.** to give (someone) such a blow. [prob. imit.]

bifid ('baɪfɪd) adj. divided into two by a cleft in the middle. [BI- + Latin findere to split]

bifocal (baɪ'fəʊk²l) adj. having two different focuses, esp. (of a lens) permitting near and distant vision.

bifocals (baɪ'fəʊk²lz) pl. n. a pair of spectacles with bifocal lenses.

bifurcate vb. ('baɪfəˌkeɪt). **1.** to fork into two branches. ∼adj. ('baɪfəˌkeɪt, -kɪt). **2.** forked into two branches. [BI- + Latin furca fork] —ˌbifur'cation n.

big (bɪg) adj. **bigger, biggest. 1.** of great or considerable size, weight, number, or capacity. **2.** having great significance; important. **3.** important through having power, wealth, etc. **4. a.** elder: my big brother. **b.** grown-up. **5.** generous: that's very big of you. **6.** extravagant; boastful: big talk. **7. too big for one's boots.** conceited; unduly self-confident. **8.** in an advanced stage of pregnancy: big with child. **9. in a big way.** in a very grand or enthusiastic way. ∼adv. Informal. **10.** boastfully; pretentiously: he talks big. **11.** on a grand scale: think big. [origin unknown]

bigamy ('bɪgəmɪ) n. the crime of marrying a person while still legally married to someone else. [BI- + Greek gamos marriage] —'**bigamist** n. —'**bigamous** adj.

big-bang theory n. a cosmological theory that suggests that the universe was created as the result of a massive explosion.

Big Brother n. a person or organization that exercises total dictatorial control. [from George Orwell's novel 1984]

big business n. large commercial organizations collectively.

big end n. Brit. the larger end of a connecting rod in an internal-combustion engine.

big game n. large animals that are hunted or fished for sport.

bighead ('bɪgˌhɛd) n. Informal. a conceited person. —'**big-'headed** adj.

bight (baɪt) n. **1.** a long curved shoreline. **2.** the slack part or a loop in a rope. [Old English byht]

bigot ('bɪgət) n. a person who is intolerant, esp. regarding religion, politics, or race. [Old French] —'**bigoted** adj. —'**bigotry** n.

big shot n. Informal. an important person.

big stick n. Informal. force or the threat of force.

big time n. **the.** Informal. the highest level of a profession, esp. entertainment. —'**big-'timer** n.

big top n. Informal. the main tent of a circus.

bigwig ('bɪgˌwɪg) n. Informal. an important person.

bijou ('biːʒuː) n., pl. **-joux** (-ʒuːz). **1.** something small and delicately worked. **2.** (modifier) small but tasteful: a bijou residence. [French: a jewel]

bike (baɪk) n. Informal. a bicycle or motorcycle.

bikini (bɪ'kiːnɪ) n. a brief two-piece swimming costume worn by women. [after Bikini atoll, from a comparison between the devastating effect of the atom-bomb test and the effect caused by women wearing bikinis]

bilateral (baɪ'lætərəl) adj. affecting or undertaken by two parties; mutual.

bilberry ('bɪlbərɪ) n., pl. **-ries.** a blue or blackish edible berry that grows on a shrub such as the whortleberry. [prob. Scandinavian]

bile (baɪl) n. **1.** a greenish fluid secreted by the liver to aid digestion of fats. **2.** irritability or peevishness. [Latin bīlis]

bilge (bɪldʒ) n. **1.** Naut. the bottom of a ship's hull. **2.** the dirty water that collects in a ship's bilge. **3.** Informal. nonsense. [prob. var. of bulge]

bilharzia (bɪl'hɑːtsɪə) n. a disease caused by infestation of the body with blood flukes. [after T. Bilharz, who discovered the blood fluke]

biliary ('bɪlɪərɪ) adj. of bile, the ducts that convey bile, or the gall bladder.

bilingual (baɪ'lɪŋgwəl) adj. **1.** able to speak two languages. **2.** expressed in two languages. ∼n. **3.** a bilingual person. —bi'lingual,ism n.

bilious ('bɪlɪəs) adj. **1.** denoting any disorder related to secretion of bile. **2.** Informal. bad-tempered; irritable. [Latin bīliōsus]

bilk (bɪlk) vb. to cheat or deceive, esp. to avoid making payment to. [perhaps var. of balk] —'**bilker** n.

bill¹ (bɪl) n. **1.** a statement of money owed for goods or services supplied. **2.** any list of items, events, etc., such as a theatre programme. **3.** a draft of a proposed new law presented to a law-making body. **4.** a printed notice or advertisement. **5.** U.S. & Canad. a piece of paper money; note. ∼vb. **6.** to send or present an account for payment to (a person). **7.** to advertise by posters. **8.** to schedule as a future programme. [Late Latin bulla a document]

bill² (bɪl) n. **1.** the projecting jaws of a bird; beak. ∼vb. **2. bill and coo.** (of lovers) to kiss and whisper amorously. [Old English *bile*]

bill³ (bɪl) *n.* **1.** a weapon with a narrow hooked blade. **2.** same as **billhook**. [Old English: sword]

billabong ('bɪlə,bɒŋ) *n. Austral.* a stagnant pool in the bed of an intermittent stream. [Aboriginal]

billboard ('bɪl,bɔːd) *n. Chiefly U.S. & Canad.* a hoarding.

billet¹ ('bɪlɪt) *n.* **1.** accommodation, esp. for a soldier, in civilian lodgings. **2.** the official requisition for such lodgings. ~*vb.* **3.** to assign a lodging to (a soldier). [Old French *billette*, from *bulle* a document]

billet² ('bɪlɪt) *n.* **1.** a chunk of wood, esp. for fuel. **2.** a small bar of iron or steel. [Old French *billette* a little log]

billet-doux (,bɪlɪ'duː) *n., pl.* **billets-doux** (,bɪlɪ'duːz). *Old-fashioned or jocular.* a love letter. [French: a sweet letter]

billhook ('bɪl,hʊk) *n.* a tool with a hooked blade, used for chopping, etc.

billiards ('bɪljədz) *n. (functioning as sing.)* a game in which a long cue is used to drive balls on a rectangular table covered with a smooth cloth and having raised cushioned edges. [Old French *billard* curved stick]

billion ('bɪljən) *n., pl.* **-lions** *or* **-lion.** **1.** (in Britain, originally) one million million: 1 000 000 000 000; 10^{12}. **2.** (in the U.S., Canada, and increasingly in Britain and elsewhere) one thousand million: 1 000 000 000; 10^9. **3.** (*often pl.*) any exceptionally large number. [French] —**billionth** *adj., n.*

billionaire (,bɪljə'nɛə) *n.* a person whose wealth exceeds a billion monetary units of his country.

bill of exchange *n.* a document instructing a third party to pay a stated sum at a designated date or on demand.

bill of fare *n.* a menu.

bill of health *n.* **1.** a certificate that confirms the health of a ship's company. **2. clean bill of health.** *Informal.* **a.** a good report of one's physical condition. **b.** a favourable account of a person's or a company's financial position.

bill of lading *n.* a document containing full particulars of goods shipped.

billow ('bɪləʊ) *n.* **1.** a large sea wave. **2.** a swelling or surging mass, as of smoke or sound. ~*vb.* **3.** to rise up or swell out. [Old Norse *bylgja*] —**'billowing** *adj., n.* —**'billowy** *adj.*

billy ('bɪlɪ) *or* **billycan** ('bɪlɪ,kæn) *n., pl.* **-lies** *or* **-lycans.** a metal can or pot for boiling water, etc., over a campfire. [Scot. *billypot*]

billy goat *n.* a male goat.

biltong ('bɪl,tɒŋ) *n. S. African.* strips of meat dried and cured in the sun. [Afrikaans]

bimbo ('bɪmbəʊ) *n., pl.* **-bos.** *Slang.* an attractive but empty-headed young woman. [origin unknown]

bimetallism (baɪ'mɛtə,lɪzəm) *n.* the use of two metals, esp. gold and silver, in fixed relative values as the standard of value and currency. —**bi'metallist** *n.*

bin (bɪn) *n.* **1.** a large container for storing something in bulk, such as coal, grain, or bottled wine. **2.** a container for rubbish, etc. [Old English *binne* basket]

binary ('baɪnərɪ) *adj.* **1.** composed of two parts. **2.** *Maths, computers.* of or expressed in a system with two as its base. **3.** containing atoms of two different elements. ~*n., pl.* **-ries.** **4.** something composed of two parts. [Late Latin *bīnārius*]

binary star *n.* a system of two stars revolving around a common centre of gravity.

bind (baɪnd) *vb.* **binding, bound.** **1.** to make or become fast or secure with or as if with a rope. **2.** to encircle with a band. **3.** to place (someone) under obligation. **4.** to impose legal obligations or duties upon (a person). **5.** to make (a bargain or agreement) irrevocable; seal. **6.** to restrain or confine with or as if with ties, as of responsibility or loyalty. **7.** to place under certain constraints: *bound by the rules.* **8.** (foll. by *up*) to bandage. **9.** to stick together or cause to stick: *egg binds fat and flour.* **10.** to enclose and fasten (the pages of a book) between covers. **11.** to provide (a garment) with an edging. ~*n.* **12.** *Informal.* a difficult or annoying situation. ~See also **bind over.** [Old English *bindan*]

binder ('baɪndə) *n.* **1.** a firm cover for holding loose sheets of paper together. **2.** a person who binds books. **3.** something used to fasten or tie, such as rope or twine. **4.** *Obs.* a machine for cutting and binding grain into sheaves.

bindery ('baɪndərɪ) *n., pl.* **-eries.** a place in which books are bound.

binding ('baɪndɪŋ) *n.* **1.** anything that binds or fastens. **2.** the covering within which the pages of a book are bound. ~*adj.* **3.** imposing an obligation or duty.

bind over *vb.* to place (a person) under a legal obligation, esp. to keep the peace.

bindweed ('baɪnd,wiːd) *n.* a plant that twines around a support.

binge (bɪndʒ) *n. Informal.* **1.** a bout of excessive drinking. **2.** excessive indulgence in anything. [prob. dialect *binge* to soak]

bingo ('bɪŋgəʊ) *n.* a gambling game in which random numbers are called out and the players cover them on their individual cards. The first to cover a given arrangement is the winner. [origin unknown]

binnacle ('bɪnək³l) *n.* a housing for a ship's compass. [Late Latin *habitāculum* dwelling-place]

binocular (bɪ'nɒkjʊlə, baɪ-) *adj.* involving or intended for both eyes: *binocular vision.* [BI- + Latin *oculus* eye]

binoculars (bɪ'nɒkjʊləz, baɪ-) *pl. n.* an optical instrument for use with both eyes, consisting of two small telescopes joined together.

binomial (baɪ'nəʊmɪəl) *n.* **1.** a mathematical expression consisting of two terms, such as $3x + 2y$. ~*adj.* **2.** referring to two names or terms. [BI- + Latin *nōmen* name]

binomial theorem *n.* a general mathematical formula that expresses any power of a binomial without multiplying out, as in $(a+b)^2 = a^2 + 2ab + b^2$.

bio- *combining form.* indicating: **1.** life or living organisms: *biogenesis*. **2.** a human life or career: *biography*. [Greek *bios* life]

bioastronautics (ˌbaɪəʊˌæstrə'nɔːtɪks) *n.* (*functioning as sing.*) the study of the effects of space flight on living organisms.

biochemistry (ˌbaɪəʊ'kemɪstrɪ) *n.* the study of the chemical compounds, reactions, etc., occurring in living organisms. —**biochemical** (ˌbaɪəʊ'kemɪk°l) *adj.* —ˌbio'chemist *n.*

biocoenosis *or U.S.* **biocenosis** (ˌbaɪəʊsiː'nəʊsɪs) *n.* the relationships between animals and plants subsisting together. [BIO- + Greek *koinōsis* sharing]

biodegradable (ˌbaɪəʊdɪ'greɪdəb°l) *adj.* (of sewage, etc.) capable of being decomposed by natural means.

bioengineering (ˌbaɪəʊˌendʒɪ'nɪərɪŋ) *n.* the design and manufacture of aids, such as artificial limbs, to help people with disabilities.

biogenesis (ˌbaɪəʊ'dʒɛnɪsɪs) *n.* the principle that a living organism must originate from a parent organism similar to itself.

biography (baɪ'ɒgrəfɪ) *n., pl.* **-phies. 1.** an account of a person's life by another. **2.** such accounts collectively. [BIO- + Greek *graphein* to write] —**bi'ographer** *n.* —**biographical** (ˌbaɪə'græfɪk°l) *adj.*

biol. 1. biological. **2.** biology.

biological (ˌbaɪə'lɒdʒɪk°l) *adj.* of or relating to biology. —**bio'logically** *adv.*

biological clock *n.* an inherent timing mechanism that controls the rhythmic repetition of processes in living organisms.

biological control *n.* the control of destructive organisms, esp. insects, by nonchemical means, such as introducing a natural predator of the pest.

biological warfare *n.* the use of living organisms or their toxic products to induce death or incapacity in humans.

biology (baɪ'ɒlədʒɪ) *n.* the study of living organisms. —**bi'ologist** *n.*

biomedicine (ˌbaɪəʊ'medɪsɪn) *n.* the medical and biological study of the effects of unusual environmental stress.

bionic (baɪ'ɒnɪk) *adj.* **1.** of or relating to bionics. **2.** (in science fiction) having physical functions augmented by electronic equipment. [BIO- + (*electro*)*nic*]

bionics (baɪ'ɒnɪks) *n.* (*functioning as sing.*) **1.** the study of biological functions in order to develop electronic equipment that operates similarly. **2.** the replacement of limbs or body parts by artificial electronically powered parts.

biophysics (ˌbaɪəʊ'fɪzɪks) *n.* (*functioning as sing.*) the physics of biological processes and the application of methods used in physics to biology. —**bio'physical** *adj.* —**biophysicist** (ˌbaɪəʊ'fɪzɪsɪst) *n.*

biopic ('baɪəʊˌpɪk) *n. Informal.* a film based on the life of a famous person. [*bio*(*graphical*) + *pic*(*ture*)]

biopsy ('baɪɒpsɪ) *n., pl.* **-sies.** examination of tissue from a living body to determine the cause or extent of a disease. [BIO- + Greek *opsis* sight]

biorhythm ('baɪəʊˌrɪðəm) *n.* a complex recurring pattern of physiological states, believed to affect physical, emotional, and mental states.

bioscope ('baɪəˌskəʊp) *n.* **1.** a kind of early film projector. **2.** *S. African.* a cinema.

biosphere ('baɪəˌsfɪə) *n.* the part of the earth's surface and atmosphere inhabited by living things.

biosynthesis (ˌbaɪəʊ'sɪnθɪsɪs) *n.* the formation of complex compounds by living organisms. —**biosynthetic** (ˌbaɪəʊsɪn'θetɪk) *adj.*

biotin ('baɪətɪn) *n.* a vitamin of the B complex, abundant in egg yolk and liver. [Greek *biotē* life]

bipartisan (ˌbaɪpɑːtɪ'zæn, baɪ'pɑːtɪˌzæn) *adj.* consisting of or supported by two political parties.

bipartite (baɪ'pɑːtaɪt) *adj.* **1.** consisting of or having two parts. **2.** affecting or made by two parties: *a bipartite agreement*.

biped ('baɪped) *n.* **1.** any animal with two feet. ~*adj. also* **bipedal** (baɪ'piːd°l, -'ped°l). **2.** having two feet. [BI- + Latin *pes, pedis* foot]

biplane ('baɪˌpleɪn) *n.* an aeroplane with two sets of wings, one above the other.

bipolar (baɪ'pəʊlə) *adj.* **1.** having two poles. **2.** having two extremes. —ˌbipo'larity *n.*

birch (bɜːtʃ) *n.* **1.** a tree with thin peeling bark and hard close-grained wood. **2. the birch.** a bundle of birch twigs or a birch rod used, esp. formerly, for flogging offenders. ~*vb.* **3.** to flog with a birch. [Old English *bierce*]

bird (bɜːd) *n.* **1.** an egg-laying vertebrate with feathers and wings. **2.** *Informal.* a person: *he's a rare bird*. **3.** *Slang, chiefly Brit.* a girl or young woman. **4. a bird in the hand.** something definite or certain. **5. birds of a feather.** people with the same ideas or interests. **6. kill two birds with one stone.** to accomplish two things with one action. [Old English *bridd*]

birdie ('bɜːdɪ) *n.* **1.** *Informal.* a bird. **2.** *Golf.* a score of one stroke under par for a hole.

birdlime ('bɜːdˌlaɪm) *n.* a sticky substance smeared on twigs to catch small birds.

bird of paradise *n.* a songbird of New Guinea, the male of which has brilliantly coloured plumage.

bird of passage *n.* **1.** a bird that migrates seasonally. **2.** a person who travels about constantly.

bird of prey *n.* a bird, such as a hawk or owl, that hunts other animals for food.

birdseed ('bɜːdˌsiːd) *n.* a mixture of various kinds of seeds for feeding caged birds.

bird's-eye view *n.* **1.** a view seen from above. **2.** a general or overall impression of something.

bird-watcher n. a person who studies wild birds in their natural surroundings.

biretta (bɪ'rɛtə) n. R.C. Church. a stiff square clerical cap. [Italian *berretta*]

Biro ('baɪrəʊ) n., pl. **-ros.** Trademark, Brit. a kind of ballpoint pen.

birth (bɜːθ) n. **1.** the process of bearing young; childbirth. **2.** the act of being born. **3.** the beginning of something; origin. **4.** ancestry: *of high birth.* **5. give birth to. a.** to bear (offspring). **b.** to produce or originate (an idea, plan, etc.). [Old Norse *byrth*]

birth certificate n. an official form stating the time and place of a person's birth.

birth control n. limitation of child-bearing by means of contraception.

birthday ('bɜːθ,deɪ) n. **1.** an anniversary of the day of one's birth. **2.** the day on which a person was born.

birthmark ('bɜːθ,mɑːk) n. a blemish on the skin formed before birth.

birthplace ('bɜːθ,pleɪs) n. the place where someone was born or where something originated.

birth rate n. the ratio of live births to population, usually expressed per 1000 population per year.

birthright ('bɜːθ,raɪt) n. privileges or possessions that a person has or is believed to be entitled to as soon as he is born.

biscuit ('bɪskɪt) n. **1.** Brit. a small flat dry sweet or plain cake of many varieties. **2.** porcelain that has been fired but not glazed. ~adj. **3.** pale brown or yellowish-grey. [Old French (*pain*) *bescuit* twice-cooked (bread)]

bisect (baɪ'sɛkt) vb. **1.** Maths. to divide into two equal parts. **2.** to cut or split into two. [BI- + Latin *secāre* to cut] —**bisection** (baɪ'sɛkʃən) n.

bisexual (baɪ'sɛksjʊəl) adj. **1.** sexually attracted by both men and women. **2.** showing characteristics of both sexes. ~n. **3.** a bisexual person. —**bisexuality** (baɪ,sɛksjʊ'ælɪtɪ) n.

bishop ('bɪʃəp) n. **1.** a clergyman having spiritual and administrative powers over a diocese. **2.** a chesspiece capable of moving diagonally. [Greek *episkopos* overseer]

bishopric ('bɪʃəprɪk) n. the see, diocese, or office of a bishop.

bismuth ('bɪzməθ) n. a brittle pinkish-white metallic element. Some compounds are used in alloys and in medicine. Symbol: Bi [German *Wismut*]

bison ('baɪs'n) n., pl. **-son.** an animal of the cattle family with a massive head, shaggy forequarters, and a humped back, formerly very common in North America and Europe. [of Germanic origin]

bisque[1] (bɪsk) n. a thick rich soup made from shellfish. [French]

bisque[2] (bɪsk) adj. **1.** pink-to-yellowish-tan. ~n. **2.** Ceramics. same as **biscuit** (sense 2). [shortened from *biscuit*]

bistre or U.S. **bister** ('bɪstə) n. a brownish-yellow pigment made by boiling the soot of wood. [French]

bistro ('biːstrəʊ) n., pl. **-tros.** a small restaurant. [French]

bit[1] (bɪt) n. **1.** a small piece, portion, or quantity. **2.** a short time or distance. **3.** a small coin. **4.** same as **bit part. 5.** a bit. rather; somewhat: *a bit dreary.* **6. a bit of.** rather: *a bit of a dope.* **7. bit by bit.** gradually. **8. do one's bit.** to make one's expected contribution. [Old English *bite*]

bit[2] (bɪt) n. **1.** a metal mouthpiece on a bridle for controlling a horse. **2.** a cutting or drilling tool, part, or head in a brace, drill, etc. [Old English *bita*]

bit[3] (bɪt) vb. the past tense of **bite.**

bit[4] (bɪt) n. Maths, computers. **1.** a single digit of binary notation, represented either by 0 or by 1. **2.** the smallest unit of information, indicating the presence or absence of a single feature. [B(INARY + DIG)IT]

bitch (bɪtʃ) n. **1.** a female dog, fox, or wolf. **2.** Slang, offensive. a malicious or spiteful woman. **3.** Informal. a difficult situation or problem. ~vb. **4.** Informal. to complain; grumble. [Old English *bicce*]

bitchy ('bɪtʃɪ) adj. bitchier, bitchiest. Informal. spiteful or malicious. —'bitchiness n.

bite (baɪt) vb. biting, bit, bitten. **1.** to grip, cut off, or tear as with the teeth or jaws. **2.** (of animals, insects, etc.) to injure by puncturing (the skin) with the teeth, fangs, etc. **3.** (of corrosive material) to eat away or into. **4.** to smart or cause to smart; sting. **5.** Angling. (of a fish) to take or attempt to take the bait or lure. **6.** to take firm hold of or act effectively upon: *turn the screw till it bites the wood.* **7.** Slang. to annoy or worry: *what's biting her?* ~n. **8.** the act of biting. **9.** a thing or amount bitten off. **10.** a wound or sting inflicted by biting. **11.** Angling. an attempt by a fish to take the bait or lure. **12.** a snack. **13.** a stinging or smarting sensation. [Old English *bītan*] —'biter n.

biting ('baɪtɪŋ) adj. **1.** piercing; keen: *a biting wind.* **2.** sarcastic; incisive.

bit part n. a very small acting role with few lines to speak.

bitten ('bɪt'n) vb. the past participle of **bite.**

bitter ('bɪtə) adj. **1.** having an unpalatable harsh taste, as the peel of an orange. **2.** showing or caused by hostility or resentment. **3.** difficult to accept: *a bitter blow.* **4.** sarcastic: *bitter words.* **5.** bitingly cold: *a bitter night.* ~n. **6.** Brit. draught beer with a slightly bitter taste. [Old English *biter*] —'bitterly adv. —'bitterness n.

bittern ('bɪtən) n. a large wading marsh bird with a booming call. [Old French *butor*]

bitters ('bɪtəz) pl. n. bitter-tasting spirits flavoured with plant extracts.

bittersweet ('bɪtə,swiːt) n. **1.** same as **woody nightshade.** ~adj. **2.** tasting of or being a mixture of bitterness and sweetness. **3.** pleasant but tinged with sadness.

bitty ('bɪtɪ) adj. -tier, -tiest. lacking unity; disjointed.

bitumen ('bɪtjʊmɪn) n. a sticky or solid

impure mixture of hydrocarbons that occurs naturally in asphalt and tar and is used in road surfacing. [Latin] —**bituminous** (bɪˈtjuːmɪnəs) *adj.*

bituminous coal *n.* a soft black coal that burns with a smoky yellow flame.

bivalent (baɪˈveɪlənt, ˈbɪvə-) *adj. Chem.* same as **divalent**. —**biˈvalency** *n.*

bivalve (ˈbaɪˌvælv) *n.* **1.** a marine mollusc, such as the oyster or mussel, with a shell consisting of two hinged valves, and gills for respiration. ~*adj.* **2.** of these molluscs.

bivouac (ˈbɪvʊˌæk, ˈbɪvwæk) *n.* **1.** a temporary encampment, as used by soldiers, mountaineers, etc. ~*vb.* -**acking**, -**acked**. **2.** to make such an encampment. [French]

biz (bɪz) *n. Informal.* business.

bizarre (bɪˈzɑː) *adj.* odd or unusual, esp. in an interesting or amusing way. [Italian *bizzarro* capricious]

bk **1.** bank. **2.** book.

Bk *Chem.* berkelium.

BL **1.** Bachelor of Law. **2.** Bachelor of Letters. **3.** Barrister-at-Law.

blab (blæb) *vb.* **blabbing**, **blabbed**. **1.** to divulge (secrets, etc.) indiscreetly. **2.** to chatter thoughtlessly; prattle. [Germanic]

blabber (ˈblæbə) *n.* **1.** a person who blabs. ~*vb.* **2.** to talk without thinking; chatter. [Middle English *blabberen*]

black (blæk) *adj.* **1.** of the colour of jet or carbon black. **2.** without light. **3.** without hope; gloomy: *the future looked black*. **4.** dirty or soiled. **5.** angry or resentful: *black looks*. **6.** unpleasant in a cynical or macabre manner: *black comedy*. **7.** (of coffee or tea) without milk or cream. **8.** wicked or harmful: *a black lie*. **9.** *Brit.* (of goods, works, etc.) being subject to boycott by trade unionists. ~*n.* **10.** a black colour. **11.** a dye or pigment producing this colour. **12.** black clothing, worn esp. in mourning. **13.** complete darkness: *the black of the night.* **14.** **in the black.** in credit or without debt. ~*vb.* **15.** same as **blacken**. **16.** to polish (shoes, etc.) with blacking. **17.** *Brit., Austral., & N.Z.* (of trade unionists) to organize a boycott of (specified goods, work, etc.). ~See also **blackout**. [Old English *blæc*] —**ˈblackness** *n.*

Black (blæk) *n.* **1.** a member of a dark-skinned race, esp. a Negro. ~*adj.* **2.** of or relating to a Black or Blacks.

blackamoor (ˈblækəˌmʊə, -ˌmɔː) *n. Archaic.* a Negro or other person with dark skin. [*Black + Moor*]

black-and-blue *adj.* (of the skin) bruised, as from a beating.

black-and-white *n.* **1.** a photograph, film, etc. in black, white, and shades of grey, rather than in colour. **2.** **in black and white. a.** in print or writing. **b.** in extremes: *she tends to see things in black and white.*

black art *n.* **the.** same as **black magic.**

black-backed gull *n.* a large common black-and-white European coastal gull.

blackball (ˈblækˌbɔːl) *n.* **1.** a negative

vote or veto. ~*vb.* **2.** to vote against. **3.** to exclude (someone) from a group, etc. [from *black ball* used formerly to veto]

black bear *n.* **1.** a bear inhabiting forests of North America. **2.** a bear of central and E Asia.

black belt *n. Judo, karate, etc.* **a.** a black belt worn by an instructor or expert. **b.** a person entitled to wear this.

blackberry (ˈblækbərɪ) *n., pl.* -**ries.** a small blackish edible fruit that grows on a woody bush with thorny stems. Also called: **bramble.**

blackbird (ˈblækˌbɜːd) *n.* a common European thrush the male of which has black plumage and a yellow bill.

blackboard (ˈblækˌbɔːd) *n.* a hard black or dark-coloured surface used for writing or drawing on with chalk, esp. in teaching.

black box *n. Informal.* a flight recorder.

blackcap (ˈblækˌkæp) *n.* a brownish-grey warbler, the male of which has a black crown.

blackcock (ˈblækˌkɒk) *n.* the male of the black grouse.

Black Country *n.* **the.** the heavily industrialized West Midlands of England.

blackcurrant (ˌblækˈkʌrənt) *n.* a small blackish edible fruit that grows in bunches on a bush.

blackdamp (ˈblækˌdæmp) *n.* air that is low in oxygen content and high in carbon dioxide as a result of an explosion in a mine.

Black Death *n.* **the.** a form of bubonic plague in Europe and Asia during the 14th century.

black economy *n.* that portion of the income of a nation that remains illegally undeclared.

blacken (ˈblækən) *vb.* **1.** to make or become black or dirty. **2.** to defame; slander.

black eye *n.* bruising round the eye.

black flag *n.* same as **Jolly Roger.**

Black Friar *n.* a Dominican friar.

blackguard (ˈblægɑːd, -gəd) *n.* an unprincipled contemptible person. [orig., a menial]

blackhead (ˈblækˌhed) *n.* **1.** a black-tipped plug of fatty matter clogging a pore of the skin. **2.** a bird with black plumage on the head.

black hole *n. Astron.* a hypothetical region of space resulting from the collapse of a star and surrounded by a gravitational field from which neither matter nor radiation can escape.

black ice *n.* a thin transparent layer of new ice on a road.

blacking (ˈblækɪŋ) *n.* any preparation for giving a black finish to shoes, metals, etc.

blackjack[1] (ˈblækˌdʒæk) *n. Chiefly U.S. & Canad.* a truncheon of leather-covered lead with a flexible shaft. [*black + jack* (implement)]

blackjack[2] (ˈblækˌdʒæk) *n.* pontoon or a similar card game. [*black + jack* (the knave)]

black lead (led) *n.* same as **graphite.**

blackleg ('blæklɛg) n. **1.** Brit. a person who continues to work or does another's job during a strike. ~vb. **-legging, -legged.** **2.** Brit. to refuse to join a strike.

blacklist ('blæk,lɪst) n. **1.** a list of persons or organizations considered untrustworthy, disloyal, etc. ~vb. **2.** to put (someone) on a blacklist.

black magic n. magic used for evil purposes.

blackmail ('blæk,meɪl) n. **1.** the act of attempting to obtain money by threatening to disclose discreditable information. **2.** the exertion of unfair pressure in an attempt to influence someone. ~vb. **3.** to obtain or attempt to obtain money from (a person) by intimidation. **4.** to attempt to influence (a person) by unfair pressure. [black + Old English māl terms] —'**black,mailer** n.

Black Maria (mə'raɪə) n. a police van for transporting prisoners.

black mark n. an indication of disapproval, failure, etc.

black market n. a place or a system for buying or selling goods or currencies illegally, esp. in violation of controls or rationing. —**black marketeer** n.

black mass n. a blasphemous travesty of the Christian Mass, used in black magic.

blackout ('blæk,aʊt) n. **1.** the extinguishing or hiding of all artificial light as a precaution against a night air attack. **2.** a momentary loss of consciousness, vision, or memory. **3.** a temporary electrical power failure. **4.** the suspension of the broadcasting of information: a news blackout. ~vb. **black out.** **5.** to extinguish (lights). **6.** to lose vision, consciousness, or memory temporarily. **7.** to stop (news, a television programme, etc.) from being broadcast.

black pepper n. a hot seasoning made by grinding the dried berries and husks of the pepper plant.

Black Power n. a movement of Black people to obtain equality with Whites.

black pudding n. a black sausage made from pig's blood, suet, etc.

Black Rod n. (in Britain) the chief usher of the House of Lords and of the Order of the Garter.

black sheep n. a person who is regarded as a disgrace or failure by his family or peer group.

Blackshirt ('blæk,ʃɜːt) n. a member of the Italian Fascist party before and during World War II.

blacksmith ('blæk,smɪθ) n. a smith who works iron with a furnace, anvil, hammer, etc.

black spot n. **1.** a place on a road where accidents frequently occur. **2.** an area where a particular situation is exceptionally bad: an unemployment black spot.

black tea n. tea made from fermented tea leaves.

blackthorn ('blæk,θɔːn) n. a thorny shrub with black twigs, white flowers, and small sour plumlike fruits.

black tie n. **1.** a black bow tie worn with a dinner jacket. **2.** (modifier) denoting an occasion when a dinner jacket should be worn.

black velvet n. a mixture of stout and champagne in equal proportions.

Black Watch n. **the.** the Royal Highland Regiment in the British Army.

black widow n. an American spider the female of which is highly venomous and commonly eats its mate.

bladder ('blædə) n. **1.** Anat. a membranous sac, usually containing liquid, esp. the urinary bladder. **2.** a hollow bag made of leather, etc., which becomes round when filled with air or liquid. **3.** a hollow saclike part in certain plants, such as seaweed. [Old English blǣdre] —'**bladdery** adj.

blade (bleɪd) n. **1.** the part of a sharp weapon, tool, etc., that forms the cutting edge. **2.** the thin flattish part of a propeller, oar, etc. **3.** the flattened part of a leaf, sepal, or petal. **4.** the long narrow leaf of a grass or related plant. [Old English blæd]

blaeberry ('bleɪbərɪ) n., pl. **-ries.** Brit. same as **whortleberry.** [dialect blae bluish + berry]

blain (bleɪn) n. a blister, blotch, or sore on the skin. [Old English blegen]

blame (bleɪm) n. **1.** responsibility for something that is wrong. **2.** an expression of condemnation. ~vb. **3.** to consider (someone) responsible for: I blame him for the failure. **4.** (foll. by on) to put responsibility for (something) on (someone): I blame the failure on him. **5.** to find fault with. **6.** be to blame. to be at fault. [Late Latin blasphēmāre to blaspheme] —'**blamable** or '**blameable** adj. —'**blameless** adj.

blameworthy ('bleɪm,wɜːðɪ) adj. deserving censure. —'**blame,worthiness** n.

blanch (blɑːntʃ) vb. **1.** to whiten. **2.** to become pale, as with sickness or fear. **3.** to prepare (meat, vegetables, etc.) by plunging them in boiling water. **4.** to cause (celery, chicory, etc.) to grow white from lack of light. [Old French blanc white]

blancmange (blə'mɒnʒ) n. a jelly-like dessert of milk, stiffened usually with cornflour. [Old French blanc manger white food]

bland (blænd) adj. **1.** dull and uninteresting. **2.** gentle and agreeable; suave. [Latin blandus flattering] —'**blandly** adv.

blandish ('blændɪʃ) vb. to persuade by mild flattery; coax. [Latin blandīrī]

blandishments ('blændɪʃmənts) pl. n. flattery intended to coax or cajole.

blank (blæŋk) adj. **1.** (of a writing surface) not written on. **2.** (of a form, etc.) with spaces left for details to be filled in. **3.** without ornament or break: a blank wall. **4.** not filled in; empty. **5.** showing no interest or expression: a blank look. **6.** devoid of ideas or inspiration: his mind went blank. ~n. **7.** an empty space. **8.** an empty space for writing in. **9.** a printed form containing such empty spaces. **10.** something characterized by incomprehension: my mind went a complete blank. **11.** a mark, often a dash, in place of a word.

12. same as **blank cartridge. 13. draw a blank.** to get no results from something. ~vb. **14.** (foll. by *out*) to cross out, blot, or obscure. [Old French *blanc* white] —**'blankly** *adv.*

blank cartridge *n.* a cartridge containing powder but no bullet.

blank cheque *n.* **1.** a signed cheque on which the amount payable has not been specified. **2.** complete freedom of action.

blanket ('blæŋkɪt) *n.* **1.** a large piece of thick cloth for use as a bed covering. **2.** a concealing cover, as of smoke, leaves, or snow. **3.** (*modifier*) applying to or covering a wide group or variety of people, conditions, situations, etc.: *blanket insurance against loss, injury, and theft.* ~vb. **4.** to cover as with a blanket. **5.** to cover a wide area; give blanket coverage to. [Old French *blancquete*]

blanket stitch *n.* a strong reinforcing stitch for the edges of blankets.

blank verse *n.* unrhymed verse.

blare (blɛə) *vb.* **1.** to sound loudly and harshly. **2.** to proclaim loudly. ~n. **3.** a loud harsh noise. [Middle English *bleren*]

blarney ('blɑːnɪ) *n.* **1.** flattering talk. ~vb. **2.** to cajole with flattery; wheedle. [after the *Blarney* Stone in SW Ireland, said to endow whoever kisses it with skill in flattery]

blasé ('blɑːzeɪ) *adj.* indifferent or bored, esp. through familiarity. [French]

blaspheme (blæs'fiːm) *vb.* **1.** to speak disrespectfully of (God or sacred things). **2.** to utter curses. [Greek *blasphēmos* evil-speaking] —**blas'phemer** *n.*

blasphemy ('blæsfɪmɪ) *n., pl.* **-mies.** behaviour or language that shows disrespect for God or sacred things. —**'blasphemous** *adj.*

blast (blɑːst) *n.* **1.** an explosion, as of dynamite. **2.** the charge used in a single explosion. **3.** a sudden strong gust of wind or air. **4.** a sudden loud sound, as of a trumpet. **5.** a violent verbal outburst, as of criticism. **6. (at) full blast.** at maximum speed, volume, etc. ~interj. **7.** *Slang.* an exclamation of annoyance. ~vb. **8.** to blow up (a rock, tunnel, etc.) with explosives. **9.** to make or cause to make a loud harsh noise. **10.** to criticize severely. [Old English *blǣst*]

blasted ('blɑːstɪd) *adj., adv. Slang.* extreme or extremely: *a blasted idiot.*

blast furnace *n.* a furnace for smelting into which a blast of preheated air is forced.

blastoff ('blɑːst,ɒf) *n.* **1.** the launching of a rocket under its own power. ~vb. **blast off. 2.** to be launched.

blatant ('bleɪt²nt) *adj.* **1.** glaringly conspicuous or obvious: *a blatant lie.* **2.** offensively noticeable; obtrusive. [coined by Edmund Spenser, poet] —**'blatantly** *adv.*

blather ('blæðə) *vb., n.* same as **blether.**

blaze¹ (bleɪz) *n.* **1.** a strong fire or flame. **2.** a very bright light or glare. **3.** an outburst (of passion, patriotism, etc.). ~vb. **4.** to burn fiercely. **5.** to shine brightly. **6.** to become stirred, as with anger or excitement. **7. blaze away.** to shoot continuously. ~See also **blazes.** [Old English *blæse*]

blaze² (bleɪz) *n.* **1.** a mark, usually indicating a path, made on a tree. **2.** a light-coloured marking on the face of an animal. ~vb. **3.** to mark (a tree, path, etc.) with a blaze. **4. blaze a trail.** to explore new territories, areas of knowledge, etc. [prob. from Middle Low German *bles* white marking]

blaze³ (bleɪz) *vb.* **blaze something abroad.** to make something widely known. [Middle Dutch *blāsen*]

blazer ('bleɪzə) *n.* a fairly lightweight jacket, often in the colours of a sports club, school, etc.

blazes ('bleɪzɪz) *pl. n. Slang, euphemistic.* hell.

blazon ('bleɪz²n) *vb.* **1.** to proclaim publicly. **2.** *Heraldry.* to describe or colour (heraldic arms) conventionally. ~n. **3.** *Heraldry.* a coat of arms. [Old French *blason* coat of arms]

bleach (bliːtʃ) *vb.* **1.** to make or become white or colourless, as by exposure to sunlight, by the action of chemical agents, etc. ~n. **2.** a bleaching agent. [Old English *blǣcan*]

bleaching powder *n.* a white powder consisting of chlorinated calcium hydroxide.

bleak (bliːk) *adj.* **1.** exposed and barren. **2.** cold and raw. **3.** offering little hope; dismal: *a bleak future.* [Old English *blāc* pale]

bleary ('blɪərɪ) *adj.* **blearier, bleariest. 1.** with eyes dimmed, as by tears or tiredness. **2.** indistinct or unclear. —**'blearily** *adv.*

bleary-eyed *or* **blear-eyed** *adj.* with eyes blurred, as with old age or after waking.

bleat (bliːt) *vb.* **1.** (of a sheep, goat, or calf) to utter its plaintive cry. **2.** to whine. ~n. **3.** the characteristic cry of sheep, goats, and calves. **4.** a weak complaint or whine. [Old English *blǣtan*]

bleed (bliːd) *vb.* **bleeding, bled** (bled). **1.** to lose or emit blood. **2.** to remove or draw blood from (a person or animal). **3.** (of plants) to exude (sap or resin), esp. from a cut. **4.** *Informal.* to obtain money, etc., from (someone), esp. by extortion. **5.** to draw liquid or gas from (a container or enclosed system). **6. my heart bleeds for you.** I am sorry for you: often used ironically. [Old English *blēdan*]

bleeding ('bliːdɪŋ) *adj., adv. Brit. slang.* extreme or extremely: *a bleeding fool.*

bleep (bliːp) *n.* **1.** a short high-pitched signal made by an electronic apparatus. **2.** same as **bleeper.** ~vb. **3.** to make a bleeping signal. **4.** to call (somebody) by means of a bleeper. [imit.]

bleeper ('bliːpə) *n.* a small portable radio receiver that makes a bleeping signal.

blemish ('blemɪʃ) *n.* **1.** a defect; flaw; stain. ~vb. **2.** to spoil or tarnish. [Old French *blemir* to make pale]

blench (blentʃ) *vb.* to shy away, as in fear; quail. [Old English *blencan* to deceive]

blend (blɛnd) *vb.* **1.** to mix or mingle (components). **2.** to mix (different varieties of tea, whisky, etc.). **3.** to look good together; harmonize. **4.** (esp. of colours) to shade gradually into each other. ~*n.* **5.** a mixture produced by blending. [Old English *blandan*]

blende (blɛnd) *n.* a mineral consisting mainly of zinc sulphide: the chief source of zinc.

blender ('blɛndə) *n.* an electrical kitchen appliance for puréeing vegetables, etc.

blenny ('blɛnɪ) *n., pl.* -nies. a small fish of coastal waters with a tapering scaleless body and long fins. [Greek *blennos* slime]

blesbok *or* **blesbuck** ('blɛs,bʌk) *n., pl.* -boks, -bok *or* -bucks, -buck. an antelope of southern Africa with a reddish-brown coat and lyre-shaped horns. [Afrikaans]

bless (blɛs) *vb.* **blessing, blessed** *or* **blest.** **1.** to make holy by means of a religious rite. **2.** to give honour or glory to (a person or thing) as holy. **3.** to call upon God to protect. **4.** to worship or adore (God). **5.** (*usually passive*) to endow with health, happiness, a talent, beauty, etc.: *blessed with immense energy.* **6. bless me!** an exclamation of surprise. **7. bless you!** said to a person who has just sneezed. [Old English *blēdsian* to sprinkle with sacrificial blood]

blessed ('blɛsɪd, blɛst) *adj.* **1.** made holy. **2.** R.C. Church. (of a person) beatified by the pope. **3.** bringing great happiness or good fortune. **4.** (blɛst). *Euphemistic.* damned: *I'm blessed if I know.*

blessing ('blɛsɪŋ) *n.* **1.** the act of invoking divine protection or aid. **2.** a short prayer before or after a meal. **3.** approval; good wishes. **4.** a happy event.

blest (blɛst) *vb.* a past of **bless.**

blether ('blɛðə) *Scot.* ~*vb.* **1.** to speak foolishly. ~*n.* **2.** foolish talk; nonsense. [Old Norse *blathr*]

blew (bluː) *vb.* the past tense of **blow.**

blight (blaɪt) *n.* **1.** any plant disease characterized by withering and shrivelling without rotting. **2.** a fungus, insect, etc., that causes blight in plants. **3.** a person or thing that spoils or prevents growth. **4.** an ugly urban district. ~*vb.* **5.** to cause to suffer a blight. **6.** to frustrate or disappoint. **7.** to destroy. [origin unknown]

blighter ('blaɪtə) *n. Brit. informal.* a despicable or irritating person or thing.

Blighty ('blaɪtɪ) *n. Brit. slang.* (used esp. by troops serving abroad) **1.** Britain; home. **2.** (*pl.* **Blighties**) (esp. in World War I) a wound that causes the recipient to be sent home to Britain. [Hindi *bilāyatī* foreign land]

blimey ('blaɪmɪ) *interj. Brit. slang.* an exclamation of surprise or annoyance. [short for *gorblimey* God blind me]

blimp¹ (blɪmp) *n.* **1.** a small nonrigid airship. **2.** *Films.* a soundproof cover fixed over a camera during shooting. [origin unknown]

blimp² (blɪmp) *n. Chiefly Brit.* a person who

is stupidly complacent and reactionary. Also called: **Colonel Blimp.** [a cartoon character]

blind (blaɪnd) *adj.* **1.** unable to see. **2.** unable or unwilling to understand: *he is blind to her faults.* **3.** not determined by reason: *blind hatred.* **4.** acting or performed without control or preparation. **5.** done without being able to see, relying on instruments for information. **6.** hidden from sight: *a blind corner.* **7.** closed at one end: *a blind alley.* **8.** completely lacking awareness or consciousness: *a blind stupor.* **9.** having no openings: *a blind wall.* ~*adv.* **10.** without being able to see ahead or using only instruments: *flying blind.* **11.** without adequate information: *to buy a house blind.* **12. blind drunk.** *Informal.* very drunk. ~*vb.* **13.** to deprive of sight permanently or temporarily. **14.** to deprive of good sense, reason, or judgment. **15.** to darken; conceal. **16.** to overwhelm by showing detailed knowledge: *to blind somebody with science.* ~*n.* **17.** a shade for a window, sometimes on a roller. **18.** any obstruction or l.indrance to sight, light, or air. **19.** a person, action, or thing that serves to deceive or conceal the truth. [Old English] —'**blinding** *adj.* —'**blindly** *adv.* —'**blindness** *n.*

blind alley *n.* **1.** an alley open at one end only. **2.** *Informal.* a situation in which no further progress can be made.

blind date *n. Informal.* a date, arranged by a third person, between two people who have not met before.

blindfold ('blaɪnd,fəʊld) *vb.* **1.** to prevent (a person or animal) from seeing by covering the eyes. ~*n.* **2.** a piece of cloth used to cover the eyes. ~*adj., adv.* **3.** having the eyes covered with a cloth. [Old English *blindfellian* to strike blind]

blind man's buff *n.* a game in which a blindfolded person tries to catch and identify the other players. [obs. *buff* a blow]

blind spot *n.* **1.** a small oval-shaped area of the retina in which vision is not experienced. **2.** a place where vision is obscured. **3.** a subject about which a person is ignorant or prejudiced.

blindworm ('blaɪnd,wɜːm) *n.* same as **slowworm.**

blink (blɪŋk) *vb.* **1.** to close and immediately reopen (the eyes or an eye), usually involuntarily. **2.** to shine intermittently or unsteadily. ~*n.* **3.** the act or an instance of blinking. **4.** a glance; glimpse. **5. on the blink.** *Slang.* not working properly. [var. of BLENCH]

blinker ('blɪŋkə) *vb.* **1.** to provide (a horse) with blinkers. **2.** to obscure or be obscured with or as with blinkers. —'**blinkered** *adj.*

blinkers ('blɪŋkəz) *pl. n. Chiefly Brit.* leather sidepieces attached to a horse's bridle to prevent sideways vision.

blinking ('blɪŋkɪŋ) *adj., adv. Informal.* extreme or extremely: *a blinking idiot.*

blip (blɪp) *n.* **1.** a repetitive sound, such as that produced by an electronic device. **2.** the spot of light on a radar screen indicating the position of an object. [imit.]

bliss (blɪs) *n.* **1.** perfect happiness; serene joy. **2.** the joy of heaven. [Old English *blīths*] —**'blissful** *adj.* —**'blissfully** *adv.*

blister ('blɪstə) *n.* **1.** a small bubble on the skin filled with a watery fluid, caused by a burn, mechanical irritation, etc. **2.** a swelling containing air or liquid, as on a painted surface. ~*vb.* **3.** to have or cause to have blisters. **4.** to attack verbally with great scorn. [Old French *blestre*] —**'blistering** *adj.*

blithe (blaɪð) *adj.* **1.** heedless; casual and indifferent. **2.** very happy or cheerful. [Old English] —**'blithely** *adv.*

blithering ('blɪðərɪŋ) *adj. Informal.* stupid; foolish: *you blithering idiot.* [var. of BLETHER]

BLitt Bachelor of Letters. [Latin *Baccalaureus Litterarum*]

blitz (blɪts) *n.* **1.** a violent and sustained attack by enemy aircraft. **2.** any intensive attack or concerted effort. ~*vb.* **3.** to attack suddenly and intensively. [see BLITZKRIEG]

Blitz (blɪts) *n.* **the.** the systematic bombing of Britain in 1940–41 by the German Air Force.

blitzkrieg ('blɪts,kriːg) *n.* a swift intensive military attack designed to defeat the opposition quickly. [German: lightning war]

blizzard ('blɪzəd) *n.* a strong wind accompanied by heavy snowfall. [origin unknown]

bloat (bləʊt) *vb.* **1.** to cause to swell, as with a liquid or air. **2.** to cause to be puffed up, as with conceit. **3.** to cure (fish, esp. herring) by half drying in smoke. [Old Norse *blautr* soaked] —**'bloated** *adj.*

bloater ('bləʊtə) *n.* a herring that has been salted in brine, smoked, and cured.

blob (blɒb) *n.* **1.** a soft mass or drop. **2.** a spot of colour, ink, etc. **3.** an indistinct or shapeless form or object. [imit.]

bloc (blɒk) *n.* a group of people or countries combined by a common interest. [French]

block (blɒk) *n.* **1.** a large solid piece of wood, stone, etc. **2.** such a piece on which particular tasks may be done, as chopping, cutting, etc. **3.** one of a set of wooden or plastic cubes as a child's toy. **4.** *Slang.* a person's head. **5.** a large building of offices, flats, etc. **6.** a group of buildings in a city bounded by intersecting streets on each side. **7.** *N.Z.* an area of bush reserved by licence for a trapper or hunter. **8.** a piece of wood, metal, etc., engraved for printing. **9.** a casing housing one or more freely rotating pulleys. See also **block and tackle.** **10.** an obstruction or hindrance. **11. a.** a quantity considered as a single unit **b.** (*as modifier*): *a block booking.* ~*vb.* **12.** to obstruct or impede by introducing an obstacle: *to block the traffic; to block up a pipe.* **13.** to impede, retard, or prevent (an action, procedure, etc.). **14.** to stamp (a title, design, etc.) on (a book cover, etc.). **15.** *Cricket.* to play (a

ball) defensively. ~See also **block out.** [Dutch *blok*] —**'blockage** *n.*

blockade (blɒ'keɪd) *n.* **1.** *Mil.* the closing off of a port or region by enemy ships or other forces to .prevent the passage of goods. ~*vb.* **2.** to impose a blockade on.

block and tackle *n.* a hoisting device in which a rope or chain is passed around a pair of blocks containing one or more pulleys.

blockbuster ('blɒk,bʌstə) *n. Informal.* **1.** a film, novel, etc., that has been or is expected to be highly successful. **2.** a large bomb used to demolish extensive areas.

blockhead ('blɒk,hed) *n.* a stupid person. —**'block,headed** *adj.*

blockhouse ('blɒk,haʊs) *n.* **1.** a concrete structure for defence or observation. **2.** (formerly) a wooden fortification with openings for defensive fire, observation, etc.

block letter *n.* a plain capital letter. Also called: **block capital.**

block out *vb.* **1.** to plan or describe (something) in a general fashion. **2.** to prevent the entry or consideration of (something).

bloke (bləʊk) *n. Brit. informal.* a man. [Shelta]

blonde *or* (*masc.*) **blond** (blɒnd) *adj.* **1.** (of hair) fair. **2.** (of a person) having fair hair and a light complexion. ~*n.* **3.** a person having light-coloured hair and skin. [Old French] —**'blondeness** *or* **'blondness** *n.*

blood (blʌd) *n.* **1.** a reddish fluid in vertebrates that is pumped by the heart through the arteries and veins. **2.** bloodshed, esp. when resulting in murder. **3.** life itself; lifeblood. **4.** relationship through being of the same family, race, or kind; kinship. **5. flesh and blood. a.** near kindred or kinship, esp. that between a parent and child. **b.** human nature: *it's more than flesh and blood can stand.* **6. in one's blood.** as a natural or inherited characteristic or talent. **7. the blood.** royal or noble descent: *a prince of the blood.* **8.** people viewed as members of a group, esp. as an invigorating force: *new blood.* **9. in cold blood.** showing no passion; ruthlessly. **10. make one's blood boil.** to cause to be angry or indignant. **11. make one's blood run cold.** to fill with horror. ~*vb.* **12.** *Hunting.* to cause (young hounds) to taste the blood of a freshly killed quarry. **13.** to initiate (a person) to war or hunting. [Old English *blōd*]

blood-and-thunder *adj.* relating to a melodramatic adventure story.

blood bank *n.* a place where blood is stored until required for transfusion.

blood bath *n.* a massacre.

blood brother *n.* a man or boy who has sworn to treat another as his brother, often in a ceremony in which their blood is mingled.

blood count *n.* determination of the

number of red and white blood corpuscles in a specific sample of blood.

bloodcurdling ('blʌd,kɜːdlɪŋ) *adj.* terrifying.

blood donor *n.* a person who gives blood to be used for transfusion.

blood group *n.* any one of the various groups into which human blood is classified.

blood heat *n.* the normal temperature of the human body, 98.4°F or 37°C.

bloodhound ('blʌd,haʊnd) *n.* a large hound, formerly used in tracking and police work.

bloodless ('blʌdlɪs) *adj.* 1. without blood. 2. conducted without violence: *a bloodless revolution.* 3. anaemic-looking; pale. 4. lacking vitality; lifeless.

blood-letting *n.* 1. the therapeutic removal of blood. 2. bloodshed, esp. in a feud.

blood money *n.* 1. compensation paid to the relatives of a murdered person. 2. money paid to a hired murderer.

blood orange *n.* a variety of orange the pulp of which is dark red when ripe.

blood poisoning *n.* same as **septicaemia.**

blood pressure *n.* the pressure exerted by the blood on the inner walls of the blood vessels.

blood relation *or* **relative** *n.* a person related to another by birth.

bloodshed ('blʌd,ʃed) *n.* slaughter; killing.

bloodshot ('blʌd,ʃɒt) *adj.* (of an eye) inflamed.

blood sport *n.* any sport involving the killing of an animal, esp. hunting.

bloodstained ('blʌd,steɪnd) *adj.* discoloured with blood.

bloodstock ('blʌd,stɒk) *n.* thoroughbred horses.

bloodstream ('blʌd,striːm) *n.* the flow of blood through the vessels of a living body.

bloodsucker ('blʌd,sʌkə) *n.* 1. an animal that sucks blood, esp. a leech. 2. *Informal.* a person who preys upon another person, esp. by extorting money.

bloodthirsty ('blʌd,θɜːstɪ) *adj.* **-thirstier, -thirstiest.** taking pleasure in bloodshed or violence.

blood vessel *n.* an artery, capillary, or vein.

bloody ('blʌdɪ) *adj.* **bloodier, bloodiest.** 1. covered with blood. 2. marked by much killing and bloodshed: *a bloody war.* 3. cruel or murderous: *a bloody tyrant.* ~*adv., adj.* 4. *Slang.* extreme or extremely: *a bloody fool.* ~*vb.* **bloodying, bloodied.** 5. to stain with blood.

Bloody Mary ('mɛərɪ) *n.* a drink consisting of tomato juice and vodka.

bloody-minded *adj. Brit. informal.* deliberately obstructive and unhelpful.

bloom (bluːm) *n.* 1. a blossom on a flowering plant. 2. the state or period when flowers open. 3. a healthy or flourishing condition; prime. 4. a youthful or healthy glow. 5. a fine whitish coating on the surface of fruits, leaves, etc. ~*vb.* 6. (of flowers) to open. 7. to bear flowers. 8. to flourish or grow. 9. to be in a healthy, glowing condition. [of Germanic origin]

bloomer[1] ('bluːmə) *n. Brit. informal.* a stupid mistake; blunder. [from BLOOMING]

bloomer[2] ('bluːmə) *n.* a medium-sized loaf with diagonal marks on top.

bloomers ('bluːməz) *pl. n.* 1. *Informal.* women's baggy knickers. 2. (formerly) loose trousers gathered at the knee worn by women. [after Mrs A. *Bloomer,* social reformer]

blooming ('bluːmɪŋ) *adv., adj. Brit. informal.* extreme or extremely: *blooming painful.* [euphemistic for *bloody*]

blossom ('blɒsəm) *n.* 1. the flower or flowers of a plant, esp. producing edible fruit. 2. the period of flowering. ~*vb.* 3. (of plants) to flower. 4. to come to a promising stage. [Old English *blōstm*]

blot (blɒt) *n.* 1. a stain or spot, esp. of ink. 2. something that spoils. 3. a stain on one's character. ~*vb.* **blotting, blotted.** 4. to stain or spot. 5. to cause a blemish in or on: *you've blotted your copybook by getting into a fight.* 6. to soak up (excess ink, etc.) by using blotting paper. 7. **blot out.** to darken or hide completely; obscure; obliterate. [Germanic]

blotch (blɒtʃ) *n.* 1. an irregular spot or discoloration. ~*vb.* 2. to become or cause to become marked by such discoloration. [prob. from *botch,* infl. by *blot*] —**'blotchy** *adj.*

blotter ('blɒtə) *n.* a sheet of blotting paper.

blotting paper *n.* a soft absorbent unsized paper, used for soaking up surplus ink.

blotto ('blɒtəʊ) *adj. Slang.* unconscious, esp. through drunkenness. [from *blot* (vb.)]

blouse (blaʊz) *n.* 1. a woman's shirtlike garment. 2. a waist-length belted jacket worn by soldiers. ~*vb.* 3. to hang or make so as to hang in full loose folds. [French]

blouson ('bluːzɒn) *n.* a tight-waisted jacket or top that blouses out. [French]

blow[1] (bləʊ) *vb.* **blowing, blew, blown.** 1. (of a current of air, the wind, etc.) to be or cause to be in motion. 2. to move or be carried by or as if by wind. 3. to expel (cigarette smoke, etc.) through the mouth or nose. 4. to force or cause (air, dust, etc.) to move something into, in, over, etc., by using an instrument or by expelling breath. 5. to breathe hard; pant. 6. to inflate with air or the breath. 7. (of wind, etc.) to make a roaring sound. 8. to cause (a wind instrument, whistle, etc.) to sound by forcing air into it or (of a wind instrument, whistle, etc.) to sound thus. 9. (often foll. by *up, down, in,* etc.) to explode, break, or disintegrate completely. 10. *Electronics.* to burn out (a fuse or valve) because of excessive current or (of a fuse or valve) to burn out. 11. to shape (glass, etc.) by forcing air or gas through the material when molten. 12. *Slang.* to spend (money) freely. 13. *Slang.* to use (an opportunity) ineffectively. **14.** *Slang.* to go suddenly away (from): *it was time to blow town.* **15.** *Slang.* to expose or betray (a secret). **16.** (*past participle* **blowed**). *Informal.* same as **damn. 17. blow hot and cold.** *Informal.* to keep changing one's attitude towards someone or something. **18. blow one's top.** *Informal.* to lose one's temper. ~*n.* **19.** the act or an instance of blowing. **20.** the sound produced by blowing. **21.** a blast of air or wind. ~See also **blow out, blow over,** etc. [Old English *blāwan*]

blow² (bləʊ) *n.* **1.** a powerful or heavy stroke with the fist, a weapon, etc. **2.** a sudden setback. **3. come to blows. a.** to fight. **b.** to result in a fight. **4.** an attacking action: *a blow for freedom.* [prob. Germanic]

blow-by-blow *adj.* explained in great detail: *a blow-by-blow account.*

blow-dry *vb.* **-drying, -dried. 1.** to style (the hair) while drying it with a hand-held hair dryer. ~*n.* **2.** this method of styling hair.

blower ('bləʊə) *n.* **1.** a mechanical device, such as a fan, that blows. **2.** *Informal.* a telephone.

blowfly ('bləʊˌflaɪ) *n., pl.* **-flies.** a fly that lays its eggs in meat.

blowhole ('bləʊˌhəʊl) *n.* **1.** the nostril of a whale. **2.** a hole in ice through which seals, etc., breathe. **3.** a vent for air or gas.

blowlamp ('bləʊˌlæmp) *n.* a small burner that produces a very hot flame, used to remove old paint, melt soft metal, etc.

blown (bləʊn) *vb.* a past participle of **blow.**

blow out *vb.* **1.** to extinguish (a flame, etc.) or (of a flame, etc.) to become extinguished. **2.** (of a tyre) to puncture suddenly. **3.** (of an oil or gas well) to lose oil or gas in an uncontrolled manner. ~*n.* **blowout. 4.** a sudden burst in a tyre. **5.** the uncontrolled escape of oil or gas from a well. **6.** *Slang.* a large filling meal.

blow over *vb.* **1.** to be forgotten. **2.** to cease or be finished: *the storm blew over.*

blowpipe ('bləʊˌpaɪp) *n.* **1.** a long tube from which pellets, poisoned darts, etc., are shot by blowing. **2.** a tube for blowing air into a flame to intensify its heat. **3.** an iron pipe used to blow glass into shape.

blow up *vb.* **1.** to explode or cause to explode. **2.** to inflate with air. **3.** to increase the importance of (something): *they blew the whole affair up.* **4.** *Informal.* to lose one's temper. **5.** *Informal.* to reprimand (someone). **6.** *Informal.* to enlarge (a photograph). **7.** to come into existence with sudden force: *a storm had blown up.* ~*n.* **blow-up. 8.** an explosion. **9.** *Informal.* an enlarged photograph.

blowy ('bləʊɪ) *adj.* **blowier, blowiest.** windy.

blowzy *or* **blowsy** ('blaʊzɪ) *adj.* **blowzier, blowziest** *or* **blowsier, blowsiest.** (of a woman) **1.** slovenly or sluttish. **2.** ruddy in complexion. [dialect *blowze* beggar girl]

blubber ('blʌbə) *vb.* **1.** to sob without restraint. **2.** to utter while sobbing. ~*n.* **3.** the fatty tissue of aquatic mammals

such as the whale. **4.** *Informal.* flabby body fat. [prob. imit.]

bludge (blʌdʒ) *Austral. & N.Z. informal.* ~*vb.* **1.** (foll. by *on*) to scrounge (from). **2.** to evade work. ~*n.* **3.** a very easy task.

bludgeon ('blʌdʒən) *n.* **1.** a stout heavy club, typically thicker at one end. ~*vb.* **2.** to hit as with a bludgeon. **3.** to force; bully; coerce. [origin unknown]

blue (bluː) *n.* **1.** a colour, such as that of a clear unclouded sky or the deep sea. **2.** a dye or pigment of this colour. **3.** blue cloth or clothing: *dressed in blue.* **4.** a sportsman who represents or has represented Oxford or Cambridge University. **5.** *Brit. informal.* a Tory. **6.** *Austral. & N.Z. slang.* an argument or fight. **7.** Also: **bluey.** *Austral. & N.Z. informal.* a court summons. **8.** *Austral. & N.Z. informal.* a mistake; error. **9. out of the blue.** unexpectedly. ~*adj.* **bluer, bluest. 10.** of the colour blue. **11.** (of the flesh) having a purple tinge, as from cold. **12.** depressed or unhappy. **13.** pornographic: *blue movies.* ~*vb.* **blueing** *or* **bluing, blued. 14.** to make, dye, or become blue. **15.** *Slang.* to spend extravagantly or wastefully. ~See also **blues.** [Old French *bleu*] —'**blueness** *n.*

blue baby *n.* a baby born with a bluish tinge to the skin because of lack of oxygen in the blood.

bluebell ('bluːˌbɛl) *n.* a woodland plant with blue bell-shaped flowers.

blueberry ('bluːbərɪ, -brɪ) *n., pl.* **-ries.** a blackish edible berry that grows on a North American shrub.

bluebird ('bluːˌbɜːd) *n.* a North American songbird with a blue plumage.

blue blood *n.* royal or aristocratic descent.

bluebook ('bluːˌbʊk) *n.* **1.** (in Britain) a government publication, usually the report of a commission. **2.** (in Canada) an annual statement of government accounts.

bluebottle ('bluːˌbɒtᵊl) *n.* **1.** a large fly with a blue body; blowfly. **2.** *Austral. & N.Z. informal.* a Portuguese man-of-war.

blue cheese *n.* cheese containing a blue mould, esp. Stilton, Roquefort, or Danish blue.

blue chip *n.* **1.** *Finance.* a stock considered reliable. **2.** (*modifier*) denoting something considered to be a valuable asset.

blue-collar *adj.* of or designating manual industrial workers.

blue-eyed boy *n. Informal, chiefly Brit.* a favourite.

blue funk *n. Slang.* a state of great terror.

blue pencil *n.* **1.** deletion or alteration of the contents of a book or other work. ~*vb.* **blue-pencil, -cilling, -cilled** *or U.S.* **-ciling, -ciled. 2.** to alter or delete parts of (a book, film, etc.).

blue peter *n.* a signal flag of blue with a white square at the centre, displayed by a vessel about to leave port.

blueprint ('bluːˌprɪnt) *n.* **1.** an original description of a plan or idea that explains how something is expected to work. **2.** a photographic print of plans, technical drawings, etc., consisting of white lines on a blue background.

blue ribbon *n.* **1.** (in Britain) a badge of blue silk worn by members of the Order of the Garter. **2.** a badge awarded as the first prize in a competition.

blues (bluːz) *pl. n.* (*sometimes functioning as sing.*) **the. 1.** a feeling of depression or deep unhappiness. **2.** a type of folk song originating among Black Americans.

bluestocking ('bluːˌstɒkɪŋ) *n. Usually disparaging.* a scholarly or intellectual woman. [from the blue worsted stockings worn by members of an 18th-cent. literary society]

bluetit ('bluːˌtɪt) *n.* a European tit with a blue crown, wings, and tail and yellow underparts.

blue whale *n.* a very large bluish-grey whalebone whale.

bluff[1] (blʌf) *vb.* **1.** to pretend to be confident about an uncertain issue in order to influence (someone). ~*n.* **2.** deliberate deception to create the impression of a strong position. **3. call someone's bluff.** to challenge someone to give proof of his claims. [Dutch *bluffen* to boast]

bluff[2] (blʌf) *n.* **1.** a steep promontory, bank, or cliff. **2.** *Canad.* a clump of trees on the prairie; copse. ~*adj.* **3.** good-naturedly frank and hearty. [prob. from Middle Dutch *blaf* broad]

bluish *or* **blueish** ('bluːɪʃ) *adj.* somewhat blue.

blunder ('blʌndə) *n.* **1.** a stupid or clumsy mistake. ~*vb.* **2.** to make stupid or clumsy mistakes. **3.** to act clumsily; stumble. [Scandinavian] —'**blundering** *n., adj.*

blunderbuss ('blʌndəˌbʌs) *n.* an obsolete short musket with large bore and flared muzzle. [Dutch *donderbus* thunder gun]

blunt (blʌnt) *adj.* **1.** (esp. of a knife) lacking sharpness. **2.** not having a sharp edge or point: *a blunt instrument.* **3.** (of people, manner of speaking, etc.) straightforward and uncomplicated. ~*vb.* **4.** to make less sharp. **5.** to diminish the sensitivity or perception of. [Scandinavian] —'**bluntly** *adv.*

blur (blɜː) *vb.* **blurring, blurred. 1.** to make or become vague or less distinct. **2.** to smear or smudge. **3.** to make (the judgment, memory, or perception) less clear; dim. ~*n.* **4.** something vague, hazy, or indistinct. **5.** a smear or smudge. [perhaps var. of *blear*] —**blurred** *adj.* —'**blurry** *adj.*

blurb (blɜːb) *n.* a promotional description, as on the jackets of books. [coined by G. Burgess, humorist & illustrator]

blurt (blɜːt) *vb.* (foll. by *out*) to utter suddenly and involuntarily. [prob. imit.]

blush (blʌʃ) *vb.* **1.** to become suddenly red in the face, esp. from embarrassment or shame. ~*n.* **2.** a sudden reddening of the face, esp. from embarrassment or shame. **3.** a rosy glow. [Old English *blȳscan*]

blusher ('blʌʃə) *n.* a cosmetic applied to the cheeks to give a rosy colour.

bluster ('blʌstə) *vb.* **1.** to speak or say

loudly or in a bullying way. **2.** (of the wind) to be gusty. ~*n.* **3.** empty threats or protests. [prob. from Middle Low German *blüsteren* to blow violently] —'**blustery** *adj.*

BM 1. Bachelor of Medicine. **2.** British Museum.

BMA British Medical Association.

B-movie *n.* a film originally made as a supporting film, now considered a genre in its own right.

BMus Bachelor of Music.

BMX *n.* **1.** bicycle motocross: stunt riding over an obstacle course on a bicycle. **2.** a bicycle designed for bicycle motocross.

BO 1. *Informal.* body odour. **2.** box office.

boa ('bəʊə) *n.* **1.** a large nonvenomous snake of Central and South America that kills its prey by constriction. **2.** a woman's long thin scarf, usually of feathers or fur. [Latin]

boa constrictor *n.* a very large snake of tropical America and the West Indies that kills its prey by constriction.

boar (bɔː) *n.* **1.** an uncastrated male pig. **2.** a wild boar. [Old English *bār*]

board (bɔːd) *n.* **1.** a long wide flat piece of sawn timber. **2.** a smaller flat piece of rigid material for a specific purpose: *ironing board.* **3.** a person's meals, provided regularly for money. **4. a.** a group of people who officially administer a company, trust, etc. **b.** any other official group, as of examiners or interviewers. **5.** stiff cardboard or similar material, used for the outside covers of a book. **6.** a flat thin rectangular sheet of composite material, such as chipboard. **7.** *Naut.* the side of a ship. **8.** a portable surface for indoor games such as chess or backgammon. **9. go by the board.** *Informal.* to be in disuse, neglected, or lost. **10. on board.** on or in a ship, aeroplane, etc. **11. the boards.** the stage. ~*vb.* **12.** to go aboard (a train or other vehicle). **13.** to attack (a ship) by forcing one's way aboard. **14.** (foll. by *up, in,* etc.) to cover with boards. **15.** to receive meals and lodging in return for money. **16. board out.** to arrange for (someone, esp. a child) to receive food and lodging away from home. **17.** (in ice hockey and box lacrosse) to bodycheck an opponent against the boards. [Old English *bord*]

boarder ('bɔːdə) *n.* a pupil who lives at school during term time.

boarding ('bɔːdɪŋ) *n.* **1.** a structure of boards. **2.** timber boards collectively. **3.** the act of embarking on an aircraft, train, ship, etc. **4.** (in ice hockey and box lacrosse) an act of bodychecking an opponent against the boards.

boarding house *n.* a private house in which accommodation and meals are provided for paying guests.

boarding school *n.* a school providing living accommodation for pupils.

boardroom ('bɔːdˌruːm, -ˌrʊm) *n.* a room where the board of directors of a company meets.

boards (bɔːdz) *pl. n.* a wooden wall forming the enclosure in which ice hockey or box lacrosse is played.

boast ('bəʊst) vb. **1.** to speak in excessively proud terms of one's possessions, superior qualities, etc. **2.** to possess (something to be proud of): *the city boasts a fine cathedral.* ∼n. **3.** a bragging statement. **4.** something that is bragged about. [origin unknown]

boastful ('bəʊstful) adj. tending to boast.

boat (bəʊt) n. **1.** a small vessel propelled by oars, paddle, sails, or motor. **2.** *Informal.* a ship. **3.** see **gravy boat, sauce boat. 4. in the same boat.** sharing the same problems. **5. miss the boat.** to lose an opportunity. **6. rock the boat.** *Informal.* to cause a disturbance in the existing situation. ∼vb. **7.** to travel or go in a boat, esp. as recreation. [Old English *bāt*]

boater ('bəʊtə) n. a stiff straw hat with a straight brim and flat crown.

boathouse ('bəʊt,haʊs) n. a shelter by the edge of a river, lake, etc., for housing boats.

boating ('bəʊtɪŋ) n. rowing, sailing, or cruising in boats as a form of recreation.

boatman ('bəʊtmən) n., pl. **-men.** a man who works on, hires out, or repairs boats.

boatswain, bo's'n, or **bosun** ('bəʊs*ə*n) n. an officer who is responsible for the maintenance of a ship and its equipment.

boat train n. a train scheduled to take passengers to or from a particular ship.

bob[1] (bɒb) vb. **bobbing, bobbed. 1.** to move or cause to move up and down repeatedly, as while floating in water. **2.** to move or cause to move with a short abrupt movement, as of the head. **3. bob up.** to appear or emerge suddenly. ∼n. **4.** a short abrupt movement, as of the head. [origin unknown]

bob[2] (bɒb) n. **1.** a hairstyle in which the hair is cut short evenly all round the head. **2.** a dangling weight on a pendulum or plumb line. ∼vb. **bobbing, bobbed. 3.** to cut (the hair) in a bob. [Middle English *bobbe* bunch of flowers]

bob[3] (bɒb) n., pl. **bob.** *Brit. informal.* (formerly) a shilling. [origin unknown]

bobbejaan ('bɒbə,jɑːn) n. *S. African.* a baboon. [Afrikaans]

bobbejaan spanner n. *S. African.* a monkey wrench.

bobbin ('bɒbɪn) n. a reel on which thread or yarn is wound. [Old French *bobine*]

bobble ('bɒb*ə*l) n. a tufted ball, usually for ornament, as on a knitted hat. [from BOB[1]]

bobby ('bɒbɪ) n., pl. **-bies.** *Informal.* a British policeman. [after Robert Peel, who set up the Metropolitan Police Force]

bobby calf n. an unweaned calf culled for slaughter.

bobby pin n. *U.S., Canad., Austral., & N.Z.* a metal hairpin.

bobsleigh ('bɒb,sleɪ) n. **1.** a sledge for racing down a steeply banked ice-covered run. ∼vb. **2.** to ride on a bobsleigh.

bobtail ('bɒb,teɪl) n. **1.** a docked tail. **2.** an animal with such a tail. ∼adj. also **bobtailed. 3.** having the tail cut short.

Boche (bɒʃ) n. *Offensive slang.* a German, esp. a German soldier. [French]

bod (bɒd) n. *Informal.* a fellow; chap: *he's a queer bod.* [short for *body*]

bode[1] (bəʊd) vb. to be an omen of (good or ill, esp. ill); portend. [Old English *bodian*]

bode[2] (bəʊd) vb. a past tense of **bide.**

bodega (bəʊ'diːgə) n. a shop in a Spanish-speaking country that sells wine. [Spanish]

bodge (bɒdʒ) vb. *Informal.* to make a mess of; botch.

bodice ('bɒdɪs) n. **1.** the upper part of a woman's dress, from the shoulder to the waist. **2.** a tight-fitting corset worn laced over a blouse, or (formerly) as a woman's undergarment. [orig. Scot. *bodies,* pl. of *body*]

bodily ('bɒdɪlɪ) adj. **1.** relating to the human body. ∼adv. **2.** by taking hold of the body: *he threw him bodily from the platform.* **3.** in person; in the flesh.

bodkin ('bɒdkɪn) n. a blunt large-eyed needle. [origin unknown]

body ('bɒdɪ) n., pl. **bodies. 1.** the entire physical structure of an animal or human. **2.** the trunk or torso. **3.** a corpse. **4.** the flesh as opposed to the spirit. **5.** the main part of anything: *the body of a vehicle.* **6.** a separate mass of water or land. **7.** a group regarded as a single entity: *a local voluntary body.* **8.** the characteristic full quality of certain wines. **9.** a person. **10. keep body and soul together.** to manage to survive. [Old English *bodig*]

body building n. regular exercising designed to enlarge the muscles.

bodycheck ('bɒdɪ,tʃɛk) *Ice hockey, etc.* ∼n. **1.** obstruction of another player. ∼vb. **2.** to deliver a bodycheck to (an opponent).

bodyguard ('bɒdɪ,gɑːd) n. a man or group of men who escort and protect someone.

body politic n. **the.** the people of a nation or the nation itself considered as a political entity.

body popping n. a dance of the 1980s characterized by schematic rhythmic movements. —**body popper** n.

body shop n. a repair yard for vehicle bodywork.

body snatcher n. (formerly) a person who robbed graves and sold the corpses for dissection.

body stocking n. **1.** a one-piece undergarment for women, covering the torso. **2.** a tightly-fitting garment covering the whole of the body, worn esp. for dancing or exercising.

body warmer n. a sleeveless quilted jerkin, worn as an outer garment.

bodywork ('bɒdɪ,wɜːk) n. the external shell of a motor vehicle.

Boer (bʊə) n. a descendant of any of the Dutch or Huguenot colonists who settled in South Africa. [Dutch]

boerbul ('bʊəbəl) n. *S. African.* a crossbred mastiff, often used as a watchdog. [Afrikaans]

boer goat n. *S. African.* a hardy native goat. [Afrikaans]

boerperd ('buə‚pɜːt) n. a rugged S African horse, often palomino. [Afrikaans]

boffin ('bɒfɪn) n. Brit. informal. a scientist. [origin unknown]

bog (bɒg) n. **1.** a wet spongy area of land. **2.** Slang. a toilet. [Gaelic bogach swamp] —**'boggy** adj. —**'bogginess** n.

bog down vb. **bogging, bogged.** to impede physically or mentally.

bogey or **bogy** ('bəʊgɪ) n. **1.** an evil or mischievous spirit. **2.** something that worries or annoys. **3.** Golf. **a.** a standard score for a hole or course that a good player should make. **b.** U.S. a score of one stroke over par on a hole. **4.** Slang. a piece of dried mucus from the nose. [prob. obs. bug an evil spirit]

bogeyman ('bəʊgɪ‚mæn) n., pl. **-men.** a person, real or imaginary, used as a threat, esp. to children.

boggle ('bɒgʲl) vb. **1.** to be surprised, confused, or alarmed: the mind boggles. **2.** to hesitate or be evasive when confronted with a problem. [prob. Scot.]

bogie or **bogy** ('bəʊgɪ) n. an assembly of wheels forming a pivoted support at either end of a railway coach. [origin unknown]

bog oak n. oak found preserved in peat bogs.

bogus ('bəʊgəs) adj. not genuine. [origin unknown]

bogy ('bəʊgɪ) n., pl. **-gies.** same as **bogey** or **bogie.**

Bohemian (bəʊ'hiːmɪən) n. **1.** a person from Bohemia; Czech. **2.** a person, esp. an artist or writer, who lives an unconventional life. ~adj. **3.** of or relating to Bohemia or its people. **4.** unconventional in appearance, behaviour, etc. —**Bo'hemian‚ism** n.

boil[1] (bɔɪl) vb. **1.** to change or cause to change from a liquid to a vapour so rapidly that bubbles of vapour are formed in the liquid. **2.** to reach or cause to reach boiling point. **3.** to cook or be cooked by the process of boiling. **4.** to bubble and be agitated like something boiling; seethe: the ocean was boiling. **5.** to be extremely angry. ~n. **6.** the state or action of boiling. ~See also **boil away, boil down, boil over.** [Latin bulla a bubble]

boil[2] (bɔɪl) n. a red painful swelling with a hard pus-filled core caused by infection of the skin. [Old English bȳle]

boil away vb. to cause (liquid) to evaporate completely by boiling or (of liquid) to evaporate completely.

boil down vb. **1.** to reduce or be reduced in quantity by boiling. **2. boil down to.** to be the essential element in.

boiler ('bɔɪlə) n. **1.** a closed vessel in which water is heated to provide heat. **2.** a domestic device to provide hot water, esp. for central heating. **3.** a large tub for boiling laundry.

boilermaker ('bɔɪlə‚meɪkə) n. a person who works with metal in heavy industry.

boiler suit n. Brit. a one-piece overall.

boiling point n. **1.** the temperature at which a liquid boils. **2.** Informal. the

condition of being angered or highly excited.

boil over vb. **1.** to overflow or cause to overflow while boiling. **2.** to burst out in anger or excitement.

boisterous ('bɔɪstərəs, -strəs) adj. **1.** noisy and lively; unruly. **2.** (of the sea, etc.) turbulent or stormy. [Middle English boistuous]

bold (bəʊld) adj. **1.** courageous, confident, and fearless. **2.** immodest or impudent: she gave him a bold look. **3.** standing out distinctly; conspicuous: a figure carved in bold relief. [Old English beald] —**'boldly** adv. —**'boldness** n.

bole (bəʊl) n. the trunk of a tree. [Old Norse bolr]

bolero (bə'lɛərəʊ) n., pl. **-ros. 1.** a Spanish dance, usually in triple time. **2.** music for this dance. **3.** (also 'bɒlərəʊ). a short open bodice-like jacket not reaching the waist. [Spanish]

boll (bəʊl) n. the fruit of such plants as flax and cotton, consisting of a rounded capsule containing the seeds. [Dutch bolle]

bollard ('bɒlɑːd, 'bɒləd) n. **1.** a strong wooden or metal post on a wharf, quay, etc., used for securing mooring lines. **2.** Brit. a small post marking a kerb or traffic island or barring cars from entering. [perhaps from bole]

bollocks ('bɒləks) or **ballocks** Taboo slang. ~pl. n. **1.** the testicles. ~interj. **2.** an exclamation of annoyance, disbelief, etc. [Old English beallucas]

Bolshevik ('bɒlʃɪvɪk) n. **1.** (formerly) a Russian Communist. **2.** any Communist. **3.** Informal, offensive. any political radical, esp. a revolutionary. [Russian Bol'shevik majority] —**'Bolshe‚vism** n. —**'Bolshevist** adj., n.

bolshie or **bolshy** ('bɒlʃɪ) Brit. informal. ~adj. **1.** difficult to manage; rebellious. **2.** politically radical or left-wing. ~n., pl. **-shies. 3.** any political radical. [from BOLSHEVIK]

bolster ('bəʊlstə) vb. **1.** to support or strengthen: to bolster morale. ~n. **2.** a long narrow pillow. **3.** any pad or support. [Old English]

bolt[1] (bəʊlt) n. **1.** a bar that can be slid into a socket to lock a door, gate, etc. **2.** a metal rod or pin that has a head and a screw thread to take a nut. **3.** a flash (of lightning). **4. a bolt from the blue.** a sudden, unexpected, and usually unwelcome event. **5.** a sudden movement, esp. in order to escape. **6.** an arrow, esp. for a crossbow. **7. shoot one's bolt.** to exhaust one's efforts. ~vb. **8.** to secure or lock with or as with a bolt. **9.** to eat hurriedly: don't bolt your food. **10.** to run away suddenly. **11.** (of a horse) to run away without control. **12.** (of cultivated plants) to produce flowers and seeds prematurely. ~adv. **13. bolt upright.** stiff and rigid. [Old English]

bolt[2] or **boult** (bəʊlt) vb. **1.** to pass (flour, a powder, etc.) through a sieve. **2.** to examine and separate. [Old French bulter]

bolt hole n. a place of escape from danger.

bomb (bɒm) n. **1.** a hollow projectile containing explosive, incendiary, or other destructive substance. **2.** an object in which an explosive device has been planted: *a car bomb*. **3.** *Brit. slang*. a large sum of money: *it cost a bomb*. **4.** *U.S. & Canad. slang*. a disastrous failure: *the new play was a total bomb*. **5. like a bomb.** *Brit. & N.Z. informal*. with great speed or success. **6. the bomb.** a hydrogen or an atom bomb considered as the ultimate destructive weapon. ~vb. **7.** to attack with or as if with a bomb or bombs; drop bombs (on). **8.** (foll. by *along*) *Informal*. to move or drive very quickly. **9.** *U.S. & Canad. slang*. to fail disastrously. [Greek *bombos* booming noise] —'**bombing** n.

bombard (bɒm'bɑːd) vb. **1.** to attack with concentrated artillery fire or bombs. **2.** to attack persistently. **3.** to attack verbally, esp. with questions. **4.** *Physics*. to direct high-energy particles or photons against (atoms, nuclei, etc.). [Old French *bombarde* stone-throwing cannon] —**bom'bardment** n.

bombardier (ˌbɒmbə'dɪə) n. **1.** *Brit*. a noncommissioned rank in the Royal Artillery. **2.** *U.S*. the member of a bomber aircrew who releases the bombs. **3.** *Canad. trademark*. a snow tractor, usually having caterpillar tracks at the rear and skis at the front.

bombast ('bɒmbæst) n. pompous and grandiloquent language. [Medieval Latin *bombāx* cotton] —**bom'bastic** adj.

Bombay duck (bɒm'beɪ) n. a fish that is eaten dried with curry dishes as a savoury. [through association with *Bombay*, port in India]

bombazine (ˌbɒmbə'ziːn, 'bɒmbəˌziːn) n. a twilled fabric, esp. one of silk and worsted. [Latin *bombyx* silk]

bomber ('bɒmə) n. **1.** a military aircraft designed to carry out bombing missions. **2.** a person who plants bombs.

bombshell ('bɒmˌʃɛl) n. a shocking or unwelcome surprise.

bona fide ('bəʊnə 'faɪdɪ) adj. **1.** genuine: *a bona fide manuscript*. **2.** undertaken in good faith: *a bona fide agreement*. [Latin]

bonanza (bə'nænzə) n. **1.** a source, usually sudden and unexpected, of luck or wealth. **2.** *U.S. & Canad*. a mine or vein rich in ore. [Spanish: calm sea, hence, good luck]

bonbon ('bɒnbɒn) n. a sweet. [French]

bond (bɒnd) n. **1.** something that binds, fastens, or holds together, such as a chain or rope. **2.** something that brings or holds people together; tie: *a bond of friendship*. **3.** (pl.) something that restrains or imprisons. **4.** a written or spoken agreement, esp. a promise. **5.** *Finance*. a certificate of debt issued in order to raise funds. **6.** *Law*. a written acknowledgment of an obligation to pay a sum or to perform a contract. **7.** *Chem*. a means by which atoms are combined in a molecule. **8. in bond.** *Commerce*. securely stored until duty is paid.

~vb. **9.** to hold or be held together, as by a rope or an adhesive; bind. **10.** to put or hold (goods) in bond. [Old Norse *band*]

bondage ('bɒndɪdʒ) n. **1.** slavery or serfdom; servitude. **2.** subjection to some influence or duty. **3.** a sexual practice in which one partner is tied or chained up.

bonded ('bɒndɪd) adj. **1.** *Finance*. consisting of, secured by, or operating under a bond or bonds. **2.** *Commerce*. in bond.

bond paper n. superior quality writing paper.

bondservant ('bɒndˌsɜːvənt) n. a serf or slave.

bone (bəʊn) n. **1.** any of the various structures that make up the skeleton in most vertebrates. **2.** the porous rigid tissue of which these parts are made. **3.** something consisting of bone or a bonelike substance. **4.** (pl.) the human skeleton. **5.** a thin strip of plastic, etc., used to stiffen corsets and brassieres. **6. have a bone to pick.** to have grounds for a quarrel. **7. make no bones about. a.** to be direct and candid about. **b.** to have no scruples about. **8. near** *or* **close to the bone.** risqué or indecent. **9. the bare bones.** the essentials. ~vb. **10.** to remove the bones from (meat for cooking, etc.). **11.** to stiffen (a corset, etc.) by inserting bones. ~See also **bone up on.** [Old English *bān*] —'**boneless** adj.

bone china n. porcelain containing powdered bone.

bone-dry adj. *Informal*. completely dry.

bone-idle adj. very idle; extremely lazy.

bone meal n. dried and ground animal bones, used as a fertilizer or in stock feeds.

boneshaker ('bəʊnˌʃeɪkə) n. *Slang*. a decrepit or rickety vehicle.

bone up on vb. *Informal*. to study intensively.

bonfire ('bɒnˌfaɪə) n. a large outdoor fire. [Middle English *bone-fire*, from the use of bones as fuel]

bongo ('bɒŋgəʊ) n., pl. **-gos** *or* **-goes**. a small bucket-shaped drum, usually one of a pair, played by beating with the fingers. [American Spanish]

bonhomie ('bɒnəmiː) n. exuberant friendliness. [French]

bonk (bɒŋk) vb. *Informal*. **1.** to have sexual intercourse. **2.** to hit. [origin unknown] —'**bonking** n.

bonkers ('bɒŋkəz) adj. *Slang, chiefly Brit*. mad; crazy. [origin unknown]

bon mot (ˌbɒn 'məʊ) n., pl. **bons mots** (ˌbɒn 'məʊ). a clever and fitting remark. [French]

bonnet ('bɒnɪt) n. **1.** *Brit., Austral., N.Z., & S. African*. the hinged metal part of a motor vehicle body that provides access to the engine. **2.** any of various hats worn, esp. formerly, by women and babies and tied with ribbons under the chin. **3.** (in Scotland) a soft cloth cap. [Old French *bonet*]

bonny ('bɒnɪ) adj. **-nier, -niest. 1.** *Scot. & N English dialect*. beautiful: *a bonny lass*. **2.** good or fine. [Latin *bonus*]

bonsai (ˈbɒnsaɪ) n., pl. **-sai.** an ornamental tree or shrub grown in a small shallow pot in order to stunt its growth. [Japanese *bon* bowl + *sai* to plant]

bontebok (ˈbɒntɪˌbʌk) n., pl. **-boks** or **-bok.** an antelope of southern Africa having a deep reddish-brown coat with a white blaze, tail, and rump patch.

bonus (ˈbəʊnəs) n. something given, paid, or received above what is due or expected. [Latin *bonus* good]

bon voyage (ˌbɒn vɔɪˈɑːʒ) interj. a phrase used to wish a traveller a pleasant journey. [French]

bony (ˈbəʊnɪ) adj. **bonier, boniest. 1.** resembling or consisting of bone. **2.** having many bones. **3.** thin or emaciated.

bonze (bɒnz) n. a Chinese or Japanese Buddhist priest or monk. [Japanese *bonsō*]

boo (buː) interj. **1.** an exclamation uttered to startle someone. **2.** a shout uttered to express dissatisfaction or contempt. ~vb. **booing, booed. 3.** to shout ''boo'' at (someone or something) as an expression of disapproval.

boob (buːb) Slang. ~n. **1.** Brit. an embarrassing mistake; blunder. **2.** a female breast. ~vb. **3.** Brit. to make a blunder. [from *booby*]

booby (ˈbuːbɪ) n., pl. **-bies. 1.** an ignorant or foolish person. **2.** a tropical marine bird related to the gannet. [Latin *balbus* stammering]

booby prize n. a mock prize given to the person with the lowest score in a competition.

booby trap n. **1.** a hidden explosive device primed so as to be set off by an unsuspecting victim. **2.** a trap for an unsuspecting person, esp. one intended as a practical joke.

boodle (ˈbuːd'l) n. Slang. money or valuables, esp. when stolen, counterfeit, or used as a bribe. [Dutch *boedel* possessions]

boogie (ˈbuːgɪ) vb. **-gieing, -gied.** Slang. to dance to pop music. [origin unknown]

boogie-woogie (ˈbʊgɪˈwʊgɪ, ˈbuːgɪˈwuːgɪ) n. a style of piano jazz using a dotted bass pattern and blues harmonies. [perhaps imit.]

boohai (buːˈhaɪ) n. **up the boohai.** N.Z. informal. thoroughly lost. [from the remote township of *Puhoi*]

boohoo (ˌbuːˈhuː) vb. **-hooing, -hooed. 1.** to sob or pretend to sob noisily. ~n., pl. **-hoos. 2.** distressed or pretended sobbing.

book (bʊk) n. **1.** a number of printed or written pages bound together along one edge and usually protected by covers. **2.** a written work or composition, such as a novel. **3.** a number of sheets of paper bound together: *an account book*. **4.** (pl.) a record of the transactions of a business or society. **5.** the libretto of an opera, musical, etc. **6.** a major division of a written composition, as of a long novel or of the Bible. **7.** a number of tickets, stamps, etc., fastened together along one edge. **8.** a record of betting transactions. **9. a closed book.** a subject that is beyond comprehension: *chemistry is a closed book to him.* **10. bring to book.** to reprimand or require (someone) to give an explanation of his conduct. **11. by the book.** according to the rules. **12. in someone's good** (or **bad**) **books.** regarded by someone with favour (or disfavour). **13. throw the book at someone. a.** to charge someone with every relevant offence. **b.** to inflict the most severe punishment on someone. ~vb. **14.** to reserve (a place, passage, etc.) or engage the services of (a performer, driver, etc.) in advance. **15.** (of a police officer) to take the name and address of (a person) for an alleged offence with a view to prosecution. **16.** (of a football referee) to take the name of (a player) who has broken the rules seriously. ~See also **book in.** [Old English *bōc*]

bookcase (ˈbʊkˌkeɪs) n. a piece of furniture containing shelves for books.

book club n. a club that sells books at low prices to members, usually by mail order.

book end n. one of a pair of supports for holding a row of books upright.

bookie (ˈbʊkɪ) n. Informal. short for **bookmaker.**

book in vb. Chiefly Brit. to register one's arrival at a hotel.

booking (ˈbʊkɪŋ) n. **1.** Chiefly Brit. a reservation, as of a table or seat. **2.** Theatre. an engagement of a performer.

bookish (ˈbʊkɪʃ) adj. **1.** fond of reading; studious. **2.** forming opinions through reading rather than experience.

book-keeping n. the skill or occupation of systematically recording business transactions. —ˈbook-ˌkeeper n.

booklet (ˈbʊklɪt) n. a thin book with paper covers.

bookmaker (ˈbʊkˌmeɪkə) n. a person who as an occupation accepts bets, esp. on horseraces. —ˈbookˌmaking n.

bookmark (ˈbʊkˌmɑːk) n. a strip of some material put between the pages of a book to mark a place.

bookplate (ˈbʊkˌpleɪt) n. a label bearing the owner's name and a design, pasted into a book.

bookstall (ˈbʊkˌstɔːl) n. a stall or stand where periodicals, newspapers, or books are sold.

bookworm (ˈbʊkˌwɜːm) n. **1.** a person devoted to reading. **2.** a small insect that feeds on the binding paste of books.

Boolean algebra (ˈbuːlɪən) n. a system of symbolic logic devised to codify nonmathematical logical operations: used in computers. [after George *Boole*, mathematician]

boom[1] (buːm) vb. **1.** to make a deep prolonged resonant sound. **2.** to prosper vigorously and rapidly: *business boomed.* ~n. **3.** a deep prolonged resonant sound. **4.** a period of high economic growth. [imit.]

boom[2] (buːm) n. **1.** Naut. a spar to which the foot of a sail is fastened to control its position. **2.** a pole carrying an overhead microphone and projected over a film or television set. **3.** a barrier across a water-way. [Dutch *boom* tree]

boomerang ('buːməˌræŋ) *n.* **1.** a curved wooden missile of Australian Aborigines which can be made to return to the thrower. **2.** an action or statement that recoils on its originator. ~*vb.* **3.** (of a plan) to recoil unexpectedly, harming its originator. [Aboriginal]

boomslang ('buːmˌslæŋ) *n.* a large greenish venomous tree-living snake of southern Africa. [Afrikaans]

boon[1] (buːn) *n.* something extremely useful, helpful, or beneficial. [Old Norse *bōn*]

boon[2] (buːn) *adj.* close or intimate: *boon companion*. [Latin *bonus* good]

boor (bʊə) *n.* an ill-mannered, clumsy, or insensitive person. [Old English *gebūr* dweller, farmer] —**'boorish** *adj.*

boost (buːst) *n.* **1.** encouragement or help: *a boost to morale.* **2.** an upward thrust or push. **3.** an increase or rise. ~*vb.* **4.** to encourage or improve: *to boost morale.* **5.** to cause to rise; increase: *to boost sales.* **6.** to advertise on a big scale. [origin unknown]

booster ('buːstə) *n.* **1.** a supplementary injection of a vaccine given to ensure that the first injection will remain effective. **2.** a radio-frequency amplifier to strengthen signals. **3.** the first stage of a multistage rocket.

boot[1] (buːt) *n.* **1.** an outer covering for the foot that extends above the ankle. **2.** *Brit., Austral., N.Z., & S. African.* an enclosed compartment of a car for holding luggage. **3.** *Informal.* a kick: *he gave the door a boot.* **4. lick someone's boots.** to behave flatteringly towards someone. **5. put the boot in.** *Slang.* **a.** to kick a person, esp. when he is already down. **b.** to finish something off with unnecessary brutality. **6. the boot.** *Slang.* dismissal from employment. ~*vb.* **7.** to kick. **8. boot out.** *Informal.* to eject forcibly. **b.** to dismiss from employment. [Middle English *bote*]

boot[2] (buːt) *n.* **to boot.** as well; in addition. [Old English *bōt* compensation]

bootee ('buːtiː, buːˈtiː) *n.* a soft shoe for a baby, esp. a knitted one.

booth (buːð, buːθ) *n., pl.* **booths** (buːðz). **1.** a small partially enclosed cubicle, such as one for telephoning (**telephone booth**) or for voting (**polling booth**). **2.** a stall, esp. a temporary one at a fair or market. [Scandinavian]

bootleg ('buːtˌleg) *vb.* **-legging, -legged.** **1.** to make, carry, or sell (illicit goods, esp. alcohol). ~*adj.* **2.** produced, distributed, or sold illicitly. [smugglers carried bottles of liquor concealed in their boots] —**'bootˌlegger** *n.*

bootless ('buːtlɪs) *adj.* of little or no use; vain; fruitless. [Old English *bōtlēas*]

bootlicker ('buːtˌlɪkə) *n. Informal.* one who seeks favour by grovelling to someone in authority.

boot sale *n.* a sale of goods from car boots in a car park hired for the occasion.

booty ('buːtɪ) *n., pl.* **-ties.** any valuable

article or articles, esp. when obtained as plunder. [Middle Low German *buite*]

booze (buːz) *Informal.* ~*n.* **1.** alcoholic drink. ~*vb.* **2.** to drink alcohol, esp. in excess. [Middle Dutch *būsen*] —**'boozy** *adj.*

boozer ('buːzə) *n. Informal.* **1.** a person who is fond of drinking. **2.** *Brit., Austral., & N.Z.* a bar or pub.

booze-up *n. Brit., Austral., & N.Z. slang.* a drinking spree.

bop (bɒp) *n.* **1.** a form of jazz with complex rhythms and harmonies. ~*vb.* **bopping, bopped.** **2.** *Informal.* to dance to pop music. [from *bebop*] —**'bopper** *n.*

boracic (bəˈræsɪk) *adj.* same as **boric.**

borage ('bɒrɪdʒ, 'bʌrɪdʒ) *n.* a Mediterranean plant with star-shaped blue flowers. The young leaves are sometimes used in salads. [Arabic *abū 'āraq*]

borax ('bɔːræks) *n.* a white mineral in crystalline form used in making glass, soap, etc. [Persian *būrah*]

Bordeaux (bɔːˈdəʊ) *n.* a red or white wine produced around Bordeaux in SW France.

border ('bɔːdə) *n.* **1.** a band or margin around or along the edge of something. **2.** the dividing line between political or geographic regions. **3.** a region straddling such a boundary. **4.** a design around the edge of something. **5.** a narrow strip of ground planted with flowers or shrubs: *a herbaceous border.* ~*vb.* **6.** to provide with a border. **7. a.** to be adjacent to; lie along the boundary of. **b.** to be nearly the same as; verge on: *his stupidity borders on madness.* [Old French *bort* side of a ship]

borderland ('bɔːdəˌlænd) *n.* **1.** land located on or near a boundary. **2.** an indeterminate state or condition.

borderline ('bɔːdəˌlaɪn) *n.* **1.** a dividing line. **2.** an indeterminate position between two conditions: *the borderline between friendship and love.* ~*adj.* **3.** on the edge of one category and verging on another: *a borderline failure.*

Borders ('bɔːdəz) *pl. n.* **the.** the area straddling the border between England and Scotland.

bore[1] (bɔː) *vb.* **1.** to produce (a hole) in (a material) with a drill, etc. **2.** to produce (a tunnel, mine shaft, etc.) as by drilling. ~*n.* **3.** a hole or tunnel in the ground, esp. one drilled in search of minerals, oil, etc. **4. a.** the hollow of a gun barrel. **b.** the diameter of this hollow; calibre. [Old English *borian*]

bore[2] (bɔː) *vb.* **1.** to tire or make weary by being dull, repetitious, or uninteresting. ~*n.* **2.** a dull or repetitious person, activity, or state. [origin unknown] —**bored** *adj.* —**'boring** *adj.*

bore[3] (bɔː) *n.* a high wave moving up a narrow estuary, caused by the tide. [Old Norse *bāra*]

bore[4] (bɔː) *vb.* the past tense of **bear**[1].

boreal forest ('bɔːrɪəl) *n.* the forest of northern latitudes, esp. in Scandinavia, Canada, and Siberia, consisting mainly of spruce and pine. [Latin *boreās* the north wind]

boredom ('bɔːdəm) n. the state of being bored.

boric ('bɔːrɪk) adj. of or containing boron.

boric acid n. a white soluble weakly acid crystalline solid used as a mild antiseptic.

born (bɔːn) vb. 1. the past participle of **bear**[1] (sense 4). 2. **not have been born yesterday.** not to be gullible or foolish. ~adj. 3. possessing certain qualities from birth: a born musician. 4. being at birth in a particular social status: ignobly born.

born-again adj. 1. having experienced conversion, esp. to evangelical Christianity. 2. showing the enthusiasm of someone newly converted to any cause: a born-again jogger.

borne (bɔːn) vb. a past participle of **bear**[1].

boron ('bɔːrɒn) n. a hard almost colourless crystalline metalloid element that occurs principally in borax and is used in hardening steel. Symbol: B [bor(ax) + (carb)on]

borough ('bʌrə) n. 1. a town, esp. (in Britain) one that forms the constituency of an MP or that was originally incorporated by royal charter. 2. any of the constituent divisions of Greater London or New York City. [Old English burg]

borrow ('bɒrəʊ) vb. 1. to obtain (something, such as money) on the understanding that it will be returned to the lender. 2. to adopt (ideas, words, etc.) from another source. [Old English borgian] —'**borrower** n. —'**borrowing** n.

borsch (bɔːʃ) or **borscht** (bɔːʃt) n. a Russian soup based on beetroot. [Russian borshch]

borstal ('bɔːstəl) n. (in Britain) an establishment in which offenders aged 15 to 21 may be detained for corrective training. [after Borstal, village in Kent where the first institution was founded]

borzoi ('bɔːzɔɪ) n. a tall dog with a narrow head and a long coat. [Russian: swift]

bosh (bɒʃ) n. Informal. meaningless talk or opinions; nonsense. [Turkish boş empty]

bosom ('bʊzəm) n. 1. the chest or breast of a person, esp. the female breasts. 2. a protective centre or part: the bosom of the family. 3. the breast considered as the seat of emotions. 4. (modifier) very dear; intimate: a bosom friend. [Old English bōsm]

boss[1] (bɒs) Informal. ~n. 1. a person in charge of or employing others. ~vb. 2. to employ, supervise, or be in charge of. 3. **boss around** or **about.** to be domineering or overbearing towards. [Dutch baas master]

boss[2] (bɒs) n. a raised knob or stud, esp. an ornamental one on a vault, shield, etc. [Old French boce]

bossa nova ('bɒsə 'nəʊvə) n. 1. a dance similar to the samba, originating in Brazil. 2. music for this dance. [Portuguese]

bossy ('bɒsɪ) adj. **bossier, bossiest.** Informal. domineering, overbearing, or authoritarian. —'**bossiness** n.

bosun ('bəʊs°n) n. Naut. same as **boatswain.**

bot. 1. botanical. 2. botany.

botany ('bɒtənɪ) n., pl. **-nies.** the study of plants, including their classification, structure, etc. [Greek botanē plant] —**botanical** (bə'tænɪk°l) or **bo'tanic** adj. —'**botanist** n.

botch (bɒtʃ) vb. 1. to spoil through clumsiness or ineptitude. 2. to repair badly or clumsily. ~n. also **botch-up.** 3. a badly done piece of work or repair. [origin unknown]

both (bəʊθ) det. 1. the two; two considered together: both dogs were dirty; both are to blame. ~conj. 2. used preceding words, phrases, or clauses joined by and: both Ellen and Keith enjoyed the play. [Old Norse bāthir]

bother ('bɒðə) vb. 1. to give annoyance, pain, or trouble to. 2. to trouble (a person) by repeatedly disturbing; pester. 3. to take the time or trouble: don't bother to come with me. ~n. 4. a state of worry, trouble, or confusion. 5. a person or thing that causes fuss, trouble, or annoyance. 6. Informal. a disturbance or fight: a spot of bother. ~interj. 7. Chiefly Brit. an exclamation of slight annoyance. [origin unknown]

botheration (ˌbɒðə'reɪʃən) interj. Informal. same as **bother.**

bothersome ('bɒðəsəm) adj. causing bother.

bothy ('bɒθɪ) n., pl. **bothies.** Chiefly Scot. 1. a hut used for temporary shelter. 2. formerly, a farmworker's quarters. [perhaps from booth]

bottle ('bɒt°l) n. 1. a vessel, often of glass and typically cylindrical with a narrow neck, for containing liquids. 2. the amount such a vessel will hold. 3. Brit. slang. courage; nerve; initiative. 4. **the bottle.** Informal. drinking of alcohol, esp. to excess. ~vb. 5. to put or place in a bottle or bottles. ~See also **bottle up.** [Late Latin buttis cask]

bottle-feed vb. **-feeding, -fed.** to feed (a baby) with milk from a bottle.

bottle-green adj. dark green.

bottleneck ('bɒt°lˌnɛk) n. 1. a narrow stretch of road or a junction at which traffic is or may be held up. 2. something that holds up progress.

bottlenose dolphin ('bɒt°lˌnəʊz) n. a grey or greenish dolphin with a bottle-shaped snout.

bottle party n. a party to which guests bring drink.

bottler ('bɒtlə) n. Austral. & N.Z. informal. an exceptional person or thing.

bottle store n. S. African & N.Z. an off-licence.

bottle up vb. to restrain (powerful emotion).

bottom ('bɒtəm) n. 1. the lowest, deepest, or farthest removed part of a thing: the bottom of a hill. 2. the least important or successful position: the bottom of a class. 3. the ground underneath a sea, lake, or river. 4. the underneath part of a thing. 5. Naut. the parts of a vessel's hull that are under water. 6. (in literary or commercial contexts) a ship. 7. the buttocks. 8. at

bottom. in reality; basically. **9. be at the bottom of.** to be the ultimate cause of. **10. get to the bottom of.** to discover the real truth about. ~*adj.* **11.** lowest or last. [Old English *botm*]

bottom drawer *n. Brit.* a woman's collection of linen, cutlery, etc., made in anticipation of marriage.

bottomless ('bɒtəmlɪs) *adj.* **1.** having no bottom. **2.** unlimited; inexhaustible. **3.** very deep.

bottom line *n.* **1.** the conclusion or main point of a process, discussion, etc. **2.** the last line of a financial statement that shows the net profit or loss of a company or organization.

bottom out *vb.* to reach the lowest point and level out.

botulism ('bɒtjʊˌlɪzəm) *n.* severe food poisoning resulting from the toxin, **botulin**, produced in imperfectly preserved food. [Latin *botulus* sausage]

bouclé ('buːkleɪ) *n.* a curled or looped yarn or fabric giving a thick knobbly effect. [French]

boudoir ('buːdwɑː, -dwɔː) *n.* a woman's bedroom or private sitting room. [French, lit.: room for sulking in]

bouffant ('buːfɒ̃) *adj.* (of a hairstyle) having extra height and width through backcombing. [French *bouffer* to puff up]

bougainvillea (ˌbuːgən'vɪlɪə) *n.* a tropical climbing plant with flowers surrounded by showy red or purple bracts. [after L. A. de *Bougainville*, navigator]

bough (baʊ) *n.* any of the main branches of a tree. [Old English *bōg*]

bought (bɔːt) *vb.* past of **buy**.

bouillon ('buːjɒn) *n.* a thin clear broth or stock. [French *bouillir* to boil]

boulder ('bəʊldə) *n.* a smooth rounded mass of rock shaped by erosion. [prob. Old Norse]

boulder clay *n.* an unstratified glacial deposit of fine clay, boulders, and pebbles.

boules (buːl) *n.* (*functioning as sing.*) a game, popular in France, played on rough surfaces with metal bowls. [French: balls]

boulevard ('buːlvɑː, -vɑːd) *n.* a wide usually tree-lined road in a city. [Middle Dutch *bolwerc* bulwark; because orig. often built on the ruins of an old rampart]

boult (bəʊlt) *vb.* same as **bolt²**.

bounce (baʊns) *vb.* **1.** (of a ball, etc.) to rebound from an impact. **2.** to cause (a ball, etc.) to hit a solid surface and spring back. **3.** to move or cause to move suddenly; spring: *she bounced up from her chair.* **4.** *Slang.* (of a bank) to send (a cheque) back or (of a cheque) to be sent back unredeemed because of lack of funds in the account. ~*n.* **5.** the action of rebounding from an impact. **6.** a leap or jump. **7.** springiness. **8.** *Informal.* vitality; vigour; resilience. **9.** *Brit.* swagger or impudence. [prob. imit.] —'**bouncy** *adj.*

bounce back *vb.* to recover one's health, good spirits, confidence, etc., easily.

bouncer ('baʊnsə) *n. Slang.* a person em-

ployed at a club, disco, etc., to prevent unwanted people from entering and to eject drunks or troublemakers.

bouncing ('baʊnsɪŋ) *adj.* vigorous and robust: *a bouncing baby.*

bound¹ (baʊnd) *vb.* **1.** past of **bind**. ~*adj.* **2.** tied as with a rope. **3.** restricted; confined: *housebound.* **4.** certain: *it's bound to happen.* **5.** compelled or obliged. **6.** (of a book) secured within a cover or binding. **7. bound up with.** closely or inextricably linked with.

bound² (baʊnd) *vb.* **1.** to move forwards by leaps or jumps. **2.** to bounce; spring away from an impact. ~*n.* **3.** a jump upwards or forwards. **4.** a bounce, as of a ball. [Old French *bond*]

bound³ (baʊnd) *vb.* **1.** to place restrictions on; limit. **2.** to form a boundary of. ~*n.* **3.** See **bounds**. [Old French *bonde*] —'**boundless** *adj.*

bound⁴ (baʊnd) *adj.* going or intending to go towards: *homeward bound.* [Old Norse *buinn*]

boundary ('baʊndərɪ, -drɪ) *n., pl.* -**ries**. **1.** something that indicates the farthest limit, as of an area. **2.** *Cricket.* **a.** the marked limit of the playing area. **b.** a stroke that hits the ball beyond this limit, scoring four or six runs.

bounden ('baʊndən) *adj.* morally obligatory: *bounden duty.*

bounder ('baʊndə) *n. Old-fashioned Brit. slang.* a morally reprehensible person; cad.

bounds (baʊndz) *pl. n.* **1.** a limit; boundary: *his ignorance knows no bounds.* **2.** something that restrains or confines, esp. the standards of a society: *within the bounds of modesty.*

bountiful ('baʊntɪfʊl) *or* **bounteous** ('baʊntɪəs) *adj.* **1.** plentiful; ample: *a bountiful supply.* **2.** giving freely; generous.

bounty ('baʊntɪ) *n., pl.* -**ties**. **1.** generosity; liberality. **2.** a generous gift. **3.** a reward or premium by a government. [Latin *bonus* good]

bouquet (buː'keɪ) *n.* **1.** a bunch of flowers, esp. a large carefully arranged one. **2.** the aroma of wine. [French]

bouquet garni ('buːkeɪ gɑː'niː) *n., pl.* **bouquets garnis** ('buːkeɪz gɑː'niː). a bunch of herbs tied together and used for flavouring soups, stews, etc. [French]

bourbon ('bɜːbən) *n.* a whiskey distilled, chiefly in the U.S., from maize. [after *Bourbon* county, Kentucky, where it was first made]

bourgeois ('bʊəʒwɑː) *Often disparaging.* ~*n., pl.* -**geois**. **1.** a member of the middle class, esp. one regarded as being conservative and materialistic. ~*adj.* **2.** characteristic of or comprising the middle class. **3.** conservative or materialistic in outlook. **4.** (in Marxist thought) dominated by capitalism. [Old French *borjois* citizen]

bourgeoisie (ˌbʊəʒwɑː'ziː) *n.* **the. 1.** the middle classes. **2.** (in Marxist thought) the capitalist ruling class.

bourn (bɔːn) *n. Chiefly S Brit.* a stream. [Old French *bodne* limit]

bourrée ('bʊəreɪ) *n.* **1.** a traditional

French dance in fast duple time. **2.** music for this dance. [French]

Bourse (buəs) *n.* a stock exchange, esp. of Paris. [French: purse]

bout (baut) *n.* **1. a.** a period of time spent doing something, such as drinking. **b.** a period of illness. **c.** a boxing or wrestling match. [obs. *bought* turn]

boutique (buːˈtiːk) *n.* a shop, esp. a small one selling fashionable clothes. [French]

bouzouki (buːˈzuːkɪ) *n.* a Greek long-necked stringed musical instrument related to the mandolin. [Modern Greek]

bovine (ˈbəʊvaɪn) *adj.* **1.** of or relating to cattle. **2.** (of people) dull, sluggish, or ugly. [Latin *bōs* ox]

bow¹ (baʊ) *vb.* **1.** to lower (one's head) or bend (one's knee or body) as a sign of respect, greeting, agreement, or shame. **2.** to bend or cause to bend. **3.** to comply or accept: *bow to the inevitable*. **4. bow and scrape.** to behave in a slavish manner. ~*n.* **5.** a lowering or bending of the head or body as a mark of respect, etc. **6. take a bow.** to acknowledge applause. ~See also **bow out.** [Old English *būgan*]

bow² (bəʊ) *n.* **1.** a weapon for shooting arrows, consisting of an arch of flexible wood, plastic, etc., bent by a string fastened at each end. **2.** a long stick across which are stretched strands of horsehair, used for playing a violin, viola, cello, etc. **3.** a decorative knot usually having two loops and two loose ends. **4.** something that is curved, bent, or arched. ~*vb.* **5.** to form or cause to form a curve or curves. **6.** to make strokes of a bow across (violin strings). [Old English *boga*]

bow³ (baʊ) *n.* **1.** *Chiefly Naut.* the front end or part of a vessel. **2.** *Rowing.* the oarsman at the bow. [prob. Low German *boog*]

bowdlerize *or* **-ise** (ˈbaʊdləˌraɪz) *vb.* to remove passages or words regarded as indecent from (a play, novel, etc.). [after Thomas *Bowdler,* who expurgated Shakespeare] —**bowdleriˈzation** *or* **-iˈsation** *n.*

bowel (ˈbaʊəl) *n.* **1.** an intestine, esp. the large intestine in man. **2.** (*pl.*) entrails. **3.** (*pl.*) the innermost part: *the bowels of the earth.* [Latin *botellus* a little sausage]

bower (ˈbaʊə) *n.* a shady leafy shelter in a wood or garden. [Old English *būr*]

bowerbird (ˈbaʊəˌbɜːd) *n.* a brightly-coloured songbird of Australia and New Guinea.

bowie knife (ˈbəʊɪ) *n.* a stout hunting knife. [after Jim *Bowie,* Texan adventurer]

bowl¹ (bəʊl) *n.* **1.** a round container open at the top, used for holding liquid or serving food. **2.** the amount a bowl will hold. **3.** the hollow part of an object, esp. of a spoon or tobacco pipe. [Old English *bolla*]

bowl² (bəʊl) *n.* **1.** a wooden ball used in the game of bowls. ~*vb.* **2.** to roll smoothly or cause to roll smoothly along the ground. **3.** *Cricket.* **a.** to send (a ball) from one's hand towards the batsman. **b.** Also: **bowl**

out. to dismiss (a batsman) by delivering a ball that breaks his wicket. **4.** to play bowls. **5. bowl along.** to move easily and rapidly, as in a car. ~See also **bowl over, bowls.**

bow-legged (ˌbəʊˈlɛgɪd, ˌbəʊˈlɛgd) *adj.* having legs that curve outwards at the knees.

bowler¹ (ˈbəʊlə) *n.* **1.** one who bowls in cricket. **2.** a player at the game of bowls.

bowler² (ˈbəʊlə) *n.* a stiff felt hat with a rounded crown and narrow curved brim. [after John *Bowler,* hatter]

bowline (ˈbəʊlɪn) *n. Naut.* **1.** a line used to keep the sail taut against the wind. **2.** a knot used for securing a loop that will not slip at the end of a piece of rope. [prob. from Middle Low German *bōlīne*]

bowling (ˈbəʊlɪŋ) *n.* **1.** a game in which a heavy ball is rolled down a long narrow alley at a group of wooden pins. **2.** *Cricket.* the act of delivering the ball to the batsman.

bow over *vb.* **1.** *Informal.* to surprise (a person) greatly, esp. in a pleasant way; astound; amaze. **2.** to knock down.

bowls (bəʊlz) *n.* (*functioning as sing.*) a game played on a very smooth area of grass in which two opponents take turns to roll biased wooden bowls as near a small bowl (the jack) as possible.

bow out (baʊ) *vb.* to retire or withdraw gracefully.

bowsprit (ˈbəʊsprɪt) *n. Naut.* a spar projecting from the bow of a sailing ship. [Middle Low German *bōch* BOW³ + *sprēt* pole]

bowstring (ˈbəʊˌstrɪŋ) *n.* the string of an archer's bow.

bow tie (bəʊ) *n.* a man's tie tied in a bow.

bow window (bəʊ) *n.* a bay window in the shape of a curve.

bow-wow *n.* **1.** (ˈbaʊˌwaʊ). a child's word for **dog.** **2.** (ˈbaʊˈwaʊ). an imitation of the bark of a dog.

box¹ (bɒks) *n.* **1.** a container made of wood, cardboard, etc., usually rectangular and having a removable or hinged lid. **2.** the contents of such a container. **3.** a separate compartment for a small group of people, as in a theatre. **4.** a compartment for a horse in a stable or a vehicle. **5.** a section of printed matter on a page, enclosed by lines or a border. **6.** a central agency to which mail is addressed and from which it is collected or redistributed: *a post-office box.* **7.** same as **penalty box. 8.** the raised seat on which the driver sits in a horse-drawn coach. **9. the box.** *Brit. informal.* television. ~*vb.* **10.** to put into a box. ~See also **box in.** [Greek *puxos* BOX³] —**ˈbox,like** *adj.*

box² (bɒks) *vb.* **1.** to fight (an opponent) in a boxing match. **2.** to engage in boxing. **3.** to hit (a person or his ears) with the fist. ~*n.* **4.** a punch with the fist, esp. on the ear. [origin unknown]

box³ (bɒks) *n.* a slow-growing evergreen tree or shrub with small shiny leaves. [Greek *puxos*]

boxer (ˈbɒksə) *n.* **1.** a man who boxes. **2.**

a medium-sized smooth-haired breed of dog with a short nose.

boxer shorts *pl. n.* men's underpants shaped like shorts but with a front opening.

box girder *n.* a girder that is hollow and square or rectangular in shape.

box in *vb.* to prevent from moving freely; confine.

boxing ('bɒksɪŋ) *n.* the act, art, or profession of fighting with the fists.

Boxing Day *n. Brit.* the first weekday after Christmas, observed as a holiday. [from the former custom of giving Christmas boxes to tradesmen on this day]

box junction *n.* (in Britain) a road junction marked with yellow crisscross lines. Vehicles may only enter it when their exit is clear.

box lacrosse *n. Canad.* lacrosse played indoors.

box office *n.* **1.** an office at a theatre, cinema, etc., where tickets are sold. **2. a.** the public appeal of an actor or production. **b.** (*as modifier*): *a box-office success.*

box pleat *n.* a flat double pleat made by folding under the fabric on either side of it.

boxroom ('bɒks,ruːm, -,rʊm) *n.* a small room in which boxes, cases, etc., may be stored.

box spring *n.* a coiled spring contained in a boxlike frame, used for mattresses, chairs, etc.

boxwood ('bɒks,wʊd) *n.* the hard closegrained yellow wood of the box tree, used to make tool handles, etc. See **box³**.

boy (bɔɪ) *n.* **1.** a male child. **2.** a man regarded as immature or inexperienced. **3.** *S. African offensive.* a Black male servant. [origin unknown] —**boyhood** *n.* —**boyish** *adj.*

boycott ('bɔɪkɒt) *vb.* **1.** to refuse to have dealings with (a person or organization) or refuse to buy (a product) as a protest or means of coercion. ~*n.* **2.** an instance of the use of boycotting. [after Captain *Boycott*, Irish land agent, a victim of such practices for refusing to reduce rents]

boyfriend ('bɔɪ,frɛnd) *n.* a male friend with whom a person is romantically or sexually involved.

Boyle's law (bɔɪlz) *n.* the principle that the pressure of a gas varies inversely with its volume at constant temperature. [after Robert *Boyle*, scientist]

boy scout *n.* See **Scout**.

BP **1.** blood pressure. **2.** British Pharmacopoeia.

bpi bits per inch (used of a computer tape).

Bq *Physics.* becquerel.

Br *Chem.* bromine.

br. **1.** branch. **2.** bronze.

Br. **1.** Breton. **2.** Britain. **3.** British.

bra (brɑː) *n.* a woman's undergarment for covering and supporting the breasts. [from *brassiere*]

braaivleis ('braɪ,fleɪs) *n. S. African.* a barbecue. [Afrikaans]

brace (breɪs) *n.* **1.** a hand tool for drilling

holes. **2.** something that steadies, binds, or holds up another thing. **3.** a beam or prop, used to stiffen a framework. **4.** a pair, esp. of game birds. **5.** either of a pair of characters, { }, used for connecting lines of printing or writing. **6.** an appliance of metal bands and wires for correcting unevenness of teeth. **7.** See **braces**. ~*vb.* **8.** to provide, strengthen, or fit with a brace. **9.** to steady or prepare (oneself) before an impact. [Latin *bracchia* arms]

brace and bit *n.* a hand tool for boring holes, consisting of a cranked handle into which a drilling bit is inserted.

bracelet ('breɪslɪt) *n.* an ornamental chain worn around the arm or wrist. [Latin *bracchium* arm]

bracelets ('breɪslɪts) *pl. n. Slang.* handcuffs.

braces ('breɪsɪz) *pl. n. Brit.* a pair of straps worn over the shoulders for holding up the trousers.

brachiopod ('breɪkɪə,pɒd, 'bræk-) *n.* an invertebrate sea animal with a coiled feeding organ and a shell consisting of two valves. [Greek *brakhiōn* arm + *pous* foot]

brachium ('breɪkɪəm, 'bræk-) *n., pl.* **-chia** (-kɪə). *Anat.* the arm, esp. the upper part. [Latin *bracchium* arm]

bracing ('breɪsɪŋ) *adj.* refreshing; stimulating; invigorating.

bracken ('brækən) *n.* **1.** a fern with large fronds. **2.** a clump of these ferns. [Old Norse]

bracket ('brækɪt) *n.* **1.** a pair of characters, [ ], ( ), or { }, used to enclose a section of writing or printing. **2.** a group or category falling within certain defined limits: *the lower income bracket.* **3.** an L-shaped or other support fixed to a wall to hold a shelf, etc. ~*vb.* **4.** to put (written or printed matter) in brackets. **5.** to group or class together. [Latin *brāca* breeches]

brackish ('brækɪʃ) *adj.* (of water) slightly salty. [Middle Dutch *brac*]

bract (brækt) *n.* a leaf, usually small and scaly, growing at the base of a flower. [Latin *bractea* thin metal plate]

brad (bræd) *n.* a small tapered nail with a small head. [Old English *brord* point]

bradawl ('bræd,ɔːl) *n.* a hand tool for making holes in wood, leather, etc.

brae (breɪ) *n. Scot.* a hill or hillside. [Middle English *bra*]

brag (bræg) *vb.* **bragging**, **bragged**. **1.** to speak arrogantly and boastfully. ~*n.* **2.** boastful talk or behaviour. **3.** a card game: an old form of poker. [origin unknown]

braggart ('brægət) *n.* **1.** a person who boasts loudly or exaggeratedly. ~*adj.* **2.** boastful.

Brahma ('brɑːmə) *n.* **1.** a Hindu god, the Creator. **2.** same as **Brahman** (sense 2).

Brahman ('brɑːmən) *n., pl.* **-mans**. **1.** Also: **Brahmin**. a member of the highest or priestly caste in the Hindu caste system. **2.** *Hinduism.* the ultimate and impersonal divine reality of the universe. [Sanskrit: prayer] —**Brahmanic** (brɑːˈmænɪk) *adj.*

braid (breɪd) *vb.* **1.** to interweave (hair,

thread, etc.); plait. **2.** to decorate with an ornamental trim or border. ~*n.* **3.** a length of hair that has been braided. **4.** narrow ornamental tape of woven silk, wool, etc. [Old English *bregdan*] —'**braiding** *n.*

Braille (breɪl) *n.* a system of writing for the blind consisting of raised dots interpreted by touch. [after Louis *Braille*, its inventor]

brain (breɪn) *n.* **1.** the soft mass of nervous tissue within the skull of vertebrates that controls and coordinates the nervous system. **2.** (*often pl.*) *Informal.* intellectual ability: *he's got brains.* **3.** *Informal.* an intelligent person. **4. on the brain.** *Informal.* constantly in mind: *I had that song on the brain.* **5. the brains.** *Informal.* a person who plans and organizes something: *who is the brains behind this scheme?* ~*vb.* **6.** *Slang.* to hit (someone) hard on the head. [Old English *brægen*]

brainchild ('breɪn,tʃaɪld) *n. Informal.* an idea or plan produced by creative thought.

brain death *n.* complete stoppage of breathing due to irreparable brain damage.

brain drain *n. Informal.* the emigration of scientists, technologists, academics, etc.

brainless ('breɪnlɪs) *adj.* stupid or foolish.

brainstorm ('breɪn,stɔːm) *n.* **1.** a sudden and violent attack of insanity. **2.** *Brit. informal.* a sudden mental aberration. **3.** *U.S. & Canad. informal.* same as **brain wave** (sense 1).

brains trust *n.* a group of knowledgeable people who discuss topics in public or on radio or television.

brain-teaser *n. Informal.* a difficult problem.

brainwash ('breɪn,wɒʃ) *vb.* to effect a radical change in the beliefs of (a person), esp. by isolation, sleeplessness, etc. —'**brain,washing** *n.*

brain wave *n.* **1.** *Informal.* a sudden idea or inspiration. **2.** a fluctuation of electrical potential in the brain.

brainy ('breɪnɪ) *adj.* **brainier, brainiest.** *Informal.* clever; intelligent.

braise (breɪz) *vb.* to cook (meat, vegetables, etc.) by cooking slowly in a closed pan with a small amount of liquid. [Old French *brese* live coals]

brak (bræk) *n. S. African.* a crossbred dog; mongrel. [Dutch]

brake[1] (breɪk) *n.* **1.** a device for slowing or stopping a vehicle. **2.** a machine or tool for crushing flax or hemp. **3.** a heavy harrow for breaking up clods. ~*vb.* **4.** to slow down or cause to slow down, by or as if by using a brake. **5.** to break up (clods) using a brake. [Middle Dutch *braeke*]

brake[2] (breɪk) *n.* an area of dense undergrowth, brushwood, etc. [Old English *bracu*]

brake[3] (breɪk) *n.* same as **bracken.**

brake horsepower *n.* the rate at which an engine does work, measured by the resistance of an applied brake.

brake light *n.* a red light at the rear of a motor vehicle that lights up when the brakes are applied.

brake lining *n.* a renewable strip of asbestos riveted to a brake shoe to increase friction.

brake shoe *n.* a curved metal casting that acts as a brake on a wheel.

bramble ('bræmb'l) *n.* **1.** a prickly plant or shrub such as the blackberry. **2.** *Scot. & N English.* a blackberry. [Old English *bræmbel*] —'**brambly** *adj.*

brambling ('bræmblɪŋ) *n.* a finch with a speckled head and back.

bran (bræn) *n.* husks of cereal grain separated from the flour. [Old French]

branch (brɑːntʃ) *n.* **1.** a secondary woody stem extending from the trunk or main branch of a tree. **2.** an offshoot or secondary part: *a branch of a deer's antlers.* **3.** a subdivision or subsidiary section of something larger or more complex: *branches of learning.* ~*vb.* **4.** (of a tree or other plant) to produce or possess branches. **5.** (of stems, roots, etc.) to grow and diverge (from another part). **6.** to divide or be divided into subsidiaries or offshoots. [Late Latin *branca* paw] —'**branch,like** *adj.*

branch off *vb.* to diverge from the main way, road, topic, etc.

branch out *vb.* to expand or extend one's interests.

brand (brænd) *n.* **1.** a particular product or a characteristic that identifies a particular producer. **2.** a particular kind or variety. **3.** an identifying mark made, usually by burning, on the skin of animals as a proof of ownership. **4.** an iron used for branding animals. **5.** a mark of disgrace. **6.** a burning or burnt piece of wood. **7.** *Archaic or poetic.* a flaming torch. ~*vb.* **8.** to label, burn, or mark with or as with a brand. **9.** to denounce; stigmatize: *they branded him a traitor.* [Old English]

brandish ('brændɪʃ) *vb.* to wave (a weapon, etc.) in a triumphant or threatening way. [Old French *brandir*]

brand-new *adj.* absolutely new.

brandy ('brændɪ) *n., pl.* **-dies.** an alcoholic spirit distilled from wine. [Dutch *brandewijn*]

brandy snap *n.* a crisp sweet biscuit, rolled into a cylinder and filled with whipped cream.

bran tub *n. Brit.* a tub containing bran in which small wrapped gifts are hidden.

brash (bræʃ) *adj.* **1.** tastelessly or offensively loud, showy, or bold. **2.** impudent. [origin unknown] —'**brashness** *n.*

brass (brɑːs) *n.* **1.** an alloy of copper and zinc. **2.** an object, ornament, or utensil made of brass. **3. a.** the large family of wind instruments including the trumpet, trombone, etc., made of brass. **b.** instruments of this family forming a section in an orchestra. **4.** same as **top brass. 5.** *N English dialect.* money. **6.** *Brit.* an engraved brass memorial tablet in a church. **7.** *Informal.* bold self-confidence; nerve. [Old English *bræs*]

brass band *n.* a group of musicians playing brass and percussion instruments.

brass hat *n. Brit. informal.* a top-ranking official, esp. a military officer.

brassica ('bræsɪkə) *n.* any plant of the cabbage and turnip family. [Latin: cabbage]

brassiere ('bræsɪə, 'bræz-) *n.* same as **bra**. [French]

brass rubbing *n.* an impression of an engraved brass tablet made by rubbing a paper placed over it with heelball or chalk.

brass tacks *pl. n.* **get down to brass tacks.** *Informal.* to discuss the realities of a situation.

brassy ('brɑːsɪ) *adj.* **brassier, brassiest.** **1.** insolent; brazen. **2.** flashy; showy. **3.** (of sound) harsh and strident. **4.** like brass, esp. in colour.

brat (bræt) *n.* a child, esp. one who is unruly. [origin unknown]

bravado (brə'vɑːdəʊ) *n.* an outward display of self-confidence; swagger. [Spanish *bravada*]

brave (breɪv) *adj.* **1.** having or displaying courage, resolution, or daring. **2.** fine; splendid: *a brave sight.* ~*n.* **3.** a warrior of a North American Indian tribe. ~*vb.* **4.** to confront with resolution or courage: *to brave the storm.* [Italian *bravo*] —'**bravery** *n.*

bravo *interj.* **1.** (brɑː'vəʊ). well done! ~*n.* **2.** (brɑː'vəʊ). (*pl.* -**vos**). a cry of "bravo." **3.** ('brɑːvəʊ). (*pl.* -**voes** or -**vos**). a hired killer or assassin. [Italian]

bravura (brə'vjʊərə, -'vʊərə) *n.* **1.** a display of boldness or daring. **2.** *Music.* brilliance of execution. [Italian]

brawl (brɔːl) *n.* **1.** a loud disagreement or fight. ~*vb.* **2.** to quarrel or fight noisily; squabble. [prob. from Dutch *brallen* to boast]

brawn (brɔːn) *n.* **1.** strong well-developed muscles. **2.** physical strength. **3.** *Brit.* a seasoned jellied loaf made from the head of a pig. [Old French *braon* meat] —'**brawny** *adj.*

bray (breɪ) *vb.* **1.** (of a donkey) to utter its characteristic loud harsh sound; heehaw. **2.** to utter something with a loud harsh sound. ~*n.* **3.** the loud harsh sound uttered by a donkey. **4.** a similar loud sound. [Old French *braire*]

braze (breɪz) *vb.* to join (two metal surfaces) by fusing brass between them. [Old French]

brazen ('breɪz²n) *adj.* **1.** shameless and bold. **2.** made of or resembling brass. **3.** having a ringing metallic sound. ~*vb.* **4.** **brazen it out.** to face and overcome a difficult or embarrassing situation boldly or shamelessly. —'**brazenly** *adv.*

brazier¹ ('breɪzɪə) *n.* a worker in brass.

brazier² ('breɪzɪə) *n.* a portable metal container for burning charcoal or coal. [French *braise* live coals]

brazil (brə'zɪl) *n.* **1.** the red wood of various tropical trees of America. **2.** same as **brazil nut.** [Old Spanish *brasa* glowing coals; referring to the redness of the wood]

brazil nut *n.* a large three-sided nut of a

tropical American tree, with a woody shell and an oily edible kernel.

breach (briːtʃ) *n.* **1.** a breaking or violation of a promise, obligation, etc. **2.** any serious disagreement or separation. **3.** a crack, break, or gap. ~*vb.* **4.** to break (a promise, law, etc). **5.** to break through or make an opening or hole in. [Old English *bræc*]

breach of promise *n. Law.* (formerly) failure to carry out one's promise to marry.

breach of the peace *n. Law.* an offence against public order causing an unnecessary disturbance of the peace.

bread (brɛd) *n.* **1.** a food made from a dough of flour or meal mixed with water or milk, usually raised with yeast and then baked. **2.** necessary food; nourishment. **3.** *Slang.* money. ~*vb.* **4.** to cover (food) with breadcrumbs before cooking. [Old English]

bread and butter *n. Informal.* a means of support; livelihood.

breadboard ('brɛd,bɔːd) *n.* **1.** a wooden board on which bread is sliced. **2.** an experimental arrangement of electronic circuits.

breadfruit ('brɛd,fruːt) *n., pl.* -**fruits** or -**fruit.** a tree of the Pacific Islands, the edible round fruit of which is eaten baked or roasted and has a texture like bread.

breadline ('brɛd,laɪn) *n.* **on the breadline.** impoverished; living at subsistence level.

breadth (brɛdθ) *n.* **1.** the extent or measurement of something from side to side; width. **2.** openness and lack of restriction, esp. of viewpoint or interest; liberality. [Old English *brād* broad]

breadwinner ('brɛd,wɪnə) *n.* a person supporting a family with his or her earnings.

break (breɪk) *vb.* **breaking, broke, broken.** **1.** to separate or become separated into two or more pieces. **2.** to damage or become damaged so as to be inoperative. **3.** to burst or cut the surface of (skin). **4.** to discontinue (a journey). **5.** to fail to observe (an agreement, promise, or law): *to break one's word.* **6.** (foll. by *with*) to discontinue an association with. **7.** to disclose or be disclosed: *he broke the news gently.* **8.** to fracture (a bone) in (a limb, etc.). **9.** to bring or come to an end: *the summer weather broke at last.* **10.** to weaken or overwhelm or be weakened or overwhelmed, as in spirit. **11.** to cut through or penetrate: *a cry broke the silence.* **12.** to improve on or surpass: *to break a record.* **13.** (often foll. by *in*) to accustom (a horse) to the bridle and saddle, to being ridden, etc. **14.** (foll. by *of*) to cause (a person) to give up (a habit): *this cure will break you of smoking.* **15.** to weaken the impact or force of: *this net will break his fall.* **16.** to decipher: *to break a code.* **17.** to lose the order of: *to break ranks.* **18.** to reduce to poverty or the state of bankruptcy. **19.** to come into being: *light broke over the mountains.* **20.** (foll. by *into*) **a.** to burst into (song, laughter, etc.). **b.** to change to (a faster pace). **21.** to open with explosives: *to break a safe.* **22.** (of waves) **a.** to strike violently. **b.** to collapse into foam or surf. **23.** *Billiards.* to scatter the balls at the start of a game. **24.** *Boxing, wrestling.* (of two fighters) to separate from a clinch. **25.** (of the male voice) to undergo a change in register, quality, and range at puberty. **26.** to interrupt the flow of current in (an electrical circuit). **27. break camp.** to pack up and leave a camp. **28. break even.** to make neither a profit nor a loss. ~*n.* **29.** the act or result of breaking; fracture. **30.** a brief respite. **31.** a sudden rush, esp. to escape: *to make a break for freedom.* **32.** any sudden interruption in a continuous action. **33.** *Brit.* a short period between classes at school. **34.** *Informal.* a fortunate opportunity, esp. to prove oneself. **35.** *Informal.* a piece of good or bad luck. **36.** *Billiards, snooker.* a series of successful shots during one turn. **37.** *Billiards, snooker.* the opening shot that scatters the placed balls. **38.** a discontinuity in an electrical circuit. **39. break of day.** the dawn. ~See also **breakaway, break down,** etc. [Old English *brecan*] —'**breakable** *adj.*

breakage ('breɪkɪdʒ) *n.* **1.** the act or result of breaking. **2.** compensation or allowance for goods damaged while in use, transit, etc.

breakaway ('breɪkə,weɪ) *n.* **1. a.** loss or withdrawal of a group of members from an association, club, etc. **b.** (*as modifier*): *a breakaway faction.* ~*vb.* **break away.** **2.** to leave hastily or escape. **3.** to withdraw or secede.

break dance *n.* **1.** an acrobatic dance style of the 1980s. ~*vb.* **break-dance.** **2.** to perform a break dance. —'**break dancing** *n.*

break down *vb.* **1.** to cease to function; become ineffective. **2.** to yield to strong emotion or tears. **3.** to crush or destroy. **4.** to have a nervous breakdown. **5.** to analyse or be subjected to analysis. ~*n.* **breakdown. 6.** an act or instance of breaking down; collapse. **7.** same as **nervous breakdown. 8.** an analysis of something into its parts.

breaker ('breɪkə) *n.* **1.** a large wave with a white crest on the open sea or one that breaks into foam on the shore. **2.** a citizens' band radio operator.

breakfast ('brɛkfəst) *n.* **1.** the first meal of the day. ~*vb.* **2.** to eat or supply with breakfast. [BREAK + FAST²]

break in *vb.* **1.** to enter a house, etc., illegally, esp. by force. **2.** to interrupt. **3.** to accustom (a person or animal) to normal duties or practice. **4.** to use or wear (new shoes or new equipment) until comfortable or running smoothly. ~*n.* **break-in. 5.** the act of illegally entering a building, esp. by thieves.

breaking and entering *n.* (formerly) the act of gaining unauthorized access to a building with intent to commit a crime.

breaking point *n.* the point at which something or someone gives way under strain.

breakneck ('breɪk,nɛk) *adj.* (of speed or pace) excessively fast and dangerous.

break off *vb.* **1.** to sever or detach. **2.** to end (a relationship or association). **3.** to stop abruptly.

break out *vb.* **1.** to begin or arise suddenly: *a riot broke out during the concert.* **2.** to make an escape, esp. from prison. **3.** (foll. by *in*) (of the skin) to erupt (in a rash or spots). ~*n.* **break-out. 4.** an escape, esp. from prison.

break through *vb.* **1.** to penetrate. **2.** to achieve success after lengthy efforts. ~*n.* **breakthrough. 3.** a significant development or discovery, esp. in science.

break up *vb.* **1.** to separate or cause to separate. **2.** to put an end to (a relationship) or (of a relationship) to come to an end. **3.** to dissolve or cause to dissolve; disrupt or be disrupted: *the meeting broke up at noon.* **4.** *Brit.* (of a school) to close for the holidays. ~*n.* **break-up. 5.** a separation or disintegration.

breakwater ('breɪk,wɔːtə) *n.* a massive wall built out into the sea to protect a shore or harbour from the force of waves.

bream (briːm) *n., pl.* **bream. 1.** a freshwater fish with a deep compressed body covered with silvery scales. **2.** a food fish of European seas. [Old French *bresme*]

breast (brɛst) *n.* **1.** either of the two soft fleshy milk-secreting glands on the chest in sexually mature human females. **2.** the front part of the body from the neck to the abdomen; chest. **3.** the corresponding part in certain other mammals. **4.** a source of nourishment. **5.** the source of human emotions. **6.** the part of a garment that covers the breast. **7. make a clean breast of something.** to confess to something. ~*vb.* **8.** to confront boldly; face: *breast the storm.* **9.** to reach the summit of: *breasting the mountain top.* [Old English *brēost*]

breastbone ('brɛst,bəʊn) *n.* same as **sternum.**

breast-feed *vb.* **-feeding, -fed.** to feed (a baby) with milk from the breast; suckle.

breastplate ('brɛst,pleɪt) *n.* a piece of armour covering the chest.

breaststroke ('brɛst,strəʊk) *n.* a swimming stroke in which the arms are extended in front of the head and swept back on either side.

breastwork ('brɛst,wɜːk) *n. Fortifications.* a temporary defensive work, usually breast-high.

breath (brɛθ) *n.* **1.** the taking in and letting out of air during breathing. **2.** a single instance of this. **3.** the air taken in or let out during breathing. **4.** the vapour, heat, or odour of air breathed out. **5.** a slight gust of air. **6.** a short pause or rest. **7.** a suggestion or slight evidence; suspicion: *a breath of scandal.* **8.** a whisper or soft sound. **9. catch one's breath. a.** to rest until breathing is normal. **b.** to stop breathing momentarily from excitement, fear, etc. **10. out of breath.** gasping for air after exertion. **11. save one's breath.** to refrain from useless talk. **12. take someone's breath away.** to overwhelm someone with surprise, etc. **13. under one's breath.** in a quiet voice or whisper. [Old English *brǣth*]

Breathalyser *or* **-lyzer** ('brɛθə,laizə) *n. Brit., trademark.* a device for estimating the amount of alcohol in the breath. [*breath* + (*an*)*alyser*] —'**breatha,lyse** *or* -,**lyze** *vb.*

breathe (briːð) *vb.* **1.** to take in oxygen and give out carbon dioxide; respire. **2.** to exist; be alive. **3.** to rest to regain breath or composure. **4.** (esp. of air) to blow lightly. **5.** to exhale or emit: *the dragon breathed fire.* **6.** to impart; instil: *to breathe confidence into the actors.* **7.** to speak softly; whisper. **8. breathe again, freely,** *or* **easily.** to feel relief. **9. breathe one's last.** to die.

breather ('briːðə) *n. Informal.* a short pause for rest.

breathing ('briːðɪŋ) *n.* **1.** the passage of air into and out of the lungs to supply the body with oxygen. **2.** the sound this makes.

breathless ('brɛθlɪs) *adj.* **1.** out of breath; gasping, etc. **2.** holding one's breath or having it taken away by excitement, etc. **3.** (esp. of the atmosphere) motionless and stifling.

breathtaking ('brɛθ,teɪkɪŋ) *adj.* causing awe or excitement.

breath test *n. Brit.* a chemical test of a driver's breath to determine the amount of alcohol he has consumed.

bred (brɛd) *vb.* past of **breed.**

breech (briːtʃ) *n.* **1.** the buttocks. **2.** the part of a firearm behind the barrel or bore. [Old English *brēc*]

breech delivery *n.* birth of a baby with the feet or buttocks appearing first.

breeches ('brɪtʃɪz, 'briː-) *pl. n.* trousers extending to the knee or just below, worn for riding, etc.

breeches buoy *n.* a life buoy with a support of a pair of short breeches, in which a person is suspended for safe transfer from a ship.

breed (briːd) *vb.* **breeding, bred. 1.** to bear (offspring). **2.** to bring up; raise. **3.** to produce or cause to produce by mating. **4.** to produce new or improved strains of (domestic animals and plants). **5.** to produce or be produced: *to breed trouble.* ~*n.* **6.** a group of animals, esp. domestic animals, within a species, that have certain clearly defined characteristics. **7.** a lineage or race. **8.** a kind, sort, or group. [Old English *brēdan*] —'**breeder** *n.*

breeder reactor *n.* a nuclear reactor that produces more fissionable material than it uses.

breeding ('briːdɪŋ) *n.* **1.** the process of bearing offspring. **2.** the process of producing plants or animals by controlled methods of reproduction. **3.** the result of good upbringing or training.

breeze[1] (briːz) *n.* **1.** a gentle or light wind. **2.** *U.S. & Canad. informal.* an easy task. ~*vb.* **3.** to move quickly or casually: *he breezed into the room.* [prob. from Old Spanish *briza*]

breeze[2] (briːz) *n.* ashes of coal, coke, or charcoal. [French *braise* live coals]

breeze block *n.* a light building brick made from the ashes of coal, coke, etc., bonded together by cement.

breezy ('briːzɪ) *adj.* **breezier, breeziest. 1.** fresh; windy. **2.** casual or carefree.

Bren gun (brɛn) *n.* an air-cooled gas-operated light machine gun used by the British in World War II. [after B*r*(*no*), Czechoslovakia, and E*n*(*field*), England, where it was made]

brent (brɛnt) *or esp. U.S.* **brant** (brænt) *n.* a small goose with a dark grey plumage.

brethren ('brɛðrɪn) *pl. n. Archaic except when referring to fellow members of a religion, society, etc.* a plural of **brother.**

Breton ('brɛt'n) *adj.* **1.** of Brittany, its people, or their language. ~*n.* **2.** a person from Brittany. **3.** the Celtic language of Brittany.

breve (briːv) *n.* an accent, ˘, placed over a vowel to indicate that it is short or is pronounced in a specified way. [Latin *brevis* short]

breviary ('briːvjərɪ) *n., pl.* -**ries.** *R.C. Church.* a book of psalms, hymns, prayers, etc., to be recited daily. [Latin *brevis* short]

brevity ('brɛvɪtɪ) *n.* **1.** a short duration; brief time. **2.** lack of verbosity. [Latin *brevis* brief]

brew (bruː) *vb.* **1.** to make (beer, ale, etc.) from malt and other ingredients by steeping, boiling, and fermentation. **2.** to prepare (a drink, such as tea) by infusing. **3.** to devise or plan: *to brew a plot.* **4.** to be in the process of being brewed. **5.** to be impending or forming: *there's a storm brewing.* ~*n.* **6.** a beverage produced by brewing, esp. tea or beer. **7.** an instance of brewing: *last year's brew.* [Old English *brēowan*] —'**brewer** *n.*

brewery ('bruərɪ) *n., pl.* -**eries.** a place where beer, ale, etc., is brewed.

briar[1] *or* **brier** ('braɪə) *n.* **1.** a shrub of S Europe, with a hard woody root (briar-root). **2.** a tobacco pipe made from this root. [French *bruyère*]

briar[2] ('braɪə) *n.* same as **brier**[1].

bribe (braɪb) *vb.* **1.** to promise, offer, or give something, often illegally, to (a person) to procure services or gain influence. ~*n.* **2.** a reward, such as money or favour, given or offered for this purpose. [Old French *briber* to beg] —'**bribery** *n.*

bric-a-brac ('brɪkə,bræk) *n.* miscellaneous small ornamental objects. [French]

brick (brɪk) *n.* **1.** a rectangular block of baked or dried clay, used in building construction. **2.** the material used to make such blocks. **3.** any rectangular block: *a brick of ice.* **4.** bricks collectively. **5.** *Informal.* a reliable, trustworthy, or helpful person. **6. drop a brick.** *Brit. informal.* to make a tactless or indiscreet remark. ~*vb.* **7.** (foll. by *in, up,* or *over*) to construct, line, pave, fill, or wall up with bricks: *to brick up a window.* [Middle Dutch *brcke*]

brickbat ('brɪk,bæt) *n.* **1.** blunt criticism. **2.** a piece of brick used as a weapon.

bricklayer ('brɪk,leɪə) *n.* a person who builds with bricks.

brick-red *adj.* reddish-brown.

bridal ('braɪd°l) *adj.* of a bride or a wedding. [Old English *brȳdealu* bride ale]

bride (braɪd) *n.* a woman who has just been or is about to be married. [Old English *brȳd*]

bridegroom ('braɪd,gruːm, -,grʊm) *n.* a man who has just been or is about to be married. [Old English *brȳdguma*]

bridesmaid ('braɪdz,meɪd) *n.* a girl or young woman who attends a bride at her wedding.

bridge[1] (brɪdʒ) *n.* **1.** a structure that provides a passage over a railway, river, etc. **2.** the hard ridge at the upper part of the nose. **3.** a dental plate containing artificial teeth that is secured to natural teeth. **4.** a platform from which a ship is piloted and navigated. **5.** a piece of wood supporting the strings of a violin, guitar, etc. ~*vb.* **6.** to build or provide a bridge over (something). **7.** to connect or reduce the distance between: *let us bridge our differences.* [Old English *brycg*]

bridge[2] (brɪdʒ) *n.* a card game for four players, based on whist, in which the trump suit is decided by bidding between the players. [origin unknown]

bridgehead ('brɪdʒ,hed) *n. Mil.* a fortified or defensive position at the end of a bridge nearest to the enemy.

bridgework ('brɪdʒ,wɜːk) *n.* a partial denture attached to the surrounding teeth.

bridging loan *n.* a loan made to cover the period between two transactions, such as the buying of another house before the sale of the first is completed.

bridle ('braɪd°l) *n.* **1.** headgear for a horse, consisting of a series of buckled straps and a metal mouthpiece (bit) by which the animal is controlled through the reins. **2.** something that curbs or restrains. ~*vb.* **3.** to put a bridle on (a horse). **4.** to restrain; curb: *he bridled his rage.* [Old English *brigdels*]

bridle path *n.* a path suitable for riding or leading horses.

Brie (briː) *n.* a soft creamy white cheese. [*Brie*, region in N France]

brief (briːf) *adj.* **1.** short in duration. **2.** short in length or extent; scanty: *a brief bikini.* **3.** terse or concise. ~*n.* **4.** a condensed statement or written synopsis. **5.** *Law.* a document containing all the facts and points of law of a case by which a solicitor instructs a barrister to represent a client. **6.** *R.C. Church.* a papal letter that is less formal than a bull. **7.** Also called: **briefing.** instructions. **8. hold a brief for.** to argue for; champion. **9. in brief.** in short; to sum up. ~*vb.* **10.** to prepare or instruct (someone) by giving him a summary of relevant facts. **11.** *English law.* **a.** to instruct (a barrister) by brief. **b.** to retain (a barrister) as counsel. [Latin *brevis*] —'**briefly** *adv.*

briefcase ('briːf,keɪs) *n.* a flat portable case for carrying papers, books, etc.

briefs (briːfs) *pl. n.* men's or women's underpants without legs.

brier[1] *or* **briar** ('braɪə) *n.* any of various thorny shrubs or other plants, such as the sweetbrier. [Old English *brēr, brǣr*]

brier[2] ('braɪə) *n.* same as **briar**[1].

brig[1] (brɪg) *n. Naut.* a two-masted square-rigger. [from BRIGANTINE]

brig[2] (brɪg) *n. Scot. & N English.* a bridge.

Brig. Brigadier.

brigade (brɪ'geɪd) *n.* **1.** a military formation smaller than a division and usually commanded by a brigadier. **2.** a group of people organized for a certain task: *a rescue brigade.* [Old French]

brigadier (,brɪgə'dɪə) *n.* a senior officer in an army, usually commanding a brigade.

brigand ('brɪgənd) *n.* a bandit, esp. a member of a gang operating in mountainous areas. [Old French]

brigantine ('brɪgən,tiːn, -,taɪn) *n.* a two-masted sailing ship, rigged square on the foremast and fore-and-aft on the mainmast. [Old Italian *brigantino* pirate ship]

bright (braɪt) *adj.* **1.** emitting or reflecting much light; shining. **2.** (of colours) intense or vivid. **3.** full of promise: *a bright future.* **4.** lively or cheerful. **5.** *Informal.* quick-witted or clever. ~*adv.* **6.** brightly: *the fire was burning bright.* [Old English *beorht*] —'**brightly** *adv.* —'**brightness** *n.*

brighten ('braɪt°n) *vb.* **1.** to make or become bright or brighter. **2.** to make or become cheerful.

brill (brɪl) *n., pl.* **brill** *or* **brills.** a European flatfish similar to the turbot. [prob. Cornish]

brilliance ('brɪljəns) *or* **brilliancy** *n.* **1.** great brightness. **2.** excellence in physical or mental ability. **3.** splendour.

brilliant ('brɪljənt) *adj.* **1.** shining with light; sparkling. **2.** (of a colour) vivid. **3.** splendid; magnificent: *a brilliant show.* **4.** of outstanding intelligence or intellect. ~*n.* **5.** a diamond cut with many facets to increase its sparkle. [French *brillant* shining]

brilliantine ('brɪljən,tiːn) *n.* a perfumed oil used to make the hair smooth and shiny. [French]

brim (brɪm) *n.* **1.** the upper rim of a cup, bowl, etc. **2.** a projecting edge of a hat. ~*vb.* **brimming, brimmed.** **3.** to be full to the brim: *eyes brimming with tears.* [Middle High German *brem*] —'**brimless** *adj.*

brimful (,brɪm'fʊl) *adj.* (foll. by *of*) filled up to the brim with.

brimstone ('brɪm,stəʊn) *n. Obs.* sulphur. [Old English *brynstān*]

brindled ('brɪnd°ld) *adj.* brown or grey streaked with a darker colour: *a brindled dog.* [Middle English *brended*]

brine (braɪn) *n.* **1.** a strong solution of salt and water, used for pickling. **2.** the sea or its water. [Old English *brīne*]

bring (brɪŋ) *vb.* **bringing, brought.** **1.** to carry, convey, or take (something or someone) to a designated place or person. **2.** to cause to happen: *responsibility brings maturity.* **3.** to cause to come to mind: *it brought back memories.* **4.** to cause to be in a certain state, position, etc.: *the punch brought him to his knees.* **5.** to make (oneself): *I couldn't bring myself to do it.* **6.** to sell for: *the painting brought £20.* **7.** *Law.* **a.** to institute (proceedings, charges, etc.). **b.** to put (evidence, etc.) before a tribunal. **8. bring forth.** to give birth to. ~See also **bring about, bring down,** etc. [Old English *bringan*]

bring about *vb.* to cause to happen: *they brought about a peaceful settlement.*

bring-and-buy sale *n.* *Brit. & N.Z.* an informal sale, often for charity, to which people bring items for sale and buy those that others have brought.

bring down *vb.* to cause to fall.

bring forward *vb.* **1.** to move (a meeting, lecture, etc.) to an earlier date or time. **2.** to present or introduce (a subject) for discussion. **3.** *Book-keeping.* to transfer (a sum) to the top of the next page or column.

bring in *vb.* **1.** to yield (income, profit, or cash). **2.** to introduce (a legislative bill, etc.). **3.** to produce or return (a verdict).

bring off *vb.* to succeed in achieving (something difficult).

bring out *vb.* **1.** to produce, publish, or have (a book) published. **2.** to expose, reveal, or cause to be seen: *she brought out the best in me.* **3.** (foll. by *in*) to cause (a person) to become covered with (a rash, spots, etc.).

bring over *vb.* to cause (a person) to change allegiances.

bring round *vb.* **1.** to restore (a person) to consciousness after a faint. **2.** to convince (another person) of an opinion or point of view.

bring to *vb.* to restore (a person) to consciousness: *the smelling salts brought her to.*

bring up *vb.* **1.** to care for and train (a child); rear. **2.** to raise (a subject) for discussion; mention. **3.** to vomit (food).

brinjal ('brɪndʒəl) *n.* (in India and Africa) same as **aubergine.** [Arabic]

brink (brɪŋk) *n.* **1.** the edge, border, or verge of a steep place. **2.** the land at the edge of a body of water. **3. on the brink of.** very near, on the point of: *on the brink of disaster.* [Middle Dutch *brinc*]

brinkmanship ('brɪŋkmənˌʃɪp) *n.* the practice of pressing a dangerous situation to the limit of safety in order to win an advantage.

briny ('braɪnɪ) *adj.* **brinier, briniest. 1.** of or like brine; salty. ~*n.* **2. the.** *Informal.* the sea.

briquette (brɪ'kɛt) *n.* a small brick made of compressed coal dust, used for fuel. [French]

brisk (brɪsk) *adj.* **1.** lively and quick; vigorous: *a brisk walk.* **2.** invigorating or sharp: *brisk weather.* ~*vb.* **3.** (foll. by *up*) to enliven; make brisk. [prob. var. of BRUSQUE]

brisket ('brɪskɪt) *n.* beef from the breast of a cow. [prob. from Old Norse]

brisling ('brɪslɪŋ) *n.* same as **sprat.** [Norwegian]

bristle ('brɪs'l) *n.* **1.** any short stiff hair, such as on a pig's back. **2.** something resembling these hairs: *toothbrush bristle.* ~*vb.* **3.** to stand up or cause to stand up like bristles. **4.** to show anger or indignation: *she bristled at the suggestion.* **5.** to be thickly covered or set: *the target bristled with arrows.* [Old English *byrst*] —'**bristly** *adj.*

Brit (brɪt) *n.* *Informal.* a British person.

Brit. 1. Britain. **2.** British.

Britannia (brɪ'tænɪə) *n.* a female warrior carrying a trident and wearing a helmet, personifying Great Britain.

Britannia metal *n.* an alloy of tin with antimony and copper.

Britannic (brɪ'tænɪk) *adj.* of Britain; British: *Her Britannic Majesty.*

britches ('brɪtʃɪz) *pl. n.* same as **breeches.**

British ('brɪtɪʃ) *adj.* **1.** of Great Britain or the British Commonwealth. **2.** relating to or denoting the English language as spoken and written in Britain. ~*n.* **3. the British.** (*functioning as pl.*) the people of Great Britain.

Briton ('brɪt'n) *n.* **1.** a person from Britain. **2.** *History.* any of the early Celtic inhabitants of S Britain. [of Celtic origin]

brittle ('brɪt'l) *adj.* **1.** easily cracked or broken; fragile. **2.** curt or irritable: *a brittle reply.* **3.** hard or sharp in quality: *a brittle laugh.* [Old English *brēotan* to break] —'**brittlely** or '**brittly** *adv.*

broach (brəʊtʃ) *vb.* **1.** to initiate (a topic) for discussion. **2.** to tap or pierce (a container) to draw off (a liquid). **3.** to open in order to begin to use. ~*n.* **4.** a tapered tool for enlarging holes. **5.** a spit for roasting meat. [Latin *brochus* projecting]

broad (brɔːd) *adj.* **1.** having great breadth or width. **2.** spacious. **3.** not detailed; general. **4.** clear and open: *broad daylight.* **5.** obvious: *broad hints.* **6.** tolerant: *a broad view.* **7.** extensive: *broad support.* **8.** vulgar or coarse. **9.** strongly marked: *a broad Yorkshire accent.* ~*n.* **10.** the broad part of something. **11.** *Slang, chiefly U.S. & Canad.* a woman. **12. the Broads.** in East Anglia, a group of shallow lakes connected by a network of rivers. [Old English *brād*] —'**broadly** *adv.*

B-road *n.* a secondary road in Britain.

broad bean *n.* the large edible flattened seed of a Eurasian bean plant.

broadcast ('brɔːdˌkɑːst) *vb.* -**casting,** -**cast** or -**casted. 1.** to transmit (announcements or programmes) on radio or television. **2.** to take part in a radio or television programme. **3.** to make widely known throughout an area: *to broadcast news.* **4.** to scatter (seed, etc.). ~*n.* **5.** a transmission or programme on radio or television. —'**broad,caster** *n.* —'**broad,casting** *n.*

broadcloth ('brɔːdˌklɒθ) *n.* a closely woven fabric of wool, worsted, cotton, or rayon with a lustrous finish, used for clothing.

broaden ('brɔːdˀn) *vb.* to make or become broad or broader; widen.

broad gauge *n.* a railway track with a greater distance between the lines than the standard gauge of 56½ in.

broad-leaved *adj.* denoting trees other than conifers; having broad rather than needle-shaped leaves.

broadloom ('brɔːd‚luːm) *n. (modifier)* of or designating carpets woven on a wide loom.

broad-minded *adj.* 1. tolerant of opposing viewpoints; liberal. 2. not easily shocked.

broadsheet ('brɔːd‚ʃiːt) *n.* a newspaper in a large format.

broadside ('brɔːd‚saɪd) *n.* 1. a strong or abusive verbal or written attack. 2. *Naval.* the simultaneous firing of all the guns on one side of a ship. 3. *Naut.* the entire side of a ship. ~*adv.* 4. with a broader side facing an object.

broadsword ('brɔːd‚sɔːd) *n.* a broad-bladed sword used for cutting rather than stabbing.

brocade (brəʊˈkeɪd) *n.* 1. a rich fabric woven with a raised design. ~*vb.* 2. to weave with such a design. [Spanish *brocado*]

broccoli ('brɒkəlɪ) *n.* a variety of cabbage with greenish flower heads eaten as a vegetable before the buds have opened. [Italian]

brochette (brɒˈʃɛt) *n.* a skewer used for holding pieces of meat or vegetables while grilling. [Old French *brochete*]

brochure ('brəʊʃjʊə, -ʃə) *n.* a pamphlet or booklet, esp. one containing introductory information or advertising. [French]

broderie anglaise ('brəʊdərɪ ɑːŋˈɡlɛz) *n.* open embroidery on white cotton, fine linen, etc. [French: English embroidery]

brogue[1] ('brəʊɡ) *n.* a broad gentle-sounding dialectal accent, esp. that used by the Irish in speaking English. [origin unknown]

brogue[2] (brəʊɡ) *n.* a sturdy walking shoe, often with ornamental perforations. [Irish Gaelic *brōg*]

broil (brɔɪl) *vb. U.S. & Canad.* same as **grill** (sense 1). [Old French *bruillir*]

broiler ('brɔɪlə) *n.* a young tender chicken suitable for roasting.

broke (brəʊk) *vb.* 1. the past tense of **break**. ~*adj.* 2. *Informal.* having no money.

broken ('brəʊkən) *vb.* 1. the past participle of **break**. ~*adj.* 2. fractured, smashed, or splintered. 3. interrupted; disturbed: *broken sleep.* 4. not functioning. 5. (of a promise or contract) violated; infringed. 6. (of the speech of a foreigner) imperfectly spoken: *broken English.* 7. Also: **broken-in.** made tame by training. 8. exhausted or weakened, as through ill-health or misfortune.

broken chord *n.* same as **arpeggio.**

broken-down *adj.* 1. worn out, as by

age or long use; dilapidated. 2. not in working order.

brokenhearted (‚brəʊkənˈhɑːtɪd) *adj.* overwhelmed by grief or disappointment.

broken home *n.* a family which does not live together because the parents are separated or divorced.

broker ('brəʊkə) *n.* 1. an agent who buys or sells goods, securities, etc.: *insurance broker.* 2. same as **stockbroker**. 3. a person who deals in second-hand goods. [Anglo-French *brocour* broacher]

brokerage ('brəʊkərɪdʒ) *n.* commission charged by a broker.

brolly ('brɒlɪ) *n., pl.* **-lies.** *Brit. informal.* an umbrella.

bromide ('brəʊmaɪd) *n.* 1. any compound of bromine with another element or radical. 2. a dose of sodium or potassium bromide given as a sedative. 3. a boring, meaningless, or obvious remark.

bromide paper *n.* a type of photographic paper coated with an emulsion of silver bromide.

bromine ('brəʊmiːn, -mɪn) *n.* a dark red liquid chemical element that gives off an irritating vapour. Symbol: Br [Greek *brōmos* bad smell]

bronchial ('brɒŋkɪəl) *adj.* of or relating to the bronchi or the smaller tubes into which they divide.

bronchitis (brɒŋˈkaɪtɪs) *n.* inflammation of the bronchial tubes, characterized by coughing, difficulty in breathing, etc.

bronchus ('brɒŋkəs) *n., pl.* **-chi** (-kaɪ). either of the two main branches of the windpipe. [Greek *bronkhos*]

bronco ('brɒŋkəʊ) *n., pl.* **-cos.** (in the U.S. and Canada) a wild or partially tamed pony of the western plains. [Spanish: wild]

brontosaurus (‚brɒntəˈsɔːrəs) *n.* a very large plant-eating four-footed dinosaur that had a long neck and long tail. [Greek *brontē* thunder + *sauros* lizard]

bronze (brɒnz) *n.* 1. an alloy of copper and smaller proportions of tin. 2. a statue, medal, or other object made of bronze. ~*adj.* 3. made of or resembling bronze. 4. yellowish-brown. ~*vb.* 5. (esp. of the skin) to make or become brown; tan. [Italian *bronzo*]

Bronze Age *n.* a phase of human culture, lasting in Britain from about 2000 to 500 B.C., during which weapons and tools were made of bronze.

bronze medal *n.* a medal awarded as third prize.

brooch (brəʊtʃ) *n.* an ornament with a hinged pin and catch, worn fastened to clothing. [Old French *broche*]

brood (bruːd) *n.* 1. a number of young animals, esp. birds, produced at one hatching. 2. all the children in a family: often used jokingly. ~*vb.* 3. (of a bird) to sit on or hatch eggs. 4. (sometimes foll. by *on* or *over*) to ponder morbidly or persistently. [Old English *brōd*] —'**brooding** *n., adj.*

broody ('bruːdɪ) *adj.* **broodier, broodiest.** 1. moody; introspective. 2. (of poultry) wishing to sit on or hatch eggs. **3.** *Informal.* (of a woman) wishing to have a baby.

brook[1] (brʊk) *n.* a natural freshwater stream smaller than a river. [Old English *brōc*]

brook[2] (brʊk) *vb.* to bear; tolerate: *she will brook no nonsense.* [Old English *brūcan*]

broom (bruːm, brʊm) *n.* **1.** a type of long-handled sweeping brush. **2.** a yellow-flowered shrub. **3. a new broom.** a newly appointed official, etc., eager to make radical changes. [Old English *brōm*]

broomstick ('bruːmˌstɪk, 'brʊm-) *n.* the long handle of a broom.

bros. *or* **Bros.** brothers.

broth (brɒθ) *n.* a soup made by boiling meat, fish, vegetables, etc., in water. [Old English *broth*]

brothel ('brɒθəl) *n.* a house where men pay to have sexual intercourse with prostitutes. [short for *brothel-house*, from Middle English *brothel* useless person]

brother ('brʌðə) *n.* **1.** a man or boy with the same parents as another person. **2.** a man belonging to the same group, trade union, etc., as another or others; fellow member. **3.** comrade; friend. **4.** *Christianity.* a member of a male religious order. [Old English *brōthor*]

brotherhood ('brʌðəˌhʊd) *n.* **1.** the state of being a brother. **2.** an association, such as a trade union. **3.** fellowship.

brother-in-law *n.*, *pl.* **brothers-in-law.** **1.** the brother of one's wife or husband. **2.** the husband of one's sister.

brotherly ('brʌðəlɪ) *adj.* of or like a brother, esp. in showing loyalty and affection.

brougham ('bruːəm, bruːm) *n.* a four-wheeled horse-drawn closed carriage with a raised outside driver's seat in front. [after Lord *Brougham*]

brought (brɔːt) *vb.* past of **bring**.

brouhaha ('bruːhɑːˌhɑː) *n.* a loud confused noise; commotion; uproar. [French]

brow (braʊ) *n.* **1.** the part of the face from the eyes to the hairline; forehead. **2.** same as **eyebrow**. **3.** the jutting top of a hill. [Old English *brū*]

browbeat ('braʊˌbiːt) *vb.* **-beating, -beat, -beaten.** to frighten (someone) with threats.

brown (braʊn) *n.* **1.** any of various dark colours, such as those of wood or earth. **2.** a dye or pigment producing these colours. ~*adj.* **3.** of the colour brown. **4.** (of bread) made from wheatmeal or wholemeal flour. **5.** deeply tanned. ~*vb.* **6.** to make (food) brown or (of food) to become brown as a result of cooking. [Old English *brūn*] —'**brownish** *or* '**browny** *adj.*

brown bear *n.* a large ferocious brownish bear inhabiting temperate forests of North America, Europe, and Asia.

brown coal *n.* same as **lignite**.

browned-off *adj. Informal, chiefly Brit.* thoroughly discouraged or disheartened; fed up.

brownie ('braʊnɪ) *n.* **1.** (in folklore) an elf said to do helpful work, esp. household

chores, at night. **2.** a small square nutty chocolate cake.

Brownie Guide *or* **Brownie** ('braʊnɪ) *n.* a member of the junior branch of the Guides.

Brownie point *n.* a notional mark to one's credit for being seen to do the right thing. [origin unknown]

browning ('braʊnɪŋ) *n. Brit.* a substance used to darken gravies.

brown paper *n.* a kind of coarse unbleached paper used for wrapping.

brown rice *n.* unpolished rice, in which the grains retain the outer yellowish-brown layer (bran).

Brown Shirt *n.* **1.** (in Nazi Germany) a storm trooper. **2.** a member of any fascist party or group.

brown sugar *n.* sugar that is unrefined or only partially refined.

brown trout *n.* a common brownish trout that occurs in the rivers of N Europe.

browse (braʊz) *vb.* **1.** to look through (a book or articles for sale) in a casual leisurely manner. **2.** (of deer, goats, etc.) to feed upon vegetation by continual nibbling. ~*n.* **3.** an instance of browsing. [French *broust* bud]

brucellosis (ˌbruːsɪ'ləʊsɪs) *n.* an infectious disease of cattle, goats, and pigs, caused by bacteria and transmittable to humans. [after Sir David *Bruce*, bacteriologist]

bruise (bruːz) *vb.* **1.** to injure (body tissue) without breaking the skin, usually with discoloration, or (of body tissue) to be injured in this way. **2.** to hurt (someone's feelings). **3.** to damage (fruit). ~*n.* **4.** a bodily injury without a break in the skin, usually with discoloration. [Old English *brȳsan*]

bruiser ('bruːzə) *n.* a strong tough person, esp. a boxer or a bully.

bruit (bruːt) *vb.* **be bruited about.** to be reported or rumoured. [French]

brunch (brʌntʃ) *n.* a meal eaten late in the morning, combining breakfast with lunch. [BR(EAKFAST) + (L)UNCH]

brunette (bruː'nɛt) *n.* a girl or woman with dark brown hair. [French]

brunt (brʌnt) *n.* the main force or shock of a blow, attack, etc.: *I had to bear the brunt of his anger.*

brush[1] (brʌʃ) *n.* **1.** a device made of bristles, hairs, wires, etc., set into a firm back or handle: used to apply paint, groom the hair, etc. **2.** the act of brushing. **3.** a brief encounter, esp. an unfriendly one. **4.** the bushy tail of a fox. **5.** an electric conductor, esp. one made of carbon, that conveys current between stationary and rotating parts of a generator, motor, etc. ~*vb.* **6.** to clean, scrub, paint, etc., with a brush. **7.** to apply or remove with a brush or brushing movement. **8.** to touch lightly and briefly. ~See also **brush aside, brush off, brush up.** [Old French *broisse*]

brush[2] (brʌʃ) *n.* a thick growth of shrubs and small trees; scrub. [Old French *broce*]

brush aside *or* **away** *vb.* to dismiss (a

suggestion or an idea) without consideration; disregard.

brushed (brʌʃt) adj. Textiles. treated with a brushing process to raise the nap and give a softer and warmer finish: brushed nylon.

brush off Slang. ~vb. 1. to dismiss and ignore (a person), esp. curtly. ~n. **brush-off. 2. give someone the brushoff.** to reject someone.

brush up vb. 1. (often foll. by on) to refresh one's knowledge or memory of (a subject). ~n. **brush-up. 2.** Brit. the act of tidying one's appearance: have a wash and brush-up.

brushwood ('brʌʃ,wʊd) n. **1.** cut or broken-off tree branches, twigs, etc. **2.** same as **brush².**

brushwork ('brʌʃ,wɜːk) n. a characteristic manner of applying paint with a brush: Rembrandt's brushwork.

brusque (bruːsk, brʊsk) adj. blunt or curt in manner or speech. [Italian brusco sour] —**'brusquely** adv. —**'brusqueness** n.

Brussels sprout ('brʌsəlz) n. a vegetable like a tiny cabbage.

brutal ('bruːt²l) adj. **1.** cruel; vicious; savage. **2.** extremely honest or coarse in speech or manner. —**bru'tality** n. —**'brutally** adv.

brutalize or **-ise** ('bruːtə,laɪz) vb. **1.** to make or become brutal. **2.** to treat (someone) brutally. —**,brutali'zation** or **-i'sation** n.

brute (bruːt) n. **1.** any animal except man; beast; lower animal. **2.** a brutal person. ~adj. **3.** wholly instinctive or physical, like that of an animal: we will never yield to brute force. **4.** without reason or intelligence. **5.** coarse and grossly sensual. [Latin brūtus irrational]

brutish ('bruːtɪʃ) adj. **1.** of or resembling a brute; animal. **2.** coarse; cruel; stupid.

bryony ('braɪənɪ) n., pl. **-nies.** a climbing plant with greenish flowers and red or black berries. [Greek bruōnia]

Brythonic (brɪ'θɒnɪk) n. **1.** the S group of Celtic languages, consisting of Welsh, Cornish, and Breton. ~adj. **2.** of this group of languages. [Welsh]

BS **1.** Bachelor of Surgery. **2.** British Standard(s).

BSc Bachelor of Science.

BSI British Standards Institution.

B-side n. the less important side of a gramophone record.

BST **1.** British Standard Time. **2.** British Summer Time.

Bt Baronet.

BT British Telecom.

btu or **BThU** British thermal unit.

bubble ('bʌb²l) n. **1.** a thin film of liquid forming a ball around air or a gas: a soap bubble. **2.** a small globule of air or a gas in a liquid or a solid. **3.** an unreliable scheme or enterprise. **4.** a dome, esp. a transparent glass or plastic one. ~vb. **5.** to form bubbles. **6.** to move or flow with a gurgling sound. **7. bubble over.** to express an

emotion freely: she was bubbling over with excitement. [imit.]

bubble and squeak n. Brit. a dish of boiled cabbage and potatoes fried together.

bubble bath n. **1.** a substance used to scent, soften, and foam in bath water. **2.** a bath with such a substance.

bubble car n. Brit. a small car with a transparent bubble-shaped top.

bubble gum n. a type of chewing gum that can be blown into large bubbles.

bubbly ('bʌblɪ) adj. **-blier, -bliest. 1.** full of or resembling bubbles. **2.** lively; animated; excited. ~n. **3.** Informal. champagne.

bubo ('bjuːbəʊ) n., pl. **-boes.** Pathol. inflammation and swelling of a lymph node, esp. in the armpit or groin. [Greek boubōn groin] —**bubonic** (bjuː'bɒnɪk) adj.

bubonic plague n. an acute infectious disease characterized by the formation of buboes.

buccaneer (,bʌkə'nɪə) n. a pirate, esp. in the Caribbean in the 17th and 18th centuries. [French boucanier]

buck¹ (bʌk) n. **1.** the male of the goat, hare, kangaroo, rabbit, and reindeer. **2.** Archaic. a spirited young man. **3.** the act of bucking. ~vb. **4.** (of a horse or other animal) to jump vertically, with legs stiff and back arched. **5.** (of a horse, etc.) to throw (its rider) by bucking. **6.** Chiefly U.S., Canad., & Austral. informal. to resist or oppose obstinately. ~See also **buck up.** [Old English bucca he-goat]

buck² (bʌk) n. U.S., Canad., & Austral. slang. a dollar. [origin unknown]

buck³ (bʌk) n. **pass the buck.** Informal. to shift blame or responsibility onto another. [prob. from buckhorn knife, placed before a player in poker to indicate that he was the next dealer]

bucket ('bʌkɪt) n. **1.** an open-topped cylindrical container. **2.** the amount a bucket will hold. **3.** a bucket-like part of a machine, such as the scoop on a mechanical shovel. **4. kick the bucket.** Slang. to die. [Old English būc]

bucket down vb. (of rain) to fall very heavily.

bucket shop n. **1.** Chiefly Brit. a travel agency specializing in cheap airline tickets. **2.** an unregistered firm of stockbrokers that engages in fraudulent speculation.

buckle ('bʌk²l) n. **1.** a clasp for fastening together two loose ends, esp. of a belt or strap. ~vb. **2.** to fasten or be fastened with a buckle. **3.** to bend or cause to bend out of shape, esp. as a result of pressure or heat. [Latin buccula cheek strap]

buckle down vb. Informal. to apply oneself with determination.

buckler ('bʌklə) n. a small round shield worn on the forearm. [Old French bocler]

buckram ('bʌkrəm) n. stiffened cotton or linen used in lining or stiffening clothes, bookbinding, etc. [Bukhara, USSR, once important for textiles]

Bucks (bʌks) Buckinghamshire.

buckshee (ˌbʌkˈʃiː) *adj. Brit. slang.* without charge; free. [from BAKSHEESH]

buckshot (ˈbʌkˌʃɒt) *n.* large lead shot used for hunting game.

buckskin (ˈbʌkˌskɪn) *n.* **1.** a strong greyish-yellow suede leather, originally made from deerskin. **2.** (*pl.*) trousers made of buckskin.

buckteeth (ˌbʌkˈtiːθ) *pl. n.* projecting upper front teeth. —**buck-toothed** (ˌbʌkˈtuːθt) *adj.*

buckthorn (ˈbʌkˌθɔːn) *n.* a thorny shrub whose berries were formerly used as a purgative.

buck up *vb. Informal.* **1.** to make or become more cheerful, confident, etc. **2.** to make haste.

buckwheat (ˈbʌkˌwiːt) *n.* **1.** a type of small black seed used as animal fodder and in making flour. **2.** the flour obtained from such seeds. [Middle Dutch *boecweite*]

bucolic (bjuːˈkɒlɪk) *adj.* **1.** of the countryside or country life; rustic. **2.** of or relating to shepherds; pastoral. ~*n.* **3.** a pastoral poem. [Greek *boukolos* cowherd]

bud (bʌd) *n.* **1.** a swelling on the stem of a plant that develops into a flower or leaf. **2.** a partially opened flower: *rosebud.* **3.** any small budlike outgrowth: *taste buds.* **4.** nip something in the bud. to put an end to something in its initial stages. ~*vb.* **budding, budded. 5.** (of plants and some animals) to produce buds. **6.** to begin to develop or grow: *a budding actor.* **7.** *Horticulture.* to graft (a bud) from one plant onto another. [Middle English *budde*]

Buddhism (ˈbʊdɪzəm) *n.* a religion founded by the Buddha that teaches that all suffering can be brought to an end by overcoming greed, hatred, and delusion. —**'Buddhist** *n., adj.*

buddleia (ˈbʌdlɪə) *n.* an ornamental shrub which has long spikes of typically purple flowers. [after A. *Buddle*, botanist]

buddy (ˈbʌdɪ) *n., pl.* **-dies. 1.** *Chiefly U.S. & Canad. informal.* a friend. **2.** a volunteer who helps and supports a person suffering from AIDS. ~*vb.* **-dying, -died. 3.** to act as a buddy to a person suffering from AIDS. [prob. var. of BROTHER]

budge (bʌdʒ) *vb.* **1.** to move slightly: *she refuses to budge off that chair.* **2.** to change or cause to change opinions: *she will not budge on any of the important issues.* [Old French *bouger*]

budgerigar (ˈbʌdʒərɪˌɡɑː) *n.* a small caged bird bred in many different-coloured varieties. [Aboriginal]

budget (ˈbʌdʒɪt) *n.* **1.** a plan of expected income and expenditure over a specified period. **2.** (*modifier*) inexpensive: *budget meals for a family.* **3.** the total amount of money allocated for a specific purpose during a specified period. ~*vb.* **4.** to enter or provide for in a budget. **5.** to plan the expenditure of (money or time). [Latin *bulga* leather pouch] —**'budgetary** *adj.*

Budget (ˈbʌdʒɪt) *n.* **the.** an annual estimate of British government expenditures and revenues and the financial plans for the following financial year.

budgie (ˈbʌdʒɪ) *n. Informal.* same as **budgerigar.**

buff¹ (bʌf) *n.* **1.** a soft thick flexible undyed leather. **2.** a cloth or pad of material used for polishing. **3. in the buff.** *Informal.* completely naked. ~*adj.* **4.** dull yellowish-brown. ~*vb.* **5.** to clean or polish (a metal, floor, shoes, etc.) with a buff. [Late Latin *būfalus* buffalo]

buff² (bʌf) *n. Informal.* an expert on or devotee of a given subject: *an opera buff.* [from the buff-coloured uniforms worn by volunteer firemen in New York City]

buffalo (ˈbʌfəˌləʊ) *n., pl.* **-loes** *or* **-lo. 1.** a type of cattle with upward-curving horns. **2.** same as **water buffalo. 3.** *U.S. & Canad.* a bison. [Greek *bous* ox]

buffer¹ (ˈbʌfə) *n.* **1.** one of a pair of spring-loaded steel pads attached at both ends of railway vehicles and at the end of a railway track to reduce shock due to contact. **2.** a person or thing that lessens shock or protects from damaging impact, circumstances, etc. **3.** *Chem.* **a.** a substance added to a solution to resist changes in its acidity or alkalinity. **b.** Also called: **buffer solution.** a solution containing such a substance. **4.** *Computers.* a device for temporarily storing data. [from BUFFET²]

buffer² (ˈbʌfə) *n. Brit. informal.* a stupid or bumbling person, esp. a man: *an old buffer.* [origin unknown]

buffer state *n.* a small and usually neutral state between two rival powers.

buffet¹ (ˈbʊfeɪ) *n.* **1.** a counter where light refreshments are served. **2.** a meal at which guests help themselves from a number of dishes.

buffet² (ˈbʌfɪt) *vb.* **-feting, -feted. 1.** to knock against or about; batter: *the ship was buffeted by huge waves.* **2.** to hit, esp. with the fist. ~*n.* **3.** a blow, esp. with a hand. [Old French *buffet* a blow]

buffet car (ˈbʊfeɪ) *n. Brit.* a railway coach where light refreshments are served.

buffoon (bəˈfuːn) *n.* a person who amuses others by silly behaviour. [Latin *būfo* toad] —**buf'foonery** *n.*

bug (bʌɡ) *n.* **1.** any of various insects having piercing and sucking mouthparts. **2.** *Chiefly U.S. & Canad.* any insect. **3.** *Informal.* a minor illness such as a stomach infection caused by a germ or virus. **4.** *Informal.* an obsessive idea or hobby; craze. **5.** *Informal.* a concealed microphone used for recording conversations, as in spying. ~*vb.* **bugging, bugged.** *Informal.* **6.** to irritate or upset (someone). **7.** to conceal a microphone in (a room or telephone). [origin unknown]

bugbear (ˈbʌɡˌbɛə) *n.* a thing that causes obsessive anxiety. [obs. *bug* an evil spirit + BEAR²]

bugger (ˈbʌɡə) *n.* **1.** *Taboo slang.* a person or thing considered to be unpleasant or difficult. **2.** *Slang.* a humorous or affectionate term for a man or child: *a friendly little bugger.* **3.** a person who practises buggery. ~*vb.* **4.** *Slang.* to tire; weary.

5. to practise buggery with. ~*interj.* **6.** *Taboo slang.* an exclamation of annoyance or disappointment. [Medieval Latin *Bulgarus* Bulgarian heretic]

bugger about *or* **around** *vb. Slang.* **1.** to fool about and waste time. **2.** to create difficulties for: *they really buggered me about when I tried to get my money back.*

bugger off *vb. Taboo slang.* to go away; depart.

bugger up *vb. Slang.* to spoil or ruin (something).

buggery (ˈbʌgərɪ) *n.* anal intercourse.

buggy (ˈbʌgɪ) *n., pl.* **-gies. 1.** a light horse-drawn carriage having two or four wheels. **2.** a lightweight folding pram for babies or young children. [origin unknown]

bugle (ˈbjuːgˀl) *Music.* ~*n.* **1.** a brass instrument used chiefly for military calls. ~*vb.* **2.** to play or sound (on) a bugle. [short for *bugle horn* ox horn, from Latin *būculus* bullock] —ˈ**bugler** *n.*

build (bɪld) *vb.* **building, built. 1.** to make, construct, or form by joining parts or materials: *to build a house.* **2.** to establish and develop: *it took ten years to build a business.* **3.** to make in a particular way or for a particular purpose: *the car was not built for speed.* **4.** (often foll. by *up*) to increase in intensity. ~*n.* **5.** physical form, figure, or proportions: *a man with an athletic build.* [Old English *byldan*]

builder (ˈbɪldə) *n.* a person who contracts for and supervises the construction of buildings.

building (ˈbɪldɪŋ) *n.* **1.** a structure, such as a house, with a roof and walls. **2.** the business of building houses, etc.

building society *n.* a cooperative banking enterprise financed by deposits on which interest is paid and from which mortgage loans are advanced on homes and real property.

build up *vb.* **1.** to construct (something) gradually, systematically, and in stages. **2.** to increase, accumulate, or strengthen, esp. by degrees: *the murmur built up to a roar.* **3.** to prepare for or gradually approach a climax. ~*n.* **build-up. 4.** a progressive increase in number or size: *the build-up of industry.* **5.** a gradual approach to a climax. **6.** extravagant publicity or praise, esp. in the form of a campaign.

built (bɪlt) *vb.* past of **build.**

built-in *adj.* **1.** incorporated as an integral part: *a built-in cupboard.* **2.** essential; inherent.

built-up *adj.* **1.** having many buildings: *a built-up area.* **2.** increased by the addition of parts: *built-up heels.*

bulb (bʌlb) *n.* **1.** the onion-shaped base of the stem of some plants, which sends down roots. **2.** a plant, such as a daffodil, which grows from a bulb. **3.** same as **light bulb. 4.** any bulb-shaped thing. [Greek *bolbos* onion] —ˈ**bulbous** *adj.*

bulge (bʌldʒ) *n.* **1.** a swelling or an outward curve on a normally flat surface. **2.** a sudden increase in number, esp. of population. ~*vb.* **3.** to swell outwards. [Latin *bulga* bag] —ˈ**bulging** *adj.*

bulimia (buˈlɪmɪə) *n.* a disorder characterized by compulsive overeating followed by vomiting. [Greek *bous* ox + *limos* hunger]

bulk (bʌlk) *n.* **1.** volume, size, or magnitude, esp. when great. **2.** the main part: *the bulk of the work is repetitious.* **3.** a large body, esp. of a person. **4.** the part of food which passes unabsorbed through the digestive system. ~*vb.* **5. bulk large.** to be or seem important or prominent. [Old Norse *bulki* cargo]

bulk buying *n.* the purchase of goods in large amounts, often at reduced prices.

bulkhead (ˈbʌlkˌhɛd) *n.* any upright wall-like partition in a ship or aeroplane. [prob. from Old Norse *bálkr* partition + *head*]

bulky (ˈbʌlkɪ) *adj.* **bulkier, bulkiest.** very large and massive, esp. so as to be unwieldy. —ˈ**bulkiness** *n.*

bull[1] (bʊl) *n.* **1.** a male of domestic cattle, esp. one that is sexually mature. **2.** the male of various other animals including the elephant and whale. **3.** a very large, strong, or aggressive person. **4.** *Stock Exchange.* a speculator who buys in anticipation of rising prices in order to make a profit on resale. **5.** *Chiefly Brit.* same as **bull's-eye** (senses 1, 2). **6. like a bull in a china shop.** clumsy. **7. take the bull by the horns.** to face and tackle a difficulty without shirking. [Old English *bula*]

bull[2] (bʊl) *n.* a ludicrously self-contradictory or inconsistent statement. [origin unknown]

bull[3] (bʊl) *n.* a formal document issued by the pope. [Latin *bulla* round object]

bulldog (ˈbʊlˌdɒg) *n.* a sturdy thickset dog with a broad head and a muscular body.

bulldog clip *n.* a clip for holding papers together, consisting of two metal clamps and a spring.

bulldoze (ˈbʊlˌdəʊz) *vb.* **1.** to move, demolish, or flatten with a bulldozer. **2.** *Informal.* to coerce (someone) into doing something by intimidation. [origin unknown]

bulldozer (ˈbʊlˌdəʊzə) *n.* a powerful tractor fitted with caterpillar tracks and a blade at the front, used for moving earth.

bullet (ˈbʊlɪt) *n.* a small metallic missile used as the projectile of a gun or rifle. [French *boulette* little ball]

bulletin (ˈbʊlɪtɪn) *n.* **1.** a broadcast summary of the news. **2.** an official statement on a matter of public interest. **3.** a periodical published by an organization for its members. [Italian *bulla* papal edict]

bullfight (ˈbʊlˌfaɪt) *n.* a public show, popular in Spain, in which a matador baits and usually kills a bull in an arena. —ˈ**bull-ˌfighter** *n.* —ˈ**bull,fighting** *n.*

bullfinch (ˈbʊlˌfɪntʃ) *n.* a common European songbird with a black head and, in the male, a pinkish breast.

bullfrog (ˈbʊlˌfrɒg) *n.* a large American frog with a loud deep croak.

bullion (ˈbʊljən) *n.* gold or silver in the form of bars and ingots. [Anglo-French: mint]

bull-necked *adj.* having a short thick neck.

bullock ('bʊlək) *n.* a gelded bull; steer. [Old English *bulluc*]

bullring ('bʊl,rɪŋ) *n.* an arena for bull-fighting.

bull's-eye *n.* **1.** the small central disc of a target or a dartboard. **2.** a shot hitting this. **3.** *Informal.* something that exactly achieves its aim. **4.** a peppermint-flavoured boiled sweet. **5.** a small circular window. **6.** a thick disc of glass set into a ship's deck, etc., to admit light. **7.** the glass boss at the centre of a sheet of blown glass. **8. a.** a convex lens used as a condenser. **b.** a lamp or lantern containing such a lens.

bullshit ('bʊl,ʃɪt) *Taboo slang.* ~*n.* **1.** exaggerated or foolish talk; nonsense. ~*vb.* **-shitting, -shitted. 2.** to talk bull-shit to: *don't bullshit me.*

bull terrier *n.* a terrier with a muscular body and a short smooth coat.

bully ('bʊlɪ) *n., pl.* **-lies. 1.** a person who hurts, persecutes, or intimidates weaker people. ~*vb.* **-lying, -lied. 2.** to hurt, intimidate, or persecute (a weaker or smaller person), esp. to make him do something. ~*interj.* **3. bully for you, him,** etc. *Informal.* well done! bravo!: now usually used sarcastically. [orig., sweetheart, fine fellow, swaggering coward, prob. from Middle Dutch *boele* lover]

bully beef *n.* canned corned beef. [French *bœuf bouilli* boiled beef]

bully-off *Hockey.* ~*n.* **1.** the method of starting play in which two opposing players stand with the ball between them and strike their sticks together three times before trying to hit the ball. ~*vb.* **bully off. 2.** to start play with a bully-off. [origin unknown]

bulrush ('bʊl,rʌʃ) *n.* **1.** a tall reedlike marsh plant with brown spiky flowers. **2.** *Bible.* same as **papyrus** (the plant). [Middle English *bulrish*]

bulwark ('bʊlwək) *n.* **1.** a wall or similar structure used as a fortification; rampart. **2.** a person or thing acting as a defence. ~*vb.* **3.** to defend or fortify with or as if with a bulwark. [Middle High German *bolwerk*]

bum[1] (bʌm) *n. Brit. slang.* the buttocks or anus. [origin unknown]

bum[2] (bʌm) *Informal, chiefly U.S. & Canad.* ~*n.* **1.** a disreputable loafer or idler. **2.** a tramp; hobo. ~*vb.* **bumming, bummed. 3.** to get by begging; cadge: *to bum a lift.* **4. bum around.** to spend time to no good purpose; loaf. ~*adj.* **5.** of poor quality; useless: *he hit a bum note.* [prob. from German *bummeln* to loaf]

bumble ('bʌmb'l) *vb.* **1.** to speak or do in a clumsy, muddled, or inefficient way. **2.** to move in a clumsy or unsteady way. [origin unknown] —'**bumbling** *adj., n.*

bumblebee ('bʌmb'l,biː) *n.* a large hairy social bee. [obs. *bumble* to buzz]

bumf (bʌmf) *n.* same as **bumph.**

bump (bʌmp) *vb.* **1.** to knock or strike (someone or something) with a jolt. **2.** to

travel or proceed in jerks and jolts. **3.** to hurt by knocking. ~*n.* **4.** an impact; knock; jolt; collision. **5.** a dull thud from an impact or collision. **6.** a lump on the body caused by a blow. **7.** a raised uneven part, as on a road surface. ~See also **bump into, bump off, bump up.** [prob. imit.] —'**bumpy** *adj.*

bumper[1] ('bʌmpə) *n.* a horizontal bar attached to the front or rear of a vehicle to protect against damage from impact.

bumper[2] ('bʌmpə) *n.* **1.** a glass or tankard, filled to the brim, esp. as a toast. **2.** an unusually large or fine example of something. ~*adj.* **3.** unusually large, fine, or abundant: *a bumper crop.* [prob. obs. *bump* to bulge]

bump into *vb. Informal.* to meet (someone) by chance; encounter (someone) unexpectedly.

bumpkin ('bʌmpkɪn) *n.* an awkward simple rustic person: *a country bumpkin.* [Dutch]

bump off *vb. Slang.* to murder (someone).

bumptious ('bʌmpʃəs) *adj.* offensively self-assertive or conceited. [prob. *bump* + *fractious*]

bump up *vb. Informal.* to increase (prices) by a large amount.

bun (bʌn) *n.* **1.** a small sweetened roll, similar to bread but often containing currants or spices. **2.** *Chiefly Scot. & N English.* a small round cake. **3.** a hairstyle in which long hair is gathered into a bun shape at the back of the head. [origin unknown]

bunch (bʌntʃ) *n.* **1.** a number of things growing, fastened, or grouped together: *a bunch of grapes; a bunch of keys.* **2.** a collection; group: *a bunch of queries.* **3.** *Informal.* a group or company: *a bunch of boys.* ~*vb.* **4.** to group or be grouped into a bunch. [origin unknown]

bundle ('bʌnd'l) *n.* **1.** a number of things or a quantity of material gathered or loosely bound together: *a bundle of sticks.* **2.** something wrapped or tied for carrying; package. **3.** *Biol.* a collection of strands of specialized tissue such as nerve fibres. **4.** *Bot.* a strand of conducting tissue within plants. ~*vb.* **5.** (foll. by *out, off, into,* etc.) to cause to go, esp. roughly or unceremoniously. **6.** to push (someone) or throw (something), esp. in a quick untidy way. [prob. from Middle Dutch *bundel*]

bundle up *vb.* to make (something) into a bundle or bundles, esp. by tying.

bun fight *n. Brit. slang.* **1.** a tea party. **2.** an official function.

bung (bʌŋ) *n.* **1.** a stopper, esp. of cork or rubber, used to close something such as a cask or flask. **2.** same as **bunghole.** ~*vb.* **3.** (foll. by *up*) *Informal.* to close or seal (something) with or as if with a bung. **4.** *Brit. slang.* to throw (something) somewhere in a careless manner; sling. [Middle Dutch *bonghe*]

bungalow ('bʌŋgə,ləʊ) *n.* a one-storey house. [Hindi *banglā*]

bunghole ('bʌŋ,həʊl) *n.* a hole in a cask or barrel through which liquid can be drained.

bungle ('bʌŋg'l) *vb.* **1.** to spoil (an operation) through clumsiness or incompetence; botch. ~*n.* **2.** a clumsy or unsuccessful performance; mistake; botch. [origin unknown] —'**bungler** *n.* —'**bungling** *adj., n.*

bunion ('bʌnjən) *n.* an inflamed swelling of the first joint of the big toe. [origin unknown]

bunk[1] (bʌŋk) *n.* **1.** a narrow shelflike bed fixed along a wall, esp. in a caravan or ship. **2.** same as **bunk bed.** [prob. from *bunker*]

bunk[2] (bʌŋk) *n. Informal.* same as **bunkum.**

bunk[3] (bʌŋk) *n.* **do a bunk.** *Brit. slang.* to make a hurried departure, usually under suspicious circumstances. [origin unknown]

bunk bed *n.* one of a pair of beds constructed one above the other to save space.

bunker ('bʌŋkə) *n.* **1.** a large storage container or tank, as for coal. **2.** an obstacle on a golf course, usually a sand-filled hollow bordered by a ridge. **3.** an underground shelter. [*Scot. bonkar*]

bunkum ('bʌŋkəm) *n.* empty talk; nonsense. [after *Buncombe,* North Carolina, alluded to in an inane speech by its Congressional representative]

bunny ('bʌnɪ) *n., pl.* -**nies.** a child's word for **rabbit.** [*Scot.* Gaelic *bun* rabbit]

bunny girl *n.* a night-club hostess whose costume includes a rabbit-like tail and ears.

Bunsen burner ('bʌns'n) *n.* a gas burner consisting of a metal tube with an adjustable air valve at the base. [after R. W. *Bunsen,* chemist]

bunting[1] ('bʌntɪŋ) *n.* **1.** a loosely woven cotton fabric used for flags. **2.** decorative flags, pennants, and streamers. [origin unknown]

bunting[2] ('bʌntɪŋ) *n.* a songbird with a short stout bill. [origin unknown]

buoy (bɔɪ; *U.S.* 'buːɪ) *n.* **1.** a brightly-coloured floating object anchored to the seabed for designating moorings, navigable channels, or obstructions in the water. ~*vb.* **2.** (foll. by *up*) to prevent from sinking: *the life belt buoyed him up.* **3.** to raise the spirits of; hearten: *the news really buoyed him up.* **4.** *Naut.* to mark (a channel or obstruction) with a buoy or buoys. [prob. Germanic]

buoyant ('bɔɪənt) *adj.* **1.** able to float in or rise to the surface of a liquid. **2.** (of a liquid or gas) able to keep a body afloat. **3.** cheerful or resilient. —'**buoyancy** *n.*

BUPA ('bjuːpə, 'buːpə) British United Provident Association: a private medical insurance scheme.

bur or **burr** (bɜː) *n.* **1.** a seed case or flower head with hooks or prickles. **2.** any plant that produces burs. [Old Norse]

burble ('bɜːb'l) *vb.* **1.** to make or utter with a bubbling sound; gurgle. **2.** to talk quickly and excitedly. [prob. imit.]

burbot ('bɜːbət) *n., pl.* -**bots** or -**bot.** a freshwater fish of the cod family that has barbels around its mouth. [Old French *bourbotte*]

burden[1] ('bɜːd'n) *n.* **1.** something that is carried; load. **2.** something that is exacting, oppressive, or difficult to bear. ~*vb.* **3.** to put or impose a burden on; load. **4.** to weigh down; oppress. [Old English *byrthen*] —'**burdensome** *adj.*

burden[2] ('bɜːd'n) *n.* **1.** a line of words recurring at the end of each verse of a song. **2.** the theme of a speech, book, etc. [Old French *bourdon*]

burdock ('bɜː,dɒk) *n.* a weed with large heart-shaped leaves, and burlike fruits. [BUR + DOCK[4]]

bureau ('bjʊərəʊ) *n., pl.* -**reaus** or -**reaux** (-rəʊz). **1.** *Chiefly Brit.* a writing desk with pigeonholes and drawers against which the writing surface can be closed when not in use. **2.** *U.S.* a chest of drawers. **3.** an office or agency, esp. one providing services for the public. **4.** *U.S.* a government department. [French]

bureaucracy (bjʊəˈrɒkrəsɪ) *n., pl.* -**cies. 1.** a system of administration based upon organization into bureaus, division of labour, a hierarchy of authority, etc. **2.** government by such a system. **3.** government officials collectively. **4.** any administration in which action is impeded by unnecessary official procedures.

bureaucrat ('bjʊərə,kræt) *n.* **1.** an official in a bureaucracy. **2.** an official who adheres rigidly to bureaucracy. —,**bureau-**'**cratic** *adj.*

burette or *U.S.* **buret** (bjʊˈret) *n.* a graduated glass tube with a stopcock on one end for dispensing known volumes of fluids. [Old French *buire* ewer]

burgeon ('bɜːdʒən) *vb.* to develop or grow rapidly; flourish. [Old French *burjon*]

burger ('bɜːgə) *n. Informal.* same as **hamburger.**

burgess ('bɜːdʒɪs) *n.* **1.** (in England) a citizen, freeman, or inhabitant of a borough. **2.** *English history.* a Member of Parliament from a borough, corporate town, or university. [Old French *burgeis*]

burgh ('bʌrə) *n.* **1.** (in Scotland until 1975) a town with a degree of self-government. **2.** *Archaic.* a borough. [Scot. form of *borough*]

burgher ('bɜːgə) *n. Archaic.* a person from a corporate town, esp. on the Continent. [German *Bürger* or Dutch *burger*]

burglar ('bɜːglə) *n.* a person who commits burglary. [Medieval Latin *burglātor*]

burglary ('bɜːglərɪ) *n., pl.* -**ries.** the crime of entering a building as a trespasser to commit theft or another offence.

burgle ('bɜːg'l) *vb.* to break into (a house, shop, etc.).

burgomaster ('bɜːgə,mɑːstə) *n.* the chief magistrate of a town in Austria, Belgium, Germany, or the Netherlands. [Dutch *burgemeester*]

burial ('berɪəl) *n.* the burying of a dead body.

burin ('bjʊərɪn) *n.* a steel chisel used for engraving metal, wood, or marble. [French]

burk or **berk** (bɜːk) *n. Brit. slang.* a stupid person; fool. [*Berkshire Hunt*, rhyming slang for *cunt*]

burl or **birl** (bɜːl) *n. Informal.* **1.** *Scot., Austral., & N.Z.* an attempt; try: *give it a burl.* **2.** *Austral. & N.Z.* a ride in a car. [from Scots *birl* to spin or turn]

burlesque (bɜː'lɛsk) *n.* **1.** an artistic work, esp. literary or dramatic, satirizing a subject by caricaturing it. **2.** *U.S. & Canad. theatre.* a bawdy comedy show of the late 19th and early 20th centuries. ~*adj.* **3.** of or characteristic of a burlesque. [Italian *burla* a jest]

burly ('bɜːlɪ) *adj.* **-lier, -liest.** large and thick of build; sturdy. [Germanic]

burn¹ (bɜːn) *vb.* **burning, burnt** or **burned. 1.** to be or set on fire. **2.** to destroy or be destroyed by fire. **3.** to damage, injure, or mark by heat: *he burnt his hand.* **4.** to die or put to death by fire. **5.** to be or feel hot: *my forehead is burning.* **6.** to smart or cause to smart: *brandy burns your throat.* **7.** to feel strong emotion, esp. anger or passion. **8.** to use for the purposes of light, heat, or power: *to burn coal.* **9.** to form by or as if by fire: *to burn a hole.* **10.** to char or become charred: *the potatoes are burning.* **11. burn one's boats** or **bridges.** to commit oneself to a particular course of action with no possibility of turning back. **12. burn one's fingers.** to suffer from having meddled or interfered. ~*n.* **13.** an injury caused by exposure to heat, electrical, chemical, or radioactive agents. **14.** a mark caused by burning. ~See also **burn out.** [Old English *beornan*]

burn² (bɜːn) *n. Scot.* a small stream; brook. [Old English *burna*]

burner ('bɜːnə) *n.* the part of a stove or lamp that produces flame or heat.

burning ('bɜːnɪŋ) *adj.* **1.** intense; passionate. **2.** urgent; crucial: *a burning problem.*

burning glass *n.* a convex lens for concentrating the sun's rays to produce fire.

burnish ('bɜːnɪʃ) *vb.* to make or become shiny or smooth by friction; polish. [Old French *brunir* to make brown]

burnous (bɜː'nuːs) *n.* a long circular cloak with a hood, worn esp. by Arabs. [Arabic *burnus*]

burn out *vb.* **1.** to become or cause to become inoperative as a result of heat or friction: *the clutch burnt out.* ~*n.* **burn-out. 2.** total exhaustion and inability to work effectively as a result of excessive demands or overwork.

burnt (bɜːnt) *vb.* **1.** a past tense and past participle of **burn¹.** ~*adj.* **2.** affected by or as if by burning; charred.

burnt sienna *n.* **1.** a reddish-brown pigment obtained by roasting raw sienna. ~*adj.* **2.** reddish-brown.

burp (bɜːp) *n.* **1.** *Informal.* a belch. ~*vb.* **2.** *Informal.* to belch. **3.** to cause (a baby) to belch. [imit.]

burr (bɜː) *n.* **1.** a whirring or humming sound. **2.** the soft trilling sound given to

the letter (r) in some English dialects. **3.** a rough edge left on metal or paper after cutting. **4.** a small hand-operated drill. [origin unknown]

burrow ('bʌrəʊ) *n.* **1.** a hole dug in the ground by a rabbit or other small animal. ~*vb.* **2.** to dig (a tunnel or hole) in, through, or under ground. **3.** to move through a place by or as by digging. **4.** to delve deeply: *he burrowed into his pockets.* **5.** to live in a burrow. [prob. var. of *borough*]

bursar ('bɜːsə) *n.* a treasurer of a school, college, or university. [Medieval Latin *bursārius* keeper of the purse]

bursary ('bɜːsərɪ) *n., pl.* **-ries.** a scholarship awarded esp. in Scottish and New Zealand schools and universities.

burst (bɜːst) *vb.* **bursting, burst. 1.** to break or cause to break open or apart suddenly and noisily; explode. **2.** to come or go suddenly and forcibly: *he burst into the room.* **3.** to be full to the point of breaking open: *bursting at the seams.* **4.** (foll. by *into*) to give vent to (something) suddenly or loudly: *to burst into song.* ~*n.* **5.** an instance of breaking open suddenly; explosion. **6.** a break; breach; rupture. **7.** a sudden increase of effort; spurt: *a burst of speed.* **8.** a sudden and violent occurrence or outbreak: *a burst of applause.* [Old English *berstan*]

burton ('bɜːt'n) *n.* **go for a burton.** *Brit. slang.* **a.** to be broken, useless, or lost. **b.** to die. [origin unknown]

bury ('bɛrɪ) *vb.* **burying, buried. 1.** to place (a corpse) in a grave. **2.** to place (something) in the earth and cover it with soil. **3.** to cover (something) from sight; hide. **4.** to occupy (oneself) with deep concentration: *to be buried in a book.* **5.** to dismiss (a feeling) from the mind: *to bury old hatreds.* [Old English *byrgan*]

bus (bʌs) *n.* **1.** a large motor vehicle designed to carry passengers between stopping places along a regular route. **2.** *Informal.* a car or aircraft that is old and shaky. **3.** *Electronics, computers.* an electrical conductor used to make a common connection between several circuits. ~*vb.* **busing, bused** or **bussing, bussed. 4.** to travel or transport by bus. **5.** *Chiefly U.S. & Canad.* to transport (children) by bus from one area to another in order to create racially integrated schools. [short for OMNIBUS]

busby ('bʌzbɪ) *n., pl.* **-bies.** a tall fur helmet worn by certain British soldiers. [origin unknown]

bush¹ (bʊʃ) *n.* **1.** a dense woody plant, smaller than a tree, with many branches; shrub. **2.** a dense cluster of such shrubs; thicket. **3.** something resembling a bush, esp. in density: *a bush of hair.* **4. the.** an uncultivated area covered with trees or shrubs in Australia, Africa, New Zealand, and Canada. **5.** *Canad.* an area on a farm on which timber is grown and cut. **6. beat about the bush.** to avoid the point at issue. [Germanic]

bush² (bʊʃ) *n.* **1.** a thin metal sleeve or tubular lining serving as a bearing. ~*vb.*

2. to fit a bush to (a casing or bearing). [Middle Dutch *busse* box]

bushbaby ('buʃ,beɪbɪ) *n., pl.* **-babies.** a small agile tree-living mammal with large eyes and a long tail.

bushed (buʃt) *adj. Informal.* extremely tired; exhausted.

bushel ('buʃəl) *n.* a British unit of dry or liquid measure equal to 8 imperial gallons. [Old French *boissel*]

bush jacket *n.* a casual jacket with four patch pockets and a belt.

bush line *n.* an airline operating in the bush country of Canada's northern regions.

bush lot *n. Canad.* same as **bush**[1] (sense 5).

bushman ('buʃmən) *n., pl.* **-men.** *Austral. & N.Z.* a person who lives or travels in the bush.

Bushman ('buʃmən) *n., pl.* **-men.** a member of a hunting and gathering people of southern Africa. [Afrikaans]

bush pilot *n. Canad.* a pilot who operates in the bush country.

bush sickness *n. N.Z.* a disease of animals caused by mineral deficiency in old bush country. —'**bush-,sick** *adj.*

bush tea *n.* a beverage prepared from the dried leaves of a shrub of southern Africa.

bush telegraph *n.* a means of spreading rumour or gossip.

bushveld ('buʃ,fɛlt, -vɛlt) *n. S. African.* bushy countryside. [Afrikaans]

bushy ('buʃɪ) *adj.* **bushier, bushiest. 1.** (of hair) thick and shaggy. **2.** covered or overgrown with bushes.

business ('bɪznɪs) *n.* **1.** a trade or profession. **2.** the purchase and sale of goods and services. **3.** a commercial or industrial establishment. **4.** commercial activity; dealings: *firms that do business with Britain.* **5.** proper or rightful concern or responsibility: *mind your own business.* **6.** an affair; matter: *it's a dreadful business.* **7.** serious work or activity: *get down to business.* **8.** a difficult or complicated matter. **9. mean business.** to be in earnest. [Old English *bisignis*]

businesslike ('bɪznɪs,laɪk) *adj.* efficient and methodical.

businessman ('bɪznɪs,mæn, -mən) *or* (*fem.*) **businesswoman** *n., pl.* **-men** *or* **-women.** a person engaged in commercial or industrial business, usually an owner or executive.

business park *n.* an area specially designated to accommodate business offices, light industry, etc.

business school *n.* an institution that offers courses to managers in aspects of business, such as marketing, finance, and law.

busker ('bʌskə) *n.* a person who entertains for money in streets or stations. [origin unknown] —**busk** *vb.*

busman's holiday ('bʌsmənz) *n. Informal.* a holiday spent doing the same as one does at work.

bust[1] (bʌst) *n.* **1.** a woman's bosom. **2.** a sculpture of the head, shoulders, and upper chest of a person. [Italian *busto* a sculpture]

bust[2] (bʌst) *Informal.* ~*vb.* **busting, busted** *or* **bust. 1.** to burst or break. **2.** (of the police) to raid or search (a place) or arrest (someone). **3.** *U.S. & Canad.* to demote in military rank. ~*adj.* **4.** broken. **5. go bust.** to become bankrupt. [from *burst*]

bustle[1] ('bʌs'l) *vb.* **1.** (often foll. by *about*) to hurry with a great show of energy or activity. ~*n.* **2.** energetic and noisy activity. [prob. obs. *buskle* to prepare] —'**bustling** *adj.*

bustle[2] ('bʌs'l) *n.* a cushion or framework worn by women in the late 19th century at the back in order to expand the skirt. [origin unknown]

bust-up *Informal.* ~*n.* **1.** a serious quarrel, esp. one ending a relationship. **2.** *Brit.* a disturbance or brawl. ~*vb.* **bust up. 3.** to quarrel and part. **4.** to disrupt (a meeting), esp. violently.

busy ('bɪzɪ) *adj.* **busier, busiest. 1.** actively or fully engaged; occupied. **2.** crowded with or characterized by activity. **3.** *Chiefly U.S. & Canad.* (of a telephone line) in use; engaged. ~*vb.* **busying, busied. 4.** to make or keep (someone, esp. oneself) busy; occupy. [Old English *bisig*] —'**busily** *adv.*

busybody ('bɪzɪ,bɒdɪ) *n., pl.* **-bodies.** a meddlesome, prying, or officious person.

but (bʌt; *unstressed* bət) *conj.* **1.** contrary to expectation: *he cut his knee but didn't cry.* **2.** in contrast; on the contrary: *I like opera but my husband doesn't.* **3.** other than: *we can't do anything but wait.* **4.** without it happening: *we never go out but it rains.* ~*prep.* **5.** except: *they saved all but one.* **6. but for.** were it not for: *but for you, we couldn't have managed.* ~*adv.* **7.** only: *I can but try; he was but a child.* ~*n.* **8.** an objection: *ifs and buts.* [Old English *būtan*]

but and ben *n. Scot.* a two-roomed cottage consisting of an outer room (**but**) and an inner room (**ben**). [Old English *būtan* outside and *binnan* inside]

butane ('bjuːteɪn, bjuː'teɪn) *n.* a colourless gas used in the manufacture of rubber and fuels. [from *butyl*]

butch (butʃ) *adj. Slang.* (of a woman or man) markedly or aggressively masculine. [from *butcher*]

butcher ('butʃə) *n.* **1.** a retailer of meat. **2.** a person who slaughters animals for meat. **3.** an indiscriminate or brutal murderer. ~*vb.* **4.** to slaughter (animals) for meat. **5.** to kill (people) indiscriminately or brutally. **6.** to make a mess of; botch. [Old French *bouchier*]

butchery ('butʃərɪ) *n., pl.* **-eries. 1.** senseless slaughter. **2.** the business of a butcher.

butler ('bʌtlə) *n.* the head manservant of a household, in charge of the wines, table, etc. [Old French *bouteille* bottle]

butt[1] (bʌt) *n.* **1.** the thicker or blunt end of something, such as the stock of a rifle. **2.** the unused end of something, esp. a cigarette; stub. **3.** *U.S. & Canad. slang.* the buttocks. [Middle English]

butt² (bʌt) *n.* **1.** a person or thing that is the target of ridicule or teasing. **2.** *Shooting, archery.* **a.** a mound of earth behind the target. **b.** (*pl.*) the target range. [Old French *but*]

butt³ (bʌt) *vb.* **1.** to strike (something or someone) with the head or horns. **2.** (foll. by *in* or *into*) to intrude, esp. into a conversation; interfere. ~*n.* **3.** a blow with the head or horns. [Old French *boter*]

butt⁴ (bʌt) *n.* a large cask for collecting or storing liquids. [Late Latin *buttis* cask]

butte (bjuːt) *n. U.S. & Canad.* an isolated steep flat-topped hill. [Old French *bute* mound behind a target]

butter ('bʌtə) *n.* **1.** an edible fatty yellow solid made from cream by churning. **2.** any substance with a butter-like consistency, such as peanut butter. ~*vb.* **3.** to put butter on or in (something). ~See also **butter up.** [Greek *bous* cow + *turos* cheese] —**'buttery** *adj.*

butter bean *n.* a large pale flat edible bean.

buttercup ('bʌtəˌkʌp) *n.* a small yellow flower.

butterfingers ('bʌtəˌfɪŋɡəz) *n.* (*functioning as sing.*) *Informal.* a person who drops things by mistake or fails to catch things.

butterflies ('bʌtəˌflaɪz) *pl. n. Informal.* a nervous feeling in the stomach.

butterfly ('bʌtəˌflaɪ) *n., pl.* **-flies. 1.** an insect with a slender body and brightly coloured wings. **2.** a person who never settles with one interest or occupation for long. **3.** a swimming stroke in which the arms are plunged forward together in large circular movements. [Old English *buttorflēoge*]

butterfly nut *n.* same as **wing nut.**

buttermilk ('bʌtəˌmɪlk) *n.* the sourish liquid remaining after the butter has been separated from milk.

butter muslin *n.* a fine loosely woven cotton material originally used for wrapping butter.

butterscotch ('bʌtəˌskɒtʃ) *n.* a hard brittle toffee made with butter, brown sugar, etc.

butter up *vb.* to flatter.

buttery ('bʌtərɪ) *n., pl.* **-teries.** *Brit.* (in some universities) a room in which food and drink are sold to students. [Latin *butta* cask]

buttock ('bʌtək) *n.* **1.** either of the two large fleshy masses that form the human rump. **2.** the corresponding part in some mammals. [perhaps from *buttuc* round slope]

button ('bʌt²n) *n.* **1.** a disc or knob of plastic, wood, etc., attached to a garment, for fastening two surfaces together by passing it through a buttonhole. **2.** a small round object, such as a sweet or badge. **3.** a small disc that operates a doorbell or machine when pressed. **4. not worth a button.** *Brit.* of no value; useless. ~*vb.* **5.** to fasten (a garment) with a button or buttons. [Old French *boton*]

buttonhole ('bʌt²nˌhəʊl) *n.* **1.** a slit in a garment through which a button is passed to fasten two surfaces together. **2.** a flower worn pinned to the lapel or in the buttonhole. ~*vb.* **3.** to detain (a person) in conversation.

button mushroom *n.* an unripe mushroom.

button up *vb.* **1.** to fasten (a garment) with a button or buttons. **2.** *Informal.* to conclude (business) satisfactorily: *she's got it all buttoned up.*

buttress ('bʌtrɪs) *n.* **1.** a construction, usually of brick or stone, built to support a wall. **2.** any support or prop. ~*vb.* **3.** to support (a wall) with a buttress. **4.** to support or sustain (an argument). [Old French *bouter* to thrust]

butty ('bʌtɪ) *n., pl.* **-ties.** *Chiefly N English dialect.* a sandwich: *a jam butty.* [French *buttered* (bread)]

butyl ('bjuːˌtaɪl, -tɪl) *n.* (*modifier*) of or containing any of four isomeric forms of the group C_4H_9: *butyl rubber.* [Latin *būtyrum* butter]

buxom ('bʌksəm) *adj.* (of a woman) healthily plump, attractive, and full-bosomed. [Middle English *buhsum* compliant]

buy (baɪ) *vb.* **buying, bought. 1.** to acquire (something) by paying a sum of money for it; purchase. **2.** to be capable of purchasing: *money can't buy love.* **3.** to acquire by any exchange or sacrifice: *to buy time by equivocation.* **4.** to bribe (someone). **5.** *Slang.* to accept (something) as true. **6.** (foll. by *into*) to purchase shares of (a company). ~*n.* **7.** a purchase: *a good buy.* [Old English *bycgan*]

buyer ('baɪə) *n.* **1.** a person who buys; customer. **2.** a person employed to buy merchandise, as for a shop or factory.

buy in *vb.* to purchase (goods) in large quantities.

buy off *vb.* to pay (someone) to drop a charge or end opposition.

buy out *vb.* **1.** to purchase the ownership of a company or property from (someone). ~*n.* **buy-out. 2.** the purchase of a company, often by its former employees.

buy up *vb.* **1.** to purchase all that is available of (something). **2.** to purchase a controlling interest in (a company).

buzz (bʌz) *n.* **1.** a rapidly vibrating humming sound, as of a bee. **2.** a low sound, as of many voices in conversation. **3.** *Informal.* a telephone call. **4.** *Informal.* a sense of excitement. ~*vb.* **5.** to make a vibrating sound like that of a prolonged *z.* **6.** (of a place) to be filled with an air of excitement: *the town buzzed with the news.* **7.** to summon (someone) with a buzzer. **8.** *Informal.* to fly an aircraft very low over (people, buildings, or another aircraft). **9. buzz about** or **around.** to move around quickly and busily. [imit.]

buzzard ('bʌzəd) *n.* a bird of prey with broad wings and tail and a soaring flight. [Latin *būteō* hawk]

buzzer ('bʌzə) *n.* an electronic device that produces a buzzing sound as a signal.

buzz off *vb. Informal, chiefly Brit.* to go away; depart.

buzz word *n. Informal.* a word, originally from a particular jargon, which becomes a popular vogue word.

bwana ('bwɑːnə) *n.* (in E Africa) a master, often used as a form of address corresponding to *sir.* [Swahili]

by (bai) *prep.* **1.** used to indicate the performer of the action of a passive verb: *seeds eaten by the birds.* **2.** used to indicate the person responsible for a creative work: *this song is by Schubert.* **3.** via; through: *enter by the back door.* **4.** used to indicate a means used: *he frightened her by hiding behind the door.* **5.** beside; next to; near: *a tree by the house.* **6.** passing the position of; past: *he drove by the old cottage.* **7.** not later than; before: *return the books by Tuesday.* **8.** used to indicate extent: *it is hotter by five degrees.* **9.** multiplied by: *four by three equals twelve.* **10.** during the passing of: *by night.* **11.** placed between measurements of the various dimensions of something: *a plank fourteen inches by seven.* ~*adv.* **12.** near: *the house is close by.* **13.** away; aside: *he put some money by each week.* **14.** passing a point near something; past: *he drove by.* ~*n., pl.* **byes. 15.** same as **bye¹.** [Old English *bī*]

by and by *adv.* presently or eventually.

by and large *adv.* in general; on the whole.

bye¹ (bai) *n.* **1.** *Sport.* status of a player or team who wins a preliminary round by virtue of having no opponent. **2.** *Cricket.* a run scored off a ball not struck by the batsman. **3. by the bye.** incidentally; by the way. [var. of *by*]

bye² (bai) *or* **bye-bye** *interj. Brit. informal.* goodbye.

by-election *or* **bye-election** *n.* an election held during the life of a parliament to fill a vacant seat.

bygone ('bai,gɒn) *adj.* **1.** past; former: *a bygone age.* ~*n.* **2.** an artefact, implement, etc., of former domestic or industrial use.

bygones ('bai,gɒnz) *pl. n.* **let bygones be bygones.** to agree to forget past quarrels.

bylaw *or* **bye-law** ('bai,lɔː) *n.* a rule made by a local authority. [prob. Scandinavian]

by-line *n.* **1.** a line under the title of a newspaper or magazine article giving the author's name. **2.** same as **touchline.**

BYO(G) *n. Austral. & N.Z.* an unlicensed restaurant at which diners may bring their own alcoholic drink. [*bring your own (grog)*]

bypass ('bai,pɑːs) *n.* **1.** a main road built to avoid a city. **2.** a secondary pipe, channel, or appliance through which the flow of a substance, such as gas or electricity, is redirected. **3.** a surgical operation in which the blood flow is redirected away from a diseased or blocked part of the heart. ~*vb.* **4.** to go around or avoid (a city, obstruction, problem, etc.). **5.** to proceed without reference to (regulations or a superior); get round; avoid.

by-play *n.* secondary action in a play, carried on apart while the main action proceeds.

by-product *n.* **1.** a secondary or incidental product of a manufacturing process. **2.** a side effect.

byre ('baiə) *n. Brit.* a shelter for cows. [Old English]

byroad ('bai,rəud) *n.* a secondary or side road.

bystander ('bai,stændə) *n.* a person present but not involved; onlooker; spectator.

byte (bait) *n. Computers.* a group of bits processed as one unit of data. [origin unknown]

byway ('bai,wei) *n.* a secondary or side road, esp. in the country.

byword ('bai,wɜːd) *n.* **1.** a person or thing regarded as a perfect example of something: *their name is a byword for good service.* **2.** a common saying; proverb.

Byzantine (bi'zæn,tain, -,tiːn, bai-; 'bizən,tiːn, -,tain) *adj.* **1.** of Byzantium, an ancient Greek city on the Bosphorus. **2.** of the Byzantine Empire, the continuation of the Roman Empire in the East. **3.** of the style of architecture developed in the Byzantine Empire, with massive domes, rounded arches, and mosaics. **4.** (of attitudes, methods, etc.) inflexible or complicated. ~*n.* **5.** an inhabitant of Byzantium.

C

c *or* **C** (siː) *n.*, *pl.* **c's**, **C's**, *or* **Cs**. **1.** the third letter of the English alphabet. **2.** the third in a series.

c 1. centi-. **2.** cubic. **3.** the speed of light in free space.

C 1. *Music.* the first note of a major scale containing no sharps or flats (**C major**). **2.** *Chem.* carbon. **3.** capacitance. **4.** Celsius. **5.** centigrade. **6.** century: *C20.* **7.** coulomb. **8.** the Roman numeral for 100.

c. 1. carat. **2.** cent(s). **3.** century *or* centuries. **4.** (*pl.* **cc.**) chapter. **5.** (used esp. preceding a date) about: *c. 1800.* [Latin *circa*] **6.** copyright.

Ca *Chem.* calcium.

ca. about. [Latin *circa*]

CA 1. California. **2.** Chartered Accountant.

cab (kæb) *n.* **1.** a taxi. **2.** the enclosed driver's compartment of a lorry, crane, or other vehicle. **3.** (formerly) a horse-drawn vehicle for public hire. [from *cabriolet*]

cabal (kəˈbæl) *n.* **1.** a small group of political intriguers. **2.** a secret plot; conspiracy. [French *cabale*]

cabaret (ˈkæbəˌreɪ) *n.* **1.** a floor show of dancing and singing at a nightclub or restaurant. **2.** a place providing such entertainment. [French: tavern]

cabbage (ˈkæbɪdʒ) *n.* **1.** a vegetable with a short thick stalk and a large head of green or reddish edible leaves. **2.** *Informal.* a person who has no mental faculties and is dependent on others. [Norman French *caboche* head]

cabbage white *n.* a large white butterfly, the larvae of which feed on the leaves of cabbages and related vegetables.

cabby *or* **cabbie** (ˈkæbɪ) *n.*, *pl.* **-bies.** *Informal.* a cab driver.

caber (ˈkeɪbə) *n. Scot.* a heavy section of trimmed tree trunk tossed in competition at Highland games. [Gaelic *cabar* pole]

cabin (ˈkæbɪn) *n.* **1.** a small simple dwelling. **2.** a room used as living quarters in a ship. **3.** a covered section in a small boat. **4.** the enclosed part of an aircraft in which the passengers or crew sit. [Late Latin *capanna* hut]

cabin boy *n.* a boy who waits on the officers and passengers of a ship.

cabin cruiser *n.* a motorboat with a cabin.

cabinet (ˈkæbɪnɪt) *n.* **1.** a piece of furniture containing shelves, cupboards, or drawers for storage or display. **2.** the outer case of a television or radio. **3.** (*often cap.*) a committee of senior government ministers or advisers to a president. [Old French *cabine* cabin]

cabinet-maker *n.* a craftsman who makes fine furniture. —**'cabinet-ˌmaking** *n.*

cabin fever *n. Canad.* acute depression resulting from being isolated or sharing cramped quarters in the wilderness.

cable (ˈkeɪbᵊl) *n.* **1.** a strong thick rope of twisted hemp or wire. **2.** a ship's anchor chain. **3.** a bundle of wires that conducts electricity: *a submarine cable.* **4.** a telegram sent abroad by submarine cable or telephone line. **5.** Also: **cable stitch.** a knitting pattern resembling a twisted rope. ~*vb.* **6.** to send (a message) to (someone) by cable. [Late Latin *capulum* halter]

cable car *n.* a vehicle which is pulled up a steep slope by a moving cable.

cablegram (ˈkeɪbᵊlˌgræm) *n.* a more formal name for **cable** (sense 4).

cable television *n.* a television service in which the subscriber's television is connected to a central receiver by cable.

caboodle (kəˈbuːdᵊl) *n.* **the whole caboodle.** *Informal.* the whole lot. [origin unknown]

caboose (kəˈbuːs) *n.* **1.** *Railways, U.S. & Canad.* a guard's van. **2.** *Naut.* a galley aboard ship. **3.** *Canad.* a mobile bunkhouse used by lumbermen. [Dutch *cabūse*]

cabriolet (ˌkæbrɪəʊˈleɪ) *n.* a small two-wheeled horse-drawn carriage with a folding hood. [French: a little skip; referring to the lightness of movement]

cacao (kəˈkɑːəʊ, -ˈkeɪəʊ) *n.* **1.** a tropical American tree with seed pods from which cocoa and chocolate are prepared. **2. cacao bean.** the seed pod; cocoa bean. [Mexican Indian *cacauatl* cacao beans]

cachalot (ˈkæʃəˌlɒt) *n.* the sperm whale. [Portuguese *cachalote*]

cache (kæʃ) *n.* **1.** a hidden store of provisions, weapons, or treasure. **2.** the place where such a store is hidden. ~*vb.* **3.** to store in a cache. [French *cacher* to hide]

cachet (ˈkæʃeɪ) *n.* **1.** prestige; distinction. **2.** an official seal on a document or letter. **3.** a distinguishing mark. [French]

cachou (ˈkæʃuː, kæˈʃuː) *n.* a lozenge eaten to sweeten the breath. [Malay *kāchu*]

cack-handed (ˌkækˈhændɪd) *adj. Informal.* **1.** clumsy. **2.** left-handed. [dialect *cack* excrement]

cackle (ˈkækᵊl) *vb.* **1.** (of a hen) to squawk with shrill broken notes. **2.** to laugh or chatter shrilly. **3.** to utter with a cackle. ~*n.* **4.** the noise or act of cackling. **5. cut the cackle.** *Informal.* to be quiet. [prob. imit.] —**'cackling** *n.*, *adj.*

cacophony (kəˈkɒfənɪ) *n.*, *pl.* **-nies.** harsh discordant sound. [Greek *kakos* bad + *phōnē* sound] —**ca'cophonous** *adj.*

cactus (ˈkæktəs) *n.*, *pl.* **-tuses** *or* **-ti** (-taɪ). a thick fleshy desert plant with spines but no leaves. [Greek *kaktos* type of thistle]

cad (kæd) *n. Brit. informal, old-fashioned.* a man who behaves dishonourably. [from *caddie*] —**'caddish** *adj.*

cadaver (kəˈdeɪvə, -ˈdɑːv-) *n. Med.* a corpse. [Latin, from *cadere* to fall]

cadaverous (kə'dævərəs) *adj.* **1.** deathly pale, like a corpse. **2.** thin and haggard.

caddie ('kædɪ) *Golf.* ~*n., pl.* **-dies. 1.** an attendant who carries clubs and other equipment for a player. ~*vb.* **-dying, -died. 2.** to act as a caddie. [from *cadet*]

caddis worm *or* **caddis** ('kædɪs) *n.* the aquatic larva of the **caddis fly**, which constructs a protective case around itself made of silk, sand, and stones.

caddy[1] ('kædɪ) *n., pl.* **-dies.** *Chiefly Brit.* a small container for tea. [Malay *kati*]

caddy[2] ('kædɪ) *n., pl.* **-dies,** *vb.* **-dying, -died.** same as **caddie**.

cadence ('keɪd'ns) *n.* **1.** the beat or measure of something rhythmic. **2.** a fall in the pitch of the voice. **3.** intonation. **4.** the close of a musical phrase. [Latin *cadere* to fall]

cadenza (kə'dɛnzə) *n.* a virtuoso solo passage during a piece of music. [Italian]

cadet (kə'dɛt) *n.* a young person training for the military services or police. [French, from Latin *caput* head] —**ca'detship** *n.*

cadge (kædʒ) *vb.* to get (food, money, or help) by sponging or begging. [origin unknown] —**'cadger** *n.*

cadi ('kɑːdɪ, 'keɪdɪ) *n., pl.* **-dis.** a judge in a Muslim community. [Arabic *qāḍī* judge]

cadmium ('kædmɪəm) *n.* a bluish-white metallic element found in zinc ores and used in electroplating and alloys. Symbol: Cd [Latin *cadmīa* zinc ore]

cadre ('kɑːdə) *n.* **1.** the nucleus of trained servicemen forming the basis of a military unit. **2.** a group of activists, esp. in the Communist Party. [Latin *quadrum* square]

caduceus (kə'djuːsɪəs) *n., pl.* **-cei** (-sɪ.aɪ). an emblem of the medical profession, showing a winged staff with two serpents twined round it. [from the staff carried by Hermes, in Greek myth. the messenger of the gods]

caecum *or U.S.* **cecum** ('siːkəm) *n., pl.* **-ca** (-kə). the pouch at the beginning of the large intestine. [short for Latin *intestinum caecum* blind intestine]

Caenozoic (ˌsiːnə'zəʊɪk) *adj.* same as **Cenozoic**.

Caerphilly (kɛə'fɪlɪ) *n.* a creamy white mild-flavoured cheese.

Caesar ('siːzə) *n.* **1.** a Roman emperor. **2.** any emperor, autocrat, or dictator. [after Gaius Julius *Caesar*, Roman general & statesman]

Caesarean, Caesarian, *or U.S.* **Cesarean, Cesarian** (sɪ'zɛərɪən) *n.* a Caesarean section.

Caesarean section *n.* surgical incision into the womb in order to deliver a baby. [from the belief that Julius Caesar was so delivered]

caesium *or U.S.* **cesium** ('siːzɪəm) *n.* a silvery-white metallic element used in photocells. Symbol: Cs [Latin *caesius* bluish-grey]

caesura (sɪ'zjʊərə) *n., pl.* **-ras** *or* **-rae** (-riː). a pause in a line of verse. [Latin: a cutting]

café ('kæfeɪ, 'kæfɪ) *n.* a small or inexpensive restaurant serving refreshments and, sometimes, meals. [French]

cafeteria (ˌkæfɪ'tɪərɪə) *n.* a self-service restaurant. [American Spanish: coffee shop]

caff (kæf) *n. Slang.* a café.

caffeine ('kæfiːn) *n.* a stimulant in tea, coffee, and cocoa. [German *Kaffee* coffee]

caftan ('kæf.tæn, -.tɑːn) *n.* same as **kaftan**.

cage (keɪdʒ) *n.* **1.** an enclosure of bars or wires, for keeping birds or animals. **2.** the enclosed platform of a lift in a mine. ~*vb.* **3.** to confine in or as in a cage. [Latin *cavea* enclosure]

cagey *or* **cagy** ('keɪdʒɪ) *adj.* **cagier, cagiest.** *Informal.* not frank; wary. [origin unknown] —**'caginess** *n.*

cagoule (kə'guːl) *n.* a lightweight usually knee-length type of anorak. [French]

cahoots (kə'huːts) *pl. n.* **in cahoots.** *Informal.* in league. [origin unknown]

caiman ('keɪmən) *n., pl.* **-mans.** same as **cayman**.

Cainozoic (ˌkaɪnəʊ'zəʊɪk, ˌkeɪ-) *adj.* same as **Cenozoic.**

cairn (kɛən) *n.* **1.** a mound of stones erected as a memorial or marker. **2.** Also: **cairn terrier.** a small rough-haired breed of terrier. [Gaelic *carn*]

cairngorm (ˌkɛən'gɔːm) *n.* a smoky yellow or brown quartz gemstone. [*Cairn Gorm* (blue cairn), mountain in Scotland]

caisson (kə'suːn, 'keɪs'n) *n.* a watertight chamber used to carry out construction work under water. [French]

cajole (kə'dʒəʊl) *vb.* to persuade by flattery; wheedle; coax. [French *cajoler*] —**ca'jolery** *n.*

cake (keɪk) *n.* **1.** a baked mixture of flour, sugar, and eggs. **2.** other food in a flat round shape: *a fish cake.* **3.** a flat, compact mass: *a cake of soap.* **4.** **go** *or* **sell like hot cakes.** *Informal.* to be sold very quickly. **5. have one's cake and eat it.** to enjoy both of two incompatible alternatives. **6. piece of cake.** *Informal.* something that is easily accomplished. ~*vb.* **7.** to form into a hardened mass or crust. [Old Norse *kaka*]

cakewalk ('keɪk.wɔːk) *n.* **1.** an old-fashioned Black American dance. **2.** *Informal.* an easy task.

cal. 1. calendar. **2.** calibre. **3.** calorie (small).

Cal. Calorie (large).

calabash ('kælə.bæʃ) *n.* **1.** a tropical American tree that produces large round gourds. **2.** the gourd. **3.** the dried hollow shell of the gourd used as a pipe or bowl. [obs. French *calabasse*]

calabrese (ˌkælə'breɪzɪ) *n.* a kind of green sprouting broccoli. [Italian]

calamine ('kælə.maɪn) *n.* a pink powder consisting chiefly of zinc oxide, used in skin lotions or ointments. [Medieval Latin *calamīna*]

calamitous (kə'læmɪtəs) *adj.* involving or resulting in a calamity; disastrous.

calamity (kə'læmɪtɪ) *n., pl.* **-ties. 1.** a

disaster or misfortune. **2.** deep distress or misery. [Latin *calamitās*]

calcareous (kælˈkɛərɪəs) *adj.* of or containing calcium carbonate. [Latin *calx* lime]

calces (ˈkælsiːz) *n.* a plural of **calx.**

calciferol (kælˈsɪfərɒl) *n.* a substance found in fish-liver oils and used in the treatment of rickets. Also called: **vitamin D₂.** [*calcif(erous* + *ergost)erol*, a substance in plants that is a source of vitamin D]

calciferous (kælˈsɪfərəs) *adj.* producing salts of calcium, esp. calcium carbonate.

calcify (ˈkælsɪˌfaɪ) *vb.* **-fying, -fied. 1.** to convert or be converted into lime. **2.** to harden by the depositing of calcium salts. [Latin *calx* lime] —**calciˈfication** *n.*

calcine (ˈkælsaɪn, -sɪn) *vb.* to oxidize (a substance) by heating or (of a substance) to be oxidized by heating. [Medieval Latin *calcināre* to heat] —**calcination** (ˌkælsɪˈneɪʃən) *n.*

calcite (ˈkælsaɪt) *n.* a colourless or white form of calcium carbonate.

calcium (ˈkælsɪəm) *n.* a soft silvery-white metallic element found in bones, teeth, limestone, and chalk. Symbol: Ca [Latin *calx* lime]

calcium carbonate *n.* a white crystalline salt found in limestone, chalk, and pearl.

calcium hydroxide *n.* a white crystalline alkali used in cement, water softening, and the neutralization of acid soils.

calcium oxide *n.* same as **quicklime.**

calculable (ˈkælkjʊləbᵊl) *adj.* that may be computed or estimated.

calculate (ˈkælkjʊˌleɪt) *vb.* **1.** to solve (a problem) by a mathematical procedure. **2.** to determine by judgment or reasoning; estimate. **3.** (*usually passive*) to aim: *calculated to annoy me.* **4.** (foll. by *on*) to rely. **5.** *U.S. dialect.* to suppose. [Latin *calculāre,* from *calculus* pebble used as a counter]

calculated (ˈkælkjʊˌleɪtɪd) *adj.* **1.** undertaken after considering the likelihood of success. **2.** premeditated: *a calculated insult.*

calculating (ˈkælkjʊˌleɪtɪŋ) *adj.* **1.** selfishly scheming. **2.** shrewd.

calculation (ˌkælkjʊˈleɪʃən) *n.* **1.** the act or result of calculating. **2.** selfish scheming.

calculator (ˈkælkjʊˌleɪtə) *n.* a small electronic device for doing mathematical calculations.

calculus (ˈkælkjʊləs) *n.* **1.** (*pl.* **-luses**) the branch of mathematics concerned with the effect on a function of an infinitesimal change in the independent variable. **2.** (*pl.* **-li** (-ˌlaɪ)). *Pathol.* same as **stone.** [Latin: pebble]

caldron (ˈkɔːldrən) *n.* same as **cauldron.**

Caledonian (ˌkælɪˈdəʊnɪən) *adj.* **1.** Scottish. ~*n.* **2.** *Literary.* a person from Scotland. [Latin *Caledonia,* the Roman name for Scotland]

calendar (ˈkælɪndə) *n.* **1.** a system for determining the beginning, length, and divisions of years. **2.** a table showing such an arrangement. **3.** a schedule of events or appointments. ~*vb.* **4.** to enter in a calendar; schedule. [Latin *kalendae* the calends]

calender (ˈkælɪndə) *n.* **1.** a machine in which paper or cloth is smoothed by passing it between rollers. ~*vb.* **2.** to smooth in such a machine. [French *calandre*]

calends or **kalends** (ˈkælɪndz) *pl. n.* (in the ancient Roman calendar) the first day of each month. [Latin *kalendae*]

calendula (kəˈlɛndjʊlə) *n.* a plant having orange-and-yellow rayed flowers. [Medieval Latin]

calf¹ (kɑːf) *n., pl.* **calves. 1.** the young of cattle. **2.** a young elephant, giraffe, buffalo, whale, or seal. **3.** same as **calfskin** (sense 2). [Old English *cealf*]

calf² (kɑːf) *n., pl.* **calves.** the back of the leg between the ankle and the knee. [Old Norse *kalfi*]

calf love *n.* temporary infatuation of an adolescent for another person.

calfskin (ˈkɑːfˌskɪn) *n.* **1.** the skin or hide of a calf. **2.** fine leather made from this.

calibrate (ˈkælɪˌbreɪt) *vb.* **1.** to measure the calibre of (something). **2.** to mark the scale or check the accuracy of (a measuring instrument). —**caliˈbration** *n.* —**ˈcaliˌbrator** *n.*

calibre or *U.S.* **caliber** (ˈkælɪbə) *n.* **1.** the diameter of the bore of a firearm or of a shell or bullet. **2.** ability; personal worth. [Arabic *qālib* shoemaker's last, mould]

calices (ˈkælɪˌsiːz) *n.* the plural of **calix.**

calico (ˈkælɪˌkəʊ) *n., pl.* **-coes** or **-cos. 1.** a white or unbleached cotton fabric. **2.** *Chiefly U.S.* a coarse printed cotton fabric. [*Calicut,* town in India]

Calif. California.

californium (ˌkælɪˈfɔːnɪəm) *n.* an artificial radioactive element. Symbol: Cf [after the University of California, where it was discovered]

caliper (ˈkælɪpə) *n. U.S.* same as **calliper.**

caliph (ˈkeɪlɪf, ˈkæl-) *n. Islam.* the title of the successors of Mohammed as rulers of the Islamic world. [Arabic *khalīfa* successor]

caliphate (ˈkeɪlɪˌfeɪt) *n.* the office, jurisdiction, or reign of a caliph.

calisthenics (ˌkælɪsˈθɛnɪks) *n.* same as **callisthenics.**

calix (ˈkeɪlɪks, ˈkæ-) *n., pl.* **calices.** a cup; chalice. [Latin]

calk (kɔːk) *vb.* same as **caulk.**

call (kɔːl) *vb.* **1.** (often foll. by *out*) to speak loudly so as to attract attention. **2.** to summon: *to call a policeman.* **3.** to visit. **4.** (often foll. by *up*) to telephone (a person). **5.** to summon to a specific office or profession. **6.** (of animals or birds) to utter (a characteristic cry). **7.** to name: *he's called Bob.* **8.** to regard as being (something specified): *I call it a waste of time; she called him a liar.* **9.** to read (a list) aloud to check for omissions or absentees. **10.** to give an order for: *to call a* *strike.* **11.** to try to predict the result of tossing a coin. **12.** to awaken: *I was called early this morning.* **13.** to cause to assemble: *to call a meeting.* **14.** *Sport.* (of an umpire or referee) to judge (a ball) to be in or out of play. **15.** *Cards.* to bid. **16.** (foll. by *for*) **a.** to require: *this problem calls for study.* **b.** to come and fetch. **17.** (foll. by *on* or *upon*) to make an appeal or request to: *they called upon him to reply.* **18. call someone's bluff.** See **bluff**[1]. **19. call to mind.** to remember or cause to be remembered. *~n.* **20.** a cry or shout. **21.** the characteristic cry of a bird or animal. **22.** a summons or invitation. **23.** a short visit: *the doctor made six calls this morning.* **24.** an inner urge to some task or profession; vocation. **25.** allure or fascination: *the call of the forest.* **26.** need, demand, or occasion: *there is no call to shout.* **27.** demand or claim: *the call of duty.* **28.** a conversation or a request for a connection by telephone. **29.** a bid or a player's turn to bid. **30.** *Sport.* a decision of an umpire or referee as to whether a ball is in or out of play. **31.** Also called: **call option.** *Stock Exchange.* an option to buy stock during a specified period. **32. on call.** available at short notice. **33. within call.** within shouting distance. *~See also* **call in, call off,** etc. [Old English *ceallian*] —**'caller** *n.*

call box *n.* a soundproof enclosure for a public telephone.

call girl *n.* a prostitute with whom appointments are made by telephone.

calligraphy (kəˈlɪgrəfɪ) *n.* handwriting, esp. beautiful handwriting. [Greek *kallos* beauty + -GRAPHY] —**cal'ligrapher** or **cal'ligraphist** *n.* —**calligraphic** (ˌkælɪˈgræfɪk) *adj.*

call in *vb.* **1.** to pay a brief visit. **2.** to demand payment of: *to call in a loan.* **3.** to take (something) out of circulation, because it is faulty. **4.** to summon to one's assistance: *to call in a specialist.*

calling (ˈkɔːlɪŋ) *n.* **1.** a strong inner urge to follow a profession or trade; vocation. **2.** an occupation, profession, or trade.

calliper or *U.S.* **caliper** (ˈkælɪpə) *n.* **1.** (*often pl.*) a measuring instrument consisting of two steel legs hinged together. **2.** a metal splint for supporting the leg. [var. of *calibre*]

callisthenics or **calisthenics** (ˌkælɪsˈθɛnɪks) *n.* light exercises designed to promote general fitness. [Greek *kalli-* beautiful + *sthenos* strength] —**callis'thenic** or **calis'thenic** *adj.*

call off *vb.* **1.** to cancel or abandon: *the game was called off.* **2.** to order to desist: *the man called off his dog.*

callosity (kəˈlɒsɪtɪ) *n., pl.* **-ties.** a callus.

callous (ˈkæləs) *adj.* **1.** insensitive. **2.** (of skin) hardened and thickened. *~vb.* **3.** *Pathol.* to make or become callous. [Latin *callōsus*] —**callously** *adv.* —**callousness** *n.*

call out *vb.* **1.** to utter loudly. **2.** to summon: *call out the troops.* **3.** to order (workers) to strike. **4.** to challenge to a duel.

callow (ˈkæləʊ) *adj.* young and inexperi-

enced; immature. [Old English *calu*] —**'callowness** *n.*

call up *vb.* **1.** to summon for active military service. **2.** to evoke. **3.** to summon (people) to action. *~n.* **call-up. 4.** a general order to report for military service.

callus (ˈkæləs) *n., pl.* **-luses. 1.** a hard or thick area of skin. **2.** an area of bony tissue formed during the healing of a broken bone. [Latin *callum* hardened skin]

calm (kɑːm) *adj.* **1.** still: *a calm sea.* **2.** windless. **3.** tranquil; serene. *~n.* **4.** an absence of disturbance or rough motion. **5.** absence of wind. **6.** tranquillity. *~vb.* **7.** (often foll. by *down*) to make or become calm. [Late Latin *cauma* heat, hence a rest during the heat of the day] —**'calmly** *adv.* —**'calmness** *n.*

calomel (ˈkæləˌmɛl, -məl) *n.* a colourless tasteless powder used as a cathartic. [Greek *kalos* beautiful + *melas* black]

Calor Gas (ˈkælə) *n. Trademark.* butane gas liquefied under pressure in containers for domestic use.

caloric (kəˈlɒrɪk) *adj.* of heat or calories.

calorie or **calory** (ˈkælərɪ) *n., pl.* **-ries.** the quantity of heat required to raise the temperature of 1 gram of water by 1°C. Also: **small calorie.** [French *calor* heat]

Calorie (ˈkælərɪ) *n.* **1.** Also: **large calorie.** a unit of heat, equal to one thousand calories. **2.** the amount of a food capable of producing one calorie of energy.

calorific (ˌkæləˈrɪfɪk) *adj.* of or generating heat.

calorimeter (ˌkæləˈrɪmɪtə) *n.* a device for measuring amounts of heat.

calumniate (kəˈlʌmnɪˌeɪt) *vb.* to slander. —**ca,lumni'ation** *n.*

calumny (ˈkæləmnɪ) *n., pl.* **-nies.** a false or malicious statement; slander. [Latin *calumnia* slander] —**calumnious** (kəˈlʌmnɪəs) *adj.*

Calvary (ˈkælvərɪ) *n.* the place just outside the walls of Jerusalem where Jesus was crucified. [Latin *calvāria* skull]

calve (kɑːv) *vb.* to give birth to (a calf).

calves (kɑːvz) *n.* the plural of **calf.**

Calvinism (ˈkælvɪˌnɪzəm) *n.* the theological system of Calvin, 16th-century French theologian, and his followers, stressing predestination and salvation solely by God's grace. —**'Calvinist** *n., adj.* —,**Calvin'istic** or ,**Calvin'istical** *adj.*

calx (kælks) *n., pl.* **calxes** or **calces.** the powdery metallic oxide left when an ore or mineral is roasted. [Latin: lime]

calypso (kəˈlɪpsəʊ) *n., pl.* **-sos.** a West Indian song with improvised topical lyrics and a syncopated rhythm. [prob. from *Calypso,* sea nymph in Greek myth.]

calyx (ˈkeɪlɪks, ˈkælɪks) *n., pl.* **calyxes** or **calyces** (ˈkælɪˌsiːz, ˈkeɪlɪ-). the sepals of a flower that protect the developing bud. [Latin: shell, husk]

cam (kæm) *n.* a rotating cylinder attached to a revolving shaft to give a back-and-forward motion to a part in contact with it. [Dutch *kam* comb]

camaraderie (ˌkæməˈrɑːdərɪ) n. familiarity and trust between friends. [French]

camber (ˈkæmbə) n. 1. a slight upward curve to the centre of a surface. ~vb. 2. to form or be formed with a camber. [Latin *camurus* curved]

Cambrian (ˈkæmbrɪən) adj. Geol. of a period of geological time about 600 million years ago.

cambric (ˈkeɪmbrɪk) n. a fine white linen fabric. [Flemish *Kamerijk* Cambrai]

Cambs (kæmbz) Cambridgeshire.

came (keɪm) vb. the past tense of **come**.

camel (ˈkæməl) n. 1. either of two humped mammals (see **dromedary, Bactrian camel**) that can survive long periods without food or water in desert regions. ~adj. 2. fawn. [Greek *kamēlos*]

camellia (kəˈmiːlɪə) n. an ornamental shrub with glossy evergreen leaves and showy white, pink, or red flowers. [after Georg Josef *Kamel*, Jesuit missionary]

camel's hair or **camelhair** (ˈkæməlˌhɛə) n. 1. the fine soft hair of a camel. 2. soft, usually tan cloth made of this hair. 3. (modifier) (of a painter's brush) made from the tail hairs of squirrels.

Camembert (ˈkæməmˌbɛə) n. a soft creamy cheese. [*Camembert*, village in Normandy]

cameo (ˈkæmɪˌəʊ) n., pl. **cameos**. 1. a brooch or ring with a profile head carved in relief. 2. an engraving upon a gem or stone with the background a different colour from the raised design. 3. a stone with such an engraving. 4. a brief but creative part in a film or play played by a well-known actor or actress. 5. a short descriptive literary work. [Italian *cammeo*]

camera (ˈkæmərə) n. 1. a photographic device in which light is allowed through a lens to form an image on light-sensitive film. 2. Television. the equipment used to convert an optical image into electrical signals. 3. **in camera**. in private. [Greek *kamara* vault]

camera obscura (ɒbˈskjʊərə) n. a darkened room with an aperture through which images of outside objects are projected onto a flat surface. [New Latin]

camiknickers (ˈkæmɪˌnɪkəz) pl. n. women's knickers attached to a camisole top.

camisole (ˈkæmɪˌsəʊl) n. a woman's underbodice with shoulder straps. [French]

camomile or **chamomile** (ˈkæməˌmaɪl) n. 1. an aromatic plant whose leaves and flowers are used medicinally. 2. **camomile tea**. a medicinal beverage made from the leaves and flowers of this plant. [Greek *khamaimēlon* earth-apple (referring to the scent of the flowers)]

camouflage (ˈkæməˌflɑːʒ) n. 1. the use of natural surroundings or artificial aids to conceal or disguise something. 2. something designed to conceal or deceive. ~vb. 3. to conceal by camouflage. [French]

camp¹ (kæmp) n. 1. a place where tents, huts, or cabins are erected. 2. temporary lodgings composed of tents, huts, or cabins. 3. a group supporting a given doctrine. 4. (modifier) suitable for use in temporary lodgings: *camp bed*. ~vb. 5. to set up a camp. 6. (often foll. by *out*) to live temporarily in or as if in a tent. [Latin *campus* field] —'**camper** n. —'**camping** n.

camp² (kæmp) Informal. ~adj. 1. effeminate or homosexual. 2. consciously artificial, vulgar, or affected. ~vb. 3. to behave or do in a camp way. 4. **camp it up**. to overact. [origin unknown] —'**campy** adj.

campaign (kæmˈpeɪn) n. 1. a series of coordinated activities designed to achieve a goal. 2. Mil. a number of operations aimed at achieving a single objective. ~vb. 3. (often foll. by *for*) to conduct or take part in a campaign. [Latin *campus* field] —**cam'paigner** n.

campanile (ˌkæmpəˈniːlɪ) n. a bell tower, not usually attached to another building. [Italian]

campanology (ˌkæmpəˈnɒlədʒɪ) n. the art of ringing bells. [Latin *campāna* bell] —ˌ**campa'nologist** n.

campanula (kæmˈpænjʊlə) n. a plant having blue or white bell-shaped flowers. [New Latin: a little bell]

camp follower n. 1. a civilian who unofficially provides services to military personnel. 2. a nonmember who supports a particular group or cause.

camphor (ˈkæmfə) n. an aromatic crystalline substance obtained from the wood of an Asian or Australian laurel (**camphor tree**): used medicinally and in mothballs. [Arabic *kāfūr*]

camphorate (ˈkæmfəˌreɪt) vb. to treat or impregnate with camphor.

campion (ˈkæmpɪən) n. a plant related to the pink, having red, pink, or white flowers. [origin unknown]

camp oven n. Austral. & N.Z. a metal pot or box with a heavy lid, used for baking over an open fire.

camp site n. a place for camping.

campus (ˈkæmpəs) n., pl. **-puses**. the grounds and buildings of a university or college. [Latin: field]

camshaft (ˈkæmˌʃɑːft) n. a shaft having one or more cams attached to it.

can¹ (kæn; unstressed kən) vb. past **could**. used to indicate: 1. ability, skill, or fitness to perform a task: *I can run*. 2. Informal. permission or the right to something: *can I have a drink?* 3. knowledge of how to do something: *he can speak three languages*. 4. possibility, opportunity, or likelihood: *my trainer says I can win the race*. [Old English *cunnan*]

can² (kæn) n. 1. a metal container, esp. for liquids. 2. Also: **canful**. the contents of a can or the amount a can will hold. 3. Slang. prison. 4. U.S. & Canad. slang. a toilet. 5. **in the can**. finished; finalized. ~vb. **canning, canned**. 6. to put (something) into a can or cans. [Old English *canne*]

Can. 1. Canada. 2. Canadian.

Canada Day n. (in Canada) July 1, a public holiday marking the anniversary of the day in 1867 when Canada became a dominion.

Canada goose n. a greyish-brown North American goose with a black neck and head and a white throat patch.

Canada jay n. a grey jay of northern N America, notorious for its stealing.

Canadian (kə'neɪdɪən) adj. **1.** of Canada or its people. ~n. **2.** a person from Canada.

Canadiana (kə,neɪdɪ'ɑːnə; Canad. -'ænə) n. objects relating to Canadian history and culture.

Canadian football n. a game like American football played on a grass pitch between teams of 12 players.

Canadianism (kə'neɪdɪə,nɪzəm) n. **1.** the Canadian national character or spirit. **2.** a linguistic feature peculiar to Canada or Canadians.

Canadianize or **-ise** (kə'neɪdɪə,naɪz) vb. to make or become Canadian.

Canadien or (fem.) **Canadienne** (kə,næd'ɪɛn) n. a French Canadian. [French: Canadian]

canaille (kæ'naɪ) n. the masses; rabble. [French, from Italian canaglia pack of dogs]

canal (kə'næl) n. **1.** an artificial waterway constructed for navigation or irrigation. **2.** a passage or duct in an animal or plant body: the alimentary canal. [Latin canna reed]

canalize or **-lise** ('kænə,laɪz) vb. **1.** to provide with or convert into a canal or canals. **2.** to give direction to or provide an outlet for. —,canali'zation or -li'sation n.

canapé ('kænəpɪ, -,peɪ) n. a small piece of bread or toast spread with a savoury topping. [French: sofa]

canard (kæ'nɑːd) n. a false report; rumour or hoax. [French: a duck]

canary (kə'neərɪ) n., pl. **-naries. 1.** a small yellow songbird often kept as a pet. ~adj. **2.** Also: **canary-yellow.** light yellow.

canasta (kə'næstə) n. a card game like rummy, using two packs of cards. [Spanish: basket (because two packs of cards are required)]

cancan ('kæn,kæn) n. a high-kicking dance performed by a female chorus. [French]

cancel ('kænsᵊl) vb. **-celling, -celled** or U.S. **-celing, -celed. 1.** to postpone (something) indefinitely; call off. **2.** to revoke or annul. **3.** to delete; cross out. **4.** to mark (a cheque or stamp) with an official stamp to prevent further use. **5.** (usually foll. by out) to counterbalance: his generosity cancelled out his past unkindness. **6.** Maths. to eliminate (common factors) from both the numerator and denominator of a fraction or equal terms from opposite sides of an equation. [Late Latin cancellāre to strike out, make like a lattice]

cancellation (,kænsɪ'leɪʃən) n. **1.** the act or an instance of cancelling. **2.** something that has been cancelled: we have a cancellation in the balcony. **3.** the marks made by cancelling.

cancer ('kænsə) n. **1.** a malignant growth or tumour, caused by abnormal and uncontrolled cell division. **2.** the disease resulting from this. **3.** an evil influence that spreads dangerously. [Latin: crab, creeping tumour] —'**cancerous** adj. —**cancroid** ('kæŋkrɔɪd) adj.

Cancer ('kænsə) n. **1.** Astrol. the fourth sign of the zodiac; the crab. **2. tropic of Cancer.** See **tropic** (sense 1).

candela (kæn'diːlə, -'deɪlə) n. the basic SI unit of luminous intensity. [Latin: candle]

candelabrum (,kændɪ'lɑːbrəm) or **candelabra** n., pl. **-bra** (-brə), **-brums,** or **-bras.** a large, branched candleholder. [Latin candela candle]

candid ('kændɪd) adj. **1.** frank and outspoken. **2.** (of a photograph) unposed or informal. [Latin candēre to be white] —'**candidly** adv. —'**candidness** n.

candidate ('kændɪ,deɪt) n. **1.** a person seeking a job or position. **2.** a person taking an examination. **3.** a person or thing regarded as suitable or likely for a particular fate or position. [Latin candidātus clothed in white] —**candidacy** ('kændɪdəsɪ) or **candidature** ('kændɪdə-tʃə) n.

candied ('kændɪd) adj. impregnated or coated with sugar.

candle ('kændᵊl) n. **1.** a stick or block of wax or tallow surrounding a wick, which is burned to produce light. **2. burn the candle at both ends.** to exhaust oneself by doing too much. **3. not hold a candle to.** Informal. to be inferior in comparison with. **4. not worth the candle.** Informal. not worth doing. [Latin candēla]

candlelight ('kændᵊl,laɪt) n. the light from a candle or candles. —'**candle,lit** adj.

Candlemas ('kændᵊlməs) n. Christianity. Feb. 2, the Feast of the Purification of the Virgin Mary.

candlepower ('kændᵊl,pauə) n. the luminous intensity of a source of light: now expressed in candelas.

candlestick ('kændᵊl,stɪk) or **candleholder** ('kændᵊl,həuldə) n. a holder for a candle.

candlewick ('kændᵊl,wɪk) adj. made of cotton or muslin with a tufted pattern.

candour or U.S. **candor** ('kændə) n. openness; frankness. [Latin candor]

candy ('kændɪ) n., pl. **-dies. 1.** Chiefly U.S. & Canad. a sweet or sweets. ~vb. **-dying, -died. 2.** (of sugar) to become or cause to become crystalline. **3.** to preserve by boiling in sugar: candied peel. [Arabic qand cane sugar]

candyfloss ('kændɪ,flɒs) n. Brit. a light fluffy mass of spun sugar, held on a stick.

candy-striped adj. having narrow coloured stripes on a white background. —**candy stripe** n.

cane (keɪn) n. **1. a.** the long flexible stem of the bamboo or any similar plant. **b.** a plant having such a stem. **2.** strips of such stems, woven to make wickerwork. **3.** the woody stem of a reed, blackberry, or loganberry. **4.** a flexible rod used to beat someone. **5.** a slender walking stick. ~vb. **6.** to beat with a cane. **7.** to make or repair with cane. [Greek kanna]

cane sugar *n.* sucrose obtained from sugar cane.

canine ('keɪnaɪn, 'kæn-) *adj.* **1.** of or like a dog. **2.** of the family of mammals including dogs, wolves, and foxes. ~*n.* **3.** an animal of the dog family. **4.** a sharp-pointed tooth between the incisors and the premolars. [Latin *canis* dog]

canister ('kænɪstə) *n.* a container, usually made of metal, in which dry food is stored. [Latin *canistrum* basket woven from reeds]

canker ('kæŋkə) *n.* **1.** an ulceration or ulcerous disease. **2.** something evil that spreads and corrupts. ~*vb.* **3.** to infect or become infected with canker. [Latin *cancer* cancerous sore] —'**cankerous** *adj.*

cankerworm ('kæŋkə,wɜːm) *n.* a moth larva harmful to fruit trees.

cannabis ('kænəbɪs) *n.* **1.** the hemp plant. **2.** the drug obtained from the dried leaves and flowers of the hemp plant. [Greek *kannabis*]

canned (kænd) *adj.* **1.** preserved in tins. **2.** *Informal.* recorded in advance. **3.** *Slang.* drunk.

cannelloni or **canneloni** (,kænɪ'ləʊnɪ) *pl. n.* tubular pieces of pasta filled with meat or cheese. [Italian]

cannery ('kænərɪ) *n., pl.* **-neries.** a place where foods are canned.

cannibal ('kænɪb'l) *n.* **1.** a person who eats human flesh. **2.** an animal that feeds on the flesh of others of its kind. [Spanish *canibales*] —'**canniba,lism** *n.*

cannibalize or **-lise** ('kænɪbə,laɪz) *vb.* to use parts from (one machine) to repair another. —,**cannibali'zation** or **-li'sation** *n.*

canning ('kænɪŋ) *n.* the process of sealing food in cans to preserve it.

cannon ('kænən) *n., pl.* **-nons** or **-non. 1.** an automatic aircraft gun. **2.** *History.* a gun consisting of a metal tube mounted on a carriage. **3.** *Billiards.* a shot in which the cue ball strikes two balls successively. ~*vb.* **4.** to rebound; collide. **5.** *Billiards.* to make a cannon. [Italian *canna* tube]

cannonade (,kænə'neɪd) *n.* **1.** continuous heavy gunfire. ~*vb.* **2.** to attack (a target) with cannon.

cannonball ('kænən,bɔːl) *n.* a heavy metal ball fired from a cannon.

cannon fodder *n.* men regarded as expendable in war.

cannot ('kænɒt, kæ'nɒt) can not.

canny ('kænɪ) *adj.* **-nier, -niest. 1.** shrewd, esp. in business. **2.** *Scot. & NE English dialect.* good or nice. [from *can* (in the sense: to know how)] —'**cannily** *adv.* —'**canniness** *n.*

canoe (kə'nuː) *n.* **1.** a light narrow open boat, propelled by one or more paddles. ~*vb.* **2.** **-noeing, -noed. 2.** to go in or transport by canoe. [Carib] —**ca'noeist** *n.*

canon[1] ('kænən) *n.* **1.** *Christianity.* a Church decree regulating morals or religious practices. **2.** (*often pl.*) a general rule or standard. **3.** *R.C. Church.* the list of the canonized saints. **4.** *R.C. Church.* the prayer in the Mass in which the Host is consecrated. **5.** a list of sacred writings recognized as genuine. **6.** a piece of music in which a melody in one part is taken up in one or more other parts successively. **7.** a list of the works of an author that are accepted as authentic. [Greek *kanōn* rule]

canon[2] ('kænən) *n.* a priest serving in a cathedral. [Late Latin *canonicus* one living under a rule]

canonical (kə'nɒnɪk'l) or **canonic** *adj.* **1.** included in a canon of writings. **2.** conforming with canon law. **3.** accepted; authoritative. **4.** of a canon (clergyman).

canonical hour *n. R.C. Church.* one of the seven prayer times appointed for each day.

canonicals (kə'nɒnɪk'lz) *pl. n.* the official clothes worn by clergy when taking services.

canonist ('kænənɪst) *n.* a specialist in canon law.

canonize or **-ise** ('kænə,naɪz) *vb.* **1.** *R.C. Church.* to declare (a person) to be a saint. **2.** to regard as a saint. **3.** to sanction by canon law. —,**canoni'zation** or **-i'sation** *n.*

canon law *n.* the codified body of laws of a Christian Church.

canoodle (kə'nuːd'l) *vb. Slang.* to kiss and cuddle. [origin unknown]

canopy ('kænəpɪ) *n., pl.* **-pies. 1.** an ornamental awning above a bed, person, or throne. **2.** a rooflike covering over an altar, niche, or door. **3.** any large or wide covering: *the sky was a grey canopy.* **4.** the part of a parachute that opens out. **5.** the transparent hood of an aircraft cockpit. ~*vb.* **-pying, -pied. 6.** to cover with a canopy. [Greek *kōnōpeion* bed with mosquito net]

canst (kænst) *vb. Archaic.* the form of **can**[1] used with the pronoun *thou.*

cant[1] (kænt) *n.* **1.** insincere talk, esp. concerning religion or morals. **2.** specialized vocabulary of a particular group, such as thieves or lawyers. ~*vb.* **3.** to use cant. [prob. from Latin *cantāre* to sing]

cant[2] (kænt) *n.* **1.** a tilted position. **2.** a sudden movement that tilts or turns something. **3.** the angle or tilt thus caused. **4.** a corner or outer angle. **5.** a slanting surface. ~*vb.* **6.** to tilt or overturn. [perhaps from Latin *canthus* iron hoop round a wheel]

can't (kænt) *vb.* can not.

cantabile (kæn'tɑːbɪlɪ) *Music.* ~*adv.* **1.** flowingly and melodiously. ~*n.* **2.** a piece or passage performed in this way. [Latin *cantāre* to sing]

cantaloupe or **cantaloup** ('kæntə,luːp) *n.* a kind of melon with ribbed warty rind and orange flesh. [*Cantaluppi*, near Rome, where first cultivated in Europe]

cantankerous (kæn'tæŋkərəs) *adj.* quarrelsome; bad-tempered. [origin unknown] —**can'tankerously** *adv.* —**can'tankerousness** *n.*

cantata (kæn'tɑːtə) *n.* a musical setting of a text, consisting of arias, duets, and choruses. [Italian]

canteen (kæn'tiːn) *n.* **1.** a restaurant

attached to a workplace or school. **2.** a small shop that provides a limited range of items to a military unit. **3. a.** a box containing cutlery. **b.** the cutlery itself. **4.** a flask for carrying water. [Italian *cantina* wine cellar]

canter (ˈkæntə) *n.* **1.** a gait of horses between a trot and a gallop in speed. ~*vb.* **2.** to move or cause to move at a canter. [short for *Canterbury trot*, the pace at which pilgrims rode to Canterbury]

canticle (ˈkæntɪkˀl) *n.* a nonmetrical hymn with a Biblical text. [Latin *canticulum*]

cantilever (ˈkæntɪˌliːvə) *n.* **1.** a beam or structural framework fixed at one end only. **2.** a part of a beam or a structure projecting outwards beyond its support. [origin unknown]

cantilever bridge *n.* a bridge made of two cantilevers which meet in the middle.

canto (ˈkæntəʊ) *n.*, *pl.* **-tos.** a main division of a long poem. [Italian: song]

canton *n.* **1.** (ˈkæntɒn, kænˈtɒn). a political division of a country, esp. Switzerland. ~*vb.* **2.** (kænˈtɒn). to divide into cantons. [Old French: corner]

Cantonese (ˌkæntəˈniːz) *n.* **1.** the Chinese dialect of Canton. **2.** (*pl.* **-ese**) a person from Canton. ~*adj.* **3.** of Canton or its dialect.

cantonment (kənˈtuːnmənt) *n.* *History.* a permanent military camp in British India. [Old French *canton* corner]

cantor (ˈkæntɔː) *n.* **1.** *Judaism.* a man employed to lead synagogue services. **2.** *Christianity.* a church choir leader. [Latin: singer]

Canuck (kəˈnʌk) *n.*, *adj.* *U.S. & Canad. informal.* Canadian. [origin unknown]

canvas (ˈkænvəs) *n.* **1.** a heavy cloth of cotton, hemp, or jute, used for sails and tents. **2. a.** a piece of cloth on which an oil painting is done. **b.** an oil painting. **3.** a tent or tents collectively. **4.** a sail or sails collectively. **5. under canvas. a.** in tents. **b.** *Naut.* with sails unfurled. [Latin *cannabis* hemp]

canvass (ˈkænvəs) *vb.* **1.** to try to get votes or support (from). **2.** to determine the opinions of (people) by conducting a survey. **3.** to investigate or discuss (something) thoroughly. ~*n.* **4.** an attempt to get opinions or votes. [prob. from obs. sense of *canvas* (to toss someone in a canvas sheet, hence, to criticize)] —**canvasser** *n.*

canyon *or* **cañon** (ˈkænjən) *n.* a gorge or ravine. [Spanish]

caoutchouc (ˈkaʊtʃʊk) *n.* same as **rubber**[1] (sense 1). [S American Indian]

cap (kæp) *n.* **1.** a soft close-fitting covering for the head. **2.** such a covering worn to identify the wearer's rank or occupation: *a nurse's cap.* **3.** a cover: *lens cap.* **4.** a top part: *the cap of a wave.* **5. a.** See **percussion cap. b.** a small amount of explosive enclosed in paper and used in a toy gun. **6.** *Sport, chiefly Brit.* **a.** a cap given to someone chosen for a representative team. **b.** a player chosen for such a team. **7.** an artificial protective top for a

tooth. **8.** a contraceptive device placed over the mouth of the womb. **9.** a mortarboard. **10. cap in hand.** humbly. ~*vb.* **capping, capped.** **11.** to cover with or as if with a cap: *snow capped the mountain.* **12.** to impose an upper level on (a tax): *rate-capping.* **13.** *Informal.* to outdo; excel. **14. to cap it all.** to provide the finishing touch. **15.** *Sport, Brit.* to select (a player) for a representative team. [Late Latin *cappa* hood]

CAP (in the EC) Common Agricultural Policy.

cap. **1.** capacity. **2.** capital. **3.** capital letter.

capability (ˌkeɪpəˈbɪlɪtɪ) *n.*, *pl.* **-ties.** **1.** the quality of being capable; ability. **2.** (*usually pl.*) potential aptitude.

capable (ˈkeɪpəbˀl) *adj.* **1.** having ability; competent. **2.** (foll. by *of*) able or having the skill (to do something): *she is capable of hard work.* **3.** (foll. by *of*) able or ready (to do something): *he seemed capable of murder.* [Latin *capere* to take] —**capably** *adv.*

capacious (kəˈpeɪʃəs) *adj.* spacious; roomy. [Latin *capere* to take] —**capaciousness** *n.*

capacitance (kəˈpæsɪtəns) *n.* **1.** the ability of a system to store electric charge. **2.** a measure of this.

capacitor (kəˈpæsɪtə) *n.* a device for storing electric charge.

capacity (kəˈpæsɪtɪ) *n.*, *pl.* **-ties.** **1.** the ability to contain, absorb, or hold. **2.** the maximum amount something can contain or absorb. **3.** mental ability. **4.** the maximum output of which an installation or producer is capable: *the factory must expand its capacity.* **5.** a position or function. **6.** *Computers.* **a.** the number of words or characters that can be stored in a storage device. **b.** the range of numbers that can be processed in a register. **7.** legal competence: *the capacity to make a will.* ~*modifier.* **8.** of the maximum amount or number possible: *a capacity crowd.* [Latin *capere* to take]

caparison (kəˈpærɪsˀn) *n.* **1.** a decorated covering for a horse. **2.** rich clothing or equipment. ~*vb.* **3.** to put a caparison on. [Old Spanish *caparazón* saddle-cloth]

cape[1] (keɪp) *n.* a short sleeveless cloak. [Late Latin *cappa*]

cape[2] (keɪp) *n.* a headland or promontory. [Latin *caput* head]

Cape (keɪp) *n.* **the.** **1.** the Cape of Good Hope. **2.** the SW region of South Africa's Cape Province.

cape pigeon *n.* a S African petrel.

caper[1] (ˈkeɪpə) *n.* **1.** a playful skip or leap. **2.** a high-spirited prank. **3. cut a caper** *or* **capers.** to skip, leap, or frolic. ~*vb.* **4.** to skip or leap about light-heartedly. [prob. from *capriole*]

caper[2] (ˈkeɪpə) *n.* **1.** a spiny trailing Mediterranean shrub with edible flower buds. **2.** (*pl.*) its pickled flower buds, used in sauces. [Greek *kapparis*]

capercaillie *or* **capercailzie** (ˌkæpəˈkeɪljɪ) *n.* a large black European woodland grouse. [Scot. Gaelic *capull coille* horse of the woods]

Cape sparrow *n.* a S African sparrow.

capillarity (ˌkæpɪˈlærɪtɪ) *n.* a phenomenon caused by surface tension and resulting in the attraction or repulsion of the surface of a liquid in contact with a solid.

capillary (kəˈpɪlərɪ) *adj.* **1.** like a hair; slender. **2.** (of tubes) having a fine bore. **3.** *Anat.* of the capillaries. ~*n.*, *pl.* **-laries. 4.** *Anat.* one of the very fine blood vessels linking the arteries and the veins. [Latin *capillus* hair]

capital¹ (ˈkæpɪtᵊl) *n.* **1.** the seat of government of a country. **2.** the total wealth owned or used in business by an individual or group. **3.** wealth used to produce more wealth. **4. make capital (out) of.** to get advantage from. **5.** (*sometimes cap.*) capitalists collectively. **6.** a capital letter. ~*adj.* **7.** *Law.* involving or punishable by death: *a capital offence.* **8.** chief or principal: *our capital concern.* **9.** designating the large letter used as the initial letter in a sentence, personal name, or place name. **10.** *Chiefly Brit.* excellent; first-rate: *a capital idea.* [Latin *caput* head]

capital² (ˈkæpɪtᵊl) *n.* the top part of a column or pillar. [Old French *capitel*, from Latin *caput* head]

capital gain *n.* profit from the sale of an asset.

capital goods *pl. n. Econ.* goods that are themselves utilized in the production of other goods.

capitalism (ˈkæpɪtəˌlɪzəm) *n.* an economic system based on the private ownership of the means of production and distribution.

capitalist (ˈkæpɪtəlɪst) *n.* **1.** a person who owns capital. **2.** *Politics.* a supporter of capitalism. ~*adj.* **3.** relating to capitalists or capitalism. —ˌcapitalˈistic *adj.*

capitalize *or* **-ise** (ˈkæpɪtəˌlaɪz) *vb.* **1.** (foll. by *on*) to take advantage of. **2.** to write or print (text) in capital letters. **3.** to convert (debt or earnings) into capital stock. **4.** to provide with capital. —ˌcapitaliˈzation *or* **-iˈsation** *n.*

capital levy *n.* a tax on capital or property as contrasted with a tax on income.

capitally (ˈkæpɪtəlɪ) *adv. Chiefly Brit.* in an excellent manner; admirably.

capital punishment *n.* the punishment of death for a crime; death penalty.

capital stock *n.* **1.** the value of the total shares that a company can issue. **2.** the total capital existing in an economy at a given time.

capital transfer tax *n.* (in Britain) a tax payable on the transfer of money or property as a gift or bequest.

capitation (ˌkæpɪˈteɪʃən) *n.* a tax of so much per person. [Latin *caput* head]

capitulate (kəˈpɪtjuˌleɪt) *vb.* to surrender under agreed conditions. [Medieval Latin *capitulare* to draw up under headings]

capitulation (kəˌpɪtjuˈleɪʃən) *n.* **1.** the act of capitulating. **2.** a document containing terms of surrender.

capo (ˈkæpəʊ) *n.*, *pl.* **-pos.** a device fitted

across the strings of a guitar or similar instrument so as to raise the pitch. [Italian *capo tasto* head stop]

capon (ˈkeɪpən) *n.* a castrated cock fowl fattened for eating. [Latin *cāpō*]

cappuccino (ˌkæpʊˈtʃiːnəʊ) *n.*, *pl.* **-nos.** coffee with steamed milk, usually sprinkled with powdered chocolate. [Italian]

caprice (kəˈpriːs) *n.* **1.** a sudden change of attitude or behaviour. **2.** a tendency to such changes. [Italian *capriccio* a shiver, caprice]

capricious (kəˈprɪʃəs) *adj.* given to sudden unpredictable changes; erratic.

Capricorn (ˈkæprɪˌkɔːn) *n.* **1.** *Astrol.* the tenth sign of the zodiac; the Goat. **2. tropic of Capricorn.** See **tropic** (sense 1). [Latin *caper* goat + *cornū* horn]

capriole (ˈkæprɪˌəʊl) *n.* **1.** an upward but not forward leap made by a horse. ~*vb.* **2.** to perform a capriole. [Latin *capreolus*, *caper* goat]

caps. 1. capital letters. **2.** capsule.

capsicum (ˈkæpsɪkəm) *n.* a kind of pepper used as a vegetable or ground to produce a spice. [Latin *capsa* box]

capsize (kæpˈsaɪz) *vb.* to overturn accidentally; upset. [origin unknown]

capstan (ˈkæpstən) *n.* **1.** a rotating cylinder round which a ship's rope or cable is wound. **2.** the rotating shaft in a tape recorder that pulls the tape past the head. [Old Provençal *cabestan*]

capstone (ˈkæpˌstəʊn) *n.* same as **copestone** (sense 2).

capsule (ˈkæpsjuːl) *n.* **1.** a soluble case of gelatin enclosing a dose of medicine. **2.** *Bot.* a plant's seed case that opens when ripe. **3.** *Anat.* a membrane or sac surrounding an organ or part. **4.** See **space capsule. 5.** (*modifier*) in a highly concise form: *a capsule summary.* [Latin *capsa* box] —ˈcapsular *adj.*

capsulize *or* **-ise** (ˈkæpsjuˌlaɪz) *vb.* **1.** to state (information) in a highly condensed form. **2.** to enclose in a capsule.

Capt. Captain.

captain (ˈkæptɪn) *n.* **1.** the person in charge of a vessel. **2.** a middle-ranking naval officer. **3.** a junior officer in the armed forces. **4.** the officer in command of a civil aircraft. **5.** the leader of a team in games. **6.** a person in command over a group or organization: *a captain of industry.* **7.** *U.S.* a policeman in charge of a precinct. ~*vb.* **8.** to be captain of. [Latin *caput* head] —ˈcaptaincy *n.*

caption (ˈkæpʃən) *n.* **1.** a title, brief explanation, or comment accompanying an illustration. **2.** a heading or title of a chapter or article. **3.** graphic material used in television presentation. ~*vb.* **4.** to provide with a caption or captions. [Latin *captiō* a seizing]

captious (ˈkæpʃəs) *adj.* tending to make trivial criticisms. [Latin *captiō* a seizing] —ˈcaptiousness *n.*

captivate (ˈkæptɪˌveɪt) *vb.* to hold the attention of by fascinating; enchant. [Latin *captīvus* captive] —ˈcaptiˌvating *adj.* —ˌcaptiˈvation *n.*

captive ('kæptɪv) n. **1.** a person or animal that is confined or restrained. ~adj. **2.** held as prisoner. **3.** restrained: a captive balloon. **4.** forced to listen or act in a particular way: a captive audience. [Latin captivus]

captivity (kæp'tɪvɪtɪ) n., pl. **-ties.** imprisonment.

captor ('kæptə) n. a person who holds another captive.

capture ('kæptʃə) vb. **1.** to take prisoner or gain control over: to capture a town. **2.** to succeed in representing (something elusive): the artist captured her likeness. **3.** Physics. (of an atomic nucleus) to acquire an additional particle. ~n. **4.** a capturing. **5.** the person or thing captured. [Latin capere to take]

capuchin ('kæpjutʃɪn, -juʃɪn) n. a S American monkey with a cowl of thick hair on the top of its head. [Italian cappuccio hood]

Capuchin ('kæpjutʃɪn, -juʃɪn) n. **1.** a friar belonging to a branch of the Franciscan Order founded in 1525. ~adj. **2.** of this order. [Italian cappuccio hood]

car (kɑː) n. **1.** a motorized road vehicle designed to carry a small number of people. **2.** the passenger compartment of a cable car, airship, lift, or balloon. **3.** Chiefly U.S. & Canad. a railway carriage or van. [Latin carra, carrum two-wheeled wagon]

caracal ('kærə,kæl) n. a lynx with reddish fur, which inhabits deserts of N Africa and S Asia. [Turkish kara kūlāk black ear]

carafe (kə'ræf, -'rɑːf) n. **1.** a wide-mouthed bottle for water or wine. **2.** the amount held by a carafe. [Arabic gharrā-fah vessel]

carambola (,kærəm'bəʊlə) n. the yellow edible star-shaped fruit of a Brazilian tree. [Spanish]

caramel ('kærəməl) n. **1.** burnt sugar, used for colouring and flavouring food. **2.** a chewy sweet made from sugar and milk. [French]

caramelize or **-ise** ('kærəmə,laɪz) vb. to turn into or be turned into caramel.

carapace ('kærə,peɪs) n. the thick hard upper shell of tortoises and crustaceans. [Spanish carapacho]

carat ('kærət) n. **1.** a unit of weight of precious stones, equal to 0.20 grams. **2.** a measure of the purity of gold in an alloy, expressed as the number of parts of gold in 24 parts of the alloy. [Arabic qīrāt weight of four grains]

caravan ('kærə,væn) n. **1.** a large enclosed vehicle designed to be pulled by a car or horse and equipped to be lived in. **2.** (in some Eastern countries) a company of traders or other travellers journeying together. ~vb. **-vanning, -vanned. 3.** Brit. to travel or have a holiday in a caravan. [Persian kārwān]

caravanserai (,kærə'vænsə,raɪ) n. (in some Eastern countries) a large inn enclosing a courtyard, providing accommodation for caravans. [Persian kārwānsarāī caravan inn]

caraway ('kærə,weɪ) n. **1.** a Eurasian

plant with small whitish flowers. **2. caraway seed.** the pungent aromatic fruit of this plant, used in cooking. [Arabic karawyā]

carbide ('kɑːbaɪd) n. a binary compound of carbon with a metal.

carbine ('kɑːbaɪn) n. a type of light rifle. [French carabine]

carbohydrate (,kɑːbəʊ'haɪdreɪt) n. any of a large group of energy-producing compounds, including sugars and starches, that contain carbon, hydrogen, and oxygen.

carbolic acid (kɑː'bɒlɪk) n. same as **phenol.**

carbon ('kɑːb'n) n. **1.** a nonmetallic element occurring in three forms, charcoal, graphite, and diamond, and present in all organic compounds. The isotope **carbon-12** is the standard for atomic weight; **carbon-14** is used in carbon dating. Symbol: C **2.** short for **carbon paper** or **carbon copy.** [Latin carbō charcoal]

carbonaceous (,kɑːbə'neɪʃəs) adj. of, resembling, or containing carbon.

carbonate n. ('kɑːbə,neɪt, -nɪt). **1.** a salt or ester of carbonic acid. ~vb. ('kɑːbə,neɪt). **2.** to fill (a drink) with carbon dioxide.

carbon black n. powdered carbon produced by partial burning of natural gas or petroleum: used in pigments and ink.

carbon copy n. **1.** a duplicate obtained by using carbon paper. **2.** Informal. a person or thing that is identical to another.

carbon dating n. a technique for finding the age of organic materials, such as wood, based on their content of the radioisotope carbon-14.

carbon dioxide n. a colourless odourless incombustible gas formed during breathing, and used in fire extinguishers.

carbonic (kɑː'bɒnɪk) adj. containing carbon.

carbonic acid n. a weak acid formed when carbon dioxide combines with water.

carboniferous (,kɑːbə'nɪfərəs) adj. yielding coal or carbon.

Carboniferous (,kɑːbə'nɪfərəs) adj. Geol. of a period of geological time about 330 million years ago, during which coal seams were formed.

carbonize or **-ise** ('kɑːbə,naɪz) vb. **1.** to turn into carbon as a result of partial burning. **2.** to coat (a substance) with carbon. —**,carboni'zation** or **-i'sation** n.

carbon monoxide n. a colourless odourless poisonous gas formed by the incomplete burning of carbon compounds.

carbon paper n. a thin sheet of paper coated on the underside with a dark waxy pigment, containing carbon, placed between two sheets of paper so that what is written or typed on the top sheet is transferred on to the bottom sheet.

carbon tetrachloride (,tetrə'klɔːraɪd) n. a colourless nonflammable liquid used as a solvent, cleaning fluid, and insecticide.

Carborundum (,kɑːbə'rʌndəm) n. Trademark. an abrasive material, esp. one consisting of silicon carbide.

carboxyl group or **radical** (kɑːˈbɒksail) n. the chemical group -COOH: the functional group in organic acids.

carboy (ˈkɑːˌbɔɪ) n. a large bottle protected by a basket or box. [Persian qarāba]

carbuncle (ˈkɑːˌbʌŋkʰl) n. 1. a large skin eruption like a boil. 2. a rounded garnet cut without facets. [Latin carbō coal] —**carbuncular** (kɑːˈbʌŋkjʊlə) adj.

carburettor (ˌkɑːbjʊˈrɛtə, ˈkɑːbjʊˌrɛtə) or U.S. **carburetor** (ˈkɑːbjʊˌreɪtə) n. a device in engines which mixes petrol with air and regulates the intake of the mixture into the engine.

carcass or **carcase** (ˈkɑːkəs) n. 1. the dead body of an animal. 2. Informal. a person's body. 3. the skeleton or framework of something. 4. the worthless remains of something. [French]

carcinogen (kɑːˈsɪnədʒən) n. any substance that produces cancer. [Greek karkinos cancer] —**carcino'genic** adj.

carcinoma (ˌkɑːsɪˈnəʊmə) n., pl. **-mas** or **-mata** (-mətə). a malignant tumour or cancer. [Greek karkinos cancer]

card¹ (kɑːd) n. 1. a piece of stiff paper or thin cardboard used for identification, reference, proof of membership, or sending greetings or messages: a birthday card. 2. one of a set of small pieces of cardboard, marked with figures or symbols, used for playing games or for fortune-telling. 3. a small rectangle of stiff plastic with identifying numbers for use as a credit card or banker's card. 4. Informal. a witty or eccentric person. 5. Also called: **racecard**. Horse racing. a daily programme of all the races at a meeting. 6. **a card up one's sleeve**. something advantageous kept in reserve until needed. 7. Computers. See **punched card**. ~See also **cards**. [Greek khartēs leaf of papyrus]

card² (kɑːd) n. 1. a machine or tool, typically a leather-covered board with wire points sticking through it, for combing fibres of cotton or wool to disentangle them before spinning. 2. a comblike tool for raising the nap on cloth. ~vb. 3. to process with such a machine or tool. [Latin carduus thistle] —**'carder** n.

cardamom (ˈkɑːdəməm) or **cardamon** n. the seeds of a tropical plant, used as a spice. [Greek kardamon cress + amōmon an Indian spice]

cardboard (ˈkɑːdˌbɔːd) n. a thin stiff board made from paper pulp.

card-carrying adj. being an official member of an organization: a card-carrying Communist.

cardiac (ˈkɑːdɪˌæk) adj. of or relating to the heart. [Greek kardia heart]

cardigan (ˈkɑːdɪgən) n. a knitted jacket or sweater with buttons up the front. [after 7th Earl of Cardigan]

cardinal (ˈkɑːdɪnʰl) n. 1. R.C. Church. any of the high-ranking clergymen who elect the pope and act as his chief counsellors. 2. a cardinal number. 3. a bright red crested North American songbird. ~adj. 4. fundamentally important; principal. 5. deep red. [Latin cardō hinge]

cardinal number or **numeral** n. a number denoting quantity but not order in a group.

cardinal points pl. n. the four main points of the compass: north, south, east, and west.

cardinal virtues pl. n. the most important moral qualities, traditionally justice, prudence, temperance, and fortitude.

card index or **file** n. an index in which each item is separately listed on systematically arranged cards.

cardiogram (ˈkɑːdɪəʊˌgræm) n. an electrocardiogram. See **electrocardiograph**.

cardiograph (ˈkɑːdɪəʊˌgrɑːf) n. 1. an instrument for recording heart movements. 2. same as **electrocardiograph**. —**cardi-ographer** n. —**cardi'ography** n.

cardiology (ˌkɑːdɪˈɒlədʒɪ) n. the branch of medicine dealing with the heart and its diseases. —**cardi'ologist** n.

cardiovascular (ˌkɑːdɪəʊˈvæskjʊlə) adj. of or relating to the heart and the blood vessels.

card reader n. a device for reading information on a punched card and transferring it to a computer storage device.

cards (kɑːdz) n. 1. **a.** any game played with cards. **b.** the playing of such a game. 2. an employee's tax and national insurance documents, held by his employer. 3. **get one's cards**. to be sacked from one's job. 4. **on the cards**. likely. 5. **play one's cards** (right). to handle a situation (cleverly). 6. **put** or **lay one's cards on the table**. to declare one's intentions.

cardsharp (ˈkɑːdˌʃɑːp) or **cardsharper** n. a professional card player who cheats.

card vote n. Brit. a vote by delegates in which each delegate's vote counts as a vote by all his constituents.

care (kɛə) vb. 1. to be worried or concerned: he is dying, and she doesn't care. 2. (foll. by for or about) to have regard or consideration for: he cares more for his hobby than his job. 3. (foll. by for) to have a desire for: would you care for tea? 4. (foll. by for) to look after or provide for. 5. to like (to do something): would you care to sit down? 6. **for all I care** or **I couldn't care less**. I am completely indifferent. ~n. 7. careful or serious attention: he does his work with care. 8. protection or charge: in the care of a doctor. 9. (often pl.) trouble; worry. 10. an object of or cause for concern. 11. caution: handle with care. 12. **care of**. at the address of: written on envelopes. 13. **in** or **into care**. Brit. made the legal responsibility of a local authority by order of a court. [Old English caru sorrow] —**'carer** n.

careen (kəˈriːn) vb. 1. to tilt over to one side. 2. Naut. to tilt (a ship) over to one side for cleaning or repairs. [Latin carina keel]

career (kəˈrɪə) n. 1. a path through life or history. 2. a profession or occupation. 3. a headlong course or path. ~vb. 4. to rush in an uncontrolled way. [Latin carrus two-wheeled wagon]

careerist (kəˈrɪərɪst) n. a person who

seeks to advance his career by any possible means. —**ca'reerism** n.

carefree ('kɛə,friː) adj. without worry or responsibility. —**'care,freeness** n.

careful ('kɛəful) adj. 1. cautious in attitude or action. 2. painstaking; exact and thorough. 3. (foll. by of, in, or about) solicitous; protective. —**'carefully** adv. —**'carefulness** n.

careless ('kɛəlɪs) adj. 1. done or acting with insufficient attention. 2. unconcerned in attitude or action. 3. carefree. —**'carelessly** adv. —**'carelessness** n.

caress (kə'rɛs) n. 1. a gentle affectionate touch or embrace. ~vb. 2. to touch gently and affectionately. [Latin cārus dear]

caret ('kærɪt) n. a symbol (ʌ) indicating the place in written or printed matter at which something is to be inserted. [Latin: there is missing]

caretaker ('kɛə,teɪkə) n. 1. a person employed to look after a place or thing. 2. (modifier) interim: a caretaker government.

careworn ('kɛə,wɔːn) adj. showing signs of care, stress, or worry: a careworn face.

cargo ('kaːgəʊ) n., pl. **-goes** or esp. U.S. **-gos.** goods carried by a ship, aircraft, or other vehicle; freight. [Spanish cargar to load]

Carib ('kærɪb) n. 1. (pl. **-ibs** or **-ib**) a member of a group of peoples of NE South America and the S West Indies. 2. their languages. [Spanish Caribe]

Caribbean (,kærɪ'biːən) adj. 1. of the Caribbean Sea and its islands. 2. of the Caribs or any of their languages. ~n. 3. the Caribbean Sea. 4. a Carib. [French]

caribou ('kærɪ,buː) n., pl. **-bous** or **-bou.** a large North American reindeer. [American Indian]

caricature ('kærɪkə,tjʊə) n. 1. a representation of a person which exaggerates his characteristic features for comic effect. 2. a ridiculously poor imitation. ~vb. 3. to make or give a caricature of. [Italian caricatura a distortion] —**'carica,turist** n.

caries ('kɛəriːz) n., pl. **-ies.** progressive decay of a bone or a tooth. [Latin: decay]

carillon (kə'rɪljən) n. 1. a set of bells usually hung in a tower and played either on a keyboard or mechanically. 2. a tune played on such bells. [French]

carinate ('kærɪ,neɪt) adj. Biol. having a keel or ridge. [Latin carīna keel]

Carlovingian (,kaːləʊ'vɪndʒɪən) adj., n. same as **Carolingian.**

Carmelite ('kaːmə,laɪt) R.C. Church. ~n. 1. a friar or nun belonging to the order of Our Lady of Carmel. ~adj. 2. of this order. [after Mount Carmel, in Palestine, where the order was founded]

carminative ('kaːmɪnətɪv) adj. 1. able to relieve flatulence. ~n. 2. a carminative drug. [Latin carmināre to card wool, comb out]

carmine ('kaːmaɪn) adj. 1. vivid red. ~n. 2. a pigment of this colour obtained from cochineal. [Arabic qirmiz kermes]

carnage ('kaːnɪdʒ) n. extensive slaughter. [Latin carō flesh]

carnal ('kaːnᵊl) adj. relating to the appetites and passions of the body. [Latin carō flesh] —**car'nality** n.

carnation (kaː'neɪʃən) n. 1. a plant with clove-scented white, pink, or red flowers. ~adj. 2. rosy pink. [Latin carō flesh]

carnelian (kaː'niːljən) n. a reddish-yellow variety of chalcedony, used as a gemstone. [Old French corneline]

carnet ('kaːneɪ) n. a customs licence permitting motorists to take their cars across certain frontiers. [French: notebook]

carnival ('kaːnɪvᵊl) n. 1. a festive period marked by merrymaking. 2. a travelling funfair. [Old Italian carnelevare a removing of meat (referring to the Lenten fast)]

carnivore ('kaːnɪ,vɔː) n. any of an order of mammals with teeth specialized for eating flesh, such as cats, dogs, and weasels. 2. any animal or plant that feeds on animals.

carnivorous (kaː'nɪvərəs) adj. feeding on flesh. [Latin carō flesh + vorāre to consume]

carob ('kærəb) n. the long brown pod of an evergreen Mediterranean tree, used as animal fodder and sometimes for human food. [Arabic al kharrūbah]

carol ('kærəl) n. 1. a joyful religious song, esp. one celebrating the birth of Christ. ~vb. **-olling, -olled** or U.S. **-oling, -oled.** 2. to sing carols. 3. to sing joyfully. [Old French]

Carolingian (,kærə'lɪndʒɪən) adj. 1. of the Frankish dynasty founded in 751 A.D. by Charlemagne. ~n. 2. a member of this dynasty. [Latin Carolus Charles; referring to kings of the dynasty]

carotid (kə'rɒtɪd) n. 1. either of the two arteries that supply blood to the head and neck. ~adj. 2. of either of these arteries. [Greek karoun to stupefy; so named because pressure on them produced unconsciousness]

carousal (kə'raʊzᵊl) n. a merry drinking party.

carouse (kə'raʊz) vb. 1. to have a merry drinking party. ~n. 2. a carousal. [German (trinken) gar aus (to drink) right out]

carousel (,kærə'sɛl, -'zɛl) n. a revolving conveyor, esp. for luggage at an airport or slides for a projector. 2. U.S. & Canad. a merry-go-round. [Italian carosello]

carp¹ (kaːp) n., pl. **carp** or **carps.** a freshwater food fish having one long dorsal fin, and two barbels on each side of the mouth. [Old French carpe]

carp² (kaːp) vb. (often foll. by at) to complain or find fault. [Old Norse karpa to boast] —**'carper** n. —**'carping** adj., n.

carpal ('kaːpᵊl) n. a wrist bone. [Greek karpos wrist]

car park n. an area or building reserved for parking cars.

carpel ('kaːpᵊl) n. the female reproductive organ of flowering plants. [Greek karpos fruit]

carpenter ('kaːpɪntə) n. 1. a person

skilled in woodwork, esp. in buildings.
~vb. **2.** to do the work of a carpenter. **3.**
to make or fit together by carpentry. [Latin
carpentum wagon]

carpentry ('kɑːpɪntrɪ) *n.* **1.** the art or
technique of working wood. **2.** the work
produced by a carpenter; woodwork.

carpet ('kɑːpɪt) *n.* **1.** a heavy fabric for
covering floors. **2.** a covering like a carpet: *a carpet of leaves.* **3. on the carpet.**
Informal. **a.** being reprimanded. **b.** under
consideration. ~vb. **4.** to cover with or
as if with a carpet. [Latin *carpere* to
pluck, card]

carpetbag ('kɑːpɪtˌbæg) *n.* a travelling
bag originally made of carpeting.

carpetbagger ('kɑːpɪtˌbægə) *n.* a politician who seeks office in a place where he
has no connections.

carpeting ('kɑːpɪtɪŋ) *n.* carpet material or
carpets in general.

car phone *n.* a telephone that operates by
cellular radio for use in a car.

carport ('kɑːˌpɔːt) *n.* a shelter for a car,
consisting of a roof supported by posts.

carpus ('kɑːpəs) *n., pl.* **-pi** (-paɪ). **1.** *Anat.*
the wrist. **2.** the set of eight bones of the
human wrist. [Greek *karpos*]

carrageen *or* **carragheen** ('kærəˌgiːn)
n. an edible red seaweed of rocky shores of
North America and N Europe. [*Carragheen,*
near Waterford, Ireland]

carriage ('kærɪdʒ) *n.* **1.** *Brit.* a railway
coach for passengers. **2.** the way a person
holds and moves his head and body. **3.** a
four-wheeled horse-drawn passenger vehicle. **4.** the moving part of a machine that
supports and shifts another part: *a typewriter carriage.* **5.** ('kærɪdʒ, 'kærɪdʒ). **a.**
the act of conveying goods. **b.** the charge
made for conveying goods. [Old French
cariage]

carriage clock *n.* a style of portable
clock, originally used by travellers.

carriageway ('kærɪdʒˌweɪ) *n.* *Brit.* the
part of a road along which traffic passes in
one direction: *a dual carriageway.*

carrier ('kærɪə) *n.* **1.** a person, thing, or
organization employed to carry goods or
passengers. **2.** a person or animal that,
without suffering from a disease, is capable of transmitting it to others. **3.** same
as **aircraft carrier.**

carrier bag *n.* *Brit.* a large paper or
plastic bag for carrying shopping.

carrier pigeon *n.* a homing pigeon used
for carrying messages.

carrion ('kærɪən) *n.* **1.** dead and rotting
flesh. **2.** something filthy or vile. [Latin
carō flesh]

carrion crow *n.* a scavenging European
crow like the rook but having a black bill.

carrot ('kærət) *n.* **1.** a long tapering orange root vegetable. **2.** something offered
as an incentive. [Greek *karōton*]

carroty ('kærətɪ) *adj.* of a reddish or
yellowish-orange colour.

carry ('kærɪ) *vb.* **-rying, -ried. 1.** to take
(something) from one place to another. **2.**
to have on one's person: *he carries a watch.*

3. to be transmitted or be a medium for
transmitting: *sound carries over water.* **4.**
to bear the weight, pressure, or responsibility of: *her efforts carry the whole
production.* **5.** to have as a quality or
result: *it carries a two-year guarantee; this
crime carries a heavy penalty.* **6.** to be
pregnant with (young). **7.** to bear (the
head or body) in a specified manner: *she
carried her head high.* **8.** to conduct (oneself) in a specified manner: *she carried
herself well.* **9.** to win over, esp. by
emotional appeal: *his words carried the
crowd.* **10.** to secure the passage of (a bill
or motion). **11.** to capture: *our troops
carried the town.* **12.** (of communications
media) to include in the contents: *this
newspaper carries no book reviews.* **13.**
Maths. to transfer (a number) from one
column of figures to the next. **14.** (of a
shop or trader) to keep in stock. **15.** (of a
ball or projectile) to travel through the air
or reach a specified point: *his first drive
carried to the green.* **16. carry the can
for.** *Informal.* to take all the blame for
something on behalf of. ~*n., pl.* **-ries. 17.**
the act of carrying. **18.** the range or
distance covered by a ball or projectile.
~See also **carry away, carry forward,** etc.
[Latin *carrum* transport wagon]

carry away *vb.* **1.** to remove forcefully.
2. (*usually passive*) to cause (a person) to
lose self-control. **3.** (*usually passive*) to
delight: *he was carried away by the music.*

carrycot ('kærɪˌkɒt) *n.* a light portable cot
for a baby.

carry forward *vb.* to transfer (an
amount) to the next column, page, or accounting period.

carry off *vb.* **1.** to remove forcefully. **2.**
to win. **3.** to handle (a situation) successfully: *he carried off the introductions well.*
4. to cause to die: *he was carried off by
pneumonia.*

carry on *vb.* **1.** to continue or persevere.
2. to conduct: *to carry on a business.* **3.**
(often foll. by *with*) *Informal.* to have an
affair. **4.** *Informal.* to cause a fuss. ~*n.*
carry-on. **5.** *Informal, chiefly Brit.* a fuss.

carry out *vb.* **1.** to put (something) into
practice. **2.** to accomplish. ~*n.* **carry-out.**
Chiefly Scot. **3.** alcohol bought for consumption elsewhere. **4.** a shop which sells
hot cooked food for consumption away
from the premises.

carry over *vb.* **1.** to postpone or defer.
2. same as **carry forward.**

carry through *vb.* **1.** to accomplish. **2.**
to enable to endure (hardship or trouble);
support.

carsick ('kɑːˌsɪk) *adj.* nauseated from riding in a car or other vehicle. —'**car,sick-
ness** *n.*

cart (kɑːt) *n.* **1.** an open horse-drawn
vehicle, usually having two wheels, used to
carry goods or passengers. **2.** any small
vehicle drawn or pushed by hand. **3. put
the cart before the horse.** to reverse the
usual order of things. ~*vb.* **4.** to carry
(something) in a cart. **5.** to carry with
effort: *to cart wood home.* [Old Norse
kartr] —'**carter** *n.*

carte blanche ('kɑːt 'blɑːntʃ) *n.*, *pl.* **cartes blanches** ('kɑːts 'blɑːntʃ). complete authority: *the government gave their negotiator carte blanche.* [French: blank paper]

cartel (kɑː'tɛl) *n.* an association of competing firms formed in order to fix prices. [German *Kartell*]

Cartesian (kɑː'tiːzɪən) *adj.* of Descartes, 17th-century French philosopher and mathematician, or his works. [*Cartesius*, Latin form of Descartes] —**Car'tesian-,ism** *n.*

Cartesian coordinates *pl. n.* a system of coordinates that defines the location of a point by its perpendicular distance from each of a set of axes intersecting at right angles.

carthorse ('kɑːt,hɔːs) *n.* a large heavily built horse kept for pulling carts or for farmwork.

Carthusian (kɑː'θjuːzɪən) *n.* **1.** a member of a strict monastic order founded in 1084. ~*adj.* **2.** of this order. [Latin *Carthusia* Chartreuse, near Grenoble]

cartilage ('kɑːtɪlɪdʒ) *n.* a strong flexible tissue forming part of the skeleton. [Latin *cartilāgō*] —**cartilaginous** (,kɑːtɪ'lædʒɪnəs) *adj.*

cartography (kɑː'tɒgrəfɪ) *n.* the skill or practice of making maps or charts. [French *carte* map, chart] —**car'tographer** *n.* —**cartographic** (,kɑːtə'græfɪk) *adj.*

carton ('kɑːt'n) *n.* **1.** a cardboard box or container. **2.** a container of waxed paper in which liquids are sold. [Italian *carta* card]

cartoon (kɑː'tuːn) *n.* **1.** a humorous or satirical drawing, usually in a newspaper or magazine. **2.** same as **comic strip.** **3.** same as **animated cartoon.** **4.** a full-size sketch for a fresco, tapestry, or mosaic. [Italian *cartone* pasteboard] —**car'toonist** *n.*

cartouche *or* **cartouch** (kɑː'tuːʃ) *n.* **1.** an ornamental tablet or panel in the form of a scroll. **2.** (in ancient Egypt) an oblong or oval figure containing royal or divine names. [French: scroll, cartridge]

cartridge ('kɑːtrɪdʒ) *n.* **1.** a metal casing containing an explosive charge, and often the bullet, for a firearm. **2.** a unit in the pick-up of a record player, which converts the movements of the stylus into electrical signals. **3.** an enclosed container of material for insertion into a device. [earlier *cartage*, var. of *cartouche* (cartridge)]

cartridge belt *n.* a belt with loops or pockets for holding cartridges.

cartridge clip *n.* a metallic container holding cartridges for an automatic firearm.

cartridge paper *n.* a type of heavy rough drawing paper.

cartwheel ('kɑːt,wiːl) *n.* **1.** the wheel of a cart, usually having wooden spokes. **2.** a sideways somersault supported by the hands with legs outstretched.

carve (kɑːv) *vb.* **1.** to cut in order to form something: *to carve wood.* **2.** to form (something) by cutting: *to carve statues.* **3.** to slice (meat) into pieces. ~See also **carve out, carve up.** [Old English *ceorfan*] —**'carver** *n.*

carve out *vb. Informal.* to make or create (a career): *he carved out his own future.*

carvery ('kɑːvərɪ) *n.*, *pl.* **-veries.** a restaurant where customers pay a set price for unrestricted helpings of meat and other food.

carve up *vb.* **1.** to cut (something) up. **2.** to divide or share out (something). ~*n.* **carve-up. 3.** *Slang.* the sharing-out of something.

carving ('kɑːvɪŋ) *n.* a figure or design produced by carving stone or wood.

carving knife *n.* a long-bladed knife for carving cooked meat.

carwash ('kɑː,wɒʃ) *n.* a place fitted with equipment for automatically washing cars.

caryatid (,kærɪ'ætɪd) *n.*, *pl.* **-ids** *or* **-ides** (-ɪ,diːz). a statue of a draped female figure used as a supporting column. [Greek *Karuatides* priestesses of Artemis at *Karuai* (Caryae), in Laconia]

Casanova (,kæsə'nəʊvə) *n.* a womanizer; philanderer. [after Giovanni *Casanova*, Italian adventurer]

casbah ('kæzbɑː) *n.* same as **kasbah.**

cascade (kæs'keɪd) *n.* **1.** a waterfall or series of waterfalls over rocks. **2.** something flowing or falling like this. ~*vb.* **3.** to flow or fall in a cascade. [Latin *cadere* to fall]

cascara (kæs'kɑːrə) *n.* **1.** the bark of a N American buckthorn, used as a laxative. **2.** the shrub it is prepared from. [Spanish: bark]

case[1] (keɪs) *n.* **1.** a single instance or example of something. **2.** a matter for discussion. **3.** a specific condition or state of affairs; situation. **4.** a set of arguments supporting an action or cause. **5.** a person attended or served by a doctor, social worker, or solicitor. **6. a.** an action or lawsuit: *he has a good case.* **b.** the evidence offered in court to support a claim. **7.** *Grammar.* any of a set of grammatical categories of nouns, pronouns, and adjectives showing the relation of that particular word to other words in the sentence: *the nominative case.* **8.** *Informal.* an eccentric. **9. in any case.** no matter what. **10. in case. a.** so as to allow for eventualities. **b.** so as to allow for the possibility that: *take your coat in case it rains.* **11. in case of.** in the event of. [Old English *casus* (grammatical) case, associated with Old French *cas* a happening; both from Latin *cadere* to fall]

case[2] (keɪs) *n.* **1.** a container, such as a box or chest. **2.** a protective outer cover. **3.** a container and its contents: *a case of ammunition.* **4.** *Printing.* a tray in which a compositor keeps individual metal types of a particular size and style. ~*vb.* **5.** to put into or enclose in a case. **6.** *Slang.* to inspect carefully (a place to be robbed). [Latin *capsa* box]

case-harden *vb.* **1.** *Metallurgy.* to form a hard surface layer on (an iron alloy). **2.** to make callous: *a case-hardened judge.*

case history *n.* a record of a person's background or medical history.

casein (ˈkeɪsiɪn, -siːn) *n.* a protein found in milk, which forms the basis of cheese. [Latin *cāseus* cheese]

case law *n.* law established by following judicial decisions made in earlier cases.

casement (ˈkeɪsmənt) *n.* **1.** a window frame hinged on one side. **2.** a window with frames hinged at the side. [prob. from Old French *encassement* frame]

casework (ˈkeɪsˌwɜːk) *n.* social work based on close study of an individual's personal history and family background. —ˈcaseˌworker *n.*

cash (kæʃ) *n.* **1.** banknotes and coins, esp. in hand or readily available. **2.** immediate payment for goods or services. **3.** (*modifier*) of, for, or paid by cash: *a cash transaction.* ~*vb.* **4.** to obtain or pay ready money for. ~See also **cash in.** [Latin *capsa* box]

cash-and-carry *adj., adv.* sold or operated on a basis of cash payment for goods that are taken away by the purchaser.

cash-book *n. Book-keeping.* a journal in which all money transactions are recorded.

cash crop *n.* a crop produced for sale rather than for subsistence.

cash desk *n.* a counter or till in a shop where purchases are paid for.

cash discount *n.* a discount granted to a purchaser who pays within a specified period.

cash dispenser *n.* a computerized device outside a bank which supplies cash when a special card is inserted and the user's code number keyed in.

cashew (ˈkæʃuː, kæˈʃuː) *n.* the edible kidney-shaped nut of a tropical American evergreen tree. [S. American Indian *acajú*]

cash flow *n.* the movement of money into and out of a business.

cashier[1] (kæˈʃɪə) *n.* a person responsible for handling cash in a bank, shop, or other business. [French *casse* money chest]

cashier[2] (kæˈʃɪə) *vb.* to dismiss with dishonour from the armed forces. [Latin *quassāre* to QUASH]

cash in *vb.* **1.** to exchange for cash. **2.** (often foll. by *on*) *Informal.* to gain a profit or advantage (from).

cashmere (ˈkæʃmɪə) *n.* **1.** a fine soft wool from goats of Kashmir. **2.** cloth made from this or similar wool.

cash on delivery *n.* a system involving cash payment to the carrier on delivery of merchandise.

cash register *n.* a till that has a mechanism for displaying and adding the prices of the goods sold.

casing (ˈkeɪsɪŋ) *n.* a protective case or covering.

casino (kəˈsiːnəʊ) *n., pl.* **-nos.** a public building or room in which gaming takes place. [Italian]

cask (kɑːsk) *n.* **1.** a strong barrel, esp. one used to hold alcoholic drink. **2.** the amount held in a cask. [Spanish *casco* helmet]

casket (ˈkɑːskɪt) *n.* **1.** a small box for valuables. **2.** *Chiefly U.S.* a coffin. [prob. from Old French *cassette* little box]

casque (kæsk) *n. Zool.* a helmet-like structure, as on the bill of most hornbills. [Spanish *casco*]

Cassandra (kəˈsændrə) *n.* anyone whose prophecies of doom are unheeded. [Trojan prophetess in Greek myth.]

cassava (kəˈsɑːvə) *n.* a starch obtained from the root of a tropical American plant: used to make tapioca. [West Indian *caçábi*]

casserole (ˈkæsəˌrəʊl) *n.* **1.** a covered dish in which food is cooked and served. **2.** any food cooked and served in such a dish: *chicken casserole.* ~*vb.* **3.** to cook or be cooked in a casserole. [French]

cassette (kæˈsɛt) *n.* **1.** a plastic container for magnetic tape, inserted into a tape deck to be played. **2.** *Photog.* a sealed case with film in it, which can be loaded quickly into a camera. [French: little box]

cassia (ˈkæsɪə) *n.* **1.** a tropical plant whose pods yield **cassia pulp,** a mild laxative. **2. cassia bark.** the cinnamon-like bark of a tropical Asian tree, used as a spice. [Greek *kasia*]

cassock (ˈkæsək) *n.* an ankle-length garment, usually black, worn by Christian priests. [Italian *casacca* a long coat]

cassowary (ˈkæsəˌwɛərɪ) *n., pl.* **-waries.** a large flightless bird of Australia and New Guinea, with a horny head crest, black plumage, and brightly coloured neck. [Malay *kèsuari*]

cast (kɑːst) *vb.* **casting, cast.** **1.** to throw with force. **2.** to reject: *he cast the idea from his mind.* **3.** to shed: *the horse cast a shoe.* **4.** to cause to appear: *to cast a shadow.* **5.** to express (doubts or aspersions). **6.** to direct (a glance): *cast your eye over this.* **7.** *Angling.* to throw (a line) into the water. **8.** to draw or choose (lots). **9.** to roll or throw (a dice). **10.** to give or deposit (a vote). **11.** to select (actors) to play parts in (a play or film). **12. a.** to shape (molten material) by pouring it into a mould. **b.** to make (an object) by such a process. **13.** to draw up (a horoscope). **14. cast a spell.** to perform magic. **15.** to formulate: *he cast his work in the form of a chart.* **16.** to twist or cause to twist. ~*n.* **17.** the act of throwing. **18.** something that is shed, such as the coil of earth left by an earthworm. **19. a.** a throw at dice. **b.** the resulting number shown. **20.** *Angling.* the casting of a line. **21.** the actors in a play collectively. **22. a.** an object made of material that has been shaped, while molten, by a mould. **b.** the mould used to shape such an object. **23.** form or appearance. **24.** a sort, kind, or style. **25.** a slight squint in the eye. **26.** *Surgery.* a rigid casing, often made of plaster of Paris, for immobilizing broken bones while they heal. **27.** a slight tinge or shade. ~See also **cast about, castaway,** etc. [Old Norse *kasta*]

cast about *vb.* to make a mental or visual search: *to cast about for a plot.*

castanets (ˌkæstəˈnɛts) *pl. n.* a musical instrument consisting of curved pieces of

castaway hollow wood, held between the fingers and thumb and clicked together: used esp. by Spanish dancers. [Spanish *castañeta*, from *castaña* chestnut]

castaway ('kɑːstə,weɪ) *n.* **1.** a person who has been shipwrecked. ~*adj.* **2.** shipwrecked.

cast back *vb.* to turn (the mind) to the past.

cast down *vb.* to make (a person) discouraged or dejected.

caste (kɑːst) *n.* **1.** any of the four major hereditary classes into which Hindu society is divided. **2.** a social class or system based on distinctions of heredity, rank, or wealth. **3. lose caste.** *Informal.* to lose one's social position. [Latin *castus* pure, unpolluted]

castellated ('kæstɪ,leɪtɪd) *adj.* having turrets and battlements, like a castle. [Medieval Latin *castellāre* to fortify as a castle] —,**castel'lation** *n.*

caster ('kɑːstə) *n.* **1.** a bottle with a perforated top for sprinkling sugar, salt, or flour. **2.** a small swivelled wheel fixed to a leg of a piece of furniture to enable it to be moved easily.

caster sugar ('kɑːstə) *n.* finely ground white sugar.

castigate ('kæstɪ,geɪt) *vb.* to rebuke or criticize severely. [Latin *castigāre* to correct] —,**casti'gation** *n.* —'**casti,gator** *n.*

casting ('kɑːstɪŋ) *n.* an object that has been cast in metal from a mould.

casting vote *n.* the deciding vote used by the chairman of a meeting when an equal number of votes are cast on each side.

cast iron *n.* **1.** iron containing so much carbon that it is brittle and must be cast into shape rather than wrought. ~*adj.* **cast-iron. 2.** made of cast iron. **3.** rigid or unchallengeable: *a cast-iron decision.*

castle ('kɑːs°l) *n.* **1.** a fortified building or set of buildings as in medieval Europe. **2.** *Chess.* same as **rook**². ~*vb.* **3.** *Chess.* to move (the king) two squares sideways and place the nearer rook on the square passed over by the king. [Latin *castellum*]

castle in the air *or* **in Spain** *n.* a hope or desire unlikely to be realized; daydream.

cast-off *adj.* **1.** abandoned or discarded: *cast-off shoes.* ~*n.* **castoff. 2.** a person or thing that has been abandoned or discarded. ~*vb.* **cast off. 3.** to abandon or discard. **4.** to untie (a ship) from a dock. **5.** to knot and remove (a row of stitches, esp. the final row) from the needle in knitting.

castor ('kɑːstə) *n.* same as **caster.**

castor oil *n.* an oil obtained from the seeds of a tall Indian plant (**castor-oil plant**) and used as a lubricant and purgative.

castrate (kæ'streɪt) *vb.* **1.** to remove the testicles of. **2.** to deprive of vigour or masculinity. [Latin *castrāre*] —**cas'tration** *n.*

cast steel *n.* steel containing varying amounts of carbon and manganese, that is cast into shape rather than wrought.

casual ('kæʒjuəl) *adj.* **1.** happening by chance. **2.** offhand: *a casual remark.* **3.** shallow or superficial: *a casual affair.* **4.** being or seeming careless or nonchalant: *he assumed a casual attitude.* **5.** for informal wear: *a casual coat.* **6.** occasional or irregular: *a casual labourer.* ~*n.* **7.** (*usually pl.*) informal clothing or footwear. **8.** an occasional worker. **9.** (*usually pl.*) a young man wearing expensive casual clothes who goes to football matches in order to start fights. [Latin *cāsus* event, chance] —'**casually** *adv.* —'**casualness** *n.*

casualty ('kæʒjuəltɪ) *n., pl.* **-ties. 1.** a person who is killed or injured in an accident or war. **2.** the hospital department treating victims of accidents. **3.** anything that is lost, damaged, or destroyed as the result of an accident or happening.

casuistry ('kæzjuɪstrɪ) *n., pl.* **-ries.** reasoning that is misleading or oversubtle. [Latin *casus* chance] —'**casuist** *n.*

cat (kæt) *n.* **1.** a small domesticated feline mammal, having thick soft fur and whiskers. **2.** any wild feline mammal, such as the lynx, lion, or tiger. **3.** *Informal.* a spiteful woman. **4.** *Slang.* a person. **5.** short for **catamaran. 6.** short for **cat-o'-nine-tails. 7. let the cat out of the bag.** to disclose a secret, often by mistake. **8. like a cat on a hot tin roof** *or* **on hot bricks.** uneasy or agitated. **9. put** *or* **set the cat among the pigeons.** to stir up trouble. **10. rain cats and dogs.** to rain very heavily. **11. the cat's pyjamas** *or* **whiskers.** an excellent person or thing. [Latin *cattus*] —'**cat,like** *adj.*

cat. catalogue.

catabolism (kə'tæbə,lɪzəm) *n.* a metabolic process in which complex molecules are broken down into simple ones with the release of energy. [Greek *kata-* down + *ballein* to throw] —**catabolic** (,kætə-'bɒlɪk) *adj.*

cataclysm ('kætə,klɪzəm) *n.* **1.** a violent upheaval. **2.** a disastrous flood. [Greek *katakluzein* to flood] —**cataclysmic** *adj.*

catacomb ('kætə,kəʊm) *n.* (*usually pl.*) an underground burial place consisting of tunnels with side recesses for tombs. [Late Latin *catacumbas*]

catafalque ('kætə,fælk) *n.* a raised platform on which a body lies in state before or during a funeral. [Italian *catafalco*]

Catalan ('kætə,læn) *n.* **1.** a language of Catalonia in NE Spain, closely related to Spanish and Provençal. **2.** a person from Catalonia. ~*adj.* **3.** of Catalonia, its inhabitants, or their language.

catalepsy ('kætə,lepsɪ) *n.* a trancelike state in which the body is rigid. [Greek *katalēpsis* a seizing] —,**cata'leptic** *adj.*

catalogue *or U.S.* **catalog** ('kætə,lɒg) *n.* **1.** a complete, usually alphabetical, list of items. **2.** a book containing details of items for sale. **3.** a list of all the books of a library. **4.** a list of events, qualities, or things considered as a group: *a catalogue of crimes.* ~*vb.* **5.** to compile a catalogue of (items). **6.** to enter (an item) in a catalogue. **7.** to list a series of (events, qualities, or things). [Greek *katalegein* to list] —'**cata,loguer** *n.*

catalpa (kə'tælpə) *n.* tree of N America and Asia, having bell-shaped whitish flowers, and long slender pods. [Carolina Creek *kutuhlpa* winged head]

catalyse *or U.S.* **-lyze** ('kætə,laız) *vb.* to influence (a chemical reaction) by catalysis.

catalysis (kə'tælısıs) *n., pl.* **-ses** (-,si:z). acceleration of a chemical reaction by the action of a catalyst. [Greek *kataluein* to dissolve] —**catalytic** (,kætə'lıtık) *adj.*

catalyst ('kætəlıst) *n.* **1.** a substance that speeds up a chemical reaction without itself undergoing any permanent chemical change. **2.** a person or thing that causes a change.

catalytic cracker *n.* a unit in an oil refinery in which mineral oils are converted into fuels by a catalytic process.

catamaran (,kætəmə'ræn) *n.* **1.** a boat with two parallel hulls. **2.** a primitive raft made of logs lashed together. [Tamil *kattumaram* tied timber]

catamite ('kætə,maıt) *n.* a boy kept as a homosexual partner. [Latin *Catamītus*, var. of *Ganymēdēs* Ganymede, cupbearer to the Gods in Greek myth.]

catapult ('kætə,pʌlt) *n.* **1.** a Y-shaped device with a loop of elastic fastened to the ends of the prongs, used mainly by children for firing stones. **2.** an ancient weapon for hurling large rocks. **3.** a device installed in warships to launch aircraft. ~*vb.* **4.** to shoot forth from or as if from a catapult. [Greek *kata-* down + *pallein* to hurl]

cataract ('kætə,rækt) *n.* **1.** a large waterfall. **2.** a downpour. **3.** *Pathol.* **a.** a condition in which the lens of the eye becomes partially or totally opaque. **b.** the opaque area. [Greek *katarassein* to dash down]

catarrh (kə'tɑː) *n.* inflammation of a mucous membrane with increased production of mucus, esp. of the nose and throat. [Greek *katarrhein* to flow down] —**ca'tarrhal** *adj.*

catastrophe (kə'tæstrəfı) *n.* **1.** a great and sudden disaster. **2.** the denouement of a play. **3.** a disastrous end. [Greek *katastrephein* to overturn] —**catastrophic** (,kætə'strɒfık) *adj.*

catatonia (,kætə'təunıə) *n.* a form of schizophrenia characterized by stupor, with outbreaks of excitement. [Greek *kata-* down + *tonos* tension] —**catatonic** (,kætə'tɒnık) *adj., n.*

cat burglar *n.* a burglar who enters buildings by climbing through upper windows.

catcall ('kæt,kɔːl) *n.* **1.** a shrill whistle or cry expressing disapproval or derision. ~*vb.* **2.** to utter such a call (at).

catch (kætʃ) *vb.* **catching, caught. 1.** to seize and hold. **2.** to capture. **3.** to ensnare or deceive. **4.** to surprise in an act: *I caught him stealing.* **5.** to strike: *the stone caught him on the side of the head.* **6.** to reach in time to board: *catch a train.* **7.** to

see or hear; attend: *did you catch the film last night?* **8.** to be infected with: *to catch a cold.* **9.** to entangle or become entangled. **10.** to fasten or be fastened. **11.** to attract: *she tried to catch his eye.* **12.** to comprehend or make out: *I couldn't catch what he said.* **13.** to captivate. **14.** to reproduce accurately: *the painter managed to catch his model's beauty.* **15.** to check suddenly: *he caught his breath in surprise.* **16.** to become alight: *the fire won't catch.* **17.** *Cricket.* to dismiss (a batsman) by catching a ball struck by him before it touches the ground. **18.** (often foll. by *at*) **a.** to grasp or attempt to grasp. **b.** to take advantage (of): *he caught at the chance.* **19. catch it.** *Informal.* to be punished. ~*n.* **20.** a catching or grasping. **21.** a device that catches and fastens. **22.** anything that is caught. **23.** the amount caught. **24.** *Informal.* a person worth having as a husband or wife. **25.** an emotional break in the voice. **26.** *Informal.* a concealed or unforeseen drawback. **27.** *Cricket.* the catching of a ball struck by a batsman before it touches the ground, resulting in him being out. **28.** *Music.* a type of round with a humorous text. ~See also **catch on, catch out, catch up.** [Latin *capere* to seize]

catching ('kætʃıŋ) *adj.* **1.** infectious. **2.** catchy.

catchment ('kætʃmənt) *n.* **1.** the act of catching or collecting water. **2.** the water so collected. **3.** *Brit.* all those served by a school or hospital in a particular catchment area.

catchment area *n.* **1.** the area of land draining into a river, basin, or reservoir. **2.** the area served by a particular school or hospital.

catch on *vb. Informal.* **1.** to become popular or fashionable. **2.** to understand.

catch out *vb. Informal, chiefly Brit.* to trap (a person) in an error.

catchpenny ('kætʃ,penı) *adj.* designed to have instant appeal in order to sell quickly: *catchpenny ornaments.*

catch phrase *n.* a well-known frequently used phrase or slogan.

catch-22 *n.* a situation in which a person is frustrated by a set of circumstances that prevent any attempt to escape from them. [from the title of a novel by J. Heller]

catch up *vb.* **1.** to pick up (something) quickly. **2.** to reach or pass (someone or something): *he caught up with him.* **3.** (usually foll. by *on* or *with*) to make up for lost ground or deal with a backlog. **4.** (*often passive*) to absorb or involve: *she was caught up in her reading.*

catchword ('kætʃ,wɜːd) *n.* **1.** same as **catch phrase. 2.** a word positioned so as to draw attention.

catchy ('kætʃı) *adj.* **catchier, catchiest.** (of a tune) easily remembered.

catechism ('kætı,kızəm) *n.* instruction on the doctrine of a Christian Church by a series of questions and answers, esp. a book containing such instruction. [Greek *katēkhizein* to catechize]

catechize *or* **-ise** ('kætı,kaız) *vb.* **1.** to

instruct in Christianity by using a catechism. **2.** to question (someone) thoroughly. [Greek *katēkhizein*] —'**catechist** *n*.

categorical (ˌkætɪ'gɒrɪk'l) *or* **categoric** *adj*. unqualified; unconditional: *a categorical statement*. —ˌcate'gorically *adv*.

categorize *or* **-ise** ('kætɪgəˌraɪz) *vb*. to place in a category. —ˌcategori'zation *or* **-i'sation** *n*.

category ('kætɪgərɪ) *n., pl.* **-ries**. a class or group of things or people possessing some quality or qualities in common. [Greek *katēgoria* assertion]

cater ('keɪtə) *vb*. **1.** (foll. by *for* or *to*) to provide what is needed or wanted for. **2.** to provide food or services: *we cater for parties*. [Anglo-Norman *acater* to buy] —'**catering** *n*.

caterer ('keɪtərə) *n*. someone who makes a living by providing food for social events such as parties or weddings.

caterpillar ('kætəˌpɪlə) *n*. **1.** the wormlike larva of a butterfly or moth, having numerous pairs of legs. **2.** *Trademark*. Also: **caterpillar track**. an endless track, driven by cogged wheels, used to propel a heavy vehicle. **3.** *Trademark*. a vehicle driven by such tracks. [prob. from Old French *catepelose* hairy cat]

caterwaul ('kætəˌwɔːl) *vb*. **1.** to make a yowling noise like a cat. ~*n*. **2.** such a noise. [imit.]

catfish ('kætˌfɪʃ) *n., pl.* **-fish** *or* **-fishes**. a freshwater fish having whisker-like barbels around the mouth.

catgut ('kætˌgʌt) *n*. a strong cord made from the dried intestines of sheep or other animals, used to string musical instruments and sports rackets.

Cath. 1. Cathedral. **2.** Catholic.

catharsis (kə'θɑːsɪs) *n., pl.* **-ses**. **1.** the relief of strong suppressed emotions, esp. through drama or psychoanalysis. **2.** purgation of the bowels. [Greek *kathairein* to purge, purify]

cathartic (kə'θɑːtɪk) *adj*. **1.** purgative. **2.** causing catharsis. ~*n*. **3.** a purgative drug.

Cathay (kæ'θeɪ) *n*. a literary or archaic name for China. [Medieval Latin *Cataya*]

cathedral (kə'θiːdrəl) *n*. the principal church of a diocese, containing the bishop's throne. [Greek *kathedra* seat]

Catherine wheel ('kæθrɪn) *n*. a firework which rotates, producing sparks and coloured flame. [after St *Catherine* of Alexandria, martyred on a spiked wheel]

catheter ('kæθɪtə) *n*. a slender flexible tube inserted into a body cavity to drain fluid. [Greek *kathienai* to insert]

cathode ('kæθəʊd) *n*. **1.** the negative electrode in an electrolytic cell. **2.** the positive terminal of a battery. [Greek *kathodos* a descent] —**cathodic** (kæ'θɒdɪk, -'θəʊ-) *adj*.

cathode rays *pl. n*. a stream of electrons emitted from the surface of a cathode in a vacuum tube.

cathode-ray tube *n*. a vacuum tube in which a beam of electrons is focused onto a

fluorescent screen to produce a visible image: used in television receivers and visual display units.

catholic ('kæθəlɪk, 'kæθlɪk) *adj*. **1.** universal; relating to all men. **2.** broad-minded; liberal. [Greek *katholikos* universal] —**catholicity** (ˌkæθə'lɪsɪtɪ) *n*.

Catholic ('kæθəlɪk, 'kæθlɪk) *Christianity*. ~*adj*. **1.** of the Roman Catholic Church. ~*n*. **2.** a member of the Roman Catholic Church.

Catholicism (kə'θɒlɪˌsɪzəm) *n*. short for **Roman Catholicism**.

cation ('kætaɪən) *n*. a positively charged ion. [Greek *kata-* down + *ienai* to go] —**cationic** (ˌkætaɪ'ɒnɪk) *adj*.

catkin ('kætkɪn) *n*. a hanging spike of very small flowers found on trees such as the birch, hazel, and willow. [obs. Dutch *katteken* kitten]

catmint ('kætˌmɪnt) *n*. a Eurasian plant with purple-spotted white flowers and scented leaves of which cats are fond. Also: **catnip**.

catnap ('kætˌnæp) *n*. **1.** a short sleep or doze. ~*vb*. **-napping, -napped**. **2.** to sleep or doze for a short time or intermittently.

cat-o'-nine-tails *n., pl.* **-tails**. a rope whip consisting of nine knotted thongs attached to a handle.

cat's cradle *n*. a game played by making patterns with a loop of string between the fingers.

Catseyes ('kætsaɪz) *pl. n. Trademark, Brit*. glass reflectors set into the road at intervals to indicate traffic lanes by reflecting light from headlights.

cat's paw *n*. a person used by another as a tool; dupe. [from the tale of a monkey who used a cat's paw to draw chestnuts out of a fire]

cattle ('kæt'l) *n*. (*functioning as pl.*) domesticated cows, bulls, or oxen. [Old French *chatel* chattel]

cattle-cake *n*. concentrated food for cattle in the form of cakelike blocks.

cattle-grid *or N.Z.* **cattle-stop** *n*. a grid covering a hole dug in a roadway, intended to prevent livestock crossing while allowing vehicles to pass unhindered.

catty ('kætɪ) *adj*. **-tier, -tiest**. *Informal*. spiteful: *a catty remark*. —'**cattiness** *n*.

catwalk ('kætˌwɔːk) *n*. a narrow pathway such as one over the stage of a theatre or along a bridge.

Caucasian (kɔː'keɪzɪən) *adj*. **1.** of the Caucasus in the SW Soviet Union. ~*n*. **2.** a person from the Caucasus. ~*adj., n*. **3.** same as **Caucasoid**.

Caucasoid ('kɔːkəˌzɔɪd) *adj*. **1.** of the predominantly light-skinned racial group of mankind, which includes the native peoples of Europe, N Africa, SW Asia, and the Indian subcontinent. ~*n*. **2.** a member of this group.

caucus ('kɔːkəs) *n., pl.* **-cuses**. **1.** *Chiefly U.S.* a local meeting of party members. **2.** *Brit*. a faction within a political party, who discuss tactics or choose candidates. **3.**

Chiefly U.S., Canad., & N.Z. a meeting of the members of one party in a legislative body. **4.** *Austral.* a group of MPs from one party who meet to discuss tactics. [prob. of American Indian origin]

caudal ('kɔːd'l) *adj.* **1.** *Anat.* of the posterior part of the body. **2.** *Zool.* like or in the position of the tail. [Latin *cauda* tail] —'**caudate** *adj.*

caught (kɔːt) *vb.* past of **catch.**

caul (kɔːl) *n. Anat.* a membrane sometimes covering a child's head at birth. [Old French *calotte* close-fitting cap]

cauldron *or* **caldron** ('kɔːldrən) *n.* a large pot used for boiling. [Latin *caldārium* hot bath]

cauliflower ('kɒlɪˌflaʊə) *n.* a variety of cabbage having a large head of crowded white flower buds, which is eaten as a vegetable. [Italian *caoli fiori* cabbage flowers]

cauliflower ear *n.* permanent swelling and distortion of the ear, caused by repeated blows usually received in boxing.

caulk (kɔːk) *vb.* to stop up (cracks, esp. the seams in the hull of a ship) with a filler. [Latin *calcāre* to trample]

causal ('kɔːz'l) *adj.* **1.** of or being a cause. **2.** relating to cause and effect. —'**causally** *adv.*

causality (kɔː'zælɪtɪ) *n., pl.* **-ties. 1. a.** the relationship of cause and effect. **b.** the principle that everything has a cause. **2.** causal agency or quality.

causation (kɔː'zeɪʃən) *n.* **1.** the production of an effect by a cause. **2.** the relationship of cause and effect.

causative ('kɔːzətɪv) *adj.* **1.** *Grammar.* (of a verb such as *persuade*) expressing cause. **2.** producing an effect. ~*n.* **3.** a causative verb.

cause (kɔːz) *n.* **1.** a person or thing that produces an effect. **2.** grounds for action; justification: *she had good cause to shout like that.* **3.** an aim or principle which an individual or group is interested in and supports: *the Communist cause.* **4. a.** a matter giving rise to a lawsuit. **b.** the lawsuit itself. ~*vb.* **5.** to be the cause of. [Latin *causa*] —'**causeless** *adj.*

cause célèbre ('kɔːz sə'lɛbrə) *n., pl.* **causes célèbres** ('kɔːz sə'lɛbrəz). a controversial legal case, issue, or person. [French]

causerie ('kɔːzərɪ) *n.* an informal talk or piece of writing. [French *causer* to chat]

causeway ('kɔːzˌweɪ) *n.* **1.** a raised path across water or marshland. **2.** a paved footpath. [Medieval Latin *cauciwey* paved way]

caustic ('kɔːstɪk) *adj.* **1.** capable of burning or corroding by chemical action: *caustic soda.* **2.** sarcastic; cutting: *a caustic reply.* ~*n.* **3.** *Chem.* a caustic substance. [Greek *kaiein* to burn] —'**caustically** *adv.* —**causticity** (kɔː'stɪsɪtɪ) *n.*

caustic soda *n.* See **sodium hydroxide.**

cauterize *or* **-ise** ('kɔːtəˌraɪz) *vb.* to burn (tissue) with a hot iron or caustic agent in order to treat a wound. [Greek *kaiein* to burn] —ˌ**cauteri'zation** *or* **-i'sation** *n.*

caution ('kɔːʃən) *n.* **1.** care or prudence, esp. in the face of danger. **2.** a warning. **3.** *Law, chiefly Brit.* a formal warning given to a person suspected of an offence. **4.** *Informal.* an amusing or surprising person or thing. ~*vb.* **5.** to warn or advise: *he cautioned against optimism.* **6.** *Law, chiefly Brit.* to give a caution to (a person). [Latin *cautiō*] —'**cautionary** *adj.*

cautious ('kɔːʃəs) *adj.* showing or having caution. —'**cautiously** *adv.*

cavalcade (ˌkævəl'keɪd) *n.* a procession of people on horseback or in cars. [Italian *cavalcare* to ride on horseback]

cavalier (ˌkævə'lɪə) *adj.* **1.** supercilious; offhand. ~*n.* **2.** a courtly gentleman. **3.** *Archaic.* an armed horseman. [Late Latin *caballārius* rider]

Cavalier (ˌkævə'lɪə) *n.* a supporter of Charles I during the English Civil War.

cavalry ('kævəlrɪ) *n., pl.* **-ries.** the part of an army originally mounted on horseback, but now often using fast armoured vehicles. [Italian *cavaliere* horseman] —'**cavalryman** *n.*

cave (keɪv) *n.* a hollow in the side of a hill or cliff, or underground. [Latin *cavus* hollow]

caveat ('keɪvɪˌæt, 'kæv-) *n.* **1.** *Law.* a formal notice requesting the court not to take a certain action without warning the person lodging the caveat. **2.** a caution. [Latin: let him beware]

cave in *vb.* **1.** to collapse inwards. **2.** *Informal.* to yield completely under pressure. ~*n.* **cave-in. 3.** the sudden collapse of a roof or piece of ground.

cavel ('keɪv'l) *n. N.Z.* a drawing of lots among miners for a good place at the coalface. [English dialect *cavel* to cast lots]

caveman ('keɪvˌmæn) *n., pl.* **-men. 1.** a Stone Age man; cave dweller. **2.** *Informal.* a man who is primitive or brutal in behaviour.

cavern ('kævən) *n.* a large cave. [Latin *cavus* hollow]

cavernous ('kævənəs) *adj.* **1.** like a cavern in vastness, depth, or hollowness: *cavernous eyes.* **2.** (of rocks) containing caverns.

caviar *or* **caviare** ('kævɪˌɑː, ˌkævɪ'ɑː) *n.* the salted roe of sturgeon, usually eaten as an appetizer. [Turkish *havyār*]

cavil ('kævɪl) *vb.* **-illing, -illed** *or U.S.* **-iling, -iled. 1.** (foll. by *at* or *about*) to raise annoying petty objections. ~*n.* **2.** a trivial objection. [Latin *cavillārī* to jeer] —'**caviller** *or U.S.* **-iler** *n.*

caving ('keɪvɪŋ) *n.* the sport of climbing in and exploring caves. —'**caver** *n.*

cavity ('kævɪtɪ) *n., pl.* **-ties. 1.** a hollow space. **2.** *Dentistry.* a decayed area on a tooth. [Latin *cavus* hollow]

cavort (kə'vɔːt) *vb.* to prance; caper. [origin unknown]

caw (kɔː) *n.* **1.** the cry of a crow, rook, or raven. ~*vb.* **2.** to make this cry. [imit.]

cay (keɪ, kiː) *n.* a small low island or bank

of sand and coral fragments. [Spanish *cayo*]

cayenne pepper *or* **cayenne** (keɪˈɛn) *n.* a very hot red spice made from the dried seeds of capsicums. [S. American Indian *quiynha*]

cayman *or* **caiman** ('keɪmən) *n.*, *pl.* **-mans.** a tropical American reptile similar to an alligator. [Carib *cayman*]

CB Citizens' Band.

CBC Canadian Broadcasting Corporation.

CBE Commander of the Order of the British Empire.

CBI Confederation of British Industry.

cc *or* **c.c.** 1. carbon copy *or* copies. 2. cubic centimetre(s).

CC 1. County Council. 2. Cricket Club.

cc. chapters.

CCTV closed-circuit television.

cd candela.

Cd *Chem.* cadmium.

CD 1. Civil Defence (Corps). 2. compact disc. 3. Diplomatic Corps. [French *Corps Diplomatique*]

Cdn. Canadian.

CDT Central Daylight Time.

Ce *Chem.* cerium.

CE 1. Church of England. 2. civil engineer.

cease (siːs) *vb.* 1. to bring or come to an end. ~*n.* 2. **without cease.** without stopping. [Latin *cessāre*]

cease-fire *n.* 1. a temporary period of truce. 2. the order to stop firing.

ceaseless ('siːslɪs) *adj.* without pause; incessant. —**'ceaselessly** *adv.*

cedar ('siːdə) *n.* 1. a coniferous tree having needle-like evergreen leaves, and erect barrel-shaped cones. 2. the wood of this tree. ~*adj.* 3. made of cedar. [Greek *kedros*]

cede (siːd) *vb.* 1. (often foll. by *to*) to transfer or surrender (territory or legal rights). 2. to concede (a point in an argument). [Latin *cēdere* to yield]

cedilla (sɪˈdɪlə) *n.* a character (ˌ) placed underneath a *c*, esp. in French or Portuguese, denoting that it is to be pronounced (s), not (k). [Spanish: little *z*]

Ceefax ('siːfæks) *n. Trademark.* the BBC teletext service.

ceilidh ('keɪlɪ) *n.* an informal social gathering with singing, dancing, and storytelling. [Gaelic]

ceiling ('siːlɪŋ) *n.* 1. the inner upper surface of a room. 2. an upper limit set on something. 3. the upper altitude to which an aircraft can climb. [origin unknown]

celandine ('sɛlənˌdaɪn) *n.* a plant with yellow flowers. [Greek *khelidōn* swallow; the plant's season was believed to parallel the migration of swallows]

celebrant ('sɛlɪbrənt) *n.* a person participating in a religious ceremony.

celebrate ('sɛlɪˌbreɪt) *vb.* 1. to hold festivities to mark (a happy event, birthday, or anniversary). 2. to perform (a solemn or religious ceremony). 3. to praise publicly. [Latin *celeber* numerous, renowned]

—ˌcele'bration *n.* —'cele,brator *n.* —'cele,bratory *adj.*

celebrated ('sɛlɪˌbreɪtɪd) *adj.* famous: *a celebrated pianist.*

celebrity (sɪˈlɛbrɪtɪ) *n.*, *pl.* **-ties.** 1. a famous person. 2. fame.

celeriac (sɪˈlɛrɪˌæk) *n.* a variety of celery with a large turnip-like root, eaten as a vegetable.

celerity (sɪˈlɛrɪtɪ) *n.* swiftness. [Latin *celeritās*]

celery ('sɛlərɪ) *n.* a Eurasian plant whose stalks are used in salads or cooked as a vegetable. [Greek *selinon* parsley]

celesta (sɪˈlɛstə) *n.* an instrument resembling a small piano in which key-operated hammers strike metal plates. [French *céleste* heavenly]

celestial (sɪˈlɛstɪəl) *adj.* 1. heavenly; divine: *celestial peace.* 2. of or relating to the sky: *celestial bodies.* [Latin *caelum* heaven]

celestial equator *n.* an imaginary circle lying on the celestial sphere in a plane perpendicular to the earth's axis.

celestial sphere *n.* an imaginary sphere of infinitely large radius enclosing the universe.

celibate ('sɛlɪbɪt) *n.* 1. a person who does not marry or have sex because he or she has taken a religious vow of chastity. 2. a person who has gone without sex for a considerable period. ~*adj.* 3. unmarried or abstaining from sex because of a religious vow of chastity. 4. having gone without sex for a considerable period. [Latin *caelebs* unmarried] —'**celibacy** *n.*

cell (sɛl) *n.* 1. a small simple room in a prison or convent. 2. any small compartment: *the cells of a honeycomb.* 3. *Biol.* the smallest unit of an organism that is able to function independently, consisting of a nucleus surrounded by cytoplasm. 4. a device which uses energy from a chemical action to produce electrical energy, usually consisting of a container with two electrodes immersed in an electrolyte. 5. a small group of persons operating as a nucleus of a larger organization: *Communist cell.* [Latin *cella* room, storeroom]

cellar ('sɛlə) *n.* 1. an underground room, usually used for storage. 2. a place where wine is stored. 3. a stock of bottled wines. [Latin *cellārium* foodstore]

cellarage ('sɛlərɪdʒ) *n.* 1. an area of a cellar. 2. a charge for storing goods in a cellar.

cello ('tʃɛləʊ) *n.*, *pl.* **-los.** a low-pitched musical instrument of the violin family, held between the knees and played by bowing the four strings. [short for *violoncello*] —'**cellist** *n.*

cellophane ('sɛləˌfeɪn) *n.* a flexible thin transparent sheeting made from cellulose and used as a moisture-proof wrapping. [*cellulose* + Greek *phainein* to shine, appear]

cellular ('sɛljʊlə) *adj.* 1. of, consisting of, or resembling a cell or cells. 2. woven with an open texture: *a cellular blanket.* 3.

designed for or using cellular radio: *a cellular phone.*

cellular radio *n.* radio communication based on a network of transmitters each serving a small area known as a "cell": used esp. in car phones.

cellule ('sɛljuːl) *n.* a very small cell.

cellulite ('sɛljuˌlaɪt) *n.* fat deposits under the skin alleged to resist dieting.

celluloid ('sɛljuˌlɔɪd) *n.* a flammable plastic made from cellulose nitrate and camphor.

cellulose ('sɛljuˌləʊz, -ˌləʊs) *n.* the main constituent of plant cell walls, used in making paper, rayon, and film.

cellulose acetate *n.* nonflammable material used in the manufacture of film, lacquers, and artificial fibres.

cellulose nitrate *n.* a compound used in plastics, lacquers, and explosives.

Celsius ('sɛlsɪəs) *adj.* denoting a measurement on the Celsius scale. [after Anders *Celsius*, astronomer who invented it]

Celsius scale *n.* a scale of temperature in which 0° represents the melting point of ice and 100° represents the boiling point of water.

Celt (kɛlt, sɛlt) *n.* 1. a person who speaks a Celtic language. 2. a member of a people inhabiting Britain, Gaul, and Spain in pre-Roman times. [Latin *Celtae*]

Celtic ('kɛltɪk, 'sɛl-) *n.* 1. a group of Indo-European languages that includes Gaelic, Welsh, and Breton. ~*adj.* 2. of the Celts or the Celtic languages. —**Celticism** ('kɛltɪˌsɪzəm, 'sɛl-) *n.*

cement (sɪ'mɛnt) *n.* 1. a fine grey powder made of limestone and clay, mixed with water and sand to make mortar or concrete. 2. something that unites, binds, or joins. 3. *Dentistry.* a material used in filling teeth. ~*vb.* 4. to join or bind with or as if with cement. 5. to cover with cement. [Latin *caementum* stone from the quarry]

cemetery ('sɛmɪtrɪ) *n., pl.* -**teries.** a place where the dead are buried, usually one not attached to a church. [Greek *koimētērion*]

cenobite ('siːnəʊˌbaɪt) *n.* same as **coenobite.**

cenotaph ('sɛnəˌtɑːf) *n.* a monument honouring a dead person or people buried elsewhere. [Greek *kenos* empty + *taphos* tomb]

Cenozoic *or* **Caenozoic** (ˌsiːnəʊ'zəʊɪk) *adj. Geol.* of the most recent geological era, characterized by the development and increase of the mammals. [Greek *kainos* recent + *zōion* animal]

censer ('sɛnsə) *n.* a container for burning incense.

censor ('sɛnsə) *n.* a person authorized to examine films, letters, or publications, in order to ban or cut anything considered obscene or objectionable. ~*vb.* 2. to ban or cut portions of (a film, letter, or publication). [Latin *cēnsēre* to consider] —**censorial** (sɛn'sɔːrɪəl) *adj.*

censorious (sɛn'sɔːrɪəs) *adj.* harshly critical. —**cen'soriously** *adv.*

censorship ('sɛnsəˌʃɪp) *n.* a practice or policy of censoring.

censure ('sɛnʃə) *n.* 1. severe disapproval. ~*vb.* 2. to criticize (someone or something) severely. [Latin *cēnsēre* to assess] —'**censurable** *adj.*

census ('sɛnsəs) *n., pl.* -**suses.** an official periodic count of a population including such information as sex, age, and occupation. [Latin *cēnsēre* to assess]

cent (sɛnt) *n.* a monetary unit worth one hundredth of the standard unit of many countries, such as the United States. [Latin *centum* hundred]

cent. 1. centigrade. 2. central. 3. century.

centaur ('sɛntɔː) *n. Greek myth.* a creature with the head, arms, and torso of a man, and the lower body and legs of a horse. [Greek *kentauros*]

centenarian (ˌsɛntɪ'nɛərɪən) *n.* 1. a person who is at least 100 years old. ~*adj.* 2. at least 100 years old. 3. of a centenarian.

centenary (sɛn'tiːnərɪ) *adj.* 1. of a period of 100 years. 2. occurring every 100 years. ~*n., pl.* -**naries.** 3. a 100th anniversary or its celebration. [Latin *centum* hundred]

centennial (sɛn'tɛnɪəl) *adj.* 1. of a period of 100 years. 2. occurring every 100 years. ~*n.* 3. *U.S. & Canad.* same as **centenary.** [Latin *centum* hundred]

center ('sɛntə) *n., vb. U.S.* same as **centre.**

centesimal (sɛn'tɛsɪməl) *n.* 1. one hundredth. ~*adj.* 2. of or divided into hundredths. [Latin *centum* hundred]

centi- *or before a vowel* **cent-** *prefix.* denoting: 1. one hundredth: *centimetre.* 2. a hundred: *centipede.* [Latin *centum* hundred]

centigrade ('sɛntɪˌgreɪd) *adj.* 1. same as **Celsius.** ~*n.* 2. a unit of angle equal to one hundredth of a right angle.

centigram *or* **centigramme** ('sɛntɪˌgræm) *n.* one hundredth of a gram.

centilitre *or U.S.* **centiliter** ('sɛntɪˌliːtə) *n.* one hundredth of a litre.

centime ('sɒnˌtiːm) *n.* a monetary unit worth one hundredth of the standard unit of many countries, such as France. [Latin *centum* hundred]

centimetre *or U.S.* **centimeter** ('sɛntɪˌmiːtə) *n.* one hundredth of a metre.

centipede ('sɛntɪˌpiːd) *n.* an arthropod having a body of many segments, each bearing one pair of legs.

central ('sɛntrəl) *adj.* 1. in, at, of, or forming the centre of something: *the central street in a city.* 2. main or principal: *the central cause of the problem.* —**centrality** (sɛn'trælɪtɪ) *n.* —'**centrally** *adv.*

central bank *n.* a national bank that acts as the government's banker, controls credit, and issues currency.

central heating *n.* a system for heating a building by means of radiators or air vents connected to a central source of heat. —**centrally heated** *adj.*

centralism ('sɛntrəˌlɪzəm) *n.* the principle

rub. ~n. **5.** a soreness caused by rubbing. [Old French *chaufer* to warm]

chafer ('tʃeɪfə) n. a large slow-moving beetle. [Old English *ceafor*]

chaff[1] (tʃɑːf) n. **1.** grain husks separated from the seeds during threshing. **2.** finely cut straw and hay used to feed cattle. **3.** something of little worth; rubbish: *separate the wheat from the chaff*. [Old English *ceaf*]

chaff[2] (tʃɑːf) n. **1.** light-hearted teasing or joking. ~vb. **2.** to tease good-naturedly. [prob. slang var. of *chafe*]

chaffinch ('tʃæfɪntʃ) n. a common European finch with black-and-white wings and, in the male, a reddish body and bluegrey head. [Old English *ceaf* CHAFF[1] + *finc* finch]

chafing dish n. a dish with a heating apparatus beneath it, for cooking or keeping food warm at the table.

chagrin ('ʃægrɪn) n. **1.** a feeling of annoyance and embarrassment. ~vb. **2.** to annoy and embarrass. [French]

chain (tʃeɪn) n. **1.** a flexible length of metal links, used for confining or connecting, or in jewellery. **2.** (*usually pl.*) anything that confines or restrains: *the chains of poverty*. **3.** a series of connected facts or events. **4.** a number of establishments, such as hotels or shops, having the same owner or management. **5.** a unit of length equal to 22 yards. **6.** *Chem.* two or more atoms or groups bonded together so that the resulting molecule, ion, or radical resembles a chain. **7.** *Geog.* a series of natural features, esp. mountain ranges. ~vb. **8.** (often foll. by *up*) to confine, tie, or fasten with or as if with a chain. [Latin *catena*]

chain gang n. *U.S.* a group of convicted prisoners chained together.

chain letter n. a letter, often with a request for and promise of money, that is sent to many people who are asked to add to or recopy it and send it on.

chain mail n. same as **mail**[2].

chain reaction n. **1.** a chemical or nuclear reaction in which the product of one step triggers the following step. **2.** a series of events, each of which causes the next. —,**chain-re'act** vb.

chain saw n. a motor-driven saw in which the cutting teeth form links in a continuous chain.

chain-smoke vb. to smoke (cigarettes) continuously, esp. lighting one from the preceding one. —**chain smoker** n.

chair (tʃɛə) n. **1.** a seat with a back on which one person sits, usually having four legs. **2.** an official position of authority or the person holding it: *questions are to be addressed to the chair*. **3.** a professorship. **4.** short for **sedan chair**. **5. take the chair**. to preside over a meeting. **6. the chair**. *Informal*. the electric chair. ~vb. **7.** to preside over (a meeting). **8.** *Brit*. to carry (a person) aloft in a sitting position after a triumph. **9.** to install in a chair of authority. [Greek *kathedra*]

chair lift n. a series of chairs suspended from a power-driven cable for carrying people, esp. skiers, up a slope.

chairman ('tʃɛəmən) n., pl. -**men.** a person who presides over a company's board of directors, a committee, or a debate. Also: **chairperson** or (*fem.*) **chairwoman.**

chaise (ʃeɪz) n. a light open horse-drawn carriage, usually with two wheels. [French]

chaise longue ('ʃeɪz 'lɒŋ) n., pl. **chaise longues** or **chaises longues** ('ʃeɪz 'lɒŋ). a long low chair with a back and single armrest. [French]

chalcedony (kæl'sɛdənɪ) n., pl. -**nies.** a form of quartz composed of very fine crystals: a semiprecious stone. [Greek *khalkēdōn* a precious stone]

chalet ('ʃæleɪ) n. **1.** a type of Swiss wooden house with wide projecting eaves. **2.** a similar house used as a ski lodge or holiday home. [French]

chalice ('tʃælɪs) n. **1.** *Poetic*. a drinking cup; goblet. **2.** *Christianity*. a gold or silver goblet containing the wine at Mass. [Latin *calix* cup]

chalk (tʃɔːk) n. **1.** a soft fine-grained white rock consisting of calcium carbonate. **2.** a piece of chalk or similar substance, often coloured, used for writing and drawing on blackboards. **3. as different as chalk and cheese.** *Informal*. totally different. **4. by a long chalk.** *Brit. informal*. by far. **5. not by a long chalk.** *Brit. informal*. by no means. ~vb. **6.** to draw or mark (something) with chalk. [Latin *calx* limestone] —'**chalky** adj. —'**chalkiness** n.

chalk up vb. *Informal*. **1.** to score or register (something). **2.** to charge or credit (money) to an account.

challenge ('tʃælɪndʒ) vb. **1.** to invite or call (someone) to take part in a contest, fight, or argument. **2.** to call (something) into question. **3.** to make demands on; stimulate: *the job challenges his ingenuity*. **4.** to order (a person) to halt and be identified. **5.** *Law*. to make formal objection to (a juror or jury). ~n. **6.** a call to engage in a contest, fight, or argument. **7.** a questioning of a statement or fact. **8.** a demanding or stimulating situation. **9.** a demand by a sentry for identification or a password. **10.** *Law*. a formal objection to a juror or jury. [Latin *calumnia* calumny] —'**challenger** n. —'**challenging** adj.

chalybeate (kə'lɪbɪɪt) adj. containing or impregnated with iron salts. [Greek *khalups* iron]

chamber ('tʃeɪmbə) n. **1.** a meeting hall, usually one used for a legislative or judicial assembly. **2.** *Archaic or poetic*. a room in a house, esp. a bedroom. **3.** a room equipped for a particular purpose: *decompression chamber*. **4.** a legislative or judicial assembly. **5.** a compartment; cavity. **6.** a compartment for a cartridge or shell in a gun. **7.** (*modifier*) of or suitable for chamber music: *a chamber concert*. ~See also **chambers.** [Latin *kamara* vault]

chamberlain ('tʃeɪmbəlɪn) n. *History*. **1.** an officer who manages the household of a king or nobleman. **2.** the treasurer of a municipal corporation. [Old French *chamberlayn*]

chambermaid ('tʃeɪmbə,meɪd) *n.* a woman employed to clean bedrooms in a hotel.

chamber music *n.* music for performance by a small group of players.

chamber of commerce *n.* (*sometimes cap.*) an organization of local businessmen to promote, regulate, and protect their interests.

chamber pot *n.* a receptacle for urine, formerly used in bedrooms.

chambers ('tʃeɪmbəz) *pl. n.* 1. a judge's room for hearing private cases not taken in open court. 2. (in England) the set of rooms used as offices by a barrister.

chameleon (kə'miːlɪən) *n.* 1. a small lizard having the ability to change colour according to its surroundings. 2. a changeable or fickle person. [Greek *khamai* on the ground + *leōn* lion]

chamfer ('tʃæmfə) *n.* 1. a bevelled surface at an edge or corner. ~*vb.* 2. to cut such a surface on (an edge or corner). [Old French *chant* edge + *fraindre* to break]

chamois ('ʃæmɪ; *for sense 1* 'ʃæmwɑː) *n.*, *pl.* **-ois.** 1. a small mountain antelope of Europe and SW Asia. 2. a soft suede leather formerly made from this animal, now obtained from sheep and goats. 3. Also: **chamois leather, shammy, chammy.** a piece of such leather or similar material, used for cleaning and polishing. ~*vb.* 4. to polish with a chamois. [Old French]

champ[1] (tʃæmp) *vb.* 1. to chew noisily. 2. **champ at the bit.** *Informal.* to be restless or impatient to do something. ~*n.* 3. the act or noise of champing. [prob. imit.]

champ[2] (tʃæmp) *n. Informal.* short for **champion** (sense 1).

champagne (ʃæm'peɪn) *n.* 1. (*sometimes cap.*) a white sparkling wine produced around Reims and Epernay, France. 2. (loosely) any similar wine. ~*adj.* 3. pale straw-coloured. [*Champagne*, region of France]

champers ('ʃæmpəz) *n.* (*functioning as sing.*) *Slang.* champagne.

champion ('tʃæmpɪən) *n.* 1. a person, plant, or animal that has defeated all others in a competition: *a chess champion.* 2. someone who defends a person or cause: *a champion of the underprivileged.* ~*adj.* 3. *N English dialect.* excellent. ~*adv.* 4. *N English dialect.* very well. ~*vb.* 5. to support: *to champion a cause.* [Latin *campus* field] —'**championship** *n.*

chance (tʃɑːns) *n.* 1. the unknown and unpredictable element that causes something to happen in one way rather than another. 2. fortune; luck; fate. 3. an opportunity or occasion. 4. a risk; gamble. 5. the extent to which something is likely to happen; probability. 6. an unpredicted event. 7. **by chance.** accidentally: *we met by chance.* 8. **on the (off) chance.** acting on the (remote) possibility. ~*vb.* 9. to risk; hazard. 10. to happen by chance: *I chanced to catch sight of her.* 11. **chance on** *or* **upon.** to come upon by accident. 12. **chance one's arm.** to attempt to do something although the chance of success may be slight. [Latin *cadere* to occur]

chancel ('tʃɑːnsəl) *n.* the part of a church containing the altar and choir. [Latin *cancellī* (pl.) lattice]

chancellery *or* **chancellory** ('tʃɑːnsələrɪ) *n.*, *pl.* **-leries** *or* **-lories.** 1. the residence or office of a chancellor. 2. the rank of a chancellor. 3. *U.S.* the office of an embassy or consulate. [Anglo-French *chancellerie*]

chancellor ('tʃɑːnsələ) *n.* 1. the head of the government in several European countries. 2. *U.S.* the president of a university. 3. *Brit. & Canad.* the honorary head of a university. [Late Latin *cancellārius* porter] —'**chancellor,ship** *n.*

Chancellor of the Exchequer *n. Brit.* the cabinet minister responsible for finance.

chancery ('tʃɑːnsərɪ) *n.*, *pl.* **-ceries.** (*usually cap.*) 1. (in England) the Lord Chancellor's court, a division of the High Court of Justice. 2. same as **chancellery.** 3. a court of public records. 4. **in chancery. a.** *Law.* (of a suit) awaiting litigation in court. **b.** in an awkward situation. [shortened from *chancellery*]

chancre ('ʃæŋkə) *n. Pathol.* a small hard growth, which is the first sign of syphilis. [French] —'**chancrous** *adj.*

chancy *or* **chancey** ('tʃɑːnsɪ) *adj.* **chancier, chanciest.** *Informal.* uncertain; risky.

chandelier (,ʃændɪ'lɪə) *n.* an ornamental branched hanging light with several candles or bulbs. [French]

chandler ('tʃɑːndlə) *n.* 1. a dealer in a specified trade or merchandise: *ship's chandler.* 2. a maker or seller of candles. [Old French *chandelle* candle] —'**chandlery** *n.*

change (tʃeɪndʒ) *vb.* 1. to make or become different; transform or be transformed. 2. to replace with or exchange for another: *to change one's name.* 3. to give and receive (something) in return: *to change places.* 4. to give or receive (money) in exchange for its equivalent sum in a smaller denomination or different currency. 5. to remove or replace the coverings of: *to change a baby; change the bed.* 6. to put on other clothes. 7. to alight from (one bus or train) and board another. ~*n.* 8. a changing or being changed. 9. a variation or modification. 10. anything that is or may be substituted for something else. 11. variety or novelty: *for a change.* 12. a different set, esp. of clothes. 13. money exchanged for its equivalent in a larger denomination or in a different currency. 14. the balance of money when the amount paid is larger than the amount due. 15. coins of a small denomination. 16. the order in which a peal of bells may be rung. 17. **get no change out of someone.** *Slang.* not to be successful in attempts to exploit someone. 18. **ring the changes.** to vary the way of doing something. ~See also **change down, changeover, change up.** [Latin *cambiāre* to exchange, barter] —'**changeful** *adj.* —'**changeless** *adj.*

changeable ('tʃeɪndʒəb'l) *adj.* 1. able to

change or be changed: *changeable weather.*
2. varying in colour when viewed from
different angles. —**,changea'bility** *n.*

change down *vb.* to select a lower gear
when driving.

changeling (ˈtʃeɪndʒlɪŋ) *n.* a child believed
to have been exchanged by fairies for the
parents' true child.

change of life *n.* the menopause.

changeover (ˈtʃeɪndʒˌəʊvə) *n.* **1.** a complete change from one system, attitude, or
product to another. ~*vb.* **change over.**
2. to adopt (a different position or attitude): *the driver and navigator changed
over.*

change up *vb.* to select a higher gear
when driving.

channel (ˈtʃænʰl) *n.* **1.** a broad strait
connecting two areas of sea. **2.** the bed or
course of a river, stream, or canal. **3.** a
navigable course through a body of water.
4. (*often pl.*) a means of access or communication: *through official channels.* **5.** a
course along which something can be directed or moved. **6.** a band of radio
frequencies assigned for the broadcasting
of a radio or television signal. **7.** a path
for an electrical signal or computer data: *a
stereo set has two channels.* **8.** a groove.
~*vb.* **-nelling, -nelled** *or U.S.* **-neling,
-neled.** **9.** to make channels in (something). **10.** to direct or convey through a
channel or channels: *information was
channelled through to them.* [Latin *canālis*
pipe, conduit]

Channel (ˈtʃænʰl) *n.* **the.** the English Channel.

channelize *or* **-ise** (ˈtʃænɪˌlaɪz) *vb.* to make
the channel of (a river) deeper or straight-
er, so that water flow is improved.
—**,channeli'zation** *or* **-i'sation** *n.*

chant (tʃɑːnt) *n.* **1.** a short simple melody
in which several words or syllables are
sung on one note. **2.** a religious song with
such a melody. **3.** a rhythmic or repetitious slogan spoken or sung, usually by
more than one person. ~*vb.* **4.** to sing or
recite (a psalm) as a chant. **5.** to intone (a
slogan). [Latin *canere* to sing] —**'chanting** *n., adj.*

chanter (ˈtʃɑːntə) *n.* the pipe on a set of
bagpipes on which the melody is played.

chanticleer (ˌtʃæntɪˈklɪə) *n.* a name for a
cock, used in fables. [Old French *chanter
cler* to sing clearly]

chanty (ˈʃæntɪ, ˈtʃæn-) *n., pl.* **-ties.** same as
shanty².

Chanukah *or* **Hanukkah** (ˈhɑːnəkə,
-nʊkə) *n.* a Jewish festival commemorating
the rededication of the temple by Judas
Maccabeus. [Hebrew]

chaos (ˈkeɪɒs) *n.* **1.** (*usually cap.*) the
disordered formless matter supposed to
have existed before the ordered universe.
2. complete disorder or confusion. [Greek
khaos] —**cha'otic** *adj.* —**cha'otically** *adv.*

chap¹ (tʃæp) *vb.* **chapping, chapped.** **1.**
(of the skin) to make or become raw and
cracked, by exposure to cold. ~*n.* **2.**

(*usually pl.*) a cracked patch on the skin.
[prob. Germanic]

chap² (tʃæp) *n. Informal.* a man or boy;
fellow. [shortened from *chapman*]

chapatti *or* **chapati** (tʃəˈpætɪ, -ˈpɑːtɪ) *n.,
pl.* **-ti, -tis,** *or* **-ties.** (in Indian cookery) a
flat thin unleavened bread. [Hindi]

chapel (ˈtʃæpʰl) *n.* **1.** a place of worship
with its own altar, in a church or cathedral. **2.** a similar place of worship in a
large house or institution. **3.** (in Britain) a
Nonconformist place of worship. **4.** the
members of a trade union in a newspaper
office, printing house, or publishing firm.
[Latin *cappa* cloak: orig. the sanctuary
where the cloak of St Martin was kept]

chaperon *or* **chaperone** (ˈʃæpəˌrəʊn) *n.*
1. an older woman who supervises a young
unmarried woman on social occasions.
~*vb.* **2.** to act as a chaperon to. [Old
French *chape* hood] —**chaperonage**
(ˈʃæpərənɪdʒ) *n.*

chaplain (ˈtʃæplɪn) *n.* a clergyman attached to a chapel or serving a military
body or institution. [Late Latin *cappella*
chapel] —**'chaplaincy** *n.*

chaplet (ˈtʃæplɪt) *n.* **1.** a garland worn on
the head. **2.** a string of beads. **3.** *R.C.
Church.* a string of prayer beads constituting one third of the rosary. [Old French
chapel hat]

chapman (ˈtʃæpmən) *n., pl.* **-men.** *Archaic.*
a travelling pedlar. [Old English *cēapman*]

chappie (ˈtʃæpɪ) *n. Informal.* a chap or
fellow.

chaps (tʃæps, ʃæps) *pl. n.* leather leggings
without a seat, worn by cowboys. [short-
ened from Spanish *chaparejos*]

chapter (ˈtʃæptə) *n.* **1.** a division of a
written work. **2.** a sequence of events: *a
chapter of disasters.* **3.** a period in a life or
history. **4.** a branch of some societies or
clubs. **5.** the body of or a meeting of the
canons of a cathedral or the members of a
monastic order. **6. chapter and verse.**
exact authority for an action or statement.
[Latin *caput* head]

char¹ (tʃɑː) *vb.* **charring, charred.** **1.** to
scorch. **2.** to reduce (wood) to charcoal by
partial burning. [short for *charcoal*]

char² *or* **charr** (tʃɑː) *n., pl.* **char, chars** *or*
charr, charrs. a troutlike fish of cold
lakes and northern seas. [origin unknown]

char³ (tʃɑː) *n.* **1.** *Informal.* short for **charwoman.** ~*vb.* **charring, charred.** **2.** *Brit.
informal.* to do cleaning as a job. [Old
English *cerran*]

char⁴ (tʃɑː) *n. Brit. slang.* tea. [Chinese
ch'a]

charabanc (ˈʃærəˌbæŋ) *n. Brit.* a coach for
sightseeing. [French: wagon with seats]

character (ˈkærɪktə) *n.* **1.** the combination of qualities distinguishing an individual person or thing. **2.** a distinguishing
quality; characteristic. **3.** moral strength:
a man of character. **4.** reputation, esp.
good reputation. **5.** a person represented
in a play, film, or story. **6.** an outstanding
person: *one of the great characters of the
century.* **7.** *Informal.* an odd or eccentric
person: *he's quite a character.* **8.** *Infor-*

mal. a person: *a shady character*. **9.** *Printing.* a single letter, numeral, or symbol used in writing or printing. **10.** *Computers.* any letter or numeral which can be represented uniquely by a binary pattern. **11.** *Genetics.* a structure, function, or attribute in an organism that is determined by a gene or genes. **12.** **in** (*or* **out of**) **character.** typical (*or* not typical) of the apparent character of a person. [Greek *kharaktēr* engraver's tool] —'**characterless** *adj.*

characteristic (ˌkærɪktəˈrɪstɪk) *n.* **1.** a distinguishing feature or quality. **2.** *Maths.* the integral part of a logarithm: *the characteristic of 2.4771 is 2.* ~*adj.* **3.** distinctive; typical. —ˌcharacter'**istically** *adv.*

characterize *or* **-ise** (ˈkærɪktəˌraɪz) *vb.* **1.** to be a characteristic of. **2.** to distinguish as a characteristic. **3.** to describe the character of. —ˌcharacteri'**zation** *or* **-i'sation** *n.*

charade (ʃəˈrɑːd) *n. Chiefly Brit.* a farce; travesty. [French]

charades (ʃəˈrɑːdz) *n.* (*functioning as sing.*) a game in which one team acts out each syllable of a word, which the other team has to guess.

charcoal (ˈtʃɑːˌkəʊl) *n.* **1.** a black form of carbon made by partially burning wood or other organic matter. **2.** a stick of this for drawing. **3.** a drawing done in charcoal. ~*adj.* **4.** Also: **charcoal-grey.** dark grey. [origin unknown]

charge (tʃɑːdʒ) *vb.* **1.** to set or ask (a price). **2.** to enter a debit against (a person or his account). **3.** to accuse (someone) formally, as of a crime in a court of law. **4.** to command; assign responsibility to: *I was charged to take the message to headquarters.* **5.** to make a rush at or sudden attack upon (a person or thing). **6.** to fill (a receptacle) with the required quantity. **7.** (often foll. by *up*) to cause (an accumulator or capacitor) to take and store electricity. **8.** to saturate with liquid or gas: *to charge water with carbon dioxide.* **9.** to fill with a feeling or mood: *the atmosphere was charged with excitement.* **10.** to load (a firearm). ~*n.* **11.** a price charged for something; cost. **12.** a formal accusation, as of a crime in a court of law. **13. a.** an onrush or attack. **b.** the call to such an attack in battle. **14.** custody or guardianship. **15.** a person or thing committed to someone's care. **16. a.** a cartridge or shell. **b.** the explosive required to discharge a firearm. **17.** the quantity of anything that a receptacle is intended to hold. **18.** *Physics.* **a.** the attribute of matter responsible for all electrical phenomena, existing in two forms, positive and negative. **b.** the total amount of electricity stored in a capacitor or an accumulator. **19.** a burden or responsibility. **20.** a command or injunction. **21.** *Heraldry.* a design depicted on heraldic arms. **22. in charge.** in command. **23. in charge of. a.** responsible for. **b.** *U.S.* under the care of. [Old French *chargier* to load]

chargeable (ˈtʃɑːdʒəbʲl) *adj.* **1.** liable to

be charged: *chargeable expenses*. **2.** liable to result in a legal charge.

chargé d'affaires (ˈʃɑːʒeɪ dæ'fɛə) *n., pl.* **chargés d'affaires** (ˈʃɑːʒeɪ, -ʒeɪz). **1.** the temporary head of a diplomatic mission in the absence of the ambassador or minister. **2.** the head of a small or unimportant diplomatic mission. [French]

charge hand *n. Brit.* a workman whose grade of responsibility is just below that of a foreman.

charge nurse *n.* the male equivalent of a hospital sister.

charger (ˈtʃɑːdʒə) *n.* **1.** a warhorse. **2.** a device for charging an accumulator.

chariot (ˈtʃærɪət) *n.* a two-wheeled horse-drawn vehicle used in ancient times for wars and races. [Old French *char* car]

charioteer (ˌtʃærɪəˈtɪə) *n.* a chariot driver.

charisma (kəˈrɪzmə) *or* **charism** (ˈkærɪzəm) *n.* **1.** the quality or power of an individual to attract, influence, or inspire people. **2.** *Christianity.* a divinely bestowed gift. [Greek *kharis* grace, favour] —**charismatic** (ˌkærɪzˈmætɪk) *adj.*

charismatic movement *n. Christianity.* a group, within an existing denomination, emphasizing divine gifts such as instantaneous healing and uttering unintelligible sounds while in a religious ecstasy.

charitable (ˈtʃærɪtəbʲl) *adj.* **1.** generous in giving to the needy. **2.** kind or lenient in one's attitude towards others. **3.** of or for charity. —'**charitably** *adv.*

charity (ˈtʃærɪtɪ) *n., pl.* **-ties. 1.** the giving of help, such as money or food, to those in need. **2.** an organization set up to provide help to those in need. **3.** help given to the needy; alms. **4.** a kindly attitude towards people. **5.** love of one's fellow human beings. [Latin *cāritās* affection]

charlatan (ˈʃɑːlətʲn) *n.* someone who claims expertise that he does not have. [Italian *ciarlare* to chatter] —'**charlatan-ism** *n.*

charleston (ˈtʃɑːlstən) *n.* a lively dance of the 1920s, characterized by twisting kicks from the knee. [after *Charleston*, South Carolina]

charlie (ˈtʃɑːlɪ) *n. Brit. informal.* a fool.

charlock (ˈtʃɑːlɒk) *n.* a weed with hairy leaves and yellow flowers. [Old English *cerlic*]

charlotte (ˈʃɑːlət) *n.* a dessert made with fruit and bread or cake crumbs: *apple charlotte*. [French]

charm (tʃɑːm) *n.* **1.** the quality of attracting, fascinating, or delighting people. **2.** a small object worn for supposed magical powers; amulet. **3.** a trinket worn on a bracelet. **4.** a magic spell. **5. like a charm.** perfectly; successfully. ~*vb.* **6.** to attract or fascinate; delight. **7.** to protect, influence, or heal, as if by magic. **8.** to influence or obtain by personal charm. [Latin *carmen* song] —'**charmer** *n.* —'**charmless** *adj.*

charming (ˈtʃɑːmɪŋ) *adj.* delightful; attractive. —'**charmingly** *adv.*

charnel house (ˈtʃɑːnʲl) *n.* (formerly) a

building or vault where corpses or bones are deposited. [Latin *carnālis* fleshly]

Charon ('kɛərən) n. *Greek myth.* the ferryman who brought the dead across the river Styx to Hades.

chart (tʃɑːt) n. **1.** a map designed to aid navigation by sea or air. **2.** an outline map on which weather information is plotted. **3.** a graph, table, or sheet of information in the form of a diagram. **4. the charts.** *Informal.* the weekly lists of the best-selling pop records. ~vb. **5.** to make a chart of. **6.** to plot the course of. **7.** to appear in the pop charts. [Greek *khartēs* papyrus]

charter ('tʃɑːtə) n. **1.** (*sometimes cap.*) a formal document granting or demanding certain rights or liberties. **2.** (*often cap.*) the fundamental principles of an organization; constitution. **3.** the hire or lease of transportation for private use. ~vb. **4.** to lease or hire by charter. **5.** to grant a charter to. [Latin *charta* leaf of papyrus]

chartered accountant n. (in Britain) an accountant who has passed the examinations of the Institute of Chartered Accountants.

Chartism ('tʃɑːtɪzəm) n. *English history.* a movement (1838–48) for social and political reforms, such as votes for all men and secret ballots, demand for which was presented to Parliament in charters. —'**Chartist** n., adj.

chartreuse (ʃɑːˈtrɜːz) n. a green or yellow liqueur made from herbs. [after *La Grande Chartreuse*, monastery near Grenoble, where the liqueur is produced]

charwoman ('tʃɑːˌwʊmən) n., pl. -**women**. *Brit.* a woman employed to clean a house.

chary ('tʃɛərɪ) adj. **charier**, **chariest**. **1.** wary; careful. **2.** sparing; mean. [Old English *cearig*] —'**chariness** n.

Charybdis (kəˈrɪbdɪs) n. a ship-devouring monster in classical mythology, identified with a whirlpool off the coast of Sicily.

chase[1] (tʃeɪs) vb. **1.** to pursue (a person, animal, or goal) persistently or quickly. **2.** (*often foll. by out, away,* or *off*) to force to run (away); drive (out). **3.** *Informal.* to court (someone) in an unsubtle manner. **4.** (*often foll. by up*) *Informal.* to pursue energetically in order to obtain results or information. **5.** *Informal.* to hurry; rush. ~n. **6.** a chasing; pursuit. **7.** *Brit.* an unenclosed area of land, originally one where wild animals were kept to be hunted. **8. the chase.** the act or sport of hunting. **9. give chase.** to set off in pursuit of (a person or animal). [Latin *capere* to take]

chase[2] (tʃeɪs) n. **1.** a rectangular metal frame into which type is locked for printing. **2.** a groove. [Latin *capsa* case, box]

chase[3] (tʃeɪs) vb. to engrave or emboss (metal). [Old French *enchasser*]

chaser ('tʃeɪsə) n. a drink drunk after another of a different kind, as beer after spirits.

chasm ('kæzəm) n. **1.** a deep crack in the ground; abyss. **2.** a wide difference in interests or feelings. [Greek *khasma*]

chassis ('ʃæsɪ) n., pl. -**sis** (-sɪz). **1.** the steel frame, wheels, and mechanical parts of a motor vehicle. **2.** a mounting for the components of an electronic device, such as a radio or television. **3.** the landing gear of an aircraft. [French]

chaste (tʃeɪst) adj. **1.** abstaining from sex outside marriage or from all sexual intercourse. **2.** (of conduct or speech) pure; decent; modest. **3.** (of style) simple. [Latin *castus* pure] —'**chastely** adv. —'**chasteness** n.

chasten ('tʃeɪs²n) vb. **1.** to correct by punishment. **2.** to subdue; restrain. [Latin *castigāre*]

chastise (tʃæsˈtaɪz) vb. **1.** to punish, esp. by beating. **2.** to scold severely. [Middle English *chastisen*] —**chastisement** ('tʃæstɪzmənt) n.

chastity ('tʃæstɪtɪ) n. **1.** the state of being chaste; purity. **2.** abstention from sexual intercourse. [Latin *castus* chaste]

chasuble ('tʃæzjʊb²l) n. *Christianity.* a long sleeveless outer vestment worn by a priest when celebrating Mass. [Late Latin *casubla* garment with a hood]

chat (tʃæt) n. **1.** informal conversation in an easy familiar manner. **2.** a songbird with a harsh chattering cry. ~vb. **chatting, chatted. 3.** to talk in an easy familiar way. ~See also **chat up.** [short for *chatter*]

chateau or **château** ('ʃætəʊ) n., pl. -**teaux** (-təʊ, -təʊz) or -**teaus**. **1.** a French country house or castle. **2.** (in the name of a wine) estate or vineyard. [French]

chatelaine ('ʃætəˌleɪn) n. **1.** (esp. formerly) the mistress of a large house or castle. **2.** *History.* a chain with keys attached worn at the waist by women. [French]

chat show n. *Brit.* a television or radio show in which guests are interviewed informally.

chattel ('tʃæt²l) n. (*often pl.*) *Property law.* a movable personal possession. [Old French *chatel*]

chatter ('tʃætə) vb. **1.** to speak about trivial matters rapidly and incessantly. **2.** (of birds or monkeys) to make rapid repetitive high-pitched noises. **3.** (of the teeth) to click together rapidly through cold or fear. ~n. **4.** idle talk; gossip. **5.** the high-pitched repetitive noise made by a bird or monkey. [imit.]

chatterbox ('tʃætəˌbɒks) n. *Informal.* a person who talks constantly about trivial matters.

chatty ('tʃætɪ) adj. -**tier**, -**tiest**. **1.** full of trivial conversation; talkative. **2.** informal and friendly; gossipy. —'**chattiness** n.

chat up vb. *Brit. informal.* **1.** to chat to (a person), usually with an ulterior motive. **2.** to talk flirtatiously to (someone).

chauffeur ('ʃəʊfə, ʃəʊˈfɜː) n. **1.** a person employed to drive a car. ~vb. **2.** to act as driver for (someone). [French: stoker] —**chauffeuse** (ʃəʊˈfɜːz) fem. n.

chauvinism ('ʃəʊvɪˌnɪzəm) n. **1.** aggressive or fanatical patriotism; jingoism. **2.** smug irrational belief that one's own race, group, or sex is superior: *male chauvinism*.

[after Nicolas *Chauvin*, French soldier under Napoleon] —'**chauvinist** *n.*, *adj.* —,**chauvin'istic** *adj.*

cheap ('tʃiːp) *adj.* **1.** costing relatively little; inexpensive. **2.** charging low prices: *a cheap hairdresser.* **3.** of poor quality; shoddy: *cheap furniture.* **4.** easily got or made; of little value: *talk is cheap.* **5.** *Informal.* mean; despicable: *a cheap liar.* ~*n.* **6. on the cheap.** *Brit. informal.* at a low cost. ~*adv.* **7.** at a low cost. [Old English *ceap* barter, price] —'**cheaply** *adv.* —'**cheapness** *n.*

cheapen ('tʃiːpən) *vb.* **1.** to make or become lower in reputation or quality. **2.** to make or become cheap or cheaper.

cheap-jack *Informal.* ~*n.* **1.** a seller of cheap and shoddy goods. ~*adj.* **2.** shoddy or inferior.

cheapskate ('tʃiːpˌskeɪt) *n.* *Informal.* a miserly person.

cheat (tʃiːt) *vb.* **1.** to deceive for gain; trick or swindle (someone). **2.** to obtain unfair advantage by trickery: *he cheats at cards.* **3.** to escape (something unpleasant) by luck or cunning: *to cheat death.* **4.** (often foll. by *on*) *Informal.* to be unfaithful to (one's spouse or lover). ~*n.* **5.** a person who cheats. **6.** a fraud; deception. [short for *escheat*] —'**cheater** *n.*

check (tʃɛk) *vb.* **1.** to examine, investigate, or make an inquiry into (something). **2.** to slow the growth or progress of. **3.** to rebuke or rebuff. **4.** to stop abruptly. **5.** *Chiefly U.S. & Canad.* to tick so as to indicate approval, correctness, or preference. **6.** (often foll. by *with*) *Chiefly U.S. & Canad.* to correspond or agree: *this report checks with the other.* **7.** *Chiefly U.S., Canad., & N.Z.* to leave in or accept for temporary custody. ~*n.* **8.** a test to ensure accuracy or progress. **9.** a means to ensure against fraud or error. **10.** a break in progress; stoppage. **11.** a rebuke or rebuff. **12.** a person or thing that restrains or halts. **13.** *U.S.* same as **tick**[1]. **14.** *U.S.* a cheque. **15.** *U.S. & Canad.* the bill in a restaurant. **16.** *Chiefly U.S. & Canad.* a tag used to identify property left in custody. **17.** a pattern of squares or crossed lines. **18.** a single square in such a pattern. **19.** fabric with such a pattern. **20.** *Chess.* the state or position of a king under direct attack. **21. in check.** under control or restraint. ~*interj.* **22.** *Chiefly U.S. & Canad.* an expression of agreement. ~See also **check in, check out, checkup.** [Old French *eschec* a check at chess]

checked (tʃɛkt) *adj.* having a pattern of squares.

checker[1] ('tʃɛkə) *U.S. & Canad.* ~*n.*, *vb.* **1.** same as **chequer.** ~*n.* **2.** same as **draughtsman** (sense 3).

checker[2] ('tʃɛkə) *n. Chiefly U.S.* **1.** a cashier. **2.** an attendant in a cloakroom or left-luggage office.

checkers ('tʃɛkəz) *n.* (functioning as sing.) *U.S. & Canad.* draughts.

check in *vb.* **1.** to register one's arrival; sign in. **2.** to register the arrival of (passengers or staff). ~*n.* **check-in. 3.** the formal registration of arrival at an airport or hotel. **4.** the place where one registers one's arrival.

check list *n.* a list to be referred to for identification or verification.

checkmate ('tʃɛkˌmeɪt) *n.* **1.** *Chess.* the winning position in which an opponent's king is under attack and unable to escape. **2.** utter defeat. ~*vb.* **3.** *Chess.* to place (an opponent's king) in checkmate. **4.** to thwart or defeat. [Arabic *shāh māt* the king is dead]

check out *vb.* **1.** to pay the bill and depart from a hotel. **2.** to depart or register one's departure from a place. **3.** to investigate, examine, or look at: *the police checked out all the statements.* **4.** *Informal.* to have a look at; inspect: *check out the wally in the pink shirt.* ~*n.* **checkout. 5.** a counter in a supermarket, where customers pay.

checkpoint ('tʃɛkˌpɔɪnt) *n.* a place where vehicles or travellers are stopped for identification or inspection.

checkup ('tʃɛkˌʌp) *n.* **1.** a thorough examination to see if a person or thing is in good condition. ~*vb.* **check up. 2.** (sometimes foll. by *on*) to investigate (something, such as a person's background).

Cheddar ('tʃɛdə) *n.* a firm orange or yellow-white cheese. [*Cheddar*, village in Somerset, where it was orig. made]

cheek (tʃiːk) *n.* **1.** either side of the face below the eye. **2.** *Informal.* impudence; effrontery. **3.** (often pl.) *Informal.* a buttock. **4. cheek by jowl.** close together; intimate. **5. turn the other cheek.** to refuse to retaliate. ~*vb.* **6.** *Informal.* to speak or behave disrespectfully to. [Old English *ceace*]

cheekbone ('tʃiːkˌbəʊn) *n.* the bone at the top of the cheek, just below the eye.

cheeky ('tʃiːkɪ) *adj.* **cheekier, cheekiest.** disrespectful; impudent. —'**cheekily** *adv.* —'**cheekiness** *n.*

cheep (tʃiːp) *n.* **1.** the short weak high-pitched cry of a young bird; chirp. ~*vb.* **2.** to utter such sounds. [imit.]

cheer (tʃɪə) *vb.* **1.** (usually foll. by *up*) to make or become happy or hopeful; comfort or be comforted. **2.** to applaud or encourage with shouts. ~*n.* **3.** a shout of applause or encouragement. **4.** state of mind; spirits (archaic except in **be of good cheer**). [Middle English (in the sense: face, welcoming aspect), from Greek *kara* head]

cheerful ('tʃɪəful) *adj.* **1.** having a happy disposition; in good spirits. **2.** pleasantly bright: *a cheerful room.* **3.** ungrudging: *cheerful help.* —'**cheerfully** *adv.* —'**cheerfulness** *n.*

cheerio (,tʃɪərɪ'əʊ) *interj. Informal, chiefly Brit.* a farewell greeting.

cheerleader ('tʃɪəˌliːdə) *n. U.S. & Canad.* a person who leads a crowd in cheers, usually at sports events.

cheerless ('tʃɪəlɪs) *adj.* dreary or gloomy.

cheers (tʃɪəz) *interj. Informal, chiefly Brit.* **1.** a drinking toast. **2.** goodbye! **3.** thanks!

cheery ('tʃɪərɪ) *adj.* **cheerier, cheeriest.** cheerful. —'**cheerily** *adv.* —'**cheeriness** *n.*

cheese[1] ('tʃiːz) n. **1.** a food made from coagulated milk curd. **2.** a block of this. **3.** a substance of similar consistency: *lemon cheese*. [Latin *cāseus*] —'**cheesy** adj.

cheese[2] ('tʃiːz) n. **big cheese.** an important person. [perhaps from Hindi *chiz* thing]

cheeseburger ('tʃiːzˌbɜːɡə) n. a hamburger cooked with a slice of cheese on top of it.

cheesecake ('tʃiːzˌkeɪk) n. **1.** a rich tart with a filling or topping which contains cream cheese. **2.** *Slang.* women, usually scantily clad, displayed for their sex appeal.

cheesecloth ('tʃiːzˌklɒθ) n. a loosely woven cotton cloth.

cheesed off adj. Brit. slang. bored, disgusted, or angry. [origin unknown]

cheeseparing ('tʃiːzˌpeərɪŋ) adj. **1.** stingy. ~n. **2.** stinginess.

cheetah ('tʃiːtə) n. a large feline of Africa and SW Asia: the swiftest mammal, having very long legs, and a black-spotted coat. [Hindi *cītā*]

chef (ʃef) n. a cook, usually the principal cook in a restaurant. [French]

chef-d'oeuvre (ˌʃeɪˈdɜːvrə) n., pl. **chefs-d'oeuvre** (ˌʃeɪˈdɜːvrə). a masterpiece. [French]

Chelsea Pensioner ('tʃelsɪ) n. an inhabitant of the Chelsea Royal Hospital in SW London, a home for old and infirm soldiers.

chem. **1.** chemical. **2.** chemist. **3.** chemistry.

chemical ('kemɪkᵊl) n. **1.** any substance used in or resulting from a reaction involving changes to atoms or molecules. ~adj. **2.** of or used in chemistry. **3.** of, made from, or using chemicals: *chemical fertilizer*. —'**chemically** adv.

chemical engineering n. the applications of chemistry in industrial processes. —**chemical engineer** n.

chemical warfare n. warfare using weapons such as gases, poisons, and defoliants.

chemin de fer (ʃəˈmæ̃ də ˈfeə) n. a gambling game, a variation of baccarat. [French: railway, referring to the fast tempo of the game]

chemise (ʃəˈmiːz) n. a woman's old-fashioned loose-fitting undergarment or dress. [Late Latin *camisa*]

chemist ('kemɪst) n. **1.** Brit. a shop selling medicines and cosmetics. **2.** Brit. a qualified dispenser of prescribed medicines. **3.** a specialist in chemistry. [Medieval Latin *alchimista* alchemist]

chemistry ('kemɪstrɪ) n. the branch of science concerned with the composition, properties, and reactions of substances.

chemotherapy (ˌkiːməʊˈθerəpɪ) n. treatment of disease by means of chemical agents.

chemurgy ('kemɜːdʒɪ) n. the branch of chemistry concerned with the industrial use of organic raw materials, esp. from farms. [*chemo-* chemical + Greek *ergon* work]

chenille (ʃəˈniːl) n. **1.** a thick soft tufty yarn. **2.** a fabric made of this. [French]

cheque or U.S. **check** (tʃek) n. a written order to someone's bank to pay money from their account to the person to whom the cheque is made out. [from *check*, in the sense: means of verification]

cheque book ('tʃekˌbʊk) n. a book of detachable blank cheques issued by a bank.

cheque card n. a plastic card issued by a bank guaranteeing payment of a customer's cheques up to a specified value.

chequer or U.S. **checker** ('tʃekə) n. **1.** a piece used in Chinese chequers. **2. a.** a pattern of squares. **b.** one of the squares in such a pattern. ~vb. **3.** to make irregular in colour or character; variegate. **4.** to mark with alternating squares of colour. ~See also **chequers.** [Middle English: chessboard]

chequered or U.S. **checkered** ('tʃekəd) adj. marked by varied fortunes: *a chequered career*.

chequers or U.S. **checkers** ('tʃekəz) n. (functioning as sing.) the game of draughts.

cherish ('tʃerɪʃ) vb. **1.** to hold dear; care for. **2.** to cling to (an idea or feeling): *to cherish a hope*. [Latin *cārus* dear]

cheroot (ʃəˈruːt) n. a cigar with both ends cut off squarely. [Tamil *curuttu* curl, roll]

cherry ('tʃerɪ) n., pl. **-ries. 1.** a small round fleshy fruit containing a hard stone. **2.** the wood of the tree bearing this fruit. ~adj. **3.** cold red. [Greek *kerasios*]

cherub ('tʃerəb) n., pl. **cherubs** or (for sense 1) **cherubim** ('tʃerəbɪm, -bɪm). **1.** Christianity. an angel, often represented as a winged child. **2.** an innocent or sweet child. [Hebrew *kĕrūbh*] —**cherubic** (tʃəˈruːbɪk) adj.

chervil ('tʃɜːvɪl) n. a Eurasian plant with aniseed-flavoured leaves used as herb. [Old English *cerfelle*]

chess (tʃes) n. a game of skill for two players using a chessboard on which chessmen are moved. The object is to checkmate the opponent's king. [Old French *esches*, pl. of *eschec* check]

chessboard ('tʃesˌbɔːd) n. a square board divided into 64 squares of two alternating colours, used for playing chess or draughts.

chessman ('tʃesˌmæn, -mən) n., pl. **-men.** a piece used in chess. [Middle English *chessemeyne* chess company]

chest (tʃest) n. **1.** the front of the body, from the neck to the belly. **2. get (something) off one's chest.** Informal. to unburden oneself of (worries or secrets) by talking about them. **3.** a heavy box for storage or shipping: *a tea chest*. [Greek *kistē* box]

chesterfield ('tʃestəˌfiːld) n. a large sofa with straight arms of the same height as the back. [after a 19th-cent. Earl of *Chesterfield*]

chestnut ('tʃesˌnʌt) n. **1.** the edible nut of a N temperate tree. **2.** the hard wood of this tree. **3.** a horse of a reddish-brown colour. **4.** Informal. an old or stale joke. ~adj. **5.** reddish-brown. [Greek *kastanea*]

chest of drawers *n.* a piece of furniture consisting of a set of drawers in a frame.

chesty (ˈtʃɛstɪ) *adj.* **chestier, chestiest.** *Brit. informal.* suffering from or symptomatic of chest disease: *a chesty cough.* —ˈ**chestiness** *n.*

cheval glass (ʃəˈvæl) *n.* a full-length mirror mounted so as to swivel within a frame. [French *cheval* support (lit.: horse)]

chevalier (ˌʃɛvəˈlɪə) *n.* **1.** a member of the French Legion of Honour. **2.** a chivalrous man. [Medieval Latin *caballārius* horseman]

Cheviot (ˈtʃiːvɪət, ˈtʃɛv-) *n.* **1.** a large British breed of sheep reared for its wool. **2.** (*often not cap.*) a rough woollen fabric. [*Cheviot* Hills on borders of England & Scotland]

chevron (ˈʃɛvrən) *n.* a V-shaped pattern or device, usually one on a military uniform to indicate rank. [Old French: rafter]

chew (tʃuː) *vb.* **1.** to work the jaws and teeth in order to grind (food). **2.** to bite repeatedly: *she chewed her nails anxiously.* **3. chew the fat** or **rag.** *Slang.* **a.** to discuss a point. **b.** to talk idly; gossip. ~*n.* **4.** the act of chewing. **5.** something that is chewed. [Old English *ceowan*]

chewing gum *n.* a flavoured gum used for chewing.

chew over *vb.* to consider carefully.

chewy (ˈtʃuːɪ) *adj.* **chewier, chewiest.** of a consistency requiring a lot of chewing.

chez (ʃeɪ) *prep.* at the home of. [French]

chianti (kɪˈæntɪ) *n.* (*sometimes cap.*) a dry red wine produced in Tuscany, Italy.

chiaroscuro (kɪˌɑːrəˈskjʊərəʊ) *n., pl.* **-ros.** the distribution of light and shade in a picture. [Italian *chiaro* clear + *oscuro* obscure]

chic (ʃiːk) *adj.* **1.** stylish or elegant. ~*n.* **2.** stylishness; fashionable good taste. [French]

chicane (ʃɪˈkeɪn) *n.* **1.** an obstacle placed on a motor-racing circuit to slow the cars down. **2.** a less common word for **chicanery.** ~*vb.* **3.** to trick by chicanery. **4.** to use chicanery. [French *chicaner* to quibble]

chicanery (ʃɪˈkeɪnərɪ) *n., pl.* **-eries.** **1.** clever but deceptive talk. **2.** a trick or deception.

chick (tʃɪk) *n.* **1.** the young of a domestic fowl or other bird. **2.** *Slang.* a girl or young woman. [short for *chicken*]

chicken (ˈtʃɪkɪn) *n.* **1.** a domestic fowl bred for its flesh or eggs. **2.** the flesh of this bird used for food. **3.** *Slang.* a coward. **4.** *Slang.* a young person: *she's no chicken.* **5. count one's chickens before they are hatched.** to be overoptimistic in acting on expectations which are not yet fulfilled. ~*adj.* **6.** *Slang.* cowardly; timid. [Old English *cicen*]

chicken feed *n. Slang.* a trifling amount of money.

chicken-hearted or **chicken-livered** *adj.* easily frightened; cowardly.

chicken out *vb. Informal.* to fail to do something through cowardice.

chickenpox (ˈtʃɪkɪnˌpɒks) *n.* an infectious viral disease usually affecting children, characterized by an itchy rash.

chicken wire *n.* wire netting.

chickpea (ˈtʃɪkˌpiː) *n.* the edible pealike seed of a Mediterranean and Asian plant. [Latin *cicer* chickpea]

chickweed (ˈtʃɪkˌwiːd) *n.* a common garden weed with small white flowers.

chicle (ˈtʃɪkᵊl) *n.* a gumlike substance used to make chewing gum. [Mexican Indian *chictli*]

chicory (ˈtʃɪkərɪ) *n., pl.* **-ries.** **1.** a plant cultivated for its leaves, which are used in salads, and for its roots. **2.** the root of this plant, roasted, dried, and used as a coffee substitute. [Greek *kikhōrion*]

chide (tʃaɪd) *vb.* **chiding, chided** or **chid** (tʃɪd); **chided, chid** or **chidden** (ˈtʃɪdᵊn). to rebuke or scold. [Old English *cīdan*]

chief (tʃiːf) *n.* **1.** the head of a group or body of people. **2. in chief.** primarily; especially. ~*adj.* **3.** most important; principal. **4.** highest in rank. [Latin *caput* head]

chiefly (ˈtʃiːflɪ) *adv.* **1.** especially or essentially. **2.** mainly; mostly.

chief petty officer *n.* a senior noncommissioned officer in a navy.

chieftain (ˈtʃiːftən, -tɪn) *n.* the leader of a tribe or clan. [Late Latin *capitāneus* commander] —ˈ**chieftaincy** or ˈ**chieftain-ˌship** *n.*

chief technician *n.* a noncommissioned officer in the Royal Air Force.

chiffchaff (ˈtʃɪfˌtʃæf) *n.* a European warbler with a yellowish-brown plumage. [imit.]

chiffon (ʃɪˈfɒn, ˈʃɪfɒn) *n.* **1.** a fine almost transparent fabric of silk or nylon. ~*adj.* **2.** made of chiffon. **3.** *Cooking.* having a very light fluffy texture. [French *chiffe* rag]

chiffonier or **chiffonnier** (ˌʃɪfəˈnɪə) *n.* **1.** a tall elegant chest of drawers. **2.** a wide low open-fronted cabinet. [French]

chignon (ˈʃiːnjɒn) *n.* a roll or knot of long hair arranged at the back of the head. [French]

chigoe (ˈtʃɪgəʊ) *n.* a tropical flea which burrows into the skin. Also: **chigger** (ˈtʃɪgə). [Carib *chigo*]

Chihuahua (tʃɪˈwɑːwɑː, -wə) *n.* a tiny short-haired dog, originally from Mexico. [after *Chihuahua*, state in Mexico]

chilblain (ˈtʃɪlˌbleɪn) *n.* an inflammation of the fingers or toes, caused by exposure to cold. [CHILL (*n.*) + BLAIN]

child (tʃaɪld) *n., pl.* **children. 1.** a boy or girl between birth and puberty. **2.** a baby or infant. **3.** an unborn baby. **4. with child.** *Old-fashioned.* pregnant. **5.** a son or daughter. **6.** a childish or immature person. **7.** a descendant: *a child of Israel.* **8.** the product of an influence or environment: *a child of nature.* [Old English *cild*] —ˈ**childless** *adj.* —ˈ**childlessness** *n.*

childbearing (ˈtʃaɪldˌbɛərɪŋ) *n.* **a.** the process of giving birth to a child. **b.** (*as modifier*): *of childbearing age.*

child benefit n. Brit. a regular government payment to parents of children up to a certain age.

childbirth ('tʃaɪld,bɜːθ) n. the act of giving birth to a child.

childhood ('tʃaɪldhʊd) n. the time or condition of being a child.

childish ('tʃaɪldɪʃ) adj. 1. of or like a child. 2. immature; silly: childish fears.

childlike ('tʃaɪld,laɪk) adj. like or befitting a child, as in being innocent or trustful.

child minder n. a person who looks after children whose parents are working.

children ('tʃɪldrən) n. the plural of **child**.

child's play n. Informal. something easy to do.

chill (tʃɪl) n. 1. a moderate coldness. 2. a feeling of coldness resulting from a cold or damp environment or from sudden fear. 3. a feverish cold. 4. a depressing influence. ~adj. 5. chilly. ~vb. 6. to make or become cold. 7. to cool (something). 8. to depress. [Old English ciele] —'**chilling** adj. —'**chillingly** adv. —'**chillness** n.

chiller ('tʃɪlə) n. 1. short for **spine-chiller**. 2. N.Z. a refrigerated storage area for meat.

chilli or **chili** ('tʃɪlɪ) n., pl. **chillies** or **chilies.** the small red or green hot-tasting pod of a type of capsicum, used in cookery, often in powdered form. [Mexican Indian]

chilli con carne (kɒn 'kɑːnɪ) n. a highly seasoned Mexican dish of meat, onions, beans, and chilli powder. [Spanish: chilli with meat]

chilly ('tʃɪlɪ) adj. **-lier, -liest.** 1. causing or feeling moderately cold. 2. without warmth; unfriendly. —'**chilliness** n.

chilly bin n. N.Z. informal. a portable insulated container with provision for packing food and drink in ice.

Chiltern Hundreds ('tʃɪltən) pl. n. (in Britain) short for **Stewardship of the Chiltern Hundreds;** a nominal office that an MP applies for in order to resign his seat.

chime (tʃaɪm) n. 1. a bell or the sound it makes when struck. Also called: **bell.** a percussion instrument consisting of a set of hanging metal tubes which are struck with a hammer. ~vb. 3. **a.** to ring (a bell) or (of a bell) to be rung. **b.** to produce (music or sounds) by chiming. 4. to indicate (time) by chiming. 5. (foll. by with) to agree or harmonize. [Latin cymbalum cymbal]

chimera or **chimaera** (kaɪ'mɪərə, kɪ-) n. 1. (often cap.) Greek myth. a fire-breathing monster with the head of a lion, body of a goat, and tail of a serpent. 2. a grotesque product of the imagination. [Greek khimaira she-goat]

chimerical (kaɪ'mɛrɪkˀl, kɪ-) or **chimeric** adj. 1. wildly fanciful; imaginary. 2. indulging in fantasies.

chimney ('tʃɪmnɪ) n. 1. a hollow vertical structure that carries smoke or steam away from a fire or engine. 2. same as **flue.** 3. a glass tube protecting the flame of an oil or gas lamp. 4. the vent of a volcano. 5. a vertical fissure in a rock face. [Greek kaminos oven]

chimney breast n. the walls surrounding the base of a chimney or fireplace.

chimneypot ('tʃɪmnɪ,pɒt) n. a short pipe on the top of a chimney.

chimney stack n. the part of a chimney projecting above a roof.

chimney sweep or **sweeper** n. a person who cleans soot from chimneys.

chimp (tʃɪmp) n. Informal. short for **chimpanzee.**

chimpanzee (,tʃɪmpæn'ziː) n. an intelligent anthropoid ape of central W Africa. [Central African dialect]

chin (tʃɪn) n. 1. the front part of the face below the lips. 2. **keep one's chin up.** Informal. to keep cheerful under difficult circumstances. 3. **take it on the chin.** Informal. to face squarely up to a defeat or difficulty. [Old English]

Chin. 1. China. 2. Chinese.

china ('tʃaɪnə) n. 1. ceramic ware of a type originally from China. 2. crockery. 3. (modifier) made of china. [Persian chīnī]

china clay n. same as **kaolin.**

Chinaman ('tʃaɪnəmən) n., pl. **-men.** Archaic or offensive. a man from China.

Chinatown ('tʃaɪnə,taʊn) n. any town outside China with a mainly Chinese population.

chinchilla (tʃɪn'tʃɪlə) n. 1. a small S American rodent bred in captivity for its soft silvery grey fur. 2. the fur of this animal. [Spanish]

chine (tʃaɪn) n. 1. the backbone. 2. a cut of meat including part of the backbone. 3. a ridge of land. ~vb. 4. to cut (meat) along the backbone. [Old French eschine]

Chinese (tʃaɪ'niːz) adj. 1. of China, its people, or their languages. ~n. 2. (pl. -nese) a person from China or a descendant of one. 3. any of the languages of China.

Chinese chequers n. (functioning as sing.) a game played with marbles or pegs on a six-pointed star-shaped board.

Chinese lantern n. a collapsible lantern made of thin paper.

Chinese leaves pl. n. the edible leaves of a Chinese plant of the cabbage family.

Chinese puzzle n. a complicated puzzle or problem.

chink¹ (tʃɪŋk) n. a fissure or crack. [Old English cine crack]

chink² (tʃɪŋk) vb. 1. to make or cause to make a light ringing sound, as by the striking of glasses or coins. ~n. 2. such a sound. [imit.]

chinless wonder ('tʃɪnlɪs) n. Brit. informal. a person, usually upper-class, lacking strength of character.

chinoiserie (ʃiːn,wɑːzə'riː, -'wɑːzəri) n. 1. a style of decorative art based on imitations of Chinese motifs. 2. an object or objects in this style. [French chinois Chinese]

Chinook (tʃɪ'nuːk, -'nʊk) n. 1. (pl. -nook or -nooks) a N American Indian people of the Pacific coast. 2. the language of this people.

Chinook salmon *n.* a Pacific salmon valued as a food fish.

chinos ('tʃiːnəʊz) *pl. n.* trousers made of a durable cotton twill cloth. [*chino*, the cloth; origin unknown]

chintz (tʃɪnts) *n.* a printed, patterned cotton fabric with a glazed finish. [Hindi *chīnt*]

chintzy ('tʃɪntsɪ) *adj.* chintzier, chintziest. 1. of, like, or covered with chintz. 2. *Brit. informal.* typical of the decor associated with the use of chintz soft furnishings.

chinwag ('tʃɪn‚wæg) *n. Brit. informal.* a chat.

chip (tʃɪp) *n.* 1. a small piece removed by chopping, cutting, or breaking. 2. a mark left after a small piece has been broken off something. 3. (in gambling) a counter used to represent money. 4. a thin strip of potato fried in deep fat. 5. *U.S. & Canad.* a potato crisp. 6. *Electronics.* a tiny wafer of semiconductor material, such as silicon, processed to form an integrated circuit. 7. a thin strip of wood or straw used for weaving hats and baskets. 8. **chip off the old block.** *Informal.* a person who resembles one of his or her parents in behaviour. 9. **have a chip on one's shoulder.** *Informal.* to be resentful or bear a grudge. 10. **have had one's chips.** *Brit. informal.* to be defeated, doomed, or killed. 11. **when the chips are down.** *Informal.* at a time of crisis. ~*vb.* **chipping, chipped.** 12. to break small pieces from or be broken off in small pieces: *will the paint chip?* 13. to break or cut into small pieces: *to chip ice.* 14. to shape by chipping. [Old English]

chip-based *adj.* using microchips.

chipboard ('tʃɪp‚bɔːd) *n.* a thin rigid board made of compressed wood particles.

chip heater *n. Austral. & N.Z.* a domestic water heater that burns chips of wood.

chip in *vb. Informal.* 1. to contribute (money) to a cause or fund. 2. to interrupt with a remark.

chipmunk ('tʃɪp‚mʌŋk) *n.* a squirrel-like striped burrowing rodent of North America and Asia. [American Indian]

chipolata (‚tʃɪpə'lɑːtə) *n. Chiefly Brit.* a small sausage. [Italian *cipolla* onion]

Chippendale ('tʃɪpən‚deɪl) *adj.* (of furniture) by or in the style of Thomas Chippendale (?1718-79): having Chinese and Gothic motifs, curved legs, and massive carving.

chirography (kaɪ'rɒɡrəfɪ) *n.* same as **calligraphy.** [Greek *kheir* hand + *graphein* to write]

chiromancy ('kaɪrə‚mænsɪ) *n.* same as **palmistry.** [Greek *kheir* hand + *manteia* prophesying]

chiropody (kɪ'rɒpədɪ) *n.* the treatment of minor foot complaints like corns. —**chiropodist** *n.*

chiropractic (‚kaɪrə'præktɪk) *n.* a system of treating bodily disorders by manipulation of the spine and other parts. [Greek *kheir* hand + *praktikos* practical] —**chiro‚practor** *n.*

chirp (tʃɜːp) *vb.* 1. (of some birds and insects) to make a short high-pitched

sound. 2. to speak in a lively fashion. ~*n.* 3. a chirping sound. [imit.]

chirpy ('tʃɜːpɪ) *adj.* chirpier, chirpiest. *Informal.* cheerful; lively. —**'chirpiness** *n.*

chirrup ('tʃɪrəp) *vb.* 1. (of some birds) to chirp repeatedly. ~*n.* 2. such a sound. [var. of *chirp*]

chisel ('tʃɪz'l) *n.* 1. a hand tool for working wood, stone, or metal, consisting of a flat steel blade sharpened at one end. ~*vb.* -elling, -elled *or U.S.* -eling, -eled. 2. to carve (a material) or form (something) with or as if with a chisel. 3. *Slang.* to cheat or get by cheating. [Latin *caesus* cut] —**'chiseller** *or U.S.* **-eler** *n.*

chit[1] (tʃɪt) *n.* 1. a voucher for a small sum of money owed. 2. Also called: **chitty.** *Chiefly Brit.* **a.** a note or memorandum. **b.** a requisition or receipt. [Hindi *cittha* note]

chit[2] (tʃɪt) *n. Facetious.* a pert, impudent, or self-confident girl. [Middle English: young animal, kitten]

chitchat ('tʃɪt‚tʃæt) *n.* gossip.

chitin ('kaɪtɪn) *n.* the tough substance forming the outer covering of the bodies of arthropods. [Greek *khitōn* tunic]

chitterlings ('tʃɪtəlɪŋz) *pl. n.* (sometimes *sing.*) the intestines of a pig or other animal prepared as a dish. [origin unknown]

chivalrous ('ʃɪvəlrəs) *adj.* 1. gallant; courteous. 2. of chivalry. —**'chivalrously** *adv.*

chivalry ('ʃɪvəlrɪ) *n., pl.* -ries. 1. the qualities expected of a medieval knight, such as courage, honour, and a readiness to help the weak. 2. courteous behaviour, esp. towards women. 3. the medieval system and principles of knighthood. [Old French *chevaler* knight] —**'chivalric** *adj.*

chive (tʃaɪv) *n.* a small Eurasian plant, whose long slender hollow leaves are used in cooking for their onion-like flavour. [Latin *caepa* onion]

chivy *or* **chivvy** ('tʃɪvɪ) *vb.* chivying, chivied *or* chivvying, chivvied. *Brit.* to harass or nag. [prob. from *Chevy Chase*, a Scottish ballad]

chloral ('klɔːrəl) *n.* 1. a colourless pungent oily liquid used to make chloral hydrate and DDT. 2. short for **chloral hydrate.**

chloral hydrate *n.* a colourless crystalline solid produced by the reaction of chloral with water and used as a sedative.

chlorate ('klɔːreɪt, -rɪt) *n.* any salt containing the ion ClO_3^-.

chloric ('klɔːrɪk) *adj.* of or containing chlorine in the pentavalent state.

chloride ('klɔːraɪd) *n.* 1. any salt of hydrochloric acid, containing the chloride ion Cl^-. 2. any compound containing a chlorine atom.

chlorinate ('klɔːrɪ‚neɪt) *vb.* 1. to combine or treat (a substance) with chlorine. 2. to disinfect (water) with chlorine. —**chlori'nation** *n.*

chlorine ('klɔːriːn) *n.* an element, a toxic

pungent greenish-yellow gas, used in water purification, and as a disinfectant and bleaching agent. Symbol: Cl

chloro- *combining form.* green. [Greek *khlōros*]

chlorofluorocarbon (ˌklɔːrəˌfluərəʊˈkɑːbˀn) *n. Chem.* any of various gaseous compounds of carbon, hydrogen, chlorine, and fluorine, used as refrigerants and aerosol propellants: some break down the ozone in the atmosphere.

chloroform (ˈklɔːrəˌfɔːm) *n.* a liquid with a sweet odour, used as a solvent and cleansing agent, and formerly as an inhalation anaesthetic. [CHLORO- + *formyl*: see FORMIC ACID]

chlorophyll *or U.S.* **chlorophyl** (ˈklɔːrəfɪl) *n.* the green pigment of plants that traps the energy of sunlight for photosynthesis: used as a colouring agent (E140) in medicines and food. [CHLORO- + Greek *phullon* leaf]

chloroplast (ˈklɔːrəʊˌplæst) *n.* one of the parts of a plant cell that contains chlorophyll. [CHLORO- + Greek *plastos* formed]

chock (tʃɒk) *n.* **1.** a block or wedge of wood used to prevent the sliding or rolling of a heavy object. ~*vb.* **2.** to fit with or secure by a chock. [origin unknown]

chock-a-block *adj., adv.* filled to capacity.

chock-full *adj.* completely full.

chocolate (ˈtʃɒkəlɪt, ˈtʃɒklɪt, -lət) *n.* **1.** a food made from roasted ground cacao seeds, usually sweetened and flavoured. **2.** a drink or sweet made from this. ~*adj.* **3.** deep brown. [Aztec *xocolatl*] —ˈchocolaty *adj.*

choice (tʃɔɪs) *n.* **1.** a choosing or selecting. **2.** the opportunity or power of choosing. **3.** a person or thing chosen or that may be chosen: *he was a possible choice.* **4.** an alternative action or possibility: *what choice did I have?* **5.** a range from which to select. ~*adj.* **6.** of superior quality: *choice wine.* [Old French *choisir* to choose] —ˈchoiceness *n.*

choir (ˈkwaɪə) *n.* **1.** an organized group of singers, usually for singing in church. **2.** the part of a church, in front of the altar, occupied by the choir. [Latin *chorus*]

choirboy (ˈkwaɪəˌbɔɪ) *n.* a young boy who sings the treble part in a church choir.

choke (tʃəʊk) *vb.* **1.** to hinder or stop the breathing of (a person or animal) by strangling or asphyxiation. **2.** to have trouble in breathing, swallowing, or speaking. **3.** to block or clog (something) up. **4.** to retard the growth or action of: *the weeds are choking my plants.* ~*n.* **5.** a device in the carburettor of a petrol engine that enriches the petrol-air mixture by reducing the air supply. **6.** *Electronics.* a device used to prevent the passage of high frequencies or to smooth the output of a rectifier. [Old English *ācēocian*] —ˈchoky *or* ˈchokey *adj.*

choke back *or* **down** *vb.* to suppress (anger, tears, or other emotions).

choker (ˈtʃəʊkə) *n.* **1.** a woman's high collar. **2.** a tightly-fitting necklace.

choke up *vb.* **1.** to block (something) completely. **2.** (*usually passive*) *Informal.* to overcome (a person) with emotion.

choko (ˈtʃəʊkəʊ) *n., pl.* **-kos.** *Austral. & N.Z.* the cucumber-like fruit of a tropical American vine. [Brazilian Indian]

choler (ˈkɒlə) *n.* anger or ill humour. [Old French]

cholera (ˈkɒlərə) *n.* a dangerous intestinal infection characterized by severe diarrhoea and cramp: caused by ingestion of contaminated water or food. [Greek *kholē* bile] —**choleraic** (ˌkɒləˈreɪk) *adj.*

choleric (ˈkɒlərɪk) *adj.* bad-tempered.

cholesterol (kəˈlestəˌrɒl) *n.* a fatty alcohol found in all animal fats, tissues, and fluids: thought to contribute to atherosclerosis. [Greek *kholē* bile + *stereos* solid]

chomp (tʃɒmp) *vb.* **1.** to chew (food) noisily. ~*n.* **2.** the act or sound of chewing in this manner.

chook (tʃʊk) *n. Informal, chiefly Austral. & N.Z.* a hen or chicken.

choose (tʃuːz) *vb.* **choosing, chose, chosen.** **1.** to select (a person, thing, or course of action) from a number of alternatives. **2.** to consider it desirable or proper: *I don't choose to read that book.* **3.** to like; please: *you may stand if you choose.* [Old English *ceosan*]

choosy (ˈtʃuːzɪ) *adj.* **choosier, choosiest.** *Informal.* particular; fussy; hard to please.

chop[1] (tʃɒp) *vb.* **chopping, chopped.** **1.** (*often foll. by down or off*) to cut (something) with a blow from an axe or other sharp tool. **2.** (*often foll. by up*) to cut into pieces. **3.** *Brit. informal.* to dispense with or reduce. **4.** *Sport.* to hit (a ball) sharply downwards. **5.** *Boxing, karate.* to hit (an opponent) with a short sharp blow. ~*n.* **6.** a cutting blow. **7.** a slice of mutton, lamb, or pork, usually including a rib. **8.** *Sport.* a sharp downward blow or stroke. **9. the chop.** *Slang, chiefly Brit.* dismissal from employment. [var. of CHAP[1]]

chop[2] (tʃɒp) *vb.* **chopping, chopped.** **chop and change.** to change one's ideas or plans repeatedly; vacillate. **2. chop logic.** to use excessively subtle or involved argument. [Old English *ceapian* to barter]

chop chop *adv. Pidgin English.* quickly.

chophouse (ˈtʃɒpˌhaʊs) *n.* a restaurant specializing in steaks, grills, and chops.

chopper (ˈtʃɒpə) *n.* **1.** *Chiefly Brit.* a small hand axe. **2.** a butcher's cleaver. **3.** *Informal.* a helicopter. **4.** a type of bicycle or motorcycle with very high handlebars. **5.** *N.Z.* a child's bicycle.

choppy (ˈtʃɒpɪ) *adj.* **-pier, -piest.** (of the sea) fairly rough. —ˈchoppiness *n.*

chops (tʃɒps) *pl. n.* **1.** the jaws; jowls. **2.** the mouth. **3. lick one's chops.** *Informal.* to anticipate something with pleasure. [origin unknown]

chopsticks (ˈtʃɒpstɪks) *pl. n.* a pair of thin sticks of ivory, wood, or plastic, used as eating utensils by the Chinese and Japanese. [pidgin English, from Chinese: quick ones]

chop suey (ˈsuːɪ) *n.* a Chinese-style dish

consisting of chopped meat, bean sprouts, and other vegetables, fried in soy sauce and served with rice. [Chinese *tsap sui* odds and ends]

choral ('kɔːrəl) *adj.* of or for a chorus or choir.

chorale *or* **choral** (kɒ'rɑːl) *n.* **1.** a slow stately hymn tune. **2.** *Chiefly U.S.* a choir or chorus. [German *Choralgesang* choral song]

chord[1] (kɔːd) *n.* **1.** *Maths.* a straight line connecting two points on a curve or curved surface. **2.** *Anat.* same as **cord.** **3.** an emotional response, usually of sympathy: *the story struck the right chord.* [Greek *khordē* string]

chord[2] (kɔːd) *n.* the simultaneous sounding of three or more musical notes. [short for *accord*]

chore (tʃɔː) *n.* **1.** a small routine task. **2.** an unpleasant task. [Old English *cierr*]

chorea (kɒ'rɪə) *n.* a disorder of the nervous system characterized by uncontrollable brief jerky movements. [Greek *khoreia* dance]

choreography (ˌkɒrɪ'ɒɡrəfɪ) *n.* **1.** the composition of dance steps and movements for ballet and other dancing. **2.** the steps and movements of a ballet or dance. **3.** the art of dancing. [Greek *khoreia* dance] —ˌchore'ographer *n.* —**choreographic** (ˌkɒrɪə'ɡræfɪk) *adj.*

chorister ('kɒrɪstə) *n.* a singer in a choir, usually a choirboy.

chortle ('tʃɔːt'l) *vb.* **1.** to chuckle gleefully. ~*n.* **2.** a gleeful chuckle. [coined by Lewis Carroll]

chorus ('kɔːrəs) *n., pl.* **-ruses.** **1.** a large choir of singers or a piece of music composed for such a choir. **2.** a body of singers or dancers who perform together. **3.** the refrain of a song. **4.** (in ancient Greece) a group of actors who commented on the action of a play. **5.** (in Elizabethan drama) **a.** the actor who spoke the prologue and epilogue. **b.** the part spoken by this actor. **6. a.** a group of people or animals producing words or sounds in unison. **b.** the words or sounds produced by such a group: *the dawn chorus.* **7. in chorus.** in unison. ~*vb.* **8.** to sing or utter (words or sounds) in unison. [Greek *khoros*]

chorus girl *n.* a girl who dances or sings in the chorus of a show or film.

chose (tʃəʊz) *vb.* the past tense of **choose.**

chosen ('tʃəʊz'n) *vb.* **1.** the past participle of **choose.** ~*adj.* **2.** selected for some special quality.

chough (tʃʌf) *n.* a large black bird of the crow family, found in parts of Europe, Asia, and Africa. [origin unknown]

choux pastry (ʃuː) *n.* a very light pastry made with eggs. [French *pâte choux* cabbage dough]

chow (tʃaʊ) *n.* **1.** *Informal.* food. **2.** a thick-coated dog with a curled tail, originally from China. [pidgin English]

chowder ('tʃaʊdə) *n. Chiefly U.S. & Canad.* a thick soup or stew containing clams or fish. [French *chaudière* kettle]

chow mein (meɪn) *n.* a Chinese-American dish, consisting of chopped meat or vegetables, fried with noodles. [Chinese]

Chr. 1. Christ. **2.** Christian.

chrism ('krɪzəm) *n.* consecrated oil used for sacramental anointing in the Greek Orthodox and Roman Catholic Churches. [Greek *khriein* to anoint]

Christ (kraɪst) *n.* **1.** Jesus of Nazareth (Jesus Christ), regarded by Christians as the Messiah of Old Testament prophecies. **2.** the Messiah of Old Testament prophecies. **3.** an image or picture of Christ. ~*interj.* **4.** *Taboo slang.* an oath expressing annoyance or surprise. [Greek *khristos* anointed one]

christen ('krɪs'n) *vb.* **1.** same as **baptize.** **2.** to give a name to (a person or thing). **3.** *Informal.* to use for the first time. [Old English *cristnian*] —**'christening** *n.*

Christendom ('krɪs'ndəm) *n.* the collective body of Christians throughout the world.

Christian ('krɪstʃən) *n.* **1.** a person who believes in and follows Jesus Christ. **2.** *Informal.* a person who possesses Christian virtues. ~*adj.* **3.** of Jesus Christ, Christians, or Christianity. **4.** (*sometimes not cap.*) exhibiting kindness or goodness.

Christian Era *n.* the period beginning with the year of Christ's birth.

Christianity (ˌkrɪstɪ'ænɪtɪ) *n.* **1.** the Christian religion. **2.** Christian beliefs or practices. **3.** same as **Christendom.**

Christianize *or* **-ise** ('krɪstʃəˌnaɪz) *vb.* **1.** to convert to Christianity. **2.** to imbue with Christian principles, spirit, or outlook. —ˌChristiani'zation *or* -i'sation *n.*

Christian name *n. Brit.* a personal name formally given to Christians at baptism: loosely used to mean any person's first name.

Christian Science *n.* the religious system founded by Mary Baker Eddy (1866), which emphasizes spiritual healing. —**Christian Scientist** *n.*

Christmas ('krɪsməs) *n.* **a.** the annual commemoration by Christians of the birth of Christ, held by most Churches to have occurred on Dec. 25. **b.** Also: **Christmas Day.** Dec. 25, as a day of secular celebrations when gifts and greetings are exchanged. [Old English *Crīstes mæsse* Mass of Christ] —**'Christmassy** *adj.*

Christmas box *n.* a tip or present given at Christmas, esp. to postmen or tradesmen.

Christmas Eve *n.* the evening or the whole day before Christmas Day.

Christmas pudding *n. Brit.* a rich steamed pudding containing suet, dried fruit, and spices.

Christmas rose *n.* an evergreen plant of S Europe and W Asia with white or pinkish winter-blooming flowers.

Christmas tree *n.* an evergreen tree or an imitation of one, decorated as part of Christmas celebrations.

chromate ('krəʊmeɪt) *n.* any salt or ester of chromic acid.

chromatic (krəˈmætɪk) adj. 1. of or in colour or colours. 2. Music. a. involving the sharpening or flattening of notes or the use of such notes. b. of the chromatic scale. [Greek khrōma colour] —chro-ˈmatically adv.

chromatics (krəʊˈmætɪks) n. (functioning as sing.) the science of colour.

chromatic scale n. a twelve-note scale including all the semitones of the octave.

chromatin (ˈkrəʊmətɪn) n. the part of the nucleus that forms the chromosomes and stains easily. [from chrome]

chromatography (ˌkrəʊməˈtɒɡrəfɪ) n. the technique of separating and analysing the components of a mixture of liquids or gases by selective adsorption. [Greek khrōma colour]

chrome (krəʊm) n. 1. another word for **chromium**. 2. anything plated with chromium. ~vb. 3. to plate or be plated with chromium. [Greek khrōma colour]

chromite (ˈkrəʊmaɪt) n. a brownish-black mineral which is the only commercial source of chromium.

chromium (ˈkrəʊmɪəm) n. a hard grey metallic element; used in steel alloys and electroplating to increase hardness and corrosion resistance. Symbol: Cr [from chrome]

chromosome (ˈkrəʊməˌsəʊm) n. any of the microscopic rod-shaped structures that appear in a cell nucleus during cell division, consisting of units (genes) that are responsible for the transmission of hereditary characteristics. [Greek khrōma colour + sōma body]

chromosphere (ˈkrəʊməˌsfɪə) n. a gaseous layer of the sun's atmosphere extending from the photosphere to the corona. [Greek khrōma colour + sphere]

chronic (ˈkrɒnɪk) adj. 1. continuing for a long time; constantly recurring. 2. (of a disease) developing slowly or lasting for a long time. 3. hardened; habitual: a chronic smoker. 4. Informal. a. very bad: the play was chronic. b. very serious: he left her in a chronic condition. [Greek khronos time] —ˈchronically adv. —chronicity (krɒˈnɪsɪtɪ) n.

chronicle (ˈkrɒnɪkˀl) n. 1. a record of events in chronological order. ~vb. 2. to record in or as if in a chronicle. [Greek khronika annals] —ˈchronicler n.

chronological (ˌkrɒnəˈlɒdʒɪkˀl) adj. 1. (esp. of a sequence of events) arranged in order of occurrence. 2. relating to or in accordance with chronology. —ˌchrono-ˈlogically adv.

chronology (krəˈnɒlədʒɪ) n., pl. -gies. 1. the determination of the proper sequence of past events. 2. the arrangement of dates or events in order of occurrence. 3. a table of events arranged in order of occurrence. [Greek khronos time + -LOGY] —chroˈnologist n.

chronometer (krəˈnɒmɪtə) n. a timepiece designed to be accurate in all conditions: used esp. at sea. [Greek khronos time + -METER]

chrysalis (ˈkrɪsəlɪs) n. the pupa of a moth

or butterfly, in a case or cocoon. [Greek khrusos gold]

chrysanthemum (krɪˈsænθəməm) n. a garden plant with brightly coloured showy flower heads in autumn. [Greek khrusos gold + anthemon flower]

chrysoberyl (ˈkrɪsəˌberɪl) n. a rare very hard greenish-yellow mineral used as a gemstone. [Greek khrusos gold + bērulios beryl]

chrysolite (ˈkrɪsəˌlaɪt) n. a brown or yellowish-green olivine: used as a gemstone. [Greek khrusos gold + lithos stone]

chrysoprase (ˈkrɪsəˌpreɪz) n. an apple-green variety of chalcedony: used as a gemstone. [Greek khrusos gold + prason leek]

chub (tʃʌb) n., pl. chub or chubs. a common European freshwater game fish of the carp family with a cylindrical dark greenish body. [origin unknown]

chubby (ˈtʃʌbɪ) adj. -bier, -biest. (esp. of the human form) plump and round. [perhaps from chub] —ˈchubbiness n.

chuck¹ (tʃʌk) vb. 1. Informal. to throw. 2. to pat (someone) affectionately under the chin. 3. Informal. (sometimes foll. by in or up) to give up; reject: he chucked up his job. ~n. 4. a throw or toss. 5. a pat under the chin. ~See also chuck off, chuck out. [origin unknown]

chuck² (tʃʌk) n. 1. Also: chuck steak. a cut of beef from the neck to the shoulder blade. 2. a device that holds a workpiece in a lathe or a tool in a drill. [var. of chock]

chuck³ (tʃʌk) n. W Canada. 1. a large body of water. 2. Also: saltchuck. the sea. [American Indian]

chuckle (ˈtʃʌkˀl) vb. 1. to laugh softly or to oneself. ~n. 2. a partly suppressed laugh. [prob. from chuck cluck]

chuck off vb. (often foll. by at) Austral. & N.Z. informal. to sneer.

chuck out vb. Informal. to throw out.

chuddy (ˈtʃʌdɪ) n. Austral. & N.Z. informal. chewing gum.

chuff (tʃʌf) n. 1. a puffing sound, as of a steam engine. ~vb. 2. to move while emitting such sounds. [imit.]

chuffed (tʃʌft) adj. Brit. slang. pleased or delighted: he was chuffed by his pay rise. [origin unknown]

chug (tʃʌɡ) n. 1. a short dull sound, as of an engine. ~vb. chugging, chugged. 2. (esp. of an engine) to operate while making such sounds. [imit.]

chukker or **chukka** (ˈtʃʌkə) n. Polo. a period of continuous play, usually 7½ minutes. [Hindi cakkar]

chum (tʃʌm) n. 1. Informal. a close friend. ~vb. chumming, chummed. 2. (usually foll. by up with) to be or become a close friend (of). [prob. from chamber fellow]

chummy (ˈtʃʌmɪ) adj. -mier, -miest. Informal. friendly. —ˈchummily adv. —ˈchumminess n.

chump (tʃʌmp) n. 1. Informal. a stupid person. 2. a thick heavy block of wood. 3. the thick blunt end of anything, esp. of a piece of meat. **4. off one's chump.** *Brit. slang.* crazy. [origin unknown]

chunk (tʃʌŋk) *n.* **1.** a thick solid piece, such as one of meat or wood. **2.** a considerable amount. [var. of CHUCK²]

chunky ('tʃʌŋkɪ) *adj.* **chunkier, chunkiest. 1.** thick and short. **2.** containing thick pieces. **3.** *Chiefly Brit.* (of clothes, esp. knitwear) made of thick bulky material. —**'chunkiness** *n.*

church (tʃɜːtʃ) *n.* **1.** a building for public Christian worship. **2.** public worship. **3.** the clergy as distinguished from the laity. **4.** (*usually cap.*) institutional religion as a political or social force: *conflict between Church and State.* **5.** (*usually cap.*) the collective body of all Christians. **6.** (*often cap.*) a particular Christian denomination or group. [Greek *kuriakon* (*dōma*) the Lord's (house)]

churchgoer ('tʃɜːtʃˌɡəʊə) *n.* a person who attends church regularly.

Church of England *n.* the reformed established state Church in England, with the sovereign as its temporal head.

Church of Scotland *n.* the established Presbyterian church in Scotland.

churchwarden (ˌtʃɜːtʃˈwɔːdᵊn) *n.* **1.** *Church of England, Episcopal Church.* one of two assistants of a parish priest who administer the secular affairs of the church. **2.** a long-stemmed tobacco pipe made of clay.

churchyard ('tʃɜːtʃˌjɑːd) *n.* the grounds round a church, used as a graveyard.

churl (tʃɜːl) *n.* **1.** a surly ill-bred person. **2.** *Archaic.* a farm labourer. [Old English *ceorl*] —**'churlish** *adj.*

churn (tʃɜːn) *n.* **1.** *Brit.* a large container for milk. **2.** a vessel or machine in which cream or whole milk is vigorously agitated to produce butter. ~*vb.* **3. a.** to agitate (milk or cream) to make butter. **b.** to make (butter) by this process. **4.** (sometimes foll. by *up*) to move with agitation. [Old English *ciern*]

churn out *vb. Informal.* to produce (something) rapidly and in large numbers.

chute¹ (ʃuːt) *n.* an inclined channel or vertical passage down which water, parcels, coal, etc., may be dropped. [Old French *cheoite* a fall]

chute² (ʃuːt) *n., vb. Informal.* short for **parachute.**

chutney ('tʃʌtnɪ) *n.* a pickle of Indian origin, made from fruit, vinegar, spices, and sugar: *mango chutney.* [Hindi *catni*]

chutzpah ('xʊtspə) *n. U.S. & Canad. informal.* shameless audacity; impudence. [Yiddish]

chyle (kaɪl) *n.* a milky fluid formed in the small intestine during digestion. [Greek *khulos* juice]

chyme (kaɪm) *n.* the thick fluid mass of partially digested food that leaves the stomach. [Greek *khumos* juice]

chypre ('ʃiːprə) *n.* a perfume made from sandalwood. [French: Cyprus]

Ci curie.

CI Channel Islands.

CIA Central Intelligence Agency; a U.S. bureau that conducts espionage and intelligence activities.

cicada (sɪˈkɑːdə) *n.* a large broad insect, most common in warm regions: the males produce a high-pitched drone. [Latin]

cicatrix ('sɪkətrɪks) *n., pl.* **cicatrices** (ˌsɪkəˈtraɪsiːz). the tissue that forms in a wound during healing; scar. [Latin: scar]

cicerone (ˌsɪsəˈrəʊnɪ, ˌtʃɪtʃ-) *n., pl.* **-nes** or **-ni** (-nɪ). a person who guides and informs sightseers. [after *Cicero*, Roman orator]

CID (in Britain) Criminal Investigation Department; the detective division of a police force.

cider ('saɪdə) *n.* an alcoholic drink made from the fermented juice of apples. [Hebrew *shēkhār* strong drink]

CIF cost, insurance, and freight (included in the price quoted).

cigar (sɪˈɡɑː) *n.* a cylindrical roll of cured tobacco leaves, for smoking. [Spanish *cigarro*]

cigarette (ˌsɪɡəˈrɛt) *n.* a short tightly rolled cylinder of tobacco, wrapped in thin paper for smoking. [French: a little cigar]

cilium ('sɪlɪəm) *n., pl.* **cilia** ('sɪlɪə). **1.** one of the short threads projecting from a cell or organism, whose rhythmic beating causes movement. **2.** an eyelash. [Latin] —**'ciliary** *adj.*

C in C *Mil.* Commander in Chief.

cinch (sɪntʃ) *n.* **1.** *Slang.* an easy task. **2.** *Slang.* a certainty. **3.** *U.S. & Canad.* same as **girth** (sense 2). [Latin *cingere* to encircle]

cinchona (sɪŋˈkəʊnə) *n.* **1.** a South American tree or shrub with medicinal bark. **2.** its dried bark which yields quinine. **3.** a drug made from cinchona bark. [after the Countess of *Chinchón*]

cincture ('sɪŋktʃə) *n.* something that encircles, esp. a belt or girdle. [Latin *cingere* to gird]

cinder ('sɪndə) *n.* **1.** a piece of material that will not burn, left after burning coal or wood. **2.** (*pl.*) ashes. [Old English *sinder*]

Cinderella (ˌsɪndəˈrɛlə) *n.* **1.** a girl who achieves fame after being obscure. **2.** a poor, neglected, or unsuccessful person or thing. [after *Cinderella*, the heroine of a fairy tale]

cine- *combining form.* indicating motion pictures or cinema: *cine camera.*

cinema ('sɪnɪmə) *n.* **1.** *Chiefly Brit.* a place designed for showing films. **2.** **the cinema. a.** the art or business of making films. **b.** films collectively. [shortened from *cinematograph*] —**cinematic** (ˌsɪnɪˈmætɪk) *adj.*

cinematograph (ˌsɪnɪˈmætəˌɡrɑːf) *Chiefly Brit.* ~*n.* **1.** a combined camera, printer, and projector. ~*vb.* **2.** to take (pictures) with a film camera. [Greek *kinēma* motion + -GRAPH] —**cinematographer** (ˌsɪnɪməˈtɒɡrəfə) *n.* —**cinematographic** (ˌsɪnɪˌmætəˈɡræfɪk) *adj.* —**cinematography** *n.*

cineraria (ˌsɪnəˈrɛərɪə) *n.* a plant grown

for its blue, purple, red, or variegated daisy-like flowers. [Latin *cinis* ashes]

cinerarium (ˌsɪnəˈrɛərɪəm) *n.*, *pl.* **-raria** (-ˈrɛərɪə). a place for keeping the ashes of the dead after cremation. [Latin *cinerārius* relating to ashes] —**cinerary** (ˈsɪnərərɪ) *adj.*

cinnabar (ˈsɪnəˌbɑː) *n.* **1.** a heavy red mineral: the chief ore of mercury. **2.** a large red-and-black European moth. ~*adj.* **3.** bright red; vermilion. [Greek *kinnabari*]

cinnamon (ˈsɪnəmən) *n.* **1.** the spice obtained from the aromatic bark of a tropical Asian tree, used for flavouring food and drink. ~*adj.* **2.** light yellowish-brown. [Hebrew *qinnamown*]

cinque (sɪŋk) *n.* the number five in cards or dice. [Old French *cinq* five]

cinquefoil (ˈsɪŋkˌfɔɪl) *n.* **1.** a plant with five-lobed compound leaves. **2.** an ornamental carving in the form of five arcs arranged in a circle. [Latin *quinquefolium* plant with five leaves]

Cinque Ports *pl. n.* an association of ports on the SE coast of England, with certain ancient duties and privileges.

cipher *or* **cypher** (ˈsaɪfə) *n.* **1.** a method of secret writing using substitution of letters according to a key. **2.** a secret message. **3.** the key to a secret message. **4.** *Obs.* the numeral zero. **5.** a person or thing of no importance; nonentity. ~*vb.* **6.** to put (a message) into secret writing. [Arabic *sifr* zero]

circa (ˈsɜːkə) *prep.* (used with a date) approximately; about: *circa 1182* B.C. [Latin]

circadian (sɜːˈkeɪdɪən) *adj.* of biological processes that occur regularly at 24-hour intervals. [Latin *circa* about + *diēs* day]

circle (ˈsɜːkʰl) *n.* **1.** a closed plane curve every point of which is equidistant from a given fixed point, the centre. **2.** the figure enclosed by such a curve. **3.** *Theatre.* the section of seats above the main level of the auditorium. **4.** something formed or arranged in the shape of a circle. **5.** a group of people sharing an interest, activity, or upbringing: *golf circles; a family circle.* **6.** a process or chain of events or parts that forms a connected whole; cycle. **7. come full circle.** to arrive back at one's starting point. ~*vb.* **8.** to move in a circle (around). **9.** to enclose in a circle; encircle. [Latin *circus*]

circlet (ˈsɜːklɪt) *n.* a small circle or ring, esp. a circular ornament worn on the head. [Old French]

circuit (ˈsɜːkɪt) *n.* **1.** a complete route or course, esp. one that is circular or that lies around an object. **2.** a complete path through which an electric current can flow. **3. a.** a periodical journey around an area, as made by judges or salesmen. **b.** the places visited on such a journey. **4.** a number of theatres or cinemas under one management. **5.** *Sport.* a series of tournaments in which the same players regularly take part: *the international tennis circuit.* **6.** *Chiefly Brit.* a motor-racing track. [Latin *circum* around + *īre* to go]

circuit breaker *n.* a device that stops the flow of current in an electrical circuit if there is a fault.

circuitous (sɜːˈkjuːɪtəs) *adj.* indirect and lengthy; roundabout: *a circuitous route.*

circuitry (ˈsɜːkɪtrɪ) *n.* **1.** the design of an electrical circuit. **2.** the system of circuits used in an electronic device.

circular (ˈsɜːkjʊlə) *adj.* **1.** of or like a circle. **2.** circuitous. **3.** (of arguments) not valid because a statement is used to prove the conclusion and the conclusion to prove the statement. **4.** travelling or occurring in a cycle. **5.** (of letters or announcements) intended for general distribution. ~*n.* **6.** a printed advertisement or notice for mass distribution. —**circularity** (ˌsɜːkjʊˈlærɪtɪ) *n.*

circularize *or* **-ise** (ˈsɜːkjʊləˌraɪz) *vb.* to distribute circulars to.

circular saw *n.* a power-driven saw in which a circular disc with a toothed edge is rotated at high speed.

circulate (ˈsɜːkjʊˌleɪt) *vb.* **1.** to send, go, or pass from place to place or person to person: *don't circulate the news.* **2.** to distribute or be distributed over a wide area. **3.** to move or cause to move through a circuit or system, returning to the starting point: *blood circulates through the body.* [Latin *circulārī*] —**circulatory** (ˌsɜːkjʊˈleɪtərɪ) *adj.*

circulating library *n. Chiefly U.S.* a library that lends out books.

circulation (ˌsɜːkjʊˈleɪʃən) *n.* **1.** the flow of blood from the heart through the arteries, and then back through the veins to the heart, where the cycle is renewed. **2.** the spreading of something to a wider group of people or area. **3.** (of air and water) free movement within an area or volume. **4. a.** the distribution of newspapers or magazines. **b.** the number of copies of an issue that are distributed. **5. in circulation. a.** (of currency) serving as a medium of exchange. **b.** (of people) active in a social or business context.

circum- *prefix.* around; surrounding; on all sides: *circumlocution.* [Latin]

circumambient (ˌsɜːkəmˈæmbɪənt) *adj.* surrounding. [Latin CIRCUM- + *ambīre* to go round]

circumcise (ˈsɜːkəmˌsaɪz) *vb.* **1.** to remove the foreskin of (a male). **2.** to incise the skin over, or remove, the clitoris of (a female). **3.** to perform such an operation as a religious rite on (someone). [Latin CIRCUM- + *caedere* to cut] —**circumcision** (ˌsɜːkəmˈsɪʒən) *n.*

circumference (səˈkʌmfərəns) *n.* **1.** the boundary of a specific area or figure, esp. of a circle. **2.** the length of a closed geometric curve, esp. of a circle. [Latin CIRCUM- + *ferre* to bear] —**circumferential** (səˌkʌmfəˈrenʃəl) *adj.*

circumflex (ˈsɜːkəmˌfleks) *n.* a mark (ˆ) placed over a vowel to show that it is pronounced in a particular way, for instance as a long vowel in French. [Latin CIRCUM- + *flectere* to bend]

circumlocution (ˌsɜːkəmləˈkjuːʃən) *n.* **1.** an indirect way of expressing something.

2. an indirect expression. —**circumlocutory** (ˌsɜːkəmˈlɒkjətrɪ) adj.

circumnavigate (ˌsɜːkəmˈnævɪˌɡeɪt) vb. to sail or fly completely around. —ˌcircumˌnaviˈgation n.

circumscribe (ˈsɜːkəmˌskraɪb) vb. **1.** to restrict within limits. **2.** to mark or set the bounds of. **3.** to draw a geometric construction around (another construction) so that the two are in contact but do not intersect. [Latin CIRCUM- + scrībere to write] —**circumscription** (ˌsɜːkəmˈskrɪpʃən) n.

circumspect (ˈsɜːkəmˌspɛkt) adj. cautious, prudent, or discreet. [Latin CIRCUM- + specere to look] —ˌcircumˈspection n. —ˈcircumˌspectly adv.

circumstance (ˈsɜːkəmstəns) n. **1.** (usually pl.) a condition that accompanies or influences an event or condition. **2.** an incident or occurrence, esp. a chance one. **3. pomp and circumstance.** formal display or ceremony. **4. under or in no circumstances.** in no case; never. **5. under the circumstances.** because of conditions; this being the case. [Latin CIRCUM- + stāre to stand]

circumstantial (ˌsɜːkəmˈstænʃəl) adj. **1.** of or dependent on circumstances. **2.** fully detailed.

circumstantial evidence n. indirect evidence that tends to establish a conclusion by inference.

circumstantiate (ˌsɜːkəmˈstænʃɪˌeɪt) vb. to support by giving particulars.

circumvent (ˌsɜːkəmˈvɛnt) vb. **1.** to avoid or get round (a rule, restriction etc.). **2.** to outwit (a person). [Latin CIRCUM- + venīre to come] —ˌcircumˈvention n.

circus (ˈsɜːkəs) n., pl. -cuses. **1.** a travelling company of entertainers such as acrobats, clowns, trapeze artists, and trained animals. **2.** a public performance given by such a company. **3.** a travelling group of professional sportsmen: a cricket circus. **4.** (in ancient Rome) an open-air stadium for chariot races or public games. **5.** Brit. an open place in a town where several streets converge. **6.** Informal. noisy or rowdy behaviour. [Greek kirkos ring]

cirrhosis (sɪˈrəʊsɪs) n. a chronic progressive disease of the liver, often caused by drinking too much alcohol. [Greek kirrhos orange-coloured]

cirrocumulus (ˌsɪrəʊˈkjuːmjʊləs) n., pl. -li (-ˌlaɪ). a high cloud of ice crystals grouped into small separate globular masses.

cirrostratus (ˌsɪrəʊˈstraːtəs) n., pl. -ti (-taɪ). a uniform layer of cloud above about 6000 metres.

cirrus (ˈsɪrəs) n., pl. -ri (-raɪ). **1.** a thin wispy fibrous cloud at high altitudes, composed of ice particles. **2.** a plant tendril. **3.** a slender tentacle in certain sea creatures. [Latin: curl]

cisalpine (sɪsˈælpaɪn) adj. on this (the southern) side of the Alps, as viewed from Rome.

cisco (ˈsɪskəʊ) n., pl. -coes or -cos. a whitefish, esp. the lake herring of cold deep lakes of North America. [American Indian]

cissy (ˈsɪsɪ) n., pl. -sies, adj. same as sissy.

Cistercian (sɪˈstɜːʃən) n. **1.** a monk or nun who follows an especially strict form of the Benedictine rule. ~adj. **2.** of or relating to this order. [Cîteaux, original home of the order]

cistern (ˈsɪstən) n. **1.** a tank for the storage of water, esp. on or within the roof of a house or connected to a WC. **2.** an underground reservoir. [Latin cista box]

citadel (ˈsɪtədᵊl, -ˌdɛl) n. a stronghold within or close to a city. [Latin cīvitās]

citation (saɪˈteɪʃən) n. **1.** the quoting of a book or author. **2.** a passage or source cited. **3.** an official commendation or award, esp. for bravery.

cite (saɪt) vb. **1.** to quote or refer to (a passage, book, or author). **2.** to mention or commend (someone) for outstanding bravery. **3.** to summon to appear before a court of law. **4.** to enumerate: he cited the king's virtues. [Old French citer to summon]

citified (ˈsɪtɪˌfaɪd) adj. Often disparaging. having the customs, manners, or dress of city people.

citizen (ˈsɪtɪzᵊn) n. **1.** a native or naturalized member of a state or nation. **2.** an inhabitant of a city or town.

citizenry (ˈsɪtɪzənrɪ) n. citizens collectively.

Citizens' Band n. a range of radio frequencies assigned officially for use by the public for private communication.

citizenship (ˈsɪtɪzənˌʃɪp) n. the condition or status of a citizen, with its rights and duties.

citrate (ˈsɪtreɪt, -rɪt; ˈsaɪtreɪt) n. any salt or ester of citric acid.

citric (ˈsɪtrɪk) adj. of or derived from citrus fruits or citric acid.

citric acid n. a weak acid found in many fruits, esp. citrus fruits, and used in pharmaceuticals and as a flavouring (**E330**).

citron (ˈsɪtrən) n. **1.** a lemon-like fruit with a thick aromatic rind, which grows on a small Asian tree. **2.** the candied rind of this fruit. [Latin citrus citrus tree]

citronella (ˌsɪtrəˈnɛlə) n. **1.** a tropical Asian grass with bluish-green lemon-scented leaves. **2.** the yellow aromatic oil obtained from this grass, used in insect repellents, soaps, and perfumes.

citrus (ˈsɪtrəs) n., pl. -ruses. **1.** any tree or shrub of a tropical and subtropical genus which includes the orange, lemon, and lime. ~adj. also **citrous**. **2.** of or relating to the plants of this genus or their fruits. [Latin: citrus tree]

city (ˈsɪtɪ) n., pl. cities. **1.** any large town. **2.** (in Britain) a town that has received this title from the Crown: usually the seat of a bishop. **3.** (in the U.S. and Canada) a large town with its own government established by charter from the state or provincial government. **4.** the people of a city collectively. [Latin cīvis citizen]

City (ˈsɪtɪ) n. **the. 1.** the area in central

London in which the United Kingdom's major financial business is transacted. **2.** the various financial institutions in this area.

city editor *n.* (on a newspaper) **1.** *Brit.* the editor in charge of business news. **2.** *U.S. & Canad.* the editor in charge of local news.

city-state *n. Ancient history.* a state consisting of a sovereign city and its dependencies.

civet ('sIvIt) *n.* **1.** a spotted catlike mammal of Africa and S Asia, which secretes a powerful-smelling fluid. **2.** this fluid, used in the manufacture of perfumes. [Arabic *zabād* civet perfume]

civic ('sIvIk) *adj.* of or relating to a city, citizens, or citizenship. —**'civically** *adv.*

civic centre *n. Brit.* a complex of public buildings, including recreational facilities and offices of local administration.

civics ('sIvIks) *n.* (*functioning as sing.*) the study of the rights and responsibilities of citizenship.

civil ('sIv²l) *adj.* **1.** of the ordinary life of citizens, as distinguished from military, legal, or ecclesiastical affairs. **2.** of or relating to the citizen as an individual: *civil rights.* **3.** of or occurring within the state or between citizens: *civil strife.* **4.** polite or courteous: *a civil manner.* [Latin *cīvis* citizen] —**'civilly** *adv.*

civil defence *n.* the organizing of civilians to deal with enemy attacks.

civil disobedience *n.* a nonviolent protest, such as a refusal to obey laws or pay taxes.

civil engineer *n.* a person qualified to design and construct public works, such as roads or harbours. —**civil engineering** *n.*

civilian (sI'vIljən) *n.* **a.** a person who is not a member of the armed forces or police. **b.** (*as modifier*): *civilian life.*

civility (sI'vIlItI) *n., pl.* **-ties. 1.** politeness or courtesy. **2.** (*often pl.*) an act of politeness.

civilization *or* **-isation** (,sIvIlaI'zeIʃən) *n.* **1.** a human society that has a complex cultural, political, and legal organization. **2.** the peoples or nations collectively who have achieved such a state. **3.** the total culture and way of life of a particular people, nation, region, or period. **4.** intellectual, cultural, and moral refinement. **5.** cities or populated areas, as contrasted with sparsely inhabited areas.

civilize *or* **-ise** ('sIvI,laIz) *vb.* **1.** to bring out of savagery or barbarism into a state of civilization. **2.** to refine, educate, or enlighten. —**'civi,lized** *or* **-ised** *adj.*

civil law *n.* **1.** the law of a state, relating to private and civilian affairs. **2.** a system of law based on that of ancient Rome.

civil list *n.* (in Britain) the annual amount given by Parliament to the royal household and the royal family.

civil marriage *n. Law.* a marriage performed by an official other than a clergyman.

civil rights *pl. n.* **1.** the personal rights of the individual citizen. **2.** (*modifier*), of,

relating to, or promoting equality in social, economic, and political rights.

civil servant *n.* a member of the civil service.

civil service *n.* the service responsible for the public administration of the government of a country. It excludes the legislative, judicial, and military branches.

civil war *n.* war between parties or factions within the same nation.

civvies ('sIvIz) *pl. n. Slang.* civilian clothes as opposed to uniform.

civvy street ('sIvI) *n. Slang.* civilian life.

Cl *Chem.* chlorine.

clack (klæk) *vb.* **1.** to make a sound like that of two pieces of wood hitting each other. ~*n.* **2.** a short sharp sound. [imit.]

clad[1] (klæd) *vb.* past of **clothe.**

clad[2] (klæd) *vb.* **cladding, clad.** to bond a metal to (another metal), esp. to form a protective coating. [special use of CLAD[1]]

cladding ('klædIŋ) *n.* **1.** a protective metal coating bonded to another metal. **2.** the material used for the outside facing of a building, etc.

cladistics (klə'dIstIks) *n.* (*functioning as sing.*) a method of grouping animals by measurable likenesses. [Greek *klādos* branch]

claim (kleIm) *vb.* **1.** to demand as being due or as one's property: *he claimed the record.* **2.** to assert as a fact: *he claimed to be telling the truth.* **3.** to call for or need; deserve: *this problem claims our attention.* **4.** to take: *the accident claimed four lives.* ~*n.* **5.** an assertion of a right; a demand for something as due. **6.** an assertion of something as true, real, or factual. **7.** a right or just title to something: *a claim to fame.* **8.** anything that is claimed, such as a piece of land staked out by a miner. **9. a.** a demand for payment in connection with an insurance claim. **b.** the sum of money demanded. [Latin *clāmāre* to shout] —**'claimant** *n.*

clairvoyance (kleə'voIəns) *n.* **1.** the alleged power of perceiving things beyond the natural range of the senses. **2.** keen intuitive understanding. [French: clear-seeing]

clairvoyant (kleə'voIənt) *adj.* **1.** of or possessing clairvoyance. ~*n.* **2.** a person claiming to have the power to foretell future events.

clam (klæm) *n.* a sea creature with a soft edible body and a shell in two parts that closes tightly. See also **clam up.** [earlier *clamshell* shell that clamps]

clamber ('klæmbə) *vb.* **1.** to climb (something) awkwardly, using hands and feet. ~*n.* **2.** a climb performed in this manner. [prob. var. of *climb*]

clammy ('klæmI) *adj.* **-mier, -miest. 1.** unpleasantly sticky; moist. **2.** (of the weather) close; humid. [Old English *clǣman* to smear] —**'clammily** *adv.* —**'clamminess** *n.*

clamour *or U.S.* **clamor** ('klæmə) *n.* **1.** a loud persistent outcry. **2.** a strong expression of collective feeling or outrage. **3.** a loud and persistent noise. ~*vb.* **4.** (often foll. by *for* or *against*) to make a loud noise or outcry; make a public demand. [Latin *clāmāre* to cry out] —**'clamorous** *adj.*

clamp[1] (klæmp) *n.* **1.** a mechanical device with movable jaws with which an object can be secured to something else. **2.** See **wheel clamp.** ~*vb.* **3.** to fix or fasten with a clamp. **4.** to immobilize (a car) by means of a wheel clamp. [Dutch or Low German *klamp*]

clamp[2] (klæmp) *n.* a mound of a harvested root crop, covered with straw and earth to protect it from winter weather. [Middle Dutch *klamp* heap]

clamp down *vb.* **1.** (often foll. by *on*) to suppress (something regarded as undesirable). ~*n.* **clampdown. 2.** a sudden restrictive measure.

clam up *vb.* **clamming, clammed.** *Informal.* to keep or become silent.

clan (klæn) *n.* **1.** a group of people interrelated by ancestry or marriage. **2.** a group of families with a common surname and a common ancestor, esp. among the Scots. **3.** a group of people united by common characteristics, aims, or interests. [Scot. Gaelic *clann*] —**'clansman** *n.*

clandestine (klænˈdɛstɪn) *adj.* secret and concealed; furtive. [Latin *clam* secretly] —**clanˈdestinely** *adv.*

clang (klæŋ) *vb.* **1.** to make a loud resounding noise, as metal when struck. ~*n.* **2.** a resounding metallic noise. [Latin *clangere*]

clanger ('klæŋə) *n.* **drop a clanger.** *Informal.* to make a conspicuous mistake.

clangour *or U.S.* **clangor** ('klæŋə, 'klæŋgə) *n.* **1.** a loud resonant oftenrepeated noise. ~*vb.* **2.** to make or produce a loud resonant noise. [Latin] —**'clangorous** *adj.*

clank (klæŋk) *n.* **1.** an abrupt harsh metallic sound. ~*vb.* **2.** to make such a sound. [imit.]

clannish ('klænɪʃ) *adj.* **1.** of or characteristic of a clan. **2.** tending to associate closely within a group to the exclusion of outsiders; cliquish.

clap[1] (klæp) *vb.* **clapping, clapped. 1.** to make a sharp abrupt sound, as of two objects struck together. **2.** to applaud (someone or something) by striking the palms of one's hands together sharply. **3.** to strike (a person) lightly with an open hand as in greeting. **4.** to place or put quickly or forcibly: *they clapped him in jail.* **5. clap eyes on.** *Informal.* to catch sight of. ~*n.* **6.** the sharp abrupt sound produced by striking one's hands together. **7.** the act of clapping, esp. in applause. **8.** a sudden sharp sound, esp. of thunder. **9.** a light blow. [Old English *clæppan*]

clap[2] (klæp) *n.* (usually preceded by *the*) *Slang.* gonorrhoea. [Old French *clapier* brothel]

clapped out *adj. Informal.* **1.** *Brit., Austral., & N.Z.* worn out; dilapidated. **2.** *Austral. & N.Z.* extremely tired; exhausted.

clapper ('klæpə) *n.* **1.** a small piece of metal hanging inside a bell, which causes it to sound when struck against its side. **2.**

go, run, *or* **move like the clappers.** *Brit. informal.* to move extremely fast.

clapperboard ('klæpə,bɔːd) *n.* a pair of hinged boards clapped together during film shooting to aid in synchronizing sound and picture prints.

claptrap ('klæp,træp) *n. Informal.* foolish or pretentious talk: *politicians' claptrap.*

claque (klæk) *n.* **1.** a group of people hired to applaud. **2.** a group of fawning admirers. [French *claquer* to clap]

claret ('klærət) *n.* **1.** a red wine, esp. a Bordeaux. ~*adj.* **2.** purplish-red. [Latin *clārus* clear]

clarify ('klærɪ,faɪ) *vb.* **-fying, -fied. 1.** to make or become clear or easy to understand. **2.** to make or become free of impurities, esp. by heating: *clarified butter.* [Latin *clārus* clear + *facere* to make] —**,clarifiˈcation** *n.*

clarinet (,klærɪˈnɛt) *n.* a keyed woodwind instrument with a single reed. [French] —**,clariˈnettist** *n.*

clarion ('klærɪən) *n.* **1.** an obsolete highpitched small-bore trumpet. **2.** the sound of such an instrument or any similar sound. ~*adj.* **3.** clear and ringing; inspiring: *a clarion call to action.* [Latin *clārus* clear]

clarity ('klærɪtɪ) *n.* clearness. [Latin *clāritās*]

clash (klæʃ) *vb.* **1.** to make a loud harsh sound, esp. by striking together. **2.** to be incompatible. **3.** to engage together in conflict. **4.** (of dates or events) to coincide. **5.** (of colours) to look inharmonious together. ~*n.* **6.** a loud harsh noise. **7.** a collision or conflict. [imit.]

clasp (klɑːsp) *n.* **1.** a fastening, such as a catch or hook, for holding things together. **2.** a firm grasp or embrace. ~*vb.* **3.** to hold in a firm grasp. **4.** to grasp tightly in one's hands or arms. **5.** to fasten together with a clasp. [origin unknown]

clasp knife *n.* a large knife with blades which fold into the handle.

class (klɑːs) *n.* **1.** a group of people or things sharing a common characteristic. **2.** a group of persons sharing a similar social and economic position. **3.** the pattern of divisions that exist within a society on the basis of social or economic status. **4. a.** a group of pupils or students who are taught together. **b.** a meeting of a group of students for tuition. **5.** one of several grades, of accommodation, quality, or attainment: *second class.* **6.** *Informal.* excellence or elegance, esp. in dress, design, or behaviour. **7.** *Biol.* any of the groups into which a phylum is divided. **8. in a class by oneself** *or* **in a class of its own.** unequalled; unparalleled. ~*vb.* **9.** to assign a place within a group, grade, or class. [Latin *classis* class, rank]

class. 1. classic(al). **2.** classification. **3.** classified.

class-conscious *adj.* aware of belonging to a particular social rank.

classic ('klæsɪk) *adj.* **1.** of the highest class, esp. in art or literature. **2.** serving as a standard or model of its kind. **3.**

characterized by simplicity, balance, regularity, and purity of form; classical. **4.** of lasting interest or significance. ~*n.* **5.** an author, artist, or work of art of the highest excellence. **6.** a creation or work considered as definitive. [Latin *classicus* of the first rank]

classical ('klæsɪk³l) *adj.* **1.** of or influenced by the ancient Greeks and Romans or their civilization. **2.** *Music.* **a.** in a style or from a period marked by stability of form, intellectualism, and restraint. **b.** denoting serious art music in general. **3.** of or in a restrained conservative style: *a classical style of painting.* **4.** (of an education) based on the humanities and the study of Latin and Greek. **5.** of the form of a language historically used for formal and literary purposes: *classical Arabic.* —'**classically** *adv.*

classicism ('klæsɪ,sɪzəm) *n.* **1.** a style based on Greek and Roman models, showing emotional restraint and regularity of form. **2.** knowledge of the culture of ancient Greece and Rome. **3.** a Greek or Latin expression. —'**classicist** *n.*

classics ('klæsɪks) *pl. n.* **1. the.** a body of literature regarded as great or lasting. **2. the.** the ancient Greek and Latin languages. **3.** (*functioning as sing.*) ancient Greek and Roman culture as a subject for academic study.

classification (,klæsɪfɪ'keɪʃən) *n.* **1.** systematic placement in categories. **2.** one of the divisions in a system of classifying. [French] —,**classifi'catory** *adj.*

classify ('klæsɪ,faɪ) *vb.* **-fying, -fied. 1.** to arrange or order by classes; categorize. **2.** *Government.* to declare (information) to be of possible aid to an enemy and therefore to be kept secret. —'**classi,fiable** *adj.*

classmate ('klɑːs,meɪt) *n.* a friend or contemporary of the same class in a school.

classroom ('klɑːs,ruːm, -,rʊm) *n.* a room in which classes are conducted, esp. in a school.

classy ('klɑːsɪ) *adj.* **classier, classiest.** *Slang.* elegant; stylish. —'**classiness** *n.*

clatter ('klætə) *vb.* **1.** to make a rattling noise, esp. as a result of movement. ~*n.* **2.** a rattling sound or noise. [Old English *clatrung* clattering]

clause (klɔːz) *n.* **1.** *Grammar.* a group of words, consisting of a subject and a predicate including a finite verb, that does not necessarily constitute a sentence. **2.** a section of a legal document such as a contract, will, or draft statute. [Latin *clausula* conclusion] —'**clausal** *adj.*

claustrophobia (,klɔːstrə'fəʊbɪə, ,klɒs-) *n.* an abnormal fear of being in a confined space. [Latin *claustrum* cloister + -PHOBIA] —,**claustro'phobic** *adj.*

clavichord ('klævɪ,kɔːd) *n.* an early keyboard instrument with a very soft tone. [Latin *clāvis* key + *chorda* string]

clavicle ('klævɪk³l) *n.* either of the two bones connecting the shoulder blades with the upper part of the breastbone; the collarbone. [Latin *clāvis* key]

claw (klɔː) *n.* **1.** a curved pointed nail on

the foot of birds, some reptiles, and certain mammals. **2.** a corresponding structure in some invertebrates, such as the pincer of a crab. ~*vb.* **3.** to scrape, tear, or dig (something or someone) with claws. **4.** to create by scratching as with claws: *to claw an opening.* [Old English *clawu*]

claw back *vb.* **1.** to get back (something) with difficulty. **2.** to recover (a part of a grant or allowance) in the form of a tax or financial penalty.

clay (kleɪ) *n.* **1.** a very fine-grained material that occurs as rock or soil. It becomes plastic when moist but hardens on heating and is used in the manufacture of bricks, ceramics, etc. **2.** earth or mud. **3.** *Poetic.* the material of the human body. [Old English *clǣg*] —'**clayey**, '**clayish**, *or* '**clay,like** *adj.*

claymore ('kleɪ,mɔː) *n.* a large two-edged broadsword used formerly by Scottish Highlanders. [Gaelic *claidheamh mòr* great sword]

clay pigeon *n.* a disc of baked clay hurled into the air from a machine as a target to be shot at.

CLC Canadian Labour Congress.

clean (kliːn) *adj.* **1.** without dirt or other impurities; unsoiled. **2.** without anything in it or on it: *a clean page.* **3.** recently washed; fresh. **4.** free of radioactive contamination. **5.** pure; morally sound: *clean living.* **6.** without objectionable language or obscenity: *good clean fun.* **7.** thorough or complete: *a clean break.* **8.** dexterous or adroit: *a clean throw.* **9.** *Sport.* played fairly and without fouls. **10.** simple and streamlined in design: *a ship's clean lines.* **11.** habitually hygienic and neat. **12.** (esp. of a driving licence) showing or having no record of offences. **13.** *Slang.* **a.** innocent; not guilty. **b.** not carrying illegal drugs, weapons, etc. ~*vb.* **14.** to make or become free of dirt: *remember to clean your teeth; the stove cleans easily.* ~*adv.* **15.** in a clean way; cleanly. **16.** *Not standard.* completely: *clean forgotten.* **17. come clean.** *Informal.* to make a revelation or confession. ~*n.* **18.** the act or an instance of cleaning: *he gave his shoes a clean.* ~See also **clean up.** [Old English *clǣne*]

clean-cut *adj.* **1.** clearly outlined; neat: *clean-cut lines of a ship.* **2.** definite.

cleaner ('kliːnə) *n.* **1.** a person, device, or substance that removes dirt, as from clothes or carpets. **2.** (*usually pl.*) a shop or firm that provides a dry-cleaning service. **3. take a person to the cleaners.** *Informal.* to rob or defraud a person.

cleanly *adv.* ('kliːnlɪ). **1.** in a fair manner. **2.** easily or smoothly. ~*adj.* ('klɛnlɪ), **-lier, -liest. 3.** habitually clean or neat. —'**cleanliness** ('klɛnlɪnɪs) *n.*

cleanse (klɛnz) *vb.* **1.** to remove dirt, filth, etc., from. **2.** to remove guilt from. —'**cleanser** *n.*

clean-shaven *adj.* (of men) having the facial hair shaved off.

clean up *vb.* **1.** to rid (something) of dirt, filth, or other impurities. **2.** to make (someone or something) orderly or presentable. **3.** to rid (a place) of undesirable people or conditions. **4.** *Informal.* to make a great profit. ~*n.* **cleanup. 5.** the process of cleaning up.

clear (klɪə) *adj.* **1.** free from darkness or obscurity; bright. **2.** (of weather) free from dullness or clouds. **3.** transparent: *clear water.* **4.** even and pure in tone or colour. **5.** without blemish or defect: *a clear skin.* **6.** easy to see or hear; distinct. **7.** free from doubt or confusion. **8.** certain in the mind; sure: *are you clear?* **9.** perceptive, alert: *clear-headed.* **10.** evident or obvious: *it is clear that he won't come now.* **11.** (of sounds or the voice) not harsh or hoarse. **12.** without qualification or limitation; complete: *a clear victory.* **13.** free of suspicion, guilt, or blame: *a clear conscience.* **14.** free of obstruction; open: *a clear passage.* **15.** free from debt or obligation. **16.** (of money) without deduction; net. ~*adv.* **17.** in a clear or distinct manner. **18.** (often foll. by *of*) not in contact (with); free: *stand clear of the gates.* ~*n.* **19.** a clear space. **20. in the clear.** free of suspicion, guilt, or blame. ~*vb.* **21.** to make or become free from darkness or obscurity. **22. a.** (of the weather) to become free from dullness, fog, or rain. **b.** (of mist or fog) to disappear. **23.** to free from impurity or blemish. **24.** to free from doubt or confusion. **25.** to rid of objects or obstructions. **26.** to make or form (a path) by removing obstructions. **27.** to free or remove (a person or thing) from something, as of suspicion, blame, or guilt. **28.** to move or pass by or over without contact: *he cleared the wall easily.* **29.** to rid (one's throat) of phlegm. **30.** to make or gain (money) as profit. **31.** to discharge or settle (a debt). **32.** (of a cheque) to pass through one's bank and be charged against one's account. **33.** to obtain or give (clearance). **34.** to permit (someone) to see or handle classified information. **35. clear the air.** to dispel tension or confusion by settling misunderstandings. ~See also **clear away, clear off,** etc. [Latin *clārus* clear] —**'clearly** *adv.*

clearance ('klɪərəns) *n.* **1.** the process or an instance of clearing: *slum clearance.* **2.** space between two parts in motion or in relative motion. **3.** permission for a vehicle or passengers to proceed. **4.** official permission to have access to secret information or areas. **5. a.** the selling of goods at reduced prices. **b.** (*as modifier*): *a clearance sale.*

clear away *vb.* to remove (dishes, etc.) from (the table) after a meal.

clear-cut *adj.* **1.** definite; not vague: *a clear-cut proposal.* **2.** clearly outlined.

clearing ('klɪərɪŋ) *n.* an area with few or no trees or shrubs in wooded or overgrown land.

clearing bank *n.* (in Britain) any bank that makes use of the central clearing house in London.

clearing house *n.* **1.** *Banking.* an institution where cheques and other commercial papers drawn on member banks are cancelled against each other so that only net balances are payable. **2.** a central

agency for the collection and distribution of information or materials.

clear off *vb. Informal.* to go away: often used imperatively.

clear out *vb.* **1.** *Informal.* to go away: often used imperatively. **2.** to remove and sort the contents of (a room or container).

clear up *vb.* **1.** to explain or solve (a mystery or misunderstanding). **2.** to put (a place or thing that is disordered) in order. **3.** (of the weather) to become brighter.

clearway ('klɪə,weɪ) *n. Brit.* a stretch of road on which motorists may stop only in an emergency.

cleat (kliːt) *n.* **1.** a wedge-shaped block attached to a structure to act as a support. **2.** a device consisting of two prongs projecting in opposite directions from a central base, used for tying ropes or lines to. [Germanic]

cleavage ('kliːvɪdʒ) *n.* **1.** *Informal.* the separation between a woman's breasts, esp. as revealed by a low-cut dress. **2.** a division or split. **3.** (of crystals) the act of splitting or the tendency to split along definite planes so as to yield smooth surfaces.

cleave[1] (kliːv) *vb.* **cleaving; cleft, cleaved,** *or* **clove; cleft, cleaved,** *or* **cloven. 1.** to split, esp. along a natural weakness. **2.** to make by or as if by cutting: *to cleave a path.* [Old English *clēofan*]

cleave[2] (kliːv) *vb.* to cling or adhere. [Old English *cleofian*]

cleaver ('kliːvə) *n.* a heavy knife or long-bladed hatchet, esp. one used by butchers.

cleavers ('kliːvəz) *n.* (*functioning as sing.*) a Eurasian plant, with small white flowers and fruits which stick to clothing. [Old English *clīfe*]

clef (klɛf) *n.* a symbol placed at the beginning of each stave indicating the pitch of the music written after it. [French]

cleft (klɛft) *vb.* **1.** past of **cleave**[1]. ~*n.* **2.** a fissure or crevice. **3.** an indentation or split in something, such as the chin, palate, etc. ~*adj.* **4.** split; divided.

cleft palate *n.* a congenital crack in the midline of the hard palate.

clematis ('klɛmətɪs, klə'meɪtɪs) *n.* a N temperate climbing plant cultivated for its large colourful flowers. [Greek *klēma* vine twig]

clement ('klɛmənt) *adj.* **1.** merciful. **2.** (of the weather) mild. [Latin *clēmēns* mild] —**'clemency** *n.*

clementine ('klɛmən,tiːn, -,taɪn) *n.* a citrus fruit resembling a tangerine. [French]

clench (klɛntʃ) *vb.* **1.** to close or squeeze together (the teeth or a fist) tightly. **2.** to grasp or grip firmly. ~*n.* **3.** a firm grasp or grip. [Old English *beclencan*]

clerestory ('klɪə,stɔːrɪ) *n., pl.* **-ries.** a row of windows in the upper part of the wall of the nave of a church above the roof of the aisle. [*clear* + *storey*]

clergy ('klɜːdʒɪ) *n., pl.* **-gies.** the collective body of ordained ministers of the Christian Church. [see CLERK]

clergyman ('klɜːdʒɪmən) n., pl. **-men.** a member of the clergy.

cleric ('klerɪk) n. a member of the clergy.

clerical ('klerɪk'l) adj. **1.** relating to or associated with the clergy: *clerical dress.* **2.** of or relating to office clerks or their work: *a clerical error.*

clerical collar n. a stiff white collar with no opening at the front, which buttons at the back of the neck; worn by the clergy in certain Churches.

clerihew ('klerɪˌhjuː) n. a form of comic or satiric verse, consisting of two couplets and containing the name of a well-known person. [after E. *Clerihew* Bentley, who invented it]

clerk (klɑːk; *U.S.* klɜːrk) n. **1.** an employee in an office, bank, or court who keeps records, files, and accounts. **2.** *U.S. & Canad.* a hotel receptionist. **3.** *Archaic.* a scholar. ~vb. **4.** to serve as a clerk. [Greek *klērikos* cleric, from *klēros* heritage] —'**clerkship** n.

clerk of the works n. an employee who oversees building work.

clever ('klevə) adj. **1.** displaying sharp intelligence or mental alertness. **2.** skilful with one's hands. **3.** smart in a superficial way. **4.** *Brit. informal.* sly; cunning. [Middle English *cliver*] —'**cleverly** adv. —'**cleverness** n.

clianthus (klɪˈænθəs) n. a plant of Australia and New Zealand with ornamental clusters of slender flowers. [prob. from Greek *kleos* glory + *anthos* flower]

cliché ('kliːʃeɪ) n. an expression, idea, action, or habit that has become trite from overuse. [French] —'**clichéd** *or* 'cli-ché'd adj.

click (klɪk) n. **1.** a short light often metallic sound. **2.** the locking member of a ratchet mechanism. ~vb. **3.** to make a clicking sound: *to click one's heels.* **4.** *Slang.* to be a great success: *that idea really clicked.* **5.** *Informal.* to become suddenly clear: *it finally clicked when her name was mentioned.* **6.** *Slang.* (of two people) to get on well together: *they clicked from their first meeting.* [imit.]

client ('klaɪənt) n. **1.** someone who seeks the advice of a professional person or organization. **2.** a customer. [Latin *cliēns* retainer]

clientele (ˌkliːɒnˈtel) n. customers or clients collectively.

cliff (klɪf) n. a steep high rock face, esp. along the seashore. [Old English *clif*]

cliffhanger ('klɪfˌhæŋə) n. a situation of imminent disaster usually occurring at the end of each episode of a serialized film. —'**cliff**ˌ**hanging** adj.

climacteric (klaɪˈmæktərɪk, ˌklaɪmækˈterɪk) n. **1.** same as **menopause.** **2.** the period in the life of a man corresponding to the menopause, during which sexual drive and fertility diminish. [Greek *klimakter* rung of a ladder]

climate ('klaɪmɪt) n. **1.** the long-term prevalent weather conditions of an area.

2. an area having a particular kind of climate. **3.** a prevailing trend: *the political climate.* [Greek *klima* inclination, region] —**climatic** (klaɪˈmætɪk) adj. —cli'**matical-ly** adv.

climax ('klaɪmæks) n. **1.** the most intense or highest point of an experience or of a series of events: *the party was the climax of the week.* **2.** a decisive moment in a dramatic or other work. **3.** an orgasm. ~vb. **4.** *Not universally accepted.* to reach or bring to a climax. [Greek *klimax* ladder] —cli'**mactic** adj.

climb (klaɪm) vb. **1.** (often foll. by *up*) to go up or ascend (stairs, a mountain, etc.). **2.** (often foll. by *along*) to progress with difficulty: *to climb along a ledge.* **3.** to rise to a higher point or intensity: *the temperature climbed.* **4.** to incline or slope upwards: *the road began to climb.* **5.** to ascend in social position. **6.** (of plants) to grow upwards by twining, using tendrils or suckers. **7.** *Informal.* (foll. by *into*) to put on or get into. ~n. **8.** the act or an instance of climbing. **9.** a place or thing to be climbed, esp. a route in mountaineering. [Old English *climban*] —'**climbable** adj. —'**climber** n. —'**climbing** n., adj.

climb down vb. **1.** (often foll. by *from*) to retreat (from an opinion or position). ~n. **climb-down.** **2.** a retreat from an opinion or position.

clime (klaɪm) n. *Poetic.* a region or its climate.

clinch (klɪntʃ) vb. **1.** to secure (a driven nail), by bending the protruding point over. **2.** to settle (something, such as an argument or bargain) in a definite way. **3.** to engage in a clinch, as in boxing or wrestling. ~n. **4.** the act of clinching. **5.** *Boxing, wrestling.* an act or an instance in which one or both competitors hold on to the other to avoid punches or regain wind. **6.** *Slang.* a lovers' embrace. [var. of *clench*]

clincher ('klɪntʃə) n. *Informal.* something decisive, such as a fact, argument, or point scored.

cling (klɪŋ) vb. **clinging, clung. 1.** (often foll. by *to*) to hold fast or adhere closely to (something), as by gripping or sticking. **2.** (foll. by *together*) to remain in contact with each other. **3.** to be or remain physically or emotionally close. [Old English *clingan*] —'**clinging** *or* '**clingy** adj.

clingfilm ('klɪŋˌfɪlm) n. a thin polythene material having the power to seal closely: used for wrapping food.

clinic ('klɪnɪk) n. **1.** a place in which outpatients are given medical treatment or advice. **2.** a similar place staffed by specialist physicians or surgeons: *eye clinic.* **3.** *Brit.* a private hospital or nursing home. **4.** the teaching of medicine to students at the bedside. [Greek *klinē* bed]

clinical ('klɪnɪk'l) adj. **1.** of or relating to a clinic. **2.** of or relating to the observation and treatment of patients directly: *clinical medicine.* **3.** scientifically detached; strictly objective: *a clinical attitude to life.* **4.** (of buildings, decoration, or furniture) plain, simple, and usually unattractive. —'**clinically** adv.

clinical thermometer *n.* a thermometer for determining the temperature of the body.

clink[1] (klɪŋk) *vb.* **1.** to make a light and sharply ringing sound. ~*n.* **2.** such a sound. [perhaps from Middle Dutch *klinken*]

clink[2] (klɪŋk) *n. Slang.* prison. [after *Clink*, a former prison in London]

clinker ('klɪŋkə) *n.* the ash and partially fused residues from a coal-fired furnace or fire. [Dutch *klinker* a type of brick]

clinker-built *adj.* (of a boat or ship) having a hull constructed with each plank overlapping the one below. [obs. *clinker* a nailing together, prob. from *clinch*]

clip[1] (klɪp) *vb.* **clipping, clipped. 1.** to cut, snip, or trim with or as if with scissors or shears, esp. in order to shorten or remove a part. **2.** *Brit.* to punch a hole in (something, esp. a ticket). **3.** to remove a short section from (a film or newspaper). **4.** to shorten (a word). **5.** *Informal.* to strike with a sharp, often slanting, blow. **6.** *Slang.* to swindle, esp. by overcharging. ~*n.* **7.** the act or process of clipping. **8.** something clipped off. **9.** a short extract from a film or newspaper. **10.** *Informal.* a sharp, often slanting, blow. **11.** *Informal.* speed: *a rapid clip.* **12.** *Austral. & N.Z.* the total quantity of wool shorn, as in one place or season. [Old Norse *klippa* to cut]

clip[2] (klɪp) *n.* **1.** any of various small implements used to hold loose articles together or to attach one article to another. **2.** an article of jewellery that can be clipped onto a dress or hat. **3.** short for **paperclip** or **cartridge clip.** ~*vb.* **clipping, clipped. 4.** to hold together tightly, as with a clip. [Old English *clyppan* to embrace]

clipboard ('klɪp,bɔːd) *n.* a portable writing board with a clip at the top for holding paper.

clip joint *n. Slang.* a place, such as a nightclub or restaurant, in which customers are overcharged.

clipper ('klɪpə) *n.* a fast sailing ship.

clippers ('klɪpəz) *pl. n.* **1.** a hand tool for clipping fingernails, etc. **2.** a hairdresser's tool for cutting short hair.

clippie ('klɪpɪ) *n. Brit. informal.* a bus conductress.

clipping ('klɪpɪŋ) *n.* something cut out, esp. an article from a newspaper; cutting.

clique (kliːk) *n.* a small exclusive group of friends or associates. [French] —**'cliquey, 'cliquy,** or **cliquish** *adj.*

clitoris ('klɪtərɪs, 'klaɪ-) *n.* a small sexually sensitive erectile organ at the upper end of the vulva. [Greek *kleitoris*] —**'clitoral** *adj.*

Cllr councillor.

cloaca (kləʊ'eɪkə) *n., pl.* **-cae** (-siː). a cavity in most animals, except higher mammals, into which the alimentary canal and the genital and urinary ducts open. [Latin: sewer]

cloak (kləʊk) *n.* **1.** a loose sleeveless outer garment, fastened at the throat and falling straight from the shoulders. **2.** something

that covers or conceals. ~*vb.* **3.** to cover with or as if with a cloak. **4.** to hide or disguise. [Medieval Latin *clocca* cloak, bell]

cloak-and-dagger *n. (modifier)* of or involving intrigue and espionage.

cloakroom ('kləʊk,ruːm, -rum) *n.* **1.** a room in which hats or coats may be temporarily left. **2.** *Brit., euphemistic.* a toilet.

clobber[1] ('klɒbə) *vb. Slang.* **1.** to batter. **2.** to defeat utterly. **3.** to criticize severely. [origin unknown]

clobber[2] ('klɒbə) *n. Brit. slang.* personal belongings, such as clothes. [origin unknown]

cloche (klɒʃ) *n.* **1.** a small glass or plastic structure used to protect young plants. **2.** a woman's close-fitting hat. [French: bell]

clock[1] (klɒk) *n.* **1.** a device for showing the time, either through pointers that revolve over a numbered dial, or through a display of figures. **2.** any clocklike device for recording or measuring something. **3.** the downy head of a dandelion that has gone to seed. **4.** short for **time clock. 5.** *Informal.* same as **speedometer** or **mileometer. 6.** *Brit. slang.* the face. **7. round the clock.** all day and all night. ~*vb.* **8.** *Brit., Austral., & N.Z. slang.* to strike, esp. on the face or head. **9.** to record (time) as with a stopwatch, esp. in the calculation of speed. **10.** *Informal.* to turn back the mileometer on (a car) illegally so that its mileage appears less. [Medieval Latin *clocca* bell]

clock[2] (klɒk) *n.* an ornamental design on the side of a sock. [origin unknown]

clock off *or* **out** *vb.* to depart from work, esp. when it involves registering the time of departure on a card.

clock on *or* **in** *vb.* to arrive at work, esp. when it involves registering the time of arrival on a card.

clock up *vb.* to record or register: *this car has clocked up 80 000 miles.*

clockwise ('klɒk,waɪz) *adv., adj.* in the direction in which the hands of a clock rotate.

clockwork ('klɒk,wɜːk) *n.* **1.** the mechanism of a spring-driven clock. **2.** any similar mechanism, as in a wind-up toy. **3. like clockwork.** with complete regularity and precision; smoothly.

clod (klɒd) *n.* **1.** a lump of earth or clay. **2.** a dull or stupid person. [Old English] —**'cloddish** *adj.*

clodhopper ('klɒd,hɒpə) *n. Informal.* **1.** a clumsy person; lout. **2.** (*usually pl.*) a large heavy shoe.

clog (klɒg) *vb.* **clogging, clogged. 1.** to obstruct or become obstructed with thick or sticky matter. **2.** to encumber; hinder. **3.** to stick in a mass. ~*n.* **4.** any of various wooden or wooden-soled shoes. **5.** something that impedes motion or action; hindrance. [origin unknown]

cloisonné (klwɑː'zɒneɪ) *n.* a design made by filling in a wire outline with coloured enamel. [French]

cloister ('klɔɪstə) *n.* **1.** a covered walk, usually around a quadrangle in a religious institution, with an open colonnade on the inside. **2.** (*sometimes pl.*) a place of religious seclusion, such as a monastery. ~*vb.* **3.** to confine or seclude in or as if in a monastery. [Medieval Latin *claustrum* monastic cell, from Latin *claudere* to close] —'**cloistered** *adj.* —'**cloistral** *adj.*

clomp (klɒmp) *n., vb.* same as **clump** (senses 2, 3).

clone (kləʊn) *n.* **1.** a group of organisms or cells of the same genetic constitution that are descended from a common ancestor by asexual reproduction. **2.** *Informal.* a person or thing that closely resembles another. ~*vb.* **3.** to produce or cause to produce a clone. **4.** *Informal.* to produce near copies of (a person or thing). [Greek *klōn* twig, shoot] —'**cloning** *n.*

clonk (klɒŋk) *vb.* **1.** to make a loud dull thud. **2.** *Informal.* to hit. ~*n.* **3.** a loud thud. [imit.]

close[1] (kləʊs) *adj.* **1.** near in space or time; in proximity. **2.** having the parts near together; dense: *a close formation.* **3.** near to the surface; short: *a close haircut.* **4.** near in relationship: *a close relative.* **5.** intimate: *a close friend.* **6.** almost equal: *a close contest.* **7.** not deviating or varying greatly from something: *a close resemblance.* **8.** careful, strict, or searching: *a close study.* **9.** confined or enclosed. **10.** shut or shut tight. **11.** oppressive, heavy, or airless: *a close atmosphere.* **12.** strictly guarded: *close custody.* **13.** secretive or reticent. **14.** miserly; not generous. **15.** restricted as to public admission or membership. **16.** hidden or secluded. ~*adv.* **17.** closely; tightly. **18.** near or in proximity. [Latin *claudere* to close] —'**closely** *adv.* —'**closeness** *n.*

close[2] (kləʊz) *vb.* **1.** to shut: *the door closed behind him.* **2.** to bar, obstruct, or fill up (an entrance, a hole, etc.): *to close a road.* **3.** to bring the parts or edges of (something, such as a wound or circuit) together or (of a wound or circuit) to be brought together. **4.** to take hold: *his hand closed over the money.* **5.** to end; terminate. **6.** (of agreements or deals) to complete or be completed successfully. **7.** to cease or cause to cease giving service: *the shop closed at six.* **8.** *Stock Exchange.* to have a value at the end of a day's trading, as specified: *steels closed two points down.* ~*n.* **9.** the act of closing. **10.** the end or conclusion: *the close of the day.* **11.** (kləʊs). *Brit.* a courtyard or quadrangle enclosed by buildings. **12.** (kləʊs). *Scot.* the entry from the street to a tenement building. ~See also **close down, close in,** etc. [Old French *clos*]

closed (kləʊzd) *adj.* **1.** blocked against entry; shut. **2.** restricted; exclusive. **3.** not open to question or debate. **4.** *Maths.* **a.** (of a curve or surface) completely enclosing an area or volume. **b.** (of a set) made up of members on which a specific operation, such as addition, gives as its result another existing member of the set. **5.** not open to public entry or membership: *a closed society.*

closed circuit *n.* a complete electrical circuit through which current can flow.

closed-circuit television *n.* a television system in which signals are transmitted from the camera to the receivers by cables or telephone links.

close down (kləʊz) *vb.* **1.** to cease or cause to cease operations. ~*n.* **closedown. 2.** *Brit. radio, television.* the end of a period of broadcasting, esp. late at night.

closed shop *n.* a contract between a trade union and an employer permitting the employment of the union's members only.

close harmony (kləʊs) *n.* a type of singing in which all parts except the bass lie close together.

close in (kləʊz) *vb.* **1.** (of days) to become shorter with the approach of winter. **2.** (foll. by *on* or *upon*) to advance on so as to encircle or surround.

close quarters (kləʊs) *pl. n.* **at close quarters. 1.** engaged in hand-to-hand combat. **2.** in close proximity; very near together.

close season (kləʊs) *n.* the period of the year when it is prohibited to kill certain game or fish.

close shave (kləʊs) *n. Informal.* a narrow escape.

closet ('klɒzɪt) *n.* **1.** a small cupboard. **2.** a small private room. **3.** short for **water closet. 4.** (*modifier*) private or secret. ~*vb.* **5.** to shut away in private, esp. for conference or meditation. [Old French *clos* enclosure]

close-up ('kləʊs,ʌp) *n.* **1.** a photograph or film or television shot taken at close range. **2.** a detailed or intimate view or examination. ~*vb.* **close up** (kləʊz). **3.** to shut entirely. **4.** to draw together: *the ranks closed up.* **5.** (of wounds) to heal completely.

close with (kləʊz) *vb.* to engage in battle with (an enemy).

closure ('kləʊʒə) *n.* **1.** the act of closing or the state of being closed. **2.** something that closes or shuts. **3.** (in a deliberative body) a procedure by which debate may be halted and an immediate vote taken. ~*vb.* **4.** (in a deliberative body) to end (debate) by closure.

clot (klɒt) *n.* **1.** a soft thick lump or mass. **2.** *Brit. informal.* a stupid person; fool. ~*vb.* **clotting, clotted. 3.** to form or cause to form into a soft thick lump or lumps. [Old English *clott*]

cloth (klɒθ) *n., pl.* **cloths** (klɒθs, klɒðz). **1.** a fabric formed by weaving, felting, or knitting fibres. **2.** a piece of such fabric used for a particular purpose, as for a dishcloth. **3.** (usually preceded by *the*) the clergy. [Old English *clāth*]

clothe (kləʊð) *vb.* **clothing, clothed** or **clad. 1.** to dress (a person). **2.** to provide with clothing. **3.** to conceal or disguise. [Old English *clāthian*]

clothes (kləʊðz) *pl. n.* **1.** articles of dress. **2.** *Chiefly Brit.* short for **bedclothes.** [Old English *clāthas,* pl. of *clāth* cloth]

clotheshorse ('kləʊðz,hɔːs) n. a frame on which to hang laundry for drying or airing.

clothesline ('kləʊðz,laɪn) n. a piece of rope from which clean washing is hung to dry.

clothes peg n. a small wooden or plastic clip for attaching washing to a clothesline.

clothier ('kləʊðɪə) n. a person who makes, sells, or deals in clothes or cloth.

clothing ('kləʊðɪŋ) n. **1.** garments collectively. **2.** something that covers or clothes.

clotted cream n. Brit. a thick cream made from scalded milk, esp. in SW England.

cloud (klaʊd) n. **1.** a mass of water or ice particles visible in the sky. **2.** any collection of particles visible in the air, esp. of smoke or dust. **3.** a large number of insects or other small animals in flight. **4.** something that darkens, threatens, or carries gloom. **5. in the clouds.** not in contact with reality. **6. on cloud nine.** Informal. elated; very happy. **7. under a cloud. a.** under reproach or suspicion. **b.** in a state of gloom or bad temper. ~vb. **8.** to make or become cloudy, overcast, or indistinct. **9.** to confuse or impair: *anxiety clouded his judgment.* **10.** to make or become gloomy or depressed. **11.** to render (liquids) milky or (of liquids) to become milky. [Old English *clūd* rock, hill] —'**cloudless** adj.

cloudburst ('klaʊd,bɜːst) n. a heavy downpour.

cloud chamber n. Physics. an apparatus for detecting high-energy particles by observing their tracks through a chamber containing a supersaturated vapour.

cloud-cuckoo-land n. a realm of fantasy or impractical notions.

cloudy ('klaʊdɪ) adj. **cloudier, cloudiest. 1.** covered with cloud or clouds. **2.** opaque or muddy. **3.** confused or unclear. —'**cloudily** adv. —'**cloudiness** n.

clough (klʌf) n. Dialect. a ravine. [Old English *clōh*]

clout (klaʊt) n. **1.** Informal. a blow, esp. with the hand. **2.** power or influence. ~vb. **3.** Informal. to give a hard blow to, esp. with the hand. [Old English *clūt* piece of cloth]

clove[1] (kləʊv) n. a dried unopened flower bud of a tropical tree of the myrtle family, used as a pungent fragrant spice. [Latin *clāvus* nail]

clove[2] (kləʊv) n. any of the segments of a compound bulb, esp. of a garlic bulb. [Old English *clufu* bulb]

clove[3] (kləʊv) vb. a past tense of **cleave**[1].

clove hitch n. a knot used for securing a rope to a spar, post, or larger rope.

cloven ('kləʊv'n) vb. **1.** a past participle of **cleave**[1]. ~adj. **2.** split; cleft; divided.

cloven hoof or **foot** n. the divided hoof of a pig, goat, cow, or deer.

clover ('kləʊvə) n. **1.** a plant with three-lobed leaves and dense flower heads. **2. in clover.** Informal. in ease or luxury. [Old English *clāfre*]

clown (klaʊn) n. **1.** a comic entertainer, usually grotesquely costumed and made up, appearing in the circus. **2.** a person who acts in a buffoon-like manner. **3.** a clumsy rude person; boor. ~vb. **4.** to perform as a clown. **5.** to play jokes or tricks. **6.** to act foolishly. [origin unknown] —'**clownish** adj.

cloy (klɔɪ) vb. to nauseate or satiate through an excess of something initially pleasurable or sweet. [Middle English, orig.: to nail, hence, to obstruct] —'**cloying** adj.

club (klʌb) n. **1.** a stout stick used as a weapon. **2.** a stick or bat used to strike the ball in various sports, esp. golf. **3.** short for **Indian club. 4.** a group or association of people with common aims or interests. **5.** the room, building, or facilities used by such a group. **6.** a building in which members go to meet, dine, read, etc. **7.** Chiefly Brit. an organization, esp. in a shop, set up as a means of saving. **8.** a playing card marked with one or more black trefoil symbols. ~vb. **clubbing, clubbed. 9.** to beat with or as if with a club. **10.** (foll. by *together*) to unite or combine (resources or efforts) for a common purpose. [Old Norse *klubba*]

club foot n. a congenital deformity of the foot.

clubhouse ('klʌb,haʊs) n. the premises of a sports or other club; a golf club.

club root n. a fungal disease of cabbages and related plants, in which the roots become thickened and distorted.

cluck (klʌk) n. **1.** the low clicking sound made by a hen or any similar sound. ~vb. **2.** (of a hen) to make a clicking sound. **3.** to express (a feeling) by making a similar sound. [imit.]

clue (kluː) n. **1.** something that helps to solve a problem or unravel a mystery. **2. not have a clue. a.** to be completely baffled. **b.** to be ignorant or incompetent. ~vb. **cluing, clued. 3.** (usually foll. by *in* or *up*) to provide with helpful information. [var. of *clew*]

clueless ('kluːlɪs) adj. Slang. helpless; stupid.

clump (klʌmp) n. **1.** a cluster, as of trees or plants. **2.** a dull heavy tread or any similar sound. ~vb. **3.** to walk or tread heavily. **4.** to gather or be gathered into clumps, clusters, or clots. [Old English *clympe*] —'**clumpy** adj.

clumsy ('klʌmzɪ) adj. **-sier, -siest. 1.** lacking in skill or physical coordination. **2.** awkwardly constructed or contrived. [Middle English *clumse* to be numb with cold] —'**clumsily** adv. —'**clumsiness** n.

clung (klʌŋ) vb. past of **cling**.

clunk (klʌŋk) n. **1.** a dull metallic sound. ~vb. **2.** to make such a sound. [imit.]

cluster ('klʌstə) n. **1.** a number of things growing, fastened, or occurring close together. **2.** a number of people or things grouped together. ~vb. **3.** to gather or be gathered in clusters. [Old English *clyster*]

clutch[1] (klʌtʃ) vb. **1.** to seize with or as if with hands or claws. **2.** to grasp or hold firmly. **3.** (usually foll. by *at*) to attempt to get hold or possession of. ~n. **4.** a device that enables two revolving shafts to be joined or disconnected, esp. one that transmits the drive from the engine to the gearbox in a vehicle. **5.** the pedal which operates the clutch in a car. **6.** a firm grasp. **7.** a hand or claw in the act of clutching: *in the clutches of a bear.* **8.** (*often pl.*) power or control: *in the clutches of the Mafia.* **9.** Also: **clutch bag.** a handbag without handles. [Old English *clyccan*]

clutch[2] (klʌtʃ) *n.* **1.** a nest of eggs laid at the same time. **2.** a brood of chickens. [Old Norse *klekja* to hatch]

clutter ('klʌtə) *vb.* **1.** (often foll. by *up*) to strew objects about (a place) in a disorderly manner. ~*n.* **2.** a disordered heap or mass of objects. **3.** a state of disorder. [Middle English *clotter*]

Clydesdale ('klaıdz,deıl) *n.* a heavy powerful carthorse, originally from Scotland.

cm centimetre.

Cm *Chem.* curium.

CMG Companion of St Michael and St George (a Brit. title).

CND Campaign for Nuclear Disarmament.

Co *Chem.* cobalt.

CO **1.** Colorado. **2.** Commanding Officer.

Co. *or* **co.** **1.** Company. **2. and co.** (kəʊ). *Informal.* and the rest of them: *Harold and co.*

Co. County.

co- *prefix.* **1.** together; joint or jointly: *coproduction.* **2.** indicating partnership or equality: *costar; copilot.* **3.** to the same or a similar degree: *coextend.* **4.** (in mathematics and astronomy) of the complement of an angle: *cosecant.* (See: also **COM-**]

c/o **1.** care of. **2.** *Book-keeping.* carried over.

coach (kəʊtʃ) *n.* **1.** a large comfortable single-decker bus used for sightseeing or long-distance travel. **2.** a large four-wheeled enclosed carriage, usually horse-drawn. **3.** a railway carriage. **4.** a trainer or instructor: *a drama coach.* **5.** a tutor who prepares students for examinations. ~*vb.* **6.** to give tuition or instruction to (a pupil). [from *Kocs*, village in Hungary where coaches were first made] —'**coach-ing** *n.*

coachman ('kəʊtʃmən) *n., pl.* -**men.** the driver of a coach or carriage.

coachwork ('kəʊtʃ,wɜːk) *n.* the body of a car.

coagulate (kəʊ'ægjʊ,leıt) *vb.* to change from a fluid state into a soft semisolid mass; clot; curdle. [Latin *coāgulāre*] —**co-'agulant** *n.* —**co₁agu'lation** *n.*

coal (kəʊl) *n.* **1.** a compact black or dark brown rock consisting largely of carbon formed from partially decomposed vegetation: a fuel and a source of coke, coal gas, and coal tar. **2.** one or more lumps of coal. **3. coals to Newcastle.** something supplied to a place where it is already plentiful. [Old English *col*]

coalesce (ˌkəʊə'les) *vb.* to unite or come together in one body or mass; fuse. [Latin *co-* together + *alēscere* to increase] —**coa-'lescence** *n.* —**coa'lescent** *adj.*

coalface ('kəʊl,feıs) *n.* the exposed seam of coal in a mine.

coalfield ('kəʊl,fiːld) *n.* an area rich in deposits of coal.

coal gas *n.* a mixture of gases produced by the distillation of bituminous coal and used for heating and lighting.

coalition (ˌkəʊə'lıʃən) *n.* a temporary alliance between groups or parties, esp. for some specific reason. [Latin *coalēscere* to coalesce]

coal scuttle *n.* a container to supply coal to a domestic fire.

coal tar *n.* a black tar, produced by the distillation of bituminous coal, used for making drugs and chemical products.

coal tit *n.* a small European songbird having a black head with a white patch on the nape.

coaming ('kəʊmıŋ) *n.* a raised frame round a ship's hatchway for keeping out water. [origin unknown]

coarse (kɔːs) *adj.* **1.** rough in texture or structure; not fine. **2.** lacking refinement or taste; indelicate; vulgar: *coarse jokes.* **3.** of inferior quality. [origin unknown] —'**coarsely** *adv.* —'**coarseness** *n.*

coarse fish *n.* any freshwater fish that is not of the salmon family. —**coarse fishing** *n.*

coarsen ('kɔːs²n) *vb.* to make or become coarse.

coast (kəʊst) *n.* **1.** the place where the land meets the sea; seaside. **2. the coast is clear.** *Informal.* the obstacles or dangers are gone. ~*vb.* **3.** to move by momentum or force of gravity, without the use of power. **4.** to proceed without great effort: *to coast to victory.* [Latin *costa* side, rib] —'**coastal** *adj.*

coaster ('kəʊstə) *n.* **1.** *Brit.* a ship used for coastal trade. **2.** a small mat placed under a bottle or glass to protect a table.

coastguard ('kəʊst,gɑːd) *n.* **1.** an organization which aids shipping, saves lives at sea, and prevents smuggling. **2.** a member of such an organization.

coastline ('kəʊst,laın) *n.* the outline of a coast.

coat (kəʊt) *n.* **1.** an outer garment with sleeves, covering the body from the shoulders to below the waist. **2.** the hair, wool, or fur of an animal. **3.** any layer that covers a surface. ~*vb.* **4.** (often foll. by *with*) to cover with a layer of (something). [Old French *cote*]

coat hanger *n.* a curved piece of wood, wire, or plastic, fitted with a hook and used to hang up clothes.

coating ('kəʊtıŋ) *n.* a layer or film spread over a surface.

coat of arms *n.* the heraldic arrangement of emblems of a person, family, or corporation.

coat of mail *n.* a protective garment made of linked metal rings or plates.

coax (kəʊks) *vb.* **1.** to persuade (someone) by tenderness, flattery, or pleading. **2.** to obtain (something) by persistent coaxing. **3.** to work on (something) carefully and patiently so as to make it function as desired: *he coaxed the engine into starting.* [obs. *cokes* a fool]

coaxial (kəʊˈæksɪəl) *adj.* **1.** having a common axis. **2.** *Electronics.* (of a cable) transmitting by means of two concentric conductors separated by an insulator.

cob (kɒb) *n.* **1.** a male swan. **2.** a thickset type of horse. **3.** short for a **corncob. 4.** *Brit.* a hazel tree or hazelnut. **5.** *Brit.* a round loaf of bread. [origin unknown]

cobalt (ˈkəʊbɔːlt) *n.* a brittle hard silvery-white metallic element used in alloys. Symbol: Co [Middle High German *kobolt* goblin; from the miners' belief that goblins placed it in the silver ore]

cobalt-blue *adj.* deep blue.

cobber (ˈkɒbə) *n. Austral. archaic. & N.Z. informal.* friend; mate: used as a term of address to males. [dialect *cob* to take a liking to someone]

cobble[1] (ˈkɒbʰl) *n.* a cobblestone.

cobble[2] (ˈkɒbʰl) *vb.* **1.** to make or mend (shoes). **2.** to put together clumsily.

cobbled (ˈkɒbʰld) *adj.* (of a street or road) paved with cobblestones.

cobbler (ˈkɒbʰl) *n.* a person who makes or mends shoes. [origin unknown]

cobblers (ˈkɒbləz) *pl. n. Brit. taboo slang.* rubbish; nonsense. [rhyming slang *cobblers' awls* balls]

cobblestone (ˈkɒbʰlˌstəʊn) *n.* a rounded stone used for paving. [from *cob*]

COBOL (ˈkəʊˌbɒl) *n.* a high-level computer programming language designed for general commercial use. [*co(mmon) b(usiness) o(riented) l(anguage)*]

cobra (ˈkəʊbrə) *n.* a highly venomous snake of tropical Africa and Asia. When alarmed it spreads the skin of its neck into a hood. [Latin *colubra* snake]

cobweb (ˈkɒbˌwɛb) *n.* **1.** a web spun by certain spiders. **2.** a single thread of such a web. [Old English (*cop)coppe* spider] —**ˈcob**ˌ**webbed** *adj.* —**ˈcob**ˌ**webby** *adj.*

cobwebs (ˈkɒbˌwɛbz) *pl. n.* mustiness, confusion, or obscurity.

coca (ˈkəʊkə) *n.* the dried leaves of a S American shrub, which contain cocaine and are chewed for their stimulating effects. [S American Indian *kúka*]

cocaine (kəˈkeɪn) *n.* an addictive drug derived from coca leaves, used as a narcotic and local anaesthetic.

coccus (ˈkɒkəs) *n., pl.* **cocci** (ˈkɒkaɪ, ˈkɒksaɪ). any spherical bacterium. [Greek *kokkos* berry, grain]

coccyx (ˈkɒksɪks) *n., pl.* **coccyges** (kɒkˈsaɪdʒiːz). a small triangular bone at the foot of the spine in human beings and some apes. [Greek *kokkux* cuckoo; from its likeness to a cuckoo's beak]

cochineal (ˌkɒtʃɪˈniːl, ˈkɒtʃɪˌniːl) *n.* **1.** a crimson substance obtained from a Mexican insect, used for colouring food and for dyeing. **2.** the insect from which the dye is obtained. [Greek *kokkos* kermes berry]

cochlea (ˈkɒklɪə) *n., pl.* **-leae** (-lɪˌiː). the

spiral tube in the internal ear, which converts sound vibrations into nerve impulses. [Greek *kokhlias* snail]

cock (kɒk) *n.* **1.** a male bird, esp. the male of the domestic fowl. **2.** a stopcock. **3.** *Taboo slang.* a penis. **4.** the hammer of a gun. **5.** *Brit. informal.* friend; mate: used as a term of address. ~*vb.* **6.** to set the hammer of (a gun) so that it is ready to fire. **7.** (sometimes foll. by *up*) to lift and turn (part of the body) in a particular direction. ~See also **cockup.** [Old English *cocc*]

cockabully (ˌkɒkəˈbʊlɪ) *n.* a small freshwater fish of New Zealand. [Maori *kokopu*]

cockade (kɒˈkeɪd) *n.* a feather or rosette worn on the hat as a badge. [French *coq* COCK]

cock-a-hoop *adj.* in very high spirits. [origin unknown]

cock-a-leekie (ˌkɒkəˈliːkɪ) *n.* a Scottish soup of chicken boiled with leeks.

cock-and-bull story *n. Informal.* an obviously improbable story, esp. one used as an excuse.

cockatoo (ˌkɒkəˈtuː, ˈkɒkəˌtuː) *n., pl.* **-toos.** **1.** a light-coloured crested parrot of Australia and the East Indies. **2.** *Austral. & N.Z.* a small farmer or settler. [Malay *kakatua*]

cockchafer (ˈkɒkˌtʃeɪfə) *n.* a large European beetle. [COCK + *chafer* beetle]

cocked hat *n.* **1.** a hat with three corners and a turned-up brim. **2. knock into a cocked hat.** *Slang.* to outdo or defeat.

cockerel (ˈkɒkərəl, ˈkɒkrəl) *n.* a young domestic cock, less than a year old.

cocker spaniel (ˈkɒkə) *n.* a small breed of spaniel. [from *cocking* hunting woodcocks]

cockeyed (ˈkɒkˌaɪd) *adj. Informal.* **1.** crooked; askew. **2.** foolish or absurd. **3.** cross-eyed.

cockfight (ˈkɒkˌfaɪt) *n.* a fight between two gamecocks fitted with sharp metal spurs.

cockle (ˈkɒkʰl) *n.* **1.** an edible bivalve shellfish that has a rounded shell with radiating ribs. **2.** its shell. **3. warm the cockles of one's heart.** to make one feel happy. [Greek *konkhule* mussel]

cockleshell (ˈkɒkʰlˌʃɛl) *n.* **1.** the shell of the cockle. **2.** a small light boat.

cockney (ˈkɒknɪ) *n.* **1.** a native of London, esp. of its East End. **2.** the urban dialect of London or its East End. ~*adj.* **3.** characteristic of cockneys or their dialect. [Middle English *cokeney* cock's egg, later applied contemptuously to townsmen]

cockpit (ˈkɒkˌpɪt) *n.* **1.** the compartment in an aircraft for the pilot and crew. **2.** the driver's compartment in a racing car. **3.** *Naut.* a space in a small vessel containing the wheel and tiller. **4.** the site of numerous battles or conflicts. **5.** an enclosure used for cockfights.

cockroach (ˈkɒkˌrəʊtʃ) *n.* an insect having an oval flattened body and long antennae: a household pest. [Spanish *cucaracha*]

cockscomb *or* **coxcomb** ('kɒks,kəʊm) *n.* **1.** the comb of a domestic cock. **2.** *Informal.* a conceited dandy.

cocksure (,kɒk'ʃʊə, -'ʃɔː) *adj.* overconfident; arrogant. [origin unknown]

cocktail ('kɒk,teɪl) *n.* **1.** any mixed drink with a spirit base. **2.** an appetizer of seafood or mixed fruits. **3.** any combination of diverse elements. [origin unknown]

cockup ('kɒk,ʌp) *Brit. slang.* ~*n.* **1.** something done badly. ~*vb.* **cock up. 2.** to botch.

cocky¹ ('kɒkɪ) *adj.* **cockier, cockiest.** excessively proud of oneself. —**'cockily** *adv.* —**'cockiness** *n.*

cocky² ('kɒkɪ) *n., pl* **cockies.** *Austral. & N.Z. informal.* short for **cockatoo** (sense 2).

coco ('kəʊkəʊ) *n., pl.* **-cos.** the coconut palm. [Portuguese *coco* grimace]

cocoa ('kəʊkəʊ) *or* **cacao** *n.* **1.** a powder made by roasting and grinding cocoa beans. **2.** a hot or cold drink made from cocoa powder and milk or water. [from CACAO]

cocoa bean *n.* a cacao seed.

cocoa butter *n.* a fatty solid obtained from cocoa beans and used for confectionery and toiletries.

coconut *or* **cocoanut** ('kəʊkə,nʌt) *n.* **1.** the fruit of a type of palm tree (**coconut palm**), which has a thick fibrous oval husk and a thin hard shell enclosing edible white flesh. The hollow centre is filled with a milky fluid (**coconut milk**). **2.** the flesh of the coconut.

coconut matting *n.* coarse matting made from the fibrous husk of the coconut.

cocoon (kə'kuːn) *n.* **1.** a silky protective envelope produced by a silkworm or other insect larva, in which the pupa develops. **2.** a protective covering. ~*vb.* **3.** to wrap in or protect as if in a cocoon. [Provençal *coucoun* eggshell]

cocotte (kəʊ'kɒt) *n.* a small fireproof dish in which individual portions of food are cooked and served. [French]

cod¹ (kɒd) *n., pl.* **cod** *or* **cods.** a food fish found in the North Atlantic. [prob. Germanic]

cod² (kɒd) *Brit. slang.* ~*vb.* **codding, codded. 1.** to make fun of. **2.** to play a trick on; hoax. ~*n.* **3.** a hoax or trick. [origin unknown]

COD cash (in the U.S. collect) on delivery.

coda ('kəʊdə) *n. Music.* the final part of a musical structure. [Italian: tail]

coddle ('kɒdəl) *vb.* **1.** to pamper or overprotect. **2.** to cook (something, esp. eggs) in water just below boiling point. [origin unknown]

code (kəʊd) *n.* **1.** a system of letters, symbols, or prearranged signals, by which information can be communicated secretly or briefly. **2.** a conventionalized set of principles or rules: *a code of behaviour.* **3.** a system of letters or digits used for identification purposes. ~*vb.* **4.** to translate or arrange into a code. [Latin *cōdex* book, wooden block]

codeine ('kəʊdiːn) *n.* an alkaloid prepared mainly from morphine, used as a painkiller and sedative. [Greek *kōdeia* head of a poppy]

codex ('kəʊdeks) *n., pl.* **codices** ('kəʊdɪ,siːz, 'kɒdɪ-).* a volume of manuscripts of an ancient text. [Latin: wooden block, book]

codfish ('kɒd,fɪʃ) *n., pl.* **-fish** *or* **-fishes.** a cod.

codger ('kɒdʒə) *n. Informal.* a man, esp. an old or eccentric one. [prob. var. of *cadger*]

codicil ('kɒdɪsɪl) *n. Law.* a supplement altering a will. [from *codex*]

codify ('kəʊdɪ,faɪ, 'kɒ-) *vb.* **-fying, -fied.** to organize or collect together (rules or procedures) systematically. —**,codifi'cation** *n.*

codling ('kɒdlɪŋ) *n.* a young cod.

cod-liver oil *n.* an oil extracted from the livers of cod and related fish, rich in vitamins A and D.

codpiece ('kɒd,piːs) *n. Hist.* a bag covering the male genitals, attached to breeches. [obs. *cod* scrotum]

codswallop ('kɒdz,wɒləp) *n. Brit. slang.* nonsense. [origin unknown]

coeducation (,kəʊedjʊ'keɪʃən) *n.* an educational system in which classes are attended by both sexes. —**,coedu'cational** *adj.*

coefficient (,kəʊɪ'fɪʃənt) *n.* **1.** *Maths.* a number or constant placed before and multiplying another quantity: *the coefficient of the term 3xyz is 3.* **2.** *Physics.* a number or constant used to calculate the behaviour of a given substance under specified conditions.

coelacanth ('siːlə,kænθ) *n.* a primitive marine bony fish, thought to be extinct until a living specimen was discovered in 1938. [Greek *koilos* hollow + *akanthos* spine]

coelenterate (sɪ'lentə,reɪt, -rɪt) *n.* any invertebrate having a saclike body with a single opening, such as jellyfishes, sea anemones, and corals. [Greek *koilos* hollow + *enteron* intestine]

coeliac *or U.S.* **celiac** ('siːlɪ,æk) *adj.* of the abdomen. [Greek *koilia* belly]

coenobite ('siːnəʊ,baɪt) *n.* a member of a religious order in a monastic community. [Greek *koinos* common + *bios* life]

coequal (kəʊ'iːkwəl) *adj., n.* equal.

coerce (kəʊ'ɜːs) *vb.* to compel or restrain by force. [Latin *co-* together + *arcēre* to enclose] —**co'ercible** *adj.* —**co'ercion** *n.*

coeval (kəʊ'iːvəl) *adj., n.* contemporary. [Latin *co-* together + *aevum* age] —**co'evally** *adv.*

coexist (,kəʊɪg'zɪst) *vb.* **1.** to exist together at the same time or in the same place. **2.** to exist together in peace despite differences. —**,coex'istence** *n.* —**,coex'istent** *adj.*

coextend (,kəʊɪk'stend) *vb.* to extend or cause to extend equally in space or time. —**,coex'tension** *n.* —**,coex'tensive** *adj.*

C of E Church of England.

coffee ('kɒfɪ) *n.* **1.** a drink made from the

roasted and ground seeds of a tall tropical shrub and water. **2.** Also called: **coffee beans.** the beanlike seeds of this shrub. **3.** the shrub yielding these seeds. ~*adj.* **4.** light brown. [Turkish *kahve*, from Arabic *qahwah* coffee, wine]

coffee bar *n.* a café; snack bar.

coffee house *n.* a place where coffee is served, esp. one that was a fashionable meeting place in 18th-century London.

coffee mill *n.* a machine for grinding roasted coffee beans.

coffee table *n.* a small low table.

coffee-table book *n.* a large, expensive, illustrated book.

coffer ('kɒfə) *n.* **1.** a chest for storing valuables. **2.** (*pl.*) a store of money. **3.** an ornamental sunken panel in a ceiling or dome. [Greek *kophinos* basket]

cofferdam ('kɒfə،dæm) *n.* a watertight enclosure pumped dry to enable construction work or ship repairs to be carried out.

coffin ('kɒfɪn) *n.* a box in which a corpse is buried or cremated. [Latin *cophinus* basket]

cog (kɒg) *n.* **1.** one of the teeth on the rim of a gearwheel. **2.** a gearwheel, esp. a small one. **3.** an unimportant member of a large organization or process. [Scandinavian]

cogent ('kəʊdʒənt) *adj.* forcefully convincing. [Latin *co-* together + *agere* to drive] —'**cogency** *n.*

cogitate ('kɒdʒɪ،teɪt) *vb.* to think deeply about (something); ponder. [Latin *cōgitāre*] —،**cogi'tation** *n.* —'**cogitative** *adj.*

cognac ('kɒnjæk) *n.* high-quality brandy distilled near Cognac in SW France.

cognate ('kɒgneɪt) *adj.* **1.** derived from a common original form: *cognate languages.* **2.** related to or descended from a common ancestor. ~*n.* **3.** a cognate word or language. **4.** a relative. [Latin *co-* same + *gnātus* born] —**cog'nation** *n.*

cognition (kɒg'nɪʃən) *n.* **1.** the processes of acquiring knowledge, including perception, intuition, and reasoning. **2.** the results of such a process. [Latin *cognōscere* to learn] —**cognitive** ('kɒgnɪtɪv) *adj.*

cognizance *or* **cognisance** ('kɒgnɪzəns, 'kɒnɪ-) *n.* **1.** knowledge; perception. **2. take cognizance of.** to take notice of; acknowledge. **3.** the range or scope of knowledge or perception. [Latin *cognōscere* to learn] —**'cognizant** *or* **'cognisant** *adj.*

cognomen (kɒg'nəʊmɛn) *n.*, *pl.* **-nomens** *or* **-nomina** (-'nɒmɪnə, -'nəʊ-). **1.** a nickname. **2.** a surname. **3.** an ancient Roman's third name or nickname. [Latin: additional name]

cognoscenti (،kɒnjəʊ'ʃɛntɪ, ،kɒgnəʊ-) *pl. n., sing.* **-te** (-ti:). (*sometimes sing.*) connoisseurs. [Italian]

cogwheel ('kɒg،wi:l) *n.* same as **gearwheel.**

cohabit (kəʊ'hæbɪt) *vb.* to live together as husband and wife, esp. without being married. [Latin *co-* together + *habitāre* to live] —**co،habi'tation** *n.*

cohere (kəʊ'hɪə) *vb.* **1.** to hold or stick firmly together. **2.** to be connected logically; be consistent. [Latin *co-* together + *haerēre* to cling]

coherent (kəʊ'hɪərənt) *adj.* **1.** capable of intelligible speech. **2.** logical and consistent. **3.** cohering or sticking together. **4.** *Physics.* (of two or more waves) having the same frequency and a constant fixed phase difference. —**co'herence** *n.*

cohesion (kəʊ'hi:ʒən) *n.* **1.** the act or state of cohering; tendency to unite. **2.** *Physics.* the force that holds together the atoms or molecules in a solid or liquid. —**co'hesive** *adj.*

cohort ('kəʊhɔːt) *n.* **1.** a band of warriors or associates. **2.** a tenth part of an ancient Roman Legion. [Latin *cohors* yard, company of soldiers]

coif *n.* **1.** (kɔɪf). a close-fitting cap worn in the Middle Ages. **2.** (kwɑːf). a hairstyle. ~*vb.* (kwɑːf), **coiffing, coiffed.** **3.** to arrange (the hair). [Late Latin *cofea* helmet, cap]

coiffeur (kwɑː'fɜː) *n.* a hairdresser. [French] —**coiffeuse** (kwɑː'fɜːz) *fem. n.*

coiffure (kwɑː'fjʊə) *n.* a hairstyle. [French]

coil[1] (kɔɪl) *vb.* **1.** to wind or be wound into loops. **2.** to move in a winding course. ~*n.* **3.** something wound in a connected series of loops. **4.** a single loop of such a series. **5.** an electrical conductor wound into a spiral, to provide inductance. **6.** a contraceptive device in the shape of a coil, inserted in the womb. [Old French *coillir* to collect together]

coil[2] (kɔɪl) *n.* **mortal coil.** the troubles of the world. [Shakespeare]

coin (kɔɪn) *n.* **1.** a metal disc or piece used as money. **2.** metal currency, coins collectively. ~*vb.* **3.** to make or stamp (coins). **4.** to make into a coin. **5.** to invent (a new word or phrase). **6. coin it in** *or* **coin money.** *Informal.* to make money rapidly. [Latin *cuneus* wedge]

coinage ('kɔɪnɪdʒ) *n.* **1.** the act of coining. **2.** coins collectively. **3.** the currency of a country. **4.** a newly invented word or phrase.

coincide (،kəʊɪn'saɪd) *vb.* **1.** to occur at the same time. **2.** to occupy the same place in space. **3.** to agree or correspond exactly. [Latin *co-* together + *incidere* to occur]

coincidence (kəʊ'ɪnsɪdəns) *n.* **1.** a chance occurrence of events remarkable either for being simultaneous or for apparently being connected. **2.** a coinciding.

coincident (kəʊ'ɪnsɪdənt) *adj.* **1.** having the same position in space or time. **2.** (usually foll. by *with*) in exact agreement; identical. —**co،inci'dental** *adj.* —**co،inci'dentally** *adv.*

coir ('kɔɪə) *n.* coconut fibre, used in making rope and matting. [Malayalam (a language of SW India) *kāyar* rope]

coitus ('kəʊɪtəs) *or* **coition** (kəʊ'ɪʃən) *n.* sexual intercourse. [Latin *coīre* to meet] —**'coital** *adj.*

coke[1] (kəʊk) *n.* **1.** a solid fuel left after the gases have been extracted from coal: used as a smokeless fuel and for smelting pig iron out of iron ore. ~*vb.* **2.** to become or convert into coke. [prob. dialect *colk* core]

coke² (kəʊk) *n. Slang.* cocaine.

col (kɒl) *n.* the lowest point of a ridge connecting two mountain peaks. [French: neck]

Col. 1. Colonel. **2.** Colorado.

cola *or* **kola** ('kəʊlə) *n.* **1.** a W African tree whose nuts yield an extract used as a tonic and in soft drinks. **2.** a sweet carbonated drink flavoured with this extract. [prob. var. of W African *kolo* nut]

colander ('kɒləndə, 'kʌl-) *n.* a bowl with a perforated bottom for straining or rinsing foods. [Latin *cōlum* sieve]

cold (kəʊld) *adj.* **1.** low in temperature: *cold weather; cold hands.* **2.** not hot enough: *this meal is cold.* **3.** lacking in affection or enthusiasm. **4.** not affected by emotion: *cold logic.* **5.** dead. **6.** (of a trail or scent in hunting) faint. **7.** (of a colour) having violet, blue, or green predominating; giving no sensation of warmth. **8.** *Slang.* unconscious. **9.** *Informal.* (of a seeker) far from the object of a search. **10. cold comfort.** little or no comfort. **11. have** *or* **get cold feet.** to be or become fearful or reluctant. **12. in cold blood.** deliberately and without mercy. **13. leave (someone) cold.** *Informal.* to fail to excite or impress (someone). **14. throw cold water on.** *Informal.* to discourage. ~*n.* **15.** the absence of heat. **16.** the sensation caused by loss or lack of heat. **17. (out) in the cold.** *Informal.* neglected; ignored. **18.** a viral infection of the nose and throat characterized by catarrh and sneezing. ~*adv.* **19.** *Informal.* unrehearsed; unprepared: *he played his part cold.* [Old English *ceald*] —'**coldly** *adv.* —'**coldness** *n.*

cold-blooded *adj.* **1.** callous or cruel. **2.** (of all animals except birds and mammals) having a body temperature that varies with that of the surroundings. —,**cold-'bloodedness** *n.*

cold chisel *n.* a toughened steel chisel.

cold cream *n.* a creamy preparation used for softening and cleansing the skin.

cold frame *n.* an unheated wooden frame with a glass top, used to protect young plants.

cold front *n. Meteorol.* the boundary line between a warm air mass and the cold air pushing it from beneath and behind.

cold-hearted *adj.* lacking in feeling or warmth; unkind. —,**cold-'heartedness** *n.*

cold shoulder *Informal.* ~*n.* **1. give someone the cold shoulder.** to snub someone. ~*vb.* **cold-shoulder. 2.** to treat with indifference.

cold sore *n.* a cluster of blisters at the margin of the lips, caused by a virus.

cold storage *n.* **1.** the storage of things in a refrigerated place. **2.** *Informal.* a state of temporary disuse; postponement: *to put an idea into cold storage.*

cold sweat *n. Informal.* coldness and sweating as a bodily reaction to fear or nervousness.

cold turkey *n. Slang.* a method of curing drug addiction by abrupt withdrawal of all doses.

cold war *n.* a state of political hostility between two countries without actual warfare.

cole (kəʊl) *n.* any of various plants such as the cabbage and rape. [Latin *caulis* cabbage]

coleslaw ('kəʊl,slɔ:) *n.* a dressed salad of shredded raw cabbage with carrots and onions. [Dutch *koolsalade* cabbage salad]

coley ('kəʊlɪ, 'kɒlɪ) *n. Brit.* an edible fish with white or grey flesh. [perhaps from *coalfish*]

colic ('kɒlɪk) *n.* severe spasmodic pain in the stomach and bowels. [Greek *kolon* COLON²] —'**colicky** *adj.*

colitis (kɒ'laɪtɪs) *n.* inflammation of the colon.

collaborate (kə'læbə,reɪt) *vb.* **1.** to work with another or others on a joint project. **2.** to cooperate with an enemy invader. [Latin *com-* together + *labōrāre* to work] —,**col,labo'ration** *n.* —**col'laborative** *adj.* —**col'labo,rator** *n.*

collage (kə'lɑːʒ, kɒ-) *n.* **1.** an art form in which compositions are made out of pieces of paper, cloth, photographs, or other materials. **2.** a composition made in this way. [French] —**col'lagist** *n.*

collagen ('kɒlədʒən) *n.* a fibrous protein found in cartilage and bone that yields gelatin on boiling. [Greek *kolla* glue]

collapse (kə'læps) *vb.* **1.** to fall down or cave in suddenly. **2.** to fail completely. **3.** to break down or fall down from lack of strength. **4.** to fold compactly, esp. for storage. ~*n.* **5.** the act or instance of falling down or falling to pieces. **6.** a sudden failure or breakdown. [Latin *collābī* to fall in ruins] —**col'lapsible** *adj.*

collar ('kɒlə) *n.* **1.** the part of a garment around the neck. **2.** a band of leather, rope, or metal placed around an animal's neck. **3.** *Biol.* a ringlike marking around the neck of a bird or animal. **4.** a cut of meat, esp. bacon, from the neck of an animal. **5.** a ring or band around a pipe, rod or shaft. ~*vb.* **6.** to seize by the collar. **7.** *Informal.* to seize; arrest; detain. **8.** to take for oneself. [Latin *collum* neck]

collarbone ('kɒlə,bəʊn) *n.* same as **clavicle.**

collate (kɒ'leɪt, kə-) *vb.* **1.** to examine and compare (texts or data) in order to note differences. **2.** to check the number and order of (the pages of a book). [Latin *com-* together + *lātus* brought] —**col'lator** *n.*

collateral (kɒ'lætərəl, kə-) *n.* **1.** security pledged for the repayment of a loan. **2.** a person, animal, or plant descended from the same ancestor as another but through a different line. ~*adj.* **3.** situated or running side by side. **4.** descended from a common ancestor but through different lines. **5.** additional but subordinate. [Latin *com-* together + *laterālis* of the side]

collation (kɒ'leɪʃən, kə-) *n.* **1.** the act or result of collating. **2.** a light meal.

colleague ('kɒliːg) *n.* a fellow worker, esp. in a profession. [Latin *collēga*]

collect[1] (kə'lɛkt) *vb.* **1.** to gather together or be gathered together. **2.** to gather (stamps, books, or other articles) as a hobby or for study. **3.** to call for or receive payment of (taxes, dues, or contributions). **4.** to regain control of (oneself or one's emotions). **5.** to fetch. [Latin *com-* together + *legere* to gather]

collect[2] ('kɒlɛkt) *n. Christianity.* a short prayer said during certain church services. [Medieval Latin *ōrātiō ad collēctam* prayer at the assembly]

collected (kə'lɛktɪd) *adj.* **1.** calm and self-controlled. **2.** brought together into one book or set of books: *the collected works of Dickens.*

collection (kə'lɛkʃən) *n.* **1.** the act or process of collecting. **2.** things collected or accumulated. **3.** a sum of money collected, as in church. **4.** regular removal of letters from a postbox.

collective (kə'lɛktɪv) *adj.* **1.** formed or assembled by collection. **2.** assembled as a group; combined. **3.** done by or characteristic of individuals acting in cooperation. ~*n.* **4.** a group of people working together on an enterprise and sharing the benefits from it. —**col'lectively** *adv.*

collective bargaining *n.* negotiation between a trade union and an employer on the wages and working conditions of the employees.

collective noun *n.* a noun that is singular in form but that refers to a group of people or things, as *crowd* or *army.*

collectivism (kə'lɛktɪ,vɪzəm) *n.* the principle of ownership of the means of production by the state or the people.

collectivize *or* **-vise** (kə'lɛktɪ,vaɪz) *vb.* to organize according to the principles of collectivism. —**col,lectivi'zation** *or* **-vi'sation** *n.*

collector (kə'lɛktə) *n.* **1.** a person who collects objects as a hobby. **2.** a person employed to collect debts, rents, or tickets.

colleen ('kɒlɪn, kɒ'liːn) *n. Irish.* a girl. [Irish Gaelic *cailín*]

college ('kɒlɪdʒ) *n.* **1.** an institution of higher or further education that is not a university. **2.** a self-governing section of certain universities. **3.** the staff and students of a college. **4.** an organized body of persons with specific rights and duties: *an electoral college.* **5.** a body organized within a particular profession, concerned with regulating standards. **6.** *Brit.* a name given to some secondary schools. [Latin *collēga* colleague]

collegian (kə'liːdʒɪən) *n.* a member of a college.

collegiate (kə'liːdʒɪɪt) *adj.* **1.** of a college or college students. **2.** (of a university) composed of various colleges.

collide (kə'laɪd) *vb.* **1.** to crash together with a violent impact. **2.** to conflict; clash; disagree. [Latin *com-* together + *laedere* to strike]

collie ('kɒlɪ) *n.* a silky-coated breed of dog used for herding sheep and cattle. [Scot., prob. from earlier *colie* black]

collier ('kɒlɪə) *n. Chiefly Brit.* **1.** a coal miner. **2.** a ship designed to transport coal.

colliery ('kɒljərɪ) *n., pl.* **-lieries.** *Chiefly Brit.* a coal mine and its buildings.

collision (kə'lɪʒən) *n.* **1.** a violent impact of moving objects; crash. **2.** the conflict of opposed ideas or wishes. [Latin *collīdere* to collide]

collocation (,kɒlə'keɪʃən) *n.* a grouping together of things in a certain order, as of the words in a sentence. —**collo,cate** *vb.*

colloid ('kɒlɔɪd) *n.* a mixture having particles of one substance suspended in a different substance. [Greek *kolla* glue] —**col'loidal** *adj.*

collop ('kɒləp) *n.* a small slice of meat. [Scandinavian]

colloquial (kə'ləʊkwɪəl) *adj.* informal; used in conversation rather than formal writing. —**col'loquially** *adv.*

colloquialism (kə'ləʊkwɪə,lɪzəm) *n.* **1.** a colloquial word or phrase. **2.** the use of colloquial words and phrases.

colloquium (kə'ləʊkwɪəm) *n., pl.* **-quiums** *or* **-quia** (-kwɪə). an academic conference or seminar. [Latin: see COLLOQUY]

colloquy ('kɒləkwɪ) *n., pl.* **-quies.** a conversation or conference. [Latin *com-* together + *loquī* to speak] —**'colloquist** *n.*

collusion (kə'luːʒən) *n.* secret or illegal agreement or cooperation; conspiracy. [Latin *collūdere* to conspire] —**col'lusive** *adj.*

collywobbles ('kɒlɪ,wɒb'lz) *pl. n. Slang.* **1.** an upset stomach. **2.** an intense feeling of nervousness. [prob. from *colic* + *wobble*]

cologne (kə'ləʊn) *n.* a perfumed toilet water. [*Cologne*, W Germany, where it was first manufactured (1709)]

colon[1] ('kəʊlən) *n., pl.* **-lons.** the punctuation mark : used before an explanation or an example, a list, or an extended quotation. [Greek *kōlon* limb, clause]

colon[2] ('kəʊlən) *n., pl.* **-lons** *or* **-la** (-lə). the part of the large intestine connected to the rectum. [Greek *kolon* large intestine] —**colonic** (kə'lɒnɪk) *adj.*

colonel ('kɜːn'l) *n.* a senior commissioned officer of land or air forces. [Old Italian *colonnello* column of soldiers] —**'colonelcy** *n.*

colonial (kə'ləʊnɪəl) *adj.* **1.** of or inhabiting a colony or colonies. ~*n.* **2.** an inhabitant of a colony.

colonial goose *n. N.Z.* an old-fashioned name for stuffed roast mutton.

colonialism (kə'ləʊnɪə,lɪzəm) *n.* the policy of acquiring and maintaining colonies, esp. for exploitation. —**co'lonialist** *n., adj.*

colonist ('kɒlənɪst) *n.* a settler in or inhabitant of a colony.

colonize *or* **-ise** ('kɒlə,naɪz) *vb.* **1.** to send colonists to or establish a colony in (an area). **2.** to settle in (an area) as colonists. —**,coloni'zation** *or* **-i'sation** *n.*

colonnade (,kɒlə'neɪd) *n.* a set of evenly spaced columns, usually supporting a roof. [French *colonne* column] —**,colon'naded** *adj.*

colony ('kɒlənɪ) *n., pl.* **-nies.** **1.** a body of

people who settle in a country distant from their homeland but still under its control. **2.** the territory occupied by such a settlement. **3.** a group of people with the same nationality or interests, forming a community in a particular place: *an artists' colony*. **4.** a group of the same type of animal or plant living or growing together. **5.** *Bacteriol.* a group of microorganisms when grown on a culture medium. [Latin *colere* to cultivate, inhabit]

colophon ('kɒlə,fɒn, -fən) *n.* a publisher's emblem on a book. [Greek *kolophōn* a finishing stroke]

color ('kʌlə) *n., vb.* U.S. same as **colour**.

Colorado beetle (,kɒlə'rɑːdəʊ) *n.* a black-and-yellow beetle that is a serious pest of potatoes. [*Colorado*, state of central U.S.]

coloration *or* **colouration** (,kʌlə'reɪʃən) *n.* colouring; arrangement of colours.

coloratura (,kɒlərə'tʊərə) *n. Music.* **1.** an elaborate and complicated vocal passage. **2.** a soprano who specializes in such music. [obs. Italian, lit.: colouring]

colossal (kə'lɒsᵊl) *adj.* **1.** of immense size; huge. **2.** *Informal.* remarkable, splendid.

colossus (kə'lɒsəs) *n., pl.* **-si** (-saɪ) *or* **-suses.** **1.** a very large statue. **2.** any huge or important person or thing. [Greek *kolossos*]

colostomy (kə'lɒstəmɪ) *n., pl.* **-mies.** an operation to form an opening from the colon onto the surface of the body, for emptying the bowel. [COLON² + Greek *stoma* mouth]

colour *or* U.S. **color** ('kʌlə) *n.* **1.** a property of things that results from the particular wavelengths of light which they reflect or give out, producing a sensation in the eye. **2.** a colour, such as red or green, that possesses hue, as opposed to black, white, or grey. **3.** a substance, such as a dye, that gives colour. **4.** the skin complexion of a person, esp. as determined by his race. **5.** the use of all the colours in painting, drawing, or photography. **6.** the distinctive tone of a musical sound. **7.** vividness or authenticity: *period colour.* **8.** semblance or pretext: *under colour of.* ~*vb.* **9.** to apply colour to (something). **10.** to give a convincing appearance to: *to colour an alibi.* **11.** to influence or distort: *anger coloured her judgment.* **12.** to become red in the face, esp. when embarrassed or annoyed. ~See also **colours.** [Latin *color*]

colour bar *n.* racial discrimination by whites against non-whites.

colour-blind *adj.* unable to distinguish between certain colours, esp. red and green. —**colour blindness** *n.*

coloured *or* U.S. **colored** ('kʌləd) *adj.* **1.** possessing colour. **2.** having a strong element of fiction or fantasy; distorted (esp. in **highly coloured**).

Coloured *or* U.S. **Colored** ('kʌləd) *n.* **1.** an individual who is not a White. **2.** in South Africa, a person of racially mixed parentage or descent. ~*adj.* **3.** of mixed White and non-White parentage.

colourful *or* U.S. **colorful** ('kʌləful) *adj.* **1.** having intense or richly varied colours. **2.** vivid, rich, or distinctive in character.

colouring *or* U.S. **coloring** ('kʌlərɪŋ) *n.* **1.** the process or art of applying colour. **2.** anything used to give colour, such as paint. **3.** appearance with regard to shade and colour. **4.** the colour of a person's complexion.

colourless *or* U.S. **colorless** ('kʌləlɪs) *adj.* **1.** without colour. **2.** dull and uninteresting: *a colourless individual.* **3.** grey or pallid in tone or hue.

colours *or* U.S. **colors** ('kʌləz) *pl. n.* **1.** the flag of a country, regiment, or ship. **2.** *Sport, Brit.* a badge or other symbol denoting membership of a team, esp. at a school or college. **3. nail one's colours to the mast.** to commit oneself publicly and irrevocably to a course of action. **4. show one's true colours.** to display one's true nature or character.

colour sergeant *n.* a sergeant who carries the regimental, battalion, or national colours.

colour supplement *n. Brit.* an illustrated magazine accompanying a newspaper.

colt (kəʊlt) *n.* **1.** a young male horse or pony. **2.** *Sport.* a young and inexperienced player; a member of a junior team. [Old English: young ass]

coltsfoot ('kəʊlts,fʊt) *n., pl.* **-foots.** a European plant with yellow daisy-like flowers and heart-shaped leaves: a common weed.

columbine ('kɒləm,baɪn) *n.* a plant that has brightly coloured flowers with five spurred petals. [Medieval Latin *columbīna herba* dovelike plant]

column ('kɒləm) *n.* **1.** an upright pillar usually having a cylindrical shaft, a base, and a capital. **2.** a form or structure in the shape of a column: *a column of air.* **3.** *Mil.* a narrow formation in which individuals or units follow one behind the other. **4. a.** a single row of type on a newspaper. **b.** a regular feature in a paper: *the fashion column.* **5.** a vertical arrangement of numbers. [Latin *columna*] —**columnar** (kə'lʌmnə) *adj.*

columnist ('kɒləmnɪst, -əmɪst) *n.* a journalist who writes a regular feature in a newspaper.

com- *or* **con-** *prefix.* used with a main word to mean: together; with; jointly: *commingle.* [Latin, from *cum* with]

coma ('kəʊmə) *n.* a state of unconsciousness from which a person cannot be aroused, caused by injury, disease, or drugs. [Greek *kōma* heavy sleep]

comatose ('kəʊmə,təʊs) *adj.* **1.** in a state of coma. **2.** drowsy; lethargic.

comb (kəʊm) *n.* **1.** a toothed strip of rigid material for disentangling or arranging hair. **2.** a tool or machine that cleans and straightens wool or cotton. **3.** a fleshy serrated crest on the head of a domestic fowl. **4.** a honeycomb. ~*vb.* **5.** to use a comb on. **6.** to search with great care: *the police combed the woods.* [Old English *camb*]

combat n. ('kɒmbæt, -bət, or kʌm-). **1.** a fight, conflict, or struggle. ~vb. (kəm-'bæt; 'kɒmbæt; 'kʌm-). **2.** to fight; to combat disease. [Latin com- with + battuere to beat] —'**combative** adj.

combatant ('kɒmbət'nt, 'kʌm-) n. **1.** a person taking part in a combat. ~adj. **2.** engaged in or ready for combat.

combe or **comb** (kuːm) n. same as **coomb**.

comber ('kəʊmə) n. **1.** a person, tool, or machine that combs wool or flax. **2.** a long curling wave; roller.

combination (,kɒmbɪ'neɪʃən) n. **1.** the act of combining or state of being combined. **2.** a union of separate parts or qualities. **3.** an alliance of people or parties. **4.** the set of numbers or letters that opens a combination lock. **5.** Maths. an arrangement of the members of a set into specified groups without regard to order in the group.

combination lock n. a lock that can only be opened when a set of dials is turned to show a specific sequence of numbers or letters.

combinations (,kɒmbɪ'neɪʃənz) pl. n. Brit. a one-piece undergarment with long sleeves and legs.

combine vb. (kəm'baɪn). **1.** to join together. **2.** to unite or cause to unite to form a chemical compound. ~n. ('kɒmbaɪn). **3.** short for **combine harvester**. **4.** an association of persons, or firms for a common purpose. [Latin com- together + bīnī two by two]

combine harvester ('kɒmbaɪn) n. a machine used to reap and thresh grain in one process.

combings ('kəʊmɪŋz) pl. n. the loose hair or fibres removed by combing.

combining form n. a part of a word that occurs only as part of a compound word, such as anthropo- in anthropology.

combo ('kɒmbəʊ) n., pl. -bos. a small group of jazz musicians.

combustible (kəm'bʌstɪb'l) adj. capable of igniting and burning easily.

combustion (kəm'bʌstʃən) n. **1.** the process of burning. **2.** a chemical reaction in which a substance combines with oxygen to produce heat and light. [Latin combūrere to burn up]

come (kʌm) vb. **coming, came, come. 1.** to move towards a place considered near to the speaker or hearer: I'll come to see you soon. **2.** to arrive or reach: we soon came to a pub. **3.** to occur: Christmas comes but once a year. **4.** to happen as a result: no good will come of this. **5.** to occur to the mind: the truth suddenly came to me. **6.** to reach a specified point, state, or situation: she comes up to my shoulder; to come to grief. **7.** to be produced: that dress comes in red. **8.** (foll. by from) to be or have been a resident or native (of): I come from London. **9.** to become: your wishes will come true. **10.** Slang. to have an orgasm. **11.** Brit. informal. to play the part of: don't come the innocent with me. **12.** (subjunctive use) when a specified time arrives: come next August. **13.** as ... as they come. the most characteristic example of a type.

14. come again? Informal. what did you say? **15. come to light.** to be revealed. ~interj. **16.** an exclamation expressing annoyance or impatience: come now! ~See also **come about, come across**, etc. [Old English cuman]

come about vb. to take place; happen.

come across vb. **1.** to meet or find by accident. **2.** to communicate the intended meaning or impression. **3.** to give a certain impression.

come at vb. to attack: he came at me with an axe.

comeback ('kʌm,bæk) n. Informal. **1.** a return to a former position or status. **2.** a response or retaliation. ~vb. **come back. 3.** to return, esp. to the memory. **4.** to become fashionable again.

come between vb. to cause the estrangement or separation of (two people).

come by vb. to find or obtain, esp. accidentally: do you ever come by any old books?

Comecon ('kɒmɪ,kɒn) n. an economic league of Soviet-oriented Communist nations. [Co(uncil for) M(utual) Econ(omic Aid)]

comedian (kə'miːdɪən) n. **1.** an entertainer who specializes in jokes or comic skits. **2.** an actor in comedy.

comedown ('kʌm,daʊn) n. **1.** a decline in status or prosperity. **2.** Informal. a disappointment. ~vb. **come down. 3.** (of prices) to become lower. **4.** to reach a decision: the report came down in favour of a pay increase. **5.** (often foll. by to) to be handed down by tradition or inheritance. **6.** (foll. by with) to begin to suffer from (illness). **7.** (foll. by on) to rebuke harshly. **8.** (foll. by to) to amount (to): it comes down to two choices. **9. come down in the world.** to lose status or prosperity.

comedy ('kɒmɪdɪ) n., pl. -dies. **1.** a humorous film, play, or broadcast. **2.** such works as a genre. **3.** (in classical literature) a play in which the main characters triumph over adversity. **4.** the humorous aspect of life or of events. [Greek kōmos village festival + aeidein to sing]

come forward vb. **1.** to offer one's services; volunteer. **2.** to present oneself.

come-hither adj. Informal. flirtatious; seductive: a come-hither look.

come in vb. **1.** to prove to be: it came in useful. **2.** to become fashionable or seasonable. **3.** to finish a race (in a certain position). **4.** to be received: news is coming in of a fire in Hull. **5.** (of money) to be received as income. **6.** to be involved in a situation: where do I come in? **7.** (foll. by for) to be the object of: she came in for a lot of criticism.

come into vb. **1.** to enter. **2.** to inherit.

comely ('kʌmlɪ) adj. -lier, -liest. good-looking; attractive. [Old English cymlic beautiful] —'**comeliness** n.

come of vb. to result from: nothing came of it.

come off vb. **1.** to emerge from a situation in a certain position: they came off badly. **2.** Informal. to take place. **3.**

Informal. to have the intended effect: *his jokes did not come off.*

come-on *n.* **1.** *Informal.* a lure or enticement. ~*vb.* **come on.** **2.** (of power or water) to start running or functioning. **3.** to make progress: *my plants are coming on nicely.* **4.** to begin: *I feel a cold coming on.* **5.** to make an entrance on stage.

come out *vb.* **1.** to be made public or revealed: *the news of her death came out last week.* **2.** to be published: *the paper comes out on Fridays.* **3.** Also: **come out of the closet.** to reveal something formerly concealed, esp. that one is a homosexual. **4.** *Chiefly Brit.* to go on strike. **5.** to declare oneself: *the council came out in favour of the project.* **6.** to end up or turn out: *he came out on top; the figures came out exactly right.* **7.** (foll. by *in*) to become covered with (a rash or spots). **8.** (foll. by *with*) to say or disclose: *you can rely on him to come out with the facts.* **9.** to enter society formally.

come over *vb.* **1.** to influence or affect: *I don't know what came over me lately.* **2.** to communicate the intended meaning or impression. **3.** to give a certain impression. **4.** to change sides or opinions. **5.** *Informal.* to feel a particular sensation: *I came over faint.*

come round *vb.* **1.** to recover consciousness. **2.** to change one's opinion.

comestibles (kə'mɛstɪb'lz) *pl. n.* food. [Latin *comedere* to eat up]

comet ('kɒmɪt) *n.* an object that travels around the sun, with a frozen nucleus and a long luminous tail. [Greek *komētēs* long-haired]

come through *vb.* to survive or endure (an illness or difficult situation) successfully.

come to *vb.* **1.** to regain consciousness. **2.** to amount to (a total figure).

come up *vb.* **1.** to be mentioned or arise: *that question will come up again.* **2.** to be about to happen: *there's a big concert coming up.* **3.** **come up against.** to come into conflict with. **4.** **come up in the world.** to rise in status. **5.** **come up to.** to meet a standard. **6.** **come up with.** to produce or propose.

come upon *vb.* to meet or encounter unexpectedly.

comeuppance (ˌkʌm'ʌpəns) *n. Informal.* deserved punishment. [from *come up* (in the sense: to appear before a court)]

comfit ('kʌmfɪt, 'kɒm-) *n.* a sugar-coated sweet. [Latin *confectum* something prepared]

comfort ('kʌmfət) *n.* **1.** a state of physical ease or wellbeing. **2.** relief from suffering or grief. **3.** a person or thing that brings ease. ~*vb.* **4.** to soothe or console. **5.** to bring physical ease. [Latin *con-* (intensive) + *fortis* strong] —**'comforting** *adj.*

comfortable ('kʌmftəb'l) *adj.* **1.** giving comfort; relaxing. **2.** at ease; free from trouble or pain. **3.** *Informal.* having or being a fairly large income. —**'comfortably** *adv.*

comforter ('kʌmfətə) *n.* **1.** *Chiefly Brit.* a woollen scarf. **2.** a baby's dummy.

comfrey ('kʌmfrɪ) *n.* a tall plant with bell-shaped blue, purplish, or white flowers. [Latin *conferva* water plant]

comfy ('kʌmfɪ) *adj.* **-fier, -fiest.** *Informal.* comfortable.

comic ('kɒmɪk) *adj.* **1.** of or relating to comedy. **2.** humorous; funny. ~*n.* **3.** a comedian. **4.** a magazine, esp. for children, containing comic strips. [Greek *kōmikos*]

comical ('kɒmɪk'l) *adj.* **1.** causing laughter. **2.** ludicrous; laughable. —**'comically** *adv.*

comic opera *n.* a play largely set to music, with comic effects or situations.

comic strip *n.* a sequence of drawings in a newspaper or magazine, telling a humorous story or an adventure.

coming ('kʌmɪŋ) *adj.* **1.** (of time or events) approaching or next. **2.** likely to be important in the future: *the coming thing.* **3.** **have it coming to one.** *Informal.* to deserve what one is about to suffer. ~*n.* **4.** arrival or approach.

comity ('kɒmɪtɪ) *n., pl.* **-ties.** friendly politeness; courtesy, esp. between nations. [Latin *cōmis* affable]

comma ('kɒmə) *n.* the punctuation mark, indicating a slight pause and used where there is a list of items or to separate the parts of a sentence. [Greek *komma* clause]

command (kə'mɑːnd) *vb.* **1.** to order or compel. **2.** to have or be in control or authority over. **3.** to deserve and get: *his nature commands respect.* **4.** to be able to see clearly as from a height. ~*n.* **5.** an order. **6.** the authority to command. **7.** knowledge; control: *a command of French.* **8.** a military or naval unit with a specific function. **9.** *Computers.* a part of a program consisting of a coded instruction to the computer to perform a specified function. [Latin *com-* (intensive) + *mandāre* to enjoin]

commandant ('kɒmənˌdænt, -ˌdɑːnt) *n.* an officer commanding a military group or establishment.

commandeer (ˌkɒmən'dɪə) *vb.* **1.** to seize for public or military use. **2.** to take arbitrarily. [Afrikaans *kommandeer*]

commander (kə'mɑːndə) *n.* **1.** an officer in command of a particular military formation or operation. **2.** a naval commissioned rank. **3.** a high-ranking member of some knightly orders.

commander in chief *n., pl.* **commanders in chief.** the officer holding supreme command of a nation's armed forces.

commanding (kə'mɑːndɪŋ) *adj.* **1.** being in charge. **2.** having the air of authority: *a commanding voice.* **3.** having a wide view.

commandment (kə'mɑːndmənt) *n.* a divine command, esp. one of the Ten Commandments of the Old Testament.

commando (kə'mɑːndəʊ) *n., pl.* **-dos** or **-does.** **a.** a military unit trained for swift, destructive raiding in enemy territory. **b.** a member of such a unit. [Dutch *commando* command]

commedia dell'arte (kɒˈmeɪdɪə dɛlˈɑːtɪ) n. a form of improvised comedy popular in Italy in the 16th century, with stock characters and a stereotyped plot. [Italian]

commemorate (kəˈmɛməˌreɪt) vb. to honour or keep alive the memory of. [Latin com- (intensive) + memorāre to remind] —**comˌmemoˈration** n. —**comˈmemorative** adj.

commence (kəˈmɛns) vb. to begin. [Latin com- (intensive) + initiāre to begin]

commencement (kəˈmɛnsmənt) n. **1.** the beginning; start. **2.** U.S. & Canad. a graduation ceremony.

commend (kəˈmɛnd) vb. **1.** to recommend. **2.** to give in charge; entrust. **3.** to praise. [Latin com- (intensive) + mandāre to entrust] —**comˈmendable** adj. —ˌcom**menˈdation** n.

commensurable (kəˈmɛnsərəbəl) adj. **1.** Maths. **a.** having a common factor. **b.** having units of the same dimensions and being related by whole numbers. **2.** measurable by the same standards. —**comˌmensuraˈbility** n.

commensurate (kəˈmɛnsərɪt) adj. **1.** corresponding in degree, amount, or value. **2.** commensurable. [Latin com- same + mēnsurāre to measure]

comment (ˈkɒmɛnt) n. **1.** a remark, criticism, or observation. **2.** talk or gossip. **3.** a note explaining or criticizing a passage in a text. ~vb. **4.** (often foll. by on) to remark or express an opinion. **5. no comment.** I decline to say anything about the matter. [Latin commentum invention]

commentary (ˈkɒməntrɪ) n., pl. -taries. **1.** a spoken accompaniment to an event, broadcast, or film. **2.** an explanatory series of notes on a text or other subject.

commentate (ˈkɒmənˌteɪt) vb. to act as a commentator.

commentator (ˈkɒmənˌteɪtə) n. **1.** a person who provides a spoken commentary for a broadcast or film, esp. of a sporting event. **2.** an expert who reports on and analyses a particular subject.

commerce (ˈkɒmɜːs) n. **1.** the purchase and sale of goods and services; trade. **2.** social relations. [Latin commercium]

commercial (kəˈmɜːʃəl) adj. **1.** of or engaged in commerce. **2.** sponsored or paid for by an advertiser: commercial television. **3.** having profit as the main aim: commercial music. ~n. **4.** a radio or television advertisement.

commercialism (kəˈmɜːʃəˌlɪzəm) n. **1.** the principles and practices of commerce. **2.** exclusive or inappropriate emphasis on profit.

commercialize or -**lise** (kəˈmɜːʃəˌlaɪz) vb. **1.** to make commercial. **2.** to exploit for profit, esp. at the expense of quality. —**comˌmercialiˈzation** or -**liˈsation** n.

commercial traveller n. same as **travelling salesman**.

commie or **commy** (ˈkɒmɪ) n., pl. -mies, adj. Informal & offensive. short for **communist**.

commination (ˌkɒmɪˈneɪʃən) n. the act of threatening divine punishment or vengeance. [Latin comminātiō]

commingle (kɒˈmɪŋgˀl) vb. to mix or be mixed.

commis (ˈkɒmɪs, ˈkɒmɪ) n., pl. -**mis**. an apprentice waiter or chef. [French]

commiserate (kəˈmɪzəˌreɪt) vb. (usually foll. by with) to feel or express sympathy or pity (for). [Latin com- together + miserārī to bewail] —**comˌmiserˈation** n.

commissar (ˈkɒmɪˌsɑː, ˌkɒmɪˈsɑː) n. (in the Soviet Union) an official of the Communist Party responsible for political education.

commissariat (ˌkɒmɪˈsɛərɪət) n. a military department in charge of food supplies. [Medieval Latin commissārius commissary]

commissary (ˈkɒmɪsərɪ) n., pl. -**saries. 1.** U.S. a shop supplying food or equipment, as in a military camp. **2.** a representative or deputy. [Medieval Latin commissārius official in charge]

commission (kəˈmɪʃən) n. **1.** a duty given to a person or group to perform. **2.** authority to perform certain duties. **3.** Mil. **a.** a document conferring a rank on an officer. **b.** the rank granted. **4.** a body or board appointed to perform certain duties: a commission of inquiry. **5.** the fee or percentage paid to an agent, esp. a salesman, for services rendered. **6.** the act of committing a sin or crime. **7. in** (or **out of**) **commission.** in good (or bad) working order. ~vb. **8.** to grant authority to. **9.** Mil. to confer a rank on. **10.** to prepare (a ship) for active service. **11.** to place an order for (something): to commission a portrait. [Latin committere to commit]

commissionaire (kəˌmɪʃəˈnɛə) n. Chiefly Brit. a uniformed doorman at a hotel, theatre, or cinema. [French]

commissioned officer n. a military officer holding rank by a commission.

commissioner (kəˈmɪʃənə) n. **1.** an appointed official in a government department or other organization. **2.** a member of a commission.

commit (kəˈmɪt) vb. -**mitting**, -**mitted. 1.** to hand over, as for safekeeping; entrust. **2. commit to memory.** to memorize. **3. commit to paper** or **writing.** to write down. **4.** to send (someone) to prison or hospital against their will. **5.** (usually passive) to pledge or bind (oneself), as to a particular cause: a committed radical. **6.** to perform (a crime or error). [Latin committere to join]

commitment (kəˈmɪtmənt) n. **1.** the act of committing or state of being committed. **2.** an obligation, responsibility, or promise that restricts freedom of action. **3.** dedication to a cause or principle.

committee (kəˈmɪtɪ) n. a group of people appointed to perform a specified service or function. [Middle English committen to entrust]

commode (kəˈməʊd) n. **1.** a chair with a hinged flap concealing a chamber pot. **2.** a chest of drawers. [French]

commodious (kəˈməʊdɪəs) adj. roomy; spacious. [Latin commodus convenient]

commodity (kə'mɒdɪtɪ) n., pl. **-ties**. something of use or profit, esp. something that can be bought or sold. [Latin *commoditās* suitability]

commodore ('kɒmə,dɔː) n. 1. *Brit.* a senior commissioned officer in the navy. 2. the president of a yacht club. [prob. from Dutch *commandeur*]

common ('kɒmən) adj. 1. belonging to two or more people: *common property*. 2. belonging to the whole community; public: *a common culture*. 3. widespread among people in general: *common decency; common knowledge*. 4. frequently encountered: *a common brand of soap*. 5. low-class, vulgar, or coarse. 6. not belonging to the upper classes: *the common man*. 7. *Maths*. belonging to two or more: *common denominator*. 8. **common or garden**. *Informal*. ordinary; usual. ~n. 9. a piece of open land belonging to all the members of a community. 10. **in common**. shared, in joint use. ~See also **commons**. [Latin *commūnis* general] —'**commonly** adv.

commonality (ˌkɒmə'nælɪtɪ) n., pl. **-ties**. 1. the sharing of common attributes. 2. the ordinary people.

commonalty ('kɒmənəltɪ) n., pl. **-ties**. 1. the ordinary people. 2. the members of an incorporated society.

commoner ('kɒmənə) n. a person who does not belong to the nobility.

common fraction n. same as **simple fraction**.

common law n. law based on judges' decisions and custom, as distinct from written laws.

common-law marriage n. a relationship regarded as a marriage, between a man and a woman who have lived together for a number of years.

Common Market n. **the**. an economic association of European countries, who make decisions on trade and agriculture. Also called: **European Community, European Economic Community**.

commonplace ('kɒmən,pleɪs) adj. 1. ordinary; everyday. 2. dull; trite: *commonplace prose*. ~n. 3. a cliché; trite remark. 4. an ordinary thing. [translation of Latin *locus commūnis* argument of wide application]

common room n. *Chiefly Brit.* a sitting room for students or staff in schools or colleges.

commons ('kɒmənz) pl. n. 1. *Brit.* shared food or rations. 2. **short commons**. reduced rations.

Commons ('kɒmənz) n. **the**. same as **House of Commons**.

common sense n. 1. good practical sense. ~adj. **common-sense**. 2. inspired by or displaying this.

common time n. *Music*. a time signature with four crotchet beats to the bar; four-four time.

commonwealth ('kɒmən,wɛlθ) n. the people of a state or nation viewed politically.

Commonwealth ('kɒmən,wɛlθ) n. **the**. 1. Official name: **the Commonwealth of Nations**. an association of sovereign states

that are or at some time have been ruled by Britain. 2. the official title of the federated states of Australia.

commotion (kə'məʊʃən) n. 1. violent disturbance; upheaval. 2. a confused noise; din. [Latin *com-* (intensive) + *movēre* to move]

communal ('kɒmjʊn'l) adj. 1. belonging to or used by a community as a whole. 2. of a commune. —'**communally** adv.

commune[1] (kə'mjuːn) vb. (usually foll. by *with*) 1. to talk intimately. 2. to experience strong emotion (for): *to commune with nature*. [Old French *comuner* to hold in common]

commune[2] ('kɒmjuːn) n. 1. a group of families or individuals living together and sharing possessions and responsibilities. 2. the smallest district of local government in Belgium, France, Italy, and Switzerland. [Latin *commūnia* things held in common]

communicable (kə'mjuːnɪkəb'l) adj. 1. capable of being communicated. 2. (of a disease) capable of being passed on readily.

communicant (kə'mjuːnɪkənt) n. *Christianity*. a person who receives Communion.

communicate (kə'mjuːnɪ,keɪt) vb. 1. to exchange (thoughts) or make known (information or feelings) by speech, writing, or other means. 2. (usually foll. by *to*) to transmit (to): *the dog communicated his fear to the other animals*. 3. to have a sympathetic mutual understanding. 4. (usually foll. by *with*) to connect: *the kitchen communicates with the dining room*. 5. *Christianity*. to receive Communion. [Latin *commūnicāre* to share] —com'**muni,cator** n. —com'**municative** adj.

communication (kə,mjuːnɪ'keɪʃən) n. 1. the imparting or exchange of information, ideas, or feelings. 2. something communicated, such as a message.

communication cord n. *Brit.* a cord or chain in a train which may be pulled by a passenger to stop the train in an emergency.

communion (kə'mjuːnjən) n. 1. a sharing of thoughts, emotions, or beliefs. 2. (foll. by *with*) strong feelings (for): *communion with nature*. 3. a religious group having common beliefs and practices. [Latin *commūnis* common]

Communion (kə'mjuːnjən) n. *Christianity*. 1. a ritual commemorating Christ's Last Supper by the consecration of bread and wine. 2. the consecrated bread and wine. ~Also called: **Holy Communion**.

communiqué (kə'mjuːnɪ,keɪ) n. an official communication or announcement. [French]

communism ('kɒmjʊ,nɪzəm) n. 1. the belief that private ownership should be abolished and all work and property should be shared by the community. 2. (*cap.*) a political movement based upon the writings of Marx that advocates communism. 3. (*cap.*) the political and social system established in countries with a ruling Communist Party, esp. in the Soviet Union. [French *communisme*]

communist ('kɒmjʊnɪst) n. **1.** a supporter of communism. **2.** (cap.) a member of a Communist party. ~adj. **3.** of or favouring communism. —**commu'nistic** adj.

community (kə'mjuːnɪtɪ) n., pl. **-ties. 1.** the people living in one locality. **2.** a group of people having cultural, or other characteristics in common: the Chinese community. **3.** a group of nations having certain interests in common. **4.** the public; society. **5.** a group of interdependent plants and animals inhabiting the same region. [Latin commūnis COMMON]

community centre n. a building used by a community for social gatherings or activities.

community charge n. the formal name for **poll tax.**

commutative (kə'mjuːtətɪv, 'kɒmjuˌteɪtɪv) adj. Maths. giving the same result irrespective of the order of the numbers or symbols; thus addition is commutative but subtraction is not.

commutator ('kɒmjuˌteɪtə) n. a device used to reverse the direction of flow of an electric current.

commute (kə'mjuːt) vb. **1.** to travel some distance regularly between one's home and one's place of work. **2.** to substitute. **3.** Law. to reduce (a sentence) to one less severe. **4.** to pay (an annuity or pension) at one time, instead of in instalments. [Latin com- mutually + mutāre to change] —**com'mutable** adj. —**commutation** (ˌkɒmjuːˈteɪʃən) n.

commuter (kə'mjuːtə) n. a person who travels a considerable distance to work, usually from the suburbs to the centre of a city.

compact¹ adj. (kəm'pækt). **1.** closely packed together. **2.** neatly fitted into a restricted space. **3.** concise; brief. ~vb. (kəm'pækt). **4.** to pack closely together; compress. ~n. ('kɒmpækt). **5.** a small flat case containing a mirror and face powder. [Latin com- together + pangere to fasten] —**com'pactly** adv. —**com'pactness** n.

compact² ('kɒmpækt) n. a contract or agreement. [Latin com- together + pacisci to contract]

compact disc ('kɒmpækt) n. a small digital audio disc on which the sound is read by an optical laser system.

companion (kəm'pænjən) n. **1.** a person who associates with or accompanies another. **2.** (esp. formerly) a woman paid to live or travel with another. **3.** one of a pair. **4.** a guidebook or handbook. [Late Latin compāniō one who eats bread with another] —**com'panionˌship** n.

companionable (kəm'pænjənəb°l) adj. sociable, friendly. —**com'panionably** adv.

companionway (kəm'pænjənˌweɪ) n. a ladder from one deck to another in a ship.

company ('kʌmpənɪ) n., pl. **-nies. 1.** a number of people gathered together; assembly. **2.** the fact of being with someone; companionship: I enjoy her company. **3.** a guest or guests. **4.** a person's associates. **5.** a business organization. **6.** a group of actors. **7.** a small unit of troops. **8.** the officers and crew of a ship. **9. keep someone company.** to accompany someone. **10. part company** to disagree or separate. [see COMPANION]

company sergeant-major n. Mil. the senior noncommissioned officer in a company.

comparable ('kɒmpərəb°l) adj. **1.** worthy of comparison. **2.** able to be compared (with). —**compara'bility** n.

comparative (kəm'pærətɪv) adj. **1.** involving comparison: comparative literature. **2.** relative: comparative peace. **3.** Grammar. the form of an adjective or adverb that indicates that the quality denoted is possessed to a greater extent. In English the comparative is marked by the suffix -er or the word more. ~n. **4.** the comparative form of an adjective or adverb. —**com'paratively** adv.

compare (kəm'pɛə) vb. **1.** (foll. by to) to regard as similar; liken: the general has been compared to Napoleon. **2.** to examine in order to observe resemblances or differences: to compare rum and gin. **3.** (usually foll. by with) to resemble: gin compares with rum in strength. **4.** to bear a specified relation when examined: this car compares badly with other cars. **5. compare notes.** to exchange opinions. ~n. **6. beyond compare.** without equal. [Latin com- together + par equal]

comparison (kəm'pærɪs°n) n. **1.** a comparing or being compared. **2.** likeness: there was no comparison between them. **3.** Grammar. the positive, comparative, and superlative forms of an adjective or adverb. **4. in comparison to or with.** compared to. **5. bear or stand comparison with.** to be able to be compared with (something else), esp. favourably.

compartment (kəm'pɑːtmənt) n. **1.** (esp. formerly) one of the sections into which a railway carriage is divided. **2.** any separate section: a compartment of the mind. **3.** a small storage space. [French compartiment]

compartmentalize or **-lise** (ˌkɒmpɑːt'ment°ˌlaɪz) vb. to put into categories, esp. to an excessive degree.

compass ('kʌmpəs) n. **1.** an instrument for finding direction, having a magnetized needle which points to magnetic north. **2.** (often pl.) an instrument used for drawing circles or measuring distances, that consists of two arms, joined at one end. **3.** limits or range: within the compass of education. [Latin com- together + passus step]

compassion (kəm'pæʃən) n. a feeling of distress and pity for the suffering or misfortune of another. [Latin com- with + pati to suffer]

compassionate (kəm'pæʃənɪt) adj. showing or having compassion. —**com'passionately** adv.

compatible (kəm'pætɪb°l) adj. **1.** (usually foll. by with) able to exist together harmoniously. **2.** (usually foll. by with) consistent: her deeds were not compatible with her ideology. **3.** (of pieces of equipment) capable of being used together. [Late Latin *compatī* to suffer with] —**com‚pati'bility** *n*.

compatriot (kəm'pætrɪət) *n*. a fellow countryman. [French *compatriote*]

compel (kəm'pɛl) *vb*. **-pelling, -pelled. 1.** to force (someone) (to be or do something). **2.** to obtain by force; exact: *to compel obedience*. [Latin *com-* together + *pellere* to drive]

compelling (kəm'pɛlɪŋ) *adj*. forceful; arousing strong interest.

compendious (kəm'pɛndɪəs) *adj*. brief but comprehensive.

compendium (kəm'pɛndɪəm) *n*., *pl*. **-diums** or **-dia** (-dɪə). **1.** *Brit*. a selection of different table games in one container. **2.** a concise but comprehensive summary. [Latin: a saving, lit.: something weighed]

compensate ('kɒmpən‚seɪt) *vb*. **1.** to make amends to (someone), esp. for loss or injury. **2.** to serve as compensation for (injury or loss). **3.** to cancel out the effects of (something). [Latin *compēnsāre*] —**compensatory** ('kɒmpən‚seɪtrɪ, kəm'pɛnsətrɪ) *adj*.

compensation (‚kɒmpən'seɪʃən) *n*. **1.** the act of making amends for something. **2.** something given as reparation for loss or injury.

compere ('kɒmpeə) *Brit*. ~*n*. **1.** a person who introduces a radio or television show, esp. a variety show. ~*vb*. **2.** to act as a compere (for). [French: godfather]

compete (kəm'piːt) *vb*. (often foll. by *with*) to take part in a contest or competition (against). [Latin *com-* together + *petere* to seek]

competence ('kɒmpɪtəns) or **competency** *n*. **1.** the condition of being capable; ability. **2.** a sufficient income to live on. **3.** the state of being legally competent or qualified.

competent ('kɒmpɪtənt) *adj*. **1.** having sufficient skill or knowledge; capable. **2.** suitable or sufficient for the purpose: *a competent answer*. [Latin *competēns*]

competition (‚kɒmpɪ'tɪʃən) *n*. **1.** the act of competing; rivalry. **2.** an event in which people compete. **3.** a series of games or sports events. **4.** the opposition offered by competitors. **5.** competitors offering opposition.

competitive (kəm'pɛtɪtɪv) *adj*. **1.** involving rivalry: *competitive sports*. **2.** of sufficiently good value to be successful against commercial rivals. **3.** characterized by an urge to compete: *a competitive personality*. —**com'petitiveness** *n*.

competitor (kəm'pɛtɪtə) *n*. a person, team, or firm, that vies or competes; rival.

compile (kəm'paɪl) *vb*. **1.** to collect and arrange (information) from various sources, esp. to form a book. **2.** *Computers*. to create (a set of machine instructions) from a high-level programming language, using a compiler. [Latin *com-* together + *pīlāre* to thrust down, pack] —**compilation** (‚kɒmpɪ'leɪʃən) *n*.

compiler (kəm'paɪlə) *n*. **1.** a person who compiles information, esp. to form a book.

2. a computer program which converts a high-level programming language into the machine language used by a computer.

complacency (kəm'pleɪsənsɪ) *n*. extreme self-satisfaction; smugness. —**com'placent** *adj*.

complain (kəm'pleɪn) *vb*. **1.** to express resentment or displeasure. **2.** (foll. by *of*) to state the presence of pain or illness: *she complained of a headache*. **3.** to make a formal protest: *she complained to the police about the noise*. [Latin *com-* (intensive) + *plangere* to bewail]

complainant (kəm'pleɪnənt) *n*. *Law*. a plaintiff.

complaint (kəm'pleɪnt) *n*. **1.** the act of complaining. **2.** a cause for complaining; grievance. **3.** a mild ailment. **4.** a formal protest.

complaisant (kəm'pleɪz°nt) *adj*. willing to please or oblige. [Latin *complacēre* to please greatly] —**com'plaisance** *n*.

complement *n*. ('kɒmplɪmənt). **1.** a person or thing that completes something. **2.** a complete amount or number: *the full complement*. **3.** the officers and crew needed to man a ship. **4.** *Grammar*. a word or words added to the verb to complete the meaning of the predicate in a sentence, as *a fool* in *He is a fool* or *that he would come* in *I hoped that he would come*. **5.** *Maths*. the angle that when added to a specified angle produces a right angle. ~*vb*. ('kɒmplɪ‚mɛnt). **6.** to complete or form a complement to. [Latin *com-* (intensive) + *plēre* to fill]

complementary (‚kɒmplɪ'mɛntrɪ) *adj*. **1.** forming a complement. **2.** forming a complete or balanced whole.

complementary medicine *n*. same as **alternative medicine**.

complete (kəm'pliːt) *adj*. **1.** having every necessary part; entire. **2.** finished. **3.** thorough; absolute: *he is a complete rogue*. **4.** perfect in quality or kind: *he is a complete scholar*. **5. complete with.** having as an extra feature or part: *a mansion complete with swimming pool*. ~*vb*. **6.** to make whole or perfect. **7.** to finish. [Latin *complēre* to fill up] —**com'pletely** *adv*. —**com'pletion** *n*.

complex ('kɒmplɛks) *adj*. **1.** made up of interconnected parts. **2.** intricate or complicated. **3.** *Maths*. of or involving complex numbers. ~*n*. **4.** a whole made up of related parts: *a sports complex*. **5.** *Psychoanal*. a group of emotional impulses that have been banished from the conscious mind but continue to influence a person's behaviour. **6.** *Informal*. an obsession or phobia: *he's got a complex about cats*. [Latin *com-* together + *plectere* to braid]

complex fraction *n*. *Maths*. a fraction in which the numerator or denominator or both contain fractions.

complexion (kəm'plɛkʃən) *n*. **1.** the colour and general appearance of a person's skin, esp. of the face. **2.** aspect, character, or nature: *the general complexion of a nation's finances*. [Latin *complexion* a combination]

complexity (kəm'plɛksɪtɪ) n., pl. **-ties.** **1.** the state or quality of being intricate or complex. **2.** something intricate; complication.

complex number n. any number of the form a + bi, where a and b are real numbers and i = √−1.

compliance (kəm'plaɪəns) n. **1.** acquiescence. **2.** a tendency to yield to others. **—com'pliant** adj.

complicate ('kɒmplɪ,keɪt) vb. to make or become complex or difficult. [Latin complicāre to fold together]
complicated ('kɒmplɪ,keɪtɪd) adj. difficult to understand or deal with.

complication (,kɒmplɪ'keɪʃən) n. **1.** a complicated or confused state of affairs. **2.** a complicating factor: her coming was a serious complication. **3.** a medical condition arising as a consequence of another.

complicity (kəm'plɪsɪtɪ) n., pl. **-ties.** the fact of being an accomplice, esp. in a criminal act.

compliment n. ('kɒmplɪmənt). **1.** a remark or praise expressing respect. **2.** (pl.) a greeting of respect or regard. ~vb. ('kɒmplɪ,mɛnt). **3.** to express admiration for; congratulate. [Italian complimento]

complimentary (,kɒmplɪ'mɛntrɪ) adj. **1.** expressing a compliment. **2.** given free, esp. as a courtesy or for publicity purposes.

comply (kəm'plaɪ) vb. **-plying, -plied.** (usually foll. by with) to act in accordance with a rule, order or request. [Spanish cumplir to complete]

component (kəm'pəʊnənt) n. **1.** a constituent part or feature of a whole. **2.** Maths. one of a set of two or more vectors whose resultant is a given vector. ~adj. **3.** forming or functioning as a part or feature; constituent. [Latin compōnere to put together]

comport (kəm'pɔːt) vb. **1.** to conduct or behave (oneself) in a specified way. **2.** (foll. by with) to suit or befit. [Latin comportāre to collect] **—com'portment** n.

compose (kəm'pəʊz) vb. **1.** to put together or make up. **2.** to be the component elements of. **3.** to create (a musical or literary work). **4.** to calm (oneself). **5.** to arrange artistically; design. **6.** Printing. to set up (type). [Latin compōnere to put in place] **—com'poser** n.

composed (kəm'pəʊzd) adj. (of people) calm; tranquil.

composite ('kɒmpəzɪt) adj. **1.** composed of separate parts. **2.** (of a plant) having flower heads made up of many small flowers, as the dandelion or daisy. **3.** Maths. capable of being factorized: a composite function. ~n. **4.** something composed of separate parts. **5.** a composite plant. [Latin compositus well arranged]

composite school n. Canad. a secondary school which offers both academic and nonacademic courses.

composition (,kɒmpə'zɪʃən) n. **1.** the act of putting together or composing. **2.** something composed. **3.** the things or parts which make up a whole. **4.** a work of

music, art, or literature. **5.** the harmonious arrangement of the parts of a work of art. **6.** a written exercise; an essay. **7.** Printing. the act or technique of setting up type.

compositor (kəm'pɒzɪtə) n. Printing. a person who sets and corrects type.

compos mentis Latin. ('kɒmpəs 'mɛntɪs) adj. of sound mind; sane.

compost ('kɒmpɒst) n. **1.** a mixture of decaying plants and manure, used as a fertilizer. **2.** soil mixed with fertilizer, used for growing plants. ~vb. **3.** to make (vegetable matter) into compost. [Latin compositus put together]

composure (kəm'pəʊʒə) n. calmness; tranquillity; serenity.

compote ('kɒmpəʊt) n. fruit stewed with sugar or in a syrup. [French]

compound[1] n. ('kɒmpaʊnd). **1.** a substance that contains atoms of two or more chemical elements held together by chemical bonds. **2.** any combination of two or more parts, features, or qualities. **3.** a word formed from two existing words or combining forms. ~vb. (kəm'paʊnd). **4.** to combine so as to create a compound. **5.** to make by combining parts or features: to compound a new plastic. **6.** to intensify by an added element: his anxiety was compounded by her crying. **7.** Law. to agree not to prosecute in return for payment: to compound a crime. ~adj. ('kɒmpaʊnd). **8.** composed of two or more parts or elements. **9.** Music. with a time in which the number of beats per bar is a multiple of three: six-four is an example of compound time. [Latin compōnere to put in order] **—com'poundable** adj.

compound[2] ('kɒmpaʊnd) n. a fenced enclosure containing buildings, such as a camp for prisoners of war. [Malay kampong village]

compound fracture n. a fracture in which the broken bone pierces the skin.

compound interest n. interest paid on both the sum invested and its accumulated interest.

compound sentence n. a sentence containing at least two clauses linked by and, or, or but.

comprehend (,kɒmprɪ'hɛnd) vb. **1.** to understand. **2.** to comprise; include. [Latin comprehendere] **—compre'hensible** adj.

comprehension (,kɒmprɪ'hɛnʃən) n. **1.** understanding. **2.** inclusion.

comprehensive (,kɒmprɪ'hɛnsɪv) adj. **1.** of broad scope or content; fully inclusive. **2.** (of car insurance) providing protection against most risks, including third-party liability, fire, theft, and damage. **3.** of the comprehensive school system. ~n. **4.** a comprehensive school.

comprehensive school n. Chiefly Brit. a secondary school for children of all abilities from the same district.

compress vb. (kəm'prɛs). **1.** to squeeze together; compress. ~n. ('kɒmprɛs). **2.** a cloth or pad applied firmly to some part of the body to relieve discomfort or reduce fever. [Latin comprimere]

compression (kəmˈprɛʃən) n. **1.** the act of compressing or state of being compressed. **2.** the reduction in volume and increase in pressure of the fuel mixture in an internal-combustion engine before ignition.

compressor (kəmˈprɛsə) n. any device that compresses a gas.

comprise (kəmˈpraɪz) vb. **1.** to be made up of: *the Council comprised 28 members.* **2.** to constitute the whole: *her singing comprised the entertainment.* [French *compris* included]

compromise (ˈkɒmprəˌmaɪz) n. **1.** settlement of a dispute by concessions on each side. **2.** the terms of such a settlement. **3.** something midway between different things. ~vb. **4.** to settle (a dispute) by making concessions. **5.** to expose (oneself or another) to disrepute. [Latin *comprōmittere* to promise at the same time] —ˈcomproˌmising adj.

Comptometer (kɒmpˈtɒmɪtə) n. *Trademark.* a high-speed calculating machine.

comptroller (kənˈtrəʊlə) n. a financial controller.

compulsion (kəmˈpʌlʃən) n. **1.** the act of compelling or the state of being compelled. **2.** something that compels. **3.** an irresistible urge to perform some action. [Latin *compellere* to compel]

compulsive (kəmˈpʌlsɪv) adj. **1.** resulting from or acting from a compulsion. **2.** irresistible or absorbing. —comˈpulsively adv.

compulsory (kəmˈpʌlsərɪ) adj. required by regulations or laws; obligatory.

compulsory purchase n. the enforced purchase of a property by a local authority or government department.

compunction (kəmˈpʌŋkʃən) n. a feeling of remorse, guilt, or regret. [Latin *compungere* to sting]

computation (ˌkɒmpjʊˈteɪʃən) n. a calculation involving numbers or quantities. —ˌcompuˈtational adj.

compute (kəmˈpjuːt) vb. to calculate (an answer or result), often with the aid of a computer. [Latin *computāre*]

computer (kəmˈpjuːtə) n. a device, usually electronic, that processes data according to a set of instructions. See **digital computer.**

computerize or **-ise** (kəmˈpjuːtəˌraɪz) vb. **1.** to equip with a computer. **2.** to control or perform (operations) by means of a computer. —comˌputeriˈzation or -iˈsation n.

comrade (ˈkɒmreɪd, -rɪd) n. **1.** a companion. **2.** a fellow member of a political party, esp. a fellow Communist. [French *camarade*] —ˈcomradely adj. —ˈcomradeˌship n.

con[1] (kɒn) *Informal.* ~n. **1.** same as **confidence trick.** ~vb. **conning, conned.** **2.** to swindle or defraud.

con[2] (kɒn) n. See **pros and cons.** [Latin *contrā* against]

con[3] (kɒn) n. *Slang.* a convict.

Con *Politics.* Conservative.

con- See **com-.**

concatenation (ˌkɒnkætɪˈneɪʃən) n. a series of linked events. [Latin *com-* together + *catēna* chain]

concave (ˈkɒnkeɪv, kɒnˈkeɪv) adj. curving inwards like the inside surface of a ball. [Latin *concavus* arched] —**concavity** (kɒnˈkævɪtɪ) n.

conceal (kənˈsiːl) vb. to keep hidden or secret. [Latin *com-* (intensive) + *cēlāre* to hide] —conˈcealment n.

concede (kənˈsiːd) vb. **1.** to admit (something) as true or correct. **2.** to give up or grant (something, such as a right). **3.** to acknowledge defeat in (a contest or argument). [Latin *concēdere*]

conceit (kənˈsiːt) n. **1.** an excessively high opinion of oneself or one's merits. **2.** *Literary.* a far-fetched or clever comparison. [see CONCEIVE]

conceited (kənˈsiːtɪd) adj. having an excessively high opinion of oneself or one's merits. —conˈceitedness n.

conceivable (kənˈsiːvəbʰl) adj. capable of being understood, believed, or imagined; possible. —conˈceivably adv.

conceive (kənˈsiːv) vb. **1.** to form in the mind; imagine; think (of). **2.** to consider in a certain way; believe: *we must do what we conceive to be right.* **3.** to become pregnant with (a child). [Latin *concipere* to take in]

concentrate (ˈkɒnsənˌtreɪt) vb. **1.** to focus all one's attention, thoughts, or efforts (on): *stop talking and concentrate on your work.* **2.** to make a liquid stronger by the removal of water from it. **3.** to bring or come together in large numbers or amounts, in one place: *power is concentrated in the hands of the rich.* ~n. **4.** a concentrated substance. [Latin *com-* same + *centrum* CENTRE] —ˈconcenˌtrated adj.

concentration (ˌkɒnsənˈtreɪʃən) n. **1.** intense mental application. **2.** the act of concentrating. **3.** something that is concentrated. **4.** the amount or proportion of a substance in a mixture or solution.

concentration camp n. a prison camp for nonmilitary prisoners, as in Nazi Germany.

concentric (kənˈsɛntrɪk) adj. having a common centre: *concentric circles.* [Latin *com-* same + *centrum* centre]

concept (ˈkɒnsɛpt) n. an idea, esp. an abstract or generalized one: *the concepts of biology.* [Latin *concipere* to conceive]

conception (kənˈsɛpʃən) n. **1.** a notion, idea, or plan. **2.** the fertilization of an egg by a sperm in the womb. **3.** origin or beginning. [Latin *concipere* to conceive]

conceptual (kənˈsɛptjʊəl) adj. of or characterized by concepts.

conceptualize or **-lise** (kənˈsɛptjʊəˌlaɪz) vb. to form a concept or idea of (something). —conˌceptualiˈzation or -liˈsation n.

concern (kənˈsɜːn) vb. **1.** to be relevant or important to. **2.** (usually foll. by *with* or *in*) to involve or interest (oneself): *he concerns himself with other people's affairs.* **3.** to worry or make anxious. ~n.

4. something that is of interest or importance to a person. **5.** regard or interest: *he felt a strong concern for her.* **6.** anxiety or worry. **7.** a business or firm. [Latin *com-* together + *cernere* to sift]

concerned (kən'sɜːnd) *adj.* **1.** interested or involved: *I shall find the boy concerned and punish him.* **2.** worried or anxious.

concerning (kən'sɜːnɪŋ) *prep.* about; regarding.

concert ('kɒnsɜːt) *n.* **1.** a performance of music by players or singers in front of an audience. **2. in concert. a.** acting with a common purpose. **b.** (of musicians or singers) performing live. [Latin *com-* together + *certāre* to strive]

concerted (kən'sɜːtɪd) *adj.* decided or planned by mutual agreement; done in co-operation: *a concerted effort.*

concertina (ˌkɒnsə'tiːnə) *n.* **1.** a small musical instrument similar to the accordion, in which two flat end pieces, joined by folds of material, are pressed together and pulled apart to force air through reeds. ~*vb.* **-naing, -naed. 2.** to collapse or fold up like a concertina. [from *concert*]

concerto (kən'tʃɛətəʊ) *n., pl.* **-tos** *or* **-ti** (-tɪ). a large-scale composition for an orchestra and one or more soloists. [Italian]

concert pitch *n.* the internationally agreed pitch to which concert instruments are tuned for performance.

concession (kən'sɛʃən) *n.* **1.** the act of yielding or conceding. **2.** something conceded. **3.** any grant of rights, land, or property by a government, local authority, or company. **4.** a reduction in price for a certain category of person: *there is a special concession for students.* **5.** *Canad.* **a.** a land subdivision in a township survey. **b.** same as **concession road.** [Latin *concēdere* to concede] —**con'cessionary** *adj.*

concessionaire (kənˌsɛʃə'nɛə) *n.* someone who holds a concession.

concession road *n. Canad.* one of a series of roads separating concessions in a township.

conch (kɒŋk, kɒntʃ) *n., pl.* **conchs** (kɒŋks) *or* **conches** ('kɒntʃɪz). **1.** a marine mollusc with a large brightly coloured spiral shell. **2.** the shell of such a mollusc. [Greek *konkhē* shellfish]

concierge (ˌkɒnsɪ'ɛəʒ) *n.* (in France) a porter or door-keeper, esp. of a block of flats. [French]

conciliate (kən'sɪlɪˌeɪt) *vb.* to overcome the hostility of; win over. [Latin *conciliāre* to bring together] —**con'cili'ation** *n.* —**con'cili,ator** *n.*

conciliatory (kən'sɪljətrɪ) *adj.* intended to placate or reconcile.

concise (kən'saɪs) *adj.* brief and to the point. [Latin *concīdere* to cut short] —**con'cisely** *adv.* —**con'ciseness** *or* **concision** (kən'sɪʒən) *n.*

conclave ('kɒnkleɪv) *n.* **1.** a secret meeting. **2.** *R.C. Church.* a private meeting of cardinals to elect a new pope. [Latin *clāvis* key]

conclude (kən'kluːd) *vb.* **1.** to come or

bring to an end. **2.** to decide by reasoning; deduce: *the judge concluded that the witness had told the truth.* **3.** to arrange or settle finally: *to conclude a treaty.* [Latin *conclūdere*]

conclusion (kən'kluːʒən) *n.* **1.** end or ending. **2.** outcome or result: *a foregone conclusion.* **3.** a final decision, opinion or judgment based on reasoning: *to come to a conclusion.* **4. in conclusion.** lastly; to sum up. **5. jump to conclusions.** to come to a conclusion too quickly, without sufficient thought or evidence.

conclusive (kən'kluːsɪv) *adj.* putting an end to doubt; decisive; final. —**con'clusively** *adv.*

concoct (kən'kɒkt) *vb.* **1.** to make by combining different ingredients. **2.** to invent or make up (a story or plan). [Latin *coquere* to cook] —**con'coction** *n.*

concomitant (kən'kɒmɪtənt) *adj.* **1.** existing or along with (something else). ~*n.* **2.** something which is concomitant. [Latin *com-* with + *comes* companion]

concord ('kɒnkɔːd) *n.* **1.** agreement or harmony. **2.** peaceful relations between nations. **3.** *Music.* a harmonious combination of musical notes. [Latin *com-* same + *cors* heart] —**con'cordant** *adj.*

concordance (kən'kɔːd'ns) *n.* **1.** a state of harmony or agreement. **2.** an alphabetical list of the principal words in a literary work, with the context and often an account of the meaning.

concordat (kən'kɔːdæt) *n.* a pact or treaty, such as one between the Vatican and another state concerning church affairs. [Latin *concordātum* something agreed]

concourse ('kɒnkɔːs) *n.* **1.** a large open space in a public place, where people can meet: *the station concourse.* **2.** a crowd; throng. [Latin *concurrere* to run together]

concrete ('kɒnkriːt) *n.* **1.** a building material made of cement, sand, stone and water that hardens to a stonelike mass. ~*adj.* **2.** specific as opposed to general. **3.** relating to things that can be perceived by the senses, as opposed to abstractions. ~*vb.* **4.** to make from or cover with concrete. [Latin *concrēscere* to grow together]

concretion (kən'kriːʃən) *n.* **1.** the act of solidifying; coalescence. **2.** a solidified mass.

concubine ('kɒŋkjʊˌbaɪn, 'kɒn-) *n.* **1.** a woman who cohabits with a man to whom she is not married. **2.** a secondary wife in polygamous societies. [Latin *concumbere* to lie together] —**concubinage** (kɒn-'kjuːbɪnɪdʒ) *n.*

concupiscence (kən'kjuːpɪsəns) *n.* strong sexual desire. [Latin *concupiscere* to covet] —**con'cupiscent** *adj.*

concur (kən'kɜː) *vb.* **-curring, -curred.** **1.** to agree; be in accord. [Latin *concurrere* to run together]

concurrence (kən'kʌrəns) *n.* **1.** agreement; accord. **2.** simultaneous occurrence.

concurrent (kən'kʌrənt) *adj.* **1.** taking place at the same time or place. **2.** meeting at, approaching, or having a common point:

concurrent lines. **3.** in agreement; harmonious.

concuss (kən'kʌs) *vb.* to subject to concussion. [Latin *concutere* to disturb greatly]

concussion (kən'kʌʃən) *n.* **1.** a jarring of the brain, caused by a blow or a fall, usually resulting in loss of consciousness. **2.** violent shaking; shock, as from impact.

condemn (kən'dɛm) *vb.* **1.** to express strong disapproval of. **2.** to pronounce sentence on in a court of law. **3.** to indicate the guilt of: *his secretive behaviour condemned him.* **4.** to judge or declare (something) unfit for use. **5.** to force into a particular state: *his disposition condemned him to boredom.* [Latin *condemnāre*] —**con'demn'nation** *n.* —**condemn'natory** *adj.*

condensation (ˌkɒndɛn'seɪʃən) *n.* **1.** the act of condensing, or the state of being condensed. **2.** anything that has condensed from a vapour, esp. on a window.

condense (kən'dɛns) *vb.* **1.** to increase the density of; compress. **2.** to express in fewer words. **3.** to change from a gas to a liquid or solid. [Latin *condēnsāre*]

condensed milk *n.* milk thickened by evaporation, with sugar added.

condenser (kən'dɛnsə) *n.* **1.** an apparatus for reducing gases to their liquid or solid form by the removal of heat. **2.** a lens that concentrates light. **3.** same as **capacitor**.

condescend (ˌkɒndɪ'sɛnd) *vb.* **1.** to behave patronizingly towards one's supposed inferiors. **2.** to do something in a way that suggests one believes it to be beneath one's own level. [Church Latin *condēscendere*] —**ˌconde'scending** *adj.* —**ˌconde'scension** *n.*

condiment ('kɒndɪmənt) *n.* any seasoning for food, such as salt, pepper, or sauces. [Latin *condīre* to pickle]

condition (kən'dɪʃən) *n.* **1.** a particular state of being: *the human condition.* **2.** something that limits or restricts; a qualification. **3.** (*pl.*) circumstances: *conditions were right for a takeover.* **4.** state of physical fitness, esp. good health: *out of condition.* **5.** an ailment: *a heart condition.* **6.** an indispensable requirement: *food is a necessary condition for survival.* **7.** a term of an agreement: *the conditions of the lease are set out.* **8. on condition that.** provided that. ~*vb.* **9.** to accustom or alter the reaction of (a person or animal) to a particular stimulus or situation. **10.** to put into a fit condition. **11.** to improve the condition of (one's hair) by use of special cosmetics. **12.** to subject to a condition. [Latin *con-* together + *dīcere* to say] —**con'ditioner** *n.* —**con'ditioning** *n.*, *adj.*

conditional (kən'dɪʃən'l) *adj.* **1.** depending on other factors. **2.** *Grammar.* expressing a condition on which something else depends: "*If he comes*" is a conditional clause in the sentence "*If he comes I shall go*".

condo ('kɒndəʊ) *n.*, *pl.* **-dos.** *U.S. & Canad. informal.* a condominium building or apartment.

condole (kən'dəʊl) *vb.* (foll. by *with*) to express sympathy with someone in grief or pain. [Latin *com-* together + *dolēre* to grieve] —**con'dolence** *n.*

condom ('kɒndəm) *n.* a rubber sheath worn on the penis during sexual intercourse to prevent conception or infection. [origin unknown]

condominium (ˌkɒndə'mɪnɪəm) *n.*, *pl.* **-ums.** **1.** joint rule or sovereignty of a state by two or more other states. **2.** *U.S. & Canad.* **a.** an apartment building in which each apartment is individually owned. **b.** an apartment in such a building. [Latin *com-* together + *dominium* ownership]

condone (kən'dəʊn) *vb.* to overlook or forgive (an offence or wrongdoing). [Latin *com-* (intensive) + *dōnāre* to donate]

condor ('kɒndɔː) *n.* a very large rare New World vulture. [S American Indian *kuntur*]

conducive (kən'djuːsɪv) *adj.* (often foll. by *to*) likely to lead to or produce (a result). [Latin *com-* together + *dūcere* to lead]

conduct *n.* ('kɒndʌkt). **1.** behaviour. **2.** the management or handling of an activity or business. ~*vb.* (kən'dʌkt). **3.** to accompany and guide (people or a party): *a conducted tour.* **4.** to carry out; organize: *conduct a survey.* **5.** to behave (oneself). **6.** to control (an orchestra or choir) by the movements of the hands or a baton. **7.** to transmit (heat or electricity). [Latin *com-* together + *dūcere* to lead]

conductance (kən'dʌktəns) *n.* the ability of a specified body to conduct electricity.

conduction (kən'dʌkʃən) *n.* the transmission of something, esp. heat or electricity, through a medium.

conductivity (ˌkɒndʌk'tɪvɪtɪ) *n.*, *pl.* **-ties.** the property of transmitting heat, electricity, or sound.

conductor (kən'dʌktə) *n.* **1.** a person who conducts an orchestra or choir. **2.** an official on a bus who collects fares. **3.** *U.S. & Canad.* a railway official in charge of a train. **4.** something that conducts electricity or heat. —**con'ductress** *fem. n.*

conduit ('kɒndɪt, -djʊɪt) *n.* a channel or tube for carrying a fluid or electrical cables. [Latin *condūcere* to lead]

cone (kəʊn) *n.* **1.** a geometric solid consisting of a circular or oval base and curved sides narrowing evenly to a point. **2.** a cone-shaped wafer shell used to contain ice cream. **3.** the reproductive fruit of conifers, made up of overlapping woody scales. **4.** a plastic cone used as a temporary traffic marker on roads. [Greek *kōnus* pine cone, geometrical cone]

confab ('kɒnfæb) *n. Informal.* a conversation or conversation.

confabulation (kən,fæbjʊ'leɪʃən) *n.* a chat or conversation. [Latin *confābulārī*]

confection (kən'fɛkʃən) *n.* **1.** any sweet food, such as a cake or a sweet. **2.** *Old-fashioned.* an elaborate article of clothing. [Latin *confectiō* a preparing]

confectioner (kənˈfɛkʃənə) n. a person who makes or sells sweets or confections.

confectionery (kənˈfɛkʃənərɪ) n., pl. **-eries.** 1. sweets and other confections collectively. 2. the art or business of a confectioner.

confederacy (kənˈfɛdərəsɪ) n., pl. **-cies.** a union of states or people joined for a common purpose. [Late Latin confoederātiō agreement]

confederate n. (kənˈfɛdərɪt) 1. a state or individual that is part of a confederacy. 2. an accomplice or conspirator. ~adj. (kənˈfɛdərɪt). 3. united; allied. ~vb. (kənˈfɛdəˌreɪt). 4. to unite in a confederacy. [Late Latin confoederāre to unite by a league]

Confederate (kənˈfɛdərɪt) adj. of or supporting those American states which withdrew from the U.S.A. in 1860-61, leading to the U.S. Civil War.

confederation (kənˌfɛdəˈreɪʃən) n. 1. the act of confederating or the state of being confederated. 2. a union or alliance of states. 3. a federation.

confer (kənˈfɜː) vb. **-ferring, -ferred.** 1. (foll. by on or upon) to grant or bestow (an honour, gift or status). 2. to consult together. [Latin com- together + ferre to bring] —con'ferment n. —con'ferrable adj.

conference (ˈkɒnfərəns) n. a meeting for consultation or discussion, esp. one with a formal agenda. [Medieval Latin conferentia]

confess (kənˈfɛs) vb. 1. (often foll. by to) to admit (a fault or crimes). 2. to admit to be true, esp. reluctantly. 3. Christianity. to declare (one's sins) to God or to a priest, so as to obtain forgiveness. [Latin confitērī to admit]

confession (kənˈfɛʃən) n. 1. something confessed. 2. an admission of one's faults, sins, or crimes. 3. **confession of faith.** a formal public statement of religious beliefs.

confessional (kənˈfɛʃənˀl) n. 1. Christianity. a small stall where a priest hears confessions. ~adj. 2. of or suited to a confession.

confessor (kənˈfɛsə) n. 1. Christianity. a priest who hears confessions and gives spiritual counsel. 2. History. a person who demonstrates his Christian religious faith by the holiness of his life: Edward The Confessor.

confetti (kənˈfɛtɪ) n. small pieces of coloured paper thrown at weddings. [Italian]

confidant or (fem.) **confidante** (ˌkɒnfɪˈdænt, ˈkɒnfɪˌdænt) n. a person to whom private matters are confided. [French confident]

confide (kənˈfaɪd) vb. 1. (usually foll. by in) to disclose (secret or personal matters) in confidence (to). 2. to entrust into another's keeping. [Latin confidere]

confidence (ˈkɒnfɪdəns) n. 1. trust in a person or thing. 2. belief in one's own abilities; self-assurance. 3. trust or a trustful relationship: take me into your confidence. 4. something confided; secret. 5. **in confidence.** as a secret.

confidence trick or U.S. & Canad. **confidence game** n. a swindle in which the victim's trust is won by the swindler.

confident (ˈkɒnfɪdənt) adj. 1. having or showing certainty; sure: confident of success. 2. sure of oneself. [Latin confidere to have complete trust in] —'confidently adv.

confidential (ˌkɒnfɪˈdɛnʃəl) adj. 1. spoken or given in confidence; private. 2. entrusted with another's secret affairs: a confidential secretary. 3. suggestive of intimacy: a confidential approach. —confiˌdentiˈality n. —confiˈdentially adv.

confiding (kənˈfaɪdɪŋ) adj. unsuspicious; trustful. —conˈfidingly adv.

configuration (kənˌfɪgjʊˈreɪʃən) n. 1. the arrangement of the parts of something. 2. the form or outline of such an arrangement. [Late Latin configūrāre to model on something]

confine vb. (kənˈfaɪn). 1. to keep within bounds; restrict. 2. to restrict the free movement of: arthritis confined him to bed. ~n. (ˈkɒnfaɪn). 3. (often pl.) a limit; boundary. [Latin fīnis boundary]

confinement (kənˈfaɪnmənt) n. 1. a confining or being confined. 2. the period of childbirth.

confirm (kənˈfɜːm) vb. 1. to prove to be true or valid; corroborate. 2. to reaffirm (something), so as to make (it) more definite, or finalize (it): he confirmed that he would appear in court. 3. to strengthen: his story confirmed my doubts. 4. to formally make valid; ratify. 5. to administer the rite of confirmation to. [Latin confirmāre]

confirmation (ˌkɒnfəˈmeɪʃən) n. 1. the act of confirming. 2. something that confirms. 3. a rite in several Christian churches that admits a baptized person to full church membership.

confirmed (kənˈfɜːmd) adj. long-established in a habit or condition: confirmed bachelor.

confiscate (ˈkɒnfɪˌskeɪt) vb. to seize (property) as a penalty. [Latin confiscāre to seize for the public treasury] —ˌconfisˈcation n.

conflagration (ˌkɒnfləˈɡreɪʃən) n. a large destructive fire. [Latin com- (intensive) + flagrāre to burn]

conflate (kənˈfleɪt) vb. to combine or blend (two or more accounts or pieces of writing) so as to form a whole. [Latin conflāre to blow together] —conˈflation n

conflict n. (ˈkɒnflɪkt). 1. a struggle or battle. 2. opposition between ideas or interests; controversy. ~vb. (kənˈflɪkt). 3. to be incompatible; clash. [Latin conflīgere to combat] —conˈflicting adj.

confluence (ˈkɒnflʊəns) n. 1. a place where rivers flow into one another. 2. a gathering. [Latin confluere to flow together] —ˈconfluent adj.

conform (kənˈfɔːm) vb. 1. (usually foll. by to) to comply with accepted standards, rules, or customs. 2. (usually foll. by *with*) to be like or in accordance with: *he conforms with my idea of a teacher.* [Latin *confirmāre* to strengthen] —**con'formist** *n., adj.*

conformation (ˌkɒnfɔːˈmeɪʃən) *n.* **1.** the general shape of an object; configuration. **2.** the arrangement of the parts of an object.

conformity (kənˈfɔːmɪtɪ) *n., pl.* -**ities.** **1.** compliance in actions or behaviour with certain accepted rules, customs, or standards. **2.** likeness; agreement.

confound (kənˈfaʊnd) *vb.* **1.** to astound; bewilder. **2.** to confuse; to fail to distinguish between. **3.** ('kɒnˈfaʊnd). **confound it!** damn it! [Latin *confundere* to mingle, pour together]

confounded (kənˈfaʊndɪd) *adj.* **1.** bewildered; confused. **2.** *Informal.* damned.

confrère ('kɒnfrɛə) *n.* a colleague; fellow worker. [Medieval Latin *confrāter*]

confront (kənˈfrʌnt) *vb.* **1.** (usually foll. by *with*) to present (with something), esp. in order to accuse or criticize. **2.** to meet face to face in hostility or defiance. **3.** (of a problem or task) to present itself to. [Latin *com-* together + *frons* forehead] —**confrontation** (ˌkɒnfrʌnˈteɪʃən) *n.*

Confucianism (kənˈfjuːʃəˌnɪzəm) *n.* the ethical system of Confucius (551–479 B.C.), the ancient Chinese philosopher, emphasizing moral order. —**Con'fucian** *n., adj.* —**Con'fucianist** *n.*

confuse (kənˈfjuːz) *vb.* **1.** to perplex or disconcert. **2.** to mix up; throw into disorder. **3.** to make unclear; complicate: *he confused his talk with irrelevant details.* **4.** to fail to distinguish between one thing and another. [Latin *confundere* to pour together] —**con'fusing** *adj.* —**con'fusingly** *adv.*

confusion (kənˈfjuːʒən) *n.* **1.** bewilderment; perplexity. **2.** disorder. **3.** lack of clarity.

confute (kənˈfjuːt) *vb.* to prove (a person or thing) to be incorrect or false. [Latin *confūtāre* to check, silence] —**confutation** (ˌkɒnfjuːˈteɪʃən) *n.*

conga ('kɒŋɡə) *n.* **1.** a Latin American dance performed by a number of people in single file. **2.** a large single-headed drum played with the hands. ~*vb.* -**gaing,** -**gaed.** **3.** to dance the conga. [American Spanish]

congeal (kənˈdʒiːl) *vb.* to change from a liquid to a semisolid state or a coagulated mass. [Latin *com-* together + *gelāre* to freeze]

congenial (kənˈdʒiːnjəl) *adj.* **1.** friendly, pleasant, or agreeable: *a congenial atmosphere to work in.* **2.** having a similar disposition or tastes; compatible. [*con-* (same) + *genial*] —**congeniality** (kənˌdʒiːnɪˈælɪtɪ) *n.*

congenital (kənˈdʒɛnɪtʔl) *adj.* (of an abnormal condition) nonhereditary but existing at birth: *congenital blindness.* [Latin *con-* together + *genitus* born] —**con'genitally** *adv.*

conger ('kɒŋɡə) *n.* a large sea eel. [Greek *gongros*]

congested (kənˈdʒɛstɪd) *adj.* **1.** crowded to excess; overfilled. **2.** (of an organ) clogged with blood. **3.** (of the nose) blocked with mucus. [Latin *congerere* to pile up] —**con'gestion** *n.*

conglomerate *n.* (kənˈɡlɒmərɪt). **1.** a thing composed of several different elements. **2.** a rock consisting of rounded pebbles or fragments held together by silica or clay. **3.** a large corporation formed by the merging of many diverse firms. ~*vb.* (kənˈɡlɒməˌreɪt). **4.** to form into a mass. ~*adj.* (kənˈɡlɒmərɪt). **5.** made up of several different elements. **6.** (of rock) consisting of rounded pebbles or fragments held together by silica or clay. [Latin *conglomerāre* to roll up] —**conˌglomerˈation** *n.*

congratulate (kənˈɡrætjʊˌleɪt) *vb.* **1.** (usually foll. by *on*) to express one's pleasure to (a person) at his success or good fortune. **2. congratulate oneself.** (often foll. by *on*) to consider oneself clever or fortunate (as a result of): *she congratulated herself on her tact.* [Latin *congrātulārī*] —**con'gratulatory** *adj.*

congratulations (kənˌɡrætjʊˈleɪʃənz) *pl. n., interj.* expressions of pleasure or joy on another's success or good fortune.

congregate ('kɒŋɡrɪˌɡeɪt) *vb.* to collect together in a body or crowd; assemble. [Latin *congregāre* to collect into a flock]

congregation (ˌkɒŋɡrɪˈɡeɪʃən) *n.* a group of worshippers. —ˌcongreˈgational *adj.*

Congregationalism (ˌkɒŋɡrɪˈɡeɪʃənəˌlɪzəm) *n.* a system of Protestant church government in which each church is self-governing. —ˌCongreˈgationalist *adj., n.*

congress ('kɒŋɡrɛs) *n.* a formal meeting of representatives of an organization, held for discussion. [Latin *com-* together + *gradī* to walk] —**congressional** (kənˈɡrɛʃənʔl) *adj.*

Congress ('kɒŋɡrɛs) *n.* the federal legislature of the U.S., consisting of the House of Representatives and the Senate. —**Congressional** (kənˈɡrɛʃənʔl) *adj.*

congruent ('kɒŋɡrʊənt) *adj.* **1.** agreeing; corresponding. **2.** *Geom.* identical in shape and size: *congruent triangles.* [Latin *congruere* to agree] —'**congruence** *n.*

congruous ('kɒŋɡrʊəs) *adj.* **1.** corresponding or agreeing. **2.** appropriate. [Latin *in congruere* to agree] —**congruity** (kənˈɡruːɪtɪ) *n.*

conical ('kɒnɪkʔl) *adj.* of or in the shape of a cone.

conic section ('kɒnɪk) *n.* a figure, either a circle, ellipse, parabola, or hyperbola, formed by the intersection of a plane and a cone.

conifer ('kəʊnɪfə, 'kɒn-) *n.* a tree or shrub bearing cones and evergreen leaves, such as the pine, spruce, fir, or larch. [Latin *cōnus* cone + *ferre* to bear] —**co'niferous** *adj.*

conjecture (kənˈdʒɛktʃə) *n.* **1.** the formation of conclusions from incomplete evidence; guessing. **2.** a guess. ~*vb.* **3.** to form (an opinion or conclusion) from incomplete evidence. [Latin *conjicere* to throw together] —con'**jectural** *adj.*

conjugal ('kɒndʒʊgᵊl) *adj.* of marriage or the relationship between husband and wife: *conjugal rights.* [Latin *conjunx* wife or husband]

conjugate *vb.* ('kɒndʒʊˌgeɪt). 1. *Grammar.* to give the conjugation of (a verb). 2. (of a verb) to undergo inflection according to a specific set of rules. ~*adj.* ('kɒndʒʊgɪt). 3. joined together in pairs; fused. 4. (of words) cognate; related in origin. ~*n.* ('kɒndʒʊgɪt). 5. one of a pair of conjugate words or things. [Latin *com*- together + *jugāre* to connect]

conjugation (ˌkɒndʒʊ'geɪʃən) *n.* 1. *Grammar.* **a.** inflection of a verb for person, number, tense, voice and mood. **b.** the complete set of the inflections of a given verb. 2. a joining.

conjunction (kən'dʒʌŋkʃən) *n.* 1. joining together; union; combination. 2. simultaneous occurrence of events; coincidence. 3. a word or group of words that connects words, phrases, or clauses; for example *and, if,* and *but.* 4. *Astron.* the apparent proximity of two heavenly bodies to each other. —con'**junctional** *adj.*

conjunctiva (ˌkɒndʒʌŋk'taɪvə) *n., pl.* -**vas** or -**vae** (-viː). the delicate mucous membrane that covers the eyeball and inner eyelid. [New Latin *membrāna conjunctīva* the conjunctive membrane] —ˌconjunc'**tival** *adj.*

conjunctive (kən'dʒʌŋktɪv) *adj.* 1. joining; connective. 2. joined. 3. used as a conjunction. ~*n.* 4. a word or words used as a conjunction. [Latin *conjungere* to join]

conjunctivitis (kənˌdʒʌŋktɪ'vaɪtɪs) *n.* inflammation of the conjunctiva.

conjuncture (kən'dʒʌŋktʃə) *n.* a combination of events, esp. a critical one.

conjure ('kʌndʒə) *vb.* 1. to practise conjuring. 2. to summon (a spirit or demon) by magic. 3. (kən'dʒʊə). to appeal earnestly to: *I conjure you to help me.* [Latin *conjūrāre* to swear together]

conjurer or **conjuror** ('kʌndʒərə) *n.* 1. a person who practises conjuring, esp. for people's entertainment. 2. a magician.

conjure up *vb.* 1. to call to mind; evoke or imagine: *he conjured up a picture of his childhood.* 2. to produce as if from nowhere.

conjuring ('kʌndʒərɪŋ) *n.* the performance of tricks that appear to defy natural laws.

conk (kɒŋk) *Slang.* ~*vb.* 1. to strike (someone) on the head or nose. ~*n.* 2. the head or nose. [prob. changed from *conch*]

conker ('kɒŋkə) *n.* same as **horse chestnut** (the nut).

conkers ('kɒŋkəz) *n.* (functioning as sing.) *Brit.* a game in which a player swings a horse chestnut (conker), threaded onto a string, against that of another player to try to break it. [dialect *conker* snail shell, orig. used in the game]

conk out *vb. Informal.* 1. (of a machine or car) to fail suddenly. 2. to tire suddenly or collapse. [origin unknown]

con man *n. Informal.* a person who swindles another by means of a confidence trick.

Conn. Connecticut.

connect (kə'nɛkt) *vb.* 1. to link or be linked. 2. to associate: *I connect him with my childhood.* 3. to put into telephone communication with. 4. to relate by birth or marriage: *she was distantly connected with the Wedgwood family.* 5. (of two public vehicles) to have the arrival of one timed to occur just before the departure of the other, for the convenient transfer of passengers. [Latin *connectere* to bind together] —con'**nective** *adj.*

connection or **connexion** (kə'nɛkʃən) *n.* 1. the act of connecting; union. 2. a link or bond. 3. a relationship or association. 4. logical sequence in thought or expression; coherence. 5. (often *pl.*) an influential acquaintance. 6. a relative. 7. **a.** an opportunity to transfer from one public vehicle to another. **b.** the vehicle scheduled to provide such an opportunity. 8. a link between two components in an electric circuit. 9. a telephone link. 10. *Slang.* a supplier of illegal drugs, such as heroin. 11. **in connection with.** with reference to; concerning: *the police want to interview him in connection with the murder.*

connective tissue *n.* body tissue that supports organs, fills the spaces between them, and forms tendons and ligaments.

conning tower ('kɒnɪŋ) *n.* the superstructure of a submarine containing the periscope and serving as an entrance when the vessel is on the surface. [*con* to steer a ship]

connivance (kə'naɪvəns) *n.* tacit encouragement of or assent to another's wrongdoing.

connive (kə'naɪv) *vb.* 1. (foll. by *at*) to give assent or encouragement to (another's wrongdoing) by pretending not to notice it. 2. to conspire. [Latin *connīvēre* to blink, hence, leave uncensured] —con'**niver** *n.*

connoisseur (ˌkɒnɪ'sɜː) *n.* a person with special knowledge or appreciation of the arts, food, or drink. [French]

connote (kɒ'nəʊt) *vb.* (of a word or phrase) to imply or suggest (associations or ideas other than the literal meaning): *the word "maiden" connotes modesty.* [Latin *con*- together + *notāre* to mark, note] —ˌconno'**tation** *n.*

connubial (kə'njuːbɪəl) *adj.* of marriage: *connubial bliss.* [Latin *cōnūbium* marriage]

conquer ('kɒŋkə) *vb.* 1. to defeat (an opponent or opponents). 2. to overcome (a difficulty or feeling). 3. to gain possession or control of by force or war. [Latin *conquīrere* to search for] —'**conquering** *adj.* —'**conqueror** *n.*

conquest ('kɒnkwɛst) *n.* 1. the act of conquering or the state of having been conquered. 2. a person or thing that has been conquered. 3. a person whose compliance or love has been won.

conquistador (kɒn'kwɪstəˌdɔː) *n., pl.* -**dors** or **conquistadores** (kɒnˌkwɪstə-

'dɔːrɛs). one of the Spanish conquerors of Mexico and Peru in the 16th century. [Spanish: conqueror]

Cons. Conservative.

consanguineous (ˌkɒnsæŋˈgwɪnɪəs) adj. having the same ancestor; closely related. [Latin con- with + sanguis blood] —ˌconsanˈguinity n.

conscience ('kɒnʃəns) n. **1.** the sense of right and wrong that governs a person's thoughts and actions. **2.** a feeling of guilt: he has a conscience about his unkind action. **3.** in (all) conscience. in fairness; justifiably. **4.** on one's conscience. causing feelings of guilt. [Latin conscire to know]

conscience money n. money paid voluntarily to relieve one's conscience.

conscience-stricken adj. feeling guilty because of having done something wrong.

conscientious (ˌkɒnʃɪˈɛnʃəs) adj. **1.** scrupulous; painstaking. **2.** governed by conscience. —ˌconsciˈentiously adv. —ˌconsciˈentiousness n.

conscientious objector n. a person who refuses to serve in the armed forces on the grounds of conscience.

conscious ('kɒnʃəs) adj. **1.** alert and awake. **2.** aware of one's surroundings and of oneself. **3.** aware (of something): I am conscious of your great kindness to me. **4.** deliberate or intentional: a conscious effort. **5.** denoting a part of the human mind that is aware of a person's self, surroundings, and thoughts, and that to a certain extent determines his choices of action. ~n. **6.** the conscious part of the mind. [Latin com- with + scire to know] —ˈconsciously adv. —ˈconsciousness n.

conscript n. ('kɒnskrɪpt). **1.** a person who is enrolled for compulsory military service. ~vb. (kənˈskrɪpt). **2.** to enrol (someone) for compulsory military service. [Latin conscriptus enrolled]

conscription (kənˈskrɪpʃən) n. compulsory military service.

consecrate ('kɒnsɪˌkreɪt) vb. **1.** to make or declare sacred or for religious use. **2.** to devote or dedicate (something) to a particular purpose. **3.** Christianity. to sanctify (bread and wine) to be received as the body and blood of Christ. [Latin consecrāre] —ˌconseˈcration n.

consecutive (kənˈsɛkjʊtɪv) adj. **1.** following in order without interruption; successive. **2.** in logical order. [Latin consecūtus] —conˈsecutively adv.

consensus (kənˈsɛnsəs) n. general or widespread agreement (esp. in consensus of opinion). [Latin consentire to agree]

consent (kənˈsɛnt) vb. **1.** to give assent or permission; agree. ~n. **2.** agreement, permission, or approval. **3.** age of consent. the age at which sexual intercourse is permitted by law. [Latin consentire to agree] —conˈsenting adj.

consequence ('kɒnsɪkwəns) n. **1.** a logical result or effect. **2.** significance or importance: it's of no consequence; a man of consequence. **3.** in consequence. as a

result. **4. take the consequences.** to accept whatever results from one's action.

consequent ('kɒnsɪkwənt) adj. **1.** following as an effect. **2.** following as a logical conclusion. [Latin consequēns following closely]

consequential (ˌkɒnsɪˈkwɛnʃəl) adj. **1.** important or significant. **2.** following as a result.

consequently ('kɒnsɪkwəntlɪ) adv. as a result; therefore.

conservancy (kənˈsɜːvənsɪ) n. environmental conservation.

conservation (ˌkɒnsəˈveɪʃən) n. **1.** protection from change, loss, or injury. **2.** protection, preservation, and careful management of the environment and natural resources. **3.** Physics. the principle that the quantity of a specified aspect of a system, such as momentum or charge, remains constant. —ˌconserˈvationist n.

conservative (kənˈsɜːvətɪv) adj. **1.** favouring the preservation of established customs and values, and opposing change. **2.** moderate or cautious: a conservative estimate. **3.** conventional in style: a conservative suit. ~n. **4.** a conservative person; conformist. —conˈservatism n.

Conservative (kənˈsɜːvətɪv) adj. **1.** of or supporting the Conservative Party, the major right-wing political party in Britain, which believes in private enterprise and capitalism. **2.** of or supporting a similar right-wing party in other countries. ~n. **3.** a supporter or member of a Conservative Party.

conservatoire (kənˈsɜːvəˌtwɑː) n. a school or college of music. [French]

conservatory (kənˈsɜːvətrɪ) n., pl. -tories. **1.** a greenhouse attached to a house. **2.** a conservatoire.

conserve vb. (kənˈsɜːv). **1.** to protect from harm, decay, or loss. **2.** to preserve (fruit or other food) with sugar. ~n. ('kɒnsɜːv, kənˈsɜːv). **3.** a preparation like jam but containing a higher proportion of fruit. [Latin conservāre to keep safe]

consider (kənˈsɪdə) vb. **1.** to think carefully about (a problem or decision). **2.** to believe to be: I consider him a fool. **3.** to have regard for or care about: consider your mother's feelings. **4.** to look at: he considered her face. **5.** to bear in mind: when buying a car consider this make. **6.** to discuss (something) in order to make a decision. [Latin consīderāre to inspect closely]

considerable (kənˈsɪdərəbˈl) adj. **1.** large enough to reckon with; important: a considerable quantity. **2.** a lot of; much: he had considerable courage. —conˈsiderably adv.

considerate (kənˈsɪdərɪt) adj. thoughtful towards other people; kind.

consideration (kənˌsɪdəˈreɪʃən) n. **1.** deliberation; contemplation. **2. take into consideration.** to bear in mind; consider. **3. under consideration.** being currently discussed. **4.** a fact to be taken into account when making a decision. **5.**

thoughtfulness for other people; kindness. **6.** payment for a service.

considered (kən'sıdəd) *adj.* **1.** presented or thought out with care: *a considered opinion.* **2.** (*with a preceding adverb*) thought of in a specified way: *highly considered.*

considering (kən'sıdərıŋ) *conj., prep.* **1.** in view of (a specified fact): *he's very fit, considering his age.* ~*adv.* **2.** *Informal.* taking into account the circumstances: *it's not bad considering.*

consign (kən'saın) *vb.* **1.** to give into the care or charge of; entrust. **2.** to put irrevocably: *he consigned the papers to the flames.* **3.** to put (in a specified place or situation): *to consign someone to jail.* **4.** to address or deliver (goods): *it was consigned to his London address.* [Latin *consignāre* to put one's seal to, sign] —,**consign'ee** *n.* —**con'signor** *n.*

consignment (kən'saınmənt) *n.* **1.** a consigning or commitment. **2.** a shipment of goods.

consist (kən'sıst) *vb.* **1.** (foll. by *of* or *in*) to be composed of. **2.** (foll. by *in* or *of*) to have as its main or only part: *his religion consists only in going to church.* [Latin *consistere* to stand firm]

consistency (kən'sıstənsı) *n., pl.* **-encies.** **1.** degree of thickness, smoothness, or firmness. **2.** conformity with previous behaviour or practice.

consistent (kən'sıstənt) *adj.* **1.** (usually foll. by *with*) showing consistency, harmony, or compatibility. **2.** holding to the same principles; constant. —**con'sistently** *adv.*

consolation (,kɒnsə'leıʃən) *n.* **1.** a consoling or being consoled. **2.** a person or thing that is a comfort in a time of sadness or distress.

console[1] (kən'səʊl) *vb.* to comfort (someone) in sadness or distress. [Latin *consōlārī*] —**con'solable** *adj.*

console[2] ('kɒnsəʊl) *n.* **1.** an ornamental bracket used to support a wall fixture. **2.** the desklike case of an organ, containing the pedals, stops, and keys. **3.** a desk or table on which the controls of an electronic system are mounted. **4.** a cabinet for a television or audio equipment, designed to stand on the floor. [Old French *consolateur* one that provides support]

consolidate (kən'sɒlı,deıt) *vb.* **1.** to combine into a whole. **2.** to make or become stronger or more stable. [Latin *consolidare* to make firm] —**con,soli'dation** *n.* —**con'soli,dator** *n.*

consommé (kən'sɒmeı) *n.* a thin clear soup made from meat juices. [French]

consonance ('kɒnsənəns) *n.* agreement or harmony, esp. of musical tones.

consonant ('kɒnsənənt) *n.* **1. a.** a speech sound made by partially or completely blocking the breath streams, as *b, l, f.* **b.** a letter representing this. ~*adj.* **2.** (foll. by *with* or *to*) consistent; in agreement. **3.** harmonious. [Latin *consonāre* to sound at the same time]

consort *vb.* (kən'sɔːt). **1.** (usually foll. by *with*) to associate (with undesirable people). ~*n.* ('kɒnsɔːt). **2.** (esp. formerly) a small group of voices or instruments. **3.** a husband or wife of a reigning monarch. [Latin *consors* partner]

consortium (kən'sɔːtıəm) *n., pl.* **-tia** (-tıə). an association of financiers or business firms. [Latin: partnership]

conspectus (kən'spektəs) *n.* **1.** an overall view; survey. **2.** a summary; résumé. [Latin: a viewing]

conspicuous (kən'spıkjʊəs) *adj.* **1.** clearly visible. **2.** noteworthy or striking: *conspicuous stupidity.* [Latin *conspicuus*] —**con'spicuously** *adv.*

conspiracy (kən'spırəsı) *n., pl.* **-cies.** **1.** a secret plan to carry out an illegal or harmful act. **2.** the act of making such plans.

conspire (kən'spaıə) *vb.* **1.** to plan (a crime) together in secret. **2.** to act together as if by design: *the elements conspired to spoil our picnic.* [Latin *conspīrāre* to plot together] —**conspirator** (kən'spırətə) *n.* —**conspiratorial** (kən,spırə'tɔːrıəl) *adj.*

constable ('kʌnstəb[1]) *n.* a police officer of the lowest rank. [Late Latin *comes stabulī* officer in charge of the stable]

constabulary (kən'stæbjʊlərı) *n., pl.* **-laries.** *Chiefly Brit.* the police force of a district or town.

constant ('kɒnstənt) *adj.* **1.** unchanging. **2.** continuous: *constant interruptions.* **3.** resolute; loyal. ~*n.* **4.** something that is unchanging. **5.** *Maths, physics.* a quantity or number which remains invariable: *the velocity of light is a constant.* [Latin *constāre* to be steadfast] —**'constancy** *n.* —**'constantly** *adv.*

constellation (,kɒnstı'leıʃən) *n.* **1.** a group of stars which form a pattern as seen from the earth and are given a name. **2.** a group of people or things. [Latin *com-* together + *stella* star]

consternation (,kɒnstə'neıʃən) *n.* a feeling of anxiety, dismay, or confusion.

constipate ('kɒnstı,peıt) *vb.* to cause constipation in. [Latin *constīpāre* to press closely together] —**'consti,pated** *adj.*

constipation (,kɒnstı'peıʃən) *n.* a condition in which the faeces are hardened making the emptying of the bowels difficult.

constituency (kən'stıtjʊənsı) *n., pl.* **-cies.** **1.** the whole body of voters who elect someone to represent them in parliament. **2.** the district that sends one representative to parliament.

constituent (kən'stıtjʊənt) *adj.* **1.** forming part of a whole; component. **2.** having the power to make or change a constitution or to elect a government: *constituent assembly.* ~*n.* **3.** a component part; ingredient. **4.** a resident of a constituency, esp. one entitled to vote. [Latin *constituere* to constitute]

constitute ('kɒnstı,tjuːt) *vb.* **1.** to form; compose: *the people who constitute a jury.* **2.** to set up (an institution) formally; found. [Latin *com-* (intensive) + *statuere* to place]

constitution (,kɒnstı'tjuːʃən) *n.* **1.** physical make-up; structure. **2.** the fundamental principles on which a state is governed. **3. the Constitution.** (in certain countries) the statute embodying such principles. **4.** a person's state of health.

constitutional (ˌkɒnstɪˈtjuːʃənˀl) *adj.* **1.** involving or related to a constitution. **2.** authorized by or in accordance with the Constitution of a nation or state: *constitutional monarchy.* **3.** inherent in the nature of a person or thing: *a constitutional weakness.* ~*n.* **4.** a regular walk taken for the benefit of one's health. —ˌ**consti'tutionally** *adv.*

constitutive (ˈkɒnstɪˌtjuːtɪv) *adj.* **1.** having power to appoint, enact, or establish. **2.** forming a part of something.

constrain (kənˈstreɪn) *vb.* **1.** to compel or force. **2.** to restrain or confine. [Latin *constringere* to bind together]

constrained (kənˈstreɪnd) *adj.* embarrassed, unnatural, or forced: *a constrained smile.*

constraint (kənˈstreɪnt) *n.* **1.** compulsion or restraint. **2.** repression of natural feelings. **3.** a forced unnatural manner. **4.** something that constrains; a restrictive condition.

constrict (kənˈstrɪkt) *vb.* **1.** to make smaller or narrower, esp. by compressing at one place. **2.** to hold in or inhibit; limit. [Latin *constringere* to tie up together] —con'strictive *adj.*

constriction (kənˈstrɪkʃən) *n.* **1.** a feeling of tightness in some part of the body, such as the chest. **2.** a narrowing. **3.** something that constricts.

constrictor (kənˈstrɪktə) *n.* **1.** a snake that coils around and squeezes its prey to kill it. **2.** a muscle that contracts an opening.

construct *vb.* (kənˈstrʌkt). **1.** to build or assemble by putting together parts systematically. **2.** to frame (an argument or sentence) mentally. **3.** *Geom.* to draw (a figure) to specified requirements. ~*n.* (ˈkɒnstrʌkt). **4.** something formulated or built systematically. **5.** a complex idea resulting from the combination of simpler ideas. [Latin *construere* to build] —con'structor *n.*

construction (kənˈstrʌkʃən) *n.* **1.** the act of constructing or manner in which a thing is constructed. **2.** something that has been constructed. **3.** the business or work of building dwellings or other structures. **4.** an interpretation: *they put a sympathetic construction on her behaviour.* **5.** *Grammar.* the way in which words are arranged in a sentence, clause, or phrase. —con'structional *adj.*

constructive (kənˈstrʌktɪv) *adj.* **1.** serving to improve; positive: *constructive criticism.* **2.** *Law.* deduced by inference; not expressed. —con'structively *adv.*

construe (kənˈstruː) *vb.* **-struing, -strued.** **1.** to interpret the meaning of (something): *you can construe that in different ways.* **2.** to analyse the grammatical structure of. **3.** to combine (words) grammatically. **4.** *Old-fashioned.* to translate literally. [Latin *construere* to build]

consul (ˈkɒnsˀl) *n.* **1.** an official appointed by a state to protect its business interests and help its citizens in a foreign city. **2.** either of two annually elected chief magistrates in ancient Rome. [Latin] —**consular** (ˈkɒnsjʊlə) *adj.* —ˈ**consul,ship** *n.*

consulate (ˈkɒnsjʊlɪt) *n.* **1.** the offices and official home of a consul. **2.** the office or period of office of a consul.

consult (kənˈsʌlt) *vb.* **1.** (often foll. by *with*) to ask advice from or discuss matters with (someone). **2.** to refer to for information: *to consult a map.* [Latin *consultāre*]

consultant (kənˈsʌltˀnt) *n.* **1.** a specialist doctor with a senior position in a hospital. **2.** a specialist who gives expert professional advice. —con'sultancy *n.*

consultation (ˌkɒnsˀlˈteɪʃən) *n.* **1.** the act of consulting. **2.** a meeting for discussion or the seeking of advice. —**consultative** (kənˈsʌltətɪv) *adj.*

consulting (kənˈsʌltɪŋ) *adj.* acting as an adviser on professional matters: *a consulting engineer.*

consulting room *n.* a room in which a doctor sees his patients.

consume (kənˈsjuːm) *vb.* **1.** to eat or drink. **2.** to obsess. **3.** to use up; waste. **4.** to destroy: *fire consumed the forest.* [Latin *com-* (intensive) + *sūmere* to take up] —con'sumable *adj.* —con'suming *adj.*

consumer (kənˈsjuːmə) *n.* a person who buys things for his own personal needs.

consumer goods *pl. n.* goods bought for personal needs rather than those required for the production of other goods or services.

consumerism (kənˈsjuːməˌrɪzəm) *n.* protection of the interests of consumers.

consummate *vb.* (ˈkɒnsjʊˌmeɪt). **1.** to bring to completion; fulfil. **2.** to make (a marriage) legal by sexual intercourse. ~*adj.* (ˈkɒnsəmɪt). **3.** supremely skilled: *a consummate artist.* **4.** complete or extreme: *a consummate fool.* [Latin *consummāre* to complete] —ˌ**consum'mation** *n.*

consumption (kənˈsʌmpʃən) *n.* **1.** a consuming or being consumed. **2.** *Econ.* purchase of goods and services for personal use. **3.** the quantity consumed. **4.** *Old-fashioned.* tuberculosis of the lungs.

consumptive (kənˈsʌmptɪv) *adj.* **1.** wasteful; destructive. **2.** of or having tuberculosis of the lungs. ~*n.* **3.** a person with tuberculosis of the lungs.

cont. **1.** contents. **2.** continued.

contact (ˈkɒntækt) *n.* **1.** the act or state of touching. **2.** the state or act of communication: *in contact; make contact.* **3.** a connection between two electrical conductors in a circuit. **4.** an acquaintance, esp. one who might be useful in business. **5.** any person who has been exposed to a contagious disease. ~*vb.* **6.** to come or be in touch or communication with. [Latin *contingere* to touch on all sides]

contact lens *n.* a small lens placed directly on the surface of the eye to correct defects of vision.

contagion (kənˈteɪdʒən) n. **1.** the spreading of disease from one person to another by contact. **2.** a contagious disease. **3.** a corrupting influence that tends to spread. [Latin *contāgiō* infection]

contagious (kənˈteɪdʒəs) adj. **1.** (of a disease) capable of being passed on by contact. **2.** (of a person) capable of passing on a transmissible disease. **3.** spreading from person to person: *her laughter was contagious.*

contain (kənˈteɪn) vb. **1.** to hold or be capable of holding: *this contains five pints.* **2.** to check or restrain (feelings or behaviour). **3.** to consist of: *the book contains three sections.* **4.** to prevent from spreading beyond fixed limits. [Latin *continēre*] —**conˈtainable** adj.

container (kənˈteɪnə) n. **1.** an object used to hold, carry, or store things in. **2.** a large standard-sized box designed for the transport of cargo by lorry or ship.

containerize or **-ise** (kənˈteɪnəˌraɪz) vb. **1.** to pack (cargo) in large standard-sized containers. **2.** to equip (a port or transportation system) to carry goods in standard-sized containers. —**conˌtaineriˈzation** or **-iˈsation** n.

containment (kənˈteɪnmənt) n. the prevention of the expansion of a hostile country or its influence.

contaminate (kənˈtæmɪˌneɪt) vb. **1.** to make impure; pollute. **2.** to make radioactive. [Latin *contamināre* to defile] —**conˈtaminant** n. —**conˌtamiˈnation** n.

contemn (kənˈtɛm) vb. Formal. to regard with contempt; scorn. [Latin *contemnere*]

contemplate (ˈkɒntɛmˌpleɪt) vb. **1.** to think about intently and at length. **2.** to meditate. **3.** to look at thoughtfully. **4.** to consider as a possibility. [Latin *contemplāre*] —**ˌcontemˈplation** n.

contemplative (ˈkɒntɛmˌpleɪtɪv, -təm-; kənˈtɛmplə-) adj. **1.** of or given to contemplation; meditative. ~n. **2.** a person dedicated to religious contemplation.

contemporaneous (kənˌtɛmpəˈreɪnɪəs) adj. existing or occurring at the same time. —**contemporaneity** (kənˌtɛmpərəˈniːɪtɪ) n.

contemporary (kənˈtɛmprərɪ) adj. **1.** living or occurring in the same period. **2.** existing or occurring at the present time. **3.** modern in style or fashion. **4.** of approximately the same age. ~n., pl. **-raries.** **5.** a person or thing living at the same time or of approximately the same age as another. [Latin *com-* together + *temporārius* relating to time]

contempt (kənˈtɛmpt) n. **1.** scorn. **2.** **hold in contempt.** to scorn or despise. **3.** deliberate disrespect for the authority of a court of law: *contempt of court.* [Latin *contemnere* to scorn]

contemptible (kənˈtɛmptɪbᵊl) adj. deserving or worthy of contempt.

contemptuous (kənˈtɛmptjuəs) adj. showing or feeling contempt; disdainful. —**conˈtemptuously** adv.

contend (kənˈtɛnd) vb. **1.** (often foll. by *with*) to compete or fight; vie. **2.** to argue earnestly. **3.** to assert. [Latin *contendere* to strive] —**conˈtender** n.

content[1] (ˈkɒntɛnt) n. **1.** (pl.) everything inside a container. **2.** (pl.) a list of chapters or divisions printed at the front of a book. **3.** the meaning or substance of a piece of writing, speech, or other work, often as distinguished from its style or form. **4.** the amount of a substance contained in a mixture: *the lead content of petrol.* [Latin *contentus* contained]

content[2] (kənˈtɛnt) adj. **1.** satisfied with things as they are. **2.** willing to accept a situation or a proposed course of action. ~vb. **3.** to satisfy (oneself or another person). ~n. **4.** peace of mind. [Latin *contentus* contented, having restrained desires] —**conˈtentment** n.

contented (kənˈtɛntɪd) adj. satisfied with one's situation or life. —**conˈtentedly** adv. —**conˈtentedness** n.

contention (kənˈtɛnʃən) n. **1.** disagreement or dispute. **2.** a point asserted in argument. **3.** **bone of contention.** a point of dispute. [Latin *contentiō*]

contentious (kənˈtɛnʃəs) adj. **1.** tending to quarrel. **2.** causing disagreement; controversial. —**conˈtentiousness** n.

contest n. (ˈkɒntɛst). **1.** a game or match in which people or teams compete. **2.** a struggle for power or control. ~vb. (kənˈtɛst). **3.** to dispute; call into question: *he decided to contest the will.* **4.** to take part in (a contest or struggle for power): *to contest an election.* [Latin *contestārī* to introduce a lawsuit] —**conˈtestable** adj.

contestant (kənˈtɛstənt) n. a person who takes part in a contest; competitor.

context (ˈkɒntɛkst) n. **1.** the parts of a piece of writing or speech that come before and after a word or passage and contribute to its full meaning: *it is unfair to quote out of context.* **2.** the circumstances relevant to an event or fact. [Latin *com-* together + *texere* to weave] —**conˈtextual** adj.

contiguous (kənˈtɪgjuəs) adj. **1.** touching; in contact. **2.** near or adjacent. [Latin *contiguus*]

continent[1] (ˈkɒntɪnənt) n. one of the earth's large landmasses (Asia, Australia, Africa, Europe, North and South America, and Antarctica). [Latin *terra continens* continuous land] —**continental** (ˌkɒntɪˈnɛntᵊl) adj.

continent[2] (ˈkɒntɪnənt) adj. **1.** able to control urination and defecation. **2.** sexually restrained; chaste. [Latin *continēre* to contain, retain] —**ˈcontinence** n.

Continent (ˈkɒntɪnənt) n. **the.** the mainland of Europe as distinct from the British Isles. —**Continental** (ˌkɒntɪˈnɛntᵊl) adj.

continental breakfast n. a light breakfast of coffee and rolls.

continental climate n. a climate with hot summers, cold winters, and little rainfall, typical of the interior of a continent.

continental drift n. Geol. the theory that the earth's continents drift gradually over the surface of the planet, due to currents in its mantle.

continental quilt n. Brit. a large quilt

used as a bed cover in place of the top sheet and blankets.

continental shelf *n.* the gently sloping shallow sea bed surrounding a continent.

contingency (kənˈtɪndʒənsɪ) *n., pl.* **-cies.** **1.** an unknown or unforeseen future event or condition. **2.** something dependent on a possible future event.

contingent (kənˈtɪndʒənt) *adj.* **1.** (often foll. by *on* or *upon*) dependent (on events or conditions not yet known); conditional. **2.** happening by chance; accidental. ~*n.* **3.** a military group that is part of a larger force. **4.** a group of people with a common interest, that represents a larger group. [Latin *contingere* to touch, befall]

continual (kənˈtɪnjʊəl) *adj.* **1.** recurring frequently. **2.** occurring without interruption; constant. [Latin *continuus* uninterrupted] —**conˈtinually** *adv.*

continuance (kənˈtɪnjʊəns) *n.* **1.** the act of continuing; continuation. **2.** duration.

continuation (kən,tɪnjʊˈeɪʃən) *n.* **1.** a part or thing added, such as a sequel. **2.** a renewal of an interrupted action or process; resumption. **3.** the act of continuing.

continue (kənˈtɪnjuː) *vb.* **-tinuing, -tinued.** **1.** to remain or cause to remain in a particular condition. **2.** to carry on (a course of action) uninterruptedly: *he continued running.* **3.** to resume after an interruption: *we'll continue after lunch.* **4.** to prolong or be prolonged: *continue the chord until it meets the tangent.* [Latin *continuāre* to join together]

continuity (,kɒntɪˈnjuːɪtɪ) *n., pl.* **-ties.** **1.** the state of being continuous or in a logical sequence. **2.** a continuous or connected whole. **3.** the smooth arrangement of scenes in a film or broadcast so that they follow each other without breaks or inconsistencies.

continuo (kənˈtɪnjʊəʊ) *n., pl.* **-tinuos.** *Music.* a continuous bass accompaniment played usually on a keyboard instrument. [Italian]

continuous (kənˈtɪnjʊəs) *adj.* unceasing: *a continuous noise.* **2.** in an unbroken series. [Latin *continuus*] —**conˈtinuously** *adv.*

continuum (kənˈtɪnjʊəm) *n., pl.* **-tinua** (-ˈtɪnjʊə) *or* **-tinuums.** a continuous series or whole ranging between two extremes: *the left-right political continuum.* [Latin]

contort (kənˈtɔːt) *vb.* to twist or bend out of shape. [Latin *contortus* intricate] —**conˈtortion** *n.*

contortionist (kənˈtɔːʃənɪst) *n.* a performer who contorts his body to entertain others.

contour (ˈkɒntʊə) *n.* **1.** the outline of a mass of land, figure, or body; a defining line. **2.** same as **contour line.** ~*vb.* **3.** to shape so as to form or follow the contour of something. **4.** to mark contour lines on. [Italian *contornare* to sketch]

contour line *n.* a line on a map or chart joining points of equal height or depth.

contra- *prefix.* **1.** against; opposing: *contraceptive.* **2.** (in music) lower in pitch: *contrabass.* [Latin *contrā* against]

contraband (ˈkɒntrə,bænd) *n.* **1.** goods that are prohibited by law from being exported or imported; smuggled goods. ~*adj.* **2.** (of goods) forbidden by law from being imported or exported; smuggled. [Spanish *contrabanda*]

contraception (,kɒntrəˈsɛpʃən) *n.* the intentional prevention of pregnancy by artificial or natural means. [CONTRA- + CONCEPTION] —**,contraˈceptive** *adj., n.*

contract *vb.* (kənˈtrækt). **1.** to make or become smaller, narrower, or shorter. **2.** (ˈkɒntrækt). to make a formal agreement with (a person or company) to do or deliver (something). **3.** to draw (the brow or muscles) together or (of the brow or muscles) to be drawn together. **4.** to become affected by (an illness). **5.** to shorten (a word or phrase) by omitting letters or syllables, usually indicated in writing by an apostrophe. ~*n.* (ˈkɒntrækt). **6.** a formal agreement between two or more parties. **7.** marriage considered as a formal agreement. [Latin *contractus* agreement] —**conˈtractible** *adj.*

contract bridge (ˈkɒntrækt) *n.* the most common variety of bridge, in which only tricks bid and won count towards the game.

contraction (kənˈtrækʃən) *n.* **1.** a contracting or being contracted. **2.** a shortening of a word or group of words, often marked by an apostrophe, for example *I've* come for *I have* come.

contractor (kənˈtræktə) *n.* a person or firm that contracts to supply materials or labour.

contract out (ˈkɒntrækt) *vb. Brit.* to agree not to take part in a scheme.

contractual (kənˈtræktjʊəl) *adj.* of or in the nature of a contract.

contradict (,kɒntrəˈdɪkt) *vb.* **1.** to declare the opposite of (a statement) to be true. **2.** (of a fact or statement) to be at variance with or in contradiction to (another). [Latin *contrā-* against + *dīcere* to speak] —**,contraˈdiction** *n.*

contradictory (,kɒntrəˈdɪktərɪ) *adj.* (of facts or statements) inconsistent or incompatible.

contradistinction (,kɒntrədɪˈstɪŋkʃən) *n.* a distinction made by contrasting different qualities. —**,contradisˈtinctive** *adj.*

contraflow (ˈkɒntrə,fləʊ) *n.* a flow, esp. of road traffic, going alongside but in an opposite direction to the usual flow.

contralto (kənˈtræltəʊ) *n., pl.* **-tos** *or* **-ti** (-tɪ). **1.** the lowest female voice. **2.** a singer with such a voice. [Italian]

contraption (kənˈtræpʃən) *n. Informal, often facetious.* a device or gadget, esp. one considered strange, elaborate, or badly made. [origin unknown]

contrapuntal (,kɒntrəˈpʌntˀl) *adj. Music.* of or in counterpoint. [Italian *contrappunto*]

contrariwise (ˈkɒntrərɪ,waɪz) *adv.* **1.** from a contrasting point of view. **2.** in the opposite way. **3.** (kənˈtrɛərɪ,waɪz). perversely.

contrary (ˈkɒntrərɪ) *adj.* **1.** opposed; completely different: *contrary ideas.* **2.** (kən-'treər). perverse; obstinate. **3.** (of the wind) unfavourable. ~*n., pl.* **-ries. 4. on** *or* **to the contrary.** in opposition to what has just been said or implied. ~*adv.* (usually foll. by *to*) **5.** in opposition or contrast (to): *contrary to popular belief.* **6.** in conflict (with): *contrary to nature.* [Latin *contrārius* opposite] —**con'trariness** *n.*

contrast *vb.* (kən'trɑːst). **1.** (often foll. by *with*) to compare or be compared in order to show the differences between (things). ~*n.* ('kɒntrɑːst). **2.** a difference which is clearly seen when two things are compared: *by contrast; in contrast to.* **3.** a person or thing showing differences when compared with another. **4.** the degree of difference between the colours or tones in a photograph or television picture. [Latin *contra-* against + *stare* to stand] —**con'trasting** *adj.*

contravene (ˌkɒntrə'viːn) *vb.* to break (a rule or law). [Latin *contra-* against + *venīre* to come] —**contravention** (ˌkɒntrə'vɛnʃən) *n.*

contretemps ('kɒntrəˌtɑːn) *n., pl.* **-temps** (-ˌtɑːnz). an awkward or embarrassing situation or mishap. [French]

contribute (kən'trɪbjuːt) *vb.* (often foll. by *to*) **1.** to give (support or money) for a common purpose or fund. **2.** to supply (ideas or opinions). **3.** to be partly responsible (for): *drink contributed to the accident.* **4.** to write (an article) for a publication. [Latin *contribuere* to collect] —**con'tribution** *n.* —**con'tributory** *adj.* —**con'tributor** *n.*

contrite (kən'traɪt, 'kɒntraɪt) *adj.* full of guilt or regret. [Latin *contrītus* worn out] —**con'tritely** *adv.* —**contrition** (kən'trɪʃən) *n.*

contrivance (kən'traɪvəns) *n.* **1.** an ingenious device. **2.** an elaborate or deceitful plan. **3.** the act or power of contriving.

contrive (kən'traɪv) *vb.* **1.** to manage (something), esp. by a trick: *he contrived to make them meet.* **2.** to invent and construct ingeniously: *he contrived a new mast for the boat.* [Old French *controver*]

control (kən'trəʊl) *vb.* **-trolling, -trolled.** **1.** to command or direct. **2.** to limit, curb, or restrain: *to control one's emotions.* **3.** to regulate or operate (a machine). ~*n.* **4.** power to direct: *under control.* **5.** a curb; check: *a frontier control.* **6.** (*pl.*) a device or apparatus used to operate a machine. **7.** a standard of comparison used in an experiment. **8.** an experiment used to verify another by having all aspects identical except for the one which is which is being tested. [Old French *conteroller* to regulate] —**con'trollable** *adj.*

controller (kən'trəʊlə) *n.* **1.** a person who directs. **2.** a person in charge of the financial side of a business or department.

control tower *n.* a tall building at an airport from which air traffic is controlled.

controversy ('kɒntrəˌvɜːsɪ, kən'trɒvəsɪ) *n., pl.* **-sies.** argument or debate concerning a matter about which there is strong disagreement. [Latin *contrā-* against +

vertere to turn] —**controversial** (ˌkɒntrə-'vɜːʃəl) *adj.*

contumacy ('kɒntjʊməsɪ) *n., pl.* **-cies.** obstinate and wilful resistance to authority. [Latin *contumāx* obstinate] —**contumacious** (ˌkɒntjʊ'meɪʃəs) *adj.*

contumely ('kɒntjʊmɪlɪ) *n., pl.* **-lies. 1.** scornful or insulting treatment. **2.** a humiliating insult. [Latin *contumēlia*]

contuse (kən'tjuːz) *vb.* to bruise. [Latin *contūsus* bruised] —**con'tusion** *n.*

conundrum (kə'nʌndrəm) *n.* **1.** a riddle whose answer contains a pun. **2.** a puzzling question or problem. [origin unknown]

conurbation (ˌkɒnɜː'beɪʃən) *n.* a large densely populated urban area formed by the growth and merging of individual towns or cities. [Latin *con-* together + *urbs* city]

convalesce (ˌkɒnvə'lɛs) *vb.* to recover from illness, injury, or an operation. [Latin *com-* (intensive) + *valēscere* to grow strong]

convalescence (ˌkɒnvə'lɛsəns) *n.* **1.** gradual return to health after illness, injury, or an operation. **2.** the period during which such recovery occurs. —**ˌconva'lescent** *n., adj.*

convection (kən'vɛkʃən) *n.* the transmission of heat caused by movement of molecules from cool regions to warmer regions of lower density. [Latin *convehere* to bring together]

convector (kən'vɛktə) *n.* a heating device from which heat is transferred to the surrounding air by convection.

convene (kən'viːn) *vb.* to gather or summon for a formal meeting. [Latin *convenīre* to assemble]

convener *or* **convenor** (kən'viːnə) *n.* a person who convenes or chairs a meeting or committee: *a convener of shop stewards.*

convenience (kən'viːnɪəns) *n.* **1.** the quality of being suitable or convenient. **2.** **at your convenience.** at a time suitable to you. **3.** an object that is useful, esp. a labour-saving device. **4.** *Euphemistic, chiefly Brit.* a toilet, esp. a public one.

convenient (kən'viːnɪənt) *adj.* **1.** suitable; opportune. **2.** easy to use. **3.** close by; handy. [Latin *convenīre* to be in accord with]

convent ('kɒnvənt) *n.* **1.** a building inhabited by a group of nuns. **2.** the nuns inhabiting such a building. **3.** a school in which the teachers are nuns. [Latin *conventus* meeting]

conventicle (kən'vɛntɪk'l) *n.* a secret or unauthorized religious meeting. [Latin *conventiculum*]

convention (kən'vɛnʃən) *n.* **1.** a large formal assembly of a group with common interests. **2.** a formal agreement or contract between persons and nations. **3.** the established view of what is thought to be proper behaviour. **4.** an accepted rule or method: *a convention used by printers.* [Latin *conventiō* an assembling]

conventional (kən'vɛnʃən'l) *adj.* **1.** following the accepted customs and lacking originality. **2.** established by accepted usage or general agreement. **3.** (of weapons or warfare) not nuclear. —**con'ventionally** adv.

conventionality (kən,venʃə'nælıtı) n., pl. -ties. **1.** the quality of being conventional. **2.** something conventional.

conventionalize or **-lise** (kən'venʃənə,laız) vb. to make conventional.

converge (kən'vɜːdʒ) vb. **1.** to move towards or meet at the same point. **2.** (of opinions or effects) to tend towards a common conclusion or result. [Latin com- together + vergere to incline] —**con'vergence** n. —**con'vergent** adj.

conversant (kən'vɜːsᵊnt) adj. (usually foll. by with) experienced (in) or familiar (with). [Latin conversāri to keep company with]

conversation (,kɒnvə'seıʃən) n. informal talk between two or more people.

conversational (,kɒnvə'seıʃənᵊl) adj. **1.** of or used in conversation: conversational French. **2.** inclined to conversation. —,conver'sationalist n.

conversation piece n. something, esp. an unusual object, that provokes conversation.

converse¹ (kən'vɜːs) vb. (often foll. by with) to have a conversation. [Latin conversāri to keep company with]

converse² ('kɒnvɜːs) adj. **1.** reversed; opposite; contrary. ~n. **2.** a statement or idea that is the opposite of another. [Latin conversus turned around] —**con'versely** adv.

conversion (kən'vɜːʃən) n. **1.** a change or adaptation in form, character, or function. **2.** a change to another belief or religion. **3.** Maths. a calculation in which a weight, volume, or distance is worked out in a different system of measurement: the conversion of miles to kilometres. **4.** Rugby. a score made after a try by kicking the ball over the crossbar from a place kick. [Latin conversiō a turning around]

convert vb. (kən'vɜːt). **1.** to change or adapt in form, character, or function. **2.** to cause (someone) to change in opinion or belief. **3.** Rugby. to make a conversion after (a try). **4.** to change (a measurement) from one system of units to another. **5.** to change (money) into a different currency. ~n. ('kɒnvɜːt). **6.** a person who has been converted to another belief or religion. [Latin convertere to turn around, alter] —**con'verter** or **con'vertor** n.

convertible (kən'vɜːtıbᵊl) adj. **1.** capable of being converted. **2.** Finance. (of a currency) freely exchangeable into other currencies. ~n. **3.** a car with a folding or removable roof.

convex ('kɒnveks, kɒn'veks) adj. curving outwards like the outside surface of a ball. [Latin convexus vaulted, rounded] —**con'vexity** n.

convey (kən'veı) vb. **1.** to carry or transport from one place to another. **2.** to communicate (a message, idea, or information). **3.** (of a channel or path) to conduct, transfer, or transmit. **4.** Law. to transfer (the title to property). [Old French conveier] —**con'veyable** adj.

conveyance (kən'veıəns) n. **1.** the act of conveying. **2.** a means of transport. **3.** Law. **a.** a transfer of the legal title to property. **b.** the document effecting such a transfer. —**con'veyancer** n. —**con'veyancing** n.

conveyor (kən'veıə) or **conveyor belt** n. an endless moving belt driven by rollers and used to transport objects, esp. in a factory.

convict vb. (kən'vıkt). **1.** to pronounce (someone) guilty of an offence. ~n. ('kɒnvıkt). **2.** a person serving a prison sentence. [Latin convictus convicted]

conviction (kən'vıkʃən) n. **1.** a convincing or being convinced. **2.** a firmly held belief or opinion. **3.** an instance of being found guilty of a crime: he had two previous convictions for assault. **4. carry conviction.** to be convincing.

convince (kən'vıns) vb. to persuade by argument or evidence. [Latin convincere to demonstrate incontrovertibly] —**con'vinced** adj. —**con'vincible** adj. —**con'vincing** adj.

convivial (kən'vıvıəl) adj. sociable; lively or festive: a convivial atmosphere. [Late Latin convīviālis] —**conviviality** (kən,vıvı'ælıtı) n.

convocation (,kɒnvə'keıʃən) n. a large formal meeting.

convoke (kən'vəuk) vb. to call (a meeting); summon. [Latin convocāre]

convoluted ('kɒnvə,luːtıd) adj. **1.** (of an argument or sentence) difficult to understand because of its complexity. **2.** coiled.

convolution (,kɒnvə'luːʃən) n. **1.** a turn, twist, or coil. **2.** an intricate or confused matter or condition. **3.** a convex fold in the surface of the brain.

convolvulus (kən'vɒlvjuləs) n., pl. -luses or -li (-,laı). a twining plant with funnel-shaped flowers and triangular leaves. [Latin]

convoy ('kɒnvɔı) n. a group of vehicles or ships travelling together. [Old French convoier to convey]

convulse (kən'vʌls) vb. **1.** to shake or agitate violently. **2.** (of muscles) to undergo violent spasms. **3.** (often foll. by with) Informal. to be overcome (with laughter or rage). [Latin con- together + vellere to pluck, pull] —**con'vulsive** adj.

convulsion (kən'vʌlʃən) n. **1.** a violent involuntary muscular contraction. **2.** a violent upheaval. **3.** (pl.) Informal. uncontrollable laughter: I was in convulsions.

cony or **coney** ('kəunı) n., pl. -nies or -neys. **a.** a rabbit; rabbit fur. [Latin cuniculus rabbit]

coo (kuː) vb. cooing, cooed. **1.** (of doves or pigeons) to make a characteristic soft throaty call. **2. bill and coo.** to murmur softly or lovingly. ~n. **3.** a cooing sound. ~interj. **4.** Brit. slang. an exclamation of surprise or amazement. [imit.] —**'cooing** adj., n.

cooee ('kuːiː) interj. a call used to attract attention. [Aboriginal]

cook (kʊk) *vb.* **1.** to prepare (food) by the action of heat or (of food) to be prepared in this way. **2.** *Slang.* to alter or falsify (figures or accounts): *to cook the books.* ~*n.* **3.** a person who prepares food for eating. ~See also **cook up.** [Latin *coquere*]

cooker (ˈkʊkə) *n.* **1.** an apparatus, heated by gas or electricity, for cooking food. **2.** *Brit.* an apple suitable for cooking but not for eating raw.

cookery (ˈkʊkərɪ) *n.* the art or practice of cooking.

cookery book *or* **cookbook** (ˈkʊkˌbʊk) *n.* a book containing recipes.

cookie (ˈkʊkɪ) *n.*, *pl.* **cookies. 1.** *U.S. & Canad.* a biscuit. **2. that's the way the cookie crumbles.** *Informal, chiefly U.S. & Canad.* that is how things inevitably are. [Dutch *koekje* little cake]

cook up *vb. Informal.* to devise or invent (a story, alibi, or scheme).

cool (kuːl) *adj.* **1.** moderately cold: *a cool day.* **2.** comfortably free of heat: *a cool room.* **3.** calm and unemotional: *a cool head.* **4.** indifferent or unfriendly: *a cool welcome.* **5.** calmly impudent. **6.** *Informal.* (of a large sum of money) without exaggeration: *a cool ten thousand.* **7.** (of a colour) having violet, blue, or green predominating. **8.** *Informal.* sophisticated or elegant; unruffled. **9.** *Informal, chiefly U.S. & Canad.* marvellous. ~*n.* **10.** coolness: *the cool of the evening.* **11.** *Slang.* calmness; composure: *don't lose your cool.* ~*vb.* (usually foll. by *down* or *off*) **12.** to make or become cooler. **13.** to calm down. [Old English *cōl*]

coolant (ˈkuːlənt) *n.* a fluid used to remove heat from a machine or system while it is working.

cool drink *n. S. African.* a soft drink.

cooler (ˈkuːlə) *n.* a container for making or keeping things cool.

coolie (ˈkuːlɪ) *n.* an unskilled Oriental labourer. [Hindi *kulī*]

cooling tower *n.* a tall hollow structure in a factory or power station, inside which hot water trickles down, becoming cool as it does so.

coomb *or* **coombe** (kuːm) *n. Chiefly southeastern English.* a short valley or deep hollow. [Old English *cumb*]

coon (kuːn) *n.* **1.** *Informal.* short for **raccoon. 2.** *Offensive slang.* a Negro or Australian Aborigine.

coop[1] (kuːp) *n.* **1.** a cage or pen for poultry or small animals. ~*vb.* **2.** (often foll. by *up* or *in*) to confine in a restricted area. [Latin *cupa* basket, cask]

coop[2] *or* **co-op** (ˈkəʊˌɒp) *n.* a cooperative society or a shop run by a cooperative society.

cooper (ˈkuːpə) *n.* a person who makes or repairs barrels or casks. [see COOP[1]]

cooperate *or* **co-operate** (kəʊˈɒpəˌreɪt) *vb.* **1.** to work or act together. **2.** to assist or be willing to assist. [Latin *co-* with + *operārī* to work] —**coˌoperˈation** *or* **coˌoperˈation** *n.*

cooperative *or* **co-operative** (kəʊˈɒprətɪv, -ˈɒprə-) *adj.* **1.** cooperating or willing to cooperate. **2.** (of an enterprise or farm) owned collectively and managed for joint economic benefit. ~*n.* **3.** a cooperative organization.

cooperative society *n.* a commercial enterprise owned and run by customers or workers, in which the profits are shared among the members.

coopt *or* **co-opt** (kəʊˈɒpt) *vb.* to add (someone) to a group by the agreement of the existing members. [Latin *cooptāre* to choose, elect]

coordinate *or* **co-ordinate** *vb.* (kəʊˈɔːdɪˌneɪt). **1.** to bring together and organize (diverse elements) into a harmonious order or relation. ~*n.* (kəʊˈɔːdɪnɪt). **2.** *Maths.* any of a set of numbers that defines the location of a point with reference to a system of axes. ~*adj.* (kəʊˈɔːdɪnɪt). **3.** of or involving coordination. **4.** of or involving the use of coordinates: *coordinate geometry.* [Latin *co-* together + *ordino* order] —**coˌordiˈnation** *or* **coˌordiˈnation** *n.* —**coˈordiˌnator** *or* **coˈordiˌnator** *n.*

coordinates *or* **co-ordinates** (kəʊˈɔːdɪnɪts) *pl. n.* matching items of clothing.

coot (kuːt) *n.* **1.** an aquatic bird like a duck, with black feathers and a white bill and forehead. **2.** a foolish person. [prob. Low German]

cop (kɒp) *Slang.* ~*n.* **1.** a policeman. **2. not much cop.** of little value or worth. ~*vb.* **3.** to take or seize. **4.** to suffer (a punishment): *you'll cop a clout if you do that!* **5. cop it.** to get into trouble or be punished. ~See also **cop out.** [perhaps from Old French *caper* to seize]

copartner (kəʊˈpɑːtnə) *n.* a partner or associate. —**coˈpartnership** *n.*

cope[1] (kəʊp) *vb.* (foll. by *with*) **1.** to contend against. **2.** to deal successfully (with); manage: *she coped well with the problem.* [Old French *coper* to strike, cut]

cope[2] (kəʊp) *n.* **1.** a large ceremonial cloak worn by some Christian priests. **2.** any covering shaped like a cope. ~*vb.* **3.** to cover with a cope. [Late Latin *cappa* hooded cloak]

cope[3] (kəʊp) *vb.* to provide (a wall) with a coping. [prob. from French *couper* to cut]

copeck (ˈkəʊpɛk) *n.* same as **kopeck.**

Copernican (kəˈpɜːnɪkən) *adj.* of the theory that the earth and the planets rotate round the sun. [after Nicolaus Copernicus, astronomer]

copestone (ˈkəʊpˌstəʊn) *n.* **1.** Also called: **coping stone.** a stone used to form a coping. **2.** the stone at the top of a building or wall.

copier (ˈkɒpɪə) *n.* a person or machine that copies.

copilot (ˈkəʊˌpaɪlət) *n.* the second pilot of an aircraft.

coping (ˈkəʊpɪŋ) *n.* the sloping top row of a wall, usually made of masonry or brick.

coping saw *n.* a handsaw with a U-shaped frame, used for cutting curves in wood.

copious ('kəʊpɪəs) *adj.* abundant; plentiful. [Latin *cōpiōsus*] —**copiously** *adv.*

cop out *Slang.* ~*vb.* **1.** to fail to assume responsibility or commit oneself. ~*n.* **copout. 2.** a way or an instance of avoiding responsibility or commitment. [prob. from COP]

copper[1] ('kɒpə) *n.* **1.** a soft reddish metallic element, used in such alloys as brass and bronze. Symbol: Cu **2.** *Informal.* any copper or bronze coin. **3.** *Chiefly Brit.* a large metal container used to boil water. ~*adj.* **4.** reddish-brown. [Latin *Cyprium aes* Cyprian metal, from Greek *Kupris* Cyprus]

copper[2] ('kɒpə) *n. Slang.* a policeman. [from COP (*vb.*)]

copper beech *n.* a cultivated European beech with reddish leaves.

copper-bottomed *adj.* financially reliable. [from the practice of coating the bottom of ships with copper to prevent the timbers rotting]

copperhead ('kɒpə,hɛd) *n.* a venomous American snake with a reddish-brown head.

copperplate ('kɒpə,pleɪt) *n.* **1.** a polished copper plate etched or engraved for printing. **2.** a print taken from such a plate. **3.** a fine handwriting based upon that used on copperplate engravings.

copper sulphate *n.* a blue crystalline copper salt used in electroplating and in plant sprays.

coppice ('kɒpɪs) *n.* a dense growth of small trees, bushes, and undergrowth. [Old French *copeiz*]

copra ('kɒprə) *n.* the dried oil-yielding kernel of the coconut. [Malayalam *koppara* coconut]

copse (kɒps) *n.* same as **coppice.** [from COPPICE]

Copt (kɒpt) *n.* **1.** a member of the Coptic Church, a part of the Christian Church which was founded in Egypt. **2.** an Egyptian descended from the ancient Egyptians. [Coptic *kyptios* Egyptian]

Coptic ('kɒptɪk) *n.* **1.** the language of the Copts, descended from Ancient Egyptian and surviving only in the Coptic Church. ~*adj.* **2.** of the Copts or their language.

copula ('kɒpjʊlə) *n., pl.* **-las** or **-lae** (-,liː). a verb, such as *be* or *seem,* that is used to link the subject with the complement of a sentence, as in *he became king; you seem tired.* [Latin: bond]

copulate ('kɒpjʊ,leɪt) *vb.* to perform sexual intercourse. [Latin *copulāre* to join together] —**copu'lation** *n.*

copy ('kɒpɪ) *n., pl.* **copies. 1.** an imitation or reproduction of an original. **2.** a single specimen of a book, magazine, or record of which there are many others exactly the same. **3.** written matter or text as distinct from graphic material in books. **4.** the text of an advertisement. **5.** *Journalism, informal.* suitable material for an article: *disasters are always good copy.* ~*vb.* **copying, copied. 6.** to make a copy (of). **7.** to imitate. [Latin *cōpia* abundance]

copybook ('kɒpɪ,bʊk) *n.* **1.** a book of

specimens of handwriting for imitation. **2. blot one's copybook.** *Informal.* to spoil one's reputation by a mistake or indiscretion. ~(*modifier*) **3.** done exactly according to the rules. **4.** trite or unoriginal.

copycat ('kɒpɪ,kæt) *n. Informal.* a person who imitates or copies another.

copyist ('kɒpɪɪst) *n.* **1.** a person who makes written copies. **2.** an imitator.

copyright ('kɒpɪ,raɪt) *n.* **1.** the exclusive legal right to reproduce and control an original literary, musical, or artistic work. ~*adj.* **2.** protected by copyright. ~*vb.* **3.** to take out a copyright on.

copy typist *n.* a typist whose job is to type from written or typed drafts rather than dictation.

copywriter ('kɒpɪ,raɪtə) *n.* a person employed to write advertising copy.

coquette (kəʊ'kɛt) *n.* a woman who flirts. [French] —**coquetry** ('kɒkɪtrɪ) *n.* —**co'quettish** *adj.*

coracle ('kɒrək*ə*l) *n.* a small roundish boat made of waterproof material stretched over a wicker frame. [Welsh *corwgl*]

coral ('kɒrəl) *n.* **1.** the stony substance formed by the skeletons of marine animals called polyps, often forming an island or reef. **2.** any of the polyps whose skeletons form coral. ~*adj.* **3.** yellowish-pink. [Greek *korallion*]

cor anglais ('kɔːr 'ɑːŋgleɪ) *n., pl.* **cors anglais** ('kɔːz 'ɑːŋglei). *Music.* an alto woodwind instrument of the oboe family. [French: English horn]

corbel ('kɔːb*ə*l) *n. Archit.* a supporting bracket projecting from a wall, usually of stone or brick. [Old French: a little raven]

corbie ('kɔːbɪ) *n. Scot.* a raven or crow. [Latin *corvus*]

cord (kɔːd) *n.* **1.** string or thin rope made of twisted strands. **2.** a ribbed fabric, esp. corduroy. **3.** *U.S. & Canad.* an electrical flex. **4.** *Anat.* a structure in the body resembling a rope: *the spinal cord.* **5.** a unit for measuring cut wood, equal to 128 cubic feet. ~*vb.* **6.** to bind with a cord or cords. ~See also **cords.** [Greek *khordē*]

corded ('kɔːdɪd) *adj.* **1.** bound or fastened with cord. **2.** (of a fabric) ribbed. **3.** (of muscles) standing out like cords.

cordial ('kɔːdɪəl) *adj.* **1.** warm and friendly: *a cordial greeting.* **2.** heartfelt or sincere: *cordial dislike.* ~*n.* **3.** a drink with a fruit base: *lime cordial.* [Latin *cor* heart] —**cordially** *adv.*

cordiality (,kɔːdɪ'ælɪtɪ) *n.* warmth of feeling.

cordite ('kɔːdaɪt) *n.* a smokeless explosive used in guns and bombs. [from *cord,* because of its stringy appearance]

cordon ('kɔːd*ə*n) *n.* **1.** a chain of police, soldiers, or ships stationed around an area to guard it. **2.** a ribbon, cord, or braid worn as insignia of honour or as an ornament. **3.** *Horticulture.* a fruit tree trained to grow as a single stem against fruit. ~*vb.* **4.** (often foll. by *off*) to put or form a cordon (around); close (off). [Old French: a little cord]

cordon bleu (,kɔːdɒn 'blɜː) *adj.* (of cookery or cooks) of the highest standard: *a cordon bleu chef*. [French: blue ribbon]

cordon sanitaire (ˌkɔːdɒn ˌsænɪˈtɛə) *n.*
1. a guarded line isolating an infected area.
2. a line of buffer states shielding a country. [French, lit.: sanitary line]

cords (kɔːdz) *pl. n.* trousers made of corduroy.

corduroy (ˈkɔːdəˌrɔɪ, ˌkɔːdəˈrɔɪ) *n.* a heavy cotton pile fabric with lengthways ribs. [origin unknown]

corduroys (ˌkɔːdəˈrɔɪz, ˈkɔːdəˌrɔɪz) *pl. n.* trousers of corduroy.

core (kɔː) *n.* **1.** the central part of certain fleshy fruits, containing the seeds. **2.** the central or essential part of something: *the core of the argument*. **3.** a piece of magnetic soft iron inside an electromagnet or transformer. **4.** *Geol.* the central part of the earth. **5.** a cylindrical sample of rock or soil, obtained by the use of a hollow drill. **6.** *Physics.* the region of a nuclear reactor containing the fissionable material. **7.** *Computers.* **a.** a ferrite ring used in a computer memory to store one bit of information. **b.** the whole memory of a computer when made up of such rings. ~*vb.* **8.** to remove the core from (fruit). [origin unknown]

co-respondent (ˌkəʊrɪˈspɒndənt) *n.* *Law.* a person alleged to have committed adultery with the person an action for divorce is being brought against (the **respondent**).

corf (kɔːf) *n., pl.* **corves** (kɔːvz). *Brit.* a wagon or basket formerly used in mines. [Middle English]

corgi (ˈkɔːgɪ) *n.* a short-legged sturdy dog. [Welsh *cor* dwarf + *ci* dog]

coriander (ˌkɒrɪˈændə) *n.* **1.** a European plant, cultivated for its aromatic seeds. **2.** the dried seeds of this plant used as a flavouring. [Greek *koriannon*]

Corinthian (kəˈrɪnθɪən) *adj.* **1.** of Corinth in Greece. **2.** of one of the five classical orders of architecture, characterized by a bell-shaped capital with carved leaf-shaped ornaments. ~*n.* **3.** a person from Corinth.

cork (kɔːk) *n.* **1.** the thick light porous outer bark of a Mediterranean oak. **2.** a piece of cork used as a stopper. **3.** *Bot.* the outer bark of a woody plant. ~*vb.* **4.** to stop up (a bottle) with a cork. **5.** (often foll. by *up*) to restrain. [prob. from Arabic *qurq*]

corkage (ˈkɔːkɪdʒ) *n.* a charge made at a restaurant for serving wine bought elsewhere.

corked (kɔːkt) *adj.* (of wine) tainted through having a decayed cork.

corker (ˈkɔːkə) *n.* *Old-fashioned slang.* a splendid or outstanding person or thing.

corkscrew (ˈkɔːkˌskruː) *n.* **1.** a device for drawing corks from bottles, usually consisting of a pointed metal spiral attached to a handle. **2.** (*modifier*) resembling a corkscrew in shape. ~*vb.* **3.** to move or cause to move in a spiral or zigzag course.

corm (kɔːm) *n.* the scaly bulblike underground stem of certain plants. [Greek *kormos* tree trunk]

cormorant (ˈkɔːmərənt) *n.* a fish-eating aquatic bird with long neck and body and a slender hooked beak. [Old French *corp* raven + *-mareng* of the sea]

corn[1] (kɔːn) *n.* **1.** *Brit.* **a.** a cereal plant such as wheat, oats, or barley. **b.** the seeds of such plants; grain. **2.** *U.S., Canad., & N.Z.* maize. **3.** *Slang.* anything, such as a song, regarded as banal or sentimental. [Old English *corn*]

corn[2] (kɔːn) *n.* a painful hardening of the skin of the toes, caused by pressure. [Latin *cornū* horn]

corncob (ˈkɔːnˌkɒb) *n.* the core of an ear of maize, to which the kernels are attached.

corncrake (ˈkɔːnˌkreɪk) *n.* a brown bird with a harsh grating cry.

cornea (ˈkɔːnɪə) *n., pl.* **-neas** *or* **-neae** (-nɪˌiː). the transparent membrane that forms the outer covering of the eyeball. [Latin *cornū* horn] —**ˈcorneal** *adj.*

corned (kɔːnd) *adj.* cooked and then preserved in salt or brine: *corned beef*.

cornelian (kɔːˈniːljən) *n.* same as **carnelian**.

corner (ˈkɔːnə) *n.* **1.** the place or angle formed by the meeting of two converging lines or surfaces. **2.** the space within the angle formed, as in a room. **3.** a remote place: *far-off corners of the globe*. **4.** any secluded or private place. **5.** the place where two streets meet. **6.** *Sports.* a free kick or shot taken from the corner of the field. **7. cut corners.** to take the shortest or easiest way at the expense of high standards. **8. turn the corner.** to pass the critical point of an illness or a difficult time. **9.** (*modifier*) on a corner: *a corner shop*. ~*vb.* **10.** to force (a person or animal) into a difficult or inescapable position. **11. a.** to acquire enough of (a commodity) to attain control of the market. **b.** to attain control of (a market) in such a manner. **12.** (of a vehicle or its driver) to turn a corner. [Latin *cornū* point, horn]

corner shop *n.* a small general shop serving a neighbourhood.

cornerstone (ˈkɔːnəˌstəʊn) *n.* **1.** a stone at the corner of a wall, uniting two intersecting walls. **2.** a stone placed at the bottom corner of a building during a ceremony to mark the start of construction. **3.** an indispensable part or basis: *the cornerstone of the whole argument*.

cornet (ˈkɔːnɪt) *n.* **1.** a brass instrument of the trumpet family. **2.** *Brit.* a cone-shaped wafer container for ice cream. [Latin *cornū* horn] —**cornetist** (kɔːˈnetɪst) *n.*

corn exchange *n.* a building where corn is bought and sold.

cornflakes (ˈkɔːnˌfleɪks) *pl. n.* a breakfast cereal made from toasted maize.

cornflour (ˈkɔːnˌflaʊə) *n.* a fine maize flour, used for thickening sauces.

cornflower (ˈkɔːnˌflaʊə) *n.* a small plant, usually with blue flowers, formerly a common weed in corn fields.

cornice (ˈkɔːnɪs) *n.* **1.** *Archit.* the projecting mouldings at the top of a column. **2.** a continuous horizontal moulding around the top of a wall or building. [Old French]

Cornish (ˈkɔːnɪʃ) *adj.* **1.** of Cornwall or its inhabitants. ~*n.* **2.** a Celtic language of Cornwall, extinct by 1800. **3. the Cornish.** (*functioning as pl.*) the people of Cornwall.

Cornish pasty (ˈpæstɪ) *n.* a pastry case with a filling of meat and vegetables.

cornucopia (ˌkɔːnjʊˈkəʊpɪə) *n.* **1.** a symbol of plenty, consisting of a horn overflowing with fruit, flowers, and corn. **2.** a great abundance. [Latin *cornū cōpiae* horn of plenty]

corny (ˈkɔːnɪ) *adj.* **cornier, corniest.** *Slang.* **1.** trite or banal. **2.** sickly sentimental.

corolla (kəˈrɒlə) *n.* the petals of a flower collectively, forming an inner envelope. [Latin: little crown]

corollary (kəˈrɒlərɪ) *n., pl.* **-laries. 1.** a proposition that follows directly from another that has been proved. **2.** a natural consequence. [Latin *corollārium* money paid for a garland]

corona (kəˈrəʊnə) *n., pl.* **-nas** *or* **-nae** (-niː). **1.** a circle of light around a luminous body, usually the moon. **2.** the outermost part of the sun's atmosphere, visible as a faint halo during a total eclipse. **3.** *Bot.* a crownlike part of some flowers on top of the seed or on the inner side of the corolla. **4.** a long cigar with blunt ends. **5.** *Physics.* an electrical glow appearing around the surface of a charged conductor. [Latin: crown]

coronary (ˈkɒrənərɪ) *adj.* **1.** *Anat.* of the arteries that supply blood to the heart. ~*n., pl.* **-naries. 2.** a coronary thrombosis. [Latin *corōnārius* belonging to a wreath or crown]

coronary thrombosis *n.* a condition where the blood flow to the heart is blocked by a clot in a coronary artery.

coronation (ˌkɒrəˈneɪʃən) *n.* the act or ceremony of crowning a monarch. [Latin *corōnāre* to crown]

coroner (ˈkɒrənə) *n.* a public official responsible for the investigation of violent, sudden, or suspicious deaths. [Anglo-French *corouner*]

coronet (ˈkɒrənɪt) *n.* **1.** a small crown worn by princes or peers. **2.** a band of jewels worn as a headdress. [Old French *coronete*]

corporal[1] (ˈkɔːpərəl) *n.* a noncommissioned officer in an army. [Old French *caporal*, from Latin *caput* head]

corporal[2] (ˈkɔːpərəl, ˈkɔːprəl) *adj.* of the body. [Latin *corpus* body]

corporal punishment *n.* punishment of a physical nature, such as caning.

corporate (ˈkɔːpərɪt) *adj.* **1.** forming a corporation; incorporated. **2.** of a business corporation or corporations: *corporate finance*. **3.** of or shared by a united group; joint. [Latin *corpus* body]

corporation (ˌkɔːpəˈreɪʃən) *n.* **1.** a large business or company. **2.** a city or town

council. **3.** *Brit. informal.* a large paunch. —ˈ**corporative** *adj.*

corporatism (ˈkɔːpərətɪzəm) *n.* organization of a state on the lines of a business enterprise, with substantial government management of the economy.

corporeal (kɔːˈpɔːrɪəl) *adj.* of the nature of the physical body; material; not spiritual. [Latin *corpus* body]

corps (kɔː) *n., pl.* **corps** (kɔːz). **1.** a military body with a specific function: *medical corps*. **2.** a body of people associated together in a particular activity: *the diplomatic corps*. [French]

corps de ballet (ˈkɔː də ˈbæleɪ) *n.* the members of a ballet company. [French]

corpse (kɔːps) *n.* a dead body, esp. of a human being. [Latin *corpus*]

corpulent (ˈkɔːpjʊlənt) *adj.* physically bulky; fat. [Latin *corpulentus*] —ˈ**corpulence** *n.*

corpus (ˈkɔːpəs) *n., pl.* **-pora** (-pərə). a body of writings, such as one by a single author or on a specific topic: *the corpus of Dickens' works*. [Latin: body]

corpuscle (ˈkɔːpʌsʲl) *n.* **1.** a red blood cell (see **erythrocyte**) or white blood cell (see **leucocyte**). **2.** any minute particle. [Latin *corpusculum* a little body] —**corpuscular** (kɔːˈpʌskjʊlə) *adj.*

corral (kɒˈrɑːl) *n.* **1.** *Chiefly U.S. & Canad.* an enclosure for cattle or horses. ~*vb.* **-ralling, -ralled. 2.** *U.S. & Canad.* to drive into a corral. [Spanish]

correct (kəˈrɛkt) *vb.* **1.** to make free from or put right errors. **2.** to indicate the errors in (something). **3.** to rebuke or punish in order to improve: *to stand corrected*. **4.** to adjust or make conform to a standard. ~*adj.* **5.** true; accurate: *the correct version*. **6.** in conformity with accepted standards: *correct behaviour*. [Latin *corrigere* to make straight] —corˈ**rective** *adj.* —corˈ**rectly** *adv.* —corˈ**rectness** *n.*

correction (kəˈrɛkʃən) *n.* **1.** an act or instance of correcting. **2.** something substituted for an error; an improvement. **3.** a reproof or punishment. —corˈ**rectional** *adj.*

correlate (ˈkɒrɪˌleɪt) *vb.* **1.** to place or be placed in a complementary or mutual relationship: *poverty can be correlated with poor health*. ~*n.* **2.** either of two things mutually related. —ˈ**correlation** *n.*

correlative (kɒˈrɛlətɪv) *adj.* **1.** having a mutual relationship; corresponding. **2.** *Grammar.* (of words, usually conjunctions) corresponding to each other and occurring regularly together, for example *neither* and *nor*.

correspond (ˌkɒrɪˈspɒnd) *vb.* **1.** (usually foll. by *with* or *to*) to be consistent or compatible (with); tally (with). **2.** (usually foll. by *to*) to be similar (to). **3.** (usually foll. by *with*) to communicate (with) by letter. [Latin *com-* together + *respondēre* to respond] —ˌcorreˈ**sponding** *adj.* —ˌcorreˈ**spondingly** *adv.*

correspondence (ˌkɒrɪˈspɒndəns) *n.* **1.** similarity. **2.** agreement or conformity. **3.**

a. communication by letters. **b.** the letters so exchanged.

correspondence course *n.* a course of study conducted by post.

correspondent (ˌkɒrɪˈspɒndənt) *n.* **1.** a person who communicates by letter. **2.** a person employed by a newspaper to report on a special subject or from a foreign country.

corridor (ˈkɒrɪˌdɔː) *n.* **1.** a passage connecting parts of a building. **2.** a strip of land or airspace that provides access through the territory of a foreign country. **3.** a passageway connecting the compartments of a railway coach. **4. corridors of power,** the higher levels of government or the Civil Service. [Old Italian *corridore*, lit.: place for running]

corrie (ˈkɒrɪ) *n.* (in Scotland) a circular hollow on a hillside. [Gaelic *coire* cauldron]

corrigendum (ˌkɒrɪˈdʒɛndəm) *n., pl.* **-da** (-də). **1.** an error to be corrected. **2.** (*sometimes pl.*) a slip of paper inserted into a book after printing, listing corrections. [Latin: that which is to be corrected]

corroborate (kəˈrɒbəˌreɪt) *vb.* to confirm or support (facts or opinions), esp. by providing fresh evidence. [Latin *com-* (intensive) + *rōborāre* to make strong] —**corˌroboˈration** *n.* —**corroborative** (kəˈrɒbərətɪv) *adj.*

corroboree (kəˈrɒbərɪ) *n. Austral.* **1.** a native gathering or dance of festive or warlike character. **2.** any noisy gathering. [Aboriginal]

corrode (kəˈrəʊd) *vb.* **1.** to eat away or be eaten away by chemical action or rusting. **2.** to destroy gradually: *jealousy corroded his happiness.* [Latin *corrōdere* to gnaw to pieces]

corrosion (kəˈrəʊʒən) *n.* **1.** the process by which something, esp. a metal, is corroded. **2.** the result of corrosion. —**corˈrosive** *adj.*

corrugate (ˈkɒruˌɡeɪt) *vb.* to fold into alternate grooves and ridges. [Latin *corrūgāre*] —**corruˈgation** *n.*

corrugated iron *n.* a thin sheet of iron or steel, formed with alternating ridges and troughs.

corrupt (kəˈrʌpt) *adj.* **1.** open to or involving bribery or other dishonest practices: *a corrupt official; corrupt practices.* **2.** morally depraved. **3.** (of a text or manuscript) made unreliable or suspect by scribal errors or alterations. ~*vb.* **4.** to become or cause to become corrupt. [Latin *corruptus* spoiled] —**corˈruptive** *adj.*

corruptible (kəˈrʌptəbʰl) *adj.* capable of being corrupted, esp. morally.

corruption (kəˈrʌpʃən) *n.* **1.** a making or being corrupt. **2.** depravity. **3.** dishonesty, esp. bribery. **4.** decay. **5.** alteration, as of a manuscript. **6.** an altered form of a word.

corsage (kɔːˈsɑːʒ) *n.* a small bouquet worn pinned to the shoulder or bosom of a dress. [Old French *cors* body]

corsair (ˈkɔːsɛə) *n.* **1.** a pirate. **2.** a

privateer. **3.** a pirate ship. [Old French *corsaire*]

corse (kɔːs) *n. Archaic.* a corpse.

corselet (ˈkɔːslɪt) *n.* a woman's one-piece undergarment, combining corset and bra. [Old French *cors* bodice]

corset (ˈkɔːsɪt) *n.* **1.** a stiffened close-fitting garment, worn by women to support or shape the torso. **2.** a similar garment worn because of injury or weakness, by either sex. [Old French: a little bodice] —**ˈcorsetry** *n.*

cortege *or* **cortège** (kɔːˈteɪʒ) *n.* a funeral procession. [Italian *corteggio*]

cortex (ˈkɔːtɛks) *n., pl.* **-tices** (-tɪˌsiːz). *Anat.* the outer layer of the brain or some other internal organ. [Latin: bark, outer layer] —**cortical** (ˈkɔːtɪkʰl) *adj.*

cortisone (ˈkɔːtɪˌzəʊn) *n.* a steroid hormone used in treating rheumatoid arthritis, allergies, and skin diseases. [*corticosterone*, a hormone]

corundum (kəˈrʌndəm) *n.* a hard mineral consisting of aluminium oxide, used as an abrasive. The ruby and sapphire are precious forms of it. [Tamil *kuruntam*]

coruscate (ˈkɒrəˌskeɪt) *vb.* to emit flashes of light; sparkle. [Latin *coruscāre* to flash] —**ˌcorusˈcation** *n.*

corvette (kɔːˈvɛt) *n.* a lightly armed escort warship. [perhaps from Middle Dutch *corf* basket, small ship]

corymb (ˈkɒrɪmb, -rɪm) *n.* a flat-topped flower cluster with the stems growing progressively shorter towards the centre. [Greek *korumbos* cluster]

cos[1] *or* **cos lettuce** (kɒs) *n.* a lettuce with a long slender head and crisp leaves. [after *Kos*, the Aegean island of its origin]

cos[2] (kɒz) cosine.

cosec (ˈkəʊsɛk) cosecant.

cosecant (kəʊˈsiːkənt) *n.* (in trigonometry) the ratio of the length of the hypotenuse to that of the opposite side in a right-angled triangle.

cosh (kɒʃ) *Brit.* ~*n.* **1.** a heavy blunt weapon, often made of hard rubber. ~*vb.* **2.** to hit on the head with a cosh. [Romany *kosh*]

cosignatory (kəʊˈsɪɡnətrɪ) *n., pl.* **-ries.** a person or country that signs a document jointly with others.

cosine (ˈkəʊˌsaɪn) *n.* (in trigonometry) the ratio of the length of the adjacent side to that of the hypotenuse in a right-angled triangle. [see CO-, SINE]

cosmetic (kɒzˈmɛtɪk) *n.* **1.** anything applied to the face or body with the intention of beautifying it. ~*adj.* **2.** used to improve the appearance of the face or body. **3.** only superficially improving: *it was a purely cosmetic measure.* [Greek *kosmētikos*, from *kosmein* to arrange]

cosmic (ˈkɒzmɪk) *adj.* **1.** of or relating to the whole universe: *cosmic laws.* **2.** occurring in or coming from outer space: *cosmic rays.*

cosmogony (kɒzˈmɒɡənɪ) *n., pl.* **-nies.** the study of the origin of the universe. [Greek *kosmos* world + *gonos* creation]

cosmology (kɒzˈmɒlədʒɪ) n. the study of the origin and nature of the universe. [Greek *kosmos* world + -LOGY] —**cosmological** (ˌkɒzməˈlɒdʒɪkˀl) adj. —**cosˈmologist** n.

cosmonaut (ˈkɒzməˌnɔːt) n. a Soviet astronaut. [Russian *kosmonavt*, from Greek *kosmos* universe + *nautēs* sailor]

cosmopolitan (ˌkɒzməˈpɒlɪtˀn) adj. 1. having lived and travelled in many countries; free of national prejudices. 2. composed of people or elements from many different countries or cultures. ~n. 3. a cosmopolitan person. [Greek *kosmos* world + *politēs* citizen] —ˌcosmoˈpolitanism n.

cosmos (ˈkɒzmɒs) n. the universe considered as an ordered system. [Greek *kosmos* order]

Cossack (ˈkɒsæk) n. 1. a member of a S Russian people, famous as horsemen and dancers. ~adj. 2. of the Cossacks: a *Cossack dance*. [Russian *kazak* vagabond]

cosset (ˈkɒsɪt) vb. to pamper or pet. [origin unknown]

cost (kɒst) n. 1. the amount of money, time, or energy required to obtain or produce something. 2. suffering or sacrifice: *I know to my cost*. 3. the amount paid for a commodity by its seller: *to sell at cost*. 4. (pl.) *Law*. the expenses of a lawsuit. 5. **at all costs**. regardless of any cost, effort, or risk involved. 6. **at the cost of**. at the expense of losing. ~vb. **costing, cost**. 7. to be obtained or obtainable in exchange for: *the ride cost one pound*. 8. to cause (someone) a loss or sacrifice: *the accident cost him dearly*. 9. to estimate the cost of producing something. [Latin *constāre* to stand at, cost]

cost accounting n. the recording and controlling of all the costs involved in running a business. —**cost accountant** n.

costermonger (ˈkɒstəˌmʌŋɡə) n. *Brit., rare*. a person who sells fruit and vegetables from a barrow. [*costard* a kind of apple + *monger* trader]

costive (ˈkɒstɪv) adj. constipated or constipating. [Old French *costivé*]

costly (ˈkɒstlɪ) adj. **-lier, -liest**. 1. expensive. 2. involving great loss or sacrifice: *a costly victory*. 3. splendid; lavish. —**ˈcostliness** n.

cost of living n. the average cost of the basic necessities of life, such as food, housing, and clothing.

costume (ˈkɒstjuːm) n. 1. a style of dressing, including all the clothes and accessories, typical of a particular country or period. 2. the clothes worn by an actor or performer: *a jester's costume*. 3. short for **swimming costume**. ~vb. 4. to provide with a costume. [Italian: dress, custom]

costume jewellery n. inexpensive but attractive jewellery.

costumier (kɒˈstjuːmɪə) n. a person who makes or supplies theatrical or fancy costumes.

cosy or *U.S.* **cozy** (ˈkəʊzɪ) adj. **-sier, -siest** or *U.S.* **-zier, -ziest**. 1. warm and snug. 2. intimate; friendly. ~n., pl. **-sies** or *U.S.*

-zies. 3. a cover for keeping things warm: *tea cosy*. [Scot.] —**ˈcosiness** or *U.S.* **ˈcoziness** n.

cot[1] (kɒt) n. 1. a bed with high sides for a baby or very young child. 2. a small portable bed. [Hindi *khāt* bedstead]

cot[2] (kɒt) n. 1. *Literary or archaic*. a small cottage. 2. a cote. [Old English]

cot[3] (kɒt) cotangent.

cotangent (kəʊˈtændʒənt) n. (in trigonometry) the ratio of the length of the adjacent side to that of the opposite side in a right-angled triangle.

cot death n. the unexplained sudden death of an infant during sleep.

cote (kəʊt) or **cot** n. a small shelter for birds or animals. [Old English]

coterie (ˈkəʊtərɪ) n. a small exclusive group of friends or people with common interests; clique. [French]

cottage (ˈkɒtɪdʒ) n. a small simple house, usually one in the country. [from COT[2]] —**ˈcottager** n.

cottage cheese n. a mild soft white cheese made from skimmed milk curds.

cottage industry n. a craft industry in which employees work at home.

cotter[1] (ˈkɒtə) n. *Machinery*. a bolt or wedge that is used to secure parts of machinery. [Middle English *cotterel*]

cotter[2] (ˈkɒtə) n. *Hist. & Scot*. a farm labourer occupying a cottage and land rent-free. [see COT[2]]

cotter pin n. *Machinery*. a split pin used to hold parts together and fastened by having the ends spread apart after it is inserted.

cotton (ˈkɒtˀn) n. 1. the soft white downy fibre surrounding the seeds of a plant grown in warm climates, used to make cloth and thread. 2. cloth or thread made from cotton fibres. [Arabic *qutn*] —**ˈcottony** adj.

cotton on vb. (often foll. by *to*) *Informal*. to understand or realize the meaning (of).

cotton wool n. *Chiefly Brit*. absorbent fluffy cotton, used for surgical dressings and to apply liquids or creams to the skin.

cotyledon (ˌkɒtɪˈliːdˀn) n. the first leaf produced by a plant embryo. [Greek *kotulē* cup]

couch (kaʊtʃ) n. 1. a piece of upholstered furniture for seating more than one person; sofa. 2. a bed on which patients of a doctor or a psychoanalyst lie during examination or treatment. ~vb. 3. to express in a particular style of language: *couched in an archaic style*. 4. *Archaic*. (of an animal) to crouch, as when preparing to leap. [Old French *coucher* to lay down]

couchette (kuːˈʃɛt) n. a bed converted from seats in a railway carriage or ship. [French]

couch grass (kaʊtʃ, kuːtʃ) n. a grassy weed with a creeping underground stem by which it spreads quickly.

cougar (ˈkuːɡə) n. same as **puma**. [S. American Indian]

cough (kɒf) vb. 1. to expel air abruptly and noisily from the lungs. 2. (of an engine or other machine) to make a sound similar to this. ~*n.* **3.** an act or sound of coughing. **4.** a condition of the lungs or throat which causes frequent coughing. [Old English *cohhetten*]

cough up *vb.* **1.** *Informal.* to give up (money or information). **2.** to bring into the mouth or eject (phlegm, food, or blood) by coughing.

could (kʊd) *vb.* used: **1.** to make the past tense of **can**[1]. **2.** to make the subjunctive mood of **can**[1], esp. in polite requests or conditional sentences: *could I see you to-night?* **3.** to indicate the suggestion of a course of action: *you could take the car if it's raining.* **4.** (often foll. by *well*) to indicate a possibility: *he could well be a spy.* [Old English *cūthe*]

couldn't (ˈkʊdᵊnt) could not.

coulomb (ˈkuːlɒm) *n.* the SI unit of electric charge. [after C.A. de *Coulomb*, physicist]

coulter (ˈkəʊltə) *n.* a vertical blade on a plough in front of the ploughshare. [Latin *culter* ploughshare, knife]

council (ˈkaʊnsəl) *n.* **1.** an assembly of people meeting for discussion or consultation. **2.** an administrative, legislative, or advisory body: *a student council.* **3.** *Brit.* the local governing authority of a town or county. **4.** (*modifier*) of, used, or provided by a local council: *council offices; a council house.* [Latin *concilium* assembly]

councillor or *U.S.* **councilor** (ˈkaʊnsələ) *n.* a member of a council.

counsel (ˈkaʊnsəl) *n.* **1.** advice or guidance. **2.** discussion; consultation: *to take counsel with a friend.* **3.** a barrister or group of barristers who conduct cases in court and advise on legal matters. ~*vb.* **-selling, -selled** or *U.S.* **-seling, -seled.** **4.** to give advice or guidance to. **5.** to recommend; urge. [Latin *consilium* deliberating body] —**counselling** or *U.S.* **counseling** *n.*

counsellor or *U.S.* **counselor** (ˈkaʊnsələ) *n.* **1.** an adviser. **2.** *U.S.* a lawyer who conducts cases in court.

count[1] (kaʊnt) *vb.* **1.** to add up or check (each thing in a group) in order to find the total: *count your change.* **2.** to recite numbers in ascending order up to and including: *I'm going to count to ten.* **3.** (often foll. by *in*) to take into account or include: *we must count him in.* **4. not counting.** excluding. **5.** to consider: *count yourself lucky.* **6.** to be important: *only winning counts nowadays.* **7.** *Music.* to keep time by counting beats. ~*n.* **8.** the act of counting. **9.** the number reached by counting: *a blood count.* **10.** *Law.* any of the separate charges in an indictment. **11. keep** or **lose count.** to keep or fail to keep an accurate record of items or events. **12. out for the count.** unconscious. ~See also **count against, countdown,** etc. [Latin *computāre* to calculate] —**countable** *adj.*

count[2] (kaʊnt) *n.* a middle-ranking European nobleman. [Latin *comes* associate]

count against *vb.* to have influence to the disadvantage of.

countdown (ˈkaʊntˌdaʊn) *n.* the act of counting backwards to zero to time exactly an operation such as the launching of a rocket.

countenance (ˈkaʊntɪnəns) *n.* **1.** the face or facial expression. ~*vb.* **2.** to support or approve. **3.** to tolerate; endure. [Latin *continentia* restraint, control]

counter[1] (ˈkaʊntə) *n.* **1.** a long narrow flat surface in a shop, cafeteria, or bank, where food is sold, goods are displayed, or business is done. **2.** a small flat disc used in various board games. **3.** a disc or token usedas an imitation coin. **4. under the counter.** (of the sale of goods) illegal. [Latin *computāre* to COMPUTE]

counter[2] (ˈkaʊntə) *n.* an apparatus that records the number of occurrences of events.

counter[3] (ˈkaʊntə) *adv.* **1.** in an opposite or opposing direction or manner. **2. run counter to.** to be in direct contrast with. ~*adj.* **3.** opposing; opposite; contrary. ~*n.* **4.** something that is contrary or opposite to something else. An opposing action. **6.** a return attack, such as a blow in boxing or a parry in fencing. ~*vb.* **7.** to say or do (something) in retaliation or response. **8.** to oppose or act against (a person or thing). **9.** to return the attack of (an opponent). [Latin *contrā* against]

counter- *prefix.* **1.** against; opposite; contrary: *counterattack.* **2.** complementary; corresponding: *counterpart.* [Latin *contrā*]

counteract (ˌkaʊntərˈækt) *vb.* to act against or neutralize by contrary action. —**counter'action** *n.* —**counter'active** *adj.*

counterattack (ˈkaʊntərəˌtæk) *n.* **1.** an attack in response to an attack. ~*vb.* **2.** to make a counterattack (against).

counterbalance *n.* (ˈkaʊntəˌbæləns). **1.** a weight or influence that balances or offsets another. ~*vb.* (ˌkaʊntəˈbæləns). **2.** to act as a counterbalance to.

counterblast (ˈkaʊntəˌblɑːst) *n.* an aggressive response to a verbal attack.

counterclockwise (ˌkaʊntəˈklɒkˌwaɪz) *adv., adj. U.S. & Canad.* same as **anticlockwise.**

counterespionage (ˌkaʊntərˈɛspɪəˌnɑːʒ) *n.* activities to counteract enemy espionage.

counterfeit (ˈkaʊntəfɪt) *adj.* **1.** made in imitation of something genuine with the intent to deceive or defraud; forged: *counterfeit money.* **2.** pretended; sham: *counterfeit affection.* ~*n.* **3.** an imitation designed to deceive or defraud. ~*vb.* **4.** to make a fraudulent imitation of. **5.** to make counterfeits. **6.** to feign. [Old French *contrefait*]

counterfoil (ˈkaʊntəˌfɔɪl) *n. Brit.* the part of a cheque or receipt retained as a record.

counterintelligence (ˌkaʊntərɪnˈtɛlɪdʒəns) *n.* activities designed to frustrate enemy espionage.

countermand (ˌkaʊntəˈmɑːnd) *vb.* to revoke or cancel (an order). [Old French *contremander*]

countermeasure (ˈkaʊntəˌmɛʒə) *n.* action taken to counteract or retaliate against some other action.

counterpane ('kaʊntə,peɪn) n. a bedspread. [Medieval Latin *culcita puncta* quilted mattress]

counterpart ('kaʊntə,pɑːt) n. 1. a person or thing that closely resembles another. 2. one of two parts that complement or correspond to each other. 3. a duplicate of a legal document.

counterpoint ('kaʊntə,pɔɪnt) n. 1. the harmonious combining of two or more parts or melodies. 2. a melody or part combined with another melody or part. ~vb. 3. to set in contrast. [Old French *contrepoint* an accompaniment set against the notes of a melody]

counterpoise ('kaʊntə,pɔɪz) vb. to oppose with something of equal effect, weight, or force; offset.

counterproductive (,kaʊntəprə'dʌktɪv) adj. having an effect contrary to the one intended.

countersign vb. ('kaʊntə,saɪn, ,kaʊntə-'saɪn). 1. to add a confirming signature to (a document already signed by another). ~n. ('kaʊntə,saɪn). 2. the signature so written.

countersink ('kaʊntə,sɪŋk) vb. -**sinking**, -**sank**, -**sunk**. 1. to enlarge the upper part of (a hole) in timber or metal, so that the head of a bolt or screw can be sunk below the surface. 2. to drive (a screw) or sink (a bolt) into such a hole.

countertenor (,kaʊntə'tɛnə) n. 1. an adult male voice with an alto range. 2. a singer with such a voice.

countess ('kaʊntɪs) n. 1. the wife or widow of a count or earl. 2. a woman of the rank of count or earl.

countless ('kaʊntlɪs) adj. too many to count.

count noun n. a noun that may be preceded by an indefinite article and can be used in the plural, as *telephone* and *thing* but not *airs and graces* or *bravery*.

count on vb. to rely or depend on.

count out vb. 1. *Informal.* to leave out; exclude. 2. (of a boxing referee) to declare (a floored boxer) defeated when he has failed to recover within a count of ten seconds.

countrified or **countryfied** ('kʌntrɪ-,faɪd) adj. rustic in appearance or manner; rural.

country ('kʌntrɪ) n., pl. -**tries**. 1. an area distinguished by its people, culture, language, or government. 2. the territory of a nation or state. 3. the people of a nation or state. 4. the part of the land that is away from cities or industrial areas; rural districts. 5. same as **country and western**. 6. **across country.** not keeping to roads. 7. **go to the country.** *Chiefly Brit.* to dissolve Parliament and hold a general election. 8. one's native land or nation of citizenship. [Medieval Latin *contrāta* (*terra*) (land) lying opposite]

country and western n. popular music in the style of White folk music of the Southern United States.

country club n. a club in the country, which has sporting and social facilities.

country dance n. a type of British folk dance in which couples face one another in a line.

countryman ('kʌntrɪmən) n., pl. -**men**. 1. a person who lives in the country. 2. a person from one's own country. —'**country,woman** fem. n.

countryside ('kʌntrɪ,saɪd) n. land away from the cities; rural areas.

county ('kaʊntɪ) n., pl. -**ties**. 1. an administrative, political, or judicial subdivision in Britain, Ireland, or the U.S.A. ~adj. 2. *Brit. informal.* upper-class; of or like the landed gentry. [Old French *conté* land belonging to a count]

coup (kuː) n. 1. a brilliant and successful stroke or action. 2. a coup d'état. [French]

coup de grâce (,kuː də 'grɑːs) n. a final or decisive stroke. [French]

coup d'état (,kuː deɪ'tɑː) n., pl. **coups d'état** (,kuːz deɪ'tɑː). a sudden violent or illegal overthrow of government. [French]

coupé ('kuːpeɪ) n. a four-seater car with a sloping back and usually two doors. [French *carrosse coupé* cut-off carriage]

couple ('kʌp'l) n. 1. two people who are married or involved in a romantic relationship. 2. two people considered as a pair, as for dancing or games. 3. **a couple of. a.** a combination of two; a pair of: *a couple of men.* **b.** *Informal.* a small number of; a few: *a couple of days.* ~pron. 4. (usually preceded by *a*) **a.** two. **b.** *Informal.* a few: *give him a couple.* ~vb. 5. to connect. 6. to have sexual intercourse. [Latin *cōpula* bond]

couplet ('kʌplɪt) n. two successive lines of verse, usually rhymed and of the same metre.

coupling ('kʌplɪŋ) n. a device for connecting things, such as railway cars or trucks.

coupon ('kuːpɒn) n. 1. a small, often detachable piece of paper entitling the holder to a discount or free gift. 2. a detachable slip that can be used as a commercial order form. 3. *Brit.* a football pools entry form. [Old French *colpon* piece cut off]

courage ('kʌrɪdʒ) n. 1. the ability to face danger, pain, or difficulty without fear. 2. **the courage of one's convictions.** the confidence to act in accordance with one's beliefs. [Latin *cor* heart]

courageous (kə'reɪdʒəs) adj. brave; showing courage. —**cou'rageously** adv.

courgette (kʊə'ʒɛt) n. a small variety of vegetable marrow. [French]

courier ('kʊərɪə) n. 1. a person who makes arrangements for or accompanies a group of travellers or tourists. 2. a messenger who carries urgent or important correspondence. [Latin *currere* to run]

course (kɔːs) n. 1. an onward movement in time or space. 2. a route or direction taken. 3. the path or channel along which a river moves. 4. an area on which a sport is played or a race is held: *a golf course.* 5. a period of time; duration: *in the course of* *the next hour.* **6.** the natural development of a sequence of events: *the illness ran its course.* **7.** a mode of conduct or action: *if you follow that course, you will fail.* **8.** a complete series of lessons or lectures in an educational curriculum. **9.** a sequence of medical treatment prescribed for a specific period of time: *a course of injections.* **10.** any of the successive parts of a meal. **11.** a continuous, usually horizontal layer of building material, such as bricks or tiles, at one level in a building. **12. as a matter of course.** as a natural or normal consequence or event. **13. in the course of.** in the process of. **14. in due course.** at the natural or appropriate time. **15. of course. a.** (*adv.*) as expected; naturally. **b.** (*interj.*) certainly; definitely. ~*vb.* **16.** to run, race, or flow. **17.** to cause (hounds) to hunt by sight rather than scent or (of hounds) to hunt (a quarry) thus. [Latin *cursus* a running]

coursebook ('kɔːs,bʊk) *n.* a book that is used as part of an educational course.

courser[1] ('kɔːsə) *n.* **1.** a person who courses hounds. **2.** a hound trained for coursing.

courser[2] ('kɔːsə) *n. Literary.* a swift horse; steed. [Old French *coursier*]

coursework ('kɔːs,wɜːk) *n.* work done by a student and assessed as part of an educational course.

coursing ('kɔːsɪŋ) *n.* hunting with hounds trained to hunt game by sight.

court (kɔːt) *n.* **1.** *Law.* **a.** a judicial body which hears and makes decisions on legal cases. **b.** the room or building in which such an assembly takes place. **2.** a marked area used for any of various ball games, such as tennis or squash. **3.** an area of ground wholly or partly surrounded by walls or buildings. **4.** a block of flats. **5.** a mansion or country house. **6.** a short street, sometimes closed at one end. **7.** the residence, household, or retinue of a sovereign. **8.** any formal assembly held by a sovereign. **9.** flattering attention (esp. in **pay court to someone**). **10. go to court.** to take legal action. **11. hold court.** to preside over a group of admirers. **12. out of court.** without a trial or legal case. ~*vb.* **13.** to attempt to gain the love of; woo. **14.** to pay attention to (someone) in order to gain favour. **15.** to try to obtain (something): *to court favour.* **16.** to make oneself open or vulnerable to; risk: *court disaster.* [Latin *cohors* cohort]

court card *n.* (in a pack of playing cards) a king, queen, or jack. [earlier *coat-card*, from the decorative coats worn by the figures depicted]

courteous ('kɜːtɪəs) *adj.* polite and considerate in manner. [Middle English *corteis* with courtly manners] —**'courteously** *adv.* —**'courteousness** *n.*

courtesan (,kɔːtɪ'zæn) *n.* (esp. formerly) a prostitute with clients of high rank. [Old French *courtisane*]

courtesy ('kɜːtɪsɪ) *n., pl.* **-sies.** **1.** politeness; good manners. **2.** a courteous act or remark. **3. by courtesy of.** with the consent of.

courthouse ('kɔːt,haʊs) *n.* a public building in which courts of law are held.

courtier ('kɔːtɪə) *n.* an attendant at a royal court.

courtly ('kɔːtlɪ) *adj.* **-lier, -liest. 1.** of or suitable for a royal court. **2.** refined in manner; gracious. —**'courtliness** *n.*

court martial *n., pl.* **court martials** or **courts martial. 1.** the trial of a member of the armed forces charged with breaking military law. ~*vb.* **court-martial, -tialling, -tialled** or *U.S.* **-tialing, -tialed. 2.** to try by court martial.

courtship ('kɔːtʃɪp) *n.* the courting of an intended spouse or mate.

court shoe *n.* a low-cut shoe for women, without laces or straps.

courtyard ('kɔːt,jɑːd) *n.* an open area of ground surrounded by walls or buildings; court.

couscous ('kuːskuːs) *n.* a spicy North African dish, consisting of a steamed semolina served with a meat stew. [Arabic *kouskous*]

cousin ('kʌz'n) *n.* the child of one's aunt or uncle. Also called: **first cousin.** [Latin *consōbrīnus*]

couture (kuː'tʊə) *n.* high-fashion designing and dressmaking. [French: sewing]

couturier (kuː'tʊərɪ,eɪ) *n.* a person who designs, makes, and sells fashion clothes for women. [French]

covalency (kəʊ'veɪlənsɪ) or *U.S.* **covalence** *n.* **1.** the ability to form a bond in which two atoms share a pair of electrons. **2.** the number of covalent bonds which a particular atom can make with others. —**co'valent** *adj.*

cove[1] (kəʊv) *n.* a small bay or inlet. [Old English *cofa*]

cove[2] (kəʊv) *n. Brit. old-fashioned & Austral. slang.* a fellow; chap. [prob. from Romany *kova*]

coven ('kʌv'n) *n.* a meeting of witches. [Latin *convenīre* to come together]

covenant ('kʌvənənt) *n.* **1.** a binding agreement; contract. **2.** *Law.* a formal sealed agreement. **3.** *Bible.* God's promise to the Israelites and their commitment to worship him alone. ~*vb.* **4.** to agree by a legal covenant. [Latin *convenīre* to come together, agree] —**'covenanter** *n.*

Covenanter ('kʌvənəntə, ,kʌvə'næntə) *n. Scot. history.* a person upholding either of two 17th-century covenants to establish and defend Presbyterianism.

Coventry ('kɒvəntrɪ) *n.* **send someone to Coventry.** to punish someone for something he has done by refusing to speak to him. [after *Coventry*, England]

cover ('kʌvə) *vb.* **1.** to place something over so as to protect or conceal. **2.** to put a garment on; clothe. **3.** to extend over or lie thickly on the surface of: *snow covered the fields.* **4.** (sometimes foll. by *up*) to screen or conceal; hide from view. **5.** to protect (an individual or group) by taking up a position from which fire may be returned if those being protected are fired upon. **6.** (foll. by *for*) to deputize for (a person). **7.**

(foll. by *for* or *up for*) to provide an alibi (for). **8.** to travel over. **9.** to keep a gun aimed at. **10.** to include or deal with: *the course covers a variety of topics.* **11.** (of a sum of money) to be enough to pay for (something). **12. a.** to insure against loss or risk. **b.** to provide for (loss or risk) by insurance. **13.** to act as reporter or photographer on (a news event) for a newspaper or magazine: *to cover sports events.* **14.** *Music.* to record a cover version of. **15.** *Sport.* to guard or obstruct (an opponent, team-mate, or area). ~*n.* **16.** anything that covers, protects, or conceals. **17.** a blanket or bedspread. **18.** a pretext, disguise, or false identity: *the thief sold brushes as a cover.* **19.** an envelope or other postal wrapping: *under plain cover.* **20.** an individual table setting, esp. in a restaurant. **21.** a cover version. **22. break cover.** to come out from a shelter or hiding place. **23. take cover.** to make for a place of safety or shelter. **24. under cover.** protected, concealed, or in secret. ~See also **cover-up.** [Latin *cooperīre* to cover completely] —**'covering** *adj., n.*

coverage ('kʌvərɪdʒ) *n. Journalism.* the amount of reporting given to a subject or event.

cover charge *n.* a fixed service charge added to the cost of the food or drink in a nightclub or restaurant.

cover girl *n.* a young woman whose picture appears on the cover of a magazine.

covering letter *n.* an accompanying letter sent as an explanation.

coverlet ('kʌvəlɪt) *n.* same as **bedspread.**

cover note *n. Brit.* a temporary certificate from an insurance company giving proof of a current policy.

covert ('kʌvət) *adj.* **1.** concealed or secret. ~*n.* **2.** a thicket or woodland providing shelter for game. **3.** *Ornithol.* any of the small feathers on the wings and tail of a bird that surround the bases of the larger feathers. [Old French: covered] —**'covertly** *adv.*

cover-up *n.* **1.** concealment or attempted concealment of a mistake or crime. ~*vb.* **cover up. 2.** to cover completely. **3.** to attempt to conceal (a mistake or crime).

cover version *n.* a version by a different artist of a previously recorded musical item.

covet ('kʌvɪt) *vb.* to long to possess (something belonging to another person). [Latin *cupiditās* cupidity]

covetous ('kʌvɪtəs) *adj.* (usually foll. by *of*) jealously longing to possess something. —**'covetously** *adv.* —**'covetousness** *n.*

covey ('kʌvɪ) *n.* **1.** a small flock of grouse or partridge. **2.** a small group of people. [Old French *cover* to sit on, hatch]

cow[1] (kaʊ) *n.* **1.** the mature female of any species of cattle. **2.** the mature female of various other mammals, including the elephant, whale, and seal. **3.** (not in technical use) any domestic species of cattle. **4.** *Informal, offensive.* a disagreeable woman. [Old English *cū*]

cow[2] (kaʊ) *vb.* to frighten or subdue, as with threats. [Old Norse *kūga* to oppress]

coward ('kaʊəd) *n.* a person who is easily frightened and avoids dangerous or difficult situations. [Latin *cauda* tail] —**'cowardly** *adj.*

cowardice ('kaʊədɪs) *n.* lack of courage; cowardly behaviour.

cowbell ('kaʊ,bɛl) *n.* a bell hung around a cow's neck.

cowboy ('kaʊ,bɔɪ) *n.* **1.** (in the U.S. and Canada) a ranch worker who herds and tends cattle, usually on horseback. **2.** a conventional character of Wild West folklore or films. **3.** *Informal.* an irresponsible or unscrupulous worker or businessman. —**'cow,girl** *fem. n.*

cowcatcher ('kaʊ,kætʃə) *n. U.S. & Canad.* a fender on the front of a locomotive to clear the track of animals or other obstructions.

cow cocky *n. Austral. & N.Z.* a one-man dairy farmer.

cower ('kaʊə) *vb.* to crouch or cringe, as in fear. [Middle Low German *kūren*]

cowl (kaʊl) *n.* **1.** a loose hood. **2.** the hooded garment of a monk. **3.** a cover fitted to a chimney to increase ventilation and prevent draughts. ~*vb.* **4.** to cover or provide with a cowl. [Latin *cucullus* hood]

cowlick ('kaʊ,lɪk) *n.* a tuft of hair which stands up over the forehead.

cowling ('kaʊlɪŋ) *n.* a streamlined detachable metal covering around an engine.

co-worker *n.* a fellow worker; associate.

cow parsley *n.* a hedgerow plant with umbrella-shaped clusters of white flowers.

cowpat ('kaʊ,pæt) *n.* a pool of cow dung.

cowpox ('kaʊ,pɒks) *n.* a contagious disease of cows, the virus of which is used to make smallpox vaccine.

cowrie or **cowry** ('kaʊrɪ) *n., pl.* **-ries.** the glossy, brightly marked shell of a marine mollusc, formerly used as money in Africa and S Asia. [Hindi *kaurī*]

cowslip ('kaʊ,slɪp) *n.* a European wild plant with yellow flowers. [Old English *cūslyppe* cow slime, dung]

cox (kɒks) *n.* **1.** a coxswain. ~*vb.* **2.** to act as coxswain of (a boat).

coxcomb ('kɒks,kəʊm) *n.* **1.** same as **cockscomb. 2.** *Obs.* a medieval jester's cap, resembling a cock's comb.

coxswain ('kɒksən, -,sweɪn) *n.* the person who steers a lifeboat or rowing boat. [*cock* a ship's boat + *swain*]

coy (kɔɪ) *adj.* **1.** affectedly shy and modest. **2.** evasive, esp. in an annoying way. [Latin *quiētus* QUIET] —**'coyly** *adv.* —**'coyness** *n.*

coyote (kɔɪ'əʊtɪ) *n., pl.* **-otes** or **-ote.** a small wolf of the deserts and prairies of North America. [Mexican Indian *coyotl*]

coypu ('kɔɪpuː) *n., pl.* **-pus** or **-pu.** an aquatic rodent, originally from South America, which resembles a small beaver and is bred for its fur. [American Indian *kóypu*]

cozen ('kʌz°n) *vb.* to cheat or trick (someone). [orig. a cant term] —**'cozenage** *n.*

Cr 1. Councillor. 2. *Chem.* chromium.

crab (kræb) *n.* 1. a crustacean with a broad flattened shell and five pairs of legs, the first pair modified into pincers. 2. short for **crab louse.** 3. **catch a crab.** *Rowing.* to make a stroke in which the oar misses the water or digs too deeply, causing the rower to fall backwards. [Old English *crabba*]

crab apple *n.* a kind of small sour apple.

crabbed ('kræbɪd) *adj.* 1. irritable; peevish. 2. (of handwriting) cramped and hard to read. [prob. from *crab*, because of its sideways movement + *crab apple*, because of its sourness]

crabby ('kræbɪ) *adj.* **-bier, -biest.** bad-tempered.

crab louse *n.* a parasitic louse that infests the pubic region in humans.

crack (kræk) *vb.* 1. to break or split without complete separation of the parts. 2. to break with a sudden sharp sound; snap. 3. to make or cause to make a sudden sharp sound: *to crack a whip.* 4. (of the voice) to become harsh or change pitch suddenly; break. 5. *Informal.* to fail or break down. 6. to yield or cease to resist: *he cracked under torture.* 7. to hit with a forceful or resounding blow. 8. to break into or force open: *to crack a safe.* 9. to solve or decipher (a code or problem). 10. *Informal.* to tell (a joke). 11. to break (a molecule) into smaller molecules or radicals by heat or catalysis as in the distillation of petroleum. 12. to open (a bottle) for drinking. 13. *Informal.* to achieve (esp. in **crack it**). ~*n.* 14. a sudden sharp noise. 15. a break or fracture without complete separation of the two parts. 16. a narrow opening or fissure. 17. *Informal.* a resounding blow. 18. **crack of dawn** or **day.** daybreak. 19. a broken or cracked tone of voice. 20. (often foll. by *at*) *Informal.* an attempt. 21. *Slang.* a gibe or joke. 22. *Slang.* a highly addictive form of cocaine. 23. **a fair crack of the whip.** *Informal.* a fair chance or opportunity. ~*adj.* 24. *Slang.* first-class; excellent: *a crack shot.* ~See also **crack down, crack up.** [Old English *cracian*]

crackbrained ('kræk,breɪnd) *adj.* idiotic or crazy: *a crackbrained scheme.*

crack down *vb.* (often foll. by *on*) 1. to take severe measures (against); become stricter (with). ~*n.* **crackdown.** 2. severe or repressive measures.

cracked (krækt) *adj.* 1. damaged by cracking. 2. harsh-sounding. 3. *Informal.* crazy.

cracker ('krækə) *n.* 1. a decorated cardboard tube that emits a bang when pulled apart, releasing a toy, a joke, or a paper hat. 2. short for **firecracker.** 3. a thin crisp biscuit, usually unsweetened. 4. *Brit. slang.* an excellent or notable thing or person.

crackers ('krækəz) *adj. Brit. slang.* insane.

cracking ('krækɪŋ) *adj.* 1. **a cracking pace.** *Informal.* a high speed. 2. **get cracking.** *Informal.* to start doing something immediately. ~*adv., adj.* 3. *Brit. infor-*

mal. first-class; excellent. ~*n.* 4. the oil-refining process in which heavy oils are broken down into smaller molecules by heat or catalysis.

crackle ('kræk⁽ə⁾l) *vb.* 1. to make a series of slight sharp popping noises. ~*n.* 2. the act or sound of crackling. —'**crackly** *adj.*

crackling ('kræklɪŋ) *n.* 1. a rapid series of slight, sharp popping noises. 2. the crisp browned skin of roast pork.

crackpot ('kræk,pɒt) *Informal.* ~*n.* 1. an eccentric person; crank. ~*adj.* 2. eccentric; crazy.

crack up *vb.* 1. to break into pieces. 2. *Informal.* to suffer a physical or mental breakdown. 3. **not all it is cracked up to be.** *Informal.* not as good as its favourable reputation would make one believe. ~*n.* **crackup.** 4. *Informal.* a physical or mental breakdown.

-cracy *n. combining form.* indicating a type of government or rule: *plutocracy; mobocracy.* See also **-crat.** [Greek *kratos* power]

cradle ('kreɪd⁽ə⁾l) *n.* 1. a baby's bed on rockers. 2. a place where something originates: *the cradle of civilization.* 3. a supporting framework or structure. 4. a platform or trolley in which workmen or ship suspended on the side of a building or ship. ~*vb.* 5. to rock or place in or as if in a cradle; hold tenderly. [Old English *cradol*]

cradle-snatcher *n.* a person who marries or has a sexual relationship with someone much younger than himself or herself.

craft (krɑːft) *n.* 1. skill or ability. 2. cunning or guile. 3. an occupation requiring skill or manual dexterity. 4. *(pl.* **craft)** a boat, ship, aircraft, or spacecraft. ~*vb.* 5. to make skilfully. [Old English *cræft* skill, strength]

craftsman ('krɑːftsmən) *n., pl.* **-men.** 1. a skilled workman; artisan. 2. a skilled artist. —'**craftsman,ship** *n.*

crafty ('krɑːftɪ) *adj.* **-tier, -tiest.** sly; shrewd; cunning. —'**craftily** *adv.* —'**craftiness** *n.*

crag (kræg) *n.* a steep rugged rock or peak. [Celtic] —'**craggy** *adj.*

crake (kreɪk) *n. Zool.* a bird of the rail family, such as the corncrake. [Old Norse, imit.]

cram (kræm) *vb.* **cramming, crammed.** 1. to force (more people or things) into (a place) than it can hold; stuff. 2. to eat or feed to excess. 3. *Informal.* to study intensively for an examination by hastily learning facts. [Old English *crammian*]

crammer ('kræmə) *n.* a person or school that prepares pupils for an examination.

cramp[1] (kræmp) *n.* 1. a sudden painful involuntary contraction of a muscle. 2. temporary stiffness of a muscle group from overexertion: *writer's cramp.* 3. severe stomach pain. ~*vb.* 4. to affect with a cramp. [Old French *crampe*]

cramp[2] (kræmp) *vb.* 1. to confine or restrict. 2. **cramp someone's style.** *Informal.* to prevent someone from using his abilities or acting freely. [Middle Dutch *crampe* hook]

cramped (kræmpt) *adj.* **1.** closed in; restricted. **2.** (of handwriting) small and irregular.

crampon ('kræmpən) *n.* one of a pair of spiked iron plates strapped to boots for climbing or walking on ice or snow. [French]

cranberry ('krænbəri, -bri) *n., pl.* **-ries.** a sour edible red berry that grows on a trailing shrub. [Low German *kraanbere* crane berry]

crane (kreɪn) *n.* **1.** a large long-necked long-legged wading bird. **2.** a machine for lifting and moving heavy objects, usually by suspending them from a movable projecting arm or beam. ~*vb.* **3.** to stretch out (the neck) in order to see something. [Old English *cran*]

crane fly *n.* a fly having long legs, slender wings, and a narrow body.

cranial ('kreɪnɪəl) *adj.* of or relating to the skull.

craniology (ˌkreɪnɪ'ɒlədʒɪ) *n.* the scientific study of the human skull. [Greek *kranion* skull + -LOGY]

cranium ('kreɪnɪəm) *n., pl.* **-niums** *or* **-nia** (-nɪə). **1.** the skull. **2.** the part of the skull that encloses the brain. [Greek *kranion*]

crank (kræŋk) *n.* **1.** a device for transmitting or converting motion, consisting of an arm projecting at right angles from a shaft. **2.** a handle incorporating a crank, used to start an engine or motor. **3.** *Informal.* **a.** an eccentric or odd person. **b.** *U.S. & Canad.* a bad-tempered person. ~*vb.* **4.** to cause to move by means of a crank. **5.** (sometimes foll. by *up*) to start (an engine or motor) by means of a crank handle. [Old English *cranc*]

crankcase ('kræŋkˌkeɪs) *n.* the metal case that encloses the crankshaft in an internal-combustion engine.

crankpin ('kræŋkˌpɪn) *n.* a short cylindrical pin in a crankshaft, to which the connecting rod is attached.

crankshaft ('kræŋkˌʃɑːft) *n.* a shaft having one or more cranks, to which the connecting rods are attached.

cranky ('kræŋkɪ) *adj.* **crankier, crankiest.** *Informal.* **1.** eccentric. **2.** *U.S., Canad., & Irish.* fussy and bad-tempered. —**'crankiness** *n.*

cranny ('krænɪ) *n., pl.* **-nies.** a narrow opening; crevice. [Old French *cran*]

crap[1] (kræp) *n.* same as **craps.**

crap[2] (kræp) *Slang.* ~*n.* **1.** nonsense. **2.** rubbish; junk. **3.** *Taboo.* faeces. ~*vb.* **crapping, crapped. 4.** *Taboo.* to defecate. [Middle English *crappe* chaff] —**'crappy** *adj.*

crape (kreɪp) *n.* same as **crepe.**

craps (kræps) *n.* (*functioning as sing.*) **1.** a gambling game using two dice. **2. shoot craps.** to play this game. [prob. from *crabs* lowest throw at dice]

crapulent ('kræpjʊlənt) *or* **crapulous** ('kræpjʊləs) *adj.* given to, suffering from, or resulting from intemperance. [Latin *crāpula* drunkenness] —**'crapulence** *n.*

crash (kræʃ) *vb.* **1.** to make or cause to

make a loud smashing noise. **2.** to drop with force and break into pieces with a loud noise. **3.** to break or smash into pieces with a loud noise. **4.** (of a business or stock exchange) to collapse or fail suddenly. **5.** to cause (a vehicle or aircraft) to collide with another vehicle, the ground, or some other object or (of vehicles or aircraft) to be involved in a collision. **6.** to move violently or noisily. **7.** (of a computer system or program) to fail suddenly because of a malfunction. **8.** *Brit. informal.* to gate-crash. ~*n.* **9.** a breaking and falling to pieces. **10.** a sudden loud noise. **11.** a collision involving a vehicle or vehicles. **12.** a sudden descent of an aircraft as a result of which it crashes. **13.** the sudden collapse of a business or stock exchange. **14.** (*modifier*) requiring or using intensive effort and all possible resources in order to accomplish something quickly: *a crash course.* [prob. Middle English *crasen* to smash + *dasshen* to strike]

crash barrier *n.* a barrier erected along the centre of a motorway, around a race-track, or at the side of a dangerous road, for safety purposes.

crash dive *n.* **1.** a sudden steep emergency dive by a submarine. ~*vb.* **crash-dive. 2.** to perform a crash dive.

crash helmet *n.* a helmet worn by motorcyclists to protect the head in case of a crash.

crashing ('kræʃɪŋ) *adj. Informal.* extreme: *a crashing bore.*

crash-land *vb.* to perform an emergency landing of (an aircraft), causing some damage, or (of an aircraft) to land in this way. —**'crash-ˌlanding** *n.*

crass (kræs) *adj.* stupid; gross. [Latin *crassus*] —**'crassly** *adv.* —**'crassness** *n.*

-crat *n. combining form.* indicating a supporter or member of a particular form of government. [Greek *-kratēs*] —**-cratic** *or* **-cratical** *adj. combining form.*

crate (kreɪt) *n.* **1.** a large container made of wooden slats, used for packing, storing, or transporting goods. **2.** *Slang.* an old car or aeroplane. ~*vb.* **3.** to pack or place in a crate. [Latin *crātis* wickerwork] —**'crateful** *n.*

crater ('kreɪtə) *n.* **1.** the bowl-shaped opening in a volcano or a geyser. **2.** a cavity formed by the impact of a meteorite or exploding bomb. **3.** a roughly circular cavity on the surface of the moon and some other planets. ~*vb.* **4.** to make or form craters in (a surface, such as the ground). [Greek *kratēr* mixing bowl]

cravat (krə'væt) *n.* a scarf worn round the neck instead of a tie. [French *cravate*]

crave (kreɪv) *vb.* **1.** (foll. by *for* or *after*) to desire intensely; long for. **2.** to beg or plead for. [Old English *crafian*] —**'craving** *n.*

craven ('kreɪv'n) *adj.* **1.** cowardly. ~*n.* **2.** a coward. [Middle English *cravant*]

craw (krɔː) *n.* **1.** the crop of a bird. **2.** the stomach of an animal. **3. stick in one's**

craw. *Informal.* to be unacceptable. [Middle English]

crawfish (ˈkrɔːˌfɪʃ) *n., pl.* **-fish** *or* **-fishes.** same as **crayfish.**

crawl (krɔːl) *vb.* **1.** to move on one's hands and knees. **2.** to proceed very slowly. **3.** to act in a servile manner; fawn. **4.** to be or feel as if overrun by crawling creatures: *the pile of refuse crawled with insects; his threats made my skin crawl.* **5.** (of insects, worms or snakes) to creep slowly. ~*n.* **6.** a slow creeping pace or motion. **7.** *Swimming.* a stroke in which the feet are kicked like paddles while each arm in turn reaches forward and pulls back through the water. [prob. from Old Norse *krafla*]

crayfish (ˈkreɪˌfɪʃ) *or esp. U.S.* **crawfish** *n., pl.* **-fish** *or* **-fishes.** a freshwater crustacean resembling a small lobster. [Old French *crevice* crab]

crayon (ˈkreɪən, -ɒn) *n.* **1.** a small stick or pencil of coloured wax, clay, or chalk. ~*vb.* **2.** to draw or colour with crayons. [Latin *crēta* chalk]

craze (kreɪz) *n.* **1.** a short-lived fashion or enthusiasm. ~*vb.* **2.** to make mad. **3.** *Ceramics, metallurgy.* to develop or cause to develop fine cracks. [prob. from Old Norse] —**crazed** *adj.*

crazy (ˈkreɪzɪ) *adj.* **-zier, -ziest.** **1.** *Informal.* insane. **2.** fantastic; ridiculous. **3.** (foll. by *about* or *over*) *Informal.* extremely fond of. —**ˈcraziness** *n.*

crazy paving *n. Brit.* a form of paving on a path, made of irregular slabs of stone.

creak (kriːk) *vb.* **1.** to make or move with a harsh squeaking sound. ~*n.* **2.** a harsh squeaking sound. [imit.] —**ˈcreaky** *adj.* —**ˈcreakiness** *n.*

cream (kriːm) *n.* **1.** the fatty part of milk, which rises to the top. **2.** anything, such as a cosmetic, resembling cream in consistency. **3.** the best part of something; pick. **4.** any of various foods resembling or containing cream. ~*adj.* **5.** yellowish-white. ~*vb.* **6.** to remove the cream from (milk). **7.** to beat (foodstuffs) to a light creamy consistency. **8.** (sometimes foll. by *off*) to take away the best part of. **9.** to prepare or cook (foodstuffs) with cream or milk. [Late Latin *crāmum*] —**ˈcreamy** *adj.*

cream cheese *n.* a rich soft white cheese made from soured cream and skimmed milk.

creamer (ˈkriːmə) *n.* a powdered substitute for cream, used in coffee.

creamery (ˈkriːmərɪ) *n., pl.* **-eries.** a place where dairy products are made or sold.

cream of tartar *n.* purified tartar, the main ingredient in baking powder.

crease (kriːs) *n.* **1.** a line or mark produced by folding, pressing, or wrinkling. **2.** a wrinkle or furrow, esp. on the face. **3.** *Cricket.* any of three lines near each wicket marking positions for the bowler or batsman. ~*vb.* **4.** to make or become wrinkled or furrowed. [Middle English *crēst*] —**ˈcreasy** *adj.*

create (kriːˈeɪt) *vb.* **1.** to cause to come into existence. **2.** to appoint to a new rank or position. **3.** to be the cause of. **4.** *Brit. slang.* to make a fuss or uproar. [Latin *creāre*]

creation (kriːˈeɪʃən) *n.* **1.** a creating or being created. **2.** something brought into existence or created.

Creation (kriːˈeɪʃən) *n. Christianity.* **the.** **1.** God's act of bringing the universe into being. **2.** the universe as thus brought into being by God.

creative (kriːˈeɪtɪv) *adj.* **1.** having the ability to create. **2.** imaginative or inventive. —**ˌcreaˈtivity** *n.*

creator (kriːˈeɪtə) *n.* a person who creates; originator.

Creator (kriːˈeɪtə) *n.* **the.** God.

creature (ˈkriːtʃə) *n.* **1.** an animal, bird, or fish. **2.** a person: usually used as a term of contempt or pity. **3.** a person or thing controlled by another.

crèche (kreʃ, kreɪʃ) *n. Chiefly Brit.* a day nursery for very young children. [French]

credence (ˈkriːdəns) *n.* belief in the accuracy or trustworthiness of a statement: *I don't give much credence to that theory.* [Latin *crēdere* to believe]

credential (krɪˈdɛnʃəl) *n.* **1.** something that entitles a person to credit or confidence. **2.** (*pl.*) a letter or certificate giving evidence of the bearer's identity or qualifications.

credibility gap *n.* the difference between claims or statements made and the true facts.

credible (ˈkrɛdɪbˀl) *adj.* **1.** capable of being believed. **2.** trustworthy. [Latin *crēdere* to believe] —**ˌcrediˈbility** *n.*

credit (ˈkrɛdɪt) *n.* **1.** praise or approval, as for an achievement or quality. **2.** a person or thing who is a source of praise or approval. **3.** influence or reputation coming from the good opinion of others. **4.** belief or confidence in someone or something. **5.** a sum of money or equivalent purchasing power, available for a person's use. **6. a.** the positive balance in a person's bank account. **b.** the sum of money that a bank makes available to a client in excess of any deposit. **7. a.** the practice of allowing a buyer to receive goods or services before payment. **b.** the time allowed for paying for such goods or services. **8.** reputation for trustworthiness in paying debts, inducing confidence among creditors. **9.** *Accounting.* **a.** acknowledgment of a sum of money by entry on the right-hand side of an account. **b.** an entry or total of entries on this side. **10.** *Education.* **a.** distinction awarded to an examination candidate obtaining good marks. **b.** certification that a section of an examination syllabus has been satisfactorily completed. **11. on credit.** with payment to be made at a future date. ~*vb.* **12.** (foll. by *with*) to attribute to; give credit for. **13.** to believe. **14.** *Accounting.* **a.** to enter (an item) as a credit in an account. **b.** to acknowledge (a payer) by making such an entry. ~See also **credits.** [Latin *crēdere* to believe]

creditable (ˈkrɛdɪtəbˀl) *adj.* deserving

credit or honour; praiseworthy. —**'creditably** adv.

credit card n. a card issued by banks or shops, allowing the holder to obtain goods and services on credit.

creditor ('kredɪtə) n. a person or company to whom money is owed.

credit rating n. an evaluation of the creditworthiness of a person or a business.

credits ('kredɪts) pl. n. a list of those responsible for the production of a record, film, or television programme.

creditworthy ('kredɪt,wɜːðɪ) adj. (of a person or a business) regarded as meriting credit on the basis of earning power and previous record of debt repayment. —**'credit,worthiness** n.

credo ('kriːdəʊ, 'kreɪ-) n., pl. **-dos**. a creed.

credulity (krɪ'djuːlɪtɪ) n. tendency to believe something on little evidence; gullibility.

credulous ('kredjʊləs) adj. 1. tending to believe something on little evidence. 2. arising from or showing credulity: credulous beliefs. [Latin crēdere to believe]

creed (kriːd) n. 1. a concise formal statement of the essential articles of Christian belief. 2. any statement or system of beliefs or principles. [Latin crēdō I believe]

creek (kriːk) n. 1. Chiefly Brit. a narrow inlet or bay. 2. U.S., Canad., Austral., & N.Z. a small stream or tributary. 3. **up the creek**. Slang. in trouble; in a difficult position. [Old Norse kriki nook]

creel (kriːl) n. a wickerwork basket used by fishermen. [Scot.]

creep (kriːp) vb. **creeping, crept.** 1. to crawl with the body near to or touching the ground. 2. to move slowly, quietly, or cautiously. 3. (of plants) to grow along the ground or over rocks. 4. to have the sensation of something crawling over the skin, as from fear or disgust: he makes my flesh creep. ~n. 5. the act of creeping or a creeping movement. 6. Slang. an obnoxious or servile person. [Old English crēopan]

creeper ('kriːpə) n. 1. a plant, such as ivy, that grows by creeping. 2. U.S. & Canad. same as **tree creeper**. 3. Informal. a shoe with a soft sole.

creeps (kriːps) pl. n. **the creeps.** Informal. a feeling of fear, repulsion, or disgust.

creepy ('kriːpɪ) adj. **creepier, creepiest.** Informal. having or causing a sensation of repulsion or fear. —**'creepiness** n.

creepy-crawly n., pl. **-crawlies**. Brit. informal. a small crawling creature.

cremate (krɪ'meɪt) vb. to burn (a corpse) to ash. [Latin cremāre] —**cre'mation** n.

crematorium (,kremə'tɔːrɪəm) n., pl. **-riums** or **-ria** (-rɪə). Brit. a building in which corpses are cremated.

crème (krɛm) n. 1. cream. 2. a thick sweet liqueur: crème de moka.

crème de menthe ('krɛm də 'mɛnθ) n. a liqueur flavoured with peppermint. [French]

crenellate or U.S. **crenelate** ('krenɪ,leɪt) vb. to supply with battlements. [Late Latin crēna a notch] —**'crenel,lated** or U.S. **'crene,lated** adj. —,**crenel'lation** or U.S. ,**crene'lation** n.

creole ('kriːəʊl) n. 1. a language that has developed from a mixture of different languages and has become the main language in a particular place. ~adj. 2. of or relating to a creole. [Spanish]

Creole ('kriːəʊl) n. 1. (in the West Indies and Latin America) a native-born person of mixed European and Negro ancestry who speaks a creole. 2. (in the Gulf States of the U.S.) a native-born person of French ancestry. 3. the French creole spoken in the Gulf States.

creosote ('krɪə,səʊt) n. 1. a thick dark liquid mixture prepared from coal tar and used as a preservative for wood. 2. a colourless liquid distilled from wood tar and used as an antiseptic. ~vb. 3. to treat (wood) with creosote. [Greek kreas flesh + sōtēr preserver]

crepe (kreɪp) n. 1. a thin light fabric with a fine ridged or crinkled surface. 2. a black mourning armband originally made of this. 3. a very thin pancake, often folded around a filling. 4. a type of sheet rubber with a wrinkled surface, used for the soles of shoes. [French]

crepe paper n. thin crinkled paper, resembling crepe and used for decorations.

crept (krept) vb. past of **creep.**

crepuscular (krɪ'pʌskjʊlə) adj. 1. of or like twilight; dim. 2. (of certain creatures) active at twilight. [Latin crepusculum dusk]

Cres. Crescent.

crescendo (krɪ'ʃendəʊ) n., pl. **-dos** or **-di** (-dɪ). 1. a gradual increase in loudness. 2. a musical passage that gradually gets louder. ~adv. 3. gradually getting louder. [Italian]

crescent ('kres³nt) n. 1. the curved shape of the moon when in its first or last quarter. 2. Chiefly Brit. a crescent-shaped street. ~adj. 3. crescent-shaped. [Latin crescere to grow]

cress (kres) n. a plant with pungent-tasting leaves, often used in salads and as a garnish. [Old English cressa]

crest (krest) n. 1. a tuft or growth of feathers, fur, or skin along the top of a bird's or animal's head. 2. the top or highest point of something. 3. an ornamental plume or emblem on top of a helmet. 4. a heraldic device used on a coat of arms, notepaper, or elsewhere. ~vb. 5. to come or rise to a high point. 6. to lie at the top of; cap. 7. to reach the top of (a hill or wave). [Latin crista] —**'crested** adj.

crestfallen ('krest,fɔːlən) adj. dejected or disheartened.

Cretaceous (krɪ'teɪʃəs) adj. Geol. of a period of geological time about 135 million years ago, at the end of which the dinosaurs died out. [Latin crēta chalk]

cretin ('kretɪn) n. 1. a person afflicted with cretinism. 2. a very stupid person.

[French, from Latin *Chrīstiānus* Christian, alluding to the humanity of such people, despite their handicaps] —'**cretinous** *adj.*

cretinism ('krɛtɪˌnɪzəm) *n.* dwarfism and mental retardation caused by a thyroid deficiency.

cretonne (krɛ'tɒn, 'krɛtɒn) *n.* a heavy printed cotton or linen fabric, used for furnishing. [French]

crevasse (krɪ'væs) *n.* a deep open crack, as in the ice of a glacier. [French]

crevice ('krɛvɪs) *n.* a narrow fissure or crack; cleft. [Latin *crepāre* to crack]

crew[1] (kruː) *n.* 1. the people who man a ship or aircraft. 2. a group of people working together: *a film crew.* 3. *Informal.* any group of people. ~*vb.* 4. to serve on (a ship) as a crew member. [Middle English *crue* reinforcement, from Latin *crescere* to increase]

crew[2] (kruː) *vb. Archaic.* a past tense of **crow**[2].

crew cut *n.* a closely cropped haircut for men.

crewel ('kruːɪl) *n.* a loosely twisted worsted yarn, used in fancy work and embroidery. [origin unknown] —'**crewelˌwork** *n.*

crew neck *n.* a plain round neckline. —'**crew-ˌneck** *or* '**crew-ˌnecked** *adj.*

crib (krɪb) *n.* 1. a baby's cradle; cot. 2. a fodder rack or manger. 3. a model of the manger scene at Bethlehem. 4. *Informal, chiefly Brit.* a translation of a foreign text or a list of answers used by students, often illicitly, as an aid in lessons or examinations. 5. short for **cribbage**. ~*vb.* **cribbing, cribbed.** 6. to confine in a small space. 7. *Informal.* to plagiarize (another's writings or thoughts). 8. *Informal.* to copy either from a crib or from someone else during a lesson or examination. [Old English *cribb*]

cribbage ('krɪbɪdʒ) *n.* a card game for two to four, in which players try to win a set number of points before their opponents. [origin unknown]

crick (krɪk) *Informal.* ~*n.* 1. a painful muscle spasm or cramp, esp. in the neck or back. ~*vb.* 2. to cause a crick in. [origin unknown]

cricket[1] ('krɪkɪt) *n.* a jumping insect like a grasshopper, which produces a chirping sound by rubbing together its forewings. [Old French *criquer* to creak, imit.]

cricket[2] ('krɪkɪt) *n.* 1. a game played by two teams of eleven players using a ball, bats, and wickets. 2. **not cricket.** *Informal.* not fair play. [Old French *criquet* wicket] —'**cricketer** *n.*

crier ('kraɪə) *n.* formerly, an official who made public announcements in a town or court.

crime (kraɪm) *n.* 1. an act prohibited and punished by law. 2. unlawful acts collectively. 3. *Informal.* a senseless or deplorable act: *destroying the rainforests is a crime against nature.* [Latin *crīmen*]

criminal ('krɪmɪnˀl) *n.* 1. a person guilty of a crime or crimes. ~*adj.* 2. of or relating to crime or its punishment.

3. *Informal.* senseless or deplorable. —**criminality** (ˌkrɪmɪ'nælɪt) *n.*

criminology (ˌkrɪmɪ'nɒlədʒɪ) *n.* the scientific study of crime. [Latin *crīmen* crime + -LOGY] —ˌcrimi'**nologist** *n.*

crimp (krɪmp) *vb.* 1. to fold or press into ridges. 2. to fold and pinch together (something, such as two pieces of metal). 3. to curl or wave (the hair) tightly with curling tongs. ~*n.* 4. the act or result of crimping. [Old English *crympan*]

Crimplene ('krɪmpliːn) *n. Trademark.* a crease-resistant synthetic fabric.

crimson ('krɪmzən) *adj.* deep vivid red. [Arabic *qirmizi* kermes (dried bodies of insects used to make a red dye)]

cringe (krɪndʒ) *vb.* 1. to shrink or flinch in fear or servility. 2. to behave in a servile or timid way. 3. *Informal.* to have a sudden feeling of embarrassment or distaste. ~*n.* 4. the act of cringing. [Old English *cringan* to yield in battle]

crinkle ('krɪŋkˀl) *vb.* 1. to wrinkle, twist, or fold. ~*n.* 2. a wrinkle, twist, or fold. [Old English *crincan* to bend] —'**crinkly** *adj.*

crinoline ('krɪn°lɪn) *n.* a petticoat stiffened with a framework of steel hoops, worn to make skirts stand out. [Latin *crīnis* hair + *lino* flax]

cripple ('krɪpˀl) *n.* 1. a person who is lame. 2. a person who is disabled or deficient in some way: *a mental cripple.* ~*vb.* 3. to make a cripple of; disable. [Old English *crypel*]

crisis ('kraɪsɪs) *n., pl.* **-ses** (-siːz). 1. a crucial stage or turning point in the course of anything. 2. a time of extreme trouble or danger. [Greek *krisis* decision]

crisp (krɪsp) *adj.* 1. dry and brittle: *crisp bacon.* 2. fresh and firm: *crisp lettuce.* 3. invigorating or bracing: *a crisp breeze.* 4. clear; sharp: *crisp reasoning.* 5. lively or brisk. 6. clean and neat. ~*vb.* 7. to make or become crisp. ~*n.* 8. *Brit.* a very thin slice of potato fried till crunchy, eaten cold as a snack. [Latin *crispus* curled] —'**crisply** *adv.* —'**crispness** *n.*

crispbread ('krɪspˌbrɛd) *n.* a thin dry biscuit made of wheat or rye.

crispy ('krɪspɪ) *adj.* **crispier, crispiest.** crisp. —'**crispiness** *n.*

crisscross ('krɪsˌkrɒs) *vb.* 1. to move in, mark with, or consist of a crosswise pattern. ~*adj.* 2. (of lines) crossing one another in different directions.

criterion (kraɪ'tɪərɪən) *n., pl.* **-ria** (-rɪə) *or* **-rions.** a standard by which something can be judged or decided. [Greek *kritērion*]

critic ('krɪtɪk) *n.* 1. a professional judge of art, music, or literature. 2. a person who finds fault and criticizes. [Greek *kritēs* judge]

critical ('krɪtɪkˀl) *adj.* 1. fault-finding or disparaging. 2. containing analytical evaluations. 3. of a critic or criticism. 4. of or forming a crisis; crucial. 5. *Physics.* denoting a constant value at which the properties of a system undergo an abrupt change: *the critical temperature at which water turns to ice.* 6. (of a nuclear power station or reactor) having reached a state in which a nuclear chain reaction becomes self-sustaining. —**critically** adv.

criticism ('krɪtɪˌsɪzəm) n. **1.** fault-finding or censure. **2.** an analysis or evaluation of a work of art or literature. **3.** the occupation of a critic. **4.** a work that sets out to evaluate or analyse.

criticize or **-ise** ('krɪtɪˌsaɪz) vb. **1.** to find fault with; censure. **2.** to evaluate or analyse (something).

critique (krɪ'tiːk) n. **1.** a critical essay or commentary. **2.** the act or art of criticizing. [French]

croak ('krəʊk) vb. **1.** (of frogs or crows) to make a low hoarse cry. **2.** to utter (something) in this manner. **3.** Slang. to die. ~n. **4.** a low hoarse utterance or sound. [Old English crǣcettan] —**croaky** adj.

Croatian (krəʊ'eɪʃən) adj. **1.** of Croatia in Yugoslavia, its people, or their dialect of Serbo-Croatian. ~n. **2.** the dialect of Croatia. **3.** a person from Croatia.

crochet ('krəʊʃeɪ, -ʃɪ) vb. **-cheting** (-ʃeɪŋ, -ʃɪŋ), **-cheted** (-ʃeɪd, -ʃɪd). **1.** to make (a piece of needlework) by looping and intertwining thread with a hooked needle. ~n. **2.** work made by crocheting. [French crochet small hook]

crock[1] (krɒk) n. an earthenware pot or jar. [Old English crocc pot]

crock[2] (krɒk) n. **old crock.** Slang, chiefly Brit. a person or thing that is old or broken-down. [Scot.]

crockery ('krɒkərɪ) n. china dishes or earthenware vessels collectively.

crocodile ('krɒkəˌdaɪl) n. **1.** a large tropical reptile with a broad head, tapering snout, huge jaws, and thick scales. **2.** Brit. informal. a line of schoolchildren walking two by two. [Greek krokodeilos lizard]

crocodile tears pl. n. an insincere show of grief; false tears. [from the belief that crocodiles wept over their prey to allure further victims]

crocus ('krəʊkəs) n., pl. **-cuses.** a plant with white, yellow, or purple flowers. [Greek krokos saffron]

croft (krɒft) n. Brit. a small enclosed plot of land, adjoining a house, worked by the tenant and his family, as in N Scotland. [Old English] —**crofter** n. —**crofting** adj., n.

croissant ('krwɑːsɒn) n. a flaky crescent-shaped bread roll. [French]

cromlech ('krɒmlɛk) n. **1.** a circle of prehistoric standing stones. **2.** (no longer in technical usage) same as **dolmen.** [Welsh]

crone (krəʊn) n. a witchlike old woman. [Old French carogne carrion]

crony ('krəʊnɪ) n., pl. **-nies.** a friend or companion. [Greek khronios long-lasting]

crook (krʊk) n. **1.** a curved or hooked thing or place: she held the puppy in the crook of her arm. **2.** a bishop's or shepherd's staff with a hooked end. **3.** Informal. a dishonest person such as a swindler or thief. ~vb. **4.** to bend or curve. [Old Norse krokr hook]

crooked ('krʊkɪd) adj. **1.** bent, winding, or twisted. **2.** set at an angle; not straight or level. **3.** Informal. dishonest or illegal. —**crookedly** adv. —**crookedness** n.

croon (kruːn) vb. **1.** to sing, hum, or speak in a soft low tone. ~n. **2.** a soft low singing or humming. [Middle Dutch crōnen to groan] —**crooner** n.

crop (krɒp) n. **1.** a cultivated plant, such as a cereal, vegetable, or fruit plant. **2.** the season's total yield of farm produce. **3.** any group of things appearing at one time: the current crop of school leavers. **4.** the handle of a thonged whip. **5.** short for **riding crop. 6.** a pouchlike part of the gullet of a bird, in which food is stored or prepared for digestion. **7.** a short cropped hairstyle. ~vb. **cropping, cropped. 8.** to cut (something) very short. **9.** to grow, bear or harvest (produce) as a crop. **10.** to clip part of (the ear or ears) of (an animal), esp. for identification. **11.** (of herbivorous animals) to feed by grazing. ~See also **crop up.** [Old English cropp]

cropper ('krɒpə) n. **come a cropper.** Informal. **a.** to fall heavily. **b.** to fail completely.

crop up vb. Informal. to occur or appear unexpectedly.

croquet ('krəʊkeɪ, -kɪ) n. a game played on a lawn in which the players hit a wooden ball through iron hoops with mallets in order to hit a peg. [French]

croquette (krəʊ'kɛt, krɒ-) n. a savoury cake of mashed potato, meat, or fish, fried in breadcrumbs. [French]

crosier or **crozier** ('krəʊʒə) n. a hooked staff carried by bishops as a symbol of office. [Old French crossier staff-bearer]

cross (krɒs) n. **1.** any structure, symbol, or mark consisting of two intersecting lines. **2.** an upright post with a bar across it, used in ancient times as a means of execution. **3.** a representation of the Cross on which Jesus Christ was executed as an emblem of Christianity. **4.** a symbol (×) used as a signature or error mark. **5. the sign of the cross.** a sign made with the hand by some Christians to represent the Cross. **6.** a medal in the shape of a cross. **7.** a monument in the shape of a cross. **8.** the place in a town or village where a cross has been set up. **9.** Biol. **a.** the process of crossing; hybridization. **b.** a hybrid. **10.** a mixture of two things. **11.** a hindrance or misfortune; affliction. **12.** Football. a pass of the ball from a wing to the middle of the field. ~vb. **13.** (sometimes foll. by over) to move or go across (something): she crossed the street to avoid him; this street crosses the main road a little further on. **14. a.** to meet and pass. **b.** (of each of two letters in the post) to be dispatched before receipt of the other. **15.** (usually foll. by out, off, or through) to cancel with a cross or with lines; delete. **16.** to place across or crosswise: to cross one's legs. **17.** to mark with a cross or crosses. **18.** Brit. to draw two parallel lines across (a cheque) and so make it payable only into a bank account. **19.** to make the sign of the cross upon (someone or something) as a blessing. **20.**

(of telephone lines) to interfere with each other so that several callers are connected together at one time. **21.** to interbreed or cross-fertilize. **22.** to thwart or oppose. **23.** *Football.* to pass (the ball) from a wing to the middle of the field. **24. cross one's fingers.** to fold one finger across another in the hope of bringing good luck. **25. cross one's heart.** to promise, esp. by making the sign of a cross over one's heart. **26. cross one's mind.** to occur to one briefly or suddenly. ~*adj.* **27.** angry; in a bad mood. **28.** lying or placed across; transverse: *a cross timber.* [Latin *crux*] —'**crossly** *adv.* —'**crossness** *n.*

Cross (krɒs) *n.* **the. 1.** the cross on which Jesus Christ was crucified. **2.** Christianity.

cross- *combining form.* **1.** indicating action from one individual or group to another: *cross-cultural; cross-refer.* **2.** indicating movement or position across something: *crosscurrent; crosstalk.* **3.** indicating a crosslike figure or intersection: *crossbones.*

crossbar ('krɒsˌbɑː) *n.* **1.** a horizontal beam across a pair of goal posts. **2.** the horizontal bar on a man's bicycle.

cross-bench *n. (usually pl.) Brit.* a seat in Parliament occupied by members belonging to neither the government nor the opposition. —'**cross-ˌbencher** *n.*

crossbill ('krɒsˌbɪl) *n.* a finch that has a bill with crossed tips.

crossbow ('krɒsˌbəʊ) *n.* a weapon consisting of a bow fixed across a wooden stock, which releases an arrow when the trigger is pulled.

crossbreed ('krɒsˌbriːd) *vb.* **-breeding, -bred. 1.** to produce (a hybrid animal or plant) by crossing two different species. ~*n.* **2.** a hybrid animal or plant.

crosscheck (ˌkrɒs'tʃɛk) *vb.* **1.** to check the accuracy of (something) by using a different method of verification from the one originally used. ~*n.* **2.** a crosschecking.

cross-country *adj., adv.* **1.** by way of open country or fields, as opposed to roads. ~*n.* **2.** a long race held over open ground.

crosscut ('krɒsˌkʌt) *adj.* **1.** cut across. ~*n.* **2.** a transverse cut or course. ~*vb.* **-cutting, -cut. 3.** to cut across.

cross-examine *vb.* **1.** *Law.* to question (a witness for the opposing side), in order to check or discredit his testimony. **2.** to question closely or relentlessly. —'**cross-exˌami'nation** *n.* —ˌ**cross-ex'aminer** *n.*

cross-eyed *adj.* having one or both eyes turning inwards towards the nose.

cross-fertilize *vb.* to fertilize (an animal or plant) by fusion of male and female reproductive cells from different individuals of the same species. —'**cross-ˌfertili'zation** *n.*

crossfire ('krɒsˌfaɪə) *n.* **1.** *Mil.* converging fire from one or more positions. **2.** a lively exchange of ideas or opinions.

crosshatch ('krɒsˌhætʃ) *vb. Drawing.* to shade with two or more sets of parallel lines that cross one another.

crossing ('krɒsɪŋ) *n.* **1.** the place where one thing crosses another. **2.** a place where a street, railway, or river may be crossed. **3.** a journey across the sea.

cross-legged ('krɒsˈlɛgɪd, -ˈlɛgd) *adj.* sitting with one leg crossed over the other.

crosspatch ('krɒsˌpætʃ) *n. Informal.* a bad-tempered person. [*cross* + obs. *patch* fool]

cross-ply *adj.* (of a motor tyre) having the fabric cords in the outer casing running diagonally to stiffen the sidewalls.

cross-purpose *n.* **at cross-purposes.** disagreeing due to a misunderstanding about the subject of the discussion.

cross-question *vb.* to cross-examine.

cross-refer *vb.* **-referring, -referred.** to refer from one part of something esp. a book, to another.

cross-reference *n.* **1.** a reference within a text to another part of the text. ~*vb.* **2.** to cross-refer.

crossroad ('krɒsˌrəʊd) *n. U.S. & Canad.* **1.** a road that crosses another road. **2.** a road that connects one main road to another.

crossroads ('krɒsˌrəʊdz) *n.* (functioning as *sing.*) **1.** the point at which roads cross one another. **2. at the crossroads.** at the point at which an important choice has to be made.

cross section *n.* **1.** *Maths.* a surface formed by cutting across a solid, usually at right angles to its longest axis. **2.** a random sample regarded as representative. —ˌ**cross-'sectional** *adj.*

cross-stitch *n.* an embroidery stitch made from two crossing stitches.

crosstalk ('krɒsˌtɔːk) *n.* **1.** unwanted signals transferred between communication channels. **2.** *Brit.* rapid or witty talk.

crosswise ('krɒsˌwaɪz) or **crossways** ('krɒsˌweɪz) *adj., adv.* **1.** across; transversely. **2.** in the shape of a cross.

crossword puzzle or **crossword** ('krɒsˌwɜːd) *n.* a puzzle in which vertically and horizontally crossing words suggested by numbered clues are written into a grid of squares.

crotch (krɒtʃ) *n.* **1. a.** the forked part of the human body between the legs. **b.** the corresponding part of a pair of trousers or pants. **2.** any forked part formed by the joining of two things. [prob. var. of *crutch*] —**crotched** *adj.*

crotchet ('krɒtʃɪt) *n. Music.* a note having the time value of a quarter of a semibreve. [Old French *crochet* little hook]

crotchety ('krɒtʃɪtɪ) *adj. Informal.* irritable; contrary.

crouch (krautʃ) *vb.* **1.** to bend low with the limbs pulled up close together. ~*n.* **2.** the act of crouching. [Old French *crochir* to become bent like a hook]

croup[1] (kruːp) *n.* inflammation of the breathing passage, usually in children, causing a hoarse cough and laboured breathing. [Middle English *croup* to cry hoarsely, prob. imit.]

croup² (kruːp) n. the hindquarters, of a horse. [Old French *croupe*]

croupier ('kruːpiə) n. a person in charge of a gaming table, who collects bets and pays out winnings. [French]

crouton ('kruːton) n. a small piece of fried or toasted bread, served in soup. [French]

crow¹ (krəʊ) n. 1. a large bird such as the raven, rook, or jackdaw, which has glossy black plumage, and a harsh call. 2. **as the crow flies.** in a straight line. [Old English *crāwa*]

crow² (krəʊ) vb. 1. (past tense **crowed** or **crew**) to utter a shrill squawking sound, as a cock. 2. (often foll. by *over*) to boast one's superiority. 3. (esp. of babies) to utter cries of pleasure. ~n. 4. a crowing sound. [Old English *crāwan*]

crowbar ('krəʊˌbɑː) n. a heavy iron lever with one end forged into a wedge shape.

crowd (kraʊd) n. 1. a large number of things or people gathered together. 2. a particular group of people, esp. considered as a set: *the crowd from the office.* 3. (preceded by *the*) the common people; the masses. ~vb. 4. to gather together in large numbers; throng. 5. to press together into a confined space. 6. to fill to excess; fill by pushing into. 7. *Informal.* to make (someone) uncomfortable by coming too close. [Old English *crūdan*] —'**crowded** adj.

crown (kraʊn) n. 1. a monarch's ornamental headdress, usually made of gold and jewels. 2. an award or honour given for merit or victory, such as a wreath for the head. 3. (formerly) a British coin worth 25 pence. 4. the highest or central point of anything arched or curved: *crown of a road.* 5. the outstanding quality or achievement: *the crown of his career.* 6. a. the enamel-covered part of a tooth projecting beyond the gum. b. a substitute crown, usually of gold or porcelain, fitted over a decayed or broken tooth. ~vb. 7. to put a crown on the head of (someone), to give them royal authority. 8. to place something on or over the top of. 9. to reward. 10. to form the summit or topmost part of. 11. to cap or put the finishing touch to (a series of events): *to crown it all, it rained too.* 12. Draughts. to promote (a draught) to a king by placing another draught on top of it. 13. to attach a crown to (a tooth). 14. *Slang.* to hit over the head. [Greek *korōnē*]

Crown (kraʊn) n. **the.** the power or institution of the monarchy.

crown colony n. a British colony whose administration is controlled by the Crown.

crown court n. *English law.* a court of criminal jurisdiction holding sessions in towns throughout England and Wales.

Crown Derby n. a type of fine porcelain made at Derby.

crown jewels pl. n. the jewellery used by a sovereign on ceremonial occasions.

crown prince n. the male heir to a sovereign throne. —**crown princess** n.

crow's feet n. wrinkles at the outer corners of the eye.

crow's nest n. a lookout platform fixed at the top of a ship's mast.

crozier ('krəʊʒə) n. same as **crosier.**

crucial ('kruːʃəl) adj. 1. of exceptional importance; critical. 2. *Slang.* very good. [Latin *crux* cross] —'**crucially** adv.

crucible ('kruːsɪbˀl) n. a pot in which metals or other substances are melted or heated to very high temperatures. [Medieval Latin *crūcibulum* night lamp]

crucifix ('kruːsɪfɪks) n. a model cross with a figure of Christ upon it. [Church Latin *crucifixus* the crucified Christ]

crucifixion (ˌkruːsɪ'fɪkʃən) n. a method of execution by fastening to a cross, normally by the hands and feet.

Crucifixion (ˌkruːsɪ'fɪkʃən) n. 1. **the.** the crucifying of Christ. 2. a representation of this.

cruciform ('kruːsɪˌfɔːm) adj. shaped like a cross.

crucify ('kruːsɪˌfaɪ) vb. **-fying, -fied.** 1. to put to death by crucifixion. 2. *Slang.* to defeat or ridicule totally. 3. to persecute or torment. [Latin *crux* cross + *fīgere* to fasten]

crud (krʌd) n. *Slang.* a sticky or encrusted substance or residue. [earlier form of *curd*] —'**cruddy** adj.

crude (kruːd) adj. 1. tasteless or vulgar. 2. in a natural or unrefined state. 3. lacking polish or skill. 4. stark; blunt. ~n. 5. short for **crude oil.** [Latin *crūdus* bloody, raw] —'**crudely** adv. —'**crudity** or '**crudeness** n.

crude oil n. unrefined petroleum.

cruel ('kruːəl) adj. 1. deliberately causing pain without pity. 2. causing pain or suffering. [Latin *crūdēlis*] —'**cruelly** adv. —'**cruelty** n.

cruet ('kruːɪt) n. 1. a small container for holding pepper, salt, vinegar, or oil at table. 2. a set of such containers on a stand. [Old French *crue* flask]

cruise (kruːz) vb. 1. to sail about from place to place for pleasure. 2. (of a vehicle, aircraft, or vessel) to travel at a moderate and efficient speed. ~n. 3. a cruising voyage. [Dutch *kruisen* to cross]

cruise missile n. a low-flying subsonic missile that is guided throughout its flight.

cruiser ('kruːzə) n. 1. a large, fast warship armed with medium-calibre weapons. 2. Also called: **cabin cruiser.** a motorboat with a cabin.

cruiserweight ('kruːzəˌweɪt) n. *Boxing.* same as **light heavyweight.**

crumb (krʌm) n. 1. a small fragment of bread, cake, or other dry foods. 2. a small bit or scrap: *a crumb of comfort.* [Old English *cruma*]

crumble ('krʌmbˀl) vb. 1. to break into crumbs or fragments. 2. to fall apart or decay. ~n. 3. *Brit.* a baked pudding consisting of a crumbly topping over stewed fruit: *apple crumble.* —'**crumbly** adj. —'**crumbliness** n.

crumby ('krʌmɪ) adj. **crumbier, crumbiest.** 1. full of crumbs. 2. same as **crummy.**

crummy ('krʌmɪ) *adj.* **-mier, -miest.** *Slang.*
1. of very bad quality; worthless. **2.** unwell or out of sorts: *I feel crummy.* [var.
spelling of *crumby*]

crumpet ('krʌmpɪt) *n. Chiefly Brit.* **1.** a
light soft yeast cake, eaten toasted and
buttered. **2.** *Slang.* sexually attractive
women collectively. [origin unknown]

crumple ('krʌmpʰl) *vb.* (often foll. by *up*)
1. to collapse or cause to collapse. **2.** to
crush or become crushed into untidy wrinkles or creases. ∼*n.* **3.** an untidy crease
or wrinkle. [obs. *crump* to bend] —**'crum-
ply** *adj.*

crunch (krʌntʃ) *vb.* **1.** to bite or chew with
a noisy crushing sound. **2.** to make or
cause to make a crisp or brittle sound.
∼*n.* **3.** the sound or act of crunching. **4.**
the crunch. *Informal.* the critical moment
or situation. [imit.] —**'crunchy** *adj.*
—**'crunchiness** *n.*

crupper ('krʌpə) *n.* **1.** a strap from the
back of a saddle that passes under a
horse's tail. **2.** the horse's rump. [Old
French *crupiere*]

crusade (kruːˈseɪd) *n.* **1.** any of the medieval military expeditions undertaken by
the Christian powers of Europe to recapture the Holy Land from the Muslims. **2.** a
vigorous campaign in favour of a cause.
∼*vb.* **3.** to engage in a crusade. [Latin
crux cross] —**cru'sader** *n.*

cruse (kruːz) *n.* a small earthenware container for liquids. [Old English]

crush (krʌʃ) *vb.* **1.** to press or squeeze so
as to injure, break, or put out of shape. **2.**
to break or grind into small particles. **3.** to
oppress or subdue by force. **4.** to extract
(liquid) by pressing. **5.** to defeat or humiliate utterly, as in argument or by a cruel
remark. **6.** to crowd; throng. ∼*n.* **7.** a
dense crowd. **8.** the act of crushing; pressure. **9.** a drink made by crushing fruit:
orange crush. **10.** *Informal.* an infatuation: *she had a crush on him.* [Old French
croissir] —**'crusher** *n.*

crush barrier *n.* a barrier put up to
separate sections of large crowds and prevent crushing.

crust (krʌst) *n.* **1. a.** the hard outer part of
bread. **b.** a piece of bread consisting mainly of this. **2.** the baked shell of a pie or
tart. **3.** any hard outer layer: *a crust of
ice.* **4.** the solid outer shell of the earth.
∼*vb.* **5.** to cover with, form, or acquire a
crust. [Latin *crūsta* hard surface, rind]

crustacean (krʌˈsteɪʃən) *n.* **1.** a usually
aquatic arthropod with a hard outer shell
and several pairs of legs, such as the
lobster, crab, or shrimp. ∼*adj.* **2.** of
crustaceans. [Latin *crūsta* shell]

crusty ('krʌstɪ) *adj.* **crustier, crustiest.**
1. having a crust. **2.** rude or irritable;
harsh. —**'crustiness** *n.*

crutch (krʌtʃ) *n.* **1.** a long staff with a rest
for the armpit, used by a lame person to
support the weight of the body. **2.** something that supports, helps, or sustains. **3.**
Brit. same as **crotch** (of the body). [Old
English *crycc*]

crutchings ('krʌtʃɪŋz) *pl. n. Austral. &*

N.Z. the wool clipped from a sheep's hindquarters.

crux (krʌks) *n., pl.* **cruxes** *or* **cruces**
('kruːsiːz). a crucial or decisive point. [Lat-
in: cross]

cry (kraɪ) *vb.* **crying, cried. 1.** (often foll.
by *out*) to make a loud vocal sound, usually
to express pain or fear or to appeal for
help. **2.** to shed tears; weep or sob. **3.**
(often foll. by *out*) to utter loudly or shout
(words of appeal, exclamation, or fear). **4.**
(often foll. by *out*) (of an animal or bird) to
utter loud characteristic sounds. **5.** (foll.
by *for*) to clamour or beg. ∼*n., pl.* **cries.**
6. the act or sound of crying; a shout,
scream, or wail. **7.** the characteristic utterance of an animal or bird. **8.** a fit of
weeping. **9.** an urgent appeal. **10.** a public demand. **11. a far cry. a.** a long way.
b. something very different. **12. in full
cry.** in eager pursuit. ∼See also **cry off.**
[Old French *crier*]

crying ('kraɪɪŋ) *adj.* **a crying shame.** something that demands immediate attention;
an injustice.

cry off *vb. Informal.* to withdraw from or
cancel (an agreement or arrangement).

cryogenics (ˌkraɪəˈdʒɛnɪks) *n.* (*with sing.
vb.*) the branch of physics concerned with
very low temperatures and their effects.
[Greek *kruos* cold + *-genēs* born] —ˌ**cryo-
'genic** *adj.*

crypt (krɪpt) *n.* a vault or underground
chamber, such as one beneath a church,
used as a burial place. [Greek *kruptē*]

cryptic ('krɪptɪk) *adj.* **1.** hidden; secret.
2. obscure in meaning. [Greek *kruptos*
concealed] —**'cryptically** *adv.*

cryptogam ('krɪptəʊˌgæm) *n.* a plant that
does not produce flowers or seeds but
reproduces by spores, such as algae,
mosses, and ferns. [Greek *kruptos* hidden
+ *gamos* marriage]

cryptography (krɪpˈtɒgrəfɪ) *n.* the art of
writing in and deciphering codes. [Greek
kruptos hidden + *-GRAPHY*] —**cryp'tographer** *n.* —**cryptographic** (ˌkrɪptəˈgræfɪk)
adj.

crystal ('krɪstʰl) *n.* **1.** a solid with a
regular shape in which the sides intersect
in a regular and symmetrical arrangement.
2. a single grain of a crystalline substance.
3. a highly transparent and brilliant type
of glass. **4.** something made of or resembling crystal. **5.** crystal glass articles collectively. **6.** *Electronics.* a crystalline element used in certain electronic devices,
such as a detector or oscillator. ∼*adj.* **7.**
like crystal; transparent: *crystal water.*
[Greek *krustallos* ice, crystal]

crystal ball *n.* the glass globe used in
crystal gazing.

crystal gazing *n.* **1.** the act of staring
into a crystal ball supposedly in order to
see future events. **2.** the act of trying to
foresee or predict. —**crystal gazer** *n.*

crystalline ('krɪstəˌlaɪn) *adj.* **1.** having
the characteristics or structure of crystals.
2. made of or containing crystals. **3.** made
of or like crystal; transparent; clear.

crystallize, -ise, *or* **crystalize, -ise**

('krɪstə‚laɪz) vb. **1.** to form or cause to form crystals. **2.** to coat with sugar. **3.** to give a definite form or expression to (an idea) or (of an idea) to assume a definite form. —‚crystalli'zation, -i'sation, or ‚crystali'zation, -i'sation n.

crystallography (‚krɪstə'lɒgrəfɪ) n. the science of crystal structure.

crystalloid ('krɪstə‚lɔɪd) n. a substance that in solution can pass through a membrane.

Cs Chem. caesium.

CSE (in Britain) Certificate of Secondary Education: an examination the first grade pass of which is an equivalent to a GCE O level.

CS gas n. a gas causing tears and painful breathing, used in civil disturbances. [initials of its U.S. inventors, Ben Carson and Roger Staughton]

CST (in the U.S. and Canada) Central Standard Time.

CT Connecticut.

CTV Canadian Television (Network Limited).

Cu Chem. copper. [Late Latin cuprum]

cu. cubic.

cub (kʌb) n. **1.** the young of certain mammals, such as the lion or bear. **2.** a young or inexperienced person. ~vb. **cubbing**, **cubbed**. **3.** to give birth to (cubs). [origin unknown]

Cub (kʌb) n. short for **Cub scout**.

cubbyhole ('kʌbɪ‚həʊl) n. a small enclosed space or room. [dialect cub cattle pen]

cube (kjuːb) n. **1.** an object with six equal square faces. **2.** the product of a number multiplied by its square: the cube of 2 is 8. ~vb. **3.** to find the cube of (a number). **4.** to shape or cut into cubes. [Greek kubos]

cube root n. the number or quantity whose cube is a given number or quantity: 2 is the cube root of 8.

cubic ('kjuːbɪk) adj. **1.** having the shape of a cube. **2. a.** having three dimensions. **b.** having the same volume as a cube with length, width, and depth each measuring the given unit: a cubic metre. **3.** Maths. involving or relating to the cubes of numbers.

cubicle ('kjuːbɪk'l) n. an enclosed compartment screened for privacy, as in a dormitory. [Latin cubiculum]

cubic measure n. a system of units for the measurement of volumes.

cubism ('kjuːbɪzəm) n. a style of art, begun in the early 20th century, in which objects are represented by geometrical shapes. —'cubist adj., n.

cubit ('kjuːbɪt) n. an ancient measure of length based on the length of the forearm. [Latin cubitum elbow, cubit]

cuboid ('kjuːbɔɪd) adj. **1.** shaped like a cube. ~n. **2.** Maths. a geometric solid whose six faces are rectangles.

Cub Scout or **Cub** n. a member of the junior branch of the Scout Association.

cuckold ('kʌkəld) n. **1.** a man whose wife has been unfaithful to him. ~vb. **2.** to make a cuckold of. [Middle English cukeweld]

cuckoo ('kʊkuː) n., pl. **cuckoos. 1.** a migratory bird with a characteristic two-note call, noted for laying its eggs in the nests of other birds. ~adj. **2.** Informal. insane or foolish. [Old French cucu, imit.]

cuckoopint ('kʊku‚paɪnt) n. a plant with arrow-shaped leaves, a pale purple spike of flowers, and scarlet berries.

cuckoo spit n. a white frothy mass produced on plants by the larvae of some insects.

cucumber ('kjuː‚kʌmbə) n. **1.** a long fruit with thin green rind and crisp white flesh, used in salads. **2. as cool as a cucumber.** calm and self-possessed. [Latin cucumis]

cud (kʌd) n. **1.** partially digested food brought back from the first stomach of ruminants to the mouth for a second chewing. **2. chew the cud.** to reflect or ponder something. [Old English cudu]

cuddle ('kʌd'l) vb. **1.** to hug or embrace fondly. **2.** (foll. by up) to lie close and snug; nestle. ~n. **3.** a fond hug, esp. when prolonged. [origin unknown] —'cuddly adj.

cudgel ('kʌdʒəl) n. a short stout stick used as a weapon. [Old English cycgel]

cue[1] (kjuː) n. **1.** a signal to an actor or musician to begin speaking, playing, or doing something. **2.** any signal, hint, or reminder. **3. on cue.** at the right moment. ~vb. **cueing, cued. 4.** to give a cue to (an actor or musician). [perhaps from the letter q, used in an actor's script to represent Latin quando when]

cue[2] (kjuː) n. **1.** a long tapering stick used to drive the balls in billiards, snooker, or pool. ~vb. **cueing, cued. 2.** to drive (a ball) with a cue. [var. of queue]

cuff[1] (kʌf) n. **1.** the end of a sleeve. **2.** U.S., Canad., & Austral. a turn-up on trousers. **3. off the cuff.** Informal. improvised; impromptu. [Middle English cuffe glove]

cuff[2] (kʌf) vb. **1.** to strike with an open hand. ~n. **2.** a blow of this kind. [origin unknown]

cuff link n. either of a pair of decorative fastenings for shirt cuffs.

cuisine (kwɪ'ziːn) n. **1.** a style or manner of cooking: French cuisine. **2.** the range of food served in a restaurant or household. [French]

cul-de-sac ('kʌldə‚sæk, 'kʊl-) n., pl. **culs-de-sac** or **cul-de-sacs.** a road with one end blocked off. [French: bottom of the bag]

culinary ('kʌlɪnərɪ) adj. of the kitchen or cookery. [Latin culina kitchen]

cull (kʌl) vb. **1.** to choose or gather; pick out. **2.** to remove or kill (the inferior or surplus) animals from (a herd). ~n. **3.** the act of culling. [Latin colligere to gather together]

culminate ('kʌlmɪ‚neɪt) vb. (usually foll. by in) to reach the highest point or climax. [Latin culmen top] —‚culmi'nation n.

culottes (kjuː'lɒts) pl. n. women's flared trousers cut to look like a skirt. [French]

culpable ('kʌlpəb'l) adj. deserving censure; blameworthy. [Latin *culpa* fault] —,culpa'bility *n*.

culprit ('kʌlprɪt) *n*. the person responsible for a particular offence or misdeed. [Anglo-French *culpable* guilty + *prit* ready]

cult (kʌlt) *n*. **1.** a specific system of religious worship. **2.** a sect devoted to the beliefs of a cult. **3.** devoted attachment to a person, idea, or activity. **4.** any popular fashion; craze. [Latin *cultus* cultivation, refinement]

cultivate ('kʌltɪ,veɪt) *vb*. **1.** to prepare (land) for the growth of crops. **2.** to grow (plants). **3.** to develop or improve (something) by giving special attention to it: *try to cultivate a sense of humour*. **4.** to try to develop a friendship with (a person). [Latin *colere* to till] —'culti,vated *adj*.

cultivation (,kʌltɪ'veɪʃən) *n*. **1.** the act of cultivating. **2.** culture or refinement.

cultivator ('kʌltɪ,veɪtə) *n*. a farm implement used to break up soil and remove weeds.

culture ('kʌltʃə) *n*. **1.** the ideas, customs, and art produced or shared by a particular society. **2.** a particular civilization at a particular period. **3.** activity or an interest in the arts in general. **4.** knowledge or refinement resulting from an interest in the arts. **5.** development or improvement by special attention or training: *physical culture*. **6.** the cultivation and rearing of plants or animals. **7.** a growth of microorganisms in a specially prepared substance. ~ *vb*. **8.** to grow (microorganisms) in a special medium. [Latin *colere* to till] —'cultural *adj*.

cultured ('kʌltʃəd) *adj*. **1.** showing or having good taste, manners, and education. **2.** artificially grown or synthesized: *cultured pearls*.

cultured pearl *n*. a pearl made to grow in the shell of an oyster, by the insertion of a foreign body.

culvert ('kʌlvət) *n*. a drain or covered channel that crosses under a road or railway. [origin unknown]

cum (kʌm) *prep*. used between nouns to indicate something with a combined nature: *a kitchen-cum-dining room*. [Latin: with]

cumbersome ('kʌmbəsəm) *or* **cumbrous** ('kʌmbrəs) *adj*. **1.** awkward because of size, weight, or shape. **2.** difficult because of extent or complexity: *a cumbersome system*.

cumin *or* **cummin** ('kʌmɪn) *n*. **1.** the sweet-smelling seeds of a Mediterranean herb, used in Indian cooking. **2.** the plant from which these seeds are obtained. [Greek *kuminon*]

cummerbund ('kʌmə,bʌnd) *n*. a wide sash, worn with a dinner jacket. [Hindi *kamarband*, from Persian *kamar* loins + *band*]

cumquat ('kʌmkwɒt) *n*. same as **kumquat**.

cumulative ('kjuːmjʊlətɪv) *adj*. growing in amount, strength, or effect by successive additions.

cumulus ('kjuːmjʊləs) *n*., *pl*. **-li** (-,laɪ). a

thick or billowing white or dark grey cloud. [Latin: mass]

cuneiform ('kjuːnɪ,fɔːm) *adj*. **1.** of or using a system of writing with wedge-shaped characters, as in several ancient languages of Mesopotamia and Persia. ~ *n*. **2.** cuneiform characters. [Latin *cuneus* wedge]

cunnilingus (,kʌnɪ'lɪŋgəs) *n*. the kissing and licking of a woman's genitals by her partner. [Latin *cunnus* vulva + *lingere* lick]

cunning ('kʌnɪŋ) *adj*. **1.** crafty and sly. **2.** made with skill; ingenious. ~ *n*. **3.** craftiness; slyness. **4.** skill or ingenuity. [Old English *cunnende*]

cunt (kʌnt) *n*. Taboo. **1.** the female genitals. **2.** *Offensive slang*. a stupid or obnoxious person. [Middle English]

cup (kʌp) *n*. **1.** a small bowl-shaped container, usually having one handle, used for drinking from. **2.** the contents of a cup. **3.** something shaped like a cup: *the cups of a bra*. **4.** a cup-shaped trophy awarded as a prize. **5.** *Brit*. a sporting contest in which a cup is awarded to the winner. **6.** a mixed drink with one ingredient as a base: *claret cup*. **7.** one's lot in life. **8. one's cup of tea.** *Informal*. one's chosen or preferred thing. ~ *vb*. **cupping, cupped. 9.** to form (something, esp. the hands) into the shape of a cup. **10.** to put into or hold as if in a cup. [Old English *cuppe*]

cupboard ('kʌbəd) *n*. a piece of furniture or a recessed area of a room, with a door concealing storage space.

cupboard love *n*. a show of love inspired only by some selfish motive.

Cup Final *n*. **1.** the annual final of the FA or Scottish Cup soccer competition. **2.** (*often not cap*.) the final of any cup competition.

Cupid ('kjuːpɪd) *n*. **1.** the Roman god of love, represented as a winged boy with a bow and arrow. **2. cupid.** a picture or statue of Cupid. [Latin *cupīdō* desire]

cupidity (kjuː'pɪdɪtɪ) *n*. strong desire for wealth or possessions. [Latin *cupere* to long for]

cupola ('kjuːpələ) *n*. **1.** a domed roof or ceiling. **2.** a small dome on the top of a roof. **3.** an armoured revolving gun turret on a warship. [Latin *cūpa* tub]

cupreous ('kjuːprɪəs) *adj*. of, containing, or resembling copper. [Latin *cuprum* copper]

cupric ('kjuːprɪk) *adj*. of or containing copper in the divalent state.

cupriferous (kjuː'prɪfərəs) *adj*. containing or yielding copper.

cupronickel (,kjuːprəʊ'nɪk'l) *n*. a copper alloy containing up to 40 per cent nickel.

cuprous ('kjuːprəs) *adj*. of or containing copper in the monovalent state.

cup tie *n*. *Sport*. an eliminating match or round between two teams in a cup competition.

cur (kɜː) *n*. **1.** a vicious mongrel dog. **2.** a despicable or cowardly person. [Middle English *kurdogge*]

curable ('kjυərəb°l) *adj.* capable of being cured. —,cura'bility *n.*

curaçao (,kjυərə'səυ) *n.* an orange-flavoured liqueur originally made in Curaçao, a Caribbean island.

curacy ('kjυərəsı) *n., pl.* -cies. the work or position of a curate.

curare (kjυ'rɑːrı) *n.* a black resin obtained from certain South American plants, used medicinally as a muscle relaxant and by some Indians as an arrow poison. [Carib *kurari*]

curate ('kjυərıt) *n.* a clergyman appointed to assist a vicar or parish priest. [Medieval Latin *cūra* spiritual oversight]

curative ('kjυərətıv) *adj.* 1. curing or able to cure. ~*n.* 2. anything able to cure.

curator (kjυə'reıtə) *n.* the administrative head of a museum or art gallery. [Latin: one who cares] —**curatorial** (,kjυərə-'tɔːrıəl) *adj.* —**cu'rator,ship** *n.*

curb (kɜːb) *n.* 1. something that restrains or holds back. 2. a raised edge that strengthens or encloses. 3. a horse's bit with an attached chain or strap, used to check the horse. ~*vb.* 4. to control or restrain with or as if with a curb. ~See also **kerb.** [Latin *curvus* curved]

curd (kɜːd) *n.* 1. (*often pl.*) a substance formed when milk coagulates, used in making cheese or as a food. 2. any similar substance: *bean curd.* [origin unknown]

curdle ('kɜːd°l) *vb.* 1. to turn into curd; coagulate. 2. **make someone's blood curdle.** to fill someone with horror.

cure (kjυə) *vb.* 1. to get rid of (an ailment or problem); heal. 2. to restore to health. 3. to preserve (meat or fish) by salting or smoking. 4. to preserve (leather or tobacco) by drying. 5. to vulcanize (rubber). ~*n.* 6. a restoration to health. 7. a course of medicinal or medical treatment that restores health. 8. a means of restoring health or improving a situation. 9. a curacy. [Latin *cūra* care]

cure-all *n.* something supposed to cure all ailments or problems.

curet *or* **curette** (kjυə'rɛt) *n.* 1. a surgical instrument for removing dead tissue or growths from the walls of body cavities. ~*vb.* -retting, -retted. 2. to scrape or clean with a curet. [French *curette*] —**cu'rettage** (,kjυərı'tɑːʒ) *n.*

curfew ('kɜːfjuː) *n.* 1. an official rule or law which states that people must stay inside their houses after a specific time at night. 2. the time set as a deadline by such a law. 3. *Hist.* the ringing of a bell at a fixed time, as a signal to people to extinguish fires and lights. [Old French *cuevrefeu* cover the fire]

Curia ('kjυərıə) *n., pl.* -riae (-rıˌiː). the papal court and government of the Roman Catholic Church. [Latin] —**'curial** *adj.*

curie ('kjυərı, -rıː) *n.* the metric unit of radioactivity. [after Marie *Curie* & her husband Pierre, physicists]

curio ('kjυərıˌəυ) *n., pl.* -rios. a rare or unusual article valued as a collector's item. [from *curiosity*]

curiosity (,kjυərı'ɒsıtı) *n., pl.* -ties. 1. an

eager desire to know; inquisitiveness. 2. something strange, rare, or fascinating.

curious ('kjυərıəs) *adj.* 1. eager to learn or know. 2. prying; nosy. 3. interesting because of oddness or novelty. [Latin *cūriōsus* taking pains over something] —**'curiously** *adv.*

curium ('kjυərıəm) *n.* a silvery-white metallic radioactive element artificially produced from plutonium. Symbol: Cm [after Pierre & Marie *Curie*]

curl (kɜːl) *vb.* 1. to twist or roll (hair) or (of hair) to grow in coils or ringlets. 2. to form into or move in a spiral or curve. 3. to play the game of curling. 4. **curl one's lip.** to show contempt by raising a corner of the lip. ~*n.* 5. a curve or coil of hair. 6. a curved or spiral shape or mark. ~See also **curl up.** [prob. from Middle Dutch *crullen* to curl] —**'curly** *adj.*

curler ('kɜːlə) *n.* 1. a pin or roller used to curl hair. 2. a person who plays curling.

curlew ('kɜːljuː) *n.* a large shore bird with a long downward-curving bill and long legs. [Old French *corlieu*]

curlicue ('kɜːlıˌkjuː) *n.* an intricate ornamental curl or twist. [*curly* + CUE²]

curling ('kɜːlıŋ) *n.* a game played on ice, in which heavy stones with handles are slid towards a target circle.

curl up *vb.* 1. to lie or sit with legs drawn up. 2. to be embarrassed or horrified.

curmudgeon (kɜː'mʌdʒən) *n.* an irritable or miserly person. [origin unknown] —**cur'mudgeonly** *adj.*

currant ('kʌrənt) *n.* 1. a small dried seedless raisin. 2. a small round acid berry which grows on shrubs, such as the redcurrant. [earlier *rayson of Corannte* raisin of Corinth]

currency ('kʌrənsı) *n., pl.* -cies. 1. the system of money or the actual coins and banknotes in use in a particular country. 2. general acceptance or use: *these theories have yet to gain much currency.* [Latin *currere* to run, flow]

current ('kʌrənt) *adj.* 1. of the immediate present; happening now: *current affairs.* 2. most recent; up-to-date. 3. commonly accepted: *current opinion.* 4. circulating and valid at present: *current coins.* ~*n.* 5. a steady flow or rate of flow of water or air in a particular direction. 6. *Physics.* a flow or rate of flow of electric charge through a conductor. 7. a general trend or drift: *currents of opinion.* [Latin *currere* to run, flow] —**'currently** *adv.*

current account *n.* a bank account from which money may be drawn at any time using a chequebook or computerized card.

curriculum (kə'rıkjυləm) *n., pl.* -la (-lə) *or* -lums. 1. a course of study in one subject at a school or college. 2. all the courses of study offered by a school or college. [Latin: course] —**cur'ricular** *adj.*

curriculum vitae ('viːtaı, 'vaıtiː) *n., pl.* **curricula vitae.** an outline of someone's personal, educational, and professional history, usually prepared for job applications. [Latin: the course of one's life]

curry¹ ('kʌrı) *n., pl.* -ries. 1. a dish of

Indian origin consisting of meat or vegetables in a hot spicy sauce. **2.** curry seasoning or sauce. **3. curry powder.** a mixture of spices used for making curry. ~*vb.* **-rying, -ried. 4.** to prepare (food) with curry powder or sauce. [Tamil *kari* sauce, relish]

curry[2] ('kʌrɪ) *vb.* **-rying, -ried. 1.** to groom (a horse). **2.** to dress and finish (leather) after it has been tanned. **3. curry favour.** to ingratiate oneself, esp. with superiors. [Old French *correer* to make ready]

currycomb ('kʌrɪ‚kəʊm) *n.* a ridged comb used for grooming horses.

curse (kɜːs) *n.* **1.** a profane or obscene expression, usually of anger; oath. **2.** an appeal to a supernatural power for harm to come to a person. **3.** harm resulting from a curse. **4.** something that causes great trouble or harm. **5. the curse.** *Informal.* menstruation or a menstrual period. ~*vb.* **cursing, cursed. 6.** to swear or swear at (someone). **7.** to call on supernatural powers to bring harm to (someone or something). **8.** to bring harm upon by a curse. [Old English *curs*]

cursed ('kɜːsɪd, kɜːst) *adj.* **1.** under a curse. **2.** deserving to be cursed; hateful.

cursive ('kɜːsɪv) *adj.* **1.** of handwriting or print in which letters are joined in a flowing style. ~*n.* **2.** a cursive letter or printing type. [Medieval Latin *cursīvus* running]

cursor ('kɜːsə) *n.* **1.** the sliding part of a slide rule or other measuring instrument. **2.** a movable point of light that shows a specific position on a visual display unit.

cursory ('kɜːsərɪ) *adj.* hasty and usually superficial; brief. [Late Latin *cursōrius* of running] —'**cursoriness** *n.*

curt (kɜːt) *adj.* so blunt and brief as to be rude. [Latin *curtus* cut short] —'**curtly** *adv.* —'**curtness** *n.*

curtail (kɜː'teɪl) *vb.* to cut short; abridge. [obs. *curtal* to dock] —**cur'tailment** *n.*

curtain ('kɜːt³n) *n.* **1.** a piece of material hung at an opening or window to shut out light or to provide privacy. **2.** something that conceals or shuts off: *a dense curtain of vegetation.* **3.** a hanging cloth that conceals all or part of a theatre stage from the audience. **4.** the end of a scene of a performance, marked by the fall or closing of the curtain. **5.** the rise or opening of the curtain at the start of a performance. ~*vb.* **6.** (sometimes foll. by *off*) to shut or conceal as with a curtain. **7.** to provide with curtains. [Late Latin *cortina*]

curtain call *n. Theatre.* the audience's summons to an actor or actors to come to the front of the stage after a performance to receive applause.

curtain-raiser *n.* **1.** *Theatre.* a short dramatic piece presented before the main play. **2.** any preliminary event.

curtains ('kɜːt³nz) *pl. n. Informal.* death or ruin; the end.

curtsy *or* **curtsey** ('kɜːtsɪ) *n., pl.* **-sies** *or* **-seys. 1.** a woman's formal gesture of greeting and respect, in which the knees are bent and the head slightly bowed.

~*vb.* **-sying, -sied** *or* **-seying, -seyed. 2.** to make a curtsy. [var. of *courtesy*]

curvaceous (kɜː'veɪʃəs) *adj. Informal.* (of a woman) having a curved shapely body.

curvature ('kɜːvətʃə) *n.* the state or degree of being curved or bent.

curve (kɜːv) *n.* **1.** a continuously bending line with no straight parts. **2.** something that curves or is curved. **3.** curvature. **4.** *Maths.* a system of points whose coordinates satisfy a given equation. **5.** a line representing data on a graph. ~*vb.* **6.** to form into or move in a curve; bend. [Latin *curvāre* to bend] —'**curvy** *adj.*

curvet (kɜː'vɛt) *n.* **1.** a horse's low leap with all four feet off the ground. ~*vb.* **-vetting, -vetted** *or* **-veting, -veted. 2.** to make such a leap. [Latin *curvāre* to bend]

curvilinear (‚kɜːvɪ'lɪnɪə) *adj.* consisting of or bounded by a curved line.

cushion ('kʊʃən) *n.* **1.** a bag filled with a soft material, used to make a seat more comfortable. **2.** anything that relieves distress, provides comfort, or absorbs shock. **3.** the resilient felt-covered rim of a billiard table. ~*vb.* **4.** to provide with cushions. **5.** to protect from injury or shock; relieve from distress. **6.** to lessen or suppress the effects of. [Latin *culcita* mattress] —'**cushiony** *adj.*

cushy ('kʊʃɪ) *adj.* **cushier, cushiest.** *Informal.* easy; comfortable. [Hindi *khush* pleasant]

cusp (kʌsp) *n.* **1.** a small point on the grinding or chewing surface of a tooth. **2.** a point or pointed end, such as one where two curves meet. **3.** *Astron.* either of the points of a crescent moon. **4.** *Astrol.* any division between houses or signs of the zodiac. [Latin *cuspis* pointed end]

cuss (kʌs) *Informal.* ~*n.* **1.** a curse; an oath. **2.** a person or animal, esp. an annoying one. ~*vb.* **3.** to swear or swear at (someone).

cussed ('kʌsɪd) *adj. Informal.* **1.** same as **cursed. 2.** obstinate or annoying. —'**cussedness** *n.*

custard ('kʌstəd) *n.* **1.** a sauce made of milk and sugar thickened with cornflour. **2.** a baked sweetened mixture of eggs and milk. [Middle English *crustade* kind of pie]

custodian (kʌ'stəʊdɪən) *n.* the person in charge of something, such as a public building. —**cus'todian‚ship** *n.*

custody ('kʌstədɪ) *n., pl.* **-dies. 1.** the act of keeping safe or guarding. **2.** the state of being held by the police; arrest. [Latin *custōs* guard, defender] —**custodial** (kʌ'stəʊdɪəl) *adj.*

custom ('kʌstəm) *n.* **1.** a usual practice or habit. **2.** the long-established habits or traditions of a society; convention. **3. a.** a practice which by long-established usage has come to have the force of law. **b.** such practices collectively: *custom and practice.* **4.** regular use of a shop or business. ~*adj.* **5.** made to the specifications of an individual customer. ~See also **customs.** [Latin *consuētūdō*]

customary ('kʌstəmərɪ) *adj.* in accordance

with custom. —'**customarily** *adv.*
—'**customariness** *n.*

custom-built *adj.* made according to the specifications of an individual customer.

customer ('kʌstəmə) *n.* **1.** a person who buys. **2.** *Informal.* a person with whom one has to deal: *a rough customer.*

custom house *n.* a government office where customs are levied.

customs ('kʌstəmz) *n. (functioning as sing. or pl.)* **1.** duty charged on imports or exports. **2.** the government department responsible for the collection of these duties. **3.** the part of a port, airport, or border, where baggage and freight are examined for dutiable goods.

cut (kʌt) *vb.* **cutting, cut. 1.** to open up or penetrate (a person or thing) with a sharp-edged instrument. **2.** (of a sharp instrument) to penetrate or open up (a person or thing). **3.** to divide or be divided with or as if with a sharp instrument. **4.** to trim. **5.** to reap or mow. **6.** (sometimes foll. by *out*) to form or shape by cutting. **7.** *Sports.* to hit (the ball) so that it spins and swerves. **8.** to hurt the feelings of (a person): *her rudeness cut me to the core.* **9.** *Informal.* to pretend not to recognize; snub. **10.** *Informal.* to absent oneself from without permission: *to cut a class.* **11.** to stop (doing something): *cut the nonsense.* **12.** to abridge or shorten. **13.** (often foll. by *down*) to reduce or curtail. **14.** to dilute or adulterate: *to cut whisky with water.* **15.** (foll. by *across* or *through*) to cross or traverse; intersect. **16.** to make a sharp or sudden change in direction; veer. **17.** to grow (teeth) through the gums. **18.** *Films.* **a.** to call a halt to a shooting sequence. **b.** (foll. by *to*) to move quickly to (another scene). **19.** *Films.* to edit (film). **20.** to switch off (a light or engine). **21.** to make (a gramophone record). **22.** *Cards.* **a.** to divide (the pack) at random into two parts after shuffling. **b.** to pick cards from a spread pack to decide the dealer, partners, or who plays first. **23. cut a dash.** to make a stylish impression. **24. cut a person dead.** *Informal.* to ignore a person completely. **25. cut and run.** *Informal.* to make a rapid escape. **26. cut both ways. a.** to have both good and bad effects. **b.** to serve both sides of an argument. **27. cut it fine.** *Informal.* to allow little margin of time or space. **28. cut no ice.** *Informal.* to fail to make an impression. **29. cut one's teeth on.** *Informal.* to acquire experience from. ~*adj.* **30.** made, detached, or shaped by cutting. **31.** reduced by cutting: *cut prices.* **32.** adulterated or diluted. **33. cut and dried.** *Informal.* settled or arranged in advance. ~*n.* **34.** the act of cutting. **35.** a stroke or incision made by cutting. **36.** a piece or part cut off: *a cut of meat.* **37.** a passage, channel, or path cut or hollowed out. **38.** an omission or deletion in a text, film, or play. **39.** a reduction, as in prices or government spending. **40.** *Informal.* a portion or share. **41.** the style in which hair or a garment is cut. **42.** a direct route; short cut. **43.** *Sports.* a stroke which makes the ball spin and swerve. **44.** *Films.* an immediate tran-

sition from one shot to the next. **45.** a refusal to recognize someone; snub. **46.** *Brit.* a canal. **47. a cut above.** *Informal.* superior to; better than. ~See also **cut across, cutback,** etc. [prob. from Old Norse]

cut across *vb.* **1.** to be contrary to (ordinary procedure or limitations); transcend. **2.** to cross or traverse, making a shorter route.

cutaneous (kjuː'teɪnɪəs) *adj.* of the skin. [Latin *cutis* skin]

cutaway ('kʌtə,weɪ) *adj.* (of a drawing or model of something) having part of the exterior omitted to reveal the interior.

cutback ('kʌt,bæk) *n.* **1.** a decrease or reduction. ~*vb.* **cut back 2.** to shorten by cutting off the end; prune. **3.** (often foll. by *on*) to decrease or make a reduction (in).

cut down *vb.* **1.** to fell. **2.** (often foll. by *on*) to decrease or make a reduction (in). **3.** to kill. **4. cut a person down to size.** to cause a person to feel less important or to be less conceited.

cute (kjuːt) *adj.* **1.** appealing or attractive, esp. in a pretty way. **2.** *Informal, chiefly U.S. & Canad.* affecting cleverness or prettiness. **3.** clever; shrewd. [from *acute*] —'**cuteness** *n.*

cut glass *n.* **1.** glass decorated by facet-cutting or grinding. **2.** (*modifier*) upper-class; refined: *a cut-glass accent.*

cuticle ('kjuːtɪk⁰l) *n.* **1.** hardened skin round the base of a fingernail or toenail. **2.** same as **epidermis.** [Latin *cuticula* skin]

cut in *vb.* **1.** to interrupt. **2.** to move in front of another vehicle, leaving too little space.

cutlass ('kʌtləs) *n.* a curved, one-edged sword formerly used by sailors. [French *coutelas*]

cutler ('kʌtlə) *n.* a person who makes or sells cutlery. [Latin *culter* knife]

cutlery ('kʌtlərɪ) *n.* knives, forks, and spoons, used for eating.

cutlet ('kʌtlɪt) *n.* **1.** a small piece of meat taken from the neck or ribs. **2.** a flat croquette of chopped meat or fish. [Old French *costelette* a little rib]

cut off *vb.* **1.** to remove or separate by cutting. **2.** to interrupt (a person who is speaking), esp. during a telephone conversation. **3.** to stop the supply of. **4.** to bring to an end. **5.** to disinherit: *cut off without a penny.* **6.** to intercept so as to prevent retreat or escape; isolate. ~*n.* **cutoff. 7.** the point at which something is cut off; limit. **8.** *Chiefly U.S.* a short cut. **9.** a device to stop the flow of a fluid in a pipe or duct.

cut out *vb.* **1.** to delete or remove. **2.** to shape or form by cutting. **3. be cut out for.** to be suited or equipped for: *you're not cut out for this job.* **4.** (of an engine) to cease to operate suddenly. **5.** (of an electrical device) to switch off, usually automatically. **6. cut it out.** *Informal.* to stop doing something. **7. have one's work cut out.** to have as much work as one can manage. ~*n.* **cutout. 8.** something that has been or is intended to be cut out from something else. **9.** a device that automatically switches off an electric circuit or engine, esp. as a safety device.

cut-price or esp. U.S. **cut-rate** adj. **1.** available at prices below the standard price. **2.** offering goods or services at prices below the standard price.

cutter ('kʌtə) n. **1.** a person or tool that cuts, esp. a person who cuts cloth for clothing. **2.** any of various small fast boats, such as a lightly-armed one used by customs officers.

cutthroat ('kʌt,θrəʊt) n. **1.** a person who cuts throats; murderer. **2.** Brit. a razor with a long blade that folds into its handle. ~adj. **3.** fierce or relentless in competition: cutthroat prices. **4.** (of a card game) played by three people: cutthroat poker.

cutting ('kʌtɪŋ) n. **1.** a piece cut from a plant for rooting or grafting. **2.** an article or photograph cut from a newspaper or magazine. **3.** the editing process of a film. **4.** an excavation for a road or railway through high ground. ~adj. **5.** designed for cutting; sharp: a cutting tool. **6.** keen; piercing: a cutting wind. **7.** likely to hurt the feelings: a cutting remark.

cuttlefish ('kʌt'l,fɪʃ) n., pl. **-fish** or **-fishes.** a flat squidlike mollusc which squirts an inky fluid when in danger. [Old English cudele]

cut up vb. **1.** to cut into pieces. **2. be cut up.** to be very upset. **3. cut up rough.** Brit. informal. to become angry or bad-tempered.

CV curriculum vitae.

cwm (kuːm) n. (in Wales) a valley. [Welsh]

cwt hundredweight.

cyanic (saɪ'ænɪk) adj. **1.** of or containing cyanogen. **2.** blue.

cyanic acid n. a colourless poisonous volatile liquid acid.

cyanide ('saɪə,naɪd) n. a highly poisonous salt of hydrocyanic acid.

cyanogen (saɪ'ænədʒɪn) n. a poisonous colourless flammable gas. [Greek kuanos dark blue]

cyanosis (,saɪə'nəʊsɪs) n. Pathol. a blue discoloration of the skin, caused by a deficiency of oxygen in the blood. [Greek kuanos dark blue]

cybernetics (,saɪbə'nɛtɪks) n. (functioning as sing.) the branch of science in which the control systems and methods of communication of electronic and mechanical devices are studied and compared to biological systems. [Greek kubernētēs steersman] —**cyber'netic** adj.

cyclamen ('sɪkləmən, -,mɛn) n. a plant having white, pink, or red flowers, with turned-back petals. [Greek kuklaminos]

cycle ('saɪk'l) n. **1.** a complete series of recurring events or phenomena. **2.** the time taken or needed for one such series. **3.** a very long period of time. **4.** a group of poems, plays, or songs about a central figure or event: the Arthurian cycle. **5.** short for **bicycle, motorcycle**. **6.** a single complete movement in an electrical, electronic, or mechanical process consisting of

a continuous repetition of such movements. ~vb. **7.** to occur in cycles. **8.** to travel by or ride a bicycle or motorcycle. [Greek kuklos]

cyclic ('saɪklɪk, 'sɪklɪk) or **cyclical** adj. **1.** recurring in cycles. **2.** (of an organic compound) containing a closed ring of atoms.

cyclist ('saɪklɪst) or U.S. **cycler** n. a person who rides a bicycle or motorcycle.

cyclo- or before a vowel **cycl-** combining form. **1.** indicating a circle or ring: cyclotron. **2.** denoting a cyclic compound: cyclopropane. [Greek kuklos cycle]

cyclometer (saɪ'klɒmɪtə) n. a device that records the number of revolutions made by a wheel and hence the distance travelled.

cyclone ('saɪkləʊn) n. **1.** a body of moving air below normal atmospheric pressure, which often brings rain; depression. **2.** a violent tropical storm; hurricane. [Greek kuklōn a turning around] —**cyclonic** (saɪ'klɒnɪk) adj.

cyclopedia or **cyclopaedia** (,saɪkləʊ'piːdɪə) n. same as **encyclopedia**.

Cyclops ('saɪklɒps) n., pl. **Cyclopes** (saɪ'kləʊpiːz) or **Cyclopses.** Classical myth. one of a race of giants having a single eye in the middle of the forehead. [Greek Kuklōps round eye]

cyclotron ('saɪklə,trɒn) n. an apparatus, used in atomic research, which accelerates charged particles by means of a strong vertical magnetic field.

cyder ('saɪdə) n. same as **cider**.

cygnet ('sɪgnɪt) n. a young swan. [Latin cygnus swan]

cylinder ('sɪlɪndə) n. **1.** a solid or hollow body with circular equal ends and straight parallel sides. **2.** any object shaped like a cylinder. **3.** the chamber in an internal-combustion engine within which the piston moves. **4.** the rotating mechanism of a revolver, containing cartridge chambers. [Greek kulindein to roll] —**cy'lindrical** adj.

cymbal ('sɪmb'l) n. a percussion instrument consisting of a thin circular piece of brass, which is clashed together with another cymbal or struck with a stick. [Greek kumbē something hollow] —**'cymbalist** n.

cyme (saɪm) n. a flower cluster which has a single flower on the end of each stem and of which the central flower blooms first. [Greek kuma anything swollen] —**'cymose** adj.

Cymric ('kɪmrɪk) n. **1.** the Welsh language. ~adj. **2.** of Wales, the Welsh, or their language.

cynic ('sɪnɪk) n. a person who believes that people always act selfishly. [Greek kuōn dog]

Cynic ('sɪnɪk) n. a member of an ancient Greek philosophical school that scorned worldly things. —**Cynicism** ('sɪnɪ,sɪzəm) n.

cynical ('sɪnɪk'l) adj. **1.** believing that people always act selfishly. **2.** sarcastic; sneering. —**'cynically** adv.

cynicism ('sɪnɪ,sɪzəm) n. **1.** the attitude

or beliefs of a cynic. **2.** a cynical action or
idea.

cynosure ('sɪnə,zjʊə, -ʃʊə) *n.* a centre of
interest or attention [Greek *Kunosoura*
dog's tail (name of the constellation of
Ursa Minor)]

cypher ('saɪfə) *n., vb.* same as **cipher**.

cypress ('saɪprəs) *n.* **1.** an evergreen tree
with dark green scalelike leaves and
rounded cones. **2.** the wood of this tree.
3. cypress branches used as a symbol of
mourning. [Greek *kuparissos*]

Cypriot ('sɪprɪət) *n.* **1.** a person from
Cyprus, an island in the E Mediterranean.
2. the dialect of Greek spoken in Cyprus.
~*adj.* **3.** of Cyprus, its inhabitants, or
dialect.

Cyrillic (sɪ'rɪlɪk) *adj.* of the Slavic alphabet
devised supposedly by Saint Cyril, now
used primarily for Russian and Bulgarian.

cyst (sɪst) *n.* **1.** *Pathol.* any abnormal
membranous sac containing fluid or diseased matter. **2.** *Anat.* any normal sac in
the body. [Greek *kustis* pouch, bag]

cystic fibrosis ('sɪstɪk) *n.* a congenital
disease, usually affecting young children,
which causes breathing disorders and malfunctioning of the pancreas.

cystitis (sɪ'staɪtɪs) *n.* inflammation of the
bladder.

-cyte *n. combining form.* indicating a
cell: *leucocyte*. [Greek *kutos* vessel]

cytology (saɪ'tɒlədʒɪ) *n.* the study of plant
and animal cells. —**cytological** (,saɪtə-
'lɒdʒɪkᵊl) *adj.* —**cy'tologist** *n.*

cytoplasm ('saɪtəʊ,plæzəm) *n.* the protoplasm of a cell excluding the nucleus.
—,**cyto'plasmic** *adj.*

czar (zɑː) *n. Chiefly U.S.* same as **tsar**.

Czech (tʃɛk) *adj.* **1.** of Bohemia, Moravia,
and, loosely, of Czechoslovakia, their people, or language. ~*n.* **2.** one of the two
closely related official languages of
Czechoslovakia (Czech and Slovak). **3.** a
person from Bohemia, Moravia, or loosely,
from Czechoslovakia.

Czechoslovak (,tʃɛkəʊ'sləʊvæk) *or*
Czechoslovakian (,tʃɛkəʊsləʊ'vækɪən)
adj. **1.** of Czechoslovakia, its peoples, or
languages. ~*n.* **2.** a person from Czechoslovakia.

D

d *or* **D** (diː) *n., pl.* **d's, D's,** *or* **Ds.** the fourth letter of the modern English alphabet.

d *Physics.* density.

D 1. *Music.* the second note of the scale of C major. **2.** *Chem.* deuterium. **3.** the Roman numeral for 500.

d. 1. daughter. **2.** *Brit.* (before decimalization) penny *or* pennies. [Latin *denarius*] **3.** died.

dab¹ (dæb) *vb.* **dabbing, dabbed. 1.** to pat lightly and quickly. **2.** to daub with short tapping strokes: *to dab the wall with paint.* **3.** to apply (a substance) with short tapping strokes. *~n.* **4.** a small amount of something soft or moist. **5.** a light stroke or tap. **6.** (*pl.*) *Slang, chiefly Brit.* fingerprints. [imit.]

dab² (dæb) *n.* a small flatfish covered with rough toothed scales. [Anglo-French *dabbe*]

dabble (ˈdæbᵊl) *vb.* **1.** (usually foll. by *in*) to deal with or work at (something) frivolously or superficially. **2.** to dip or splash (the fingers or feet) in a liquid. [prob. from Dutch *dabbelen*] —**ˈdabbler** *n.*

dab hand *n. Brit. informal.* a person who is particularly skilled at something: *a dab hand at chess.* [origin unknown]

da capo (dɑː ˈkɑːpəʊ) *adv. Music.* to be repeated from the beginning. [Italian]

dace (deɪs) *n., pl.* **dace** *or* **daces.** a freshwater fish of the carp family. [Old French *dars* dart]

dachshund (ˈdæksˌhʊnd) *n.* a long-bodied short-legged dog. [German *Dachs* badger + *Hund* dog]

dactyl (ˈdæktɪl) *n. Prosody.* a metrical foot of three syllables, one long followed by two short (‒◡◡). [Greek *daktulos* finger, comparing the finger's three joints to the three syllables] —**ˈdacˈtylic** *adj.*

dad (dæd) *or* **daddy** *n. Informal.* father. [from child's *da da*]

Dada (ˈdɑːdɑː) *or* **Dadaism** (ˈdɑːdɑːˌɪzəm) *n.* an art movement of the early 20th century that systematically used arbitrary and absurd concepts. [French: hobbyhorse] —**ˈDadaist** *n., adj.*

daddy-longlegs *n. Brit. informal.* a crane fly.

dado (ˈdeɪdəʊ) *n., pl.* **-does** *or* **-dos. 1.** the lower part of an interior wall that is decorated differently from the upper part. **2.** *Archit.* the part of a pedestal between the base and the cornice. [Italian: die, die-shaped pedestal]

daemon (ˈdiːmən) *n.* **1.** a demigod. **2.** the guardian spirit of a place or person.

daffodil (ˈdæfədɪl) *n.* **1.** a widely cultivated Eurasian plant with spring-blooming yellow flowers. *~adj.* **2.** brilliant yellow. [var. of Latin *asphodelus* asphodel]

daft (dɑːft) *adj. Informal, chiefly Brit.* foolish or frivolous. [Old English *gedæfte* gentle, foolish]

dag (dæg) *n. N.Z. informal.* a person with a good sense of humour. [origin unknown]

dagger (ˈdægə) *n.* **1.** a short stabbing weapon with a pointed blade. **2.** a character (†) used to indicate a cross-reference. **3. at daggers drawn.** in a state of open hostility. **4. look daggers.** to glare with hostility. [origin unknown]

daguerreotype (dəˈgɛrəʊˌtaɪp) *n.* a type of early photograph produced on chemically treated silver. [after L. *Daguerre*, its inventor]

dahlia (ˈdeɪljə) *n.* a herbaceous plant with showy flowers. [after Anders *Dahl*, botanist]

Dáil Éireann (ˌdɔɪl ˈɛərən) *or* **Dáil** *n.* (in the Republic of Ireland) the lower chamber of parliament. [Irish *dáil* assembly + *Éireann* of Eire]

daily (ˈdeɪlɪ) *adj.* **1.** occurring every day or every weekday. *~n., pl.* **-lies.** **2.** a daily newspaper. **3.** *Brit.* a charwoman. *~adv.* **4.** every day. [Old English *dæglic*]

dainty (ˈdeɪntɪ) *adj.* **-tier, -tiest. 1.** delicate or elegant. **2.** choice: *a dainty morsel.* *~n., pl.* **-ties. 3.** a delicacy. [Old French *deintié*] —**ˈdaintily** *adv.*

daiquiri (ˈdaɪkɪrɪ, ˈdæk-) *n., pl.* **-ris.** an iced drink containing rum, lime juice, and sugar. [after *Daiquiri*, town in Cuba]

dairy (ˈdɛərɪ) *n., pl.* **dairies. 1.** a company or shop that sells milk and milk products. **2.** a place where milk and cream are stored or made into butter and cheese. **3.** (*modifier*) of milk or milk products: *dairy butter.* [Old English *dæge* servant girl]

dais (ˈdeɪɪs, deɪs) *n.* a raised platform in a hall, used by speakers. [Old French *deis*]

daisy (ˈdeɪzɪ) *n., pl.* **-sies. 1.** a small low-growing flower with a yellow centre and pinkish-white outer rays. **2.** any of various similar flowers. [Old English *dægeseġe* day's eye]

daisywheel (ˈdeɪzɪˌwiːl) *n.* a disc-shaped part of the printer of a word processor with many radiating spokes, each with a character on the end.

dal (dɑːl) *n.* same as **dhal.**

Dalai Lama (ˈdælaɪ ˈlɑːmə) *n.* the chief lama and (until 1959) ruler of Tibet.

dale (deɪl) *n.* an open valley. [Old English *dæl*]

dally (ˈdælɪ) *vb.* **-lying, -lied. 1.** to dawdle. **2. dally with.** to amuse oneself with; trifle with. [Anglo-French *dalier* to gossip] —**ˈdalliance** *n.*

Dalmatian (dælˈmeɪʃən) *n.* a large dog with a smooth white coat and black spots.

dal segno (ˈdæl ˈsɛnjəʊ) *adv. Music.* repeat from the point marked. [Italian]

dam¹ (dæm) *n.* **1.** a barrier built across a river to create a body of water. **2.** a reservoir of water created by such a barrier. *~vb.* **damming, dammed. 3.** (often foll. by *up*) to restrict by a dam. [prob.

from Middle Low German]

dam² (dæm) *n.* the female parent of an animal, esp. a sheep or horse. [var. of *dame*]

damage ('dæmɪdʒ) *n.* **1.** injury or harm to a person or thing. **2.** *Informal.* cost: *what's the damage?* ~*vb.* **3.** to cause damage to. [Latin *damnum* injury, loss] —'**damaging** *adj.*

damages ('dæmɪdʒɪz) *pl. n. Law.* money to be paid as compensation for injury or loss.

damask ('dæməsk) *n.* **1.** a fabric with a pattern woven into it, used for table linen, curtains, etc. ~*adj.* **2.** greyish-pink. [*Damascus*, where fabric orig. made]

dame (deɪm) *n.* **1.** *Slang, chiefly Scot., U.S., & Canad.* a woman. **2.** *Brit.* the role of a comic old woman in a pantomime, usually played by a man. **3.** (formerly) a woman of rank or dignity; lady. [Latin *domina* lady]

Dame (deɪm) *n.* (in Britain) the title of a woman who has been awarded the Order of the British Empire or another order of chivalry.

damn (dæm) *interj.* **1.** *Slang.* an exclamation of annoyance. ~*adv., adj.* **2.** *Slang.* extreme or extremely: *a damn good pianist.* ~*vb.* **3.** to condemn as bad or worthless. **4.** to curse. **5.** to condemn to hell or eternal punishment. **6.** to prove (someone) guilty: *damning evidence.* **7. damn with faint praise.** to praise so unenthusiastically that the effect is condemnation. ~*n.* **8. not give a damn.** *Informal.* not care. [Latin *damnum* loss, injury]

damnable ('dæmnəb³l) *adj.* hateful; detestable. —'**damnably** *adv.*

damnation (dæm'neɪʃən) *interj.* **1.** an exclamation of anger. ~*n.* **2.** *Theol.* eternal punishment.

damned (dæmd) *adj.* **1.** condemned to hell. ~*adv., adj. Slang.* **2.** extreme or extremely: *a damned good try.* **3.** used to indicate amazement or refusal: *damned if I care.*

damnedest ('dæmdɪst) *n.* **do one's damnedest.** *Informal.* to do one's utmost.

damp (dæmp) *adj.* **1.** slightly wet. ~*n.* **2.** slight wetness; moisture. ~*vb.* **3.** to make slightly wet. **4.** (often foll. by *down*) to stifle or deaden: *to damp one's ardour.* **5.** (often foll. by *down*) to reduce the flow of air to (a fire) to make it burn more slowly. [Middle Low German *damp* steam] —'**damply** *adv.* —'**dampness** *n.*

dampcourse ('dæmp,kɔːs) *n.* a layer of impervious material in a wall, to stop moisture rising.

dampen ('dæmpən) *vb.* **1.** to stifle; deaden. **2.** to make damp.

damper ('dæmpə) *n.* **1. put a damper on.** to produce a depressing or stultifying effect on. **2.** a movable plate to regulate the draught in a stove or furnace. **3.** the pad in a piano or harpsichord that deadens the vibration of each string as its key is released.

damsel ('dæmz³l) *n. Archaic or poetic.* a young woman. [Old French *damoisele*]

damson ('dæmzən) *n.* a small blue-black

edible plumlike fruit that grows on a tree. [Latin *prūnum damascēnum* Damascus plum]

dan (dæn) *n. Judo, karate.* **1.** any of the 10 black-belt grades of proficiency. **2.** a competitor entitled to dan grading. [Japanese]

dance (dɑːns) *vb.* **1.** to move the feet and body rhythmically in time to music. **2.** to perform (a particular dance): *to dance a jig.* **3.** to skip or leap. **4.** to move in a rhythmical way: *the fairy lights danced in the breeze.* **5. dance attendance on someone.** to attend someone solicitously. ~*n.* **6.** a social meeting arranged for dancing. **7.** a series of rhythmical steps and movements in time to music. **8.** a piece of music in the rhythm of a particular dance. [Old French *dancier*] —'**dancer** *n.* —'**dancing** *n., adj.*

D and C *n. Med.* dilatation of the cervix and curettage of the uterus: a minor operation to clear the womb or remove tissue for diagnosis.

dandelion ('dændɪ,laɪən) *n.* a plant with yellow rayed flowers and deeply notched leaves. [Old French *dent de lion* tooth of a lion, referring to its leaves]

dander ('dændə) *n.* **get one's dander up.** *Informal.* to become annoyed or angry. [from *dandruff*]

dandified ('dændɪ,faɪd) *adj.* dressed like or resembling a dandy.

dandle ('dænd³l) *vb.* to move (a young child) up and down on one's knee or in one's arms. [origin unknown]

dandruff ('dændrəf) *n.* loose scales of dry dead skin shed from the scalp. [origin unknown]

dandy ('dændɪ) *n., pl.* **-dies. 1.** a man who is greatly concerned with the elegance of his appearance. ~*adj.* **-dier, -diest. 2.** *Informal.* very good or fine. [origin unknown]

dandy-brush *n.* a stiff brush used for grooming a horse.

Dane (deɪn) *n.* a person from Denmark.

danger ('deɪndʒə) *n.* **1.** the state of being vulnerable to injury or loss; risk. **2.** a person or thing that may cause injury or pain. **3.** a likelihood that something unpleasant will happen. [Middle English *daunger* power, hence power to inflict injury]

danger money *n.* extra money paid to compensate for the risks involved in dangerous jobs.

dangerous ('deɪndʒərəs) *adj.* causing danger; perilous. —'**dangerously** *adv.*

dangle ('dæŋg³l) *vb.* **1.** to hang or cause to hang freely. **2.** to display (something attractive) as an enticement. [prob. imit.]

Danish ('deɪnɪʃ) *adj.* **1.** of Denmark, its people, or their language. ~*n.* **2.** the official language of Denmark.

Danish blue *n.* a white cheese with blue veins.

Danish pastry *n.* a rich puff pastry filled with apple, almond paste, icing, etc.

dank (dæŋk) *adj.* (esp. of cellars or caves)

daphne ('dæfnɪ) n. a shrub with small bell-shaped flowers. [Greek: laurel]

dapper ('dæpə) adj. neat in dress and bearing. [Middle Dutch]

dappled ('dæp²ld) adj. marked with spots of a different colour; mottled. [origin unknown]

dapple-grey n. a horse with a grey coat having spots of a darker colour.

Darby and Joan ('dɑːbɪ; dʒəʊn) n. an elderly happily married couple. [couple in 18th-cent. ballad]

dare (dɛə) vb. 1. to be courageous enough to try (to do something). 2. to challenge (a person to do something) as proof of courage. 3. **I dare say.** a. it is quite possible (that). b. probably. ~n. 4. a challenge to do something as proof of courage. [Old English durran]

daredevil ('dɛə,dɛv²l) n. 1. a recklessly bold person. ~adj. 2. reckless; daring; bold.

daring ('dɛərɪŋ) adj. 1. bold or adventurous. ~n. 2. courage in taking risks; boldness. —'**daringly** adv.

dark (dɑːk) adj. 1. having little or no light. 2. (of a colour) reflecting or transmitting little light: dark brown. 3. (of the complexion or hair) not fair; swarthy; brunette. 4. gloomy. 5. sinister; evil: a dark purpose. 6. unenlightened: a dark period in our history. 7. secret or mysterious. ~n. 8. absence of light; darkness. 9. night or nightfall. 10. **in the dark.** in ignorance. [Old English deorc] —'**darkly** adv. —'**darkness** n.

Dark Continent n. **the.** a term for Africa when it was relatively unexplored by Europeans.

darken ('dɑːkən) vb. 1. to make or become dark or darker. 2. to make angry or sad.

dark horse n. a person who reveals unexpected talents.

darkroom ('dɑːk,ruːm, -,rʊm) n. a room in which photographs are processed in darkness or safe light.

darling ('dɑːlɪŋ) n. 1. a person very much loved. 2. a favourite. ~adj. 3. beloved. 4. pleasing: a darling man. [Old English dēorling]

darn[1] (dɑːn) vb. 1. to mend (a hole or a garment) with a series of interwoven stitches. ~n. 2. a patch of darned work on a garment. [origin unknown]

darn[2] (dɑːn) interj., adj., adv., vb., n. Euphemistic. same as **damn**.

darnel ('dɑːn²l) n. a weed that grows in grain fields. [origin unknown]

dart (dɑːt) n. 1. a small narrow pointed missile that is thrown or shot, as in the game of darts. 2. a sudden quick movement. 3. a tapered tuck made in dressmaking. ~vb. 4. to move or throw swiftly and suddenly. [Germanic] —'**darting** adj.

dartboard ('dɑːt,bɔːd) n. a circular board used as the target in the game of darts.

darts (dɑːts) n. (functioning as sing.) a game in which darts are thrown at a dartboard.

Darwinism ('dɑːwɪn,ɪzəm) or **Darwinian theory** n. the theory of the origin of animal and plant species by evolution. —**Dar'winian** adj., n. —'**Darwinist** n., adj.

dash (dæʃ) vb. 1. to move hastily; rush. 2. to hurl; crash: he dashed the cup to the floor. 3. to frustrate: his hopes were dashed. ~n. 4. a sudden quick movement. 5. a small admixture: a dash of cream. 6. panache; style: he rides with dash. 7. the punctuation mark —, used to indicate a change of subject or to enclose a parenthetical remark. 8. the symbol (–), used in combination with the symbol dot (.) in Morse code. 9. Athletics, chiefly U.S. & Canad. the sprint. ~See also **dash off.** [Middle English daschen, dassen]

dashboard ('dæʃ,bɔːd) n. the instrument panel in a car, boat, or aircraft.

dasher ('dæʃə) n. Canad. the ledge along the top of the boards of an ice hockey rink.

dashing ('dæʃɪŋ) adj. 1. spirited; lively: a dashing young man. 2. stylish; showy.

dash off vb. to write down or finish off hastily.

dassie ('dæsɪ) n. a hyrax, esp. a rock hyrax. [Afrikaans]

dastardly ('dæstədlɪ) adj. mean and cowardly. [Middle English]

dat. dative.

data ('deɪtə, 'dɑːtə) n. 1. a series of observations, measurements, or facts; information. 2. Computers. the numbers, digits, characters, and symbols operated on by a computer. [Latin: (things) given]

data base n. a store of information in a form that can be easily handled by a computer.

data capture n. a process for converting information into a form that can be handled by a computer.

data processing n. a sequence of operations performed on data, esp. by a computer, in order to extract or interpret information.

date[1] (deɪt) n. 1. a specified day of the month. 2. the particular day or year when an event happened. 3. a. an appointment, esp. with a person of the opposite sex. b. the person with whom the appointment is made. 4. **to date.** up to now. ~vb. 5. to mark (a letter, cheque, etc.) with the date. 6. to assign a date of occurrence or creation to. 7. (foll. by from or back to) to have originated (at a specified time). 8. to reveal the age of: that dress dates her. 9. to make or become old-fashioned: good films hardly date at all. 10. Informal, chiefly U.S. & Canad. to be a boyfriend or girlfriend of. [Latin data to give, as in epistula data Romae letter handed over at Rome] —'**dated** adj.

date[2] (deɪt) n. the dark-brown, sweet tasting fruit of the date palm. [Greek daktulos finger]

dateless ('deɪtlɪs) adj. likely to remain

fashionable or interesting regardless of age.

date line *n.* the line approximately following the 180° meridian from Greenwich, on the east side of which the date is one day earlier than on the west.

date palm *n.* a tall palm grown in tropical regions for its fruit.

date stamp *n.* a rubber stamp with movable figures for recording the date.

dative ('deɪtɪv) *n.* in certain languages, including Latin and German, the form of the noun that expresses the indirect object. [Latin *datīvus*]

datum ('deɪtəm, 'dɑːtəm) *n., pl.* **-ta.** a single piece of information; fact. [Latin: something given]

daub (dɔːb) *vb.* **1.** to smear or spread (paint, mud, etc.), esp. carelessly. **2.** to paint (a picture) clumsily or badly. ~*n.* **3.** an unskilful or crude painting. **4.** something daubed on. [Old French *dauber* to paint]

daughter ('dɔːtə) *n.* **1.** a female child. **2.** a girl or woman who comes from a certain place or is connected with a certain thing: *a daughter of the church.* ~(*modifier*) **3.** *Biol.* denoting a cell, chromosome, etc. produced by the division of one of its own kind. **4.** *Physics.* (of a nuclide) formed from another nuclide by radioactive decay. [Old English *dohtor*] —'**daughterly** *adj.*

daughter-in-law *n., pl.* **daughters-in-law.** the wife of one's son.

daunt (dɔːnt) *vb.* to frighten or dishearten. [Latin *domitāre* to tame] —'**daunting** *adj.*

dauntless ('dɔːntlɪs) *adj.* fearless; not discouraged.

dauphin ('dɔːfɪn) *n.* (from 1349–1830) the eldest son of the king of France. [Old French: orig. a family name]

davenport ('dævən,pɔːt) *n.* **1.** *Chiefly Brit.* a writing desk with drawers at the side. **2.** *U.S. & Canad.* a large sofa, esp. one convertible into a bed. [sense 1 supposedly after Captain *Davenport,* who commissioned the first ones]

davit ('dævɪt, 'deɪ-) *n.* a cranelike device on a ship, usually one of a pair, for suspending or lowering a lifeboat. [Anglo-French *daviot* from *Davi* David]

Davy Jones's locker ('deɪvɪ 'dʒəʊnzɪz) *n.* the ocean's bottom, regarded as the grave of those lost or buried at sea. [origin unknown]

Davy lamp *n.* same as **safety lamp.** [after Sir Humphrey *Davy,* chemist]

dawdle ('dɔːd⁰l) *vb.* **1.** to be slow or lag behind. **2.** to waste time. [origin unknown]

dawn (dɔːn) *n.* **1.** daybreak. **2.** the beginning of something. ~*vb.* **3.** to begin to grow light after the night. **4.** to begin to develop or appear. **5.** (usually foll. by *on* or *upon*) to become apparent (to). [Old English *dagian* to dawn]

dawn chorus *n.* the singing of birds at dawn.

day (deɪ) *n.* **1.** the period of 24 hours from one midnight to the next. **2.** the period of light between sunrise and sunset. **3.** the part of a day occupied with regular activity, esp. work. **4.** a period or point in time: *in days gone by; in Shakespeare's day.* **5.** (*often cap.*) a day of special observance: *Christmas Day.* **6.** a time of success or recognition: *his day will come.* **7.** a struggle or issue: *the day is lost.* **8.** **all in a day's work.** part of one's normal activity. **9.** **at the end of the day.** in the final reckoning. **10.** **call it a day.** to stop work or other activity. **11.** **day in, day out.** every day without changing. **12.** **that'll be the day. a.** that is most unlikely to happen. **b.** I look forward to that. [Old English *dæg*]

day bed *n.* a narrow couchlike bed.

daybreak ('deɪ,breɪk) *n.* the time in the morning when light first appears.

daydream ('deɪ,driːm) *n.* **1.** a pleasant fantasy indulged in while awake. ~*vb.* **2.** to indulge in idle fantasy. —'**day,dreamer** *n.*

daylight ('deɪ,laɪt) *n.* **1.** light from the sun. **2.** daytime. **3.** daybreak. **4.** **see daylight.** to realize that the end of a difficult task is approaching. ~See also **daylights.**

daylight robbery *n. Informal.* blatant overcharging.

daylights ('deɪ,laɪts) *pl. n.* **1.** **beat the living daylights out of someone.** to beat someone soundly. **2.** **scare the living daylights out of someone.** to frighten someone greatly.

daylight-saving time *n.* time set one hour ahead of the local standard time, to provide extra daylight in the evening in summer.

day release *n. Brit.* a system whereby workers go to college one day a week for vocational training.

day return *n.* a reduced fare for a train or bus journey travelling both ways in one day.

day room *n.* a communal living room in a residential institution, such as a hospital.

day-to-day *adj.* routine; everyday.

daze (deɪz) *vb.* **1.** to stun, esp. by a blow or shock. ~*n.* **2.** a state of confusion or shock: *in a daze.* [Old Norse]

dazzle ('dæz⁰l) *vb.* **1.** to blind temporarily by sudden excessive light. **2.** to amaze, as with brilliance. ~*n.* **3.** bright light that dazzles. [from *daze*] —'**dazzling** *adj.* —'**dazzlingly** *adv.*

dB *or* **db** decibel(s).

DBE Dame Commander of the Order of the British Empire.

DC **1.** *Music.* da capo. **2.** direct current. **3.** District of Columbia.

DCB Dame Commander of the Order of the Bath.

DCM *Brit. mil.* Distinguished Conduct Medal.

DD Doctor of Divinity.

D-day *n.* the day selected for the start of some operation. [after *D(ay)-day,* the day of the Allied invasion of Europe on June 6, 1944]

DDR Deutsche Demokratische Republik (East Germany; GDR).

DDS *or* **DDSc** Doctor of Dental Surgery *or* Science.

DDT *n.* dichlorodiphenyltrichloroethane; an insecticide.

DE Delaware.

de- *prefix.* indicating: **1.** removal: *deforest; dethrone.* **2.** reversal: *decode; desegregate.* **3.** departure from: *decamp.* [Latin]

deacon ('di:kən) *n. Christianity.* **1.** (in episcopal churches) an ordained minister ranking immediately below a priest. **2.** (in some Protestant churches) a lay official who assists the minister. [Greek *diakonos* servant]

deaconess ('di:kənɪs) *n. Christianity.* a female member of the laity with duties similar to those of a deacon.

deactivate (di:'æktɪ̩veɪt) *vb.* **1.** to make (an explosive device) inoperative. **2.** to become less radioactive.

dead (dɛd) *adj.* **1.** no longer alive. **2.** inanimate. **3.** no longer in use or relevant: *a dead issue; a dead language.* **4.** unresponsive. **5.** (of a limb) numb. **6.** no longer burning: *dead coals.* **7.** complete: *a dead stop.* **8.** *Informal.* very tired. **9.** (of a place) lacking activity. **10.** *Electronics.* **a.** drained of electric charge. **b.** not connected to a source of electric charge. **11.** *Sport.* (of a ball) out of play. **12. dead from the neck up.** *Informal.* stupid. **13. dead to the world.** *Informal.* fast asleep; in a drunken stupor. ~*n.* **14.** a period during which coldness or darkness is most intense: *the dead of winter.* ~*adv.* **15.** extremely: *dead easy.* **16.** suddenly: *stop dead.* **17. dead on.** exactly right. [Old English]

deadbeat ('dɛd̩bi:t) *n. Informal, chiefly U.S. & Canad.* a lazy or socially undesirable person.

dead beat *adj. Informal.* exhausted.

dead duck *n. Slang.* something that is doomed to failure.

deaden ('dɛd̩n) *vb.* **1.** to make less sensitive, intense, or lively. **2.** to make less resonant. —'**deadening** *adj.*

dead end *n.* **1.** a cul-de-sac. **2.** a situation in which further progress is impossible.

deadhead ('dɛd̩hɛd) *U.S. & Canad.* ~*n.* **1.** *Informal.* a person who uses a free ticket, as for the theatre. **2.** *Informal.* a commercial vehicle travelling empty. **3.** *Slang.* a dull person. **4.** a log sticking out of the water. ~*vb.* **5.** *Informal.* to drive (an empty commercial vehicle). **6.** to remove dead flower heads from plants.

dead heat *n.* a tie for first place between two or more participants in a race or contest.

dead letter *n.* a law or rule that is no longer enforced.

deadline ('dɛd̩laɪn) *n.* a time limit.

deadlock ('dɛd̩lɒk) *n.* **1.** a state of affairs in which further action between two opposing forces is impossible. ~*vb.* **2.** to bring to a deadlock.

dead loss *n. Informal.* a useless person or thing.

deadly ('dɛdlɪ) *adj.* **-lier, -liest. 1.** likely to cause death. **2.** *Informal.* extremely boring. ~*adv., adj.* **3.** like or suggestive of death. **4.** extremely.

deadly nightshade *n.* a poisonous plant with purple bell-shaped flowers and black berries.

dead man's handle *or* **pedal** *n.* a safety switch on a piece of machinery that allows operation only while depressed by the operator.

dead march *n.* solemn funeral music played to accompany a procession.

dead marine *n. Austral. & N.Z. informal.* an empty beer bottle.

dead-nettle *n.* a plant with leaves resembling nettles but lacking stinging hairs.

deadpan ('dɛd̩pæn) *adj., adv.* with a deliberately emotionless face or manner.

dead reckoning *n.* a method of establishing one's position using the distance and direction travelled.

dead set *adv.* **1.** absolutely: *he is dead set against going to Spain.* ~*n.* **2.** a serious attempt or effort.

dead weight *n.* **1.** a heavy weight or load. **2.** the difference between the loaded and the unloaded weights of a ship.

dead wood *n. Informal.* a useless person or persons.

deaf (dɛf) *adj.* **1.** unable to hear. **2. deaf to.** refusing to listen or take notice of. [Old English] —'**deafness** *n.*

deaf-and-dumb *adj. Offensive.* unable to hear or speak.

deafen ('dɛf°n) *vb.* to make deaf, esp. momentarily by a loud noise. —'**deafeningly** *adv.*

deaf-mute *n.* a person who is unable to hear or speak.

deal[1] (di:l) *vb.* **dealing, dealt. 1.** (often foll. by *out*) to apportion or distribute. **2.** to inflict (a blow) on. **3.** *Slang.* to sell any illegal drug. **4. deal in.** to engage in commercially. ~*n.* **5.** a transaction or agreement. **6.** a particular type of treatment received: *a fair deal.* **7.** a large amount (esp. in a **good** or **great deal**). **8.** *Cards.* a player's turn to distribute the cards. **9. big deal.** *Slang.* an important matter: often used sarcastically. ~*See also* **deal with.** [Old English *dǣlan*] —'**dealer** *n.*

deal[2] (di:l) *n.* **1.** a plank of softwood timber. **2.** the sawn wood of various coniferous trees. [Middle Low German *dele* plank]

dealignment ('di:ə̩laɪnmənt) *n.* the process by which voters abandon traditional loyalties to a political party or social class.

dealings ('di:lɪŋz) *pl. n.* transactions or business relations.

dealt (dɛlt) *vb.* past of **deal**[1].

deal with *vb.* **1.** to take action on: *to deal with each problem in turn.* **2.** to be concerned with: *the book deals with architecture.* **3.** to do business with.

dean (di:n) *n.* **1.** the chief administrative

official of a college or university faculty. **2.** *Chiefly Church of England.* the chief administrator of a cathedral or collegiate church. [Late Latin *decānus* one set over ten persons]

deanery (ˈdiːnərɪ) *n., pl.* **-eries. 1.** the office or residence of a dean. **2.** the parishes presided over by a rural dean.

dear (dɪə) *adj.* **1.** beloved; precious. **2.** used in conventional forms of address, as in *Dear Sir.* **3. a.** highly priced. **b.** charging high prices. **4. dear to.** important or close to. ~*interj.* **5.** used in exclamations of surprise or dismay, such as *Oh dear!* ~*n.* **6.** (*often used in direct address*) someone regarded with affection. ~*adv.* **7.** dearly. [Old English *dēore*] —ˈ**dearly** *adv.*

dearth (dɜːθ) *n.* an inadequate amount; scarcity. [Middle English *derthe*]

death (dɛθ) *n.* **1.** the permanent end of all functions of life in an organism. **2.** an instance of this: *his death ended an era.* **3.** ending or destruction. **4.** (*usually cap.*) a personification of death, usually a skeleton holding a scythe. **5. at death's door.** likely to die soon. **6. catch one's death (of cold).** *Informal.* to contract a severe cold. **7. like death warmed up.** *Informal.* very ill. **8. put to death.** to execute. **9. to death. a.** until dead. **b.** very much. [Old English]

deathbed (ˈdɛθˌbɛd) *n.* the bed in which a person dies or is about to die.

deathblow (ˈdɛθˌbləʊ) *n.* a thing or event that destroys hope, esp. suddenly.

death certificate *n.* a document issued by a medical practitioner certifying the death of a person and stating the cause if known.

death duty *n.* a tax on property inheritances, in Britain replaced by capital transfer tax since 1975.

deathless (ˈdɛθlɪs) *adj.* immortal, esp. because of greatness.

deathly (ˈdɛθlɪ) *adj.* **1.** resembling death: *a deathly quiet.* **2.** deadly.

death rate *n.* the ratio of deaths in an area or group to the population of that area or group.

death's-head *n.* a human skull or a representation of one.

deathtrap (ˈdɛθˌtræp) *n.* a place or vehicle considered very unsafe.

death warrant *n.* **1.** the official authorization for carrying out a sentence of death. **2. sign one's (own) death warrant.** to cause one's own destruction.

deathwatch beetle (ˈdɛθˌwɒtʃ) *n.* a beetle that bores into wood and produces a tapping sound.

deb (dɛb) *n. Informal.* a debutante.

debacle (deɪˈbɑːkᵊl, dɪ-) *n.* a disastrous collapse or defeat; rout. [French]

debag (diːˈbæg) *vb.* **-bagging, -bagged.** *Brit. slang.* to remove the trousers from (someone) by force.

debar (dɪˈbɑː) *vb.* **-barring, -barred.** to exclude; bar. —de'**barment** *n.*

debase (dɪˈbeɪs) *vb.* to lower in quality, character, or value; adulterate. [see DE-, BASE²] —de'**basement** *n.*

debate (dɪˈbeɪt) *n.* **1.** a formal discussion, as in a legislative body, in which opposing arguments are put forward. **2.** discussion. ~*vb.* **3.** to discuss (a motion), esp. in a formal assembly. **4.** to deliberate upon (a course of action). [Old French *debatre*] —de'**batable** *adj.*

debauch (dɪˈbɔːtʃ) *n.* an instance of extreme dissipation. [Old French *desbaucher* to corrupt] —de'**bauchery** *n.*

debauched (dɪˈbɔːtʃt) *adj.* leading a life of depraved self-indulgence.

debenture (dɪˈbɛntʃə) *n.* a long-term bond, bearing fixed interest and usually unsecured, issued by a company or governmental agency. [Latin *dēbentur mihi* there are owed to me] —de'**bentured** *adj.*

debenture stock *n.* shares issued by a company, guaranteeing a fixed return at regular intervals.

debilitate (dɪˈbɪlɪˌteɪt) *vb.* to make feeble; weaken. [Latin *dēbilis* weak] —de,bili'**tation** *n.*

debility (dɪˈbɪlɪtɪ) *n., pl.* **-ties.** weakness or infirmity.

debit (ˈdɛbɪt) *n.* **1.** acknowledgment of a sum owing by entry on the left side of an account. ~*vb.* **2. a.** to record (an item) as a debit in an account. **b.** to charge (an account) with a debt. [Latin *dēbitum* debt]

debonair *or* **debonnaire** (ˌdɛbəˈnɛə) *adj.* **1.** suave and refined. **2.** carefree and cheerful. [Old French]

debouch (dɪˈbaʊtʃ) *vb.* **1.** (esp. of troops) to move into a more open space. **2.** (of a river, glacier, etc.) to flow into a larger area or body. [Old French *dé-* from + *bouche* mouth] —de'**bouchment** *n.*

debrief (diːˈbriːf) *vb.* to elicit a report from (a soldier, diplomat, etc.) after a mission or event. —de'**briefing** *n.*

debris *or* **débris** (ˈdeɪbriː, ˈdɛbrɪ) *n.* **1.** fragments of something destroyed; rubble. **2.** a collection of loose material derived from rocks. [French]

debt (dɛt) *n.* **1.** something owed, esp. money. **2. bad debt.** a debt that has little prospect of being paid. **3.** the state of owing something (esp. in **in debt, in someone's debt**). [Latin *dēbitum*]

debt of honour *n.* a debt that is morally but not legally binding.

debtor (ˈdɛtə) *n.* a person who owes a financial obligation.

debug (diːˈbʌg) *vb.* **-bugging, -bugged.** *Informal.* **1.** to remove concealed microphones from (a room). **2.** to locate and remove defects in (a device or system). **3.** to remove insects from.

debunk (diːˈbʌŋk) *vb. Informal.* to expose the pretensions or falseness of. [DE- + BUNK²]

debut (ˈdeɪbjuː, ˈdɛbjuː) *n.* the first public appearance of a performer.

debutante (ˈdɛbjuˌtɑːnt, -ˌtænt) *n.* a young upper-class woman who is formally presented to society. [French]

Dec. December.

decade ('dɛkeɪd) *n.* **1.** a period of ten years. **2.** a group of ten. [Greek *deka* ten]

decadence ('dɛkədəns) *n.* a state of deterioration of morality or culture. [Medieval Latin *dēcadentia* a falling away] —'**decadent** *adj., n.*

decaffeinated (diː'kæfɪˌneɪtɪd) *adj.* (of coffee, etc.) with caffeine removed.

decagon ('dɛkəˌgon) *n.* a polygon with ten sides. [Greek *deka* ten + *gōnia* angle] —**decagonal** (dɪ'kægən⁷l) *adj.*

decahedron (ˌdɛkə'hiːdrən) *n.* a solid figure with ten plane faces. [Greek *deka* ten + *hedra* base] —ˌdeca'**hedral** *adj.*

decalitre *or U.S.* **decaliter** ('dɛkəˌliːtə) *n.* a measure of volume equivalent to 10 litres.

Decalogue ('dɛkəˌlog) *n.* same as **Ten Commandments.** [Greek *deka* ten + *logos* word]

decametre *or U.S.* **decameter** ('dɛkəˌmiːtə) *n.* a measure of length equivalent to 10 metres.

decamp (dɪ'kæmp) *vb.* **1.** to depart secretly or suddenly. **2.** to leave a camp; break camp.

decant (dɪ'kænt) *vb.* **1.** to pour (a liquid, esp. wine) from one container to another. **2.** to rehouse (people) while their homes are being refurbished. [Medieval Latin *de-* from + *canthus* spout, rim]

decanter (dɪ'kæntə) *n.* a stoppered bottle into which a drink is poured for serving.

decapitate (dɪ'kæpɪˌteɪt) *vb.* to behead. [Latin *de-* from + *caput* head] —deˌcapi-'**tation** *n.*

decapod ('dɛkəˌpod) *n.* **1.** a creature such as a crab or lobster, which has five pairs of walking limbs. **2.** a creature such as a squid or cuttlefish, which has eight short tentacles and two longer ones. [Greek *deka* ten + *pous* foot]

decarbonize *or* **-ise** (diː'kɑːbəˌnaɪz) *vb.* to remove carbon from (an internal-combustion engine). —deˌcarboni'**zation** *or* **-i'sation** *n.*

decathlon (dɪ'kæθlon) *n.* an athletic contest in which each athlete competes in ten different events: 100m sprint, long jump, shot put, high jump, 400m, 110m hurdles, discus, pole vault, javelin, and 1500m. [Greek *deka* ten + *athlon* contest] —de'**cathlete** *n.*

decay (dɪ'keɪ) *vb.* **1.** to decline gradually in health, prosperity, or excellence; deteriorate. **2.** to rot or cause to rot. **3.** *Physics.* (of an atomic nucleus) to undergo radioactive disintegration. ~*n.* **4.** the process of decline, as in health or mentality. **5.** the state brought about by this process. **6.** *Physics.* disintegration of a nucleus, occurring spontaneously or as a result of electron capture. [Latin *de-* from + *cadere* to fall]

decease (dɪ'siːs) *n. Formal.* death. [Latin *dēcēdere* to depart]

deceased (dɪ'siːst) *adj.* **a.** *Formal.* dead. **b.** (*as n.*): *the deceased.*

deceit (dɪ'siːt) *n.* behaviour intended to deceive.

deceitful (dɪ'siːtful) *adj.* full of deceit.

deceive (dɪ'siːv) *vb.* **1.** to mislead by lying. **2. deceive oneself.** to delude oneself. **3.** to be unfaithful to (one's sexual partner). [Latin *dēcipere* to ensnare, cheat]

decelerate (diː'sɛləˌreɪt) *vb.* to slow down. [*de-* + (*ac*)*celerate*] —deˌceler'a-**tion** *n.*

December (dɪ'sɛmbə) *n.* the twelfth month of the year. [Latin: the tenth month (the Roman year began with March)]

decencies ('diːsənsɪz) *pl. n.* generally accepted standards of good behaviour.

decency ('diːsənsɪ) *n.* conformity to the prevailing standards of what is right.

decennial (dɪ'sɛnɪəl) *adj.* **1.** lasting for ten years. **2.** occurring every ten years.

decent ('diːs⁷nt) *adj.* **1.** polite or respectable. **2.** proper; fitting. **3.** conforming to conventions of sexual behaviour. **4.** good or adequate: *a decent wage.* **5.** *Informal.* kind; generous. [Latin *decēns* suitable] —'**decently** *adv.*

decentralize *or* **-ise** (diː'sɛntrəˌlaɪz) *vb.* to reorganize into smaller more autonomous units. —deˌcentrali'**zation** *or* **-i'sation** *n.*

deception (dɪ'sɛpʃən) *n.* **1.** the act of deceiving someone or the state of being deceived. **2.** something that deceives; trick.

deceptive (dɪ'sɛptɪv) *adj.* likely or designed to deceive. —de'**ceptively** *adv.* —de'**ceptiveness** *n.*

deci- *prefix.* one tenth: *decimetre.* [Latin *decimus* tenth]

decibel ('dɛsɪˌbɛl) *n.* a unit for measuring the intensity of a sound. [see DECI-, BEL]

decide (dɪ'saɪd) *vb.* **1.** (foll. by *on* or *about*) to reach a decision: *decide what you want; he decided to go.* **2.** to cause to reach a decision. **3.** to settle (a contest or question). **4.** (foll. by *for* or *against*) to pronounce a formal verdict. [Latin *dēcīdere* to cut off]

decided (dɪ'saɪdɪd) *adj.* **1.** unmistakable. **2.** determined; resolute. —de'**cidedly** *adv.*

deciduous (dɪ'sɪdjʊəs) *adj.* **1.** (of a tree) shedding all leaves annually. **2.** (of antlers or teeth) being shed at the end of a period of growth. [Latin: falling off]

decilitre *or U.S.* **deciliter** ('dɛsɪˌliːtə) *n.* a measure of volume equivalent to one-tenth of a litre.

decimal ('dɛsɪməl) *n.* **1.** a fraction with an unwritten denominator of a power of ten. It is indicated by a decimal point before the numerator: $\cdot 2 = \frac{2}{10}$. ~*adj.* **2.** relating to or using powers of ten. **3.** expressed as a decimal. [Latin *decima* a tenth]

decimal currency *n.* a system of currency in which the units are parts or powers of ten.

decimalize *or* **-ise** ('dɛsɪməˌlaɪz) *vb.* to change (a system or number) to the decimal system. —ˌdecimali'**zation** *or* **-i'sation** *n.*

decimal point *n.* the dot between the

unit and the fraction of a number in the decimal system.

decimal system *n.* a number system in general use with a base of ten, in which numbers are expressed by combinations of the digits 0 to 9.

decimate ('dɛsɪˌmeɪt) *vb.* to destroy or kill a large proportion of. [Latin *decimāre*] —ˌdeci'mation *n.*

decimetre *or U.S.* **decimeter** ('dɛsɪˌmiːtə) *n.* one tenth of a metre.

decipher (dɪ'saɪfə) *vb.* **1.** to make out the meaning of (something obscure or illegible). **2.** to convert from code into plain text. —de'cipherable *adj.*

decision (dɪ'sɪʒən) *n.* **1.** a judgment, conclusion, or resolution. **2.** the act of making up one's mind. **3.** firmness of purpose or character. [Latin *decisio* a cutting off]

decisive (dɪ'saɪsɪv) *adj.* **1.** influential; conclusive. **2.** having the ability to make decisions, esp. quickly. —de'cisively *adv.* —de'cisiveness *n.*

deck (dɛk) *n.* **1.** an area of a ship that forms a floor, at any level. **2.** a similar area in a bus. **3. a.** the platform that supports the turntable and pick-up of a record player. **b.** same as **tape deck. 4.** *Chiefly U.S.* a pack of (playing cards). **5.** *Computers.* a collection of punched cards relevant to a particular program. **6. clear the decks.** *Informal.* to prepare for action, as by removing obstacles. ~*vb.* **7.** (often foll. by *out*) to dress or decorate. [Middle Dutch *dec* a covering]

deck chair *n.* a folding chair consisting of a wooden frame suspending a length of canvas.

deck hand *n.* a seaman assigned duties on the deck of a ship.

deckle edge ('dɛk'l) *n.* a rough edge on paper, often left as ornamentation. [the *deckle* is the frame that holds the pulp in paper making] —'deckle-'edged *adj.*

declaim (dɪ'kleɪm) *vb.* **1.** to make (a speech) loudly and dramatically. **2. declaim against.** to protest against loudly and publicly. [Latin *dēclāmāre*] —declamation (ˌdɛklə'meɪʃən) *n.* —declamatory (dɪ'klæmətrɪ) *adj.*

declaration (ˌdɛklə'reɪʃən) *n.* **1.** an emphatic statement. **2.** a formal announcement. —declaratory (dɪ'klærətrɪ) *adj.*

declare (dɪ'klɛə) *vb.* **1.** to announce publicly or officially: *war was declared.* **2.** to state officially that (a person, fact, etc.) is as specified: *he declared him fit.* **3.** to state emphatically. **4.** (often foll. by *for* or *against*) to make known one's opinion. **5.** to acknowledge (dutiable goods or income) for tax purposes. **6.** *Cards.* to decide (the trump suit) by making the winning bid. **7.** *Cricket.* to close an innings voluntarily before all ten wickets have fallen. [Latin *dēclārāre* to make clear]

declassify (diː'klæsɪˌfaɪ) *vb.* -fying, -fied. to release (a document or information) from the security list. —deˌclassifi'cation *n.*

declension (dɪ'klɛnʃən) *n.* *Grammar.* changes in the form of nouns, pronouns, or adjectives to show case, number, and gender. [Latin *dēclīnātiō* a bending aside, hence variation]

declination (ˌdɛklɪ'neɪʃən) *n.* **1.** *Astron.* the angular distance of a star or planet north or south from the celestial equator. **2.** the angle made by a compass needle with the direction of the geographical north pole.

decline (dɪ'klaɪn) *vb.* **1.** to refuse, esp. politely. **2.** to grow smaller; diminish. **3.** *Grammar.* to list the inflections of (a noun, pronoun, or adjective). ~*n.* **4.** gradual deterioration or loss. **5.** a movement downward; diminution. **6.** *Archaic.* a slowly progressive disease, such as tuberculosis. [Latin *dēclīnāre* to bend away]

declivity (dɪ'klɪvɪtɪ) *n., pl.* -ties. a downward slope. [Latin *dēclīvitās*] —de'clivitous *adj.*

declutch (diː'klʌtʃ) *vb.* to disengage the clutch of a motor vehicle.

decoct (dɪ'kɒkt) *vb.* to extract the essence from (a substance) by boiling. [Latin *dēcoquere* to boil down] —de'coction *n.*

decode (diː'kəʊd) *vb.* to convert from code into ordinary language. —de'coder *n.*

decoke (diː'kəʊk) *vb.* same as **decarbonize.**

décolletage (ˌdeɪkɒl'tɑːʒ) *n.* a low-cut dress or neckline. [French]

décolleté (deɪ'kɒlteɪ) *adj.* (of a woman's garment) low-cut. [French]

decompose (ˌdiːkəm'pəʊz) *vb.* **1.** to rot. **2.** to break up constituent parts. —decomposition (ˌdiːkɒmpə'zɪʃən) *n.*

decompress (ˌdiːkəm'prɛs) *vb.* **1.** to relieve of pressure. **2.** to return (a diver) to normal atmospheric pressure. —ˌdecom'pression *n.*

decompression sickness *n.* a condition of severe pain and difficulty in breathing caused by a sudden change in atmospheric pressure.

decongestant (ˌdiːkən'dʒɛstənt) *n.* a drug that relieves nasal congestion.

decontaminate (ˌdiːkən'tæmɪˌneɪt) *vb.* to render harmless by the removal of poisons, radioactivity, etc. —ˌdeconˌtami'nation *n.*

décor *or* **decor** ('deɪkɔː) *n.* a style or scheme of interior decoration and furnishings in a room or house. [French]

decorate ('dɛkəˌreɪt) *vb.* **1.** to ornament; adorn. **2.** to paint or wallpaper. **3.** to confer a mark of distinction, esp. a medal, upon. [Latin *decorāre*] —'decorative *adj.* —'decoˌrator *n.*

Decorated style *n.* a 14th-century style of English architecture characterized by geometrical tracery and floral decoration.

decoration (ˌdɛkə'reɪʃən) *n.* **1.** an addition that makes something more attractive or ornate. **2.** the way in which a room or building is decorated. **3.** something, esp. a medal, conferred as a mark of honour.

decorous ('dɛkərəs) *adj.* polite, calm, and sensible in behaviour. [Latin *decōrus*] —'decorously *adv.* —'decorousness *n.*

decorum (dɪˈkɔːrəm) *n.* decorous behaviour.

decoy *n.* (ˈdiːkɔɪ, dɪˈkɔɪ). **1.** a person or thing used to lure someone into danger. **2.** an image of a bird or animal, used to lure game into a trap or within shooting range. ~*vb.* (dɪˈkɔɪ). **3.** to lure by or as if by means of a decoy. [prob. from Dutch *de kooi* the cage]

decrease *vb.* (dɪˈkriːs). **1.** to diminish or cause to diminish in size, strength, or quantity. ~*n.* (ˈdiːkriːs, dɪˈkriːs). **2.** a diminution; reduction. **3.** the amount by which something has been diminished. [Latin *dēcrescere* to grow less] —**deˈcreasingly** *adv.*

decree (dɪˈkriː) *n.* **1.** a law made by someone in authority. **2.** a judgment of a court. ~*vb.* **decreeing, decreed. 3.** to order by decree. [Latin *dēcrētum* ordinance]

decree absolute *n.* the final decree in divorce proceedings, which leaves the parties free to remarry.

decree nisi (ˈnaɪsaɪ) *n.* a provisional decree in divorce proceedings, which will later be made absolute unless cause is shown why it should not. [Latin *nisi* unless]

decrepit (dɪˈkrɛpɪt) *adj.* weakened or worn out by age or long use. [Latin *crepāre* to creak] —**deˈcrepiˌtude** *n.*

decrescendo (ˌdiːkrɪˈʃɛndəʊ) *n., adv.* same as **diminuendo.** [Italian]

decretal (dɪˈkriːtˀl) *n.* R.C. Church. a papal decree. [Late Latin *dēcrētālis*]

decry (dɪˈkraɪ) *vb.* **-crying, -cried.** to express open disapproval of. [Old French *descrier*]

dedicate (ˈdɛdɪˌkeɪt) *vb.* **1.** (often foll. by *to*) to devote (oneself, one's time, etc.) wholly to a special purpose or cause. **2.** (foll. by *to*) to address a book, etc., to a person as a token of affection or respect. **3.** (foll. by *to*) to play (a record) on radio for someone as a greeting. **4.** to set apart for sacred uses. [Latin *dēdicāre* to announce]

dedicated (ˈdɛdɪˌkeɪtɪd) *adj.* **1.** devoted to a particular purpose or cause. **2.** *Computers.* designed to fulfil one function.

dedication (ˌdɛdɪˈkeɪʃən) *n.* **1.** wholehearted devotion. **2.** an inscription in a book dedicating it to a person.

deduce (dɪˈdjuːs) *vb.* to work out; infer. [Latin *de-* away + *dūcere* to lead] —**deˈducible** *adj.*

deduct (dɪˈdʌkt) *vb.* to subtract (a number, quantity, or part). [Latin *dēdūcere* to deduce]

deductible (dɪˈdʌktɪbˀl) *adj.* **1.** capable of being deducted. **2.** *U.S.* tax-deductible.

deduction (dɪˈdʌkʃən) *n.* **1.** the act or process of deducting or subtracting. **2.** something that is deducted. **3.** *Logic.* **a.** a process of reasoning by which a conclusion necessarily follows from a set of general premises. **b.** a conclusion reached by this process. —**deˈductive** *adj.*

deed (diːd) *n.* **1.** something that is done or performed; act. **2.** a notable achievement.

3. action as opposed to words. **4.** *Law.* a legal document, esp. to effect a conveyance or transfer of property. [Old English *dēd*]

deed box *n.* a strong box in which deeds and other documents are kept.

deed poll *n.* *Law.* a deed made by one party only, esp. to change one's name.

deejay (ˈdiːˌdʒeɪ) *n. Informal.* a disc jockey. [from the initials *DJ* (disc jockey)]

deem (diːm) *vb.* to judge or consider: *take whatever measures are deemed necessary.* [Old English *dēman*]

deemster (ˈdiːmstə) *n.* either of the two justices in the Isle of Man.

deep (diːp) *adj.* **1.** extending or situated far down from a surface: *a deep pool.* **2.** extending or situated far inwards, backwards, or sideways. **3.** of a specified dimension downwards, inwards, or backwards: *six feet deep.* **4.** coming from or penetrating to a great depth. **5.** difficult to understand. **6.** of great intensity: *deep trouble.* **7.** deep in. immersed in: *deep in study.* **8.** (of a colour) intense or dark. **9.** low in pitch: *a deep voice.* **10.** go off the deep end. *Informal.* to lose one's temper. **11.** in deep water. *Informal.* in a tricky position or in trouble. ~*n.* **12.** any deep place on land or under water. **13.** the deep. **a.** *Poetic.* the ocean. **b.** *Cricket.* the area of the field relatively far from the pitch. **14.** the most profound, intense, or central part: *the deep of winter.* ~*adv.* **15.** late: *deep into the night.* **16.** profoundly or intensely. [Old English *dēop*] —**ˈdeeply** *adv.*

deepen (ˈdiːpˀn) *vb.* to make or become deeper or more intense.

deep-freeze *n.* **1.** same as **freezer.** ~*vb.* **-freezing, -froze, -frozen. 2.** to freeze or keep in a deep-freeze.

deep-laid *adj.* (of a plan) carefully worked out and kept secret.

deep-rooted *or* **deep-seated** *adj.* (of ideas, beliefs, etc.) firmly fixed or held.

deer (dɪə) *n., pl.* **deer** *or* **deers.** a hoofed ruminant mammal with antlers in the male. [Old English *dēor* beast]

deerstalker (ˈdɪəˌstɔːkə) *n.* a hat, peaked in front and behind, with earflaps.

de-escalate (diːˈɛskəˌleɪt) *vb.* to reduce the intensity of (a problem or situation). —**de-ˌescaˈlation** *n.*

def (dɛf) *adj.* **deffer, deffest.** *Slang.* very good. [perhaps from *definitive*]

deface (dɪˈfeɪs) *vb.* to spoil the surface or appearance of; disfigure. —**deˈfacement** *n.*

de facto (deɪ ˈfæktəʊ) *adv.* **1.** in fact. ~*adj.* **2.** existing in fact, whether legally recognized or not. [Latin]

defalcate (ˈdiːfælˌkeɪt) *vb. Law.* to misappropriate funds entrusted to one. [Medieval Latin *dēfalcāre* to cut off] —**ˌdefalˈcation** *n.*

defame (dɪˈfeɪm) *vb.* to attack the good reputation of. [Latin *diffāmāre* to spread by unfavourable report] —**defamation** (ˌdɛfəˈmeɪʃən) *n.* —**defamatory** (dɪˈfæmətrɪ) *adj.*

default (dɪˈfɔːlt) n. **1.** a failure to do something, esp. to meet a financial obligation or to appear in court. **2. by default.** because of lack of prevention or opposition. **3. in default of.** in the absence of. ~vb. **4.** (often foll. by on or in) to fail to fulfil an obligation, esp. to make payment when due. [Old French defaillir to fail]

defeat (dɪˈfiːt) vb. **1.** to overcome; win a victory over. **2.** to thwart or frustrate. ~n. **3.** the act of defeating or state of being defeated. [Old French desfaire to undo, ruin]

defeatism (dɪˈfiːtɪzəm) n. a ready acceptance or expectation of defeat. —deˈfeatist n., adj.

defecate (ˈdɛfɪˌkeɪt) vb. to discharge waste from the body through the anus. [Latin dēfaecāre] —ˌdefeˈcation n.

defect n. (ˈdiːfɛkt). **1.** an imperfection or blemish. ~vb. (dɪˈfɛkt). **2.** to desert one's country or cause to join the opposing forces. [Latin dēficere to forsake, fail] —deˈfection n. —deˈfector n.

defective (dɪˈfɛktɪv) adj. having a flaw; imperfect.

defence or U.S. **defense** (dɪˈfɛns) n. **1.** resistance against attack. **2.** something that provides such resistance. **3.** a plea, essay, etc., in support of something. **4.** a country's military resources. **5.** Law. a defendant's denial of the truth of a charge. **6.** Law. the defendant and his legal advisers collectively. **7.** Sport. (usually preceded by the) the players in a team whose function is to prevent the opposing team from scoring. **8.** (pl.) fortifications. [Latin dēfendere to defend] —deˈfenceless or U.S. deˈfenseless adj.

defend (dɪˈfɛnd) vb. **1.** to protect from harm or danger. **2.** to support in the face of criticism, esp. by argument. **3.** to represent (a defendant) in court. **4.** to protect (a title or championship) against a challenge. [Latin dēfendere to ward off] —deˈfender n.

defendant (dɪˈfɛndənt) n. a person against whom an action is brought in a court of law.

defensible (dɪˈfɛnsɪbˈl) adj. capable of being defended because believed to be right.

defensive (dɪˈfɛnsɪv) adj. **1.** intended for defence. **2.** rejecting criticisms of oneself. ~n. **3. on the defensive.** in a position of defence, as in being ready to reject criticism. —deˈfensively adv.

defer¹ (dɪˈfɜː) vb. -ferring, -ferred. to delay (something) until a future time; postpone. [Old French differer to be different, postpone] —deˈferment or deˈferral n.

defer² (dɪˈfɜː) vb. -ferring, -ferred. (foll. by to) to yield (to) or comply with the wishes (of). [Latin dēferre to bear down]

deference (ˈdɛfərəns) n. **1.** compliance with the wishes of another. **2.** courteous regard; respect.

deferential (ˌdɛfəˈrɛnʃəl) adj. showing respect. —ˌdeferˈentially adv.

defiance (dɪˈfaɪəns) n. open resistance to authority or opposition. —deˈfiant adj.

deficiency (dɪˈfɪʃənsɪ) n., pl. -cies. **1.** the state of being deficient. **2.** a lack or shortage.

deficiency disease n. any condition, such as scurvy, produced by a lack of vitamins or other essential substances.

deficient (dɪˈfɪʃənt) adj. **1.** lacking some essential. **2.** inadequate in quantity or quality. [Latin dēficere to fall short]

deficit (ˈdɛfɪsɪt, dɪˈfɪsɪt) n. the amount by which a sum is lower than that expected or required. [Latin: there is lacking]

defile¹ (dɪˈfaɪl) vb. **1.** to make (something) filthy or polluted. **2.** to violate or damage (something holy or respected). [Old French defouler to trample underfoot, abuse] —deˈfilement n.

defile² (ˈdiːfaɪl, dɪˈfaɪl) n. **1.** a narrow pass or gorge. ~vb. **2.** to march in single file. [French défiler to file off]

define (dɪˈfaɪn) vb. **1.** to state precisely the meaning of. **2.** to describe the nature of. **3.** (often passive) to show clearly the outline of. **4.** to fix with precision; specify. [Latin dēfīnīre to set bounds to] —deˈfinable adj.

definite (ˈdɛfɪnɪt) adj. **1.** clear and exact in meaning. **2.** having precise limits. **3.** known for certain. [Latin dēfīnītus limited, distinct] —ˈdefinitely adv.

definite article n. Grammar. the word "the".

definition (ˌdɛfɪˈnɪʃən) n. **1.** a statement of the meaning of a word or phrase. **2.** a description of the essential qualities of something. **3.** the quality of being clear and distinct. **4.** sharpness of outline.

definitive (dɪˈfɪnɪtɪv) adj. **1.** serving to decide finally. **2.** most reliable or authoritative.

deflate (diːˈfleɪt) vb. **1.** to collapse or cause to collapse through the release of gas. **2.** to take away the self-esteem or conceit from. **3.** Econ. to cause deflation of (an economy). [de- + (in)flate]

deflation (diːˈfleɪʃən) n. **1.** Econ. a reduction in economic activity resulting in lower levels of output and investment. **2.** a feeling of sadness following excitement. —deˈflationary adj.

deflect (dɪˈflɛkt) vb. to turn or cause to turn aside from a course. [Latin dēflectere] —deˈflection n. —deˈflector n.

deflower (diːˈflaʊə) vb. Literary. to deprive (a woman) of virginity.

defoliate (diːˈfəʊlɪˌeɪt) vb. to deprive (a plant) of leaves. [Latin de- from + folium leaf] —deˈfoliant n. —deˌfoliˈation n.

deform (dɪˈfɔːm) vb. **1.** to make misshapen or distorted. **2.** to make ugly; disfigure. [Latin de- from + forma shape, beauty]

deformed (dɪˈfɔːmd) adj. disfigured or misshapen.

deformity (dɪˈfɔːmɪtɪ) n., pl. -ties. **1.** Pathol. a distortion of an organ or part. **2.** a deformed condition.

defraud (dɪˈfrɔːd) vb. to take away or withhold money, rights, etc., from (a person) by fraud.

defray (dɪˈfreɪ) vb. to provide money for (costs or expenses). [Old French *deffroier* to pay expenses] —**deˈfrayal** n.

defrock (diːˈfrɒk) vb. to deprive (a priest) of ecclesiastical status.

defrost (diːˈfrɒst) vb. 1. to make or become free of frost or ice. 2. to thaw, esp. through removal from a deep-freeze.

deft (dɛft) adj. quick and neat in movement; dexterous. [Middle English (in the sense: gentle): var. of *daft*] —**ˈdeftly** adv. —**ˈdeftness** n.

defunct (dɪˈfʌŋkt) adj. no longer existing or operative. [Latin *defungī* to discharge (one's obligations), die]

defuse or U.S. (sometimes) **defuze** (diːˈfjuːz) vb. 1. to remove the triggering device of (an explosive device). 2. to remove the cause of tension from (a crisis, etc.).

defy (dɪˈfaɪ) vb. **-fying, -fied.** 1. to resist openly and boldly. 2. to elude, esp. in a baffling way. 3. *Formal.* to challenge (someone to do something). [Old French *desfier*]

degenerate adj. (dɪˈdʒɛnərɪt). 1. having deteriorated to a lower mental, moral, or physical level; degraded. ~n. (dɪˈdʒɛnərɪt). 2. a degenerate person. ~vb. (dɪˈdʒɛnəˌreɪt). 3. to become degenerate. [Latin *dēgener* departing from its kind, ignoble] —**deˈgeneracy** n.

degeneration (dɪˌdʒɛnəˈreɪʃən) n. 1. the process of degenerating. 2. *Biol.* the loss of specialization or function by organisms.

degrade (dɪˈɡreɪd) vb. 1. to reduce to dishonour or disgrace. 2. to reduce in status or quality. 3. *Chem.* to decompose into atoms or smaller molecules. [Latin *de-* from + *gradus* rank, degree] —**degradation** (ˌdɛɡrəˈdeɪʃən) n. —**deˈgrading** adj.

degree (dɪˈɡriː) n. 1. a stage in a scale of relative amount or intensity: *a high degree of competence.* 2. an academic award conferred by a university or college on successful completion of a course. 3. any of three categories of seriousness of a burn. 4. (in the U.S.) any of the categories into which a crime is divided according to seriousness. 5. *Grammar.* any of the forms of an adjective used to indicate relative amount or intensity. 6. a unit of temperature. Symbol: ° 7. a measure of angle equal to one three-hundred-and-sixtieth of the circumference of a circle. Symbol: ° 8. a unit of latitude or longitude. Symbol: ° 9. **by degrees.** little by little; gradually. [Latin *de-* down + *gradus* step]

dehisce (dɪˈhɪs) vb. (of fruits, anthers, etc.) to burst open spontaneously. [Latin *dēhiscere* to split open] —**deˈhiscence** n. —**deˈhiscent** adj.

dehumanize or **-ise** (diːˈhjuːməˌnaɪz) vb. 1. to deprive of human qualities. 2. to render mechanical or routine. —**deˌhumaniˈzation** or **-iˈsation** n.

dehydrate (diːˈhaɪdreɪt) vb. 1. to cause to lose water. 2. to deprive (the body) of water. —**ˌdehyˈdration** n.

de-ice (diːˈaɪs) vb. to free of ice. —**deˈicer** n.

deify (ˈdiːɪˌfaɪ, ˈdeɪ-) vb. **-fying, -fied.** 1. to exalt to the position of a god. 2. to accord divine honour or worship to. [Latin *deus* god + *facere* to make] —**ˌdeifiˈcation** n.

deign (deɪn) vb. to think it worthy of oneself (to do something); condescend. [Latin *dignārī* to consider worthy]

deism (ˈdiːɪzəm, ˈdeɪ-) n. belief in the existence of God based on natural reason, rather than revelation. —**ˈdeist** n., adj. —**deˈistic** adj.

deity (ˈdiːɪtɪ, ˈdeɪ-) n., pl. **-ties.** 1. a god or goddess. 2. the state of being divine. [Latin *deus* god]

Deity (ˈdiːɪtɪ, ˈdeɪ-) n. **the.** God.

déjà vu (ˈdeɪʒæ ˈvuː) n. a feeling of having experienced before something that is actually happening now. [French: already seen]

dejected (dɪˈdʒɛktɪd) adj. miserable; despondent; downhearted. [Latin *dēicere* to cast down] —**deˈjectedly** adv. —**deˈjection** n.

de jure (deɪ ˈdʒʊəreɪ) adv. according to law. [Latin]

deke (diːk) *Canad. slang.* ~vb. 1. (in ice hockey or box lacrosse) to draw (a defending player) out of position by faking a shot or movement. ~n. 2. such a shot or movement. [from *decoy*]

dekko (ˈdɛkəʊ) n., pl. **-kos.** *Brit. slang.* a look (esp. in **have a dekko**). [Hindi]

Del. Delaware.

delay (dɪˈleɪ) vb. 1. to put (something) off to a later time. 2. to slow up or cause to be late. 3. to be irresolute in doing something. 4. to linger; dawdle. ~n. 5. the act of delaying. 6. a period of inactivity or waiting before something happens or continues. [Old French *des-* off + *laier* to leave]

delectable (dɪˈlɛktəbəl) adj. delightful. [Latin *dēlectāre* to delight]

delectation (ˌdiːlɛkˈteɪʃən) n. *Formal.* great pleasure and enjoyment.

delegate n. (ˈdɛlɪɡɪt). 1. a person chosen to act for others, esp. at a conference or meeting. ~vb. (ˈdɛlɪˌɡeɪt). 2. to entrust (duties or powers) to another person. 3. to authorize (a person) as representative. [Latin *dēlēgāre* to send on a mission]

delegation (ˌdɛlɪˈɡeɪʃən) n. 1. a group chosen to represent others. 2. the act of delegating.

delete (dɪˈliːt) vb. to remove or cross out (something printed or written). [Latin *dēlēre*] —**deˈletion** n.

deleterious (ˌdɛlɪˈtɪərɪəs) adj. harmful; injurious. [Greek *dēlētērios*]

Delft (dɛlft) n. tin-glazed earthenware which originated in Delft in the Netherlands typically with blue decoration on a white ground.

deliberate adj. (dɪˈlɪbərɪt). 1. carefully thought out in advance; intentional. 2. careful and unhurried: *a deliberate pace.* ~vb. (dɪˈlɪbəˌreɪt). 3. to consider (something) deeply; think over. [Latin *dēlīberā-*

re] —de'liberately adv. —de'liberative adj.

deliberation (dɪˌlɪbəˈreɪʃən) n. 1. careful consideration. 2. (pl.) formal discussions. 3. calmness and absence of hurry.

delicacy (ˈdɛlɪkəsɪ) n., pl. -cies. 1. fine or subtle quality or workmanship. 2. fragile, graceful beauty. 3. something that is considered particularly nice to eat. 4. frail health. 5. refinement of feeling, manner, or appreciation. 6. need for tactful or sensitive handling.

delicate (ˈdɛlɪkɪt) adj. 1. fine or subtle in quality or workmanship. 2. having a fragile beauty. 3. (of colour, smell, or taste) pleasantly subtle. 4. easily damaged; fragile. 5. precise or sensitive in action: a delicate mechanism. 6. requiring tact: a delicate situation. 7. showing regard for the feelings of others. [Latin dēlicātus affording pleasure] —'delicately adv.

delicatessen (ˌdɛlɪkəˈtɛsᵊn) n. a shop selling unusual or imported foods, already cooked or prepared. [German Delikatessen delicacies]

delicious (dɪˈlɪʃəs) adj. 1. very appealing, esp. to taste or smell. 2. extremely enjoyable. [Latin dēliciae delights] —de'liciously adv.

delight (dɪˈlaɪt) vb. 1. to please greatly. 2. delight in. to take great pleasure in. ~n. 3. extreme pleasure. 4. something or someone that causes this. [Latin dēlectāre] —de'lightful adj. —de'lightfully adv.

delimit (diːˈlɪmɪt) vb. to mark or prescribe the limits of. —deˌlimi'tation n.

delineate (dɪˈlɪnɪˌeɪt) vb. 1. to show by drawing. 2. to describe in words. [Latin dēlīneāre to sketch out] —deˌline'ation n.

delinquent (dɪˈlɪŋkwənt) n. 1. someone, esp. a young person, guilty of an offence. ~adj. 2. guilty of an offence. [Latin dēlinquēns offending] —de'linquency n.

deliquesce (ˌdɛlɪˈkwɛs) vb. (esp. of certain salts) to dissolve in water absorbed from the air. [Latin dēliquēscere] —ˌdeli'quescence n. —ˌdeli'quescent adj.

delirious (dɪˈlɪrɪəs) adj. 1. suffering from delirium. 2. wildly excited, esp. with joy. —de'liriously adv.

delirium (dɪˈlɪrɪəm) n. 1. a state of excitement and mental confusion, often with hallucinations. 2. violent excitement. [Latin: madness]

delirium tremens (ˈtrɛmɛnz, ˈtriː-) n. a condition caused by chronic alcoholism, characterized by delirium, trembling, and vivid hallucinations. [New Latin: trembling delirium]

deliver (dɪˈlɪvə) vb. 1. to carry (goods or mail) to a destination. 2. (often foll. by over or up) to hand over. 3. (often foll. by from) to release or rescue (from captivity or danger). 4. to aid in the birth of (offspring). 5. to present (a speech, etc.). 6. to strike (a blow) suddenly. 7. Informal. Also: deliver the goods. to produce something promised. [Latin de- from + līberāre to free] —de'liverance n.

delivery (dɪˈlɪvərɪ) n., pl. -eries. 1. a. the act of delivering goods or mail. b. something that is delivered. 2. the act of giving birth to a child. 3. manner or style, esp. in public speaking.

dell (dɛl) n. a small wooded hollow. [Old English]

delouse (diːˈlaʊs, -ˈlaʊz) vb. to rid (a person or animal) of lice.

Delphic (ˈdɛlfɪk) adj. obscure or ambiguous, like the ancient Greek oracle at Delphi.

delphinium (dɛlˈfɪnɪəm) n., pl. -iums or -ia (-ɪə). a plant with spikes of blue flowers. [Greek delphis dolphin]

delta (ˈdɛltə) n. 1. the fourth letter in the Greek alphabet (Δ or δ). 2. the flat area at the mouth of some rivers where the main stream splits up into several tributaries.

delta wing n. a triangular aircraft wing.

delude (dɪˈluːd) vb. to deceive. [Latin dēlūdere]

deluge (ˈdɛljuːdʒ) n. 1. a great flood of water. 2. torrential rain. 3. an overwhelming number. ~vb. 4. to flood. 5. to overwhelm. [Latin dīluere to wash away]

Deluge (ˈdɛljuːdʒ) n. the. same as the **Flood**.

delusion (dɪˈluːʒən) n. 1. a mistaken idea or belief. 2. Psychiatry. a belief held in the face of evidence to the contrary, that is resistant to all reason. 3. the state of being deluded. —de'lusive adj. —de'lusory (dɪˈluːsərɪ) adj. [Latin]

de luxe (də ˈlʌks, ˈlʊks) adj. rich or sumptuous; superior in quality: the de luxe model of a car. [French]

delve (dɛlv) vb. 1. to research deeply or intensively (for information). 2. Archaic. to dig. [Old English delfan]

demagnetize or **-ise** (diːˈmægnəˌtaɪz) vb. to remove magnetic properties. —deˌmagneti'zation or -i'sation n.

demagogue or U.S. (sometimes) **demagog** (ˈdɛməˌgɒg) n. a political agitator who appeals to the prejudice and passions of the mob. [Greek dēmagōgos people's leader] —ˌdema'gogic adj. —'demaˌgogy n.

demand (dɪˈmɑːnd) vb. 1. to request peremptorily. 2. to require as just, urgent, etc.: the situation demands attention. 3. to claim as a right. ~n. 4. a peremptory request. 5. something that requires special effort or sacrifice. 6. Econ. willingness and ability to purchase goods and services. 7. in demand. sought after. 8. on demand. as soon as requested. [Latin dēmandāre to commit to]

demanding (dɪˈmɑːndɪŋ) adj. requiring great patience, skill, etc.: a demanding job.

demarcation (ˌdiːmɑːˈkeɪʃən) n. the act of establishing limits or boundaries, esp. between the kinds of work performed by members of different trade unions. [Spanish demarcar to appoint the boundaries of]

demean (dɪˈmiːn) vb. to lower (someone, esp. oneself) in dignity, status, or character; debase. [see DE-, MEAN²]

demeanour or U.S. **demeanor** (dɪˈmiːnə) n. the way a person behaves.

[Old French *de-* (intensive) + *mener* to lead]

demented (dɪˈmɛntɪd) *adj.* mad; insane. [Late Latin *dēmentāre* to drive mad] —**deˈmentedly** *adv.*

dementia (dɪˈmɛnʃə, -ʃɪə) *n.* a state of serious mental deterioration. [Latin: madness]

demerara sugar (ˌdɛməˈrɛərə) *n.* brown crystallized cane sugar from the West Indies. [after *Demerara*, a region of Guyana]

demerit (diːˈmɛrɪt) *n.* 1. a fault. 2. *U.S. & Canad.* a mark given against a student for failure or misconduct.

demesne (dɪˈmeɪn, -ˈmiːn) *n.* 1. land surrounding a house or manor. 2. *Property law.* the possession of one's own property or land. 3. domain; region. [Old French *demeine*]

demi- *prefix.* 1. half: *demirelief.* 2. of less than full size, status, or rank: *demigod.* [Latin *dīmīdius* half]

demigod (ˈdɛmɪˌɡɒd) *n.* 1. **a.** a being who is part mortal, part god. **b.** a lesser deity. 2. a godlike person.

demijohn (ˈdɛmɪˌdʒɒn) *n.* a large bottle with a short narrow neck, often encased in wickerwork. [prob. from French *dame-jeanne*]

demilitarize *or* **-ise** (diːˈmɪlɪtəˌraɪz) *vb.* to remove any military presence from: *demilitarized zone.* —**deˌmilitariˈzation** *or* **-iˈsation** *n.*

demimonde (ˌdɛmɪˈmɒnd) *n.* 1. (esp. in the 19th century) women considered to be outside respectable society, esp. on account of sexual promiscuity. 2. any group considered not wholly respectable. [French: half-world]

demise (dɪˈmaɪz) *n.* 1. *Euphemistic, formal.* death. 2. *Property law.* a transfer of an estate by lease. ~*vb.* 3. *Property law.* to transfer for a limited period; lease. [Old French *demis* dismissed]

demisemiquaver (ˈdɛmɪˌsɛmɪˌkweɪvə) *n. Music.* a note having the time value of one thirty-second of a semibreve.

demo (ˈdɛməʊ) *n., pl.* **-os.** *Informal.* 1. short for **demonstration** (sense 1). 2. a demonstration record or tape.

demob (diːˈmɒb) *vb.* **-mobbing, -mobbed.** *Brit. informal.* to demobilize.

demobilize *or* **-ise** (diːˈməʊbɪˌlaɪz) *vb.* to release from the armed forces. —**deˌmobiliˈzation** *or* **-iˈsation** *n.*

democracy (dɪˈmɒkrəsɪ) *n., pl.* **-cies.** 1. government by the people or their elected representatives. 2. a political or social unit governed ultimately by all its members. 3. social equality. [Greek *dēmokratia*]

democrat (ˈdɛməˌkræt) *n.* 1. an advocate of democracy. 2. a member or supporter of a democratic party or movement.

Democrat (ˈdɛməˌkræt) *n. U.S. politics.* a member or supporter of the Democratic Party. —ˌDemoˈcratic *adj.*

democratic (ˌdɛməˈkrætɪk) *adj.* 1. of or relating to the principles of democracy. 2. upholding democracy or the interests of the common people. —ˌdemoˈcratically *adv.*

demodulation (ˌdiːmɒdjʊˈleɪʃən) *n. Electronics.* the process by which an output wave or signal is obtained having the characteristics of the original modulating wave or signal.

demography (dɪˈmɒɡrəfɪ) *n.* the study of human populations. [Greek *dēmos* the populace + -GRAPHY] —**demographic** (ˌdiːməˈɡræfɪk, ˌdɛmə-) *adj.*

demolish (dɪˈmɒlɪʃ) *vb.* 1. to tear down or break up (buildings). 2. to put an end to (an argument, etc.). 3. *Facetious.* to eat up. [Latin *dēmōlīrī* to throw down] —**deˈmolisher** *n.* —**demolition** (ˌdɛməˈlɪʃən) *n.*

demon (ˈdiːmən) *n.* 1. an evil spirit. 2. a person, obsession, etc., thought of as evil. 3. a person extremely skilful in or devoted to a given activity: *a demon at cycling.* 4. same as **daemon** (sense 1). [Greek *daimōn* spirit, fate] —**demonic** (dɪˈmɒnɪk) *adj.*

demonetize *or* **-ise** (diːˈmʌnɪˌtaɪz) *vb.* to withdraw (a coin, etc.) from use as currency. —**deˌmonetiˈzation** *or* **-iˈsation** *n.*

demoniac (dɪˈməʊnɪˌæk) *or* **demoniacal** (ˌdiːməˈnaɪəkʔl) *adj.* 1. suggesting inner possession: *the demoniac fire of genius.* 2. frantic; frenzied. —ˌdemoˈniacally *adv.*

demonolatry (ˌdiːməˈnɒlətrɪ) *n.* the worship of demons. [*demon* + Greek *latreia* worship]

demonology (ˌdiːməˈnɒlədʒɪ) *n.* the study of demons or demonic beliefs. [*demon* + -LOGY]

demonstrable (ˈdɛmənstrəbʔl, dɪˈmɒn-) *adj.* able to be proved. —**ˈdemonstrably** *adv.*

demonstrate (ˈdɛmənˌstreɪt) *vb.* 1. to show or prove by reasoning or evidence. 2. to reveal the existence of: *the plan later demonstrated a serious flaw.* 3. to display and explain the workings of (a machine, product, etc.). 4. to show support or protest by public parades or rallies. [Latin *dēmonstrāre* to point out]

demonstration (ˌdɛmənˈstreɪʃən) *n.* 1. a manifestation of support or protest by public parades or rallies. 2. proof. 3. an explanation, illustration, or experiment showing how something works. 4. a show of emotion.

demonstrative (dɪˈmɒnstrətɪv) *adj.* 1. tending to express one's feelings unreservedly. 2. **demonstrative of.** giving proof of. 3. *Grammar.* denoting a word used to point out the person or thing referred to, such as *this* and *those.* —**deˈmonstratively** *adv.*

demonstrator (ˈdɛmənˌstreɪtə) *n.* 1. a person who demonstrates machines, products, etc. 2. a person who takes part in a public demonstration.

demoralize *or* **-ise** (dɪˈmɒrəˌlaɪz) *vb.* to undermine the morale of; dishearten. —**deˌmoraliˈzation** *or* **-iˈsation** *n.*

demote (dɪˈməʊt) *vb.* to lower in rank or position; relegate. [DE- + (PRO)MOTE] —**deˈmotion** *n.*

demotic (dɪˈmɒtɪk) *adj.* of or relating to the common people. [Greek *dēmotikos*]

demur (dɪˈmɜː) *vb.* **-murring, -murred. 1.** to show reluctance; object. ~*n.* **2. without demur.** without objecting. [Latin *dēmorārī*]

demure (dɪˈmjʊə) *adj.* quiet, reserved, and rather shy. [perhaps from Old French *demorer* to delay, linger] —**deˈmurely** *adv.* —**deˈmureness** *n.*

demurrer (dɪˈmʌrə) *n. Law.* a pleading that admits an opponent's point but denies its relevance.

demystify (diːˈmɪstɪˌfaɪ) *vb.* **-fying, -fied.** to remove the mystery from; make clear. —**deˌmystifiˈcation** *n.*

den (dɛn) *n.* **1.** the home of a wild animal; lair. **2.** a small secluded room in a home, often used for a hobby. **3.** a site or haunt: *a den of vice.* [Old English *denn*]

denarius (dɪˈnɛərɪəs) *n., pl.* **-narii** (-ˈnɛərɪ-ˌaɪ). a silver coin of ancient Rome, often called a penny in translation. [Latin]

denary (ˈdiːnərɪ) *adj.* calculated by tens; decimal. [Latin *dēnārius*]

denationalize *or* **-ise** (diːˈnæʃənˌlaɪz) *vb.* to transfer (an industry or a service) from public to private ownership. —**deˌnationaliˈzation** *or* **-iˈsation** *n.*

denature (diːˈneɪtʃə) *vb.* **1.** to change the nature of. **2.** to make (alcohol) unfit to drink by adding nauseous substances.

dendrology (dɛnˈdrɒlədʒɪ) *n.* the study of trees. [Greek *dendron* tree + -LOGY]

Dene (ˈdɛnɪ) *pl. n.* the North American Indian peoples of the Northwest Territories in Canada. [American Indian]

dengue (ˈdɛŋɡɪ) *n.* a viral disease transmitted by mosquitoes, characterized by headache, fever, pains in the joints, and rash. [prob. of African origin]

denial (dɪˈnaɪəl) *n.* **1.** a statement that something is not true. **2.** a rejection of a request. **3.** a refusal to acknowledge; disowning.

denier (ˈdɛnɪˌeɪ, ˈdɛnjə) *n.* a unit of weight used to measure the fineness of silk and man-made fibres. [Old French: coin]

denigrate (ˈdɛnɪˌɡreɪt) *vb.* to criticize unfairly; belittle. [Latin *dēnigrāre* to make very black] —**deniˈgration** *n.* —**ˈdeniˌgrator** *n.*

denim (ˈdɛnɪm) *n.* **1.** a hard-wearing cotton fabric used for trousers, work clothes, etc. **2.** (*pl.*) jeans made of denim. [French (*serge*) *de Nîmes* (serge) of Nîmes, in S France]

denizen (ˈdɛnɪzən) *n.* **1.** an inhabitant; resident. **2.** a plant or animal established in a place to which it is not native. [Old French *denzein*]

denominate (dɪˈnɒmɪˌneɪt) *vb.* to give a specific name to; designate. [Latin *dēnōminare*]

denomination (dɪˌnɒmɪˈneɪʃən) *n.* **1.** a group having a distinctive interpretation of a religious faith. **2.** a grade or unit of value, weight, measure, etc. **3.** a name. —**deˌnomiˈnational** *adj.*

denominator (dɪˈnɒmɪˌneɪtə) *n.* the divisor of a fraction, as 8 in ⅜.

denote (dɪˈnəʊt) *vb.* **1.** to be a sign of; designate. **2.** (of a word or phrase) to have as a literal or obvious meaning. [Latin *dēnotāre* to mark] —**denoˈtation** *n.*

denouement *or* **dénouement** (deɪˈnuːmɒn) *n.* the final outcome or solution, esp. in a play or book. [French]

denounce (dɪˈnaʊns) *vb.* **1.** to condemn openly or vehemently. **2.** to give information against. [Latin *dēnuntiāre* to make an official proclamation, threaten]

dense (dɛns) *adj.* **1.** thickly crowded or closely packed. **2.** impenetrable: *dense smoke.* **3.** stupid; dull. [Latin *densus* thick] —**ˈdensely** *adv.*

density (ˈdɛnsɪtɪ) *n., pl.* **-ties. 1.** the degree to which something is filled or occupied: *a high population density.* **2.** a measure of the compactness of a substance, expressed as its mass per unit volume. **3.** a measure of a physical quantity per unit of length, area, or volume.

dent (dɛnt) *n.* **1.** a hollow in a surface, as made by a blow. ~*vb.* **2.** to make a dent in. [var. of *dint*]

dental (ˈdɛntʰl) *adj.* of or relating to the teeth or dentistry. [Latin *dēns* tooth]

dental floss *n.* a waxed thread used to remove food particles from between the teeth.

dental surgeon *n.* same as **dentist.**

dentate (ˈdɛnteɪt) *adj.* having teeth or toothlike processes. [Latin *dentātus*]

dentifrice (ˈdɛntɪfrɪs) *n.* paste or powder for cleaning the teeth. [Latin *dens* tooth + *fricāre* to rub]

dentine (ˈdɛntiːn) *n.* the calcified tissue comprising the bulk of a tooth. [Latin *dens* tooth]

dentist (ˈdɛntɪst) *n.* a person qualified to practise dentistry. [French *dentiste*]

dentistry (ˈdɛntɪstrɪ) *n.* the branch of medicine concerned with the teeth and gums.

dentition (dɛnˈtɪʃən) *n.* the arrangement, type, and number of teeth in a species. [Latin *dentitiō* a teething]

denture (ˈdɛntʃə) *n.* (*often pl.*) a partial or full set of artificial teeth. [French *dent* tooth]

denude (dɪˈnjuːd) *vb.* to make bare; strip. —**ˌdenuˈdation** *n.*

denumerable (dɪˈnjuːmərəbʰl) *adj. Maths.* countable.

denunciation (dɪˌnʌnsɪˈeɪʃən) *n.* open condemnation; denouncing. [Latin *dēnuntiāre* to proclaim]

deny (dɪˈnaɪ) *vb.* **-nying, -nied. 1.** to declare (a statement) to be untrue. **2.** to refuse to give or allow: *we were denied access to the information.* **3.** to refuse to acknowledge; disown. [Latin *dēnegāre*]

deodar (ˈdiːəʊˌdɑː) *n.* a Himalayan cedar with drooping branches. [Hindi]

deodorant (diːˈəʊdərənt) *n.* a substance applied to the body to suppress or mask the odour of perspiration.

deodorize *or* **-ise** (diːˈəʊdəˌraɪz) *vb.* to

remove or disguise the odour of. —de-
¡odori'zation *or* **-i'sation** *n.*

dep. **1.** department. **2.** departure.

depart (dɪ'pɑːt) *vb.* **1.** to leave. **2.** to
differ; vary: *to depart from normal procedure.* [Old French *departir*]

departed (dɪ'pɑːtɪd) *adj. Euphemistic.*
dead.

department (dɪ'pɑːtmənt) *n.* **1.** a specialized division of a large organization, such
as a business, store, or university. **2.** a
major subdivision of the administration of
a government. **3.** an administrative division in several countries, such as France.
4. *Informal.* a specialized sphere of activity: *wine-making is my wife's department.*
[French *département*] —**departmental**
(¡diːpɑːt'mentᵊl) *adj.*

department store *n.* a large shop divided into departments selling many kinds of
goods.

departure (dɪ'pɑːtʃə) *n.* **1.** the act of
departing. **2.** a variation from previous
custom. **3.** a course of action or venture:
selling is a new departure for him.

depend (dɪ'pend) *vb.* **1.** (foll. by *on* or
upon) to put trust (in); rely (on). **2.**
(usually foll. by *on* or *upon*) to be influenced or determined (by): *it all depends on
you.* **3.** (foll. by *on* or *upon*) to rely (on)
for income or support. [Latin *dēpendēre* to
hang from]

dependable (dɪ'pendəbᵊl) *adj.* able to be
depended on; reliable. —**de¡penda'bility**
n. —**de'pendably** *adv.*

dependant (dɪ'pendənt) *n.* a person who
depends on another for financial support.

dependence (dɪ'pendəns) *n.* **1.** the state
or fact of being dependent, esp. for support
or help. **2.** reliance.

dependency (dɪ'pendənsɪ) *n., pl.* **-cies.**
1. a territory subject to a state on which it
does not border. **2.** *Psychol.* overreliance
on another person or on a drug.

dependent (dɪ'pendənt) *adj.* **1.** depending on a person or thing for aid or support.
2. dependent on *or* **upon.** influenced or
conditioned by.

depict (dɪ'pɪkt) *vb.* **1.** to represent by
drawing, painting, etc. **2.** to describe in
words. [Latin *dēpingere*] —**de'piction** *n.*

depilatory (dɪ'pɪlətrɪ) *adj.* **1.** able or serving to remove hair. ~*n., pl.* **-ries.** a
chemical used to remove hair. [Latin
dēpilāre to pull out the hair]

deplete (dɪ'pliːt) *vb.* **1.** to use up (supplies or money). **2.** to reduce in number.
[Latin *dēplēre* to empty out] —**de'pletion** *n.*

deplorable (dɪ'plɔːrəbᵊl) *adj.* very bad.
—**de'plorably** *adv.*

deplore (dɪ'plɔː) *vb.* to express or feel
strong disapproval of. [Latin *dēplōrāre* to
weep bitterly]

deploy (dɪ'plɔɪ) *vb.* to organize (troops or
resources) into a position ready for immediate and effective action. [Latin
displicāre to unfold] —**de'ployment** *n.*

deponent (dɪ'pəʊnənt) *n. Law.* a person

who makes an affidavit or a deposition.
[Latin *dēpōnēns* putting down]

depopulate (dɪ'pɒpjʊˌleɪt) *vb.* to cause to
be reduced in population. —**de¡popu'lation** *n.*

deport (dɪ'pɔːt) *vb.* **1.** to remove forcibly
from a country. **2. deport oneself.** to
behave oneself in a specified manner. [Lat-
in *dēportāre* to carry away, banish]

deportation (¡diːpɔː'teɪʃən) *n.* the act of
expelling someone from a country.

deportee (¡diːpɔː'tiː) *n.* a deported person.

deportment (dɪ'pɔːtmənt) *n.* the manner
in which a person behaves, esp. in physical
bearing: *military deportment.* [Old French
deporter to conduct (oneself)]

depose (dɪ'pəʊz) *vb.* **1.** to remove from an
office or position of power. **2.** *Law.* to
testify on oath. [Latin *dēpōnere* to put
aside]

deposit (dɪ'pɒzɪt) *vb.* **1.** to put down. **2.**
to entrust for safekeeping. **3.** to place
(money) in a bank or similar institution to
earn interest or for safekeeping. **4.** to lay
down naturally: *the river deposits silt.*
~*n.* **5. a.** the entrusting of money to a
bank or similar institution. **b.** the money
so entrusted. **6.** money given in part payment or as security. **7.** an accumulation of
sediments, minerals, etc. [Latin *dēpositus*
put down]

deposit account *n. Brit.* a bank account
that earns interest.

depositary (dɪ'pɒzɪtrɪ) *n., pl.* **-taries.** a
person or group to whom something is
entrusted for safety.

deposition (¡depə'zɪʃən) *n.* **1.** *Law.* the
sworn statement of a witness used in court
in his absence. **2.** the act of deposing. **3.**
the act of depositing. **4.** something deposited. [Late Latin *dēpositiō* a laying down,
testimony]

depositor (dɪ'pɒzɪtə) *n.* a person who
places or has money on deposit, esp. in a
bank.

depository (dɪ'pɒzɪtrɪ) *n., pl.* **-ries.** **1.** a
store for furniture, valuables, etc. **2.** same
as **depositary.**

depot ('depəʊ) *n.* **1.** a storehouse or warehouse. **2.** *Chiefly Brit.* a building used for
the storage and servicing of buses or railway engines. **3.** *Chiefly U.S. & Canad.* a
bus or railway station. [French]

deprave (dɪ'preɪv) *vb.* to make morally
bad; corrupt. [Latin *dēprāvāre* to distort,
corrupt] —**de'praved** *adj.*

depravity (dɪ'prævɪtɪ) *n., pl.* **-ties.** moral
corruption.

deprecate ('deprɪˌkeɪt) *vb.* to express disapproval of; protest against. [Latin
dēprecārī to avert, ward off] —**¡depre'cation** *n.* —'**deprecatory** *adj.*

depreciate (dɪ'priːʃɪˌeɪt) *vb.* **1.** to decline
in value or price. **2.** to deride or criticize.
[Latin *de-* down + *pretium* price] —**depre-
ciatory** (dɪ'priːʃɪətrɪ) *adj.*

depreciation (dɪ¡priːʃɪ'eɪʃən) *n.* **1.** *Accounting.* the reduction in value of a fixed
asset through use, obsolescence, etc. **2.**
the act or an instance of belittling. **3.** a

decrease in the exchange value of a currency.

depredation (ˌdɛprɪ'deɪʃən) n. plundering; pillage. [Latin *dēpraedāre* to plunder]

depress (dɪ'prɛs) vb. **1.** to lower (someone's) spirits; make gloomy. **2.** to lower (prices). **3.** to push down. [Old French *depresser*] —**de'pressing** adj. —**de'pressingly** adv.

depressant (dɪ'prɛs²nt) adj. **1.** Med. able to reduce nervous or functional activity. ~n. **2.** a depressant drug.

depressed (dɪ'prɛst) adj. **1.** low in spirits; downcast. **2.** pressed down or flattened. **3.** characterized by economic hardship, such as unemployment: a depressed area.

depression (dɪ'prɛʃən) n. **1.** a mental state characterized by feelings of gloom and inadequacy. **2.** an economic condition characterized by substantial unemployment, low output and investment; slump. **3.** Meteorol. a body of moving air below normal atmospheric pressure, which often brings rain. **4.** a sunken place.

Depression (dɪ'prɛʃən) n. the. the worldwide economic depression of the early 1930s.

deprive (dɪ'praɪv) vb. (foll. by of) to prevent from possessing or enjoying. [Latin de- from + prīvāre to deprive of] —**deprivation** (ˌdɛprɪ'veɪʃən) n.

deprived (dɪ'praɪvd) adj. lacking adequate living conditions, education, etc.: deprived inner-city areas.

depth (dɛpθ) n. **1.** the distance downwards, backwards, or inwards. **2.** intensity of emotion. **3.** profundity of character or thought. **4.** intensity of colour. **5.** lowness of pitch. **6.** (pl.) **a.** a remote inaccessible region: the depths of the country. **b.** the most severe part: the depths of winter. **c.** a low moral state. **7.** out of one's depth. **a.** in water deeper than one is tall. **b.** beyond the range of one's competence or understanding. [Middle English dep deep]

depth charge n. a bomb used to attack submarines that explodes at a preset depth of water.

deputation (ˌdɛpjʊ'teɪʃən) n. a body of people appointed to represent others.

depute (dɪ'pjuːt) vb. to appoint (someone) to act on one's behalf. [Late Latin *dēputāre* to assign, allot]

deputize or **-ise** ('dɛpjʊˌtaɪz) vb. to act as deputy.

deputy ('dɛpjʊtɪ) n., pl. **-ties. a.** a person appointed to act on behalf of another. **b.** (as modifier): the deputy chairman. [Old French deputer to appoint]

derail (dɪ'reɪl) vb. to cause (a train) to go off the rails. —**de'railment** n.

derange (dɪ'reɪndʒ) vb. **1.** to make insane. **2.** to throw into disorder. [Old French desrengier] —**de'rangement** n.

derby ('dɜːbɪ) n., pl. **-bies.** U.S. & Canad. a bowler hat.

Derby ('dɑːbɪ; U.S. 'dɜːrbɪ) n., pl. **-bies. 1. the.** an annual horse race run at Epsom Downs, Surrey. **2. local derby.** a sporting event between teams from the same area. [after the Earl of Derby, who founded the race in 1780]

Derby. Derbyshire.

deregulate (diː'rɛgjʊleɪt) vb. to remove regulations or controls from. —**deˌregu'lation** n.

derelict ('dɛrɪlɪkt) adj. **1.** deserted or abandoned, as by an owner or occupant. **2.** falling into ruins. ~n. **3.** a social outcast or vagrant. [Latin *dērelinquere* to abandon]

dereliction (ˌdɛrɪ'lɪkʃən) n. **1. dereliction of duty.** wilful neglect of one's duty. **2.** the state of being abandoned.

derestrict (ˌdiːrɪ'strɪkt) vb. to make (a road) free from speed limits. —**dere'striction** n.

deride (dɪ'raɪd) vb. to speak of or treat with contempt or ridicule. [Latin *dērīdēre* to laugh to scorn] —**derision** (dɪ'rɪʒən) n.

de rigueur (də rɪ'ɡɜː) adj. required by fashion. [French, lit.: of strictness]

derisive (dɪ'raɪsɪv) adj. mocking; scornful. —**de'risively** adv.

derisory (dɪ'raɪsərɪ) adj. so small or inadequate that it is not worth serious consideration.

derivation (ˌdɛrɪ'veɪʃən) n. the origin or descent of something, such as a word.

derivative (dɪ'rɪvətɪv) adj. **1.** based on other sources; not original. ~n. **2.** a word, idea, etc., that is derived from another. **3.** Maths. the rate of change of one quantity with respect to another.

derive (dɪ'raɪv) vb. (usually foll. by from) to draw or be drawn (from) in source or origin. [Old French]

dermatitis (ˌdɜːmə'taɪtɪs) n. inflammation of the skin. [Greek derma skin]

dermatology (ˌdɜːmə'tɒlədʒɪ) n. the branch of medicine concerned with the skin. [Greek derma skin + -LOGY] —**derma'tologist** n.

derogate ('dɛrəˌɡeɪt) vb. (foll. by from) to cause to seem inferior; detract from. [Latin *dērogāre* to diminish] —**dero'gation** n.

derogatory (dɪ'rɒɡətrɪ) adj. intentionally offensive.

derrick ('dɛrɪk) n. **1.** a simple crane that has lifting tackle slung from a boom. **2.** the framework erected over an oil well to enable drill tubes to be raised and lowered. [Derrick, celebrated hangman]

derring-do ('dɛrɪŋ'duː) n. Archaic or literary. boldness or bold action. [Middle English durring don daring to do]

derv (dɜːv) n. Brit. diesel oil, when used for road transport. [d(iesel) e(ngine) r(oad) v(ehicle)]

dervish ('dɜːvɪʃ) n. a member of a Muslim religious order noted for a frenzied, ecstatic, whirling dance. [Persian darvīsh mendicant monk]

desalination (diːˌsælɪ'neɪʃən) n. the process of removing salt, esp. from sea water.

descant ('dɛskænt) n. **1.** a decorative counterpoint added above a basic melody. ~adj. **2.** of the highest member in a family of musical instruments: *a descant recorder*. [Latin *dis-* apart + *cantus* song]

descend (dɪ'sɛnd) *vb.* **1.** to move down (a slope, staircase, etc.). **2.** to move to a lower level, pitch, etc.; fall. **3. be descended from.** to be connected by a blood relationship to (a dead person). **4.** to sink to (a shameful action). **5. descend on.** to visit unexpectedly. [Latin *dēscendere*]

descendant (dɪ'sɛndənt) *n.* a person or animal when described as descended from an individual, race, or species.

descendent (dɪ'sɛndənt) *adj.* descending.

descent (dɪ'sɛnt) *n.* **1.** the act of descending. **2.** a downward slope. **3.** a path or way leading downwards. **4.** derivation from an ancestor; lineage. **5.** a degeneration. **6.** (often foll. by *on*) a sudden arrival or attack.

describe (dɪ'skraɪb) *vb.* **1.** to give an account of (something or someone) in words. **2.** to trace the outline of (a circle, etc.). [Latin *dēscrībere* to copy off, write out]

description (dɪ'skrɪpʃən) *n.* **1.** a statement or account that describes. **2.** the act of describing. **3.** sort: *reptiles of every description.*

descriptive (dɪ'skrɪptɪv) *adj.* characterized by or containing description. —**de'scriptively** *adv.*

descry (dɪ'skraɪ) *vb.* **-scrying, -scried.** **1.** to catch sight of. **2.** to discover by looking carefully. [Old French *descrier* to proclaim]

desecrate ('dɛsɪ,kreɪt) *vb.* to violate the sacred character of (an object or place). [DE- + CONSECRATE] —,dese'cration *n.*

desegregate (diː'sɛgrɪ,geɪt) *vb.* to end racial segregation in (a public institution). —,desegre'gation *n.*

deselect (,diːsɪ'lɛkt) *vb. Brit. politics.* (of a constituency organization) to refuse to select (an MP) for re-election. —,dese'lection *n.*

desert¹ ('dɛzət) *n.* a region that has little or no vegetation because of low rainfall. [Latin *dēserere* to abandon]

desert² (dɪ'zɜːt) *vb.* **1.** to abandon (a person or place) without intending to return. **2.** *Chiefly mil.* to abscond from (a post or duty) with no intention of returning. [Latin *dēserere:* see DESERT¹] —**de'serter** *n.* —**de'sertion** *n.*

desertification (,dɛzɜːtɪfɪ'keɪʃən) *n.* a process by which fertile land turns into desert.

deserts (dɪ'zɜːts) *pl. n.* just rewards or punishment. [Old French *deserte*]

deserve (dɪ'zɜːv) *vb.* to be entitled to or worthy of; merit. [Latin *dēservīre* to serve devotedly]

deserved (dɪ'zɜːvd) *adj.* rightfully earned; warranted. —**deservedly** (dɪ'zɜːvɪdlɪ) *adv.*

deserving (dɪ'zɜːvɪŋ) *adj.* (often foll. by *of*) worthy, esp. of praise or help.

deshabille (,deɪzæ'biːl) *n.* same as **dishabille**.

desiccate ('dɛsɪ,keɪt) *vb.* to remove most of the water from; dry. [Latin *dēsiccāre* to

dry up] —'desic,cated *adj.* —,desic'cation *n.*

design (dɪ'zaɪn) *vb.* **1.** to work out the structure or form of (something), as by making a sketch or plans. **2.** to plan and make (something) artistically. **3.** to intend (something) for a specific purpose; plan. ~*n.* **4.** a preliminary drawing. **5.** the arrangement or features of an artistic or decorative work: *the design of the desk is Chippendale.* **6.** a finished artistic or decorative creation. **7.** the art of designing. **8.** an intention; purpose. **9. have designs on.** to plot to gain possession of. [Latin *dēsignāre* to mark out, describe]

designate *vb.* ('dɛzɪg,neɪt). **1.** to give a name to; entitle. **2.** to select (someone) for an office or duty; appoint. ~*adj.* ('dɛzɪgnɪt). **3.** appointed, but not yet in office: *a minister designate.* [Latin *dēsignātus* marked out]

designation (,dɛzɪg'neɪʃən) *n.* **1.** something that designates, such as a name. **2.** the act of designating.

designedly (dɪ'zaɪnɪdlɪ) *adv.* by intention.

designer (dɪ'zaɪnə) *n.* **1.** a person who draws up original sketches or plans from which things are made. **2.** (*modifier*) designed by a well-known fashion designer: *designer jeans.*

designing (dɪ'zaɪnɪŋ) *adj.* scheming.

desirable (dɪ'zaɪərəb'l) *adj.* **1.** worthy of desire: *a desirable residence.* **2.** arousing sexual desire. —de,sira'bility *n.* —de'sirably *adv.*

desire (dɪ'zaɪə) *vb.* **1.** to long for; crave. **2.** to request. ~*n.* **3.** a wish or longing. **4.** a request. **5.** sexual appetite. **6.** a person or thing that is desired. [Latin *dēsīderāre*]

desirous (dɪ'zaɪərəs) *adj.* (foll. by *of*) having a desire (for).

desist (dɪ'zɪst) *vb.* (often foll. by *from*) to stop or abstain. [Latin *dēsistere*]

desk (dɛsk) *n.* **1.** a piece of furniture with a writing surface and usually drawers. **2.** a service counter in a public building, such as a hotel. **3.** the section of a newspaper or television station responsible for a particular subject: *the news desk.* [Latin *discus* disc, dish]

desktop ('dɛsk,tɒp) *n.* (*modifier*) denoting a computer system small enough to use at a desk but sophisticated enough to produce print-quality documents: *desktop publishing.*

desolate *adj.* ('dɛsəlɪt). **1.** uninhabited; deserted. **2.** laid waste. **3.** without hope. **4.** dismal; depressing. ~*vb.* ('dɛsə,leɪt). **5.** to deprive (a place) of inhabitants. **6.** to lay waste. **7.** to make (someone) wretched or forlorn. [Latin *dēsōlāre* to leave alone] —'desolately *adv.* —'desolateness *n.*

desolation (,dɛsə'leɪʃən) *n.* **1.** ruin or devastation. **2.** solitary misery; wretchedness.

despair (dɪ'spɛə) *vb.* **1.** to lose or give up hope: *I despair of his coming.* ~*n.* **2.** total loss of hope. [Old French *despoir* hopelessness]

despatch (dɪ'spætʃ) *vb., n.* same as **dispatch**.

desperado (ˌdɛspə'rɑːdəʊ) *n., pl.* **-does** or **-dos.** a reckless person ready to commit any violent illegal act. [prob. pseudo-Spanish]

desperate ('dɛsprɪt) *adj.* **1.** careless of danger, as from despair. **2.** (of an action) undertaken as a last resort. **3.** very grave: *in desperate need.* **4.** (often foll. by *for*) having a great need or desire. [Latin *dēspērāre* to have no hope] —**'desperately** *adv.*

desperation (ˌdɛspə'reɪʃən) *n.* **1.** desperate recklessness. **2.** the state of being desperate.

despicable ('dɛspɪkəb'l, dɪ'spɪk-) *adj.* worthy of being despised; contemptible. —**'despicably** *adv.*

despise (dɪ'spaɪz) *vb.* to look down on with contempt. [Latin *dēspicere* to look down]

despite (dɪ'spaɪt) *prep.* in spite of. [Old French *despit*]

despoil (dɪ'spɔɪl) *vb. Formal.* to plunder. [Latin *dēspoliāre*] —**despoliation** (dɪˌspəʊlɪ'eɪʃən) *n.*

despondent (dɪ'spɒndənt) *adj.* downcast or disheartened. [Latin *dēspondēre* to lose heart] —**de'spondency** *n.* —**de'spondently** *adv.*

despot ('dɛspɒt) *n.* any person in power, esp. a ruler, who acts tyrannically. [Greek *despotēs* lord, master] —**des'potic** *adj.* —**des'potically** *adv.*

despotism ('dɛspəˌtɪzəm) *n.* **1.** absolute or tyrannical government. **2.** tyrannical behaviour.

dessert (dɪ'zɜːt) *n.* the sweet, usually last course of a meal. [French]

dessertspoon (dɪ'zɜːtˌspuːn) *n.* a spoon between a tablespoon and a teaspoon in size.

destination (ˌdɛstɪ'neɪʃən) *n.* the place to which something or someone is going.

destine ('dɛstɪn) *vb.* to set apart (for a certain purpose); intend. [Latin *dēstināre* to appoint]

destiny ('dɛstɪnɪ) *n., pl.* **-nies. 1.** the future destined for a person or thing. **2.** the predetermined course of events. **3.** the power that predetermines the course of events. [Old French *destiner* to destine]

destitute ('dɛstɪˌtjuːt) *adj.* lacking the means to live; totally impoverished. [Latin *dēstituere* to leave alone] —ˌdesti-'tution *n.*

destroy (dɪ'strɔɪ) *vb.* **1.** to ruin; demolish. **2.** to put an end to. **3.** to kill (an animal). **4.** to crush or defeat. [Latin *dēstruere* to pull down]

destroyer (dɪ'strɔɪə) *n.* **1.** a small heavily armed warship. **2.** a person or thing that destroys.

destruct (dɪ'strʌkt) *vb.* **1.** to destroy (one's own equipment) for safety. **2.** (of equipment) to be destroyed, for safety, by those in control. ~*adj.* **3.** capable of destroying itself or the object containing it: *destruct mechanism.*

destructible (dɪ'strʌktɪb'l) *adj.* capable of being destroyed.

destruction (dɪ'strʌkʃən) *n.* **1.** the act of destroying something or state of being destroyed. **2.** a cause of ruin. [Latin *dēstructiō* a pulling down]

destructive (dɪ'strʌktɪv) *adj.* **1.** causing or tending to cause destruction. **2.** intended to discredit, without positive suggestions: *destructive criticism.* —**de'structively** *adv.*

desuetude (dɪ'sjuːɪˌtjuːd) *n.* the condition of not being in use. [Latin *dēsuēscere* to lay aside a habit]

desultory ('dɛsəltrɪ) *adj.* **1.** passing from one thing to another in a fitful way. **2.** random: *a desultory thought.* [Latin *de-* from + *salīre* to jump] —**'desultorily** *adv.*

detach (dɪ'tætʃ) *vb.* **1.** to disengage and separate. **2.** *Mil.* to separate (a small unit) from a larger. [Old French *destachier*] —**de'tachable** *adj.*

detached (dɪ'tætʃt) *adj.* **1.** standing apart; not attached: *a detached house.* **2.** showing no emotional involvement.

detachment (dɪ'tætʃmənt) *n.* **1.** indifference; aloofness. **2.** *Mil.* a small unit separated from its main body.

detail ('diːteɪl) *n.* **1.** an item that is considered separately; particular. **2.** an item that is unimportant: *passengers' comfort was regarded as a detail.* **3.** treatment of particulars: *this essay includes too much detail.* **4.** a small section of a work of art, when considered in isolation. **5.** *Chiefly mil.* a. personnel assigned a specific duty. **b.** the duty. **6. in detail.** including all the important particulars. ~*vb.* **7.** to list fully. **8.** *Chiefly mil.* to select (personnel) for a specific duty. [Old French *detailler* to cut in pieces]

detailed ('diːteɪld) *adj.* having many details.

detain (dɪ'teɪn) *vb.* **1.** to delay (someone). **2.** to confine or hold (someone) in custody. [Latin *dētinēre*] —**detainee** (ˌdiːteɪ'niː) *n.* —**de'tainment** *n.*

detect (dɪ'tɛkt) *vb.* **1.** to perceive or notice. **2.** to discover the existence or presence of (something likely to elude observation). [Latin *dētegere* to uncover] —**de'tectable** *adj.* —**de'tector** *n.*

detection (dɪ'tɛkʃən) *n.* **1.** the act of discovering or the fact of being discovered. **2.** the act or process of extracting information.

detective (dɪ'tɛktɪv) *n.* **a.** a police officer who investigates crimes. **b.** same as **private detective.**

détente (deɪ'tɑːnt) *n.* the easing of tension between nations. [French]

detention (dɪ'tɛnʃən) *n.* **1.** imprisonment, esp. of a suspect awaiting trial. **2.** a form of punishment in which a pupil is detained after school.

detention centre *n.* a place where young people may be detained for short periods by order of a court.

deter (dɪ'tɜː) *vb.* **-terring, -terred.** to discourage (someone) from doing something or prevent (something) from occurring, by instilling fear, doubt, or anxiety. [Latin *dēterrēre*]

detergent (dɪ'tɜːdʒənt) *n.* **1.** a chemical cleansing agent, widely used in industry, laundering, etc. ~*adj.* **2.** having cleansing power. [Latin *dētergēns* wiping off]

deteriorate (dɪ'tɪərɪəˌreɪt) *vb.* to become worse. [Latin *dēterior* worse] —**de,terio-'ration** *n.*

determinant (dɪ'tɜːmɪnənt) *adj.* **1.** serving to determine. ~*n.* **2.** a factor that influences or determines. **3.** *Maths.* a square array of elements that represents the sum of certain products of these elements.

determinate (dɪ'tɜːmɪnɪt) *adj.* **1.** definitely limited or fixed. **2.** determined.

determination (dɪˌtɜːmɪ'neɪʃən) *n.* **1.** the condition of being determined; resoluteness. **2.** the act of making a decision. **3.** the act of fixing the quality, limit, or position of something.

determine (dɪ'tɜːmɪn) *vb.* **1.** to settle (an argument or a question) conclusively. **2.** to conclude, esp. after observation or consideration. **3.** to fix in scope, variety, etc.: *the river determined the edge of the property.* **4.** to make a decision. [Latin *dētermināre* to set boundaries to]

determined (dɪ'tɜːmɪnd) *adj.* of unwavering mind; resolute; firm. —**de'terminedly** *adv.*

determiner (dɪ'tɜːmɪnə) *n. Grammar.* a word, such as *the* or *all,* that determines the object to which a noun phrase refers.

determinism (dɪ'tɜːmɪˌnɪzəm) *n.* the philosophical doctrine that all events are determined by preceding events, and so freedom of choice is illusory. —**de'terminist** *n.,* *adj.*

deterrent (dɪ'tɛrənt) *n.* **1.** something that deters. **2.** a weapon, esp. nuclear, held by one state to deter attack by another. ~*adj.* **3.** tending to deter. [Latin *dēterrēns* hindering] —**de'terrence** *n.*

detest (dɪ'tɛst) *vb.* to dislike intensely. [Latin *dētestārī*] —**de'testable** *adj.*

detestation (ˌdiːtɛs'teɪʃən) *n.* intense hatred.

dethrone (dɪ'θrəʊn) *vb.* to remove from a throne or deprive of any high position. —**de'thronement** *n.*

detonate ('dɛtəˌneɪt) *vb.* to cause (an explosive device) to explode or (of an explosive device) to explode. [Latin *dētonāre* to thunder down] —ˌdeto'na-tion *n.*

detonator ('dɛtəˌneɪtə) *n.* a small amount of explosive, or a device, such as an electrical generator, used to set off an explosion.

detour ('diːtʊə) *n.* a deviation from a direct route or course of action. [French]

detoxify (diː'tɒksɪˌfaɪ) *vb.* -**fying,** -**fied.** to remove poison from. —de,toxifi'ca-tion *n.*

detract (dɪ'trækt) *vb.* (foll. by *from*) to diminish: *her anger detracts from her beauty.* [Latin *dētrahere* to pull away, disparage] —**de'tractor** *n.* —**de'traction** *n.*

detriment ('dɛtrɪmənt) *n.* disadvantage or damage. [Latin *dētrimentum* a rubbing off] —ˌdetri'mental *adj.*

detritus (dɪ'traɪtəs) *n.* **1.** a loose mass of stones and silt worn away from rocks. **2.** debris. [Latin: a rubbing away] —**de'trital** *adj.*

de trop (də 'trəʊ) *adj.* not wanted; in the way. [French]

detumescence (ˌdiːtjʊ'mɛsəns) *n.* the subsidence of a swelling. [Latin *dētumescere* to cease swelling]

deuce[1] (djuːs) *n.* **1.** a playing card or dice with two spots. **2.** *Tennis.* a tied score that requires one player to gain two successive points to win the game. [Latin *duo* two]

deuce[2] (djuːs) *Informal.* ~*interj.* **1.** an expression of annoyance or frustration. ~*n.* **2. the deuce.** used for emphasis in such phrases as **what the deuce, where the deuce.** [prob. special use of DEUCE[1] in the sense: lowest throw at dice]

deuterium (djuː'tɪərɪəm) *n.* a stable isotope of hydrogen. Symbol: D or [2]H [Greek *deuteros* second; because it is the second heaviest hydrogen isotope]

deuterium oxide *n.* same as **heavy wa-ter.**

Deutschmark ('dɔɪtʃˌmɑːk) *or* **Deutsche Mark** ('dɔɪtʃə) *n.* the standard monetary unit of West Germany. [German: German mark]

devalue (diː'væljuː) *vb.* -**valuing,** -**valued. 1.** to reduce the exchange value of (a currency). **2.** to reduce the value of (something or someone). —**de,valu'ation** *n.*

devastate ('dɛvəˌsteɪt) *vb.* **1.** to lay waste; destroy. **2.** to shock or upset greatly. [Latin *dēvastāre*] —**'devas'tation** *n.*

develop (dɪ'vɛləp) *vb.* **1.** to grow or bring to a later, more elaborate, or more advanced stage. **2.** to make or become gradually clearer or more widely known. **3.** to come or bring into existence: *he developed a new faith in God.* **4.** to follow as a result of something: *a row developed after her remarks.* **5.** to contract (an illness). **6.** to improve the value or change the use of (land). **7.** to exploit the natural resources of (a country or region). **8.** *Photog.* to treat (exposed film) with chemical solutions in order to produce a visible image. [Old French *desveloper* to unwrap]

developer (dɪ'vɛləpə) *n.* **1.** a person who develops property. **2.** *Photog.* a chemical used to develop photographs or films.

developing country *n.* a poor or non-industrial country that is seeking to develop its resources by industrialization.

development (dɪ'vɛləpmənt) *n.* **1.** the process of growing or developing. **2.** the product of developing. **3.** a fact or event that changes a situation. **4.** an area of land that has been developed. —**de,velop-'mental** *adj.*

development area *n.* (in Britain) an area which has experienced economic depression and which is given government assistance to establish new industry.

deviant ('diːvɪənt) *adj.* **1.** deviating from what is considered acceptable behaviour.

~*n.* **2.** a person whose behaviour deviates from what is considered to be acceptable. —'**deviance** *n.*

deviate ('diːvɪˌeɪt) *vb.* **1.** to differ (from others) in belief or thought. **2.** to turn aside (from a course of action). [Late Latin *dēviāre* to turn aside from the direct road] —ˌ**devi'ation** *n.*

device (dɪ'vaɪs) *n.* **1.** a machine or tool used for a specific task. **2.** *Euphemistic.* a bomb. **3.** a scheme or trick. **4.** a design or emblem. **5. leave someone to his own devices.** to leave someone alone to do as he wishes. [Old French *devis* contrivance & *devise* intention]

devil ('dɛv'l) *n.* **1. the Devil.** *Theol.* the chief spirit of evil and enemy of God. **2.** any evil spirit. **3.** a person regarded as wicked or ill-natured. **4.** a person: *poor devil.* **5.** a person regarded as daring: *be a devil!* **6.** *Informal.* something difficult or annoying. **7. between the devil and the deep blue sea.** between equally undesirable alternatives. **8. give the devil his due.** to acknowledge the talent or success of an unpleasant person. **9. talk of the devil!** used when an absent person who has been the subject of conversation appears. **10. the devil.** used for emphasis in such phrases as **what the devil, where the devil.** ~*vb.* **-illing, -illed** *or U.S.* **-iling, -iled.** **11.** to prepare (food) by coating with a highly flavoured spiced mixture. **12.** *Chiefly Brit.* to do routine literary work, esp. for a lawyer or author. [Greek *diabolos* enemy, accuser]

devilish ('dɛvəlɪʃ) *adj.* **1.** diabolic; fiendish. ~*adv., adj.* **2.** *Informal.* extreme or extremely: *devilish good food.* —'**devilishly** *adv.*

devil-may-care *adj.* reckless; happy-go-lucky.

devilment ('dɛv'lmənt) *n.* devilish or mischievous conduct.

devilry ('dɛv'lrɪ) *n.* **1.** reckless fun or mischief. **2.** wickedness.

devil's advocate *n.* a person who advocates an opposing or unpopular view for the sake of argument.

devious ('diːvɪəs) *adj.* **1.** not sincere or straightforward. **2.** (of a route or course of action) indirect. [Latin *dēvius* lying to one side of the road] —'**deviously** *adv.*

devise (dɪ'vaɪz) *vb.* **1.** to work out (something) in one's mind. **2.** *Law.* to dispose of (real property) by will. [Old French *deviser* to divide]

devoid (dɪ'vɔɪd) *adj.* (foll. by *of*) destitute (of); free (from). [Old French *devoider* to remove]

devolution (ˌdiːvə'luːʃən) *n.* a transfer of authority from a central government or organization to regional departments or administration. [Medieval Latin *dēvolūtiō* a rolling down] —ˌ**devo'lutionist** *n., adj.*

devolve (dɪ'vɒlv) *vb.* (foll. by *on, upon* or *to*) to pass or cause to pass to a successor or substitute, as duties or power. [Latin *dēvolvere* to roll down]

Devonian (də'vəʊnɪən) *adj.* **1.** *Geol.* of a

period of geological time about 405 million years ago. **2.** of or relating to Devon.

devote (dɪ'vəʊt) *vb.* to apply or dedicate (oneself, money, etc.) to some pursuit or cause. [Latin *dēvovēre* to vow]

devoted (dɪ'vəʊtɪd) *adj.* **1.** feeling or demonstrating loyalty or devotion. **2.** (foll. by *to*) dedicated or consecrated. —de'**votedly** *adv.*

devotee (ˌdɛvə'tiː) *n.* **1.** a person ardently enthusiastic about something, such as a sport. **2.** a zealous follower of a religion.

devotion (dɪ'vəʊʃən) *n.* **1.** strong attachment to or affection for a cause or person. **2.** religious zeal; piety. **3.** (*pl.*) religious observance or prayers. —de'**votional** *adj.*

devour (dɪ'vaʊə) *vb.* **1.** to eat up greedily. **2.** to engulf and destroy. **3.** to read avidly. [Latin *dēvorāre* to gulp down] —de'**vouring** *adj.*

devout (dɪ'vaʊt) *adj.* **1.** deeply religious. **2.** sincere. [Latin *dēvōtus* faithful] —de'**voutly** *adv.*

dew (djuː) *n.* drops of water condensed on a cool surface at night from vapour in the air. [Old English *dēaw*] —'**dewy** *adj.*

dewclaw ('djuːˌklɔː) *n.* a nonfunctional claw on a dog's leg.

Dewey Decimal System ('djuːɪ) *n.* a system of library book classification with ten main subject classes. [after Melvil Dewey, educator]

dewlap ('djuːˌlæp) *n.* a loose fold of skin hanging under the throat in cattle, dogs, etc. [Middle English *dew* + *lap* hanging flap]

dew-worm *n.* a large earthworm used as fishing bait.

dexter ('dɛkstə) *adj.* of or on the right side of a shield, etc., from the bearer's point of view. [Latin]

dexterity (dɛk'stɛrɪtɪ) *n.* **1.** skill in using one's hands. **2.** mental quickness. [Latin *dexteritās* aptness, readiness]

dexterous ('dɛkstrəs) *adj.* possessing or done with dexterity. —'**dexterously** *adv.*

dextrin ('dɛkstrɪn) *or* **dextrine** ('dɛkstrɪn, -triːn) *n.* a sticky substance obtained from starch: used as a thickening agent in food. [French *dextrine*]

dextrose ('dɛkstrəʊz, -trəʊs) *n.* a glucose occurring in fruit, honey, and in the blood of animals.

DF Defender of the Faith.

DFC Distinguished Flying Cross.

DFM Distinguished Flying Medal.

dg decigram.

dhal *or* **dal** (dɑːl) *n.* the nutritious pealike seed of a tropical shrub. [Hindi]

dharma ('dɑːmə) *n.* **1.** *Hinduism.* moral law or behaviour. **2.** *Buddhism.* ideal truth. [Sanskrit]

dhoti ('dəʊtɪ) *n., pl.* **-tis.** a long loincloth worn by men in India. [Hindi]

DHSS (in Britain) Department of Health and Social Security.

di- *prefix.* **1.** twice; two; double: *dicotyledon.* **2.** containing two specified atoms or groups of atoms: *carbon dioxide.* [Greek]

diabetes (ˌdaɪəˈbiːtiːz) n. an illness characterized by excretion of an abnormal amount of urine containing an excess of sugar, caused by a deficiency of insulin. [Greek: a passing through]

diabetic (ˌdaɪəˈbɛtɪk) adj. **1.** of or having diabetes. ~n. **2.** a person who has diabetes.

diabolic (ˌdaɪəˈbɒlɪk) adj. **1.** of the devil; satanic. **2.** extremely cruel or wicked. [Greek diabolos devil]

diabolical (ˌdaɪəˈbɒlɪkəl) adj. Informal. **1.** excruciatingly bad. **2.** extreme: a diabolical liberty. —ˌdiaˈbolically adv.

diabolism (daɪˈæbəˌlɪzəm) n. **a.** witchcraft or sorcery. **b.** worship of devils. —diˈabolist n.

diaconate (daɪˈækənɪt, -ˌneɪt) n. the position or period of office of a deacon. [Late Latin diāconātus] —diˈaconal adj.

diacritic (ˌdaɪəˈkrɪtɪk) n. a sign placed above or below a character or letter to indicate phonetic value or stress. [Greek diakritikos serving to distinguish]

diadem (ˈdaɪəˌdɛm) n. a royal crown, esp. a light jewelled circlet. [Greek: royal headdress]

diaeresis or esp. U.S. **dieresis** (daɪˈɛrɪsɪs) n., pl. **-ses** (-ˌsiːz). the mark ¨ placed over the second of two adjacent vowels to indicate that it is to be pronounced separately, as in naïve. [Greek: a division]

diagnose (ˈdaɪəɡˌnəʊz) vb. to determine by diagnosis.

diagnosis (ˌdaɪəɡˈnəʊsɪs) n., pl. **-ses** (-siːz). the discovery and identification of diseases from the examination of symptoms. [Greek: a distinguishing] —**diagnostic** (ˌdaɪəɡˈnɒstɪk) adj.

diagonal (daɪˈæɡənˈl) adj. **1.** Maths. connecting any two vertices in a polygon that are not adjacent. **2.** slanting. ~n. **3.** a diagonal line, plane, or pattern. [Greek dia- through + gōnia angle] —diˈagonally adv.

diagram (ˈdaɪəˌɡræm) n. a sketch or plan demonstrating the form or workings of something. [Greek diagraphein to mark out] —**diagrammatic** (ˌdaɪəɡrəˈmætɪk) adj.

dial (ˈdaɪəl) n. **1.** the face of a clock or watch, marked with divisions representing units of time. **2.** the graduated disc on a measuring instrument. **3.** the control on a radio or television set used to change the station. **4.** a numbered disc on a telephone that is rotated a set distance for each digit of a number. ~vb. **dialling, dialled** or U.S. **dialing, dialed.** **5.** to try to establish a telephone connection with (someone) by indicating (his number) on the dial. [Latin diēs day]

dialect (ˈdaɪəˌlɛkt) n. a form of a language spoken in a particular area, distinguished by its vocabulary, grammar, and pronunciation. [Greek dialektos speech, dialect] —ˌdiaˈlectal adj.

dialectic (ˌdaɪəˈlɛktɪk) n. **1.** logical debate by question and answer to resolve differences between two views. **2.** the art of

logical argument. [Greek dialektikē (tekhnē) (the art) of argument] —ˌdiaˈlectical adj.

dialling tone or U.S. & Canad. **dial tone** n. a continuous sound heard over a telephone, indicating that a number can be dialled.

dialogue or U.S. (often) **dialog** (ˈdaɪəˌlɒɡ) n. **1.** conversation between two people. **2.** a conversation in a literary or dramatic work. **3.** a discussion between representatives of two nations or groups. [Greek dia- between + legein to speak]

dialysis (daɪˈælɪsɪs) n., pl. **-ses** (-ˌsiːz). **1.** Med. the filtering of blood through a semipermeable membrane to remove waste products. **2.** the separation of the particles in a solution by filtering through a semipermeable membrane. [Greek dialuein to tear apart, dissolve] —ˈdiaˌlyser or -ˌlyzer n. —**dialytic** (ˌdaɪəˈlɪtɪk) adj.

diamagnetism (ˌdaɪəˈmæɡnɪˌtɪzəm) n. the phenomenon exhibited by substances that are repelled by both poles of a magnet.

diamanté (ˌdaɪəˈmæntɪ) adj. decorated with glittering bits of material, such as sequins. [French]

diameter (daɪˈæmɪtə) n. **a.** a straight line through the centre of a circle or sphere. **b.** the length of such a line. [Greek dia- through + metron measure]

diametric (ˌdaɪəˈmɛtrɪk) or **diametrical** adj. **1.** of or relating to a diameter. **2.** completely opposed. —**diaˈmetrically** adv.

diamond (ˈdaɪəmənd) n. **1.** a usually colourless exceptionally hard precious stone of crystallized carbon. **2.** Geom. a figure with four sides of equal length forming two acute and two obtuse angles. **3.** a playing card marked with one or more red lozenge-shaped symbols. **4.** Baseball. the playing field. [Latin adamas the hardest iron or steel, diamond]

diamond wedding n. the 60th anniversary of a marriage.

diapason (ˌdaɪəˈpeɪzˈn) n. Music. **1.** either of two stops found throughout the range of a pipe organ. **2.** the range of an instrument or voice. [Greek: through all (the notes)]

diaper (ˈdaɪəpə) n. U.S. & Canad. a nappy. [Medieval Greek diaspros pure white]

diaphanous (daɪˈæfənəs) adj. (of fabrics) fine and translucent. [Greek diaphanēs transparent]

diaphragm (ˈdaɪəˌfræm) n. **1.** Anat. the muscular partition that separates the abdominal cavity and chest cavity. **2.** same as **cap** (sense 8). **3.** a device to control the amount of light entering an optical instrument. **4.** a thin vibrating disc to convert sound signals to electrical signals or vice versa, as in telephones. [Greek dia- across + phragma fence]

diapositive (ˌdaɪəˈpɒzɪtɪv) n. a positive transparency; slide.

diarist (ˈdaɪərɪst) n. a person who writes a diary, esp. one that is published.

diarrhoea or esp. U.S. **diarrhea** (ˌdaɪəˈrɪə) n. frequent and copious discharge of abnormally liquid faeces. [Greek *dia-*through + *rhein* to flow]

diary ('daɪərɪ) *n., pl.* **-ries.** **1.** a record of daily events, appointments, or observations. **2.** a book for this. [Latin *diēs* day]

Diaspora (daɪ'æspərə) *n.* **1.** the dispersion of the Jews after the Babylonian conquest of Palestine. **2.** a dispersion of people originally belonging to one nation. [Greek: a scattering]

diastase ('daɪə,steɪs, -,steɪz) *n.* an enzyme that hydrolyses starch to maltose. [Greek *diastasis* a separation]

diatom ('daɪətəm) *n.* a microscopic unicellular alga. [Greek *diatomos* cut in two]

diatomic (,daɪə'tɒmɪk) *adj.* **a.** containing two atoms. **b.** containing two characteristic groups or atoms.

diatonic (,daɪə'tɒnɪk) *adj.* of or relating to any scale of five tones and two semitones produced by playing the white keys of a keyboard instrument. [Greek *diatonos* extending]

diatribe ('daɪə,traɪb) *n.* a bitter critical attack. [Greek *dia-* through + *tribein* to rub]

dibble ('dɪb'l) *n.* a small hand tool used to make holes in the ground for bulbs, seeds, or roots. [origin unknown]

dice (daɪs) *n., pl.* **dice.** **1.** a small cube, each of whose sides has a different number of spots (1 to 6), used in games of chance. ~*vb.* **2.** to cut (food) into small cubes. **3. dice with death.** to take a risk. [orig. pl. of DIE²]

dicey ('daɪsɪ) *adj.* **dicier, diciest.** *Informal, chiefly Brit.* dangerous; tricky.

dichotomy (daɪ'kɒtəmɪ) *n., pl.* **-mies.** division into two parts or classifications, esp. when they are opposed. [Greek *dicha* in two + *temnein* to cut] —**di'chotomous** *adj.*

dichromatic (,daɪkrəʊ'mætɪk) *adj.* having two colours. [Greek *di-* double + *khrōma* colour]

dick (dɪk) *n. Slang.* **1.** *Taboo.* a penis. **2. clever dick.** *Brit.* an opinionated person. [*Dick* familiar form of *Richard*]

dickens ('dɪkɪnz) *n. Informal, euphemistic.* used for emphasis in such phrases as **what the dickens.** [from the name *Dickens*]

Dickensian (dɪ'kenzɪən) *adj.* **1.** of Charles Dickens (1812–70), English novelist. **2.** denoting poverty, distress, and exploitation, as depicted in the novels of Dickens.

dicky¹ ('dɪkɪ) *n., pl.* **dickies.** **1.** a false shirt front. **2.** Also called: **dicky bow.** *Brit.* a bow tie. **3.** Also called: **dicky-bird.** a child's word for a bird. [from *Dick* (name)]

dicky² ('dɪkɪ) *adj.* **dickier, dickiest.** *Brit. informal.* shaky or weak: *a dicky heart.* [origin unknown]

dicotyledon (,daɪkɒtɪ'liːd'n) *n.* a flowering plant with two seed leaves.

Dictaphone ('dɪktə,fəʊn) *n. Trademark.* a tape recorder for recording dictation for subsequent typing.

dictate *vb.* (dɪk'teɪt). **1.** to say (letters, speeches, etc.) aloud for transcription by another person. **2.** to give (commands) authoritatively. **3.** to seek to impose one's will on others. ~*n.* ('dɪkteɪt). **4.** an authoritative command. **5.** a guiding principle: *the dictates of reason.* [Latin *dictāre* to say repeatedly]

dictation (dɪk'teɪʃən) *n.* **1.** the act of dictating material to be taken down in writing. **2.** the material dictated. **3.** the act of giving authoritative commands.

dictator (dɪk'teɪtə) *n.* **1.** a ruler who is not bound by a constitution or laws. **2.** a person who behaves in a tyrannical manner. —**dic'tatorship** *n.*

dictatorial (,dɪktə'tɔːrɪəl) *adj.* **1.** of or characteristic of a dictator. **2.** tyrannical; overbearing. —**dicta'torially** *adv.*

diction ('dɪkʃən) *n.* the manner of enunciating words and sounds. [Latin *dīcere* to speak]

dictionary ('dɪkʃənərɪ) *n., pl.* **-aries.** **1. a.** a book that consists of an alphabetical list of words with their meanings. **b.** a similar book giving equivalent words in two languages. **2.** a reference book listing terms and giving information about a particular subject. [Late Latin *dictiō* word]

dictum ('dɪktəm) *n., pl.* **-tums** *or* **-ta** (-tə). **1.** a formal statement; pronouncement. **2.** a popular saying or maxim. [Latin]

did (dɪd) *vb.* the past tense of **do¹.**

didactic (dɪ'dæktɪk) *adj.* **1.** intended to instruct, esp. excessively. **2.** morally instructive. [Greek *didaktikos* skilled in teaching] —**di'dactically** *adv.* —**di'dacticism** *n.*

diddle ('dɪd'l) *vb. Informal.* to swindle. [Jeremy *Diddler*, a scrounger in a 19th-cent. play] —'**diddler** *n.*

didgeridoo (,dɪdʒərɪ'duː) *n. Music.* a native deep-toned Australian wind instrument. [imit.]

didn't ('dɪd'nt) did not.

die¹ (daɪ) *vb.* **dying, died.** **1.** (of an organism) to cease all biological activity permanently. **2.** (of something inanimate) to cease to exist. **3.** (often foll. by *away, down,* or *out*) to lose strength, power, or energy by degrees. **4.** to stop working: *the engine died.* **5. be dying.** to be eager for something or to do something). **6. be dying of.** *Informal.* to be nearly overcome with (laughter, boredom, etc.). **7. die hard.** to change or disappear only slowly: *old habits die hard.* ~See also **die down, die out.** [Old English *dīegan*]

die² (daɪ) *n.* **1.** a shaped block used to cut or form metal. **2.** a casting mould. **3. the die is cast.** an irrevocable decision has been taken. [Latin *dare* to give, play]

die down *vb.* **1.** to lose strength or power by degrees. **2.** to become calm.

die-hard *n.* a person who resists change.

dielectric (,daɪɪ'lektrɪk) *n.* **1.** a substance of very low electrical conductivity; insulator. ~*adj.* **2.** having the properties of a dielectric. [Greek *dia-* through + *electric*]

die out *or* **off** *vb.* to become extinct or disappear after a gradual decline.

diesel ('diːz'l) *n.* **1.** same as **diesel engine. 2.** a vehicle driven by a diesel engine.

3. *Informal.* diesel oil. [after R. *Diesel*, engineer]

diesel-electric *n.* a locomotive with a diesel engine driving an electric generator.

diesel engine *n.* an internal-combustion engine in which atomized fuel oil is ignited by compression.

diesel oil *or* **fuel** *n.* a fuel obtained from petroleum distillation, used in diesel engines.

diet[1] (ˈdaɪət) *n.* **1.** the food that a person or animal regularly eats. **2.** a specific allowance or selection of food, to control weight or for health reasons: *a salt-free diet.* ~*vb.* **3.** to follow a special diet so as to lose weight. [Greek *diaita* mode of living] —ˈ**dietary** *adj.* —ˈ**dieter** *n.*

diet[2] (ˈdaɪət) *n.* a legislative assembly in various countries. [Medieval Latin *diēta* public meeting]

dietary fibre *n.* fibrous substances in fruits and vegetables that aid digestion.

dietetic (ˌdaɪəˈtɛtɪk) *adj.* prepared for special dietary requirements.

dietetics (ˌdaɪəˈtɛtɪks) *n.* (*functioning as sing.*) the study of food intake and preparation.

dietician (ˌdaɪəˈtɪʃən) *n.* a person who specializes in dietetics.

differ (ˈdɪfə) *vb.* **1.** to be dissimilar in quality, nature, or degree. **2.** to disagree. [Latin *differre* to scatter, be different]

difference (ˈdɪfərəns) *n.* **1.** the state or quality of being unlike. **2.** a specific instance of being unlike. **3.** a disagreement or argument. **4.** the result of the subtraction of one number or quantity from another. **5. make a difference.** to have an effect. **6. split the difference. a.** to compromise. **b.** to divide a remainder equally.

different (ˈdɪfərənt) *adj.* **1.** partly or completely unlike. **2.** new or unusual. —ˈ**differently** *adv.*

differential (ˌdɪfəˈrɛnʃəl) *adj.* **1.** of, relating to, or using a difference. **2.** *Maths.* involving differentials. ~*n.* **3.** a factor that differentiates between two comparable things. **4.** *Maths.* a minute difference between values in a scale. **5.** *Chiefly Brit.* the difference between rates of pay for different types of labour, esp. within an industry.

differential calculus *n.* the branch of calculus concerned with the study, evaluation, and use of derivatives and differentials.

differential gear *n.* the gear in the driving axle of a road vehicle that permits one driving wheel to rotate faster than the other, when cornering.

differentiate (ˌdɪfəˈrɛnʃɪˌeɪt) *vb.* **1.** to serve to distinguish (one thing from another). **2.** (often foll. by *between*) to perceive or make a difference (in or between); discriminate. **3.** *Maths.* to determine the derivative of a function or variable. —ˌ**differˌentiˈation** *n.*

difficult (ˈdɪfɪkˀlt) *adj.* **1.** not easy to do, understand, or solve. **2.** troublesome; not easily pleased or satisfied: *a difficult child.* **3.** full of hardships or trials.

difficulty (ˈdɪfɪkˀltɪ) *n.*, *pl.* **-ties.** **1.** the quality of being difficult. **2.** a problem that is hard to deal with. **3.** (*often pl.*) a troublesome or embarrassing situation, esp. a financial one. **4.** (*often pl.*) an objection or obstacle. **5.** lack of ease; awkwardness. [Latin *difficultās*]

diffident (ˈdɪfɪdənt) *adj.* lacking self-confidence; shy. [Latin *dis-* not + *fīdere* to trust] —ˈ**diffidence** *n.* —ˈ**diffidently** *adv.*

diffract (dɪˈfrækt) *vb.* to cause to undergo diffraction. —**difˈfractive** *adj.*

diffraction (dɪˈfrækʃən) *n.* **1.** *Physics.* a deviation in the direction of a wave at the edge of an obstacle in its path. **2.** the formation of light and dark fringes by the passage of light through a small aperture. [Latin *diffringere* to shatter]

diffuse *vb.* (dɪˈfjuːz). **1.** to spread in all directions. **2.** to cause to undergo diffusion. ~*adj.* (dɪˈfjuːs). **3.** spread out over a wide area. **4.** lacking conciseness. [Latin *diffūsus* spread abroad] —**diffusible** (dɪˈfjuːzɪbˀl) *adj.*

diffusion (dɪˈfjuːʒən) *n.* **1.** the act of diffusing or the fact of being diffused; dispersion. **2.** *Physics.* the random thermal motion of atoms and molecules in gases, liquids, and some solids. **3.** *Physics.* the transmission or reflection of light, in which the radiation is scattered in many directions.

dig (dɪg) *vb.* **digging, dug.** **1.** (often foll. by *up*) to cut into, break up, and turn over or remove (earth, etc.), esp. with a spade. **2.** to excavate (a hole or tunnel) by digging, usually with an implement or (of animals) with claws. **3.** (foll. by *out* or *up*) to obtain by digging. **4.** (foll. by *out* or *up*) to find by effort or searching: *to dig out facts.* **5.** (foll. by *in* or *into*) to thrust or jab. **6.** *Informal.* to like or understand. ~*n.* **7.** the act of digging. **8.** a thrust or poke. **9.** a cutting remark. **10.** an archaeological excavation. ~*See also* **dig in.** [Middle English *diggen*]

digest *vb.* (dɪˈdʒɛst, daɪ-). **1.** to subject (food) to a process of digestion. **2.** to assimilate mentally. ~*n.* (ˈdaɪdʒɛst). **3.** a comprehensive and systematic compilation of information, often condensed. [Latin *dīgerere* to divide] —di**ˈgestible** *adj.*

digestion (dɪˈdʒɛstʃən, daɪ-) *n.* **1.** the process of breaking down food into easily absorbed substances. **2.** the body's system for doing this.

digestive (dɪˈdʒɛstɪv, daɪ-) *adj.* relating to digestion.

digestive biscuit *n.* a biscuit made from wholemeal flour.

digger (ˈdɪgə) *n.* **1.** a machine used for excavation. **2.** *Austral. & N.Z. informal.* an Australian or New Zealander: often used as a friendly term of address.

dig in *vb.* **1.** to mix (compost or fertilizer) into the soil by digging. **2.** *Informal.* to begin to eat vigorously. **3. dig oneself in.** *Informal.* to entrench oneself. **4. dig one's heels in.** *Informal.* to refuse to move or be persuaded.

digit (ˈdɪdʒɪt) n. **1.** a finger or toe. **2.** any numeral from 0 to 9. [Latin *digitus* toe, finger]

digital (ˈdɪdʒɪtˀl) adj. **1.** representing data as a series of numerical values. **2.** displaying information as numbers rather than with a dial. **3.** of or possessing digits. —ˈdigitally adv.

digital audio tape n. magnetic tape on which sound is recorded digitally, giving high-fidelity reproduction.

digital clock or **watch** n. a clock or watch in which the time is indicated by digits rather than by hands on a dial.

digital computer n. a computer in which the input consists of numbers, letters, etc., that are represented internally in binary notation.

digitalis (ˌdɪdʒɪˈteɪlɪs) n. a drug prepared from foxglove leaves: used as a heart stimulant. [Latin: relating to a finger (from the shape of the foxglove flowers)]

digital recording n. a sound recording process that converts audio or analogue signals into a series of pulses.

digitate (ˈdɪdʒɪˌteɪt) adj. **1.** (of leaves) having leaflets in the form of a spread hand. **2.** (of animals) having digits.

digitize or **-ise** (ˈdɪdʒɪˌtaɪz) vb. to transcribe (data) into a digital form for processing by a computer. —ˈdigiˌtizer or -iser n.

dignified (ˈdɪgnɪˌfaɪd) adj. characterized by dignity of manner; noble.

dignify (ˈdɪgnɪˌfaɪ) vb. -fying, -fied. **1.** to add distinction to. **2.** to add a semblance of dignity to (something or someone) by the use of a pretentious name or title. [Latin *dignus* worthy + *facere* to make]

dignitary (ˈdɪgnɪtərɪ) n., pl. -taries. a person of high official position or rank.

dignity (ˈdɪgnɪtɪ) n., pl. -ties. **1.** serious, calm, and controlled behaviour or manner. **2.** the quality of being worthy of honour. **3.** sense of self-importance: *he considered the job beneath his dignity.* **4.** high rank, esp. in government or the church. [Latin *dignus* worthy]

digraph (ˈdaɪgrɑːf) n. two letters used to represent a single sound, such as *gh* in *tough*.

digress (daɪˈgres) vb. to depart from the main subject in speech or writing. [Latin *digressus* turned aside] —diˈgression n.

digs (dɪgz) pl. n. Brit. informal. lodgings. [from *diggings*, perhaps referring to where one *digs* or works]

dihedral (daɪˈhiːdrəl) adj. having or formed by two intersecting planes.

dike (daɪk) n., vb. same as **dyke**.

dilapidated (dɪˈlæpɪˌdeɪtɪd) adj. (of a building) having fallen into ruin. [Latin *dīlapidāre* to waste] —diˌlapiˈdation n.

dilate (daɪˈleɪt) vb. **1.** to make or become wider or larger. **2.** to speak or write at length. [Latin *dīlātāre* to spread out] —diˈlation or dilatation (ˌdaɪləˈteɪʃən) n.

dilatory (ˈdɪlətrɪ) adj. **1.** (of a person) tending to delay or waste time. **2.** (of an

action) intended to waste time or defer action. [Late Latin *dīlātōrius*] —ˈdilatorily adv. —ˈdilatoriness n.

dildo (ˈdɪldəʊ) n., pl. -dos. an object used as a substitute for an erect penis. [origin unknown]

dilemma (dɪˈlemə, daɪ-) n. a situation necessitating a choice between two equally undesirable alternatives. [Greek *di-* double + *lēmma* proposition]

dilettante (ˌdɪlɪˈtæntɪ) n., pl. -tantes or -tanti (-ˈtæntɪ). a person whose interest in a subject, esp. art, is superficial rather than serious. [Italian] —ˌdiletˈtantism n.

diligent (ˈdɪlɪdʒənt) adj. **1.** careful and persevering in carrying out tasks or duties. **2.** carried out with care and perseverance: *diligent work.* [Latin *dīligere* to value] —ˈdiligence n. —ˈdiligently adv.

dill (dɪl) n. an aromatic herb used for flavouring. [Old English *dile*]

dilly-dally (ˌdɪlɪˈdælɪ) vb. -lying, -lied. Informal. to loiter or vacillate. [reduplication of *dally*]

dilute (daɪˈluːt) vb. **1.** to make (a liquid) less concentrated, esp. by adding water. **2.** to make (a quality, etc.) weaker in force or effect. ~adj. **3.** Chem. (of a solution) having a low concentration. [Latin *dīluere*] —diˈlution n.

diluvial (daɪˈluːvɪəl, dɪ-) or **diluvian** adj. of a flood, esp. the great Flood described in Genesis. [Latin *dīluere* to wash away]

dim (dɪm) adj. dimmer, dimmest. **1.** badly illuminated. **2.** not clearly seen; faint. **3.** not seeing clearly. **4.** mentally dull. **5.** not clear in the mind; obscure: *a dim memory.* **6.** lacking in brightness. **7. take a dim view of.** to disapprove of. ~vb. dimming, dimmed. **8.** to become or cause to become dim. **9.** to cause to seem less bright. **10.** U.S. & Canad. same as **dip** (sense 4). [Old English *dimm*] —ˈdimly adv. —ˈdimness n.

dime (daɪm) n. a coin of the U.S. and Canada worth ten cents. [Latin *decem* ten]

dimension (dɪˈmenʃən) n. **1.** (often pl.) a measurement of the size of something in a particular direction, such as the length, width, height, or diameter. **2.** (pl.) scope; extent. **3.** aspect: *a new dimension to politics.* [Latin *dīmensiō* an extent] —diˈmensional adj.

dimer (ˈdaɪmə) n. Chem. a molecule made up of two identical molecules bonded together.

diminish (dɪˈmɪnɪʃ) vb. **1.** to make or become smaller, fewer, or less. **2.** Music. to decrease (a minor interval) by a semitone. **3.** to reduce in authority or status. [Latin *dēminuere* + archaic *minish* to lessen]

diminuendo (dɪˌmɪnjʊˈendəʊ) Music. ~n., pl. -dos. **1. a.** a gradual decrease in loudness. **b.** a passage affected by a diminuendo. ~adv. **2.** gradually decreasing in loudness. [Italian]

diminution (ˌdɪmɪˈnjuːʃən) n. reduction; decrease. [Latin *dēminūtiō*]

diminutive (dɪˈmɪnjʊtɪv) adj. **1.** very small; tiny. **2.** Grammar. **a.** denoting an affix added to a word to convey the meaning *small* or *unimportant* or to express affection. **b.** denoting a word formed by the addition of a diminutive affix. ~*n.* **3.** *Grammar.* a diminutive word or affix. —**di'minutiveness** *n.*

dimmer ('dɪmə) *n.* **1.** a device for dimming an electric light. **2.** *U.S.* **a.** a dipped headlight on a road vehicle. **b.** a parking light on a car.

dimple ('dɪmp'l) *n.* **1.** a small natural dent, esp. on the cheeks or chin. ~*vb.* **2.** to produce dimples by smiling. [Middle English *dympull*]

dimwit ('dɪm,wɪt) *n. Informal.* a stupid person. —**dim-'witted** *adj.*

din (dɪn) *n.* **1.** a loud discordant confused noise. ~*vb.* **dinning, dinned.** **2. din something into someone.** to instil something into someone by constant repetition. [Old English *dynn*]

dinar ('diːnɑː) *n.* a monetary unit of Yugoslavia and various Middle Eastern and North African countries. [Latin *dēnārius* a Roman coin]

Dincs *or* **DINKS** (dɪŋks) double income no children (*or* kids): used of couples.

dine (daɪn) *vb.* **1.** to eat dinner. **2.** (foll. by *on, off,* or *upon*) to make one's meal (of): *the guests dined upon roast beef.* [Old French *disner*]

diner ('daɪnə) *n.* **1.** a person eating a meal, esp. in a restaurant. **2.** *Chiefly U.S. & Canad.* a small cheap restaurant. **3.** short for **dining car.**

dinette (daɪ'nɛt) *n.* an alcove or small room for use as a dining room.

ding (dɪŋ) *vb.* **1.** to ring, esp. with tedious repetition. ~*n.* **2.** an imitation of the sound of a bell. [prob. imit.]

ding-dong *n.* **1.** (,dɪŋ'dɒŋ). the sound of a bell. **2.** ('dɪŋdɒŋ). a violent exchange of blows or words. [imit.]

dinges ('dɪŋəs) *n. S. African informal.* a jocular word for something whose name is unknown or forgotten; thingumabob. [Dutch *dinges* thing]

dinghy ('dɪŋɪ) *n., pl.* **-ghies.** a small boat, powered by sail, oars, or outboard motor. [Hindi or Bengali *dingi*]

dingle ('dɪŋg'l) *n.* a small wooded dell. [origin unknown]

dingo ('dɪŋgəʊ) *n., pl.* **-goes.** a wild dog of Australia. [Aboriginal]

dingy ('dɪndʒɪ) *adj.* **-gier, -giest.** **1.** dull, neglected, and drab. **2.** dirty; discoloured. [origin unknown] —'**dinginess** *n.*

dining car *n.* a railway coach in which meals are served.

dining room *n.* a room where meals are eaten.

dinkum ('dɪŋkəm) *adj. Austral. & N.Z. informal.* **1.** genuine or right: *a fair dinkum offer.* **2. dinkum oil.** the truth. [English dialect: work]

dinky ('dɪŋkɪ) *adj.* **dinkier, dinkiest.** *Brit. informal.* small and neat; dainty. [dialect *dink* neat]

dinner ('dɪnə) *n.* **1.** a meal taken in the evening. **2.** a meal taken at midday, esp.

when it is the main meal of the day. **3.** a formal social occasion at which an evening meal is served. [Old French *disner* to dine]

dinner jacket *n.* a man's semiformal evening jacket without tails, usually black.

dinner service *n.* a set of matching dishes suitable for serving a meal.

dinosaur ('daɪnə,sɔː) *n.* any of a large order of extinct prehistoric reptiles many of which were gigantic. [Greek *deinos* fearful + *sauros* lizard]

dint (dɪnt) *n.* **by dint of.** by means of: *by dint of hard work.* [Old English *dynt*]

diocesan (daɪ'ɒsɪs'n) *adj.* of or relating to a diocese.

diocese ('daɪəsɪs) *n.* the district under the jurisdiction of a bishop. [Greek *dioikēsis* administration]

diode ('daɪəʊd) *n.* **1.** a semiconductor device for converting alternating current to direct current. **2.** an electronic valve with two electrodes between which a current can flow only in one direction. [Greek *di*-double + *hodos* a way, road]

dioecious (daɪ'iːʃəs) *adj.* (of plants) having the male and female reproductive organs on separate plants. [Greek *di*- twice + *oikia* house]

Dionysian (,daɪə'nɪzɪən) *adj.* wild or orgiastic. [*Dionysus,* Greek god of wine and revelry]

dioptre *or U.S.* **diopter** (daɪ'ɒptə) *n.* a unit for measuring the refractive power of a lens. [Greek *dia*- through + *opsesthai* to see]

diorama (,daɪə'rɑːmə) *n.* **1.** a miniature three-dimensional scene, in which models of figures are seen against a background. **2.** a picture made up of illuminated translucent curtains, viewed through an aperture. [Greek *dia*- through + *horama* view]

dioxide (daɪ'ɒksaɪd) *n.* an oxide containing two oxygen atoms per molecule.

dip (dɪp) *vb.* **dipping, dipped.** **1.** to plunge or be plunged quickly or briefly into a liquid. **2.** to undergo a slight decline, esp. temporarily: *sales dipped in November.* **3.** to slope downwards. **4.** to switch (car headlights) from the main to the lower beam. **5.** to immerse (farm animals) briefly in a chemical to rid them of insects. **6.** to lower or be lowered briefly. **7.** to plunge a container or one's hands into something, esp. to obtain an object. ~*n.* **8.** the act of dipping. **9.** a brief swim. **10.** a liquid chemical in which farm animals are dipped. **11.** a depression, esp. in a landscape. **12.** a momentary sinking down. **13.** a creamy mixture into which pieces of food are dipped before being eaten. **14.** a candle made by plunging a wick into wax. ~*See also* **dip into.** [Old English *dyppan*]

Dip Ed (in Britain) Diploma in Education.

diphtheria (dɪp'θɪərɪə) *n.* a contagious disease producing fever and difficulty in breathing and swallowing. [Greek *diphthera* leather; from the membrane that forms in the throat]

diphthong ('dɪfθɒŋ) *n.* a vowel sound, occupying a single syllable, in which the speaker's tongue moves continuously from one position to another, as in the pronunciation of *a* in *late*. [Greek *di-* double + *phthongos* sound]

dip into *vb.* **1.** to draw upon: *he dipped into his savings.* **2.** to read passages at random from (a book or journal).

diploma (dɪˈpləʊmə) *n.* a document conferring a qualification or recording successful completion of a course of study. [Latin: official document, lit.: letter folded double]

diplomacy (dɪˈpləʊməsɪ) *n.* **1.** the conduct of the relations of one state with another by peaceful means. **2.** skill in the management of international relations. **3.** tact or skill in dealing with people.

diplomat (ˈdɪpləˌmæt) *n.* an official, such as an ambassador, engaged in diplomacy.

diplomatic (ˌdɪpləˈmætɪk) *adj.* **1.** of or relating to diplomacy. **2.** skilled in negotiating between states. **3.** tactful in dealing with people. [French *diplomatique* concerning the documents of diplomacy; see DIPLOMA] —**diplo'matically** *adv.*

diplomatic immunity *n.* the freedom from legal action and exemption from taxation which diplomats have in the country where they are working.

dipole (ˈdaɪˌpəʊl) *n.* **1.** two equal but opposite electric charges or magnetic poles separated by a small distance. **2.** a molecule that has two such charges or poles. —**di'polar** *adj.*

dipper (ˈdɪpə) *n.* **1.** a ladle used for dipping. **2.** a songbird that inhabits fast-flowing streams.

dipsomania (ˌdɪpsəʊˈmeɪnɪə) *n.* a compulsive desire to drink alcoholic beverages. [Greek *dipsa* thirst + *mania* madness] —**dipso'maniac** *n., adj.*

dipstick (ˈdɪpˌstɪk) *n.* a rod with notches on it dipped into a container to indicate the fluid level.

dip switch *n.* a device for dipping car headlights.

dipterous (ˈdɪptərəs) *adj.* having two wings or winglike parts. [Greek *dipteros* two-winged]

diptych (ˈdɪptɪk) *n.* a painting on two hinged panels. [Greek *di-* double + *ptuchē* a panel]

dire (ˈdaɪə) *adj.* **1.** desperate; urgent: *dire need.* **2.** likely to bring disaster; ominous. [Latin *dīrus* ominous]

direct (dɪˈrɛkt) *vb.* **1.** to conduct or control the affairs of. **2.** to give orders with authority to (a person or group). **3.** to tell (someone) the way to a place. **4.** to address (a letter, package, remarks, etc.). **5.** to provide guidance to (actors, cameramen, etc.) in (a play or film). ~*adj.* **6.** without evasion; straightforward. **7.** shortest; straight: *a direct route.* **8.** without intervening persons or agencies: *a direct link.* **9.** honest; frank. **10.** precise; exact: *a direct quotation.* **11.** diametrical: *the direct opposite.* **12.** in an unbroken line of descent: *a direct descendant.* ~*adv.* **13.** directly; straight. [Latin *dīrigere* to guide] —**di'rectness** *n.*

direct access *n.* a method of reading data from a computer file without reading through the file from the beginning.

direct current *n.* an electric current that flows in one direction only.

direction (dɪˈrɛkʃən) *n.* **1.** the course or line along which a person or thing moves, points, or lies. **2.** management or guidance. **3.** the work of a stage or film director.

directional (dɪˈrɛkʃənˀl) *adj.* **1.** of or showing direction. **2.** *Electronics.* (of an aerial) transmitting or receiving radio waves more effectively in some directions than in others.

directions (dɪˈrɛkʃənz) *pl. n.* instructions for doing something or for reaching a place.

directive (dɪˈrɛktɪv) *n.* an instruction; order.

directly (dɪˈrɛktlɪ) *adv.* **1.** in a direct manner. **2.** at once; without delay. **3.** (often foll. by *before* or *after*) immediately; just. ~*conj.* **4.** as soon as.

direct object *n. Grammar.* a noun, pronoun, or noun phrase denoting the person or thing receiving the direct action of a verb. For example, *a book* in *They bought Anne a book.*

director (dɪˈrɛktə) *n.* **1.** a person or thing that directs or controls. **2.** a member of the governing board of a business or an institution, trust, etc. **3.** the person responsible for the artistic and technical aspects of the making of a film or television programme. —**direc'torial** *adj.* —**di'rector,ship** *n.*

directorate (dɪˈrɛktərɪt) *n.* **1.** a board of directors. **2.** the position of director.

directory (dɪˈrɛktrɪ) *n., pl.* **-ries.** a book listing names, addresses, and telephone numbers of individuals or firms.

direct speech *n.* the reporting of what someone has said by quoting the exact words.

direct tax *n.* a tax paid by the person or organization on which it is levied.

dirge (dɜːdʒ) *n.* **1.** a chant of lamentation for the dead. **2.** any mournful song. [Latin *dīrige* direct (imperative), opening word of antiphon used in the office of the dead]

dirigible (ˈdɪrɪdʒɪbˀl) *adj.* **1.** able to be steered. ~*n.* **2.** same as **airship.** [Latin *dīrigere* to direct]

dirk (dɜːk) *n.* a dagger, formerly worn by Scottish Highlanders. [Scot. *durk*]

dirndl (ˈdɜːndˀl) *n.* **1.** a woman's dress with a full gathered skirt and fitted bodice. **2.** a gathered skirt of this kind. [from German]

dirt (dɜːt) *n.* **1.** any unclean substance, such as mud; filth. **2.** loose earth; soil. **3. a.** packed earth, cinders, etc., used to make a racetrack. **b.** (*as modifier*): *a dirt track.* **4.** obscene speech or writing. [Old Norse *drit* excrement]

dirt-cheap *adj., adv. Informal.* at an extremely low price.

dirty (ˈdɜːtɪ) *adj.* **dirtier, dirtiest. 1.** covered or marked with dirt; filthy. **2. a.** obscene: *dirty books.* **b.** sexually clandestine: *a dirty weekend.* **3.** causing one to become grimy: *a dirty job.* **4.** (of a colour) not clear and bright. **5.** unfair, dishonest, or unkind. **6.** revealing dislike or anger: *a dirty look.* **7.** (of weather) rainy or stormy. **8. dirty work.** unpleasant or illicit activity. ~*n.* **9. do the dirty on.** *Informal.* to behave meanly towards. ~*vb.* **dirtying, dirtied. 10.** to make dirty; soil. —**'dirtiness** *n.*

dis- *prefix.* indicating: **1.** reversal: *disconnect.* **2.** negation or lack: *dissimilar; disgrace.* **3.** removal or release: *disembowel.* [Latin]

disability (ˌdɪsəˈbɪlɪtɪ) *n., pl.* **-ties. 1.** the condition of being physically or mentally impaired. **2.** something that disables; handicap.

disable (dɪsˈeɪbʰl) *vb.* to make ineffective, unfit, or incapable, as by crippling. —**disˈabled** *adj.* —**disˈablement** *n.*

disabuse (ˌdɪsəˈbjuːz) *vb.* (foll. by *of*) to rid (someone) of a mistaken idea.

disadvantage (ˌdɪsədˈvɑːntɪdʒ) *n.* **1.** an unfavourable circumstance, thing, or situation: *at a disadvantage.* **2.** injury, loss, or detriment. —**ˌdisadvanˈtageous** *adj.*

disadvantaged (ˌdɪsədˈvɑːntɪdʒd) *adj.* socially or economically deprived.

disaffected (ˌdɪsəˈfɛktɪd) *adj.* having lost loyalty to or affection for someone or something; alienated. —**ˌdisafˈfection** *n.*

disagree (ˌdɪsəˈɡriː) *vb.* **-greeing, -greed.** (often foll. by *with*) **1.** to dissent in opinion or dispute (about an idea or fact). **2.** to fail to correspond; conflict. **3.** to cause physical discomfort to: *curry disagrees with me.*

disagreeable (ˌdɪsəˈɡrɪəbʰl) *adj.* **1.** (of a person) not likable; bad-tempered or disobliging. **2.** (of an incident or situation) not to one's liking; unpleasant. —**ˌdisaˈgreeably** *adv.*

disagreement (ˌdɪsəˈɡriːmənt) *n.* **1.** refusal or failure to agree. **2.** a failure to correspond. **3.** an argument or dispute.

disallow (ˌdɪsəˈlaʊ) *vb.* to reject as untrue or invalid; cancel.

disappear (ˌdɪsəˈpɪə) *vb.* **1.** to cease to be visible; vanish. **2.** to go away or become lost, esp. without explanation. **3.** to cease to exist. —**ˌdisapˈpearance** *n.*

disappoint (ˌdɪsəˈpɔɪnt) *vb.* **1.** to fail to meet the expectations or hopes of; let down. **2.** to prevent the fulfilment of (a plan, etc.); frustrate. [Old French *desapointier*] —**ˌdisapˈpointed** *adj.* —**ˌdisapˈpointing** *adj.*

disappointment (ˌdɪsəˈpɔɪntmənt) *n.* **1.** the feeling of being disappointed. **2.** a person or thing that disappoints.

disapprobation (ˌdɪsæprəʊˈbeɪʃən) *n.* disapproval.

disapprove (ˌdɪsəˈpruːv) *vb.* (often foll. by *of*) to consider wrong or bad. —**ˌdisapˈproval** *n.* —**ˌdisapˈproving** *adj.*

disarm (dɪsˈɑːm) *vb.* **1.** to deprive of weapons. **2.** to win the confidence or affection of. **3.** (of a nation) to decrease the size and capability of one's armed forces.

disarmament (dɪsˈɑːməmənt) *n.* the reduction of fighting capability by a nation.

disarming (dɪsˈɑːmɪŋ) *adj.* tending to neutralize hostility or suspicion. —**disˈarmingly** *adv.*

disarrange (ˌdɪsəˈreɪndʒ) *vb.* to throw into disorder. —**ˌdisarˈrangement** *n.*

disarray (ˌdɪsəˈreɪ) *n.* **1.** confusion and lack of discipline. **2.** extreme untidiness. ~*vb.* **3.** to throw into confusion.

disassociate (ˌdɪsəˈsəʊʃɪˌeɪt, -sɪ-) *vb.* same as **dissociate.** —**ˌdisasˌsociˈation** *n.*

disaster (dɪˈzɑːstə) *n.* **1.** an occurrence that causes great distress or destruction. **2.** a thing, project, etc., that fails or has been ruined. [Italian *disastro*] —**disˈastrous** *adj.* —**disˈastrously** *adv.*

disavow (ˌdɪsəˈvaʊ) *vb.* to deny connection with or responsibility for (something). —**ˌdisaˈvowal** *n.*

disband (dɪsˈbænd) *vb.* to cease to function or cause to stop functioning as a unit or group. —**disˈbandment** *n.*

disbelieve (ˌdɪsbɪˈliːv) *vb.* **1.** to reject as false or lying. **2.** (foll. by *in*) to have no faith (in). —**ˌdisbeˈlief** *n.*

disburse (dɪsˈbɜːs) *vb.* to pay out. [Old French *desborser*] —**disˈbursement** *n.*

disc (dɪsk) *n.* **1.** a flat circular object. **2.** a gramophone record. **3.** *Anat.* a circular flat structure in the body, esp. between the vertebrae. **4.** *Computers.* same as **disk.** [Latin *discus* discus]

discard (dɪsˈkɑːd) *vb.* **1.** to get rid of (something or someone) as useless or undesirable. **2.** *Cards.* to play (a card of little value) when unable to follow suit. [DIS- + *card* (the playing card)]

disc brake *n.* a brake in which two pads rub against a flat disc.

discern (dɪˈsɜːn) *vb.* to see or be aware of (something) clearly. [Latin *discernere* to divide] —**disˈcernible** *adj.*

discerning (dɪˈsɜːnɪŋ) *adj.* having or showing good judgment. —**disˈcernment** *n.*

discharge *vb.* (dɪsˈtʃɑːdʒ) **1.** to release or allow to go. **2.** to dismiss (someone) from duty or employment. **3.** to fire (a gun). **4.** to cause to pour forth: *the boil discharges pus.* **5.** to remove (the cargo) from a boat, etc.; unload. **6.** to meet the demands of (an office, obligation, etc.). **7.** to relieve oneself of (a responsibility or debt). **8.** *Physics.* to take or supply electrical current from (a cell or battery). **9.** *Law.* to release (a prisoner from custody, etc.). ~*n.* (ˈdɪstʃɑːdʒ, dɪsˈtʃɑːdʒ). **10.** something that is discharged. **11.** dismissal or release from an office, job, institution, etc. **12.** a pouring forth of a fluid; emission. **13.** *Physics.* a conduction of electricity through a gas.

disciple (dɪˈsaɪpʰl) *n.* **1.** a follower of the doctrines of a teacher. **2.** one of the personal followers of Christ during his earthly life. [Latin *discipulus* pupil]

disciplinarian (ˌdɪsɪplɪˈnɛərɪən) *n.* a person who practises strict discipline.

disciplinary (ˈdɪsɪˌplɪnərɪ) *adj.* of or imposing discipline; corrective.

discipline ('dɪsɪplɪn) *n.* **1.** training imposed for the improvement of physical powers, self-control, etc. **2.** systematic training in obedience. **3.** the state of improved behaviour resulting from such training. **4.** punishment. **5.** a branch of learning or instruction. ~*vb.* **6.** to improve or attempt to improve the behaviour or orderliness of (oneself or another) by training, conditions, or rules. **7.** to punish. [Latin *disciplīna* teaching]

disc jockey *n.* a person who announces and plays recorded pop music on a radio programme or at a disco.

disclaim (dɪs'kleɪm) *vb.* **1.** to deny (responsibility for or knowledge of something). **2.** to give up (any claim to).

disclaimer (dɪs'kleɪmə) *n.* a repudiation or denial.

disclose (dɪs'kləʊz) *vb.* **1.** to make known. **2.** to allow to be seen. —**dis'closure** *n.*

disco ('dɪskəʊ) *n., pl.* **-cos. 1.** an occasion at which people dance to pop records. **2.** a nightclub or other public place where such dances are held. **3.** mobile equipment for providing music for a disco.

discolour *or U.S.* **discolor** (dɪs'kʌlə) *vb.* to change in colour; fade or stain. —**dis,colour'ation** *n.*

discomfit (dɪs'kʌmfɪt) *vb.* **1.** to make uneasy or confused. **2.** to frustrate the plans of. [Old French *desconfire* to destroy] —**dis'comfiture** *n.*

discomfort (dɪs'kʌmfət) *n.* **1.** an inconvenience, distress, or mild pain. **2.** something that disturbs or deprives of ease.

discommode (,dɪskə'məʊd) *vb.* to cause inconvenience. [DIS- + obs. *commode* to suit] —**,discom'modious** *adj.*

discompose (,dɪskəm'pəʊz) *vb.* to disturb; disconcert. —**,discom'posure** *n.*

disconcert (,dɪskən'sɜːt) *vb.* to disturb the confidence or self-possession of; upset, embarrass, or take aback. —**,discon'certing** *adj.*

disconnect (,dɪskə'nekt) *vb.* **1.** to undo or break the connection between two things. **2.** to stop the supply of (gas or electricity to a building). —**,discon'nection** *n.*

disconnected (,dɪskə'nektɪd) *adj.* (of speech or ideas) not logically connected; incoherent.

disconsolate (dɪs'kɒnsəlɪt) *adj.* sad beyond comfort. [Medieval Latin *disconsōlātus*] —**dis'consolately** *adv.*

discontent (,dɪskən'tent) *n.* lack of contentment, as with one's condition or lot in life. —**,discon'tented** *adj.* —**,discon'tentedly** *adv.*

discontinue (,dɪskən'tɪnjuː) *vb.* **-uing, -ued.** to come or bring to an end; stop.

discontinuous (,dɪskən'tɪnjʊəs) *adj.* characterized by interruptions; intermittent. —**,disconti'nuity** *n.*

discord ('dɪskɔːd) *n.* **1.** lack of agreement or harmony between people. **2.** harsh confused sounds. **3.** a combination of musical notes that lacks harmony. [Latin *discors* at variance]

discordant (dɪs'kɔːd²nt) *adj.* **1.** at variance; disagreeing. **2.** harsh in sound; inharmonious. —**dis'cordance** *n.*

discotheque ('dɪskəʊ,tek) *n.* same as **disco.** [French]

discount *vb.* (dɪs'kaʊnt, 'dɪskaʊnt). **1.** to leave (something) out of account as being unreliable, prejudiced, or irrelevant. **2.** to deduct (an amount or percentage) from the price of something. ~*n.* ('dɪskaʊnt). **3.** a deduction from the full amount of a price. **4. at a discount.** below the regular price.

discountenance (dɪs'kaʊntɪnəns) *vb.* to make (someone) ashamed or confused.

discourage (dɪs'kʌrɪdʒ) *vb.* **1.** to deprive of the will to persist in something. **2.** to oppose by expressing disapproval. —**dis'couragement** *n.* —**dis'couraging** *adj.*

discourse *n.* ('dɪskɔːs, dɪs'kɔːs). **1.** conversation. **2.** a formal treatment of a subject in speech or writing. ~*vb.* (dɪs'kɔːs). **3.** (foll. by *on* or *upon*) to speak or write (about) at length. [Medieval Latin *discursus* argument]

discourteous (dɪs'kɜːtɪəs) *adj.* showing bad manners; rude. —**dis'courteously** *adv.* —**dis'courtesy** *n.*

discover (dɪ'skʌvə) *vb.* **1.** to be the first to find or find out about. **2.** to learn about for the first time. **3.** to find after study or search. —**dis'coverer** *n.*

discovery (dɪ'skʌvərɪ) *n., pl.* **-eries. 1.** the act of discovering. **2.** a person, place, or thing that has been discovered.

discredit (dɪs'kredɪt) *vb.* **1.** to damage the reputation of (someone). **2.** to cause (an idea) to be disbelieved or distrusted. ~*n.* **3.** something that causes disgrace. —**dis'creditable** *adj.*

discreet (dɪ'skriːt) *adj.* **1.** careful to avoid embarrassment, esp. by keeping confidences secret; tactful. **2.** unobtrusive. [Old French *discret*] —**dis'creetly** *adv.*

discrepancy (dɪ'skrepənsɪ) *n., pl.* **-cies.** a conflict or variation between facts, figures, or claims. [Latin *discrepāre* to differ in sound] —**dis'crepant** *adj.*

discrete (dɪs'kriːt) *adj.* separate or distinct. [Latin *discrētus* separated] —**dis'creteness** *n.*

discretion (dɪ'skreʃən) *n.* **1.** the quality of behaving so as to avoid social embarrassment or distress. **2.** freedom or authority to make judgments and to act as one sees fit: *use your own discretion.* **3. age or years of discretion.** the age at which one is thought able to manage one's own affairs. —**dis'cretionary** *adj.*

discriminate (dɪ'skrɪmɪ,neɪt) *vb.* **1.** (usu. foll. by *against* or *in favour of*) to single out a particular person or group, etc., for special disfavour or favour. **2.** (foll. by *between* or *among*) to recognize or understand the difference (between). [Latin *discrimināre* to divide] —**dis'crimi,nating** *adj.*

discrimination (dɪ,skrɪmɪ'neɪʃən) *n.* **1.** unfair treatment of a person, racial group, minority, etc., based on prejudice. **2.** subtle appreciation in matters of taste. **3.** the ability to see fine distinctions.

discriminatory (dɪˈskrɪmɪnətrɪ) *adj.* based on prejudice.

discursive (dɪˈskɜːsɪv) *adj.* passing from one topic to another. [Latin *discursus* a running to and fro]

discus (ˈdɪskəs) *n. Field sports.* a disc-shaped object with a heavy middle, thrown by athletes. [Greek *diskos*]

discuss (dɪˈskʌs) *vb.* **1.** to consider (something) by talking it over. **2.** to treat (a subject) in speech or writing. [Latin *discutere* to dash to pieces] —**dis'cussion** *n.*

disdain (dɪsˈdeɪn) *n.* **1.** a feeling of superiority and dislike; contempt. ~*vb.* **2.** to refuse with disdain: *she disdained to reply.* [Old French *desdeign*] —**dis'dainful** *adj.* —**dis'dainfully** *adv.*

disease (dɪˈziːz) *n.* **1.** an illness or sickness. **2.** a corresponding condition in plants. [Old French *desaise*] —**dis'eased** *adj.*

diseconomy (ˌdɪsɪˈkɒnəmɪ) *n. Econ.* a disadvantage, such as higher costs, resulting from the scale on which an enterprise operates.

disembark (ˌdɪsɪmˈbɑːk) *vb.* to land or cause to land from a ship, aircraft, or bus. —**disembarkation** (dɪsˌembɑːˈkeɪʃən) *n.*

disembodied (ˌdɪsɪmˈbɒdɪd) *adj.* **1.** lacking a body. **2.** seeming not to be attached to or come from anyone. —**disem'bodiment** *n.*

disembowel (ˌdɪsɪmˈbaʊəl) *vb.* **-elling, -elled** *or U.S.* **-eling, -eled.** to remove the entrails of. —**disem'bowelment** *n.*

disenchant (ˌdɪsɪnˈtʃɑːnt) *vb.* to free (someone) from or as if from an enchantment; disillusion. —**disen'chantment** *n.*

disengage (ˌdɪsɪnˈɡeɪdʒ) *vb.* **1.** to release or become released from a connection, obligation, etc. **2.** *Mil.* to withdraw from close action. —**disen'gagement** *n.*

disentangle (ˌdɪsɪnˈtæŋɡ'l) *vb.* **1.** to release from entanglement or confusion. **2.** to unravel or work out. —**disen'tanglement** *n.*

disequilibrium (ˌdɪsiːkwɪˈlɪbrɪəm) *n.* a loss or absence of stability or balance.

disestablish (ˌdɪsɪˈstæblɪʃ) *vb.* to deprive (a church, custom, institution, etc.) of established status. —**dises'tablishment** *n.*

disfavour *or U.S.* **disfavor** (dɪsˈfeɪvə) *n.* **1.** disapproval or dislike. **2.** the state of being disapproved of or disliked.

disfigure (dɪsˈfɪɡə) *vb.* to spoil the appearance or shape of. —**dis'figurement** *n.*

disfranchise (dɪsˈfræntʃaɪz) *or* **disenfranchise** *vb.* to deprive (a person) of the right to vote or other rights of citizenship. —**disfranchisement** (dɪsˈfræntʃɪzmənt) *n.*

disgorge (dɪsˈɡɔːdʒ) *vb.* **1.** to throw out (food) from the throat; vomit. **2.** to discharge (contents).

disgrace (dɪsˈɡreɪs) *n.* **1.** a condition of shame, loss of reputation, or dishonour. **2.** a shameful person or thing. **3.** exclusion

from confidence or trust: *he is in disgrace with his father.* ~*vb.* **4.** to bring shame upon (oneself or others). —**dis'graceful** *adj.* —**dis'gracefully** *adv.*

disgruntled (dɪsˈɡrʌnt'ld) *adj.* sulky or discontented. [DIS- + obs. *gruntle* to complain] —**dis'gruntlement** *n.*

disguise (dɪsˈɡaɪz) *vb.* **1.** to change the appearance or manner in order to conceal the identity of (someone or something). **2.** to misrepresent (something) in order to obscure its actual nature or meaning. ~*n.* **3.** a mask, costume, or manner that disguises. **4.** the state of being disguised. [Old French *desguisier*] —**dis'guised** *adj.*

disgust (dɪsˈɡʌst) *vb.* **1.** to sicken or fill with loathing. ~*n.* **2.** a great loathing or distaste. [Old French *desgouster*] —**dis'gusted** *adj.* —**dis'gusting** *adj.*

dish (dɪʃ) *n.* **1.** a container used for holding or serving food, esp. an open shallow container. **2.** the food in a dish. **3.** a particular kind of food. **4.** something resembling a dish. **5.** short for **dish aerial. 6.** *Informal.* an attractive person. ~*vb.* **7.** to make concave. **8.** *Brit. informal.* to ruin or spoil. ~See also **dish out, dish up.** [Old English *disc*]

dishabille (ˌdɪsæˈbiːl) *or* **deshabille** *n.* the state of being partly dressed. [French *déshabillé*]

dish aerial *n. Brit.* a microwave aerial, used esp. in radar, radio telescopes, and satellite broadcasting, consisting of a concave dish-shaped reflector.

disharmony (dɪsˈhɑːmənɪ) *n.* lack of agreement or harmony. —**disharmonious** (ˌdɪshɑːˈməʊnɪəs) *adj.*

dishcloth (ˈdɪʃˌklɒθ) *n.* a cloth for washing dishes.

dishearten (dɪsˈhɑːt'n) *vb.* to weaken or destroy the hope, courage, or enthusiasm of. —**dis'heartened** *adj.* —**dis'heartening** *adj.*

dishevelled *or U.S.* **disheveled** (dɪˈʃev'ld) *adj.* (of a person's hair, clothes, or general appearance) disordered and untidy. [Old French *deschevelé*]

dishonest (dɪsˈɒnɪst) *adj.* not honest or fair. —**dis'honestly** *adv.* —**dis'honesty** *n.*

dishonour *or U.S.* **dishonor** (dɪsˈɒnə) *vb.* **1.** to treat with disrespect. **2.** to refuse to pay (a cheque, etc.). ~*n.* **3.** a lack of honour or respect. **4.** a state of shame or disgrace. **5.** something that causes a loss of honour. —**dis'honourable** *adj.* —**dis'honourably** *adv.*

dish out *vb.* **1.** *Informal.* to distribute. **2.** **dish it out.** to inflict punishment.

dish up *vb.* to serve (food).

dishwasher (ˈdɪʃˌwɒʃə) *n.* a machine for washing dishes, cutlery, etc.

dishwater (ˈdɪʃˌwɔːtə) *n.* **1.** water in which dishes have been washed. **2.** like **dishwater.** (of tea) very weak.

dishy (ˈdɪʃɪ) *adj.* **dishier, dishiest.** *Informal, chiefly Brit.* good-looking.

disillusion (ˌdɪsɪˈluːʒən) *vb.* **1.** to destroy the illusions or false ideas of (someone).

~*n. also* **disillusionment. 2.** the state of being disillusioned.

disincentive (ˌdɪsɪn'sɛntɪv) *n.* something that acts as a deterrent.

disinclined (ˌdɪsɪn'klaɪnd) *adj.* unwilling. —**disinclination** (ˌdɪsɪnklɪ'neɪʃən) *n.*

disinfect (ˌdɪsɪn'fɛkt) *vb.* to rid of harmful germs, esp. by chemical means. —ˌ**disin-**ˈ**fection** *n.*

disinfectant (ˌdɪsɪn'fɛktənt) *n.* a substance that destroys harmful germs.

disinformation (ˌdɪsɪnfə'meɪʃən) *n.* false information intended to mislead.

disingenuous (ˌdɪsɪn'dʒɛnjʊəs) *adj.* not sincere. —ˌ**disin**ˈ**genuously** *adv.*

disinherit (ˌdɪsɪn'hɛrɪt) *vb. Law.* to deprive (an heir) of inheritance. —ˌ**disin-**ˈ**heritance** *n.*

disintegrate (dɪs'ɪntɪˌgreɪt) *vb.* **1.** to break into fragments; shatter. **2.** to lose cohesion; break up: *the marriage disintegrated.* **3.** *Physics.* **a.** to undergo nuclear fission or include nuclear fission in. **b.** same as **decay** (sense 3). —**dis,inte**ˈ**gration** *n.*

disinter (ˌdɪsɪn'tɜː) *vb.* -**terring,** -**terred. 1.** to dig up. **2.** to bring to light; expose.

disinterested (dɪs'ɪntrɪstɪd) *adj.* **1.** free from bias; objective. **2.** *Not universally accepted.* feeling or showing a lack of interest; uninterested. —**dis**ˈ**interest** *n.*

disjointed (dɪs'dʒɔɪntɪd) *adj.* having no coherence; disconnected.

disjunctive (dɪs'dʒʌŋktɪv) *adj.* serving to disconnect or separate.

disk (dɪsk) *n.* **1.** *Chiefly U.S. & Canad.* same as **disc. 2.** *Computers.* a storage device, consisting of a stack of plates coated with a magnetic layer, which rotates rapidly as a single unit. [see DISC]

disk drive *n. Computers.* the unit that controls the mechanism for handling a floppy disk.

dislike (dɪs'laɪk) *vb.* **1.** to consider unpleasant or disagreeable. ~*n.* **2.** a feeling of aversion.

dislocate ('dɪsləˌkeɪt) *vb.* **1.** to displace (a bone or joint) from its normal position. **2.** to disrupt or shift out of place. —ˌ**dis-**loˈ**cation** *n.*

dislodge (dɪs'lɒdʒ) *vb.* to remove (something) from a previously fixed position.

disloyal (dɪs'lɔɪəl) *adj.* not loyal; deserting one's allegiance. —**dis**ˈ**loyalty** *n.*

dismal ('dɪzməl) *adj.* **1.** causing gloom or depression. **2.** *Informal.* of poor quality. [Medieval Latin *diēs malī* unlucky days] —ˈ**dismally** *adv.*

dismantle (dɪs'mænt'l) *vb.* **1.** to take apart. **2.** to demolish piece by piece. [Old French *desmanteler*]

dismay (dɪs'meɪ) *vb.* **1.** to fill with alarm or depression. ~*n.* **2.** consternation or agitation. [Old French *des-* (intensive) + *esmayer* to frighten]

dismember (dɪs'mɛmbə) *vb.* **1.** to remove the limbs of. **2.** to cut to pieces. —**dis-**ˈ**memberment** *n.*

dismiss (dɪs'mɪs) *vb.* **1.** to discharge from employment. **2.** to allow (someone) to

leave. **3.** to put out of one's mind; no longer think about. **4.** to decline further hearing to (a claim or lawsuit). **5.** *Cricket.* to bowl out (a side) for a particular number of runs. [Latin *dis-* from + *mittere* to send] —**dis**ˈ**missal** *n.* —**dis**ˈ**missive** *adj.*

dismount (dɪs'maʊnt) *vb.* **1.** to get off a horse or bicycle. **2.** to take apart.

disobedient (ˌdɪsə'biːdɪənt) *adj.* refusing to obey. —ˌ**diso**ˈ**bedience** *n.*

disobey (ˌdɪsə'beɪ) *vb.* to neglect or refuse to obey (someone, an order, etc.).

disobliging (ˌdɪsə'blaɪdʒɪŋ) *adj.* unwilling to help; unaccommodating.

disorder (dɪs'ɔːdə) *n.* **1.** a state of untidiness and disorganization. **2.** public violence or rioting. **3.** an illness. —**dis**ˈ**ordered** *adj.*

disorderly (dɪs'ɔːdəlɪ) *adj.* **1.** untidy and disorganized. **2.** uncontrolled; unruly. **3.** *Law.* violating public peace.

disorganize *or* -**ise** (dɪs'ɔːgəˌnaɪz) *vb.* to disrupt the arrangement or system of. —**dis,organi**ˈ**zation** *or* -**i**ˈ**sation** *n.*

disorientate (dɪs'ɔːrɪɛnˌteɪt) *or* **disorient** *vb.* to cause (someone) to lose his bearings. —**dis,orien**ˈ**tation** *n.*

disown (dɪs'əʊn) *vb.* to deny any connection with (someone).

disparage (dɪ'spærɪdʒ) *vb.* **1.** to speak contemptuously of. **2.** to damage the reputation of. [Old French *desparagier*] —**dis-**ˈ**paragement** *n.* —**dis**ˈ**paraging** *adj.*

disparate ('dɪspərɪt) *adj.* utterly different in kind. [Latin *disparāre* to divide] —**disparity** (dɪ'spærɪtɪ) *n.*

dispassionate (dɪs'pæʃənɪt) *adj.* uninfluenced by emotion; objective. —**dis**ˈ**passionately** *adv.*

dispatch *or* **despatch** (dɪ'spætʃ) *vb.* **1.** to send off to a destination or to perform a task. **2.** to carry out (a duty or task) promptly. **3.** to murder. ~*n.* **4.** an official communication or report, sent in haste. **5.** a report sent to a newspaper by a correspondent. **6.** murder. **7. with dispatch.** quickly. [Italian *dispacciare*]

dispatch rider *n.* a motorcyclist or (formerly) horseman who carries despatches.

dispel (dɪ'spɛl) *vb.* -**pelling,** -**pelled.** to disperse or drive away. [Latin *dispellere*]

dispensable (dɪ'spɛnsəb'l) *adj.* not essential; expendable.

dispensary (dɪ'spɛnsərɪ) *n., pl.* -**ries.** a place where medicine is dispensed.

dispensation (ˌdɪspɛn'seɪʃən) *n.* **1.** the act of distributing or dispensing. **2.** *Chiefly R.C. Church.* permission to dispense with an obligation of church law. **3.** any exemption from an obligation. **4.** an administrative system. **5.** the ordering of life and events by God.

dispense (dɪ'spɛns) *vb.* **1.** to distribute in portions. **2.** to prepare and distribute (medicine), esp. on prescription. **3.** to administer (the law, etc.). **4. dispense with.** to do away with or manage without. [Latin *dispendere* to weigh out] —**dis-**ˈ**penser** *n.*

disperse (dɪ'spɜːs) *vb.* **1.** to scatter over

a wide area. **2.** to leave or cause to leave a gathering. **3.** to separate (light) into its different wavelengths. **4.** to spread (news, etc.). **5.** to separate (particles) throughout a solid, liquid, or gas. [Latin *dispergere* to scatter widely] —**dis'persal** or **dis'persion** n.

dispirit (dɪ'spɪrɪt) vb. to make downhearted. —**dis'pirited** adj. —**dis'piriting** adj.

displace (dɪs'pleɪs) vb. **1.** to move from the usual location. **2.** to remove from office.

displaced person n. a person removed from his home or country, esp. by war or revolution.

displacement (dɪs'pleɪsmənt) n. **1.** the act of displacing. **2.** the weight or volume displaced by a body in a fluid.

display (dɪ'spleɪ) vb. **1.** to show or exhibit. **2.** to disclose; reveal. ~n. **3.** the act of exhibiting or displaying. **4.** something exhibited or displayed. **5.** an exhibition. **6.** *Electronics*. a device capable of representing information visually, as on a screen. **7.** *Zool.* a pattern of behaviour by which an animal attracts attention while courting, defending its territory, etc. [Anglo-French *despleier* to unfold]

displease (dɪs'pliːz) vb. to annoy or offend (someone). —**displeasure** (dɪs'plɛʒə) n.

disport (dɪ'spɔːt) vb. **disport oneself.** to indulge oneself in pleasure. [Anglo-French]

disposable (dɪ'spəʊzəb'l) adj. **1.** designed for disposal after use: *disposable cups*. **2.** available for use if needed: *disposable assets*.

disposal (dɪ'spəʊz'l) n. **1.** the act or means of getting rid of something. **2.** at one's disposal. available for use.

dispose (dɪ'spəʊz) vb. **1.** (foll. by *of*) **a.** to deal with or settle. **b.** to give, sell, or transfer to another. **c.** to throw away. **d.** to kill. **2.** to make willing or receptive. **3.** to place in a certain order. [Latin *dispōnere* to set in different places]

disposition (ˌdɪspə'zɪʃən) n. **1.** a person's usual temperament. **2.** a tendency or habit. **3.** arrangement; layout.

dispossess (ˌdɪspə'zɛs) vb. to take away (something, esp. property) from. —**dispos'sessed** adj. —**dispos'session** n.

disproportion (ˌdɪsprə'pɔːʃən) n. lack of proportion or equality.

disproportionate (ˌdɪsprə'pɔːʃənɪt) adj. out of proportion; unequal. —**dispro'portionately** adv.

disprove (dɪs'pruːv) vb. to show (an assertion or claim) to be incorrect.

dispute vb. (dɪ'spjuːt). **1.** to argue or quarrel about (something). **2.** to doubt the validity of. **3.** to fight over possession of. ~n. (dɪ'spjuːt, 'dɪspjuːt). **4.** an argument. [Latin *disputāre* to discuss] —**dispu'tation** n. —**dispu'tatious** adj.

disqualify (dɪs'kwɒlɪˌfaɪ) vb. **-fying, -fied.** **1.** to debar from a contest. **2.** to make ineligible, as for entry to an examination. —**dis,qualifi'cation** n.

disquiet (dɪs'kwaɪət) n. **1.** a feeling of anxiety or uneasiness. ~vb. **2.** to make (someone) anxious. —**dis'quieting** adj. —**dis'quietude** n.

disregard (ˌdɪsrɪ'gɑːd) vb. **1.** to give little or no attention to; ignore. ~n. **2.** lack of attention or respect.

disrepair (ˌdɪsrɪ'pɛə) n. the condition of being worn out or in poor working order.

disreputable (dɪs'rɛpjʊtəb'l) adj. having or causing a bad reputation. —**dis'reputably** adv.

disrepute (ˌdɪsrɪ'pjuːt) n. a loss or lack of good reputation.

disrespect (ˌdɪsrɪ'spɛkt) n. contempt; lack of respect. —**disre'spectful** adj.

disrobe (dɪs'rəʊb) vb. to undress.

disrupt (dɪs'rʌpt) vb. to interrupt the progress of. [Latin *disruptus* burst asunder] —**dis'ruption** n. —**dis'ruptive** adj.

dissatisfy (dɪs'sætɪsˌfaɪ) vb. **-fying, -fied.** to fail to satisfy; disappoint. —**dissatis'faction** n.

dissect (dɪ'sɛkt, daɪ-) vb. **1.** to cut open and examine (a dead body). **2.** to examine critically and minutely. [Latin *dissecāre*] —**dis'section** n.

dissemble (dɪ'sɛmb'l) vb. to conceal one's real motives or emotions by pretence. [Latin *dissimulāre*] —**dis'sembler** n.

disseminate (dɪ'sɛmɪˌneɪt) vb. to scatter about. [Latin *dissēmināre*] —**dis,semi'nation** n.

dissension (dɪ'sɛnʃən) n. disagreement, esp. when leading to a quarrel. [Latin *dissentīre* to dissent]

dissent (dɪ'sɛnt) vb. **1.** to disagree. **2.** *Christianity*. to reject the doctrines of an established church. ~n. **3.** a difference of opinion. **4.** *Christianity*. separation from an established church. [Latin *dissentīre* to disagree] —**dis'senter** n. —**dis'senting** adj.

Dissenter (dɪ'sɛntə) n. *Christianity, chiefly Brit.* a Protestant who refuses to conform to the established church.

dissentient (dɪ'sɛnʃənt) adj. dissenting from the opinion of the majority.

dissertation (ˌdɪsə'teɪʃən) n. **1.** a written thesis, usually required for a higher degree. **2.** a long formal speech. [Latin *dissertāre* to debate]

disservice (dɪs'sɜːvɪs) n. an ill turn; wrong.

dissident ('dɪsɪdənt) adj. **1.** disagreeing; dissenting. ~n. **2.** a person who disagrees, esp. with the government. [Latin *dissidēre* to be remote from] —**'dissidence** n.

dissimilar (dɪ'sɪmɪlə) adj. not alike; different. —**dissimi'larity** n.

dissimulate (dɪ'sɪmjʊˌleɪt) vb. to conceal one's real feelings by pretence. —**dis,simu'lation** n.

dissipate ('dɪsɪˌpeɪt) vb. **1.** to waste or squander. **2.** to scatter or break up. [Latin *dissipāre* to disperse]

dissipated ('dɪsɪˌpeɪtɪd) adj. indulging without restraint in the pursuit of pleasure; debauched.

dissipation (ˌdɪsɪˈpeɪʃən) n. **1.** the process of dissipating. **2.** unrestrained indulgence in physical pleasures.

dissociate (dɪˈsəʊʃɪˌeɪt, -sɪ-) vb. **1.** to break the association between (people, organizations, etc.). **2.** to regard or treat as separate. —**disˌsociˈation** n.

dissoluble (dɪˈsɒljʊbˈl) adj. same as **soluble**. [Latin *dissolūbilis*] —**disˌsoluˈbility** n.

dissolute (ˈdɪsəˌluːt) adj. given to dissipation; debauched. [Latin *dissolūtus* loose]

dissolution (ˌdɪsəˈluːʃən) n. **1.** destruction by breaking up and dispersing. **2.** the termination of a meeting or assembly, such as Parliament. **3.** the termination of a formal or legal relationship, such as a business or marriage.

dissolve (dɪˈzɒlv) vb. **1.** to become or cause to become liquid; melt. **2.** to bring to an end. **3.** to dismiss (a meeting, Parliament, etc.). **4.** to collapse emotionally: *to dissolve into tears.* **5.** to lose or cause to lose distinctness. **6.** *Films, television.* to fade out one scene and replace with another to make two scenes merge imperceptibly. [Latin *dissolvere* to make loose]

dissonance (ˈdɪsənəns) n. **1.** a discordant combination of sounds. **2.** lack of agreement or consistency. —**ˈdissonant** adj.

dissuade (dɪˈsweɪd) vb. to deter (someone) by persuasion from a course of action, policy, etc. [Latin *dissuādēre*] —**disˈsuasion** n.

dissyllable (dɪˈsɪləbˈl) or **disyllable** n. a word of two syllables. —**dissyllabic** (ˌdɪsɪˈlæbɪk) or **disyllabic** (ˌdaɪsɪˈlæbɪk) adj.

distaff (ˈdɪstɑːf) n. the rod on which wool, flax, etc., is wound for spinning. [Old English *distæf*]

distaff side n. the female side of a family.

distance (ˈdɪstəns) n. **1.** the space between two points. **2.** the state of being apart. **3.** a distant place. **4.** remoteness in manner. **5. the distance.** the most distant part of the visible scene. **6. go the distance.** *Boxing.* to complete a bout without being knocked out. **7. keep one's distance.** to maintain a reserved attitude to another person. ~vb. **8. distance oneself** or **be distanced from.** to separate oneself or be separated mentally from. **9.** to outstrip.

distant (ˈdɪstənt) adj. **1.** far apart. **2.** separated by a specified distance: *five miles distant.* **3.** apart in relationship: *a distant cousin.* **4.** going to a faraway place. **5.** remote in manner; aloof. **6.** abstracted: *a distant look.* [Latin *disapart + stāre* to stand] —**ˈdistantly** adv.

distaste (dɪsˈteɪst) n. a dislike; aversion.

distasteful (dɪsˈteɪstfʊl) adj. unpleasant or offensive. —**disˈtastefulness** n.

distemper[1] (dɪsˈtempə) n. a highly contagious viral disease of animals, esp. dogs. [Latin *dis-* apart + *temperāre* to regulate]

distemper[2] (dɪsˈtempə) n. **1.** paint mixed with water, glue, size, etc.: used for poster,

mural, and scene painting. ~vb. **2.** to paint (something) with distemper. [Latin *dis-*(intensive) + *temperāre* to mingle]

distend (dɪsˈtɛnd) vb. to expand by pressure from within; swell; inflate. [Latin *distendere*] —**disˈtensible** adj. —**disˈtension** n.

distich (ˈdɪstɪk) n. *Prosody.* a unit of two verse lines. [Greek *di-* two + *stikhos* row, line]

distil or *U.S.* **distill** (dɪsˈtɪl) vb. **-tilling, -tilled. 1.** to subject to or obtain by distillation. **2.** to give off (a substance) in drops. **3.** to extract the essence of. [Latin *de-* down + *stillāre* to drip]

distillate (ˈdɪstɪlɪt) n. a concentrated essence.

distillation (ˌdɪstɪˈleɪʃən) n. **1.** the process of evaporating a liquid and condensing its vapour. **2.** purification or separation of mixtures by using different evaporation rates or boiling points of their components. **3.** a concentrated essence.

distiller (dɪsˈtɪlə) n. a person or company that makes spirits.

distillery (dɪsˈtɪlərɪ) n., pl. **-eries.** a place where alcoholic drinks are made by distillation.

distinct (dɪsˈtɪŋkt) adj. **1.** easily sensed or understood; clear. **2.** not the same; different. **3.** sharp; clear. **4.** recognizable; unequivocal. [Latin *distinctus*] —**disˈtinctly** adv.

distinction (dɪsˈtɪŋkʃən) n. **1.** the act of distinguishing or differentiating. **2.** a distinguishing feature. **3.** the state of being different or distinguishable. **4.** special honour, recognition, or fame. **5.** excellence of character. **6.** a symbol of honour or rank.

distinctive (dɪsˈtɪŋktɪv) adj. easily recognizable; characteristic. —**disˈtinctively** adv. —**disˈtinctiveness** n.

distingué (dɪsˈtæŋɡeɪ) adj. distinguished or noble. [French]

distinguish (dɪsˈtɪŋɡwɪʃ) vb. **1.** (foll. by *between* or *among*) to make, show, or recognize a difference (between or among); differentiate (between). **2.** to be a distinctive feature of; characterize. **3.** to make out; perceive. **4. distinguish oneself.** to make oneself noteworthy. [Latin *distinguere* to separate] —**disˈtinguishable** adj. —**disˈtinguishing** adj.

distinguished (dɪsˈtɪŋɡwɪʃt) adj. **1.** noble or dignified in appearance. **2.** famous.

distort (dɪsˈtɔːt) vb. **1.** to twist out of shape; deform. **2.** to alter or misrepresent (facts). **3.** *Electronics.* to reproduce or amplify (a signal) inaccurately. [Latin *distorquēre* to turn different ways] —**disˈtorted** adj. —**disˈtortion** n.

distract (dɪsˈtrækt) vb. **1.** to draw the attention of (a person) away from something. **2.** to confuse or trouble (a person). **3.** to amuse or entertain. [Latin *distrahere* to pull in different directions]

distraction (dɪsˈtrækʃən) n. **1.** something that diverts the attention. **2.** something that serves as an entertainment. **3.** mental turmoil.

distrain (dɪ'streɪn) vb. Law. to seize (personal property) as security for a debt. [Latin *di-* apart + *stringere* to draw tight] —**dis'traint** n.

distrait (dɪ'streɪ) adj. absent-minded; abstracted. [French]

distraught (dɪ'strɔːt) adj. distracted or agitated. [obs. *distract*]

distress (dɪ'strɛs) vb. **1.** to cause mental pain to; upset badly. ～n. **2.** mental pain; anguish. **3.** physical or financial trouble. **4. in distress.** in dire need of help. [Latin *districtus* divided in mind] —**dis'tressing** adj. —**dis'tressingly** adv.

distressed (dɪ'strɛst) adj. **1.** much troubled; upset. **2.** in financial difficulties; poor. **3.** (of furniture or fabric) having signs of ageing artificially applied.

distributary (dɪ'strɪbjʊtrɪ) n., pl. **-taries.** one of several outlet streams draining a river, esp. on a delta.

distribute (dɪ'strɪbjuːt) vb. **1.** to give out in shares; dispense. **2.** to hand out or deliver. [Latin *distribuere*]

distribution (ˌdɪstrɪ'bjuːʃən) n. **1.** the act of distributing. **2.** arrangement or location. **3.** the process of satisfying the demand for goods and services.

distributive (dɪ'strɪbjʊtɪv) adj. **1.** characterized by or relating to distribution. **2.** Maths. of a rule that the same result is produced when multiplication is performed on a set of numbers as when performed on the members of the set individually.

distributor (dɪ'strɪbjʊtə) n. **1.** a wholesaler engaged in the distribution of goods to retailers in a specific area. **2.** the device in a petrol engine that distributes the electric current to the sparking plugs.

district ('dɪstrɪkt) n. **1.** an area of land regarded as an administrative or geographical unit. **2.** any region or area: *country districts; a shopping district*. [Medieval Latin *districtus* area of jurisdiction]

district high school n. (in New Zealand) a school in a rural area providing both primary and secondary education.

district nurse n. (in Britain) a nurse appointed to attend patients in their homes within a particular district.

distrust (dɪs'trʌst) vb. **1.** to regard as untrustworthy. ～n. **2.** suspicion; doubt. —**dis'trustful** adj.

disturb (dɪ'stɜːb) vb. **1.** to intrude on; interrupt. **2.** to disarrange. **3.** to upset; trouble. **4.** to inconvenience. [Latin *disturbāre*] —**dis'turbing** adj. —**dis'turbingly** adv.

disturbance (dɪ'stɜːbəns) n. **1.** an interruption or intrusion. **2.** an unruly outburst or tumult.

disturbed (dɪ'stɜːbd) adj. Psychiatry. emotionally upset, troubled, or maladjusted.

disunite (ˌdɪsjuː'naɪt) vb. to set at variance; estrange. —**dis'union** n. —**dis'unity** n.

disuse (dɪs'juːs) n. the condition of being unused; neglect.

disyllable ('daɪˌsɪləb'l) n. same as **dissyllable.**

ditch (dɪtʃ) n. **1.** a narrow channel dug in the earth for drainage or irrigation. ～vb. **2.** Slang. to abandon. [Old English *dīc*]

dither ('dɪðə) vb. **1.** Chiefly Brit. to be uncertain or indecisive. **2.** Chiefly U.S. to be agitated. ～n. **3.** Chiefly Brit. a state of indecision or agitation. [Middle English *didder*] —**'ditherer** n. —**'dithery** adj.

dithyramb ('dɪθɪˌræm, -ˌræmb) n. **1.** (in ancient Greece) a passionate choral hymn in honour of Dionysus. **2.** any utterance or a piece of writing that resembles this. [Greek *dithurambos*] —ˌdithy'rambic adj.

ditto ('dɪtəʊ) n., pl. **-tos.** **1.** the aforementioned; the above; the same. Used in lists, etc., to avoid repetition, and symbolized by two small marks („) placed under the thing repeated. ～adv. **2.** in the same way. [Italian (dialect) *detto* said]

ditty ('dɪtɪ) n., pl. **-ties.** a short simple song or poem. [Latin *dictāre* to say repeatedly]

diuretic (ˌdaɪjʊ'rɛtɪk) n. a drug that increases the flow of urine. [Greek *dia-* through + *ourein* to urinate]

diurnal (daɪ'ɜːn'l) adj. **1.** happening during the day or daily. **2.** (of animals) active during the day. [Latin *diurnus*]

diva ('diːvə) n., pl. **-vas** or **-ve** (-vɪ). a distinguished female singer; prima donna. [Latin: a goddess]

divalent (daɪ'veɪlənt, ˌdaɪ'veɪ-) adj. Chem. **1.** having a valency of two. **2.** having two valencies. —**di'valency** n.

divan (dɪ'væn) n. **a.** a backless sofa or couch. **b.** a bed resembling such a couch. [Turkish *dīvān*]

dive (daɪv) vb. **diving, dived** or U.S. **dove** (dəʊv), **dived.** **1.** to plunge headfirst into water. **2.** (of a submarine or diver) to submerge under water. **3.** to fly in a steep nose-down descending path. **4.** to rush or reach for quickly: *he dived for the ball.* **5.** (foll. by *in* or *into*) **a.** to put (one's hand) quickly or forcefully (into). **b.** to start doing (something) enthusiastically. ～n. **6.** a headlong plunge into water. **7.** the act of diving. **8.** a steep nose-down descent of an aircraft or a bird. **9.** Slang. a disreputable bar or club. [Old English *dȳfan*]

dive bomber n. a military aircraft designed to release bombs on a target during a dive. —**'dive-bomb** vb.

diver ('daɪvə) n. **1.** a person who works or explores underwater. **2.** a person who dives for sport.

diverge (daɪ'vɜːdʒ) vb. **1.** to separate and go in different directions. **2.** to be at variance; differ. **3.** to deviate (from a prescribed course). [Latin *dis-* apart + *vergere* to turn] —**di'vergence** n. —**di'vergent** adj.

divers ('daɪvəz) det. Archaic or literary. various; sundry. [Latin *dīversus* turned in different directions]

diverse (daɪ'vɜːs, 'daɪvɜːs) adj. **1.** having variety; assorted. **2.** distinct in kind. [Latin *dīversus* turned in different directions]

diversify (daɪ'vɜːsɪˌfaɪ) vb. **-fying, -fied.**

1. to create different forms of; vary. **2.** (of an enterprise) to vary (products or operations) in order to spread risk or expand. [Latin *dīversus* different + *facere* to make] —**di,versifi'cation** *n.*

diversion (daɪ'vɜːʃən) *n.* **1.** the act of diverting from a specified course. **2.** *Chiefly Brit.* an official detour used by traffic when a main route is closed. **3.** something that distracts from business, etc.; amusement. —**di'versionary** *adj.*

diversity (daɪ'vɜːsɪtɪ) *n.* **1.** the quality of being different or varied. **2.** a point of difference.

divert (daɪ'vɜːt) *vb.* **1.** to deflect. **2.** to entertain; amuse. **3.** to distract the attention of. [Latin *dīvertere* to turn aside]

diverticulitis (,daɪvə,tɪkjʊ'laɪtɪs) *n.* an illness causing abdominal pain, resulting from inflammation within pouches that have formed in the wall of the colon. [Latin *dīverticulum* path, track]

divertimento (dɪ,vɜːtɪ'mɛntəʊ) *n., pl.* **-ti** (-tɪ). a piece of entertaining music. [Italian]

divertissement (dɪ'vɜːtɪsmənt) *n.* a brief entertainment or diversion. [French]

divest (daɪ'vɛst) *vb.* **1.** to strip (of clothes). **2.** to deprive or dispossess. [earlier *devest*]

divide (dɪ'vaɪd) *vb.* **1.** to separate into parts. **2.** to share or be shared out in parts. **3.** to disagree or cause to disagree: *the whole village was divided over the issue.* **4.** to keep apart or be a boundary between. **5.** to categorize; classify. **6.** to calculate how many times one number can be contained in another. ~*n.* **7.** *Chiefly U.S. & Canad.* an area of high ground separating drainage basins. **8.** a division; split. [Latin *dīvidere* to force apart]

dividend ('dɪvɪ,dɛnd) *n.* **1.** a sum of money representing part of the profit made, paid by a company to its shareholders. **2.** something extra; a bonus. **3.** a number to be divided by another number. [Latin *dīvidendum* what is to be divided]

divider (dɪ'vaɪdə) *n.* a screen placed so as to divide a room into separate areas.

dividers (dɪ'vaɪdəz) *pl. n.* compasses with two pointed arms, used for measuring lines or dividing them.

divination (,dɪvɪ'neɪʃən) *n.* the art or practice of discovering future events or unknown things, as though by supernatural powers.

divine (dɪ'vaɪn) *adj.* **1.** of God or a god. **2.** godlike. **3.** *Informal.* splendid; perfect. ~*n.* **4.** a priest who is learned in theology. ~*vb.* **5.** to discover (something) by intuition or guessing. [Latin *dīvus* a god] —**di'vinely** *adv.* —**di'viner** *n.*

diving bell *n.* a diving apparatus with an open bottom, supplied with compressed air.

diving board *n.* a platform from which swimmers may dive.

diving suit *n.* a waterproof suit used by divers, having a helmet and an air supply.

divining rod *n.* a forked twig said to move when held over ground in which water or metal is to be found.

divinity (dɪ'vɪnɪtɪ) *n., pl.* **-ties.** **1.** the state of being divine. **2.** a god. **3.** theology.

divisible (dɪ'vɪzɪb'l) *adj.* capable of being divided. —**di,visi'bility** *n.*

division (dɪ'vɪʒən) *n.* **1.** the act of dividing or sharing out. **2.** one of the parts into which something is divided. **3.** a part of an organization that has been made into a unit for administrative or other reasons. **4.** a formal vote in Parliament. **5.** a difference of opinion. **6.** the mathematical operation of dividing. **7.** *Army.* a major formation containing the necessary arms to sustain independent combat. [Latin *dīvidere* to divide] —**di'visional** *adj.*

division sign *n.* the symbol ÷, placed between the dividend and the divisor to indicate division, as in $12 ÷ 6 = 2$.

divisive (dɪ'vaɪsɪv) *adj.* tending to cause disagreement or dissension.

divisor (dɪ'vaɪzə) *n.* a number to be divided into another number.

divorce (dɪ'vɔːs) *n.* **1.** the legal ending of a marriage. **2.** a separation, esp. one that is total. ~*vb.* **3.** to separate or be separated by divorce. **4.** to remove or separate. [Latin *dīvertere* to separate]

divorcée (dɪvɔː'siː) *or* (*masc.*) **divorcé** (dɪ'vɔːseɪ) *n.* a person who is divorced.

divulge (daɪ'vʌldʒ) *vb.* to make known; disclose. [Latin *dīvulgāre*] —**di'vulgence** *n.*

divvy ('dɪvɪ) *Informal.* ~*n., pl.* **-vies.** **1.** *Brit.* a dividend. ~*vb.* **-vying, -vied.** **2.** (foll. by *up*) to divide and share.

dixie ('dɪksɪ) *n. Chiefly mil.* a large metal pot for cooking. [Hindi *degcī*]

Dixie ('dɪksɪ) *n.* the southern states of the U.S. Also called: **Dixieland.** [origin unknown]

DIY *or* **d.i.y.** (in Britain) do-it-yourself.

dizzy ('dɪzɪ) *adj.* **-zier, -ziest.** **1.** feeling giddy. **2.** mentally confused. **3.** tending to cause giddiness or bewilderment. ~*vb.* **-zying, -zied.** **4.** to make dizzy. [Old English *dysig* silly] —**dizzily** *adv.* —**dizziness** *n.*

DJ *or* **dj 1.** disc jockey. **2.** dinner jacket.

djinni *or* **djinny** (dʒɪ'niː, 'dʒɪnɪ) *n., pl.* **djinn** (dʒɪn). same as **jinni.**

dl decilitre.

DLitt *or* **DLit 1.** Doctor of Letters. **2.** Doctor of Literature. [Latin *Doctor Litterarum*]

dm decimetre.

DM Deutsche Mark.

DMus Doctor of Music.

DNA deoxyribonucleic acid, the main constituent of the chromosomes of all organisms.

D-notice *n. Brit.* an official notice sent to newspapers prohibiting the publication of certain security information. [from their administrative classification letter]

do¹ (duː; *unstressed* dʊ, də) *vb.* **does, doing, did, done.** **1.** to perform or complete (a deed or action): *to do a portrait.* **2.** to be suitable; suffice. **3.** to provide; serve: *this restaurant doesn't do lunch on Sundays.* **4.** to make tidy, elegant, or ready: *to do* one's hair. **5.** to improve: *that hat does nothing for you.* **6.** to find an answer to (a problem or puzzle). **7.** to conduct oneself: *do as you please.* **8.** to cause or produce: *complaints do nothing to help.* **9.** to give or render: *do me a favour.* **10.** to work at, esp. as a course of study or a job. **11.** to perform (a play, etc.); act. **12.** to mimic. **13.** to travel at a specified speed, esp. as a maximum. **14.** to travel (a distance). **15.** used: **a.** to form questions: *do you agree?* **b.** to intensify positive statements and commands: *I do like your new house; do hurry!* **c.** to form negative statements or commands: *do not leave me here alone!* **d.** to replace an earlier verb: *he likes you as much as I do.* **16.** *Informal.* to visit (a place) as a tourist. **17.** *Slang.* to serve (a period of time) as a prison sentence. **18.** *Informal.* to cheat or rob. **19.** *Slang.* **a.** to arrest. **b.** to convict of a crime. **20.** *Slang, chiefly Brit.* to assault. **21.** *Slang.* to take or use (drugs). **22. make do.** to manage with whatever is available. ~*n., pl.* **dos** *or* **do's. 23.** *Informal, chiefly Brit. & N.Z.* a festive gathering; party. **24. do's and don'ts.** *Informal.* rules. ~See also **do away with, do by,** etc. [Old English *dōn*]

do² (dəʊ) *n., pl.* **dos.** same as **doh.**

doable ('duːəbəl) *adj.* capable of being done.

do away with *vb.* **1.** to kill or destroy. **2.** to abolish.

Doberman pinscher ('dəʊbəmən 'pɪnʃə) *or* **Doberman** *n.* a large dog with a glossy black-and-tan coat. [German]

do by *vb.* *Informal.* to treat in the manner specified: *he felt badly done by.*

doc (dɒk) *n. Informal.* same as **doctor.**

docile ('dəʊsaɪl) *adj.* easy to manage; submissive. [Latin *docilis* easily taught] —**docilely** *adv.* —**docility** (dəʊ'sɪlɪtɪ) *n.*

dock¹ (dɒk) *n.* **1.** an enclosed area of water where ships are loaded, unloaded, or repaired. **2.** a wharf or pier. ~*vb.* **3.** to moor or be moored at a dock. **4.** to link (two spacecraft) together in space or (of two spacecraft) to link together in space. [Middle Dutch *docke*]

dock² (dɒk) *vb.* **1.** to remove part of (an animal's tail) by cutting through the bone. **2.** to deduct (an amount) from (a person's wages). [Middle English *dok*]

dock³ (dɒk) *n.* an enclosed space in a court of law where the accused person sits or stands. [Flemish *dok* sty]

dock⁴ (dɒk) *n.* a weed with broad leaves. [Old English *docce*]

docker ('dɒkə) *n. Brit.* a man employed in the loading or unloading of ships.

docket ('dɒkɪt) *n.* **1.** *Chiefly Brit.* a piece of paper accompanying a package or other delivery, stating contents, delivery instructions, etc. ~*vb.* **2.** to fix a docket to (a package, etc.). [origin unknown]

dockyard ('dɒk,jɑːd) *n.* a place with docks and equipment where ships are built or repaired.

doctor ('dɒktə) *n.* **1.** a person licensed to practise medicine. **2.** a person who has been awarded a higher academic degree in

any field of knowledge. **3.** *Chiefly U.S. & Canad.* a person licensed to practise dentistry or veterinary medicine. ~*vb.* **4.** *Informal.* to practise medicine. **5.** to make different in order to deceive. **6.** to poison or drug (food or drink). **7.** *Informal.* to castrate (a cat, dog, etc.). [Latin: teacher] —**'doctoral** *adj.*

doctorate ('dɒktrɪt) *n.* the highest academic degree in any field of knowledge.

doctrinaire (,dɒktrɪ'nɛə) *adj.* stubbornly insistent on the observation of the niceties of a theory without regard to practicality.

doctrine ('dɒktrɪn) *n.* **1.** a body of teachings of a religious, political, or philosophical group. **2.** a principle or body of principles that is taught or advocated. [Latin *doctrīna* teaching] —**doctrinal** (dɒk'traɪnəl) *adj.*

docudrama ('dɒkjʊ,drɑːmə) *n.* a film or television programme based on true events, presented in a dramatized form.

document *n.* ('dɒkjʊmənt). **1.** a piece of paper, booklet, etc., providing information, esp. of an official nature. ~*vb.* ('dɒkjʊ,mɛnt). **2.** to record or report (something) in detail, as in the press or on television. **3.** to support (a claim) with evidence. [Latin *documentum* a lesson]

documentary (,dɒkjʊ'mɛntrɪ) *n., pl.* -**ries. 1.** a film or television programme presenting the facts about a particular subject. **2.** of or based on documents: *documentary evidence.*

documentation (,dɒkjʊmɛn'teɪʃən) *n.* **1.** the act of supplying with documents or references. **2.** the documents or references supplied.

dodder ('dɒdə) *vb.* to move unsteadily; totter. [var. of earlier *dadder*] —**'dodderer** *n.* —**'doddery** *adj.*

doddle ('dɒdəl) *n. Brit. informal.* something easily accomplished. [origin unknown]

dodecagon (dəʊ'dɛkə,gɒn) *n.* a polygon with twelve sides. [Greek *dōdeka* twelve]

dodecahedron (,dəʊdɛkə'hiːdrən) *n.* a solid figure with twelve plane faces.

dodge (dɒdʒ) *vb.* **1.** to avoid (a blow, discovery, etc.) by moving suddenly. **2.** to evade by cleverness or trickery. ~*n.* **3.** a plan contrived to deceive. **4.** a sudden evasive movement. [origin unknown]

Dodgem ('dɒdʒəm) *n. Trademark.* an electrically propelled vehicle driven and bumped against similar cars in a rink at a funfair.

dodger ('dɒdʒə) *n.* a person who evades or shirks something.

dodgy ('dɒdʒɪ) *adj.* **dodgier, dodgiest.** *Brit., Austral., & N.Z. informal.* **1.** difficult or dangerous. **2.** unreliable; tricky.

dodo ('dəʊdəʊ) *n., pl.* **dodos** *or* **dodoes. 1.** a large flightless extinct bird. **2. as dead as a dodo.** irretrievably defunct or out of date. [Portuguese *duodo* stupid]

do down *vb.* to belittle or humiliate: *don't do yourself down.*

doe (dəʊ) *n., pl.* **does** *or* **doe.** the female of the deer, hare, or rabbit. [Old English *dā*]

DOE (in Britain) Department of the Environment.

doek (dʊk) n. S. African informal. a square of cloth worn on the head. [Afrikaans]

doer ('duːə) n. an active or energetic person.

does (dʌz) vb. third person singular of the present tense of **do**[1].

doff (dɒf) vb. to take off or lift (one's hat) in salutation. [Old English dōn of]

do for vb. Informal. 1. to cause the ruin, death, or defeat of. 2. to do housework for. 3. **do well for oneself.** to thrive or succeed.

dog (dɒg) n. 1. a domesticated canine mammal occurring in many different breeds. 2. any other member of the dog family, such as the dingo or coyote. 3. the male of animals of the dog family. 4. a mechanical device for gripping. 5. Informal. a fellow; chap: you lucky dog! 6. U.S. & Canad. informal. something unsatisfactory or inferior. 7. **a dog's life.** a wretched existence. 8. **dog eat dog.** ruthless competition. 9. **like a dog's dinner.** dressed smartly and ostentatiously. 10. **put on the dog.** U.S. & Canad. informal. to behave pretentiously. ~vb. **dogging, dogged.** 11. to follow (someone) closely. 12. to trouble; plague. ~See also **dogs.** [Old English docga]

dog biscuit n. a hard biscuit for dogs.

dog box n. N.Z. informal. same as **doghouse** (sense 2).

dogcart ('dɒgˌkɑːt) n. a light horse-drawn two-wheeled vehicle.

dog collar n. 1. a collar for a dog. 2. Informal. a clerical collar.

dog days pl. n. the hottest period of the summer. [in ancient times reckoned from the heliacal rising of the Dog Star]

doge (dəʊdʒ) n. (formerly) the chief magistrate of Venice or Genoa. [Latin dux leader]

dog-eared adj. 1. (of a book) having pages folded down at the corner. 2. shabby or worn.

dog-end n. Informal. a cigarette end.

dogfight ('dɒgˌfaɪt) n. 1. close-quarters combat between fighter aircraft. 2. any rough fight.

dogfish ('dɒgˌfɪʃ) n., pl. **-fish** or **-fishes.** a small shark.

dogged ('dɒgɪd) adj. obstinately determined; tenacious. —'**doggedly** adv. —'**doggedness** n.

doggerel ('dɒgərəl) n. poorly written, usually comic, verse. [Middle English dogerel worthless]

doggo ('dɒgəʊ) adv. **lie doggo.** Brit. informal. to hide and keep quiet. [prob. from dog]

doggy or **doggie** ('dɒgɪ) n., pl. **-gies.** 1. a child's word for a dog. ~adj. **-gier, -giest.** 2. of or like a dog. 3. fond of dogs.

doggy bag n. a bag in which leftovers from a meal may be taken away for a dog.

doghouse ('dɒgˌhaʊs) n. 1. U.S. & Canad. a kennel. 2. **in the doghouse.** Informal. in disfavour.

dogie, dogy, or **dogey** ('dəʊgɪ) n., pl. **-gies** or **-geys.** U.S. & Canad. a motherless calf. [from dough-guts, because they were fed on flour-and-water paste]

dog in the manger n. a person who prevents others from using something he has no use for.

dogleg ('dɒgˌleg) n. a sharp bend.

dogma ('dɒgmə) n. a doctrine or system of doctrines proclaimed by authority as true. [Greek: opinion]

dogmatic (dɒg'mætɪk) adj. 1. (of a statement or opinion) forcibly asserted as if unchallengeable. 2. (of a person) prone to making such statements. —dog'**matically** adv. —'**dogma,tism** n.

do-gooder n. Informal. a well-intentioned person, esp. a naive or impractical one.

dog paddle n. a swimming stroke in which the hands are paddled in imitation of a swimming dog.

dog rose n. a wild rose with pink or white flowers. [from the belief that its root was effective against the bite of a mad dog]

dogs (dɒgz) pl. n. 1. **go to the dogs.** Informal. to go to ruin physically or morally. 2. **let sleeping dogs lie.** to leave things undisturbed. 3. **the dogs.** Brit. informal. greyhound racing.

dogsbody ('dɒgzˌbɒdɪ) n., pl. **-bodies.** Informal. a person who carries out menial tasks for others.

dog-tired adj. Informal. exhausted.

dogtooth violet ('dɒgˌtuːθ) n. a plant of North America with yellow flowers, or a European plant with purple flowers.

dogtrot ('dɒgˌtrɒt) n. a gently paced trot.

dogwatch ('dɒgˌwɒtʃ) n. either of two watches aboard ship, from four to six p.m. or from six to eight p.m.

doh or **do** (dəʊ) n. Music. 1. the note D. 2. (in tonic sol-fa) the first degree of any major scale.

doily or **doyley** ('dɔɪlɪ) n., pl. **-lies** or **-leys.** a decorative mat of lace or lacelike paper, etc., laid on plates. [after Doily, a London draper]

do in vb. Slang. 1. to kill. 2. to exhaust.

doings ('duːɪŋz) n. 1. (functioning as pl.) deeds or actions. 2. (functioning as sing.) Informal. anything of which the name is not known or is left unsaid.

do-it-yourself n. the practice of constructing and repairing things oneself, esp. as a hobby.

doldrums ('dɒldrəmz) n. **the.** 1. a depressed state of mind. 2. a state of inactivity. 3. a belt of sea along the equator noted for absence of winds. [prob. from Old English dol dull]

dole (dəʊl) n. 1. (usually preceded by the) Brit. informal. money received from the state while out of work. 2. **on the dole.** Brit. informal. receiving such money. ~vb. 3. (foll. by out) to distribute (something), esp. in small portions. [Old English dǣl share]

doleful ('dəʊlfʊl) adj. dreary; mournful.

[from Latin *dolēre* to lament] —**'dolefully**
adv. —**'dolefulness** *n.*

doll (dɒl) *n.* **1.** a small model of a human
being, used as a toy. **2.** *Slang.* a girl or
young woman, esp. a pretty one. [prob.
from *Doll*, pet name for *Dorothy*]

dollar ('dɒlə) *n.* the standard monetary
unit of the U.S., Canada, and various other
countries. [Low German *daler*]

dollop ('dɒləp) *n.* *Informal.* a semisolid
lump. [origin unknown]

doll up *vb. Slang.* to dress in a stylish or
showy manner: *all dolled up.*

dolly ('dɒlɪ) *n., pl.* **-lies. 1.** a child's word
for a **doll. 2.** *Films, etc.* a wheeled support
on which a camera may be mounted. **3.**
Also called: **dolly bird.** *Slang, chiefly
Brit.* an attractive and fashionable girl.

dolman sleeve ('dɒlmən) *n.* a sleeve
that is very wide at the armhole and tapers
to a tight wrist. [Turkish]

dolmen ('dɒlmɛn) *n.* a prehistoric monument consisting of a horizontal stone supported by vertical stones, thought to be a
tomb. [French]

dolomite ('dɒlə,maɪt) *n.* a mineral consisting of calcium magnesium carbonate. [after
Déodat de *Dolomieu*, mineralogist]

dolorous ('dɒlərəs) *adj.* causing or involving pain or sorrow. [Latin *dolor* pain]

dolphin ('dɒlfɪn) *n.* a mammal smaller than
a whale and larger than a porpoise, with a
beaklike snout. [Greek *delphin-, delphis*]

dolphinarium (,dɒlfɪ'nɛərɪəm) *n.* an
aquarium for dolphins, esp. one in which
they give public displays.

dolt (dəʊlt) *n.* a stupid person. [prob.
related to Old English *dol* stupid] —**'dolt-
ish** *adj.*

domain (də'meɪn) *n.* **1.** a field of knowledge or activity. **2.** land under one ruler or
government. [French *domaine*]

dome (dəʊm) *n.* **1.** a hemispherical roof.
2. something shaped like this. [Latin
domus house]

domed (dəʊmd) *adj.* shaped like a dome.

Domesday Book *or* **Doomsday Book**
('du:mz,deɪ) *n. History.* the record of a
survey of the land of England carried out
by the commissioners of William I in 1086.

domestic (də'mɛstɪk) *adj.* **1.** of the home
or family. **2.** enjoying home or family life.
3. (of an animal) bred or kept as a pet or
for the supply of food. **4.** of one's own
country or a specific country: *domestic and
foreign affairs.* ~*n.* **5.** a household servant. [Latin *domesticus* belonging to the
house] —**do'mestically** *adv.*

domesticate (də'mɛstɪ,keɪt) *vb.* **1.** to
bring or keep (wild animals or plants)
under control or cultivation. **2.** to accustom (someone) to home life. —**do,mesti-
'cation** *n.*

domesticity (,dəʊmɛ'stɪsɪtɪ) *n., pl.* **-ties.**
1. home life. **2.** devotion to home life.

domestic science *n.* the study of cooking, needlework, and other household
skills.

domicile ('dɒmɪ,saɪl) *n.* **1.** a dwelling
place. **2.** a permanent legal residence.

~*vb.* **3.** to establish (someone) in a dwelling place. [Latin *domus* house] —**domicili-
ary** (,dɒmɪ'sɪlɪərɪ) *adj.*

dominant ('dɒmɪnənt) *adj.* **1.** having primary authority or influence. **2.** predominant: *the dominant topic of the day.* **3.**
Genetics. (in a pair of genes) designating
the gene that produces a particular character in an organism. ~*n.* **4.** *Music.* the
fifth degree of a scale. —**'dominance** *n.*

dominate ('dɒmɪ,neɪt) *vb.* **1.** to control or
govern. **2.** to tower above (surroundings).
3. to predominate. [Latin *dominārī* to be
lord over] —**'domi,nating** *adj.* —**,domi-
'nation** *n.*

domineering (,dɒmɪ'nɪərɪŋ) *adj.* arrogant;
tyrannical. [Dutch *domineren*]

Dominican¹ (də'mɪnɪkən) *n.* **1.** a friar or
nun of an order founded by Saint Dominic.
~*adj.* **2.** of the Dominican order.

Dominican² (də'mɪnɪkən) *adj.* **1.** of the
Dominican Republic or Dominica. ~*n.* **2.**
a person from the Dominican Republic or
Dominica.

dominion (də'mɪnjən) *n.* **1.** rule; authority. **2.** the land governed by one ruler or
government. **3.** (formerly) a self-
governing division of the British Empire.
[Latin *dominium* ownership]

domino¹ ('dɒmɪ,nəʊ) *n., pl.* **-noes.** a small
rectangular block marked with dots, used
in dominoes. [Italian, perhaps from *domino!* master!, said by the winner]

domino² ('dɒmɪ,nəʊ) *n., pl.* **-noes** *or* **-nos.** a
large hooded cloak worn with an eye mask
at a masquerade. [Latin *dominus* lord,
master]

dominoes ('dɒmɪ,nəʊz) *n.* (*functioning as
sing.*) a game in which dominoes with
matching halves are laid together.

domkop ('dɒm,kɒp) *n. S. African slang.* an
idiot; thickhead. [Afrikaans]

don¹ (dɒn) *vb.* **donning, donned.** to put on
(clothing). [Middle English]

don² (dɒn) *n.* **1.** *Brit.* a member of the
teaching staff at a university or college. **2.**
a Spanish gentleman or nobleman. [Latin
dominus lord]

Don (dɒn) *n.* a Spanish title equivalent to
Mr.

Doña ('dɒnjə) *n.* a Spanish title equivalent
to *Mrs* or *Madam.*

donate (dəʊ'neɪt) *vb.* to give (something),
esp. to a charity.

donation (dəʊ'neɪʃən) *n.* **1.** the act of
donating. **2.** a contribution. [Latin *dōnum*
gift]

donder ('dɒnə) *S. African slang.* ~*vb.* **1.**
to beat (someone) up. ~*n.* **2.** a wretch;
swine. [Dutch *donderen* to swear; bully]

done (dʌn) *vb.* **1.** the past participle of
do¹. 2. be *or* **have done with.** to end
relations with. ~*interj.* **3.** an expression
of agreement, as on the settlement of a
bargain. ~*adj.* **4.** completed. **5.** cooked
enough. **6.** used up. **7.** socially acceptable: *the done thing.* **8.** *Informal.* cheated;
tricked. **9. done for.** *Informal.* **a.** dead or
almost dead. **b.** in serious difficulty. **10.
done in** *or* **up.** *Informal.* exhausted.

doner kebab ('dɔːnə) n. a dish of grilled minced lamb, served in a split slice of unleavened bread.

donga ('dɒŋɡə) n. S. African, Austral., & N.Z. a steep-sided gully created by soil erosion. [Afrikaans]

donjon ('dʌndʒən) n. the heavily fortified central tower of a castle. [archaic var. of dungeon]

Don Juan ('dɒn 'dʒuːən) n. a successful seducer of women. [after the legendary Spanish philanderer]

donkey ('dɒŋkɪ) n. 1. a long-eared member of the horse family. 2. a person who is considered to be stupid or stubborn. [origin unknown]

donkey jacket n. a thick hip-length jacket, usually navy blue, with a waterproof panel across the shoulders.

donkey's years pl. n. Informal. a long time.

donkey-work n. 1. groundwork. 2. drudgery.

Donna ('dɒnə) n. an Italian title equivalent to Madam.

donnish ('dɒnɪʃ) adj. resembling a university don; pedantic or fussy.

donor ('dəʊnə) n. 1. a person who makes a donation. 2. Med. a person who gives blood, organs, etc., for use in the treatment of another person. [Latin dōnāre to give]

donor card n. a card carried to show that the body parts specified may be used for transplants after the carrier's death.

Don Quixote ('dɒn kiː'həʊtɪ; 'kwɪksət) n. an impractical idealist. [after the hero of Cervantes' Don Quixote de la Mancha]

don't (dəʊnt) do not.

doodle ('duːd'l) Informal. ~vb. 1. to scribble or draw aimlessly. ~n. 2. a shape or picture drawn aimlessly. [orig., a foolish person]

doodlebug ('duːd'l‚bʌɡ) n. a robot bomb invented by the Germans in World War II. Also called: V-1. [prob. DOODLE + BUG]

doom (duːm) n. 1. death or a terrible fate. ~vb. 2. to destine or condemn to death or a terrible fate. [Old English dōm]

doomsday or **domesday** ('duːmz‚deɪ) n. 1. the day on which the Last Judgment will occur. 2. any day of reckoning. [Old English dōmes dæg Judgment Day]

door (dɔː) n. 1. a hinged or sliding panel for closing the entrance to a room, cupboard, etc. 2. a doorway or entrance. 3. a means of access or escape: a door to success. 4. **lay at someone's door**. to lay the blame or responsibility) on someone. 5. **out of doors**. in the open air. [Old English duru]

doorjamb ('dɔː‚dʒæm) n. one of the two vertical posts forming the sides of a door frame. Also called: **doorpost**.

doorman ('dɔː‚mæn, -mən) n., pl. -**men**. a man employed to be on duty at the doors of certain public buildings.

doormat ('dɔː‚mæt) n. 1. a mat, placed at an entrance, for wiping dirt from shoes. 2. Informal. a person who offers little resistance to ill-treatment.

doorstep ('dɔː‚stɛp) n. 1. a step in front of a door. 2. Informal. a thick slice of bread.

doorstop ('dɔː‚stɒp) n. a device which prevents a door from moving or from striking a wall.

door-to-door adj. 1. (of selling) from one house to the next. 2. (of journeys) direct.

doorway ('dɔː‚weɪ) n. an opening into a building or room.

dope (dəʊp) n. 1. Slang. an illegal drug, usually cannabis. 2. a drug, esp. one administered to a racehorse or greyhound to affect its performance. 3. Informal. a slow-witted person. 4. Informal. confidential information. 5. a thick liquid, such as a lubricant. ~vb. 6. to administer a drug to. [Dutch doop sauce]

dopey or **dopy** ('dəʊpɪ) adj. **dopier, dopiest**. 1. Informal. half-asleep, as when under the influence of a drug. 2. Slang. silly.

doppelgänger ('dɒp'l‚ɡɛŋə) n. Legend. a ghostly duplicate of a living person. [German Doppelgänger double-goer]

Doppler effect ('dɒplə) n. a change in the apparent frequency of a sound or light wave as a result of relative motion between the observer and the source. [after C. J. Doppler, physicist]

Doric ('dɒrɪk) adj. of or denoting a classical order of architecture characterized by a heavy fluted column and a simple capital. [Doris, in ancient Greece]

dormant ('dɔːmənt) adj. 1. temporarily quiet, inactive, or not being used. 2. Biol. alive but in a resting condition. [Latin dormīre to sleep] —'**dormancy** n.

dormer or **dormer window** ('dɔːmə) n. a window that projects from a sloping roof. [Latin dormītōrium dormitory]

dormitory ('dɔːmɪtrɪ) n., pl. -**ries**. 1. a large room, esp. at a school, containing several beds. 2. U.S. a building, esp. at a college, providing living accommodation. 3. (modifier) Brit. denoting an area from which most of the residents commute to work: a dormitory suburb. [Latin dormītōrium, from dormīre to sleep]

Dormobile ('dɔːməʊ‚biːl) n. Trademark. a vanlike vehicle specially equipped for living in while travelling.

dormouse ('dɔː‚maʊs) n., pl. -**mice**. a small rodent resembling a mouse with a furry tail. [origin unknown]

dorp (dɔːp) n. S. African. a small town or village. [Dutch]

dorsal ('dɔːs'l) adj. Anat., zool. relating to the back. [Latin dorsum back]

dory ('dɔːrɪ) n., pl. -**ries**. a spiny-finned food fish. Also called: **John Dory**. [French dorée gilded]

dose (dəʊs) n. 1. a specific quantity of a medicine taken at one time. 2. Informal. something unpleasant to experience: a dose of influenza. 3. the total energy of radiation absorbed. 4. Slang. a sexually transmitted infection. ~vb. 5. to administer a dose to (someone). [Greek dosis a giving] —'**dosage** n.

dosing strip n. (in New Zealand) an area for treating dogs suspected of having hydatid disease.

doss down (dɒs) vb. Brit. slang. to sleep, esp. on a makeshift bed. [origin unknown]

dosshouse ('dɒs,haʊs) n. Brit. slang. a cheap lodging house for homeless people.

dossier ('dɒsɪ,eɪ) n. a collection of papers about a subject or person. [French]

dot (dɒt) n. 1. a small round mark; spot; point. 2. the symbol (·) used, in combination with the symbol for *dash* (—), in Morse code. 3. **on the dot.** at exactly the arranged time. ~vb. **dotting, dotted.** 4. to mark with a dot. 5. to scatter or intersperse: *bushes dotting the plain.* 6. **dot one's i's and cross one's t's.** *Informal.* to pay meticulous attention to detail. [Old English *dott* head of a boil]

dotage ('dəʊtɪdʒ) n. feebleness of mind as a result of old age. [Middle English *doten* to dote]

dotard ('dəʊtəd) n. a person who is weak-minded through senility.

dote (dəʊt) vb. (foll. by *on* or *upon*) to love to an excessive or foolish degree. [Middle English *doten*]

dotterel ('dɒtrəl) n. a plover with white bands around the head and neck. [Middle English *dotrelle*]

dottle ('dɒt³l) n. the tobacco left in a pipe after smoking. [obs. *dot* lump]

dotty ('dɒtɪ) adj. **-tier, -tiest.** *Slang, chiefly Brit.* slightly crazy. [from *dot*] —**'dottiness** n.

double ('dʌb³l) adj. 1. as much again in size, strength, number, etc.: *a double portion.* 2. composed of two equal or similar parts. 3. designed for two users: *a double room.* 4. folded in two; composed of two layers. 5. stooping: *bent double.* 6. ambiguous: *a double meaning.* 7. false, deceitful, or hypocritical: *a double life.* 8. (of flowers) having more than the normal number of petals. 9. *Music.* (of an instrument) sounding an octave lower: *a double bass.* ~adv. 10. twice over; twofold. ~n. 11. twice the number, amount, size, etc. 12. a double measure of spirits. 13. a duplicate or counterpart, esp. a person who closely resembles another. 14. a bet on two horses in different races in which any winnings from the first race are placed on the horse in the later race. 15. **at** or **on the double.** quickly or immediately. ~vb. 16. to make or become twice as much. 17. to bend or fold (material, etc.). 18. to play two parts or serve two roles. 19. to turn sharply. 20. *Bridge.* to make a call that will double certain scoring points if the preceding bid becomes the contract. 21. (foll. by *for*) to act as substitute. ~See also **double back, doubles, double up.** [Latin *duplus* twofold] —**'doubler** n.

double agent n. a spy employed by two mutually antagonistic countries.

double back vb. to go back in the opposite direction: *to double back on one's tracks.*

double-barrelled or U.S. **-barreled** adj. 1. (of a gun) having two barrels. 2.

Brit. (of surnames) having hyphenated parts.

double bass (beɪs) n. a stringed instrument, the largest and lowest member of the violin family.

double-breasted adj. (of a garment) having overlapping fronts.

double-check vb. to check again; verify.

double chin n. a fold of fat under the chin.

double cream n. thick cream with a high fat content.

double-cross vb. 1. to cheat or betray. ~n. 2. an instance of double-crossing; betrayal.

double-dealing n. action characterized by treachery or deceit.

double-decker n. 1. *Chiefly Brit.* a bus with two passenger decks. 2. *Informal.* **a.** a thing or structure with two layers. **b.** (*as modifier*): *a double-decker sandwich.*

double Dutch n. *Brit. informal.* incomprehensible language; gibberish.

double-edged adj. 1. (of a remark) having two possible interpretations, esp. being malicious though apparently innocuous. 2. (of a knife) having a cutting edge on either side of the blade.

double entendre (ɑːn'tɑːndrə) n. a word or phrase that can be interpreted in two ways, esp. with one meaning that is indelicate. [obs. French]

double entry n. a book-keeping system in which any commercial transaction is entered as a debit in one account and as a credit in another.

double glazing n. two panes of glass in a window, fitted to reduce heat loss.

double-jointed adj. having unusually flexible joints.

double knitting n. a medium thickness of knitting wool.

double negative n. a construction, considered ungrammatical, in which two negatives are used where one is needed, as in *I wouldn't never have believed it.*

double pneumonia n. pneumonia affecting both lungs.

double-quick adj. 1. very quick; rapid. ~adv. 2. in a very quick or rapid manner.

doubles ('dʌb³lz) n. (*functioning as sing.*) a game between two pairs of players.

double standard n. a set of principles that allows greater freedom to one person or group than to another.

doublet ('dʌblɪt) n. 1. (formerly) a man's close-fitting jacket, with or without sleeves. 2. **a.** a pair of similar things. **b.** one of such a pair. [Old French]

double take n. (esp. in comedy) a delayed reaction by a person to a remark or situation.

double talk n. deceptive or ambiguous talk.

doublethink ('dʌb³l,θɪŋk) n. deliberate, perverse, or unconscious acceptance of conflicting facts or principles.

double time n. 1. a doubled wage rate sometimes paid for overtime work. 2. *Music.* two beats per bar.

double up vb. **1.** to bend or cause to bend in two. **2.** to share a room or bed designed for one person or family.

doubloon (dʌˈbluːn) n. a former Spanish gold coin. [Spanish doblón]

doubly (ˈdʌblɪ) adv. **1.** to or in a double degree, quantity, or measure. **2.** in two ways.

doubt (daʊt) n. **1.** uncertainty about the truth, facts, or existence of something. **2.** an unresolved difficulty or point. **3. give someone the benefit of the doubt.** to presume innocent someone suspected of guilt. **4. no doubt.** almost certainly. ~vb. **5.** to be inclined to disbelieve. **6.** to distrust or be suspicious of. [Latin dubitāre] —ˈdoubter n.

doubtful (ˈdaʊtful) adj. **1.** unlikely; improbable. **2.** feeling doubt; uncertain. —ˈdoubtfully adv. —ˈdoubtfulness n.

doubtless (ˈdaʊtlɪs) adv. **1.** certainly. **2.** probably.

douche (duːʃ) n. **1.** a stream of water directed onto or into the body for cleansing or medical purposes. **2.** an instrument for applying a douche. ~vb. **3.** to cleanse or treat by means of a douche. [French]

dough (dəʊ) n. **1.** a thick mixture of flour and water or milk, used for making bread, pastry, etc. **2.** Slang. money. [Old English dāg]

doughnut (ˈdəʊnʌt) n. a small cake of sweetened dough cooked in hot fat.

doughty (ˈdaʊtɪ) adj. **-tier, -tiest.** hardy; resolute. [Old English dohtig]

do up vb. **1.** to wrap and make into a bundle: to do up a parcel. **2.** to fasten or be fastened. **3.** to renovate or redecorate.

dour (dʊə) adj. sullen. [prob. from Latin dūrus hard] —ˈdourness n.

douse or **dowse** (daʊs) vb. **1.** to drench with water or other liquid. **2.** to put out (a light). [origin unknown]

dove (dʌv) n. **1.** a bird with a heavy body, small head, and short legs. **2.** Politics. a person opposed to war. [Old English]

dovecote (ˈdʌvˌkəʊt) or **dovecot** (ˈdʌvˌkɒt) n. a structure for housing pigeons.

dove-grey adj. greyish-brown.

dovetail (ˈdʌvˌteɪl) n. **1.** Also called: **dovetail joint.** a joint containing wedge-shaped tenons. ~vb. **2.** to fit together closely or neatly.

dowager (ˈdaʊədʒə) n. **1. a.** a widow possessing property or a title obtained from her husband. **b.** (as modifier): the dowager duchess. **2.** a wealthy or dignified elderly woman. [Old French douagiere]

dowdy (ˈdaʊdɪ) adj. **-dier, -diest.** (esp. of a woman or a woman's dress) shabby or old-fashioned. [Middle English dowd slut] —ˈdowdily adv. —ˈdowdiness n.

dowel (ˈdaʊəl) n. a wooden or metal peg that fits into two corresponding holes to join two adjacent parts. [Middle Low German dövel plug]

dower (ˈdaʊə) n. **1.** the life interest in a part of her husband's estate allotted to a widow by law. **2.** Archaic. a dowry. [Latin dōs gift]

dower house n. a house for the use of a widow, often on her deceased husband's estate.

do with vb. **1. could** or **can do with.** to find useful; benefit from: I could do with a good night's sleep. **2. have to do with.** to be involved in or connected with. **3. to do with.** concerning; related to. **4. to put or place:** what did you do with my coat?

do without vb. to manage without.

down¹ (daʊn) prep. **1.** used to indicate movement from a higher to a lower position. **2.** at a lower or further level or position on, in, or along: he ran down the street. ~adv. **3.** downwards; at or to a lower level or position. **4.** used with many verbs when the result of the verb's action is to lower or destroy its object: knock down. **5.** used with several verbs to indicate intensity or completion: calm down. **6.** immediately: cash down. **7.** on paper: write this down. **8.** arranged; scheduled. **9.** away from a more important place. **10.** reduced to a state of lack: down to the last pound. **11.** lacking a specified amount: 3 down. **12.** lower in price. **13.** from an earlier to a later time. **14.** to a finer state: to grind down. **15.** Sport. being a specified number of points or goals behind an opponent. **16.** (of a person) being inactive, owing to illness: down with flu. **17. down with...!** away with...!: down with the king! ~adj. **18.** depressed. **19.** relating to a train from a more important place or one regarded as higher: the down line. **20.** made in cash: a down payment. ~vb. **21.** Informal. to drink, esp. quickly. **22.** to bring (someone) down, esp. by tackling. ~n. **23.** a poor period: ups and downs. **24. have a down on.** Informal. to bear ill will towards. [Old English dūne]

down² (daʊn) n. **1.** soft fine feathers. **2.** soft fine hair. [Old Norse] —ˈdowny adj.

down-and-out adj. **1.** without any means of livelihood; poor and, often, socially outcast. ~n. **2.** a person who is destitute and, often, homeless.

downbeat (ˈdaʊnˌbiːt) n. **1.** Music. the first beat of a bar. ~adj. Informal. **2.** depressed; gloomy. **3.** relaxed.

downcast (ˈdaʊnˌkɑːst) adj. **1.** dejected. **2.** (of the eyes) directed downwards.

downer (ˈdaʊnə) n. Slang. **1.** a barbiturate, tranquillizer, or narcotic. **2. on a downer.** in a state of depression.

downfall (ˈdaʊnˌfɔːl) n. **1.** a sudden loss of position or reputation. **2.** the cause of this.

downgrade (ˈdaʊnˌgreɪd) vb. to reduce in importance or value.

downhearted (ˌdaʊnˈhɑːtɪd) adj. discouraged; dejected.

downhill (ˈdaʊnˈhɪl) adj. **1.** going or sloping down. ~adv. **2.** towards the bottom of a hill; downwards. **3. go downhill.** Informal. to deteriorate.

Downing Street (ˈdaʊnɪŋ) n. the prime minister or the British Government. [after the street in London which contains the official residence of the prime minister and the chancellor of the exchequer]

down-market *adj.* cheap, having little prestige, and poor in quality.

down payment *n.* the deposit paid on an item purchased on hire-purchase, mortgage, etc.

downpour ('daun,pɔː) *n.* a heavy continuous fall of rain.

downright ('daun,raɪt) *adv., adj.* extreme or extremely: *downright rude.*

downs (daunz) *pl. n.* rolling upland, esp. in the chalk areas of S England.

downside ('daunsaɪd) *n.* the disadvantageous aspect of a situation: *the downside of twentieth-century living.*

Down's syndrome (daunz) *n. Pathol.* a genetic disorder characterized by a flat face and nose, slanting eyes, and mental retardation. [after John *Langdon-Down*, physician]

downstairs ('daun'stɛəz) *adv.* 1. down the stairs; to or on a lower floor. ~*n.* 2. a lower or ground floor.

downstream ('daun'striːm) *adv., adj.* in or towards the lower part of a stream; with the current.

down-to-earth *adj.* sensible; practical; realistic.

downtown ('daun'taun) *Chiefly U.S., Canad., & N.Z.* ~*n.* 1. the central or lower part of a city, esp. the main commercial area. ~*adv.* 2. towards, to, or into this area.

downtrodden ('daun,trɒdᵊn) *adj.* oppressed and lacking the will to resist.

down under *Informal.* ~*n.* 1. Australia or New Zealand. ~*adv.* 2. in or to Australia or New Zealand.

downward ('daunwəd) *adj.* 1. descending from a higher to a lower level, condition, or position. ~*adv.* 2. same as **downwards.** —'**downwardly** *adv.*

downwards ('daunwədz) *or* **downward** *adv.* 1. from a higher to a lower place, level, etc. 2. from an earlier time or source to a later.

downwind ('daun'wɪnd) *adv., adj.* in the same direction towards which the wind is blowing; with the wind from behind.

dowry ('dauərɪ) *n., pl.* -**ries.** the property brought by a woman to her husband at marriage. [Latin *dōs* gift]

dowse (dauz) *vb.* to search for underground water or minerals using a divining rod. [origin unknown] —'**dowser** *n.*

doxology (dɒk'sɒlədʒɪ) *n., pl.* -**gies.** a hymn, verse, or form of words in Christian liturgy glorifying God. [Greek *doxologos* uttering praise]

doyen ('dɔɪən) *n.* the senior member of a group, profession, or society. [French] —**doyenne** (dɔɪ'ɛn) *fem. n.*

doz. dozen.

doze (dauz) *vb.* 1. to sleep lightly or intermittently. 2. (foll. by *off*) to fall into a light sleep. ~*n.* 3. a short sleep. [prob. from Old Norse *dūs* lull]

dozen ('dʌzᵊn) *det.* 1. twelve or a group of twelve: *two dozen oranges.* ~*n., pl.* **doz-**

ens *or* **dozen.** 2. **talk nineteen to the dozen.** to talk without stopping. [Latin *duodecim*] —'**dozenth** *adj.*

dozy ('dauzɪ) *adj.* **dozier, doziest.** 1. drowsy. 2. *Brit. informal.* stupid.

DP 1. data processing. 2. displaced person.

DPhil *or* **DPh** Doctor of Philosophy.

DPP (in Britain) Director of Public Prosecutions.

Dr 1. Doctor. 2. Drive.

drab (dræb) *adj.* **drabber, drabbest.** 1. dull; dingy. 2. cheerless; dreary. 3. light olive-brown. [Old French *drap* cloth] —'**drabness** *n.*

drachm (dræm) *n. Brit.* one eighth of a fluid ounce. [var. of *dram*]

drachma ('drækmə) *n., pl.* -**mas** *or* -**mae** (-miː). 1. the standard monetary unit of Greece. 2. a silver coin of ancient Greece. [Greek *drakhmē* a handful]

draconian (dreɪ'kəunɪən) *adj.* harsh. [after *Draco*, Athenian statesman]

draft (drɑːft) *n.* 1. a plan, sketch, or drawing of something. 2. a preliminary outline of a book, speech, etc. 3. a written order for payment of money by a bank. 4. *U.S.* selection for compulsory military service. 5. detachment of personnel from one place to another, esp. for a specific task. ~*vb.* 6. to draw up an outline or plan of. 7. to detach (personnel) from one place to another, esp. for a specific task. 8. *U.S.* to select for compulsory military service. ~*n., vb.* 9. *U.S.* same as **draught.** [var. of *draught*]

drag (dræg) *vb.* **dragging, dragged.** 1. to pull with force, esp. along the ground. 2. (foll. by *away* or *from*) to persuade (someone) or force (oneself) to come away. 3. to trail on the ground. 4. to bring (oneself or someone else) with effort or difficulty. 5. to linger behind. 6. (often foll. by *on* or *out*) to last, prolong, or be prolonged tediously: *his talk dragged on for hours.* 7. to search (a river) with a dragnet or hook. 8. *Informal.* to draw (on a cigarette). 9. **drag one's feet.** *Informal.* to act with deliberate slowness. ~*n.* 10. an implement, such as a dragnet, used for dragging. 11. a person or thing that slows up progress. 12. *Aeronautics.* the resistance to the motion of a body passing through air. 13. *Informal.* a person or thing that is very tedious. 14. women's clothes worn by a man (esp. in **in drag**). 15. *Informal.* a draw on a cigarette. ~See also **drag up.** [Old English *dragan*]

draggle ('drægᵊl) *vb.* to make or become wet or dirty by trailing on the ground. [Middle English]

dragnet ('dræg,nɛt) *n.* a net used to scour the bottom of a pond or river, as when searching for something.

dragoman ('drægəumən) *n., pl.* -**mans** *or* -**men.** (in Middle Eastern countries) a professional interpreter or guide. [Arabic *targumān*]

dragon ('drægən) *n.* 1. a mythical fire-breathing monster with a scaly reptilian body, wings, claws, and a long tail. 2. *Informal.* a fierce woman. 3. **chase the**

dragon. *Slang.* to smoke opium or heroin. [Greek *drakōn*]

dragonfly ('drægən,flaɪ) *n., pl.* **-flies.** a brightly coloured insect with a long slender body and two pairs of wings.

dragoon (drə'guːn) *n.* **1.** a heavily armed cavalryman. ~*vb.* **2.** to coerce; force. [French *dragon*]

drag race *n.* a race in which specially built or modified cars or motorcycles are timed over a measured course. —**drag racing** *n.*

drag up *vb. Informal.* to revive (an unpleasant fact or story).

drain (dreɪn) *n.* **1.** a pipe or channel that carries off water or sewage. **2.** a cause of continuous diminution in resources or energy: *a drain on one's resources.* **3. down the drain.** wasted. ~*vb.* **4.** (often foll. by *off*) to draw off or remove (liquid) from. **5.** (often foll. by *away*) to flow (away) or filter (off). **6.** to dry or be emptied as a result of liquid running off or flowing away. **7.** to drink the entire contents of (a glass or cup). **8.** to make constant demands on (resources, energy, etc.); exhaust. **9.** (of a river) to carry off the surface water from (an area). [Old English *drēahnian*]

drainage ('dreɪnɪdʒ) *n.* **1.** the process or a method of draining. **2.** a system of watercourses or drains.

draining board *n.* a sloping grooved surface at the side of a sink, used for draining washed dishes.

drainpipe ('dreɪn,paɪp) *n.* a pipe for carrying off rainwater or sewage.

drainpipes ('dreɪn,paɪps) *pl. n.* very narrow trousers.

drake (dreɪk) *n.* the male of a duck. [origin unknown]

dram (dræm) *n.* **1.** a small amount of spirits, esp. whisky. **2.** one sixteenth of an ounce (avoirdupois). **3.** *U.S.* one eighth of an apothecaries' ounce; 60 grains. [Greek *drakhmē*; see DRACHMA]

drama ('drɑːmə) *n.* **1.** a work to be performed by actors; play. **2.** the genre of literature represented by works intended for the stage. **3.** the art of the writing and production of plays. **4.** a situation that is highly emotional, tragic, or turbulent. [Greek: something performed]

dramatic (drə'mætɪk) *adj.* **1.** of drama. **2.** like a drama in suddenness, emotional impact, etc. **3.** striking; effective. **4.** acting or performed in a flamboyant way. —**dra'matically** *adv.*

dramatics (drə'mætɪks) *n.* **1.** (*functioning as sing. or pl.*) the art of acting or producing plays. **2.** (*usually functioning as pl.*) exaggerated, theatrical behaviour.

dramatis personae ('drɑːmətɪs pə-'səʊnaɪ) *pl. n.* the characters in a play. [New Latin]

dramatist ('dræmətɪst) *n.* a playwright.

dramatize *or* **-tise** ('dræmə,taɪz) *vb.* **1.** to put into dramatic form. **2.** to express (something) in a dramatic or exaggerated way. —**,dramati'zation** *or* **-ti'sation** *n.*

drank (dræŋk) *vb.* the past tense of **drink.**

drape (dreɪp) *vb.* **1.** to cover with material or fabric, usually in folds. **2.** to hang or arrange, esp. in folds. **3.** to place casually and loosely. ~*See also* **drapes.** [Old French *draper*]

draper ('dreɪpə) *n. Brit.* a dealer in fabrics and sewing materials.

drapery ('dreɪpərɪ) *n., pl.* **-peries. 1.** fabric or clothing arranged and draped. **2.** (*pl.*) curtains. **3.** fabrics and cloth collectively.

drapes (dreɪps) *pl. n. Chiefly U.S. & Canad.* curtains.

drastic ('dræstɪk) *adj.* extreme or forceful; severe. [Greek *drastikos*] —**'drastically** *adv.*

drat (dræt) *interj. Slang.* an exclamation of annoyance. [prob. alteration of *God rot*]

draught *or U.S.* **draft** (drɑːft) *n.* **1.** a current of air, esp. in an enclosed space. **2. a.** the act of pulling a load by a vehicle or animal. **b.** (*as modifier*): *a draught horse.* **3.** a portion of liquid to be drunk, esp. a dose of medicine. **4.** an instance of drinking; a gulp or swallow. **5. on draught.** (of beer) drawn from a cask. **6.** one of the flat discs used in the game of draughts. *U.S.* and *Canad.* equivalent: **checker. 7. feel the draught.** to be short of money. [prob. Old Norse *drahtr*]

draught beer *n.* beer stored in a cask.

draughtboard ('drɑːft,bɔːd) *n.* a square board divided into 64 squares, used for playing draughts.

draughts (drɑːfts) *n.* (*functioning as sing.*) a game for two players using a draughtboard and 12 draughtsmen each. [pl. of *draught* (in obs. sense: a chess move)]

draughtsman *or U.S.* **draftsman** ('drɑːftsmən) *n., pl.* **-men. 1.** a person employed to prepare detailed scale drawings of machinery, buildings, etc. **2.** a person skilled in drawing. **3.** *Brit.* any of the flat discs used in the game of draughts. *U.S.* and *Canad.* equivalent: **checker.** —**'draughtsman,ship** *n.*

draughty *or U.S.* **drafty** ('drɑːftɪ) *adj.* **draughtier, draughtiest** *or U.S.* **draftier, draftiest.** exposed to draughts of air. —**'draughtily** *adv.* —**'draughtiness** *n.*

draw (drɔː) *vb.* **drawing, drew, drawn. 1.** to depict or sketch (a figure, picture, etc.) in lines, as with a pencil or pen. **2.** to cause (a person or thing) to move towards one or away from a place by pulling. **3.** to bring, take, or pull (something) out, as from a drawer, holster, etc. **4.** to take (liquid) out of a cask, etc., by means of a tap. **5.** to move, esp. in a specified direction: *to draw alongside.* **6.** to attract: *to draw attention.* **7.** to cause to flow: *to draw blood.* **8.** to formulate or derive: *to draw conclusions.* **9.** (of a chimney) to induce or allow a draught to carry off smoke. **10.** to take from a source: *to draw money from the bank.* **11.** to earn: *draw interest.* **12.** to choose at random. **13.** *Archery.* to bend (a bow) by pulling the string. **14.** (of tea) to steep in boiling water. **15.** to disembowel. **16.** to cause (pus) to discharge from an abscess or wound. **17.** (of two teams or contestants) to finish a game with an equal number of points; tie. **18.** *Naut.* (of a vessel) to require (a specified depth) in which to float. ~*n.* **19.** *Informal.* an event, act, etc., that attracts a large audience. **20.** a raffle or lottery. **21.** something taken at random, as a ticket in a lottery. **22.** a contest or game ending in a tie. ~See also **drawback**, **draw in**, etc. [Old English *dragan*]

drawback ('drɔː,bæk) *n.* **1.** a disadvantage or hindrance. ~*vb.* **draw back.** **2.** to retreat. **3.** to turn aside from an undertaking.

drawbridge ('drɔː,brɪdʒ) *n.* a bridge that may be raised to prevent access or to enable vessels to pass.

drawer *n.* **1.** (drɔː). a boxlike container in a chest, table, etc., made for sliding in and out. **2.** ('drɔːə). a person or thing that draws.

drawers (drɔːz) *pl. n. Old-fashioned.* an undergarment worn below the waist.

draw in *vb.* **1.** (of a train) to arrive at a station. **2. the nights are drawing in.** the hours of daylight are becoming shorter.

drawing ('drɔːɪŋ) *n.* **1.** a picture or plan made by means of lines on a surface, esp. with a pencil or pen. **2.** the art of making drawings; draughtsmanship.

drawing pin *n. Brit.* a short tack with a broad smooth head for fastening papers to a drawing board, etc.

drawing room *n.* a room where visitors are received and entertained.

drawl (drɔːl) *vb.* **1.** to speak or utter (words) slowly, esp. prolonging the vowel sounds. ~*n.* **2.** the way of speech of someone who drawls. [prob. frequentative of *drawl*] —**'drawling** *adj.*

drawn (drɔːn) *vb.* **1.** the past participle of **draw.** ~*adj.* **2.** haggard, tired, or tense in appearance.

draw off *vb.* to cause (a liquid) to flow from something.

draw on *vb.* **1.** to use or exploit (a source, fund, etc.). **2.** to come near: *winter draws on.* **3.** to lead (someone) further; entice (someone).

draw out *vb.* **1.** to extend. **2.** to cause (a person) to talk freely. **3.** (foll. by *of*) to elicit (information) (from). **4.** (of hours of daylight) to become longer. **5.** (of a train) to leave a station.

drawstring ('drɔː,strɪŋ) *n.* a cord run through a hem around an opening, so that when it is pulled tighter, the opening closes.

draw up *vb.* **1.** (of a vehicle) to come to a halt. **2.** to formulate and write out: *to draw up a contract.* **3. draw oneself up.** to straighten oneself.

dray (dreɪ) *n.* a low cart used for carrying heavy loads. [Old English *dræge* dragnet]

dread (drɛd) *vb.* **1.** to anticipate with apprehension or terror. ~*n.* **2.** great fear. **3.** *Slang.* a Rastafarian. [Old English *ondrǣdan*]

dreadful ('drɛdful) *adj.* **1.** extremely disagreeable, shocking, or bad. **2.** extreme: *a*

dreadful waste of time. —**'dreadfully** *adv.*

dreadnought ('drɛd,nɔːt) *n.* a battleship armed with heavy guns.

dream (driːm) *n.* **1.** mental activity, usually an imagined series of events, occurring during sleep. **2.** a sequence of imaginative thoughts indulged in while awake. **3.** a cherished hope; aspiration. **4.** a vain hope. **5.** a person or thing that is as pleasant or seemingly unreal as a dream. ~*vb.* **dreaming, dreamt** (drɛmt) *or* **dreamed. 6.** to experience (a dream). **7.** to indulge in daydreams. **8.** to be unrealistic. **9.** (foll. by *of* or *about*) to have an image (of) or fantasy (about) in or as if in a dream. **10.** (foll. by *of*) to consider the possibility (of). ~*adj.* **11.** ideal: *dream kitchen.* [Old English *drēam* song] —**'dreamer** *n.*

dream up *vb.* to invent by ingenuity and imagination: *to dream up an excuse.*

dreamy ('driːmɪ) *adj.* **dreamier, dreamiest. 1.** vague or impractical. **2.** relaxing; gentle: *dreamy music.* **3.** *Informal.* wonderful. —**'dreamily** *adv.* —**'dreaminess** *n.*

dreary ('drɪərɪ) *adj.* **drearier, dreariest.** sad or dull; boring. [Old English *drēorig* gory] —**'drearily** *adv.* —**'dreariness** *n.*

dredge¹ (drɛdʒ) *n.* **1.** a machine used to scoop or suck up material from a riverbed, etc. ~*vb.* **2.** to remove material from (a riverbed, etc.) by means of a dredge. **3.** to search for (a submerged object) with or as if with a dredge. [origin unknown] —**'dredger** *n.*

dredge² (drɛdʒ) *vb.* to sprinkle (food) with flour, etc. [Old French *dragie*] —**'dredger** *n.*

dredge up *vb. Informal.* to bring (something) to notice, esp. with effort and from an obscure source.

dregs (drɛgz) *pl. n.* **1.** solid particles that settle at the bottom of some liquids. **2.** the worst or most despised elements: *the dregs of society.* [Old Norse *dregg*]

drench (drɛntʃ) *vb.* **1.** to make completely wet. **2.** to give medicine to (an animal). ~*n.* **3.** a dose of medicine given to an animal. [Old English *drencan* to cause to drink] —**'drenching** *n., adj.*

Dresden ('drɛzdən) *or* **Dresden china** *n.* delicate and decorative porcelain made near Dresden, East Germany.

dress (drɛs) *vb.* **1.** to put clothes on. **2.** to put on formal clothes. **3.** to arrange merchandise in (a shop window). **4.** to arrange (the hair). **5.** to apply protective covering to (a wound). **6.** to cover (a salad) with dressing. **7.** to prepare (fowl or fish) by cleaning, gutting, etc. **8.** to put a finish on (stone, metal, etc.). **9.** *Mil.* to bring (troops) into line *or* (of troops) to come into line: *dress ranks.* ~*n.* **10.** a one-piece garment for a woman or girl, consisting of a skirt and bodice. **11.** complete style of clothing: *military dress.* **12.** (*modifier*) suitable for a formal occasion: *a dress shirt.* ~See also **dress up.** [Old French *drecier*]

dressage ('drɛsɑːʒ) *n.* **a.** the training of a

horse to perform manoeuvres in response to the rider's body signals. **b.** the manoeuvres performed. [French]

dress circle n. the first gallery in a theatre.

dresser[1] ('drɛsə) n. **1.** a set of shelves, usually also with cupboards, for storing or displaying dishes. **2.** U.S. a chest of drawers. [Old French *drecier* to arrange]

dresser[2] ('drɛsə) n. **1.** a person who dresses in a specified way: *a fashionable dresser*. **2.** Theatre. a person employed to assist actors with their costumes. **3.** Brit. a person who assists a surgeon.

dressing ('drɛsɪŋ) n. **1.** a sauce for salad. **2.** U.S. & Canad. same as **stuffing** (sense 2). **3.** a covering for a wound. **4.** fertilizer spread on land. **5.** size used for stiffening textiles.

dressing-down n. Informal. a severe scolding.

dressing gown n. a robe worn before dressing or for lounging.

dressing room n. **1.** Theatre. a room backstage where an actor changes and makes up. **2.** any room used for changing clothes.

dressing table n. a piece of bedroom furniture with a mirror and a set of drawers.

dressmaker ('drɛsˌmeɪkə) n. a person who makes clothes for women. —'**dress-ˌmaking** n.

dress rehearsal n. **1.** the last rehearsal of a play, using costumes, lighting, etc., as for the first night. **2.** any full-scale practice.

dress shirt n. a man's evening shirt, worn as part of formal evening dress.

dress suit n. a man's evening suit.

dress up vb. **1.** to attire (oneself or another) in smart, glamorous, or stylish clothes. **2.** to put fancy dress on. **3.** to improve the appearance or impression of: *to dress up the facts*.

dressy ('drɛsɪ) adj. **dressier, dressiest.** **1.** (of clothes or occasions) elegant. **2.** (of persons) dressing stylishly. —'**dressi-ness** n.

drew (druː) vb. the past tense of **draw.**

drey or **dray** (dreɪ) n. a squirrel's nest. [origin unknown]

dribble ('drɪb°l) vb. **1.** to flow or allow to flow in a thin stream or drops. **2.** to allow saliva to trickle from the mouth. **3.** (in soccer, basketball, hockey, etc.) to propel (the ball) by repeatedly tapping it with the hand, foot, or a stick. ~n. **4.** a small quantity of liquid falling in drops or flowing in a thin stream. **5.** a small supply. **6.** an act of dribbling. [obs. *drib*, var. of *drip*] —'**dribbler** n.

driblet or **dribblet** ('drɪblɪt) n. a small amount. [obs. *drib* to fall bit by bit]

dried (draɪd) vb. past of **dry.**

drier[1] ('draɪə) adj. a comparative of **dry.**

drier[2] ('draɪə) n. same as **dryer**[1].

driest ('draɪɪst) adj. a superlative of **dry.**

drift (drɪft) vb. **1.** to be carried along by currents of air or water. **2.** to move

aimlessly from one place or activity to another. **3.** to wander away from a fixed course or point. **4.** (of snow) to accumulate in heaps. ~n. **5.** something piled up by the wind or current, as a snowdrift. **6.** tendency or meaning: *the drift of the argument*. **7.** a general movement or development: *the drift of workers away from the countryside*. **8.** the extent to which a vessel or aircraft is driven off course by winds, etc. **9.** a general tendency of a mass of water to flow in the direction of the prevailing winds. **10.** a controlled four-wheel skid used to take bends at high speed. [Old Norse]

drifter ('drɪftə) n. **1.** a person who moves aimlessly from place to place. **2.** a boat used for drift-net fishing.

drift net n. a fishing net that is allowed to drift with the tide.

driftwood ('drɪftˌwʊd) n. wood floating on or washed ashore by the sea or other body of water.

drill[1] (drɪl) n. **1.** a machine or tool for boring holes. **2.** Mil. training in procedures or movements, as for parades. **3.** strict and often repetitious training. **4.** Informal. correct procedure. ~vb. **5.** to pierce, bore, or cut (a hole) in (material) with or as if with a drill. **6.** to instruct or be instructed in military procedures or movements. **7.** to teach by rigorous exercises or training. [Middle Dutch *drillen*]

drill[2] (drɪl) n. **1.** a machine for planting seeds in rows. **2.** a furrow in which seeds are sown. **3.** a row of seeds planted by means of a drill. ~vb. **4.** to plant (seeds) by means of a drill. [origin unknown]

drill[3] (drɪl) n. a hard-wearing cotton cloth, used for uniforms. [German *Drillich* thread]

drill[4] (drɪl) n. a monkey of W Africa, related to the mandrill. [West African]

drilling platform n. a structure which supports the machinery and equipment, together with the stores, etc., required for drilling an offshore oil well.

drilling rig n. **1.** the complete machinery, equipment, and structures needed to drill an oil well. **2.** a mobile drilling platform used for exploratory offshore drilling.

drily ('draɪlɪ) adv. same as **dryly.**

drink (drɪŋk) vb. **drinking, drank, drunk.** **1.** to swallow (a liquid). **2.** to consume alcohol, esp. to excess. **3.** to bring (oneself) into a specified condition by consuming alcohol: *he drank himself to death*. **4.** (foll. by *to*) to drink a toast. **5.** **drink someone's health.** to salute someone with a toast. **6.** to soak up (liquid). **7.** (foll. by *in*) to pay close attention to. ~n. **8.** liquid suitable for drinking. **9.** a portion of liquid for drinking. **10.** alcohol or its habitual or excessive consumption. **11.** **the drink.** Informal. the sea. [Old English *drincan*] —'**drinkable** adj. —'**drinker** n.

drink-driving n. (modifier) relating to driving a car after drinking alcohol: *a drink-driving charge*.

drip (drɪp) vb. **dripping, dripped.** **1.** to fall or let fall in drops. ~n. **2.** the falling of drops of liquid. **3.** the sound made by falling drops. **4.** *Informal.* an inane, insipid person. **5.** *Med.* an apparatus for the intravenous drop-by-drop administration of a solution. [Old English *dryppan*]

drip-dry *adj.* **1.** designating clothing that will dry free of creases if hung up when wet. ~*vb.* **-drying, -dried.** to dry or become dry thus.

drip-feed *vb.* **-feeding, -fed. 1.** to feed (someone) a liquid drop by drop, esp. intravenously. ~*n.* **2.** same as **drip** (sense 5).

dripping ('drɪpɪŋ) *n.* the fat that exudes from meat while it is being roasted or fried.

drive (draɪv) *vb.* **driving, drove, driven. 1.** to guide the movement of (a vehicle). **2.** to transport or be transported in a vehicle. **3.** to compel to work excessively hard. **4.** to goad into a specified state: *pressure of work drove him to despair.* **5.** to push or propel. **6.** to cause (an object) to make (a hole or crack). **7.** to move rapidly by striking or throwing with force. **8.** *Sport.* to hit (a ball) very hard and straight. **9.** *Golf.* to strike (the ball) with a driver. **10.** to chase (game) from cover. **11.** to rush or dash violently, esp. against an obstacle. **12.** to transact with vigour: *he drives a hard bargain.* **13. drive home. a.** to cause to penetrate to the fullest extent. **b.** to make clear by special emphasis. ~*n.* **14.** a journey in a driven vehicle. **15.** a road for vehicles, esp. a private road leading to a house. **16.** a united effort towards a common goal. **17.** *Brit.* a large gathering of people to play cards. **18.** energy, ambition, or initiative. **19.** *Psychol.* a motive or interest, such as sex or ambition. **20.** a sustained and powerful military offensive. **21.** the means by which force, motion, etc., is transmitted in a mechanism: *fluid drive.* **22.** *Sport.* a hard straight shot or stroke. [Old English *drīfan*]

drive at *vb. Informal.* to intend or mean: *what are you driving at?*

drive-in *adj.* **1.** denoting a public facility or service used by patrons in their cars: *a drive-in bank.* ~*n.* **2.** *Chiefly U.S. & Canad.* a cinema used in such a manner.

drivel ('drɪvˀl) *n.* **1.** foolish talk. ~*vb.* **-elling, -elled** *or U.S.* **-eling, -eled. 2.** to speak foolishly. **3.** to allow (saliva) to flow from the mouth. [Old English *dreflian* to slaver]

driven ('drɪvˀn) *vb.* the past participle of **drive.**

driver ('draɪvə) *n.* **1.** a person who drives a vehicle. **2. in the driver's seat.** in a position of control. **3.** *Golf.* a club used for tee shots.

driveway ('draɪv,weɪ) *n.* a path for vehicles, often connecting a house with a public road.

driving licence *n.* an official document authorizing a person to drive a motor vehicle.

drizzle ('drɪzˀl) *n.* **1.** very light rain. ~*vb.* **2.** to rain lightly. [Old English *drēosan* to fall] —'**drizzly** *adj.*

droll (drəʊl) *adj.* amusing in a quaint manner; comical. [Old French *drôle* scamp] —'**drollery** *n.* —'**drolly** *adv.*

dromedary ('drʌmədərɪ) *n., pl.* **-daries.** a camel with a single hump. [Greek *dromas* running]

drone[1] (drəʊn) *n.* **1.** a male honeybee whose sole function is to mate with the queen. **2.** a person who lives off the work of others. [Old English *drān*]

drone[2] (drəʊn) *vb.* **1.** to make a monotonous low dull sound. **2.** (foll. by *on*) to talk in a monotonous tone, esp. without stopping. ~*n.* **3.** a monotonous low dull sound. **4.** a single-reed pipe in a set of bagpipes. [related to DRONE[1]]

drool (druːl) *vb.* **1.** (foll. by *over*) to show excessive enthusiasm for or pleasure in. **2.** same as **drivel** (senses 2 and 3). [prob. alteration of *drivel*]

droop (druːp) *vb.* **1.** to sag or allow to sag, as from weakness. **2.** to be overcome by weariness. [Old Norse *drūpa*] —'**drooping** *adj.*

drop (drɒp) *n.* **1.** a small quantity of liquid forming a round shape. **2.** a very small quantity of liquid: *a drop of tea.* **3.** something shaped like a drop: *peppermint drops; pearl drops.* **4.** the act of falling. **5.** a decrease in amount or value. **6.** the vertical distance that anything may fall. **7.** the act of unloading troops or supplies by parachute. ~*vb.* **dropping, dropped. 8.** (of liquids) to fall or allow to fall in globules. **9.** to fall or allow (something) to fall vertically. **10.** to sink or fall to the ground, as from a blow or weariness. **11.** (foll. by *back, behind,* etc.) to move in a specified manner or direction. **12.** (foll. by *in* or *by*) *Informal.* to pay someone a casual visit. **13.** to decrease in amount, strength, or value. **14.** to sink to a lower position. **15.** (foll. by *into*) to pass easily into a condition: *to drop into a habit.* **16.** to mention casually: *to drop a hint.* **17.** to leave out in speaking: *to drop one's h's.* **18.** to set down (passengers or goods). **19.** to send: *drop me a line.* **20.** to discontinue: *let's drop the matter.* **21.** to cease to associate with. **22.** (of animals) to give birth to (offspring). **23.** *Slang, chiefly U.S. & Canad.* to lose (money). **24.** *Sport.* to omit (a player) from a team. **25.** to lose (a game or point). ~See also **drop off, drop-out, drops.** [Old English *dropian*] —'**droplet** *n.*

drop curtain *n. Theatre.* a curtain that can be raised and lowered onto the stage.

drop-in *n.* (*modifier*) denoting a social service or meeting place provided where people may attend if and when they please.

drop off *vb.* **1.** to grow smaller or less. **2.** to set down (passengers or goods). **3.** *Informal.* to fall asleep.

dropout ('drɒp,aʊt) *n.* **1.** a student who does not complete a course of study. **2.** a person who rejects conventional society. ~*vb.* **drop out.** (often foll. by *of*) **3.** to abandon or withdraw (from a school, job, etc.).

dropper ('drɒpə) *n.* a small tube with a rubber bulb at one end for dispensing drops of liquid.

droppings ('drɒpɪŋz) *pl. n.* the dung of certain animals, such as rabbits or birds.

drops (drɒps) *pl. n.* any liquid medication applied by means of a dropper.

drop scone *n.* a flat spongy cake made by dropping a spoonful of batter on a hot griddle.

dropsy ('drɒpsɪ) *n.* an illness in which watery fluid collects in the tissues or in a body cavity. [Middle English *ydropesie*, from Greek *hudōr* water] —'**dropsical** *adj.*

droshky ('drɒʃkɪ) *or* **drosky** ('drɒskɪ) *n., pl.* **-kies.** an open four-wheeled carriage, formerly used in Russia. [Russian]

dross (drɒs) *n.* **1.** the scum formed on the surfaces of molten metals. **2.** worthless matter; waste. [Old English *drōs* dregs]

drought (draut) *n.* a prolonged period of scanty rainfall. [Old English *drūgoth*]

drove[1] (drəuv) *vb.* the past tense of **drive.**

drove[2] (drəuv) *n.* **1.** a herd of livestock being driven together. **2.** (*pl.*) a moving crowd of people. [Old English *drāf* herd]

drover ('drəuvə) *n.* a person who drives sheep or cattle.

drown (draun) *vb.* **1.** to die or kill by immersion in liquid. **2.** to get rid of (one's sorrows) temporarily by drinking alcohol. **3.** to drench thoroughly. **4.** (sometimes foll. by *out*) to render (a sound) inaudible by making a loud noise. [prob. from Old English *druncnian*]

drowse (drauz) *vb.* to be sleepy, dull, or sluggish. [prob. from Old English *drūsian* to sink]

drowsy ('drauzɪ) *adj.* **drowsier, drowsiest.** **1.** heavy with sleepiness. **2.** inducing sleep; soporific. —'**drowsily** *adv.* —'**drowsiness** *n.*

drub (drʌb) *vb.* **drubbing, drubbed.** **1.** to beat as with a stick. **2.** to defeat utterly, as in a contest. [prob. from Arabic *dáraba* to beat] —'**drubbing** *n.*

drudge (drʌdʒ) *n.* **1.** a person who works hard at wearisome menial tasks. ~*vb.* **2.** to toil at such tasks. [origin unknown]

drudgery ('drʌdʒərɪ) *n.* hard, menial, and monotonous work.

drug (drʌg) *n.* **1.** any substance used in the treatment, prevention, or diagnosis of disease. **2.** a chemical substance, esp. a narcotic, taken for the effects it produces. **3. drug on the market.** a commodity available in excess of demand. ~*vb.* **drugging, drugged.** **4.** to mix a drug with (food or drink). **5.** to administer a drug to (a person or an animal) in order to induce sleepiness or unconsciousness. [Old French *drogue*]

drug addict *n.* a person who is dependent on narcotic drugs.

drugget ('drʌgɪt) *n.* a coarse fabric used as a floor covering. [French *droguet*]

druggist ('drʌgɪst) *n. U.S. & Canad.* a pharmacist.

drugstore ('drʌg,stɔː) *n. U.S. & Canad.* a shop where medical prescriptions are made up and a wide variety of goods and usually light meals are sold.

Druid ('druːɪd) *n.* a member of an ancient order of priests in Gaul, Britain, and Ireland in the pre-Christian era. [Latin *druides*] —**Dru'idic** *or* **Dru'idical** *adj.*

drum (drʌm) *n.* **1.** a percussion instrument sounded by striking a skin stretched across the opening of a hollow cylinder. **2.** the sound produced by a drum. **3.** an object that resembles a drum in shape, such as a large spool or a cylindrical container. **4.** same as **eardrum.** ~*vb.* **drumming, drummed.** **5.** to play (music) on a drum. **6.** to tap rhythmically or regularly. **7.** to instil by constant repetition: *these facts had been drummed into him.* ~See also **drum up.** [Middle Dutch *tromme*] —'**drummer** *n.*

drumbeat ('drʌm,biːt) *n.* the sound made by beating a drum.

drumhead ('drʌm,hed) *n.* the part of a drum that is struck.

drum machine *n.* a synthesizer programmed to reproduce the sound of percussion instruments.

drum major *n.* the noncommissioned officer who commands the corps of drums of a military band and who is in command of both the drums and the band when paraded together.

drum majorette (ˌmeɪdʒə'ret) *n.* a girl who marches at the head of a procession, twirling a baton.

drumstick ('drʌm,stɪk) *n.* **1.** a stick used for playing a drum. **2.** the lower joint of the leg of a cooked fowl.

drum up *vb.* to obtain (support or business) by solicitation or canvassing.

drunk (drʌŋk) *vb.* **1.** the past participle of **drink.** ~*adj.* **2.** intoxicated with alcohol to the extent of losing control over normal functions. **3.** overwhelmed by strong influence or emotion. ~*n.* **4.** a person who is drunk.

drunkard ('drʌŋkəd) *n.* a person who is frequently or habitually drunk.

drunken ('drʌŋkən) *adj.* **1.** intoxicated. **2.** habitually drunk. **3.** caused by or relating to alcoholic intoxication: *a drunken brawl.* —'**drunkenly** *adv.* —'**drunkenness** *n.*

drupe (druːp) *n.* a fleshy fruit with a stone, such as the peach, plum, or cherry. [Greek *druppa* olive]

dry (draɪ) *adj.* **drier, driest** *or* **dryer, dryest.** **1.** lacking moisture; not wet. **2.** having little or no rainfall. **3.** having the water drained away or evaporated: *a dry river.* **4.** not providing milk: *a dry cow.* **5.** (of the eyes) free from tears. **6.** *Informal.* thirsty. **7.** eaten without butter, jam, etc.: *dry toast.* **8.** (of wine) not sweet. **9.** consisting of solid as opposed to liquid substances. **10.** lacking interest: *a dry book.* **11.** lacking warmth: *a dry greeting.* **12.** (of humour) shrewd and keen in a sarcastic or laconic way. **13.** prohibiting the sale of alcoholic liquor: *a dry area.* ~*vb.* **drying, dried.** **14.** to make or become dry. **15.** to preserve (food) by removing the moisture. ~*n., pl.* **drys** *or* **dries.** **16.** *Brit. informal.* a Conservative politician who is a hardliner. ~See also **dry out, dry up**. [Old English *drýge*] —**'dryness** *n.*

dryad ('draɪəd, -æd) *n. Greek myth.* a nymph of the woods. [Greek *drus* tree]

dry battery *n.* an electric battery consisting of two or more dry cells.

dry cell *n.* an electric cell in which the electrolyte is in the form of a paste to prevent it from spilling.

dry-clean *vb.* to clean (clothes, etc.) with a solvent other than water. —**,dry-'cleaner** *n.* —**,dry-'cleaning** *n.*

dry dock *n.* a dock that can be pumped dry for work on a ship's bottom.

dryer[1] ('draɪə) *n.* an apparatus for removing moisture by forced draught, heating, or centrifuging.

dryer[2] ('draɪə) *adj.* same as **drier**[1].

dry fly *n. Angling.* **a.** an artificial fly designed to be floated on the surface of the water. **b.** (*as modifier*): *dry-fly fishing*.

dry ice *n.* solid carbon dioxide used as a refrigerant.

dryly *or* **drily** ('draɪlɪ) *adv.* in a dry manner.

dry measure *n.* a unit or system of units for measuring dry goods.

dry out *vb.* **1.** to make or become dry. **2.** to undergo or cause to undergo treatment for alcoholism or drug addiction.

dry rot *n.* **1.** crumbling and drying of timber, caused by certain fungi. **2.** a fungus causing this decay.

dry run *n. Informal.* a rehearsal.

dry-stone *adj.* (of a wall) made without mortar.

dry up *vb.* **1.** to become unproductive; fail. **2.** to dry (dishes, cutlery, etc.) with a tea towel after they have been washed. **3.** *Informal.* to stop speaking.

DSc Doctor of Science.

DSC *Mil.* Distinguished Service Cross.

DSM *Mil.* Distinguished Service Medal.

DSO *Brit. mil.* Distinguished Service Order.

DSW (in New Zealand) Department of Social Welfare.

DT's *Informal.* delirium tremens.

dual ('djuːəl) *adj.* **1.** relating to or denoting two. **2.** twofold; double. [Latin *duo* two] —**duality** (djuː'ælɪtɪ) *n.*

dual carriageway *n. Brit.* a road on which traffic travelling in opposite directions is separated by a central strip of turf or concrete.

dub[1] (dʌb) *vb.* **dubbing, dubbed.** **1.** to give (a person or place) a name or nickname. **2.** to make (a person) a knight by tapping him on the shoulder with a sword. [Old English *dubbian*]

dub[2] (dʌb) *vb.* **dubbing, dubbed.** **1.** to provide (a film) with a new soundtrack, esp. in a different language. **2.** to provide (a film or tape) with a soundtrack. ~*n.* **3.** *Music.* a style of record production associated with reggae, involving exaggeration of instrumental parts, the use of echo, etc. [shortened from *double*]

dubbin ('dʌbɪn) *n. Brit.* a greasy preparation applied to leather to soften it and make it waterproof. [*dub* to dress leather]

dubious ('djuːbɪəs) *adj.* **1.** marked by or causing doubt. **2.** uncertain; doubtful. **3.** of doubtful quality; untrustworthy. [Latin *dubius* wavering] —**dubiety** (djuː'baɪɪtɪ) *n.* —**'dubiously** *adv.*

ducal ('djuːk'l) *adj.* of a duke.

ducat ('dʌkət) *n.* a former European gold or silver coin. [Old Italian *ducato*]

duchess ('dʌtʃɪs) *n.* **1.** the wife or widow of a duke. **2.** a woman who holds the rank of duke in her own right. [Old French *duchesse*]

duchy ('dʌtʃɪ) *n., pl.* **duchies.** the territory of a duke or duchess. [Old French *duché*]

duck[1] (dʌk) *n., pl.* **ducks** *or* **duck.** **1.** a water bird with short legs, webbed feet, and a broad blunt bill. **2.** the flesh of this bird, used as food. **3.** the female of such a bird. **4.** Also: **ducks.** *Brit. informal.* dear: used as a term of address. **5.** *Cricket.* a score of nothing. **6.** **like water off a duck's back.** without effect. [Old English *dūce*]

duck[2] (dʌk) *vb.* **1.** to move (the head or body) quickly downwards, to escape observation or evade a blow. **2.** to plunge suddenly under water. **3.** *Informal.* to dodge or escape (a duty, etc.). [Middle English]

duck-billed platypus *n.* an amphibious mammal of E Australia with dense fur, a broad bill and tail, and webbed feet.

duckboard ('dʌk,bɔːd) *n.* a board laid so as to form a path over muddy ground.

duckling ('dʌklɪŋ) *n.* a young duck.

ducks and drakes *n.* (*functioning as sing.*) **1.** a game in which a flat stone is bounced across the surface of water. **2.** **play ducks and drakes with.** *Informal.* to use recklessly; squander.

ducky *or* **duckie** ('dʌkɪ) *n., pl.* **duckies.** *Brit. informal.* dear: a term of endearment.

duct (dʌkt) *n.* **1.** a tube, pipe, or canal by means of which a fluid or gas is conveyed. **2.** a bodily passage conveying secretions or excretions. [Latin *dūcere* to lead]

ductile ('dʌktaɪl) *adj.* **1.** (of a metal) able to be hammered into sheets or drawn out into wires. **2.** easily led or influenced. [Latin *ductilis*] —**ductility** (dʌk'tɪlɪtɪ) *n.*

ductless gland ('dʌktlɪs) *n. Anat.* same as **endocrine gland.**

dud (dʌd) *Informal.* ~*n.* **1.** a person or thing that proves ineffectual. **2.** (*pl.*) Old-fashioned. clothes. ~*adj.* **3.** bad or useless. [origin unknown]

dude (djuːd) *n. Informal.* **1.** *Western U.S. & Canad.* a city dweller, esp. one holidaying on a ranch. **2.** *U.S. & Canad.* a dandy. **3.** *U.S. & Canad.* a fellow; chap. [origin unknown]

dudgeon ('dʌdʒən) *n.* **in high dudgeon.** angry or resentful. [origin unknown]

due (djuː) *adj.* **1.** expected or scheduled to be present or arrive. **2.** immediately payable. **3.** owed as a debt. **4.** fitting; proper.

5. due to. attributable to or caused by. ~*n.* **6.** something that is owed, required, or due. **7. give a person his due.** to allow a person what is deserved or acknowledge his good points. ~*adv.* **8.** directly or exactly: *due north.* [Latin *debēre* to owe]

duel ('dju:əl) *n.* **1.** a formal prearranged combat with deadly weapons between two people, to settle a quarrel. ~*vb.* **duelling, duelled** or *U.S.* **dueling, dueled.** **2.** to fight in a duel. [Latin *duellum,* poetical var. of *bellum* war] —'**duellist** *n.*

duenna (dju:'ɛnə) *n.* (esp. in Spain) an elderly woman acting as chaperon to girls. [Spanish *dueña*]

dues (dju:z) *pl. n.* charges for membership of a club or organization.

duet (dju:'ɛt) *n.* **1.** a musical composition for two performers. **2.** a pair of performers. [Latin *duo* two] —**du'ettist** *n.*

duff[1] (dʌf) *n.* a pudding boiled in a cloth bag. [N English var. of *dough*]

duff[2] (dʌf) *vb.* **1.** (foll. by *up*) *Brit. slang.* to beat (a person) severely. **2.** *Golf, informal.* to bungle (a shot). ~*adj.* **3.** *Brit. informal.* bad or useless: *a duff engine.* [prob. from *duffer*]

duffel or **duffle** ('dʌf'l) *n.* **1.** same as **duffel coat.** **2.** a heavy woollen cloth. [after *Duffel,* Belgian town]

duffel bag *n.* a cylindrical drawstring canvas bag.

duffel coat *n.* a wool coat, usually with a hood and fastened with toggles.

duffer ('dʌfə) *n. Informal.* a dull or incompetent person. [origin unknown]

dug[1] (dʌg) *vb.* past of **dig.**

dug[2] (dʌg) *n.* a teat or udder. [Scandinavian]

dugong ('du:gɒn) *n.* a whalelike mammal occurring in tropical waters. [Malay *duyong*]

dugout ('dʌg,aʊt) *n.* **1.** a canoe made by hollowing out a log. **2.** *Mil.* a covered excavation dug to provide shelter. **3.** (at a sports ground) the covered bench where managers and substitutes sit.

duiker or **duyker** ('daɪkə) *n., pl.* **-kers** or **-ker.** **1.** a small African antelope. **2.** *S. African.* a long-tailed cormorant. [Dutch *duiker* diver]

duke (dju:k) *n.* **1.** a nobleman of high rank. **2.** the prince or ruler of a small principality or duchy. [Latin *dux* leader] —'**dukedom** *n.*

dulcet ('dʌlsɪt) *adj.* (of a sound) soothing or pleasant. [Latin *dulcis* sweet]

dulcimer ('dʌlsɪmə) *n.* a tuned percussion instrument consisting of a set of strings stretched over a sounding board and struck with hammers. [Old French *doulcemer*]

dull (dʌl) *adj.* **1.** lacking in interest. **2.** slow to understand; stupid. **3.** (of a blade) lacking sharpness. **4.** (of an ache) not acute, intense, or piercing. **5.** (of weather) not bright or clear. **6.** lacking in spirit; listless. **7.** (of colour) lacking brilliance; sombre. **8.** not loud or clear; muffled. ~*vb.* **9.** to make or become dull. [Old English *dol*] —'**dullness** *n.* —'**dully** *adv.*

dullard ('dʌləd) *n.* a dull or stupid person.

dulse (dʌls) *n.* a seaweed with large red edible fronds. [Irish *duilesc* seaweed]

duly ('dju:lɪ) *adv.* **1.** in a proper manner. **2.** at the proper time.

dumb (dʌm) *adj.* **1.** lacking the power to speak. **2.** lacking the power of human speech: *dumb animals.* **3.** temporarily bereft of the power to speak: *struck dumb.* **4.** done or performed without speech. **5.** *Informal.* **a.** dim-witted. **b.** foolish. [Old English] —'**dumbly** *adv.*

dumbbell ('dʌm,bɛl) *n.* **1.** an exercising weight consisting of a short bar with a heavy ball or disc at either end. **2.** *Slang, chiefly U.S. & Canad.* a fool.

dumbfound or **dumfound** (dʌm'faʊnd) *vb.* to strike dumb with astonishment; amaze. [*dumb* + (*con*)*found*]

dumb show *n.* meaningful gestures.

dumbstruck ('dʌm,strʌk) *adj.* temporarily deprived of speech through shock or surprise.

dumbwaiter ('dʌm,weɪtə) *n.* **1.** *Brit.* **a.** a stand placed near a dining table to hold food. **b.** a revolving circular tray placed on a table to hold food. **2.** a lift for carrying food, rubbish, etc., between floors.

dumdum ('dʌm,dʌm) or **dumdum bullet** *n.* a soft-nosed bullet that expands on impact and inflicts extensive wounds. [after *Dum-Dum,* town near Calcutta where orig. made]

dummy ('dʌmɪ) *n., pl.* **-mies. 1.** a figure representing the human form, used for displaying clothes, as a target, etc. **2.** a copy of an object, often lacking some essential feature of the original. **3.** *Slang.* a stupid person. **4.** a person who appears to act for himself while acting on behalf of another. **5.** *Bridge.* **a.** the hand exposed on the table by the declarer's partner and played by the declarer. **b.** the declarer's partner. **6.** *Brit.* a rubber teat for babies to suck. **7.** (*modifier*) counterfeit; sham. [from *dumb*]

dummy run *n.* an experimental run; practice; rehearsal.

dump (dʌmp) *vb.* **1.** to drop or let fall heavily or in a mass. **2. a.** *Informal.* to dispose of (something or someone) without subtlety or proper care. **b.** to dispose of (nuclear waste). **3.** *Commerce.* to market (goods) in bulk and at low prices, esp. abroad, in order to maintain a high price in the home market. **4.** *Computers.* to record (the contents of the memory) on a storage device at a series of points during a computer run. ~*n.* **5.** a place where waste materials are dumped. **6.** *Informal.* a dirty, unattractive place. **7.** *Mil.* a place where weapons or supplies are stored. [prob. from Old Norse]

dumpling ('dʌmplɪŋ) *n.* **1.** a small ball of dough cooked and served with stew. **2.** a round pastry case filled with fruit: *apple dumpling.* **3.** *Informal.* a short plump person. [obs. *dump* lump]

dumps (dʌmps) *pl. n.* **down in the dumps.** *Informal.* in a state of melancholy or depression. [prob. from Midddle Dutch *domp haze*]

dumpy ('dʌmpɪ) *adj.* **dumpier, dumpiest.** short and plump. [perhaps related to *dumpling*]

dun¹ (dʌn) *vb.* **dunning, dunned. 1.** to press (a debtor) for payment. ~*n.* **2.** a demand for payment. [origin unknown]

dun² (dʌn) *adj.* **dunner, dunnest.** brownish-grey. [Old English *dunn*]

dunce (dʌns) *n.* a person who is stupid or slow to learn. [*Dunses,* term of ridicule applied to the followers of John *Duns Scotus,* scholastic theologian]

dunderhead ('dʌndə,hɛd) *n.* a slow-witted person. [prob. from Dutch *donder* thunder + *head*]

dune (djuːn) *n.* a mound or ridge of drifted sand. [Middle Dutch]

dung (dʌŋ) *n.* excrement of animals; manure. [Old English]

dungarees (,dʌŋgə'riːz) *pl. n.* trousers with a bib attached. [*Dungrī,* district of Bombay, where the fabric originated]

dungeon ('dʌndʒən) *n.* a prison cell, often underground. [Old French *donjon*]

dunghill ('dʌŋ,hɪl) *n.* a heap of dung.

dunk (dʌŋk) *vb.* **1.** to dip (a biscuit, etc.) in a drink or soup before eating it. **2.** to submerge (something) in liquid. [Old High German *dunkōn*]

dunlin ('dʌnlɪn) *n.* a small sandpiper with a brown back. [from DUN²]

dunnock ('dʌnək) *n.* same as **hedge sparrow.** [from DUN²]

duo ('djuːəʊ) *n., pl.* **duos. 1.** a pair of performers. **2.** *Informal.* a pair of closely connected individuals. [Latin: two]

duodecimal (,djuːəʊ'dɛsɪməl) *adj.* relating to twelve or twelfths. [Latin *duodecim* twelve]

duodenum (,djuːəʊ'diːnəm) *n., pl.* **-na** (-nə) *or* **-nums.** the first part of the small intestine, just below the stomach. [Medieval Latin *intestinum duodenum digitorum* intestine of twelve fingers' length] —**duo'denal** *adj.*

duologue *or U.S. (sometimes)* **duolog** ('djuːə,lɒg) *n.* a part or all of a play in which the speaking roles are limited to two actors. [Latin DUO + (MONO)LOGUE]

dupe (djuːp) *vb.* **1.** to deceive; cheat; fool. ~*n.* **2.** a person who is easily deceived. [French]

duple ('djuːp³l) *adj.* **1.** same as **double. 2.** *Music.* having two beats in a bar. [Latin *duplus* double]

duplex ('djuːplɛks) *n.* **1.** *U.S. & Canad.* **a.** an apartment on two floors. **b.** a semidetached house. ~*adj.* **2.** having two parts. [Latin: twofold]

duplicate *adj.* ('djuːplɪkɪt). **1.** copied exactly from an original. **2.** existing as a pair or in pairs. ~*n.* ('djuːplɪkɪt). **3.** an exact copy. **4.** something additional of the same kind. **5. in duplicate.** in two exact copies. ~*vb.* ('djuːplɪ,keɪt). **6.** to make a replica of. **7.** to do again (something that has already been done). **8.** to make double.

[Latin *duplicāre* to double] —,dupli'cation *n.* —'dupli,cator *n.*

duplicity (djuː'plɪsɪtɪ) *n.* deception; double-dealing. [Old French *duplicite*]

Dur. Durham.

durable ('djʊərəb³l) *adj.* long-lasting; enduring. [Latin *dūrāre* to last] —,dura'bility *n.*

durable goods *pl. n.* goods that require infrequent replacement. Also called: **durables.**

duration (djʊ'reɪʃən) *n.* the length of time that something lasts. [Latin *dūrāre* to last]

durbar ('dɜːbɑː, ,dɜː'bɑː) *n.* **a.** (formerly) the court of a native ruler or a governor in India. **b.** a reception at such a court. [Hindi *darbār*]

duress (djʊ'rɛs, djʊə-) *n.* compulsion by use of force or threat: *he agreed to be chairman under duress.* [Latin *dūrus* hard]

during ('djʊərɪŋ) *prep.* throughout or within the limit of (a period of time). [Latin *dūrāre* to last]

dusk (dʌsk) *n.* the time just before nightfall when it is almost dark. [Old English *dox*]

dusky ('dʌskɪ) *adj.* **duskier, duskiest. 1.** dark in colour. **2.** dim or shadowy. —'duskily *adv.* —'duskiness *n.*

dust (dʌst) *n.* **1.** dry fine powdery material, such as particles of dirt. **2.** the remains of a dead person. **3. kick up a dust.** *Informal.* to raise a disturbance. **4. shake the dust off one's feet.** to depart angrily. **5. throw dust in someone's eyes.** to confuse or mislead someone. ~*vb.* **6.** to remove dust from (furniture) by wiping. **7.** to sprinkle (something) with dust or some other powdery substance. [Old English]

dustbin ('dʌst,bɪn) *n.* a large, usually cylindrical container for household rubbish.

dust bowl *n.* a dry area in which the surface soil is exposed to wind erosion.

dustcart ('dʌst,kɑːt) *n.* a road vehicle for collecting refuse.

dust cover *n.* **1.** same as **dustsheet. 2.** same as **dust jacket.**

duster ('dʌstə) *n.* a cloth used for dusting.

dust jacket *or* **cover** *n.* a removable paper cover used to protect a book.

dustman ('dʌstmən) *n., pl.* **-men.** *Brit.* a man whose job is to collect household refuse.

dustpan ('dʌst,pæn) *n.* a short-handled hooded shovel into which dust is swept from floors.

dustsheet ('dʌst,ʃiːt) *n.* *Brit.* a large cloth used to protect furniture from dust.

dust-up *n.* *Informal.* a fight or argument.

dusty ('dʌstɪ) *adj.* **dustier, dustiest. 1.** covered with dust. **2.** (of a colour) tinged with grey.

Dutch (dʌtʃ) *n.* **1.** the language of the Netherlands. **b. the Dutch.** (*functioning as pl.*) the people of the Netherlands. ~*adj.* **3.** of the Netherlands, their inhabitants, or their language. ~*adv.* **4. go Dutch.** *Informal.* to go on an outing where each person pays his own expenses.

Dutch auction *n.* an auction in which the price is lowered by stages until a buyer is found.

Dutch barn *n. Brit.* a farm building consisting of a steel frame and a curved roof.

Dutch courage *n.* false courage gained from drinking alcohol.

Dutch elm disease *n.* a fungal disease of elm trees.

Dutchman ('dʌtʃmən) *n., pl.* **-men.** **1.** a person from the Netherlands. **2.** *S. African offensive.* an Afrikaner.

Dutch oven *n.* **1.** an iron or earthenware container with a cover, used for stews, etc. **2.** a metal box, open in front, for cooking in front of an open fire.

Dutch treat *n. Informal.* an outing where each person pays his own expenses.

Dutch uncle *n. Informal.* a person who criticizes or reproves frankly and severely.

duteous ('djuːtɪəs) *adj. Formal or archaic.* dutiful; obedient.

dutiable ('djuːtɪəb²l) *adj.* (of goods) requiring payment of duty.

dutiful ('djuːtɪful) *adj.* showing or resulting from a sense of duty. —**'dutifully** *adv.*

duty ('djuːtɪ) *n., pl.* **-ties.** **1.** a task that a person is bound to perform for moral or legal reasons. **2.** respect or obedience owed to parents, older people, etc. **3.** the force that binds one morally or legally to one's obligations. **4.** a government tax, esp. on imports. **5. on** (or **off**) **duty.** at (or not at) work. [Anglo-French *dueté*]

duty-bound *adj.* morally obliged.

duty-free *adj., adv.* with exemption from customs or excise duties.

duty-free shop *n.* a shop, esp. at an airport, that sells certain goods at duty-free prices.

duvet ('duːveɪ) *n.* same as **continental quilt.** [French]

duvet jacket *n.* a down-filled jacket.

dwaal (dwɑːl) *n. S. African.* a state of befuddlement; daze. [Afrikaans]

dwarf (dwɔːf) *n., pl.* **dwarfs** or **dwarves** (dwɔːvz). **1.** an abnormally undersized person. **2.** (*modifier*) denoting an animal or plant much below the average size for the species. **3.** (in folklore) a small ugly manlike creature, often possessing magical powers. ~*vb.* **4.** to cause (someone or something) to seem small by being much larger. [Old English *dweorg*]

dwell (dwel) *vb.* **dwelling, dwelt** or **dwelled.** *Formal, literary.* to live as a permanent resident. [Old English *dwellan* to seduce, get lost] —**'dweller** *n.*

dwelling ('dwelɪŋ) *n. Formal, literary.* a place of residence.

dwell on or **upon** *vb.* to think, speak, or write at length about (something).

dwindle ('dwɪnd²l) *vb.* to grow less in size, intensity, or number. [Old English *dwīnan*]

Dy *Chem.* dysprosium.

dye (daɪ) *n.* **1.** a staining or colouring substance. **2.** the colour produced by dyeing. ~*vb.* **dyeing, dyed. 3.** to colour or stain (fabric, hair, etc.) by the application of a dye. [Old English *dēag*] —**'dyer** *n.*

dyed-in-the-wool *adj.* uncompromising or unchanging in attitude or opinion.

dying ('daɪɪŋ) *vb.* **1.** the present participle of **die**¹. ~*adj.* **2.** relating to or occurring at the moment of death: *a dying wish.*

dyke¹ or esp. *U.S.* **dike** (daɪk) *n.* **1.** an embankment to prevent flooding. **2.** a ditch. **3.** *Scot.* a dry-stone wall. ~*vb.* **4.** to enclose or drain (land) with a dyke. [Old English *dic* ditch]

dyke² or **dike** (daɪk) *n. Slang.* a lesbian. [origin unknown]

dynamic (daɪ'næmɪk) *adj.* **1.** characterized by force of personality, ambition, and energy. **2.** of or concerned with energy or forces that produce motion. [Greek *dunamis* power] —**dy'namically** *adv.*

dynamics (daɪ'næmɪks) *n.* **1.** (functioning as *sing.*) the branch of mechanics concerned with the forces that change or produce the motions of bodies. **2.** (functioning as *pl.*) those forces that produce change in any field or system. **3.** (functioning as *pl.*) *Music.* the various degrees of loudness present in a performance.

dynamism ('daɪnə‚mɪzəm) *n.* the forcefulness of an energetic personality.

dynamite ('daɪnə‚maɪt) *n.* **1.** an explosive consisting of nitroglycerin mixed with an absorbent substance. **2.** *Informal.* a spectacular or potentially dangerous person or thing: *the new singer is dynamite.* ~*vb.* **3.** to mine or blow (something) up with dynamite. [Greek *dunamis* power]

dynamo ('daɪnə‚məʊ) *n., pl.* **-mos.** a device for converting mechanical energy into electrical energy. [short for *dynamoelectric machine*]

dynamoelectric (‚daɪnəməʊ'lektrɪk) *adj.* of the conversion of mechanical into electrical energy or vice versa.

dynamometer (‚daɪnə'mɒmɪtə) *n.* an instrument for measuring mechanical power.

dynast ('dɪnəst) *n.* a ruler, esp. a hereditary one. [Greek *dunasthai* to be powerful]

dynasty ('dɪnəstɪ) *n., pl.* **-ties.** **1.** a sequence of hereditary rulers. **2.** any sequence of powerful leaders of the same family. [Greek *dunastēs* dynast] —**dynastic** (dɪ'næstɪk) *adj.*

dyne (daɪn) *n.* the cgs unit of force; the force that imparts an acceleration of 1 centimetre per second per second to a mass of 1 gram. [Greek *dunamis* power]

dysentery ('dɪs²ntrɪ) *n.* infection of the intestine causing severe diarrhoea with mucus and blood. [Greek *dusentera* bad bowels]

dysfunction (dɪs'fʌŋkʃən) *n. Med.* any disturbance or abnormality in the function of an organ or part.

dyslexia (dɪs'leksɪə) *n.* a developmental disorder causing impaired ability to read. [Greek *dus-* not + *legein* to speak] —**dys'lexic** *adj., n.*

dysmenorrhoea or esp. *U.S.* **dysmenorrhea** (‚dɪsmenə'rɪə) *n.* painful or difficult menstruation. [Greek *dus-* bad + *rhoiā* a flowing]

dyspepsia (dɪsˈpɛpsɪə) *n.* indigestion. [Greek *dus-* bad + *pepsis* digestion] —**dysˈpeptic** *adj., n.*

dysprosium (dɪsˈprəʊsɪəm) *n.* a metallic element of the lanthanide series. Symbol:

Dy [Greek *dusprositos* difficult to get near]

dystrophy (ˈdɪstrəfɪ) *n.* See **muscular dystrophy.** [Greek *dus-* not + *trophē* food]

dz. dozen.

E

e *or* **E** (iː) *n., pl.* **e's, E's,** *or* **Es.** the fifth letter of the English alphabet.

e *Maths.* a number used as the base of natural logarithms. Approximate value: 2.718 282...

E **1.** *Music.* the third note of the scale of C major. **2.** East. **3.** English. **4.** *Physics.* **a.** energy. **b.** electromotive force.

E- *prefix.* used with numbers indicating an EC standard, as of pack size or recognized food additive.

each (iːtʃ) *det.* **1.** every (one) of two or more considered individually: *each day; each gave according to his ability.* ~*adv.* **2.** for, to, or from each one; apiece: *four apples each.* **3. each other.** one another. **4. each way.** (of a bet) made on a horse or other contestant either winning or coming second or third. [Old English *ǽlc*]

eager ('iːɡə) *adj.* showing or feeling great desire; keen. [Latin *acer* sharp, keen] —'**eagerly** *adv.* —'**eagerness** *n.*

eager beaver *n. Informal.* an extremely hard-working person.

eagle ('iːɡ'l) *n.* **1.** a bird of prey having large broad wings and strong soaring flight. **2.** *Golf.* a score of two strokes under par for a hole. [Latin *aquila*]

eagle-eyed *adj.* having keen or piercing eyesight.

eaglet ('iːɡlɪt) *n.* a young eagle.

ear¹ (ɪə) *n.* **1.** the organ of hearing. **2.** the external, visible part of the ear. **3.** sensitivity to musical or other sounds: *a good ear for music.* **4.** attention; consideration: *lend me your ears.* **5. all ears.** listening carefully. **6. fall on deaf ears.** to be ignored. **7. in one ear and out the other.** heard but unheeded. **8. keep** *or* **have one's ear to the ground.** to be well informed about current trends. **9. out on one's ear.** *Informal.* dismissed unceremoniously. **10. play by ear. a.** *Informal.* to act according to the demands of a situation. **b.** to play without written music. **11. turn a deaf ear.** to be deliberately unresponsive. **12. up to one's ears.** *Informal.* deeply involved. [Old English *ēare*]

ear² (ɪə) *n.* the part of a cereal plant, such as wheat or barley, that contains the seeds. [Old English *ēar*]

earache ('ɪərˌeɪk) *n.* pain in the ear.

eardrum ('ɪəˌdrʌm) *n.* the thin membrane separating the external ear from the middle ear.

earl (ɜːl) *n.* (in Britain) a nobleman ranking below a marquess and above a viscount. [Old English *eorl*] —'**earldom** *n.*

Earl Marshal *n.* (in Britain) an officer who presides over the College of Heralds and organizes ceremonies.

early ('ɜːlɪ) *adj., adv.* **-lier, -liest. 1.** before the expected or usual time. **2.** in the first part of a period. **3.** in a period far back in time. **4.** in the near future. [Old English *ǽrlīce*]

Early English *n.* a style of architecture used in England in the 12th and 13th centuries, characterized by lancet arches and tracery.

earmark ('ɪəˌmɑːk) *vb.* **1.** to set (something) aside for a specific purpose. **2.** to make an identification mark on the ear of (a domestic animal). ~*n.* **3.** such a mark of identification.

earn (ɜːn) *vb.* **1.** to gain or be paid (money) in return for work. **2.** to acquire or deserve through behaviour or action: *this action earned the condemnation of the world's press.* **3.** (of securities or investments) to gain (interest or profit). [Old English *earnian*] —'**earner** *n.*

earnest¹ ('ɜːnɪst) *adj.* **1.** serious in mind or intention. ~*n.* **2. in earnest.** with serious or sincere intentions. [Old English *eornost*] —'**earnestly** *adv.* —'**earnestness** *n.*

earnest² ('ɜːnɪst) *n.* a part payment given in advance as a guarantee of the remainder, esp. to confirm a contract. [Old French *erres* pledges]

earnings ('ɜːnɪŋz) *pl. n.* **1.** money earned. **2.** profits or investment income.

earphone ('ɪəˌfəʊn) *n.* a device or one of a pair of devices for converting electric currents into sound, worn over the ear.

ear-piercing *adj.* loud or shrill.

earplug ('ɪəˌplʌg) *n.* a piece of soft material placed in the ear to keep out noise or water.

earring ('ɪəˌrɪŋ) *n.* an ornament for the lobe of the ear.

earshot ('ɪəˌʃɒt) *n.* the range within which sound may be heard: *out of earshot.*

ear-splitting *adj.* loud or shrill.

earth (ɜːθ) *n.* **1.** (sometimes *cap.*) the planet that we live on, the third planet from the sun, the only one on which life is known to exist. **2.** the inhabitants of this planet. **3.** land; ground. **4.** soil. **5.** the hole in which a fox lives. **6.** a connection between an electric circuit and the earth. **7. come down to earth.** to return to reality. **8. on earth.** (used for emphasis): *what on earth are you doing?* **9. run to earth.** to hunt down: *they ran him to earth on the Costa del Sol.* ~*vb.* **10.** to connect (a circuit) to earth. ~*See also* **earth up.** [Old English *eorthe*]

earthbound ('ɜːθˌbaʊnd) *adj.* **1.** confined to the earth. **2.** heading towards the earth.

earth closet *n.* a type of lavatory in which earth is used to cover excreta.

earthen ('ɜːθən) *adj.* made of earth or baked clay: *earthen pots.*

earthenware ('ɜːθənˌwɛə) *n.* dishes, mugs, etc., made of baked clay.

earthly ('ɜːθlɪ) *adj.* **-lier, -liest. 1.** of the earth as opposed to heaven; materialistic;

worldly. **2.** *Informal.* conceivable or possible: *they haven't got an earthly chance of winning.*

earthquake ('ɜːθ,kweɪk) *n.* a series of vibrations at the earth's surface caused by movement of the earth's crust.

earth science *n.* any science, such as geology, concerned with the structure, age, etc., of the earth.

earth up *vb.* to cover (part of a plant) with soil to protect it from frost, light, etc.

earthward ('ɜːθwəd) *adj.* directed towards the earth.

earthwards ('ɜːθwədz) *adv.* towards the earth.

earthwork ('ɜːθ,wɜːk) *n.* a fortification made of earth.

earthworm ('ɜːθ,wɜːm) *n.* any of numerous worms which burrow in the soil.

earthy ('ɜːθɪ) *adj.* **earthier, earthiest. 1.** of or like earth. **2.** unrefined, coarse, or crude. —'**earthiness** *n.*

ear trumpet *n.* a trumpet-shaped instrument held to the ear: an old form of hearing aid.

earwig ('ɪə,wɪg) *n.* an insect with pincers at the tip of its abdomen. [Old English *ēare* ear + *wicga* beetle]

ease (iːz) *n.* **1.** lack of difficulty. **2.** freedom from discomfort or worry. **3.** rest, leisure, or relaxation. **4.** freedom from poverty. **5. at ease. a.** *Mil.* (of a soldier) standing in a relaxed position with the feet apart. **b.** in a relaxed attitude or frame of mind. ~*vb.* **6.** to make or become less difficult or severe. **7.** to relieve (a person) of worry or care. **8.** to move into or out of a place or situation with careful manipulation. **9.** (often foll. by *off* or *up*) to lessen or cause to lessen in severity, pressure, tension, or strain. [Old French *aise*]

easel ('iːz'l) *n.* a frame for supporting an artist's canvas, a display, or a blackboard. [Dutch *ezel* ass]

easement ('iːzmənt) *n. Property law.* the right of making limited use of a neighbour's land, as for a right of way.

easily ('iːzɪlɪ) *adv.* **1.** with ease; without difficulty. **2.** almost certainly: *easily the best.*

east (iːst) *n.* **1.** the direction along a line of latitude towards the sunrise, at 90° to north. **2. the east.** any area lying in or towards the east. ~*adj.* **3.** situated in, moving towards, or facing the east. **4.** (esp. of the wind) from the east. ~*adv.* **5.** in, to, or towards the east. [Old English]

East (iːst) *n.* **the. 1.** the continent of Asia; the Orient. **2.** the countries under Communist rule in the E hemisphere. ~*adj.* **3.** of or denoting the eastern part of a country or region.

eastbound ('iːst,baʊnd) *adj.* going towards the east.

Easter ('iːstə) *n.* **1.** *Christianity.* a festival, in the spring, commemorating the Resurrection of Christ. **2.** the time of the year when this is celebrated. [Old English *ēastre*]

Easter egg *n.* a chocolate egg given at Easter.

easterly ('iːstəlɪ) *adj.* **1.** of or in the east. ~*adv., adj.* **2.** towards the east. **3.** from the east: *an easterly wind.*

eastern ('iːstən) *adj.* **1.** situated in or towards the east. **2.** facing or moving towards the east.

eastern hemisphere *n.* the half of the globe that contains Europe, Asia, Africa, and Australia.

eastward ('iːstwəd) *adj., adv. also* **eastwards. 1.** towards the east. ~*n.* **2.** the eastward part, direction, etc.

easy ('iːzɪ) *adj.* **easier, easiest. 1.** not difficult. **2.** free from pain, care, or anxiety. **3.** tolerant and undemanding; easygoing. **4.** readily influenced; pliant: *an easy victim.* **5.** moderate: *an easy pace.* **6.** *Informal.* ready to fall in with any suggestion made: *you decide what to do, I'm easy.* ~*adv.* **7.** *Informal.* in an easy or relaxed manner. **8. easy does it.** *Informal.* go slowly and carefully. **9. go easy.** to exercise moderation: *go easy on the salt, it's bad for your heart.* **10. take it easy. a.** to avoid stress or undue hurry. **b.** to remain calm. [Old French *aisié*] —'**easiness** *n.*

easy chair *n.* a comfortable upholstered armchair.

easy-going ('iːzɪ'gəʊɪŋ) *adj.* relaxed in manner or attitude; very tolerant.

eat (iːt) *vb.* **eating, ate, eaten. 1.** to take (food) into the mouth and swallow it. **2.** (often foll. by *away, into,* or *up*) to destroy or use up partly or wholly: *the damp had eaten away the woodwork.* **3.** to take (a meal): *we eat at six.* **4.** *Informal.* to cause to worry; make anxious: *what's eating you?* ~See also **eat out, eat up.** [Old English *etan*] —'**eater** *n.*

eatable ('iːtəb'l) *adj.* fit or suitable for eating.

eating ('iːtɪŋ) *n.* **1.** food in relation to quality or taste: *this fruit makes excellent eating.* ~*adj.* **2.** suitable for eating uncooked: *eating apples.*

eat out *vb.* to eat at a restaurant.

eat up *vb.* **1.** to eat or consume entirely: *eat up your breakfast.* **2.** *Informal.* to affect grossly: *eaten up by jealousy.*

eau de Cologne (,əʊ də kə'ləʊn) *n.* See **cologne.** [French: water of Cologne]

eau de vie (,əʊ də 'viː) *n.* brandy or other spirits. [French: water of life]

eaves (iːvz) *pl. n.* the edge of a sloping roof that overhangs the walls. [Old English *efes*]

eavesdrop ('iːvz,drɒp) *vb.* **-dropping, -dropped.** to listen secretly to private conversation. [Old English *yfesdrype* water dripping from the eaves] —'**eaves,dropper** *n.*

ebb (ɛb) *vb.* **1.** (of tide water) to flow back or recede. **2.** to fall away or decline. ~*n.* **3.** the flowing back of the tide from high to low water. **4. at a low ebb.** in a state of weakness. [Old English *ebba*]

ebony ('ɛbənɪ) *n., pl.* **-onies. 1.** the hard dark wood of various tropical and subtropical trees. **2.** a black colour. [Greek *ebenos* ebony]

ebullient (ɪ'bʌljənt) *adj.* overflowing with enthusiasm or excitement. [Latin *ēbullīre* to bubble forth, be boisterous] —e'**bullience** *n.*

EC European Community.

eccentric (ɪk'sɛntrɪk) *adj.* **1.** unconventional or odd. **2.** situated away from the centre or the axis. **3.** not having a common centre: *eccentric circles.* ~*n.* **4.** a person who deviates from normal behaviour. [Greek *ek-* away from + *kentron* centre] —ec'**centrically** *adv.*

eccentricity (ˌɛksɛn'trɪsɪtɪ) *n., pl.* **-ties.** **1.** unconventional behaviour. **2.** deviation from a circular path or orbit.

ecclesiastic (ɪˌkliːzɪ'æstɪk) *n.* **1.** a clergyman. ~*adj.* **2.** of or associated with the Christian Church or clergy. [Greek *ekklēsia* assembly]

ecclesiastical (ɪˌkliːzɪ'æstɪkəl) *adj.* of or relating to the Christian Church.

ECG electrocardiogram.

echelon ('ɛʃəˌlɒn) *n.* **1.** a level of power, influence, or responsibility: *the upper echelons.* **2.** *Mil.* a formation in which units follow one another but are offset to allow each a line of fire ahead. [French *échelon* rung of a ladder]

echidna (ɪ'kɪdnə) *n.* a spine-covered egg-laying mammal of Australia and New Guinea, with a long snout and claws. Also called: **spiny anteater.** [Greek *ekhidna*]

echinoderm (ɪ'kaɪnəʊˌdɜːm) *n.* any of various marine animals with a five-part symmetrical body, such as starfish, sea urchins, and sea cucumbers. [Greek *ekhinos* sea urchin + *derma* skin]

echo ('ɛkəʊ) *n., pl.* **-oes. 1. a.** the reflection of sound by a solid object. **b.** the sound so reflected. **2.** a repetition or imitation of another's opinions. **3.** something that evokes memories. **4.** the signal reflected by a radar target. ~*vb.* **-oing, -oed. 5.** to resound or cause to resound with an echo. **6.** (of sounds) to repeat by echoes; reverberate. **7.** (of persons) to repeat (words or opinions) in imitation, agreement, or flattery. [Greek *ēkhō*] —'**echoing** *adj.*

echo chamber *n.* a room with walls that reflect sound, used for acoustic measurements and as a recording studio when echo effects are required.

echoic (ɛ'kəʊɪk) *adj.* **1.** of or like an echo. **2.** sounding like something else; imitative.

echolocation (ˌɛkəʊləʊ'keɪʃən) *n.* determination of an object's position by measuring the time taken for an echo to return from it.

echo sounder *n.* a navigation device that determines depth by measuring the time taken for a pulse of sound to reach the sea bed and for the echo to return. —**echo sounding** *n.*

éclair (eɪ'klɛə, ɪ'klɛə) *n.* a finger-shaped cake of choux pastry, filled with cream and covered with chocolate. [French: lightning (prob. because it does not last long)]

éclat (eɪ'klɑː) *n.* **1.** brilliant success or

effect. **2.** showy display. **3.** acclaim. [French]

eclectic (ɪ'klɛktɪk) *adj.* **1.** selecting from various styles, ideas, or methods. **2.** composed of elements so selected. ~*n.* **3.** a person who favours an eclectic approach. [Greek *eklegein* to select] —e'**clectically** *adv.* —**eclecticism** (ɪ'klɛktɪˌsɪzəm) *n.*

eclipse (ɪ'klɪps) *n.* **1.** the obscuring of one celestial body by another. A solar eclipse occurs when the moon passes between the sun and the earth; a **lunar eclipse** when the earth passes between the sun and the moon. **2.** a loss of importance, power, or fame: *the management has suffered an eclipse.* ~*vb.* **3.** to cause an eclipse of. **4.** to overshadow or surpass. [Greek *ekleipsis* a forsaking]

ecliptic (ɪ'klɪptɪk) *n. Astron.* the great circle on the celestial sphere representing the apparent annual path of the sun relative to the stars.

eclogue ('ɛklɒg) *n.* a short poem on a rural theme. [Greek *eklogē* selection]

eco- *combining form.* denoting ecology or ecological: *ecocide; ecosphere.*

ecology (ɪ'kɒlədʒɪ) *n.* the study of the relationships between living organisms and their environment. [Greek *oikos* house] —**ecological** (ˌiːkə'lɒdʒɪkəl) *adj.* —e'**cologist** *n.*

econ. economic(s).

economic (ˌiːkə'nɒmɪk, ˌɛkə-) *adj.* **1.** of or relating to an economy, economics, or finance. **2.** *Brit.* capable of being produced, operated, or sold for profit; profitable. **3.** *Informal.* inexpensive; cheap.

economical (ˌiːkə'nɒmɪkəl, ˌɛkə-) *adj.* **1.** using the minimum required; not wasteful. **2.** frugal; thrifty. —**eco'nomically** *adv.*

economics (ˌiːkə'nɒmɪks, ˌɛkə-) *n.* **1.** (*functioning as sing.*) the social science concerned with the production and consumption of goods and services and the commercial activities of a society. **2.** (*functioning as pl.*) financial aspects.

economist (ɪ'kɒnəmɪst) *n.* a person who specializes in economics.

economize *or* **-ise** (ɪ'kɒnəˌmaɪz) *vb.* to limit or reduce (expense or waste). —e,conomi'**zation** *or* -i'**sation** *n.*

economy (ɪ'kɒnəmɪ) *n., pl.* **-mies. 1.** careful management of resources; thrift. **2.** a means or instance of this. **3.** the complex of activities concerned with the production, distribution, and consumption of goods and services. **4.** the management of the resources, finances, income, and expenditure of a community, business enterprise, etc. **5.** a class of air travel, cheaper than first class. **6.** (*modifier*) purporting to offer a larger quantity for a lower price: *an economy pack.* [Greek *oikos* house + *nemein* to manage]

ecosystem ('iːkəʊˌsɪstəm, 'ɛkəʊ-) *n. Ecology.* a system involving the interactions between a community and its nonliving environment.

ecru ('ɛkruː) *adj.* greyish-yellow. [French]

ecstasy ('ɛkstəsɪ) *n., pl.* **-sies. 1.** a state of exalted delight or joy; rapture. **2.** *Slang.*

3,4-methylenedioxymethamphetamine: a powerful drug which acts as a stimulant and which can produce hallucinations. [Greek *ekstasis* displacement, trance] —**ec-static** (ek'stætɪk) *adj.*

ECT electroconvulsive therapy.

ectoplasm ('ɛktəʊˌplæzəm) *n. Spiritualism.* the substance that supposedly exudes from the body of a medium during a trance. [Greek *ektos* outside + *plasm*] —ˌecto-'plasmic *adj.*

ECU ('eɪkjuː) *n.* European Currency Unit: a unit of currency based on the composite value of several different currencies in the Common Market.

ecumenical (ˌiːkjʊ'mɛnɪkᵊl, ˌɛk-) *adj.* 1. of or relating to the Christian Church throughout the world. 2. tending to promote unity among Churches. [Greek *oikoumenikos* of the inhabited world] —ˌecu'menically *adv.*

eczema ('ɛksɪmə) *n. Pathol.* a skin inflammation with blisters that scale, crust, or weep, often accompanied by intense itching. [Greek *ek-* out + *zein* to boil]

ed. 1. edited. 2. (*pl.* **eds.**) edition. 3. (*pl.* **eds.**) editor. 4. educated. 5. education.

Edam ('iːdæm) *n.* a round yellow cheese with a red waxy covering. [after *Edam*, in Holland]

eddy ('ɛdɪ) *n., pl.* **-dies.** 1. a movement in air, water, or other fluid in which the current doubles back on itself. ~*vb.* **-dying, -died.** 2. to move or cause to move against the main current. [prob. Old Norse]

edelweiss ('eɪd'lˌvaɪs) *n.* a small alpine flowering plant having white woolly leaves surrounding the flowers. [German: noble white]

Eden ('iːd'n) *n.* 1. Also called: **Garden of Eden.** *Bible.* the garden in which Adam and Eve were placed at the Creation. 2. a place of great delight or contentment. [Hebrew *'ēdhen* place of pleasure]

edentate (iː'dɛnteɪt) *n.* 1. any of an order of mammals which have few or no teeth, such as anteaters, sloths, and armadillos. ~*adj.* 2. of or relating to this order. [Latin *ēdentātus* lacking teeth]

edge (ɛdʒ) *n.* 1. a border, brim, or margin. 2. a line along which two faces or surfaces of a solid meet. 3. the sharp cutting side of a blade. 4. keenness, sharpness, or urgency. 5. **have the edge on.** to have a slight advantage over. 6. **on edge.** nervously irritable or excited. 7. **set (someone's) teeth on edge.** to make (someone) acutely irritated. ~*vb.* 8. to provide an edge or border for. 9. to shape or trim the edge or border of (something). 10. (foll. by *in, through,* etc.) to push (one's) way gradually. 11. to sharpen (a knife, etc.). [Old English *ecg*]

edgeways ('ɛdʒˌweɪz) *or esp. U.S. & Canad.* **edgewise** ('ɛdʒˌwaɪz) *adv.* 1. with the edge forwards or uppermost. 2. on, by, with, or towards the edge. 3. **get a word in edgeways.** to interrupt a conversation in which someone else is talking continuously.

edging ('ɛdʒɪŋ) *n.* anything placed along an edge to finish it, esp. as an ornament.

edgy ('ɛdʒɪ) *adj.* **edgier, edgiest.** nervous, irritable, tense, or anxious. —'**edginess** *n.*

edible ('ɛdɪb'l) *adj.* fit to be eaten; eatable. [Latin *edere* to eat] —ˌedi'bility *n.*

edict ('iːdɪkt) *n.* a decree or order issued by any authority. [Latin *ēdīcere* to declare]

edifice ('ɛdɪfɪs) *n.* 1. a building, esp. a large or imposing one. 2. an elaborate organization. [Latin *aedificāre* to build]

edify ('ɛdɪˌfaɪ) *vb.* **-fying, -fied.** to improve the morality or understanding of (a person) by instruction. [Latin *aedificāre* to build] —ˌedifi'cation *n.* —'ediˌfying *adj.*

edit ('ɛdɪt) *vb.* 1. to prepare (text) for publication by checking and improving its accuracy or clarity. 2. to be in charge of (a publication, esp. a periodical). 3. to prepare (a film, tape, etc.) by rearranging or selecting material. 4. (often foll. by *out*) to remove (parts of a text, film, etc.).

edition (ɪ'dɪʃən) *n.* 1. one of a number of printings of a book or other publication, issued at separate times with alterations or amendments. 2. *Printing.* the entire number of copies of a book or other publication printed at one time.

editor ('ɛdɪtə) *n.* 1. a person who edits. 2. a person in overall charge of a newspaper or periodical. 3. a person in charge of one section of a newspaper or periodical. 4. a person in overall control of a television or radio programme. [Latin *ē-* out + *dāre* to give] —'editorˌship *n.*

editorial (ˌɛdɪ'tɔːrɪəl) *adj.* 1. of editing or editors. 2. of or expressed in an editorial. ~*n.* 3. an article in a newspaper expressing the opinion of the editor or the publishers. —ˌedi'torially *adv.*

EDP electronic data processing.

EDT Eastern Daylight Time.

educate ('ɛdjʊˌkeɪt) *vb.* 1. to impart knowledge by formal instruction to (a pupil); teach. 2. to provide schooling for. 3. to improve or develop (a person, taste, skills, etc.). [Latin *ēducāre* to rear, educate] —'educable *adj.* —ˌeduca'bility *n.* —'educative *adj.*

educated ('ɛdjʊˌkeɪtɪd) *adj.* 1. having an education, esp. a good one. 2. displaying culture, taste, and knowledge. 3. based on experience: *an educated guess.*

education (ˌɛdjʊ'keɪʃən) *n.* 1. the process of acquiring knowledge. 2. the knowledge acquired. 3. the process of imparting knowledge, esp. at a school, college, or university. 4. the theory of teaching and learning. —ˌedu'cational *adj.* —ˌedu'cationalist *or* ˌedu'cationist *n.*

Edwardian (ɛd'wɔːdɪən) *adj.* of or characteristic of the reign of King Edward VII (1901–10).

EEC European Economic Community (the Common Market).

EEG electroencephalogram.

eel (iːl) *n.* a fish with a long snakelike

body, a smooth slimy skin, and reduced fins. [Old English *ǣl*]

e'en (iːn) *adv., n. Poetic or archaic.* short for **even** or evening.

e'er (ɛə) *adv. Poetic or archaic.* short for **ever**.

eerie ('ɪərɪ) *adj.* **eerier, eeriest.** uncannily frightening or disturbing; weird. [prob. from Old French *earg* cowardly] —**'eerily** *adv.* —**'eeriness** *n.*

efface (ɪ'feɪs) *vb.* **1.** to obliterate or make dim: *to efface a memory.* **2.** to make (oneself) inconspicuous. **3.** to rub out; erase. [French *effacer* to obliterate or face] —**ef'facement** *n.*

effect (ɪ'fɛkt) *n.* **1.** a change or state of affairs produced by a cause; result. **2.** power to influence or produce a result. **3.** the condition of being operative: *problems arose in putting the proposals into effect.* **4.** the overall impression. **5.** basic meaning or purpose: *comments to the effect that it was disgraceful; words to that effect.* **6.** an impression, usually contrived: *he's only doing it for effect.* **7. in effect.** for all practical purposes: *in effect, there is no alternative.* **8. take effect.** to begin to produce results. ~*vb.* **9.** to cause to occur; accomplish. [Latin *efficere* to accomplish]

effective (ɪ'fɛktɪv) *adj.* **1.** producing a desired result. **2.** operative. **3.** impressive: *an effective speech.* **4.** (of a military force) equipped and prepared for action. —**ef'fectively** *adv.* —**ef'fectiveness** *n.*

effects (ɪ'fɛkts) *pl. n.* **1.** personal belongings. **2.** lighting, sounds, etc., to accompany a stage, film, or broadcast production.

effectual (ɪ'fɛktjʊəl) *adj.* **1.** producing an intended result; effective. **2.** (of documents, etc.) having legal force. —**ef'fectually** *adv.*

effeminate (ɪ'fɛmɪnɪt) *adj.* (of a man) displaying characteristics typical of a woman. [Latin *fēmina* woman] —**ef'feminacy** *n.*

efferent ('ɛfərənt) *adj. Physiol.* carrying outwards, esp. from the brain or spinal cord. [Latin *efferre* to bear off]

effervescent (ˌɛfə'vɛsənt) *adj.* **1.** (of a liquid) giving off bubbles of gas. **2.** (of a person or a person's behaviour) lively and enthusiastic. [Latin *effervescere*] —**effer'vescence** *n.*

effete (ɪ'fiːt) *adj.* **1.** weak or decadent. **2.** (of animals or plants) no longer capable of reproduction. [Latin *effētus* exhausted by bearing] —**ef'feteness** *n.*

efficacious (ˌɛfɪ'keɪʃəs) *adj.* producing an intended result; effective. [Latin *efficere* to achieve] —**efficacy** ('ɛfɪkəsɪ) *n.*

efficient (ɪ'fɪʃənt) *adj.* functioning or producing effectively and with the least waste of effort; competent. [Latin *efficiēns* effecting] —**ef'ficiency** *n.* —**ef'ficiently** *adv.*

effigy ('ɛfɪdʒɪ) *n., pl.* **-gies.** **1.** a portrait, esp. as a monument. **2.** a crude representation of someone, as a focus for contempt or ridicule: *the prime minister was burned in effigy.* [Latin *effingere* to portray]

efflorescence (ˌɛflɔː'rɛsᵊns) *n.* **1.** a bursting forth or flowering. **2.** *Chem., geol.* a change that occurs as a result of loss of water or crystallization. **3.** a powdery substance formed in this way. [Latin *efflōrēscere* to blossom] —**efflo'rescent** *adj.*

effluence ('ɛfluəns) *or* **efflux** ('ɛflʌks) *n.* **1.** a flowing out. **2.** something that flows out.

effluent ('ɛfluənt) *n.* **1.** liquid discharged as waste, as from an industrial plant or sewage works. **2.** a stream that flows out of another body of water. ~*adj.* **3.** flowing out. [Latin *effluere* to flow out]

effluvium (ɛ'fluːvɪəm) *n., pl.* **-via** (-vɪə). an unpleasant smell, as a gaseous waste or decaying matter. [Latin *a flowing out*]

effort ('ɛfət) *n.* **1.** physical or mental exertion. **2.** a determined attempt. **3.** achievement: *a great literary effort.* [Latin *fortis* strong] —**'effortless** *adj.*

effrontery (ɪ'frʌntərɪ) *n., pl.* **-eries.** shameless or insolent boldness. [Late Latin *effrons* putting forth one's forehead]

effusion (ɪ'fjuːʒən) *n.* **1.** an unrestrained outpouring in speech or words. **2.** a being poured out. [Latin *effundere* to shed]

effusive (ɪ'fjuːsɪv) *adj.* extravagantly demonstrative of emotion; gushing. —**ef'fusively** *adv.* —**ef'fusiveness** *n.*

EFL English as a Foreign Language.

eft (ɛft) *n. Dialect or archaic.* a newt. [Old English *efeta*]

EFTA ('ɛftə) European Free Trade Association.

EFTPOS ('ɛftpɒs) electronic funds transfer at point of sale.

e.g. for example. [Latin *exempli gratia*]

egad (ɪ'gæd) *interj. Archaic.* a mild oath. [prob. var. of *Ah God!*]

egalitarian (ɪˌgælɪ'tɛərɪən) *adj.* **1.** denoting or upholding the equality of mankind. ~*n.* **2.** an adherent of egalitarian principles. [French *égal* equal] —**e,gali'tarianism** *n.*

egg (ɛg) *n.* **1.** the oval or round reproductive body laid by the females of birds, reptiles, and other creatures, containing a developing embryo. **2.** a hen's egg used as food. **3.** any female reproductive cell; ovum. **4. put all one's eggs in one basket.** to stake everything on a single venture. **5. teach one's grandmother to suck eggs.** *Informal.* to presume to teach someone something that he knows already. **6. with egg on one's face.** *Informal.* made to look ridiculous. [Old Norse]

egg cup *n.* a small cup for holding a boiled egg.

egghead ('ɛgˌhɛd) *n. Informal.* an intellectual person.

eggnog (ˌɛg'nɒg) *n.* a drink made of raw eggs, milk, sugar, spice, and brandy or rum. Also called: **egg flip.** [*egg* + *nog* strong ale]

egg on *vb.* to encourage (someone) to do something foolish or daring. [Old English *eggian*]

eggplant ('ɛg,plɑːnt) n. U.S. & Canad. same as **aubergine**.

eggshell ('ɛg,ʃɛl) n. **1.** the hard porous outer layer of a bird's egg. **2.** (modifier) (of paint) having a very slight sheen.

eglantine ('ɛglən,taɪn) n. same as **sweetbrier**. [Latin acus needle]

ego ('iːgəʊ) n., pl. **egos. 1.** the self of an individual person; the conscious subject. **2.** egotism; conceit. [Latin: I]

egocentric (,iːgəʊ'sɛntrɪk) adj. selfcentred. —,**egocen'tricity** n.

egoism ('iːgəʊ,ɪzəm, 'ɛg-) or **egotism** ('iːgə,tɪzəm, 'ɛg-) n. **1.** excessive concern for one's own interests. **2.** an excessively high opinion of oneself. —'**egoist** or '**egotist** n. —,**ego'istic** or ,**ego'tistic** adj.

ego trip n. Informal. something undertaken to boost a person's own image of himself.

egregious (ɪ'griːdʒəs) adj. outstandingly bad; flagrant. [Latin ēgregius outstanding (lit.: standing out from the herd)]

egress ('iːgrɛs) n. **1.** the act of going out. **2.** a way out; exit. **3.** the right to go out. [Latin ēgredī to come out]

egret ('iːgrɪt) n. a wading bird like a heron, with long white feathery plumes. [Old French aigrette]

Egyptian (ɪ'dʒɪpʃən) adj. **1.** of or relating to Egypt. **2.** of or characteristic of the ancient Egyptians, their language, or their culture. ~n. **3.** a person from Egypt. **4.** the language of the ancient Egyptians.

Egyptology (,iːdʒɪp'tɒlədʒɪ) n. the study of the culture of ancient Egypt. —,**Egyp'tologist** n.

eh (eɪ) interj. an exclamation used to express questioning surprise or to seek repetition or confirmation.

eider or **eider duck** ('aɪdə) n. a large sea duck of the N hemisphere. [Old Norse æthr]

eiderdown ('aɪdə,daʊn) n. **1.** the breast down of the female eider duck, used, esp. formerly, for stuffing quilts or other kinds of bed covers. **2.** a thick, warm cover for a bed, stuffed with down.

eight (eɪt) n. **1.** the cardinal number that is the sum of one and seven. **2.** a numeral, 8, VIII, representing this number. **3.** something consisting of eight units. **4.** Rowing. **a.** a racing shell propelled by eight oarsmen. **b.** the crew. ~det. **5.** amounting to eight. [Old English eahta] —**eighth** (eɪtθ) adj., n.

eighteen ('eɪ'tiːn) n. **1.** the cardinal number that is the sum of ten and eight. **2.** a numeral, 18, XVIII, representing this number. **3.** something consisting of 18 units. ~det. **4.** amounting to eighteen. —'**eigh'teenth** adj., n.

eightfold ('eɪt,fəʊld) adj. **1.** having eight times as many. **2.** composed of eight parts. ~adv. **3.** by eight times as much.

eightsome reel ('eɪtsəm) n. a Scottish dance for eight people.

eighty ('eɪtɪ) n., pl. **eighties. 1.** the cardinal number that is the product of ten and eight. **2.** a numeral, 80, LXXX, representing this number. **3.** (pl.) the numbers 80-89, esp. the 80th to the 89th year of a person's life or of a century. **4.** something consisting of 80 units. —det. **5.** amounting to eighty. —'**eightieth** adj., n.

einsteinium (aɪn'staɪnɪəm) n. a radioactive metallic element artificially produced from plutonium. Symbol: Es [after Albert Einstein, physicist]

eisteddfod (aɪ'stɛdfəd) n. a Welsh festival with competitions in music, poetry, drama, and art. [Welsh: session]

either ('aɪðə, 'iːðə) det. **1.** one or the other (of two): either is acceptable. **2.** both one and the other: at either end of the table. ~conj. **3.** used preceding two or more possibilities joined by "or". ~adv. **4.** (with a negative) used to indicate that the clause immediately preceding is a partial reiteration of a previous clause: John isn't a liar, but he isn't exactly honest either. [Old English ǣgther]

ejaculate (ɪ'dʒækjʊ,leɪt) vb. **1.** to discharge (semen) in orgasm. **2.** Literary. to utter abruptly; blurt out. [Latin ējaculārī to hurl out] —e,jacu'lation n. —e'jaculatory adj.

eject (ɪ'dʒɛkt) vb. **1.** to force out; expel or emit. **2.** to compel (a person) to leave; evict. **3.** to leave an aircraft rapidly in mid-flight, using an ejection seat. [Latin ejicere] —e'jection n. —e'jective adj. —e'jector n.

ejection seat or **ejector seat** n. a seat, esp. in a military aircraft, that ejects the occupant in an emergency.

eke out (iːk) vb. **1.** to make (a supply) last for a long time by frugal use. **2.** to support (existence) with difficulty. **3.** to add to (something insufficient), esp. with difficulty. [obs. eke to enlarge]

elaborate adj. (ɪ'læbərɪt). **1.** with a lot of fine details; complex. ~vb. (ɪ'læbə,reɪt). **2.** (often foll. by on or upon) to add detail to an account; expand upon. **3.** to work out in detail; develop. [Latin ēlabōrāre to take pains] —e'laborately adv. —e,labo'ration n.

élan (eɪ'lɑːn) n. style and vigour. [French]

eland ('iːlənd) n. a large spiral-horned antelope of southern Africa. [Dutch eland elk]

elapse (ɪ'læps) vb. (of time) to pass by. [Latin ēlābī to slip away]

elastic (ɪ'læstɪk) adj. **1.** capable of returning to its original shape after stretching, compression, or other deformation. **2.** adaptable or tolerant: they take an elastic view of what counts as right. **3.** quick to recover from fatigue or dejection. **4.** springy: an elastic walk. **5.** made of elastic. ~n. **6.** tape, cord, or fabric containing flexible rubber. [Greek elastikos propellent] —e'lastically adv. —e'lasticated adj. —elas'ticity n.

elastic band n. a rubber band.

elate (ɪ'leɪt) vb. to fill with high spirits, pride, or optimism. [Latin elatus carried away] —e'lated adj. —e'latedly adv. —e'lation n.

elbow ('ɛlbəʊ) n. **1.** the joint between the upper arm and the forearm. **2.** the part of a garment that covers the elbow. ~*vb.* **3.** to make (one's way) by shoving or jostling. **4.** to knock or shove (someone) with one's elbow. [Old English *elnboga*]

elbow grease *n. Facetious.* vigorous physical labour, esp. hard rubbing.

elbow room *n.* sufficient scope to move or to function.

elder¹ ('ɛldə) *adj.* **1.** born earlier; senior. ~*n.* **2.** an older person; one's senior. **3.** a senior member of a tribe, who has authority. **4.** (in certain Protestant Churches) a lay officer. [Old English *eldra*]

elder² ('ɛldə) *n.* a shrub or small tree with clusters of small white flowers and dark purple berry-like fruits. [Old English *ellern*]

elderberry ('ɛldə,bɛrɪ) *n., pl.* **-ries.** **1.** the fruit of the elder. **2.** same as **elder**².

elderly ('ɛldəlɪ) *adj.* (of people) quite old; past middle age. —**'elderliness** *n.*

elder statesman *n.* a respected influential older person, esp. a politician.

eldest ('ɛldɪst) *adj.* oldest, esp. the oldest child. [Old English *eldesta*]

El Dorado (ɛl dɔ'rɑːdəʊ) *n.* **1.** a fabled city in South America, supposedly rich in treasure. **2.** Also: **eldorado.** any place of great riches or fabulous opportunity. [Spanish: the golden (place)]

eldritch ('ɛldrɪtʃ) *adj. Poetic, Scot.* unearthly; weird. [origin unknown]

elect (ɪ'lɛkt) *vb.* **1.** to choose (someone) by voting. **2.** to choose or decide: *he elected not to go.* ~*adj.* **3.** voted into office but not yet installed: *the President elect.* **4.** chosen; elite. [Latin *ēligere* to select] —**e'lectable** *adj.*

elect. *or* **elec.** **1.** electric(al). **2.** electricity.

election (ɪ'lɛkʃən) *n.* **1.** the selection by vote of a person or persons for a position, esp. a political office. **2.** a public vote. **3.** the act or an instance of choosing.

electioneer (ɪ,lɛkʃə'nɪə) *vb.* to be active in a political election or campaign. —**e,lection'eering** *n.*

elective (ɪ'lɛktɪv) *adj.* **1.** of or based on selection by vote. **2.** having the power to elect. **3.** optional.

elector (ɪ'lɛktə) *n.* **1.** someone who is eligible to vote in an election. **2.** (*cap.*) (in the Holy Roman Empire) any of the German princes who were entitled to elect a new emperor. —**e'lectoral** *adj.*

electorate (ɪ'lɛktərɪt) *n.* **1.** the body of all qualified voters. **2.** the rank or territory of an elector of the Holy Roman Empire.

electric (ɪ'lɛktrɪk) *adj.* **1.** produced by, producing, transmitting, or powered by electricity. **2.** very tense or exciting: *the atmosphere was electric.* ~*n.* **3.** (*pl.*) electric appliances. [Greek *ēlektron* amber (because friction causes amber to become electrically charged)]

electrical (ɪ'lɛktrɪk°l) *adj.* of or concerned with electricity. —**e'lectrically** *adv.*

electrical engineering *n.* the branch of engineering concerned with practical applications of electricity and electronics. —**electrical engineer** *n.*

electric chair *n.* (in the U.S.) an electrified chair for executing criminals.

electric eel *n.* an eel-like freshwater fish of N South America, able to stun or kill its prey with a powerful electric shock.

electric eye *n.* same as **photocell.**

electric field *n. Physics.* a region of space surrounding a charged particle within which another charged particle experiences a force.

electric guitar *n.* an electrically amplified guitar.

electrician (ɪlɛk'trɪʃən, ,iːlɛk-) *n.* a person whose occupation is to install and repair electrical equipment.

electricity (ɪlɛk'trɪsɪtɪ, ,iːlɛk-) *n.* **1.** a form of energy associated with stationary or moving electrons, ions, or other charged particles. **2.** the science of electricity. **3.** an electric current. **4.** emotional tension or excitement.

electrify (ɪ'lɛktrɪ,faɪ) *vb.* **-fying, -fied.** **1.** to adapt or equip (a system, device, etc.) for operation by electrical power. **2.** to charge with or subject to electricity. **3.** to startle or excite intensely. —**e,lectrifi'cation** *n.*

electro (ɪ'lɛktrəʊ) *n., pl.* **-tros.** short for **electroplate.**

electro- *or sometimes before a vowel* **electr-** *combining form.* electric or electrically: *electrodynamic.* [Greek *ēlektron* amber: see ELECTRIC]

electrocardiograph (ɪ,lɛktrəʊ'kɑːdɪəʊ,grɑːf) *n.* an instrument for making tracings (**electrocardiograms**) recording the electrical activity of the heart.

electrocute (ɪ'lɛktrə,kjuːt) *vb.* to kill or execute (someone) by an electric shock. [*electro-* + (*exe*)*cute*] —**e,lectro'cution** *n.*

electrode (ɪ'lɛktrəʊd) *n.* a conductor through which an electric current enters or leaves an electrolyte, an electric arc, or an electronic valve or tube.

electrodynamics (ɪ,lɛktrəʊdaɪ'næmɪks) *n.* (*functioning as sing.*) the branch of physics concerned with the interactions between electrical and mechanical forces.

electroencephalograph (ɪ,lɛktrəʊɛn-'sɛfələ,grɑːf) *n.* an instrument for making tracings (**electroencephalograms**) recording the electrical activity of the brain.

electrolysis (ɪlɛk'trɒlɪsɪs) *n.* **1.** the conduction of electricity by an electrolyte, esp. the use of this process to induce chemical changes. **2.** the destruction of living tissue, such as hair roots, by an electric current.

electrolyte (ɪ'lɛktrəʊ,laɪt) *n.* a solution or molten substance that conducts electricity. —**electrolytic** (ɪ,lɛktrəʊ'lɪtɪk) *adj.*

electromagnet (ɪ,lɛktrəʊ'mægnɪt) *n.* a magnet consisting of a coil of wire wound round an iron core through which a current is passed.

electromagnetic (ɪ,lɛktrəʊmæg'nɛtɪk) *adj.* **1.** of or operated by an electromagnet. **2.** of or relating to electromagnetism. —**e,lectromag'netically** *adv.*

electromagnetism (ɪ,lɛktrəʊ'mægnɪ,tɪzɔm) *n.* magnetism produced by electric current.

electromotive (ɪˌlɛktrəʊˈməʊtɪv) *adj.* of or producing an electric current.

electromotive force *n. Physics.* **1.** a source of energy that can cause current to flow in an electrical circuit. **2.** the rate at which energy is drawn from such a source when unit current flows through the circuit, measured in volts.

electron (ɪˈlɛktrɒn) *n. Physics.* an elementary particle in all atoms that has a negative electrical charge.

electronegative (ɪˌlɛktrəʊˈnɛɡətɪv) *adj. Physics.* **1.** having a negative charge. **2.** tending to gain or attract electrons.

electronic (ɪlɛkˈtrɒnɪk, ˌiːlɛk-) *adj.* **1.** of or concerned with electronics or electrons. **2.** making use of electronic systems: *electronic shopping.* —**elecˈtronically** *adv.*

electronics (ɪlɛkˈtrɒnɪks, ˌiːlɛk-) *n. (functioning as sing.)* the science and technology concerned with the development, behaviour, and applications of devices and circuits that are operated by the actions of electrons.

electron microscope *n.* a powerful microscope that uses electrons, rather than light, to produce a magnified image.

electron tube *n.* an electrical device in which a flow of electrons between electrodes takes place.

electronvolt (ɪˌlɛktrɒnˈvəʊlt) *n. Physics.* a unit of energy equal to the work done on an electron accelerated through a potential difference of 1 volt.

electroplate (ɪˈlɛktrəʊˌpleɪt) *vb.* **1.** to plate (an object) by electrolysis. ~*n.* **2.** electroplated articles collectively.

electropositive (ɪˌlɛktrəʊˈpɒzɪtɪv) *adj. Physics.* **1.** having a positive electric charge. **2.** tending to release electrons.

electrostatics (ɪˌlɛktrəʊˈstætɪks) *n. (functioning as sing.)* the branch of physics concerned with static electricity. —**eˌlectroˈstatic** *adj.*

elegant (ˈɛlɪɡənt) *adj.* **1.** tasteful in dress, style, or design. **2.** dignified and graceful. **3.** cleverly simple. [Latin *ēlegāns* tasteful] —**ˈelegance** *n.*

elegiac (ˌɛlɪˈdʒaɪək) *adj.* **1.** of or like an elegy. **2.** lamenting; mournful. —ˌ**eleˈgiacally** *adv.*

elegy (ˈɛlɪdʒɪ) *n., pl.* **-gies.** a mournful poem or song, esp. a lament for the dead. [Greek *elegos* lament]

element (ˈɛlɪmənt) *n.* **1.** one of the fundamental components making up a whole. **2.** *Chem.* any of the 105 known substances that cannot be separated into simple substances by chemical means. **3.** a distinguishable section of a social group. **4.** the most favourable environment for an animal or plant. **5.** the situation in which a person is happiest: *she was in her element at the keyboard.* **6.** a metal part in an electrical device, such as a heater, that changes the electric current into heat. **7.** one of the four substances thought in ancient and medieval cosmology to constitute the universe (earth, air, water, or fire). **8.** (*pl.*) atmospheric conditions, esp. wind, rain, and cold. **9.** (*pl.*) the basic principles of something. **10.** *Christianity.* the bread and wine in the Eucharist. [Latin *elementum*]

elemental (ˌɛlɪˈmɛntˀl) *adj.* **1.** fundamental; basic. **2.** of or like primitive powerful natural forces or passions. **3.** denoting or relating to wind, rain, or other atmospheric conditions.

elementary (ˌɛlɪˈmɛntrɪ) *adj.* denoting or relating to the first principles of a subject; introductory or fundamental.

elementary particle *n. Physics.* any of several entities, such as electrons, neutrons, or protons, that are less complex than atoms.

elementary school *n.* **1.** *Brit.* same as **primary school.** **2.** *U.S. & Canad.* a state school for the first six to eight years of a child's education.

elephant (ˈɛlɪfənt) *n., pl.* **-phants** or **-phant.** the largest living four-legged animal which has a long flexible nose (**trunk**) and two tusks of ivory. The **African elephant** has large flapping ears and a less humped back than the **Indian elephant** of S and SE Asia. [Greek *elephas*]

elephantiasis (ˌɛlɪfənˈtaɪəsɪs) *n. Pathol.* a skin disease, caused by parasitic worms, in which the affected parts of the body become extremely enlarged.

elephantine (ˌɛlɪˈfæntaɪn) *adj.* resembling an elephant, esp. in being huge, clumsy, or ponderous.

elevate (ˈɛlɪˌveɪt) *vb.* **1.** to lift (something) to a higher place. **2.** to raise (someone or something) in rank or status. **3.** to put (someone) on a higher cultural plane; uplift. [Latin *ēlevāre*]

elevation (ˌɛlɪˈveɪʃən) *n.* **1.** the act of elevating or the state of being elevated. **2.** the height of something, esp. above sea level. **3.** a raised area; height. **4.** a drawing to scale of the external face of a building.

elevator (ˈɛlɪˌveɪtə) *n.* **1.** a person or thing that elevates. **2.** a mechanical hoist. **3.** *U.S. & Canad.* a lift. **4.** *Chiefly U.S. & Canad.* a building for storing grain.

eleven (ɪˈlɛvˀn) *n.* **1.** the cardinal number that is the sum of ten and one. **2.** a numeral, 11, XI, representing this number. **3.** something consisting of 11 units. **4.** (*functioning as sing. or pl.*) a team of 11 players in football, cricket, etc. [Old English *endleofan*] —**eˈleventh** *adj.*

eleven-plus *n.* (in Britain, esp. formerly) an examination taken by children aged 11 or 12 that determines the type of secondary education a child will be given.

elevenses (ɪˈlɛvˀnzɪz) *pl. n.* (*sometimes functioning as sing.*) *Brit. informal.* a mid-morning snack.

elf (ɛlf) *n., pl.* **elves.** (in folklore) a small mischievous fairy. [Old English *ælf*] —**ˈelfish** *or* **ˈelvish** *adj.*

elfin (ˈɛlfɪn) *adj.* small and delicate: *elfin features.*

elicit (ɪˈlɪsɪt) *vb.* to give rise to; evoke: *elicit a sharp retort.* [Latin *ēlicere*]

elide (ɪˈlaɪd) vb. to omit a syllable or vowel from a spoken word. [Latin *ēlīdere* to knock]

eligible (ˈɛlɪdʒəbˀl) adj. **1.** fit, worthy, or qualified, as for office. **2.** *Old-fashioned.* desirable as a spouse. [Latin *ēligere* to elect] —ˌeligiˈbility n.

eliminate (ɪˈlɪmɪˌneɪt) vb. **1.** to get rid of. **2.** to leave out of consideration; ignore. **3.** to remove (a competitor or team) from a contest. **4.** *Slang.* to murder (someone) in cold blood. —eˌlimiˈnation n.

elision (ɪˈlɪʒən) n. omission of a syllable or vowel from a spoken word. [Latin *ēlīdere* to elide]

elite or **élite** (ɪˈliːt, eɪ-) n. (sometimes functioning as pl.) the most powerful, rich, or gifted members of a group or community. [French]

elitism (ɪˈliːtɪzəm, eɪ-) n. **1.** the belief that society should be governed by a small group of people who are superior to everyone else. **2.** pride in being one of an elite. —eˈlitist n., adj.

elixir (ɪˈlɪksə) n. **1.** an imaginary substance that is supposed to be capable of prolonging life and changing base metals into gold. **2.** a liquid medicine with syrup. [Arabic]

Elizabethan (ɪˌlɪzəˈbiːθən) adj. **1.** of or relating to the reign of Queen Elizabeth I of England (1558-1603). **2.** of the style of architecture used in England during the reign of Queen Elizabeth I.

elk (ɛlk) n., pl. **elks** or **elk.** a large deer of N Europe and Asia with broad antlers. [Old English *eolh*]

ellipse (ɪˈlɪps) n. a closed curve shaped like a flattened circle, formed by an inclined plane through a cone.

ellipsis (ɪˈlɪpsɪs) n., pl. **-ses** (-siːz). **1.** the omission of a word or words from a sentence. **2.** *Printing.* three dots (...) indicating an omission. [Greek *en* in + *leipein* to leave]

ellipsoid (ɪˈlɪpsɔɪd) n. *Geom.* a surface whose plane sections are ellipses or circles.

elliptical (ɪˈlɪptɪkˀl) or **elliptic** adj. **1.** oval-shaped. **2.** (of speech or writing) obscure or ambiguous.

elm (ɛlm) n. **1.** a tree with serrated leaves and winged fruits. **2.** its hard heavy wood. [Old English]

elocution (ˌɛləˈkjuːʃən) n. the art of speaking clearly in public. [Latin *e-* out + *loquī* to speak] —eloˈcutionary adj. —eloˈcutionist n.

elongate (ˈiːlɒŋɡeɪt) vb. to make or become longer; stretch. [Latin *ē-* away + *longē* (adv.) far] —ˈelongated adj. —ˌelonˈgation n.

elope (ɪˈləʊp) vb. (of two people) to run away secretly to get married. [Anglo-French *aloper*]

eloquence (ˈɛləkwəns) n. **1.** the ability to speak or write in a skilful and convincing way. **2.** the art of speaking or writing in such a way.

eloquent (ˈɛləkwənt) adj. **1.** (of speech or writing) fluent and persuasive. **2.** visibly or vividly expressive: *an eloquent yawn.* [Latin *e-* out + *loquī* to speak] —ˈeloquently adv.

else (ɛls) det. **1.** in addition; more: *there is nobody else here.* **2.** other; different: *where else could he be?* ~adv. **3. or else. a.** if not, then: *go away or else I won't finish my work.* **b.** or something terrible will result: used as a threat: *sit down, or else!* [Old English *elles*]

elsewhere (ˌɛlsˈwɛə) adv. in or to another place.

ELT English Language Teaching.

elucidate (ɪˈluːsɪˌdeɪt) vb. to make (something obscure or difficult) clear; clarify. [Late Latin *ēlūcidāre* to enlighten] —eˌluciˈdation n. —eˈluciˌdative adj.

elude (ɪˈluːd) vb. **1.** to escape from (someone or something) by cleverness or quickness. **2.** to escape discovery or understanding by; baffle: *the solution eluded her.* [Latin *ēlūdere* to deceive] —**elusion** (ɪˈluːʒən) n.

elusive (ɪˈluːsɪv) adj. **1.** difficult to catch. **2.** difficult to remember. ~Also: **eˈlusory.** —eˈlusiveness n.

elver (ˈɛlvə) n. a young eel. [var. of *eelfare* eel-journey]

elves (ɛlvz) n. the plural of **elf.**

elvish (ˈɛlvɪʃ) adj. same as **elfish:** see **elf.**

Elysium (ɪˈlɪzɪəm) n. **1.** *Greek myth.* the dwelling place of the blessed after death. **2.** a state or place of perfect bliss. [Greek *Ēlusion pedion* Elysian (that is, blessed) fields]

em (ɛm) n. *Printing.* the square of a body of any size of type, used as a unit of measurement. [from the name of the letter *M*]

emaciated (ɪˈmeɪsɪˌeɪtɪd) adj. abnormally thin. [Latin *macer* thin] —eˌmaciˈation n.

emanate (ˈɛməˌneɪt) vb. to issue or proceed from or as from a source: *these ideas emanate from Henry Kissinger; a dim light emanated from the room.* [Latin *ēmānāre* to flow out] —ˌemaˈnation n.

emancipate (ɪˈmænsɪˌpeɪt) vb. to free (a person or section of society) from social, political, or legal restrictions. [Latin *ēmancipāre* to give independence (to a son)] —eˈmanciˌpated adj. —eˌманciˈpation n.

emasculate (ɪˈmæskjʊˌleɪt) vb. **1.** to remove the testicles of; castrate. **2.** to deprive (someone or something) of power or strength. [Latin *ēmasculāre*] —eˈmascuˌlated adj. —eˌmascuˈlation n.

embalm (ɪmˈbɑːm) vb. to treat (a dead body) with preservatives. [Old French *embaumer*] —emˈbalmment n.

embankment (ɪmˈbæŋkmənt) n. a manmade ridge of earth or stone that carries a road or railway or confines a waterway.

embargo (ɛmˈbɑːɡəʊ) n., pl. **-goes. 1.** a government order prohibiting the departure or arrival of merchant ships in the ports of a country. **2.** any legal stoppage of commerce. **3.** a restraint or prohibition. ~vb. **-going, -goed. 4.** to lay an embargo upon. [Spanish *embargar*]

embark (ɛmˈbɑːk) vb. **1.** to board (a ship or aircraft). **2.** (usually foll. by *on* or *upon*) to begin a new project or venture. [Old French *em-* into + *barca* boat] —ˌem-ˈbarˈkation n.

embarrass (ɪmˈbærəs) vb. **1.** to cause (someone) to feel ashamed or self-conscious. **2.** to involve (someone) in financial difficulties. **3.** *Archaic.* to hamper. [Italian *imbarrare* to confine within bars] —emˈbarrassed adj. —emˈbarrassing adj. —emˈbarrassingly adv. —emˈbarrassment n.

embassy (ˈɛmbəsɪ) n., pl. **-sies**. **1.** the residence or place of business of an ambassador. **2.** an ambassador and his entourage collectively. **3.** any important or official mission. [Old French *ambaisada*]

embattled (ɪmˈbætˈld) adj. **1.** prepared for battle. **2.** beset with difficulties.

embed (ɪmˈbɛd) vb. **-bedding, -bedded. 1.** (usually foll. by *in*) to fix or become fixed firmly in a surrounding solid mass. **2.** to fix or retain (a thought or idea) in the mind.

embellish (ɪmˈbɛlɪʃ) vb. **1.** to beautify; adorn. **2.** to make (a story) more interesting by adding often fictitious detail. [Old French *embelir*] —emˈbellishment n.

ember (ˈɛmbə) n. a glowing or smouldering piece of coal or wood, as in a dying fire. [Old English *æmyrge*]

embezzle (ɪmˈbɛzˈl) vb. to steal (money or property that has been entrusted to one). [Anglo-French *embeseiller* to destroy] —emˈbezzlement n. —emˈbezzler n.

embitter (ɪmˈbɪtə) vb. to make (a person) bitter. —emˈbittered adj. —emˈbitterment n.

emblazon (ɪmˈbleɪzˈn) vb. **1.** to portray heraldic arms on. **2.** to make bright or splendid, as with colours or flowers. **3.** to proclaim or publicize: *her feat was emblazoned on the front page.* —emˈblazoned adj. —emˈblazonment n.

emblem (ˈɛmbləm) n. a visible object or representation that symbolizes a quality, type, or group. [Greek *emblēma* insertion] —ˌemblemˈatic adj.

embody (ɪmˈbɒdɪ) vb. **-bodying, -bodied. 1.** to be an example of or express (an idea, principle, or other abstract concept). **2.** (often foll. by *in*) to collect in a comprehensive whole. —emˈbodiment n.

embolden (ɪmˈbəʊldˈn) vb. to make bold.

embolism (ˈɛmbəˌlɪzəm) n. the blocking of a blood vessel by an embolus.

embolus (ˈɛmbələs) n., pl. -li (-ˌlaɪ). a blood clot, air bubble or other stoppage that blocks a small blood vessel. [Greek *embolos* stopper]

emboss (ɪmˈbɒs) vb. to mould or carve (a decoration) on (a surface) so that it stands out from the surface. [Old French *embocer*] —emˈbossed adj. —emˈbossment n.

embrace (ɪmˈbreɪs) vb. **1.** (of a person) to clasp (another person) in the arms, or (of two people) to clasp each other, as in affection or greeting; hug. **2.** to accept eagerly: *to embrace new ideas.* **3.** to com-

prise: *the proposal embraces many previous suggestions.* ~n. **4.** the act of embracing. [Latin *im-* in + *bracchia* arms]

embrasure (ɪmˈbreɪʒə) n. **1.** a door or window having splayed sides on the interior. **2.** an opening in a battlement or fortified wall, for shooting through. [French] —emˈbrasured adj.

embrocation (ˌɛmbrəʊˈkeɪʃən) n. a liniment or lotion. [Greek *brokhē* a moistening]

embroider (ɪmˈbrɔɪdə) vb. **1.** to do decorative needlework on something, such as a tablecloth or piece of clothing. **2.** to add fictitious detail to (a story). [Old French *embroder*] —emˈbroiderer n.

embroidery (ɪmˈbrɔɪdərɪ) n., pl. -deries. **1.** the art or a piece of decorative needlework done usually on cloth or canvas. **2.** embellishment in reporting a story.

embroil (ɪmˈbrɔɪl) vb. **1.** to involve oneself or another person in problems or difficulties. **2.** to throw (affairs) into confusion; complicate. [French *embrouiller*] —emˈbroilment n.

embryo (ˈɛmbrɪˌəʊ) n., pl. -bryos. **1.** an unborn animal or human being in the early stages of development, in humans up to approximately the end of the second month of pregnancy. **2.** something in an early stage of development: *an embryo of an idea.* [Greek *embruon*]

embryology (ˌɛmbrɪˈɒlədʒɪ) n. the scientific study of embryos.

embryonic (ˌɛmbrɪˈɒnɪk) adj. **1.** of or relating to an embryo. **2.** in an early stage.

emend (ɪˈmɛnd) vb. to make corrections or improvements in (a text). [Latin *ē-* out + *mendum* a mistake] —ˌemenˈdation n.

emerald (ˈɛmərəld, ˈɛmrəld) n. **1.** a green transparent variety of beryl; highly valued as a gem. **2.** its clear green colour. [Greek *smaragdos*]

Emerald Isle n. the. *Poetic.* Ireland.

emerge (ɪˈmɜːdʒ) vb. (often foll. by *from*) **1.** to come into view, as from concealment or obscurity. **2.** to come out of or live through (a difficult experience, etc.). **3.** to become apparent: *it emerged that she was in London all the time.* [Latin *ēmergere* to rise up from] —eˈmergence n. —eˈmergent adj.

emergency (ɪˈmɜːdʒənsɪ) n., pl. -cies. **1.** an unforeseen or sudden occurrence, esp. of danger demanding immediate action. **2.** *N.Z.* a reserve player. **3. state of emergency.** a condition, declared by a government, in which martial law applies.

emeritus (ɪˈmɛrɪtəs) adj. retired, but retaining one's title on an honorary basis: *a professor emeritus.* [Latin *merēre* to deserve]

emery (ˈɛmərɪ) n. a hard greyish-black mineral used for smoothing and polishing. [Greek *smuris* powder for rubbing]

emery board n. a strip of cardboard coated with crushed emery, for filing one's nails.

emetic (ɪˈmɛtɪk) adj. **1.** causing vomiting. ~n. **2.** a substance that causes vomiting. [Greek *emetikos*]

EMF electromotive force.

emigrate ('ɛmɪˌgreɪt) *vb.* to leave one's native country to settle in another. [Latin *ēmigrāre*] —'**emigrant** *n., adj.* —ˌemi'**gration** *n.*

émigré ('ɛmɪˌgreɪ) *n.* someone who has left his native country for political reasons. [French]

eminence ('ɛmɪnəns) *n.* **1.** a position of superiority or fame. **2.** a high or raised piece of ground.

Eminence ('ɛmɪnəns) *n., pl.* -**nences.** (preceded by *Your* or *His*) a title used to address or refer to a cardinal.

éminence grise (ˌeɪmɪnɒns 'griːz) *n., pl.* **éminences grises** (ˌeɪmɪnɒns 'griːz). a person who wields power and influence unofficially. [French, lit.: grey eminence, orig. applied to Père Joseph, secretary of Cardinal Richelieu]

eminent ('ɛmɪnənt) *adj.* distinguished, powerful, and famous. [Latin *ēminēre* to stand out]

emir (ɛ'mɪə) *n.* (in the Islamic world) an independent ruler or chieftain. [Arabic *'amir* commander] —e'**mirate** *n.*

emissary ('ɛmɪsərɪ) *n., pl.* -**saries.** an agent sent on a mission by a government or head of state. [Latin *ēmissārius*]

emission (ɪ'mɪʃən) *n.* **1.** the act of emitting something. **2.** energy, in the form of heat, light, radio waves, etc., emitted from a source. **3.** a discharge; something emitted. —e'**missive** *adj.*

emit (ɪ'mɪt) *vb.* **emitting, emitted. 1.** to give or send forth (heat, light, or a smell). **2.** to utter (a sound). [Latin *ēmittere* to send out]

Emmenthal *or* **Emmental** ('ɛmən,tɑːl) *n.* a hard Swiss cheese with holes in it. [after *Emmenthal*, valley in Switzerland]

emollient (ɪ'mɒljənt) *adj.* **1.** softening or soothing to the skin. ~*n.* **2.** any preparation that has this effect. [Latin *ēmollīre* to soften]

emolument (ɪ'mɒljʊmənt) *n.* profit from employment; fees or wages. [Latin *ēmolumentum* benefit; orig., fee paid to a miller]

emote (ɪ'məʊt) *vb.* to display exaggerated emotion, as in acting.

emotion (ɪ'məʊʃən) *n.* any strong feeling, as of joy or fear. [Latin *ēmovēre* to disturb]

emotional (ɪ'məʊʃən'l) *adj.* **1.** of or denoting emotion or the emotions. **2.** readily or excessively affected by emotion. **3.** appealing to or arousing emotion: *an emotional argument.* —e'**motional,ism** *n.* —e'**motionally** *adv.*

emotive (ɪ'məʊtɪv) *adj.* **1.** tending to or designed to arouse emotion. **2.** of or characterized by emotion.

empanel (ɪm'pæn'l) *vb.* -**elling, -elled** *or* *U.S.* -**eling, -eled.** *Law.* to enter on a list (names of persons for jury service).

empathy ('ɛmpəθɪ) *n.* the power of imaginatively entering into and understanding another person's feelings. [Greek *empatheia* affection, passion] —ˌempa'**thetic** *adj.*

emperor ('ɛmpərə) *n.* a monarch who rules an empire. [Latin *imperāre* to command]

emperor penguin *n.* an Antarctic penguin with orange-yellow patches on the neck: the largest penguin.

emphasis ('ɛmfəsɪs) *n., pl.* -**ses** (-siːz). **1.** special importance or significance given to something, such as an object or idea. **2.** stress on a particular syllable, word, or phrase in speaking. **3.** force or intensity of expression. [Greek]

emphasize *or* -**ise** ('ɛmfə,saɪz) *vb.* to give emphasis or prominence to; stress.

emphatic (ɪm'fætɪk) *adj.* **1.** expressed, spoken, or done with emphasis. **2.** forceful and positive: *an emphatic personality.* **3.** important or significant: *the emphatic points in an argument.* [Greek *emphainein* to display] —em'**phatically** *adv.*

emphysema (ˌɛmfɪ'siːmə) *n. Pathol.* a condition in which the air sacs of the lungs are grossly enlarged. [Greek *emphusēma* a swelling up]

empire ('ɛmpaɪə) *n.* **1.** a group of peoples and territories under the rule of a single person or sovereign state. **2.** supreme power; sovereignty. **3.** a large industrial organization that is directed or owned by one person. [Latin *imperāre* to command]

empire-builder *n. Informal.* a person who seeks extra power by increasing the number of his staff. —'**empire-,building** *n., adj.*

empirical (ɛm'pɪrɪk'l) *adj.* **1.** derived from experiment and observation rather than from theory or from first principles by logic. **2.** (of medical treatment) based on practical experience rather than scientific proof. [Greek *empeirikos* practised] —em'**pirically** *adv.*

empiricism (ɛm'pɪrɪ,sɪzəm) *n. Philosophy.* the doctrine that all knowledge derives from experience. —em'**piricist** *n.*

emplacement (ɪm'pleɪsmənt) *n.* **1.** a prepared position for a gun. **2.** the act of putting something in place.

emplane (ɪm'pleɪn) *vb.* to board or put on board an aeroplane.

employ (ɪm'plɔɪ) *vb.* **1.** to engage the services of (a person) in return for money; hire. **2.** to provide work or occupation for; keep busy. **3.** to use as a means: *to employ secret measures to achieve one's ends.* ~*n.* **4.** the state of being employed: *the company has 20 000 workers in its employ.* [Old French *emploier*] —em'**ployable** *adj.*

employee *or U.S.* **employe** (ɛm'plɔɪiː, ˌɛmplɔɪ'iː) *n.* a person who is hired to work for another in return for payment.

employer (ɪm'plɔɪə) *n.* a person or company that employs workers.

employment (ɪm'plɔɪmənt) *n.* **1.** the act of employing or state of being employed. **2.** a person's work or occupation.

emporium (ɛm'pɔːrɪəm) *n., pl.* -**riums** *or* -**ria** (-rɪə). a large retail shop with a wide variety of merchandise. [Latin, from Greek *emporos* merchant]

empower (ɪm'paʊə) vb. to give (someone) the power or authority to do something.

empress ('ɛmprɪs) n. 1. the wife or widow of an emperor. 2. a woman who rules an empire. [Latin *imperātrix*]

empty ('ɛmptɪ) adj. -tier, -tiest. 1. containing nothing. 2. without inhabitants; unoccupied. 3. without purpose, substance, or value: *an empty life*. 4. insincere or trivial: *empty words*. 5. *Informal*. drained of energy or emotion. 6. *Maths, logic*. (of a set or class) containing no members. ~vb. -tying, -tied. 7. to make or become empty. 8. to remove (the contents) of something: *to empty the rubbish out of the bin*. ~n., pl. -ties. 9. an empty container, esp. a bottle. [Old English *æmtig*] —'**emptiness** n.

empty-handed adj. having gained nothing: *they returned from the talks empty-handed*.

empty-headed adj. lacking sense; frivolous.

empyrean (ˌɛmpaɪ'riːən) n. 1. *Archaic*. the highest part of the heavens. 2. *Poetic*. the sky. [Greek *empurios* fiery] —ˌempy-'**real** adj.

emu ('iːmjuː) n. a large Australian flightless bird with long legs. [Portuguese *ema* ostrich]

emulate ('ɛmjʊˌleɪt) vb. to attempt to equal or surpass by imitating. [Latin *aemulus* competing with] —ˌemu'**lation** n. —'**emulative** adj. —'**emuˌlator** n.

emulous ('ɛmjʊləs) adj. 1. desiring to equal or surpass another. 2. arising from emulation.

emulsify (ɪ'mʌlsɪˌfaɪ) vb. -fying, -fied. to make or form into an emulsion. —e'**mulsiˌfier** n. —eˌmulsifi'**cation** n.

emulsion (ɪ'mʌlʃən) n. 1. a mixture of two liquids one of which is dispersed in the other. 2. *Photog*. a light-sensitive coating for paper or film. 3. a type of water-based paint. [Latin *ēmulgēre* to milk out] —e'**mulsive** adj.

en (ɛn) n. *Printing*. a unit of measurement, half the width of an em.

enable (ɪn'eɪbʔl) vb. 1. to provide (someone) with the means, opportunity, or authority (to do something). 2. to make possible: *the porous shell enables oxygen to pass in*.

enact (ɪn'ækt) vb. 1. to establish by law; decree: *to enact a bill*. 2. to represent as in a play. —en'**actment** n.

enamel (ɪ'næməl) n. 1. a coloured glassy coating on the surface of articles made of metal, glass, or pottery. 2. an enamel-like paint or varnish. 3. the hard white substance that covers each tooth. ~vb. -elling, -elled or *U.S.* -eling, -eled. 4. to decorate or cover with or as if with enamel. [Old French *esmail*]

enamoured or *U.S.* **enamored** (ɪn'æməd) adj. (foll. by *of*) inspired with love; captivated. [Latin *amor* love]

en bloc (ɒn 'blɒk) adv. as a whole; all together. [French]

enc. 1. enclosed. 2. enclosure.

encamp (ɪn'kæmp) vb. *Formal*. to set up or cause to set up in a camp. —en'**campment** n.

encapsulate (ɪn'kæpsjʊˌleɪt) vb. 1. to enclose or be enclosed as in a capsule. 2. to put in a concise form; abridge. —enˌcapsu'**lation** n.

encase (ɪn'keɪs) vb. to place or enclose as in a case. —en'**casement** n.

encaustic (ɪn'kɔːstɪk) *Ceramics, etc.* ~adj. 1. decorated by burning colours onto or into a surface. ~n. 2. the process or a product of burning in colours. [Greek *enkaiein* to burn in]

enceinte (ɒn'sænt) adj. pregnant. [French]

encephalitis (ˌɛnsɛfə'laɪtɪs) n. inflammation of the brain. [Greek *en*- in + *kephalē* head] —**encephalitic** (ˌɛnsɛfə'lɪtɪk) adj.

encephalogram (ɛn'sɛfələˌgræm) n. short for **electroencephalogram**; see **electroencephalograph**. [Greek *en*- in + *kephalē* head + *gramma* drawing]

enchain (ɪn'tʃeɪn) vb. 1. to bind with chains. 2. to captivate (the attention).

enchant (ɪn'tʃɑːnt) vb. 1. to delight; charm. 2. to cast a spell on; bewitch. [Latin *incantāre*] —en'**chanted** adj. —en'**chantment** n. —en'**chantress** fem. n.

encircle (ɪn'sɜːkʔl) vb. to form a circle around; surround. —en'**circlement** n.

enclave ('ɛnkleɪv) n. a part of a country entirely surrounded by foreign territory. [Latin *in*- in + *clavis* key]

enclose (ɪn'kləʊz) vb. 1. to surround completely: *the garden is enclosed with a seven foot fence*. 2. to include along with something else: *I have enclosed a cheque for ten pounds*.

enclosure (ɪn'kləʊʒə) n. 1. the act of enclosing or state of being enclosed. 2. an area of land enclosed as by a fence. 3. something, such as a cheque, enclosed with a letter.

encomium (ɛn'kəʊmɪəm) n., pl. -miums or -mia (-mɪə). a formal expression of praise. [Latin]

encompass (ɪn'kʌmpəs) vb. 1. to enclose within a circle; surround. 2. to include comprehensively: *this book encompasses the whole range of knowledge*.

encore ('ɒŋkɔː) interj. 1. again: used by an audience to demand a short extra performance. ~n. 2. an extra performance in response to enthusiastic demand. ~vb. 3. to demand an extra performance of or by. [French]

encounter (ɪn'kaʊntə) vb. 1. to meet (someone) unexpectedly. 2. to meet (an enemy) in battle or contest. 3. to be faced with: *we encountered many difficulties on our journey*. ~n. 4. a casual or unexpected meeting. 5. a contest. [Latin *in*- in + *contrā* against, opposite]

encourage (ɪn'kʌrɪdʒ) vb. 1. to inspire (someone) with the confidence (to do something). 2. to stimulate (something or someone) by approval or help. [French *encourager*] —en'**couragement** n. —en'**couraging** adj.

encroach (ɪnˈkrəʊtʃ) *vb*. (often foll. by *on* or *upon*) to intrude gradually on someone's rights or on a piece of land. [Old French *encrochier* to seize] —en'**croachment** *n*.

encrust (ɪnˈkrʌst) *vb*. to cover (a surface) with a layer of something, such as jewels or ice —ˌencrus'**tation** *n*.

encumber (ɪnˈkʌmbə) *vb*. 1. to hinder or impede; hamper: *she was encumbered with heavy parcels; his stupidity encumbers his efforts to learn.* 2. to burden, as with debts. [Old French *en-* into + *combre* a barrier]

encumbrance (ɪnˈkʌmbrəns) *n*. a thing that impedes or is burdensome; hindrance.

ency., **encyc.**, *or* **encycl.** encyclopedia.

encyclical (enˈsɪklɪkˀl) *n*. 1. a letter sent by the pope to all Roman Catholic bishops. ~*adj*. 2. (of letters) for general circulation. [Greek *kuklos* circle]

encyclopedia *or* **encyclopaedia** (enˌsaɪkləʊˈpiːdɪə) *n*. a book or set of books, often in alphabetical order, that contains facts about many different subjects or about one particular subject. [Greek *enkuklios* general + *paideia* education]

encyclopedic *or* **encyclopaedic** (enˌsaɪkləʊˈpiːdɪk) *adj*. (of knowledge or information) very full and thorough; comprehensive.

end (end) *n*. 1. one of the two extreme points of something, such as a road. 2. the surface at one of the two extreme points of an object: *a pencil with a rubber at one end.* 3. the extreme extent or limit of something: *that hedge marks the end of my garden.* 4. the most distant place or time that can be imagined: *the ends of the earth.* 5. the last part of something: *I cried at the end of the film.* 6. a remnant or fragment: *a cigarette end.* 7. death; destruction. 8. the purpose of an action: *she'll stop at nothing to achieve her ends.* 9. *Sport.* either of the two defended areas of a playing field. 10. **in the end.** finally. 11. **make (both) ends meet.** to spend no more than the money one has. 12. **no end (of).** *Informal.* (used for emphasis): *I had no end of work.* 13. **on end.** *Informal.* without pause or interruption. 14. **the end.** *Slang.* the worst, esp. beyond the limits of endurance. ~*vb*. 15. to bring or come to a finish; conclude. 16. **end it all.** *Informal.* to commit suicide. ~See also **end up.** [Old English *ende*]

endanger (ɪnˈdeɪndʒə) *vb*. to put in danger; risk —en'**dangered** *adj*.

endear (ɪnˈdɪə) *vb*. to cause to be beloved. —en'**dearing** *adj*.

endearment (ɪnˈdɪəmənt) *n*. an affectionate word or phrase.

endeavour *or* *U.S.* **endeavor** (ɪnˈdɛvə) *vb*. 1. to try (to do something). ~*n*. 2. an effort to do something. [Middle English *endeveren*]

endemic (enˈdɛmɪk) *adj*. present within a localized area or peculiar to a particular group of people: *an endemic disease.* [Greek *en-* in + *dēmos* the people] —en'**demically** *adv*.

ending (ˈendɪŋ) *n*. 1. the act of bringing to

or reaching an end. 2. the last part of something. 3. the last part of a word.

endive (ˈendaɪv) *n*. a plant with crisp curly leaves, used in salads. [Old French]

endless (ˈendlɪs) *adj*. 1. having no end; eternal or infinite. 2. continuing too long or continually recurring. 3. with the ends joined: *an endless belt.* —'**endlessly** *adv*.

endmost (ˈendˌməʊst) *adj*. nearest the end.

endocrine (ˈendəʊˌkraɪn) *adj*. of or denoting endocrine glands or their secretions. [Greek *endon* within + *krinein* to separate]

endocrine gland *n*. any of the glands that secrete hormones directly into the bloodstream, such as the pituitary.

endogenous (enˈdɒdʒɪnəs) *adj*. *Biol*. developing or originating from within.

endorsation (ˌendɔːˈseɪʃən) *n*. *Canad*. approval or support.

endorse *or* **indorse** (ɪnˈdɔːs) *vb*. 1. to give approval or sanction to. 2. to sign the back of (a document) to specify the payee. 3. *Chiefly Brit*. to record a conviction on (a driving licence). [Old French *endosser* to put on the back] —en'**dorsement** *n*.

endow (ɪnˈdaʊ) *vb*. 1. to provide with or bequeath a source of permanent income. 2. **endowed with.** provided (with qualities, characteristics, etc.). [Old French *endouer*]

endowment (ɪnˈdaʊmənt) *n*. 1. the money given to an institution, such as a hospital. 2. the act or process of endowing. 3. (*usually pl.*) natural talents or qualities.

endowment assurance *or* **insurance** *n*. a life insurance that pays a specified sum directly to the policyholder at a designated date or to his beneficiary should he die before this date.

endpaper (ˈendˌpeɪpə) *n*. either of two leaves at the front and back of a book pasted to the inside of the cover.

end product *n*. the final result of a process.

endue (ɪnˈdjuː) *vb*. **-duing, -dued.** (usually foll. by *with*) to provide with some quality or trait. [Latin *in-* in + *dūcere* to lead]

end up *vb*. 1. to turn out to be. 2. to arrive (somewhere) by a roundabout route.

endurance (ɪnˈdjʊərəns) *n*. 1. the capacity, state, or an instance of enduring. 2. the ability to withstand strain or hardship.

endure (ɪnˈdjʊə) *vb*. 1. to undergo (strain or hardship) without yielding; bear. 2. to tolerate. 3. to last. [Latin *indūrāre* to harden] —en'**durable** *adj*.

enduring (ɪnˈdjʊərɪŋ) *adj*. permanent; lasting.

endways (ˈendˌweɪz) *or* *esp. U.S. & Canad.* **endwise** (ˈendˌwaɪz) *adv*. 1. having the end forwards or upwards. ~*adj*. 2. standing or lying end to end.

enema (ˈenɪmə) *n*. *Med*. 1. the injection of liquid into the rectum to evacuate the bowels, medicate, or nourish. 2. the liquid so injected. [Greek *enienai* to send in]

enemy (ˈenəmɪ) *n., pl.* **-mies.** 1. a person hostile or opposed to a policy, cause, person, or group. 2. an adversary; opposing military force. **3.** a hostile nation or people. **4.** something that harms or opposes. [Latin *inimicus* hostile]

energetic (ˌenəˈdʒetɪk) *adj.* showing energy; vigorous. —ˌener'getically *adv.*

energize *or* **-ise** ('enəˌdʒaɪz) *vb.* to cause to have energy; invigorate.

energy ('enədʒɪ) *n., pl.* **-gies. 1.** capacity for intense activity; vigour. **2.** intensity or vitality of action or expression; forcefulness. **3.** *Physics.* the capacity to do work and overcome resistance. [Greek *energeia* activity]

enervate ('enəˌveɪt) *vb.* to deprive of strength or vitality. [Latin *ēnervāre* to remove the nerves from] —'ener,vating *adj.* —ˌener'vation *n.*

enfant terrible (ˌɒnfɒn təˈriːblə) *n., pl.* **enfants terribles** (ˌɒnfɒn təˈriːblə). a person who is unconventional or indiscreet. [French, lit.: terrible child]

enfeeble (ɪnˈfiːbʳl) *vb.* to make (someone or something) weak. —en'feeblement *n.*

enfilade (ˌenfɪˈleɪd) *Mil.* ~*n.* **1.** gunfire directed along the length of a formation. ~*vb.* **2.** to attack (a formation) with enfilade. [French *enfiler* to thread on string]

enfold (ɪnˈfəʊld) *vb.* **1.** to cover (something) by wrapping something else around it. **2.** to embrace.

enforce (ɪnˈfɔːs) *vb.* **1.** to ensure that (a law or decision) is obeyed. **2.** to impose (obedience) by force. **3.** to emphasize or reinforce (an argument). —en'forceable *adj.* —en'forcement *n.*

enfranchise (ɪnˈfræntʃaɪz) *vb.* **1.** to grant (someone) the right to vote. **2.** to free as from slavery. **3.** (in England) to give (a town or city) the right to be represented in Parliament. —en'franchisement *n.*

Eng. 1. England. **2.** English.

engage (ɪnˈgeɪdʒ) *vb.* **1.** to employ (someone). **2.** to reserve (a room, seat, etc.). **3.** to involve (a person or his attention) intensely. **4.** to draw (somebody) into conversation. **5.** to take part: *she engages in many sports.* **6.** to promise (to do something). **7.** *Mil.* to begin a battle with (an enemy). **8.** to bring (part of a machine or other mechanism) into operation. **9.** to undergo or cause to undergo interlocking, as of the components of a driving mechanism, such as a gear train. [Old French *en-* in + *gage* a pledge]

engaged (ɪnˈgeɪdʒd) *adj.* **1.** pledged to be married. **2.** occupied or busy: *the toilet is engaged.* **3.** (of a telephone line) in use.

engagement (ɪnˈgeɪdʒmənt) *n.* **1.** a business or social appointment. **2.** a pledge of marriage. **3.** a limited period of employment, esp. in the performing arts. **4.** a battle.

engaging (ɪnˈgeɪdʒɪŋ) *adj.* pleasing, charming, or winning. —en'gagingly *adv.*

engender (ɪnˈdʒendə) *vb.* to produce or cause (a particular feeling, atmosphere, or situation) to occur. [Latin *ingenerāre*]

engine ('endʒɪn) *n.* **1.** any machine designed to convert energy into mechanical

work. **2.** a railway locomotive. [Latin *ingenium* nature, talent]

engineer (ˌendʒɪˈnɪə) *n.* **1.** a person trained in any branch of engineering. **2.** *U.S. & Canad.* the driver of a railway locomotive. **3.** an officer responsible for a ship's engines. **4.** a member of the armed forces trained in engineering and construction work. ~*vb.* **5.** to cause or plan (an event or situation) in a clever or devious manner. **6.** to design or construct as a professional engineer.

engineering (ˌendʒɪˈnɪərɪŋ) *n.* the profession of applying scientific principles to the design and construction of engines, cars, buildings, bridges, roads, and electrical machines.

English ('ɪŋglɪʃ) *n.* **1.** the official language of Britain, the U.S., most of the Commonwealth, and certain other countries. **2. the English.** (*functioning as pl.*) the people of England collectively. ~*adj.* **3.** of or relating to England, its people, or the English language.

English horn *n. Music.* see **cor anglais.**

Englishman ('ɪŋglɪʃmən) *or* (*fem.*) **Englishwoman** *n., pl.* **-men** *or* **-women.** a person from England.

engorge (ɪnˈgɔːdʒ) *vb.* **1.** to eat (food) greedily. **2.** *Pathol.* to congest with blood.

engrave (ɪnˈgreɪv) *vb.* **1.** to carve or etch (a design or inscription) onto (a block, plate, or other printing surface). **2.** to print (designs or characters) from a plate so made. **3.** to fix deeply or permanently in the mind. [*en-* in + *obs. grave* to carve] —en'graver *n.*

engraving (ɪnˈgreɪvɪŋ) *n.* **1.** the art of an engraver. **2.** a printing surface that has been engraved. **3.** a print made from this.

engross (ɪnˈgrəʊs) *vb.* **1.** to occupy one's attention completely; absorb. **2.** to write out in large legible handwriting or in legal form. [*en-* in + Latin *grossus* thick] —en'grossed *adj.* —en'grossing *adj.*

engulf (ɪnˈgʌlf) *vb.* **1.** to immerse, plunge or swallow up: *flames engulfed the house.* **2.** (*often passive*) to overwhelm: *engulfed by debts.*

enhance (ɪnˈhɑːns) *vb.* to intensify or increase in quality, value or power; improve. [Old French *enhaucier*] —en'hancement *n.*

enigma (ɪˈnɪgmə) *n.* a person, thing, or situation that is mysterious or puzzling. [Greek *ainissesthai* to speak in riddles] —enigmatic (ˌenɪgˈmætɪk) *adj.* —ˌenig'matically *adv.*

enjoin (ɪnˈdʒɔɪn) *vb.* **1.** to order (someone) to do something. **2.** to impose (a particular kind of behaviour) on someone. **3.** *Law.* to prohibit (a person) from some act by an injunction. [Old French *enjoindre*]

enjoy (ɪnˈdʒɔɪ) *vb.* **1.** to receive pleasure from; take joy in. **2.** to have the benefit of; use. **3.** to have as a condition; experience. **4. enjoy oneself.** to have a good time. [Old French *enjoir*] —en'joyable *adj.* —en'joyably *adv.* —en'joyment *n.*

enkindle (ɪnˈkɪndʳl) *vb.* **1.** to set on fire. **2.** to excite or arouse.

enlarge (ɪnˈlɑːdʒ) vb. **1.** to make or grow larger; increase or expand. **2.** to make (a photographic print) larger. **3. enlarge on** or **upon**. to speak or write (about) in greater detail. —**enˈlargement** n. —**enˈlarger** n.

enlighten (ɪnˈlaɪtᵊn) vb. **1.** to give information or understanding to; instruct. **2.** to free from prejudice, ignorance, or superstition. —**enˈlightened** adj.

enlightenment (ɪnˈlaɪtᵊnmənt) n. the act of enlightening or the state of being enlightened.

enlist (ɪnˈlɪst) vb. **1.** to enter the armed forces. **2.** to engage or secure (a person or his support) for a cause or venture. —**enˈlistment** n.

enliven (ɪnˈlaɪvᵊn) vb. to make lively, cheerful, or bright. —**enˈlivening** adj.

en masse (ɒn ˈmæs) adv. in a group or mass; as a whole; all together. [French]

enmesh (ɪnˈmɛʃ) vb. to catch in or as if in a net; entangle.

enmity (ˈɛnmɪtɪ) n., pl. **-ties.** a feeling of hostility or ill will, as between enemies. [Latin inimīcus hostile]

ennoble (ɪˈnəʊbᵊl) vb. **1.** to make (something) noble; dignify. **2.** to raise (someone) to a noble rank. —**enˈnoblement** n.

ennui (ˈɒnwiː) n. a feeling of boredom and dissatisfaction resulting from lack of activity or excitement. [French]

enormity (ɪˈnɔːmɪtɪ) n., pl. **-ties. 1.** the quality of extreme wickedness. **2.** an act of great wickedness. **3.** Not universally accepted. vastness of size or extent.

enormous (ɪˈnɔːməs) adj. unusually large in size, extent, or degree. [Latin ē- out of, away from + norma rule, pattern] —**eˈnormously** adv.

enough (ɪˈnʌf) det. **1.** sufficient to answer a need or demand. **2. that's enough!** that will do: used to stop someone behaving in a particular way. ~adv. **3.** as much as necessary. **4.** very or quite; rather. **5.** especially: oddly enough. **6.** just adequately; tolerably: he did it well enough. [Old English genōh]

en passant (ɒn pæˈsɑːnt) adv. in passing; by the way. [French]

enquire (ɪnˈkwaɪə) vb. same as **inquire.** —**enˈquiry** n.

enrage (ɪnˈreɪdʒ) vb. to put (someone) into a rage. —**enˈraged** adj.

enrapture (ɪnˈræptʃə) vb. to fill (someone) with delight; enchant.

enrich (ɪnˈrɪtʃ) vb. **1.** to increase the wealth of. **2.** to improve in quality, colour or flavour. —**enˈriched** adj. —**enˈrichment** n.

enrol or U.S. **enroll** (ɪnˈrəʊl) vb. **-rolling, -rolled. 1.** to record (someone's name) in a list. **2.** to become or cause to become a member; enlist. —**enˈrolment** n.

en route (ɒn ˈruːt) adv. on or along the way. [French]

ensconce (ɪnˈskɒns) vb. to settle firmly or comfortably. [en- in + sconce fortification]

ensemble (ɒnˈsɒmbᵊl) n. **1.** all the parts of something considered together. **2.** a person's complete costume; outfit. **3.** the cast of a play. **4.** Music. a group of musicians playing together. [French: together]

enshrine (ɪnˈʃraɪn) vb. **1.** to enclose as in a shrine. **2.** to hold as sacred; cherish.

enshroud (ɪnˈʃraʊd) vb. to cover or hide as with a shroud.

ensign (ˈɛnsəm) n. **1.** (also ˈɛnsən). a flag flown by a ship to indicate nationality. **2.** any flag, standard, or banner. **3.** (in the U.S. Navy) a commissioned officer of the lowest rank. **4.** (formerly, in the British infantry) a commissioned officer of the lowest rank. [Latin insignia badges]

ensilage (ˈɛnsɪlɪdʒ) n. **1.** the process of storing green fodder in a silo. **2.** silage.

enslave (ɪnˈsleɪv) vb. to make a slave of (someone). —**enˈslavement** n.

ensnare (ɪnˈsnɛə) vb. to catch or trap as in a snare. —**enˈsnarement** n.

ensue (ɪnˈsjuː) vb. **-suing, -sued. 1.** to come next. **2.** to occur as a consequence; result. [Latin in- in + sequī to follow] —**enˈsuing** adj.

en suite (ɒn ˈswiːt) adv. forming a unit: a room with a bathroom en suite. [French, lit.: in sequence]

ensure (ɛnˈʃʊə) or esp. U.S. **insure** vb. **1.** to make certain or sure; guarantee. **2.** to make safe or secure; protect.

ENT Med. ear, nose, and throat.

entablature (ɛnˈtæblətʃə) n. Archit. the part of a classical temple above the columns, having an architrave, a frieze, and a cornice. [Italian intavolatura something put on a table, hence, something laid flat]

entail (ɪnˈteɪl) vb. **1.** to bring about or impose inevitably: this task entails careful thought. **2.** Property law. to restrict (the descent of an estate) to designated heirs. ~n. **3.** Property law. **a.** an entailed estate. **b.** the order of descent for an entailed estate. [Middle English en- in + taille limitation]

entangle (ɪnˈtæŋgᵊl) vb. **1.** to catch or involve in or as if in a tangle; ensnare or enmesh. **2.** to make complicated; confuse. **3.** to involve in difficulties. —**enˈtanglement** n.

entente (ɒnˈtɒnt) n. short for **entente cordiale.** [French: understanding]

entente cordiale (kɔːdɪˈɑːl) n. a friendly understanding between two or more countries. [French: cordial understanding]

enter (ˈɛntə) vb. **1.** to come or go into (a particular place). **2.** to penetrate or pierce: the bullet entered her leg. **3.** to join (a party or organization). **4.** to become involved or take part (in): to enter a competition; to enter into an agreement. **5.** to record (an item, a name, etc.) in a journal, list, etc. **6.** to present or submit: to enter a proposal. **7.** Theatre. to come on stage: enter Juliet. **8.** to begin; start: to enter upon a new career. **9.** to place (evidence) before a court of law. [Latin intrāre]

enteric (ɛnˈtɛrɪk) adj. intestinal. [Greek enteron intestine]

enter into vb. 1. to be considered as a necessary part of (one's plans). 2. to be in sympathy with.

enteritis (ˌɛntəˈraɪtɪs) n. inflammation of the intestine.

enterprise (ˈɛntəˌpraɪz) n. 1. a company or firm. 2. a project or undertaking, esp. one that requires boldness or effort. 3. boldness and energy. [Old French *entreprendre* to undertake]

enterprising (ˈɛntəˌpraɪzɪŋ) adj. full of boldness and initiative. —**enter,prising-ly** adv.

entertain (ˌɛntəˈteɪn) vb. 1. to provide amusement for (a person or audience). 2. to show hospitality to (guests). 3. to consider (an idea or suggestion). [Old French *entre-* mutually + *tenir* to hold]

entertainer (ˌɛntəˈteɪnə) n. any person who entertains, esp. professionally.

entertaining (ˌɛntəˈteɪnɪŋ) adj. diverting; amusing.

entertainment (ˌɛntəˈteɪnmənt) n. an act, production, etc., that entertains.

enthral or U.S. **enthrall** (ɪnˈθrɔːl) vb. -thralling, -thralled. to hold the attention or interest of (someone). —**en'thralling** adj. —**en'thralment** n.

enthrone (ɛnˈθrəʊn) vb. 1. to place (someone) on a throne. 2. to praise or honour. —**en'thronement** n.

enthuse (ɪnˈθjuːz) vb. to feel or show or cause to feel or show enthusiasm.

enthusiasm (ɪnˈθjuːzɪˌæzəm) n. ardent and lively interest or eagerness. [Greek *enthousiazein* to be possessed by a god]

enthusiast (ɪnˈθjuːzɪˌæst) n. a person motivated by enthusiasm; fanatic. —**en,thusi'astic** adj. —**en,thusi'astically** adv.

entice (ɪnˈtaɪs) vb. to attract by exciting hope or desire; tempt. [Old French *enticier*] —**en'ticement** n. —**en'ticing** adj.

entire (ɪnˈtaɪə) adj. 1. whole; complete. 2. without reservation or exception. 3. not broken or damaged. 4. undivided; continuous. [Latin *integer* whole] —**en'tirely** adv.

entirety (ɪnˈtaɪərɪtɪ) n., pl. -ties. 1. completeness. 2. a thing that is entire. 3. **in its entirety**, as a whole.

entitle (ɪnˈtaɪtᵊl) vb. 1. to give (a person) the right to do or have something; qualify; allow. 2. to give a name or title to (a book, film, etc.). —**en'titlement** n.

entity (ˈɛntɪtɪ) n., pl. -ties. 1. something having real or distinct existence. 2. existence or being. [Latin *esse* to be]

entomb (ɪnˈtuːm) vb. 1. to place (a corpse) in a tomb; bury. 2. to serve as a tomb for. —**en'tombment** n.

entomology (ˌɛntəˈmɒlədʒɪ) n. the branch of science concerned with the study of insects. [Greek *entomon* insect] —**entomological** (ˌɛntəməˈlɒdʒɪkᵊl) adj. —**ento'mologist** n.

entourage (ˈɒntuˌrɑːʒ) n. a group of people who assist an important person or group of people. [French *entourer* to surround]

entr'acte (ɒnˈtrækt) n. 1. an interval between two acts of a play. 2. (esp. formerly) an entertainment during such an interval. [French]

entrails (ˈɛntreɪlz) pl. n. 1. the internal organs of a person or animal; intestines. 2. the innermost parts of anything. [Latin *interānea* intestines]

entrance¹ (ˈɛntrəns) n. 1. the act of entering; entry. 2. a place for entering, such as a door. 3. the right of entering. 4. the coming of an actor onto a stage.

entrance² (ɪnˈtrɑːns) vb. 1. to fill with delight; enchant. 2. to put into a trance. —**en'trancement** n. —**en'trancing** adj.

entrant (ˈɛntrənt) n. a person who enters a university, competition, etc.

entrap (ɪnˈtræp) vb. -trapping, -trapped. 1. to catch as in a trap. 2. to trick into danger or difficulty. —**en'trapment** n.

entreat (ɪnˈtriːt) vb. to ask (someone) earnestly to do something. [Old French *entraiter*]

entreaty (ɪnˈtriːtɪ) n., pl. -treaties. an earnest request or petition; plea.

entrecôte (ˈɒntrəˌkəʊt) n. a beefsteak cut from between the ribs. [French]

entrée (ˈɒntreɪ) n. 1. the right of entry. 2. a dish served before a main course. 3. *Chiefly U.S.* the main course. [French]

entrench (ɪnˈtrɛntʃ) vb. 1. to fix or establish firmly: *strongly entrenched ideas*. 2. to construct a defensive position by digging trenches around it. —**en'trenched** adj. —**en'trenchment** n.

entrepreneur (ˌɒntrəprəˈnɜː) n. the owner of a business who, by risk and initiative, attempts to make profits. [French] —**,entrepre'neurial** adj.

entropy (ˈɛntrəpɪ) n., pl. -pies. 1. a thermodynamic quantity that changes by an amount equal to the heat absorbed or emitted divided by the thermodynamic temperature. 2. lack of pattern or organization; disorder. [Greek *entropē* a turning towards]

entrust (ɪnˈtrʌst) vb. 1. (usually foll. by *with*) to invest or charge (with a duty or responsibility). 2. (often foll. by *to*) to give (something) into the care of someone.

entry (ˈɛntrɪ) n., pl. -tries. 1. the act of entering; entrance. 2. a place for entering, such as a door. 3. the right of entering. 4. the act of recording an item in a journal, account, etc. 5. an item so recorded. 6. a person, horse, car, etc., entering a competition. 7. the competitors collectively.

entwine (ɪnˈtwaɪn) vb. to twist together or around (something else).

E number n. any of a series of numbers with the prefix E indicating a specific food additive recognized by the EC.

enumerate (ɪˈnjuːməˌreɪt) vb. 1. to name one by one; list. 2. to count. 3. *Canad.* to compile the voting list for an area. [Latin *e-* out + *numerāre* to count] —**e,numer'ation** n. —**e'numerative** adj. —**e'num-e,rator** n.

enunciate (ɪˈnʌnsɪˌeɪt) vb. 1. to pronounce (words) clearly. 2. to state precisely or formally. [Latin *ēnuntiāre* to declare] —**e,nunci'ation** n.

enuresis (ˌɛnjuˈriːsɪs) n. involuntary discharge of urine, esp. during sleep. [Greek *en-* in + *ouron* urine] —**enuretic** (ˌɛnjuˈrɛtɪk) adj.

envelop (ɪnˈvɛləp) vb. to cover, surround, or enclose. [Old French *envoluper*] —**en'velopment** n.

envelope (ˈɛnvəˌləʊp, ˈɒn-) n. **1.** a flat covering of paper, that can be sealed, used to enclose a letter, etc. **2.** any covering or wrapper. **3.** *Biol.* any enclosing structure, such as a shell or skin. **4.** the bag enclosing gas in a balloon. **5.** *Maths.* a curve or surface that is tangential to each one of a group of curves or surfaces. [French *enveloppe* to wrap round]

enviable (ˈɛnvɪəbˀl) adj. exciting envy; fortunate or privileged. —**'enviably** adv.

envious (ˈɛnvɪəs) adj. feeling, showing, or resulting from envy. —**'enviously** adv.

environment (ɪnˈvaɪrənmənt) n. **1.** external conditions or surroundings in which people live. **2.** *Ecology*. the external surroundings in which a plant or animal lives, which influence its development. [French *environs* surroundings] —**en,viron'mental** adj.

environmentalist (ɪnˌvaɪrənˈmɛntəlɪst) n. a person concerned with the protection and preservation of the natural environment.

environs (ɪnˈvaɪrənz) pl. n. a surrounding area, esp. the outskirts of a city.

envisage (ɪnˈvɪzɪdʒ) vb. **1.** to form a mental image of; visualize. **2.** to conceive of as a possibility in the future. [French *en-* in + *visage* face]

envoy[1] (ˈɛnvɔɪ) n. **1.** a diplomat ranking next below an ambassador. **2.** a messenger or representative. [French *envoyer* to send]

envoy[2] (ˈɛnvɔɪ) n. a brief concluding stanza in a ballade. [Old French]

envy (ˈɛnvɪ) n., pl. **-vies. 1.** a feeling of discontent aroused by the possessions, achievements, or qualities of another. **2.** an object of envy. —vb. **-vying, -vied. 3.** to be envious of (a person or thing). [Latin *invidia*] —**'envyingly** adv.

enzyme (ˈɛnzaɪm) n. any of a group of complex proteins, that act as catalysts in specific biochemical reactions. [Greek *en-* in + *zumē* leaven] —**enzymatic** (ˌɛnzaɪˈmætɪk) adj.

Eocene (ˈiːəʊˌsiːn) adj. of an epoch of geological time about 55 million years ago. [Greek *ēōs* dawn + *kainos* new]

Eolithic (ˌiːəʊˈlɪθɪk) adj. of or denoting the early part of the Stone Age, characterized by the use of crude stone tools.

EP n. an extended-play gramophone record.

epaulette (ˈɛpəˌlɛt) n. a piece of ornamental material on the shoulder of a garment, esp. a military uniform. [French]

epergne (ɪˈpɜːn) n. an ornamental centrepiece for a table. [prob. from French *épargne* a saving]

ephedrine (ɪˈfɛdrɪn) n. an alkaloid used

for the treatment of asthma and hay fever. [*Ephedra*, genus of plants which produce it]

ephemeral (ɪˈfɛmərəl) adj. lasting only for a short time. [Greek *hēmera* day]

epic (ˈɛpɪk) n. **1.** a long narrative poem recounting the deeds of a legendary hero. **2.** a book, poem, or film having qualities associated with an epic. —adj. **3.** of or characteristic of an epic. [Greek *epos* word, song]

epicene (ˈɛpɪˌsiːn) adj. **1.** having the characteristics of both sexes. **2.** sexless. **3.** effeminate. [Greek *epikoinos* common to many]

epicentre or U.S. **epicenter** (ˈɛpɪˌsɛntə) n. the point on the earth's surface immediately above the origin of an earthquake. [Greek *epi* above + *kentron* point]

epicure (ˈɛpɪˌkjʊə) n. a person who enjoys consuming good food and drink. [after *Epicurus*; see EPICUREAN] —**'epicur,ism** n.

epicurean (ˌɛpɪkjʊˈriːən) adj. **1.** devoted to sensual pleasures, esp. food and drink. ~n. **2.** an epicure; gourmet. —**epicu'reanism** n.

Epicurean (ˌɛpɪkjʊˈriːən) adj. **1.** of or relating to the philosophy of Epicurus, who held that the highest good is pleasure. ~n. **2.** a follower of the philosophy of Epicurus. —**Epicu'reanism** n.

epidemic (ˌɛpɪˈdɛmɪk) adj. **1.** (esp. of a disease) affecting many persons in an area. ~n. **2.** a widespread occurrence of a disease. **3.** a rapid development or spread of something: *an epidemic of strikes*. [Greek *epi* among + *dēmos* people] —**epidemically** adv.

epidemiology (ˌɛpɪˌdiːmɪˈɒlədʒɪ) n. the branch of medical science concerned with epidemic diseases. —**epi,demi'ologist** n.

epidermis (ˌɛpɪˈdɜːmɪs) n. the thin protective outer layer of the skin. [Greek *epi* upon + *derma* skin] —**epi'dermal** adj.

epidiascope (ˌɛpɪˈdaɪəˌskəʊp) n. an optical device for projecting a magnified image onto a screen. [Greek *epi* upon + *dia* through + *skopein* to look]

epidural (ˌɛpɪˈdjʊərəl) adj. **1.** upon or outside the outermost membrane covering the brain and spinal cord (**dura mater**). ~n. **2 a.** injection of anaesthetic into the space outside the dura mater, the outermost membrane enveloping the spinal cord. **b.** anaesthesia induced by this method. [Greek *epi* upon + *dura mater*]

epiglottis (ˌɛpɪˈglɒtɪs) n. a thin flap that covers the entrance to the larynx during swallowing. [Greek *epi* upon + *glōtta* tongue] —**epi'glottal** adj.

epigram (ˈɛpɪˌgræm) n. **1.** a witty remark. **2.** a short poem with a witty ending. [Greek *epi* upon + *graphein* to write] —**epigram'matic** adj.

epigraph (ˈɛpɪˌgrɑːf) n. **1.** a quotation at the beginning of a book. **2.** an inscription on a monument or building. [Greek *epi* upon + *graphein* to write]

epilepsy (ˈɛpɪˌlɛpsɪ) n. a disorder of the central nervous system characterized by periodic loss of consciousness with or without convulsions. [Greek *epi* upon + *lambanein* to take]

epileptic (ˌɛpɪˈlɛptɪk) *adj.* **1.** of or having epilepsy. ~*n.* **2.** a person who has epilepsy.

epilogue (ˈɛpɪˌlɒg) *n.* **1.** a speech addressed to the audience by an actor at the end of a play. **2.** a short postscript to any literary work. [Greek *epi* upon + *logos* word, speech]

Epiphany (ɪˈpɪfənɪ) *n.*, *pl.* **-nies.** a Christian festival held on Jan. 6, commemorating, in the Western Church, the manifestation of Christ to the Magi. [Greek *epi* to + *phainein* to show]

episcopacy (ɪˈpɪskəpəsɪ) *n.*, *pl.* **-cies.** **1.** government of a Church by bishops. **2.** same as **episcopate**.

episcopal (ɪˈpɪskəpˀl) *adj.* of, denoting, governed by, or relating to bishops. [Greek *episkopos* overseer]

Episcopal (ɪˈpɪskəpˀl) *adj.* of or denoting the Episcopal Church of Scotland and the U.S.

episcopalian (ɪˌpɪskəˈpeɪlɪən) *adj. also* **episcopal.** **1.** practising or advocating Church government by bishops. ~*n.* **2.** an advocate of such Church government. —ˌepiscoˈpalianism *n.*

Episcopalian (ɪˌpɪskəˈpeɪlɪən) *adj.* belonging to or denoting the Episcopal Church. ~*n.* **2.** a member of this Church.

episcopate (ɪˈpɪskəpɪt) *n.* **1.** the office, status, or term of office of a bishop. **2.** bishops collectively.

episode (ˈɛpɪˌsəʊd) *n.* **1.** an event or series of events. **2.** any of the sections into which a novel, radio programme, or television programme is divided. **3.** an incident that forms part of a narrative but may be a digression from the main story. [Greek *epi-* (in addition) + *eisodios* coming in]

episodic (ˌɛpɪˈsɒdɪk) *or* **episodical** *adj.* **1.** resembling or relating to an episode. **2.** irregular or sporadic. —ˌepiˈsodically *adv.*

epistemology (ɪˌpɪstɪˈmɒlədʒɪ) *n.* the theory of knowledge, esp. the critical study of its validity, methods, and scope. [Greek *epistēmē* knowledge] —**epistemological** (ɪˌpɪstɪməˈlɒdʒɪkˀl) *adj.* —eˌpisteˈmologist *n.*

epistle (ɪˈpɪsˀl) *n. Sometimes humorous.* a letter. **2.** a literary work in letter form, esp. a poem. [Greek *epistolē*]

Epistle (ɪˈpɪsˀl) *n. New Testament.* any of the letters written by the apostles. **2.** a reading chosen from one of the Epistles, part of the Eucharistic service in many Christian Churches.

epistolary (ɪˈpɪstələrɪ) *adj.* **1.** relating to, conducted by, or contained in letters. **2.** (of a novel) presented in the form of a series of letters.

epitaph (ˈɛpɪˌtɑːf) *n.* **1.** a commemorative inscription on a tombstone. **2.** a commemorative speech or written passage. [Greek *epi* upon + *taphos* tomb]

epithelium (ˌɛpɪˈθiːlɪəm) *n.*, *pl.* **-lia** (-lɪə). an animal cellular tissue covering the external and internal surfaces of the body.

[Greek *epi* upon + *thēlē* nipple] —ˌepiˈthelial *adj.*

epithet (ˈɛpɪˌθɛt) *n.* a descriptive word or phrase added to a person's name. [Greek *epitithenai* to add] —ˌepiˈthetic *adj.*

epitome (ɪˈpɪtəmɪ) *n.* **1.** a person or thing that is a typical example of a characteristic or class; personification. **2.** a summary, esp. of a written work. [Greek *epitemnein* to abridge]

epitomize *or* **-ise** (ɪˈpɪtəˌmaɪz) *vb.* to be or make an epitome of.

EPNS electroplated nickel silver.

epoch (ˈiːpɒk) *n.* **1.** the beginning of a new or distinctive period. **2.** a long period of time marked by some predominant characteristic; era. **3.** *Geol.* a unit of time within a period during which a series of rocks is formed. [Greek *epokhē* cessation] —**epochal** (ˈɛpɒkˀl) *adj.*

eponym (ˈɛpənɪm) *n.* the name of the person from which the name of a place or thing is derived. [Greek *epōnumos* giving a significant name] —**eponymous** (ɪˈpɒnɪməs) *adj.*

EPOS electronic point of sale.

epoxy (ɪˈpɒksɪ) *Chem.* ~*adj.* **1.** of or containing an oxygen atom joined to two different groups that are themselves joined to other groups. **2.** of or consisting of an epoxy resin. ~*n.*, *pl.* **epoxies.** **3.** an epoxy resin. [Greek *epi* upon + *oxy(gen)*]

epoxy resin *n.* a tough resistant thermosetting synthetic resin, used in laminates and adhesives.

Epsom salts (ˈɛpsəm) *n.* (*functioning as sing. or pl.*) a medicinal preparation of hydrated magnesium sulphate, used to empty the bowels. [after *Epsom*, a town in England]

equable (ˈɛkwəbˀl) *adj.* **1.** even-tempered; placid. **2.** unvarying; uniform: *an equable climate.* [Latin *aequābilis*] —ˈequably *adv.*

equal (ˈiːkwəl) *adj.* **1.** identical in size, quantity, degree, or intensity. **2.** having identical privileges, rights, or status. **3.** having uniform effect or application: *equal opportunities.* **4.** evenly balanced or proportioned. **5.** (usually foll. by *to*) having the necessary strength, ability, or means (for): *to be equal to one's work.* ~*n.* **6.** a person or thing equal to another. ~*vb.* **equalling, equalled** *or U.S.* **equaling, equaled. 7.** to be equal to; match. **8.** to make or do something equal to: *to equal the world record.* [Latin *aequālis*] —ˈequally *adv.*

equality (ɪˈkwɒlɪtɪ) *n.*, *pl.* **-ties.** the state of being equal.

equalize *or* **-ise** (ˈiːkwəˌlaɪz) *vb.* **1.** to make equal or uniform. **2.** (in sports) to reach the same score as one's opponent or opponents. —ˌequaliˈzation *or* -iˈsation *n.*

equal opportunity *n.* the offering of employment or promotion equally to all, without discrimination as to sex, race, colour, etc.

equanimity (ˌɛkwəˈnɪmɪtɪ) *n.* calmness of

mind or temper; composure. [Latin *aequus* even + *animus* mind, spirit]

equate (ɪˈkweɪt) *vb.* **1.** to make or regard as equivalent. **2.** *Maths.* to indicate the equality of; form an equation from. —e**'quatable** *adj.*

equation (ɪˈkweɪʒən) *n.* **1.** a mathematical statement that two expressions are equal. **2.** the act of equating. **3.** a representation of a chemical reaction using symbols of the elements.

equator (ɪˈkweɪtə) *n.* **1.** an imaginary circle around the earth at an equal distance from the North Pole and the South Pole. **2.** *Astron.* See **celestial equator.** [Medieval Latin (*circulus*) *aequātor* (*diei et noctis*) (circle) that equalizes (the day and night)]

equatorial (ˌɛkwəˈtɔːrɪəl) *adj.* of, like, or existing at or near the equator.

equerry (ɪˈkwɛrɪ) *n., pl.* **-ries.** an officer of the royal household who acts as a personal attendant to a member of the royal family. [alteration (through infl. of Latin *equus* horse) of earlier *escuirie*, from Old French: stable]

equestrian (ɪˈkwɛstrɪən) *adj.* **1.** of or relating to horses and riding. **2.** on horseback; mounted. ~*n.* **3.** a person skilled in riding. [Latin *equus* horse] —e**'questrian‚ism** *n.*

equiangular (ˌiːkwɪˈæŋɡjʊlə) *adj.* having all angles equal.

equidistant (ˌiːkwɪˈdɪstənt) *adj.* equally distant. —‚equi**'distance** *n.*

equilateral (ˌiːkwɪˈlætərəl) *adj.* **1.** having all sides of equal length. ~*n.* **2.** a geometric figure having all sides of equal length.

equilibrium (ˌiːkwɪˈlɪbrɪəm) *n., pl.* **-ria** (-rɪə). **1.** a stable condition in which forces cancel one another. **2.** a state of mental and emotional balance; composure. [Latin *aequi-* equal + *lībra* balance]

equine (ˈɛkwaɪn) *adj.* of or resembling a horse.

equinoctial (ˌiːkwɪˈnɒkʃəl) *adj.* **1.** relating to or occurring at an equinox. ~*n.* **2.** a storm at or near an equinox. **3.** same as **celestial equator.**

equinoctial circle *or* **line** *n.* same as **celestial equator.**

equinox (ˈiːkwɪ‚nɒks) *n.* either of the two occasions when day and night are of equal length: the **vernal equinox** occurs around March 21 and the **autumnal equinox** around Sept. 23. [Latin *aequi-* equal + *nox* night]

equip (ɪˈkwɪp) *vb.* **equipping, equipped. 1.** to furnish (with necessary supplies). **2.** to provide with abilities, understanding, etc.: *her son was never equipped to be a scholar.* [Old French *eschiper* to fit out (a ship)]

equipage (ˈɛkwɪpɪdʒ) *n.* **1.** the stores and equipment of a military unit. **2.** a horse-drawn carriage with liveried footmen.

equipment (ɪˈkwɪpmənt) *n.* **1.** an equipping. **2.** the items so provided. **3.** a set of tools or devices used for a particular purpose; kit.

equipoise (ˈɛkwɪ‚pɔɪz) *n.* **1.** even balance

of weight; equilibrium. **2.** a counterbalance.

equitable (ˈɛkwɪtəbʰl) *adj.* **1.** fair; just. **2.** *Law.* relating to or valid in equity, as distinct from law. —**'equitably** *adv.*

equitation (ˌɛkwɪˈteɪʃən) *n.* riding and horsemanship. [Latin *equitāre* to ride]

equities (ˈɛkwɪtɪz) *pl. n.* same as **ordinary shares.**

equity (ˈɛkwɪtɪ) *n., pl.* **-ties. 1.** the quality of being impartial; fairness. **2.** *Law.* a system of jurisprudence founded on principles of natural justice and fair conduct that supplements common law. [Latin *aequus* level, equal]

Equity (ˈɛkwɪtɪ) *n.* *Brit.* the actors' trade union.

equiv. equivalent.

equivalent (ɪˈkwɪvələnt) *adj.* **1.** equal in value, quantity, significance, etc. **2.** having the same or a similar effect or meaning. ~*n.* **3.** something that is equivalent. [Latin *aequi-* equal + *valēre* to be worth] —e**'quivalence** *n.*

equivocal (ɪˈkwɪvəkʰl) *adj.* **1.** capable of varying interpretations; ambiguous. **2.** deliberately misleading or vague. **3.** of doubtful character or sincerity. [Latin *aequi* equal + *vōx* voice] —e**'quivocally** *adv.*

equivocate (ɪˈkwɪvə‚keɪt) *vb.* to use equivocal language in order to deceive someone or to avoid speaking the truth. —e‚quivo**'cation** *n.* —e**'quivo‚cator** *n.*

er (ə, ɜː) *interj.* a sound made when hesitating in speech.

Er *Chem.* erbium.

ER 1. Queen Elizabeth. [Latin *Elizabeth Regina*] **2.** King Edward. [Latin *Eduardus Rex*]

era (ˈɪərə) *n.* **1.** a period of time considered as distinctive; epoch. **2.** an extended period of time measured from a fixed point: *the Christian era.* **3.** the beginning of a new or distinctive period. **4.** *Geol.* a major division of time. [Latin *aera* counters, pieces of brass money]

eradicate (ɪˈrædɪ‚keɪt) *vb.* to destroy (something) completely; root out. [Latin *e-* out + *rādīx* root] —e**'radicable** *adj.* —e‚radi**'cation** *n.* —e**'radi‚cator** *n.*

erase (ɪˈreɪz) *vb.* **1.** to obliterate or rub out (something written). **2.** to destroy all traces of (something). **3.** to remove (a recording) from (magnetic tape). [Latin *e-* out + *rādere* to scrape] —e**'rasable** *adj.*

eraser (ɪˈreɪzə) *n.* an object, such as a piece of rubber, for erasing something written.

erasure (ɪˈreɪʒə) *n.* **1.** an erasing. **2.** the place or mark where something has been erased.

erbium (ˈɜːbɪəm) *n.* a soft silvery-white element of the lanthanide series of metals. Symbol: Er [after *Ytterby*, Sweden]

ere (ɛə) *conj., prep.* *Poetic.* before. [Old English *ǣr*]

erect (ɪˈrɛkt) *adj.* **1.** upright in posture or position. **2.** *Physiol.* (of the penis, clitoris, or nipples) firm or rigid after swelling with blood, esp. as a result of sexual excitement.

~*vb.* **3.** to build. **4.** to raise to an upright position. **5.** to found or form; set up. [Latin *ērigere* to set up] —**e'rection** *n.*

erectile (ɪ'rɛktaɪl) *adj. Physiol.* (of an organ, such as the penis) capable of becoming erect.

eremite ('ɛrɪ,maɪt) *n.* a Christian hermit. [Greek *erēmos* lonely] —**eremitic** (,ɛrɪ'mɪtɪk) *adj.*

erg (ɜːg) *n.* the cgs unit of work or energy. [Greek *ergon* work]

ergo ('ɜːgəʊ) *conj.* therefore. [Latin]

ergonomics (,ɜːgə'nɒmɪks) *n.* (*functioning as sing.*) the study of the relationship between workers and their environment. [Greek *ergon* work + (*eco*)*nomics*] —,**ergo'nomic** *adj.*

ergot ('ɜːgət, -gɒt) *n.* **1.** a disease of a cereal, such as rye, caused by a fungus. **2.** the dried fungus used in medicine. [French]

Erin ('ɪərɪn, 'ɛərɪn) *n. Archaic or poetic.* Ireland. [Irish Gaelic]

ermine ('ɜːmɪn) *n., pl.* **-mines** *or* **-mine. 1.** the stoat in northern regions, where it has a white winter coat. **2.** the fur of this animal, used to trim state robes of judges, nobles, etc. [Medieval Latin *Armenius* (*mūs*) Armenian (mouse)]

erne *or* **ern** (ɜːn) *n.* a fish-eating sea eagle. [Old English *earn*]

Ernie ('ɜːnɪ) *n.* (in Britain) a computer that randomly selects winning numbers of Premium Bonds. [acronym of *Electronic Random Number Indicator Equipment*]

erode (ɪ'rəʊd) *vb.* **1.** to wear down or away or become worn down or away. **2.** to deteriorate or cause to deteriorate. [Latin *e-* away + *rōdere* to gnaw]

erogenous (ɪ'rɒdʒɪnəs) *adj.* **1.** sensitive to sexual stimulation. **2.** arousing sexual desire or giving sexual pleasure. [Greek *erōs* love + *-genē* born]

erosion (ɪ'rəʊʒən) *n.* the wearing away of rocks or soil by the action of water, ice, or wind. —**e'rosive** *or* **e'rosional** *adj.*

erotic (ɪ'rɒtɪk) *adj.* of, concerning, or arousing sexual desire or giving sexual pleasure. [Greek *erōs* love] —**e'rotical-ly** *adv.*

erotica (ɪ'rɒtɪkə) *pl. n.* explicitly sexual literature or art.

eroticism (ɪ'rɒtɪ,sɪzəm) *n.* **1.** erotic quality or nature. **2.** the use of sexually arousing symbolism in literature or art. **3.** sexual excitement or desire.

err (ɜː) *vb.* **1.** to make a mistake. **2.** to sin. [Latin *errāre*]

errand ('ɛrənd) *n.* **1.** a short trip to get or do something for someone. **2.** the purpose of such a trip. [Old English *ærende*]

errant ('ɛrənt) *adj.* **1.** *Archaic or literary.* wandering in search of adventure: *a knight errant.* **2.** erring or straying from the right course. [Latin *iter* journey] —**'errantry** *n.*

erratic (ɪ'rætɪk) *adj.* **1.** irregular or unpredictable: *erratic behaviour.* **2.** having no fixed course. ~*n.* **3.** a rock that has been transported by glacial action. [Latin *errāre* to wander] —**er'ratically** *adv.*

erratum (ɪ'rɑːtəm) *n., pl.* **-ta** (-tə). an error in writing or printing. [Latin]

erroneous (ɪ'rəʊnɪəs) *adj.* based on or containing error; incorrect. —**er'roneous-ly** *adv.*

error ('ɛrə) *n.* **1.** a mistake or inaccuracy. **2.** an incorrect belief or wrong judgment. **3.** the condition of deviating from accuracy or correctness. **4.** *Maths, statistics.* a measure of the difference between some quantity and an approximation of it. [Latin *errāre* to err]

ersatz ('ɛəzæts) *adj.* **1.** made in imitation. ~*n.* **2.** an ersatz substance. [German *ersetzen* to substitute]

Erse (ɜːs) *n.* **1.** Gaelic. ~*adj.* **2.** of or relating to the Gaelic language. [Lowland Scots *Erisch* Irish]

erstwhile ('ɜːst,waɪl) *adj.* **1.** former. ~*adv.* **2.** *Archaic.* formerly.

eruct (ɪ'rʌkt) *or* **eructate** *vb.* to belch. [Latin *e-* out + *ructāre* to belch] —**eructation** (,ɪrʌk'teɪʃən, ,ɪːrʌk-) *n.*

erudite ('ɛrʊ,daɪt) *adj.* having or showing scholarship; learned. [Latin *ērudīre* to polish] —**erudition** (,ɛrʊ'dɪʃən) *n.*

erupt (ɪ'rʌpt) *vb.* **1.** to eject (steam, water, and volcanic material) violently or (of volcanic material, etc.) to be so ejected. **2.** (of a blemish) to appear on the skin. **3.** to burst forth suddenly and violently. [Latin *e-* out + *rumpere* to burst] —**e'ruptive** *adj.* —**e'ruption** *n.*

erysipelas (,ɛrɪ'sɪpɪləs) *n.* an acute disease of the skin, with fever and raised purplish patches. [Greek *erusi-* red + *-pelas* skin]

erythrocyte (ɪ'rɪθrəʊ,saɪt) *n.* a red blood cell that transports oxygen through the body. [Greek *eruthros* red + *kutos* hollow vessel]

Es *Chem.* einsteinium.

escalate ('ɛskə,leɪt) *vb.* to increase or be increased in extent, intensity, or magnitude. [from *escalator*] —,**esca'lation** *n.*

escalator ('ɛskə,leɪtə) *n.* a moving staircase consisting of stair treads fixed to a conveyor belt. [Latin *scāla* ladder]

escalator clause *n.* a clause in a contract stipulating an adjustment in wages, prices, etc., esp. in relation to the cost of living.

escallop (ɛ'skɒləp) *n.* same as **scallop.**

escalope ('ɛskə,lɒp) *n.* a thin slice of meat, usually veal. [Old French: shell]

escapade ('ɛskə,peɪd) *n.* an adventure, esp. mischievous or unlawful. [French]

escape (ɪ'skeɪp) *vb.* **1.** to get away or break free from (confinement). **2.** to manage to avoid (something dangerous, unpleasant, or difficult). **3.** (of gases, liquids, etc.) to leak gradually. **4.** to elude; be forgotten by: *the figure escapes me.* **5.** to be articulated involuntarily from: *a cry escaped his lips.* ~*n.* **6.** the act of escaping or state of having escaped. **7.** avoidance of injury, harm, etc. **8.** a means of escape. **9.** a means of distraction or relief: *hill walking provides an escape for city* *dwellers.* **10.** a leakage. [Late Latin *e-* out + *cappa* cloak] —**es₁cap'ee** *n.*

escapement (ɪ'skeɪpmənt) *n.* a mechanism used in timepieces to provide periodic impulses to the pendulum or balance.

escape road *n.* a road, as on a hill, into which a car can be driven if the brakes fail.

escape velocity *n.* the minimum velocity necessary for a particle, space vehicle, etc. to escape from the gravitational field of the earth or other celestial body.

escapism (ɪ'skeɪpɪzəm) *n.* an inclination to retreat from unpleasant reality, as through fantasy. —**es'capist** *n., adj.*

escapologist (₁eskə'pɒlədʒɪst) *n.* an entertainer who specializes in freeing himself from chains, ropes, etc. —**esca'pology** *n.*

escarpment (ɪ'skɑːpmənt) *n.* **1.** the long continuous steep face of a ridge or mountain. **2.** a steep artificial slope in front of a fortified place. [French *escarpe*]

eschatology (₁eskə'tɒlədʒɪ) *n.* the branch of theology concerned with the end of the world. [Greek *eskhatos* last] —**eschatological** (₁eskətə'lɒdʒɪkʰl) *adj.*

escheat (ɪs'tʃiːt) *Law.* ~*n.* **1.** formerly, the reversion of property to the Crown or feudal lord in the absence of legal heirs. **2.** the property so reverting. ~*vb.* **3.** to take (land) or (of land) to revert by escheat. [Old French *escheoir* to fall to the lot of]

eschew (ɪs'tʃuː) *vb.* to keep clear of or abstain from (something disliked or harmful); avoid. [Old French *eschiver*] —**es'chewal** *n.*

escort *n.* ('eskɔːt). **1.** one or more persons or vehicles accompanying another or others for protection or as a mark of honour. **2.** a person who accompanies another of the opposite sex on a social occasion. ~*vb.* (ɪs'kɔːt). **3.** to accompany or attend as an escort. [French *escorte*]

escritoire (₁eskrɪ'twɑː) *n.* a writing desk with compartments and drawers. [Medieval Latin *scriptōrium* writing room in a monastery]

escudo (ɛ'skuːdəʊ) *n., pl.* **-dos.** the standard monetary unit of Portugal. [Spanish: shield]

esculent ('eskjulənt) *n.* **1.** any edible substance. ~*adj.* **2.** edible. [Latin *ēsculentus* good to eat]

escutcheon (ɪ'skʌtʃən) *n.* **1.** a shield, esp. displaying a coat of arms. **2. blot on one's escutcheon.** a stain on one's honour. [Latin *scūtum* shield]

Eskimo ('eskɪ₁məʊ) *n.* **1.** (*pl.* **-mos** or **-mo**) a member of a group of peoples who live in N Canada, Greenland, Alaska, and E Siberia. The Eskimos are more properly referred to as the **Inuit. 2.** the language of these peoples. ~*adj.* **3.** of or relating to the Eskimos. [prob. from American Indian *esquimantsic* eaters of raw flesh]

Eskimo dog *n.* a large powerful breed of dog with a long thick coat and curled tail, used by the Eskimos to pull sledges.

ESN educationally subnormal.

esoteric (₁esəʊ'tɛrɪk) *adj.* understood by only a small number of people, esp. because they have a special knowledge. [Greek *esōterō* inner] —**eso'terically** *adv.*

ESP extrasensory perception.

esp. especially.

espadrille (₁espə'drɪl) *n.* a light canvas shoe with a braided cord sole. [French]

espalier (ɪ'spæljə) *n.* **1.** a shrub or fruit tree trained to grow flat. **2.** the trellis on which such plants are trained. [French]

esparto *or* **esparto grass** (ɛ'spɑːtəʊ) *n., pl.* **-tos.** any of various grasses of S Europe and N Africa, used to make ropes, mats, etc. [Greek *spartos* a kind of rush]

especial (ɪ'spɛʃəl) *adj. Formal.* same as **special.** [Latin *speciālis* individual]

especially (ɪ'spɛʃəlɪ) *adv.* **1.** particularly: *I love fruit, especially apples.* **2.** more than usually.

Esperanto (₁espə'ræntəʊ) *n.* an international artificial language. [lit.: the one who hopes, pseudonym of Dr L. L. Zamenhof, its inventor] —**Espe'rantist** *n., adj.*

espionage ('espɪə₁nɑːʒ) *n.* **1.** the use of spies to obtain secret information, esp. by governments. **2.** the act of spying. [French]

esplanade (₁esplə'neɪd) *n.* a long open level stretch of ground, esp. beside the seashore or in front of a fortified place. [French]

espousal (ɪ'spaʊzʰl) *n.* **1.** adoption or support: *an espousal of new beliefs.* **2.** (*sometimes pl.*) *Archaic.* a marriage or betrothal ceremony.

espouse (ɪ'spaʊz) *vb.* **1.** to adopt or give support to (a cause, ideal, etc.). **2.** *Archaic.* (esp. of a man) to marry. [Latin *spōnsāre*]

espresso (ɛ'sprɛsəʊ) *n., pl.* **-sos. 1.** coffee made by forcing steam or boiling water through ground coffee. **2.** a machine for making coffee in this way. [Italian: pressed]

esprit (ɛ'spriː) *n.* spirit, liveliness, or wit. [French]

esprit de corps (ɛ'spriː də 'kɔː) *n.* consciousness of and pride in belonging to a particular group. [French]

espy (ɪ'spaɪ) *vb.* **espying, espied.** to catch sight of; detect. [Old French *espier*]

Esq. esquire.

esquire (ɪ'skwaɪə) *n.* **1.** *Chiefly Brit.* a title of respect, usually abbreviated *Esq.*, placed after a man's name. **2.** (in medieval times) the attendant of a knight. [Late Latin *scūtārius* shield bearer]

ESRO ('ezrəʊ) *n.* European Space Research Organization.

essay *n.* ('eseɪ; *sense 2 also* ɛ'seɪ). **1.** a short literary composition. **2.** an attempt. ~*vb.* (ɛ'seɪ). **3.** to attempt (something). [Old French *essai* an attempt]

essayist ('eseɪɪst) *n.* a person who writes essays.

essence ('esʰns) *n.* **1.** the basic, central, and most important feature of something which determines its identity. **2.** the most distinctive element of a thing. **3.** a concentrated liquid used to flavour food. **4.** a perfume. **5. in essence.** essentially. **6. of the essence.** vitally important. [Latin *esse* to be]

essential (ɪˈsɛnʃəl) *adj.* **1.** vitally important; absolutely necessary. **2.** basic; fundamental. ~*n.* **3.** something fundamental or indispensable. —**esˈsentially** *adv.*

essential oil *n.* any of various volatile oils in plants, having the odour or flavour of the plant from which they are extracted. [Latin *stabilis* firm, stable]

EST 1. (in the U.S. and Canada) Eastern Standard Time. **2.** electric-shock treatment.

est. 1. established. **2.** estimate(d).

establish (ɪˈstæblɪʃ) *vb.* **1.** to create or set up (an organization, etc.) on a permanent basis. **2.** to make secure or permanent in a certain place, job, etc. **3.** to prove correct: *establish a fact.* **4.** to cause (a principle) to be accepted: *establish a precedent.* **5.** to give (a Church) the status of a national institution. [Latin *stabilis* firm, stable]

establishment (ɪˈstæblɪʃmənt) *n.* **1.** the act of establishing or state of being established. **2. a.** a business organization or other institution. **b.** a place of business. **3.** the staff of an organization. **4.** a body of employees.

Establishment (ɪˈstæblɪʃmənt) *n.* **the.** a group of people having authority within a society: usually seen as conservative.

estate (ɪˈsteɪt) *n.* **1.** a large piece of landed property, esp. in the country. **2.** *Chiefly Brit.* a large area of property development, esp. of new houses or factories. **3.** *Law.* property or possessions, esp. of a deceased person. **4.** an order or class in a political community: the lords spiritual (**first estate**), lords temporal or peers (**second estate**), and commons (**third estate**). [Latin *status* condition]

estate agent *n.* **1.** *Brit.* an agent concerned with the valuation, lease, and sale of property. **2.** the administrator of a large landed property.

estate car *n. Brit.* a car which has a long body with a door at the back end and luggage space behind the rear seats.

estate duty *n.* same as **death duty.**

esteem (ɪˈstiːm) *vb.* **1.** to have great respect or high regard for (someone). **2.** *Formal.* to judge or consider: *I esteem him nothing but a fool.* ~*n.* **3.** high regard or respect; good opinion. [Latin *aestimāre* to assess the worth of] —**esˈteemed** *adj.*

ester (ˈɛstə) *n. Chem.* a compound produced by the reaction between an acid and an alcohol. [German]

estimable (ˈɛstɪməbˀl) *adj.* worthy of respect.

estimate *vb.* (ˈɛstɪˌmeɪt). **1.** to form an approximate idea of (size, cost, etc.); calculate roughly. **2.** to form an opinion about; judge. **3.** to submit (an approximate price) for (a job) to a prospective client. ~*n.* (ˈɛstɪmɪt). **4.** an approximate calculation. **5.** a statement of the likely charge for certain work. **6.** an opinion. [Latin *aestimāre* to assess the worth of] —**ˈestiˌmator** *n.*

estimation (ˌɛstɪˈmeɪʃən) *n.* **1.** a considered opinion; judgment. **2.** the act of estimating.

estrange (ɪˈstreɪndʒ) *vb.* to antagonize (someone previously friendly); alienate. [Latin *extrāneus* foreign] —**esˈtranged** *adj.* —**esˈtrangement** *n.*

estuary (ˈɛstjʊərɪ) *n.* the widening channel of a river where it nears the sea. [Latin *aestus* tide] —**ˈestuarine** *adj.*

ETA estimated time of arrival.

et al. 1. and elsewhere. [Latin *et alibi*] **2.** and others. [Latin *et alii*]

etc. et cetera.

et cetera *or* **etcetera** (ɪt ˈsɛtrə) *n. and vb. substitute.* **1.** and the rest; and others; and so forth. **2.** or the like; or something similar. [Latin *et* and + *cetera* the other (things)]

etceteras (ɪtˈsɛtrəz) *pl. n.* miscellaneous extra things or persons.

etch (ɛtʃ) *vb.* **1.** to wear away the surface of (a metal, glass, etc.) by the action of an acid. **2.** to cut (a design or pattern) on (a metal or other printing plate) by the action of acid. **3.** to imprint vividly: *the horror of the crash was etched on her memory.* [Dutch *etsen*] —**ˈetcher** *n.*

etching (ˈɛtʃɪŋ) *n.* **1.** the art or process of preparing or printing etched designs. **2.** an etched plate. **3.** an impression made from an etched plate.

eternal (ɪˈtɜːnˀl) *adj.* **1.** without beginning or end; lasting for ever. **2.** (*often cap.*) a name applied to God. **3.** unchanged by time: *eternal truths.* **4.** seemingly unceasing: *eternal bickering.* [Latin *aeternus*] —**eˈternally** *adv.*

eternal triangle *n.* an emotional or sexual relationship in which there are conflicts between a man and two women or a woman and two men.

eternity (ɪˈtɜːnɪtɪ) *n., pl.* **-ties. 1.** endless or infinite time. **2.** the state of being eternal. **3.** the timeless existence after death. **4.** a seemingly endless period of time: *I waited for what seemed like an eternity.*

eternity ring *n.* a ring given as a token of lasting affection, esp. one set all around with stones to symbolize continuity.

ethane (ˈiːθeɪn) *n.* a flammable gaseous alkane obtained from natural gas and petroleum: used as a fuel. [from *ethyl*]

ethanoic acid (ˌɛθəˈnəʊɪk) *n.* same as **acetic acid.**

ethanol (ˈɛθəˌnɒl) *n.* same as **alcohol** (sense 1).

ethene (ˈɛθiːn) *n.* same as **ethylene.**

ether (ˈiːθə) *n.* **1.** a colourless volatile highly flammable liquid: used as a solvent and anaesthetic. **2.** the medium formerly believed to fill all space and to transmit electromagnetic waves. **3.** the upper regions of the atmosphere; clear sky. **4.** Also (for senses 2 and 3): **aether.** [Greek *aithein* to burn]

ethereal (ɪˈθɪərɪəl) *adj.* **1.** extremely delicate or refined. **2.** heavenly; spiritual. [Greek *aithēr* ether] —**eˈthereally** *adv.*

ethic ('εθɪk) *n.* a moral principle or set of moral values held by an individual or group. [Greek *ēthos* custom]

ethical ('εθɪk*ə*l) *adj.* 1. of or based on a system of moral beliefs about right and wrong. 2. in accordance with principles of professional conduct. 3 of or relating to ethics. —'**ethically** *adv.*

ethics ('εθɪks) *n.* 1. (*functioning as pl.*) a code of behaviour, esp. of a particular group, profession, or individual. 2. (*functioning as pl.*) the moral fitness of a decision, course of action, etc. 3. (*functioning as sing.*) the study of the moral value of human conduct.

Ethiopian (ˌiːθɪ'əupɪən) *adj.* 1. of Ethiopia. ~*n.* 2. a person from Ethiopia.

ethnic ('εθnɪk) *or* **ethnical** *adj.* 1. of or relating to a human group having racial, religious, and linguistic characteristics in common. 2. characteristic of another culture, esp. a peasant one: *ethnic music.* [Greek *ethnos* race] —'**ethnically** *adv.*

ethnocentric (ˌεθnəʊ'sεntrɪk) *adj.* of or relating to the belief that one's own nation, culture, or group is intrinsically superior. —**ethnocentricity** (ˌεθnəʊsεn'trɪsɪtɪ) *n.*

ethnology (εθ'nɒlədʒɪ) *n.* the branch of anthropology that deals with races and peoples and their relations to one another. —**ethnological** (ˌεθnə'lɒdʒɪk*ə*l) *adj.* —**eth'nologist** *n.*

ethos ('iːθɒs) *n.* the distinctive spirit and attitudes of a people, culture, etc. [Greek]

ethyl ('iːθaɪl, 'εθɪl) *n.* (*modifier*) of, consisting of, or containing the monovalent group C_2H_5–. [from *ether*]

ethyl alcohol *n.* same as **alcohol** (sense 1).

ethylene ('εθɪˌliːn) *or* **ethene** ('εθiːn) *n.* a colourless flammable gaseous alkene used to make polythene and other chemicals.

etiolate ('iːtɪəʊˌleɪt) *vb.* 1. *Bot.* to whiten (a green plant) through lack of sunlight. 2. to become or cause to become pale and weak. [French *étioler*] —ˌ**etio'lation** *n.*

etiology (ˌiːtɪ'ɒlədʒɪ) *n.*, *pl.* -**gies.** 1. the study of causation. 2. the study of the cause of diseases. [Greek *aitia* cause + -LOGY] —**etiological** (ˌiːtɪə'lɒdʒɪk*ə*l) *adj.*

etiquette ('εtɪˌkεt) *n.* 1. the customs or rules of behaviour regarded as correct in social life. 2. a conventional code of practice in certain professions. [French]

Eton collar ('iːt*ə*n) *n.* a broad stiff white collar worn outside a Eton jacket.

Eton crop *n.* a very short mannish hairstyle worn by women in the 1920s.

Eton jacket *n.* a waist-length jacket, open in front, formerly worn by pupils of Eton College.

Etruscan (ɪ'trʌskən) *n.* 1. a member of an ancient people of Etruria in central Italy. 2. the language of the Etruscans. ~*adj.* 3. of Etruria or the Etruscans.

étude ('eɪtjuːd) *n.* a short musical composition for a solo instrument, esp. for exercise or exploiting virtuosity. [French]

etymology (ˌεtɪ'mɒlədʒɪ) *n.*, *pl.* -**gies.** 1. the study of the sources and development

of words. 2. an account of the source and development of a word. [Greek *etumon* basic meaning + -LOGY] —**etymological** (ˌεtɪmə'lɒdʒɪk*ə*l) *adj.* —ˌ**ety'mologist** *n.*

Eu *Chem.* europium.

eucalyptus (ˌjuːkə'lɪptəs) *or* **eucalypt** ('juːkəˌlɪpt) *n.*, *pl.* -**lyptuses, -lypti** (-'lɪptaɪ), *or* -**lypts.** any of a mostly Australian genus of trees, widely cultivated for timber and gum, and for the medicinal oil in their leaves (**eucalyptus oil**). [Greek *eu-* well + *kaluptos* covered]

Eucharist ('juːkərɪst) *n.* 1. the Christian sacrament commemorating Christ's Last Supper by the consecration of bread and wine. 2. the consecrated elements of bread and wine. [Greek *eukharistos* thankful] —ˌ**Eucha'ristic** *adj.*

Euclidean *or* **Euclidian** (juː'klɪdɪən) *adj.* denoting a system of geometry based on the rules of Euclid, 3rd-century B.C. Greek mathematician.

eugenics (juː'dʒεnɪks) *n.* (*functioning as sing.*) the study of methods of improving the human race, esp. by selective breeding. [Greek *eugenēs* well-born] —**eu'genic** *adj.* —**eu'genically** *adv.* —**eu'genicist** *n.*

eulogize *or* -**gise** (ˈjuːləˌdʒaɪz) *vb.* to praise (a person or thing) highly in speech or writing. —ˌ**eulo'gistic** *adj.*

eulogy ('juːlədʒɪ) *n.*, *pl.* -**gies.** 1. a speech or piece of writing praising a person or thing, esp. a person who has recently died. 2. high praise. [Greek]

eunuch ('juːnək) *n.* a man who has been castrated, esp. (formerly) a guard in a harem. [Greek *eunoukhos* bedchamber attendant]

euphemism ('juːfɪˌmɪzəm) *n.* an inoffensive word or phrase substituted for one considered offensive or upsetting, such as *departed* for *dead.* [Greek *eu-* well + *phēmē* speech] —ˌ**euphe'mistic** *adj.* —ˌ**euphe'mistically** *adv.*

euphonious (juː'fəʊnɪəs) *adj.* pleasing to the ear.

euphonium (juː'fəʊnɪəm) *n.* a brass musical instrument with four valves. [*euph(ony* + *harm)onium*]

euphony ('juːfənɪ) *n.*, *pl.* -**nies.** a pleasing sound, esp. in speech. [Greek *eu-* well + *phōnē* voice]

euphoria (juː'fɔːrɪə) *n.* a feeling of great elation, esp. when exaggerated. [Greek *eu-* well + *pherein* to bear] —**euphoric** (juː'fɒrɪk) *adj.*

euphuism ('juːfjuːˌɪzəm) *n.* an artificial high-flown prose style. [after *Euphues*, prose romance by John Lyly] —ˌ**euphu'istic** *adj.*

Eur. Europe(an).

Eurasian (jʊə'reɪʒən) *adj.* 1. of Europe and Asia. 2. of mixed European and Asian descent. ~*n.* 3. a person of mixed European and Asian descent.

Euratom (jʊə'rætɒm) *n.* European Atomic Energy Community.

eureka (jʊ'riːkə) *interj.* an exclamation of triumph on discovering or solving something. [Greek *heurēka* I have found (it)]

eurhythmics or esp. U.S. **eurythmics** (juːˈrɪðmɪks) n. (functioning as sing.) a system of training through physical movement to music. [Greek eu- well + rhuthmos rhythm]

Euro- (ˈjʊərəʊ) or before a vowel **Eur-** combining form. Europe or European.

European (ˌjʊərəˈpɪən) adj. 1. of or relating to Europe. 2. native to Europe. ~n. 3. a person from Europe. 4. a person of European descent. 5. S. African. any White person. —**Euroˈpeanˌism** n.

European Community or **European Economic Community** n. formal names for the **Common Market**.

europium (juˈrəʊpɪəm) n. a silvery-white element of the lanthanide series. Symbol: Eu [after Europe]

Eustachian tube (juːˈsteɪʃən) n. a tube that connects the middle ear with the pharynx and equalizes the pressure between the two sides of the eardrum. [after Bartolomeo Eustachio, anatomist]

euthanasia (ˌjuːθəˈneɪzɪə) n. the act of killing someone painlessly, esp. to relieve suffering from an incurable illness. [Greek: easy death]

eV electronvolt.

evacuate (ɪˈvækjʊˌeɪt) vb. 1. to send (people) away (from a place of danger) to a place of safety: children in London were evacuated to the country during the Second World War. 2. to make empty. 3. Physiol. to discharge (waste) from (the body). [Latin ēvacuāre to empty] —eˌvacuˈation n. —eˌvacuˈee n.

evade (ɪˈveɪd) vb. 1. to get away from or avoid (imprisonment, captors, etc.). 2. to get around, shirk, or dodge (the law, a duty, etc.). 3. to avoid answering (a question). [Latin ēvādere to go forth]

evaluate (ɪˈvæljʊˌeɪt) vb. 1. to ascertain or set the value of. 2. to judge the quality of. [French évaluer] —eˌvaluˈation n.

evanesce (ˌevəˈnes) vb. Formal. to fade gradually from sight; vanish. [Latin ēvānēscere]

evanescent (ˌevəˈnesᵊnt) adj. quickly fading away; ephemeral or transitory. —ˌevaˈnescence n.

evangelical (ˌiːvænˈdʒelɪkᵊl) Christianity. ~adj. 1. of or following from the Gospels. 2. of certain Protestant sects which emphasize personal conversion and faith in atonement through the death of Christ as a means of salvation. ~n. 3. a member of an evangelical sect. [Greek evangelion good news] —ˌevanˈgelicalism n. —ˌevanˈgelically adv.

evangelism (ɪˈvændʒɪˌlɪzəm) n. the practice of spreading the Christian gospel.

evangelist (ɪˈvændʒɪlɪst) n. a preacher, sometimes itinerant. —eˌvangeˈlistic adj.

Evangelist (ɪˈvændʒɪlɪst) n. any of the writers of the Gospels: Matthew, Mark, Luke, or John.

evangelize or **-lise** (ɪˈvændʒɪˌlaɪz) vb. to preach the Christian gospel (to). —eˌvangeliˈzation or **-liˈsation** n.

evaporate (ɪˈvæpəˌreɪt) vb. 1. to change

from a liquid or solid to a vapour. 2. to lose or cause to lose liquid by vaporization leaving a more concentrated residue. [Latin e- out + vapor steam] —eˈvaporable adj. —eˌvapoˈration n.

evaporated milk n. thick unsweetened tinned milk from which some of the water has been evaporated.

evasion (ɪˈveɪʒən) n. 1. the act of evading, esp. a duty, responsibility, etc., by cunning or illegal means: tax evasion. 2. cunning or deception used to dodge a question, duty, etc.

evasive (ɪˈveɪsɪv) adj. 1. seeking to evade; not straightforward: an evasive answer. 2. avoiding or seeking to avoid trouble or difficulties: evasive action. —eˈvasively adv.

eve (iːv) n. 1. the evening or day before some special event. 2. the period immediately before an event: the eve of war. 3. Archaic. evening. [var. of EVEN²]

even¹ (ˈiːvᵊn) adj. 1. level and regular; flat. 2. on the same level or in the same plane (as). 3. without fluctuation; regular; constant. 4. not easily excited; calm: an even temper. 5. equally balanced between two sides. 6. equal in number, quantity, etc. 7. a. (of a number) divisible by two. b. indicated by such a number: the even pages. 8. denoting alternatives, events, etc., that have an equal probability: an even chance of winning or losing. 9. equal, as in score; level. 10. **even money** or **evens**. a bet in which the winnings are exactly the same as the amount staked. 11. **get even (with)**. Informal. to exact revenge (on); settle accounts (with). ~adv. 12. (intensifier; used to suggest that the content of a statement is unexpected or paradoxical): even an idiot can do that. 13. (intensifier; used with comparative forms): even better. 14. used to introduce a word that is stronger and more accurate than one already used: they appeared satisfied, even happy, with the outcome. 15. used preceding a hypothesis to emphasize that whether or not the condition is fulfilled, the statement remains valid: even if she died he wouldn't care. 16. **even so**. in spite of any assertion to the contrary: nevertheless. 17. **even though**. despite the fact that. ~See also **even out**, **even up**. [Old English efen] —ˈevenly adv. —ˈevenness n.

even² (ˈiːvᵊn) n. Archaic. 1. eve. 2. evening. [Old English æfen]

even-handed adj. fair; impartial.

evening (ˈiːvnɪŋ) n. 1. the latter part of the day, esp. from late afternoon until nightfall. 2. the latter or concluding period: the evening of one's life. ~adj. 3. of or in the evening. [Old English æfnung]

evening dress n. clothes for a formal occasion during the evening.

evening primrose n. a plant having yellow flowers that open in the evening.

evening star n. a planet, usually Venus, seen shining brightly in the west just after sunset.

even out vb. to make or become even, as by the removal of bumps, inequalities, etc.

evensong (ˈiːvᵊnˌsɒŋ) *n. Church of England.* the daily evening service. Also called: **Evening Prayer.**

event (ɪˈvɛnt) *n.* **1.** anything that takes place, esp. something important; an incident. **2.** the actual or final outcome (esp. in **in the event**). **3.** any one contest in a sporting programme. **4. at all events** *or* **in any event.** whatever happens. **5. in the event of.** if (such a thing) happens. **6. in the event that.** if it should happen that. [Latin *ēvenīre* to happen]

eventful (ɪˈvɛntfʊl) *adj.* full of exciting or important incidents.

eventide (ˈiːvᵊnˌtaɪd) *n. Archaic or poetic.* evening.

eventing (ɪˈvɛntɪŋ) *n. Chiefly Brit.* riding competitions (esp. **three-day events**), usually involving cross-country riding, jumping, and dressage.

eventual (ɪˈvɛntʃʊəl) *adj.* happening in due course; ultimate. —**eˈventually** *adv.*

eventuality (ɪˌvɛntʃʊˈælɪtɪ) *n., pl.* **-ties.** a possible event, occurrence, or result.

eventuate (ɪˈvɛntʃʊˌeɪt) *vb.* (often foll. by *in*) to result ultimately (in).

even up *vb.* to make or become equal.

ever (ˈɛvə) *adv.* **1.** at any time: *did you ever meet her?* **2.** always: *ever optimistic.* **3.** used to give emphasis: *come as fast as ever you can.* **4.** *Informal, chiefly Brit.* (intensifier, in **ever so, ever such,** and **ever such a**). [Old English *ǣfre*]

evergreen (ˈɛvəˌgriːn) *adj.* **1.** (of certain trees and shrubs) bearing foliage throughout the year. ~*n.* **2.** an evergreen tree or shrub.

everlasting (ˌɛvəˈlɑːstɪŋ) *adj.* **1.** never coming to an end; eternal. **2.** lasting so long or occurring so often as to become tedious. ~*n.* **3.** eternity. **4.** a type of flower that retains its colour when dried. —ˌ**everˈlastingly** *adv.*

evermore (ˌɛvəˈmɔː) *adv.* all time to come.

every (ˈɛvrɪ) *det.* **1.** each one without exception: *every person in the room.* **2.** the greatest or best possible: *every hope.* **3.** each: *every third day.* **4. every bit.** (used in comparisons with *as*) just; equally. **5. every other.** each alternate. [Old English *ǣfre*]

everybody (ˈɛvrɪˌbɒdɪ) *pron.* every person; everyone.

everyday (ˈɛvrɪˌdeɪ) *adj.* **1.** happening each day. **2.** commonplace or usual. **3.** suitable for or used on ordinary days.

Everyman (ˈɛvrɪˌmæn) *n.* the ordinary person; common man. [after the central figure in a medieval morality play]

everyone (ˈɛvrɪˌwʌn) *pron.* every person; everybody.

everything (ˈɛvrɪˌθɪŋ) *pron.* **1.** the whole; all things: *everything went smoothly.* **2.** the thing that is most important: *money isn't everything.*

everywhere (ˈɛvrɪˌwɛə) *adv.* to or in all parts or places.

evict (ɪˈvɪkt) *vb.* to expel (a tenant) from property by process of law; turn out. [Latin *ēvincere* to vanquish utterly] —**eˈviction** *n.*

evidence (ˈɛvɪdəns) *n.* **1.** ground for belief or disbelief; data on which to base proof. **2.** a mark or sign that makes evident. **3.** *Law.* matter produced before a court of law in an attempt to prove or disprove a point in issue. **4. in evidence.** on display; apparent. ~*vb.* **5.** to make evident; show clearly.

evident (ˈɛvɪdənt) *adj.* easy to see or understand; apparent. [Latin *vidēre* to see] —ˈ**evidently** *adv.*

evidential (ˌɛvɪˈdɛnʃəl) *adj.* of, serving as, or based on evidence. —ˌ**eviˈdentially** *adv.*

evil (ˈiːvᵊl) *adj.* **1.** morally wrong; wicked. **2.** causing harm. **3.** very unpleasant: *an evil smell.* ~*n.* **4.** wickedness. **5.** a force of wickedness. [Old English *yfel*] —ˈ**evilly** *adv.* —ˈ**evilness** *n.*

evildoer (ˈiːvᵊlˌduːə) *n.* a person who does evil. —ˈ**evilˌdoing** *n.*

evil eye *n.* **the.** a look superstitiously supposed to have the power of inflicting harm.

evince (ɪˈvɪns) *vb.* to make evident; show (something) clearly. [Latin *ēvincere* to overcome]

eviscerate (ɪˈvɪsəˌreɪt) *vb.* to remove the internal organs of; disembowel. [Latin *e-* out + *viscera* entrails] —**eˌviscerˈation** *n.*

evocation (ˌɛvəˈkeɪʃən) *n.* the act of evoking. —**evocative** (ɪˈvɒkətɪv) *adj.*

evoke (ɪˈvəʊk) *vb.* **1.** to call or summon up (a memory, feeling, etc.), esp. from the past. **2.** to provoke; elicit. [Latin *ēvocāre* to call forth]

evolution (ˌiːvəˈluːʃən) *n.* **1.** *Biol.* a gradual change in the characteristics of a population of animals or plants over successive generations. **2.** a gradual development, esp. to a more complex form. **3.** the act of throwing off, as heat, gas, vapour, etc. **4.** *Mil.* an exercise carried out in accordance with a set procedure. [Latin *ēvolūtiō* an unrolling] —ˌ**evoˈlutionary** *adj.*

evolve (ɪˈvɒlv) *vb.* **1.** to develop gradually. **2.** (of animal or plant species) to undergo evolution. **3.** to give off (heat, gas, vapour, etc.). [Latin *ēvolvere* to unfold]

ewe (juː) *n.* a female sheep. [Old English *ēowu*]

ewer (ˈjuːə) *n.* a large jug with a wide mouth. [Latin *aqua* water]

ex[1] (ɛks) *prep.* **1.** *Finance.* excluding; without: *ex dividend.* **2.** *Commerce.* sold from: *ex warehouse.* [Latin: out of, from]

ex[2] (ɛks) *n. Informal.* one's former wife or husband.

ex- *prefix.* **1.** out of; outside; from: *exodus.* **2.** former: *ex-wife.* [Latin]

exacerbate (ɛkˈsæsəˌbeɪt) *vb.* to make (pain, emotion, or a situation) worse. [Latin *acerbus* bitter] —**exˌacerˈbation** *n.*

exact (ɪgˈzækt) *adj.* **1.** correct in every detail; strictly accurate. **2.** precise, as opposed to approximate. **3.** based on measurement and the formulation of laws:

an exact science. ~*vb.* **4.** to force (payment of); extort. **5.** to demand as a right; insist upon. [Latin *exigere* to demand]

exacting (ɪgˈzæktɪŋ) *adj.* making rigorous or excessive demands.

exaction (ɪgˈzækʃən) *n.* **1.** an exacting. **2.** an extortion. **3.** a sum or payment exacted.

exactitude (ɪgˈzæktɪˌtjuːd) *n.* the quality of being exact; precision; accuracy.

exactly (ɪgˈzæktlɪ) *adv.* **1.** in an exact manner; accurately or precisely. **2.** in every respect; just. **3.** just so! precisely!

exaggerate (ɪgˈzædʒəˌreɪt) *vb.* **1.** to regard or represent as greater than is true. **2.** to make greater, more noticeable, etc. [Latin *exaggerāre* to heap up] —**exˈaggerˌated** *adj.* —**exˈaggerˌatedly** *adv.* —**exˌaggerˈation** *n.*

exalt (ɪgˈzɔːlt) *vb.* **1.** to elevate in rank, dignity, etc. **2.** to praise highly. **3.** to fill with joy or delight. [Latin *exaltāre* to raise] —**exˈalted** *adj.* —ˌ**exalˈtation** *n.*

exam (ɪgˈzæm) *n.* short for **examination**.

examination (ɪgˌzæmɪˈneɪʃən) *n.* **1.** the act of examining. **2.** *Education.* written exercises, oral questions, or practical tasks set to test a candidate's knowledge and skill. **3.** *Med.* physical inspection of a patient. **4.** *Law.* the formal interrogation of a person on oath.

examine (ɪgˈzæmɪn) *vb.* **1.** to inspect carefully or in detail; investigate. **2.** *Education.* to test the knowledge of (a candidate) in (a subject) by written or oral questions. **3.** *Med.* to investigate the state of health of (a patient). **4.** *Law.* to interrogate (a person) formally on oath. [Latin *exāmināre* to weigh] —**exˌamiˈnee** *n.* —**exˈaminer** *n.*

example (ɪgˈzɑːmpʰl) *n.* **1.** a specimen that is typical of its group; sample. **2.** a person, action, or thing that is worthy of imitation. **3.** a precedent or model. **4.** a punishment or the person punished regarded as a warning to others. **5. for example.** as an illustration. [Latin *exemplum*]

exasperate (ɪgˈzɑːspəˌreɪt) *vb.* to cause great irritation to. [Latin *exasperāre* to make rough] —**exˈasperˌated** *adj.* —**exˈasperˌating** *adj.* —**exˈasperˌation** *n.*

ex cathedra (ˈɛks kəˈθiːdrə) *adj., adv.* **1.** with authority. **2.** *R.C. Church.* (of doctrines of faith or morals) defined by the pope as infallibly true. [Latin: from the chair]

excavate (ˈɛkskəˌveɪt) *vb.* **1.** to unearth (buried objects) methodically to discover information about the past. **2.** to remove (soil) by digging. **3.** to make (a hole) in (solid matter) by hollowing. [Latin *excavare* to make hollow] —ˌ**excaˈvation** *n.* —**ˈexcaˌvator** *n.*

exceed (ɪkˈsiːd) *vb.* **1.** to be greater in degree or quantity. **2.** to go beyond the limit of. [Latin *excēdere* to go beyond]

exceedingly (ɪkˈsiːdɪŋlɪ) *adv.* very; extremely.

excel (ɪkˈsɛl) *vb.* **-celling, -celled. 1.** to be superior to (another or others); surpass.

2. (foll. by *in* or *at*) to be outstandingly good. [Latin *excellere* to rise up]

excellence (ˈɛksələns) *n.* the quality of being exceptionally good. —**ˈexcellent** *adj.*

Excellency (ˈɛksələnsɪ) *or* **Excellence** *n., pl.* **-lencies** *or* **-lences.** (usually preceded by *Your, His,* or *Her*) a title used to address a high-ranking official, such as an ambassador.

except (ɪkˈsɛpt) *prep.* **1.** Also: **except for.** other than; apart from. **2. except that.** (*conj.*) but for the fact that. ~*conj.* **3.** *Archaic.* unless. ~*vb.* **4.** to leave out; exclude. [Latin *excipere* to take out]

excepting (ɪkˈsɛptɪŋ) *prep.* except.

exception (ɪkˈsɛpʃən) *n.* **1.** the act of excepting or fact of being excepted; omission. **2.** anything excluded from or not in conformance with a general rule, principle, class, etc. **3. take exception.** (usually foll. by *to*) to make objections to.

exceptionable (ɪkˈsɛpʃənəbʰl) *adj.* open to objection.

exceptional (ɪkˈsɛpʃənʰl) *adj.* **1.** forming an exception. **2.** having much more than average intelligence, ability, or skill.

excerpt *n.* (ˈɛksɜːpt). **1.** a passage taken from a book, speech, etc.; extract. ~*vb.* (ɛkˈsɜːpt). **2.** to take (a passage) from a book, speech, etc. [Latin *excerptum* (something) picked out] —**exˈcerption** *n.*

excess *n.* (ɪkˈsɛs). **1.** the state or act of going beyond normal or permitted limits. **2.** an immoderate or abnormal amount. **3.** the amount, number, etc., by which one thing exceeds another. **4.** overindulgence or intemperance. **5. in excess of.** more than. **6. to excess.** immoderately. ~*adj.* (ˈɛksɛs). **7.** more than normal, necessary, or permitted: *excess weight.* [Latin *excēdere* to go beyond] —**exˈcessive** *adj.* —**exˈcessively** *adv.*

excess luggage *or* **baggage** *n.* luggage that is more in weight or number of pieces than an airline, etc., will carry free.

exchange (ɪksˈtʃeɪndʒ) *vb.* **1.** to give up or transfer (one thing) for an equivalent. **2.** to give and receive (information, ideas, etc.). **3.** to replace (one thing) with another, esp. to replace unsatisfactory goods. ~*n.* **4.** the act of exchanging. **5.** anything given or received as an equivalent or substitute for something else. **6.** an argument. **7.** Also called: **telephone exchange.** a centre in which telephone lines are interconnected. **8.** a place where securities or commodities are traded, esp. by brokers or merchants. **9.** the system by which commercial debts are settled, esp. by bills of exchange, without direct payment of money. **10.** a transfer of sums of money of equivalent value, as between different currencies. [Latin *cambīre* to barter] —**exˈchangeable** *adj.*

exchange rate *n.* the rate at which the currency unit of one country may be exchanged for that of another.

exchequer (ɪksˈtʃɛkə) *n.* (often cap.) *Government.* (in Britain and certain other* countries) the accounting department of the Treasury. [Old French *eschequier*]

excise[1] (ˈɛksaɪz) *n.* **1.** a tax on goods, such as spirits, produced for the home market. **2.** *Brit.* that section of the government service responsible for the collection of excise, now the Board of Customs and Excise. [Latin *assidēre* to sit beside, assist in judging]

excise[2] (ɪkˈsaɪz) *vb.* **1.** to delete (a passage). **2.** to remove (an organ or part) surgically. [Latin *excidere* to cut down] —**excision** (ɪkˈsɪʒən) *n.*

exciseman (ˈɛksaɪzˌmæn) *n.*, *pl.* **-men.** *Brit.* (formerly) a government agent who collected excise and prevented smuggling.

excitable (ɪkˈsaɪtəbᵊl) *adj.* easily excited; volatile. —**ex**ˌcita**ˈbility** *n.*

excite (ɪkˈsaɪt) *vb.* **1.** to arouse (a person), esp. to pleasurable anticipation or nervous agitation. **2.** to arouse (an emotion, response, etc.); evoke. **3.** to cause; stir up: *to excite suspicion.* **4.** to arouse sexually. **5.** *Physiol.* to cause a response in (an organ, tissue, or part). **6.** to raise (an atom, molecule, etc.) to a higher energy level. [Latin *excitāre* to stimulate] —**ex**ˈcited *adj.* —**ex**ˈcitedly *adv.*

excitement (ɪkˈsaɪtmənt) *n.* **1.** the state of being excited. **2.** a person or thing that excites.

exciting (ɪkˈsaɪtɪŋ) *adj.* causing excitement; stirring; stimulating. —**ex**ˈciting**ly** *adv.*

exclaim (ɪkˈskleɪm) *vb.* to cry out or speak suddenly or excitedly, as from surprise, delight, horror, etc. [Latin *exclāmāre*]

exclamation (ˌɛkskləˈmeɪʃən) *n.* **1.** an abrupt or excited cry or utterance. **2.** the act of exclaiming. —**exclamatory** (ɪkˈsklæmətrɪ) *adj.*

exclamation mark *or U.S.* **point** *n.* the punctuation mark ! used after exclamations and vehement commands.

exclude (ɪkˈskluːd) *vb.* **1.** to keep out; prevent from entering. **2.** to leave out of consideration. [Latin *exclūdere*] —**ex**ˈclu**sion** *n.*

excluding (ɪkˈskluːdɪŋ) *prep.* excepting.

exclusive (ɪkˈskluːsɪv) *adj.* **1.** excluding all else. **2.** not shared: *exclusive rights.* **3.** catering for a privileged minority, esp. a fashionable clique. **4.** *exclusive to.* limited to; found only in. **5.** not including the numbers, dates, etc., mentioned. **6.** *exclusive of.* except for; not taking account of. ~*n.* **7.** a story reported in only one newspaper. —**ex**ˈclusive**ly** *adv.* —**ex**ˈclusiveness *or* exclusivity (ˌɛksklˈsɪvɪtɪ) *n.*

excommunicate (ˌɛkskəˈmjuːnɪˌkeɪt) *vb.* to sentence (a member of the Church) to exclusion from membership and the sacraments of the Church. [Late Latin *excommūnicāre* to exclude from the community] —ˌexcom**ˌmuni**ˈcation *n.*

excoriate (ɪkˈskɔːrɪˌeɪt) *vb.* **1.** to strip skin from (a person or animal). **2.** to censure severely. [Late Latin *excoriāre* to strip, flay] —**ex**ˌcori**ˈation** *n.*

excrement (ˈɛkskrɪmənt) *n.* waste matter discharged from the body; faeces. [Latin

excernere to sift, excrete] —**excremental** (ˌɛkskrɪˈmentᵊl) *adj.*

excrescence (ɪkˈskrɛsᵊns) *n.* a protuberance, esp. an outgrowth from a part of the body. [Latin *excrēscere* to grow out] —**ex**ˈcrescent *adj.*

excreta (ɪkˈskriːtə) *pl. n.* urine and faeces discharged from the body.

excrete (ɪkˈskriːt) *vb.* to discharge (waste matter, such as urine, sweat, or faeces) from the body. [Latin *excernere* to discharge] —**ex**ˈcretion *n.* —**ex**ˈcretory *adj.*

excruciating (ɪkˈskruːʃɪˌeɪtɪŋ) *adj.* **1.** unbearably painful; agonizing. **2.** *Humorous.* very bad: *an excruciating pun.* [Latin *excruciāre* to torture] —**ex**ˈcruci**atingly** *adv.*

exculpate (ˈɛkskʌlˌpeɪt) *vb.* to free from blame or guilt. [Latin *ex* from + *culpa* fault]

excursion (ɪkˈskɜːʃən) *n.* a short outward and return journey, esp. for sightseeing, etc.; outing. [Latin *excurrere* to run out]

excursive (ɪkˈskɜːsɪv) *adj.* tending to digress; rambling. [Latin *excurrere* to run forth]

excuse *vb.* (ɪkˈskjuːz) **1.** to put forward a reason or justification for (an action, fault, or offending person). **2.** to pardon (a person) or overlook (a fault). **3.** to make allowances for: *to excuse someone's ignorance.* **4.** to exempt from a task, obligation, etc. **5.** to allow to leave. **6. be excused.** *Euphemistic.* to go to the lavatory. **7. excuse me!** an expression used to catch someone's attention or to apologize for an interruption, disagreement, etc. ~*n.* (ɪkˈskjuːs) **8.** an explanation offered in defence of some fault or as a reason for not fulfilling an obligation, etc. [Latin *ex* out + *causa* cause, accusation] —**ex**ˈcusable *adj.*

ex-directory *adj. Chiefly Brit.* not listed in a telephone directory by request.

execrable (ˈɛksɪkrəbᵊl) *adj.* of very poor quality. [see EXECRATE] —**ˈex**ecrably *adv.*

execrate (ˈɛksɪˌkreɪt) *vb.* **1.** to loathe; detest. **2.** to denounce. **3.** to curse (a person or thing). [Latin *exsecrārī* to curse] —ˌexe**ˈcration** *n.*

execute (ˈɛksɪˌkjuːt) *vb.* **1.** to put (a condemned person) to death. **2.** to carry out; accomplish. **3.** to produce: *to execute a drawing.* **4.** *Law.* to render (a deed) effective, as by signing. **5.** to carry out the terms of (a contract, will, etc.). [Old French *executer*] —**exe**ˌcuter *n.*

execution (ˌɛksɪˈkjuːʃən) *n.* **1.** the act of executing. **2.** the carrying out or undergoing of a sentence of death. **3.** the manner in which something is performed; technique.

executioner (ˌɛksɪˈkjuːʃənə) *n.* an official charged with carrying out the death sentence.

executive (ɪgˈzɛkjʊtɪv) *n.* **1.** a person or group responsible for the administration of a project or business. **2.** the branch of government responsible for carrying out laws, decrees, etc. ~*adj.* **3.** having the function of carrying plans, orders, laws, etc., into effect. **4.** *Informal.* very expensive or exclusive: *executive housing.*

executor (ɪɡˈzɛkjʊtə) *n. Law.* a person appointed by a testator to carry out his will. —**ex,ecu'torial** *adj.* —**ex'ecutrix** *fem. n.*

exegesis (ˌɛksɪˈdʒiːsɪs) *n., pl.* **-ses** (-siːz). explanation of a text, esp. of the Bible. [Greek *exēgeisthai* to interpret]

exemplar (ɪɡˈzɛmplə, -plɑː) *n.* **1.** a person or thing to be copied; model. **2.** a typical specimen; example. [Latin *exemplum* example]

exemplary (ɪɡˈzɛmplərɪ) *adj.* **1.** fit for imitation; model. **2.** serving as a warning; admonitory. **3.** representative; typical.

exemplify (ɪɡˈzɛmplɪˌfaɪ) *vb.* **-fying, -fied.** **1.** to show by example. **2.** to serve as an example of. [Latin *exemplum* example + *facere* to make] —**ex,emplifi'cation** *n.*

exempt (ɪɡˈzɛmpt) *vb.* **1.** to release (someone) from an obligation, tax, etc. ~*adj.* **2.** not subject to an obligation, tax, etc. [Latin *exemptus* removed] —**ex'emption** *n.*

exequies (ˈɛksɪkwɪz) *pl. n., sing.* **-quy.** funeral rites. [Latin *exequiae*]

exercise (ˈɛksəˌsaɪz) *n.* **1.** physical exertion, esp. for training or keeping fit. **2.** mental or other activity, esp. to develop a skill. **3.** a set of movements, tasks, etc., designed to improve or test one's ability. **4.** the performance of a function: *the exercise of one's rights.* **5.** (*usually pl.*) *Mil.* a manoeuvre or simulated combat operation. ~*vb.* **6.** to put into use; employ. **7.** to take exercise or perform exercises. **8.** to practise using in order to develop or train. **9.** to make use of: *to exercise one's rights.* **10.** (*often passive*) to worry or vex: *to be exercised about a decision.* **11.** *Mil.* to carry out simulated combat, manoeuvres, etc. [Latin *exercēre* to drill] —**'exer,ciser** *n.*

exert (ɪɡˈzɜːt) *vb.* **1.** to use (influence, authority, etc.) forcefully or effectively. **2. exert oneself.** to make a special effort. [Latin *exserere* to thrust out] —**ex'ertion** *n.*

exeunt (ˈɛksɪˌʌnt) *Latin.* they go out: used as a stage direction.

exeunt omnes (ˈɒmneɪz) *Latin.* they all go out: used as a stage direction.

ex gratia (ˈɡreɪʃə) *adj.* given as a favour where no legal obligation exists: *an ex gratia payment.* [New Latin: out of kindness]

exhale (ɛksˈheɪl, ɪɡˈzeɪl) *vb.* **1.** to expel (breath or smoke) from the lungs; breathe out. **2.** to give off (air, fumes, etc.) or (of air, etc.) to be given off. [Latin *exhālāre*] —**,exha'lation** *n.*

exhaust (ɪɡˈzɔːst) *vb.* **1.** to tire out. **2.** to use up (supplies or resources) totally. **3.** to empty (a container) by drawing off (the contents). **4.** to develop or discuss (a topic) so thoroughly that no more remains to be said. **5.** to remove gas from (a vessel, etc.). ~*n.* **6.** gases ejected from an engine as waste products. **7.** the parts of an

engine through which exhausted gases pass. [Latin *exhaurīre* to draw out] —**ex'hausted** *adj.* —**ex'hausting** *adj.*

exhaustion (ɪɡˈzɔːstʃən) *n.* **1.** extreme tiredness. **2.** the act of exhausting or state of being exhausted.

exhaustive (ɪɡˈzɔːstɪv) *adj.* comprehensive; thorough. —**ex'haustively** *adv.*

exhibit (ɪɡˈzɪbɪt) *vb.* **1.** to display (something) to the public. **2.** to show: *the child exhibited signs of distress.* ~*n.* **3.** an object exhibited to the public. **4.** *Law.* a document or object produced in court as evidence. [Latin *exhibēre* to hold forth] —**ex'hibitor** *n.*

exhibition (ˌɛksɪˈbɪʃən) *n.* **1.** a public display of art, skills, etc. **2.** the act of exhibiting or the state of being exhibited. **3. make an exhibition of oneself.** to behave so foolishly that one attracts public attention. **4.** *Brit.* a scholarship awarded to a student at a university or school.

exhibitioner (ˌɛksɪˈbɪʃənə) *n. Brit.* a student who has been awarded an exhibition.

exhibitionism (ˌɛksɪˈbɪʃəˌnɪzəm) *n.* **1.** a compulsive desire to attract attention to oneself. **2.** a compulsive desire to expose one's genitals publicly. —**,exhi'bitionist** *n.*

exhilarate (ɪɡˈzɪləˌreɪt) *vb.* to make lively and cheerful. [Latin *exhilarāre*] —**ex,hila'ration** *n.*

exhort (ɪɡˈzɔːt) *vb.* to urge (someone) earnestly. [Latin *exhortārī*] —**ex'hortative** *or* **ex'hortatory** *adj.* —**,exhor'tation** *n.*

exhume (ɛksˈhjuːm) *vb.* to dig up (something buried, esp. a corpse). [Latin *ex* out + *humus* the ground] —**exhumation** (ˌɛkshjuːˈmeɪʃən) *n.*

exigency (ˈɛksɪdʒənsɪ, ɪɡˈzɪdʒənsɪ) *n., pl.* **-gencies.** **1.** (*often pl.*) an urgent demand or need. **2.** an emergency. [Latin *exigere* to require] —**'exigent** *adj.*

exiguous (ɪɡˈzɪɡjʊəs, ɪkˈsɪɡ-) *adj.* scanty; meagre. [Latin *exiguus*] —**exiguity** (ˌɛksɪˈɡjuːɪtɪ) *n.*

exile (ˈɛɡzaɪl, ˈɛksaɪl) *n.* **1.** a prolonged, usually enforced absence from one's country. **2.** the official expulsion of a person from his native land. **3.** a person banished or living away from his country. ~*vb.* **4.** to expel from one's country; banish. [Latin *exsilium*]

exist (ɪɡˈzɪst) *vb.* **1.** to have being or reality; be. **2.** to eke out a living. **3.** to be living; live. **4.** to be present under specified conditions or in a specified place. [Latin *exsistere* to step forth] —**ex'isting** *adj.*

existence (ɪɡˈzɪstəns) *n.* **1.** the fact or state of existing; being. **2.** the continuance of life; living. **3.** everything that exists. —**ex'istent** *adj.*

existential (ˌɛɡzɪˈstɛnʃəl) *adj.* **1.** of or relating to existence, esp. human existence. **2.** *Philosophy.* known by experience rather than reason. **3.** of or relating to existentialism.

existentialism (ˌɛɡzɪˈstɛnʃəˌlɪzəm) *n.* a modern philosophical movement stressing personal experience and responsibility of the individual, who is seen as a free agent. —**exis¦tentialist** *adj.*, *n.*

exit ('ɛgzɪt, 'ɛksɪt) *n.* **1.** a way out. **2.** the act of going out. **3.** *Theatre.* the act of going offstage. **4.** *Brit.* a point at which vehicles may leave or join a motorway. ~*vb.* **5.** to go away or out; depart. **6.** *Theatre.* to go offstage: used as a stage direction. [Latin *exīre* to go out]

exocrine ('ɛksəʊ,kraɪn) *adj.* of a gland, such as the sweat gland, that discharges its product through a duct. [Greek *exō* outside + *krinein* to separate]

exodus ('ɛksədəs) *n.* the departure of a large number of people. [Greek *ex* out + *hodos* way]

Exodus ('ɛksədəs) *n.* **the.** the departure of the Israelites from Egypt.

ex officio ('ɛks ə'fɪʃɪəʊ) *adv.*, *adj.* by right of position or office. [Latin]

exonerate (ɪg'zɒnə,reɪt) *vb.* to absolve from blame or a criminal charge. [Latin *exonerāre* to free from a burden] —**ex¦oner'ation** *n.*

exorbitant (ɪg'zɔːbɪt'nt) *adj.* (of prices, demands, etc.) excessive; immoderate. [Latin *ex* out, away + *orbita* track] —**ex'orbitantly** *adv.*

exorcise *or* **-cize** ('ɛksɔː,saɪz) *vb.* to expel (evil spirits) from (a person or place), by prayers and religious rites. [Greek *ex* out + *horkos* oath] —**'exorcism** *n.* —**'exorcist** *n.*

exordium (ɛk'sɔːdɪəm) *n.*, *pl.* **-diums** *or* **-dia** (-dɪə). an introductory part, esp. of a speech or treatise. [Latin *exōrdīrī* to begin]

exoskeleton (,ɛksəʊ'skɛlɪt'n) *n.* the protective or supporting structure covering the outside of the body of many animals, for example insects or crabs.

exotic (ɪg'zɒtɪk) *adj.* **1.** originating in a foreign country; not native. **2.** having a strange allure or beauty. ~*n.* **3.** an exotic thing, esp. a plant. [Greek *exō* outside] —**ex'otically** *adv.*

exotica (ɪg'zɒtɪkə) *pl. n.* exotic objects, esp. as a collection.

expand (ɪk'spænd) *vb.* **1.** to make or become greater in extent, size, or scope. **2.** to spread out; unfold. **3.** (often foll. by *on*) to enlarge (on a story, topic, etc.). **4.** to become increasingly relaxed, friendly, and talkative. **5.** *Maths.* to express (a function or expression) as the sum or product of terms. [Latin *expandere* to spread out] —**ex'pandable** *adj.*

expanse (ɪk'spæns) *n.* an uninterrupted wide area; stretch: *an expanse of blue sky.*

expansible (ɪk'spænsəb'l) *adj.* able to expand or be expanded.

expansion (ɪk'spænʃən) *n.* **1.** the act of expanding. **2.** the amount by which something expands. **3.** an increase or development, esp. in the activities of a company.

expansionism (ɪk'spænʃə,nɪzəm) *n.* the practice of expanding the economy or territory of a country. —**ex'pansionist** *n.*, *adj.*

expansive (ɪk'spænsɪv) *adj.* **1.** able or tending to expand. **2.** wide; extensive. **3.** friendly, open, and talkative. —**ex'pansiveness** *n.*

expatiate (ɪk'speɪʃɪ,eɪt) *vb.* (foll. by *on* or *upon*) to speak or write at length (on a topic). [Latin *exspatiārī* to digress] —**ex,pati'ation** *n.*

expatriate (ɛks'pætrɪt) *adj.* **1.** resident outside one's native country. **2.** exiled. ~*n.* **3.** a person living outside his native country **4.** an exile. [Latin *ex* out, away + *patria* native land] —**ex,patri'ation** *n.*

expect (ɪk'spɛkt) *vb.* **1.** to regard as likely. **2.** to look forward to or be waiting for. **3.** to require (something) as an obligation: *the teacher expects us to work late.* **4. be expecting.** *Informal.* to be pregnant. [Latin *exspectāre* to watch for]

expectancy (ɪk'spɛktənsɪ) *n.* **1.** something expected, esp. on the basis of a norm: *his life expectancy was 30 years.* **2.** anticipation; expectation.

expectant (ɪk'spɛktənt) *adj.* **1.** expecting or hopeful. **2.** pregnant. —**ex'pectantly** *adv.*

expectation (,ɛkspɛk'teɪʃən) *n.* **1.** the state of expecting or of being expected. **2.** (*usually pl.*) something looked forward to, whether feared or hoped for. **3.** an attitude of expectancy or hope.

expectorant (ɪk'spɛktərənt) *Med.* ~*adj.* **1.** helping the bringing up of phlegm from the respiratory passages. ~*n.* **2.** an expectorant medicine.

expectorate (ɪk'spɛktə,reɪt) *vb.* to cough up (phlegm from the respiratory passages); spit. [Latin *expectorāre* to drive from the breast, expel] —**ex,pecto'ration** *n.*

expediency (ɪk'spiːdɪənsɪ) *or* **expedience** *n.*, *pl.* **-encies** *or* **-ences. 1.** appropriateness; suitability. **2.** the use of methods that are advantageous rather than fair or just.

expedient (ɪk'spiːdɪənt) *adj.* **1.** suitable to the circumstances; appropriate. **2.** inclined towards methods that are advantageous rather than fair or just. ~*n.* **3.** something that achieves a particular purpose. [Latin *expediēns* setting free; see EXPEDITE]

expedite ('ɛkspɪ,daɪt) *vb.* **1.** to facilitate the progress of; hasten. **2.** to do quickly. [Latin *expedīre* to free the feet]

expedition (,ɛkspɪ'dɪʃən) *n.* **1.** an organized journey or voyage, esp. for exploration. **2.** the people and equipment comprising an expedition. **3.** promptness. [Latin *expedīre* to prepare, expedite] —**,expe'ditionary** *adj.*

expeditious (,ɛkspɪ'dɪʃəs) *adj.* done with speed and efficiency; prompt; quick.

expel (ɪk'spɛl) *vb.* **-pelling, -pelled. 1.** to drive out with force. **2.** to dismiss from a school, club, etc., permanently. [Latin *expellere*]

expend (ɪk'spɛnd) *vb.* to spend or use up (time, energy, or money). [Latin *expendere* to weigh out, pay]

expendable (ɪk'spɛndəb'l) *adj.* **1.** not worth preserving. **2.** able to be sacrificed to achieve an objective, esp. a military one.

expenditure (ɪk'spɛndɪtʃə) *n.* **1.** something expended, esp. money. **2.** the amount expended.

expense (ɪk'spɛns) n. **1.** a particular payment of money; expenditure. **2.** money needed for individual purchases; cost. **3.** (pl.) money spent in the performance of a job, etc. **4.** something requiring money for its purchase or upkeep. **5. at the expense of.** to the detriment of. [Latin expēnsus weighed out]

expense account n. **1.** an arrangement by which an employee's expenses are refunded by his employer. **2.** a record of such expenses.

expensive (ɪk'spɛnsɪv) adj. high-priced; costly; dear. —**ex'pensiveness** n.

experience (ɪk'spɪərɪəns) n. **1.** direct personal participation. **2.** a particular incident, feeling, etc., that a person has undergone. **3.** accumulated knowledge, esp. of practical matters. ∼vb. **4.** to participate in or undergo. **5.** to be moved by; feel. [Latin experīrī to prove]

experienced (ɪk'spɪərɪənst) adj. skilful or knowledgeable from extensive participation.

experiential (ɪkˌspɪərɪ'ɛnʃəl) adj. Philosophy. relating to or derived from experience.

experiment n. (ɪk'spɛrɪmənt). **1.** a test or investigation to provide evidence for or against a hypothesis. **2.** an attempt at something new or original. ∼vb. (ɪk'spɛrɪˌment). **3.** to make an experiment or experiments. [Latin experīrī to test] —**exˌperimen'tation** n. —**ex'periˌmenter** n.

experimental (ɪkˌspɛrɪ'mɛntəl) adj. **1.** relating to, based on, or having the nature of experiment. **2.** tentative or provisional. —**exˌperi'mentally** adv.

expert ('ɛkspɜːt) n. **1.** a person who has extensive skill or knowledge in a particular field. ∼adj. **2.** skilful or knowledgeable. **3.** of, involving, or done by an expert. [Latin expertus known by experience] —**'expertly** adv.

expertise (ˌɛkspɜː'tiːz) n. special skill, knowledge, or judgment. [French]

expiate ('ɛkspɪˌeɪt) vb. to atone for (sin or wrongdoing); make amends for. [Latin expiāre] —**ˌexpi'ation** n.

expiration (ˌɛkspɪ'reɪʃən) n. **1.** the finish of something; expiry. **2.** the act, process, or sound of breathing out. —**expiratory** (ɪk'spaɪərətrɪ) adj.

expire (ɪk'spaɪə) vb. **1.** to finish or run out; come to an end. **2.** to breathe out (air). **3.** to die. [Latin exspīrāre to breathe out]

expiry (ɪk'spaɪərɪ) n., pl. **-ries.** a coming to an end, esp. of a contract period.

explain (ɪk'spleɪn) vb. **1.** to make (something) comprehensible, esp. by giving a clear and detailed account of it. **2.** to justify or attempt to justify (oneself) by reasons for one's actions. **3. explain away.** to offer excuses or reason for (mistakes). [Latin explānāre to flatten, make clear]

explanation (ˌɛksplə'neɪʃən) n. **1.** the act of explaining. **2.** something that explains.

explanatory (ɪk'splænətrɪ) adj. serving or intended to serve as an explanation.

expletive (ɪk'spliːtɪv) n. an exclamation or swearword; an oath or sound expressing emotion rather than meaning. [Latin explēre to fill up]

explicable ('ɛksplɪkəbᵊl, ɪk'splɪk-) adj. capable of being explained.

explicate ('ɛksplɪˌkeɪt) vb. Formal. to make clear; explain. [Latin explicāre to unfold] —**ˌexpli'cation** n.

explicit (ɪk'splɪsɪt) adj. **1.** precisely and clearly expressed, leaving nothing to implication. **2.** leaving little to the imagination; graphically detailed. **3.** openly expressed. [Latin explicitus unfolded] —**ex'plicitly** adv.

explode (ɪk'spləʊd) vb. **1.** to burst with great violence; blow up. **2.** (of a gas) to undergo a sudden violent expansion as a result of a fast chemical or nuclear reaction. **3.** to react suddenly or violently with emotion. **4.** (esp. of a population) to increase rapidly. **5.** to show (a theory, etc.) to be baseless. [Latin explōdere to drive off by clapping]

exploit n. ('ɛksplɔɪt). **1.** a notable deed or feat. ∼vb. (ɪk'splɔɪt). **2.** to take advantage of (a person, situation, etc.) for one's own ends. **3.** to make the best use of. [Old French] —**ˌexploi'tation** n. —**ex'ploiter** n.

explore (ɪk'splɔː) vb. **1.** to examine or investigate, esp. systematically. **2.** to travel into (unfamiliar regions), esp. for scientific purposes. [Latin ex out + plōrāre to cry aloud] —**exploration** (ˌɛksplɔː'reɪʃən) n. —**exploratory** (ɪk'splɔrətrɪ) adj. —**ex'plorer** n.

explosion (ɪk'spləʊʒən) n. **1.** an exploding. **2.** a violent release of energy resulting from a rapid chemical or nuclear reaction. **3.** a sudden or violent outburst of activity, noise, emotion, etc. **4.** a rapid increase.

explosive (ɪk'spləʊsɪv) adj. **1.** able, liable, or tending to explode. **2.** potentially violent: an explosive situation. ∼n. **3.** a substance capable of exploding. —**ex'plosiveness** n.

expo ('ɛkspəʊ) n., pl. **-pos.** short for **exposition** (sense 3).

exponent (ɪk'spəʊnənt) n. **1.** (usually foll. by of) a person who advocates (an idea, cause, etc.). **2.** a person or thing that explains or interprets. **3.** Maths. a number or variable placed as a superscript to another number indicating how many times the number is to be multiplied by itself. [Latin expōnere to expound]

exponential (ˌɛkspəʊ'nɛnʃəl) adj. **1.** Maths. of or involving numbers raised to an exponent. **2.** Informal. very rapid. —**ˌexpo'nentially** adv.

export n. ('ɛkspɔːt). **1.** (often pl.) goods or services sold to a foreign country. ∼vb. (ɪk'spɔːt, 'ɛkspɔːt). **2.** to sell (goods or services) or ship (goods) to a foreign country. [Latin exportāre to carry away] —**ex'porter** n.

expose (ɪk'spəʊz) vb. **1.** to uncover

(something previously covered). **2.** to reveal (something previously hidden), esp. when disreputable. **3.** (foll. by *to*) to make vulnerable (to attack or criticism). **4.** to leave (a person or thing) unprotected in a potentially harmful situation. **5.** (foll. by *to*) to give (a person) an introduction to or experience of something new. **6.** *Photog.* to subject (a film) to light. **7. expose oneself.** to display one's sexual organs in public. [Latin *expōnere* to set out]

exposé (εks'pəʊzeɪ) *n.* the bringing of a scandal, crime, etc., to public notice. [French]

exposed (ɪk'spəʊzd) *adj.* **1.** not concealed; displayed for viewing. **2.** without shelter from the elements. **3.** vulnerable.

exposition (,εkspə'zɪʃən) *n.* **1.** a systematic explanation of a subject. **2.** the act of expounding or setting forth a viewpoint. **3.** a large public exhibition. **4.** *Music.* the first statement of the themes of a movement. [Latin *expōnere* to display]

expository (ɪk'spɒzɪtrɪ) *adj.* explanatory.

ex post facto (ˈɛks pəʊst ˈfæktəʊ) *adj.* having retrospective effect. [Latin *ex* from + *post* afterwards + *factus* done]

expostulate (ɪk'spɒstjʊ,leɪt) *vb.* (usually foll. by *with*) to reason (with), esp. in order to dissuade. **b.** [Latin *expostulāre* to require] —**ex,postu'lation** *n.* —**ex'postulatory** *adj.*

exposure (ɪk'spəʊʒə) *n.* **1.** the act of exposing or the condition of being exposed. **2.** lack of shelter from the weather, esp. the cold. **3.** *Photog.* **a.** the act of exposing a film to light. **b.** an area on a film that has been exposed. **4.** *Photog.* **a.** the intensity of light falling on a film multiplied by the time for which it is exposed. **b.** a combination of lens aperture and shutter speed used in taking a photograph. **5.** appearance before the public, as on television.

exposure meter *n.* *Photog.* an instrument for measuring the intensity of light so that suitable camera settings can be determined.

expound (ɪk'spaʊnd) *vb.* to explain (a theory) in detail. [Latin *expōnere* to set forth]

express (ɪk'sprεs) *vb.* **1.** to transform (ideas) into words; utter. **2.** to show: *her face expressed disapproval.* **3.** to indicate through a symbol or formula. **4.** to squeeze out juice, etc. **5. express oneself.** to communicate one's thoughts or ideas. ~*adj.* **6.** explicitly stated. **7.** particular. **8.** of or for rapid transportation of people, mail, etc. ~*n.* **9.** a fast train stopping at only a few stations. **10.** *Chiefly U.S. & Canad.* a system for sending mail rapidly. ~*adv.* **11.** by express delivery. [Latin *exprimere* to force out] —**ex'pressible** *adj.*

expression (ɪk'sprεʃən) *n.* **1.** transforming ideas into words. **2.** a showing of emotion without words. **3.** communication of emotion through music, painting, etc. **4.** a look on the face that indicates mood or emotion. **5.** the choice of words, intonation, etc., in communicating. **6.** a particular phrase used conventionally to express

something. **7.** *Maths.* a variable, function, or some combination of these. —**ex'pressionless** *adj.*

expressionism (ɪk'sprεʃə,nɪzəm) *n.* an artistic and literary movement in the early 20th century, which sought to express emotions rather than to represent the physical world. —**ex'pressionist** *n., adj.*

expressive (ɪk'sprεsɪv) *adj.* **1.** of or full of expression. **2.** (foll. by *of*) suggestive (of): *a look expressive of love.* **3.** having a particular meaning or force.

expressway (ɪk'sprεs,weɪ) *n.* a motorway.

expropriate (εks'prəʊprɪ,eɪt) *vb.* to deprive (an owner) of (property). [Medieval Latin *expropriāre* to deprive of possessions] —**ex,propri'ation** *n.* —**ex'propri,ator** *n.*

expulsion (ɪk'spʌlʃən) *n.* the act of expelling or the fact of being expelled. [Latin *expellere* to expel] —**ex'pulsive** *adj.*

expunge (ɪk'spʌndʒ) *vb.* to delete or erase; blot out. [Latin *expungere* to blot out] —**expunction** (ɪk'spʌŋkʃən) *n.*

expurgate (ˈεkspə,geɪt) *vb.* to amend (a piece of writing) by removing (offensive sections). [Latin *expurgāre* to clean out] —**,expur'gation** *n.* —**'expur,gator** *n.*

exquisite (ɪk'skwɪzɪt, 'εkskwɪzɪt) *adj.* **1.** showing unusual delicacy and craftsmanship. **2.** extremely beautiful. **3.** sensitive; discriminating: *exquisite taste.* **4.** intense or sharp in feeling: *exquisite pain.* [Latin *exquīsitus* excellent] —**ex'quisitely** *adv.*

ex-serviceman *or* (*fem.*) **ex-servicewoman** *n., pl.* **-men** *or* **-women.** a person who has served in the armed forces.

extant (εk'stænt, 'εkstənt) *adj.* still in existence; surviving. [Latin *exstāns* standing out]

extemporaneous (ɪk,stεmpə'reɪnɪəs) *or* **extemporary** (ɪk'stεmpərərɪ) *adj.* spoken or performed without preparation. —**ex,tempo'raneously** *or* **ex'temporarily** *adv.*

extempore (ɪk'stεmpərɪ) *adv., adj.* without planning or preparation. [Latin *ex tempore* instantaneously]

extemporize *or* **-rise** (ɪk'stεmpə,raɪz) *vb.* to perform, speak, or compose (an act, speech, or piece of music) without preparation. —**ex,tempori'zation** *or* **-ri'sation** *n.*

extend (ɪk'stεnd) *vb.* **1.** to draw out or be drawn out; stretch. **2.** to last for a certain time: *his schooling extended for three years.* **3.** to reach a certain point in time or distance: *the land extends five miles.* **4.** to exist or occur: *the trees extended throughout the area.* **5.** to increase (a building) in size. **6.** to broaden the meaning or scope of: *the law was extended.* **7.** to present or offer: *to extend greetings.* **8.** to stretch forth (an arm, etc.). [Latin *extendere* to stretch out] —**ex'tendible** *or* **ex'tendable** *adj.*

extended family *n.* a social unit in which parents, children, grandparents, and other relatives live as a family unit.

extensible (ɪkˈstɛnsɪbˀl) *adj.* capable of being extended.

extension (ɪkˈstɛnʃən) *n.* **1.** the act of extending or the condition of being extended. **2.** a room or rooms added to an existing building. **3.** something that can be extended or that extends another object: *an extension ladder.* **4.** the length, range, etc., of something. **5.** an additional telephone connected to the same line as another. **6.** a delay in the date originally set for payment of a debt or completion of a contract. **7.** a service by which the facilities of an educational establishment are offered to outsiders.

extensive (ɪkˈstɛnsɪv) *adj.* **1.** having a large extent, area, degree, etc. **2.** widespread. —**exˈtensively** *adv.*

extensor (ɪkˈstɛnsə) *n.* any muscle that stretches or extends an arm, leg, or other part of the body.

extent (ɪkˈstɛnt) *n.* **1.** the range over which something extends. **2.** an area or volume.

extenuate (ɪkˈstɛnjʊˌeɪt) *vb.* to represent (an offence or fault) as less serious than it appears, by giving reasons that partly excuse it. [Latin *extenuāre* to make thin] —**exˈtenuˌating** *adj.* —**ex̩tenuˈation** *n.*

exterior (ɪkˈstɪərɪə) *n.* **1.** a part or surface that is on the outside. **2.** the outward appearance of a person. **3.** a film scene shot outside. ~*adj.* **4.** of, situated on, or suitable for the outside. **5.** coming or acting from without. [Latin comp. of *exterus* on the outside]

exterior angle *n.* **1.** an angle of a polygon contained between one side extended and the adjacent side. **2.** any of the four angles formed outside two straight lines by a straight line cutting across them.

exterminate (ɪkˈstɜːmɪˌneɪt) *vb.* to destroy (living things) completely. [Latin *extermināre* to drive away] —**ex̩termiˈnation** *n.* —**exˈtermiˌnator** *n.*

external (ɪkˈstɜːnˀl) *adj.* **1.** of, situated on, or suitable for the outside. **2.** coming or acting from without. **3.** of or involving foreign nations. **4.** of or designating a medicine applied to the outside of the body. **5.** *Anat.* situated on or near the outside of the body. **6.** (of a student) studying a university subject, but not attending a university. ~*n.* **7.** (*often pl.*) an external circumstance or aspect, esp. one that is superficial. [Latin *externus*] —**ˌexterˈnality** *n.* —**exˈternally** *adv.*

externalize or **-ise** (ɪkˈstɜːnəˌlaɪz) *vb.* to make external; give outward shape or expression to. —**ex̩ternaliˈzation** or **-iˈsation** *n.*

extinct (ɪkˈstɪŋkt) *adj.* **1.** (of an animal or plant species) having died out. **2.** quenched or extinguished. **3.** (of a volcano) no longer liable to erupt. [Latin *exstinguere* to extinguish]

extinction (ɪkˈstɪŋkʃən) *n.* **1.** the act of making extinct or the state of being extinct. **2.** the act of extinguishing or the state of being extinguished. **3.** complete destruction.

extinguish (ɪkˈstɪŋgwɪʃ) *vb.* **1.** to put out or quench (a fire or light). **2.** to remove or destroy entirely. [Latin *exstinguere*] —**exˈtinguishable** *adj.* —**exˈtinguisher** *n.*

extirpate (ˈɛkstəˌpeɪt) *vb.* **1.** to destroy completely. **2.** to pull up; uproot. [Latin *exstirpāre* to root out] —**ˌextirˈpation** *n.*

extol or *U.S.* **extoll** (ɪkˈstəʊl) *vb.* **-tolling, -tolled.** to praise lavishly; exalt. [Latin *extollere* to elevate]

extort (ɪkˈstɔːt) *vb.* to secure (money or favours) by intimidation, violence, or the misuse of authority. [Latin *extorquēre* to wrest away] —**exˈtortion** *n.*

extortionate (ɪkˈstɔːʃənɪt) *adj.* **1.** (of prices) excessive. **2.** (of persons) using extortion. —**exˈtortionately** *adv.*

extra (ˈɛkstrə) *adj.* **1.** being more than what is usual or expected; additional. ~*n.* **2.** a person or thing that is additional. **3.** something for which an additional charge is made. **4.** an additional edition of a newspaper. **5.** *Films.* a person temporarily engaged, usually for crowd scenes. **6.** *Cricket.* a run not scored from the bat. ~*adv.* **7.** unusually; exceptionally. [prob. from *extraordinary*]

extra- *prefix.* outside or beyond an area or scope: *extrasensory; extraterritorial.* [Latin]

extract *vb.* (ɪkˈstrækt). **1.** to pull out or uproot by force. **2.** to remove or separate. **3.** to derive (pleasure, information, etc.) from some source. **4.** *Informal.* to extort (money, etc.). **5.** to obtain (a substance) from a material by digestion, distillation, mechanical separation, etc. **6.** to copy out (an article, passage, etc.) from a publication. **7.** to determine the value of (the root of a number). ~*n.* (ˈɛkstrækt). **8.** something extracted, such as a passage from a book, etc. **9.** a preparation containing the concentrated essence of a material. [Latin *extrahere* to draw out] —**exˈtraction** *n.* —**exˈtractive** *adj.* —**exˈtractor** *n.*

extracurricular (ˌɛkstrəkəˈrɪkjʊlə) *adj.* not part of the set curriculum.

extradite (ˈɛkstrəˌdaɪt) *vb.* **1.** to surrender (an alleged offender) for trial to a foreign state. **2.** to obtain the extradition of. [Latin *ex* away + *trāditiō* a handing over] —**ˈextraˌditable** *adj.* —**ˌextraˈdition** *n.*

extramarital (ˌɛkstrəˈmærɪtˀl) *adj.* (esp. of sexual relations) occurring outside marriage.

extramural (ˌɛkstrəˈmjʊərəl) *adj.* connected with but outside the normal courses of a university or college. [Latin *extra* beyond + *mūrus* wall]

extraneous (ɪkˈstreɪnɪəs) *adj.* **1.** not essential. **2.** not pertinent; irrelevant. **3.** coming from outside. [Latin *extrāneus* external]

extraordinary (ɪkˈstrɔːdˀnrɪ) *adj.* **1.** very unusual or surprising. **2.** not in an established manner or order. **3.** employed for particular purposes. [Latin *extraordinārius* beyond what is usual] —**exˈtraordinarily** *adv.*

extrapolate (ɪkˈstræpəˌleɪt) *vb. Maths.*

estimate (a value of a function or measurement) beyond the known values, by the extension of a curve. [EXTRA- + -*polate*, as in *interpolate*] —**ex,trapo'lation** *n.*

extrasensory (ˌɛkstrəˈsɛnsərɪ) *adj.* of or relating to extrasensory perception.

extrasensory perception *n.* the supposed ability to obtain information without the use of normal sensory channels.

extravagant (ɪkˈstrævɪɡənt) *adj.* 1. spending money excessively. 2. going beyond usual bounds: *extravagant praise*. 3. exorbitant in price. [Latin *extra* beyond + *vagārī* to wander] —**ex'travagance** *n.*

extravaganza (ɪkˌstrævəˈɡænzə) *n.* 1. an elaborately staged light entertainment. 2. any fanciful display, literary composition, etc. [Italian: *extravaganza*]

extreme (ɪkˈstriːm) *adj.* 1. being of a high or the highest degree or intensity. 2. immoderate. 3. very strict or severe; drastic. 4. farthest or outermost. ~*n.* 5. (*often pl.*) either of the two limits of a scale or range. 6. **go to extremes.** to be unreasonable in speech or action. 7. **in the extreme.** to the highest or further degree: *her manner was friendly in the extreme.* [Latin *extrēmus* outermost] —**ex'tremely** *adv.*

extreme unction *n. R.C. Church.* a sacrament in which a person who dying is anointed by a priest.

extremist (ɪkˈstriːmɪst) *n.* 1. a person who favours or resorts to immoderate methods, esp. in being politically radical. ~*adj.* 2. of or characterized by immoderate actions, opinions, etc. —**ex'tremism** *n.*

extremity (ɪkˈstrɛmɪtɪ) *n., pl.* **-ties.** 1. the farthest point. 2. the greatest degree. 3. an extreme condition, as of misfortune. 4. (*pl.*) hands and feet.

extricate (ˈɛkstrɪˌkeɪt) *vb.* to free from complication or difficulty; disentangle. [Latin *extrīcāre*] —**'extricable** *adj.* —ˌex-tri'cation *n.*

extrinsic (ɛkˈstrɪnsɪk) *adj.* 1. not included within; extraneous. 2. originating or acting from outside. [Latin *exter* outward + *secus* alongside] —**ex'trinsically** *adv.*

extrovert (ˈɛkstrəˌvɜːt) *Psychol.* ~*adj.* 1. concerned more with external reality than inner feelings. ~*n.* 2. such a person. [*extro-* (var. of EXTRA-, contrasting with *intro-*) + Latin *vertere* to turn] —**'extro-ˌverted** *adj.*

extrude (ɪkˈstruːd) *vb.* 1. to squeeze or force out. 2. to produce (moulded sections of plastic, metal, etc.) by forcing through a shaped die. [Latin *extrūdere* to thrust out] —**ex'truded** *adj.* —**ex'trusion** *n.*

exuberant (ɪɡˈzjuːbərənt) *adj.* 1. full of vigour and high spirits. 2. growing luxuriantly or in profusion. [Latin *exūberāns* abounding] —**ex'uberance** *n.*

exude (ɪɡˈzjuːd) *vb.* 1. to release or be released through pores, incisions, etc., as sweat or sap. 2. to make apparent by mood or behaviour. [Latin *exsūdāre*] —**exudation** (ˌɛksjʊˈdeɪʃən) *n.*

exult (ɪɡˈzʌlt) *vb.* to be joyful or jubilant.

[Latin *exsultāre* to jump for joy] —**exulta-tion** (ˌɛɡzʌlˈteɪʃən) *n.* —**ex'ultant** *adj.*

eye (aɪ) *n.* 1. the organ of sight in man and animals. 2. (*often pl.*) the ability to see; vision. 3. the external part of an eye, often including the area around it. 4. a look, glance, or gaze. 5. attention or observation. 6. ability to judge or appreciate: *an eye for antiques.* 7. (*often pl.*) opinion, judgment, or authority: *in the eyes of the law.* 8. resembling an eye, such as the bud on a potato tuber. 9. a small hole, as at one end of a sewing needle. 10. a small area of calm in the centre of a hurricane or tornado. 11. **all eyes.** *Informal.* acutely vigilant. 12. **(all) my eye.** *Informal.* nonsense. 13. **an eye for an eye.** retributive or vengeful justice. 14. **have eyes for.** to be interested in. 15. **in one's mind's eye.** imagined or remembered vividly. 16. **in the public eye.** exposed to public curiosity. 17. **keep an eye on.** to take care of. 18. **keep an eye open** *or* **out (for).** to watch with special attention (for). 19. **keep one's eyes skinned** *or* **peeled.** to watch vigilantly (for). 20. **clap, lay,** *or* **set eyes on.** to see: *I haven't clapped eyes on her all day.* 21. **look (someone) in the eye.** to look openly and without embarrassment at (someone). 22. **make sheep's eyes (at).** *Old-fashioned.* to ogle amorously. 23. **more than meets the eye.** hidden motives, meaning, or facts. 24. **see eye to eye (with).** to agree (with). 25. **shut one's eyes (to)** *or* **turn a blind eye (to).** to pretend not to notice. 26. **up to one's eyes (in).** extremely busy (with). 27. **with an eye to.** with the intention of. 28. **with one's eyes open.** in full knowledge of all the facts. 29. **with one's eyes shut.** with great ease, esp. through familiarity. ~*vb.* **eyeing** *or* **eying, eyed.** 30. to look at carefully or warily. ~**See also eye up.** [Old English *ēage*] —**'eyeless** *adj.* —**'eye-like** *adj.*

eyeball (ˈaɪˌbɔːl) *n.* 1. the entire ball-shaped part of the eye. 2. **eyeball to eyeball.** in close confrontation.

eyebrow (ˈaɪˌbraʊ) *n.* 1. the bony ridge over each eye. 2. the arch of hair on this ridge. 3. **raise an eyebrow.** to show doubt or disapproval.

eye-catching *adj.* tending to attract attention; striking. —**'eye-ˌcatcher** *n.*

eye dog *n. N.Z.* a dog trained to control sheep by staring fixedly at them.

eyeful (ˈaɪˌful) *n. Informal.* 1. a view or gaze. 2. an attractive sight, esp. a woman.

eyeglass (ˈaɪˌɡlɑːs) *n.* a lens for aiding defective vision.

eyehole (ˈaɪˌhəʊl) *n.* 1. the cavity that contains the eyeball. 2. a hole to look through; peephole.

eyelash (ˈaɪˌlæʃ) *n.* any of the short hairs that grow from the edge of the eyelids.

eyelet (ˈaɪlɪt) *n.* 1. a small hole for a lace or cord to be passed through. 2. a small metal ring reinforcing such a hole.

eyelevel (ˈaɪˌlɛvəl) *adj.* level with a person's eyes: *an eyelevel grill.*

eyelid (ˈaɪˌlɪd) *n.* either of the two folds of skin that can be moved to cover the eyes.

eyeliner (ˈaɪˌlaɪnə) *n.* a cosmetic used to outline the eyes.

eye-opener *n. Informal.* something startling or revealing.

eyepiece (ˈaɪˌpiːs) *n.* the lens in an optical instrument nearest the eye of the observer.

eye shadow *n.* a coloured cosmetic worn on the upper eyelids.

eyeshot (ˈaɪˌʃɒt) *n.* range of vision; view.

eyesight (ˈaɪˌsaɪt) *n.* the ability to see.

eyesore (ˈaɪˌsɔː) *n.* something very ugly.

eyestrain (ˈaɪˌstreɪn) *n.* fatigue or irritation of the eyes, from excessive use or from uncorrected defects of vision.

eyetooth (ˌaɪˈtuːθ) *n., pl.* **-teeth.** **1.** either of the two canine teeth in the upper jaw. **2. give one's eyeteeth for.** to go to any lengths to achieve or obtain (something).

eye up *vb.* to look at (someone) in a way that indicates sexual interest.

eyewash (ˈaɪˌwɒʃ) *n.* **1.** a lotion for the eyes. **2.** *Informal.* nonsense; rubbish.

eyewitness (ˈaɪˌwɪtnɪs) *n.* a person present at an event who can describe what happened.

eyrie (ˈɪərɪ, ˈɛərɪ, ˈaɪərɪ) *n.* **1.** the nest of an eagle, built in a high inaccessible place. **2.** any high isolated position. [Latin *ārea* open field, hence, nest]

F

f *or* **F** (ɛf) *n., pl.* **f's, F's,** *or* **Fs.** the sixth letter of the English alphabet.

f **1.** *Music.* forte: an instruction to play loudly. **2.** *Physics.* frequency. **3.** *Maths.* function (of). **4.** *Physics.* femto-.

f, f /, *or* **f:** f- number.

F **1.** *Music.* the fourth note of the scale of C major. **2.** Fahrenheit. **3.** farad(s). **4.** *Chem.* fluorine. **5.** *Physics.* force. **6.** franc(s).

f. *or* **F.** **1.** fathom(s). **2.** female. **3.** *Grammar.* feminine. **4.** (*pl.* **ff.** *or* **FF.**) folio. **5.** (*pl.* **ff.**) following (page).

fa (fɑː) *n. Music.* same as **fah.**

FA (in Britain) Football Association.

Fabian ('feɪbɪən) *adj.* **1.** cautious; using delaying tactics as a policy. ~*n.* **2.** a member of the Fabian Society which seeks to establish socialism by gradual reforms. [after *Fabius,* Roman general, who wore out Hannibal's strength while avoiding a pitched battle] —'**Fabian,ism** *n.*

fable ('feɪb'l) *n.* **1.** a short moral story, esp. one with animals as characters. **2.** a false, fictitious, or improbable account. **3.** a story about mythical characters or events. **4.** legends or myths collectively. [Latin *fābula* story]

fabled ('feɪb'ld) *adj.* made famous in fable.

Fablon ('fæblɒn) *n. Trademark.* a brand of adhesive-backed plastic used for covering surfaces.

fabric ('fæbrɪk) *n.* **1.** any cloth made from yarn or fibres by weaving, knitting, or felting. **2.** a structure or framework: *the fabric of society.* **3.** the walls, floor, and roof of a building. [Latin *faber* craftsman]

fabricate ('fæbrɪ,keɪt) *vb.* **1.** to make or build. **2.** to invent (a story or lie). [Latin *fabrica* workshop] —,**fabri'cation** *n.*

fabulous ('fæbjʊləs) *adj.* almost unbelievable; astounding; legendary. **2.** *Informal.* extremely good. **3.** of or based upon fable: *a fabulous beast.* [Latin *fābulōsus* celebrated in fable] —'**fabulously** *adv.*

façade (fə'sɑːd) *n.* **1.** the front of a building. **2.** a front or outer appearance, esp. a deceptive one. [French]

face (feɪs) *n.* **1.** the front of the head from the forehead to the lower jaw. **2. a.** one's expression: *a sad face.* **b.** a distorted expression to indicate disgust or defiance. **3.** appearance or pretence (esp. in **put a bold, good, bad,** etc., **face on**). **4.** dignity (esp. in **lose** *or* **save face**). **5.** *Informal.* impudence. **6.** the front or main side of an object, building, etc. **7.** the dial of a clock or watch. **8.** the functional side of an object, as of a tool or playing card. **9.** the exposed area of a mine from which coal or ore may be mined. **10.** Also called: **typeface.** *Printing.* the style of the type. **11. in the face of.** despite. **12. on the face of it.** to all appearances. **13. set one's face against.** to oppose with determination.

14. show one's face. to make an appearance. **15. to someone's face.** directly and openly. ~*vb.* **16.** to look or be situated (in a specified direction). **17.** to be opposite. **18.** to be confronted by. **19.** to provide with a surface of a different material. ~See also **face up to.** [Latin *faciēs* form]

face card *n.* a court card.

faceless ('feɪslɪs) *adj.* without identity; anonymous.

face-lift *n.* cosmetic surgery for tightening sagging skin and smoothing wrinkles on the face.

facer ('feɪsə) *n. Brit. informal.* a difficulty or problem.

face-saving *adj.* maintaining dignity or prestige. —'**face-,saver** *n.*

facet ('fæsɪt) *n.* **1.** any of the surfaces of a cut gemstone. **2.** an aspect, as of a personality. [French]

facetious (fə'siːʃəs) *adj.* joking, or trying to be amusing, esp. at inappropriate times. [Old French *facetie* witticism] —fa-'**cetiously** *adv.*

face up to *vb.* to accept (an unpleasant fact or reality).

face value *n.* apparent worth or meaning: *she took the remark at face value.*

facia ('feɪʃɪə) *n.* same as **fascia.**

facial ('feɪʃəl) *adj.* **1.** of the face. ~*n.* **2.** a beauty treatment for the face. —'**facially** *adv.*

facile ('fæsaɪl) *adj.* (of a remark, argument, etc.) superficial and showing lack of real thought. [Latin *facilis* easy]

facilitate (fə'sɪlɪ,teɪt) *vb.* to assist the progress of. —fa,**cili'tation** *n.*

facility (fə'sɪlɪtɪ) *n., pl.* **-ties.** **1.** ease of action or performance. **2.** ready skill or ease. **3.** (*often pl.*) the means or equipment needed for an activity. [Latin *facilis* easy]

facing ('feɪsɪŋ) *n.* **1.** a piece of material used esp. to conceal the seam of a garment. **2.** (*usually pl.*) contrasting collar and cuffs on a jacket. **3.** an outer layer of material applied to the surface of a wall.

facsimile (fæk'sɪmɪlɪ) *n.* **1.** an exact copy. **2.** a telegraphic system for transmitting an exact copy of a document. [Latin *fac simile!* make something like it!]

fact (fækt) *n.* **1.** an event or thing known to have happened or existed. **2.** a truth that can be proved from experience or observation. **3.** a piece of information. **4. after** (*or* **before**) **the fact.** *Criminal law.* after (or before) the commission of the offence. **5. as a matter of fact** *or* **in fact.** in reality or actuality. **6. fact of life.** an inescapable truth, esp. an unpleasant one. See also **facts of life.** [Latin *factum* something done]

faction ('fækʃən) *n.* **1.** a small dissenting group of people within a larger body. **2.**

strife within a group. [Latin *factiō* a making] —**'factional** *adj.*

factitious (fæk'tɪʃəs) *adj.* artificial rather than natural. [Latin *facticius*]

factor ('fæktə) *n.* **1.** an element that contributes to a result. **2.** *Maths.* one of two or more integers whose product is a given integer: *2 and 3 are factors of 6.* **3.** (in Scotland) the manager of an estate. [Latin: one who acts]

factorial (fæk'tɔːrɪəl) *Maths.* ~*n.* **1.** the product of all the integers from one to a given integer. ~*adj.* **2.** of factorials or factors.

factorize or **-rise** ('fæktə,raɪz) *vb. Maths.* to resolve (an integer) into factors. —,**factori'zation** or **-ri'sation** *n.*

factory ('fæktrɪ) *n., pl.* **-ries.** a building or buildings containing a plant assembly for the manufacture of goods. [Late Latin *factorium*, from *facere* to make]

factory farm *n.* a farm in which animals are intensively reared using modern industrial methods. —**factory farming** *n.*

factory ship *n.* a vessel that processes fish supplied by a fleet.

factotum (fæk'təʊtəm) *n.* a person employed to do all kinds of work. [Latin *fac! do! + tōtum* all]

facts of life *pl. n.* **the.** the details of sexual behaviour and reproduction.

factual ('fæktjʊəl) *adj.* **1.** of facts. **2.** real; actual. —**'factually** *adv.*

faculty ('fæk^əltɪ) *n., pl.* **-ties.** **1.** one of the inherent powers of the mind or body, such as memory, sight, or hearing. **2.** any ability or power. **3. a.** a department within a university or college. **b.** its staff. **c.** *Chiefly U.S. & Canad.* all the staff of a university, school, or college. [Latin *facultās* capability]

fad (fæd) *n. Informal.* **1.** an intense but short-lived fashion. **2.** a personal whim. [origin unknown] —**'faddish** or **'faddy** *adj.*

fade (feɪd) *vb.* **1.** to lose or cause to lose brightness, colour, or strength. **2.** (usually foll. by *away* or *out*) to vanish slowly. [Middle English *fade* dull]

fade in *vb.* to increase gradually, as vision or sound in a film or broadcast.

fade out *vb.* to decrease gradually, as vision or sound in a film or broadcast.

faeces or *esp. U.S.* **feces** ('fiːsiːz) *pl. n.* bodily waste matter discharged through the anus. [Latin: dregs] —**faecal** or *esp. U.S.* **fecal** ('fiːk^əl) *adj.*

Faeroese or **Faroese** (,fɛərəʊ'iːz) *adj.* **1.** of the Faeroes, islands in the N Atlantic, their inhabitants, or their language. ~*n.* **2.** the language of the Faeroes. **3.** (*pl.* -**ese**) a person from the Faeroes.

faff (fæf) *vb.* (often foll. by *about*) *Brit. informal.* to dither or fuss. [origin unknown]

fag[1] (fæg) *n.* **1.** *Informal.* a boring or wearisome task. **2.** *Brit.* (esp. formerly) a young public school boy who performs menial chores for an older boy. ~*vb.* **fagging, fagged. 3.** (often foll. by *out*)

Informal. to become or make exhausted by hard work. **4.** *Brit.* to do menial chores in a public school. [origin unknown]

fag[2] (fæg) *n. Brit. slang.* a cigarette. [origin unknown]

fag[3] (fæg) *n. Slang, chiefly U.S. & Canad.* short for **faggot**[2].

fag end *n.* **1.** the last and worst part. **2.** *Brit. informal.* the stub of a cigarette.

faggot[1] or *esp. U.S.* **fagot** ('fægət) *n.* **1.** a ball of chopped liver bound with herbs and bread. **2.** a bundle of sticks. [Old French]

faggot[2] ('fægət) *n. Slang, chiefly U.S. & Canad.* a male homosexual. [special use of FAGGOT[1]]

fah or **fa** (fɑː) *n. Music.* **1.** the note F. **2.** (in tonic sol-fa) the fourth degree of any major scale.

Fah. or **Fahr.** Fahrenheit.

Fahrenheit ('færən,haɪt) *adj.* of or measured according to the scale of temperature in which 32° represents the melting point of ice and 212° the boiling point of water. [after Gabriel *Fahrenheit*, physicist]

faïence (faɪ'ɑːns) *n.* tin-glazed earthenware. [*Faenza*, N Italy, where made]

fail (feɪl) *vb.* **1.** to be unsuccessful in an attempt. **2.** to stop operating. **3.** to judge or be judged as being below the officially accepted standard required in (a course or examination). **4.** to prove disappointing or useless to (someone). **5.** to neglect or be unable (to do something). **6.** to go bankrupt. ~*n.* **7.** a failure to attain the required standard. **8. without fail.** definitely. [Latin *fallere* to disappoint]

failing ('feɪlɪŋ) *n.* **1.** a weak point. ~*prep.* **2.** in default of: *failing a solution, the problem will have to wait.*

fail-safe *adj.* **1.** designed to return to a safe condition in the event of a failure or malfunction. **2.** safe from failure; foolproof.

failure ('feɪljə) *n.* **1.** the act or an instance of failing. **2.** a person or thing that is unsuccessful. **3.** nonperformance of something required or expected. **4.** cessation of normal operation: *a power failure.* **5.** an insufficiency: *crop failure.* **6.** the fact of not reaching the required standard in an examination or test. **7.** bankruptcy.

fain (feɪn) *adv.* **1.** *Archaic.* gladly. ~*adj.* **2.** *Obs.* **a.** willing. **b.** compelled. [Old English *fægen*]

faint (feɪnt) *adj.* **1.** lacking clarity, brightness, or volume. **2.** lacking conviction or force. **3.** feeling dizzy or weak. **4.** timid (esp. in **faint-hearted**). ~*vb.* **5.** to lose consciousness. ~*n.* **6.** a sudden loss of consciousness. [Old French *faindre* to be idle] —**'faintly** *adv.*

fair[1] (fɛə) *adj.* **1.** free from discrimination or dishonesty. **2.** in conformity with rules. **3.** light in colour. **4.** beautiful. **5.** quite good. **6.** unblemished. **7.** (of the wind) favourable. **8.** fine or cloudless. **9. fair and square.** in a correct or just way. ~*adv.* **10.** in a fair way. **11.** absolutely or squarely; quite. [Old English *fæger*] —**'fairness** *n.*

fair[2] (fɛə) *n.* **1.** a travelling entertainment

with sideshows, rides, and amusements. **2.** an exhibition of goods produced by a particular industry to promote business. [Latin *fēriae* holidays]

fairground (ˈfɛəˌɡraʊnd) *n.* an open space used for a fair.

fairing (ˈfɛərɪŋ) *n.* an external metal structure fitted around parts of an aircraft, car, etc., to reduce drag. [*fair* to streamline]

Fair Isle *n.* an intricate multicoloured knitted pattern. [after one of the Shetland Islands where this type of pattern originated]

fairly (ˈfɛəlɪ) *adv.* **1.** moderately. **2.** as deserved; justly. **3.** positively: *the hall fairly rang with applause.*

fair play *n.* a conventional standard of honourable behaviour.

fair sex *n.* **the.** women collectively.

fairway (ˈfɛəˌweɪ) *n.* **1.** (on a golf course) the mown areas between tees and greens. **2.** *Naut.* a navigable channel.

fair-weather *adj.* not reliable in difficult situations: *fair-weather friend.*

fairy (ˈfɛərɪ) *n., pl.* **fairies.** **1.** an imaginary supernatural being with magical powers. **2.** *Slang.* a male homosexual. [Old French *faerie* fairyland, from *feie* fairy]

fairy godmother *n.* a benefactress.

fairyland (ˈfɛərɪˌlænd) *n.* **1.** the imaginary domain of the fairies. **2.** an enchanted or wonderful place.

fairy lights *pl. n.* small coloured electric bulbs used as decoration, esp. on a Christmas tree.

fairy ring *n.* a ring of dark grass caused by fungi.

fairy tale *or* **story** *n.* **1.** a story about fairies or other mythical beings. **2.** a highly improbable account.

fait accompli (ˌfeɪt əˈkɒmpliː) *n.* something already done and beyond alteration. [French]

faith (feɪθ) *n.* **1.** strong belief in something, esp. without proof. **2.** a specific system of religious beliefs. **3.** complete confidence or trust, as in a person or remedy. **4.** loyalty. **5. bad faith.** dishonesty. **6. good faith.** honesty. ~*adj.* **7.** using or relating to the supposed ability to cure bodily ailments by means of religious faith: *a faith healer.* [Latin *fidēs* trust, confidence]

faithful (ˈfeɪθfʊl) *adj.* **1.** remaining true or loyal. **2.** maintaining sexual loyalty to one's lover or spouse. **3.** consistently reliable. **4.** accurate. ~*n.* **5. the faithful. a.** the believers in a religious faith. **b.** loyal followers. —ˈ**faithfully** *adv.* —ˈ**faithfulness** *n.*

faithless (ˈfeɪθlɪs) *adj.* treacherous or disloyal.

fake (feɪk) *vb.* **1.** to cause (something not genuine) to appear real or more valuable by fraud. **2.** to pretend to have (an illness, emotion, etc.). ~*n.* **3.** an object, person, or act that is not genuine. ~*adj.* **4.** not genuine. [prob. from Italian *facciare* to make or do]

fakir (ˈfeɪkɪə, fəˈkɪə) *n.* **1.** a member of any

religious order of Islam. **2.** a Hindu holy man. [Arabic *faqīr* poor]

falcon (ˈfɔːlkən) *n.* a type of bird of prey that can be trained to hunt small game. [Late Latin *falcō* hawk]

falconry (ˈfɔːlkənrɪ) *n.* **1.** the art of training falcons to hunt. **2.** the sport of hunting with falcons. —ˈ**falconer** *n.*

fall (fɔːl) *vb.* **falling, fell, fallen.** **1.** to descend by the force of gravity from a higher to a lower place. **2.** to drop suddenly from an erect position. **3.** to collapse to the ground. **4.** to become less or lower in number or quality. **5.** to slope downwards. **6.** to be badly wounded or killed. **7.** to yield to temptation or sin. **8.** to yield to attack. **9.** to lose power or status. **10.** to pass into a specified condition: *fall asleep.* **11.** to adopt a despondent expression: *her face fell.* **12.** to occur; take place: *night fell.* **13.** to occur at a specified place: *the accent falls on the last syllable.* **14.** (foll. by *to*) to be inherited (by). **15. fall short. a.** to prove inadequate. **b.** (often foll. by *of*) to fail to reach (a standard). ~*n.* **16.** an instance of falling. **17.** something that falls: *a fall of snow.* **18.** *Chiefly U.S. & Canad.* autumn. **19.** (*often pl.*) a waterfall. **20.** a decrease in value or number. **21.** a decline in status or importance. **22.** a capture or overthrow: *the fall of the city.* **23.** *Wrestling.* a scoring move, pinning both shoulders of one's opponent to the floor for a specified period. ~See also **fall about, fall away,** etc. [Old English *feallan*]

Fall (fɔːl) *n.* **the.** *Theol.* Adam's sin of disobedience and the state of innate sinfulness following from this for himself and all mankind.

fall about *vb.* to laugh in an uncontrolled manner.

fallacy (ˈfæləsɪ) *n., pl.* **-cies.** **1.** an incorrect or misleading notion based on inaccurate facts or invalid reasoning. **2.** unsound reasoning. [Latin *fallere* to deceive] —**fallacious** (fəˈleɪʃəs) *adj.*

fall away *vb.* **1.** to become less: *their supporters fell away.* **2.** to slope down.

fall back *vb.* **1.** to retreat. **2.** (foll. by *on* or *upon*) to have recourse (to).

fall behind *vb.* **1.** to fail to keep up. **2.** to be in arrears, as with a payment.

fall down *vb.* **1.** to drop suddenly or collapse. **2.** (often foll. by *on*) *Informal.* to fail.

fallen (ˈfɔːlən) *vb.* **1.** the past participle of **fall.** ~*adj.* **2.** having sunk in reputation: *a fallen woman.* **3.** killed in battle.

fall for *vb.* **1.** to become infatuated with (a person). **2.** to be deceived by (a lie or trick).

fall guy *n. Informal.* **1.** the victim of a confidence trick. **2.** a scapegoat.

fallible (ˈfælɪbᵊl) *adj.* **1.** capable of being mistaken. **2.** liable to mislead. [Latin *fallere* to deceive] —ˌ**falli'bility** *n.*

fall in *vb.* **1.** to collapse. **2.** to adopt a military formation, esp. as a soldier taking his place in a line. **3.** (often foll. by *with*) **a.** to meet and join. **b.** to agree with or support a person or suggestion.

falling star *n. Informal.* a meteor.

fall off *vb.* **1.** to drop unintentionally to the ground from (a high object, bicycle, etc.). **2.** to diminish in size or intensity.

fall on *vb.* **1.** to attack or snatch (an army, booty, etc.). **2. fall on one's feet.** to emerge unexpectedly well from a difficult situation.

Fallopian tube (fəˈləʊpɪən) *n.* either of a pair of slender tubes through which ova pass from the ovaries to the uterus in female mammals. [after Gabriello *Fallopio*, anatomist]

fallout (ˈfɔːlˌaʊt) *n.* **1.** radioactive material in the atmosphere following a nuclear explosion. ~*vb.* **fall out.** **2.** *Informal.* to disagree. **3.** to occur. **4.** *Mil.* to leave a disciplinary formation.

fallow[1] (ˈfæləʊ) *adj.* (of land) left unseeded after being ploughed to regain fertility for a crop. [Old English *fealga*]

fallow[2] (ˈfæləʊ) *adj.* light yellowish-brown. [Old English *fealu*]

fallow deer *n.* a species of deer with a reddish coat with white spots in summer.

fall through *vb.* to fail.

fall to *vb.* **1.** to begin some activity, as eating, working, or fighting. **2.** to devolve on (a person): *the task fell to me.*

false (fɔːls) *adj.* **1.** not in accordance with the truth or facts. **2.** irregular or invalid: *a false start.* **3.** untruthful or false: *a false account.* **4.** artificial; fake. **5.** misleading or deceptive. **6.** treacherous. **7.** forced or insincere: *a false smile.* **8.** based on mistaken ideas. ~*adv.* **9.** in a dishonest manner (esp. in **play someone false**). [Old English *fals*] —**ˈfalsely** *adv.* —**ˈfalseness** *n.*

falsehood (ˈfɔːls.hʊd) *n.* **1.** the quality of being untrue. **2.** a lie.

false pretences *pl. n.* **under false pretences.** so as to mislead people about one's true intentions.

falsetto (fɔːlˈsɛtəʊ) *n., pl.* -**tos.** a voice pitch higher than normal, esp. of a male tenor. [Italian]

falsies (ˈfɔːlsɪz) *pl. n. Informal.* pads worn to exaggerate the size of a woman's breasts.

falsify (ˈfɔːlsɪˌfaɪ) *vb.* -**fying,** -**fied.** to make (a report or evidence) false by alteration in order to deceive. [Latin *falsus* false + *facere* to make] —**falsification** (ˌfɔːlsɪfɪˈkeɪʃən) *n.*

falsity (ˈfɔːlsɪtɪ) *n., pl.* -**ties.** **1.** the state of being false. **2.** a lie.

falter (ˈfɔːltə) *vb.* **1.** to be hesitant, weak, or unsure. **2.** to move unsteadily. **3.** to utter hesitantly. [origin unknown] —**ˈfaltering** *adj.*

fame (feɪm) *n.* **1.** the state of being widely known or recognized. **2.** *Archaic.* public report. [Latin *fāma* report]

famed (feɪmd) *adj.* famous or renowned.

familial (fəˈmɪlɪəl) *adj.* of or relating to the family.

familiar (fəˈmɪljə) *adj.* **1.** well-known. **2.** frequent or customary: *a familiar excuse.* **3.** (foll. by *with*) acquainted. **4.** friendly; intimate. **5.** more intimate than is accept-able; presumptuous. ~*n.* **6.** a supernatural spirit supposed to attend a witch. **7.** a friend. [Latin *familia* family] —**faˈmiliarly** *adv.* —**familiarity** (fəˌmɪlɪˈærɪtɪ) *n.*

familiarize *or* -**rise** (fəˈmɪljəˌraɪz) *vb.* to make (oneself or someone else) fully acquainted with a particular subject. —**faˌmiliariˈzation** *or* -**riˈsation** *n.*

family (ˈfæmɪlɪ, ˈfæmlɪ) *n., pl.* -**lies.** **1.** a social group consisting of parents and their offspring. **2.** one's wife or husband and one's children. **3.** one's children. **4.** a group descended from a common ancestor. **5.** all the people living together in one household. **6.** any group of related things or beings, esp. when scientifically categorized. **7.** *Biol.* any of the taxonomic groups into which an order is divided and which contains one or more genera. **8. in the family way.** *Informal.* pregnant. [Latin *familia*]

Family Allowance *n.* **1.** (in Britain) a former name for **child benefit.** **2.** (in Canada) an allowance paid by the Federal Government to the parents of dependent children.

family benefit *n. N.Z.* a child allowance paid to the mothers of children under 18.

family credit *n. Brit.* an allowance paid to families whose earnings from full-time work are low.

family man *n.* a man who is married and has children, esp. one who is devoted to his family.

family name *n.* a surname, esp. when regarded as representing the family honour.

family planning *n.* the control of the number of children in a family, esp. by the use of contraceptives.

family support *n. N.Z.* a top-up of family income in certain circumstances where there are dependent children.

family tree *n.* a chart showing the genealogical relationships of a family.

famine (ˈfæmɪn) *n.* a severe shortage of food. [Latin *famēs* hunger]

famish (ˈfæmɪʃ) *vb.* **be famished** *or* **famishing.** to be very hungry. [Latin *famēs* famine]

famous (ˈfeɪməs) *adj.* **1.** known to or recognized by many people. **2.** *Informal.* excellent; splendid. [Latin *fāmōsus*] —**famously** *adv.*

fan[1] (fæn) *n.* **1.** any device for creating a current of air, esp. a rotating device of blades attached to a central hub. **2.** a folding semicircular series of flat segments of paper or ivory, waved in the hand to cool oneself. **3.** something shaped like such a fan, such as the tail of certain birds. ~*vb.* **fanning, fanned.** **4.** to cause a current of air to blow upon, as by means of a fan. **5.** to agitate or move (air) with or as if with a fan. **6.** (often foll. by *out*) to spread out in the shape of a fan. [Latin *vannus*]

fan[2] (fæn) *n.* a devotee of a pop star, sport, or hobby. [from *fanatic*]

fanatic (fəˈnætɪk) *n.* **1.** a person whose enthusiasm for something is extreme. **2.**

Informal. a person devoted to a particular hobby or pastime. **~adj.** *also* **fanatical.** 3. excessively dedicated. [Latin *fānāticus* belonging to a temple, hence, inspired by a god, frenzied] —**fa'natically** *adv.* —**fa-'nati,cism** *n.*

fan belt *n.* the belt that drives a cooling fan in a car engine.

fancier ('fænsɪə) *n.* a person with a special interest in something: *a pigeon fancier.*

fanciful ('fænsɪful) *adj.* 1. not based on fact. 2. made in a curious or imaginative way. 3. indulging in fancy. —**'fancifully** *adv.*

fan club *n.* an organized group of admirers of a particular pop singer or star.

fancy ('fænsɪ) *adj.* **-cier, -ciest.** 1. special, unusual, and elaborate. 2. (often used ironically) superior in quality. 3. higher than expected: *fancy prices.* **~n.,** *pl.* **-cies.** 4. a sudden capricious idea. 5. a sudden or irrational liking for a person or thing. 6. imagination. **~vb.** **-cying, -cied.** 7. to picture in the imagination. 8. to suppose: *I fancy it will rain.* 9. (reflexive) to have a high opinion of oneself. 10. *Informal.* to have a wish for. 11. *Brit. informal.* to be physically attracted to (another person). **~interj.** 12. Also: **fancy that!** an exclamation of surprise. [Middle English *fantsy*] —**'fancily** *adv.*

fancy dress *n.* costume worn at parties, representing a historical or fictional figure.

fancy-free *adj.* not in love.

fancy goods *pl. n.* small decorative gifts.

fancy man *n. Slang.* 1. a woman's lover. 2. a pimp.

fancy woman *n. Slang.* a mistress or prostitute.

fancywork ('fænsɪ,wɜːk) *n.* ornamental needlework.

fandango (fæn'dæŋɡəʊ) *n., pl.* **-gos.** an old Spanish dance in triple time. [Spanish]

fanfare ('fænfɛə) *n.* a flourish or short tune played on brass instruments. [French]

fang (fæŋ) *n.* 1. the long pointed tooth of a poisonous snake through which poison is injected. 2. the canine tooth of a carnivorous mammal. [Old English *fang* what is caught, prey]

fanjet ('fæn,dʒɛt) *n.* same as **turbofan.**

fanlight ('fæn,laɪt) *n.* a semicircular window over a door or window.

fanny ('fænɪ) *n., pl.* **-nies.** *Slang.* 1. *Brit. taboo.* the female genitals. 2. *Chiefly U.S. & Canad.* the buttocks. [origin unknown]

fantail ('fæn,teɪl) *n.* 1. a breed of domestic pigeon having a large tail like a fan. 2. a flycatcher of Australia, New Zealand, and SE Asia with a broad fan-shaped tail.

fantasia (fæn'teɪzɪə) *n.* 1. any musical composition of a free or improvisatory nature. 2. a potpourri of popular tunes. [Italian: fancy]

fantasize *or* **-sise** ('fæntə,saɪz) *vb.* to indulge in extravagant or fantastic daydreams (about something).

fantastic (fæn'tæstɪk) *adj.* 1. strange or

fanciful in appearance or conception. 2. unrealistic or absurd. 3. *Informal.* very large or very good.

fantasy ('fæntəsɪ) *n., pl.* **-sies.** 1. imagination unrestricted by reality. 2. a whimsical or far-fetched notion. 3. a daydream. 4. a highly elaborate imaginative creation. 5. literature with a large fantasy content. 6. *Music.* same as **fantasia.** [Greek *phantazein* to make visible]

fan vaulting *n. Archit.* vaulting having ribs that radiate like those of a fan from the top of a capital.

far (fɑː) *adv., adj.* **farther** *or* **further, farthest** *or* **furthest.** 1. at, to, or from a great distance. 2. at or to a remote time: *far in the future.* 3. to a considerable degree: *far better.* 4. **as far as. a.** to the degree or extent that. **b.** to the distance or place of. **c.** *Informal.* with reference to. 5. **by far.** by a considerable margin. 6. **far and away.** by a very great margin. 7. **far and wide.** everywhere. 8. **go far. a.** to be successful. **b.** to be sufficient or last long: *the wine didn't go far.* 9. **go too far.** to exceed reasonable limits. 10. **so far. a.** up to the present moment. **b.** up to a certain point, extent, or degree. **~adj.** 11. remote in space or time: *in the far past.* 12. extending a great distance. 13. more distant: *the far end of the room.* 14. **far from.** in a degree or state remote from: *he is far from happy.* [Old English *feorr*]

farad ('færəd) *n. Physics.* the derived SI unit of electric capacitance. [after Michael Faraday, physicist]

faraway ('fɑːrə,weɪ) *adj.* 1. very distant. 2. absent-minded.

farce (fɑːs) *n.* 1. a broadly humorous play based on improbable situations. 2. the genre of comedy of this kind. 3. a ludicrous situation or action. [Latin *farcire* to stuff, interpolate passages (in plays)] —**'farcical** *adj.*

fare (fɛə) *n.* 1. the sum charged or paid for conveyance in a bus, train, or plane. 2. a paying passenger. 3. a range of food and drink. **~vb.** 4. to get on (as specified): *he fared well.* [Old English *faran*]

Far East *n.* **the.** the countries of E Asia. —**Far Eastern** *adj.*

fare stage *n.* 1. a section of a bus journey for which a set charge is made. 2. the bus stop marking the end of such a section.

farewell (,fɛə'wɛl) *interj.* 1. goodbye; adieu. **~n.** 2. a parting salutation. 3. an act of departure.

far-fetched *adj.* unlikely.

far-flung *adj.* 1. widely distributed. 2. far distant; remote.

farinaceous (,færɪ'neɪʃəs) *adj.* 1. having a mealy texture. 2. containing starch. [Latin *fār* coarse meal]

farm (fɑːm) *n.* 1. a tract of land, usually with a house and buildings, cultivated as a unit or used to rear livestock. 2. a unit of land or water devoted to the growing or rearing of some particular type of fruit, animal, or fish: *a salmon farm.* **~vb.** 3. **a.** to cultivate (land). **b.** to rear (stock) on a farm. **4.** to engage in agricultural work as a way of life. **5.** to collect the moneys due and retain the profits from (a tax district or business). ~See also **farm out.** [Old French *ferme* rented land]

farmer ('fɑːmə) *n.* a person who owns or manages a farm.

farm hand *n.* a person who is hired to work on a farm.

farmhouse ('fɑːm,haʊs) *n.* a house attached to a farm.

farming ('fɑːmɪŋ) *n.* the business or skill of agriculture.

farm out *vb.* **1.** to send (work) to be done by another person or firm. **2.** to put (a child) into the care of a private individual.

farmstead ('fɑːm,stɛd) *n.* a farm and its main buildings.

farmyard ('fɑːm,jɑːd) *n.* an area surrounded by or adjacent to farm buildings.

far-off *adj.* remote in space or time; distant.

far-out *adj. Slang.* **1.** bizarre or avant-garde. **2.** wonderful.

far-reaching *adj.* extensive in influence, effect, or range.

farrier ('færɪə) *n. Chiefly Brit.* a person who shoes horses. [Latin *ferrārius* smith]

farrow ('færəʊ) *n.* **1.** a litter of piglets. ~*vb.* **2.** (of a sow) to give birth to (a litter). [Old English *fearh*]

far-seeing *adj.* having shrewd judgment.

far-sighted *adj.* **1.** possessing prudence and foresight. **2.** long-sighted.

fart (fɑːt) *Taboo.* ~*n.* **1.** an emission of intestinal gas from the anus. ~*vb.* **2.** to break wind. [Middle English *farten*]

farther ('fɑːðə) *adv.* **1.** to or at a greater distance in space or time. **2.** in addition. ~*adj.* **3.** more distant or remote in space or time. **4.** additional. [Middle English]

farthermost ('fɑːðə,məʊst) *adj.* most distant or remote.

farthest ('fɑːðɪst) *adv.* **1.** to or at the greatest distance in space or time. ~*adj.* **2.** most distant in space or time. **3.** most extended. [Middle English *ferthest*]

farthing ('fɑːðɪŋ) *n.* a former British coin worth a quarter of an old penny. [Old English *fēorthing*]

farthingale ('fɑːðɪŋ,geɪl) *n.* a hoop worn under skirts, esp. in the Elizabethan period. [Old Spanish *verdugo* rod]

fasces ('fæsiːz) *pl. n., sing.* **-cis** (-sɪs). (in ancient Rome) a bundle of rods containing an axe with its blade protruding; a symbol of a magistrate's power. [Latin]

fascia or **facia** ('feɪʃə) *n., pl.* **-ciae** (-ʃɪ,iː). **1.** the flat surface above a shop window. **2.** *Archit.* a flat band or surface. **3.** *Brit.* the outer panel which covers the dashboard of a motor vehicle. [Latin: band]

fascinate ('fæsɪ,neɪt) *vb.* **1.** to attract and delight by arousing interest. **2.** to render motionless, as by arousing terror or awe. [Latin *fascinum* a bewitching] —**'fasci,nating** *adj.* —**,fasci'nation** *n.*

Fascism ('fæʃɪzəm) *n.* **1.** the authoritarian nationalistic political movement in Italy (1922–43). **2.** (*sometimes not cap.*) any ideology or movement like this. [Italian *fascio* political group] —**'Fascist** *n., adj.*

fashion ('fæʃən) *n.* **1.** style in clothes or behaviour, esp. the latest style. **2.** manner of performance: *in a striking fashion.* **3. after** or **in a fashion.** in some manner, but not very well: *I mended it, after a fashion.* ~*vb.* **4.** to form or shape. [Latin *facere* to make]

fashionable ('fæʃənəb'l) *adj.* **1.** conforming to fashion; in vogue. **2.** of or patronized by people of fashion: *a fashionable café.* —**'fashionably** *adv.*

fast¹ (fɑːst) *adj.* **1.** acting or moving or capable of acting or moving quickly. **2.** accomplished in or lasting a short time. **3.** adapted to or facilitating rapid movement: *the fast lane.* **4.** (of a clock or watch) indicating a time in advance of the correct time. **5.** given to an active dissipated life. **6.** firmly fixed, fastened, or shut. **7.** steadfast; constant (esp. in **fast friends**). **8.** that will not fade. **9.** *Photog.* requiring a relatively short exposure. **10. a fast one.** *Informal.* an unscrupulous trick (esp. in **pull a fast one**). ~*adv.* **11.** quickly; rapidly. **12.** soundly; deeply: *fast asleep.* **13.** firmly; tightly: *stuck fast.* **14. play fast and loose.** to behave in an insincere or unreliable manner. [Old English *fæst* strong, tight]

fast² (fɑːst) *vb.* **1.** to abstain from eating, esp. as a religious observance. ~*n.* **2.** a period of fasting. [Old English *fæstan*]

fast-breeder reactor *n.* a nuclear reactor that produces more fissionable material than it consumes.

fasten ('fɑːs'n) *vb.* **1.** to make or become secure or joined. **2.** to close by fixing firmly in place or locking. **3.** (usually foll. by *on* or *upon*) to direct (one's attention) in a concentrated way. **4.** (usually foll. by *on*) to take a firm hold of. [Old English *fæstnian*] —**'fastener** *n.*

fastening ('fɑːs'nɪŋ) *n.* something that fastens, such as a clasp or lock.

fast food *n.* food, such as hamburgers, that is prepared and served very quickly.

fastidious (fæ'stɪdɪəs) *adj.* **1.** excessively particular about details. **2.** easily disgusted. [Latin *fastīdiōsus* scornful] —**fas'tidiously** *adv.* —**fas'tidiousness** *n.*

fast lane *n.* **1.** the outside lane on a motorway for overtaking or travelling fast. **2.** *Informal.* the quickest but most competitive route to success.

fastness ('fɑːstnɪs) *n.* a stronghold; fortress.

fast-track *adj.* taking the quickest but most competitive route to success or personal advancement: *fast-track executives.*

fat (fæt) *adj.* **fatter, fattest** **1.** having more flesh on the body than is thought necessary or desirable; overweight. **2.** containing a lot of fat: *fat bacon.* **3.** thick: *a fat volume.* **4.** profitable. **5.** fertile or productive. **6.** *Slang.* very little or none (esp. in **a fat chance, a fat lot of good**). ~*n.* **7.** extra or unwanted flesh on the body. **8.** a greasy or oily substance obtained from animals or plants and used in cooking. **9. the fat is in the fire.** an action has been taken from which dire consequences are expected. **10. the fat of the land.** the best that is obtainable. [Old English *fætt*] —**'fatless** *adj.* —**'fatness** *n.*

fatal ('feɪt'l) *adj.* **1.** resulting in death: *a fatal accident.* **2.** bringing ruin. [Latin *fātum* fate] —**'fatally** *adv.*

fatalism ('feɪtə,lɪzəm) *n.* the belief that all events are predetermined so that man is powerless to alter his destiny. —**'fatalist** *n.* —**,fatal'istic** *adj.* —**,fatal'istically** *adv.*

fatality (fə'tælɪtɪ) *n., pl.* **-ties. 1.** a death caused by an accident or disaster. **2.** the power of causing death or disaster.

fate (feɪt) *n.* **1.** the ultimate agency that predetermines the course of events. **2.** the inevitable fortune that befalls a person or thing. **3.** death or downfall. [Latin *fātum*]

fated ('feɪtɪd) *adj.* **1.** destined: *we were fated to dislike each other.* **2.** doomed to death or destruction.

fateful ('feɪtful) *adj.* having important, and usually disastrous, consequences. —**'fatefully** *adv.*

fathead ('fæt,hed) *n. Informal.* a stupid person; fool. —**'fat,headed** *adj.*

father ('fɑːðə) *n.* **1.** a male parent. **2.** a person who founds a line or family; forefather. **3.** any male acting in a paternal capacity. **4.** a male who originates something: *the father of modern psychology.* **5.** a leader of an association or council: *a city father.* ~*vb.* **6.** to procreate (offspring). **7.** to create, found, etc. [Old English *fæder*] —**'fatherhood** *n.*

Father ('fɑːðə) *n.* **1.** God. **2.** any of the early writers on Christian doctrine. **3.** a title used for Christian priests.

father-in-law *n., pl.* **fathers-in-law.** the father of one's wife or husband.

fatherland ('fɑːðə,lænd) *n.* a person's native country.

fatherly ('fɑːðəlɪ) *adj.* kind or protective, like a father.

Father's Day *n.* a day observed in honour of fathers.

fathom ('fæðəm) *n.* **1.** a unit of length equal to six feet, used to measure depths of water. ~*vb.* **2.** to penetrate (a mystery or problem). **3.** to measure the depth of. [Old English *fæthm*] —**'fathomable** *adj.*

fathomless ('fæðəmlɪs) *adj.* too deep or difficult to fathom.

fatigue (fə'tiːg) *n.* **1.** physical or mental exhaustion due to exertion. **2.** the weakening of a material subjected to alternating stresses. **3.** any of the mainly domestic duties performed by military personnel. **4.** (*pl.*) special clothing worn to carry out such duties. ~*vb.* **-tiguing, -tigued. 5.** to make or become weary or exhausted. [Latin *fatigāre* to tire]

fat stock *n.* livestock fattened and ready for market.

fatten ('fæt'n) *vb.* to grow or cause to grow fat or fatter. —**'fattening** *adj.*

fatty ('fætɪ) *adj.* **-tier, -tiest. 1.** containing or derived from fat. **2.** greasy; oily. ~*n., pl.* **-ties.** *Informal.* a fat person.

fatty acid *n.* any of a class of organic acids some of which, such as stearic acid, are found in animal or vegetable fats.

fatuity (fə'tjuːɪtɪ) *n., pl.* **-ties. 1.** complacent silliness. **2.** a fatuous remark.

fatuous ('fætjʊəs) *adj.* complacently silly. [Latin *fatuus*] —**'fatuously** *adv.*

faucet ('fɔːsɪt) *n.* **1.** a tap fitted to a barrel. **2.** *U.S. & Canad.* a tap. [Old French]

fault (fɔːlt) *n.* **1.** a failing or defect; flaw. **2.** a mistake or error. **3.** responsibility for something wrong. **4.** *Geol.* a fracture in the earth's crust with displacement of the rocks on either side. **5.** *Tennis, squash, etc.* an invalid serve. **6.** (in showjumping) a penalty mark for failing to clear, or refusing, a fence. **7. at fault.** guilty of error; culpable. **8. find fault with.** to seek out minor imperfections in. **9. to a fault.** excessively. ~*vb.* **10.** *Geol.* to undergo or cause to undergo a fault. **11.** to criticize or blame. [Latin *fallere* to fail] —**'faultless** *adj.* —**'faultlessly** *adv.*

fault-finding *n.* continual criticism.

faulty ('fɔːltɪ) *adj.* **faultier, faultiest.** defective or imperfect. —**'faultily** *adv.* —**'faultiness** *n.*

faun (fɔːn) *n.* (in Roman legend) a rural god represented as a man with a goat's ears, horns, and hind legs. [Latin *Faunus* god of forests]

fauna ('fɔːnə) *n., pl.* **-nas** or **-nae** (-niː). all the animal life of a given place or time. [Latin *Fauna* a goddess of living things]

faux pas (,fəʊ 'pɑː) *n., pl.* **faux pas** (,fəʊ 'pɑːz). a social blunder. [French]

favour or *U.S.* **favor** ('feɪvə) *n.* **1.** an approving attitude; goodwill. **2.** an act performed out of goodwill or generosity. **3.** partiality. **4.** in (or out of) favour. regarded with approval (or disapproval). **5. in favour of. a.** approving. **b.** to the benefit of. ~*vb.* **6.** to regard with especial kindness. **7.** to treat with partiality. **8.** to support; advocate. **9.** *Informal.* to resemble: *he favours his father.* [Latin *favēre* to protect]

favourable or *U.S.* **favorable** ('feɪvərəb'l) *adj.* **1.** advantageous, encouraging, or promising. **2.** giving consent. —**'favourably** or *U.S.* **'favorably** *adv.*

favourite or *U.S.* **favorite** ('feɪvərɪt) *adj.* **1.** most liked. ~*n.* **2.** a person or thing regarded with especial preference or liking. **3.** *Sport.* a competitor thought likely to win. [Latin *favēre* to protect]

favouritism or *U.S.* **favoritism** ('feɪvərɪ,tɪzəm) *n.* the practice of giving special treatment to a person or group.

fawn[1] (fɔːn) *n.* **1.** a young deer aged under one year. ~*adj.* **2.** light greyish-brown. [Latin *fētus* offspring]

fawn[2] (fɔːn) *vb.* (often foll. by *on* or *upon*) **1.** to seek attention (from someone) by cringing and flattering. **2.** (esp. of dogs) to try to please by a show of extreme friendliness. [Old English *fægnian* to be glad] —**'fawning** *adj.*

fax (fæks) *n.* **1.** short for **facsimile.** ~*vb.* **2.** to send (a document) by a telegraphic facsimile system.

FBI (in the U.S.) Federal Bureau of Investigation.

FD Defender of the Faith: one of the titles of the British sovereign. [Latin *Fidei Defensor*]

Fe *Chem.* iron. [Latin *ferrum*]

fealty ('fiːəltɪ) *n., pl.* **-ties.** (in feudal society) the loyalty sworn to a lord by his vassal. [Latin *fidēlitās* fidelity]

fear (fɪə) *n.* **1.** a feeling of distress or alarm caused by impending danger or pain. **2.** a cause of this feeling. **3.** awe; reverence: *fear of God.* **4.** possibility: *little fear of them refusing.* **5. no fear.** *Informal.* certainly not. ~*vb.* **6.** to be afraid (to do something) or of (a person or thing). **7.** to revere; respect. **8.** to be politely sorry: *I fear that you have not won.* **9.** (foll. by *for*) to feel anxiety about something. [Old English] —'**fearless** *adj.* —'**fearlessly** *adv.*

fearful ('fɪəful) *adj.* **1.** afraid. **2.** causing fear. **3.** *Informal.* very unpleasant. —'**fearfully** *adv.*

fearsome ('fɪəsəm) *adj.* frightening.

feasible ('fiːzəb'l) *adj.* able to be done; possible. [Anglo-French *faisible*] —,**feasi'bility** *n.* —'**feasibly** *adv.*

feast (fiːst) *n.* **1.** a large and sumptuous meal. **2.** a periodic religious celebration. **3.** something extremely pleasing: *a feast for the eyes.* ~*vb.* **4. a.** to eat a feast. **b.** (usually foll. by *on*) to enjoy the eating of. **5.** to give a feast to. **6.** to delight: *feast one's eyes.* [Latin *festus* joyful]

feat (fiːt) *n.* a remarkable, skilful, or daring action. [Anglo-French *fait*]

feather ('fɛðə) *n.* **1.** any of the flat light structures forming the plumage of birds, each consisting of a shaft with barbs on either side. **2. feather in one's cap.** a cause for pleasure at one's achievements. ~*vb.* **3.** to fit, cover, or supply with feathers. **4.** *Rowing.* to turn (an oar) parallel to the water between strokes, in order to lessen wind resistance. **5. feather one's nest.** to provide oneself with comforts. [Old English *fether*] —'**feathered** *adj.* —'**feathery** *adj.*

feather bed *n.* **1.** a mattress filled with feathers or down. ~*vb.* **featherbed, -bedding, -bedded.** **2.** to pamper; spoil.

featherbrain ('fɛðə,breɪn) *n.* a frivolous or forgetful person. —'**feather,brained** *adj.*

featherweight ('fɛðə,weɪt) *n.* **1.** something very light or of little importance. **2.** a professional boxer weighing up to 126 pounds or an amateur boxer weighing up to 57 kg. **3.** an amateur wrestler weighing up to 137 pounds.

feature ('fiːtʃə) *n.* **1.** any one of the parts of the face, such as the nose, chin, or mouth. **2.** a prominent or distinctive part, as of a landscape. **3.** the principal film in a cinema programme. **4.** an item appearing at intervals in a newspaper or magazine. **5.** a prominent story in a newspaper. ~*vb.* **6.** to have as a feature or make a feature of. **7.** to give prominence to. [Anglo-French *feture*] —'**featureless** *adj.*

Feb. February.

febrile ('fiːbraɪl) *adj.* of or relating to fever; feverish. [Latin *febris* fever]

February ('fɛbrʊərɪ) *n., pl.* **-aries.** the second month of the year. [Latin *Februārius mēnsis* month of expiation]

feckless ('fɛklɪs) *adj.* feeble; weak; ineffectual. [obs. *feck* value, effect]

fecund ('fiːkənd, 'fɛk-) *adj.* **1.** fertile. **2.** intellectually productive. [Latin *fēcundus*] —**fecundity** (fɪ'kʌndɪtɪ) *n.*

fecundate ('fiːkən,deɪt, 'fɛk-) *vb.* to make fruitful; fertilize. [Latin *fēcundāre* to fertilize]

fed (fɛd) *vb.* the past of **feed.**

federal ('fɛdərəl) *adj.* **1.** of a form of government in which power is divided between one central and several regional governments. **2.** of the central government of a federation. [Latin *foedus* league] —'**federa,lism** *n.* —'**federalist** *n., adj.*

Federal ('fɛdərəl) *adj.* of or supporting the Union government during the American Civil War.

Federal Government *n.* the national government of a federated state, such as that of Canada located in Ottawa.

federalize or **-lise** ('fɛdərə,laɪz) *vb.* **1.** to unite in a federal union. **2.** to subject to federal control. —,**federali'zation** or **-li'sation** *n.*

federate *vb.* ('fɛdə,reɪt). **1.** to unite in a federal union. ~*adj.* ('fɛdərɪt). **2.** federated. —'**federative** *adj.*

federation (,fɛdə'reɪʃən) *n.* **1.** the union of several provinces, states, etc. **2.** any alliance or confederacy.

fed up *adj. Informal.* annoyed or bored.

fee (fiː) *n.* **1.** a payment asked by professional people or public servants for their services. **2.** a charge made for a privilege: *an entrance fee.* **3.** *Property law.* an interest in land capable of being inherited. The interest can be with unrestricted rights (**fee simple**) or restricted (**fee tail**). [Old French *fie*]

feeble ('fiːb'l) *adj.* **1.** lacking in physical or mental strength. **2.** unconvincing: *feeble excuses.* [Old French *feble*] —'**feebly** *adv.*

feeble-minded *adj.* mentally defective.

feed (fiːd) *vb.* **feeding, fed. 1.** to give food to: *to feed the cat.* **2.** to give as food: *to feed meat to the cat.* **3.** to eat food: *the horses feed at noon.* **4.** to provide food for. **5.** to provide what is necessary for the continued existence, operation, or growth of: *feed one's imagination; the flames were fed by the escaping gas.* ~*n.* **6.** the act of feeding. **7.** food, esp. that of animals or babies. **8.** *Informal.* a meal. [Old English *fēdan*]

feedback ('fiːd,bæk) *n.* **1.** the return of part of the output of an electronic circuit to its input. **2.** the return of part of the sound output of a loudspeaker to the microphone, so that a high-pitched whistle is produced. **3.** information in response to an inquiry or experiment.

feeder ('fiːdə) n. **1.** a child's feeding bottle or bib. **2.** a tributary channel. **3.** a road or transport service that links secondary areas to the main traffic network.

feel (fiːl) vb. **feeling, felt. 1.** to have a physical or emotional sensation of (something): to feel anger. **2.** to become aware of or examine (something) by touching. **3.** to sense (esp. in **feel (it) in one's bones**). **4.** to believe: she felt it was right. **5.** (foll. by for) to show compassion (towards). **6.** (often foll. by up) Slang. to pass one's hands over the sexual organs of. **7. feel like.** to have an inclination (for something or doing something). **8. feel up to.** to be fit enough for (something or doing something). ~n. **9.** the act of feeling. **10.** an impression: a homely feel. **11.** the sense of touch. **12.** an instinctive aptitude: she's got a feel for this sort of work. [Old English fēlan]

feeler ('fiːlə) n. **1.** an organ in certain animals, such as an antenna, that is sensitive to touch. **2.** a remark designed to probe the reactions of others.

feeling ('fiːlɪŋ) n. **1.** an emotional reaction: a feeling of panic. **2.** (pl.) emotional sensitivity (esp. in **hurt the feelings of**). **3.** an emotional disturbance, esp. anger: a lot of bad feeling. **4.** intuitive appreciation and understanding: a feeling for words. **5.** an intuition: I had a feeling that something was wrong. **6.** opinion; view: what is his feeling on the matter? **7.** sympathy; pity. **8. a.** the ability to experience physical sensations, such as heat. **b.** the sensation so experienced. **9.** atmosphere; impression: a feeling of warmth. —**'feelingly** adv.

feet (fiːt) n. **1.** the plural of **foot. 2. be run or rushed off one's feet.** to be very busy. **3. feet of clay.** a weakness that is not widely known. **4. have (or keep) one's feet on the ground.** to be practical and reliable. **5. put one's feet up.** to take a rest. **6. stand on one's own feet.** to be independent. **7. sweep off one's feet.** to fill with enthusiasm.

feign (feɪn) vb. to pretend: to feign innocence. [Old French] —**feigned** adj.

feint[1] (feɪnt) n. **1.** a mock attack or movement designed to distract an adversary, as in boxing or fencing. ~vb. **2.** to make a feint. [Old French feindre to feign]

feint[2] (feɪnt) n. Printing. a narrow rule used for ruled paper. [var. of faint]

feldspar ('feldˌspɑː, 'felˌspɑː) or **felspar** n. a hard mineral that is the principal constituent of igneous rocks. [German] —**feldspathic** (feldˈspæθɪk, felˈspæθ-) or **fel'spathic** adj.

felicitate (fɪˈlɪsɪˌteɪt) vb. to congratulate. —**feˌliciˈtation** n.

felicity (fɪˈlɪsɪtɪ) n., pl. **-ties. 1.** happiness. **2.** appropriate expression or style. [Latin fēlīcitās happiness] —**feˈlicitous** adj.

feline ('fiːlaɪn) adj. **1.** of or belonging to the cat family. **2.** like a cat, esp. in stealth or grace. ~n. **3.** any member of the cat

family; a cat. [Latin fēlēs cat] —**felinity** (frɪˈlɪnɪtɪ) n.

fell[1] (fel) vb. the past tense of **fall**.

fell[2] (fel) vb. **1.** to cut or knock down: to fell a tree. **2.** Needlework. to fold under and sew flat (the edges of a seam). [Old English fellan]

fell[3] (fel) adj. **1.** Archaic. cruel or deadly. **2. one fell swoop.** a single destructive action or occurrence. [Middle English fel]

fell[4] (fel) n. (often pl.) Scot. & N English. a mountain, hill, or moor. [Old Norse fjall]

fellatio (frɪˈleɪʃɪəʊ) n. a sexual activity in which the penis is stimulated by the partner's mouth. [Latin fellāre to suck]

felloe ('feləʊ) or **felly** ('felɪ) n., pl. **-loes** or **-lies.** a segment or the whole rim of a wooden wheel. [Old English felge]

fellow ('feləʊ) n. **1.** a man or boy. **2.** (often pl.) a companion; associate. **3.** a member of the governing body at any of various universities or colleges. **4.** a postgraduate research student. **5.** a person in the same group, class, or condition. **6.** one of a pair; counterpart. [Old English fēolaga]

Fellow ('feləʊ) n. a member of any of various learned societies.

fellow feeling n. sympathy existing between people who have shared similar experiences.

fellowship ('feləʊˌʃɪp) n. **1.** the state of sharing mutual interests or activities. **2.** a society of people sharing mutual interests or activities. **3.** companionship; friendship. **4.** Education. a financed research post providing study facilities.

fellow traveller n. a non-Communist who sympathizes with Communism.

felon ('felən) n. Criminal law. (formerly) a person who has committed a felony. [Old French: villain]

felony ('felənɪ) n., pl. **-nies.** Criminal law. (formerly) a serious crime, such as murder or arson. —**felonious** (frɪˈləʊnɪəs) adj.

felspar ('felˌspɑː) n. same as **feldspar**.

felt[1] (felt) vb. the past of **feel**.

felt[2] (felt) n. **1.** a matted fabric of wool, made by working the fibres together under pressure. ~vb. **2.** to make into or cover with felt. **3.** to become matted. [Old English]

felt-tip pen n. a pen whose writing point is made from pressed fibres.

fem. 1. female. **2.** feminine.

female ('fiːmeɪl) adj. **1.** of the sex producing offspring. **2.** of or characteristic of a woman. **3.** (of reproductive organs such as the ovary and carpel) capable of producing female gametes. **4.** (of flowers) lacking stamens. **5.** having an internal cavity into which a projecting male counterpart may be fitted: a female thread. ~n. **6.** a female animal or plant. [Latin fēmina a woman]

feminine ('femɪnɪn) adj. **1.** characteristic of a woman. **2.** possessing qualities considered typical of or appropriate to a woman. **3.** effeminate; womanish. **4.** Grammar. belonging to a gender of nouns that includes all kinds of referents as well as some female referents. [Latin *fēmina* a woman] —,femi'ninity *n.*

feminism ('fɛmɪ,nɪzəm) *n.* a doctrine or movement that advocates equal rights for women. —'**feminist** *n., adj.*

femme fatale (,fæm fə'tɑːl) *n., pl.* **femmes fatales** (,fæm fə'tɑːlz). an alluring or seductive woman who causes men distress. [French]

femur ('fiːmə) *n., pl.* **femurs** or **femora** ('fɛmərə). the thighbone. [Latin: thigh] —'**femoral** *adj.*

fen (fɛn) *n.* low-lying flat marshy land. [Old English *fenn*]

fence (fɛns) *n.* **1.** a barrier that encloses an area such as a garden or field, usually made of posts connected by wire rails or boards. **2.** *Slang.* a dealer in stolen property. **3.** an obstacle for a horse to jump in steeplechasing or showjumping. **4.** *Machinery.* a guard or guide, esp. in a circular saw or plane. **5.** (**sit**) **on the fence.** (to be) unwilling to commit oneself. ~*vb.* **6.** to construct a fence on or around (a piece of land). **7.** (foll. by *in* or *off*) to close in or separate off with or as if with a fence. **8.** to fight using swords or foils. **9.** to evade a question. [Middle English *fens*, from *defens* defence]

fencing ('fɛnsɪŋ) *n.* **1.** the sport of fighting with foils. **2.** materials used for making fences.

fend (fɛnd) *vb.* **1.** (foll. by *for*) to give support (to someone, esp. oneself). **2.** (usually foll. by *off*) to ward off or turn aside (blows, questions, etc.). [Middle English *fenden*]

fender ('fɛndə) *n.* **1.** a low metal frame which confines falling coals to the hearth. **2.** a soft but solid object, such as a coil of rope, hung over the side of a vessel to prevent damage when docking. **3.** *U.S. & Canad.* the wing of a car.

fenestration (,fɛnɪ'streɪʃən) *n.* the arrangement of windows in a building. [Latin *fenestra* windows]

Fenian ('fiːnɪən, 'fɪnjən) *n.* (formerly) a member of an Irish revolutionary organization founded to fight for an independent Ireland. [after *Fiann* Irish folk hero] —'**Fenianism** *n.*

fennel ('fɛn°l) *n.* a strong-smelling yellow-flowered umbelliferous plant whose seeds, leaves, and root are used in cookery. [Old English *fenol*]

fenugreek ('fɛnjʊ,griːk) *n.* a heavily scented Mediterranean leguminous plant cultivated for its aromatic seeds. [Old English *fēnogrēcum*]

feoff (fiːf) *n.* same as **fief**. [Anglo-French]

feral ('fɪərəl) *adj.* **1.** (of animals and plants) existing in a wild state. **2.** savage; brutal. [Latin *ferus* savage]

fermata (fə'mɑːtə) *n., pl.* **-tas** or **-te** (-tɪ). *Music.* same as **pause** (sense 4). [Italian]

ferment *n.* ('fɜːment). **1.** commotion; unrest. **2.** any substance, such as yeast, that causes fermentation. ~*vb.* (fə'mɛnt). **3.** to undergo or cause to undergo fermentation. [Latin *fermentum* yeast]

fermentation (,fɜːmɛn'teɪʃən) *n.* a chemi-

cal reaction in which an organic molecule splits into simpler substances, esp. the conversion of sugar to ethyl alcohol by yeast.

fermium ('fɜːmɪəm) *n.* an element artificially produced by neutron bombardment of plutonium. Symbol: Fm [after Enrico *Fermi*, physicist]

fern (fɜːn) *n.* a flowerless plant with roots, stems, and fronds that reproduces by spores. [Old English *fearn*] —'**ferny** *adj.*

ferocious (fə'rəʊʃəs) *adj.* savagely fierce or cruel. [Latin *ferox*] —**ferocity** (fə'rɒsɪtɪ) *n.*

ferret ('fɛrɪt) *n.* **1.** a domesticated albino variety of the polecat bred for hunting rats and rabbits. ~*vb.* **2.** to hunt (rabbits or rats) with ferrets. **3.** to search around. **4. ferret out. a.** to drive from hiding. **b.** to find by persistent investigation. [Latin *fur* thief]

ferric ('fɛrɪk) *adj.* of or containing iron in the trivalent state. [Latin *ferrum* iron]

Ferris wheel ('fɛrɪs) *n.* a fairground wheel with seats freely suspended from its rim. [after G.W.G. *Ferris*, engineer]

ferroconcrete (,fɛrəʊ'kɒŋkriːt) *n.* same as **reinforced concrete**.

ferrous ('fɛrəs) *adj.* of or containing iron in the divalent state. [Latin *ferrum* iron]

ferruginous (fə'ruːdʒɪnəs) *adj.* **1.** (of minerals, rocks, etc.) containing iron. **2.** rust-coloured. [Latin *ferrum* iron]

ferrule ('fɛruːl) *n.* a metal ring or cap placed over the end of a stick for added strength. [Latin *viria* bracelet]

ferry ('fɛrɪ) *n., pl.* **-ries.** **1.** a boat for transporting passengers and usually vehicles across a body of water, esp. as a regular service. **2.** such a service. ~*vb.* **-rying, -ried.** **3.** to transport or go by ferry. **4.** to convey (passengers or goods). [Old English *ferian* to carry] —'**ferryman** *n.*

fertile ('fɜːtaɪl) *adj.* **1.** capable of producing offspring. **2.** (of land) capable of an abundant growth of plants. **3.** *Biol.* capable of development. **4.** producing many offspring; prolific. **5.** highly productive: *a fertile brain.* **6.** *Physics.* (of a substance) able to be transformed into fissile or fissionable material. [Latin *fertilis*] —**fertility** (fɜː'tɪlɪtɪ) *n.*

fertilize or **-lise** ('fɜːtɪ,laɪz) *vb.* **1.** to provide (an animal or plant) with sperm or pollen to bring about fertilization. **2.** to supply (soil) with nutrients. **3.** to make fertile. —,**fertili'zation** or -li'**sation** *n.*

fertilizer or **-liser** ('fɜːtɪ,laɪzə) *n.* any substance, such as manure, added to soil to increase its productivity.

fervent ('fɜːvənt) or **fervid** ('fɜːvɪd) *adj.* intensely sincere and passionate. [Latin *fervēre* to boil] —'**fervently** *adv.*

fervour or *U.S.* **fervor** ('fɜːvə) *n.* great intensity of feeling or belief. [Latin *fervēre* to boil]

fescue ('fɛskjuː) *n.* a widely grown pasture and lawn grass. [Old French *festu*]

festal ('fɛst°l) *adj.* festive. [Latin *festum* holiday]

fester ('fɛstə) vb. **1.** to form or cause to form pus. **2.** to rot; decay. **3.** to grow worse and develop increasing bitterness or hatred: *his anger festered inwardly.* [Old French *festre* suppurating sore]

festival ('fɛstɪvᵊl) n. **1.** a day or period set aside for celebration. **2.** an organized series of special events and performances: *a festival of drama.* [Latin *festivus* joyful]

festive ('fɛstɪv) adj. appropriate to or characteristic of a holiday or celebration. [Latin *festivus* joyful]

festivity (fɛs'tɪvɪtɪ) n., pl. **-ties. 1.** happy celebration; merriment. **2.** (*pl.*) celebrations.

festoon (fɛ'stuːn) n. **1.** a decorative chain of flowers or ribbons suspended in loops. **2.** a representation of this, as in architecture. ~vb. **3.** to decorate with festoons. **4.** to form into festoons. [Italian *festone* ornament for a feast]

feta ('fɛtə) n. a Greek white sheep cheese. [Modern Greek]

fetch[1] (fɛtʃ) vb. **1.** to go after and bring back. **2.** to cost or sell for (a certain price). **3.** to utter (a sigh or groan). **4.** *Informal.* to deal (a blow or slap). **5. fetch and carry.** to perform menial tasks. ~n. **6.** a trick or stratagem. [Old English *feccan*]

fetch[2] (fɛtʃ) n. the ghost or apparition of a living person. [origin unknown]

fetching ('fɛtʃɪŋ) adj. *Informal.* attractive.

fetch up vb. **1.** *Informal.* to arrive or end up. **2.** *Slang.* to vomit food.

fête or **fete** (feɪt) n. **1.** an event, usually outdoors, with stalls, competitions, etc., held to raise money for charity. ~vb. **2.** to honour or entertain regally. [French]

fetid ('fɛtɪd, 'fiː-) adj. having a stale nauseating smell, as of decay. [Latin *fētēre* stink]

fetish ('fɛtɪʃ, 'fiː-) n. **1.** something, esp. an inanimate object, that is believed to have magical powers. **2. a.** a form of behaviour in which sexual satisfaction is derived from handling an object. **b.** any object that is involved in such behaviour. **3.** any object, activity, etc., to which one is excessively devoted. [Portuguese *feitiço* sorcery] —'**fetish,ism** n. —'**fetishist** n.

fetlock ('fɛt,lɒk) n. **1.** a projection behind and above a horse's hoof. **2.** the tuft of hair growing from this part. [Middle English *fetlak*]

fetter ('fɛtə) n. **1.** (*often pl.*) a chain or bond fastened round the ankle. **2.** (*usually pl.*) a check or restraint. ~vb. **3.** to restrict. **4.** to bind in fetters. [Old English *fetor*]

fettle ('fɛtᵊl) n. state of health or spirits (esp. in **in fine fettle**). [Old English *fetel* belt]

fetus or **foetus** ('fiːtəs) n., pl. **-tuses.** the embryo of a mammal in the later stages of development. [Latin: offspring] —'**fetal** or '**foetal** adj.

feu (fjuː) n. *Scots Law.* a right to the use of land in return for a fixed annual payment (**feu duty**). [Old French]

feud (fjuːd) n. **1.** long and bitter hostility between two families, clans, or individuals. ~vb. **2.** to carry on a feud. [Old French *feide*]

feudal ('fjuːdᵊl) adj. of or characteristic of feudalism. [Medieval Latin *feudum* fief]

feudalism ('fjuːdə,lɪzəm) n. the legal and social system in medieval Europe, in which vassals were protected by their lords, and were required to serve under them in war. Also called: **feudal system.**

fever ('fiːvə) n. **1.** an abnormally high body temperature, accompanied by a fast pulse rate, shivering, and nausea. **2.** any of various diseases characterized by a high temperature. **3.** intense nervous excitement. ~vb. **4.** to affect with or as if with fever. [Latin *febris*] —'**fevered** adj.

feverish ('fiːvərɪʃ) adj. **1.** suffering from fever. **2.** in a state of restless excitement. —'**feverishly** adv.

fever pitch n. a state of intense excitement.

few (fjuː) det. **1.** hardly any: *few men are so cruel.* **2.** (preceded by *a*) a small number of: *a few drinks.* **3. a good few.** *Informal.* several. **4. few and far between.** scarce. **5. quite a few.** *Informal.* several. [Old English *fēawa*]

fey (feɪ) adj. **1.** whimsically strange. **2.** clairvoyant. **3.** *Chiefly Scot.* doomed. [Old English *fæge* marked out for death]

fez (fɛz) n., pl. **fezzes.** an originally Turkish brimless red cap, shaped like a truncated cone and with a tassel. [Turkish]

ff *Music.* fortissimo. See **f**

ff. and the following (pages, lines, etc.).

fiancé or (*fem.*) **fiancée** (fɪ'ɒnseɪ) n. a person who is engaged to be married. [Old French *fiancier* to promise, betroth]

fiasco (fɪ'æskəʊ) n., pl. **-cos** or **-coes.** a ridiculous or humiliating failure. [Italian: flask; sense development obscure]

fiat ('faɪæt) n. **1.** official sanction. **2.** an arbitrary order. [Latin: let it be done]

fib (fɪb) n. **1.** a trivial and harmless lie. ~vb. **fibbing, fibbed. 2.** to tell such a lie. [origin unknown] —'**fibber** n.

fibre or *U.S.* **fiber** ('faɪbə) n. **1.** a natural or synthetic thread that may be spun into yarn. **2.** essential substance or nature. **3.** strength of character (esp. in **moral fibre**). **4.** a fibrous substance, such as bran, as part of someone's diet: *dietary fibre.* [Latin *fibra* filament, entrails] —'**fibrous** adj.

fibreboard ('faɪbə,bɔːd) n. a building material made of compressed wood.

fibreglass ('faɪbə,glɑːs) n. **1.** material consisting of matted fine glass fibres, used as insulation. **2.** a light strong material made by bonding fibreglass with a synthetic resin; used for boats and car bodies.

fibre optics n. (*functioning as sing.*) the transmission of information modulated on light down very thin flexible fibres of glass. —**fibre optic** adj.

fibril ('faɪbrɪl) n. a small fibre.

fibrillation (,faɪbrɪ'leɪʃən) n. **1.** a local and uncontrollable twitching of muscle fibres. **2.** irregular twitchings of the muscular wall of the heart.

fibrin ('fıbrın) *n.* a white insoluble elastic protein formed when blood clots.

fibroid ('faıbrɔıd) *adj.* **1.** *Anat.* (of structures or tissues) containing or resembling fibres. ~*n.* **2.** a benign tumour derived from fibrous connective tissue.

fibrosis (faı'brəusıs) *n.* the formation of an abnormal amount of fibrous tissue.

fibrositis (,faıbrə'saıtıs) *n.* inflammation of white fibrous tissue, esp. of muscle sheaths.

fibula ('fıbjulə) *n., pl.* **-lae** (-,liː) *or* **-las.** the outer and thinner of the two bones between the knee and ankle of the human leg. [Latin: a clasp] —**'fibular** *adj.*

fiche (fiːʃ) *n.* See **microfiche.**

fickle ('fık³l) *adj.* changeable in purpose, affections, etc. [Old English ficol deceitful] —**'fickleness** *n.*

fiction ('fıkʃən) *n.* **1.** literary works invented by the imagination, such as novels. **2.** an invented story or explanation. **3.** *Law.* something assumed to be true for the sake of convenience, though probably false. [Latin fictiō a fashioning] —**'fictional** *adj.*

fictionalize *or* **-lise** ('fıkʃənə,laız) *vb.* to make into fiction.

fictitious (fık'tıʃəs) *adj.* **1.** not genuine: *a fictitious name.* **2.** of or in fiction.

fiddle ('fıd³l) *n.* **1.** *Informal or disparaging.* the violin. **2.** a violin played as a folk instrument. **3.** *Brit. informal.* a dishonest action or scheme. **4. on the fiddle.** *Informal.* engaged in an illegal or fraudulent undertaking. **5. fit as a fiddle.** *Informal.* in very good health. **6. play second fiddle.** *Informal.* to play a subordinate part. ~*vb.* **7.** to play (a tune) on the fiddle. **8.** (often foll. by *with*) to move or touch (something) restlessly or nervously. **9.** (often foll. by *about* or *around*) *Informal.* to waste time. **10.** *Informal.* to do (something) by illegal or dishonest means. **11.** *Informal.* to falsify (accounts). [Old English fithele]

fiddle-faddle ('fıd³l,fæd³l) *n., interj.* nonsense. [reduplication of *fiddle*]

fiddler ('fıdlə) *n.* **1.** a person who plays the fiddle. **2.** a small burrowing crab. **3.** *Informal.* a petty rogue.

fiddlesticks ('fıd³l,stıks) *interj.* an expression of annoyance or disagreement.

fiddling ('fıdlıŋ) *adj.* insignificant.

fiddly ('fıdlı) *adj.* **-dlier, -dliest.** small and awkward to do or handle.

fidelity (fı'delıtı) *n., pl.* **-ties. 1.** loyalty to a person, belief, or cause. **2.** faithfulness to one's spouse or lover. **3.** accuracy in reporting detail. **4.** *Electronics.* the degree to which an amplifier or radio accurately reproduces the input signal. [Latin fidēs faith]

fidget ('fıdʒıt) *vb.* **1.** to move about restlessly. **2.** (often foll. by *with*) to make restless or uneasy movements (with something). ~*n.* **3.** (often *pl.*) a state of restlessness: *he's got the fidgets.* **4.** a person who fidgets. [earlier fidge] —**'fidgety** *adj.*

fiduciary (fı'duːʃıərı) *Law.* ~*n.* **1.** a person bound to act for another's benefit, as a trustee. ~*adj.* **2. a.** having the nature of a trust. **b.** of or relating to a trust or trustee. [Latin fidūcia trust]

fie (faı) *interj. Obs. or facetious.* an exclamation of distaste or mock dismay. [Old French fi]

fief (fiːf) *n.* (in feudal Europe) the property or fee granted to a vassal by his lord in return for service. [Old French fief]

field (fiːld) *n.* **1.** an area of uncultivated grassland; meadow. **2.** a piece of cleared land used for pasture or growing crops. **3.** a marked off area on which sports or athletic competitions are held. **4.** an area that is rich in minerals or other natural resources: *a coalfield.* **5. a.** all the competitors in a competition. **b.** the competitors in a competition excluding the favourite. **6.** a battlefield. **7.** *Cricket.* the fielders collectively. **8.** a wide or open expanse: *a field of snow.* **9.** an area of human activity or knowledge: *his field is physics.* **10.** a place away from the laboratory or classroom where practical work is done. **11.** the surface or background, as of a flag. **12.** *Physics.* In full: **field of force.** the region surrounding a body, such as a magnet, within which it can exert a force on another similar body not in contact with it. **13. play the field.** *Informal.* to disperse one's interests among a number of activities, people, or objects. ~*adj.* **14.** *Mil.* of equipment or personnel for operations in the field: *a field gun.* ~*vb.* **15.** *Sport.* to catch or return (the ball) as a fielder. **16.** *Sport.* to send (a player or team) onto the field to play. **17.** *Sport.* (of a player or team) to act or take turn as a fielder or fielders. **18.** *Informal.* to deal with successfully: *field a question.* [Old English feld]

field day *n.* **1.** *Mil.* a day devoted to manoeuvres or exercises. **2.** *Informal.* a day or time of exciting activity.

fielder ('fiːldə) *n. Cricket, etc.* a member of the fielding side.

field event *n.* a competition, such as the discus, that takes place on a field as opposed to the track.

fieldfare ('fiːld,feə) *n.* a type of large thrush. [Old English feldefare]

field glasses *pl. n.* binoculars.

field hockey *n. U.S. & Canad.* hockey played on a field, as distinguished from ice hockey.

field marshal *n.* an officer holding the highest rank in certain armies.

fieldmouse ('fiːld,maus) *n., pl.* **-mice.** a nocturnal mouse of woods and fields that has yellowish-brown fur.

field officer *n.* an officer holding the rank of major, lieutenant colonel, or colonel.

fieldsman ('fiːldzmən) *n., pl.* **-men.** *Cricket.* a fielder.

field sports *pl. n.* sports carried on in the countryside, such as hunting or fishing.

field trip *n.* an expedition, as by students, to study something at first hand.

fieldwork ('fiːld,wɜːk) *n. Mil.* a temporary

structure used in fortifying a place or position.

field work *n.* an investigation made in the field as opposed to the classroom or laboratory. —**field worker** *n.*

fiend (fiːnd) *n.* **1.** an evil spirit. **2.** a cruel, brutal, or spiteful person. **3.** *Informal.* a person who is intensely interested in or fond of something: *a fresh-air fiend.* [Old English *fēond*] —**fiendish** *adj.* —**fiendishly** *adv.*

Fiend (fiːnd) *n.* **the.** the devil; Satan.

fierce (fɪəs) *adj.* **1.** having a violent and unrestrained nature. **2.** wild or turbulent. **3.** intense or strong. [Latin *ferus*] —**fiercely** *adv.*

fiery (ˈfaɪərɪ) *adj.* **fierier, fieriest. 1.** composed of or like fire: *clouds of fiery gas; a fiery red.* **2.** easily angered: *a fiery temper.* **3.** (of food) producing a burning sensation. —**fierily** *adv.* —**fieriness** *n.*

fiesta (fɪˈestə) *n.* (esp. in Spain and Latin America) **1.** a religious festival or celebration. **2.** a carnival. [Spanish]

FIFA (ˈfiːfə) International Association Football Federation. [French *Fédération Internationale de Football Association*]

fife (faɪf) *n.* a small high-pitched flute, used esp. in military bands. [Old High German *pfīfa*]

fifteen (ˈfɪfˈtiːn) *n.* **1.** the cardinal number that is the sum of ten and five. **2.** a numeral, 15, XV, representing this number. **3.** something represented by or consisting of 15 units. **4.** a rugby football team. ~*det.* **5.** amounting to fifteen: *fifteen jokes.* —**fifteenth** *adj., n.*

fifth (fɪfθ) *adj., n.* See **five.**

fifth column *n.* any group that secretly helps the enemies of its own country or organization. —**fifth columnist** *n.*

fifty (ˈfɪftɪ) *n., pl.* **-ties. 1.** the cardinal number that is the product of ten and five. **2.** a numeral, 50, L, representing this number. **3.** something represented by or consisting of 50 units. **4.** amounting to fifty: *fifty people.* —**fiftieth** *adj., n.*

fifty-fifty *adj., adv. Informal.* in equal parts.

fig (fɪg) *n.* **1.** a soft sweet fruit full of tiny seeds, which grows on a **fig tree. 2.** something negligible: *I don't care a fig for your opinion.* [Latin *ficus* fig tree]

fig. 1. figurative(ly). **2.** figure.

fight (faɪt) *vb.* **fighting, fought. 1.** to struggle against (an enemy) in battle or physical combat. **2.** to struggle to overcome or destroy: *to fight racism.* **3.** to carry on (a battle or contest). **4.** to uphold (a cause) by struggling: *to fight for freedom.* **5.** to make (a way) by fighting. **6. fight it out.** to contend until a decisive result is obtained. **7. fight shy.** to avoid. ~*n.* **8.** a battle. **9.** a quarrel or contest. **10.** resistance (esp. in **put up a fight**). **11.** a boxing match. ~See also **fight off.** [Old English *feohtan*]

fighter (ˈfaɪtə) *n.* **1.** a professional boxer. **2.** a person who has determination. **3.** *Mil.* an armed aircraft for destroying other aircraft.

fighting chance *n.* a slight chance of success dependent on a struggle.

fight off *vb.* **1.** to repulse; repel. **2.** to struggle to avoid or repress: *to fight off a cold.*

fig leaf *n.* a representation of a leaf of the fig tree used in sculpture to cover the genitals of nude figures.

figment (ˈfɪgmənt) *n.* a fantastic notion or fabrication: *a figment of the imagination.* [Latin *fingere* to shape]

figuration (ˌfɪgəˈreɪʃən) *n.* **1.** ornamentation. **2.** a figurative representation. **3.** the act of decorating with a design.

figurative (ˈfɪgərətɪv) *adj.* **1.** involving a figure of speech; not literal; metaphorical. **2.** using or filled with figures of speech. —**figuratively** *adv.*

figure (ˈfɪgə) *n.* **1.** a written symbol for a number. **2.** an amount expressed numerically. **3.** (*pl.*) calculations with numbers. **4.** visible shape or form; outline. **5.** a slim bodily shape (esp. in **keep** *or* **lose one's figure**). **6.** a well-known person: *a national figure.* **7.** the impression created by a person's behaviour: *she cut a poor figure.* **8.** a representation in painting or sculpture, esp. of the human form. **9.** an illustration or diagram in a text. **10.** a decorative pattern. **11.** a predetermined set of movements in dancing or skating. **12.** *Geom.* any combination of points, lines, curves, or planes. **13.** *Music.* a characteristic short pattern of notes. ~*vb.* **14.** to calculate (sums or amounts). **15.** *U.S., Canad., & N.Z. informal.* to consider. **16.** (usually foll. by *in*) to be included: *his name figures in the article.* **17.** *Informal.* to accord with expectation: *it figures that he wouldn't come.* ~See also **figure out.** [Latin *figūra* a shape]

figured (ˈfɪgəd) *adj.* **1.** decorated with a design. **2.** *Music.* ornamental.

figurehead (ˈfɪgəˌhɛd) *n.* **1.** a person nominally having a prominent position, but no real authority. **2.** a carved bust on the bow of some sailing vessels.

figure of speech *n.* an expression of language, such as metaphor, by which the literal meaning of a word is not employed.

figure out *vb. Informal.* to work out; solve or understand.

figure skating *n.* ice skating in which the skater traces outlines of selected patterns. —**figure skater** *n.*

figurine (ˌfɪgəˈriːn) *n.* a small carved or moulded figure; statuette. [French]

filament (ˈfɪləmənt) *n.* **1.** the thin wire inside a light bulb that emits light. **2.** *Electronics.* a high-resistance wire forming the cathode in some valves. **3.** a single strand of fibre. **4.** *Bot.* the stalk of a stamen. [Latin *fīlum* thread] —**filamentary** (ˌfɪləˈmɛntrɪ) *adj.*

filbert (ˈfɪlbət) *n.* the edible rounded brown nuts of the cultivated hazel. [after St Philbert, because the nuts are ripe around his feast day, Aug. 22]

filch (fɪltʃ) *vb.* to steal small amounts. [Middle English *filchen* to steal, attack]

file¹ (faɪl) *n.* **1.** a folder or box used to keep

documents in order. **2.** the documents, etc., kept in this way. **3.** documents or information about a specific subject or person. **4.** a line of people in marching formation, one behind another. **5.** *Computers.* an organized collection of related records. **6. on file.** recorded for reference, as in a file. ~*vb.* **7.** to place (a document) in a file. **8.** to place (a legal document) on public or official record. **9.** to bring (a suit, esp. a divorce suit) in a court of law. **10.** to submit (copy) to a newspaper. **11.** to march or walk in a file or files. [Latin *filum* a thread]

file² ('faɪl) *n.* **1.** a hand tool consisting of a steel blade with small cutting teeth on its faces: used for shaping or smoothing. ~*vb.* **2.** to shape or smooth (a surface) with a file. [Old English]

filial ('fɪlɪəl) *adj.* of or suitable to a son or daughter: *filial affection.* [Latin *filius* son]

filibuster ('fɪlɪˌbʌstə) *n.* **1.** the process of obstructing legislation by means of long speeches. **2.** a legislator who engages in such obstruction. ~*vb.* **3.** to obstruct (legislation) with such delaying tactics. [prob. from Dutch *vrijbuiter* pirate]

filigree ('fɪlɪˌgriː) *n.* **1.** delicate ornamental work of twisted gold, silver, or other wire. ~*adj.* **2.** made of filigree. [Latin *filum* thread + *grānum* grain]

filings ('faɪlɪŋz) *pl. n.* shavings or particles removed by a file: *iron filings.*

Filipino (ˌfɪlɪ'piːnəʊ) *n., pl.* **-nos. 1.** a person from the Philippines. ~*adj.* **2.** of or relating to the Philippines or their inhabitants.

fill (fɪl) *vb.* (often foll. by *up*) **1.** to make or become full. **2.** to occupy the whole of. **3.** to plug (a gap or crevice). **4.** to meet (a requirement or need) satisfactorily. **5.** to cover (a page or blank space) with writing or drawing. **6.** to hold and perform the duties of (an office or position). **7.** to appoint or elect an occupant to (an office or position). **8. fill the bill.** *Informal.* to be suitable or adequate. ~*n.* **9.** one's fill. the quantity needed to satisfy one. ~See also **fill in, fill out,** etc. [Old English *fyllan*]

filler ('fɪlə) *n.* **1.** a paste used for filling in cracks or holes in a surface before painting. **2.** *Journalism.* an item to fill space between more important articles.

fillet ('fɪlɪt) *n.* **1.** a piece of boneless meat or fish. **2.** a thin strip of ribbon or lace worn in the hair or around the neck. **3.** *Archit.* a narrow flat moulding. ~*vb.* **4.** to cut or prepare (meat or fish) as a fillet. [Latin *filum* thread]

fill in *vb.* **1.** to complete (a form or drawing). **2.** to act as a substitute. **3.** to put material into (a hole) as to make it level with a surface. **4.** *Informal.* to give (a person) fuller details.

filling ('fɪlɪŋ) *n.* **1.** the substance or thing used to fill a space or container: *pie filling.* **2.** *Dentistry.* any of various substances for inserting into the prepared cavity of a tooth. ~*adj.* **3.** (of food or a meal) substantial and satisfying.

filling station *n.* a place where petrol and other supplies for motorists are sold.

fillip ('fɪlɪp) *n.* **1.** something that adds stimulation or enjoyment. **2.** the action of holding a finger towards the palm with the thumb and suddenly releasing it with a snapping sound. [imit.]

fill out *vb.* **1.** to make or become plumper, thicker, or rounder. **2.** to make more substantial. **3.** *Chiefly U.S. & Canad.* to fill in (a form or application).

fill up *vb.* **1.** to complete (a form or application). **2.** to make or become full.

filly ('fɪlɪ) *n., pl.* **-lies. 1.** a young female horse. **2.** *Informal.* a lively young woman. [Old Norse *fylja*]

film (fɪlm) *n.* **1. a.** a photographed sequence of images of moving objects providing the optical illusion of continuous movement when projected onto a screen. **b.** a form of entertainment composed of such a sequence of images. **2.** a thin flexible strip of cellulose coated with a photographic emulsion, used to make negatives and transparencies. **3.** a thin coating or layer. **4.** a thin sheet of any material, as of plastic for packaging. **5.** a fine haze, mist, or blur. ~*vb.* **6. a.** to photograph with a cine camera. **b.** to make a film of (a screenplay or event). **7.** (often foll. by *over*) to cover or become covered with a film. [Old English *filmen* membrane]

filmset ('fɪlmˌsɛt) *vb.* **-setting, -set.** *Brit.* to set (type matter) by exposing type characters onto photographic film from which printing plates are made.

film star *n.* a popular film actor or actress.

film strip *n.* a strip of film composed of different images projected separately as slides.

filmy ('fɪlmɪ) *adj.* **filmier, filmiest. 1.** transparent or gauzy. **2.** hazy; blurred. —**'filmily** *adv.* —**'filminess** *n.*

Filofax ('faɪləʊˌfæks) *n. Trademark.* a type of loose-leaf ring binder, used as a portable personal filing system.

filter ('fɪltə) *n.* **1.** a porous substance, such as paper or sand, that allows fluid to pass but retains solid particles. **2.** any device containing such a porous substance, esp. a tip on the mouth end of a cigarette. **3.** any electronic or acoustic device that blocks signals of certain frequencies while allowing others to pass. **4.** any transparent disc of gelatin or glass used to reduce the intensity of given frequencies from the light leaving a lamp or entering a camera. **5.** *Brit.* a traffic signal which permits vehicles to turn either left or right when the main signals are red. ~*vb.* **6.** (often foll. by *out*) to remove or separate (particles) from (a liquid or gas) by a filter. **7** (foll. by *through*) to pass (through a filter or something like a filter). [Medieval Latin *filtrum* piece of felt used as a filter]

filter out *or* **through** *vb.* to become known gradually; leak.

filter paper *n.* a porous paper used for filtering liquids.

filter tip *n.* **1.** an attachment to the mouth end of a cigarette for trapping impurities. **2.** a cigarette with such an attachment. —'**filter-,tipped** adj.

filth (filθ) n. **1.** foul or disgusting dirt; refuse. **2.** vulgarity or obscenity. [Old English fȳlth] —'**filthiness** n. —'**filthy** adj.

filtrate ('filtreit) n. **1.** a liquid or gas that has been filtered. ~vb. **2.** to filter. [Medieval Latin filtrāre to filter] —**fil'tration** n.

fin (fin) n. **1.** any of the winglike projections from a fish's body enabling it to balance and swim. **2.** Brit. a vertical surface to which the rudder is attached at the rear of an aeroplane. **3.** (pl.) a swimmer's flippers. [Old English finn] —**finned** adj.

fin. **1.** finance. **2.** financial.

finagle (fi'neig°l) vb. Informal. to use or achieve by craftiness or trickery. [origin unknown] —**fi'nagler** n.

final ('fain°l) adj. **1.** of or occurring at the end; last. **2.** having no possibility of further discussion, action, or change. ~n. **3.** a deciding contest between the winners of previous rounds in a competition. ~See also **finals**. [Latin fīnis limit, boundary] —**fi'nality** n. —'**finally** adv.

finale (fi'nɑːlɪ) n. the concluding part of a dramatic performance or musical composition. [Italian]

finalist ('fainəlist) n. a contestant who has reached the last stage of a competition.

finalize or **-lise** ('fainə,laiz) vb. to put into final form; settle. —,**finali'zation** or **-li'sation** n.

finals ('fain°lz) pl. n. **1.** the deciding part of a competition. **2.** Education. the last examinations in an academic course.

finance ('fainæns, 'fainæns) n. **1.** the system of money, credit, and investment. **2.** funds or the provision of funds. **3.** (pl.) financial condition. ~vb. **4.** to provide or obtain funds for. [Old French finer to end, settle by payment]

financial (fi'nænʃəl, fai-) adj. **1.** of or relating to finance or finances. **2.** of or relating to people who manage money. **3.** Austral. & N.Z. informal. having money; in funds. —**fi'nancially** adv.

financial year n. Brit. any annual accounting period, such as that of the British Government which ends on April 5.

financier (fi'nænsɪə, fai-) n. a person who is engaged in large-scale financial operations.

finch (fintʃ) n. any of various songbirds with a short stout bill, such as the bullfinch or chaffinch. [Old English finc]

find (faind) vb. **finding, found. 1.** to discover by chance. **2.** to discover by search or effort. **3.** to realize: he found that nobody knew. **4.** to consider: I find this wine a little sour. **5.** to experience or feel: found comfort in his words. **6.** Law. to determine an issue and pronounce a verdict (upon): the court found the accused guilty. **7.** to reach (a target): the bullet found its mark. **8.** to provide, esp. with difficulty. **9. find one's feet.** to become capable or confident. ~n. **10.** a person or

thing that is found, esp. a valuable discovery. [Old English findan]

finder ('faində) n. **1.** a person or thing that finds. **2.** a small telescope fitted to a larger one. **3.** Photog. short for **viewfinder.**

finding ('faindiŋ) n. (often pl.) the conclusion reached after an inquiry or investigation.

find out vb. **1.** to gain knowledge of (something); learn. **2.** to detect the crime, deception, etc., of (someone).

fine¹ (fain) adj. **1.** very good of its kind. **2.** superior in skill: a fine violinist. **3.** (of weather) clear and dry. **4.** Informal. quite well: I feel fine. **5.** satisfactory; acceptable: that's fine by me. **6.** of delicate or careful workmanship. **7.** abstruse or subtle: a fine point. **8.** very thin or slender: fine hair. **9.** very small: fine print. **10.** (of edges or blades) sharp. **11.** ornate, showy, or smart. **12.** good-looking. **13.** Informal. disappointing or terrible: a fine mess. ~adv. **14.** Informal. all right: that suits me fine. **15.** finely. ~vb. **16.** (often foll. by down or away) to make or become smaller, finer, thinner, etc. [Latin fīnis end, boundary, as in fīnis honōrum the highest degree of honour] —'**finely** adv.

fine² (fain) n. **1.** an amount of money exacted as a penalty. **2. in fine.** in conclusion. ~vb. **3.** to impose a fine on. [Old French fin]

fine art n. **1.** art produced chiefly for its appeal to the sense of beauty. **2.** (often pl.) any of the fields in which such art is produced, such as painting, sculpture, and engraving.

fine-drawn adj. **1.** (of arguments or distinctions) subtle. **2.** (of wire) drawn out until very fine.

finery ('fainəri) n. elaborate or showy decoration, esp. clothing and jewellery.

fines herbes ('fiːnz 'ɛːb) pl. n. finely chopped mixed herbs, used to flavour omelettes. [French]

finespun ('fain'spʌn) adj. **1.** spun or drawn out to a fine thread. **2.** excessively subtle.

finesse (fi'nɛs) n. **1.** elegant skill. **2.** subtlety and tact in handling difficult situations. **3.** Bridge, whist. an attempt to win a trick when opponents hold a high card in the suit led by playing a lower card. ~vb. **4.** to bring about with finesse. **5.** to play (a card) as a finesse. [Old French]

fine-tooth comb or **fine-toothed comb** n. **1.** a comb with fine teeth set closely together. **2. go over with a fine-tooth(ed) comb.** to examine very thoroughly.

fine-tune vb. to make fine adjustments to (something) so that it works really well.

finger ('fiŋgə) n. **1.** any of the digits of the hand, often excluding the thumb. **2.** the part of a glove made to cover a finger. **3.** something that resembles a finger in shape or function. **4.** a quantity of liquid in a glass as deep as a finger is wide. **5. get one's finger out.** Brit. informal. to begin or speed up activity, esp. after initial delay. **6. put one's finger on.** to identify precisely. **7. put the finger on.** *U.S. & N.Z. informal.* to inform on or identify, esp. for the police. **8. twist around one's little finger.** to have easy and complete influence over. ~*vb.* **9.** to touch or manipulate with the fingers; handle. **10.** to use one's fingers in playing (a musical instrument). [Old English] —'**fingerless** *adj.*

fingerboard ('fɪŋɡə,bɔːd) *n.* the long strip of hard wood on a violin, guitar, etc., upon which the strings are stopped by the fingers.

finger bowl *n.* a small bowl of water for rinsing the fingers at table during a meal.

fingering ('fɪŋɡərɪŋ) *n.* **1.** the technique of using one's fingers in playing a musical instrument. **2.** the numerals in a musical part indicating this.

fingernail ('fɪŋɡə,neɪl) *n.* a thin horny translucent plate covering part of the upper surface of the end of each finger.

fingerprint ('fɪŋɡə,prɪnt) *n.* **1.** an impression of the pattern of ridges on the inner surface of the end of each finger and thumb. ~*vb.* **2.** to take an inked impression of the fingerprints of (a person). **3.** to take a sample of the DNA of (a person).

fingerstall ('fɪŋɡə,stɔːl) *n.* a protective covering for a finger.

fingertip ('fɪŋɡə,tɪp) *n.* **1.** the end of a finger. **2. have at one's fingertips.** to know or understand thoroughly.

finicky ('fɪnɪkɪ) *or* **finicking** *adj.* **1.** excessively particular; fussy. **2.** overelaborate. [earlier *finical,* from FINE¹]

finis ('fɪnɪs) *n.* the end: used at the end of books. [Latin]

finish ('fɪnɪʃ) *vb.* **1.** to bring to an end; conclude or stop. **2.** to be at or come to the end; use up. **3.** to bring to a desired or complete condition. **4.** to put a particular surface texture on (wood, cloth, or metal). **5.** (often foll. by *off*) to destroy or defeat completely. **6.** (foll. by *with*) to end a relationship. ~*n.* **7.** the final stage or part; end. **8.** death or absolute defeat. **9.** the surface texture of wood, cloth, or metal. **10.** a thing or event that completes. [Latin *fīnīre*]

finishing school *n.* a private school for girls that teaches social graces.

finite ('faɪnaɪt) *adj.* **1.** having limits in size, space, or time. **2.** *Maths, logic.* having a countable number of elements. **3.** *Grammar.* denoting any form of a verb inflected for person, number, and tense. [Latin *fīnītus* limited]

Finn (fɪn) *n.* a person from Finland.

Finnish ('fɪnɪʃ) *adj.* **1.** of or characteristic of Finland, the Finns, or their language. ~*n.* **2.** the official language of Finland.

fino ('fiːnəʊ) *n.* a very dry sherry. [Spanish]

fiord (fjɔːd) *n.* same as **fjord**.

fipple flute ('fɪp'l) *n.* an end-blown flute with a plug (**fipple**) at the mouthpiece, such as the recorder or flageolet.

fir (fɜː) *n.* a pyramidal coniferous tree with single needle-like leaves and erect cones. [Old English *furh*]

fire ('faɪə) *n.* **1.** the state of combustion in which inflammable material burns, producing heat, flames, and often smoke. **2.** burning coal or wood, esp. in a hearth to heat a room. **3.** a destructive uncontrolled burning that destroys building, crops, etc. **4.** an electric or gas device for heating a room. **5.** the act of discharging weapons. **6.** a rapid volley: *a fire of questions.* **7.** intense passion; ardour. **8. catch fire.** to ignite. **9. on fire. a.** burning. **b.** ardent or eager. **10. open fire.** to start firing a gun, artillery, etc. **11. play with fire.** to be involved in something risky. **12. set fire to** *or* **set on fire. a.** to ignite. **b.** to arouse or excite. **13. set the Thames on fire.** *Informal.* to cause a great sensation. **14. under fire.** being attacked, as by weapons or by harsh criticism. ~*vb.* **15.** to discharge (a firearm). **16.** to detonate (an explosive device). **17.** *Informal.* to dismiss from employment. **18.** *Ceramics.* to bake in a kiln to harden the clay. **19.** to kindle or be kindled. **20.** (of an internal-combustion engine) undergo ignition. **21.** to provide with fuel. **22.** to arouse to strong emotion. **23.** to glow or cause to glow. [Old English *fȳr*]

fire alarm *n.* a device to give warning of fire.

firearm ('faɪər,ɑːm) *n.* a weapon, such as a pistol, from which a projectile can be discharged by an explosion.

fireball ('faɪə,bɔːl) *n.* **1.** ball-shaped lightning. **2.** the hot ionized gas at the centre of a nuclear explosion. **3.** a large bright meteor. **4.** *Slang.* an energetic person.

firebomb ('faɪə,bɒm) *n.* same as **incendiary** (sense 5).

firebrand ('faɪə,brænd) *n.* **1.** a piece of burning wood. **2.** a person who causes unrest.

firebreak ('faɪə,breɪk) *n.* a strip of open land in a forest to stop the advance of a fire.

firebrick ('faɪə,brɪk) *n.* a heat-resistant brick, used for lining furnaces, flues, and fireplaces.

fire brigade *n. Chiefly Brit.* an organized body of firemen.

fire clay *n.* a heat-resistant clay used in making firebricks and furnace linings.

firecracker ('faɪə,krækə) *n.* a small cardboard container filled with explosive powder.

firedamp ('faɪə,dæmp) *n.* an explosive mixture of hydrocarbons, chiefly methane, formed in coal mines.

firedog ('faɪə,dɒg) *n.* an andiron.

fire door *n.* a door made of noncombustible material that prevents a fire spreading within a building.

fire-eater *n.* **1.** a performer who simulates the swallowing of fire. **2.** a belligerent person.

fire engine *n.* a vehicle that carries firemen and fire-fighting equipment to a fire.

fire escape *n.* a metal staircase or ladder on the outside of a building for escape in the event of fire.

fire-extinguisher n. a portable device for spraying water, foam, or powder to extinguish a fire.

firefly ('faɪə,flaɪ) n., pl. **-flies.** a beetle that glows in the dark.

fireguard ('faɪə,gɑːd) n. a screen made of wire mesh put before an open fire to protect against sparks.

fire hall n. Canad. a fire station.

fire hydrant n. an outlet from a water main in the street, from which firemen can draw water.

fire irons pl. n. metal fireside implements; poker, shovel, and tongs.

fireman ('faɪəmən) n., pl. **-men.** 1. a person who fights fires; member of a fire brigade. 2. (on steam locomotives) the man who stokes the fire. 3. a stoker.

fireplace ('faɪə,pleɪs) n. an open recess at the base of a chimney for a fire; hearth.

fireplug ('faɪə,plʌg) n. Chiefly U.S. & N.Z. same as **fire hydrant.**

fire power n. Mil. the amount of fire that can be delivered by a unit or weapon.

fire raiser n. a person who deliberately sets fire to property. —**fire raising** n.

fire ship n. a vessel loaded with explosives, set on fire and left to drift among an enemy's warships.

fireside ('faɪə,saɪd) n. the hearth.

fire station n. a building where firefighting vehicles and equipment are stationed.

firetrap ('faɪə,træp) n. a building that would burn easily or one without fire escapes.

firewater ('faɪə,wɔːtə) n. any alcoholic spirit.

firework ('faɪə,wɜːk) n. a device in which combustible materials are ignited to produce coloured sparks and sometimes bangs.

fireworks ('faɪə,wɜːks) pl. n. 1. a show in which fireworks are let off. 2. Informal. a burst of temper.

firing ('faɪərɪŋ) n. 1. the process of baking ceramics in a kiln. 2. a discharge of a firearm. 3. something used as fuel.

firing line n. 1. Mil. the positions from which fire is delivered. 2. the leading or most vulnerable position in an activity.

firm[1] (fɜːm) adj. 1. not soft or yielding to a touch or pressure. 2. securely in position; stable. 3. definitely established: a firm date. 4. having determination or strength: firm leadership. ~adv. 5. in an unyielding manner: he stood firm. ~vb. 6. to make or become firm. [Latin firmus] —'**firmly** adv. —'**firmness** n.

firm[2] (fɜːm) n. 1. a business partnership. 2. any commercial enterprise. [Spanish firma signature]

firmament ('fɜːməmənt) n. Literary. the sky; heavens. [Late Latin firmāmentum]

first (fɜːst) adj. 1. coming before all others. 2. preceding all others in order; 1st. 3. rated, graded, or ranked above all other levels. 4. denoting the lowest forward ratio of a gearbox in a motor vehicle. 5. Music. denoting the highest voice part in a chorus or one of the sections of an orches-

tra: the first violins. ~n. 6. the person or thing coming before all others. 7. the beginning; outset. 8. Education, chiefly Brit. an honours degree of the highest class. 9. the lowest forward ratio of a gearbox in a motor vehicle. ~adv. 10. Also: **firstly.** before anything else: do this first. 11. for the first time: I've loved you since I first saw you. [Old English fyrest]

first aid n. immediate medical assistance given in an emergency.

first-born adj. 1. eldest of the children in a family. ~n. 2. the eldest child in a family.

first class n. 1. the class or grade of the best or highest value or quality. ~adj. 2. of the best or highest class or grade. 3. excellent. 4. of or denoting the most comfortable class of accommodation in a hotel, aircraft, or train. 5. (in Britain) of letters that are handled faster than second-class letters. ~adv. **first-class.** 6. by first-class mail, means of transportation, etc.

first-day cover n. Philately. an envelope postmarked on the first day of the issue of its stamps.

first-degree burn n. Pathol. the least severe type of burn, in which the skin surface is red and painful.

first-foot Chiefly Scot. ~n. 1. the first person to enter a household in the New Year. ~vb. 2. to visit (someone) as first-foot. —'**first-'footing** n.

first fruits pl. n. 1. the first results or profits of an undertaking. 2. fruit that ripens first.

first-hand adj., adv. 1. from the original source. 2. **at first hand.** directly.

first lady n. (often caps.) (in the U.S.) the wife of the president.

firstly ('fɜːstlɪ) adv. same as **first.**

first mate n. an officer second in command to the captain of a merchant ship.

first night n. the first public performance of a play or other production.

first offender n. a person convicted of a criminal offence for the first time.

first officer n. same as **first mate.**

first person n. a grammatical category of pronouns and verbs used by the speaker to refer to himself.

first-rate adj. of the best quality; excellent.

firth (fɜːθ) n. a narrow inlet of the sea. [Old Norse fjörthr]

fiscal ('fɪskˀl) adj. 1. of or relating to government finances, esp. tax revenues. 2. of financial matters. [Latin fiscālis concerning the state treasury]

fish (fɪʃ) n., pl. **fish** or **fishes.** 1. a cold-blooded animal with a backbone, gills, and usually fins and a skin covered in scales, that lives in water. 2. the flesh of fish used as food. 3. Informal. a person of little emotion or intelligence. 4. **drink like a fish.** to drink alcohol to excess. 5. **have other fish to fry.** to have other more important concerns. 6. **like a fish out of water.** ill at ease in an unfamiliar situation. ~vb. 7. to attempt to catch fish. 8.

to fish in (a particular area of water). **9.** to grope for and find with some difficulty: *I fished the book out of the bottom of my bag.* **10.** (foll. by *for*) to seek something indirectly: *to fish for compliments.* [Old English *fisc*]

fish cake *n.* a fried flattened ball of flaked fish mixed with mashed potatoes.

fisherman ('fɪʃəmən) *n., pl.* **-men.** a person who fishes as a profession or for sport.

fishery ('fɪʃərɪ) *n., pl.* **-eries. 1. a.** the industry of catching, processing, and selling fish. **b.** a place where this is carried on. **2.** a place where fish are reared. **3.** a fishing ground.

fish-eye lens *n. Photog.* a lens with a highly curved protruding front that covers almost 180°.

fishfinger ('fɪʃ'fɪŋɡə) *n.* an oblong piece of fish coated in breadcrumbs.

fishing ('fɪʃɪŋ) *n.* the occupation of catching fish.

fishing rod *n.* a long tapered flexible pole for use with a fishing line and, usually, a reel.

fish meal *n.* ground dried fish used as feed for farm animals or as a fertilizer.

fishmonger ('fɪʃ,mʌŋɡə) *n. Chiefly Brit.* a retailer of fish.

fishnet ('fɪʃ,nɛt) *n.* an open mesh fabric resembling netting.

fishplate ('fɪʃ,pleɪt) *n.* a flat piece of metal joining one rail or beam to the next, esp. on railway tracks.

fishtail ('fɪʃ,teɪl) *n.* a nozzle having a long narrow slot at the top, placed over a Bunsen burner to produce a thin fanlike flame.

fishwife ('fɪʃ,waɪf) *n., pl.* **-wives.** a coarse scolding woman.

fishy ('fɪʃɪ) *adj.* **fishier, fishiest. 1.** of or suggestive of fish. **2.** *Informal.* suspicious or questionable. —'**fishily** *adv.*

fissile ('fɪsaɪl) *adj.* **1.** *Brit.* capable of undergoing nuclear fission. **2.** tending to split.

fission ('fɪʃən) *n.* **1.** the act or process of splitting into parts. **2.** *Biol.* a form of asexual reproduction involving a division into two or more equal parts. **3.** short for **nuclear fission.** [Latin *fissiō* a splitting] —'**fissionable** *adj.*

fissure ('fɪʃə) *n.* any long narrow cleft or crack, esp. in a rock. [Latin *fissus* split]

fist (fɪst) *n.* a hand with the fingers clenched into the palm, as for hitting. [Old English *fȳst*]

fisticuffs ('fɪstɪ,kʌfs) *pl. n.* combat with the fists. [prob. from obs. *fisty* with the fist + CUFF²]

fistula ('fɪstjʊlə) *n. Pathol.* an abnormal opening between one hollow organ and another or between a hollow organ and the surface of the skin. [Latin: tube, ulcer]

fit¹ (fɪt) *vb.* **fitting, fitted. 1.** to be appropriate or suitable for. **2.** to be of the correct size or shape for. **3.** to adjust in order to make appropriate. **4.** to try clothes on (someone) in order to make adjustments if necessary. **5.** to make com-

petent or ready. **6.** to correspond with the facts or circumstances. ~*adj.* **fitter, fittest. 7.** appropriate. **8.** in good health. **9.** worthy or deserving. ~*n.* **10.** the manner in which something fits. ~See also **fit in, fit out.** [prob. from Middle Dutch *vitten*] —'**fitly** *adv.* —'**fitness** *n.*

fit² (fɪt) *n.* **1.** a sudden attack or convulsion, such as an epileptic seizure. **2.** a sudden short burst or spell: *a fit of coughing; fits of depression.* **3. by** or **in fits (and starts).** in spasmodic spells. **4. have a fit.** *Informal.* to become very angry. [Old English *fitt* conflict]

fitful ('fɪtfʊl) *adj.* occurring in irregular spells. —'**fitfully** *adv.*

fit in *vb.* **1.** to give a place or time to (someone or something). **2.** to belong or conform, esp. after adjustment.

fitment ('fɪtmənt) *n.* **1.** an accessory attached to a machine. **2.** *Chiefly Brit.* a detachable part of the furnishings of a room.

fit out *vb.* to equip.

fitted ('fɪtɪd) *adj.* **1.** designed for excellent fit: *a fitted bodice.* **2.** (of a carpet) covering a floor completely. **3. a.** (of furniture) built to fit a particular space. **b.** (of a room) equipped with fitted furniture. **4.** (of sheets) having ends that are elasticated to fit tightly over a mattress.

fitter ('fɪtə) *n.* **1.** a person who is skilled in the assembly and adjustment of machinery. **2.** a person who fits a garment for a particular person.

fitting ('fɪtɪŋ) *adj.* **1.** appropriate or proper. ~*n.* **2.** an accessory or part. **3.** (*pl.*) furnishings or accessories in a building. **4.** the trying on of clothes so that they can be adjusted to fit. —'**fittingly** *adv.*

five (faɪv) *n.* **1.** the cardinal number that is the sum of four and one. **2.** a numeral, 5, V, representing this number. **3.** the amount or quantity that is one greater than four. **4.** something representing or consisting of five units, such as a playing card with five symbols on it. ~*det.* **5.** amounting to five. ~See also **fives.** [Old English *fīf*] —**fifth** (fɪfθ) *adj., n.*

five-eighth *n. Austral. & N.Z.* a rugby player positioned between the halfbacks and three-quarters.

fivefold ('faɪv,fəʊld) *adj.* **1.** having five times as many or as much. **2.** composed of five parts. ~*adv.* **3.** five times as many or as much.

fivepins ('faɪv,pɪnz) *n.* (functioning as sing.) a bowling game played esp. in Canada.

fiver ('faɪvə) *n. Brit. informal.* a five-pound note.

fives (faɪvz) *n.* (functioning as sing.) a ball game similar to squash but played with bats or the hands.

fix (fɪks) *vb.* **1.** to make or become firm, stable, or secure. **2.** to place permanently. **3.** to settle definitely; decide. **4.** to hold or direct (eyes, etc.) steadily. **5.** to rivet or transfix: *he fixed the woman with his gaze.* **6.** to make rigid: *to fix one's jaw.* **7.** to repair. **8.** *Informal.* to influence (a person,

etc.) unfairly, as by bribery. **9.** *Informal.*
to give (someone) his just deserts: *that'll
fix him.* **10.** *Informal, chiefly U.S. &
Canad.* to prepare: *to fix a meal.* **11.**
Photog. to treat (a film, plate, or paper)
with fixer to make the image permanent.
12. to convert (atmospheric nitrogen) into
nitrogen compounds. **13.** *Slang.* to inject a
narcotic drug. ~*n.* **14.** *Informal.* a predicament; dilemma. **15.** the ascertaining of
the navigational position, as of a ship, by
radar, etc. **16.** *Slang.* an injection of a
narcotic. ~See also **fix up.** [Latin *fixus*
fixed]

fixation (fɪkˈseɪʃən) *n.* **1.** a preoccupation
or obsession. **2.** *Psychol.* a strong attachment of a person to another person or an
object in early life. **3.** *Chem.* the conversion of nitrogen in the air into a compound,
esp. a fertilizer. —**fixˈated** *adj.*

fixative (ˈfɪksətɪv) *n.* **1.** a fluid sprayed
over drawings to prevent smudging. **2.** a
substance added to a perfume to make it
less volatile.

fixed (fɪkst) *adj.* **1.** attached or placed so
as to be immovable. **2.** stable: *fixed prices.*
3. steadily directed: *a fixed expression.* **4.**
established as to relative position: *a fixed
point.* **5.** always at the same time. **6.** (of
ideas) firmly maintained. **7.** *Informal.*
equipped or provided for, as with money or
possessions. **8.** *Informal.* illegally arranged: *a fixed trial.* —**fixedly** (ˈfɪksɪdlɪ)
adv.

fixed star *n.* an extremely distant star
that appears to be almost stationary.

fixer (ˈfɪksə) *n.* **1.** *Photog.* a solution used
to make an image permanent. **2.** *Slang.* a
person who makes arrangements, esp. illegally.

fixity (ˈfɪksɪtɪ) *n., pl.* **-ties.** the state or
quality of being fixed.

fixture (ˈfɪkstʃə) *n.* **1.** an object firmly
fixed in place, esp. a household appliance.
2. a person regarded as fixed in a particular place or position. **3.** *Chiefly Brit.* **a.** a
sports match. **b.** the date of it.

fix up *vb.* **1.** to arrange. **2.** (often foll. by
with) to provide.

fizz (fɪz) *vb.* **1.** to make a hissing or
bubbling sound. **2.** (of a drink) to produce
bubbles of carbon dioxide. ~*n.* **3.** a
hissing or bubbling sound. **4.** effervescence. **5.** any effervescent drink. [imit.]
—**fizzy** *adj.* —**fizziness** *n.*

fizzle (ˈfɪzᵊl) *vb.* **1.** to make a hissing or
bubbling sound. **2.** (often foll. by *out*)
Informal. to fail or die out, esp. after a
promising start. [prob. from obs. *fist* to
break wind]

fjord (fjɔːd) *n.* a long narrow inlet of the
sea between high cliffs, esp. in Norway.
[Norwegian, from Old Norse *fjörthr*]

FL or **Fla.** Florida.

fl. **1.** floor. **2.** fluid.

flab (flæb) *n.* unsightly or unwanted fat on
the body. [from *flabby*]

flabbergast (ˈflæbəˌgɑːst) *vb.* (*usually
passive*) *Informal.* to amaze utterly;
astound. [origin unknown]

flabby (ˈflæbɪ) *adj.* **-bier, -biest.** **1.** loose

or yielding: *flabby muscles.* **2.** having
flabby flesh. **3.** weak. [alteration of
flappy from *flap*] —**flabbiness** *n.*

flaccid (ˈflæksɪd) *adj.* soft and limp. [Latin
flaccidus] —**flacˈcidity** *n.*

flag[1] (flæg) *n.* **1.** a piece of cloth often
attached to a pole, used as an emblem or
for signalling. **2.** *Brit., Austral., & N.Z.* the
part of a taximeter that is raised when a
taxi is for hire. ~*vb.* **flagging, flagged.**
3. to mark with a tag or sticker. **4.** (often
foll. by *down*) to signal (a vehicle) to stop.
5. to send (information) by flag. [origin
unknown]

flag[2] (flæg) *n.* any of various plants that
have long swordlike leaves, esp. an iris.
[origin unknown]

flag[3] (flæg) *vb.* **flagging, flagged.** **1.** to
lose enthusiasm or energy. **2.** to become
limp; droop. [origin unknown] —**flagging**
adj.

flag[4] (flæg) *n.* **1.** short for **flagstone.**
~*vb.* **flagging, flagged.** **2.** to pave with
flagstones.

flag day *n.* a day on which money is
collected by a charity and small stickers
are given to contributors.

flagellate *vb.* (ˈflædʒɪˌleɪt). **1.** to whip.
~*adj.* (ˈflædʒɪlɪt). **2.** possessing one or
more flagella. **3.** whiplike. [Latin *flagellāre* to whip] —**flagelˈlation** *n.*

flagellum (fləˈdʒɛləm) *n., pl.* **-la** (-lə) or
-lums. **1.** *Biol.* a long whiplike outgrowth
that acts as an organ of movement. **2.** *Bot.*
a long thin shoot or runner. [Latin: a little
whip]

flageolet (ˌflædʒəˈlɛt) *n.* a high-pitched
musical instrument of the recorder family.
[French]

flag of convenience *n.* a foreign flag
flown by a ship registered in that country
to gain financial or legal advantage.

flag of truce *n.* a white flag indicating
an invitation to an enemy to negotiate.

flagon (ˈflægən) *n.* **1.** a large bottle of
wine, cider, etc. **2.** a container for liquids
with a handle, spout, and narrow neck.
[Late Latin *flascō* flask]

flagpole (ˈflægˌpəʊl) or **flagstaff** (ˈflæg-
ˌstɑːf) *n.* a pole on which a flag is flown.

flagrant (ˈfleɪgrənt) *adj.* openly outrageous. [Latin *flagrāre* to blaze, burn]
—**flagrancy** *n.*

flagship (ˈflægˌʃɪp) *n.* **1.** a ship aboard
which the commander of a fleet is quartered. **2.** the most important ship belonging to a shipping company.

flagstone (ˈflægˌstəʊn) *n.* a flat slab of
hard stone for paving. [Old Norse *flaga*
slab]

flag-waving *n.* *Informal.* an emotional
appeal to patriotic feeling.

flail (fleɪl) *n.* **1.** an implement used for
threshing grain, consisting of a long handle
with a free-swinging bar attached to it.
~*vb.* **2.** to beat with or as if with a flail.
3. to thresh about: *with arms flailing.*
[Latin *flagellum* whip]

flair (fleə) *n.* **1.** natural ability; talent. **2.**
originality and stylishness. [French]

flak (flæk) n. **1.** anti-aircraft fire. **2.** adverse criticism. [German *Fl(ieger)a(b-wehr)k(anone)* aircraft defence gun]

flake (fleɪk) n. **1.** a small thin piece chipped off an object or substance. **2.** a small piece: *a flake of snow.* ~vb. **3.** to peel or cause to peel off in flakes. **4.** to break into small thin pieces: *simmer the fish until it flakes easily.* [Old Norse] —**'flaky** adj.

flake out vb. *Informal.* to collapse or fall asleep as through extreme exhaustion.

flambé ('flɑːmbeɪ) adj. (of food) served in flaming brandy, etc. [French]

flamboyant (flæm'bɔɪənt) adj. **1.** elaborate or extravagant; showy. **2.** exuberant or ostentatious: *flamboyant gestures.* [French: flaming] —**flam'boyance** n.

flame (fleɪm) n. **1.** a hot luminous body of burning gas coming in flickering streams from burning material. **2.** (*often pl.*) the state of burning: *to burst into flames.* **3.** a strong reddish-orange colour. **4.** intense passion. ~vb. **5.** to burn brightly. **6.** to become red or fiery. **7.** to become angry or excited. [Latin *flamma*]

flamenco (flə'mɛŋkəʊ) n., pl. **-cos.** a very rhythmical type of dance music for vocal soloist and guitar. [Spanish]

flame-thrower n. a weapon that ejects a stream or spray of burning fluid.

flaming ('fleɪmɪŋ) adj. **1.** burning with flames. **2.** glowing brightly. **3.** intense; heated: *a flaming row.* **4.** *Informal.* damned: *you flaming idiot.*

flamingo (flə'mɪŋgəʊ) n., pl. **-gos** or **-goes.** a large wading bird with pink-and-red plumage and long thin legs. [Portuguese]

flammable ('flæməb°l) adj. easily set on fire; inflammable. —**flamma'bility** n.

flan (flæn) n. an open pastry or sponge tart filled with fruit or a savoury mixture. [French]

flange (flændʒ) n. a projecting collar or rim on an object for strengthening it or for attaching it to another object. [origin unknown]

flank (flæŋk) n. **1.** the side of a man or animal between the ribs and the hip. **2.** a cut of beef from the flank. **3.** the side of a naval or military formation. ~vb. **4.** to be positioned at the side of (a person or thing). [Old French *flanc*]

flannel ('flæn°l) n. **1.** a soft light woollen fabric used for clothing. **2.** (*pl.*) trousers made of flannel. **3.** *Brit.* a small piece of towelling cloth used to wash the face. **4.** *Brit. informal.* evasive talk that avoids giving any commitment or direct answer. ~vb. **-nelling, -nelled** or U.S. **-neling, -neled.** **5.** *Brit. informal.* to flatter or talk evasively. [Welsh *gwlân* wool]

flannelette (ˌflæn°l'ɛt) n. a cotton imitation of flannel.

flap (flæp) vb. **flapping, flapped.** **1.** to move backwards and forwards or up and down, like a bird's wings in flight. **2.** *Informal.* to become agitated or flustered. ~n. **3.** the action of or noise made by flapping. **4.** a piece of material attached at one edge and usually used to cover an

opening, as on a pocket. **5.** a hinged section of an aircraft wing that is raised or lowered to control the aircraft's speed. **6.** *Informal.* a state of panic or agitation. [prob. imit.]

flapjack ('flæpˌdʒæk) n. a chewy biscuit made with rolled oats.

flapper ('flæpə) n. (in the 1920s) a young unconventional woman.

flare (flɛə) vb. **1.** to burn with an unsteady or sudden bright flame. **2.** (of temper, violence, or trouble) to break out suddenly. **3.** to spread outwards from a narrow to a wider shape. ~n. **4.** an unsteady flame. **5.** a sudden burst of flame. **6. a.** a blaze of light used to illuminate, signal distress, alert, etc. **b.** the device producing such a blaze. **7.** a spreading shape. [origin unknown]

flare up vb. **1.** to burst suddenly into fire. **2.** *Informal.* to burst into anger.

flash (flæʃ) n. **1.** a sudden short blaze of intense light or flame. **2.** a sudden occurrence or display, esp. one suggestive of brilliance: *a flash of understanding.* **3.** a very brief time: *over in a flash.* **4.** a short unscheduled news announcement. **5.** *Chiefly Brit.* an emblem on a uniform or vehicle to identify its military formation. **6.** *Photog.* short for **flashlight.** **7. flash in the pan.** a project, person, etc., that enjoys only short-lived success. ~adj. **8.** *Informal.* ostentatious or vulgar. **9.** *Informal.* relating to the criminal underworld. **10.** brief and rapid: *flash freezing.* ~vb. **11.** to burst or cause to burst suddenly into flame. **12.** to emit or cause to emit light suddenly or intermittently. **13.** to move very fast. **14.** to come rapidly (into the mind or vision). **15. a.** to signal very fast: *to flash a message.* **b.** to signal by use of a light, such as car headlights. **16.** *Informal.* to display ostentatiously: *to flash money around.* **17.** *Informal.* to show briefly. **18.** *Brit. slang.* to expose oneself indecently. [origin unknown] —**'flasher** n.

flashback ('flæʃˌbæk) n. a transition in a novel, film, etc., to an earlier event.

flashbulb ('flæʃˌbʌlb) n. *Photog.* a small light bulb that produces a bright flash of light.

flash flood n. a sudden short-lived torrent.

flashing ('flæʃɪŋ) n. a weatherproof material used to cover the joins in a roof.

flashlight ('flæʃˌlaɪt) n. **1.** *Photog.* the brief bright light emitted by a flashbulb. **2.** *Chiefly U.S. & Canad.* a torch.

flash point n. **1.** the lowest temperature at which the vapour above a liquid can be ignited. **2.** a critical time beyond which a situation will inevitably erupt into violence.

flashy ('flæʃɪ) adj. **flashier, flashiest.** gaudy and ostentatious. —**'flashily** adv. —**'flashiness** n.

flask (flɑːsk) n. **1.** a bottle with a narrow neck, esp. used in a laboratory. **2.** a small flat container for alcoholic drink designed to be carried in a pocket. **3.** See **vacuum flask.** [Medieval Latin *flasca, flasco*]

flat¹ (flæt) *adj.* **flatter, flattest. 1.** horizontal; level: *a flat roof.* **2.** even or smooth: *a flat surface.* **3.** lying stretched out at full length. **4.** (of a tyre) deflated. **5.** (of shoes) having an unraised heel. **6.** without qualification; total: *a flat denial.* **7.** fixed: *a flat rate.* **8.** neither more nor less; exact: *a flat thirty minutes.* **9.** unexciting: *a flat joke.* **10.** without variation or emotion: *a flat voice.* **11.** (of drinks) having lost effervescence. **12.** (of a battery) fully discharged. **13.** (of paint) without gloss. **14.** *Music.* **a.** denoting a note that has been lowered in pitch by one chromatic semitone: *B flat.* **b.** (of an instrument, voice, etc.) out of tune by being too low in pitch. *~adv.* **15.** in or into a level or flat position: *he held his hand out flat.* **16.** completely; absolutely. **17.** exactly: in *three minutes flat.* **18.** *Music.* **a.** lower than a standard pitch. **b.** too low in pitch: *she sings flat.* **19. fall flat (on one's face).** to fail to achieve a desired effect. **20. flat out.** *Informal.* with maximum speed and effort. *~n.* **21.** a flat object or part. **22.** (*often pl.*) low-lying land, esp. a marsh. **23.** (*often pl.*) a mud bank exposed at low tide. **24.** *Music.* **a.** an accidental that lowers the pitch of a note by one semitone. Usual symbol: ♭ **b.** a note affected by this accidental. **25.** *Theatre.* a wooden frame covered with painted canvas, used to form part of a stage setting. **26.** a punctured car tyre. **27.** (*often cap.; preceded by the*) *Chiefly Brit.* the season of flat racing. [Old Norse *flatr*] —**'flatly** *adv.*

flat² (flæt) *n.* a set of rooms forming a home entirely on one floor of a building. [Old English *flett* floor, hall, house]

flatboat ('flæt,bəʊt) *n.* a flat-bottomed boat for transporting goods on a canal.

flatfish ('flæt,fɪʃ) *n., pl.* **-fish** or **-fishes.** a sea fish, such as the sole, which has a flat body with both eyes on the uppermost side.

flat-footed (,flæt'fʊtɪd) *adj.* **1.** having less than the usual degree of arching in the insteps of the feet. **2.** *Informal.* clumsy or insensitive.

flatiron ('flæt,aɪən) *n.* (formerly) an iron for pressing clothes that was heated by being placed on a stove.

flatlet ('flætlɪt) *n.* a small flat.

flat racing *n.* the racing of horses on racecourses without jumps.

flat spin *n.* **1.** an aircraft spin in which the longitudinal axis is more nearly horizontal than vertical. **2.** *Informal.* a state of confusion.

flatten ('flæt²n) *vb.* **1.** to make or become flat or flatter. **2.** *Informal.* **a.** to knock down or injure. **b.** to crush or subdue.

flatter ('flætə) *vb.* **1.** to praise insincerely, esp. in order to win favour. **2.** to show to advantage: *that dress flatters her.* **3.** to make (a person) appear more attractive than in reality. **4.** to gratify the vanity of (a person). **5. flatter oneself.** to believe, perhaps mistakenly, something good about oneself. [Old French *flater* to lick, fawn upon] —**'flatterer** *n.*

flattery ('flætərɪ) *n., pl.* **-teries.** excessive or insincere praise.

flatulent ('flætjʊlənt) *adj.* **1.** suffering from or caused by too much gas in the stomach or intestines. **2.** pretentious. [Latin *flatus* blowing] —**'flatulence** *n.*

flatworm ('flæt,wɜːm) *n.* a worm, such as a tapeworm, with a flattened body.

flaunt (flɔːnt) *vb.* to display (possessions, oneself, etc.) ostentatiously. [origin unknown]

flautist ('flɔːtɪst) *n.* a player of the flute. [Italian *flautista*]

flavour or *U.S.* **flavor** ('fleɪvə) *n.* **1.** taste perceived in food or liquid in the mouth. **2.** a distinctive quality or atmosphere. *~vb.* **3.** to impart a flavour to. [Old French *flaour*] —**'flavourless** or *U.S.* **'flavorless** *adj.*

flavouring or *U.S.* **flavoring** ('fleɪvərɪŋ) *n.* a substance used to flavour food.

flaw (flɔː) *n.* **1.** an imperfection or blemish. **2.** a mistake in something that makes it invalid: *a flaw in the argument.* [prob. from Old Norse *flaga* stone slab] —**flawed** *adj.* —**'flawless** *adj.*

flax (flæks) *n.* **1.** a plant that has blue flowers and is cultivated for its seeds and the fibres of its stems. **2.** this fibre, made into linen fabrics. **3.** *N.Z.* a swamp plant producing a fibre that is used by Maoris for decorative work, baskets, etc. [Old English *fleax*]

flaxen ('flæksən) *adj.* **1.** of flax. **2.** pale yellow: *flaxen hair.*

flay (fleɪ) *vb.* **1.** to strip off the skin of, esp. by whipping. **2.** to attack with savage criticism. [Old English *flēan*]

flea (fliː) *n.* **1.** a small wingless jumping insect feeding on the blood of mammals and birds. **2. flea in one's ear.** *Informal.* a sharp rebuke. [Old English *flēah*]

fleabite ('fliː,baɪt) *n.* **1.** the bite of a flea. **2.** a slight annoyance or discomfort.

flea-bitten *adj.* **1.** bitten by or infested with fleas. **2.** *Informal.* shabby or decrepit.

flea market *n.* an open-air market selling cheap second-hand goods.

fleapit ('fliː,pɪt) *n. Informal.* a shabby cinema or theatre.

fleck (flɛk) *n.* **1.** a small marking or streak. **2.** a speck: *a fleck of dust.* *~vb.* **3.** to speckle. [prob. from Old Norse *flekkr* stain, spot]

fled (flɛd) *vb.* the past of **flee.**

fledged (flɛdʒd) *adj.* **1.** (of young birds) able to fly. **2.** qualified and competent: *a fully fledged instructor.* [Old English *-flycge*, as in *unflycge* unfledged]

fledgling or **fledgeling** ('flɛdʒlɪŋ) *n.* a young bird that has grown feathers.

flee (fliː) *vb.* **fleeing, fled. 1.** to run away from (a place, danger, etc.). **2.** to run or move quickly. [Old English *flēon*]

fleece (fliːs) *n.* **1.** the coat of wool that covers a sheep. **2.** the wool removed from a sheep at one shearing. **3.** sheepskin or a fabric with soft pile, used as a lining for coats, etc. *~vb.* **4.** to defraud or charge exorbitantly. **5.** same as **shear** (sense 1). [Old English *fléos*] —**'fleecy** *adj.*

fleecie ('fliːsɪ) *n. N.Z.* a person who collects fleeces after shearing and prepares them for baling.

fleet[1] (fliːt) *n.* **1.** a number of warships organized as a tactical unit. **2.** all the warships of a nation. **3.** a number of vehicles under the same ownership. [Old English *fléot*]

fleet[2] (fliːt) *adj.* rapid in movement; swift. [prob. from Old English *fléotan* to float]

fleet chief petty officer *n.* a noncommissioned officer in a navy.

fleeting ('fliːtɪŋ) *adj.* rapid and soon passing: *a fleeting glimpse.* —**'fleetingly** *adv.*

Fleming ('flɛmɪŋ) *n.* a person from Flanders or Flemish-speaking Belgium.

Flemish ('flɛmɪʃ) *n.* **1.** one of the two official languages of Belgium. **2.** the **Flemish.** (*functioning as pl.*) the Flemings collectively. ~*adj.* **3.** of or characteristic of Flanders, the Flemings, or their language.

flesh (flɛʃ) *n.* **1.** the soft part of the body of an animal or human, esp. muscular tissue. **2.** *Informal.* excess weight; fat. **3.** the edible tissue of animals as opposed to that of fish or, sometimes, fowl. **4.** the thick soft part of a fruit or vegetable. **5.** the human body and its physical or sensual nature as opposed to the soul. **6.** mankind in general. **7.** a yellowish-pink colour. **8. in the flesh.** in person; actually present. **9. one's own flesh and blood.** one's own family. [Old English *flǽsc*]

fleshly ('flɛʃlɪ) *adj.* **-lier, -liest. 1.** relating to the body; carnal: *fleshly desire.* **2.** worldly as opposed to spiritual.

fleshpots ('flɛʃˌpɒts) *pl. n. Often facetious.* **1.** luxurious living. **2.** places where bodily desires are gratified. [from the Biblical use as applied to Egypt (Exodus 16:3)]

flesh wound (wuːnd) *n.* a wound affecting superficial tissues.

fleshy ('flɛʃɪ) *adj.* **fleshier, fleshiest. 1.** plump. **2.** resembling flesh. **3.** *Bot.* (of some fruits) thick and pulpy. —**'fleshiness** *n.*

fleur-de-lis *or* **fleur-de-lys** (ˌflɜːdə'liː) *n., pl.* **fleurs-de-lis** *or* **fleurs-de-lys** (ˌflɜːdə'liːz). a representation of a lily with three distinct petals. [Old French *flor de lis* lily flower]

flew (fluː) *vb.* the past tense of **fly**[1].

flews (fluːz) *pl. n.* the fleshy hanging upper lip of a bloodhound or similar dog. [origin unknown]

flex (flɛks) *n.* **1.** *Brit.* a flexible insulated electric cable. ~*vb.* **2.** to bend. **3.** to contract (a muscle) or (of a muscle) to contract. [Latin *flexus* bent, winding]

flexible ('flɛksɪb'l) *adj.* **1.** able to be bent easily without breaking. **2.** adaptable to changing circumstances. —**ˌflexi'bility** *n.* —**'flexibly** *adv.*

flexitime ('flɛksɪˌtaɪm) *n.* a system permitting flexibility of working hours at the beginning or end of the day, provided an agreed total is worked.

flibbertigibbet ('flɪbətɪˌdʒɪbɪt) *n.* an irresponsible, silly, gossipy person. [origin unknown]

flick (flɪk) *vb.* **1.** to touch or move with or as if with the finger or hand in a quick jerky movement. **2.** (foll. by *through*) to look at (a book or magazine) quickly or idly. ~*n.* **3.** a tap or quick stroke with the fingers, a whip, etc. [imit.]

flicker ('flɪkə) *vb.* **1.** to shine with an unsteady or intermittent light. **2.** to move quickly to and fro. ~*n.* **3.** an unsteady or brief light. **4.** a brief or faint indication of emotion. [Old English *flicorian*]

flick knife *n.* a knife with a retractable blade that springs out when a button is pressed.

flicks (flɪks) *pl. n. Slang, old-fashioned.* the cinema.

flier *or* **flyer** ('flaɪə) *n.* **1.** a person or thing that flies or moves very fast. **2.** an aviator.

flight[1] (flaɪt) *n.* **1.** the act or manner of flying. **2.** a journey made by a flying animal or object. **3.** a group of flying birds or aircraft. **4.** an aircraft flying on a scheduled journey. **5.** a mental soaring above the everyday world: *a flight of fancy.* **6.** a feather or plastic attachment to an arrow or dart. **7.** a set of stairs between one landing and the next. [Old English *flyht*]

flight[2] (flaɪt) *n.* **1.** the act of running away, as from danger. **2. put to flight.** to cause to run away. **3. take (to) flight.** to run away. [Old English *flyht* (unattested)]

flight deck *n.* **1.** the crew compartment in an airliner. **2.** the upper deck of an aircraft carrier from which aircraft take off.

flightless ('flaɪtlɪs) *adj.* (of certain birds and insects) unable to fly.

flight lieutenant *n.* a junior commissioned officer in an air force.

flight recorder *n.* an electronic device in an aircraft for storing information concerning its performance in flight. It is often used to determine the cause of a crash. Also called: **black box.**

flight sergeant *n.* a noncommissioned officer in an air force.

flighty ('flaɪtɪ) *adj.* **flightier, flightiest.** frivolous and irresponsible. —**'flightiness** *n.*

flimsy ('flɪmzɪ) *adj.* **-sier, -siest. 1.** not strong or substantial. **2.** light and thin: *a flimsy dress.* **3.** unconvincing; weak: *a flimsy excuse.* [origin unknown] —**'flimsily** *adv.* —**'flimsiness** *n.*

flinch (flɪntʃ) *vb.* **1.** to draw back suddenly, as from pain; wince. **2.** (foll. by *from*) to shrink from; avoid: *he never flinched from his duty.* [Old French *flenchir*]

fling (flɪŋ) *vb.* **flinging, flung. 1.** to throw with force. **2.** to put or send without warning: *to fling someone into jail.* **3.** to move or go hurriedly or violently: *he flung his arms up.* **4.** to put (something) somewhere hurriedly or carelessly. **5.** (usually foll. by *into*) to apply (oneself) with vigour (to). ~*n.* **6.** a short spell of self-indulgent enjoyment. **7.** a vigorous Scottish reel: *a Highland fling.* [Old Norse]

flint (flɪnt) *n.* **1.** a very hard stone that produces sparks when struck with steel. **2.** any piece of flint, esp. one used as a primitive tool. **3.** a small piece of an iron alloy, used in cigarette lighters. [Old English] —**flinty** *adj.*

flintlock (ˈflɪntˌlɒk) *n.* an obsolete gun in which the powder was lit by a spark produced by a flint.

flip (flɪp) *vb.* **flipping, flipped. 1.** to throw (something light or small) carelessly. **2.** to throw (an object such as a coin) so that it turns in the air. **3.** (foll. by *through*) to look at (a book or magazine) idly. **4.** Also: **flip one's lid.** *Slang.* to fly into an emotional outburst. ~*n.* **5.** a snap or tap, usually with the fingers. **6.** any alcoholic drink containing beaten egg. ~*adj.* **7.** *Informal.* flippant or pert. [prob. imit.]

flip-flop *n.* a rubber-soled sandal attached to the foot by a thong between the big toe and the next toe. [reduplication of *flip*]

flippant (ˈflɪpənt) *adj.* treating serious matters with inappropriate light-heartedness or lack of respect. [prob. from *flip*] —**ˈflippancy** *n.*

flipper (ˈflɪpə) *n.* **1.** the flat broad limb of seals, whales, and other aquatic animals specialized for swimming. **2.** (*often pl.*) either of a pair of rubber paddle-like devices worn on the feet as an aid in swimming.

flirt (flɜːt) *vb.* **1.** to behave amorously towards someone without emotional commitment. **2.** (foll. by *with*) to deal playfully or carelessly (with something dangerous or serious). ~*n.* **3.** a person who flirts. [origin unknown] —**flirˈtation** *n.* —**ˈflirˈtatious** *adj.*

flit (flɪt) *vb.* **flitting, flitted. 1.** to fly or move along rapidly and lightly. **2.** to pass quickly: *a memory flitted into his mind.* **3.** *Scot. & N English dialect.* to move house. **4.** *Brit. informal.* to depart hurriedly and stealthily in order to avoid debts. ~*n.* **5.** the act of flitting. [Old Norse *flytja* to carry]

flitch (flɪtʃ) *n.* a side of pork salted and cured. [Old English *flicce*]

flitter (ˈflɪtə) *vb.* same as **flutter.**

flittermouse (ˈflɪtəˌmaʊs) *n., pl.* **-mice.** *Dialect.* a bat.

float (fləʊt) *vb.* **1.** to rest on the surface of a fluid without sinking. **2.** to move lightly or freely across a surface or through air or water. **3.** to move about aimlessly, esp. in the mind: *vague ideas floated through his head.* **4. a.** to launch (a commercial enterprise, etc.). **b.** to offer for sale on the stock market. **5.** *Finance.* to allow (a currency) to fluctuate against other currencies. ~*n.* **6.** *Angling.* an indicator attached to a baited line that moves when a fish bites. **7.** a structure allowing an aircraft to land on water. **8.** a motor vehicle used to carry a tableau in a parade. **9.** a small delivery vehicle: *a milk float.* **10.** *Austral. & N.Z.* a vehicle for transporting horses. **11.** a sum of money used to

cover small expenses or provide change. **12.** the hollow floating ball of a ballcock. [Old English *flotian*]

floatation (fləʊˈteɪʃən) *n.* same as **flotation.**

floating (ˈfləʊtɪŋ) *adj.* **1.** moving about; not settled: *a floating population.* **2.** (of an organ or part) displaced or abnormally movable: *a floating kidney.* **3.** uncommitted: *floating voters.* **4.** *Finance.* **a.** (of capital) available for current use. **b.** (of a currency) free to fluctuate against other currencies.

floating rib *n.* a lower rib not attached to the breastbone.

floats (fləʊts) *pl. n. Theatre.* footlights.

flocculent (ˈflɒkjʊlənt) *adj.* like wool; in tufts. [Latin *floccus* FLOCK²] —**ˈflocculence** *n.*

flock¹ (flɒk) *n.* (*sometimes functioning as pl.*) **1.** a group of animals of one kind, esp. sheep or birds. **2.** a large number of people. **3.** a body of Christians regarded as the pastoral charge of a priest. ~*vb.* **4.** to gather together or move in large numbers. [Old English *flocc*]

flock² (flɒk) *n.* **1.** waste from fabrics such as cotton or wool used for stuffing mattresses. **2.** very small tufts of wool applied to wallpaper to give a raised pattern. [Latin *floccus* tuft of wool]

floe (fləʊ) *n.* See **ice floe.** [prob. from Norwegian *flo* slab, layer]

flog (flɒg) *vb.* **flogging, flogged. 1.** to beat harshly, esp. with a whip or stick. **2.** *Brit. slang.* to sell. **3. flog a dead horse.** *Chiefly Brit.* to waste one's energy. [prob. from Latin *flagellāre*]

flood (flʌd) *n.* **1.** an overflowing of water on an area that is normally dry. **2.** a great outpouring: *a flood of words.* **3.** the rising of the tide from low to high water. **4.** *Theatre.* short for **floodlight.** ~*vb.* **5.** (of water) to cover (land) or (of land) to be covered. **6.** to fill to overflowing: *cheap goods flooded the market.* **7.** to flow; surge: *relief flooded through him.* **8.** to supply excess petrol to (a petrol engine) so that it cannot work properly. **9.** to bleed profusely from the womb. [Old English *flōd*]

Flood (flʌd) *n. Old Testament.* **the.** the flood from which Noah and his family and livestock were saved in the ark (Genesis 7–8).

floodgate (ˈflʌdˌgeɪt) *n.* **1.** a gate used to control the flow of water. **2.** (*often pl.*) a control against an outpouring of emotion.

floodlight (ˈflʌdˌlaɪt) *n.* **1.** a lamp that casts a broad intense light, used in the theatre or to illuminate sports grounds or the exterior of buildings. ~*vb.* **-lighting, -lit. 2.** to illuminate by floodlight.

floor (flɔː) *n.* **1.** the inner lower surface of a room. **2.** a storey of a building. **3.** a flat bottom surface: *the sea floor.* **4.** that part of a legislative hall in which debate is conducted. **5.** the right to speak in a legislative body (esp. in **get, have,** *or* **be given the floor**). **6.** a minimum limit. ~*vb.* **7.** to cover with or construct a floor.

8. to knock to the ground. **9.** *Informal.* to disconcert or defeat. [Old English *flōr*]

floorboard ('flɔː,bɔːd) *n.* one of the boards forming a floor.

flooring ('flɔːrɪŋ) *n.* **1.** the material used in making a floor. **2.** a floor.

floor plan *n.* a scale drawing of the arrangement of rooms on one floor of a building.

floor show *n.* a series of entertainments, such as singing and dancing, in a nightclub.

floozy, floozie, *or* **floosie** ('fluːzɪ) *n., pl.* **-zies** *or* **-sies.** *Slang.* a disreputable woman. [origin unknown]

flop (flɒp) *vb.* **flopping, flopped. 1.** to bend, fall, or collapse loosely or carelessly. **2.** to fall or move with a sudden noise. **3.** *Informal.* to fail: *the scheme flopped.* ~*n.* **4.** the act of flopping. **5.** *Informal.* a complete failure. [var. of *flap*] —**floppy** *adj.*

floppy disk *n.* a flexible magnetic disk that stores data in the memory of a digital computer.

flora ('flɔːrə) *n.* all the plant life of a given place or time. [*Flōra*, Roman goddess of flowers]

floral ('flɔːrəl) *adj.* decorated with or consisting of flowers or patterns of flowers.

Florentine ('flɒrən,taɪn) *adj.* **1.** of or relating to Florence, in Italy. ~*n.* **2.** a person from Florence.

floret ('flɔːrɪt) *n.* a small flower, esp. one of many making up a composite flower. [Old French *florete*]

floribunda (,flɒrɪ'bʌndə) *n.* a cultivated hybrid rose whose flowers grow in large sprays. [New Latin *flōribundus* flowering freely]

florid ('flɒrɪd) *adj.* **1.** having a red or flushed complexion. **2.** excessively ornate; flowery. [Latin *flōridus* blooming]

florin ('flɒrɪn) *n.* a former British coin, equivalent to ten (new) pence. [Old Italian *fiorino* Florentine coin]

florist ('flɒrɪst) *n.* a person who grows or deals in flowers.

floss (flɒs) *n.* **1.** fine silky fibres, such as those obtained from silkworm cocoons. **2.** See **dental floss.** [prob. from Old French *flosche* down] —**flossy** *adj.*

flotation *or* **floatation** (fləʊ'teɪʃən) *n.* the launching or financing of a commercial enterprise by bond or share issues.

flotilla (flə'tɪlə) *n.* a small fleet or a fleet of small vessels. [Spanish]

flotsam ('flɒtsəm) *n.* **1.** wreckage from a ship found floating. **2. flotsam and jetsam. a.** odds and ends. **b.** homeless or vagrant people. [Anglo-French *floteson*]

flounce¹ (flaʊns) *vb.* **1.** to move or go with emphatic movements. ~*n.* **2.** the act of flouncing. [Scandinavian]

flounce² (flaʊns) *n.* an ornamental gathered ruffle on a garment. [Old French *froncir* to wrinkle]

flounder¹ ('flaʊndə) *vb.* **1.** to move with difficulty, as in mud. **2.** to behave or speak in an awkward, confused way. [prob. a blend of FOUNDER + BLUNDER]

flounder² ('flaʊndə) *n., pl.* **-der** *or* **-ders.** an edible flatfish. [Scandinavian]

flour ('flaʊə) *n.* **1.** a powder prepared by grinding grain, esp. wheat. ~*vb.* **2.** to sprinkle (food or utensils) with flour. [Middle English *flur* "flower", i.e. best part] —**floury** *adj.*

flourish ('flʌrɪʃ) *vb.* **1.** to thrive; prosper. **2.** to be at the peak of development. **3.** to wave with sweeping strokes. ~*n.* **4.** a dramatic waving or sweeping movement: *he drew his knife with a flourish.* **5.** an ornamental curly line in writing. **6.** a grandiose passage of music. [Latin *flōrēre* to flower] —**flourishing** *adj.*

flout (flaʊt) *vb.* to show contempt (for). [prob. from Middle English *flouten* to play the flute]

flow (fləʊ) *vb.* **1.** (of liquids) to move in a stream. **2.** (of blood; electricity, etc.) to circulate. **3.** to move steadily and smoothly: *traffic flowing down the street.* **4.** to be produced effortlessly: *ideas flowed from her pen.* **5.** to hang freely: *her hair flowed down her back.* **6.** to be abundant: *wine flows at their parties.* **7.** (of tide water) to rise. ~*n.* **8.** the act, rate, or manner of flowing: *a fast flow.* **9.** a continuous stream or discharge. **10.** the advancing of the tide. [Old English *flōwan*]

flow chart *or* **sheet** *n.* a diagrammatic representation of the sequence of operations in an industrial process, computer program, etc.

flower ('flaʊə) *n.* **1.** the part of a plant that is, usually, brightly coloured, and quickly fades, producing seeds. **2.** a plant grown for its colourful flowers. **3.** the best or finest part. **4. in flower.** with flowers open. ~*vb.* **5.** to produce flowers; bloom. **6.** to reach full growth or maturity. [Latin *flōs*]

flowered ('flaʊəd) *adj.* decorated with flowers or a floral design.

flowerpot ('flaʊə,pɒt) *n.* a pot in which plants are grown.

flowery ('flaʊərɪ) *adj.* **1.** decorated with flowers or floral patterns. **2.** (of language or style) elaborate. —**floweriness** *n.*

flown (fləʊn) *vb.* the past participle of **fly¹.**

flu (fluː) *n. Informal.* short for **influenza.**

fluctuate ('flʌktjʊ,eɪt) *vb.* to change frequently and erratically: *prices fluctuated.* [Latin *fluctus* a wave] —**fluctu'ation** *n.*

flue (fluː) *n.* a shaft, tube, or pipe, as in a chimney, used to carry off smoke or gas. [origin unknown]

fluent ('fluːənt) *adj.* **1.** able to speak or write with ease: *a fluent reader; fluent in French.* **2.** spoken or written with ease. [Latin *fluere* to flow] —**'fluency** *n.* —**'fluently** *adv.*

fluff (flʌf) *n.* **1.** soft light particles, such as the down of cotton or wool. **2.** *Informal.* a mistake, esp. in speaking or reading lines. ~*vb.* **3.** to make or become soft and puffy. **4.** *Informal.* to make a mistake in performing. [prob. from earlier *flue* downy matter] —**'fluffiness** *n.* —**'fluffy** *adj.*

fluid ('fluːɪd) *n.* **1.** a substance, such as a liquid or gas, that can flow and has no fixed shape. ~*adj.* **2.** capable of flowing and easily changing shape. **3.** constantly changing or apt to change. [Latin *fluere* to flow] —**flu'idity** *n.*

fluid ounce *n.* **1.** *Brit.* one twentieth of an Imperial pint. **2.** *U.S.* one sixteenth of a U.S. pint.

fluke[1] (flu:k) *n.* an accidental stroke of luck. [origin unknown] —**'fluky** *adj.*

fluke[2] (flu:k) *n.* **1.** a flat bladelike projection at the end of the arm of an anchor. **2.** either of the two lobes of the tail of a whale. [perhaps a special use of FLUKE[3] (in the sense: a flounder, flatfish)]

fluke[3] (flu:k) *n.* any parasitic flatworm, such as the liver fluke. [Old English *flōc*]

flummery ('flʌmərɪ) *n.*, *pl.* **-meries. 1.** *Informal.* meaningless flattery. **2.** *Chiefly Brit.* a cold pudding of oatmeal and milk. [Welsh *llymru*]

flummox ('flʌməks) *vb.* to perplex or bewilder. [origin unknown]

flung (flʌŋ) *vb.* the past of **fling.**

flunk (flʌŋk) *vb. Informal, chiefly U.S., Canad., & N.Z.* to fail (an examination, course, etc.). [origin unknown]

flunky *or* **flunkey** ('flʌŋkɪ) *n.*, *pl.* **flunkies** *or* **flunkeys. 1.** a servile follower. **2.** a person who performs menial tasks. **3.** a manservant in livery. [origin unknown]

fluor ('flu:ɔ:) *n.* same as **fluorspar.** [Latin: a flowing; so called from its use as a metallurgical flux]

fluoresce (,fluə'rɛs) *vb.* to exhibit fluorescence.

fluorescence (,fluə'rɛsəns) *n.* **1.** *Physics.* the emission of light from atoms or molecules that are bombarded by particles, such as electrons, or by radiation from a separate source. **2.** the radiation emitted as a result of fluorescence. [from *fluor*] —,**fluo'rescent** *adj.*

fluorescent lamp *n.* a lamp in which ultraviolet radiation from an electrical gas discharge causes a thin layer of phosphor on a tube's inside surface to fluoresce.

fluoridate ('fluərɪ,deɪt) *vb.* to add fluoride to (water) as protection against tooth decay. —,**fluori'dation** *n.*

fluoride ('fluə,raɪd) *n.* any compound containing fluorine and another element or radical.

fluorinate ('fluərɪ,neɪt) *vb.* to treat or combine with fluorine. —,**fluori'nation** *n.*

fluorine ('fluəri:n) *n.* a toxic pungent pale yellow gas that is the most reactive of all the elements. Symbol: F

fluoroscopy (fluə'rɒskəpɪ) *n.* same as **radioscopy.**

fluorspar ('fluə,spɑ:), **fluor,** *or U.S. & Canad.* **fluorite** *n.* a white or colourless mineral, consisting of calcium fluoride in crystalline form: the chief ore of fluorine.

flurry ('flʌrɪ) *n.*, *pl.* **-ries. 1.** a sudden commotion. **2.** a light gust of wind or rain or fall of snow. ~*vb.* **-rying, -ried. 3.** to confuse or bewilder. [obs. *flurr* to scatter]

flush[1] (flʌʃ) *vb.* **1.** to blush or cause to blush. **2.** to send a volume of water quickly through (a pipe) or into (a toilet)

for cleansing. **3.** (*usually passive*) to elate: *flushed with success.* ~*n.* **4.** a rosy colour, esp. in the cheeks. **5.** a sudden flow, as of water. **6.** a feeling of elation: *in the first flush of enthusiasm.* **7.** freshness: *the flush of youth.* [perhaps from FLUSH[3]]

flush[2] (flʌʃ) *adj.* **1.** level with another surface. **2.** *Informal.* having plenty of money. ~*adv.* **3.** so as to be level. [prob. from FLUSH[1] (in the sense: spring out)]

flush[3] (flʌʃ) *vb.* to rouse (game) and put to flight. [Middle English *flusshen*]

flush[4] (flʌʃ) *n.* (in poker and similar games) a hand containing only one suit. [Latin *fluxus* flux]

fluster ('flʌstə) *vb.* **1.** to make or become nervous or upset. ~*n.* **2.** a state of confusion or agitation. [Old Norse]

flute (flu:t) *n.* **1.** a wind instrument consisting of a tube of wood or metal with holes in the side stopped either by the fingers or keys. The breath is directed across a mouth hole in the side. **2.** *Archit.* a rounded shallow groove. ~*vb.* **3.** to produce or utter (sounds) in the tone of a flute. **4.** to make grooves in. [Old French *flahute*] —**'fluty** *adj.*

fluting ('flu:tɪŋ) *n.* a design or decoration of flutes on a column.

flutter ('flʌtə) *vb.* **1.** to wave rapidly. **2.** (of birds or butterflies) to flap the wings. **3.** to move with an irregular motion. **4.** *Pathol.* (of the heart) to beat abnormally rapidly. **5.** to move about restlessly. ~*n.* **6.** a quick flapping or vibrating motion. **7.** a state of nervous excitement or confusion. **8.** excited interest; stir. **9.** *Brit. informal.* a modest bet. **10.** *Pathol.* an abnormally rapid beating of the heart. **11.** *Electronics.* a slow variation in pitch in a sound-reproducing system. [Old English *floteri-an*]

fluvial ('flu:vɪəl) *adj.* of or occurring in a river: *fluvial deposits.* [Latin *fluvius* river]

flux (flʌks) *n.* **1.** a flow or discharge. **2.** continuous change; instability. **3.** a substance mixed with a metal oxide to assist in fusion. **4.** *Physics.* **a.** the rate of flow of particles, energy, or a fluid. **b.** the strength of a field in a given area: *magnetic flux.* [Latin *fluxus* a flow]

fly[1] (flaɪ) *vb.* **flying, flew, flown. 1.** (of birds, aircraft, etc.) to move through the air using aerodynamic forces. **2.** to travel over (an area of land or sea) in an aircraft. **3.** to operate (an aircraft). **4.** to float, flutter, display or be displayed in the air: *they flew the flag.* **5.** to transport or be transported through the air by aircraft, wind, etc. **6.** to move very quickly or suddenly: *the door flew open.* **7.** to pass swiftly: *time flies.* **8.** to escape from (an enemy or a place); flee. **9.** (foll. by *at* or *upon*) to attack a person. **10. fly a kite.** to release information or take a step in order to test public opinion. **11. fly high.** *Informal.* to have a high aim. **12. let fly.** *Informal.* **a.** to lose one's temper: *she really let fly at him.* **b.** to throw (an object). ~*n.*, *pl.* **flies. 13.** (*often pl.*) a closure that conceals a zip, buttons, or other fastening, as on trousers. **14.** a flap forming the entrance to a tent. **15.** (*pl.*) *Theatre.* the space above the stage, used for storing scenery. [Old English *flēogan*]

fly² (flaɪ) *n., pl.* **flies. 1.** any two-winged insect, esp. the housefly, characterized by active flight. **2.** any of various similar but unrelated insects, such as the dragonfly. **3.** *Angling.* a lure made from a fish-hook dressed with feathers to resemble a fly. **4. fly in the ointment.** *Informal.* a slight flaw that detracts from value or enjoyment. **5. fly on the wall.** a person who watches others, while not being noticed himself. **6. there are no flies on him, her,** etc. *Informal.* he, she, etc., is no fool. [Old English *flēoge*]

fly³ (flaɪ) *adj. Slang, chiefly Brit.* knowing and sharp; smart. [origin unknown]

flyaway ('flaɪəˌweɪ) *adj.* **1.** (of hair or clothing) fine and fluttering. **2.** frivolous.

flyblown ('flaɪˌbləʊn) *adj.* **1.** covered with blowfly eggs. **2.** contaminated; tainted.

fly-by-night *Informal.* ~*adj.* **1.** unreliable or untrustworthy, esp. in finance. ~*n.* **2.** an untrustworthy person.

flyer ('flaɪə) *n.* same as **flier.**

fly-fish *vb. Angling.* to fish using artificial flies as lures. —'**fly-ˌfishing** *n.*

flying ('flaɪɪŋ) *adj.* **1.** hurried: *a flying visit.* **2.** designed for fast action. **3.** hanging, waving, or floating freely: *flying hair.* ~*n.* **4.** the act of piloting, navigating, or travelling in an aircraft.

flying boat *n.* a seaplane in which the fuselage consists of a hull that provides buoyancy.

flying buttress *n.* a buttress supporting a wall by an arch that transmits the thrust outwards and downwards.

flying colours *pl. n.* conspicuous success; triumph: *he passed his test with flying colours.*

flying fish *n.* a fish of warm and tropical seas, with enlarged winglike pectoral fins used for gliding above the water.

flying fox *n.* **1.** any large fruit bat of tropical Africa and Asia. **2.** *Austral. & N.Z.* a cable mechanism used for transportation across a river, gorge, etc.

flying officer *n.* a junior commissioned officer in an air force.

flying saucer *n.* any unidentified disc-shaped flying object alleged to come from outer space.

flying squad *n.* a small group of police or soldiers ready to move into action quickly.

flying start *n.* **1.** a start to a race in which the competitor is already travelling at speed as he passes the starting line. **2.** any promising beginning.

flying wing *n.* (in Canadian football) the twelfth player, who has a variable position behind the scrimmage line.

flyleaf ('flaɪˌliːf) *n., pl.* **-leaves.** the inner leaf of the endpaper of a book.

flyover ('flaɪˌəʊvə) *n. Brit.* an intersection of two roads at which one is carried over the other by a bridge.

flypaper ('flaɪˌpeɪpə) *n.* paper with a sticky and poisonous coating, hung up to trap flies.

fly-past *n.* a ceremonial flight of aircraft over a given area.

fly sheet *n.* a piece of canvas drawn over the ridgepole of a tent to form an outer roof.

fly spray *n.* a liquid used to destroy flies, sprayed from an aerosol.

flyweight ('flaɪˌweɪt) *n.* **1. a.** a professional boxer weighing up to 112 pounds. **b.** an amateur boxer weighing up to 51 kg. **2.** an amateur wrestler weighing up to 115 pounds.

flywheel ('flaɪˌwiːl) *n.* a heavy wheel that smooths the operation of a machine by making it work at a steady speed.

Fm *Chem.* fermium.

FM frequency modulation.

f-number *n. Photog.* the ratio of the effective diameter of a lens to its focal length.

foal (fəʊl) *n.* **1.** the young of a horse or related animal. ~*vb.* **2.** to give birth to (a foal). [Old English *fola*]

foam (fəʊm) *n.* **1.** a mass of small bubbles of gas formed on the surface of a liquid, such as by agitation. **2.** frothy saliva. **3.** any of a number of light cellular solids made by creating bubbles of gas in a material such as plastic or rubber, when it is liquid. ~*vb.* **4.** to produce or cause to produce foam; froth. **5.** to be very angry (esp. in **foam at the mouth**). [Old English *fām*] —'**foamy** *adj.*

fob (fɒb) *n.* **1.** a chain by which a pocket watch is attached to a waistcoat. **2.** a small pocket in a man's waistcoat, for holding a watch. [Germanic]

f.o.b. *or* **FOB** *Commerce.* free on board.

fob off *vb.* **fobbing, fobbed. 1.** to pretend to satisfy (a person) with lies or excuses. **2.** to dispose of (goods) by trickery. [prob. from German *foppen* to trick]

focal ('fəʊk°l) *adj.* **1.** of or relating to a focus. **2.** situated at or measured from the focus.

focal length *n.* the distance from the focal point of a lens or mirror to the surface of the mirror or the centre of the lens.

focal point *n.* **1.** the point where the rays of light from a lens or mirror meet. **2.** the centre of attention or interest.

focus ('fəʊkəs) *n., pl.* **-cuses** *or* **-ci** (-saɪ). **1.** a point of convergence of light or sound waves, or a point from which they appear to diverge. **2.** same as **focal point** *or* **focal length. 3.** *Optics.* the state of an optical image when it is distinct or the state of an instrument producing this image. **4.** a point upon which attention or activity is concentrated. **5.** *Geom.* a fixed reference point on the concave side of a conic section, used when defining its eccentricity. ~*vb.* **-cusing, -cused** *or* **-cussing, -cussed. 6.** to bring or come to a focus or into focus. **7.** (often foll. by *on*) to concentrate. [Latin: hearth, fireplace]

fodder ('fɒdə) *n.* bulk feed for livestock, esp. hay or straw. [Old English *fōdor*]

foe (fəʊ) n. *Formal or literary.* an enemy. [Old English *fāh* hostile]

FoE *or* **FOE** Friends of the Earth.

foetid ('fɛtɪd, 'fiː-) adj. same as **fetid**.

foetus ('fiːtəs) n., pl. **-tuses.** same as **fetus**.

fog (fɒg) n. **1.** a mass of droplets of condensed water vapour suspended in the air, often greatly reducing visibility. **2.** *Photog.* a blurred area on a developed negative, print, or transparency. ~vb. **fogging, fogged. 3.** to envelop or become enveloped with or as if with fog. [prob. from Old Norse] —'**foggy** adj.

fog bank n. a distinct mass of fog, esp. at sea.

fogbound ('fɒgˌbaʊnd) adj. prevented from operation by fog.

foghorn ('fɒgˌhɔːn) n. a mechanical instrument sounded at intervals as a warning to ships in fog.

fogy *or* **fogey** ('fəʊgɪ) n., pl. **-gies** *or* **-geys.** an extremely old-fashioned person (esp. in **old fogy**). [origin unknown] —'**fogyish** *or* '**fogeyish** adj.

foible ('fɔɪbʲl) n. a slight peculiarity or minor weakness; idiosyncrasy. [obs. French form of *faible* feeble]

foil[1] (fɔɪl) vb. to baffle or frustrate (a person or an attempt). [Middle English *foilen* to trample]

foil[2] (fɔɪl) n. **1.** metal in the form of very thin sheets. **2.** a person or thing that gives contrast to another. [Latin *folia* leaves]

foil[3] (fɔɪl) n. a light slender flexible sword tipped by a button. [origin unknown]

foist (fɔɪst) vb. (often foll. by *off* or *on*) to pass off (something inferior) as genuine or valuable. [prob. from obs. Dutch *vuisten* to enclose in one's hand]

fold[1] (fəʊld) vb. **1.** to bend double so that one part covers another. **2.** to bring together and intertwine (the arms or legs). **3.** (often foll. by *up* or *in*) to enclose in a surrounding material. **4.** (foll. by *in*) to clasp (a person) in the arms. **5.** Also: **fold in.** to mix (ingredients) by gently turning one over the other with a spoon. **6.** *Informal.* to collapse; fail. ~n. **7.** a piece or section that has been folded. **8.** a mark, crease, or hollow made by folding. **9.** a bend in stratified rocks that results from movements within the earth's crust. [Old English *fealdan*]

fold[2] (fəʊld) n. **1.** a small enclosure for sheep. **2.** a church or the members of it. [Old English *falod*]

folder ('fəʊldə) n. a binder or file for holding loose papers.

folding door n. a door with two or more vertical hinged leaves that can be folded one against another.

foliaceous (ˌfəʊlɪ'eɪʃəs) adj. **1.** like a leaf. **2.** *Geol.* consisting of thin layers. [Latin *foliāceus*]

foliage ('fəʊlɪɪdʒ) n. **1.** the green leaves of a plant. **2.** sprays of leaves used for decoration. [Old French *fuellage*]

foliation (ˌfəʊlɪ'eɪʃən) n. **1.** *Bot.* **a.** the process of producing leaves. **b.** the state of being in leaf. **2.** a leaflike decoration.

folio ('fəʊlɪəʊ) n., pl. **-lios. 1.** a sheet of paper folded in half to make two leaves for a book. **2.** a book of the largest common size made up of such sheets. **3. a.** a leaf of paper numbered on the front side only. **b.** the page number of a book. ~adj. **4.** of or made in the largest book size, common esp. in earlier centuries: *a folio edition.* [Latin phrase *in foliō* in a leaf]

folk (fəʊk) n., pl. **folk** *or* **folks. 1.** (*functioning as pl.; often pl. in form*) people in general, esp. those of a particular group or class: *country folk.* **2.** (*functioning as pl.; usually pl. in form*) *Informal.* members of a family. **3.** (*functioning as sing.*) *Informal.* short for **folk music. 4.** a people or tribe. ~adj. **5.** originating from or traditional to the common people of a country: *a folk song.* [Old English *folc*]

folk dance n. **1.** a traditional rustic dance. **2.** music for such a dance.

folk etymology n. the gradual change in the form of a word through the influence of a more familiar word, as for example *crayfish* from its Middle English form *crevis.*

folklore ('fəʊkˌlɔː) n. the unwritten literature of a people as expressed in stories and songs.

folk music n. **1.** music that is passed on from generation to generation. **2.** any music composed in this idiom.

folk song n. **1.** a song which has been handed down among the common people. **2.** a modern song which reflects the folk idiom. —**folk singer** n.

folksy ('fəʊksɪ) adj. **-sier, -siest.** of or like ordinary people; simple and unpretentious, sometimes affectedly so.

follicle ('fɒlɪkʲl) n. any small sac or cavity in the body: *hair follicle.* [Latin *folliculus* small bag] —**follicular** (fɒ'lɪkjʊlə) adj.

follow ('fɒləʊ) vb. **1.** to go or come after. **2.** to accompany: *she followed her sister everywhere.* **3.** to come after as a logical or natural consequence. **4.** to keep to the course or track of. **5.** to act in accordance with: *to follow instructions.* **6.** to accept the ideas or beliefs of (a previous authority). **7.** to understand (an explanation). **8.** to have a keen interest in: *to follow athletics.* [Old English *folgian*]

follower ('fɒləʊə) n. **1.** a person who accepts the teachings of another: *a follower of Marx.* **2.** a supporter, as of a sport or team.

following ('fɒləʊɪŋ) adj. **1.** about to be mentioned. **2.** (of winds or currents) moving in the same direction as a vessel. ~n. **3.** a group of supporters or enthusiasts.

follow-on *Cricket.* ~n. **1.** an immediate second innings forced on a team scoring a prescribed number of runs fewer than its opponents in the first innings. ~vb. **follow on. 2.** to play a follow-on.

follow up vb. **1.** to investigate (a person, evidence, etc.) closely. **2.** to continue (action) after a beginning, esp. to increase its effect. ~n. **follow-up. 3.** something done to reinforce an initial action.

folly ('fɒlɪ) n., pl. **-lies. 1.** the quality of being foolish. **2.** a foolish action, idea, etc. **3.** a building in the form of a castle, temple, etc., built to satisfy a fancy. [Old French folie madness]

foment (fə'mɛnt) vb. to encourage or instigate (trouble, discord, etc.). [Latin fōmentum a poultice] —**fomentation** (ˌfəʊmɛn-'teɪʃən) n.

fond (fɒnd) adj. **1.** (foll. by of) having a liking (for). **2.** loving; tender. **3.** indulgent: a fond mother. **4.** (of hopes, wishes, etc.) cherished but unlikely to be realized. [Middle English fonnen to be foolish] —**'fondly** adv. —**'fondness** n.

fondant ('fɒndənt) n. **1.** a thick flavoured paste of sugar and water. **2.** a sweet made of this mixture. [French]

fondle ('fɒnd'l) vb. to touch or stroke tenderly. [obs. fond to fondle]

fondue ('fɒndjuː) n. a Swiss dish, consisting of melted cheese into which small pieces of bread are dipped. [French]

font (fɒnt) n. a large bowl in a church for baptismal water. [Latin fons fountain]

fontanelle or chiefly U.S. **fontanel** (ˌfɒntə'nɛl) n. Anat. any of the soft membranous gaps between the bones of the skull in a fetus or infant. [Old French fontanele a little spring]

food (fuːd) n. **1.** any substance that can be taken into the body by a living organism and changed into energy and body tissue. **2.** nourishment in more or less solid form: food and drink. [Old English fōda]

food chain n. Ecology. a series of organisms in a community, each member of which feeds on another in the chain and is in turn eaten.

food poisoning n. an acute illness caused by food that is contaminated by bacteria.

foodstuff ('fuːdˌstʌf) n. any substance that can be used as food.

fool[1] (fuːl) n. **1.** a person who lacks sense or judgment. **2.** a person who is made to appear ridiculous. **3.** (formerly) a professional jester living in a royal or noble household. **4. act** or **play the fool.** to deliberately act foolishly. ~vb. **5.** to deceive (someone), esp. in order to make ridiculous. **6.** (foll. by with, around with, or about with) Informal. to act or play (with) irresponsibly or aimlessly. **7.** to speak or act in a playful or jesting manner. [Latin follis bellows]

fool[2] (fuːl) n. Chiefly Brit. a dessert made from a purée of fruit with cream. [perhaps from FOOL[1]]

foolery ('fuːlərɪ) n., pl. **-eries.** foolish behaviour.

foolhardy ('fuːlˌhɑːdɪ) adj. **-hardier, -hardiest.** heedlessly rash or adventurous. [Old French fol foolish + hardi bold] —**'fool,hardily** adv. —**'fool,hardiness** n.

foolish ('fuːlɪʃ) adj. **1.** unwise; silly. **2.** ridiculous or absurd. —**'foolishly** adv. —**'foolishness** n.

foolproof ('fuːlˌpruːf) adj. Informal. **1.** proof against failure. **2.** (esp. of machines, etc.) proof against human misuse or error.

foolscap ('fuːlzˌkæp) n. Chiefly Brit. a size of paper, 13½ by 17 inches. [from the watermark of a fool's (i.e. dunce's) cap formerly used on it]

fool's errand n. a fruitless undertaking.

fool's paradise n. illusory happiness.

foot (fut) n., pl. **feet. 1.** the part of the leg below the ankle joint that is in contact with the ground during standing and walking. **2.** the part of a garment covering a foot. **3.** a unit of length equal to 12 inches (0.3048 metre). **4.** any part resembling a foot in form or function: the foot of a chair. **5.** the lower part of something; bottom: the foot of a hill; the foot of the list. **6.** Archaic. infantry. **7.** Prosody. a group of two or more syllables in which one syllable has the major stress, forming the basic unit of poetic rhythm. **8. one foot in the grave.** Informal. near to death. **9. on foot.** walking. **10. put one's best foot forward. a.** to try to do one's best. **b.** to hurry. **11. put one's foot down.** Informal. to act firmly. **12. put one's foot in it.** Informal. to blunder tactlessly. **13. under foot.** on the ground; beneath one's feet. ~vb. **14. foot it. a.** to walk. **b.** to dance. **15. foot the bill.** to pay the entire cost of something. ~See also **feet.** [Old English fōt] —**'footless** adj.

footage ('fʊtɪdʒ) n. **1.** a length in feet. **2.** the extent of film exposed.

foot-and-mouth disease n. a highly infectious viral disease of cattle, pigs, sheep, and goats, in which blisters form in the mouth and on the feet.

football ('fʊtˌbɔːl) n. **1.** any of various games played with a ball in which two teams compete to kick, head or propel the ball into each other's goal. **2.** the ball used in any of these games. —**'football,baller** n.

football pools pl. n. same as **pools.**

footbridge ('fʊtˌbrɪdʒ) n. a narrow bridge for the use of pedestrians.

footfall ('fʊtˌfɔːl) n. the sound of a footstep.

foothill ('fʊtˌhɪl) n. (often pl.) a relatively low hill at the foot of a mountain.

foothold ('fʊtˌhəʊld) n. **1.** a ledge or other place where a foot can be securely positioned, as during climbing. **2.** a secure position from which further progress may be made.

footing ('fʊtɪŋ) n. **1.** basis or foundation: get this on an official footing. **2.** the relationship between two people or groups: on an equal footing. **3.** a secure grip by or for the feet.

footle ('fuːt'l) vb. (often foll. by around or about) Informal. to loiter aimlessly. [prob. from French foutre to copulate with] —**'footling** adj.

footlights ('fʊtˌlaɪts) pl. n. Theatre. lights set in a row along the front of the stage floor.

footloose ('fʊtˌluːs) adj. free to go or do as one wishes.

footman ('fʊtmən) n., pl. **-men.** a male servant in livery.

footnote ('fʊt,nəʊt) n. a note printed at the bottom of a page.

footpad ('fʊt,pæd) n. Archaic. a highwayman, on foot rather than horseback.

footpath ('fʊt,pɑːθ) n. a narrow path for walkers only.

footplate ('fʊt,pleɪt) n. Chiefly Brit. a platform in the cab of a locomotive on which the crew stand to operate the controls.

footprint ('fʊt,prɪnt) n. an indentation or outline of the foot on a surface.

footsie ('fʊtsɪ) n. Informal. flirtation involving the touching together of feet.

footsore ('fʊt,sɔː) adj. having sore or tired feet, esp. from much walking.

footstep ('fʊt,stɛp) n. 1. a step in walking. 2. the sound made by walking. 3. a footmark. 4. **follow in someone's footsteps.** to continue the example of another.

footstool ('fʊt,stuːl) n. a low stool used for supporting the feet of a seated person.

footwear ('fʊt,wɛə) n. anything worn to cover the feet.

footwork ('fʊt,wɜːk) n. skilful use of the feet, as in sports or dancing.

fop (fɒp) n. a man who is excessively concerned with fashion. [perhaps from Middle English foppe fool] —'**foppery** n. —'**foppish** adj.

for (fɔː; unstressed fə) prep. 1. directed or belonging to: there's a phone call for you. 2. to the advantage of: I only did it for you. 3. in the direction of: heading for the border. 4. over a span of (time or distance): working for six days. 5. in favour of: vote for me. 6. in order to get: I do it for money. 7. designed to meet the needs of: these kennels are for puppies. 8. at a cost of: I got it for 10p. 9. in place of: a substitute for the injured player. 10. because of: she wept for pure relief. 11. with regard to the usual characteristics of: it's cool for this time of year. 12. concerning: desire for money. 13. as being: I know that for a fact. 14. at a specified time: a date for the next evening. 15. to do or partake of: an appointment for supper. 16. in the duty or task of: that's for him to say. 17. to allow of: too big a job for us to handle. 18. despite: she's a good wife, for all her nagging. 19. in order to preserve, retain, etc.: to fight for survival. 20. as a direct equivalent to: word for word. 21. in order to become or enter: to train for the priesthood. 22. in recompense for: I paid for it last week. 23. **for it.** Brit. informal. liable for punishment or blame: you'll be for it if she catches you. ~conj. 24. because; seeing that: I couldn't stay, for the area was violent. [Old English]

forage ('fɒrɪdʒ) n. 1. food for horses or cattle, esp. hay or straw. 2. the act of searching for food or provisions. ~vb. 3. to search (the countryside or a town) for food, etc. 4. to obtain by searching about. [Old French fourrage]

forage cap n. a soldier's undress cap.

foramen (fɒ'reɪmɛn) n., pl. -ramina (-'ræmɪnə) or -ramens. a natural hole, esp. one in a bone through which nerves pass. [Latin]

forasmuch as (fərəz'mʌtʃ) conj. Archaic or legal. seeing that; since.

foray ('fɒreɪ) n. 1. a short raid or incursion. 2. a first attempt at new undertaking. [Middle English forrayen to pillage]

forbade (fə'bæd, -'beɪd) or **forbad** (fə'bæd) vb. the past tense of **forbid.**

forbear¹ (fɔː'bɛə) vb. -bearing, -bore, -borne. to cease or refrain (from doing something). [Old English forberan] —**for'bearance** n.

forbear² ('fɔː,bɛə) n. same as **forebear.**

forbid (fə'bɪd) vb. -bidding, -bade or -bad, -bidden or -bid. to prohibit (a person) in a forceful or authoritative manner (from doing or having something). [Old English forbēodan]

forbidding (fə'bɪdɪŋ) adj. severe, unfriendly, or threatening.

forbore (fɔː'bɔː) vb. the past tense of **forbear¹.**

forborne (fɔː'bɔːn) vb. the past participle of **forbear¹.**

force¹ (fɔːs) n. 1. strength or power: the force of the blow. 2. exertion or the use of exertion against a person or thing that resists. 3. Physics. an influence that changes a body from a state of rest to one of motion or changes its rate of motion. Symbol: F 4. a. intellectual or moral influence: the force of his argument. b. a person or thing with such influence: he was a force in the land. 5. vehemence or intensity: she spoke with great force. 6. a group of people organized for particular duties or tasks: a workforce; police force. 7. **in force.** a. (of a law) having legal validity. b. in great strength or numbers. ~vb. 8. to compel (a person, group, etc.) to do something through effort, superior strength, etc. 9. to acquire or produce through effort, superior strength, etc.: force a confession. 10. to propel or drive despite resistance. 11. to break down or open (a lock, door, etc.). 12. to impose or inflict: he forced his views on them. 13. to cause (plants or farm animals) to grow at an increased rate. 14. to strain to the utmost: to force the voice. [Latin fortis strong]

force² (fɔːs) n. (in N England) a waterfall. [Old Norse fors]

forced (fɔːst) adj. 1. done because of force: forced labour. 2. false or unnatural: a forced smile. 3. due to an emergency: a forced landing.

force-feed vb. -feeding, -fed. to force (a person or animal) to swallow food.

forceful ('fɔːsfʊl) adj. 1. powerful. 2. persuasive or effective. —'**forcefully** adv.

forcemeat ('fɔːs,miːt) n. a mixture of chopped ingredients used for stuffing. [from force (see FARCE) + meat]

forceps ('fɔːsɛps) n., pl. -ceps. a surgical instrument in the form of a pair of pincers. [Latin formus hot + capere to seize]

forcible ('fɔːsəb°l) adj. 1. done by, involving, or having force. 2. convincing or effective: *a forcible argument.* —'**forcibly** *adv.*

ford (fɔːd) *n.* **1.** a shallow area in a river that can be crossed by car, on horseback, etc. ~*vb.* **2.** to cross (a river) over a shallow area. [Old English] —'**fordable** *adj.*

fore (fɔː) *adj.* **1.** (*usually in combination*) at, in, or towards the front: *the forelegs of a horse.* ~*n.* **2.** the front part. **3. fore and aft.** located at both ends of a vessel: *a fore-and-aft rig.* **4. to the fore.** to the front or conspicuous position. [Old English]

fore- *prefix.* **1.** before in time or rank: *forefather.* **2.** at or near the front: *forecourt.* [Old English]

forearm[1] ('fɔːr,ɑːm) *n.* the part of the arm from the elbow to the wrist.

forearm[2] (fɔːr'ɑːm) *vb.* to prepare or arm (someone) in advance.

forebear *or* **forbear** ('fɔː,bɛə) *n.* an ancestor.

foreboding (fɔː'bəʊdɪŋ) *n.* a strong feeling that something bad is going to happen.

forecast ('fɔː,kɑːst) *vb.* **-casting, -cast** *or* **-casted.** **1.** to predict or calculate (weather, events, etc.), in advance. ~*n.* **2.** a statement of probable future weather calculated from meteorological data. **3.** a prediction. —'**fore,caster** *n.*

forecastle, fo'c's'le, *or* **fo'c'sle** ('fəʊksᵊl) *n.* the part of a vessel at the bow, formerly where the crew was quartered.

foreclose (fɔː'kləʊz) *vb. Law.* to take possession of property bought with borrowed money because repayment has not been made: *the bank foreclosed on me.* [Old French *for-* out + *clore* to close] —**foreclosure** (fɔː'kləʊʒə) *n.*

forecourt ('fɔː,kɔːt) *n.* a courtyard in front of a building, as one in a filling station.

forefather ('fɔː,fɑːðə) *n.* an ancestor.

forefinger ('fɔː,fɪŋgə) *n.* the finger next to the thumb. Also called: **index finger.**

forefoot ('fɔː,fʊt) *n., pl.* **-feet.** either of the front feet of an animal.

forefront ('fɔː,frʌnt) *n.* **1.** the extreme front. **2.** the position of most prominence or action.

foregather (fɔː'gæðə) *vb.* same as **forgather.**

forego[1] (fɔː'gəʊ) *vb.* **-going, -went, -gone.** to precede in time, place, etc. [Old English *foregān*]

forego[2] (fɔː'gəʊ) *vb.* **-going, -went, -gone.** same as **forgo.**

foregoing (fɔː'gəʊɪŋ) *adj.* (esp. of writing or speech) going before; preceding.

foregone conclusion ('fɔː,gɒn) *n.* an inevitable result.

foreground ('fɔː,graʊnd) *n.* **1.** the part of a scene nearest the viewer. **2.** a conspicuous position.

forehand ('fɔː,hænd) *Tennis, squash, etc.* ~*adj.* **1.** (of a stroke) made with the palm of the hand facing the direction of the stroke. ~*n.* **2.** a forehand stroke.

forehead ('fɒrɪd, 'fɔː,hɛd) *n.* the part of

the face between the natural hairline and the eyes. [Old English *forhēafod*]

foreign ('fɒrɪn) *adj.* **1.** of, located in, or coming from another country, area, or people. **2.** dealing or concerned with another country, area, or people: *a foreign office.* **3.** not familiar; strange. **4.** in an abnormal place or position: *foreign matter.* [Latin *foris* outside]

foreigner ('fɒrɪnə) *n.* **1.** a person from a foreign country. **2.** an outsider.

foreign minister *or* **secretary** *n.* (*often caps.*) a cabinet minister who is responsible for a country's dealings with other countries.

foreign office *n.* the ministry of a country that is concerned with dealings with other states.

foreknowledge (fɔː'nɒlɪdʒ) *n.* knowledge of something before it actually happens.

foreleg ('fɔː,lɛg) *n.* either of the front legs of an animal.

forelock ('fɔː,lɒk) *n.* a lock of hair growing or falling over the forehead.

foreman ('fɔːmən) *n., pl.* **-men.** **1.** a person who supervises other workmen. **2.** *Law.* the principal juror.

foremast ('fɔː,mɑːst) *n.* the mast nearest the bow of a vessel.

foremost ('fɔː,məʊst) *adj., adv.* first in time, place, rank, etc. [Old English *forma* first]

forenoon ('fɔː,nuːn) *n.* the daylight hours before noon.

forensic (fə'rɛnsɪk) *adj.* used in or connected with a court of law. [Latin *forēnsis* public] —**fo'rensically** *adv.*

forensic medicine *n.* the application of medical knowledge to the purposes of the law, as in determining the cause of death.

foreordain (,fɔːrɔː'deɪn) *vb.* to determine (events, etc.) in the future.

forepaw ('fɔː,pɔː) *n.* either of the front feet of an animal.

foreplay ('fɔː,pleɪ) *n.* sexual stimulation before intercourse.

forerunner ('fɔː,rʌnə) *n.* **1.** a person or thing that precedes another. **2.** a person or thing coming in advance to herald the arrival of someone or something.

foresail ('fɔː,seɪl) *n.* the main sail on the foremast of a vessel.

foresee (fɔː'siː) *vb.* **-seeing, -saw, -seen.** to see or know beforehand. —**fore'seeable** *adj.*

foreshadow (fɔː'ʃædəʊ) *vb.* to show, indicate, or suggest in advance; presage.

foreshore ('fɔː,ʃɔː) *n.* the part of the shore that lies between the limits for high and low tides.

foreshorten (fɔː'ʃɔːtᵊn) *vb.* to represent (a line, form, or object) as shorter than it really is in accordance with perspective.

foresight ('fɔː,saɪt) *n.* **1.** provision for or insight into future problems, needs, etc. **2.** the front sight on a firearm.

foreskin ('fɔː,skɪn) *n. Anat.* the prepuce.

forest ('fɒrɪst) *n.* **1.** a large wooded area having a thick growth of trees and plants. **2.** the trees of such an area. **3.** *N.Z.* an area planted with pines or other trees that are not native to the country. [Medieval Latin *forestis* unfenced woodland, from Latin *foris* outside] —**'forested** adj.

forestall (fɔː'stɔːl) vb. to delay, stop, or guard against beforehand. [Middle English *forestallen* to waylay]

forestation (ˌfɒrɪ'steɪʃən) n. the planting of trees over a wide area.

forester ('fɒrɪstə) n. a person skilled in forestry or in charge of a forest.

forestry ('fɒrɪstrɪ) n. **1.** the science of planting and caring for trees. **2.** the management of forests.

foretaste ('fɔːˌteɪst) n. an early but limited experience of something to come.

foretell (fɔː'tɛl) vb. **-telling, -told.** to tell or indicate (an event, a result, etc.) beforehand.

forethought ('fɔːˌθɔːt) n. thoughtful anticipation of future events: *I wished I'd had the forethought to bring a flask of coffee.*

foretoken ('fɔːˌtəʊkən) n. a sign of a future event.

for ever or **forever** (fə'rɛvə) adv. **1.** without end; everlastingly. **2.** at all times.

forewarn (fɔː'wɔːn) vb. to warn beforehand.

foreword ('fɔːˌwɜːd) n. an introductory statement to a book.

forfeit ('fɔːfɪt) n. **1.** something lost or given up as a penalty for a fault, mistake, etc. ~vb. **2.** to lose or be liable to lose in consequence of a mistake, fault, etc. ~adj. **3.** surrendered or liable to be surrendered as a penalty. [Old French *forfet* offence] —**'forfeiture** n.

forgather or **foregather** (fɔː'gæðə) vb. to gather together; assemble.

forgave (fə'geɪv) vb. the past tense of **forgive.**

forge¹ (fɔːdʒ) n. **1.** a place in which metal is worked by heating and hammering; smithy. **2.** a hearth or furnace used for heating metal. ~vb. **3.** to shape (metal) by heating and hammering. **4.** to make a fraudulent imitation of (a signature, etc.). [Old French *forgier* to construct] —**'forger** n.

forge² (fɔːdʒ) vb. **1.** to move at a steady pace. **2. forge ahead.** to increase speed or progress; take the lead. [origin unknown]

forgery ('fɔːdʒərɪ) n., pl. **-geries. 1.** the act of reproducing something for a fraudulent purpose. **2.** something forged, such as an antique.

forget (fə'gɛt) vb. **-getting, -got, -gotten. 1.** to fail to remember (someone or something once known). **2.** to neglect, either by mistake or on purpose. **3.** to leave behind by mistake. **4. forget oneself. a.** to act in an improper manner. **b.** to be unselfish. [Old English *forgietan*] —**for'gettable** adj.

forgetful (fə'gɛtfʊl) adj. **1.** tending to forget. **2.** inattentive (to) or neglectful (of). —**for'getfully** adv.

forget-me-not n. a low-growing plant with clusters of small blue flowers.

forgive (fə'gɪv) vb. **-giving, -gave, -given. 1.** to cease to feel anger and resentment towards (a person who has offended) or at (an offending deed). **2.** to pardon (a mistake). **3.** to free from (a debt). [Old English *forgiefan*]

forgiveness (fə'gɪvnɪs) n. the act of forgiving or the state of being forgiven.

forgiving (fə'gɪvɪŋ) adj. willing to forgive.

forgo or **forego** (fɔː'gəʊ) vb. **-going, -went, -gone.** to give up or do without. [Old English *forgān*]

forgot (fə'gɒt) vb. **1.** the past tense of **forget. 2.** *Archaic or dialect.* a past participle of **forget.**

forgotten (fə'gɒt'n) vb. a past participle of **forget.**

fork (fɔːk) n. **1.** a small usually metal implement with long thin prongs on the end of a handle, used for lifting food to the mouth. **2.** a larger similar-shaped agricultural tool, used for lifting, digging, etc. **3.** a pronged part of any machine, device, etc. **4.** (of a road, river, etc.) **a.** a division into two or more branches. **b.** the point where the division begins. **c.** such a branch. ~vb. **5.** to pick up, dig, etc., with a fork. **6.** to be divided into two or more branches. **7.** to take one or other branch at a fork in a road, etc. [Latin *furca*]

forked (fɔːkt) adj. **1.** having a fork or forklike parts. **2.** zigzag: *forked lightning.*

fork-lift truck n. a vehicle with two horizontal prongs that can be raised and lowered for transporting and unloading goods.

fork out vb. *Slang.* to pay, esp. with reluctance.

forlorn (fə'lɔːn) adj. **1.** miserable or cheerless. **2.** forsaken. **3.** desperate: *the last forlorn attempt.* [Old English *forloren* lost] —**for'lornly** adv.

forlorn hope n. **1.** a hopeless enterprise. **2.** a faint hope. [changed (by folk etymology) from Dutch *verloren hoop* lost troop]

form (fɔːm) n. **1.** the shape or configuration of something. **2.** a visible person or animal. **3.** the particular mode in which a thing or person manifests itself: *water in the form of ice.* **4.** a type or kind: *imprisonment is a form of punishment.* **5.** a printed document, esp. one with spaces in which to insert facts or answers. **6.** physical or mental condition. **7.** the previous record of a horse, athlete, etc. **8.** *Brit. slang.* a criminal record. **9.** *Education, chiefly Brit.* a group of children who are taught together. **10.** procedure; etiquette: *good form.* **11.** a prescribed order of words. **12.** *Brit.* a bench. **13.** a hare's nest. **14.** any of the various ways in which a word may be spelt or inflected. ~vb. **15.** to give shape or to take shape, esp. a particular shape. **16.** to come or bring into existence: *ice formed on the lake.* **17.** to make or construct or be made or constructed. **18.** to train or mould by instruction or example. **19.** to acquire or develop: *to form a habit; to form an opinion.* **20.** to be an element of: *this plank will form a bridge.* [Latin *forma* shape, model]

formal ('fɔːməl) *adj.* **1.** of or following established conventions: *a formal document; formal language.* **2.** characterized by conventional forms of ceremony and behaviour: *a formal dinner.* **3.** suitable for occasions organized according to conventional ceremony: *formal dress.* **4.** methodical; organized: *a formal approach to the subject.* **5.** symmetrical in form: *a formal garden.* **6.** relating to the form of something as distinguished from its substance. **7.** logically deductive: *formal proof.* [Latin *formālis*] —**'formally** *adv.*

formaldehyde (fɔː'mældɪˌhaɪd) *n.* a colourless poisonous pungent gas, used as formalin and in synthetic resins. [*form(ic)* + *aldehyde*]

formalin ('fɔːməlɪn) *n.* a solution of formaldehyde in water, used as a disinfectant and as a preservative for biological specimens.

formalism ('fɔːməˌlɪzəm) *n.* scrupulous or excessive adherence to outward form at the expense of content. —**'formalist** *n.*

formality (fɔː'mælɪtɪ) *n., pl.* **-ties. 1.** a requirement of custom or etiquette: *let's get the formalities over.* **2.** a necessary procedure without real effect: *the interview was just a formality.* **3.** strict observance of ceremony.

formalize *or* **-lise** ('fɔːməˌlaɪz) *vb.* **1.** to make official or valid. **2.** to give a definite form to. —**ˌformali'zation** *or* **-li'sation** *n.*

format ('fɔːmæt) *n.* **1.** the shape, size, and general appearance of a publication. **2.** style or arrangement, as of a television programme. **3.** *Computers.* the arrangement of data to comply with a computer's input device. ~*vb.* **-matting, -matted. 4.** to arrange in a specified format. [Latin *formātus* formed]

formation (fɔː'meɪʃən) *n.* **1.** the act of giving or taking form or existence. **2.** something that is formed. **3.** the manner in which something is arranged. **4.** an arrangement of people or things acting as a unit, such as a troop of soldiers. **5.** a series of rocks with certain characteristics in common.

formative ('fɔːmətɪv) *adj.* **1.** of or relating to formation, development, or growth: *formative years.* **2.** shaping; moulding: *a formative experience.*

former ('fɔːmə) *adj.* **1.** belonging to or occurring in an earlier time: *former glory.* **2.** having been at a previous time: *a former colleague.* ~*n.* **3. the former.** the first or first mentioned of two.

formerly ('fɔːməlɪ) *adv.* in the past.

Formica (fɔː'maɪkə) *n. Trademark.* a hard laminated plastic used esp. for heat-resistant surfaces.

formic acid ('fɔːmɪk) *n.* an acid derived from ants. [Latin *formīca* ant]

formidable ('fɔːmɪdəbˀl) *adj.* **1.** arousing fear or dread. **2.** extremely difficult to defeat, overcome, manage, etc. [Latin *formīdō* fear] —**'formidably** *adv.*

formless ('fɔːmlɪs) *adj.* without a definite shape or form; amorphous.

formula ('fɔːmjʊlə) *n., pl.* **-las** *or* **-lae** (-ˌliː).

1. a group of letters, numbers, or other symbols which represents a mathematical or scientific rule. **2.** an established form of words, as used in religious ceremonies, legal proceedings, etc. **3.** a method or rule for doing something, often one proved to be successful. **4.** *U.S. & Canad.* a powder used to make a milky drink for babies. **5.** *Motor racing.* the category in which a car competes, judged according to engine size. [Latin *forma* form] —**formulaic** (ˌfɔːmjʊ'leɪɪk) *adj.*

formulary ('fɔːmjʊlərɪ) *n., pl.* **-laries.** a book of prescribed formulas.

formulate ('fɔːmjʊˌleɪt) *vb.* **1.** to express in a formula. **2.** to plan or describe precisely and clearly. —**ˌformu'lation** *n.*

fornicate ('fɔːnɪˌkeɪt) *vb.* to commit fornication. [Latin *fornix* vault, brothel situated therein] —**'forni,cator** *n.*

fornication (ˌfɔːnɪ'keɪʃən) *n.* voluntary sexual intercourse outside marriage.

forsake (fə'seɪk) *vb.* **-saking, -sook, -saken. 1.** to withdraw support or friendship from. **2.** to give up (something valued or enjoyed). [Old English *forsacan*]

forsooth (fə'suːθ) *adv. Archaic.* in truth; indeed. [Old English *forsōth*]

forswear (fɔː'swɛə) *vb.* **-swearing, -swore, -sworn. 1.** to reject or renounce with determination. **2.** to perjure (oneself). [Old English *forswearian*]

forsythia (fɔː'saɪθɪə) *n.* a shrub with yellow flowers which appear in spring before the foliage. [after William *Forsyth*, botanist]

fort (fɔːt) *n.* **1.** a fortified enclosure, building, or position. **2. hold the fort.** *Informal.* to keep things in operation during someone's absence. [Latin *fortis* strong]

forte[1] ('fɔːteɪ) *n.* something at which a person excels. [Latin *fortis* strong]

forte[2] ('fɔːtɪ) *adv. Music.* loudly. [Italian]

forth (fɔːθ) *adv.* **1.** *Formal or archaic.* forward, out, or away: *they put forth their conclusions; they set forth for the New World.* **2. and so forth.** and so on. [Old English]

forthcoming (ˌfɔːθ'kʌmɪŋ) *adj.* **1.** about to appear or happen: *his forthcoming book.* **2.** available. **3.** (of a person) willing to be communicative.

forthright ('fɔːθˌraɪt) *adj.* direct and outspoken.

forthwith (ˌfɔːθ'wɪθ) *adv.* at once.

fortification (ˌfɔːtɪfɪ'keɪʃən) *n.* **1.** the act of fortifying. **2.** (*pl.*) walls, mounds, etc., used to fortify a place.

fortify ('fɔːtɪˌfaɪ) *vb.* **-fying, -fied. 1.** to make (a place) defensible, as by building walls. **2.** to strengthen physically, mentally, or morally. **3.** to add alcohol to (wine), in order to produce sherry, port, etc. **4.** to increase the nutritious value of (a food), as by adding vitamins. [Latin *fortis* strong + *facere* to make]

fortissimo (fɔː'tɪsɪˌməʊ) *adv. Music.* very loudly. [Italian]

fortitude ('fɔːtɪˌtjuːd) *n.* strength and

firmness of mind. [Latin *fortitūdō* courage]

fortnight ('fɔːt,naɪt) *n.* a period of 14 consecutive days; two weeks. [Old English *fēowertiene niht* fourteen nights]

fortnightly ('fɔːt,naɪtlɪ) *Chiefly Brit.* ~*adj.* **1.** occurring or appearing once each fortnight. ~*adv.* **2.** once a fortnight.

FORTRAN ('fɔːtræn) *n.* a high-level computer programming language. [*for(mula) tran(slation)*]

fortress ('fɔːtrɪs) *n.* a large fort or fortified town. [Latin *fortis* strong]

fortuitous (fɔː'tjuːɪtəs) *adj.* happening by chance, esp. by a lucky chance. [Latin *fortuitus*] —**for'tuitously** *adv.*

fortunate ('fɔːtʃənɪt) *adj.* **1.** having good luck. **2.** occurring by good luck. —**'fortunately** *adv.*

fortune ('fɔːtʃən) *n.* **1.** wealth or material prosperity. **2.** a power regarded as being responsible for human affairs. **3.** luck, esp. when favourable. **4.** (*often pl.*) a person's destiny. [Latin *fors* chance]

fortune-teller *n.* a person who claims to predict events in other people's lives.

forty ('fɔːtɪ) *n., pl.* -**ties. 1.** the cardinal number that is the product of ten and four. **2.** a numeral, 40, XL, representing this number. **3.** something representing or consisting of 40 units. ~*det.* **4.** amounting to forty: *forty thieves.* —**'fortieth** *adj., n.*

forty winks *n.* (*functioning as sing. or pl.*) *Informal.* a short light sleep; nap.

forum ('fɔːrəm) *n.* **1.** a meeting or medium for the open discussion of subjects of public interest. **2.** (in ancient Roman cities) an open space serving as a marketplace and centre of public business. [Latin]

forward ('fɔːwəd) *adj.* **1.** directed or moving ahead. **2.** at, in, or near the front. **3.** presumptuous or impudent. **4.** well developed or advanced. **5.** of or relating to the future or favouring change. **6.** *Commerce.* relating to fulfilment at a future date. ~*n.* **7.** an attacking player in any of various sports, such as soccer. ~*adv.* **8.** same as **forwards.** ~*vb.* **9.** to send on to an ultimate destination: *the letter was forwarded.* **10.** to advance or promote: *to forward one's career.* [Old English *foreweard*]

forwards ('fɔːwədz) *or* **forward** *adv.* **1.** towards or at a place ahead or in advance, esp. in space but also in time. **2.** towards the front.

fosse *or* **foss** (fɒs) *n.* a ditch or moat, esp. one dug as a fortification. [Latin *fossa*]

fossick ('fɒsɪk) *vb. Austral. & N.Z.* **1.** to search for gold or precious stones in abandoned workings, rivers, etc. **2.** to search for (something). [prob. from English dialect *fussock* to bustle about]

fossil ('fɒsˀl) *n.* **1.** remains of a plant or animal that existed in a past geological age, occurring in the form of mineralized bones, shells, etc. ~*adj.* **2.** of, like, or being a fossil. **3.** formed by the decomposition of prehistoric organisms: *fossil fuel.* [Latin *fossilis* dug up]

fossil fuel *n.* any naturally occurring fuel,

such as coal, formed by the decomposition of prehistoric organisms.

fossilize *or* -**lise** ('fɒsɪ,laɪz) *vb.* **1.** to convert or be converted into a fossil. **2.** to become antiquated or inflexible.

foster ('fɒstə) *vb.* **1.** to promote the growth or development of. **2.** to bring up (a child not one's own). ~*adj.* **3.** of or involved in the fostering of a child: *foster home.* [Old English *fōstrian* to feed] —**'fostering** *n.*

fought (fɔːt) *vb.* the past of **fight.**

foul (faʊl) *adj.* **1.** offensive to the senses; revolting. **2.** stinking. **3.** full of dirt or offensive matter. **4.** obscene; vulgar: *foul language.* **5.** unfair: *to resort to foul means.* **6.** (of weather) unpleasant. **7.** blocked with dirt or foreign matter: *a foul drain.* **8.** *Informal.* disgustingly bad. ~*n.* **9.** *Sport.* a violation of the rules. ~*vb.* **10.** to make dirty or polluted. **11.** to become or cause to become entangled. **12.** to become or cause to become clogged. **13.** *Sport.* to commit a foul against (an opponent). ~*adv.* **14. fall foul of.** to come into conflict with. [Old English *fūl*]

foul play *n.* **1.** unfair conduct, esp. with violence. **2.** a violation of the rules in a game.

foul up *vb.* **1.** *Informal.* to bungle. **2.** to contaminate. **3.** to block or choke.

found[1] (faʊnd) *vb.* the past of **find.**

found[2] (faʊnd) *vb.* **1.** to bring into being or establish (something, such as an institution). **2.** to lay the foundation of (a building). **3.** (foll. by *on* or *upon*) to have a basis (in). [Latin *fundus* bottom] —**'founder** *n.*

found[3] (faʊnd) *vb.* **1.** to cast (metal or glass) by melting and pouring into a mould. **2.** to make (articles) in this way. [Latin *fundere* to melt] —**'founder** *n.*

foundation (faʊn'deɪʃən) *n.* **1.** that on which something is founded. **2.** (*often pl.*) a construction below the ground that distributes the load of a building, wall, etc. **3.** the base on which something stands. **4.** the act of founding. **5.** an endowment for the support of an institution, such as a college. **6.** an institution supported by an endowment. **7.** a cosmetic used as a base for make-up.

foundation stone *n.* a stone laid at a ceremony to mark the foundation of a new building.

founder ('faʊndə) *vb.* **1.** (of a ship) to sink. **2.** to break down or fail: *the project foundered.* **3.** to sink into or become stuck in soft ground. **4.** (of a horse) to stumble or go lame. [Old French *fondrer* to submerge]

foundling ('faʊndlɪŋ) *n.* an abandoned infant whose parents are not known. [Middle English *foundeling*]

foundry ('faʊndrɪ) *n., pl.* -**ries.** a place in which metal castings are produced.

fount[1] (faʊnt) *n.* *Poetic.* a spring or fountain. **2.** a source. [from *fountain*]

fount[2] (faʊnt, fɒnt) *n.* *Printing.* a complete set of type of one style and size. [Old French *fonte* a founding, casting]

fountain ('faʊntɪn) n. 1. a jet or spray of water. 2. a structure from which such a jet or a number of such jets spurt. 3. a natural spring of water. 4. a cascade of sparks, lava, etc. 5. a principal source. [Latin *fons* spring]

fountainhead ('faʊntɪnˌhɛd) n. a principal or original source.

fountain pen n. a pen the nib of which is supplied with ink from a cartridge or a reservoir in its barrel.

four (fɔː) n. 1. the cardinal number that is the sum of three and one. 2. a numeral, 4, IV, representing this number. 3. something representing or consisting of four units. 4. *Rowing.* a. a racing shell propelled by four oarsmen. b. the crew of such a shell. ~*det.* 5. amounting to four: *four times*. [Old English *fēower*] —**fourth** *adj., n.*

fourfold ('fɔːˌfəʊld) adj. 1. equal to or having four times as many or as much. 2. composed of four parts. ~*adv.* 3. by or up to four times as many or as much.

four-in-hand n. a road vehicle drawn by four horses and driven by one driver.

four-letter word n. any of several short English words referring to sex or excrement: regarded generally as offensive or obscene.

four-poster n. a bed with posts at each corner supporting a canopy and curtains.

fourscore (ˌfɔː'skɔː) det. *Archaic.* eighty.

foursome ('fɔːsəm) n. 1. a set of four. 2. *Golf.* a game between two pairs of players.

foursquare (ˌfɔː'skwɛə) adv. 1. squarely; firmly. ~*adj.* 2. solid and strong.

four-stroke adj. designating an internal-combustion engine in which the piston makes four strokes for every explosion.

fourteen ('fɔː'tiːn) n. 1. the cardinal number that is the sum of ten and four. 2. a numeral, 14, XIV, representing this number. 3. something represented by or consisting of 14 units. ~*det.* 4. amounting to fourteen: *fourteen cats*. —'**four'teenth** *adj., n.*

fourth dimension n. 1. the dimension of time, which in addition to three spatial dimensions specifies the position of a point or particle. 2. the concept in science fiction of an extra dimension. —ˌfourth-di'mensional *adj.*

fourth estate n. the press.

fowl (faʊl) n. 1. a domesticated bird such as a chicken. 2. any other bird that is used as food or hunted as game. 3. the meat of fowl. 4. *Archaic.* a bird. ~*vb.* 5. to hunt or snare wildfowl. [Old English *fugol*]

fox (fɒks) n., pl. **foxes** or **fox**. 1. a doglike wild animal with a pointed muzzle and a bushy tail. 2. its reddish-brown or grey fur. 3. a person who is cunning and sly. ~*vb.* 4. *Informal.* to perplex or deceive. 5. to cause (paper) to become discoloured with spots or (of paper) to become discoloured. [Old English]

foxglove ('fɒksˌglʌv) n. a plant with spikes of purple or white thimble-like flowers. [Old English]

foxhole ('fɒksˌhəʊl) n. *Mil.* a small pit dug to provide shelter against hostile fire.

foxhound ('fɒksˌhaʊnd) n. a breed of short-haired hound, usually kept for hunting foxes.

fox-hunting n. the sport of hunting foxes with hounds.

fox terrier n. either of two breeds of small tan-black-and-white terrier, the wire-haired and the smooth.

foxtrot ('fɒksˌtrɒt) n. 1. a ballroom dance in quadruple time. ~*vb.* -**trotting**, -**trotted**. 2. to perform this dance.

foxy ('fɒksɪ) adj. **foxier**, **foxiest**. 1. of or resembling a fox, esp. in craftiness. 2. reddish-brown. —'**foxily** adv. —'**foxiness** n.

foyer ('fɔɪeɪ) n. an entrance hall as in a hotel, theatre, or cinema. [French: fireplace]

fp forte-piano.

FP 1. fire plug. 2. freezing point.

Fr 1. Christianity: a. Father. b. Frater. [Latin: brother] 2. *Chem.* francium.

fr. 1. franc. 2. from.

fracas ('frækɑː) n. a noisy quarrel; brawl. [French]

fraction ('frækʃən) n. 1. *Maths.* a ratio of two expressions or numbers other than zero. 2. any part or subdivision. 3. a small piece; fragment. 4. *Chem.* a component of a mixture separated by distillation. [Latin *fractus* broken] —'**fractional** adj. —'**fractionally** adv.

fractious ('frækʃəs) adj. peevishly irritable. [obs. *fraction* discord]

fracture ('fræktʃə) n. 1. breaking, esp. the breaking or cracking of a bone. ~*vb.* 2. to break, esp. to break (a bone) or (of a bone) to become broken. [Latin *frangere* to break] —'**fractural** adj.

fragile ('frædʒaɪl) adj. 1. able to be broken easily. 2. in a weakened physical state. [Latin *fragilis*] —**fragility** (frə'dʒɪlɪtɪ) n.

fragment n. ('frægmənt). 1. a piece broken off. 2. an incomplete piece: *fragments of a novel*. ~*vb.* (fræg'mɛnt). 3. to break into fragments. [Latin *fragmentum*] —ˌfrag'men'tation n.

fragmentary ('frægməntrɪ) adj. made up of fragments; disconnected.

fragrance ('freɪgrəns) n. 1. a pleasant odour. 2. the state of being fragrant.

fragrant ('freɪgrənt) adj. having a pleasant smell. [Latin *frāgrāre* to emit a smell]

frail (freɪl) adj. 1. physically weak and delicate. 2. fragile: *a frail craft*. 3. easily tempted. [Old French *frele*]

frailty ('freɪltɪ) n., pl. -**ties**. 1. physical or moral weakness. 2. (*often pl.*) a fault symptomatic of moral weakness.

frame (freɪm) n. 1. an open structure that gives shape and support to something, such as a building. 2. an enclosing case or border into which something is fitted: *the frame of a picture*. 3. the system around which something is built up: *the frame of government*. 4. the structure of the human body. 5. a condition; state (esp. in **frame of mind**). 6. one of a series of exposures on film used in making motion pictures. **7.** a television picture scanned by electron beams at a particular frequency. **8.** *Snooker, etc.* **a.** the wooden triangle used to set up the balls. **b.** the balls when set up. **c.** a single game. **9.** short for **cold frame. 10.** *Slang.* a frame-up. ~*vb.* **11.** to construct by fitting parts together. **12.** to draw up the plans: *to frame a policy.* **13.** to compose: *to frame a reply.* **14.** to provide or enclose with a frame: *to frame a picture.* **15.** *Slang.* to conspire to incriminate (someone) on a false charge. [Old English *framian* to avail]

frame of reference *n.* **1.** a set of standards that determines behaviour. **2.** any set of planes or curves, such as the three coordinate axes, used to locate a point in space.

frame-up *n. Slang.* a conspiracy to incriminate someone on a false charge.

framework ('freim,wɜːk) *n.* **1.** a structural plan or basis of a project. **2.** a structure supporting something.

franc (fræŋk) *n.* the standard monetary unit of France and various other countries. [Latin *Rex Francōrum* King of the Franks, inscribed on 14th-century francs]

franchise ('fræntʃaɪz) *n.* **1.** (usually preceded by *the*) the right to vote, esp. for a member of parliament. **2.** any exemption, privilege, or right granted by a public authority. **3.** *Commerce.* authorization granted to a distributor to market a manufacturer's products. ~*vb.* **4.** *Commerce, chiefly U.S. & Canad.* to grant (a person, firm, etc.) a franchise. [Old French *franchir* to set free]

Franciscan (fræn'sɪskən) *n.* a member of a Christian religious order of friars or nuns founded by Saint Francis of Assisi.

francium ('frænsɪəm) *n.* an unstable radioactive element of the alkali-metal group. Symbol: Fr [from *France*, because first found there]

Franco- ('fræŋkəʊ) *combining form.* indicating France or French: *Franco-Prussian.* [Medieval Latin *Francus*]

frank (fræŋk) *adj.* **1.** honest and straightforward in speech or attitude. Also called: **outspoken** **2.** outspoken or blunt. **3.** open; undisguised: *frank interest.* ~*vb.* **4.** *Chiefly Brit.* to put a mark on (a letter), ensuring free carriage. ~*n.* **5.** an official mark affixed to a letter ensuring free delivery. [Medieval Latin *francus* free] —'**frankly** *adv.* —'**frankness** *n.*

Frank (fræŋk) *n.* a member of the West Germanic peoples who in the late 4th century A.D. gradually conquered most of Gaul. [Old English *Franca*]

Frankenstein ('fræŋkɪn,staɪn) *n.* a thing that destroys its creator. Also called: **Frankenstein's monster.** [after Baron *Frankenstein*, who created a monster from parts of corpses in the novel by Mary Shelley]

frankfurter ('fræŋk,fɜːtə) *n.* a smoked sausage of pork or beef. [short for German *Frankfurter Wurst* sausage from *Frankfurt*]

frankincense ('fræŋkɪn,sɛns) *n.* an aromatic gum resin burnt as incense. [Old French *franc* free, pure + *encens* incense]

Frankish ('fræŋkɪʃ) *n.* **1.** the ancient West Germanic language of the Franks. ~*adj.* **2.** of the Franks or their language.

frantic ('fræntɪk) *adj.* **1.** distracted with fear, pain, joy, etc. **2.** marked by or showing frenzy: *frantic efforts.* [Latin *phrenēticus* mad] —'**frantically** *adv.*

frappé ('fræpeɪ) *adj.* (esp. of drinks) chilled. [French]

fraternal (frə'tɜːnᵊl) *adj.* **1.** of a brother; brotherly. **2.** designating twins that developed from two separate fertilized ova. [Latin *frāter* brother] —**fra'ternally** *adv.*

fraternity (frə'tɜːnɪtɪ) *n., pl.* **-ties. 1.** a body of people united in interests, aims, etc. **2.** brotherliness. **3.** *U.S. & Canad.* a society of male students.

fraternize *or* **-nise** ('frætə,naɪz) *vb.* (often foll. by *with*) to associate on friendly terms. —,**fraterni'zation** *or* -**ni'sation** *n.*

fratricide ('frætrɪ,saɪd) *n.* **1.** the act of killing one's brother. **2.** a person who kills his brother. [Latin *frater* brother + *caedere* to kill] —,**fratri'cidal** *adj.*

Frau (frau) *n., pl.* **Frauen** ('frauən) *or* **Fraus.** a married German woman: a title equivalent to *Mrs.* [German]

fraud (frɔːd) *n.* **1.** deliberate deception or cheating intended to gain an advantage. **2.** an act of such deception. **3.** *Informal.* a person who acts in a false or deceitful way. [Latin *fraus*]

fraudulent ('frɔːdjʊlənt) *adj.* **1.** acting with intent to deceive. **2.** proceeding from fraud. [Latin *fraudulentus*] —'**fraudulence** *n.*

fraught (frɔːt) *adj.* **1.** (foll. by *with*) filled: *a venture fraught with peril.* **2.** *Informal.* showing or producing tension or anxiety. [Middle Dutch *vrachten*]

Fräulein ('frɔɪlaɪn) *n., pl.* **-lein** *or* **-leins.** an unmarried German woman: a title equivalent to *Miss.* [German]

fray[1] (freɪ) *n.* **1.** a noisy quarrel or brawl. **2.** any challenging conflict. [short for *affray*]

fray[2] (freɪ) *vb.* **1.** to wear away into loose threads, esp. at an edge. **2.** to make or become strained or irritated. [French *frayer* to rub]

frazil ('freɪzɪl) *n.* small pieces of ice that form in water moving turbulently enough to prevent the formation of a sheet of ice. [French *fraisil* cinders]

frazzle ('fræzᵊl) *n. Informal.* the state of being exhausted: *worn to a frazzle.* [prob. from Middle English *faselen* to fray]

freak (friːk) *n.* **1.** a person, animal, or plant that is abnormal or deformed. **2.** an object, event, etc., that is abnormal. **3.** *Informal.* a person who acts or dresses in a markedly unconventional way. **4.** *Informal.* a person who is ardently fond of something specified: *a jazz freak.* ~*adj.* **5.** abnormal: *a freak storm.* [origin unknown] —'**freakish** *adj.* —'**freaky** *adj.*

freak out *vb. Informal.* to be or cause to be in a heightened emotional state.

freckle ('frek'l) *n.* **1.** a small brownish spot on the skin. ~*vb.* **2.** to mark or become marked with freckles. [Old Norse *freknur*] —'**freckled** *adj.*

free (friː) *adj.* **freer, freest. 1.** able to act at will; not under compulsion or restraint. **2.** not enslaved or confined. **3.** (foll. by *from*) not subject (to): *free from pain.* **4.** (of a country, etc.) independent. **5.** exempt from external direction: *free will.* **6.** not subject to conventional constraints: *free verse.* **7.** not exact or literal: *a free translation.* **8.** provided without charge: *free entertainment.* **9.** (often foll. by *of* or *with*) ready or generous in using or giving: *free with advice.* **10.** not occupied or in use; available: *a free cubicle.* **11.** (of a person) not busy. **12.** open or available to all. **13.** not fixed or joined; loose: *the free end of a chain.* **14.** without obstruction or impediment: *free passage.* **15.** *Chem.* chemically uncombined: *free nitrogen.* **16. free and easy.** casual or tolerant. **17. make free with.** to behave too familiarly towards. ~*adv.* **18.** in a free manner; freely. **19.** without charge or cost. ~*vb.* **freeing, freed. 20.** to set at liberty; release. **21.** to remove obstructions or impediments from. **22.** (often foll. by *of* or *from*) to relieve or rid (of obstacles, pain, etc.). [Old English *frēo*] —'**freely** *adv.*

-free *adj.* combining form. free from: *trouble-free; lead-free petrol.*

freebie ('friːbɪ) *n. Slang.* something provided without charge.

freeboard ('friːˌbɔːd) *n.* the space or distance between the deck of a vessel and the waterline.

freebooter ('friːˌbuːtə) *n.* a pirate. [Dutch *vrijbuit* booty]

freeborn ('friːˌbɔːn) *adj.* not born in slavery.

Free Church *n. Chiefly Brit.* any Protestant Church other than the Established Church.

freedman ('friːdˌmæn) *n., pl.* **-men.** a man who has been freed from slavery.

freedom ('friːdəm) *n.* **1.** the state of being free, esp. to enjoy political and civil liberties. **2.** (usually foll. by *from*) exemption or immunity: *freedom from taxation.* **3.** liberation, as from slavery. **4.** the right or privilege of unrestricted access: *the freedom of a city.* **5.** self-government or independence. **6.** the power to order one's own actions. **7.** ease or frankness of manner. **8.** excessive familiarity.

free enterprise *n.* an economic system in which commercial organizations compete for profit with little state control.

free fall *n.* **1.** free descent of a body in which gravity is the only force acting on it. **2.** the part of a parachute descent before the parachute opens.

free-for-all *n. Informal.* a disorganized brawl or argument involving all those present.

free hand *n.* **1.** unrestricted freedom to act: *they gave her a free hand to run her*

department. ~*adj., adv.* **freehand. 2.** (done) by hand without the use of guiding instruments.

freehold ('friːˌhəʊld) *Property law.* ~*n.* **1.** tenure by which land is held without restrictions and for life. ~*adj.* **2.** of or held by freehold. —'**free,holder** *n.*

free house *n. Brit.* a public house not bound to sell only one brewer's products.

free kick *n. Soccer.* a place kick awarded for a foul or infringement.

freelance ('friːˌlɑːns) *n.* **1.** a self-employed person, esp. a writer or artist, who is hired to do specific assignments. ~*vb.* **2.** to work as a freelance. ~*adj., adv.* **3.** of or as a freelance. [orig. applied to a mercenary soldier]

freeloader ('friːˌləʊdə) *n. Slang.* a person who habitually depends on others for food, shelter, etc.

free love *n.* sexual relationships without fidelity to a single partner.

freeman ('friːmən) *n., pl.* **-men. 1.** a person who is not a slave. **2.** a person who enjoys a privilege, such as the freedom of a city.

free-market *adj.* denoting an economic system which allows supply and demand to regulate prices and wages.

Freemason ('friːˌmeɪs'n) *n.* a member of a widespread secret order, pledged to brotherliness and mutual aid. Sometimes shortened to **Mason.** —'**Free,masonry** *n.*

free-range *adj. Chiefly Brit.* kept or produced in natural conditions.

freesia ('friːzɪə) *n.* a bulbous plant with tubular fragrant flowers. [after F. H. T. *Freese*, physician]

free space *n.* a region that has no gravitational and electromagnetic fields.

freestanding (ˌfriːˈstændɪŋ) *adj.* not attached to or supported by another object.

freestyle ('friːˌstaɪl) *n.* **1.** a competition, as in swimming, in which each participant may use a style of his or her choice. **2.** Also called: **all-in wrestling.** a style of professional wrestling with no internationally agreed set of rules.

freethinker (ˌfriːˈθɪŋkə) *n.* a person who forms his ideas independently of authority, esp. in matters of religion.

free trade *n.* international trade that is free of such government interference as protective tariffs.

free verse *n.* unrhymed verse without a metrical pattern.

freeway ('friːˌweɪ) *n. U.S.* an expressway.

freewheel (ˌfriːˈwiːl) *n.* **1.** a device in the rear hub of a bicycle wheel that permits it to rotate freely while the pedals are stationary. ~*vb.* **2.** to coast.

free will *n.* **1.** the apparent human ability to make choices that are not externally determined. **2.** the ability to make a choice without outside coercion: *he left of his own free will.*

Free World *n.* **the.** the non-Communist countries collectively.

freeze (friːz) *vb.* **freezing, froze, frozen. 1.** to change (a liquid) into a solid as a result of a reduction in temperature, or (of a liquid) to solidify in this way. **2.** to cover or become covered with ice. **3.** to fix fast or become fixed (to something) because of frost. **4.** to preserve (food) by subjection to extreme cold. **5.** to feel or cause to feel the effects of extreme cold. **6.** to die of extreme cold. **7.** to become or make motionless through fear, shock, etc. **8.** to cause (moving film) to stop at a particular frame. **9.** to become formal, haughty, etc., in manner. **10.** to fix (prices, incomes, etc.) at a particular level. **11.** to forbid by law the exchange or collection of (loans, assets, etc.). ~*n.* **12.** the act of freezing or state of being frozen. **13.** *Meteorol.* a spell of temperatures below freezing point. **14.** the fixing of incomes, prices, etc., by legislation. [Old English *frēosan*]

freeze-dry *vb.* **-drying, -dried.** to preserve (a substance) by rapid freezing and subsequently drying in a vacuum.

freezer ('friːzə) *n.* an insulated cabinet for cold-storage of perishable foodstuffs.

freezing point *n.* the temperature below which a liquid turns into a solid.

freezing works *n. Austral. & N.Z.* a slaughterhouse at which animal carcasses are frozen for export.

freight (freit) *n.* **1. a.** commercial transport. **b.** the price charged for such transport. **c.** goods transported by this means. **2.** *Chiefly Brit.* a ship's cargo or part of it. ~*vb.* **3.** to transport (goods) by freight. **4.** to load with goods for transport. [Middle Dutch *vrecht*]

freighter ('freitə) *n.* a ship or aircraft designed for transporting cargo.

French (frentʃ) *n.* **1.** the official language of France: also an official language of Switzerland, Belgium, Canada, and certain other countries. **2. the French.** (*functioning as pl.*) the people of France collectively. ~*adj.* **3.** of France, the French, or their language. [Old English *Frencisc* Frankish]

French bread *n.* white bread in a long slender loaf.

French Canadian *n.* a Canadian citizen whose native language is French.

French chalk *n.* a variety of talc used to mark cloth or remove grease stains.

French dressing *n.* a salad dressing made from oil and vinegar with seasonings.

French fries *pl. n. Chiefly U.S. & Canad.* chips.

French horn *n. Music.* a valved brass instrument coiled into a spiral.

Frenchify ('frentʃɪˌfaɪ) *vb.* **-fying, -fied.** *Informal.* to make or become French in appearance, etc.

French leave *n.* an unauthorized absence or departure.

French letter *n. Brit. slang.* a condom.

French polish *n.* a shellac varnish for wood, giving a high gloss.

French seam *n.* a seam in which the edges are enclosed.

French windows *pl. n. Brit.* a pair of

casement windows extending to floor level and opening onto a balcony or garden.

frenetic (frɪˈnetɪk) *adj.* distracted or frantic. [Greek *phrenitis* insanity] —**freˈnetically** *adv.*

frenzy ('frenzɪ) *n., pl.* **-zies. 1.** violent mental derangement. **2.** wild excitement or agitation. **3.** a bout of wild or agitated activity: *a frenzy of preparations.* [Late Latin *phrēnēsis* madness, from Greek *phrēn* mind] —**ˈfrenzied** *adj.*

Freon ('friːɒn) *n. Trademark.* any of a group of gas or liquid chemical compounds of methane with chlorine and fluorine: used as refrigerants, aerosol propellants, and solvents.

frequency ('friːkwənsɪ) *n., pl.* **-cies. 1.** the state of being frequent. **2.** the number of times that an event occurs within a given period. **3.** *Physics.* the number of times that a periodic function or vibration repeats itself in a specified time.

frequency distribution *n.* statistical data arranged to show the frequency with which the possible values of a variable occur.

frequency modulation *n.* a method of transmitting information by varying the frequency carrier wave in accordance with the amplitude of the input signal.

frequent *adj.* ('friːkwənt). **1.** recurring at short intervals. **2.** habitual. ~*vb.* (frɪˈkwent). **3.** to visit habitually. [Latin *frequēns* numerous] —**ˈfrequently** *adv.*

frequentative (frɪˈkwentətɪv) *Grammar.* ~*adj.* **1.** denoting a verb or an affix meaning repeated action. ~*n.* **2.** a frequentative verb or affix.

fresco ('freskəʊ) *n., pl.* **-coes** or **-cos. 1.** a method of wall-painting using watercolours on wet plaster. **2.** a painting done in this way. [Italian]

fresh (freʃ) *adj.* **1.** newly made, acquired, etc. **2.** novel; original: *a fresh outlook.* **3.** most recent: *fresh developments.* **4.** further; additional: *fresh supplies.* **5.** not canned, frozen, or otherwise preserved. **6.** (of water) not salt. **7.** bright and clear: *a fresh morning.* **8.** chilly or invigorating: *a fresh breeze.* **9.** not tired; alert. **10.** not worn or faded: *fresh colours.* **11.** having a healthy or ruddy appearance. **12.** just arrived: *fresh from the presses.* **13.** youthful or inexperienced. **14.** *Informal.* presumptuous or disrespectful. ~*adv.* **15.** recently: *fresh-cut flowers.* [Old English *fersc*] —**ˈfreshly** *adv.* —**ˈfreshness** *n.*

freshen ('freʃən) *vb.* **1.** to make or become fresh or fresher. **2.** (often foll. by *up*) to refresh (oneself), esp. by washing. **3.** (of the wind) to increase.

fresher ('freʃə) or **freshman** ('freʃmən) *n., pl.* **-ers** or **-men.** a first-year student at college or university.

freshet ('freʃɪt) *n.* **1.** the sudden overflowing of a river. **2.** a stream of fresh water emptying into the sea.

freshwater ('freʃˌwɔːtə) *n. (modifier)* of or living in fresh water.

fret[1] (fret) *vb.* **fretting, fretted. 1.** to distress or be distressed. **2.** to rub or wear away. **3.** to feel or give annoyance or vexation. ~*n*. **4.** a state of irritation or anxiety. [Old English *fretan* to eat]

fret² (frɛt) *n*. **1.** a repetitive geometrical figure, esp. one used as an ornamental border. ~*vb*. **fretting, fretted. 2.** to ornament with fret or fretwork. [Old French *frete* interlaced design used on a shield]

fret³ (frɛt) *n*. any of several small metal bars set across the fingerboard of a musical instrument, such as a guitar, as a guide to fingering. [origin unknown]

fretful ('frɛtful) *adj*. peevish, irritable, or upset. —'**fretfully** *adv*.

fret saw *n*. a fine-toothed saw with a long thin narrow blade, used for cutting designs in thin wood or metal.

fretwork ('frɛt,wɜːk) *n*. decorative geometrical carving or openwork.

Freudian ('frɔɪdɪən) *adj*. of or relating to Sigmund Freud (1856–1939), Austrian psychiatrist, or his ideas. —'**Freudian,ism** *n*.

Freudian slip *n*. a slip of the tongue that may reveal an unconscious thought.

Fri. Friday.

friable ('fraɪəb'l) *adj*. easily broken up. [Latin *friāre* to crumble] —,**fria'bility** *n*.

friar ('fraɪə) *n*. a member of any of various men's religious orders of the Roman Catholic Church. [Latin *frāter* brother]

friar's balsam *n*. a compound with a camphor-like smell, used as an inhalant.

friary ('fraɪərɪ) *n., pl*. **-aries.** a house of friars.

fricassee ('frɪkəsɪ) *n*. stewed meat, esp. chicken or veal, served in a thick white sauce. [Old French]

fricative ('frɪkətɪv) *n*. **1.** a consonant produced by friction of breath through a partly closed mouth, such as (f) or (z). ~*adj*. **2.** relating to or denoting a fricative. [Latin *fricāre* to rub]

friction ('frɪkʃən) *n*. **1.** a resistance encountered when one body moves relative to another body with which it is in contact. **2.** the act of rubbing one object against another. **3.** disagreement or conflict. [Latin *fricāre* to rub] —'**frictional** *adj*.

Friday ('fraɪdɪ) *n*. **1.** the sixth day of the week; fifth day of the working week. **2.** See **man Friday.** [Old English *Frīgedæg*]

fridge (frɪdʒ) *n*. short for **refrigerator.**

fried (fraɪd) *vb*. the past of **fry¹.**

friend (frɛnd) *n*. **1.** a person known well to another and regarded with liking, affection, and loyalty. **2.** an ally in a fight or cause. **3.** a patron or supporter. **4. make friends (with).** to become friendly (with). [Old English *frēond*] —'**friendless** *adj*. —'**friendship** *n*.

Friend (frɛnd) *n*. a member of the Society of Friends; Quaker.

friendly ('frɛndlɪ) *adj*. **-lier, -liest. 1.** showing or expressing liking, goodwill, or trust. **2.** on the same side; not hostile. **3.** tending or disposed to help or support. ~*n., pl*. **-lies. 4.** *Sport*. a match played for its own sake. —'**friendliness** *n*.

friendly society *n. Brit*. an association

of people who pay regular dues in return for old-age pensions, sickness benefits, etc.

frier ('fraɪə) *n*. same as **fryer.** See **fry¹.**

frieze (friːz) *n*. **1.** any ornamental band on a wall. **2.** *Archit*. the horizontal band between the architrave and cornice of a classical temple. [French *frise*]

frigate ('frɪgɪt) *n*. **1.** *Brit*. a warship smaller than a destroyer. **2.** a medium-sized warship of the 18th and 19th centuries. [French *frégate*]

fright (fraɪt) *n*. **1.** sudden fear or alarm. **2.** a sudden alarming shock. **3.** *Informal*. a grotesque or ludicrous person or thing. [Old English *fryhto*]

frighten ('fraɪt'n) *vb*. **1.** to terrify; scare. **2.** to drive or force to go (away, off, out, in, etc.) by making afraid. —'**frighteningly** *adv*.

frightful ('fraɪtful) *adj*. **1.** very alarming or horrifying. **2.** unpleasant, annoying, or extreme: *a frightful hurry*. —'**frightfully** *adv*.

frigid ('frɪdʒɪd) *adj*. **1.** formal or stiff in behaviour or temperament. **2.** (esp. of women) lacking sexual responsiveness. **3.** characterized by physical coldness: *a frigid zone*. [Latin *frigidus* cold] —**fri'gidity** *n*.

frill (frɪl) *n*. **1.** a gathered strip of cloth sewn on at one edge only, as ornament. **2.** (*often pl*.) *Informal*. a superfluous or pretentious thing; affectation: *he made a plain speech with no frills*. [origin unknown] —**frilled** *adj*. —'**frilly** *adj*.

fringe (frɪndʒ) *n*. **1.** an edging consisting of hanging threads, tassels, etc. **2.** an outer edge; periphery. **3.** (*modifier*) unofficial; not conventional in form: *fringe theatre*. **4.** *Chiefly Brit*. a section of the front hair cut short over the forehead. ~*vb*. **5.** to adorn with a fringe. **6.** to be a fringe for. [Latin *fimbria* fringe, border]

fringe benefit *n*. an additional advantage, esp. a benefit that supplements an employee's regular pay.

frippery ('frɪpərɪ) *n., pl*. **-peries. 1.** ornate or showy clothing or adornment. **2.** trifles; trivia. [Old French *frepe* frill, rag]

Frisian ('frɪʒən) *n*. **1.** a language spoken in the NW Netherlands. **2.** a speaker of this language. ~*adj*. **3.** of or relating to this language or its speakers. [Latin *Frīsiī* people of northern Germany]

frisk (frɪsk) *vb*. **1.** to leap, move about, or act in a playful manner. **2.** *Informal*. to search (someone) by feeling for concealed weapons, etc. ~*n*. **3.** a playful movement. **4.** *Informal*. an instance of frisking a person. [Old French *frisque*]

frisky ('frɪskɪ) *adj*. **friskier, friskiest.** lively, high-spirited, or playful. —'**friskily** *adv*.

frisson ('friːsɒn) *n*. a shiver; thrill. [French]

fritter¹ ('frɪtə) *vb*. (usually foll. by *away*) to waste: *to fritter away time*. [obs. *fitter* to break into small pieces]

fritter² ('frɪtə) *n*. a piece of food, such as apple, that is dipped in batter and fried in deep fat. [Latin *frīgere* to fry]

frivolous ('frɪvələs) *adj*. **1.** not serious or

sensible in content, attitude, or behaviour. **2.** unworthy of serious or sensible treatment: *frivolous details.* [Latin *frivolus*] —**frivolity** (frɪˈvɒlɪtɪ) *n.*

frizz (frɪz) *vb.* **1.** (of hair) to form or cause (hair) to form tight curls. ~*n.* **2.** hair that has been frizzed. [French *friser* to curl] —**frizzy** *adj.*

frizzle[1] (ˈfrɪzˀl) *vb.* **1.** to form (hair) into tight crisp curls. ~*n.* **2.** a tight curl. [prob. related to Old English *frīs* curly]

frizzle[2] (ˈfrɪzˀl) *vb.* to scorch or be scorched until crisp or shrivelled up. [prob. blend of *fry + sizzle*]

frock (frɒk) *n.* **1.** a girl's or woman's dress. **2.** a loose garment, such as a peasant's smock. [Old French *froc*]

frock coat *n.* a man's skirted coat, as worn in the 19th century.

frog[1] (frɒg) *n.* **1.** an amphibian having a short squat tailless body with a moist smooth skin and very long hind legs specialized for hopping. **2. a frog in one's throat.** phlegm on the vocal cords that affects one's speech. [Old English *frogga*]

frog[2] (frɒg) *n.* (*often pl.*) a decorative fastening of looped braid, as on a military uniform. [origin unknown] —**ˈfrogging** *n.*

frog[3] (frɒg) *n.* horny material in the centre of the sole of a horse's foot. [origin unknown]

frogman (ˈfrɒgmən) *n., pl.* **-men.** a swimmer equipped with a rubber suit, flippers, and breathing equipment for working underwater.

frogmarch (ˈfrɒgˌmɑːtʃ) *Chiefly Brit.* ~*n.* **1.** a method of carrying a resisting person in which each limb is held and the victim is face downwards. ~*vb.* **2.** to carry in a frogmarch or cause to move forward unwillingly.

frogspawn (ˈfrɒgˌspɔːn) *n.* a mass of frogs' eggs surrounded by protective jelly.

frolic (ˈfrɒlɪk) *n.* **1.** a light-hearted occasion. **2.** light-hearted activity; gaiety. ~*vb.* **-icking, -icked. 3.** to caper about. [Dutch *vrolijk*]

frolicsome (ˈfrɒlɪksəm) *adj.* merry and playful.

from (frɒm; *unstressed* frəm) *prep.* **1.** indicating the original location, situation, etc.: *from behind the bushes.* **2.** in a period of time starting at: *he lived from 1910 to 1970.* **3.** indicating the distance between two things or places: *a hundred miles from here.* **4.** indicating a lower amount: *from five to fifty pounds.* **5.** showing the model of: *painted from life.* **6.** used with a verbal noun to mark prohibition, etc.: *nothing prevents him from leaving.* **7.** because of: *exhausted from his walk.* [Old English *fram*]

frond (frɒnd) *n.* **1.** the compound leaf of a fern. **2.** the leaf of a palm. [Latin *frōns*]

front (frʌnt) *n.* **1.** that part or side that is forward, or most often seen or used. **2.** a position or place directly before or ahead. **3.** the beginning, opening, or first part. **4.** the position of leadership. **5.** a promenade at a seaside resort. **6.** *Mil.* **a.** the total area in which opposing armies face each other.

b. the space in which a military unit is operating. **7.** *Meteorol.* the dividing line between two air masses of different origins. **8.** outward aspect: *a bold front.* **9.** *Informal.* a business or other activity serving as a respectable cover for another, usually criminal, organization. **10.** also called: **front man.** a nominal leader of an organization. **11.** a particular field of activity: *on the wages front.* **12.** a group of people with a common goal: *a national liberation front.* ~*adj.* **13.** of, at, or in the front. ~*vb.* **14.** to face (onto). **15.** to be a front of or for. **16.** to appear as a presenter in (a television show). **17.** to be the leader of (a band) onstage. [Latin *frōns* forehead, foremost part]

frontage (ˈfrʌntɪdʒ) *n.* **1.** the façade of a building or the front of a plot of ground. **2.** the extent of the front of a shop, plot of land, etc.

frontal (ˈfrʌntˀl) *adj.* **1.** of, at, or in the front. **2.** of or relating to the forehead. [Latin *frōns* forehead]

front bench *n.* the leadership of either the Government or Opposition in the House of Commons or in various other legislative assemblies. —**ˌfront-ˈbencher** *n.*

frontier (ˈfrʌntɪə, frʌnˈtɪə) *n.* **1.** the region of a country bordering on another or a line marking such a boundary. **2.** the edge of the settled area of a country. **3.** (*often pl.*) the limit of knowledge in a particular field. [Old French *front* part which is opposite]

frontispiece (ˈfrʌntɪsˌpiːs) *n.* an illustration facing the title page of a book. [Late Latin *frontispicium* façade]

frontrunner (ˈfrʌntˌrʌnə) *n. Informal.* the leader or a favoured contestant in a race or election.

frost (frɒst) *n.* **1.** a white deposit of ice particles. **2.** an atmospheric temperature of below freezing point, producing this deposit. ~*vb.* **3.** to cover with frost. **4.** to kill or damage (plants) with frost. [Old English]

frostbite (ˈfrɒstˌbaɪt) *n.* destruction of tissues, esp. of the fingers, ears, toes, and nose, by freezing. —**ˈfrostˌbitten** *adj.*

frosted (ˈfrɒstɪd) *adj.* (of glass) having the surface roughened so that it cannot be seen through clearly.

frosting (ˈfrɒstɪŋ) *n. Chiefly U.S. & Canad.* icing.

frosty (ˈfrɒstɪ) *adj.* **frostier, frostiest. 1.** characterized by frost: *a frosty night.* **2.** covered by frost. **3.** lacking warmth or enthusiasm: *a frosty reception.* —**ˈfrostily** *adv.* —**ˈfrostiness** *n.*

froth (frɒθ) *n.* **1.** a mass of small bubbles of air or a gas in a liquid. **2.** a mixture of saliva and air bubbles formed at the lips in certain diseases, such as rabies. ~*vb.* **3.** to produce or cause to produce froth. [Old Norse *frotha*] —**ˈfrothy** *adj.*

frown (fraʊn) *vb.* **1.** to draw the brows together and wrinkle the forehead in worry, anger, or concentration. **2.** (foll. by *on* or *upon*) to look disapprovingly (upon). ~*n.* **3.** the act of frowning. **4.** a look of disapproval or displeasure. [Old French *froigner*]

frowsty ('frausti) *adj.* ill-smelling; stale; musty. [from *frowzy*]

frowzy *or* **frowsy** ('frauzi) *adj.* **frowzier, frowziest,** *or* **frowsier, frowsiest. 1.** slovenly or unkempt in appearance. **2.** ill-smelling; frowsty. [origin unknown]

froze (frouz) *vb.* the past tense of **freeze.**

frozen ('frouz'n) *vb.* **1.** the past participle of **freeze.** ~*adj.* **2.** turned into or covered with ice. **3.** killed or stiffened by extreme cold. **4.** (of food) preserved by a freezing process. **5. a.** (of prices or wages) arbitrarily pegged at a certain level. **b.** (of business assets) not convertible into cash. **6.** motionless: *he was frozen with horror.*

FRS (in Britain) Fellow of the Royal Society.

fructify ('frʌktɪˌfaɪ) *vb.* **-fying, -fied.** to bear or cause to bear fruit. [Latin *frūctus* fruit + *facere* to produce]

fructose ('frʌktəus) *n.* a crystalline sugar occurring in honey and many fruits. [Latin *frūctus* fruit]

frugal ('fruːg'l) *adj.* **1.** practising economy; thrifty. **2.** not costly; meagre. [Latin *frūgī* useful, temperate] —**fru'gality** *n.* —**frugally** *adv.*

fruit (fruːt) *n.* **1.** *Bot.* the ripened ovary of a flowering plant, containing one or more seeds. **2.** any fleshy part of a plant that supports the seeds and is edible, such as the strawberry. **3.** any plant product useful to man, including grain and vegetables. **4.** (*often pl.*) the result of an action or effort. ~*vb.* **5.** to bear fruit. [Latin *frūctus* enjoyment, fruit]

fruiterer ('fruːtərə) *n.* Chiefly *Brit.* a fruit dealer or seller.

fruitful ('fruːtful) *adj.* **1.** producing good and useful results: *a fruitful discussion.* **2.** bearing fruit in abundance. —**'fruitfully** *adv.*

fruition (fruːˈɪʃən) *n.* **1.** the attainment of something worked for or desired. **2.** the act or condition of bearing fruit. [Latin *fruī* to enjoy]

fruitless ('fruːtlɪs) *adj.* **1.** yielding nothing of value; unproductive. **2.** without fruit. —**'fruitlessly** *adv.*

fruit machine *n. Brit.* a gambling machine that pays out when certain combinations of diagrams, usually of fruit, appear on a dial.

fruit sugar *n.* same as **fructose.**

fruity ('fruːtɪ) *adj.* **fruitier, fruitiest. 1.** of or like fruit. **2.** (of a voice) mellow or rich. **3.** *Informal, chiefly Brit.* full of earthy humour. —**'fruitiness** *n.*

frump (frʌmp) *n.* a woman who is dowdy and unattractive. [Middle Dutch *verrompelen* to wrinkle] —**'frumpish** *or* **'frumpy** *adj.*

frustrate (frʌˈstreɪt) *vb.* **1.** to hinder or prevent (the efforts, plans, or desires) of. **2.** to upset or anger (a person) by presenting insuperable difficulties: *the lack of facilities depressed and frustrated him.* [Latin *frustrāre* to cheat] —**frus'trating** *adj.* —**frus'tration** *n.*

frustrated (frʌˈstreɪtɪd) *adj.* dissatisfied or unfulfilled.

frustum ('frʌstəm) *n., pl.* **-tums** *or* **-ta** (-tə). *Geom.* the part of a solid, such as a cone or pyramid, contained between the base and a plane parallel to the base that intersects the solid. [Latin: piece]

fry [1] (fraɪ) *vb.* **frying, fried. 1.** to cook or be cooked in fat or oil, usually over direct heat. ~*n., pl.* **fries. 2.** a dish of something fried, esp. the offal of a specified animal: *pig's fry.* **3.** Also: **fry-up.** *Brit. informal.* a dish of mixed fried food. [Latin *frīgere* to fry] —**'fryer** *or* **'frier** *n.*

fry [2] (fraɪ) *pl. n.* **1.** the young of various species of fish. **2.** See **small fry.** [Old French *freier* to spawn]

frying pan *n.* **1.** a long-handled shallow pan used for frying. **2. out of the frying pan into the fire.** from a bad situation to a worse one.

f-stop ('ɛfˌstɒp) *n.* any of the settings for the f-number of a camera.

ft. foot *or* feet.

fuchsia ('fjuːʃə) *n.* a shrub widely cultivated for its showy drooping purple, red, or white flowers. [after Leonhard *Fuchs*, botanist]

fuck (fʌk) *Taboo.* ~*vb.* **1.** to have sexual intercourse with (someone). ~*n.* **2.** an act of sexual intercourse. **3.** *Slang.* a partner in sexual intercourse. **4. not give a fuck.** not to care at all. ~*interj.* **5.** *Offensive.* an expression of strong disgust or anger. [Germanic] —**'fucking** *n., adj., adv.*

fuck off *vb. Offensive taboo slang.* to go away.

fuck up *vb. Offensive taboo slang.* to make a mess of (something).

fuddle ('fʌd'l) *vb.* **1.** to cause to be confused or intoxicated. ~*n.* **2.** a confused state. [origin unknown]

fuddy-duddy ('fʌdɪˌdʌdɪ) *n., pl.* **-dies.** *Informal.* a person, esp. an elderly one, who is extremely conservative or dull. [origin unknown]

fudge [1] (fʌdʒ) *n.* a soft sweet made from sugar, butter, and milk. [origin unknown]

fudge [2] (fʌdʒ) *vb.* to make (an issue or problem) less clear deliberately; misrepresent. [origin unknown]

fuel (fjʊəl) *n.* **1.** any substance burned for heat or power, such as coal or petrol. **2.** the material that produces energy in a nuclear reactor. **3.** something that nourishes or builds up emotion or action. ~*vb.* **fuelling, fuelled** *or* U.S. **fueling, fueled. 4.** to supply with or receive fuel. [Old French *feu* fire]

fuel cell *n.* a cell in which chemical energy is converted directly into electrical energy.

fug (fʌg) *n. Chiefly Brit.* a hot stale atmosphere. [origin unknown] —**'fuggy** *adj.*

fugitive ('fjuːdʒɪtɪv) *n.* **1.** a person who flees. ~*adj.* **2.** fleeing, esp. from arrest or pursuit. **3.** not permanent; fleeting. [Latin *fugere* to take flight]

fugue (fjuːg) *n.* a musical form consisting

of a theme repeated above or below the continuing first statement. [French] —**'fugal** adj.

Führer or **Fuehrer** ('fjʊərə) n. a leader; the title taken by Hitler. [German]

fulcrum ('fʊlkrəm) n., pl. **-crums** or **-cra** (-krə). the pivot about which a lever turns. [Latin: foot of a couch]

fulfil or U.S. **fulfill** (fʊl'fɪl) vb. **-filling**, **-filled**. 1. to bring about the achievement of (a desire or promise). 2. to carry out (a request). 3. to satisfy (demands or conditions). 4. **fulfil oneself**. to achieve one's potential. [Old English *fulfyllan*] —**ful'filment** or U.S. **ful'fillment** n.

full[1] (fʊl) adj. 1. holding as much as possible. 2. abundant in supply: *full of energy*. 3. having consumed enough food or drink. 4. (esp. of the face or figure) rounded or plump. 5. complete: *a full dozen*. 6. with all privileges or rights: *a full member*. 7. (foll. by *of*) engrossed (with): *full of his own projects*. 8. *Music*. powerful or rich in volume and sound. 9. (of a skirt) containing a large amount of fabric. 10. **full of oneself**. full of pride or conceit. 11. **full up**. filled to capacity. ~adv. 12. completely; entirely. 13. directly; right: *he hit him full in the stomach*. 14. very; extremely (esp. in **full well**). ~n. 15. **in full**. without omitting or shortening. 16. **to the full**. thoroughly; fully. [Old English] —**'fullness** or esp. U.S. **'fulness** n.

full[2] (fʊl) vb. to make (cloth) more compact during manufacture through shrinking and beating. [Old French *fouler*]

fullback ('fʊl,bæk) n. *Soccer, hockey, & rugby*. a defensive player.

full-blooded adj. 1. having great vigour or enthusiasm. 2. (esp. of horses) of unmixed ancestry.

full-blown adj. fully developed.

full-bodied adj. having a full rich flavour or quality.

fuller's earth ('fʊləz) n. a natural absorbent clay used for fulling cloth.

full-frontal adj. *Informal*. exposing the genitals to full view.

full house n. 1. a theatre filled to capacity. 2. (in bingo) the set of numbers needed to win.

full-length n. (*modifier*) 1. showing the complete human figure. 2. not abridged.

full moon n. the phase of the moon when it is visible as a fully illuminated disc.

full pitch or **toss** n. *Cricket*. a bowled ball that reaches the batsman without bouncing.

full-scale n. (*modifier*) 1. (of a plan) of actual size. 2. using all resources; all-out.

full stop n. the punctuation mark (.) used at the end of a sentence and after abbreviations. Also called (esp. U.S. and Canad.): **period**.

full-time adj. 1. for the entire time appropriate to an activity: *a full-time job*. ~adv. **full time**. 2. on a full-time basis: *he works full time*.

fully ('fʊlɪ) adv. 1. to the greatest degree or extent. 2. amply; adequately. 3. at least: *it was fully an hour before she came*.

fully fashioned adj. (of stockings or knitwear) shaped and seamed so as to fit closely.

fulmar ('fʊlmə) n. a heavily built short-tailed sea bird of polar regions. [Scandinavian]

fulminate ('fʌlmɪ,neɪt) vb. (often foll. by *against*) to criticize or denounce angrily and vehemently. [Latin *fulmen* lightning that strikes] —**,fulmi'nation** n.

fulsome ('fʊlsəm) adj. distastefully excessive or insincere: *fulsome compliments*.

fumble ('fʌmb'l) vb. (often foll. by *for* or *with*) 1. to use the hands clumsily or grope about blindly. 2. to say or do awkwardly. ~n. 3. the act of fumbling. [prob. Scandinavian]

fume (fjuːm) vb. 1. to be overcome with anger or fury. 2. to give off (fumes) or (of fumes) to be given off, esp. during a chemical reaction. 3. to treat with fumes. ~n. 4. (often *pl.*) a pungent or toxic vapour, gas, or smoke. [Latin *fūmus* smoke, vapour]

fumigate ('fjuːmɪ,geɪt) vb. to treat (something contaminated) with fumes. [Latin *fūmus* smoke + *agere* to drive] —**,fumi'gation** n.

fun (fʌn) n. 1. a source of enjoyment, amusement or diversion. 2. pleasure, gaiety, or merriment. 3. jest or sport (esp. in **in** or **for fun**). 4. **make fun of** or **poke fun at**. to ridicule or deride. [obs. *fon* to make a fool of]

function ('fʌŋkʃən) n. 1. the natural action or intended purpose of a person or thing. 2. an official or formal social gathering. 3. a factor dependent upon another or other factors. 4. *Maths*. a quantity, the value of which depends on the varying value of another quantity. ~vb. 5. to operate; work. 6. (foll. by *as*) to perform the action or role of (something or someone else). [Latin *functiō*]

functional ('fʌŋkʃən'l) adj. 1. of or performing a function. 2. practical rather than decorative. 3. working. 4. *Med*. affecting a function of an organ without structural change. —**'functionally** adv.

functionalism ('fʌŋkʃənə,lɪzəm) n. the theory that the form of a thing should be determined by its use. —**'functionalist** n., adj.

functionary ('fʌŋkʃənərɪ) n., pl. **-aries**. a person acting in an official capacity, as for a government; an official.

fund (fʌnd) n. 1. a reserve of money set aside for a certain purpose. 2. a supply or store of something; stock. ~vb. 3. to provide money to. 4. to convert (short-term debt) into long-term debt bearing fixed interest. ~See also **funds**. [Latin *fundus* the bottom, piece of land]

fundamental (,fʌndə'ment'l) adj. 1. of or forming a foundation; basic. 2. essential; primary. ~n. 3. a principle that serves as the basis of an idea or system. 4. the lowest note of a harmonic series. —**,funda'mentally** adv.

fundamentalism (ˌfʌndəˈmentəˌlɪzəm) n. **1.** *Christianity.* the view that the Bible is literally true. **2.** *Islam.* a movement favouring strict observance of Islamic law. —ˌfundaˈmentalist n., adj.

fundamental particle n. same as **elementary particle.**

funds (fʌndz) pl. n. money that is readily available.

funeral (ˈfjuːnərəl) n. **1.** a ceremony at which a dead person is buried or cremated. **2.** *Informal.* problem; affair: *that's your funeral.* ~adj. **3.** of or for a funeral. [Latin *fūnus*] —ˈfunerary adj.

funeral director n. an undertaker.

funereal (fjuːˈnɪərɪəl) adj. suggestive of a funeral; gloomy or mournful. —fuˈnereally adv.

funfair (ˈfʌnˌfɛə) n. *Brit.* an amusement park.

fungicide (ˈfʌndʒɪˌsaɪd) n. a substance that destroys fungi. [*fungus* + Latin *caedere* to kill] —ˌfungiˈcidal adj.

fungoid (ˈfʌŋɡɔɪd) adj. resembling a fungus.

fungous (ˈfʌŋɡəs) adj. appearing suddenly and spreading quickly like a fungus.

fungus (ˈfʌŋɡəs) n., pl. **fungi** (ˈfʌŋɡaɪ) or **funguses.** any of a division of plants that do not have leaves or roots, and reproduce by spores, including moulds, yeasts, and mushrooms. [Latin] —ˈfungal adj.

funicular (fjuːˈnɪkjʊlə) n. a railway up the side of a mountain, consisting of two cars at either end of a cable passing round a driving wheel at the summit. Also called: **funicular railway.** [Latin *fūnis* rope]

funk[1] (fʌŋk) *Informal, chiefly Brit.* ~n. **1.** Also called: **blue funk.** a state of nervousness, fear, or depression. **2.** a coward. ~vb. **3.** to avoid doing something through fear. [origin unknown]

funk[2] (fʌŋk) n. a type of Black dance music with a strong beat. [from *funky*]

funky (ˈfʌŋkɪ) adj. **-kier, -kiest.** (of jazz or pop) passionate; soulful. [from obs. *funk* to smoke tobacco, perhaps referring to music that is smelly, i.e. earthy]

funnel (ˈfʌnˀl) n. **1.** a hollow utensil with a wide mouth tapering to a small hole, used for pouring liquids into a narrow-necked vessel. **2.** a smokestack, as on a steamship. ~vb. **-nelling, -nelled** or *U.S.* **-neling, -neled. 3.** to move or cause to move through or as if through a funnel. [Old Provençal *fonilh*]

funny (ˈfʌnɪ) adj. **-nier, -niest. 1.** causing amusement or laughter; humorous. **2.** peculiar; odd. **3.** suspicious or dubious (esp. in **funny business**). **4.** *Informal.* faint or ill. —ˈfunnily adv. —ˈfunniness n.

funny bone n. a sensitive area near the elbow where the nerve is close to the surface of the skin.

fur (fɜː) n. **1.** the dense coat of fine silky hairs on many mammals. **2.** the skin of certain animals, with the hair left on. **3.** a garment made of fur. **4. make the fur fly.** to cause a scene or disturbance. **5.** *Informal.* a whitish coating on the tongue,

caused by illness. **6.** *Brit.* a deposit on the insides of waterpipes or kettles, caused by hard water. ~vb. **furring, furred. 7.** (often foll. by *up*) to cover or become covered with a furlike deposit. [Old French *fuerre* sheath]

furbelow (ˈfɜːbɪˌləʊ) n. **1.** a flounce or ruffle. **2.** (*often pl.*) showy ornamentation. [French dialect *farbella* a frill]

furbish (ˈfɜːbɪʃ) vb. (often foll. by *up*) to brighten up; renovate. [Old French *fourbir* to polish]

furcate (ˈfɜːkeɪt) vb. **1.** to divide into two parts. ~adj. **2.** forked: *furcate branches.* [Latin *furca* a fork] —**furˈcation** n.

Furies (ˈfjʊərɪz) pl. n., sing. **Fury.** *Classical myth.* the goddesses of vengeance, who pursued unpunished criminals.

furious (ˈfjʊərɪəs) adj. **1.** extremely angry or annoyed. **2.** violent or unrestrained, as in speed or energy. —**ˈfuriously** adv.

furl (fɜːl) vb. to roll up (an umbrella, flag, or sail) neatly and securely. [Old French *ferm* tight + *lier* to bind]

furlong (ˈfɜːˌlɒŋ) n. a unit of length equal to 220 yards (201.168 metres). [Old English *furh* furrow + *lang* long]

furlough (ˈfɜːləʊ) n. leave of absence from military duty. [Dutch *verlof*]

furnace (ˈfɜːnɪs) n. **1.** an enclosed chamber in which heat is produced to destroy refuse or smelt ores. **2.** a very hot place. [Latin *fornax*]

furnish (ˈfɜːnɪʃ) vb. **1.** to provide (a house or room) with furniture, etc. **2.** to supply. [Old French *fournir*]

furnishings (ˈfɜːnɪʃɪŋz) pl. n. furniture, carpets, and fittings with which a room or house is furnished.

furniture (ˈfɜːnɪtʃə) n. **1.** the movable articles that equip a room or house. **2.** the equipment necessary for a ship or factory. **3.** locks and handles for use on doors. [Old French *fournir* to equip]

furore (fjʊˈrɔːrɪ) or esp. *U.S.* **furor** (ˈfjʊərɔː) n. a very angry or excited reaction by people to something: *the present furore over drugs.* [Latin: frenzy]

furrier (ˈfʌrɪə) n. a person who makes or sells fur garments. [Middle English *fourour*]

furrow (ˈfʌrəʊ) n. **1.** a long narrow trench made in the ground by a plough. **2.** any long deep groove, esp. a deep wrinkle on the forehead. ~vb. **3.** to become wrinkled. **4.** to make furrows in (land). [Old English *furh*]

furry (ˈfɜːrɪ) adj. **-rier, -riest.** like or covered with fur or something furlike.

further (ˈfɜːðə) adv. **1.** in addition; furthermore. **2.** to a greater degree or extent. **3.** to or at a more advanced point. **4.** to or at a greater distance in time or space. ~adj. **5.** additional; more. **6.** more distant or remote in time or space. ~vb. **7.** to assist the progress of (something). [Old English *furthor*] —**ˈfurtherance** n.

further education n. (in Britain) formal education beyond school other than at a university or polytechnic.

furthermore ('fɜːðə,mɔː) *adv.* in addition.

furthest ('fɜːðɪst) *adv.* **1.** to the greatest degree or extent. **2.** to or at the greatest distance in time or space; farthest. ~*adj.* **3.** most distant in time or space; farthest.

furtive ('fɜːtɪv) *adj.* characterized by stealth; sly and secretive. [Latin *furtīvus* stolen] —'**furtively** *adv.*

fury ('fjʊərɪ) *n., pl.* **-ries. 1.** violent anger. **2.** an outburst of such anger. **3.** uncontrolled violence: *the fury of the storm.* **4.** a person with a violent temper. **5.** See **Furies. 6. like fury.** *Informal.* energetically; powerfully. [Latin *furere* to be furious]

furze (fɜːz) *n.* gorse. [Old English *fyrs*] —'**furzy** *adj.*

fuse¹ *or U.S.* **fuze** (fjuːz) *n.* **1.** a lead containing an explosive, used to fire an explosive charge. ~*vb.* **2.** to equip with such a fuse. [Latin *fūsus* spindle] —'**fuseless** *adj.*

fuse² (fjuːz) *n.* **1.** a protective device for safeguarding electric circuits, containing a wire that melts and breaks the circuit when the current exceeds a certain value. ~*vb.* **2.** *Brit.* to fail or cause to fail as a result of a fuse blowing. **3.** to equip (a plug or circuit) with a fuse. **4.** to join or become combined. **5.** to become or cause to become liquid, esp. by the action of heat. **6.** to unite or become united by melting. [Latin *fūsus* melted, cast]

fuselage ('fjuːzɪ,lɑːʒ) *n.* the main body of an aircraft. [French]

fusible ('fjuːzəb'l) *adj.* capable of being melted.

fusilier (,fjuːzɪ'lɪə) *n.* (formerly) an infantryman armed with a light musket: a term still used in the names of certain British regiments. [French]

fusillade (,fjuːzɪ'leɪd) *n.* **1.** a rapid continual discharge of firearms. **2.** a sudden outburst, as of criticism. [French *fusiller* to shoot]

fusion ('fjuːʒən) *n.* **1.** the act or process of melting together. **2.** something produced by fusing. **3.** a kind of popular music that is a blend of two or more styles, such as jazz and funk. **4.** See **nuclear fusion.** [Latin *fūsiō* a melting]

fuss (fʌs) *n.* **1.** nervous activity or agitation. **2.** complaint or objection: *he made a fuss over the bill.* **3.** an exhibition of affection or admiration: *they made a great fuss over the new baby.* ~*vb.* **4.** to worry unnecessarily. **5.** to be excessively concerned over trifles. **6.** (usually foll. by *over*) to show great or excessive concern or

affection (for). **7.** to bother (a person). [origin unknown]

fusspot ('fʌs,pɒt) *n. Brit. informal.* a person who fusses unnecessarily.

fussy ('fʌsɪ) *adj.* **fussier, fussiest. 1.** inclined to fuss. **2.** very particular about detail. **3.** overelaborate. —'**fussily** *adv.*

fustian ('fʌstɪən) *n.* **1.** (formerly) a hard-wearing fabric of cotton mixed with flax or wool. **2.** pompous talk or writing. [Old French]

fusty ('fʌstɪ) *adj.* **-tier, -tiest. 1.** smelling of damp or mould. **2.** old-fashioned. [Middle English *fust* wine cask] —'**fustiness** *n.*

futile ('fjuːtaɪl) *adj.* **1.** having no effective result; unsuccessful. **2.** pointless; trifling. [Latin *futtilis* pouring out easily] —**futility** (fjuː'tɪlɪtɪ) *n.*

future ('fjuːtʃə) *n.* **1.** the time yet to come. **2.** undetermined events that will occur in that time. **3.** the condition of a person or thing at a later date. **4.** *Grammar.* a tense of verbs used when the action described is to occur after the time of utterance. **5. in future.** from now on. ~*adj.* **6.** that is yet to come or be. **7.** of or expressing time yet to come. **8.** destined to become. **9.** *Grammar.* in or denoting the future as a tense of verbs. ~See also **futures.** [Latin *fūtūrus* about to be]

future perfect *Grammar.* ~*adj.* **1.** denoting a tense of verbs describing an action that will have been performed by a certain time. ~*n.* **2.** the future perfect tense.

futures ('fjuːtʃəz) *pl. n.* commodities bought or sold at an agreed price for delivery at a specified future date.

futurism ('fjuːtʃə,rɪzəm) *n.* an art movement that replaced traditional aesthetic values with the characteristics of the machine age. —'**futurist** *n., adj.*

futuristic (,fjuːtʃə'rɪstɪk) *adj.* **1.** of design or technology that appears to belong to some future time. **2.** of futurism.

futurity (fjuː'tjʊərɪtɪ) *n., pl.* **-ties. 1.** future. **2.** a future event.

futurology (,fjuːtʃə'rɒlədʒɪ) *n.* the study or prediction of the future of mankind.

fuzz¹ (fʌz) *n.* a mass or covering of fine or curly hairs, fibres, etc. [prob. from Low German *fussig* loose]

fuzz² (fʌz) *n. Slang.* the police or a policeman. [origin unknown]

fuzzy ('fʌzɪ) *adj.* **fuzzier, fuzziest. 1.** of, resembling, or covered with fuzz. **2.** unclear or distorted. **3.** (of hair) tightly curled. —'**fuzzily** *adv.* —'**fuzziness** *n.*

G

g or **G** (dʒiː) n., pl. **g's, G,s** or **Gs.** the seventh letter of the English alphabet.

g 1. gallon(s). **2.** gram(s). **3.** acceleration due to gravity.

G 1. *Music.* the fifth note of the scale of C major. **2.** gravity. **3.** good. **4.** *Slang, chiefly U.S.* grand (a thousand dollars or pounds).

Ga *Chem.* gallium.

GA or **Ga.** Georgia.

gab (gæb) *Informal.* ~vb. **gabbing, gabbed. 1.** to talk idly or too much; chatter. ~n. **2.** idle talk. **3. gift of the gab.** ability to talk glibly or persuasively. [prob. from Irish Gaelic *gob* mouth]

gabble ('gæb³l) vb. **1.** to speak rapidly and indistinctly. ~n. **2.** rapid and indistinct speech. [Middle Dutch *gabbelen*]

gaberdine ('gæbə,diːn, ,gæbə'diːn) n. **1.** a twill-weave worsted, cotton, or viscose fabric. **2.** a coat or other garment made of this. [Old French *gauvardine* pilgrim's garment]

gable ('geɪb³l) n. the triangular upper part of a wall between the sloping ends of a ridged roof. [prob. from Old Norse *gafl*] —'**gabled** adj.

gad (gæd) vb. **gadding, gadded.** (often foll. by *about* or *around*) to go about in search of pleasure; gallivant. [obs. *gadling* companion]

gadabout ('gædə,baʊt) n. *Informal.* a person who restlessly seeks amusement.

gadfly ('gæd,flaɪ) n., pl. **-flies. 1.** a large fly that bites livestock. **2.** a constantly irritating person. [obs. *gad* sting]

gadget ('gædʒɪt) n. a small mechanical device or appliance. [origin unknown] —'**gadgetry** n.

gadoid ('geɪdɔɪd) adj. **1.** of or belonging to the cod family of marine fishes. ~n. **2.** any gadoid fish. [New Latin *gadus* cod]

gadolinium (,gædə'lɪnɪəm) n. a silvery-white metallic element of the rare-earth group. Symbol: Gd [after Johan *Gadolin*, mineralogist]

gadwall ('gæd,wɔːl) n., pl. **-walls** or **-wall.** a duck related to the mallard. The male has a grey body and black tail. [origin unknown]

gadzooks (gæd'zuːks) interj. *Archaic.* a mild oath. [perhaps from *God's hooks* (the nails of the cross) from *Gad* archaic euphemism for God]

Gael (geɪl) n. a Gaelic-speaker of Scotland, Ireland, or the Isle of Man. [Gaelic *Gaidheal*] —'**Gaeldom** n.

Gaelic ('geɪlɪk, 'gæl-) n. **1.** any of the closely related Celtic languages of Scotland, Ireland, or the Isle of Man. ~adj. **2.** of the Celtic people of Scotland, Ireland, or the Isle of Man, or their language.

gaff¹ (gæf) n. **1.** *Angling.* a stiff pole with a stout hook attached for landing large fish. **2.** *Naut.* a spar hoisted to support a fore-and-aft sail. ~vb. **3.** *Angling.* to hook or land (a fish) with a gaff. [Provençal *gaf* boat hook]

gaff² (gæf) n. **blow the gaff.** *Brit. slang.* to divulge a secret. [origin unknown]

gaffe (gæf) n. a social blunder. [French]

gaffer ('gæfə) n. **1.** an old man: often used affectionately. **2.** *Informal, chiefly Brit.* a boss or foreman. **3.** *Informal.* the senior electrician on a television or film set. [from *godfather*]

gag¹ (gæg) vb. **gagging, gagged. 1.** to stop up (a person's mouth), usually with a piece of cloth, to prevent him from speaking or crying out. **2.** to deprive of free speech. **3.** to retch or cause to retch. **4.** to struggle for breath; choke. ~n. **5.** something, usually a piece of cloth, stuffed into or tied across the mouth. **6.** any restraint on free speech. **7.** *Parliamentary procedure.* same as **closure** (sense 3). [Middle English *gaggen*]

gag² (gæg) *Informal.* ~n. **1.** a joke, usually one told by a professional comedian. **2.** a hoax or practical joke. ~vb. **gagging, gagged. 3.** to tell jokes. [origin unknown]

gaga ('gɑːgɑː) adj. *Informal.* **1.** senile; doting. **2.** slightly crazy. [French]

gage¹ (geɪdʒ) n. **1.** something given as security; pledge. **2.** (formerly) a glove or other object thrown down to indicate a challenge to combat. [Old French]

gage² (geɪdʒ) n. short for **greengage.**

gage³ (geɪdʒ) n., vb. *U.S.* same as **gauge.**

gaggle ('gæg³l) n. **1.** a flock of geese. **2.** *Informal.* a disorderly group of people. [Germanic]

gaiety ('geɪətɪ) n., pl. **-ties. 1.** the condition of being merry. **2.** festivity; merry-making. **3.** colourful bright appearance.

gaily ('geɪlɪ) adv. **1.** in a lively manner; merrily. **2.** with bright colours.

gain (geɪn) vb. **1.** to acquire (something desirable); obtain. **2.** to win in competition: *to gain the victory.* **3.** to increase, improve, or advance: *the car gained speed.* **4.** (usually foll. by *on* or *upon*) to get nearer (to) or catch up (on). **5.** to get to; reach: *the steamer gained port.* **6.** (of a timepiece) to become or be too fast. ~n. **7.** something won or acquired; profit; advantage. **8.** an increase in size or amount. **9.** a gaining; attainment; acquisition. **10.** *Electronics.* the ratio of the output signal of an amplifier to the input signal, usually measured in decibels. [Old French *gaaignier*]

gainful ('geɪnfʊl) adj. profitable; lucrative. —'**gainfully** adv.

gainsay (geɪn'seɪ) vb. **-saying, -said.** *Archaic or literary.* to deny; contradict. [Middle English *gainsaien,* from *gain-* against + *saien* to say]

gait (geɪt) n. **1.** manner of walking. **2.** (of

horses and dogs) the pattern of footsteps at a particular speed, such as a trot. [var. of *gate*]

gaiter ('geɪtə) *n.* (*often pl.*). a cloth or leather covering for the leg or ankle. [French *guêtre*]

gal (gæl) *n. Slang.* a girl.

gal. gallon.

gala ('gɑːlə, 'geɪlə) *n.* **1.** a celebration; festival. **2.** *Chiefly Brit.* a sporting occasion with competitions in several events: *a swimming gala.* [Old French *galer* to make merry]

galactic (gə'læktɪk) *adj.* of the Galaxy or other galaxies.

galantine ('gælən,tiːn) *n.* a dish of white meat which is boned, cooked, and served cold in jelly. [Old French]

galaxy ('gæləksɪ) *n., pl.* **-axies. 1.** a star system held together by gravitational attraction. **2.** a splendid gathering of famous or distinguished people. [Middle English (in the sense: the Milky Way): from Greek *gala* milk]

Galaxy ('gæləksɪ) *n.* **the.** the spiral galaxy that contains the solar system. Also called: the **Milky Way.**

gale (geɪl) *n.* **1.** a strong wind, specifically one of force 8 on the Beaufort scale. **2.** (*often pl.*) a loud outburst: *gales of laughter.* [origin unknown]

galena (gə'liːnə) *or* **galenite** (gə'liːnaɪt) *n.* a soft bluish-grey mineral consisting of lead sulphide: the chief source of lead. [Latin: lead ore]

Galia melon ('gæliə) *n.* a kind of melon with a raised network texture on the skin and aromatic flesh.

gall¹ (gɔːl) *n.* **1.** *Informal.* impudence. **2.** bitterness; rancour. **3.** something bitter or disagreeable. **4.** *Physiol., obs.* same as **bile.** [Old Norse]

gall² (gɔːl) *n.* **1.** a sore on the skin caused by chafing. **2.** something that causes annoyance. **3.** annoyance. ~*vb.* **4.** to chafe (the skin) by rubbing. **5.** to annoy. [Germanic]

gall³ (gɔːl) *n.* an abnormal outgrowth in plant tissue caused by parasitic insects, fungi, or bacteria. [Latin *galla*]

gall. gallon.

gallant *adj.* ('gælənt). **1.** brave and noble. **2.** (gə'lænt, 'gælənt). (of a man) attentive to women; chivalrous. **3.** imposing; stately: *a gallant ship.* ~*n.* ('gælənt, gə'lænt). **4.** a woman's lover or suitor. **5.** a dashing or fashionable young man who pursues women. [Old French *galer* to make merry] —**'gallantly** *adv.*

gallantry ('gæləntrɪ) *n., pl.* **-ries. 1.** conspicuous courage. **2.** polite attentiveness to women. **3.** a gallant action or phrase.

gall bladder *n.* a muscular sac, attached to the liver, that stores bile.

galleon ('gæliən) *n.* a large, three-masted sailing ship used from the 15th to the 18th centuries. [Spanish *galeón*]

gallery ('gælərɪ) *n., pl.* **-leries. 1.** a covered passageway open on one or both sides. **2.** a balcony running along or around the inside wall of a church, hall, or other building. **3.** *Theatre.* **a.** an upper floor that projects from the rear and contains the cheapest seats. **b.** the audience seated there. **4.** a long narrow room: *a shooting gallery.* **5.** a room or building for exhibiting works of art. **6.** an underground passage. **7.** a group of spectators, as at a golf match. **8. play to the gallery.** to try to gain approval by appealing to popular taste. [Old French *galerie*]

galley ('gælɪ) *n.* **1.** a ship propelled by oars or sails, used in ancient or medieval times. **2.** the kitchen of a ship, boat, or aircraft. **3.** *Printing.* **a.** a tray for holding composed type. **b.** short for **galley proof.** [Old French *galie*]

galley proof *n.* a printer's proof taken from type in a galley, used to make corrections before the type is made up into pages.

galley slave *n.* **1.** a criminal or slave forced to row in a galley. **2.** *Informal.* a drudge.

galliard ('gæljəd) *n.* **1.** a lively dance in triple time for two persons, popular in the 16th and 17th centuries. **2.** music for this dance. [Old French *gaillard*]

Gallic ('gælɪk) *adj.* **1.** French. **2.** of ancient Gaul or the Gauls.

Gallicism ('gælɪ,sɪzəm) *n.* a word or idiom borrowed from French.

gallinaceous (,gælɪ'neɪʃəs) *adj.* of an order of birds, including poultry, pheasants, and grouse, having a heavy rounded body. [Latin *gallina* hen]

galling ('gɔːlɪŋ) *adj.* annoying or bitterly humiliating.

gallium ('gæliəm) *n.* a silvery metallic element used in high-temperature thermometers and semiconductors. Symbol: Ga [Latin *gallus* cock, translation of French *coq* in the name of its discoverer, *Lecoq* de Boisbaudran]

gallivant ('gælɪ,vænt) *vb.* to go about in search of pleasure. [perhaps from *gallant*]

gallon ('gælən) *n.* **1.** *Brit.* a unit of capacity equal to 4.55 litres. **2.** *U.S.* a unit of capacity equal to 3.79 litres. [Old Northern French *galon*]

gallop ('gæləp) *vb.* **1.** (of a horse) to run fast with a two-beat stride in which all four legs are off the ground at once. **2.** to ride (a horse) at a gallop. **3.** to move or progress rapidly. ~*n.* **4.** the fast two-beat gait of horses. **5.** a galloping. [Old French *galoper*]

gallows ('gæləʊz) *n., pl.* **-lowses** *or* **-lows. 1.** a wooden structure consisting of two upright posts with a crossbeam, used for hanging criminals. **2. the gallows.** execution by hanging. [Old Norse *galgi*]

gallstone ('gɔːl,stəʊn) *n.* a small hard mass formed in the gall bladder or its ducts.

Gallup Poll ('gæləp) *n.* a sampling of the views of a representative cross section of the population, used to forecast voting. [after G.H. *Gallup*, statistician]

galop ('gæləp) *n.* **1.** a 19th-century dance in quick duple time. **2.** music for this dance. [French]

galore (gəˈlɔː) det. in abundance: food and drink galore. [Irish Gaelic go leór to sufficiency]

galoshes (gəˈlɒʃɪz) pl. n. (sometimes sing.) a pair of waterproof overshoes. [Old French]

galumph (gəˈlʌmpf, -ˈlʌmf) vb. Informal. to leap or move about clumsily or joyfully. [prob. a blend of GALLOP + TRIUMPH]

galvanic (gælˈvænɪk) adj. 1. of or producing an electric current by chemical means, as in a battery. 2. Informal. stimulating, startling, or energetic.

galvanism (ˈgælvəˌnɪzəm) n. Obs. electricity produced by chemical means, as in a battery. [after Galvani, physiologist]

galvanize or **-ise** (ˈgælvəˌnaɪz) vb. 1. to stimulate; excite; startle. 2. to cover (metal) with a protective zinc coating. 3. to stimulate by an electric current. —ˌgalvaniˈzation or -iˈsation n.

galvanometer (ˌgælvəˈnɒmɪtə) n. a sensitive instrument for detecting or measuring small electric currents.

gambit (ˈgæmbɪt) n. 1. Chess. an opening move in which a piece, usually a pawn, is sacrificed to gain an advantageous position. 2. an opening line or move intended to gain an advantage. [Italian gambetto a tripping up]

gamble (ˈgæmb°l) vb. 1. to play games of chance to win money or prizes. 2. to risk or bet (something) on the outcome of an event or sport. 3. (often foll. by on) to act with the expectation of: to gamble on its being a sunny day. 4. (often foll. by away) to lose by gambling. ~n. 5. a risky act or venture. 6. a bet or wager. [prob. var. of GAME¹] —ˈgambler n. —ˈgambling n.

gamboge (gæmˈbəʊdʒ, -ˈbuːʒ) n. a gum resin obtained from a tropical Asian tree, used as a yellow pigment and as a purgative. [from Cambodia (now Kampuchea), where first found]

gambol (ˈgæmb°l) vb. -bolling, -bolled or U.S. -boling, -boled. 1. to jump about playfully; frolic. ~n. 2. a gambolling; frolic. [French gambade]

game¹ (geɪm) n. 1. an amusement or pastime. 2. a contest with rules. 3. a single period of play in such a contest. 4. the score needed to win a contest. 5. a single contest in a series; match. 6. (pl.; often cap.) an event consisting of various sporting contests, usually in athletics: Olympic Games. 7. equipment needed for playing certain games: a compendium of games. 8. style or ability in playing a game. 9. a proceeding practised like a game: the game of politics. 10. an activity undertaken in a spirit of levity: marriage is just a game to him. 11. wild animals, birds, or fish, hunted for sport or food. 12. the flesh of such animals, used as food. 13. an object of pursuit: fair game. 14. Informal. work or occupation. 15. Informal. a trick or scheme: what's your game? 16. Slang, chiefly Brit. prostitution: on the game. 17. **give the game away.** to reveal one's intentions or a secret. 18. **make (a) game of.** to make fun of; mock. 19. **play the game.** to behave fairly. 20. **the game is up.** the

scheme or trick has been found out and so cannot succeed. ~adj. 21. Informal. full of fighting spirit; plucky. 22. (usually foll. by for) Informal. prepared or ready; willing: I'm game for a try. ~vb. 23. to play games of chance for money; gamble. [Old English gamen] —ˈgamely adv. —ˈgameness n.

game² (geɪm) adj. lame: a game leg. [prob. from Irish cam crooked]

gamecock (ˈgeɪmˌkɒk) n. a cock bred and trained for fighting.

gamekeeper (ˈgeɪmˌkiːpə) n. a person employed to take care of game on an estate.

game laws pl. n. laws governing the hunting and preservation of game.

gamesmanship (ˈgeɪmzmənˌʃɪp) n. Informal. the art of winning by cunning practices without actually cheating.

gamester (ˈgeɪmstə) n. a gambler.

gamete (ˈgæmiːt, gəˈmiːt) n. a cell that can fuse with another in reproduction. [Greek gametē wife] —**gametic** (gəˈmɛtɪk) adj.

gamin (ˈgæmɪn) n. a street urchin. [French]

gamine (gæˈmiːn) n. a slim and boyish girl or young woman. [French]

gaming (ˈgeɪmɪŋ) n. gambling.

gamma (ˈgæmə) n. the third letter in the Greek alphabet (Γ, γ).

gamma radiation n. electromagnetic radiation of shorter wavelength and higher energy than x-rays.

gamma rays pl. n. streams of gamma radiation.

gammon (ˈgæmən) n. 1. a cured or smoked ham. 2. the hindquarter of a side of bacon. [Old French gambon leg]

gammy (ˈgæmɪ) adj. -mier, -miest. Brit. slang. (of the leg) lame. [dialect var. of GAME²]

gamp (gæmp) n. Brit. informal. an umbrella. [after Mrs Gamp, in Dickens' Martin Chuzzlewit]

gamut (ˈgæmət) n. 1. entire range or scale, as of emotions. 2. Music. a. a scale. b. the whole range of notes. [Medieval Latin, from gamma, the lowest note of the hexachord as established by Guido d'Arezzo + ut (now, doh), the first of the notes of the scale ut, re, mi, fa, sol, la, si]

gamy or **gamey** (ˈgeɪmɪ) adj. **gamier, gamiest.** having the smell or flavour of game.

gander (ˈgændə) n. 1. a male goose. 2. Informal. a quick look: take a gander. [Old English gandra, ganra]

gang¹ (gæŋ) n. 1. a group of people who associate together, usually for criminal purposes. 2. an organized group of workmen. 3. a set of tools arranged to work in co-ordination. ~vb. 4. to become or act as a gang. ~See also **gang up.** [Old English: journey]

gang² (gæŋ) vb. Scot. to go or walk. [Old English gangan]

gangland (ˈgæŋˌlænd, -lənd) n. the criminal underworld.

gangling (ˈgæŋglɪŋ) or **gangly** adj. lanky

and awkward in movement. [see GANG²]

ganglion ('gæŋglɪən) n., pl. **-glia** (-glɪə) or **-glions.** a collection of nerve cells outside the brain and spinal cord. [Greek: cystic tumour] —**gangli'onic** adj.

gangplank ('gæŋ,plæŋk) n. Naut. a portable bridge for boarding and leaving a ship.

gangrene ('gæŋgriːn) n. **1.** decay of tissue due to the blood supply being interrupted by disease or injury. ~vb. **2.** to affect or become affected with gangrene. [Greek gangraina an eating sore] —**gangrenous** ('gæŋgrɪnəs) adj.

gangster ('gæŋstə) n. a member of an organized gang of criminals.

gangue (gæŋ) n. valueless material in an ore. [German Gang vein of metal, course]

gang up vb. (often foll. by on or against) Informal. to combine in a group (against).

gangway ('gæŋ,weɪ) n. **1.** same as **gangplank.** **2.** an opening in a ship's side to take a gangplank. **3.** Brit. an aisle between rows of seats. ~interj. **4.** clear a path!

gannet ('gænɪt) n. **1.** a heavily built marine bird with white plumage and dark wingtips. **2.** Slang. a greedy person. [Old English ganot]

ganoid ('gænɔɪd) adj. **1.** (of the scales of certain fishes) consisting of an inner bony layer covered with an enamel-like substance. **2.** (of a fish) having such scales. ~n. **3.** a ganoid fish. [Greek ganos brightness]

gantry ('gæntrɪ) n., pl. **-tries.** **1.** a bridgelike framework used to support something, such as a travelling crane or signals over a railway track. **2.** the framework tower used to position and service a large rocket on its launching pad. [Latin cantherius supporting frame, pack ass]

gaol (dʒeɪl) n., vb. Brit. same as **jail.** —**'gaoler** n.

gap (gæp) n. **1.** a break or opening in something. **2.** a break in continuity; interruption; interval. **3.** Chiefly U.S. a gorge or ravine. **4.** a divergence or difference; disparity: the generation gap. [Old Norse] —**'gappy** adj.

gape (geɪp) vb. **1.** to stare in wonder with the mouth open. **2.** to open the mouth wide, as in yawning. **3.** to be or become wide open: the crater gaped under his feet. ~n. **4.** a wide opening. **5.** a stare of astonishment. [Old Norse gapa] —**'gaping** adj.

garage ('gærɑːʒ, -rɪdʒ) n. **1.** a building used to house motor vehicles. **2.** an establishment in which vehicles are sold and repaired, and which also sells petrol and diesel oil. ~vb. **3.** to put into or keep in a garage. [French]

garage sale n. a sale of household items held at a person's home, usually in the garage.

garb (gɑːb) n. **1.** clothes, usually the distinctive attire of an occupation or group: clerical garb. **2.** external appearance. ~vb. **3.** to clothe. [Old French]

garbage ('gɑːbɪdʒ) n. **1.** worthless, useless, or unwanted matter. **2.** U.S. & Canad. rubbish. [prob. from Anglo-French]

garble ('gɑːbʰl) vb. **1.** to jumble (a story or quotation) unintentionally. **2.** to distort the meaning of (a text) by making misleading omissions. [Old Italian garbellare to strain, sift]

garçon (gɑː'sɒn) n. a waiter. [French]

garda ('gɑːdə) n., pl. **gardai** ('gɑːdɪ). a member of the police force of the Republic of Ireland. [Irish Gaelic: guard]

garden ('gɑːdʰn) n. **1.** Brit. an area of land usually next to a house, for growing flowers, fruit, or vegetables. **2.** (often pl.) a cultivated area of land open to the public, sometimes part of a park: botanical gardens. **3. lead (a person) up the garden path.** Informal. to mislead or deceive. ~vb. **4.** to work in or take care of (a garden or plot of land). [Old French gardin] —**'gardener** n. —**'gardening** n.

garden centre n. a place where gardening tools and equipment, and plants are sold.

garden city n. Brit. a planned town of limited size surrounded by countryside.

gardenia (gɑː'diːnɪə) n. **1.** an evergreen shrub or tree cultivated for its large fragrant waxy white flowers. **2.** its flower. [after Dr Alexander Garden, botanist]

gargantuan (gɑː'gæntjʊən) adj. huge; enormous. [after Gargantua, a giant in Rabelais' Gargantua and Pantagruel]

gargle ('gɑːgʰl) vb. **1.** to rinse the mouth and throat with (a liquid) by slowly breathing out through the liquid. ~n. **2.** the liquid used for gargling. **3.** the sound made by gargling. [Old French gargouille throat]

gargoyle ('gɑːgɔɪl) n. a waterspout carved in the form of a grotesque face or figure and projecting from a roof gutter. [Old French gargouille gargoyle, throat]

garish ('gɛərɪʃ) adj. crudely bright or colourful; gaudy. [obs. gaure to stare] —**'garishly** adv. —**'garishness** n.

garland ('gɑːlənd) n. **1.** a wreath of flowers and leaves worn round the head or neck or hung up. ~vb. **2.** to adorn with a garland or garlands. [Old French garlande]

garlic ('gɑːlɪk) n. the bulb of a plant of the onion family, made up of small, pungent, strong-smelling segments, that are used in cooking. [Old English gārlēac] —**'garlicky** adj.

garment ('gɑːmənt) n. **1.** (often pl.) an article of clothing. **2.** outer covering. [Old French garniment]

garner ('gɑːnə) vb. to gather or store as in a granary. [Latin grānum grain]

garnet ('gɑːnɪt) n. a hard glassy red, yellow, or green silicate mineral: its red form is used as a gemstone. [Old French grenat red, from pome grenate POMEGRANATE]

garnish ('gɑːnɪʃ) vb. **1.** to decorate; trim. **2.** to decorate (food) with something to improve its appearance or flavour. ~n. **3.** a decoration; trimming. **4.** something added to food to improve its appearance or its flavour. [Old French garnir to adorn, equip]

garret ('gærɪt) n. an attic in a house. [Old French: watchtower]

garrison ('gærɪsˀn) n. **1.** the troops who maintain and guard a base or fort. **2.** the place itself. ~vb. **3.** to station (troops) in (a fort or base). [Old French garir to defend]

garrotte or **garotte** (gə'rɒt) n. **1.** a Spanish method of execution by strangling. **2.** a cord, wire, or iron collar, used to strangle someone. ~vb. **3.** to execute with the garrotte. **4.** to strangle. [Spanish garrote]

garrulous ('gærʊləs) adj. constantly chattering; talkative. [Latin garrīre to chatter] —'**garrulousness** or **garrulity** (gæ'ruːlɪtɪ) n.

garter ('gɑːtə) n. **1.** a band, usually of elastic, worn round the leg to hold up a sock or stocking. **2.** U.S. & Canad. a suspender. [Old French gartier]

Garter ('gɑːtə) n. **the Order of the Garter.** the highest order of British knighthood.

garter stitch n. knitting in which all the rows are knitted in plain stitch.

gas (gæs) n., pl. **gases** or **gasses**. **1.** a substance which does not resist change of shape and will expand indefinitely to fill any container. **2.** any substance that is gaseous at room temperature and atmospheric pressure. **3.** a fossil fuel in the form of a gas, used as a source of heat. **4.** a gaseous anaesthetic. **5.** Mining. firedamp or the explosive mixture of firedamp and air. **6.** U.S., Canad., Austral., & N.Z. petrol. **7. step on the gas.** Informal. **a.** to accelerate a motor vehicle. **b.** to hurry. **8.** a poisonous gas used against an enemy or rioters. **9.** Informal. idle talk or boasting. **10.** Slang. an entertaining person or thing: his latest record is a gas. ~vb. **gases** or **gasses, gassing, gassed. 11.** to subject to gas fumes so as to asphyxiate or render unconscious. **12.** Informal. to talk in an idle or boastful way. [coined from Greek khaos atmosphere]

gasbag ('gæs,bæg) n. Informal. a person who talks idly or too much.

gas chamber or **oven** n. an airtight room which is filled with poison gas to kill people or animals.

gaseous ('gæsɪəs, -ʃəs, -ʃɪəs, 'geɪ-) adj. of or like a gas.

gas gangrene n. gangrene resulting from infection of a wound by bacteria that cause gas bubbles in the surrounding tissues.

gash (gæʃ) vb. **1.** to make a long deep cut in; slash. ~n. **2.** a long deep cut. [Old French garser to scratch; wound]

gasholder ('gæs,həʊldə) n. a large tank for storing gas prior to distribution to users.

gasify ('gæsɪ,faɪ) vb. **-fying, -fied.** to change into a gas. —,**gasifi'cation** n.

gasket ('gæskɪt) n. a piece of paper, rubber, or metal sandwiched between the faces of a metal joint to provide a seal. [prob. from French garcette rope's end]

gaslight ('gæs,laɪt) n. **1.** a lamp in which light is produced by burning gas. **2.** the light produced by such a lamp.

gasman ('gæs,mæn) n., pl. **-men.** a man employed to read household gas meters and install or repair gas fittings, etc.

gas mask n. a mask fitted with a chemical filter to protect the wearer from breathing in harmful gases.

gas meter n. an apparatus for measuring and recording the amount of gas passed through it.

gasoline or **gasolene** ('gæsə,liːn) n. U.S. & Canad. petrol.

gasometer (gæs'ɒmɪtə) n. same as **gasholder.**

gasp (gɑːsp) vb. **1.** to draw in the breath sharply or with difficulty. **2.** (foll. by after or for) to crave. **3.** to utter breathlessly. ~n. **4.** a short convulsive intake of breath. [Old Norse geispa to yawn]

gas ring n. a hollow perforated metal ring fed with gas for cooking.

gassy ('gæsɪ) adj. **-sier, -siest. 1.** filled with, containing, or resembling gas. **2.** Informal. full of idle or vapid talk. —'**gassiness** n.

gastric ('gæstrɪk) adj. of the stomach.

gastric juice n. a digestive fluid secreted by the stomach.

gastric ulcer n. an ulcer of the mucous membrane lining the stomach.

gastritis (gæs'traɪtɪs) n. inflammation of the stomach.

gastroenteritis (,gæstrəʊ,entə'raɪtɪs) n. inflammation of the stomach and intestines.

gastronomy (gæs'trɒnəmɪ) n. the art of good eating. [Greek gastēr stomach + nomos law] —**gastronomic** (,gæstrə-'nɒmɪk) adj.

gastropod ('gæstrə,pɒd) or **gasteropod** n. a mollusc, such as a snail, whelk, or slug, having a single flattened muscular foot. [Greek gastēr stomach + -podos footed] —**gastropodous** (gæs'trɒpədəs) adj.

gasworks ('gæs,wɜːks) n. (functioning as sing.) a plant in which coal gas is made.

gate (geɪt) n. **1.** a movable barrier, usually hinged, for closing an opening in a wall or fence. **2.** an opening where there is a gate. **3.** any means of entrance or access. **4. a.** the number of people admitted to a sporting event or entertainment. **b.** the total entrance money received from them. **5.** Electronics. a circuit having one or more input terminals and one output terminal, the output being determined by the combination of input signals. **6.** a slotted metal frame that controls the positions of the gear lever in a motor vehicle. [Old English geat]

gâteau ('gætəʊ) n., pl. **-teaux** (-təʊz). a large rich layered cake. [French]

gate-crash vb. Informal. to gain entry to (a party or other event) without invitation. —'**gate-,crasher** n.

gatehouse ('geɪt,haʊs) n. a building at or above a gateway.

gate-leg table or **gate-legged table** n. a table with leaves supported by hinged legs that can swing back to let the leaves drop from the frame.

gateway ('geɪtˌweɪ) n. 1. an entrance that may be closed by a gate. 2. a means of entry or access: *Bombay, gateway to India.*

gather ('gæðə) vb. 1. to assemble. 2. to collect or be collected gradually. 3. to learn from information given; conclude. 4. to pick or harvest. 5. to bring close (to). 6. to increase gradually in force, speed, or intensity. 7. to wrinkle (one's brow). 8. to prepare or make ready: *to gather one's wits.* 9. to draw (material) into small folds or tucks. 10. (of a boil or other sore) to come to a head; form pus. ~n. 11. a small fold in material; tuck. [Old English *gadrian*]

gathering ('gæðərɪŋ) n. 1. a group of people or things that are gathered together; assembly. 2. *Sewing.* a series of gathers in material.

GATT (gæt) n. General Agreement on Tariffs and Trade.

gauche (gəʊʃ) adj. lacking ease of manner; socially awkward. [French] —**gaucherie** (ˌgəʊʃə'riː, 'gəʊʃərɪ) n.

gaucho ('gaʊtʃəʊ) n., pl. -chos. a cowboy of the South American pampas. [American Spanish]

gaudy ('gɔːdɪ) adj. gaudier, gaudiest. bright or colourful in a vulgar manner. [Middle English *gaude* trinket] —**gaudily** adv. —**gaudiness** n.

gauge (geɪdʒ) vb. 1. to measure the amount or condition of. 2. to estimate; judge. ~n. 3. a scale or standard of measurement. 4. an instrument for measuring a quantity: *a pressure gauge.* 5. a standard or means for assessing. 6. capacity or extent. 7. the diameter of the barrel of a gun. 8. the thickness of sheet metal or the diameter of wire. 9. the distance between the rails of a railway track or between parallel wheels. 10. a measure of the fineness of woven or knitted fabric. [Old French] —**gaugeable** adj.

Gaul (gɔːl) n. 1. a native of ancient Gaul. 2. a Frenchman.

gaunt (gɔːnt) adj. 1. bony and emaciated in appearance. 2. (of places) bleak or desolate. [origin unknown] —**gauntness** n.

gauntlet[1] ('gɔːntlɪt) n. 1. a medieval armoured glove. 2. a heavy glove with a long cuff. 3. **take up** (or **throw down**) **the gauntlet.** to accept (or offer) a challenge. [Old French *gantelet*]

gauntlet[2] ('gɔːntlɪt) n. **run the gauntlet. a.** to be forced to run between, and be struck by, two rows of men: a former military punishment. **b.** to endure an onslaught, as of criticism. [Swedish *gatlopp* passageway]

gauss (gaʊs) n., pl. gauss. the cgs unit of magnetic flux density. [after K. F. *Gauss,* mathematician]

gauze (gɔːz) n. 1. a transparent, loosely-woven cloth. 2. any thin openwork material, such as wire. [French *gaze*] —**gauzy** adj.

gave (geɪv) vb. the past tense of **give.**

gavel ('gævəl) n. a small hammer used by a judge, auctioneer, or chairman to call for order or attention. [origin unknown]

gavotte or **gavot** (gə'vɒt) n. 1. an old formal dance in quadruple time. 2. music for this dance. [French]

gawk (gɔːk) vb. 1. to stare stupidly; gape. ~n. 2. a clumsy stupid person. [Old Danish *gaukr*]

gawky ('gɔːkɪ) adj. gawkier, gawkiest. clumsy or ungainly; awkward. —**gawkiness** n.

gawp (gɔːp) vb. (often foll. by *at*) *Brit. slang.* to stare stupidly; gape. [Middle English *galpen*]

gay (geɪ) adj. 1. **a.** homosexual. **b.** (*as n.*): *a group of gays.* 2. carefree and merry: *a gay temperament.* 3. brightly coloured: *a gay hat.* 4. licentious. [Old French *gai*] —**gayness** n.

gaze (geɪz) vb. 1. to look long and fixedly. ~n. 2. a fixed look. [Swedish dialect *gasa* to gape at]

gazebo (gə'ziːbəʊ) n., pl. -bos or -boes. a summerhouse or pavilion with a good view. [perhaps a pseudo-Latin coinage based on *gaze*]

gazelle (gə'zɛl) n., pl. -zelles or -zelle. a small graceful usually fawn-coloured antelope of Africa and Asia. [Arabic *ghazāl*]

gazette (gə'zɛt) n. 1. a newspaper. 2. *Brit.* an official publication containing announcements. ~vb. 3. *Brit.* to announce something in a gazette. [French]

gazetteer (ˌgæzɪ'tɪə) n. a book or section of a book that lists and describes places.

gazump (gə'zʌmp) vb. *Brit.* to raise the price of a house after agreeing a price verbally with (an intending buyer). [origin unknown]

GB Great Britain.

GBE (Knight or Dame) Grand Cross of the British Empire (a Brit. title).

GBH grievous bodily harm.

GC George Cross (a Brit. award for bravery).

GCB (Knight) Grand Cross of the Bath (a Brit. title).

GCE (in Britain) 1. General Certificate of Education. 2. *Informal.* any subject taken for a GCE examination.

GCMG (Knight or Dame) Grand Cross of the Order of St Michael and St George (a Brit. title).

GCSE (in Britain) General Certificate of Secondary Education.

GCVO (Knight or Dame) Grand Cross of the Royal Victorian Order (a Brit. title).

Gd *Chem.* gadolinium.

GDP gross domestic product.

Ge *Chem.* germanium.

gear (gɪə) n. 1. a toothed wheel that engages with another or with a rack in order to change the speed or direction of transmitted motion. 2. a mechanism for transmitting motion by gears. 3. the engagement or particular setting of a system of gears: *in gear; high gear.* 4. clothing or personal belongings. 5. equipment for a particular task. 6. **out of gear.** out of order. ~vb. 7. to adapt (one thing) so as to fit in with another: *to gear our output to current demand*. **8.** to equip with or connect by gears. [Old Norse *gervi*]

gearbox ('gɪə,bɒks) *n*. the metal casing enclosing a set of gears in a motor vehicle.

gearing ('gɪərɪŋ) *n*. a system of gears designed to transmit motion.

gear lever or *U.S.* or *Canad.* **gearshift** ('gɪə,ʃɪft) *n*. a lever used to engage or change gears in a motor vehicle.

gearwheel ('gɪə,wiːl) *n.* same as **gear** (sense 1).

gecko ('gɛkəʊ) *n., pl.* **geckos** or **geckoes**. a small tropical lizard. [Malay *ge'kok*]

gee[1] (dʒiː) *interj.* an exclamation to a horse to encourage it to start or go faster. Also: **gee up!** [origin unknown]

gee[2] (dʒiː) *interj. U.S. & Canad. informal.* a mild exclamation. Also: **gee whiz**. [euphemism for *Jesus*]

geelbek ('xiːl,bɛk) *n. S. African.* an edible marine fish with yellow jaws. [Afrikaans]

geese (giːs) *n.* the plural of **goose**[1].

geezer ('giːzə) *n. Informal.* a man, usually an eccentric old man. [prob. dialect pronunciation of *guiser*, a mummer]

Geiger counter ('gaɪgə) or **Geiger-Müller counter** ('mʊlə) *n.* an instrument for detecting and measuring radiation. [after Hans *Geiger*, physicist]

geisha ('geɪʃə) *n., pl.* **-sha** or **-shas.** a professional female companion for men in Japan, trained in music, dancing, and conversation. [Japanese]

gel (dʒɛl) *n.* **1.** jelly-like colloid in which a liquid is dispersed through a solid: *nondrip paint is a gel.* ~*vb.* **gelling, gelled. 2.** to become or cause to become a gel. **3.** same as **jell.** [from *gelatin*]

gelatin ('dʒɛlətɪn) or **gelatine** ('dʒɛlə,tiːn) *n.* **1.** a clear water-soluble protein made by boiling animal hides and bones: used in foods, glue, and photographic emulsions. **2.** an edible jelly made of this. [Latin *gelāre* to freeze]

gelatinize or **-ise** (dʒɪ'lætɪ,naɪz) *vb.* to make or become gelatinous. —**ge,latini-'zation** or **-i'sation** *n.*

gelatinous (dʒɪ'lætɪnəs) *adj.* of or like jelly.

geld (gɛld) *vb.* **gelding, gelded** or **gelt** (gɛlt). to castrate (a horse or other animal). [Old Norse *geldr* barren]

gelding ('gɛldɪŋ) *n.* a castrated male horse. [Old Norse *geldingr*]

gelignite ('dʒɛlɪg,naɪt) *n.* a type of dynamite used for blasting. [*gelatin* + Latin *ignis* fire]

gem (dʒɛm) *n.* **1.** a precious stone used as a decoration; jewel. **2.** a highly-valued person or thing. ~*vb.* **gemming, gemmed. 3.** to ornament with gems. [Latin *gemma* bud, precious stone] —**'gemmy** *adj.*

geminate *adj.* ('dʒɛmɪnɪt, -,neɪt). **1.** combined in pairs: *a geminate leaf.* ~*vb.* ('dʒɛmɪ,neɪt). **2.** to arrange or be arranged in pairs. [Latin *gemināre* to double] —**,gemi'nation** *n.*

Gemini ('dʒɛmɪ,naɪ, -,niː) *n.* the third sign of the zodiac; the Twins.

gemma ('dʒɛmə) *n., pl.* **-mae** (-miː). a budlike outgrowth in mosses that detaches from the parent and grows into a new individual. [Latin: bud]

gen (dʒɛn) *n. Brit. informal.* information: *give me the gen on your latest project.* See also **gen up.** [from gen(*eral information*)]

Gen. General.

-gen *suffix forming nouns.* **1.** producing or that which produces: *hydrogen.* **2.** something produced: *carcinogen.* [Greek *-genēs* born]

gendarme ('ʒɒndɑːm) *n.* a member of the French police force. [French]

gender ('dʒɛndə) *n.* **1.** the classification of nouns in certain languages as masculine, feminine, or neuter. **2.** *Informal.* the state of being male, female, or neuter. [Latin *genus* kind]

gene (dʒiːn) *n.* a unit composed of DNA forming part of a chromosome, by which inherited characteristics are transmitted from parent to offspring. [German *Gen*]

-gene *suffix forming nouns.* same as **-gen.**

genealogy (,dʒiːnɪ'ælədʒɪ) *n., pl.* **-gies. 1.** the direct descent of an individual or group from an ancestor. **2.** the study of the evolutionary development of animals and plants. **3.** a chart showing the descent of an individual or group. [Greek *genea* race] —**genealogical** (,dʒiːnɪə'lɒdʒɪk[ə]l) *adj.* —**,gene'alogist** *n.*

general ('dʒɛnərəl, 'dʒɛnrəl) *adj.* **1.** common; widespread. **2.** of, affecting, or including all or most of the members of a group. **3.** not specialized: *general office work.* **4.** including various or miscellaneous items: *general knowledge; a general store.* **5.** not definite; vague: *the general idea.* **6.** true in most cases; usual. **7.** highest in authority or rank: *general manager; consul general.* ~*n.* **8.** a very senior military officer. **9.** the head of a religious order. **10.** *in general.* generally; mostly or usually. [Latin *generālis*]

general anaesthetic *n.* See **anaesthesia.**

general election *n.* **1.** an election in which representatives are chosen in all constituencies of a state. **2.** *U.S. & Canad.* a national, state, or provincial election.

generalissimo (,dʒɛnərə'lɪsɪ,məʊ, ,dʒɛnrə-) *n., pl.* **-mos.** a supreme commander of combined armed forces. [Italian]

generality (,dʒɛnə'rælɪtɪ) *n., pl.* **-ties. 1.** a principle or observation having general application. **2.** the state of being general. **3.** *Archaic.* the majority.

generalization or **-isation** (,dʒɛnrəlaɪ-'zeɪʃən) *n.* **1.** a principle or statement with general application. **2.** a generalizing.

generalize or **-ise** ('dʒɛnrə,laɪz) *vb.* **1.** to form (general principles or conclusions) from (specific instances); infer. **2.** to speak in generalities. **3.** (*usually passive*) to make widely used or known.

generally ('dʒɛnrəlɪ) *adv.* **1.** usually; as a rule. **2.** commonly or widely. **3.** not specifically; broadly.

general practitioner *n.* a doctor who

does not specialize but has a medical practice (**general practice**) in which he treats all illnesses.

general-purpose adj. having a variety of uses.

general staff n. officers who assist commanders in the planning and execution of military operations.

general strike n. a strike by all or most of the workers of a country, area, or town.

generate ('dʒɛnəˌreɪt) vb. to produce or bring into being; create. [Latin generāre to beget]

generation (ˌdʒɛnə'reɪʃən) n. 1. production or reproduction. 2. a successive stage in descent of people or animals. 3. the average time between two generations of a species: about 35 years for humans. 4. all the people of approximately the same age. 5. production of electricity or heat. 6. (modifier) belonging to a specified generation or stage of development: a third-generation American; a second-generation computer.

generation gap n. the difference in outlook and the lack of understanding between people of different generations.

generative ('dʒɛnərətɪv) adj. 1. of production. 2. capable of producing or originating.

generator ('dʒɛnəˌreɪtə) n. 1. a device for converting mechanical energy into electrical energy. 2. an apparatus for producing a gas.

generic (dʒɪ'nɛrɪk) adj. 1. of a whole class or group; general. 2. Biol. of a genus: the generic name. [Latin genus kind, race]

generosity (ˌdʒɛnə'rɒsɪtɪ) n., pl. -ties. 1. the quality of being generous. 2. a generous act.

generous ('dʒɛnərəs, 'dʒɛnrəs) adj. 1. ready to give freely; unselfish. 2. free from pettiness in character and mind. 3. full or plentiful: a generous portion. [Latin generōsus nobly born] —'**generously** adv.

genesis ('dʒɛnɪsɪs) n., pl. -ses (-ˌsiːz). a beginning or origin of anything. [Greek]

Genesis ('dʒɛnɪsɪs) n. the first book of the Bible.

genetic (dʒɪ'nɛtɪk) adj. of genetics, genes, or the origin of something. [from genesis] —ge'**netically** adv.

genetic code n. Biochem. the order in which the four nucleic acid bases of DNA are arranged in the molecule for transmitting genetic information to the cells.

genetic engineering n. alteration of the DNA of a cell as a means of manufacturing animal proteins or producing new breeds of plants or animals.

genetic fingerprinting n. the use of a person's unique pattern of DNA, which can be obtained from blood, saliva, or tissue, as a means of identification. —**genetic fingerprint** n.

genetics (dʒɪ'nɛtɪks) n. (functioning as sing.) the study of heredity and variation in organisms. —ge'**neticist** n.

Geneva Convention (dʒɪ'niːvə) n. the international agreement formulated in 1864 at Geneva, establishing a code for wartime treatment of the sick, wounded, and prisoners of war.

genial ('dʒiːnjəl, -nɪəl) adj. 1. cheerful, easy-going, and friendly. 2. pleasantly warm, so as to give life, growth, or health. [Latin genius guardian deity] —**geniality** (ˌdʒiːnɪ'ælɪtɪ) n. —'**genially** adv.

genie ('dʒiːnɪ) n., pl. -nies or -nii (-nɪˌaɪ). 1. (in fairy stories) a servant who appears by magic and fulfils a person's wishes. 2. same as **jinni**. [Arabic jinni demon]

genital ('dʒɛnɪtˈl) adj. of the sexual organs or reproduction. [Latin genitālis concerning birth]

genitals ('dʒɛnɪtˈlz) or **genitalia** (ˌdʒɛnɪ'teɪlɪə, -'teɪljə) pl. n. the external sexual organs.

genitive ('dʒɛnɪtɪv) Grammar. ~adj. 1. denoting a grammatical case used to indicate a relation of ownership or association. ~n. 2. a. the genitive case. b. a word in this case. [Latin genetivus relating to birth]

genius ('dʒiːnɪəs, -njəs) n., pl. -uses or (for sense 5) **genii** ('dʒiːnɪˌaɪ). 1. a person with exceptional ability in a particular subject or activity. 2. such ability. 3. the distinctive spirit of something. 4. a person considered as exerting influence of a certain sort: an evil genius. 5. Roman myth. a. the guiding spirit who attends a person from birth to death. b. the guardian spirit of a place. [Latin]

genocide ('dʒɛnəʊˌsaɪd) n. the deliberate killing of a people or nation. [Greek genos race + Latin caedere to kill] —ˌgeno'**cid-al** adj.

genre ('ʒɑːnrə) n. 1. kind or type of literary, musical, or artistic work. 2. a kind of painting depicting incidents from everyday life. [French]

gent (dʒɛnt) n. Informal. short for **gentle-man**.

genteel (dʒɛn'tiːl) adj. 1. affectedly proper, refined, or polite. 2. respectable, polite, and well-bred. 3. appropriate to polite or fashionable society. [French gentil well-born] —gen'**teelly** adv.

gentian ('dʒɛnʃən) n. a mountain plant with usually blue showy flowers. [Latin gentiāna]

gentian violet n. a violet solution used as an antiseptic and in the treatment of burns.

Gentile ('dʒɛntaɪl) n. 1. a person who is not a Jew. 2. a heathen or pagan. ~adj. 3. not Jewish. 4. pagan or heathen. [Latin gentilis belonging to the same tribe]

gentility (dʒɛn'tɪlɪtɪ) n., pl. -ties. 1. respectability and good manners. 2. affected politeness. 3. noble birth or ancestry. [Old French]

gentle ('dʒɛntˈl) adj. 1. mild or kindly in character. 2. temperate; moderate: a gentle breeze. 3. gradual: a gentle slope. 4. easily controlled; tame. 5. Archaic. of good breeding; noble: gentle blood. 6. Archaic. gallant; chivalrous. [Latin gentilis belonging to the same family] —**'gentleness** n. —**'gently** adv.

gentlefolk ('dʒɛnt'l,fəuk) or **gentlefolks** pl. n. people regarded as being of good breeding.

gentleman ('dʒɛnt'lmən) n., pl. **-men**. **1.** a man who comes from a family of high social position. **2.** a cultured, courteous, and well-bred man. **3.** a polite name for a man. —**'gentlemanly** adj.

gentrification (,dʒɛntrɪfɪ'keɪʃən) n. Brit. a process by which middle-class people take up residence in a traditionally working-class area, changing its character. —**'gentri,fy** vb.

gentry ('dʒɛntrɪ) n. **1.** Brit. persons just below the nobility in social rank. **2.** people of a particular class, usually one considered to be inferior. [Old French genterie]

gents (dʒɛnts) n. (functioning as sing.) Brit. informal. a men's public lavatory.

genuflect ('dʒɛnju,flɛkt) vb. to bend the knee as a sign of reverence or deference. [Latin genu knee + flectere to bend] —**,genu'flection** or esp. Brit. **,genu'flexion** n.

genuine ('dʒɛnjuɪn) adj. **1.** not fake; authentic. **2.** sincere. [Latin genuīnus inborn] —**'genuinely** adv. —**'genuineness** n.

gen up vb. **genning, genned.** (often foll. by on) Brit. informal. to make or become fully informed (about).

genus ('dʒiːnəs) n., pl. **genera** ('dʒɛnərə) or **genuses**. **1.** Biol. a group into which a family of animals or plants is divided and which contains one or more species. **2.** Logic. a class of objects that can be divided into two or more groups. **3.** a class or group. [Latin: race]

geocentric (,dʒiːəʊ'sɛntrɪk) adj. **1.** having the earth as its centre. **2.** measured as from the centre of the earth.

geode ('dʒiːəʊd) n. a cavity, lined with crystals, within a rock. [Greek geoeidēs earthlike] —**geodic** (dʒiː'ɒdɪk) adj.

geodesic (,dʒiːəʊ'dɛsɪk, -'diː-) adj. **1.** relating to the geometry of curved surfaces. ~n. **2.** the shortest line between two points on a curved surface.

geodesy (dʒiː'ɒdɪsɪ) n. the study of the shape and size of the earth. [Greek gē earth + daiein to divide] —**ge'odesist** n.

geog. **1.** geographic(al). **2.** geography.

geographical mile n. same as **nautical mile**.

geography (dʒɪ'ɒɡrəfɪ) n., pl. **-phies**. **1.** the study of the earth's surface, including physical features, climate, and population. **2.** the physical features of a region. [Greek gē earth + -GRAPHY] —**ge'ographer** n. —**geographical** (,dʒɪə'ɡræfɪk'l) or **geo'graphic** adj.

geoid ('dʒiːɔɪd) n. the earth considered as a hypothetical ellipsoid with its surface corresponding to the mean sea level.

geol. **1.** geologic(al). **2.** geologist. **3.** geology.

geology (dʒɪ'ɒlədʒɪ) n. **1.** the study of the origin, structure, and composition of the earth. **2.** the geological features of an area. [Greek gē earth + -LOGY] —**geological** (,dʒɪə'lɒdʒɪk'l) or **,geo'logic** adj. —**ge'ologist** n.

geometric (,dʒɪə'mɛtrɪk) or **geometrical** adj. **1.** of geometry. **2.** consisting of or characterized by geometric forms, such as circles, triangles, and straight lines. —**,geo'metrically** adv.

geometric progression n. a sequence of numbers, each of which differs from the succeeding one by a constant ratio, as 1, 2, 4, 8, ...

geometry (dʒɪ'ɒmɪtrɪ) n. the branch of mathematics concerned with points, lines, curves, and surfaces. [Greek geōmetrein to measure the land] —**ge,ome'trician** n.

Geordie ('dʒɔːdɪ) n. Brit. **1.** a person from Tyneside. **2.** the Tyneside dialect.

George Cross (dʒɔːdʒ) n. a British award for bravery, esp. of civilians.

georgette or **georgette crepe** (dʒɔː-'dʒɛt) n. a thin crepe fabric. [after Mme Georgette, a French dressmaker]

Georgian ('dʒɔːdʒən) adj. **1.** of any of the kings of Great Britain called George, or their reigns (1714-1830; 1910-52): Georgian architecture. **2.** of the Georgian SSR, its people, or their language. **3.** of Georgia, U.S., or its inhabitants. **4.** (of furniture) in the style prevalent in Britain during the 18th century. ~n. **5.** the official language of the Georgian SSR. **6.** a person from the Georgian SSR. **7.** a person from Georgia, U.S.

geostationary (,dʒiːəʊ'steɪʃənərɪ) adj. (of a satellite) orbiting so as to remain over the same point on the earth's surface.

geothermal (,dʒiːəʊ'θɜːməl) adj. of or using the heat in the earth's interior.

geotropism (dʒɪ'ɒtrə,pɪzəm) n. the response of a plant part to the force of gravity. [Greek gē earth + tropos a turning] —**geotropic** (,dʒiːəʊ'trɒpɪk) adj.

geranium (dʒɪ'reɪnɪəm) n. **1.** a cultivated plant of the pelargonium family, having scarlet, pink, or white showy flowers. **2.** a plant having divided leaves and pink or purplish flowers. [Latin: cranesbill]

gerbil ('dʒɜːbɪl) n. a burrowing rodent of the deserts of Asia and Africa. [French]

gerfalcon ('dʒɜː,fɔːlkən, -,fɔːkən) n. same as **gyrfalcon**.

geriatrics (,dʒɛrɪ'ætrɪks) n. (functioning as sing.) the branch of medicine concerned with the diseases affecting elderly people. —**,geri'atric** n., adj. —**,geria'trician** n.

germ (dʒɜːm) n. **1.** a microorganism, usually one that causes disease. **2.** (often pl.) the beginning form of something which may develop: the germs of revolution. **3.** a simple structure that can develop into a complete organism. [Latin germen sprout, seed]

german ('dʒɜːmən) adj. **1.** having the same parents as oneself: brother-german. **2.** being a first cousin: cousin-german. [Latin germānus of the same race]

German ('dʒɜːmən) n. **1.** the language of East and West Germany and Austria and one of the languages of Switzerland. **2.** a

person from East or West Germany. ~*adj.*
3. of Germany, its people, or their language.

germander (dʒɜːˈmændə) *n.* a European plant having two-lipped flowers with a very small upper lip. [Greek *khamai* on the ground + *drus* oak tree]

germane (dʒɜːˈmeɪn) *adj.* (usually foll. by *to*) relevant. [var. of *german*]

Germanic (dʒɜːˈmænɪk) *n.* **1.** a branch of the Indo-European family of languages that includes English, German, and the Scandinavian languages. **2.** the language from which these languages developed. ~*adj.* **3.** of this group of languages. **4.** of the German language or any people that speaks a Germanic language. **5.** (formerly) German.

germanium (dʒɜːˈmeɪnɪəm) *n.* a brittle grey metalloid element that is a semiconductor: used in transistors. Symbol: Ge [after *Germany*]

German measles *n.* (functioning as sing.) same as **rubella.**

German shepherd dog *n.* same as **Alsatian.**

German silver *n.* same as **nickel silver.**

germ cell *n.* a sexual reproductive cell.

germicide (ˈdʒɜːmɪˌsaɪd) *n.* a substance that kills germs. [*germ* + Latin *caedere* to kill] —ˌgermiˈcidal *adj.*

germinal (ˈdʒɜːmɪnˀl) *adj.* **1.** of or like germs or a germ cell. **2.** of or in the earliest stage of development.

germinate (ˈdʒɜːmɪˌneɪt) *vb.* **1.** to sprout or to cause (a seed) to sprout. **2.** to grow or cause to grow; develop. [Latin *germināre* to sprout] —ˈgerminative *adj.* —ˌgermiˈnation *n.*

germ warfare *n.* the military use of disease-spreading bacteria against an enemy.

gerontology (ˌdʒɛrɒnˈtɒlədʒɪ) *n.* the scientific study of ageing and the problems of elderly people. [Greek *gerōn* old man + -LOGY] —ˌgeronˈtologist *n.*

gerrymander (ˈdʒɛrɪˌmændə) *vb.* **1.** to divide the constituencies of (a voting area) so as to give one party an unfair advantage. ~*n.* **2.** a gerrymandering. [from Elbridge *Gerry*, U.S. politician + (*sala*)*mander*, from the salamander-like outline of a reshaped electoral district]

gerund (ˈdʒɛrənd) *n.* a noun formed from a verb, ending in *-ing*, denoting an action or state. [Latin *gerundum* something to be carried on]

gerundive (dʒɪˈrʌndɪv) *n.* (in Latin grammar) an adjective formed from a verb, with the sense "that should be done". [Late Latin *gerundium* gerund]

gesso (ˈdʒɛsəʊ) *n.* plaster used for painting or in sculpture. [Italian]

Gestapo (ɡɛˈstɑːpəʊ) *n.* the secret state police of Nazi Germany. [German *Ge-(heime) Sta(ats)po(lizei)* secret state police]

gestate (ˈdʒɛsteɪt) *vb.* **1.** to carry (a developing young) in the womb during pregnancy. **2.** to develop (a plan or idea) in the

mind. **3.** to be gestating. [Latin *gestare*] —gesˈtation *n.*

gesticulate (dʒɛˈstɪkjʊˌleɪt) *vb.* to express by or make gestures. [Latin *gesticulārī*] —geˌsticuˈlation *n.*

gesture (ˈdʒɛstʃə) *n.* **1.** a motion of the hands, head, or body to express or emphasize an idea or emotion. **2.** something said or done to indicate intention, or as a formality. ~*vb.* **3.** to gesticulate. [Latin *gestus*] —ˈgestural *adj.*

get (ɡɛt) *vb.* **getting, got. 1.** to come into possession of; receive or earn. **2.** to bring or fetch. **3.** to contract (an illness). **4.** to capture or seize: *the police got him.* **5.** to become or cause to become as specified: *to get one's hair cut; get wet.* **6.** to prepare: *to get a meal.* **7.** to hear or understand: *I didn't get your meaning.* **8.** to learn or master by study. **9.** (often foll. by *to*) to come (to) or arrive (at): *we got home safely.* **10.** to catch or enter: *to get a train.* **11.** to persuade: *get him to leave.* **12.** to reach by calculation: *add 2 and 2 and you will get 4.* **13.** to receive a broadcast signal. **14.** to communicate with (a person or place), as by telephone. **15.** (foll. by *to*) *Informal.* to have an emotional effect (on): *that music really gets me.* **16.** *Informal.* to annoy: *her voice gets me.* **17.** *Informal.* to baffle. **18.** *Informal.* to hit: *the blow got him in the back.* **19.** *Informal.* to be revenged on. **20.** *Informal.* to have the better of: *your extravagant habits will get you in the end.* **21.** (foll. by present participle) *Informal.* to begin: *get moving.* **22.** (used as a command) *Informal.* go! **23. get with child.** *Archaic.* to make pregnant. ~*n.* **24.** *Brit. slang.* same as **git.** ~See also **get about, get across,** etc. [Old English *gietan*]

get about *or* **around** *vb.* **1.** to move around. **2.** to be socially active. **3.** (of news or rumour) to circulate.

get across *vb.* to be or cause to be understood.

get at *vb.* **1.** to gain access to. **2.** to imply: *what are you getting at?* **3.** to annoy persistently; criticize: *stop getting at him.* **4.** to try to influence by bribery or threats: *someone had got at the witness before the trial.*

get away *vb.* **1.** to escape; leave. **2.** to start. **3. get away with. a.** to steal and escape with (something). **b.** to do (something wrong) without being caught or punished. ~*interj.* **4.** an exclamation of disbelief. ~*n.* **getaway. 5.** the act of escaping, usually by criminals. **6.** (*modifier*) used to escape: *a getaway car.*

get back *vb.* **1.** to regain. **2.** (often foll. by *to*) to return to a former state or activity. **3.** (foll. by *at*) to retaliate (against). **4. get one's own back.** *Informal.* to get one's revenge.

get by *vb.* **1.** to go past or overtake. **2.** *Informal.* to manage in spite of difficulties. **3.** to be just acceptable. **4.** to be accepted or permitted: *that book will never get by the authorities.*

get in *vb.* **1.** to enter a vehicle. **2.** to arrive. **3.** to bring inside: *get the milk in.*

4. to insert or slip in: *he got his suggestion in before anyone else.* **5.** to gather (crops). **6.** to be elected. **7.** to get a place at university or college. **8.** (foll. by *on*) to join in (an activity).

get off *vb.* **1.** to escape the consequences of an action. **2.** to be or cause to be acquitted. **3.** to leave or move away from or cause to leave or move away from (a thing or place). **4.** to remove: *get your coat off.* **5.** to go to sleep. **6.** to send (letters) or (of letters) to be sent. **7. get off with.** *Brit. informal.* to begin a romantic or sexual relationship (with).

get on *vb.* **1.** Also: **get onto.** to board or cause to board (a vehicle). **2.** to grow late or (of time) to elapse: *it's getting on and I must go.* **3.** to grow old. **4.** (foll. by *for*) to approach (a time, age, or amount): *she is getting on for seventy.* **5.** to make progress, manage, or fare: *how did you get on in your exam?* **6.** (often foll. by *with*) to have a friendly relationship: *he gets on well with people.* **7.** (foll. by *with*) to continue to do: *get on with your work!*

get out *vb.* **1.** to leave or escape or cause to leave or escape. **2.** to make or become known. **3.** to express with difficulty. **4.** to gain something, usually of significance or value: *she got a confession out of him; what do we get out of the deal?* **5.** (foll. by *of*) to avoid or cause to avoid: *she always gets out of swimming.*

get over *vb.* **1.** to cross or surmount (something). **2.** to recover from (an illness or shock). **3.** to overcome (a problem). **4.** to appreciate fully: *I can't get over seeing you again.* **5.** to communicate effectively. **6.** (foll. by *with*) to bring (something necessary but unpleasant) to an end: *let's get this job over with quickly.*

get round *or* **around** *vb.* **1.** to circumvent or overcome. **2.** *Informal.* to win over; cajole: *she can get round anyone.* **3.** (foll. by *to*) to come to at length: *I'll get round to that job in an hour.* **4.** (of information or gossip) to circulate.

get through *vb.* **1.** to succeed or cause to succeed in an examination or test. **2.** to bring or come to a destination after overcoming problems: *we got through the blizzards to the survivors.* **3.** to contact by telephone. **4.** to use up (money or supplies). **5.** to complete or cause to complete (a task or process): *to get a bill through Parliament.* **6.** (foll. by *to*) to succeed in making (a person) understand: *I can't get through to him.*

get-together *n.* **1.** *Informal.* a small informal social gathering. ~*vb.* **get together. 1.** (of people) to meet socially. **2.** to discuss in order to reach an agreement.

get up *vb.* **1.** to rise or cause to rise from bed. **2.** to rise to one's feet; stand up. **3.** to ascend or cause to ascend. **4.** to intensify or cause to intensify: *the wind got up at noon.* **5.** *Informal.* to dress in a particular way, usually elaborately. **6.** *Informal.* to devise or create: *to get up an entertainment for Christmas.* **7.** *Informal.* to study or improve one's knowledge of: *I must get up my history.* **8.** (foll. by *to*) *Informal.* to

be involved in: *he's always getting up to mischief.* ~*n.* **get-up.** *Informal.* **9.** a costume or outfit.

get-up-and-go *n.* *Informal.* energy or drive.

geyser ('gi:zə; *U.S.* 'gaizər) *n.* **1.** a spring that discharges steam and hot water. **2.** *Brit.* a domestic gas water heater. [Icelandic *Geysir*]

ghastly ('gɑ:stlɪ) *adj.* -**lier**, -**liest**. **1.** *Informal.* very unpleasant. **2.** deathly pale. **3.** *Informal.* extremely unwell. **4.** terrifying; horrible. ~*adv.* **5.** unhealthily; sickly: *ghastly pale.* [Old English *gāstlīc* spiritual] —'**ghastliness** *n.*

ghat (gɔ:t) *n.* (in India) **1.** stairs leading down to a river. **2.** a mountain pass. [Hindi]

ghee (gi:) *n.* clarified butter used in Indian cookery. [Hindi]

gherkin ('gɜ:kɪn) *n.* a small pickled cucumber. [Dutch]

ghetto ('gɛtəʊ) *n., pl.* -**tos** *or* -**toes**. **1.** an area of slums inhabited by a deprived minority. **2.** an area or community that is segregated or isolated. **3.** an area in a European city to which Jews were formerly restricted. [Italian]

ghetto blaster *n.* *Informal.* a large portable cassette recorder with built-in speakers.

ghillie ('gɪlɪ) *n.* same as **gillie.**

ghost (gəʊst) *n.* **1.** the disembodied spirit of a dead person, supposed to haunt the living. **2.** a faint trace: *a ghost of a smile.* **3.** a faint secondary image in an optical instrument, esp. one on a television screen. **4. give up the ghost.** to die. ~*vb.* **5.** short for **ghostwrite.** [Old English *gāst*] —'**ghost,like** *adj.* —'**ghostly** *adj.*

ghost town *n.* a deserted town.

ghostwrite ('gəʊst,raɪt) *vb.* -**writing**, -**wrote**, -**written**. to write (an article or book) on behalf of a person who is then credited as author. —'**ghost,writer** *n.*

ghoul (gu:l) *n.* **1.** a person interested in morbid or disgusting things. **2.** (in Muslim legend) a demon that eats corpses. [Arabic *ghūl*] —'**ghoulish** *adj.* —'**ghoulishly** *adv.*

GHQ *Mil.* General Headquarters.

ghyll (gɪl) *n.* same as **gill**³.

GI *n., pl.* **GIs** *or* **GI's.** *U.S. informal.* **1.** a soldier in the U.S. Army. ~*adj.* **2.** of or for the U.S. armed forces. [abbrev. of *government issue*]

giant ('dʒaɪənt) *n.* **1.** Also (fem.): **giantess** ('dʒaɪəntɪs). a mythical figure of superhuman size and strength. **2.** a person or thing of exceptional size, ability, or importance. ~*adj.* **3.** remarkably large. **4.** (of an atom or ion or its structure) having large numbers of particles present in a crystal lattice, with each particle exerting a strong force of attraction on those near to it: *all metals have a giant structure.* [Greek *gigas*]

giant panda *n.* See **panda.**

gibber ('dʒɪbə) *vb.* to utter rapidly and unintelligibly; prattle. [imit.]

gibberish ('dʒɪbərɪʃ) n. rapid, incomprehensible talk; nonsense.

gibbet ('dʒɪbɪt) n. **1. a.** a wooden structure like a gallows, from which the bodies of executed criminals were formerly hung to public view. **b.** a gallows. ~vb. **2.** to hang on a gibbet. **3.** to expose to public scorn. [Old French]

gibbon ('gɪbˀn) n. a small agile tree-dwelling ape of the forests of S Asia. [French]

gibbous ('gɪbəs) adj. **1.** (of the moon or a planet) more than half but less than fully illuminated. **2.** hunchbacked. **3.** bulging. [Latin gibba hump]

gibe or **jibe** (dʒaɪb) vb. **1.** to jeer or scoff (at); taunt. ~n. **2.** a jeer; taunt. [perhaps from Old French giber to treat roughly]

giblets ('dʒɪblɪts) pl. n. (sometimes sing.) the gizzard, liver, heart, and neck of a fowl. [Old French gibelet stew of game birds]

gidday (gə'daɪ) interj. Austral. & N.Z. informal. same as **good day.**

giddy ('gɪdɪ) adj. **-dier, -diest. 1.** affected with a reeling sensation; dizzy. **2.** tending to cause dizziness. **3.** impulsive; scatterbrained. [Old English gydig mad, frenzied, possessed by God] —'**giddiness** n.

gie (giː) vb. Scot. to give.

gift (gɪft) n. **1.** a present. **2.** a special ability or power; talent. **3.** the power or right to give: in the gift of. **4. look a gift-horse in the mouth.** to find fault with a gift or favour. ~vb. **5.** to present (something) as a gift to (a person). [Old English]

gifted ('gɪftɪd) adj. having natural talent or aptitude: a gifted musician.

giftwrap ('gɪft,ræp) vb. **-wrapping, -wrapped.** to wrap (a gift) attractively.

gig¹ (gɪg) n. **1.** a light open two-wheeled one-horse carriage. **2.** Naut. a light ship's boat. **3.** a long light rowing boat, used for racing. [origin unknown]

gig² (gɪg) n. **1.** a single performance by jazz or pop musicians. ~vb. **gigging, gigged. 2.** to play a gig or gigs. [origin unknown]

giga- ('gɪgə, 'gaɪgə) combining form. **1.** denoting 10⁹: gigavolt. **2.** Computers. denoting 2³⁰: gigabyte. [Greek gigas giant]

gigantic (dʒaɪ'gæntɪk) adj. enormous. [Greek gigantikos] —**gi'gantically** adv.

giggle ('gɪgˀl) vb. **1.** to laugh nervously or foolishly. ~n. **2.** such a laugh. **3.** Informal. an amusing person or thing. [imit.] —'**giggly** adj.

gigolo ('ʒɪgə,ləʊ) n., pl. **-los.** a man who is kept by an older woman to be her escort or lover. [French]

gigot ('dʒɪgət) n. a leg of lamb or mutton. [French]

gild (gɪld) vb. **gilding, gilded** or **gilt. 1.** to cover with or as if with gold. **2. gild the lily. a.** to adorn unnecessarily something already beautiful. **b.** to praise someone excessively. **3.** to give a falsely attractive appearance to. [Old English gyldan]

gill¹ (gɪl) n. **1.** the breathing organ of most aquatic animals. **2.** a radiating structure

on the underside of the cap of a mushroom. [Old Norse] —**gilled** adj.

gill² (dʒɪl) n. a unit of liquid measure equal to one quarter of a pint. [Old French gille vat, tub]

gill³ or **ghyll** (gɪl) n. Dialect. **1.** a narrow stream; rivulet. **2.** a wooded ravine. [Old Norse gil steep-sided valley]

gillie or **ghillie** ('gɪlɪ) n., pl. **-lies.** Scot. a sportsman's attendant or guide for hunting or fishing. [Scot. Gaelic gille boy, servant]

gills (gɪlz) pl. n. **1.** (sometimes sing.) the wattle of birds such as domestic fowl. **2.** a person's cheeks and jowls. **3. green about the gills.** Informal. looking or feeling sick.

gilt¹ (gɪlt) vb. **1.** past of **gild.** ~n. **2.** gold or a substance like it, used in gilding. **3.** a gilt-edged security. ~adj. **4.** covered with gilt; gilded.

gilt² (gɪlt) n. a young sow. [Old Norse gyltr]

gilt-edged adj. denoting government securities on which interest payments and final repayments are guaranteed.

gimbals ('dʒɪmbˀlz, 'gɪm-) pl. n. a device, consisting of two or three pivoted rings at right angles to each other, that allows a ship's instrument to remain level despite the ship's movement. [Old French gemel double finger ring]

gimcrack ('dʒɪm,kræk) adj. **1.** showy but cheap; shoddy. ~n. **2.** a cheap showy object. [origin unknown]

gimlet ('gɪmlɪt) n. **1.** a small hand tool with a pointed spiral tip, used for boring holes in wood. ~adj. **2. gimlet-eyed.** having a piercing glance. [Old French guimbelet]

gimmick ('gɪmɪk) n. Informal. something designed to attract attention or publicity. [origin unknown] —'**gimmickry** n. —'**gimmicky** adj.

gimp (gɪmp) n. a tapelike trimming. [prob. from Dutch]

gin¹ (dʒɪn) n. an alcoholic drink distilled from malted grain and flavoured with juniper berries. [Dutch genever, from Latin jūniperus juniper]

gin² (dʒɪn) n. **1.** a machine in which a vertical shaft is turned by horses driving a horizontal beam in a circle. **2.** a machine of this type used for separating seeds from raw cotton. **3.** a noose of thin strong wire for catching small mammals. ~vb. **ginning, ginned. 4.** to free (cotton) of seeds with a gin. **5.** to snare (game) with a gin. [Middle English gyn]

gin³ (gɪn) vb. **ginning, gan** (gæn), **gun** (gʌn). Archaic. to begin.

ginger ('dʒɪndʒə) n. **1.** the underground stem of a tropical plant, powdered and used as a spice or sugared and eaten as a sweet. **2.** a light reddish-brown colour. **3.** Informal. vigour. [Old French gingivre] —'**gingery** adj.

ginger ale n. a nonalcoholic fizzy drink flavoured with ginger extract.

ginger beer n. a drink made by fermenting a mixture of syrup and root ginger.

gingerbread ('dʒɪndʒə,brɛd) n. **1.** a moist brown cake or biscuit flavoured with ginger. **2.** showy but unsubstantial ornamentation.

ginger group *n. Chiefly Brit.* a group within a larger group that enlivens or radicalizes its parent body.

gingerly ('dʒɪndʒəlɪ) *adv.* **1.** carefully or cautiously. ~*adj.* **2.** careful or cautious. [perhaps from Old French *gensor* dainty]

ginger snap *or* **nut** *n.* a crisp biscuit flavoured with ginger.

gingham ('gɪŋəm) *n.* a cotton fabric, usually woven in a checked or striped design. [Malay *ginggang* striped cloth]

gingivitis (ˌdʒɪndʒɪ'vaɪtɪs) *n.* inflammation of the gums. [Latin *gingiva* gum]

ginkgo ('gɪŋkgəʊ) *n., pl.* **-goes.** an ornamental Chinese tree with fan-shaped leaves and fleshy yellow fruit. [Japanese]

ginormous (dʒaɪ'nɔːməs) *adj. Informal.* very large. [*gi*(*gantic*) + (*e*)*normous*]

gin palace *n.* (formerly) a gaudy drinking house.

gin rummy (dʒɪn) *n.* a version of rummy in which a player may finish if the odd cards in his hand total less than ten points. [GIN + *rummy*]

ginseng ('dʒɪnsɛŋ) *n.* the forked aromatic root of a plant of China and N America or a substance obtained from this, believed to possess tonic and energy-giving properties. [Mandarin Chinese *jen shen*]

gip (dʒɪp) *n.* same as **gyp.**

Gipsy ('dʒɪpsɪ) *n., pl.* **-sies.** (*sometimes not cap.*) same as **Gypsy.**

giraffe (dʒɪ'rɑːf, -'ræf) *n.* a large ruminant mammal of the African savannas: the tallest mammal, with very long legs and neck and a spotted yellowy skin. [Arabic *zarāfah*]

gird (gɜːd) *vb.* **girding, girded** *or* **girt. 1.** to put a belt or girdle around (the waist or hips). **2.** to secure with or as if with a belt: *to gird on one's armour.* **3.** to surround. **4. gird (up) one's loins.** to prepare oneself for action. [Old English *gyrdan*]

girder ('gɜːdə) *n.* a large timber or steel beam used in the construction of bridges and buildings.

girdle[1] ('gɜːd³l) *n.* **1.** a woman's elastic corset covering the waist and hips. **2.** anything that surrounds. **3.** a belt. **4.** *Anat.* an encircling structure or part: the *pelvic girdle.* ~*vb.* **5.** to put a girdle on or around. **6.** to surround. [Old English *gyrdel*]

girdle[2] ('gɜːd³l) *n. Scot. & N English dialect.* same as **griddle.**

girl (gɜːl) *n.* **1.** a female child. **2.** a young woman. **3.** *Informal.* a sweetheart or girlfriend. **4.** *Informal.* a woman of any age. **5.** a female employee, usually a servant. [Middle English *girle*] —'**girl,hood** *n.* —'**girlish** *adj.*

girlfriend ('gɜːl,frɛnd) *n.* **1.** a female friend with whom a person is romantically or sexually involved. **2.** any female friend.

Girl Guide *n.* See **Guide.**

girlie ('gɜːlɪ) *n.* (*modifier*) *Informal.* featuring nude or scantily dressed women: a *girlie magazine.*

giro ('dʒaɪrəʊ) *n., pl.* **-ros. 1.** a system of transferring money within a bank or post office, directly from one account into another. **2.** *Brit. informal.* a social security payment by giro cheque. [Greek *guros* circuit]

girt[1] (gɜːt) *vb.* past of **gird.**

girt[2] (gɜːt) *vb.* to bind or encircle; gird.

girth (gɜːθ) *n.* **1.** the distance around something; circumference. **2.** a band around a horse's belly to keep the saddle in position. [Old Norse *gjörth* belt]

gist (dʒɪst) *n.* the point or substance of a matter. [Anglo-French, as in *cest action gist en* this action consists in]

git (gɪt) *n. Brit. slang.* a contemptible person. [from *get* (in the sense: *to beget*, hence *a bastard, fool*)]

give (gɪv) *vb.* **giving, gave, given. 1.** to present (something that is one's own) voluntarily to another. **2.** (often foll. by *for*) to transfer (something, usually money) in exchange or payment: *to give fifty pounds for a painting.* **3.** to hand over temporarily to another: *I gave the porter my bags.* **4.** to grant or provide: *give me some advice.* **5.** to administer: *to give a reprimand.* **6.** to award or attribute: *they gave her the blame.* **7.** to be a source of: *he gives no trouble.* **8.** to impart: *to give news.* **9.** to utter or emit: *to give a shout.* **10.** to perform, make, or do: *the car gave a jolt.* **11.** to sacrifice or devote: *he gave his life for his country.* **12.** to concede: *I will give you this game.* **13.** *Informal.* to happen: *what gives?* **14.** (often foll. by *to*) to cause; lead: *she gave me to believe that she would come.* **15.** to organize or put on (an entertainment). **16.** to yield or break under pressure: *this seat will give if you sit on it.* **17. give or take.** plus or minus: *three thousand, give or take a few hundred.* ~*n.* **18.** tendency to yield under pressure; resilience. ~*See also* **give away, give in,** etc. [Old English *giefan*] —'**giver** *n.*

give-and-take *n.* **1.** mutual concessions and cooperation. **2.** a smoothly flowing exchange of ideas and talk.

give away *vb.* **1.** to donate as a gift. **2.** to reveal. **3.** to present (a bride) formally to her husband in a marriage ceremony. ~*n.* **giveaway. 4.** a usually unintentional disclosure. **5.** (*modifier*) very cheap or free: *giveaway prices; a giveaway supplement.*

give in *vb.* **1.** to yield; admit defeat. **2.** to hand (something) in.

given ('gɪv³n) *vb.* **1.** past participle of **give.** ~*adj.* **2.** specific or previously stated. **3.** assumed as a premise. **4.** *Maths.* known or determined independently: *a given volume.* **5. given to.** inclined to.

give off *vb.* to emit or discharge: *the mothballs gave off an acrid odour.*

give out *vb.* **1.** to emit or discharge. **2.** to make known: *he gave out that he would resign.* **3.** to distribute: *they gave out leaflets.* **4.** to become exhausted; fail: *the light gave out.*

give over *vb.* **1.** to transfer to the custody of another. **2.** to set aside for a specific purpose: *the day was given over to work.* **3.** *Informal.* to cease: *give over fighting!*

give up *vb.* **1.** to abandon hope (for). **2.** to renounce or relinquish (something): *I have given up smoking; he gave up his job.* **3.** to surrender: *the escaped convict gave himself up.* **4.** to admit defeat or failure. **5.** to devote completely (to): *she gave herself up to caring for the sick.*

gizzard ('gɪzəd) *n.* the thick-walled part of a bird's stomach, in which hard food is broken up. [Old French *guisier* fowl's liver]

glacé ('glæsɪ) *adj.* **1.** crystallized or candied: *glacé cherries.* **2.** (of leather or cloth) having a glossy finish. [French: iced]

glacial ('gleɪsɪəl, -ʃəl) *adj.* **1.** characterized by masses of ice. **2.** of or produced by a glacier. **3.** extremely cold; icy. **4.** unfriendly.

glacial period *n.* **1.** any period of time during which a large part of the earth's surface was covered with ice, due to the advance of glaciers. **2.** (*often caps.*) the Pleistocene epoch.

glaciate ('gleɪsɪˌeɪt) *vb.* **1.** to cover with glaciers or masses of ice. **2.** to subject to the effects of glaciers. —ˌglaci'ation *n.*

glacier ('glæsɪə, 'gleɪs-) *n.* a slowly moving mass of ice formed by an accumulation of snow. [Latin *glaciēs* ice]

glad (glæd) *adj.* **gladder, gladdest. 1.** happy and pleased. **2.** causing happiness. **3.** (foll. by *to*) very willing: *he was glad to help.* [Old English *glæd*] —'**gladly** *adv.* —'**gladness** *n.*

gladden ('glædᵊn) *vb.* to make or become glad.

glade (gleɪd) *n.* an open place in a forest. [origin unknown]

glad eye *n. Informal.* an inviting or seductive glance: *give someone the glad eye.*

gladiator ('glædɪˌeɪtə) *n.* (in ancient Rome) a man trained to fight in arenas to provide entertainment. [Latin: swordsman] —**gladiatorial** (ˌglædɪə'tɔːrɪəl) *adj.*

gladiolus (ˌglædɪ'əʊləs) *n., pl.* -**lus, -li** (-laɪ), *or* -**luses.** a plant having sword-shaped leaves and spikes of funnel-shaped brightly coloured flowers. [Latin: a small sword]

glad rags *pl. n. Informal.* best clothes.

gladsome ('glædsəm) *adj. Archaic.* joyous or cheerful.

glair (gleə) *n.* **1.** white of egg, used as a size, glaze, or adhesive. **2.** any substance like or made from this. [Old French *glaire*]

glamour *or U.S.* (*sometimes*) **glamor** ('glæmə) *n.* **1.** alluring charm; fascination. **2.** fascinating beauty. [Scot. var. of *grammar* (hence a spell, since occult practices were popularly associated with learning)] —'**glamorize** *or* -ise *vb.* —'**glamorous** *adj.*

glance (glɑːns) *vb.* **1.** to look hastily or

briefly. **2.** (foll. by *over or through*) to look over briefly: *to glance through a report.* **3.** to glint or gleam: *the sun glanced on the water.* **4.** (usually foll. by *off*) to be deflected (off an object struck) at an oblique angle: *the arrow glanced off the tree.* ~*n.* **5.** a hasty or brief look. **6.** a flash or glint of light. **7.** a glancing off. [Middle English *glacen* to strike obliquely] —'**glancing** *adj.*

gland (glænd) *n.* **1.** an organ that synthesizes and secretes chemical substances for the body to use or eliminate. **2.** an organ in plants that synthesizes and secretes a particular substance. [Latin *glāns* acorn]

glanders ('glændəz) *n.* (*functioning as sing.*) a highly infectious, often fatal disease of horses, characterized by inflammation and ulceration of the air passages, skin, and lymph glands. [Latin *glandulae* little acorns]

glandular ('glændjʊlə) *adj.* of, like, or affecting a gland or glands.

glandular fever *n.* an acute infectious viral disease characterized by fever, sore throat, and painful swollen lymph nodes.

glare (gleə) *vb.* **1.** to stare angrily. **2.** (of light or colour) to be too bright. ~*n.* **3.** an angry stare. **4.** a dazzling light or brilliance. [Middle English]

glaring ('gleərɪŋ) *adj.* **1.** conspicuous: *a glaring omission.* **2.** dazzling or garish. —'**glaringly** *adv.*

glasnost ('glæsˌnɒst) *n.* a policy of public frankness and accountability, esp. that developed in the USSR under Mikhail Gorbachov. [Russian: openness]

glass (glɑːs) *n.* **1.** a hard brittle transparent or translucent solid, consisting of metal silicates or similar compounds. **2.** something made of glass, such as a drinking vessel or a mirror. **3.** the amount contained in a drinking glass: *he drank a glass of wine.* **4.** glassware collectively. ~*vb.* **5.** to fit or cover with glass. [Old English *glæs*]

glass-blowing *n.* the process of shaping a mass of molten glass by blowing air into it through a tube. —'**glass-ˌblower** *n.*

glasses ('glɑːsɪz) *pl. n.* a pair of lenses for correcting faulty vision, in a frame that rests on the nose and hooks behind the ears.

glasshouse ('glɑːsˌhaʊs) *n.* **1.** *Brit.* same as **greenhouse. 2.** *Informal, chiefly Brit.* a military detention centre.

glass wool *n.* fine glass fibres in a wool-like mass, used in insulation and filtering.

glassy ('glɑːsɪ) *adj.* **glassier, glassiest. 1.** like glass in smoothness or transparency. **2.** expressionless: *a glassy stare.*

Glaswegian (glæz'wiːdʒən) *adj.* **1.** of Glasgow, a city in Scotland, or its inhabitants. ~*n.* **2.** a person from Glasgow. **3.** the Glasgow dialect.

glaucoma (glɔː'kəʊmə) *n.* an eye disease in which increased pressure in the eyeball causes gradual loss of sight. [Greek *glaukos* silvery, bluish-green] —**glau'comatous** *adj.*

glaze (gleɪz) *vb.* **1.** to fit or cover with

glass. **2.** *Ceramics.* to cover with a vitreous coating, rendering impervious to liquid. **3.** to cover (foods) with a shiny coating, such as beaten egg or syrup. **4.** to make glossy or shiny. **5.** (sometimes foll. by *over*) to become glassy: *his eyes were glazing over.* ~*n.* **6.** *Ceramics.* **a.** a vitreous coating. **b.** the substance used to produce this. **7.** a smooth lustrous finish on a fabric. **8.** something used to give a glossy surface to foods: *a syrup glaze.* [Middle English *glasen*] —**glazed** *adj.* —**glazing** *n.*

glazier ('gleızıə) *n.* a person who fits windows or doors with glass. —**glaziery** *n.*

gleam (gliːm) *n.* **1.** a small beam or glow of light. **2.** a brief or dim indication: *a gleam of hope.* ~*vb.* **3.** to send forth a small beam of light. **4.** to appear briefly. [Old English *glǣm*] —**gleaming** *adj.*

glean (gliːn) *vb.* **1.** to gather (something) bit by bit: *to glean information.* **2.** to gather (the useful remnants of a crop) after harvesting. [Old French *glener*] —**gleaner** *n.*

gleanings ('gliːnıŋz) *pl. n.* things which are gleaned.

glebe (gliːb) *n. Brit.* land granted to a clergyman as part of his benefice. [Latin *glaeba*]

glee (gliː) *n.* **1.** great merriment; joy. **2.** a type of song sung by three or more unaccompanied voices. [Old English *gléo*]

gleeful ('gliːful) *adj.* full of glee; merry. —**gleefully** *adv.* —**gleefulness** *n.*

glen (glɛn) *n.* a deep narrow mountain valley. [Scot. Gaelic *gleann*]

glengarry (glɛn'gærı) *n., pl.* **-ries.** a brimless Scottish cap with a crease down the crown. [after *Glengarry*, Scotland]

glib (glıb) *adj.* **glibber, glibbest.** fluent and easy, often in an insincere or deceptive way: *glib promises.* [prob. from Middle Low German *glibberich* slippery] —**glibly** *adv.* —**glibness** *n.*

glide (glaıd) *vb.* **1.** to move easily and smoothly. **2.** to pass gradually and imperceptibly: *to glide into sleep.* **3.** (of an aircraft) to land without engine power. **4.** to fly a glider. **5.** to cause to glide. ~*n.* **6.** a smooth easy movement. **7.** a manoeuvre in which an aircraft descends gently without engine power. [Old English *glīdan*] —**gliding** *adj., n.*

glider ('glaıdə) *n.* an aircraft which does not use an engine, but flies by floating on air currents.

glide time *n. N.Z.* same as **flexitime**.

glimmer ('glımə) *vb.* **1.** (of a light) to glow faintly or flickeringly. **2.** to be indicated faintly: *hope glimmered in his face.* ~*n.* **3.** a glow or twinkle of light. **4.** a faint indication. [Middle English]

glimpse (glımps) *n.* **1.** a brief or incomplete view: *to catch a glimpse of the sea.* **2.** a vague indication. ~*vb.* **3.** to catch sight of momentarily. [Germanic]

glint (glınt) *vb.* **1.** to gleam brightly. ~*n.* **2.** a bright gleam. [prob. from Old Norse]

glissade (glı'sɑːd, -'seıd) *n.* **1.** a gliding step in ballet. **2.** a controlled slide down a

snow slope. ~*vb.* **3.** to perform a glissade. [French]

glisten ('glıs'n) *vb.* **1.** (of a wet or glossy surface) to gleam by reflecting light. **2.** (of light) to reflect brightly: *the sunlight glistens on wet leaves.* [Old English *glisnian*]

glitch (glıtʃ) *n.* a sudden malfunction in an electronic system. [Yiddish *glitsh* a slip]

glitter ('glıtə) *vb.* **1.** (of a surface) to reflect light in bright flashes. **2.** (of light) to be reflected in bright flashes. **3.** (usually foll. by *with*) to be showy or glamorous with: *the show glitters with famous actors.* ~*n.* **4.** sparkle or brilliance. **5.** show and glamour. **6.** tiny pieces of shiny decorative material. **7.** *Canad.* ice formed from freezing rain. [Old Norse *glitra*] —**glittering** *adj.* —**glittery** *adj.*

glitzy ('glıtsı) *adj.* **glitzier, glitziest.** *Slang.* showily attractive. [prob. from German *glitzern* to glitter]

gloaming ('gləumıŋ) *n. Scot. or poetic.* twilight or dusk. [Old English *glōmung*]

gloat (gləut) *vb.* **1.** (often foll. by *over*) to look (at) or think (of) with malicious pleasure. ~*n.* **2.** a gloating. [prob. Scandinavian]

glob (glɒb) *n. Informal.* a rounded mass of thick fluid. [prob. from *globe*, infl. by *blob*]

global ('gləub'l) *adj.* **1.** worldwide. **2.** comprehensive; total. —**globally** *adv.*

globe (gləub) *n.* **1.** a sphere on which a map of the world is drawn. **2. the globe.** the earth. **3.** a spherical object, such as a glass lampshade or fishbowl. [Latin *globus*]

globeflower ('gləub,flauə) *n.* a plant having yellow, white, or orange spherical flowers.

globetrotter ('gləub,trɒtə) *n.* a habitual worldwide traveller. —**globe,trotting** *n., adj.*

globular ('glɒbjulə) *adj.* **1.** shaped like a globe or globule. **2.** consisting of globules.

globule ('glɒbjuːl) *n.* a small globe, usually a drop of liquid. [Latin *globulus*]

globulin ('glɒbjulın) *n.* a simple protein found in living tissue.

glockenspiel ('glɒkən,spiːl, -,ʃpiːl) *n.* a percussion instrument consisting of tuned metal plates played with a pair of small hammers. [German *Glocken* bells + *Spiel* play]

gloom (gluːm) *n.* **1.** partial or total darkness. **2.** depression or melancholy. ~*vb.* **3.** to make or become gloomy. [Middle English *gloumben* to look sullen]

gloomy ('gluːmı) *adj.* **gloomier, gloomiest.** **1.** dark or dismal. **2.** causing depression or gloom: *gloomy news.* **3.** despairing; sad. —**gloomily** *adv.* —**gloominess** *n.*

glorify ('glɔːrı,faı) *vb.* **-fying, -fied.** **1.** to make glorious. **2.** to exalt in worship. **3.** to extol. **4.** to make (something) seem more splendid than it is. —**glorification** *n.*

glorious ('glɔːrıəs) *adj.* **1.** having or full of glory; illustrious. **2.** conferring glory: *a glorious victory.* **3.** brilliantly beautiful.

4. delightful or enjoyable. —**'gloriously** *adv.* —**'gloriousness** *n.*

glory ('glɔːrɪ) *n., pl.* **-ries. 1.** exaltation, praise, or honour. **2.** something worthy of praise: *crowning glory.* **3.** adoration or worship: *glory be to God.* **4.** splendour: *the glory of the king's reign.* **5.** the beauty and bliss of heaven. **6.** extreme happiness or prosperity. **7.** a saint's halo. ~*vb.* **-rying, -ried. 8.** (often foll. by *in*) to triumph or exalt. [Latin *glōria*]

glory box *n. Austral. & N.Z.* a box in which a young woman stores her trousseau.

glory hole *n.* a cupboard or storeroom, usually one which is very untidy.

Glos Gloucestershire.

gloss[1] (glɒs) *n.* **1.** lustre or sheen of a surface. **2.** a superficially attractive appearance. **3.** a paint giving a shiny finish. **4.** a cosmetic used to give a sheen. ~*vb.* **5.** to make glossy. **6.** (often foll. by *over*) to conceal (an error, failing, or awkward moment) by minimizing it. [prob. Scandinavian]

gloss[2] (glɒs) *n.* **1.** an explanatory comment added in the margin or text of a manuscript or book. ~*vb.* **2.** to add glosses to. [Latin *glōssa* unusual word requiring explanatory note]

glossary ('glɒsərɪ) *n., pl.* **-ries.** an alphabetical list of technical or special words in a book, with explanations. [Late Latin *glossārium*; see GLOSS[2]]

glossy ('glɒsɪ) *adj.* **glossier, glossiest. 1.** smooth and shiny; lustrous. **2.** superficially attractive. **3.** (of a magazine) produced on shiny paper. —**'glossily** *adv.* —**'glossiness** *n.*

glottal stop *n.* a speech sound produced by tightly closing and then opening the glottis.

glottis ('glɒtɪs) *n., pl.* **-tises** *or* **-tides** (-tɪ,diːz). the vocal apparatus of the larynx, consisting of the vocal cords and the opening between them. [Greek *glōtta* tongue] —**'glottal** *adj.*

glove (glʌv) *n.* **1.** (*often pl.*) a shaped covering for the hand with individual sheaths for each finger and the thumb. **2.** a protective hand cover worn in various sports, such as boxing. ~*vb.* **3.** to cover with or as if with gloves. [Old English *glōfe*]

glover ('glʌvə) *n.* a maker or seller of gloves.

glow (gləʊ) *n.* **1.** light emitted as a result of great heat. **2.** a steady light without flames. **3.** brilliance of colour. **4.** brightness of complexion. **5.** a feeling of wellbeing or satisfaction. **6.** intensity of emotion. ~*vb.* **7.** to emit a steady light without flames. **8.** to shine intensely. **9.** to experience a feeling of wellbeing or satisfaction: *to glow with pride.* **10.** (esp. of the complexion) to show a strong bright colour. **11.** to be very hot. [Old English *glōwan*]

glower ('glaʊə) *vb.* **1.** to stare angrily. ~*n.* **2.** an angry stare. [origin unknown]

glow-worm *n.* a European beetle, the females and larvae of which have organs producing a soft greenish light.

gloxinia (glɒk'sɪnɪə) *n.* a tropical plant cultivated for its white, red, or purple bell-shaped flowers. [after Benjamin P. *Gloxin,* botanist]

glucose ('gluːkəʊz, -kəʊs) *n.* a white crystalline sugar found in plant and animal tissues. [Greek *gleukos* sweet wine]

glue (gluː) *n.* **1.** a natural or synthetic adhesive. ~*vb.* **gluing** *or* **glueing, glued. 2.** to join or stick together as with glue. **3.** (foll. by *to*) to pay full attention to: *her eyes were glued to the TV screen.* [Late Latin *glūs*] —**'gluey** *adj.*

glue-sniffing *n.* the inhaling of the fumes of certain types of glue to produce intoxicating or hallucinatory effects. —**'glue-,sniffer** *n.*

glum (glʌm) *adj.* **glummer, glummest.** morose or sullen; gloomy. [var. of *gloom*] —**'glumly** *adv.* —**'glumness** *n.*

glut (glʌt) *n.* **1.** an excessive supply. **2.** a glutting or being glutted. ~*vb.* **glutting, glutted. 3.** to feed or fill beyond capacity. **4.** to supply (a market) with a commodity in excess of the demand for it. [prob. from Old French *gloutir* to swallow]

gluten ('gluːt'n) *n.* a protein present in cereal grains, such as wheat. [Latin: glue]

glutinous ('gluːtɪnəs) *adj.* gluelike in texture; sticky.

glutton[1] ('glʌt'n) *n.* **1.** someone who eats and drinks too much. **2.** a person who has a great capacity for something: *a glutton for punishment.* [Latin *gluttīre* to swallow] —**'gluttonous** *adj.*

glutton[2] ('glʌt'n) *n.* same as **wolverine.** [translation of German *Vielfass* great eater]

gluttony ('glʌtənɪ) *n., pl.* **-tonies.** the act or practice of eating too much.

glyceride ('glɪsə,raɪd) *n.* an ester of glycerol.

glycerin ('glɪsərɪn) *or* **glycerine** ('glɪsərɪin, ,glɪsə'riːn) *n.* a nontechnical name for **glycerol.** [Greek *glukeros* sweet]

glycerol ('glɪsə,rɒl) *n.* a colourless odourless syrupy liquid: a by-product of soap manufacture, used as a solvent, antifreeze, sweetener (**E422**), and in explosives.

glycogen ('glaɪkəʊdʒən) *n.* a starchlike carbohydrate consisting of glucose units: the form in which carbohydrate is stored in animals. —**glycogenic** (,glaɪkəʊ'dʒɛnɪk) *adj.*

glycolysis (glaɪ'kɒlɪsɪs) *n. Biochem.* the breakdown of glucose by enzymes, with the release of energy.

GM (in Britain) George Medal.

gm gramme.

G-man *n., pl.* **G-men.** *U.S. slang.* an FBI agent.

GMT Greenwich Mean Time.

gnarled (nɑːld) *or* **gnarly** *adj.* rough, twisted, and knobby, usually through age.

gnash (næʃ) *vb.* **1.** to grind (the teeth) together in pain or anger. ~*n.* **2.** the act of gnashing. [Old Norse]

gnat (næt) *n.* a small fragile biting two-winged insect. [Old English *gnætt*]

gnaw (nɔː) *vb.* **gnawing, gnawed; gnawed** *or* **gnawn.** **1.** to bite or chew constantly so as to wear away bit by bit. **2.** to form by gnawing: *to gnaw a hole.* **3.** to erode (something). **4.** (often foll. by *at*) to cause constant distress or anxiety (to). [Old English *gnagan*]

gneiss (naɪs) *n.* a coarse-grained layered metamorphic rock. [German *Gneis*]

gnome (nəʊm) *n.* **1.** a legendary creature said to live in the depths of the earth and guard buried treasure. **2.** the statue of a gnome in a garden. **3.** *Facetious.* an international banker or financier: *gnomes of Zürich.* [French]

gnomic ('nəʊmɪk, 'nɒm-) *adj.* of aphorisms; pithy.

gnostic ('nɒstɪk) *adj.* of or having knowledge. [Greek *gnōstikos* of knowledge]

Gnosticism ('nɒstɪˌsɪzəm) *n.* a religious movement characterized by a belief in intuitive spiritual knowledge: regarded as a heresy by the Christian Church. —'**Gnostic** *n., adj.*

GNP gross national product.

gnu (nuː) *n., pl.* **gnus** *or* **gnu.** a sturdy antelope of the African savannas, having an oxlike head. [Xhosa *ngu*]

go (gəʊ) *vb.* **going, went, gone.** **1.** to move or proceed to or from a place: *go home.* **2.** to depart: *we'll have to go at eleven.* **3.** to start in a race: often used in commands. **4.** to make regular journeys: *this train service goes to the east coast.* **5.** to operate or function: *the radio won't go.* **6.** to do or become as specified: *his face went red; the gun went bang.* **7.** to be or continue to be in a specified state: *to go hungry.* **8.** to lead or proceed as specified: *this path goes to the river; go to sleep.* **9.** (takes an *infinitive*) to serve or contribute: *this letter goes to prove my point.* **10.** to follow a specified course; fare: *the lecture went badly.* **11.** to be allotted to a particular purpose or recipient: *his money went on drink.* **12.** to be sold: *the necklace went for fifty pounds.* **13.** to be ranked: *this meal is good as my meals go.* **14.** to blend or harmonize: *that colour doesn't go with your hair.* **15.** (foll. by *by* or *under*) to be known (by a name or disguise). **16.** to have a usual place: *those books go on this shelf.* **17.** (of words or music) to be expressed or sung: *how does that song go?* **18.** to fail or break down: *my eyesight is going; the ladder went at the critical moment.* **19.** to die: *the old man went at 2 a.m.* **20.** (often foll. by *by*) **a.** (of time or distance) to elapse: *the hours go by so slowly.* **b.** to be guided (by). **21.** to occur: *happiness does not always go with riches.* **22.** to be eliminated or given up: *this entry must go to save space.* **23.** to be spent or finished: *all his money has gone.* **24.** to attend: *go to school.* **25.** to join a stated profession: *go on the stage.* **26.** (foll. by *to*) to have recourse (to): *to go to arbitration.* **27.** (foll. by *to*) to subject or put oneself (to): *she goes to great pains to please him.* **28.** to proceed up to or beyond certain limits: *you will go too far one day.* **29.** to be acceptable: *anything goes.* **30.** to

carry authority: *what the boss says goes.* **31.** *Nonstandard.* to say: *Then she goes, "shut up!"* **32.** (foll. by *into*) to be contained in: *four goes into twelve three times.* **33.** (often foll. by *for*) to endure or last out: *we can't go for much longer without water.* **34.** **be going.** to intend or be going to start (doing or happening): *what's going to happen to us?* **35.** **go and.** *Informal.* to be so foolish or unlucky as to: *then she had to go and lose her hat.* **36.** **go it alone.** *Informal.* to act or proceed without help. **37.** **go one better.** *Informal.* to surpass or outdo (someone). **38.** **let go a.** to relax one's hold (on); release. **b.** to discuss or consider no further. **39.** **let oneself go. a.** to act in an uninhibited manner. **b.** to lose interest in one's appearance. **40.** **to go. a.** remaining. **b.** *U.S. & Canad. informal.* (of food sold in a restaurant) for taking away. ~*n., pl.* **goes.** **41.** the act of going. **42.** an attempt: *he had a go at the stamp business.* **43.** an attack, usually verbal: *she had a real go at them.* **44.** a turn: *it's my go next.* **45.** *Informal.* the quality of being active and energetic: *she has a lot of go.* **46.** *Informal.* hard or energetic work: *it's all go.* **47.** *Informal.* a success: *he made a go of it.* **48.** **from the word go.** *Informal.* from the very beginning. **49.** **no go.** *Informal.* impossible or futile: *it's no go, I'm afraid.* **50.** **on the go.** *Informal.* active and energetic. ~*adj.* **51.** *Informal.* functioning and ready for action: *all systems are go.* ~See also **go about, go against**, etc. [Old English *gān*]

go about *vb.* **1.** to busy oneself with: *to go about one's duties.* **2.** to tackle (a problem or task). **3.** to circulate: *there's a lot of flu going about.*

goad (gəʊd) *n.* **1.** a sharp pointed stick for driving cattle. **2.** a spur or incitement. ~*vb.* **3.** to drive as if with a goad; spur. [Old English *gād*]

go against *vb.* **1.** to be contrary to (principles or beliefs). **2.** to be unfavourable to (a person): *the case went against him.*

go-ahead *n.* **1.** (usually preceded by *the*) *Informal.* permission to proceed. ~*adj.* **2.** enterprising or ambitious.

goal (gəʊl) *n.* **1.** an aim or object. **2.** the end point of a journey or race. **3.** *Sport.* the space into which players try to propel the ball or puck to score. **4.** *Sport.* **a.** a successful attempt at scoring. **b.** the score so made. [origin unknown] —'**goalless** *adj.*

goalie ('gəʊlɪ) *n. Informal.* a goalkeeper.

goalkeeper ('gəʊlˌkiːpə) *n. Sport.* a player at the goal whose duty is to prevent the ball or puck from entering it.

goal line *n. Sport.* the line marking each end of the pitch, on which the goals stand.

goalpost ('gəʊlˌpəʊst) *n.* **1.** either of two uprights supporting the crossbar of a goal. **2. move the goalposts.** to change the aims of an activity to ensure the desired results.

goat (gəʊt) *n.* **1.** a sure-footed ruminant mammal with hollow horns. **2.** *Informal.* a lecherous man. **3.** a foolish person. **4.** **get**

someone's goat. *Slang.* to annoy someone. [Old English *gāt*] —'**goatish** *adj.*

go at *vb.* **1.** to make an energetic attempt at (something). **2.** to attack vehemently.

goatee (gəʊ'tiː) *n.* a pointed tuftlike beard.

goatherd ('gəʊt,hɜːd) *n.* a person employed to tend or herd goats.

goatskin ('gəʊt,skɪn) *n.* **1.** the hide of a goat. **2.** something made from this, such as leather or a container for wine.

goatsucker ('gəʊt,sʌkə) *n. U.S. & Canad.* same as **nightjar**.

gob[1] (gob) *n.* **1.** a lump or chunk of a soft substance. ∼*vb.* **gobbing, gobbed.** **2.** *Brit. informal.* to spit. [Old French *gobe* lump]

gob[2] (gob) *n. Slang, chiefly Brit.* the mouth. [origin unknown]

go back *vb.* **1.** to return. **2.** (often foll. by *to*) to originate (in): *the links with France go back to the Norman Conquest.* **3.** (foll. by *on*) to change one's mind about; repudiate: *go back on one's word.*

gobbet ('gobɪt) *n.* a chunk or lump. [Old French *gobet*]

gobble[1] ('gob'l) *vb.* (often foll. by *up*) to eat (food) hastily and greedily. [prob. from GOB[1]]

gobble[2] ('gob'l) *n.* **1.** the loud rapid gurgling sound made by male turkeys. ∼*vb.* **2.** to make this sound. [prob. imit.]

gobbledegook *or* **gobbledygook** ('gob'ldɪ,guːk) *n.* pretentious or unintelligible language or jargon. [whimsical formation from GOBBLE[2]]

gobbler ('goblə) *n. Informal.* a male turkey.

go-between *n.* a person who acts as intermediary for two people or groups.

goblet ('goblɪt) *n.* a drinking vessel with a base and stem but without handles. [Old French *gobelet* a little cup]

goblin ('goblɪn) *n.* (in folklore) a small grotesque creature, malevolent towards human beings. [Old French]

goby ('gəʊbɪ) *n., pl.* **-by** *or* **-bies.** a small spiny-finned fish having ventral fins modified into a sucker. [Latin *gōbius* gudgeon]

go by *vb.* **1.** to pass: *as the years go by.* **2.** to be guided by: *in the darkness we could only go by the stars; don't go by appearances.* ∼*n.* **go-by.** *Slang.* a deliberate snub or slight: *she gave me the go-by.*

go-cart *n.* same as **go-kart.**

god (god) *n.* **1.** a supernatural being, worshipped as the controller of the universe or some aspect of life or as the personification of some force. **2.** an image of such a deity. **3.** a person or thing to which excessive attention is given: *money was his god.* **4.** a man who has qualities regarded as making him superior to other men. **5.** (*pl.*) the gallery of a theatre. [Old English] —'**goddess** *fem. n.*

God (god) *n.* **1.** the sole Supreme Being, Creator and ruler of all, in monotheistic religions. ∼*interj.* an oath or exclamation of surprise or annoyance.

godchild ('god,tʃaɪld) *n., pl.* **-children.** a

person who is sponsored by adults at baptism.

goddaughter ('god,dɔːtə) *n.* a female godchild.

godetia (gə'diːʃə) *n.* a plant grown for its showy flowers. [after C. H. *Godet*, botanist]

godfather ('god,fɑːðə) *n.* **1.** a male godparent. **2.** the head of a Mafia family or other criminal ring.

God-fearing *adj.* pious; devout.

godforsaken ('godfə,seɪkən) *adj.* desolate; dreary; forlorn.

Godhead ('god,hɛd) *n.* **1.** the nature and condition of being God. **2. the Godhead.** God.

godless ('godlɪs) *adj.* **1.** wicked or unprincipled. **2.** irreligious. —'**godlessness** *n.*

godly ('godlɪ) *adj.* **-lier, -liest.** religious; pious; devout. —'**godliness** *n.*

godmother ('god,mʌðə) *n.* a female godparent.

godown ('gəʊ,daʊn) *n.* (in the Far East) a warehouse. [Malay *godong*]

godparent ('god,pɛərənt) *n.* a person who stands sponsor to a child at baptism.

godsend ('god,sɛnd) *n.* a person or thing that comes unexpectedly but is very welcome.

godson ('god,sʌn) *n.* a male godchild.

Godspeed ('god'spiːd) *interj.* an expression of good wishes for a person's safe journey and success.

godwit ('godwɪt) *n.* a shore bird having long legs and an upturned bill. [origin unknown]

goer ('gəʊə) *n.* **1.** a person who attends something regularly: *a filmgoer.* **2.** an energetic person.

go for *vb.* **1.** to go somewhere in order to have or fetch: *he went for a drink.* **2.** to seek to obtain: *I'd go for that job if I were you.* **3.** to like: *I really go for that idea of yours.* **4.** to attack. **5.** to be considered to be of a stated importance or value: *his experience went for nothing when he was made redundant.*

go-getter *n. Informal.* an ambitious enterprising person. —,**go-'getting** *adj.*

goggle ('gog'l) *vb.* **1.** to stare with bulging eyes. **2.** (of the eyes) to bulge. ∼*n.* **3.** a bulging stare. **4.** (*pl.*) close-fitting protective spectacles. [Middle English *gogelen* to look aside] —'**goggle-,eyed** *adj.*

gogglebox ('gog'l,boks) *n. Brit. slang.* a television set.

go-go dancer *n.* a scantily dressed woman who performs erotic dance routines in a nightclub or bar.

Goidelic (gɔɪ'dɛlɪk) *n.* **1.** the group of Celtic languages, consisting of Irish Gaelic, Scottish Gaelic, and Manx. ∼*adj.* **2.** of this group of languages. [Old Irish *Goídel*]

go in *vb.* **1.** (of the sun) to become hidden behind a cloud. **2. go in for. a.** to enter as a competitor. **b.** to adopt as an activity or principle: *she went in for nursing.*

going ('gəʊɪŋ) *n.* **1.** a departure. **2.** the

condition of the ground with regard to walking or riding: *muddy going.* **3.** *Informal.* speed or progress: *we made good going on the trip.* ~*adj.* **4.** thriving: *a going concern.* **5.** current or accepted: *the going rate.* **6.** available: *the best going.*

going-over *n., pl.* **goings-over.** *Informal.* **1.** a thorough examination or investigation. **2.** a scolding or thrashing.

goings-on *pl. n. Informal.* actions or events, usually when mysterious or disapproved of.

go into *vb.* **1.** to start a career in: *to go into publishing.* **2.** to investigate. **3.** to discuss: *we won't go into that now.* **4.** to be admitted to: *she went into hospital.* **5.** to enter a specified state: *she went into hysterics.*

goitre *or U.S.* **goiter** (ˈgɔɪtə) *n. Pathol.* a swelling of the thyroid gland in the neck. [French]

go-kart *n.* a small four-wheeled motor vehicle, used for racing.

gold (gəʊld) *n.* **1.** a bright yellow precious metal: used as a monetary standard and in jewellery and plating. Symbol: Au **2.** a coin or coins made of this metal. **3.** money; wealth. **4.** something precious or beautiful. **5.** short for **gold medal.** ~*adj.* **6.** deep yellow. [Old English]

goldcrest (ˈgəʊldˌkrɛst) *n.* a small warbler having a bright yellow-and-black crown.

gold-digger *n.* **1.** a person who prospects or digs for gold. **2.** *Informal.* a woman who uses her sexual attractions to get gifts and money.

gold dust *n.* gold in the form of small particles or powder.

golden (ˈgəʊldən) *adj.* **1.** of the colour of gold: *golden hair.* **2.** made of or containing gold: *a golden statue.* **3.** happy or prosperous: *golden days.* **4.** (*sometimes cap.*) (of anniversaries) the 50th: *Golden Jubilee; golden wedding.* **5.** *Informal.* very successful or destined for success: *the golden girl of tennis.* **6.** very valuable or advantageous: *a golden opportunity.*

golden age *n.* the most flourishing and outstanding period in the history of an art or nation: *the golden age of poetry.*

golden eagle *n.* a large mountain eagle of the N hemisphere, having golden-brown plumage on the back.

golden handshake *n. Informal.* money given to an employee, either on retirement or to compensate for loss of employment.

golden mean *n.* the middle course between extremes.

golden retriever *n.* a breed of retriever with a silky wavy coat of a golden colour.

goldenrod (ˌgəʊldənˈrɒd) *n.* a plant having spikes of small yellow flowers.

golden rule *n.* **1.** the rule of conduct, formulated by Christ, that one should do as one would wish to be done by. **2.** any important principle.

golden syrup *n. Brit.* a light golden-coloured treacle.

goldfinch (ˈgəʊldˌfɪntʃ) *n.* a European finch, the male of which has yellow-and-black wings.

goldfish (ˈgəʊldˌfɪʃ) *n., pl.* **-fish** *or* **-fishes.** a gold or orange-red freshwater fish, widely kept as a pond or aquarium fish.

gold foil *n.* thin gold sheet that is thicker than gold leaf.

gold leaf *n.* very thin gold sheet made by rolling or hammering gold and used for gilding.

gold medal *n.* a medal of gold, awarded to the winner of a competition or race.

gold plate *n.* **1.** a thin coating of gold, usually produced by electroplating. **2.** tableware made of gold. —ˌgold-ˈplate *vb.*

gold rush *n.* a large-scale migration of people to a territory where gold has been found.

goldsmith (ˈgəʊldˌsmɪθ) *n.* a person who makes or sells articles made from gold.

gold standard *n.* a monetary system in which the basic currency unit equals a specified weight of gold.

golf (gɒlf) *n.* **1.** a game played on a large open course, the object of which is to hit a ball using clubs, with as few strokes as possible, into each of usually 18 holes. ~*vb.* **2.** to play golf. [origin unknown] —ˈgolfer *n.*

golf club *n.* **1.** a long-shafted club used to strike a golf ball. **2. a.** an association of golf players. **b.** the premises of such an association.

golf course *or* **links** *n.* an area of ground laid out for golf.

Goliath (gəˈlaɪəθ) *n.* a Biblical giant.

golliwog (ˈgɒlɪˌwɒg) *n.* a soft doll with a black face, usually made of cloth. [from a doll in a series of American children's books]

golly (ˈgɒlɪ) *interj.* an exclamation of mild surprise. [orig. a euphemism for *God*]

goloshes (gəˈlɒʃɪz) *pl. n.* same as **galoshes.**

gonad (ˈgɒnæd) *n.* an animal organ in which reproductive cells are produced, such as a testis or ovary. [Greek *gonos* seed]

gondola (ˈgɒndələ) *n.* **1.** a long narrow flat-bottomed boat with a high ornamented stem: traditionally used on the canals of Venice. **2.** a car suspended from an airship, balloon, or cable car. [Italian]

gondolier (ˌgɒndəˈlɪə) *n.* a man who rows a gondola.

gone (gɒn) *vb.* **1.** the past participle of **go.** ~*adj.* **2.** ended; past. **3.** lost; ruined. **4.** dead. **5.** used up. **6.** *Informal.* having been pregnant (for a specified time): *six months gone.* **7.** (usually foll. by *on*) *Slang.* in love with.

goner (ˈgɒnə) *n. Slang.* a person about to die or a thing beyond help or recovery.

gonfalon (ˈgɒnfələn) *n.* a banner hanging from a crossbar, usually ending in streamers. [Germanic]

gong (gɒŋ) *n.* **1.** a rimmed metal disc that produces a note when struck. **2.** *Brit. slang.* a medal. [Malay]

gonorrhoea *or esp. U.S.* **gonorrhea** (ˌgɒnəˈrɪə) *n.* a venereal disease characterized by inflammation and a discharge from the genital organs. [Greek *gonos* semen + *rhoia* flux]

goo (guː) *n. Informal.* **1.** a sticky substance. **2.** sickly sentiment. [origin unknown]

good (gʊd) *adj.* **better, best.** **1.** having admirable, pleasing, superior, or desirable qualities: *a good teacher.* **2.** morally excellent; virtuous: *a good man.* **3.** suitable for a purpose: *a good winter coat.* **4.** beneficial: *vegetables are good for you.* **5.** not ruined or decayed: *the meat is still good.* **6.** kindly or generous: *you are good to him.* **7.** valid or genuine: *I would not do this without good reason.* **8.** honourable or held in high esteem: *a good family.* **9.** financially sound: *a good investment.* **10.** competent or talented: *he's good at science.* **11.** obedient or well-behaved: *a good dog.* **12.** reliable or recommended: *a good make of clothes.* **13.** giving material pleasure: *the good life.* **14.** complete; full: *I took a good look round the house.* **15.** opportune: *a good time to ask for a rise.* **16.** satisfying or enjoyable: *a good rest.* **17.** newest or of the best quality: *keep the good plates for guests.* **18.** fairly large, extensive, or long: *a good distance away.* **19.** ample: *a good supply of food.* **20. as good as.** virtually; practically: *as good as new.* ~*interj.* **21.** an exclamation of approval or pleasure. ~*n.* **22.** moral or material advantage; benefit or profit: *what is the good of worrying?* **23.** positive moral qualities; virtue. **24.** (*sometimes cap.*) moral qualities seen as an abstract entity: *the conflict between Good and Evil.* **25.** a good thing. **26. for good (and all).** forever; permanently: *I have left them for good.* **27. good for** *or* **on you.** well done or well said: a term of congratulation. **28. make good. a.** to recompense or repair damage or injury. **b.** to be successful. **c.** to fulfil (something intended or promised). ~See also **goods.** [Old English *gōd*]

Good Book *n.* the Bible.

goodbye (ˌgʊdˈbaɪ) *interj.* **1.** farewell: an expression used on parting. ~*n.* **2.** a parting; farewell: *I said my goodbyes.* [from *God be with ye*]

good day *interj.* an expression of greeting or farewell used during the day.

good-for-nothing *n.* **1.** an irresponsible or worthless person. ~*adj.* **2.** irresponsible; worthless.

Good Friday *n.* the Friday before Easter, observed by Christians as a commemoration of the Crucifixion of Jesus.

goodies (ˈgʊdɪz) *pl. n.* any things considered particularly desirable.

goodly (ˈgʊdlɪ) *adj.* **-lier, -liest. 1.** considerable: *a goodly amount.* **2.** *Obs.* attractive, pleasing, or fine. —**ˈgoodliness** *n.*

good morning *interj.* an expression of greeting or farewell used in the morning.

good-natured *adj.* tolerant and kindly.

goodness (ˈgʊdnɪs) *n.* **1.** the quality of

being good. **2.** kindness. **3.** virtue. ~*interj.* **4.** an exclamation of surprise.

good night *interj.* an expression of farewell, used in the evening or at night.

goods (gʊdz) *pl. n.* **1.** movable personal property. **2.** merchandise. **3.** *Chiefly Brit.* freight. **4. deliver the goods.** *Informal.* to do that which is expected or required. **5. have the goods on someone.** *U.S. & Canad. slang.* to know something incriminating about someone.

Good Samaritan *n.* a person who helps another in difficulty or distress. [from a parable in Luke 10:30-37]

Good Shepherd *n. New Testament.* a title given to Jesus Christ in John 10:11-12.

good-tempered *adj.* of a tolerant, kindly, and generous disposition.

good turn *n.* a helpful and friendly act.

goodwill (ˌgʊdˈwɪl) *n.* **1.** benevolence; kindly feeling. **2.** willingness or acquiescence. **3.** the popularity and good reputation of a well-established business, considered as a valuable asset.

goody (ˈgʊdɪ) *interj.* **1.** a child's exclamation of pleasure. ~*n., pl.* **goodies. 2.** *Informal.* the hero in a film or book. **3.** See **goodies.**

goody-goody *n., pl.* **-goodies. 1.** *Informal.* a smugly virtuous person. ~*adj.* **2.** smugly virtuous.

gooey (ˈguːɪ) *adj.* **gooier, gooiest.** *Informal.* **1.** sticky, soft, and often sweet. **2.** sentimental.

goof (guːf) *Informal.* ~*n.* **1.** a foolish error. **2.** a stupid person. ~*vb.* **3.** to bungle (something); botch. **4.** (often foll. by *about* or *around*) to fool (around); mess (about). [prob. from dialect *goff* simpleton]

go off *vb.* **1.** to stop functioning: *the lights suddenly went off.* **2.** to explode. **3.** (of an alarm) to sound. **4.** to occur as specified: *the meeting went off well.* **5.** to leave (a place): *the actors went off stage.* **6.** to fall asleep. **7.** *Brit. informal.* (of food) to become stale or rotten. **8.** *Brit. informal.* to stop liking.

goofy (ˈguːfɪ) *adj.* **goofier, goofiest.** *Informal.* foolish; silly. —**ˈgoofiness** *n.*

googly (ˈguːglɪ) *n., pl.* **-lies.** *Cricket.* a ball bowled so as to change direction unexpectedly on the bounce. [origin unknown]

goon (guːn) *n.* **1.** a stupid person. **2.** *U.S. informal.* a hired thug. [dialect *gooney* fool + U.S. cartoon character Alice the *Goon*]

go on *vb.* **1.** to continue or proceed. **2.** to happen: *there's something strange going on.* **3.** *Theatre.* to make an entrance on stage. **4.** to talk. **5.** to criticize or nag: *stop going on at me!*

goosander (guːˈsændə) *n.* a duck of Europe and North America, having a dark head and white body in the male, and a sharp serrated beak. [prob. from *goose* + Old Norse *önd* (genitive *andar*) duck]

goose¹ (guːs) *n., pl.* **geese. 1.** a web-footed long-necked migratory bird typically larger than a duck. **2.** the female of such a bird, as opposed to the male (gander). **3.** *Informal.* a silly person. **4.** the flesh of the goose, used as food. **5. cook someone's goose.** *Informal.* to spoil someone's chances or plans completely. [Old English *gōs*]

goose² (guːs) *Slang.* ~*vb.* **1.** to prod (a person) playfully in the bottom. ~*n., pl.* **gooses. 2.** such a prod. [from the jabbing of a goose's bill]

gooseberry ('guzbərı, -brı) *n., pl.* **-ries. 1.** the edible yellow-green berries of a Eurasian shrub. **2. play gooseberry.** *Brit. informal.* to be an unwanted single person accompanying a couple.

goose flesh *n.* the bumpy condition of the skin due to cold or fear, in which the muscles at the base of the hair follicles contract, making the hair bristle. Also: **goose pimples.**

goosegog ('guzgɒg) *n. Brit. informal.* a gooseberry.

goose step *n.* **1.** a military march step in which the leg is swung rigidly to an exaggerated height. ~*vb.* **goose-step, -stepping, -stepped. 2.** to march in goose step.

go out *vb.* **1.** to be extinguished or cease to function: *the fire has gone out.* **2.** to cease to be fashionable or popular: *that style went out ages ago!* **3.** (of a broadcast) to be transmitted. **4.** to go to entertainments or social functions. **5.** (usually foll. by *with* or *together*) to spend time (with someone) regularly as a couple.

go over *vb.* **1.** to be received in a specified manner: *the concert went over well.* **2.** to examine and emend or repair as necessary: *he went over the accounts; can you go over my car, please?* **3.** to rehearse or revise: *I'll go over my lines before the play.*

gopher ('gəufə) *n.* **1.** an American burrowing rodent having wide cheek pouches. **2.** same as **ground squirrel. 3.** a burrowing tortoise of North America. [origin unknown]

Gordian knot ('gɔːdɪən) *n.* **cut the Gordian knot.** to solve a complicated problem by bold or forceful action. [*Gordius*, in Greek legend, who tied a knot that Alexander the Great cut with a sword]

gore¹ (gɔː) *n.* blood shed from a wound. [Old English *gor* dirt]

gore² (gɔː) *vb.* (of an animal) to pierce or stab (a person or another animal) with a horn or tusk. [prob. from Old English *gār* spear]

gore³ (gɔː) *n.* **1.** a tapering piece of material in a garment, sail, or umbrella. ~*vb.* **2.** to make into or with a gore or gores. [Old English *gāra*] —**gored** *adj.*

gorge (gɔːdʒ) *n.* **1.** a deep ravine. **2.** the contents of the stomach. **3.** *Archaic.* the gullet. **4. make one's gorge rise.** to induce feelings of disgust or resentment. ~*vb.* **5.** to eat (food) ravenously. **6.** to stuff (oneself) with food. [Latin *gurges* whirlpool]

gorgeous ('gɔːdʒəs) *adj.* **1.** strikingly beautiful or attractive. **2.** *Informal.* extremely pleasant or fine: *gorgeous weath-*

er. [Old French *gorgias* elegant] —**'gorgeously** *adv.*

Gorgon ('gɔːgən) *n.* **1.** *Greek myth.* one of three monstrous sisters who had live snakes for hair, and were so horrifying that anyone looking on them was turned to stone. **2.** (*often not cap.*) *Informal.* an ugly, fierce, or unpleasant woman. [Greek *gorgos* terrible]

Gorgonzola (,gɔːgən'zəulə) *n.* a semihard blue-veined cheese of sharp flavour. [after *Gorgonzola*, Italian town where it originated]

gorilla (gə'rɪlə) *n.* the largest anthropoid ape, inhabiting the forests of central W Africa. It is stocky with a short muzzle and coarse dark hair. [Greek *Gorillai*, an African tribe renowned for their hairy appearance]

gormless ('gɔːmlɪs) *adj. Brit. informal.* stupid; dull. [obs. *gaumless*]

go round *vb.* **1.** to be sufficient: *is there enough food to go round?* **2.** to circulate (in): *measles is going round the school.* **3.** to be long enough to encircle: *will that belt go round you?*

gorse (gɔːs) *n.* an evergreen shrub which has yellow flowers and thick green spines instead of leaves. [Old English *gors*] —**'gorsy** *adj.*

gory ('gɔːrɪ) *adj.* **gorier, goriest. 1.** horrific or bloodthirsty: *a gory tale.* **2.** involving bloodshed: *a gory battle.* **3.** covered in gore. —**'goriness** *n.*

gosh (gɒʃ) *interj.* an exclamation of mild surprise or wonder. [euphemistic for *God*]

goshawk ('gɒs,hɔːk) *n.* a large, swift, short-winged hawk. [Old English *gōshafoc*]

gosling ('gɒzlɪŋ) *n.* a young goose. [Old Norse *gæslingr*]

go-slow *n. Brit.* a deliberate slowing of the rate of production by workers as a tactic in industrial conflict.

gospel ('gɒspʰl) *n.* **1.** Also called: **gospel truth.** an unquestionable truth: *to take someone's word as gospel.* **2.** a doctrine held to be of great importance. **3.** Black religious music originating in the churches of the Southern U.S. **4.** the story of Christ's life and teachings. [Old English *gōd* good + *spell* message]

Gospel ('gɒspʰl) *n.* one of the first four books of the New Testament, namely Matthew, Mark, Luke, and John.

gossamer ('gɒsəmə) *n.* **1.** a very fine fabric. **2.** a filmy cobweb often seen on foliage or floating in the air. [prob. Middle English *gos* goose + *soer* summer; referring to *St Martin's summer*, a period in November when goose was eaten and cobwebs abound]

gossip ('gɒsɪp) *n.* **1.** idle chat. **2.** a conversation involving chatter about other people. **3.** a person who habitually talks about others, usually maliciously. ~*vb.* **4.** (often foll. by *about*) to talk idly or maliciously (about other people). [Old English *godsibb* godparent, applied to a woman's female friends at the birth of a child] —**'gossipy** *adj.*

got (gɒt) *vb.* **1.** the past of **get.** **2. have got. a.** to possess. **b.** (*takes an infinitive*) used to express necessity: *I've got to get a new coat.*

Goth (gɒθ) *n.* **1.** a member of an East Germanic people who invaded many parts of the Roman Empire from the 3rd to the 5th century. **2.** a rude or barbaric person. [Greek *Gothoi*]

Gothic ('gɒθɪk) *adj.* **1.** of or resembling the style of architecture used in W Europe from the 12th to the 16th centuries, characterized by pointed arches, ribbed vaults, and flying buttresses. **2.** (*sometimes not cap.*) of or in a literary style characterized by gloom, horror, and the supernatural, popular in the late 18th century. **3.** of the Goths or their language. **4.** (*sometimes not cap.*) primitive and barbarous. ~*n.* **5.** Gothic architecture or art. **6.** the extinct language of the ancient Goths. **7.** a heavy ornate script typeface much used from about the 15th to 18th centuries. —'**Gothi-,cism** *n.*

go through *vb.* **1.** to be approved: *the amendment went through.* **2.** to use up; exhaust: *we went through our supplies in a day.* **3.** to examine: *he went through the figures.* **4.** to suffer: *she went through great pain.* **5.** to rehearse or revise: *go through the details again.* **6.** to search: *she went through the cupboards.* **7.** (foll. by *with*) to bring to a successful conclusion, often by persistence.

go together *vb.* **1.** to be mutually suited; harmonize: *the colours go well together.* **2.** *Informal.* (of two people) to be romantically involved with each other.

gotten ('gɒt'n) *vb. U.S.* a past participle of **get.**

gouache (gʊ'ɑːʃ) *n.* **1.** a painting technique using opaque watercolours bound with glue. **2.** the paint used in this technique. **3.** a painting done by this method. [French]

Gouda ('gaʊdə) *n.* a flat round mild Dutch cheese, orig. made in the town of Gouda.

gouge (gaʊdʒ) *vb.* **1.** (usually foll. by *out*) to scoop or force (something) out of its position. **2.** (sometimes foll. by *out*) to cut (a hole or groove) in (something) with a pointed object. ~*n.* **3.** a type of chisel with a curved blade for cutting holes or grooves. **4.** a mark or groove made by gouging. [French]

goulash ('guːlæʃ) *n.* a rich stew, originating in Hungary and highly seasoned with paprika. [Hungarian *gulyás hus* herdsman's meat]

go up *vb.* **1.** to move to a higher place or level: *prices are going up.* **2.** to be destroyed: *the house went up in flames.*

gourd (gʊəd) *n.* **1.** the fruit of a plant of the cucumber family, whose dried shells are used for ornaments or drinking cups. **2.** a plant bearing this fruit. **3.** a container made from a dried gourd shell. [Old French *gourde*]

gourmand ('gʊəmənd) *n.* a person devoted to eating and drinking, usually to excess. [Old French *gourmant*]

gourmet ('gʊəmeɪ) *n.* a connoisseur of good food and drink. [French]

gout (gaʊt) *n.* **1.** a disease characterized by painful inflammation of certain joints, esp. of the big toe. **2.** *Archaic.* a drop or splash. [Latin *gutta* a drop] —'**gouty** *adj.*

Gov. *or* **gov.** **1.** government. **2.** governor.

govern ('gʌv'n) *vb.* **1.** to direct and control the policy and affairs of (an organization or nation); rule. **2.** to exercise restraint over; control: *to govern one's temper.* **3.** to decide or determine (something): *what governed his decision to leave?* **4.** (of a word) to determine the inflection of (another word). [Latin *gubernāre* to steer] —'**governable** *adj.*

governance ('gʌvənəns) *n.* **1.** government, control, or authority. **2.** the action, manner, or system of governing.

governess ('gʌvənɪs) *n.* a woman employed in a private household to teach and train the children.

government ('gʌvənmənt, 'gʌvəmənt) *n.* **1.** the exercise of political authority over a country or state. **2.** the system by which a country or state is ruled: *tyrannical government.* **3.** (sometimes *cap.*) the executive policy-making body of a country or state. **4.** regulation; direction. —**governmental** (,gʌvən'ment'l, ,gʌvə'ment'l) *adj.*

governor ('gʌvənə) *n.* **1.** an official governing a province or region. **2.** the representative of the Crown in a British colony. **3.** *Brit.* the senior administrator of a society, institution, or prison. **4.** the chief executive of a U.S. state. **5.** a device that automatically controls the speed of an engine. **6.** *Brit. informal.* one's father or employer. —'**governor,ship** *n.*

governor general *n., pl.* **governors general** *or* **governor generals. 1.** the representative of the Crown in a Commonwealth dominion. **2.** *Brit.* a governor with authority over other governors.

Govt Government.

go with *vb.* **1.** to accompany. **2.** to blend or harmonize: *that new wallpaper goes well with the furniture.* **3.** to belong with: *a company car goes with the job.* **4.** (of two people) to be romantically involved with each other.

go without *vb. Chiefly Brit.* to be denied or deprived of (something): *if you don't like your tea, you can go without.*

gown (gaʊn) *n.* **1.** a woman's long formal dress. **2.** a surgeon's overall. **3.** a loose wide official robe worn by clergymen, judges, lawyers, and academics. **4.** the members of a university collectively. [Late Latin *gunna* garment made of fur]

goy (gɔɪ) *n., pl.* **goyim** ('gɔɪm) *or* **goys.** *Slang.* a Jewish word for a **Gentile.** [Yiddish]

GP general practitioner.

GPO general post office.

grab (græb) *vb.* **grabbing, grabbed. 1.** to seize hold of (something). **2.** to seize illegally or unscrupulously. **3.** to take (food, drink, or rest) hurriedly: *to grab a meal.* **4.** *Informal.* to interest; impress.

~*n.* **5.** a grabbing. **6.** a mechanical device for gripping objects. [prob. from Middle Dutch *grabben*]

grace (greɪs) *n.* **1.** elegance and beauty of movement, form, or expression. **2.** a pleasing or charming quality. **3.** goodwill or favour. **4.** a delay granted for the completion of a task or payment of a debt. **5.** courtesy; decency. **6.** *Christian theol.* the free and unmerited favour of God shown towards man. **7.** a short prayer of thanks for a meal. **8. airs and graces.** affected manner. **9. with (a) bad grace.** unwillingly or grudgingly. **10. with (a) good grace.** willingly or ungrudgingly. ~*vb.* **11.** to add grace: *flowers graced the room.* **12.** to honour or favour: *to grace a party with one's presence.* [Latin *grātia*]

Grace (greɪs) *n.* (preceded by *Your, His,* or *Her*) a title of a duke, duchess, or archbishop.

grace-and-favour *n.* (*modifier*) *Brit.* (of a house or flat) owned by the sovereign and granted rent-free to someone.

graceful ('greɪsfʊl) *adj.* characterized by beauty of movement, style, or form. —'**gracefully** *adv.* —'**gracefulness** *n.*

graceless ('greɪslɪs) *adj.* **1.** lacking manners. **2.** lacking elegance.

grace note *n. Music.* a merely ornamental note, usually printed in small type.

Graces ('greɪsɪz) *pl. n. Greek myth.* three sister goddesses, givers of charm and beauty.

gracious ('greɪʃəs) *adj.* **1.** showing kindness and courtesy. **2.** condescendingly polite. **3.** characterized by elegance, ease, and indulgence: *gracious living.* **4.** compassionate. ~*interj.* **5.** an expression of mild surprise or wonder. —'**graciously** *adv.* —'**graciousness** *n.*

gradation (grə'deɪʃən) *n.* **1.** a series of systematic stages; gradual progression. **2.** (*often pl.*) a stage in such a series or progression. **3.** an arranging in stages or a gradual progression. —**gra'date** *vb.* —**gra'dational** *adj.*

grade (greɪd) *n.* **1.** a position or degree in a scale of quality, rank, or size. **2.** a group of people or things of the same category. **3.** a stage in a course of progression. **4.** a mark or rating indicating a student's level of achievement. **5.** *U.S. & Canad.* a class or year in a school. **6. make the grade.** *Informal.* **a.** to reach the required standard. **b.** to succeed. ~*vb.* **7.** to arrange according to quality or rank. **8.** to give a grade to. **9.** to change or blend (something) gradually; merge. **10.** to level (ground or a road) to a suitable gradient. [Latin *gradus* step]

gradient ('greɪdɪənt) *n.* **1.** Also (esp. U.S.): **grade.** a sloping part of a railway, road, or path. **2.** Also (esp. U.S. and Canad.): **grade.** a measure of the steepness of such a slope. **3.** a measure of the change in something, such as the angle of a curve, over a specified distance. [Latin *gradiēns* stepping]

gradual ('grædjʊəl) *adj.* occurring, developing, or moving in small stages: *a gradual improvement; a gradual slope.* [Latin *gradus* a step] —'**gradually** *adv.*

gradualism ('grædjʊə,lɪzəm) *n.* the policy of seeking to change something gradually. —'**gradualist** *n., adj.*

graduate *n.* ('grædjʊɪt). **1.** a person who holds a university or college degree. **2.** *U.S. & Canad.* a student who has completed a course of studies at a high school and received a diploma. **3.** *U.S. & Canad.* same as **postgraduate.** ~*vb.* ('grædjʊ,eɪt). **4.** to receive a degree or diploma. **5.** to mark (a measuring flask or instrument) with units of measurement. **6.** to group according to type or quality. **7.** (often foll. by *to*) to change by degrees (from something to something else). [Latin *gradus* a step]

graduation (,grædjʊ'eɪʃən) *n.* **1.** a graduating or being graduated. **2.** the ceremony at which degrees and diplomas are conferred. **3.** a mark or marks indicating measure on an instrument or container.

Graeco-Roman *or esp. U.S.* **Greco-Roman** (,griːkəʊ'rəʊmən) *adj.* having Greek and Roman influences.

graffiti (græ'fiːtɪ) *pl. n.* (sometimes functioning as sing.) drawings or words scribbled or sprayed on walls or posters. [Italian: little scratches]

graft[1] (grɑːft) *n.* **1. a.** a small piece of tissue from one plant that is made to unite with another plant so that they grow together as one. **b.** a plant produced by this method. **2.** *Surgery.* a piece of tissue transplanted to an area of the body in need of the tissue. **3.** grafting. ~*vb.* **4.** to join part of one plant onto another plant so that they grow together as one. **5.** to transplant (tissue) or (of tissue) to be transplanted. **6.** to attach or incorporate or become attached or incorporated: *modern methods grafted onto old ideas.* [Greek *grapheion* stylus]

graft[2] (grɑːft) *n.* **1.** *Informal.* hard work. **2.** the obtaining of money by taking advantage of one's position. ~*vb.* **3.** *Informal.* to work hard. **4.** to acquire by or practise graft. [origin unknown]

Grail (greɪl) *n.* See **Holy Grail.**

grain (greɪn) *n.* **1.** the small hard seedlike fruit of a cereal plant. **2.** a mass of such fruits gathered for food. **3.** cereal plants in general. **4.** a small hard particle: *a grain of sand.* **5. a.** the arrangement of the fibres, layers, or particles in wood, leather, or stone. **b.** the pattern or texture resulting from this. **6.** a very small amount: *a grain of truth.* **7. go against the grain.** to be contrary to one's natural inclinations. ~*vb.* **8.** to form or cause to form into grains. **9.** to give a granular or roughened appearance or texture to. **10.** to paint or stain in imitation of the grain of wood or leather. [Latin *grānum*] —'**grainy** *adj.*

grallatorial (,grælə'tɔːrɪəl) *adj.* of or relating to long-legged wading birds. [Latin *grallātor* one who walks on stilts]

gram or **gramme** (græm) *n.* a metric unit of mass equal to one thousandth of a kilogram. [Greek *gramma* small weight]

gram. **1.** grammar. **2.** grammatical.

gramineous (grə'mınıəs) *adj.* of or like grass. Also: **graminaceous** (ˌgræmı'neıʃəs). [Latin *grāmen* grass]

graminivorous (ˌgræmı'nıvərəs) *adj.* (of animals) feeding on grass. [Latin *grāmen* grass + *vorāre* to swallow]

grammar ('græmə) *n.* **1.** the branch of linguistics that deals with the form, function, and order of words. **2.** a systematic description of the generally accepted rules of a language. **3.** a book containing such a description. **4.** one's language with regard to observance of the grammatical rules: *the teacher told him to watch his grammar.* [Greek *gramma* letter]

grammarian (grə'meərıən) *n.* a person who studies or writes about grammar for a living.

grammar school *n.* **1.** *Brit.* (esp. formerly) a secondary school providing an education with an academic bias. **2.** *U.S.* same as **elementary school**. **3.** *Austral.* a private school, usually one controlled by a church. **4.** *N.Z.* a secondary school forming part of the public education system.

grammatical (grə'mætık³l) *adj.* **1.** of grammar. **2.** (of a sentence) following the rules of grammar. —**gram'matically** *adv.*

gramme (græm) *n.* same as **gram**.

gramophone ('græmə,fəʊn) *n.* an old-fashioned type of record player. [inversion of *phonogram*]

grampus ('græmpəs) *n.*, *pl.* **-puses. 1.** a dolphin-like mammal with a blunt snout. **2.** a person who puffs or breathes heavily. [Old French *gras* fat + *pois* fish]

gran (græn) *n.* *Informal.* a grandmother.

granary ('grænərı; *U.S.* 'greınərı) *n.*, *pl.* **-ries. 1.** a building for storing threshed grain. **2.** a region that produces a large amount of grain. [Latin *grānārium*]

grand (grænd) *adj.* **1.** large or impressive in size or appearance; magnificent: *grand scenery; a grand feast.* **2.** dignified or haughty. **3.** designed to impress: *grand gestures.* **4.** *Informal.* excellent; wonderful. **5.** comprehensive; complete: *a grand total.* **6.** worthy of respect: *a grand old man.* **7.** most important; chief: *the grand arena.* ~*n.* **8.** See **grand piano**. **9.** (*pl.* **grand**) *Slang.* a thousand pounds or dollars. [Latin *grandis*] —**'grandly** *adv.*

grand- *prefix.* (in designations of kinship) one generation older or younger than: *grandfather; grandson.* [French]

grandam ('grændəm, -dæm) *or* **grandame** ('grændeım, -dəm) *n.* *Archaic.* a grandmother. [Anglo-French GRAND- + *dame* lady, mother]

grandchild ('græn,tʃaıld) *n.*, *pl.* **-children.** the son or daughter of one's child.

granddad ('græn,dæd) *or* **granddaddy** *n.*, *pl.* **-dads** *or* **-daddies.** *Informal.* a grandfather.

granddaughter ('græn,dɔːtə) *n.* a daughter of one's son or daughter.

grand duke *n.* a prince or nobleman who rules a territory, state, or principality. —**grand duchess** *fem.* *n.* —**grand duchy** *n.*

grande dame (grɒnd'dɑːm) *n.* a woman regarded as the most experienced or venerable member of her profession or group. [French]

grandee (græn'diː) *n.* **1.** a high-ranking Spanish or Portuguese noble. **2.** a person of high station. [Spanish *grande*]

grandeur ('grændʒə) *n.* **1.** personal greatness, dignity, or nobility. **2.** magnificence; splendour.

grandfather ('græn,fɑːðə, 'grænd-) *n.* the father of one's father or mother.

grandfather clock *n.* a long-pendulum clock in a tall standing wooden case.

grandiloquent (græn'dıləkwənt) *adj.* pompous or inflated in language. [Latin *grandiloquus*] —**gran'diloquence** *n.*

grandiose ('grændı,əʊs) *adj.* **1.** pretentiously grand. **2.** on a large or impressive scale. [French] —**grandiosity** (ˌgrændı'ɒsıtı) *n.*

grand jury *n.* *Law, chiefly U.S.* a jury which investigates accusations of crime to ascertain whether the evidence is adequate to bring a prosecution.

grandma ('grænd,mɑː), **grandmama**, *or* **grandmamma** ('grænmə,mɑː) *n.* *Informal.* a grandmother.

grand mal (grɒn 'mæl) *n.* a form of epilepsy characterized by loss of consciousness and violent convulsions. [French: great illness]

grandmaster ('grænd,mɑːstə) *n.* a leading exponent of any of various arts, such as chess.

grandmother ('græn,mʌðə, 'grænd-) *n.* the mother of one's father or mother.

Grand National *n.* **the.** an annual steeplechase run at Aintree, Liverpool.

grandnephew ('græn,nevjuː, -,nefjuː, 'grænd-) *n.* a great-nephew.

grandniece ('græn,niːs, 'grænd-) *n.* a great-niece.

grand opera *n.* an opera that has a serious plot and no spoken dialogue.

grandpa ('græn,pɑː) *or* **grandpapa** ('grænpə,pɑː) *n.* *Informal.* a grandfather.

grandparent ('græn,peərənt, 'grænd-) *n.* the father or mother of either of one's parents.

grand piano *n.* a large piano in which the strings are arranged horizontally.

Grand Prix (grɒn 'priː) *n.* any of a series of formula motor races to determine the annual Drivers' World Championship. [French: great prize]

grandsire ('græn,saıə, 'grænd-) *n.* *Archaic.* a grandfather.

grandson ('grænsʌn, 'grænd-) *n.* a son of one's son or daughter.

grandstand ('græn,stænd, 'grænd-) *n.* the main block of seats commanding the best view at a sports ground.

grand tour *n.* **1.** (formerly) an extended tour of continental Europe. **2.** *Informal.* a sightseeing trip or tour of inspection.

grange (greındʒ) *n.* *Chiefly Brit.* a farmhouse or country house with its farm buildings. [Anglo-French *graunge*]

granite ('grænɪt) n. a very hard igneous rock consisting of quartz and feldspars: widely used for building. [Italian *granito* grained]

granivorous (græ'nɪvərəs) adj. (of animals) feeding on seeds and grain. [Latin *grānum* grain + *vorāre* to swallow]

granny or **grannie** ('grænɪ) n., pl. **-nies.** *Informal.* a grandmother.

granny flat n. self-contained accommodation in or adjoining a house, suitable for an elderly parent.

granny knot n. a reef knot with the ends crossed the wrong way, making it liable to slip or jam.

grant (grɑːnt) vb. **1.** to consent to perform or fulfil: *to grant a wish.* **2.** to permit as a favour: *to grant an interview.* **3.** to admit as true: *I grant it was a stupid mistake.* **4.** to bestow formally. **5. take for granted. a.** to accept (something) as true and not requiring verification. **b.** to take advantage of (something) without due appreciation. ~n. **6.** a sum of money provided by a government or public fund to a person or organization for a specific purpose. **7.** a privilege or right that has been granted. [Old French *graunter*]

Granth (grʌnt) n. the sacred scripture of the Sikhs. [Hindi]

grant-in-aid n., pl. **grants-in-aid.** a sum of money granted by one government to a lower level of government for a programme.

granular ('grænjʊlə) adj. **1.** of, like, or containing granules. **2.** having a grainy surface. —**granularity** (ˌgrænjʊ'lærɪtɪ) n.

granulate ('grænjʊˌleɪt) vb. **1.** to make into grains: *granulated sugar.* **2.** to make or become roughened in surface texture. —ˌgranu'lation n.

granule ('grænjuːl) n. a small grain. [Late Latin *grānulum* a small grain]

grape (greɪp) n. a round, sweet, juicy berry with a purple or green skin: eaten raw, dried to make raisins, currants, or sultanas, or used to make wine. [Old French *grape* bunch of grapes]

grapefruit ('greɪpˌfruːt) n., pl. **-fruit** or **-fruits.** a large round citrus fruit with yellow rind and juicy slightly bitter edible pulp.

grape hyacinth n. a plant with clusters of rounded blue flowers like tiny grapes.

grapeshot ('greɪpˌʃɒt) n. ammunition for cannons consisting of a cluster of iron balls that scatter after firing.

grapevine ('greɪpˌvaɪn) n. **1.** a vine cultivated for its grapes. **2.** *Informal.* an unofficial means of relaying information from person to person.

graph (grɑːf) n. **1.** a drawing showing the relation between certain sets of numbers or quantities by means of a series of dots or lines plotted with reference to a set of axes. ~vb. **2.** to draw or represent in a graph. [short for *graphic formula*]

-graph n. combining form. **1.** an instrument that writes or records: *telegraph.* **2.** a writing or record: *autograph.* [Greek *graphein* to write] —**graphic** or **-graphi-**

cal adj. combining form. —**graphically** adv. combining form.

graphic ('græfɪk) or **graphical** adj. **1.** vividly described: *a graphic account of the disaster.* **2.** of writing: *graphic symbols.* **3.** *Maths.* of or using a graph: *a graphic representation of the figures.* [Greek *graphikos*] —**graphically** adv.

graphic arts pl. n. the visual arts based on drawing or the use of line.

graphics ('græfɪks) n. **1.** (functioning as sing.) the process or art of drawing in accordance with mathematical rules. **2.** (functioning as pl.) the illustrations in a magazine or book, or in a television or film production. **3.** (functioning as pl.) *Computers.* information displayed in the form of diagrams or graphs.

graphite ('græfaɪt) n. a soft black form of carbon used in pencils, as a lubricant, and as a moderator in nuclear reactors. [German *Graphit*]

graphology (græ'fɒlədʒɪ) n. the study of handwriting, usually to analyse the writer's character. —**gra'phologist** n.

graph paper n. paper printed with intersecting lines for drawing graphs or diagrams.

-graphy n. combining form. indicating: **1.** a form of writing or representing: *calligraphy; photography.* **2.** an art or descriptive science: *choreography; oceanography.* [Greek *graphein* to write]

grapnel ('græpn'l) n. **1.** a device with several hooks at one end, which is used to grasp or secure an object. **2.** a small anchor with several hooks. [Old French *grapin*]

grapple ('græp'l) vb. **1.** to come to grips with (someone) in hand-to-hand combat. **2.** (foll. by *with*) to try to cope (with): *to grapple with a problem.* **3.** to secure with a grapple. ~n. **4.** a hook or instrument by which something is secured, such as a grapnel. **5. a.** a gripping or seizing, as in wrestling. **b.** a grip or hold. [Old French *grappelle* a little hook]

grappling iron or **hook** n. a grapnel.

grasp (grɑːsp) vb. **1.** to grip (something) firmly as with the hands. **2.** (sometimes foll. by *at*) to try to seize. **3.** to understand. ~n. **4.** a grip or clasp, as of a hand. **5.** total rule or possession. **6.** understanding; comprehension. [Low German *grapsen*]

grasping ('grɑːspɪŋ) adj. greedy; avaricious.

grass (grɑːs) n. **1.** any of a family of plants having jointed stems sheathed by long narrow leaves, such as cereals and bamboo. **2.** a small plant of this family eaten by animals or used for lawns or sports fields. **3.** a lawn. **4.** pasture land. **5.** *Slang.* marijuana. **6.** *Brit. slang.* a person who informs, usually on criminals. **7. let the grass grow under one's feet.** to waste time or opportunity. ~vb. **8.** to cover or become covered with grass. **9.** to feed with grass. **10.** (usually foll. by *on*) *Brit. slang.* to inform (on someone), usually

to the police. [Old English *græs*]
—**'grassy** *adj.*

grass hockey *n.* in W Canada, field
hockey, as contrasted with ice hockey.

grasshopper ('grɑːs,hɒpə) *n.* an insect
with long hind legs adapted for leaping.

grassland ('grɑːs,lænd) *n.* **1.** land covered with grass. **2.** pasture land.

grass roots *pl. n.* **1.** ordinary people as
distinct from the leadership of a group or
organization. **2.** the essentials.

grass snake *n.* a harmless European
snake having a brownish-green body with
variable markings.

grass widow *or (masc.)* **grass widower**
n. a person whose husband or wife is
regularly away for a time. [perhaps an
allusion to a grass bed as representing an
illicit relationship]

grate[1] (greɪt) *vb.* **1.** to reduce to shreds by
rubbing against a rough surface: *to grate
carrots.* **2.** to produce or cause to produce
a harsh rasping sound by scraping (something) against another object or surface.
3. (foll. by *on* or *upon*) to annoy. [Old
French *grater*] —**'grater** *n.*

grate[2] (greɪt) *n.* **1.** a framework of metal
bars for holding fuel in a fireplace or
furnace. **2.** a fireplace. **3.** same as **grating**[1]. [Latin *crātis* hurdle]

grateful ('greɪtfʊl) *adj.* **1.** feeling or showing gratitude. **2.** pleasant or welcome: *a
grateful rest.* [Latin *grātus*] —**'gratefully**
adv.

gratify ('grætɪ,faɪ) *vb.* **-fying, -fied.** **1.** to
satisfy or please. **2.** to indulge (a desire or
whim). [Latin *grātus* grateful + *facere* to
make] —**,gratifi'cation** *n.*

grating[1] ('greɪtɪŋ) *n.* a framework of metal
bars in the form of a grille set into a wall or
pavement.

grating[2] ('greɪtɪŋ) *adj.* **1.** (of sounds)
harsh and rasping. **2.** annoying; irritating.
~*n.* **3.** (*often pl.*) something produced by
grating.

gratis ('greɪtɪs, 'grætɪs, 'grɑːtɪs) *adv., adj.*
without payment; free. [Latin]

gratitude ('grætɪ,tjuːd) *n.* a feeling of
thankfulness for gifts or favours. [Latin
grātus grateful]

gratuitous (grə'tjuːɪtəs) *adj.* **1.** given or
received without charge or obligation. **2.**
without cause; unjustified. [Latin *grātuī-
tus*] —**gra'tuitously** *adv.* —**gra'tuitous-
ness** *n.*

gratuity (grə'tjuːɪtɪ) *n., pl.* **-ties.** money
given for services rendered; tip.

grav (græv) *n.* a unit of acceleration equal
to the standard acceleration of free fall.

grave[1] (greɪv) *n.* **1.** a place for the burial
of a corpse, usually underground. **2.** *Poetic.* (often preceded by *the*) death. **3. make
(someone) turn in his grave.** to do something that would have shocked a person
now dead. [Old English *græf*]

grave[2] (greɪv) *adj.* **1.** serious and solemn: *a
grave look.* **2.** full of or threatening danger: *a grave situation.* **3.** important; crucial: *grave matters of state.* **4.** (of colours)
sober or dull. **5.** (grɑːv) of an accent (`)

over vowels, denoting that the letter is
pronounced with a special quality (as in
French), or in a manner that gives the
vowel status as a syllable (as in English
agèd). ~*n.* (grɑːv). **6.** a grave accent.
[Latin *gravis*] —**'gravely** *adv.*

gravel ('græv°l) *n.* **1.** a mixture of rock
fragments and pebbles that is coarser than
sand. **2.** *Pathol.* small rough stones in the
kidneys or bladder. ~*vb.* **-elling, -elled** *or
U.S.* **-eling, -eled.** **3.** to cover with gravel.
4. to perplex. [Old French *gravele*]

gravelly ('græv°lɪ) *adj.* **1.** of, like, or full
of gravel. **2.** (of a voice) harsh and grating.

graven ('greɪv°n) *adj.* strongly fixed.

graven image *n. Chiefly Bible.* a carved
image used as an idol.

Graves (grɑːv) *n. (functioning as sing.)*
(*sometimes not cap.*) a dry, usually white
wine from the district around Bordeaux,
France.

gravestone ('greɪv,stəʊn) *n.* a stone
marking a grave.

graveyard ('greɪv,jɑːd) *n.* a cemetery or
burial ground.

gravid ('grævɪd) *adj. Med.* pregnant. [Latin
gravis heavy]

gravimeter (grə'vɪmɪtə) *n.* **1.** an instrument for measuring the force of gravity.
2. an instrument for measuring relative
density. [French *gravimètre*] —**gravimet-
ric** (,grævɪ'mɛtrɪk) *adj.* —**gra'vimetry** *n.*

gravitate ('grævɪ,teɪt) *vb.* **1.** *Physics.* to
move under the influence of gravity. **2.**
(usually foll. by *to* or *towards*) to be
influenced or drawn, as by strong impulses.

gravitation (,grævɪ'teɪʃən) *n.* **1.** the force
of attraction that bodies exert on one
another as a result of their mass. **2.** the
process or result of this interaction.
—**,gravi'tational** *adj.*

gravity ('grævɪtɪ) *n., pl.* **-ties.** **1.** the force
that attracts bodies towards the centre of a
celestial body, such as the earth or moon.
2. the property of having weight. **3.** same
as **gravitation.** **4.** seriousness or importance. **5.** solemn or dignified manner or
conduct. [Latin *gravitās* weight]

gravy ('greɪvɪ) *n., pl.* **-vies.** **a.** the juices
that come from meat during cooking. **b.**
the sauce made by thickening and flavouring these juices. [Old French *gravé*]

gravy boat *n.* a small boat-shaped vessel
for serving gravy or sauce.

gravy train *n. Slang.* a job or scheme that
produces good money or gains for little
effort.

gray (greɪ) *adj., n., vb. Chiefly U.S.* grey.

grayling ('greɪlɪŋ) *n., pl.* **-ling** *or* **-lings.** a
silvery-grey freshwater food fish resem-
bling the salmon.

graze[1] (greɪz) *vb.* to allow (cattle) to feed
on growing plants or (of animals) to feed
thus. [Old English *grasian*]

graze[2] (greɪz) *vb.* **1.** (often foll. by *against*
or *along*) to brush (against) gently in passing. **2.** to break the skin of (a part of the
body) by scraping. ~*n.* **3.** a grazing. **4.**

an abrasion made by grazing. [prob. special use of GRAZE¹]

grazier ('greɪzɪə) n. a rancher or farmer who keeps cattle or sheep on grazing land.

grazing ('greɪzɪŋ) n. land where grass is grown for livestock to feed upon.

grease (griːs, griːz) n. **1.** soft melted animal fat. **2.** any thick oily substance. ~vb. **3.** to soil, coat, or lubricate with grease. **4. grease the palm** (or **hand**) **of.** Slang. to bribe. [Latin crassus thick]

greasepaint ('griːsˌpeɪnt) n. theatrical make-up.

greasy ('griːsɪ, -zɪ) adj. **greasier, greasiest. 1.** coated or soiled with grease. **2.** containing or like grease. **3.** unctuous in manner. —**'greasiness** n.

greasy wool n. untreated wool still retaining the lanolin; used for waterproof clothing.

great (greɪt) adj. **1.** large in size. **2.** large in number: a great crowd. **3.** long in duration: a great wait. **4.** larger than others of its kind: the great auk. **5.** extreme or more than usual: great worry. **6.** of importance or consequence: a great decision. **7.** of exceptional talents or achievements: a great writer. **8.** heroic; noble: great deeds. **9.** illustrious or eminent: a great history. **10.** impressive or striking: a great show of wealth. **11.** active or enthusiastic: a great reader. **12.** (often foll. by at) skilful: a great carpenter; you are great at singing. **13.** Informal. excellent. [Old English] —**'greatly** adv. —**'greatness** n.

great- prefix. (in designations of kinship) two generations older or younger than: great-grandparent; great-grandchild.

great auk n. an extinct large flightless auk.

great-aunt n. an aunt of one's father or mother; a grandparent's sister.

Great Britain n. the mainland part of the British Isles; England, Scotland, and Wales.

great circle n. a circular section of a sphere that has a radius equal to that of the sphere.

greatcoat ('greɪtˌkəʊt) n. a heavy overcoat.

Great Dane n. a very large breed of dog with a short smooth coat.

great-nephew n. a son of one's nephew or niece; grandson of one's brother or sister. —**ˌgreat-'niece** fem. n.

Great Russian n. **1.** Linguistics. the Russian language. **2.** a member of the chief East Slavonic people of Russia. ~adj. **3.** of this people or their language.

Greats (greɪts) pl. n. (at Oxford University) **1.** the Honours course in classics and philosophy. **2.** the final examinations at the end of this course.

great seal n. (often caps.) the principal seal of a nation or sovereign, used to authenticate documents of the highest importance.

great tit n. a Eurasian bird with yellow-and-black underparts and a black-and-white head.

great-uncle n. an uncle of one's father or mother; a grandparent's brother.

Great War n. same as **World War I.**

greave (griːv) n. (often pl.) a piece of armour for the shin. [Old French greve]

grebe (griːb) n. an aquatic bird with lobed toes and a vestigial tail. [French]

Grecian ('griːʃən) adj. **1.** (of beauty or architecture) conforming to ancient Greek ideals. ~adj., n. **2.** same as **Greek.**

greed (griːd) n. **1.** excessive desire for food. **2.** any excessive desire.

greedy ('griːdɪ) adj. **greedier, greediest. 1.** excessively desirous of food. **2.** (foll. by for) eager (for): greedy for success. [Old English grædig] —**'greedily** adv.

Greek (griːk) n. **1.** the official language of Greece. **2.** a person from Greece. **3. it's (all) Greek to me.** Informal. I find it incomprehensible. ~adj. **4.** of Greece, the Greeks, or the Greek language.

Greek cross n. a cross with each of the four arms of the same length.

green (griːn) n. **1.** a colour, such as that of fresh grass, that lies between yellow and blue in the spectrum. **2.** something of this colour. **3.** a small area of grassy public land. **4.** an area of smooth turf kept for a special purpose: a putting green. **5.** (pl.) the leaves and stems of certain plants, eaten as a vegetable. **6.** (sometimes cap.) a person who supports environmentalist issues. ~adj. **7.** green in colour. **8.** vigorous; flourishing: a green old age. **9.** envious or jealous. **10.** inexperienced or gullible. **11.** characterized by foliage or green plants: a green wood; a green salad. **12.** denoting a unit of account used to make payments to agricultural producers within the EEC: green pound. **13.** (sometimes cap.) of or concerned with conservation and improvement of the environment: in a political context. **14.** fresh, raw, or unripe: green bananas. **15.** unhealthily pale: he was green after his boat trip. **16.** (of meat) not smoked or cured: green bacon. **17.** (of timber) not dried or seasoned. ~vb. **18.** to make or become green. [Old English grēne] —**'greenish** or **'greeny** adj. —**'greenness** n.

green bean n. a bean plant having narrow green edible pods.

green belt n. a protected zone of parkland or open country surrounding a town or city.

green card n. an insurance document covering motorists against accidents abroad.

Green Cross Code n. Brit. a road safety code for children.

greenery ('griːnərɪ) n., pl. **-eries.** green foliage.

green-eyed adj. jealous or envious.

greenfinch ('griːnˌfɪntʃ) n. a European finch, the male of which has olive-green plumage with yellow patches on the wings and tail.

green fingers pl. n. skill in growing plants.

greenfly ('griːnˌflaɪ) n., pl. **-flies.** a green

aphid commonly occurring as a pest on plants.

greengage ('griːnˌgeɪdʒ) n. a green sweet variety of plum. [after Sir W. *Gage*, botanist]

greengrocer ('griːnˌgrəʊsə) n. *Chiefly Brit.* a retail trader in fruit and vegetables. —'**green**ˌ**grocery** n.

greenhorn ('griːnˌhɔːn) n. an inexperienced person; novice. [orig. an animal with *green* (that is, young) horns]

greenhouse ('griːnˌhaʊs) n. a building with glass walls and roof for the cultivation of plants under controlled conditions.

greenhouse effect n. the gradual rise in temperature in the earth's atmosphere due to heat being absorbed from the sun and being unable to leave the atmosphere.

greenkeeper ('griːnˌkiːpə) n. a person responsible for maintaining a golf course or bowling green.

green light n. **1.** a signal to go. **2.** permission to proceed with a project.

green paper n. (*often caps.*) (in Britain) a government document containing policy proposals to be discussed.

green pepper n. the green unripe fruit of the sweet pepper, eaten as a vegetable.

green pound n. See **green** (sense 12).

greenroom ('griːnˌruːm, -ˌrʊm) n. (esp. formerly) a backstage room in a theatre where performers may rest or receive visitors.

greenshank ('griːnˌʃæŋk) n. a large European sandpiper with greenish legs.

greenstick fracture ('griːnˌstɪk) n. a fracture in which the bone is partly bent and splinters only on the outer side of the bend.

greensward ('griːnˌswɔːd) n. *Archaic or literary.* an area of fresh green turf.

green tea n. a tea made from leaves that have been dried quickly without fermenting.

Greenwich Mean Time ('grɪnɪdʒ) n. the local time of the 0° meridian passing through Greenwich, England: a basis for calculating times throughout most of the world.

greet¹ (griːt) vb. **1.** to address or meet with expressions of friendliness or welcome. **2.** to receive in a specified manner: *her remarks were greeted by silence.* **3.** to be immediately noticeable to: *the smell of bread greeted him.* [Old English grētan]

greet² (griːt) *Scot. or dialect.* ~vb. **1.** to weep; lament. ~n. **2.** weeping; lamentation. [Old English grētan]

greeting ('griːtɪŋ) n. **1.** the act or words of welcoming on meeting. **2.** (*pl.*) an expression of friendly salutation.

gregarious (grɪ'gɛərɪəs) adj. **1.** enjoying the company of others. **2.** (of animals) living together in herds or flocks. [Latin grex flock] —gre'**gariousness** n.

Gregorian calendar (grɪ'gɔːrɪən) n. the revision of the calendar introduced in 1582 by Pope Gregory XIII and still widely used.

Gregorian chant n. same as **plainsong.**

gremlin ('grɛmlɪn) n. an imaginary imp

jokingly blamed for malfunctions in machinery. [origin unknown]

grenade (grɪ'neɪd) n. a small bomb filled with explosive or gas, thrown by hand or fired from a rifle. [Spanish: pomegranate]

grenadier (ˌgrɛnə'dɪə) n. *Mil.* **1.** (in the British Army) a member of the senior regiment of infantry in the Household Brigade (the **Grenadier Guards**). **2.** (formerly) a soldier trained to throw grenades. [French]

grew (gruː) vb. the past tense of **grow.**

grey or U.S. **gray** (greɪ) adj. **1.** of a colour between black and white. **2.** (of hair) having partly turned white. **3.** dismal or dark; gloomy. **4.** dull or boring. **5.** having grey hair. **6.** ancient; venerable. ~n. **7.** a grey colour. **8.** grey cloth or clothing. **9.** an animal, usually a horse, that is grey or whitish. ~vb. **10.** to become or make grey. [Old English grǣg] —'**greyish** adj. —'**greyness** n.

Grey Friar n. a Franciscan friar.

greyhound ('greɪˌhaʊnd) n. a tall slender swift breed of dog.

greylag or **greylag goose** ('greɪˌlæg) n. a large grey Eurasian goose. [*lag* because it migrates later than other species]

grey matter n. **1.** the grey nerve tissue of the brain and spinal cord. **2.** *Informal.* intellect.

grey squirrel n. a grey-furred squirrel, native to E North America but now common in Britain.

grid (grɪd) n. **1.** See **gridiron. 2.** a network of crossing parallel lines on a map, plan, or graph paper for locating points. **3. the grid.** the national network of cables or pipes by which electricity, gas, or water is distributed. **4.** *Electronics.* an electrode that controls the flow of electrons between the cathode and anode of a valve. [from *gridiron*]

griddle ('grɪd'l) n. **1.** a thick round iron plate placed on top of a cooker and used to cook food. ~vb. **2.** to cook (food) on a griddle. [Old French gridil]

gridiron ('grɪdˌaɪən) n. **1.** a utensil of parallel metal bars, used to grill food. **2.** the field of play in American football. [Middle English gredire]

grief (griːf) n. **1.** deep or intense sorrow. **2.** something that causes keen distress. **3. come to grief.** *Informal.* to end unsuccessfully or disastrously.

grievance ('griːv'ns) n. **1.** a real or imaginary cause for complaint. **2.** a feeling of resentment at having been unfairly treated.

grieve (griːv) vb. to feel or cause to feel great sorrow or distress. [Old French grever] —**grieved** adj. —'**grieving** n., adj.

grievous ('griːvəs) adj. **1.** very severe or painful: *a grievous injury.* **2.** very serious; heinous: *a grievous sin.* **3.** showing or marked by grief. **4.** causing grief. —'**grievously** adv.

grievous bodily harm n. *Criminal law.* serious injury caused by one person to another.

griffin ('grɪfɪn), **griffon,** or **gryphon** n. a mythical winged monster with an eagle's head and a lion's body. [Old French *grifon*]

griffon ('grɪf'n) n. **1.** a small wire-haired breed of dog. **2.** a large vulture having a pale plumage with black wings. [French]

grill (grɪl) vb. **1.** to cook (food) by direct heat under a grill or over a hot fire, or (of food) to be cooked in this way. **2.** (usually passive) to torment with or as if with extreme heat: *grilled by the scorching sun*. **3.** Informal. to subject to relentless questioning. ~n. **4.** a device on a cooker that radiates heat downwards for grilling food. **5.** a gridiron for cooking food. **6.** grilled food. **7.** See **grillroom.** [Latin *crāticula* fine wickerwork] —**grilled** adj. —**grilling** n.

grille or **grill** (grɪl) n. **1.** a metal or wooden grating, used as a screen or partition. **2.** Also called: **radiator grille.** a grating that lets cooling air into the radiator of a motor vehicle. [Latin *crāticula* fine hurdlework]

grillroom ('grɪl,ruːm, -,rʊm) n. a restaurant specializing in grilled foods.

grilse (grɪls) n., pl. **grilses** or **grilse.** a salmon on its first return from the sea to fresh water. [origin unknown]

grim (grɪm) adj. **grimmer, grimmest. 1.** stern; resolute: *grim determination*. **2.** harsh or forbidding: *a grim castle*. **3.** harshly ironic or sinister: *grim laughter*. **4.** cruel, severe, or ghastly: *a grim accident*. **5.** Informal. unpleasant; disagreeable. [Old English *grimm*] —**grimly** adv. —**grimness** n.

grimace (grɪ'meɪs) n. **1.** an ugly or distorted facial expression, as of wry humour, disgust, or pain. ~vb. **2.** to contort the face. [French]

grimalkin (grɪ'mælkɪn, -'mɔːl-) n. an old female cat. [*grey* + *malkin*, short for *Maud*]

grime (graɪm) n. **1.** ingrained dirt, soot, or filth. ~vb. **2.** to make very dirty. [Middle Dutch] —**grimy** adj. —**griminess** n.

grin (grɪn) vb. **grinning, grinned. 1.** to smile broadly, revealing the teeth, or express (something) by such a smile: *to grin a welcome*. **2.** to draw back the lips revealing the teeth in a snarl or grimace. **3. grin and bear it.** Informal. to suffer hardship without complaint. ~n. **4.** a broad smile. **5.** a snarl or grimace. [Old English *grennian*] —**grinning** adj., n.

grind (graɪnd) vb. **grinding, ground. 1.** to reduce or be reduced to small particles by pounding or rubbing: *to grind corn*. **2.** to smooth, sharpen, or polish by friction: *to grind a knife*. **3.** (of two objects) to scrape or be scraped together with a harsh rasping sound. **4.** (often foll. by *down*) to oppress or tyrannize. **5.** to operate (a machine) by turning a handle. **6.** (foll. by *out*) to produce in a routine or uninspired manner: *he ground out his weekly article for the paper*. **7.** Informal. to study or work laboriously. ~n. **8.** Informal. laborious work or study. **9.** a specific size of ground particles. **10.** the act or sound of grinding. [Old English *grindan*]

grinder ('graɪndə) n. **1.** a machine that grinds. **2.** a molar tooth.

grindstone ('graɪnd,stəʊn) n. **1.** a revolving stone disc used for sharpening, grinding, or polishing. **2. keep** or **have one's nose to the grindstone.** to work hard and steadily.

grip (grɪp) n. **1.** a grasping and holding firmly: *he lost his grip on the slope*. **2.** the strength or way in which something is grasped: *a tight grip*. **3.** understanding or mastery of a subject or problem. **4. get** or **come to grips.** (often foll. by *with*) **a.** to deal with (a problem or subject). **b.** to tackle (an assailant). **5.** a handle. **6.** a travelling bag or holdall. **7.** a hairgrip. ~vb. **gripping, gripped. 8.** to take hold of firmly or tightly. **9.** to hold the interest or attention of: *to grip an audience*. [Old English *gripe*] —**gripping** adj.

gripe (graɪp) vb. **1.** Informal. to complain persistently. **2.** to cause or suffer sudden intense pain in the bowels. ~n. **3.** (usually pl.) a sudden intense pain in the bowels; colic. **4.** Informal. a complaint. [Old English *grīpan*]

grippe (grɪp) n. a former name for **influenza.** [French]

grisly ('grɪzlɪ) adj. **-lier, -liest.** causing horror or dread; gruesome. [Old English *grislic*] —**grisliness** n.

grist (grɪst) n. **1.** grain intended to be or that has been ground. **2. grist to** (or **for**) **the** (or **one's**) **mill.** anything that can be turned to profit or advantage. [Old English *grīst*]

gristle ('grɪs'l) n. cartilage present in meat. [Old English] —**gristly** adj.

grit (grɪt) n. **1.** small hard particles of sand, earth, or stone. **2.** coarse sandstone. **3.** indomitable courage or resolution. ~vb. **gritting, gritted. 4.** to clench or grind (the teeth) together. **5.** to cover (a surface, such as icy roads) with grit. [Old English *grēot*] —**gritter** n. —**gritty** adj.

grits (grɪts) pl. n. hulled or coarsely ground grain. [Old English *grytt*]

grizzle ('grɪz'l) vb. Informal, chiefly Brit. (esp. of a child) to fret; whine. [Germanic]

grizzled ('grɪz'ld) adj. **1.** streaked or mixed with grey. **2.** having grey hair.

grizzly ('grɪzlɪ) adj. **-zlier, -zliest. 1.** greyish; grizzled. ~n., pl. **-zlies. 2.** See **grizzly bear.**

grizzly bear n. a large N American variety of the brown bear: its fur has cream or white tips on the back, giving it a grizzled appearance.

groan (grəʊn) n. **1.** a long deep cry of pain, grief, or disapproval. **2.** a sound like a groan. **3.** Informal. a grumble or complaint. ~vb. **4.** to utter a long deep cry of pain, grief, or disapproval. **5.** to make a sound like a groan. **6.** (usually foll. by *beneath* or *under*) to be weighed down (by). **7.** Informal. to complain or grumble. [Old English *grānian*] —**groaning** adj., n.

groat (grəʊt) n. an obsolete British silver coin worth four old pennies. [Middle Dutch *groot*]

groats (grəʊts) *pl. n.* the hulled and crushed grain of various cereals. [Old English *grot* particle]

grocer ('grəʊsə) *n.* a dealer in foodstuffs and household supplies. [Old French *grossier*]

groceries ('grəʊsəriz) *pl. n.* merchandise sold by a grocer.

grocery ('grəʊsəri) *n., pl.* **-ceries.** the business or premises of a grocer.

grog (grɒg) *n.* **1.** diluted spirit, usually rum, as an alcoholic drink. **2.** *Austral. & N.Z. informal.* any alcoholic drink. [Old *Grog*, nickname of Edward Vernon, British admiral, who in 1740 issued naval rum diluted with water]

groggy ('grɒgi) *adj.* **-gier, -giest.** *Informal.* faint, weak, or dizzy. —'**grogginess** *n.*

grogram ('grɒgrəm) *n.* a coarse fabric of silk mixed with wool or mohair. [French]

groin (grɔin) *n.* **1.** the part of the body where the abdomen joins the legs. **2.** *Chiefly U.S.* same as **groyne.** **3.** *Archit.* a curved edge formed where two intersecting vaults meet. ~*vb.* **4.** *Archit.* to build with groins. [origin unknown]

grommet ('grɒmit) *or* **grummet** *n.* a rubber, plastic, or metal ring or eyelet. [obs. French *gourmer* bridle]

groom (gruːm, grʊm) *n.* **1.** a person employed to clean and look after horses. **2.** See **bridegroom. 3.** an officer of a royal or noble household. ~*vb.* **4.** to make or keep (one's clothes or appearance) clean and tidy. **5.** to clean and smarten (a horse or other animal). **6.** to train for a particular task or occupation: *to groom someone for the Presidency.* [Middle English *grom* manservant]

groomsman ('gruːmzmən, 'grʊmz-) *n., pl.* **-men.** a man who attends the groom at a wedding, usually the best man.

groove (gruːv) *n.* **1.** a long narrow furrow cut into a surface. **2.** the spiral channel in a gramophone record. **3.** a habitual existence or routine. ~*vb.* **4.** to form or cut a groove in. [Dutch *groeve*]

groovy ('gruːvi) *adj.* **groovier, grooviest.** *Dated slang.* attractive, fashionable, or exciting.

grope (grəʊp) *vb.* **1.** (usually foll. by *for*) to feel about uncertainly (for something). **2.** (usually foll. by *for* or *after*) to search uncertainly (for a solution or expression). **3.** to find (one's way) by groping. **4.** *Slang.* to fondle (someone's) body in a sexual way. ~*n.* **5.** a groping. [Old English *grāpian*]

grosbeak ('grəʊs,biːk, 'grɒs-) *n.* a finch with a large powerful bill. [French *grosbec*]

grosgrain ('grəʊ,grein) *n.* a heavy ribbed silk or rayon fabric. [French]

gros point (grəʊ) *n.* **1.** a cross-stitch in embroidery. **2.** work done in this stitch. [French]

gross (grəʊs) *adj.* **1.** repulsively fat. **2.** with no deductions for tax or the weight of the container; total: *gross sales; 150kg gross weight.* **3.** very coarse or vulgar. **4.** outrageously wrong; flagrant: *gross ineffi-* ciency. **5.** lacking in perception, sensitivity, or discrimination: *gross judgments.* **6.** thick; luxuriant. ~*n.* **7.** (*pl.* **gross**). twelve dozen. **8.** (*pl.* **grosses**). the entire amount or weight. ~*vb.* **9.** to earn as total revenue, before deductions. [Old French *gros* large] —'**grossly** *adv.* —'**grossness** *n.*

gross domestic product *n.* the total value of all goods and services produced domestically by a nation during a year.

gross national product *n.* the total value of all final goods and services produced annually by a nation. It is equivalent to gross domestic product plus net investment income from abroad.

gross profit *n. Accounting.* the difference between total revenue from sales and the total cost of purchases or materials.

grotesque (grəʊ'tɛsk) *adj.* **1.** strangely distorted; bizarre. **2.** of the grotesque in art. **3.** absurdly incongruous; ludicrous. ~*n.* **4.** an artistic style in which parts of human, animal, and plant forms are distorted and mixed, or a work of art in this style. **5.** a grotesque person or thing. [Old Italian (*pittura*) *grottesca* cave painting]

grotto ('grɒtəʊ) *n., pl.* **-toes** *or* **-tos.** **1.** a small picturesque cave. **2.** a construction in the form of a cave. [Old Italian *grotta*]

grotty ('grɒti) *adj.* **-tier, -tiest.** *Brit. slang.* **1.** nasty or unattractive. **2.** in bad condition. [from *grotesque*]

grouch (grautʃ) *Informal.* ~*vb.* **1.** to complain; grumble. ~*n.* **2.** a persistent complaint. **3.** a person who is always grumbling. [Old French *grouchier*] —'**grouchy** *adj.*

ground[1] (graʊnd) *n.* **1.** the land surface. **2.** earth or soil. **3.** (*pl.*) the land around a building. **4.** (*sometimes pl.*) an area given over to a purpose: *football ground; fishing grounds.* **5.** land having a particular characteristic: *high ground.* **6.** matter for consideration or discussion: *the report covered a lot of ground.* **7.** a viewpoint, as in an argument or controversy: *give ground; stand one's ground; shift one's ground.* **8.** advantage, as in a competition: *gain ground; lose ground.* **9.** (*often pl.*) reason; justification: *grounds for complaint.* **10.** a substance applied to a wall or canvas to prevent it reacting with or absorbing the paint. **11.** the background colour of a painting. **12.** (*pl.*) sediment or dregs. **13.** *U.S. & Canad.* an electrical earth. **14. break new ground.** to do something that has not been done before. **15. common ground.** an agreed basis for identifying issues in an argument. **16. cut the ground from under someone's feet.** to anticipate someone's action or argument and thus deprive it of force. **17. (down) to the ground.** *Brit. informal.* completely; absolutely: *it suited him down to the ground.* **18. get (something) off the ground.** to start (something). **19. into the ground.** to exhaustion or excess. **20.** (*modifier*) on or concerned with the ground: *ground frost; ground forces.* ~*vb.* **21.** to place on the ground. **22.** to instruct in the basics. **23.** to provide a basis for; establish. **24.** to confine (an aircraft or pilot) to the ground. **25.** *U.S. & Canad.* to connect (a circuit or electrical device) to an earth. **26.** *Naut.* to run (a vessel) aground. [Old English *grund*]

ground² (graʊnd) *vb.* **1.** past of **grind.** ~*adj.* **2.** having a surface produced by grinding. **3.** reduced to fine particles by grinding.

ground bass (beɪs) *n. Music.* a short melodic bass line that is repeated over and over again.

ground control *n.* the personnel and equipment on the ground that monitor the progress of aircraft or spacecraft.

ground cover *n.* dense low plants that grow over the surface of the ground.

ground floor *n.* the floor of a building level or almost level with the ground.

grounding (ˈgraʊndɪŋ) *n.* a foundation, esp. the basic general knowledge of a subject.

ground ivy *n.* an aromatic creeping plant with scalloped leaves and purplish-blue flowers.

groundless (ˈgraʊndlɪs) *adj.* without reason or justification: *his suspicions were groundless.*

groundnut (ˈgraʊndˌnʌt) *n.* **1.** the small edible underground tuber of a North American climbing plant. **2.** a peanut.

groundsel (ˈgraʊnsəl) *n.* a weed with heads of small yellow flowers. [Old English *gundeswilge*]

groundsheet (ˈgraʊndˌʃiːt) *n.* a waterproof sheet placed on the ground in a tent to keep out damp.

groundsman (ˈgraʊndzmən) *n., pl.* **-men.** a person employed to maintain a sports ground or park.

ground squirrel *n.* a burrowing rodent resembling a chipmunk, found in N America, E Europe, and Asia.

ground swell *n.* smooth heavy waves caused by a distant storm or earthquake.

groundwork (ˈgraʊndˌwɜːk) *n.* preliminary work as a foundation or basis.

group (gruːp) *n.* **1.** a number of people or things considered as a collective unit. **2.** a small band of players or singers, esp. of pop music. **3.** an association of companies under a single ownership. **4.** an air force unit larger than a squadron. **5.** *Chem.* two or more atoms that are bound together in a molecule and behave as a single unit: *a methyl group -CH₃.* **6.** a vertical column of elements in the periodic table that all have similar properties: *the halogen group.* ~*vb.* **7.** to place (things or people) in a group, or (of things or people) to form into a group. [French *groupe*]

group captain *n.* a middle-ranking officer in certain air forces.

groupie (ˈgruːpɪ) *n. Slang.* an ardent fan of a celebrity.

group therapy *n. Psychol.* the treatment of people by bringing them together to share their problems in group discussion.

grouse¹ (graʊs) *n., pl.* **grouse** or **grouses.** a game bird with a stocky body and feathered legs and feet. [origin unknown]

grouse² (graʊs) *vb.* **1.** to grumble; complain. ~*n.* **2.** a persistent complaint. [origin unknown]

grouse³ (graʊs) *adj. Austral. & N.Z. slang.* fine; excellent. [origin unknown]

grout (graʊt) *n.* **1.** a thin mortar for filling joints between tiles or masonry. ~*vb.* **2.** to fill (joints) with grout. [Old English *grūt*]

grove (grəʊv) *n.* a small wood or group of trees. [Old English *grāf*]

grovel (ˈgrɒv²l) *vb.* **-elling, -elled** or *U.S.* **-eling, -eled.** **1.** to humble or abase oneself. **2.** to lie or crawl face downwards, as in fear or humility. [Middle English *on grufe* on the face]

grow (grəʊ) *vb.* **growing, grew, grown.** **1.** (of a living thing) to increase in size and develop physically: *warthogs grow up to 1.5m long; she decided to let her hair grow.* **2.** (of a plant) to exist: *nettles can grow almost anywhere.* **3.** (usually foll. by *from* or *out of*) to originate: *the idea for her novel grew out of a childhood memory.* **4.** to increase in size or degree: *the population grew rapidly.* **5.** (esp. of emotions or physical states) to develop or become gradually: *it was growing cold.* **6.** to cultivate (plants): *we tried growing leeks.* **7.** to let (hair or nails) develop: *he had grown a moustache.* ~See also **grow on, grow out of,** etc. [Old English *grōwan*]

growing pains *pl. n.* pains in muscles or joints sometimes experienced by growing children.

growl (graʊl) *vb.* **1.** (of animals, esp. when hostile) to utter low rumbling sounds: *the dog growled.* **2.** to utter (words) in a gruff or angry manner. ~*n.* **3.** the act or sound of growling. [Old French *grouller* to grumble] —ˈgrowlingly *adv.*

grown (grəʊn) *adj.* developed or advanced: *fully grown; half-grown.*

grown-up *adj.* **1.** having reached maturity; adult. **2.** of or suitable for an adult. ~*n.* **3.** an adult.

grow on *vb.* to become progressively more acceptable or pleasant to.

grow out of *vb.* to become too big or mature for: *she soon grew out of her girlish ways.*

growth (grəʊθ) *n.* **1.** the process of growing. **2.** an increase in size, number, or significance. **3.** something grown or growing: *a new growth of hair.* **4.** any abnormal tissue, such as a tumour. **5.** (*modifier*) characterized by growth: *a growth industry.*

grow up *vb.* to reach maturity; become adult.

groyne or esp. *U.S.* **groin** (grɔɪn) *n.* a wall or breakwater built out from a shore to control erosion. [Old French *groign* snout]

grub (grʌb) *vb.* **grubbing, grubbed.** **1.** (often foll. by *up* or *out*) to search for and pull up (roots or stumps) by digging in the ground. **2.** to dig up the surface of (soil). **3.** (often foll. by *in* or *among*) to search carefully. ~*n.* **4.** the short legless larva of certain insects, esp. beetles. **5.** *Slang.* food. [Germanic]

grubby ('grʌbɪ) *adj.* **-bier, -biest.** dirty; slovenly. —**'grubbily** *adv.* —**'grubbiness** *n.*

grudge (grʌdʒ) *n.* **1.** a persistent feeling of resentment, esp. one due to an insult or injury. ~*vb.* **2.** to give unwillingly. **3.** to resent or envy (someone else's success or possessions). [Old French *grouchier* to grumble] —**'grudging** *adj.*

gruel ('gruːəl) *n.* thin porridge made by boiling meal, esp. oatmeal, in water or milk. [Old French]

gruelling *or U.S.* **grueling** ('gruːəlɪŋ) *adj.* extremely severe or tiring. [obs. *gruel* to punish]

gruesome ('gruːsəm) *adj.* inspiring horror and disgust. [Scandinavian]

gruff (grʌf) *adj.* **1.** rough or surly in manner or speech. **2.** (of a voice) low and throaty. [Germanic] —**'gruffly** *adv.* —**'gruffness** *n.*

grumble ('grʌmbəl) *vb.* **1.** to utter (complaints) in a nagging way. **2.** to make low dull rumbling sounds. ~*n.* **3.** a complaint; grouse. **4.** a low rumbling sound. [Middle Low German *grommelen*] —**'grumbler** *n.* —**'grumbling** *adj., n.*

grumpy ('grʌmpɪ) *adj.* **grumpier, grumpiest.** peevish; sulky. [imit.] —**'grumpily** *adv.* —**'grumpiness** *n.*

grunt (grʌnt) *vb.* **1.** (esp. of pigs) to emit a low short gruff noise. **2.** to express something gruffly: *he grunted his answer.* ~*n.* **3.** the characteristic low short gruff noise of pigs, or a similar sound, as of disgust. [Old English *grunnettan*]

Gruyère ('gruːjɛə) *n.* a hard flat pale yellow cheese, with holes. [after *Gruyère*, Switzerland, where it originated]

gryphon ('grɪf'n) *n.* same as **griffin.**

G-string *n.* **1.** a strip of cloth worn between the legs and attached to a waistband. **2.** *Music.* a string tuned to G.

G-suit *n.* a close-fitting pressurized garment that is worn by the crew of high-speed aircraft. [from *g(ravity) suit*]

GT gran turismo: a touring car; usually a fast sports car with a hard fixed roof.

guanaco (gwɑːˈnɑːkəʊ) *n., pl.* **-cos.** a cud-chewing South American mammal related to the llama. [S American Indian *huanacu*]

guano ('gwɑːnəʊ) *n., pl.* **-nos.** the dried excrement of fish-eating sea birds: used as a fertilizer. [S American Indian *huano dung*]

guarantee (ˌgærənˈtiː) *n.* **1.** a formal assurance, esp. in writing, that a product or service will meet certain standards or specifications. **2.** a guarantor. **3.** something that makes a specified condition or outcome certain. **4.** same as **guaranty.** ~*vb.* **-teeing, -teed. 5.** to take responsibility for (someone else's debts or obligations). **6.** to serve as a guarantee for. **7.** to secure: *a small deposit will guarantee any dress.* **8.** (usually foll. by *from* or *against*) to undertake to protect or keep secure, as against injury or loss. **9.** to ensure: *good planning will guarantee suc-*

cess. **10.** to promise or make certain. [Germanic]

guarantor (ˌgærənˈtɔː) *n.* a person who gives or is bound by a guarantee or guaranty.

guaranty ('gærəntɪ) *n., pl.* **-ties. 1.** a pledge of responsibility for fulfilling another person's obligations in case of that person's default. **2.** a thing given or taken as security for a guaranty.

guard (gɑːd) *vb.* **1.** to watch over or shield (a person or thing) from danger or harm; protect. **2.** to keep watch over (a prisoner or other potentially dangerous person or thing), as to prevent escape. **3.** to control: *to guard one's tongue.* **4.** (usually foll. by *against*) to take precautions. ~*n.* **5.** a person or group who protect or watch over people or things. **6.** a person or group of people, such as soldiers, who form a ceremonial escort. **7.** *Brit.* the official in charge of a train. **8.** the act or duty of protecting or supervising. **9.** a device or part of a machine designed to protect the user against injury. **10.** anything that provides protection: *a guard against infection.* **11.** the posture of defence or readiness in sports such as fencing and boxing. **12. off** (one's) **guard.** having one's defences down; unprepared. **13. on** (one's) **guard.** prepared to face danger or difficulties. **14. stand guard.** (of a sentry) to keep watch. [Old French *garder* to protect]

guarded ('gɑːdɪd) *adj.* cautious or noncommittal: *a guarded reply.* —**'guardedly** *adv.*

guardhouse ('gɑːd,haʊs) *or* **guardroom** ('gɑːd,ruːm,-,rʊm) *n. Mil.* a military police office in which prisoners can be detained.

guardian ('gɑːdɪən) *n.* **1.** one who looks after, protects, or defends: *the guardian of public morals.* **2.** someone legally appointed to manage the affairs of a person incapable of acting for himself, as a minor or person of unsound mind. —**'guardian,ship** *n.*

guardsman ('gɑːdzmən) *n., pl.* **-men. 1.** a member of a regiment responsible for ceremonial duties. **2.** a guard.

guard's van *n. Railways, Brit. & N.Z.* the van in which the guard travels.

guava ('gwɑːvə) *n.* the edible fruit of a tropical American tree, having yellow skin and pink pulp. [S American Indian]

gubernatorial (ˌgjuːbənəˈtɔːrɪəl) *adj. Chiefly U.S.* of or relating to a governor. [Latin *gubernātor* governor]

gudgeon[1] ('gʌdʒən) *n.* a small slender European freshwater fish: used as bait by anglers. [Old French *goujon*]

gudgeon[2] ('gʌdʒən) *n.* **1.** the socket of a hinge, which fits around the pin. **2.** *Naut.* one of two or more looplike sockets, into which the pins of a rudder are fitted. [Old French *goujon*]

guelder-rose ('gɛldə,rəʊz) *n.* a Eurasian shrub with clusters of white flowers. [from *Gelderland*, province of Holland]

Guernsey ('gɜːnzɪ) *n.* **1.** a breed of dairy cattle producing rich creamy milk, originating from Guernsey, in the Channel Islands. **2.** (*not cap.*) a seaman's knitted woollen sweater.

guerrilla *or* **guerilla** (gə'rılə) *n.* a member of an irregular usually politically motivated armed force that fights regular forces. [Spanish]

guess (gɛs) *vb.* **1.** to form an estimate or conclusion (about something), without proper knowledge: *guess what we're having for dinner.* **2.** to arrive at a correct estimate of (something) by guessing: *he guessed my age.* **3.** *Informal, chiefly U.S. & Canad.* to think or suppose (something): *I guess I'll go now.* ~*n.* **4.** an estimate or conclusion arrived at by guessing: *a bad guess.* [prob. Old Norse]

guesswork ('gɛs,wɜːk) *n.* **1.** a set of conclusions or estimates arrived at by guessing. **2.** the process of making guesses.

guest (gɛst) *n.* **1.** a person who is entertained or taken out to eat and paid for by another. **2.** a person who receives hospitality at the home of another. **3.** a performer or speaker taking part in an event, show, or film by special invitation. **4.** a patron of a hotel or restaurant. ~*vb.* **5.** (in theatre and broadcasting) to be a guest: *to guest on a show.* [Old English *giest*]

guesthouse ('gɛst,haʊs) *n.* a private home or boarding house offering accommodation.

guff (gʌf) *n. Slang.* ridiculous talk. [imit.]

guffaw (gʌ'fɔː) *n.* **1.** a crude and boisterous laugh. ~*vb.* **2.** to laugh or express (something) in this way. [imit.]

guidance ('gaɪdⁿs) *n.* **1.** leadership, instruction, or direction. **2.** counselling or advice on educational, vocational, or psychological matters.

guide (gaɪd) *vb.* **1.** to lead the way for (a person). **2.** to control the movement or course of; steer. **3.** to supervise or instruct (a person). **4.** to direct the affairs of (a person, company, or nation). **5.** to influence (a person) in his actions or opinions: *let truth guide you.* ~*n.* **6.** a person or thing that guides. **7.** a person, usually paid, who conducts tour expeditions. **8.** a model or criterion, as in moral standards or accuracy. **9.** same as **guidebook.** **10.** a book that explains the fundamentals of a subject or skill. **11.** any device that directs the motion of a tool or machine part. [Germanic]

Guide (gaɪd) *n.* a member of the organization for girls equivalent to the Scouts.

guidebook ('gaɪd,bʊk) *n.* a handbook with information for visitors to a place.

guided missile *n.* a missile having a course controlled either by radio signals or by internal homing devices.

guide dog *n.* a dog specially trained to accompany a blind person, enabling that person to move about safely.

guideline ('gaɪd,laɪn) *n.* a principle put forward to set standards or determine a course of action.

guild (gɪld) *n.* **1.** an organization, club, or fellowship. **2.** (in medieval Europe) an association of men in the same trade or craft. [Old Norse]

guilder ('gɪldə) *n., pl.* **-ders** *or* **-der.** **1.** the standard monetary unit of the Netherlands. **2.** any of various former coins of Germany, Austria, or the Netherlands. [Middle Dutch *gulden*]

guildhall ('gɪld,hɔːl) *n. Brit.* **1.** the hall of a guild or corporation. **2.** a town hall.

guile (gaɪl) *n.* crafty character or behaviour. [Old French] —**'guileful** *adj.* —**'guileless** *adj.*

guillemot ('gɪlɪ,mɒt) *n.* a northern oceanic diving bird with black-and-white plumage and a long narrow bill. [French]

guillotine ('gɪlə,tiːn) *n.* **1.** a device for beheading people, consisting of a weighted blade set between two upright posts. **2.** a device with a blade for cutting paper or sheet metal. **3.** (in Parliament) a method of hastening the progress of a bill by dividing it into parts, which must be completely dealt with by a specified time. ~*vb.* **4.** to behead (a person) by guillotine. **5.** (in Parliament) to limit debate on (a bill) by the guillotine. [after J. I. *Guillotin*, who advocated its use]

guilt (gɪlt) *n.* **1.** the fact or state of having done wrong. **2.** remorse or self-reproach caused by feeling that one has done something wrong. [Old English *gylt*]

guiltless ('gɪltlɪs) *adj.* free of all responsibility for wrongdoing or crime; innocent.

guilty ('gɪltɪ) *adj.* **guiltier, guiltiest.** **1.** responsible for an offence or misdeed. **2.** *Law.* judged to have committed an offence: *the accused was found guilty.* **3.** showing, feeling, or characterized by guilt. —**'guiltily** *adv.*

guinea ('gɪnɪ) *n.* **1.** the sum of £1.05 (21 shillings), used in quoting professional fees. **2.** a former British gold coin worth this amount. [the coin was orig. made of gold from Guinea]

guinea fowl *n.* a domestic bird with a heavy rounded body and speckled plumage.

guinea pig *n.* **1.** a tailless S American rodent, commonly kept as a pet or used in scientific experiments. **2.** a person used for experimentation. [origin unknown]

guipure (gɪ'pjʊə) *n.* heavy lace that has its pattern connected by threads, rather than supported on a net mesh. [French]

guise (gaɪz) *n.* **1.** semblance or pretence: *under the guise of friendship.* **2.** external appearance in general. [Old French]

guitar (gɪ'tɑː) *n.* a plucked stringed instrument, usually with six strings, a flat back, and a long neck with a fretted fingerboard. [Spanish *guitarra*] —**gui'tarist** *n.*

Gulag ('guːlæg) *n.* the department of the Soviet security service which runs prisons and labour camps. [Russian *G(lavnoye) U(pravleniye Ispravitelno-Trudovykh) Lag(erei)* Main Administration for Corrective Labour Camps]

gulch (gʌltʃ) *n. U.S. & Canad.* a narrow ravine with a fast stream running through it. [origin unknown]

gulf (gʌlf) *n.* **1.** a large deep bay. **2.**

something that divides or separates people, such as a lack of understanding. [Greek *kolpos*]

Gulf Stream *n.* a warm ocean current flowing northeastwards from the Gulf of Mexico towards NW Europe.

gull (gʌl) *n.* a large sea bird with long pointed wings and a mostly white plumage. [Celtic]

gullet ('gʌlɪt) *n.* the muscular tube through which food passes from the throat to the stomach. [Latin *gula* throat]

gullible ('gʌlɪbªl) *adj.* easily tricked. —ˌgulli'bility *n.*

gully *or* **gulley** ('gʌlɪ) *n., pl.* **-lies** *or* **leys**. **1.** a channel or small valley originally worn away by running water. **2.** *Cricket.* **a.** a fielding position slightly behind and to the right of the batsman. **b.** a fielder in this position. [French *goulet* neck of a bottle]

gulp (gʌlp) *vb.* **1.** to swallow (food or drink) rapidly in large mouthfuls. **2.** (foll. by *back*) to stifle: *to gulp back sobs.* **3.** to gasp or breathe in violently, for example when nervous or when swimming. ~*n.* **4.** the act of gulping. **5.** the quantity taken in a gulp. [imit.]

gum[1] (gʌm) *n.* **1.** a sticky substance obtained from certain plants, which hardens on exposure to air and dissolves in water. **2.** a sticky substance used as an adhesive; glue. **3.** short for **chewing gum** or **bubble gum.** **4.** a gumtree. **5.** *Chiefly Brit.* a gumdrop. ~*vb.* **gumming, gummed. 6.** to stick (something) together or in place with gum. ~See also **gum up.** [Old French *gomme*]

gum[2] (gʌm) *n.* the fleshy tissue that covers the bases of the teeth. [Old English *gōma* jaw]

gum arabic *n.* a gum obtained from certain acacia trees, used in the manufacture of ink, food thickeners, and pills.

gumboil ('gʌmˌbɔɪl) *n.* an abscess on the gum.

gumboots ('gʌmˌbuːts) *pl. n.* same as **Wellington boots.**

gumdrop ('gʌmˌdrɒp) *n.* a small hard transparent jelly-like sweet.

gummy[1] ('gʌmɪ) *adj.* **-mier, -miest. 1.** sticky or tacky. **2.** producing gum.

gummy[2] ('gʌmɪ) *adj.* **-mier, -miest.** toothless.

gumption ('gʌmpʃən) *n. Brit. informal.* common sense; resourcefulness; initiative. [origin unknown]

gumtree ('gʌmˌtriː) *n.* **1.** any of various trees that yield gum, such as the eucalyptus. **2. up a gumtree.** *Informal.* in an awkward position; in difficulties.

gum up *vb.* **1.** to cover (something) with a gumlike substance. **2. gum up the works.** *Informal.* to make a mess of something.

gun (gʌn) *n.* **1.** a weapon with a metallic tube or barrel from which a missile is fired, usually by force of an explosion. **2.** a member of a shooting party. **3.** a device used to project something under pressure: *a spray gun.* **4.** *U.S. slang.* a gunman. **5. jump the gun.** *Informal.* to act premature-

ly. **6. stick to one's guns.** *Informal.* to maintain one's opinions or intentions in spite of opposition. ~*vb.* **gunning, gunned. 7.** (foll. by *down*) to shoot (someone) with a gun. **8.** to press hard on the accelerator of (an engine). ~See also **gun for.** [Middle English *gonne*]

gunboat ('gʌnˌbəʊt) *n.* a small ship carrying mounted guns.

gunboat diplomacy *n.* diplomacy conducted by threats of military intervention.

guncotton ('gʌnˌkɒtªn) *n.* a form of cellulose nitrate used as an explosive.

gun dog *n.* **1.** a dog trained to locate or retrieve birds or animals that have been shot in a hunt. **2.** a dog belonging to any breed traditionally used for these activities.

gunfire ('gʌnˌfaɪə) *n.* the repeated firing of one or more guns.

gun for *vb.* **1.** to search for (someone) in order to reprimand, punish, or kill him. **2.** to try earnestly for (something): *he was gunning for promotion.*

gunge (gʌndʒ) *n. Informal.* sticky or congealed matter. [imit.] —'**gungy** *adj.*

gunk (gʌŋk) *n. Informal.* slimy, oily, or filthy matter. [perhaps imit.]

gunman ('gʌnmən) *n., pl.* **-men.** a man who uses a gun to commit a crime.

gunmetal ('gʌnˌmetªl) *n.* **1.** a type of bronze containing copper, tin, and zinc. ~*adj.* **2.** dark grey.

gunnel ('gʌnªl) *n.* same as **gunwale.**

gunner ('gʌnə) *n.* a serviceman who works with, uses, or specializes in guns.

gunnery ('gʌnərɪ) *n.* the art and science of the efficient design and use of large guns.

gunny ('gʌnɪ) *n. Chiefly U.S.* **1.** a coarse hard-wearing fabric, made from jute and used for sacks. **2.** (*pl.* **-nies**) a sack made from this fabric. [Hindi]

gunpoint ('gʌnˌpɔɪnt) *n.* **at gunpoint.** being under or using the threat of being shot.

gunpowder ('gʌnˌpaʊdə) *n.* an explosive mixture of potassium nitrate, charcoal, and sulphur.

gunrunning ('gʌnˌrʌnɪŋ) *n.* the smuggling of guns and ammunition into a country. —'**gun**ˌ**runner** *n.*

gunshot ('gʌnˌʃɒt) *n.* **1.** bullets fired from a gun. **2.** the sound of a gun being fired. **3.** the range of a gun: *out of gunshot.*

gunslinger ('gʌnˌslɪŋə) *n. Slang.* a gunfighter or gunman in the frontier days of the American West.

gunstock ('gʌnˌstɒk) *n.* the wooden handle to which the barrel of a rifle is attached.

gunwale ('gʌnªl) *n. Naut.* the top of the side of a boat or ship. [*wale* ridge of planking orig. supporting guns]

guppy ('gʌpɪ) *n., pl.* **-pies.** a small brightly coloured freshwater fish of the Caribbean area: a popular aquarium fish. [after R. J. L. *Guppy,* who gave specimens to the British Museum]

gurgle ('gɜːgªl) *vb.* **1.** (of water) to make low bubbling noises when flowing. **2.** to make low throaty bubbling noises: *the* *baby gurgled with delight.* ~*n.* **3.** the sound of gurgling. [origin unknown]

Gurkha ('gɜːkə) *n.* **1.** a member of a Hindu people living mainly in Nepal. **2.** a member of a Gurkha regiment in the British Army. [Sanskrit]

gurnard ('gɜːnəd) *n., pl.* **-nard** *or* **-nards.** a sea fish with a heavily armoured head and finger-like pectoral fins. [Old French *gornard*]

guru ('guruː) *n.* **1.** a Hindu or Sikh religious teacher or leader. **2.** a leader or adviser of a movement: *the feminist guru.* [Hindi]

gush (gʌʃ) *vb.* **1.** to pour out suddenly and profusely. **2.** to act or utter (something) in an overenthusiastic manner. ~*n.* **3.** a sudden copious flow of liquid. **4.** an extravagant and insincere expression of admiration. [prob. imit.] —**'gushing** *or* **'gushy** *adj.*

gusher ('gʌʃə) *n.* **1.** someone who gushes. **2.** a spurting oil well.

gusset ('gʌsɪt) *n.* a piece of material sewn into a garment to strengthen it. [Old French *gousset*]

gust (gʌst) *n.* **1.** a sudden blast of wind. **2.** a sudden rush of smoke or rain. **3.** an outburst of emotion. ~*vb.* **4.** to blow in gusts. [Old Norse *gustr*] —**'gusty** *adj.*

gusto ('gʌstəʊ) *n.* vigorous enjoyment: *the aria was sung with great gusto.* [Spanish: taste]

gut (gʌt) *n.* **1.** same as **intestine.** **2.** (*pl.*) the internal organs of a person or an animal. **3.** *Slang.* the belly; paunch. **4.** short for **catgut.** **5.** a silky fibrous substance extracted from silkworms and used in the manufacture of fishing tackle. **6.** (*pl.*) *Informal.* courage, willpower, or daring; forcefulness. **7.** (*pl.*) *Informal.* the essential part: *the guts of a problem.* ~*vb.* **gutting, gutted.** **8.** to remove the internal organs from (a dead animal or fish). **9.** (of a fire) to destroy the inside of (a building). ~*adj.* **10.** *Informal.* basic, essential, or natural: *the gut problem; a gut reaction.* [Old English *gutt*]

gutless ('gʌtlɪs) *adj. Informal.* lacking courage or determination.

gutsy ('gʌtsɪ) *adj.* **gutsier, gutsiest.** *Slang.* **1.** gluttonous; greedy. **2.** courageous; bold.

gutta-percha ('gʌtə'pɜːtʃə) *n.* a whitish rubber substance derived from various tropical Asian trees: used in electrical insulation and dentistry. [Malay]

gutter ('gʌtə) *n.* **1.** a channel on the roof of a building or running alongside the kerb of a road, used to collect and carry away rainwater. **2.** *Tenpin bowling.* one of the channels running down either side of an alley. **3. the gutter.** a poverty-stricken, degraded, or criminal environment. ~*vb.* **4.** (of a candle) to melt away as the wax forms channels and runs down in drops. **5.** (of a flame) to flicker and be about to go out. [Latin *gutta* a drop] —**'guttering** *n.*

gutter press *n.* the section of the popular press that seeks sensationalism in its coverage.

guttersnipe ('gʌtə,snaɪp) *n.* a child who spends most of his time in the streets, usually in a slum area.

guttural ('gʌtərəl) *adj.* **1.** *Phonetics.* pronounced at the back of the throat. **2.** harsh-sounding. [Latin *guttur* gullet]

guy[1] (gaɪ) *n.* **1.** *Informal.* a man or boy. **2.** (*pl.*) *Chiefly U.S.* people of either sex: *I'll see you guys next week.* **3.** *Brit.* a crude model of Guy Fawkes, that is burnt on top of a bonfire on Guy Fawkes Day (November 5). ~*vb.* **4.** to make fun of (someone). [short for *Guy* Fawkes, who plotted to blow up the Houses of Parliament]

guy[2] (gaɪ) *n.* **1.** a rope, chain, or wire for anchoring, steadying, or guiding an object. ~*vb.* **2.** to anchor, steady, or guide (an object) with a guy or guys. [prob. Low German]

guzzle ('gʌzᵊl) *vb.* to eat or drink excessively or greedily. [origin unknown]

gybe *or* **jibe** (dʒaɪb) *Naut.* ~*vb.* **1.** (of a fore-and-aft sail) to swing suddenly from one side of a ship or boat to the other. **2.** (of a ship or boat) to change course by letting the sail gybe. ~*n.* **3.** an instance of gybing. [obs. Dutch *gijben*]

gym (dʒɪm) *n.* short for **gymnasium** *or* **gymnastics.**

gymkhana (dʒɪm'kɑːnə) *n. Chiefly Brit.* an event in which horses and riders take part in various races and contests. [Hindi *gendkhānā* ball house]

gymnasium (dʒɪm'neɪzɪəm) *n.* a large room containing equipment such as bars, weights, and ropes, for physical training. [Greek *gumnazein* to exercise naked]

gymnast ('dʒɪmnæst) *n.* a person who is skilled or trained in gymnastics. —**gym'nastic** *adj.*

gymnastics (dʒɪm'næstɪks) *n.* **1.** (*functioning as sing.*) practice or training in exercises that develop physical strength and agility. **2.** (*functioning as pl.*) gymnastic exercises.

gym shoes *pl. n.* same as **plimsolls.**

gymslip ('dʒɪm,slɪp) *n.* a tunic or pinafore dress formerly worn by schoolgirls as part of a school uniform.

gynaecology *or U.S.* **gynecology** (ˌgaɪnɪ'kɒlədʒɪ) *n.* the branch of medicine concerned with diseases and conditions specific to women. [Greek *gunē* women + -LOGY] —**gynaecological** *or U.S.* **gyneco'logical** (ˌgaɪnɪkə'lɒdʒɪkᵊl) *adj.* —** gynae'cologist** *or U.S.* **gyne'cologist** *n.*

gyp *or* **gip** (dʒɪp) *n.* **give someone gyp.** *Brit. & N.Z. slang.* to cause someone severe pain: *his back was giving him gyp.* [prob. a contraction of *gee up*!]

gypsum ('dʒɪpsəm) *n.* a mineral used in making plaster of Paris. [Greek *gupsos*]

Gypsy *or* **Gipsy** ('dʒɪpsɪ) *n., pl.* **-sies.** a member of a travelling people scattered throughout Europe and North America. [from *Egyptian*, since they were thought to have come orig. from Egypt]

gyrate (dʒaɪ'reɪt) *vb.* to rotate or spiral about a fixed point or axis. [Greek *guros* circle] —**gyration** (dʒaɪ'reɪʃən) *n.*

gyrfalcon ('dʒɜːˌfɔːlkən) *n.* a very large rare falcon of northern regions. [Old French *gerfaucon*]

gyro ('dʒaɪrəʊ) *n., pl.* **-ros.** short for **gyroscope.**

gyrocompass ('dʒaɪrəʊˌkʌmpəs) *n.* a non-magnetic compass that uses a motor-driven gyroscope to indicate true north. [Greek *guros* circle + *compass*]

gyroscope ('dʒaɪrəˌskəʊp) *n.* a device containing a disc rotating on an axis that can turn freely in any direction, so that the disc maintains the same position regardless of the movement of the surrounding structure. [Greek *guros* circle + *scope*]

H

h *or* **H** (eɪtʃ) *n., pl.* **h's, H's,** *or* **Hs.** the eighth letter of the English alphabet.

H *Chem.* hydrogen.

h. *or* **H.** **1.** height. **2.** hour.

ha¹ *or* **hah** (hɑː) *interj.* an exclamation expressing derision, triumph or surprise.

ha² hectare.

habeas corpus (ˈheɪbɪəs ˈkɔːpəs) *n. Law.* a writ ordering a person to be brought before a judge, so as to decide whether his detention is lawful. [Latin: you may have the body]

haberdasher (ˈhæbəˌdæʃə) *n. Brit.* a dealer in small articles for sewing, such as buttons and ribbons. [Anglo-French *hapertas* small items of merchandise] —**ˈhaberˌdashery** *n.*

habiliments (həˈbɪlɪmənts) *pl. n.* dress or attire. [Old French *habillement*]

habit (ˈhæbɪt) *n.* **1.** a tendency to act in a particular way. **2.** established custom; usual practice. **3.** mental disposition or attitude: *a good working habit of mind.* **4.** the costume of a nun or monk. [Latin *habitus* custom]

habitable (ˈhæbɪtəbəl) *adj.* suitable to be lived in. —ˌhabitaˈbility *n.*

habitant (ˈhæbɪtənt) *n.* an early French settler in Canada or Louisiana or a descendant of one, esp. a farmer.

habitat (ˈhæbɪˌtæt) *n.* the natural home of an animal or plant. [Latin: it inhabits]

habitation (ˌhæbɪˈteɪʃən) *n.* **1.** occupation of a dwelling place: *unfit for human habitation.* **2.** a dwelling place.

habit-forming *adj.* tending to become a habit or addiction.

habitual (həˈbɪtjʊəl) *adj.* **1.** done regularly and repeatedly: *the habitual Sunday walk.* **2.** by habit: *a habitual drinker.* —**haˈbitually** *adv.*

habituate (həˈbɪtjʊˌeɪt) *vb.* to accustom: *habituated to the timetable.* —**haˌbituˈation** *n.*

habitué (həˈbɪtjʊˌeɪ) *n.* a frequent visitor to a place. [French]

hachure (hæˈfjʊə) *n.* shading of short lines drawn on a map to indicate the degree of steepness of a hill. [French]

hacienda (ˌhæsɪˈɛndə) *n.* (in Spanish-speaking countries) a ranch or large estate with a house on it. [Spanish]

hack¹ (hæk) *vb.* **1.** to chop roughly or violently. **2.** to cut and clear (a way) through undergrowth. **3.** (in sport) to foul (an opposing player) by kicking his shins. **4.** to cough in short dry bursts. ~*n.* **5.** a cut or gash. **6.** a tool, such as a pick. **7.** a chopping blow. **8.** a kick on the shins, as in rugby. [Old English *haccian*]

hack² (hæk) *n.* **1.** a horse kept for riding, often one for hire. **2.** *Brit.* a country ride on horseback. **3.** a person who produces mediocre literary work. ~*vb.* **4.** *Brit.* to ride (a horse) cross-country for pleasure. ~*adj.* **5.** banal, mediocre, or unoriginal: *hack writing.* [short for *hackney*]

hacker (ˈhækə) *n. Slang.* a computer enthusiast, esp. one who through a personal computer breaks into the computer system of a company or government. —**ˈhackery** *n.*

hackles (ˈhækəlz) *pl. n.* **1.** anger or resentment: *to make one's hackles rise.* **2.** the hairs or feathers on the back of the neck of certain animals or birds, which rise when they are angry. [Middle English *hakell*]

hackney (ˈhæknɪ) *n.* **1.** a taxi. **2.** same as **hack²** (sense 1). [prob. after *Hackney*, London, where horses were formerly raised]

hackneyed (ˈhæknɪd) *adj.* (of a word or phrase) used so often as to be trite.

hacksaw (ˈhækˌsɔː) *n.* a small saw for cutting metal.

had (hæd) *vb.* past of **have.**

haddock (ˈhædək) *n., pl.* **-dock.** a North Atlantic food fish. [origin unknown]

hadedah *or* **hadeda** (ˈhɑːdɪˌdɑː) *n.* a large grey-green S. African ibis. [imit.]

Hades (ˈheɪdiːz) *n. Greek myth.* the underworld abode of the souls of the dead.

hadj (hædʒ) *n.* same as **hajj.**

hadji (ˈhædʒɪ) *n., pl.* **hadjis.** same as **hajji.**

hadn't (ˈhædənt) had not.

haemal *or U.S.* **hemal** (ˈhiːməl) *adj.* of the blood. [Greek *haima* blood]

haematic *or U.S.* **hematic** (hiːˈmætɪk) *adj.* relating to or containing blood.

haematology *or U.S.* **hematology** (ˌhiːməˈtɒlədʒɪ) *n.* the branch of medical science concerned with the blood. [Greek *haima* blood + -LOGY]

haemoglobin *or U.S.* **hemoglobin** (ˌhiːməʊˈɡləʊbɪn) *n.* a protein in red blood cells that carries oxygen from the lungs to the tissues. [Greek *haima* blood + Latin *globus* ball]

haemophilia *or U.S.* **hemophilia** (ˌhiːməʊˈfɪlɪə) *n.* a hereditary disorder, usually affecting males, in which the blood does not clot properly. [Greek *haima* blood + *philos* loving] —ˌhaemoˈphiliac *n.*

haemorrhage *or U.S.* **hemorrhage** (ˈhemərɪdʒ) *n.* **1.** profuse bleeding from ruptured blood vessels. ~*vb.* **2.** to bleed profusely. [Greek *haima* blood + *rhēgnunai* to burst]

haemorrhoids *or U.S.* **hemorrhoids** (ˈheməˌrɔɪdz) *pl. n. Pathol.* swollen veins in the wall of the anus. [Greek *haimorrhoos* discharging blood]

haeremai (ˈhaɪrəˌmaɪ) *interj. N.Z.* an expression of greeting or welcome. [Maori]

hafnium (ˈhæfnɪəm) *n.* a metallic element found in zirconium ores. Symbol: Hf [after *Hafnia,* Latin name of Copenhagen]

haft (hɑːft) n. the handle of an axe, knife, or dagger. [Old English hæft]

hag (hæg) n. **1.** an unpleasant or ugly old woman. **2.** a witch. [Old English hægtesse witch] —**'haggish** adj.

haggard ('hægəd) adj. looking careworn or gaunt. [Old French hagard]

haggis ('hægɪs) n. a Scottish dish made from sheep's or calf's offal, oatmeal, suet, and seasonings boiled in a skin made from the animal's stomach. [origin unknown]

haggle ('hæg'l) vb. to bargain or wrangle (over a price); barter. [Scandinavian]

hagiography (ˌhægɪ'ɒgrəfɪ) n., pl. -**phies.** the writing of lives of the saints. [Greek hagios holy + graphein to write] —ˌhagi-'**ographer** n.

hagiology (ˌhægɪ'ɒlədʒɪ) n., pl. -**gies.** literature about the lives and legends of saints. [Greek hagios holy + -LOGY]

hag-ridden adj. tormented or distressed.

hah (hɑː) interj. same as **ha¹**.

ha-ha¹ ('hɑː'hɑː) or **haw-haw** ('hɔː'hɔː) interj. a written representation of the sound of laughter.

ha-ha² (hɑːhɑː) n. a ditch, with one side made into a retaining wall, that borders a garden or park, and allows an uninterrupted view from within. [French]

haiku ('haɪkuː) n., pl. -**ku.** a Japanese verse form in 17 syllables. [Japanese]

hail¹ (heɪl) n. **1.** small pellets of ice falling from thunderclouds. **2.** words, ideas, missiles, etc., directed with force and in great quantity: a hail of abuse. ~vb. **3.** to fall as hail: it's hailing. **4.** to fall or cause to fall like hail: blows hailed down on him. [Old English hægl]

hail² (heɪl) vb. **1.** to call out to; greet: she hailed John excitedly. **2.** to acclaim or acknowledge: they hailed him as their hero. **3.** to stop (a taxi) by shouting or gesturing. **4. hail from.** to be a native of: she hails from India. ~n. **5. within hailing distance.** within hearing range. ~interj. **6.** Poetic. an exclamation of greeting. [Old Norse heill healthy]

hail-fellow-well-met adj. genial and familiar in an offensive way.

Hail Mary n. R.C. Church. a prayer to the Virgin Mary.

hailstone ('heɪlˌstəʊn) n. a pellet of hail.

hailstorm ('heɪlˌstɔːm) n. a storm during which hail falls.

hair (hɛə) n. **1.** any of the threadlike outgrowths on the skin of mammals. **2.** a mass of such outgrowths, as on a person's head or an animal's body. **3.** Bot. a threadlike growth from the outer layer of a plant. **4.** a very small distance or margin: to lose by a hair. Informal. to annoy someone. **5. get in someone's hair.** **6. hair of the dog.** an alcoholic drink taken as a cure for a hangover. **7. let one's hair down.** to enjoy oneself without restraint. **8. not turn a hair.** to show no reaction. **9. split hairs.** to make petty and unnecessary distinctions. [Old English hær] —'**hairless** adj.

hairdo ('hɛəˌduː) n., pl. -**dos.** the style of a person's hair.

hairdresser ('hɛəˌdrɛsə) n. **1.** a person who cuts and styles hair. **2.** a hairdresser's premises. —'**hairˌdressing** n.

hairgrip ('hɛəˌgrɪp) n. Chiefly Brit. a small bent clasp used to fasten the hair.

hairline ('hɛəˌlaɪn) n. **1.** the natural margin formed by hair. **2. a.** a crack or line. **b.** (as modifier): a hairline crack.

hairpiece ('hɛəˌpiːs) n. a section of false hair added to one's real hair.

hairpin ('hɛəˌpɪn) n. a thin U-shaped pin used to fasten the hair.

hairpin bend n. a bend in the road that curves very sharply.

hair-raising adj. causing horror; terrifying.

hair's-breadth n. an extremely small margin or distance.

hair shirt n. a shirt made of horsehair cloth worn against the skin as a penance.

hair slide n. a decorative clasp used to fasten the hair.

hairsplitting ('hɛəˌsplɪtɪŋ) n. **1.** the act of making petty distinctions. ~adj. **2.** characterized by petty distinctions.

hairspring ('hɛəˌsprɪŋ) n. a fine spring in some clocks and watches which regulates the timekeeping.

hairstyle ('hɛəˌstaɪl) n. the cut and arrangement of the hair. —'**hairˌstylist** n.

hair trigger n. a trigger that responds to the slightest pressure.

hairy ('hɛərɪ) adj. **hairier, hairiest.** **1.** covered with hair. **2.** Slang. dangerous, exciting, and difficult. —'**hairiness** n.

hajj or **hadj** (hædʒ) n. the pilgrimage a Muslim makes to Mecca.

hajji or **hadji** ('hædʒɪ) n., pl. **hajjis** or **hadjis.** a Muslim who has made a pilgrimage to Mecca.

haka ('hɑːkə) n. N.Z. **1.** a Maori war chant accompanied by gestures. **2.** a similar chant by a sports team.

hake (heɪk) n., pl. **hake** or **hakes.** a food fish with a long body and a large head. [origin unknown]

halal or **hallal** (hɑː'lɑːl) n. meat from animals that have been slaughtered according to Muslim law. [Arabic]

halberd ('hælbəd) n. Hist. a tall spear that includes an axe blade and a pick. [Middle High German helm handle + barde axe]

halcyon ('hælsɪən) adj. peaceful, gentle, and calm: halcyon days. [Greek alkuōn kingfisher]

hale (heɪl) adj. healthy and robust: hale and hearty. [Old English hæl]

half (hɑːf) n., pl. **halves** (hɑːvz). **1.** either of two equal or corresponding parts that together make up a whole. **2.** the fraction equal to one divided by two. **3.** half a pint, esp. of beer. **4.** Sport. one of two equal periods of play in a game. **5.** a half-price ticket. **6. by halves.** without being thorough: we don't do things by halves. **7. go halves.** to share expenses. ~det. **8.** being a half or approximately a half: half the kingdom. ~adj. **9.** incomplete: he only *did a half job on it.* ~*adv.* **10.** to the amount or extent of a half. **11.** partially; to an extent: *half dead with exhaustion.* **12. by half.** to an excessive degree: *he's too arrogant by half.* **13. not half.** *Informal.* **a.** *Brit.* very; indeed: *he isn't half stupid.* **b.** yes, indeed. [Old English *healf*]

half-and-half *adj.* half one thing and half another thing.

halfback ('hɑːf,bæk) *n. Sport.* a player positioned immediately behind the forwards.

half-baked *adj. Informal.* foolish; poorly planned: *half-baked ideas.*

half board *n.* the daily provision by a hotel of bed, breakfast, and evening meal.

half-bottle *n.* a bottle of spirits or wine that contains half the quantity of a standard bottle.

half-breed *n.* a person whose parents are of different races.

half-brother *n.* the son of either one's mother or father by another partner.

half-caste *n.* a person whose parents are of different races.

half-cock *n.* **go off at half-cock** or **half-cocked.** to fail because of inadequate preparation.

half-crown or **half-a-crown** *n.* a former British coin worth two shillings and sixpence (12½p).

half-cut *adj. Brit. slang.* rather drunk.

half-day *n.* a day when one works only in the morning or only in the afternoon.

half-dozen *n.* six.

half-hearted *adj.* without enthusiasm or determination. —,**half-'heartedly** *adv.*

half-hitch *n.* a knot made by passing the end of a piece of rope around itself and through the loop so made.

half-hour *n.* **1.** a period of 30 minutes. **2.** the point of time 30 minutes after the beginning of an hour. —,**half-'hourly** *adv., adj.*

half-life *n.* the time taken for radioactive material to lose half its radioactivity.

half-light *n.* a dim light, as at dawn or dusk.

half-mast *n.* the halfway position of a flag on a mast as a sign of mourning.

half measures *pl. n.* inadequate actions or solutions: *we don't want any half measures.*

half-moon *n.* **1.** the moon when half its face is illuminated. **2.** the time at which a half-moon occurs. **3.** something shaped like a half-moon.

half-nelson *n.* a wrestling hold in which a wrestler places an arm under his opponent's arm from behind and exerts pressure with his palm on the back of his opponent's neck.

halfpenny or **ha'penny** ('heɪpnɪ, 'hɑːf-,penɪ) *n., pl.* **-pennies.** a former British coin worth half a penny.

half-pie *adj. N.Z. informal.* badly planned; not properly thought out: *a half-pie scheme.* [Maori *pai* good]

half-price *adj., adv.* for half the normal

price: *half-price strawberries; children travel half-price.*

half-sister *n.* the daughter of either one's mother or father by another partner.

half term *n. Brit. education.* a short holiday midway through a term.

half-timbered *adj.* (of a building) having an exposed timber framework filled with brick or plaster.

half-time *n. Sport.* an interval between the two halves of a game.

half-title *n.* the first right-hand page of a book, with only the title on it.

halftone ('hɑːf,təʊn) *n.* a photographic illustration in which the image is composed of a large number of black and white dots.

half-track *n.* a vehicle with caterpillar tracks on the rear wheels.

half-truth *n.* a partially true statement. —,**half-'true** *adj.*

halfway (,hɑːf'weɪ) *adv., adj.* **1.** at or to half the distance. **2.** in or of an incomplete manner. **3. meet someone halfway.** to compromise with someone.

halfway house *n.* **1.** a place to rest midway on a journey. **2.** the halfway stage in any process: *adolescence is the halfway house between childhood and maturity.*

halfwit ('hɑːf,wɪt) *n.* a foolish or feeble-minded person. —,**half'witted** *adj.*

halibut ('hælɪbət) *n.* the largest flatfish: a very important food fish. [Middle English *hali* holy (because it was eaten on holy days) + *butte* flatfish]

halitosis (,hælɪ'təʊsɪs) *n.* the condition of having offensive-smelling breath. [Latin *hālitus* breath]

hall (hɔːl) *n.* **1.** an entry area to other rooms in a house. **2.** a building or room for public meetings, dances, etc. **3.** a residential building in a college or university. **4.** the great house of an estate; manor. **5.** a large dining room in a college or university. **6.** the large room of a castle or stately home. [Old English *heall*]

hallelujah, halleluiah (,hælɪ'luːjə), or **alleluia** (,ælɪ'luːjə) *interj.* an exclamation of praise to God. [Hebrew *hellēl* to praise + *yāh* the Lord]

hallmark ('hɔːl,mɑːk) *n.* **1.** *Brit.* an official seal stamped on gold, silver, or platinum articles to guarantee purity and date of manufacture. **2.** a typical feature. **3.** a mark of authenticity or excellence. ~*vb.* **4.** to stamp with a hallmark. [after Goldsmiths' *Hall* in London, where items were stamped]

hallo (hə'ləʊ) *interj., n.* same as **hello.**

halloo (hə'luː) *interj.* a shout used to call hounds at a hunt. [perhaps var. of *hallow* to encourage hounds by shouting]

hallowed ('hæləʊd) *adj.* **1.** regarded as holy: *hallowed ground.* **2.** worshipped; respected. [Old English *hālgian*]

Hallowe'en or **Halloween** (,hæləʊ'iːn) *n.* Oct. 31, the eve of All Saints' Day. [*all hallow even* all saints eve]

hallucinate (hə'luːsɪ,neɪt) *vb.* to seem to

see something that is not really there. [Latin *ālūcinārī*]

hallucination (həˌluːsɪˈneɪʃən) *n.* the experience of seeming to see something that is not really there. —**halˈlucinatory** *adj.*

hallucinogen (həˈluːsɪnəˌdʒɛn) *n.* any drug that causes hallucinations. —**halˌlucinoˈgenic** *adj.*

hallway (ˈhɔːlˌweɪ) *n.* an entrance area.

halo (ˈheɪləʊ) *n., pl.* **-loes** *or* **-los.** **1.** a ring of light around the head of a sacred figure. **2.** a circle of refracted light around the sun or moon. ~*vb.* **-loes** *or* **-los, -loing, -loed.** **3.** to surround with a halo. [Latin *halōs* circular threshing floor]

halogen (ˈhæləˌdʒɛn) *n.* any of the non-metallic chemical elements fluorine, chlorine, bromine, iodine, and astatine which form salts when combined with metal. [Greek *hals* salt + *-genēs* born]

halt (hɔːlt) *n.* **1.** a temporary standstill. **2.** a military command to stop. **3.** *Chiefly Brit.* a minor railway station without a building. **4. call a halt to.** to put an end to; stop. ~*vb.* **5.** to come to a stop or bring (someone or something) to a stop. [German *halten* to stop]

halter (ˈhɔːltə) *n.* **1.** headgear for a horse, usually with a rope for leading. ~*vb.* **2.** to put a halter on (a horse). [Old English *hælfter*]

halterneck (ˈhɔːltəˌnɛk) *n.* a woman's top or dress which fastens behind the neck, leaving the back and arms bare.

halting (ˈhɔːltɪŋ) *adj.* hesitant: *halting speech.*

halve (hɑːv) *vb.* **1.** to divide (something) into two equal parts. **2.** to reduce (something) by half, as by cutting. **3.** *Golf.* to draw with one's opponent on (a hole or round).

halyard *or* **halliard** (ˈhæljəd) *n.* *Naut.* a line for hoisting or lowering a sail, flag, or spar. [Middle English *halier*]

ham¹ (hæm) *n.* **1.** the rear of a pig between buttock and upper thigh. **2.** the meat from this part. [Old English *hamm*]

ham² (hæm) *n.* **1.** *Theatre, informal.* **a.** an actor who overacts and exaggerates the part. **b.** (*as modifier*): *a ham actor.* **2.** *Informal.* an amateur radio operator. ~*vb.* **hamming, hammed. 3. ham it up.** *Informal.* to overact. [special use of HAM¹]

hamba (ˈhæmbə) *interj.* *S. African, usually offensive.* go away.

hamburger (ˈhæmˌbɜːgə) *n.* a flat round of minced beef, often served in a bread roll. [*Hamburger steak* (steak in the fashion of *Hamburg, Germany*)]

ham-fisted *or* **ham-handed** *adj.* *Informal.* clumsy.

hamlet (ˈhæmlɪt) *n.* a small village. [Old French *hamelet*]

hammer (ˈhæmə) *n.* **1.** a hand tool consisting of a heavy metal head on the end of a handle, used for driving in nails, beating metal, etc. **2.** the part of a gun that causes the bullet to shoot when the trigger is pulled. **3.** *Field sports.* **a.** a heavy metal ball attached to a flexible wire: thrown in competitions. **b.** the sport of throwing the

hammer. **4.** an auctioneer's gavel. **5.** the striking mechanism in a piano. **6. come** *or* **go under the hammer.** to be on sale at auction. **7. hammer and tongs.** with great vigour and emotion. ~*n.* **8.** to hit with or as if with a hammer. **9.** (foll. by *in* or *into*) to force (facts or ideas) into someone through constant repetition. **10.** to feel or sound like hammering: *the rain hammered down.* **11.** (foll. by *away*) to work at (something) constantly: *she hammered away at her essay for five hours.* **12.** *Brit.* to criticize severely. **13.** *Informal.* to defeat. [Old English *hamor*]

hammer and sickle *n.* the emblem on the flag of the Soviet Union, representing the industrial workers and the peasants.

hammerhead (ˈhæməˌhɛd) *n.* a fierce shark with a hammer-shaped head.

hammer out *vb.* to settle (differences) with great effort.

hammertoe (ˈhæməˌtəʊ) *n.* a condition causing the toe to be permanently bent at the joint.

hammock (ˈhæmək) *n.* a hanging bed of canvas or net. [Spanish *hamaca*]

hamper¹ (ˈhæmpə) *vb.* to impede the progress of (someone or something). [origin unknown]

hamper² (ˈhæmpə) *n.* **1.** a large basket, usually with a cover. **2.** *Brit.* a selection of food and drink packed in a hamper or other container. [Middle English *hanaper* a small basket]

hamster (ˈhæmstə) *n.* a rodent with a stocky body, short tail, and cheek pouches. [German]

hamstring (ˈhæmˌstrɪŋ) *n.* **1.** one of the tendons at the back of the knee. ~*vb.* **-stringing, -strung. 2.** to hinder. [*ham* in the sense: leg]

hand (hænd) *n.* **1.** the part of the body at the end of the arm, consisting of a thumb, four fingers, and a palm. **2. a.** the cards dealt in one round of a card game. **b.** one round of a card game. **3.** an influence: *the hand of God.* **4.** a part in some activity: *he had a hand in the victory.* **5.** assistance: *can I give you a hand?* **6.** a pointer on a dial or gauge, esp. on a clock. **7.** consent to marry someone: *he asked for her hand in marriage.* **8.** a position indicated by its location to the side of an object or the observer: *on the right hand.* **9.** a contrasting aspect or condition: *on the other hand.* **10.** source: *a story heard at third hand.* **11.** a person who creates something: *a good hand at baking.* **12.** a manual worker. **13.** a member of a ship's crew. **14.** a person's handwriting: *the letter was in his own hand.* **15.** a round of applause: *let's give him a big hand.* **16.** a unit of length equalling four inches, used for measuring the height of horses. **17. by hand. a.** by manual rather than mechanical means. **b.** by messenger: *the letter was delivered by hand.* **18. from hand to mouth.** with no food or money in reserve: *living from hand to mouth.* **19. hand in glove.** in close association. **20. hand over fist.** steadily and quickly: *he makes money hand over fist.* **21. in hand. a.** under control. **b.**

receiving attention: *the job in hand.* **c.** available in reserve: *he arrived with half an hour in hand.* **22. keep one's hand in.** to continue to practise something. **23. (near) at hand.** very close. **24. on hand.** close by; available. **25. out of hand. a.** beyond control. **b.** decisively, without possible reconsideration: *he rejected my suggestion out of hand.* **26. show one's hand.** to reveal one's plans. **27. to hand.** accessible. ~*vb.* **28.** to transmit or offer by the hand or hands. **29. hand it to someone.** to give credit to someone. ~See also **hand down, hand on,** etc., **hands.** [Old English] —'**handless** *adj.*

handbag ('hænd,bæg) *n.* a woman's small bag carried to contain personal articles.

handball ('hænd,bɔːl) *n.* a game in which players strike a ball against a wall with their hands.

handbill ('hænd,bɪl) *n.* a small printed notice for distribution by hand.

handbook ('hænd,bʊk) *n.* a reference manual giving practical information on a subject.

handbrake ('hænd,breɪk) *n.* a brake operated by a hand lever.

handcart ('hænd,kɑːt) *n.* a simple cart pushed or drawn by hand.

handcrafted ('hænd,krɑːftɪd) *adj.* made by handicraft.

handcuff ('hænd,kʌf) *vb.* **1.** to put handcuffs on (a person). ~*n.* **2.** (*pl.*) a linked pair of locking metal rings used for securing prisoners.

hand down *vb.* **1.** to bequeath. **2.** to pass (an outgrown garment) on from one member of a family to a younger one. **3.** *U.S. & Canad. law.* to announce (a verdict).

handful ('hændfʊl) *n., pl.* **-fuls. 1.** the amount that can be held in the hand. **2.** a small number. **3.** *Informal.* a person or animal that is difficult to control.

handicap ('hændɪ,kæp) *n.* **1.** a physical, mental, or social impairment. **2.** something that hampers or hinders. **3. a.** a contest in which competitors are given advantages or disadvantages in an attempt to equalize their chances. **b.** the advantage or disadvantage given. **4.** *Golf.* the number of strokes by which a player's averaged score exceeds par for the course. ~*vb.* **-capping, -capped. 5.** to be an impediment to (someone). [prob. *hand in cap,* a lottery game in which players drew forfeits from a cap]

handicapped ('hændɪ,kæpt) *adj.* physically or mentally disabled.

handicraft ('hændɪ,krɑːft) *n.* **1.** a skill performed with the hands, such as weaving. **2.** the work so produced.

handiwork ('hændɪ,wɜːk) *n.* **1.** the result of someone's work or activity. **2.** work produced by hand.

handkerchief ('hæŋkətʃɪf, -tʃiːf) *n.* a small square of fabric used to wipe the nose.

handle ('hænd'l) *n.* **1.** the part of an object that is held or operated in order that it may be used. **2.** *Slang.* a person's name. **3.** a reason for doing something: *his background served as a handle for their mock-*

ery. **4. fly off the handle.** *Informal.* to become suddenly extremely angry. ~*vb.* **5.** to hold, move, operate or touch with the hands. **6.** to control: *my wife handles my investments.* **7.** to manage successfully: *a secretary must be able to handle clients.* **8.** to discuss (a subject). **9.** to deal with in a specified way: *I was handled with great tact.* **10.** to trade or deal in (specified merchandise). **11.** to react in a specified way: *the car handles well.* [Old English] —'**handling** *n.*

handlebars ('hænd'l,bɑːz) *pl. n.* a metal bar with handles at each end, used for steering a bicycle or motorcycle.

handler ('hændlə) *n.* **1.** a person who trains and controls an animal. **2.** a person who handles something: *a baggage handler.*

handmade (,hænd'meɪd) *adj.* made by hand, not by machine.

handmaiden (,hænd'meɪd'n) *or* **handmaid** *n.* *Archaic.* a female servant.

hand-me-down *n.* *Informal.* something, esp. an outgrown garment, passed down from one person to another.

hand on *vb.* to pass (something) to the next person in a succession.

hand-out *n.* **1.** clothing, food, or money given to a needy person. **2.** a leaflet, free sample, etc., given out to publicize something. **3.** a statement distributed to the press or an audience to confirm or replace an oral presentation. ~*vb.* **hand out. 4.** to distribute.

hand over *vb.* to surrender possession of or transfer (something).

hand-pick *vb.* to select (a person) with great care, as for a special job. —,**handpicked** *adj.*

handrail ('hænd,reɪl) *n.* a rail alongside a stairway, to provide support.

hands (hændz) *pl. n.* **1.** power or keeping: *your welfare is in his hands.* **2. change hands.** to pass from the possession of one person to another. **3. have one's hands full.** to be completely occupied. **4. off one's hands.** no longer one's responsibility. **5. on one's hands.** for which one is responsible: *I've got too much on my hands.* **6. wash one's hands of.** to have nothing more to do with. **7. win hands down.** to win easily.

handset ('hænd,sɛt) *n.* a telephone mouthpiece and earpiece mounted as a single unit.

handshake ('hænd,ʃeɪk) *n.* the act of grasping and shaking a person's hand, as a greeting or when agreeing on a deal.

handsome ('hændsəm) *adj.* **1.** (esp. of a man) good-looking. **2.** well-proportioned; stately: *a handsome room.* **3.** liberal; generous: *a handsome allowance.* [obs. *handsom* easily handled]

hands-on *adj.* involving practical experience of equipment: *hands-on training in computers.*

handspring ('hænd,sprɪŋ) *n.* a gymnastic feat in which a person leaps forwards or backwards into a handstand and then onto his feet.

handstand ('hænd,stænd) *n.* the act of

supporting the body on the hands in an upside-down position.

hand-to-hand *adj., adv.* (of combat) at close quarters.

hand-to-mouth *adj., adv.* with barely enough money or food to satisfy immediate needs.

handwork ('hænd,wɜːk) *n.* work done by hand rather than by machine.

handwriting ('hænd,raɪtɪŋ) *n.* **1.** writing by hand rather than by typing or printing. **2.** a person's characteristic writing style. —'**hand,written** *adj.*

handy ('hændɪ) *adj.* **handier, handiest. 1.** conveniently within reach. **2.** easy to handle or use. **3.** skilful with one's hands. —'**handily** *adv.*

handyman ('hændɪ,mæn) *n., pl.* -**men.** a man who is skilled in odd jobs.

hang (hæŋ) *vb.* **hanging, hung. 1.** to fasten or be fastened from above. **2.** to place (something) in position as by a hinge so as to allow free movement: *to hang a door.* **3.** to hover: *a pall of smoke hung over the city.* **4.** (foll. by *over*) to worry: *the threat of redundancy hung over them.* **5.** (*p.t. & p.p.* **hanged**) to suspend or be suspended by the neck until dead. **6.** to decorate with something suspended, such as pictures. **7.** to fasten to a wall: *to hang wallpaper.* **8.** to exhibit or be exhibited in an art gallery. **9.** to allow to droop: *to hang one's head.* **10.** (of cloth or clothing) to drape: *her skirt hangs well.* **11.** (*p.t. & p.p.* **hanged**) *Slang.* to damn: used in mild curses or interjections. **12. hang fire.** to procrastinate. ~*n.* **13.** the way in which something hangs. **14.** *Slang.* a damn: *I don't give a hang.* **15. get the hang of something.** *Informal.* to understand the technique of doing something. ~See also **hang about, hang back,** etc. [Old English *hangian*]

hang about *or* **around** *vb.* **1.** to waste time; loiter. **2.** (foll. by *with*) to frequent the company (of someone).

hangar ('hæŋə) *n.* a large building for storing aircraft. [French]

hang back *vb.* to be reluctant to do something.

hangdog ('hæŋ,dɒg) *adj.* downcast, furtive, or guilty in appearance or manner.

hanger ('hæŋə) *n.* **1.** same as **coat hanger. 2.** a person who hangs something: *paperhanger.*

hanger-on *n., pl.* **hangers-on.** an unwanted follower.

hang-glider *n.* an unpowered aircraft consisting of a large cloth wing stretched over a light framework from which the pilot hangs in a harness. —'**hang,gliding** *n.*

hangi ('hʌŋiː) *n.* N.Z. **1.** an open-air cooking pit. **2.** the food cooked in it. **3.** the social gathering at the resultant meal. [Maori]

hanging ('hæŋɪŋ) *n.* **1.** the act or practice of putting a person to death by suspending the body by the neck. **2.** a decorative drapery hung on a wall.

hangman ('hæŋmən) *n., pl.* -**men.** an official who carries out a sentence of hanging.

hangnail ('hæŋ,neɪl) *n.* a piece of skin partly torn away from the base or side of a fingernail.

hang on *vb.* **1.** *Informal.* to wait: *hang on for a few minutes.* **2.** to continue or persist with effort or difficulty. **3.** to grasp or hold. **4.** to depend on: *everything hangs on this deal.* **5.** to listen attentively to: *he hangs on her every word.*

hang out *vb.* **1.** to suspend, be suspended, or lean. **2.** *Informal.* to frequent a place: *where does Richard hang out these days?* **3. let it all hang out.** *Informal, chiefly U.S.* to relax completely; act or speak freely. ~*n.* **hang-out. 4.** *Informal.* a place that one frequents.

hangover ('hæŋ,əʊvə) *n.* the aftereffects of drinking too much alcohol.

hang together *vb.* **1.** to be united. **2.** to be consistent: *your statements don't quite hang together.*

hang up *vb.* **1.** to replace (a telephone receiver) at the end of a conversation. **2.** to put on a hook or hanger. ~*n.* **hang-up. 3.** *Informal.* an emotional or psychological preoccupation or problem.

hank (hæŋk) *n.* a loop, coil, or skein, as of rope or wool. [Old Norse]

hanker ('hæŋkə) *vb.* (foll. by *for* or *after*) to have a yearning. [prob. from Dutch dialect *hankeren*] —'**hankering** *n.*

hanky *or* **hankie** ('hæŋkɪ) *n., pl.* **hankies.** *Informal.* short for **handkerchief.**

hanky-panky ('hæŋkɪ'pæŋkɪ) *n. Informal.* **1.** illicit sexual relations. **2.** dubious or foolish behaviour. [var. of *hocus-pocus*]

Hanoverian (,hænə'vɪərɪən) *adj.* of or relating to the British royal house ruling from 1714 to 1901. [after *Hanover,* Germany]

Hansard ('hænsɑːd) *n.* the official verbatim report of the proceedings of the British or Canadian parliament. [after L. *Hansard,* its original compiler]

Hanseatic League (,hænsɪ'ætɪk) *n.* a commercial organization of towns in N Germany formed in the 14th century to protect and control trade.

hansom ('hænsəm) *n.* a two-wheeled one-horse carriage with a fixed hood. Also called: **hansom cab.** [after its designer J. A. *Hansom*]

Hants (hænts) Hampshire.

Hanukkah ('hɑːnəkə, -nʊ,kɑː) *n.* same as **Chanukah.**

haphazard (hæp'hæzəd) *adj.* done at random; careless; slipshod. [Old Norse *happ* good luck + *hazard*] —**hap'hazardly** *adv.*

hapless ('hæplɪs) *adj.* unfortunate; wretched. [Old Norse *happ* good luck]

happen ('hæp'n) *vb.* **1.** to take place; occur. **2.** (foll. by *to*) (of some unforeseen event, such as death) to fall to the lot (of): *if anything happens to me it'll be your fault.* **3.** to chance (to be or do something): *I happen to know him.* **4.** to be the case, esp. by chance: *it happens that I know him.* [obs. *hap*]

happening ('hæpəniŋ, 'hæpniŋ) n. **1.** an event. **2.** an improvised or spontaneous performance consisting of bizarre events.

happy ('hæpi) adj. **-pier, -piest. 1.** feeling or expressing joy; pleased. **2.** causing joy or gladness: *the happiest day of my life.* **3.** fortunate: *the happy position of not having to work.* [Old Norse *happ* good luck] —'**happily** adv. —'**happiness** n.

happy-go-lucky adj. carefree or easygoing.

hara-kiri (,hærə'kırı) n. (formerly, in Japan) ritual suicide by disembowelment when disgraced or under sentence of death. [Japanese *hara* belly + *kiri* cut]

harangue (hə'ræŋ) vb. **1.** to address (a person or group) in an angry or forcefully persuasive way. ~n. **2.** a forceful or angry speech. [Old Italian *aringa* public speech]

harass ('hærəs, hə'ræs) vb. to trouble, torment, or confuse by continual persistent attacks, questions, or problems. [French *harasser*] —'**harassed** adj. —'**harassment** n.

harbinger ('haːbındʒə) n. a person or thing that announces or indicates the approach of something: *a harbinger of doom.* [Old French *herbergere*]

harbour or U.S. **harbor** ('haːbə) n. **1.** a sheltered port. **2.** a place of refuge or safety. ~vb. **3.** to maintain secretly: *to harbour a grudge.* **4.** to give shelter to: *to harbour a criminal.* [Old English *here* army + *beorg* shelter]

harbour master n. an official in charge of a harbour.

hard (haːd) adj. **1.** firm or rigid. **2.** difficult to do or understand: *a hard sum.* **3.** showing or requiring considerable effort or application: *hard work.* **4.** harsh; cruel: *a hard fate.* **5.** causing pain, sorrow, or hardship: *hard times.* **6.** tough or violent: *a hard man.* **7.** forceful: *a hard knock.* **8.** cool or uncompromising: *we took a long hard look at our profit factor.* **9.** indisputable; real: *hard facts.* **10.** (of water) containing calcium salts which stop soap lathering freely. **11.** practical, shrewd, or calculating: *he is a hard man in business.* **12.** harsh: *hard light.* **13.** (of currency) high and stable in exchange value. **14.** (of alcoholic drink) being a spirit rather than a wine or beer. **15.** (of a drug) highly addictive. **16.** short for **hard-core. 17.** *Phonetics.* denoting the consonants *c* and *g* when they are pronounced as in *cat* and *got.* **18.** politically extreme: *the hard left.* **19. hard of hearing.** slightly deaf. **20. hard up.** *Informal.* in need of money. ~adv. **21.** with great energy or force: *the team always played hard.* **22.** with great intensity: *she thought hard.* **23. hard by.** close by. **24. hard put (to it).** scarcely having the capacity (to do something). ~n. **25. have a hard on.** *Taboo slang.* to have an erection of the penis. [Old English *heard*] —'**hardness** n.

hard-and-fast adj. (of rules) invariable or strict.

hardback ('haːd,bæk) n. **1.** a book with stiff covers. ~adj. **2.** of or denoting a hardback.

hard-bitten adj. *Informal.* tough and realistic.

hardboard ('haːd,bɔːd) n. stiff board made in thin sheets of compressed sawdust and woodchips.

hard-boiled adj. **1.** (of an egg) boiled until solid. **2.** *Informal.* tough and realistic.

hard cash n. money or payment in money, as opposed to payment by cheque, credit, etc.

hard copy n. computer output printed on paper.

hard core n. **1.** the members of a group who most resist change. **2.** broken stones used to form a foundation for a road. ~adj. **hard-core. 3.** (of pornography) depicting sexual acts in explicit detail.

hard disk n. *Computers.* an inflexible disk in a sealed container.

harden ('haːd'n) vb. **1.** to make or become hard; freeze, stiffen, or set. **2.** to make or become tough or unfeeling. **3.** to make or become stronger or firmer. **4.** *Commerce.* (of prices or a market) to cease to fluctuate.

hardened ('haːd'nd) adj. toughened; seasoned: *a hardened criminal.*

hard-headed adj. tough, realistic, or shrewd; not moved by sentiment.

hardhearted (,haːd'haːtıd) adj. unkind or intolerant.

hardihood ('haːdı,hʊd) n. courage or daring.

hard labour n. *Criminal law.* (formerly) the penalty of compulsory physical labour imposed in addition to a sentence of imprisonment.

hard line n. an uncompromising policy. —,**hard'liner** n.

hardly ('haːdlı) adv. **1.** scarcely; barely: *we hardly knew the family.* **2.** *Ironic.* not at all: *he will hardly incriminate himself.* **3.** with difficulty: *I can hardly keep my eyes open.*

hard pad n. (in dogs) an abnormal increase in the thickness of the foot pads: a sign of distemper.

hard palate n. the bony front part of the roof of the mouth.

hard-pressed adj. **1.** in difficulties. **2.** closely pursued.

hard science n. one of the natural or physical sciences, such as physics, chemistry, or biology.

hard sell n. an aggressive insistent technique of selling.

hardship ('haːdʃıp) n. **1.** conditions of life difficult to endure. **2.** something that causes suffering.

hard shoulder n. *Brit.* a surfaced verge running along the edge of a motorway for emergency stops.

hardtack ('haːd,tæk) n. a kind of hard saltless biscuit, formerly eaten by sailors.

hardware ('haːd,wɛə) n. **1.** metal tools or implements, esp. cutlery or cooking utensils. **2.** *Computers.* the physical equipment used in a computer system. **3.** heavy military equipment, such as tanks and missiles.

hard-wired adj. (of a circuit or instruction) permanently wired into a computer.

hardwood ('haːd,wʊd) n. the wood of a deciduous tree such as oak, beech, or ash.

hardy ('haːdɪ) adj. **-dier, -diest. 1.** having a tough constitution; robust. **2.** (of plants) able to live out of doors throughout the winter. [Old French hardi emboldened] —'**hardiness** n.

hare (hɛə) n., pl. **hares** or **hare. 1.** a mammal which is larger than a rabbit and has longer ears and legs. ~vb. **2.** (foll. by off or after) Brit. informal. to run fast or wildly. [Old English hara]

harebell ('hɛə,bɛl) n. a blue bell-shaped flower.

harebrained ('hɛə,breɪnd) adj. foolish; badly thought out: harebrained schemes.

harelip ('hɛə,lɪp) n. a slight split in the midline of the upper lip.

harem ('hɛərəm, haː'riːm) n. **1.** a Muslim man's wives and concubines collectively. **2.** the part of an Oriental house reserved for wives and concubines. [Arabic harīm forbidden (place)]

haricot bean or **haricot** ('hærɪkəʊ) n. a white edible bean, which can be dried. [French]

hark (haːk) vb. to listen; pay attention: Hark, the cocks are crowing. [Old English heorcnian]

hark back vb. to return (to an earlier subject in speech or thought): he keeps harking back to his music-hall days.

harlequin ('haːlɪkwɪn) n. Theatre. a stock comic character, usually wearing a diamond-patterned multicoloured costume and a black mask. ~adj. **2.** in varied colours. [Old French]

harlequinade (,haːlɪkwɪ'neɪd) n. **1.** Theatre. a play in which harlequin has a leading role. **2.** buffoonery.

harlot ('haːlət) n. a prostitute. [Old French herlot rascal] —'**harlotry** n.

harm (haːm) n. **1.** physical, moral, or mental injury. ~vb. **2.** to injure physically, morally, or mentally. [Old English hearm]

harmful ('haːmfʊl) adj. causing or tending to cause harm; injurious.

harmless ('haːmlɪs) adj. not causing or tending to cause harm.

harmonic (haː'mɒnɪk) adj. **1.** of, producing, or characterized by harmony; harmonious. ~n. **2.** Music. overtone. ~See also **harmonics.** [Latin harmonicus relating to harmony] —har'**monically** adv.

harmonica (haː'mɒnɪkə) n. a small wind instrument in which reeds enclosed in a narrow oblong box are made to vibrate by blowing and sucking.

harmonics (haː'mɒnɪks) n. (functioning as sing.) the science of musical sounds.

harmonious (haː'məʊnɪəs) adj. **1.** (esp. of colours or sounds) fitting together well. **2.** agreeing. **3.** tuneful or melodious.

harmonium (haː'məʊnɪəm) n. a musical keyboard instrument in which air from pedal-operated bellows causes the reeds to vibrate.

harmonize or **-nise** ('haːmə,naɪz) vb. **1.** to sing or play in harmony, as with another singer or player. **2.** to make or become harmonious.

harmony ('haːmənɪ) n., pl. **-nies. 1.** Music. an agreeable combination of notes sounded simultaneously. **2.** agreement in action, opinion, or feeling. **3.** the way parts combine well together or into a whole. [Greek harmonia]

harness ('haːnɪs) n. **1.** an arrangement of straps fitted to a horse so that it can be attached to a cart. **2.** something resembling this, for attaching something to a person's body: a parachute harness. **3. in harness.** at one's routine work. ~vb. **4.** to put a harness on (a horse or other animal). **5.** to control something in order to use its energy: to harness the waves. [Old French harneis baggage]

harp (haːp) n. **1.** a large upright triangular stringed instrument played by plucking the strings with the fingers. ~vb. **2.** (foll. by on) to speak in a persistent and tedious manner (about a subject). [Old English hearpe] —'**harpist** n.

harpoon (haː'puːn) n. **1.** a barbed missile attached to a long cord and hurled or fired when hunting whales, etc. ~vb. **2.** to spear with a harpoon. [prob. from Dutch harpoen]

harpsichord ('haːpsɪ,kɔːd) n. a stringed keyboard instrument, triangular in shape, with strings that are plucked mechanically. [Late Latin harpa harp + Latin chorda string]

harpy ('haːpɪ) n., pl. **-pies.** a cruel grasping woman. [Greek Harpuiai the Harpies, lit.: snatchers]

harridan ('hærɪd⁰n) n. a scolding old woman; nag. [origin unknown]

harrier [1] ('hærɪə) n. **1.** a cross-country runner. **2.** a smallish hound used originally for hare-hunting. [from hare]

harrier [2] ('hærɪə) n. a bird of prey with broad wings and long legs and tail.

harrow ('hærəʊ) n. **1.** an implement used to break up clods of soil. ~vb. **2.** to draw a harrow over (land). [Old Norse]

harrowing ('hærəʊɪŋ) adj. very distressing.

harry ('hærɪ) vb. **-rying, -ried.** to harass; worry. [Old English hergian]

harsh (haːʃ) adj. **1.** rough or grating to the senses. **2.** stern, severe, or cruel: harsh punishment. [prob. Scandinavian] —'**harshly** adv. —'**harshness** n.

hart (haːt) n., pl. **harts** or **hart.** the male of the deer, esp. the red deer. [Old English heorot]

hartebeest ('haːtɪ,biːst) n. a large African antelope with curved horns and a fawn-coloured coat. [Dutch]

harum-scarum ('hɛərəm'skɛərəm) adj. **1.** reckless. ~adv. **2.** recklessly. ~n. **3.** an impetuous person. [origin unknown]

harvest ('haːvɪst) n. **1.** the gathering of a ripened crop. **2.** the crop itself. **3.** the season for gathering crops. **4.** the product of an effort or action. ~*vb.* **5.** to gather (a ripened crop). [Old English *hærfest*]

harvester ('hɑːvɪstə) *n.* **1.** a harvesting machine, esp. a combine harvester. **2.** a person who harvests.

harvest moon *n.* the full moon occurring nearest to the autumn equinox.

harvest mouse *n.* a very small reddish-brown mouse that lives in cornfields or hedgerows.

has (hæz) *vb.* third person singular of the present tense of **have.**

has-been *n. Informal.* a person who is no longer popular or successful.

hash[1] (hæʃ) *n.* **1.** a dish of diced cooked meat, vegetables, etc., reheated: *cornbeef hash.* **2.** a reworking of old material. **3. make a hash of.** *Informal.* to mess up or destroy. **4. settle someone's hash.** *Informal.* to subdue or silence someone. [Old French *hacher* to chop up]

hash[2] (hæʃ) *n. Slang.* short for **hashish.**

hashish ('hæʃiːʃ, -ɪʃ) *n.* a drug made from the dried flower tops of the hemp plant, smoked for its intoxicating effects. [Arabic]

hasn't ('hæzᵊnt) has not.

hasp (hɑːsp) *n.* a metal fastening consisting of a hinged strap with a slot that fits over a staple and is secured by a pin, bolt, or padlock. [Old English *hæpse*]

hassle ('hæsᵊl) *Informal.* ~*n.* **1.** a great deal of trouble. **2.** a prolonged argument. ~*vb.* **3.** to cause annoyance or trouble to (someone); harass. [origin unknown]

hassock ('hæsək) *n.* a firm upholstered cushion for kneeling on in church. [Old English *hassuc* matted grass]

haste (heɪst) *n.* **1.** speed, esp. in an action. **2.** the act of hurrying in a careless manner. **3. make haste.** to hurry; rush. ~*vb.* **4.** *Poetic.* to hasten. [Old French]

hasten ('heɪsᵊn) *vb.* **1.** to hurry or cause to hurry; rush. **2.** to be anxious (to say something).

hasty ('heɪstɪ) *adj.* **-tier, -tiest. 1.** rapid; swift; quick. **2.** too quick; rash. —'**hastily** *adv.*

hat (hæt) *n.* **1.** a head covering, esp. one with a brim and a shaped crown. **2.** *Informal.* a role or capacity: *I'm wearing my teacher's hat today.* **3. keep something under one's hat.** to keep something secret. **4. pass the hat round.** to collect money for a cause. **5. take off one's hat to someone.** to admire or congratulate someone. [Old English *hætt*]

hatband ('hæt,bænd) *n.* a band or ribbon around the base of the crown of a hat.

hatch[1] (hætʃ) *vb.* **1.** to cause (the young of various animals, esp. birds) to emerge from the egg or (of young birds, etc.) to emerge from the egg. **2.** (of eggs) to break and release the young animal within. **3.** to contrive or devise (a plot). [Germanic]

hatch[2] (hætʃ) *n.* **1.** a covering for a hatchway. **2. a.** short for **hatchway. b.** a door in an aircraft or spacecraft. **3.** Also called: **serving hatch.** an opening in a wall between a kitchen and a dining area. [Old English *hæcc*]

hatch[3] (hætʃ) *vb.* *Drawing, engraving, etc.* to mark (a figure, etc.) with fine parallel or crossed lines to indicate shading. [Old French *hacher* to chop] —'**hatching** *n.*

hatchback ('hætʃ,bæk) *n.* a car that has a sloping rear with a single door that is lifted to open.

hatchet ('hætʃɪt) *n.* **1.** a short axe used for chopping wood, etc. **2.** (*modifier*) narrow and sharp: *a hatchet face.* **3. bury the hatchet.** to cease hostilities and become reconciled. [Old French *hachette*]

hatchet man *n. Informal.* a person who carries out unpleasant tasks on behalf of an employer.

hatchway ('hætʃ,weɪ) *n.* an opening in the deck of a vessel to provide access below.

hate (heɪt) *vb.* **1.** to dislike (someone or something) intensely; detest. **2.** to be unwilling (to do something): *I hate to bother you.* ~*n.* **3.** intense dislike. **4.** *Informal.* a person or thing that is hated: *ironing is my pet hate.* [Old English *hatian*]

hateful ('heɪtfʊl) *adj.* causing or deserving hate; loathsome.

hatred ('heɪtrɪd) *n.* intense dislike; enmity.

hatter ('hætə) *n.* **1.** a person who makes and sells hats. **2. mad as a hatter.** eccentric.

hat trick *n.* **1.** *Cricket.* the achievement of a bowler in taking three wickets with three successive balls. **2.** any achievement of three successive goals, victories, etc.

hauberk ('hɔːbɜːk) *n.* a long sleeveless coat of mail. [Old French *hauberc*]

haughty ('hɔːtɪ) *adj.* **-tier, -tiest.** having or showing arrogance. [Latin *altus* high] —'**haughtily** *adv.* —'**haughtiness** *n.*

haul (hɔːl) *vb.* **1.** to drag (something) with effort. **2.** to transport, as in a lorry. **3.** *Naut.* to alter the course of (a vessel). ~*n.* **4.** the act of dragging with effort. **5.** goods obtained by theft or robbery. **6.** a distance of travelling: *a long haul.* [Old French *haler*]

haulage ('hɔːlɪdʒ) *n.* **1.** the business of transporting goods. **2.** a charge for transporting goods.

haulier ('hɔːljə) *n. Brit.* a person or firm that transports goods by road.

haulm (hɔːm) *n.* the stalks of beans, peas, potatoes, etc., collectively. [Old English *healm*]

haunch (hɔːntʃ) *n.* **1.** the human hip or fleshy hindquarter of an animal. **2.** the leg and loin of an animal, used for food. [Old French *hanche*]

haunt (hɔːnt) *vb.* **1.** to visit (a person or place) in the form of a ghost. **2.** to recur to the memory or thoughts of: *he was haunted by the fear of insanity.* **3.** to visit (a place) frequently. ~*n.* **4.** a place visited frequently. [Old French *hanter*]

haunted ('hɔːntɪd) *adj.* **1.** (of a place) frequented or visited by ghosts. **2.** (of a person) obsessed or worried.

haunting ('hɔːntɪŋ) *adj.* poignantly sentimental; eerily evocative.

hautboy ('əʊbɔɪ) *n. Archaic.* an oboe. [French *haut* high + *bois* wood]

haute couture ('əʊt kuː'tʊə) n. high fashion. [French].

hauteur (əʊ'tɜː) n. pride; haughtiness. [French *haut* high]

have (hæv) vb. **has, having, had. 1.** to possess: *he has two cars; he has dark hair.* **2.** to receive, take, or obtain: *she had a present; have a look.* **3.** to hold in the mind: *to have an idea.* **4.** to possess a knowledge of: *I have no German.* **5.** to experience: *to have a shock.* **6.** to suffer from: *to have a cold.* **7.** to gain control of or advantage over: *you have me on that point.* **8.** Slang. to cheat or outwit: *I've been had.* **9.** to show: *have mercy on me.* **10.** to take part in; hold: *to have a conversation.* **11.** to cause, compel, or require to (be, do, or be done): *have my shoes mended.* **12.** (foll. by *to*) used to express compulsion or necessity: *I had to run quickly to escape him.* **13.** to eat or drink. **14.** *Taboo slang.* to have sexual intercourse with. **15.** to tolerate or allow: *I won't have all this noise.* **16.** to receive as a guest: *to have people to stay.* **17.** to be pregnant with or bear (offspring). **18.** (*takes a past participle*) used to form past tenses: *I have gone; I had gone.* **19. have had it.** *Informal.* **a.** to be exhausted or killed. **b.** to have lost one's last chance. **20. have it off.** *Taboo, Brit. slang.* to have sexual intercourse. ~n. **21.** (*pl.*) *Informal.* people who have wealth, security, etc.: *the haves and the have-nots.* ~See also **have on, have out,** etc. [Old English *habban*]

haven ('heɪv'n) n. **1.** a place of safety. **2.** a harbour for shipping. [Old English *hæfen*]

haven't ('hæv'nt) have not.

have on vb. **1.** to wear: *she had a blue dress on.* **2.** to have a commitment: *what do you have on this afternoon?* **3.** *Informal.* to trick or tease: *he's having you on.* **4.** to have (information, esp. when incriminating) about (a person): *she's got something on him.*

have out vb. to settle (a matter), esp. by fighting or by frank discussion: *we decided to have it out.*

haver ('heɪvə) vb. **1.** *Scot. & N English dialect.* to talk nonsense. **2.** to dither. [origin unknown]

haversack ('hævə,sæk) n. a canvas bag carried on the back or shoulder. [French *havresac*]

have up vb. to cause to appear for trial: *he was had up for breaking and entering.*

havoc ('hævək) n. **1.** *Informal.* confusion; chaos. **2.** destruction; devastation; ruin. **3. play havoc with.** to cause a great deal of damage or confusion to. [Old French *havot* pillage]

haw[1] (hɔː) n. the fruit of the hawthorn. [Old English *haga*]

haw[2] (hɔː) vb. **hum and haw.** to hesitate in speaking. [imit.]

hawk[1] (hɔːk) n. **1.** a bird of prey with short rounded wings and a long tail. **2.** a person who advocates warlike policies. ~vb. **3.** to hunt with falcons or hawks.

[Old English *hafoc*] —'**hawkish** adj. —'**hawk,like** adj.

hawk[2] (hɔːk) vb. to offer (goods) for sale, as in the street. [from *hawker* pedlar]

hawk[3] (hɔːk) vb. **1.** to clear the throat noisily. **2.** to force (phlegm) up from the throat. [imit.]

hawker ('hɔːkə) n. a person who travels from place to place selling goods. [prob. from Middle Low German *höken* to peddle]

hawk-eyed adj. having extremely keen eyesight.

hawser ('hɔːzə) n. *Naut.* a large heavy rope. [Anglo-French *hauceour*]

hawthorn ('hɔː,θɔːn) n. a thorny tree or shrub with white or pink flowers and reddish fruits. [Old English *haguthorn*]

hay (heɪ) n. **1.** grass cut and dried as fodder. **2. hit the hay.** *Slang.* to go to bed. **3. make hay while the sun shines.** to take full advantage of an opportunity. [Old English *hieg*]

hay fever n. an allergic reaction to pollen, which causes sneezing, runny nose, and watery eyes.

haystack ('heɪ,stæk) or **hayrick** n. a large pile of hay built in the open and covered with thatch.

haywire ('heɪ,waɪə) adj. **go haywire.** *Informal.* to stop functioning properly.

hazard ('hæzəd) n. **1.** exposure or vulnerability to injury, loss, etc. **2. at hazard.** at risk; in danger. **3.** a thing likely to cause injury, loss, etc. **4.** *Golf.* an obstacle such as a bunker. ~vb. **5.** to risk. **6.** to venture (a guess). [Arabic *az-zahr* the die]

hazardous ('hæzədəs) adj. involving great risk.

haze (heɪz) n. **1.** *Meteorol.* reduced visibility as a result of condensed water vapour, dust, etc., in the air. **2.** confused or unclear understanding or feeling. [from *hazy*]

hazel ('heɪz'l) n. **1.** a shrub with edible rounded nuts. ~adj. **2.** greenish-brown: *hazel eyes.* [Old English *hæsel*]

hazelnut ('heɪz'l,nʌt) n. the nut of a hazel shrub, which has a smooth shiny hard shell.

hazy ('heɪzɪ) adj. **-zier, -ziest.** misty; indistinct; vague. [origin unknown] —'**hazily** adv. —'**haziness** n.

Hb haemoglobin.

HB *Brit.* (of pencil lead) hard-black: denoting a medium-hard lead.

H-bomb n. short for **hydrogen bomb.**

he (hiː; unstressed ɪ) pron. refers to: **1.** a male person or animal. **2.** a person or animal of unknown or unspecified sex: *a member may vote as he sees fit.* ~n. **3.** a male person or animal: *a he-goat.* [Old English]

He *Chem.* helium.

HE His *or* Her Excellency.

head (hɛd) n. **1.** the upper or front part of the body that contains the brain, eyes, mouth, nose, and ears. **2.** something resembling a head in form or function, such as the top of a tool. **3.** the person commanding most authority within a group or an organization. **4.** the position of leadership or command. **5.** the most forward part of a thing; front: *the head of a queue.* **6.** the highest part of a thing; upper end: *the head of the pass.* **7.** the froth on the top of a glass of beer. **8.** aptitude, intelligence, and emotions: *she has a good head for figures.* **9.** (*pl.* **head**) a person or animal considered as a unit: *the show was two pounds per head; six hundred head of cattle.* **10.** *Bot.* the top part of a plant, where the leaves or flowers grow in a cluster. **11.** a culmination or crisis: *increasing anti-British feeling came to a head in the 1890's.* **12.** the pus-filled tip of a pimple or boil. **13.** the source of a river or stream. **14.** a headland or promontory: *Beachy Head.* **15.** the side of a coin that usually bears a portrait of the head of a monarch, etc. **16.** a headline or heading. **17.** pressure of water or steam in an enclosed space. **18.** part of a computer or tape recorder that can read, write, or erase information. **19.** *Informal.* short for **headmaster, headmistress,** *or* **head teacher. 20.** *Informal.* short for **headache. 21. give someone his head.** to allow someone greater freedom or responsibility. **22. go to one's head. a.** (of an alcoholic drink) to make one tipsy. **b.** to make one conceited: *his success has gone to his head.* **23. head over heels (in love).** very much (in love). **24. keep one's head.** to remain calm. **25. not make head nor tail of.** not to understand (a problem, etc.). **26. off one's head.** *Slang.* insane or delirious. **27. on one's own head.** at a one's own risk. **28. over someone's head. a.** to a higher authority: *he went straight to the director, over the head of his immediate boss.* **b.** beyond a person's comprehension. **29. put (our, their,** etc.**) heads together.** *Informal.* to consult together. **30. turn someone's head.** to make someone conceited. *~vb.* **31.** to be at the front or top of: *to head the field.* **32.** to be in charge of. **33.** (often foll. by *for*) to go or cause to go (towards): *where are you heading?* **34.** *Soccer.* to propel (the ball) by striking it with the head. **35.** to provide with a heading. *~See also* **head off, heads.** [Old English *hēafod*]

headache ('hɛd,eɪk) *n.* **1.** a continuous pain in the head. **2.** *Informal.* any cause of worry, difficulty, or annoyance.

head-banger *n. Slang.* **1.** a person who shakes his head violently to the beat of heavy-metal music. **2.** a crazy or stupid person.

headboard ('hɛd,bɔːd) *n.* a vertical board at the head of a bed.

headdress ('hɛd,drɛs) *n.* any head covering, esp. an ornate one.

headed ('hɛdɪd) *adj.* **1.** having a head or heads: *two-headed; bullet-headed.* **2.** having a heading: *headed notepaper.*

header ('hɛdə) *n.* **1.** *Soccer.* the action of striking a ball with the head. **2.** *Informal.* a headlong fall or dive.

headfirst ('hɛd'fɜːst) *adv.* **1.** with the head foremost; headlong. **2.** rashly.

headgear ('hɛd,gɪə) *n.* hats collectively.

head-hunting *n.* **1.** the practice among certain peoples of removing the heads of enemies they have killed and preserving them as trophies. **2.** (of companies) the practice of actively searching for new high-level personnel. —'**head-,hunter** *n.*

heading ('hɛdɪŋ) *n.* **1.** a title for a page, chapter, etc. **2.** a division, as of a speech. **3.** *Mining.* a horizontal tunnel.

headland ('hɛdlənd) *n.* a narrow area of land jutting out into a sea.

headlight ('hɛd,laɪt) *or* **headlamp** *n.* a powerful light on the front of a vehicle.

headline ('hɛd,laɪn) *n.* **1.** a phrase in heavy large type at the top of a newspaper or magazine article indicating the subject. **2.** (*pl.*) the main points of a television or radio news broadcast.

headlong ('hɛd,lɒŋ) *adv., adj.* **1.** with the head foremost; headfirst. **2.** with great haste.

headmaster (,hɛd'mɑːstə) *or* (*fem.*) **headmistress** *n.* the principal of a school.

head off *vb.* **1.** to intercept and force to change direction: *to head off the stampede.* **2.** to prevent or forestall.

head-on *adv., adj.* **1.** front foremost: *a head-on collision.* **2.** with directness or without compromise: *in his usual head-on fashion.*

headphones ('hɛd,fəʊnz) *pl. n.* two small sound receivers held against the ears by a flexible metallic strap passing over the head, worn to listen to the radio or recorded music without other people hearing it.

headquarters (,hɛd'kwɔːtəz) *pl. n.* (*sometimes functioning as sing.*) any centre from which operations are directed, as in the police.

headroom ('hɛd,rʊm, -,ruːm) *or* **headway** *n.* the height of a bridge, room, etc.; clearance.

heads (hɛdz) *adv.* with the side of a coin uppermost which has a portrait of a head on it.

headship ('hɛdʃɪp) *n.* the position or state of being a leader, esp. the head teacher of a school.

headshrinker ('hɛd,ʃrɪŋkə) *n. Slang.* a psychiatrist.

headstall ('hɛd,stɔːl) *n.* the part of a bridle that fits round a horse's head.

head start *n.* an initial advantage in a competitive situation.

headstone ('hɛd,stəʊn) *n.* a memorial stone at the head of a grave.

headstrong ('hɛd,strɒŋ) *adj.* self-willed; obstinate.

head teacher *n.* the principal of a school.

headwaters ('hɛd,wɔːtəz) *pl. n.* the tributary streams of a river in the area in which it rises.

headway ('hɛd,weɪ) *n.* **1.** progress: *he made no headway with the problem.* **2.** motion forward: *the vessel made no headway.* **3.** same as **headroom.**

headwind ('hɛd,wɪnd) *n.* a wind blowing directly against the course of an aircraft or ship.

heady ('hɛdɪ) *adj.* **headier, headiest. 1.** (of an experience or period of time) extremely exciting. **2.** (of alcoholic drink) intoxicating. **3.** rash; impetuous.

heal (hiːl) *vb.* **1.** (of a wound) to repair by natural processes, as by scar formation. **2.** to restore (someone) to health. **3.** to repair (a rift in a personal relationship or an emotional wound). [Old English *hælan*] —'**healer** *n.* —'**healing** *n., adj.*

health (hɛlθ) *n.* **1.** the state of being bodily and mentally vigorous and free from disease. **2.** the general condition of body and mind: *in poor health.* **3.** the condition of an organization, society, etc.: *the economic health of a nation.* [Old English]

health centre *n.* the surgery and offices of the doctors in a district.

health food *n.* vegetarian food, produced without chemicals, eaten for its benefit to health.

healthful ('hɛlθful) *adj.* same as **healthy** (senses 1–3).

health visitor *n.* (in Britain) a nurse employed to visit people such as mothers of babies and the elderly in their homes.

healthy ('hɛlθɪ) *adj.* **healthier, healthiest. 1.** having or showing good health. **2.** likely to produce good health. **3.** sound: *the company's finances are not very healthy.* **4.** *Informal.* considerable: *a healthy sum.* —'**healthily** *adv.* —'**healthiness** *n.*

heap (hiːp) *n.* **1.** a collection of articles or mass of material gathered in a pile. **2.** (*often pl.*) *Informal.* a large number or quantity. ~*adv.* **3. heaps.** much: *he was heaps better.* ~*vb.* **4.** to collect into a pile. **5.** to give abundantly: *the critics heaped him with praise.* [Old English]

hear (hɪə) *vb.* **hearing, heard** (hɜːd). **1.** to perceive (a sound) with the sense of hearing. **2.** to listen to: *did you hear what I said?* **3.** to be informed of (something): *I heard you were leaving.* **4.** *Law.* to give a hearing to (a case). **5.** (foll. by *of*) to allow: *she wouldn't hear of it.* **6. hear from.** to receive a letter or telephone call from. **7. hear! hear!** an exclamation of approval. [Old English *hieran*] —'**hearer** *n.*

hearing ('hɪərɪŋ) *n.* **1.** the sense by which sound is perceived. **2.** an opportunity for someone to be listened to. **3.** the range within which sound can be heard; earshot. **4.** the investigation of a matter by a court of law.

hearing aid *n.* a small amplifier worn by a partially deaf person in or behind the ear to improve hearing.

hearken ('hɑːkən) *vb. Archaic.* to listen. [Old English *heorcnian*]

hearsay ('hɪəˌseɪ) *n.* gossip; rumour.

hearse (hɜːs) *n.* a large car used to carry a coffin at a funeral. [Latin *hirpex* harrow]

heart (hɑːt) *n.* **1.** a hollow muscular organ whose contractions pump the blood throughout the body. **2.** this organ considered as the centre of emotions, esp. love. **3.** tenderness or pity: *you have no heart.* **4.** courage or spirit. **5.** the most central

part or important part: *the heart of the matter.* **6.** (of vegetables, such as cabbage) the inner compact part. **7.** the breast: *she held him to her heart.* **8.** a shape representing the heart, with two rounded lobes at the top meeting in a point at the bottom. **9. a.** a red heart-shaped symbol on a playing card. **b.** a card with one or more of these symbols or (*when pl.*) the suit of cards so marked. **10. break someone's heart.** to cause someone to grieve very deeply, esp. by ending a love affair. **11. by heart.** by memorizing. **12. have a change of heart.** to experience a profound change of outlook or attitude. **13. have one's heart in one's mouth.** to be full of apprehension, excitement, or fear. **14. have the heart.** to have the necessary will or callousness (to do something): *I didn't have the heart to tell him.* **15. set one's heart on something.** to have something as one's ambition. **16. take heart.** to become encouraged. **17. take something to heart.** to take something seriously or be upset about something. **18. wear one's heart on one's sleeve.** to show one's feelings openly. **19. with all one's heart.** deeply and sincerely. [Old English *heorte*]

heartache ('hɑːtˌeɪk) *n.* intense anguish or mental suffering.

heart attack *n.* an instance of abnormal heart functioning causing sudden severe chest pain.

heartbeat ('hɑːtˌbiːt) *n.* one complete pulsation of the heart.

heartbreak ('hɑːtˌbreɪk) *n.* intense and overwhelming grief, esp. after the end of a love affair. —'**heart,breaking** *adj.* —'**heart,broken** *adj.*

heartburn ('hɑːtˌbɜːn) *n.* a burning sensation beneath the breastbone caused by inflammation of the gullet.

hearten ('hɑːt'n) *vb.* to make cheerful. —'**heartening** *adj.*

heart failure *n.* **1.** a condition in which the heart is unable to pump an adequate amount of blood to the tissues. **2.** sudden stopping of the heartbeat, resulting in death.

heartfelt ('hɑːtˌfɛlt) *adj.* sincerely and strongly felt.

hearth (hɑːθ) *n.* **1.** the floor of a fireplace. **2.** this as a symbol of the home. [Old English *heorth*]

heartless ('hɑːtlɪs) *adj.* unkind or cruel. —'**heartlessly** *adv.*

heart-rending *adj.* causing great mental pain and sorrow.

heart-searching *n.* examination of one's feelings or conscience.

heartstrings ('hɑːtˌstrɪŋz) *pl. n. Often facetious.* deep emotions: *a sentimental film that tugs at the heartstrings.* [orig. referring to the tendons supposed to support the heart]

heart-throb *n. Brit.* an object of infatuation, esp. a male film star or pop star.

heart-to-heart *adj.* **1.** (of a talk) concerned with personal problems or intimate feelings. ~*n.* **2.** an intimate conversation.

heart-warming adj. inspiring feelings of happiness.

heartwood ('hɑːtˌwʊd) n. the central core of dark hard wood in tree trunks, consisting of nonfunctioning tissue.

hearty ('hɑːtɪ) adj. **heartier, heartiest. 1.** warm and unreserved in manner. **2.** vigorous and heartfelt: a hearty dislike. **3.** (of a meal) substantial and nourishing. —'**heartily** adv.

heat (hiːt) n. **1.** the state of being hot. **2.** the energy transferred as a result of a difference in temperature. **3.** hot weather: the heat of summer. **4.** intensity of feeling: the heat of rage. **5.** the most intense part: the heat of the battle. **6.** Sport. a preliminary eliminating contest in a competition. **7. in** or **on heat.** (of some female mammals) sexually receptive. ~vb. **8.** to make or become hot or warm. [Old English hǣtu] —'**heating** n.

heated ('hiːtɪd) adj. impassioned or highly emotional. —'**heatedly** adv.

heater ('hiːtə) n. a device for supplying heat.

heath (hiːθ) n. **1.** Brit. a large open area, usually with sandy soil, low shrubs, and heather. **2.** a low-growing evergreen shrub with small bell-shaped pink or purple flowers. [Old English hǣth]

heathen ('hiːðən) n., pl. **-thens** or **-then. 1.** a person who does not acknowledge the God of Christianity, Judaism, or Islam; pagan. ~adj. **2.** of or relating to heathen peoples. [Old English]

heather ('hɛðə) n. a low-growing evergreen shrub with clusters of small bell-shaped pinkish-purple or white flowers. [origin unknown]

Heath Robinson (hiːθ 'rɒbɪnsən) adj. (of a mechanical device) absurdly complicated in design for a simple function. [after William Heath Robinson, cartoonist]

heatstroke ('hiːtˌstrəʊk) n. same as **sunstroke.**

heat wave n. a spell of unusually hot weather.

heave (hiːv) vb. **heaving, heaved** or **hove. 1.** to lift or move (something) with a great effort. **2.** to throw (something heavy) with effort. **3.** to utter (a sigh) noisily or unhappily. **4.** to rise and fall heavily. **5.** (p.t. & p.p. **hove**) Naut. **a.** to move in a specified direction: to heave in sight. **b.** (of a vessel) to pitch or roll. **6.** to vomit or retch. ~n. **7.** the act of heaving. [Old English hebban]

heaven ('hɛvən) n. **1.** the abode of God and the angels and of the righteous after death. **2.** (pl.) the sky. **3.** a place or state of happiness. **4.** (sing. or pl.) God or the gods, used in exclamatory phrases: for heaven's sake. [Old English heofon]

heavenly ('hɛvənlɪ) adj. **1.** Informal. wonderful. **2.** of or occurring in space: a heavenly body. **3.** of or relating to heaven.

heave to vb. to stop (a vessel) or (of a vessel) to stop, as by trimming the sails.

heavy ('hɛvɪ) adj. **heavier, heaviest. 1.** of comparatively great weight. **2.** with a relatively high density: lead is a heavy metal. **3.** great in yield, quality, or quantity: heavy traffic. **4.** considerable: heavy emphasis. **5.** hard to fulfil: heavy demands. **6.** sad or dejected: heavy at heart. **7.** coarse or broad: heavy features. **8.** (of soil) with a high clay content. **9.** solid or fat: a heavy build. **10.** (of an industry) engaged in the large-scale manufacture of large objects or extraction of raw materials. **11.** serious; grave. **12.** Mil. (of guns, etc.) large and powerful. **13.** dull and uninteresting: a heavy style. **14.** excessive: a heavy drinker. **15.** (of cakes or bread) insufficiently raised. **16.** deep and loud: a heavy thud. **17.** (of music, literature, etc.) not immediately comprehensible or appealing. **18.** Slang. (of rock music) having a powerful beat. **19.** clumsy and slow: heavy going. **20.** cloudy or overcast: heavy skies. **21.** not easily digestible: a heavy meal. **22.** Slang. using, or prepared to use, violence or brutality. ~n., pl. **heavies. 23.** Slang. a large strong man hired to threaten violence or deter others by his presence. **24. a.** a villainous role. **b.** an actor who plays such a part. **25. the heavies.** Informal. serious newspapers. ~adv. **26.** heavily: time hangs heavy. [Old English hefig] —'**heavily** adv. —'**heaviness** n.

heavy-duty adj. (modifier) made to withstand hard wear, bad weather, etc.

heavy-handed adj. clumsy; harsh and oppressive.

heavy-hearted adj. sad; melancholy.

heavy hydrogen n. same as **deuterium.**

heavy metal n. a type of rock music with a strong beat and amplified instrumental effects.

heavy water n. water formed of oxygen and deuterium.

heavyweight ('hɛvɪˌweɪt) n. **1.** a professional boxer weighing over 175 pounds or an amateur weighing over 81 kg. **2.** a professional wrestler weighing over 209 pounds or an amateur weighing over 220 pounds. **3.** a person who is heavier than average. **4.** Informal. an important or highly influential person.

Heb. or **Hebr.** Hebrew (language).

Hebraic (hɪ'breɪɪk) adj. of or relating to the Hebrews or their language or culture.

Hebrew ('hiːbruː) n. **1.** the ancient language of the Hebrews, revived as the official language of Israel. **2.** a member of an ancient Semitic people; an Israelite. ~adj. **3.** of the Hebrews or their language. [Hebrew 'ibhrī one from beyond (the river)]

heck (hɛk) interj. a mild exclamation of surprise, irritation, etc. [euphemistic for hell]

heckle ('hɛkəl) vb. to interrupt (a public speaker) with comments, questions, or taunts. [form of hackle] —'**heckler** n.

hectare ('hɛktɑː) n. one hundred ares (10 000 square metres or 2.471 acres). [French]

hectic ('hɛktɪk) adj. involving a great deal of activity or excitement. [Greek hektikos hectic, consumptive]

hector ('hɛktə) vb. **1.** to bully or torment.

~n. **2.** a blustering bully. [after *Hector* (son of Priam)]

he'd (hiːd; *unstressed* iːd, hid, id) he had *or* he would.

hedge (hedʒ) n. **1.** a row of shrubs or bushes forming a boundary. **2.** a barrier or protection against something, esp. against the risk of loss on an investment. ~vb. **3.** to avoid making a decision by making noncommittal statements. **4.** to guard against the risk of loss in (a bet or disagreement), by supporting the opposition as well. [Old English *hecg*]

hedgehog (ˈhedʒˌhɒg) n. a small mammal with a protective covering of spines.

hedgehop (ˈhedʒˌhɒp) vb. **-hopping,** **-hopped.** (of an aircraft) to fly close to the ground, as in crop spraying. —**ˈhedgeˌhopping** n.

hedgerow (ˈhedʒˌrəʊ) n. a hedge of shrubs or low trees bordering a field.

hedge sparrow n. a small brownish songbird.

hedonism (ˈhiːdəˌnɪzəm, ˈhed-) n. the doctrine that the pursuit of pleasure is the most important thing in life. [Greek *hēdonē* pleasure] —**ˈhedonist** n. —ˌhe-donˈistic adj.

heebie-jeebies (ˈhiːbɪˈdʒiːbɪz) pl. n. the. *Slang.* nervous apprehension. [coined by W. De Beck, cartoonist]

heed (hiːd) n. **1.** careful attention; notice: *take heed of these warnings.* ~vb. **2.** to pay close attention to (a warning or piece of advice). [Old English *hēdan*]

heedless (ˈhiːdlɪs) adj. taking no notice; careless or thoughtless. —**ˈheedlessly** adv.

heehaw (ˌhiːˈhɔː) interj. a representation of the braying sound of a donkey.

heel[1] (hiːl) n. **1.** the back part of the foot. **2.** the part of a stocking or sock designed to fit the heel. **3.** the outer part of a shoe underneath the heel. **4.** *Slang.* a contemptible person. **5. at one's heels.** following closely behind one. **6. cool** *or* **kick one's heels.** to be kept waiting. **7. down at heel.** shabby. **8. take to one's heels.** to run off. **9. to heel.** under control, as a dog walking by a person's heel. ~vb. **10.** to repair or replace the heel of (a shoe or boot). [Old English *hēla*]

heel[2] (hiːl) vb. (of a vessel) to lean over; list. [Old English *hieldan*]

heelball (ˈhiːlˌbɔːl) n. **a.** a mixture of beeswax and lampblack used by shoemakers. **b.** a similar substance used to take brass rubbings.

hefty (ˈheftɪ) adj. **heftier, heftiest.** *Informal.* **1.** big and strong. **2.** bulky or heavy: *a hefty package.* **3.** involving a large amount of money: *a hefty fine.*

hegemony (hɪˈgɛmənɪ) n., pl. **-nies.** domination of one power or state within a league, confederation, etc. [Greek *hēgemonia*]

Hegira (ˈhedʒɪrə) n. the flight of Mohammed from Mecca to Medina in 622 A.D.; the starting point of the Muslim era. [Arabic *hijrah* flight]

heifer (ˈhefə) n. a young cow. [Old English *heahfore*]

height (haɪt) n. **1.** the vertical distance from the bottom of something to the top. **2.** the vertical distance of a place above sea level. **3.** relatively great altitude. **4.** the topmost point; summit. **5.** the period of greatest intensity: *the height of the battle.* **6.** an extreme example: *the height of rudeness.* [Old English *hiehthu*]

heighten (ˈhaɪt²n) vb. to make or become more intense. —**ˈheightened** adj.

height of land n. *U.S. & Canad.* a ridge of high ground dividing two river basins.

heinous (ˈheɪnəs, ˈhiː-) adj. evil; atrocious. [Old French *haineus*]

heir (εə) n. the person legally succeeding to the property of a deceased person. [Latin *hērēs*] —**ˈheiress** fem. n.

heir apparent n., pl. **heirs apparent.** a person whose right to succeed to certain property cannot be defeated.

heirloom (ˈεəˌluːm) n. an object that has been in a family for generations. [*heir* + *lome* tool]

heir presumptive n. *Property law.* a person who expects to succeed to an estate but whose right may be defeated by the birth of an heir nearer in blood to the ancestor.

held (held) vb. past of **hold**[1].

helical (ˈhelɪk²l) adj. of or like a helix; spiral.

helicopter (ˈhelɪˌkɒptə) n. an aircraft, propelled by rotating overhead blades, that is capable of hovering, vertical flight, and horizontal flight in any direction. [Greek *helix* spiral + *pteron* wing]

heliograph (ˈhiːlɪəˌgrɑːf) n. an instrument with mirrors and a shutter used for sending messages in Morse code by reflecting the sun's rays. [Greek *hēlios* sun + -GRAPHY]

heliotrope (ˈhiːlɪəˌtrəʊp, ˈheljə-) n. a plant with small fragrant purple flowers. [Greek *hēlios* sun + *trepein* to turn]

heliport (ˈhelɪˌpɔːt) n. an airport for helicopters. [*heli(copter)* + *port*]

helium (ˈhiːlɪəm) n. a very light colourless odourless inert gas. Symbol: He [Greek *hēlios* sun; because first detected in the solar spectrum]

helix (ˈhiːlɪks) n., pl. **helices** *or* **helixes.** a spiral. [Greek *spiral*]

hell (hel) n. **1.** (in Christianity and some other religions) the place or state of eternal punishment of the wicked after death. **2.** (in various religions and cultures) the abode of the spirits of the dead. **3.** *Informal.* a situation that causes suffering or extreme difficulty: *war is hell.* **4. come hell or high water.** *Informal.* whatever difficulties may arise. **5. for the hell of it.** *Informal.* for the fun of it. **6. give someone hell.** *Informal.* **a.** to give someone a severe reprimand or punishment. **b.** to be a torment to someone. **7. hell for leather.** at great speed. **8. the hell.** *Informal.* **a.** used for emphasis in such phrases as **what the hell. b.** an expression of strong disagreement: *the hell I will.*

~*interj.* **9.** *Informal.* an exclamation of anger or surprise. [Old English]

he'll (hiːl; *unstressed* iːl, hil, ıl) he will *or* he shall.

hellbent (ˌhɛl'bɛnt) *adj. Informal.* rashly intent: *hellbent on revenge.*

hellebore ('hɛlıˌbɔː) *n.* a plant with showy flowers and poisonous parts. [Greek *helleboros*]

Hellene ('hɛliːn) *n.* a Greek.

Hellenic (hɛ'lɛnık, -'liː-) *adj.* **1.** of the Greeks or their language. **2.** of or relating to ancient Greece during the classical period (776-323 B.C.).

Hellenism ('hɛlıˌnızəm) *n.* **1.** the principles and ideals of classical Greek civilization. **2.** the spirit or national character of the Greeks. —'**Hellenist** *n.*

Hellenistic (ˌhɛlı'nıstık) *adj.* of Greek civilization during the period 323-30 B.C.,

hellfire ('hɛl,faıə) *n.* the torment of hell, envisaged as eternal fire.

hellish ('hɛlıʃ) *adj. Informal.* very unpleasant.

hello, hallo, *or* **hullo** (hɛ'ləʊ, hə-; 'hɛləʊ) *interj.* **1.** an expression of greeting or surprise. **2.** a call used to attract attention. ~*n., pl.* **-los. 3.** the act of saying "hello". [French *holà*]

Hell's Angel *n.* a member of a motorcycle gang noted for their lawless behaviour.

helm (hɛlm) *n.* **1.** *Naut.* the wheel or entire apparatus by which a vessel is steered. **2. at the helm.** in a position of leadership or control. [Old English *helma*] —'**helmsman** *n.*

helmet ('hɛlmıt) *n.* a piece of protective headgear worn by soldiers, policemen, firemen, divers, etc. [Old French *helme*]

helot ('hɛlət, 'hiː-) *n.* a serf or slave. [Greek *Heilōtes* serfs, lit.: inhabitants of Helos]

help (hɛlp) *vb.* **1.** to assist (someone to do something). **2.** to contribute to: *to help the relief operations.* **3.** to improve a situation: *crying won't help.* **4. a.** to refrain from: *we can't help wondering who he is.* **b.** to be responsible for: *I can't help it if it rains.* **5.** to serve (a customer). **6. help oneself.** to take something, esp. food or drink, for oneself, without being served. ~*n.* **7.** the act of helping. **8.** a person or thing that helps, esp. a farm worker or domestic servant. **9.** a remedy: *there's no help for it.* ~*interj.* **10.** used to ask for assistance. ~See also **help out.** [Old English *helpan*] —'**helper** *n.*

helpful ('hɛlpfʊl) *adj.* giving help. —'**helpfully** *adv.* —'**helpfulness** *n.*

helping ('hɛlpıŋ) *n.* a single portion of food.

helpless ('hɛlplıs) *adj.* **1.** unable to manage independently. **2.** made weak: *they were helpless from giggling.*

helpline ('hɛlp,laın) *n.* a telephone line set aside for callers to contact an organization for help with a problem.

helpmate ('hɛlp,meıt) *or* **helpmeet**

('hɛlp,miːt) *n.* a companion and helper, esp. a spouse.

help out *vb.* to assist (someone) by sharing the burden or cost of something.

helter-skelter ('hɛltə'skɛltə) *adj.* **1.** haphazard or careless. ~*adv.* **2.** in a haphazard or careless manner. ~*n.* **3.** *Brit.* a high spiral slide at a fairground. [prob. imit.]

hem[1] (hɛm) *n.* **1.** the bottom edge of a garment, folded under and stitched down. ~*vb.* **hemming, hemmed. 2.** to provide (a garment) with a hem. ~See also **hem in.** [Old English *hemm*]

hem[2] (hɛm) *n.* **1.** a representation of the sound of clearing the throat, used to gain attention. ~*vb.* **hemming, hemmed. 2.** to utter this sound. **3. hem and haw.** to hesitate in speaking.

he-man *n., pl.* **-men.** *Informal.* a strongly built muscular man.

hemi- *prefix.* half: *hemisphere.* [Greek]

hem in *vb.* to enclose or confine (someone).

hemipterous (hı'mıptərəs) *adj.* of an order of insects with sucking or piercing mouthparts. [Greek *hēmi* half + *pteron* wing]

hemisphere ('hɛmıˌsfıə) *n.* one half of a sphere, esp. of the earth (**northern** and **southern hemisphere**) or of the brain. —**hemispherical** (ˌhɛmı'sfɛrık'l) *adj.*

hemline ('hɛm,laın) *n.* the level to which the hem of a skirt or dress hangs.

hemlock ('hɛm,lɒk) *n.* a poisonous drug derived from a plant with spotted stems and small white flowers. [Old English *hymlic*]

hemp (hɛmp) *n.* **1.** an Asian plant with tough fibres. **2.** the fibre of this plant, used to make canvas and rope. **3.** a narcotic drug obtained from this plant. [Old English *hænep*] —'**hempen** *adj.*

hen (hɛn) *n.* the female of any bird, esp. of the domestic fowl. [Old English *henn*]

hence (hɛns) *adv.* **1.** for this reason; therefore. **2.** from this time: *a year hence.* **3.** *Archaic.* from here. [Old English *hionane*]

henceforth (ˌhɛns'fɔːθ) *or* **henceforward** *adv.* from now on.

henchman ('hɛntʃmən) *n., pl.* **-men.** a faithful attendant or supporter. [Middle English *hengestman*]

henge (hɛndʒ) *n.* a circular monument, often containing a circle of stones, dating from the Neolithic and Bronze Ages. [from *Stonehenge*]

henna ('hɛnə) *n.* **1.** a reddish dye, obtained from a shrub or tree of Asia and N Africa which is used to colour hair. ~*vb.* **2.** to dye (the hair) with henna. [Arabic *hinnā'*]

hen party *n. Informal.* a party at which only women are present.

henpecked ('hɛn,pɛkt) *adj.* (of a man) harassed by the persistent nagging of his wife.

henry ('hɛnrı) *n., pl.* **-ry, -ries,** *or* **-rys.** the derived SI unit of electric inductance. Symbol: H [after Joseph *Henry*, physicist]

hepatic ('hɪ'pætɪk) *adj.* of the liver. [Greek *hēpar* liver]

hepatitis (ˌhepə'taɪtɪs) *n.* inflammation of the liver.

heptagon ('heptəgən) *n.* a polygon with seven sides. [Greek *heptagōnos* having seven angles] —**heptagonal** (hep'tægənˀl) *adj.*

heptathlon (hep'tæθlon) *n.* an athletic contest for women in which athletes compete in seven different events: 100 m hurdles, shot put, high jump, 200 m, long jump, javelin, and 800 m.

her (hɜː; *unstressed* hə, ə) *pron.* refers to: **1.** a female person or animal: *he loves her.* **2.** things personified as feminine, such as ships and nations. ~*det.* **3.** of, belonging to, or associated with her: *her hair.* [Old English *hire*]

herald ('herəld) *n.* **1.** a person who announces important news. **2.** *Often literary.* a forerunner. ~*vb.* **3.** to precede: *his rise to power heralded the end of the liberal era.* **4.** to announce publicly. [Germanic] —**heraldic** (he'rældɪk) *adj.*

heraldry ('herəldrɪ) *n., pl.* -**ries.** the study of coats of arms, the tracing of genealogies, etc.

herb (hɜːb) *n.* **1.** a plant whose parts above ground die back at the end of the growing season. **2.** an aromatic plant, such as parsley or rosemary, that is used in cookery and medicine. [Latin *herba* grass, green plants] —**herbal** *adj.* —**herby** *adj.*

herbaceous (hɜː'beɪʃəs) *adj.* designating plants that are fleshy rather than woody.

herbaceous border *n.* a flower bed that contains perennials rather than annuals.

herbage ('hɜːbɪdʒ) *n.* herbaceous plants collectively, esp. those on which animals graze.

herbalist ('hɜːbˀlɪst) *n.* a person who grows or specializes in the use of medicinal herbs.

herbicide ('hɜːbɪˌsaɪd) *n.* a chemical that destroys plants, esp. weeds. [Latin *herba* plant + *caedere* to kill]

herbivore ('hɜːbɪˌvɔː) *n.* an animal that feeds on plants. [Latin *herba* plant + *vorāre* to swallow] —**herbivorous** (hɜː-'bɪvərəs) *adj.*

herculean (ˌhɜːkjʊ'liːən) *adj.* **1.** (of a task) requiring tremendous effort or strength. **2.** resembling Hercules, hero of classical myth, in strength or courage.

herd (hɜːd) *n.* **1.** a large group of mammals, esp. cattle living and feeding together. **2.** *Often disparaging.* a large group of people. ~*vb.* **3.** to collect or be collected into or as if into a herd. [Old English *heord*]

herd instinct *n. Psychol.* the inborn tendency to associate with others and follow the group's behaviour.

herdsman ('hɜːdzmən) *n., pl.* -**men.** *Chiefly Brit.* a man who looks after a herd of animals.

here (hɪə) *adv.* **1.** in, at, or to this place, point, case, or respect: *we come here every summer.* **2. here and there.** at several places in or throughout an area. **3. here's to.** a formula used in proposing a toast. **4. neither here nor there.** of no relevance. ~*n.* **5.** this place: *they leave here tonight.* [Old English *hēr*]

hereabouts ('hɪərəˌbaʊts) *or* **hereabout** *adv.* in this region.

hereafter (hɪər'ɑːftə) *adv.* **1.** *Formal or law.* in a subsequent part of this document, matter or case. **2.** at some time in the future. ~*n.* **3. the. a.** life after death. **b.** the future.

hereby (ˌhɪə'baɪ) *adv.* (used in official statements and documents) by means of or as a result of this.

hereditable (hɪ'redɪtəbˀl) *adj.* same as **heritable.**

hereditary (hɪ'redɪtrɪ) *adj.* **1.** transmitted genetically from one generation to another. **2.** *Law.* descending to succeeding generations by inheritance.

heredity (hɪ'redɪtɪ) *n., pl.* -**ties.** the transmission from one generation to another of genetic factors that determine individual characteristics. [Latin *hērēditās* inheritance]

herein (ˌhɪər'ɪn) *adv. Formal or law.* in this place, matter, or document.

hereinafter (ˌhɪərɪn'ɑːftə) *adv. Formal or law.* from this point on in this document, matter, or case.

hereof (ˌhɪər'ɒv) *adv. Formal or law.* of or concerning this.

heresy ('herəsɪ) *n., pl.* -**sies.** **1.** an opinion contrary to the principles of a religion. **2.** any belief thought to be contrary to official or established theory. [Greek *hairein* to choose]

heretic ('herɪtɪk) *n.* **1.** *Now chiefly R.C. Church.* a person who maintains beliefs contrary to the established teachings of the Church. **2.** a person who holds unorthodox opinions in any field. —**heretical** (hɪ'retɪkˀl) *adj.*

hereto (ˌhɪə'tuː) *adv. Formal or law.* to this place, matter, or document.

heretofore (ˌhɪətʊ'fɔː) *adv. Formal or law.* until now.

hereupon (ˌhɪərə'pɒn) *adv.* following immediately after this; at this stage.

herewith (ˌhɪə'wɪð, -'wɪθ) *adv. Formal.* together with this: *we send you herewith your statement of account.*

heritable ('herɪtəbˀl) *adj.* capable of being inherited.

heritage ('herɪtɪdʒ) *n.* **1.** something inherited at birth. **2.** anything that has been transmitted from the past or handed down by tradition. **3.** the evidence of the past, such as historical sites, considered as the inheritance of present-day society.

hermaphrodite (hɜː'mæfrəˌdaɪt) *n.* an animal, flower, or person that has both male and female reproductive organs. [after *Hermaphroditus*, son of Hermes and Aphrodite, who merged with the nymph Salmacis to form one body] —**hermaphroditic** (hɜːˌmæfrə'dɪtɪk) *adj.*

hermetic (hɜːˈmɛtɪk) *adj.* sealed so as to be airtight. [after the Greek God *Hermes*, traditionally the inventor of a magic seal] —**herˈmetically** *adv.*

hermit (ˈhɜːmɪt) *n.* a person living in solitude, esp. for religious reasons. [Greek *erēmos* lonely]

hermitage (ˈhɜːmɪtɪdʒ) *n.* **1.** the dwelling of a hermit. **2.** any retreat.

hermit crab *n.* a small crab that lives in empty shells of other shellfish.

hernia (ˈhɜːnɪə) *n.* protrusion of an organ or part through the lining of the body cavity in which it is normally situated. [Latin]

hero (ˈhɪərəʊ) *n., pl.* **-roes. 1.** a man distinguished by exceptional courage, nobility, etc. **2.** a man who is idealized for possessing superior qualities in any field. **3.** the principal male character in a novel, play, etc. [Greek *hērōs*]

heroic (hɪˈrəʊɪk) *adj.* **1.** of, like, or befitting a hero. **2.** courageous but desperate. **3.** treating of heroes and their deeds. —**heˈroically** *adv.*

heroics (hɪˈrəʊɪks) *pl. n.* extravagant or melodramatic language or behaviour.

heroin (ˈhɛrəʊɪn) *n.* a highly addictive narcotic derived from morphine. [prob. from *hero*, referring to its aggrandizing effect on the personality]

heroine (ˈhɛrəʊɪn) *n.* **1.** a woman distinguished by exceptional courage, nobility, etc. **2.** a woman who is idealized for possessing superior qualities in any field. **3.** the principal female character in a novel, play, etc.

heroism (ˈhɛrəʊˌɪzəm) *n.* the state or quality of being a hero.

heron (ˈhɛrən) *n.* a wading bird with a long neck and grey or white plumage. [Old French *hairon*]

heronry (ˈhɛrənrɪ) *n., pl.* **-ries.** a colony of breeding herons.

hero worship *n.* admiration for heroes or idealized persons.

herpes (ˈhɜːpiːz) *n.* any of several inflammatory diseases of the skin. [Greek *herpein* to creep]

herpes simplex (ˈsɪmplɛks) *n.* an acute viral disease causing clusters of watery blisters. [New Latin: simple herpes]

herpes zoster (ˈzɒstə) *n.* same as **shingles.** [New Latin: girdle herpes]

Herr (hɛə) *n., pl.* **Herren** (ˈhɛrən). a German title of address equivalent to *Mr.* [German]

herring (ˈhɛrɪŋ) *n., pl.* **-rings** *or* **-ring.** an important food fish of northern seas, with a long silver-coloured body. [Old English *hǣring*]

herringbone (ˈhɛrɪŋˌbəʊn) *n.* a pattern consisting of rows of short parallel strokes slanting in alternate directions to form a series of zigzags.

herring gull *n.* a common gull that has a white plumage with black-tipped wings.

hers (hɜːz) *pron.* **1.** something belonging to her: *hers is the nicest dress; that cat is hers.* **2. of hers.** belonging to her.

herself (həˈsɛlf) *pron.* **1. a.** the reflexive

form of *she* or *her: she taught herself to type.* **b.** (used for emphasis: *the queen herself signed.* **2.** her normal self: *she looks herself again after the operation.*

Herts (hɑːts) Hertfordshire.

hertz (hɜːts) *n., pl.* **hertz.** the derived SI unit of frequency. [after H. R. *Hertz*, physicist]

he's he is *or* he has.

hesitant (ˈhɛzɪtənt) *adj.* wavering, hesitating, or irresolute. —**ˈhesitancy** *n.*

hesitate (ˈhɛzɪˌteɪt) *vb.* **1.** to be slow in acting; be uncertain. **2.** to be reluctant (to do something): *I hesitate to use the word "squandered".* **3.** to stammer or pause in speaking. [Latin *haesitāre*] —ˌhesiˈtation *n.*

hessian (ˈhɛsɪən) *n.* a coarse jute fabric similar to sacking. [after *Hesse*, Germany]

hetero- *combining form.* other, another, or different: *heterosexual.* [Greek *heteros* other]

heterodox (ˈhɛtərəʊˌdɒks) *adj.* at variance with established or accepted doctrines or beliefs. [HETERO- + Greek *doxa* opinion] —ˈheteroˌdoxy *n*

heterodyne (ˈhɛtərəʊˌdaɪn) *Electronics.* ~*vb.* **1.** to combine (two alternating signals) so as to produce two signals with frequencies corresponding to the sum and the difference of the original frequencies. ~*adj.* **2.** produced or operating by heterodyning two signals. [HETERO- + Greek *dunamis* power]

heterogeneous (ˌhɛtərəʊˈdʒiːnɪəs) *adj.* composed of unrelated parts. [HETERO- + Greek *genos* sort] —**heterogeneity** (ˌhɛtərəʊdʒɪˈniːɪtɪ) *n.*

heteromorphic (ˌhɛtərəʊˈmɔːfɪk) *adj.* *Biol.* **1.** differing from the normal form. **2.** (esp. of insects) having different forms at different stages of the life cycle. [HETERO- + Greek *morphē* form] —ˌhetero**ˈmorphism** *n.*

heterosexual (ˌhɛtərəʊˈsɛksjʊəl) *n.* **1.** a person who is sexually attracted to members of the opposite sex. ~*adj.* **2.** (of a person) sexually attracted to members of the opposite sex. **3.** (of a sexual relationship) between a man and a woman. —ˌhetero**ˌsexuˈal**ity *n.*

het up *adj. Informal.* angry; excited: *don't get het up.* [dialect for *heated*]

heuristic (hjʊəˈrɪstɪk) *adj.* (of a method of teaching) allowing students to learn things for themselves by trial and error. [Greek *heuriskein* to discover]

hew (hjuː) *vb.* **hewing, hewed, hewed** *or* **hewn. 1.** to strike (stone or wood) with cutting blows, as with an axe. **2.** to carve (something) from a substance: *huge figures hewn out of stone.* [Old English *hēawan*]

hex (hɛks) *n.* **a.** short for **hexadecimal notation.** **b.** (as modifier): *hex code.*

hexa- *or before a vowel* **hex-** *combining form.* six: *hexameter.* [Greek *hex* SIX]

hexadecimal notation (ˌhɛksəˈdɛsɪməl) *n.* a number system with a base of 16, the numbers 10-15 being represented by the letters A-F.

hexagon ('hɛksəgən) n. Geom. a plane shape with six sides. —**hex'agonal** adj.

hexagram ('hɛksə,græm) n. Geom. a star formed by extending the sides of a regular hexagon to meet at six points.

hexameter (hɛk'sæmɪtə) n. Prosody. a verse line consisting of six metrical feet.

hey (heɪ) interj. **1.** an expression indicating surprise, dismay, discovery, etc. **2. hey presto.** an exclamation used by conjurers at the climax of a trick. [imit.]

heyday ('heɪ,deɪ) n. the time of most power, popularity, or vigour: he was a bit of a heart-throb in his heyday. [prob. based on hey]

Hf Chem. hafnium.

Hg Chem. mercury.

HGV (in Britain) heavy goods vehicle.

HH 1. His (or Her) Highness. **2.** His Holiness (title of the Pope).

hi (haɪ) interj. Informal. hello. [prob. from how are you?]

HI Hawaii.

hiatus (haɪ'eɪtəs) n., pl. **-tuses** or **-tus.** a break or interruption in continuity. [Latin: gap, cleft]

hiatus hernia n. protrusion of the stomach through the diaphragm at the hole for the gullet.

hibernate ('haɪbə,neɪt) vb. (of some animals) to pass the winter in a dormant condition. [Latin hībernāre to spend the winter] —**hiber'nation** n.

Hibernia (haɪ'bɜːnɪə) n. Poetic. Ireland. —**Hi'bernian** adj., n.

hibiscus (hɪ'bɪskəs) n., pl. **-cuses.** a plant with largely brightly coloured flowers. [Greek hibiskos marsh mallow]

hiccup ('hɪkʌp) n. **1.** a spasm of the diaphragm producing a sudden breathing in of air resulting in a characteristic sharp sound. **2.** (pl.) the state of having such spasms. **3.** Informal. a minor difficulty. ~vb. **-cuping, -cuped** or **-cupping, -cupped. 4.** to make a hiccup or hiccups. ~Also: **hiccough** ('hɪkʌp). [imit.]

hick (hɪk) n. Informal, chiefly U.S. & Canad. an unsophisticated country person. [after Hick, familiar form of Richard]

hickory ('hɪkərɪ) n., pl. **-ries. 1.** a North American tree with edible nuts. **2.** the hard wood of this tree. [American Indian pawcohiccora]

hidden ('hɪdən) vb. **1.** the past participle of hide[1]. —adj. **2.** concealed or obscured: a hidden meaning.

hide[1] (haɪd) vb. **hiding, hid, hidden** or **hid. 1.** to conceal (oneself or an object) from view or discovery: to hide from the police. **2.** to obscure: clouds hide the sun. **3.** to keep (information or one's feelings) secret. ~n. **4.** Brit. a place of concealment, disguised to appear as part of its surrounding, used by hunters, birdwatchers, etc. [Old English hȳdan]

hide[2] (haɪd) n. the skin of an animal, either tanned or raw. [Old English hȳd]

hide-and-seek n. a game in which one player covers his eyes while the others hide, and he then tries to find them.

hideaway ('haɪdə,weɪ) n. a hiding place or secluded spot.

hidebound ('haɪd,baʊnd) adj. restricted by petty rules or a conservative attitude.

hideous ('hɪdɪəs) adj. extremely ugly or unpleasant. [Old French hisdos]

hide-out n. a hiding place.

hiding[1] ('haɪdɪŋ) n. **1.** a state of concealment: in hiding. **2. hiding place.** a place of concealment.

hiding[2] ('haɪdɪŋ) n. Informal. a flogging; beating.

hie (haɪ) vb. **hieing** or **hying, hied.** Archaic or poetic. to hurry. [Old English hīgian to strive]

hierarchy ('haɪə,rɑːkɪ) n., pl. **-chies. 1.** a system of persons or things arranged in a graded order. **2. the hierarchy.** the people in power in any organization. [Late Greek hierarkhēs high priest] —**hier'archical** adj.

hieroglyphic (,haɪərə'glɪfɪk) adj. **1.** of or relating to a form of writing using picture symbols, as used in ancient Egypt. ~n. also **hieroglyph. 2.** a symbol that is difficult to decipher. **3.** a picture or symbol representing an object, idea, or sound. [Greek hieros holy + gluphein to carve]

hieroglyphics (,haɪərə'glɪfɪks) n. (functioning as sing. or pl.) **1.** a form of writing, as used in ancient Egypt, in which pictures or symbols are used to represent objects, ideas, or sounds. **2.** writing that is difficult to decipher.

hi-fi ('haɪ,faɪ) n. Informal. **1.** a set of high-quality sound-reproducing equipment. **2. a.** short for **high fidelity. b.** (as modifier): hi-fi equipment.

higgledy-piggledy ('hɪgˈldɪ'pɪgˈldɪ) adj., adv. Informal. in a jumble. [origin unknown]

high (haɪ) adj. **1.** being a relatively great distance from top to bottom: a high building. **2.** situated at a relatively great distance above sea level: a high plateau. **3.** being a specified distance from top to bottom: three feet high. **4.** coming up to a specified level: knee-high. **5.** being at its peak: high noon. **6.** of greater than average height: a high collar. **7.** greater than usual in intensity or amount: a high wind; high mileage. **8.** (of a sound) acute in pitch. **9.** (of food) slightly decomposed, regarded as enhancing the flavour of game. **10.** very important: the high priestess. **11.** intensely emotional: high drama. **12.** elated; cheerful: high spirits. **13.** Informal. under the influence of alcohol or drugs. **14.** luxurious or extravagant: high life. **15.** advanced in complexity: high finance. **16.** formal and elaborate: High Mass. **17. high and dry.** stranded; destitute. **18. high and mighty.** Informal. arrogant. **19. high opinion.** a favourable opinion. ~adv. **20.** at or to a height: flying high. ~n. **21.** a high level. **22.** same as **anticyclone. 23. on a high.** Informal. **a.** in a state of intoxication by alcohol or drugs. **b.** in a state of great excitement and happiness. [Old English hēah]

highball ('haɪ,bɔːl) n. Chiefly U.S. a long

iced drink consisting of spirits with soda water, etc.

highbrow ('haɪˌbraʊ) *Often disparaging.* ~*n.* **1.** a person of scholarly tastes. ~*adj.* **2.** appealing to highbrows.

highchair ('haɪˌtʃɛə) *n.* a long-legged chair with a table-like tray, used for a child at mealtimes.

High Church *n.* **1.** the movement within the Church of England stressing the importance of ceremony and ritual. ~*adj.* **High-Church. 2.** of or relating to this movement.

high commissioner *n.* the senior diplomatic representative sent by one Commonwealth country to another.

high country *n.* **the.** *N.Z.* sheep pastures in the foothills of the Southern Alps.

High Court *n.* (in England, Wales, Australia, and New Zealand) the supreme court dealing with civil law cases.

higher education *n.* education and training at colleges, universities, and polytechnics.

higher-up *n. Informal.* a person of higher rank.

highest common factor *n.* the largest number that divides equally into each member of a group of numbers.

high explosive *n.* an extremely powerful chemical explosive, such as TNT or gelignite.

highfalutin (ˌhaɪfə'luːtɪn) *adj. Informal.* pompous or pretentious. [-*falutin* perhaps var. of *fluting*]

high fidelity *n.* **a.** the electronic reproduction of sound with little or no distortion. **b.** (*as modifier*): *a high-fidelity amplifier.*

high-flier *or* **high-flyer** *n.* **1.** a person who is extremely ambitious. **2.** a person of great ability in a career. —'**high-**ˌ**flying** *adj.*

high-flown *adj.* extravagant or pretentious: *high-flown ideas.*

high frequency *n.* a radio frequency lying between 30 and 3 megahertz.

High German *n.* the standard German language.

high-handed *adj.* tactlessly overbearing and inconsiderate. —ˌ**high-**'**handedness** *n.*

highjack ('haɪˌdʒæk) *vb., n.* same as **hijack.**

high jump *n.* **the. 1.** an athletic event in which competitors have to jump over a high bar. **2.** *Brit. informal.* a severe reprimand or punishment: *you're for the high jump when your mother finds out.*

Highland ('haɪlənd) *n.* (*modifier*) of or denoting the Highlands, a mountainous region of NW Scotland. —'**Highlander** *n.*

Highland cattle *n.* cattle with shaggy reddish-brown hair and long horns.

Highland fling *n.* an energetic Scottish solo dance.

highlands ('haɪləndz) *n.* relatively high ground.

high-level language *n.* a computer-

programming language that is close to human language.

highlight ('haɪˌlaɪt) *n.* **1.** Also called: **high spot.** the most exciting or memorable part of something. **2.** an area of the lightest tone in a painting or photograph. **3.** (*pl.*) a lightened streak in the hair produced by bleaching. ~*vb.* **4.** to bring emphasis to: *this problem was highlighted in her book.*

highly ('haɪlɪ) *adv.* **1.** extremely: *highly disappointed.* **2.** with great approbation: *they spoke highly of her.*

highly strung *or U.S. & Canad.* **high-strung** *adj.* tense and easily upset.

High Mass *n.* a solemn and elaborate Mass.

high-minded *adj.* having high moral principles.

Highness ('haɪnɪs) *n.* (preceded by *Your, His,* or *Her*) a title used to address or refer to a royal person.

high-pitched *adj.* (of a sound, esp. a voice) pitched high in tone.

high-powered *adj.* dynamic and energetic.

high-pressure *adj. Informal.* (of selling) persuasive in an aggressive and persistent manner.

high priest *n.* the head of a cult. —**high priestess** *fem. n.*

high-rise *adj.* of or relating to a building that has many storeys: *a high-rise block.*

high-risk *adj.* denoting a group or area that is particularly subject to a danger.

highroad ('haɪˌrəʊd) *n.* a main road.

high school *n.* a secondary school.

high seas *pl. n.* the open seas, which are outside the authority of any one nation.

high season *n.* the most popular time of year at a holiday resort, etc.

high-spirited *adj.* vivacious, bold, or lively.

high tea *n. Brit.* an early evening meal consisting of a cooked dish, bread, cakes and tea.

high-tech *adj.* See **hi-tech.**

high-tension *n.* (*modifier*) carrying a relatively high voltage.

high tide *n.* the tide at its highest level.

high time *adv. Informal.* the latest possible time: *it's high time you left.*

high treason *n.* an act of treason directly affecting a sovereign or state.

high-water mark *n.* **1.** the level reached by sea water at high tide or a river in flood. **2.** the highest point of any process.

highway ('haɪˌweɪ) *n.* **1.** a public road that everyone may use. **2.** *Chiefly U.S. & Canad.* a main road, esp. one that connects towns.

highwayman ('haɪweɪmən) *n., pl.* **-men.** (formerly) a robber, usually on horseback, who held up travellers on public roads.

hijack *or* **highjack** ('haɪˌdʒæk) *vb.* **1.** to seize control of or divert (a vehicle) while in transit: *to hijack an aircraft.* ~*n.* **2.** an instance of hijacking. [origin unknown] —'**hi**ˌ**jacker** *or* '**high**ˌ**jacker** *n.*

hike (haɪk) vb. **1.** to walk a long way in the country, usually for pleasure. **2.** to pull up; hitch up. **3.** (foll. by *up*) to raise (prices). ~n. **4.** a long walk. **5.** a rise in price. [origin unknown] —'**hiker** n.

hilarious (hɪˈlɛərɪəs) adj. very funny. [Greek *hilaros* cheerful] —hi'**lariously** adv. —**hilarity** (hɪˈlærɪtɪ) n.

hill (hɪl) n. **1.** a natural elevation of the earth's surface, less high than a mountain. **2.** a heap or mound. **3.** an incline; slope. [Old English *hyll*] —'**hilly** adj.

hillbilly (ˈhɪlˌbɪlɪ) n., pl. -**lies.** 1. *Usually disparaging.* an unsophisticated person from the mountainous areas in the southeastern U.S. **2.** same as **country and western.** [*hill* + *Billy* (the nickname)]

hillock (ˈhɪlək) n. a small hill or mound.

hilt (hɪlt) n. **1.** the handle or shaft of a sword, dagger or knife. **2. to the hilt.** to the full: *he plays the role to the hilt.* [Old English]

hilum (ˈhaɪləm) n., pl. -**la** (-lə). *Bot.* a scar on a seed marking its point of attachment to the seed vessel. [Latin: trifle]

him (hɪm; *unstressed* ɪm) pron. refers to a male person or animal: *they needed him; she gave him an assignment.* [Old English]

himself (hɪmˈsɛlf; *unstressed* ɪmˈsɛlf) pron. **1. a.** the reflexive form of *he* or *him: he introduced himself.* **b.** used for emphasis: *the king himself waved to me.* **2.** his normal self: *he seems himself once more.*

hind[1] (haɪnd) adj. **hinder, hindmost.** situated at the back: *a hind leg.* [Old English *hindan* at the back]

hind[2] (haɪnd) n., pl. **hinds** or **hind.** the female of the deer, esp. the red deer. [Old English]

hinder[1] (ˈhɪndə) vb. to get in the way of (someone or something). [Old English *hindrian*]

hinder[2] (ˈhaɪndə) adj. situated at the back; posterior. [Old English]

Hindi (ˈhɪndɪ) n. **1.** a language or group of dialects of N central India. **2.** a formal literary dialect of this language, the official language of India. [Old Persian *Hindu* the river Indus]

hindmost (ˈhaɪndˌməʊst) adj. furthest back; last.

hindquarters (ˈhaɪndˌkwɔːtəz) pl. n. the rear of a four-legged animal.

hindrance (ˈhɪndrəns) n. **1.** an obstruction or snag. **2.** the act of hindering.

hindsight (ˈhaɪndˌsaɪt) n. the ability to understand, after something has happened, what should have been done.

Hindu (ˈhɪnduː, hɪnˈduː) n., pl. -**dus.** 1. a person who practises Hinduism. ~adj. 2. relating to Hinduism.

Hinduism (ˈhɪnduːˌɪzəm) n. the dominant religion of India, which involves the worship of many gods, a caste system, and belief in reincarnation.

Hindustani (ˌhɪnduːˈstɑːnɪ) n. a group of northern Indian languages that includes Hindi and Urdu.

hinge (hɪndʒ) n. **1.** a device for holding together two parts so that one can swing freely. ~vb. **2.** (foll. by *on*) to depend on: *the future of the company hinges on your decision.* **3.** to fit a hinge to (something). [prob. Germanic] —**hinged** adj.

hinny (ˈhɪnɪ) n., pl. -**nies.** the offspring of a male horse and a female donkey. [Greek *hinnos*]

hint (hɪnt) n. **1.** a suggestion given in an indirect or subtle manner. **2.** a helpful piece of advice. **3.** a small amount: *a hint of garlic.* ~vb. **4.** (sometimes foll. by *at*) to suggest indirectly: *this hints at the truth.* [origin unknown]

hinterland (ˈhɪntəˌlænd) n. **1.** land lying behind a coast or the shore of a river. **2.** an area near and dependent on a large city, esp. a port. [German *hinter* behind + *land* LAND]

hip[1] (hɪp) n. either side of the body below the waist and above the thigh. [Old English *hype*]

hip[2] (hɪp) n. the berry-like brightly coloured fruit of a rose bush. Also called: **rosehip.** [Old English *héopa*]

hip[3] (hɪp) interj. an exclamation used to introduce cheers: *hip, hip, hurrah.* [origin unknown]

hip[4] (hɪp) adj. **hipper, hippest.** *Slang.* following the latest trends. [var. of earlier *hep*]

hip bath n. a portable bath in which the bather sits.

hipbone (ˈhɪpˌbəʊn) n. either of the two bones that form the sides of the pelvis.

hip-hop (ˈhɪpˌhɒp) n. a U.S. pop culture movement of the 1980s, comprising rap music, graffiti, and break dancing.

hippie or **hippy** (ˈhɪpɪ) n. (esp. during the 1960s) a person whose behaviour and dress imply a rejection of conventional values. [from HIP[4]]

hippo (ˈhɪpəʊ) n., pl. -**pos.** *Informal.* short for **hippopotamus.**

Hippocratic oath (ˌhɪpəʊˈkrætɪk) n. an oath taken by a doctor to observe a code of medical ethics. [after *Hippocrates,* Greek physician]

hippodrome (ˈhɪpəˌdrəʊm) n. **1.** a music hall, variety theatre, or circus. **2.** (in ancient Greece or Rome) an open-air course for horse and chariot races. [Greek *hippos* horse + *dromos* race]

hippopotamus (ˌhɪpəˈpɒtəməs) n., pl. -**muses** or -**mi** (-ˌmaɪ). a very large mammal with thick wrinkled skin and short legs, which lives around the rivers of tropical Africa. [Greek: river horse]

hippy[1] (ˈhɪpɪ) adj. -**pier, -piest.** *Informal.* having large hips.

hippy[2] (ˈhɪpɪ) n., pl. -**pies.** same as **hippie.**

hipsters (ˈhɪpstəz) pl. n. *Brit.* trousers cut so that the top encircles the hips.

hire (ˈhaɪə) vb. **1.** to acquire the temporary use of (a thing) or the services of (a person) in exchange for payment. **2.** to employ (a person) for wages. **3.** (foll. by *out*) to provide (something) or the services of (oneself or others) for payment. **4.** (foll. by *out*) *Chiefly Brit.* to pay independent contractors for (work to be done). ~n. **5.**

the act of hiring. **6. for hire.** available to be hired. [Old English *hȳrian*]

hireling ('haɪəlɪŋ) *n. Disparaging.* a person who works only for money.

hire-purchase *n. Brit.* a system in which a buyer takes possession of merchandise on payment of a deposit and completes the purchase by paying a series of instalments while the seller retains ownership until the final instalment is paid.

hirsute ('hɜːsjuːt) *adj.* hairy. [Latin *hirsūtus* shaggy]

his (hɪz; *unstressed* ɪz) *det.* **1.** of, belonging to, or associated with him: *his knee.* ~*pron.* **2.** something belonging to him: *his is on the left; that book is his.* **3. of his.** belonging to him. [Old English]

Hispanic (hɪ'spænɪk) *adj.* **1.** of or derived from Spain or the Spanish. ~*n.* **2.** *U.S.* a U.S. citizen of Latin-American descent. [Latin *Hispania* Spain]

hiss (hɪs) *n.* **1.** a sound like that of a prolonged *s.* **2.** such a sound as an exclamation of contempt. ~*vb.* **3.** to utter a hiss. **4.** to express with a hiss: *she hissed her disapproval.* **5.** to show derision or anger towards (a speaker or performer) by hissing. [imit.]

histamine ('hɪstə,miːn) *n.* a chemical compound released by the body tissues in allergic reactions. [Greek *histos* tissue + *amine*]

histogram ('hɪstə,græm) *n.* a statistical graph that represents the frequency of values of a quantity by vertical rectangles of varying heights and widths. [prob. *histo(ry)* + Greek *grammē* line]

histology (hɪ'stɒlədʒɪ) *n.* the study of the tissues of an animal or plant. [Greek *histos* tissue + -LOGY]

historian (hɪ'stɔːrɪən) *n.* a person who writes or studies history.

historic (hɪ'stɒrɪk) *adj.* famous in history; significant: *a historic decision.*

historical (hɪ'stɒrɪk'l) *adj.* **1.** occuring in history. **2.** based on history; *a historical novel.* **3.** belonging to or typical of the study of history: *historical methods.*

historicism (hɪ'stɒrɪ,sɪzəm) *n.* **1.** the belief that natural laws govern historical events. **2.** excessive emphasis on history and past styles.

historicity (,hɪstə'rɪsɪtɪ) *n.* historical authenticity.

historiographer (hɪ,stɔːrɪ'ɒgrəfə) *n.* a historian employed to write the history of a group or public institution. —**hi,stori'ography** *n.*

history ('hɪstrɪ) *n., pl.* **-ries. 1.** a record or account of past events and developments. **2.** all that is preserved of the past, esp. in written form. **3.** the study of interpreting past events. **4.** the past events or previous experiences, of a place, thing, or person: *the house had a strange history.* **5.** a play that depicts historical events. [Greek *historia* inquiry]

histrionic (,hɪstrɪ'ɒnɪk) *adj.* **1.** excessively dramatic: *histrionic gestures.* ~*n.* **2.** (*pl.*) melodramatic displays of temperament. [Latin *histriō* actor]

hit (hɪt) *vb.* **hitting, hit. 1.** to deal a blow to (a person or thing). **2.** to come into violent contact with: *the car hit the tree.* **3.** to propel (a ball) by striking. **4.** *Cricket.* to score (runs). **5.** to affect (a person, place, or thing) adversely: *his illness hit him very hard.* **6.** to reach: *unemployment hit a new high.* **7. hit the bottle.** *Slang.* to start drinking excessive amounts of alcohol. **8. hit the road.** *Informal.* to set out on a journey. ~*n.* **9.** an impact or collision. **10.** a shot or blow that reaches its target. **11.** *Informal.* a person or thing that gains wide appeal: *she's a hit with everyone.* ~See also **hit off, hit on, hit out at.** [Old English *hittan*]

hit-and-run *adj.* denoting a motor-vehicle accident in which the driver leaves the scene without stopping to give assistance or inform the police.

hitch (hɪtʃ) *n.* **1.** a temporary or minor impediment. **2.** a knot that can be undone by pulling against the direction of the strain that holds it. ~*vb.* **3.** (foll. by *up*) to pull up (one's trousers, etc.) with a quick jerk. **4.** *Informal.* to obtain (a ride) by hitchhiking. **5.** to fasten with a knot or tie. **6. get hitched.** *Slang.* to get married. [origin unknown]

hitchhike ('hɪtʃ,haɪk) *vb.* to travel by obtaining free lifts in motor vehicles. —**'hitch,hiker** *n.*

hi-tech *adj.* using sophisticated, esp. electronic technology.

hither ('hɪðə) *adv. Old-fashioned.* towards this place: *come hither.* [Old English *hider*]

hitherto (,hɪðə'tuː) *adv.* until this time: *hitherto, there have been no problems.*

hit list *n. Informal.* **1.** a list of people to be murdered. **2.** a list of targets to be eliminated: *a hit list of pits to be closed.*

hit man *n.* a hired assassin.

hit off *vb.* **hit it off.** *Informal.* to have a good relationship with someone.

hit on *or* **upon** *vb.* to think of (an idea or a solution).

hit-or-miss *adj. Informal.* random; haphazard. Also: **hit-and-miss.**

hit out at *vb.* **1.** to direct blows forcefully and vigorously at (someone). **2.** to make a verbal attack upon (someone).

HIV human immunodeficiency virus.

hive (haɪv) *n.* **1.** a structure in which bees live. **2. hive of activity.** a place showing signs of great industry. [Old English *hȳf*]

hive off *vb.* to transfer (profitable activities of a nationalized industry) back to private ownership.

hives (haɪvz) *n.* (*functioning as sing. or pl.*) *Pathol.* an allergic reaction in which itchy red or whitish raised patches develop on the skin. [origin unknown]

HM Her (*or* His) Majesty.

HMI (in Britain) Her (*or* His) Majesty's Inspector; a government official who examines and supervises schools.

H.M.S. *or* **HMS** Her (*or* His) Majesty's Ship.

HMSO (in Britain) Her (*or* His) Majesty's Stationery Office.

HNC (in Britain) Higher National Certificate; a qualification recognized by many national technical and professional institutions.

HND (in Britain) Higher National Diploma; a qualification in a technical subject equivalent to an ordinary degree.

Ho *Chem.* holmium.

hoar (hɔː) *adj. Archaic.* hoary. [Old English *hār*]

hoard (hɔːd) *n.* **1.** an accumulated store of money, food, etc., hidden away for future use. ~*vb.* **2.** to gather or accumulate (money, food, etc.). [Old English *hord*] —'**hoarder** *n.*

hoarding ('hɔːdɪŋ) *n.* a large board at the side of a road, used for displaying advertising posters. [Old French *hourd* palisade]

hoarfrost ('hɔːˌfrɒst) *n.* a deposit of ice crystals formed on the ground by condensation at temperatures below freezing point.

hoarse (hɔːs) *adj.* having a husky voice, as through illness or too much shouting. [Old Norse] —'**hoarsely** *adv.* —'**hoarseness** *n.*

hoary ('hɔːrɪ) *adj.* **hoarier, hoariest. 1.** having grey or white hair. **2.** ancient.

hoax (həʊks) *n.* **1.** a deception, esp. a practical joke. ~*vb.* **2.** to deceive or play a joke on (someone). [prob. from *hocus* to trick]

hob (hɒb) *n.* the flat top part of a cooking stove, or a separate flat surface, containing hotplates or burners. [perhaps from *hub*]

hobble ('hɒbʲl) *vb.* **1.** to walk with a lame awkward movement. **2.** to fetter the legs of (a horse) in order to restrict its movement. [prob. from Low German]

hobby ('hɒbɪ) *n., pl.* **-bies.** an activity pursued in one's spare time for pleasure or relaxation. [prob. var. of name *Robin*]

hobbyhorse ('hɒbɪˌhɔːs) *n.* **1.** a favourite topic: *on one's hobbyhorse.* **2.** a toy consisting of a stick with a figure of a horse's head at one end. **3.** a figure of a horse attached to a performer's waist in a morris dance.

hobgoblin (ˌhɒbˈgɒblɪn) *n.* a mischievous goblin. [*hob* var. of the name *Rob* + GOBLIN]

hobnail ('hɒbˌneɪl) *n. Old-fashioned.* **a.** a short nail with a large head for protecting the soles of heavy footwear. **b.** (*as modifier*): *hobnail boots.* [*hob* in archaic sense: peg]

hobnob ('hɒbˌnɒb) *vb.* **-nobbing, -nobbed.** to socialize or talk informally: *hobnobbing with the aristocracy.* [*hob* or *nob* to drink to one another in turns]

hobo ('həʊbəʊ) *n., pl.* **-boes** or **-bos.** *Chiefly U.S. & Canad.* a tramp; vagrant. [origin unknown]

Hobson's choice ('hɒbsʲnz) *n.* the choice of taking what is offered or nothing at all. [after Thomas *Hobson*, liveryman who gave his customers no choice]

hock¹ (hɒk) *n.* the joint in the leg of a horse or similar animal that corresponds to the human ankle. [Old English *hōhsinu* heel sinew]

hock² (hɒk) *n.* a white wine from the German Rhine. [German *Hochheimer*]

hock³ (hɒk) *Informal.* ~*vb.* **1.** to pawn or pledge. ~*n.* **2. in hock. a.** in pawn. **b.** in prison. **c.** in debt. [Dutch *hok* prison, debt]

hockey ('hɒkɪ) *n.* **1.** a game played on a field by two teams of 11 players who try to hit a ball into their opponents' goal using long sticks curved at the end. **2.** same as **ice hockey.** [origin unknown]

hocus-pocus ('həʊkəsˈpəʊkəs) *n. Informal.* trickery. [dog Latin: an exclamation used by conjurers]

hod (hɒd) *n.* an open wooden box attached to a pole, for carrying bricks or mortar. [Old French *hotte* pannier]

hodgepodge ('hɒd3ˌpɒd3) *n. Chiefly U.S. & Canad.* same as **hotchpotch.**

Hodgkin's disease ('hɒdʒkɪnz) *n.* a malignant disease that causes enlargement of the lymph nodes, spleen, and liver. [after Thomas *Hodgkin*, physician]

hoe (həʊ) *n.* **1.** a long-handled implement used to loosen the soil or to weed. ~*vb.* **hoeing, hoed. 2.** to scrape or weed with a hoe. [Germanic]

hog (hɒg) *n.* **1.** a castrated male pig. **2.** *U.S. & Canad.* any mammal of the pig family. **3.** *Informal.* a greedy person. **4. go the whole hog.** *Slang.* to do something thoroughly or unreservedly. ~*vb.* **hogging, hogged. 5.** *Slang.* to take more than one's share of (something). [Old English *hogg*]

Hogmanay (ˌhɒgməˈneɪ) *n.* New Year's Eve in Scotland. [prob. from Old French *aguillanneuf* a New Year's Eve gift]

hogshead ('hɒgzˌhed) *n.* a large cask. [origin unknown]

hogwash ('hɒgˌwɒʃ) *n.* nonsense.

ho-ho ('həʊˈhəʊ) *interj.* a written representation of the sound of laughter.

hoick (hɔɪk) *vb.* to raise abruptly and sharply. [origin unknown]

hoi polloi ('hɔɪ pəˈlɔɪ) *n.* the masses; the common people. [Greek: the many]

hoist (hɔɪst) *vb.* **1.** to raise or lift up, esp. by mechanical means. ~*n.* **2.** any apparatus or device for lifting things. [prob. from Low German]

hoity-toity (ˌhɔɪtɪˈtɔɪtɪ) *adj. Informal.* arrogant or haughty. [obs. *hoit* to romp]

hokonui (ˌhəʊkəˈnuːiː) *n. N.Z.* illicit whisky. [after *Hokonui*, district in New Zealand]

hokum ('həʊkəm) *n. Slang, chiefly U.S. & Canad.* **1.** claptrap; bunk. **2.** obvious sentimental material in a play or film. [prob. a blend of *hocus-pocus* & *bunkum*]

hold¹ (həʊld) *vb.* **holding, held. 1.** to keep (an object or a person) with or within the hands or arms; clasp. **2.** to support: *to hold a drowning man's head above water.* **3.** to maintain or be maintained in a specified state: *to hold firm.* **4.** to set aside or reserve: *they will hold our tickets until tomorrow.* **5.** to restrain: *hold that man* *until the police come.* **6.** to remain unbroken: *that cable won't hold much longer.* **7.** (of the weather) to remain dry and bright. **8.** to keep (the attention of): *to hold an audience; to hold someone's attention.* **9.** to engage in or carry on: *to hold a meeting.* **10.** to have the ownership or possession of: *he holds a law degree; who's holding the ace?* **11.** to have responsibility for: *to hold office.* **12.** to have the capacity for: *the carton will hold eight books.* **13.** to be able to control the outward effects of drinking (alcohol): *he can't hold his liquor.* **14.** to remain or cause to remain committed: *hold him to his promise.* **15.** to claim: *he holds that the theory is incorrect.* **16.** to remain valid or true: *the old philosophies don't hold nowadays.* **17.** to consider in a specified manner: *I hold him very dear.* **18.** to defend successfully: *hold the fort against the attack.* **19.** *Music.* to sustain the sound of (a note). ~*n.* **20.** the act or a method of holding fast or grasping something or someone. **21.** something to hold onto for support. **22.** controlling influence: *she has a hold on him.* **23. with no holds barred.** with all limitations removed. ~See also **hold back, hold down,** etc. [Old English *healdan*] —'**holder** *n.*

hold² (həuld) *n.* the space in a ship or aircraft for storing cargo. [var. of *hole*]

holdall ('həuld,ɔːl) *n. Brit.* a large strong travelling bag.

hold back *vb.* **1.** to restrain (someone) or refrain from doing something: *police held back the crowds; I held back from telling him the full truth.* **2.** to withhold: *he held back part of the payment.*

hold down *vb.* **1.** to restrain or control someone. **2.** *Informal.* to manage to keep: *to hold down two jobs at once.*

hold forth *vb.* to speak for a long time.

hold in *vb.* to curb, control, or conceal (one's feelings).

holding ('həuldɪŋ) *n.* **1.** land held under a lease. **2.** property to which the holder has legal title, such as land, stocks, or shares.

holding company *n.* a company with controlling shareholdings in one or more other companies.

holding paddock *n. Austral & N.Z.* a paddock in which cattle or sheep are kept temporarily, as when awaiting sale.

hold off *vb.* **1.** to keep (an attacker or attacking force) at a distance. **2.** to refrain (from doing something): *he held off making a final decision.*

hold on *vb.* **1.** to maintain a firm grasp (of something or someone). **2.** (foll. by *to*) to keep or retain: *hold on to those stamps as they'll soon be valuable.* **3.** *Informal.* to wait, esp. on the telephone.

hold out *vb.* **1.** to offer (something). **2.** to last: *I hope my luck holds out.* **3.** to continue to stand firm, refusing to succumb to persuasion. **4. hold out for.** to wait patiently for (the fulfilment of one's demands). **5. hold out on someone.** *Informal.* to keep from telling someone some important information.

hold over *vb.* to defer or postpone: *the*

decision has been held over until the next meeting.

hold-up *n.* **1.** an armed robbery. **2.** a delay; stoppage. ~*vb.* **hold up. 3.** to delay; hinder. **4.** to support (an object). **5.** to detain and rob someone, using a weapon. **6.** to exhibit or present (something) as an example.

hold with *vb.* approve of: *I don't hold with blood sports.*

hole (həul) *n.* **1.** an area hollowed out in a solid. **2.** an opening in or through something. **3.** an animal's burrow. **4.** *Informal.* an unattractive town or other place. **5.** *Informal.* a fault or error: *there's a hole in your argument.* **6. pick holes in.** to point out faults in. **7.** *Slang.* a difficult and embarrassing situation. **8.** (on a golf course) any one of the divisions of a course (usually 18) represented by the distance between the tee and the cavity on the green into which the ball is to be played. **9. make a hole in.** to use a great amount of (one's money or food supply). ~*vb.* **10.** to make a hole or holes in (something). [Old English *hol*] —'**holey** *adj.*

hole-and-corner *adj. Informal.* furtive or secretive.

hole in the heart *n.* a congenital defect of the heart, in which there is an abnormal opening in the partition between the left and right halves.

hole up *vb. Informal.* to go into hiding.

holiday ('hɒlɪ,deɪ) *n.* **1.** (*often pl.*) *Chiefly Brit.* a period in which a break is taken from work or studies for rest or recreation. **2.** a day on which work is suspended by law or custom, such as a bank holiday. ~*vb.* **3.** *Chiefly Brit.* to spend a holiday. [Old English *hāligdæg* holy day]

holier-than-thou *adj.* offensively self-righteous.

Holiness ('həulɪnɪs) *n.* (preceded by *His* or *Your*) a title reserved for the pope.

holism ('həulɪzəm) *n.* **1.** the view that a whole is greater than the sum of its parts. **2.** (in medicine) consideration of the complete person in the treatment of disease. [Greek *holos* whole] —ho'**listic** *adj.*

hollandaise sauce (,hɒlən'deɪz, 'hɒlən-,deɪz) *n.* a rich sauce of egg yolks, butter, vinegar, and lemon juice. [French *sauce hollandaise* Dutch sauce]

holler ('hɒlə) *Informal.* ~*vb.* **1.** to shout or yell. ~*n.* **2.** a shout; call. [French *holà* stop!]

hollow ('hɒləu) *adj.* **1.** having a hole or space within; not solid. **2.** concave: *hollow cheeks.* **3.** (of sounds) as if echoing in a hollow space. **4.** without substance or validity: *a hollow claim; a hollow laugh.* ~*adv.* **5. beat someone hollow.** *Brit. informal.* to defeat someone thoroughly. ~*n.* **6.** a cavity or space in something. **7.** a dip in the land. ~*vb.* (often foll. by *out*) **8.** to form a hole or cavity in. [Old English *holh* cave] —'**hollowly** *adv.*

holly ('hɒlɪ) *n.* a tree or shrub with bright red berries and shiny evergreen leaves with prickly edges, used for Christmas decorations. [Old English *holegn*]

hollyhock ('hɒlɪˌhɒk) n. a tall plant with white, yellow, red, or purple flowers. [*holy* + obs. *hock* mallow]

holmium ('hɒlmɪəm) n. a silver-white metallic element. Symbol: Ho [after *Holmia* Stockholm]

holm oak n. an evergreen oak tree with prickly leaves resembling holly.

holocaust ('hɒləˌkɔːst) n. destruction or loss of life on a massive scale. [Greek *holos* whole + *kaiein* to burn]

hologram ('hɒləˌgræm) n. a three-dimensional photographic image produced by means of a split laser beam. [Greek *holos* whole + *grammē* line]

holograph ('hɒləˌgrɑːf) n. a book or document handwritten by its author. [Greek *holos* whole + *graphein* to write]

holography (hɒ'lɒgrəfɪ) n. the science or practice of producing holograms. [Greek *holos* whole + -GRAPHY] —**holographic** (ˌhɒlə'græfɪk) adj. —**holo·graphically** adv.

hols (hɒlz) pl. n. Brit. school slang. holidays.

holster ('hɒʊlstə) n. a sheathlike leather case for a pistol, worn attached to a belt. [Germanic]

holt (hɒʊlt) n. the lair of an otter. [from HOLD²]

holy ('hɒʊlɪ) adj. **-lier, -liest. 1.** of or associated with God or a deity; sacred. **2.** devout or virtuous. [Old English *hālig*] —**holiness** n.

Holy Communion n. Christianity. a church service in which people take bread and wine in remembrance of Christ's Last Supper and His atonement for the sins of the world.

Holy Ghost n. **the.** same as **Holy Spirit.**

Holy Grail n. **the.** (in medieval legend) the bowl used by Jesus at the Last Supper. [*grail* from Medieval Latin *gradālis* bowl]

Holy Land n. **the.** Palestine.

holy of holies n. **1.** any place of special sanctity. **2.** the innermost compartment of the Jewish tabernacle.

holy orders pl. n. the status of an ordained Christian minister.

Holy See n. **the.** R.C. Church. the see of the pope as bishop of Rome.

Holy Spirit n. **the.** Christianity. the third person of the Trinity.

Holy Week n. Christianity. the week before Easter Sunday.

homage ('hɒmɪdʒ) n. a public show of respect or honour towards someone or something: *in his final number he paid homage to his hero Oscar Peterson.* [Latin *homo* man]

home (hɒʊm) n. **1.** the place where one lives. **2.** the country or area of one's birth. **3.** the place where something is invented or started: *the home of the cuckoo clock.* **4.** a building or organization set up to care for people in a certain category, such as orphans or the aged. **5.** Sport. one's own ground: *the match is at home.* **6.** the objective towards which a player strives in certain games and sports. **7. at home. a.**

in one's own home or country. **b.** at ease. **c.** receiving visitors. **8. home and dry.** Brit. slang. definitely safe or successful. ~adj. **9.** of one's home, birthplace, or native country; domestic. **10.** (of an activity) done in one's house: *home taping.* **11.** Sport. played on one's own ground: *a home game.* ~adv. **12.** to or at home: *I'll be home tomorrow.* **13.** to or on the point: *that remark hit home.* **14.** to the fullest extent: *hammer the nail home.* **15. bring something home to someone.** to make something clear to someone. ~vb. **16.** (foll. by *in* or *on*) to be directed towards (a goal or target). **17.** (of birds) to return home accurately from a distance. [Old English *hām*] —**homeless** adj., n. —**homelessness** n.

Home Counties pl. n. the counties surrounding London.

home economics n. (functioning as sing. or pl.) the study of diet, budgeting, child care, and other subjects concerned with running a home.

home farm n. Brit. a farm that was attached to and provided food for a large country house.

Home Guard n. a part-time military force of volunteers recruited for the defence of the United Kingdom in World War II.

home help n. Brit. a person employed by a local authority to do housework in a person's home.

homeland ('hɒʊmˌlænd) n. **1.** the country from which the ancestors of a person or group came. **2.** the official name in S Africa for a **Bantustan.**

homely ('hɒʊmlɪ) adj. **-lier, -liest. 1.** characteristic of or suited to the ordinary home; unpretentious. **2.** (of a person) **a.** Brit. warm and domesticated. **b.** Chiefly U.S. & Canad. unattractive. —**homeliness** n.

home-made adj. (esp. of foods) made at home or on the premises.

Home Office n. Brit. government. the department responsible for law and order, immigration, and other domestic affairs.

homeopathy or **homoeopathy** (ˌhɒmɪ-'ɒpəθɪ) n. a method of treating disease by the use of small amounts of a drug that produces symptoms of the disease in healthy people. [Greek *homoios* similar + *patheia* suffering] —**homeopath** ('hɒmɪəˌpæθ) n. —**homeopathic** (ˌhɒmɪə'pæθ-ɪk) adj.

homeostasis or **homoeostasis** (ˌhɒ-mɪəʊ'stæsɪs) n. the tendency of an organism to achieve a stable metabolic state by compensating automatically for violent changes in the environment and other disruptions. [Greek *homoios* similar + *stasis* standing]

Homeric (hɒʊ'mɛrɪk) adj. of or relating to Homer, Greek epic poet (circa 800 B.C.).

home rule n. self-government in domestic affairs.

Home Secretary n. Brit. government. the head of the Home Office.

homesick ('hɒʊmˌsɪk) adj. melancholy at

being away from home and family. —**'home,sickness** n.

homespun ('həʊm,spʌn) *adj.* (of philosophies or opinions) plain and unsophisticated.

homestead ('həʊm,stɛd, -stɪd) n. **1.** a farmhouse and the adjoining land. **2.** (in the western U.S. & Canada) a house and adjoining tract of land (originally often 160 acres) that was granted by the government for development as a farm. Homesteads are exempt from seizure or sale for debt.

homesteader ('həʊm,stɛdə) n. (in the western U.S. & Canada) a person who lives on and farms a homestead.

home truths pl. n. unpleasant facts told to a person about himself.

home unit n. Austral. & N.Z. a self-contained residence which is part of a block of such residences.

homeward ('həʊmwəd) adj. **1.** going home. ~adv. also **homewards. 2.** towards home.

homework ('həʊm,wɜːk) n. **1.** school work done at home. **2.** any preparatory study.

homicide ('hɒmɪ,saɪd) n. **1.** the killing of a human being by another person. **2.** a person who kills another. [Latin *homo* man + *caedere* to slay] —,**homi'cidal** adj.

homily ('hɒmɪlɪ) n., pl. **-lies.** a moralizing talk or piece of writing. [Greek *homilia* discourse] —,**homi'letic** adj.

homing ('həʊmɪŋ) n. (*modifier*) **1.** Zool. denoting the ability to return home after travelling great distances. **2.** (of a missile) capable of guiding itself onto a target.

homing pigeon n. a pigeon developed for its homing instinct, used for racing.

hominid ('hɒmɪnɪd) n. any member of the family of primates that includes modern man and the extinct forerunners of man. ~adj. **2.** of or belonging to this family. [Latin *homo* man]

hominoid ('hɒmɪ,nɔɪd) adj. **1.** of or like man; manlike. ~n. **2.** a manlike animal. [Latin *homo* man]

hominy ('hɒmɪnɪ) n. Chiefly U.S. coarsely ground maize prepared as a food by boiling in milk or water. [prob. American Indian]

homogeneous (,hɒmə'dʒiːnɪəs) adj. composed of similar parts. [Greek *homos* same + *genos* kind] —**homogeneity** (,hɒmədʒɪ-'niːɪtɪ) n.

homogenize or **-nise** (hɒ'mɒdʒɪ,naɪz) vb. **1.** to break up the fat globules in (milk) so that they are evenly distributed. **2.** to make homogeneous.

homogenous (hɒ'mɒdʒɪnəs) adj. having a similar structure because of common ancestry.

homograph ('hɒmə,grɑːf) n. a word spelt the same as another, but having a different meaning, such as *bear* (to carry) and *bear* (the animal). [Greek *homos* same + *graphein* to write]

homologous (hɒ'mɒləgəs) adj. **1.** having a related or similar position or structure. **2.** Biol. (of organs and parts) deriving from the same origin but having different functions: *the wing of a bat and the arm of a monkey are homologous.* [Greek *homos* same + *logos* ratio]

homology (hɒ'mɒlədʒɪ) n. the condition of being homologous.

homonym ('hɒmənɪm) n. a word pronounced and spelt the same as another, but having a different meaning, such as *novel* (a book) and *novel* (new).

homophobia (,həʊməʊ'fəʊbɪə) n. intense hatred or fear of homosexuals. [*homo*(*sexual*) + *phobia*]

homophone ('hɒmə,fəʊn) n. a word pronounced the same as another, but having a different meaning or spelling or both, such as *bear* and *bare*. [Greek *homos* same + *phōnē* sound]

Homo sapiens ('sæpɪ,ɛnz) n. the name for modern man as a species. [Latin *homo* man + *sapiens* wise]

homosexual (,həʊməʊ'sɛksjʊəl, ,hɒm-) n. **1.** a person who is sexually attracted to members of the same sex. ~adj. **2.** (of a person) sexually attracted to members of the same sex. **3.** (of a sexual relationship) between members of the same sex. [Greek *homos* same] —,**homo,sexu'ality** n.

homy or esp. U.S. **homey** ('həʊmɪ) adj. **homier, homiest.** like a home; cosy.

Hon. Honourable (title).

hone (həʊn) n. **1.** a fine whetstone for sharpening. ~vb. **2.** to sharpen with or as if with a hone. [Old English *hān* stone]

honest ('ɒnɪst) adj. **1.** not given to lying, cheating, or stealing; trustworthy. **2.** just or fair: *honest wages.* **3.** genuine; sincere; without pretensions: *an honest attempt.* [Latin *honōs* esteem]

honestly ('ɒnɪstlɪ) adv. **1.** in an honest manner. **2.** truly: *I honestly don't believe it.*

honesty ('ɒnɪstɪ) n., pl. **-ties. 1.** the condition of being honest. **2.** a plant with flattened silvery pods which are used for indoor decoration.

honey ('hʌnɪ) n. **1.** a sweet edible sticky substance made by bees from nectar. **2.** Chiefly U.S. & Canad. a term of endearment. **3.** Informal, chiefly U.S. & Canad. something very good of its kind: *a honey of a role.* [Old English *huneg*]

honeybee ('hʌnɪ,biː) n. a bee widely domesticated as a source of honey and beeswax.

honeycomb ('hʌnɪ,kəʊm) n. a waxy structure, constructed by bees in a hive, that consists of many six-sided cells in which honey is stored.

honeydew ('hʌnɪ,djuː) n. a sugary substance excreted by aphids and similar insects.

honeydew melon n. a melon with yellow skin and sweet pale flesh.

honeyed ('hʌnɪd) adj. Poetic. flattering or soothing: *honeyed words.*

honeymoon ('hʌnɪ,muːn) n. **1.** a holiday taken by a newly married couple. **2.** the early, usually calm period of a relationship or enterprise. ~vb. **3.** to take a honeymoon. [traditionally, referring to the feelings of married couples as changing with the phases of the moon] —**'honey,moon-er** n.

honeysuckle ('hʌnɪˌsʌk³l) n. a climbing shrub with sweet-smelling white, yellow, or pink flowers. [Old English *hunigsūce*]

honk (hɒŋk) n. **1.** the sound made by a motor horn. **2.** the sound made by a goose. ~vb. **3.** to make or cause (something) to make a honking sound.

honky-tonk ('hɒŋkɪˌtɒŋk) n. **1.** U.S. & Canad. slang. a cheap disreputable nightclub or dance hall. **2.** a style of ragtime piano-playing, esp. on a tinny-sounding piano. [rhyming compound based on HONK]

honorarium (ˌɒnəˈrɛərɪəm) n., pl. **-iums** or **-ia** (-ɪə) a voluntary fee paid for a service which is usually free. [Latin *honorarium* (*donum*) honorary gift]

honorary ('ɒnərərɪ) adj. **a.** held or given only as an honour, without the normal privileges or duties: *an honorary degree.* **b.** (of a secretary, treasurer, etc.) unpaid.

honorific (ˌɒnəˈrɪfɪk) adj. showing respect.

honour or U.S. **honor** ('ɒnə) n. **1.** the quality of being firm in one's moral principles. **2. a.** fame or glory. **b.** a person who wins this for his country, school, etc. **3.** great respect or esteem, or an outward sign of this. **4.** a privilege or pleasure: *it is an honour to serve you.* **5.** (of a woman) chastity. **6.** *Bridge, whist.* any of the top four or five cards in a suit. **7.** *Golf.* the right to tee off first. **8. in honour of.** out of respect for. **9. on one's honour.** under a moral obligation. ~vb. **10.** to hold someone in respect. **11.** to give (someone) a symbol of honour. **12.** to accept and then pay (a cheque or bill). **13.** to keep (one's promise); fulfil (a previous agreement). [Latin *honor* esteem]

Honour ('ɒnə) n. (preceded by *Your, His,* or *Her*) a title used to address or refer to certain judges.

honourable or U.S. **honorable** ('ɒnərəb³l) adj. **1.** possessing high principles. **2.** worthy of honour or esteem. —**'honourably** adv.

Honourable ('ɒnərəb³l) adj. **the.** a title of respect placed before a name: used of various officials, of the children of certain peers, and in Parliament by one member speaking of another.

honours or U.S. **honors** ('ɒnəz) pl. n. **1.** observances of respect, esp. at a funeral. **2.** (in a university degree course) a rank or mark of the highest academic standard: *an honours degree.* **3. do the honours.** to serve as host or hostess, as by serving food or drinks.

hooch (huːtʃ) n. Informal. alcoholic drink, esp. illicitly distilled spirits. [American Indian]

hood¹ (hʊd) n. **1.** a loose head covering either attached to a cloak or coat or made as a separate garment. **2.** U.S. & Canad. the bonnet of a car. **3.** the folding roof of a convertible car or a pram. ~vb. **4.** to cover with or as if with a hood. [Old

English *hōd*] —**'hooded** adj. —**'hood-ˌlike** adj.

hood² (hʊd) n. Slang. short for **hoodlum.**

hooded crow n. a crow that has a grey body and black head, wings, and tail.

hoodlum ('huːdləm) n. **1.** a petty gangster. **2.** a lawless youth. [origin unknown]

hoodoo ('huːduː) n., pl. **-doos. 1.** same as **voodoo. 2.** Informal. bad luck. **3.** Informal. a person or thing that brings bad luck.

hoodwink ('hʊdˌwɪŋk) vb. to dupe; trick. [orig., to cover the eyes with a hood]

hooey ('huːɪ) n. Slang. nonsense. [origin unknown]

hoof (huːf) n., pl. **hooves** or **hoofs. 1.** the horny covering of the end of the foot in the horse, deer, and certain other mammals. ~vb. **2. hoof it.** Slang. to walk. [Old English *hōf*] —**'hoofed** adj.

hoo-ha ('huːˌhɑː) n. a noisy commotion or fuss. [origin unknown]

hook (hʊk) n. **1.** a curved piece of metal used to hang, hold, or pull something. **2.** something resembling a hook, such as a sharp bend in a river or a sharply curved strip of land. **3.** *Boxing.* a short swinging blow with the elbow bent. **4.** *Cricket, golf.* a shot that causes the ball to go to the player's left. **5. by hook or by crook.** by any means: *I'll get there by hook or by crook.* **6. hook, line, and sinker.** Informal. completely: *he fell for it hook, line, and sinker.* Slang. to free someone from obligation or guilt. **8. sling one's hook.** Brit. slang. to leave. ~vb. **9.** to fasten with or as if with a hook. **10.** to catch (a fish) on a hook. **11.** *Cricket, etc.* to play (a ball) with a hook. **12.** *Rugby.* to obtain and pass (the ball) backwards from a scrum, using the feet. [Old English *hōc*]

hookah ('hʊkə) n. an oriental pipe for smoking marijuana or tobacco, with a long flexible stem connected to a container of water through which smoke is drawn and cooled. [Arabic *huqqah*]

hooked (hʊkt) adj. **1.** bent like a hook. **2. hooked on. a.** Slang. addicted to: *hooked on cocaine.* **b.** obsessed with: *hooked on video games.*

hooker ('hʊkə) n. **1.** Slang. a prostitute. **2.** *Rugby.* a player in the front row of a scrum whose main job is to hook the ball.

hook-up n. the linking of broadcasting equipment or stations to transmit a special programme.

hookworm ('hʊkˌwɜːm) n. a bloodsucking worm with hooked mouthparts.

hooligan ('huːlɪgən) n. Slang. a rough lawless young person. [origin unknown] —**'hooliganism** n.

hoop (huːp) n. **1.** a rigid circular band of metal or wood. **2.** a child's toy shaped like a hoop and rolled on the ground or whirled around the body. **3.** *Croquet.* any of the iron arches through which the ball is driven. **4.** a large ring often with paper stretched over it through which performers or animals jump in the circus. **5. go or be put through the hoops.** to be subjected to an ordeal. ~vb. **6.** to surround (something) with a hoop. [Old English *hōp*] —**hooped** *adj*.

hoopla ('huːplɑː) *n. Brit.* a fairground game in which a player tries to throw a hoop over an object and so win it.

hoopoe ('huːpuː) *n.* a bird having a pinkish-brown plumage with black-and-white wings and a fanlike crest. [imit.]

hooray (huː'reɪ) *interj., n.* same as **hurrah**.

Hooray Henry ('huːˌreɪ 'hɛnrɪ) *n., pl.* **Hooray Henries** or **-rys.** a young upper-class man with affectedly hearty voice and manners.

hoot[1] (huːt) *n.* **1.** the mournful wavering cry of some owls. **2.** a similar sound, such as that of a car horn. **3.** a jeer of derision. **4.** *Informal.* an amusing person or thing. ~*vb.* **5.** to jeer or yell contemptuously at someone. **6.** to drive (speakers or performers on stage) off by hooting. **7.** to make a hoot. **8.** *Brit.* to blow (a horn). [imit.]

hoot[2] (huːt) *n. Austral & N.Z. slang.* money.

hooter ('huːtə) *n. Chiefly Brit.* **1.** a device that hoots, such as a car horn. **2.** *Slang.* a nose.

Hoover ('huːvə) *n.* **1.** *Trademark.* a vacuum cleaner. ~*vb.* **2.** to vacuum-clean (a carpet).

hooves (huːvz) *n.* a plural of **hoof.**

hop[1] (hɒp) *vb.* **hopping, hopped. 1.** to jump forwards or upwards on one foot. **2.** (of frogs, birds, etc.) to move forwards in short jumps. **3.** to jump over something. **4.** *Informal.* to move quickly (in, on, out of, etc.): *hop on a bus.* **5. hop it.** *Brit. slang.* to go away. ~*n.* **6.** an instance of hopping. **7.** *Informal.* an informal dance. **8.** *Informal.* a short journey, usually in an aircraft. **9. on the hop.** *Informal.* **a.** active or busy: *he keeps me on the hop.* **b.** *Brit.* unawares or unprepared: *you've caught me on the hop.* [Old English *hoppian*]

hop[2] (hɒp) *n.* a climbing plant with green conelike flowers. See also **hops.** [Dutch *hoppe*]

hope (həʊp) *n.* **1.** a feeling of desire for something, usually with confidence in the possibility of its fulfilment: *his hope for peace was justified.* **2.** a reasonable ground for this feeling: *there is still hope.* **3.** a person or thing that gives cause for hope. **4.** a thing, situation, or event that is desired: *my hope is that prices will fall.* ~*vb.* **5.** to desire (something), usually with some possibility of fulfilment: *I hope to tell you.* **6.** to trust or believe: *we hope that this is satisfactory.* [Old English *hopa*]

hopeful ('həʊpfʊl) *adj.* **1.** having or expressing hope. **2.** inspiring hope; promising. ~*n.* **3.** a person considered to be on the brink of success: *a young hopeful.*

hopefully ('həʊpfʊlɪ) *adv.* **1.** in a hopeful manner. **2.** *Informal.* it is hoped: *hopefully they will be married soon.*

hopeless ('həʊplɪs) *adj.* **1.** having or offering no hope. **2.** impossible to solve. **3.** *Informal.* without skill or ability: *I'm hopeless at maths.*

hopper ('hɒpə) *n.* **1.** a funnel-shaped device from which solid materials can be

discharged into a receptacle below. **2.** a hopping insect.

hops (hɒps) *pl. n.* the dried flowers of the hop plant, used to give a bitter taste to beer.

hopscotch ('hɒpˌskɒtʃ) *n.* a children's game in which a player throws a stone to land in one of a pattern of squares marked on the ground and then hops over to it to pick it up. [*hop* + obs. *scotch* a line, scratch]

horde (hɔːd) *n.* a vast crowd; throng; mob. [Turkish *ordū* camp]

horehound ('hɔːˌhaʊnd) *n.* a plant that produces a bitter juice formerly used as a cough medicine. [Old English *hārhūne*]

horizon (hə'raɪz'n) *n.* **1.** the apparent line that divides the earth and the sky. **2.** (*pl.*) the limits of scope, interest, or knowledge. [Greek *horizein* to limit]

horizontal (ˌhɒrɪ'zɒnt'l) *adj.* **1.** parallel to the plane of the horizon; level; flat. **2.** *Econ.* relating to identical stages of commercial activity: *horizontal integration.* ~*n.* **3.** a horizontal plane, position, or line. —ˌhori'zontally *adv.*

hormone ('hɔːməʊn) *n.* **1.** a chemical substance produced in an endocrine gland and transported in the blood to a certain tissue, on which it has a specific effect. **2.** a similar substance produced by a plant that is essential for growth. **3.** a synthetic substance having the same effects. [Greek *hormōn*] —**hor'monal** *adj.*

horn (hɔːn) *n.* **1.** either of a pair of permanent bony outgrowths on the heads of animals such as cattle and antelopes. **2.** any hornlike projection, such as the eye-stalk of a snail. **3.** the antler of a deer. **4.** the hard substance of which horns are made. **5.** a musical wind instrument made from horn. **6.** any musical instrument consisting of a pipe or tube of brass fitted with a mouthpiece. **7.** a device, as on a vehicle, for producing a warning or signalling noise. ~*vb.* **8.** to provide with a horn or horns. [Old English] —**horned** *adj.*

hornbeam ('hɔːnˌbiːm) *n.* a tree with hard white wood.

hornbill ('hɔːnˌbɪl) *n.* a tropical bird having a very large bill with a bony protuberance.

hornblende ('hɔːnˌblɛnd) *n.* a green to black mineral containing aluminium, calcium, sodium, magnesium, and iron.

hornet ('hɔːnɪt) *n.* **1.** a large wasp that can inflict a severe sting. **2. hornet's nest.** a strongly unfavourable reaction: *I seem to have stirred up a hornet's nest.* [Old English *hyrnetu*]

horn of plenty *n.* same as **cornucopia.**

hornpipe ('hɔːnˌpaɪp) *n.* **1.** a solo dance, traditionally performed by sailors. **2.** music for this dance.

horny ('hɔːnɪ) *adj.* **hornier, horniest. 1.** of, like, or hard as horn. **2.** *Slang.* aroused sexually.

horology (hɒ'rɒlədʒɪ) *n.* the art of making clocks and watches or of measuring time. [Greek *hōra* hour + -LOGY] —**horological** (ˌhɒrə'lɒdʒɪk'l) *adj.*

horoscope ('hɒrəˌskəʊp) n. **1.** the prediction of a person's future based on the positions of the planets, sun, and moon at the time of birth. **2.** a diagram showing the positions of the planets, sun, and moon at a particular time and place. [Greek *hōra* HOUR + *skopos* observer]

horrendous (hɒ'rɛndəs) adj. same as **horrific**. [Latin *horrendus* fearful]

horrible ('hɒrɪbʰl) adj. **1.** causing horror; dreadful. **2.** disagreeable. [Latin *horribilis*] —**'horribly** adv.

horrid ('hɒrɪd) adj. **1.** disagreeable; unpleasant: *a horrid meal.* **2.** *Informal.* unkind. [Latin *horridus* prickly]

horrific (hɒ'rɪfɪk, hə-) adj. provoking horror; horrible. —**hor'rifically** adv.

horrify ('hɒrɪˌfaɪ) vb. **-fying, -fied.** to cause feelings of horror in (someone); shock (someone) greatly.

horror ('hɒrə) n. **1.** extreme fear; terror; dread. **2.** intense hatred. **3.** a thing or person causing fear, loathing, or distaste. **4.** (*modifier*) having a frightening subject: *a horror film.* [Latin: a trembling with fear]

horrors ('hɒrəz) pl. n. **the.** *Slang.* a fit of depression or anxiety.

hors d'oeuvre (ɔː 'dɜːvrə) n., pl. **hors d'oeuvre** or **hors d'oeuvres** ('dɜːvrə). an appetizer, usually served before the main meal. [French]

horse (hɔːs) n. **1.** a solid-hoofed domesticated mammal used for pulling carts, etc., and for riding. **2.** the adult male of this species; stallion. **3.** (*functioning as pl.*) cavalry: *a regiment of horse.* **4.** *Gymnastics.* a padded apparatus on legs, used for vaulting. **5. be** or **get on one's high horse.** *Informal.* to act haughtily. **6. the horse's mouth.** the most reliable source: *I got it straight from the horse's mouth.* [Old English *hors*]

horse around or **about** vb. *Informal.* to indulge in horseplay.

horseback ('hɔːsˌbæk) n. a horse's back: *on horseback.*

horsebox ('hɔːsˌbɒks) n. *Brit.* a van or trailer used for transporting horses.

horse brass n. a decorative brass ornament, originally attached to a horse's harness.

horse chestnut n. **1.** a tree with broad leaves and brown shiny inedible nuts enclosed in a spiky case. **2.** the nut of this tree.

horseflesh ('hɔːsˌflɛʃ) n. **1.** horses collectively: *a good judge of horseflesh.* **2.** the flesh of a horse as food.

horsefly ('hɔːsˌflaɪ) n., pl. **-flies.** a large fly which sucks the blood of horses, cattle, and people.

horsehair ('hɔːsˌheə) n. hair from the tail or mane of a horse, used in upholstery.

horse laugh n. a coarse or raucous laugh.

horseman ('hɔːsmən) n., pl. **-men. 1.** a man who is skilled in riding. **2.** a man riding a horse. —**'horsemanˌship** n. —**'horseˌwoman** fem. n.

horseplay ('hɔːsˌpleɪ) n. rough or rowdy play.

horsepower ('hɔːsˌpaʊə) n. a unit of power (equivalent to 745.7 watts), used to measure the power of an engine.

horseradish ('hɔːsˌrædɪʃ) n. a plant with a white strong-tasting root, which is used to make a sauce.

horse sense n. same as **common sense.**

horseshoe ('hɔːsˌʃuː) n. **1.** a piece of iron shaped like a U nailed to the bottom of a horse's hoof to protect the foot. **2.** an object of similar shape.

horsetail ('hɔːsˌteɪl) n. a plant with small dark toothlike leaves.

horsewhip ('hɔːsˌwɪp) n. **1.** a whip with a long thong, used for managing horses. ~vb. **-whipping, -whipped. 2.** to flog (a person or animal) with such a whip.

horsy or **horsey** ('hɔːsɪ) adj. **horsier, horsiest. 1.** of or relating to horses: *a horsy smell.* **2.** devoted to horses: *the horsy set.* **3.** like a horse: *a horsy face.*

hortatory ('hɔːtətrɪ) or **hortative** ('hɔːtətɪv) adj. encouraging. [Latin *hortārī* to encourage]

horticulture ('hɔːtɪˌkʌltʃə) n. the art of cultivating gardens. [Latin *hortus* garden + *culture*] —**ˌhortiˈcultural** adj. —**ˌhortiˈculturist** n.

hosanna (həʊ'zænə) interj. an exclamation of praise to God. [Hebrew *hōshi 'āh nnā* save now, we pray]

hose[1] (həʊz) n. **1.** a flexible pipe, for conveying a liquid or gas. ~vb. **2.** to wash or water (a person or thing) with a hose. [later use of HOSE[2]]

hose[2] (həʊz) n. **1.** stockings, socks, and tights collectively. **2.** *History.* a man's garment covering the legs and reaching up to the waist. [Old English *hosa*]

hosiery ('həʊzɪərɪ) n. stockings, socks, and knitted underclothing collectively.

hospice ('hɒspɪs) n. **1.** a nursing home that specializes in caring for the terminally ill. **2.** *Archaic.* a place of shelter for travellers, esp. one kept by a religious order. [Latin *hospes* guest]

hospitable ('hɒspɪtəbʰl, hɒ'spɪt-) adj. welcoming to guests or strangers. [Medieval Latin *hospitāre* receive as a guest] —**'hospitably** adv.

hospital ('hɒspɪtʰl) n. an institution for the medical or psychiatric care and treatment of patients. [Latin *hospes* guest]

hospitality (ˌhɒspɪ'tælɪtɪ) n., pl. **-ties.** kindness in welcoming strangers or guests.

hospitalize or **-lise** ('hɒspɪtəˌlaɪz) vb. to admit or send (a person) into a hospital. —ˌhospitaliˈzation or **-liˈsation** n.

hospitaller or U.S. **hospitaler** ('hɒspɪtələ) n. a member of a religious order dedicated to hospital work, ambulance services, etc.

host[1] (həʊst) n. **1.** a person who receives or entertains guests, esp. in his own home. **2.** the compere of a radio or television programme. **3.** *Biol.* an animal or plant in or on which a parasite lives. **4.** *Old-fashioned.* the owner or manager of an inn.

~*vb.* **5.** to be the host of (a party or programme): *to host one's own show.* [Latin *hospes* guest, host]

host² (həʊst) *n.* a great number; multitude. [Latin *hostis* stranger]

Host (həʊst) *n. Christianity.* the bread used in Holy Communion. [Latin *hostia* victim]

hostage ('hɒstɪdʒ) *n.* a person held by another or others as security for the fulfilment of certain terms. [Old French *hoste* guest]

hostel ('hɒst'l) *n.* **1.** a building providing overnight accommodation, as for homeless people. **2.** same as **youth hostel. 3.** *Brit.* a supervised lodging house for nurses, students, etc. [Medieval Latin *hospitāle* hospice] —'**hosteller** *or U.S.* '**hosteler** *n.*

hostelry ('hɒstəlrɪ) *n., pl.* -ries. *Archaic or facetious.* an inn.

hostel school *n. Canad.* same as **residential school.**

hostess ('həʊstɪs) *n.* **1.** a woman acting as host. **2.** a woman who receives and entertains patrons of a club, restaurant, or dance hall.

hostile ('hɒstaɪl) *adj.* **1.** unfriendly and aggressive. **2.** antagonistic; opposed: *hostile to new developments.* **3.** of or relating to an enemy. [Latin *hostis* enemy]

hostility (hɒ'stɪlɪtɪ) *n., pl.* -ties. **1.** unfriendly and aggressive feelings or behaviour. **2.** (*pl.*) fighting; warfare.

hot (hɒt) *adj.* **hotter, hottest. 1.** having a relatively high temperature. **2.** having a temperature higher than desirable. **3.** causing a burning sensation on the tongue: *a hot curry.* **4.** expressing or feeling intense emotion, such as anger or lust. **5.** (of a contest or conflict) intense or vehement. **6.** recent; new: *hot from the press.* **7.** much favoured: *a hot favourite.* **8.** *Informal.* having a dangerously high level of radioactivity. **9.** *Slang.* stolen or otherwise illegally obtained. **10.** (of a colour) intense; striking: *hot pink.* **11.** following closely: *hot on the scent.* **12.** *Informal.* dangerous or unpleasant: *they're making it hot for me here.* **13.** (in various games) very near the answer. **14. hot on.** *Informal.* **a.** strict about: *the police are hot on drunk driving.* **b.** particularly knowledgeable about. **15. hot under the collar.** *Informal.* aroused with anger, annoyance, or resentment. **16. in hot water.** *Informal.* in trouble. ~See also **hot up.** [Old English *hāt*] —'**hotly** *adv.*

hot air *n. Informal.* empty and usually boastful talk.

hotbed ('hɒt,bed) *n.* a place offering ideal conditions for the growth of an idea or activity, esp. one considered bad: *a hotbed of crime.*

hot-blooded *adj.* passionate or excitable.

hotchpotch ('hɒtʃ,pɒtʃ) *or esp. U.S. & Canad.* **hodgepodge** *n.* a jumbled mixture. [French *hotchpot* shake pot]

hot cross bun *n.* a yeast bun marked with a cross and traditionally eaten on Good Friday.

hot dog *n.* a long roll split lengthways with a hot sausage inside.

hotel (həʊ'tel) *n.* a commercially run establishment providing lodging and meals for guests. [French]

hotelier (hɒ'telɪeɪ) *n.* an owner or manager of a hotel.

hotfoot ('hɒt,fʊt) *adv.* with all possible speed.

hot-gospeller *n. Informal.* a revivalist preacher with a highly enthusiastic delivery.

hot-headed *adj.* impetuous, rash, or hot-tempered. —,**hot-'headedness** *n.*

hothouse ('hɒt,haʊs) *n.* a greenhouse in which the temperature is maintained at a fixed level.

hot line *n.* a direct telephone link between heads of government for emergency use.

hot money *n.* capital that is transferred from one financial centre to another seeking the best opportunity for short-term gain.

hotplate ('hɒt,pleɪt) *n.* **1.** an electrically heated plate on a cooker. **2.** a portable device on which food can be kept warm.

hotpot ('hɒt,pɒt) *n. Brit.* a casserole of meat and vegetables covered with a layer of potatoes.

hot rod *n.* a car with an engine that has been modified to produce increased power.

hot seat *n.* **1. in the hot seat.** *Informal.* in a difficult and responsible position. **2.** *U.S. slang.* the electric chair.

hot stuff *n. Informal.* **1.** a person, object, or activity considered attractive, exciting, or important. **2.** pornographic or erotic books, plays, films, etc.

Hottentot ('hɒt'n,tɒt) *n.* **1.** (*pl.* -**tot** *or* -**tots**) a member of a race of people of southern Africa which is now almost extinct. **2.** any of the languages of this people. [Afrikaans]

hot up *vb.* **hotting, hotted.** *Informal.* **1.** to make or become more exciting, active, or intense. **2.** same as **soup up.**

hot-water bottle *n.* a rubber container, designed to be filled with hot water and used for warming a bed.

hound (haʊnd) *n.* **1.** a dog used for hunting: *a deerhound.* **2.** a despicable person. ~*vb.* **3.** to pursue relentlessly: *hounded by the press.* [Old English *hund*]

hour ('aʊə) *n.* **1.** a period of time equal to 60 minutes; 1/24th of a day. **2.** any of the points on the face of a clock or watch that indicate intervals of 60 minutes: *the bus leaves on the hour.* **3.** the time. **4.** the time allowed for or used for something: *the lunch hour.* **5.** a special moment: *our finest hour.* **6.** the distance covered in an hour: *we live an hour from the city.* ~See also **hours.** [Latin *hōra*]

hourglass ('aʊə,glɑːs) *n.* a device consisting of two transparent sections linked by a narrow channel, containing a quantity of sand that takes an hour to trickle from one section to the other.

houri ('hʊərɪ) *n., pl.* -ris. (in Muslim belief)

any of the nymphs of Paradise. [Arabic *haurā'* woman with dark eyes]

hourly ('auəlɪ) *adj.* **1.** of, occurring, or done once every hour. **2.** measured by the hour: *an hourly rate.* **3.** frequent. ~*adv.* **4.** once every hour. **5.** by the hour: *hourly paid.* **6.** frequently. **7.** at any moment: *we expect him hourly.*

hours ('auəz) *pl. n.* **1.** a period regularly appointed for work or business. **2.** one's times of rising and going to bed: *he keeps late hours.* **3.** an indefinite time: *we talked for hours.* **4.** R.C. Church. prayers recited at seven specified times of the day.

house *n.* (haus), *pl.* **houses** ('hauzɪz). **1.** a building used as a home; dwelling. **2.** the people in a house. **3.** a building for some specific purpose: *schoolhouse.* **4.** a family or dynasty: *the House of York.* **5.** a commercial company: *a publishing house.* **6.** a law-making body or the hall where it meets. **7.** *Astrol.* any of the 12 divisions of the zodiac. **8.** a division of a large school: *house captain.* **9.** the audience in a theatre or cinema. **10.** *Informal.* a brothel. **11. get on like a house on fire.** *Informal.* (of people) to get on very well together. **12. on the house.** (usually of drinks) paid for by the management. **13. put one's house in order.** to settle or organize one's affairs. ~*vb.* (hauz). **14.** to provide (someone) with or serve (someone) as accommodation. **15.** to contain or cover (something). [Old English *hūs*]

house arrest *n.* confinement to one's own home rather than in prison.

houseboat ('haus,bəut) *n.* a stationary boat used as a home.

housebound ('haus,baund) *adj.* unable to leave one's house, usually because of illness.

housebreaking ('haus,breɪkɪŋ) *n. Criminal law.* the act of entering a building as a trespasser for an unlawful purpose. —'**house,breaker** *n.*

housecoat ('haus,kəut) *n.* a woman's loose robelike informal garment.

housefly ('haus,flaɪ) *n., pl.* -**flies.** a common fly often found in houses.

household ('haus,həuld) *n.* **1.** all the people living together in one house. **2.** (*modifier*) relating to the running of a household: *household management.*

householder ('haus,həuldə) *n.* a person who owns or rents a house.

household name *or* **word** *n.* a person or thing that is very well known.

housekeeper ('haus,kiːpə) *n.* a person employed to run someone else's household.

housekeeping ('haus,kiːpɪŋ) *n.* **1.** the running of a household. **2.** money allotted for this.

house lights *pl. n.* the lights in the auditorium of a theatre or cinema.

housemaid ('haus,meɪd) *n.* a female servant employed to do housework.

housemaid's knee *n.* a fluid-filled swelling of the kneecap.

houseman ('hausmən) *n., pl.* -**men.** *Med.* a junior doctor in a hospital.

house martin *n.* a swallow with a slightly forked tail.

House music *or* **House** *n.* a type of disco music of the late 1980s, based on funk, with fragments of other recordings edited in electronically.

House of Commons *n.* (in Britain and Canada) the lower chamber of Parliament.

House of Keys *n.* the lower chamber of the law-making body of the Isle of Man.

House of Lords *n.* (in Britain) the upper chamber of Parliament, composed of the peers of the realm.

house party *n.* **1.** a party, usually in a country house, at which guests are invited to stay for several days. **2.** the guests who are invited.

house-proud *adj.* excessively concerned with the appearance, cleanliness, and tidiness of one's house.

houseroom ('haus,rum, -,ruːm) *n.* **not give something houseroom.** not to want to have something in one's house.

housetops ('haus,tops) *pl. n.* **shout** *or* **proclaim something from the housetops.** to announce something publicly.

house-train *vb. Brit.* to train (a pet) to urinate and defecate outside.

house-warming *n.* a party given after moving into a new home.

housewife ('haus,waɪf) *n., pl.* -**wives.** a woman who runs her own household and does not have a paid job. —'**housewifely** *adj.*

housework ('haus,wɜːk) *n.* the work of running a home, such as cleaning, cooking, and shopping.

housing ('hauzɪŋ) *n.* **1.** houses collectively. **2.** the job of providing people with accommodation. **3.** a part designed to contain and support a component or mechanism: *a wheel housing.*

hove (həuv) *vb. Chiefly naut.* a past of **heave.**

hovel ('hɒv'l) *n.* a dirty or untidy dwelling place. [origin unknown]

hover ('hɒvə) *vb.* **1.** to remain suspended in one place, as hawks do by rapidly beating their wings. **2.** to linger uncertainly in a place. **3.** to be in a state of indecision. [Middle English *hoveren*]

hovercraft ('hɒvə,krɑːft) *n.* a vehicle that is able to travel across both land and water on a cushion of air.

how (hau) *adv.* **1.** in what way, by what means: *how did it happen? tell me how he did it.* **2.** to what extent: *how tall is he?* **3.** how good, how well, what...like: *how did she sing? how was the holiday?* **4. how about?** used to suggest something: *how about a cup of tea?* **5. how are you?** what is your state of health? **6. how's that? a.** what is your opinion?: *I'll give you it for a fiver - how's that?* **b.** *Cricket.* Also written: **howzat** (hau'zæt). (an appeal to the umpire) is the batsman out? [Old English *hu*]

howdah ('haudə) *n.* a seat for riding on an elephant's back. [Hindi *haudah*]

however (hau'ɛvə) *adv.* **1.** still; nevertheless: *I don't want to go - however, I will make the effort.* **2.** by whatever means: *get there however you can.* **3.** (*with an adjective or adverb*) no matter how: *however long it takes, finish it.*

howitzer ('haʊɪtsə) *n.* a cannon with a short barrel and a steep angle of fire. [Czech *houfnice* stone-sling]

howl (haʊl) *n.* **1.** the long plaintive cry of a wolf or hound. **2.** a similar cry of pain or sorrow. **3.** a loud burst of laughter. ~*vb.* **4.** to express (something) in a howl or utter such cries. **5.** (of the wind, etc.) to make a wailing noise. [Middle English *houlen*]

howl down *vb.* to prevent (a speaker) from being heard by shouting disapprovingly.

howler ('haʊlə) *n. Informal.* a glaring mistake.

howling ('haʊlɪŋ) *adj. Informal.* great: *a howling success.*

hoy (hɔɪ) *interj.* a cry used to attract someone's attention. [var. of *hey*]

hoyden ('hɔɪd'n) *n.* a wild boisterous girl; tomboy. [perhaps from Middle Dutch *heidijn* heathen] —**'hoydenish** *adj.*

HP or **h.p.** **1.** *Brit.* hire-purchase. **2.** horsepower.

HQ or **h.q.** headquarters.

hr hour.

HRH Her (or His) Royal Highness.

HRT hormone replacement therapy.

hub (hʌb) *n.* **1.** the central portion of a wheel, through which the axle passes. **2.** the focal point of a place. [prob. var. of *hob*]

hubble-bubble ('hʌb'l'bʌb'l) *n.* **1.** same as **hookah.** **2.** turmoil. **3.** a gargling sound. [imit.]

hubbub ('hʌbʌb) *n.* a confused noise of many voices. **2.** tumult; uproar. [prob. from Irish *hooboobbes*]

hubby ('hʌbɪ) *n., pl.* **-bies.** *Informal.* a husband.

hubris ('hjuːbrɪs) *n.* pride or arrogance. [Greek] —**hu'bristic** *adj.*

huckster ('hʌkstə) *n.* **1.** a person who uses aggressive methods of selling. **2.** *Now rare.* a person who sells small articles or fruit in the street. [prob. from Middle Dutch *hoekster*]

huddle ('hʌd'l) *n.* **1.** a heaped or crowded mass of people or things. **2. go into a huddle.** *Informal.* to have a private conference. ~*vb.* **3.** (of a group of people) to crowd or nestle closely together. **4.** (of a person) to hunch (oneself), as through cold. [origin unknown]

hue (hjuː) *n.* **1.** the feature of colour that enables an observer to classify it as red, blue, etc. **2.** a shade of a colour. [Old English *hīw* beauty]

hue and cry *n.* a loud public outcry. [Old French *hue* outcry]

huff (hʌf) *n.* **1.** a passing mood of anger or resentment: *in a huff.* ~*vb.* **2.** to blow or puff heavily. **3.** *Draughts* to remove (an opponent's draught) from the board for failure to make a capture. **4. huffing and**

puffing. empty threats or objections; bluster. [imit.] —**'huffy** *adj.* —**'huffily** *adv.*

hug (hʌg) *vb.* **hugging, hugged. 1.** to clasp (someone or something) tightly, usually with affection. **2.** to keep close to (a shore or the kerb). ~*n.* **3.** a tight or fond embrace. [prob. Scandinavian]

huge (hjuːdʒ) *adj.* extremely large. [Old French *ahuge*] —**'hugely** *adv.*

huggermugger ('hʌgə,mʌgə) *Archaic.* ~*n.* **1.** confusion or secrecy. ~*adj., adv.* **2.** in confusion. [origin unknown]

Huguenot ('hjuːgə,nɒʊ, -,nɒt) *n.* a French Calvinist of the 16th or 17th centuries. [French]

huh (hʌ) *interj.* an exclamation of derision, bewilderment, or inquiry.

hui ('huːɪ) *n. N.Z.* **1.** a Maori social gathering. **2.** any party. [Hawaiian]

hula ('huːlə) *n.* a Hawaiian dance performed by a woman. [Hawaiian]

hulk (hʌlk) *n.* **1.** the body of an abandoned ship. **2.** *Disparaging.* a large ungainly person or thing. [Old English *hulc*]

hulking ('hʌlkɪŋ) *adj.* big and ungainly.

hull (hʌl) *n.* **1.** the main body of a boat. **2.** the outer covering of a fruit or seed such as a pea or bean. **3.** the leaves round the stem of a strawberry, raspberry, or similar fruit. ~*vb.* **4.** to remove the hulls from (fruit or seeds). [Old English *hulu*]

hullabaloo (,hʌləbə'luː) *n., pl.* **-loos.** a loud confused noise; commotion. [*hallo* + Scot. *baloo* lullaby]

hullo (hʌ'lʌʊ) *interj., n.* same as **hello.**

hum (hʌm) *vb.* **humming, hummed. 1.** to make a low continuous vibrating sound. **2.** (of a person) to sing with the lips closed. **3.** to utter an indistinct sound, as in hesitation. **4.** *Slang.* to be in a state of feverish activity: *an area humming with shoppers.* **5.** *Slang.* to smell unpleasant. **6. hum and haw.** to hesitate in speaking. ~*n.* **7.** a low continuous murmuring sound. **8.** an unpleasant smell. ~*interj., n.* **9.** an indistinct sound of hesitation. [imit.]

human ('hjuːmən) *adj.* **1.** of or relating to people: *human nature.* **2.** having the qualities of people as opposed to animals, divine beings, or machines: *human failings.* **3.** kind or considerate. ~*n.* **4.** a human being. [Latin *hūmānus*]

human being *n.* a man, woman, or child.

humane (hjuː'meɪn) *adj.* **1.** showing kindness and sympathy. **2.** inflicting as little pain as possible: *a humane killing.* **3.** civilizing or liberal: *humane studies.* [var. of *human*]

humanism ('hjuːmə,nɪzəm) *n.* the rejection of religion in favour of a belief in the advancement of humanity by its own efforts. —**'humanist** *n., adj.* —**,human'istic** *adj.*

humanitarian (hjuː,mænɪ'tɛərɪən) *adj.* **1.** having the interests of mankind at heart. ~*n.* **2.** a person who has the interests of mankind at heart. —**hu,mani'tarianism** *n.*

humanity (hjuː'mænɪtɪ) *n., pl.* **-ties. 1.** the human race. **2.** the quality of being human. **3.** kindness or mercy. **4.** (*pl.*) the study of literature, philosophy, and the arts.

humanize *or* **-nise** ('hjuːmə,naɪz) *vb.* to make human or humane. —**,humani'za-tion** *or* **-ni'sation** *n.*

humankind (,hjuːmən'kaɪnd) *n.* the human race; humanity.

humanly ('hjuːmənlɪ) *adv.* by human powers or means: *as fast as is humanly possible.*

humanoid ('hjuːmə,nɔɪd) *adj.* **1.** like a human being in appearance. ~*n.* **2.** (in science fiction) a robot or creature resembling a human being.

human rights *pl. n.* the basic rights of individuals to liberty, justice, etc.

humble ('hʌmb'l) *adj.* **1.** conscious of one's failings. **2.** unpretentious; lowly: *a humble cottage; my humble opinion.* ~*vb.* **3.** to cause to become humble; humiliate. [Latin *humilis* low] —**'humbly** *adv.*

humble pie *n.* **eat humble pie.** to be forced to behave humbly; be humiliated. [earlier *an umble pie*, from *numbles* offal of a deer]

humbug ('hʌm,bʌg) *n.* **1.** *Brit.* a hard peppermint sweet with a striped pattern. **2.** a person or thing that deceives. **3.** nonsense. [origin unknown]

humdinger ('hʌm,dɪŋə) *n. Slang.* an excellent person or thing. [origin unknown]

humdrum ('hʌm,drʌm) *adj.* ordinary; dull. [prob. based on *hum*]

humerus ('hjuːmərəs) *n., pl.* **-meri** (-mə,raɪ). the bone from the shoulder to the elbow. [Latin *umerus*] —**'humeral** *adj.*

humid ('hjuːmɪd) *adj.* moist; damp. [Latin *ūmidus*]

humidex ('hjuːmɪ,dɛks) *n. Canad.* a system of measuring discomfort showing the combined effect of humidity and temperature.

humidify (hjuː'mɪdɪ,faɪ) *vb.* **-fying, -fied.** to make the air in (a room) more humid or damp. —**hu'midi,fier** *n.*

humidity (hjuː'mɪdɪtɪ) *n.* **1.** dampness. **2.** a measure of the amount of moisture in the air.

humiliate (hjuː'mɪlɪ,eɪt) *vb.* to lower or hurt the dignity or pride of: *he humiliated her in front of her friends.* [Latin *humilis* humble] —**hu'mili,ating** *adj.* —**hu,mili'ation** *n.*

humility (hjuː'mɪlɪtɪ) *n.* the quality of being humble.

hummingbird ('hʌmɪŋ,bɜːd) *n.* a very small American bird with a brilliant plumage, long slender bill, and powerful wings that hum as they vibrate.

hummock ('hʌmək) *n.* a hillock. [origin unknown]

humorist ('hjuːmərɪst) *n.* a person who speaks or writes in a humorous way.

humorous ('hjuːmərəs) *adj.* funny; comical; amusing. —**'humorously** *adv.*

humour *or U.S.* **humor** ('hjuːmə) *n.* **1.** the quality of being funny. **2.** the ability to appreciate or express things that are humorous: *a good sense of humour.* **3.** situa-tions, speech, or writings that are humorous. **4.** a state of mind; mood: *good humour.* **5.** any of various fluids in the body: *aqueous humour.* ~*vb.* **6.** to indulge: *he bought it to humour his wife.* [Latin *humor liquid*] —**'humourless** *adj.*

hump (hʌmp) *n.* **1.** a rounded lump on the ground. **2.** a rounded deformity of the back. **3.** a rounded lump on the back of a camel or related animal. **4. the hump.** *Brit. informal.* a fit of sulking: *what's he got the hump about?* ~*vb.* **5.** *Slang.* to carry or heave. [prob. from *humpbacked*]

humpback ('hʌmp,bæk) *n.* **1.** same as **hunchback. 2.** Also called: **humpback whale.** a large whalebone whale with a hump on its back. **3.** Also called: **hump-back bridge.** *Brit.* a road bridge with a sharp slope on either side. —**'hump-,backed** *adj.*

humph (hʌmf) *interj.* an exclamation of annoyance or indecision.

humus ('hjuːməs) *n.* a dark brown or black mass of partially decomposed plant and animal matter in the soil. [Latin: soil]

Hun (hʌn) *n., pl.* **Huns** *or* **Hun. 1.** a member of any of several Asiatic peoples who invaded the Roman Empire in the 4th and 5th centuries A.D. **2.** *Offensive, informal.* (esp. in World War I) a German. [Old English *Hūnas*]

hunch (hʌntʃ) *n.* **1.** an intuitive guess or feeling. **2.** same as **hump.** ~*vb.* **3.** to draw (oneself or one's shoulders) up or together. [origin unknown]

hunchback ('hʌntʃ,bæk) *n.* a person who has an abnormal curvature of the spine. —**'hunch,backed** *adj.*

hundred ('hʌndrəd) *n., pl.* **-dreds** *or* **-dred. 1.** the cardinal number that is the product of ten and ten. **2.** a numeral, 100, C, representing this number. **3.** (*often pl.*) a large but unspecified number, amount, or quantity. **4.** (*pl.*) the 100 years of a specified century: *in the sixteen hundreds.* ~*det.* **5.** amounting to a hundred. [Old English] —**'hundredth** *adj., n.*

hundreds and thousands *pl. n.* tiny beads of coloured sugar, used in decorating cakes.

hundredweight ('hʌndrəd,weɪt) *n., pl.* **-weights** *or* **-weight. 1.** *Brit.* a unit of weight equal to 112 pounds (50.802 kg). **2.** *U.S. & Canad.* a unit of weight equal to 100 pounds (45.359 kg). **3.** a metric unit of weight equal to 50 kilograms.

hung (hʌŋ) *vb.* **1.** past of **hang** (except in the sense of *to execute*). ~*adj.* **2.** (of a parliament or jury) with no side having a clear majority. **3. hung over.** *Informal.* suffering the effects of a hangover.

Hungarian (hʌŋ'gɛərɪən) *n.* **1.** the official language of Hungary. **2.** a person from Hungary. ~*adj.* **3.** of or relating to Hungary, its people, or their language.

hunger ('hʌŋgə) *n.* **1.** a feeling of emptiness or weakness caused by lack of food. **2.** desire or craving: *a hunger for power.* ~*vb.* **3.** (foll. by *for* or *after*) to have a great desire (for). [Old English]

hunger strike *n.* a voluntary fast undertaken, usually by a prisoner, as a means of protest.

hungry (ˈhʌŋgrɪ) adj. -grier, -griest. 1. desiring food. 2. (foll. by for) having a craving, desire, or need for: hungry for news. 3. expressing greed, craving, or desire: hungry eyes. —ˈhungrily adv.

hunk (hʌŋk) n. 1. a large piece: a hunk of cheese. 2. Slang. a sexually attractive man. [prob. related to Flemish hunke]

hunkers (ˈhʌŋkəz) pl. n. haunches. [origin unknown]

hunt (hʌnt) vb. 1. to seek out and kill (animals) for food or sport. 2. (often foll. by for) to search (for): to hunt for a book. 3. (often foll. by down) to track in an attempt to capture (someone): to hunt down a criminal. ~n. 4. the act or an instance of hunting. 5. a party organized for the pursuit of wild animals for sport. 6. the members of such a party. [Old English huntian] —ˈhunting n.

hunter (ˈhʌntə) n. 1. a person or animal that seeks out and kills or captures game. 2. a person who looks carefully for something: a bargain-hunter. 3. a horse used in hunting. 4. a watch with a hinged metal lid or case to protect the glass.

huntsman (ˈhʌntsmən) n., pl. -men. 1. a person who hunts. 2. a person who trains hounds and manages them during a hunt.

hurdle (ˈhɜːdᵊl) n. 1. Athletics. one of a number of light barriers over which runners leap in certain events. 2. an obstacle: the next hurdle in his career. ~vb. 3. to jump (a hurdle). [Old English hyrdel] —ˈhurdler n.

hurdy-gurdy (ˈhɜːdɪˈɡɜːdɪ) n., pl. hurdy-gurdies. a mechanical musical instrument, such as a barrel organ. [prob. imit.]

hurl (hɜːl) vb. 1. to throw (something) with great force. 2. to utter (something) with force; yell: to hurl insults. [prob. imit.]

hurling (ˈhɜːlɪŋ) or **hurley** n. a traditional Irish game resembling hockey.

hurly-burly (ˈhɜːlɪˈbɜːlɪ) n. confusion or commotion. [obs. hurling uproar]

hurrah (hʊˈrɑː) or **hooray** interj., n. a cheer of joy or victory. [prob. from German hurra]

hurricane (ˈhʌrɪkᵊn) n. a severe, often destructive storm, esp. a tropical cyclone. [Spanish huracán]

hurricane lamp n. a paraffin lamp with a glass covering.

hurried (ˈhʌrɪd) adj. done with great or excessive haste. —ˈhurriedly adv.

hurry (ˈhʌrɪ) vb. -rying, -ried. 1. to hasten; rush: hurry home. 2. to speed up the completion or progress of: if you hurry your work you will make mistakes. ~n. 3. haste. 4. urgency or eagerness: in my hurry to get here I forgot my glasses. 5. in a hurry. Informal. a. easily: you won't beat him in a hurry. b. willingly: we won't go there again in a hurry. [prob. imit.]

hurt (hɜːt) vb. hurting, hurt. 1. to cause physical or mental injury to: don't hurt me. 2. to cause someone to feel pain: my leg hurts. 3. Informal. to feel pain: I'm hurt-ing all over. ~n. 4. physical or mental pain or suffering. ~adj. 5. injured or pained: a hurt knee; a hurt look. [Old French hurter to knock against] —ˈhurtful adj.

hurtle (ˈhɜːtᵊl) vb. to move very quickly or violently. [Middle English hurtlen]

husband (ˈhʌzbənd) n. 1. a woman's partner in marriage. ~vb. 2. to use (resources, finances, etc.) thriftily. [Old English húsbonda]

husbandry (ˈhʌzbəndrɪ) n. 1. farming. 2. management of resources.

hush (hʌʃ) vb. 1. to make silent; quieten; soothe. ~n. 2. stillness; silence. ~interj. 3. a plea or demand for silence. [earlier husht quiet!] —**hushed** adj.

hush-hush adj. Informal. (esp. of official work) secret; confidential.

hush money n. Slang. money given to a person to ensure that something is kept secret.

hush up vb. to suppress information or rumours about (something).

husk (hʌsk) n. 1. the outer covering of certain fruits and seeds. ~vb. 2. to remove the husk from. [prob. from Middle Dutch húskijn house]

husky¹ (ˈhʌskɪ) adj. huskier, huskiest. 1. (of a voice) slightly hoarse. 2. Informal. (of a man) big and strong. [prob. from husk, from the toughness of a corn husk] —ˈhuskily adv.

husky² (ˈhʌskɪ) n., pl. huskies. an Arctic sled dog with a thick coat and a curled tail. [prob. based on eskimo]

hussar (hʊˈzɑː) n. a member of a light cavalry regiment. [Hungarian huszár]

hussy (ˈhʌsɪ, -zɪ) n., pl. -sies. a shameless or promiscuous woman. [from hussif housewife]

hustings (ˈhʌstɪŋz) pl. n. the proceedings at a parliamentary election. [Old Norse hús house + thing assembly]

hustle (ˈhʌsᵊl) vb. 1. to shove (someone) roughly or furtively: he hustled her out of sight. 2. to deal with (something) hurriedly: to hustle legislation through. 3. U.S. & Canad. slang. (of a prostitute) to solicit clients. ~n. 4. lively activity; bustle. [Dutch husselen to shake]

hut (hʌt) n. a small house or shelter. [French hutte]

hutch (hʌtʃ) n. a cage for small animals. [Old French huche]

hyacinth (ˈhaɪəsɪnθ) n. a plant with bell-shaped sweet-smelling flowers. [Greek huakinthos]

hyaena (haɪˈiːnə) n. same as **hyena**.

hybrid (ˈhaɪbrɪd) n. 1. an animal or plant resulting from a cross between two different types of animal or plant. 2. anything of mixed ancestry. ~adj. 3. of mixed origin. [Latin hibrida]

hybridize or **-ise** (ˈhaɪbrɪˌdaɪz) vb. to produce or cause (species) to produce hybrids; crossbreed. —ˌhybridiˈzation or -iˈsation n.

hydatid disease (ˈhaɪdətɪd) n. a condition caused by the presence of bladder-like cysts (**hydatids**) in the liver, lungs, or brain. [Greek *hudatis* watery sac]

hydra ('haɪdrə) *n.* **1.** a freshwater polyp with tentacles around the mouth. **2.** a persistent trouble. [Greek *hudra* water serpent]

hydrangea (haɪ'dreɪndʒə) *n.* a shrub with large clusters of white, pink, or blue flowers. [Greek *hudōr* water + *angeion* vessel]

hydrant ('haɪdrənt) *n.* an outlet from a water main, from which water can be tapped for fighting fires.

hydrate ('haɪdreɪt) *Chem.* ~*n.* **1.** a compound containing water chemically combined with a substance: *chloral hydrate.* ~*vb.* **2.** to treat or impregnate (a substance) with water or (of a substance) to be treated or impregnated with water. —**hy'dration** *n.*

hydraulic (haɪ'drɒlɪk) *adj.* operated by pressure transmitted through a pipe by a liquid, such as water or oil. [Greek *hudōr* water + *aulos* pipe] —**hy'draulically** *adv.*

hydraulics (haɪ'drɒlɪks) *n.* (*functioning as sing.*) the study of the mechanical properties of fluids as they apply to practical engineering.

hydride ('haɪdraɪd) *n. Chem.* a compound of hydrogen with another element.

hydro[1] ('haɪdrəʊ) *n., pl.* -**dros.** *Brit.* a hotel offering facilities for hydropathic treatment.

hydro[2] ('haɪdrəʊ) *adj.* short for **hydroelectric.**

hydro- *or before a vowel* **hydr-** *combining form.* **1.** indicating water or fluid: *hydrodynamics.* **2.** indicating hydrogen in a chemical compound: *hydrochloric acid.* [Greek *hudōr* water]

hydrocarbon (ˌhaɪdrəʊ'kɑːb'n) *n. Chem.* a compound containing only carbon and hydrogen.

hydrocephalus (ˌhaɪdrəʊ'sefələs) *n.* accumulation of fluid within the cavities of the brain. [Greek *hudōr* water + *kephalē* head] —**hydrocephalic** (ˌhaɪdrəʊsɪ'fælɪk) *adj.*

hydrochloric acid (ˌhaɪdrə'klɒrɪk) *n. Chem.* a solution of hydrogen chloride in water: a strong acid used in many industrial and laboratory processes.

hydrodynamics (ˌhaɪdrəʊdaɪ'næmɪks, -dɪ-) *n.* (*functioning as sing.*) the branch of science concerned with the mechanical properties of fluids.

hydroelectric (ˌhaɪdrəʊɪ'lektrɪk) *adj.* **1.** generated by the pressure of falling water: *hydroelectric power.* **2.** of the generation of electricity by water pressure: *a hydroelectric scheme.* —**hydroelectricity** (ˌhaɪdrəʊɪlek'trɪsɪtɪ) *n.*

hydrofoil ('haɪdrə,fɔɪl) *n.* **1.** a fast light vessel the hull of which is raised out of the water on one or more pairs of fins. **2.** any of these fins.

hydrogen ('haɪdrɪdʒən) *n. Chem.* a colourless gas that burns easily and is the lightest element in the universe. It occurs in water and in most organic compounds. Symbol: H [HYDRO- + -*gen* (producing); because its combustion produces water] —**hydrogenous** (haɪ'drɒdʒɪnəs) *adj.*

hydrogenate (haɪ'drɒdʒɪ,neɪt) *vb. Chem.* to combine (a substance) with hydrogen: *hydrogenated vegetable oil.* —,**hydrogen'ation** *n.*

hydrogen bomb *n.* an extremely powerful bomb in which energy is released by fusion of hydrogen nuclei to give helium nuclei.

hydrogen peroxide *n.* a colourless oily unstable liquid chemical used as a bleach.

hydrogen sulphide *n.* a colourless poisonous gas with an odour of rotten eggs.

hydrography (haɪ'drɒgrəfɪ) *n.* the study of the oceans, seas, and rivers. —**hy'drographer** *n.* —**hydrographic** (ˌhaɪdrə'græfɪk) *adj.*

hydrology (haɪ'drɒlədʒɪ) *n.* the study of the distribution, conservation, and use, of the water of the earth and its atmosphere.

hydrolysis (haɪ'drɒlɪsɪs) *n. Chem.* a process of decomposition in which a compound reacts with water to produce other compounds. [Greek *hudōr* water + *lusis* loosening]

hydrometer (haɪ'drɒmɪtə) *n.* an instrument for measuring the density of a liquid.

hydropathy (haɪ'drɒpəθɪ) *n.* a method of treating disease by the use of large quantities of water both internally and externally. [Greek *hudōr* water + *patheia* suffering] —**hydropathic** (ˌhaɪdrəʊ'pæθɪk) *adj.*

hydrophilic (ˌhaɪdrəʊ'fɪlɪk) *adj. Chem.* tending to dissolve in or mix with water: *a hydrophilic colloid.*

hydrophobia (ˌhaɪdrə'fəʊbɪə) *n.* **1.** same as **rabies.** **2.** (esp. of a person with rabies) a fear of drinking fluids. —,**hydro'phobic** *adj.*

hydroplane ('haɪdrəʊ,pleɪn) *n.* **1.** a motorboat that raises its hull out of the water at high speeds. **2.** a fin on the hull of a submarine for controlling its vertical motion.

hydroponics (ˌhaɪdrəʊ'pɒnɪks) *n.* (*functioning as sing.*) a method of growing plants in gravel, etc., through which water containing the necessary nutrients is pumped. [HYDRO- + (*geo*)*ponics* science of agriculture]

hydrosphere ('haɪdrə,sfɪə) *n.* the watery part of the earth's surface.

hydrostatics (ˌhaɪdrəʊ'stætɪks) *n.* (*functioning as sing.*) the branch of science concerned with the properties and behaviour of fluids that are not in motion. —,**hydro'static** *adj.*

hydrotherapy (ˌhaɪdrəʊ'θerəpɪ) *n. Med.* the treatment of certain diseases by the external application of water.

hydrous ('haɪdrəs) *adj.* containing water.

hydroxide (haɪ'drɒksaɪd) *n. Chem.* a compound containing a hydroxyl group or ion.

hydroxyl (haɪ'drɒksɪl) *n.* (*modifier*) *Chem.* of or containing the monovalent group -OH or the ion OH⁻: *a hydroxyl group or radical.*

hyena *or* **hyaena** (haɪ'iːnə) *n.* a meat-eating doglike mammal of Africa and S Asia. [Greek *hus* hog]

hygiene ('haɪdʒiːn) *n.* **1.** clean or healthy practices: *personal hygiene.* **2.** Also called: **hygienics.** the science concerned with the maintenance of health. [Greek *hugieinē*] —**hy'gienic** *adj.* —**hy'gienically** *adv.* —**'hygienist** *n.*

hygrometer (haɪ'grɒmɪtə) *n.* an instrument for measuring humidity. [Greek *hugros* wet]

hygroscope ('haɪgrə,skəʊp) *n.* a device that indicates the humidity of the air without measuring it. [Greek *hugros* wet + *skopein* to observe]

hygroscopic (,haɪgrə'skɒpɪk) *adj.* (of a substance) tending to absorb water from the air.

hymen ('haɪmɛn) *n. Anat.* a membrane that partly covers the entrance to the vagina and is usually ruptured when sexual intercourse takes place for the first time. [Greek: membrane]

hymenopterous (,haɪmɪ'nɒptərəs) *adj.* of or belonging to an order of insects with two pairs of membranous wings. [Greek *humen* membrane + *pteron* wing]

hymn (hɪm) *n.* a Christian song of praise sung to God or a saint. [Greek *humnos*]

hymnal ('hɪmn°l) *n.* a book of hymns. Also: **hymn book.**

hymnody ('hɪmnədɪ) *n.* **1.** the composition or singing of hymns. **2.** hymns collectively.

hymnology (hɪm'nɒlədʒɪ) *n.* the study of hymn composition. —**hym'nologist** *n.*

hype (haɪp) *Slang.* ~*n.* **1.** intensive or exaggerated publicity or sales promotion. ~*vb.* **2.** to market or promote (a commodity) using intensive or exaggerated publicity. [origin unknown]

hyped up *adj. Old-fashioned slang.* stimulated or excited by or as if by drug.

hyper ('haɪpə) *adj. Informal.* overactive; overexcited.

hyper- *prefix.* above, over, or in excess: *hypercritical.* [Greek *huper* over]

hyperactive (,haɪpər'æktɪv) *adj.* abnormally active.

hyperbola (haɪ'pɜːbələ) *n. Geom.* a conic section formed by a plane that cuts a cone at a steeper angle to its base than its side. [Greek *huperbolē*]

hyperbole (haɪ'pɜːbəlɪ) *n.* a deliberate exaggeration used for effect: *he embraced her a thousand times.* [Greek *huper* over + *ballein* to throw]

hyperbolic (,haɪpə'bɒlɪk) *or* **hyperbolical** *adj.* of a hyperbola or a hyperbole.

hypercritical (,haɪpə'krɪtɪk°l) *adj.* excessively critical.

hyperglycaemia *or U.S.* **hyperglycemia** (,haɪpəglaɪ'siːmɪə) *n. Pathol.* an abnormally large amount of sugar in the blood. [Greek *huper* over + *glukus* sweet]

hypermarket ('haɪpə,mɑːkɪt) *n.* a huge self-service store. [translation of French *hypermarché*]

hypersensitive (,haɪpə'sɛnsɪtɪv) *adj.* **1.** having unduly vulnerable feelings. **2.** ab-

normally sensitive to an allergen, a drug, or high or low temperatures.

hypersonic (,haɪpə'sɒnɪk) *adj.* having a speed of at least five times the speed of sound.

hypertension (,haɪpə'tɛnʃən) *n. Pathol.* abnormally high blood pressure.

hypertrophy (haɪ'pɜːtrəfɪ) *n., pl.* **-phies.** enlargement of an organ or part resulting from an increase in the size of the cells. [Greek *huper* over + *trophe* nourishment]

hyperventilation (,haɪpə,vɛntɪ'leɪʃən) *n.* an increase in the rate of breathing at rest. —,**hyper'venti,late** *vb.*

hyphen ('haɪf°n) *n.* the punctuation mark (-), used to separate parts of compound words and between syllables of a word split between two consecutive lines. [Greek *huphen* together]

hyphenate ('haɪf°,neɪt) *vb.* to separate (words) with a hyphen. —,**hyphen'a-tion** *n.*

hypnosis (hɪp'nəʊsɪs) *n.* an artificially induced state of relaxation in which the mind is more than usually receptive to suggestion.

hypnotherapy (,hɪpnəʊ'θɛrəpɪ) *n.* the use of hypnosis in the treatment of emotional and mental problems.

hypnotic (hɪp'nɒtɪk) *adj.* **1.** of or producing hypnosis or sleep. **2.** having an effect resembling hypnosis: *a hypnotic voice.* ~*n.* **3.** a drug that induces sleep. [Greek *hupnos* sleep] —**hyp'notically** *adv.*

hypnotism ('hɪpnə,tɪzəm) *n.* **1.** the practice of hypnosis. **2.** the process of inducing hypnosis. —**'hypnotist** *n.*

hypnotize *or* **-tise** ('hɪpnə,taɪz) *vb.* **1.** to induce hypnosis in (a person). **2.** to charm or beguile; fascinate.

hypo- *or before a vowel* **hyp-** *prefix.* beneath; less than: *hypodermic.* [Greek *hupo* under]

hypoallergenic (,haɪpəʊ,ælə'dʒɛnɪk) *adj.* not likely to cause an allergic reaction.

hypocaust ('haɪpə,kɔːst) *n.* an ancient Roman heating system in which hot air circulated under the floor and between double walls. [Latin *hypocaustum*]

hypochondria (,haɪpə'kɒndrɪə) *n.* abnormal anxiety concerning one's health. [Late Latin: abdomen, supposedly the seat of melancholy]

hypochondriac (,haɪpə'kɒndrɪ,æk) *n.* a person suffering from hypochondria.

hypocrisy (hɪ'pɒkrəsɪ) *n., pl.* **-sies.** **1.** the practice of claiming to have standards or beliefs that are contrary to one's real character or actual behaviour. **2.** an act or instance of this.

hypocrite ('hɪpəkrɪt) *n.* a person who pretends to be what he is not. [Greek *hupokrinein* to pretend] —,**hypo'critical** *adj.*

hypodermic (,haɪpə'dɜːmɪk) *adj.* **1.** used for injecting. ~*n.* **2.** a hypodermic syringe or needle.

hypodermic syringe *n. Med.* a syringe consisting of a hollow cylinder, a piston, and a hollow needle, used for withdrawing blood samples or injecting drugs under the skin.

hypotension (ˌhaɪpəʊˈtɛnʃən) n. *Pathol.* abnormally low blood pressure.

hypotenuse (haɪˈpɒtɪˌnjuːz) n. the side in a right-angled triangle that is opposite the right angle. [Greek *hupoteinousa grammē* subtending line]

hypothermia (ˌhaɪpəʊˈθɜːmɪə) n. *Pathol.* an abnormally low body temperature, as a result of exposure to cold weather.

hypothesis (haɪˈpɒθɪsɪs) n., pl. **-ses** (-ˌsiːz). a suggested explanation for a group of facts, accepted either as a basis for further verification or as likely to be true. [Greek *hupotithenai* to propose, lit.: put under] —**hyˈpotheˌsize** or **-ise** vb.

hypothetical (ˌhaɪpəˈθɛtɪkᵊl) adj. assumed or thought to exist. —ˌhypoˈthetically adv.

hyssop (ˈhɪsəp) n. **1.** an aromatic herb used in folk medicine. **2.** a Biblical plant, used for sprinkling in the ritual practices of the Hebrews. [Greek *hussōpos*]

hysterectomy (ˌhɪstəˈrɛktəmɪ) n., pl. **-mies.** surgical removal of the womb. [Greek *hustera* womb + *temnein* to cut]

hysteria (hɪˈstɪərɪə) n. **1.** a mental disorder marked by emotional outbursts and, often, symptoms such as paralysis. **2.** any frenzied emotional state, as of laughter or crying. [Greek *hustera* womb: from the belief that hysteria in women originated in disorders of the womb]

hysteric (hɪˈstɛrɪk) n. a hysterical person.

hysterical (hɪˈstɛrɪkᵊl) adj. **1.** suggesting hysteria: *hysterical cries.* **2.** suffering from hysteria. **3.** *Informal.* wildly funny. —hysˈterically adv.

hysterics (hɪˈstɛrɪks) n. (*functioning as pl. or sing.*) **1.** an attack of hysteria. **2.** *Informal.* wild uncontrollable bursts of laughter.

Hz hertz.

I

i *or* **I** (aɪ) *n., pl.* **i's, I's,** *or* **Is.** the ninth letter and third vowel of the English alphabet.

i the imaginary number √−1.

I[1] (aɪ) *pron.* used by a speaker or writer to refer to himself as the subject of a verb. [Old English *ic*]

I[2] **1.** *Chem.* iodine. **2.** the Roman numeral for one.

I. 1. Independent. **2.** Institute. **3.** International. **4.** Island; Isle.

IA *or* **Ia.** Iowa.

iamb (ˈaɪæm) *or* **iambus** (aɪˈæmbəs) *n., pl.* **iambs** *or* **iambuses.** *Prosody.* a metrical foot of two syllables, a short one followed by a long one. [Greek *iambos*]

iambic (aɪˈæmbɪk) *Prosody.* ~*adj.* **1.** of or using an iamb. ~*n.* **2.** a metrical foot, line, or stanza consisting of iambs.

IBA (in Britain) Independent Broadcasting Authority.

Iberian (aɪˈbɪərɪən) *n.* **1.** a person from the Iberian Peninsula in SW Europe; a Spaniard or Portuguese. ~*adj.* **2.** of the Iberian Peninsula, its inhabitants, or any of their languages.

ibex (ˈaɪbɛks) *n., pl.* **ibexes** *or* **ibex.** a wild goat of the mountainous regions of Europe, Asia, and North Africa, which has large backward-curving horns. [Latin: chamois]

ibid. (referring to a book, page, or passage previously cited) in the same place. [Latin *ibidem* in the same place]

ibis (ˈaɪbɪs) *n., pl.* **ibises** *or* **ibis.** a large wading bird with a long thin curved bill. [Egyptian *hby*]

Ibo (ˈiːbəʊ) *n.* **1.** (*pl.* **Ibos** *or* **Ibo**) a member of an African people of S Nigeria. **2.** their language.

ICBM intercontinental ballistic missile.

ice (aɪs) *n.* **1.** water that has frozen and become solid. **2.** a portion of ice cream. **3. break the ice.** to relax the atmosphere, esp. between strangers. **4. on ice.** in readiness or reserve. **5. on thin ice.** unsafe; dangerous. ~*vb.* **6.** (often foll. by *up or over*) to form ice; freeze. **7.** to cool or chill with ice. **8.** to cover (a cake) with icing. [Old English *īs*] —**iced** *adj.*

ice age *n.* same as **glacial period.**

iceberg (ˈaɪsbɜːɡ) *n.* **1.** a large mass of ice floating in the sea. **2. tip of the iceberg.** the small visible part of a problem that is much larger. [prob. Middle Dutch *ijsberg* ice mountain]

iceberg lettuce *n.* a type of lettuce with very crisp pale leaves tightly enfolded.

icebox (ˈaɪsˌbɒks) *n.* **1.** a compartment in a refrigerator for making or storing ice. **2.** an insulated cabinet packed with ice for keeping food cold. **3.** *U.S. & Canad.* a refrigerator.

icebreaker (ˈaɪsˌbreɪkə) *n.* a ship designed to break through ice.

icecap (ˈaɪsˌkæp) *n.* a thick mass of glacial ice that permanently covers an area.

ice cream *n.* a sweet frozen food, made from cream, milk, or a custard base, flavoured in various ways.

ice field *n.* a large expanse of floating sea ice.

ice floe *n.* a sheet of ice, of variable size, floating in the sea.

ice hockey *n.* a game played on ice by two teams wearing skates, who try to drive a flat puck into their opponents' goal with long sticks.

Icelandic (aɪsˈlændɪk) *adj.* **1.** of Iceland, its people, or their language. ~*n.* **2.** the official language of Iceland.

ice lolly *n. Brit. informal.* a water ice or an ice cream on a stick.

ice pack *n.* **1.** a bag or folded cloth containing crushed ice, applied to a part of the body to reduce swelling. **2.** same as **pack ice.**

ice skate *n.* **1.** a boot with a steel blade fitted to the sole which enables the wearer to glide over ice. ~*vb.* **ice-skate. 2.** to glide over ice on ice skates. —**ˈice-ˌskater** *n.*

ichthyology (ˌɪkθɪˈɒlədʒɪ) *n.* the study of fishes. [Greek *ikhthus* fish + -LOGY] —**ichthyological** (ˌɪkθɪəˈlɒdʒɪkˀl) *adj.* —ˌ**ichthyˈologist** *n.*

ICI Imperial Chemical Industries.

icicle (ˈaɪsɪkˀl) *n.* a hanging spike of ice formed by dripping water freezing as it falls. [*ice* + Old English *gicel* icicle]

icing (ˈaɪsɪŋ) *n.* **1.** Also (esp. U.S. and Canad.): **frosting.** a mixture of sugar and water or egg whites used to coat and decorate cakes. **2. icing on the cake.** an unexpected extra or bonus. **3.** the formation of ice on a ship or aircraft.

icing sugar *n. Brit.* a very finely ground sugar used for making icing or sweets.

icon (ˈaɪkɒn) *n.* a picture of Christ, the Virgin Mary, or a saint, venerated in the Orthodox Church. [Greek *eikōn* image]

iconoclast (aɪˈkɒnəˌklæst) *n.* **1.** a person who attacks established or traditional ideas or principles. **2.** a destroyer of religious images or objects. [Late Greek *eikōn* icon + *klastes* breaker] —**iˌcono-ˈclastic** *adj.* —**iˈconoˌclasm** *n.*

icosahedron (ˌaɪkɒsəˈhiːdrən) *n., pl.* **-drons** *or* **-dra** (-drə). a solid figure with 20 faces. [Greek *eikosi* twenty + -*edron* -sided]

icy (ˈaɪsɪ) *adj.* **icier, iciest. 1.** made of, covered with, or containing ice. **2.** like ice. **3.** freezing or very cold. **4.** cold or reserved in manner; aloof. —**ˈicily** *adv.* —**ˈiciness** *n.*

id (ɪd) *n. Psychoanal.* the primitive instincts and energies in the unconscious mind that underlie all psychological impulses. [Latin: it]

ID **1.** Idaho. **2.** identification.

'd (aɪd) I had *or* I would.

idea (aɪ'dɪə) *n.* **1.** any product of mental activity; thought. **2.** the thought of something: *the idea appals me.* **3.** a belief; opinion. **4.** a scheme, intention, or plan. **5.** a vague notion; inkling: *he had no idea of the truth.* **6.** a person's conception of something: *her idea of honesty is not the same as mine.* **7.** aim or purpose: *the idea of the game is to discover the murderer.* **8.** *Philosophy.* (in Plato) a universal model of which all things in the same class are only imperfect imitations. [Greek: model, outward appearance]

ideal (aɪ'dɪəl) *n.* **1.** a conception of something that is perfect. **2.** a person or thing considered to represent perfection. **3.** something existing only as an idea. ~*adj.* **4.** conforming to an ideal: *he is the ideal person for the job.* **5.** of, involving, or existing only as an idea; imaginary: *an ideal world.* —**i'deally** *adv.*

idealism (aɪ'dɪə,lɪzəm) *n.* **1.** belief in or striving towards ideals. **2.** the tendency to represent things in their ideal forms, rather than as they are. **3.** *Philosophy.* the doctrine that material objects and the external world do not exist in reality, but are creations of the mind. —**i'dealist** *n.* —**i,deal'istic** *adj.*

idealize *or* **-ise** (aɪ'dɪə,laɪz) *vb.* to consider or represent (something) as ideal or more nearly perfect than is true. —**i,deali-'zation** *or* **-i'sation** *n.*

idée fixe (ˌiːdeɪ 'fiːks) *n., pl.* **idées fixes** (ˌiːdeɪ 'fiːks). a fixed idea; obsession. [French]

idem (ˈaɪdɛm, ˈɪdɛm) *pron., adj.* the same: used to refer to an article, chapter, or book previously cited. [Latin]

identical (aɪ'dɛntɪkəl) *adj.* **1.** that is the same: *we got the identical hotel room as last year.* **2.** exactly alike or equal. **3.** (of twins) developed from a single fertilized ovum that has split into two, and thus of the same sex and very much alike. [Latin *idem* the same] —**i'dentically** *adv.*

identification (aɪ,dɛntɪfɪ'keɪʃən) *n.* **1.** an identifying or being identified. **2.** something that identifies a person or thing.

identification parade *n.* a group of persons, including one suspected of a crime, assembled to discover whether a witness can identify the suspect.

identify (aɪ'dɛntɪ,faɪ) *vb.* **-fying, -fied.** **1.** to prove or recognize as being a certain person or thing; determine the identity of. **2.** to consider or treat as the same. **3.** to connect or associate closely: *he was identified with a revolutionary group.* **4.** (often foll. by *with*) to understand and sympathize with a person or group because one regards oneself as having characteristics in common with them. —**i'denti,fiable** *adj.*

identikit (aɪ'dɛntɪ,kɪt) *n. Trademark.* a composite picture, assembled from descriptions given, of a person wanted by the police.

identity (aɪ'dɛntɪtɪ) *n., pl.* **-ties.** **1.** the state of being a specified person or thing:

the identity of the killer is still unknown. **2.** the individual characteristics by which a person or thing is recognized; individuality or personality. **3.** the state of being the same: *linked by the identity of their tastes.* **4.** *Maths.* Also called: **identity element.** a member of a set that when combined with any other member of the set, leaves it unchanged: the identity for multiplication of numbers is 1. [Latin *idem* the same]

ideogram (ˈɪdɪəʊ,græm) *or* **ideograph** (ˈɪdɪəʊ,grɑːf) *n.* a character or symbol that directly represents a concept or thing, rather than the sounds that form its name. [Greek *idea* idea + *gramma* a drawing]

ideology (ˌaɪdɪ'ɒlədʒɪ) *n., pl.* **-gies.** the doctrines, opinions, or way of thinking of a person, group, or nation. [from *ideo-* + -LOGY] —**ideological** (ˌaɪdɪə'lɒdʒɪkʰl) *adj.* —**ˌide'ologist** *n.*

ides (aɪdz) *n.* (*functioning as sing.*) (in the ancient Roman calendar) the 15th day in March, May, July, and October and the 13th of the other months. [Latin *īdūs*]

idiocy (ˈɪdɪəsɪ) *n., pl.* **-cies.** **1.** (*not in technical usage*) severe mental retardation. **2.** foolishness; stupidity. **3.** a foolish act or remark.

idiom (ˈɪdɪəm) *n.* **1.** a group of words which, when used together, have a different meaning from the one suggested by the individual words, e.g. *it was raining cats and dogs.* **2.** linguistic usage that is grammatical and natural to native speakers. **3.** the characteristic vocabulary or usage of a specific person or group. **4.** the characteristic artistic style of an individual or school. [Greek *idios* private, separate] —**idiomatic** (ˌɪdɪə'mætɪk) *adj.*

idiosyncrasy (ˌɪdɪəʊ'sɪŋkrəsɪ) *n., pl.* **-sies.** a personal peculiarity, habit, or type of behaviour; quirk. [Greek *idios* private, separate + *sunkrasis* mixture] —**idiosyncratic** (ˌɪdɪəʊsɪŋ'krætɪk) *adj.*

idiot (ˈɪdɪət) *n.* **1.** a person with severe mental retardation. **2.** a foolish or senseless person. [Greek *idiōtēs* private person, ignoramus] —**idiotic** (ˌɪdɪ'ɒtɪk) *adj.* —**,idi'otically** *adv.*

idle (ˈaɪdʰl) *adj.* **1.** unemployed or unoccupied; inactive. **2.** not operating or being used. **3.** not wanting to work; lazy. **4.** frivolous or trivial: *idle pleasures.* **5.** ineffective or vain: *it would be idle to look for a solution now.* **6.** without basis; unfounded: *idle rumours.* ~*vb.* **7.** (often foll. by *away*) to waste or pass (time) in idleness; be idle. **8.** (of an engine) to run at low speed without transmitting any power. [Old English *īdel*] —**idleness** *n.* —**idler** *n.* —**idly** *adv.*

idol (ˈaɪdʰl) *n.* **1.** an image of a god used as an object of worship. **2.** an object of excessive devotion or admiration. [Latin: image]

idolatry (aɪ'dɒlətrɪ) *n.* **1.** the worship of idols. **2.** excessive devotion or reverence. —**i'dolater** *n.* —**i'dolatrous** *adj.*

idolize *or* **-ise** (ˈaɪdə,laɪz) *vb.* **1.** to admire or revere greatly. **2.** to worship as an idol. —**,idoli'zation** *or* **-i'sation** *n.*

idyll *or U.S.* (*sometimes*) **idyl** (ˈɪdɪl) *n.* **1.** a poem or prose work describing a simple, pleasant rural or pastoral scene. **2.** such a scene. [Greek *eidullion*] —**i'dyllic** *adj*.

i.e. that is to say. [Latin *id est*]

if (if) *conj.* **1.** in the event that, or on condition that: *if you try hard it might work.* **2.** used to introduce an indirect question to which the answer is either *yes* or *no*; whether: *I asked if I could help.* **3.** even though: *an attractive if awkward girl.* **4.** used to introduce an unfulfilled wish, with *only: if only you had told me.* —*n.* **5.** a condition or stipulation: *I won't have any ifs or buts.* [Old English *gif*]

iffy ('ɪfɪ) *adj. Informal.* full of uncertainty.

igloo ('ɪgluː) *n., pl.* **-loos.** a dome-shaped Eskimo house, built of blocks of solid snow. [Eskimo *igldu*]

igneous ('ɪgnɪəs) *adj.* **1.** (of rocks) formed by volcanic action. **2.** of or like fire. [Latin *ignis* fire]

ignis fatuus ('ɪgnɪs 'fætjʊəs) *n., pl.* **ignes fatui** ('ɪgniːz 'fætjʊˌaɪ). same as **will-o'-the-wisp.** [Medieval Latin, lit.: foolish fire]

ignite (ɪg'naɪt) *vb.* to catch fire or set fire to. [Latin *ignis* fire] —**ig'nitable** *or* **ig'nitible** *adj*.

ignition (ɪg'nɪʃən) *n.* **1.** an igniting or the process of igniting. **2.** the system used to ignite the fuel in an internal-combustion engine.

ignoble (ɪg'nəʊbᵊl) *adj.* **1.** dishonourable; base; despicable. **2.** of low birth or origins. [Latin *in-* not + *nobilis* noble] —**ig'nobly** *adv*.

ignominy ('ɪgnəˌmɪnɪ) *n., pl.* **-minies.** disgrace or public shame; dishonour. [Latin *ignōminia* disgrace] —**igno'minious** *adj*.

ignoramus (ˌɪgnə'reɪməs) *n., pl.* **-muses.** an ignorant person; fool. [Latin, lit.: we have no knowledge of]

ignorance ('ɪgnərəns) *n.* lack of knowledge or education; the state of being ignorant.

ignorant ('ɪgnərənt) *adj.* **1.** lacking in knowledge or education; unenlightened. **2.** (often foll. by *of*) lacking in awareness or knowledge (of): *ignorant of the law.* **3.** uncouth through lack of knowledge or awareness: *an ignorant remark.*

ignore (ɪg'nɔː) *vb.* to refuse to notice; disregard deliberately. [Latin *ignōrāre* not to know]

iguana (ɪ'gwɑːnə) *n.* a large tropical tree lizard of the W Indies and S America having a greyish-green body with a row of spines along the back. [S American Indian *iwana*]

ikebana (ˌiːkə'bɑːnə) *n.* the Japanese art of flower arrangement. [Japanese]

IL Illinois.

il- same as **in-¹** and **in-².**

ileum ('ɪlɪəm) *n.* the third and lowest part of the small intestine. [Latin *Ilium* flank, groin]

ilex ('aɪlɛks) *n.* **1.** same as **holly. 2.** same as **holm oak.** [Latin]

ilium ('ɪlɪəm) *n., pl.* **-ia** (-ɪə). the uppermost

and widest of the three sections of the hipbone.

ilk (ɪlk) *n.* a type; class; sort: *people of that ilk should not be allowed here.* [Old English *ilca* the same family]

ill (ɪl) *adj.* **worse, worst. 1.** not in good health; sick. **2.** bad, harmful, or hostile: *ill effect; ill will.* **3.** promising an unfavourable outcome: *ill omen.* **4. ill at ease.** unable to relax; uncomfortable. —*n.* **5.** evil or harm; misfortune; trouble. —*adv.* **6.** badly, wrongly: *the title ill befits him.* **7.** with difficulty; hardly: *he can ill afford the money.* [Old Norse *illr* bad]

ill. **1.** illustrated. **2.** illustration.

Ill. Illinois.

I'll (aɪl) I will *or* I shall.

ill-advised *adj.* **1.** (of a person) acting without reasonable care or thought. **2.** (of a plan or action) badly thought out; unwise.

ill-bred *adj.* badly brought up; lacking good manners. —**ill-'breeding** *n*.

ill-disposed *adj.* (often foll. by *towards*) unfriendly or unsympathetic; malicious.

illegal (ɪ'liːgᵊl) *adj.* unlawful; against the law. —**il'legally** *adv*. —**ille'gality** *n*.

illegible (ɪ'lɛdʒɪbᵊl) *adj.* unable to be read or deciphered. —**il,legi'bility** *n*.

illegitimate (ˌɪlɪ'dʒɪtɪmɪt) *adj.* **1.** born of parents who were not married to each other at the time of birth; bastard. **2.** illegal; unlawful. —**ille'gitimacy** *n*.

ill-fated *adj.* doomed or unlucky.

ill-favoured *adj.* unattractive or repulsive in appearance.

ill-founded *adj.* not based on proper proof or evidence.

ill-gotten *adj.* obtained dishonestly or illegally: *ill-gotten gains.*

ill-health *n.* the condition of being unwell; poor health.

illiberal (ɪ'lɪbərəl) *adj.* **1.** narrow-minded; prejudiced; intolerant. **2.** not generous; mean. **3.** lacking in culture or refinement. —**il,liber'ality** *n*.

illicit (ɪ'lɪsɪt) *adj.* **1.** same as **illegal. 2.** not allowed or approved by the social customs of a country: *illicit sexual relations.*

illiterate (ɪ'lɪtərɪt) *adj.* **1.** unable to read and write. **2.** uneducated or ignorant: *scientifically illiterate.* —*n.* **3.** an illiterate person. —**il'literacy** *n*.

ill-mannered *adj.* having bad manners; rude.

illness ('ɪlnɪs) *n.* **1.** a disease or indisposition; sickness. **2.** a state of ill health.

illogical (ɪ'lɒdʒɪkᵊl) *adj.* **1.** senseless or unreasonable. **2.** not following logical principles. —**illogicality** (ɪˌlɒdʒɪ'kælɪtɪ) *n*. —**il'logically** *adv*.

ill-starred *adj.* unlucky; unfortunate; ill-fated.

ill-timed *adj.* happening at or done at an unsuitable time.

ill-treat *vb.* to treat (someone or something) cruelly or harshly; maltreat. —**ill-'treatment** *n*.

illuminant (ɪ'luːmɪnənt) *n.* **1.** something

that gives off light. ~*adj.* **2.** giving off light.

illuminate (ɪˈluːmɪˌneɪt) *vb.* **1.** to give light to; light up. **2.** to make easily understood; clarify: *the book illuminates many obscure points.* **3.** to decorate with lights. **4.** to decorate (an initial letter or manuscript) with designs of gold, silver, or bright colours. [Latin *illūmināre* to light up] —**ilˈlumiˌnating** *adj.* —**ilˈluminative** *adj.*

illumination (ɪˌluːmɪˈneɪʃən) *n.* **1.** an illuminating or being illuminated. **2.** a source of light; lighting. **3.** (*pl.*) *Chiefly Brit.* lights used as decorations in streets or towns. **4.** the decoration in colours, gold, or silver used on some manuscripts.

illumine (ɪˈluːmɪn) *vb.* same as **illuminate.**

illusion (ɪˈluːʒən) *n.* **1.** a false appearance or deceptive impression of reality: *the mirror gives an illusion of depth.* **2.** a false or misleading idea or belief; delusion. [Latin *illūsiō* deceit] —**ilˈlusory** *or* **ilˈlusive** *adj.*

illusionist (ɪˈluːʒənɪst) *n.* a conjurer; magician who performs sleight-of-hand tricks.

illustrate (ˈɪləˌstreɪt) *vb.* **1.** to clarify or explain by use of examples or comparisons. **2.** to be an example of. **3.** to explain or decorate (a book or text) with pictures. [Latin *illustrare* to make light, explain] —**ˈillusˌtrative** *adj.* —**ˈillusˌtrator** *n.*

illustration (ˌɪləˈstreɪʃən) *n.* **1.** pictorial matter used to explain or decorate a text. **2.** an example: *an illustration of his ability.* **3.** an illustrating or being illustrated.

illustrious (ɪˈlʌstrɪəs) *adj.* glorious; famous and distinguished. [Latin *illustris* bright, famous]

ill will *n.* hostile feeling; enmity; antagonism.

I'm (aɪm) I am.

im- same as **in-**[1] and **in-**[2].

image (ˈɪmɪdʒ) *n.* **1.** a representation of a person or thing, esp. in sculpture. **2.** an optical reproduction of an object, formed by the lens of an eye or camera or by a mirror. **3.** a person or thing that resembles another closely; double or copy. **4.** a mental picture; idea produced by the imagination or memory. **5.** the appearance or impression given to the public by a person or organization: *a politician's image.* **6.** a personification of a specified quality; epitome: *the image of good breeding.* **7.** a simile or metaphor. ~*vb.* **8.** to picture in the mind; imagine. **9.** to mirror or reflect an image of. **10.** to portray or describe. [Latin *imāgō*]

imagery (ˈɪmɪdʒrɪ, -dʒərɪ) *n., pl.* **-ries. 1.** figurative or descriptive language in a literary work. **2.** images collectively, esp. statues or carvings. **3.** mental images.

imaginary (ɪˈmædʒɪnərɪ, -dʒɪnrɪ) *adj.* **1.** existing in the imagination; unreal. **2.** *Maths.* relating to the square root of a negative number.

imagination (ɪˌmædʒɪˈneɪʃən) *n.* **1.** the faculty or action of producing mental images of what is not present or in one's experience. **2.** mental creative ability.

imaginative (ɪˈmædʒɪnətɪv) *adj.* **1.** produced by or showing a creative imagination. **2.** having a vivid imagination.

imagine (ɪˈmædʒɪn) *vb.* **1.** to form a mental image of. **2.** to think, believe, or guess: *I can't imagine what's happened to him.* [Latin *imāginārī*] —**imˈaginable** *adj.*

imago (ɪˈmeɪɡəʊ) *n., pl.* **imagoes** *or* **imagines** (ɪˈmædʒəˌniːz). an adult sexually mature insect. [Latin: likeness]

imam (ɪˈmɑːm) *n. Islam.* **1.** a leader of congregational prayer in a mosque. **2.** the title of some Muslim leaders. [Arabic]

imbalance (ɪmˈbæləns) *n.* a lack of balance as in emphasis or proportion: *the political imbalance of the programme.*

imbecile (ˈɪmbɪˌsiːl) *n.* **1.** *Psychol.* a person of abnormally low intelligence. **2.** *Informal.* an extremely stupid person. ~*adj.* **3.** of or like an imbecile. **4.** stupid or senseless: *an imbecile thing to do.* [Latin *imbēcillus* feeble] —**imbecility** (ˌɪmbɪˈsɪlɪtɪ) *n.*

imbed (ɪmˈbed) *vb.* **-bedding, -bedded.** same as **embed.**

imbibe (ɪmˈbaɪb) *vb.* **1.** to drink (esp. alcoholic drinks). **2.** *Literary.* to take in or assimilate (ideas): *to imbibe the spirit of the Renaissance.* [Latin *imbibere*]

imbroglio (ɪmˈbrəʊlɪˌəʊ) *n., pl.* **-glios.** a confusing and complicated situation. [Italian *imbrogliare* to confuse]

imbue (ɪmˈbjuː) *vb.* **-buing, -bued.** (usually foll. by *with*) **1.** to instil or inspire (with ideals or principles). **2.** *Rare.* to saturate, esp. with dye. [Latin *imbuere*]

IMF International Monetary Fund.

imitate (ˈɪmɪˌteɪt) *vb.* **1.** to copy the manner or style of or take as a model: *many writers imitated the language of Shakespeare.* **2.** to mimic or impersonate, esp. for humour. **3.** to make a copy or reproduction of; duplicate. [Latin *imitārī*] —**ˈimitable** *adj.* —**ˈimiˌtator** *n.*

imitation (ˌɪmɪˈteɪʃən) *n.* **1.** the act or practice of imitating. **2.** an instance or product of imitating, such as a copy of the manner of a person. **3.** a copy of a genuine article; counterfeit. ~*adj.* **4.** made to resemble something which is usually superior or more expensive: *imitation leather.*

imitative (ˈɪmɪtətɪv) *adj.* **1.** imitating or tending to copy. **2.** copying or reproducing an original, esp. in an inferior manner: *imitative painting.* **3.** same as **onomatopoeic.**

immaculate (ɪˈmækjʊlɪt) *adj.* **1.** completely clean or tidy: *his clothes were immaculate.* **2.** completely flawless: *an immaculate rendering of the symphony.* [Latin *in-* not + *macula* blemish] —**imˈmaculately** *adv.*

immanent (ˈɪmənənt) *adj.* **1.** inherent; remaining within. **2.** (of God) present throughout the universe. [Latin *immanēre* to remain in] —**ˈimmanence** *n.*

immaterial (ˌɪməˈtɪərɪəl) *adj.* **1.** of no real importance; inconsequential. **2.** not formed of matter; spiritual.

immature (ˌɪməˈtjʊə, -ˈtʃʊə) *adj.* **1.** not

fully grown or developed. **2.** without wisdom, insight, or emotional stability, due to lack of maturity —**imma'turity** n.

immeasurable (ɪˈmɛʒərəbˀl) adj. too great to be measured; limitless. —**im'measurably** adv.

immediate (ɪˈmiːdɪət) adj. **1.** taking place without delay: an immediate reaction. **2.** next or nearest in space, time, or relationship: our immediate neighbour. **3.** present; current: the immediate problem is food. [Latin in- not + mediāre to be in the middle] —**im'mediacy** n. —**im'mediately** adv.

immemorial (ˌɪmɪˈmɔːrɪəl) adj. originating in the distant past; ancient: this has been the custom since time immemorial.

immense (ɪˈmɛns) adj. **1.** unusually large; huge. **2.** Informal. very good. [Latin immensus unmeasured] —**im'mensely** adv. —**im'mensity** n.

immerse (ɪˈmɜːs) vb. **1.** (often foll. by in) to plunge or dip into liquid. **2.** (often passive; often foll. by in) to involve deeply; engross: to immerse oneself in a problem. **3.** to baptize by dipping the whole body into water. [Latin immergere] —**im'mersion** n.

immersion heater n. an electrical device in a domestic hot-water tank for heating the water in which it is immersed.

immigrant (ˈɪmɪɡrənt) n. a person who immigrates.

immigrate (ˈɪmɪˌɡreɪt) vb. to come to a foreign country in order to settle there. [Latin immigrāre to go into] —**immi'gration** n.

imminent (ˈɪmɪnənt) adj. likely to happen soon. [Latin imminēre to project over] —**'imminence** n.

immiscible (ɪˈmɪsɪbˀl) adj. (of liquids) incapable of being mixed: oil and water are immiscible. —**im,misci'bility** n.

immobile (ɪˈməʊbaɪl) adj. **1.** not moving; motionless. **2.** not able to move or be moved; fixed. —**immobility** (ˌɪməʊˈbɪlɪtɪ) n.

immobilize or **-lise** (ɪˈməʊbɪˌlaɪz) vb. to make immobile: to immobilize a car. —**im,mobili'zation** or **-li'sation** n.

immoderate (ɪˈmɒdərɪt) adj. lacking in moderation; excessive: immoderate demands. —**im'moderately** adv.

immodest (ɪˈmɒdɪst) adj. **1.** indecent; improper. **2.** bold, impudent, or conceited. —**im'modesty** n.

immolate (ˈɪməʊˌleɪt) vb. to kill or offer as a sacrifice. [Latin immolāre] —**immo'lation** n.

immoral (ɪˈmɒrəl) adj. **1.** morally wrong; corrupt: nuclear energy is dangerous and immoral. **2.** sexually depraved or promiscuous: an immoral seducer of young girls. —**immorality** (ˌɪməˈrælɪtɪ) n.

immortal (ɪˈmɔːtˀl) adj. **1.** living forever. **2.** having everlasting fame; remembered throughout time. **3.** everlasting; perpetual. ~n. **4.** an immortal being. **5.** (often pl.) a person who is remembered enduringly, esp. an author. —**immortality** (ˌɪmɔːˈtælɪtɪ) n.

immortalize or **-ise** (ɪˈmɔːtəˌlaɪz) vb. **1.** to give everlasting fame to, as by treating in a literary work. **2.** to give immortality to.

immovable (ɪˈmuːvəbˀl) adj. **1.** that cannot be moved; immobile. **2.** unyielding; steadfast. **3.** unaffected by feeling; impassive. **4.** unchanging; unalterable. **5.** Law. (of property) consisting of land or houses. —**im,mova'bility** n. —**im'movably** adv.

immune (ɪˈmjuːn) adj. **1.** protected against a specific disease by inoculation or as the result of natural resistance. **2.** (foll. by to) unsusceptible (to) or secure (against): immune to inflation. **3.** exempt from obligation or penalty. [Latin immūnis exempt from a public service]

immunity (ɪˈmjuːnɪtɪ) n., pl. **-ties.** **1.** the ability of an organism to resist disease, by producing its own antibodies or as a result of inoculation. **2.** freedom from obligation or duty, esp. exemption from tax or legal liability.

immunize or **-nise** (ˈɪmjʊˌnaɪz) vb. to make immune, esp. by inoculation. —**immuni'zation** or **-ni'sation** n.

immunodeficiency (ˌɪmjʊnəʊdɪˈfɪʃənsɪ) n. a deficiency in or breakdown of a person's immune system.

immunology (ˌɪmjʊˈnɒlədʒɪ) n. the branch of medicine concerned with the study of immunity. —**immuno'logical** adj. —**immu'nologist** n.

immure (ɪˈmjʊə) vb. Archaic or literary. **1.** to imprison. **2.** to shut (oneself) away from society. [Latin im- in + mūrus wall]

immutable (ɪˈmjuːtəbˀl) adj. unchangeable or unchanging; ageless: immutable laws. —**im,muta'bility** n.

imp (ɪmp) n. **1.** a small demon. **2.** a mischievous child. [Old English impa bud, hence offspring, child]

imp. **1.** imperative. **2.** imperfect.

impact n. (ˈɪmpækt). **1.** the act of one object striking another; collision. **2.** the force of a collision. **3.** the effect or impression made by something. ~vb. (ɪmˈpækt). **4.** to press (an object) firmly into (another object) or (of two objects) to be pressed firmly together. [Latin impactus pushed against] —**im'paction** n.

impacted (ɪmˈpæktɪd) adj. (of a tooth) unable to grow out because of being wedged against another tooth below the gum.

impair (ɪmˈpɛə) vb. to damage or weaken in strength or quality: his hearing was impaired by an accident. [Old French empeirer to make worse] —**im'pairment** n.

impala (ɪmˈpɑːlə) n., pl. **-las** or **-la.** an African antelope with lyre-shaped horns, that can move with enormous leaps. [Zulu]

impale (ɪmˈpeɪl) vb. (often foll. by on, upon, or with) to pierce through or fix with a sharp instrument: they impaled his severed head on a spear. [Latin im- on + pālus pole] —**im'palement** n.

impalpable (ɪmˈpælpəbˀl) adj. **1.** imperceptible to the touch: impalpable shadows. **2.** difficult to understand; abstruse. —**im,palpa'bility** n.

impanel (ɪmˈpæn'l) vb. **-elling, -elled** or U.S. **-eling, -eled.** Chiefly U.S. to empanel.

impart (ɪmˈpɑːt) vb. **1.** to communicate (information or knowledge); tell. **2.** to give (a specified quality): *to impart flavour.* [Latin *im-* on + *partīre* to share]

impartial (ɪmˈpɑːʃəl) adj. fair; unbiased. **—impartiality** (ɪmˌpɑːʃɪˈælɪtɪ) n. **—impartially** adv.

impassable (ɪmˈpɑːsəb'l) adj. (of terrain or roads) not able to be travelled through or over. **—imˌpassaˈbility** n.

impasse (ˈæmpɑːs) n. a situation in which progress or escape is impossible. [French]

impassioned (ɪmˈpæʃənd) adj. filled with passion; fiery; ardent: *an impassioned appeal.*

impassive (ɪmˈpæsɪv) adj. not feeling or expressing emotion; calm or reserved. **—imˈpassively** adv. **—ˌimpasˈsivity** n.

impasto (ɪmˈpæstəʊ) n. the technique of applying paint thickly, so that brush marks are evident. [Italian]

impatience (ɪmˈpeɪʃəns) n. **1.** lack of patience; intolerance of or annoyance with anything that causes delay. **2.** restless eagerness to do or have something. **—imˈpatient** adj. **—imˈpatiently** adv.

impeach (ɪmˈpiːtʃ) vb. **1.** Brit. criminal law. to accuse of treason or serious crime. **2.** Chiefly U.S. to charge (a public official) with an offence committed in office. **3.** to challenge or question (a person's honesty or honour). [Late Latin *impedicāre* to entangle] **—imˈpeachable** adj. **—imˈpeachment** n.

impeccable (ɪmˈpɛkəb'l) adj. without flaw or error; faultless: *an impeccable record.* [Latin *in-* not + *peccāre* to sin] **—imˈpeccably** adv.

impecunious (ˌɪmpɪˈkjuːnɪəs) adj. without money; penniless. [Latin *in-* not + *pecūniōsus* wealthy]

impedance (ɪmˈpiːd'ns) n. the total effective resistance in an electric circuit to the flow of an alternating current.

impede (ɪmˈpiːd) vb. to restrict or retard in action or progress; obstruct. [Latin *impedīre*]

impediment (ɪmˈpɛdɪmənt) n. **1.** a hindrance or obstruction. **2.** a physical defect, esp. one of speech.

impedimenta (ɪmˌpɛdɪˈmɛntə) pl. n. any objects that impede progress, esp. the baggage and equipment carried by an army.

impel (ɪmˈpɛl) vb. **-pelling, -pelled. 1.** to urge or force (a person) to an action. **2.** to push, drive, or force into motion. [Latin *impellere* to drive forward]

impending (ɪmˈpɛndɪŋ) adj. (esp. of something threatening) about to happen. [Latin *impendēre* to overhang]

impenetrable (ɪmˈpɛnɪtrəb'l) adj. **1.** incapable of being passed through or penetrated: *an impenetrable forest.* **2.** incapable of being understood; incomprehensible. **3.** not receptive to ideas or influence: *impenetrable ignorance.* **—imˌpenetraˈbility** n. **—imˈpenetrably** adv.

impenitent (ɪmˈpɛnɪtənt) adj. not sorry or penitent; unrepentant. **—imˈpenitence** n.

imper. imperative.

imperative (ɪmˈpɛrətɪv) adj. **1.** extremely urgent; essential. **2.** commanding or authoritative: *an imperative tone of voice.* **3.** Grammar. denoting a mood of verbs used in giving orders. ~n. **4.** Grammar. the imperative mood. [Latin *imperāre* to command]

imperceptible (ˌɪmpəˈsɛptɪb'l) adj. too slight, subtle, or gradual to be noticed. **—ˌimperˈceptibly** adv.

imperf. imperfect.

imperfect (ɪmˈpɜːfɪkt) adj. **1.** having faults or errors. **2.** not complete. **3.** Grammar. denoting a tense of verbs describing continuous, incomplete, or repeated past actions. ~n. **4.** Grammar. the imperfect tense. **—imˈperfectly** adv.

imperfection (ˌɪmpəˈfɛkʃən) n. **1.** the state of being imperfect. **2.** a fault or defect.

imperial (ɪmˈpɪərɪəl) adj. **1.** of an empire, emperor, or empress. **2.** majestic; commanding. **3.** exercising supreme authority; imperious. **4.** (of weights or measures) conforming to the standards of a system formerly official in Great Britain. [Latin *imperium* authority]

imperialism (ɪmˈpɪərɪəˌlɪzəm) n. **1.** the policy or practice of extending a country's influence over other territories by conquest, colonization, or economic domination. **2.** an imperial system, authority, or government. **—imˈperialist** adj., n. **—imˌperiaˈlistic** adj.

imperil (ɪmˈpɛrɪl) vb. **-illing, -illed** or U.S. **-iling, -iled.** to put in danger.

imperious (ɪmˈpɪərɪəs) adj. domineering; overbearing. [Latin *imperium* power] **—imˈperiously** adv.

impermanent (ɪmˈpɜːmənənt) adj. not permanent; fleeting. **—imˈpermanence** n.

impermeable (ɪmˈpɜːmɪəb'l) adj. (of a substance) not allowing the passage of a fluid. **—imˌpermeaˈbility** n.

impermissible (ˌɪmpəˈmɪsɪb'l) adj. not allowed.

impersonal (ɪmˈpɜːsən'l) adj. **1.** without reference to any individual person; objective: *an impersonal assessment.* **2.** without human warmth or sympathy; unemotional: *an impersonal manner.* **3.** Grammar. **a.** (of a verb) having no subject, as in *it is raining.* **b.** (of a pronoun) not referring to a person. **—impersonality** (ɪmˌpɜːsəˈnælɪtɪ) n. **—imˈpersonally** adv.

impersonate (ɪmˈpɜːsəˌneɪt) vb. **1.** to pretend to be (another person). **2.** to imitate the character or mannerisms of (another person) for entertainment. **—imˌpersonˈation** n. **—imˈpersonˌator** n.

impertinent (ɪmˈpɜːtɪnənt) adj. rude; insolent; impudent. [Latin *impertinēns* not belonging] **—imˈpertinence** n.

imperturbable (ˌɪmpəˈtɜːbəb'l) adj. not easily upset; calm; unruffled. **—ˌimperˌturbaˈbility** n. **—ˌimperˈturbably** adv.

impervious (ɪmˈpɜːvɪəs) adj. **1.** not able

to be penetrated; impermeable. **2.** (foll. by *to*) not able to be affected or influenced by: *impervious to argument*.

impetigo (ˌɪmpɪˈtaɪgəʊ) *n.* a contagious skin disease causing spots or pimples. [Latin: scabby eruption]

impetuous (ɪmˈpɛtjʊəs) *adj.* **1.** acting without consideration; rash; impulsive. **2.** done in rashness or haste. [Late Latin *impetuōsus* violent] —**impetuosity** (ɪmˌpɛtjʊˈɒsɪtɪ) *n.*

impetus (ˈɪmpɪtəs) *n., pl.* **-tuses. 1.** an incentive or impulse; stimulus. **2.** *Physics.* the force that starts a body moving or that tends to resist changes in its speed or direction once it is moving. [Latin: attack]

impi (ˈɪmpɪ) *n., pl.* **-pi** or **-pies.** a group of Zulu warriors. [Zulu]

impiety (ɪmˈpaɪtɪ) *n.* lack of respect or religious reverence.

impinge (ɪmˈpɪndʒ) *vb.* (usually foll. by *on* or *upon*) to encroach or infringe: *to impinge on someone's time*. [Latin *impingere* to dash against] —**imˈpingement** *n.*

impious (ˈɪmpɪəs) *adj.* **1.** lacking piety or religious reverence. **2.** lacking respect.

impish (ˈɪmpɪʃ) *adj.* of or like an imp; mischievous. —**impishness** *n.*

implacable (ɪmˈplækəbəl) *adj.* **1.** incapable of being appeased or pacified. **2.** inflexible; intractable. —**imˌplacaˈbility** *n.* —**imˈplacably** *adv.*

implant *vb.* (ɪmˈplɑːnt) **1.** to fix firmly in the mind, instil: *to implant sound moral principles.* **2.** to plant or embed; fix firmly. **3.** *Surgery.* to graft or insert (a tissue or hormone) into the body. ~*n.* (ˈɪmplɑːnt) **4.** anything implanted in the body, such as a tissue graft. —ˌimplanˈtation *n.*

implausible (ɪmˈplɔːzəbəl) *adj.* not easy to believe; unlikely. —**imˌplausiˈbility** *n.*

implement *n.* (ˈɪmplɪmənt) **1.** a piece of equipment; tool or utensil: *gardening implements.* ~*vb.* (ˈɪmplɪˌmɛnt) **2.** to carry out; put into action: *to implement a plan.* [Late Latin *implēmentum*, lit.: a filling up] —ˌimplemenˈtation *n.*

implicate (ˈɪmplɪˌkeɪt) *vb.* **1.** to show to be involved, esp. in a crime. **2.** to imply. [Latin *implicāre* to involve]

implication (ˌɪmplɪˈkeɪʃən) *n.* **1.** something that is implied. **2.** an implying or being implied.

implicit (ɪmˈplɪsɪt) *adj.* **1.** implied; expressed indirectly. **2.** absolute and unquestioning: *implicit trust.* **3.** contained, although not stated openly: *to bring out the anger implicit in the argument.* [Latin *implicitus*] —**imˈplicitly** *adv.*

implied (ɪmˈplaɪd) *adj.* hinted at or suggested; not directly expressed: *an implied criticism.*

implode (ɪmˈpləʊd) *vb.* to collapse inwards. [*im-* in + (*ex*)*plode*]

implore (ɪmˈplɔː) *vb.* to beg (someone) earnestly (to do something); plead for (something). [Latin *implōrāre*]

imply (ɪmˈplaɪ) *vb.* **-plying, -plied. 1.** to express or indicate by a hint; suggest. **2.**

to suggest or involve as a necessary consequence. [Old French *emplier*]

impolite (ˌɪmpəˈlaɪt) *adj.* discourteous; rude. —ˌimpoˈliteness *n.*

impolitic (ɪmˈpɒlɪtɪk) *adj.* ill-advised; unwise.

imponderable (ɪmˈpɒndərəbəl, -drəbəl) *adj.* **1.** unable to be weighed or assessed. ~*n.* **2.** something difficult or impossible to assess.

import *vb.* (ɪmˈpɔːt, ˈɪmpɔːt). **1.** to bring in (esp. goods or services) from another country. **2.** *Rare.* to signify; mean: *to import doom.* ~*n.* (ˈɪmpɔːt). **3.** (*often pl.*) something imported. **4.** importance: *a work of great import.* **5.** meaning. **6.** *Canad. slang.* a sportsman who is not native to the area where he plays. [Latin *importāre* to carry in] —**imˈporter** *n.*

important (ɪmˈpɔːtˀnt) *adj.* **1.** of great significance, value, or consequence. **2.** of social significance; eminent; esteemed: *an important man in the town.* **3.** (usually foll. by *to*) of great concern (to); valued highly (by): *your wishes are important to me.* [Medieval Latin *importāre* to signify, from Latin: to carry in] —**imˈportance** *n.*

importation (ˌɪmpɔːˈteɪʃən) *n.* **1.** an importing or being imported. **2.** something imported.

importunate (ɪmˈpɔːtjʊnɪt) *adj.* persistent or demanding; insistent.

importune (ɪmˈpɔːtjuːn, ˌɪmpɔːˈtjuːn) *vb.* to harass with persistent requests; demand of (someone) insistently. [Latin *importūnus* tiresome] —**imporˈtunity** *n.*

impose (ɪmˈpəʊz) *vb.* (usually foll. by *on* or *upon*) **1.** to establish (a rule, condition, etc.) as something to be obeyed or complied with; enforce. **2.** to force (oneself) on others. **3.** to take advantage of (a person or quality): *to impose on someone's kindness.* **4.** *Printing.* to arrange (pages) in the correct order for printing. **5.** to pass off deceptively. [Latin *impōnere* to place upon]

imposing (ɪmˈpəʊzɪŋ) *adj.* grand or impressive: *an imposing building.*

imposition (ˌɪmpəˈzɪʃən) *n.* **1.** the act of imposing. **2.** something imposed, esp. unfairly on someone. **3.** a task set as a school punishment. **4.** the arrangement of pages for printing.

impossibility (ɪmˌpɒsəˈbɪlɪtɪ) *n., pl.* **-ties. 1.** the state or quality of being impossible. **2.** something that is impossible.

impossible (ɪmˈpɒsəbəl) *adj.* **1.** incapable of being done, or of happening. **2.** absurd or inconceivable; unreasonable. **3.** *Informal.* intolerable; outrageous: *those children are impossible.* —**imˈpossibly** *adv.*

impostor (ɪmˈpɒstə) *n.* a person who deceives others, esp. by assuming a false identity. [Late Latin: deceiver]

imposture (ɪmˈpɒstʃə) *n.* deception, esp. by assuming a false identity.

impotent (ˈɪmpətənt) *adj.* **1.** lacking sufficient strength; ineffective or powerless. **2.** (of males) unable to perform sexual intercourse. —**ˈimpotence** *n.*

impound (ɪmˈpaʊnd) *vb.* **1.** to confine (an

animal) in a pound. **2.** to take legal possession of; confiscate.

impoverish (ɪmˈpɒvərɪʃ) vb. to make poor or diminish the quality of: *to impoverish society by cutting the grant to the arts.* [Old French *empovrir*] —**imˈpoverishment** n.

impracticable (ɪmˈpræktɪkəbᵊl) adj. **1.** incapable of being put into practice; not feasible. **2.** unsuitable for a desired use; unfit. —**imˌpracticaˈbility** n.

impractical (ɪmˈpræktɪkᵊl) adj. **1.** not practical or workable: *an impractical solution.* **2.** not having practical skills. —**impracticality** (ɪmˌpræktɪˈkælɪtɪ) n.

imprecate (ˈɪmprɪˌkeɪt) vb. **1.** to swear or curse. **2.** to invoke or bring down (evil or a curse). [Latin *imprecārī* to invoke] —**imˈpreˈcation** n. —**ˈimpreˌcatory** adj.

imprecise (ˌɪmprɪˈsaɪs) adj. not precise; inexact or inaccurate. —**imprecision** (ˌɪmprɪˈsɪʒən) n.

impregnable (ɪmˈprɛgnəbᵊl) adj. **1.** unable to be broken into or taken by force: *an impregnable castle.* **2.** unable to be affected or overcome: *impregnable self-confidence.* [Old French *imprenable*] —**imˌpregnaˈbility** n.

impregnate (ˈɪmprɛgˌneɪt) vb. **1.** to saturate, soak, or fill throughout. **2.** to imbue or permeate. **3.** to make pregnant; fertilize. [Latin *in-* in + *praegnans* pregnant] —**ˌimpregˈnation** n.

impresario (ˌɪmprɪˈsɑːrɪˌəʊ) n., pl. **-sarios.** the director or manager of a theatre or music company. [Italian]

impress¹ vb. (ɪmˈprɛs). **1.** to make a strong, lasting, or favourable impression on: *I am impressed by your work.* **2.** to imprint or stamp by pressure: *to impress a seal in wax.* **3.** (often foll. by *on*) to stress (something to a person); emphasize. ~n. (ˈɪmprɛs). **4.** an impressing. **5.** a mark produced by impressing. [Latin *imprimere* to press into] —**imˈpressible** adj.

impress² (ɪmˈprɛs) vb. to force (a person) into service in the army or navy. [see *IM-²*, *PRESS²*]

impression (ɪmˈprɛʃən) n. **1.** an effect produced in the mind by a person or thing: *I don't think I made a very good impression at the interview.* **2.** an imprint or mark produced by pressing. **3.** a vague idea or belief: *I had the impression we had met before.* **4.** a strong, favourable, or remarkable effect. **5.** *Printing.* **a.** the act or result of printing from type or plates. **b.** the number of copies of a publication printed at one time. **6.** an impersonation for entertainment.

impressionable (ɪmˈprɛʃənəbᵊl) adj. easily impressed or influenced: *an impressionable age.* —**imˌpressionaˈbility** n.

impressionism (ɪmˈprɛʃəˌnɪzəm) n. (*often cap.*) a style of painting developed in 19th-century France, with the aim of reproducing the immediate impression or mood of things, especially the effects of light and atmosphere, rather than form or structure. —**imˈpressionist** n. —**imˌpressionˈistic** adj.

impressive (ɪmˈprɛsɪv) adj. capable of impressing, esp. by size, magnificence, or importance. —**imˈpressively** adv.

imprimatur (ˌɪmprɪˈmeɪtə, -ˈmɑː-) n. sanction or approval for something to be printed, usually given by the Roman Catholic Church. [New Latin: let it be printed]

imprint n. (ˈɪmprɪnt). **1.** a mark or impression produced by pressing, printing, or stamping. **2.** the publisher's name and address, often with the date of publication, printed on the title page of a book. ~vb. (ɪmˈprɪnt). **3.** to produce (a mark or impression) on (a surface) by pressing, printing, or stamping: *to imprint a seal on wax.* **4.** to establish firmly; impress: *to imprint the details on one's mind.*

imprison (ɪmˈprɪzən) vb. to confine in or as if in prison. —**imˈprisonment** n.

improbable (ɪmˈprɒbəbᵊl) adj. not likely or probable; doubtful; unlikely. —**imˌprobaˈbility** n. —**imˈprobably** adv.

improbity (ɪmˈprəʊbɪtɪ) n., pl. **-ties.** dishonesty or wickedness.

impromptu (ɪmˈprɒmptjuː) adj. **1.** unrehearsed; improvised. ~adv. **2.** in a spontaneous or improvised way: *he spoke impromptu.* ~n. **3.** something that is impromptu. **4.** a short piece of instrumental music resembling improvisation. [Latin *in promptū* in readiness]

improper (ɪmˈprɒpə) adj. **1.** indecent; unseemly. **2.** irregular or incorrect. —**imˈproperly** adv.

improper fraction n. a fraction in which the numerator is greater than the denominator, as ⁷⁄₆.

impropriety (ˌɪmprəˈpraɪɪtɪ) n., pl. **-ties.** **1.** indecency; indecorum. **2.** an improper act or use.

improve (ɪmˈpruːv) vb. **1.** to make or become better in quality. **2.** (usually foll. by *on* or *upon*) to achieve a better standard or quality in comparison (with): *to improve on last year's crop.* [Anglo-French *emprouer* to turn to profit] —**imˈprovable** adj.

improvement (ɪmˈpruːvmənt) n. **1.** the act of improving or the state of being improved. **2.** a change that improves something or adds to its value. **3.** *Austral. & N.Z.* a building on a piece of land, adding to its value.

improvident (ɪmˈprɒvɪdənt) adj. **1.** not providing for the future; thriftless. **2.** incautious or rash. —**imˈprovidence** n.

improvise (ˈɪmprəˌvaɪz) vb. **1.** to do or make quickly from whatever is available, without previous planning. **2.** to perform (a play or piece of music) composing as one goes along. [Latin *imprōvīsus* unforeseen] —**ˌimproviˈsation** n.

imprudent (ɪmˈpruːdᵊnt) adj. rash, heedless, or indiscreet. —**imˈprudence** n.

impudent (ˈɪmpjʊdənt) adj. impertinent or insolent. [Latin *impudēns* shameless] —**ˈimpudence** n. —**ˈimpudently** adv.

impugn (ɪmˈpjuːn) vb. to challenge or attack as false; criticize. [Latin *impugnāre* to fight against] —**imˈpugnment** n.

impulse (ˈɪmpʌls) n. **1.** an impelling force

or motion; thrust; impetus. **2.** a sudden desire, whim, or inclination. **3.** an instinctive drive; urge. **4.** *Physics.* **a.** the product of a force acting on a body and the time for which it acts. **b.** the change in the momentum of a body as a result of a force acting upon it. **5.** *Physiol.* a stimulus transmitted in a nerve or muscle. [Latin *impulsus* incitement]

impulsive (ımˈpʌlsıv) *adj.* **1.** tending to act on impulse: *an impulsive man.* **2.** done on impulse. **3.** forceful, inciting, or impelling.

impunity (ımˈpjuːnıtı) *n., pl.* **-ties.** exemption from punishment or unpleasant consequences: *done with impunity.* [Latin *impūnis* unpunished]

impure (ımˈpjʊə) *adj.* **1.** combined with something else; tainted or adulterated. **2.** dirty or unclean. **3.** immoral; obscene.

impurity (ımˈpjʊərıtı) *n., pl.* **-ties.** **1.** the quality of being impure. **2.** an impure thing or element: *impurities in the water.*

impute (ımˈpjuːt) *vb.* **1.** to attribute or ascribe (blame or a crime) to a person. **2.** to attribute to a source or cause: *I impute your success to nepotism.* [Latin *in-* in + *putāre* to think] —**impuˈtation** *n.*

in (ın) *prep.* **1.** inside; within: *in the room.* **2.** at a place where there is: *in the shade.* **3.** indicating a state, situation, or condition: *in silence.* **4.** when (a period of time) has elapsed: *come back in one year.* **5.** using: *written in code.* **6.** wearing: *the man in the blue suit.* **7.** with regard to a specified activity or occupation: *in journalism.* **8.** while performing the action of: *in crossing the street he was run over.* **9.** having as purpose: *in honour of the president.* **10.** (of certain animals) pregnant with: *in calf.* **11.** into: *she fell in the water.* **12.** **have it in one.** (often foll. by an infinitive) to have the ability (to do something). **13. in that** *or* **in so far as.** (*conj.*) because or to the extent that: *I regret my remark in that it upset you.* ~*adv.* **14.** in or into a particular place; indoors: *come in.* **15.** at one's home or place of work: *he's not in at the moment.* **16.** fashionable or popular: *bright colours are in this year.* **17.** in office or power: *the Conservatives got in at the last election.* **18.** so as to enclose: *block in.* **19.** (in certain games) so as to take one's turn of the play: *you have to get the other side out before you go in.* **20.** *Brit.* (of a fire) alight. **21.** indicating prolonged activity, esp. by a large number: *teach-in; sit-in.* **22. in for.** about to experience (something, esp. something unpleasant): *you're in for a shock.* **23. in on.** acquainted with or sharing in: *I was in on all his plans.* **24. in with.** friendly with. **25. have (got) it in for.** to wish or intend harm towards. ~*adj.* **26.** fashionable; modish: *the in thing to do.* ~*n.* **27. ins and outs.** the detailed points or facts (of a situation). [Old English]

In *Chem.* indium.

IN Indiana.

in. inch(es).

in-¹, il-, im-, *or* **ir-** *prefix.* **a.** not; non-:

incredible; illegal; imperfect; irregular. **b.** lack of: *inexperience.* [Latin]

in-², il-, im-, *or* **ir-** *prefix.* in; into; towards; within; on: *infiltrate.* [from *in*]

inability (ˌınəˈbılıtı) *n.* the fact of not being able to do something.

in absentia Latin. (ın æbˈsɛntıə) *adv.* in the absence of (someone indicated).

inaccessible (ˌınækˈsɛsəb²l) *adj.* **1.** impossible or very difficult to reach: *the most inaccessible parts of the jungle.* **2.** (of a person) unapproachable. —**ˌinacˌcessiˈbility** *n.*

inaccuracy (ınˈækjʊrəsı) *n., pl.* **-cies.** **1.** lack of accuracy; imprecision. **2.** an error or mistake. —**inˈaccurate** *adj.*

inaction (ınˈækʃən) *n.* lack of action; inertia.

inactive (ınˈæktıv) *adj.* **1.** idle; not active. **2.** *Chem.* (of a substance) having little or no reactivity. —**inacˈtivity** *n.*

inadequate (ınˈædıkwıt) *adj.* **1.** not adequate; insufficient. **2.** not capable; incompetent. —**inˈadequacy** *n.* —**inˈadequately** *adv.*

inadmissible (ˌınədˈmısəb²l) *adj.* not allowable or acceptable.

inadvertent (ˌınədˈvɜːt²nt) *adj.* resulting from heedless action; unintentional. —**inadˈvertence** *n.* —**inadˈvertently** *adv.*

inadvisable (ˌınədˈvaızəb²l) *adj.* unwise; not sensible.

inalienable (ınˈeıljənəb²l) *adj.* not able to be taken away or transferred to another: *the inalienable rights of the citizen.*

inamorata (ınˌæməˈrɑːtə) *or (masc.)* **inamorato** (ınˌæməˈrɑːtəʊ) *n., pl.* **-tas** *or (masc.)* **-tos.** a sweetheart or lover. [Italian]

inane (ıˈneın) *adj.* senseless or silly: *inane remarks.* [Latin *inānis* empty] —**inanity** (ıˈnænıtı) *n.*

inanimate (ınˈænımıt) *adj.* lacking the qualities of living beings: *inanimate objects.*

inanition (ˌınəˈnıʃən) *n.* emptiness or weakness, esp. from lack of food. [Latin *inānis* empty]

inapplicable (ˌınæˈplıkəb²l) *adj.* not suitable or relevant.

inapposite (ınˈæpəzıt) *adj.* not appropriate; unsuitable. —**inˈappositeness** *n.*

inappropriate (ˌınəˈprəʊprııt) *adj.* not suitable or proper.

inapt (ınˈæpt) *adj.* **1.** inappropriate. **2.** lacking skill. —**inˈaptiˌtude** *n.*

inarticulate (ˌınɑːˈtıkjʊlıt) *adj.* unable to express oneself clearly or well.

inasmuch as (ˌınəzˈmʌtʃ) *conj.* **1.** since; because. **2.** in so far as.

inattentive (ˌınəˈtɛntıv) *adj.* not paying attention.

inaudible (ınˈɔːdəb²l) *adj.* not loud enough to be heard.

inaugural (ınˈɔːgjʊərəl) *adj.* **1.** of or for an inauguration. ~*n.* **2.** a speech made at an inauguration.

inaugurate (ınˈɔːgjʊˌreıt) *vb.* **1.** to begin officially or formally. **2.** to place in office formally and ceremonially. **3.** to open or celebrate the first public use of ceremonially: *to inaugurate a factory*. [Latin *inaugurāre* to take omens, hence to install in office after taking auguries] **—in,augu'ra tion** *n.* **—in'augu,rator** *n.*

inauspicious (,ɪnɔː'spɪʃəs) *adj.* unlucky.

inboard ('ɪn,bɔːd) *adj.* **1.** (of a boat's motor or engine) situated within the hull. **2.** situated close to the fuselage of an aircraft. ~*adv.* **3.** within the sides of or towards the centre of a vessel or aircraft.

inborn ('ɪn'bɔːn) *adj.* existing from birth; congenital; innate.

inbred ('ɪn'brɛd) *adj.* **1.** produced as a result of inbreeding. **2.** deeply ingrained; innate: *inbred good manners*.

inbreed ('ɪn'briːd) *vb.* **-breeding, -bred.** to breed from closely related individuals. **—'in'breeding** *n., adj.*

inbuilt ('ɪn'bɪlt) *adj.* (of a quality or feeling) present from the beginning: *inbuilt limitations.*

inc. 1. including. **2.** inclusive. **3.** income. **4.** increase.

Inc. (esp. U.S.) incorporated.

incalculable (ɪn'kælkjʊləb'l) *adj.* unable to be predicted or determined. **—in,calcula'bility** *n.*

incandescent (,ɪnkæn'dɛs'nt) *adj.* glowing with heat; red-hot or white-hot. [Latin *incandescere* to glow] **—,incan'descence** *n.*

incandescent lamp *n.* a lamp that contains a filament which is electrically heated to incandescence.

incantation (,ɪnkæn'teɪʃən) *n.* **1.** ritual chanting of magic words or sounds. **2.** a magic spell. [Latin *incantāre* to repeat magic formulas] **—in'cantatory** *adj.*

incapable (ɪn'keɪpəb'l) *adj.* **1.** (foll. by *of*) not capable; lacking the ability to. **2.** powerless; helpless: *drunk and incapable.*

incapacitate (,ɪnkə'pæsɪ,teɪt) *vb.* to deprive of power, strength, or capacity; disable.

incapacity (,ɪnkə'pæsɪtɪ) *n., pl.* **-ties. 1.** lack of power, strength, or capacity; disability. **2.** *Law.* legal disqualification or ineligibility.

incarcerate (ɪn'kɑːsə,reɪt) *vb.* to confine or imprison. [Latin *in-* in + *carcer* prison] **—in,carcer'ation** *n.*

incarnate *adj.* (ɪn'kɑːnɪt). **1.** possessing bodily form, esp. the human form: *a devil incarnate.* **2.** personified or typified: *stupidity incarnate.* ~*vb.* (ɪn'kɑːneɪt). **3.** to give a bodily or concrete form to. **4.** to be representative or typical of. [Late Latin *incarnāre* to make flesh]

incarnation (,ɪnkɑː'neɪʃən) *n.* **1.** the act of embodying or state of being embodied, esp. in human form. **2.** a person or thing that typifies some quality or idea.

Incarnation (,ɪnkɑː'neɪʃən) *n. Christian theol.* the assuming of a human body by Jesus as the Son of God.

incautious (ɪn'kɔːʃəs) *adj.* (of a person or action) careless or rash.

incendiary (ɪn'sɛndɪərɪ) *adj.* **1.** relating to the illegal burning of property or goods. **2.** tending to create strife or violence. **3.** designed to cause fires, as certain bombs. ~*n., pl.* **-aries. 4.** a person who illegally sets fire to property or goods; arsonist. **5.** a bomb that is designed to start fires. [Latin *incendere* to kindle] **—in'cendia,rism** *n.*

incense¹ ('ɪnsɛns) *n.* **1.** an aromatic substance burnt for its fragrant odour, esp. in religious ceremonies. **2.** the odour or smoke so produced. ~*vb.* **3.** to burn incense to (a deity). **4.** to perfume or fumigate with incense. [Church Latin *incensum*]

incense² (ɪn'sɛns) *vb.* to enrage greatly. [Latin *incensus* set on fire]

incentive (ɪn'sɛntɪv) *n.* **1.** a motivating influence; stimulus. **2.** an additional payment made to employees to increase production. ~*adj.* **3.** inciting to action. [Latin: setting the tune]

inception (ɪn'sɛpʃən) *n.* the beginning of a project. [Latin *incipere* to begin]

incessant (ɪn'sɛs'nt) *adj.* unceasing; continual. [Latin *in-* not + *cessāre* to cease] **—in'cessantly** *adv.*

incest ('ɪnsɛst) *n.* sexual intercourse between two persons who are too closely related to marry. [Latin *in-* not + *castus* chaste] **—in'cestuous** *adj.*

inch (ɪntʃ) *n.* **1.** a unit of length equal to one twelfth of a foot or 2.54cm. **2.** *Meteorol.* the amount of rain or snow that would cover a surface to a depth of one inch. **3.** a very small distance, degree, or amount. **4. every inch.** in every way; completely: *every inch an aristocrat.* **5. inch by inch.** gradually; little by little. **6. within an inch of one's life.** almost to death. ~*vb.* **7.** to move or be moved very slowly or gradually: *the car inched forward.* [Old English *ynce*]

inchoate (ɪn'kəʊɪt) *adj.* **1.** just beginning. **2.** undeveloped; half-formed. [Latin *incohāre* to make a beginning]

incidence ('ɪnsɪdəns) *n.* **1.** extent or frequency of occurrence: *a high incidence of death from pneumonia.* **2.** *Physics.* the arrival of a beam of light or particles at a surface. **3.** *Geom.* the partial overlapping of two figures or a figure and a line.

incident ('ɪnsɪdənt) *n.* **1.** an occurrence, event, or episode, esp. a minor, subsidiary, or related one. **2.** a relatively insignificant event that might have serious consequences. **3.** a public disturbance. ~*adj.* **4.** (foll. by *to*) likely to occur in connection with: *the dangers are incident to a policeman's job.* **5.** (of a beam of light or particles) arriving at or striking a surface. [Latin *incidere* to happen]

incidental (,ɪnsɪ'dɛnt'l) *adj.* **1.** happening in connection with or resulting from something more important. **2.** secondary or minor: *incidental expenses.* ~*n.* **3.** (*often pl.*) a minor expense, event, or action. **—,inci'dentally** *adv.*

incidental music *n.* background music for a film or play.

incinerate (ɪn'sɪnə,reɪt) *vb.* to burn up

completely; reduce to ashes. [Latin *in-* to + *cinis* ashes] **—in₁ciner'ation** *n.*

incinerator (ɪn'sɪnə₁reɪtə) *n.* a furnace or other device for incinerating something.

incipient (ɪn'sɪpɪənt) *adj.* just starting to be or happen. [Latin *incipere* to begin]

incise (ɪn'saɪz) *vb.* to cut into (something) with a sharp tool. [Latin *incīdere* to cut into]

incision (ɪn'sɪʒən) *n.* a cut, esp. one made during a surgical operation.

incisive (ɪn'saɪsɪv) *adj.* keen, penetrating, or sharp.

incisor (ɪn'saɪzə) *n.* a sharp cutting tooth at the front of the mouth.

incite (ɪn'saɪt) *vb.* to stir up or provoke to action. [Latin *in-* in, on + *citāre* to excite] **—in'citement** *n.*

incivility (₁ɪnsɪ'vɪlɪtɪ) *n., pl.* **-ties.** **1.** rudeness. **2.** an impolite act or remark.

incl. **1.** including. **2.** inclusive.

inclement (ɪn'klɛmənt) *adj.* (of weather) stormy or severe. **—in'clemency** *n.*

inclination (₁ɪnklɪ'neɪʃən) *n.* **1.** a particular disposition or tendency; a liking: *I've no inclination for such dull work.* **2.** the degree of incline from a horizontal or vertical plane. **3.** a slope or slant. **4.** *Surveying.* the angular distance of the horizon below the plane of observation.

incline *vb.* (ɪn'klaɪn). **1.** to deviate from a vertical or horizontal plane; slope or slant. **2.** to have or cause to have a certain tendency or disposition: *that does not incline me to think that you are right.* **3.** to bend or lower (part of the body, esp. the head). **4. incline one's ear.** to listen favourably. ~*n.* ('ɪnklaɪn). **5.** an inclined surface or slope. [Latin *inclīnāre* to cause to lean] **—in'clined** *adj.*

inclined plane *n.* a sloping plane used to enable a load to be raised or lowered by pushing or sliding, which requires less force than lifting.

include (ɪn'kluːd) *vb.* **1.** to have as part of the whole; be made up of or contain. **2.** to put in as part of a set, group, or category. [Latin *in-* in + *claudere* to close]

inclusion (ɪn'kluːʒən) *n.* **1.** an including or being included. **2.** something included.

inclusive (ɪn'kluːsɪv) *adj.* **1.** (foll. by *of*) including: *capital inclusive of profit.* **2.** including the limits specified: *Monday to Friday inclusive.* **3.** comprehensive.

incognito (₁ɪnkɒg'niːtəʊ) *adv., adj.* **1.** under an assumed name or appearance; in disguise. ~*n., pl.* **-tos.** **2.** a person who is incognito. **3.** the pretended identity of such a person. [Latin *incognitus* unknown]

incognizant (ɪn'kɒgnɪzənt) *adj.* (foll. by *of*) unaware of. **—in'cognizance** *n.*

incoherent (₁ɪnkəʊ'hɪərənt) *adj.* **1.** not logically connected or ordered. **2.** unable to express oneself clearly. **—₁inco'herence** *n.*

income ('ɪnkʌm, 'ɪnkəm) *n.* the total amount of money earned from work or obtained from other sources over a given period of time.

income support *n.* (in Britain) an allowance paid by the government to people with a very low income.

income tax *n.* a personal tax levied on annual income.

incoming ('ɪn₁kʌmɪŋ) *adj.* **1.** coming in; entering. **2.** about to come into office; succeeding.

incommensurable (₁ɪnkə'mɛnʃərəb'l) *adj.* **1.** incapable of being judged, measured, or compared. **2.** *Maths.* not having a common divisor other than 1, such as 2 and √-5. **—₁incom₁mensura'bility** *n.*

incommensurate (₁ɪnkə'mɛnʃərɪt) *adj.* **1.** (often foll. by *with*) inadequate; disproportionate: *gains incommensurate with the risk involved.* **2.** incommensurable.

incommode (₁ɪnkə'məʊd) *vb.* to bother, disturb, or inconvenience. [Latin *incommodus* inconvenient]

incommodious (₁ɪnkə'məʊdɪəs) *adj.* inconveniently small; cramped.

incommunicado (₁ɪnkə₁mjuːnɪ'kɑːdəʊ) *adv., adj.* not permitted to communicate with other people, as while in solitary confinement. [Spanish]

incomparable (ɪn'kɒmpərəb'l) *adj.* beyond or above comparison; unequalled. **—in'comparably** *adv.*

incompatible (₁ɪnkəm'pætəb'l) *adj.* incapable of existing together in harmony; conflicting or inconsistent. **—₁incom₁pati'bility** *n.*

incompetent (ɪn'kɒmpɪtənt) *adj.* **1.** not possessing the necessary ability or skill to carry out a task. **2.** *Law.* not legally qualified: *an incompetent witness.* ~*n.* **3.** an incompetent person. **—in'competence** *n.*

incomplete (₁ɪnkəm'pliːt) *adj.* **1.** not finished. **2.** not whole.

incomprehension (ɪn₁kɒmprɪ'hɛnʃən) *n.* inability to understand. **—in₁compre'hensible** *adj.*

inconceivable (₁ɪnkən'siːvəb'l) *adj.* unable to be imagined or considered. **—₁incon₁ceiva'bility** *n.*

inconclusive (₁ɪnkən'kluːsɪv) *adj.* not conclusive or decisive.

incongruous (ɪn'kɒŋgrʊəs) *adj.* out of place; inappropriate: *an incongruous figure among the tourists.* **—in'congruously** *adv.* **—incongruity** (₁ɪnkɒŋ'gruːɪtɪ) *n.*

inconnu ('ɪnkənjuː, -nuː) *n.* Canad. a whitefish of arctic waters. [French]

inconsequential (ɪn₁kɒnsɪ'kwɛnʃəl) *or* **inconsequent** (ɪn'kɒnsɪkwənt) *adj.* **1.** not following logically as a consequence. **2.** trivial or insignificant. **—in₁conse'quentially** *adv.*

inconsiderable (₁ɪnkən'sɪdərəb'l) *adj.* **1.** relatively small. **2.** not worth considering; insignificant. **—₁incon'siderably** *adv.*

inconsiderate (₁ɪnkən'sɪdərɪt) *adj.* lacking in care or thought for others; thoughtless. **—₁incon'siderateness** *n.*

inconsistent (₁ɪnkən'sɪstənt) *adj.* **1.** unstable or changeable in behaviour or mood. **2.** containing contradictory elements: *an inconsistent argument.* **3.** not in accordance: *actions inconsistent with high office.* —**,incon'sistency** *n.*

inconsolable (,ınkən'səʊləb'l) *adj.* that cannot be comforted. —**,incon'solably** *adv.*

inconspicuous (,ınkən'spıkjʊəs) *adj.* not easily noticed or seen; attracting little attention.

inconstant (ın'kɒnstənt) *adj.* **1.** not constant; variable. **2.** fickle. —**in'constancy** *n.*

incontestable (,ınkən'tɛstəb'l) *adj.* not able to be disputed.

incontinent (ın'kɒntınənt) *adj.* **1.** unable to control the bladder and bowels. **2.** lacking self-restraint, esp. sexually. [Latin *in-* not + *continere* to restrain] —**in'continence** *n.*

incontrovertible (ın,kɒntrə'vɜːtəb'l) *adj.* absolutely certain; undeniable. —**in,controvertibly** *adv.*

inconvenience (,ınkən'viːnıəns) *n.* **1.** a state or instance of trouble or difficulty. ~*vb.* **2.** to cause trouble or difficulty to (a person). —**incon'venient** *adj.*

incorporate *vb.* (ın'kɔːpə,reɪt). **1.** to include or be included as part of a united whole. **2.** to form a united whole or mass; merge or blend. **3.** to form into a corporation. ~*adj.* (ın'kɔːpərɪt). **4.** incorporated. [Latin *in-* in + *corpus* body] —**in'corpo,rated** *adj.* —**in,corpo'ration** *n.*

incorporeal (,ınkɔː'pɔːrıəl) *adj.* without material form, substance, or existence. —**incorporeity** (ın,kɔːpə'riːıtı) *n.*

incorrect (,ınkə'rɛkt) *adj.* **1.** wrong: *an incorrect answer.* **2.** not proper: *incorrect behaviour.* —**incor'rectly** *adv.*

incorrigible (ın'kɒrıdʒəb'l) *adj.* (of a person or behaviour) beyond correction or reform; incurably bad. —**in,corrigi'bility** *n.* —**in'corrigibly** *adv.*

incorruptible (,ınkə'rʌptəb'l) *adj.* **1.** incapable of being corrupted; honest. **2.** not subject to decay. —**,incor,rupti'bility** *n.*

increase *vb.* (ın'kriːs). **1.** to make or become greater in size, degree, or frequency. ~*n.* ('ınkriːs). **2.** an increasing or becoming increased. **3.** the amount by which something increases. **4. on the increase.** increasing, esp. in frequency. [Latin *in-* in + *crescere* to grow] —**in'creasingly** *adv.*

incredible (ın'krɛdəb'l) *adj.* **1.** unbelievable. **2.** *Informal.* marvellous; amazing. —**in,credi'bility** *n.* —**in'credibly** *adv.*

incredulity (,ınkrı'djuːlıtı) *n.* unwillingness to believe; scepticism.

incredulous (ın'krɛdjʊləs) *adj.* not prepared or willing to believe something; unbelieving.

increment ('ınkrımənt) *n.* **1.** the amount by which something increases. **2.** *Maths.* a small positive or negative change in a variable or function. [Latin *incrēmentum* increase] —**incremental** (,ınkrı'mɛnt'l) *adj.*

incriminate (ın'krımı,neıt) *vb.* **1.** to imply or suggest the guilt of (someone). **2.** to charge (someone) with a crime. [Late Lat-

in *incrīmināre* to accuse] —**in,crimi'nation** *n.* —**in'criminatory** *adj.*

incrust (ın'krʌst) *vb.* same as **encrust.**

incubate ('ınkjʊ,beıt) *vb.* **1.** (of birds) to hatch (eggs) by sitting on them. **2.** to cause (bacteria) to develop, esp. in an incubator or culture medium. **3.** (of disease germs) to remain inactive in an animal or human before causing disease. **4.** to develop gradually. [Latin *incubāre*] —**in cu'bation** *n.*

incubator ('ınkjʊ,beıtə) *n.* **1.** *Med.* an apparatus used to care for prematurely born babies. **2.** an apparatus for hatching birds' eggs or growing bacterial cultures.

incubus ('ınkjʊbəs) *n., pl.* **-bi** (-,baı) *or* **-buses. 1.** a demon believed in folklore to have sexual intercourse with sleeping women. **2.** a nightmare. [Latin *incubāre* to lie upon]

inculcate ('ınkʌl,keıt, ın'kʌlkeıt) *vb.* to instil (an idea, habit, or value) in a person by insistent repetition. [Latin *inculcāre* to tread upon] —**,incul'cation** *n.*

inculpate ('ınkʌl,peıt, ın'kʌlpeıt) *vb.* to incriminate. [Latin *in-* on + *culpāre* to blame]

incumbency (ın'kʌmbənsı) *n., pl.* **-cies.** the office, duty, or tenure of an incumbent.

incumbent (ın'kʌmbənt) *adj.* **1.** *Formal.* (often foll. by *on* or *upon* and an infinitive) resting on one as a duty; obligatory: *it is incumbent on me to attend.* ~*n.* **2.** a person who holds an office, esp. a clergyman holding a benefice. [Latin *incumbere* to lie upon]

incur (ın'kɜː) *vb.* **-curring, -curred.** to bring (something undesirable) upon oneself. [Latin *incurrere* to run into]

incurable (ın'kjʊərəb'l) *adj.* **1.** not capable of being cured or changed: *an incurable disease; incurable optimism.* ~*n.* **2.** a person with an incurable disease. —**in,cura'bility** *n.* —**in'curably** *adv.*

incurious (ın'kjʊərıəs) *adj.* indifferent or uninterested. —**in'curiously** *adv.*

incursion (ın'kɜːʃən) *n.* **1.** a sudden or brief invasion. **2.** an inroad or encroachment: *buying a car made a considerable incursion into our savings.* [Latin *incursiō* attack] —**incursive** (ın'kɜːsıv) *adj.*

ind. 1. independent. **2.** index. **3.** indicative. **4.** indirect. **5.** industrial.

Ind. 1. Independent. **2.** India. **3.** Indian. **4.** Indiana. **5.** Indies.

indaba (ın'dɑːbə) *n.* **1.** (among native peoples of southern Africa) a meeting to discuss a serious topic. **2.** *S. African informal.* a matter of concern or for discussion; problem. [Zulu]

indebted (ın'dɛtɪd) *adj.* **1.** owing gratitude for help or favours; obligated. **2.** owing money. —**in'debtedness** *n.*

indecent (ın'diːs'nt) *adj.* **1.** morally or sexually offensive. **2.** unseemly or improper: *they married in indecent haste.* —**in'decency** *n.* —**in'decently** *adv.*

indecipherable (,ındı'saıfərəb'l) *adj.* not able to be read.

indecisive (,ındı'saısıv) *adj.* **1.** unable to

make decisions; wavering. **2.** not decisive or conclusive: *an indecisive argument*. —**indecision** (ˌɪndɪˈsɪʒən) *or* ˌindeˈcisiveness *n*.

indeed (ɪnˈdiːd) *adv.* **1.** certainly; actually: *indeed, it may never happen*. **2.** truly, very: *that is indeed amazing*. **3.** in fact; what is more: *a comfortable, indeed wealthy family*. —*interj.* **4.** an expression of doubt or surprise.

indef. indefinite.

indefatigable (ˌɪndɪˈfætɪgəbəl) *adj.* unable to be tired out; unflagging. [Latin *in-* not + *fatigāre* to tire] —**indeˈfatigably** *adv.*

indefensible (ˌɪndɪˈfɛnsəbəl) *adj.* **1.** (of behaviour or statements) unable to be justified or supported. **2.** (of places or buildings) incapable of defence against attack. —**indeˌfensiˈbility** *n*.

indefinable (ˌɪndɪˈfaɪnəbəl) *adj.* not able to be fully described or explained.

indefinite (ɪnˈdɛfɪnɪt) *adj.* **1.** without exact limits; indeterminate: *an indefinite number*. **2.** vague or unclear. —**inˈdefinitely** *adv.*

indefinite article *n. Grammar.* a determiner that does not limit or specify the noun to which it refers, such as *a, an,* or *some.*

indelible (ɪnˈdɛlɪbəl) *adj.* **1.** incapable of being erased or obliterated. **2.** making indelible marks: *indelible ink.* [Latin *in-* not + *delēre* to destroy] —**inˈdelibly** *adv.*

indelicate (ɪnˈdɛlɪkɪt) *adj.* **1.** coarse, crude, or rough. **2.** offensive, embarrassing, or tasteless. —**inˈdelicacy** *n*.

indemnify (ɪnˈdɛmnɪˌfaɪ) *vb.* **-fying, -fied.** **1.** to secure against loss, damage, or liability; insure. **2.** to compensate for loss or damage; reimburse. —**inˌdemnifiˈcation** *n*.

indemnity (ɪnˈdɛmnɪtɪ) *n., pl.* **-ties.** **1.** compensation for loss or damage; reimbursement. **2.** insurance against loss or damage. **3.** legal exemption from penalties incurred. [Latin *in-* not + *damnum* damage]

indent *vb.* (ɪnˈdɛnt) **1.** to place (written matter) in from the margin. **2.** to write out (a document) in duplicate. **3.** *Chiefly Brit.* (foll. by *for, on,* or *upon*) to order (goods, esp. foreign merchandise) by an official order form. **4.** to notch (an edge or border); make jagged. **5.** to bind (an apprentice) by indenture. —*n.* (ˈɪnˌdɛnt). **6.** *Chiefly Brit.* an official order for goods, esp. foreign merchandise. [Latin *in-* in + *dēns* tooth]

indentation (ˌɪndɛnˈteɪʃən) *n.* **1.** a hollow, notch, or cut, as on an edge or on a coastline. **2.** an indenting or being indented. **3.** Also: **indention.** the leaving of space or the amount of space left between a margin and the start of an indented line.

indenture (ɪnˈdɛntʃə) *n.* **1.** a deed, contract, or sealed agreement. **2.** (*often pl.*) a contract binding an apprentice to his master. —*vb.* **3.** to enter into an agreement by indenture. **4.** to bind (an apprentice) by indenture.

independent (ˌɪndɪˈpɛndənt) *adj.* **1.** free from the influence or control of others. **2.** not dependent on anything else for function or validity; separate. **3.** not relying on the support, esp. financial support, of others. **4.** capable of acting for oneself or on one's own: *a very independent little girl*. **5.** of or having a private income large enough to enable one to live without working: *independent means.* **6.** *Maths.* (of a variable) not dependent on another variable. ~*n.* **7.** an independent person or thing. **8.** a politician who does not represent any political party. —**indeˈpendence** *n.* —**indeˈpendently** *adv.*

independent school *n.* (in Britain) a school that is neither financed nor controlled by the government or local authorities.

indescribable (ˌɪndɪˈskraɪbəbəl) *adj.* beyond description; too intense or extreme for words. —**indeˈscribably** *adv.*

indestructible (ˌɪndɪˈstrʌktəbəl) *adj.* not able to be destroyed; very strong.

indeterminate (ˌɪndɪˈtɜːmɪnɪt) *adj.* **1.** uncertain in extent, amount, or nature. **2.** left doubtful; inconclusive: *an indeterminate reply.* **3.** *Maths.* **a.** having no numerical meaning, as %. **b.** (of an equation) having more than one variable and an unlimited number of solutions. —**indeˈterminable** *adj.* —**indeˈterminacy** *n.*

index (ˈɪndɛks) *n., pl.* **-dexes** *or* **-dices** (-dɪˌsiːz). **1.** an alphabetical list of names or subjects mentioned in a text, usually at the back, and indicating where they are referred to. **2.** a file or catalogue, as in a library, which enables a book or reference to be found. **3.** an indication or sign. **4.** a pointer, needle, or other indicator on an instrument. **5.** *Maths.* **a.** same as **exponent. b.** a superscript number placed to the left of a radical sign indicating the root to be extracted: *the index of $\sqrt[3]{8}$ is 3.* **6.** a number indicating the level of wages or prices as compared with some standard value. **7.** a number or ratio indicating a specific characteristic or property: *refractive index.* ~*vb.* **8.** to put an index in (a book). **9.** to enter (a word or item) in an index. **10.** to make index-linked. [Latin: pointer]

indexation (ˌɪndɛkˈseɪʃən) *or* **index-linking** *n.* the act of making wages, pensions, or interest rates index-linked.

index finger *n.* the finger next to the thumb. Also called: **forefinger.**

index-linked *adj.* (of pensions, wages, or interest rates) directly related to the cost-of-living index and rising or falling accordingly.

Indiaman (ˈɪndɪəmən) *n., pl.* **-men.** (formerly) a merchant ship engaged in trade with India.

Indian (ˈɪndɪən) *n.* **1.** a person from the Republic of India, a subcontinent of Asia. **2.** an American Indian. ~*adj.* **3.** of India, its inhabitants, or any of their languages. **4.** of the American Indians or any of their languages.

Indian club *n.* a heavy bottle-shaped club, usually swung in pairs for exercise.

Indian corn *n.* same as **maize.**

Indian file *n.* same as **single file**.

Indian hemp *n.* same as **hemp**.

Indian ink *or esp. U.S. & Canad.* **India ink** (ˈɪndɪə) *n.* a black ink made from lampblack.

Indian list *n. Informal.* (in Canada) a list of persons to whom spirits may not be sold.

Indian summer *n.* **1.** a period of unusually warm weather, esp. in the autumn. **2.** a period of tranquillity or of renewed productivity towards the end of something, esp. a person's life.

India paper *n.* a thin soft opaque printing paper originally made in the Orient.

Indic (ˈɪndɪk) *adj.* **1.** of a branch of Indo-European consisting of many of the languages of India, including Sanskrit, Hindi, and Urdu. ~*n.* **2.** this group of languages.

indicate (ˈɪndɪˌkeɪt) *vb.* **1.** to be or give a sign or symptom of; imply: *cold hands indicate a warm heart.* **2.** to point out or show. **3.** to state briefly; suggest. **4.** (of measuring instruments) to show a reading of. **5.** (*usually passive*) to recommend or require: *surgery seems to be indicated for this patient.* [Latin *indicāre*] —**ˌindiˈcation** *n.*

indicative (ɪnˈdɪkətɪv) *adj.* **1.** (foll. by *of*) acting as a sign of; suggesting: *indicative of trouble ahead.* **2.** *Grammar.* denoting a mood of verbs used to make a statement. ~*n.* **3.** *Grammar.* the indicative mood.

indicator (ˈɪndɪˌkeɪtə) *n.* **1.** something that acts as a sign or indication: *an indicator of public opinion.* **2.** an instrument or device, such as a gauge, that registers or measures something. **3.** a device for turning left or right, esp. two pairs of lights that flash. **4.** *Chem.* a substance used to indicate the completion of a chemical reaction, usually by a change of colour.

indices (ˈɪndɪˌsiːz) *n.* a plural of **index**.

indict (ɪnˈdaɪt) *vb.* to charge (a person) formally with a crime, esp. in writing; accuse. [Latin *in-* against + *dictāre* to declare] —**inˈdictable** *adj.*

indictment (ɪnˈdaɪtmənt) *n.* **1.** *Criminal law.* a formal charge of crime, esp. in writing; accusation. **2.** a serious criticism; denunciation: *a striking indictment of our educational system.*

indie (ˈɪndɪ) *n. Informal.* an independent record company.

indifference (ɪnˈdɪfrəns) *n.* **1.** lack of concern or interest: *years of official indifference.* **2.** lack of importance; insignificance: *a matter of indifference to me.*

indifferent (ɪnˈdɪfrənt) *adj.* **1.** (often foll. by *to*) showing no concern or interest: *he was indifferent to my pleas.* **2.** unimportant; immaterial. **3. a.** of only average standard or quality; mediocre. **b.** not at all good; poor. **4.** showing or having no preferences; impartial. [Latin *indifferēns* making no distinction]

indigenous (ɪnˈdɪdʒɪnəs) *adj.* (often foll. by *to*) originating or occurring naturally (in a country or area); native: *the indigenous population.* [Latin *indigenus*]

indigent (ˈɪndɪdʒənt) *adj.* so poor as to lack even necessities; very needy. [Latin *indigēre* to need] —**ˈindigence** *n.*

indigestible (ˌɪndɪˈdʒɛstəbᵊl) *adj.* difficult or impossible to digest. —**ˌindiˌgestiˈbility** *n.*

indigestion (ˌɪndɪˈdʒɛstʃən) *n.* difficulty in digesting food, accompanied by stomach pain, heartburn, and belching.

indignant (ɪnˈdɪgnənt) *adj.* feeling or showing indignation. [Latin *indignārī* to be displeased with] —**inˈdignantly** *adv.*

indignation (ˌɪndɪgˈneɪʃən) *n.* anger aroused by something felt to be unfair, unworthy, or wrong.

indignity (ɪnˈdɪgnɪtɪ) *n., pl.* **-ties.** injury to one's self-esteem or dignity; humiliation.

indigo (ˈɪndɪˌgəʊ) *n., pl.* **-gos** *or* **-goes.** **1.** a blue dye originally obtained from plants but now made synthetically. ~*adj.* **2.** deep violet-blue. [Spanish, from Greek *Indikos* of India]

indirect (ˌɪndɪˈrɛkt) *adj.* **1.** not going in a direct course or line; roundabout: *an indirect route.* **2.** not done or caused directly; secondary: *indirect benefits.* **3.** not coming straight to the point; devious: *an indirect question.*

indirect object *n. Grammar.* the person or thing indirectly affected by the action of a verb and its direct object, as *John* in the sentence *I bought John a newspaper.*

indirect speech *n.* same as **reported speech.**

indirect tax *n.* a tax levied on goods or services which is paid indirectly by being added to the price.

indiscernible (ˌɪndɪˈsɜːnəbᵊl) *adj.* not able or scarcely able to be seen.

indiscipline (ɪnˈdɪsɪplɪn) *n.* lack of discipline.

indiscreet (ˌɪndɪˈskriːt) *adj.* not discreet; incautious or tactless.

indiscretion (ˌɪndɪˈskrɛʃən) *n.* **1.** the lack of discretion. **2.** an indiscreet act or remark.

indiscriminate (ˌɪndɪˈskrɪmɪnɪt) *adj.* **1.** lacking discrimination or careful choice; random: *indiscriminate slaughter.* **2.** jumbled; confused: *an indiscriminate mixture.* —**ˌindisˈcriminately** *adv.* —**ˌindisˌcrimiˈnation** *n.*

indispensable (ˌɪndɪˈspɛnsəbᵊl) *adj.* absolutely necessary; essential: *in my job a telephone is indispensable.* —**ˌindisˌpensaˈbility** *n.*

indisposed (ˌɪndɪˈspəʊzd) *adj.* **1.** sick or ill. **2.** unwilling. [Latin *indispositus* disordered] —**indisposition** (ˌɪndɪspəˈzɪʃən) *n.*

indisputable (ˌɪndɪˈspjuːtəbᵊl) *adj.* beyond doubt; certain.

indistinct (ˌɪndɪˈstɪŋkt) *adj.* unable to be seen or heard clearly. —**ˌindisˈtinctly** *adv.*

indistinguishable (ˌɪndɪˈstɪŋgwɪʃəbᵊl) *adj.* so similar as to be difficult to tell apart.

indite (ɪnˈdaɪt) *vb. Archaic.* to put into words and write. [Latin *indīcere* to declare]

indium (ˈɪndɪəm) *n.* a rare soft silvery

metallic element. Symbol: In [Latin *indicum* indigo]

individual (ˌɪndɪˈvɪdjʊəl) *adj.* **1.** of, relating to, or meant for a single person or thing: *individual tuition.* **2.** separate or distinct from others of its kind; specific: *please mark the individual pages.* **3.** characterized by unusual and striking qualities; unique. ~*n.* **4.** a single person, esp. when regarded as distinct from others: *the freedom of the individual.* **5.** *Biol.* a single animal or plant, esp. as distinct from a species. **6.** *Informal.* a person: *a most obnoxious individual.* [Latin *indīviduus* indivisible] —ˌindiˈvidually *adv.*

individualism (ˌɪndɪˈvɪdjʊəˌlɪzəm) *n.* **1.** the principle of leading one's life in one's own way. **2.** egoism. **3.** same as **laissez faire.** —ˌindiˈvidualist *n.* —ˌindiˌvidualˈistic *adj.*

individuality (ˌɪndɪˌvɪdjʊˈælɪtɪ) *n., pl.* -ties. **1.** distinctive or unique character or personality: *a work of great individuality.* **2.** the qualities that distinguish one person or thing from another. **3.** a separate existence.

individualize or **-ise** (ˌɪndɪˈvɪdjʊəˌlaɪz) *vb.* to make individual or distinctive in character.

indivisible (ˌɪndɪˈvɪzəbʰl) *adj.* **1.** unable to be divided. **2.** *Maths.* leaving a remainder when divided by a given number.

indoctrinate (ɪnˈdɒktrɪˌneɪt) *vb.* to teach (someone) systematically to accept a doctrine or opinion uncritically. —inˌdoctriˈnation *n.*

Indo-European (ˈɪndəʊ-) *adj.* **1.** of a family of languages that includes most of the European and some of the Asian languages. ~*n.* **2.** the Indo-European family of languages.

indolent (ˈɪndələnt) *adj.* disliking work; lazy; idle. [Latin *indolēns* not feeling pain] —ˈindolence *n.*

indomitable (ɪnˈdɒmɪtəbʰl) *adj.* (of a quality) difficult or impossible to defeat or discourage: *indomitable pride; an indomitable spirit.* [Latin *indomitus* untamable]

Indonesian (ˌɪndəʊˈniːzɪən) *adj.* **1.** of Indonesia, a republic in SE Asia, its people, or their language. ~*n.* **2.** a person from Indonesia.

indoor (ˈɪnˌdɔː) *adj.* situated, happening, or used inside a building: *an indoor pool.*

indoors (ˌɪnˈdɔːz) *adv., adj.* inside or into a building.

indorse (ɪnˈdɔːs) *vb.* same as **endorse.**

indrawn (ˌɪnˈdrɔːn) *adj.* drawn or pulled in: *an indrawn breath.*

indubitable (ɪnˈdjuːbɪtəbʰl) *adj.* not able to be doubted; definite. [Latin *in-* not + *dubitāre* to doubt] —inˈdubitably *adv.*

induce (ɪnˈdjuːs) *vb.* **1.** to persuade or use influence on. **2.** to cause or bring about. **3.** *Med.* to cause (labour) to begin by the use of drugs or other means. **4.** *Logic, obs.* to draw (a general conclusion) from particular instances. **5.** to produce (an electromotive force or electrical current) by induction. **6.** to transmit (magnetism) by

induction. [Latin *indūcere* to lead in] —inˈducible *adj.*

inducement (ɪnˈdjuːsmənt) *n.* **1.** the act of inducing. **2.** a means of inducing; incentive.

induct (ɪnˈdʌkt) *vb.* **1.** to bring in formally or install in a job, rank, or position. **2.** (foll. by *to* or *into*) to introduce to or initiate in knowledge of (a profession). [Latin *inductus* led in]

inductance (ɪnˈdʌktəns) *n.* the property of an electric circuit as a result of which an electromotive force is created by a change of current in the same or in a neighbouring circuit.

induction (ɪnˈdʌkʃən) *n.* **1.** an inducting or being inducted. **2.** the act of inducing (labour). **3.** (in an internal-combustion engine) the drawing in of mixed air and fuel from the carburettor to the cylinder. **4.** *Logic.* a process of reasoning by which a general conclusion is drawn from particular instances. **5.** the process by which electrical or magnetic properties are transferred, without physical contact, from one circuit or body to another. **6.** a formal introduction or entry into an office or position. —inˈductional *adj.*

induction coil *n.* a transformer for producing a high voltage from a low voltage. It consists of a soft-iron core, a primary coil of few turns, and a concentric secondary coil of many turns.

inductive (ɪnˈdʌktɪv) *adj.* **1.** of or operated by electrical or magnetic induction. **2.** *Logic.* of or using induction: *inductive reasoning.*

inductor (ɪnˈdʌktə) *n.* a device designed to create inductance in an electrical circuit.

indue (ɪnˈdjuː) *vb.* **-duing, -dued.** same as **endue.**

indulge (ɪnˈdʌldʒ) *vb.* **1.** (often foll. by *in*) to yield to or gratify (a whim or desire for): *to indulge in new clothes.* **2.** to yield to the wishes of; pamper: *to indulge a child.* **3.** to allow (oneself) the pleasure of something: *he indulged himself.* **4.** *Informal.* to take alcoholic drink. [Latin *indulgēre* to concede]

indulgence (ɪnˈdʌldʒəns) *n.* **1.** an indulging or being indulgent. **2.** a pleasure that is indulged in. **3.** liberal or tolerant treatment. **4.** something granted as a favour or privilege. **5.** *R.C. Church.* a remission of the temporal punishment for sin after its guilt has been forgiven.

indulgent (ɪnˈdʌldʒənt) *adj.* indulging or tending to indulge; kind or lenient often to excess. —inˈdulgently *adv.*

industrial (ɪnˈdʌstrɪəl) *adj.* **1.** of or derived from industry. **2.** employed or used in industry. **3.** relating to or concerned with industry: *industrial conditions.*

industrial action *n.* *Brit.* action, such as a strike or go-slow, taken by employees in industry to protest about pay, working conditions, or redundancies.

industrial estate *n.* *Brit.* an area of land set aside for industrial and business use.

industrialism (ɪnˈdʌstrɪəˌlɪzəm) *n.* an organization of society characterized by large-scale manufacturing industry rather than trade or farming.

industrialist (ɪn'dʌstrɪəlɪst) *n.* a person who owns or controls large amounts of money or property in industry.

industrialize *or* **-lise** (ɪn'dʌstrɪəˌlaɪz) *vb.* to develop industry on a large scale in (a country or region). —**inˌdustrialiˈzation** *or* **-liˈsation** *n.*

industrious (ɪn'dʌstrɪəs) *adj.* hard-working; diligent.

industry ('ɪndəstrɪ) *n., pl.* **-tries.** 1. the work and process involved in manufacture: *Japanese industry is making increasing use of robots.* 2. a branch of commercial enterprise concerned with the manufacture of a specified product: *the steel industry.* 3. the quality of working hard; diligence. [Latin *industrius* active]

inebriate *vb.* (ɪn'iːbrɪˌeɪt). 1. to make drunk; intoxicate. ~*n.* (ɪn'iːbrɪt). 2. a person who is drunk, esp. habitually. ~*adj.* (ɪn'iːbrɪt) *also* **inebriated.** 3. drunk, esp. habitually. [Latin *ēbrius* drunk] —**inˌebriˈation** *n.*

inedible (ɪn'ɛdɪb³l) *adj.* not fit to be eaten.

ineducable (ɪn'ɛdjʊkəb³l) *adj.* incapable of being educated, esp. on account of mental retardation.

ineffable (ɪn'ɛfəb³l) *adj.* too great or intense to be expressed in words; unutterable. [Latin *in-* not + *effābilis* utterable] —**inˈeffably** *adv.*

ineffective (ˌɪnɪ'fɛktɪv) *adj.* having no effect.

ineffectual (ˌɪnɪ'fɛktʃʊəl) *adj.* having no effect or an inadequate effect: *ineffectual struggles.*

inefficient (ˌɪnɪ'fɪʃənt) *adj.* wasteful, incompetent, or ineffective. —**inefˈficiency** *n.*

inelegant (ɪn'ɛlɪgənt) *adj.* lacking elegance or refinement.

ineligible (ɪn'ɛlɪdʒəb³l) *adj.* not qualified for or entitled to something.

ineluctable (ˌɪnɪ'lʌktəb³l) *adj.* incapable of being avoided; inescapable. [Latin *in-* not + *ēluctārī* to escape]

inept (ɪn'ɛpt) *adj.* 1. awkward, clumsy, or incompetent. 2. not suitable or fitting; out of place. [Latin *in-* not + *aptus* fitting] —**inˈeptiˌtude** *n.*

inequable (ɪn'ɛkwəb³l) *adj.* 1. unfair. 2. not uniform.

inequality (ˌɪnɪ'kwɒlɪtɪ) *n., pl.* **-ties.** 1. the lack of equality. 2. an instance of this. 3. lack of smoothness or regularity of a surface. 4. *Maths.* a statement indicating that the value of one quantity or expression is not equal to another.

inequitable (ɪn'ɛkwɪtəb³l) *adj.* unjust or unfair.

ineradicable (ˌɪnɪ'rædɪkəb³l) *adj.* not able to be removed or rooted out: *an ineradicable disease.*

inert (ɪn'ɜːt) *adj.* 1. with no inherent power to move or to resist motion. 2. inactive, lazy, or sluggish. 3. having only a limited ability to react chemically; unreactive. [Latin *iners* unskilled]

inertia (ɪn'ɜːʃə) *n.* 1. the state of being inert; disinclination to move or act. 2. *Physics.* the tendency of a body to remain still or continue moving unless a force is applied to it. —**inˈertial** *adj.*

inertia selling *n.* the illegal practice of sending unrequested goods to householders, followed by a bill for the goods if they do not return them.

inescapable (ˌɪnɪ'skeɪpəb³l) *adj.* not able to be avoided.

inessential (ˌɪnɪ'sɛnʃəl) *adj.* 1. not necessary. ~*n.* 2. an unnecessary thing.

inestimable (ɪn'ɛstɪməb³l) *adj.* not able to be estimated; immeasurable.

inevitable (ɪn'ɛvɪtəb³l) *adj.* 1. unavoidable; sure to happen; certain. 2. *Informal.* so regular as to be predictable: *the inevitable cup of tea.* ~*n.* 3. (often preceded by *the*) something that is unavoidable. [Latin *in-* not + *ēvītāre* to avoid] —**inˌeviˈtaˈbility** *n.* —**inˈevitably** *adv.*

inexact (ˌɪnɪg'zækt) *adj.* not exact or accurate.

inexcusable (ˌɪnɪk'skjuːzəb³l) *adj.* too bad to be justified or tolerated.

inexhaustible (ˌɪnɪg'zɔːstəb³l) *adj.* incapable of being used up; endless.

inexorable (ɪn'ɛksərəb³l) *adj.* 1. (of a person) not able to be moved by entreaty or persuasion. 2. (of a thing) that cannot be prevented from continuing or progressing; relentless: *an inexorable trend.* [Latin *in-* not + *exōrāre* to prevail upon] —**inˈexorably** *adv.*

inexpensive (ˌɪnɪk'spɛnsɪv) *adj.* not expensive; cheap.

inexperience (ˌɪnɪk'spɪərɪəns) *n.* lack of experience. —**inexˈperienced** *adj.*

inexpert (ɪn'ɛkspɜːt) *adj.* not expert; lacking skill.

inexpiable (ɪn'ɛkspɪəb³l) *adj.* (of sin) incapable of being atoned for; unpardonable.

inexplicable (ˌɪnɪk'splɪkəb³l) *adj.* not able to be explained.

inexpressible (ˌɪnɪk'sprɛsəb³l) *adj.* (of a feeling) too strong to be expressed in words.

in extremis *Latin.* (ɪn ɪk'striːmɪs) *adv.* 1. in dire straits. 2. at the point of death.

inextricable (ˌɪnɛks'trɪkəb³l) *adj.* 1. not able to be escaped from: *an inextricable dilemma.* 2. not able to be disentangled or separated: *an inextricable knot.* —**inexˈtricably** *adv.*

inf. 1. *Also:* **Inf.** infantry. 2. infinitive. 3. informal. 4. information.

infallible (ɪn'fæləb³l) *adj.* 1. incapable of error. 2. not liable to fail; certain: *an infallible cure.* 3. (of the Pope) incapable of error in setting forth matters of doctrine on faith and morals. —**inˌfalliˈbility** *n.* —**inˈfallibly** *adv.*

infamous ('ɪnfəməs) *adj.* having a bad reputation; notorious.

infamy ('ɪnfəmɪ) *n., pl.* **-mies.** 1. the state of being infamous. 2. an infamous act or event. [Latin *infāmis* of evil repute]

infancy ('ɪnfənsɪ) *n., pl.* **-cies.** 1. the state or period of being an infant. 2. an early stage of growth or development: *this research is still in its infancy*. **3.** *Law.* the state or period of being a minor.

infant ('ɪnfənt) *n.* **1.** a very young child; baby. **2.** *Law.* same as **minor** (sense 4). **3.** *Brit.* a young schoolchild. **4.** (*modifier*) **a.** of or relating to young children or infancy. **b.** designed or intended for young children: *infant school*. ~*adj.* **5.** in an early stage of development: *an infant science*. [Latin *infāns*, lit.: speechless]

infanta (ɪn'fæntə) *n.* **1.** (formerly) a daughter of a king of Spain or Portugal. **2.** the wife of an infante. [Spanish and Portuguese]

infante (ɪn'fæntɪ) *n.* (formerly) any son of a king of Spain or Portugal, except the heir to the throne. [Spanish and Portuguese]

infanticide (ɪn'fæntɪˌsaɪd) *n.* the killing of an infant. [*-icide* from Latin *caedere* to kill]

infantile ('ɪnfənˌtaɪl) *adj.* **1.** like a child in action or behaviour; childishly immature. **2.** of infants or infancy.

infantile paralysis *n.* same as **poliomyelitis.**

infantry ('ɪnfəntrɪ) *n., pl.* **-tries.** soldiers who fight on foot. [Italian *infanteria*]

infant school *n.* *Brit.* a school for children aged between 5 and 7.

infatuate (ɪn'fætjʊˌeɪt) *vb.* to inspire or fill with an intense and unreasoning passion. [Latin *infatuāre*] —**inˌfatuˈation** *n.*

infatuated (ɪn'fætjʊˌeɪtɪd) *adj.* (often foll. by *with*) carried away by an intense and unreasoning passion for someone.

infect (ɪn'fɛkt) *vb.* **1.** to cause infection in; contaminate (a person or thing) with a germ or virus or its consequent disease. **2.** to taint or contaminate. **3.** to affect, esp. adversely, with an opinion or feeling as if by contagion: *I was infected by his pessimism.* [Latin *inficere* to stain]

infection (ɪn'fɛkʃən) *n.* **1.** contamination of a person or thing by a germ or virus or its consequent disease. **2.** the resulting physical condition. **3.** an infectious disease. **4.** something that infects.

infectious (ɪn'fɛkʃəs) *adj.* **1.** (of a disease) capable of being transmitted without actual contact; caused by microorganisms, such as bacteria or viruses. **2.** causing or transmitting infection. **3.** tending to spread from one person to another: *infectious mirth.*

infectious hepatitis *n.* an acute viral disease causing inflammation of the liver, fever, and jaundice.

infectious mononucleosis *n.* same as **glandular fever.**

infelicity (ˌɪnfɪ'lɪsɪtɪ) *n., pl.* **-ties.** **1.** the state or quality of being unhappy or unfortunate. **2.** an instance of bad luck; misfortune. **3.** something, esp. a remark or expression, that is inapt. —ˌinfe'licitous *adj.*

infer (ɪn'fɜː) *vb.* **-ferring, -ferred.** **1.** to conclude by reasoning from evidence; deduce. **2.** *Not universally accepted.* to imply or suggest. [Latin *inferre* to bring into] —in'ferable *or* in'ferrable *adj.*

inference ('ɪnfərəns) *n.* **1.** the act or process of reaching a conclusion by reasoning from evidence. **2.** an inferred conclusion or deduction.

inferential (ˌɪnfə'rɛnʃəl) *adj.* of or based on inference.

inferior (ɪn'fɪərɪə) *adj.* **1.** lower in value or quality. **2.** lower in rank, position, or status; subordinate. **3.** of poor quality; second-rate. **4.** lower in position; situated beneath. **5.** *Printing.* (of a character) printed at the foot of an ordinary character. ~*n.* **6.** a person inferior to another, esp. in rank. [Latin: lower] —**inferiority** (ɪnˌfɪərɪ'ɒrɪtɪ) *n.*

inferiority complex *n.* *Psychiatry.* a disorder arising from a feeling of inferiority to others, characterized by aggressiveness or extreme shyness.

infernal (ɪn'fɜːnəl) *adj.* **1.** of or relating to hell. **2.** wicked and cruel; diabolic; fiendish: *infernal experiments.* **3.** *Informal.* irritating: *stop that infernal noise.* [Latin *infernus* lower]

inferno (ɪn'fɜːnəʊ) *n., pl.* **-nos.** **1.** (*sometimes cap.;* usually preceded by *the*) hell; the infernal region. **2.** a place or situation resembling hell, usually because it is crowded and noisy. **3.** a raging fire. [Late Latin *infernus* hell]

infertile (ɪn'fɜːtaɪl) *adj.* **1.** not capable of producing offspring; sterile. **2.** (of land) not productive; barren. —**infertility** (ˌɪnfə'tɪlɪtɪ) *n.*

infest (ɪn'fɛst) *vb.* (of vermin or parasites) to inhabit or overrun (a place, plant, etc.) in unpleasantly large numbers: *the place was infested by rats.* [Latin *infestāre* to molest] —ˌinfes'tation *n.*

infidel ('ɪnfɪdəl) *n.* **1.** a person who has no religious belief; unbeliever. **2.** a person who rejects a specific religion, esp. Christianity or Islam. ~*adj.* **3.** of unbelievers or unbelief. [Latin *infidēlis* unfaithful]

infidelity (ˌɪnfɪ'dɛlɪtɪ) *n., pl.* **-ties.** **1.** unfaithfulness to another, esp. one's husband or wife. **2.** an act or instance of unfaithfulness.

infield ('ɪnˌfiːld) *n.* **1.** *Cricket.* the area of the field near the pitch. **2.** *Baseball.* the area of the playing field enclosed by the base lines. —'inˌfielder *n.*

infighting ('ɪnˌfaɪtɪŋ) *n.* **1.** rivalry or quarrelling between members of the same group or organization. **2.** *Boxing.* combat at close quarters.

infiltrate ('ɪnfɪlˌtreɪt) *vb.* **1.** *Mil.* to pass undetected through (an enemy-held line or position). **2.** to enter or cause to enter (an organization) gradually and in secret, so as to gain influence or control: *they infiltrated the party structure.* **3.** to pass (a liquid or gas) through (a substance) by filtering or (of a liquid or gas) to pass through (a substance) by filtering. —ˌinfil'tration *n.* —'infilˌtrator *n.*

infin. infinitive.

infinite ('ɪnfɪnɪt) *adj.* **1.** having no limits or boundaries in time, space, extent, or size. **2.** extremely or immeasurably great or numerous: *infinite wealth.* **3.** *Maths.*

having an unlimited or uncountable number of digits, factors, or terms. —'**infinitely** adv.

infinitesimal (,ɪnfɪnɪ'tesɪməl) adj. **1.** infinitely or immeasurably small. **2.** Maths. of or involving a small change in the value of a variable that approaches zero as a limit. ~n. **3.** Maths. an infinitesimal quantity.

infinitive (ɪn'fɪnɪtɪv) n. Grammar. a form of the verb which is not inflected for tense or person and is used without a particular subject. In English, the infinitive usually consists of the word to followed by the verb.

infinitude (ɪn'fɪnɪˌtjuːd) n. **1.** the state or quality of being infinite. **2.** an infinite extent or quantity.

infinity (ɪn'fɪnɪtɪ) n., pl. **-ties. 1.** the state or quality of being infinite. **2.** endless time, space, or quantity. **3.** an infinitely great number or amount. **4.** Maths. the concept of a value greater than any finite numerical value.

infirm (ɪn'fɜːm) adj. weak in health or body, esp. from old age.

infirmary (ɪn'fɜːmərɪ) n., pl. **-ries.** a place for the treatment of the sick or injured; hospital.

infirmity (ɪn'fɜːmɪtɪ) n., pl. **-ties. 1.** the state or quality of being infirm. **2.** physical weakness or debility; frailty.

infix (ɪn'fɪks, 'ɪnˌfɪks) vb. **1.** to fix firmly in. **2.** to instil or impress on the mind by repetition. —ˌ**infix'ation** or **infixion** (ɪn'fɪkʃən) n.

in flagrante delicto (ɪn fləˈɡræntɪ dɪˈlɪktəʊ) adv. Chiefly law. in the very act of committing the offence; red-handed. [Latin]

inflame (ɪn'fleɪm) vb. **1.** to arouse or become aroused to violent emotion, esp. anger. **2.** to increase or intensify; aggravate. **3.** to produce inflammation in (a tissue, organ, or part) or (of a tissue, organ, or part) to become inflamed. **4.** to set or be set on fire.

inflammable (ɪn'flæməbᵊl) adj. **1.** liable to catch fire; flammable. **2.** easily aroused to anger or passion. —ˌ**inflamma'bility** n.

inflammation (ˌɪnfləˈmeɪʃən) n. **1.** the reaction of living tissue to injury or infection, characterized by heat, redness, swelling, and pain. **2.** an inflaming or being inflamed.

inflammatory (ɪn'flæmətrɪ) adj. **1.** tending to arouse violence or strong emotion. **2.** characterized by or caused by inflammation.

inflatable (ɪn'fleɪtəbᵊl) adj. **1.** capable of being inflated. ~n. **2.** any object, made of strong plastic or rubber, which can be inflated.

inflate (ɪn'fleɪt) vb. **1.** to expand or cause to expand by filling with gas or air. **2.** to give an impression of greater importance than is justified; puff up: to have an inflated opinion of oneself. **3.** to cause inflation of (prices or money) or (of prices or money) to undergo inflation. [Latin inflāre to blow into]

inflation (ɪn'fleɪʃən) n. **1.** an inflating or

being inflated. **2.** Econ. a progressive increase in the general level of prices brought about by an increase in the amount of money in circulation or by increases in costs. **3.** Informal. the rate of increase of prices. —in'**flationary** adj.

inflect (ɪn'flɛkt) vb. **1.** Grammar. to change (the form of a word) by inflection. **2.** to change (the voice) in tone or pitch; modulate. **3.** to bend or curve. [Latin inflectere to curve, alter] —in'**flective** adj.

inflection or **inflexion** (ɪn'flɛkʃən) n. **1.** modulation of the voice. **2.** Grammar. a change in the form of a word, signalling change in such grammatical functions as tense or number. **3.** an angle or bend. **4.** an inflecting or being inflected. **5.** Maths. a change in curvature from concave to convex or vice versa. —in'**flectional** or in'**flexional** adj.

inflexible (ɪn'flɛksəbᵊl) adj. **1.** obstinate; unyielding: dogmatically inflexible in the face of change. **2.** unalterable; fixed: inflexible schedules. **3.** rigid; stiff: inflexible joints. —inˌ**flexi'bility** n.

inflict (ɪn'flɪkt) vb. **1.** (often foll. by on or upon) to impose (something unwelcome or unpleasant, such as pain) upon (a person). **2.** to deal out (a blow or wound). [Latin infligere to strike (something) against] —in'**fliction** n. —in'**flictor** n.

in-flight adj. provided during flight in an aircraft: in-flight meals.

inflorescence (ˌɪnflɔː'rɛsəns) n. **1.** the part of a plant that consists of the flower-bearing stalks. **2.** the arrangement of the flowers on the stalks. **3.** the process of flowering; blossoming. [Latin in- into + flōrescere to bloom]

inflow ('ɪnˌfləʊ) n. **1.** something, such as a liquid or gas, that flows in. **2.** the act of flowing in; influx.

influence ('ɪnfluəns) n. **1.** an effect of one person or thing on another. **2.** the power of a person or thing to have such an effect. **3.** power resulting from ability, wealth, or position. **4.** a person or thing having influence. **5. under the influence.** Informal. drunk. ~vb. **6.** to persuade or induce. **7.** to have an effect upon (actions or events); affect. [Latin influere to flow into]

influential (ˌɪnflʊ'ɛnʃəl) adj. having or exerting influence.

influenza (ˌɪnflʊ'ɛnzə) n. a highly contagious viral disease characterized by fever, muscular pains, and inflammation of the breathing passages. [Italian: influence, hence incursion, epidemic]

influx ('ɪnˌflʌks) n. **1.** the arrival or entry of many people or things. **2.** the act of flowing in; inflow. [Latin influere to flow into]

info ('ɪnfəʊ) n. Informal. short for **information.**

inform (ɪn'fɔːm) vb. **1.** (often foll. by of or about) to give information to; tell. **2.** (often foll. by of or about) to make knowledgeable (about) or familiar (with). **3.** (often foll. by against or on) to give information incriminating someone, esp. to the police. **4.** to impart some essential or formative characteristic to. **5.** to animate or inspire. [Latin *informāre* to describe] —**in'formed** *adj.*

informal (ɪn'fɔːməl) *adj.* **1.** not of a formal, official, or stiffly conventional nature; relaxed and friendly: *an informal interview.* **2.** appropriate to everyday life or use rather than formal occasions: *informal clothes.* **3.** (of speech or writing) appropriate to ordinary conversation rather than to formal written language. —**informality** (ˌɪnfɔː'mælɪtɪ) *n.* —**in'formally** *adv.*

informant (ɪn'fɔːmənt) *n.* a person who gives information.

information (ˌɪnfə'meɪʃən) *n.* **1.** knowledge acquired in any manner; facts. **2.** *Computers.* **a.** the meaning given to data by the way it is interpreted. **b.** same as **data** (sense 2).

information technology *n.* the production, storage, and communication of information using computers and microelectronics.

information theory *n.* the study of the processes of communication and the transmission of information.

informative (ɪn'fɔːmətɪv) *adj.* providing information; instructive.

informer (ɪn'fɔːmə) *n.* a person who informs against someone, esp. a criminal.

infra dig ('ɪnfrə 'dɪg) *adj. Informal.* beneath one's dignity. [Latin *infrā dignitātem*]

infrared (ˌɪnfrə'rɛd) *adj.* **1.** of or using rays with a wavelength just beyond the red end of the visible spectrum. ~*n.* **2.** the infrared part of the spectrum. [Latin *infra* beneath]

infrasonic (ˌɪnfrə'sɒnɪk) *adj.* having a frequency below the range audible to the human ear. [Latin *infra* beneath]

infrastructure ('ɪnfrəˌstrʌktʃə) *n.* **1.** the basic structure of an organization or system. **2.** the stock of facilities, services, and equipment in a country, including factories, roads, and schools, that are needed for it to function properly. [Latin *infra* beneath]

infrequent (ɪn'friːkwənt) *adj.* not happening often; only occasional. —**in'frequently** *adv.*

infringe (ɪn'frɪndʒ) *vb.* **1.** to violate or break (a law or agreement). **2.** (foll. by *on* or *upon*) to encroach or trespass on: *the children infringed on our privacy.* [Latin *infringere* to break off] —**in'fringement** *n.*

infuriate (ɪn'fjʊərɪˌeɪt) *vb.* to anger; annoy. [Medieval Latin *infuriāre*] —**in'furiˌating** *adj.* —**in'furiˌatingly** *adv.*

infuse (ɪn'fjuːz) *vb.* **1.** (often foll. by *into*) to instil or impart (a quality). **2.** (foll. by *with*) to inspire: *she infused them with new hope.* **3.** to soak or be soaked in order to extract flavour or other properties. [Latin *infundere* to pour into]

infusible (ɪn'fjuːzəb'l) *adj.* that cannot be fused or melted. —**in,fusi'bility** *n.*

infusion (ɪn'fjuːʒən) *n.* **1.** the act of infus-ing. **2.** something infused. **3.** an extract obtained by soaking.

ingenious (ɪn'dʒiːnjəs) *adj.* made or contrived with skill and originality; clever. [Latin *ingenium* natural ability]

ingénue ('ænʒeɪˌnjuː) *n.* an artless, innocent, or inexperienced young woman, esp. as a role played by an actress. [French]

ingenuity (ˌɪndʒɪ'njuːɪtɪ) *n.* inventive talent; cleverness. [Latin *ingenuitās* a freeborn condition; meaning infl. by INGENIOUS]

ingenuous (ɪn'dʒɛnjʊəs) *adj.* **1.** naive, artless, or innocent. **2.** candid; frank; straightforward. [Latin *ingenuus* freeborn, virtuous]

ingest (ɪn'dʒɛst) *vb.* to take (food or liquid) into the body. [Latin *ingerere* to put into] —**in'gestion** *n.*

ingle ('ɪŋg'l) *n. Archaic or dialect.* a fire in a room or a fireplace. [prob. Scot. Gaelic *aingeal* fire]

inglenook ('ɪŋg'lˌnʊk) *n. Brit.* a corner by a fireplace; chimney corner.

ingoing ('ɪnˌgəʊɪŋ) *adj.* going in; entering.

ingot ('ɪŋgət) *n.* a piece of metal cast in a form suitable for storage, usually a bar. [origin unknown]

ingrained *or* **engrained** (ɪn'greɪnd) *adj.* **1.** (of a habit, feeling, or belief) deeply impressed or instilled. **2.** (esp. of dirt) worked into or through the fibre or pores. [*dyed in grain* dyed with kermes through the fibre]

ingratiate (ɪn'greɪʃɪˌeɪt) *vb.* (often foll. by *with*) to act so as to bring (oneself) into favour with (someone). [Latin *in-* in + *grātia* favour] —**in'gratiˌating** *adj.*

ingratitude (ɪn'grætɪˌtjuːd) *n.* lack of gratitude; ungratefulness.

ingredient (ɪn'griːdɪənt) *n.* a component of a mixture or compound, esp. in cooking. [Latin *ingrediēns* going into]

ingress ('ɪngrɛs) *n.* **1.** the act of going or coming in. **2.** the right or permission to enter. [Latin *ingressus*]

ingrowing ('ɪnˌgrəʊɪŋ) *adj.* (esp. of a toenail) growing abnormally into the flesh.

ingrown ('ɪnˌgrəʊn, ɪn'grəʊn) *adj.* (esp. of a toenail) grown abnormally into the flesh.

inhabit (ɪn'hæbɪt) *vb.* to live or dwell in; occupy. [Latin *inhabitāre*] —**in'habitable** *adj.*

inhabitant (ɪn'hæbɪtənt) *n.* a person or animal that is a permanent resident of a particular place or region.

inhalant (ɪn'heɪlənt) *n.* a medicinal preparation inhaled for its therapeutic effect.

inhale (ɪn'heɪl) *vb.* to draw (breath, smoke, or vapour) into the lungs; breathe in. [Latin *in-* in + *halāre* to breathe] —**inhalation** (ˌɪnhə'leɪʃən) *n.*

inhaler (ɪn'heɪlə) *n.* a device for sending out therapeutic vapours for inhalation, esp. one for relieving nasal congestion.

inharmonious (ˌɪnhɑː'məʊnɪəs) *adj.* lacking harmony; discordant; disagreeing.

inhere (ɪn'hɪə) *vb.* (foll. by *in*) to be an inseparable part (of). [Latin *inhaerēre* to stick in]

inherent (ɪn'hɪərənt, -'hɛr-) *adj.* existing as

an inseparable part; intrinsic. —**in'herent**ly adv.

inherit (ɪn'hɛrɪt) vb. **1.** to receive money, property, or a title by succession or under a will. **2.** to receive (a characteristic) from an earlier generation by heredity: he inherited the disease from his father. **3.** to receive (a position or situation) from a predecessor: the government inherited a work economy. [Old French enheriter] —**in'heritor** n.

inheritable (ɪn'hɛrɪtəb'l) adj. **1.** capable of being transmitted by heredity from one generation to a later one. **2.** capable of being inherited.

inheritance (ɪn'hɛrɪtəns) n. **1.** Law. **a.** hereditary succession to an estate or title. **b.** the right of an heir to succeed on the death of an ancestor. **2.** the act of inheriting. **3.** something inherited or to be inherited; heritage. **4.** the fact of receiving characteristics from an earlier generation by heredity.

inhibit (ɪn'hɪbɪt) vb. **1.** to restrain or hinder (an impulse or desire). **2.** to prohibit or prevent: it inhibits progress. **3.** Chem. to stop, prevent, or decrease the rate of (a chemical reaction). [Latin inhibēre] —**in'hibited** adj.

inhibition (ˌɪnɪ'bɪʃən, ˌɪnhɪ-) n. **1.** an inhibiting or being inhibited. **2.** Psychol. a mental condition in which the expression and behaviour of an individual become restricted by emotional resistance. **3.** the process of stopping or retarding a chemical reaction.

inhospitable (ˌɪnhɒ'spɪtəb'l, ɪn'hɒs-) adj. **1.** not hospitable; unfriendly. **2.** (of a place or climate) not easy to live in; harsh.

inhuman (ɪn'hjuːmən) adj. Also: **inhumane** (ˌɪnhjuː'meɪn). unfeeling; cruel; brutal. **2.** not human.

inhumanity (ˌɪnhjuː'mænɪtɪ) n., pl. **-ties. 1.** lack of humane qualities. **2.** an inhumane act.

inimical (ɪ'nɪmɪk'l) adj. **1.** adverse or unfavourable: inimical to change. **2.** not friendly; hostile. [Latin in- not + amīcus friendly]

inimitable (ɪ'nɪmɪtəb'l) adj. incapable of being imitated; unique. —**in'imitably** adv.

iniquity (ɪ'nɪkwɪtɪ) n., pl. **-ties. 1.** lack of justice or righteousness; wickedness. **2.** a wicked act; sin. [Latin inīquus unfair] —**in'iquitous** adj.

initial (ɪ'nɪʃəl) adj. **1.** of or at the beginning. ~n. **2.** the first letter of a word, esp. a person's name. **3.** Printing. a large letter set at the beginning of a chapter or work. ~vb. **-tialling, -tialled** or U.S. **-tialing, -tialed. 3.** to sign with one's initials, esp. to indicate approval; endorse. [Latin initium beginning] —**in'itially** adv.

initiate vb. (ɪ'nɪʃɪˌeɪt). **1.** to begin or set going: to initiate peace talks. **2.** to accept (new members) into an organization or social group, through often secret ceremonies. **3.** to teach fundamentals of a skill or knowledge to. ~n. (ɪ'nɪʃɪɪt, -ˌeɪt). **4.** a person who has been initiated, esp. recent-

ly. **5.** a beginner; novice. [Latin initiāre to begin] —**i,niti'ation** n. —**i'niti,ator** n.

initiative (ɪ'nɪʃɪətɪv) n. **1.** a first step; commencing move: a peace initiative. **2.** the right or power to initiate something: he has the initiative. **3.** enterprise: try to show some initiative. **4. on one's own initiative.** without being prompted.

inject (ɪn'dʒɛkt) vb. **1.** Med. to introduce (a fluid) into the body (of a person or animal) by means of a syringe. **2.** (foll. by into) to introduce (a new element): to inject humour into a scene. [Latin injicere to throw in] —**in'jection** n.

injudicious (ˌɪndʒuː'dɪʃəs) adj. showing poor judgment; unwise.

injunction (ɪn'dʒʌŋkʃən) n. **1.** Law. an order issued by a court to a person or group, esp. to refrain from some act. **2.** an authoritative command. [Latin injungere to enjoin] —**in'junctive** adj.

injure (ˈɪndʒə) vb. **1.** to hurt physically or mentally. **2.** to do wrong to (a person), esp. by an injustice. —**'injured** adj.

injurious (ɪn'dʒʊərɪəs) adj. **1.** causing harm. **2.** abusive, slanderous, or libellous.

injury (ˈɪndʒərɪ) n., pl. **-ries. 1.** physical hurt. **2.** a specific instance of this: a leg injury. **3.** harm done to the feelings. [Latin injūria injustice]

injury time n. Football, rugby, etc. extra playing time added on to compensate for time spent attending to injured players during the match.

injustice (ɪn'dʒʌstɪs) n. **1.** unfairness; lack of justice. **2.** an unjust act.

ink (ɪŋk) n. **1.** a black or coloured liquid used for printing, writing, and drawing. **2.** a dark brown fluid squirted into the water for self-concealment by an octopus or cuttlefish. ~vb. **3.** to mark with ink. **4.** to coat (a printing surface) with ink. [Old French enque]

inkling (ˈɪŋklɪŋ) n. a hint; vague idea or suspicion. [Middle English inclen to hint at]

inkstand (ˈɪŋkˌstænd) n. a stand or tray on which are kept writing tools and containers for ink.

inkwell (ˈɪŋkˌwɛl) n. a small container for ink, often fitted into the surface of a desk.

inky (ˈɪŋkɪ) adj. **inkier, inkiest. 1.** like ink, esp. in colour; dark or black. **2.** of or stained with ink. —**'inkiness** n.

inlaid (ɪn'leɪd) adj. **1.** set in another material so that the surfaces are smooth and flat, as a design in wood. **2.** having such a design: an inlaid table.

inland adj. (ˈɪnlənd). **1.** of or in the interior of a country or region, away from a sea or border. **2.** Chiefly Brit. operating within a country or region; domestic: inland trade. ~n. (ˈɪnˌlænd, -lənd). **3.** the interior of a country or region. ~adv. (ˈɪnˌlænd, -lənd). **4.** towards or into the interior of a country or region.

Inland Revenue n. (in Britain and New Zealand) a government department that administers and collects major direct taxes, such as income tax.

in-law n. **1.** a relative by marriage.

~*adj.* **2.** related by marriage: *a father-in-law.*

inlay *vb.* (ɪnˈleɪ), **-laying, -laid. 1.** to decorate (an article, esp. of furniture) by inserting pieces of wood, ivory, or metal so that the surfaces are smooth and flat. ~*n.* (ˈɪnˌleɪ). **2.** *Dentistry.* a filling shaped to fit a cavity. **3.** decoration made by inlaying. **4.** an inlaid article.

inlet (ˈɪnlɪt) *n.* **1.** a narrow strip of water which goes from a sea or lake into the land or between two islands. **2.** a passage or valve through which a substance, esp. a fluid, enters a machine.

in loco parentis Latin. (ɪn ˈlɒkəʊ pəˈrɛntɪs) in place of a parent: said of a person acting in a parental capacity.

inmate (ˈɪnˌmeɪt) *n.* a person who is confined to an institution such as a prison or hospital.

inmost (ˈɪnˌməʊst) *adj.* same as **innermost.**

inn (ɪn) *n.* a pub or small hotel providing food and accommodation. [Old English]

innards (ˈɪnədz) *pl. n. Informal.* the internal organs of the body, esp. the entrails. [var. of *inwards*]

innate (ɪˈneɪt, ˈɪneɪt) *adj.* existing from birth, rather than acquired; natural; inborn: *an innate talent.* [Latin *innascī* to be born in] —**inˈnately** *adv.*

inner (ˈɪnə) *adj.* **1.** happening or located inside or further inside: *an inner room.* **2.** of the mind or spirit: *inner calm.* **3.** more profound; less apparent: *the inner meaning.* **4.** exclusive or private: *inner regions of the party.* ~*n.* **5.** *Archery.* **a.** the red innermost ring on a target. **b.** a shot which hits this ring.

inner city *n.* the parts of a city in or near its centre, where there are often social and economic problems such as unemployment and inadequate housing.

inner man *or (fem.)* **inner woman** *n.* **1.** the mind or soul. **2.** *Jocular.* the stomach.

innermost (ˈɪnəˌməʊst) *adj.* **1.** furthest within; central. **2.** most intimate or private.

inner tube *n.* an inflatable rubber tube inside a pneumatic tyre casing.

innings (ˈɪnɪŋz) *n.* **1.** (*functioning as sing.*) *Cricket, baseball.* **a.** the batting turn of a player or team. **b.** the runs scored during such a turn. **2.** a period of opportunity or action.

innkeeper (ˈɪnˌkiːpə) *n.* an owner or manager of an inn.

innocence (ˈɪnəsəns) *n.* the quality or state of being innocent. [Latin *innocentia* harmlessness]

innocent (ˈɪnəsənt) *adj.* **1.** not tainted with evil; sinless; pure. **2.** not guilty of a particular crime; blameless. **3.** (foll. by *of*) free of; lacking: *innocent of all knowledge of history.* **4.** harmless or innocuous: *an innocent game.* **5.** naive or artless. ~*n.* **6.** an innocent person, esp. a young child or a naive adult. —**ˈinnocently** *adv.*

innocuous (ɪˈnɒkjʊəs) *adj.* having no adverse or harmful effect; harmless. [Latin *innocuus*]

innovate (ˈɪnəˌveɪt) *vb.* to invent or begin to apply new methods or ideas. [Latin *innovāre* to renew] —**ˈinnoˌvative** *or* **ˈinnoˌvatory** *adj.* —**ˈinnoˌvator** *n.*

innovation (ˌɪnəˈveɪʃən) *n.* **1.** something newly introduced, such as a new method or device. **2.** the act of innovating.

innuendo (ˌɪnjʊˈɛndəʊ) *n., pl.* **-dos** *or* **-does.** an indirect or subtle reference, esp. one which is malicious, derogatory, or disapproving; insinuation. [Latin: by hinting]

Innuit (ˈɪnjuːɪt) *n.* same as **Inuit.**

innumerable (ɪˈnjuːmərəbᵊl) *adj.* too many to be counted; extremely numerous. —**inˈnumerably** *adv.*

innumerate (ɪˈnjuːmərɪt) *adj.* having no knowledge or understanding of mathematics or science. —**inˈnumeracy** *n.*

inoculate (ɪˈnɒkjʊˌleɪt) *vb.* **1.** to inject a vaccine or serum into (a person or animal) in order to create immunity to a disease. **2.** to introduce (microorganisms, esp. bacteria) into (a culture medium). [Latin *inoculāre* to implant] —**inˌocuˈlation** *n.*

inoffensive (ˌɪnəˈfɛnsɪv) *adj.* causing no harm or annoyance; unobjectionable.

inoperable (ɪnˈɒpərəbᵊl) *adj. Surgery.* that cannot safely be operated on: *an inoperable tumour.*

inopportune (ɪnˈɒpəˌtjuːn) *adj.* badly timed or inappropriate.

inordinate (ɪnˈɔːdɪnɪt) *adj.* **1.** exceeding normal limits; excessive: *an inordinate number of old people died of cold this winter.* **2.** unrestrained, as in behaviour or emotion: *inordinate fury.* [Latin *inordinātus* disordered] —**inˈordinately** *adv.*

inorganic (ˌɪnɔːˈɡænɪk) *adj.* **1.** not having the structure or characteristics of living organisms; not organic. **2.** of or denoting chemical compounds that do not contain carbon. **3.** not resulting from or produced by growth; artificial: *inorganic fertilizers.*

inorganic chemistry *n.* the branch of chemistry concerned with the elements and compounds which do not contain carbon.

inpatient (ˈɪnˌpeɪʃənt) *n.* a patient living in the hospital where he is being treated.

input (ˈɪnˌpʊt) *n.* **1.** that which is put in. **2.** a resource required for industrial production, such as money, labour, or power. **3.** *Computers.* the data fed into a computer. ~*vb.* **4.** to insert (data) into a computer.

inquest (ˈɪnˌkwɛst) *n.* **1.** an official inquiry, esp. into the cause of an unexplained, sudden, or violent death, held by a coroner. **2.** *Informal.* an investigation or discussion. [Latin *in-* into + *quaesītus* investigation]

inquietude (ɪnˈkwaɪɪˌtjuːd) *n.* restlessness, uneasiness, or anxiety.

inquire *or* **enquire** (ɪnˈkwaɪə) *vb.* **1. a.** to seek information (about); ask: *she inquired his age; she inquired about rates of pay.* **b.** (foll. by *of*) to ask (a person) for information: *I'll inquire of my aunt when she is coming.* **2.** (often foll. by *into*) to make an investigation. [Latin *inquīrere*] —**inˈquirer** *or* **enˈquirer** *n.* —**inˈquiry** *or* **enˈquiry** *n.*

inquisition (ˌɪnkwɪˈzɪʃən) *n.* **1.** a deep or searching inquiry. **2.** an official inquiry, esp. one held by a jury before an officer of the Crown. —ˌinquiˈsitional *adj.*

Inquisition (ˌɪnkwɪˈzɪʃən) *n. History.* a tribunal of the Roman Catholic Church (1232–1820) founded to suppress heresy.

inquisitive (ɪnˈkwɪzɪtɪv) *adj.* **1.** excessively curious, esp. about other people's business; prying. **2.** eager to learn; inquiring. —inˈquisitively *adv.* —inˈquisitiveness *n.*

inquisitor (ɪnˈkwɪzɪtə) *n.* **1.** a person who inquires, esp. deeply, searchingly, or ruthlessly. **2.** (*often cap.*) an officer of the Inquisition.

inquisitorial (ɪnˌkwɪzɪˈtɔːrɪəl) *adj.* **1.** of or resembling inquisition or an inquisitor. **2.** offensively curious; prying. —inˌquisiˈtorially *adv.*

in re (ɪn ˈreɪ) *prep.* in the matter of; concerning. [Latin]

INRI Jesus of Nazareth, king of the Jews (the inscription placed over Christ's head during the Crucifixion). [Latin *Iesus Nazarenus Rex Judaeorum*]

inroad (ˈɪnˌrəʊd) *n.* **1.** a sudden hostile attack; raid. **2.** an encroachment or intrusion: *my gambling has made great inroads on my savings.*

inrush (ˈɪnˌrʌʃ) *n.* a sudden and overwhelming inward flow; influx.

ins. **1.** inches. **2.** insurance.

insane (ɪnˈseɪn) *adj.* **1.** mentally ill; crazy; of unsound mind. **2.** irresponsible; very foolish; stupid: *an insane plan.* —inˈsanely *adv.*

insanitary (ɪnˈsænɪtrɪ) *adj.* dirty; unhealthy.

insanity (ɪnˈsænɪtɪ) *n., pl.* **-ties. 1.** the state of being insane. **2.** utter folly; stupidity.

insatiable (ɪnˈseɪʃəbəl, -ʃɪə-) *adj.* not able to be satisfied; greedy or unappeasable. —inˌsatiaˈbility *n.* —inˈsatiably *adv.*

inscribe (ɪnˈskraɪb) *vb.* **1.** to mark or engrave (words, symbols, or letters) on (a surface such as stone or paper). **2.** to enter (a name) on a list. **3.** to write one's name, and sometimes a brief dedication, on (a book or work of art) before presentation to another person. **4.** to draw (a geometric construction) inside another construction so that the two are in contact at as many points as possible but do not intersect. [Latin *inscribere*]

inscription (ɪnˈskrɪpʃən) *n.* **1.** something inscribed, esp. words carved or engraved on a coin, tomb, or ring. **2.** a signature or brief dedication in a book or on a work of art.

inscrutable (ɪnˈskruːtəbəl) *adj.* mysterious or enigmatic; incomprehensible. [Latin *in-* not + *scrūtārī* to examine] —inˌscrutaˈbility *n.*

insect (ˈɪnsɛkt) *n.* **1.** a small air-breathing invertebrate with a body divided into head, thorax, and abdomen, three pairs of legs, and (in most species) two pairs of wings. **2.** (loosely) any similar invertebrate, such as a spider, tick, or centipede.

[Latin *insectum* (animal that has been) cut into]

insecticide (ɪnˈsɛktɪˌsaɪd) *n.* a substance used to destroy insect pests. [*-icide* from Latin *caedere* to kill] —inˌsectiˈcidal *adj.*

insectivore (ɪnˈsɛktɪˌvɔː) *n.* **1.** any of an order of small primitive mammals which feed on invertebrates. The group includes shrews, moles, and hedgehogs. **2.** any animal or plant that feeds on insects. [*insect* + Latin *vorāre* to swallow] —insecˈtivorous *adj.*

insecure (ˌɪnsɪˈkjʊə) *adj.* **1.** anxious or afraid; not confident or certain. **2.** not adequately protected: *an insecure fortress.* **3.** unstable or shaky. —inseˈcurity *n.*

inseminate (ɪnˈsɛmɪˌneɪt) *vb.* to impregnate (a female) with semen. [Latin *in-* + *sēmen* seed] —inˌsemiˈnation *n.*

insensate (ɪnˈsɛnseɪt, -sɪt) *adj.* **1.** lacking sensation or consciousness. **2.** insensitive; unfeeling. **3.** foolish; senseless.

insensible (ɪnˈsɛnsɪbəl) *adj.* **1.** lacking sensation or consciousness. **2.** (foll. by *of* or *to*) unaware of or indifferent to: *insensible to suffering.* **3.** same as **imperceptible.** —inˌsensiˈbility *n.*

insensitive (ɪnˈsɛnsɪtɪv) *adj.* unaware of or not responsive to other people's feelings.

inseparable (ɪnˈsɛprəbəl) *adj.* **1.** constantly together because of mutual liking: *the two girls became inseparable friends.* **2.** too closely connected to be separated.

insert *vb.* (ɪnˈsɜːt). **1.** to place or fit (something) inside something else. **2.** to introduce into text or a speech. ~*n.* (ˈɪnsɜːt). **3.** something inserted, esp. a printed sheet bearing advertising, placed loose between the leaves of a magazine. [Latin *inserere* to plant in]

insertion (ɪnˈsɜːʃən) *n.* **1.** the act of inserting. **2.** something inserted, such as an advertisement in a newspaper.

in-service *adj.* denoting training that is given to employees during the course of employment: *an in-service course.*

inset *vb.* (ɪnˈsɛt), **-setting, -set. 1.** to place in or within; insert. ~*n.* (ˈɪnˌsɛt). **2.** something inserted. **3.** *Printing.* a small map or diagram set within the borders of a larger one.

inshore (ˈɪnˈʃɔː) *adj.* **1.** in or on the water, but close to the shore: *inshore weather.* ~*adv., adj.* **2.** towards the shore from the water: *we swam inshore; an inshore wind.*

inside *n.* (ˈɪnˈsaɪd). **1.** the inner side or part of something. **2.** the side of a path away from the road. **3.** (*also pl.*) *Informal.* the stomach and bowels. **4. inside out.** with the inside facing outwards. **5. know inside out.** to know thoroughly. ~*prep.* (ˌɪnˈsaɪd). **6.** in or to the interior of; within. **7.** in a period of time less than: *I'll be back inside an hour.* ~*adj.* (ˈɪnˌsaɪd). **8.** on or of the inside: *an inside door.* **9.** arranged or provided by someone within an organization, esp. illicitly: *inside information.* ~*adv.* (ˌɪnˈsaɪd). **10.** on, in, or to the inside; indoors. **11.** *Slang.* in or into prison.

inside job n. Informal. a crime committed with the assistance of someone employed by or trusted by the victim.

insider (ˌɪnˈsaɪdə) n. a member of a specified group or organization who therefore has exclusive information about it.

insider dealing n. the illegal practice of a person on the stock exchange or in the civil service taking advantage of early confidential information in order to deal in shares for personal profit.

insidious (ɪnˈsɪdɪəs) adj. working in a subtle or apparently harmless way, but nevertheless dangerous or deadly: insidious propaganda; an insidious illness. [Latin insidiae an ambush] —**inˈsidiously** adv. —**inˈsidiousness** n.

insight (ˈɪnˌsaɪt) n. 1. the ability to perceive clearly or deeply the inner nature of things. 2. a penetrating understanding, as of a complex situation or problem.

insignia (ɪnˈsɪgnɪə) n., pl. -nias or -nia. a badge or emblem of membership, office, or dignity. [Latin: badges]

insignificant (ˌɪnsɪgˈnɪfɪkənt) adj. having little or no importance; trivial or relatively small. —**ˌinsigˈnificance** n.

insincere (ˌɪnsɪnˈsɪə) adj. lacking sincerity; hypocritical. —**ˌinsinˈcerely** adv. —**insincerity** (ˌɪnsɪnˈsɛrɪtɪ) n.

insinuate (ɪnˈsɪnjʊˌeɪt) vb. 1. to suggest indirectly by allusion, hints, or innuendo. 2. to get (someone, esp. oneself) into a position by gradual manoeuvres: insinuating himself into her favour. [Latin insinuāre to wind one's way into]

insinuation (ɪnˌsɪnjʊˈeɪʃən) n. 1. an indirect or devious hint or suggestion. 2. an act or the practice of insinuating.

insipid (ɪnˈsɪpɪd) adj. 1. lacking spirit or interest; boring. 2. lacking taste; unpalatable. [Latin in- not + sapidus full of flavour] —**inˈsipidity** n.

insist (ɪnˈsɪst) vb. (often foll. by on or upon) 1. to make a determined demand (for): he insisted on his rights. 2. to express a convinced belief (in) or assertion (of): I insist that he is innocent. [Latin insistere to stand upon, urge]

insistent (ɪnˈsɪstənt) adj. 1. making continual and persistent demands. 2. demanding attention; compelling: the insistent cry of a bird. —**inˈsistence** n. —**inˈsistently** adv.

in situ Latin. (ɪn ˈsɪtjuː) adv., adj. in the original position.

in so far or U.S. **insofar** (ˌɪnsəʊˈfɑː) adv. (usually foll. by as) to the degree or extent (that).

insole (ˈɪnˌsəʊl) n. 1. the inner sole of a shoe or boot. 2. a loose additional inner sole used to give extra warmth or to make a shoe fit.

insolent (ˈɪnsələnt) adj. insulting; disrespectful. [Latin in- not + solēre to be accustomed] —**ˈinsolence** n. —**ˈinsolently** adv.

insoluble (ɪnˈsɒljʊbᵊl) adj. 1. incapable of being dissolved. 2. incapable of being solved. —**inˌsoluˈbility** n.

insolvent (ɪnˈsɒlvənt) adj. 1. unable to pay debts; bankrupt. ~n. 2. a person who is insolvent; bankrupt. —**inˈsolvency** n.

insomnia (ɪnˈsɒmnɪə) n. chronic inability to sleep. [Latin in- not + somnus sleep] —**inˈsomniˌac** n., adj.

insomuch (ˌɪnsəʊˈmʌtʃ) adv. 1. (foll. by as or that) to such an extent or degree. 2. (foll. by as) because of the fact (that); inasmuch (as).

insouciant (ɪnˈsuːsɪənt) adj. carefree or unconcerned; light-hearted. [French] —**inˈsouciance** n.

inspan (ɪnˈspæn) vb. -spanning, -spanned. Chiefly S. African. 1. to harness (animals) to (a vehicle); yoke. 2. to press (people) into service. [Middle Dutch inspannen]

inspect (ɪnˈspɛkt) vb. 1. to examine closely, esp. for faults or errors. 2. to examine officially. [Latin inspicere] —**inˈspection** n.

inspector (ɪnˈspɛktə) n. 1. a person who inspects, esp. an official who examines for compliance with regulations or standards. 2. a police officer ranking below a superintendent and above a sergeant.

inspectorate (ɪnˈspɛktərɪt) n. 1. the position or duties of an inspector. 2. a body of inspectors.

inspiration (ˌɪnspɪˈreɪʃən) n. 1. stimulation of the mind or feelings to activity or creativity. 2. a person or thing that causes this state. 3. an inspired idea or action. —**ˌinspiˈrational** adj.

inspire (ɪnˈspaɪə) vb. 1. to stimulate (a person) to activity or creativity. 2. (foll. by with or to) to arouse (with a particular emotion or to a particular reaction): he inspires confidence. [Latin in- into + spīrāre to breathe]

inst. instant (this month).

instability (ˌɪnstəˈbɪlɪtɪ) n. lack of stability or steadiness.

install (ɪnˈstɔːl) vb. 1. to place (equipment) in position and connect and adjust it for use. 2. to place (a person) formally in a position or rank. 3. to settle (a person, esp. oneself) in a position or state: she installed herself in an armchair. [Medieval Latin installāre] —**installation** (ˌɪnstəˈleɪʃən) n.

installment plan n. U.S. same as **hirepurchase**. Also (Canad.) **instalment plan**.

instalment or U.S. **installment** (ɪnˈstɔːlmənt) n. 1. one of the portions into which a debt is divided for payment at regular intervals. 2. a portion of something that is issued, broadcast, or published in parts. [prob. from Old French estal something fixed]

instance (ˈɪnstəns) n. 1. a case or particular example. 2. **for instance**. as an example. 3. a specified stage in proceedings: step: in the first instance. 4. urgent request or demand: at the instance of. ~vb. 5. to cite as an example. [Latin instantia a being close upon]

instant (ˈɪnstənt) n. 1. a very brief time; moment. 2. a particular moment: at the same instant. ~adj. 3. immediate. 4. (of foods) that can be prepared very quickly and easily: *instant coffee.* **5.** urgent or pressing. **6.** of the present month: *a letter of the 7th instant.* [Latin *instāns* present, pressing closely]

instantaneous (ˌɪnstənˈteɪnɪəs) *adj.* occurring or done in an instant; immediate: *instantaneous death.* —ˌinstan'taneously *adv.*

instantly ('ɪnstəntlɪ) *adv.* immediately; at once.

instead (ɪnˈstɛd) *adv.* **1.** as a replacement or substitute for the person or thing mentioned. **2. instead of.** in place of or as an alternative to. [*in stead* in place]

instep ('ɪnˌstɛp) *n.* **1.** the middle section of the human foot, forming the arch between the ankle and toes. **2.** the part of a shoe or stocking covering this.

instigate ('ɪnstɪˌgeɪt) *vb.* **1.** to bring about by incitement: *to instigate rebellion.* **2.** to urge on to some action. [Latin *instigāre*] —ˌinsti'gation *n.* —'insti,gator *n.*

instil or *U.S.* **instill** (ɪnˈstɪl) *vb.* -stilling, -stilled. **1.** to introduce (an idea or feeling) gradually. **2.** *Rare.* to pour in or inject drop by drop. [Latin *instillāre* to pour in a drop at a time] —ˌinstil'lation *n.* —in'stiller *n.*

instinct ('ɪnstɪŋkt) *n.* **1.** the inborn tendency of a person or animal to behave in a particular way without the need for thought: *maternal instinct.* **2.** natural reaction: *my first instinct was to hit him.* **3.** intuition: *she knew by instinct that he was lying.* [Latin *instinctus* roused] —in'stinctive *adj.* —in'stinctively *adv.*

institute ('ɪnstɪˌtjuːt) *vb.* **1.** to organize; establish. **2.** to initiate: *to institute a practice.* **3.** to install in a position or office. ~*n.* **4.** an organization founded for particular work, especially research or teaching. **5.** the building where such an organization is situated. **6.** a rule, custom, or precedent. [Latin *instituere*]

institution (ˌɪnstɪˈtjuːʃən) *n.* **1.** an instituting or being instituted. **2.** an organization founded for a specific purpose, such as a hospital or college. **3.** an established custom, law, or principle: *the institution of marriage.* **4.** *Informal.* a well-established person or feature: *he has become a local institution.*

institutional (ˌɪnstɪˈtjuːʃənˀl) *adj.* **1.** of or relating to an institution: *institutional care.* **2.** dull, routine, and uniform: *institutional meals.* —ˌinsti'tutional,ism *n.*

institutionalize (ˌɪnstɪˈtjuːʃənəˌlaɪz) *vb.* **1.** to place in an institution. **2.** (*often passive*) to subject (a person) to institutional life, often causing apathy and dependence on routine. **3.** to make or become an institution: *institutionalized religion.*

instruct (ɪnˈstrʌkt) *vb.* **1.** to direct to do something; order. **2.** to teach (someone) how to do (something). [Latin *instruere*]

instruction (ɪnˈstrʌkʃən) *n.* **1.** a direction; order. **2.** the process or act of teaching; education. —in'structional *adj.*

instructions (ɪnˈstrʌkʃənz) *pl. n.* clear and detailed information, in written form, on how to do something: *read the instructions before you switch on the engine.*

instructive (ɪnˈstrʌktɪv) *adj.* serving to instruct or enlighten; conveying information.

instructor (ɪnˈstrʌktə) *n.* **1.** someone who instructs; teacher. **2.** *U.S. & Canad.* a college teacher ranking below assistant professor. —in'structress *fem. n.*

instrument ('ɪnstrəmənt) *n.* **1.** a tool or implement, esp. one used for precision work. **2.** *Music.* any of various devices that can be played to produce musical sounds. **3.** an important factor in something: *her evidence was an instrument in his arrest.* **4.** *Informal.* a person used by another to gain an end. **5.** a device for measuring, indicating, or controlling: *the pilot watched the panel of instruments.* **6.** a formal legal document. [Latin *instrūmentum*]

instrumental (ˌɪnstrəˈmɛntˀl) *adj.* **1.** serving as a means or factor. **2.** of or done with an instrument: *instrumental error.* **3.** played by or composed for musical instruments.

instrumentalist (ˌɪnstrəˈmɛntəlɪst) *n.* a person who plays a musical instrument.

instrumentation (ˌɪnstrəmɛnˈteɪʃən) *n.* **1.** the instruments specified in a musical score or arrangement. **2.** same as **orchestration.** **3.** the use or provision of instruments or tools.

instrument panel *n.* a panel on which instruments are mounted in a vehicle or on a machine.

insubordinate (ˌɪnsəˈbɔːdɪnɪt) *adj.* not submissive to authority; disobedient or rebellious. —**insubordination** (ˌɪnsəˌbɔːdɪˈneɪʃən) *n.*

insubstantial (ˌɪnsəbˈstænʃəl) *adj.* **1.** not substantial; flimsy, fine, or slight. **2.** imaginary; unreal.

insufferable (ɪnˈsʌfərəbˀl) *adj.* intolerable; unendurable. —in'sufferably *adv.*

insufficient (ˌɪnsəˈfɪʃənt) *adj.* not enough for a particular purpose; inadequate. —ˌinsuf'ficiency *n.* —ˌinsuf'ficiently *adv.*

insular ('ɪnsjʊlə) *adj.* **1.** not responsive to change or new influences; narrowminded. **2.** of or like an island. [Latin *insula* island] —**insularity** (ˌɪnsjʊˈlærɪtɪ) *n.*

insulate ('ɪnsjʊˌleɪt) *vb.* **1.** to prevent the transmission of electricity, heat, or sound to or from (a place or body) by surrounding with a nonconducting material. **2.** to isolate or set apart. [Late Latin *insulātus* made into an island] —'insu,lator *n.*

insulation (ˌɪnsjʊˈleɪʃən) *n.* **1.** material used to insulate something. **2.** the act of insulating.

insulin ('ɪnsjʊlɪn) *n.* a hormone, secreted in the pancreas, that controls the amount of sugar in the blood. [Latin *insula* islet (of tissue in the pancreas)]

insult *vb.* (ɪnˈsʌlt). **1.** to treat or speak to rudely; offend. ~*n.* ('ɪnsʌlt). **2.** an offensive remark or action. **3.** a person or thing producing the effect of an insult: *some* *television is an insult to intelligence.* [Latin *insultāre* to jump upon]

insuperable (ɪnˈsuːpərəbʳl) *adj.* incapable of being overcome; insurmountable. —**in-ˌsupera'bility** *n.*

insupportable (ˌɪnsəˈpɔːtəbʳl) *adj.* **1.** incapable of being endured; intolerable. **2.** incapable of being upheld or justified; indefensible: *an insupportable accusation.*

insurance (ɪnˈʃʊərəns) *n.* **1. a.** the business of providing financial protection in the event of loss, damage, or death. **b.** the state of having such protection. **c.** Also called: **insurance policy.** the policy providing such protection. **d.** the amount paid by the insurance company in the event of loss, damage, or death. **e.** the amount paid in return for such protection. **2.** a means of safeguarding against risk or injury.

insure (ɪnˈʃʊə) *vb.* **1.** (often foll. by *against*) to guarantee or protect (against risk or loss). **2.** (often foll. by *against*) to issue (a person) with an insurance policy or take out an insurance policy (on): *his house was heavily insured against fire.* **3.** *Chiefly U.S.* same as **ensure.** —**in'surable** *adj.* —**in,sura'bility** *n.*

insured (ɪnˈʃʊəd) *n.* **the.** the person covered by an insurance policy.

insurer (ɪnˈʃʊərə) *n.* a person or company that sells insurance.

insurgent (ɪnˈsɜːdʒənt) *adj.* **1.** rebellious or in revolt against an established authority. ~*n.* **2.** a person who takes part in a rebellion. [Latin *insurgēns* rising] —**in-'surgence** *n.*

insurmountable (ˌɪnsəˈmaʊntəbʳl) *adj.* impossible to overcome: *insurmountable problems.*

insurrection (ˌɪnsəˈrɛkʃən) *n.* the act of rebelling against an established authority; insurgence. [Latin *insurgere* to rise up] —**insur'rectionist** *n., adj.*

int. 1. internal. **2.** Also: **Int.** international.

intact (ɪnˈtækt) *adj.* untouched; left complete or perfect. [Latin *intactus*] —**in-'tactness** *n.*

intaglio (ɪnˈtɑːlɪ,əʊ) *n., pl.* **-lios** or **-li** (-ljiː). **1.** a seal or gem ornamented with an engraved design. **2.** a design carved into the surface of the material used. [Italian] —**intagliated** (ɪnˈtɑːlɪ,eɪtd) *adj.*

intake (ˈɪn,teɪk) *n.* **1.** a thing or a quantity taken in: *an intake of students.* **2.** the act of taking in. **3.** the opening through which fluid enters a pipe or fuel or air enters an engine.

intangible (ɪnˈtændʒɪbʳl) *adj.* **1.** incapable of being perceived by touch. **2.** vague or indefinable; difficult for the mind to grasp: *intangible ideas.* —**in,tangi'bility** *n.*

integer (ˈɪntɪdʒə) *n.* any positive or negative whole number or zero, as opposed to a number with fractions or decimals. [Latin: untouched]

integral (ˈɪntɪɡrəl) *adj.* **1.** (often foll. by *to*) being an essential part (of a whole). **2.** whole; complete. **3.** *Maths.* **a.** of or involving an integral. **b.** involving or being an integer. ~*n.* **4.** *Maths.* the sum of a large

number of minute quantities, summed either between stated limits (**definite integral**) or in the absence of limits (**indefinite integral**).

integral calculus *n.* the branch of calculus concerned with the determination of integrals and their use in solving differential equations.

integrand (ˈɪntɪ,ɡrænd) *n.* a mathematical function to be integrated.

integrate (ˈɪntɪ,ɡreɪt) *vb.* **1.** to make or be made into a whole; incorporate or be incorporated. **2.** to designate (an institution) for use by all races or groups; desegregate. **3.** to amalgamate (a racial or religious group) with an existing community. **4.** *Maths.* to determine the integral of a function or variable. [Latin *integrāre*] —**inte'gration** *n.*

integrated circuit *n.* a very small electronic circuit consisting of an assembly of elements made from a single chip of semiconducting material.

integrity (ɪnˈtɛɡrɪtɪ) *n.* **1.** adherence to moral principles; honesty. **2.** the quality of being unimpaired; soundness. **3.** unity; wholeness: *cultural integrity.* [Latin *integritās*]

integument (ɪnˈtɛɡjʊmənt) *n.* any outer protective covering, such as a skin, rind, or shell. [Latin *integumentum*] —**in,tegu-'mental** or **in,tegu'mentary** *adj.*

intellect (ˈɪntɪ,lɛkt) *n.* **1.** the ability to understand, think, and reason. **2.** a particular person's mind or intelligence, esp. a brilliant one: *his intellect is wasted on that job.* **3.** *Informal.* a person who has a brilliant mind. [Latin *intellectus* comprehension]

intellectual (ˌɪntɪˈlɛktjʊəl) *adj.* **1.** of, involving, or appealing to the intellect: *intellectual literature.* **2.** having a highly developed intellect. ~*n.* **3.** a person who has a highly developed intellect. —**intel-ˌlectu'ality** *n.* —**intel'lectually** *adv.*

intelligence (ɪnˈtɛlɪdʒəns) *n.* **1.** the ability to understand, learn, and think things out quickly. **2.** *Old-fashioned.* news; information. **3.** the collection of secret information, esp. for military purposes. **4.** a group or department that gathers or deals with such information. [Latin *intellegere* to choose between]

intelligence quotient *n.* a measure of the intelligence of a person. The quotient is calculated by dividing a person's mental age by his actual age and multiplying the result by 100.

intelligent (ɪnˈtɛlɪdʒənt) *adj.* **1.** having or showing intelligence; clever: *an intelligent child; an intelligent guess.* **2.** (of computerized functions, weapons, etc.) able to initiate or modify action in the light of ongoing events. —**in'telligently** *adv.*

intelligentsia (ɪnˌtɛlɪˈdʒɛntsɪə) *n.* (usually preceded by *the*) the educated or intellectual people in a society. [Russian *intelligentsiya*]

intelligible (ɪnˈtɛlɪdʒəbʳl) *adj.* able to be understood; comprehensible. —**in,telligi'bility** *n.*

intemperate (ɪnˈtɛmpərɪt) *adj.* **1.** drinking alcohol too much or too often. **2.** unrestrained: *intemperate rage.* **3.** extreme or severe: *an intemperate climate.* —**inˈtemperance** *n.*

intend (ɪnˈtɛnd) *vb.* **1.** to propose or plan (something or to do something); have as one's purpose: *I intend to go out.* **2.** (often foll. by *for*) to design or destine (for a certain purpose or person): *the money was intended for you.* **3.** to mean to express or indicate: *no criticism was intended.* [Latin *intendere* to stretch forth]

intended (ɪnˈtɛndɪd) *adj.* **1.** planned or future. ~*n.* **2.** *Informal.* a person whom one is to marry; fiancé or fiancée.

intense (ɪnˈtɛns) *adj.* **1.** of very great force, strength, degree, or amount: *intense heat.* **2.** characterized by deep or forceful feelings: *an intense person.* [Latin *intensus* stretched] —**inˈtensely** *adv.* —**inˈtenseness** *n.*

intensifier (ɪnˈtɛnsɪˌfaɪə) *n.* a word, esp. an adjective or adverb, that intensifies the meaning of the word or phrase that it modifies, for example *very* or *extremely.*

intensify (ɪnˈtɛnsɪˌfaɪ) *vb.* **-fying, -fied.** to make or become intense or more intense. —**intensification** (ɪnˌtɛnsɪfɪˈkeɪʃən) *n.*

intensity (ɪnˈtɛnsɪtɪ) *n., pl.* **-ties. 1.** the state or quality of being intense. **2.** extreme force, degree, or amount. **3.** *Physics.* the amount or degree of strength of electricity, heat, light, or sound per unit area of volume.

intensive (ɪnˈtɛnsɪv) *adj.* **1.** of or characterized by intensity; thorough: *intensive training.* **2.** using one specified factor more than others: *labour-intensive.* **3.** *Agriculture.* designed to increase production from a particular area: *an intensive agricultural programme.* **4.** *Grammar.* of a word giving emphasis, for example *very* in *the very same.* —**inˈtensively** *adv.* —**inˈtensiveness** *n.*

intensive care *n.* thorough, continuously supervised treatment of an acutely ill patient in a hospital.

intent (ɪnˈtɛnt) *n.* **1.** something that is intended; aim; purpose. **2.** *Law.* the will or purpose to commit a crime: *lurking with intent.* **3.** **to all intents and purposes.** in almost every respect; virtually. ~*adj.* **4.** having one's attention firmly fixed; absorbed: *an intent look.* **5.** (foll. by *on* or *upon*) having the fixed intention of; strongly resolved on: *intent on getting it right.* [Late Latin *intentus* aim] —**inˈtently** *adv.* —**inˈtentness** *n.*

intention (ɪnˈtɛnʃən) *n.* something intended; a plan, idea, or purpose: *she had no intention of going; motivated by good intentions.*

intentional (ɪnˈtɛnʃənˀl) *adj.* done on purpose; deliberate. —**inˈtentionally** *adv.*

inter (ɪnˈtɜː) *vb.* **-terring, -terred.** to place (a body) in the earth; bury. [Latin *in-* into + *terra* earth]

inter- *prefix.* **1.** between or among: *international.* **2.** together, mutually, or reciprocally: *interdependent; interchange.* [Latin]

interact (ˌɪntərˈækt) *vb.* to act on or in close relation with each other. —**ˌinterˈaction** *n.* —**ˌinterˈactive** *adj.*

inter alia Latin. (ˈɪntər ˈeɪlɪə) *adv.* among other things.

interbreed (ˌɪntəˈbriːd) *vb.* **-breeding, -bred. 1.** to breed within a single family or strain so as to produce particular characteristics in the offspring. **2.** same as **crossbreed** (sense 1).

intercede (ˌɪntəˈsiːd) *vb.* to act as a mediator in order to end a disagreement; plead on another's behalf: *to intercede in the strike; I interceded for him with his father.* [Latin *inter-* between + *cēdere* to move]

intercept *vb.* (ˌɪntəˈsɛpt). **1.** to stop or seize on the way from one place to another; prevent from arriving or proceeding. **2.** *Maths.* to mark off or include (part of a line, curve, plane, or surface) between two points or lines. ~*n.* (ˈɪntəˌsɛpt). **3.** *Maths.* **a.** a point at which two figures intersect. **b.** the distance from the origin to the point at which a line, curve, or surface cuts a coordinate axis. [Latin *intercipere* to seize before arrival] —**ˌinterˈception** *n.* —**ˌinterˈceptor** *n.*

intercession (ˌɪntəˈsɛʃən) *n.* **1.** the act of interceding. **2.** prayer offered to God on behalf of others. —**ˌinterˈcessor** *n.*

interchange *vb.* (ˌɪntəˈtʃeɪndʒ). **1.** to change places or cause to change places; exchange; switch. ~*n.* (ˈɪntəˌtʃeɪndʒ). **2.** the act of interchanging; exchange. **3.** a motorway junction of interconnecting roads and bridges designed to prevent streams of traffic crossing one another. —**ˌinterˈchangeable** *adj.* —**ˌinterˈchangeably** *adv.*

inter-city *adj.* (in Britain) denoting a fast rail service between main towns.

intercom (ˈɪntəˌkɒm) *n.* an internal telephone system for communicating within a building or vehicle. [short for *intercommunication*]

intercommunicate (ˌɪntəkəˈmjuːnɪˌkeɪt) *vb.* **1.** to communicate mutually. **2.** (of two rooms) to interconnect. —**ˌintercomˌmuniˈcation** *n.*

intercommunion (ˌɪntəkəˈmjuːnjən) *n.* association between Churches, involving esp. mutual reception of Holy Communion.

interconnect (ˌɪntəkəˈnɛkt) *vb.* to connect with one another. —**ˌintercon'nected** *adj.* —**ˌintercon'nection** *n.*

intercontinental (ˌɪntəˌkɒntɪˈnɛntˀl) *adj.* travelling between or linking continents.

intercourse (ˈɪntəˌkɔːs) *n.* **1.** same as **sexual intercourse. 2.** communication or dealings between individuals or groups. [Latin *intercurrere* to run between]

interdenominational (ˌɪntədɪˌnɒmɪˈneɪʃənˀl) *adj.* among or involving more than one denomination of the Christian Church.

interdepartmental (ˌɪntəˌdiːpɑːtˈmɛntˀl) *adj.* of or between different departments.

interdependent (ˌɪntədɪˈpɛndənt) *adj.* dependent on one another. —**ˌinterdeˈpendence** *n.*

interdict *n.* (ˈɪntəˌdɪkt). **1.** *R.C. Church.*

the exclusion of a person or place from certain sacraments, although not from communion. **2.** *Law.* an official prohibition or restraint. ~*vb.* (ˌɪntəˈdɪkt). **3.** to place under legal or ecclesiastical sanction; prohibit or forbid. [Latin *interdicere* to forbid] —ˌinterˈdiction *n.* —ˌinterˈdictory *adj.*

interdisciplinary (ˌɪntəˈdɪsɪˌplɪnərɪ) *adj.* involving two or more academic disciplines.

interest (ˈɪntrɪst) *n.* **1.** curiosity or concern about something or someone. **2.** the power of causing this: *to have great interest.* **3.** something in which one is interested; a hobby or pursuit. **4.** (*often pl.*) advantage: *in one's own interest.* **5.** (*often pl.*) a right, share, or claim, esp. in a business or property. **6.** money paid for the use of credit or borrowed money: *he borrowed money at 25 per cent interest.* **7.** (*often pl.*) a group of people with common aims: *the landed interest.* ~*vb.* **8.** to arouse the curiosity or concern of. **9.** to cause to become interested or involved in something. [Latin: it concerns]

interested (ˈɪntrɪstɪd) *adj.* **1.** showing or having interest. **2.** personally involved: *the interested parties met to discuss the business.*

interesting (ˈɪntrɪstɪŋ) *adj.* causing interest; absorbing. —ˈinterestingly *adv.*

interface *n.* (ˈɪntəˌfeɪs). **1.** *Physical chem.* a surface that forms the boundary between two liquids or chemical phases that cannot be mixed. **2.** a common boundary between two things: *the interface between technology and design.* **3.** an electrical circuit linking one device, esp. a computer, with another. ~*vb.* (ˌɪntəˈfeɪs). **4.** to connect or be connected with by interface.

interfacing (ˈɪntəˌfeɪsɪŋ) *n.* **1.** a piece of fabric sewn beneath the facing of a garment to give shape and firmness. **2.** same as **interlining.**

interfere (ˌɪntəˈfɪə) *vb.* **1.** (often foll. by *in*) to meddle: *your mother always interferes in our business.* **2.** (foll. by *with*) to clash with; hinder: *child-bearing may interfere with your career.* **3.** (foll. by *with*) *Euphemistic.* to assault sexually. **4.** *Physics.* to produce or cause to produce interference. [Old French *s'entreferir* to collide] —ˌinterˈfering *adj.*

interference (ˌɪntəˈfɪərəns) *n.* **1.** the act of interfering. **2.** *Physics.* the meeting of two waves which reinforce or neutralize each other depending on whether they are in or out of phase. **3.** any undesired signal that interferes with the reception of radio waves.

interferon (ˌɪntəˈfɪərɒn) *n. Biochem.* a protein made by cells in response to virus infection that prevent the growth of the virus.

interfuse (ˌɪntəˈfjuːz) *vb.* **1.** to mix or become mixed; intermingle. **2.** to blend or fuse together. —ˌinterˈfusion *n.*

interim (ˈɪntərɪm) *adj.* **1.** temporary or provisional: *interim measures to deal with the emergency.* ~*n.* **2. in the interim.**

during the intervening time. [Latin: meanwhile]

interior (ɪnˈtɪərɪə) *n.* **1.** a part or region that is inside: *the interior of the earth.* **2.** the central area of a country or continent, furthest from the sea. **3.** a picture of the inside of a room or building. **4.** the inside of a building or room, with respect to design and decoration. ~*adj.* **5.** of, situated on, or suitable for the inside; inner. **6.** coming or acting from within; internal. **7.** of a nation's domestic affairs; internal. **8.** mental or spiritual: *interior development.* [Latin]

interior angle *n.* an angle of a polygon contained between two adjacent sides.

interior decoration *n.* **1.** the decoration and furnishings of the interior of a room or house. **2.** Also called: **interior design.** the art or business of planning this.

interj. interjection.

interject (ˌɪntəˈdʒɛkt) *vb.* to interpose abruptly; interrupt with: *she interjected clever remarks.* [Latin *interjicere* to place between]

interjection (ˌɪntəˈdʒɛkʃən) *n.* a word or phrase which is used on its own and which expresses sudden emotion; exclamation.

interlace (ˌɪntəˈleɪs) *vb.* to join together by crossing over, as if woven: *interlaced fingers.*

interlard (ˌɪntəˈlɑːd) *vb.* to insert in or occur throughout: *to interlard one's writing with foreign phrases.*

interlay (ˌɪntəˈleɪ) *vb.* **-laying, -laid.** to insert (layers) between; interpose: *to interlay gold among the silver.*

interleaf (ˈɪntəˌliːf) *n., pl.* **-leaves.** a blank leaf inserted between the other leaves of a book. —ˌinterˈleave *vb.*

interleukin (ˌɪntəˈluːkɪn) *n.* a substance obtained from white blood cells that stimulates their activity against infection and may be used to fight some forms of cancer.

interline[1] (ˌɪntəˈlaɪn) *or* **interlineate** (ˌɪntəˈlɪnɪˌeɪt) *vb.* to write or print (matter) between the lines of (a text or book).

interline[2] (ˌɪntəˈlaɪn) *vb.* to provide (a part of a garment) with a second lining, esp. of stiffened material.

interlining (ˈɪntəˌlaɪnɪŋ) *n.* the material used to interline parts of garments.

interlink (ˌɪntəˈlɪŋk) *vb.* to connect together.

interlock *vb.* (ˌɪntəˈlɒk). **1.** to join or be joined firmly together. ~*n.* (ˈɪntəˌlɒk). **2.** a device used to prevent a mechanism from operating independently or unsafely. **3.** a closely knitted fabric. ~*adj.* (ˈɪntəˌlɒk). **4.** closely knitted.

interlocutor (ˌɪntəˈlɒkjʊtə) *n.* a person who takes part in a conversation. [Latin *inter-* between + *loqui* to talk]

interlocutory (ˌɪntəˈlɒkjʊtrɪ) *adj.* **1.** *Law.* pronounced during the course of legal proceedings; provisional: *an interlocutory injunction.* **2.** of dialogue; conversational.

interloper (ˈɪntəˌləʊpə) *n.* a person who

interferes in other people's affairs; intruder.

interlude ('ɪntə,luːd) n. **1.** a period of time or different activity between longer periods or events; interval. **2. a.** a pause between the acts of a play. **b.** a brief piece of music or other entertainment performed during this pause. [Latin *inter-* between + *lūdus* play]

intermarry (,ɪntə'mærɪ) vb. **-rying, -ried. 1.** (of different races, religions, or social groups) to become connected by marriage. **2.** to marry within one's own family or tribe. **—,inter'marriage** n.

intermediary (,ɪntə'miːdɪərɪ) n., pl. **-aries. 1.** a person who tries to bring about agreement between two parties in dispute. **2.** a medium or means. **~adj. 3.** acting as an intermediary. **4.** intermediate.

intermediate adj. (,ɪntə'miːdɪt). **1.** occurring between two points or extremes; in between. **~n.** (,ɪntə'miːdɪt). **2.** something intermediate. **3.** a substance formed between the first and final stages of a chemical process. **~vb.** (,ɪntə'miːdɪ,eɪt). **4.** to act as an intermediary. [Latin *inter-* between + *medius* middle] **—,inter-,medi'ation** n.

interment (ɪn'tɜːmənt) n. an interring; burial.

intermezzo (,ɪntə'mɛtsəʊ) n., pl. **-zos** or **-zi** (-tsiː). **1.** a short piece of instrumental music performed between the acts of a play or opera. **2. a.** a short composition between two longer movements in an extended musical work. **b.** a similar composition intended for independent performance. [Italian]

interminable (ɪn'tɜːmɪnəb³l) adj. seemingly endless because of monotony: *an interminable lecture.* **—in'terminably** adv.

intermingle (,ɪntə'mɪŋg³l) vb. to mix together.

intermission (,ɪntə'mɪʃən) n. a pause, esp. an interval between parts of a film, play, etc. [Latin *intermittere* to leave off, cease]

intermittent (,ɪntə'mɪt³nt) adj. occurring at regular or irregular intervals; not continuous. **—,inter'mittently** adv.

intern vb. (ɪn'tɜːn). **1.** to confine within a country or a limited area, esp. during wartime. **~n.** (ɪn'tɜːn), also **interne. 2.** Chiefly U.S. a medical student or recent graduate undergoing practical training in a working environment. [Latin *internus* internal] **—in'ternment** n.

internal (ɪn'tɜːn³l) adj. **1.** of, situated on, or suitable for the inside; inner. **2.** coming or acting from within an organization: *an internal reorganization.* **3.** spiritual or mental: *internal conflict.* **4.** of a nation's domestic affairs: *internal politics.* **5.** affecting or relating to the inside of the body: *internal bleeding.* [Latin *internus*] **—in'ternally** adv.

internal-combustion engine n. an engine in which power is produced by the explosion of a fuel-and-air mixture within the cylinders.

international (,ɪntə'næʃən³l) adj. **1.** of or involving two or more nations. **2.** controlling or legislating for several nations: *an international court.* **3.** available for use by all nations: *international waters.* **~n. 4.** *Sport.* **a.** a contest between two national teams. **b.** a member of a national team. **—,inter,nation'ality** n. **—,inter'nationally** adv.

International (,ɪntə'næʃən³l) n. any of several international socialist organizations.

internationalism (,ɪntə'næʃənə,lɪzəm) n. the ideal or practice of cooperation and understanding for the good of all nations. **—,inter'nationalist** n.

International Phonetic Alphabet n. a series of signs and letters for the representation of human speech sounds.

internecine (,ɪntə'niːsaɪn) adj. destructive to both sides: *internecine war.* [Latin *internecāre* to destroy]

internee (,ɪntɜː'niː) n. a person who is interned.

internist (ɪn'tɜːnɪst) n. a physician who specializes in internal medicine.

interpenetrate (,ɪntə'pɛnɪ,treɪt) vb. to penetrate (something) thoroughly; pervade. **—,inter,pene'tration** n.

interplanetary (,ɪntə'plænɪtrɪ) adj. between planets.

interplay ('ɪntə,pleɪ) n. the reciprocal action and reaction of things on each other.

Interpol ('ɪntə,pɒl) International Criminal Police Organization: an association of over 100 national police forces, devoted chiefly to fighting international crime.

interpolate (ɪn'tɜːpə,leɪt) vb. **1.** to insert (a comment or passage) into (a conversation or text). **2.** *Maths.* to estimate (a value of a function) between the values already known. [Latin *interpolāre* to give a new appearance to] **—in,terpo'lation** n.

interpose (,ɪntə'pəʊz) vb. **1.** to place (something) between or among other things. **2.** to interrupt (with comments or questions). **3.** to put forward so as to interrupt: *he ended the discussion by interposing a veto.* [Latin *inter-* between + *pōnere* to put] **—,interpo'sition** n.

interpret (ɪn'tɜːprɪt) vb. **1.** to explain the meaning of; elucidate. **2.** to construe the significance of: *to interpret a smile as an invitation.* **3.** to convey the meaning of (a poem, song, etc.) in performance. **4.** to act as an interpreter; translate orally. [Latin *interpretārī*] **—in'terpretive** adj.

interpretation (ɪn,tɜːprɪ'teɪʃən) n. **1.** the act or result of interpreting or explaining. **2.** the expression of a person's conception of a play, dance, or other work of art through acting or performing. **3.** explanation, as of a historical site, provided by the use of original objects, visual display material, etc.

interpreter (ɪn'tɜːprɪtə) n. **1.** a person who translates orally from one language into another. **2.** *Computers.* a program that translates a statement in a source program to machine language and executes it before translating and executing the next statement.

interpretive centre n. a building situated at a place of interest, such as a country park or historical site, that provides information about the site by showing videos, exhibiting objects, etc.

interracial (ˌɪntəˈreɪʃəl) *adj.* between or among people of different races.

interregnum (ˌɪntəˈrɛgnəm) *n., pl.* **-nums** or **-na** (-nə). a period when a state lacks its usual government, esp. the interval between the end of one ruler's reign and the beginning of the next. [Latin *inter-* between + *regnum* reign] —ˌinterˈregnal *adj.*

interrelate (ˌɪntərɪˈleɪt) *vb.* to connect (two or more things) or (of two or more things) to become connected to each other: *these courses interrelate; all three factors are interrelated.* —ˌinterreˈlation *n.* —ˌinterreˈlation,ship *n.*

interrogate (ɪnˈtɛrəˌgeɪt) *vb.* to question (someone) closely. [Latin *interrogāre*] —inˌterroˈgation *n.* —inˈterro,gator *n.*

interrogative (ˌɪntəˈrɒgətɪv) *adj.* **1.** asking or having the nature of a question: *an interrogative look.* **2.** used in asking a question: *an interrogative pronoun.* ~*n.* **3.** an interrogative word, phrase, sentence, or construction.

interrogatory (ˌɪntəˈrɒgətərɪ) *adj.* **1.** expressing or involving a question. ~*n., pl.* **-tories. 2.** a question or interrogation.

interrupt (ˌɪntəˈrʌpt) *vb.* **1.** to break into (a conversation or discussion) by questions or comment. **2.** to break the continuity of (an action or event) or hinder (a person) by intrusion. [Latin *inter-* between + *rumpere* to break] —ˌinterˈrupted *adj.* —ˌinterˈruptive *adj.*

interrupter or **interruptor** (ˌɪntəˈrʌptə) *n.* a device for opening and closing an electric circuit.

interruption (ˌɪntəˈrʌpʃən) *n.* **1.** something that interrupts, such as a comment or question. **2.** an interval or intermission. **3.** the act of interrupting or the state of being interrupted.

interscholastic (ˌɪntəskəˈlæstɪk) *adj.* occurring between two or more schools: *an interscholastic competition.*

intersect (ˌɪntəˈsɛkt) *vb.* **1.** to divide or mark off (a place, area, or surface) by passing through or across. **2.** (esp. of roads) to cross (each other). [Latin *intersecāre* to divide]

intersection (ˌɪntəˈsɛkʃən) *n.* **1.** a point at which things intersect, esp. a road junction. **2.** the act of intersecting or the state of being intersected. **3.** *Maths.* **a.** a point or set of points common to two or more geometric figures. **b.** the set of elements that are common to two sets. —ˌinterˈsectional *adj.*

interspace (ˌɪntəˈspeɪs) *vb.* to make or occupy a space between.

intersperse (ˌɪntəˈspɜːs) *vb.* **1.** to scatter among, between, or on. **2.** to mix (something) with other things scattered here and there. [Latin *inter-* between + *spargere* to sprinkle] —**interspersion** (ˌɪntəˈspɜːʃən) *n.*

interstellar (ˌɪntəˈstɛlə) *adj.* between or among stars.

interstice (ɪnˈtɜːstɪs) *n.* (*usually pl.*) **1.** a small gap or crack between things. **2.** *Physics.* the space between adjacent atoms in a crystal lattice. [Latin *interstitium* interval]

intertwine (ˌɪntəˈtwaɪn) *vb.* to twist together.

interval (ˈɪntəvəl) *n.* **1.** the period of time between two events. **2.** the distance between two things. **3.** *Brit.* a short period between parts of a play, concert, etc.; intermission. **4.** *Music.* the difference of pitch between two notes. **5. at intervals. a.** now and then: *turn the chicken at intervals.* **b.** with a certain amount of space between: *plant the seeds at intervals of six inches.* [Latin *intervallum,* lit.: space between two palisades]

intervene (ˌɪntəˈviːn) *vb.* **1.** (often foll. by *in*) to come between two people or groups in order to prevent conflict or settle a dispute. **2.** (foll. by *in* or *between*) to come or be among or between. **3.** (of an event) to disturb or hinder a course of action: *neither bill became law because the general election intervened.* [Latin *intervenīre* to come between]

intervention (ˌɪntəˈvɛnʃən) *n.* the act of intervening, esp. by one state in the affairs of another. —ˌinterˈventionist *n., adj.*

interview (ˈɪntəˌvjuː) *n.* **1.** a formal discussion, esp. one in which an employer assesses a job applicant. **2.** a conversation in which a well-known person is asked about his or her views, career, etc., by a reporter. ~*vb.* **3.** to conduct an interview with (someone). [Old French *entrevue*] —ˌinterviewˈee *n.* —ˈinter,viewer *n.*

interwar (ˌɪntəˈwɔː) *adj.* of or happening in the period between World War I and World War II.

interweave (ˌɪntəˈwiːv) *vb.* **-weaving, -wove** or **-weaved; -woven** or **-weaved.** to weave together; connect intimately.

intestate (ɪnˈtɛsteɪt, -tɪt) *adj.* **1.** (of a person) not having made a will. ~*n.* **2.** a person who dies without having made a will. [Latin *intestātus*] —inˈtestacy *n.*

intestine (ɪnˈtɛstɪn) *n.* the part of the alimentary canal between the stomach and the anus. See **large intestine, small intestine.** [Latin *intestīnus* internal] —inˈtestinal *adj.*

intimacy (ˈɪntɪməsɪ) *n., pl.* **-cies. 1.** close or warm friendship; personal relationship. **2.** (*often pl.*) *Euphemistic.* sexual relations.

intimate[1] (ˈɪntɪmɪt) *adj.* **1.** characterized by a close or warm personal relationship: *an intimate friend.* **2.** deeply personal, private, or secret. **3.** *Euphemistic.* having sexual relations . **4.** (of knowledge) extensive and detailed. **5.** having a friendly quiet atmosphere: *an intimate nightclub.* ~*n.* **6.** a close friend. [Latin *intimus* innermost] —ˈintimately *adv.*

intimate[2] (ˈɪntɪˌmeɪt) *vb.* to make (something) known in an indirect way: *she had already intimated her disapproval.* [Late Latin *intimāre* to proclaim] —ˌintiˈmation *n.*

intimidate (ɪnˈtɪmɪˌdeɪt) vb. to frighten (someone) by threats, esp. in order to subdue or influence. [Latin *in-* in + *timidus* fearful] —**inˈtimiˌdating** adj. —**inˌtimiˈdation** n.

into (ˈɪntuː; unstressed ˈɪntə) prep. 1. to the inner part of: *they went into the house.* 2. to the middle of so as to be surrounded by: *into the bushes.* 3. against; up against: *he drove into a wall.* 4. used to indicate the result of a change: *he changed into a monster.* 5. Maths. used to indicate division: *three into six is two.* 6. Informal. interested in: *I'm really into Freud.*

intolerable (ɪnˈtɒlərəb⁰l) adj. more than can be endured. —**inˈtolerably** adv.

intolerant (ɪnˈtɒlərənt) adj. refusing to accept practices and beliefs that differ from one's own. —**inˈtolerance** n.

intonation (ˌɪntəʊˈneɪʃən) n. 1. the sound pattern produced by variations in the voice. 2. the act of intoning. 3. Music. the capacity to play or sing in tune. —**intoˈnational** adj.

intone (ɪnˈtəʊn) or **intonate** (ˈɪntəʊˌneɪt) vb. 1. to speak or recite (a chant or prayer) in a monotonous tone. 2. to speak with a particular tone. [Medieval Latin *intonare*]

in toto Latin. (ɪn ˈtəʊtəʊ) adv. totally; entirely.

intoxicant (ɪnˈtɒksɪkənt) n. 1. something, such as an alcoholic drink, that causes intoxication. ~adj. 2. causing intoxication.

intoxicate (ɪnˈtɒksɪˌkeɪt) vb. 1. (of an alcoholic drink) to make (a person) drunk; inebriate. 2. to stimulate or excite to a point beyond self-control. [Latin *in-* in + *toxicum* poison] —**inˈtoxiˌcating** adj.

intoxication (ɪnˌtɒksɪˈkeɪʃən) n. 1. drunkenness; inebriation. 2. great elation.

intractable (ɪnˈtræktəb⁰l) adj. 1. (of a person) difficult to influence or direct. 2. (of a problem or illness) difficult to solve, alleviate, or cure. —**inˌtractaˈbility** n. —**inˈtractably** adv.

intramural (ˌɪntrəˈmjʊərəl) adj. Chiefly U.S. & Canad. operating within or involving those within boundaries, esp. of a school or college: *intramural sports.* [Latin *intra-* inside + *mūrus* wall]

intransigent (ɪnˈtrænsɪdʒənt) adj. 1. uncompromising; obstinately maintaining an attitude. ~n. 2. an intransigent person, esp. in politics. [Latin *in-* not + *transigere* to settle] —**inˈtransigence** n.

intransitive (ɪnˈtrænsɪtɪv) adj. denoting a verb that does not require a direct object. —**inˈtransitively** adv.

intrapreneur (ˌɪntrəprəˈnɜː) n. a person who while remaining within a larger organization uses entrepreneurial skills to develop new services or systems as a subsidiary of the organization. [*intra-* inside + (*entre*)*preneur*]

intrauterine (ˌɪntrəˈjuːtəraɪn) adj. situated within the womb. [Latin *intra-* inside + *uterus* womb]

intrauterine device n. a contraceptive device in the shape of a coil, inserted into the womb.

intravenous (ˌɪntrəˈviːnəs) adj. Anat. within a vein: *an intravenous injection.* [Latin *intra-* inside + *vēna* vein] —**intraˈvenously** adv.

in-tray n. a tray used in offices for incoming letters or documents requiring attention.

intrepid (ɪnˈtrɛpɪd) adj. fearless; daring; bold. [Latin *in-* not + *trepidus* fearful] —**intreˈpidity** n. —**inˈtrepidly** adv.

intricate (ˈɪntrɪkɪt) adj. 1. difficult to sort out; involved: *an intricate problem.* 2. full of complicated detail: *intricate patterns.* [Latin *intrīcāre* to entangle] —**ˈintricacy** n. —**ˈintricately** adv.

intrigue vb. (ɪnˈtriːg), **-triguing**, **-trigued**. 1. to make interested or curious: *the idea seemed to intrigue her.* 2. to plot secretly or dishonestly; conspire. ~n. (ˈɪntriːg, ɪnˈtriːg). 3. secret plotting. 4. a secret love affair. [French *intriguer*] —**inˈtriguing** adj. —**inˈtriguingly** adv.

intrinsic (ɪnˈtrɪnsɪk) adj. 1. essential to the real nature of a thing; inherent: *dependency is an intrinsic part of love.* 2. Anat. situated within or peculiar to a part: *intrinsic muscles.* [Latin *intrinsecus* inwardly] —**inˈtrinsically** adv.

intro (ˈɪntrəʊ) n., pl. **-tros.** Informal. short for **introduction.**

introduce (ˌɪntrəˈdjuːs) vb. 1. to present (someone) by name (to another person). 2. to present (a radio or television programme). 3. (foll. by *to*) to cause to experience for the first time: *to introduce a visitor to beer.* 4. to present for consideration or approval: *to introduce a bill in parliament.* 5. to bring into use; establish: *to introduce decimal currency.* 6. (foll. by *with*) to start: *he introduced his talk with some music.* [Latin *intrōdūcere* to bring inside] —**introˈducible** adj.

introduction (ˌɪntrəˈdʌkʃən) n. 1. the act of introducing. 2. a presentation of one person to another or others. 3. a preliminary part, as of a book or musical composition. 4. a book that explains the basic facts about a particular subject to a beginner.

introductory (ˌɪntrəˈdʌktrɪ) adj. serving as an introduction; preliminary.

introit (ˈɪntrɔɪt) n. R.C. Church, Church of England. a short prayer said or sung as the celebrant is entering the sanctuary to celebrate Mass or Holy Communion. [Latin *introitus* entrance]

introspection (ˌɪntrəˈspɛkʃən) n. the examining of one's own thoughts, impressions, and feelings. [Latin *intrōspicere* to look within] —**introˈspective** adj.

introversion (ˌɪntrəˈvɜːʃən) n. Psychol. the directing of interest inwards towards one's own thoughts and feelings rather than towards the external world or making social contacts.

introvert (ˈɪntrəˌvɜːt) Psychol. ~adj. 1. concerned more with one's inner feelings than with external reality. ~n. 2. such a person. [Latin *intrō-* inward + *vertere* to turn] —**intro,verted** *adj.*

intrude (ɪn'truːd) *vb.* (foll. by *on* or *upon*) to put forward or interpose (oneself or one's views) abruptly or without invitation. [Latin *intrūdere* to thrust in] —**in'truder** *n.*

intrusion (ɪn'truːʒən) *n.* **1.** the act of intruding; an unwelcome visit, etc.: *an intrusion on one's privacy.* **2. a.** the forcing of molten rock into spaces in the overlying strata. **b.** molten rock formed in this way. —**in'trusive** *adj.*

intrust (ɪn'trʌst) *vb.* same as **entrust**.

intuition (,ɪntjʊ'ɪʃən) *n.* instinctive knowledge of or belief about something without conscious reasoning: *my intuition told me to stay away.* [Latin *intuērī* to gaze upon] —,**intu'itional** *adj.*

intuitive (ɪn'tjuːɪtɪv) *adj.* of, possessing, or resulting from intuition: *an intuitive awareness.* —**in'tuitively** *adv.*

Inuit or **Innuit** ('ɪnjuːɪt) *n., pl.* **-it** or **-its.** an Eskimo of North America or Greenland. [Eskimo *inuit* people]

Inuktitut (ɪ'nʊktə,tʊt) *n. Canad.* the language of the Inuit.

inundate ('ɪnʌn,deɪt) *vb.* **1.** to cover completely with water; swamp. **2.** to overwhelm, as if with a flood: *to be inundated with requests.* [Latin *inundāre*] —,**inun'dation** *n.*

inure (ɪ'njʊə) *vb.* **be inured** or **inure oneself to something.** to be or become hardened to something. [Middle English *enuren* to accustom] —**in'urement** *n.*

invade (ɪn'veɪd) *vb.* **1.** to enter (a country or territory) by military force. **2.** to occupy in large numbers: *the town was invaded by football supporters.* **3.** to encroach upon (privacy, etc.). [Latin *invādere*] —**in'vader** *n.*

invalid[1] ('ɪnvə,liːd, -lɪd) *n.* **1.** a person who is disabled or chronically ill. ~*adj.* **2.** sick; disabled. ~*vb.* **3.** *Chiefly Brit.* to dismiss (a member of the armed forces) from active service because of illness. [Latin *in-* not + *validus* strong] —'**invalid,ism** *n.*

invalid[2] (ɪn'vælɪd) *adj.* **1.** not valid; having no legal force: *an invalid cheque.* **2.** (of an argument, result, etc.) not valid because it has been based on a mistake. —,**inva'lidity** *n.* —**in'validly** *adv.*

invalidate (ɪn'vælɪ,deɪt) *vb.* **1.** to prove (an argument, result, etc.) to be wrong. **2.** to take away the legal force of (a contract). —**in,vali'dation** *n.*

invaluable (ɪn'væljʊəb*ə*l) *adj.* having great value that is impossible to calculate; priceless.

invariable (ɪn'vɛərɪəb*ə*l) *adj.* unchanging; always the same. —**in'variably** *adv.*

invasion (ɪn'veɪʒən) *n.* **1.** the act of invading with armed forces. **2.** any intrusion: *an invasion of privacy.* —**invasive** (ɪn'veɪsɪv) *adj.*

invective (ɪn'vɛktɪv) *n.* a verbal attack, esp. of a bitterly abusive or sarcastic kind. [Latin *invectus* carried in]

inveigh (ɪn'veɪ) *vb.* (foll. by *against*) to

criticize (something) harshly. [Latin *invehī*, lit.: to be carried in, hence, assail]

inveigle (ɪn'veɪg*ə*l) *vb.* to coax or manipulate (someone) into an action or situation. [Old French *avogler* to blind, deceive] —**in'veiglement** *n.*

invent (ɪn'vɛnt) *vb.* **1.** to create or devise (a machine, game, etc.). **2.** to make up (a story, excuse, etc.). [Latin *invenīre* to find] —**in'ventor** *n.*

invention (ɪn'vɛnʃən) *n.* **1.** the act of inventing. **2.** something that is invented. **3.** creative power; inventive skill. **4.** *Euphemistic.* a fabrication; lie: *his story is a malicious invention.*

inventive (ɪn'vɛntɪv) *adj.* creative; ingenious; resourceful.

inventory ('ɪnvəntrɪ) *n., pl.* **-tories. 1.** a detailed list of articles, goods, etc., in a particular place. ~*vb.* **-torying, -toried. 2.** to enter (items) in an inventory; make a list of. [Medieval Latin *inventōrium*]

inverse (ɪn'vɜːs, 'ɪnvɜːs) *adj.* **1.** opposite in effect, sequence, direction, etc. **2.** *Maths.* (of a relationship) containing two variables such that an increase in one results in a decrease in the other. ~*n.* **3.** *Maths.* an inverse element.

inversion (ɪn'vɜːʃən) *n.* **1.** the act of inverting or state of being inverted. **2.** something inverted, esp. a reversal of order, mutual functions, etc.: *an inversion of their previous relationship.* —**in'versive** *adj.*

invert *vb.* (ɪn'vɜːt). **1.** to turn upside down or inside out. **2.** to reverse in effect, sequence, or direction. ~*n.* ('ɪnvɜːt). **3.** a homosexual. [Latin *in-* in + *vertere* to turn] —**in'vertible** *adj.*

invertebrate (ɪn'vɜːtɪbrɪt) *n.* **1.** any animal without a backbone, such as an insect, worm, or octopus. ~*adj.* **2.** of or designating invertebrates.

inverted comma *n.* same as **quotation mark**.

invest (ɪn'vɛst) *vb.* **1.** (often foll. by *in*) to put (money into an enterprise) with the expectation of profit. **2.** (often foll. by *in*) to devote (time, effort, etc., to a project). **3.** (foll. by *in*) *Informal.* to buy: *she invested in a new dress.* **4.** (often foll. by *in*) to install someone (in an official position). **5.** to give power or authority to: *to invest new rights in the monarchy.* **6.** (foll. by *in* or *with*) to provide (a person with qualities): *he was invested with great common sense.* **7.** (foll. by *with*) *Usually poetic.* to cover, as if with a coat: *when spring invests the trees with leaves.* [Medieval Latin *investīre* to clothe] —**in'vestor** *n.*

investigate (ɪn'vɛstɪ,geɪt) *vb.* to inquire into (a situation or problem) thoroughly in order to discover the truth: *the inspector had come to investigate a murder; we set out to investigate the mood of the community.* [Latin *investīgāre* to search after] —**in'vesti,gative** *adj.* —**in'vesti,gator** *n.*

investigation (ɪn,vɛstɪ'geɪʃən) *n.* a careful search or examination in order to discover facts.

investiture (ɪn'vɛstɪtʃə) n. the act of presenting someone with an official title.

investment (ɪn'vɛstmənt) n. **1.** the act of investing. **2.** money invested. **3.** something, such as a business, in which money is invested.

investment trust n. a financial enterprise that invests its subscribed capital in a wide range of securities for its investors' benefit.

inveterate (ɪn'vɛtərɪt) adj. **1.** deep-rooted or ingrained: an inveterate feeling of hostility. **2.** confirmed in a habit or practice: an inveterate smoker. [Latin inveterātus of long standing] —**in'veteracy** n.

invidious (ɪn'vɪdɪəs) adj. likely to cause resentment or unpopularity: an invidious task. [Latin invidia envy]

invigilate (ɪn'vɪdʒɪˌleɪt) vb. Brit. to supervise people who are sitting an examination, esp. to prevent cheating. [Latin invigilāre to watch over] —**in,vigi'lation** n. —**in'vigi,lator** n.

invigorate (ɪn'vɪgəˌreɪt) vb. to give vitality and vigour to; refresh: to be invigorated by fresh air. [Latin in- + vigor vigour] —**in'vigor,ating** adj.

invincible (ɪn'vɪnsəb'l) adj. incapable of being defeated: an army of invincible strength. [Latin in- not + vincere to conquer] —**in,vinci'bility** n. —**in'vincibly** adv.

inviolable (ɪn'vaɪələb'l) adj. that must not be violated; sacred: an inviolable oath. —**in,viola'bility** n.

inviolate (ɪn'vaɪəlɪt) adj. free from violation, injury, disturbance, etc. —**in'violacy** n.

invisible (ɪn'vɪzəb'l) adj. **1.** not able to be seen by the eye: invisible rays. **2.** concealed from sight; hidden. **3.** Econ. relating to services, such as insurance and freight, rather than goods: invisible earnings. —**in,visi'bility** n. —**in'visibly** adv.

invitation (ˌɪnvɪ'teɪʃən) n. **1.** a request to attend a dance, meal, etc. **2.** the card or paper on which an invitation is written.

invite vb. (ɪn'vaɪt). **1.** to ask (a person) in a friendly or polite way (to do something, attend an event, etc.). **2.** to make a request for, esp. publicly or formally: to invite applications. **3.** to bring on or provoke: you invite disaster by your actions. **4.** to tempt. ~n. ('ɪnvaɪt). **5.** Informal. an invitation. [Latin invītāre]

inviting (ɪn'vaɪtɪŋ) adj. tempting; alluring; attractive.

in vitro (ɪn 'viːtrəʊ) adv., adj. (of biological processes or reactions) made to occur outside the body of the organism in an artificial environment. [New Latin, lit.: in glass]

invocation (ˌɪnvə'keɪʃən) n. **1.** the act of invoking. **2.** a prayer to God or another deity asking for help, forgiveness, etc. —**invocatory** (ɪn'vɒkətrɪ) adj.

invoice ('ɪnvɔɪs) n. **1.** a document issued by a seller to a buyer listing the goods or services supplied and stating the sum of money due. ~vb. **2.** to present (a customer) with an invoice. [Old French envois, pl. of envoi message]

invoke (ɪn'vəʊk) vb. **1.** to call on (God or another deity) for help, inspiration, etc. **2.** to put (a law or penalty) into use: the union invoked the dispute procedure. **3.** to implore or beg (help, etc.). **4.** to summon (a spirit) by uttering magic words. [Latin invocāre to appeal to]

involuntary (ɪn'vɒləntrɪ) adj. **1.** carried out without one's conscious wishes; unintentional. **2.** Physiol. (esp. of a movement or muscle) performed or acting without conscious control. —**in'voluntarily** adv.

involute ('ɪnvəˌluːt) adj. also **involuted. 1.** complex, intricate, or involved. **2.** rolled inwards or curled in a spiral. ~n. **3.** Geom. the curve described by the free end of a thread as it is wound around another curve on the same plane. [Latin involūtus]

involve (ɪn'vɒlv) vb. **1.** to include as a necessary part. **2.** to have an effect on: the investigation involved many innocent people. **3.** to implicate: many people were involved in the crime. **4.** to make complicated: the situation was further involved by her disappearance. [Latin in- + volvere to roll] —**in'volvement** n.

invulnerable (ɪn'vʌlnərəb'l) adj. incapable of being wounded or damaged. —**in,vulnera'bility** n.

inward ('ɪnwəd) adj. **1.** directed towards the middle of something. **2.** situated within; inside. **3.** of the mind or spirit: inward meditation. ~adv. **4.** same as **inwards.**

inwardly ('ɪnwədlɪ) adv. **1.** within the private thoughts or feelings; secretly: inwardly troubled, he kept smiling. **2.** not aloud: to laugh inwardly. **3.** in or on the inside; internally.

inwards ('ɪnwədz) or **inward** adv. towards the inside or middle of something.

inwrought (ˌɪn'rɔːt) adj. worked or woven into material, esp. decoratively.

Io Chem. ionium.

iodide ('aɪəˌdaɪd) n. a compound containing an iodine atom, such as methyl iodide.

iodine ('aɪəˌdiːn) n. Chem. a bluish-black element found in seaweed and used in medicine, photography, and dyeing. Symbol: I [Greek iōdēs rust-coloured, but mistakenly derived from ion violet]

iodize or **-dise** ('aɪəˌdaɪz) vb. to treat with iodine. —**iodi'zation** or **-di'sation** n.

IOM Isle of Man.

ion ('aɪən, -ɒn) n. an electrically charged atom or group of atoms formed by the loss or gain of one or more electrons. [Greek, lit.: going]

ion exchange n. the process in which ions are exchanged between a solution and an insoluble solid. It is used to soften water.

ionic (aɪ'ɒnɪk) adj. of or in the form of ions.

Ionic (aɪ'ɒnɪk) adj. of an order of classical architecture distinguished by ornamental scrolls on the capitals.

ionize or **-ise** ('aɪəˌnaɪz) vb. to change or become changed into ions. —**ioni'zation** or **-i'sation** n.

ionosphere (aɪ'ɒnəˌsfɪə) n. a region of

ionized layers of air in the earth's upper atmosphere, which reflects radio waves. —**ionospheric** (aɪˌɒnəˈsfɛrɪk) *adj.*

iota (aɪˈəʊtə) *n.* **1.** the ninth letter in the Greek alphabet (I, ι). **2.** a very small amount; jot: *I don't feel one iota of guilt.*

IOU *n.* a written promise or reminder to pay a debt. [representing *I owe you*]

IOW Isle of Wight.

IPA International Phonetic Alphabet.

ipecac (ˈɪpɪˌkæk) *or* **ipecacuanha** (ˌɪpɪˌkækjuˈænə) *n.* a drug prepared from the dried roots of a South American plant, used to induce vomiting. [S. American Indian *ipekaaguéne*]

ipso facto (ˈɪpsəʊ ˈfæktəʊ) *adv.* by that very fact or act. [Latin]

IQ intelligence quotient.

Ir *Chem.* iridium.

IRA Irish Republican Army.

Iranian (ɪˈreɪnɪən) *n.* **1.** a person from Iran, in SW Asia. **2.** a branch of the Indo-European family of languages, including Persian. ~*adj.* **3.** of Iran, its inhabitants, or their language.

Iraqi (ɪˈrɑːkɪ) *adj.* **1.** of Iraq, in SW Asia, its inhabitants, or their language. ~*n., pl.* **-qis. 2.** a person from Iraq.

irascible (ɪˈræsɪbᵊl) *adj.* easily angered; irritable. [Latin *īra* anger] —**i,rasci'bility** *n.* —**i'rascibly** *adv.*

irate (aɪˈreɪt) *adj.* very angry; furious. [Latin *īrātus* enraged]

ire (ˈaɪə) *n. Literary.* anger. [Latin *īra*]

iridaceous (ˌɪrɪˈdeɪʃəs) *adj.* of or belonging to the iris family.

iridescent (ˌɪrɪˈdɛsᵊnt) *adj.* having or displaying a spectrum of colours that shimmer and change. [Latin *irid-* iris] —**iri'descence** *n.*

iridium (aɪˈrɪdɪəm, ɪˈrɪd-) *n.* a hard yellowish-white chemical element that occurs in platinum ores and is used as an alloy with platinum. Symbol: Ir [Latin *irid-* iris]

iris (ˈaɪrɪs) *n.* **1.** the coloured muscular membrane in the eye that surrounds and controls the size of the pupil. **2.** a tall plant with long pointed leaves and large flowers. [Greek: rainbow]

Irish (ˈaɪrɪʃ) *adj.* **1.** of Ireland, its people, their Celtic language, or their dialect of English. ~*n.* **2. the Irish.** (*functioning as pl.*) the people of Ireland. **3.** same as **Irish Gaelic. 4.** the dialect of English spoken in Ireland.

Irish coffee *n.* hot coffee mixed with Irish whiskey and topped with double cream.

Irish Gaelic *n.* the Celtic language of Ireland.

Irish moss *n.* same as **carragéen.**

irk (ɜːk) *vb.* to irritate, vex, or annoy. [Middle English *irken* to grow weary]

irksome (ˈɜːksəm) *adj.* annoying, tiresome, or tedious.

iron (ˈaɪən) *n.* **1.** a strong silvery-white metallic element, widely used for structural and engineering purposes. Symbol: Fe **2.** any of certain tools made of iron, esp. a

small electrically heated device with a weighted flat bottom for pressing clothes. **3.** any of various golf clubs with metal heads. **4.** a splintlike support for a malformed leg. **5.** great strength or resolve: *a will of iron.* **6. strike while the iron is hot.** to act at an opportune moment. ~*adj.* **7.** very hard or merciless: *iron determination.* **8.** very strong: *an iron constitution.* ~*vb.* **9.** to smooth (clothes or fabric) by removing (creases) using a heated iron. ~See also **iron out, irons.** [Old English *īren*]

Iron Age *n.* the period that began in the Middle East about 1100 B.C. during which iron tools and weapons were used.

ironclad *adj.* (ˌaɪənˈklæd). **1.** covered or protected with iron: *an ironclad warship.* ~*n.* (ˈaɪənˌklæd). **2.** a large wooden 19th-century warship with armoured plating.

Iron Curtain *n.* the guarded border between the countries of the Soviet bloc and the rest of Europe.

ironic (aɪˈrɒnɪk) *or* **ironical** *adj.* of, characterized by, or using irony. —**i'ronically** *adv.*

ironing board *n.* a narrow board, usually on legs, with a suitable covering on which to iron clothes.

iron lung *n.* an airtight metal cylinder enclosing the entire body up to the neck and providing artificial respiration.

iron maiden *n.* a medieval instrument of torture, consisting of a hinged case (often shaped in the form of a woman) lined with iron spikes.

ironmaster (ˈaɪənˌmɑːstə) *n. Brit.* a manufacturer of iron.

ironmonger (ˈaɪənˌmʌŋgə) *n. Brit.* a person who deals in hardware. —**'iron,mongery** *n.*

iron out *vb.* to settle (a problem or difficulty) as a result of negotiations or discussions.

iron pyrites (ˈpaɪraɪts) *n.* same as **pyrite.**

iron rations *pl. n.* emergency food supplies, esp. for military personnel in action.

irons (ˈaɪənz) *pl. n.* **1.** fetters or chains. **2. have several irons in the fire.** to be involved in many projects.

ironstone (ˈaɪənˌstəʊn) *n.* **1.** any rock consisting mainly of an iron-bearing ore. **2.** a tough durable earthenware.

ironwood (ˈaɪənˌwʊd) *n.* **1.** any of various trees, such as hornbeam, with exceptionally hard wood. **2.** the wood of any of these trees.

ironwork (ˈaɪənˌwɜːk) *n.* work done in iron, esp. decorative work.

ironworks (ˈaɪənˌwɜːks) *n.* (*sometimes functioning as sing.*) a building in which iron is smelted, cast, or wrought.

irony (ˈaɪrənɪ) *n., pl.* **-nies. 1.** the mildly sarcastic use of words to imply the opposite of what they normally mean. **2.** a situation or result that is the direct opposite of what was expected or intended. [Greek *eirōneía*]

irradiate (ɪˈreɪdɪˌeɪt) *vb.* **1.** *Physics.* to subject to or treat with light or other electromagnetic radiation. **2.** to make clear or bright intellectually or spiritually; illumine. **3.** same as **radiate** (sense 1). —**ir₁radi'ation** n.

irrational (ɪ'ræʃənᵊl) adj. **1.** inconsistent with reason; illogical; absurd. **2.** incapable of reasoning. **3.** Maths. (of an equation or expression) involving radicals or fractional exponents. —**ir₁ration'ality** n. —**ir'rationally** adv.

irrational number n. any real number that cannot be expressed as the ratio of two integers, such as π.

irreconcilable (ɪ'rɛkⁿn₁saɪləbᵊl) adj. not able to be brought into agreement; opposed; incompatible. —**ir₁recon₁cila'bility** n.

irrecoverable (₁ɪrɪ'kʌvərəbᵊl) adj. not able to be recovered, remedied, or rectified.

irredeemable (₁ɪrɪ'diːməbᵊl) adj. **1.** (of bonds or shares) incapable of being bought back directly or paid off. **2.** (of paper money) not convertible into coin. **3.** irreparable; hopeless.

irredentist (₁ɪrɪ'dɛntɪst) n. a person who favours the acquisition of territory that was once part of his country. [Italian irredenta unredeemed] —**irre'dentism** n.

irreducible (₁ɪrɪ'djuːsɪbᵊl) adj. not able to be brought to a simpler or reduced form. —**irre₁duci'bility** n.

irrefutable (ɪ'rɛfjʊtəbᵊl, ₁ɪrɪ'fjuːtəbᵊl) adj. impossible to deny or disprove.

irregular (ɪ'rɛgjʊlə) adj. **1.** uneven in shape, position, arrangement, etc. **2.** not occurring at expected or equal intervals: an irregular pulse. **3.** not conforming to accepted practice or routine; unconventional. **4.** (of a word) not following the usual pattern of formation in a language. **5.** (of troops) not belonging to regular forces. ~n. **6.** a soldier not in a regular army. —**irregularity** (ɪ₁rɛgjʊ'lærɪtɪ) n. —**ir'regularly** adv.

irrelevant (ɪ'rɛləvᵊnt) adj. not connected with the matter at hand. —**ir'relevance** or **ir'relevancy** n.

irreligious (₁ɪrɪ'lɪdʒəs) adj. **1.** lacking religious faith. **2.** indifferent or opposed to religion.

irremediable (₁ɪrɪ'miːdɪəbᵊl) adj. not able to be remedied; incurable.

irremovable (₁ɪrɪ'muːvəbᵊl) adj. not able to be removed. —**irre₁mova'bility** n.

irreparable (ɪ'rɛpərəbᵊl) adj. not able to be put right or remedied: irreparable damage to her reputation. —**ir₁repara'bility** n.

irreplaceable (₁ɪrɪ'pleɪsəbᵊl) adj. not able to be replaced: an irreplaceable antique.

irrepressible (₁ɪrɪ'prɛsəbᵊl) adj. not capable of being repressed, controlled, or restrained. —**irre₁pressi'bility** n. —**ir-re'pressibly** adv.

irreproachable (₁ɪrɪ'prəʊtʃəbᵊl) adj. blameless; faultless. —**irre₁proacha'bility** n.

irresistible (₁ɪrɪ'zɪstəbᵊl) adj. **1.** not able to be resisted or refused; overpowering: an irresistible impulse. **2.** very fascinating or alluring: an irresistible woman. —**irre₁sisti'bility** n. —**irre'sistibly** adv.

irresolute (ɪ'rɛzə₁luːt) adj. unable to make decisions; hesitating. —**ir₁reso'lution** n.

irrespective (₁ɪrɪ'spɛktɪv) adj. **irrespective of.** without taking account of; regardless of.

irresponsible (₁ɪrɪ'spɒnsəbᵊl) adj. **1.** not showing or done with due care for the consequences of one's actions or attitudes; reckless. **2.** not capable of bearing responsibility. —**irre₁sponsi'bility** n. —**irre'sponsibly** adv.

irretrievable (₁ɪrɪ'triːvəbᵊl) adj. not able to be retrieved, recovered, or repaired. —**irre₁trieva'bility** n. —**irre'trievably** adv.

irreverence (ɪ'rɛvərəns) n. **1.** lack of due respect; disrespect. **2.** a disrespectful remark or act. —**ir'reverent** adj.

irreversible (₁ɪrɪ'vɜːsəbᵊl) adj. not able to be reversed or put right again: the damage may be irreversible. —**irre'versibly** adv.

irrevocable (ɪ'rɛvəkəbᵊl) adj. not able to be changed or undone: an irrevocable loss. —**ir'revocably** adv.

irrigate ('ɪrɪ₁geɪt) vb. **1.** to supply (land) with water through ditches or pipes, esp. to promote the growth of food crops. **2.** Med. to bathe or wash out (a bodily part or wound). [Latin irrigāre] —**irri'gation** n. —**'irri₁gator** n.

irritable ('ɪrɪtəbᵊl) adj. **1.** easily annoyed or angered. **2.** (of all living organisms) capable of responding to such stimuli as heat, light, and touch. **3.** Pathol. abnormally sensitive. —**irrita'bility** n.

irritant ('ɪrɪtᵊnt) adj. **1.** causing irritation; irritating. ~n. **2.** something that irritates, esp. a substance that causes a part of the body to become tender or inflamed.

irritate ('ɪrɪ₁teɪt) vb. **1.** to annoy or anger (someone). **2.** Biol. to stimulate (an organ) to respond in a characteristic manner. **3.** Pathol. to cause (a bodily organ or part) to become inflamed or tender. [Latin irrītāre to provoke] —**irri'tation** n.

irrupt (ɪ'rʌpt) vb. to enter forcibly or suddenly. [Latin irrumpere] —**ir'ruption** n. —**ir'ruptive** adj.

is (ɪz) vb. third person singular of the present tense of **be.** [Old English]

isallobar (aɪ'sælə₁bɑː) n. a line on a map connecting places with equal pressure changes. [Greek isos equal + allos other + baros weight]

ISBN International Standard Book Number.

isinglass ('aɪzɪŋ₁glɑːs) n. **1.** a gelatin made from the air bladders of freshwater fish. **2.** same as **mica.** [Middle Dutch huysenblase sturgeon bladder]

Isl. 1. Island. **2.** Isle.

Islam ('ɪzlɑːm) n. **1.** Also called: **Islamism.** the religion of Muslims, teaching that there is only one God and that Mohammed is his prophet. **2. a.** Muslims collectively and their civilization. **b.** the countries where the Muslim religion is predominant. [Arabic: surrender (to God)] —**Is'lamic** adj.

island ('aɪlənd) n. **1.** a mass of land that is completely surrounded by water. **2.** something isolated, detached, or surrounded: *a traffic island.* [Old English *īgland*]

islander (ˈaɪləndə) *n.* a person who lives on an island.

isle (aɪl) *n. Poetic except when cap. and part of place name.* an island, esp. a small one.

islet (ˈaɪlɪt) *n.* a small island.

ism (ˈɪzəm) *n. Informal, often used to show contempt.* a doctrine, system, or practice, esp. one whose name ends in *-ism: communism; fascism.*

isn't (ˈɪzᵊnt) is not.

iso- *or before a vowel* **is-** *combining form.* equal or identical: *isomagnetic.* [Greek *isos* equal]

isobar (ˈaɪsəʊˌbɑː) *n.* **1.** a line on a map connecting places of equal atmospheric pressure. **2.** *Physics.* any of two or more atoms that have the same mass number but different atomic numbers. [Greek *isobarēs* of equal weight] —**ˌisoˈbaric** *adj.* —**ˈisobarˌism** *n.*

isochronal (aɪˈsɒkrənᵊl) *or* **isochronous** *adj.* **1.** equal in length of time. **2.** occurring at equal time intervals. [Greek *isos* equal + *khronos* time] —**iˈsochroˌnism** *n.*

isohel (ˈaɪsəʊˌhɛl) *n.* a line on a map connecting places with an equal period of sunshine. [Greek *isos* equal + *hēlios* sun]

isohyet (ˌaɪsəʊˈhaɪɪt) *n.* a line on a map connecting places having equal rainfall. [Greek *isos* equal + *huetos* rain]

isolate (ˈaɪsəˌleɪt) *vb.* **1.** to place apart; cause to be alone. **2.** *Med.* to quarantine (a person or animal) having a contagious disease. **3.** to obtain (a compound) in an uncombined form. [Latin *insulātus,* lit.: made into an island] —**ˌisoˈlation** *n.*

isomer (ˈaɪsəmə) *n. Chem.* a substance with the same molecules as another but a different atomic arrangement. —**isomeric** (ˌaɪsəˈmɛrɪk) *adj.*

isometric (ˌaɪsəʊˈmɛtrɪk) *or* **isometrical** *adj.* **1.** having equal dimensions or measurements. **2.** *Physiol.* of or relating to muscular contraction that does not produce shortening of the muscle. **3.** (of a method of projecting a drawing in three dimensions) having the three axes equally inclined and all lines drawn to scale. [Greek *isometria*] —**ˌisoˈmetrically** *adv.*

isomorphism (ˌaɪsəʊˈmɔːˌfɪzəm) *n.* **1.** *Biol.* similarity of form, as in different generations of the same life cycle. **2.** *Chem.* the existence of two or more substances of different composition in a similar crystalline form. **3.** *Maths.* a one-to-one correspondence between the elements of two or more sets. —**ˈisoˌmorph** *n.* —**ˌisoˈmorphic** *or* **ˌisoˈmorphous** *adj.*

isosceles (aɪˈsɒsɪˌliːz) *adj.* (of a triangle) having two sides of equal length. [Greek *isos* equal + *skelos* leg]

isotherm (ˈaɪsəʊˌθɜːm) *n.* a line on a map linking places of equal temperature. Also called: **isothermal, isothermal line.**

isotope (ˈaɪsəˌtəʊp) *n.* one of two or more atoms with the same atomic number but different atomic weights. [Greek *isos* equal + *topos* place] —**isotopic** (ˌaɪsəˈtɒpɪk) *adj.* —**isotopy** (aɪˈsɒtəpɪ) *n.*

isotropic (ˌaɪsəʊˈtrɒpɪk) *or* **isotropous** (aɪˈsɒtrəpəs) *adj.* having uniform physical properties, such as elasticity or conduction in all directions. —**iˈsotropy** *n.*

Israeli (ɪzˈreɪlɪ) *n., pl.* **-lis** *or* **-li.** **1.** a person from Israel, in SW Asia. ~*adj.* **2.** of Israel or its inhabitants.

Israelite (ˈɪzrɪəˌlaɪt) *n. Bible.* a member of the ethnic group claiming descent from Jacob; a Hebrew.

issue (ˈɪʃjuː) *n.* **1.** the act of sending or giving out something. **2.** something issued, such as an edition of stamps or a magazine. **3.** the act of emerging; outflow. **4.** something flowing out, such as a river. **5.** a place of outflow; outlet. **6.** the descendants of a person; offspring. **7.** a topic of interest or discussion. **8.** an important subject requiring a decision. **9.** a consequence; result. **10. at issue. a.** under discussion. **b.** in disagreement. **11. force the issue.** to compel decision on some matter. **12. join issue.** to join in controversy. **13. take issue.** to disagree. ~*vb.* **-suing, -sued. 14.** to come forth or emerge. **15.** to send out; put into circulation. **16.** to publish. **17.** to be a consequence; result. **18.** (foll. by *in*) to end or terminate. **19.** (foll. by *with*) to supply officially with. [Old French *eissue* way out] —**ˈissuable** *adj.*

isthmus (ˈɪsməs) *n., pl.* **-muses** *or* **-mi** (-maɪ). a narrow strip of land connecting two relatively large land areas. [Greek *isthmos*] —**ˈisthmoid** *adj.*

it (ɪt) *pron.* (*subjective or objective*) **1.** refers to a nonhuman, animal, plant, or inanimate thing, or sometimes to a small baby: *it looks dangerous; give it a bone.* **2.** refers to something unspecified or implied or to a previous or understood clause, phrase, or word: *it is impossible; I knew it.* **3.** used to represent human life or experience in respect of the present situation: *how's it going?; to brazen it out.* **4.** used as the subject of impersonal verbs: *it is raining; it's Tuesday.* **5.** *Informal.* the crucial or ultimate point: *the steering failed and I thought that was it.* ~*n.* **6.** *Informal.* **a.** sexual intercourse. **b.** sex appeal. [Old English *hit*]

i.t.a. *or* **ITA** initial teaching alphabet: a partly phonetic alphabet used to teach reading.

Italian (ɪˈtæljən) *n.* **1.** the official language of Italy and one of the official languages of Switzerland. **2.** a person from Italy. ~*adj.* **3.** of Italy, its inhabitants, or their language.

Italianate (ɪˈtæljəˌneɪt) *or* **Italianesque** (ɪˌtæljəˈnɛsk) *adj.* Italian in style or character.

italic (ɪˈtælɪk) *adj.* **1.** of or denoting a style of printing type in which the characters slant to the right. ~*n.* **2.** (*often pl.*) italic type or print. [Latin *Italicus* of Italy (where it was first used)]

italicize *or* **-ise** (ɪˈtælɪˌsaɪz) *vb.* to print (text) in italic type. —**iˌtaliciˈzation** *or* **-iˈsation** *n.*

itch (ɪtʃ) *n.* **1.** an irritation or tickling sensation of the skin. **2.** a restless desire. **3.** any skin disorder, such as scabies, characterized by intense itching. ~*vb.* **4.** to feel an irritating or tickling sensation. **5.** to have a restless desire (to do something): *I was itching to get away.* **6. have itchy feet.** to be restless; have a desire to travel. [Old English *giccean*] —'**itchy** *adj.* —'**itchiness** *n.*

it'd ('ɪt²d) it would *or* it had.

item ('aɪtəm) *n.* **1.** a thing or unit, esp. one included in a list or collection. **2.** *Bookkeeping.* an entry in an account. **3.** a piece of information: *a news item.* [Latin: in like manner]

itemize *or* **-ise** ('aɪtə̩maɪz) *vb.* to put on a list or make a list of. —̩**itemi'zation** *or* **-i'sation** *n.*

iterate ('ɪtə̩reɪt) *vb.* to say or do again. [Latin *iterum* again] —̩**iter'ation** *n.* —'**iterative** *adj.*

itinerant (aɪ'tɪnərənt) *adj.* **1.** working for a short time in various places, esp. as a casual labourer. ~*n.* **2.** an itinerant worker or other person. [Latin *iter* a journey]

itinerary (aɪ'tɪnərərɪ) *n.,* *pl.* **-aries. 1.** a detailed plan of travel; route. **2.** a record of a journey. **3.** a guidebook for travellers.

-itis *suffix forming nouns.* indicating inflammation of a specified part: *tonsillitis.* [Greek *-itēs* belonging to]

it'll ('ɪt²l) it will *or* it shall.

its (ɪts) *det.* **1.** of, belonging to, or associat-ed in some way with it: *its left rear wheel; I can see its logical consequence.* ~*pron.* **2.** something belonging to it: *its over there.*

it's (ɪts) it is *or* it has.

itself (ɪt'sɛlf) *pron.* **1. a.** the reflexive form of *it*: *the dog scratched itself.* **b.** (used for emphasis): *even the money itself won't convince me.* **2.** its normal or usual self: *my cat doesn't seem itself these days.*

ITV (in Britain) Independent Television.

IU(C)D intrauterine (contraceptive) device.

I've (aɪv) I have.

ivories ('aɪvərɪz) *pl. n. Slang.* **1.** the keys of a piano. **2.** the teeth. **3.** dice.

ivory ('aɪvərɪ) *n.,* *pl.* **-ries. 1.** a hard smooth creamy white type of bone that makes up a major part of the tusks of elephants. ~*adj.* **2.** yellowish-white. [Latin *ebur* ivory] —'**ivory-̩like** *adj.*

ivory tower ('taʊə) *n.* seclusion or withdrawal from practical matters or from the problems of everyday life. —̩**ivory-'towered** *adj.*

IVR International Vehicle Registration.

ivy ('aɪvɪ) *n.,* *pl.* **ivies. 1.** a woody climbing or trailing plant with evergreen leaves and black berry-like fruits. **2.** any of various other climbing or creeping plants, such as the poison ivy. [Old English *ifig*]

ixia ('ɪksɪə) *n.* a southern African plant of the iris family with showy ornamental funnel-shaped flowers. [Greek *ixos* mistletoe]

J

j *or* **J** (dʒeɪ) *n.*, *pl.* **j's, J's,** *or* **Js.** the tenth letter of the English alphabet.

J joule(s).

jab (dʒæb) *vb.* **jabbing, jabbed. 1.** to poke sharply. **2.** to punch with quick short blows. ~*n.* **3.** a sharp poke. **4.** a quick short punch. **5.** *Informal.* an injection: *a polio jab.* [var. of *job*]

jabber ('dʒæbə) *vb.* **1.** to speak very quickly and excitedly; chatter. ~*n.* **2.** quick, excited chatter. [imit.]

jabot ('ʒæbəʊ) *n.* a frill or ruffle on the front of a blouse or shirt. [French]

jacaranda (,dʒækə'rændə) *n.* a tropical American tree with sweet-smelling wood and pale purple flowers. [American Indian]

jack (dʒæk) *n.* **1.** a mechanical device used to raise a heavy weight, such as a motor vehicle. **2.** a playing card with a picture of a pageboy on it. **3.** *Bowls.* a small white bowl at which the players aim with their own bowls. **4.** *Electrical engineering.* a socket designed for the insertion of a plug. **5.** a flag flown at the bow of a ship, showing the ship's nationality. **6.** Also called: **jackstone.** one of the pieces used in the game of jacks. **7. every man jack.** everyone without exception. ~See also **jack in, jacks, jack up.** [from short form of *John*]

jackal ('dʒækɔːl) *n.* a wild doglike animal of Africa and Asia, which has a yellowish-grey coat, long legs, and pointed ears and which feeds on the decaying flesh of dead animals. [Persian *shagāl*]

jackanapes ('dʒækə,neɪps) *n.* (*functioning as sing.*) an impertinent person. [lit.: Jack of the ape, nickname of first Duke of Suffolk, whose badge showed an ape's ball and chain]

jackass ('dʒæk,æs) *n.* **1.** a male donkey. **2.** a fool. [*jack* (male) + *ass*]

jackboot ('dʒæk,buːt) *n.* **1.** a leather military boot, reaching up to or above the knee. **2. under the jackboot of.** under the harsh rule of.

jackdaw ('dʒæk,dɔː) *n.* a large black-and-grey bird of Europe and Asia, which is related to the crow. [*jack* + *daw*, obs. name for jackdaw]

jacket ('dʒækɪt) *n.* **1.** a short coat with a front opening and long sleeves. **2.** same as **dust jacket. 3.** the skin of a potato. [Old French *jaquet*]

Jack Frost *n.* frost represented as a person.

jack in *vb. Slang.* to abandon (an attempt or enterprise).

jack-in-office *n.* a self-important petty official.

jack-in-the-box *n.* a toy consisting of a figure on a tight spring in a box, which springs out when the lid is opened.

jackknife ('dʒæk,naɪf) *n.*, *pl.* **-knives. 1.** a knife with a blade that can be folded into the handle. **2.** a dive in which the diver bends at the waist in midair. ~*vb.* **3.** (of an articulated lorry) to go out of control in such a way that the trailer swings round at a sharp angle to the cab.

jack of all trades *n.*, *pl.* **jacks of all trades.** a person who can do many different kinds of work; handyman.

jackpot ('dʒæk,pɒt) *n.* **1.** the most valuable prize in an accumulated stake that may be won in a game or lottery. **2. hit the jackpot.** *Informal.* to achieve great success through luck. [prob. from *jack* (playing card)]

jack rabbit *n.* a hare of W North America with long hind legs and large ears. [*jackass-rabbit,* referring to its long ears]

jacks (dʒæks) *n.* (*functioning as sing.*) a game in which bone or metal pieces are thrown and then picked up between throws of a small ball. Also called: **jackstones.** [*jackstones,* var. of *checkstones* pebbles]

Jack Tar *n. Now chiefly literary.* a sailor.

jack up *vb.* **1.** to raise (a heavy weight, such as a motor vehicle) with a jack. **2.** *Slang.* to inject oneself with a drug. **3.** to increase (prices or salaries).

Jacobean (,dʒækə'bɪən) *adj.* **1.** *History.* relating to James I of England and Ireland or to the period of his rule (1603–25). **2.** of the style of furniture or architecture current at this time. [Latin *Jacōbus* James]

Jacobite ('dʒækə,baɪt) *n. History.* a supporter of James II of England, Scotland, and Ireland and his descendants. [Latin *Jacōbus* James]

Jacquard ('dʒækɑːd) *n.* **1.** a fabric in which the design is incorporated into the weave. **2.** a loom on which this fabric is produced. [after Joseph M. *Jacquard,* its inventor]

Jacuzzi (dʒə'kuːzɪ) *n. Trademark.* a large circular bath fitted with a mechanism that makes the water swirl around.

jade¹ (dʒeɪd) *n.* **1.** a hard, usually green, semiprecious stone used for making ornaments and jewellery. ~*adj.* **2.** of the colour of green jade. [obs. Spanish *piedra de ijada* colic stone, because it was believed to cure colic]

jade² (dʒeɪd) *n. Old-fashioned.* a disreputable woman. [origin unknown]

jaded ('dʒeɪdɪd) *adj.* tired and unenthusiastic; weary.

Jaffa ('dʒæfə, 'dʒɑː-) *n.* a large orange with a thick skin. [after *Jaffa,* port in W Israel]

jag¹ (dʒæg) *n. Informal.* same as **jab** (sense 5). [origin unknown]

jag² (dʒæg) *n. Slang.* **1.** a bout of drinking. **2.** a period of uncontrolled activity: *a crying jag.* [origin unknown]

jagged ('dʒægɪd) *adj.* having an uneven

edge with sharp points. [from *jag* a sharp point]

jaguar ('dʒægjʊə) *n.* a large catlike animal of south and central America, similar to the leopard but with larger spots on its coat. [S American Indian]

jail *or* **gaol** (dʒeɪl) *n.* **1.** a prison. ~*vb.* **2.** to confine (someone) in prison. [Old French *jaiole* cage]

jailbird *or* **gaolbird** ('dʒeɪlˌbɜːd) *n.* a person who is or has often been in jail.

jailer *or* **gaoler** ('dʒeɪlə) *n.* a person in charge of prisoners in a jail.

jake (dʒeɪk) *adj.* **she's jake.** *Austral. & N.Z. slang.* it is all right. [origin unknown]

jalap ('dʒæləp) *n.* the dried and powdered root of a Mexican climbing plant, used as a purgative. [Mexican Spanish *jalapa*]

jalopy (dʒə'lɒpɪ) *n., pl.* **-lopies.** *Informal.* a dilapidated old car. [origin unknown]

jalousie ('ʒæluˌziː) *n.* a window blind or shutter made of horizontal slats of wood. [Old French *gelosie*]

jam¹ (dʒæm) *vb.* **jamming, jammed. 1.** to cram or wedge (a thing or people) into a place or against a thing: *to jam paper into an incinerator.* **2.** to crowd, pack, or congest: *cars jammed the roads.* **3.** to make or become stuck or locked. **4.** (foll. by *on*) to activate suddenly: *to jam on the brakes.* **5.** *Radio.* to prevent the clear reception of (radio communications) by transmitting other signals on the same frequency. **6.** *Slang.* to play in a jam session. ~*n.* **7.** a crowd or congestion in a confined space: *a traffic jam.* **8.** *Informal.* a difficult situation: *to help a friend out of a jam.* **9.** same as **jam session.** [prob. imit.]

jam² (dʒæm) *n.* a food made from fruit boiled with sugar until the mixture sets, used for spreading on bread. [perhaps from JAM¹ (the act of squeezing)]

jamb (dʒæm) *n.* a side post of a doorframe or window frame. [Old French *jambe* leg, jamb]

jamboree (ˌdʒæmbə'riː) *n.* **1.** a party or spree. **2.** a large gathering of Scouts. [origin unknown]

jammy ('dʒæmɪ) *adj.* **-mier, -miest. 1.** covered with jam. **2.** *Brit. slang.* lucky: *you jammy so-and-so!*

jam-packed *adj.* filled to capacity.

jam session *n. Slang.* an improvised performance by jazz or rock musicians. [prob. from JAM¹]

Jan. January.

jandal ('dʒænd'l) *n. N.Z.* same as **flip-flop.**

jangle ('dʒæŋg'l) *vb.* **1.** to make or cause (something) to make a harsh unpleasant ringing noise. **2.** to produce an irritating or unpleasant effect on: *the accident jangled his nerves.* [Old French *jangler*]

janitor ('dʒænɪtə) *n. Chiefly Scot., U.S., & Canad.* the caretaker of a school, university, hospital, or apartment block. [Latin: doorkeeper]

January ('dʒænjʊərɪ) *n., pl.* **-aries.** the first month of the year. [Latin *Jānuārius*]

japan (dʒə'pæn) *n.* **1.** a glossy black lacquer, originally from the Orient, which is used on wood or metal. ~*vb.* **-panning, -panned. 2.** to lacquer (something) with japan.

Japanese (ˌdʒæpə'niːz) *adj.* **1.** of Japan, its people, or their language. ~*n.* **2.** (*pl.* **-nese**) a person from Japan. **3.** the official language of Japan.

jape (dʒeɪp) *n.* a joke or prank. [origin unknown]

japonica (dʒə'pɒnɪkə) *n.* **1.** a Japanese shrub with red flowers and yellowish fruit. **2.** same as **camellia.** [New Latin *Japonia* Japan]

jar¹ (dʒɑː) *n.* **1.** a wide-mouthed container that is usually cylindrical and made of glass. **2.** *Brit. informal.* a glass of beer. [Arabic *jarrah* large earthen vessel]

jar² (dʒɑː) *vb.* **jarring, jarred. 1.** to have an irritating or unpleasant effect: *their laughing jarred on his nerves.* **2.** to vibrate or cause (something) to vibrate. **3.** to make or cause (something) to make a harsh unpleasant noise. **4.** to clash: *our beliefs jar.* ~*n.* **5.** a jolt or shock. [prob. imit.] —**'jarring** *adj.*

jardinière (ˌʒɑːdɪ'njɛə) *n.* **1.** an ornamental pot or stand for plants. **2.** a garnish of fresh vegetables for a dish of meat. [French]

jargon ('dʒɑːgən) *n.* **1.** specialized language concerned with a particular subject, profession, or group. **2.** pretentious language. [Old French]

jasmine ('dʒæzmɪn) *n.* a shrub or climbing plant with sweet-smelling white, yellow, or red flowers. [Persian *yāsmīn*]

jasper ('dʒæspə) *n.* a red, yellow, brown, or dark green opaque variety of quartz, used as a gemstone and for ornamental decoration. [Greek *iaspis*]

jaundice ('dʒɔːndɪs) *n.* **1.** a condition in which the skin becomes yellow due to the abnormal presence of bile pigments in the blood. ~*vb.* **2.** to distort (someone's judgment) adversely: *jealousy had jaundiced his mind.* **3.** to affect (someone) with or as if with jaundice. [French *jaune* yellow] —**'jaundiced** *adj.*

jaunt (dʒɔːnt) *n.* **1.** a short pleasurable excursion; outing. ~*vb.* **2.** to go on such an excursion. [origin unknown]

jaunting car *n.* a light two-wheeled one-horse car, formerly widely used in Ireland.

jaunty ('dʒɔːntɪ) *adj.* **-tier, -tiest. 1.** sprightly and cheerful: *a jaunty step.* **2.** smart: *a jaunty hat.* [French *gentil* noble] —**'jauntily** *adv.*

Javanese (ˌdʒɑːvə'niːz) *adj.* **1.** of the island of Java, in Indonesia. ~*n.* **2.** (*pl.* **-nese**) a person from Java. **3.** the language of Java.

javelin ('dʒævlɪn) *n.* **1.** a long pointed spear thrown in a sports competition. **2.** **the javelin.** the sport of throwing the javelin. [Old French *javeline*]

jaw (dʒɔː) *n.* **1.** either of the two bony structures in the head that hold the teeth and frame the mouth. **2.** the lower part of the face below the mouth. **3.** either of a pair of hinged or sliding parts of a machine or tool that are designed to grip an object.

4. *Slang.* a long conversation. ~*vb.* **5.** *Slang.* to chat; gossip. [prob. Old French *joue* cheek]

jawbone ('dʒɔː,bəun) *n.* the bone in the lower jaw of a person or animal.

jaws (dʒɔːz) *pl. n.* **1.** the narrow opening of some confined place such as a gorge. **2.** a dangerous or threatening position: *the jaws of death.*

jay (dʒeı) *n.* a bird of Europe and Asia with a pinkish-brown body and blue-and-black wings. [Old French *jai*]

jaywalking ('dʒeı,wɔːkıŋ) *n.* the act of crossing a road in a dangerous or careless manner. [*jay* (in sense: a foolish person)] —'**jay,walker** *n.*

jazz (dʒæz) *n.* **1.** a kind of popular music of Black American origin, which has an exciting rhythm and usually features a lot of improvisation. **2.** *Slang.* other related things: *legal papers and all that jazz.* ~*vb.* **3.** to play or dance to jazz music. [origin unknown]

jazz up *vb. Informal.* **1.** to liven up (a piece of music) with jazzy qualities. **2.** to make (something) more colourful, appealing, or lively.

jazzy ('dʒæzı) *adj.* **-zier, -ziest. 1.** colourful and stylish: *a jazzy tie.* **2.** of or like jazz.

JCB *n. Trademark.* a machine with a hydraulically operated shovel on the front and a digger arm on the back, used in building. [initials of Joseph Cyril Bamford, its manufacturer]

jealous ('dʒeləs) *adj.* **1.** suspicious or fearful of being displaced by a rival. **2.** envious: *jealous of her success.* **3.** (foll. by *of*) possessive and watchful in the protection of: *jealous of one's reputation.* **4.** resulting from jealousy: *a jealous rage.* [Late Latin *zēlus* emulation] —'**jealously** *adv.*

jealousy ('dʒeləsı) *n., pl.* **-ousies.** the state or quality of being jealous.

Jean Baptiste (,ʒɒn bæ'tiːst) *n. Canad. slang.* a French Canadian. [French]

jeans (dʒiːnz) *pl. n.* trousers for casual wear, usually made of denim. [from *jean* fustian fabric from Genoa]

Jeep (dʒiːp) *n. Trademark.* a small road vehicle with four-wheel drive. [perhaps *general-purpose* (*vehicle*), infl. by Eugene the *Jeep*, creature in a comic strip]

jeer (dʒıə) *vb.* **1.** to laugh or scoff (at a person or thing). ~*n.* **2.** a cry of derision. [origin unknown] —'**jeering** *adj., n.*

Jehovah (dʒı'həuvə) *n. Bible.* a personal name of God. [Hebrew *Yahweh*]

Jehovah's Witness *n.* a member of a Christian Church of American origin, the followers of which believe that the end of the present world system of government is near.

jejune (dʒı'dʒuːn) *adj.* **1.** simple and unsophisticated. **2.** dull and uninteresting: *a jejune film.* [Latin *jējūnus* empty]

jejunum (dʒı'dʒuːnəm) *n. Anat.* the part of the small intestine between the duodenum and the ileum. [Latin]

Jekyll and Hyde ('dʒɛk²l; haıd) *n.* a person with two distinct personalities, one good and the other evil. [after the character in a novel by R.L. Stevenson]

jell *or* **gel** (dʒɛl) *vb.* **1.** to become thick and jelly-like. **2.** to take on a definite form: *his ideas have jelled.* [from *jelly*]

jellaba *or* **jellabah** ('dʒɛləbə) *n.* a loose cloak with a hood, worn by many Arab men. [Arabic *jallabah*]

jelly ('dʒɛlı) *n., pl.* **-lies. 1.** a fruit-flavoured clear dessert set with gelatin. **2.** a food made from the juice of fruit boiled with sugar, usually spread on bread. **3.** a savoury food preparation set with gelatin. ~*vb.* **-lying, -lied. 4.** to prepare (food) in a jelly. [Latin *gelare* to freeze] —'**jellied** *adj.* —'**jelly-like** *adj.*

jellyfish ('dʒɛlı,fıʃ) *n., pl.* **-fish.** a sea creature with an umbrella-shaped body and trailing tentacles.

jemmy ('dʒemı) *or U.S.* **jimmy** *n., pl.* **-mies.** a short steel crowbar, used by burglars to prise open doors and windows. [from short form of *James*]

jenny ('dʒenı) *n., pl.* **-nies. 1.** the female of certain animals or birds, such as a donkey, ass, or wren. **2.** short for **spinning jenny.** [from the name *Jenny*]

jeopardize *or* **-ise** ('dʒepə,daız) *vb.* to put (something) in danger; risk: *he jeopardized his job by being persistently late.*

jeopardy ('dʒepədı) *n.* danger of injury, loss, or death: *his health was in jeopardy.* [Old French *jeu parti*, lit.: divided game, hence uncertain issue]

jerbil ('dʒɜːbıl) *n.* same as **gerbil.**

jerboa (dʒɜː'bəuə) *n.* a small rodent of Asia and N Africa, with long hind legs specialized for jumping. [Arabic *yarbū'*]

jeremiad (,dʒerı'maıəd) *n.* a long mournful complaint. [French *jérémiade*, referring to the Lamentations of Jeremiah in the Old Testament]

jerk¹ (dʒɜːk) *vb.* **1.** to move with an irregular or spasmodic motion. **2.** to throw, twist, pull, or push (something) abruptly or spasmodically. ~*n.* **3.** an abrupt or spasmodic movement. **4.** an irregular jolting motion: *the car moved with a jerk.* **5.** *Slang, chiefly U.S. & Canad.* a stupid or ignorant person. [prob. var. of *yerk* to pull stitches tight]

jerk² (dʒɜːk) *vb.* to preserve (beef) by cutting it into thin strips and drying it in the sun. [S. American Indian]

jerkin ('dʒɜːkın) *n.* a short jacket. [origin unknown]

jerky ('dʒɜːkı) *adj.* **jerkier, jerkiest.** having an irregular jolting motion: *the bus ride was a bit jerky.* —'**jerkily** *adv.* —'**jerkiness** *n.*

Jerry ('dʒerı) *n., pl.* **-ries.** *Brit. slang.* **1.** a German. **2.** Germans collectively.

jerry-built *adj.* (of houses) built badly with cheap materials. —'**jerry,builder** *n.*

jerry can *n.* a flat-sided can used for storing or transporting motor fuel or water. [from *Jerry* German soldier]

jersey ('dʒɜːzı) *n.* **1.** a knitted garment

covering the upper part of the body. **2.** a machine-knitted slightly elastic cloth of wool, silk, or nylon, used for clothing. [after *Jersey* because of the woollen sweaters worn by the fishermen]

Jersey ('dʒɜːzɪ) *n.* a breed of reddish-brown dairy cattle producing milk with a high butterfat content. [after *Jersey*, island in the English Channel]

Jerusalem artichoke (dʒə'ruːsələm) *n.* a small yellowish-white vegetable that grows underground. [altered from Latin *girasole* sunflower]

jest (dʒɛst) *n.* **1.** something done or said for amusement; joke. **2.** playfulness; fun: *spoken in jest.* ~*vb.* **3.** to act or speak in an amusing way. [var. of *gest* exploit]

jester ('dʒɛstə) *n.* a professional clown employed by a king or nobleman during the Middle Ages.

Jesuit ('dʒɛzjʊɪt) *n.* a member of a Roman Catholic religious order founded by Ignatius Loyola in 1534. [New Latin *Jēsuita*] —ˌJesuˈitical *adj.*

Jesus ('dʒiːzəs) *n.* **1.** Also called: **Jesus Christ, Jesus of Nazareth.** the founder of Christianity, believed by Christians to be the Son of God. ~*interj.* **2.** *Taboo slang.* an oath expressing intense surprise or dismay. [Hebrew *Hehōshūa* God is help]

jet¹ (dʒɛt) *n.* **1.** a thin stream of liquid or gas forced out of a small hole. **2.** an outlet or nozzle through which such a stream is forced out. **3.** a jet-propelled aircraft. ~*vb.* **jetting, jetted. 4.** to come out in a jet: *water jetted from the hose.* **5.** to transport or be transported by jet aircraft. [Old French *jeter* to throw]

jet² (dʒɛt) *n.* a hard black mineral that takes a brilliant polish and is used in jewellery. [Old French *jaiet*]

jet-black *adj.* deep black.

jet engine *n.* an engine that uses jet propulsion for forward thrust, esp. one fitted to an aircraft.

jet lag *n.* a general feeling of fatigue often experienced by aircraft passengers who have crossed several time zones in relatively few hours.

jet-propelled *adj.* **1.** driven by jet propulsion. **2.** *Informal.* very fast.

jet propulsion *n.* propulsion by means of a jet of air or gas, esp. when the exhaust gases provide the forward thrust.

jetsam ('dʒɛtsəm) *n.* **1.** the portion of a ship's cargo thrown overboard to lighten her during a storm. **2.** See **flotsam** (sense 2). [from *jettison*]

jet set *n.* rich and fashionable people who travel widely for pleasure. —'jet-ˌsetter *n.* —'jet-ˌsetting *n., adj.*

jettison ('dʒɛtɪs'n, -z'n) *vb.* **1.** to abandon: *to jettison old clothes.* **2.** to throw (cargo) overboard. [Latin *jactātiō* a tossing about]

jetty ('dʒɛtɪ) *n., pl.* **-ties. 1.** a structure built from a shore out into the water to direct currents or protect a harbour. **2.** a landing pier; dock. [Old French *jetee*]

Jew (dʒuː) *n.* **1.** a descendant of the ancient Israelites. **2.** a person whose religion is Judaism. **3.** *Offensive.* a miserly

person. [Hebrew *yehūdāh* Judah] —'**Jewess** *fem. n.*

jewel ('dʒuːəl) *n.* **1.** a precious or semiprecious stone; gem. **2.** a person or thing regarded as precious or special. **3.** a gemstone used as part of the machinery of a watch. ~*vb.* **-elling, -elled** *or U.S.* **-eling, -eled. 4.** to decorate (something) with jewels. [Old French *jouel*]

jeweller *or U.S.* **jeweler** ('dʒuːələ) *n.* a person who makes, sells, and repairs jewellery.

jewellery *or U.S.* **jewelry** ('dʒuːəlrɪ) *n.* objects such as rings, necklaces, or bracelets, worn for decoration.

Jewish ('dʒuːɪʃ) *adj.* of Jews or Judaism.

Jewry ('dʒʊərɪ) *n.* Jews collectively.

jew's-harp *n.* a small musical instrument held between the teeth and played by plucking a steel tongue with one's finger.

Jezebel ('dʒɛzəˌbɛl) *n.* a shameless or scheming woman. [after the wife of Ahab, in the Bible]

jib¹ (dʒɪb) *n.* **1.** *Naut.* any triangular sail set forward of the foremast of a vessel. **2. the cut of one's jib.** one's manner or style. [origin unknown]

jib² (dʒɪb) *vb.* **jibbing, jibbed.** *Chiefly Brit.* **1.** (of an animal) to stop short and refuse to go forwards: *the horse jibbed at the jump.* **2. jib at.** to object to: *I thought she would jib at the new working methods.* **3.** *Naut.* same as **gybe.** [origin unknown]

jib³ (dʒɪb) *n.* the projecting arm of a crane. [prob. from *gibbet*]

jib boom *n. Naut.* a spar forming an extension of the bowsprit of a ship.

jibe¹ (dʒaɪb) *vb., n. Naut.* same as **gybe.**

jibe² (dʒaɪb) *vb.* same as **gibe.**

jiffy ('dʒɪfɪ) *or* **jiff** *n., pl.* **jiffies** *or* **jiffs.** *Informal.* a very short time: *I'll be back in a jiffy.* [origin unknown]

Jiffy bag *n. Trademark.* a large padded envelope.

jig (dʒɪg) *n.* **1.** a lively folk dance. **2.** music for this dance. **3.** a mechanical device that holds and locates a component during machining. ~*vb.* **jigging, jigged. 4.** to dance a jig. **5.** to jerk up and down rapidly. **6.** to drill or cut (a workpiece) in a jig. [origin unknown]

jigger ('dʒɪgə) *n.* a small whisky glass.

jiggered ('dʒɪgəd) *adj. Informal.* damned; blowed: *I'm jiggered if he'll get away with it.* [prob. euphemism for *buggered*]

jiggery-pokery ('dʒɪgərɪ'pəʊkərɪ) *n. Informal, chiefly Brit.* dishonest or deceitful behaviour. [Scot. dialect *joukery-pawkery*]

jiggle ('dʒɪg'l) *vb.* **1.** to move up and down or to and fro with a short jerky motion. ~*n.* **2.** a short jerky motion. [frequentative of *jig*]

jigsaw ('dʒɪgˌsɔː) *n.* **1.** Also called: **jigsaw puzzle.** a puzzle in which the player has to put together a picture that has been cut into irregularly shaped interlocking pieces. **2.** a mechanical saw with a fine steel blade for cutting along curved or irregular lines in sheets of material. [*jig* (to jerk up and down) + SAW¹]

jilt (dʒɪlt) *vb.* to leave or reject (a lover) without previous warning. [dialect *jillet* flighty girl]

Jim Crow (ˈdʒɪm ˈkrəʊ) *n. U.S.* **1.** the policy or practice of segregating Black people. **2.** *Offensive.* a Black person. [from name of song]

jimjams (ˈdʒɪmˌdʒæmz) *pl. n.* **1.** *Slang.* same as **delirium tremens. 2.** a state of nervous tension or anxiety. [whimsical formation]

jingle (ˈdʒɪŋgᵊl) *vb.* **1.** to ring lightly and repeatedly. ~*n.* **2.** a sound of metal jingling. **3.** a short song or tune used to advertise a product on radio or television or in a cinema. [prob. imit.]

jingo (ˈdʒɪŋgəʊ) *n., pl.* **-goes. 1.** a person who boasts loudly of his patriotism and favours an aggressive warlike foreign policy. **2. by jingo.** *Old-fashioned.* an exclamation of surprise. [after the use of *by Jingo!* in a 19th-cent. song]

jingoism (ˈdʒɪŋgəʊˌɪzəm) *n.* aggressive patriotism. —ˈjingoˈistic *adj.*

jink (dʒɪŋk) *vb.* to move swiftly in order to dodge someone: *when they saw me they jinked behind the trees.* [Scot.]

jinks (dʒɪŋks) *pl. n.* in **high jinks.** boisterous or mischievous behaviour. [origin unknown]

jinni, jinnee, *or* **djinni** (dʒɪˈniː) *n., pl.* **jinn** *or* **djinn** (dʒɪn). a spirit in Muslim mythology that could take on human or animal form. [Arabic]

jinx (dʒɪŋks) *n.* **1.** an unlucky force, person, or thing. ~*vb.* **2.** to be or put a jinx on. [perhaps from Greek *iunx* wryneck, a bird used in magic]

jitterbug (ˈdʒɪtəˌbʌg) *n.* **1.** a fast jerky American dance that was popular in the 1940s. ~*vb.* **-bugging, -bugged. 2.** to dance the jitterbug.

jitters (ˈdʒɪtəz) *pl. n.* **the.** *Informal.* a feeling of extreme nervousness experienced before an important event: *I had a bad case of the jitters before the audition.* [origin unknown] —ˈjittery *adj.*

jive (dʒaɪv) *n.* **1.** a lively jerky dance that was popular in the 1940s and 1950s. **2.** *Slang, chiefly U.S.* misleading or deceptive talk. ~*vb.* **3.** to dance the jive. **4.** *Slang, chiefly U.S.* to mislead or deceive (someone). [origin unknown] —ˈjiver *n.*

Jnr Junior.

job (dʒɒb) *n.* **1.** an occupation; paid employment. **2.** a piece of work; task. **3.** an object worked on or a result produced from working: *you made a good job of the paintwork.* **4.** a duty: *her job was to cook the dinner.* **5.** *Informal.* a difficult task: *I had a job to contact him.* **6.** a state of affairs: *to make the best of a bad job.* **7.** *Informal.* a crime, esp. a robbery. **8. just the job.** exactly what is required. **9. on the job.** actively engaged in one's employment. ~*vb.* **jobbing, jobbed. 10.** to do piecework or casual jobs. [origin unknown] —ˈjobber *n.* —ˈjobbing *adj.* —ˈjobless *adj.*

Jobcentre (ˈdʒɒbˌsɛntə) *or* **job centre** *n. Brit.* a government office in which people can consult displayed advertisements of available jobs.

job lot *n.* a miscellaneous collection of articles sold together.

Job's comforter (dʒəʊbz) *n.* a person who, while pretending to be sympathetic, succeeds only in adding to someone's distress. [after *Job* in the Bible]

job sharing *n.* an arrangement by which a job is shared by two part-time workers.

Jock (dʒɒk) *n. Slang.* a Scot.

jockey (ˈdʒɒkɪ) *n.* **1.** a person who rides horses in races, esp. as a profession. ~*vb.* **2.** to ride (a horse) in a race. **3. jockey for position.** to try to obtain an advantage by skilful manoeuvring. [from the name *Jock*]

jockstrap (ˈdʒɒkˌstræp) *n.* an elasticated belt with a pouch to support the genitals worn by male athletes. Also called: **athletic support.** [slang *jock* penis]

jocose (dʒəˈkəʊs) *adj.* playful or humorous. [Latin *jocus* joke] —joˈcosely *adv.*

jocular (ˈdʒɒkjʊlə) *adj.* **1.** (of a person) often joking; good-humoured. **2.** (of a remark) meant lightly or humorously. [Latin *joculus* little joke] —jocularity (ˌdʒɒkjʊˈlærɪtɪ) *n.* —ˈjocularly *adv.*

jocund (ˈdʒɒkənd) *adj. Literary.* cheerful; merry. [Latin *jūcundus* pleasant]

jodhpurs (ˈdʒɒdpəz) *pl. n.* riding breeches loose-fitting around the thighs and tight fitting from the knees to the ankles. [*Jodhpur*, town in NW India]

jog (dʒɒg) *vb.* **jogging, jogged. 1.** to run at a gentle pace for physical exercise. **2.** (foll. by *along*) to continue in a plodding way: *she has no ambition, she just jogs along.* **3.** to nudge slightly. **4. jog someone's memory.** to remind someone of something. ~*n.* **5.** the act of jogging. **6.** a slight nudge. [prob. var. of *shog* to shake] —ˈjogger *n.* —ˈjogging *n.*

joggle (ˈdʒɒgᵊl) *vb.* **1.** to shake or move with a slightly jolting motion. ~*n.* **2.** the act of joggling. [frequentative of *jog*]

jog trot *n.* an easy bouncy gait, midway between a walk and a trot.

john (dʒɒn) *n. Slang, chiefly U.S. & Canad.* a toilet. [special use of the name]

John Bull *n.* **1.** England represented as a person. **2.** a typical Englishman.

johnny (ˈdʒɒnɪ) *n., pl.* **-nies.** *Brit. informal.* a man or boy; chap.

Johnny Canuck (kəˈnʌk) *n. Canad. informal.* **1.** Canada represented as a person. **2.** a typical Canadian.

joie de vivre (ʒwa: də ˈviːvrə) *n.* joy of living; enjoyment of life. [French]

join (dʒɔɪn) *vb.* **1.** to come or bring together. **2.** to become a member of (a club, organization, or society). **3.** to meet (someone) as a companion: *I'll join you later.* **4.** to become part of: *join the queue.* **5.** to unite (two people) in marriage. **6.** to connect (two points), for example with a straight line. ~*n.* **7.** a joint; seam. See also **join in, join up.** [Latin *jungere* to yoke]

joiner ('dʒɔɪnə) n. Chiefly Brit. a person skilled in making finished woodwork, such as windows and stairs.

joinery ('dʒɔɪnərɪ) n. 1. the skill or craft of a joiner. 2. work made by a joiner.

join in vb. to take part in (an activity).

joint (dʒɔɪnt) n. 1. a junction of two or more parts or objects. 2. Anat. the junction between two or more bones. 3. a piece of meat suitable for roasting. 4. Slang. a building or place, for example a bar or nightclub. 5. Slang. a cannabis cigarette. **6. out of joint. a.** (of a bone) knocked out of its normal position. **b.** Informal. out of order. ~adj. 7. shared by or belonging to two or more people: joint property. ~vb. **8.** to provide (something) with a joint or joints. **9.** to cut or divide (meat) into joints. —'**jointed** adj. —'**jointly** adv.

joint-stock company n. Brit. a business enterprise whose capital is owned jointly by shareholders.

jointure ('dʒɔɪntʃə) n. Law. property settled on a wife by her husband for her use after his death. [Latin junctūra a joining]

join up vb. 1. to become a member of a military organization; enlist. 2. to connect (two or more things).

joist (dʒɔɪst) n. a beam made of timber, steel, or reinforced concrete, used in the construction of floors or roofs. [Old French giste]

jojoba (həʊˈhəʊbə) n. a shrub with seeds that contain an oil which is used in cosmetics. [Mexican Spanish]

joke (dʒəʊk) n. 1. a humorous story. 2. something that is said or done for fun. 3. a ridiculous or humorous circumstance. 4. a person or thing inspiring ridicule or amusement. **5. no joke.** a situation that is difficult or serious: it's no joke trying to bring up a child on your own. ~vb. **6.** to tell jokes. **7.** to speak or act facetiously. **8. joking apart.** seriously: said after there has been joking in a discussion. [Latin jocus] —'**jokey** adj. —'**jokingly** adv.

joker ('dʒəʊkə) n. 1. a person who jokes a lot. 2. Slang. an incompetent person: that joker earns a lot more than me. 3. an extra playing card in a pack, which in many card games can replace any other card.

jollification (ˌdʒɒlɪfɪˈkeɪʃən) n. a merry festivity.

jollity ('dʒɒlɪtɪ) n. the condition of being jolly.

jolly ('dʒɒlɪ) adj. **-lier, -liest. 1.** full of good humour. **2.** having or provoking gaiety and merrymaking. ~adv. **3.** Brit. extremely: that's jolly kind of you. ~vb. **-lying, -lied. 4.** (foll. by along) Informal. to try to keep (someone) cheerful by flattery or coaxing. [Old French jolif] —'**jolliness** n.

Jolly Roger n. the traditional pirate flag, consisting of a white skull and crossbones on a black background.

jolt (dʒəʊlt) vb. **1.** to bump against (someone or something) with a jarring blow. **2.** to move in a jerking manner. **3.** to surprise or shock: it jolted me seeing them just then.

~n. **4.** a sudden jerking movement. **5.** an emotional shock. [origin unknown]

Jonah ('dʒəʊnə) n. a person believed to bring bad luck to those around him. [after Jonah in the Bible]

jonquil ('dʒɒŋkwɪl) n. a kind of narcissus with long sweet-smelling yellow or white flowers. [French jonquille]

josh (dʒɒʃ) Slang, chiefly U.S. & Canad. ~vb. **1.** to tease (someone). ~n. **2.** a teasing joke. [origin unknown]

joss (dʒɒs) n. a Chinese idol. [Portuguese deos god]

joss stick n. a stick of dried perfumed paste, giving off a sweet smell when burnt as incense.

jostle ('dʒɒs'l) vb. **1.** to bump or push (someone) roughly. **2.** to compete with someone: jostling for first place. ~n. **3.** the act of jostling. [Old French jouster to joust]

jot (dʒɒt) vb. jotting, jotted. **1.** (foll. by down) to write a brief note of: jot down this message. ~n. **2.** the least bit: I don't care a jot whether she comes or not. [Greek iōta]

jotter ('dʒɒtə) n. a small notebook.

jotting ('dʒɒtɪŋ) n. something jotted down.

joual (ʒwɑːl) n. nonstandard Canadian French dialect, as associated with ill-educated speakers. [French]

joule (dʒuːl) n. the derived SI unit of work or energy. Symbol: J [after J. P. Joule, physicist]

journal ('dʒɜːn'l) n. **1.** a newspaper or magazine. **2.** a book in which a record of a person's daily activities is recorded. [Latin diurnālis daily]

journalese (ˌdʒɜːn'lˈiːz) n. a superficial style of writing regarded as typical of newspapers and magazines.

journalism ('dʒɜːn'lˌɪzəm) n. **1.** the profession of collecting, writing, and publishing news through newspapers and magazines or by radio and television. **2.** newspapers and magazines collectively. —'**journalist** n. —ˌjourna'**listic** adj.

journey ('dʒɜːnɪ) n. **1.** the act of travelling from one place to another. **2. a.** the distance travelled in a journey. **b.** the time taken to make a journey. ~vb. **3.** to make a journey. [Old French journee a day, a day's travelling]

journeyman ('dʒɜːnɪmən) n., pl. **-men. 1.** a qualified craftsman who works at his trade in the employment of another. **2.** a competent workman. [journey in obs. sense: a day's work]

joust (dʒaʊst) History. ~n. **1.** a combat with lances between two mounted knights. ~vb. **2.** to take part in such a tournament. [Old French jouster]

Jove (dʒəʊv) n. **1.** Jupiter (the god). **2. by Jove.** Old-fashioned. an exclamation of surprise or excitement.

jovial ('dʒəʊvɪəl) adj. happy and cheerful. [Latin joviālis (of the planet) Jupiter] —joviality (ˌdʒəʊvɪˈælɪtɪ) n. —'**jovially** adv.

jowl[1] (dʒaʊl) n. **1.** the lower jaw. **2.** (pl.)

cheeks. **3. cheek by jowl.** See **cheek.** [Old English *ceafl* jaw] —**jowled** *adj.*

jowl² (dʒaʊl) *n.* fatty flesh hanging from the lower jaw. [Old English *ceole* throat]

joy (dʒɔɪ) *n.* **1.** a deep feeling of happiness and contentment. **2.** something causing such a feeling. **3.** *Brit. informal.* success; satisfaction: *I went for a loan, but got no joy.* [Latin *gaudium* joy]

joyful ('dʒɔɪfʊl) *adj.* **1.** full of joy; elated. **2.** expressing or producing joy: *a joyful look; a joyful occasion.* —**joyfully** *adv.*

joyless ('dʒɔɪlɪs) *adj.* having or producing no joy or pleasure.

joyous ('dʒɔɪəs) *adj.* **1.** having a happy nature or mood. **2.** joyful.

joy ride *n.* **1.** a ride taken for pleasure in a stolen car, usually driven recklessly. ~*vb.* **joy-ride, -riding, -rode, -ridden. 2.** to take such a ride. —**joyriding** *n.*

joystick ('dʒɔɪ,stɪk) *n.* the control lever of an aircraft or a computer.

JP Justice of the Peace.

Jr Junior.

jube (dʒuːb) *n. Austral. & N.Z. informal.* same as **jujube.**

jubilant ('dʒuːbɪlənt) *adj.* feeling or expressing great joy. [Latin *jūbilāre* to give a joyful cry]

jubilation (,dʒuːbɪ'leɪʃən) *n.* a feeling of great happiness.

jubilee ('dʒuːbɪ,liː) *n.* **1.** a special anniversary, esp. a 25th or 50th one. **2.** a time of rejoicing. [Old French *jubile,* ult. from Hebrew *yōbhēl* ram's horn, used for proclamation]

Judaic (dʒuː'deɪɪk) *adj.* of the Jews or Judaism.

Judaism ('dʒuːdeɪ,ɪzəm) *n.* **1.** the religion of the Jews, based on the Old Testament and the Talmud. **2.** the religious and cultural traditions of the Jews.

Judas ('dʒuːdəs) *n.* a person who betrays a friend; traitor. [after *Judas* Iscariot in the Bible]

judder ('dʒʌdə) *Informal, chiefly Brit.* ~*vb.* **1.** to shake or vibrate: *the car juddered to a halt.* ~*n.* **2.** a shaking or vibrating motion. [prob. blend of *jar* (jolt) + *shudder*]

judge (dʒʌdʒ) *n.* **1.** a public official with authority to hear cases and pass sentences in a court of law. **2.** a person appointed to determine the result of a competition. **3.** a person whose opinion on a particular subject is usually reliable: *a good judge of character.* ~*vb.* **4.** to hear and decide upon (a case at law). **5.** to pass judgment on (someone). **6.** to decide (something) after inquiry. **7.** to determine the result of (a competition). **8.** to appraise (something) critically. **9.** to believe (something to be the case): *he judged that it was safe to proceed.* [Latin *jūdex* a judge]

judgment or **judgement** ('dʒʌdʒmənt) *n.* **1.** the faculty of being able to make critical distinctions and achieve a balanced viewpoint. **2. a.** the verdict pronounced by a court of law. **b.** an obligation arising as a result of such a verdict. **3.** the formal decision of one or more judges of a competition. **4.** a particular decision formed in a case in dispute. **5.** criticism or censure. **6. against one's better judgment.** contrary to what one thinks is sensible. —**judgmental** or **judgemental** (dʒʌdʒ'mentˀl) *adj.*

Judgment ('dʒʌdʒmənt) *n.* same as **Last Judgment.**

Judgment Day *n.* the occasion of the Last Judgment by God at the end of the world.

judicature ('dʒuːdɪkətʃə) *n.* **1.** the administration of justice. **2.** the office, function, or power of a judge. **3.** a group of judges.

judicial (dʒuː'dɪʃəl) *adj.* **1.** of judges, courts, or the administration of justice. **2.** having qualities appropriate to a judge: *a judicial mind.* [Latin *jūdicium* judgment] —**ju'dicially** *adv.*

judiciary (dʒuː'dɪʃərɪ) *n.* the branch of the central authority in a state that administers justice.

judicious (dʒuː'dɪʃəs) *adj.* having or showing good judgment; sensible.

judo ('dʒuːdəʊ) *n.* a sport derived from jujitsu, in which the object is to force an opponent to submit using the minimum of physical effort. [Japanese *jū* gentleness + *dō* art]

jug (dʒʌg) *n.* **1.** a container for holding or pouring liquids, usually with a handle and a lip. **2.** the amount of liquid held by a jug. **3.** *Slang.* jail. ~*vb.* **jugging, jugged. 4.** to stew (hare) in an earthenware container. [origin unknown]

juggernaut ('dʒʌgə,nɔːt) *n.* **1.** *Brit.* a very large heavy lorry. **2.** any terrible force that demands complete self-sacrifice. [Hindi *Japannath* lord of the world]

juggle ('dʒʌgˀl) *vb.* **1.** to throw and catch (several objects) continuously so that most are in the air at the same time. **2.** to manipulate (facts or figures) to suit one's purpose. **3.** to keep (several activities) in progress at the same time. [Old French *jogler* to perform as a jester] —**'juggler** *n.*

jugular ('dʒʌgjʊlə) *n.* a large vein in the neck that carries blood to the heart from the head. Also called: **jugular vein.** [Latin *jugulum* throat]

juice (dʒuːs) *n.* **1.** any liquid that occurs naturally in or is secreted by plant or animal tissue: *orange juice.* **2.** *Informal.* **a.** petrol. **b.** electricity. [Old French *jus*]

juicy ('dʒuːsɪ) *adj.* **juicier, juiciest. 1.** full of juice. **2.** provocatively interesting; spicy: *juicy gossip.*

jujitsu (dʒuː'dʒɪtsuː) *n.* the traditional Japanese system of unarmed self-defence, perfected by the samurai. [Japanese *jū* gentleness + *jutsu* art]

juju ('dʒuː,dʒuː) *n.* **1.** a magic charm or fetish used in parts of west Africa by certain tribes. **2.** the power associated with a juju. [prob. from W African *djudju* evil spirit, fetish]

jujube ('dʒuː,dʒuːb) *n.* a chewy sweet made of flavoured gelatin. [Medieval Latin *jujuba*]

jukebox ('dʒuːk,bɒks) *n.* an automatic record player in which records may be selected by inserting coins and pressing appropriate buttons. [*juke* (from a Black American language) bawdy]

jukskei ('juk,skeɪ) *n. S. African.* a game in which a peg is thrown over a fixed distance at a stake driven into the ground. [Afrikaans]

Jul. July.

Julian calendar ('dʒuːljən) *n.* the calendar introduced by Julius Caesar in 46 B.C., in which leap years occurred every fourth year and in every centenary year.

julienne (,dʒuːli'ɛn) *adj.* **1.** (of vegetables or meat) cut into thin shreds. ∼*n.* **2.** a clear soup containing thinly shredded vegetables. [French]

July (dʒuː'laɪ) *n., pl.* **-lies.** the seventh month of the year. [after *Julius* Caesar]

jumble ('dʒʌmb'l) *vb.* **1.** to mingle (objects) in a state of disorder. **2.** to remember (something) in a confused form. ∼*n.* **3.** a disordered mass or state. **4.** *Brit.* articles donated for a jumble sale. [origin unknown]

jumble sale *n. Brit.* a sale, usually of second-hand articles, in aid of charity.

jumbo ('dʒʌmbəʊ) *n.* **1.** (*modifier*) *Informal.* very large: *a jumbo box of detergent.* **2.** (*pl.* **-bos**) short for **jumbo jet.** [after a famous elephant exhibited by P.T. Barnum]

jumbo jet *n. Informal.* a type of large jet-propelled airliner.

jump (dʒʌmp) *vb.* **1.** to leap or spring into the air by using the muscles in the legs and feet. **2.** to leap over (an obstacle): *to jump a gap.* **3.** to cause to leap over an obstacle: *to jump a horse over a hedge.* **4.** to proceed hastily: *she jumped into a taxi.* **5.** to jerk with astonishment or surprise: *she jumped when she heard the explosion.* **6.** (of prices) to rise suddenly or abruptly. **7.** to pass over (intervening matter): *she jumped a few lines and then continued reading.* **8.** to change (from one subject to another). **9.** (of a train) to come off (the rails). **10.** (of the stylus of a record player) to be jerked out of the groove. **11.** *Slang.* to be lively: *the party was jumping.* **12.** *Informal.* to attack without warning: *thieves jumped the old man.* **13.** *Informal.* (of a driver or a motor vehicle) to pass through (a red traffic light). **14. jump down someone's throat.** *Informal.* to speak sharply to someone. **15. jump to it.** *Informal.* to begin something quickly and efficiently. ∼*n.* **16.** the act or an instance of jumping. **17.** a space, distance, or obstacle to be jumped. **18.** *Sport.* any of several contests involving a jump: *the high jump.* **19.** a sudden rise: *the jump in prices last month.* **20.** a sudden change from one subject to another: *the professor made an unexpected jump in his lecture.* **21.** a sudden jerk, as a reaction of surprise. **22.** a step or degree: *one jump ahead.* **23.** *Films.* a break in continuity in the normal sequence of shots. **24. take a running jump.** *Brit. informal.* a contemptuous expression of dismissal. ∼See also **jump at,** **jump on.** [prob. imit.]

jump at *vb.* to be glad to accept: *I would jump at the chance of going.*

jumped-up *adj. Informal.* having suddenly risen in significance and appearing arrogant: *a jumped-up office boy.*

jumper¹ ('dʒʌmpə) *n.* **1.** *Chiefly Brit.* a knitted garment covering the upper part of the body. **2.** *U.S. & Canad.* a pinafore dress. [obs. *jump* man's loose jacket]

jumper² ('dʒʌmpə) *n.* **1.** a short piece of wire used to make an electrical connection, usually temporarily. **2.** a person or animal that jumps.

jump jet *n. Informal.* a fixed-wing jet aircraft that is capable of landing and taking off vertically.

jump leads (liːdz) *pl. n.* two heavy cables used to start a motor vehicle with a flat battery by connecting the flat battery to the battery of another vehicle.

jump on *vb. Informal.* to reprimand or attack (someone) suddenly and forcefully.

jump-start *vb.* **1.** to start the engine of (a motor vehicle) by pushing or rolling it and then engaging the gears or (of a motor vehicle) to start in this way. ∼*n.* **2.** the act of starting a motor vehicle in this way.

jump suit *n.* a one-piece garment of combined trousers and top.

jumpy ('dʒʌmpɪ) *adj.* **jumpier, jumpiest.** **1.** nervous or apprehensive. **2.** moving jerkily.

Jun. **1.** June. **2.** Junior.

junction ('dʒʌŋkʃən) *n.* **1.** a place where several routes, lines, or roads meet, link, or cross each other: *a railway junction.* **2.** a point on a motorway where traffic may leave or join it. **3.** *Electronics.* a point where wires are joined. [Latin *junctiō* joining]

juncture ('dʒʌŋktʃə) *n.* a point in time, esp. a critical one: *we don't want to risk an industrial dispute at this juncture.*

June (dʒuːn) *n.* the sixth month of the year. [prob. from Latin *Junius* of the goddess Juno]

jungle ('dʒʌŋg'l) *n.* **1.** a forest area in a hot country with luxuriant vegetation. **2.** any dense or tangled vegetation. **3.** a place of intense struggle for survival: *the concrete jungle.* [Hindi]

junior ('dʒuːnjə) *adj.* **1.** lower in rank or position: *a junior partner.* **2.** younger in years: *my sister is junior to me by ten years.* **3.** *Brit.* of schoolchildren between the ages of 7 and 11 approximately. **4.** *U.S.* of the third year of a four-year course at college or high school. ∼*n.* **5.** a person holding a low rank or position. **6.** a person younger than a particular person: *she married a man eight years her junior.* **7.** *Brit.* a junior schoolchild. **8.** *U.S.* a junior student. [Latin: younger]

Junior ('dʒuːnjə) *adj. Chiefly U.S.* being the younger: usually used after a name to distinguish between two people of the same name: *Douglas Fairbanks, Junior.*

juniper ('dʒuːnɪpə) *n.* a low-growing evergreen shrub or tree with purple berries which are used as a flavouring in making gin. [Latin *jūniperus*]

junk¹ (dʒʌŋk) *n.* **1.** discarded objects collectively. **2.** *Informal.* **a.** rubbish generally.

b. nonsense: *the play was absolute junk.* **3.** *Slang.* narcotic drugs, esp. heroin. [Middle English *jonke* old useless rope]

junk² (dʒʌŋk) *n.* a Chinese sailing boat with a flat bottom and square sails. [Portuguese *junco* from Javanese *jon*]

junket ('dʒʌŋkɪt) *n.* **1.** a sweet dessert made of flavoured milk set with rennet. **2.** a feast. **3.** an excursion made by a public official and paid for out of public funds. ~*vb.* **4.** to have a feast. **5.** (of a public official) to go on an excursion paid for out of public funds. [Middle English: rush basket, hence custard served on rushes]

junk food *n.* food with a low nutritional value.

junkie ('dʒʌŋkɪ) *n. Informal.* a drug addict.

junta ('dʒʌntə) *n.* (functioning as sing. or pl.) a group of military officers holding the power in a country after a revolution. [Spanish: council]

Jupiter ('dʒuːpɪtə) *n.* **1.** the king of the Roman gods. **2.** the largest planet.

Jurassic (dʒʊˈræsɪk) *adj. Geol.* of the geological period about 180 million years ago, during which dinosaurs flourished. [after the *Jura* (Mountains) in W central Europe]

juridical (dʒʊˈrɪdɪkˀl) *adj.* of law or the administration of justice; legal. [Latin *iūs* law + *dicere* to say]

jurisdiction (ˌdʒʊərɪsˈdɪkʃən) *n.* **1.** the right or power to administer justice and to apply laws. **2.** the exercise or extent of such right or power. **3.** authority in general. [Latin *jūrisdictiō*]

jurisprudence (ˌdʒʊərɪsˈpruːdˀns) *n.* the science or philosophy of law. [Latin *jūris prūdentia*]

jurist ('dʒʊərɪst) *n.* a person who is expert in the science of law. [French *juriste*]

juror ('dʒʊərə) *n.* a member of a jury. [Old French *jurer* to take an oath]

jury ('dʒʊərɪ) *n., pl.* **-ries.** **1.** a group of twelve people sworn to deliver a true verdict according to the evidence upon a case presented in a court of law. **2.** a group of people appointed to judge a competition. [Old French *jurer* to swear]

jury box *n.* an enclosure where the jury sits in a court of law.

jury-rigged *adj. Chiefly naut.* set up in a makeshift manner. [origin unknown]

just (dʒʌst) *adv.* **1.** used to indicate an action performed in the very recent past: *I have just closed the door.* **2.** at this very instant: *he's just coming in to land.* **3.** no more than; only: *just an ordinary car.* **4.** exactly: *that's just what I mean.* **5.** barely: *he just got there in time.* **6. just about.** a. at the point of starting (to do something). **b.** almost: *I've just about had enough.* **7. just a moment, second,** or **minute.** an

expression requesting someone to wait for a short time. **8. just now. a.** a short time ago: *he left on the bus just now.* **b.** at the present time: *we're very busy just now.* **9. just so. a.** an expression used to indicate agreement. **b.** arranged with precision: *when we arrived everything was just so.* ~*adj.* **10.** fair or impartial in action or judgment: *a just decision.* **11.** rightly given: *a just reward.* **12.** well-founded: *just criticism.* [Latin *jūs* justice] —'**justly** *adv.* —'**justness** *n.*

justice ('dʒʌstɪs) *n.* **1.** the quality of being just. **2.** the administration of law according to prescribed and accepted principles. **3.** conformity to the law. **4.** a judge. **5.** short for **justice of the peace.** **6.** good reason: *she complained bitterly, and with justice.* **7. bring to justice.** to capture, try, and punish (a criminal). **8. do justice to. a.** to show to full advantage: *the picture did not do justice to her beauty.* **b.** to show full appreciation of (something) by action: *he did justice to the meal.* **9. do oneself justice.** to make full use of one's abilities: *he didn't do himself justice in the exam.* [Latin *jūstitia*]

justice of the peace *n.* a magistrate who is authorized to act as a judge in a local court of law.

justiciary (dʒʌˈstɪʃərɪ) *n., pl.* **-aries.** an administrator of justice; judge.

justify ('dʒʌstɪˌfaɪ) *vb.* **-fying, -fied.** **1.** to prove (something) to be just or valid; show (something) to be reasonable: *his behaviour justifies our suspicion.* **2.** to show (someone) to be free from blame; absolve. **3.** to arrange (text) when typing or printing so that both margins are straight. [Latin *justificāre*] —'**justiˌfiable** *adj.* —'**justiˌfiably** *adv.* —**justification** (ˌdʒʌstɪfɪˈkeɪʃən) *n.*

jut (dʒʌt) *vb.* **jutting, jutted.** (foll. by *out*) to stick out beyond the surface or main part of something. [var. of JET¹]

jute (dʒuːt) *n.* a fibre obtained from the bark of an East Indian plant and used in making rope, sacks, and mats. [Bengali *jhuto*]

juvenile ('dʒuːvɪˌnaɪl) *adj.* **1.** young, youthful, or immature. **2.** suitable for young people: *juvenile pastimes.* ~*n.* **3.** a young person. **4.** an actor who performs youthful roles. [Latin *juvenīlis*]

juvenile delinquent *n.* a young person who is guilty of a crime. —**juvenile delinquency** *n.*

juxtapose (ˌdʒʌkstəˈpəʊz) *vb.* to place (things or ideas) close together or side by side. [Latin *juxta* next to + *position*] —ˌ**juxtapoˈsition** *n.*

K

k *or* **K** (keɪ) *n.*, *pl.* **k's**, **K's**, *or* **Ks**. the 11th letter of the English alphabet.

K **1.** kelvin(s). **2.** *Chess.* king. **3.** *Chem.* potassium. [New Latin *kalium*] **4.** one thousand. [from KILO-] **5.** *Computers.* originally or strictly, a unit of 1024 words, bits, or bytes.

Kaffir ('kæfə) *n.* **1.** *Offensive.* (in Africa) a Black African. **2.** an old name for the Xhosa language. [Arabic *kāfir* infidel]

kaftan *or* **caftan** ('kæftæn) *n.* a long coatlike garment worn by men in eastern countries and by women and men in western countries. [Turkish *qaftān*]

kahawai ('kɑːhəwaɪ, 'kɑːwaɪ) *n.* a New Zealand food and game fish. [Maori]

kai (kaɪ) *n. N.Z. informal.* food. [Maori]

kaiser ('kaɪzə) *n. History.* a German or Austro-Hungarian emperor. [German, from Latin *Caesar* emperor]

kaka ('kɑːkə) *n.* a green parrot of New Zealand with a long compressed bill. [Maori]

kakapo ('kɑːkə,pəʊ) *n.*, *pl.* **-pos.** a ground-living parrot of New Zealand that resembles an owl. [Maori]

kalashnikov (kə'læʃnɪ,kɒf) *n.* a Russian-made sub-machine-gun used by terrorists and guerrillas. [Russian]

kale (keɪl) *n.* a variety of cabbage with crinkled leaves. [Old English *cāl*]

kaleidoscope (kə'laɪdə,skəʊp) *n.* a tube-shaped toy that contains loose pieces of coloured paper or glass reflected by mirrors so that various symmetrical patterns form when the tube is twisted. [Greek *kalos* beautiful + *eidos* form + *skopein* to look at] —**kaleidoscopic** (kə,laɪdə-'skɒpɪk) *adj.*

kalends ('kælɪndz) *pl. n.* same as **calends.**

kaleyard ('keɪl,jɑːd) *n. Scot.* a vegetable garden. [lit.: cabbage garden]

Kamasutra (,kɑːmə'suːtrə) *n.* **the.** an ancient Hindu text on erotic pleasure. [Sanskrit *kāma* love + *sūtra* thread, rule]

kamikaze (,kæmɪ'kɑːzɪ) *n.* **1.** (in World War II) a Japanese pilot who performed suicidal missions. **2.** (*modifier*) (of an action) undertaken or (of a person) undertaking an action in the knowledge that it will result in the death or injury of the person performing it: *a kamikaze attack.* [Japanese *kami* divine + *kaze* wind]

Kamloops trout ('kæmluːps) *n.* a bright silvery rainbow trout common in British Columbia, Canada.

Kan. Kansas.

kangaroo (,kæŋgə'ruː) *n.*, *pl.* **-roos.** a large Australian animal with powerful hind legs used for leaping and, in the female, a pouch for carrying her babies in. [prob. Aboriginal]

kangaroo court *n.* an unofficial court, for example one set up by strikers to judge strikebreakers.

kaolin ('keɪəlɪn) *n.* a fine white clay used in making porcelain and as a poultice. [*Kaoling,* Chinese mountain where supplies for Europe were first obtained]

kapok ('keɪpɒk) *n.* a silky fibre obtained from a tropical tree and used for stuffing pillows and padding sleeping bags. [Malay]

kaput (kæ'pʊt) *adj. Informal.* **a.** ruined: *now all our plans are kaput.* **b.** broken: *this record player seems to be kaput.* [German *kaputt*]

karakul ('kærək°l) *n.* **1.** a sheep of central Asia the lambs of which have soft curled dark hair. **2.** the fur prepared from these lambs. [Russian]

karate (kə'rɑːtɪ) *n.* a Japanese system of unarmed combat, in which punches, chops, and kicks are made with the hands, feet, elbows, and legs. [Japanese: empty hand]

Karitane (,kærɪ'tɑːnɪ) *n. N.Z.* a nurse for babies; nanny. [from former child-care hospital at *Karitane,* New Zealand]

karma ('kɑːmə) *n. Hinduism, Buddhism.* the totality of a person's actions in one life seen as affecting or deciding his fate in the next. [Sanskrit: action, effect]

karoo *or* **karroo** (kə'ruː) *n.*, *pl.* **-roos.** a dry tableland of southern Africa, with semidesert vegetation. [Afrikaans]

kart (kɑːt) *n.* same as **go-kart.**

kasbah *or* **casbah** ('kæzbɑː) *n.* the citadel of a North African city. [Arabic *kasba* citadel]

katydid ('keɪtɪ,dɪd) *n.* a large green grasshopper of North America. [imit.]

kauri ('kaʊrɪ) *n.* a New Zealand coniferous tree cultivated for its wood and resin. [Maori]

kayak ('kaɪæk) *n.* **1.** a canoe-like boat used by Eskimos, consisting of a frame covered with animal skins. **2.** a fibreglass or canvas-covered canoe of similar design. [Eskimo]

kazoo (kə'zuː) *n.*, *pl.* **-zoos.** a simple musical instrument, consisting of a metal tube open at both ends with a membrane-covered hole in one side, which vibrates with a buzzing sound when the player hums into it. [prob. imit.]

KBE Knight Commander of the Order of the British Empire.

kbyte *Computers.* kilobyte.

kcal kilocalorie.

kea ('kɪə) *n.* a large parrot of New Zealand with a brownish-green plumage. [Maori]

kebab (kə'bæb) *n.* a dish consisting of small pieces of meat and vegetables, usually threaded onto skewers and grilled. [Arabic *kabāb* roast meat]

kedge (kedʒ) *Naut.* ~*vb.* **1.** to draw (a ship) along by hauling in on the cable of a light anchor, or (of a ship) to be drawn in this fashion. ~*n.* **2.** a light anchor used for kedging. [Middle English *caggen* to fasten]

kedgeree (ˌkɛdʒəˈriː) *n. Chiefly Brit.* a dish consisting of rice, fish, and eggs. [Hindi]

keek (kiːk) *n., vb. Scot.* same as **peep**[1]. [prob. from Middle Dutch *kīken* to look]

keel (kiːl) *n.* **1.** one of the main lengthways steel or timber pieces along the base of a ship, to which the frames are fastened. **2. on an even keel.** well balanced; steady. [Old Norse *kjǫlr*]

keelhaul (ˈkiːlˌhɔːl) *vb.* **1.** to rebuke (someone) harshly. **2.** to drag (someone) under the keel of a ship as a punishment.

keel over *vb.* **1.** (of an object) to turn upside down; capsize. **2.** *Informal.* (of a person) to collapse suddenly.

keelson *or* **kelson** (ˈkɛlsən) *n.* a lengthways beam fastened to the keel of a ship for strength. [prob. from Low German *kielswin*, keel swine]

keen[1] (kiːn) *adj.* **1.** eager or enthusiastic. **2.** (foll. by *on*) fond of; devoted to: *keen on golf.* **3.** intellectually acute: *a keen wit.* **4.** (of sight, smell, or hearing) capable of recognizing fine distinctions. **5.** (of a knife or blade) having a sharp cutting edge. **6.** extremely cold and penetrating: *a keen wind.* **7.** intense or strong: *a keen desire.* **8.** *Chiefly Brit.* extremely low so as to be competitive: *keen prices.* [Old English *cēne*] —ˈ**keenly** *adv.* —ˈ**keenness** *n.*

keen[2] (kiːn) *vb.* **1.** to lament the dead. ~*n.* **2.** a lament for the dead. [Irish Gaelic *caoine*]

keep (kiːp) *vb.* **keeping, kept.** **1.** to have or retain possession of (something). **2.** to have temporary charge of: *keep my watch for me.* **3.** to store in a customary place: *I keep my books in the desk.* **4.** to remain or cause (someone or something) to remain in a specified state or condition: *keep quiet.* **5.** to continue or cause (someone) to continue: *keep in step.* **6.** to look after or maintain for use, pleasure, or profit: *to keep chickens.* **7.** to support (someone) financially. **8.** to detain (someone). **9.** not to give away: *to keep a secret.* **10.** (of food) to stay in good condition for a certain time: *fish doesn't keep very well.* **11.** to observe (a religious festival) with rites or ceremonies. **12.** to maintain by writing regular records in: *to keep a diary.* **13.** to stay (in, on, or at a place or position): *keep to the path.* **14.** to associate with: *to keep bad company.* **15.** *Chiefly Brit.* to have habitually in stock: *this shop keeps all kinds of wool.* **16. how are you keeping?** are you well? ~*n.* **17.** the cost of food and other everyday expense: *to pay one's keep.* **18.** the main tower within the walls of a medieval castle or fortress. **19. for keeps.** *Informal.* permanently. ~See also **keep at, keep away,** etc. [Old English *cēpan* to observe]

keep at *vb.* **1.** to persist in (an activity). **2.** to compel (a person) to continue doing (a task).

keep away *vb.* (often foll. by *from*) to refrain or prevent (someone) from going (somewhere).

keep back *vb.* to refuse to reveal (something).

keep down *vb.* **1.** to hold (a group of people) under control. **2.** to cause (numbers or costs) not to increase. **3.** to lie low. **4.** to cause (food) to stay in the stomach; not vomit.

keeper (ˈkiːpə) *n.* **1.** a person in charge of animals in a zoo. **2.** a person in charge of a museum, collection, or section of a museum. **3.** a person in charge of other people, such as a warder in a jail. **4.** short for **goalkeeper** or **wicketkeeper**.

keep fit *n.* exercises designed to promote physical fitness if performed regularly.

keep from *vb.* **1.** to restrain (oneself or someone else) from (doing something). **2.** to preserve or protect (someone) from (something).

keeping (ˈkiːpɪŋ) *n.* **1. in keeping with.** suitable or appropriate to or for. **2. out of keeping with.** unsuitable or inappropriate to or for.

keep off *vb.* **1.** to stay or cause (someone) to stay at a distance (from). **2.** not to eat or drink or to prevent (someone) from eating or drinking (something). **3.** to avoid or cause (someone) to avoid (a topic).

keep on *vb.* **1.** to persist in (doing something): *keep on running.* **2.** to continue to employ: *the firm kept on only ten men.* **3.** (foll. by *about*) to persist in talking about. **4.** (foll. by *at*) to nag (a person).

keep out *vb.* **1.** to remain or cause (someone) to remain outside. **2.** (foll. by *of*) **a.** to cause (someone) to remain unexposed to (an unpleasant situation). **b.** to avoid: *keep out of trouble.*

keepsake (ˈkiːpˌseɪk) *n.* a gift kept in memory of the giver.

keep to *vb.* **1.** to adhere to: *to keep to a promise.* **2.** to be confined to: *she kept to her bed when she had flu.* **3. keep oneself to oneself.** to avoid the company of others. **4. keep to oneself. a.** to avoid the company of others. **b.** to refrain from disclosing (information).

keep up *vb.* **1.** to maintain (prices, standards, or one's morale) at the present level. **2.** to maintain in good condition. **3. keep up with. a.** to maintain a pace set by (someone). **b.** to remain informed about: *to keep up with developments.* **c.** to remain in contact with (someone). **d. keep up with the Joneses.** *Informal.* to compete with one's friends or neighbours in material possessions.

keg (kɛg) *n.* a small barrel in which beer is transported and stored. [Scandinavian]

kelp (kɛlp) *n.* a large brown seaweed rich in iodine and potash. [origin unknown]

kelpie (ˈkɛlpɪ) *n.* (in Scottish folklore) a water spirit in the form of a horse. [origin unknown]

kelson (ˈkɛlsən) *n.* same as **keelson.**

kelt (kɛlt) *n.* a salmon that has recently spawned. [origin unknown]

Kelt (kɛlt) *n.* same as **Celt.**

kelvin ('kɛlvɪn) *n. Physics.* the basic SI unit of thermodynamic temperature. [after William Thomson *Kelvin*, physicist]

Kelvin scale *n. Physics.* a thermodynamic temperature scale in which the zero is absolute zero.

ken (kɛn) *n.* **1. beyond one's ken.** beyond one's range of knowledge. ~*vb.* **kenning, kenned** or **kent. 2.** *Scot. & northern English dialect.* to know. [Old English *cennan*]

kendo ('kɛndəʊ) *n.* the Japanese art of fencing with pliable bamboo poles or, sometimes, real swords. [Japanese]

kennel ('kɛn²l) *n.* **1.** a hutlike shelter for a dog. **2.** (*pl.*) an establishment where dogs are bred, trained, or boarded. ~*vb.* **-nelling, -nelled** or *U.S.* **-neling, -neled. 3.** to keep (a dog) in a kennel. [Latin *canis* dog]

kepi ('keɪpiː) *n.* a military cap with a circular top and a horizontal peak. [French]

kept (kɛpt) *vb.* **1.** past of **keep. 2. kept woman** or **man.** a person financially supported by someone in return for sexual favours.

kerb or *U.S. & Canad.* **curb** (kɜːb) *n.* a line of stone or concrete forming an edge between a pavement and a roadway. [Old French *courbe* bent]

kerb crawling *n.* the act of driving slowly beside a kerb in order to entice someone into the car for sexual purposes. —**kerb crawler** *n.*

kerbstone or *U.S. & Canad.* **curbstone** ('kɜːb,stəʊn) *n.* one of a series of stones that form a kerb.

kerchief ('kɜːtʃɪf) *n.* a piece of cloth worn over the head or round the neck. [Old French]

kêrel ('kɛərəl) *n. S. African.* a young man. [Afrikaans]

kerfuffle (kə'fʌf²l) *n. Informal, chiefly Brit.* a commotion. [Scot. *curfuffle, carfuffle*]

kermes ('kɜːmɪz) *n.* the dried bodies of female scale insects, used as a red dyestuff. [Arabic *qirmiz*]

kernel ('kɜːn²l) *n.* **1.** the edible seed of a nut or fruit within the shell or stone. **2.** the grain of a cereal, such as wheat, consisting of the seed in a hard husk. **3.** the central or essential part of something: *the kernel of the plan.* [Old English *cyrnel*]

kerosene ('kɛrə,siːn) *n. Chiefly U.S. & Canad.* same as **paraffin** (sense 1). [Greek *kēros* wax]

kestrel ('kɛstrəl) *n.* a small falcon that feeds on small animals such as mice. [Old French *cresserele*]

ketch (kɛtʃ) *n.* a two-masted sailing ship. [Middle English *cache*]

ketchup ('kɛtʃəp) *n.* a thick cold sauce containing vinegar: *tomato ketchup.* [Chinese *kōetsiap* brine of pickled fish]

ketone ('kiːtəʊn) *n. Chem.* any of a class of compounds with the general formula R′COR″. [German *Keton,* from *Aketon* acetone]

kettle ('kɛt²l) *n.* **1.** a metal container with a handle and spout, for boiling water. **2. a different kettle of fish.** a different matter entirely. **3. a fine kettle of fish.** a difficult or awkward situation. [Old Norse *ketill*]

kettledrum ('kɛt²l,drʌm) *n.* a percussion instrument consisting of a hollow bowl shape covered with a skin or membrane and supported on a tripod.

key[1] (kiː) *n.* **1.** a specially shaped metal instrument, for moving the bolt of a lock so as to lock or unlock a door, suitcase, etc. **2.** an instrument that is turned to operate a valve, clock winding mechanism, etc. **3.** any of a set of levers pressed to operate a typewriter, computer, or musical keyboard instrument. **4.** a scale of musical notes that starts at one specific note. **5.** something that is crucial in providing an explanation or interpretation. **6.** (*modifier*) of great importance: *a key issue.* **7.** a means of achieving a desired end: *the key to happiness.* **8.** a list of explanations of symbols, codes, or abbreviations. **9.** pitch: *he spoke in a low key.* ~*vb.* **10.** (foll. by *to*) to harmonize with: *to key one's actions to the prevailing mood.* **11.** to adjust or fasten (something) with a key or some similar device. **12.** same as **keyboard.** ~See also **key in.** [Old English *cǣg*]

key[2] (kiː) *n.* same as **cay.**

keyboard ('kiː,bɔːd) *n.* **1.** a set of keys on a typewriter, computer, or musical keyboard instrument. ~*vb.* **2.** to set (text) in type using a keyboard machine. —**'key,boarder** *n.*

keyed up *adj.* very excited or nervous.

key grip *n.* the person in charge of moving and setting up camera tracks and scenery in a film or television studio.

keyhole ('kiː,həʊl) *n.* an opening in a lock through which a key may be passed to engage the lock mechanism.

key in *vb.* to enter (information or instructions) into a computer by means of a keyboard.

key money *n.* a sum of money required from a new tenant of a house or flat before he moves in.

Keynesian ('keɪnzɪən) *adj.* of the economic theories of J.M. Keynes, who argued that governments should fund public works to maintain full employment, accepting if necessary the consequence of inflation.

keynote ('kiː,nəʊt) *n.* **1. a.** a central or determining idea in a speech or literary work. **b.** (*as modifier*): *a keynote speech.* **2.** the note upon which a scale or key is based.

keypad ('kiː,pæd) *n.* a small panel with a set of buttons for operating a teletext system, electronic calculator, etc.

keyring ('kiː,rɪŋ) *n.* a metal ring, often decorative, for keeping keys on.

key signature *n. Music.* a group of sharps or flats at the beginning of each stave line to indicate the key.

keystone ('kiː,stəʊn) *n.* **1.** the central stone at the top of an arch. **2.** something that is necessary to connect other related things.

kg kilogram(s).

KG (in Britain) Knight of the Order of the Garter.

KGB the Soviet secret police. [Russian *Komitet gosudarstvennoi bezopasnosti* State Security Committee]

khaki ('kɑːkɪ) *adj.* **1.** dull yellowish-brown. ~*n.* **2.** a hard-wearing fabric of this colour, used for military uniforms. [Urdu, from Persian: dusty]

khan (kɑːn) *n.* a title of respect in Afghanistan and central Asia. [Turkish]

kHz kilohertz.

kia ora (ˌkiːə 'ɔːrə) *interj.* N.Z. good luck! [Maori]

kibbutz (kɪ'bʊts) *n., pl.* **kibbutzim** (ˌkɪbʊt'siːm). a farm, factory, or other workplace in Israel, owned and administered communally by its members. [Modern Hebrew *qibbūs* gathering]

kibosh ('kaɪˌbɒʃ) *n.* **put the kibosh on.** *Slang.* to put a stop to. [origin unknown]

kick (kɪk) *vb.* **1.** to drive, push, or hit with the foot or feet. **2.** to strike out with the feet, as in swimming. **3.** to raise a leg high, as in dancing. **4.** (of a firearm) to recoil when fired. **5.** *Soccer.* to score (a goal) by a kick. **6.** *Informal.* to object or resist: *she's for ever kicking against the system.* **7.** *Informal.* to be active and in good health: *alive and kicking.* **8.** *Informal.* to free oneself of (an addiction): *to kick the heroin habit.* **9. kick someone upstairs.** to promote someone to a higher but effectively powerless position. ~*n.* **10.** a thrust or blow with the foot. **11.** any of certain rhythmic leg movements used in swimming. **12.** the recoil of a firearm. **13.** *Informal.* an exciting effect: *we get a kick out of going to the races; she only does it for kicks.* **14.** *Informal.* power or force. **15. kick in the teeth.** *Slang.* a humiliating rebuff. ~*See also* **kick about, kick off,** etc. [Middle English *kiken*]

kick about *or* **around** *vb. Informal.* **1.** to treat (someone) harshly. **2.** to discuss (ideas) informally. **3.** to wander aimlessly. **4.** to lie neglected or forgotten: *there's a copy of that book kicking about somewhere.*

kickback ('kɪkˌbæk) *n.* **1.** a strong reaction. **2.** part of an income paid to a person in return for an opportunity to make a profit, often by some illegal arrangement.

kick off *vb.* **1.** to start play in a game of football by kicking the ball from the centre of the field. **2.** *Informal.* to commence (a discussion, event, etc.). ~*n.* **kickoff.** **3. a.** the kick that officially starts a game of football. **b.** the time when the first kick is due to take place. **4.** *Informal.* the time when an event is due to begin.

kick out *vb. Informal.* to dismiss (someone) or throw (someone) out forcefully.

kickstand ('kɪkˌstænd) *n.* a short metal bar on a motorcycle, which when kicked into a vertical position holds the cycle upright when stationary.

kick-start *n. also* **kick-starter. 1.** a pedal on a motorcycle that is kicked downwards

to start the engine. ~*vb.* **2.** to start (a motorcycle) in this way.

kick up *vb. Informal.* to cause (trouble).

kid¹ (kɪd) *n.* **1.** a young goat. **2.** soft smooth leather made from the hide of a kid. **3.** *Informal.* **a.** a young person; child. **b.** (*modifier*) younger: *my kid brother.* ~*vb.* **kidding, kidded. 4.** (of a goat) to give birth to (young). [Old Norse]

kid² (kɪd) *vb.* **kidding, kidded.** *Informal.* **1.** to tease or deceive (someone) for fun. **2.** to fool (oneself) into believing something: *don't kid yourself that no-one else knows.* [prob. from KID¹] —**'kidder** *n.*

kiddie ('kɪdɪ) *n. Informal.* a child.

kid gloves *pl. n.* **handle someone with kid gloves.** to treat someone with great tact.

kidnap ('kɪdnæp) *vb.* **-napping, -napped** *or U.S.* **-naping, -naped.** to capture and hold (a person), usually for ransom. [KID¹ + obs. *nap* to steal] —**'kidnapper** *or U.S.* **-naper** *n.*

kidney ('kɪdnɪ) *n.* **1.** either of two bean-shaped organs at the back of the abdominal cavity. They filter waste products from the blood, which are excreted as urine. **2.** the kidneys of certain animals used as food. [origin unknown]

kidney bean *n.* a reddish-brown kidney-shaped bean, eaten as a vegetable.

kidney machine *n.* a machine carrying out the functions of damaged human kidneys.

kidology (kɪ'dɒlədʒɪ) *n. Brit. informal.* the practice of bluffing or deception in order to gain a psychological advantage over someone.

kill (kɪl) *vb.* **1.** to cause the death of (a person or animal). **2.** to put an end to: *to kill someone's interest.* **3.** to make (time) pass quickly while waiting for something. **4.** *Informal.* to cause (someone) pain or discomfort: *my shoes are killing me.* **5.** *Informal.* to quash or veto: *the bill was killed in the House of Lords.* **6.** *Informal.* to overcome (someone) with attraction, laughter, or surprise: *she was dressed to kill.* **7. kill oneself.** *Informal.* to overexert oneself. **8. kill two birds with one stone.** to achieve two results with one action. ~*n.* **9.** the act of causing death at the end of a hunt or bullfight. **10.** the animal or animals killed during a hunt. **11. in at the kill.** present when something comes to a dramatic end with unpleasant results for someone else. [Middle English *cullen*] —**'killer** *n.*

killer whale *n.* a ferocious black-and-white toothed whale, most common in cold seas.

killing ('kɪlɪŋ) *Informal.* ~*adj.* **1.** very tiring: *a killing pace.* **2.** extremely funny. **3.** causing death; fatal. ~*n.* **4.** the act of causing death; slaying. **5. make a killing.** to make a sudden financial gain.

killjoy ('kɪlˌdʒɔɪ) *n.* a person who spoils other people's pleasure.

kiln (kɪln) *n.* a large oven for burning, drying, or processing something, such as porcelain or bricks. [Latin *culina* kitchen]

kilo ('kiːləʊ) *n.*, *pl.* **kilos.** short for **kilogram** or **kilometre.**

kilo- *prefix.* **1.** denoting 10^3 (1000): *kilometre.* **2.** (in computers) denoting 2^{10} (1024): *kilobyte.* In computer usage, *kilo-* is restricted to sizes of storage (e.g. *kilobit*) when it means 1024; in other computer contexts it retains its usual meaning of 1000. [Greek *khilioi* thousand]

kilobyte ('kɪləˌbaɪt) *n. Computers.* 1024 bytes.

kilocalorie ('kɪləˌkælərɪ) *n.* same as **Calorie.**

kilocycle ('kɪləˌsaɪkʰl) *n.* an old word for **kilohertz.**

kilogram or **kilogramme** ('kɪləˌgræm) *n.* **1.** one thousand grams. **2.** the basic SI unit of mass.

kilohertz ('kɪləˌhɜːts) *n.* one thousand hertz; one thousand cycles per second.

kilojoule ('kɪləˌdʒuːl) *n.* one thousand joules.

kilolitre or *U.S.* **kiloliter** ('kɪləˌliːtə) *n.* one thousand litres.

kilometre or *U.S.* **kilometer** ('kɪləˌmiːtə, kɪ'lɒmɪtə) *n.* one thousand metres.

kiloton ('kɪləˌtʌn) *n.* **1.** one thousand tons. **2.** an explosive power equal to the power of 1000 tons of TNT.

kilovolt ('kɪləˌvəʊlt) *n.* one thousand volts.

kilowatt ('kɪləˌwɒt) *n.* one thousand watts.

kilowatt-hour *n.* a unit of energy equal to the work done by a power of 1000 watts in one hour.

kilt (kɪlt) *n.* **1.** a knee-length pleated tartan skirt, worn by men in Highland dress and by women and girls. ~*vb.* **2.** to put pleats in (cloth). [Scandinavian] —**'kilted** *adj.*

kimono (kɪ'məʊnəʊ) *n.*, *pl.* **-nos.** a loose sashed ankle-length garment with wide sleeves, worn in Japan. [Japanese: clothing]

kin (kɪn) *n.* **1.** a person's relatives collectively. **2.** See **next of kin.** [Old English *cyn*]

kind[1] (kaɪnd) *adj.* **1.** considerate, friendly, and helpful: *a kind neighbour; a kind thought.* **2.** cordial; courteous: *kind regards.* [Old English *gecynde* natural, native]

kind[2] (kaɪnd) *n.* **1.** a class or group having characteristics in common: *two of a kind.* **2.** essential nature or character: *the difference is one of kind rather than degree.* **3. in kind. a.** (of payment) in goods or services rather than in money. **b.** with something of the same sort: *to return an insult in kind.* **4. kind of.** to a certain extent; loosely: *kind of hard; a kind of socialist.* **5. of a kind.** of poorer quality or standard than is wanted or expected. [Old English *gecynd* nature]

kindergarten ('kɪndəˌgɑːtʰn) *n.* a school for young children, usually between the ages of 4 and 6. [from German, lit.: children's garden]

kind-hearted *adj.* kindly; readily sympathetic.

kindle ('kɪndʰl) *vb.* **1.** to set (a fire) alight or (of a fire) to start to burn. **2.** to arouse or be aroused: *the project kindled his interest.* [Old Norse *kynda*]

kindling ('kɪndlɪŋ) *n.* material for starting a fire, such as dry wood or straw.

kindly ('kaɪndlɪ) *adj.* **-lier, -liest. 1.** having a warm-hearted nature. **2.** pleasant: *a kindly climate.* ~*adv.* **3.** in a considerate or humane way. **4.** please: *will you kindly behave yourself!* **5. not take kindly to.** to react unfavourably towards. —**'kindliness** *n.*

kindness ('kaɪndnɪs) *n.* **1.** the quality of being kind. **2.** a kind or helpful act.

kindred ('kɪndrɪd) *adj.* **1.** having similar qualities. **2.** related by blood or marriage. **3. kindred spirit.** a person with whom one has something in common. ~*n.* **4.** relationship by blood or marriage. **5.** similarity in character. **6.** a person's relatives collectively. [Middle English *kinred*]

kine (kaɪn) *pl. n. Archaic.* cows or cattle. [Old English *cȳna* of cows]

kinematics (ˌkɪnɪ'mætɪks) *n.* (*functioning as sing.*) *Physics.* the study of the motion of bodies without reference to mass or force. [Greek *kinēma* movement] —**ˌkine'matic** *adj.*

kinetic (kɪ'nɛtɪk) *adj.* relating to or caused by motion. [Greek *kinein* to move] —**ki'netically** *adv.*

kinetic art *n.* art, such as sculpture, that moves or has moving parts.

kinetic energy *n. Physics.* the energy of motion of a body equal to the work it would do if it were brought to rest.

kinetics (kɪ'nɛtɪks) *n.* (*functioning as sing.*) *Physics.* the branch of mechanics concerned with the study of bodies in motion.

king (kɪŋ) *n.* **1.** a male ruler of a monarchy. **2.** a ruler or chief: *king of the fairies.* **3.** a person, animal, or thing considered as the best or most important of its kind: *king of the jungle.* **4.** a playing card with a picture of a king on it. **5.** the most important chess piece. **6.** *Draughts.* a piece which has moved entirely across the board and been crowned and which may therefore move backwards as well as forwards. [Old English *cyning*] —**'kingship** *n.*

King Charles spaniel (tʃɑːlz) *n.* a small spaniel with a black-and-tan coat. [after *Charles* II of England, who popularized the breed]

kingcup ('kɪŋˌkʌp) *n. Brit.* a yellow-flowered plant; marsh marigold.

kingdom ('kɪŋdəm) *n.* **1.** a territory or state ruled by a king or queen. **2.** any of the three groups into which natural objects may be divided: *the animal, plant, and mineral kingdoms.* **3.** an area of activity: *the kingdom of the mind.*

kingfisher ('kɪŋˌfɪʃə) *n.* a fish-eating bird with a greenish-blue and orange plumage. [orig. *king's fisher*]

kingklip ('kɪŋˌklɪp) *n.* an edible eel-like marine fish of S. Africa. [Afrikaans]

king-of-arms *n.*, *pl.* **kings-of-arms.** a person holding the highest rank of heraldic office.

kingpin (ˈkɪŋˌpɪn) n. **1.** the most important person in an organization. **2.** a pivot pin that provides a steering joint in a motor vehicle.

king-size or **king-sized** adj. larger than a standard size.

kink (kɪŋk) n. **1.** a twist or bend in something such as a rope or hair. **2.** a flaw or quirk in someone's personality. [Dutch]

kinky (ˈkɪŋkɪ) adj. **kinkier, kinkiest. 1.** Slang. given to unusual or deviant sexual practices. **2.** tightly looped or curled.

kinsfolk (ˈkɪnzˌfəʊk) pl. n. one's family or relatives.

kinship (ˈkɪnʃɪp) n. **1.** blood relationship. **2.** the state of having common characteristics.

kinsman (ˈkɪnzmən) n., pl. **-men.** a relation by blood or marriage. **—ˈkinsˌwoman** fem. n.

kiosk (ˈkiːɒsk) n. **1.** a small booth from which cigarettes, newspapers, and sweets are sold. **2.** Chiefly Brit. a telephone box. [French kiosque bandstand, from Persian kūshk pavilion]

kip (kɪp) Brit. slang. ~n. **1.** sleep: to get some kip. **2.** a bed. ~vb. **kipping, kipped. 3.** to sleep or take a nap. **4.** kip down. to sleep in a makeshift bed. [origin unknown]

kipper (ˈkɪpə) n. **1.** a herring that has been cleaned, salted, and smoked. ~vb. **2.** to cure (a herring) by salting and smoking it. [Old English cypera]

kirk (kɜːk) n. Scot. a church. [Old Norse kirkja]

Kirsch (kɪəʃ) or **Kirschwasser** (ˈkɪəʃˌvɑːsə) n. a brandy distilled from black cherries. [German Kirschwasser cherry water]

kismet (ˈkɪzmɛt, ˈkɪs-) n. fate or destiny. [Persian qismat]

kiss (kɪs) vb. **1.** to touch with the lips as an expression of love, greeting or respect. **2.** to join lips with another person as an act of love or desire. **3.** to touch lightly: the sunlight kissed her cheek. ~n. **4.** a caress with the lips. **5.** a light touch. [Old English cyssan] **—ˈkissable** adj.

kissagram (ˈkɪsəˌɡræm) n. a greetings service in which a person is employed to present greetings by kissing the person celebrating.

kiss curl n. Brit. a circular curl of hair pressed flat against the cheek or forehead.

kisser (ˈkɪsə) n. Slang. the mouth or face.

kiss of life n. **the.** mouth-to-mouth resuscitation in which a person blows gently into the mouth of an unconscious person.

kit[1] (kɪt) n. **1.** a set of tools or supplies for use together or for a purpose: a first-aid kit. **2.** the container for such a set. **3.** a set of parts ready to be assembled: a model aeroplane kit. **4.** clothing and other personal effects, such as those of a soldier: a safari kit. ~See also **kit out.** [Middle Dutch kitte tankard]

kit[2] (kɪt) n. N.Z. a shopping bag made of string. [Maori]

kitbag (ˈkɪtˌbæɡ) n. a canvas or other bag for a serviceman's kit.

kitchen (ˈkɪtʃɪn) n. a room equipped for preparing and cooking food. [Late Latin coquīna]

kitchenette (ˌkɪtʃɪˈnɛt) n. a small kitchen or part of a room equipped for use as a kitchen.

kitchen garden n. a garden where vegetables and sometimes also fruit are grown.

kitchen tea n. Austral. & N.Z. a party held before a wedding to which guests bring kitchen equipment as presents.

kite (kaɪt) n. **1.** a light frame covered with a thin material flown in the wind at the end of a length of string. **2.** a bird of prey with a long forked tail and large wings. [Old English cȳta]

Kite mark n. Brit. the official mark in the form of a kite on articles approved by the British Standards Institution.

kith (kɪθ) n. **kith and kin.** one's friends and relations. [Old English cȳthth]

kit out or **up** vb. **kitting, kitted.** Chiefly Brit. to provide (someone or something) with clothes, furniture, or equipment.

kitsch (kɪtʃ) n. tawdry, vulgarized, or pretentious art or literature, usually with popular appeal. [from German] **—ˈkitschy** adj.

kitten (ˈkɪtᵊn) n. **1.** a young cat. **2. have kittens.** Brit. informal. to react with disapproval or anxiety: she had kittens when she got the bill. [Old French caton]

kittenish (ˈkɪtᵊnɪʃ) adj. lively and coyly flirtatious.

kittiwake (ˈkɪtɪˌweɪk) n. an oceanic gull with pale grey black-tipped wings and a square-cut tail. [imit.]

kitty[1] (ˈkɪtɪ) n., pl. **-ties.** a diminutive or affectionate name for a **kitten** or **cat.**

kitty[2] (ˈkɪtɪ) n., pl. **-ties. 1.** the pool in certain gambling games. **2.** any shared fund of money. [prob. from KIT[1]]

kiwi (ˈkiːwiː) n., pl. **kiwis. 1.** a nocturnal flightless bird of New Zealand having a long beak, stout legs, and no tail. **2.** Informal except in N.Z. a New Zealander. **3.** N.Z. informal. a lottery. [Maori]

kiwi fruit n. an edible fruit with a fuzzy brown skin and green flesh.

kJ kilojoule.

klaxon (ˈklæksᵊn) n. a type of loud horn used on fire engines and ambulances as a warning signal. [former trademark]

kleptomania (ˌklɛptəʊˈmeɪnɪə) n. Psychol. a strong impulse to steal. [Greek kleptein to steal + mania madness] **—ˌkleptoˈmaniˌac** n.

klipspringer (ˈklɪpˌsprɪŋə) n. a small agile antelope inhabiting rocky regions of Africa south of the Sahara. [Afrikaans]

km kilometre.

knack (næk) n. **1.** a skilful way of doing something. **2.** an innate talent or aptitude. [prob. from Middle English knak sharp knock]

knacker (ˈnækə) Brit. ~n. **1.** a person who buys up old horses for slaughter.

~*vb.* **2.** *Slang.* to tire: *she was knackered after the climb.* [origin unknown]

knapsack ('næp₁sæk) *n.* a canvas or leather bag carried strapped on the back or shoulder. [Low German *knappen* to eat + *sack* bag]

knapweed ('næp₁wiːd) *n.* any of several plants with purplish thistle-like flowers. [Middle English *knopwed*]

knave (neɪv) *n.* **1.** *Archaic.* a dishonest man. **2.** *Cards.* the jack. [Old English *cnafa*] —'**knavish** *adj.*

knavery ('neɪvərɪ) *n., pl.* **-eries.** dishonest conduct; trickery.

knead (niːd) *vb.* **1.** to work and press (a soft substance, such as dough) into a smooth mixture with the hands. **2.** to squeeze or press with the hands. [Old English *cnedan*] —'**kneader** *n.*

knee (niː) *n.* **1.** the joint of the leg between the thigh and the lower leg. **2.** the area around this joint. **3.** the upper surface of a sitting person's thigh: *the child sat on her mother's knee.* **4.** the part of a garment that covers the knee. **5.** **bring someone to his knees.** to force someone into submission. ~*vb.* **kneeing, kneed.** **6.** to strike, nudge, or push with the knee. [Old English *cnēow*]

kneecap ('niː₁kæp) *n.* **1.** *Anat.* a small flat triangular bone in front of and protecting the knee. ~*vb.* **-capping, -capped.** **2.** (of terrorists) to shoot (a person) in the kneecap.

knee-deep *adj.* **1.** so deep as to reach or cover the knees. **2. a.** sunk to the knees: *knee-deep in sand.* **b.** deeply involved: *knee-deep in work.*

knee-high *adj.* as high as the knee.

knee-jerk *n.* **1.** *Physiol.* a sudden involuntary kick of the lower leg caused by a sharp tap on the tendon just below the kneecap. ~*modifier.* **kneejerk.** **2.** made or occurring as a predictable and automatic response: *a kneejerk reaction.*

kneel (niːl) *vb.* **kneeling, knelt** or **kneeled.** **1.** to rest, fall, or support oneself on one's knees. ~*n.* **2.** the act or position of kneeling. [Old English *cnēowlian*] —'**kneeler** *n.*

knell (nɛl) *n.* **1.** the sound of a bell rung to announce a death or a funeral. **2.** something that indicates death or destruction. ~*vb.* **3.** to ring a knell. **4.** to proclaim by a tolling bell. [Old English *cnyll*]

knelt (nɛlt) *vb.* past of **kneel.**

knew (njuː) *vb.* the past tense of **know.**

knickerbockers ('nɪkə₁bɒkəz) *pl. n.* baggy breeches fastened with a band at the knee or above the ankle. [after Diedrich *Knickerbocker,* fictitious author of Washington Irving's *History of New York*]

knickers ('nɪkəz) *pl. n.* a woman's or girl's undergarment covering the lower trunk and having separate legs or leg-holes. [contraction of *knickerbockers*]

knick-knack ('nɪk₁næk) *n.* a small ornament or trinket. [reduplication of obs. *knack* a toy]

knife (naɪf) *n., pl.* **knives** (naɪvz). **1.** a cutting instrument or weapon consisting of a sharp-edged blade of metal fitted into a handle. ~*vb.* **2.** to stab or kill with a knife. [Old English *cnīf*] —'**knife₁like** *adj.*

knife edge *n.* **1.** the sharp cutting edge of a knife. **2.** a critical point in the development of a situation.

knight (naɪt) *n.* **1.** a man who has been given a knighthood in recognition of his achievements. **2.** (in medieval Europe) a person who served his lord as a mounted and heavily armed soldier. **3.** a chess piece, usually shaped like a horse's head. **4.** a champion of a lady or of a cause or principle. ~*vb.* **5.** to make (a man) a knight. [Old English *cniht* servant]

knight errant *n., pl.* **knights errant.** (esp. in medieval romance) a knight who wanders in search of deeds of courage, chivalry, etc. —**knight errantry** *n.*

knighthood ('naɪthʊd) *n.* an honorary title given to a man by the British sovereign in recognition of his achievements.

knightly ('naɪtlɪ) *adj.* of, resembling, or befitting a knight. —'**knightliness** *n.*

knit (nɪt) *vb.* **knitting, knitted** or **knit.** **1.** to make (a garment) by looping (wool) using long eyeless needles or a knitting machine. **2.** to join together closely. **3.** to draw (the brows) together or (of the brows) to come together, as in frowning or concentrating. ~*n.* **4.** a fabric made by knitting. [Old English *cnyttan* to tie in] —'**knitter** *n.*

knitting ('nɪtɪŋ) *n.* knitted work or the process of producing it.

knitwear ('nɪt₁wɛə) *n.* sweaters or other knitted clothes.

knives (naɪvz) *n.* the plural of **knife.**

knob (nɒb) *n.* **1.** a rounded projection from a surface, such as a rotating switch on a radio. **2.** a rounded handle of a door or drawer. **3.** a small amount of butter or lard. [Middle Low German *knobbe* knot in wood] —'**knobbly** *adj.* —'**knob₁like** *adj.*

knock (nɒk) *vb.* **1.** to give a blow or push to. **2.** to rap sharply with the knuckles: *to knock at the door.* **3.** to make by striking: *to knock a hole in the wall.* **4.** to collide (with). **5.** to bring into a certain condition by hitting: *to knock someone unconscious.* **6.** *Informal.* to criticize adversely. **7.** to emit a regular banging sound as a result of a fault: *the engine was knocking badly.* **8. knock on the head.** to prevent the further development of (a plan). ~*n.* **9. a.** a blow, push, or rap: *he gave the table a knock.* **b.** the sound so caused. **10.** the sound of knocking in an engine or bearing. **11.** *Informal.* a misfortune, rebuff, or setback. **12.** *Informal.* criticism. ~See also **knock about, knock back,** etc. [Old English *cnocian*]

knock about or **around** *vb.* **1.** to wander or travel about: *he's knocked about the world.* **2.** (foll. by *with*) to associate. **3.** to treat brutally: *he knocks his wife about.* **4.** to consider or discuss informally. ~*adj.* **knockabout. 5.** boisterous: *knockabout farce.*

knock back *vb. Informal.* **1.** to drink

quickly. **2.** to cost: *how much did the meal knock you back?* **3.** to reject or refuse: *you can't knock back such an offer.* ~*n.* **knockback. 4.** *Slang.* a refusal or rejection.

knock down *vb.* **1.** to strike to the ground with a blow, as in boxing. **2.** (in auctions) to declare an article sold. **3.** to demolish. **4.** *Informal.* to reduce (a price). ~*adj.* **knockdown. 5.** powerful: *a knockdown argument.* **6.** *Chiefly Brit.* cheap: *a knockdown price.* **7.** easily dismantled: *knockdown furniture.*

knocker (ˈnɒkə) *n.* **1.** a metal object attached to a door by a hinge and used for knocking. **2.** (*usually pl.*) *Slang.* a female breast.

knock-knees *pl. n.* legs that are bent inwards at the knees. —,**knock-ˈkneed** *adj.*

knock off *vb.* **1.** *Informal.* to finish work: *we knocked off an hour early.* **2.** *Informal.* to make or do hastily or easily: *to knock off a novel in a week.* **3.** *Informal.* to take (an amount) off the price of (an article): *I'll knock off 10% if you pay cash.* **4.** *Slang.* to kill. **5.** *Slang.* to stop doing something, used as a command: *knock it off!*

knock-on *Rugby.* ~*n.* **1.** the infringement of playing the ball forward with the hand or arm. ~*vb.* **knock on. 2.** to play (the ball) forward with the hand or arm.

knock-on effect *n.* the indirect result of an action or decision.

knockout (ˈnɒkˌaʊt) *n.* **1.** the act of rendering someone unconscious. **2.** *Boxing.* a blow that renders an opponent unable to continue after the referee has counted to ten. **3.** a competition in which competitors are eliminated progressively. **4.** *Informal.* a person or thing that is very impressive or attractive: *she's a knockout.* ~*vb.* **knock out. 5.** to render (someone) unconscious. **6.** *Boxing.* to defeat (an opponent) by a knockout. **7.** to destroy: *the radars were completely knocked out.* **8.** to eliminate from a knockout competition. **9.** *Informal.* to amaze: *I was knocked out by that new song.*

knock up *vb.* **1.** Also: **knock together.** *Informal.* to assemble quickly: *to knock up a set of shelves.* **2.** *Brit. informal.* to waken: *to knock someone up early.* **3.** *Slang.* to make pregnant. **4.** to practise before a game of tennis, squash, or badminton. ~*n.* **knock-up. 5.** a practice session at tennis, squash, or badminton.

knoll (nəʊl) *n.* a small rounded hill. [Old English *cnoll*]

knot (nɒt) *n.* **1.** a fastening formed by looping and tying pieces of rope, cord, or string. **2.** a tangle, as in hair. **3.** a decorative bow, as of ribbon. **4.** a small cluster or huddled group. **5.** a bond: *the marriage knot.* **6. a.** a hard mass of wood where a branch joins the trunk of a tree. **b.** a cross section of this visible in timber. **7.** a sensation of constriction, caused by tension or nervousness: *his stomach was tying itself in knots.* **8.** a unit of speed used by ships and aircraft, equal to one nautical

mile per hour. **9. at a rate of knots.** very fast. **10. tie someone in knots.** to completely perplex someone. ~*vb.* **knotting, knotted. 11.** to tie or fasten in a knot. **12.** to form into a knot. **13.** to entangle or become entangled. [Old English *cnotta*] —ˈ**knotted** *adj.* —ˈ**knotless** *adj.*

knothole (ˈnɒtˌhəʊl) *n.* a hole in a piece of wood where a knot has been.

knotty (ˈnɒtɪ) *adj.* **-tier, -tiest. 1.** full of knots. **2.** extremely difficult or intricate: *a knotty problem.*

know (nəʊ) *vb.* **knowing, knew, known. 1.** to be or feel certain of the truth or accuracy of (a fact, answer, or piece of information). **2.** to be acquainted with: *she's known him five years.* **3.** to have a grasp of: *he knows French.* **4.** to understand or be aware of (something, or how to do or be something): *I know how to repair that.* **5.** to experience: *to know poverty.* **6.** to be intelligent, informed, or sensible enough (to do something): *she knew not to go home yet.* **7.** to be able to distinguish: *to know right from wrong.* **8. know what's what.** to know how one thing or things in general work. **9. you never know.** things are uncertain. ~*n.* **10. in the know.** *Informal.* aware or informed. [Old English *gecnāwan*] —ˈ**knowable** *adj.*

know-all *n.* *Informal, disparaging.* a person who pretends or appears to know a lot more than other people.

know-how *n.* *Informal.* ingenuity, aptitude, or skill.

knowing (ˈnəʊɪŋ) *adj.* **1.** suggesting secret knowledge: *she gave him a knowing glance.* **2.** wise, shrewd, or clever. **3.** deliberate. —ˈ**knowingly** *adv.* —ˈ**knowingness** *n.*

knowledge (ˈnɒlɪdʒ) *n.* **1.** the facts or experiences known by a person or group of people. **2.** the state of knowing. **3.** specific information about a subject. **4. to my knowledge.** as I understand it.

knowledgeable *or* **knowledgable** (ˈnɒlɪdʒəbˀl) *adj.* possessing or showing much knowledge; well-informed. —ˈ**knowledgeably** *or* ˈ**knowledgably** *adv.*

known (nəʊn) *vb.* **1.** the past participle of **know.** ~*adj.* **2.** identified: *a known criminal.*

knuckle (ˈnʌkˀl) *n.* **1.** a joint of a finger. **2.** the knee joint of a calf or pig. **3. near the knuckle.** *Informal.* approaching indecency. ~See also **knuckle down, knuckle under.** [Middle English]

knuckle down *vb.* *Informal.* to apply oneself diligently: *to knuckle down to some work.*

knuckle-duster *n.* (*often pl.*) a metal bar or set of linked rings fitted over the knuckles for inflicting injury by a blow with the fist.

knuckle under *vb.* to give way under pressure or authority; yield.

knurl (nɜːl) *n.* a small ridge, often one of a series. [prob. from *knur* a knot in wood]

KO *or* **k.o.** (ˈkeɪˈəʊ) *vb.* **KO'ing, KO'd; k.o.'ing, k.o.'d. 1.** to knock out. ~*n.,* *pl.* **KO's** *or* **k.o.'s.** a knockout.

koala *or* **koala bear** (kəʊˈɑːlə) *n.* a slow-moving Australian tree-dwelling marsupial with dense greyish fur. [Aboriginal]

kohl (kəʊl) *n.* a cosmetic powder used to darken the area around the eyes. *[Arabic]

kohlrabi (kəʊlˈrɑːbɪ) *n., pl.* **-bies.** a type of cabbage whose thickened stem is eaten as a vegetable. [Italian *cavolo* cabbage + *rapa* turnip]

kokanee (kəʊˈkænɪ) *n.* a freshwater salmon of lakes and rivers in W North America. [*Kokanee* Creek, in British Columbia]

kola (ˈkəʊlə) *n.* same as **cola.**

kolkhoz (kɒlˈhɔːz) *n.* a Russian collective farm. [Russian]

komatik (ˈkəʊmætɪk) *n.* Canad. a sledge with wooden runners and crossbars bound with rawhide. [Eskimo]

kook (kuːk) *n.* U.S. & Canad. informal. an eccentric or foolish person. [prob. from *cuckoo*] —**kooky** or **kookie** *adj.*

kookaburra (ˈkʊkəˌbʌrə) *n.* a large Australian kingfisher with a cackling cry. [Aboriginal]

kopeck (ˈkəʊpɛk) *n.* a Soviet monetary unit worth one hundredth of a rouble. [Russian *kopeika*]

Koran (kɔːˈrɑːn) *n.* the sacred book of Islam, believed by Muslims to be the infallible word of God dictated to Mohammed. [Arabic *qur'ān* reading, book] —**Ko'ranic** *adj.*

Korean (kəˈriːən) *adj.* **1.** of Korea in SE Asia, its people, or their language. ~*n.* **2.** a person from Korea. **3.** the official language of North and South Korea.

kosher (ˈkəʊʃə) *adj.* **1.** Judaism. conforming to religious law: esp. (of food) prepared in accordance with the dietary laws. **2.** Informal. legitimate, genuine, or proper. ~*n.* **3.** kosher food. [Yiddish]

kowhai (ˈkəʊwaɪ) *n.* a small tree of New Zealand and Chile with clusters of yellow flowers. [Maori]

kowtow (ˌkaʊˈtaʊ) *vb.* **1.** to touch the forehead to the ground in deference. **2.** to be servile (towards). ~*n.* **3.** the act of kowtowing. [Chinese *k'o* to strike, knock + *t'ou* head]

kph kilometres per hour.

Kr Chem. krypton.

kraal (krɑːl) *n.* **1.** a Southern African hut village surrounded by a stockade. **2.** S. African. an enclosure for livestock. [Afrikaans]

krans (krɑːns) *n.* S. African. a sheer rock face. [Afrikaans]

kremlin (ˈkrɛmlɪn) *n.* the citadel of any Russian city. [Russian *kreml*]

Kremlin (ˈkrɛmlɪn) *n.* the central government of the Soviet Union.

krill (krɪl) *n., pl.* **krill.** a small shrimplike crustacean. [Norwegian *kril* young fish]

krona (ˈkrəʊnə) *n., pl.* **-nor** (-nə). the standard monetary unit of Sweden. [Swedish, from Latin *corōna* crown]

krone (ˈkrəʊnə) *n., pl.* **-ner** (-nə). the standard monetary unit of Denmark or Norway. [Danish or Norwegian, from Latin *corōna* crown]

krugerrand (ˈkruːgəˌrænd) *n.* a one-ounce gold coin minted in South Africa. [Paul *Kruger*, Boer statesman + *rand*]

krypton (ˈkrɪptɒn) *n.* an inert gaseous element occurring in trace amounts in air and used in fluorescent lights and lasers. Symbol: Kr [Greek *kruptos* hidden]

KS Kansas.

Kt Knight.

kudos (ˈkjuːdɒs) *n.* (functioning as sing.) acclaim, glory, or prestige. [Greek]

kudu or **koodoo** (ˈkuːduː) *n.* either of two spiral-horned African antelopes. [Afrikaans]

Ku Klux Klan (ˌkuː klʌks ˈklæn) *n.* a secret organization of White Protestant Americans who use violence against Blacks and Jews. [prob. based on Greek *kuklos* circle + *clan*] —**Ku Klux Klanner** (ˈklænə) *n.*

kukri (ˈkʊkrɪ) *n.* a heavy curved knife used by Gurkhas. [Hindi]

kulak (ˈkuːlæk) *n.* a property-owning Russian peasant. [Russian]

kumera or **kumara** (ˈkuːmərə) *n.* N.Z. the sweet potato. [Maori]

kümmel (ˈkʊməl) *n.* a German liqueur flavoured with aniseed and cumin. [from German]

kumquat (ˈkʌmkwɒt) *n.* a citrus fruit resembling a very small orange. [Mandarin Chinese *chin chü* golden orange]

kung fu (ˈkʌŋ ˈfuː) *n.* a Chinese martial art combining principles of karate and judo. [Chinese: martial art]

kuri (ˈkuːrɪ) *n.* N.Z. a mongrel dog. [Maori]

kW kilowatt.

kwashiorkor (ˌkwæʃɪˈɔːkə) *n.* severe malnutrition of young children, caused by not eating enough protein. [native word in Ghana]

kWh kilowatt-hour.

KWIC (kwɪk) keyword in context.

KWOC (kwɒk) keyword out of context.

KY or **Ky.** Kentucky.

kyle (kaɪl) *n.* Scot. a narrow strait or channel: *Kyle of Lochalsh.* [Gaelic *caol* narrow]

L

l or **L** (ɛl) n., pl. **l's, L's,** or **Ls.** 1. the 12th letter of the English alphabet. 2. something shaped like an L.

l litre.

L 1. large. 2. Latin. 3. learner driver. 4. Usually written: £ pound. [Latin *libra*] 5. the Roman numeral for 50.

L. or **l.** 1. lake. 2. left. 3. length. 4. (*pl.* **LL.** or **ll.**) line.

la (lɑː) n. *Music.* same as **lah.**

La *Chem.* lanthanum.

LA 1. Los Angeles. 2. Also: **La.** Louisiana.

laager (ˈlɑːgə) n. (in Africa) a camp defended by a circular formation of wagons. [Afrikaans *lager*]

lab (læb) n. *Informal.* short for **laboratory.**

Lab. *Politics.* Labour.

label (ˈleɪbəl) n. 1. a piece of card or other material attached to an object to show its contents, ownership, use, or destination. 2. a brief descriptive term given to a person, group, or school of thought: *the label "Romantic" is applied to many kinds of poetry.* ~vb. **-belling, -belled** or *U.S.* **-beling, -beled.** 3. to fasten a label to. 4. to describe or classify in a word or phrase. [Old French *label* ribbon]

labial (ˈleɪbɪəl) adj. 1. of or near the lips. 2. *Phonetics.* relating to a speech sound made using the lips. ~n. 3. *Phonetics.* a speech sound such as English *p* or *m*, that involves the lips. [Latin *labium* lip]

labiate (ˈleɪbɪˌeɪt, -ɪt) n. 1. any of a family of plants with square stems, aromatic leaves, and a two-lipped flower, such as mint or thyme. ~adj. 2. of this family. [Latin *labium* lip]

labium (ˈleɪbɪəm) n., pl. **-bia** (-bɪə). 1. a lip or liplike structure. 2. any one of the four lip-shaped folds of the vulva. [Latin: lip]

laboratory (ləˈbɒrətrɪ; *U.S.* ˈlæbrəˌtɔːrɪ) n., pl. **-ries.** a building or room equipped for conducting scientific research or for teaching practical science. [Latin *labōrāre* to work]

laborious (ləˈbɔːrɪəs) adj. involving great exertion or long effort. —**laˈboriously** adv.

labour or *U.S.* **labor** (ˈleɪbə) n. 1. productive work, esp. physical toil done for wages. 2. the people involved in this, as opposed to management. 3. difficult work or a difficult job. 4. the final stage of pregnancy, leading to childbirth. ~vb. 5. to perform labour; work. 6. to strive or work hard (for something). 7. (usually foll. by *under*) to be burdened (by) or be at a disadvantage (because of): *to labour under a misapprehension.* 8. to make one's way with difficulty. 9. to deal with too persistently: *to labour a point.* [Latin *labor*]

Labour Day n. a public holiday in honour of labour, held in Britain on May 1.

laboured or *U.S.* **labored** (ˈleɪbəd) adj. showing effort.

labourer or *U.S.* **laborer** (ˈleɪbərə) n. a person engaged in physical work.

labour exchange n. *Brit.* an old name for employment office.

Labour Party n. 1. the major left-wing political party in Britain, which believes in democratic socialism and social equality. 2. any similar party in various other countries.

Labrador or **Labrador retriever** (ˈlæbrəˌdɔː) n. a powerfully-built breed of dog with a short dense black or golden coat.

laburnum (ləˈbɜːnəm) n. a small ornamental tree that has clusters of yellow drooping flowers. It is highly poisonous. [Latin]

labyrinth (ˈlæbərɪnθ) n. 1. a mazelike network of tunnels or paths, either natural or man-made. 2. any complex or confusing system. 3. the interconnecting cavities of the internal ear. [Greek *laburinthos*] —ˌlabyˈrinthine adj.

lac (læk) n. a resinous substance secreted by certain insects (**lac insects**), used in the manufacture of shellac. [Hindi *lākh* resin]

lace (leɪs) n. 1. a delicate decorative fabric made from threads woven in an open web of patterns. 2. a cord or string drawn through eyelets to fasten a shoe or garment. ~vb. 3. to fasten (shoes) with a lace. 4. to draw (a cord or thread) through holes as when tying shoes. 5. to add a dash of spirits to (a beverage). 6. to intertwine; interlace. [Latin *laqueus* noose]

lacerate (ˈlæsəˌreɪt) vb. 1. to tear (the flesh) jaggedly. 2. to hurt (the feelings). [Latin *lacerāre* to tear] —ˌlacerˈation n.

lace up vb. 1. to fasten (clothes or footwear) with laces. ~adj. **lace-up.** 2. (of footwear) to be fastened with laces. ~n. **lace-up.** 3. a lace-up shoe or boot.

lachrymal (ˈlækrɪməl) adj. same as **lacrimal.**

lachrymose (ˈlækrɪˌməʊs) adj. 1. given to weeping; tearful. 2. mournful; sad. [Latin *lacrima* a tear]

lacing (ˈleɪsɪŋ) n. *Informal.* a severe beating.

lack (læk) n. 1. an insufficiency, shortage, or absence of something required or desired: *lack of privacy.* ~vb. 2. (often foll. by *in* or *for*) to be deficient (in) or have need (of): *lacking in taste.* [related to Middle Dutch *laken* to be wanting]

lackadaisical (ˌlækəˈdeɪzɪkəl) adj. 1. lacking vitality and purpose. 2. lazy, esp. in a dreamy way. [earlier *lackadaisy*]

lackey (ˈlækɪ) n. 1. a servile follower; hanger-on. 2. a liveried male servant or valet. [Catalan *lacayo, alacayo*]

lacklustre or *U.S.* **lackluster** (ˈlækˌlʌstə) adj. lacking force, brilliance, or vitality.

laconic (ləˈkɒnɪk) *adj.* (of a person's speech) using few words; terse. [Greek *Lakōnikos* Spartan; referring to the Spartans' terseness of speech] —**laˈconically** *adv.*

lacquer (ˈlækə) *n.* **1.** a hard glossy coating made by dissolving natural or synthetic resins in a solvent that evaporates quickly. **2.** a black resinous substance, obtained from certain trees (**lacquer trees**), used to give a hard glossy finish to wooden furniture. **3.** a clear sticky substance for spraying onto the hair to hold a style in place. ~*vb.* **4.** to apply lacquer to. [Portuguese *laca* lac]

lacrimal or **lachrymal** (ˈlækrɪməl) *adj.* of or relating to tears or to the glands that secrete tears. [Latin *lacrima* a tear]

lacrosse (ləˈkrɒs) *n.* a sport in which two teams try to propel a ball into each other's goal using long-handled pouched sticks. [French: the hooked stick]

lactate¹ (ˈlækteɪt) *n.* an ester or salt of lactic acid.

lactate² (ˈlækteɪt) *vb.* (of mammals) to secrete milk.

lactation (lækˈteɪʃən) *n.* **1.** the secretion of milk from the mammary glands. **2.** the period during which milk is secreted.

lacteal (ˈlæktɪəl) *adj.* **1.** of or like milk. **2.** (of lymphatic vessels) conveying or containing chyle. ~*n.* **3.** any of the lymphatic vessels that convey chyle from the small intestine to the blood. [Latin *lacteus* of milk]

lactic (ˈlæktɪk) *adj.* relating to or derived from milk. [Latin *lac* milk]

lactic acid *n.* a colourless syrupy acid found in sour milk and used as a preservative (**E270**) for foodstuffs.

lactose (ˈlæktəʊs) *n.* a white crystalline sugar occurring in milk.

lacuna (ləˈkjuːnə) *n., pl.* **-nae** (-niː) or **-nas.** a gap or missing part in a book or manuscript. [Latin *lacūna* pool, cavity]

lacy (ˈleɪsɪ) *adj.* **lacier, laciest.** of or like lace.

lad (læd) *n.* **1.** a boy or young man. **2.** *Informal.* any male. [perhaps from Old Norse]

ladder (ˈlædə) *n.* **1.** a portable framework with two long parallel pieces of wood, metal, or rope connected by steps, for climbing up or down. **2.** any system thought of as having a series of ascending stages: *the social ladder.* **3.** *Chiefly Brit.* a line of connected stitches that have come undone in tights or stockings. ~*vb.* **4.** *Chiefly Brit.* to cause a line of interconnected stitches (in stockings) to undo, as by snagging, or (of a stocking) to come undone in this way. [Old English *hlǣdder*]

ladder back *n.* a chair in which the back is made of horizontal slats between two uprights.

lade *vb.* (leɪd) *vb.* **lading, laded, laden** or **laded.** **1.** to put cargo on board (a ship) or (of a ship) to take on cargo. **2.** (foll. by *with*) to burden or load. [Old English *hladen* to load]

laden (ˈleɪd²n) *vb.* **1.** a past participle of **lade.** ~*adj.* **2.** loaded. **3.** burdened.

la-di-da or **lah-di-dah** (ˌlɑːdɪˈdɑː) *adj. Informal.* affected or pretentious in speech or manners. [mockingly imit. of affected speech]

ladies or **ladies' room** *n.* (functioning as *sing.*) *Informal.* a women's public toilet.

lading (ˈleɪdɪŋ) *n.* a load; cargo; freight.

ladle (ˈleɪd²l) *n.* **1.** a long-handled spoon with a deep bowl for serving soup, stew, etc. ~*vb.* **2.** to serve out as with a ladle. [Old English *hlædel*]

ladle out *vb. Informal.* to distribute (money, gifts, etc.) generously.

lady (ˈleɪdɪ) *n., pl.* **-dies. 1.** a woman regarded as having the characteristics of a good family and high social position. **2.** a polite name for a woman. ~*adj.* **3.** female: *a lady doctor.* [Old English *hlǣfdīge* kneader of bread]

Lady (ˈleɪdɪ) *n., pl.* **-dies. 1.** (in Britain) a title of honour borne by various classes of women of the peerage. **2. Our Lady.** a title of the Virgin Mary.

ladybird (ˈleɪdɪˌbɜːd) *n.* a small red beetle with black spots. [after Our *Lady*, the Virgin Mary]

Lady Day *n.* March 25, the feast of the Annunciation of the Virgin Mary: a quarter day in England, Wales, and Ireland.

lady-in-waiting *n., pl.* **ladies-in-waiting.** a lady who attends a queen or princess.

lady-killer *n. Informal.* a man who is or believes he is irresistible to women.

ladylike (ˈleɪdɪˌlaɪk) *adj.* like or befitting a lady; refined and fastidious.

Ladyship (ˈleɪdɪʃɪp) *n.* (preceded by *Your* or *Her*) a title used to address or refer to a peeress except a duchess.

lady's-slipper *n.* an orchid with reddish or purple flowers.

lag¹ (læg) *vb.* **lagging, lagged. 1.** (often foll. by *behind*) to hang (back) or fall (behind) in movement, progress, or development. **2.** to fall away in strength or intensity. ~*n.* **3.** a slowing down or falling behind. **4.** the interval of time between two events, esp. between an action and its effect. [origin unknown]

lag² (læg) *n. Slang.* a convict or ex-convict. [origin unknown]

lag³ (læg) *vb.* **lagging, lagged. 1.** to cover (a pipe, cylinder, or boiler) with lagging to prevent loss of heat. ~*n.* **2.** the insulating casing of a steam cylinder or boiler. [Scandinavian]

lager (ˈlɑːgə) *n.* a light-bodied beer. [German *Lagerbier* beer for storing]

laggard (ˈlægəd) *n.* a person who lags behind.

lagging (ˈlægɪŋ) *n.* insulating material wrapped around pipes, boilers, or tanks to prevent loss of heat.

lagoon (ləˈguːn) *n.* a body of water cut off from the open sea by coral reefs or sand bars. [Latin *lacūna* pool]

lah (lɑː) *n. Music.* (in tonic sol-fa) the sixth note of any major scale.

laid (leɪd) *vb.* the past of **lay**[1].

laid-back *adj.* relaxed in style or character.

laid paper *n.* paper with a regular mesh impressed upon it.

lain (leɪn) *vb.* the past participle of **lie**[2].

lair (lɛə) *n.* **1.** the resting place of a wild animal. **2.** *Informal.* a place of seclusion or hiding. [Old English *leger*]

laird (lɛəd) *n. Scot.* a landowner, esp. of a large estate. [Scots var. of *lord*]

laissez faire or **laisser faire** (ˌlɛseɪ ˈfɛə) *n.* the doctrine of unrestricted freedom in commerce, esp. for private interests. [French, lit.: let (them) act]

laity (ˈleɪɪtɪ) *n.* **1.** laymen, as distinguished from clergymen. **2.** all the people who do not belong to a specific profession. [from LAY[3]]

lake[1] (leɪk) *n.* an expanse of water entirely surrounded by land. [Latin *lacus*]

lake[2] (leɪk) *n.* **1.** a bright pigment produced by combining organic colouring matter with an inorganic compound. **2.** a red dye obtained by combining a metallic compound with cochineal. [var. of *lac*]

Lake District *n.* a region of lakes and mountains in NW England. Also called: **Lakeland, the Lakes.**

lake trout *n.* a yellow-spotted trout of the Great Lakes region of Canada.

lakh (lɑːk) *n.* (in India) 100 000, esp. referring to this sum of rupees. [Hindi *lākh*]

lam[1] (læm) *vb.* **lamming, lammed.** *Slang.* to thrash or beat. [Scandinavian]

lam[2] (læm) *n.* **on the lam.** *U.S. & Canad. slang.* making an escape. [origin unknown]

lama (ˈlɑːmə) *n.* a Buddhist priest or monk in Mongolia or Tibet. [Tibetan *blama*]

lamb (læm) *n.* **1.** the young of a sheep. **2.** the meat of a young sheep eaten as food. **3.** someone who is innocent, gentle, and good. ~*vb.* **4.** (of a ewe) to give birth. [Old English]

Lamb (læm) *n.* **the.** a title given to Christ.

lambaste (læmˈbeɪst) or **lambast** (læmˈbæst) *vb.* **1.** to beat (someone) severely. **2.** to reprimand (someone). [LAM[1] + BASTE[3]]

lambent (ˈlæmbənt) *adj.* **1.** (of a flame or light) flickering softly over a surface. **2.** (of wit or humour) light or brilliant. [Latin *lambere* to lick] —**ˈlambency** *n.*

lambskin (ˈlæmˌskɪn) *n.* the skin of a lamb, usually with the wool still on, used to make coats, slippers, etc.

lame (leɪm) *adj.* **1.** disabled or crippled in the legs or feet. **2.** weak; unconvincing: *a lame excuse.* ~*vb.* **3.** to make lame. [Old English *lama*] —**ˈlamely** *adv.* —**ˈlameness** *n.*

lamé (ˈlɑːmeɪ) *n.* a fabric interwoven with threads of metal. [Old French *lame* gold or silver thread]

lame duck *n.* a person who is unable to cope without the help of other people.

lament (ləˈmɛnt) *vb.* **1.** to feel or express sorrow, remorse, or regret (for or over). ~*n.* **2.** an expression of sorrow. **3.** a poem or song in which a death is lamented. [Latin *lāmentum*] —ˌlamenˈtation *n.*

lamentable (ˈlæməntəbªl) *adj.* deplorable or distressing. —ˈlamentably *adv.*

lamented (ləˈmɛntɪd) *adj.* grieved for: usually said of someone dead.

lamina (ˈlæmɪnə) *n., pl.* **-nae** (-ˌniː). a thin plate, esp. of bone or mineral. [Latin: thin plate] —ˈlaminar *adj.*

laminate *vb.* (ˈlæmɪˌneɪt). **1.** to make (material in sheet form) by bonding together thin sheets. **2.** to split or be split into thin sheets. **3.** to beat or press (metal) into thin sheets. **4.** to cover with a thin sheet of material. ~*n.* (ˈlæmɪˌneɪt, -nɪt). **5.** a material made by bonding sheets together. ~*adj.* (ˈlæmɪˌneɪt, -nɪt). **6.** composed of lamina; laminated. —ˌlamiˈnation *n.*

laminated (ˈlæmɪˌneɪtɪd) *adj.* **1.** composed of many layers bonded together. **2.** covered with a thin protective layer of plastic.

Lammas (ˈlæməs) *n.* Aug. 1, formerly observed in England as a harvest festival: a quarter day in Scotland. [Old English *hlāfmæsse* loaf mass]

lamp (læmp) *n.* **1.** a device that produces illumination: *an electric lamp; a gas lamp; an oil lamp.* **2.** a device that produces radiation, esp. for therapeutic purposes: *an ultraviolet lamp.* [Greek *lampein* to shine]

lampblack (ˈlæmpˌblæk) *n.* a fine black soot used as a pigment in paint and ink.

lampoon (læmˈpuːn) *n.* **1.** a satire ridiculing a person. ~*vb.* **2.** to attack or satirize (someone) in a lampoon. [French *lampon*] —**lamˈpooner** or **lamˈpoonist** *n.*

lamppost (ˈlæmpˌpəʊst) *n.* a metal or concrete pole supporting a lamp in a street.

lamprey (ˈlæmprɪ) *n.* an eel-like fish with a round sucking mouth for clinging to and feeding on the blood of other fish. [Late Latin *lamprēda*]

Lancastrian (læŋˈkæstrɪən) *n.* **1.** a person from Lancashire or Lancaster. **2.** a supporter of the house of Lancaster in the Wars of the Roses (1455-85). ~*adj.* **3.** of Lancashire or Lancaster. **4.** of the house of Lancaster.

lance (lɑːns) *n.* **1.** a long weapon with a pointed head used by horsemen. ~*vb.* **2.** to pierce (an abscess or boil) with a lancet. **3.** to pierce with or as with a lance. [Latin *lancea*]

lance corporal *n.* a noncommissioned officer of the lowest rank in the British Army.

lanceolate (ˈlɑːnsɪəˌleɪt, -lɪt) *adj.* narrow and tapering to a point at each end, as certain leaves. [Latin *lanceola* small lance]

lancer (ˈlɑːnsə) *n.* (formerly) a cavalryman armed with a lance.

lancers (ˈlɑːnsəz) *n.* (*functioning as sing.*) **1.** a quadrille. **2.** music for this dance.

lancet (ˈlɑːnsɪt) *n.* **1.** a pointed surgical knife with two sharp edges. **2.** short for **lancet arch** or **lancet window**. [Old French: small lance]

lancet arch *n.* a narrow acutely pointed arch.

lancet window n. a narrow window with a lancet arch.

lancewood ('lɑːns,wʊd) n. a New Zealand tree with slender leaves.

Lancs (læŋks) Lancashire.

land (lænd) n. **1.** the solid part of the surface of the earth as distinct from seas and lakes. **2.** ground, esp. with reference to its use or quality: *arable land*. **3.** rural or agricultural areas: *life on the land*. **4.** *Law.* ground owned as property. **5.** a country, region, or area: *native land*. ~vb. **6.** to come down or bring (something) down to earth after a flight or jump. **7.** to transfer (something) or go from a ship to the shore: *land the cargo*. **8.** to come to or touch shore. **9.** (in Canada) to be legally admitted to the country as an immigrant. **10.** *Angling.* to retrieve (a hooked fish) from the water. **11.** *Informal.* to obtain: *to land a job.* **12.** *Informal.* to deliver (a blow or punch). ~See also **land up.** [Old English] —'**landless** adj.

land agent n. a person in charge of a landed estate.

landau ('lændɔː) n. a four-wheeled horse-drawn carriage with two folding hoods. [after *Landau* (a town in Germany), where first made]

landed ('lændɪd) adj. **1.** owning land: *landed gentry*. **2.** consisting of land: *a landed estate*.

landfall ('lænd,fɔːl) n. the act of sighting or nearing land, esp. from the sea.

land girl n. a girl or woman who does farm work, esp. in wartime.

land-holder n. a person who owns or occupies land. —'**land-,holding** adj., n.

landing ('lændɪŋ) n. **1.** the floor area at the top of a flight of stairs. **2.** the act of coming to land, esp. after a sea voyage. **3.** a place of disembarkation.

landing field n. an area of land on which aircraft land and from which they take off.

landing gear n. the undercarriage of an aircraft.

landlady ('lænd,leɪdɪ) n., pl. -**dies.** **1.** a woman who owns and leases property. **2.** a woman who owns or runs a lodging house or pub.

landlocked ('lænd,lɒkt) adj. (of a country) completely surrounded by land.

landlord ('lænd,lɔːd) n. **1.** a man who owns and leases property. **2.** a man who owns or runs a lodging house or pub.

landlubber ('lænd,lʌbə) n. *Naut.* any person without experience at sea.

landmark ('lænd,mɑːk) n. **1.** a prominent object in or feature of a particular landscape. **2.** an important or unique decision, event, fact, or discovery: *the discovery of penicillin was a landmark in medicine.*

landmass ('lænd,mæs) n. a large continuous area of land, as opposed to seas or islands.

land mine n. *Mil.* an explosive device placed in the ground, usually detonated when someone steps on it or drives over it.

landowner ('lænd,əʊnə) n. a person who owns land. —'**land,owning** n., adj.

landscape ('lænd,skeɪp) n. **1.** an extensive area of scenery as viewed from a single place. **2.** a painting, drawing, or photograph depicting natural scenery. ~vb. **3.** to improve the natural features of (an area of land). [Middle Dutch *lantscap* region]

landscape gardening n. the art of laying out grounds in imitation of natural scenery. —**landscape gardener** n.

landslide ('lænd,slaɪd) n. **1.** Also called: **landslip. a.** the sliding of a large mass of rocks and soil down the side of a mountain or cliff. **b.** the material dislodged in this way. **2.** an overwhelming electoral victory.

land up vb. to arrive at a final point or condition.

landward ('lændwəd) adj. **1.** lying, facing, or moving towards land. **2.** in the direction of the land. ~adv. also **landwards.** **3.** towards land.

lane (leɪn) n. **1.** a narrow road between buildings, hedges, or fences. **2.** any well-defined track or course, as for traffic in a road, or for ships or aircraft. **3.** one of the parallel strips into which a running track or swimming bath is divided for races. [Old English *lane, lanu*]

lang. language.

language ('læŋgwɪdʒ) n. **1.** a system of expression by spoken sounds or conventional symbols. **2.** the faculty for the use of such systems. **3.** the language of a particular nation or people. **4.** any other means of communicating: *the language of love.* **5.** the specialized vocabulary used by a particular group: *medical language.* **6.** a particular manner or style of verbal expression: *your language is disgusting.* **7.** *Computers.* See **programming language.** [Latin *lingua* tongue]

language laboratory n. a room in a school or college equipped with tape recorders, etc., for learning foreign languages.

languid ('læŋgwɪd) adj. **1.** lacking energy or enthusiasm. **2.** sluggish; inactive. [Latin *languēre* to languish] —'**languidly** adv.

languish ('læŋgwɪʃ) vb. **1.** to suffer deprivation, hardship, or neglect: *to languish in prison.* **2.** to lose or diminish in strength or energy. **3.** (often foll. by *for*) to be listless with desire; pine. [Latin *languēre*] —'**languishing** adj.

languor ('læŋgə) n. **1.** laziness or weariness. **2.** dreaminess and relaxation. **3.** oppressive stillness. [Latin *languēre* to languish] —'**languorous** adj.

lank (læŋk) adj. **1.** (of hair) long and limp. **2.** thin or gaunt. [Old English *hlanc* loose]

lanky ('læŋkɪ) adj. **lankier, lankiest.** ungracefully tall and thin. —'**lankiness** n.

lanolin ('lænəlɪn) n. a yellowish sticky substance extracted from wool: used in some ointments. [Latin *lāna* wool + *oleum* oil]

lantern ('læntən) n. **1.** a light with a transparent protective case. **2.** a structure on top of a dome or roof with windows for light or air. **3.** the upper part of a lighthouse that houses the light. [Greek *lampein* to shine]

lantern jaw *n.* a long hollow jaw that gives the face a drawn appearance. —**'lantern-,jawed** *adj.*

lanthanide series (ˈlænθəˌnaɪd) *n.* a class of 15 chemically related elements (**lanthanides**) with atomic numbers from 57 (lanthanum) to 71 (lutetium).

lanthanum (ˈlænθənəm) *n.* a silvery-white metallic element of the lanthanide series: used in electronic devices and glass manufacture. Symbol: La [Greek *lanthanein* to lie unseen]

lanyard (ˈlænjəd) *n.* 1. a cord worn around the neck to hold a whistle or knife. 2. *Naut.* a line for extending or tightening rigging. [Old French *lasne* strap]

laodicean (ˌleɪəʊdɪˈsɪən) *adj.* indifferent, esp. in religious matters. [referring to the early Christians of Laodicea (Revelation 3:14–16)]

lap¹ (læp) *n.* 1. the area formed by the upper surface of the thighs of a seated person. 2. a protected place or environment: *in the lap of luxury.* 3. the part of a person's clothing that covers the lap. 4. **drop in someone's lap.** to give someone the responsibility of. [Old English *læppa* flap]

lap² (læp) *n.* 1. one circuit of a racecourse or track. 2. a stage or part of a journey. 3. **a.** an overlapping part. **b.** the extent of overlap. ~*vb.* 4. to overtake (an opponent) in a race so as to be one or more circuits ahead. 5. to wrap or fold (around or over): *he lapped a bandage around his wrist.* 6. to envelop in: *he lapped his wrist in a bandage.* 7. to place or lie partly or completely over or project beyond. 8. (*usually passive*) to envelop or surround with comfort, love, or peace: *lapped in luxury.* [prob. same as LAP¹]

lap³ (læp) *vb.* **lapping, lapped.** 1. (of small waves) to wash against the shore or a boat) with light splashing sounds. 2. (often foll. by *up*) (esp. of animals) to scoop (a liquid) into the mouth with the tongue. ~*n.* 3. the act or sound of lapping. ~See also **lap up.** [Old English *lapian*]

lapdog (ˈlæpˌdɒg) *n.* a small pet dog.

lapel (ləˈpɛl) *n.* the part on the front of a garment, such as a jacket, that folds back towards the shoulders. [from LAP¹]

lapidary (ˈlæpɪdərɪ) *n., pl.* **-daries.** 1. a person who cuts, polishes, or deals in gemstones. ~*adj.* 2. of or relating to gemstones or the work of a lapidary. [Latin *lapidārius* from *lapis* stone]

lapis lazuli (ˈlæpɪs ˈlæzjʊˌlaɪ) *n.* 1. a brilliant blue mineral used as a gemstone. 2. its deep blue colour. [Latin *lapis* stone + Medieval Latin *lazulī* azure]

lap joint *n.* a joint made by overlapping parts and fastening them together.

lap of honour *n.* a ceremonial circuit of a racing track by the winner of a race.

Lapp (læp) *n.* 1. Also: **Laplander.** a member of a nomadic people living chiefly in N Scandinavia. 2. the language of this peo-

ple. ~*adj.* 3. of this people or their language.

lappet (ˈlæpɪt) *n.* 1. a small hanging flap or piece of lace. 2. a lobelike hanging structure in some invertebrate animals. [LAP¹ + -*et* diminutive suffix]

lapse (læps) *n.* 1. a temporary drop in standard as a result of forgetfulness or lack of concentration. 2. a moment or instance of bad behaviour, esp. by someone who is usually well-behaved. 3. a break in occurrence or usage: *a lapse of five weeks between letters.* 4. a gradual decline to a lower degree, condition, or state: *a lapse from high office.* 5. *Law.* the termination of some right, interest, or privilege, as by neglecting to claim, exercise, or renew it. ~*vb.* 6. to drop in standard or fail to maintain a norm. 7. to decline gradually in status, condition, or degree. 8. to be discontinued, esp. through negligence. 9. (usually foll. by *into*) to drift (into a condition): *to lapse into sleep.* 10. (often foll. by *from*) to turn away (from beliefs or norms). 11. (of time) to slip away. [Latin *lāpsus* error] —**lapsed** *adj.*

laptop (ˈlæpˌtɒp) *n. (modifier)* (of a computer) small and light enough to be held on the user's lap.

lap up *vb.* 1. to eat or drink. 2. to accept (information or attention) eagerly: *he laps up stories.*

lapwing (ˈlæpˌwɪŋ) *n.* a bird of the plover family with a crested head. Also called: **peewit.** [Old English *hlēapewince* plover]

larboard (ˈlɑːbəd) *n., adj. Naut.* an old word for **port**². [*laddeborde* (changed to *larboard* by association with *starboard*), from *laden* to load + *borde* board]

larceny (ˈlɑːsɪnɪ) *n., pl.* **-nies.** *Law.* theft. [Old French *larcin*] —**larcenist** *n.*

larch (lɑːtʃ) *n.* 1. a coniferous tree with needle-like leaves and egg-shaped cones. 2. the wood of this tree. [Latin *larix*]

lard (lɑːd) *n.* 1. the soft white fat obtained from pigs and prepared for use in cooking. ~*vb.* 2. to prepare (lean meat or poultry) by inserting small strips of bacon or fat before cooking. 3. to add unnecessary material to (speech or writing). [Latin *lāridum* bacon fat]

larder (ˈlɑːdə) *n.* a room or cupboard, used as a store for food. [Old French *lardier*]

lardy cake (ˈlɑːdɪ) *n. Brit.* a sweet cake made of bread dough, lard, sugar, and dried fruit.

large (lɑːdʒ) *adj.* 1. having a relatively great size, quantity, or extent; big. 2. of wide or broad scope, capacity, or range; comprehensive: *large change.* ~*n.* 3. **at large. a.** (of a dangerous criminal or wild animal) free; not confined. **b.** as a whole; in general. **c.** in full detail. [Latin *largus* ample] —**largeness** *n.*

large intestine *n.* the part of the alimentary canal consisting of the caecum, colon, and rectum.

largely (ˈlɑːdʒlɪ) *adv.* principally; to a great extent.

large-scale *adj.* 1. wide-ranging or extensive. **2.** (of maps and models) constructed or drawn to a big scale.

largess *or* **largesse** (lɑːˈdʒɛs) *n.* the generous giving of gifts, favours, or money. [Old French]

largish (ˈlɑːdʒɪʃ) *adj.* fairly large.

largo (ˈlɑːgəʊ) *Music.* ~*adv.* **1.** slowly and stately. ~*n., pl.* **-gos. 2.** a piece or passage to be performed in this way. [Italian]

lariat (ˈlærɪət) *n. U.S. & Canad.* **1.** a lasso. **2.** a rope for tethering animals. [Spanish *la reata* the lasso]

lark[1] (lɑːk) *n.* a small brown songbird, esp. the skylark. [Old English *lāwerce*]

lark[2] (lɑːk) *Informal.* ~*n.* **1.** a carefree adventure or frolic. **2.** a harmless piece of mischief. ~*vb.* **3. lark about.** to have a good time frolicking or playing pranks. [orig. slang] —**larkish** *or* **larky** *adj.*

larkspur (ˈlɑːkˌspɜː) *n.* a plant with blue, pink, or white spurred flowers. [LARK[1] + *spur*]

larva (ˈlɑːvə) *n., pl.* **-vae** (-viː). an immature free-living form of many animals that develops into a different adult form by metamorphosis. [New Latin] —**larval** *adj.*

laryngeal (ˌlærɪnˈdʒiːəl) *adj.* of or relating to the larynx.

laryngitis (ˌlærɪnˈdʒaɪtɪs) *n.* inflammation of the larynx.

larynx (ˈlærɪŋks) *n.* a hollow organ forming part of the air passage to the lungs: it contains the vocal cords. [Greek *larunx*]

lasagne *or* **lasagna** (ləˈzænjə, -ˈsæn-) *n.* **1.** a form of pasta consisting of wide flat sheets. **2.** a dish made from layers of lasagne, meat, and cheese. [Italian, from Latin *lasanum* cooking pot]

lascivious (ləˈsɪvɪəs) *adj.* **1.** lustful; lecherous. **2.** producing sexual desire. [Latin *lascīvia* wantonness] —**lasˈciviously** *adv.*

laser (ˈleɪzə) *n.* a device for converting light of mixed frequencies into an intense narrow beam of light of the same frequency. [from *l*ight *a*mplification by *s*timulated *e*mission of *r*adiation]

laser printer *n.* a quiet, high-quality computer printer which uses a laser beam shining on light-sensitive paper to produce characters.

lash[1] (læʃ) *n.* **1.** a sharp cutting blow from a whip. **2.** the flexible end of a whip. **3.** an eyelash. ~*vb.* **4.** to hit (a person or thing) sharply with a whip, esp. formerly as punishment. **5.** (of rain or waves) to beat forcefully against. **6.** to attack (someone) with words of ridicule or scolding. **7.** to flick or wave sharply to and fro: *the panther lashed his tail.* **8.** to urge as with a whip: *to lash the audience into a violent mood.* ~See also **lash out.** [possibly imit.]

lash[2] (læʃ) *vb.* to bind or secure with rope, string, or cord. [Latin *laqueus* noose]

lashing[1] (ˈlæʃɪŋ) *n.* **1.** a flogging. **2.** a scolding.

lashing[2] (ˈlæʃɪŋ) *n.* rope, string, or cord used for binding or securing.

lashings (ˈlæʃɪŋz) *pl. n. Brit. informal.* large amounts; lots: *lashings of cream.*

lash out *vb.* **1.** to burst into or resort to verbal or physical attack. **2.** *Informal.* to spend (money) extravagantly.

lass (læs) *n.* a girl or young woman. [origin unknown]

Lassa fever (ˈlæsə) *n.* a serious viral disease of Central West Africa, characterized by high fever and muscular pains. [after *Lassa*, the Nigerian village where it was first identified]

lassie (ˈlæsɪ) *n. Informal.* a little lass; girl.

lassitude (ˈlæsɪˌtjuːd) *n.* physical or mental weariness. [Latin *lassus* tired]

lasso (læˈsuː, ˈlæsəʊ) *n., pl.* **-sos** *or* **-soes. 1.** a long rope with a running noose at one end, esp. used for roping horses and cattle. ~*vb.* **-soing, -soed. 2.** to catch as with a lasso. [Spanish, from Latin *laqueus* noose] —**lasˈsoer** *n.*

last[1] (lɑːst) *adj.* **1.** being, happening, or coming at the end or after all others. **2.** most recent: *last Thursday.* **3.** only remaining: *one's last cigarette.* **4.** most extreme; utmost. **5.** least suitable or likely: *he was the last person I would have chosen.* ~*adv.* **6.** after all others. **7.** most recently: *he was last seen in the mountains.* **8.** as the last or latest item. ~*n.* **9.** the **last. a.** a person or thing that is last. **b.** the final moment; end. **10.** the final appearance, mention, or occurrence: *we've seen the last of him.* **11. at last.** in the end; finally. **12. at long last.** finally, after difficulty or delay. [var. of Old English *latest, lætest*]

last[2] (lɑːst) *vb.* **1.** to remain in being (for a length of time); continue: *his hatred lasted for several years.* **2.** to be sufficient for the needs of (a person) for (a length of time): *it will last us until Friday.* **3.** to remain fresh, uninjured, or unaltered (for a certain time): *she lasted for three hours underground.* ~See also **last out.** [Old English *læstan*]

last[3] (lɑːst) *n.* the wooden or metal form on which a shoe or boot is made or repaired. [Old English *lāst* footprint]

last-ditch *adj.* done as a last resort: *a last-ditch effort.*

lasting (ˈlɑːstɪŋ) *adj.* permanent or enduring.

Last Judgment *n.* the. *Theol.* God's verdict on the destinies of all human beings at the end of the world.

lastly (ˈlɑːstlɪ) *adv.* **1.** at the end or at the last point. **2.** finally.

last-minute *adj.* given or done at the latest possible time: *last-minute preparations.*

last name *n.* same as **surname.**

last out *vb.* **1.** to be sufficient for one's needs: *will our supplies last out?* **2.** to endure or survive: *some old people don't last out the winter.*

last rites *pl. n. Christianity.* religious rites for those close to death.

last straw *n.* a small incident, irritation, or

setback that coming after others is too much to cope with.

Last Supper *n.* **the.** the meal eaten by Christ with his disciples on the night before his Crucifixion.

lat. latitude.

Lat. Latin.

latch (lætʃ) *n.* **1.** a fastening for a gate or door that consists of a bar that may be slid or lowered into a groove, hole, or notch. **2.** a spring-loaded door lock that can be opened by a key from outside. ~*vb.* **3.** to fasten, fit, or be fitted as with a latch. [Old English *læccan* to seize]

latchkey child ('lætʃ,kiː) *n.* a child who has to let himself in at home after school, as his parents are out at work.

latch on *vb. Informal.* **1.** (often foll. by *to*) to attach oneself (to): *to latch on to new ideas.* **2.** to understand: *it took me a while to latch on.*

late (leɪt) *adj.* **1.** occurring or arriving after the correct or expected time: *the train was late.* **2.** occurring or being at a relatively advanced time: *a late marriage.* **3.** towards or near the end: *the late evening.* **4.** at an advanced time in the evening or at night: *it was late.* **5.** recent: *his late remarks on industry.* **6.** having died recently: *my late grandfather.* **7.** former: *the late manager of this firm.* **8. of late.** recently. ~*adv.* **9.** after the correct or expected time: *he arrived late.* **10.** at a relatively advanced age: *she married late.* **11.** recently: *as late as yesterday he was selling books.* **12. late in the day. a.** at a late or advanced stage. **b.** too late. [Old English *læt*] —**'lateness** *n.*

lateen (lə'tiːn) *adj. Naut.* denoting a rig with a triangular sail bent to a yard hoisted to the head of a low mast. [French *voile latine* Latin sail]

Late Greek *n.* the Greek language from about the 3rd to the 8th centuries A.D.

Late Latin *n.* the form of written Latin used from the 3rd to the 7th centuries A.D.

lately ('leɪtlɪ) *adv.* in recent times; of late.

latent ('leɪt°nt) *adj.* lying hidden and not yet developed within a person or thing. [Latin *latēre* to lie hidden] —**'latency** *n.*

later ('leɪtə) *adj., adv.* **1.** the comparative of **late.** ~*adv.* **2.** afterwards.

lateral ('lætərəl) *adj.* **1.** of or relating to the side or sides. ~*n.* **2.** a lateral object, part, passage, or movement. [Latin *latus* side] —**'laterally** *adv.*

lateral thinking *n.* a way of solving problems by apparently illogical methods.

latest ('leɪtɪst) *adj., adv.* **1.** the superlative of **late.** ~*adj.* **2.** most recent, modern, or new: *the latest fashions.* ~*n.* **3. at the latest.** no later than the time specified.

latex ('leɪtɛks) *n.* a milky fluid produced by many plants which is used in the manufacture of rubber. [Latin: liquid]

lath (lɑːθ) *n., pl.* **laths** (lɑːðz, lɑːθs). one of several thin narrow strips of wood used as a supporting framework for plaster or tiles. [Old English *lætt*]

lathe (leɪð) *n.* a machine for shaping metal

or wood, in which the workpiece is turned against a fixed tool. [possibly Old Norse]

lather ('lɑːðə) *n.* **1.** foam formed by soap or detergent in water. **2.** foamy sweat, as of a horse. **3.** *Informal.* a state of agitation. ~*vb.* **4.** to coat or become coated with lather. **5.** to form a lather. **6.** *Informal.* to beat; flog. [Old English *lēathor* soap] —**'lathery** *adj.*

Latin ('lætɪn) *n.* **1.** the language of ancient Rome and the Roman Empire. **2.** a member of any of those peoples whose languages are derived from Latin. ~*adj.* **3.** of or relating to the Latin language. **4.** of or relating to those peoples whose languages are derived from Latin. **5.** of or relating to the Roman Catholic Church. [Latin *Latīnus* of Latium]

Latin America *n.* those areas of South and Central America whose official languages are Spanish and Portuguese.

latish ('leɪtɪʃ) *adj., adv.* rather late.

latitude ('lætɪ,tjuːd) *n.* **1. a.** an angular distance measured in degrees north or south of the equator. **b.** (*often pl.*) a region considered with regard to its distance from the equator. **2.** scope for freedom of action and thought. [Latin *lātus* broad] —**,lati'tudinal** *adj.*

latitudinarian (,lætɪ,tjuːdɪ'nɛərɪən) *adj.* **1.** liberal, esp. in religious matters. ~*n.* **2.** a person with latitudinarian views.

latrine (lə'triːn) *n.* a toilet, as in a barracks or camp. [Latin *lavātrīna* bath]

latter ('lætə) *adj.* **1.** near or nearer the end: *the latter part of a film.* **2.** more advanced in time or sequence; later. ~*n.* **3. the latter.** the second or second mentioned of two. [Old English *lætra*]

latter-day *adj.* present-day; modern.

latterly ('lætəlɪ) *adv.* recently; lately.

lattice ('lætɪs) *n.* **1.** Also called: **lattice-work.** an open framework of strips of wood or metal, arranged to form an ornamental pattern. **2.** a gate, screen, or fence formed of such a framework. **3.** an array of atoms, ions, or molecules in a crystal or an array of points indicating their positions in space. ~*vb.* **4.** to make, adorn, or supply with a lattice. [Old French *latte* lath] —**'latticed** *adj.*

laud (lɔːd) *Literary.* ~*vb.* **1.** to praise or glorify. ~*n.* **2.** praise or glorification. [Latin *laudāre* to praise]

laudable ('lɔːdəb°l) *adj.* deserving praise; commendable; admirable —,**lauda'bil-ity** *n.* —**'laudably** *adv.*

laudanum ('lɔːd°nəm) *n.* a tincture of opium. [New Latin]

laudatory ('lɔːdətrɪ) *adj.* (of speech or writing) expressing praise.

laugh (lɑːf) *vb.* **1.** to express mirth or amusement, typically by producing an inarticulate voiced noise. **2.** to utter or express with laughter: *he laughed his derision at the play.* **3.** to bring or force (someone, esp. oneself) into a certain condition by laughter: *he laughed himself sick.* **4. laugh at.** to make fun (of); jeer (at). **5. laugh up one's sleeve.** to laugh secretly. ~*n.* **6.** the act or an instance of laughing.

7. a manner of laughter. **8.** *Informal.* a person or thing that causes laughter: *that holiday was a laugh.* **9. the last laugh.** final success after previous defeat. ~See also **laugh off.** [Old English *læhan, hliehhen*] —'**laughingly** *adv.*

laughable ('lɑːfəbªl) *adj.* **1.** producing scorn; ludicrous. **2.** arousing laughter.

laughing gas *n.* nitrous oxide used as an anaesthetic: it may cause laughter and exhilaration when inhaled.

laughing stock *n.* an object of humiliating ridicule.

laugh off *vb.* to treat (something serious or difficult) lightly.

laughter ('lɑːftə) *n.* the action of or noise produced by laughing. [Old English *hleahtor*]

launch[1] (lɔːntʃ) *vb.* **1.** to move (a vessel) into the water, esp. for the first time. **2. a.** to start off or set in motion: *to launch a scheme.* **b.** to put (a new product) on the market. **3.** to involve (oneself) totally and enthusiastically: *to launch oneself into work.* **4.** to set (a rocket, missile, or spacecraft) into motion. **5. launch into.** to start talking or writing (about). **6.** (usually foll. by *out*) to start (out) on a new enterprise. ~*n.* **7.** an act or instance of launching. [Late Latin *lanceāre* to use a lance, hence, to set in motion] —'**launcher** *n.*

launch[2] (lɔːntʃ) *n.* an open motorboat. [Malay *lancharan* boat, from *lanchar* speed]

launching pad *or* **launch pad** *n.* a platform from which a spacecraft, rocket, or missile is launched.

launder ('lɔːndə) *vb.* **1.** to wash and often also iron (clothes and linen). **2.** to make (money illegally obtained) appear to be legally gained by passing it through foreign banks or legitimate enterprises. [Latin *lavāre* to wash]

Launderette (,lɔːndə'rɛt, lɔːn'drɛt) *Brit. & N.Z. trademark.* an establishment where clothes can be washed and dried, using coin-operated machines. Also called (U.S., Canad., and N.Z.): **Laundromat.**

laundry ('lɔːndrɪ) *n., pl.* **-dries. 1.** a place where clothes and linen are washed and ironed. **2.** the clothes or linen to be laundered or that have been laundered.

laureate ('lɔːrɪɪt) *adj.* **1.** *Literary.* crowned with laurel leaves as a sign of honour. ~*n.* **2.** short for **poet laureate.** [Latin *laurea* laurel] —'**laureate,ship** *n.*

laurel ('lɒrəl) *n.* **1.** a small Mediterranean evergreen tree with glossy leaves. **2.** (*pl.*) a wreath of laurel, worn on the head as an emblem of victory or honour in classical times. **3.** (*pl.*) honour, distinction, or fame. **4. look to one's laurels.** to be on guard against one's rivals. **5. rest on one's laurels.** to be satisfied with what one has already achieved and stop striving for further success. [Latin *laurus, laurea*]

Laurentian (lɔː'rɛnʃən) *adj.* of or near the St Lawrence River.

Laurentian Shield *n.* same as **Canadian Shield.**

lav (læv) *n. Brit. informal.* short for **lavatory.**

lava ('lɑːvə) *n.* **1.** molten rock flowing from volcanoes. **2.** any rock formed by the solidification of lava. [Latin *lavāre* to wash]

lavatorial (,lævə'tɔːrɪəl) *adj.* characterized by frequent reference to excretion: *lavatorial humour.*

lavatory ('lævətrɪ) *n., pl.* **-ries.** same as **toilet.** [Latin *lavāre* to wash]

lavender ('lævəndə) *n.* **1.** a shrub or plant cultivated for its mauve or blue flowers and as the source of a fragrant oil (**oil of lavender**). **2.** its dried flowers, used to perfume clothes. **3.** a pale or light bluish-purple colour. [Medieval Latin *lavendula*]

lavender water *n.* a light perfume made from lavender.

lavish ('lævɪʃ) *adj.* **1.** great in quantity or richness: *lavish decoration.* **2.** very generous in giving. **3.** extravagant; wasteful: *lavish expenditure.* ~*vb.* **4.** to give or to spend very generously or in great quantities. [Old French *lavasse* torrent] —'**lavishly** *adv.*

law (lɔː) *n.* **1.** a rule or set of rules regulating the relationship between the state and its subjects, and the conduct of subjects towards one another. **2.** a rule or body of rules made by the legislature or other authority. **3.** the condition and control enforced by such rules. **4. law and order.** the policy of strict enforcement of the law, esp. against crime and violence. **5.** a rule of conduct: *a law of etiquette.* **6. the law. a.** the legal or judicial system. **b.** the profession or practice of law. **c.** *Informal.* the police or a policeman. **7.** Also called: **law of nature.** a generalization based on a recurring fact or event. **8.** the science or knowledge of law; jurisprudence. **9.** a general principle, formula, or rule in mathematics, science, or philosophy: *the laws of thermodynamics.* **10. the Law.** the laws contained in the first five books of the Old Testament. **11. go to law.** to resort to legal proceedings on some matter. **12. lay down the law.** to speak in an authoritative manner. [Old English *lagu*]

law-abiding *adj.* obeying the laws: *a law-abiding citizen.*

lawbreaker ('lɔː,breɪkə) *n.* a person who breaks the law. —'**law,breaking** *n., adj.*

lawful ('lɔːful) *adj.* allowed, recognized, or sanctioned by law; legal. —'**lawfully** *adv.*

lawgiver ('lɔː,gɪvə) *n.* **1.** the giver of a code of laws. **2.** Also called: **lawmaker.** a maker of laws. —'**law,giving** *n., adj.*

lawless ('lɔːlɪs) *adj.* **1.** breaking the law, esp. in a wild or violent way: *lawless violence.* **2.** not having laws. —'**lawlessness** *n.*

Law Lords *pl. n.* members of the House of Lords who sit as the highest court of appeal.

lawn[1] (lɔːn) *n.* a flat area of mown grass. [Old French *lande*]

lawn[2] (lɔːn) *n.* a fine linen or cotton fabric.

[prob. from *Laon*, town in France where made]

lawn mower *n.* a hand-operated or power-operated machine for cutting grass on lawns.

lawn tennis *n.* **1.** tennis played on a grass court. **2.** same as **tennis**.

lawrencium (lɒ'rɛnsɪəm) *n.* an element artificially produced from californium. Symbol: Lr [after Ernest O. *Lawrence*, physicist]

lawsuit ('lɔːˌsuːt) *n.* a proceeding in a court of law brought by one party against another.

lawyer ('lɔːjə, 'lɔɪə) *n.* a member of the legal profession, esp. a solicitor.

lax (læks) *adj.* lacking firmness; not strict. [Latin *laxus* loose] — **laxity** *n.*

laxative ('læksətɪv) *n.* **1.** a medicine that eases the emptying of the bowels. ~*adj.* **2.** easing the emptying of the bowels. [Latin *laxāre* to loosen]

lay[1] (leɪ) *vb.* **laying, laid. 1.** to put in a low or horizontal position; cause to lie: *to lay a cover on a bed.* **2.** to place, put, or be in a particular state or position: *he laid his finger on his lips.* **3.** to establish as a basis: *to lay a foundation for discussion.* **4.** to place in position: *to lay a carpet.* **5.** to arrange (a table) for a meal. **6.** to prepare (a fire) by arranging fuel in the grate. **7.** (of birds, esp. the domestic hen) to produce (eggs). **8.** to put forward: *he laid his case before the magistrate.* **9.** to attribute: *all the blame was laid on him.* **10.** to arrange, devise, or prepare: *to lay a trap.* **11.** to make (a bet) with (someone): *I lay you five to one on Prince.* **12.** *Taboo slang.* to have sexual intercourse with. **13. lay bare.** to reveal or explain: *he laid bare his plans.* **14. lay hold of.** to seize or grasp. **15. lay oneself open.** to make oneself vulnerable (to criticism or attack). **16. lay open.** to reveal or disclose. ~*n.* **17.** the manner or position in which something lies or is placed. **18.** *Taboo slang.* **a.** an act of sexual intercourse. **b.** a sexual partner. ~See also **lay aside, lay down,** etc. [Old English *lecgan*]

lay[2] (leɪ) *vb.* the past tense of **lie**[2].

lay[3] (leɪ) *adj.* **1.** of or involving people who are not clergymen. **2.** nonprofessional or nonspecialist. [Greek *laos* people]

lay[4] (leɪ) *n.* a short narrative poem, esp. one intended to be sung. [Old French *lai*]

layabout ('leɪəˌbaʊt) *n.* a lazy person; loafer.

lay aside *vb.* **1.** to store or reserve for future use. **2.** to abandon or reject.

lay-by *n. Brit.* a place for drivers to stop at the side of a main road.

lay down *vb.* **1.** to place on the ground or a surface. **2.** to sacrifice: *to lay down one's life.* **3.** to formulate (a rule or principle). **4.** to record (plans) on paper. **5.** to store or stock: *to lay down wine.*

layer ('leɪə) *n.* **1.** a single thickness of some substance, such as a stratum or a coating on a surface. **2.** a laying hen. **3.** *Horticulture.* a shoot or branch that forms its own root while still attached to the

parent plant. ~*vb.* **4.** to form or make a layer of (something). **5.** to take root or cause to take root as a layer. [from LAY[1]]

layette (leɪ'ɛt) *n.* a complete set of clothing, bedclothes, and other accessories for a newborn baby. [Middle Dutch *laege* box]

lay figure *n.* **1.** an artist's jointed dummy, used esp. for studying effects of drapery. **2.** a person considered to be subservient or unimportant. [Dutch *leeman*, lit.: joint-man]

lay in *vb.* to accumulate and store: *we must lay in food for the party.*

lay into *vb. Informal.* to attack or scold (someone) severely.

layman ('leɪmən) *or (fem.)* **laywoman** *n., pl.* **-men** *or* **-women. 1.** a person who is not a clergyman. **2.** a person who does not have specialized knowledge of a subject: *science for the layman.*

lay off *vb.* **1.** to suspend (an employee) from work with the intention of re-employing later. **2.** *Informal.* to leave (a person, thing, or activity) alone: *lay off me, will you!* ~*n.* **lay-off. 3.** a period of imposed unemployment.

lay on *vb.* **1.** to provide or supply: *to lay on entertainment.* **2. lay it on thick.** *Slang.* to exaggerate, esp. when flattering.

lay out *vb.* **1.** to arrange or spread out. **2.** to prepare (a corpse) for burial. **3.** to plan or design: *to lay out a garden.* **4.** *Informal.* to spend (money), esp. lavishly. **5.** *Informal.* to knock (someone) unconscious. ~*n.* **layout. 6.** the arrangement or plan of something, such as a building. **7.** the arrangement of written material and photographs in a book, newspaper, or magazine.

lay reader *n.* **1.** *Church of England.* a person licensed to conduct religious services other than the Eucharist. **2.** *R.C. Church.* a layman chosen to read the epistle at Mass.

lay up *vb.* **1.** to store or reserve for future use. **2.** *Informal.* to confine through illness: *laid up with a bad cold.*

laze (leɪz) *vb.* **1.** to be idle or lazy. **2.** (often foll. by *away*) to spend (time) in idleness. ~*n.* **3.** the act or an instance of idling. [from *lazy*]

lazy ('leɪzɪ) *adj.* **lazier, laziest. 1.** not inclined to work or exert oneself. **2.** encouraging or causing inactivity. **3.** moving in a sluggish manner: *a lazy river.* [origin unknown] — **lazily** *adv.* — **laziness** *n.*

lazybones ('leɪzɪˌbəʊnz) *n. Informal.* a lazy person.

lb pound (weight). [Latin *libra*]

lbw *Cricket.* leg before wicket.

lc 1. in the place cited. [Latin *loco citato*] **2.** *Printing.* lower case.

LCD 1. liquid crystal display. **2.** Also: **lcd.** lowest common denominator.

lcm *or* **LCM** lowest common multiple.

lea (liː) *n.* **1.** *Poetic.* a meadow or field. **2.** grassland. [Old English *lēah*]

LEA Local Education Authority.

leach (liːtʃ) *vb.* **1.** to remove or be removed from a substance by a liquid passing through it. **2.** to lose soluble substances by the action of a liquid passing through. [possibly Old English *leccan* to water]

lead[1] (liːd) *vb.* **leading, led. 1.** to show the way to (an individual or a group) by going with or ahead: *lead the party into the garden.* **2.** to guide or be guided by holding or pulling: *he led the horse by its reins.* **3.** to cause to act, feel, think, or behave in a certain way: *he led me to believe that he would go.* **4.** (of a road, route, or way) to serve as the means of reaching a place. **5.** to guide, control, or direct: *to lead an army.* **6.** to direct the course of (water, a rope, or wire) along or as if along a channel. **7.** to have the principal part in (something): *to lead a discussion.* **8.** to go at the head of or have the top position in (something): *he leads his class in geography.* **9.** (foll. by *with*) to have as the most important item: *the newspaper led with the royal birth.* **10.** *Music, Brit.* to play first violin in (an orchestra). **11.** to pass or spend: *I lead a miserable life.* **12.** to begin a round of cards by putting down (the first card). ~*n.* **13.** the first, foremost, or most prominent place. **14.** example or leadership: *the class followed the teacher's lead.* **15.** an advantage over others: *the runner had a lead of twenty yards.* **16.** an indication; clue: *the police are following up several leads.* **17.** a leash. **18.** the act of playing the first card in a round of cards or the card so played. **19.** the principal role in a play, film, or other production, or the person playing such a role. **20.** the most important news story in a newspaper: *the scandal was the lead in the papers.* **21.** a wire, cable, or other conductor for making an electrical connection. ~*adj.* **22.** acting as a leader or lead: *lead singer.* ~See also **lead off, lead on,** etc. [Old English *lǣdan*]

lead[2] (led) *n.* **1.** a heavy toxic bluish-white metallic element: used in alloys, cable sheaths, paints, and as a radiation shield. Symbol: Pb **2. a.** graphite used for drawing. **b.** a thin stick of this as the core of a pencil. **3.** a lead weight suspended on a line, used to take soundings of the depth of water. **4.** lead weights or shot, as used in cartridges or fishing lines. **5.** a thin strip of lead for holding small panes of glass or pieces of stained glass. **6.** (*pl.*) **a.** thin sheets or strips of lead used as a roof covering. **b.** a roof covered with such sheets. **7.** Also called: **leading.** *Printing.* a thin strip of type metal, used esp. formerly for spacing between lines. ~*adj.* **8.** of, relating to, or containing lead. ~*vb.* **9.** to surround, cover, or secure with lead or leads. [Old English]

leaden ('led'n) *adj.* **1.** heavy or sluggish: *leaden steps.* **2.** gloomy, spiritless, or lifeless. **3.** made of lead. **4.** of a dull greyish colour: *a leaden sky.*

leader ('liːdə) *n.* **1.** a person who rules, guides, or inspires others; head. **2.** *Music.* the principal first violinist of an orchestra who acts as the conductor's deputy. **3.** the leading horse or dog in a team. **4.** *Chiefly Brit.* the leading editorial in a newspaper. Also: **leading article. 5.** a strip of blank film or tape at the beginning of a reel. **6.** *Bot.* any of the long slender shoots that grow from the stem or branch of a tree. —'**leader,ship** *n.*

lead-in ('liːd,ɪn) *n.* an introduction to a subject.

leading ('liːdɪŋ) *adj.* **1.** principal or primary: *the leading role.* **2.** in the first position: *the leading car.*

leading aircraftman *n. Brit. Air Force.* the rank above aircraftman. —**leading aircraftwoman** *fem. n.*

leading light *n.* an important or outstanding person in an organization or campaign.

leading note *n. Music.* same as **subtonic.**

leading question *n.* a question put in such a way as to suggest the desired answer, such as *What do you think of the horrible effects of pollution?*

lead off (liːd) *vb.* to begin.

lead on (liːd) *vb.* to lure or entice (someone), esp. into trouble or wrongdoing.

lead pencil (led) *n.* a pencil containing a thin stick of a graphite compound.

lead poisoning (led) *n.* acute or chronic poisoning by lead.

lead time (liːd) *n. Manufacturing.* the time between the design of a product and its production.

lead up to (liːd) *vb.* **1.** to act as a preliminary or introduction to. **2.** to approach (a topic) gradually or cautiously.

leaf (liːf) *n., pl.* **leaves** (liːvz). **1.** one of the flat usually green blades attached to the stem of a plant. **2.** leaves collectively. **3. in leaf.** (of shrubs or trees) having a full complement of leaves. **4.** one of the sheets of paper in a book. **5.** a hinged, sliding, or detachable part, such as an extension to a table. **6. take a leaf out of** (or **from**) **someone's book.** to imitate someone in a particular course of action. **7. turn over a new leaf.** to begin a new and improved course of behaviour. ~*vb.* **8.** (usually foll. by *through*) to turn (pages) casually or hurriedly. **9.** (of plants) to produce leaves. [Old English] —'**leafless** *adj.*

leafage ('liːfɪdʒ) *n.* the leaves of plants.

leaflet ('liːflɪt) *n.* **1.** a printed and usually folded sheet of paper for distribution, usually free, for advertising or information. **2.** one of the divisions of a compound leaf. **3.** any small leaf. ~*vb.* **4.** to distribute leaflets (to).

leaf mould *n.* a rich soil consisting of decayed leaves.

leafy ('liːfɪ) *adj.* **leafier, leafiest. 1.** covered with leaves. **2.** resembling a leaf or leaves.

league[1] (liːg) *n.* **1.** an association of people or nations formed to promote the interests of its members. **2.** an association of sporting clubs that organizes matches between member teams. **3.** a class, category, or level: *he is not in the same league.* **4. in league (with).** working or planning together with. ~*vb.* **leaguing, leagued. 5.** to form or be formed into a league. [Latin *ligāre* to bind]

league[2] (liːg) *n.* an obsolete unit of distance of varying length: commonly equal to 3 miles. [Late Latin *leuga, leuca*]

leak (liːk) *n.* **1. a.** a crack or hole that allows the accidental escape or entrance as of fluid or light. **b.** such escaping or entering fluid or light. **2.** the loss of current from an electrical conductor because of faulty insulation. **3.** a disclosure of secret information. **4.** the act or an instance of leaking. **5.** *Slang.* urination. ~*vb.* **6.** to enter or escape or allow to enter or escape through a crack or hole. **7.** to disclose (secret information) or (of secret information) to be disclosed. [Old Norse] —**'leaky** *adj.*

leakage ('liːkɪdʒ) *n.* **1.** the act or an instance of leaking. **2.** something that escapes or enters by a leak.

lean[1] (liːn) *vb.* **leaning; leant** *or* **leaned.** **1.** (foll. by *against, on,* or *upon*) to rest or cause to rest against a support. **2.** to bend or cause to bend from an upright position. **3.** (foll. by *to* or *towards*) to have or express a tendency or preference. ~*n.* **4.** the condition of bending from an upright position. ~See also **lean on.** [Old English *hleonian, hlinian*]

lean[2] (liːn) *adj.* **1.** (esp. of a person) having no surplus flesh or bulk. **2.** (of meat) having little or no fat. **3.** (of a period) sparse, difficult, or causing hardship: *the lean years.* ~*n.* **4.** the part of meat that contains little or no fat. [Old English *hlǣne*] —**'leanness** *n.*

leaning ('liːnɪŋ) *n.* a tendency or inclination.

lean on *vb.* **1.** *Informal.* to put pressure on (someone) as by threats. **2.** to depend on (someone) for help and advice.

leant (lɛnt) *vb.* past of **lean**[1].

lean-to *n., pl.* -**tos.** a building with a sloping roof attached to another building or a wall.

leap (liːp) *vb.* **leaping; leapt** (lɛpt) *or* **leaped.** **1.** to jump suddenly from one place to another. **2.** (often foll. by *at*) to move or react quickly. **3.** to jump over. ~*n.* **4.** the act of jumping. **5.** an abrupt change or increase: *a leap in costs.* **6. a leap in the dark.** an action performed without knowledge of the consequences. **7. by leaps and bounds.** with unexpectedly rapid progress. [Old English *hlēapan*]

leapfrog ('liːp,frɒg) *n.* **1.** a children's game in which each player in turn leaps over the others' bent backs. ~*vb.* -**frogging, -frogged. 2. a.** to play leapfrog. **b.** to leap over (something). **3.** to advance by jumps or stages.

leap year *n.* a calendar year of 366 days, February 29 (**leap day**) being the additional day, that occurs every four years.

learn (lɜːn) *vb.* **learning; learnt** (lɜːnt) *or* **learned** (lɜːnd). **1.** to gain knowledge of (something) or acquire skill in (some art or practice). **2.** to memorize (something). **3.** to gain by experience, example, or practice: *she learned how to cope over the years.* **4.** (often foll. by *of* or *about*) to become informed; find out: *his parents learnt of the accident by chance.* [Old English *leornian*] —**'learnable** *adj.* —**'learner** *n.*

learned ('lɜːnɪd) *adj.* **1.** having great knowledge. **2.** involving or characterized by scholarship: *learned journals.*

learning ('lɜːnɪŋ) *n.* knowledge gained by studying.

lease (liːs) *n.* **1.** a contract by which an owner grants the use of buildings or land to another person for a named period, usually for rent. **2.** a prospect of renewed energy, health, or happiness: *a new lease of life.* ~*vb.* **3.** to give or take (land or buildings) by lease. [Old French *laissier* to let go]

leasehold ('liːs,həʊld) *n.* **1.** land or property held under a lease. **2.** the holding of such property under lease. —**'lease,holder** *n.*

leash (liːʃ) *n.* **1.** a length of leather or chain used to walk or control a dog or other animal; lead. **2. straining at the leash.** eagerly impatient to begin something. ~*vb.* **3.** to control as by a leash. [Old French *laissier* to loose (hence, to let a dog run on a leash)]

least (liːst) *det.* **1. the.** the superlative of *little: you have the least talent of anyone.* **2. at least.** if nothing else: *you should at least try.* **3. at the least.** at the minimum: *at the least you should earn a hundred pounds.* **4. not in the least.** not at all: *I don't mind in the least.* ~*adj.* **5. the least.** superlative of **little:** *they travel the least.* ~*adj.* **6.** of very little importance. [Old English *lǣst,* superlative of *lǣssa* less]

leastways ('liːst,weɪz) *or* U.S. & Canad. **leastwise** *adv. Informal.* at least; anyway.

leather ('lɛðə) *n.* **1.** the skin of an animal made smooth and flexible by tanning and removing the hair. ~*adj.* **2.** made of leather. ~*vb.* **3.** to cover with leather. **4.** to whip as with a leather strap. [Old English *lether-* (in compound words)]

leatherjacket ('lɛðə,dʒækɪt) *n.* the tough-skinned larva of certain craneflies, which destroy the roots of grasses.

leathery ('lɛðərɪ) *adj.* having the appearance or texture of leather, esp. in toughness.

leave[1] (liːv) *vb.* **leaving, left. 1.** to go away (from a person or place). **2.** to cause to remain behind, often by mistake, in a place: *he often leaves his keys in his coat.* **3.** to cause to be or remain in a specified state: *paying the bill left him penniless.* **4.** to stop attending or belonging to a particular organization or institution: *to leave a political movement.* **5.** to break off from consuming or doing something: *the things we have left undone.* **6.** to result in; cause: *childhood problems often leave emotional scars.* **7.** to allow (someone) to do something without interfering: *leave the shopping to her.* **8.** to be survived by (members of one's family): *he leaves a wife and two children.* **9.** to bequeath: *he left his investments to his children.* **10.** to have as a remainder: *37−14 leaves 23.* **11. leave (someone) alone. a.** to stop annoying (someone). **b.** to permit to stay or be alone. [Old English *lǣfan*] ~See also **leave off, leave out.**

leave[2] (liːv) *n.* **1.** permission to be absent,

as from work: *leave of absence.* **2.** the duration of such absence: *ten days' leave.* **3.** permission to do something: *he was granted leave to speak.* **4. on leave.** officially excused from work or duty. **5. take (one's) leave (of).** to say farewell (to). [Old English *lēaf*]

leaven ('lɛv°n) *n. also* **leavening.** **1.** any substance, such as yeast, that produces fermentation in dough and causes it to rise. **2.** an influence that produces a gradual change. ~*vb.* **3.** to cause fermentation in (dough). **4.** to spread through, causing a gradual change. [Latin *levāre* to raise]

leave off *vb.* **1.** to stop; cease. **2.** to stop wearing or using.

leave out *vb.* to omit or exclude: *we'll have to leave out the next scene.*

leaves (liːvz) *n.* the plural of **leaf.**

leave-taking *n.* a departing; a farewell.

leavings ('liːvɪŋz) *pl. n.* something remaining, such as food on a plate, residue, or refuse.

Lebensraum ('leɪbənz,raʊm) *n.* territory claimed by a nation or state because it is necessary for survival or growth. [German: living space]

lecherous ('lɛtʃərəs) *adj.* (of a man) having or showing strong and uncontrolled sexual desire. [Old French *lechier* to lick] —'**lecher** *n.* —'**lechery** *n.*

lecithin ('lɛsɪθɪn) *n. Biochem.* a yellow-brown compound found in plant and animal tissues, esp. egg yolk: used in making cosmetics and inks, and as an emulsifier and stabilizer (**E322**) in foods. [Greek *lekithos* egg yolk]

lectern ('lɛktən) *n.* a sloping reading desk, esp. in a church. [Latin *legere* to read]

lecture ('lɛktʃə) *n.* **1.** a talk on a particular subject given or read to an audience. **2.** a lengthy rebuke or scolding. ~*vb.* **3.** to give or read a lecture to an audience or class. **4.** to rebuke (someone) at length. [Latin *legere* to read] —'**lecturer** *n.* —'**lectureship** *n.*

led (lɛd) *vb.* the past of **lead**[1].

LED *Electronics.* light-emitting diode: a semiconductor that gives out light when an electric current is applied to it.

ledge (lɛdʒ) *n.* **1.** a narrow horizontal surface that projects from a wall or window. **2.** a narrow shelflike projection on a cliff or mountain. [possibly Middle English *leggen* to lay]

ledger ('lɛdʒə) *n. Book-keeping.* the principal book in which the commercial transactions of a company are recorded. [possibly Middle English *leggen* to lay (because kept in a specific place)]

ledger line *n. Music.* a short line above or below the staff used to indicate the pitch of notes higher or lower than the range of the staff.

lee (liː) *n.* **1.** a sheltered part or side; the side away from the direction from which the wind is blowing. ~*adj.* **2.** *Naut.* on, at, or towards the side away from the wind: *on a lee shore.* [Old English *hlēow* shelter]

leech (liːtʃ) *n.* **1.** a worm which has a

sucker at each end of the body and feeds on the blood or tissues of other animals. **2.** a person who lives off another person; parasite. [Old English *lǣce, lȳce*]

leek (liːk) *n.* a vegetable of the onion family with a slender white bulb and broad flat overlapping leaves: the national emblem of Wales. [Old Engilsh *lēac*]

leer (lɪə) *vb.* **1.** to give a sneering or suggestive look or grin. ~*n.* **2.** such a look. [Old English *hlēor* cheek]

leery ('lɪərɪ) *adj.* **leerier, leeriest** **1.** *Now chiefly dialect.* knowing or sly. **2.** *Slang.* (foll. by *of*) suspicious or wary. [possibly obs. sense (to look askance) of *leer*]

lees (liːz) *pl. n.* the sediment from an alcoholic drink. [plural of obs. *lee* from Old French]

leet (liːt) *n. Scot.* a list of candidates for an office. [possibly Anglo-French *litte,* var. of LIST[1]]

leeward ('liːwəd; *Naut.* 'luːəd) *Chiefly naut.* ~*adj.* **1.** of, in, or moving to the quarter towards which the wind blows. ~*n.* **2.** the side towards the lee. ~*adv.* **3.** towards the lee.

leeway ('liː,weɪ) *n.* **1.** room for free movement within limits, as in action or expenditure. **2.** sideways drift of a boat or aircraft.

left[1] (lɛft) *adj.* **1.** of or designating the side of something or someone that faces west when the front is turned towards the north. **2.** worn on a left hand or foot. **3.** of or relating to the political left. ~*adv.* **4.** on or in the direction of the left. ~*n.* **5.** a left side, direction, position, area, or part. **6.** (*often cap.*) the people who support the political ideals of socialism rather than capitalism. **7.** *Boxing.* **a.** a blow with the left hand. **b.** the left hand. [Old English *left* idle, weak]

left[2] (lɛft) *vb.* the past of **leave**[1].

left-hand *adj.* **1.** of, on, or towards the left. **2.** for the left hand.

left-handed *adj.* **1.** using the left hand with greater ease than the right. **2.** performed with the left hand. **3.** designed for use by the left hand. **4.** awkward or clumsy. **5.** ambiguous or insincere: *a left-handed compliment.* **6.** turning from right to left; anticlockwise. ~*adv.* **7.** with the left hand. —,**left-'hander** *n.*

leftist ('lɛftɪst) *adj.* **1.** of or relating to the political left or its principles. ~*n.* **2.** a person who supports the political left. —'**leftism** *n.*

left-luggage office *n. Brit.* a place at a railway station or airport where luggage may be left for a small charge.

leftover ('lɛft,əʊvə) *n.* **1.** (*often pl.*) an unused portion, as of material or of cooked food. ~*adj.* **2.** left as an unused portion.

leftward ('lɛftwəd) *adj., adv. also* **leftwards.** on or towards the left.

left wing *n.* **1.** (*often cap.*) the more radical or progressive section, esp. of a political party. **2.** *Sports.* **a.** the left-hand side of the field. **b.** a player positioned in this area in certain games. ~*adj.* **left-**

wing. 3. of, belonging to, or relating to the political left wing. —**left-'winger** n.

lefty ('lɛftɪ) n., pl. **lefties.** Informal. **1.** a left-winger. **2.** Chiefly U.S. & Canad. a left-handed person.

leg (lɛg) n. **1.** either of the two lower limbs in humans, or any similar structure in animals that is used for movement or support. **2.** this part of an animal, used for food: leg of lamb. **3.** something similar to a leg in appearance or function, such as one of the supports of a chair. **4.** a branch of a forked object. **5.** the part of a garment that covers the leg. **6.** a section of a journey. **7.** a single stage, lap, or length in a relay race. **8.** one of a series of games, matches, or parts of games. **9.** Cricket. the side of the field to the left of and behind a right-handed batsman as he faces the bowler. **10. not have a leg to stand on.** Informal. to have no reasonable basis for an opinion or argument. **11. on his, its,** etc., **last legs.** (of a person or thing) worn out; exhausted. **12. pull someone's leg.** Informal. to tease or make fun of someone. **13. shake a leg.** Informal. to hurry up. **14. stretch one's legs.** to stand up or walk around, esp. after sitting for some time. ~vb. **legging, legged. 15. leg it.** Informal. to walk, run, or hurry. [Old Norse leggr]

legacy ('lɛgəsɪ) n., pl. **-cies. 1.** money or personal property left to someone by a will. **2.** something handed down by a predecessor. [Medieval Latin lēgātia commission]

legal ('liːg'l) adj. **1.** established by or founded upon law; lawful. **2.** of or relating to law. **3.** relating to or characteristic of lawyers. [Latin lēgālis, from lēx law] —**'legally** adv.

legal aid n. financial assistance available to people who are unable to meet the full cost of legal proceedings.

legalese (ˌliːgə'liːz) n. the conventional language in which legal documents are written.

legalism ('liːgəˌlɪzəm) n. strict adherence to the letter of the law. —**'legalist** n., adj. —ˌlegal'istic adj.

legality (lɪ'gælɪtɪ) n., pl. **-ties.** the state or quality of being legal or lawful.

legalize or **-ise** ('liːgəˌlaɪz) vb. to make lawful or legal. —ˌlegali'zation or -i'sation n.

legal tender n. currency that a creditor must by law accept to pay a debt.

legate ('lɛgɪt) n. a messenger, esp. one representing the Pope. [Latin lēgāre to delegate]

legation (lɪ'geɪʃən) n. **1.** a diplomatic mission headed by a minister. **2.** the official residence and office of a diplomatic minister.

legato (lɪ'gɑːtəʊ) Music. ~adv. **1.** smoothly and evenly. ~n., pl. **-tos. 2.** a style of playing with no gaps between notes. [Italian]

leg before wicket n. Cricket. a dismissal on the grounds that a batsman has been struck on the leg by a bowled ball that

otherwise would have hit the wicket. Abbrev.: **lbw.**

legend ('lɛdʒənd) n. **1.** a popular story handed down from earlier times which may or may not be true. **2.** such stories collectively. **3.** modern stories about a famous person which may or may not be true: the Monroe legend. **4.** a person whose fame makes him seem exceptional: a legend in his own lifetime. **5.** an inscription, as on a coin or beneath a coat of arms. **6.** an explanation on a table, map, or chart, of the symbols used. [Medieval Latin legenda passages to be read, from Latin legere to read]

legendary ('lɛdʒəndrɪ) adj. **1.** of or relating to legend. **2.** celebrated or described in legend: legendary knights of long ago. **3.** very famous: legendary skill.

legerdemain (ˌlɛdʒədə'meɪn) n. **1.** same as **sleight of hand. 2.** cunning deception. [Old French: light of hand]

leger line ('lɛdʒə) n. same as **ledger line.**

leggings ('lɛgɪŋz) pl. n. **1.** an extra outer covering for the lower legs. **2.** close-fitting trousers for women or children.

leggy ('lɛgɪ) adj. **1.** having unusually long legs. **2.** (of a plant) having a long weak stem.

leghorn ('lɛgˌhɔːn) n. **1.** a type of Italian wheat straw that is woven into hats. **2.** any hat made from this straw. [English name for Livorno, in W central Italy]

Leghorn (lɛ'gɔːn) n. a breed of domestic fowl.

legible ('lɛdʒəb'l) adj. (of handwriting) able to be read. [Latin legere to read] —ˌlegi'bility n. —'legibly adv.

legion ('liːdʒən) n. **1.** a unit in the ancient Roman army of infantry with supporting cavalry of three to six thousand men. **2.** any large military force: the French Foreign Legion. **3.** (often pl.) any very large number. [Latin legere to choose] —**'legionary** adj., n.

legionnaire (ˌliːdʒə'nɛə) n. (often cap.) a member of a legion.

Legionnaire's disease (ˌliːdʒə'nɛəz) n. a serious bacterial infection, with symptoms similar to pneumonia. [after the outbreak at a meeting of the American Legion in Philadelphia in 1976]

legislate ('lɛdʒɪsˌleɪt) vb. **1.** to make or pass laws. **2.** to bring into effect by legislation. [Latin lēx, lēgis law + latus past participle of ferre to bring] —**'legisˌlator** n.

legislation (ˌlɛdʒɪs'leɪʃən) n. **1.** the act or process of making laws. **2.** the laws so made.

legislative ('lɛdʒɪslətɪv) adj. **1.** of or relating to legislation or a legislature. **2.** having the power or function of legislating: a legislative assembly.

legislature ('lɛdʒɪsˌleɪtʃə) n. a body of persons empowered to make and repeal laws.

legitimate adj. (lɪ'dʒɪtɪmɪt). **1.** authorized by or in accordance with law: legitimate business. **2** based on correct or acceptable principles of reasoning: a legiti-

mate argument. **3.** (of a child) born of parents legally married to each other. **4.** of, relating to, or ruling by hereditary right: *a legitimate monarch.* **5.** of or relating to serious drama as distinct from films, television, or vaudeville. ~*vb.* (lɪ'dʒɪtɪ,meɪt). **6.** to make, pronounce, or show to be legitimate. [Medieval Latin *légitimātus* made legal] —**le'gitimacy** *n.* —**le'git-imately** *adv.*

legitimize *or* **-mise** (lɪ'dʒɪtɪ,maɪz) *vb.* to make (something) legitimate; legalize. —**le-,gitimi'zation** *or* **-mi'sation** *n.*

Lego ('lɛgəʊ) *n. Trademark.* a construction toy consisting of plastic bricks that fit together with studs. [Danish *leg godt* play well]

leg-pull *n. Brit. informal.* a practical joke.

legroom ('lɛg,ruːm) *n.* room to move one's legs comfortably, as in a car.

leguaan ('lɛgʊ,ɑːn) *n.* a large amphibious S African lizard. [Dutch *leguaan*]

legume ('lɛgjuːm, lɪ'gjuːm) *n.* **1.** the fruit of leguminous plants; a pod. **2.** any of various table vegetables, esp. beans or peas. [Latin *legere* to pick (a crop)]

leguminous (lɪ'gjuːmɪnəs) *adj.* of or relating to any family of flowering plants having pods (or legumes) as fruits.

lei (leɪ) *n.* (in Hawaii) a garland of flowers, worn around the neck. [Hawaiian]

Leics Leicestershire.

leisure ('lɛʒə) *n.* **1.** time or opportunity for ease, relaxation, or hobbies. **2. at leisure. a.** having free time. **b.** not occupied. **c.** without hurrying. **3. at one's leisure.** when one has free time. [Old French, from Latin *licēre* to be allowed] —**'leisured** *adj.*

leisure centre *n.* a building providing facilities, such as a swimming pool, gym, and café, for a range of leisure pursuits.

leisurely ('lɛʒəlɪ) *adj.* **1.** unhurried; relaxed. ~*adv.* **2.** in a relaxed way. —**'leisureliness** *n.*

leitmotiv *or* **leitmotif** ('laɪtməʊ,tiːf) *n.* **1.** *Music.* a recurring melodic phrase used to suggest a character, thing, or idea. **2.** an often repeated image in a literary work. [German: leading motif]

lekker ('lɛkə) *adj. S. African slang.* pleasing, enjoyable, or likable. [Afrikaans]

lemming ('lɛmɪŋ) *n.* **1.** a small rodent of northern and arctic regions, noted for rushing into the sea in large groups and drowning. **2.** a member of any group following an unthinking course towards destruction. [Norwegian]

lemon ('lɛmən) *n.* **1.** a yellow oval edible fruit with juicy acidic flesh that grows on an evergreen tree in warm and tropical regions. **2.** a pale yellow colour. **3.** *Slang.* a person or thing considered to be useless or defective. [Arabic *laymūn*] —**'lemony** *adj.*

lemonade (,lɛmə'neɪd) *n.* a drink made from lemon juice, sugar, and water or from carbonated water, citric acid, and sweetener.

lemon sole *n.* a European flatfish valued as food.

lemon squash *n. Brit.* a drink made from a sweetened lemon concentrate and water.

lemur ('liːmə) *n.* an animal of Madagascar, related to the monkeys, with a foxy face and long tail, that lives in trees and is active at night. [Latin *lemurēs* ghosts]

lend (lɛnd) *vb.* **lending, lent. 1.** to permit the use of (something) on the condition that it is returned. **2.** to provide (money) temporarily, often at interest. **3.** to contribute (something, esp. some abstract quality): *her presence lent beauty.* **4. lend an ear.** to listen. **5. lend oneself** *or* **itself.** to be appropriate for: *the novel lends itself to serialization.* [Old English *lǣn* loan] —**'lender** *n.*

length (lɛŋθ) *n.* **1.** the extent or measurement of something from end to end. **2.** a specified distance, esp. between two positions: *the length of a race.* **3.** a period of time, as between specified limits or moments. **4.** a piece of something narrow and long: *a length of tubing.* **5.** the quality, state, or fact of being long rather than short. **6.** *(usually pl.)* the amount of trouble taken in doing something: *to go to great length.* **7.** *Prosody, phonetics.* the duration of a vowel or syllable. **8. at length. a.** after a long interval or period of time. **b.** in great detail. [Old English *lengthu*]

lengthen ('lɛŋθən) *vb.* to make or become longer.

lengthways ('lɛŋθ,weɪz) *or* **lengthwise** ('lɛŋθ,waɪz) *adv., adj.* in, according to, or along the direction of length.

lengthy ('lɛŋθɪ) *adj.* **lengthier, lengthiest.** very long or tiresome. —**'lengthily** *adv.* —**'lengthiness** *n.*

lenient ('liːnɪənt) *adj.* tolerant, not strict or severe. [Latin *lēnis* soft] —**'leniency** *n.* —**'leniently** *adv.*

lenity ('lɛnɪtɪ) *n., pl.* **-ties.** the state or quality of being lenient.

lens (lɛnz) *n.* **1.** a piece of glass or other transparent material with a curved surface or surfaces, used to bring together or spread rays of light passing through it: used in cameras, telescopes, and spectacles. **2.** *Anat.* a transparent structure in the eye, behind the iris, that focuses images on the retina. [Latin *lēns* lentil]

lent (lɛnt) *vb.* the past of **lend.**

Lent (lɛnt) *n. Christianity.* the period from Ash Wednesday to Easter Saturday, observed as a time of penance and fasting. [Old English *lencten, lengten* spring, lit.: lengthening (of hours of daylight)] —**'Lenten** *adj.*

lentil ('lɛntɪl) *n.* any of the small seeds of a leguminous Asian plant, which are cooked and eaten in soups and vegetable dishes. [Latin *lēns* lentil]

lento ('lɛntəʊ) *Music.* ~*adv.* **1.** slowly. ~*n., pl.* **-tos. 2.** a movement or passage performed slowly. [Italian]

Leo ('liːəʊ) *n. Astrol.* the fifth sign of the zodiac: the Lion.

leonine ('liːə,naɪn) *adj.* of or like a lion. [Latin *leō* lion]

leopard ('lɛpəd) *n.* a large African and

Asian mammal of the cat family, usually having a tawny yellow coat with black spots. Also called: **panther**. [Greek *leōn* lion + *pardos* pard]

leotard ('liːə,tɑːd) n. a tight-fitting garment covering the body from the shoulders to the thighs and worn by acrobats, ballet dancers, and people doing exercises. [after Jules *Léotard*, acrobat]

leper ('lɛpə) n. **1.** a person who has leprosy. **2.** a person who is avoided. [Greek *lepros* scaly]

lepidopteran (,lɛpɪ'dɒptərən) n., pl. **-terans** or **-tera** (-tərə). **1.** any of a large order of insects, including the butterflies and moths, typically having two pairs of wings covered with fragile scales. ~adj. also **lepidopterous**. **2.** of this order. [Greek *lepis* scale + *pteron* wing]

lepidopterist (,lɛpɪ'dɒptərɪst) n. a person who studies or collects moths and butterflies.

leprechaun ('lɛprə,kɔːn) n. (in Irish folklore) a mischievous elf. [Irish Gaelic *leipreachān*]

leprosy ('lɛprəsɪ) n. Pathol. a chronic infectious disease, characterized by painful inflamed lumps beneath the skin and disfigurement and wasting of affected parts. —**leprous** adj.

lepton ('lɛptɒn) n. Physics. any of a group of elementary particles with weak interactions. [Greek *leptos* thin]

lesbian ('lɛzbɪən) n. **1.** a female homosexual. ~adj. **2.** of or characteristic of lesbians. [*Lesbos*, Greek Aegean island] —**lesbianism** n.

lese-majesty ('liːz'mædʒɪstɪ) n. **1.** an offence against the sovereign power in a state; treason. **2.** a slight against authority or position. [from Latin *laesa mājestās* wounded majesty]

lesion ('liːʒən) n. **1.** any structural change in an organ or tissue resulting from injury or disease. **2.** an injury or wound. [Late Latin *laesiō* injury]

less (lɛs) det. **1.** the comparative of **little** (sense 1): *less sugar; less spirit than before*. **2.** *Not universally accepted.* fewer. **3.** (usually preceded by *no*) lower in rank or importance: *no less a man than the president*. **4. less of.** to a smaller extent or degree: *we see less of John these days*. ~adv. **5.** the comparative of **a little**: *she walks less than she should*. ~prep. **6.** subtracting; minus: *three weeks less a day*. [Old English *lǣssa* (adj.), *lǣs* (adv., n.)]

lessee (lɛ'siː) n. a person to whom a lease is granted. [Old French *lesser* to lease]

lessen ('lɛs°n) vb. to make or become less.

lesser ('lɛsə) adj. not as great in quantity, size, or worth.

lesson ('lɛs°n) n. **1. a.** a unit, or single period of instruction in a subject; class. **b.** the content of such a unit. **2.** material assigned for individual study. **3.** something from which useful knowledge or principles can be learned; example: *his patience is a lesson to us all*. **4.** an experience that serves as a warning or example: *let that be a lesson to you*. **5.** a passage of

Scripture read aloud from the Bible during a church service. [Latin *lēctiō*, from *legere* to read]

lessor ('lɛsɔː, lɛ'sɔː) n. a person who grants a lease of property.

lest (lɛst) conj. **1.** so as to prevent any possibility that: *keep down lest anyone see us*. **2.** in case: *he was alarmed lest she should find out*. [Old English *lǣste*]

let¹ (lɛt) vb. **letting, let. 1.** to allow: *she lets him roam around*. **2.** used as an auxiliary to express: **a.** a request, proposal, or command, or to convey a warning or threat: *let's get on; just let me catch you here again!* **b.** an assumption or hypothesis: *let "a" equal "b"*. **c.** resigned acceptance of the inevitable: *let the worst happen*. **3.** to allow someone to rent (property or accommodation). **4.** to allow or cause the movement of (something) in a specified direction: *to let air out of a tyre*. **5. let alone.** not to mention: *I can't afford wine, let alone champagne*. **6. let alone** or **be.** stop annoying or interfering with: *let the poor cat alone*. **7. let go.** to relax one's hold (on). **8. let loose.** to allow (a person or animal) to leave or escape. ~n. **9.** Brit. the act of letting property or accommodation. ~See also **let down, let off**, etc. [Old English *lǣtan* to permit]

let² (lɛt) n. **1.** Tennis, squash, etc. a minor infringement or obstruction of the ball, requiring a point to be replayed. **2. without let or hindrance.** without obstruction. [Old English *lettan* to hinder]

let down vb. **1.** to fail to satisfy the expectations of (someone); disappoint. **2.** to lower. **3.** to shorten (the hem) so as to lengthen (a dress, skirt, or trousers). **4.** to deflate: *to let down a tyre*. ~n. **letdown. 5.** a disappointment.

lethal ('liːθəl) adj. able to cause or causing death. [Latin *lētum* death] —**lethally** adv.

lethargy ('lɛθədʒɪ) n., pl. **-gies. 1.** sluggishness or dullness. **2.** an abnormal lack of energy. [Greek *lēthargos* drowsy] —**lethargic** (lɪ'θɑːdʒɪk) adj. —**lethargically** adv.

let off vb. **1.** to excuse from (work or other responsibilities): *I'll let you off homework for a week*. **2.** Informal. to allow to get away without or with less than the expected punishment: *I'll let you off with a warning this time*. **3.** to explode or fire (a bomb, gun, or firework). **4.** to release (liquid, air, or steam).

let on vb. Informal. **1.** to allow (something, such as a secret) to be known; reveal. **2.** to pretend: *she let on she didn't know me*.

let out vb. **1.** to emit: *to let out a howl*. **2.** to allow to leave; release. **3.** to reveal (a secret). **4.** to make (property) available for people to rent. **5.** to make (a garment) larger, as by reducing the seams. ~n. **let-out. 6.** a chance to escape.

letter ('lɛtə) n. **1.** a written or printed message, usually enclosed in an envelope and sent by post. **2.** any of a set of conventional symbols used in writing or printing a language: character of the alphabet. **3.** the strict meaning of an agreement or document; exact wording: *the letter of the law.* **4. to the letter.** precisely: *I followed her instructions to the letter.* ~*vb.* **5.** to write or mark letters on (a sign). [Latin *littera* letter of the alphabet] —**'lettering** *n.*

letter bomb *n.* an explosive device in an envelope or parcel that explodes when the envelope or parcel is opened.

letter box *n. Chiefly Brit.* **1.** a slot through which letters are delivered to a building. **2.** Also called: **pillar box, postbox.** a public box into which letters and postcards are put for collection.

lettered ('lɛtəd) *adj.* **1.** well educated. **2.** printed or marked with letters.

letterhead ('lɛtə,hɛd) *n.* a sheet of writing paper with the name and address of a person, company, or organization printed at the top.

letter of credit *n.* a letter issued by a bank entitling the bearer to draw money from other banks.

letterpress ('lɛtə,prɛs) *n.* a method of printing in which ink is transferred from raised surfaces to paper by pressure.

letters ('lɛtəz) *n. (functioning as sing. or pl.)* **1.** literary knowledge, ability, or learning: *a man of letters.* **2.** literary culture in general.

letters patent *pl. n.* See **patent** (senses 1, 3).

lettuce ('lɛtɪs) *n.* a plant cultivated in many varieties for its large edible leaves, which are eaten in salads. [Latin *lactūca* milk, because of its milky juice]

let up *vb.* **1.** to diminish or stop. **2.** (foll. by *on*) *Informal.* to be less harsh (towards someone). ~*n.* **let-up. 3.** *Informal.* a lessening.

leucocyte ('luːkə,saɪt) *n.* any of the various large white cells in the blood of vertebrates. [Greek *leukos* white + *kutos* vessel]

leukaemia *or esp. U.S.* **leukemia** (luː-'kiːmɪə) *n.* an acute or chronic disease characterized by overproduction of white blood cells. [Greek *leukos* white + *haima* blood]

levee[1] ('lɛvɪ) *n. U.S.* **1.** an embankment alongside a river, produced naturally or constructed to prevent flooding. **2.** a quay. [French, from Latin *levāre* to raise]

levee[2] ('lɛvɪ, 'lɛveɪ) *n.* a formal reception held by a sovereign just after rising from bed. [French, from Latin *levāre* to raise]

level ('lɛv'l) *adj.* **1.** on a horizontal plane. **2.** having a surface of completely equal height. **3.** being of the same height as something else: *the sunflowers were level with the porch roof.* **4.** equal to or even with (something or someone else): *production will keep level with population growth.* **5.** not inconsistent or irregular: *a level pulse.* **6. one's level best.** the best one can do. ~*vb.* **-elling, -elled** *or U.S.* **-eling, -eled. 7.** (sometimes foll. by *off*) to make (a surface) horizontal, level, or even. **8.** to make (two or more people or things) equal, as in position or status. **9.** to raze to the ground. **10.** to direct (a gaze, accusa-

tion, or criticism) emphatically at someone. **11.** (often foll. by *at*) to aim (a weapon) horizontally. ~*n.* **12.** a horizontal line or plane. **13.** a device, such as a spirit level, for determining whether a surface is horizontal. **14.** position or status in a scale of values: *low-level nuclear waste.* **15.** amount or degree of progress; stage: *primary school level.* **16.** a specified vertical position: *roof level.* **17.** a horizontal line or plane from which measurement of height is based: *sea level.* **18.** a flat even surface or area of land. **19.** a degree or intensity reached on a measurable or notional scale: *noise level.* **20. on the level.** *Informal.* sincere or genuine. [Latin *lībella*, diminutive of *lībra* scales]

level crossing *n. Brit.* a point at which a railway and a road cross.

level-headed *adj.* even-tempered, balanced, and reliable.

lever ('liːvə) *n.* **1.** a rigid bar pivoted about a fulcrum, used to transfer a force to a load and usually to provide a mechanical advantage. **2.** a bar, such as a crowbar, used to move a heavy object or to prise something open. **3.** a means of exerting pressure in order to accomplish something: *industrial action may be threatened as a political lever.* ~*vb.* **4.** to prise or move (an object) with a lever. [Latin *levāre*]

leverage ('liːvərɪdʒ) *n.* **1.** the action of a lever. **2.** the mechanical advantage gained by using a lever. **3.** strategic advantage.

leveret ('lɛvərɪt) *n.* a young hare. [Latin *lepus* hare]

leviathan (lɪ'vaɪəθən) *n.* **1.** *Bible.* a sea monster. **2.** any huge or powerful thing. [Hebrew *liwyāthān*]

Levis ('liːvaɪz) *pl. n. Trademark.* denim jeans.

levitate ('lɛvɪ,teɪt) *vb.* to rise or cause to rise and float in the air, usually by using supernatural powers. [Latin *levis* light] —,**levi'tation** *n.*

levity ('lɛvɪtɪ) *n., pl.* **-ties.** the quality of being light-hearted about serious matters. [Latin *levis* light]

levy ('lɛvɪ) *vb.* **levying, levied. 1.** to impose and collect (a tax, tariff, or fine). **2.** to conscript troops for service. ~*n., pl.* **levies. 3. a.** the act of imposing and collecting a tax, tariff, or fine. **b.** the money so raised. **4.** troops conscripted for service. [Latin *levāre* to raise]

lewd (luːd) *adj.* characterized by or intended to excite crude sexual desire; obscene. [Old English *lǣwde* ignorant]

lexical ('lɛksɪk'l) *adj.* **1.** of or relating to the vocabulary of a language. **2.** of or relating to a lexicon. —**'lexically** *adv.*

lexicography (,lɛksɪ'kɒɡrəfɪ) *n.* the process or profession of writing or compiling dictionaries. —**lexi'cographer** *n.*

lexicon ('lɛksɪkən) *n.* **1.** a dictionary, esp. one of an ancient language such as Greek. **2.** the vocabulary of a language or of an individual. [Greek *lexis* word]

ley (leɪ, liː) *n.* land temporarily under grass. [var. of *lea*]

Leyden jar ('laɪd'n) *n. Physics.* an early

type of capacitor consisting of a glass jar with the lower part of the inside and outside coated with tinfoil. [Leiden (*Leyden*), city in the Netherlands]

Li *Chem.* lithium.

liability (ˌlaɪəˈbɪlɪtɪ) *n., pl.* **-ties. 1.** the state of being liable. **2.** a financial obligation. **3.** a person or thing that is a hindrance or disadvantage.

liable (ˈlaɪəbᵊl) *adj.* **1.** legally obliged or responsible; answerable. **2.** given to or at risk from a condition: *liable to colds.* **3.** *Not universally accepted.* probable or likely: *it's liable to happen soon.* [Old French *lier* to bind, from Latin *ligāre*]

liaise (lɪˈeɪz) *vb.* (usually foll. by *with*) to communicate and maintain contact with.

liaison (lɪˈeɪzɒn) *n.* **1.** communication and contact between groups or units. **2.** a secretive or adulterous sexual relationship. [Old French *lier* to bind, from Latin *ligāre*]

liana (lɪˈɑːnə) *n.* a woody climbing and twining plant of tropical forests. [French]

liar (ˈlaɪə) *n.* a person who tells lies.

lib (lɪb) *n. Informal.* short for **liberation**: used in the name of certain movements: *women's lib; gay lib.*

Lib. Liberal.

libation (laɪˈbeɪʃən) *n.* **a.** the pouring-out of wine in honour of a deity. **b.** the wine so poured out. [Latin *lībāre* to pour an offering of drink]

libel (ˈlaɪbᵊl) *n.* **1.** *Law.* the publication of something false which damages a person's reputation. **2.** any damaging or unflattering representation or statement. ~*vb.* **-belling, -belled** or *U.S.* **-beling, -beled. 3.** *Law.* to make or publish a false damaging statement or representation about (a person). [Latin *libellus* a little book] —**libellous** or **libelous** *adj.*

liberal (ˈlɪbərəl, ˈlɪbrəl) *adj.* **1.** relating to or having social and political views that favour progress and reform. **2.** giving and generous in temperament or behaviour. **3.** tolerant of other people. **4.** abundant; lavish: *a liberal helping of cream.* **5.** not strict; free: *a liberal translation.* **6.** (of an education) designed to develop general cultural interests and intellectual ability. ~*n.* **7.** a person who has liberal ideas or opinions. [Latin *līber* free] —**liberalism** *n.* —**liberally** *adv.*

Liberal (ˈlɪbərəl, ˈlɪbrəl) *n.* **1.** a member or supporter of a political party that favours progress and reform. ~*adj.* **2.** of or relating to such a party.

liberality (ˌlɪbəˈrælɪtɪ) *n., pl.* **-ties. 1.** generosity; bounty. **2.** the quality or condition of being broad-minded.

liberalize or **-ise** (ˈlɪbərəˌlaɪz, ˈlɪbrə-) *vb.* to make or become liberal. —**liberalization** or **-isation** *n.*

liberate (ˈlɪbəˌreɪt) *vb.* **1.** to free (someone) from social prejudices or injustices. **2.** to give liberty to; make free. **3.** to release (a country) from enemy occupation. —**liberation** *n.* —**liberator** *n.*

liberated (ˈlɪbəˌreɪtɪd) *adj.* **1.** not bound by traditional sexual and social roles: *a liberated woman.* **2.** given liberty. **3.** released from enemy occupation.

libertine (ˈlɪbəˌtiːn, -ˌtaɪn) *n.* **1.** a person who is promiscuous and unscrupulous. ~*adj.* **2.** promiscuous and unscrupulous. [Latin *lībertus* freed]

liberty (ˈlɪbətɪ) *n., pl.* **-ties. 1.** the power of choosing, thinking, and acting for oneself; freedom from control or restriction. **2.** the right or privilege of access to a particular place; freedom. **3.** (*often pl.*) a social action regarded as being familiar, forward, or improper. **4. at liberty.** free, unoccupied, or unrestricted. **5. take liberties** (**with**). to be overfamiliar (towards someone). [Latin *lībertās*, from *līber* free]

libidinous (lɪˈbɪdɪnəs) *adj.* characterized by excessive sexual desire. —**li·bidinously** *adv.*

libido (lɪˈbiːdəʊ) *n., pl.* **-dos. 1.** *Psychoanal.* psychic energy from the id. **2.** sexual urge or desire. [Latin: desire] —**libidinal** (lɪˈbɪdɪnᵊl) *adj.*

Libra (ˈliːbrə) *n. Astrol.* the seventh sign of the zodiac. [Latin]

librarian (laɪˈbreərɪən) *n.* a person in charge of or assisting in a library. —**li·brarian,ship** *n.*

library (ˈlaɪbrərɪ) *n., pl.* **-braries. 1.** a room or set of rooms where books and other literary materials are kept. **2.** a collection of literary materials, films, tapes, or gramophone records, kept for borrowing or reference. **3.** the building or institution that houses such a collection. **4.** a set of books published as a series, often in a similar format. **5.** *Computers.* a collection of standard programs, usually stored on disk. [Latin *liber* book]

libretto (lɪˈbretəʊ) *n., pl.* **-tos** or **-ti** (-tiː). a text written for an opera. [Italian: little book] —**li·brettist** *n.*

lice (laɪs) *n.* the plural of **louse.**

licence or *U.S.* **license** (ˈlaɪsəns) *n.* **1.** a document giving official permission to do something. **2.** formal permission or exemption. **3.** intentional disregard of conventional rules to achieve a certain effect: *poetic licence.* **4.** excessive freedom. [Latin *licet* it is allowed]

license (ˈlaɪsəns) *vb.* **1.** to grant or give a licence for (something, such as the sale of alcohol). **2.** to give permission to or for. —**licensable** *adj.*

licensee (ˌlaɪsənˈsiː) *n.* a person who holds a licence, esp. one to sell alcoholic drink.

licentiate (laɪˈsenʃɪɪt) *n.* a person who holds a certificate of competence to practise a certain profession.

licentious (laɪˈsenʃəs) *adj.* sexually unrestrained or promiscuous. [Latin *licentia* licence] —**li·centiousness** *n.*

lichee (ˌlaɪˈtʃiː) *n.* same as **lychee.**

lichen (ˈlaɪkən, ˈlɪtʃən) *n.* any of various small plants which are formed by the association of a fungus and an alga that grow in patches on tree trunks, bare ground, rocks, and stone walls. [Greek *leikhein* to lick]

lich gate or **lych gate** (lɪtʃ) *n.* a roofed

licit ('lɪsɪt) *adj.* lawful; permitted. [Latin *licēre* to be permitted]

lick (lɪk) *vb.* **1.** to pass the tongue over in order to taste, wet, or clean. **2.** to flicker over or round (something): *the flames licked around the door.* **3.** *Informal.* **a.** to defeat. **b.** to thrash. **4. lick into shape.** to put into a satisfactory condition. **5. lick one's wounds.** to retire after a defeat. ~*n.* **6.** an instance of passing the tongue over something. **7.** a small amount: *a lick of paint.* **8.** *Informal.* a hit; blow. **9.** *Informal.* a fast pace: *he was going at quite a lick.* **10. a lick and a promise.** something hastily done, esp. a hurried wash. [Old English *liccian*]

licorice ('lɪkərɪs) *n. U.S. & Canad.* same as **liquorice.**

lid (lɪd) *n.* **1.** a removable or hinged cover: *a saucepan lid.* **2.** short for **eyelid. 3. put the (tin) lid on.** *Informal.* to put an end to. [Old English *hlid*] —**'lidded** *adj.*

lido ('liːdəʊ) *n., pl.* **-dos.** *Brit.* a public place of recreation, including a swimming pool. [*Lido,* island bathing beach near Venice]

lie[1] (laɪ) *vb.* **lying, lied. 1.** to speak untruthfully with intent to mislead or deceive. **2.** to convey a false impression or practise deception: *the camera does not lie.* ~*n.* **3.** an untrue statement deliberately used to mislead. **4.** something that is deliberately intended to deceive. **5. give the lie to.** **a.** to disprove. **b.** to accuse of lying. [Old English *lyge* (n.), *lēogan* (vb.)]

lie[2] (laɪ) *vb.* **lying, lay, lain. 1.** (often foll. by *down*) to place oneself or be in a prostrate position, horizontal to the ground. **2.** to be situated, esp. on a horizontal surface: *the pencil is lying on the desk; India lies to the south of Russia.* **3.** to be and remain (in a particular state or condition): *to lie dormant.* **4.** to stretch or extend: *the city lies before us.* **5.** (usually foll. by *in*) to exist or consist in: *strength lies in unity.* **6.** (foll. by *with*) to be or rest (with): *the ultimate decision lies with you.* ~*n.* **7.** the manner, place, or style in which something is situated. **8.** the hiding place or lair of an animal. **9. lie of the land.** the way in which a situation is developing. ~See also **lie down, lie in.** [Old English *licgan*]

lied (liːd) *n., pl.* **lieder** ('liːdə) *Music.* a musical setting for solo voice and piano of a romantic or lyrical poem. [German: song]

lie detector *n. Informal.* a device used to measure the blood pressure, pulse rate, etc., of someone being questioned, which is thought to increase when the person is lying.

lie down *vb.* **1.** to place oneself or be in a horizontal position in order to rest. **2.** to accept without protest or opposition: *I won't take bureaucratic bullying lying down.* ~*n.* **lie-down.** a rest.

liege (liːdʒ) *adj.* **1.** (of a lord) owed feudal allegiance: *liege lord.* **2.** (of a vassal or servant) owing feudal allegiance: *a liege subject.* **3.** faithful; loyal. ~*n.* **4.** a liege lord. **5.** a subject. [Old French *lige*]

lie in *vb.* **1.** to remain in bed late in the morning. ~*n.* **lie-in. 2.** a long stay in bed in the morning.

lien ('liːən, liːn) *n. Law.* a right to retain possession of another's property until a debt is paid. [Latin *ligāmen* bond]

lieu (ljuː, luː) *n.* **in lieu of.** instead of. [Latin *locus* place]

lieutenant (lefˈtɛnənt; *U.S.* luːˈtɛnənt) *n.* **1.** a junior officer in the army or navy, or in the U.S. police force. **2.** a person who holds an office in subordination to or in place of a superior. [Old French, lit.: place-holding] —**lieuˈtenancy** *n.*

lieutenant colonel *n.* an officer in an army, air force, or marine corps.

lieutenant commander *n.* an officer in a navy.

lieutenant general *n.* a senior officer in an army, air force, or marine corps.

lieutenant governor *n.* **1.** a deputy governor. **2.** (in Canada) the representative of the Crown in a province.

life (laɪf) *n., pl.* **lives** (laɪvz). **1.** the state or quality that distinguishes living beings from dead ones, characterized chiefly by metabolism, growth, and the ability to reproduce and respond to stimuli. **2.** the period between birth and death or between birth and the present time. **3.** a living person or being: *to save a life.* **4.** the remainder or extent of one's life. **5.** *Informal.* a sentence of imprisonment for life, now taken to be approximately fifteen years. **6.** the amount of time that something is active or functioning: *the life of a battery.* **7.** a present condition, state, or mode of existence: *my life is very dull here.* **8.** a biography. **9.** a characteristic state or mode of existence: *town life.* **10.** the sum or course of human events and activities. **11.** liveliness or high spirits: *full of life.* **12.** a source of strength, animation, or vitality: *he was the life of the show.* **13.** all living things, taken as a whole: *there is no life on Mars; plant life.* **14. a matter of life and death.** a matter of extreme urgency. **15. as large as life.** *Informal.* real and living. **16. not on your life.** *Informal.* certainly not. **17. to the life.** (of a copy of a painting or drawing) resembling the original exactly. **18. true to life.** faithful to reality. [Old English *līf*]

life assurance *n.* insurance that provides for a sum of money to be paid to the policyholder at a certain age or to the widow or children on the death of the policyholder. Also called: **life insurance.**

life belt *n.* an inflatable ring used to keep a person afloat when in danger of drowning.

lifeblood ('laɪf,blʌd) *n.* **1.** the blood vital to life. **2.** something that is essential in order to exist, develop, or be successful.

lifeboat ('laɪf,bəʊt) *n.* a boat used for rescuing people at sea or escaping from a sinking ship.

life buoy *n.* a buoyant device for keeping people afloat in an emergency.

gate to a churchyard, formerly used as a temporary shelter for a coffin. [Old English *līc* corpse]

life cycle n. the series of changes occuring in each generation of an animal or plant.

lifeguard ('laɪf,gɑːd) n. a person at a beach or pool to guard people against drowning.

life jacket n. an inflatable sleeveless jacket worn to keep a person afloat when in danger of drowning.

lifeless ('laɪflɪs) adj. 1. inanimate; dead. 2. having no vitality or animation. 3. unconscious.

lifelike ('laɪf,laɪk) adj. closely resembling or representing life.

lifeline ('laɪf,laɪn) n. 1. a rope used for life-saving. 2. a single means of contact, communication, or support on which a person or an area relies.

lifelong ('laɪf,lɒŋ) adj. lasting for or as if for a lifetime.

life peer n. Brit. a peer whose title lapses at his death.

life preserver n. 1. Brit. a bludgeon kept for self-defence. 2. U.S. & Canad. a life belt or life jacket.

lifer ('laɪfə) n. Informal. a prisoner sentenced to imprisonment for life.

life raft n. a raft for emergency use at sea.

life-saver n. 1. same as **lifeguard**. 2. Informal. a person or thing that gives help in time of need. —**'life-,saving** adj., n.

life science n. any of the sciences concerned with the structure and behaviour of living organisms, such as biology, botany, or zoology.

life-size or **life-sized** adj. representing actual size.

lifestyle ('laɪf,staɪl) n. a set of attitudes, habits, and possessions regarded as fashionable and desirable or associated with a particular person or group.

life-support adj. of or providing the equipment to sustain life in an unnatural environment, such as in space, or in severe illness.

lifetime ('laɪf,taɪm) n. the length of time a person is alive.

lift (lɪft) vb. 1. to rise or cause to rise upwards to a higher place: to lift a sack. 2. to move upwards: to lift one's eyes. 3. to raise in status or estimation: his position lifted him from the common crowd. 4. to revoke or cancel: to lift tax restrictions. 5. to take (plants or underground crops) out of the ground for harvesting. 6. to disappear by lifting or as if by lifting: the fog lifted. 7. Informal. to plagiarize (music or a piece of writing). ~n. 8. the act or an instance of lifting. 9. the power or force available or used for lifting. 10. a. Brit. a platform, compartment, or cage raised or lowered in a vertical shaft to transport people or goods to another floor in a building. b. See **chair lift, ski lift**. 11. a ride in a car or other vehicle for part or all of a passenger's journey. 12. a rise in morale or feeling of cheerfulness. 13. aid; help. [Old Norse]

liftoff ('lɪft,ɒf) n. the initial movement of a rocket from its launching pad.

ligament ('lɪgəmənt) n. Anat. a band of tough tissue that connects various bones or cartilages. [Latin ligāre to bind]

ligature ('lɪgətʃə, -,tʃʊə) n. 1. the act of binding or tying up. 2. a link, bond, or tie. 3. Printing. a character of two or more joined letters, such as fi, ffi. 4. Music. a slur or group of notes connected by it. ~vb. 5. to bind with a ligature. [Latin ligāre to bind]

light¹ (laɪt) n. 1. the medium of illumination that makes sight possible. 2. electromagnetic radiation that is capable of causing a visual sensation. 3. anything that illuminates, such as a lamp or candle. 4. See **traffic light**. 5. a particular quality or type of light: a good light for reading. 6. a. daylight. b. daybreak; dawn. 7. anything that lets in light, such as a window. 8. an aspect or view: he saw it in a different light. 9. mental understanding or spiritual insight: suddenly he saw the light. 10. an outstanding person: a leading light of the movement. 11. brightness of countenance, esp. a sparkle in the eyes. 12. a. something that ignites, such as a spark or flame. b. something used for igniting, such as a match. 13. See **lighthouse**. 14. **come to light**. to become known or visible. 15. **in (the) light of**. taking into account. 16. **see the light**. to understand. 17. **see the light (of day)**. a. to come into being. b. to come to public notice. ~adj. 18. full of light; well-lighted. 19. (of a colour) pale; not dark: light blue. ~vb. **lighting, lighted** or **lit**. 20. to ignite. 21. (often foll. by up) to illuminate or cause to illuminate. 22. to guide or lead by light. ~See also **light up**. [Old English lēoht] —**'lightish** adj.

light² (laɪt) adj. 1. not heavy; weighing relatively little. 2. relatively low in density, strength, amount, degree, etc.: light rain; light metal. 3. lacking sufficient weight. 4. without burdens, difficulties, or problems: a light heart. 5. graceful or agile: light fingers. 6. not bulky or clumsy: light weapons. 7. not serious or profound; entertaining: light music. 8. frivolous or capricious. 9. loose in morals. 10. dizzy or unclear: a light head. 11. (of bread or cake) spongy or well leavened. 12. easily digested: a light meal. 13. relatively low in alcohol: a light wine. 14. (of a vessel, lorry, or other transport) a. designed to carry light loads. b. not loaded. 15. carrying light arms or equipment: light infantry. 16. **make light of**. to treat as insignificant or trifling. ~adv. 17. with little equipment or luggage: to travel light. ~vb. **lighting, lighted** or **lit**. 18. (esp. of birds) to settle or land after flight. 19. (foll. by on or upon) to discover by chance. ~See also **lights**. [Old English lēoht] —**'lightish** adj. —**'lightly** adv. —**'lightness** n.

light bulb n. a hollow rounded glass fitting containing a gas and a thin metal filament that gives out light when an electric current is passed through it.

lighten¹ ('laɪt'n) vb. 1. to become or make light. 2. to shine; glow. 3. (of lightning) to flash.

lighten[2] ('lait'n) vb. **1.** to make or become less heavy. **2.** to make or become less burdensome. **3.** to make or become more cheerful or lively.

lighter[1] ('laitə) n. a small portable device for lighting cigarettes, etc.

lighter[2] ('laitə) n. a flat-bottomed barge used in loading or unloading a ship. [probably from Middle Dutch]

light-fingered adj. skilful at thieving, esp. by picking pockets.

light flyweight n. **1.** an amateur boxer weighing not more than 48 kg. **2.** an amateur wrestler weighing not more than 48 kg.

light-footed adj. having a light tread.

light-headed adj. **1.** giddy; feeling faint or slightly delirious. **2.** frivolous.

light-hearted adj. cheerful or carefree in mood or disposition. —**light-'heartedly** adv.

light heavyweight n. **1. a.** a professional boxer weighing 160–175 pounds. **b.** an amateur boxer weighing 75–81 kg. **2. a.** a professional wrestler weighing not more than 198 pounds. **b.** an amateur wrestler weighing not more than 90 kg.

lighthouse ('lait,haus) n. a tower with a light to guide and warn ships of obstructions.

lighting ('laitiŋ) n. **1.** the act or quality of illumination. **2.** the apparatus for and design of artificial light effects to a stage, film, or television set.

lighting-up time n. the time when vehicles are required by law to have their lights on.

light middleweight n. an amateur boxer weighing 67–71 kg.

lightning ('laitniŋ) n. **1.** a flash of light in the sky caused by a discharge of electricity. **2.** (modifier) fast and sudden: a lightning raid. [var. of lightening]

lightning conductor or **rod** n. a metal strip attached to the highest part of a building to provide a safe path to earth for lightning discharges.

light pen n. a penlike photoelectric device that in conjunction with a computer can be used to draw lines or identify symbols on a VDU screen.

lights (laits) pl. n. the lungs of sheep, bullocks, and pigs, used for feeding pets. [because of the light weight of the lungs]

lightship ('lait,ʃip) n. a moored ship equipped as a lighthouse.

lights out n. the time when those resident at an institution, such as soldiers in barracks, are expected to retire to bed.

light up vb. **1.** to illuminate. **2.** to make or become cheerful or animated: her face lit up when they arrived. **3.** to light a cigarette or pipe.

lightweight ('lait,weit) adj. **1.** of relatively light weight. **2.** not serious. ~n. **3.** a person or animal of relatively light weight. **4. a.** a professional boxer weighing 130–135 pounds. **b.** an amateur boxer weighing 57–60 kg. **5. a.** a professional wrestler weighing not more than 154

pounds. **b.** an amateur wrestler weighing not more than 68 kg. **6.** Informal. a person of little importance or influence.

light welterweight n. an amateur boxer weighing 60–63.5 kg.

light year n. Astron. the distance travelled by light in one mean solar year, i.e. 9.4607×10^{15} metres.

ligneous ('lignias) adj. of or resembling wood. [Latin lignum wood]

lignite ('lignait) n. a brown sedimentary rock with woody texture: used as a fuel.

lignum vitae ('lignam 'vaiti:) n. a tropical American tree with heavy resinous wood. [Late Latin, lit.: wood of life]

like[1] (laik) adj. **1.** similar; resembling. ~prep. **2.** similar to; similarly to; in the manner of: acting like a maniac; he's so like his father. **3.** such as: there are lots of games—like draughts, for instance. ~adv. **4.** Dialect. likely. ~conj. **5.** Not universally accepted. as though; as if: you look like you've just seen a ghost. **6.** Not universally accepted. in the same way as: she doesn't dance like you do. ~n. **7.** the equal or counterpart of a person or thing. **8.** the like. similar things: dogs, foxes, and the like. **9.** the likes or like of. people or things similar to (someone or something specified): we don't want the likes of you around here. [Old English gelíc]

like[2] (laik) vb. **1.** to find (something) enjoyable or find it enjoyable (to do something). **2.** to be fond of. **3.** to prefer or wish (to do something): we would like you to go. **4.** to feel disposed or inclined; choose; wish. ~n. **5.** (usually pl.) a favourable feeling, desire, or preference. [Old English lícian] —**'likable** or **'likeable** adj.

likelihood ('laikli,hud) n. chance; probability.

likely ('laikli) adj. **1.** tending or inclined; apt: likely to rain. **2.** probable: a likely result. **3.** appropriate for a purpose or activity. ~adv. **4.** probably or presumably. **5.** not likely. Informal. definitely not. [Old Norse líkligr]

like-minded adj. agreeing in opinions.

liken ('laikən) vb. to see or represent as the same or similar; compare.

likeness ('laiknis) n. **1.** the condition of being alike. **2.** an image created of a person or thing. **3.** an imitative appearance; semblance.

likewise ('laik,waiz) adv. **1.** in addition; moreover; also. **2.** similarly.

liking ('laikiŋ) n. **1.** fondness. **2.** a preference, inclination, or pleasure.

lilac ('lailək) n. **1.** a shrub or small tree that has large sprays of purple or white fragrant flowers. ~adj. **2.** light purple. [Persian nílak bluish]

Lilliputian (,lili'pju:ʃiən) n. **1.** a tiny person or being. ~adj. **2.** tiny; very small. [Lilliput, an imaginary country of tiny people in Swift's Gulliver's Travels]

Lilo ('lai,ləʊ) n., pl. **-los**. Trademark. a type of inflatable plastic mattress.

lilt (lilt) n. **1.** a pleasing musical quality in a speaking voice. **2.** (in music) a jaunty rhythm. **3.** a graceful rhythmic motion. ~*vb.* **4.** (of a voice, tune, or song) to rise and fall in a pleasant way. **5.** to move gracefully and rhythmically. [origin unknown] —'**lilting** *adj.*

lily ('lɪlɪ) *n., pl.* **lilies. 1.** any perennial plant of a N temperate genus, such as the tiger lily, with scaly bulbs and showy white or coloured flowers. **2.** the bulb or flower of any of these plants. **3.** any of various similar plants, such as the water lily. [Latin *lilium*]

lily-livered *adj.* cowardly; timid.

lily of the valley *n., pl.* **lilies of the valley.** a small plant with spikes of fragrant white bell-shaped flowers.

limb[1] (lɪm) *n.* **1.** an arm, leg, or wing. **2.** any of the main branches of a tree. **3. out on a limb. a.** in a precarious or questionable position. **b.** *Brit.* isolated, esp. because of unpopular opinions. [Old English *lim*] —'**limbless** *adj.*

limb[2] (lɪm) *n.* the apparent outer edge of the sun, a moon, or a planet. [Latin *limbus* edge]

limber[1] ('lɪmbə) *adj.* **1.** capable of being easily bent; pliant. **2.** able to move or bend the body freely; agile. [origin unknown]

limber[2] ('lɪmbə) *n.* **1.** part of a gun carriage, consisting of an axle, pole, and two wheels. ~*vb.* **2.** to attach the limber (to a gun). [Middle English *lymour* shaft of a gun carriage]

limber up *vb.* (esp. in sports) to exercise in preparation.

limbo[1] ('lɪmbəʊ) *n., pl.* -**bos. 1.** (*often cap.*) *R.C. Church.* (formerly) the supposed region intermediate between heaven and hell for the unbaptized. **2.** an imaginary place for lost, forgotten, or unwanted persons or things. **3.** an unknown intermediate place or condition: *in limbo.* [Medieval Latin *in limbo* on the border (of hell)]

limbo[2] ('lɪmbəʊ) *n., pl.* -**bos.** a West Indian dance in which dancers lean backwards and pass under a horizontal bar which is gradually lowered. [origin unknown]

lime[1] (laɪm) *n.* **1.** *Agriculture.* calcium hydroxide spread as a dressing on acidic land. ~*vb.* **2.** to spread a calcium compound upon (land). [Old English *līm*]

lime[2] (laɪm) *n.* the round oval fruit of a small Asian citrus tree with acid fleshy pulp rich in vitamin C. [Arabic *līmah*]

lime[3] (laɪm) *n.* a European linden tree planted for ornament. [Old English *lind* linden]

lime-green *adj.* greenish-yellow.

limekiln ('laɪm,kɪln) *n.* a kiln in which calcium carbonate is burned to produce quicklime.

limelight ('laɪm,laɪt) *n.* **1. the.** a position of public attention or notice: *in the limelight.* **2. a.** a type of lamp, formerly used in stage lighting, in which lime is heated to white heat. **b.** brilliant white light produced in this way.

limerick ('lɪmərɪk) *n.* a form of comic verse consisting of five lines. [allegedly from *will you come up to Limerick?* a refrain sung between nonsense verses at a party]

limestone ('laɪm,stəʊn) *n.* rock consisting mainly of calcium carbonate: used as a building stone and in making cement.

limey ('laɪmɪ) *n. U.S. & Canad. slang.* **1.** a British person. **2.** a British sailor or ship. [from *lime-juicer*, because British sailors drank lime juice as a protection against scurvy]

limit ('lɪmɪt) *n.* **1.** (*sometimes pl.*) the ultimate extent, degree, or amount of something: *the limit of endurance.* **2.** (*often pl.*) the boundary or edge of a specific area: *the city limits.* **3.** the largest quantity or amount allowed. **4. the limit.** *Informal.* a person or thing that is intolerably exasperating. ~*vb.* **5.** to restrict or confine, as to area, extent, or time. [Latin *līmes* boundary] —'**limitable** *adj.*

limitation (,lɪmɪ'teɪʃən) *n.* **1.** something that limits a quality or achievement. **2.** the act of limiting or the condition of being limited.

limited ('lɪmɪtɪd) *adj.* **1.** having a limit; restricted. **2.** without fullness or scope; narrow. **3.** (of governing powers or sovereignty) restricted, by or as if by a constitution, laws, or an assembly: *limited government.* **4.** *Chiefly Brit.* (of a business enterprise) owned by shareholders whose liability for the enterprise's debts is restricted.

limn (lɪm) *vb.* to represent in drawing or painting. [Latin *inlūmināre* to brighten]

limousine ('lɪmə,ziːn, ,lɪmə'ziːn) *n.* any large and luxurious car. [French, lit.: cloak]

limp[1] (lɪmp) *vb.* **1.** to walk with an uneven step, esp. with a weak or injured leg. **2.** to advance in a labouring or faltering manner. ~*n.* **3.** an uneven walk or progress. [Old English *lemphealt*] —'**limping** *adj., n.*

limp[2] (lɪmp) *adj.* **1.** not firm or stiff. **2.** not energetic or vital. **3.** (of the binding of a book) not stiffened with boards. [prob. Scandinavian] —'**limply** *adv.*

limpet ('lɪmpɪt) *n.* **1.** a sea creature that has a conical shell and clings tightly to rocks with its muscular foot. **2.** (*modifier*) denoting certain weapons that are attached to their targets by magnetic or adhesive properties and resist removal: *limpet mines.* [Old English *lempedu*]

limpid ('lɪmpɪd) *adj.* **1.** clear or transparent. **2.** (of speech or writing) clear and easy to understand. [Latin *limpidus* clear] —lim'**pidity** *n.*

limy[1] ('laɪmɪ) *adj.* **limier, limiest.** of, like, or smeared with birdlime.

limy[2] ('laɪmɪ) *adj.* **limier, limiest.** of or tasting of lime (the fruit).

linage ('laɪnɪdʒ) *n.* **1.** the number of lines in written or printed matter. **2.** payment according to the number of lines.

linchpin ('lɪntʃ,pɪn) *n.* **1.** a pin placed through an axle to keep a wheel in position. **2.** a person or thing regarded as essential: *the linchpin of the company.* [Old English *lynis*]

Lincs (lɪŋks) Lincolnshire.

linctus ('lɪŋktəs) *n., pl.* -**tuses.** a soothing syrupy cough mixture. [Latin p.p. of *lingere* to lick]

linden ('lɪndən) n. a large tree with heart-shaped leaves and fragrant yellowish flowers. See also **lime³**. [Old English *linde* lime tree]

line¹ (laɪn) n. **1.** a narrow continuous mark, as one made by a pencil or brush. **2.** a thin indented mark or wrinkle. **3.** a straight or curved continuous trace having no breadth that is produced by a moving point. **4.** a boundary: *the county line*. **5.** *Sport.* **a.** a white band indicating division on a field or track. **b.** a mark or imaginary mark at which a race begins or ends. **6.** a specified point of change or limit: *the dividing line between sanity and madness*. **7.** the edge or contour of a shape: *the line of a building*. **8.** anything long, flexible, and thin, such as a wire or string: *a fishing line*. **9.** a telephone connection: *a direct line to New York*. **10.** a conducting wire, cable, or circuit for electric-power transmission or telecommunications. **11.** a system of travel or transportation: *a shipping line*. **12.** a route between two points on a railway. **13.** *Chiefly Brit.* a railway track. **14.** a course or direction of movement or advance: *the line of flight of a bullet*. **15.** a course or method of action or behaviour: *take a new line with him*. **16.** a policy or prescribed course of action or way of thinking: *bring into line*. **17.** a field of study, interest, or occupation: *this book is in your line*. **18.** alignment; true: *in line*. **19.** one kind of product or article: *a nice line in hats*. **20.** a row of people or things. **21.** a row of words printed or written across a page. **22.** a unit of verse consisting of words in a single row. **23.** one of a number of narrow horizontal bands forming a television picture. **24.** *Music.* any of the five horizontal marks that make up the stave. **25.** the most forward defensive position: *the front line*. **26.** a formation of ships or soldiers abreast of each other. **27.** the combatant forces of certain armies and navies. **28.** *U.S. & Canad.* a queue. **29. all along the line.** at every stage in a series. **30. draw the line (at).** to object (to) or set a limit (on): *her father draws the line at her coming in after midnight*. **31. drop someone a line.** to send someone a short note. **32. get a line on.** *Informal.* to obtain information about. **33. in line for.** to be a candidate for: *he's in line for a directorship*. **34. in line with.** conforming to. **35. lay** *or* **put on the line. a.** to speak frankly and directly. **b.** to risk (one's career or reputation) on something. ~*vb.* **36.** to mark with a line or lines. **37.** to be or put as a border to: *tulips lined the lawns*. **38.** to place in or form a row, series, or alignment. ~See also **lines, line-up**. [Old French *ligne* & Old English *līn*, from Latin *linea* flaxen, *linum* flax] **—lined** *adj.*

line² (laɪn) *vb.* **1.** to attach an inside covering to (a garment or curtain). **2.** to cover or fit the inside of: *to line the walls with books*. **3.** to fill: *line one's pockets with money*. [Latin *linum* flax]

lineage ('lɪnɪɪdʒ) *n.* direct descent from an ancestor.

lineal ('lɪnɪəl) *adj.* **1.** being in a direct line of descent from an ancestor. **2.** of or derived from direct descent. **3.** linear. [Latin *linea* line]

lineament ('lɪnɪəmənt) *n.* (*often pl.*) a facial outline or distinctive feature. [Latin *lineare* to draw a line]

linear ('lɪnɪə) *adj.* **1.** of, in, along, or relating to a line. **2.** of or relating to length. **3.** resembling, represented by, or consisting of a line or lines. **—linearity** (ˌlɪnɪ'ærɪtɪ) *n.*

linear measure *n.* a unit or system of units for the measurement of length.

lineation (ˌlɪnɪ'eɪʃən) *n.* **1.** the act of marking with lines. **2.** an arrangement of lines.

line drawing *n.* a drawing made with lines only.

linen ('lɪnɪn) *n.* **1.** a hard-wearing fabric woven from the spun fibres of flax. **2.** yarn or thread spun from flax fibre. **3.** things, such as sheets or tablecloths, made from linen cloth or from cotton. [Latin *linum* flax]

line of fire *n.* the flight path of a missile discharged from a firearm.

line printer *n.* an electromechanical device that prints a line of characters at a time: used in printing and in computer systems.

liner¹ ('laɪnə) *n.* **1.** a passenger ship or aircraft, esp. one that is part of a commercial fleet. **2.** Also called: **eyeliner.** a cosmetic used to outline the eyes.

liner² ('laɪnə) *n.* something used as a lining: *a plastic bin liner*.

lines (laɪnz) *pl. n.* **1.** the words of a theatrical role: *he forgot his lines*. **2.** *Informal, chiefly Brit.* a marriage certificate: *marriage lines*. **3.** a school punishment of writing the same sentence or phrase out a specified number of times. **4. read between the lines.** to understand or find an implicit meaning in addition to the obvious one.

linesman ('laɪnzmən) *n., pl.* **-men.** an official who helps the referee or umpire in various sports, by indicating when the ball has gone out of play.

line-up *n.* **1.** a row or arrangement of people or things for a particular purpose: *the line-up for the football match*. **2.** the members of such a row or arrangement. ~*vb.* **line up. 3.** to form, put into, or organize a line-up.

ling¹ (lɪŋ) *n., pl.* **ling** *or* **lings.** a northern coastal food fish with a long slender body. [prob. Low German]

ling² (lɪŋ) *n.* heather. [Old Norse *lyng*]

linger ('lɪŋɡə) *vb.* **1.** to delay or prolong departure. **2.** to remain just alive for some time before death. **3.** to spend a long time doing or considering something. [Old English *lengan*] **—'lingering** *adj.*

lingerie ('lænʒərɪ) *n.* women's underwear and nightwear. [French, from Latin *līneus* linen]

lingo ('lɪŋɡəʊ) *n., pl.* **-goes.** *Informal.* any foreign or unfamiliar language or jargon. [possibly from LINGUA FRANCA]

lingua franca ('lɪŋɡwə 'fræŋkə) *n., pl.*

lingua francas *or* **linguae francae** ('lɪŋgwɪː 'frænsiː). **1.** a language used for communication among people of different mother tongues. **2.** any system of communication providing mutual understanding. [Italian: Frankish tongue]

lingual ('lɪŋgwəl) *adj.* **1.** *Anat.* of the tongue. **2.** *Rare.* of language or languages. **3.** articulated with the tongue. —**lingually** *adv.*

linguist ('lɪŋgwɪst) *n.* **1.** a person who is skilled in foreign languages. **2.** a person who studies linguistics. [Latin *lingua* tongue]

linguistic (lɪŋ'gwɪstɪk) *adj.* **1.** of language. **2.** of linguistics. —**linguistically** *adv.*

linguistics (lɪŋ'gwɪstɪks) *n.* (*functioning as sing.*) the scientific study of language.

liniment ('lɪnɪmənt) *n.* a medicated liquid, usually containing an oil, applied to the skin to relieve pain or stiffness. [Latin *linere* to smear]

lining ('laɪnɪŋ) *n.* **1.** material used to line a garment or curtain. **2.** any interior covering: *the stomach lining.*

link (lɪŋk) *n.* **1.** any of the separate rings, loops, or pieces that form a chain. **2.** an emotional or logical relationship between people or things; association. **3.** a connecting part or episode. **4.** any of various types of communications connection: *a rail link; radio link.* **5.** a unit of length equal to one hundredth of a chain. ~*vb.* **6.** (often foll. by *up*) to connect with or as if with links. **7.** to connect by association. [Old Norse]

linkage ('lɪŋkɪdʒ) *n.* **1.** the act of linking or the state of being linked. **2.** a system of links.

linkman ('lɪŋkmən) *n.*, *pl.* **-men.** a presenter of a television or radio programme consisting of a number of outside broadcasts from different locations.

links (lɪŋks) *pl. n.* short for **golf links.** See **golf course.** [Old English *hlincas* plural of *hlinc* ridge]

link-up *n.* a joining together of two systems or groups.

linnet ('lɪnɪt) *n.* a brownish finch: the male has a red breast and forehead. [Old French *linotte*, from *līnum* flax (because the bird feeds on flaxseeds)]

lino ('laɪnəʊ) *n.* short for **linoleum.**

linocut ('laɪnəʊˌkʌt) *n.* **1.** a design cut in relief on a block of linoleum. **2.** a print made from such a block.

linoleum (lɪ'nəʊlɪəm) *n.* a floor covering made of hessian or jute coated with powdered cork. [Latin *līnum* flax + *oleum* oil]

Linotype ('laɪnəʊˌtaɪp) *n. Trademark.* a typesetting machine that casts an entire line on one piece of metal.

linseed ('lɪnˌsiːd) *n.* the seed of flax. [Old English *līnsǣd*, *līn* flax + *sǣd* seed]

linseed oil *n.* a yellow oil extracted from seeds of the flax plant. It is used in making oil paints, printer's ink, linoleum, and varnish.

linsey-woolsey ('lɪnzɪ'wʊlzɪ) *n.* a thin rough fabric of linen and wool or cotton.

[prob. from *Lindsey*, village in Suffolk where first made + *wool*]

lint (lɪnt) *n.* **1.** an absorbent cotton or linen fabric with the nap raised on one side, used to dress wounds. **2.** shreds of yarn or cloth. [prob. Latin *linteus* made of linen, from *līnum* flax]

lintel ('lɪntəl) *n.* a horizontal beam, as over a door or window. [prob. ultimately from Latin *līmes* boundary]

lion ('laɪən) *n.* **1.** a large predatory mammal of the cat family found in Africa and India, with a tawny yellow coat and, in the male, a shaggy mane. **2.** a courageous strong person. **3. the lion's share.** the largest portion. [Latin *leo*] —**lioness** *fem. n.*

lion-hearted *adj.* very brave; courageous.

lionize *or* **-ise** ('laɪəˌnaɪz) *vb.* to treat as or make into a celebrity.

lip (lɪp) *n.* **1.** *Anat.* either of the two fleshy folds surrounding the mouth. **2.** any structure resembling a lip, such as the rim of a jug. **3.** *Slang.* impudent talk or backchat. **4. bite one's lip.** to stifle one's feelings. **5. keep a stiff upper lip.** to maintain one's composure during a time of trouble. **6. lick** *or* **smack one's lips.** to anticipate or recall something with glee or relish. [Old English *lippa*]

lip-read ('lɪpˌriːd) *vb.* **-reading, -read** (-ˌrɛd). to interpret (words) by lip-reading.

lip-reading *n.* a method used by the deaf to comprehend spoken words by interpreting movements of the speaker's lips. —**lip-reader** *n.*

lip service *n.* support or respect expressed but not practised.

lipstick ('lɪpˌstɪk) *n.* a cosmetic for colouring the lips, usually in the form of a stick.

liquefy ('lɪkwɪˌfaɪ) *vb.* **-fying, -fied.** (esp. of a gas) to become or cause to become liquid. [Latin *liquefacere* to make liquid] —**liquefaction** (ˌlɪkwɪ'fækʃən) *n.*

liqueur (lɪ'kjʊə) *n.* a highly flavoured sweetened spirit, intended to be drunk after a meal. [French]

liquid ('lɪkwɪd) *n.* **1.** a substance in a physical state in which it does not resist change of shape but does resist change of size. ~*adj.* **2.** of or being a liquid: *liquid wax.* **3.** shining, transparent, or brilliant: *liquid eyes.* **4.** flowing, fluent, or smooth. **5.** (of assets) in the form of money or easily convertible into money. [Latin *liquēre* to be fluid] —**liquidity** *n.*

liquidate ('lɪkwɪˌdeɪt) *vb.* **1.** to settle or pay off (a debt or claim). **2.** to terminate the operations of (a commercial firm) by assessment of debts and appropriation of assets to settle them. **3.** to convert (assets) into cash. **4.** to eliminate or kill. —**liquidator** *n.*

liquidation (ˌlɪkwɪ'deɪʃən) *n.* **1. a.** the winding-up of a business firm by selling its assets to pay off its debts. **b. go into liquidation.** (of a business firm) to have its affairs so terminated. **2.** destruction; elimination.

liquid crystal display *n.* a display of numbers, as on a calculator, using cells containing a liquid with crystalline properties, that change their reflectivity when an electric field is applied to them.

liquidize *or* **-dise** ('lɪkwɪˌdaɪz) *vb.* **1.** to make or become liquid; liquefy. **2.** to pulverize (food) in a liquidizer so as to produce a fluid.

liquidizer *or* **-diser** ('lɪkwɪˌdaɪzə) *n.* a kitchen appliance with blades for puréeing food.

liquid measure *n.* a unit or system of units for measuring volumes of liquids or their containers.

liquid oxygen *n.* oxygen liquefied by cooling: used in rocket fuels.

liquid paraffin *n.* an oily liquid obtained by petroleum distillation and used as a laxative.

liquor ('lɪkə) *n.* **1.** spirits or other alcoholic drinks. **2.** any liquid in which food has been cooked. [Latin *liquēre* to be liquid]

liquorice *or* *U.S. & Canad.* **licorice** ('lɪkərɪs, -ərɪʃ) *n.* **1.** the dried root of a Mediterranean plant, used as a laxative and in confectionery. **2.** a sweet having a liquorice flavour. [Greek *glukus* sweet + *rhiza* root]

lira ('lɪərə) *n., pl.* **lire** ('lɪərɪ) *or* **liras.** **1.** the standard monetary unit of Italy. **2.** the standard monetary unit of Turkey. [Italian, from Latin *lībra* pound]

lisle (laɪl) *n.* a strong fine cotton thread or fabric. [after *Lisle* (now Lille), in France]

lisp (lɪsp) *n.* **1.** a speech defect in which *s* and *z* are pronounced like the *th* sounds in English *thin* and *then* respectively. ~*vb.* **2.** to speak or pronounce (something) with a lisp. [Old English *wlisp* lisping (adj.), imit.]

lissom *or* **lissome** ('lɪsəm) *adj.* supple in the limbs or body; lithe; agile. [var. of *lithesome*, from *lithe* + *-some* of a specific nature]

list[1] (lɪst) *n.* **1.** an item-by-item record of names or things, usually written one under the other. ~*vb.* **2.** to make a list of. **3.** to include in a list. [Old English *līst*] —**listing** *n.*

list[2] (lɪst) *vb.* **1.** (esp. of ships) to lean over to one side. ~*n.* **2.** the act or an instance of leaning to one side. [origin unknown]

listed building *n.* (in Britain) a building protected from demolition or alteration because of its special historical or architectural interest.

listen ('lɪs'n) *vb.* **1.** to concentrate on hearing something. **2.** to take heed; pay attention: *I warned you but you wouldn't listen.* [Old English *hlysnan*] —**listener** *n.*

listen in *vb.* (often foll. by *on* or *to*) to listen secretly to a conversation or communication.

listeriosis (lɪˌstɪərɪˈəʊsɪs) *n.* a serious form of food poisoning, caused by bacteria of the genus *Listeria.* Its symptoms can include meningitis. [after Joseph *Lister*, English surgeon]

listless ('lɪstlɪs) *adj.* having or showing no interest or energy. [*list* desire] —**'listlessly** *adv.*

list price *n.* the selling price of merchandise as quoted in a catalogue or advertisement.

lists (lɪsts) *pl. n.* **1.** *History.* the enclosed field of combat at a tournament. **2.** any arena of conflict or controversy. **3. enter the lists.** to engage in a conflict or controversy. [plural of Old English *līst* border]

lit (lɪt) *vb.* the past of **light**[1] and **light**[2].

lit. 1. literal(ly). **2.** literary. **3.** literature.

litany ('lɪtənɪ) *n., pl.* **-nies. 1.** *Christianity.* a prayer consisting of a series of invocations, each followed by the same response. **2.** any tedious recital. [Late Greek *litaneia* prayer]

litchi (ˌlaɪˈtʃiː) *n.* same as **lychee.**

liter ('liːtə) *n. U.S.* same as **litre.**

literacy ('lɪtərəsɪ) *n.* **1.** the ability to read and write. **2.** the ability to use language proficiently.

literal ('lɪtərəl) *adj.* **1.** in exact accordance with the explicit meaning of a word or text. **2.** word for word: *a literal translation.* **3.** dull, factual, or prosaic. **4.** true; actual. ~*n.* **5.** a misprint or misspelling in a text. [Latin *littera* letter] —**'literally** *adv.*

literalism ('lɪtərəlˌɪzəm) *n.* the tendency to take words and statements in their literal sense. —**'literalist** *n.*

literary ('lɪtrərɪ) *adj.* **1.** of or characteristic of literature: *a literary style.* **2.** knowledgeable about literature. **3.** (of a word) formal; not colloquial. [Latin *litterārius* concerning reading & writing] —**'literariness** *n.*

literate ('lɪtərɪt) *adj.* **1.** able to read and write. **2.** educated; learned. ~*n.* **3.** a literate person. [Latin *litterātus* learned]

literati (ˌlɪtəˈrɑːtiː) *pl. n.* literary or scholarly people. [Latin]

literature ('lɪtərɪtʃə, 'lɪtrɪ-) *n.* **1.** written material such as poetry, novels, or essays. **2.** the body of written work of a particular culture or people: *Scandinavian literature.* **3.** written or printed matter of a particular type or genre: *scientific literature.* **4.** the art or profession of a writer. **5.** *Informal.* printed matter on any subject. [Latin *litterātūra* writing]

lithe (laɪð) *adj.* flexible or supple. [Old English (in the sense: gentle; later: supple)]

lithium ('lɪθɪəm) *n.* a soft silvery element of the alkali metal series: the lightest known metal. Symbol: Li [Greek *lithos* stone]

litho ('laɪθəʊ) *n., pl.* **-thos,** *adj., adv.* short for **lithography, lithograph, lithographic,** or **lithographically.**

lithograph ('lɪθəˌɡrɑːf) *n.* **1.** a print made by lithography. ~*vb.* **2.** to reproduce (pictures or text) by lithography. —**lithographic** (ˌlɪθəˈɡræfɪk) *adj.* —**ˌlithoˈgraphically** *adv.*

lithography (lɪˈθɒɡrəfɪ) *n.* a method of printing from a metal or stone surface on which the printing areas are made ink-receptive. [Greek *lithos* stone + *graphein* to write] —**li'thographer** n.

litigant ('lɪtɪgənt) n. a party to a lawsuit.

litigate ('lɪtɪ,geɪt) vb. 1. to bring or contest (a claim or action) in a lawsuit. 2. to engage in legal proceedings. [Latin *līs*, *lit-* lawsuit + *agere* to carry on] —**'liti,gator** n.

litigation (,lɪtɪ'geɪʃən) n. the process of bringing or contesting a lawsuit.

litigious (lɪ'tɪdʒəs) adj. frequently going to law.

litmus ('lɪtməs) n. a soluble powder obtained from certain lichens. It turns red under acid conditions and blue under basic conditions. Absorbent paper treated with it (**litmus paper**) is used as an indicator. [possibly Scandinavian]

litotes ('laɪtəʊ,tiːz) n., pl. **-tes.** understatement for effect, as in "She was not a little upset" meaning "She was extremely upset". [Greek *litos* small]

litre or U.S. **liter** ('liːtə) n. one cubic decimetre. [Greek *litra* a unit of weight]

litter ('lɪtə) n. 1. small refuse or waste materials carelessly dropped in public places. 2. a disordered or untidy collection of objects. 3. a group of animals produced at one birth. 4. straw or hay used as bedding for animals. 5. a means of conveying people, esp. sick or wounded people, consisting of a light bed or seat held between parallel sticks. ~vb. 6. to make (a place) untidy by strewing (refuse). 7. to scatter (objects) about or (of objects) to lie around or upon (anything) in an untidy fashion. 8. (of animals) to give birth to (offspring). 9. to provide (an animal) with straw or hay for bedding. [Latin *lectus* bed]

litter lout or U.S. & Canad. **litterbug** ('lɪtə,bʌg) n. Slang. a person who tends to drop refuse in public places.

little ('lɪt'l) det. 1. a small quantity, extent, or duration of: *the little hope there is left*; *little damage was done.* 2. **make little of.** to regard or treat as insignificant; dismiss. 3. **think little of.** to have a low opinion of. ~adj. 4. of small or less than average size. 5. young: *a little boy.* 6. endearingly familiar: *my husband's little ways.* 7. contemptible, mean, or disagreeable: *your filthy little mind.* ~adv. 8. (usually preceded by *a*) to a small extent or degree; not a lot: *to laugh a little.* 9. (used preceding a verb) not at all, or hardly: *he little realized his fate.* 10. not much or often: *we go there very little now.* 11. **little by little.** by small degrees. ~See also **less, lesser, least.** [Old English *lȳtel*]

little people pl. n. Folklore. small supernatural beings, such as elves.

littoral ('lɪtərəl) adj. 1. of or by the shore. ~n. 2. a coastal region. [Latin *lītus* shore]

liturgy ('lɪtədʒɪ) n., pl. **-gies.** the forms of public services officially prescribed by a Church. [Greek *leitourgia*, from *leit-* people + *ergon* work] —**li'turgical** adj.

livable or **liveable** ('lɪvəb'l) adj. (foll. by *with*) tolerable or pleasant to live (with).

live[1] (lɪv) vb. 1. to show the characteristics

of life; be alive. 2. to remain alive or in existence. 3. to exist in a specified way: *to live poorly.* 4. to reside or dwell: *to live in London.* 5. to continue or last: *the pain still lives in her memory.* 6. (foll. by *on*, *upon*, or *by*) to support one's style of life; subsist: *to live by writing.* 7. (foll. by *with*) to endure the effects (of a crime or mistake). 8. to pass or spend (one's life). 9. to enjoy life to the full: *he knows how to live.* 10. to put into practice in one's daily life; express: *he lives religion every day.* 11. **live and let live.** to be tolerant. ~See also **live down, live in,** etc. [Old English *libban, lifian*]

live[2] (laɪv) adj. 1. showing the characteristics of life. 2. of current interest; controversial: *a live issue.* 3. actual: *a real live cowboy.* 4. (of a coal or ember) glowing or burning. 5. loaded or capable of exploding: *a live bomb.* 6. Radio, television. transmitted at the time of performance, rather than being a recording: *a live show.* 7. (of a record) recorded during a performance. 8. connected to a source of electric power: *a live circuit.* ~adv. 9. during, at, or in the form of a live performance. [shortened from *on live* alive]

live down (lɪv) vb. to withstand the effects of (a crime or mistake) by waiting until others forget or forgive it.

live in (lɪv) vb. 1. to dwell at one's place of employment, as in a hotel. ~adj. **live-in.** 2. resident: *a live-in nanny; her live-in boyfriend.*

livelihood ('laɪvlɪ,hʊd) n. occupation or employment.

livelong ('lɪv,lɒŋ) adj. Chiefly poetic. long or seemingly long: *all the livelong day.*

lively ('laɪvlɪ) adj. **-lier, -liest.** 1. full of life or vigour. 2. vivacious or animated. 3. vivid. —**'liveliness** n.

liven ('laɪv'n) vb. (usually foll. by *up*) to make or become lively; enliven.

liver[1] ('lɪvə) n. 1. a large glandular organ which process nutrients for use by the body and which secretes bile and removes certain poisons. 2. the liver of certain animals used as food. 3. a reddish-brown colour. [Old English *lifer*]

liver[2] ('lɪvə) n. a person who lives in a specified way: *a fast liver.*

liveried ('lɪvərɪd) adj. wearing livery.

liverish ('lɪvərɪʃ) adj. 1. Informal. having a disorder of the liver. 2. disagreeable; peevish.

liver sausage n. a sausage containing liver.

liverwort ('lɪvə,wɜːt) n. a plant growing in wet places and resembling green seaweeds or leafy mosses. [late Old English *liferwyrt*]

livery ('lɪvərɪ) n., pl. **-eries.** 1. the identifying uniform of a servant. 2. distinctive dress or outward appearance. 3. the stabling, keeping, or hiring out of horses for money. [Old French *livrée* allocation, from Latin *līberāre* to set free]

lives (laɪvz) n. the plural of **life.**

livestock ('laɪv,stɒk) n. (functioning as

sing. or pl.) cattle, horses, and similar animals kept on a farm.

live together (lɪv) *vb.* (of an unmarried couple) to dwell in the same house; cohabit.

live up (lɪv) *vb.* (foll. by *to*) to fulfil (an expectation, obligation, or principle).

live wire (laɪv) *n.* **1.** *Informal.* an energetic or enterprising person. **2.** a wire carrying an electric current.

livid (ˈlɪvɪd) *adj.* **1.** *Informal.* angry or furious. **2.** of a greyish colour. [Latin *līvēre* to be black and blue]

living (ˈlɪvɪŋ) *adj.* **1.** possessing life; not dead or inanimate. **2.** currently in use or valid: *living language.* **3.** seeming to be real: *a living image.* **4.** (of animals or plants) existing in the present age. **5.** very: *the living daylights.* ~*n.* **6.** the condition of being alive. **7.** the manner of one's life: *fast living.* **8.** one's financial means. **9.** *Church of England.* a benefice. **10.** (*modifier*) of or like everyday life: *living conditions.* **11.** (*modifier*) of or involving those now alive: *in living memory.*

living room *n.* a room in a private house or flat used for relaxation and entertainment.

living wage *n.* a wage adequate for a worker to live on and support a family in reasonable comfort.

lizard (ˈlɪzəd) *n.* a reptile with an elongated body, four limbs, and a long tail. [Latin *lacerta*]

ll. lines (of written matter).

llama (ˈlɑːmə) *n.* a domesticated South American mammal of the camel family, that is used as a beast of burden and is valued for its hair, flesh, and hide. [American Indian]

LLB Bachelor of Laws. [Latin *Legum Baccalaureus*]

lo (ləʊ) *interj.* look! see! (now often in **lo and behold**). [Old English *lā*]

loach (ləʊtʃ) *n.* a carplike freshwater fish with a long narrow body and barbels around the mouth. [Old French *loche*]

load (ləʊd) *n.* **1.** something to be borne or conveyed; weight. **2.** the amount borne or conveyed. **3.** something that weighs down, oppresses, or burdens: *that's a load off my mind.* **4.** *Electronics.* the power delivered by a machine, generator, or circuit. **5.** an external force applied to a component or mechanism. **6. a load of.** *Informal.* a quantity of: *a load of nonsense.* **7. get a load of.** *Informal.* to pay attention to. ~*vb.* **8.** to place or receive (cargo or goods) upon (a ship or vehicle). **9.** to burden or oppress. **10.** to supply in abundance: *load with gifts.* **11.** to cause to be biased: *to load a question.* **12.** to put an ammunition charge into (a firearm). **13.** *Photog.* to position (a film) in (a camera). **14.** to weight or bias (a roulette wheel or dice). **15.** *Computers.* to transfer (a program) to a memory. ~*See also* **loads.** [Old English *lād* course; in meaning, infl. by *lade*] —**loader** *n.*

loaded (ˈləʊdɪd) *adj.* **1.** carrying a load. **2.** (of dice or a roulette wheel) weighted or

otherwise biased. **3.** (of a question or statement) containing a hidden trap or implication. **4.** charged with ammunition. **5.** *Slang.* wealthy. **6.** *Slang, chiefly U.S. & Canad.* drunk.

loads (ləʊdz) *pl. n. Informal.* (often foll. by *of*) a lot.

loadstar (ˈləʊdˌstɑː) *n.* same as **lodestar.**

loadstone (ˈləʊdˌstəʊn) *n.* same as **lodestone.**

loaf[1] (ləʊf) *n., pl.* **loaves** (ləʊvz). **1.** a shaped mass of baked bread. **2.** any shaped or moulded mass of food, such as sugar or cooked meat. **3.** *Slang.* the head; sense: *use your loaf!* [Old English *hlāf*]

loaf[2] (ləʊf) *vb.* to loiter or lounge around in an idle way. [possibly from *loafer*]

loafer (ˈləʊfə) *n.* **1.** a person who avoids work; idler. **2.** *Chiefly U.S. & Canad.* a moccasin-like shoe. [possibly German *Landläufer* vagabond]

loam (ləʊm) *n.* rich soil consisting of sand, clay, and decaying organic material. [Old English *lām*] —**loamy** *adj.*

loan (ləʊn) *n.* **1.** the act of lending: *the loan of a car.* **2.** property lent, esp. money lent at interest for a period of time. **3. on loan.** lent out; borrowed. ~*vb.* **4.** to lend (something, esp. money). [Old Norse *lān*]

loath *or* **loth** (ləʊθ) *adj.* (usually foll. by *to*) reluctant or unwilling. [Old English *lāth* (in the sense: hostile)]

loathe (ləʊð) *vb.* to feel strong hatred or disgust for. [Old English *lāthian*]

loathing (ˈləʊðɪŋ) *n.* abhorrence; disgust.

loathsome (ˈləʊðsəm) *adj.* causing loathing; abhorrent.

loaves (ləʊvz) *n.* the plural of **loaf**[1].

lob (lɒb) *Sport.* ~*n.* **1.** a ball struck or bowled in a high arc. ~*vb.* **lobbing, lobbed.** **2.** to hit or kick (a ball) in a high arc. **3.** *Informal.* to throw. [prob. Low German]

lobar (ˈləʊbə) *adj.* of or affecting a lobe.

lobate (ˈləʊbeɪt) *adj.* with or like lobes.

lobby (ˈlɒbɪ) *n., pl.* **-bies.** **1.** a room or corridor used as an entrance hall or vestibule. **2.** *Chiefly Brit.* a hall in a legislative building used for meetings between legislators and members of the public. **3.** *Chiefly Brit.* one of two corridors in a legislative building in which members vote. **4.** a group of persons who attempt to influence legislators on behalf of a particular interest. ~*vb.* **-bying, -bied.** **5.** to attempt to influence (legislators) in the formulation of policy. [Old High German *lauba* arbor, from *laub* leaf]

lobbyist (ˈlɒbɪɪst) *n.* a person employed by a particular interest to lobby.

lobe (ləʊb) *n.* **1.** any rounded projection forming part of a larger structure. **2.** the fleshy lower part of the external ear. **3.** any subdivision of a bodily organ. [Greek *lobos* lobe of the ear or of the liver]

lobelia (ləʊˈbiːlɪə) *n.* a plant with red, blue, white, or yellow five-lobed flowers with the three lower lobes forming a lip. [Matthias de *Lobel*, botanist]

lobola (lɔːˈbɔːlə) *n.* (in southern Africa) an

African custom by which a bridegroom's family makes a payment in cattle or cash to the bride's family shortly before the marriage. [Zulu]

lobotomy (ləʊˈbɒtəmɪ) n., pl. **-mies.** surgical cutting of nerves in the frontal lobe of the brain: used in the treatment of severe mental disorders. [Greek *lobos* lobe + *tomē* a cutting]

lobscouse (ˈlɒbˌskaʊs) n. a sailor's stew of meat, vegetables, and hardtack. [possibly dialect *lob* to boil + *scouse* broth]

lobster (ˈlɒbstə) n., pl. **-sters** or **-ster. 1.** a large crustacean found on rocky sea shores and with the first pair of limbs modified as large pincers. **2.** its edible flesh. [Old English *loppestre*, from *loppe* spider]

lobster pot n. a round basket made of open slats, used to catch lobsters.

local (ˈləʊkəl) adj. **1.** characteristic of or associated with a particular locality or area. **2.** of or relating to a particular place or point in space. **3.** Med. of, affecting, or confined to a limited area or part: a *local anaesthetic.* **4.** (of a train or bus) stopping at all stations or stops. ~n. **5.** an inhabitant of a specified locality: *the locals support him.* **6.** Brit. informal. a pub close to one's home. [Latin *locus* place] —'**locally** adv.

local anaesthetic n. Med. See **anaesthesia.**

local authority n. Brit. & N.Z. the governing body of a county or district.

locale (ləʊˈkɑːl) n. the place where something happens or has happened. [French, from Latin *locus* place]

local government n. government of the affairs of counties, towns, and districts by locally elected political bodies.

locality (ləʊˈkælɪtɪ) n., pl. **-ties. 1.** a neighbourhood or area. **2.** the site or scene of an event.

localize or **-ise** (ˈləʊkəˌlaɪz) vb. to restrict or confine (something) to a particular place.

locate (ləʊˈkeɪt) vb. **1.** to discover the whereabouts of; find. **2.** to situate or place: *located on the edge of the city.* **3.** U.S. & Canad. to become established or settled.

location (ləʊˈkeɪʃən) n. **1.** a site or position; situation. **2.** the act of locating or the state of being located. **3.** a place outside a studio where filming is done: *shot on location.* **4.** (in South Africa) a Black African or Coloured township. [Latin *locare* to place]

loc. cit. (in textual annotation) loco citato. [Latin: in the place cited]

loch (lɒx) n. **1.** Scot. a lake. **2.** a long narrow arm of the sea in Scotland. [Gaelic]

loci (ˈləʊsaɪ) n. the plural of **locus.**

lock[1] (lɒk) n. **1.** a device fitted to a door, drawer, lid, etc., to keep it closed and prevent unauthorized access. **2.** a section of a canal or river that may be closed off by gates to control the water level and the raising and lowering of vessels that pass through it. **3.** the jamming or fastening together of parts. **4.** Brit. the extent to

which a vehicle's front wheels will turn: *this car has a good lock.* **5.** a mechanism that detonates the charge of a gun. **6. lock, stock, and barrel.** completely; entirely. **7.** any wrestling hold in which a wrestler seizes a part of his opponent's body. **8.** Also called: **lock forward.** Rugby. a player in the second row of the scrum. ~vb. **9.** to fasten (a door, gate, etc.) or (of a door, etc.) to become fastened so as to prevent entry or exit. **10.** to secure (a building) by locking all doors and windows. **11.** to fix or become fixed together securely or inextricably. **12.** to become or cause to become rigid or immovable: *the front wheels of the car locked.* **13.** to clasp or entangle (someone or each other) in a struggle or embrace. ~See also **lock out, lock in.** [Old English *loc*]

lock[2] (lɒk) n. **1.** a strand or curl of hair. **2.** (pl.) Chiefly literary. hair. [Old English *loc*]

locker (ˈlɒkə) n. a small compartment that may be locked, as for temporarily storing clothes and valuables.

locket (ˈlɒkɪt) n. a small ornamental case, usually on a necklace or chain, that holds a picture or keepsake. [French *loquet* latch]

lockjaw (ˈlɒkˌdʒɔː) n. Pathol. a nontechnical name for **trismus** and (often) **tetanus.**

lock out vb. **1.** to prevent from entering by locking a door. **2.** to prevent (employees) from working during an industrial dispute, as by closing a factory. ~n. **lockout. 3.** the closing of a place of employment by an employer, in order to bring pressure on employees to agree to terms.

locksmith (ˈlɒkˌsmɪθ) n. a person who makes or repairs locks.

lock up vb. **1.** to imprison or confine. **2.** to lock or secure the doors and windows of (a building). ~n. **lockup. 3.** a jail. **4.** Brit. a small shop with no attached quarters for the owner. **5.** Brit. a garage or store separate from the main premises. ~adj. **lock-up. 6.** Brit. & N.Z. (of premises) without living quarters: a *lock-up shop.*

loco[1] (ˈləʊkəʊ) n. Informal. a locomotive.

loco[2] (ˈləʊkəʊ) adj. Slang, chiefly U.S. insane. [Spanish: crazy]

locomotion (ˌləʊkəˈməʊʃən) n. the act or power of moving. [Latin *locō* from a place + *motion*]

locomotive (ˌləʊkəˈməʊtɪv) n. **1.** a self-propelled engine used for pulling trains. ~adj. **2.** of locomotion.

locum (ˈləʊkəm) n. Chiefly Brit. a person who stands in temporarily for a doctor or clergyman. [Medieval Latin *locum tenens* (someone) holding the place (of another)]

locus (ˈləʊkəs) n., pl. **loci.** Maths. a set of points or lines whose location satisfies or is determined by one or more specified conditions: *the locus of points equidistant from a given point is a circle.* [Latin]

locust (ˈləʊkəst) n. **1.** an insect, related to the grasshopper, of warm and tropical regions, which travels in vast swarms, stripping large areas of vegetation. **2.** a

North American leguminous tree with prickly branches; the carob tree. [Latin *locusta*]

locution (ləʊˈkjuːʃən) *n.* **1.** a word, phrase, or expression. **2.** manner or style of speech. [Latin *locūtiō* an utterance]

lode (ləʊd) *n.* a vein of metallic ore. [Old English *lād* course]

lodestar (ˈləʊdˌstɑː) *n.* **1.** a star, esp. the North Star, used in navigation or astronomy as a point of reference. **2.** something that serves as a guide.

lodestone (ˈləʊdˌstəʊn) *n.* **1. a.** magnetite that is naturally magnetic. **b.** a piece of this, which can be used as a magnet. **2.** a person or thing regarded as a focus of attraction.

lodge (lɒdʒ) *n.* **1.** *Chiefly Brit.* a small house at the entrance to the grounds of a country mansion, usually occupied by a gatekeeper. **2.** a house or cabin used occasionally, as for some seasonal activity: *a ski lodge.* **3.** a room for the use of porters in a university or college. **4.** a local branch of certain societies. **5.** a beaver's home. ~*vb.* **6.** to provide or be provided with rented accommodation. **7.** to live temporarily in rented accommodation. **8.** to implant or embed or be implanted or embedded: *the bullet lodged close to his spine.* **9.** to deposit or leave for safety or storage: *documents lodged with my solicitor.* **10.** to bring (a charge or accusation) against someone: *to lodge a complaint.* **11.** (often foll. by *in* or *with*) to place (authority or power) in the control of (someone). [Old French *loge*]

lodger (ˈlɒdʒə) *n.* a person who pays rent in return for accommodation in someone else's house.

lodging (ˈlɒdʒɪŋ) *n.* **1.** a temporary residence. **2.** (*pl.*) a rented room or rooms in another person's house.

loess (ˈləʊɪs) *n.* a fine-grained soil, found esp. in river valleys, originally deposited by the wind. [Swiss German *lösch* loose]

loft (lɒft) *n.* **1.** the space inside a roof. **2.** a gallery, esp. one for the choir in a church. **3.** a room over a stable used to store hay. **4.** a raised house or coop in which pigeons are kept. **5.** *Golf.* **a.** the angle from the vertical made by the club face to give elevation to a ball. **b.** the height reached by a struck ball. ~*vb.* **6.** *Sport.* to strike or kick (a ball) high in the air. [Old Norse *lopt* air, ceiling]

lofty (ˈlɒftɪ) *adj.* **loftier, loftiest. 1.** of majestic or imposing height. **2.** exalted or noble. **3.** haughty or supercilious. —**loftily** *adv.* —**loftiness** *n.*

log[1] (lɒg) *n.* **1.** a section of the trunk or a main branch of a tree, when stripped of branches. **2. a.** a detailed record of a voyage of a ship or aircraft. **b.** a record of the hours flown by pilots and aircrews. **c.** a book in which these records are kept; logbook. **3.** a device consisting of a float with an attached line, formerly used to measure the speed of a ship. **4. sleep like a log.** to sleep without stirring or being disturbed. ~*vb.* **logging, logged. 5.** to saw logs from (trees). **6.** to enter (a distance or event) in a logbook or log. [origin unknown]

log[2] (lɒg) *n.* short for **logarithm.**

loganberry (ˈləʊgənbərɪ) *n., pl.* -ries. a purplish-red fruit, similar to a raspberry, that grows on a trailing prickly plant. [after James H. *Logan,* who first grew it]

logarithm (ˈlɒgəˌrɪðəm) *n.* the exponent indicating the power to which a fixed number, the base, must be raised to obtain a given number or variable. [Greek *logos* ratio + *arithmos* number] —**logarithmic** *adj.*

logbook (ˈlɒgˌbʊk) *n.* **1.** a book containing the official record of trips made by a ship or aircraft. **2.** *Brit. informal.* the registration document of a car.

loggerhead (ˈlɒgəˌhed) *n.* **1.** a large-headed turtle occurring in most seas. **2. at loggerheads.** engaged in dispute or confrontation. [prob. dialect *logger* wooden block + *head*]

loggia (ˈlɒdʒə) *n.* a covered gallery on the side of a building. [Italian]

logging (ˈlɒgɪŋ) *n.* the work of felling, trimming, and transporting timber. —**logger** *n.*

logic (ˈlɒdʒɪk) *n.* **1.** the branch of philosophy concerned with analysing the patterns of reasoning. **2.** a particular system or method of reasoning. **3.** reasoned thought or argument, as distinguished from irrationality. **4.** the relationship and interdependence of a series of events or facts. **5.** *Electronics, computers.* the principles underlying the units in a computer system that produce results from data. [Greek *logikos* concerning speech or reasoning]

logical (ˈlɒdʒɪkᵊl) *adj.* **1.** relating to or characteristic of logic. **2.** using or deduced from the principles of logic: *a logical conclusion.* **3.** capable of or using clear or valid reasoning. **4.** reasonable because of facts or events: *the logical candidate.* —**logically** *adv.*

logician (lɒˈdʒɪʃən) *n.* a person who specializes in or is skilled at logic.

logistics (lɒˈdʒɪstɪks) *n.* (*functioning as sing. or pl.*) the detailed planning and organization of a large complex operation, such as a military campaign. [French *loger* to lodge] —**logistic** *or* **logistical** *adj.* —**logistically** *adv.*

log jam *n. Chiefly U.S. & Canad.* **1.** a blockage caused by the crowding together of logs floating in a river. **2.** a deadlock.

logo (ˈləʊgəʊ, ˈlɒg-) *n., pl.* -os. a trademark, company emblem, or similar device. [shortened from *logotype* badge, symbol]

-logy *n. combining form.* **1.** indicating the science or study of: *musicology.* **2.** indicating writing or discourse: *trilogy; phraseology; martyrology.* [Greek *logos* word] —**logical** *or* -**logic** *adj. combining form.* —**logist** *n. combining form.*

loin (lɔɪn) *n.* **1.** *Anat.* the lower back and sides between the pelvis and the ribs. **2.** a cut of meat from this part of an animal. ~See also **loins.** [Old French *loigne*]

loincloth (ˈlɔɪnˌklɒθ) *n.* a piece of cloth worn round the loins.

loins (lɔɪnz) *pl. n.* **1.** the hips and the inner surface of the legs where they join the body. **2.** *Euphemistic.* the genitals.

loiter ('lɔɪtə) *vb.* to stand or act aimlessly or idly. [possibly Middle Dutch *lōteren* to wobble]

loll (lɒl) *vb.* **1.** to lie, lean, or lounge in a lazy manner. **2.** to hang or allow to hang loosely. [possibly imit.]

lollipop ('lɒlɪ,pɒp) *n.* **1.** a boiled sweet or toffee stuck on a small wooden stick. **2.** *Brit.* an ice lolly. [possibly dialect *lolly* the tongue + POP²]

lollipop man *or* **lady** *n. Brit. informal.* a person holding a circular sign on a pole who stops traffic so that children may cross the road.

lollop ('lɒləp) *vb. Chiefly Brit.* to walk or run with a clumsy or relaxed bouncing movement. [prob. *loll* + *-op* as in gallop]

lolly ('lɒlɪ) *n.*, *pl.* **-lies. 1.** *Informal.* a lollipop. **2.** *Brit.* short for **ice lolly. 3.** *Brit., Austral., & N.Z. slang.* money. **4.** *Austral. & N.Z. informal.* a sweet. [shortened from *lollipop*]

London pride ('lʌndən) *n.* a saxifrage plant with a rosette of leaves and pink flowers.

lone (ləʊn) *adj.* **1.** unaccompanied; solitary: *a lone figure.* **2.** isolated: *a lone house.* **3.** unmarried or widowed: *a lone parent.* [the mistaken division of *alone* into *a lone*]

lonely ('ləʊnlɪ) *adj.* **-lier, -liest. 1.** unhappy as a result of being without companions. **2.** causing or resulting from the state of being alone: *a lonely existence.* **3.** isolated or unfrequented: *lonely moorland.* —'**loneliness** *n.*

lonely hearts *adj.* of or for people who wish to find a congenial companion or marriage partner: *a lonely hearts advertisement.*

loner ('ləʊnə) *n. Informal.* a person who prefers to be alone.

lonesome ('ləʊnsəm) *adj.* **1.** *Chiefly U.S. & Canad.* lonely. **2.** causing feelings of loneliness: *an owl's lonesome cry.*

long¹ (lɒŋ) *adj.* **1.** having relatively great extent in space or duration in time. **2.** of a specified extent or duration: *three hours long.* **3.** consisting of a large number of items or parts: *a long list.* **4.** having greater than the average or expected range, extent, or duration: *a long match.* **5.** seeming to occupy a greater time than is really so: *she spent a long afternoon waiting.* **6.** *Informal.* (foll. by *on*) plentifully supplied or endowed (with): *long on good ideas.* **7.** *Phonetics, prosody.* (of a vowel) of relatively considerable duration. **8.** from end to end; lengthwise. **9.** *Finance.* having large holdings of securities or commodities in anticipation of rising prices. **10. in the long run.** ultimately; after or over a period of time. ~*adv.* **11.** for a certain time or period: *how long will it last?* **12.** for or during an extensive period of time: *long into the next year.* **13.** a considerable amount of time: *long before I met you; long ago.* **14. as** *or* **so long as. a.**

for or during just the length of time that. **b.** provided that; if. ~*n.* **15.** anything that is long. **16. before long.** soon. **17. for long.** for a long time. **18. the long and the short of it.** the essential points or facts. [Old English *lang*] —'**longish** *adj.*

long² (lɒŋ) *vb.* (foll. by *for* or an infinitive) to have a strong desire. [Old English *langian*]

long. longitude.

long- *adv.* (*in combination*) for or lasting a long time: *long-established; long-lasting.*

longboat ('lɒŋ,bəʊt) *n.* the largest boat carried aboard a commercial ship.

longbow ('lɒŋ,bəʊ) *n.* a large powerful hand-drawn bow.

long-distance *n.* (*modifier*) **1.** covering relatively long distances: *a long-distance driver.* **2.** (of telephone calls) connecting points a relatively long way apart.

longevity (lɒn'dʒɛvɪtɪ) *n.* long life. [Latin *longus* long + *aevum* age]

longhand ('lɒŋ,hænd) *n.* ordinary handwriting, as opposed to typing or shorthand.

longing ('lɒŋɪŋ) *n.* **1.** a prolonged unfulfilled desire. ~*adj.* **2.** having or showing desire: *a longing look.* —'**longingly** *adv.*

longitude ('lɒndʒɪ,tjuːd, 'lɒŋgɪ-) *n.* distance in degrees east or west of the prime meridian at 0°. [Latin *longitūdō* length]

longitudinal (,lɒndʒɪ'tjuːdɪn²l, ,lɒŋgɪ-) *adj.* **1.** of longitude or length. **2.** placed or extended lengthways.

long johns *pl. n. Informal.* long underpants.

long jump *n.* an athletic contest of covering the farthest distance with a running jump from a fixed mark.

long-lived *adj.* having long life, existence, or currency.

long-playing *adj.* of or relating to an LP.

long-range *adj.* **1.** of or extending into the future: *a long-range weather forecast.* **2.** (of vehicles, aircraft, or weapons) capable of covering great distances.

longship ('lɒŋ,ʃɪp) *n.* a narrow open boat with oars and a square sail, used by the Vikings.

longshore drift ('lɒŋ,ʃɔː) *n.* the movement of material along a beach, caused by the fact that waves approach the shore at an oblique angle.

longshoreman ('lɒŋ,ʃɔːmən) *n.*, *pl.* **-men.** *U.S. & Canad.* a docker.

long shot *n.* **1.** a bet against heavy odds. **2.** an undertaking, guess, or possibility with little chance of success. **3. by a long shot.** by any means: *he still hasn't finished by a long shot.*

long-sighted *adj.* **1.** able to see distant objects in focus. **2.** far-sighted.

long-standing *adj.* existing for a long time.

long-suffering *adj.* enduring trouble or unhappiness without complaint.

long-term *adj.* lasting or extending over a long time: *long-term prospects.*

longtime ('lɒŋ,taɪm) *adj.* of long standing: *his longtime friend.*

long ton n. See **ton**[1] (sense 1).

long wave n. a radio wave with a wavelength greater than 1000 metres.

longways ('lɒŋ,weɪz) or U.S. & Canad. **longwise** adv. lengthways.

long-winded (,lɒŋ'wɪndɪd) adj. tiresomely long. —,**long-'windedness** n.

loo (luː) n., pl. **loos**. Brit. informal. a toilet. [possibly from French lieux d'aisance water closet]

loofah ('luːfə) n. the dried fibrous interior of a type of gourd, used as a sponge. [Arabic lūf]

look (lʊk) vb. 1. (often foll. by at) to direct the eyes (towards): to look at the sea. 2. (often foll. by at) to direct one's attention (towards): let's look at the circumstances. 3. to give the impression of being; seem: that looks interesting. 4. to face in a particular direction: the house looks north. 5. to expect or hope (to do something): I look to hear from you soon. 6. (foll. by for) to search or seek: I looked for you everywhere. 7. (foll. by into) to carry out an investigation. 8. to direct a look at (someone) in a specified way: she looked her rival up and down. 9. to accord in appearance with (something): to look one's age. 10. **look alive, lively, sharp,** or **smart.** to hurry up; get busy. 11. **look here.** an expression used to attract someone's attention or add emphasis to a statement. ~n. 12. an instance of looking: a look of despair. 13. a view or sight (of something): let's have a look. 14. (often pl.) appearance to the eye or mind; aspect: the look of innocence; I don't like the looks of this place. 15. style; fashion: the new look for spring. ~conj. 16. an expression demanding attention or showing annoyance: look, I've had enough of this. ~See also **look after, look back,** etc. [Old English lōcian] —'**looker** n.

look after vb. to take care of.

lookalike ('lʊkə,laɪk) n. a person or thing that is the double of another, often well-known, person or thing.

look back vb. 1. to cast one's mind to the past. 2. **never looked back.** was extremely successful: after his first book was published, he never looked back.

look down vb. (often foll. by on or upon) to express or show contempt (for).

look forward to vb. to wait or hope for, esp. with pleasure.

look-in Informal. ~n. 1. a chance to be chosen or join in: she never got a look-in. ~vb. **look in.** 2. to pay a short visit.

looking glass n. a mirror.

look on vb. 1. to be a spectator at an event or incident. 2. to consider or regard: she looked on the affair as a joke. —,**looker-'on** n.

lookout ('lʊk,aʊt) n. 1. the act of keeping watch against danger or for an opportunity: on the lookout. 2. a person or persons keeping such a watch, as on a ship. 3. a strategic point from which a watch is kept. 4. Informal. worry or concern: that's his lookout. 5. Chiefly Brit. chances or prospect: a poor lookout. ~vb. **look out.** 6. to

be careful. 7. to be on the watch: look out for my mother at the station. 8. to search for and find: I've looked out the books you asked for. 9. (foll. by on or over) to face in a particular direction: the house looks out over the moor.

look over vb. 1. to inspect or examine. ~n. **look-over.** 2. an inspection.

look-see n. Slang. a brief inspection or look.

look up vb. 1. to discover (something required to be known) by checking in a reference book. 2. to improve: things are looking up. 3. (foll. by to) to have respect (for): I looked up to her because of her wisdom. 4. to visit (a person): I'll look you up when I'm in town.

loom[1] (luːm) n. an apparatus for weaving yarn into cloth. [var. of Old English gelōma tool]

loom[2] (luːm) vb. 1. to come into view indistinctly with an enlarged and often threatening aspect. 2. (of an event) to seem ominously close. [possibly East Frisian lomen to move slowly]

loon (luːn) n. U.S. & Canad. a diver (the bird). [Scandinavian]

loony ('luːnɪ) Slang. ~adj. **loonier, looniest.** 1. lunatic; insane. 2. foolish or ridiculous. ~n., pl. **loonies.** 3. a foolish or insane person. [shortened from lunatic]

loop (luːp) n. 1. the round or oval shape formed by a line that curves around to cross itself. 2. any round or oval-shaped thing that is closed or nearly closed. 3. Electronics. a closed circuit through which a signal can circulate. 4. a flight manoeuvre in which an aircraft flies in a complete vertical circle. 5. a continuous strip of cinema film or tape. 6. Computers. a series of instructions in a program, performed repeatedly until some specified condition is satisfied. ~vb. 7. to make a loop in or of (a line, string, or thread). 8. to fasten or encircle with a loop. 9. Also: **loop the loop.** to cause (an aircraft) to perform a loop or (of an aircraft) to perform a loop. [origin unknown]

loophole ('luːp,həʊl) n. an ambiguity or omission, as in a law, by which one can avoid a penalty or responsibility.

loopy ('luːpɪ) adj. **loopier, loopiest.** Informal. slightly mad, crazy.

loose (luːs) adj. 1. free or released from confinement or restraint. 2. not close, compact, or tight in structure or arrangement. 3. not fitted or fitting closely: loose clothing is cooler. 4. not bundled, fastened, or put in a container: loose nails. 5. inexact; imprecise: a loose translation. 6. (of cash) readily available: loose change. 7. promiscuous, immoral, or dissolute. 8. lacking a sense of responsibility or propriety: loose talk. 9. **the loose.** Rugby. the part of play when the forwards close round the ball in a ruck or loose scrum. 10. **on the loose.** free from confinement or restraint. ~adv. 11. in a loose manner; loosely. ~vb. 12. to set free or release, as from restraint or obligation: until that hold of law is loosed. 13. to unfasten or untie: he loosed the strap. 14. to make or become less strict, tight, firmly attached, or compact. **15.** to let fly (a bullet, arrow, or other missile). [Old Norse *lauss* free] —'**loosely** adv. —'**looseness** n.

loosebox ('lu:s,bɒks) n. an enclosed stall with a door in which an animal can be kept.

loose-jointed adj. supple and easy in movement.

loose-leaf adj. (of a binder) capable of being opened to allow removal and addition of pages.

loosen ('lu:s'n) vb. **1.** to make or become less tight or fixed: *loosen the screws.* **2.** (often foll. by *up*) to make or become less firm, compact, or rigid: *loosen up the soil.* **3.** to untie. **4.** (often foll. by *up*) to make or become less strict or severe: *as sexual attitudes loosened up.*

loot (lu:t) n. **1.** goods stolen in wartime or during riots. **2.** *Informal.* money. ~vb. **3.** to rob (a city) during war or riots. **4.** to steal (money or goods) during war or riots. [Hindi *lūt*] —'**looter** n.

lop (lɒp) vb. **lopping, lopped.** (usually foll. by *off*) **1.** to sever (parts) from a tree or body. **2.** to cut out or eliminate from as excessive. [Middle English *loppe* branches cut off]

lope (ləʊp) vb. **1.** to move or run with a long swinging stride or gait. ~n. **2.** a long steady gait or stride. [Old Norse *hlaupa* to leap]

lop-eared adj. (of animals) having ears that droop.

lopsided (,lɒp'saɪdɪd) adj. greater in weight, height, or size on one side.

loquacious (lɒ'kweɪʃəs) adj. having a tendency to talk a great deal. [Latin *loquī* to speak] —**loquacity** (lɒ'kwæsɪtɪ) n.

lord (lɔːd) n. **1.** a person who has power or authority over others, such as a monarch or master. **2.** a male member of the nobility. **3.** (in medieval Europe) a feudal superior. **4. my lord.** a respectful form of address used to a judge, bishop, or nobleman. ~vb. **5. lord it over someone.** to act in a superior manner towards someone. [Old English *hlāford* bread keeper]

Lord (lɔːd) n. **1.** *Christianity.* a title given to God or Jesus Christ. **2.** *Brit.* a title given to certain male peers. **3.** *Brit.* a title given to certain high officials and judges. ~interj. **4.** an exclamation of dismay or surprise: *Good Lord!*

Lord Chancellor n. *Brit. government.* the cabinet minster who is head of the judiciary and Speaker of the House of Lords.

Lord Chief Justice n. (in England and Wales) the judge who is second only to the Lord Chancellor and president of one division of the High Court of Justice.

Lord Lieutenant n. **1.** (in Britain) the representative of the Crown in a county. **2.** (formerly) the British viceroy in Ireland.

lordly ('lɔːdlɪ) adj. **-lier, -liest. 1.** haughty; arrogant; proud. **2.** of or suitable to a lord. —'**lordliness** n.

Lord Mayor n. the mayor in the City of London and in certain other boroughs.

Lord Privy Seal n. (in Britain) the senior cabinet minister without official duties.

Lords (lɔːdz) n. **the.** short for **House of Lords.**

lordship ('lɔːdʃɪp) n. the position or authority of a lord.

Lordship ('lɔːdʃɪp) n. (preceded by *Your* or *His*) *Brit.* a title used to address or refer to a bishop, a judge of the high court, or any peer except a duke.

Lord's Prayer n. **the.** the prayer taught by Jesus Christ to his disciples.

Lords Spiritual pl. n. (in Britain) the Anglican archbishops and senior bishops who are members of the House of Lords.

Lord's Supper n. **the.** same as **Holy Communion.**

Lords Temporal pl. n. **the.** (in Britain) peers other than bishops in their capacity as members of the House of Lords.

lore (lɔː) n. collective knowledge or wisdom on a particular subject. [Old English *lār*]

lorgnette (lɔː'njet) n. a pair of spectacles or opera glasses mounted on a handle. [French, from *lorgner* to squint]

lorry ('lɒrɪ) n., pl. **-ries.** a large motor vehicle designed to carry heavy loads. [possibly dialect *lurry* to pull]

lose (lu:z) vb. **losing, lost. 1.** to part with or come to be without, as through theft, accident, or carelessness. **2.** to fail to keep or maintain: *to lose one's balance.* **3.** to suffer the loss or deprivation of: *to lose a parent.* **4.** to get rid off: *try to lose weight.* **5.** to fail to get or make use of: *to lose a chance.* **6.** to be defeated, as in a fight or game. **7.** to fail to see, hear, or understand: *I lost the gist of his speech.* **8.** to waste: *to lose money gambling.* **9.** to wander from so as to be unable to find: *to lose one's way.* **10.** to cause the loss of: *his delay lost him the battle.* **11.** to allow to go astray or out of sight: *we lost him in the crowd.* **12.** to absorb or engross: *he was lost in contemplation.* **13.** to cause the death or destruction of: *two men were lost in the attack.* **14.** to outdistance or escape from: *he soon lost his pursuers.* **15.** (of a timepiece) to run slow (by a specified amount). [Old English *losian* to perish]

lose out vb. *Informal.* **1.** to be defeated or unsuccessful. **2. lose out on.** to fail to secure or make use of: *we lost out on the sale.*

loser ('lu:zə) n. **1.** a person or thing that loses. **2.** *Informal.* a person or thing that seems destined to be taken advantage of or fail: *a born loser.*

losing ('lu:zɪŋ) adj. unprofitable; failing: *the business was a losing concern.*

loss (lɒs) n. **1.** the act or an instance of losing. **2.** the disadvantage or deprivation resulting from losing: *a loss of reputation.* **3.** the person, thing, or amount lost: *a large loss.* **4. at a loss. a.** uncertain what to do; bewildered. **b.** with income less than outlay: *the firm was running at a loss.* [Old English *lōsian* to be destroyed]

loss leader n. an article offered below cost to attract customers.

lost (lɒst) vb. **1.** the past of **lose.** ~adj.

2. unable to be found or recovered. **3.** unable to find one's way. **4.** confused or bewildered: *he is lost in discussions of theory.* **5.** (sometimes foll. by *on*) not utilized, noticed, or understood (by): *rational arguments are lost on her.* **6.** no longer possessed or existing because of defeat, misfortune, or the passage of time: *a lost art.* **7.** (foll. by *in*) engrossed (in): *he was lost in his book.* **8.** morally fallen: *a lost woman.* **9.** damned: *a lost soul.*

lost cause *n.* a cause with no chance of success.

lot (lɒt) *pron.* **1.** (*functioning as sing. or pl.; preceded by a*) a great number or quantity: *a lot to do; a lot of people.* ~*n.* **2.** a collection of things or people: *a nice lot of youngsters.* **3.** destiny or fortune: *it falls to my lot to be poor.* **4.** any object, such as a straw or slip of paper, drawn from others at random to make a selection or choice: *draw lots; cast lots.* **5.** the use of lots in making a choice: *chosen by lot.* **6.** an item or set of items for sale in an auction. **7.** *Chiefly U.S. & Canad.* an area of land: *a parking lot.* **8. a bad lot.** an unpleasant or disreputable person. **9. cast or throw in one's lot with someone.** to join with voluntarily and share the fortunes of someone. **10. the lot.** the entire amount or number. ~*adv.* **11.** (*preceded by a*) *Informal.* to a considerable extent, degree, or amount: *to delay a lot.* ~See also **lots.** [Old English *hlot*]

loth (ləʊθ) *adj.* same as **loath.**

Lothario (ləʊˈθɑːrɪˌəʊ) *n., pl.* -**os.** a seducer. [after a character in a play]

lotion (ˈləʊʃən) *n.* a liquid preparation having a soothing, cleansing, or antiseptic action, applied to the skin. [Latin *lōtiō* a washing]

lots (lɒts) *Informal.* ~*pl. n.* **1.** (often foll. by *of*) great numbers or quantities: *lots of people; lots of cats.* ~*adv.* **2.** a great deal.

lottery (ˈlɒtərɪ) *n., pl.* -**teries.** **1.** a game of chance in which tickets are sold, which may later qualify the holder for a prize. **2.** an endeavour the success of which is regarded as a matter of luck. [Middle Dutch *loterije*]

lotto (ˈlɒtəʊ) *n.* a game of chance in which numbers are drawn and called out, while the players cover the corresponding numbers on cards, the winner being the first to cover all the numbers or a particular row. [Italian]

lotus (ˈləʊtəs) *n.* **1.** (in Greek mythology) a fruit that induces dreamy forgetfulness in those who eat it. **2.** any of several water lilies of tropical Africa and Asia, regarded as sacred. **3.** a symbolic representation of such a plant. [Greek *lōtos*]

lotus-eater *n.* one who lives in lazy forgetfulness.

lotus position *n.* a seated cross-legged position with each foot on top of the opposite thigh, used in yoga and meditation.

loud (laʊd) *adj.* **1.** (of sound) relatively great in volume: *a loud shout.* **2.** making or able to make sounds of relatively great volume: *a loud voice.* **3.** insistent and emphatic: *loud protests.* **4.** (of colours or patterns) harsh to look at. **5.** noisy, vulgar, and offensive. ~*adv.* **6.** in a loud manner. **7. out loud.** audibly. [Old English *hlud*] —ˈ**loudly** *adv.* —ˈ**loudness** *n.*

loud-hailer *n.* a portable loudspeaker with a built-in amplifer and microphone.

loudspeaker (ˌlaʊdˈspiːkə) *n.* a device for converting electrical signals into sounds.

lough (lɒx, lɒk) *n.* **1.** *Irish.* a lake. **2.** a long narrow arm of the sea in Ireland. [Irish *loch* lake]

lounge (laʊndʒ) *vb.* **1.** (often foll. by *about* or *around*) to sit, lie, walk, or stand in a relaxed manner. **2.** to pass (time) lazily or idly. ~*n.* **3.** a communal room in a hotel, ship, or airport, used for waiting or relaxing in. **4.** *Chiefly Brit.* a living room in a private house. **5.** *Brit.* a more expensive bar in a pub or hotel. **6.** the act of lounging. [origin unknown]

lounge suit *n.* a man's suit of matching jacket and trousers worn for the normal business day.

lour (ˈlaʊə) *vb.* same as **lower²**.

lourie (ˈlaʊrɪ) *n.* a type of African bird with bright plumage. [Afrikaans]

louse (laʊs) *n.* **1.** (*pl.* **lice**) a wingless bloodsucking insect which infests man and some animals. **2.** (*pl.* **louses**) *Slang.* an unpleasant or mean person. [Old English *lūs*]

louse up *vb. Slang.* to ruin or spoil.

lousy (ˈlaʊzɪ) *adj.* **lousier, lousiest.** **1.** *Slang.* very mean or unpleasant. **2.** *Slang.* inferior or bad. **3.** *Slang.* ill or unwell. **4.** infested with lice.

lout (laʊt) *n.* a crude or oafish person; boor. [possibly Old English *lūtan* to stoop] —ˈ**loutish** *adj.*

louvre *or U.S.* **louver** (ˈluːvə) *n.* **a.** any of a set of horizontal slats in a door or window, sloping outwards to throw off rain and admit air. **b.** the slats and frame supporting them. [Old French *lovier*] —ˈ**louvred** *or U.S.* ˈ**louvered** *adj.*

lovage (ˈlʌvɪdʒ) *n.* a European herb with greenish-white flowers. [Old French *luvesche*, from Latin *ligusticum*, lit.: Ligurian (plant)]

love (lʌv) *vb.* **1.** to have a great fondness and affection for a person or thing. **2.** to have passionate desire for a particular person. **3.** to like or desire (to do something) very much. ~*n.* **4.** an intense emotion of affection, warmth, and regard towards a person or thing. **5.** a deep feeling of sexual attraction and desire. **6.** wholehearted liking for or pleasure in something. **7.** a beloved person: often used as an endearment. **8.** *Brit. informal.* a term of address, not necessarily for a person regarded as likable. **9.** (in tennis, squash, etc.) a score of zero. **10. fall in love.** to become in love. **11. for love or money.** by any means. **12. in love.** in a state of strong emotional attachment and usually sexual attraction. **13. make love to. a.** to have sexual intercourse with. **b.** *Now archaic.* to court. [Old English *lufu*] —ˈ**lovable** *or* ˈ**loveable** *adj.*

lovebird ('lʌv,bɜːd) n. any of several small African parrots often kept as cagebirds.

lovebite ('lʌv,baɪt) n. a temporary red mark left on a person's skin by a partner's biting or sucking it during lovemaking.

love child n. Euphemistic. a child whose parents have not been married to each other.

loveless ('lʌvlɪs) adj. without love: a loveless marriage.

love-lies-bleeding n. a plant with drooping spikes of small red flowers.

love life n. the part of a person's life consisting of romantic or sexual relationships.

lovelorn ('lʌv,lɔːn) adj. miserable because of unrequited love or unhappiness in love.

lovely ('lʌvlɪ) adj. -lier, -liest. 1. very attractive or beautiful. 2. highly pleasing or enjoyable: a lovely time. ~n., pl. -lies. 3. Slang. a lovely woman. —'loveliness n.

lovemaking ('lʌv,meɪkɪŋ) n. 1. sexual play and activity between lovers, including sexual intercourse. 2. Archaic. courtship.

lover ('lʌvə) n. 1. a person who has a sexual relationship with another person outside marriage. 2. (often pl.) either of the people involved in a love affair. 3. someone who loves a specified person or thing: a cat-lover.

lovesick ('lʌv,sɪk) adj. pining or languishing because of love. —'love,sickness n.

lovey-dovey (,lʌvɪ'dʌvɪ) adj. making a sentimental or showy display of affection.

loving ('lʌvɪŋ) adj. feeling or showing love and affection. —'lovingly adv.

loving cup n. a large two-handled cup out of which people drink in turn at a banquet.

low¹ (ləʊ) adj. 1. having a relatively small distance from base to top: a low building. 2. situated at a relatively short distance above the ground, sea level, or the horizon: low cloud. 3. of less than usual height, depth, degree, or cost: low temperature; low prices. 4. (of numbers) small. 5. involving or containing a relatively small amount of something: a low supply. 6. having little value or quality: of low grade. 7. coarse or vulgar: a low conversation. 8. inferior in culture or status. 9. in a physically or mentally depressed or weakened state. 10. low-necked: a low dress. 11. with a hushed tone: a low whisper. 12. Music. of or having a relatively low pitch. 13. (of latitudes) situated not far north or south of the equator. 14. having little or no money. 15. unfavourable: a low opinion. 16. deep: a low bow. 17. (of a gear) providing a relatively low forward speed for a given engine speed. ~adv. 18. in a low position, level, degree, or intensity: to bring someone low. 19. at a low pitch; deep: to sing low. 20. cheaply: to buy low. 21. lay low. a. to cause to fall by a blow. b. to overcome, defeat, or destroy. 22. lie low. to keep or be concealed or quiet. ~n. 23. a low position, level, or degree: an all-time low. 24. an area of low atmospheric pressure; a depression. [Old Norse lāgr] —'lowness n.

low² (ləʊ) n. also **lowing**. 1. the sound uttered by cattle; moo. ~vb. 2. to make or express by a low or moo. [Old English hlōwan]

lowborn (,ləʊ'bɔːn) adj. Now rare. of ignoble or common parentage.

lowbrow ('ləʊ,braʊ) Disparaging. ~n. 1. a person who has uncultivated or nonintellectual tastes. ~adj. 2. of or for such a person.

Low Church n. the school of thought in the Church of England stressing evangelical beliefs and practices. —,Low-'Church adj.

low comedy n. comedy characterized by slapstick and physical action.

Low Countries pl. n. Belgium, Luxembourg, and the Netherlands.

low-down Informal. ~adj. 1. mean, underhand, or despicable. ~n. lowdown. 2. the. information.

lower¹ ('ləʊə) adj. 1. being below one or more other things: the lower shelf. 2. reduced in amount or value: a lower price. 3. Lower. Geol. denoting the early part of a period or formation. ~vb. 4. to bring, put, or cause to move down: lower one's eyes. 5. to reduce or bring down in estimation, dignity, or value: to lower oneself. 6. to reduce or be reduced: to lower one's confidence. 7. to make quieter or reduce the pitch of. 8. to become less.

lower² or **lour** ('laʊə) vb. (of the sky or weather) to be overcast and menacing. [Middle English louren to scowl] —'lowering or 'louring adj.

lower case ('ləʊə) n. (in printing) small letters, as opposed to capital letters. —,lower-'case adj.

lower class ('ləʊə) n. the class with the lowest position in society. —,lower-'class adj.

lower house ('ləʊə) n. one of the houses of a parliament that has two chambers: usually the larger and more representative.

lowest common denominator n. Maths. the smallest integer or polynomial that is exactly divisible by each denominator of a set of fractions.

lowest common multiple n. Maths. the smallest number or quantity that is exactly divisible by each member of a set of numbers or quantities.

low frequency n. any radio frequency lying between 300 and 30 kilohertz.

Low German n. a language of N Germany, spoken in rural areas.

low-key or **low-keyed** adj. 1. having a low intensity or tone. 2. restrained or subdued.

lowland ('ləʊlənd) n. 1. relatively low ground. 2. (often pl.) a low generally flat region. ~adj. 3. of a lowland or lowlands. —'lowlander n.

Lowland ('ləʊlənd) n. (modifier) of the Lowlands, a low generally flat region of S Central Scotland or the dialects of English spoken there. —'Lowlander n.

lowly ('ləʊlɪ) adj. -lier, -liest. 1. humble or low in position, rank, or status. 2.

simple, unpretentious, or plain. —**'lowliness** n.

Low Mass n. a simplified form of Mass that is spoken rather than sung.

low-minded adj. having a vulgar or crude mind. —**low-'mindedness** n.

low-pitched adj. 1. pitched low in tone. 2. (of a roof) having a shallow slope.

low profile n. a position or attitude deliberately avoiding prominence or publicity.

low-spirited adj. depressed or dejected.

low-tech adj. 1. of or using low technology. 2. in the style of interior design using items associated with low technology.

low technology n. simple unsophisticated technology that is limited to the production of basic necessities.

low tide n. the tide when it is at its lowest level or the time at which it reaches this.

low water n. 1. low tide. 2. the state of any stretch of water at its lowest level.

loyal ('lɔɪəl) adj. 1. faithful to one's friends, country, or government. 2. of or expressing loyalty. [Latin *lēgālis* legal] —**'loyally** adv.

loyalist ('lɔɪəlɪst) n. a patriotic supporter of his sovereign or government. —**'loyalism** n.

Loyalist ('lɔɪəlɪst) n. (in Northern Ireland) any of the Protestants wishing to retain Ulster's link with Britain.

loyalty ('lɔɪəltɪ) n., pl. -ties. 1. the quality of being loyal. 2. a feeling of friendship or duty towards someone or something.

lozenge ('lɒzɪndʒ) n. 1. Med. a medicated tablet held in the mouth until it has dissolved. 2. Geom. a rhombus. [Old French *losange*]

LP n. a record, usually 12 inches in diameter, which is played at 33⅓ revolutions per minute and normally holds about 20 or 25 minutes of sound on each side. [shortened from *long player*]

L-plate n. Brit. a red "L" on a white square fixed to the front and back of a motor vehicle to show that the driver has not passed the driving test.

Lr Chem. lawrencium.

LSD n. lysergic acid diethylamide; an illegal hallucinogenic drug.

L.S.D., £.s.d., or **l.s.d.** pounds, shillings, pence. [Latin *librae, solidi, denarii*]

Lt Lieutenant.

Ltd Limited (Liability).

Lu Chem. lutetium.

lubber ('lʌbə) n. 1. a big, awkward, or stupid person. 2. short for **landlubber**. [prob. Old Norse] —**'lubberly** adj., adv. —**'lubberliness** n.

lubricant ('luːbrɪkənt) n. a lubricating substance, such as oil.

lubricate ('luːbrɪ,keɪt) vb. 1. to cover or treat with an oily substance so as to lessen friction. 2. to make greasy, slippery, or smooth. [Latin *lūbricāre* to make slippery] —**,lubri'cation** n.

lubricious (luː'brɪʃəs) adj. Formal or literary. lewd. [Latin *lūbricus* slippery]

lucerne (luː'sɜːn) n. Brit. same as **alfalfa**.

lucid ('luːsɪd) adj. 1. readily understood; clear. 2. shining or glowing. 3. of or relating to a period of normality between periods of insanity or delirium. [Latin *lūcidus* full of light] —**lu'cidity** n. —**'lucidly** adv.

Lucifer ('luːsɪfə) n. Satan. [Latin *Lūcifer* light-bearer, from *lūx* light + *ferre* to bear]

luck (lʌk) n. 1. events that are beyond control and seem subject to chance; fortune. 2. success or good fortune. 3. **down on one's luck**. having so little luck as to be suffering hardships. 4. **no such luck**. Informal. unfortunately not. 5. **try one's luck**. to attempt something that is uncertain. [Middle Dutch *luc*]

luckless ('lʌklɪs) adj. unfortunate; unlucky.

lucky ('lʌkɪ) adj. **luckier, luckiest.** 1. having or bringing good fortune. 2. happening by chance, esp. as desired. —**'luckily** adv.

lucky dip n. Brit. a box filled with sawdust containing small prizes for which children search.

lucrative ('luːkrətɪv) adj. profitable.

lucre ('luːkə) n. Usually facetious. money or wealth: filthy lucre. [Latin *lucrum* gain]

Luddite ('lʌdaɪt) n. Brit. 1. any of the textile workers opposed to mechanization, who organized machine-breaking between 1811 and 1816. 2. any opponent of industrial change or innovation. ~adj. 3. of the Luddites. [after Ned Ludd, who destroyed machinery]

ludicrous ('luːdɪkrəs) adj. absurd or ridiculous. [Latin *lūdus* game] —**'ludicrously** adv.

ludo ('luːdəʊ) n. Brit. a simple board game in which players advance counters by throwing dice. [Latin: I play]

luff (lʌf) vb. 1. Naut. to head (a sailing vessel) into the wind so that her sails flap. 2. to move the jib of (a crane) in order to shift a load. [Old French *lof*]

lug¹ (lʌg) vb. **lugging, lugged.** to carry or drag (something heavy) with great effort. [prob. Old Norse]

lug² (lʌg) n. 1. a projecting piece by which something is connected, supported, or lifted. 2. Informal or Scot. an ear. [Scots: ear]

luggage ('lʌgɪdʒ) n. suitcases, trunks, and bags. [possibly LUG¹, influenced by *baggage*]

lugger ('lʌgə) n. Naut. a small working boat with a four-sided fore-and-aft sail. [origin unknown]

lugubrious (lʊ'guːbrɪəs) adj. excessively mournful. [Latin *lūgēre* to grieve]

lugworm ('lʌg,wɜːm) n. a worm living in burrows on sandy shores: much used as bait. [origin unknown]

lukewarm (,luːk'wɔːm) adj. 1. (of a liquid) moderately warm; tepid. 2. having or expressing little enthusiasm or conviction. [prob. Old English *hlēow* warm]

lull (lʌl) vb. **1.** to soothe (a person or animal) by soft sounds or motions. **2.** to calm (someone or someone's fears or suspicions) by deception. ~n. **3.** a short period of calm. [possibly imit. of crooning sounds]

lullaby ('lʌlə,baɪ) n., pl. **-bies.** a quiet song to lull a child to sleep. [possibly a blend of lull + goodbye]

lumbago (lʌm'beɪɡəʊ) n. pain in the lower back; backache. [Latin lumbus loin]

lumbar ('lʌmbə) adj. of, in, or near the part of the body between the lowest ribs and the hipbones. [Latin lumbus loin]

lumbar puncture n. Med. insertion of a hollow needle into the lower spinal cord to withdraw fluid for diagnosis.

lumber[1] ('lʌmbə) n. **1.** Brit. useless household articles that are stored away. **2.** Chiefly U.S. & Canad. logs; sawn timber. ~vb. **3.** Brit. informal. to burden with something unpleasant or tedious. **4.** to fill up or encumber with useless household articles. **5.** Chiefly U.S. & Canad. to convert trees into marketable timber. [possibly a n. use of LUMBER[2]]

lumber[2] ('lʌmbə) vb. to move or proceed in an awkward heavy manner. [Middle English lomeren] —**'lumbering** adj.

lumberjack ('lʌmbə,dʒæk) n. (esp. in North America) a person whose work involves felling trees and transporting the timber.

luminary ('luːmɪnərɪ) n., pl. **-naries. 1.** a famous person who enlightens or influences others. **2.** Literary. something, such as the sun or moon, that gives off light.

luminescence (,luːmɪ'nesəns) n. Physics. the emission of light at low temperatures by any process other than incandescence. —,lumi'nescent adj.

luminous ('luːmɪnəs) adj. **1.** reflecting or giving off light: luminous colours. **2.** (not in technical use) luminescent: luminous paint. **3.** enlightening or wise. [Latin lūmen light] —**luminosity** (,luːmɪ'nɒsɪtɪ) n.

lump[1] (lʌmp) n. **1.** a small solid mass without definite shape. **2.** Pathol. any small swelling or tumour. **3.** Informal. an awkward, heavy, or stupid person. **4.** the **lump.** Brit. self-employed workers in the building trade considered collectively. **5.** (modifier) in the form of a lump or lumps: lump sugar. **6. a lump in one's throat.** a tight dry feeling in one's throat, usually caused by great emotion. ~vb. **7.** to grow into lumps or become lumpy. **8.** (often foll. by together) to consider as a single group, often without justification. [prob. related to Scandinavian dialect lump block]

lump[2] (lʌmp) vb. Informal. to tolerate or put up with: you'll just have to lump it. [origin unknown]

lumpectomy (,lʌm'pektəmɪ) n., pl. **-mies.** the surgical removal of a tumour in a breast. [lump + Greek tomē a cutting]

lumpish ('lʌmpɪʃ) adj. stupid, clumsy, or heavy. —**'lumpishness** n.

lump sum n. a relatively large sum of money, paid at one time.

lumpy ('lʌmpɪ) adj. **lumpier, lumpiest.** full of or having lumps. —**'lumpiness** n.

lunacy ('luːnəsɪ) n., pl. **-cies. 1.** (formerly) any severe mental illness. **2.** foolishness.

lunar ('luːnə) adj. of, occurring on, or used on the moon: lunar module. [Latin lūna moon]

lunatic ('luːnətɪk) adj. **1.** Archaic. insane. **2.** foolish; eccentric. ~n. **3.** a person who is insane. [Latin lūna moon]

lunatic asylum n. Offensive. a home or hospital for the mentally ill.

lunatic fringe n. the members of a group who adopt views regarded as extreme.

lunch (lʌntʃ) n. **1.** a meal eaten during the middle of the day. ~vb. **2.** to eat lunch. [shortened from luncheon]

luncheon ('lʌntʃən) n. a lunch, often a formal one. [prob. var. of nuncheon, from Middle English none noon + schench drink]

luncheon meat n. a ground mixture of meat (often pork) and cereal, usually tinned.

luncheon voucher n. a voucher worth a specified amount issued to employees and accepted by some restaurants as payment for food.

lunchroom ('lʌntʃ,ruːm) n. Chiefly Canad. a room where lunch is served or where students or employees may eat lunches they bring.

lung (lʌŋ) n. the part of the body that allows an animal or bird to breathe air. Humans have two lungs, contained within the chest cavity. [Old English lungen]

lunge (lʌndʒ) n. **1.** a sudden forward motion. **2.** Fencing. a thrust made by advancing the front foot and straightening the back leg. ~vb. **3.** to move with a lunge. **4.** Fencing. to make a lunge. [French allonger to stretch out (one's arm)]

lungfish ('lʌŋ,fɪʃ) n., pl. **-fish** or **-fishes.** a freshwater fish with an air-breathing lung.

lupin ('luːpɪn) n. a plant with large spikes of brightly coloured flowers and flattened pods. [Latin lupīnus wolfish; from the belief that it ravenously exhausted the soil]

lupine ('luːpaɪn) adj. of or like a wolf. [Latin lupus wolf]

lupus ('luːpəs) n. an ulcerous skin disease. [Latin: wolf; so called because it rapidly eats away the affected part]

lurch[1] (lɜːtʃ) vb. **1.** to lean or tilt suddenly to one side. **2.** to stagger. ~n. **3.** a lurching. [origin unknown]

lurch[2] (lɜːtʃ) n. **leave someone in the lurch.** to desert someone in trouble. [French lourche a game similar to backgammon]

lurcher ('lɜːtʃə) n. a crossbred hunting dog trained to hunt silently. [obs. lurch to prowl]

lure (lʊə) vb. **1.** (sometimes foll. by away or into) to tempt or attract by the promise of reward. ~n. **2.** a person or thing that lures. **3.** Angling. a brightly coloured artificial spinning bait. **4.** Falconry. a feathered decoy to which small pieces of meat can be attached. [Old French *loirre* falconer's lure]

lurid ('luərɪd) *adj.* **1.** vivid in shocking detail; sensational. **2.** horrible in savagery or violence. **3.** glaring in colour. [Latin *lūridus* pale yellow] —'**luridly** *adv.*

lurk (lɜːk) *vb.* **1.** to move stealthily or be concealed, as for evil purposes. **2.** to be present in an unobtrusive way; be latent. [prob. frequentative of *lour*]

lurking ('lɜːkɪŋ) *adj.* lingering but almost unacknowledged: *a lurking suspicion.*

luscious ('lʌʃəs) *adj.* **1.** extremely pleasurable to taste or smell. **2.** very attractive. [perhaps short for *delicious*]

lush[1] (lʌʃ) *adj.* **1.** (of vegetation) abounding in lavish growth. **2.** luxurious, elaborate, or opulent. [Latin *laxus* loose]

lush[2] (lʌʃ) *n.* Slang, chiefly U.S. & Canad. an alcoholic. [origin unknown]

lust (lʌst) *n.* **1.** a strong sexual desire. **2.** a strong desire or drive: *a lust for power.* ~*vb.* **3.** (often foll. by *after* or *for*) to have a lust (for). [Old English] —'**lustful** *adj.* —'**lustfully** *adv.*

lustre *or U.S.* **luster** ('lʌstə) *n.* **1.** reflected light; sheen. **2.** radiance or brilliance of light. **3.** great splendour of accomplishment or beauty. **4.** a shiny metallic surface on some pottery and porcelain. [Latin *lustrāre* to make bright] —'**lustrous** *adj.*

lusty ('lʌstɪ) *adj.* **lustier, lustiest. 1.** having or characterized by robust health. **2.** strong or invigorating. —'**lustily** *adv.* —'**lustiness** *n.*

lute (luːt) *n.* an ancient plucked stringed instrument with a long fingerboard and a body shaped like a sliced pear. [Arabic *al 'ūd,* lit.: the wood]

lutetium (luː'tiːʃɪəm) *n.* a silvery-white metallic element of the lanthanide series. Symbol: Lu [*Lūtētia* ancient name of Paris]

Lutheran ('luːθərən) *n.* **1.** a follower of Luther (1483-1546), German leader of the Reformation, or a member of a Lutheran Church. ~*adj.* **2.** of or relating to Luther, his doctrines, or any of the Churches that follow these doctrines. —'**Lutheranism** *n.*

lux (lʌks) *n.,* pl. **lux.** the SI unit of illumination. [Latin: light]

luxe (lʌks, luks) *n.* See **de luxe.**

luxuriant (lʌg'zjuərɪənt) *adj.* **1.** rich and abundant; lush. **2.** very elaborate or ornate. [Latin *luxuriāre* to abound to excess] —**lux'uriance** *n.* —**lux'uriantly** *adv.*

luxuriate (lʌg'zjuərɪ‚eit) *vb.* **1.** (foll. by *in*) to take self-indulgent pleasure; revel. **2.** to flourish profusely.

luxurious (lʌg'zjuərɪəs) *adj.* **1.** characterized by luxury. **2.** enjoying or devoted to luxury.

luxury ('lʌkʃərɪ) *n.,* pl. **-ries. 1.** indulgence in and enjoyment of rich, comfortable, and sumptuous living. **2.** something considered an indulgence rather than a necessity. **3.** (*modifier*) relating to, indicating, or supplying luxury: *a luxury liner.* [Latin *luxuria* excess]

LV luncheon voucher.

lyceum (laɪ'sɪəm) *n.* (now chiefly in the names of buildings) a public building for events such as concerts and lectures. [Latin: a school in ancient Athens]

lychee (‚laɪ'tʃiː) *n.* the fruit of a Chinese tree, which has a whitish juicy pulp. [Cantonese *lai chi*]

lych gate (lɪtʃ) *n.* same as **lich gate.**

Lycra ('laɪkrə) *n. Trademark.* a synthetic elastic fabric and fibre used for tight-fitting garments, such as swimming costumes.

lye (laɪ) *n.* **1.** a caustic solution obtained from wood ash. **2.** a concentrated solution of sodium hydroxide or potassium hydroxide. [Old English *lēag*]

lying ('laɪɪŋ) *vb.* the present participle of **lie**[1] and **lie**[2].

lying-in *n.,* pl. **lyings-in.** confinement in childbirth.

lymph (lɪmf) *n.* the almost colourless fluid, containing chiefly white blood cells, that comes from the tissues of the body. [Latin *lympha* water] —**lym'phatic** *adj.*

lymphatic system *n.* a network of fine vessels by which lymph circulates throughout the body.

lymph node *n.* any of many bean-shaped masses of tissue in the lymphatic system that help to protect against infection.

lymphocyte ('lɪmfəʊ‚saɪt) *n.* a type of white blood cell. [*lymph* + Greek *kutos* vessel]

lynch (lɪntʃ) *vb.* (of a mob) to kill (a person) for some supposed offence without a trial. [after Capt. William *Lynch* of Virginia, USA] —'**lynching** *n.*

lynx (lɪŋks) *n.,* pl. **lynxes** or **lynx.** a mammal of the cat family, with grey-brown mottled fur, tufted ears, and a short tail. [Greek *lunx*]

lynx-eyed *adj.* having keen sight.

lyre ('laɪə) *n.* an ancient Greek U-shaped stringed instrument, similar to a harp but plucked with a plectrum. [Greek *lura*]

lyrebird ('laɪə‚bɜːd) *n.* either of two pheasant-like Australian birds: during courtship displays, the male spreads its tail into the shape of a lyre.

lyric ('lɪrɪk) *adj.* **1.** (of poetry) **a.** expressing the writer's personal feelings. **b.** having the form and manner of a song. **2.** of or relating to such poetry. **3.** (of a singing voice) light and melodic. ~*n.* **4.** a short poem of songlike quality. **5.** (*pl.*) the words of a popular song. [Greek *lura* lyre] —'**lyrically** *adv.*

lyrical ('lɪrɪk²l) *adj.* **1.** same as **lyric** (senses 1, 2). **2.** enthusiastic; effusive.

lyricism ('lɪrɪ‚sɪzəm) *n.* **1.** the quality or style of lyric poetry. **2.** emotional outpouring.

lyricist ('lɪrɪsɪst) *n.* a person who writes the words for a song, opera, or musical.

M

m *or* **M** (ɛm) *n.*, *pl.* **m's, M's,** *or* **Ms.** the 13th letter of the English alphabet.

m **1.** metre(s). **2.** mile(s). **3.** milli-. **4.** million. **5.** minute(s).

M **1.** mach. **2.** *Currency.* mark(s). **3.** medium. **4.** mega-. **5.** (in Britain) motorway. **6.** the Roman numeral for 1000.

m. **1.** male. **2.** married. **3.** masculine. **4.** meridian. **5.** month.

M. **1.** Majesty. **2.** Master. **3.** (in titles) Member. **4.** (*pl.* **MM.** *or* **MM**) *French.* Monsieur.

ma (mɑː) *n. Informal.* a mother.

MA **1.** Massachusetts. **2.** Master of Arts.

ma'am (mæm, mɑːm; *unstressed* məm) *n.* short for **madam:** used as a title of respect.

mac *or* **mack** (mæk) *n. Brit. informal.* a mackintosh.

Mac (mæk) *n. Chiefly U.S. & Canad.* an informal term of address to a man. [Gaelic *mac* son of]

macabre (məˈkɑːbrə) *adj.* gruesome; ghastly; grim. [French]

macadam (məˈkædəm) *n.* a road made of compressed layers of small broken stones, esp. one bound together with tar or asphalt. [after John *McAdam,* engineer] —**maˈcadamˌize** *or* **-ˌise** *vb.*

macaque (məˈkɑːk) *n.* any of various Asian and African monkeys with cheek pouches and either a short tail or no tail. [W African *makaku*]

macaroni (ˌmækəˈrəʊnɪ) *n.*, *pl.* **-nis** *or* **-nies.** **1.** pasta tubes made from wheat flour. **2.** (in 18th-century Britain) a dandy. [Italian (dialect) *maccarone*]

macaroon (ˌmækəˈruːn) *n.* a sweet biscuit made of ground almonds. [French *macaron*]

macaw (məˈkɔː) *n.* a large tropical American parrot with a long tail and brilliant plumage. [Portuguese *macau*]

mace¹ (meɪs) *n.* **1.** a club with a spiked metal head used in the Middle Ages. **2.** a ceremonial staff carried by certain officials. [prob. Vulgar Latin *mattea*]

mace² (meɪs) *n.* a spice made from the dried outer casing of the nutmeg. [Latin *macir*]

macebearer (ˈmeɪsˌbɛərə) *n.* a person who carries a mace in processions or ceremonies.

macerate (ˈmæsəˌreɪt) *vb.* **1.** to soften or be softened by soaking. **2.** to become or cause to become thin. [Latin *mācerāre* to soften] —**ˌmacerˈation** *n.*

Mach (mæk) *n.* short for **Mach number.**

machete (məˈʃɛtɪ, -ˈʃeɪ-) *n.* a broad heavy knife used for cutting or as a weapon. [Spanish]

Machiavellian (ˌmækɪəˈvɛlɪən) *adj.* cunning, amoral, and opportunist. [after *Machiavelli,* political philosopher] —**ˌMachiaˈvellianˌism** *n.*

machinate (ˈmækɪˌneɪt) *vb.* to contrive, plan, or devise (schemes, plots, etc.) [Latin *māchinārī* to plan] —**ˌmachiˈnation** *n.*

machine (məˈʃiːn) *n.* **1.** an assembly of components arranged so as to perform a particular task and usually powered by electricity. **2.** a vehicle, such as a car or aircraft. **3.** a system within an organization that controls activities and policies: *the party machine.* ~*vb.* **4.** to shape, cut, or make (something) using a machine. [Latin *māchina* machine, from Greek *makhana* pulley] —**maˈchinable** *adj.*

machine gun *n.* **1.** a rapid-firing automatic gun, using small-arms ammunition. ~*vb.* **machine-gun, -gunning, -gunned.** **2.** to shoot or fire at with a machine gun.

machine language *n.* instructions for a computer in binary or hexadecimal code.

machinery (məˈʃiːnərɪ) *n.*, *pl.* **-eries.** **1.** machines, machine parts, or machine systems collectively. **2.** the mechanism of a machine.

machine shop *n.* a workshop in which machine tools are operated.

machine tool *n.* a power-driven machine, such as a lathe, for cutting and shaping metal, wood, or plastic.

machinist (məˈʃiːnɪst) *n.* **1.** a person who operates machines to cut or process materials. **2.** a maker or repairer of machines.

machismo (mæˈkɪzməʊ, -ˈtʃɪz-) *n.* strong or exaggerated masculinity. [Spanish *macho* male]

Mach number (mæk) *n.* (*often not cap.*) the ratio of the speed of a body in a particular medium to the speed of sound in that medium. [after Ernst *Mach,* physicist]

macho (ˈmætʃəʊ) *adj.* **1.** strongly or exaggeratedly masculine. ~*n.*, *pl.* **machos. 2.** machismo. [from *machismo*]

mack (mæk) *n. Brit. informal.* same as **mac.**

mackerel (ˈmækrəl) *n.*, *pl.* **-rel** *or* **-rels.** an edible sea fish with a greenish-blue body marked with wavy dark bands on the back. [Old French *maquerel*]

mackintosh *or* **macintosh** (ˈmækɪnˌtɒʃ) *n.* **1.** a raincoat made of rubberized cloth. **2.** such cloth. **3.** any raincoat. [after Charles *Macintosh,* who invented it]

macramé (məˈkrɑːmɪ) *n.* a type of ornamental work made by knotting and weaving coarse thread. [Turkish *makrama* towel]

macro- *or before a vowel* **macr-** *combining form.* large, long, or great: *macroscopic.* [Greek *makros*]

macrobiotics (ˌmækrəʊbaɪˈɒtɪks) *n.* (*functioning as sing.*) a dietary system which advocates whole grains and vegetables grown without chemical additives. [Greek *makros* long + *biotos* life] —**ˌmacrobiˈotic** *adj.*

macrocarpa (ˌmækrəʊˈkɑːpə) *n.* a large

New Zealand coniferous tree. [Greek *makros* large + *karpos* fruit]

macrocosm ('mækrǝ,kɒzǝm) *n.* a complex structure, such as the universe or society, regarded as a whole. [Greek *makros* large + *kosmos* great world]

macromolecule (,mækrǝʊ'mɒlɪ,kjuːl) *n.* any very large molecule, such as a protein or synthetic polymer.

macron ('mækrɒn) *n.* a mark (ˉ) placed over a letter to represent a long vowel. [Greek *makros* long]

macroscopic (,mækrǝʊ'skɒpɪk) *adj.* 1. large enough to be visible to the naked eye. 2. comprehensive; concerned with large units. [Greek *makros* large + *skopein* to look at]

macula ('mækjʊlǝ) *n.*, *pl.* **-ulae** (-jʊ,liː). *Anat.* a small spot or area of distinct colour, such as a freckle. [Latin]

mad (mæd) *adj.* **madder, maddest.** 1. mentally deranged; insane. 2. senseless; foolish. 3. (often foll. by *at*) *Informal.* angry. 4. (foll. by *about, on,* or *over*) wildly enthusiastic (about) or fond (of). 5. extremely excited or confused; frantic: *a mad rush.* 6. (of animals) **a.** unusually ferocious: *a mad buffalo.* **b.** afflicted with rabies. 7. **like mad.** *Informal.* with great energy, enthusiasm, or haste. [Old English *gemǣded* made insane] —**'madness** *n.*

madam ('mædǝm) *n.*, *pl.* **madams** or (for sense 1) **mesdames.** 1. a polite term of address for a woman. 2. a woman who runs a brothel. 3. *Brit. informal.* a precocious or pert girl. [Old French *ma dame* my lady]

madame ('mædǝm) *n.*, *pl.* **mesdames.** a French title equivalent to *Mrs.*

madcap ('mæd,kæp) *adj.* 1. impulsive, reckless, or lively. ~*n.* 2. an impulsive, reckless, or lively person.

madden ('mæd³n) *vb.* to make or become mad or angry. —**'maddening** *adj.*

madder ('mædǝ) *n.* 1. a plant with small yellow flowers and a red fleshy root. 2. a dark reddish-purple dye formerly obtained from its root. 3. an artificial pigment of this colour. [Old English *mædere*]

made (meɪd) *vb.* 1. the past of **make.** ~*adj.* 2. produced or shaped as specified: *handmade.* 3. **get** or **have it made.** *Informal.* to be assured of success.

Madeira (mǝ'dɪǝrǝ) *n.* a fortified white wine from Madeira, an island in the N Atlantic.

mademoiselle (,mædmwɑ'zɛl) *n.*, *pl.* **mesdemoiselles.** 1. a French title equivalent to *Miss.* 2. a French teacher or governess.

made-up *adj.* 1. invented; fictional. 2. wearing make-up. 3. put together. 4. (of a road) surfaced with tarmac or concrete.

madhouse ('mæd,haʊs) *n.* *Informal.* 1. a mental hospital. 2. a state of uproar or confusion.

madly ('mædlɪ) *adv.* 1. in an insane or foolish manner. 2. with great speed and energy. 3. *Informal.* extremely or excessively: *I love you madly.*

madman ('mædmǝn) or (*fem.*) **mad-**

woman *n.*, *pl.* **-men** or **-women.** a person who is insane.

Madonna (mǝ'dɒnǝ) *n.* 1. *Chiefly R.C. Church.* the Virgin Mary. 2. (*sometimes not cap.*) a picture or statue of the Virgin Mary. [Italian: my lady]

madrigal ('mædrɪg²l) *n.* a type of 16th- or 17th-century part song for unaccompanied voices. [Medieval Latin *mātricāle* primitive] —**'madrigalist** *n.*

maelstrom ('meɪlstrǝm) *n.* a large powerful whirlpool. [Old Dutch *malen* to whirl round + *stroom* stream]

maenad ('miːnæd) *n.* 1. *Classical history.* a female disciple of Dionysus, Greek god of wine. 2. a frenzied woman. [Greek *mainas* madwoman]

maestro ('maɪstrǝʊ) *n.*, *pl.* **-tri** (-trɪ) or **-tros.** 1. a distinguished music teacher, conductor, or musician. 2. any master of an art. [Italian: master]

mae west (meɪ) *n.* *Slang.* an inflatable life jacket. [after *Mae West,* actress renowned for her generous bust]

Mafia ('mæfɪǝ) *n.* **the.** a secret criminal organization founded in Sicily, and carried to the U.S. by Italian immigrants. [Sicilian dialect, lit.: hostility to the law]

mafioso (,mæfɪ'ǝʊsǝʊ) *n.*, *pl.* **-sos** or **-si** (-sɪ). a member of the Mafia.

magazine (,mægǝ'ziːn) *n.* 1. a periodic paperback publication containing written pieces and illustrations. 2. a television or radio programme made up of short nonfictional items. 3. a metal case holding several cartridges used in some automatic firearms. 4. a place for storing weapons, explosives, or military equipment. 5. a stock of ammunition. 6. a rack for automatically feeding slides through a projector. [Arabic *makhāzin* storehouses]

magenta (mǝ'dʒɛntǝ) *adj.* deep purplish-red. [after *Magenta,* Italy]

maggot ('mægǝt) *n.* the limbless larva of various insects, esp. the housefly and blowfly. [earlier *mathek*] —**'maggoty** *adj.*

magi ('meɪdʒaɪ) *pl. n.*, *sing.* **magus** ('meɪgǝs). 1. See **magus.** 2. **the three Magi.** *Christianity.* the wise men from the East who came to do homage to the infant Jesus (Matthew 2:1–12). [see MAGUS]

magic ('mædʒɪk) *n.* 1. the supposed invocation of supernatural powers to influence events; sorcery. 2. tricks done to entertain; conjuring. 3. any mysterious or extraordinary quality or power. 4. **like magic.** very quickly. ~*adj. also* **magical.** 5. of magic. 6. possessing or considered to possess mysterious powers. 7. unaccountably enchanting. 8. *Informal.* wonderful; marvellous. ~*vb.* **-icking, -icked.** 9. to transform or produce as if by magic. 10. (foll. by *away*) to cause to disappear as if by magic. [Greek *magikē* witchcraft] —**'magically** *adv.*

magician (mǝ'dʒɪʃǝn) *n.* 1. a conjurer. 2. a person with magic powers.

magic lantern *n.* an early type of slide projector.

magisterial (,mædʒɪ'stɪǝrɪǝl) *adj.* 1. commanding; authoritative. **2.** of a magistrate. [Latin *magister* master] —**magisterially** *adv.*

magistracy ('mædʒɪstrəsɪ) *n., pl.* **-cies. 1.** the office or function of a magistrate. **2.** magistrates collectively.

magistrate ('mædʒɪˌstreɪt) *n.* **1.** a public officer concerned with the administration of law. **2.** same as **justice of the peace.** [Latin *magister* master]

magistrates' court *n.* (in England) a court that deals with minor crimes, certain civil actions, and preliminary hearings.

magma ('mægmə) *n., pl.* **-mas** or **-mata** (-mətə). hot molten rock within the earth's crust which sometimes finds its way to the surface where it solidifies to form igneous rock. [Greek: salve made by kneading]

Magna Carta ('mægnə 'kɑːtə) *n. English history.* the charter granted by King John at Runnymede in 1215, recognizing the rights and privileges of the barons, church, and freemen. [Medieval Latin: great charter]

magnanimous (mæg'nænɪməs) *adj.* generous and noble. [Latin *magnanimus* greatsouled] —**magnanimity** (ˌmægnə'nɪmɪtɪ) *n.* —**mag'nanimously** *adv.*

magnate ('mægneɪt) *n.* a person of power and rank, esp. in industry. [Late Latin *magnates* great men]

magnesia (mæg'niːʒə) *n.* a white tasteless substance used as an antacid and laxative; magnesium oxide. [Greek *Magnēsia,* of *Magnēs,* ancient mineral-rich region]

magnesium (mæg'niːzɪəm) *n.* a light silvery-white metallic element that burns with an intense white flame. Symbol: Mg [from *magnesia*]

magnet ('mægnɪt) *n.* **1.** a piece of iron, steel, or lodestone that has the property of attracting iron to it. **2.** a person or thing that exerts a great attraction. [Greek *magnēs*]

magnetic (mæg'nɛtɪk) *adj.* **1.** of, producing, or operated by means of magnetism. **2.** of or like a magnet. **3.** capable of being magnetized. **4.** exerting a powerful attraction: *a magnetic personality.* —**mag'netically** *adv.*

magnetic disk *n.* a computer storage disk.

magnetic field *n.* an area around a magnet in which its power of attraction is felt.

magnetic mine *n.* a mine which detonates when a magnetic field such as that generated by the metal of a ship's hull is detected.

magnetic needle *n.* a slender magnetized rod used in certain instruments, such as the magnetic compass, for indicating the direction of a magnetic field.

magnetic north *n.* the direction in which a compass needle points, at an angle from the direction of true (geographic) north.

magnetic pole *n.* either of two variable points on the earth's surface towards which a magnetic needle points.

magnetic storm *n.* a sudden severe disturbance of the earth's magnetic field, caused by emission of charged particles from the sun.

magnetic tape *n.* a long plastic strip coated with a magnetic substance, and used to record sound or video signals or to store information in computers.

magnetism ('mægnɪˌtɪzəm) *n.* **1.** the property of attraction displayed by magnets. **2.** the branch of physics concerned with magnetic phenomena. **3.** powerful personal charm.

magnetite ('mægnɪˌtaɪt) *n.* a black magnetizable mineral that is an important source of iron.

magnetize or **-ise** ('mægnɪˌtaɪz) *vb.* **1.** to make (a substance or object) magnetic. **2.** to attract strongly. —**'magnet,izable** or **-,isable** *adj.* —**,magneti'zation** or **-i'sation** *n.*

magneto (mæg'niːtəʊ) *n., pl.* **-tos.** a small electric generator in which the magnetic field is produced by a permanent magnet. [short for *magnetoelectric generator*]

magnetron ('mægnɪˌtrɒn) *n.* an electronic valve used with a magnetic field to generate microwave oscillations, esp. for use in radar. [*magnet* + *electron*]

Magnificat (mæg'nɪfɪˌkæt) *n. Christianity.* the hymn of the Virgin Mary (Luke 1:46-55), used as a canticle. [from its opening word]

magnification (ˌmægnɪfɪ'keɪʃən) *n.* **1.** the act of magnifying or the state of being magnified. **2.** the degree to which something is magnified. **3.** a magnified copy of something.

magnificent (mæg'nɪfɪs*ə*nt) *adj.* **1.** splendid or impressive in appearance. **2.** superb or very fine: *a magnificent performance.* [Latin *magnificus* great in deeds] —**mag'nificence** *n.* —**mag'nificently** *adv.*

magnify ('mægnɪˌfaɪ) *vb.* **-fying, -fied. 1.** to increase in apparent size, as through the action of a lens or microscope. **2.** to exaggerate: *don't magnify your troubles.* **3.** *Archaic.* to glorify. [Latin *magnificāre* to praise]

magnifying glass or **magnifier** ('mægnɪˌfaɪə) *n.* a convex lens used to produce an enlarged image of an object.

magniloquent (mæg'nɪləkwənt) *adj.* (of speech) lofty in style; grandiloquent. [Latin *magnus* great + *loqui* to speak] —**mag'niloquence** *n.*

magnitude ('mægnɪˌtjuːd) *n.* **1.** relative importance: *a problem of the first magnitude.* **2.** relative size or extent. **3.** *Astron.* the apparent brightness of a celestial body expressed on a numerical scale on which bright stars have a low value. [Latin *magnitūdō* size]

magnolia (mæg'nəʊlɪə) *n.* an Asian and North American tree or shrub with white, pink, purple, or yellow showy flowers. [after Pierre *Magnol,* botanist]

magnox ('mægnɒks) *n.* an alloy composed mainly of magnesium, used in fuel elements of some nuclear reactors (**magnox reactors**). [from *mag(nesium) n(o) ox(idation)*]

magnum (ˈmægnəm) n., pl. **-nums.** a wine bottle of twice the normal size. [Latin: a big thing]

magnum opus n. a great work of art or literature, esp. the greatest single work of an artist. [Latin]

magpie (ˈmægˌpaɪ) n. **1.** a bird of the crow family with black-and-white plumage, a long tail, and a chattering call. **2.** Brit. a person who hoards small objects. [from Mag, dim. of Margaret + pie, obs. name for the magpie]

magus (ˈmeɪgəs) n., pl. **magi. 1.** a Zoroastrian priest. **2.** an astrologer or magician of ancient times. [Old Persian magus magician]

Magyar (ˈmægjɑː) n. **1.** (pl. **-yars**) a member of the main ethnic group of Hungary. **2.** the Hungarian language. ~adj. **3.** of the Magyars or their language.

maharajah or **maharaja** (ˌmɑːhəˈrɑːdʒə) n. an Indian prince. esp. any of the rulers of the former native states. [Hindi: great rajah]

maharani or **maharanee** (ˌmɑːhəˈrɑːnɪ) n. the wife of a maharajah. [Hindi: great rani]

maharishi (ˌmɑːhəˈriːʃɪ, məˈhɑːrɪʃɪ) n. Hinduism. a teacher of religious and mystical knowledge. [Hindi: great sage]

mahatma (məˈhɑːtmə) n. (sometimes cap.) a person revered for his holiness or wisdom. [Sanskrit mahā great + ātman soul]

mahjong or **mah-jongg** (ˌmɑːˈdʒɒŋ) n. a game of Chinese origin, usually played by four people, using tiles bearing various designs. [Chinese, lit.: sparrows]

mahogany (məˈhɒgənɪ) n., pl. **-nies. 1.** the hard reddish-brown wood of any of several tropical trees. ~adj. **2.** reddish-brown. [origin unknown]

mahout (məˈhaʊt) n. (in India and the East Indies) an elephant driver or keeper. [Hindi mahāut]

maid (meɪd) n. **1.** a female servant. **2.** Archaic or literary. a young unmarried girl; maiden. [form of maiden]

maiden (ˈmeɪdᵊn) n. **1.** Archaic or literary. a young unmarried girl, esp. a virgin. **2.** Horse racing. a horse that has never won a race. **3.** (modifier) unmarried: a maiden aunt. **4.** (modifier) first; earliest: a maiden voyage. [Old English mægden] —**maidenhood** n. —**maidenly** adj.

maidenhair fern (ˈmeɪdᵊnˌhɛə) n. a fern with delicate hairlike fronds of small pale green leaflets.

maidenhead (ˈmeɪdᵊnˌhɛd) n. **1.** the hymen. **2.** virginity; maidenhood.

maiden name n. a woman's surname before marriage.

maiden over n. Cricket. an over in which no runs are scored.

maid of honour n. **1.** an unmarried lady attending a queen or princess. **2.** U.S. & Canad. the principal unmarried attendant of a bride.

maidservant (ˈmeɪdˌsɜːvənt) n. a female servant.

mail[1] (meɪl) n. **1.** letters and packages transported and delivered by the post office. **2.** the postal system. **3.** a single collection or delivery of mail. **4.** a train, ship, or aircraft that carries mail. ~vb. **5.** Chiefly U.S. & Canad. to send by mail. [Old French male bag]

mail[2] (meɪl) n. flexible armour consisting of riveted metal rings or links. [Old French maille mesh] —**mailed** adj.

mailbag (ˈmeɪlˌbæg) n. a large bag for transporting or delivering mail.

mail coach n. Hist. a fast stagecoach designed primarily for carrying mail.

mailing list n. a register of names and addresses to which information or advertising matter is sent by post.

mail order n. a system of buying and selling goods by post.

mailshot (ˈmeɪlˌʃɒt) n. a posting of circulars, leaflets, or other advertising to a selected large number of people at once.

maim (meɪm) vb. to mutilate, cripple, or disable. [Old French mahaignier to wound]

main (meɪn) adj. **1.** chief or principal. ~n. **2.** a principal pipe or line in a system used to distribute water, electricity, or gas. **3.** (pl.) the main distribution network for water, gas, or electricity. **4.** great strength or force (now esp. in (with) **might and main**). **5.** Literary. the open ocean. **6.** Archaic. the mainland. **7. in the main.** on the whole. [Old English mægen strength]

mainbrace (ˈmeɪnˌbreɪs) n. Naut. **1.** the rope that controls the movement of the spar of a ship's mainsail. **2. splice the mainbrace.** See **splice.**

main clause n. Grammar. a clause that can stand alone as a sentence.

mainframe (ˈmeɪnˌfreɪm) n. Computers. a high-speed general-purpose computer, with a large store capacity.

mainland (ˈmeɪnlənd) n. the main part of a land mass as opposed to an island.

main line n. **1.** Railways. the trunk route between two points, usually fed by branch lines. ~vb. **mainline. 2.** Slang. to inject a drug into a vein.

mainly (ˈmeɪnlɪ) adv. for the most part; principally.

mainmast (ˈmeɪnˌmɑːst) n. Naut. the chief mast of a sailing vessel with two or more masts.

mainsail (ˈmeɪnˌseɪl; Naut. ˈmeɪnsᵊl) n. Naut. the largest and lowermost sail on the mainmast.

mainspring (ˈmeɪnˌsprɪŋ) n. the chief cause or motive of something.

mainstay (ˈmeɪnˌsteɪ) n. a chief support.

mainstream (ˈmeɪnˌstriːm) n. the main current (of a river or cultural trend).

mainstreeting (ˈmeɪnˌstriːtɪŋ) n. Canad. the practice of a politician walking about a town or city to try to gain votes.

maintain (meɪnˈteɪn) vb. **1.** to continue or retain; keep in existence. **2.** to keep in proper or good condition. **3.** to enable (a person) to support a style of living: the money maintained us for a month. **4.** (takes a clause as object) to assert: she maintained that the plan was bound to fail.

5. to defend against contradiction; uphold: *she maintained her innocence.* [from Latin *manū tenēre* to hold in the hand]

maintenance (ˈmeɪntɪnəns) *n.* **1.** the act of maintaining or the state of being maintained. **2.** a means of support; livelihood. **3.** *Law.* financial provision ordered to be made by way of periodical payments or a lump sum, as for a spouse after a divorce.

maisonette (ˌmeɪzəˈnɛt) *n.* a flat with more than one floor. [French, diminutive of *maison* house]

maître d'hôtel (ˌmɛtrə dəʊˈtɛl) *n., pl.* **maîtres d'hôtel.** a head waiter. [French]

maize (meɪz) *n.* a tall annual grass cultivated for its yellow edible grains, which are used for food and as a source of oil. [Spanish *maiz*]

Maj. Major.

majesty (ˈmædʒɪstɪ) *n.* **1.** great stateliness of bearing; grandeur. **2.** supreme power or authority. [Latin *mājestās*] —**maˈjestic** *adj.* —**maˈjestically** *adv.*

Majesty (ˈmædʒɪstɪ) *n., pl.* **-ties.** (preceded by *Your, His, Her,* or *Their*) a title used to address or refer to a sovereign or the wife or widow of a sovereign.

majolica (məˈdʒɒlɪkə, məˈjɒl-) *or* **maiolica** (məˈjɒlɪkə) *n.* a type of porous pottery glazed with bright metallic oxides that was extensively made in Renaissance Italy. [Italian, from Late Latin *Mājorica* Majorca]

major (ˈmeɪdʒə) *n.* **1.** a middle-ranking military officer. **2.** (often preceded by *the*) *Music.* a major key, chord, mode, or scale. **3.** a person who has reached the age of legal majority. **4.** *U.S., Canad., Austral., & N.Z.* the principal field of study of a student. ~*adj.* **5.** of greater size, number, or importance. **6.** very serious or significant. **7.** main or principal. **8.** *Music.* (of a scale) **a.** having notes separated by a whole tone, except for the third and fourth degrees, and seventh and eighth degrees, which are separated by a semitone. **b.** of or based on the major scale: *a major key.* ~*vb.* **9.** (usually foll. by *in*) *U.S., Canad., Austral., & N.Z.* to do one's principal study (in a particular subject): *to major in English literature.* [Latin: greater]

major-domo (-ˈdəʊməʊ) *n., pl.* **-mos.** the chief steward or butler of a great household. [Medieval Latin *mājor domūs* head of the household]

majorette (ˌmeɪdʒəˈrɛt) *n.* one of a group of girls who practise formation marching and baton twirling.

major general *n.* a senior military officer.

majority (məˈdʒɒrɪtɪ) *n., pl.* **-ties.** **1.** the greater number or part of something. **2.** (in an election) the number of votes or seats by which the strongest party or candidate beats the combined opposition or the runner-up. **3.** the largest party or group that votes together in an assembly. **4.** full legal age. **5. in the majority.** forming or part of the greater number of something. [Medieval Latin *mājorītās*]

make (meɪk) *vb.* **making, made. 1.** to bring into being by shaping, changing, or combining materials or ideas; form. **2.** to draw up; establish: *to make one's will.* **3.** to bring about or produce: *don't make a noise.* **4.** to compel or induce: *please make him go away.* **5.** to appoint: *they made him chairman.* **6.** to come into a specified state or condition: *to make merry.* **7.** to become: *he will make a good teacher.* **8.** to cause or ensure the success of: *your news has made my day.* **9.** to amount to: *5 and 5 make 10.* **10.** to serve as or be suitable for: *that piece of cloth will make a coat.* **11.** to prepare for use: *to make a bed.* **12.** to be the essential element in: *charm makes a good salesman.* **13.** to carry out, effect, or do. **14.** (foll. by *to*, *as if to*, or *as though to*) to act with the intention or with a show of doing something: *he made as if to hit her.* **15.** to use for a specified purpose: *I will make this town my base.* **16.** to deliver: *to make a speech.* **17.** to consider to be: *what time do you make it?* **18.** to cause to seem or represent as being. **19.** to acquire: *to make friends.* **20.** to engage in: *to make war.* **21.** to travel: *we can make a hundred miles by nightfall.* **22.** to arrive in time for: *he didn't make the first act of the play.* **23.** to win or score. **24.** *Informal.* to gain a place or position on or in: *to make the headlines.* **25. make a day, night,** etc., **of it.** to cause an activity to last a day, night, etc. **26. make eyes at.** to flirt with or ogle. **27. make it.** *Informal.* to succeed. **28. make like.** *Slang, chiefly U.S. & Canad.* **a.** to imitate. **b.** to pretend. ~*n.* **29.** manufacturer; brand. **30.** the way in which something is made. **31. on the make.** *Slang.* out for profit or conquest. ~See also **make away, make for,** etc. [Old English *macian*] —**ˈmaker** *n.*

make away *vb.* **1.** to depart in haste. **2. make away with. a.** to steal. **b.** to kill or get rid of.

make believe *vb.* **1.** to pretend. ~*n.* **make-believe. 2.** a fantasy or pretence.

make for *vb.* **1.** to head towards. **2.** to prepare to attack. **3.** to help bring about.

make of *vb.* to interpret as the meaning of: *what do you make of it all?*

make off *vb.* **1.** to go or run away in haste. **2. make off with.** to steal or abduct.

make out *vb.* **1.** to perceive. **2.** to understand. **3.** to write out: *he made out a cheque.* **4.** to attempt to establish or prove: *he made me out to be a liar.* **5.** to pretend: *he made out that he could cook.* **6.** to manage.

Maker (ˈmeɪkə) *n.* a title given to God.

makeshift (ˈmeɪkˌʃɪft) *adj.* serving as a temporary substitute.

make-up *n.* **1.** cosmetics, such as powder or lipstick. **2.** the cosmetics used by an actor to adapt his appearance. **3.** the arrangement of the parts of something. **4.** mental or physical constitution. ~*vb.* **make up. 5.** to form or constitute: *these arguments make up the case for the defence.* **6.** to devise or compose, sometimes with the intent to deceive: *to make up an excuse.* **7.** to supply what is lacking in; complete: *these extra people will make up* *our numbers.* **8.** (foll. by *for*) to compensate or atone (for). **9.** to settle (differences) amicably (often in **make it up**). **10.** to apply cosmetics to (the face). **11. make up to.** *Informal.* **a.** to make friendly overtures to. **b.** to flirt with.

makeweight ('meɪk,weɪt) *n.* **1.** something put on a scale to make up a required weight. **2.** an unimportant person or thing added to make up a lack.

making ('meɪkɪŋ) *n.* **1.** the act or process of producing something. **2. be the making of.** to cause the success of. **3. in the making.** in the process of becoming or being made.

makings ('meɪkɪŋz) *pl. n.* potentials, qualities, or materials: *he had the makings of a leader.*

mal- *combining form.* bad or badly; wrong or wrongly: *maladjusted; malfunction.* [Latin *malus* bad, *male* badly]

malachite ('mælə,kaɪt) *n.* a green mineral used as a source of copper, and for making ornaments. [Greek *molokhitis*]

maladjustment (,mælə'dʒʌstmənt) *n. Psychol.* a failure to meet the demands of society, such as coping with problems and social relationships. —,**malad'justed** *adj.*

maladminister (,mæləd'mɪnɪstə) *vb.* to administer badly, inefficiently, or dishonestly. —,**malad,minis'tration** *n.*

maladroit (,mælə'drɔɪt) *adj.* clumsy, awkward, or tactless. [French *mal* badly + ADROIT] —,**mala'droitly** *adv.* —,**mala'droitness** *n.*

malady ('mælədɪ) *n., pl.* **-dies.** any disease or illness. [Latin *male habitus* in poor condition]

malaise (mæ'leɪz) *n.* a feeling of unease, mild sickness, or depression. [Old French *mal* bad + *aise* ease]

malapropism ('mæləprop,ɪzəm) *n.* the comic misuse of a word by confusion with one of similar sound, as in *under the affluence of alcohol.* [after Mrs *Malaprop* in Sheridan's play *The Rivals*]

malaria (mə'lɛərɪə) *n.* a disease with recurring attacks of fever, caused by the bite of a mosquito. [Italian *mala aria* bad air] —**ma'larial** *adj.*

malarkey (mə'lɑːkɪ) *n. Slang.* nonsense; rubbish. [origin unknown]

Malay (mə'leɪ) *n.* **1.** a member of a people living chiefly in Malaysia and Indonesia. **2.** the language of this people. ~*adj.* **3.** of the Malays or their language.

Malayan (mə'leɪən) *adj.* **1.** of or from the Malay peninsula in SE Asia. ~*n.* **2.** a person from the Malay peninsula.

malcontent ('mælkən,tɛnt) *n.* a person who is discontented with the existing situation. [Old French]

male (meɪl) *adj.* **1.** of the sex that can fertilize female reproductive cells. **2.** of or characteristic of a man. **3.** for or composed of men or boys: *a male choir.* **4.** (of flowers) bearing stamens but lacking a pistil. **5.** *Electronics, engineering.* having a projecting part or parts that fit into a hollow counterpart: *a male plug.* ~*n.* **6.** a

male person, animal, or plant. [Latin *masculus* masculine] —'**maleness** *n.*

male chauvinism *n.* the belief, held by certain men, that men are superior to women. —**male chauvinist** *n., adj.*

malediction (,mælɪ'dɪkʃən) *n.* the utterance of a curse against someone or something. [Latin *maledictiō* a reviling] —,**mal-e'dictory** *adj.*

malefactor ('mælɪ,fæktə) *n.* a criminal; wrongdoer. [Latin *malefacere* to do evil] —,**male'faction** *n.*

malevolent (mə'lɛvələnt) *adj.* wishing evil to others; malicious. [Latin *malevolens*] —**ma'levolence** *n.* —**ma'levolently** *adv.*

malfeasance (mæl'fiːz²ns) *n. Law.* wrongful or illegal behaviour, esp. by a public official. [Old French *mal faisant* evil-doing]

malformation (,mælfɔː'meɪʃən) *n.* **1.** the condition of being faulty or abnormal in form or shape. **2.** *Pathol.* a deformity, esp. when congenital. —**mal'formed** *adj.*

malfunction (mæl'fʌŋkʃən) *vb.* **1.** to function imperfectly or fail to function. ~*n.* **2.** failure to function or defective functioning.

malice ('mælɪs) *n.* the desire to do harm or cause mischief. [Latin *malus* evil] —**ma'licious** *adj.*

malice aforethought *n. Law.* a deliberate intention to do something unlawful.

malign (mə'laɪn) *adj.* **1.** evil in influence, intention, or effect. ~*vb.* **2.** to slander or defame. [Latin *malignus* spiteful]

malignant (mə'lɪgnənt) *adj.* **1.** seeking to harm others. **2.** tending to cause great harm; injurious. **3.** *Pathol.* (of a tumour) uncontrollable or resistant to therapy. [Late Latin *malignāre* to behave spitefully] —**ma'lignancy** *n.*

malignity (mə'lɪgnɪtɪ) *n.* the condition of being malign or deadly.

malinger (mə'lɪŋgə) *vb.* to pretend or exaggerate illness, esp. to avoid work. [French *malingre* sickly] —**ma'lingerer** *n.*

mall (mɔːl, mæl) *n.* **1.** a shaded avenue, esp. one open to the public. **2.** a street or shopping centre closed to vehicles. [after *the Mall*, in St James's Park, London]

mallard ('mælɑːd) *n., pl.* **-lard** *or* **-lards.** a common N hemisphere duck, the male of which has a dark green head. [Old French *mallart*]

malleable ('mælɪəb²l) *adj.* **1.** (esp. of metal) able to be worked, hammered, or shaped without breaking. **2.** able to be influenced. [Medieval Latin *malleābilis*] —,**mallea'bility** *n.* —'**malleably** *adv.*

mallet ('mælɪt) *n.* **1.** a hammer with a large, often wooden head. **2.** a long stick with a head like a hammer used to strike the ball in croquet or polo. [Old French *maillet* wooden hammer]

mallow ('mæləʊ) *n.* any of a group of European plants, having purple, pink, or white flowers. [Latin *malva*]

malmsey ('mɑːmzɪ) *n.* a sweet Madeira wine. [from *Monembasia*, Greek port]

malnutrition (,mælnjuː'trɪʃən) *n.* physical

weakness resulting from insufficient food or unbalanced diet.

malodorous (mæl'əudərəs) adj. having a bad smell.

malpractice (mæl'præktɪs) n. illegal, unethical, or negligent professional conduct.

malt (mɔːlt) n. **1.** cereal grain, such as barley, that is kiln-dried after it has germinated by soaking in water. **2.** See **malt whisky.** ~vb. **3.** to make into or become malt. [Old English mealt] —'**malty** adj.

Maltese (mɔːl'tiːz) adj. **1.** of Malta, an island in the Mediterranean, its inhabitants, or their language. ~n. **2.** (pl. -tese) a person from Malta. **3.** the language of Malta.

Maltese cross n. a cross with triangular arms that taper towards the centre, sometimes having indented outer sides.

Malthusian (mæl'θjuːzɪən) adj. of the theory stating that increases in population tend to exceed increases in the food supply and that therefore sexual restraint should be exercised. [after T. R. Malthus, economist]

maltose ('mɔːltəʊz) n. a sugar formed by the action of enzymes on starch. [malt + -ose indicating a sugar]

maltreat (mæl'triːt) vb. to treat badly, cruelly, or violently. [French maltraiter] —**mal'treatment** n.

malt whisky n. whisky made from malted barley.

malversation (ˌmælvɜː'seɪʃən) n. Rare. professional or public misconduct. [French malverser to behave badly]

mam (mæm) n. Informal or dialect. same as **mother.**

mama or esp. U.S. **mamma** (mə'mɑː) n. Old-fashioned, informal. same as **mother.** [reduplication of childish syllable ma]

mamba ('mæmbə) n. a poisonous tropical African tree snake. [Zulu im-amba]

mambo ('mæmbəʊ) n., pl. -bos. a modern Latin American dance resembling the rumba. [American Spanish]

mammal ('mæməl) n. any warm-blooded vertebrate animal, the female of which produces milk to feed her young. [Latin mamma breast] —**mammalian** (mæ'meɪlɪən) adj., n.

mammary gland ('mæmərɪ) n. any of the milk-producing glands in mammals, such as a woman's breast or a cow's udder. [Latin mamma breast]

mammon ('mæmən) n. wealth regarded as a source of evil and corruption, personified in the New Testament as a false god (**Mammon**). [New Testament Greek mammōnas wealth]

mammoth ('mæməθ) n. **1.** a large extinct elephant with a hairy coat and long curved tusks. ~adj. **2.** gigantic. [Russian ma‾mot]

man (mæn) n., pl. **men. 1.** an adult male human being, as distinguished from a woman. **2.** a human being of either sex; person: all men are born equal. **3.** human beings collectively; mankind. **4.** a human being regarded as representative of a particular period or category: medieval man; Nean-

derthal man. **5.** an adult male human being with qualities associated with the male, such as courage or virility: take it like a man. **6.** a subordinate, servant, or employee. **7.** (usually pl.) a member of the armed forces who is not an officer, (as in **officers and men**). **8.** a member of a group or team. **9.** a husband, boyfriend, or male lover. **10.** a movable piece in various games, such as draughts. **11.** S. African slang. any person. **12. as one man.** with unanimous action or response. **13. he's your man.** he's the person needed. **14. man and boy.** from childhood. **15. sort out the men from the boys.** to discover who can cope with difficult or dangerous situations and who cannot. **16. to a man.** without exception. ~vb. **manning, manned. 17.** to provide with sufficient men for operation or defence. **18.** to take one's place at or near in readiness for action. [Old English mann] —'**manhood** n.

Man. Manitoba.

manacle ('mænək'l) n. **1.** (usually pl.) a shackle, handcuff, or fetter, used to secure a prisoner or convict. ~vb. **2.** to put manacles on. [Latin manus hand]

manage ('mænɪdʒ) vb. **1.** to be in charge (of); administer: to manage a shop. **2.** to succeed in being able (to do something); contrive. **3.** to have room or time for: can you manage dinner tomorrow? **4.** to exercise control or domination over. **5.** to struggle on despite difficulties, esp. financial ones. **6.** to wield or handle (a weapon). [Italian maneggiare to train (esp. horses)] —'**manageable** adj.

management ('mænɪdʒmənt) n. **1.** the people responsible for running an organization or business. **2.** managers or employers collectively. **3.** the technique or practice of managing or controlling.

manager ('mænɪdʒə) n. **1.** a person who manages an organization or business. **2.** a person who controls the business affairs of an actor or entertainer. **3.** a person in charge of a sports team. —ˌ**manage'ress** fem. n.

managerial (ˌmænɪ'dʒɪərɪəl) adj. of a manager or management.

mañana (mə'njɑːnə) n., adv. **a.** tomorrow. **b.** some other and later time. [Spanish]

man-at-arms n., pl. **men-at-arms.** a soldier, esp. a medieval soldier.

manatee (ˌmænə'tiː) n. a large plant-eating mammal occurring in tropical coastal waters of the Atlantic. [Carib Manattoui]

Manchu (mæn'tʃuː) n., pl. **-chus** or **-chu.** a member of a Mongoloid people of Manchuria, a region of NE China, who conquered China in the 17th century, ruling until 1912.

Mancunian (mæŋ'kjuːnɪən) n. **1.** a person from Manchester, a city in NW England. ~adj. **2.** of Manchester. [Medieval Latin Mancunium Manchester]

mandala ('mændələ) n. Hindu & Buddhist art. a circular design symbolizing the universe. [Sanskrit: circle]

mandarin ('mændərɪn) n. **1.** (in the Chinese Empire) a member of a senior grade of the bureaucracy. **2.** a high-ranking official with extensive powers. **3.** a person of standing and influence, as in literary or intellectual circles. **4.** a small citrus fruit resembling the tangerine. [Sanskrit *mantrin* counsellor]

Mandarin Chinese *or* **Mandarin** *n.* the official language of China since 1917.

mandate ('mændeɪt) *n.* **1.** an official or authoritative command. **2.** *Politics.* the political authority given to a government or an elected representative through an electoral victory. **3.** (*often cap.*) Also: **mandated territory.** (formerly) a territory administered by one country on behalf of an international body. ~*vb.* **4.** to assign (territory) to a nation under a mandate. **5.** to delegate authority to. [Latin *mandāre* to command]

mandatory ('mændətrɪ) *adj.* **1.** having the nature or powers of a mandate. **2.** obligatory; compulsory. —'**mandatorily** *adv.*

mandible ('mændɪbʲl) *n.* **1.** the lower jawbone in vertebrates. **2.** either of the jawlike mouthparts of an insect. **3.** either part of the bill of a bird, esp. the lower part. [Late Latin *mandibula* jaw]

mandolin (,mændə'lɪn) *n.* a musical instrument with four pairs of strings stretched over a small light body: usually played with a plectrum. [Italian *mandolino*, dim.]

mandrake ('mændreɪk) *n.* a plant with a forked root. It was formerly thought to have magic powers and a narcotic was prepared from its root. [Latin *mandragoras*]

mandrel *or* **mandril** ('mændrəl) *n.* **1.** a spindle on which the piece being worked on is supported during machining. **2.** a shaft on which a machining tool is mounted. [perhaps from French *mandrin* lathe]

mandrill ('mændrɪl) *n.* a monkey of W Africa. The male has red and blue markings on its face and buttocks. [*man* + *drill* an Old-World monkey]

mane (meɪn) *n.* **1.** the long hair that grows from the neck in such mammals as the lion and horse. **2.** long thick human hair. [Old English *manu*] —**maned** *adj.*

manège *or* **manege** (mæ'neɪʒ) *n.* **1.** the art of training horses and riders. **2.** a riding school. [Italian *maneggiare* to manage]

maneuver (mə'nuːvə) *n., vb. U.S.* same as **manoeuvre.**

man Friday *n.* **1.** a loyal male servant or assistant. **2.** Also: **girl Friday, person Friday.** any factotum, esp. in an office. [after the native in *Robinson Crusoe*]

manful ('mænful) *adj.* resolute, strong; manly. —'**manfully** *adv.*

manganese ('mæŋgə,niːz) *n.* a brittle greyish-white metallic element: used in making steel. Symbol: Mn [prob. altered form of Medieval Latin *magnesia*]

mange (meɪndʒ) *n.* a skin disease of domestic animals, characterized by itching and loss of hair. [Old French *mangeue* itch]

mangelwurzel ('mæŋgʲl,wɜːzʲl) *n.* a vari-

ety of beet with a large yellowish root. [German *Mangold* beet + *Wurzel* root]

manger ('meɪndʒə) *n.* a trough or box in a stable or barn from which horses or cattle feed. [Old French *maingeure*]

mangetout ('mɒnʒ,tuː) *n.* a variety of garden pea with an edible pod. [French: eat all]

mangle[1] ('mæŋgʲl) *vb.* **1.** to mutilate or destroy by cutting, crushing, or tearing. **2.** to ruin; spoil. [Norman French *mangler* maim] —'**mangled** *adj.*

mangle[2] ('mæŋgʲl) *n.* **1.** a machine for pressing or squeezing water out of washed clothes, consisting of two heavy rollers between which the clothes are passed. ~*vb.* **2.** to put through a mangle. [Dutch *mangel*]

mango ('mæŋgəʊ) *n., pl.* **-goes** *or* **-gos.** the egg-shaped edible fruit of a tropical Asian tree, with a smooth rind and sweet juicy flesh. [Malay *mangā*]

mangrove ('mæŋgrəʊv, 'mæn-) *n.* a tropical evergreen tree or shrub with intertwining aerial roots that forms dense thickets along coasts. [older *mangrow* (changed through infl. of *grove*), from Portuguese *mangue*]

mangy ('meɪndʒɪ) *adj.* **-gier, -giest.** **1.** having or caused by mange. **2.** scruffy or shabby. —'**mangily** *adv.* —'**manginess** *n.*

manhandle ('mæn,hændʲl) *vb.* **1.** to handle or push (someone) about roughly. **2.** to move or do by manpower rather than by machinery.

manhole ('mæn,həʊl) *n.* a hole with a detachable cover, through which a person can enter a sewer or pipe to inspect or repair it.

man-hour *n.* a unit of work in industry, equal to the work done by one person in one hour.

manhunt ('mæn,hʌnt) *n.* an organized search, usually by police, for a wanted man or fugitive.

mania ('meɪnɪə) *n.* **1.** a mental disorder characterized by great or violent excitement. **2.** obsessional enthusiasm or partiality. [Greek: madness] —**manic** ('mænɪk) *adj., n.*

-mania *n. combining form.* indicating extreme or abnormal excitement aroused by something: *kleptomania.*

maniac ('meɪnɪ,æk) *n.* **1.** a wild disorderly person. **2.** a person who has a great craving or enthusiasm for something. [Late Latin *maniacus* belonging to madness] —**maniacal** (mə'naɪəkʲl) *adj.*

manic-depressive (,mænɪkdɪ'presɪv) *Psychiatry.* ~*adj.* **1.** denoting a mental disorder characterized by an alternation between extreme euphoria and deep depression. ~*n.* **2.** a person afflicted with this disorder.

manicure ('mænɪ,kjʊə) *n.* **1.** cosmetic care of the hands and fingernails, as by trimming the nails. ~*vb.* **2.** to care for (the hands and fingernails) in this way. [Latin *manus* hand + *cūra* care] —'**mani,curist** *n.*

manifest ('mænɪˌfɛst) *adj.* **1.** easily noticed, obvious. ~*vb.* **2.** to show plainly. **3.** to be evidence of. **4.** (of a disembodied spirit) to appear in visible form. ~*n.* **5.** a customs document containing particulars of a ship and its cargo. **6.** a list of cargo and passengers on an aeroplane. [Latin *manifestus* plain] —ˌmanifeˈstation *n.*

manifesto (ˌmænɪˈfɛstəʊ) *n.*, *pl.* -toes or -tos. a public declaration of intent or policy as issued by a political party. [Italian]

manifold ('mænɪˌfəʊld) *adj. Formal.* **1.** of several different kinds; multiple. **2.** having many different forms or features. ~*n.* **3.** a pipe with a number of inlets or outlets, esp. one in a car engine. [Old English *manigfeald*]

manikin ('mænɪkɪn) *n.* a little man; dwarf or child. [Dutch *manneken*]

manila or **manilla** (mə'nɪlə) *n.* a strong usually brown paper used to make envelopes. [after *Manila*, in the Philippines]

man in the street *n.* the average person.

manipulate (mə'nɪpjʊˌleɪt) *vb.* **1.** to handle or use skilfully. **2.** to control (something or someone) cleverly or deviously. [Latin *manipulus* handful] —maˌnipuˈlation *n.*

mankind (ˌmæn'kaɪnd) *n.* **1.** human beings collectively. **2.** men collectively.

manly ('mænlɪ) *adj.* -lier, -liest. **1.** possessing qualities, such as vigour or courage, generally regarded as appropriate to a man; masculine. **2.** characteristic of a man. —'manliness *n.*

man-made *adj.* made by man; artificial.

manna ('mænə) *n.* **1.** *Bible.* the miraculous food which sustained the Israelites in the wilderness (Exodus 16:14–36). **2.** a windfall (esp. in **manna from heaven**). [Hebrew *mān*]

manned (mænd) *adj.* having a human staff or crew: *a manned spaceflight.*

mannequin ('mænɪkɪn) *n.* **1.** a woman who wears the clothes displayed at a fashion show; model. **2.** a life-size dummy of the human body used to fit or display clothes. [French]

manner ('mænə) *n.* **1.** a way of doing or being. **2.** a person's bearing and behaviour. **3.** the style or customary way of doing something: *sculpture in the Greek manner.* **4.** type or kind. **5. in a manner of speaking.** in a way; so to speak. **6. to the manner born.** naturally fitted to a specified role or activity. [Old French *maniere*]

mannered ('mænəd) *adj.* **1.** having idiosyncrasies or mannerisms; affected. **2.** having manners as specified: *ill-mannered.*

mannerism ('mænəˌrɪzəm) *n.* **1.** a distinctive and individual gesture or trait. **2.** adherence to a distinctive or affected manner, esp. in art or literature.

mannerly ('mænəlɪ) *adj.* well-mannered; polite. —'mannerliness *n.*

manners ('mænəz) *pl. n.* **1.** social conduct. **2.** a socially acceptable way of behaving.

mannish ('mænɪʃ) *adj.* (of a woman) displaying qualities regarded as typical of a man.

manoeuvre or *U.S.* **maneuver** (mə'nuːvə) *n.* **1.** a contrived, complicated, and possibly deceptive plan or action. **2.** a movement or action requiring dexterity and skill. **3.** (*pl.*) military or naval exercises, usually on a large scale. **4.** a change in course of a ship or aircraft, esp. a complicated one. ~*vb.* **5.** to contrive or accomplish with skill or cunning. **6.** to manipulate situations in order to gain some end. **7.** to perform a manoeuvre or manoeuvres. [French, from Medieval Latin *manuopera* manual work] —ma'noeuvrable or *U.S.* ma'neuverable *adj.* —maˌnoeuvra'bility or *U.S.* maˌneuvra'bility *n.*

man-of-war *n.*, *pl.* **men-of-war**. **1.** a warship. **2.** short for **Portuguese man-of-war**.

manor ('mænə) *n.* **1.** (in medieval Europe) the lands and property controlled by a lord. **2.** a manor house. **3.** a landed estate. **4.** *Brit. slang.* a police district. [Old French *manoir* dwelling] —**manorial** (mə'nɔːrɪəl) *adj.*

manor house *n.* a large country house, esp. one that was originally part of a medieval manor.

manpower ('mænˌpaʊə) *n.* the number of people needed or available for a job.

manqué ('mɒŋkeɪ) *adj.* unfulfilled; would-be: *an actor manqué.* [French, lit.: having missed]

mansard ('mænsɑːd) *n.* a roof having two slopes on both sides and both ends, the lower slopes being steeper than the upper. [after François *Mansart*, architect]

manse (mæns) *n.* (in certain Christian Churches) the house provided for a minister. [Medieval Latin *mansus* dwelling]

manservant ('mænˌsɜːvənt) *n.*, *pl.* **menservants.** a male servant, esp. a valet.

mansion ('mænʃən) *n.* **1.** a large and imposing house. **2.** (*pl.*) *Brit.* a block of flats. [Latin *mansio* a remaining]

manslaughter ('mænˌslɔːtə) *n. Law.* the unlawful but not deliberately planned killing of one human being by another.

mantel ('mænt'l) *n.* a wooden or stone frame around a fireplace. [variant of *mantle*]

mantelpiece ('mænt'lˌpiːs) *n.* a shelf above a fireplace often forming part of the mantel. Also: **mantel shelf, chimney-piece.**

mantilla (mæn'tɪlə) *n.* a woman's lace or silk scarf covering the shoulders and head, worn esp. in Spain. [Spanish *manta* cloak]

mantis ('mæntɪs) *n.*, *pl.* -tises or -tes (-tiːz). a carnivorous insect with a long body and large eyes that rests with the first pair of legs raised as if in prayer. Also: **praying mantis.** [Greek: prophet]

mantissa (mæn'tɪsə) *n.* the fractional part of a common logarithm: *the mantissa of 2.4771 is .4771.* [Latin: something added]

mantle ('mænt'l) *n.* **1.** *Archaic.* a loose wrap or cloak. **2.** anything that covers completely or envelops. **3.** a small mesh dome used to increase illumination in a gas or oil lamp by becoming incandescent. **4.** *Geol.* the part of the earth between the crust and the core. ~*vb.* **5.** to spread over or become spread over. [Latin *mantellum*]

mantra ('mæntrə, 'mʌn-) *n.* **1.** *Hinduism.* a Vedic psalm of praise. **2.** *Hinduism, Buddhism.* any sacred word or syllable used as an object of concentration. [Sanskrit: speech, instrument of thought]

manual ('mænjʊəl) *adj.* **1.** of a hand or hands. **2.** operated or done by hand. **3.** physical as opposed to mental: *manual labour.* **4.** by human labour rather than automatic or computer-aided means. ~*n.* **5.** a book of instructions or information. **6.** *Music.* one of the keyboards on an organ. [Latin *manus* hand] —'**manually** *adv.*

manufacture (ˌmænjʊ'fæktʃə) *vb.* **1.** to process or make (a product) from a raw material, esp. as a large-scale operation using machinery. **2.** to invent or concoct (evidence, an excuse, etc.). ~*n.* **3.** the production of goods, esp. by industrial processes. [Latin *manus* hand + *facere* to make] —ˌmanu'facturer *n.* —ˌmanu-'facturing *n., adj.*

manuka ('mɑːnukə) *n.* a New Zealand tree with strong elastic wood and aromatic leaves. [Maori]

manumit (ˌmænjʊ'mɪt) *vb.* -mitting, -mitted. to free from slavery. [Latin *manūmittere* to release] —**manumission** (ˌmænjʊ'mɪʃən) *n.*

manure (mə'njʊə) *n.* **1.** animal excrement used as a fertilizer. ~*vb.* **2.** to spread manure upon (fields or soil). [Anglo-French *mainoverer*]

manuscript ('mænjʊˌskrɪpt) *n.* **1.** a book or other document written by hand. **2.** the original handwritten or typed version of a book or article as submitted by an author for publication. [Medieval Latin *manūscriptus* handwritten]

Manx (mæŋks) *adj.* **1.** of the Isle of Man (an island in the Irish Sea) or its inhabitants. ~*n.* **2.** an almost extinct Celtic language of the Isle of Man. **3. the Manx.** (*functioning as pl.*) the people of the Isle of Man. [Scandinavian] —'**Manxman** *n.* —'**Manx**ˌ**woman** *n.*

Manx cat *n.* a short-haired tailless variety of cat.

many ('mɛnɪ) *det.* **1. a.** a large number of: *many times; too many to count.* **b.** (as *pron.*; functioning as pl.): *many are seated already; take as many as you want.* **2.** (foll. by a, an, or another, and a sing. noun) each of a considerable number of: *many a man.* ~*n.* **3. the many.** the majority of mankind, esp. the common people. [Old English *manig*]

Maoism ('maʊɪzəm) *n.* Communism as interpreted in the theories and policies of Mao Tse-tung (1893–1976), Chinese statesman. —'**Maoist** *n., adj.*

Maori ('maʊrɪ) *n.* **1.** (pl. -ris or -ri) a member of the Polynesian people living in New Zealand since before the arrival of European settlers. **2.** the language of this people. ~*adj.* **3.** of this people or their language.

map (mæp) *n.* **1.** a diagrammatic representation of the earth's surface or part of it, showing the geographical distributions or positions of features such as roads, towns, relief and rainfall. **2.** a diagrammatic representation of the stars or of the surface of a celestial body. **3.** *Maths.* same as **function.** **4. put on the map.** to make (a town or company) well-known. ~*vb.* **mapping, mapped.** **5.** to make a map of. **6.** *Maths.* to represent or transform (a function, figure, or set). ~See also **map out.** [Latin *mappa* cloth]

maple ('meɪpˀl) *n.* **1.** any of various trees or shrubs with winged seeds borne in pairs and lobed leaves. **2.** the hard wood of any of these trees. ~See also **sugar maple.** [Old English *mapeltrēow* maple tree]

maple leaf *n.* the leaf of the maple tree, the national emblem of Canada.

maple syrup *n.* a very sweet syrup made from the sap of the sugar maple.

map out *vb.* to plan or design.

mapping ('mæpɪŋ) *n. Maths.* same as **function.**

maquis (mɑː'kiː) *n., pl.* -**quis** (-'kiː). (*often cap.*) **1.** the French underground movement that fought against the German occupying forces in World War II. **2.** a member of this movement. [French]

mar (mɑː) *vb.* **marring, marred.** to cause harm to; spoil or impair. [Old English *merran*]

Mar. March.

marabou ('mærəˌbuː) *n.* **1.** a large black-and-white African stork. **2.** a down feather of this bird, used to trim garments. [Arabic *murābit* holy man]

maraca (mə'rækə) *n.* a shaken percussion instrument, usually one of a pair, consisting of a gourd or plastic shell filled with dried seeds or pebbles. [Brazilian Portuguese]

marae (mɑː'raɪ) *n. N.Z.* a traditional Maori meeting place. [Maori]

maraschino (ˌmærə'skiːnəʊ, -'ʃiːnəʊ) *n.* a liqueur made from a type of sour cherry having a taste like bitter almonds. [Italian]

maraschino cherry *n.* a cherry preserved in maraschino.

marathon ('mærəθən) *n.* **1.** a race on foot of 26 miles 385 yards (42.195 kilometres). **2.** any long or arduous task. [referring to the feat of the messenger said to have run 26 miles from Marathon to Athens to bring the news of victory in 490 B.C.]

maraud (mə'rɔːd) *vb.* to wander or raid in search of plunder. [French *marauder* to prowl] —**ma'rauder** *n.* —**ma'rauding** *adj.*

marble ('mɑːbˀl) *n.* **1.** a hard limestone rock, which usually has a mottled appearance and can be given a high polish. **2.** a block or work of art of marble. **3.** a small round glass ball used in playing marbles. ~*vb.* **4.** to mottle with variegated streaks in imitation of marble. [Greek *marmaros*] —'**marbled** *adj.*

marbles ('mɑːbˀlz) *n.* (*functioning as sing.*)

a game in which marbles are rolled at one another, similar to bowls.

marbling ('mɑːblɪŋ) n. 1. a mottled effect or pattern resembling marble. 2. the streaks of fat in lean meat.

marc (mɑːk) n. 1. the remains of grapes or other fruit that have been pressed for wine-making. 2. a brandy distilled from these. [French]

marcasite ('mɑːkə,saɪt) n. 1. a pale yellow form of iron pyrites used in jewellery. 2. a cut and polished form of steel used for making jewellery. [Arabic marqashītā]

march[1] (mɑːtʃ) vb. 1. to walk with stately or regular steps, usually in a procession or military formation. 2. to make (a person or group) proceed. 3. to traverse by marching. ~n. 4. a regular stride. 5. a long or exhausting walk. 6. advance; progression (as of time). 7. a distance covered by marching. 8. a piece of music, as for a march. 9. **steal a march on.** to gain an advantage over, esp. by a trick. [Old French marchier to tread] —'**marcher** n.

march[2] (mɑːtʃ) n. a border or boundary or the land lying along it, often of disputed ownership. [Old French marche]

March (mɑːtʃ) n. the third month of the year. [Latin Martius (month) of Mars]

March hare n. a hare during its breeding season in March, noted for its wild and excitable behaviour (esp. in **mad as a March hare**).

marching orders pl. n. 1. military orders, giving instructions about a march. 2. Informal. dismissal, esp. from employment.

marchioness ('mɑːʃənɪs) n. 1. a woman who holds the rank of marquis. 2. the wife or widow of a marquis. [Medieval Latin marchionissa]

marchpane ('mɑːtʃ,peɪn) n. Archaic. marzipan. [French]

Mardi Gras ('mɑːdɪ 'grɑː) n. the festival of Shrove Tuesday, celebrated in some cities with great revelry. [French: fat Tuesday]

mare[1] (mɛə) n. the adult female of a horse or zebra. [Old English]

mare[2] ('mɑːreɪ) n., pl. **maria** ('mɑːrɪə). a huge dry plain on the surface of the moon or Mars, visible as dark markings. [Latin: sea]

mare's-nest ('mɛəz,nɛst) n. a discovery imagined to be important but proving worthless.

margarine (,mɑːdʒə'riːn, ,mɑːg-) n. a substitute for butter, prepared from vegetable and animal fats. [Greek margaron pearl]

marge (mɑːdʒ) n. Brit. informal. margarine.

margin ('mɑːdʒɪn) n. 1. an edge or rim; border. 2. the blank space surrounding the text on a page. 3. an additional amount or one beyond the minimum necessary: they won by a small margin; a margin of error. 4. a limit. 5. Econ. the minimum return below which an enterprise becomes unprofitable. [Latin margō border]

marginal ('mɑːdʒɪn'l) adj. 1. of, in, on, or forming a margin. 2. close to a limit, esp. a lower limit: marginal legal ability. 3. not considered central or important; insignifi-

cant. 4. Econ. relating to goods or services produced and sold at the margin of profitability: marginal cost. 5. Politics, chiefly Brit. & N.Z. of or designating a constituency in which elections tend to be won by small margins: a marginal seat. 6. designating agricultural land on the edge of fertile areas. ~n. 7. Politics, chiefly Brit. & N.Z. a marginal constituency. —'**marginally** adv.

marginalia (,mɑːdʒɪ'neɪlɪə) pl. n. notes in the margin of a book, manuscript, or letter.

margrave ('mɑː,greɪv) n. a German nobleman ranking above a count. [Middle Dutch markgrave count of the frontier]

marguerite (,mɑːgə'riːt) n. a garden plant with flowers resembling large daisies. [French]

marigold ('mærɪ,gəʊld) n. any of various plants cultivated for their yellow or orange flowers. [from Mary (the Virgin) + gold]

marijuana or **marihuana** (,mærɪ'wɑːnə) n. the dried leaves and flowers of the hemp plant, used as a drug, esp. in cigarettes. [Mexican Spanish]

marimba (mə'rɪmbə) n. a percussion instrument consisting of a set of hardwood plates placed over tuned metal resonators, played with soft-headed sticks. [West African]

marina (mə'riːnə) n. a harbour for yachts and other pleasure boats. [Latin: marine]

marinade (,mærɪ'neɪd) n. 1. a mixture of oil, wine, vinegar, etc., in which meat or fish is soaked before cooking. 2. meat or fish soaked in this. ~vb. 3. same as **marinate**. [French]

marinate ('mærɪ,neɪt) vb. to soak in marinade. [Italian marinare to pickle]

marine (mə'riːn) adj. 1. of, found in, or relating to the sea. 2. of shipping or navigation. 3. used or adapted for use at sea. ~n. 4. a soldier trained to serve on land or at sea. 5. a country's shipping or navy collectively: the merchant marine. [Latin marīnus of the sea]

mariner ('mærɪnə) n. a seaman.

marionette (,mærɪə'nɛt) n. a puppet whose limbs are moved by strings. [French, from the name Marion]

marital ('mærɪt'l) adj. of or relating to marriage. [Latin marītus married] —'**maritally** adv.

maritime ('mærɪ,taɪm) adj. 1. of or relating to shipping. 2. of, near, or living near the sea. [Latin maritimus of the sea]

marjoram ('mɑːdʒərəm) n. a plant with sweet-scented leaves, used for seasoning food and in salads. [Medieval Latin marjorana]

mark[1] (mɑːk) n. 1. a visible impression on a surface, such as a spot or scratch. 2. a sign, symbol, or other indication that distinguishes something. 3. a written or printed symbol, as for punctuation. 4. a letter, number, or percentage used to grade academic work. 5. a thing that indicates position; marker. 6. a desired standard: up to the mark. 7. an indication of some quality: a mark of respect. 8. a target or goal. 9. impression or influence: this book displays the mark of its author's admiration of Kafka. **10.** (often cap.) (in trade names) a model, brand, or type. **11. make one's mark.** to achieve recognition. **12. on your mark** or **marks.** a command given to runners in a race to prepare themselves at the starting line. ~vb. **13.** to make or receive (a visible impression, trace, or stain) on (a surface). **14.** to characterize or distinguish. **15.** (often foll. by off or out) to set boundaries or limits (on). **16.** to select, designate, or doom: to mark someone as a criminal. **17.** to label, esp. to indicate price. **18.** to pay attention to: mark my words. **19.** to observe; notice. **20.** to grade or evaluate (scholastic work). **21.** to stay close to (an opponent) to hamper his play. **22. mark time. a.** to move the feet alternately as in marching but without advancing. **b.** to wait for something more interesting to happen. ~See also **markdown**, **mark-up**. [Old English mearc mark] —'**marker** n.

mark² (maːk) n. **1.** See **Deutschmark**. **2.** the standard monetary unit of East Germany. [Old English marc unit of weight of precious metal]

markdown ('maːk,daun) n. **1.** a price reduction. ~vb. **mark down. 2.** to reduce in price.

marked (maːkt) adj. **1.** obvious or noticeable. **2.** singled out, esp. as the target of attack: a marked man. —**markedly** ('maːkɪdlɪ) adv.

market ('maːkɪt) n. **1.** an occasion at which people meet to buy and sell merchandise. **2.** a place at which a market is held. **3.** the trading opportunities provided by a particular group of people: the foreign market. **4.** demand for a particular product. **5.** short for **stock market**. **6. be in the market for.** to wish to buy. **7. on the market.** available for purchase. **8. seller's** (or **buyer's**) **market.** a market characterized by excess demand (or supply) and thus favourable to sellers (or buyers). ~vb. **9.** to offer or produce for sale. [Latin mercārī to trade] —'**marketable** adj.

market garden n. Chiefly Brit. a place where fruit and vegetables are grown for sale. —**market gardener** n.

marketing ('maːkɪtɪŋ) n. the part of a business which controls the way that goods or services are sold.

market maker n. Stock Exchange. someone who uses his firm's money to create a market for a stock: formerly done by a jobber, but a market maker can deal directly with the public.

marketplace ('maːkɪt,pleɪs) n. **1.** a place where a public market is held. **2.** the commercial world of buying and selling.

market price n. the prevailing price at which goods may be bought or sold.

market research n. the study of influences upon customer behaviour and the analysis of market characteristics and trends.

market town n. Chiefly Brit. a town that holds a market, esp. an agricultural centre.

marking ('maːkɪŋ) n. **1.** the arrangement

of colours on an animal or plant. **2.** assessment and correction of pupils' or students' written work by teachers.

marksman ('maːksmən) n., pl. -**men.** a person skilled in shooting. —'**marksmanship** n.

mark-up n. **1.** an amount added to the cost of a commodity to provide the seller with a profit. ~vb. **mark up. 2.** to add a percentage for profit to the cost of (a commodity).

marl (maːl) n. a fine-grained rock consisting of clay, limestone, and silt: used as a fertilizer. [Late Latin margila] —'**marly** adj.

marlin ('maːlɪn) n., pl. -**lin** or -**lins.** a large fish with a very long upper jaw, found in warm and tropical seas. [after marlinspike (because of its long jaw)]

marlinespike or **marlinspike** ('maːlɪn,spaɪk) n. Naut. a pointed metal tool used in separating strands of rope. [Dutch marlijn]

marmalade ('maːmə,leɪd) n. jam made from citrus fruits, esp. oranges. [Portuguese marmelo quince]

marmoreal (maːˈmɔːrɪəl) adj. of or like marble. [Latin marmoreus]

marmoset ('maːmə,zɛt) n. a small South American monkey with a long hairy tail. [Old French marmouset grotesque figure]

marmot ('maːmət) n. any of various burrowing rodents of Europe, Asia, and North America. They are heavily built and have coarse fur. [French marmotte]

maroon¹ (məˈruːn) vb. **1.** to abandon ashore, esp. on an island. **2.** to isolate without resources. [American Spanish cimarrón wild]

maroon² (məˈruːn) adj. dark purplish-red. [French: chestnut]

marque (maːk) n. a brand of product, esp. of a car. [French]

marquee (maːˈkiː) n. a large tent used for entertainment, exhibition, etc. [French marquise]

marquess ('maːkwɪs) n. **1.** (in the British Isles) a nobleman ranking between a duke and an earl. **2.** See **marquis**.

marquetry ('maːkɪtrɪ) n., pl. -**quetries.** a pattern of inlaid veneers of wood or metal used chiefly as ornamentation in furniture. [Old French marqueter to inlay]

marquis ('maːkwɪs, maːˈkiː) n., pl. -**quises** or -**quis.** (in various countries) a nobleman ranking above a count, corresponding to a British marquess. [Old French marchis count of the frontier]

marquise (maːˈkiːz) n. **1.** (in various countries) a marchioness. **2.** a gemstone cut in a pointed oval shape. [French]

marram grass ('mærəm) n. a grass that grows on sandy shores: often planted to stabilize sand dunes. [Old Norse marálmr]

marriage ('mærɪdʒ) n. **1.** the state or relationship of being husband and wife: the institution of marriage. **2.** the contract made by a man and woman to live as husband and wife. **3.** the ceremony formalizing this union; wedding.

marriageable (ˈmærɪdʒəbᵊl) *adj.* suitable for marriage, usually with reference to age.

marriage guidance *n.* advice given to couples who have problems in their married life.

married (ˈmærɪd) *adj.* **1.** having a husband or wife. **2.** of marriage or married persons. ~*n.* **3.** (*usually pl.*) a married person (esp. in **young marrieds**).

marrow (ˈmærəʊ) *n.* **1.** the fatty tissue that fills the cavities of bones. **2.** *Brit.* short for **vegetable marrow**. [Old English *mærg*]

marrowfat (ˈmærəʊˌfæt) *or* **marrow pea** *n.* a variety of large pea.

marry¹ (ˈmærɪ) *vb.* **-rying, -ried. 1.** to take (someone as one's husband or wife) in marriage. **2.** to join or give in marriage. **3.** (sometimes foll. by *up*) to fit together or align (two things); join. [Latin *marītāre*]

marry² (ˈmærɪ) *interj. Archaic.* an exclamation of surprise or anger. [euphemistic for the Virgin *Mary*]

Mars (mɑːz) *n.* **1.** the Roman god of war. **2.** the fourth planet from the sun.

Marsala (mɑːˈsɑːlə) *n.* a dark sweet dessert wine from Marsala, a port in Sicily.

Marseillaise (ˌmɑːseɪˈjeɪz, -sɔˈleɪz) *n.* **the.** the French national anthem. [French (*chanson*) *marseillaise* song of Marseilles (first sung in Paris by the battalion of Marseilles)]

marsh (mɑːʃ) *n.* low poorly drained land that is wet, muddy, and sometimes flooded. [Old English *merisc*] —**'marshy** *adj.*

marshal (ˈmɑːʃəl) *n.* **1.** (in some armies and air forces) an officer of the highest rank. **2.** an officer who organizes or controls ceremonies or public events. **3.** (formerly in England) an officer of the royal family or court. ~*vb.* **-shalling, -shalled** *or U.S.* **-shaling, -shaled. 4.** to arrange in order: *to marshal the facts.* **5.** to assemble and organize (people or vehicles) in readiness for onward movement. **6.** to guide or lead, esp. in a ceremonious way. [Old French *mareschal*] —**'marshalcy** *n.*

marshalling yard *n. Railways.* a place where railway wagons are shunted and made up into trains.

Marshal of the Royal Air Force *n.* the highest rank in the Royal Air Force.

marsh gas *n.* a gas largely composed of methane formed when plants decay in the absence of air.

marshmallow (ˌmɑːʃˈmæləʊ) *n.* a spongy pink or white sweet.

marsh mallow *n.* a plant that grows in salt marshes and has pale pink flowers. It was formerly used to make marshmallows.

marsupial (mɑːˈsjuːpɪəl) *n.* **1.** any mammal whose young are born in an immature state and continue development in a pouch on the mother's body. They include the opossums and kangaroos. ~*adj.* **2.** of or like a marsupial. [Latin *marsupium* purse]

mart (mɑːt) *n.* a market or trading centre. [Middle Dutch: market]

Martello tower (mɑːˈtɛləʊ) *n.* a small circular tower for coastal defence. [after Cape *Mortella* in Corsica]

marten (ˈmɑːtɪn) *n., pl.* **-tens** *or* **-ten. 1.** any of several agile weasel-like mammals with bushy tails and golden-brown to blackish fur. **2.** the highly valued fur of these animals. [Middle Dutch *martren*]

martial (ˈmɑːʃəl) *adj.* of or characteristic of war, soldiers, or the military life. [Latin *martiālis* of Mars, god of war]

martial art *n.* any of various philosophies and techniques of self-defence originating in the Far East, such as judo or karate.

martial law *n.* rule of law maintained by the military in the absence of civil law.

Martian (ˈmɑːʃən) *adj.* **1.** of the planet Mars. ~*n.* **2.** an inhabitant of Mars, in science fiction.

martin (ˈmɑːtɪn) *n.* a bird of the swallow family with a square or slightly forked tail. [prob. after St *Martin,* or because the birds were believed to migrate at Martinmas]

martinet (ˌmɑːtɪˈnɛt) *n.* a person who maintains strict discipline. [after General *Martinet,* drillmaster under Louis XIV]

martingale (ˈmɑːtɪnˌɡeɪl) *n.* a strap from the reins to the girth of a horse, preventing it from carrying its head too high. [French]

martini (mɑːˈtiːnɪ) *n.* **1.** (*often cap.*) *Trademark.* an Italian vermouth. **2.** a cocktail of gin and vermouth.

Martinmas (ˈmɑːtɪnməs) *n.* the feast of St Martin on Nov. 11; a quarter day in Scotland.

martyr (ˈmɑːtə) *n.* **1.** a person who suffers death rather than renounce his religious beliefs. **2.** a person who suffers greatly or dies for a cause or belief. **3.** a martyr to. suffering constantly from: *a martyr to rheumatism.* ~*vb.* **4.** to make a martyr of. [Late Greek *martur-* witness] —**'martyrdom** *n.*

marvel (ˈmɑːvᵊl) *vb.* **-velling, -velled** *or U.S.* **-veling, -veled. 1.** to be filled with surprise or wonder. ~*n.* **2.** something that causes wonder. [Old French *merveille*]

marvellous *or U.S.* **marvelous** (ˈmɑːvᵊləs) *adj.* **1.** causing great wonder or surprise; extraordinary. **2.** excellent; splendid. —**'marvellously** *or U.S.* **'marvelously** *adv.*

Marxism (ˈmɑːksɪzəm) *n.* the economic and political theories of Karl Marx (1818–83), German political philosopher, holding that class struggle is the basic agency of historical change, and that capitalism will be superseded by communism. —**'Marxist** *n., adj.*

marzipan (ˈmɑːzɪˌpæn) *n.* a paste made from ground almonds, sugar, and egg whites. [Italian *marzapane*]

masc. masculine.

mascara (mæˈskɑːrə) *n.* a cosmetic for darkening the eyelashes. [Spanish: mask]

mascot (ˈmæskət) *n.* a person, animal, or thing considered to bring good luck. [French *mascotte*]

masculine (ˈmæskjʊlɪn) *adj.* **1.** possessing

qualities or characteristics considered typical of or appropriate to a man; manly. **2.** unwomanly. **3.** *Grammar.* denoting a gender of nouns that includes some male animate things. **4.** *Prosody.* denoting a rhyme between pairs of single final stressed syllables. [Latin *masculinus*] —₁**mascu'linity** *n.*

maser ('meɪzə) *n.* a device for amplifying microwaves, working on the same principle as a laser. [*m(icrowave) a(mplification by) s(timulated) e(mission of) r(adiation)*]

mash (mæʃ) *n.* **1.** a soft pulpy mass. **2.** *Agriculture.* a feed of bran, meal, or malt mixed with water and fed to horses, cattle, or poultry. **3.** *Brit. informal.* mashed potatoes. ~*vb.* **4.** to beat or crush into a mash. [Old English *mæsc*] —**mashed** *adj.*

mask (mɑːsk) *n.* **1.** any covering for the whole or a part of the face worn for amusement, protection, or disguise. **2.** behaviour that hides one's true feelings: *a mask of indifference.* **3.** a moulded likeness of a face or head, such as a death mask. **4.** *Surgery.* a sterile gauze covering for the nose and mouth worn to minimize the spread of germs. **5.** a device placed over the nose and mouth to facilitate or prevent inhalation of a gas. **6.** the face or head of an animal such as a fox. ~*vb.* **7.** to cover with or put on a mask. **8.** to conceal; disguise: *to mask an odour.* [Arabic *maskharah* clown] —**masked** *adj.*

masking tape *n.* an adhesive tape used to protect surfaces surrounding an area to be painted.

masochism ('mæsə,kɪzəm) *n.* **1.** *Psychiatry.* a condition in which pleasure, esp. sexual pleasure, is derived from pain or from being humiliated. **2.** a tendency to take pleasure from one's own suffering. [after Leopold von Sacher *Masoch*, novelist] —**masochist** *n., adj.* —₁**maso'chistic** *adj.*

mason ('meɪs'n) *n.* a person skilled in building with stone. [Old French *masson*]

Mason ('meɪs'n) *n.* short for **Freemason**.

Masonic (mə'sɒnɪk) *adj.* of Freemasons or Freemasonry.

masonry ('meɪsənrɪ) *n.* **1.** the craft of a mason. **2.** stonework or brickwork.

Masonry ('meɪsənrɪ) *n.* short for **Freemasonry**.

masque (mɑːsk) *n.* a dramatic entertainment of the 16th to 17th centuries, consisting of dancing, dialogue, and song. [var. of *mask*] —**masquer** *n.*

masquerade (₁mæskə'reɪd) *n.* **1.** a deceptive show; pretence. **2.** a party at which the guests wear masks and costumes. ~*vb.* **3.** to pretend to be someone or something else. [Spanish *mascara* mask]

mass (mæs) *n.* **1.** a large coherent body of matter without a definite shape. **2.** a collection of the component parts of something: *a mass of fibres.* **3.** a large amount or number, as of people. **4.** the main part or majority. **5.** the size of a body; bulk. **6.** *Physics.* a physical quantity expressing the amount of matter in a body. **7.** (in painting or drawing) an area of unified colour,

shade, or intensity. ~*(modifier)* **8.** done or occurring on a large scale: *mass hysteria.* **9.** consisting of a mass or large number, esp. of people: *a mass meeting.* ~*vb.* **10.** to form (people or things) or (of people or things) to join together into a mass. ~See also **masses**. [Latin *massa*]

Mass (mæs, mɑːs) *n.* **1.** (in the Roman Catholic Church and certain other Christian churches) the celebration of the Eucharist. **2.** a musical setting of parts of the Eucharistic service. [Church Latin *missa*]

Mass. Massachusetts.

massacre ('mæsəkə) *n.* **1.** the wanton or savage killing of large numbers of people. **2.** *Informal.* an overwhelming defeat. ~*vb.* **3.** to kill indiscriminately in large numbers. **4.** *Informal.* to defeat overwhelmingly. [Old French]

massage ('mæsɑːʒ) *n.* **1.** the act of kneading or rubbing parts of the body to promote circulation, suppleness, or relaxation. ~*vb.* **2.** to give a massage to. **3.** to manipulate (statistics or evidence) to produce a desired result. [French *masser* to rub]

massasauga (₁mæsə'sɔːgə) *n.* a North American venomous snake with a horny rattle at the end of the tail. [after the *Missisauga* River, Ontario, Canada]

masses ('mæsɪz) *pl. n.* **1.** (preceded by *the*) the body of common people. **2.** (often foll. by *of*) *Informal, chiefly Brit.* great numbers or quantities: *masses of food.*

masseur (mæ'sɜː) *or (fem.)* **masseuse** (mæ'sɜːz) *n.* a person who gives massages.

massif ('mæsiːf) *n.* a series of connected masses of rock forming a mountain range. [French]

massive ('mæsɪv) *adj.* **1.** (of objects) large, bulky, heavy, and usually solid. **2.** impressive or imposing. **3.** intensive or considerable: *a massive dose.* [French *massif*] —**'massively** *adv.*

mass-market *adj.* of, for, or appealing to a large number of people; popular: *mass-market paperbacks.*

mass media *pl. n.* the means of communication that reach large numbers of people, such as television, newspapers, and radio.

mass noun *n.* a noun that refers to an extended substance rather than to each of a set of objects, e.g., *water* as opposed to *lake.*

mass number *n.* the total number of protons and neutrons in the nucleus of an atom.

mass-produce *vb.* to manufacture standardized goods on a large scale by means of extensive mechanization. —₁**mass-pro'duced** *adj.*

mass spectrometer *n.* an instrument for analysing the composition of a sample of material, in which ions, produced from the sample, are separated by electric or magnetic fields according to their ratios of charge to mass.

mast[1] (mɑːst) *n.* **1.** *Naut.* any vertical spar for supporting sails, radar equipment, etc., above the deck of a vessel. **2.** any upright

pole used as a support: *a television mast.*
3. before the mast. *Naut.* as an apprentice
seaman. [Old English mæst]

mast² (mɑːst) *n.* the fruit of forest trees,
such as beech or oak, used as food for pigs.
[Old English mæst]

mastaba ('mæstəbə) *n.* a mudbrick superstructure above tombs in ancient Egypt.
[Arabic: bench]

mastectomy (mæ'stɛktəmɪ) *n., pl.* **-mies.**
the surgical removal of a breast.

master ('mɑːstə) *n.* **1.** the man in authority, such as the head of a household, the
employer of servants, or the owner of
slaves or animals. **2.** a person with exceptional skill at a certain thing. **3.** a person
who has complete control of a situation. **4.**
a craftsman fully qualified to practise his
trade and to train others. **5.** an original
copy or tape from which duplicates are
made. **6.** a player of a game, esp. chess or
bridge, who has won a specified number of
tournament games. **7.** a highly regarded
teacher or leader. **8.** a graduate holding a
master's degree. **9.** the chief officer
aboard a merchant ship. **10.** *Chiefly Brit.*
a male teacher. **11.** the superior person or
side in a contest. **12.** (*often cap.*) the heir
apparent of a Scottish viscount or baron:
the Master of Ballantrae. ~(*modifier*)
13. overall or controlling: *master plan.* **14.**
designating a mechanism that controls others: *master switch.* **15.** main; principal:
master bedroom. ~*vb.* **16.** to become
thoroughly proficient in. **17.** to overcome;
defeat. [Latin *magister* teacher]

Master ('mɑːstə) *n.* a title of address for a
boy who is not old enough to be called *Mr.*

masterful ('mɑːstəfʊl) *adj.* **1.** having or
showing mastery. **2.** fond of playing the
master; imperious. —'**masterfully** *adv.*

master key *n.* a key that opens all the
locks of a set; passkey.

masterly ('mɑːstəlɪ) *adj.* showing the skill
befitting a master; expert.

mastermind ('mɑːstə,maɪnd) *vb.* **1.** to
plan and direct (a complex undertaking).
~*n.* **2.** a person of great intelligence, esp.
one who directs an undertaking.

Master of Arts *n.* a degree, usually
postgraduate and in a nonscientific subject, or its holder.

master of ceremonies *n.* a person who
presides over a public ceremony, formal
dinner, or entertainment, introducing the
events and performers.

Master of Science *n.* a degree, usually
postgraduate and in a scientific subject, or
its holder.

Master of the Rolls *n.* (in England) the
senior civil judge in the country and the
head of the Public Record Office.

masterpiece ('mɑːstə,piːs) *or* **master-
work** ('mɑːstə,wɜːk) *n.* **1.** an outstanding
work or performance. **2.** the most outstanding piece of work of an artist or
craftsman.

masterstroke ('mɑːstə,strəʊk) *n.* an outstanding piece of strategy, skill, or talent.

mastery ('mɑːstərɪ) *n., pl.* **-teries.** **1.** out-

standing skill; expertise. **2.** the power of
command; control.

masthead ('mɑːst,hɛd) *n.* **1.** *Naut.* the
head of a mast. **2.** the name of a newspaper or periodical printed at the top of
the front page.

mastic ('mæstɪk) *n.* **1.** an aromatic resin
obtained from a Mediterranean tree and
used to make varnishes and lacquers. **2.**
any of several putty-like substances used
as a filler, adhesive, or seal. [Greek
mastikhē]

masticate ('mæstɪ,keɪt) *vb.* to chew
(food). [Greek *mastikhan* to grind the
teeth] —,**masti'cation** *n.*

mastiff ('mæstɪf) *n.* a breed of large powerful short-haired dog, usually fawn or brindled. [Latin *mansuētus* tame]

mastitis (mæ'staɪtɪs) *n.* inflammation of a
breast or an udder.

mastodon ('mæstə,dɒn) *n.* an extinct
elephant-like mammal. [New Latin, lit.:
breast-tooth, referring to the nipple-
shaped projections on the teeth]

mastoid ('mæstɔɪd) *adj.* **1.** shaped like a
nipple or breast. ~*n.* **2.** a nipple-like
projection of the temporal bone behind the
ear. **3.** *Informal.* mastoiditis. [Greek
mastos breast]

mastoiditis (,mæstɔɪ'daɪtɪs) *n.* inflammation of the mastoid.

masturbate ('mæstə,beɪt) *vb.* to fondle
the genitals of (oneself or another) to cause
sexual pleasure. [Latin *masturbārī*]
—,**mastur'bation** *n.*

mat¹ (mæt) *n.* **1.** a thick flat piece of fabric
used as a floor covering, a place to wipe
one's shoes, etc. **2.** a smaller pad of
material used to protect a surface from
heat or scratches from an object placed
upon it. **3.** a large piece of thick padded
material put on the floor as a surface for
wrestling, gymnastics, etc. ~*vb.* **matting,
matted. 4.** to tangle or become tangled
into a dense mass. [Old English *matte*]

mat² (mæt) *adj.* having a dull, lustreless, or
roughened surface. [French, lit.: dead]

matador ('mætə,dɔː) *n.* the bullfighter
armed with a sword, who attempts to kill
the bull. [Spanish, from *matar* to kill]

matai ('mɑːtaɪ) *n.* a New Zealand tree, the
wood of which is used for building timber.
[Maori]

match¹ (mætʃ) *n.* **1.** a formal game or
sports event in which people or teams
compete. **2.** a person or thing able to
provide competition for another: *she's met
her match.* **3.** a person or thing that
resembles, harmonizes with, or is equivalent to another. **4.** a person or thing that is
an exact copy or equal of another. **5.** a
partnership between a man and a woman,
as in marriage. **6.** a person regarded as a
possible partner in marriage. ~*vb.* **7.** to
fit (parts) together. **8.** (sometimes foll. by
up) to resemble, harmonize with, or equal
(one another or something else). **9.** (sometimes foll. by *with* or *against*) to compare
in order to determine which is the superior.
10. (often foll. by *with* or *against*) to
arrange a competition between. **11.** to find

a match for. [Old English *gemæcca* spouse] —**'matching** *adj.*

match[2] (mætʃ) *n.* **1.** a thin strip of wood or cardboard tipped with a chemical that ignites when scraped against a rough or specially treated surface. **2.** a fuse used to fire cannons' explosives. [Old French *meiche*]

matchbox ('mætʃ,bɒks) *n.* a small box for holding matches.

matchless ('mætʃlɪs) *adj.* unequalled.

matchmaker ('mætʃ,meɪkə) *n.* a person who introduces people in the hope that they will form a couple. —**'match,making** *n., adj.*

match play *n. Golf.* scoring according to the number of holes won and lost.

match point *n. Sport.* the final point needed to win a match.

matchstick ('mætʃ,stɪk) *n.* **1.** the wooden part of a match. ~*adj.* **2.** (esp. of drawn figures) thin and straight: *matchstick men.*

matchwood ('mætʃ,wʊd) *n.* **1.** wood suitable for making matches. **2.** splinters.

mate[1] (meɪt) *n.* **1.** the sexual partner of an animal. **2.** a marriage partner. **3. a.** *Informal, chiefly Brit., Austral., & N.Z.* a friend: often used to any male in direct address. **b.** an associate or colleague: *a classmate.* **4.** one of a pair of matching items. **5.** *Naut.* any officer below the master on a commercial ship. **6.** (in some trades) an assistant: *a plumber's mate.* ~*vb.* **7.** to pair (a male and female animal) or (of animals) to pair for reproduction. **8.** to marry. **9.** to join as a pair. [Low German]

mate[2] (meɪt) *n., vb. Chess.* same as **checkmate.**

mater ('meɪtə) *n. Brit. slang.* mother: often used facetiously. [Latin]

material (mə'tɪərɪəl) *n.* **1.** the substance of which a thing is made; component matter. **2.** things needed for a particular activity: *writing materials.* **3.** ideas or notes that a finished work may be based on. **4.** cloth. ~*adj.* **5.** composed of physical substance. **6.** of or affecting economic or physical wellbeing: *material ease.* **7.** of physical rather than spiritual interests. **8.** (often foll. by *to*) relevant. ~See also **materials.** [Latin *māteria* matter]

materialism (mə'tɪərɪə,lɪzəm) *n.* **1.** interest in and desire for money or possessions rather than spiritual or ethical values. **2.** *Philosophy.* the doctrine that matter is the only reality. —**ma'terialist** *n.* —**ma,terial'istic** *adj.*

materialize or **-ise** (mə'tɪərɪə,laɪz) *vb.* **1.** *Not universally accepted.* to become fact; actually happen. **2.** to appear or cause to appear after being invisible: *trees materialized out of the gloom.* **3.** to take shape; become tangible. —**ma,teriali'zation** or **-i'sation** *n.*

materially (mə'tɪərɪəlɪ) *adv.* to a significant extent; considerably.

materials (mə'tɪərɪəlz) *pl. n.* the equipment necessary for a particular activity.

materiel or **matériel** (mə,tɪərɪ'ɛl) *n.* the materials and equipment of an organization, esp. of a military force. [French]

maternal (mə'tɜːn³l) *adj.* **1.** of or characteristic of a mother. **2.** related through the mother's side of the family: *his maternal uncle.* [Latin *māter* mother] —**ma'ternally** *adv.*

maternity (mə'tɜːnɪtɪ) *n.* **1.** motherhood. **2.** motherliness. **3.** (*modifier*) relating to pregnant women: *maternity leave.*

mate's rates *pl. n. N.Z. informal.* reduced charges offered to a friend or colleague: *a plumber friend did the job at mate's rates.*

matey ('meɪtɪ) *adj. Brit. informal.* friendly or intimate.

math (mæθ) *n. U.S. & Canad. informal.* short for **mathematics.**

mathematical (,mæθə'mætɪk³l) *adj.* **1.** using, used in, or relating to mathematics. **2.** having the precision of mathematics. —**,mathe'matically** *adv.*

mathematician (,mæθəmə'tɪʃən) *n.* an expert or specialist in mathematics.

mathematics (,mæθə'mætɪks) *n.* **1.** (*functioning as sing.*) a group of related sciences, including algebra, geometry, and calculus, which use a specialized notation to study number, quantity, shape, and space. **2.** (*functioning as sing. or pl.*) numerical calculations involved in the solution of a problem. [Greek *mathēma* a science]

maths (mæθs) *n.* (*functioning as sing.*) *Brit. informal.* short for **mathematics.**

matinée ('mætɪ,neɪ) *n.* an afternoon performance of a play or film. [French]

matinée coat or **jacket** *n.* a short coat for a baby.

matins ('mætɪnz) *n.* (*functioning as sing. or pl.*) *Christianity.* an early morning service in various Churches. [Latin *mātūtīnus* of the morning]

matriarch ('meɪtrɪ,ɑːk) *n.* the female head of a tribe or family. [Latin *māter* mother + Greek *arkhein* to rule] —**,matri,archal** *adj.*

matriarchy ('meɪtrɪ,ɑːkɪ) *n., pl.* **-chies.** a form of social organization in which a female is head of the family or society, and descent and kinship are traced through the female line.

matricide ('mætrɪ,saɪd, 'meɪ-) *n.* **1.** the act of killing one's mother. **2.** a person who kills his mother. [Latin *māter* mother + *caedere* to kill] —**,matri'cidal** *adj.*

matriculate (mə'trɪkjʊ,leɪt) *vb.* to enrol or be enrolled in a college or university. [Medieval Latin *mātrīculāre* to register] —**ma,tricu'lation** *n.*

matrilineal (,mætrɪ'lɪnɪəl, ,meɪ-) *adj.* relating to descent through the female line.

matrimony ('mætrɪmənɪ) *n., pl.* **-nies.** **1.** the state of being married. **2.** the ceremony of marriage. [Latin *mātrimōnium* wedlock] —**matrimonial** (,mætrɪ'məʊnɪəl) *adj.*

matrix ('meɪtrɪks) *n., pl.* **matrices** ('meɪtrɪ,siːz) or **matrixes.** **1.** a substance, situation, or environment in which something has its origin, takes form, or is enclosed. **2.** the rock in which fossils or pebbles are embedded. **3.** a mould, esp. one used in printing. **4.** *Maths.* a rectangular array of elements set out in rows and columns. [Latin: womb]

matron ('meɪtrən) n. **1.** a staid or dignified married woman. **2.** a woman in charge of the domestic or medical arrangements in an institution. **3.** Brit. (formerly) the administrative head of the nursing staff in a hospital. [Latin mātrōna] —'**matronly** adj.

matron of honour n., pl. **matrons of honour.** a married woman attending a bride.

matt or **matte** (mæt) adj. same as **mat²**.

matted ('mætɪd) adj. tangled into a thick mass.

matter ('mætə) n. **1.** that which makes up something, esp. a physical object; material. **2.** substance that occupies space and has mass, as distinguished from substance that is mental or spiritual. **3.** substance of a specified type: vegetable matter. **4.** (sometimes foll. by of or for) thing; affair; concern; question: a matter of taste. **5.** a quantity or amount: a matter of a few pence. **6.** the content of written or verbal material as distinct from its style or form. **7.** written material in general: advertising matter. **8.** a secretion or discharge, such as pus. **9. for that matter.** as regards that. **10. no matter. a.** regardless of; irrespective of: no matter what the excuse, you must not be late. **b.** interj. it is unimportant. **11. the matter.** wrong; the trouble: there's nothing the matter. ~vb. **12.** to be of consequence or importance. [Latin māteria cause, substance]

matter of fact n. **1. as a matter of fact.** actually; in fact. ~adj. **matter-of-fact. 2.** unimaginative or emotionless: he gave a matter-of-fact account of the murder.

matting ('mætɪŋ) n. a coarsely woven fabric used as a floor covering and packing material.

mattock ('mætək) n. a type of large pick that has one flat, horizontal end to its blade, used for loosening soil. [Old English mattuc]

mattress ('mætrɪs) n. a large flat cushion with a strong cover, filled with cotton, foam rubber, etc., and often including coiled springs, used as a bed or as part of a bed. [Arabic almatrah place where something is thrown]

maturate ('mætjʊ͵reɪt) vb. **1.** to mature or bring to maturity. **2.** (of a wound etc.) to discharge pus. —͵matu'**ration** n.

mature (mə'tjʊə) adj. **1.** fully developed physically or mentally; grown-up. **2.** (of plans or theories) fully considered; perfected. **3.** due or payable: a mature insurance policy. **4.** (of fruit, wine, or cheese) ripe or fully aged. ~vb. **5.** to make or become mature. **6.** (of bills or bonds) to become due for payment or repayment. [Latin mātūrus early, developed] —ma'**turity** n.

matzo ('mætsəʊ) n., pl. **matzos.** a large very thin biscuit of unleavened bread, traditionally eaten by Jews during Passover. [Hebrew matsāh]

maudlin ('mɔːdlɪn) adj. foolishly tearful or sentimental, as when drunk. [Middle English Maudelen Mary Magdalene, often shown weeping]

maul (mɔːl) vb. **1.** to handle clumsily; paw. **2.** to batter or tear. ~n. **3.** a heavy two-handed hammer. **4.** Rugby. a loose scrum. [Latin malleus hammer]

maunder ('mɔːndə) vb. to move, talk, or act aimlessly or idly. [origin unknown]

Maundy money ('mɔːndɪ) n. specially minted coins given by the British sovereign in a symbolic almsgiving ceremony on the Thursday before Easter (**Maundy Thursday**).

mausoleum (͵mɔːsə'lɪəm) n. a large stately tomb. [Greek mausōleion, the tomb of king Mausolus]

mauve (məʊv) adj. light purple. [Latin malva mallow]

maverick ('mævərɪk) n. **1.** a person of independent or unorthodox views. **2.** (in the U.S. and Canada) an unbranded stray calf. [after Samuel A. Maverick, Texas rancher]

maw (mɔː) n. the mouth, throat, or stomach of an animal, esp. of a voracious animal. [Old English maga]

mawkish ('mɔːkɪʃ) adj. falsely sentimental, esp. in a weak or maudlin way. [obs. mawk maggot] —'**mawkishness** n.

max. maximum.

maxi ('mæksɪ) adj. **1.** (of a garment) very long. **2.** large or considerable. [from maximum]

maxilla (mæk'sɪlə) n., pl. **-lae** (-liː). **1.** the upper jawbone in vertebrates. **2.** any part of the mouth in insects and other arthropods. [Latin: jaw] —**max'illary** adj.

maxim ('mæksɪm) n. a brief expression of a general truth, principle, or rule of conduct. [Latin maxima, in the phrase maxima prōpositiō basic axiom]

maximal ('mæksɪməl) adj. of or being a maximum; the greatest possible.

maximize or **-ise** ('mæksɪ͵maɪz) vb. to make as high or great as possible; increase to a maximum. —͵maximi'**zation** or **-i'sation** n.

maximum ('mæksɪməm) n., pl. **-mums** or **-ma** (-mə). **1.** the greatest possible amount or degree. **2.** the highest value of a variable quantity. ~adj. **3.** of, being, or showing a maximum or maximums. [Latin: greatest]

maxwell ('mækswəl) n. the cgs unit of magnetic flux. [after J. C. Maxwell, physicist]

may¹ (meɪ) vb. past **might.** used as an auxiliary to indicate or express: **1.** that permission is requested by or granted to someone: he may go. **2.** (often foll. by well) possibility: the rope may well break. **3.** ability or capacity, esp. in questions: may I help you? **4.** a strong wish: long may she reign. [Old English mæg, from magan to be able]

may² or **may tree** (meɪ) n. Brit. same as **hawthorn.** [from May]

May (meɪ) n. the fifth month of the year.

[Latin *Maius* (month) of *Maia*, Roman goddess]

Maya (ˈmaɪə) *n.* **1.** (*pl.* **-ya** *or* **-yas**) a member of an American Indian people of Central America, once having an advanced civilization. **2.** the language of this people. —ˈ**Mayan** *n., adj.*

maybe (ˈmeɪbiː) *adv.* perhaps.

Mayday (ˈmeɪˌdeɪ) *n.* the international radiotelephone distress signal. [phonetic spelling of French *m'aider* help me]

May Day *n.* the first day of May, traditionally a celebration of the coming of spring: in some countries now a holiday in honour of workers.

mayfly (ˈmeɪˌflaɪ) *n., pl.* **-flies.** a short-lived insect with large transparent wings.

mayhem (ˈmeɪhɛm) *n.* **1.** any violent destruction or confusion. **2.** *Law.* the maiming of a person. [Anglo-French *mahem* injury]

mayn't (ˈmeɪənt, meɪnt) may not.

mayonnaise (ˌmeɪəˈneɪz) *n.* a thick creamy sauce made from egg yolks, oil, and vinegar. [French]

mayor (mɛə) *n.* the civic head of a municipal council in many countries. [Latin *maior* greater] —ˈ**mayoral** *adj.*

mayoralty (ˈmɛərəltɪ) *n., pl.* **-ties.** the office or term of office of a mayor.

mayoress (ˈmɛərɪs) *n.* **1.** *Chiefly Brit.* the wife of a mayor. **2.** a female mayor.

maypole (ˈmeɪˌpəʊl) *n.* a tall pole around which people dance during May-Day celebrations.

May queen *n.* a girl chosen to preside over May-Day celebrations.

maze (meɪz) *n.* **1.** a complex network of paths or passages designed to puzzle those walking through it. **2.** a similar system represented diagrammatically as a pattern of lines. **3.** any confusing network of streets or paths. **4.** a state of confusion. [from *amaze*]

mazurka (məˈzɜːkə) *n.* **1.** a Polish national dance in triple time. **2.** music for this dance. [Polish]

MB **1.** Bachelor of Medicine. **2.** *Computers.* megabyte.

MBE Member of the Order of the British Empire (a Brit. title).

MC **1.** Master of Ceremonies. **2.** (in the U.S.) Member of Congress. **3.** (in Britain) Military Cross.

MCC (in Britain) Marylebone Cricket Club.

MCh Master of Surgery. [Latin *Magister Chirurgiae*]

Md *Chem.* mendelevium.

MD **1.** Doctor of Medicine. [Latin *Medicinae Doctor*] **2.** Managing Director. **3.** Also: **Md.** Maryland.

MDT (in the U.S. and Canada) Mountain Daylight Time.

me¹ (miː; *unstressed* mɪ) *pron.* (*objective*) **1.** refers to the speaker or writer: *that shocks me.* ~*n.* **2.** *Informal.* the personality of the speaker or writer or something that expresses it: *the real me.* [Old English]

me² (miː) *n.* same as **mi.**

ME **1.** Also: **Me.** Maine. **2.** Middle English. **3.** myalgic encephalomyelitis: painful muscles and general weakness sometimes persisting long after a viral illness.

mea culpa (ˈmeɪɑː ˈkʊlpɑː) an acknowledgment of guilt. [Latin, lit.: my fault]

mead¹ (miːd) *n.* a wine made from fermented honey, often with spices added. [Old English *medu*]

mead² (miːd) *n.* *Archaic or poetic.* a meadow. [Old English *mæd*]

meadow (ˈmɛdəʊ) *n.* **1.** an area of grassland, often used for hay or for grazing of animals. **2.** a low-lying piece of grassland, often near a river. [Old English *mædwe*]

meadowsweet (ˈmɛdəʊˌswiːt) *n.* a plant with dense heads of small fragrant cream-coloured flowers.

meagre *or U.S.* **meager** (ˈmiːgə) *adj.* **1.** deficient in amount, quality, or extent. **2.** thin or emaciated. [Old French *maigre*]

meal¹ (miːl) *n.* **1.** any of the regular occasions, such as breakfast or dinner, when food is served and eaten. **2.** the food served and eaten. **3. make a meal of.** *Informal.* to perform (a task) with unnecessarily great effort. [Old English *mæl*]

meal² (miːl) *n.* **1.** the edible part of a grain or pulse (excluding wheat) ground to a coarse powder. **2.** *Scot.* oatmeal. **3.** *Chiefly U.S.* maize flour. [Old English *melu*] —ˈ**mealy** *adj.*

mealie (ˈmiːlɪ) *n.* (*often pl.*) *S. African.* same as **maize.** [Afrikaans, from Latin *milium* millet]

meals-on-wheels *n.* (*functioning as sing.*) (in Britain) a service taking hot meals to the elderly or infirm in their own homes.

meal ticket *n.* *Slang.* a person or situation providing a source of livelihood or income. [from orig. U.S. sense of ticket entitling holder to a meal]

mealy-mouthed *adj.* hesitant or afraid to speak plainly; not outspoken.

mean¹ (miːn) *vb.* **meaning, meant. 1.** to intend to convey or express. **2.** to intend: *she didn't mean to hurt it.* **3.** to say or do in all seriousness: *the boss means what he says.* **4.** (often foll. by *for*) to destine or design (for a certain person or purpose): *she was meant for greater things.* **5.** to denote; signify; represent. **6.** to produce; cause: *the weather will mean long traffic delays.* **7.** to foretell: *those dark clouds mean rain.* **8.** to have the importance of: *money means nothing to him.* **9. mean well.** to have good intentions. [Old English *mænan*]

mean² (miːn) *adj.* **1.** *Chiefly Brit.* miserly, ungenerous, or petty. **2.** despicable, ignoble, or callous: *a mean action.* **3.** poor or shabby: *a mean abode.* **4.** *Informal, chiefly U.S. & Canad.* bad-tempered; vicious. **5.** *Informal.* ashamed: *he felt mean about not letting the children stay out late.* **6.** *Slang.* excellent; skilful: *he plays a mean trombone.* **7. no mean. a.** of high quality: *no mean performer.* **b.** difficult: *no mean*

feat. [Old English *gemǽne* common]
—'**meanly** *adv.* —'**meanness** *n.*

mean[3] (miːn) *n.* **1.** the middle point, state, or course between limits or extremes. **2.** *Maths.* **a.** the mid-point between the highest and lowest number in a set. **b.** the average. ~*adj.* **3.** intermediate in size or quantity. **4.** occurring halfway between extremes or limits; average. [Late Latin *mediānus* median]

meander (mɪ'ændə) *vb.* **1.** to follow a winding course. **2.** to wander without definite aim or direction. ~*n.* **3.** a curve or bend, as in a river. **4.** a winding course or movement. [Greek *Maiandros* the River Maeander]

mean deviation *n. Statistics.* the difference between an observed value of a variable and its mean.

meanie *or* **meany** ('miːnɪ) *n. Informal.* **1.** *Chiefly Brit.* a miserly person. **2.** *Chiefly U.S.* a nasty ill-tempered person.

meaning ('miːnɪŋ) *n.* **1.** the sense or significance of a word, sentence, or symbol. **2.** the inner, symbolic, or true interpretation, value, or message: *the meaning of life.* ~*adj.* **3.** expressive of some sense or intention: *a meaning look.*

meaningful ('miːnɪŋfʊl) *adj.* **1.** having great meaning or validity. **2.** eloquent; expressive: *a meaningful silence.*

meaningless ('miːnɪŋlɪs) *adj.* futile or empty of meaning.

means (miːnz) *n.* **1.** (*functioning as sing. or pl.*) the medium, method, or instrument used to obtain a result or achieve an end: *a means of communication.* **2.** (*functioning as pl.*) income: *a man of means.* **3. by all means.** without hesitation or doubt; certainly. **4. by means of.** with the use or help of. **5. by no** *or* **not by any means.** on no account; in no way.

means test *n.* the checking of a person's income to determine whether he qualifies for financial aid.

meant (mɛnt) *vb.* past of **mean**[1].

meantime ('miːn,taɪm) *n.* **1.** the intervening period *in the meantime.* ~*adv.* **2.** same as **meanwhile.**

mean time *or* **mean solar time** *n.* the times, at a particular place, measured so as to give 24-hour days (mean solar days) throughout a year.

meanwhile ('miːn,waɪl) *adv.* **1.** during the intervening period. **2.** at the same time, esp. in another place.

meany ('miːnɪ) *n., pl.* **meanies.** same as **meanie.**

measles ('miːz°lz) *n.* (*functioning as sing.*) a highly contagious viral disease common in children, characterized by fever and a rash of small red spots. See also **German measles.** [Low German *masele* spot on the skin]

measly ('miːzlɪ) *adj.* **-slier, -sliest. 1.** *Informal.* meagre in quality or quantity. **2.** having or relating to measles.

measure ('mɛʒə) *n.* **1.** the extent, quantity, amount, or degree of something, as determined by measurement or calculation. **2.** a device for measuring distance, volume,

etc., such as a graduated scale or container. **3.** a system or unit of measurement: *metric measure.* **4.** degree or extent: *a measure of freedom.* **5.** (*often pl.*) a particular action intended to achieve an effect. **6.** a legislative bill, act, or resolution. **7.** *Music.* another word for **bar**[1] (sense 11). **8.** *Prosody.* poetic rhythm or cadence; metre. **9.** a metrical foot. **10.** *Archaic.* a dance. **11. for good measure.** as an extra precaution or beyond requirements. **12. made to measure.** (of clothes) made to fit an individual purchaser. ~*vb.* **13.** (*often foll. by up*) to determine the size, amount, etc., of by measurement. **14.** to make a measurement. **15.** to estimate or determine. **16.** to function as a measurement of: *the ohm measures electrical resistance.* **17.** to bring into competition or conflict with: *he measured his strength against that of his opponent.* **18.** to be as specified in extent, amount, etc.: *the room measures six feet.* ~See also **measure up.** [Latin *mēnsūra*] —'**measurable** *adj.*

measured ('mɛʒəd) *adj.* **1.** slow or stately. **2.** carefully considered; deliberate.

measurement ('mɛʒəmənt) *n.* **1.** the act or process of measuring. **2.** an amount, extent, or size determined by measuring. **3.** a system of measures based on a particular standard.

measures ('mɛʒəz) *pl. n.* rock strata that contain a particular type of deposit: *coal measures.*

measure up *vb.* (usually foll. by *to*) to fulfil (expectations or standards).

meat (miːt) *n.* **1.** the flesh of animals used as food. **2.** the essence or gist. [Old English *mete*] —'**meatless** *adj.*

meatball ('miːt,bɔːl) *n.* minced beef, shaped into a ball before cooking.

meaty ('miːtɪ) *adj.* **meatier, meatiest. 1.** of, like, or full of meat. **2.** heavily built; fleshy or brawny. **3.** full of import or interest: *a meaty discussion.*

Mecca ('mɛkə) *n.* (*sometimes not cap.*) a place that attracts many visitors. [after *Mecca,* holy city of Islam]

mech. 1. mechanical. **2.** mechanics.

mechanic (mɪ'kænɪk) *n.* a person skilled in maintaining or operating machinery or motors. [Greek *mēkhanē* machine]

mechanical (mɪ'kænɪk°l) *adj.* **1.** made, performed, or operated by machinery. **2.** concerned with machines or machinery. **3.** relating to or operated by physical forces. **4.** of or concerned with mechanics. **5.** (of a gesture or response) automatic; lacking thought or feeling. —**me'chanically** *adv.*

mechanical drawing *n.* a drawing to scale of a machine or architectural plan from which dimensions can be taken.

mechanical engineering *n.* the branch of engineering concerned with the design, construction, and operation of machines.

mechanics (mɪ'kænɪks) *n.* **1.** (*functioning as sing.*) the branch of science concerned with the equilibrium or motion of bodies. **2.** (*functioning as sing.*) the science of designing, constructing, and operating machines. **3.** the technical aspects of something.

mechanism ('mɛkə,nızəm) n. **1.** a system of moving parts that performs some function, esp. in a machine. **2.** any mechanical device or part of such a device. **3.** a process or technique: *the defence mechanism.* —ˌmecha'nistic *adj.*

mechanize *or* **-ise** ('mɛkə,naız) vb. **1.** to equip (a factory or industry) with machinery. **2.** to make mechanical or automatic. **3.** to equip (an army) with motorized or armoured vehicles. —ˌmechani'zation *or* -i'sation n.

med. 1. medical. **2.** medicine. **3.** medieval. **4.** medium.

MEd Master of Education.

medal ('mɛd⁰l) n. a small flat piece of metal bearing an inscription or image, given as an award or in commemoration of some outstanding event. [French *médaille*]

medallion (mı'dæljən) n. **1.** a round ornament worn on a chain round the neck. **2.** a large medal. **3.** a decorative device resembling a medal, used in architecture. [Italian *medaglia* medal]

medallist *or* *U.S.* **medalist** ('mɛd⁰lıst) n. *Chiefly sport.* a winner of a medal or medals.

meddle ('mɛd⁰l) vb. (foll. by *with* or *in*) to interfere annoyingly. [Old French *medler*] —'meddler n. —'meddlesome *adj.*

media ('miːdıə) n. **1.** a plural of medium. **2.** the mass media collectively.

mediaeval (ˌmɛdı'iːv⁰l) *adj.* same as medieval.

media event n. an event that is staged for or exploited by the mass media.

medial ('miːdıəl) *adj.* of or situated in the middle. [Latin *medius* middle] —'medially *adv.*

median ('miːdıən) n. **1.** a middle point, plane, or part. **2.** *Geom.* a straight line joining one vertex of a triangle to the midpoint of the opposite side. **3.** *Statistics.* the middle value in a frequency distribution, below and above which lie values with equal total frequencies. [Latin *medius* middle]

mediate vb. ('miːdı,eıt). **1.** (usually foll. by *between* or *in*) to intervene (between parties or in a dispute) in order to bring about agreement. **2.** to resolve (differences) by mediation. **3.** to be in an intermediate position. ~*adj.* ('miːdııt). **4.** occurring as a result of or dependent upon mediation. [Late Latin *mediāre* to be in the middle] —ˌmedi'ation n. —'medi,ator n.

medic ('mɛdık) n. *Informal.* a doctor, medical orderly, or medical student. [from MEDICAL]

medical ('mɛdık⁰l) *adj.* **1.** of or relating to the science of medicine or to the treatment of patients without surgery. ~n. **2.** *Informal.* a medical examination. [Latin *medicus* physician] —'medically *adv.*

medical certificate n. **1.** a document stating the result of a satisfactory medical examination. **2.** a doctor's certificate giving evidence of a person's unfitness for work.

medicament (mı'dıkəmənt) n. a medicine.

medicate ('mɛdı,keıt) vb. **1.** to treat (a patient) with a medicine. **2.** to add a medication to (a bandage or shampoo). [Latin *medicāre* to heal] —'medicative *adj.*

medication (ˌmɛdı'keıʃən) n. **1.** treatment with drugs or remedies. **2.** a drug or remedy.

medicinal (mı'dısın⁰l) *adj.* relating to or having therapeutic properties. —me'dicinally *adv.*

medicine ('mɛdısın, 'mɛdsın) n. **1.** any substance used in treating or alleviating the symptoms of disease. **2.** the science of preventing, diagnosing, or curing disease. **3.** any nonsurgical branch of medical science. **4. take one's medicine.** to accept a deserved punishment. [Latin *medicīna (ars)* (art) of healing]

medicine man n. (among certain peoples) a person believed to have supernatural powers of healing.

medico ('mɛdı,kəʊ) n., pl. **-cos.** *Informal.* a doctor or medical student.

medieval *or* **mediaeval** (ˌmɛdı'iːv⁰l) *adj.* **1.** of, relating to, or in the style of the Middle Ages. **2.** *Informal.* old-fashioned; primitive. [New Latin *medium aevum* the middle age] —ˌmedi'evalist *or* ˌmedi'aevalist n.

Medieval Greek n. the Greek language from the 7th to 13th century A.D.

Medieval Latin n. the Latin language as used throughout Europe in the Middle Ages.

mediocre (ˌmiːdı'əʊkə) *adj.* average or ordinary in quality. [Latin *mediocris* moderate] —mediocrity (ˌmiːdı'ɒkrıtı) n.

meditate ('mɛdı,teıt) vb. **1.** (foll. by *on* or *upon*) to think about something deeply. **2.** to reflect deeply on spiritual matters. **3.** to plan, consider, or think of doing (something). [Latin *meditārī* to reflect upon] —'meditative *adj.* —'medi,tator n.

meditation (ˌmɛdı'teıʃən) n. **1.** the act of meditating; reflection. **2.** contemplation of spiritual matters, esp. as a religious practice.

Mediterranean (ˌmɛdıtə'reınıən) n. **1.** short for the **Mediterranean Sea,** the sea between S Europe, N Africa, and SW Asia. ~*adj.* **2.** of, relating to, or near the Mediterranean Sea. [Latin *medius* middle + *terra* land]

medium ('miːdıəm) *adj.* **1.** midway between extremes; average. ~n., pl. **-dia** *or* **-diums. 2.** a middle state, degree, or condition: *the happy medium.* **3.** an intervening substance or agency for transmitting or producing an effect. **4.** a means for communicating information or news to the public. **5.** a person who can supposedly communicate with the dead. **6.** the substance or surroundings in which an organism naturally lives or grows. **7.** *Art.* the category of a work of art, as determined by its materials: *her works in the photographic medium.* [Latin *medius* middle]

medium wave *n.* a radio wave with a wavelength between 100 and 1000 metres.

medlar ('medlə) *n.* the fruit of a small Eurasian tree, which resembles the crab apple and is not edible until it has begun to decay. [Old French *medlier*]

medley ('medlı) *n.* 1. a mixture of various elements. 2. a musical composition consisting of various tunes arranged as a continuous whole. 3. *Swimming.* a race in which a different stroke is used for each length. [Old French from *medler* to mix, quarrel]

medulla (mɪ'dʌlə) *n., pl.* **-las** *or* **-lae** (-liː). 1. *Anat.* the innermost part of an organ or structure. 2. *Anat.* the lower stalklike section of the brain. 3. *Bot.* the central pith of a plant stem. [Latin: marrow] —**me'dullary** *adj.*

medusa (mɪ'djuːzə) *n., pl.* **-sas** *or* **-sae** (-ziː). jellyfish. [*Medusa*, the Gorgon, whose hair was snakes]

meek (miːk) *adj.* patient, long-suffering, or submissive. [related to Old Norse *mjūkr* amenable] —**'meekly** *adv.*

meerkat ('mɪəˌkæt) *n.* a South African mongoose. [Dutch: sea-cat]

meerschaum ('mɪəʃəm) *n.* 1. a white, heat-resistant, claylike mineral. 2. a tobacco pipe with a bowl made of this mineral. [German *Meerschaum*, lit.: sea foam]

meet[1] (miːt) *vb.* **meeting, met.** 1. to come together (with), either by design or by accident; encounter. 2. to come into contact with (something or each other). 3. to come to or be at the place of arrival of: *to meet a train.* 4. to make the acquaintance of or be introduced to (someone or each other). 5. (of people) to gather together for a purpose: *the committee meets once a month.* 6. to come into the presence of (someone or each other) as opponents. 7. to cope with effectively; satisfy: *to meet someone's demands.* 8. (sometimes foll. by *with*) to experience; suffer: *he met his death in a road accident.* 9. **more to this than meets the eye.** there is more involved in this than appears. ~*n.* 10. the assembly of hounds and huntsmen prior to a hunt. 11. a sports meeting. [Old English *mētan*]

meet[2] (miːt) *adj. Archaic.* proper, fitting, or correct. [Old English *gemēte*]

meeting ('miːtɪŋ) *n.* 1. an act of coming together; encounter. 2. an assembly or gathering. 3. a sporting competition, as of athletes, or of horse racing.

mega ('megə) *adj. Slang.* extremely good, great, or successful.

mega- *combining form.* 1. denoting 10[6]: *megawatt.* 2. (in computer technology) denoting 2[20] (1 048 576): *megabyte.* 3. large or great: *megalith.* 4. *Informal.* greatest: *megastar.* [Greek *megas* huge, powerful]

megabyte ('megəˌbaɪt) *n. Computers.* 2[20] or 1 048 576 bytes.

megadeath ('megəˌdeθ) *n.* the death of a million people, esp. in a nuclear war or attack.

megahertz ('megəˌhɜːts) *n., pl.* **megahertz.** one million hertz.

megajoule ('megəˌdʒuːl) *n.* one million joules.

megalith ('megəlɪθ) *n.* a stone of great size, esp. one forming part of a prehistoric monument. —ˌmega'lithic *adj.*

megalomania (ˌmegələʊ'meɪnɪə) *n.* 1. a mental illness characterized by delusions of power. 2. *Informal.* a craving for power. [Greek *megas* great + *mania* madness] —ˌmegalo'maniac *adj., n.*

megaphone ('megəˌfəʊn) *n.* a funnel-shaped instrument used to amplify the voice.

megapode ('megəˌpəʊd) *n.* any of various ground-living birds of Australia, New Guinea, and adjacent islands. Their eggs incubate in mounds of sand or rotting vegetation. [Greek *megas* great + *-podoa* footed]

megaton ('megəˌtʌn) *n.* an explosive power, esp. of a nuclear weapon, equal to the power of one million tons of TNT.

megawatt ('megəˌwɒt) *n.* one million watts.

meiosis (maɪ'əʊsɪs) *n., pl.* **-ses** (-ˌsiːz). a type of cell division in which reproductive cells are produced, each containing half the chromosome number of the parent nucleus. [Greek *meiōn* less]

melamine ('meləˌmiːn) *n.* a colourless crystalline compound used in making synthetic resins. [German *Melamin*]

melancholia (ˌmelən'kəʊlɪə) *n.* an old name for depression.

melancholy ('melənkəlɪ) *n., pl.* **-cholies.** 1. a tendency to gloominess or depression. 2. a sad thoughtful state of mind. ~*adj.* 3. characterized by, causing, or expressing sadness. [Greek *melas* black + *kholē* bile] —**melancholic** (ˌmelən'kɒlɪk) *adj., n.*

melange *or* **mélange** (meɪ'lɒnʒ) *n.* a mixture; confusion. [French *mêler* to mix]

melanin ('melənɪn) *n.* a black pigment present in the hair, skin, and eyes of man and animals. [Greek *melas* black]

melanoma (ˌmelə'nəʊmə) *n., pl.* **-mas** *or* **-mata** (-mətə). *Pathol.* a tumour composed of darkly pigmented cells. [Greek *melas* black + *-oma*, modelled on *carcinoma*]

Melba toast ('melbə) *n.* very thin crisp toast. [after Dame Nellie *Melba*, singer]

meld (meld) *vb.* to merge. [blend of *melt* + *weld*]

melee *or* **mêlée** ('meleɪ) *n.* a noisy riotous fight or brawl. [French, from *mêler* to mix]

mellifluous (mɪ'lɪflʊəs) *adj.* (of sounds or utterances) smooth or honeyed; sweet. [Latin *mel* honey + *fluere* to flow]

mellow ('meləʊ) *adj.* 1. (esp. of fruits) full-flavoured; sweet; ripe. 2. (esp. of wines) well-matured. 3. (esp. of colours or sounds) soft or rich. 4. kind-hearted, esp. through maturity or old age. 5. genial, as through the effects of alcohol. 6. (of soil) soft and loamy. ~*vb.* 7. to make or become mellow. [origin unknown]

melodeon (mɪ'ləʊdɪən) *n. Music.* 1. a small accordion. 2. a keyboard instrument like a harmonium. [German *Melodie* melody]

melodic (mɪˈlɒdɪk) *adj.* **1.** of or relating to melody. **2.** melodious. **—meˈlodically** *adv.*

melodious (mɪˈləʊdɪəs) *adj.* **1.** tuneful and pleasant to the ear. **2.** of or relating to melody; melodic. **—meˈlodiousness** *n.*

melodrama (ˈmɛləˌdrɑːmə) *n.* **1.** a play or film characterized by extravagant action and emotion. **2.** overdramatic emotion or behaviour. [Greek *melos* song + *drame* drama] **—melodramatic** (ˌmɛlədrəˈmætɪk) *adj.* **—ˌmelodraˈmatics** *pl. n.*

melody (ˈmɛlədɪ) *n., pl.* **-dies. 1.** *Music.* a succession of notes forming a distinctive sequence; tune. **2.** sounds that are pleasant because of tone or arrangement, esp. words of poetry. [Greek *melōidia*]

melon (ˈmɛlən) *n.* the large edible fruit of various trailing plants, which has a hard rind and juicy flesh. [Greek *mēlon* apple]

melt (mɛlt) *vb.* **1.** to change from a solid into a liquid as a result of the action of heat. **2.** to dissolve: *these scones melt in the mouth.* **3.** (often foll. by *away*) to disappear; fade. **4.** (often foll. by *into*) to blend or cause to blend gradually. **5.** to make or become emotional or sentimental; soften. [Old English *meltan* to digest] **—ˈmeltingly** *adv.*

meltdown (ˈmɛltˌdaʊn) *n.* (in a nuclear reactor) the melting of the fuel rods, with the possible escape of radioactivity.

melting point *n.* the temperature at which a solid turns into a liquid.

melting pot *n.* a place or situation in which many races, ideas, etc., are mixed.

meltwater (ˈmɛltˌwɔːtə) *n.* melted snow or ice.

member (ˈmɛmbə) *n.* **1.** a person who belongs to a group or organization such as a club or political party. **2.** any part of a plant or animal, such as a limb or petal. [Latin *membrum* limb, part]

Member of Parliament *n.* a member of the House of Commons or similar legislative body, as in many Commonwealth countries.

membership (ˈmɛmbəʃɪp) *n.* **1.** the members of an organization collectively. **2.** the number of members. **3.** the state of being a member.

membrane (ˈmɛmbreɪn) *n.* a pliable sheetlike tissue that covers, lines, or connects plant and animal organs or cells. [Latin *membrāna* skin covering a part of the body] **—membranous** (ˈmɛmbrənəs) *adj.*

memento (mɪˈmɛntəʊ) *n., pl.* **-tos** *or* **-toes.** something that reminds one of past events; a souvenir. [Latin, imperative of *meminisse* to remember]

memento mori (ˈmɔːriː) *n., pl.* **memento mori.** an object intended to remind people of death. [Latin: remember you must die]

memo (ˈmɛməʊ) *n., pl.* **memos.** short for **memorandum.**

memoir (ˈmɛmwɑː) *n.* a biography or historical account, esp. one based on personal knowledge. [Latin *memoria* memory]

memoirs (ˈmɛmwɑːz) *pl. n.* **1.** a collection of reminiscences about a period or series of events, written from personal experience. **2.** an autobiography.

memorabilia (ˌmɛmərəˈbɪlɪə) *pl. n., sing.* **-rabile** (-ˈræbɪlɪ). objects connected with famous people or events.

memorable (ˈmɛmərəbˈl) *adj.* worth remembering or easily remembered. [Latin *memorāre* to remember] **—ˈmemorably** *adv.*

memorandum (ˌmɛməˈrændəm) *n., pl.* **-dums** *or* **-da** (-də). **1.** a written statement, record, or communication. **2.** a note of things to be remembered. **3.** *Law.* a short written summary of the terms of a transaction. [Latin: (something) to be remembered]

memorial (mɪˈmɔːrɪəl) *adj.* **1.** serving to preserve the memory of the dead or a past event. ~*n.* **2.** something, such as a statue, serving as a remembrance of someone or something. [Late Latin *memoriāle* a reminder]

memorize *or* **-ise** (ˈmɛməˌraɪz) *vb.* to commit to memory; learn by heart.

memory (ˈmɛmərɪ) *n., pl.* **-ries. 1.** the ability of the mind to store and recall past sensations, thoughts, and knowledge: *he can do it from memory.* **2.** the sum of everything retained by the mind. **3.** a particular recollection of an event or person. **4.** the time over which recollection extends: *within his memory.* **5.** commemoration: *in memory of our leader.* **6.** the state of being remembered, as after death. **7.** a part of a computer in which information is stored. [Latin *memoria*]

memsahib (ˈmɛmˌsɑːɪb) *n.* (formerly, in India) a term of respect used for a European married woman. [*ma'am* + *sahib*]

men (mɛn) *n.* the plural of **man.**

menace (ˈmɛnɪs) *vb.* **1.** to threaten with violence or danger. ~*n.* **2.** a threat; a source of danger. **3.** *Informal.* a nuisance. [Latin *minax* threatening] **—ˈmenacing** *adj.*

ménage (meɪˈnɑːʒ) *n.* a household. [French]

ménage à trois (meɪˈnɑːʒ ɑː ˈtrwɑː) *n., pl.* **ménages à trois** (meɪˈnɑːʒ ɑː ˈtrwɑː). a sexual arrangement involving a married couple and the lover of one of them. [French, lit.: household of three]

menagerie (mɪˈnædʒərɪ) *n.* a collection of wild animals kept for exhibition. [French]

mend (mɛnd) *vb.* **1.** to repair (something broken or not working). **2.** to heal or recover. **3.** to improve; become better. ~*n.* **4.** a mended area, esp. on a garment. **5. on the mend.** becoming better, esp. in health. [from *amend*]

mendacity (mɛnˈdæsɪtɪ) *n.* the tendency to be untruthful. [Latin *mendāx* untruthful] **—mendacious** (mɛnˈdeɪʃəs) *adj.*

mendelevium (ˌmɛndɪˈliːvɪəm) *n.* an artificially produced radioactive element. Symbol: Md [after D. I. *Mendeleyev*, chemist]

Mendel's laws (ˈmɛndˈlz) *pl. n.* the principles of heredity proposed by Gregor Mendel (1822–84), Austrian monk and botanist. —'**Mendel**,**ism** n.

mendicant ('mɛndɪkənt) adj. **1.** begging. **2.** (of a member of a religious order) dependent on charity for food. ~n. **3.** a mendicant friar. **4.** a beggar. [Latin mendīcus beggar]

meneer (mə'nɪə) n. a S. African title of address equivalent to sir or Mr. [Afrikaans]

menfolk ('mɛn,fʊk) pl. n. men collectively, esp. the men of a particular family.

menhir ('mɛnhɪə) n. a single standing stone, dating from prehistoric times. [Breton men stone + hir long]

menial ('miːnɪəl) adj. **1.** involving or doing boring work of low status. ~n. **2.** a domestic servant. [Old French meinie household]

meninges (mɪ'nɪndʒiːz) pl. n., sing. **meninx** ('miːnɪŋks). the three membranes that envelop the brain and spinal cord. [Greek, plural of meninx membrane]

meningitis (,mɛnɪn'dʒaɪtɪs) n. inflammation of the membranes that surround the brain or spinal cord, caused by infection.

meniscus (mɪ'nɪskəs) n., pl. **-nisci** (-'nɪsaɪ) or **-niscuses**. **1.** the curved upper surface of a liquid standing in a tube, produced by the surface tension. **2.** a crescent-shaped lens. [Greek mēniskos crescent]

menopause ('mɛnəʊ,pɔːz) n. the period during which a woman's menstrual cycle ceases, normally at an age of 45 to 50. [Greek mēn month + pausis halt] —,**meno**'**pausal** adj.

menorah (mɪ'nɔːrə) n. Judaism. a seven-branched candelabrum used as an emblem of Judaism. [Hebrew: candlestick]

menses ('mɛnsiːz) n., pl. **menses.** same as **menstruation.** [Latin, plural of mensis month]

menstruate ('mɛnstrʊ,eɪt) vb. to undergo menstruation. [Latin menstruāre, from mensis month] —'**menstrual** adj.

menstruation (,mɛnstrʊ'eɪʃən) n. the approximately monthly discharge of blood from the womb in nonpregnant women of childbearing age.

mensuration (,mɛnsjə'reɪʃən) n. **1.** the study of the measurement of geometric magnitudes such as length. **2.** the act or process of measuring. [Late Latin mēnsūra measure]

mental ('mɛntʲl) adj. **1.** of, done by, or involving the mind. **2.** affected by mental illness: a mental patient. **3.** concerned with mental illness: a mental hospital. **4.** Slang. insane. [Latin mēns mind] —'**mentally** adv.

mental handicap n. any intellectual disability resulting from injury to or abnormal development of the brain. —**mentally handicapped** adj.

mentality (mɛn'tælɪt) n., pl. **-ties.** a way of thinking; mental inclination or character.

menthol ('mɛnθɒl) n. an organic compound found in peppermint oil and used as an antiseptic, in inhalants, and as a painkiller. [Latin mentha mint] —'**mentho,lated** adj.

mention ('mɛnʃən) vb. **1.** to refer to or speak about briefly or incidentally. **2.** to acknowledge or honour. **3. not to mention (something).** to say nothing of (something too obvious to mention). ~n. **4.** a recognition or acknowledgment. **5.** a slight reference or allusion. [Latin mentiō a calling to mind]

mentor ('mɛntɔː) n. an adviser or guide. [Mentor, adviser of Telemachus in the Odyssey]

menu ('mɛnjuː) n. **1.** a list of dishes served at a meal or that can be ordered in a restaurant. **2.** a list of options displayed on a visual display unit from which the operator can choose. [French menu small, detailed (list)]

MEP (in Britain) Member of the European Parliament.

Mephistopheles (,mɛfɪ'stɒfɪ,liːz) n. a devil in medieval mythology to whom Faust sold his soul. —**Mephistophelean** (,mɛfɪstə'fiːlɪən) adj.

mercantile ('mɜːkən,taɪl) adj. of trade or traders; commercial. [Italian mercante merchant]

Mercator projection (mɜː'keɪtə) n. a way of drawing maps in which latitude and longitude form a rectangular grid, scale being exaggerated with increasing distance from the equator. [after G. Mercator, cartographer]

mercenary ('mɜːsɪnərɪ, -sɪnrɪ) adj. **1.** influenced by greed or desire for gain. **2.** of or relating to a mercenary or mercenaries. ~n., pl. **-naries.** **3.** a soldier hired to fight for a foreign army. [Latin mercēs wages]

mercerize or **-ise** ('mɜːsə,raɪz) vb. to treat (cotton yarn) with an alkali to make it strong and shiny. [after John Mercer, maker of textiles]

merchandise ('mɜːtʃəndaɪz) n. **1.** commercial goods; commodities. ~vb. **2.** to engage in the commercial purchase and sale of (goods or services); trade.

merchant ('mɜːtʃənt) n. **1.** a person who buys and sells goods for profit; trader. **2.** Chiefly Scot., U.S., & Canad. a person engaged in retail trade. **3.** Slang. a person dealing in something undesirable: a gossip merchant. **4.** (modifier) **a.** of the merchant navy: a merchant sailor. **b.** of or concerned with trade: a merchant ship. [Latin mercārī to trade]

merchant bank n. Brit. a financial institution that deals primarily with foreign trade and business finance. —**merchant banker** n.

merchantman ('mɜːtʃəntmən) n., pl. **-men.** a merchant ship.

merchant navy n. the ships or crew engaged in a nation's commercial shipping.

merciful ('mɜːsɪful) adj. showing or giving mercy; compassionate. —'**mercifully** adv.

merciless ('mɜːsɪlɪs) adj. without mercy; pitiless, cruel, or heartless. —'**mercilessly** adv.

mercurial (mɜː'kjʊərɪəl) adj. **1.** volatile; lively: a mercurial temperament. **2.** of or containing mercury. [Latin mercuriālis

mercuric ('mɜːˈkjʊərɪk) *adj.* of or containing mercury in the divalent state.

mercurous ('mɜːkjʊrəs) *adj.* of or containing mercury in the monovalent state.

mercury ('mɜːkjʊrɪ) *n., pl.* **-ries.** a heavy silvery-white toxic liquid metallic element: used in thermometers, barometers, mercury-vapour lamps, and dental amalgams. Symbol: Hg [Latin *Mercurius*, messenger of Jupiter]

Mercury ('mɜːkjʊrɪ) *n.* **1.** *Roman myth.* the messenger of the gods. **2.** the second smallest planet and the nearest to the sun.

mercy ('mɜːsɪ) *n., pl.* **-cies.** **1.** compassionate treatment of or attitude towards an offender or enemy who is in one's power. **2.** the power to show mercy. a relieving or welcome occurrence. **4. at the mercy of.** in the power of. [Latin *mercēs* recompense]

mercy killing *n.* same as **euthanasia.**

mere[1] (mɪə) *adj.* being nothing more than something specified: *a mere child.* [Latin *merus* pure] —**'merely** *adv.*

mere[2] (mɪə) *n. Dialect or archaic.* a lake. [Old English *mere* sea, lake]

meretricious (ˌmɛrɪˈtrɪʃəs) *adj.* superficially or garishly attractive but of no real value. [Latin *merētrix* prostitute]

merganser (mɜːˈgænsə) *n., pl.* **-sers** or **-ser.** a large crested marine diving duck. [Latin *mergere* to plunge + *anser* goose]

merge (mɜːdʒ) *vb.* **1.** to combine, esp. so as to become part of a larger whole. **2.** to blend or cause to blend; fuse. [Latin *mergere* to plunge]

merger ('mɜːdʒə) *n.* the act of merging, esp. the combination of two or more companies.

meridian (məˈrɪdɪən) *n.* **1.** one of the imaginary lines joining the north and south poles at right angles to the equator, designated by degrees of longitude from 0° at Greenwich to 180°. **2.** the peak; zenith: *the meridian of his achievements.* [Latin *merīdiēs* midday]

meridional (məˈrɪdɪən'l) *adj.* **1.** of or along a meridian. **2.** of or in the south, esp. of Europe.

meringue (məˈræŋ) *n.* **1.** stiffly beaten egg whites mixed with sugar and baked. **2.** a small cake of this mixture. [French]

merino (məˈriːnəʊ) *n., pl.* **-nos.** **1.** a breed of sheep with long fine wool. **2.** the yarn made from this wool. [Spanish]

merit ('mɛrɪt) *n.* **1.** worth or superior quality; excellence. **2.** (*often pl.*) a good or admirable quality or act. **3.** a mark of worth or excellence. **4. on its merits.** on its intrinsic qualities or virtues. ~*vb.* **5.** to be worthy of; deserve. [Latin *meritum* reward]

meritocracy (ˌmɛrɪˈtɒkrəsɪ) *n., pl.* **-cies.** a social system based on rule by persons of superior talents or intellect.

meritorious (ˌmɛrɪˈtɔːrɪəs) *adj.* praiseworthy; showing merit. [Latin *meritōrius* earning money]

merlin ('mɜːlɪn) *n.* a small falcon with dark plumage. [Old French *esmerillon*]

mermaid ('mɜːˌmeɪd) *n.* an imaginary sea creature with a woman's head and upper body and a fish's tail. [*mere* sea + *maid*] —**'mer,man** *masc. n.*

merry ('mɛrɪ) *adj.* **-rier, -riest.** **1.** cheerful; jolly. **2.** *Brit. informal.* slightly drunk. **3. make merry.** to revel; be festive. [Old English *merige* agreeable] —**'merrily** *adv.* —**'merriment** *n.*

merry-go-round *n.* **1.** a fairground roundabout. **2.** a whirl of activity.

merrymaking ('mɛrɪˌmeɪkɪŋ) *n.* fun, revelry, or festivity. —**'merry,maker** *n.*

mésalliance (meˈzælɪəns) *n.* a marriage with a person of lower social status. [French]

mescal (meˈskæl) *n.* a spineless globe-shaped cactus of Mexico and the southwestern U.S. [Mexican Indian *mexcalli*]

mescaline ('meskəˌliːn) *n.* a hallucinogenic drug derived from the button-like top of the mescal cactus.

mesdames ('meɪˌdæm) *n.* the plural of **madame** and **madam** (sense 1).

mesdemoiselles (ˌmeɪdmwɑˈzɛl) *n.* the plural of **mademoiselle.**

mesembryanthemum (mɪˌzɛmbrɪˈænθɪməm) *n.* a plant with fleshy leaves and bright flowers with rayed petals. [Greek *mesēmbria* noon + *anthemon* flower]

mesh (meʃ) *n.* **1.** a network; net. **2.** an open space between the strands of a network. **3.** (*often pl.*) the strands surrounding these spaces. **4.** anything that ensnares or holds like a net. ~*vb.* **5.** to entangle or become entangled. **6.** (of gear teeth) to engage. **7.** to work in harmony. [prob. Dutch *maesche*]

mesmerize *or* **-ise** ('mɛzməˌraɪz) *vb.* **1.** *Archaic.* to hypnotize. **2.** to hold (someone) as if spellbound. —**'mesmer,ism** *n.*

Mesolithic (ˌmɛsəʊˈlɪθɪk) *adj.* of the middle period of the Stone Age, in Europe from about 12 000 to 3000 B.C. [Greek *misos* middle + *lithos* stone]

meson ('miːzɒn) *n.* any of a group of elementary particles that has a mass between those of an electron and a proton. [*meso-* from Greek *misos* middle + *-on*, indicating an elementary particle]

mesosphere ('mɛsəʊˌsfɪə) *n.* the atmospheric layer above the stratosphere.

Mesozoic (ˌmɛsəʊˈzəʊɪk) *adj. Geol.* of or denoting a geological era that began 225 000 000 years ago and lasted about 155 000 000 years; the era of the dinosaurs. [Greek *misos* middle + *zōion* animal]

mess (mɛs) *n.* **1.** a state of confusion or untidiness, esp. if dirty or unpleasant. **2.** *Informal.* a dirty or untidy person or thing. **3.** *Archaic.* a portion of soft or semiliquid food. **4.** a place where service personnel eat or take recreation. **5.** a group of people, usually servicemen, who eat together. ~*vb.* **6.** (often foll. by *up*) to muddle or dirty. **7.** (often foll. by *with*) to interfere; meddle. **8.** (often foll. by *with* or *together*) *Mil.* to group together for eating. [Old French *mes* dish of food]

mess about *or* **around** *vb.* **1.** to occupy oneself trivially; potter. **2.** to interfere or meddle (with). **3.** (often foll. by *with*) *Chiefly U.S.* to engage in adultery.

message ('mɛsɪdʒ) n. **1.** a communication from one person or group to another. **2.** an implicit meaning, as in a work of art. **3.** a religious or political belief that someone attempts to communicate to others: *the Christian message of salvation.* **4. get the message.** *Informal.* to understand. [Old French, from Latin *mittere* to send]

messages ('mɛsɪdʒɪz) pl. n. *Scot. & NE English dialect.* household shopping.

messenger ('mɛsɪndʒə) n. a person who takes messages from one person or group to another. [Old French]

Messiah (mɪ'saɪə) n. **1.** *Judaism.* the awaited king of the Jews, to be sent by God to free them. **2.** *Christianity.* Jesus Christ, when regarded in this role. **3.** a liberator of a country or people. [Hebrew *māshīah* anointed] —**Messianic** (,mɛsɪ'ænɪk) adj.

messieurs ('mɛsəz) n. the plural of **monsieur.**

mess jacket n. a waist-length jacket, worn by officers in the mess for formal dinners.

mess kit n. *Mil.* eating utensils used esp. in the field.

Messrs ('mɛsəz) n. the plural of **Mr.**

messy ('mɛsɪ) adj. **messier, messiest.** dirty, confused, or untidy. —**messily** adv. —**messiness** n.

met (mɛt) vb. past of **meet**[1].

met. 1. meteorological. **2.** metropolitan.

metabolism (mɪ'tæbə,lɪzəm) n. the chemical processes that occur in living organisms, resulting in growth, production of energy, and elimination of waste. [Greek *metaballein* to change] —**metabolic** (,mɛtə'bɒlɪk) adj.

metabolize or **-ise** (mɪ'tæbə,laɪz) vb. to produce or be produced by metabolism.

metacarpus (,mɛtə'kɑːpəs) n., pl. **-pi** (-paɪ). the set of five long bones in the hand between the wrist and the fingers. [Greek *meta* after + *karpus* wrist] —**,meta'carpal** adj., n.

metal ('mɛt[']l) n. **1. a.** a chemical element, such as iron or copper, that is lustrous and ductile, forms positive ions, and is a good conductor of heat and electricity. **b.** an alloy, such as brass or steel, containing one or more of these elements. **2.** short for **road metal. 3.** (pl.) the rails of a railway. ~adj. **4.** made of metal. ~vb. **-alling, -alled** or *U.S.* **-aling, -aled. 5.** to fit or cover with metal. **6.** to make or mend (a road) with road metal. [Greek *metallon*]

metallic (mɪ'tælɪk) adj. **1.** of or consisting of metal. **2.** suggestive of a metal: *a metallic click; metallic lustre.*

metalliferous (,mɛt[']'lɪfərəs) adj. containing a metallic element. [Latin *metallum* metal + *ferre* to bear]

metallography (,mɛtə'lɒgrəfɪ) n. the study of the composition and structure of metals.

metalloid ('mɛtə,lɔɪd) n. a nonmetallic element, such as arsenic or silicon, that has some of the properties of a metal.

metallurgy (mɛ'tælədʒɪ) n. the scientific study of the extraction and alloying of metals and of their structure and properties. [*metal* + Greek *-urgia*, from *ergon* work] —**metallurgist** (mɛ'tælədʒɪst, 'mɛtə,lɜːdʒɪst) n.

metalwork ('mɛt[']l,wɜːk) n. **1.** the craft of working in metal. **2.** articles made from metal. —**'metal,worker** n.

metamorphic (,mɛtə'mɔːfɪk) adj. **1.** of metamorphosis or metamorphism. **2.** (of rocks) altered considerably from the original structure and composition by pressure and heat.

metamorphism (,mɛtə'mɔːfɪzəm) n. **1.** the process by which metamorphic rocks are formed. **2.** same as **metamorphosis.**

metamorphose (,mɛtə'mɔːfəʊz) vb. to change from one state or thing into something different.

metamorphosis (,mɛtə'mɔːfəsɪs) n., pl. **-ses** (-,siːz). **1.** a complete change of physical form or substance. **2.** a complete change of character or appearance. **3.** *Zool.* the change of form that accompanies transformation into an adult in certain animals, for example the butterfly or frog. [Greek: transformation, from *meta* after + *morphē* form]

metaphor ('mɛtəfə) n. a figure of speech in which a word or phrase is applied to an object or action that it does not literally denote in order to imply a resemblance, for example *he is a lion in battle.* [Greek *metapherein* to transfer] —**metaphorical** (,mɛtə'fɒrɪk[']l) adj. —**metaphorically** (,mɛtə'fɒrɪkəlɪ) adv.

metaphysical (,mɛtə'fɪzɪk[']l) adj. **1.** of metaphysics. **2.** (popularly) abstract, abstruse, or unduly theoretical.

Metaphysical (,mɛtə'fɪzɪk[']l) adj. denoting certain 17th-century poets who combined intense feeling with elaborate imagery.

metaphysics (,mɛtə'fɪzɪks) n. (functioning as sing.) **1.** the philosophical study of the nature of reality. **2.** (popularly) abstract or subtle discussion or reasoning. [Greek *ta meta ta phusika* the things after the physics, from the arrangement of subjects treated in the works of Aristotle]

metastasis (mɪ'tæstəsɪs) n., pl. **-ses** (-,siːz). *Pathol.* the spreading of a disease, esp. cancer, from one part of the body to another. [Greek: transition]

metatarsus (,mɛtə'tɑːsəs) n., pl. **-si** (-saɪ). the set of five long bones in the foot between the toes and the ankle. [Greek *meta* after + *tarsos* instep] —**,meta'tarsal** adj., n.

metathesis (mɪ'tæθəsɪs) n., pl. **-ses** (-,siːz). the transposition of two sounds or letters in a word or of two words in a sentence. [Greek *metatithenai* to transpose]

metazoan (,mɛtə'zəʊən) n. **1.** any animal having a body composed of many cells: includes all animals except sponges and protozoans. ~adj. **2.** of the metazoans. [Greek *meta* denoting change + *-zoa* indicating a group of animals]

mete (miːt) *vb.* (usually foll. by *out*) *Formal.* to distribute or allot (something, often unpleasant). [Old English *metan*]

meteor ('miːtɪə) *n.* **1.** a small meteoroid that has entered the earth's atmosphere. **2.** Also: **shooting star.** the bright streak of light appearing in the sky due to a meteroid burning up because of friction as it falls through the atmosphere. [Greek *meteōros* lofty]

meteoric (ˌmiːtɪ'ɒrɪk) *adj.* **1.** of or relating to meteors. **2.** like a meteor in brilliance, speed, or transience. —ˌmete'orically *adv.*

meteorite ('miːtɪəˌraɪt) *n.* the rocklike remains of a meteoroid that has fallen on earth.

meteoroid ('miːtɪəˌrɔɪd) *n.* any of the small celestial bodies that are thought to orbit the sun. When they enter the earth's atmosphere, they become visible as meteors.

meteorol. *or* **meteor.** **1.** meteorological. **2.** meteorology.

meteorology (ˌmiːtɪə'rɒlədʒɪ) *n.* the study of the earth's atmosphere, esp. of weather-forming processes and for weather forecasting. —**meteorological** (ˌmiːtɪərə'lɒdʒɪkᵊl) *adj.* —ˌmeteor'ologist *n.*

meter[1] ('miːtə) *n.* **1.** any device that measures and records a quantity, such as of gas, current, or voltage that has passed through it during a specified period. **2.** See **parking meter.** ~*vb.* **3.** to measure (a rate of flow) with a meter. [Old English *metan* to measure]

meter[2] ('miːtə) *n. U.S.* same as **metre**[1] and **metre**[2].

-meter *n. combining form.* **1.** indicating an instrument for measuring: *barometer.* **2.** *Prosody.* indicating a verse having a specified number of feet: *pentameter.* [Greek *metron* measure]

methadone ('mɛθəˌdəʊn) *n.* a drug similar to morphine but less habit-forming. [(*di*)*meth*(*yl*) + *a*(*mino*) + *d*(*iphenyl*) + *-one*, indicating a ketone]

methane ('miːθeɪn) *n.* a colourless odourless flammable gas, the main constituent of natural gas. [*meth*(*yl*) + *-one*, indicating an alkane]

methane series *n.* a series of saturated hydrocarbons with the general formula C_nH_{2n+2}.

methanol ('mɛθəˌnɒl) *n.* a colourless poisonous liquid used as a solvent and fuel. Also: **methyl alcohol.** [*methane* + *-ol*, indicating alcohol]

methinks (mɪ'θɪŋks) *vb. past* **methought.** (takes a clause as object) *Archaic.* it seems to me.

method ('mɛθəd) *n.* **1.** a way of doing something, esp. a systematic or regular one. **2.** orderliness of thought or action. **3.** (often pl.) the techniques of a particular field or subject. [Greek *methodos*, lit.: a going after]

Method ('mɛθəd) *n.* (sometimes not cap.) an acting technique in which the actor bases his role on the inner motivation of the character played.

methodical (mɪ'θɒdɪkᵊl) *adj.* characterized by method or orderliness; systematic. —me'thodically *adv.*

Methodist ('mɛθədɪst) *n.* **1.** a member of any of the Christian Nonconformist denominations that derive from the beliefs and practices of John Wesley and his followers. ~*adj.* **2.** of or relating to Methodists or their Church. —'Methodism *n.*

methodology (ˌmɛθə'dɒlədʒɪ) *n., pl.* **-gies.** **1.** the system of methods and principles used in a particular discipline. **2.** the philosophical study of method. —methodological (ˌmɛθədə'lɒdʒɪkᵊl) *adj.*

methought (mɪ'θɔːt) *vb. Archaic.* the past tense of **methinks.**

meths (mɛθs) *n. Chiefly Brit., Austral., & N.Z. informal.* methylated spirits.

methyl ('miːθaɪl, 'mɛθɪl) *n.* (modifier) of or containing the monovalent group of atoms CH_3. [from *methylene*]

methyl alcohol *n.* same as **methanol.**

methylate ('mɛθɪˌleɪt) *vb.* to mix with methanol.

methylated spirits *n.* (functioning as sing. or pl.) alcohol that has been rendered undrinkable by the addition of methanol and a violet dye. Also: **methylated spirit.**

methylene ('mɛθɪˌliːn) *n.* (modifier) of, consisting of, or containing the divalent group of atoms $=CH_2$: *a methylene group or radical.* [Greek *methu* wine + *hulē* wood + *-ene*, indicating a double bond]

meticulous (mɪ'tɪkjʊləs) *adj.* very precise about details; painstaking. [Latin *meticulōsus* fearful] —me'ticulously *adv.*

métier ('mɛtɪeɪ) *n.* **1.** a profession or trade. **2.** a person's strong point or speciality. [French]

Métis (me'tiːs) *n., pl.* **-tis** (-'tiːs, -'tiːz). a person of mixed parentage, esp. the offspring of a North American Indian and a French Canadian. [French] —**Métisse** (me'tiːs) *fem. n.*

metonymy (mɪ'tɒnɪmɪ) *n., pl.* **-mies.** the substitution of a word referring to an attribute for the thing that is meant, e.g. *the crown,* used to refer to a monarch. [Greek *meta-*, indicating change + *onoma* name]

metre[1] *or U.S.* **meter** ('miːtə) *n.* the basic SI unit of length equal to approximately 1.094 yards. [same as METRE[2]]

metre[2] *or U.S.* **meter** ('miːtə) *n.* **1.** *Prosody.* the rhythmic arrangement of syllables in verse, usually according to the number and kind of feet in a line. **2.** *Music, chiefly U.S.* the rhythmic arrangement of the beat in a piece of music. [Latin *metron* measure]

metre-kilogram-second *n.* See **mks units.**

metric ('mɛtrɪk) *adj.* of or relating to the metre or metric system.

metrical ('mɛtrɪkᵊl) *or* **metric** *adj.* **1.** of or relating to measurement. **2.** of or in poetic metre. —'metrically *adv.*

metricate ('mɛtrɪˌkeɪt) *vb.* to convert (a

measuring system or instrument) to metric units. —, **metri′cation** n.

metric system n. any decimal system of units based on the metre. For scientific purposes SI units are used.

metric ton n. (not in technical use) a tonne.

metro ('metrəʊ) n., pl. **-ros**. an urban, usually underground, railway system in certain cities, such as Paris. [French, from *chemin de fer métropolitain* metropolitan railway]

metronome ('metrə,nəʊm) n. a device which indicates the tempo of music by producing a clicking sound from a pendulum with an adjustable period of swing. [Greek *metron* measure + *nomos* law]

metropolis (mɪ'trɒpəlɪs) n. the main city of a country or region. [Greek *mētēr* mother + *polis* city]

metropolitan (,metrə'pɒlɪtən) adj. **1.** of or characteristic of a metropolis. **2.** constituting a city and its suburbs. **3.** of or belonging to the home territories of a country, as opposed to overseas territories: *metropolitan France*. ~n. **4.** Christianity. the senior clergyman, esp. an archbishop, in charge of an ecclesiastical province. **5.** an inhabitant of a large city.

-metry n. combining form. indicating the process or science of measuring: *geometry*. [Greek *metron* measure] —**metric** adj. combining form.

mettle ('met'l) n. **1.** courage; spirit. **2.** character. **3. on one's mettle.** roused to making one's best efforts. [var. of *metal*]

MeV million electronvolts (10^6 electronvolts).

mevrou (mə'frəʊ) n. a S. African title of address equivalent to *madam* or *Mrs*. [Afrikaans]

mew[1] (mjuː) n. **1.** the characteristic high-pitched cry of a cat. ~vb. **2.** to make such a sound. [imit.]

mew[2] (mjuː) n. a seagull. [Old English *mǣw*]

mewl (mjuːl) vb. **1.** (esp. of a baby) to cry weakly; whimper. ~n. **2.** such a cry. [imit.]

mews (mjuːz) n. (functioning as sing. or pl.) Chiefly Brit. a yard or street lined by buildings originally used as stables but now often converted into dwellings. [plural of *mew* orig. referring to royal stables built on the site of hawks' mews (cages)]

Mex. **1.** Mexican. **2.** Mexico.

Mexican ('meksɪkən) adj. **1.** of or relating to Mexico, in Central America. ~n. **2.** a person from Mexico.

mezzanine ('mezə,niːn, 'metsə,niːn) n. an intermediate storey, esp. a low one between the ground and first floor of a building. [Italian *mezzano* middle]

mezzo ('metsəʊ) adv. Music. moderately; quite: *mezzo piano*. [Italian: half]

mezzo-soprano n., pl. **-nos**. **1.** a female voice intermediate between a soprano and contralto. **2.** a singer with such a voice.

mezzotint ('metsəʊ,tɪnt) n. **1.** a method of engraving a copper plate by scraping and

burnishing the roughened surface. **2.** a print made from a plate so treated. [Italian *mezzotinto* half tint]

mf Music. moderately loud. [Italian *mezzo forte*]

mg milligram.

Mg Chem. magnesium.

M. Glam Mid Glamorgan.

Mgr **1.** manager. **2.** monseigneur. **3.** monsignor.

MHz megahertz.

mi or **me** (miː) n. Music. (in tonic sol-fa) the third degree of any major scale.

MI **1.** Michigan. **2.** Military Intelligence.

MI5 Military Intelligence, section five; the counterintelligence agency of the British Government.

MI6 Military Intelligence, section six; the intelligence and espionage agency of the British Government.

miaow (mɪ'aʊ, mjaʊ) vb. **1.** (of a cat) to make a characteristic crying sound. ~interj. **2.** an imitation of this sound.

miasma (mɪ'æzmə) n., pl. **-mata** (-mətə) or **-mas**. an unwholesome or foreboding atmosphere. [Greek: defilement]

mica ('maɪkə) n. any of a group of minerals consisting of silicates of aluminium or potassium found in flakelike crystals. They have a high resistance to electricity and heat. [Latin: crumb]

mice (maɪs) n. the plural of **mouse**.

Mich. **1.** Michaelmas. **2.** Michigan.

Michaelmas ('mɪk'lməs) n. Sept. 29, the feast of St Michael the archangel; in England, Ireland, and Wales, one of the four quarter days.

Michaelmas daisy n. Brit. a composite plant with small purple, pink, or white flowers in autumn.

Mick (mɪk) n. (sometimes not cap.) Offensive slang. an Irishman. [nickname for *Michael*]

mickey ('mɪkɪ) n. **take the mickey (out of).** Informal. to tease. [origin unknown]

Mickey Finn n. Slang. a drink containing a drug to make the drinker unconscious. [origin unknown]

mickle ('mɪk'l) or **muckle** ('mʌk'l) Archaic or Scot. & N English dialect. ~adj. **1.** great or abundant. ~adv. **2.** much; greatly. ~n. **3.** a great amount. [Old Norse *mikell*]

micro ('maɪkrəʊ) n., pl. **-os**. short for **microcomputer** and **microprocessor**.

micro- or **micr-** combining form. **1.** small or minute: *microdot*. **2.** involving the use of a microscope: *microscopy*. **3.** denoting one millionth of a unit: *microsecond*. [Greek *mikros* small]

microbe ('maɪkrəʊb) n. any microscopic organism, esp. a disease-causing bacterium. [MICRO- + Greek *bios* life] —**mi′crobial** or **mi′crobic** adj.

microbiology (,maɪkrəʊbaɪ'ɒlədʒɪ) n. the branch of biology involving the study of microorganisms.

microchemistry (,maɪkrəʊ'kemɪstrɪ) n.

chemical experimentation with minute quantities of material.

microchip ('maɪkrəʊˌtʃɪp) n. same as **chip** (sense 6).

microcircuit ('maɪkrəʊˌsɜːkɪt) n. a miniature electronic circuit in which a number of permanently connected components are contained in one small chip of semiconducting material.

microcomputer (ˌmaɪkrəʊkəm'pjuːtə) n. a computer in which the central processing unit is contained in one or more silicon chips.

microcosm ('maɪkrəʊˌkɒzəm) n. **1.** a miniature representation of something. **2.** man regarded as epitomizing the universe. [Greek *mikros kosmos* little world] —ˌmicro'cosmic adj.

microdot ('maɪkrəʊˌdɒt) n. a greatly reduced photographic copy (about the size of a pinhead) of a document.

microelectronics (ˌmaɪkrəʊɪlek'trɒnɪks) n. (functioning as sing.) the branch of electronics concerned with microcircuits.

microfiche ('maɪkrəʊˌfiːʃ) n. a sheet of film, usually the size of a filing card, on which publications can be recorded in miniaturized form. [French, from MICRO- + *fiche* small card]

microfilm ('maɪkrəʊˌfɪlm) n. **1.** a strip of film on which books or documents can be recorded in miniaturized form. ~vb. **2.** to photograph (a page or document) on microfilm.

microlight ('maɪkrəʊˌlaɪt) n. a very small private aircraft with large wings.

micrometer (maɪ'krɒmɪtə) n. an instrument for the accurate measurement of small distances or angles.

microminiaturization or **-isation** (ˌmaɪkrəʊˌmɪnɪtʃərəɪ'zeɪʃən) n. the production and use of very small electronic components.

micron ('maɪkrɒn) n. a unit of length equal to one millionth of a metre. [Greek *mikros* small]

microorganism (ˌmaɪkrəʊ'ɔːɡəˌnɪzəm) n. any organism, such as a virus or bacterium, of microscopic size.

microphone ('maɪkrəˌfəʊn) n. a device for converting sound into electrical energy.

microprocessor (ˌmaɪkrəʊ'prəʊsesə) n. Computers. a single integrated circuit which acts as the central processing unit in a small computer.

microscope ('maɪkrəˌskəʊp) n. **1.** an optical instrument that uses a lens or combination of lenses to produce a magnified image of a small, close object. **2.** any instrument, such as the electron microscope, for producing a magnified visual image of a small object.

microscopic (ˌmaɪkrə'skɒpɪk) adj. **1.** too small to be seen except with a microscope. **2.** very small; minute. **3.** of or using a microscope. —ˌmicro'scopically adv.

microsecond ('maɪkrəʊˌsekənd) n. one millionth of a second.

microstructure ('maɪkrəʊˌstrʌktʃə) n.

structure on a microscopic scale, such as that of a metal or a cell.

microsurgery (ˌmaɪkrəʊ'sɜːdʒərɪ) n. intricate surgery performed using a special microscope and miniature precision instruments.

microwave ('maɪkrəˌweɪv) n. **1.** electromagnetic radiation in the wavelength range 0.3 to 0.001 metres: used in radar and cooking. **2.** short for **microwave oven.** ~vb. **3.** to cook in a microwave oven.

microwave detector n. N.Z. a device used by police for recording the speed of a motorist.

microwave oven n. an oven which uses microwaves to cook food quickly.

micturate ('mɪktjʊˌreɪt) vb. to urinate. [Latin *micturire* to desire to urinate] —**micturition** (ˌmɪktjʊ'rɪʃən) n.

mid¹ (mɪd) n. Archaic. the middle. [Old English]

mid² or **'mid** (mɪd) prep. Poetic. amid.

mid- combining form. indicating a middle part, point, time, or position: midday; mid-April; mid-Victorian.

midair (ˌmɪd'ɛə) n. some point above ground level, in the air.

midday ('mɪd'deɪ) n. the middle of the day; noon.

midden ('mɪdˈn) n. Archaic or dialect. a dunghill or pile of refuse. [Old Norse]

middle ('mɪdˈl) adj. **1.** equally distant from the ends or outer edge of something; central. **2.** intermediate in status or situation: middle management. **3.** between the early and late parts of a time sequence. **4.** not extreme, esp. in size; medium. ~n. **5.** an area or point equal in distance from the ends or edge or in time between the early and late parts. **6.** an intermediate part or section, such as the waist. [Old English *middel*]

middle age n. the period of life between youth and old age, usually considered to occur between the ages of 40 and 60. —ˌmiddle-'aged adj.

Middle Ages n. the. European history. **1.** (broadly) the period from the fall of the W Roman Empire in 476 A.D. to the Italian Renaissance. **2.** (narrowly) the period from about 1000 A.D. to the 15th century.

Middle America n. the U.S. middle class, esp. those groups that are politically conservative.

middlebrow ('mɪdˈlˌbraʊ) Disparaging. ~n. **1.** a person with conventional tastes and limited cultural appreciation. ~adj. **2.** of or appealing to middlebrows.

middle C n. Music. the note written on the first ledger line below the treble staff or the first ledger line above the bass staff.

middle class n. **1.** the social class between the working and upper classes. It consists of business and professional people. ~adj. **middle-class.** **2.** of or characteristic of the middle class.

middle ear n. the sound-conducting part of the ear immediately inside the eardrum.

Middle East n. the area around the E

Mediterranean, esp. Israel and the Arab countries from Turkey to North Africa and eastwards to Iran. —**Middle Eastern** *adj.*

Middle English *n.* the English language from about 1100 to about 1450.

Middle High German *n.* High German from about 1200 to about 1500.

Middle Low German *n.* Low German from about 1200 to about 1500.

middleman ('mɪd'l,mæn) *n., pl.* -**men.** 1. a trader engaged in the distribution of goods from producer to consumer. 2. an intermediary.

middle name *n.* 1. a name between a person's first name and surname. 2. a characteristic quality for which a person is known: *caution is my middle name.*

middle-of-the-road *adj.* 1. not extreme, esp. in political views; moderate. 2. of or denoting popular music of wide general appeal.

middle school *n. Brit.* a school for children aged between 8 or 9 and 12 or 13.

middleweight ('mɪd'l,weɪt) *n.* 1. a professional boxer weighing up to 160 pounds or an amateur weighing up to 75 kg. 2. a professional wrestler weighing up to 176 pounds or an amateur weighing up to 82 kg.

middling ('mɪdlɪŋ) *adj.* 1. mediocre in quality or size. 2. **fair to middling.** neither good nor bad, esp. in health. ~*adv.* 3. *Informal.* moderately: *middling well.*

Middx. Middlesex.

midfield (,mɪd'fiːld) *n. Soccer.* the area between the two opposing defences.

midge (mɪdʒ) *n.* a mosquito-like insect occurring in dancing swarms, esp. near water. [Old English *mycge*] —**midgy** *adj.*

midget ('mɪdʒɪt) *n.* 1. a dwarf whose skeleton and features are of normal proportions. 2. something small of its kind. [*midge* + *-et* small]

mid-heavyweight *n.* a professional wrestler weighing up to 209 pounds or an amateur weighing up to 100kg.

midi- *combining form.* of medium or middle size or length: *midibus.*

midi system ('mɪdɪ) *n.* a complete set of compact hi-fi sound equipment designed as a single unit.

midland ('mɪdlənd) *adj.* the central or inland part of a country.

Midlands ('mɪdləndz) *n. (functioning as pl. or sing.)* **the.** the central counties of England.

midmost ('mɪd,məʊst) *adj., adv.* in the middle or midst.

midnight ('mɪd,naɪt) *n.* 1. the middle of the night; 12 o'clock at night. 2. **burn the midnight oil.** to work or study late into the night.

midnight sun *n.* the sun visible at midnight during the summer inside the Arctic and Antarctic circles.

mid-off *n. Cricket.* the fielding position on the off side closest to the bowler.

mid-on *n. Cricket.* the fielding position on the on side closest to the bowler.

midpoint ('mɪd,pɔɪnt) *n.* 1. the point on a

line equally distant from either end. 2. a point in time halfway between the beginning and end of an event.

midriff ('mɪdrɪf) *n.* 1. the middle part of the human body between waist and chest. 2. *Anat.* same as **diaphragm** (sense 1). [Old English *midhrif* mid belly]

midshipman ('mɪd,ʃɪpmən) *n., pl.* -**men.** a junior naval officer.

midships ('mɪd,ʃɪps) *adv., adj. Naut.* See **amidships.**

midst (mɪdst) *n.* 1. **in our midst.** among us. 2. **in the midst of.** surrounded by; at a point during.

midsummer ('mɪd'sʌmə) *n.* 1. the middle or height of summer. 2. same as **summer solstice.**

Midsummer Day *or* **Midsummer's Day** *n.* June 24, the feast of St John the Baptist; in England, Ireland, and Wales, one of the four quarter days.

midway *adj.* ('mɪd,weɪ). 1. in or at the middle of the distance; halfway. ~*adv.* (,mɪd'weɪ). 2. to the middle of the distance.

midweek ('mɪd'wiːk) *n.* the middle of the week.

Midwest ('mɪd'wɛst) *n.* the N central part of the U.S. —**'Mid'western** *adj.*

mid-wicket *n. Cricket.* the fielding position on the on side, roughly the same distance from both wickets, and halfway towards the boundary.

midwife ('mɪd,waɪf) *n., pl.* -**wives** (-,waɪvz). a nurse qualified to deliver babies and to care for women before, during, and after childbirth. [Old English *mid* with + *wif* woman] —**midwifery** ('mɪd-,wɪfərɪ) *n.*

midwinter ('mɪd'wɪntə) *n.* 1. the middle or depth of winter. 2. same as **winter solstice.**

mien (miːn) *n. Literary.* a person's manner, bearing, or appearance. [prob. from obs. *demean* appearance]

miff (mɪf) *vb. Informal.* to take offence or offend. [possibly imit. of bad temper] —**miffed** *adj.*

might[1] (maɪt) *vb.* used as an auxiliary: 1. making the past tense or subjunctive mood of **may**: *he might have come.* 2. (often foll. by *well*) expressing possibility: *he might well come.* In this sense *might* looks to the future and functions as a weak form of *may.* See **may**[1] (sense 2). [Old English *miht*]

might[2] (maɪt) *n.* 1. great power, strength, or vigour. 2. (**with**) **might and main.** See **main.** [Old English *miht*]

mighty ('maɪtɪ) *adj.* **mightier, mightiest.** 1. powerful or strong. 2. very large; vast. 3. very great in extent or importance. ~*adv.* 4. *Informal, chiefly U.S. & Canad.* very: *mighty tired.* —**'mightily** *adv.* —**'mightiness** *n.*

mignonette (,mɪnjə'nɛt) *n.* a plant with spikes of small fragrant greenish-white flowers. [French, diminutive of *mignon* dainty]

migraine ('miːgreɪn, 'maɪ-) *n.* a throbbing

headache usually affecting only one side of the head and commonly accompanied by nausea and visual disturbances. [French, from Greek *hemi* half + *kranion* head]

migrant ('maigrənt) *n.* **1.** a person or animal that moves from one place to another. ~*adj.* **2.** moving from one place to another: *migrant workers.*

migrate (mai'greit) *vb.* **1.** to go from one place to settle in another, esp. in a foreign country. **2.** (of living creatures, esp. birds) to journey between different habitats at specific times of the year. [Latin *migrāre* to change one's abode] —**mi'gration** *n.* —**migratory** ('maigrətri) *adj.*

mikado (mi'ka:dəʊ) *n., pl.* **-dos.** (*often cap.*) *Archaic.* the Japanese emperor. [Japanese]

mike (maik) *n. Informal.* a microphone.

mil (mil) *n.* **1.** a unit of length equal to one thousandth of an inch. **2.** *Photog.* short for **millimetre**: *35-mil film.* [Latin *millēsimus* thousandth]

milady (mi'leidi) *n., pl.* **-dies.** (formerly) a continental title for an English gentlewoman.

milch (miltʃ) *n. modifier* (esp. of cattle) yielding milk. [Old English *-milce* (in compounds)]

mild (maild) *adj.* **1.** (of a taste or sensation) not strong; bland. **2.** gentle or temperate in character, climate, or behaviour. **3.** not extreme; moderate: *mild amusement.* **4.** feeble; unassertive: *a mild protest.* ~*n.* **5.** *Brit.* a dark beer flavoured with fewer hops than bitter. [Old English *milde*]

mildew ('mil,dju:) *n.* **1.** a disease of plants caused by a parasitic fungus. **2.** same as **mould²**. ~*vb.* **3.** to affect or become affected with mildew. [Old English *mildēaw* honey dew] —**'mil,dewy** *adj.*

mild steel *n.* strong tough steel containing a small quantity of carbon.

mile (mail) *n.* **1.** Also: **statute mile.** a unit of length used in English-speaking countries, equal to 1760 yards. 1 mile is equivalent to 1.60934 kilometres. **2.** See **nautical mile. 3.** (*often pl.*) *Informal.* a great distance; great deal: *he missed by a mile.* **4.** a race extending over a mile. ~*adv.* **5. miles.** very much: *that's miles better.* [Latin *mīlia* (*passuum*) a thousand (paces)]

mileage ('mailidʒ) *n.* **1.** a distance expressed in miles. **2.** the total number of miles that a motor vehicle has travelled. **3.** the number of miles a motor vehicle will travel on one gallon of fuel. **4.** *Informal.* use, benefit, or service provided by something.

mileometer or **milometer** (mai'lɒmitə) *n.* a device that records the number of miles that a vehicle has travelled.

milepost ('mail,pəʊst) *n. Chiefly U.S. & Canad.* a signpost that shows the distance in miles to or from a place.

miler ('mailə) *n.* an athlete, horse, etc., that runs or specializes in races of one mile.

milestone ('mail,stəʊn) *n.* **1.** a stone pillar that shows the distance in miles to or from a place. **2.** a significant event in a life or history.

milfoil ('mil,foil) *n.* same as **yarrow.** [Latin *mille* thousand + *folium* leaf]

milieu ('mi:ljɜ:) *n., pl.* **milieus** or **milieux** ('mi:ljɜ:z). surroundings, location, or setting. [French]

militant ('militənt) *adj.* **1.** aggressive or vigorous, esp. in the support of a cause. **2.** warring; engaged in warfare. ~*n.* **3.** a militant person. [Latin *mīlitāre* to be a soldier] —**'militancy** *n.* —**'militantly** *adv.*

militarism ('militə,rizəm) *n.* **1.** military spirit; pursuit of military ideals. **2.** a belief in maintaining a strong military organization in aggressive readiness for war. —**'militarist** *n.*

military ('militri) *adj.* **1.** of or relating to the armed forces or war. **2.** of or characteristic of soldiers. ~*n., pl.* **-taries** or **-tary. 3.** (*preceded by the*) the armed services, esp. the army. [Latin *mīles* soldier] —**'militarily** *adv.*

military police *n.* a corps within an army that performs police duties.

militate ('mili,teit) *vb.* (usually foll. by *against* or *for*) (of facts or events) to have influence or effect: *the evidence militated against his release.*

militia (mi'liʃə) *n.* a body of citizen (as opposed to professional) soldiers enlisted for service in emergency only. [Latin: soldiery] —**mi'litiaman** *n.*

milk (milk) *n.* **1. a.** a whitish fluid secreted by the mammary glands of mature female mammals and used for feeding their young. **b.** the milk of cows, goats, etc., used by man as a food. **2.** any similar fluid, such as the juice of a coconut. ~*vb.* **3.** to draw milk from the udder of (an animal). **4.** to extract as much money, help, or value as possible from: *to milk a situation of its news value.* [Old English *milc*] —**'milker** *n.* —**'milkiness** *n.* —**'milky** *adj.*

milk-and-water *adj.* weak, feeble, or insipid.

milk bar *n.* a snack bar at which milk drinks and light refreshments are served.

milk chocolate *n.* chocolate that has been made with milk, having a creamy taste.

milk float *n. Brit.* a small electrically powered vehicle used to deliver milk to houses.

milkmaid ('milk,meid) *n.* a girl or woman who milks cows.

milkman ('milkmən) *n., pl.* **-men.** a man who delivers milk to people's houses.

milk of magnesia *n.* a suspension of magnesium hydroxide in water, used as an antacid and laxative.

milk pudding *n. Chiefly Brit.* a pudding made by cooking milk with a grain, esp. rice.

milk round *n. Brit.* **1.** a route along which a milkman regularly delivers milk. **2.** a regular series of visits, esp. as made by recruitment officers from industry to colleges.

milk run *n. Aeronautics, informal.* a routine and uneventful flight. [from a milk-man's safe and regular routine]

milk shake *n.* a cold frothy drink made of milk, flavouring, and sometimes ice cream, whisked together.

milksop ('mɪlk‚sɒp) *n.* a feeble or ineffectual man or youth.

milk tooth *n.* any of the first teeth to come through; a baby tooth.

Milky Way *n.* **the.** the diffuse band of light stretching across the night sky that consists of millions of distant stars. [translation of Latin *via lactea*]

mill (mɪl) *n.* **1.** a factory. **2.** any of various processing or manufacturing machines, esp. one that grinds, presses, or rolls. **3.** a small device for grinding solids: *a pepper mill.* **4. go** *or* **be put through the mill.** to have an unpleasant experience or ordeal. ~*vb.* **5.** to grind, press, or otherwise process in or as if in a mill. **6.** to groove or flute the edge of (a coin). **7.** (often foll. by *about* or *around*) to move about in a confused manner. [Latin *molere* to grind]

millennium (mɪ'lɛnɪəm) *n.,* pl. **-niums** *or* **-nia** (-nɪə). **1. the.** *Christianity.* the period of a thousand years of Christ's awaited reign upon earth. **2.** any period of one thousand years. **3.** a time of peace and happiness, esp. in the distant future. [Latin *mille* thousand + *annus* year] —**mil'len-nial** *adj.*

millepede ('mɪlɪ‚piːd) *n.* same as **milli-pede**.

miller ('mɪlə) *n.* a person who keeps, operates, or works in a mill, esp. a corn mill.

miller's thumb *n.* a small freshwater European fish with a flattened body. [from the alleged likeness of the fish's head to a thumb]

millesimal (mɪ'lɛsɪməl) *adj.* **1. a.** denoting a thousandth. **b.** (*as n.*): *a millesimal.* **2.** of or consisting of a thousandth. [Latin *mīllēsimus*]

millet ('mɪlɪt) *n.* a cereal grass cultivated for its edible grain and as animal fodder. [Latin *milium*]

milli- *prefix.* denoting 10⁻³: *millimetre.* [Latin *mille* thousand]

milliard ('mɪljɑːd) *n. Brit.* (no longer in technical use) a thousand million. [French]

millibar ('mɪlɪ‚bɑː) *n.* a unit of atmospheric pressure equal to 100 newtons per square metre.

milligram *or* **milligramme** ('mɪlɪ‚græm) *n.* one thousandth of a gram. [French]

millilitre *or U.S.* **milliliter** ('mɪlɪ‚liːtə) *n.* one thousandth of a litre.

millimetre *or U.S.* **millimeter** ('mɪlɪ‚miːtə) *n.* one thousandth of a metre.

milliner ('mɪlɪnə) *n.* a person who makes or sells women's hats. [orig. *Milaner,* a native of Milan, once famous for its fancy goods] —**'millinery** *n.*

million ('mɪljən) *n.,* pl. **-lions** *or* **-lion. 1.** the cardinal number that is the product of 1000 multiplied by 1000: 1 000 000; 10⁶. **2.** (*often pl.*) *Informal.* an extremely large but unspecified number: *I have millions of*

things to do. [early Italian *millione*] —**'millionth** *n., adj.*

millionaire (‚mɪljə'nɛə) *n.* a person whose assets are worth at least a million of the standard monetary units of his country. —**‚million'airess** *fem. n.*

millipede *or* **millepede** ('mɪlɪ‚piːd) *n.* a small crawling animal with a cylindrical many-segmented body, each segment of which bears two pairs of legs. [Latin *mille* thousand + *pēs* foot]

millisecond ('mɪlɪ‚sɛkənd) *n.* one thousandth of a second.

millpond ('mɪl‚pɒnd) *n.* a pool which provides water to turn a millwheel.

millrace ('mɪl‚reɪs) *n.* the current of water that turns a millwheel.

millstone ('mɪl‚stəʊn) *n.* **1.** one of a pair of heavy flat stones that are rotated one against the other to grind grain. **2.** a heavy burden, such as a responsibility or obligation.

millstream ('mɪl‚striːm) *n.* a stream of water used to turn a millwheel.

millwheel ('mɪl‚wiːl) *n.* a wheel, esp. a waterwheel, that drives a mill.

milometer (maɪ'lɒmɪtə) *n.* same as **mile-ometer**.

milord (mɪ'lɔːd) *n.* (formerly) a continental title used for an English gentleman. [French, from *my lord*]

milt (mɪlt) *n.* the testis, sperm, or semen of a fish. [Old English *milte* spleen]

mime (maɪm) *n.* **1.** a theatrical technique of acting using only gesture and bodily movement and not words. **2.** a performer specializing in this. **3.** a dramatic presentation using such a technique. ~*vb.* **4.** to express (an idea or message) in actions or gestures without speech. **5.** (of musicians) to perform as if singing or playing music that is actually prerecorded. [Greek *mimos* imitator] —**'mimer** *n.*

Mimeograph ('mɪmɪə‚grɑːf) *n.* **1.** *Trade-mark.* an office machine for printing multiple copies from a stencil. ~*vb.* **2.** to print copies using this machine.

mimetic (mɪ'mɛtɪk) *adj.* **1.** of or relating to imitation. **2.** *Biol.* of or showing mimicry. [Greek *mimeisthai* to imitate]

mimic ('mɪmɪk) *vb.* **-icking, -icked. 1.** to imitate (a person or manner), esp. for satirical effect; ape. **2.** to take on the appearance of: *certain flies mimic wasps.* **3.** to copy closely or in a servile manner. ~*n.* **4.** a person or an animal, such as a parrot, that is clever at mimicking. [Greek *mimikos*]

mimicry ('mɪmɪkrɪ) *n.,* pl. **-ries. 1.** the act or art of copying or imitating closely; mimicking. **2.** *Biol.* the resemblance shown by one animal species to another, which protects it from predators.

mimosa (mɪ'məʊsə, -zə) *n.* a tropical shrub with ball-like clusters of typically yellow flowers. [Latin *mīmus* mime, because the plant's sensitivity to touch imitates the similar reaction of animals]

min. 1. minimum. **2.** minute *or* minutes.

Min. 1. Minister. **2.** Ministry.

mina (ˈmaɪnə) n. same as **myna**.

minaret (ˌmɪnəˈrɛt, ˈmɪnəˌrɛt) n. a slender tower of a mosque with one or more balconies. [Arabic manārat lamp]

minatory (ˈmɪnətrɪ) adj. threatening or menacing. [Latin minārī to threaten]

mince (mɪns) vb. **1.** to chop, grind, or cut into very small pieces. **2.** to soften or moderate: I didn't mince my words. **3.** to walk or speak in an affected dainty manner. ~n. **4.** Chiefly Brit. minced meat. [Old French, from Late Latin minūtia smallness] —ˈmincer n.

mincemeat (ˈmɪnsˌmiːt) n. **1.** a mixture of dried fruit and spices used esp. for filling pies. **2. make mincemeat of.** Informal. to defeat completely.

mince pie n. a small round pastry tart filled with mincemeat.

mincing (ˈmɪnsɪŋ) adj. (of a person) affectedly elegant in gait, manner, or speech.

mind (maɪnd) n. **1.** the part of a person responsible for thought, feelings, and intention. **2.** intelligence as opposed to feelings or wishes. **3.** recollection or remembrance: it comes to mind. **4.** a person considered as an intellectual being: great minds. **5.** condition, state, or manner of feeling or thought: a depressed state of mind. **6.** an inclination, desire, or purpose: I have a mind to go. **7.** attention or thoughts: keep your mind on your work. **8.** a sound mental state; sanity: she's out of her mind. **9. change one's mind.** to alter one's decision or opinion. **10. in two minds.** undecided; wavering. **11. make up one's mind.** to decide (something or to do something). **12. on one's mind.** in one's thoughts. ~vb. **13.** to take offence at: do you mind if I smoke? **14.** to pay attention to (something): to mind one's own business. **15.** to make certain; ensure: mind you tell her. **16.** to take care of: mind the shop. **17.** to be cautious or careful about (something): mind how you go. ~See also **mind out.** [Old English gemynd mind]

minded (ˈmaɪndɪd) adj. having a mind, inclination, or intention as specified: politically minded.

minder (ˈmaɪndə) n. **1.** Slang. an aide or assistant, esp. one employed as a bodyguard or public relations officer for someone. **2.** short for **child minder.**

mindful (ˈmaɪndfʊl) adj. (usually foll. by of) keeping aware; heedful: mindful of your duty.

mindless (ˈmaɪndlɪs) adj. **1.** stupid or careless. **2.** requiring little or no intellectual effort. **3.** heedless: mindless of the danger. —ˈmindlessly adv. —ˈmindlessness n.

mind out vb. Brit. to be careful or pay attention.

mind-reader n. a person seemingly able to make out the thoughts of another.

mind's eye n. the imagination.

mine¹ (maɪn) pron. **1.** something or someone belonging to or associated with me: mine is best. **2. of mine.** belonging to or associated with me. ~det. **3.** Archaic.

same as **my**: mine eyes; mine host. [Old English mīn]

mine² (maɪn) n. **1.** a place where minerals, esp. coal, ores, or precious stones are dug from the ground. **2.** any deposit of ore or minerals. **3.** a lucrative source or abundant supply: a mine of information. **4.** a type of bomb designed to destroy ships, vehicles, or personnel, usually laid beneath the ground or in water. ~vb. **5.** to dig into (the earth) for (minerals). **6.** to dig (minerals) from the ground. **7.** to make (a hole or tunnel) by digging or boring. **8.** to place explosive mines in position below the surface of (the sea or land). [Old French]

mine dump n. S. African. a large mound of residue, esp. from gold-mining operations.

minefield (ˈmaɪnˌfiːld) n. **1.** an area of ground or water containing explosive mines. **2.** a subject or situation full of hidden problems.

minelayer (ˈmaɪnˌleɪə) n. a warship or aircraft for carrying and laying mines.

miner (ˈmaɪnə) n. a person who works in a mine, esp. a coal mine.

mineral (ˈmɪnərəl, ˈmɪnrəl) n. **1.** a naturally occurring solid inorganic substance with a characteristic chemical composition and structure. **2.** any inorganic matter. **3.** any substance obtained by mining, esp. a metal or ore. **4.** (often pl.) Brit. short for **mineral water. 5.** Brit. a soft drink containing carbonated water and flavourings. ~adj. **6.** of, containing, or resembling minerals. [Medieval Latin minera mine, ore]

mineral acid n. any acid which can be produced from a mineral.

mineralogy (ˌmɪnəˈrælədʒɪ) n. the scientific study of minerals. —**mineralogical** (ˌmɪnərəˈlɒdʒɪkˌl) adj. —ˌminerˈalogist n.

mineral water n. water containing dissolved mineral salts or gases.

minestrone (ˌmɪnɪˈstrəʊnɪ) n. a soup made from a variety of vegetables and pasta. [Italian, from minestrare to serve]

minesweeper (ˈmaɪnˌswiːpə) n. a naval vessel equipped to clear mines.

Ming (mɪŋ) adj. of or relating to Chinese porcelain from the time of the Ming dynasty, which ruled China from 1368 to 1644.

mingle (ˈmɪŋgˌl) vb. **1.** to mix or cause to mix. **2.** (often foll. by with) to come into close association. [Old English mengan to mix]

mingy (ˈmɪndʒɪ) adj. **-gier, -giest.** Brit. informal. miserly or niggardly. [prob. a blend of mean + stingy]

mini (ˈmɪnɪ) adj. **1.** small; miniature. **2.** (of a skirt or dress) very short; thigh-length. ~n., pl. **minis. 3.** something very small of its kind, esp. a miniskirt.

mini- combining form. smaller or shorter than the standard size: minibus; miniskirt. [from miniature & minimum]

miniature (ˈmɪnɪtʃə) n. **1.** a model or representation on a very small scale. **2.** a very small painting, esp. a portrait. **3. in miniature.** on a small scale. ~adj. **4.** greatly reduced in size. **5.** on a small scale. [Medieval Latin miniāre to paint red (in illuminating manuscripts) from *minium* red lead] —'**miniaturist** *n.*

miniaturize *or* -**ise** ('mɪnɪtʃə,raɪz) *vb.* to make or construct (something, esp. electronic components) to a very small size.

minibus ('mɪnɪ,bʌs) *n.* a small bus.

minicab ('mɪnɪ,kæb) *n. Brit.* an ordinary car used as a taxi.

minicomputer (,mɪnɪkəm'pjuːtə) *n.* a small digital computer which is more powerful than a microcomputer.

minim ('mɪnɪm) *n.* 1. a unit of fluid measure equal to one sixtieth of a drachm; a drop. 2. *Music.* a note with the time value of half a semibreve. [Latin *minimus* smallest]

minimalism ('mɪnɪmə,lɪzəm) *n.* 1. a type of music based on the repetition of simple elements. 2. design or style using the simplest and fewest elements to create the maximum effect. —'**minimalist** *adj., n.*

minimize *or* -**ise** ('mɪnɪ,maɪz) *vb.* 1. to reduce to or estimate at the least possible degree or amount. 2. to rank or treat at less than the true worth; belittle.

minimum ('mɪnɪməm) *n., pl.* -**mums** *or* -**ma** (-mə). 1. the least possible amount, degree, or quantity. 2. the least amount recorded, allowed, or reached. 3. (*modifier*) being the least possible amount, or allowed: *minimum age.* ~*adj.* 4. of or relating to a minimum or minimums. [Latin *minimus* least] —'**minimal** *adj.* —'**minimally** *adv.*

minimum lending rate *n.* the minimum rate at which a central bank, such as the Bank of England, will lend money.

minimum wage *n.* the lowest wage that an employer is permitted to pay by law or union contract.

mining ('maɪnɪŋ) *n.* 1. the act, process, or industry of extracting coal or other metals from the earth. 2. *Mil.* the process of laying mines.

minion ('mɪnjən) *n.* a servile follower or subordinate. [French *mignon* darling]

miniseries ('mɪnɪ,sɪərɪːz) *n., pl.* -**series.** a television programme in several parts that is shown on consecutive days over a short period.

miniskirt ('mɪnɪ,skɜːt) *n.* a very short skirt.

minister ('mɪnɪstə) *n.* 1. (esp. in Presbyterian and some Nonconformist Churches) a clergyman. 2. a head of a government department. 3. any diplomatic agent accredited to a foreign government or head of state. 4. a person who acts as the agent or servant of a person or thing. ~*vb.* 5. (often foll. by *to*) to attend to the needs (of); take care (of). [Latin: servant] —**ministerial** (,mɪnɪ'stɪərɪəl) *adj.*

minister of state *n.* (in the British Parliament) a minister, usually below cabinet rank, appointed to assist a senior minister.

Minister of the Crown *n. Brit.* any Government minister of cabinet rank.

ministration (,mɪnɪ'streɪʃən) *n.* 1. the act or an instance of serving or giving aid. 2. the act or an instance of ministering religiously. [Latin *ministrāre* to wait upon]

ministry ('mɪnɪstrɪ) *n., pl.* -**tries.** 1. the profession or duties of a minister of religion. 2. ministers considered as a group. 3. the tenure of a minister. 4. **a.** a government department headed by a minister. **b.** the buildings of such a department.

mink (mɪŋk) *n., pl.* **mink** *or* **minks.** 1. a mammal of Europe, Asia, and North America, resembling a large stoat. 2. its highly valued fur. 3. a garment made of this, esp. a woman's coat or stole. [Scandinavian]

Minn. Minnesota.

minneola (,mɪnɪ'əʊlə) *n.* a juicy citrus fruit that is a cross between a tangerine and a grapefruit.

minnow ('mɪnəʊ) *n., pl.* -**nows** *or* -**now.** a small slender European freshwater fish. [Old English *myne*]

Minoan (mɪ'nəʊən) *adj.* of or denoting the Bronze Age culture of Crete from about 3000 B.C. to about 1100 B.C. [*Minos* in Greek myth, king of Crete]

minor ('maɪnə) *adj.* 1. lesser or secondary in amount or importance. 2. below the age of legal majority. 3. *Music.* **a.** (of a scale) having a semitone between the second and third and fifth and sixth degrees (**natural minor**). **b.** relating to or employing notes from the minor scale: *the key of D minor; a minor seventh.* ~*n.* 4. a person below the age of legal majority. 5. *U.S. & Canad. education.* a subsidiary subject. 6. *Music.* a minor key, chord, mode, or scale. ~*vb.* 7. (usually foll. by *in*) *U.S. education.* to take a minor. [Latin: less, smaller]

minority (maɪ'nɒrɪtɪ, mɪ-) *n., pl.* -**ties.** 1. the smaller of two parts, factions, or groups. 2. a group that is different, esp. racially or politically, from a larger group of which it is a part. 3. **a.** the state of being a minor. **b.** the period during which a person is below legal age. 4. (*modifier*) relating to or being a minority: *a minority opinion.*

minster ('mɪnstə) *n. Brit.* any of certain cathedrals and large churches, usually originally connected to a monastery. [Church Latin *monastērium* monastery]

minstrel ('mɪnstrəl) *n.* 1. a medieval singer and musician. 2. a performer in a minstrel show. [Old French *menestral*]

minstrel show *n.* a theatrical entertainment consisting of songs and dances performed by actors wearing black face make-up.

mint[1] (mɪnt) *n.* 1. any of various plants with aromatic leaves used for seasoning and flavouring. 2. a sweet flavoured with mint. [Greek *minthē*] —'**minty** *adj.*

mint[2] (mɪnt) *n.* 1. a place where money is coined by governmental authority. 2. a very large amount of money. ~*adj.* 3. in **mint condition.** in perfect condition; as if new. ~*vb.* 4. to make (coins) by stamping metal. 5. to invent (esp. phrases or words). [Latin *monēta* money, mint]

minuet (,mɪnju'ɛt) *n.* 1. a stately court dance of the 17th and 18th centuries in triple time. 2. music for this dance. [French *menuet* dainty]

minus ('maɪnəs) *prep.* 1. reduced by the

subtraction of: *four minus two* (written 4 –
2). **2.** *Informal.* deprived of; lacking: *minus the trimmings.* ~*adj.* **3. a.** indicating
or involving subtraction: *a minus sign.* **b.**
Also: **negative.** less than zero: *a minus
number.* **4.** *Education.* slightly below the
standard of a particular grade: *a B minus.*
5. denoting a negative electric charge. ~*n.*
6. short for **minus sign.** **7.** a negative
quantity. **8.** *Informal.* something detri-
mental or negative. [Latin, neuter of *minor,* less]

minuscule ('mɪnəˌskjuːl) *adj.* very small.
[Latin (*littera*) *minuscula* very small (letter)]

minus sign *n.* the symbol –, indicating
subtraction or a negative quantity.

minute[1] ('mɪnɪt) *n.* **1.** 60 seconds; one
sixtieth of an hour. **2.** a measure of angle
equal to one sixtieth of a degree. **3.** any
very short period of time; moment. **4.** the
distance that can be travelled in a minute:
it's only two minutes away. **5. up to the
minute.** the very latest or newest. ~*vb.*
6. to record in minutes: *to minute a meeting.* ~See also **minutes.** [Medieval Latin
minūta noun use of Latin *minūtus* minute
(small)]

minute[2] (maɪˈnjuːt) *adj.* **1.** very small;
tiny. **2.** unimportant; petty. **3.** precise or
detailed. [Latin *minūtus,* past participle of
minuere to diminish] —**miˈnutely** *adv.*

minutes ('mɪnɪts) *pl. n.* an official record
of the proceedings of a meeting or conference.

minute steak ('mɪnɪt) *n.* a small piece of
steak that can be cooked quickly.

minutiae (mɪˈnjuːʃɪˌiː) *pl. n., sing.* -**tia**
(-ʃɪə). small, precise, or trifling details.
[Late Latin, plural of *minūtia* smallness]

minx (mɪŋks) *n.* a bold, flirtatious, or
scheming woman. [origin unknown]

Miocene ('maɪəˌsiːn) *adj. Geol.* of the epoch of geological time about 25 million
years ago. [Greek *meiōn* less + *kainos*
new]

miracle ('mɪrək'l) *n.* **1.** an event contrary
to the laws of nature and attributed to a
supernatural cause. **2.** any amazing or
wonderful event. **3.** a marvellous example
of something: *a miracle of engineering.*
[Latin *mīrārī* to wonder at]

miracle play *n.* a medieval play based on
a biblical story or the life of a saint.

miraculous (mɪˈrækjʊləs) *adj.* **1.** like a
miracle; marvellous. **2.** surprising or remarkable.

mirage (mɪˈrɑːʒ) *n.* **1.** an image of a
distant object or sheet of water, often
inverted or distorted, caused by atmospheric refraction by hot air. **2.** something
illusory. [French from (*se*) *mirer* to be
reflected]

mire ('maɪə) *n.* **1.** a boggy or marshy area.
2. mud, muck, or dirt. ~*vb.* **3.** to sink or
cause to sink in a mire. **4.** to make dirty or
muddy. [Old Norse *mýrr*]

mirror ('mɪrə) *n.* **1.** a surface, such as
glass coated with a metal film, that reflects
an image of an object placed in front of it.
2. a thing that reflects or depicts some-

thing else. ~*vb.* **3.** to reflect, represent,
or depict faithfully: *he mirrors his teacher's ideals.* [Latin *mīrārī* to wonder at]

mirror ball *n.* a large revolving ball covered with small pieces of mirror glass so
that it reflects light in changing patterns:
used in discos and ballrooms.

mirror image *n.* an image or object that
has left and right reversed as if seen in a
mirror.

mirth (mɜːθ) *n.* laughter, gaiety, or merriment. [Old English *myrgth*] —**'mirthful**
adj. —**'mirthless** *adj.*

MIRV (mɜːv) multiple independently tar-
geted re-entry vehicle: a missile that has
several warheads, each one being aimed at
a different target.

mis- *prefix.* **1.** wrong or bad; wrongly or
badly: *misunderstanding; mislead.* **2.** lack
of; not: *mistrust.* [Old English *mis(se)*-]

misadventure (ˌmɪsədˈvɛntʃə) *n.* **1.** an
unlucky event; misfortune. **2.** *Law.* accidental death not due to crime or negligence.

misaligned (ˌmɪsəˈlaɪnd) *adj.* not properly
aligned; out of true. —**ˌmisaˈlignment** *n.*

misalliance (ˌmɪsəˈlaɪəns) *n.* an unsuitable
alliance or marriage.

misanthrope ('mɪzənˌθrəʊp) *or* **misan-
thropist** (mɪˈzænθrəpɪst) *n.* a person who
dislikes or distrusts people in general.
[Greek *misos* hatred + *anthrōpos* man]
—**misanthropic** (ˌmɪzənˈθrɒpɪk) *adj.*
—**misanthropy** (mɪˈzænθrəpɪ) *n.*

misapply (ˌmɪsəˈplaɪ) *vb.* -**plying, -plied.**
to apply wrongly or badly. —**misapplica-
tion** (ˌmɪsæplɪˈkeɪʃən) *n.*

misapprehend (ˌmɪsæprɪˈhɛnd) *vb.* to
misunderstand. —**misapprehension** (ˌmɪs-
æprɪˈhɛnʃən) *n.*

misappropriate (ˌmɪsəˈprəʊprɪˌeɪt) *vb.* to
take (money) for a wrong or dishonest use;
embezzle or steal. —**ˌmisapˌpropriˈa-
tion** *n.*

misbegotten (ˌmɪsbɪˈgɒt'n) *adj.* **1.** conceived, planned, or designed badly or with
dishonourable motives or aims. **2.** *Literary or dialect.* illegitimate; bastard.

misbehave (ˌmɪsbɪˈheɪv) *vb.* to behave
badly. —**misbehaviour** *or U.S.* **misbe-
havior** (ˌmɪsbɪˈheɪvjə) *n.*

miscalculate (ˌmɪsˈkælkjʊˌleɪt) *vb.* to calculate wrongly. —**ˌmiscalcuˈlation** *n.*

miscall (ˌmɪsˈkɔːl) *vb.* to call by the wrong
name.

miscarriage (mɪsˈkærɪdʒ) *n.* **1.** (*also*
'mɪskær-). spontaneous expulsion of a fetus from the womb, esp. before the 20th
week of pregnancy. **2.** an act of misman-
agement or failure: *a miscarriage of justice.*

miscarry (mɪsˈkærɪ) *vb.* -**rying, -ried.** **1.**
to expel a fetus prematurely from the
womb. **2.** to fail.

miscast (ˌmɪsˈkɑːst) *vb.* -**casting, -cast.**
(*often passive*) to cast (a role or an actor)
in (a play or film) inappropriately: *Falstaff
was miscast; he was miscast as Othello.*

miscegenation (ˌmɪsɪdʒɪˈneɪʃən) *n.* inter-
breeding of races, esp. where differences

of colour are involved. [Latin *miscēre* to mingle + *genus* race]

miscellaneous (ˌmɪsəˈleɪnɪəs) *adj.* composed of or containing a variety of things; mixed. [Latin *miscēre* to mix]

miscellany (mɪˈsɛlənɪ; *U.S.* ˈmɪsəˌleɪnɪ) *n., pl.* **-nies.** (*sometimes pl.*) a miscellaneous collection of items, esp. essays or poems.

mischance (mɪsˈtʃɑːns) *n.* **1.** bad luck. **2.** a stroke of bad luck.

mischief (ˈmɪstʃɪf) *n.* **1.** wayward but not malicious behaviour that causes trouble or irritation. **2.** a playful inclination to behave in this way. **3.** injury or harm caused by a person or thing. **4.** a source of trouble or difficulty. [Old French *meschief*, from *mes-* MIS- + *chef* end]

mischievous (ˈmɪstʃɪvəs) *adj.* **1.** inclined to acts of mischief. **2.** teasing; slightly malicious. **3.** intended to cause harm. —ˈmischievously *adv.*

miscible (ˈmɪsɪbᵊl) *adj.* capable of mixing: *miscible with water.* [Latin *miscēre* to mix] —ˌmisciˈbility *n.*

misconception (ˌmɪskənˈsɛpʃən) *n.* a false or mistaken view, opinion, or attitude.

misconduct (mɪsˈkɒndʌkt) *n.* behaviour, such as adultery or professional negligence, that is regarded as immoral or unethical.

misconstrue (ˌmɪskənˈstruː) *vb.* **-struing, -strued.** to interpret mistakenly. —**misconstruction** (ˌmɪskənˈstrʌkʃən) *n.*

miscreant (ˈmɪskrɪənt) *n.* a wrongdoer or villain. [Old French *mescreant* unbelieving]

misdeal (ˌmɪsˈdiːl) *vb.* **-dealing, -dealt** (-ˈdɛlt). **1.** to deal out cards incorrectly. ~*n.* **2.** a faulty deal.

misdeed (ˌmɪsˈdiːd) *n.* an evil or illegal action.

misdemeanour or *U.S.* **misdemeanor** (ˌmɪsdɪˈmiːnə) *n.* **1.** a minor wrongdoing. **2.** *Criminal law.* (formerly) an offence less serious than a felony.

misdirect (ˌmɪsdɪˈrɛkt) *vb.* to give (a person) wrong directions or instructions. —ˌmisdiˈrection *n.*

mise en scène (ˌmiːz ɒn ˈseɪn) *n.* **1.** the stage setting and scenery in a play. **2.** the environment of an event. [French]

miser (ˈmaɪzə) *n.* a person who hoards money or possessions, often living miserably. [Latin: wretched] —ˈmiserly *adj.*

miserable (ˈmɪzərəbᵊl) *adj.* **1.** unhappy or depressed; wretched. **2.** causing misery or discomfort: *a miserable life.* **3.** sordid or squalid: *miserable living conditions.* **4.** mean; stingy. [Latin *miserābilis*] —ˈmiserableness *n.* —ˈmiserably *adv.*

misericord (mɪˈzɛrɪˌkɔːd) *n.* a ledge projecting from the underside of the hinged seat of a choir stall in a church, on which the occupant can support himself while standing. [Latin *miserēre* to pity + *cor* heart]

misery (ˈmɪzərɪ) *n., pl.* **-eries.** **1.** intense unhappiness or suffering. **2.** a cause of such unhappiness. **3.** squalid or poverty-stricken conditions. **4.** *Brit. informal.* a person who is habitually depressed: *he is such a misery.* [Latin *miser* wretched]

misfire (ˌmɪsˈfaɪə) *vb.* **1.** (of a firearm) to fail to fire as expected. **2.** (of a motor engine or vehicle) to fail to fire at the appropriate time. **3.** to fail to operate or occur as intended. ~*n.* **4.** the act or an instance of misfiring.

misfit (ˈmɪsˌfɪt) *n.* **1.** a person not suited to a particular social environment. **2.** something that does not fit or fits badly.

misfortune (mɪsˈfɔːtʃən) *n.* **1.** bad luck. **2.** an unfortunate event.

misgiving (mɪsˈɡɪvɪŋ) *n.* (*often pl.*) a feeling of uncertainty, apprehension, or doubt.

misgovern (ˌmɪsˈɡʌvən) *vb.* to govern badly. —ˌmisˈgovernment *n.*

misguided (ˌmɪsˈɡaɪdɪd) *adj.* mistaken or unwise in opinion or action.

mishandle (ˌmɪsˈhændᵊl) *vb.* to handle or treat badly or inefficiently.

mishap (ˈmɪsˌhæp) *n.* an unfortunate accident.

mishear (ˌmɪsˈhɪə) *vb.* **-hearing, -heard** (-ˈhɜːd). to fail to hear correctly.

mishit *Sport.* ~*n.* (ˈmɪsˌhɪt). **1.** a faulty shot or stroke. ~*vb.* (ˌmɪsˈhɪt), **-hitting, -hit.** **2.** to hit (a ball) with a faulty stroke.

mishmash (ˈmɪʃˌmæʃ) *n.* a confused collection or mixture. [reduplication of *mash*]

misinform (ˌmɪsɪnˈfɔːm) *vb.* to give incorrect information to. —**misinformation** (ˌmɪsɪnfəˈmeɪʃən) *n.*

misinterpret (ˌmɪsɪnˈtɜːprɪt) *vb.* to interpret badly, misleadingly, or incorrectly. —ˌmisinˌterpreˈtation *n.*

misjudge (ˌmɪsˈdʒʌdʒ) *vb.* to judge wrongly or unfairly. —ˈmisˈjudgment or ˌmisˈjudgement *n.*

mislay (mɪsˈleɪ) *vb.* **-laying, -laid.** to lose (something) temporarily, esp. by forgetting where it is.

mislead (mɪsˈliːd) *vb.* **-leading, -led.** to give false or confusing information to. —misˈleading *adj.*

mismanage (ˌmɪsˈmænɪdʒ) *vb.* to organize, run, or handle (something) badly or wrongly. —ˌmisˈmanagement *n.*

mismatch (ˌmɪsˈmætʃ) *vb.* **1.** to match badly, esp. in marriage. ~*n.* **2.** a bad match.

misnamed (ˌmɪsˈneɪmd) *adj.* badly or incorrectly named.

misnomer (ˌmɪsˈnəʊmə) *n.* **1.** an incorrect or unsuitable name for a person or thing. **2.** the use of the wrong name. [Old French *mesnomer* to misname]

misogyny (mɪˈsɒdʒɪnɪ, maɪ-) *n.* hatred of women. [Greek *misos* hatred + *gunē* woman] —miˈsogynist *n.* —miˈsogynous *adj.*

misplace (ˌmɪsˈpleɪs) *vb.* **1.** to put (something) in the wrong place, esp. to lose (something) temporarily by forgetting where it was placed. **2.** (*often passive*) to bestow (trust or affection) unadvisedly.

misprint *n.* (ˈmɪsˌprɪnt). **1.** an error in printing. ~*vb.* (ˌmɪsˈprɪnt). **2.** to print (a letter) incorrectly.

misprision (mɪsˈprɪʒən) *n. Law.* the con-

mispronounce (ˌmɪsprəˈnaʊns) vb. to pronounce (a word) wrongly. —**mispronunciation** (ˌmɪsprəˌnʌnsɪˈeɪʃən) n.

misquote (ˌmɪsˈkwəʊt) vb. to quote inaccurately. —ˌmisquoˈtation n.

misread (ˌmɪsˈriːd) vb. -reading, -read (-ˈred). 1. to read incorrectly. 2. to misinterpret.

misrepresent (ˌmɪsreprɪˈzɛnt) vb. to represent wrongly or inaccurately.

misrule (ˌmɪsˈruːl) vb. 1. to govern inefficiently or without justice. ~n. 2. inefficient or unjust government. 3. disorder.

miss[1] (mɪs) vb. 1. to fail to reach, hit, meet, find, or attain (some aim or target). 2. to fail to be present for: *to miss an appointment.* 3. to fail to see, hear, understand, or perceive. 4. to fail to take advantage of: *to miss an opportunity.* 5. to discover or regret the loss or absence of: *she missed him.* 6. to escape or avoid (something, esp. a danger), usually narrowly: *he missed death by inches.* ~n. 7. a failure to reach, hit, etc. 8. **give** (**something**) **a miss.** *Informal.* to avoid (something): *give the pudding a miss.* ~See also **miss out.** [Old English *missan*]

miss[2] (mɪs) n. *Informal.* an unmarried woman or girl. [from *mistress*]

Miss (mɪs) n. a title of an unmarried woman or girl, usually used before the surname.

Miss. Mississippi.

missal (ˈmɪsəl) n. *R.C. Church.* a book containing the prayers and rites of the Masses for a complete year. [Church Latin *missale,* from *missa* Mass]

misshapen (ˌmɪsˈʃeɪpən) adj. badly shaped; deformed.

missile (ˈmɪsaɪl) n. 1. any object or weapon that is thrown, launched, or fired at a target. 2. a rocket with an exploding warhead, used as a weapon. [Latin *mittere* to send]

missing (ˈmɪsɪŋ) adj. 1. not present; absent or lost. 2. not able to be traced and not known to be dead: *nine men were missing after the attack.*

missing link n. 1. any missing section or part in a series. 2. (usually preceded by *the*) a hypothetical extinct animal, formerly thought to be intermediate between the apes and man.

mission (ˈmɪʃən) n. 1. a specific task or duty assigned to a person or group of people. 2. a person's vocation. 3. a group of persons representing or working for a particular country or organization in a foreign country. 4. a group of people sent by a church to a foreign country to do religious and social work. 5. a building in which missionary work is performed. 6. the dispatch of aircraft or spacecraft to achieve a particular task. 7. a charitable centre that offers shelter or aid to the destitute or underprivileged. [Latin *mittere* to send]

missionary (ˈmɪʃənərɪ) n., pl. -aries. a member of a religious mission.

missis *or* **missus** (ˈmɪsɪz, -ɪs) n. 1. (usually preceded by *the*) *Informal.* one's wife or the wife of the person addressed or referred to. 2. an informal term of address for a woman. [spoken version of *mistress*]

missive (ˈmɪsɪv) n. a formal or official letter. [Latin *mittere* to send]

miss out vb. 1. to leave out; overlook. 2. (often foll. by *on*) to fail to take part in something enjoyable or beneficial: *you missed out on the celebrations.*

misspell (ˌmɪsˈspɛl) vb. -spelling, -spelt *or* -spelled. to spell (a word or words) wrongly.

misspend (ˌmɪsˈspɛnd) vb. -spending, -spent. to spend thoughtlessly or wastefully.

missy (ˈmɪsɪ) n., pl. missies. *Informal.* an affectionate or disparaging form of address to a girl.

mist (mɪst) n. 1. a thin fog. 2. a fine spray of liquid, such as that produced by an aerosol container. 3. condensed water vapour on a surface. 4. something that causes haziness or lack of clarity, such as a film of tears. ~vb. 5. to cover or be covered with mist. [Old English] —ˈmisty adj. —ˈmistiness n.

mistake (mɪˈsteɪk) n. 1. an error or blunder. 2. a misconception or misunderstanding. ~vb. -taking, -took, -taken. 3. to misunderstand; misinterpret: *she mistook his meaning.* 4. (foll. by *for*) to interpret as or confuse with: *she mistook his direct manner for honesty.* 5. to choose badly or incorrectly: *he mistook his path.* [Old Norse *mistaka* to take erroneously]

mistaken (mɪˈsteɪkən) adj. 1. wrong in opinion or judgment. 2. arising from error in opinion or judgment: *a mistaken viewpoint.*

mister (ˈmɪstə) n. (*sometimes cap.*) an informal form of address for a man. [variant of *master*]

Mister (ˈmɪstə) n. the full form of **Mr.**

mistime (ˌmɪsˈtaɪm) vb. to time (an action or utterance) wrongly.

mistle thrush *or* **missel thrush** (ˈmɪsəl) n. a large European thrush with a brown back and spotted breast. [Old English *mistel* mistletoe]

mistletoe (ˈmɪsəlˌtəʊ) n. a Eurasian evergreen shrub with waxy white berries: grows as a parasite on various trees. [Old English *mistel* mistletoe + *tān* twig]

mistook (mɪˈstʊk) vb. the past tense of **mistake.**

mistral (ˈmɪstrəl, mɪˈstrɑːl) n. a strong cold dry northerly wind of S France. [Provençal, from Latin *magistrālis* masterful]

mistreat (ˌmɪsˈtriːt) vb. to treat badly. —ˌmisˈtreatment n.

mistress (ˈmɪstrɪs) n. 1. a woman who has a continuing sexual relationship with a man she is not married to. 2. a woman in a position of authority, ownership, or control. 3. a woman having control over something specified: *mistress of her own destiny.* 4. *Chiefly Brit.* short for **schoolmistress.** [Old French *maistresse*]

mistrial (mɪsˈtraɪəl) n. a trial made void because of some error.

mistrust (ˌmɪsˈtrʌst) vb. 1. to have doubts or suspicions about (someone or something). ~n. 2. distrust. —ˌmisˈtrustful adj. —misˈtrustfully adv.

misunderstand (ˌmɪsʌndəˈstænd) vb. -standing, -stood. to fail to understand properly.

misunderstanding (ˌmɪsʌndəˈstændɪŋ) n. 1. a failure to understand properly. 2. a disagreement.

misunderstood (ˌmɪsʌndəˈstʊd) adj. not properly or sympathetically understood: a misunderstood adolescent.

misuse n. (ˌmɪsˈjuːs), also **misusage**. 1. erroneous, improper, or unorthodox use: misuse of words. 2. cruel or inhumane treatment. ~vb. (ˌmɪsˈjuːz) 3. to use wrongly. 4. to treat badly or harshly.

mite[1] (maɪt) n. any of numerous very small creatures of the spider family some of which live as parasites. [Old English mite]

mite[2] (maɪt) n. 1. a very small particle, creature, or object. 2. a very small sum of money. 3. a mite. Informal. somewhat: he's a mite foolish. [Middle Dutch mīte]

mitigate (ˈmɪtɪˌgeɪt) vb. to make or become less severe or harsh; moderate. [Latin mītis mild + agere to make] —ˈmitiˌgating adj. —ˌmitiˈgation n.

mitosis (maɪˈtəʊsɪs, mɪ-) n. a method of cell division, in which the nucleus divides into two daughter nuclei, each containing the same number of chromosomes as the parent nucleus. [Greek mitos thread]

mitre or U.S. **miter** (ˈmaɪtə) n. 1. Christianity. the liturgical headdress of a bishop or abbot, consisting of a tall pointed cleft cap. 2. Also: **mitre joint**. a corner joint formed by cutting bevels of equal angles at the ends of each piece of material. ~vb. 3. to make a mitre joint between (two pieces of material). 4. to confer a mitre upon: a mitred abbot. [Greek mitra turban]

mitt (mɪt) n. 1. a glovelike hand covering that does not cover the fingers. 2. short for **mitten**. 3. Slang. a hand. 4. a baseball glove. [from mitten]

mitten (ˈmɪtᵊn) n. a glove with one section for the thumb and a single section for the fingers. [Old French mitaine]

mix (mɪks) vb. 1. to combine or blend into one mass. 2. to become or have the capacity to become combined or joined: some chemicals do not mix. 3. to form (something) by combining constituents: to mix cement. 4. to do at the same time: to mix study and pleasure. 5. to be outgoing in social situations: Pauline mixed well. 6. Music. to balance and adjust (individual performers' parts) to make an overall sound by electronic means. ~n. 7. the result of mixing; mixture. 8. a mixture of ingredients, esp. one commercially prepared for making a cake. 9. Music. the sound produced by mixing. ~See also **mix-up**. [Latin miscēre to mix] —**mixed** adj.

mixed bag n. Informal. something composed of diverse elements, characteristics, or people.

mixed blessing n. an event or situation with both advantages and disadvantages.

mixed doubles pl. n. Tennis, badminton. a doubles game with a man and a woman as partners on each side.

mixed farming n. combined arable and livestock farming (on **mixed farms**).

mixed grill n. a dish of several kinds of grilled meat, tomatoes, and mushrooms.

mixed marriage n. a marriage between persons of different races or religions.

mixed metaphor n. a combination of incongruous metaphors, as when the Nazi jackboots sing their swan song.

mixed-up adj. in a state of mental confusion.

mixer (ˈmɪksə) n. 1. Informal. a person considered in relation to his ability to mix socially. 2. a kitchen appliance, usually electrical, used for mixing foods. 3. a drink such as ginger ale or fruit juice used in preparing cocktails.

mixture (ˈmɪkstʃə) n. 1. something mixed; a result of mixing. 2. a combination of different things, such as feelings: she watched with a mixture of disgust and fascination. 3. Chem. a substance consisting of two or more substances mixed together without any chemical bonding between them.

mix-up n. 1. a confused condition or situation. ~vb. **mix up**. 2. to make into a mixture. 3. to confuse: Tom mixes John up with Bill. 4. (foll. by in or with; usually passive) to involve (in an activity or group, esp. one that is illegal): mixed up in the drugs racket.

mizzenmast (ˈmɪzᵊn̩ˌmɑːst; Naut. ˈmɪzᵊnˌməst) n. Naut. (on a vessel with three or more masts) the third mast from the bow. [Italian mezzano middle + mast]

mks units pl. n. a metric system of units based on the metre, kilogram, and second; it forms the basis of the SI units.

ml 1. mile. 2. millilitre.

ML Medieval Latin.

MLitt Master of Letters. [Latin Magister Litterarum]

Mlle or **Mlle.**, pl. **Mlles** or **Mlles.** the French equivalent of Miss. [from Mademoiselle]

MLR minimum lending rate.

mm millimetre.

Mme, pl. **Mmes.** the French equivalent of Mrs. [from Madame, Mesdames]

MMus Master of Music.

Mn Chem. manganese.

MN Minnesota.

mnemonic (nɪˈmɒnɪk) adj. 1. aiding or meant to aid one's memory. ~n. 2. something, such as a verse, to assist memory. [Greek mnēmōn mindful] —mneˈmonically adv.

mo (məʊ) n. Informal, chiefly Brit. short for **moment** (sense 1).

Mo Chem. molybdenum.

MO 1. Medical Officer. 2. Also: **Mo.** Missouri.

m.o. *or* **MO** 1. mail order. 2. money order.

moa ('məʊə) *n.* any of various recently extinct large flightless birds of New Zealand resembling the ostrich. [Maori]

moan (məʊn) *n.* 1. a low prolonged mournful sound expressive of suffering or pleading. 2. any similar sound, esp. that made by the wind. 3. *Informal.* a grumble or complaint. ~*vb.* 4. to utter in a low mournful manner. 5. to make a sound like a moan. 6. *Informal.* to grumble or complain. [Old English *mǣnan* to grieve over] —'**moaner** *n.*

moat (məʊt) *n.* a wide water-filled ditch surrounding a fortified place, such as a castle. [Old French *motte* mound]

mob (mɒb) *n.* 1. a riotous or disorderly crowd of people. 2. *Informal.* any group of people. 3. the masses. 4. *Slang.* a gang of criminals. 5. *Austral. & N.Z.* a flock or herd of animals. 6. **mobs of.** *Austral. & N.Z. informal.* lots of. ~*vb.* **mobbing, mobbed.** 7. to attack in a group resembling a mob. 8. to surround, esp. in order to acclaim. [shortened from Latin *mōbile vulgus* the fickle populace]

mobcap ('mɒb,kæp) *n.* a woman's 18th-century cotton cap with a pouched crown. [obs. *mob* woman, esp. loose-living + *cap*]

mobile ('məʊbaɪl) *adj.* 1. having freedom of movement; movable. 2. changing quickly in expression: *a mobile face.* 3. *Sociol.* (of individuals or social groups) moving within and between classes, occupations, and localities. ~*n.* 4. a sculpture suspended in midair with delicately balanced parts that are set in motion by air currents. [Latin *mōbilis*] —**mobility** (məʊ'bɪlɪtɪ) *n.*

mobilize *or* **-lise** ('məʊbɪ,laɪz) *vb.* 1. to prepare for war or another emergency by organizing (resources and armed services). 2. to organize for a purpose. —,**mobili'za-tion** *or* **-li'sation** *n.*

moccasin ('mɒkəsɪn) *n.* a shoe of soft leather originally worn by North American Indians. [American Indian]

mocha ('mɒkə) *n.* 1. a dark brown coffee originally imported from the port of Mocha in Arabia. 2. a flavouring made from coffee and chocolate.

mock (mɒk) *vb.* 1. to behave with scorn or contempt towards (a person or thing). 2. to imitate, esp. in fun; mimic. 3. to deceive, disappoint, or delude. 4. to defy or frustrate. ~*n.* 5. a counterfeit; imitation. 6. (*often pl.*) *Informal.* (in England and Wales) school examinations taken as practice before public exams. ~*adj.* 7. sham or counterfeit. 8. serving as an imitation or substitute, esp. for practice purposes: *a mock battle.* ~See also **mock-up.** [Old French *mocquer*] —'**mocking** *n., adj.*

mockers ('mɒkəz) *pl. n.* **put the mockers on.** *Informal.* to ruin the chances of success of. [possibly from *mock*]

mockery ('mɒkərɪ) *n., pl.* **-eries.** 1. ridicule, contempt, or derision. 2. an imitation or pretence, esp. a derisive one. 3. a

person or thing that is mocked. 4. a person, thing, or action that is inadequate.

mock-heroic *adj.* (of a literary work, esp. a poem) imitating the style of heroic poetry in order to satirize an unheroic subject.

mockingbird ('mɒkɪŋ,bɜːd) *n.* an American songbird which can mimic the song of other birds.

mock orange *n.* a shrub with white fragrant flowers like those of the orange.

mock turtle soup *n.* an imitation turtle soup made from a calf's head.

mock-up *n.* a working full-scale model of a machine or apparatus for test or research purposes.

mod¹ (mɒd) *n. Brit.* a member of a group of teenagers, originally in the mid-1960s, noted for their clothes-consciousness. [from *modernist*]

mod² (mɒd) *n.* an annual Highland Gaelic meeting with musical and literary competitions. [Gaelic *mōd* assembly]

MOD (in Britain) Ministry of Defence.

mod. 1. moderate. 2. modern.

modal ('məʊd³l) *adj.* 1. of or relating to mode or manner. 2. *Grammar.* (of a verb form or auxiliary verb) expressing a distinction of mood, such as that between possibility and actuality: *in English, "can" and "might" are modal verbs.* 3. *Music.* of or relating to a mode. —**modality** (məʊ-'dælɪtɪ) *n.*

mod cons *pl. n. Informal.* modern conveniences, such as hot water and heating.

mode (məʊd) *n.* 1. a manner or way of doing, acting, or existing. 2. the current fashion or style. 3. *Music.* any of the various scales of notes within one octave. [Latin *modus* manner]

model ('mɒd³l) *n.* 1. a representation, usually on a smaller scale, of something such as a device or structure. 2. **a.** a standard to be imitated. **b.** (*as modifier*): *a model wife.* 3. a representative form, style, or pattern. 4. a person who poses for a sculptor, painter, or photographer. 5. a person who wears clothes to display them to prospective buyers; mannequin. 6. a design or style of a particular product. ~*vb.* **-elling, -elled** *or U.S.* **-eling, -eled.** 7. to make a model of (something or someone). 8. to form in clay or wax; mould. 9. to display (clothing and accessories) as a mannequin. 10. to plan or create according to a model or models. [Latin *modulus*, diminutive of *modus* mode]

modem ('məʊdɛm) *n. Computers.* a device for connecting two computers by a telephone line, consisting of a modulator that converts computer signals into audio signals and a corresponding demodulator. [from *mo(dulator)* *dem(odulator)*]

moderate *adj.* ('mɒdərɪt). 1. not extreme or excessive. 2. not violent; mild or temperate. 3. of average quality or extent: *moderate success.* ~*n.* ('mɒdərɪt). 4. a person who holds moderate views, esp. in politics. ~*vb.* ('mɒdə,reɪt). 5. to become or cause to become less extreme or violent.

6. to preside over a meeting, discussion, etc. [Latin *moderārī* to restrain]

moderation (ˌmɒdəˈreɪʃən) *n.* **1.** the state or an instance of being moderate. **2.** the act of moderating. **3. in moderation.** within moderate or reasonable limits.

moderato (ˌmɒdəˈrɑːtəʊ) *adv. Music.* **1.** at a moderate tempo. **2.** with restraint: *allegro moderato.* [Italian]

moderator (ˈmɒdəˌreɪtə) *n.* **1.** *Presbyterian Church.* a minister appointed to preside over a Church court, synod, or general assembly. **2.** a presiding officer at a public or legislative assembly. **3.** a material, such as heavy water, used for slowing down neutrons in nuclear reactors.

modern (ˈmɒdən) *adj.* **1.** of the present or a recent time; contemporary. **2.** of contemporary styles or schools of art, literature, and music, esp. those of an experimental kind. ∼*n.* **3.** a contemporary person. [Late Latin *modernus*, from *modus* mode] —**moˈdernity** *n.*

Modern English *n.* the English language since about 1450.

modernism (ˈmɒdəˌnɪzəm) *n.* modern tendencies, thoughts, or styles, or support of these. —**ˈmodernist** *n., adj.*

modernize *or* **-ise** (ˈmɒdəˌnaɪz) *vb.* **1.** to make modern in style, methods, or equipment: *to modernize rolling stock.* **2.** to adopt modern ways or ideas. —ˌmoderniˈzation *or* -iˈsation *n.*

modern pentathlon *n.* an athletic contest consisting of five different events: horse riding with jumps, fencing with electric épée, freestyle swimming, pistol shooting, and cross-country running.

modest (ˈmɒdɪst) *adj.* **1.** having a humble opinion of oneself or one's accomplishments. **2.** reserved or shy. **3.** not ostentatious or pretentious. **4.** not extreme or excessive. **5.** decorous or decent. [Latin *modestus* moderate] —**ˈmodestly** *adv.* —**ˈmodesty** *n.*

modicum (ˈmɒdɪkəm) *n.* a small amount. [Latin]

modifier (ˈmɒdɪˌfaɪə) *n. Grammar.* a word or phrase that qualifies the sense of another word; for example, the noun *alarm* is a modifier of *clock* in *alarm clock.*

modify (ˈmɒdɪˌfaɪ) *vb.* **-fying, -fied.** **1.** to change or alter slightly. **2.** to make less extreme or uncompromising. **3.** *Grammar.* (of a word or phrase) to bear the relation of modifier to (another word or phrase). [Latin *modus* measure + *facere* to make] —ˌmodifiˈcation *n.*

modish (ˈməʊdɪʃ) *adj.* in the current fashion or style. —**ˈmodishly** *adv.*

modiste (məʊˈdiːst) *n.* a fashionable dressmaker or milliner. [French]

modulate (ˈmɒdjʊˌleɪt) *vb.* **1.** to change the tone, pitch, or volume of (one's voice). **2.** to adjust or regulate the degree of. **3.** *Music.* to change from one key to another. **4.** *Physics, electronics.* to superimpose the amplitude, frequency, or phase of a wave or signal onto another wave or signal. [Latin *modulārī* to modulate] —ˌmoduˈlation *n.*

module (ˈmɒdjuːl) *n.* **1.** a standard self-contained unit or item, such as an assembly of electronic components or a standardized piece of furniture, that can be used in combination with other units. **2.** *Astronautics.* a self-contained separable unit making up a spacecraft. **3.** *Education.* a short course of study that together with other such courses counts towards a qualification. [Latin *modulus*, diminutive of *modus* mode] —**ˈmodular** *adj.*

modulus (ˈmɒdjʊləs) *n., pl.* **-li** (-ˌlaɪ). *Physics.* a coefficient expressing a specified property, for instance elasticity, of a specified substance. [Latin]

modus operandi (ˈməʊdəs ˌɒpəˈrændaɪ) *n., pl.* **modi operandi** (ˈməʊdaɪ ˌɒpəˈrændaɪ). procedure; method of operating. [Latin]

modus vivendi (ˈməʊdəs vɪˈvɛndaɪ) *n., pl.* **modi vivendi** (ˈməʊdaɪ vɪˈvɛndaɪ). a working arrangement between conflicting interests; practical compromise. [Latin: way of living]

mog (mɒg) *or* **moggy** *n., pl.* **mogs** *or* **moggies.** *Brit. slang.* a cat. [dialect, orig. a pet name for a cow]

mogul (ˈməʊgʌl) *n.* an important or powerful person.

Mogul (ˈməʊgʌl) *adj.* of or relating to a Muslim dynasty of Indian emperors established in 1526. [Persian *mughul* Mongolian]

MOH (in Britain) Medical Officer of Health.

mohair (ˈməʊˌhɛə) *n.* **1.** the long soft silky hair of the Angora goat. **2.** a fabric made from yarn of this hair and cotton or wool. [Arabic *mukhayyar*, lit.: choice]

Mohammedan (məʊˈhæmɪdˀn) *n., adj.* another word (not in Muslim use) for **Muslim.**

mohican (məʊˈhiːkən) *n.* a punk hairstyle in which the head is shaved at the sides and the remaining strip of hair is worn stiffly erect. [after the *Mohicans*, American Indians]

moiety (ˈmɔɪtɪ) *n., pl.* **-ties.** **1.** a half. **2.** one of two parts or divisions of something. [Old French *moitié*]

moire (mwɑː) *n.* a fabric, usually silk, with a watered effect. [French (earlier) *mouaire* mohair]

moiré (ˈmwɑːreɪ) *adj.* **1.** with a watered or wavelike pattern. ∼*n.* **2.** such a pattern, impressed on fabrics. **3.** any fabric with such a pattern. **4.** Also: **moiré pattern.** a pattern seen when two geometrical patterns, such as grids, are visually superimposed. [French]

moist (mɔɪst) *adj.* **1.** slightly damp or wet. **2.** saturated with or suggestive of moisture. [Old French]

moisten (ˈmɔɪsˀn) *vb.* to make or become moist.

moisture (ˈmɔɪstʃə) *n.* water diffused as vapour or condensed on or in objects.

moisturize *or* **-ise** (ˈmɔɪstʃəˌraɪz) *vb.* to add moisture to (the air or the skin). —**ˈmoisturˌizer** *or* **-ˌiser** *n.*

moke (məʊk) *n. Brit. slang.* a donkey. [origin unknown]

mol *Chem.* mole³.

mol. **1.** molecular. **2.** molecule.

molar (ˈməʊlə) *n.* **1.** any of the back teeth specialized for grinding in man and other mammals. ~*adj.* **2.** of any of these teeth. [Latin *mola* millstone]

molasses (məˈlæsɪz) *n.* (*functioning as sing.*) **1.** the thick brown uncrystallized bitter syrup obtained from sugar during refining. **2.** *U.S. & Canad.* same as **treacle** (sense 1). [Portuguese *melaço*]

mold (məʊld) *n., vb. U.S.* same as **mould**.

mole¹ (məʊl) *n. Pathol.* a small dark raised spot on the skin.

mole² (məʊl) *n.* **1.** a small burrowing mammal with velvety, typically dark fur and forearms specialized for digging. **2.** *Informal.* a spy who has infiltrated an organization and become a trusted member of it. [Middle Dutch *mol*]

mole³ (məʊl) *n.* the basic SI unit of amount of substance; the amount that contains as many elementary entities as there are atoms in 0.012 kilogram of carbon-12. [German *Mol*, short for *Molekül* molecule]

mole⁴ (məʊl) *n.* **1.** a breakwater. **2.** a harbour protected by a breakwater. [Latin *mōlēs* mass]

molecular (məˈlɛkjʊlə) *adj.* of or relating to molecules.

molecular compound *n.* a compound in which the atoms are linked by covalent bonds to form molecules.

molecular formula *n.* a chemical formula indicating the number and type of atoms in a molecule, but not its structure: NH_3 is the molecular formula of ammonia.

molecular weight *n.* the sum of all the atomic weights of the atoms in a molecule.

molecule (ˈmɒlɪˌkjuːl) *n.* **1.** the simplest unit of a chemical compound that can exist, consisting of two or more atoms held together by chemical bonds. **2.** a very small particle. [New Latin *mōlēcula*, diminutive of Latin *mōlēs* mass]

molehill (ˈməʊlˌhɪl) *n.* **1.** the small mound of earth thrown up by a burrowing mole. **2. make a mountain out of a molehill.** to exaggerate an unimportant matter out of all proportion.

molest (məˈlɛst) *vb.* **1.** to disturb or annoy (someone) by hostile interference. **2.** to accost or attack, (esp. a woman or child) with the intention of assaulting sexually. [Latin *molestāre* to annoy] —**molestation** (ˌməʊlɛˈsteɪʃən) *n.* —**moˈlester** *n.*

moll (mɒl) *n. Slang.* **1.** the female accomplice of a gangster. **2.** a prostitute. [from *Moll*, familiar form of *Mary*]

mollify (ˈmɒlɪˌfaɪ) *vb.* **-fying, -fied.** to pacify; soothe. [Latin *mollis* soft + *facere* to make] —, **mollifiˈcation** *n.*

mollusc or *U.S.* **mollusk** (ˈmɒləsk) *n.* any of various invertebrates with a soft unsegmented body and often a shell. The group includes snails, slugs, clams, mussels, squid, and octopuses. [Latin *molluscus*]

mollycoddle (ˈmɒlɪˌkɒdˀl) *vb.* **1.** to treat

with indulgent care; pamper. ~*n.* **2.** a pampered person. [from *Molly* girl's name + *coddle*]

Molotov cocktail (ˈmɒləˌtɒf) *n.* an elementary incendiary weapon, usually a bottle of petrol with a short delay fuse or wick; petrol bomb. [after V. M. *Molotov*, Soviet statesman]

molt (məʊlt) *vb., n. U.S.* same as **moult**.

molten (ˈməʊltən) *adj.* liquefied; melted.

molto (ˈmɒltəʊ) *adv. Music.* very: *allegro molto; molto adagio.* [Italian]

molybdenum (mɒˈlɪbdənəm) *n.* a very hard silvery-white metallic element used in alloys, esp. to harden and strengthen steels. Symbol: Mo [Greek *molubdos* lead]

mom (mɒm) *n. Informal, chiefly U.S. & Canad.* same as **mother**.

moment (ˈməʊmənt) *n.* **1.** a short indefinite period of time. **2.** a specific instant or point in time: *at that moment the phone rang.* **3. the moment.** the present point of time: *at the moment it's fine.* **4.** import, significance, or value: *a matter of greatest moment.* **5.** *Physics.* **a.** a tendency to produce motion, esp. rotation about a point or axis. **b.** the product of a physical quantity, such as force or mass, and its distance from a fixed reference point. [Latin *mōmentum* movement]

momentary (ˈməʊməntrɪ) *adj.* lasting for only a moment; temporary. —**ˈmomentarily** *adv.*

moment of truth *n.* a moment when a person or thing is put to the test.

momentous (məʊˈmɛntəs) *adj.* of great significance. —**moˈmentousness** *n.*

momentum (məʊˈmɛntəm) *n., pl.* **-ta** (-tə) or **-tums.** **1.** *Physics.* the product of a body's mass and its velocity. **2.** the impetus of a moving body. **3.** driving power or strength. [Latin: movement]

momma (ˈmɒmə) *n. Chiefly U.S.* an informal or childish word for **mother**.

Mon. Monday.

mon- *combining form.* See **mono-**.

monad (ˈmɒnæd, ˈməʊ-) *n.* **1.** *Philosophy.* any fundamental singular metaphysical entity. **2.** a single-celled organism. **3.** an atom, ion, or radical with a valency of one. [Greek *monas* unit]

monandrous (mɒˈnændrəs) *adj.* **1.** having only one male sexual partner over a period of time. **2.** *Biol.* having only one stamen (in each flower). [Greek *monos* sole + *anēr* man]

monarch (ˈmɒnək) *n.* a sovereign head of state, esp. a king, queen, or emperor, who rules usually by hereditary right. [Greek *monos* sole + *arkhos* ruler] —**monarchical** (mɒˈnɑːkɪkˀl) or **moˈnarchic** *adj.* —**ˈmonarchism** *n.* —**ˈmonarchist** *n., adj.*

monarchy (ˈmɒnəkɪ) *n., pl.* **-chies.** **1.** a form of government in which supreme authority is vested in a single and usually hereditary figure, such as a king. **2.** a country reigned over by a monarch.

monastery (ˈmɒnəstrɪ) *n., pl.* **-teries.** the residence of a religious community, esp. of monks. [Greek *monazein* to live alone]

monastic (mə'næstɪk) *adj.* **1.** of or relating to monasteries, monks, or nuns. **2.** resembling this sort of life; ascetic. —**monasticism** (mə'næstɪ,sɪzəm) *n.*

monatomic (,mɒnə'tɒmɪk) *adj. Chem.* **1.** (of an element) consisting of single atoms. **2.** (of a compound or molecule) having only one atom or group that can be replaced in a reaction.

Monday ('mʌndɪ) *n.* the second day of the week; first day of the working week. [Old English *mōnandæg* moon's day]

monetarism ('mʌnɪtə,rɪzəm) *n.* **1.** the theory that inflation is caused by an excess quantity of money in an economy. **2.** an economic policy based on this theory and a belief in the efficiency of free market forces. —**'monetarist** *n., adj.*

monetary ('mʌnɪtrɪ) *adj.* of money or currency. [Latin *monēta* money]

money ('mʌnɪ) *n.* **1.** a medium of exchange that functions as legal tender. **2.** the official currency, in the form of banknotes or coins, issued by a government. **3.** (*Law or archaic. pl.* **moneys** *or* **monies**) a financial sum or income. **4.** an unspecified amount of wealth: *money to lend.* **5. for one's money.** in one's opinion. **6. one's money's worth.** full value for the money one has paid for something. **7. put money on.** to place a bet on. [Latin *monēta*]

moneybags ('mʌnɪ,bægz) *n.* (functioning as sing.) *Informal.* a very rich person.

moneychanger ('mʌnɪ,tʃeɪndʒə) *n.* a person engaged in the business of exchanging currencies or money.

moneyed *or* **monied** ('mʌnɪd) *adj.* having a great deal of money; rich.

money-grubbing *adj. Informal.* seeking greedily to obtain money. —**'money,grubber** *n.*

moneylender ('mʌnɪ,lendə) *n.* a person who lends money at interest as a living.

moneymaker ('mʌnɪ,meɪkə) *n.* **1.** a person who is intent on accumulating money. **2.** a person or thing that is or might be profitable. —**'money,making** *adj., n.*

money-spinner *n. Informal.* an enterprise, idea, or thing that is a source of wealth.

monger ('mʌngə) *n.* **1.** a trader or dealer: *ironmonger.* **2.** a promoter of something: *warmonger.* [Old English *mangere*]

mongol ('mɒŋg'l) *n.* (not in technical use) a person affected by Down's syndrome. —**'mongo,loid** *n., adj.*

Mongolian (mɒŋ'gəʊlɪən) *adj.* **1.** of Mongolia, a region in E Central Asia, its people, or their language. ~*n.* **2.** a person from Mongolia. **3.** the language of Mongolia.

mongolism ('mɒŋgə,lɪzəm) *n. Pathol.* a former name (not in technical use) for **Down's syndrome.** [the condition produces facial features similar to those of the Mongoloid peoples]

Mongoloid ('mɒŋgə,lɔɪd) *adj.* of a major racial group of mankind, characterized by yellowish skin, straight black hair, and slanting eyes: includes most of the people of Asia, the American Indians, and the Eskimos.

mongoose ('mɒŋ,guːs) *n., pl.* **-gooses.** a small long-tailed predatory mammal of Asia and Africa that kills snakes. [from Marathi (a language of India) *mangūs*]

mongrel ('mʌŋgrəl) *n.* **1.** a plant or animal, esp. a dog, of mixed or unknown breeding. ~*adj.* **2.** of mixed origin, breeding, or character. [from obs. *mong* mixture]

monied ('mʌnɪd) *adj.* same as **moneyed.**

monies ('mʌnɪz) *n. Law, archaic.* a plural of **money.**

monism ('mɒnɪzəm) *n. Philosophy.* the doctrine that reality consists of only one basic substance or element, such as mind or matter. [Greek *monos* sole] —**'monist** *n., adj.*

monition (məʊ'nɪʃən) *n.* a warning or caution. [Latin *monēre* to warn]

monitor ('mɒnɪtə) *n.* **1.** a person or piece of equipment that warns, checks, controls, or keeps a continuous record of something. **2.** *Education.* a pupil assisting a teacher with various duties. **3.** a television set or loudspeaker used in a studio for checking what is being transmitted or recorded. **4.** a large predatory lizard inhabiting warm regions of Africa, Asia, and Australia. ~*vb.* **5.** to act as a monitor of. **6.** to observe or record (the condition or performance of a person or thing). **7.** to check (a broadcast) for acceptable quality or content. [Latin *monēre* to advise] —**monitorial** (,mɒnɪ'tɔːrɪəl) *adj.*

monitory ('mɒnɪtrɪ) *adj.* warning or admonishing.

monk (mʌŋk) *n.* a male member of a religious community bound by vows of poverty, chastity, and obedience. [Greek *monos* alone] —**'monkish** *adj.*

monkey ('mʌŋkɪ) *n.* **1.** any of numerous long-tailed primates excluding lemurs and tarsiers. **2.** any primate except man. **3.** a naughty or mischievous child. **4.** *Slang.* £500 or $500. ~*vb.* **5.** (usually foll. by *around, with,* etc.) to meddle, fool, or tinker. [origin unknown]

monkey business *n. Informal.* mischievous, suspect, or dishonest behaviour or acts.

monkey nut *n. Brit.* a peanut.

monkey puzzle *n.* a South American coniferous tree with branches shaped like a candelabrum and stiff sharp leaves.

monkey tricks *or U.S.* **monkey shines** *pl. n. Informal.* mischievous behaviour or acts.

monkey wrench *n.* a wrench with adjustable jaws.

monkshood ('mʌŋkshʊd) *n.* a poisonous plant with hooded blue-purple flowers.

mono ('mɒnəʊ) *adj.* **1.** short for **monophonic.** ~*n.* **2.** monophonic sound.

mono- *or before a vowel* **mon-** *combining form.* **1.** one; single: *monorail.* **2.** indicating that a chemical compound contains a single specified atom or group: *monoxide.* [Greek *monos* alone]

monobasic (,mɒnəʊ'beɪsɪk) *adj. Chem.* (of an acid, such as hydrogen chloride) having only one replaceable hydrogen atom per molecule.

monochromatic (ˌmɒnəʊkrəʊˈmætɪk) *adj.* (of light or other electromagnetic radiation) having only one wavelength.

monochrome (ˈmɒnəˌkrəʊm) *adj.* **1.** *Photog., T.V.* black-and-white. ~*n.* **2.** a painting or drawing done in a range of tones of a single colour. [Greek *monokhrōmos* of one colour]

monocle (ˈmɒnəkᵊl) *n.* a lens for correcting defective vision of one eye, held in position by the facial muscles. [MONO- + Latin *oculus* eye] —ˈ**monocled** *adj.*

monocline (ˈmɒnəʊˌklaɪn) *n.* a fold in stratified rocks in which the strata are inclined in the same direction from the horizontal. [MONO- + Greek *klīnein* to lean] —ˌ**monoˈclinal** *adj., n.*

monoclinic (ˌmɒnəʊˈklɪnɪk) *adj. Crystallog.* of the crystal system characterized by three unequal axes, one pair of which are not at right angles to each other.

monoclonal antibody (ˌmɒnəʊˈkləʊnᵊl) *n.* an antibody produced from a single clone of cells grown in a culture.

monocotyledon (ˌmɒnəʊˌkɒtɪˈliːdᵊn) *n.* any flowering plant with a single embryonic seed leaf, such as the grasses, lilies, palms, and orchids.

monocular (mɒˈnɒkjʊlə) *adj.* having or intended for the use of only one eye. [Late Latin *monoculus* one-eyed]

monody (ˈmɒnədɪ) *n., pl.* **-dies.** **1.** (in Greek tragedy) an ode sung by a single actor. **2.** *Music.* a style of composition consisting of a single vocal part, usually with accompaniment. [MONO- + Greek *aeidein* to sing] —ˈ**monodist** *n.*

monoecious (mɒˈniːʃəs) *adj.* **1.** (of some flowering plants) having the male and female reproductive organs in separate flowers on the same plant. **2.** (of some animals and lower plants) hermaphrodite. [MONO- + Greek *oikos* house]

monogamy (mɒˈnɒgəmɪ) *n.* the state or practice of having only one husband or wife at a time. [MONO- + Greek *gamos* marriage] —mɒˈ**nogamous** *adj.*

monogram (ˈmɒnəˌgræm) *n.* a design of one or more letters, esp. initials, on clothing, stationery, etc. [Greek *monogrammatos* consisting of one letter]

monograph (ˈmɒnəˌgrɑːf) *n.* a paper, book, or other work concerned with a single subject or aspect of a subject.

monolingual (ˌmɒnəʊˈlɪŋgwəl) *adj.* knowing or expressed in only one language.

monolith (ˈmɒnəlɪθ) *n.* **1.** a large block of stone or anything that resembles one in appearance, solidity, or size. **2.** a statue, obelisk, or column cut from one block of stone. [Greek *monolithos* made from a single stone] —ˌ**monoˈlithic** *adj.*

monologue (ˈmɒnəˌlɒg) *n.* **1.** a long speech made by one actor in a play or film; soliloquy. **2.** a dramatic piece for a single performer. **3.** any long speech by one person, esp. when interfering with conversation. [Greek *monologos* speaking alone]

monomania (ˌmɒnəʊˈmeɪnɪə) *n.* an obses-

sion with one thing or idea. —ˌ**monoˈmaniˌac** *n., adj.*

monomer (ˈmɒnəmə) *n. Chem.* a compound whose molecules can join together to form a polymer.

monomial (mɒˈnəʊmɪəl) *n. Maths.* an expression consisting of a single term, such as 5*ax*. [MONO- + (*bin*)*omial*]

mononucleosis (ˌmɒnəʊˌnjuːklɪˈəʊsɪs) *n.* **infectious mononucleosis.** same as **glandular fever.**

monophonic (ˌmɒnəʊˈfɒnɪk) *adj.* (of a system of broadcasting, recording, or reproducing sound) using only one channel between source and loudspeaker. Often shortened to **mono.**

monoplane (ˈmɒnəˌpleɪn) *n.* an aeroplane with only one pair of wings.

monopolize *or* **-lise** (məˈnɒpəˌlaɪz) *vb.* **1.** to have full control or use of, to the exclusion of others. **2.** to hold a monopoly of (a market or commodity).

monopoly (məˈnɒpəlɪ) *n., pl.* **-lies.** **1.** exclusive control of the market supply of a product or service. **2. a.** an enterprise exercising this control. **b.** the product or service so controlled. **3.** *Law.* the exclusive right granted to a person or company by the state to trade in a specified commodity or area. **4.** exclusive control, possession, or use of something. [MONO- + Greek *pōlein* to sell] —moˈ**nopolist** *n.* —ˌ**monoˈpolistic** *adj.*

Monopoly (məˈnɒpəlɪ) *n. Trademark.* a board game for two to six players who deal in "property" as they move tokens around the board.

monorail (ˈmɒnəʊˌreɪl) *n.* a single-rail railway.

monosaccharide (ˌmɒnəʊˈsækəˌraɪd) *n.* a simple sugar, such as glucose, that cannot be broken down into other sugars.

monosodium glutamate (ˌmɒnəʊˈsəʊdɪəm ˈgluːtəˌmeɪt) *n.* a substance which enhances protein flavours: used as a food additive.

monosyllable (ˈmɒnəˌsɪləbᵊl) *n.* a word of one syllable. —**monosyllabic** (ˌmɒnəsɪˈlæbɪk) *adj.*

monotheism (ˈmɒnəʊθiːˌɪzəm) *n.* the belief or doctrine that there is only one God. —ˈ**mono**ˌ**theist** *n., adj.* —ˌ**monotheˈistic** *adj.*

monotone (ˈmɒnəˌtəʊn) *n.* **1.** a single unvaried pitch level in speech or sound. **2.** speech without change of pitch. **3.** lack of variety in style or expression. ~*adj.* **4.** unvarying.

monotonous (məˈnɒtənəs) *adj.* tedious, esp. because of repetition. —moˈ**notonously** *adv.*

monotony (məˈnɒtənɪ) *n., pl.* **-nies.** **1.** wearisome routine; dullness. **2.** lack of variety in pitch or cadence.

monovalent (ˌmɒnəʊˈveɪlənt) *adj. Chem.* **1.** having a valency of one. **2.** having only one valency. —ˌ**monoˈvalence** *or* ˌ**mono**ˈ**valency** *n.*

monoxide (mɒˈnɒksaɪd) *n.* an oxide that contains one oxygen atom per molecule.

Monseigneur (ˌmɒnsɛnˈjɜː) n., pl. **Messeigneurs** (ˌmeɪsɛnˈjɜː). a title given to French prelates and princes. [French, lit.: my lord]

monsieur (məsˈjɜː) n., pl. **messieurs.** a French title of address equivalent to *sir* or *Mr.* [lit.: my lord]

Monsignor (mɒnˈsiːnjə) n., pl. **Monsignors** or **Monsignori** (ˌmɒnsiːˈnjɔːrɪ). R.C. Church. an ecclesiastical title attached to certain offices. [Italian]

monsoon (mɒnˈsuːn) n. **1.** a seasonal wind of S Asia from the southwest in summer and from the northeast in winter. **2.** the rainy season when the SW monsoon blows, from about April to October. [Arabic *mawsim* season]

mons pubis (ˈmɒnz ˈpjuːbɪs) n., pl. **montes pubis** (ˈmɒntiːz). the fatty flesh in human males over the junction of the pubic bones. [New Latin: hill of the pubes]

monster (ˈmɒnstə) n. **1.** an imaginary beast, usually frightening in appearance. **2.** a person, animal, or plant with a marked deformity. **3.** a cruel, wicked, or inhuman person. **4.** a very large person, animal, or thing. [Latin *monstrum* portent]

monstrance (ˈmɒnstrəns) n. R.C. Church. a vessel in which the consecrated Host is exposed for adoration. [Latin *mōnstrāre* to show]

monstrosity (mɒnˈstrɒsɪtɪ) n., pl. **-ties. 1.** an outrageous or ugly person or thing. **2.** the state or quality of being monstrous.

monstrous (ˈmɒnstrəs) adj. **1.** hideous or unnatural in size or character. **2.** (of plants and animals) abnormal in structure. **3.** outrageous, atrocious, or shocking. **4.** huge. **5.** of or like a monster. —**ˈmonstrously** adv.

mons veneris (ˈmɒnz ˈvɛnərɪs) n., pl. **montes veneris** (ˈmɒntiːz). the fatty flesh in human females over the junction of the pubic bones. [New Latin: hill of Venus]

Mont. Montana.

montage (mɒnˈtɑːʒ) n. **1.** the creation of pictures from miscellaneous elements, such as other pictures or photographs. **2.** such a composition. **3.** a method of film editing by juxtaposition or partial superimposition of several shots to form a single image. **4.** a film sequence of this kind. [French]

month (mʌnθ) n. **1.** one of the twelve divisions (**calendar months**) of the calendar year. **2.** a period of time extending from one date to a corresponding date in the next calendar month. **3.** a period of four weeks or of 30 days. [Old English *mōnath*]

monthly (ˈmʌnθlɪ) adj. **1.** occurring, done, or payable once every month. **2.** lasting or valid for a month. ~adv. **3.** once a month. ~n., pl. **-lies. 4.** a book or periodical published once a month.

monument (ˈmɒnjʊmənt) n. **1.** something, such as a statue or building, erected in commemoration of a person or event. **2.** a tomb or tombstone. **3.** an exceptional example: *his lecture was a monument of tedium.* [Latin *monumentum*]

monumental (ˌmɒnjʊˈmɛntəl) adj. **1.** like a monument, esp. in large size, endurance, or importance. **2.** of or being a monument. **3.** *Informal.* extreme: *monumental stupidity.*

moo (muː) vb. **1.** (of a cow) to make a characteristic deep long sound; low. ~interj. **2.** this sound.

mooch (muːtʃ) vb. Slang. **1.** (often with *around*) to loiter or walk aimlessly. **2.** to cadge. [possibly Old French *muchier* to skulk]

mood[1] (muːd) n. **1.** a temporary state of mind or temper: *a cheerful mood.* **2.** a sullen or gloomy state of mind, esp. when temporary: *she's in a mood.* **3.** a prevailing atmosphere or feeling. **4. in the mood.** inclined to do or have (something). [Old English *mōd* mind, feeling]

mood[2] (muːd) n. Grammar. a form of a verb indicating whether the verb expresses a fact (indicative mood), a wish or supposition (subjunctive mood), or a command (imperative mood). [same as MOOD[1], influenced by *mode*]

moody (ˈmuːdɪ) adj. **moodier, moodiest. 1.** sullen, sulky, or gloomy. **2.** temperamental or changeable. —**ˈmoodily** adv. —**ˈmoodiness** n.

Moog (muːg) n. Music, trademark. a type of synthesizer. [after Robert *Moog*, engineer]

mooi (mɔɪ) adj. S. African slang. pleasing; nice. [Afrikaans]

mooli (ˈmuːlɪ) n. a type of large white radish. [E African native name]

moon (muːn) n. **1.** the natural satellite of the earth. **2.** this satellite as it is seen during its revolution around the earth, esp. at one of its phases: *new moon; full moon.* **3.** any natural satellite of a planet. **4.** a month. **5. over the moon.** *Informal.* extremely happy; ecstatic. ~vb. **6.** (often foll. by *away* or *around*) to be idle in a listless way or to idle (time) away. [Old English *mōna*] —**ˈmoonless** adj.

moonbeam (ˈmuːnˌbiːm) n. a ray of moonlight.

moon-faced adj. having a round face.

moonlight (ˈmuːnˌlaɪt) n. **1.** light from the sun received on earth after reflection by the moon. **2.** (modifier) illuminated by the moon: *a moonlight walk.* ~vb. **-lighting, -lighted. 3.** Informal. to work at a secondary job, esp. at night and illegally. —**ˈmoonˌlighter** n.

moonlight flit n. Brit. informal. a hurried departure at night to avoid paying rent.

moonlit (ˈmuːnlɪt) adj. illuminated by the moon.

moonscape (ˈmuːnˌskeɪp) n. the surface of the moon or a representation of it.

moonshine (ˈmuːnˌʃaɪn) n. **1.** moonlight. **2.** U.S. & Canad. illegally distilled or smuggled whisky. **3.** foolish talk or thought.

moonshot (ˈmuːnˌʃɒt) n. the launching of a spacecraft to the moon.

moonstone (ˈmuːnˌstəʊn) n. a white translucent form of feldspar, used as a gem.

moonstruck ('muːnˌstrʌk) *adj.* deranged or mad.

moony ('muːnɪ) *adj.* **moonier, mooniest.** *Informal.* dreamy or listless.

moor[1] (mʊə, mɔː) *n.* an expanse of open ground, usually covered with heather, coarse grass, and bracken. [Old English *mōr*]

moor[2] (mʊə, mɔː) *vb.* to secure (a ship or boat) with cables, ropes, or anchors or (of a ship or boat) to be secured in this way. [Germanic] —'**moorage** *n.*

Moor (mʊə, mɔː) *n.* a member of a Muslim people of North Africa who ruled Spain between the 8th and 15th centuries. [Greek *Mauros*] —'**Moorish** *adj.*

moorhen ('mʊəˌhɛn, 'mɔː-) *n.* a waterfowl with black plumage and a red bill.

mooring ('mʊərɪŋ, 'mɔː-) *n.* **1.** a place for anchoring a vessel. **2.** (*pl.*) *Naut.* the ropes and anchors used in mooring a vessel.

moorland ('mʊələnd) *n.* *Brit.* an area of moor.

moose (muːs) *n., pl.* **moose.** a large North American deer with large flattened antlers; the American elk. [American Indian]

moot (muːt) *adj.* **1.** subject or open to debate: *a moot point.* ~*vb.* **2.** to suggest or bring up for debate. ~*n.* **3.** (in Anglo-Saxon England) a local administrative assembly. [Old English *gemōt*]

mop (mɒp) *n.* **1.** a tool with a long handle and a head made of twists of cotton or sponge, used for washing or polishing floors, and for washing dishes. **2.** something resembling this, such as a tangle of hair. ~*vb.* **mopping, mopped. 3.** to clean or soak up as with a mop. ~See also **mop up.** [Latin *mappa* napkin]

mope (məʊp) *vb.* **1.** to be gloomy or apathetic. **2.** to move or act in an aimless way. ~*n.* **3.** a gloomy person. [possibly *mope* fool]

moped ('məʊpɛd) *n.* *Brit.* a light motor-cycle not over 50cc. [*motor* + *pedal*]

mopes (məʊps) *pl. n.* **the.** low spirits.

mopoke ('məʊˌpəʊk) *n.* **1.** a small spotted owl of Australia and New Zealand. **2.** *Austral. & N.Z. slang.* a slow or lugubrious person. [imit. of the bird's cry]

moppet ('mɒpɪt) *n.* same as **poppet.** [obs. *mop* rag doll]

mop up *vb.* **1.** to clean with a mop. **2.** *Informal.* to complete (a task). **3.** *Mil.* to clear (remaining enemy forces) after a battle, by killing them or taking them prisoner.

moquette (mɒ'kɛt) *n.* a thick velvety fabric used for carpets and upholstery. [French]

moraine (mɒ'reɪn) *n.* a mass of debris, carried by glaciers and forming ridges and mounds when deposited. [French]

moral ('mɒrəl) *adj.* **1.** concerned with or relating to the distinction between good and bad or right and wrong behaviour: *moral sense.* **2.** based on a sense of right and wrong: *moral duty.* **3.** having psychological rather than physical effects: *moral support.* ~*n.* **4.** the lesson to be obtained from a fable or event. **5.** (*pl.*) principles of behaviour in accordance with standards of right and wrong. [Latin *mōrālis* relating to morals or customs] —'**morally** *adv.*

morale (mɒ'rɑːl) *n.* the degree of confidence or optimism of a person or group. [French]

moralist ('mɒrəlɪst) *n.* **1.** a person who seeks to regulate the morals of others. **2.** a person who lives in accordance with moral principles. —ˌ**moral'istic** *adj.*

morality (mə'rælɪtɪ) *n., pl.* -**ties. 1.** the quality of being moral. **2.** conformity, or degree of conformity, to moral ideals. **3.** a system of moral principles.

morality play *n.* a medieval type of drama concerned with the conflict between personified virtues and vices.

moralize *or* -**lise** ('mɒrəˌlaɪz) *vb.* **1.** to make moral pronouncements. **2.** to interpret or explain in a moral sense. **3.** to improve the morals of.

moral philosophy *n.* the branch of philosophy dealing with morals.

morass (mə'ræs) *n.* **1.** a tract of swampy low-lying land. **2.** a disordered, confusing, or muddled state of affairs. [Old French *marais* marsh]

moratorium (ˌmɒrə'tɔːrɪəm) *n., pl.* -**ria** (-rɪə) *or* -**riums. 1.** a legally authorized postponement of the payment of a debt. **2.** an agreed suspension of activity. [Latin *mora* delay]

moray (mɒ'reɪ) *n.* a voracious marine coastal eel marked with brilliant colours. [Greek *muraina*]

morbid ('mɔːbɪd) *adj.* **1.** having an unusual interest in death or unpleasant events. **2.** gruesome. **3.** relating to or characterized by disease. [Latin *morbus* illness] —'**mor'bidity** *n.* —'**morbidly** *adv.*

mordant ('mɔːd'nt) *adj.* **1.** sarcastic or caustic. ~*n.* **2.** a substance used in dyeing to fix colours. **3.** an acid or other corrosive fluid used to etch lines on a printing plate. [Latin *mordēre* to bite]

more (mɔː) *det.* **1.** the comparative of **much** or **many**: *more joy than you know; even more are dying.* **2.** additional; further: *no more bananas.* **3. more of.** to a greater extent or degree: *more of a nuisance.* ~*adv.* **4.** used to form the comparative of some adjectives and adverbs: *more quickly.* **5.** the comparative of **much**: *people listen to the radio more now.* **6. more or less. a.** as an estimate; approximately. **b.** to an unspecified extent or degree: *the party was ruined, more or less.* [Old English *māra*]

moreish *or* **morish** ('mɔːrɪʃ) *adj.* *Informal.* (of food) causing a desire for more.

morel (mɒ'rɛl) *n.* an edible mushroom with a pitted cap. [French *morille*]

morello (mə'rɛləʊ) *n., pl.* -**los.** a variety of small dark sour cherry. [Italian *morello* blackish]

moreover (mɔː'rəʊvə) *adv.* in addition to what has already been said.

morepork ('mɔːˌpɔːk) *n.* *Chiefly N.Z.* same as **mopoke.**

mores ('mɔːreɪz) *pl. n.* the customs and conventions embodying the fundamental values of a community. [Latin: customs]

morganatic (ˌmɔːɡəˈnætɪk) *adj.* of or designating a marriage between a person of high rank and a person of low rank, by which the latter is not elevated to the higher rank and any children have no rights to inherit the higher party's titles or property. [Latin *morganáticum* morning-gift after consummation representing the husband's only liability]

morgue (mɔːɡ) *n.* **1.** a mortuary. **2.** *Informal.* a store of clippings and back numbers used for reference in a newspaper. [French]

moribund ('mɒrɪˌbʌnd) *adj.* **1.** near death. **2.** without force or vitality. [Latin *mori* to die]

Morisco (məˈrɪskəʊ) *n., pl.* **-cos** or **-coes.** **1.** a Spanish Moor. ~*adj.* **2.** Moorish. [Spanish *Moro* Moor]

morish ('mɔːrɪʃ) *adj.* same as **moreish.**

Mormon ('mɔːmən) *n.* **1.** a member of the Church of Jesus Christ of Latter-day Saints, founded in 1830 in New York by Joseph Smith. ~*adj.* **2.** of the Mormons, their Church, or their beliefs. —'**Mormonism** *n.*

morn (mɔːn) *n. Poetic.* morning. [Old English *morgen*]

mornay ('mɔːneɪ) *adj.* denoting a cheese sauce: *eggs mornay.* [after Philippe de *Mornay,* Huguenot leader]

morning ('mɔːnɪŋ) *n.* **1.** the first part of the day, ending at noon. **2.** daybreak; dawn. **3. the morning after.** *Informal.* the aftereffects of excess, esp. a hangover. **4.** (*modifier*) of or in the morning: *morning coffee.* [from *morn,* on the model of *evening*]

morning dress *n.* formal day dress for men, comprising a cutaway frock coat (**morning coat**), usually with grey trousers and top hat.

morning-glory *n., pl.* **-ries.** a tropical climbing plant with trumpet-shaped blue, pink, or white flowers, which close in late afternoon.

mornings ('mɔːnɪŋz) *adv. Informal.* in the morning, esp. regularly, or during every morning.

morning sickness *n.* nausea occurring shortly after rising in early pregnancy.

morning star *n.* a planet, usually Venus, seen just before sunrise.

Moroccan (məˈrɒkən) *adj.* **1.** of or denoting Morocco, a kingdom in NW Africa, or its inhabitants. ~*n.* **2.** a person from Morocco.

morocco (məˈrɒkəʊ) *n.* a fine soft leather made from goatskins. [after *Morocco,* where it was orig. made]

moron ('mɔːrɒn) *n.* **1.** a foolish or stupid person. **2.** a person having an intelligence quotient of between 50 and 70. [Greek *mōros* foolish] —**moronic** (məˈrɒnɪk) *adj.*

morose (məˈrəʊs) *adj.* ill-tempered or gloomy. [Latin *mōrōsus* peevish] —**mo-'rosely** *adv.*

morpheme ('mɔːfiːm) *n. Linguistics.* a speech element having a meaning or grammatical function that cannot be subdivided into further such elements.

morphine ('mɔːfiːn) *or* **morphia** ('mɔːfɪə) *n.* a drug extracted from opium: used in medicine as an anaesthetic and sedative. [*Morpheus,* in Greek myth, the god of sleep & dreams]

morphology (mɔːˈfɒlədʒɪ) *n.* the form and structure of anything, esp. organisms or words. —**morphological** (ˌmɔːfəˈlɒdʒɪkˀl) *adj.*

morris dance ('mɒrɪs) *n.* an old English folk dance usually performed by men (**morris men**) adorned with bells. [Middle English *moreys daunce* Moorish dance]

morrow ('mɒrəʊ) *n.* (usually preceded by *the*) *Archaic or poetic.* **1.** the next day. **2.** the morning. [Old English *morgen* morning]

Morse code (mɔːs) *n.* a code used internationally for transmitting messages. Letters and numbers are represented by groups of dots and dashes, or by shorter and longer sounds. [after Samuel *Morse,* inventor]

morsel ('mɔːsˀl) *n.* **1.** a small slice or mouthful of food. **2.** a small piece; bit. [Old French *mors* a bite]

mortal ('mɔːtˀl) *adj.* **1.** (of living beings, esp. humans) subject to death. **2.** of or involving life or the world. **3.** causing death; fatal: *a mortal blow.* **4.** deadly or unrelenting: *a mortal enemy.* **5.** of or like the fear of death: *mortal terror.* **6.** great or very intense: *mortal pain.* **7.** conceivable or possible: *there was no mortal reason to go.* **8.** *Slang.* long and tedious: *for three mortal hours.* ~*n.* **9.** a mortal being. **10.** *Informal.* a person: *a mean mortal.* [Latin *mors* death] —'**mortally** *adv.*

mortality (mɔːˈtælɪtɪ) *n., pl.* **-ties.** **1.** the condition of being mortal. **2.** great loss of life, as in war or disaster. **3.** the number of deaths in a given period.

mortal sin *n. Christianity.* a sin regarded as involving total loss of grace.

mortar ('mɔːtə) *n.* **1.** a mixture of cement or lime or both with sand and water, used as a bond between bricks or stones. **2.** a cannon with a short barrel that fires shells in high arcs. **3.** a vessel, usually bowl-shaped, in which substances are crushed with a pestle. ~*vb.* **4.** to join (bricks or stones) with mortar. **5.** to fire on with mortars. [Latin *mortárium* basin in which mortar is mixed]

mortarboard ('mɔːtəˌbɔːd) *n.* **1.** a black tasselled academic cap with a flat square top. **2.** a small square board with a handle on the underside for carrying mortar.

mortgage ('mɔːɡɪdʒ) *n.* **1.** a conditional pledging of property, such as a house, as security for the repayment of a loan. **2.** the deed effecting such a transaction. **3.** the loan itself. ~*vb.* **4.** to convey (property) by mortgage. [Old French, lit.: dead pledge]

mortician (mɔːˈtɪʃən) n. Chiefly U.S. same as **undertaker**.

mortify (ˈmɔːtɪˌfaɪ) vb. **-fying, -fied. 1.** to humiliate or cause to feel shame. **2.** Christianity. to subdue and bring under control (one's emotions, the body, etc.) by self-denial. **3.** to become gangrenous. [Latin mors death + facere to do] —**mortification** (ˌmɔːtɪfɪˈkeɪʃən) n. —ˈmortiˌfying adj.

mortise or **mortice** (ˈmɔːtɪs) n. **1.** a slot or recess cut into a piece of wood or stone to receive a matching projection (tenon) on another piece, or a mortise lock. ~vb. **2.** to cut a slot or recess in (a piece of wood or stone) **3.** to join (two pieces of wood or stone) by means of a mortise and tenon. [Old French mortoise]

mortise lock n. a lock set into the edge of a door so that the mechanism of the lock is enclosed by the door.

mortuary (ˈmɔːtjʊərɪ) n., pl. **-aries.** a building where dead bodies are kept before cremation or burial. [Latin mortuārius of the dead]

mosaic (məˈzeɪɪk) n. a design or decoration made up of small pieces of coloured glass or stone. [Greek mousikē (an art) presided over by the Muses]

Mosaic (məˈzeɪɪk) adj. of or relating to Moses or the laws and traditions ascribed to him.

moselle (məʊˈzɛl) n. a German white wine from the valley of the river Moselle.

mosey (ˈməʊzɪ) vb. Informal. (often foll. by along or on) to amble. [origin unknown]

Moslem (ˈmɒzləm) n., pl. **-lems** or **-lem,** adj. same as **Muslim**.

mosque (mɒsk) n. a Muslim place of worship. [Arabic masjid temple]

mosquito (məˈskiːtəʊ) n., pl. **-toes** or **-tos.** a two-winged insect, the females of which pierce the skin of man and animals to suck their blood. [Spanish, diminutive of mosca fly]

mosquito net n. a fine curtain or net to keep mosquitoes out.

moss (mɒs) n. **1.** a very small flowerless plant typically growing in dense mats on trees, rocks, or moist ground. **2.** Scot. & N English. a peat bog or marsh. [Old English mos swamp] —ˈmossy adj.

mossie (ˈmɒsɪ) n. same as **cape sparrow**.

moss rose n. a variety of rose that has a mossy stem and fragrant pink flowers.

most (məʊst) det. **1.** a great majority of; nearly all: most of it is finished. **2. the most.** the superlative of **many** and **much**: you have the most money. **3. at (the) most.** at the maximum: that girl is four at the most. **4. make the most of.** to use to the best advantage: she made the most of the chance. ~adv. **5. the most.** used to form the superlative of some adjectives and adverbs: the most beautiful daughter of all. **6.** the superlative of **much. 7.** very; exceedingly: a most absurd story. [Old English mǣst or mǣst]

mostly (ˈməʊstlɪ) adv. **1.** almost entirely; chiefly. **2.** on many or most occasions; usually.

Most Reverend n. (in Britain) a courtesy title applied to archbishops.

mot (məʊ) n. short for **bon mot**. [French: word]

MOT 1. Brit. & N.Z. Ministry of Transport (Brit., now Transport Industries). **2.** Brit. the MOT test or test certificate.

mote (məʊt) n. a tiny speck. [Old English mot]

motel (məʊˈtɛl) n. a roadside hotel for motorists. [motor + hotel]

motet (məʊˈtɛt) n. a polyphonic religious song for choir. [Old French, diminutive of mot word]

moth (mɒθ) n. any of numerous chiefly nocturnal insects resembling butterflies, that typically have stout bodies with antennae of various shapes (but not clubbed). [Old English moththe]

mothball (ˈmɒθˌbɔːl) n. **1.** a small ball of camphor or naphthalene placed in stored clothing to repel clothes moths. **2. put in mothballs.** to postpone work on (a project or activity). ~vb. **3.** to take (something) out of operation but maintain it for future use. **4.** to postpone work on (a project or activity).

moth-eaten adj. **1.** decayed, decrepit, or outdated. **2.** eaten away by or as if by moths.

mother (ˈmʌðə) n. **1.** a female who has given birth to offspring. **2.** (often cap., esp. as a term of address) a person's own mother. **3.** motherly qualities, such as maternal affection: it appealed to the mother in her. **4.** a female or thing that creates, nurtures, or protects something. **5.** a title given to certain members of female religious orders. **6.** (modifier) native or innate: mother wit. ~vb. **7.** to give birth to or produce. **8.** to nurture or protect. [Old English mōdor] —ˈmotherless adj. —ˈmotherly adj.

Mother Carey's chicken (ˈkɛərɪz) n. same as **stormy petrel**. [origin unknown]

mother country n. **1.** the original country of colonists or settlers. **2.** a person's native country.

Mother Goose n. the imaginary author of a collection of nursery rhymes. [translated from French Contes de ma mère l'Oye (1697)]

motherhood (ˈmʌðəˌhʊd) n. the state of being a mother.

Mothering Sunday (ˈmʌðərɪŋ) n. Brit. the fourth Sunday in Lent, when mothers traditionally receive presents from their children. Also called: **Mother's Day**.

mother-in-law n., pl. **mothers-in-law.** the mother of one's wife or husband.

motherland (ˈmʌðəˌlænd) n. a person's native country.

mother-of-pearl n. a hard iridescent substance that forms the inner layer of the shells of certain molluscs, such as the oyster.

Mother's Day n. **1.** See **Mothering Sunday. 2.** U.S. & Canad. the second Sunday in May, observed as a day in honour of mothers.

mother superior *n., pl.* **mother superiors** or **mothers superior.** the head of a community of nuns.

mother tongue *n.* the language first learned by a child.

mothproof ('mɒθ,pruːf) *adj.* **1.** (esp. of clothes) chemically treated so as to repel clothes moths. ~*vb.* **2.** to make mothproof.

motif (məʊ'tiːf) *n.* **1.** a distinctive idea, esp. a theme elaborated on in a piece of music or literature. **2.** a recurring shape in a design. **3.** a single decoration, such as a symbol or name on a piece of clothing. [French: motive]

motion ('məʊʃən) *n.* **1.** the process of continual change in the position of an object; movement. **2.** a movement or action, esp. of part of the human body; a gesture. **3. a.** the capacity for movement. **b.** a manner of movement, esp. walking; gait. **4.** a formal proposal to be discussed and voted on in a debate or meeting. **5.** *Brit.* **a.** the evacuation of the bowels. **b.** excrement. **6. go through the motions.** to do something mechanically or without sincerity. **7. set in motion.** to make operational or start functioning. ~*vb.* **8.** to signal or direct (a person) by a movement or gesture. [Latin *movēre* to move] —'**motionless** *adj.*

motion picture *n. U.S. & Canad.* a film; movie.

motivate ('məʊtɪ,veɪt) *vb.* to give incentive to. —,**moti'vation** *n.*

motive ('məʊtɪv) *n.* **1.** the reason for a certain course of action, whether conscious or unconscious. **2.** same as **motif** (sense 2). ~*adj.* **3.** of or causing motion: *a motive force.* [Late Latin *mōtīvus* moving]

motive power *n.* **1.** any source of energy used to produce motion. **2.** the means of supplying power to an engine or vehicle.

mot juste (,məʊ 'ʒuːst) *n., pl.* **mots justes** (,məʊ 'ʒuːst). the appropriate word or expression. [French]

motley ('mɒtlɪ) *adj.* **1.** made up of disparate elements. **2.** multicoloured. ~*n.* **3.** *History.* the costume of a jester. [perhaps Old English *mot* speck]

motocross ('məʊtə,krɒs) *n.* the sport of motorcycle racing across rough ground. [*moto(r)* + *cross(-country)*]

motor ('məʊtə) *n.* **1.** the engine, esp. an internal-combustion engine, of a vehicle. **2.** a machine that converts energy, esp. electrical energy, into mechanical energy. **3.** *Chiefly Brit.* a car. ~*adj.* **4.** producing or causing motion. **5.** powered by or relating to a motor. ~*vb.* **6.** to travel by car. **7.** *Informal.* to move fast. [Latin *movēre* to move] —'**moto,rize** *or* **-ise** *vb.*

motorbicycle ('məʊtə,baɪsɪk²l) *n.* **1.** a motorcycle. **2.** a moped.

motorbike ('məʊtə,baɪk) *n. Informal.* a motorcycle.

motorboat ('məʊtə,bəʊt) *n.* any boat powered by a motor.

motorcade ('məʊtə,keɪd) *n.* a procession of cars carrying important people. [*motor* + (*caval*)*cade*]

motorcar ('məʊtə,kɑː) *n.* a more formal word for **car.**

motorcycle ('məʊtə,saɪk²l) *n.* a two-wheeled vehicle that is driven by a petrol engine. —'**motor,cyclist** *n.*

motorist ('məʊtərɪst) *n.* a driver of a car.

motorman ('məʊtəmən) *n., pl.* **-men.** the driver of an electric train.

motor scooter *n.* a light motorcycle with small wheels and an enclosed engine.

motor vehicle *n.* a road vehicle driven by an engine.

motorway ('məʊtə,weɪ) *n. Brit.* a dual carriageway for fast-moving traffic, with no stopping permitted and no crossroads.

Motown ('məʊ,taʊn) *n.* music combining rhythm and blues and pop. [*Mo(tor) Town*, nickname for Detroit]

motte (mɒt) *n. History.* a mound on which a castle was built. [Old French]

MOT test *n.* (in Britain) a compulsory annual test of the roadworthiness of motor vehicles over a certain age.

mottle ('mɒt²l) *vb.* to colour with streaks or blotches of different shades. [from *motley*] —'**mottled** *adj.*

motto ('mɒtəʊ) *n., pl.* **-toes** *or* **-tos.** **1.** a short saying expressing the guiding maxim or ideal of a family or organization, esp. when part of a coat of arms. **2.** a verse or maxim contained in a paper cracker. **3.** a quotation prefacing a book or chapter of a book. [Italian]

mould[1] *or U.S.* **mold** (məʊld) *n.* **1.** a shaped cavity used to give a definite form to fluid or plastic material. **2.** a frame on which something may be constructed. **3.** something made in or on a mould. **4.** shape, form, design, or pattern. **5.** specific nature, character, or type. ~*vb.* **6.** to make in a mould. **7.** to shape or form, as by using a mould. **8.** to influence or direct: *to mould opinion.* [Latin *modulus* a small measure]

mould[2] *or U.S.* **mold** (məʊld) *n.* a coating or discoloration caused by various fungi that develop in a damp atmosphere on food, fabrics, and walls. [Northern English dialect *mowlde* mouldy]

mould[3] *or U.S.* **mold** (məʊld) *n.* loose soil, esp. when rich in organic matter. [Old English *molde*]

mouldboard *or U.S.* **moldboard** ('məʊld,bɔːd) *n.* the curved blade of a plough, which turns over the furrow.

moulder *or U.S.* **molder** ('məʊldə) *vb.* (often foll. by *away*) to crumble or cause to crumble, as through decay. [from MOULD[2]]

moulding *or U.S.* **molding** ('məʊldɪŋ) *n.* **1.** a shaped outline, such as one used on cornices. **2.** a shaped strip made of wood or stone.

mouldy *or U.S.* **moldy** ('məʊldɪ) *adj.* **-dier, -diest.** **1.** covered with mould. **2.** stale or musty, esp. from age or lack of use. **3.** *Slang.* boring; dull.

moult *or U.S.* **molt** (məʊlt) *vb.* **1.** (of birds and animals) to shed (feathers, hair, or cuticle) so that they can be replaced by a new growth. ~n. **2.** the periodic process of moulting. [Latin *mūtāre* to change]

mound (maʊnd) *n.* **1.** a raised mass of earth, debris, etc. **2.** any heap or pile. **3.** a small natural hill. **4.** an artificial ridge of earth, stone, etc., as used for defence. [origin unknown]

mount¹ (maʊnt) *vb.* **1.** to climb or ascend (stairs or a slope). **2.** to get up on (a horse, a platform, etc.). **3.** (often foll. by *up*) to increase; accumulate: *excitement mounted.* **4.** to fix onto a backing, setting, or support: *to mount a photograph.* **5.** to organize and stage (a campaign, a play, etc.). ~n. **6.** a backing, setting, or support onto which something is fixed. **7.** a horse for riding. [same as MOUNT²]

mount² (maʊnt) *n.* a mountain or hill: used in literature and (when cap.) in proper names: *Mount Everest.* [Latin *mons* mountain]

mountain (ˈmaʊntɪn) *n.* **1.** a natural upward projection of the earth's surface, higher and steeper than a hill. **2.** a huge heap or mass: *a mountain of papers.* **3.** anything of great quantity or size. **4.** a surplus of a commodity, esp. in the European Community: *a butter mountain.* [Latin *mons*]

mountain ash *n.* any of various trees, such as the rowan, with clusters of small white flowers and bright red berries.

mountain bike *n.* a type of bicycle with straight handlebars and heavy-duty tyres.

mountain cat *n.* any of various wild feline mammals, such as the bobcat, lynx, or puma.

mountaineer (ˌmaʊntɪˈnɪə) *n.* **1.** a person who climbs mountains. ~vb. **2.** to climb mountains. —ˌmountainˈeering *n.*

mountain goat *n.* any wild goat inhabiting mountainous regions.

mountain lion *n.* a puma.

mountainous (ˈmaʊntɪnəs) *adj.* **1.** having many mountains: *a mountainous region.* **2.** like a mountain, esp. in size.

mountain sickness *n.* nausea, headache, and shortness of breath caused by climbing to high altitudes.

mountebank (ˈmaʊntɪˌbæŋk) *n.* **1.** (formerly) a person who sold quack medicines in public places. **2.** a charlatan; fake. [Italian *montambanco* a climber on a bench]

mounted (ˈmaʊntɪd) *adj.* riding horses: *mounted police.*

Mountie or **Mounty** (ˈmaʊntɪ) *n., pl.* **Mounties.** *Informal.* a member of the Royal Canadian Mounted Police. [from *mounted*]

mounting (ˈmaʊntɪŋ) *n.* same as **mount¹** (sense 6).

mourn (mɔːn) *vb.* to feel or express sadness for the death or loss of (someone or something). [Old English *murnan*] —ˈmourner *n.*

mournful (ˈmɔːnfʊl) *adj.* **1.** evoking grief; sorrowful. **2.** gloomy; sad. —ˈmournfully *adv.*

mourning (ˈmɔːnɪŋ) *n.* **1.** sorrow or grief, esp. over a death. **2.** the conventional symbols of grief, such as the wearing of black. **3.** the period of time during which a death is officially mourned. ~adj. **4.** of or relating to mourning.

mouse *n.* (maʊs), *pl.* **mice** (maɪs). **1.** any of numerous small long-tailed rodents that are similar to but smaller than rats. **2.** a quiet, timid, or cowardly person. **3.** *Computers.* a hand-held device used to control cursor movements and computing functions without keying. ~vb. (maʊz). **4.** to stalk and catch (mice). [Old English *mūs*]

mouser (ˈmaʊzə, ˈmaʊsə) *n.* a cat or other animal that is used to catch mice.

mousetrap (ˈmaʊsˌtræp) *n.* **1.** a spring-loaded trap for killing mice. **2.** *Brit. informal.* cheese of indifferent quality.

moussaka (muˈsɑːkə) *n.* a dish originating in the Balkan States, consisting of meat, aubergines, and tomatoes, topped with cheese sauce. [Modern Greek]

mousse (muːs) *n.* **1.** a light creamy dessert made with eggs, cream, and fruit set with gelatin. **2.** a similar dish made from fish or meat. **3.** short for **styling mousse.** [French: froth]

moustache or *U.S.* **mustache** (məˈstɑːʃ) *n.* unshaved hair growing on the upper lip. [French, from Italian *mostaccio*]

mousy or **mousey** (ˈmaʊsɪ) *adj.* **mousier**, **mousiest.** **1.** resembling a mouse, esp. in hair colour. **2.** shy or ineffectual. —ˈmousiness *n.*

mouth *n.* (maʊθ), *pl.* **mouths** (maʊðz). **1.** the opening through which many animals take in food and issue vocal sounds. **2.** the visible part of the mouth; lips. **3.** a person regarded as a consumer of food: *four mouths to feed.* **4.** a particular manner of speaking: *a foul mouth.* **5.** *Informal.* boastful, rude, or excessive talk: *he is all mouth.* **6.** the point where a river issues into a sea or lake. **7.** an opening, such as that of a bottle, tunnel, or gun. **8. down in the mouth.** in low spirits. ~vb. (maʊð). **9.** to speak or say (something) insincerely, esp. in public. **10.** to form (words) with movements of the lips but without speaking. [Old English *mūth*]

mouthful (ˈmaʊθˌfʊl) *n., pl.* **-fuls.** **1.** as much as is held in the mouth at one time. **2.** a small quantity, as of food. **3.** a long word or phrase that is difficult to say. **4.** *Brit. informal.* an abusive response.

mouth organ *n.* same as **harmonica.**

mouthpiece (ˈmaʊθˌpiːs) *n.* **1.** the part of a wind instrument into which the player blows. **2.** the part of a telephone receiver into which a person speaks. **3.** a person or publication expressing the views of an organization.

mouthwash (ˈmaʊθˌwɒʃ) *n.* a medicated solution for gargling and cleansing the mouth.

mouthwatering (ˈmaʊθˌwɔːtərɪŋ) *adj.* (of food) making one want to eat it, because it looks or smells delicious.

movable or **moveable** (ˈmuːvəbᵊl) *adj.* **1.** able to be moved; not fixed. **2.** (of a festival, esp. Easter) varying in date from year to year. ~*n.* **3.** (*often pl.*) a movable article, esp. a piece of furniture.

move (muːv) *vb.* **1.** to go or take from one place to another; change in position. **2.** to change (one's dwelling or place of business). **3.** to be or cause to be in motion; stir. **4.** (of machines) to work or operate. **5.** to cause (to do something); prompt: *public opinion moved the government to action.* **6.** to begin to act: *move soon or we'll lose the order.* **7.** to associate oneself with a specified social circle: *to move in exalted spheres.* **8.** to make progress. **9.** to arouse affection, pity, or compassion in; touch. **10.** (in board games) to change the position of (a piece). **11.** (of merchandise) to be disposed of by being bought. **12.** to suggest (a proposal) formally, as in debating or parliamentary procedure. **13.** to cause (the bowels) to evacuate or (of the bowels) to be evacuated. ~*n.* **14.** the act of moving; movement. **15.** one of a sequence of actions, usually part of a plan; manoeuvre. **16.** the act of moving one's residence or place of business. **17.** (in board games) **a.** a player's turn to move his piece. **b.** a manoeuvre of a piece. **18. get a move on.** *Informal.* to hurry up. **19. on the move.** travelling from place to place. [Latin *movēre*]

move in *vb.* **1.** Also: **move into.** to start to live or be based in (a new residence or place of business). **2.** (*often foll. by on*) *Informal.* to try to gain power or influence (over).

movement ('muːvmənt) *n.* **1.** the act, process, or an instance of moving. **2.** the manner of moving. **3. a.** a group of people with a common ideology. **b.** the organized action of such a group. **4.** a trend or tendency. **5.** the driving and regulating mechanism of a watch or clock. **6.** (*often pl.*) a person's location and activities during a specific time. **7. a.** the evacuation of the bowels. **b.** the matter evacuated. **8.** *Music.* a principal self-contained section of a large-scale work, such as a symphony.

mover ('muːvə) *n.* **1.** *Informal.* a person, business, idea, etc., that is advancing or progressing. **2.** a person who moves a proposal, as in a debate. **3.** *U.S. & Canad.* a removal firm or a person who works for one.

movie ('muːvɪ) *n. Informal.* same as **film** (sense 1).

moving ('muːvɪŋ) *adj.* **1.** arousing or touching the emotions. **2.** changing or capable of changing position. —'**movingly** *adv.*

moving staircase *or* **stairway** *n.* an escalator.

mow (məʊ) *vb.* **mowing, mowed, mowed** *or* **mown.** **1.** to cut down (grass or crops). **2.** to cut the growing vegetation of (a field or lawn). [Old English *māwan*] —'**mower** *n.*

mow down *vb.* to kill in large numbers, esp. by gunfire.

mown (məʊn) *vb.* the past participle of **mow.**

mozzarella (ˌmɒtsə'rɛlə) *n.* a moist white curd cheese originally made in Italy from buffalo milk. [Italian]

mp *Music.* moderately soft. [Italian *mezzo piano*]

MP 1. Member of Parliament. **2.** Military Police. **3.** Mounted Police.

mpg miles per gallon.

mph miles per hour.

MPhil Master of Philosophy.

Mr ('mɪstə) *n., pl.* **Messrs.** a title used before a man's name or before some office that he holds: *Mr Brown; Mr President.* [from *mister*]

Mrs ('mɪsɪz) *n., pl.* **Mrs** *or* **Mesdames.** a title used before the name of a married woman. [from *mistress*]

Ms (mɪz) *n.* a title used before the name of a woman to avoid indicating whether she is married or not.

MS 1. Mississippi. **2.** multiple sclerosis.

MS. *or* **ms.,** *pl.* **MSS.** *or* **mss.** manuscript.

MSc Master of Science.

MSC (in Britain) Manpower Services Commission.

MSG monosodium glutamate.

MST (in the U.S. and Canada) Mountain Standard Time.

Mt Mount: *Mt Everest.*

MT Montana.

MTech (in the U.S. and Canada) Master of Technology.

much (mʌtʃ) *det.* **1.** (*usually used with a negative*) a great quantity or degree of: *there isn't much honey left.* **2.** *Informal.* rather excessive. **3. make much of. a.** (*used with a negative*) to make sense of: *he couldn't make much of her babble.* **b.** to give importance to: *she made much of this fact.* **4. not much of.** not to any appreciable degree or extent: *he's not much of an actor.* **5. not up to much.** *Informal.* of a low standard: *this beer is not up to much.* ~*adv.* **6.** considerably: *they're much better now.* **7.** practically; nearly: *it's much the same.* **8.** (*usually used with a negative*) often; a great deal: *it doesn't happen much in this country.* **9.** (**as**) **much as.** even though; although: *much as I'd like to, I can't come.* ~See also **more** and **most.** [Old English *mycel*]

muchness ('mʌtʃnɪs) *n.* **much of a muchness.** *Brit.* very similar.

mucilage ('mjuːsɪlɪdʒ) *n.* **1.** a sticky preparation, such as gum, used as an adhesive. **2.** a glutinous substance secreted by certain plants. [Late Latin *mūcilāgo* mouldy juice] —**mucilaginous** (ˌmjuːsɪ-'lædʒɪnəs) *adj.*

muck (mʌk) *n.* **1.** farmyard dung or decaying vegetable matter. **2.** dirt or filth. **3.** *Slang, chiefly Brit.* rubbish. **4. make a muck of.** *Slang, chiefly Brit.* to ruin or spoil. ~*vb.* **5.** to spread manure upon (fields). **6.** to soil or pollute. **7.** (*usually foll. by up*) *Brit. slang.* to ruin or spoil. **8.** (*often foll. by out*) to clear muck from. [prob. Old Norse] —'**mucky** *adj.*

muck about *vb. Brit. slang.* **1.** to waste time; misbehave. **2.** (*often foll. by with*) to interfere with, annoy, or waste the time of.

muck in *vb. Brit. slang.* to share duties or work (with other people).

muckraking ('mʌk,reɪkɪŋ) n. seeking out and exposing scandal concerning public figures. —**'muck,raker** n.

mucksweat ('mʌk,swɛt) n. Brit. informal. profuse sweat.

mucous membrane n. a mucus-secreting membrane that lines body cavities or passages.

mucus ('mjuːkəs) n. the slimy protective secretion of the mucous membranes. [Latin: nasal secretions] —**mucosity** (mjuːˈkɒsɪtɪ) n. —**'mucous** adj.

mud (mʌd) n. 1. soft wet earth, as found on the ground after rain or at the bottom of ponds. 2. (**someone's**) **name is mud.** Informal. (someone) is disgraced. 3. **throw mud at.** Informal. slander; vilify. ~adj. 4. made from mud or dried mud. [prob. Low German mudde]

mud bath n. 1. a medicinal bath in heated mud. 2. a dirty or muddy occasion or state.

muddle ('mʌdˀl) vb. 1. (often foll. by up) to mix up (objects or items). 2. to confuse. ~n. 3. a state of physical or mental confusion. [possibly Middle Dutch moddelen to make muddy] —**'muddled** adj.

muddleheaded (,mʌdˀl'hɛdɪd) adj. mentally confused or vague.

muddle through vb. Chiefly Brit. to succeed in spite of lack of organization.

muddy ('mʌdɪ) adj. **-dier, -diest.** 1. covered or filled with mud. 2. not clear or bright: muddy colours. 3. cloudy: a muddy liquid. 4. (esp. of thoughts) confused or vague. ~vb. **-dying, -died.** 5. to become or cause to become muddy. —**'muddily** adv. —**'muddiness** n.

mud flat n. an area of low muddy land that is covered at high tide but not at low tide.

mud flow n. the rapid downhill movement of a mass of mud, typically in the shape of a tongue.

mudguard ('mʌd,gɑːd) n. a curved part of a bicycle or other vehicle attached above the wheels to reduce the amount of water or mud thrown up by them.

mudpack ('mʌd,pæk) n. a cosmetic astringent paste containing fuller's earth.

mudslinging ('mʌd,slɪŋɪŋ) n. casting malicious slurs on an opponent, esp. in politics. —**'mud,slinger** n.

muesli ('mjuːzlɪ) n. a mixture of rolled oats, nuts, and fruit, eaten with milk. [Swiss German]

muezzin (muːˈɛzɪn) n. Islam. the official of a mosque who calls the faithful to prayer from the minaret. [Arabic mu'adhdhin]

muff[1] (mʌf) n. an open-ended cylinder of fur or cloth into which the hands are placed for warmth. [prob. Dutch mof]

muff[2] (mʌf) vb. 1. to perform (an action) awkwardly. 2. to bungle (a shot or catch). [origin unknown]

muffin ('mʌfɪn) n. 1. Brit. a thick round baked yeast roll, usually toasted and served with butter. 2. U.S. & Canad. a

small cup-shaped sweet bread roll, usually eaten hot with butter. [origin unknown]

muffin man n. Brit. (formerly) an itinerant seller of muffins.

muffle ('mʌfˀl) vb. 1. (often foll. by up) to wrap up in a scarf or coat esp. for warmth. 2. to deaden (a sound or noise), esp. by wrapping. 3. to prevent (the expression of something) by (someone). [prob. Old French moufle mitten]

muffler ('mʌflə) n. 1. a thick scarf worn for warmth. 2. U.S. & Canad. a device to deaden sound, esp. one on a car exhaust; silencer.

mufti ('mʌftɪ) n. civilian dress, esp. as worn by a person who normally wears a military uniform. [Arabic]

mug[1] (mʌg) n. 1. a large drinking cup with a handle, usually cylindrical and made of earthenware. 2. Also called: **mugful.** the quantity held by a mug or its contents. [prob. Scandinavian]

mug[2] (mʌg) n. 1. Slang. a person's face or mouth. 2. Slang. a gullible person, esp. one who is swindled easily. 3. **a mug's game.** a worthless activity. ~vb. **mugging, mugged.** 4. Informal. to attack or rob (someone) violently. [possibly same as MUG[1]] —**'mugger** n.

muggins ('mʌgɪnz) n. (functioning as sing.) Brit. slang. **a.** a simpleton. **b.** a title used humorously to refer to oneself. [prob. from surname Muggins]

muggy ('mʌgɪ) adj. **-gier, -giest.** (of weather or air) unpleasantly warm and humid. [dialect mug drizzle] —**'mugginess** n.

mug shot n. Informal. a photograph of a person's face, esp. one resembling a police-file picture.

mug up vb. Brit. slang. to study (a subject) hard, esp. for an exam. [origin unknown]

Muhammadan (muˈhæməd'n) n., adj. (not in Muslim use) same as **Muslim.**

mujaheddin or **mujahedeen** (,muːdʒə-hə'diːn) pl. n. (preceded by the) fundamentalist Muslim guerrillas. [Arabic mujāhi-dīn fighters]

mukluk ('mʌklʌk) n. a soft boot, usually of sealskin, worn by Inuits. [Eskimo muklok large seal]

mulatto (mjuːˈlætəʊ) n., pl. **-tos** or **-toes.** a person having one Black and one White parent. [Spanish mulato young mule]

mulberry ('mʌlbərɪ, -brɪ) n., pl. **-ries.** 1. a tree with edible blackberry-like fruit, the leaves of which are used to feed silkworms. 2. the fruit of any of these trees. ~adj. 3. dark purple. [Latin mōrum mulberry]

mulch (mʌltʃ) n. 1. a mixture of half-rotten vegetable matter and peat used to protect the roots of plants or enrich the soil. ~vb. 2. to cover (the surface of land) with mulch. [obs. mulch soft]

mule[1] (mjuːl) n. 1. the sterile offspring of a male donkey and a female horse, used as a beast of burden. 2. a machine that spins cotton into yarn. [Latin mūlus]

mule[2] (mjuːl) n. a backless shoe or slipper. [Latin mulleus a magistrate's shoe]

muleteer (ˌmjuːlɪˈtɪə) *n.* a person who drives mules.

mulish (ˈmjuːlɪʃ) *adj.* stubborn; obstinate.

mull[1] (mʌl) *vb.* (often foll. by *over*) to study or ponder. [prob. from *muddle*]

mull[2] (mʌl) *vb.* to heat (wine or ale) with sugar and spices. [origin unknown] —**mulled** *adj.*

mull[3] (mʌl) *n. Scot.* a promontory. [prob. Gaelic *maol*]

mullah (ˈmʊlə) *n.* (formerly) a Muslim scholar, teacher, or religious leader. [Arabic *mawlā* master]

mullet (ˈmʌlɪt) *n.* any of various marine food fishes such as the red mullet. [Greek *mullos*]

mulligatawny (ˌmʌlɪɡəˈtɔːnɪ) *n.* a curry-flavoured soup of Anglo-Indian origin. [Tamil *milakutanni* pepper water]

mullion (ˈmʌlɪən) *n.* a slender vertical bar between the casements or panes of a window. [Old French *moinel*] —**mullioned** *adj.*

multi- *combining form.* **1.** many or much: *multimillion.* **2.** more than one: *multistorey.* [Latin *multus* much, many]

multicoloured (ˌmʌltɪˈkʌləd) *adj.* having many colours.

multicultural (ˌmʌltɪˈkʌltʃərəl) *adj.* of or for the cultures of several different races.

multifarious (ˌmʌltɪˈfɛərɪəs) *adj.* having many parts of great variety. [Late Latin *multifārius* manifold]

multiflora rose (ˌmʌltɪˈflɔːrə) *n.* a climbing rose with clusters of small fragrant flowers.

multiform (ˈmʌltɪˌfɔːm) *adj.* having many shapes or forms.

multilateral (ˌmʌltɪˈlætərəl) *adj.* **1.** of or involving more than two nations or parties: *a multilateral pact.* **2.** having many sides.

multilingual (ˌmʌltɪˈlɪŋɡwəl) *adj.* **1.** able to speak more than two languages. **2.** written or expressed in more than two languages.

multimedia (ˌmʌltɪˈmiːdɪə) *pl. n.* the combined use of media such as television and slides.

multimillionaire (ˌmʌltɪˌmɪljəˈnɛə) *n.* a person with a fortune of several million pounds, dollars, etc.

multinational (ˌmʌltɪˈnæʃənˀl) *adj.* **1.** (of a large business company) operating in several countries. ~*n.* **2.** such a company.

multiparous (mʌlˈtɪpərəs) *adj.* producing many offspring at one birth. [New Latin *multiparus*]

multiple (ˈmʌltɪpˀl) *adj.* **1.** having or involving more than one part, individual, or element. ~*n.* **2.** the product of a given number or polynomial and any other one: *6 is a multiple of 2.* [Latin *multiplus*] —**ˈmultiply** *adv.*

multiple-choice *adj.* having a number of possible answers given from which the correct one must be chosen.

multiple sclerosis *n.* a chronic progressive disease of the central nervous system, resulting in speech and visual disorders,

multiplex (ˈmʌltɪˌplɛks) *adj.* having many elements; complex. [Latin: having many folds]

multiplicand (ˌmʌltɪplɪˈkænd) *n.* a number to be multiplied by another number, the **multiplier.**

multiplication (ˌmʌltɪplɪˈkeɪʃən) *n.* **1.** a mathematical operation, equivalent to adding a number to itself a specified number of times. For instance, 4 multiplied by 3 equals 12 (i.e. 4+4+4). **2.** the act of multiplying or state of being multiplied.

multiplication sign *n.* the symbol ×, placed between numbers to be multiplied.

multiplication table *n.* a table giving the results of multiplying two numbers together.

multiplicity (ˌmʌltɪˈplɪsɪtɪ) *n., pl.* **-ties. 1.** a large number or great variety. **2.** the state of being multiple.

multiplier (ˈmʌltɪˌplaɪə) *n.* a number by which another number (the **multiplicand**) is multiplied.

multiply (ˈmʌltɪˌplaɪ) *vb.* **-plying, -plied. 1.** to increase or cause to increase in number, quantity, or degree. **2.** to combine (two numbers or quantities) by multiplication. **3.** to increase in number by reproduction. [Latin *multiplicāre*]

multipurpose (ˌmʌltɪˈpɜːpəs) *adj.* having many uses: *a multipurpose gadget.*

multiracial (ˌmʌltɪˈreɪʃəl) *adj.* comprising people of many races. —ˌmulti'racial·ism *n.*

multistage (ˈmʌltɪˌsteɪdʒ) *adj.* (of a rocket or missile) having several stages, each of which can be jettisoned after it has burnt out.

multistorey (ˌmʌltɪˈstɔːrɪ) *adj.* (of a building) having many storeys.

multitrack (ˈmʌltɪˌtræk) *adj.* (in sound recording) using tape containing two or more tracks.

multitude (ˈmʌltɪˌtjuːd) *n.* **1.** a large gathering of people. **2.** *the.* the common people. **3.** a large number. [Latin *multitūdō*] —ˌmulti'tudinous *adj.*

multi-user *adj.* (of a computer) capable of being used by several people at once.

mum[1] (mʌm) *n.* **1.** *Informal, chiefly Brit.* same as **mother.** **2.** *Austral. & N.Z. informal.* same as **wife.** [a child's word]

mum[2] (mʌm) *adj.* **1.** silent. ~*n.* **2. mum's the word.** keep quiet (about something). [suggestive of closed lips]

mumble (ˈmʌmbˀl) *vb.* **1.** to utter indistinctly, as with the mouth partly closed. ~*n.* **2.** an indistinct or low utterance or sound. [Middle English *momelen,* from MUM[2]]

mumbo jumbo (ˈmʌmbəʊ) *n., pl.* **mumbo jumbos. 1.** foolish religious ritual or incantation. **2.** meaningless or unnecessarily complicated language. **3.** an object of superstitious awe or reverence. [prob. from West African *mama dyumbo,* name of a tribal god]

mummer (ˈmʌmə) *n.* one of a group of

masked performers in a folk play or mime. [Old French *momer* to mime]

mummery ('mʌmərɪ) *n., pl.* **-meries.** 1. a performance by mummers. 2. hypocritical or ostentatious ceremony.

mummify ('mʌmɪˌfaɪ) *vb.* to preserve (a body) as a mummy. —ˌmummifiˈcation *n.*

mummy[1] ('mʌmɪ) *n., pl.* **-mies.** an embalmed body as prepared for burial in ancient Egypt. [Persian *mūm* wax]

mummy[2] ('mʌmɪ) *n., pl.* **-mies.** *Chiefly Brit.* a child's word for **mother.** [var. of MUM[1]]

mumps (mʌmps) *n.* (*functioning as sing. or pl.*) an acute contagious viral disease in which the glands below the ear swell and are painful. [obs. *mump* to grimace]

munch (mʌntʃ) *vb.* to chew (food) steadily, esp. with a crunching noise. [imit.]

mundane (mʌn'deɪn) *adj.* 1. everyday, ordinary, or banal. 2. relating to the world or worldly matters. [Latin *mundus* world]

mung bean (mʌŋ) *n.* an E Asian bean plant grown for forage and for its edible seeds which are used as a source of bean sprouts for cookery. [Tamil *mūngu*]

municipal (mjuː'nɪsɪp°l) *adj.* of or relating to a town or city or its local government. [Latin *mūnicipium* a free town]

municipality (mjuːˌnɪsɪ'pælɪtɪ) *n., pl.* **-ties.** 1. a city, town, or district enjoying local self-government. 2. the governing body of such a unit.

munificent (mjuː'nɪfɪsənt) *adj.* 1. (of a person) generous; bountiful. 2. (of a gift) liberal. [Latin *mūnus* gift + *facere* to make] —muˈnificence *n.*

muniments ('mjuːnɪmənts) *pl. n. Law.* the title deeds and other documentary evidence relating to the title to land. [Latin *munire* to defend]

munitions (mjuː'nɪʃənz) *pl. n.* (*sometimes sing.*) military equipment and stores, esp. ammunition.

muon ('mjuːɒn) *n.* a positive or negative elementary particle with a mass 207 times that of an electron. [short for *mu meson*]

mural ('mjʊərəl) *n.* 1. a large painting on a wall. ~*adj.* 2. of or relating to a wall. [Latin *mūrus* wall] —ˈmuralist *n.*

murder ('mɜːdə) *n.* 1. the unlawful premeditated killing of one human being by another. 2. *Informal.* something dangerous, difficult, or unpleasant: *driving around London is murder.* 3. *cry blue murder. Informal.* to make an outcry. 4. *get away with murder. Informal.* to do as one pleases. ~*vb.* 5. to kill (someone) unlawfully with premeditation or during the commission of a crime. 6. *Informal.* to destroy; ruin: *he murdered that soliloquy.* 7. *Informal.* to beat decisively: *the home team murdered their opponents.* [Old English *morthor*] —ˈmurderer *n.* —ˈmurderess *fem. n.* —ˈmurderous *adj.*

murk (mɜːk) *n.* gloomy darkness. [Old Norse *myrkr* darkness]

murky ('mɜːkɪ) *adj.* **murkier, murkiest.** 1. gloomy or dark. 2. cloudy or impenetrable as with smoke or fog. 3. obscure and

suspicious; shady: *murky goings-on; her murky past.* —ˈmurkily *adv.* —ˈmurkiness *n.*

murmur ('mɜːmə) *n.* 1. a continuous low indistinct sound, as of distant voices. 2. an indistinct utterance: *a murmur of satisfaction.* 3. a complaint; grumble: *he made no murmur at my suggestion.* 4. *Med.* an abnormal soft blowing sound heard usually over the chest: *a heart murmur.* ~*vb.* 5. to utter (something) in a murmur. 6. to complain. [Latin *murmurāre* to rumble] —ˈmurmuring *n., adj.* —ˈmurmurous *adj.*

murrain ('mʌrɪn) *n.* any plaguelike disease in cattle. [Old French *morir* to die]

mus. 1. museum. 2. music. 3. musical.

MusB *or* **MusBac** Bachelor of Music.

muscat ('mʌskət) *n.* 1. any of various grapevines that produce sweet white grapes used for making wine or raisins. 2. same as **muscatel.** [Old Provençal *musc* musk]

muscatel (ˌmʌskə'tɛl) *n.* 1. a rich sweet wine made from muscat grapes. 2. the grape or raisin from a muscat vine. [Old Provençal *muscat* musky]

muscle ('mʌs°l) *n.* 1. a tissue composed of bundles of elongated cells capable of contraction and relaxation to produce movement in an organ or part. 2. an organ composed of muscle tissue. 3. strength or force. ~*vb.* 4. (often foll. by *in* or *on*) *Informal.* to force one's way (in). [Medical Latin *musculus* little mouse]

muscle-bound *adj.* having overdeveloped and inelastic muscles.

muscleman ('mʌs°lˌmæn) *n., pl.* **-men.** 1. a man with highly developed muscles. 2. a henchman employed to intimidate or use violence upon victims.

Muscovite ('mʌskəˌvaɪt) *n.* 1. a person from Moscow. ~*adj.* 2. of or relating to Moscow.

muscular ('mʌskjʊlə) *adj.* 1. having well-developed muscles; brawny. 2. of, relating to, or consisting of muscle. —**muscularity** (ˌmʌskjʊ'lærɪtɪ) *n.*

muscular dystrophy *n.* a genetic disease characterized by progressive deterioration and wasting of muscle fibres.

musculature ('mʌskjʊlətʃə) *n.* the arrangement of muscles in an organ, part, or organism.

MusD *or* **MusDoc** Doctor of Music.

muse[1] (mjuːz) *vb.* (sometimes foll. by *on* or *about*) to reflect (about) or ponder (on), usually in silence. [Old French *muser*]

muse[2] (mjuːz) *n.* (often preceded by *the*) a goddess that inspires a creative artist, esp. a poet. [Greek *Mousa* a Muse]

Muse (mjuːz) *n. Greek myth.* any of nine sister goddesses, each of whom was regarded as the protectress of a different art or science.

museum (mjuː'zɪəm) *n.* a building where objects of historical, artistic, or scientific interest are exhibited and preserved. [Greek *Mouseion* home of the Muses]

museum piece *n. Informal.* a person or thing regarded as antiquated.

mush[1] (mʌʃ) *n.* **1.** a soft pulpy mass or consistency. **2.** *Informal.* cloying sentimentality. [obs. *moose* porridge]

mush[2] (mʌʃ) *Canad. ~interj.* **1.** an order to dogs in a sled team to start up or go faster. *~vb.* **2.** to travel by or drive a dogsled. [possibly imperative of French *marcher* to advance]

mushroom (ˈmʌʃrʊm) *n.* **1.** an edible fungus consisting of a cap at the end of a stem. **2.** something resembling a mushroom in shape or rapid growth. *~vb.* **3.** to grow rapidly: *demand mushroomed overnight.* [Late Latin *mussiriō*]

mushroom cloud *n.* the large mushroom-shaped cloud produced by a nuclear explosion.

mushy (ˈmʌʃɪ) *adj.* **mushier, mushiest.** **1.** soft and pulpy. **2.** *Informal.* excessively sentimental.

music (ˈmjuːzɪk) *n.* **1.** an art form consisting of sequences of sounds organized melodically, harmonically, and rhythmically. **2.** such sounds, esp. when produced by singing or musical instruments. **3.** any written or printed representation of musical sounds. **4.** any sequence of sounds perceived as pleasing or harmonious. **5.** **face the music.** *Informal.* to confront the consequences of one's actions. [Greek *mousikē* (*tekhnē*) (art) in the protection of the Muses]

musical (ˈmjuːzɪkʰl) *adj.* **1.** of or used in music. **2.** harmonious; melodious: *musical laughter.* **3.** talented in or fond of music. **4.** involving or set to music. *~n.* **5.** a play or film having dialogue interspersed with songs and dances. **—musicality** (ˌmjuːzɪˈkælɪtɪ) *n.* **—ˈmusically** *adv.*

musical box *n.* a box containing a mechanical instrument that plays tunes when the box is opened.

musical chairs *n.* (*functioning as sing.*) a game in which whenever the music stops, the player who fails to find a chair is out of the game.

music centre *n.* a single hi-fi unit containing a turntable, radio, and cassette player.

music hall *n. Chiefly Brit.* **1.** a variety entertainment consisting of songs and comic turns. **2.** a theatre at which such entertainments are staged.

musician (mjuːˈzɪʃən) *n.* a person who plays or composes music, esp. as a profession. **—muˈsicianship** *n.*

musicology (ˌmjuːzɪˈkɒlədʒɪ) *n.* the scholarly study of music. **—ˌmusiˈcologist** *n.*

musk (mʌsk) *n.* **1.** a strong-smelling glandular secretion of the male musk deer, used in perfumery. **2.** any similar substance produced by animals, plants, or manufactured synthetically. [Persian *mush*]

musk deer *n.* a small central Asian mountain deer. The male secretes musk.

muskeg (ˈmʌs.kɛg) *n. Chiefly Canad.* an area of undrained boggy land. [American Indian: grassy swamp]

musket (ˈmʌskɪt) *n.* a long-barrelled muzzle-loading shoulder gun, a forerunner of the rifle. [Italian *moschetto* arrow, earlier: sparrow hawk] **—ˌmuskeˈteer** *n.*

muskmelon (ˈmʌskˌmɛlən) *n.* any of several varieties of melon, such as the cantaloupe and honeydew.

musk ox *n.* a large ox, which has a dark shaggy coat, downward-curving horns, and emits a musky smell.

muskrat (ˈmʌskˌræt) *n., pl.* **-rats** *or* **-rat.** **1.** a North American beaver-like amphibious rodent. **2.** the brown fur of this animal.

musk rose *n.* a Mediterranean rose, cultivated for its white musk-scented flowers.

musky (ˈmʌskɪ) *adj.* **muskier, muskiest.** resembling the smell of musk; having a heady or pungent sweet aroma. **—ˈmuskiness** *n.*

Muslim (ˈmʊzlɪm, ˈmʌz-) *or* **Moslem** *n., pl.* **-lims** *or* **-lim.** **1.** a follower of the religion of Islam. *~adj.* **2.** of or relating to Islam. [Arabic, lit.: one who surrenders]

muslin (ˈmʌzlɪn) *n.* a fine plain-weave cotton fabric. [French *mousseline*]

musquash (ˈmʌskwɒʃ) *n.* same as **muskrat**, esp. the fur. [American Indian]

muss (mʌs) *vb. U.S. & Canad. informal.* (often foll. by *up*) to make untidy; rumple. [prob. a blend of *mess* + *fuss*]

mussel (ˈmʌsˀl) *n.* any of various bivalves, esp. the edible mussel, which has a dark slightly elongated shell and lives attached to rocks. [Latin *musculus,* diminutive of *mūs* mouse]

must[1] (mʌst) *vb.* used as an auxiliary to express or indicate: **1.** obligation or necessity: *I must go to the bank.* In this sense, *must* does not form a negative. If used with a negative infinitive it indicates obligatory prohibition. **2.** the probable correctness of a statement: *he must be there by now.* **3.** inevitability: *all good things must come to an end.* **4.** resolution: *I must finish this.* **5.** conviction or certainty on the part of the speaker: *you must be joking.* *~n.* **6.** an essential or necessary thing: *strong shoes are a must for hill walking.* [Old English *mōste*]

must[2] (mʌst) *n.* the pressed juice of grapes or other fruit ready for fermentation. [Latin *mustum* new wine]

mustache (məˈstɑːʃ) *n. U.S.* same as **moustache.**

mustachio (məˈstɑːʃɪˌəʊ) *n., pl.* **-chios.** (*often pl.*) *Often humorous.* a moustache, esp. when bushy or elaborately shaped. [Italian *mostaccio*] **—musˈtachioed** *adj.*

mustang (ˈmʌstæŋ) *n.* a small breed of horse, often wild or half wild, found in the southwestern U.S. [Mexican Spanish *mestengo*]

mustard (ˈmʌstəd) *n.* **1.** any of several plants with yellow flowers and slender pods: cultivated for their pungent seeds. **2.** a paste made from the powdered seeds of any of these plants and used as a condiment. **3.** a brownish-yellow colour. [Old French *moustarde*]

mustard and cress *n.* seedlings of white mustard and garden cress, used in salads, and as a garnish.

mustard gas n. an oily liquid whose poisonous vapour is used in chemical warfare. It causes blindness, burns, and sometimes death.

mustard plaster n. Med. a mixture of powdered black mustard seeds applied to the skin for its counterirritant effects.

muster ('mʌstə) vb. **1.** to call (people, esp. soldiers) or (of people) to be called together for duty or inspection. **2.** (sometimes foll. by up) to summon or gather: to muster one's arguments. ~n. **3.** an assembly of military personnel for duty or inspection. **4.** a collection, assembly, or gathering. **5. pass muster.** to be acceptable. [Latin monstrāre to show]

musty ('mʌstɪ) adj. **-tier, -tiest. 1.** smelling or tasting old, stale, or mouldy. **2.** old-fashioned, dull, or hackneyed: musty ideas. [perhaps var. of obs. moisty] —'mustily adv. —'mustiness n.

mutable ('mjuːtəbᵊl) adj. able to or tending to change. [Latin mūtāre to change] —,muta'bility n.

mutant ('mjuːtᵊnt) n. **1.** an animal, organism, or gene that has undergone mutation. ~adj. **2.** of mutation.

mutate (mjuː'teɪt) vb. to undergo or cause to undergo mutation. [Latin mutare to change]

mutation (mjuː'teɪʃən) n. **1.** a change or alteration. **2.** a change in the chromosomes or genes of a cell which may affect the structure and development of the resultant offspring. **3.** a physical characteristic, or the organism resulting from this type of chromosomal change.

mute (mjuːt) adj. **1.** not giving out sound or speech; silent. **2.** unable to speak; dumb. **3.** unspoken or unexpressed. **4.** (of a letter in a word) silent. ~n. **5.** a person who is unable to speak. **6.** any of various devices used to soften the tone of stringed or brass instruments. **7.** a silent letter. ~vb. **8.** to reduce the volume of (a musical instrument) by means of a mute or soft pedal. **9.** to subdue the strength of (a colour, lighting, emotion, or activity): their criticism was muted; a muted blue shirt. [Latin mūtus silent] —'mutely adv. —'muteness n.

mute swan n. a Eurasian swan with a pure white plumage and an orange-red bill.

muti ('muːtɪ) n. S. African. medicine, esp. herbal. [Zulu]

mutilate ('mjuːtɪ,leɪt) vb. **1.** to deprive of a limb or essential part; maim. **2.** to expurgate or otherwise damage (a text). [Latin mutilāre to cut off] —,muti'lation n. —'muti,lator n.

mutineer (,mjuːtɪ'nɪə) n. a person who mutinies.

mutinous ('mjuːtɪnəs) adj. **1.** openly rebellious. **2.** characteristic or indicative of mutiny.

mutiny ('mjuːtɪnɪ) n., pl. **-nies. 1.** open rebellion against constituted authority, esp. by seamen or soldiers against their officers. ~vb. **-nying, -nied. 2.** to engage in mutiny. [Old French mutin rebellious]

mutt (mʌt) n. Slang. **1.** a foolish or stupid person. **2.** a mongrel dog. [from mutton-head]

mutter ('mʌtə) vb. **1.** to utter (something) in a low and indistinct tone. **2.** to grumble. ~n. **3.** a muttered sound or complaint. [Middle English moteren] —'muttering n., adj.

mutton ('mʌtᵊn) n. **1.** the flesh of mature sheep, used as food. **2. mutton dressed as lamb.** an older person dressed up to look young. [Medieval Latin multō]

muttonchops ('mʌtᵊn,tʃɒps) pl. n. side whiskers trimmed in the shape of chops.

muttonhead ('mʌtᵊn,hɛd) n. Slang. a stupid or ignorant person; fool.

mutual ('mjuːtʃʊəl) adj. **1.** experienced or expressed by each of two or more people about the other; reciprocal: mutual distrust. **2.** Informal. common to or shared by both: a mutual friend. **3.** denoting an organization, such as an insurance company, in which the policyholders or investors share the profits and expenses and there are no shareholders. [Latin mūtuus reciprocal] —mutuality (,mjuːtʃʊ'ælɪtɪ) n. —'mutually adv.

Muzak ('mjuːzæk) n. Trademark. recorded light music played in places such as restaurants and factories.

muzzle ('mʌzᵊl) n. **1.** the projecting part of an animal's face, usually the jaws and nose. **2.** a guard or strap fitted over an animal's nose and jaws to prevent it biting or eating. **3.** the front end of a gun barrel. ~vb. **4.** to prevent from being heard or noticed. **5.** to put a muzzle on (an animal). [Old French muse snout]

muzzy ('mʌzɪ) adj. **-zier, -ziest. 1.** blurred or hazy. **2.** confused or befuddled. [origin unknown] —'muzzily adv. —'muzziness n.

MW 1. megawatt. **2.** Radio. medium wave.

Mx Physics. maxwell.

my (maɪ) det. **1.** of, belonging to, or associated with the speaker or writer (me): my own ideas. **2.** used in various forms of address: my lord. ~interj. **3.** an exclamation of surprise or awe: my, how you've grown! [var. of Old English mīn]

mycelium (maɪ'siːlɪəm) n., pl. **-lia** (-lɪə). the mass forming the body of a fungus. [Greek mukēs mushroom + hēlos nail]

Mycenaean (,maɪsɪ'niːən) adj. of or relating to the Aegean civilization of Mycenae, a city in S Greece (1400 to 1100 B.C.).

mycology (maɪ'kɒlədʒɪ) n. the study of fungi. [Greek mukēs mushroom + -LOGY]

myelin ('maɪɪlɪn) n. a white tissue forming an insulating sheath around certain nerve fibres. [Greek muelos marrow]

myeloma (,maɪə'ləʊmə) n., pl. **-mas** or **-mata** (-mətə). a tumour of the bone marrow. [Greek mus muscle + -oma, modelled on carcinoma]

myna, mynah, or **mina** ('maɪnə) n. a tropical Asian starling which can mimic human speech. [Hindi mainā]

Mynheer (mə'nɪə) n. a Dutch title of address equivalent to *Sir* or *Mr.* [Dutch *mijnheer* my lord]

myocardium (ˌmaɪəʊˈkɑːdɪəm) *n., pl.* **-dia** (-dɪə). the muscular tissue of the heart. [Greek *mus* muscle + *kardia* heart] —ˌ**myoˈcardial** *adj.*

myopia (maɪˈəʊpɪə) *n.* inability to see distant objects clearly because the images are focused in front of the retina; short-sightedness. [Greek *muōps* short-sighted] —**myopic** (maɪˈɒpɪk) *adj.*

myriad (ˈmɪrɪəd) *adj.* **1.** innumerable. ~*n.* (*also used in pl.*) **2.** a large indefinite number. [Greek *murias* ten thousand]

myriapod (ˈmɪrɪəˌpɒd) *n.* an arthropod with a long segmented body and many walking limbs, such as a centipede. [Greek *murias* ten thousand + *pous* foot]

myrmidon (ˈmɜːmɪˌdɒn, -dᵊn) *n.* a follower or henchman. [after the followers of Achilles in Greek myth]

myrrh (mɜː) *n.* the aromatic resin of an African or Asian shrub or tree, used in perfume, incense, and medicine. [Greek *murrha*]

myrtle (ˈmɜːtᵊl) *n.* an evergreen shrub with pink or white flowers and aromatic blue-black berries. [Greek *murtos*]

myself (maɪˈsɛlf) *pron.* **1.** the reflexive form of *I* or *me.* **2.** I or me in person, as distinct from anyone else: *I myself know of no answer.* **3.** my usual self: *I'm not myself today.*

mysterious (mɪˈstɪərɪəs) *adj.* **1.** characterized by or indicative of mystery. **2.** puzzling, curious. —**mysˈteriously** *adv.*

mystery (ˈmɪstrɪ) *n., pl.* **-teries.** **1.** an unexplained or inexplicable event or phenomenon. **2.** a person or thing that arouses curiosity or suspense because of an unknown, obscure, or enigmatic quality. **3.** a story or film which arouses suspense and curiosity because of facts concealed. **4.** a religious rite, such as the Eucharist in Christianity. [Greek *mustērion* secret rites]

mystery play *n.* (in the Middle Ages) a type of drama based on the life of Christ.

mystery tour *n.* an excursion to an unspecified destination.

mystic (ˈmɪstɪk) *n.* **1.** a person who achieves mystical experience. ~*adj.* **2.** same as **mystical.** [*mustēs* one who has been initiated]

mystical (ˈmɪstɪkᵊl) *adj.* **1.** relating to or characteristic of mysticism. **2.** *Christianity.* having a sacred significance that is beyond human understanding. **3.** having occult or metaphysical significance. —ˈ**mystically** *adv.*

mysticism (ˈmɪstɪˌsɪzəm) *n.* **1.** belief in or experience of a reality beyond normal human understanding or experience. **2.** the use of prayer and meditation in an attempt to achieve direct intuitive experience of the divine.

mystify (ˈmɪstɪˌfaɪ) *vb.* **-fying, -fied.** **1.** to confuse, bewilder, or puzzle. **2.** to make obscure. —ˌ**mystifiˈcation** *n.* —ˈ**mystiˌfying** *adj.*

mystique (mɪˈstiːk) *n.* an aura of mystery, power, and awe that surrounds a person or thing.

myth (mɪθ) *n.* **1. a.** a story about superhuman beings of an earlier age, usually of how natural phenomena or social customs came into existence. **b.** same as **mythology** (senses 1, 3). **2.** a person or thing whose existence is fictional or unproven. [Greek *muthos* fable]

myth. **1.** mythological. **2.** mythology.

mythical (ˈmɪθɪkᵊl) *or* **mythic** *adj.* **1.** of or relating to myth. **2.** imaginary or fictitious. —ˈ**mythically** *adv.*

mythology (mɪˈθɒlədʒɪ) *n., pl.* **-gies.** **1.** myths collectively, esp. those associated with a particular culture or person. **2.** a body of stories about a person, institution, etc. **3.** the study of myths. —**mythological** (ˌmɪθəˈlɒdʒɪkᵊl) *adj.*

myxoedema *or U.S.* **myxedema** (ˌmɪksɪˈdiːmə) *n.* a disease resulting from underactivity of the thyroid gland, characterized by puffy eyes, face, and hands and mental sluggishness. [Greek *muxa* mucus + *oidēma* swelling]

myxomatosis (ˌmɪksəməˈtəʊsɪs) *n.* an infectious and usually fatal viral disease of rabbits causing swellings and tumours. [Greek *muxa* mucus + *-oma* denoting tumour + *-osis* denoting disease]

N

n *or* **N** (ɛn) *n., pl.* **n's, N's,** *or* **Ns.** the 14th letter of the English alphabet.

n[1] **1.** nano-. **2.** neutron.

n[2] (ɛn) *det.* an indefinite number: *there are n objects in the box.* —**nth** (ɛnθ) *adj.*

N 1. *Chess.* knight. **2.** newton(s). **3.** *Chem.* nitrogen. **4.** North. **5.** nuclear: *N plant.*

n. **1.** neuter. **2.** noun.

N. 1. National(ist). **2.** Navy. **3.** New. **4.** Norse.

Na *Chem.* sodium. [Latin *natrium*]

NA North America.

NAAFI *or* **Naafi** ('næfɪ) *n.* **1.** Navy, Army, and Air Force Institutes. **2.** a canteen or shop run by this organization for military personnel.

naartjie ('nɑːtʃɪ) *n. S. African.* a tangerine. [Afrikaans]

nab (næb) *vb.* **nabbing, nabbed.** *Informal.* **1.** to arrest (someone). **2.** to catch (someone) doing something wrong. [perhaps Scandinavian]

nabob ('neɪbɒb) *n.* **1.** *Informal.* a rich or important person. **2.** (formerly) a European who made a fortune in India. **3.** same as **nawab.** [Hindi *nawwāb*; see NAWAB]

nacre ('neɪkə) *n.* same as **mother-of-pearl.** [Arabic *naqqārah* shell, drum] —**nacreous** ('neɪkrɪəs) *adj.*

nadir ('neɪdɪə, 'næ-) *n.* **1.** the point in the sky directly below an observer and opposite the zenith. **2.** the lowest point of anything. [Arabic *nazīr as-samt,* lit.: opposite the zenith]

nae (neɪ) *or* **na** (nɑː) *det., adv. Scot.* same as **no**[2] *or* **not.**

naevus *or U.S.* **nevus** ('niːvəs) *n., pl.* **-vi** (-vaɪ). a birthmark or mole. [Latin]

naff (næf) *adj. Brit. slang.* inferior or useless. [perhaps back slang from *fan,* short for *fanny*]

nag[1] (næg) *vb.* **nagging, nagged.** **1.** to scold or find fault constantly. **2.** (foll. by *at*) to be a constant source of discomfort or worry to. ~*n.* **3.** a person who nags. [Scandinavian] —**'nagging** *adj., n.*

nag[2] (næg) *n.* **1.** *Often disparaging.* a horse. **2.** a small riding horse. [Germanic]

naiad ('naɪæd) *n., pl.* **-ads** *or* **-ades** (-ˌdiːz). *Greek myth.* a water nymph. [Greek *nāias* water nymph]

naïf (nɑː'iːf) *adj.* same as **naive.**

nail (neɪl) *n.* **1.** a piece of metal with a point at one end and a head at the other, hit with a hammer to join two objects together. **2.** the horny covering of the upper tips of the fingers and toes. **3. hit the nail on the head.** to say something exactly correct or accurate. **4. on the nail.** at once: *she paid on the nail.* ~*vb.* **5.** to attach (something) with nails. **6.** *Informal.* to arrest or catch (someone). [Old English *nægl*]

nailfile ('neɪlˌfaɪl) *n.* a small metal file, used to trim the nails.

nail polish *or* **varnish** *or esp. U.S.* **enamel** *n.* a cosmetic lacquer applied to the nails.

naive, naïve (nɑː'iːv, naɪ'iːv), *or* **naïf** *adj.* **1.** innocent and credulous. **2.** lacking developed powers of reasoning or criticism: *a naive argument.* [French, from Latin *nātīvus* native] —**na'ively, na'ïvely,** *or* **na'ïfly** *adv.*

naivety (naɪ'iːvtɪ), **naiveté,** *or* **naiveté** (ˌnɑːiːv'teɪ) *n.* the state or quality of being naive.

naked ('neɪkɪd) *adj.* **1.** having the body unclothed. **2.** having no covering: *a naked flame.* **3.** with no concealment: *the naked facts.* **4.** unaided by special equipment: *visible to the naked eye.* **5.** with no protection. [Old English *nacod*] —**'nakedly** *adv.* —**'nakedness** *n.*

namby-pamby (ˌnæmbɪ'pæmbɪ) *adj.* insipidly sentimental or prim. [nickname of Ambrose Phillips, pastoral poet]

name (neɪm) *n.* **1.** a word or term by which a person or thing is known. **2.** mere outward appearance as opposed to fact: *ruler in name only.* **3.** an abusive word or phrase considered descriptive of someone: *to call someone names.* **4.** reputation, usually good reputation: *he's made quite a name for himself.* **5.** a famous person: *a big name in the music world.* **6. in the name of a. a.** for the sake of: *in the name of peace.* **b.** by the authority of: *in the name of the law.* **7. name of the game.** the most significant or important aspect of something. **8. to one's name.** in one's possession: *I haven't a penny to my name.* ~*vb.* **9.** to give a name to. **10.** to refer to by name; cite: *he named three French poets.* **11.** to ban (an MP) from the House of Commons by mentioning him formally by name as being guilty of disorderly conduct. **12.** to fix or specify: *they have named a date for the meeting.* **13.** to appoint: *he was named Journalist of the Year.* **14. name names.** to cite people in order to blame or accuse them. **15. name the day.** to choose the day for one's wedding. [Old English *nama*]

name day *n. R.C. Church.* the feast day of a saint whose name one bears.

name-dropping *n. Informal.* the practice of referring to famous people as though they were friends, in order to impress others.

nameless ('neɪmlɪs) *adj.* **1.** without a name. **2.** unspecified: *persons who shall remain nameless.* **3.** too horrible to mention: *nameless terror.*

namely ('neɪmlɪ) *adv.* that is to say.

nameplate ('neɪmˌpleɪt) *n.* a panel on or next to a door bearing the occupant's name and, sometimes, profession.

namesake ('neɪm,seɪk) *n.* a person or thing with the same name as another. [prob. orig. *for the name's sake*]

nan bread *or* **naan** (nɑːn) *n.* (in Indian cookery) a slightly leavened bread in a large flat leaf shape. [Hindi]

nancy ('nænsɪ) *n., pl.* **-cies.** an effeminate or homosexual boy or man. Also called: **nance, nancy boy.** [from the girl's name]

nankeen (næŋ'kiːn) *n.* **1.** a buff-coloured cotton fabric. ~*adj.* **2.** pale greyish-yellow. [after *Nanking*, China, where it originated]

nanny ('nænɪ) *n., pl.* **-nies.** **1.** a child's nursemaid. **2.** Also: **nana, nan.** a child's word for **grandmother.** [child's name for a nurse]

nanny goat *n.* a female goat.

nano- ('nænəʊ) *combining form.* denoting one billionth (10^{-9}): *nanosecond.* [Latin *nānus* dwarf]

nap[1] (næp) *vb.* **napping, napped.** **1.** to sleep for a short while; doze. **2. catch someone napping.** to catch someone off guard. ~*n.* **3.** a doze. [Old English *hnappian*]

nap[2] (næp) *n.* the raised fibres of velvet or similar cloth; doze. [prob. Middle Dutch *noppe*]

nap[3] (næp) *n.* **1.** a card game similar to whist. **2.** *Horse racing.* a tipster's choice for a certain winner. ~*vb.* **napping, napped.** **3.** *Horse racing.* to name (a horse) as a likely winner. [shortened from *Napoleon*]

napalm ('neɪpɑːm, 'næ-) *n.* **1.** a thick and highly incendiary liquid, used in firebombs and flame-throwers. ~*vb.* **2.** to attack (people or places) with napalm. [*na(ph-thene)* + *palm(itate)* salt of palmitic acid]

nape (neɪp) *n.* the back of the neck. [origin unknown]

naphtha ('næfθə, 'næp-) *n. Chem.* a liquid mixture distilled from coal tar or petroleum: used as a solvent and in petrol. [Greek]

naphthalene ('næfθə,liːn, 'næp-) *n. Chem.* a white crystalline substance distilled from coal tar or petroleum, used in mothballs, dyes, and explosives. [*naphtha* + *alcohol* + *-ene*]

napkin ('næpkɪn) *n.* **1.** a piece of cloth or paper used while eating to protect the clothes or to wipe the mouth. **2.** same as **nappy. 3.** same as **sanitary towel.** [Latin *mappa* cloth]

nappy ('næpɪ) *n., pl.* **-pies.** *Brit.* a piece of soft absorbent material wrapped around the waist and between the legs of a baby to absorb its excrement. [from *napkin*]

narcissism ('nɑːsɪ,sɪzəm) *n.* an exceptional interest in or admiration for oneself. [after *Narcissus,* a youth in Gk myth., who fell in love with his reflection] —,**narcis-'sistic** *adj.*

narcissus (nɑː'sɪsəs) *n., pl.* **-cissi** (-'sɪsaɪ). a yellow, orange, or white flower with a crown surrounded by spreading segments. [Greek *nárkissos,* possibly from *narkē* numbness, because of narcotic properties attributed to the plant]

narcosis (nɑː'kəʊsɪs) *n.* unconsciousness caused by a narcotic or general anaesthetic. [Greek *narkē* numbness]

narcotic (nɑː'kɒtɪk) *n.* **1.** a drug, such as opium or morphine, that produces numbness and drowsiness. ~*adj.* **2.** of narcotics or narcosis. [Greek *narkē* numbness]

nard (nɑːd) *n.* **1.** same as **spikenard. 2.** a plant whose aromatic roots were formerly used in medicine. [Greek *nárdos*]

nark (nɑːk) *Slang.* ~*n.* **1.** *Brit., Austral.,* & *N.Z.* an informer or spy: *copper's nark.* **2.** *Brit.* someone who complains in an irritating or whining manner. ~*vb.* **3.** *Brit., Austral.,* & *N.Z.* to annoy. [prob. from Romany *nāk* nose]

narky ('nɑːkɪ) *adj.* **narkier, narkiest.** *Slang.* irritable, complaining, or sarcastic.

narrate (nə'reɪt) *vb.* **1.** to tell (a story); relate. **2.** to speak in accompaniment of (a film). [Latin *narrāre* to recount] —**nar'ra-tor** *n.*

narration (nə'reɪʃən) *n.* **1.** a narrating. **2.** a narrated account or story.

narrative ('nærətɪv) *n.* **1.** an account of events. **2.** the part of a literary work that relates events. ~*adj.* **3.** telling a story: *a narrative poem.* **4.** of narration: *narrative art.*

narrow ('nærəʊ) *adj.* **1.** small in breadth in comparison to length. **2.** limited in range or extent: *in a narrow sense.* **3.** limited in outlook: *a narrow mind.* **4.** with little margin: *a narrow escape.* ~*vb.* **5.** to make or become narrow. ~See also **narrows.** [Old English *nearu*] —**'narrowly** *adv.* —**'narrowness** *n.*

narrow boat *n.* a long bargelike canal boat.

narrow gauge *n.* **1.** a railway track with less than 56½ inches between the lines. ~*adj.* **narrow-gauge. 2.** denoting a railway with a narrow gauge.

narrow-minded *adj.* bigoted, intolerant, or prejudiced. —,**narrow-'mindedness** *n.*

narrows ('nærəʊz) *pl. n.* a narrow part of a strait, river, or current.

narwhal ('nɑːwəl) *n.* an arctic whale, the male of which has a long spiral tusk. [Old Norse *nāhvalr,* from *nār* corpse + *hvalr* whale]

NASA ('næsə) (in the U.S.) National Aeronautics and Space Administration.

nasal ('neɪz²l) *adj.* **1.** of the nose. **2.** (of a sound) pronounced with air passing through the nose. **3.** (of a voice) characterized by nasal sounds. [Latin *nāsus* nose] —**'nasally** *adv.*

nasalize *or* **-lise** ('neɪz²,laɪz) *vb.* to pronounce or speak nasally.

nascent ('næs²nt, 'neɪ-) *adj.* starting to grow or develop. [Latin *nāscī* to be born]

nasturtium (nə'stɜːʃəm) *n.* a plant with yellow, red, or orange trumpet-shaped flowers. [Latin: kind of cress]

nasty ('nɑːstɪ) *adj.* **-tier, -tiest. 1.** unpleasant: *a nasty smell.* **2.** dangerous or painful: *a nasty wound.* **3.** (of a person) spiteful or ill-natured. ~*n., pl.* **-ties. 4.** something unpleasant: *a video nasty.*

[prob. related to Dutch *nestig* dirty] —'**nastily** *adv.* —'**nastiness** *n.*

nat. **1.** national. **2.** nationalist.

natal ('neɪt'l) *adj.* of or relating to birth. [Latin *nātālis* of one's birth]

nation ('neɪʃən) *n.* a large body of people of one or more cultures or races, organized into a single state: *the Australian nation*. [Latin *nātiō* birth, tribe]

national ('næʃən'l) *adj.* **1.** of a nation as a whole. **2.** characteristic of a particular nation: *the national dress of Poland.* ~*n.* **3.** a citizen of a particular country: *Greek nationals.* **4.** a national newspaper. —'**nationally** *adv.*

national anthem *n.* a patriotic song adopted by a nation for use on public occasions.

national debt *n.* the total outstanding borrowings of a nation's central government.

national grid *n. Brit.* **1.** a network of high-voltage power lines linking major electric power stations. **2.** the arrangement of vertical and horizontal lines on an ordnance survey map.

National Health Service *n.* (in Britain) the system of national medical services, financed mainly by taxation.

national insurance *n.* (in Britain) state insurance based on contributions from employees and employers, providing payments to the unemployed, the sick, and the retired.

nationalism ('næʃənə‚lɪzəm) *n.* **1.** a policy of national independence. **2.** patriotism, sometimes to an excessive degree. —'**nationalist** *n., adj.* —‚**national'istic** *adj.*

nationality (‚næʃə'nælɪtɪ) *n., pl.* **-ties. 1.** the fact of being a citizen of a particular nation. **2.** a nation.

nationalize *or* **-lise** ('næʃənə‚laɪz) *vb.* to put (an industry or a company) under state control. —‚**nationali'zation** *or* **-li'sation** *n.*

national park *n.* an area of countryside protected by a national government for its scenic or environmental importance.

national service *n. Chiefly Brit.* compulsory military service.

National Socialism *n. German history.* the doctrines and practices of the Nazis, involving the supremacy of Hitler, anti-Semitism, state control of the economy, and national expansion. —**National Socialist** *n., adj.*

national superannuation *n. N.Z.* a government pension paid to people of 65 years and over; retirement pension.

National Trust *n.* (in Britain) an organization concerned with the preservation of historic buildings and areas of natural beauty.

nationwide ('neɪʃən‚waɪd) *adj.* covering or available to the whole of a nation; national.

native ('neɪtɪv) *adj.* **1.** relating to a place where a person was born: *native language.* **2.** natural or inborn: *native wit.* **3.** born in a specified place: *a native Indian.* **4.** (foll. by *to*) originating in: *tigers are native to*

India. **5.** relating to the original inhabitants of a country: *the native state of New Zealand.* **6. go native.** (of a settler) to adopt the lifestyle of the local population. ~*n.* **7.** a person born in a specified place: *a native of Geneva.* **8.** an indigenous animal or plant: *the llama is a native of Peru.* **9.** a member of the original people of a country, as opposed to colonial immigrants. [Latin *nātīvus* innate, natural, from *nascī* to be born]

nativity (nə'tɪvɪtɪ) *n., pl.* **-ties.** birth or origin. [Late Latin *nātīvitas* birth]

Nativity (nə'tɪvɪtɪ) *n.* **1.** the birth of Christ. **2.** the feast of Christmas commemorating this.

NATO *or* **Nato** ('neɪtəʊ) North Atlantic Treaty Organization: an international organization established for purposes of collective security.

natter ('nætə) *Chiefly Brit. informal.* ~*vb.* **1.** to talk idly and at length; chatter. ~*n.* **2.** a long idle chat. [dialect *gnatter* to grumble, imit.]

natterjack ('nætə‚dʒæk) *n.* a greyish-brown toad with reddish warty lumps. [origin unknown]

natty ('nætɪ) *adj.* **-tier, -tiest.** *Informal.* smart; spruce. [dialect *net* neat] —'**nattily** *adv.*

natural ('nætʃrəl) *adj.* **1.** of, existing in, or produced by nature: *natural science; natural cliffs.* **2.** in accordance with human nature. **3.** as is normal or to be expected: *the natural course of events.* **4.** not acquired; inborn: *a natural talent.* **5.** being so through inborn qualities: *a natural leader.* **6.** genuine or spontaneous. **7.** lifelike: *she looked more natural without make-up.* **8.** not affected by man; wild: *in the natural state this animal is not ferocious.* **9.** being or made from organic material; not synthetic: *a natural fibre like wool.* **10.** born out of wedlock: *his natural son.* **11.** related by blood: *her natural parents.* **12.** *Music.* not sharp or flat: *F natural.* ~*n.* **13.** *Informal.* a person or thing regarded as certain for success or selection: *the horse was a natural for first place.* **14.** *Music.* **a.** an accidental cancelling a previous sharp or flat. **b.** a note affected by this accidental. —'**naturalness** *n.*

natural gas *n.* a gaseous mixture, consisting mainly of methane, found below ground; used widely as a fuel.

natural history *n.* the study of animals and plants in the wild state.

naturalism ('nætʃrə‚lɪzəm) *n.* a movement in art and literature advocating detailed realism. —‚**natural'istic** *adj.*

naturalist ('nætʃrəlɪst) *n.* **1.** a person who studies botany or zoology. **2.** a person who advocates or practises naturalism.

naturalize *or* **-lise** ('nætʃrə‚laɪz) *vb.* **1.** to give citizenship to (a person of foreign birth). **2.** to cause (a foreign word or custom) to be adopted in another place. **3.** to introduce (a plant or animal from another region) and cause it to adapt to local conditions. —‚**naturali'zation** *or* **-li'sation** *n.*

natural logarithm *n.* a logarithm which has the irrational number e as a base.

naturally ('nætʃrəlɪ) *adv.* **1.** of course; surely. **2.** in a natural or normal way. **3.** instinctively.

natural number *n.* a positive integer, such as 1, 2, 3, 4, and so on.

natural philosophy *n.* physics.

natural resources *pl. n.* naturally occurring materials such as coal, oil, and minerals.

natural science *n.* any of the sciences dealing with the study of the physical world, including biology, physics, chemistry, and geology, or these sciences collectively.

natural selection *n.* a process resulting in the survival of those animals or plants that are best adapted to their environment.

natural wastage *n.* the reduction in number of employees through not replacing those who leave, rather than by dismissing employees or making them redundant.

nature ('neɪtʃə) *n.* **1.** fundamental qualities; essential character. **2.** the whole system of the existence, forces, and events of the physical world that are not controlled by man. **3.** disposition: *a sweet nature.* **4.** the basic biological needs of the body. **5.** sort: *a problem of a serious nature.* **6. by nature.** innately. **7. call of nature.** *Informal.* the need to urinate or defecate. **8. in the nature of.** essentially; by way of: *this call is in the nature of a reminder.* [Latin *nātūra,* from *nascī* to be born]

nature reserve *n.* an area of land that is preserved and managed in order to protect its animal and plant life.

nature study *n.* the study of animals and plants by direct observation.

nature trail *n.* a path through countryside, signposted to draw attention to natural features of interest.

naturism ('neɪtʃə,rɪzəm) *n.* same as **nudism.** —'**naturist** *n., adj.*

naught (nɔːt) *n.* **1.** *Archaic or literary.* nothing. **2.** *Chiefly U.S.* same as **nought.** ~*adv.* **3.** *Archaic or literary.* not at all: *it matters naught.* [Old English *nāwiht*]

naughty ('nɔːtɪ) *adj.* **-tier, -tiest. 1.** (usually of children) mischievous or disobedient. **2.** mildly indecent; titillating: *naughty pictures.* [(orig.: needy, poor) from *naught*] —'**naughtily** *adv.* —'**naughtiness** *n.*

nausea ('nɔːzɪə, -sɪə) *n.* **1.** the feeling that precedes vomiting. **2.** revulsion. [Greek: seasickness, from *naus* ship]

nauseate ('nɔːzɪ,eɪt, -sɪ-) *vb.* **1.** to arouse feelings of revulsion in (someone). **2.** to cause (someone) to feel sick. —'**nause,ating** *adj.*

nauseous ('nɔːzɪəs, -sɪəs) *adj.* **1.** as if about to be sick: *I feel nauseous.* **2.** sickening.

nautical ('nɔːtɪk'l) *adj.* of ships, navigation, or sailors. [Greek *nautikos,* from *naus* ship]

nautical mile *n.* a unit of length, used in navigation, equal to 1852 metres (6076.103 feet).

nautilus ('nɔːtɪləs) *n., pl.* **-luses** *or* **-li** (-,laɪ). a sea creature with a shell and tentacles. [Greek *nautilos* sailor]

naval ('neɪv'l) *adj.* **1.** of or having a navy. **2.** of or relating to ships. [Latin *nāvis* ship]

nave[1] (neɪv) *n.* the central space in a church. [Latin *nāvis* ship, from the similarity of shape]

nave[2] (neɪv) *n.* the hub of a wheel. [Old English *nafu, nafa*]

navel ('neɪv'l) *n.* the slight hollow in the centre of the abdomen, where the umbilical cord was attached. [Old English *nafela*]

navel orange *n.* a sweet orange that has a navel-like hollow at the top.

navigable ('nævɪgəb'l) *adj.* **1.** wide, deep, or safe enough to be sailed through: *a navigable river.* **2.** that can be steered: *a navigable raft.*

navigate ('nævɪ,geɪt) *vb.* **1.** to direct or plot the course of (a ship or an aircraft). **2.** to travel over or through (water, air, or land) in a ship, aircraft, or vehicle. **3.** *Informal.* to direct (oneself) carefully or safely: *he navigated his way to the bar.* **4.** (of a passenger in a vehicle) to give directions to the driver. [Latin *nāvis* ship + *agere* to drive] —,**navi'gation** *n.* —,**navi'gational** *adj.* —'**navi,gator** *n.*

navvy ('nævɪ) *n., pl.* **-vies.** *Brit. informal.* a labourer on a building site or road. [from *navigator* builder of a *navigation* (in the sense: canal)]

navy ('neɪvɪ) *n., pl.* **-vies. 1.** the warships of a nation. **2.** the branch of a country's armed services comprising such ships, their crews, and all their supporting services. ~*adj.* **3.** short for **navy-blue.** [Latin *nāvis* ship]

navy-blue *adj.* dark blue. [from the colour of the British naval uniform]

nawab (nə'wɑːb) *n.* (formerly) a Muslim ruler or powerful landowner in India. [Hindi *nawwāb* from Arabic *nuwwāb,* plural of *na'ib* viceroy]

nay (neɪ) *interj.* **1.** same as **no**[1]: archaic or dialect except in voting. ~*n.* **2.** a person who votes against a motion. ~*adv.* **3.** used for emphasis: *there were hundreds, nay, thousands of people there.* [Old Norse *nei*]

Nazarene (,næzə'riːn) *n.* **1.** an old name for a Christian or (when preceded by *the*) for Jesus Christ. **2.** a person from Nazareth in N Israel. ~*adj.* **3.** of Nazareth.

Nazi ('nɑːtsɪ) *n., pl.* **-zis. 1.** a member of the National Socialist German Workers' Party, which seized political control in Germany in 1933 under Adolf Hitler. ~*adj.* **2.** of or relating to the Nazis. [German, phonetic spelling of the first two syllables of *Nationalsozialist* National Socialist] —'**Nazism** *n.*

Nb *Chem.* niobium.

NB 1. Nebraska. **2.** New Brunswick. **3.** note well. [Latin *nota bene*]

NC North Carolina.

NCO noncommissioned officer.

Nd *Chem.* neodymium.

ND *or* **N.Dak.** North Dakota.

NDT (in Canada) Newfoundland Daylight Time.

Ne *Chem.* neon.

NE northeast(ern).

ne- *combining form.* See **neo-**: *Nearctic.*

Neanderthal man (nɪˈændə,tɑːl) *n.* a type of primitive man of late Palaeolithic Europe. [after *Neandertal*, a valley in Germany]

neap (niːp) *n.* short for **neap tide**. [Old English, as in *nēpflōd* neap tide]

Neapolitan (,nɪəˈpɒlɪt²n) *n.* **1.** a person from Naples, a city in SW Italy. ~*adj.* **2.** of Naples. [Greek *Neapolis* new town]

neap tide *n.* a tide that occurs at the first and last quarter of the moon when there is the smallest rise and fall in tidal level.

near (nɪə) *prep.* **1.** at or to a place or time not far away from. ~*adv.* **2.** at or to a place or time not far away. **3.** short for **nearly**: *I was damn near killed.* ~*adj.* **4.** at or in a place or time not far away: *in the near future.* **5.** with little margin: *a near escape.* **6.** closely connected or intimate: *a near relation.* ~*vb.* **7.** to draw close (to): *we're nearing home.* ~*n.* **8.** the left side of a horse or vehicle. [Old English *nēar* (adv.), comparative of *nēah* close] —ˈnearness *n.*

nearby (ˈnɪəˌbaɪ) *adj.* (ˌnɪəˈbaɪ) *adv.* not far away; close at hand.

Near East *n.* same as **Middle East**.

nearly (ˈnɪəlɪ) *adv.* **1.** almost. **2. not nearly**. nowhere near: *not nearly enough.*

near miss *n.* **1.** a bomb or shot that does not quite hit the target. **2.** any attempt that just fails to succeed. **3.** an incident in which two aircraft or vehicles narrowly avoid collision.

nearside (ˈnɪəˌsaɪd) *n.* **1.** *Chiefly Brit.* the side of a vehicle that is nearer the kerb. **2.** the left side of an animal.

near-sighted (ˌnɪəˈsaɪtɪd) *adj.* same as **short-sighted**.

near thing *n. Informal.* an event or action whose outcome is nearly a failure, nearly a success, or nearly a disaster.

neat (niːt) *adj.* **1.** clean and tidy. **2.** smoothly or competently done: *a neat job.* **3.** (of alcoholic drinks) undiluted. **4.** *Slang, chiefly U.S. & Canad.* admirable; excellent. [Latin *nitidus* clean] —ˈneatly *adv.* —ˈneatness *n.*

neaten (ˈniːt²n) *vb.* to make neat.

neath *or* **'neath** (niːθ) *prep. Archaic.* short for **beneath**.

neb (nɛb) *n. Archaic or dialect.* the beak of a bird or the nose of an animal. [Old English *nebb*]

Nebr. Nebraska.

nebula (ˈnɛbjʊlə) *n., pl.* **-lae** (-,liː). *Astron.* a mass of particles and gases visible as a hazy luminous or dark patch. [Latin: mist, cloud] —ˈnebular *adj.*

nebulous (ˈnɛbjʊləs) *adj.* lacking definite form or content; vague.

necessaries (ˈnɛsɪsərɪz) *pl. n.* essential items: *the necessaries of life.*

necessarily (ˌnɛsɪˈsɛrɪlɪ, ˌnɛsɪˈsɛrɪlɪ) *adv.* **1.** as a certainty: *he won't necessarily come.* **2.** inevitably: *I was necessarily detained.*

necessary (ˈnɛsɪsərɪ) *adj.* **1.** indispensable; required. **2.** inevitable: *the necessary consequences.* ~*n.* **3.** (preceded by *the*) *Informal.* the money required for a particular purpose. **4. do the necessary**. *Informal.* to do something that is necessary in a particular situation. ~See also **necessaries**. [Latin *necessārius* indispensable]

necessitate (nɪˈsɛsɪˌteɪt) *vb.* to compel or require.

necessitous (nɪˈsɛsɪtəs) *adj.* very needy.

necessity (nɪˈsɛsɪtɪ) *n., pl.* **-ties**. **1.** something needed: *necessities of life.* **2.** a set of circumstances that inevitably requires a certain result: *it is a matter of necessity to wear formal clothes when meeting the Queen.* **3.** the state or quality of being obligatory or unavoidable. **4.** urgent requirement. **5.** poverty or want. **6. of necessity**. inevitably.

neck (nɛk) *n.* **1.** the part of the body connecting the head with the rest of the body. **2.** the part of a garment around the neck. **3.** the narrow part of something, such as a bottle or violin. **4.** the length of a horse's head and neck taken as the distance by which one horse beats another in a race: *to win by a neck.* **5.** *Informal.* impudence. **6. get it in the neck**. *Informal.* to be reprimanded or punished severely. **7. neck and neck**. absolutely level in a race or competition. **8. neck of the woods**. *Informal.* a particular area: *what brings you to this neck of the woods?* **9. save someone's neck**. *Informal.* to help someone out of a difficult or dangerous situation. **10. stick one's neck out**. *Informal.* to risk criticism or ridicule by speaking one's mind. **11.** (of two people) *Informal.* to kiss each other passionately. [Old English *hnecca*]

neckband (ˈnɛk,bænd) *n.* a band around the neck of a garment.

neckerchief (ˈnɛkətʃɪf, -,tʃiːf) *n.* a piece of cloth worn round the neck. [*neck* + *kerchief*]

necklace (ˈnɛklɪs) *n.* **1.** a decorative chain, band, or cord, often with beads or jewels, worn around the neck, usually by women. **2.** (in South Africa) a tyre soaked in petrol, placed round a person's neck, and set on fire in order to burn the person to death.

neckline (ˈnɛk,laɪn) *n.* the shape or position of the upper edge of a dress or top.

necktie (ˈnɛk,taɪ) *n. U.S.* same as **tie** (sense 8).

necromancy (ˈnɛkrəʊ,mænsɪ) *n.* black magic; sorcery. [Greek *nekros* corpse + *mantis* prophet] —ˈnecro,mancer *n.*

necrophilia (,nɛkrəʊˈfɪlɪə) *n.* sexual attraction for or sexual intercourse with dead bodies. [Greek *nekros* corpse + *philos* loving]

necropolis (nɛ'krɒpəlɪs) n. a cemetery. [Greek *nekros* dead + *polis* city]

necrosis (nɛ'krəʊsɪs) n. 1. *Biol., Med.* the death of cells in the body, as from an interruption of the blood supply. 2. *Bot.* death of plant tissue due to disease or frost. [Greek *nekros* corpse] —**necrotic** (nɛ'krɒtɪk) *adj.*

nectar ('nɛktə) n. 1. a sugary fluid produced by flowers and collected by bees. 2. *Classical myth.* the drink of the gods. 3. any delicious drink. [Greek *néktar*]

nectarine ('nɛktərɪn) n. a smooth-skinned variety of peach. [apparently from *nectar*]

ned (nɛd) n. *Slang.* a hooligan. [origin unknown]

NEDC National Economic Development Council. Also (informal): **Neddy** ('nɛdɪ).

neddy ('nɛdɪ) n., pl. **-dies.** a child's word for a **donkey.** [from *Ned*, pet form of *Edward*]

née or **nee** (neɪ) adj. indicating the maiden name of a married woman: *Jane Bloggs, née Blandish.* [French: past participle (fem.) of *naître* to be born]

need (niːd) vb. 1. to be in want of: *to need money.* 2. to be obliged: *you need to do more work.* 3. used to express necessity or obligation and does not add -*s* when used with singular nouns or pronouns: *need he go?* ~n. 4. the condition of lacking something: *he has need of a new coat.* 5. a requirement: *the need for vengeance.* 6. necessity: *no need to be frightened.* 7. distress: *a friend in need.* 8. poverty or destitution: *the money will go to those areas where need is greatest.* ~See also **needs.** [Old English *nēad, nied*]

needful ('niːdfʊl) adj. 1. necessary; required. ~n. 2. **the needful.** *Informal.* what is necessary, usually money.

needle ('niːd'l) n. 1. a pointed slender piece of metal with a hole in it through which thread is passed for sewing. 2. a rod with a point at one end, used in knitting. 3. same as **stylus.** 4. *Med.* the long hollow pointed part of a hypodermic syringe, which is inserted into the body. 5. a long narrow stiff leaf: *pine needles.* 6. a pointer on the scale of a measuring instrument. 7. short for **magnetic needle.** 8. *Informal.* anger or intense rivalry, usually in a sporting encounter. 9. **have** or **get the needle.** *Brit. informal.* to be annoyed. ~vb. 10. *Informal.* to goad or provoke. [Old English *nǣdl*]

needlecord ('niːd'l,kɔːd) n. a finely-ribbed corduroy fabric.

needlepoint ('niːd'l,pɔɪnt) n. 1. embroidery done on canvas. 2. lace made by needles on a paper pattern.

needless ('niːdlɪs) adj. not required; unnecessary. —**needlessly** adv.

needlewoman ('niːd'l,wʊmən) n., pl. **-women.** a woman who does needlework.

needlework ('niːd'l,wɜːk) n. sewing and embroidery.

needs (niːdz) adv. 1. (preceded or foll. by *must*) of necessity: *we must needs go.* ~pl. n. 2. what is required: *his needs are modest.*

needy ('niːdɪ) adj. **needier, neediest.** in need of financial support; poor.

ne'er (nɛə) adv. *Poetic.* never.

ne'er-do-well n. 1. an irresponsible or lazy person. ~adj. 2. useless; worthless: *your ne'er-do-well schemes.*

nefarious (nɪ'fɛərɪəs) adj. evil; wicked. [Latin *nē* not + *fās* divine law]

neg. negative.

negate (nɪ'geɪt) vb. 1. to invalidate: *that negates all our efforts.* 2. to deny the existence of. [Latin *negāre*]

negation (nɪ'geɪʃən) n. 1. the opposite or absence of something. 2. a negative thing or condition. 3. a negating.

negative ('nɛgətɪv) adj. 1. expressing a refusal or denial: *a negative answer.* 2. lacking positive qualities, such as enthusiasm or optimism. 3. measured in a direction opposite to that regarded as positive. 4. *Med.* indicating absence of the condition for which a test was made. 5. same as **minus** (sense 3b). 6. *Physics.* **a.** (of an electric charge) having the same electrical charge as an electron. **b.** (of a body or system) having a negative electric charge; having an excess of electrons. 7. short for **electronegative.** 8. of a photographic negative. ~n. 9. a statement or act of denial or refusal. 10. a word or expression with a negative meaning, such as *not.* 11. *Photog.* a piece of photographic film, exposed and developed, bearing an image with a reversal of tones or colours, from which positive prints are made. 12. a quantity less than zero. 13. **in the negative.** indicating denial or refusal. —**negatively** adv.

negativism ('nɛgətɪv,ɪzəm) n. 1. a tendency to be unconstructively critical. 2. any sceptical system of thought. —**negativist** n., adj.

neglect (nɪ'glɛkt) vb. 1. to fail to give due care or attention to: *to neglect a child.* 2. to fail (to do something) through carelessness: *he neglected to tell her.* 3. to disregard: *to neglect one's duty.* ~n. 4. lack of due care or attention: *the child starved through neglect.* 5. the state of being neglected. [Latin *neglegere*]

neglectful (nɪ'glɛktfʊl) adj. careless; negligent.

negligee or **negligée** ('nɛglɪ,ʒeɪ) n. a woman's light, usually lace-trimmed dressing gown. [French]

negligent ('nɛglɪdʒənt) adj. 1. lacking attention or concern. 2. careless or nonchalant. —**negligence** n. —**negligently** adv.

negligible ('nɛglɪdʒəb'l) adj. so small or unimportant as to be not worth considering.

negotiable (nɪ'gəʊʃəb'l) adj. 1. able to be negotiated: *salary is negotiable.* 2. (of a bill of exchange or promissory note) legally transferable.

negotiate (nɪ'gəʊʃɪ,eɪt) vb. 1. to talk with others in order to reach (an agreement). 2. to succeed in passing round or over (a place or a problem). [Latin *negōtium* busi-

ness, from *nec* not + *ōtium* leisure] —**ne-
,goti'ation** n. —**ne'goti,ator** n.

Negress ('niːgrɪs) n. a female Negro.

negritude ('niːgrɪ,tjuːd, 'neg-) n. **1.** the
fact of being a Negro. **2.** awareness and
cultivation of Negro culture.

Negro ('niːgrəʊ) n., pl. -**groes**. **1.** a member of any of the dark-skinned peoples of
Africa and their descendants elsewhere.
~*adj.* **2.** of Negroes. [Latin *niger* black]

Negroid ('niːgrɔɪd) *adj.* **1.** of or belonging
to one of the major racial groups of mankind, characterized by brown-black skin,
crisp curly hair, a short broad nose, and
full lips. ~*n.* **2.** a member of this racial
group.

neigh (neɪ) n. **1.** the high-pitched cry of a
horse. ~*vb.* **2.** to make this sound. [Old
English *hnǣgan*]

neighbour or U.S. **neighbor** ('neɪbə) n.
1. a person who lives near or next to
another. **2.** a person, thing, or country
near or next to another. ~*vb.* **3.** (often
foll. by *on*) to be or live close (to). [Old
English *nēah* near + *būr, gebūr* dweller]
—'**neighbouring** or U.S. '**neighboring**
adj.

neighbourhood or U.S. **neighborhood**
('neɪbə,hʊd) n. **1.** the immediate environment; surroundings. **2.** a district where
people live. **3.** the people in a district. **4.**
(*modifier*) in and for a district: *a neighbourhood watch scheme.* **5. in the neighbourhood of.** approximately.

neighbourly or U.S. **neighborly**
('neɪbəlɪ) *adj.* kind, friendly, or helpful.

neither ('naɪðə, 'niːðə) *det.* **1.** not one nor
the other (of two): *neither option appeals
to me; neither can win.* ~*conj.* **2. a.** (used
preceding alternatives joined by *nor*) not:
neither John nor Mary went. **b.** same as
nor (sense 2). ~*adv.* **3.** *Not standard.*
same as **either** (sense 4). [Old English
nǣwther]

nelson ('nelsən) n. a wrestling hold in
which a wrestler places his arm or arms
under his opponent's arm or arms from
behind and exerts pressure with his palms
on the back of his opponent's neck. [from
a proper name]

nematode ('nemə,təʊd) n. a slender unsegmented cylindrical worm. [Greek *nēma*
thread + *eidos* shape]

nemesis ('nemɪsɪs) n., pl. -**ses** (-,siːz). any
agency of retribution and vengeance.
[Greek *neémein* to distribute what is due]

neo- or *sometimes before a vowel* **ne-**
combining form. new, recent, or a modern
form: *neoclassicism.* [Greek *neos* new]

neoclassicism (,niːəʊ'klæsɪ,sɪzəm) n. a
late 18th- and early 19th-century style in
architecture and art, based on classical
models. —**neoclassical** (,niːəʊ'klæsɪk²l)
adj.

neodymium (,niːəʊ'dɪmɪəm) n. *Chem.* a
toxic silvery-white metallic element of the
lanthanide series. Symbol: Nd [NEO- +
didymium a compound orig. thought to be
an element]

Neolithic (,niːə'lɪθɪk) *adj. Geol.* of the cultural period that lasted in Europe from

about 4000 to 2400 B.C. and was characterized by primitive farming and the use of
polished stone and flint tools and weapons.
[NEO- + Greek *lithos* stone]

neologism (nɪ'ɒlə,dʒɪzəm) n. a newly
coined word, or an established word used
in a new sense. [NEO- + Greek *logos* word]

neon ('niːɒn) n. **1.** *Chem.* a colourless
odourless rare gas, used in illuminated
signs and lights. Symbol: Ne **2.** (*modifier*)
of or illuminated by neon: *neon sign.*
[Greek *neon* new]

neonatal (,niːəʊ'neɪt²l) *adj.* relating to the
first few weeks of a baby's life. —'**neo-
,nate** n.

neon light n. a glass tube containing
neon, which gives a pink or red glow when
a voltage is applied.

neophyte ('niːəʊ,faɪt) n. **1.** a beginner.
2. a person newly converted to a religious
faith. **3.** a novice in a religious order.
[Greek *neos* new + *phuton* a plant]

Nepali (nɪ'pɔːlɪ) or **Nepalese** (,nepə'liːz)
n. **1.** the official language of Nepal. **2.** (*pl.*
-**pali**, -**palis**, or -**palese**) a person from
Nepal. ~*adj.* **3.** of Nepal, its inhabitants,
or their language.

nephew ('nevjuː, 'nef-) n. a son of one's
sister or brother. [Latin *nepôs*]

nephritis (nɪ'fraɪtɪs) n. inflammation of a
kidney. [Greek *nephros* kidney]

nepotism ('nepə,tɪzəm) n. favouritism
shown to relatives or close friends by those
with power. [Italian *nepote* nephew]

Neptune ('neptjuːn) n. **1.** the Roman god
of the sea. **2.** the eighth planet from the
sun.

neptunium (nep'tjuːnɪəm) n. *Chem.* a silvery metallic element synthesized in the
production of plutonium. Symbol: Np [af-
ter *Neptune*, the planet]

nerine (nɪ'raɪnɪ) n. a plant, originally from
South Africa, with pink, red, or orange
flowers. [after *Nerine* Roman water
nymph]

nervate ('nɜːveɪt) *adj.* (of leaves) having
veins.

nerve (nɜːv) n. **1.** a cordlike bundle of
fibres that conducts impulses between the
brain and other parts of the body. **2.**
bravery and determination. **3. lose one's
nerve.** to lose self-confidence and become
afraid about what one is doing. **4.** *Informal.* impudence: *what a nerve.* **5.** *strain
every nerve.* to make every effort (to do
something). ~*vb.* **6. nerve oneself.** to
prepare oneself (to do something difficult
or unpleasant). ~*See also* **nerves.** [Latin
nervus]

nerve cell n. same as **neuron.**

nerve centre n. **1.** a group of nerve
cells associated with a specific function.
2. a centre of control: *the nerve centre of
the BBC.*

nerve gas n. a poisonous gas which has a
paralysing effect and which can be fatal.

nerveless ('nɜːvlɪs) *adj.* **1.** (of a person)
fearless. **2.** (of fingers) without feeling;
numb.

nerve-racking or **nerve-wracking** adj. very distressing or harrowing.

nerves ('nɜːvz) pl. n. Informal. 1. the imagined source of emotional control: my nerves won't stand it. 2. anxiety or tension: she's all nerves. 3. **get on someone's nerves.** to irritate someone.

nervous ('nɜːvəs) adj. 1. excitable; highly strung. 2. apprehensive or worried. 3. of or containing nerves: nervous tissue. 4. affecting the nerves: a nervous disease. —'**nervously** adv. —'**nervousness** n.

nervous breakdown n. a mental illness in which the patient ceases to function properly, often accompanied by severely impaired concentration, anxiety, and lack of self-esteem.

nervous system n. the apparatus that controls the thoughts, feelings, and movements of animals, and which consists of a network of nerve cells (see **neuron**).

nervy ('nɜːvi) adj. **nervier, nerviest.** Brit. informal. excitable or nervous.

-ness suffix forming nouns chiefly from adjectives and participles. indicating state, condition, or quality: greatness; selfishness. [Old English -nes]

nest (nɛst) n. 1. a place or structure in which birds or other animals lay eggs or give birth to young. 2. a cosy or secluded place. 3. a set of things of graduated sizes, designed to fit together: a nest of tables. ~vb. 4. (of a bird or other animal) to make or inhabit a nest. 5. Computers. to position (data) within other data at different ranks or levels. [Old English]

nest egg n. a fund of money kept in reserve; savings.

nestle ('nɛs²l) vb. 1. to snuggle or cuddle closely. 2. to be in a sheltered position: houses nestling on the hillside. [Old English nestlian]

nestling ('nɛstlɪŋ, 'nɛslɪŋ) n. a young bird not yet able to fly.

net¹ (nɛt) n. 1. an openwork fabric of string, thread, or wire; mesh. 2. a piece of net, used to protect or hold things or to trap animals. 3. a strategy intended to trap people: the murderer slipped through the police net. 4. Tennis, badminton, volleyball. a strip of net that divides the playing area into two equal parts. 5. the goal in soccer or hockey. ~vb. **netting, netted.** 6. to catch (a fish or other animal) in a net. [Old English net]

net² or **nett** (nɛt) adj. 1. remaining after all deductions, as for taxes and expenses: net profit. 2. (of weight) excluding the weight of wrapping or container. 3. final; conclusive: a net result. ~vb. **netting, netted.** 4. to yield or earn (a sum) as clear profit. [French net neat]

netball ('nɛt,bɔːl) n. a game for two teams of seven players (usually women). Points are scored by shooting the ball through a net hanging from a ring at the top of a pole.

nether ('nɛðə) adj. lower or under: nether regions. [Old English nither down]

nethermost ('nɛðə,məʊst) adj. lowest.

nether world n. 1. the underworld. 2. hell. ~Also called: **nether regions.**

net profit n. gross profit minus all operating expenses such as wages and overheads.

nett (nɛt) adj., vb. same as **net²**.

netting ('nɛtɪŋ) n. a fabric or structure made of net.

nettle ('nɛt²l) n. 1. a plant having spiky leaves with stinging hairs. 2. **grasp the nettle.** to attempt something with boldness and courage. ~vb. 3. to irritate. [Old English netele]

nettle rash n. a skin condition, usually caused by an allergy, in which itchy red or whitish raised patches appear.

network ('nɛt,wɜːk) n. 1. an interconnected group or system: a network of shops. 2. a system of intersecting lines, roads, veins, etc. 3. Radio & TV. a group of broadcasting stations that all transmit the same programme at the same time. 4. Electronics, computers. a system of interconnected components or circuits. ~vb. 5. Radio & TV. to broadcast (a programme) over a network.

neural ('njʊərəl) adj. of a nerve or the nervous system.

neuralgia (njʊ'rældʒə) n. severe pain along a nerve. —**neu'ralgic** adj.

neuritis (njʊ'raɪtɪs) n. inflammation of a nerve or nerves.

neurology (njʊ'rɒlədʒɪ) n. Med. the study of the nervous system. —**neurological** (,njʊərə'lɒdʒɪk²l) adj. —**neu'rologist** n.

neuron ('njʊərɒn) or **neurone** ('njʊərəʊn) n. a cell specialized to conduct nerve impulses.

neurosis (njʊ'rəʊsɪs) n., pl. **-ses** (-siːz). a mental disorder producing hysteria, anxiety, depression, or obsessive behaviour.

neurosurgery (,njʊərəʊ'sɜːdʒərɪ) n. Med. the branch of surgery concerned with the nervous system. —**neuro'surgeon** n. —,**neuro'surgical** adj.

neurotic (njʊ'rɒtɪk) adj. 1. tending to be emotionally unstable. 2. afflicted by neurosis. ~n. 3. a person afflicted with a neurosis or tending to be emotionally unstable.

neuter ('njuːtə) adj. 1. Grammar. denoting a gender of nouns which are neither male nor female. 2. (of animals and plants) sexually underdeveloped. ~n. 3. Grammar. **a.** the neuter gender. **b.** a neuter noun. 4. a sexually underdeveloped female insect, such as a worker bee. 5. a castrated animal. ~vb. 6. to castrate (an animal). [Latin ne not + uter either (of two)]

neutral ('njuːtrəl) adj. 1. not taking any side in a war or dispute. 2. of or belonging to a neutral party or country. 3. of no distinctive quality or type. 4. (of a colour) **a.** having no hue: neutral shoe cream. **b.** dull, but harmonizing with most other colours, for example fawn or grey. 5. same as **neuter** (sense 2). 6. Chem. neither acidic nor alkaline. 7. Physics. having zero charge or potential. ~n. 8. a neutral person or nation. 9. the position of the controls of a gearbox that leaves the gears unconnected to the engine. [Latin *neutrālis* of neuter gender] —**neutrality** (nju:ˈtrælɪtɪ) *n.*

neutralize *or* **-ise** (ˈnju:trəˌlaɪz) *vb.* **1.** to render ineffective by counteracting. **2.** to make electrically or chemically neutral. **3.** to make (a country) neutral by international agreement: *the great powers neutralized Belgium in the 19th century.* —ˌneutrali-**'zation** *or* **-i'sation** *n.*

neutrino (nju:ˈtri:nəʊ) *n., pl.* **-nos.** *Physics.* an elementary particle with zero rest mass and a spin of ½. [Italian, diminutive of *neutrone* neutron]

neutron (ˈnju:trɒn) *n. Physics.* a neutral elementary particle of about the same mass as a proton. [*neutral,* on the model of *electron*]

neutron bomb *n.* a nuclear weapon, designed to cause little blast or radioactive contamination, which destroys all life in the target area.

Nev. Nevada.

never (ˈnɛvə) *adv.* **1.** at no time; not ever. **2.** certainly not; not at all. **3.** Also: **well I never!** surely not! [Old English *næfre*]

nevermore (ˌnɛvəˈmɔ:) *adv. Literary.* never again.

never-never *n.* **the.** *Brit. informal.* the hire-purchase system of buying.

never-never land *n.* an imaginary idyllic place.

nevertheless (ˌnɛvəðəˈlɛs) *adv.* in spite of that; however; yet.

new (nju:) *adj.* **1.** recently made, brought into being, or acquired: *a new dress.* **2.** of a kind never before existing; novel: *a new concept in marketing.* **3.** recently discovered: *a new comet.* **4.** recently introduced to or inexperienced in a place or situation: *new to this game.* **5.** fresh; additional: *send some new troops.* **6.** unknown: *this is new to me.* **7.** (of a cycle) beginning again: *a new year.* **8.** (of crops) harvested early: *new potatoes.* **9.** changed for the better: *she returned a new woman.* ~*adv.* **10.** recently, newly: *new-laid eggs.* ~See also **news.** [Old English *nīowe*] —**'newish** *adj.* —**'newness** *n.*

New Age Music *or* **New Age** *n.* a type of gentle, melodic popular music originating in the U.S. in the late 1980s, which takes in elements of jazz, folk, and classical music and is played largely on synthesizers and acoustic instruments.

newborn (ˈnju:ˌbɔ:n) *adj.* recently or just born.

New Canadian *n. Canad.* a recent immigrant to Canada.

new chum *n. Austral. & N.Z. informal.* a recent British immigrant.

newcomer (ˈnju:ˌkʌmə) *n.* a person who has recently arrived or started to participate in something.

newel (ˈnju:əl) *n.* **1.** Also called: **newel post.** the post at the top or bottom of a flight of stairs that supports the handrail. **2.** the central pillar of a winding staircase. [Old French *nouel* knob]

newfangled (ˈnju:ˈfæŋg²ld) *adj.* objectionably or unnecessarily modern. [Middle English *newefangel* liking new things]

New Jerusalem *n. Christianity.* heaven.

New Latin *n.* the form of Latin used since the Renaissance, mainly for scientific names.

newly (ˈnju:lɪ) *adv.* **1.** recently. **2.** again; anew: *newly raised hopes.*

newlyweds (ˈnju:lɪˌwɛdz) *pl. n.* a recently married couple.

new maths *n.* (*functioning as sing.*) *Brit.* an approach to mathematics in which basic set theory is introduced at an elementary level.

new moon *n.* the moon when it appears as a narrow crescent at the beginning of its cycle.

news (nju:z) *n.* (*functioning as sing.*) **1.** important or interesting new happenings. **2.** information about such events, reported in the mass media. **3. the news.** a television or radio programme presenting such information. **4.** interesting or important new information: *that's news to me.* **5.** a person or thing widely reported in the mass media: *she is news in the film world.*

newsagent (ˈnju:zˌeɪdʒənt) *or U.S.* **newsdealer** *n.* a shopkeeper who sells newspapers and magazines.

newscast (ˈnju:zˌkɑ:st) *n.* a radio or television broadcast of the news. [*news* + (*broad)cast*] —**'news,caster** *n.*

news conference *n.* same as **press conference.**

newsflash (ˈnju:zˌflæʃ) *n.* a brief item of important news, which interrupts a radio or television programme.

newsletter (ˈnju:zˌlɛtə) *n.* a periodical bulletin issued to members of a group.

newspaper (ˈnju:zˌpeɪpə) *n.* a weekly or daily publication consisting of folded sheets and containing news, features, and advertisements.

newspeak (ˈnju:ˌspi:k) *n.* the language of politicians and officials regarded as deliberately ambiguous and misleading. [from *1984,* a novel by George Orwell]

newsprint (ˈnju:zˌprɪnt) *n.* an inexpensive wood-pulp paper used for newspapers.

newsreader (ˈnju:zˌri:də) *n.* a news announcer on radio or television.

newsreel (ˈnju:zˌri:l) *n.* a short film with a commentary which presents current events.

newsroom (ˈnju:zˌru:m, -ˌrʊm) *n.* a room in a newspaper office or broadcasting station where news is received and prepared for publication or broadcasting.

newsstand (ˈnju:zˌstænd) *n.* a portable stand from which newspapers are sold.

New Style *n.* the present method of reckoning dates using the Gregorian calendar.

newsworthy (ˈnju:zˌwɜ:ðɪ) *adj.* sufficiently interesting to be reported as news.

newsy (ˈnju:zɪ) *adj.* **newsier, newsiest.** (of a letter) full of news.

newt (nju:t) *n.* a small amphibious creature with a long slender body and tail and short legs. [mistaken division of *an ewt; ewt,* from Old English *eveta* eft]

New Testament *n.* the part of the Christian Bible dealing with the life and teachings of Christ and his followers.

newton ('njuːtˀn) n. the SI unit of force that gives an acceleration of 1 metre per second per second to a mass of 1 kilogram. [after Sir Isaac *Newton*, scientist]

new town n. (in Britain) a town planned as a complete unit and built with government sponsorship.

New World n. **the.** the Americas; the western hemisphere.

New Year n. the first day or days of the year in various calendars, usually a holiday.

New Year's Day n. January 1, celebrated as a holiday in many countries.

New Year's Eve n. December 31.

next (nɛkst) adj. **1.** immediately following: *send in the next patient.* **2.** immediately adjoining: *the next room.* **3.** closest to in degree: *the next-best thing.* ~adv. **4.** at a time immediately to follow: *the patient to be examined next.* **5. next to. a.** adjacent to: *the house next to ours.* **b.** following in degree: *next to my wife, I love you most.* **c.** almost: *next to nothing.* ~prep. **6.** next to. [Old English *nēhst*, superlative of *nēah* near]

next door adj., adv. in, at, or to the adjacent house or flat: *my next-door neighbour; she lives next door.*

next of kin n. a person's closest relative.

nexus ('nɛksəs) n., pl. **nexus. 1.** a means of connection; link; bond. **2.** a connected group or series. [Latin, from *nectere* to bind]

NF (in Britain) National Front.

Nfld. or **NF** Newfoundland.

ngati ('ŋɑːtɪ) n., pl. **ngati.** N.Z. a tribe or clan. [Maori]

NH New Hampshire.

NHS (in Britain) National Health Service.

Ni Chem. nickel.

NI (in Britain) National Insurance.

nib (nɪb) n. the writing point of a pen. [origin unknown]

nibble ('nɪbˀl) vb. (often foll. by *at*) **1.** (of small animals) to take small repeated bites (of). **2.** (of a person) to take dainty or cautious bites: *to nibble at a cake.* **3.** to bite gently: *he nibbled her ear lobe.* ~n. **4.** Informal. a light hurried meal. **5.** a nibbling. [related to Low German *nibbelen*]

nibs (nɪbz) n. **his** or **her nibs.** Slang. a mock title used of an important or self-important person. [origin unknown]

nice (naɪs) adj. **1.** pleasant. **2.** kind: *a nice gesture.* **3.** good or satisfactory: *they made a nice job of it.* **4.** subtle; precise: *a nice distinction.* [(orig.: foolish) Latin *nescius* ignorant] —**'nicely** adv. —**'niceness** n.

nicety ('naɪsɪtɪ) n., pl. **-ties. 1.** a subtle point: *a nicety of etiquette.* **2.** a refinement or delicacy: *the niceties of first-class travel.* **3. to a nicety.** precisely.

niche (nɪtʃ, niːʃ) n. **1.** a recess in a wall for a statue or ornament. **2.** a position exactly suitable for the person occupying it: *he found his niche in politics.* [Old French *nichier* to nest]

Nichrome ('naɪkrəʊm) n. *Trademark.* an alloy containing nickel, iron, and chromium, used in electrical heating elements and furnaces.

nick (nɪk) n. **1.** a small notch or cut. **2.** *Brit. slang.* a prison or police station. **3.** *Informal.* condition: *in good nick.* **4. in the nick of time.** just in time. ~vb. **5.** to chip or cut (something or oneself). **6.** *Slang, chiefly Brit.* **a.** to steal (something). **b.** to arrest (someone). [possibly Middle English *nocke* nock]

nickel ('nɪkˀl) n. **1.** *Chem.* a silvery-white metallic element that is often used in alloys. Symbol: Ni **2.** a U.S. or Canadian coin worth five cents. [German *Kupfernickel*, lit.: copper demon; it was mistakenly thought to contain copper]

nickelodeon (ˌnɪkə'ləʊdɪən) n. *U.S.* an early type of jukebox. [*nickel* + (*mel*)*odeon*]

nickel silver n. an alloy containing copper, zinc, and nickel.

nicker ('nɪkə) n., pl. **-er.** *Brit. slang.* a pound sterling. [origin unknown]

nick-nack ('nɪkˌnæk) n. same as **knick-knack.**

nickname ('nɪkˌneɪm) n. **1.** a familiar, pet, or derisory name given to a person or place. ~vb. **2.** to call (a person or place) by a nickname: *Bruce Springsteen, nicknamed the Boss.* [mistaken division of *an ekename* an additional name]

nicotine ('nɪkəˌtiːn) n. a poisonous alkaloid found in tobacco. [after J. *Nicot*, who introduced tobacco into France] —**nicotinic** (ˌnɪkə'tɪnɪk) adj.

nictitating membrane ('nɪktɪˌteɪtɪŋ) n. (in reptiles, birds, and some mammals) a thin fold of skin under the eyelid that can be drawn across the eye.

niece (niːs) n. a daughter of one's sister or brother. [Latin *neptis* granddaughter]

niff (nɪf) *Brit. slang.* ~n. **1.** a stink. ~vb. **2.** to stink. [possibly from *sniff*] —**'niffy** adj.

nifty ('nɪftɪ) adj. **-tier, -tiest.** *Informal.* pleasing, apt, or stylish. [origin unknown]

niggard ('nɪgəd) n. a stingy person. [possibly Old Norse]

niggardly ('nɪgədlɪ) adj. **1.** stingy. **2.** meagre: *a niggardly salary.* —**'niggardliness** n.

nigger ('nɪgə) n. **1.** *Offensive.* a Negro or other dark-skinned person. **2. nigger in the woodpile.** a hidden snag. [Spanish *negro*]

niggle ('nɪgˀl) vb. **1.** to irritate or worry (someone). **2.** to find fault continually; fuss. ~n. **3.** a small worry or doubt. **4.** a trivial objection or complaint. [Scandinavian] —**'niggling** adj.

nigh (naɪ) adj., adv., prep. *Archaic, poetic, or dialect.* near. [Old English *nēah*, *nēh*]

night (naɪt) n. **1.** the period of darkness that occurs each 24 hours, between sunset and sunrise. **2.** (modifier) of, occurring, or working at night: *a night nurse.* **3.** the period between sunset and bedtime; evening. **4.** the time between bedtime and morning. **5.** an evening designated for a specific activity: *parents' night*. **6.** nightfall or dusk. **7. make a night of it.** to celebrate the whole evening. ~See also **nights**. [Old English *niht*]

nightcap ('naɪt,kæp) *n.* **1.** a bedtime drink. **2.** a soft cap formerly worn in bed.

nightclub ('naɪt,klʌb) *n.* a place of entertainment open until late at night, usually offering food, drink, a floor show and dancing.

nightdress ('naɪt,drɛs) *n. Brit.* a loose dress worn in bed by women or girls.

nightfall ('naɪt,fɔːl) *n.* the approach of darkness; dusk.

nightgown ('naɪt,gaʊn) *n.* same as **nightdress.**

nightie ('naɪtɪ) *n. Informal.* short for **nightdress.**

nightingale ('naɪtɪŋ,geɪl) *n.* a brownish bird which is well known for its musical song, usually heard at night. [Old English *nihtegale* night singer]

nightjar ('naɪt,dʒɑː) *n.* a nocturnal bird with large eyes. [*night* + JAR², so called from its discordant cry]

nightlife ('naɪt,laɪf) *n.* the entertainment and social activities available at night in a town or city: *the New York nightlife*.

night-light *n.* a dim light burning at night.

nightlong ('naɪt,lɒŋ) *adj., adv.* throughout the night.

nightly ('naɪtlɪ) *adj.* **1.** happening each night. ~*adv.* **2.** each night.

nightmare ('naɪt,mɛə) *n.* **1.** a terrifying or deeply distressing dream. **2.** a terrifying or unpleasant experience. **3.** a thing that is feared: *my nightmare is being buried alive*. [*night* + Old English *mare, mære* evil spirit] ~'**night,marish** *adj.*

nights (naɪts) *adv. Informal.* at night or on most nights: *he works nights*.

night safe *n.* a safe built into the outside wall of a bank, in which customers can deposit money when the bank is closed.

night school *n.* an educational institution that holds classes in the evening.

nightshade ('naɪt,ʃeɪd) *n.* a plant of the family that includes the deadly nightshade. [Old English *nihtscada*]

nightshirt ('naɪt,ʃɜːt) *n.* a long loose shirt-like garment worn in bed mainly by men and boys.

night soil *n. Archaic.* human excrement collected at night from cesspools or privies.

nightspot ('naɪt,spɒt) *n. Informal.* a nightclub.

night-time *n.* the time from sunset to sunrise.

night watch *n.* **1.** a watch or guard kept at night for security. **2.** the period of time this watch is kept. **3.** a night watchman.

night watchman *n.* a person who keeps guard at night on a factory or other building.

nihilism ('naɪɪ,lɪzəm) *n.* a total denial of all established authority and institutions.

[Latin *nihil* nothing] ~'**nihilist** *n., adj.* ~,**nihil'istic** *adj.*

-nik *suffix forming nouns.* indicating a person associated with a particular state or quality: *beatnik*. [Russian]

nil (nɪl) *n.* nothing: used esp. as a score in games. [Latin]

nimble ('nɪmb'l) *adj.* **1.** agile and quick in movement. **2.** mentally alert or acute. [Old English *næmel* quick to grasp, & *numol* quick at seizing] ~'**nimbly** *adv.*

nimbus ('nɪmbəs) *n., pl.* **-bi** (-baɪ) *or* **-buses.** a dark grey rain cloud. [Latin: cloud]

nincompoop ('nɪnkəm,puːp, 'nɪŋ-) *n.* a stupid person. [origin unknown]

nine (naɪn) *n.* **1.** the cardinal number that is the sum of one and eight. **2.** a numeral, 9, IX, representing this number. **3.** something consisting of nine units. **4. dressed up to the nines.** *Informal.* elaborately dressed. **5.** 999. (in Britain) the telephone number of the emergency services. ~*det.* **6.** amounting to nine. [Old English *nigon*] ~**ninth** (naɪnθ) *adj., n.*

nine-days wonder *n.* something that arouses great interest, but only for a short period.

ninefold ('naɪn,fəʊld) *adj.* **1.** having nine times as many. **2.** having nine parts. ~*adv.* **3.** by nine times as much.

ninepins ('naɪn,pɪnz) *n.* (*functioning as sing.*) the game of skittles.

nineteen ('naɪn'tiːn) *n.* **1.** the cardinal number that is the sum of ten and nine. **2.** a numeral, 19, XIX, representing this number. **3.** something consisting of nineteen units. **4. talk nineteen to the dozen.** to talk very fast. ~*det.* **5.** amounting to nineteen. ~'**nine'teenth** *adj., n.*

nineteenth hole *n. Golf, slang.* the bar in a golf clubhouse. [from its being the next objective after a standard 18-hole round]

ninety ('naɪntɪ) *n., pl.* **-ties.** **1.** the cardinal number that is the product of ten and nine. **2.** a numeral, 90, XC, representing this number. **3.** (*pl.*) the numbers 90—99, esp. the 90th to the 99th year of a person's life or of a century. **4.** something consisting of ninety units. ~*det.* **5.** amounting to ninety. ~'**nine'tieth** *adj., n.*

ninny ('nɪnɪ) *n., pl.* **-nies.** a stupid person. [possibly from *an innocent*]

niobium (naɪ'əʊbɪəm) *n. Chem.* a white superconductive metallic element. Symbol: Nb [Latin, after *Niobe* (daughter of Tantalus); because it occurred in tantalite]

nip¹ (nɪp) *vb.* **nipping, nipped. 1.** to pinch or squeeze. **2.** (foll. by *along, up, out*, etc.) *Brit. informal.* to hurry; dart. **3.** to bite lightly. **4.** (of the cold) to affect (someone) with a stinging sensation. **5.** to check the growth of (something): *nip it in the bud*. ~*n.* **6.** a pinch or light bite. **7.** coldness: *a nip in the air*. [Old Norse]

nip² (nɪp) *n.* a small drink of spirits. [from *nipperkin* a vessel holding a half-pint or less]

nipper ('nɪpə) *n. Informal, chiefly Brit.* a child.

nipple ('nɪp³l) n. the small projection in the centre of each breast, which in females contains the outlet of the milk ducts. [possibly from *neb* peak, tip]

nippy ('nɪpɪ) adj. **-pier, -piest. 1.** (of weather) frosty or chilly. **2.** Brit. informal. **a.** quick; nimble. **b.** (of a motor vehicle) small and relatively powerful.

nirvana (nɪəˈvɑːnə, nɜː-) n. Buddhism, Hinduism. the ultimate state of spiritual enlightenment and bliss attained by extinction of all desires and individual existence. [Sanskrit: extinction]

Nissen hut ('nɪs³n) n. a tunnel-shaped military shelter made of corrugated steel. [after Lt Col. Peter *Nissen*, mining engineer]

nit[1] (nɪt) n. the egg or larva of a louse. [Old English *hnitu*]

nit[2] (nɪt) n. Informal, chiefly Brit. short for **nitwit**.

nit-picking Informal. ~n. **1.** a concern with insignificant details, usually with the intention of finding fault. ~adj. **2.** showing such concern; fussy.

nitrate ('naɪtreɪt) Chem. ~n. **1.** a salt or ester of nitric acid. **2.** a fertilizer containing nitrate salts. ~vb. **3.** to treat with nitric acid or a nitrate. **4.** to convert or be converted into a nitrate. —**ni'tration** n.

nitre or U.S. **niter** ('naɪtə) n. Chem. same as **potassium nitrate**. [Latin *nitrum*]

nitric ('naɪtrɪk) adj. Chem. of or containing nitrogen.

nitric acid n. Chem. a colourless corrosive liquid widely used in industry.

nitride ('naɪtraɪd) n. a compound of nitrogen with a more electropositive element.

nitrify ('naɪtrɪˌfaɪ) vb. **-fying, -fied.** Chem. **1.** to treat (a substance) or cause (a substance) to react with nitrogen. **2.** to treat (soil) with nitrates. **3.** to convert (ammonium compounds) into nitrates by oxidation. —ˌnitrifi'cation n.

nitrite ('naɪtraɪt) n. a salt or ester of nitrous acid.

nitro- or before a vowel **nitr-** combining form. indicating that: **1.** a chemical compound contains the univalent group, -NO₂: *nitrobenzene*. **2.** a chemical compound is a nitrate ester: *nitrocellulose*. [Greek *nitron* nitre]

nitrogen ('naɪtrədʒən) n. Chem. a colourless odourless gaseous element that forms four-fifths of the air and is an essential part of all animal and plant life. Symbol: N —**nitrogenous** (naɪˈtrɒdʒɪnəs) adj.

nitrogen cycle n. the natural cycle by which nitrates in the soil, derived from dead organic matter, are absorbed by plants and reduced to nitrates again when the plants and the animals feeding on them die and decay.

nitrogen fixation n. the conversion of atmospheric nitrogen into nitrogen compounds by soil bacteria.

nitroglycerin (ˌnaɪtrəʊˈɡlɪsərɪn) or **nitroglycerine** (ˌnaɪtrəʊˈɡlɪsəˌriːn) n. Chem. a thick pale yellow explosive liquid made from glycerol and nitric and sulphuric acids.

nitrous ('naɪtrəs) adj. Chem. derived from or containing nitrogen in a low valency state.

nitrous acid n. Chem. a weak acid known only in solution and in the form of nitrite salts.

nitrous oxide n. Chem. a colourless gas used as an anaesthetic.

nitty-gritty ('nɪtɪˈɡrɪtɪ) n. the. Informal. the basic facts of a matter or situation. [possibly rhyming compound from *grit*]

nitwit ('nɪtˌwɪt) n. Informal. a stupid person. [possibly NIT[1] + WIT[1]]

NJ New Jersey.

NM or **N. Mex.** New Mexico.

no[1] (nəʊ) interj. **1.** used to express denial, disagreement, or refusal. ~n., pl. **noes** or **nos. 2.** an answer or vote of no. **3.** a person who votes in the negative. [Old English *nā*]

no[2] (nəʊ) det. **1.** not any, not a, or not one: *I have no money; no excuse.* **2.** not at all: *he's no fool.* **3.** (foll. by comparative adjectives and adverbs) not: *no taller than a child.* **4. no way!** an expression of emphatic refusal or denial. [Old English *nān* none]

No[1] or **Noh** (nəʊ) n., pl. **No** or **Noh.** the stylized classic drama of Japan, using music and dancing. [Japanese *nō* talent]

No[2] Chem. nobelium.

No. or **no.**, pl. **Nos.** or **nos.** number. [French *numéro*]

n.o. Cricket. not out.

nob (nɒb) n. Slang, chiefly Brit. a person of wealth or social distinction. [origin unknown]

no-ball n. Cricket. an improperly bowled ball, for which the batting side scores a run.

nobble ('nɒb³l) vb. Brit. slang. **1.** to disable (a racehorse) to stop it from winning. **2.** to outwit (a person) by underhand means. **3.** to bribe or threaten (a person). **4.** to steal. [*nobbler*, a false division of *an hobbler* one who hobbles horses]

nobelium (nəʊˈbiːlɪəm) n. Chem. a radioactive element produced artificially from curium. Symbol: No [after *Nobel* Institute, Stockholm, where it was discovered]

Nobel prize (nəʊˈbɛl) n. a prize for outstanding contributions to chemistry, physics, physiology and medicine, literature, economics, and peace that may be awarded annually. [after Alfred *Nobel*, chemist & philanthropist]

nobility (nəʊˈbɪlɪtɪ) n. **1.** the quality of being noble; dignity. **2.** the class of people who hold titles and high social rank.

noble ('nəʊb³l) adj. **1.** having or showing high moral qualities: *a noble deed.* **2.** belonging to a class of people who hold titles and high social rank. **3.** imposing; magnificent: *a noble palace.* **4.** Chem. (of certain metals) resisting oxidation. ~n. **5.** a person who holds a title and high social rank. [Latin *nōbilis*, orig. capable of being known, hence well-known] —**'nobly** adv.

noble gas n. any of the unreactive gaseous elements helium, neon, argon, krypton, xenon, and radon.

nobleman ('nəʊb'lmən) or (fem.) **noblewoman** n., pl. **-men** or **-women**. a person of noble rank; peer; aristocrat.

noblesse oblige (nəʊˈbles əʊˈbliːʒ) n. Often ironic. the obligation of nobility to be honourable and kind. [French, lit.: nobility obliges]

nobody ('nəʊbədɪ) pron. 1. no person; no-one. ~n., pl. **-bodies**. 2. an insignificant person.

nock (nɒk) n. 1. a notch on an arrow that fits on the bowstring. 2. a groove at either end of a bow that holds the bowstring. [related to Swedish nock tip]

no-claim bonus n. a reduction on an insurance premium, usually one covering a motor vehicle, if no claims have been made within a specified period. Also called: **no-claims bonus**.

nocturnal (nɒkˈtɜːn'l) adj. 1. of the night. 2. (of animals) active at night. [Latin nox night]

nocturne ('nɒktɜːn) n. a short dreamy piece of music.

nod (nɒd) vb. **nodding, nodded**. 1. to lower and raise (the head) briefly, to express agreement or greeting. 2. to express by nodding: she nodded approval. 3. to sway or bend forwards and back. 4. to let the head fall forwards through drowsiness; be drowsy. 5. **nodding acquaintance**. a slight knowledge (of a subject or person). ~n. 6. a quick down-and-up movement of the head, in agreement. 7. **land of Nod**. an imaginary land of sleep. [origin unknown]

noddle ('nɒd'l) n. Informal, chiefly Brit. the head or brains. [origin unknown]

noddy ('nɒdɪ) n., pl. **-dies**. 1. a tropical tern with a dark plumage. 2. a fool. [perhaps from obs. noddy foolish, drowsy]

node (nəʊd) n. 1. a knot or knob. 2. Bot. the point on a plant stem from which the leaves grow. 3. Physics. a point in a vibrating body at which there is practically no vibration. 4. Maths. a point at which a curve crosses itself. 5. Astron. either of the two points at which the orbit of a body intersects the path of the sun or the orbit of another body. 6. Anat. any natural bulge or swelling: lymph node. [Latin nōdus knot] —**'nodal** adj.

nod off vb. Informal. to fall asleep.

nodule ('nɒdjuːl) n. 1. a small rounded lump, knot, or node. 2. a knoblike growth on the root of a plant such as clover, which contains nitrogen-fixing bacteria. [Latin nōdulus] —**'nodular** adj.

Noel or **Noël** (nəʊˈel) n. (in carols and on cards) same as **Christmas**. [French, from Latin nātālis a birthday]

nog (nɒg) n. an alcoholic drink containing beaten egg. [origin unknown]

noggin ('nɒgɪn) n. 1. Informal. the head.

2. a small quantity of spirits. [origin unknown]

no-go area n. a district in a town that is barricaded off and which the police or army can only enter by force.

noise (nɔɪz) n. 1. a sound, usually a loud or disturbing one. 2. clamour; din. 3. an undesired electrical disturbance in a signal. 4. (pl.) conventional utterances conveying a reaction: sympathetic noises. ~vb. 5. **be noised abroad**. (of news or gossip) to be spread. [Latin nausea seasickness]

noiseless ('nɔɪzlɪs) adj. making little or no sound. —**'noiselessly** adv.

noisette (nwɑːˈzet) n. a hazelnut chocolate. [French]

noisome ('nɔɪsəm) adj. 1. (of smells) offensive. 2. harmful or poisonous. [obs. noy, var. of annoy]

noisy ('nɔɪzɪ) adj. **noisier, noisiest**. 1. making a lot of noise. 2. (of a place) full of noise. —**'noisily** adv.

nomad ('nəʊmæd) n. 1. a member of a tribe who move from place to place to find pasture and food. 2. a wanderer. [Greek nomas wandering for pasture] —**no'madic** adj.

no-man's-land n. land between boundaries, esp. an unoccupied zone between opposing forces.

nom de plume ('nɒm də 'pluːm) n., pl. **noms de plume** ('nɒm də pluːm). same as **pen name**. [French]

nomenclature (nəʊˈmenklətʃə) n. the system of names used in a particular subject. [Latin nōmenclātūra list of names]

nominal ('nɒmɪn'l) adj. 1. in name only: the nominal leader. 2. very small in comparison with real worth: a nominal fee. [Latin nōmen name]

nominalism ('nɒmɪn'ˌlɪzəm) n. the philosophical theory that a general word, such as dog, is merely a name and does not denote a real object. —**'nominalist** n.

nominal value n. same as **par value**.

nominate ('nɒmɪˌneɪt) vb. 1. to propose (someone) as a candidate. 2. to appoint (someone) to an office or position. [Latin nōmen name] —**ˌnomi'nation** n.

nominative ('nɒmɪnətɪv) Grammar. ~adj. 1. denoting a case of nouns and pronouns in some languages such as Latin, that identifies the subject of a verb. ~n. 2. a. the nominative case. b. a word in this case. [Latin nōminātīvus belonging to naming]

nominee (ˌnɒmɪˈniː) n. a person who is nominated to an office or as a candidate.

non- prefix. indicating: 1. negation: nonexistent. 2. refusal or failure: noncooperation. 3. exclusion from a specified class: nonfiction. 4. lack or absence: nonevent. [Latin nōn not]

nonage ('nəʊnɪdʒ) n. 1. Law. the state of being under full legal age. 2. immaturity.

nonagenarian (ˌnəʊnədʒɪˈneərɪən) n. a person who is from 90 to 99 years old. [Latin nōnāginta ninety]

---

nonagon ('nɒnəˌgɒn) n. a polygon having nine sides. —**nonagonal** (nɒn'ægən'l) adj.

nonaligned (ˌnɒnə'laɪnd) adj. (of a country) not part of a major alliance or power bloc. —ˌnona'lignment n.

nonce (nɒns) n. **for the nonce.** for the present. [a mistaken division of for then anes, for the once]

nonce word n. a word coined for a single occasion.

nonchalant ('nɒnʃələnt) adj. casually unconcerned or indifferent. [French, from nonchaloir to lack warmth] —'**nonchalance** n. —'**nonchalantly** adv.

non-com ('nɒnˌkɒm) n. short for **noncommissioned officer.**

noncombatant (nɒn'kɒmbətənt) n. a member of the armed forces whose duties do not include fighting, such as a chaplain or surgeon.

noncommissioned officer (ˌnɒnkə-'mɪʃənd) n. (in the armed forces) a person who is appointed as a subordinate officer, from the lower ranks, rather than by a commission.

noncommittal (ˌnɒnkə'mɪt'l) adj. not committing oneself to any particular opinion.

non compos mentis ('nɒn 'kɒmpəs 'mɛntɪs) adj. of unsound mind. [Latin: not in control of one's mind]

nonconductor (ˌnɒnkən'dʌktə) n. a substance that is a poor conductor of heat, electricity, or sound.

nonconformist (ˌnɒnkən'fɔːmɪst) n. **1.** a person who does not conform to generally accepted patterns of behaviour or thought. ~adj. **2.** (of behaviour or ideas) not conforming to accepted patterns. —ˌnoncon-'formity n.

Nonconformist (ˌnɒnkən'fɔːmɪst) n. **1.** a Protestant who does not belong to the Church of England. ~adj. **2.** of or denoting Nonconformists.

noncontributory (ˌnɒnkən'trɪbjʊtrɪ) adj. denoting a pension scheme for employees, the premiums of which are paid entirely by the employer.

nondescript ('nɒndɪˌskrɪpt) adj. having no outstanding features. [NON- + Latin dēscriptus, past participle of dēscrībere to copy]

none (nʌn) pron. (functioning as sing. or pl.) **1.** not any: none of us went; none of it looks edible. **2.** no-one; nobody: there were none to tell the tale. **3.** none the. (foll. by a comparative adj.) in no degree: she was none the worse for her ordeal. [Old English nān, lit.: not one]

nonentity (nɒn'ɛntɪtɪ) n., pl. -ties. an insignificant person or thing.

nonetheless (ˌnʌnðə'lɛs) adv. nevertheless.

nonevent (ˌnɒnɪ'vɛnt) n. a disappointing or insignificant occurrence which was expected to be important.

nonferrous (nɒn'fɛrəs) adj. denoting a metal other than iron.

nonflammable (nɒn'flæməb'l) adj. not easily set on fire.

nonintervention (ˌnɒnɪntə'vɛnʃən) n. refusal to intervene in the affairs of others.

nonmetal (nɒn'mɛt'l) n. Chem. a chemical element that forms acidic oxides and is a poor conductor of heat and electricity. —**nonmetallic** (ˌnɒnmɪ'tælɪk) adj.

nonmoral (nɒn'mɒrəl) adj. not involving morality; neither moral nor immoral.

no-nonsense (ˌnəʊ'nɒnsəns) adj. sensible, practical, and straightforward: a severe no-nonsense look.

nonpareil ('nɒnpərəl, ˌnɒnpə'reɪl) n. a person or thing that is unsurpassed. [French, from NON- + pareil similar]

nonplussed or U.S. **nonplused** (nɒn-'plʌst) adj. perplexed. [Latin nōn plūs no further]

nonproliferation (ˌnɒnprəˌlɪfər'eɪʃən) n. limitation of the production or spread of something such as nuclear or chemical weapons.

nonalcoholic	nondrip	nonparticipation
nonbeliever	nondriver	nonpartisan
nonbelligerent	nonessential	nonparty
non-Catholic	nonexecutive	nonpaying
non-Christian	nonexistent	nonpayment
nonclassified	nonfattening	nonplaying
noncombustible	nonfiction	nonpractising
noncommercial	nonfulfilment	nonprofessional
noncommunicable	nonfunctional	non-profit-making
noncommunist	nongovernmental	nonracial
noncompetitive	noninfectious	nonreader
noncompliance	nonintellectual	nonrecognition
noncompulsory	noniron	nonrenewable
noncontagious	nonmalignant	nonresident
noncontroversial	nonmember	nonreturnable
noncooperation	non-native	nonscientific
noncustodial	non-negotiable	nonsectarian
nondenominational	non-nuclear	nonsegregated
nondiscrimination	nonobservance	
nondrinker	nonoperational	

nonrepresentational (ˌnɒnreprɪˈzenˈteɪʃənˀl) *adj. Art.* same as **abstract**.

nonsense (ˈnɒnsəns) *n.* **1.** something that has or makes no sense; unintelligible language. **2.** foolish behaviour: *she'll stand no nonsense.* —**nonsensical** (nɒnˈsensɪkˀl) *adj.*

non sequitur (ˈnɒn ˈsekwɪtə) *n.* a statement having little or no relevance to what preceded it. [Latin: it does not follow]

nonstandard (nɒnˈstændəd) *adj.* denoting words, expressions, or pronunciations that are not regarded as correct by educated native speakers of a language.

nonstarter (nɒnˈstɑːtə) *n.* a person or an idea that has little chance of success.

nonstick (ˈnɒnˈstɪk) *adj.* (of saucepans, etc.) coated with a substance that prevents food sticking to them.

nonstop (ˈnɒnˈstɒp) *adj., adv.* without a stop: *a nonstop flight; she talks nonstop.*

non-U (nɒnˈjuː) *adj. Brit. informal.* (of language or behaviour) not characteristic of the upper classes.

nonunion (nɒnˈjuːnjən) *adj.* **1.** (of a company) not employing union labour: *a nonunion shop.* **2.** not belonging to a trade union.

nonvoter (nɒnˈvəʊtə) *n.* **1.** a person who does not vote. **2.** a person not eligible to vote.

nonvoting (nɒnˈvəʊtɪŋ) *adj. Finance.* (of shares) not entitling the holder to vote at company meetings.

noodle (ˈnuːdˀl) *n. U.S. & Canad. slang.* the head. [a blend of *noddle* & *noodles*]

noodles (ˈnuːdˀlz) *pl. n.* ribbon-like strips of pasta. [German *Nudeln*]

nook (nʊk) *n.* **1.** a corner or recess. **2.** a secluded or sheltered place. [origin unknown]

noon (nuːn) *n.* the middle of the day; 12 o'clock. [Latin *nōna* (*hōra*) ninth hour (orig. 3 p.m., the ninth hour from sunrise)]

noonday (ˈnuːnˌdeɪ) *n.* midday; noon.

no-one *or* **no one** *pron.* no person; nobody.

noose (nuːs) *n.* **1.** a loop in the end of a rope, tied with a slipknot, such as one used to hang people. **2. put one's head in a noose.** to bring about one's own downfall. [Latin *nōdus* node]

nor (nɔː; *unstressed* nə) *conj.* **1.** (used to join alternatives, the first of which is preceded by *neither*) and not: *neither up nor down.* **2.** (foll. by a verb) and not...either: *I'm not rich nor am I famous.* [contraction of Old English *nōther*]

nordic (ˈnɔːdɪk) *adj. Skiing.* of competitions in cross-country racing and ski-jumping.

Nordic (ˈnɔːdɪk) *adj.* of the tall blond blue-eyed long-headed people of Scandinavia. [French *nordique* of the north]

norm (nɔːm) *n.* a standard that is required, desired, or regarded as normal. [Latin *norma* carpenter's square]

normal (ˈnɔːmˀl) *adj.* **1.** usual; regular; typical: *the normal level.* **2.** free from mental or physical disorder. **3.** *Geom.* same as **perpendicular** (sense 1). ~*n.* **4.** the usual, regular, or typical state, degree, or form. **5.** *Geom.* a perpendicular line or plane. [Latin *normālis* conforming to the carpenter's square] —**normality** (nɔːˈmælɪtɪ) *or esp. U.S.* ˈ**normalcy** *n.*

normalize *or* **-ise** (ˈnɔːməˌlaɪz) *vb.* **1.** to make or become normal. **2.** to bring into conformity with a standard. —ˌnormaliˈzation *or* -iˈsation *n.*

normally (ˈnɔːməlɪ) *adv.* **1.** as a rule; usually. **2.** in a normal manner.

Norman (ˈnɔːmən) *n.* **1.** a person from Normandy in N France, esp. one of the people who conquered England in 1066. **2.** same as **Norman French.** ~*adj.* **3.** of the Normans or their dialect of French. **4.** denoting or having the style of architecture used in Britain from the Norman Conquest in 1066 until the 12th century, with rounded arches and massive masonry walls.

Norman French *n.* the medieval Norman and English dialect of Old French.

normative (ˈnɔːmətɪv) *adj.* of or establishing a norm or standard: *normative grammar.*

Norn (nɔːn) *n. Norse myth.* any of the three virgin goddesses of fate. [Old Norse]

Norse (nɔːs) *adj.* **1.** of ancient and medieval Scandinavia. **2.** of Norway. ~*n.* **3. a.** the N group of Germanic languages spoken in Scandinavia. **b.** any one of these languages, esp. in their ancient or medieval forms.

Norseman (ˈnɔːsmən) *n., pl.* **-men.** same as **Viking.**

north (nɔːθ) *n.* **1.** one of the four cardinal points of the compass, at 0° or 360°, that is opposite south. **2.** the direction along a meridian towards the North Pole. **3.** the direction in which a compass needle points; magnetic north. **4. the north.** (*often cap.*) any area lying in or towards the north. ~*adj.* **5.** in or towards the north. **6.** from the north: *a north wind.* ~*adv.* **7.** in, to, or towards the north. [Old English]

North (nɔːθ) *n.* **the. 1.** the northern part of England, generally regarded as reaching the southern boundaries of Yorkshire, Derbyshire, and Cheshire. **2.** (in the U.S.) the states north of the Mason-Dixon Line that were known as the Free States during the Civil War. **3.** the economically and techni-

---

nonsexist	nonspecialist	nontransferable
nonsexual	nonswimmer	nonverbal
nonslip	nontaxable	nonvintage
nonsmoker	nonteaching	nonviolence
nonsoluble	nontechnical	nonviolent
nonspeaking	nontoxic	non-White

cally advanced countries of the world. ~*adj.* **4.** of or denoting the northern part of a country or area.

Northants (nɔː'θænts) Northamptonshire.

North Country *n.* **the.** same as **North** (sense 1).

northeast (ˌnɔːθ'iːst; *Naut.* ˌnɔːr'iːst) *n.* **1.** the direction midway between north and east. **2. the northeast.** (*often cap.*) any area lying in or towards the northeast. ~*adj.* also **northeastern. 3.** (*sometimes cap.*) of or denoting that part of a country or area which lies in the northeast. **4.** in, towards, or facing the northeast. **5.** from the northeast: *a northeast wind.* ~*adv.* **6.** in, to, or towards the northeast. —ˌnorth'easterly *adj., adv., n.*

Northeast (ˌnɔːθ'iːst) *n.* **the.** the northeastern part of England, esp. Northumberland and Durham.

northeaster (ˌnɔːθ'iːstə; *Naut.* ˌnɔːr'iːstə) *n.* a strong wind or storm from the northeast.

northerly ('nɔːðəlɪ) *adj.* **1.** of or in the north. ~*adv., adj.* **2.** towards the north. **3.** from the north: *a northerly wind.*

northern ('nɔːðən) *adj.* **1.** of, in, or towards the north. **2.** from the north. **3.** (*sometimes cap.*) of or characteristic of the North. —'northern, most *adj.*

Northerner ('nɔːðənə) *n.* a person from the north of a country or area.

northern hemisphere *n.* that half of the globe lying north of the equator.

northern lights *pl. n.* same as **aurora borealis.**

Northman ('nɔːθmən) *n., pl.* -men. same as **Viking.**

North Pole *n.* the northernmost point on the earth's axis, at a latitude of 90°N, which has very low temperatures.

North-Sea gas *n.* (in Britain) natural gas obtained from deposits below the North Sea.

North Star *n.* **the.** same as **Pole Star.**

Northumb. Northumberland.

northward ('nɔːθwəd; *Naut.* 'nɔːðəd) *adj., adv.* also **northwards. 1.** towards the north. ~*n.* **2.** the northward part or direction.

northwest (ˌnɔːθ'wɛst; *Naut.* ˌnɔː'wɛst) *n.* **1.** the direction midway between north and west. **2.** (*often cap.*) any area lying in or towards the northwest. ~*adj.* also **northwestern. 3.** (*sometimes cap.*) of or denoting that part of a country or area which lies in the northwest. **4.** in or towards the northwest. ~*adv.* **5.** in, to, or towards the northwest. —ˌnorth'westerly *adj., adv., n.*

Northwest (ˌnɔːθ'wɛst) *n.* **the.** the northwestern part of England, esp. Lancashire and the Lake District.

northwester (ˌnɔːθ'wɛstə; *Naut.* ˌnɔː'wɛstə) *n.* a strong wind or storm from the northwest.

Norwegian (nɔː'wiːdʒən) *adj.* **1.** of Norway, its language, or its people. ~*n.* **2.** the language of Norway. **3.** a person from Norway.

Nos. *or* **nos.** numbers.

nose (nəʊz) *n.* **1.** the organ situated above the mouth, used for smelling and breathing. **2.** the sense of smell. **3.** the odour or bouquet of something such as wine. **4.** instinctive skill in finding something: *he had a nose for good news stories.* **5.** the front part of a vehicle. **6. get up someone's nose.** *Informal.* to annoy someone. **7. keep one's nose clean.** to stay out of trouble. **8. look down one's nose at.** *Informal.* to be disdainful of. **9. pay through the nose.** *Informal.* to pay a high price. **10. put someone's nose out of joint.** *Informal.* to make someone envious by doing what he would have liked to do or had expected to do. **11. rub someone's nose in it.** *Informal.* to remind someone unkindly of a failing or error. **12. turn up one's nose at.** *Informal.* to show contempt for. **13. win by a nose.** to win by a narrow margin. **14. with one's nose in the air.** haughtily. ~*vb.* **15.** (foll. by *out*) to discover (a secret) by prying. **16.** to move forward slowly and carefully: *we nosed the car into the garage.* **17.** (foll. by *around* or *about*) to pry or snoop. [Old English *nosu*]

nosebag ('nəʊzˌbæg) *n.* a bag containing feed, fastened around the head of a horse.

noseband ('nəʊzˌbænd) *n.* the part of a horse's bridle that goes around the nose.

nosebleed ('nəʊzˌbliːd) *n.* bleeding from the nose.

nose cone *n.* the cone-shaped front section of a missile or spacecraft.

nose dive *n.* **1.** (of an aircraft) a sudden plunge with the nose pointing downwards. **2.** *Informal.* a sudden drop: *prices took a nose dive.* ~*vb.* **nose-dive. 3.** to take a nose dive.

nosegay ('nəʊzˌgeɪ) *n.* a small bunch of flowers; posy. [*nose* + *gay* (archaic) toy]

nosey ('nəʊzɪ) *adj.* same as **nosy.**

nosh (nɒʃ) *Slang.* ~*n.* **1.** food. ~*vb.* **2.** to eat. [Yiddish]

nosh-up *n. Brit. slang.* a large meal.

nostalgia (nɒ'stældʒə, -dʒɪə) *n.* **1.** a sentimental yearning for the past. **2.** homesickness. [Greek *nostos* a return home + *algios* pain] —**nos'talgic** *adj.* —**nos'talgically** *adv.*

nostril ('nɒstrɪl) *n.* either of the two openings at the end of the nose. [Old English *nosu* nose + *thyrel* hole]

nostrum ('nɒstrəm) *n.* **1.** a quack medicine. **2.** a favourite remedy. [Latin: our own (make)]

nosy *or* **nosey** ('nəʊzɪ) *adj.* **nosier, nosiest.** *Informal.* prying or inquisitive. —'nosiness *n.*

nosy parker *n. Informal, chiefly Brit.* a prying person. [arbitrary use of surname *Parker*]

not (nɒt) *adv.* **1.** used to negate the sentence, phrase, or word that it modifies: *I will not stand for it.* **2. not that.** which is not to say that: *he's left me —not that I care.* [Old English *nāwiht*, from *nā* no + *wiht* creature, thing]

nota bene ('nəʊtə 'biːnɪ) note well; take note. [Latin]

notable ('nəʊtəb'l) *adj.* **1.** worthy of being noted; remarkable; distinguished. ~*n.* **2.** a notable person. [Latin *notāre* to note] —ˌnota'bility *n.* —'notably *adv.*

notary public *or* **notary** ('nəʊtərɪ) *n., pl.* **notaries public** *or* **notaries.** a public official, usually a solicitor, who is legally authorized to attest and certify documents. [Latin *notarius* one who makes notes, a clerk]

notation (nəʊ'teɪʃən) *n.* a series of signs or symbols used to represent quantities or elements in a specialized system such as music or mathematics. [Latin *notāre* to note]

notch (nɒtʃ) *n.* **1.** a V-shaped cut; nick. **2.** *Informal.* a step or level: *my esteem for her went up a notch.* ~*vb.* **3.** to cut a notch in. **4.** (foll. by *up*) *Informal.* to score or achieve: *he notched up a victory.* [mistaken division of *an otch*, from Old French *oche* notch]

note (nəʊt) *n.* **1.** a brief record in writing for future reference. **2.** a brief informal letter. **3.** an official written communication, as from a government or from a doctor. **4.** a critical comment or explanation in a book. **5.** short for **banknote. 6.** a particular feeling or atmosphere: *a note of sarcasm.* **7.** a distinctive vocal sound, as of a type of animal. **8.** a written symbol representing the pitch and duration of a musical sound. **9.** *Chiefly Brit.* a musical sound of a particular pitch. **10.** *Chiefly Brit.* a key on a piano, organ, or other keyboard instrument. **11.** a sound used as a signal or warning: *the note to retreat was sounded.* **12.** short for **promissory note. 13. of note. a.** distinguished or famous. **b.** important: *nothing of note.* **14. strike the right note.** to behave appropriately. **15. take note of.** to pay attention to. ~*vb.* **16.** to notice; perceive; pay attention to: *they noted every movement.* **17.** to make a written note of: *she noted the date in her diary.* **18.** to remark upon: *I note that you do not wear shoes.* [Latin *nota* sign]

notebook ('nəʊt,bʊk) *n.* a book for writing in.

notecase ('nəʊt,keɪs) *n.* same as **wallet.**

noted ('nəʊtɪd) *adj.* celebrated; famous: *a noted sculptor.*

notelet ('nəʊtlɪt) *n.* a folded card with a printed design on the front, for writing a short letter.

notepaper ('nəʊt,peɪpə) *n.* paper for writing letters.

noteworthy ('nəʊt,wɜːðɪ) *adj.* worthy of notice; notable.

nothing ('nʌθɪŋ) *pron.* **1.** not anything: *I saw nothing.* **2.** a matter of no importance: *don't worry, it's nothing.* **3.** absence of meaning, value, or worth: *to amount to nothing.* **4.** zero; nought. **5. have** *or* **be nothing to do with.** to have no connection with. **6. nothing but.** no more than; only. **7. nothing doing.** *Informal.* an expression of dismissal or refusal. **8. nothing less than.** downright; truly: *nothing less than*

tragic. **9. think nothing of something.** to regard something as easy or natural. ~*adv.* **10.** not at all: *he looked nothing like his brother.* ~*n.* **11.** *Informal.* a person or thing of no importance or significance. [Old English *nāthing*, *nān thing*]

nothingness ('nʌθɪŋnɪs) *n.* **1.** nonexistence. **2.** unconsciousness. **3.** total insignificance.

notice ('nəʊtɪs) *n.* **1.** observation; attention: *to escape notice.* **2. take notice.** to pay attention. **3. take no notice of.** to ignore or disregard. **4.** a displayed placard or announcement giving information. **5.** advance notification of something such as intention to end a contract of employment: *I handed in my notice this morning.* **6. at short notice.** with very little notification. **7.** a theatrical or literary review: *the play received very good notices.* ~*vb.* **8.** to become aware (of); perceive; note. **9.** to point out or remark upon. [Latin *nōtus* known]

noticeable ('nəʊtɪsəb'l) *adj.* easily seen or detected. —'noticeably *adv.*

notice board *n. Brit.* a board on which notices are displayed.

notifiable ('nəʊtɪ,faɪəb'l) *adj.* denoting certain infectious diseases, outbreaks of which must be reported to the public health authorities.

notification (,nəʊtɪfɪ'keɪʃən) *n.* **1.** the act of notifying someone of something. **2.** a formal announcement.

notify ('nəʊtɪ,faɪ) *vb.* **-fying, -fied.** to tell: *you should notify the bank of your change of address.* [Latin *nōtus* known + *facere* to make]

notion ('nəʊʃən) *n.* **1.** a vague idea; impression. **2.** an idea or opinion. **3.** a whim. [Latin *nōtiō* a becoming acquainted (with)]

notional ('nəʊʃən'l) *adj.* not real; hypothetical or imaginary: *a notional tax credit.*

notorious (nəʊ'tɔːrɪəs) *adj.* well known for some bad reason. [Medieval Latin *notōrius* well known] —**notoriety** (,nəʊtə'raɪɪtɪ) *n.* —no'toriously *adv.*

not proven ('prəʊv'n) *adj.* a verdict in Scottish courts, given when there is insufficient evidence to convict the accused.

no-trump *Cards.* ~*n.* **1.** a bid or hand without trumps. ~*adj.* **2.** (of a hand) suitable for playing without trumps.

Notts (nɒts) Nottinghamshire.

notwithstanding (,nɒtwɪθ'stændɪŋ) *prep.* **1.** in spite of. ~*adv.* **2.** nevertheless.

nougat ('nuːgɑː) *n.* a hard chewy pink or white sweet containing chopped nuts. [French, from Latin *nux* nut]

nought (nɔːt) *n.* **1.** same as **zero.** ~*n., adj., adv.* **2.** same as **naught.** [Old English *nōwiht*, from *ne* not, no + *ōwiht* something]

noughts and crosses *n.* (*functioning as sing.*) *Brit.* a game in which two players, one using a nought, the other a cross, alternately mark squares formed by two pairs of crossed lines, the winner being the first to get three of his symbols in a row.

noun (naʊn) *n.* a word that refers to a

person, place, or thing. [Latin *nōmen* name]

nourish ('nʌrɪʃ) *vb.* **1.** to provide (a person or animal) with the food necessary for life and growth. **2.** to encourage or foster (an idea or feeling). [Latin *nūtrīre* to feed] —**'nourishing** *adj.*

nourishment ('nʌrɪʃmənt) *n.* **1.** a nourishing substance; food. **2.** a nourishing or being nourished.

nous (naʊs) *n. Old-fashioned Brit. slang.* common sense. [Greek: mind]

nouveau riche (,nuːvəʊ 'riːʃ) *n., pl.* **nouveaux riches** (,nuːvəʊ 'riːʃ). a person who has become wealthy recently and is regarded as vulgar. [French: new rich]

nouvelle cuisine ('nuːvel kwiː'ziːn) *n.* a style of preparing food, often raw or only lightly cooked, with unusual combinations of flavours. [French: new cooking]

Nov. November.

nova ('nəʊvə) *n., pl.* **-vae** (-viː) *or* **-vas.** a star that undergoes an explosion and fast increase of brightness, then gradually decreases to its original brightness. [New Latin *nova* (*stella*) new (star)]

novel[1] ('nɒv'l) *n.* a long fictional story in prose, dealing with character, action, and thought. [Latin *novella* (*narrātiō*) new (story)]

novel[2] ('nɒv'l) *adj.* fresh; new; original: *a novel suggestion.* [Latin *novus* new]

novelette (,nɒvə'let) *n.* a short novel, usually one regarded as slight, trivial, or sentimental.

novelist ('nɒvəlɪst) *n.* a writer of novels.

novella (nəʊ'velə) *n., pl.* **-las** *or* **-le** (-leɪ). a short narrative tale or short novel. [Italian]

novelty ('nɒv'ltɪ) *n., pl.* **-ties.** **1.** the quality of being new and interesting. **2.** a new or unusual experience. **3.** a small cheap toy or trinket.

November (nəʊ'vembə) *n.* the eleventh month of the year. [Latin: ninth month]

novena (nəʊ'viːnə) *n., pl.* **-nae** (-niː). *R.C. Church.* a devotion consisting of prayers or services on nine consecutive days. [Latin *novem* nine]

novice ('nɒvɪs) *n.* **1.** a beginner. **2.** a person who has entered a religious order but has not yet taken vows. [Latin *novus* new]

novitiate *or* **noviciate** (nəʊ'vɪʃɪt, -ˌeɪt) *n.* **1.** the period of being a novice. **2.** the part of a monastery or convent where the novices live.

now (naʊ) *adv.* **1.** at or for the present time. **2.** immediately: *do it now.* **3.** in these times; nowadays. **4.** given the present circumstances: *now we'll have to stay to the end.* **5. a.** used as a hesitation word: *now, I can't really say.* **b.** used for emphasis: *now listen to this.* **c.** used at the end of a command: *run along now.* **6. just now. a.** very recently: *he left just now.* **b.** very soon: *I'm going just now.* **7. now and again** *or* **then.** occasionally. **8. now now!** an exclamation used to tell someone off or to calm someone. ~*conj.* **9.** (often foll. by *that*) seeing that: *now you're here, you can*

help me. ~*n.* **10.** the present time: *now is the time to go.* [Old English nū]

nowadays ('naʊə,deɪz) *adv.* in these times: *most companies use computers nowadays.*

Nowel *or* **Nowell** (nəʊ'el) *n.* same as **Noel.**

nowhere ('nəʊwɛə) *adv.* **1.** in, at, or to no place; not anywhere. **2. getting nowhere.** *Informal.* making no progress. **3. nowhere near.** far from; not nearly. ~*n.* **4. in the middle of nowhere.** (of a place) completely isolated.

nowise ('nəʊ,waɪz) *adv.* in no way; not at all.

nowt (naʊt) *n. N English dialect.* nothing. [from *naught*]

noxious ('nɒkʃəs) *adj.* poisonous or harmful. [Latin *noxius* harmful]

nozzle ('nɒz'l) *n.* a projecting spout from which fluid is discharged. [diminutive of *nose*]

Np *Chem.* neptunium.

NS **1.** New Style (method of reckoning dates). **2.** Nova Scotia.

NSPCC (in Britain) National Society for the Prevention of Cruelty to Children.

NST (in Canada) Newfoundland Standard Time.

NT **1.** (in Britain) National Trust. **2.** New Testament.

-n't not: added to *be* or *have*, or auxiliary verbs: *can't; don't; isn't.*

nth (enθ) *adj.* See **n**[2].

nuance (njuː'ɑːns, 'njuːɑːns) *n.* a subtle difference, as in colour, meaning, or tone. [French]

nub (nʌb) *n.* the point or gist: *the nub of a story.* [Middle Low German *knubbe* KNOB]

nubble ('nʌb'l) *n.* a small lump. [from *nub*] —**'nubbly** *adj.*

nubile ('njuːbaɪl) *adj.* (of a young woman) **1.** sexually attractive. **2.** old enough or mature enough for marriage. [Latin *nūbere* to marry]

nuclear ('njuːklɪə) *adj.* **1.** of an atomic nucleus: *nuclear fission.* **2.** of atoms or nuclear energy: *a nuclear weapon; nuclear war.*

nuclear bomb *n.* a bomb whose force is due to uncontrolled nuclear fusion or fission.

nuclear energy *n. Chem., physics.* energy released during a nuclear reaction as a result of fission or fusion.

nuclear family *n. Sociol., anthropol.* a family consisting only of parents and their offspring.

nuclear fission *n. Nuclear physics.* the splitting of an atomic nucleus, either spontaneously or by bombardment by a neutron: used in atomic bombs and nuclear power plants.

nuclear fusion *n. Nuclear physics.* the combination of two nuclei to form a heavier nucleus with the release of energy: used in hydrogen bombs.

nuclear physics *n.* (functioning *as sing.*) the branch of physics concerned with the structure of the nucleus and the behaviour of its particles.

nuclear power n. power produced by a nuclear reactor.

nuclear reaction n. Physics. a process in which the structure and energy content of an atomic nucleus is changed by interaction with another nucleus or particle.

nuclear reactor n. Nuclear physics. a device in which a nuclear reaction is maintained and controlled to produce nuclear energy.

nuclear winter n. a period of low temperatures and little light that has been suggested would occur after a nuclear war.

nucleate adj. ('njuːklɪɪt, -ˌeɪt). **1.** having a nucleus. ~vb. ('njuːklɪˌeɪt). **2.** to form a nucleus.

nuclei ('njuːklɪˌaɪ) n. the plural of **nucleus**.

nucleic acid (njuːˈkliːɪk, -ˈkleɪ-) n. Biochem. a complex compound with a high molecular weight: a vital constituent of all living cells.

nucleon ('njuːkliˌɒn) n. Physics. a proton or neutron.

nucleonics (ˌnjuːklɪˈɒnɪks) n. (functioning as sing.) the branch of physics concerned with the applications of nuclear energy. —ˌnucleˈonic adj.

nucleus ('njuːklɪəs) n., pl. **-clei. 1.** a central thing around which others are grouped; core. **2.** a centre of growth or development: the nucleus of an idea. **3.** Physics. the positively charged centre of an atom, made of protons and neutrons, about which electrons orbit. **4.** Biol. the part of a cell that contains the chromosomes and associated molecules that control the characteristics and growth of the cell. **5.** Chem. a fundamental group of atoms in a molecule serving as the base structure for related compounds. [Latin: kernel]

nude (njuːd) adj. **1.** completely undressed. ~n. **2.** a naked figure in painting, sculpture, or photography. **3. in the nude.** naked. [Latin nūdus] —ˈnudity n.

nudge (nʌdʒ) vb. **1.** to push (someone) gently with the elbow to get attention. **2.** to push (something or someone) lightly: as I drove out, I just nudged the gatepost. ~n. **3.** a gentle poke or push. [origin unknown]

nudism ('njuːdɪzəm) n. the practice of not wearing clothes, for reasons of health. —ˈnudist n., adj.

nugatory ('njuːgətrɪ) adj. **1.** of little value; trifling. **2.** not valid: a nugatory law. [Latin nugae trifling things]

nugget ('nʌgɪt) n. **1.** a small lump of gold in its natural state. **2.** something small but valuable: a nugget of information. [origin unknown]

nuisance ('njuːsəns) n. a person or thing that causes annoyance or bother. [Old French nuire to injure]

nuke (njuːk) Slang, chiefly U.S. ~vb. **1.** to attack with nuclear weapons. ~n. **2.** a nuclear bomb.

null (nʌl) adj. **1. null and void.** without legal force. **2. null set.** Maths. a set with no members. [Latin nullus none] —ˈnullity n.

nullify ('nʌlɪˌfaɪ) vb. **-fying, -fied. 1.** to make (something) ineffective; cancel out. **2.** to make (something) legally void. [Latin nullus of no account + facere to make] —ˌnullifiˈcation n.

numb (nʌm) adj. **1.** deprived of feeling through cold, shock, or fear. **2.** unable to move; paralysed. ~vb. **3.** to make numb; deaden, shock, or paralyse. [Middle English nomen, lit.: taken (with paralysis)] —ˈnumbly adv. —ˈnumbness n.

number ('nʌmbə) n. **1.** a concept of quantity that is or can be derived from a single unit, a sum of units, or zero. **2.** the symbol used to represent a number; numeral. **3.** a numeral or string of numerals used to identify a person or thing: a telephone number. **4.** the person or thing so identified: she was number seven in the race. **5.** sum or quantity: a large number of people. **6.** one of a series, as of a magazine. **7.** a self-contained piece of pop or jazz music. **8.** a group of people: he was not one of our number. **9.** Informal. an admired article: that little number is by Dior. **10.** Grammar. classification of words depending on how many persons or things are referred to. **11.** any number of. many. **12. beyond** or **without number.** innumerable. **13. have someone's number.** Informal. to have discovered someone's true character or intentions. **14. one's number is up.** Brit. Informal. one is about to die. ~vb. **15.** to assign a number to: number the pages of your essay. **16.** to add up to; total: the guests numbered seventy. **17.** to include in a group: they were numbered among the worst hit. **18. one's days are numbered.** something unpleasant, such as death, is likely to happen to one soon. [Latin numerus]

number crunching n. Computers. the large-scale processing of numerical data.

numberless ('nʌmbəlɪs) adj. too many to be counted.

number one n. **1.** Informal. oneself: look after number one. **2.** Informal. the best-selling pop record in any one week. ~adj. **3.** first in importance, urgency, or quality: number one priority.

numberplate ('nʌmbəˌpleɪt) n. a plate on the front or back of a motor vehicle showing the registration number.

Number Ten n. 10 Downing Street, the British prime minister's official London residence.

numbskull ('nʌmˌskʌl) n. same as **numskull.**

numeral ('njuːmərəl) n. a symbol or group of symbols used to express a number. [Latin numerus number]

numerate ('njuːmərɪt) adj. able to do basic arithmetic. —ˈnumeracy n.

numeration (ˌnjuːməˈreɪʃən) n. **1.** the act or process of numbering or counting. **2.** a system of numbering.

numerator ('njuːməˌreɪtə) n. Maths. the number above the line in a fraction.

numerical (njuːˈmerɪkᵊl) adj. measured or expressed in numbers: numerical value. —nuˈmerically adv.

numerology (ˌnjuːməˈrɒlədʒɪ) n. the study of numbers and of their supposed influence on human affairs.

numerous (ˈnjuːmərəs) adj. 1. many: on numerous occasions. 2. having many parts: a numerous collection.

numinous (ˈnjuːmɪnəs) adj. 1. arousing spiritual or religious emotions. 2. mysterious or awe-inspiring. [Latin numen divine will]

numismatics (ˌnjuːmɪzˈmætɪks) n. (functioning as sing.) the study or collection of coins or medals. [Greek nomisma piece of currency] —**numismatist** (njuːˈmɪzmətɪst) n.

numskull or **numbskull** (ˈnʌmˌskʌl) n. a stupid person.

nun (nʌn) n. a female member of a religious order. [Late Latin nonna]

nuncio (ˈnʌnʃɪˌəʊ, -sɪ-) n., pl. **-cios.** R.C. Church. a papal ambassador. [Latin nuntius messenger]

nunnery (ˈnʌnərɪ) n., pl. **-neries.** a convent.

nunny bag (ˈnʌnɪ) n. Canad. (in Newfoundland) a small sealskin haversack. [probably from Scot. dialect noony lunch]

nuptial (ˈnʌpʃəl, -tʃəl) adj. relating to marriage: nuptial vows. [Latin nuptiae marriage]

nuptials (ˈnʌpʃəlz, -tʃəlz) pl. n. a wedding.

nurd (nɜːd) n. Slang. a stupid and feeble person. [origin unknown] —**ˈnurdish** adj.

nurse (nɜːs) n. 1. a person trained to tend the sick and infirm and assist doctors. 2. short for **nursemaid.** ~vb. 3. to tend (the sick). 4. (of a woman) to feed (a baby) at the breast. 5. (of a baby) to feed at its mother's breast. 6. to try to cure (an ailment). 7. to clasp fondly: she nursed the child in her arms. 8. to harbour; foster: to nurse a grudge. [Latin nūtrīre to nourish] —**ˈnursing** n., adj.

nursemaid (ˈnɜːsˌmeɪd) or **nurserymaid** n. a woman employed to look after children.

nursery (ˈnɜːsrɪ) n., pl. **-ries.** 1. a room in a house, set apart for children. 2. an establishment providing daycare for babies and young children. 3. a place where plants and young trees are grown for sale.

nurseryman (ˈnɜːsrɪmən) n., pl. **-men.** a person who owns or works in a nursery in which plants are grown.

nursery rhyme n. a short traditional verse or song for children.

nursery school n. a school for young children, usually from three to five years old.

nursery slopes pl. n. gentle slopes used by beginners in skiing.

nursery stakes pl. n. a race for two-year-old horses.

nursing home n. a private hospital or home for aged or infirm persons.

nurture (ˈnɜːtʃə) n. 1. the act or process of promoting the development of a child or young plant. ~vb. 2. to promote the development of (a child or young plant). 3. to encourage the development of (a person, project, or idea). [Latin nūtrīre to nourish]

nut (nʌt) n. 1. a dry one-seeded fruit that grows inside a hard shell. 2. the edible inner part of such a fruit. 3. Slang. an eccentric or insane person. 4. Slang. the head. 5. a small piece of metal with a hole in it, that screws on to a bolt. 6. Brit. a small piece of coal. 7. **do one's nut.** Brit. slang. to be very angry. 8. **off one's nut.** Slang. mad or foolish. 9. **a hard** or **tough nut to crack.** a person or thing that presents difficulties. ~See also **nuts.** [Old English hnutu]

nutcase (ˈnʌtˌkeɪs) n. Slang. an insane person.

nutcracker (ˈnʌtˌkrækə) n. a device for cracking the shells of nuts. Also: **nutcrackers.**

nuthatch (ˈnʌtˌhætʃ) n. a songbird that feeds on insects, seeds, and nuts. [notehache nut hatchet, from its habit of splitting nuts]

nutmeg (ˈnʌtˌmɛg) n. a spice made from the seed of a tropical tree. [Old French nois muguede musk-scented nut]

nutria (ˈnjuːtrɪə) n. coypu fur. [Latin lūtra otter]

nutrient (ˈnjuːtrɪənt) n. 1. a substance that provides nourishment. ~adj. 2. providing nourishment. [Latin nūtrīre to nourish]

nutriment (ˈnjuːtrɪmənt) n. a substance providing nourishment. [Latin nūtrīmentum]

nutrition (njuːˈtrɪʃən) n. 1. the process in animals and plants of taking in and absorbing nutrients. 2. a nourishing. 3. the study of nutrition. [Latin nūtrīre to nourish] —**nuˈtritional** adj. —**nuˈtritionist** n.

nutritious (njuːˈtrɪʃəs) adj. nourishing. [Latin nūtrix nurse]

nutritive (ˈnjuːtrɪtɪv) adj. of nutrition; nutritious.

nuts (nʌts) adj. Slang. 1. insane. 2. **nuts about.** very fond of or enthusiastic about.

nuts and bolts pl. n. Informal. the essential or practical details.

nutshell (ˈnʌtˌʃel) n. **in a nutshell.** in essence; briefly.

nutter (ˈnʌtə) n. Brit. slang. an insane person.

nutty (ˈnʌtɪ) adj. **-tier, -tiest.** 1. containing nuts. 2. like nuts. 3. Slang. insane. 4. **nutty about.** Informal. very enthusiastic about. —**ˈnuttiness** n.

nux vomica (ˈnʌks ˈvɒmɪkə) n. the seed of a tree, which contains strychnine. [Medieval Latin: vomiting nut]

nuzzle (ˈnʌzˈl) vb. to push or rub gently with the nose or snout. [from nose]

NV Nevada.

NW northwest(ern).

NWT Northwest Territories (of Canada).

NY or **N.Y.** New York.

NYC New York City.

nylon (ˈnaɪlɒn) n. a synthetic material used for clothing, stockings, and other products. [orig. a trademark]

nylons ('nailɒnz) *pl. n.* stockings made of nylon.

nymph (nɪmf) *n.* **1.** *Myth.* a spirit of nature, represented as a beautiful maiden. **2.** *Chiefly poetic.* a beautiful young woman. **3.** a wingless larval form resembling that of the adult in the development of certain insects. [Greek *numphē*]

nymphet ('nɪmfɪt) *n.* a girl who is sexually precocious and desirable.

nympho ('nɪmfəʊ) *n., pl.* **-phos.** *Informal.* short for **nymphomaniac**.

nymphomaniac (ˌnɪmfə'meɪnɪæk) *n.* a woman who has a neurotic compulsion to have sexual intercourse with many men. [Greek *numphē* nymph + *mania* madness] —ˌnympho'mania *n.*

N.Z., NZ, *or* **N. Zeal.** New Zealand.

O

o *or* **O** (əʊ) *n., pl.* **o's, O's,** *or* **Os. 1.** the 15th letter of the English alphabet. **2.** same as **nought.**

O¹ 1. *Chem.* oxygen. **2.** Old.

O² (əʊ) *interj.* same as **oh:** *O God! O for the wings of a dove!*

o. *or* **O. 1.** octavo. **2.** old.

O. Ocean.

o' (ə) *prep. Informal or archaic.* shortened form of **of:** *a cup o' tea.*

oaf (əʊf) *n.* a stupid or clumsy person. [var. of Old English ælf elf] —**'oafish** *adj.*

oak (əʊk) *n.* **1.** a large forest tree with hard wood, acorns as fruits, and lobed leaves. **2.** the wood of this tree, used as building timber and for making furniture. [Old English āc] —**'oaken** *adj.*

oak apple *or* **gall** *n.* a brownish round lump or ball produced on oak trees by certain wasps.

Oaks (əʊks) *n. (functioning as sing.)* **the.** a horse race for fillies held annually at Epsom. [named after an estate near Epsom]

oakum ('əʊkəm) *n.* loose fibre obtained by unravelling old rope, used esp. for caulking seams in wooden ships. [Old English ācuma lit.: off-combings]

OAP (in Britain) old age pension *or* pensioner.

oar (ɔː) *n.* **1.** a long pole with a broad blade, used for rowing a boat. **2. put** *or* **stick one's oar in.** to interfere or interrupt. [Old English ār]

oarsman ('ɔːzmən) *n., pl.* **-men.** a man who rows. —**'oarsmanship** *n.*

oasis (əʊ'eɪsɪs) *n., pl.* **-ses** (-siːz). **1.** a fertile patch in a desert. **2.** a place or situation offering relief in the midst of difficulty or dullness. [Greek]

oast (əʊst) *n. Chiefly Brit.* **1.** a kiln for drying hops. **2.** Also called: **oast house.** a building containing such kilns. [Old English āst]

oat (əʊt) *n.* **1.** a hard cereal grown as food. **2.** *(usually pl.)* the edible grain of this cereal. **3. sow one's (wild) oats.** to indulge in adventure or promiscuity during youth. [Old English āte] —**'oaten** *adj.*

oatcake ('əʊtˌkeɪk) *n.* a thin unleavened biscuit made of oatmeal.

oath (əʊθ) *n., pl.* **oaths** (əʊðz). **1.** a solemn promise, esp. to tell the truth in a court of law. **2.** the form of such a promise. **3.** an offensive or blasphemous expression; a swearword. **4. on** *or* **under oath.** having made a solemn promise to tell the truth, esp. in a court of law. [Old English āth]

oatmeal ('əʊtˌmiːl) *n.* **1.** a coarse flour made by grinding oats. ~*adj.* **2.** greyish-yellow.

ob. (on tombstones) he (*or* she) died. [Latin *obiit*]

obbligato (ˌɒblɪ'gɑːtəʊ) *Music.* ~*adj.* **1.** not to be omitted in performance. ~*n., pl.* **-tos. 2.** an essential part or accompaniment: *with oboe obbligato.* [Italian]

obdurate ('ɒbdjʊrɪt) *adj.* not easily moved; hardhearted or obstinate. [Latin *obdūrāre* to make hard] —**'obduracy** *n.*

OBE Officer of the Order of the British Empire.

obedient (ə'biːdɪənt) *adj.* obeying or willing to obey. [Latin *oboediens*] —**o'bedience** *n.* —**o'bediently** *adv.*

obeisance (əʊ'beɪsəns) *n.* **1.** an attitude of respect or homage. **2.** a gesture of respect, such as a curtsy. [Old French *obéissant*] —**o'beisant** *adj.*

obelisk ('ɒbɪlɪsk) *n.* **1.** a four-sided stone pillar that tapers towards a pyramidal top. **2.** *Printing.* same as **dagger** (sense 2). [Greek *obeliskos* a little spit]

obese (əʊ'biːs) *adj.* very fat. [Latin *obēsus*] —**o'besity** *n.*

obey (ə'beɪ) *vb.* **1.** to carry out (instructions or orders); be obedient. **2.** to behave or act in accordance with: *to obey one's conscience.* [Latin *oboedīre*]

obfuscate ('ɒbfʌsˌkeɪt) *vb.* **1.** to obscure or darken. **2.** to confuse or bewilder. [Latin *ob-* (intensive) + *fuscāre* to blacken] —ˌobfus'cation *n.* —**'obfusˌcatory** *adj.*

obituary (ə'bɪtjʊərɪ) *n., pl.* **-aries.** a published announcement of a death, usually with a short biography of the dead person. [Latin *obitus* death] —**o'bituarist** *n.*

obj. 1. objection. **2.** *Grammar.* objec t(ive).

object¹ ('ɒbdʒɪkt) *n.* **1.** a thing that can be touched or seen. **2.** a person or thing seen as a focus for feelings, actions, or thought: *the object of her dislike.* **3.** an aim or purpose. **4.** *Philosophy.* that which can be perceived by the mind, as contrasted with the thinking subject. **5.** *Grammar.* a noun, pronoun, or noun phrase that receives the action of a verb or is governed by a preposition. **6. no object.** not a hindrance or obstacle: *money is no object.* [Late Latin *objectus* something thrown before (the mind)]

object² (əb'dʒɛkt) *vb.* **1.** to state as an objection. **2.** (often foll. by *to*) to state an objection (to); present an argument (against). [Latin *ob-* against + *jacere* to throw] —**ob'jector** *n.*

objection (əb'dʒɛkʃən) *n.* **1.** an expression or feeling of opposition or dislike. **2.** a reason for objecting.

objectionable (əb'dʒɛkʃənəb³l) *adj.* unpleasant, offensive, or obnoxious.

objective (əb'dʒɛktɪv) *adj.* **1.** having existence independent of the mind; real. **2.** undistorted by personal feelings or bias: *an objective opinion.* **3.** of or relating to actual facts as opposed to thoughts or feelings: *objective evidence.* **4.** *Grammar.* denoting a case of nouns and pronouns, that identifies the direct object of a verb or preposition. ~*n*. **5.** a goal; aim. **6.** an actual fact; reality. **7.** *Grammar*. the objective case. **8.** *Optics*. the lens nearest to the object observed in an optical instrument. —**objectival** (ˌɒbdʒɛkˈtaɪvəl) *adj*. —**ob'jectively** *adv*. —ˌob'jec'tivity *n*.

object lesson *n*. a practical demonstration of some principle or ideal.

objet d'art (ˌɒbʒeɪ 'dɑː) *n*., *pl*. **objets d'art** (ˌɒbʒeɪ 'dɑː). a small object considered to be of artistic worth. [French: object of art]

oblate ('ɒbleɪt) *adj*. *Geom*. (of a spheroid) flattened at the poles: *the earth is an oblate sphere*. [New Latin *oblātus* lengthened]

oblation (ɒ'bleɪʃən) *n*. **1.** *Christianity*. the offering of bread and wine to God at Communion. **2.** any offering made for religious purposes. [Medieval Latin *oblātus* offered] —**ob'lational** *adj*.

obligate ('ɒblɪˌgeɪt) *vb*. to bind (someone) morally or legally to do something: *I felt obligated to pay for the damage*. —**ob'liga-tive** *adj*.

obligation (ˌɒblɪ'geɪʃən) *n*. **1.** a moral or legal duty. **2.** the binding power of such a duty. **3.** indebtedness for a service or favour.

obligatory (ɒ'blɪgətrɪ) *adj*. legally or morally binding; required or compulsory.

oblige (ə'blaɪdʒ) *vb*. **1.** to compel (someone) by legal, moral, or physical means to do something. **2.** to make indebted or grateful to someone by doing a favour: *I am obliged to you for your help*. **3.** to do a favour to (someone): *she obliged the guests with a song*. [Latin *ob-* towards + *ligāre* to bind]

obliging (ə'blaɪdʒɪŋ) *adj*. willing to be helpful; accommodating. —**o'bligingly** *adv*.

oblique (ə'bliːk) *adj*. **1.** at an angle; slanting; sloping. **2.** *Geom*. (of lines or planes) neither perpendicular nor parallel to one another. **3.** indirect or evasive. **4.** *Grammar*. denoting any case other than the nominative or vocative. ~*n*. **5.** something that is oblique. **6.** same as **solidus**. [Latin *oblīquus*] —**o'bliquely** *adv*. —**o'bliqueness** *n*.

oblique angle *n*. an angle that is not a right angle or any multiple of a right angle.

obliterate (ə'blɪtəˌreɪt) *vb*. to destroy every trace of; wipe out completely. [Latin *oblitterāre*] —**oˌblite'ration** *n*.

oblivion (ə'blɪvɪən) *n*. **1.** the condition of being forgotten or disregarded: *old crafts such as thatching are gradually sinking into oblivion*. **2.** the state of being unaware or unconscious: *the oblivion of sleep*. [Latin *oblīviō* forgetfulness]

oblivious (ə'blɪvɪəs) *adj*. (usually foll. by *of*) unaware or forgetful. —**ob'livious-ness** *n*.

oblong ('ɒbˌlɒŋ) *adj*. **1.** having an elongated, rectangular shape. ~*n*. **2.** a figure or object having this shape. [Latin *oblongus*]

obloquy ('ɒblɒkwɪ) *n*., *pl*. **-quies. 1.** verbal abuse or censure. **2.** disgrace brought about by this. [Latin *obloquium* contradiction]

obnoxious (əb'nɒkʃəs) *adj*. extremely unpleasant. [Latin *obnoxius*] —**ob'noxious-ness** *n*.

oboe ('əʊbəʊ) *n*. a double-reeded woodwind instrument with a penetrating nasal tone. [French *haut bois*, lit.: high wood (referring to its pitch)] —**'oboist** *n*.

obs. obsolete.

obscene (əb'siːn) *adj*. **1.** offensive to accepted standards of decency or modesty. **2.** *Law*. tending to deprave or corrupt: *obscene publications*. **3.** disgusting; repulsive. [Latin *obscēnus* inauspicious] —**ob-scenity** (əb'sɛnɪtɪ) *n*.

obscure (əb'skjʊə) *adj*. **1.** unclear or indistinct: *an obscure shape*. **2.** not well known: *an obscure opera*. **3.** not easily understood: *an obscure point of theology*. ~*vb*. **4.** to make unclear or vague. **5.** to cover or cloud over. [Latin *obscūrus* dark] —**obscuration** (ˌɒbskjʊ'reɪʃən) *n*. —**ob-'scurity** *n*.

obsequies ('ɒbsɪkwɪz) *pl. n.*, *sing*. **-quy.** funeral rites. [Medieval Latin *obsequiae*]

obsequious (əb'siːkwɪəs) *adj*. ingratiating or servile; fawning. [Latin *obsequiōsus* compliant] —**ob'sequiousness** *n*.

observance (əb'zɜːvəns) *n*. **1.** the observing of a law or custom. **2.** a ritual, ceremony, or practice, esp. of a religion.

observant (əb'zɜːvənt) *adj*. paying close attention to detail; watchful or perceptive.

observation (ˌɒbzə'veɪʃən) *n*. **1.** the act or power of observing; the state of being observed. **2.** a comment or remark. **3.** detailed examination of something before analysis, diagnosis, or interpretation: *the patient was under observation*. **4.** the facts learned from observing. —ˌobser'va-tional *adj*.

observatory (əb'zɜːvətrɪ) *n*., *pl*. **-ries.** a building specially designed and equipped for meteorological and astronomical observation.

observe (əb'zɜːv) *vb*. **1.** to see; perceive: *we have observed that you steal*. **2.** to watch or pay attention to (something) carefully. **3.** to make scientific observations of (something). **4.** to make a comment or remark: *the speaker observed that times had changed*. **5.** to abide by or keep (a law or custom). [Latin *observāre*] —**ob'servable** *adj*. —**ob'server** *n*.

obsess (əb'sɛs) *vb*. (often passive and foll. by *with* or *by*) to preoccupy completely; haunt. [Latin *obsessus* besieged] —**ob'ses-sive** *adj*.

obsession (əb'sɛʃən) *n*. **1.** *Psychiatry*. a persistent idea or impulse, often associated with anxiety and mental illness. **2.** any persistent preoccupation, idea, or feeling. —**ob'sessional** *adj*.

obsidian (ɒb'sɪdɪən) *n*. a dark glassy volcanic rock. [after *Obsius*, the discoverer of a stone resembling obsidian]

obsolescent (ˌɒbsə'lɛs'nt) *adj*. becoming obsolete or out of date. —ˌobso'les-cence *n*.

obsolete (ˈɒbsəˌliːt) *adj.* no longer used; out of date. [Latin *obsolētus* worn out]

obstacle (ˈɒbstək²l) *n.* a person or thing that obstructs or hinders progress. [Latin *obstāculum*, from *ob-* against + *stāre* to stand]

obstetrician (ˌɒbstɪˈtrɪʃən) *n.* a doctor who specializes in obstetrics.

obstetrics (ɒbˈstɛtrɪks) *n.* (*functioning as sing.*) the branch of medicine concerned with pregnancy and childbirth. [Latin *obstetrix* a midwife] —**obˈstetric** *adj.*

obstinate (ˈɒbstɪnɪt) *adj.* 1. holding stubbornly to a particular opinion or course of action. 2. resisting treatment; persistent: *an obstinate fever.* [Latin *obstinātus*] —**ˈobstinacy** *n.* —**ˈobstinately** *adv.*

obstreperous (əbˈstrɛpərəs) *adj.* noisy, boisterous, or unruly. [Latin *ob-* against + *strepere* to roar]

obstruct (əbˈstrʌkt) *vb.* 1. to block (a way) with an obstacle. 2. to make (progress or activity) difficult; impede. 3. to block a clear view of. [Latin: built against] —**obˈstructive** *adj.*, *n.* —**obˈstructiveness** *n.*

obstruction (əbˈstrʌkʃən) *n.* 1. a person or thing that obstructs. 2. an obstructing or being obstructed. 3. *Sport.* the act of unfairly impeding an opposing player.

obstructionist (əbˈstrʌkʃənɪst) *n.* a person who deliberately obstructs legal or parliamentary business. —**obˈstructionism** *n.*

obtain (əbˈteɪn) *vb.* 1. to gain possession of; get. 2. to be customary or accepted: *a new law obtains in this case.* [Latin *obtinēre* to take hold of] —**obˈtainable** *adj.*

obtrude (əbˈtruːd) *vb.* 1. to push (oneself or one's opinions) on others in an unwelcome way. 2. to be or make unpleasantly noticeable. [Latin *obtrūdere*] —**obtrusion** (əbˈtruːʒən) *n.*

obtrusive (əbˈtruːsɪv) *adj.* 1. obtruding or tending to obtrude. 2. sticking out; protruding. —**obˈtrusiveness** *n.*

obtuse (əbˈtjuːs) *adj.* 1. mentally slow or emotionally insensitive. 2. *Maths.* (of an angle) between 90° and 180°. 3. not sharp or pointed; of blunt shape. [Latin *obtūsus* dulled] —**obˈtuseness** *n.*

obverse (ˈɒbvɜːs) *n.* 1. a counterpart or opposite. 2. the side of a coin that bears the main design. 3. the front, top, or main surface of anything. [Latin *obversus* turned towards]

obviate (ˈɒbvɪˌeɪt) *vb.* to anticipate and prevent (a problem or difficulty) by effective measures: *he destroyed the letter to obviate any suspicion that might fall on him.* [Latin *obviāre*]

obvious (ˈɒbvɪəs) *adj.* easy to see or understand; evident. [Latin *obvius*] —**ˈobviously** *adv.* —**ˈobviousness** *n.*

ocarina (ˌɒkəˈriːnə) *n.* a small egg-shaped wind instrument with a mouthpiece and finger holes. [Italian: little goose]

occasion (əˈkeɪʒən) *n.* 1. a particular happening or event or the time at which it happens. 2. (*sometimes foll. by for*) a need or reason (to do or be something); grounds:

I had no occasion to complain. 3. a suitable time or opportunity (to do something). 4. a special event, time, or celebration: *the party was quite an occasion.* 5. **on occasion.** every so often. 6. **rise to the occasion.** to meet the special demands of a situation. ∼*vb.* 7. to cause; esp. incidentally. [Latin *occāsiō* a falling down]

occasional (əˈkeɪʒən²l) *adj.* 1. happening from time to time; not frequent or regular. 2. of, for, or on special occasions. —**ocˈcasionally** *adv.*

Occident (ˈɒksɪdənt) *n.* the western hemisphere, esp. Europe and America. [Latin *occidere* to fall (with reference to the setting sun)] —**Occidental** (ˌɒksɪˈdɛnt²l) *adj.*

occiput (ˈɒksɪˌpʌt) *n.* the back of the head or skull. [Latin *ob-* at the back of + *caput* head] —**ocˈcipital** *adj.*

occlude (əˈkluːd) *vb.* 1. to block or stop up (a passage or opening); obstruct. 2. to shut in or out. 3. *Chem.* (of a solid) to absorb and retain (a gas or other substance). [Latin *occlūdere*] —**ocˈclusion** *n.*

occluded front *n. Meteorol.* the front formed when the cold front of a depression overtakes a warm front, raising the warm air from ground level.

occult (ɒˈkʌlt, ˈɒkʌlt) *adj.* 1. involving mystical or supernatural phenomena or powers. 2. beyond ordinary human understanding. 3. secret or esoteric. ∼*n.* 4. **the occult.** the knowledge and study of occult phenomena and powers. [Latin *occultus* hidden, secret]

occupancy (ˈɒkjʊpənsɪ) *n.*, *pl.* **-cies.** 1. the act of occupying; taking or keeping possession of a property. 2. the period of time during which one is an occupant of a property.

occupant (ˈɒkjʊpənt) *n.* a person or thing occupying a dwelling, position, or place.

occupation (ˌɒkjʊˈpeɪʃən) *n.* 1. a person's job or profession. 2. any activity on which time is spent by a person. 3. an occupying or being occupied. 4. the control of a country by a foreign military power. —**ˌoccuˈpational** *adj.*

occupational therapy *n. Med.* creative activity, such as a craft or hobby, to help a patient recover from an illness.

occupier (ˈɒkjʊˌpaɪə) *n. Brit.* a person who is in possession or occupation of a house or land.

occupy (ˈɒkjʊˌpaɪ) *vb.* **-pying, -pied.** 1. to live, stay or work in (a house, flat or office). 2. (*often passive*) to keep (a person or his mind) busy. 3. (*often passive*) to take up (time or space): *this seat is occupied.* 4. to take and hold possession of forcibly: *students occupied the college buildings.* 5. to fill or hold (a position or office). [Latin *occupāre* to seize hold of]

occur (əˈkɜː) *vb.* **-curring, -curred.** 1. to happen; take place. 2. to be found or be present; exist. 3. **occur to.** to come into the mind of; suggest itself to. [Latin *occurrere* to run up to]

occurrence (əˈkʌrəns) *n.* 1. something that occurs; a happening; event. 2. the act or fact of occurring: *a crime of frequent occurrence.*

ocean (ˈəʊʃən) *n.* **1.** the body of salt water covering about 70 per cent of the earth's surface. **2.** one of the five principal divisions of this, the Atlantic, Pacific, Indian, Arctic, and Antarctic. **3.** a huge quantity or expanse: *an ocean of replies.* **4.** *Literary.* the sea. [from *Oceanus*, Greek god of the stream believed to flow round the earth] **—oceanic** (ˌəʊʃɪˈænɪk) *adj.*

ocean-going *adj.* (of a ship or boat) suited for travel on the open ocean.

oceanography (ˌəʊʃəˈnɒɡrəfɪ) *n.* the study of oceans and their environment. **—ˌoceanˈographer** *n.*

ocelot (ˈɒsɪˌlɒt, ˈəʊ-) *n.* a large cat of Central and South America that has a dark-spotted yellow-grey coat. [Mexican Indian *ocelotl* jaguar]

och (ɒx) *interj. Scot. & Irish.* an expression of surprise, annoyance, or disagreement.

ochre *or U.S.* **ocher** (ˈəʊkə) *n.* **1.** a yellow or reddish-brown earth used as a pigment. **~***adj.* **2.** moderate yellow-orange to orange. [Greek *ōkhros* pale yellow]

o'clock (əˈklɒk) *adv.* used after a number to specify an hour: *four o'clock in the morning.*

OCR optical character reader *or* recognition.

oct. octavo.

Oct. October.

octagon (ˈɒktəɡən) *n.* a polygon having eight sides. [Greek *oktagōnos* having eight angles] **—octagonal** (ɒkˈtæɡənˀl) *adj.*

octahedron (ˌɒktəˈhiːdrən) *n., pl.* **-drons** *or* **-dra** (-drə). a solid figure having eight plane faces.

octane (ˈɒkteɪn) *n.* a liquid hydrocarbon found in petroleum.

octane number *or* **rating** *n.* a number indicating the antiknock quality of a petrol.

octave (ˈɒktɪv) *n.* **1. a.** the musical interval between the first note and the eighth note of a major or minor scale. **b.** the higher of these two notes. **c.** the series of notes filling this interval. **2.** *Prosody.* a rhythmic group of eight lines of verse. [Latin *octo* eight]

octavo (ɒkˈteɪvəʊ) *n., pl.* **-vos.** **1.** a book size resulting from folding a sheet of paper of a standard size to form eight leaves. **2.** a book or sheet of this size. [New Latin *in octavo* in an eighth (of a sheet)]

octet (ɒkˈtɛt) *n.* **1.** any group of eight, esp. singers or musicians. **2.** a piece of music composed for eight performers. [Latin *octo* eight]

October (ɒkˈtəʊbə) *n.* the tenth month of the year. [Latin *octo* eight, since it was the eighth month in Roman reckoning]

octogenarian (ˌɒktəʊdʒɪˈnɛərɪən) *n.* **1.** a person between 80 and 89 years old. **~***adj.* **2.** of an octogenarian. [Latin *octōgēnārius* containing eighty]

octopus (ˈɒktəpəs) *n., pl.* **-puses.** a sea creature with a soft oval body and eight

long suckered tentacles. [Greek *oktōpous* having eight feet]

ocular (ˈɒkjʊlə) *adj.* of or relating to the eyes or sight. [Latin *oculus* eye]

oculist (ˈɒkjʊlɪst) *n.* an old name for an ophthalmologist.

OD (ˌəʊˈdiː) *Informal.* **~***n.* **1.** an overdose of a drug. **~***vb.* **OD'ing, OD'd.** **2.** to take an overdose of a drug.

odalisque (ˈəʊdəlɪsk) *n.* a female slave in a harem. [Turkish *ōdalik*]

odd (ɒd) *adj.* **1.** unusual or peculiar. **2.** occasional or incidental: *odd jobs.* **3.** leftover or additional: *odd bits of wool.* **4. a.** not divisible by two. **b.** indicated by an odd number: *graphs are on odd pages.* **5.** being part of a pair or set when the other or others are missing: *an odd sock.* **6.** somewhat more than the round numbers specified: *fifty-odd pounds: ten pounds and some odd change.* **7.** out of the way: *in odd corners.* **8. odd man out.** a person or thing excluded from others forming a group or unit. **~**See also **odds.** [Old Norse *oddi* triangle, point] **—oddly** *adv.* **—ˈoddness** *n.*

oddball (ˈɒdˌbɔːl) *n. Informal.* a strange or eccentric person.

oddity (ˈɒdɪtɪ) *n., pl.* **-ties.** **1.** an odd person or thing. **2.** an odd characteristic; peculiarity.

oddment (ˈɒdmənt) *n.* (*often pl.*) an odd piece or thing; leftover.

odds (ɒdz) *pl. n.* **1.** (foll. by *on* or *against*) the probability, expressed as a ratio, that something will or will not happen: *the odds against the outsider are a hundred to one.* **2.** the difference, expressed as a ratio, between the money placed on a bet and the amount that would be received as winning payment: *he was offering odds of five to one.* **3.** the likelihood that a certain state of affairs will be so: *the odds are that he is drunk.* **4.** the advantage that one contender is judged to have over another: *all the odds are in his favour.* **5.** it makes no odds. *Brit.* it does not matter. **6. at odds.** in conflict or at variance. **7. over the odds.** more than is expected or necessary.

odds and ends *pl. n.* miscellaneous articles.

odds-on *adj.* having a better than even chance of winning.

ode (əʊd) *n.* a lyric poem, usually addressed to a particular subject, with lines of varying lengths and metres. [Greek *ōidē* song]

odious (ˈəʊdɪəs) *adj.* offensive; hateful. [see ODIUM]

odium (ˈəʊdɪəm) *n.* widespread dislike or disapproval of a person or action. [Latin]

odometer (ɒˈdɒmɪtə, əʊ-) *n. U.S. & Canad.* same as **mileometer.** [Greek *hodos* way + -METER]

odoriferous (ˌəʊdəˈrɪfərəs) *adj.* having or giving off a fragrant odour.

odour *or U.S.* **odor** (ˈəʊdə) *n.* **1.** a particular and distinctive scent or smell. **2.** repute or regard (in **in good odour, in bad odour**). [Latin *odor*] **—ˈodorous** *adj.* **—ˈodourless** *adj.*

odyssey ('ɒdɪsɪ) *n.* a long eventful journey.

OECD Organization for Economic Cooperation and Development.

oedema *or* **edema** (ɪ'diːmə) *n., pl.* **-mata** (-mətə). *Pathol.* an abnormal accumulation of fluid in the tissues of the body, causing swelling. [Greek *oidēma* swelling]

Oedipus complex ('iːdɪpəs) *n.* *Psychoanal.* the usually unconscious sexual desire of a child, esp. a male child, for the parent of the opposite sex. —**'oedipal** *adj.*

o'er (ɔː, 'əʊə) *prep., adv. Poetic.* over.

oesophagus (iː'sɒfəgəs) *n., pl.* **-gi** (-ˌgaɪ). the tube through which food travels from the throat to the stomach; gullet. [Greek *oisophagos*] —**oesophageal** (iːˌsɒfə'dʒiːəl) *adj.*

oestrogen ('iːstrədʒən, 'estrə-) *n.* a female sex hormone that controls the reproductive cycle, and prepares the body for pregnancy. [from *oestrus* + *-gen* (suffix) producing]

oestrus ('iːstrəs, 'estrəs) *n.* a regularly occurring period of fertility and sexual receptivity in the reproductive cycle of most female mammals, except humans; heat. [Greek *oistros* gadfly, hence frenzy]

of (ɒv) *prep.* **1.** belonging to; situated in or coming from; because of: *citizens of London; to die of hunger.* **2.** used after words or phrases expressing quantities: *a pint of milk.* **3.** specifying an amount or value: *a height of two metres.* **4.** made up of, containing, or characterized by: *a rod of iron; a man of some depth.* **5.** used with a verbal noun to link it with a following noun that is either the subject or the object of the verb: *the breathing of a fine swimmer* (subject); *the breathing of clean air* (object). **6.** at a given distance or space of time from: *within a mile of the town; within ten minutes of leaving.* **7.** used to indicate identity or closer definition: *the city of Naples; a speech on the subject of archaeology.* **8.** about; concerning: *think of me.* **9.** *U.S.* before the hour of: *a quarter of nine.* [Old English]

off (ɒf) *prep.* **1.** so as to be no longer in contact with something: *to lift a cup off the table.* **2.** so as to be no longer attached to or associated with something else: *to take the tax off potatoes.* **3.** away from: *we swerved off the road.* **4.** situated near to or leading away from: *just off the High Street.* **5.** no longer having a liking for: *I've gone off you.* **6.** no longer using: *he has been taken off the antibiotics.* ~*adv.* **7.** so as to deactivate or disengage: *turn off the radio.* **8. a.** so as to get rid of: *sleep off a hangover.* **b.** as a reduction in price: *he took ten per cent off.* **9.** spent away from work or other duties: *take the afternoon off.* **10.** away; at a distance: *the girl ran off; the ship was 10 miles off.* **11.** away in the future: *August is less than a week off.* **12.** so as to be no longer taking place: *the match has been called off.* **13.** removed from contact with something: *she took her clothes off.* **14. off and on.** now and then: *he comes here off and on.* ~*adj.* **15.** not

on; no longer operating: *turn the television off.* **16.** cancelled or postponed: *the meeting is off.* **17.** in a specified condition, esp. regarding money or provisions: *I'd be better off without this job; how are you off for money?* **18.** not up to the usual standard: *an off year for good wine.* **19.** no longer on the menu: *haddock is off.* **20.** (of food or drink) having gone bad or sour: *this milk is off.* ~*n.* **21.** *Cricket.* the side of the field to the right of a right-handed batsman when he is facing the bowler. [var. of *of*]

off. **1.** office. **2.** officer. **3.** official.

offal ('ɒf'l) *n.* **1.** the edible internal parts of an animal, such as the heart or liver. **2.** refuse; rubbish. [*off* + *fall*, referring to parts cut off]

offbeat ('ɒfˌbiːt) *adj.* unusual, unconventional, or eccentric.

off colour *adj.* **1.** *Chiefly Brit.* slightly ill; unwell. **2.** indecent or indelicate; risqué.

offcut ('ɒfˌkʌt) *n.* a piece of paper, wood, or fabric remaining after the main pieces have been cut.

offence *or U.S.* **offense** (ə'fɛns) *n.* **1.** a breaking of a law or rule; crime. **2.** annoyance or anger. **3.** a cause of annoyance or anger. **4.** attack; assault. **5. give offence.** to cause annoyance or anger. **6. take offence.** to feel hurt or offended.

offend (ə'fɛnd) *vb.* **1.** to hurt the feelings of (a person); insult. **2.** to be disagreeable to; disgust: *the smell offended him.* **3.** to commit a crime. [Latin *offendere*] —**of'fender** *n.* —**of'fending** *adj.*

offensive (ə'fɛnsɪv) *adj.* **1.** unpleasant or disgusting to the senses: *an offensive smell.* **2.** causing annoyance or anger; insulting. **3.** for the purpose of attack rather than defence. ~*n.* **4.** (usually preceded by *the*) an attitude or position of aggression. **5.** an attack or hostile action. —**of'fensively** *adv.*

offer ('ɒfə) *vb.* **1.** to present for acceptance or rejection: *I offered him a cup of tea.* **2.** to provide: *this stream offers the best fishing.* **3.** to present itself: *if an opportunity should offer.* **4.** to be willing (to do something): *he offered to help me.* **5.** to put forward (a proposal, information, or opinion) for consideration: *have you any advice to offer?* **6.** to present for sale. **7.** to propose as payment; bid. **8.** (often foll. by *up*) to present (a prayer or sacrifice) as an act of worship. **9.** to show readiness for: *to offer resistance.* ~*n.* **10.** something that is offered. **11.** the act of offering. **12. on offer.** for sale at a reduced price. [Latin *offerre* to present]

offering ('ɒfərɪŋ) *n.* **1.** something that is offered. **2.** a contribution to the funds of a religious organization. **3.** a sacrifice to a god.

offertory ('ɒfətərɪ) *n., pl.* **-tories.** *Christianity.* **1.** the part of a church service when the bread and wine for communion are offered for consecration. **2.** the collection of money at this service. **3.** the prayers said or sung while the worshippers' offerings are being brought to the altar.

offhand (ˌɒf'hænd) *adj. also* **offhanded,**

adv. **1.** curt or casual in manner: *offhand behaviour.* **2.** without preparation; impromptu: *I can't give you an answer offhand.* —₁**off'handedness** *n.*

office ('ɒfɪs) *n.* **1.** a room, set of rooms, or building in which business, professional duties or clerical work are carried out. **2.** a room or department of an organization dealing with particular business: *the architect's office approved the plans.* **3.** the group of persons working in an office: *it was a happy office until she came.* **4.** (*cap. when part of a name*) a government department or agency: *Office of Fair Trading.* **5.** a position of trust or authority, as in a government: *to run for office.* **6.** duty or function: *the office of an administrator.* **7.** (*often pl.*) something done for another: *through his good offices.* **8.** a place where tickets, information, or some service can be obtained: *a ticket office.* **9.** *Christianity.* (*often pl.*) a religious ceremony or service. **10. in** (*or* **out of**) **office.** (of a government) in (*or* out of) power. [Latin *officium* service, duty]

officer ('ɒfɪsə) *n.* **1.** a person in the armed services, or on a nonnaval ship, who holds a position of authority. **2.** a policeman. **3.** a person holding a position of authority in a government or organization.

official (ə'fɪʃəl) *adj.* **1.** of an office or position of authority: *in an official capacity.* **2.** sanctioned by or derived from authority: *an official statement.* **3.** formal or ceremonial: *an official dinner.* ~*n.* **4.** a person holding a position of authority. —**of'ficially** *adv.*

officialdom (ə'fɪʃəldəm) *n.* officials or bureaucrats collectively.

officialese (ə₁fɪʃə'liːz) *n.* language typical of official documents, esp. when wordy or pompous.

Official Receiver *n.* an officer appointed by the government to deal with the affairs of a bankrupt person or company.

officiate (ə'fɪʃɪ₁eɪt) *vb.* **1.** to perform the duties of an office; act in an official capacity. **2.** to conduct a religious or other ceremony. —**of₁fici'ation** *n.* —**of'fici₁ator** *n.*

officious (ə'fɪʃəs) *adj.* offering unwanted advice or services; interfering. [Latin *officiōsus* kindly] —**of'ficiousness** *n.*

offing ('ɒfɪŋ) *n.* **1.** the part of the sea that can be seen from the shore. **2. in the offing.** not far off; likely to occur soon.

off key *adj., adv.* **1.** *Music.* out of tune. **2.** out of keeping; not quite suitable or fitting.

off-licence *n. Brit.* **1.** a shop or a counter in a shop where alcoholic drink is sold for consumption elsewhere. **2.** a licence permitting such sales.

off-line *adj.* (of computer equipment) not directly connected to or controlled by the central processing unit of a computer.

off-load *vb.* to get rid of (something unpleasant), usually by giving it to someone else.

off-peak *adj.* (of services) used at times other than those of greatest demand.

off-putting *adj. Brit. informal.* arousing dislike; distracting or disconcerting.

offset *n.* ('ɒf₁sɛt). **1. a.** a printing method in which the impression is made onto a surface, such as a rubber roller, which transfers it to the paper. **b.** (*as modifier*): *offset letterpress.* **2.** *Bot.* a short runner in certain plants that produces roots and shoots at the tip. ~*vb.* (₁ɒf'sɛt), **-setting, -set.** **3.** to counterbalance or compensate for. **4.** to print (something) using the offset process.

offshoot ('ɒf₁ʃuːt) *n.* **1.** a shoot growing from the main stem of a plant. **2.** something that has developed from something else.

offshore (₁ɒf'ʃɔː) *adj., adv.* **1.** away from or at some distance from the shore. ~*adj.* **2.** sited or conducted at sea: *offshore industries.*

offside *adj., adv.* (₁ɒf'saɪd). **1.** *Sport.* in a position illegally ahead of the ball when it is played. ~*n.* ('ɒf₁saɪd). **2.** (usually preceded by *the*) *Chiefly Brit.* the side of a vehicle nearest the centre of the road.

offspring ('ɒf₁sprɪŋ) *n.* **1.** the immediate descendant or descendants of a person or animal. **2.** a product, outcome, or result.

off-the-peg *adj.* (of clothing) ready to wear; not produced especially for the person buying.

oft (ɒft) *adv. Archaic or poetic.* short for **often.** [Old English]

often ('ɒfⁿn) *adv.* **1.** frequently; much of the time. **2. as often as not.** quite frequently. **3. every so often.** occasionally. **4. more often than not.** in more than half the instances. [Middle English var. of *oft*]

ogee arch ('əʊdʒiː) *n.* a pointed arch made with an S-shaped curve on each side. [prob. from Old French]

ogle ('əʊg'l) *vb.* to stare at (someone) lustfully. [prob. from Low German]

ogre ('əʊgə) *n.* **1.** (in folklore) a man-eating giant. **2.** any monstrous or cruel person. [French] —**'ogreish** *adj.* —**'ogress** *fem. n.*

oh (əʊ) *interj.* an exclamation of surprise, pain, pleasure, fear, or annoyance.

OH Ohio.

ohm (əʊm) *n.* the SI unit of electric resistance. [after Georg Simon *Ohm*, physicist]

OHMS (in Britain and the Commonwealth) On Her (*or* His) Majesty's Service.

oil (ɔɪl) *n.* **1.** any of a number of viscous liquids with a smooth sticky feel, which are usually flammable, insoluble in water, and are obtained from plants, animals, or mineral deposits by synthesis. **2.** same as **petroleum.** **3.** a substance derived from petroleum and used for lubrication. **4.** *Brit.* paraffin as a domestic fuel. **5.** (*often pl.*) oil colour or paint. **6.** an oil painting. ~*vb.* **7.** to lubricate with oil or apply oil to. **8. oil the wheels.** to make things run smoothly. [Latin *oleum* (olive) oil]

oil cake *n.* compressed linseed from which the oil has been extracted, used as livestock feed.

oilcloth ('ɔɪl₁klɒθ) *n.* cloth made waterproof by treating with oil or a synthetic resin.

oilfield (ˈɔɪlˌfiːld) n. an area containing reserves of oil.

oilfired (ˈɔɪlˌfaɪəd) adj. using oil as fuel.

oil paint n. a thick paint made of pigment ground in linseed oil.

oil painting n. 1. a picture painted with oil paints. 2. the art of painting with oil paints.

oil rig n. a structure used as a base when drilling an oil well.

oilskin (ˈɔɪlˌskɪn) n. 1. a cotton fabric treated with oil to make it waterproof. 2. (often pl.) a protective outer garment of this fabric.

oil slick n. a mass of floating oil covering an area of water.

oil well n. a well bored into the earth or sea bed to a supply of oil.

oily (ˈɔɪlɪ) adj. **oilier, oiliest.** 1. soaked or covered with oil. 2. of, containing, or like oil. 3. flatteringly servile or fawning. —ˈoiliness n.

oink (ɔɪŋk) interj. the grunt of a pig or an imitation of this.

ointment (ˈɔɪntmənt) n. a smooth greasy substance applied to the skin to heal or protect, or as a cosmetic. [Latin unguentum unguent]

OK Oklahoma.

O.K. (ˌəʊˈkeɪ) Informal. ~interj. 1. an expression of approval or agreement. ~adj., adv. 2. in good or satisfactory condition. ~vb. **O.K.ing** (ˌəʊˈkeɪɪŋ), **O.K.ed** (ˌəʊˈkeɪd). 3. to approve or endorse. ~n., pl. **O.K.s.** 4. approval or agreement. [perhaps from oll k(orrect), jocular alteration of all correct]

okapi (əʊˈkɑːpɪ) n., pl. -pis or -pi. an African mammal related to the giraffe, but with a shorter neck, a reddish coat, and white stripes on the legs. [from a Central African word]

okay (ˌəʊˈkeɪ) interj., adj., adv., vb., n. same as **O.K.**

Okla. Oklahoma.

okra (ˈəʊkrə) n. a tall plant with long green pods that are used as food. [West African]

old (əʊld) adj. 1. having lived or existed for a long time: an old man; an old tradition. 2. of or relating to advanced years or a long life: old age. 3. decrepit or senile. 4. worn with age or use: old clothes. 5. having lived or existed for a specified period: six years old. 6. earlier or earliest of two or more things with the same name: the old edition; the Old Testament. 7. designating the form of a language in which the earliest known records are written: Old English. 8. familiar through long acquaintance or repetition: an old friend; an old excuse. 9. (often preceded by good) dear: used as a term of affection or familiarity: good old George. 10. skilled through long experience (esp. in **an old hand**). 11. out of date; unfashionable. 12. remote in origin or time of origin: an old culture. 13. former; previous: my old house was small. 14. of long standing: an old member. 15. sensible, wise, or mature: old beyond one's years. 16. very: a high old time. 17. **good old days.** an earlier period of time regarded as better than the present. ~n. 18. an earlier or past time: in days of old. [Old English eald] —ˈoldish adj. —ˈoldness n.

old age pension n. a former name for **retirement pension.** —**old age pensioner** n.

Old Bailey (ˈbeɪlɪ) n. the Central Criminal Court of England.

old boy n. 1. (sometimes caps.) Brit. a male ex-pupil of a school. 2. Informal, chiefly Brit. **a.** a familiar form of address used to refer to a man. **b.** an old man.

old country n. the country of origin of an immigrant or an immigrant's ancestors.

olden (ˈəʊldᵊn) adj. Archaic or poetic. old: in olden days.

Old English n. the English language of the Anglo-Saxons, spoken from the fifth century A.D. to about 1100. Also called: **Anglo-Saxon.**

Old English sheepdog n. a breed of large sheepdog with a thick shaggy coat.

old-fashioned adj. 1. belonging to or favoured by former times; outdated: old-fashioned ideas. 2. favouring or adopting the styles or ideas of a former time: an old-fashioned romantic.

old flame n. Informal, old-fashioned. a former sweetheart.

Old French n. the French language in its earliest forms, from about the 9th century up to about 1400.

old guard n. 1. a group that works for a long-established or old-fashioned cause. 2. the conservative element in a party or group. [after Napoleon's imperial guard]

old hat adj. old-fashioned or trite.

Old High German n. a group of West Germanic dialects that developed into modern German; High German up to about 1200.

oldie (ˈəʊldɪ) n. Informal. an old joke, song, film or person.

old lady n. Informal. one's mother or wife.

old maid n. 1. a woman regarded as unlikely ever to marry; spinster. 2. Informal. a prim, fussy, or excessively cautious person.

old man n. 1. Informal. one's father or husband. 2. an affectionate form of address used to a man.

old master n. 1. one of the great European painters of the period 1500 to 1800. 2. a painting by one of these.

old moon n. a phase of the moon between last quarter and new moon, when it appears as a waning crescent.

Old Nick (nɪk) n. Informal. Satan.

old school n. a group of people favouring traditional or conservative ideas or practices.

old school tie n. the system of mutual help supposed to operate among the former pupils of public schools.

Old Style n. the former method of reckoning dates using the Julian calendar.

Old Testament n. the first part of the

Christian Bible, containing the sacred Scriptures of the Hebrews.

old-time *adj.* of or relating to a former time; old-fashioned: *old-time dancing.*

old wives' tale *n.* a belief, usually superstitious or foolish, passed on by word of mouth as a piece of traditional wisdom.

old woman *n.* **1.** *Informal.* one's mother or wife. **2.** a timid, fussy, or cautious person. —**old-'womanish** *adj.*

Old World *n.* that part of the world that was known before the discovery of the Americas; the eastern hemisphere.

old-world *adj.* of or characteristic of former times; quaint or traditional.

oleaginous (ˌəʊlɪ'ædʒɪnəs) *adj.* like or producing oil; oily. [Latin *oleāginus*]

oleander (ˌəʊlɪ'ændə) *n.* an evergreen Mediterranean shrub with fragrant white, pink, or purple flowers. [Medieval Latin]

O level *n. Brit.* **1.** the basic level of the General Certificate of Education. **2.** a pass in a particular subject at O level: *he has eight O levels.*

olfactory (ɒl'fæktrɪ) *adj.* of the sense of smell. [Latin *olere* to smell + *facere* to make]

oligarch ('ɒlɪˌgɑːk) *n.* a member of an oligarchy.

oligarchy ('ɒlɪˌgɑːkɪ) *n., pl.* -chies. **1.** government by a small group of people. **2.** a state or organization so governed. **3.** a small body of individuals ruling such a state or organization. [Greek *oligos* few + *arkhein* to rule] —**oli'garchic** *or* ˌoli-'garchical** *adj.*

Oligocene ('ɒlɪgəʊˌsiːn, ɒ'lɪg-) *adj. Geol.* of the epoch of geological time about 35 million years ago. [Greek *oligos* little + *kainos* new]

olive ('ɒlɪv) *n.* **1.** an evergreen mediterranean tree. **2.** the fruit of this tree, eaten as a relish or pressed to make olive oil. ~*adj.* **3.** yellow-green. [Latin *oliva*]

olive branch *n.* peace offering: *to hold out the olive branch.*

olive-green *adj.* deep yellowish-green.

olive oil *n.* a green or yellow oil pressed from ripe olives and used in cooking and medicines.

Olympiad (ə'lɪmpɪˌæd) *n.* **1.** a staging of the modern Olympic Games. **2.** an international contest in chess or other games.

Olympian (ə'lɪmpɪən) *adj.* **1.** of Mount Olympus or the classical Greek gods. **2.** majestic or godlike. ~*n.* **3.** a god of Mount Olympus.

Olympic (ə'lɪmpɪk) *adj.* of the Olympic Games.

Olympic Games *n.* (*functioning as sing. or pl.*) **1.** an ancient Greek festival, held every fourth year in honour of Zeus, consisting of games and festivities. **2.** Also called: **the Olympics.** the modern revival of these games, consisting of international athletic and sporting contests held every four years in a selected country.

OM Order of Merit (a Brit. title).

ombudsman ('ɒmbʊdzmən) *n., pl.* -men. an official who investigates citizens' com-

plaints against the government or its servants. [Swedish: commissioner]

omega ('əʊmɪgə) *n.* **1.** the 24th and last letter of the Greek alphabet (Ω, ω). **2.** the ending or last of a series.

omelette *or esp. U.S.* **omelet** ('ɒmlɪt) *n.* a dish of beaten eggs cooked in a flat pan and often folded round a savoury filling. [French]

omen ('əʊmən) *n.* **1.** a thing or occurrence regarded as a sign of future happiness or disaster. **2.** prophetic significance: *bird of ill omen.* [Latin]

ominous ('ɒmɪnəs) *adj.* foreboding evil. [Latin *ōminōsus*] —**'ominously** *adv.*

omission (əʊ'mɪʃən) *n.* **1.** something that has been omitted or neglected. **2.** an omitting or having been omitted.

omit (əʊ'mɪt) *vb.* omitting, omitted. **1.** to fail to include; leave out. **2.** to fail (to do something). [Latin *omittere*]

omnibus ('ɒmnɪˌbʌs, -bəs) *n., pl.* -buses. **1.** a bus. **2.** a collection of works by one author or several works on a similar topic, reprinted in one volume. ~*adj.* **3.** consisting of or dealing with several different things at once: *an omnibus programme.* [Latin, lit.: for all]

omnipotent (ɒm'nɪpətənt) *adj.* having very great or unlimited power. [Latin *omnipotens* all-powerful] —**om'nipotence** *n.*

omnipresent (ˌɒmnɪ'prɛzʲnt) *adj.* (esp. of a god) present in all places at the same time. [Latin *omnis* all] —ˌomni'presence** *n.*

omniscient (ɒm'nɪsɪənt) *adj.* knowing or seeming to know everything. [Latin *omnis* all + *scire* to know] —**om'niscience** *n.*

omnivorous (ɒm'nɪvərəs) *adj.* **1.** eating any type of food. **2.** taking in or assimilating everything indiscriminately: *an omnivorous reader.* [Latin *omnivorus* all-devouring] —**omnivore** ('ɒmnɪˌvɔː) *n.* —**om'nivorousness** *n.*

on (ɒn) *prep.* **1.** in contact with the surface of; at the upper surface of: *an apple on the ground; a mark on the tablecloth.* **2.** attached to: *a puppet on a string.* **3.** carried with: *I've no money on me.* **4.** near to or along the side of: *a house on the sea.* **5.** within the time limits of (a day or date): *he arrived on Thursday.* **6.** being performed upon or relayed through the medium of: *a waltz played on the violin; what's on television?* **7.** at the occasion of: *on his retirement.* **8.** immediately after or at the same time as: *on entering I spotted him.* **9.** through the use of: *he lives on bread; cars run on petrol.* **10. a.** regularly taking (a drug): *she's on the pill.* **b.** addicted to: *he's on heroin.* **11.** by means of (a mode of transport): *on foot; on horseback.* **12.** in the process or course of: *on a journey; on strike.* **13.** concerned with or relating to: *a programme on jazz.* **14.** (of as statement or action): having as basis or grounds: *I have it on good authority.* **15.** charged to: *the drinks are on me.* **16.** staked as a bet: *ten pounds on that horse.* **17.** (used with an *adj.* preceded by *the*) indicating the manner or way in which an action is carried out: *on the sly*; *on the cheap.* ~*adv.* **18.** in operation; functioning: *the radio's been on all night.* **19.** attached to, surrounding, or placed in contact with something: *the girl had nothing on.* **20.** taking place: *what's on tonight?* **21.** continuously or persistently: *don't keep on about it; the play went on all afternoon.* **22.** towards or forwards: *we drove on towards London; march on!* **23. on and off.** intermittently; from time to time. **24. on and on.** without ceasing; continually. ~*adj.* **25.** functioning; operating: *the on position on a radio.* **26.** *Informal.* performing: *I'm on in five minutes.* **27.** *Informal.* definitely taking place: *the match is on for Friday.* **28.** *Informal.* tolerable, practicable or acceptable: *your plan just isn't on.* **29. on at.** *Informal.* nagging: *she was always on at her husband.* ~*n.* **30.** *Cricket.* the side of the field to the left of and behind a right-handed batsman. [Old English *an, on*]

onager (ˈɒnədʒə) *n., pl.* **-gri** (-ˌgraɪ) *or* **-gers.** a wild ass of Persia. [Greek *onagros*]

onanism (ˈəʊnəˌnɪzəm) *n.* **1.** withdrawal in sexual intercourse before ejaculation. **2.** masturbation. [after *Onan:* see Genesis 38:9]

ONC (in Britain) Ordinary National Certificate.

once (wʌns) *adv.* **1.** one time; on one occasion only. **2.** at some past time, but no longer: *I could speak French once.* **3.** by one degree (of relationship): *a cousin once removed.* **4.** ever; at all: *if you once forget it.* **5. once and for all.** conclusively; for the last time. **6. once in a while.** occasionally; now and then. **7. once or twice.** a few times. **8. once upon a time.** used to begin fairy tales and children's stories. ~*conj.* **9.** as soon as: *once you begin, you'll enjoy it.* ~*n.* **10.** one occasion or case: *you may do it, this once.* **11. all at once. a.** suddenly. **b.** simultaneously. **12. at once. a.** immediately. **b.** simultaneously. **13. for once.** this time, even if at no other time. [Middle English *ones, anes*]

once-over *n. Informal.* a quick examination or appraisal.

oncoming (ˈɒnˌkʌmɪŋ) *adj.* coming nearer in space or time; approaching.

oncogene (ˈɒŋkəʊˌdʒiːn) *n.* a gene present in all cells, that when abnormally activated can cause cancer. [Greek *onkos* tumour + *-gen* (suffix) producing]

OND (in Britain) Ordinary National Diploma.

one (wʌn) *det.* **1.** single; lone; not two or more: *one drink; one at a time.* **2.** only; unique: *he's the one man who can do it; one of a kind.* **3.** a specified (person or thing) as distinct from another or others of its kind: *raise one hand and then the other; which one is correct?* **4.** a certain, indefinite, or unspecified (time): *one day you'll be sorry.* **5.** *Informal.* an emphatic word for **a** or **an:** *it was one hell of a fight.* **6.** (**all**) **in one.** combined; united. **7. all one.** of no consequence: *it's all one to me.* **8. at one.** (often foll. by *with*) in a state of agreement or harmony. **9. one and all.** everyone, without exception. **10. one by one.** one at a time; individually. **11. one or two.** a few. ~*pron.* **12.** an indefinite person regarded as typical of every person: *one can't say any more than that.* **13.** any indefinite person: *one can catch fine trout in this stream.* ~*n.* **14.** the smallest natural number and first cardinal number. **15.** a numeral, 1 or I, representing this number. **16.** *Informal.* a joke or story: *have you heard the one about the actress and the bishop?* **17.** something consisting of one unit or represented by the number one. [Old English *ān*]

one another *pron.* each other; each one the other: *they dislike one another.*

one-armed bandit *n. Informal.* a fruit machine operated by pulling down a lever at one side.

one-horse *adj. Informal.* small or insignificant: *a one-horse town.*

one-liner *n. Informal.* a short joke or witty remark.

oneness (ˈwʌnnɪs) *n.* **1.** agreement. **2.** uniqueness. **3.** sameness.

one-night stand *n.* **1.** a performance given only once at any one place. **2.** *Informal.* a sexual encounter lasting only one evening or night.

one-off *n. Brit.* something that happens or is made only once.

onerous (ˈɒnərəs, ˈəʊ-) *adj.* laborious or burdensome. [Latin *onus* load] —ˈonerousness *n.*

oneself (wʌnˈsɛlf) *pron.* **1.** the reflexive form of *one.* **2.** one's normal or usual self: *one doesn't feel oneself after such an experience.*

one-sided *adj.* **1.** considering or favouring only one side of a matter or problem: *a one-sided account.* **2.** having all the advantage on one side: *a one-sided race.*

one-stop *adj.* having or providing a range of related services or goods in one place: *a one-stop shop.*

one-time *adj.* at some time in the past; former.

one-to-one *adj.* **1.** (of two or more things) corresponding exactly. **2.** denoting a relationship or encounter in which someone is involved with only one other person: *one-to-one tuition.* **3.** *Maths.* involving the pairing of each member of one set with only one member of another set, without remainder.

one-track *adj. Informal.* obsessed with one idea or subject: *a one-track mind.*

one-up *adj. Informal.* having an advantage or lead over another. —ˌone-ˈupmanship *n.*

one-way *adj.* **1.** moving or allowing travel in one direction only: *one-way traffic.* **2.** involving no reciprocal obligation or action: *a one-way relationship.*

ongoing (ˈɒnˌgəʊɪŋ) *adj.* in progress; continuing: *ongoing projects.*

onion (ˈʌnjən) *n.* **1.** a vegetable with an edible bulb having a pungent odour and taste. **2. know one's onions.** *Brit. slang.* to be fully acquainted with a subject. [Latin *unio*] —ˈoniony *adj.*

on-line *adj.* (of computer equipment) directly connected to and controlled by the central processing unit of a computer.

onlooker (ˈɒnˌlʊkə) *n.* a person who observes without taking part. —**ˈonˌlooking** *adj.*

only (ˈəʊnlɪ) *adj.* **1.** alone of its or their kind: *the only men left in town were too old to bear arms.* **2.** (of a child) having no brother or sisters. **3.** unique by virtue of superiority; best: *flying is the only way to travel.* **4. one and only.** incomparable: *the one and only Diana Ross.* ~*adv.* **5.** without anyone or anything else being included; alone: *you have one choice only; only a genius can do that.* **6.** merely or just: *it's only Henry.* **7.** no more or no greater than: *we met only an hour ago.* **8.** merely: *I returned, only to find him gone.* **9.** not earlier than; not until: *I only found out yesterday.* **10. if only** or **if...only.** used to introduce a wish or hope. **11. only too.** *adj.* extremely: *he was only too pleased to help.* ~*conj.* **12.** but; however: *play outside, only don't go into the street.* [Old English *ānlīc*]

o.n.o. or near(est) offer.

onomatopoeia (ˌɒnəˌmætəˈpiːə) *n.* the formation or use of a word whose sound imitates the sound of the noise or action represented, such as *hiss.* [Greek *onoma* name + *poiein* to make] —**ˌonoˌmatoˈpoeic** or **onomatopoetic** (ˌɒnəˌmætəpəʊˈɛtɪk) *adj.*

onrush (ˈɒnˌrʌʃ) *n.* a forceful forward rush or flow; surge.

onset (ˈɒnˌsɛt) *n.* a start; beginning.

onshore (ˈɒnˈʃɔː) *adj., adv.* **1.** towards the land: *an onshore gale.* **2.** on land; not at sea.

onside (ˌɒnˈsaɪd) *adj., adv. Sport.* (of a player) in a legal position, as when behind the ball or with a required number of opponents between oneself and the opposing team's goal line.

onslaught (ˈɒnˌslɔːt) *n.* a violent attack. [Middle Dutch *aenslag*]

Ont. Ontario.

onto or **on to** (ˈɒntʊ) *prep.* **1.** to a position that is on: *step onto the train.* **2.** having become aware of (something): *the police are onto us.* **3.** into contact with: *get onto the factory.*

ontology (ɒnˈtɒlədʒɪ) *n. Philosophy.* the study of the nature of being. [Greek *ōn* being + -LOGY] —**ontological** (ˌɒntəˈlɒdʒɪkəl) *adj.*

onus (ˈəʊnəs) *n., pl.* **onuses.** a responsibility, task, or burden. [Latin: burden]

onward (ˈɒnwəd) *adj.* **1.** directed or moving forward. ~*adv.* also **onwards.** **2.** continuing; progressing.

onyx (ˈɒnɪks) *n.* a kind of quartz with alternating coloured layers, used as a gemstone. [Greek: fingernail (so called from its veined appearance)]

oodles (ˈuːdəlz) *pl. n. Informal.* great quantities: *oodles of money.* [origin unknown]

Ookpik (ˈuːkpɪk) *n. Canad. trademark.* a sealskin doll resembling an owl, used

abroad as a symbol of Canadian handicrafts.

oolite (ˈəʊəˌlaɪt) *n.* a limestone made up of tiny grains of calcium carbonate. [New Latin *oolītēs,* lit.: egg stone] —**oolitic** (ˌəʊəˈlɪtɪk) *adj.*

oomiak or **oomiac** (ˈuːmɪˌæk) *n.* same as **umiak.**

oompah (ˈuːmˌpɑː) *n.* a representation of the sound made by a deep brass instrument, esp. in brass band music.

oomph (ʊmf) *n. Informal.* enthusiasm, vigour, or energy. [origin unknown]

oops (ʊps, uːps) *interj.* an exclamation of surprise or of apology when someone makes a slight accident or makes a mistake.

ooze[1] (uːz) *vb.* **1.** to flow or leak out slowly; seep. **2.** to exude or emit moisture. **3.** to overflow with (a feeling or quality): *to ooze charm.* ~*n.* **4.** a slow flowing or leaking. [Old English *wōs* juice] —**ˈoozy** *adj.*

ooze[2] (uːz) *n.* a soft thin mud, such as that found at the bottom of a lake, river, or sea. [Old English *wāse* mud]

op. opus.

opacity (əʊˈpæsɪtɪ) *n., pl.* **-ties. 1.** the state or quality of being opaque. **2.** obscurity of meaning; unintelligibility.

opal (ˈəʊpəl) *n.* a precious stone, usually milky or bluish in colour, with iridescent reflections. [Greek *opallios*]

opalescent (ˌəʊpəˈlɛsənt) *adj.* iridescent like opal. —**ˌopalˈescence** *n.*

opaque (əʊˈpeɪk) *adj.* **1.** not able to be seen through; not transparent or translucent. **2.** hard to understand; unintelligible. [Latin *opācus* shady]

op. cit. (in textual annotations) in the work cited. [Latin *opere citato*]

OPEC (ˈəʊpɛk) Organization of Petroleum-Exporting Countries.

open (ˈəʊpən) *adj.* **1.** not closed, fastened, or blocked up. **2.** not enclosed, covered, or wrapped. **3.** extended, expanded, or unfolded: *an open flower.* **4.** ready for business: *the shops are open till five.* **5.** (of a job) available: *the position is no longer open.* **6.** unobstructed by buildings or trees: *open countryside.* **7.** free to all to join in, enter, or use: *an open competition.* **8.** (of a season or period) not restricted for purposes of hunting game of various kinds. **9.** not decided or finalized: *an open question.* **10.** ready to consider new ideas: *an open mind.* **11.** frank; candid. **12.** liberal or generous: *an open hand.* **13.** undisguised; manifest: *open disregard of the law.* **14.** unprotected; susceptible: *you will leave yourself open to attack.* **15.** having spaces or gaps: *open ranks; an open texture.* **16.** *Music.* **a.** (of a string) not stopped with the finger. **b.** (of a note) played on such a string. **17.** *Sport.* (of a goal or court) unguarded or relatively unprotected. **18.** (of a wound) exposed to the air. ~*vb.* **19.** to make or become open: *to open a window.* **20.** to make or become accessible or unobstructed: *to open a road; to open a parcel.* **21.** to extend, expand, or unfold: *to open a newspaper.* **22.** to set or be set in action; start: *to open the batting; to open a shop.* **23.** to arrange for (a bank account), usually by making an initial deposit. **24.** to declare open ceremonially or officially. ~*n.* **25. the open.** any wide or unobstructed area. **26.** *Sport.* a competition which all may enter. [Old English] —**'opener** *n.* —**'openly** *adv.* —**'openness** *n.*

open air *n.* the place or space where the air is unenclosed; outdoors.

open-and-shut *adj.* easily decided or solved; obvious: *an open-and-shut case.*

opencast mining (ˈəʊpˌnˌkɑːst) *n. Brit.* mining by excavating from the surface. [*open* + archaic *cast* ditch, cutting]

open day *n.* a special occasion on which a school, university, or other institution is open for the public to visit.

open-ended *adj.* without definite limits; unrestricted: *an open-ended contract.*

open-eyed *adj.* **1.** with the eyes wide open, as in amazement. **2.** watchful; alert.

open-handed *adj.* generous.

open-hearted *adj.* **1.** kindly; generous. **2.** frank; candid.

open-heart surgery *n.* surgical repair of the heart during which the heart is exposed and the blood circulation is maintained mechanically.

open house *n.* a situation in which people allow friends or visitors to come to their house whenever they want to.

opening (ˈəʊpənɪŋ) *n.* **1.** the act of making or becoming open. **2.** a hole or gap. **3.** the beginning or first part of something. **4.** the first performance of a theatrical production. **5.** an opportunity or chance.

opening time *n. Brit.* the time at which public houses can legally open for business.

open letter *n.* a letter, esp. one of protest, addressed to an individual but published in a newspaper or magazine for all to read.

open-minded *adj.* having a mind receptive to new ideas; unprejudiced.

open-mouthed *adj.* gaping in surprise.

open-plan *adj.* having no or few dividing walls between areas: *an open-plan office.*

open prison *n.* a prison in which the prisoners are not locked up, thus extending the range of work they can do.

open secret *n.* something that is supposed to be secret but is widely known.

Open University *n.* (in Britain) a university teaching by means of television and radio lectures, correspondence courses, and summer schools.

open up *vb.* **1.** to make or become accessible: *the motorway opened up the remoter areas.* **2.** to speak freely or without self-restraint. **3.** to start firing a gun or guns. **4.** *Informal.* (of a motor vehicle) to accelerate.

open verdict *n.* a finding by a coroner's jury of death without stating the cause.

opera[1] (ˈɒpərə, ˈɒprə) *n.* **1.** a dramatic work in which most or all of the text is sung to orchestral accompaniment. **2.** the branch of music or drama relating to operas. **3.** a theatre where opera is performed. [Latin: work]

opera[2] (ˈɒpərə) *n.* a plural of **opus.**

operable (ˈɒpərəb²l, ˈɒprə-) *adj.* **1.** capable of being treated by a surgical operation. **2.** capable of being operated. **3.** capable of being put into practice. —**ˌoperaˈbility** *n.*

opera glasses *pl. n.* small low-powered binoculars used by audiences in theatres.

opera house *n.* a theatre specially designed for the performance of operas.

operand (ˈɒpəˌrænd) *n. Maths.* a quantity, variable, or function upon which an operation is performed.

operate (ˈɒpəˌreɪt) *vb.* **1.** to function or cause to function. **2.** to control the functioning of. **3.** to manage, direct, or run (a business or system). **4.** to perform a surgical operation (upon a person or animal). **5.** to produce a desired effect. **6.** to conduct military or naval operations. [Latin *operārī* to work]

operatic (ˌɒpəˈrætɪk) *adj.* **1.** of or relating to opera. **2.** overdramatic or exaggerated.

operating theatre or *U.S.* **room** *n.* a room in which surgical operations are performed.

operation (ˌɒpəˈreɪʃən) *n.* **1.** the act or method of operating. **2.** the condition of being in action: *similar schemes are in operation elsewhere.* **3.** an action or series of actions done to produce a particular result. **4.** *Surgery.* a surgical prodeudure carried out to remove, replace, or repair a diseased or damaged part of the body. **5.** a military or naval campaign or manoeuvre. **6.** *Maths.* any procedure, such as addition, in which a number is derived from another number or numbers by applying specific rules.

operational (ˌɒpəˈreɪʃənˀl) *adj.* **1.** of or relating to an operation. **2.** in working order and ready for use.

operations research *n.* the analysis of problems in business and industry. Also called: **operational research.**

operative (ˈɒpərətɪv) *adj.* **1.** in force, effect, or operation. **2.** (of a word) particularly relevant or significant: *"if" is the operative word.* **3.** of or relating to a surgical operation. ~*n.* **4.** a worker with a special skill.

operator (ˈɒpəˌreɪtə) *n.* **1.** a person who operates a machine or instrument, esp. a telephone switchboard. **2.** a person who runs a business. **3.** a financial speculator. **4.** *Informal.* a person who manipulates affairs and other people. **5.** *Maths.* any symbol, term or letter used to indicate or express a specific operation or process.

operculum (əʊˈpɜːkjʊləm) *n., pl.* **-la** (-lə) or **-lums.** a covering flap or lidlike structure in animals or plants. [Latin: lid]

operetta (ˌɒpəˈrɛtə) *n.* a type of comic or light-hearted opera.

ophthalmia (ɒfˈθælmɪə) *n.* inflammation of the eyeball or conjunctiva. [Greek *ophthalmos* eye]

ophthalmic (ɒfˈθælmɪk) *adj*. of or relating to the eye.

ophthalmic optician *n*. See **optician**.

ophthalmology (ˌɒfθælˈmɒlədʒɪ) *n*. the branch of medicine concerned with the eye and its diseases. —ˌ**ophthalˈmologist** *n*.

ophthalmoscope (ɒfˈθælmə‚skəʊp) *n*. an instrument for examining the interior of the eye.

opiate (ˈəʊpɪɪt) *n*. **1.** a narcotic or sedative drug containing opium. **2.** something that has a tranquillizing or stupefying effect.

opine (əʊˈpaɪn) *vb*. to hold or express an opinion: *he opined that it was a mistake.* [Latin *opīnāri*]

opinion (əˈpɪnjən) *n*. **1.** belief not founded on certainty or proof but on what seems probable. **2.** evaluation or estimation of a person or thing. **3.** an evaluation or judgment given by an expert: *a medical opinion.* **4. a matter of opinion.** a point open to question. [Latin *opīniō* belief]

opinionated (əˈpɪnjə‚neɪtɪd) *adj*. holding obstinately to one's own opinions; dogmatic.

opinion poll *n*. same as **poll** (sense 3).

opium (ˈəʊpɪəm) *n*. **1.** an addictive narcotic drug made from the seed capsules of the opium poppy: used in medicine as a pain-killer and sedative. **2.** something having a tranquillizing or stupefying effect. [Greek *opion* poppy juice]

opossum (əˈpɒsəm) *n*., *pl.* **-sums** *or* **-sum.** **1.** a thick-furred American marsupial, with a long snout and a hairless prehensile tail. **2.** *Austral. & N.Z.* a similar Australian animal, such as a phalanger. [American Indian *aposoum*]

opp. opposite.

opponent (əˈpəʊnənt) *n*. a person who opposes another in a contest, battle, or argument. [Latin *oppōnere* to oppose]

opportune (ˈɒpə‚tjuːn) *adj*. **1.** happening at a time that is suitable or advantageous: *an opportune interruption.* **2.** (of time) suitable for a particular purpose: *an opportune moment.* [Latin *opportūnus*, from *ob*-to + *portus* harbour (orig.: coming to the harbour, obtaining timely protection)]

opportunist (ˌɒpəˈtjuːnɪst) *n*. **1.** a person who adapts his actions to take advantage of opportunities and circumstances without regard for principles. ~*adj*. **2.** taking advantage of opportunities and circumstances in this way. —ˌ**oppor'tunism** *n*. —ˌ**opportu'nistic** *adj*.

opportunity (ˌɒpəˈtjuːnɪtɪ) *n*., *pl.* **-ties.** **1.** a favourable combination of circumstances. **2.** a good chance or prospect.

opposable (əˈpəʊzəb'l) *adj*. **1.** capable of being opposed. **2.** (of the thumb) capable of touching the tip of all the other fingers.

oppose (əˈpəʊz) *vb*. **1.** to be against (something) in speech or action; resist strongly. **2.** to contrast or counterbalance. **3.** to place opposite or facing. [Latin *oppōnere*] —op'posing *adj*.

opposite (ˈɒpəzɪt, -sɪt) *adj*. **1.** situated on the other or further side. **2.** facing or going in contrary directions: *opposite ways.* **3.** completely different; exactly contrary. **4.** *Maths.* (of a side in a triangle) facing a specified angle. ~*n*. **5.** a person or thing that is opposite; antithesis. ~*prep*. **6.** facing; across from. ~*adv*. **7.** in an opposite position: *she lives opposite.* —'**oppositeness** *n*.

opposite number *n*. a person holding an equivalent position in another group or organization.

opposition (ˌɒpəˈzɪʃən) *n*. **1.** an opposing or being opposed. **2.** hostility, resistance or disagreement. **3.** a person or group antagonistic or opposed to another. **4.** a political party or group opposed to the ruling party or government. **5.** *Astrol.* a diametrically opposite position of two heavenly bodies.

oppress (əˈprɛs) *vb*. **1.** to subjugate by cruelty or force. **2.** to make anxious or uncomfortable. [Latin *ob*- against + *premere* to press] —op'pression *n*. —op'pressor *n*.

oppressive (əˈprɛsɪv) *adj*. **1.** cruel, harsh, or tyrannical. **2.** constricting or depressing. **3.** (of weather) hot and humid. —op'pressiveness *n*.

opprobrium (əˈprəʊbrɪəm) *n*. **1.** the state of being abused or scornfully criticized. **2.** a cause of disgrace or shame. [Latin *ob*-against + *probrum* a shameful act] —op'probrious *adj*.

oppugn (əˈpjuːn) *vb*. to call into question; dispute. [Latin *ob*- against + *pugnāre* to fight]

opt (ɒpt) *vb*. (often foll. by *for*) to show preference (for) or choose (to do something). [Latin *optāre* to choose]

optic (ˈɒptɪk) *adj*. of the eye or vision. [Greek *optos* visible]

optical (ˈɒptɪk'l) *adj*. **1.** of or involving light or optics. **2.** of the eye or the sense of sight; optic. **3.** (of a lens) helping vision.

optical character reader *n*. a computer device enabling letters and numbers to be optically scanned and input to a storage device.

optical fibre *n*. a thin flexible glass fibre used in fibre optics to transmit information.

optician (ɒpˈtɪʃən) *n*. a general name used to refer to: **a. an ophthalmic optician.** one qualified to examine the eyes and prescribe and supply spectacles and contact lenses. **b. a dispensing optician.** one who supplies and fits spectacle frames and lenses, but is not qualified to prescribe lenses.

optics (ˈɒptɪks) *n*. (functioning as sing.) the science dealing with light and vision.

optimism (ˈɒptɪ‚mɪzəm) *n*. **1.** the tendency to take the most hopeful view in all matters. **2.** the doctrine of the ultimate triumph of good over evil. [Latin *optimus* best] —'optimist *n*. —ˌopti'mistic *adj*. —ˌopti'mistically *adv*.

optimize *or* **-mise** (ˈɒptɪ‚maɪz) *vb*. to make the most of.

optimum (ˈɒptɪməm) *n*., *pl.* **-ma** (-mə) *or* **-mums.** **1.** the most favourable conditions or best compromise possible. ~*adj*. **2.** most favourable or advantageous; best:

optimum conditions. [Latin: the best (thing)]

option ('ɒpʃən) *n.* **1.** an act of choosing or deciding. **2.** the power or liberty to choose. **3.** an exclusive right, usually for a limited period, to buy or sell something at a future date: *a six-month option on the Canadian rights to this book.* **4.** something that is or may be chosen. **5. keep** *or* **leave one's options open.** not to commit oneself. **6. soft option.** an easy alternative. [Latin *optāre* to choose]

optional ('ɒpʃənᵊl) *adj.* possible but not compulsory; open to choice.

optometrist (ɒp'tɒmɪtrɪst) *n.* a person qualified to examine the eyes and prescribe and supply spectacles and contact lenses. **—op'tometry** *n.*

opt out *vb.* (often foll. by *of*) to choose not to be involved (in) or part (of).

opulent ('ɒpjʊlənt) *adj.* **1.** having or indicating wealth. **2.** abundant or plentiful. [Latin *opulens*] **—'opulence** *n.*

opus ('əʊpəs) *n., pl.* **opuses** *or* **opera.** an artistic creation, esp. a musical work by a particular composer, numbered in order of publication: *Beethoven's opus 61.* [Latin: a work]

or (ɔː) *conj.* used to join: **1.** alternatives: *do you want to go out or stay at home?* **2.** rephrasings of the same thing: *twelve, or a dozen.* [Middle English contraction of *other*]

OR Oregon.

oracle ('ɒrəkᵊl) *n.* **1.** a shrine in ancient Greece or Rome at which gods were consulted through the medium of a priest or priestess for advice or prophecy. **2.** a prophecy or statement made by an oracle. **3.** any person belived to indicate future action with infallible authority. [Latin *ōrāculum*]

Oracle ('ɒrəkᵊl) *n. Trademark.* Optional Reception of Announcements by Coded Line Electronics: the teletext service of Independent Television.

oracular (ɒ'rækjʊlə) *adj.* **1.** of or like an oracle. **2.** wise and prophetic. **3.** mysterious or ambiguous.

oral ('ɔːrəl, 'ɒrəl) *adj.* **1.** spoken or verbal; using spoken words. **2.** of or for use in the mouth: *an oral thermometer.* **3.** (of a drug) to be taken by mouth: *an oral contraceptive.* **~n.** **4.** an examination in which the questions and answers are spoken rather than written. [Latin *ōs, oris* mouth] **—'orally** *adv.*

orange ('ɒrɪndʒ) *n.* **1.** a round reddish-yellow juicy citrus fruit. **2.** the evergreen tree on which it grows. **~adj.** **3.** of a colour between red and yellow. [Arabic *nāranj*]

orangeade (ˌɒrɪndʒ'eɪd) *n.* a usually fizzy orange-flavoured drink.

orange blossom *n.* the flowers of the orange tree, traditionally worn by brides.

Orangeman ('ɒrɪndʒmən) *n., pl.* **-men.** a member of a political society founded in Ireland in 1795 to uphold Protestantism. [after William, prince of *Orange,* later William III]

orangery ('ɒrɪndʒərɪ, -dʒrɪ) *n., pl.* **-eries.** a conservatory or greenhouse in which orange trees are grown in cooler climates.

orang-utan (ˌɔːræŋ'uːtæn) *or* **orang-outang** (ˌɔːræŋ'uːtæŋ) *n.* a large ape of the forests of Sumatra and Borneo, with shaggy reddish-brown hair and long arms. [Malay *ōrang* man + *hūtan* forest]

oration (ɔː'reɪʃən) *n.* **1.** a formal or ceremonial public speech. **2.** any lengthy or pompous speech. [Latin *ōrātiō*]

orator ('ɒrətə) *n.* a person who gives an oration, esp. one skilled in rhetoric.

oratorio (ˌɒrə'tɔːrɪəʊ) *n., pl.* **-rios.** a musical composition for soloists, chorus, and orchestra, based on a religious theme. [Italian]

oratory[1] ('ɒrətrɪ) *n.* the art or skill of public speaking. [Latin (*ars*) *ōrātōria* (the art of) public speaking]

oratory[2] ('ɒrətrɪ) *n., pl.* **-ries.** a small room or building, set apart for private prayer. [Latin *ōrāre* to pray]

orb (ɔːb) *n.* **1.** an ornamental sphere with a cross on top, carried by a king or queen in important ceremonies. **2.** a sphere; globe. **3.** *Poetic.* the eye. **4.** *Obs. or poetic.* a heavenly body, such as the sun. [Latin *orbis* circle, disc]

orbit ('ɔːbɪt) *n.* **1.** the curved path followed by something, such as a heavenly body or spacecraft, in its motion around another body. **2.** a range or sphere of action or influence. **3.** the eye socket. **~vb.** **4.** to move around (a heavenly body) in an orbit. **5.** to send (a satellite or spacecraft) into orbit. [Latin *orbis* circle] **—'orbital** *adj.*

Orcadian (ɔː'keɪdɪən) *n.* **1.** a person from the Orkneys. **~adj.** **2.** of the Orkneys. [Latin *Orcades* the Orkney Islands]

orchard ('ɔːtʃəd) *n.* an area of land on which fruit trees are grown. [Old English *orceard*]

orchestra ('ɔːkɪstrə) *n.* **1.** a large group of musicians whose members play a variety of different instruments. **2.** Also called: **orchestra pit.** the space, in front of or under the stage, reserved for musicians in a theatre. [Greek: the space in the theatre for the chorus] **—orchestral** (ɔː'kestrəl) *adj.*

orchestrate ('ɔːkɪˌstreɪt) *vb.* **1.** to score or arrange (a piece of music) for orchestra. **2.** to arrange (something) in order to produce a particular result: *he orchestrated the whole event.* **—ˌorches'tration** *n.*

orchid ('ɔːkɪd) *n.* a plant having flowers of unusual shapes and beautiful colours, usually with one lip-shaped petal which is larger than the other two. [Greek *orkhis* testicle; because of the shape of its roots]

ordain (ɔː'deɪn) *vb.* **1.** to consecrate (someone) as a priest. **2.** to decree, order, or enact with authority. [Late Latin *ordināre*] **—or'dainment** *n.*

ordeal (ɔː'diːl) *n.* **1.** a severe or trying experience. **2.** *History.* a method of trial in which the accused person was subjected to physical danger. [Old English *ordāl, ordēl* verdict]

order (ˈɔːdə) n. **1.** a state in which everything is arranged logically, comprehensibly, or naturally. **2.** an arrangement of things in succession; sequence: *alphabetical order.* **3.** an established or customary system of society: *after 1945 a new world order was constructed.* **4.** a peaceful or harmonious condition of society: *order reigned in the streets.* **5.** a social class or rank: *the lower orders.* **6.** *Biol.* a grouping that ranks below a class and above a family in animal or plant classification. **7.** an instruction that must be obeyed; command. **8.** kind or sort: *skills of the highest order.* **9. a.** an instruction to supply something in return for payment. **b.** the thing supplied. **10.** a written instruction to pay money: *a banker's order.* **11.** a procedure followed by an assembly or meeting. **12.** (*usually cap.*) Also called: **religious order.** a religious community who bind themselves by vows in order to devote themselves to the pursuit of religious aims. **13.** a group of people distinguished by a particular honour awarded for service or merit. **14.** a style of architecture, usually one of the five major classical styles of architecture classified by the type of columns used. **15.** *Christianity.* **a.** any rank in the Christian clergy. **b.** the office of an ordained Christian minister. **16. a tall order.** something difficult or demanding. **17. in order. a.** in sequence. **b.** properly arranged. **c.** appropriate or fitting. **18. in order that.** (*conj.*) so that. **19. in order to.** (*prep.*) so that it is possible to: *to eat in order to live.* **20. keep order.** to maintain or enforce order. **21. on order.** having been ordered but not yet delivered. **22. out of order. a.** not in sequence. **b.** not working. **c.** not following the rules or customary procedure. **23. to order.** according to a buyer's specifications. ~*vb.* **24.** to give a command (to do something). **25.** to request (something) to be supplied in return for payment. **26.** to command to move or go (to a specified place): *they ordered her into the house.* **27.** to arrange (things) in their proper places. ~*interj.* **28.** an exclamation demanding that orderly behaviour be restored. [Latin *ordō*]

orderly (ˈɔːdəlɪ) *adj.* **1.** tidy, methodical, or well-organized. **2.** well-behaved; law-abiding. ~*n., pl.* **-lies. 3.** *Med.* a male hospital attendant. **4.** *Mil.* a soldier whose duty is to carry orders or perform minor tasks for a more senior officer. —ˈorderliness *n.*

Order of Merit *n. Brit.* an order awarded for outstanding achievement in any field.

order paper *n.* a list indicating the order of business, esp. in Parliament.

ordinal (ˈɔːdɪnˀl) *or* **ordinal number** *n.* a number indicating relative position in a sequence, such as *first, second, third.*

ordinance (ˈɔːdɪnəns) *n.* an authoritative regulation, decree, or practice. [Latin *ordināre* to set in order]

ordinarily (ˈɔːdˀnrɪlɪ) *adv.* in ordinary circumstances; usually; normally.

ordinary (ˈɔːdˀnrɪ) *adj.* **1.** customary or usual. **2.** familiar, everyday, or unexceptional. **3.** uninteresting or commonplace. ~*n., pl.* **-naries. 4.** *R.C. Church.* the parts of the Mass that do not vary from day to day. **5. out of the ordinary.** unusual. [Latin *ordinārius* orderly]

Ordinary level *n.* same as **O level.**

ordinary rating *n.* a rank in the Royal Navy equivalent to that of a private in the army.

ordinary seaman *n.* a seaman of the lowest rank.

ordinary shares *pl. n. Brit.* shares issued by a company entitling their holders to a dividend according to the profits of the company and to a claim on net assets.

ordinate (ˈɔːdɪnɪt) *n. Maths.* the vertical coordinate of a point in a two-dimensional system of coordinates. [Latin *ordināre* to arrange in order]

ordination (ˌɔːdɪˈneɪʃən) *n.* the act or ceremony of making someone a member of the clergy.

ordnance (ˈɔːdnəns) *n.* **1.** weapons and other military supplies. **2. the.** a government department dealing with military supplies. [var. of *ordinance*]

Ordnance Survey *n.* the British government organization that produces detailed maps of Britain and Ireland.

Ordovician (ˌɔːdəˈvɪʃɪən) *adj. Geol.* of the period of geological time about 500 million years ago. [Latin *Ordovices*, ancient Celtic tribe in N Wales]

ordure (ˈɔːdjʊə) *n.* excrement; dung. [Old French *ord* dirty]

ore (ɔː) *n.* rock or mineral from which valuable substances such as metals can be extracted. [Old English *ār, ōra*]

Oreg. Oregon.

oregano (ˌɒrɪˈgɑːnəʊ) *n.* a sweet-smelling herb used as seasoning. [Greek *origanon* an aromatic herb]

organ (ˈɔːgən) *n.* **1.** a musical keyboard instrument in which sound is produced by means of pipes of different lengths, through which air is forced. **2.** a part in animals and plants that is adapted to perform a particular function. **3.** a means of communication, such as a newspaper issued by a specialist group or party. **4.** *Euphemistic.* a penis. [Greek *organon* tool]

organdie (ˈɔːgəndɪ) *n.* a fine, slightly stiff cotton fabric. [French *organdi*]

organ-grinder *n.* an entertainer who plays a barrel organ in the streets.

organic (ɔːˈgænɪk) *adj.* **1.** of, produced by, or found in plants or animals. **2.** relating to an organ or organs of an animal or plant. **3.** of or grown with fertilizers or pesticides produced from animal or vegetable matter. **4.** of or belonging to the class of chemical compounds that are formed from carbon. **5.** systematically arranged or organized: *an organic whole.* —orˈganically *adv.*

organic chemistry *n.* the branch of chemistry dealing with carbon compounds.

organism (ˈɔːgəˌnɪzəm) *n.* **1.** an animal or plant. **2.** anything resembling a living creature in structure, behaviour, or complexity.

organist ('ɔːgənɪst) n. a person who plays the organ.

organization or **-isation** (ˌɔːgənaɪ'zeɪʃən) n. 1. an organized group of people, such as a club, society, union, or business. 2. the act of organizing. 3. the administrative or executive structure of a political party or business. —ˌorgani'zational or -i'sational adj.

organize or **-ise** ('ɔːgəˌnaɪz) vb. 1. to form (parts or elements of something) into a structured whole; coordinate or arrange methodically. 2. to make plans and arrange for (something). 3. to enlist (the workers in a factory or business) in a trade union: organized labour. 4. to form an organization or trade union. [Medieval Latin organizare] —'organ,izer or -ˌiser n.

organza (ɔː'gænzə) n. a thin stiff fabric of silk, cotton, or synthetic fibre. [origin unknown]

orgasm ('ɔːgæzəm) n. the most intense point during sexual excitement. [Greek orgasmos] —or'gasmic adj.

orgy ('ɔːdʒɪ) n., pl. **-gies**. 1. a wild party involving promiscuous sexual activity and excessive drinking. 2. an act of immoderate or frenzied indulgence: an orgy of destruction. [Greek orgia secret rites] —ˌorgi'astic adj.

oriel window or **oriel** ('ɔːrɪəl) n. a window built out from the wall of a house at an upper level. [Old French oriol gallery]

orient n. ('ɔːrɪənt). 1. Poetic. the east. ~vb. ('ɔːrɪˌɛnt). 2. to adjust or align (oneself or one's ideas) according to surroundings or circumstances. 3. to position or set (a map or chart) with relation to the points of the compass or other specific directions. 4. **be oriented to** or **towards**. to have a particular interest in; concentrate one's efforts on: the union is oriented towards welfare capitalism. [Latin oriēns rising (sun)]

Orient ('ɔːrɪənt) n. **the**. East Asia.

oriental (ˌɔːrɪ'ɛntʰl) adj. eastern.

Oriental (ˌɔːrɪ'ɛntʰl) adj. 1. of the Orient. ~n. 2. a person from the Orient.

orientate ('ɔːrɪɛnˌteɪt) vb. Not universally accepted. same as **orient**.

orientation (ˌɔːrɪɛn'teɪʃən) n. 1. the adjustment or alignment of oneself or one's ideas to surroundings or circumstances. 2. positioning with relation to the points of the compass or other specific directions. 3. Chiefly U.S. & Canad. information or training needed to understand a new situation or environment: an orientation course.

orienteering (ˌɔːrɪɛn'tɪərɪŋ) n. a sport in which contestants race on foot over a cross-country course consisting of checkpoints found with the aid of a map and compass. [Swedish orientering]

orifice ('ɒrɪfɪs) n. an opening; vent or aperture. [Latin ōs mouth + facere to make]

orig. 1. origin. 2. original(ly).

origami (ˌɒrɪ'gɑːmɪ) n. the art, originally Japanese, of folding paper intricately into decorative shapes. [Japanese ori a fold + kami paper]

origin ('ɒrɪdʒɪn) n. 1. a primary source; root: the origin of a word. 2. the beginning of something; starting point: the origin of the war. 3. (pl.) ancestry or parentage. 4. Maths. the point at which the horizontal and vertical axes intersect. [Latin orīgō beginning]

original (ə'rɪdʒɪnʰl) adj. 1. first; earliest; initial: my original idea was to do it all myself. 2. fresh and unusual; novel: an original concept. 3. able to think of or carry out new ideas or concepts: a very original writer. 4. being the first and genuine form of something, from which a copy or translation is made: translated from the original French. ~n. 5. the first and genuine form of something, from which others are copied or translated: the original is in the British Museum. 6. a person or thing used as a model in art or literature. —**originality** (əˌrɪdʒɪ'nælɪtɪ) n. —o'riginally adv.

original sin n. a state of sin believed by some Christians to be inborn in all human beings as a result of Adam's disobedience.

originate (ə'rɪdʒɪˌneɪt) vb. to come or bring (something) into being. —**origination** (əˌrɪdʒɪ'neɪʃən) n. —o'rigiˌnator n.

oriole ('ɔːrɪˌəʊl) n. a songbird with a long pointed bill and a mostly yellow-and-black plumage. [Latin aureolus golden]

ormolu ('ɔːməˌluː) n. a gold-coloured alloy of copper, tin, or zinc, used to decorate furniture and other articles. [French or moulu ground gold]

ornament n. ('ɔːnəmənt). 1. anything that adorns someone or something; decoration. 2. decorations collectively: she was totally without ornament. 3. a small decorative object: a china ornament. 4. a person whose character or talent makes them an asset to society or the group to which they belong: an ornament of the firm. ~vb. ('ɔːnəˌment). 5. to furnish with ornaments or act as an ornament to; adorn. [Latin ornāmentum] —**ornamental** (ˌɔːnə'mentʰl) adj. —**ornamentation** (ˌɔːnəmen'teɪʃən) n.

ornate (ɔː'neɪt) adj. 1. heavily or elaborately decorated. 2. (of style in writing) overelaborate; using many literary expressions. [Latin ornāre to decorate] —or'nately adv.

ornithology (ˌɔːnɪ'θɒlədʒɪ) n. the study of birds. [Greek ornis bird] —**ornithological** (ˌɔːnɪθə'lɒdʒɪkʰl) adj. —ˌorni'thologist n.

orotund ('ɒrəʊˌtʌnd) adj. 1. (of the voice) resonant; booming. 2. (of speech or writing) pompous; containing many long or formal words. [Latin ore rotundo with rounded mouth]

orphan ('ɔːfən) n. 1. a child whose parents are dead. ~vb. 2. to deprive (someone) of his parents. [Greek orphanos]

orphanage ('ɔːfənɪdʒ) n. an institution for orphans and abandoned children.

orrery ('ɒrərɪ) n., pl. **-ries**. a mechanical model of the solar system in which the planets can be moved around the sun. [orig. made for Earl of *Orrery*]

orris (ˈɒrɪs) *n.* **1.** a kind of iris that has fragrant roots. **2.** Also: **orrisroot.** the root of this plant prepared and used as perfume. [var. of *iris*]

orthodontics (ˌɔːθəʊˈdɒntɪks) *n.* (*functioning as sing.*) the branch of dentistry concerned with correcting irregularities of the teeth. [Greek *orthos* straight + *odōn* tooth] —ˌortho'dontic *adj.* —ˌortho'dontist *n.*

orthodox (ˈɔːθəˌdɒks) *adj.* conforming with traditional or established standards in religion, behaviour, or attitudes. [Greek *orthos* correct + *doxa* belief] —ˈorthoˌdoxy *n.*

Orthodox (ˈɔːθəˌdɒks) *adj.* of the Orthodox Church of Eastern Europe.

Orthodox Church *n.* the Christian Church dominant in Eastern Europe, with the Greek Patriarch of Constantinople as its head.

orthography (ɔːˈθɒɡrəfɪ) *n.* **1.** spelling considered to be correct. **2.** the study of spelling. [Greek *orthos* straight + *graphein* to write] —**orthographic** (ˌɔːθəʊˈɡræfɪk) *adj.*

orthopaedics or *U.S.* **orthopedics** (ˌɔːθəʊˈpiːdɪks) *n.* (*functioning as sing.*) the branch of surgery concerned with disorders of the bones and joints. [Greek *orthos* straight + *pais* child] —ˌortho'paedic or *U.S.* ˌortho'pedic *adj.* —ˌortho'paedist or *U.S.* ˌortho'pedist *n.*

ortolan (ˈɔːtələn) *n.* a European songbird eaten as a delicacy. [Latin *hortulus* a little garden]

Os *Chem.* osmium.

OS **1.** Ordnance Survey. **2.** outsize(d).

Oscar (ˈɒskə) *n.* any of several small gold statuettes awarded annually in the U.S. for outstanding achievements in films. [said to have been named after a remark made by an official that it reminded him of his uncle Oscar]

oscillate (ˈɒsɪˌleɪt) *vb.* **1.** to swing repeatedly back and forth. **2.** to waver between two extremes of opinion, attitude, or behaviour. **3.** *Physics.* (of an electric current) to vary between minimum and maximum values. [Latin *oscillāre* to swing] —oscillation (ˌɒsɪˈleɪʃən) *n.* —ˈoscilˌlator *n.*

oscilloscope (ɒˈsɪləˌskəʊp) *n.* an instrument that produces a visual representation of an oscillating electric current on the screen of a cathode-ray tube.

osier (ˈəʊzɪə) *n.* **1.** a willow tree whose flexible branches or twigs are used for making baskets and furniture. **2.** a twig or branch from this tree. [Old French]

osmium (ˈɒzmɪəm) *n.* a very hard brittle bluish-white metal, the heaviest known element. Symbol: Os [Greek *osmē* smell, from its penetrating odour]

osmosis (ɒzˈməʊsɪs) *n.* **1.** the diffusion of liquids through a membrane until they are mixed. **2.** the process by which people influence each other gradually and subtly. [Greek *ōsmos* push]

osprey (ˈɒspreɪ) *n.* a large fish-eating bird

of prey, with a dark back and whitish head and underparts. [Old French *ospres*, apparently from Latin *ossifraga*, lit.: bonebreaker]

osseous (ˈɒsɪəs) *adj.* consisting of, containing, or like bone. [Latin *os* bone]

ossify (ˈɒsɪˌfaɪ) *vb.* **-fying, -fied.** **1.** to change into bone; harden. **2.** to become rigid, inflexible, or unprogressive: *a bureaucratic and ossified system.* [Latin *os* bone + *facere* to make] —**ossification** (ˌɒsɪfɪˈkeɪʃən) *n.*

ostensible (ɒˈstɛnsɪbʰl) *adj.* apparent; seeming; alleged: *the ostensible cause of the war.* [Latin *ostendere* to show] —os'tensibly *adv.*

ostensive (ɒˈstɛnsɪv) *adj.* directly showing or pointing out: *an ostensive definition.* [Latin *ostendere* to show]

ostentation (ˌɒstɛnˈteɪʃən) *n.* pretentious, showy, or vulgar display. —ˌosten'tatious *adj.* —ˌosten'tatiously *adv.*

osteoarthritis (ˌɒstɪəʊɑːˈθraɪtɪs) *n.* chronic inflammation of the joints, causing pain and stiffness. [Greek *osteon* bone + *arthritis*]

osteopathy (ˌɒstɪˈɒpəθɪ) *n.* a system of healing based on the manipulation of bones or muscle. [Greek *osteon* bone + *patheia* suffering] —**osteopath** (ˈɒstɪəˌpæθ) *n.*

osteoporosis (ˌɒstɪəʊpɔːˈrəʊsɪs) *n.* brittleness of the bones, caused by lack of calcium. [Greek *osteon* bone + *póros* passage]

ostler (ˈɒslə) *n.* *Archaic.* a stableman at an inn. [var. of *hostler*, from *hostel*]

ostracize or **-ise** (ˈɒstrəˌsaɪz) *vb.* to exclude or banish (a person) from a particular group or from society. [Greek *ostrakizein* to select someone for banishment by voting on potsherds] —**ostracism** *n.*

ostrich (ˈɒstrɪtʃ) *n.* **1.** a large fast-running flightless African bird with powerful two-toed feet and dark feathers. **2.** a person who refuses to recognize an unpleasant truth. [Greek *strouthion*]

OT Old Testament.

OTC (in Britain) Officers' Training Corps.

other (ˈʌðə) *det.* **1.** being the remaining (one or ones) in a group of which one or some have been specified: *I'll read the other sections of the paper later; one walks while the other rides.* **2.** being a different one or ones from the one or ones already specified or understood: *no other man but you.* **3.** additional; further: *I need one other thing.* **4.** every other. every alternate: *it buzzes every other minute.* **5.** other than a. apart from: *a lady other than his wife.* **b.** different from: *he couldn't be other than what he is.* **6.** or other. (preceded by a word or phrase with *some*) used to add vagueness to the preceding word or phrase: *he's somewhere or other; for some reason or other.* **7.** the other day. a few days ago. ~*pron.* **8.** another person or thing: *show me one other.* ~*adv.* **9.** otherwise; differently: *they couldn't behave other than they do.* [Old English *ōther*] —ˈotherness *n.*

other ranks *pl. n.* Chiefly *Brit.* (in the armed forces) all those who do not hold a commissioned rank.

otherwise ('ʌðə,waɪz) *conj.* **1.** or else; if not, then: *go home — otherwise your mother will worry.* ~*adv.* **2.** differently: *I wouldn't have thought otherwise.* **3.** in other respects: *an otherwise hopeless situation.* ~*adj.* **4.** different: *the facts are otherwise.* ~*pron.* **5. or otherwise.** or not; or the opposite: *I have no ideas, brilliant or otherwise.*

otherworldly (,ʌðə'wɜːldlɪ) *adj.* of or concerned with the spiritual world.

otiose ('əʊtɪ,əʊs, -,əʊz) *adj.* serving no useful purpose: *otiose language.* [Latin *ōtiōsus* leisured]

OTT *Brit. slang.* over the top.

otter ('ɒtə) *n.* a small freshwater fish-eating animal with smooth brown fur, a streamlined body, and webbed feet. [Old English *otor*]

ottoman ('ɒtəmən) *n., pl.* **-mans.** a low padded seat without back or arms, usually in the form of a chest. [French *ottomane*, fem. of *Ottoman*]

Ottoman ('ɒtəmən) *adj.* **1.** *History.* of the Ottomans or the Ottoman Empire, the former Turkish empire which lasted from the late 13th century until the end of World War I. ~*n., pl.* **-mans.** **2.** a member of a Turkish people forming this empire. [Arabic *Othmānī*]

ou (əʊ) *n. S. African slang.* a man. [Afrikaans]

OU 1. the Open University. **2.** Oxford University.

oubaas ('əʊ,bɑːs) *n. S. African.* a man in authority. [Afrikaans *ou* + *baas* boss]

ouch (aʊtʃ) *interj.* an exclamation of sharp sudden pain.

ought[1] (ɔːt) *vb.* (foll. by *to*) used to express: **1.** duty or obligation: *you ought to pay.* **2.** advisability: *you ought to see a doctor.* **3.** probability or expectation: *you ought to finish this by Friday.* **4.** a desire on the part of the speaker: *you ought to come next week.* [Old English *āhte*]

ought[2] (ɔːt) *n.* same as **nought** (zero). [mistaken division of *a nought* as *an ought*]

oughtn't ('ɔːt*ə*nt) ought not.

Ouija board *or* **Ouija** ('wiːdʒə) *n. Trademark.* a board on which are marked the letters of the alphabet. Answers to questions are spelt out by a pointer and are supposedly formed by spirits during séances. [French *oui* yes + German *ja* yes]

ouma ('əʊmɑː) *n. S. African.* **1.** grandmother, often as a title with a surname. **2.** *Slang.* any elderly woman. [Afrikaans]

ounce (aʊns) *n.* **1.** a unit of weight equal to one sixteenth of a pound. **2.** short for **fluid ounce.** **3.** a small amount: *he hasn't an ounce of sense.* [Latin *uncia* a twelfth]

oupa ('əʊpɑː) *n. S. African.* **1.** grandfather, often as a title with a surname. **2.** *Slang.* any elderly man. [Afrikaans]

our ('aʊə) *det.* **1.** of, belonging to, or associated with us: *our parents.* **2.** a

formal word for *my* used by monarchs. [Old English *ūre*]

Our Father *n.* same as the **Lord's Prayer.**

ours ('aʊəz) *pron.* **1.** something belonging to us: *ours have blue tags; the brown car is ours.* **2. of ours.** belonging to us.

ourself (aʊə'sɛlf) *pron. Archaic.* a formal word for *myself* used by monarchs.

ourselves (aʊə'sɛlvz) *pron.* **1. a.** the reflexive form of *we* or *us*: *we hurt ourselves.* **b.** used for emphasis: *we ourselves will finish it.* **2.** our usual selves: *we are not ourselves today.* **3.** *Not standard.* used instead of *we* or *us* in compound noun phrases: *other people and ourselves.*

ousel ('uːz*ə*l) *n.* same as **ouzel.**

oust (aʊst) *vb.* to force (someone) out of a position; supplant or expel. [Anglo-Norman *ouster*]

out (aʊt) *adv., adj.* **1.** away from a place; outside: *get out at once; she rushed out of the house.* **2.** used to indicate exhaustion or extinction: *the sugar's run out; put the light out.* **3.** absent from one's home or place of work for a short time: *I came while you were out.* **4.** public; revealed: *the secret is out.* **5.** available to the public: *the book is being brought out next May.* **6.** (of the sun, stars, or moon) visible. **7.** in bloom: *the roses are out now.* **8.** not in fashion, favour, or current usage: *long skirts are out this year.* **9.** excluded from consideration: *that plan is out.* **10.** not allowed: *smoking on duty is out.* **11.** not working: *the radio's out.* **12.** on strike. **13.** out of consciousness: *she passed out.* **14.** used to indicate a burst of activity as indicated by a verb: *fever broke out.* **15.** out of existence: *the mistakes were scored out.* **16.** to the fullest extent: *spread out.* **17.** loudly; clearly: *calling out.* **18.** (foll. by *for* or *to*) desirous of or intent on (something or doing something): *I'm out for as much money as I can get; they're out to get me.* **19.** to a conclusion; completely: *he worked it out.* **20.** (preceded by a superlative) existing: *the friendliest dog out.* **21.** used up: *our supplies are completely out.* **22.** inaccurate or discrepant: *out by six pence.* **23.** not in office or authority: *he was voted out.* **24.** (of a period of time) completed: *before the year is out.* **25.** *Obs.* (of a young woman) in or into society: *Lucinda had a large party when she came out.* **26.** *Sport.* (of a player) dismissed from play. **27. out of. a.** at or to a point outside: *out of his reach.* **b.** away from; not in: *stepping out of line; out of focus.* **c.** because of; motivated by: *out of jealousy.* **d.** from (a material or source): *made out of plastic.* **e.** no longer having any (of a substance or material): *we're out of sugar.* **f.** no longer in a specified state or condition: *out of work; out of practice.* ~*adj.* **28.** directed or indicating direction outwards: *the out tray.* ~*prep.* **29.** *Non-standard or U.S.* out of; out through: *he ran out the door.* ~*interj.* **30. a.** an exclamation of dismissal. **b.** (in signalling and radio) an expression used to signal that the speaker is signing off: *over and out!* **31. out with it.** a command to someone to make something known immediately, without missing any details. ~n. **32.** *Chiefly U.S.* a method of escape from a difficult situation. **33.** *Baseball.* an instance of causing a batter or base runner to be out. [Old English *ūt*]

out- **1.** excelling or surpassing in a particular action: *outlast; outlive.* **2.** at or from a point away, outside: *outpost; outpatient.* **3.** going away, outward: *outcrop; outgrowth.*

outage ('autɪdʒ) *n.* a period of power failure.

out-and-out *adj.* absolute; thorough: *an out-and-out cheat.*

outback ('aut,bæk) *n.* the remote bush country of Australia.

outbid (,aut'bɪd) *vb.* **-bidding, -bidded** or **-bid.** to offer a higher price than (another person).

outboard motor ('aut,bɔːd) *n.* a portable petrol engine that can be attached externally to the stern of a boat to propel it.

outbreak ('aut,breɪk) *n.* a sudden occurrence of disease or war.

outbuilding ('aut,bɪldɪŋ) *n.* same as **outhouse.**

outburst ('aut,bɜːst) *n.* **1.** a sudden strong expression of emotion. **2.** a sudden period of violent activity: *an outburst of drunken violence.*

outcast ('aut,kɑːst) *n.* a person who is rejected or excluded from a particular group or from society.

outclass (,aut'klɑːs) *vb.* to surpass (someone) in performance or quality.

outcome ('aut,kʌm) *n.* the result or consequence of something.

outcrop ('aut,krɒp) *n.* part of a rock formation that sticks out of the earth.

outcry ('aut,kraɪ) *n., pl.* **-cries.** a widespread or vehement protest.

outdated (,aut'deɪtɪd) *adj.* old-fashioned or obsolete.

outdistance (,aut'dɪstəns) *vb.* **1.** to surpass (someone) in a particular activity. **2.** to leave (other competitors) behind in a race.

outdo (,aut'duː) *vb.* **-doing, -did, -done.** to surpass (someone) in performance.

outdoor ('aut,dɔː) *adj.* **1.** taking place, existing, or intended for use in the open air: *outdoor games; outdoor clothes.* **2.** fond of the outdoors: *he's the outdoor type.*

outdoors (,aut'dɔːz) *adv.* **1.** in the open air; outside. ~n. **2.** the world outside or far away from buildings; the open air.

outer ('autə) *adj.* **1.** exterior; external. **2.** further from the middle. ~n. **3.** *Archery.* **a.** the white outermost ring on a target. **b.** a shot that hits this ring.

outermost ('autə,məust) *adj.* furthest from the centre or middle.

outer space *n.* space beyond the atmosphere of the earth.

outface (aut'feɪs) *vb.* to subdue or disconcert (someone) by staring.

outfield ('aut,fiːld) *n.* **1.** *Cricket.* the area of the field far from the pitch. **2.** *Baseball.* the area of the playing field beyond the

lines connecting first, second, and third bases. —'**out,fielder** *n.*

outfit ('aut,fɪt) *n.* **1.** a set of clothes worn together. **2.** *Informal.* a group of people working together as a unit. **3.** a set of equipment for a particular task; kit.

outfitter ('aut,fɪtə) *n. Old-fashioned.* a supplier of men's clothes.

outflank (,aut'flæŋk) *vb.* **1.** to go around and beyond the flank of (an opposing army). **2.** to get the better of (someone).

outflow ('aut,fləu) *n.* **1.** anything that flows out, such as liquid or money. **2.** the amount that flows out.

outfox (,aut'fɒks) *vb.* to surpass (someone) in cunning.

outgoing ('aut,gəuɪŋ) *adj.* **1.** leaving: *outgoing mail; the outgoing president.* **2.** friendly and sociable.

outgoings ('aut,gəuɪŋz) *pl. n.* expenses.

outgrow (,aut'grəu) *vb.* **-growing, -grew, -grown.** **1.** to grow too large for (clothes or shoes). **2.** to lose (a way of behaving or thinking) in the course of becoming more mature. **3.** to grow larger or faster than (someone).

outgrowth ('aut,grəuθ) *n.* **1.** a thing growing out of a main body; offshoot. **2.** a natural development, result, or consequence.

outhouse ('aut,haus) *n.* a building near to, but separate from, a main building.

outing ('autɪŋ) *n.* a trip or excursion.

outlandish (aut'lændɪʃ) *adj.* grotesquely unconventional; bizarre.

outlast (,aut'lɑːst) *vb.* to last longer than.

outlaw ('aut,lɔː) *n.* **1.** a criminal who is a fugitive from the law. ~vb. **2.** to declare (a person) to be an outlaw. **3.** to ban.

outlay ('aut,leɪ) *n.* an expenditure of money, effort, or time.

outlet ('autlɪt) *n.* **1.** a means of expressing one's feelings: *an outlet for his anger.* **2. a.** a market for a product. **b.** a shop or organization selling the goods of a particular producer or wholesaler. **3.** an opening permitting escape or release.

outline ('aut,laɪn) *n.* **1.** a general explanation or description of something, which does not give all the details. **2.** (*usually pl.*) the important features of something. **3.** the line by which an object or figure is or appears to be bounded. **4.** a drawing showing only the external lines of an object. ~vb. **5.** to draw the outline of (something). **6.** to give the main features or general idea of (something).

outlive (,aut'lɪv) *vb.* **1.** to live longer than (someone). **2.** to live beyond (a date or period): *he outlived the century.*

outlook ('aut,luk) *n.* **1.** a mental attitude. **2.** the probable condition or outcome of something; prospect: *the weather outlook.* **3.** the view from a place.

outlying ('aut,laɪɪŋ) *adj.* far out from a central point.

outmanoeuvre or *U.S.* **outmaneuver** (,autmə'nuːvə) *vb.* to gain an advantage over (someone) by skilful manoeuvring.

outmatch (ˌaʊtˈmætʃ) vb. to surpass or outdo (someone).

outmoded (ˌaʊtˈməʊdɪd) adj. no longer fashionable or widely accepted.

outnumber (ˌaʊtˈnʌmbə) vb. to exceed in number: *we outnumbered them twelve to one.*

out of bounds adj., adv. 1. (foll. by to) not to be entered by; barred to: *out of bounds to civilians.* 2. outside specified or prescribed limits.

out-of-date adj., adv. outmoded; old-fashioned.

out of doors adv. in the open air; outside.

out of pocket adj. having lost money: *I was £10 out of pocket after paying for their drinks.*

out-of-the-way adj. 1. remote or secluded. 2. unusual.

outpace (ˌaʊtˈpeɪs) vb. 1. to go faster than (someone). 2. to surpass or outdo (someone).

outpatient (ˈaʊtˌpeɪʃənt) n. a patient who receives treatment at a hospital but who is not staying there.

outpost (ˈaʊtˌpəʊst) n. 1. Mil. a settlement stationed at a distance from the area occupied by a major formation. 2. an outlying settlement or position.

outpouring (ˈaʊtˌpɔːrɪŋ) n. 1. (pl.) a passionate outburst. 2. the amount of something that pours out.

output (ˈaʊtˌpʊt) n. 1. the amount produced: *a weekly output.* 2. Electronics. the power, voltage, or current delivered by a circuit or component. 3. Computers. the information produced by a computer. ~vb. **-putting, -putted** or **-put.** 4. Computers. to cause (data) to be emitted as output.

outrage (ˈaʊtˌreɪdʒ) n. 1. deep indignation, anger, or resentment. 2. an extremely vicious or cruel act; gross violation of decency, morality, or honour. ~vb. 3. to cause deep indignation, anger, or resentment in (someone). [French *outré* beyond]

outrageous (aʊtˈreɪdʒəs) adj. 1. immoderate in behaviour. 2. grossly offensive to decency, morality, or honour; shocking or unacceptable. —**outˈrageously** adv.

outrank (ˌaʊtˈræŋk) vb. to be of higher rank than (someone).

outré (ˈuːtreɪ) adj. eccentric or bizarre; outrageous. [French]

outrider (ˈaʊtˌraɪdə) n. a person who rides a motorcycle or horse in front of or beside a car or carriage as an attendant or guard.

outrigger (ˈaʊtˌrɪgə) n. 1. a framework projecting over the side of a boat or canoe to provide stability. 2. a boat or canoe equipped with such a framework.

outright adj. (ˈaʊtˌraɪt). 1. complete; total: *an outright villain.* 2. straightforward; direct: *outright hostility.* ~adv. (ˌaʊtˈraɪt). 3. completely: *the government has banned it outright.* 4. openly: *ask outright.* 5. instantly: *he was killed outright.*

outrun (ˌaʊtˈrʌn) vb. **-running, -ran, -run.** 1. to run faster or further than (someone). 2. to exceed (something).

outsell (ˌaʊtˈsɛl) vb. **-selling, -sold.** to be sold in greater quantities than (another product).

outset (ˈaʊtˌsɛt) n. a start; beginning: *this plan was a failure from the outset.*

outshine (ˌaʊtˈʃaɪn) vb. **-shining, -shone.** to surpass (someone) in excellence.

outside prep. (ˌaʊtˈsaɪd). 1. on or to the exterior of: *outside the house.* 2. beyond the limits of: *outside his capabilities.* 3. apart from; other than: *no-one knows outside us.* ~adj. (ˈaʊtˌsaɪd). 4. situated on the exterior: *an outside lavatory.* 5. remote; unlikely: *an outside chance.* 6. coming from outside a particular group or organization: *outside influences.* ~adv. (ˌaʊtˈsaɪd). 7. outside a specified thing or place; out of doors. 8. Slang. not in prison. ~n. (ˈaʊtˌsaɪd). 9. the external side or surface of something. 10. **at the outside.** Informal. at the very most: *two days at the outside.*

outside broadcast n. Radio, television. a broadcast not made from a studio.

outsider (ˌaʊtˈsaɪdə) n. 1. a person excluded from a group. 2. a contestant thought unlikely to win a race.

outsize (ˈaʊtˌsaɪz) adj. also **outsized.** 1. very large or larger than normal. ~n. 2. an outsize garment or person.

outskirts (ˈaʊtˌskɜːts) pl. n. outlying areas.

outsmart (ˌaʊtˈsmɑːt) vb. Informal. same as **outwit.**

outspan (ˈaʊtˌspæn) S. African. ~n. 1. an area on a farm kept available for travellers to rest and refresh their animals. ~vb. **-spanning, -spanned.** 2. to unharness or unyoke (animals). [Afrikaans *uit* out + *spannen* to stretch]

outspoken (ˌaʊtˈspəʊkən) adj. 1. candid or bold in speech. 2. spoken candidly: *her outspoken comments.*

outspread (ˈaʊtˌsprɛd) adj. spread or stretched out; extended or expanded.

outstanding (ˌaʊtˈstændɪŋ) adj. 1. superior; excellent. 2. prominent, remarkable, or striking. 3. unsettled, unpaid, or unresolved. —**outˈstandingly** adv.

outstation (ˈaʊtˌsteɪʃən) n. a station or post in a remote region.

outstay (ˌaʊtˈsteɪ) vb. same as **overstay.**

outstretch (ˌaʊtˈstrɛtʃ) vb. to extend or expand; stretch out.

outstrip (ˌaʊtˈstrɪp) vb. **-stripping, -stripped.** 1. to surpass (someone) in a particular activity. 2. to go faster than (someone).

outtake (ˈaʊtˌteɪk) n. an unreleased take from a recording session, film, or television programme.

outvote (ˌaʊtˈvəʊt) vb. to defeat (someone) by a majority of votes.

outward (ˈaʊtwəd) adj. 1. apparent or superficial: *outward appearances.* 2. of or relating to the outside: *outward shape.* 3. (of a journey) away from a place to which one intends to return. ~adv. also **out-**

wards. 4. in an outward direction; towards the outside. —**'outwardly** adv.

outweigh (ˌaʊt'weɪ) vb. **1.** to be more important, significant, or influential than. **2.** to be heavier than.

outwit (ˌaʊt'wɪt) vb. **-witting, -witted.** to gain an advantage over (someone) by cunning or ingenuity.

outworks ('aʊt,wɜːks) pl. n. defences which lie outside main defensive works.

ouzel or **ousel** ('uːz'l) n. same as **dipper** (the bird). [Old English ōsle]

ouzo ('uːzəʊ) n., pl. **ouzos.** a strong aniseed-flavoured alcoholic drink from Greece. [Modern Greek ouzon]

ova ('əʊvə) n. the plural of **ovum.**

oval ('əʊv'l) adj. **1.** egg-shaped. ~n. **2.** anything that is oval in shape, such as a sports ground. [Latin ōvum egg]

ovary ('əʊvərɪ) n., pl. **-ries. 1.** a reproductive organ in women and female animals in which eggs are produced. **2.** Bot. the lower part of a pistil, containing the ovules. [Latin ōvum egg] —**ovarian** (əʊ-'veərɪən) adj.

ovate ('əʊveɪt) adj. shaped like an egg. [Latin ōvātus egg-shaped]

ovation (əʊ'veɪʃən) n. an enthusiastic reception with prolonged applause. [Latin ovātiō rejoicing]

oven ('ʌv'n) n. an enclosed heated compartment or receptacle for baking or roasting food, drying substances, or firing ceramics. [Old English ofen]

over ('əʊvə) prep. **1.** directly above; on the top of; across the top or upper surface of: over one's head. **2.** on or to the other side of: over the river. **3.** during or throughout (a period of time). **4.** throughout the whole extent of: to travel over England. **5.** by means of (an instrument of telecommunication): over the radio. **6.** more than: over a century ago. **7.** concerning; about: an argument over nothing. **8.** while occupied in: discussing business over dinner. **9.** having recovered from the effects of: she is not over her husband's death yet. **10. all over someone.** Informal. extremely affectionate or attentive towards someone. **11. over and above.** added to; in addition to. ~adv. **12.** in a state, condition, or position over something: to climb over. **13.** so as to cause (someone) to fall: knocking over a policeman. **14.** at or to a point across an intervening space. **15.** covering the whole area: the world over. **16.** from beginning to end: to read a document over. **17. all over. a.** finished. **b.** over one's entire body. **c.** typically: that's you all over. **18. over again.** once more. **19. over and over (again).** repeatedly. ~interj. **20.** (in signalling and radio) it is now your turn to speak. ~adj. **21.** finished; no longer in progress: the fight is over. ~adv., adj. **22.** remaining; surplus: with

six left over. ~n. **23.** Cricket. **a.** a series of six or eight balls bowled by a bowler from the same end of the pitch. **b.** the play during this. [Old English ofer]

over- prefix. **1.** excessive or excessively: overcharge; overdue. **2.** superior in rank: overlord. **3.** indicating location or movement above: overhang. **4.** downwards from above: overthrow.

overact (ˌəʊvər'ækt) vb. to act in an exaggerated manner.

overall adj. ('əʊvər,ɔːl). **1.** from one end to the other: the overall length. **2.** including everything; total: the overall cost. ~adv. (ˌəʊvər'ɔːl). **3.** in general; on the whole. ~n. ('əʊvər,ɔːl). **4.** Brit. a coat-shaped work garment worn over ordinary clothes as a protection against dirt. **5.** (pl.) work trousers with a front flap or jacket attached, worn over ordinary clothes as a protection against dirt and wear.

overarm ('əʊvər,ɑːm) Sport, esp. cricket. ~adj. **1.** bowled, thrown, or performed with the arm raised above the shoulder. ~adv. **2.** with the arm raised above the shoulder.

overawe (ˌəʊvər'ɔː) vb. to subdue (someone) by affecting him with a feeling of awe.

overbalance (ˌəʊvə'bæləns) vb. to lose one's balance.

overbearing (ˌəʊvə'beərɪŋ) adj. **1.** domineering or dictatorial. **2.** of particular or overriding importance: an overbearing need.

overblown (ˌəʊvə'bləʊn) adj. inflated or excessive: overblown pride.

overboard ('əʊvə,bɔːd) adv. **1.** from on board a vessel into the water. **2. go overboard.** Informal. **a.** to be extremely enthusiastic. **b.** to go to extremes. **3. throw overboard.** to reject or abandon (an idea or a plan).

overcast ('əʊvə,kɑːst) adj. (of the sky or weather) cloudy.

overcharge (ˌəʊvə'tʃɑːdʒ) vb. to charge too high a price.

overcoat ('əʊvə,kəʊt) n. a warm heavy coat worn in cold weather.

overcome (ˌəʊvə'kʌm) vb. **-coming, -came, -come. 1.** (of an emotion or a feeling) to affect (someone) strongly or make (someone) powerless: overcome by exhaustion. **2.** to deal successfully with or control (a problem or feeling). **3.** to defeat (someone) in a conflict.

overdo (ˌəʊvə'duː) vb. **-doing, -did, -done. 1.** to do (something) to excess. **2.** to exaggerate or overplay (something). **3.** to cook (something) too long. **4. overdo it** or **things.** to overtax one's strength.

overdose n. ('əʊvə,dəʊs). **1.** an excessive dose of a drug. ~vb. (ˌəʊvə'dəʊs). **2.** to take an excessive dose of a drug.

overdraft ('əʊvə,drɑːft) n. **1.** a withdraw-

---

overabundance	overburden	overcook
overactive	overcautious	overcrowded
overambitious	overcompensate	overdeveloped
overanxious	overconfident	

al of money in excess of the credit balance in one's bank account. **2.** the amount of money withdrawn thus.

overdraw (ˌəʊvəˈdrɔː) *vb.* **-drawing, -drew, -drawn. a. be overdrawn.** to have drawn money from one's bank account in excess of the credit balance. **b.** to draw money from (one's bank account) in excess of the credit balance.

overdress *vb.* (ˌəʊvəˈdrɛs). **1.** to dress too elaborately or formally. ~*n.* (ˈəʊvəˌdrɛs). **2.** a dress that may be worn over a jumper or blouse.

overdrive (ˈəʊvəˌdraɪv) *n.* a very high gear in a motor vehicle, used at high speeds to reduce wear.

overdue (ˌəʊvəˈdjuː) *adj.* past the due time for arrival, occurrence, or payment.

overestimate *vb.* (ˌəʊvərˈɛstɪˌmeɪt). **1.** to estimate too highly. ~*n.* (ˌəʊvərˈɛstɪmɪt). **2.** an estimate that is too high. —**overestimation** (ˌəʊvərˌɛstɪˈmeɪʃən) *n.*

overflow *vb.* (ˌəʊvəˈfləʊ), **-flowing, -flowed, -flown. 1.** to flow over (a brim). **2.** to be filled beyond capacity so as to spill over. **3.** (foll. by *with*) to be filled with an emotion: *overflowing with love.* **4.** to spread over; flood. ~*n.* (ˈəʊvəˌfləʊ). **5.** something that overflows, usually a liquid. **6.** an outlet that enables surplus liquid to be drained off. **7.** the amount by which a limit or capacity is exceeded.

overgraze (ˌəʊvəˈɡreɪz) *vb.* to graze (land) too intensively so that it is damaged and no longer provides nourishment.

overgrown (ˌəʊvəˈɡrəʊn) *adj.* covered over with plants or weeds: *an overgrown path.*

overhang *vb.* (ˌəʊvəˈhæŋ), **-hanging, -hung. 1.** to project or hang over beyond (something). ~*n.* (ˈəʊvəˌhæŋ). **2.** an overhanging part or object.

overhaul *vb.* (ˌəʊvəˈhɔːl). **1.** to examine (a system or an idea) carefully for faults. **2.** to make repairs or adjustments to (a vehicle or machine). **3.** to overtake (a vehicle or person). ~*n.* (ˈəʊvəˌhɔːl). **4.** a thorough examination and repair.

overhead (ˈəʊvəˌhɛd, ˌəʊvəˈhɛd) *adj., adv.* above head height.

overhead projector *n.* a projector that throws an enlarged image of a transparency onto a surface above and behind the person using it.

overheads (ˈəʊvəˌhɛdz) *pl. n.* the general costs of running a business, such as rent, electricity, and stationery.

overhear (ˌəʊvəˈhɪə) *vb.* **-hearing, -heard** (-ˈhɜːd). to hear (a speaker or remark) unintentionally or without the knowledge of the speaker.

overheat (ˌəʊvəˈhiːt) *vb.* **1.** to make or

become too hot. **2.** to make (someone) very agitated or irritated. **3.** to stimulate (the economy) excessively.

overjoyed (ˌəʊvəˈdʒɔɪd) *adj.* extremely pleased.

overkill (ˈəʊvəˌkɪl) *n.* **1.** a capability to kill or destroy which far exceeds that necessary to achieve victory. **2.** any treatment that is greater than that required: *the media coverage of this event amounts to overkill.*

overlap *vb.* (ˌəʊvəˈlæp), **-lapping, -lapped. 1.** (of two things) to extend or lie partly over (each other). **2.** to coincide partly in time or subject: *our holidays overlap by two days.* ~*n.* (ˈəʊvəˌlæp). **3.** a part that overlaps. **4.** the amount or length of something overlapping.

overlay *vb.* (ˌəʊvəˈleɪ), **-laying, -laid. 1.** to cover (a surface) with an applied decoration: *ebony overlaid with silver.* ~*n.* (ˈəʊvəˌleɪ). **2.** something that is laid over something else; a covering. **3.** an applied decoration or layer, for example of gold leaf.

overleaf (ˌəʊvəˈliːf) *adv.* on the other side of the page.

overlie (ˌəʊvəˈlaɪ) *vb.* **-lying, -lay, -lain. 1.** to lie on (something or someone). **2.** to smother (a baby or newborn animal) by lying on it.

overload *vb.* (ˌəʊvəˈləʊd). **1.** to put too large a load on or in (something). ~*n.* (ˈəʊvəˌləʊd). **2.** an excessive load.

overlook (ˌəʊvəˈlʊk) *vb.* **1.** to fail to notice (something). **2.** to disregard (misbehaviour or a fault) deliberately or indulgently. **3.** to give a view of (something) from above: *the house overlooks the bay.*

overlord (ˈəʊvəˌlɔːd) *n.* a supreme lord or master.

overly (ˈəʊvəlɪ) *adv.* too; excessively.

overmuch (ˌəʊvəˈmʌtʃ) *adv., adj.* too much; very much.

overnight *adv.* (ˌəʊvəˈnaɪt). **1.** during the night. **2.** in or as if in the course of one night; suddenly: *the situation changed overnight.* ~*adj.* (ˈəʊvəˌnaɪt). **3.** done in, occurring in, or lasting the night: *an overnight stop.* **4.** staying for one night: *an overnight guest.* **5.** for use during a single night: *an overnight bag.* **6.** occurring in or as if in the course of one night; sudden: *an overnight success.*

overpass (ˈəʊvəˌpɑːs) *n.* same as **flyover** (the road).

overplay (ˌəʊvəˈpleɪ) *vb.* **1.** to overemphasize (something). **2. overplay one's hand.** to overestimate the worth or strength of one's position.

overpower (ˌəʊvəˈpaʊə) *vb.* **1.** to conquer or subdue (someone) by superior force. **2.**

overeager	overexert	overindulge
overeat	overexpose	overpaid
overemotional	overfeed	overpopulated
overemphasize	overfill	overpopulation
overenthusiastic	overfond	
overexcited	overfull	

to have such a strong effect on (someone) as to make him helpless or ineffective: *the smell overpowered me.* —**‚over'powering** *adj.*

overprint *vb.* (‚əʊvə'prɪnt). **1.** to print (additional matter or another colour) onto (something already printed). ~*n.* ('əʊvə‚prɪnt). **2.** additional matter or another colour printed onto something already printed.

overrate (‚əʊvə'reɪt) *vb.* to have too high an opinion of.

overreach (‚əʊvə'riːtʃ) *vb.* **1.** to defeat or thwart (oneself) by attempting to do or gain too much. **2.** to gain an advantage over (someone) by trickery.

overreact (‚əʊvərɪ'ækt) *vb.* to react excessively. —**overreaction** (‚əʊvərɪ'ækʃən) *n.*

override (‚əʊvə'raɪd) *vb.* **-riding, -rode, -ridden. 1.** to set aside or disregard (a person or a person's decisions) with superior authority or power. **2.** to supersede or replace (something). —**‚over'riding** *adj.*

overrule (‚əʊvə'ruːl) *vb.* **1.** to disallow the arguments of (a person) by the use of authority. **2.** to rule or decide against (an argument or decision).

overrun (‚əʊvə'rʌn) *vb.* **-running, -ran, -run. 1.** to spread over (a place) rapidly: *the city is overrun by rats.* **2.** to conquer (territory) rapidly by force of number. **3.** to extend or run beyond a limit: *the meeting overran by an hour.*

overseas *adv.* (‚əʊvə'siːz). **1.** across the sea; abroad. ~*adj.* ('əʊvə'siːz). **2.** of, to, from, or situated in countries across the sea. ~*n.* (‚əʊvə'siːz). **3.** (*functioning as sing.*) *Informal.* a foreign country or foreign countries collectively.

oversee (‚əʊvə'siː) *vb.* **-seeing, -saw, -seen.** to watch over and direct (someone or something); supervise. —**'over‚seer** *n.*

oversew (‚əʊvə'səʊ) *vb.* **-sewing, -sewed; -sewn** *or* **-sewed.** to sew (two edges) with stitches that pass over them both.

oversexed (‚əʊvə'sɛkst) *adj.* having an excessive preoccupation with sexual activity.

overshadow (‚əʊvə'ʃædəʊ) *vb.* **1.** to make (someone or something) seem insignificant or less important by comparison. **2.** to cast a gloom over (an occasion).

overshoe ('əʊvə‚ʃuː) *n.* a protective shoe worn over an ordinary shoe.

overshoot (‚əʊvə'ʃuːt) *vb.* **-shooting, -shot.** to go beyond (a mark or target): *the plane overshot the runway.*

overshot ('əʊvə‚ʃɒt) *adj.* (of a water wheel) driven by a flow of water that passes over the wheel.

oversight ('əʊvə‚saɪt) *n.* a mistake made through failure to notice something.

oversleep (‚əʊvə'sliːp) *vb.* **-sleeping, -slept.** to sleep beyond the intended time for getting up.

overspend (‚əʊvə'spɛnd) *vb.* **-spending, -spent.** to spend more than one can afford.

overspill ('əʊvə‚spɪl) *n.* an arrangement by which people from overcrowded cities are rehoused in smaller towns.

overstate (‚əʊvə'steɪt) *vb.* to state (something) too strongly; overemphasize. —**'over‚statement** *n.*

overstay (‚əʊvə'steɪ) *vb.* **overstay one's welcome.** to stay as a guest longer than pleases the host or hostess.

overstep (‚əʊvə'stɛp) *vb.* **-stepping, -stepped.** to go beyond (a certain limit).

overstrung (‚əʊvə'strʌŋ) *adj.* too highly strung; tense.

oversubscribe (‚əʊvəsəb'skraɪb) *vb.* to subscribe or apply for (something) in excess of the available supply.

overt (əʊ'vɜːt) *adj.* done or shown in an open and obvious way: *overt hostility.* [Old French] —**o'vertly** *adv.*

overtake (‚əʊvə'teɪk) *vb.* **-taking, -took, -taken. 1.** *Chiefly Brit.* to move past (another vehicle or person) travelling in the same direction. **2.** to do better than (someone) after catching up with him. **3.** to come upon (someone) suddenly or unexpectedly: *night overtook him.*

overtax (‚əʊvə'tæks) *vb.* **1.** to impose too great a strain on (oneself). **2.** to tax (people) too heavily.

over the top *adj. Brit. slang.* excessive; beyond the usual or acceptable bounds of behaviour.

overthrow *vb.* (‚əʊvə'θrəʊ), **-throwing, -threw, -thrown. 1.** to bring about the downfall of (a ruler or government) by force. **2.** to replace (standards or values). ~*n.* ('əʊvə‚θrəʊ). **3.** downfall; destruction.

overtime ('əʊvə‚taɪm) *n.* **1.** work at a regular job done in addition to regular working hours. **2.** pay for such work. ~*adv.* **3.** in addition to one's regular working hours: *to work overtime.*

overtone ('əʊvə‚təʊn) *n.* **1.** an additional meaning or hint: *overtones of despair.* **2.** *Music, acoustics.* any of the tones, with the exception of the principal or lowest one, that make up a musical sound.

overture ('əʊvə‚tjʊə) *n.* **1.** *Music.* a piece of orchestral music played at the beginning of an opera, oratorio, or ballet, musical comedy, or film, often containing the main musical themes of the work. **2.** (*pl.*) opening moves towards a new relationship or agreement: *friendly overtures.* [Late Latin *apertūra* opening]

overturn (‚əʊvə'tɜːn) *vb.* **1.** to turn over or upside down. **2.** to overrule or reverse (a legal decision). **3.** to overthrow or destroy (a government).

overview ('əʊvə‚vjuː) *n.* a general survey.

overweening (‚əʊvə'wiːnɪŋ) *adj.* (of opinions or qualities) excessive; immoderate: *overweening pride.* [obs. *ween* to think]

---

overpriced   overripe   oversimplify
overprotective   oversensitive   overuse

overweight (ˌəʊvəˈweɪt) *adj.* weighing more than is usual, allowed, or healthy.

overwhelm (ˌəʊvəˈwɛlm) *vb.* 1. to overpower the thoughts, emotions, or senses of (someone): *overwhelmed by horror.* 2. to overcome (people) with irresistible force: *the army overwhelmed the city.* —ˌover-ˈwhelming *adj.* —ˌoverˈwhelmingly *adv.*

overwork *vb.* (ˌəʊvəˈwɜːk). 1. to work too hard or too long. 2. to use (something) too much: *to overwork an excuse.* ~*n.* (ˈəʊvəˌwɜːk). 3. excessive work.

overwrought (ˌəʊvəˈrɔːt) *adj.* full of nervous tension; agitated.

oviduct (ˈəʊvɪˌdʌkt) *n.* *Anat.* the tube through which eggs are conveyed from an ovary. [Latin *ōvum* egg]

oviform (ˈəʊvɪˌfɔːm) *adj.* *Biol.* shaped like an egg. [Latin *ōvum* egg]

ovine (ˈəʊvaɪn) *adj.* of or resembling a sheep. [Latin *ovis* sheep]

oviparous (əʊˈvɪpərəs) *adj.* *Zool.* producing eggs that hatch outside the body of the mother. [Latin *ōvum* egg + *-parus* bearing]

ovoid (ˈəʊvɔɪd) *adj.* egg-shaped.

ovulate (ˈɒvjʊˌleɪt) *vb.* *Biol.* to produce or discharge eggs from an ovary. —ovulation (ˌɒvjʊˈleɪʃən) *n.*

ovule (ˈɒvjuːl) *n.* 1. *Bot.* the part of a plant that contains the egg cell and develops into the seed after fertilization. 2. *Zool.* an immature ovum. [Latin *ōvum* egg]

ovum (ˈəʊvəm) *n., pl.* **ova.** an unfertilized female egg cell. [Latin: egg]

owe (əʊ) *vb.* 1. to be under an obligation to pay (someone) to the amount of: *you owe me a pound.* 2. to be in debt: *he still owes for his house.* 3. (foll. by *to*) to have as a result of: *I owe my success to my teacher.* 4. to feel an obligation to do or give: *I owe you an apology.* [Old English *āgan* to have]

owing (ˈəʊɪŋ) *adj.* 1. owed; due. 2. **owing to.** because of; on account of.

owl (aʊl) *n.* a bird of prey which has a flat face, large eyes, and a small hooked beak, and which is active at night. [Old English *ūle*] —ˈowlish *adj.*

own (əʊn) *det.* (*preceded by a possessive*) 1. used to emphasize that something belongs to a particular person: *John's own idea; I'll use my own.* 2. **come into one's own.** to fulfil one's potential. 3. **hold one's own.** to have the necessary ability to deal successfully with a situation: *she can hold her own in an argument.* 4. **on one's own.** **a.** without help. **b.** by oneself; alone. ~*vb.* 5. to have (something) as one's possession. 6. (often foll. by *up, to,* or *up to*) to confess or admit; acknowledge. [Old English *āgen*] —ˈowner *n.* —ˈownership *n.*

owner-occupier *n.* someone who owns the house in which he lives.

own goal *n.* 1. *Soccer.* a goal scored by a player accidentally playing the ball into his own team's net. 2. *Informal.* any action that results in disadvantage to the person who took it or to his associates.

ox (ɒks) *n., pl.* **oxen.** a castrated bull used

for pulling heavy loads and for meat. [Old English *oxa*]

oxalic acid (ɒkˈsælɪk) *n.* a colourless poisonous acid found in many plants. [Latin *oxalis* garden sorrel]

Oxbridge (ˈɒksˌbrɪdʒ) *n.* the British universities of Oxford and Cambridge considered together.

oxen (ˈɒksən) *n.* the plural of **ox.**

oxeye (ˈɒksˌaɪ) *n.* a daisy-like flower with yellow rays and a dark centre.

Oxfam (ˈɒksˌfæm) Oxford Committee for Famine Relief.

oxidation (ˌɒksɪˈdeɪʃən) *n.* the act or process of oxidizing.

oxide (ˈɒksaɪd) *n.* a compound of oxygen with another element. [French *ox(ygène)* + *(ac)ide*]

oxidize *or* **-ise** (ˈɒksɪˌdaɪz) *vb.* to undergo or cause (a substance) to undergo a chemical reaction with oxygen, as in burning or rusting. —ˌoxidiˈzation *or* -iˈsation *n.*

Oxon (ˈɒksən) Oxfordshire.

Oxon. (in degree titles) of Oxford University. [Latin *Oxoniensis*]

Oxonian (ɒkˈsəʊnɪən) *adj.* 1. of Oxford or Oxford University. ~*n.* 2. a member of Oxford University. 3. a person from Oxford, a city in England.

oxtail (ˈɒksˌteɪl) *n.* the tail of an ox, used in soups and stews.

oxyacetylene (ˌɒksɪəˈsɛtɪˌliːn) *n.* a mixture of oxygen and acetylene, used in blowlamps for cutting or welding metals at high temperatures.

oxygen (ˈɒksɪdʒən) *n.* a colourless odourless gaseous element essential to life processes and to combustion. Symbol: O [Greek *oxus* sharp + *-genēs* producing: from former belief that all acids contained oxygen]

oxygenate (ˈɒksɪdʒɪˌneɪt) *vb.* to treat or combine with oxygen: *to oxygenate blood.*

oxygen tent *n.* *Med.* a transparent enclosure covering a bedridden patient, into which oxygen is released to aid breathing.

oxymoron (ˌɒksɪˈmɔːrɒn) *n.* a figure of speech in which contradictory terms are used together, for example *cruel kindness.* [Greek *oxus* sharp + *mōros* stupid]

oyez *or* **oyes** (ˈəʊˈjɛs) *interj.* a cry usually uttered three times by a public crier or court official, for silence and attention. [Old French *oyez* hear!]

oyster (ˈɔɪstə) *n.* 1. an edible shellfish of which some types produce pearls. 2. **the world is your oyster.** you are in a position where there is every possible chance of personal advancement and satisfaction. ~*adj.* 3. greyish-white. [Greek *ostreon*]

oystercatcher (ˈɔɪstəˌkætʃə) *n.* a wading bird with black-and-white plumage and a long stout red bill.

oz *or* **oz.** ounce. [Italian *onza*]

ozone (ˈəʊzəʊn) *n.* 1. a form of oxygen with a strong odour, formed by an electric discharge in the atmosphere. 2. *Informal.* clean bracing air, as found at the seaside. [Greek *ozein* to smell]

P

p or **P** (piː) *n.*, *pl.* **p's**, **P's**, or **Ps.** 1. the 16th letter of the English alphabet. 2. **mind one's p's and q's.** to be careful to behave correctly and use polite language.

p 1. (in Britain) penny *or* pence. 2. *Music.* quietly. [Latin *piano*]

P 1. *Chem.* phosphorus. 2. (on road signs) parking. 3. *Chess.* pawn.

p. 1. (*pl.* **pp.**) page. 2. per.

pa (pɑː) *n. Informal.* father.

Pa *Chem.* protactinium.

PA 1. Also: **Pa.** Pennsylvania. 2. personal assistant. 3. public-address system.

p.a. yearly. [Latin *per annum*]

pace[1] (peɪs) *n.* 1. **a.** a single step in walking. **b.** the distance covered by a step. 2. speed of walking or running. 3. rate of proceeding at some other activity: *to live at a fast pace.* 4. manner of walking; gait. 5. **keep pace with.** to proceed at the same speed as. 6. **put someone through his paces.** to test someone's ability. 7. **set the pace.** to determine the speed at which a group proceeds. ~*vb.* 8. to set the pace for (the competitors) in a race. 9. to walk with regular slow or fast paces, often in anxiety or impatience: *to pace up and down.* 10. (foll. by *out*) to measure by paces. [Latin *passūs* step]

pace[2] (ˈpeɪsɪ) *prep.* with due respect to: used to express polite disagreement. [Latin, from *pāx* peace]

pacemaker (ˈpeɪsˌmeɪkə) *n.* 1. an electronic device implanted in the body, next to the heart, in order to regulate the heartbeat. 2. a competitor who leads the other competitors during part of a race, causing that part of the race to be run at a particular speed.

pachyderm (ˈpækɪˌdɜːm) *n.* a large thick-skinned mammal, such as an elephant or rhinoceros. [Greek *pakhus* thick + *derma* skin]

pacific (pəˈsɪfɪk) *adj.* tending to bring peace; peaceful. [Latin *pāx* peace + *facere* to make]

Pacific (pəˈsɪfɪk) *n.* 1. Also called: **Pacific Ocean.** the world's largest and deepest ocean, lying between Asia and Australia and North and South America. ~*adj.* 2. of the Pacific Ocean or its islands.

pacifier (ˈpæsɪˌfaɪə) *n. U.S. & Canad.* a baby's dummy.

pacifism (ˈpæsɪˌfɪzəm) *n.* the belief that violence of any kind is unjustifiable and that one should not participate in war. —**pacifist** *n., adj.*

pacify (ˈpæsɪˌfaɪ) *vb.* **-fying, -fied.** to bring or restore (a person or country) to a state of peace or calm. [Old French *pacifier*; see PACIFIC] —**pacification** (ˌpæsɪfɪˈkeɪʃən) *n.*

pack[1] (pæk) *n.* 1. a bundle or load carried on the back of a person or an animal. 2. *Chiefly Brit.* a complete set of playing cards. 3. a group of animals that hunt together: *a pack of hounds.* 4. *Rugby.* the forwards of a team. 5. an organized group of Cub Scouts or Brownie Guides. 6. *Chiefly U.S. & Canad.* same as **packet** (sense 1). 7. any collection of people or things: *a pack of lies.* 8. same as **rucksack** or **backpack.** 9. Also called: **face pack.** a cream treatment that cleanses and tones the skin. ~*vb.* 10. to put (articles) in (a container), such as clothes in a suitcase. 11. to roll (articles) up into a bundle. 12. to press tightly together; cram: *the hall was packed out.* 13. (foll. by *off*) to send away hastily: *the children were packed off to bed.* 14. *Slang.* to be capable of inflicting (a blow): *he packs a mean punch.* 15. *U.S. informal.* to carry (a gun) habitually. 16. **send someone packing.** *Informal.* to dismiss someone abruptly. ~See also **pack in, pack up.** [origin unknown]

pack[2] (pæk) *vb.* to fill (a committee, jury, or audience) with one's own supporters. [perhaps from *pact*]

package (ˈpækɪdʒ) *n.* 1. a wrapped or boxed object or group of objects. 2. **a.** a proposition, offer, or thing for sale in which separate items are presented together as a unit. **b.** (*as modifier*): *a package holiday.* 3. *U.S. & Canad.* same as **packet** (sense 1). ~*vb.* 4. to put (something) into a package. —**packaging** *n.*

packet (ˈpækɪt) *n.* 1. a container made of cardboard, paper, or plastic, often together with its contents: *a packet of biscuits.* 2. a small parcel. 3. Also: **packet boat.** a boat that transports mail, passengers, or goods on a fixed short route. 4. *Slang.* a large sum of money: *to cost a packet.* [Old French *pacquet*]

packhorse (ˈpækˌhɔːs) *n.* a horse used to transport goods.

pack ice *n.* a large area of floating ice, consisting of pieces that have become massed together.

pack in *vb. Informal.* to stop doing (something): *that's enough noise, pack it in.*

packing (ˈpækɪŋ) *n.* material, such as paper or plastic, used to cushion packed goods.

packthread (ˈpækˌθrɛd) *n.* a strong thread for sewing or tying up packages.

pack up *vb.* 1. to put (articles) away in a proper or suitable place. 2. *Informal.* to stop doing (something). 3. (of a machine) to fail to operate; break down.

pact (pækt) *n.* a formal agreement between two or more parties. [Latin *pactum*]

pad[1] (pæd) *n.* 1. a thick piece of soft material used to make something comfortable, give it shape, or protect it. 2. a number of sheets of paper fastened together along one edge. 3. the fleshy cushion-like underpart of an animal's paw. 4. a level surface or flat-topped structure, such as a launching pad. 5. the floating leaf of the water lily. 6. *Slang.* a person's residence. ~vb. **padding, padded. 7.** to line, stuff, or fill (something) out with soft material, in order to make it comfortable, give it shape, or protect it. **8. pad out.** to lengthen (a speech or piece of writing) with unnecessary words or pieces of information. [origin unknown]

pad² (pæd) vb. **padding, padded. 1.** to walk with a soft or muffled step. **2.** to travel (a route) on foot; tramp: *to pad around the country.* [Middle Dutch *pad* path]

padded cell n. a room with padded walls in a psychiatric hospital, in which violent patients are placed.

padding ('pædɪŋ) n. **1.** any soft material used to pad something. **2.** unnecessary words or information put into a speech or written work to make it longer.

paddle¹ ('pæd²l) n. **1.** a short light oar with a flat blade at one or both ends, used without a rowlock. **2.** a blade of a water wheel or paddle wheel. **3.** a paddle wheel used to propel a boat. ~vb. **4.** to propel (a boat) with a paddle. **5.** to swim with short rapid strokes, like a dog. **6.** U.S. & Canad. *informal.* to spank. [origin unknown]

paddle² ('pæd²l) vb. **1.** to walk barefoot in shallow water. **2.** to dabble (one's fingers, hands, or feet) in water. ~n. **3.** the act of paddling in water. [origin unknown]

paddle steamer n. a ship propelled by paddle wheels turned by a steam engine.

paddle wheel n. a large wheel fitted with paddles, turned by an engine to propel a ship.

paddock ('pædək) n. **1.** a small enclosed field, usually near a house or stable. **2.** (in horse racing) the enclosure in which horses are paraded and mounted before a race. [Old English *pearruc* enclosure]

paddy¹ ('pædɪ) n., pl. **-dies. 1.** Also: **paddy field.** a field planted with rice. **2.** rice as a growing crop or when harvested but not yet milled. [Malay *pādī*]

paddy² ('pædɪ) n., pl. **-dies.** Brit. informal. a fit of temper. [from *Paddy,* informal name for an Irishman]

padlock ('pæd,lɒk) n. **1.** a detachable lock with a pivoted U-shaped bar, which can be used to secure a door or lid by passing this bar through a ring or hoop. ~vb. **2.** to fasten (something) with a padlock. [origin unknown]

padre ('pɑːdrɪ) n. *Informal.* a chaplain to the armed forces. [via Spanish or Italian from Latin *pater* father]

paean ('piːən) n. a song of praise, triumph, or joy. [Greek *paiān*]

paediatrician or U.S. **pediatrician** (,piːdɪə'trɪʃən) n. a doctor who specializes in children's diseases.

paediatrics or U.S. **pediatrics** (,piːdɪ-'ætrɪks) n. (functioning as sing.) the branch of medicine concerned with children and their diseases. [Greek *pais, paid-* child + *iatros* physician] —,paedi'atric or U.S. ,pedi'atric adj.

paedophile or U.S. **pedophile** ('piːdəʊ-

,faɪl) n. a person who is sexually attracted to children.

paedophilia or U.S. **pedophilia** (,piːdəʊ-'fɪlɪə) n. the condition of being sexually attracted to children. [Greek *pais, paid-* child + *philos* loving]

paella (paɪ'ɛlə) n. a Spanish dish made from rice, shellfish, chicken, and vegetables. [Catalan]

pagan ('peɪgən) n. **1.** a person who is not a Christian, Jew, or Muslim. **2.** a person without any religion; heathen. ~adj. **3.** of pagans. **4.** irreligious. [Church Latin *pāgānus* civilian (hence, not a soldier of Christ)] —'**paganism** n.

page¹ (peɪdʒ) n. **1.** one side of one of the leaves of a book, newspaper, or magazine. **2.** one of the leaves of a book, newspaper, or magazine. **3.** an episode, phase, or period: *a glorious page in our history.* [Latin *pāgina*]

page² (peɪdʒ) n. **1.** a boy employed to run errands for the guests in a hotel or club. **2.** a youth in attendance at official functions or ceremonies, such as weddings. **3.** Medieval history. a boy in training for knighthood. ~vb. **4.** to call out the name of (a person), often using a loudspeaker system, so as to give him a message. [Greek *pais* child]

pageant ('pædʒənt) n. **1.** an outdoor show portraying scenes from history. **2.** any magnificent display or procession. [perhaps from *pāgina* scene of a play]

pageantry ('pædʒəntrɪ) n. spectacular display or ceremony.

pageboy ('peɪdʒ,bɔɪ) n. **1.** a smooth medium-length hairstyle with the ends of the hair curled under. **2.** same as **page².**

pagination (,pædʒɪ'neɪʃən) n. the numbering of the pages of a book, manuscript, etc. in sequence.

pagoda (pə'gəʊdə) n. a Far Eastern temple, usually an ornate pyramid-shaped tower with many storeys. [Portuguese *pagode*]

paid (peɪd) vb. **1.** past of **pay. 2. put paid to.** Chiefly Brit. & N.Z. to end or destroy: *breaking his leg put paid to his hopes of running in the Olympics.*

pail (peɪl) n. **1.** a bucket. **2.** Also called: **pailful.** the amount contained in a pail: *a pail of water.* [Old English *pægel*]

pain (peɪn) n. **1.** physical hurt or discomfort caused by injury or illness. **2.** emotional suffering or mental distress. **3. on pain of.** subject to the penalty of: *they were ordered not to cross the borders, on pain of death.* **4.** Also called: **pain in the neck.** Informal. a person or thing that is annoying or irritating. ~vb. **5.** to cause (a person) hurt, grief, or anxiety. **6.** Informal. to annoy; irritate. ~See also **pains.** [Latin *poena* punishment] —'**painless** adj.

pained (peɪnd) adj. having or suggesting pain or distress: *a pained expression.*

painful ('peɪnfʊl) adj. **1.** causing pain; distressing: *a painful duty.* **2.** affected with pain: *a painful toe.* **3.** tedious or difficult: *progress is rather painful.* **4.** Informal. extremely bad: *a painful performance.* —'**painfully** adv.

painkiller ('peɪnˌkɪlə) *n.* a pill or other form of medicine that relieves pain.

pains (peɪnz) *pl. n.* care or trouble: *she takes great pains with her work.*

painstaking ('peɪnzˌteɪkɪŋ) *adj.* extremely careful as to fine detail. —**pains·takingly** *adv.*

paint (peɪnt) *n.* **1.** a substance used for decorating or protecting a surface, usually consisting of a solid pigment suspended in a liquid that dries to form a hard coating. **2.** a dry film of paint on a surface. **3.** *Informal.* face make-up. ~*vb.* **4.** to make (a picture) of (a figure, landscape, etc.) with paint applied to paper or canvas. **5.** to coat (a surface) with paint, as in decorating. **6.** to apply (liquid) to (a surface): *she painted the cut with antiseptic.* **7.** to apply make-up to (the face). **8.** to describe vividly in words: *she paints a dismal picture of the future.* **9. paint the town red.** *Informal.* to celebrate uninhibitedly. [Latin *pingere* to paint]

paintbrush ('peɪntˌbrʌʃ) *n.* a brush used to apply paint.

painted lady *n.* a butterfly with pale brownish-red mottled wings.

painter[1] ('peɪntə) *n.* **1.** a person who paints surfaces of buildings as a trade. **2.** an artist who paints pictures.

painter[2] ('peɪntə) *n.* a rope attached to the bow of a boat for tying it up. [prob. from Old French *penteur* strong rope]

painting ('peɪntɪŋ) *n.* **1.** a picture produced by using paint. **2.** the art of producing pictures by applying paints to paper or canvas. **3.** the act of applying paint to a surface.

pair (pɛə) *n.* **1.** two identical or similar things matched for use together: *a pair of socks.* **2.** two people, animals, or things used or grouped together: *a pair of horses; a pair of scoundrels.* **3.** an object considered to be two identical or similar things joined together: *a pair of trousers.* **4.** a male and a female animal of the same species kept for breeding purposes. **5.** *Parliament.* two opposed members who both agree not to vote on a specified motion. **6.** two playing cards of the same denomination. **7.** one member of a matching pair: *I can't find the pair to this glove.* ~*vb.* **8.** to group (people or things) in matching pairs. **9.** (foll. by *off*) to separate into groups of two. [Latin *pār* equal]

paisley pattern *or* **paisley** ('peɪzlɪ) *n.* **1.** a pattern of small curving shapes with intricate detailing. **2.** a fine wool fabric traditionally printed with this pattern. [after *Paisley*, town in Scotland]

pajamas (pə'dʒɑːməz) *pl. n.* U.S. pyjamas.

pakeha ('pɑːkɪˌhɑː) *n., pl.* **pakeha** *or* **pakehas.** *N.Z.* a person of European descent, as distinct from a Maori. [Maori]

Paki ('pækɪ) *Brit. slang, offensive.* ~*n.* **1.** a Pakistani or person of Pakistani descent. ~*adj.* **2.** Pakistani or of Pakistani descent.

Pakistani (ˌpɑːkɪ'stɑːnɪ) *adj.* **1.** of or relating to Pakistan. ~*n.* **2.** a person from Pakistan.

pal (pæl) *Informal.* ~*n.* **1.** a close friend;

comrade. ~*vb.* **palling, palled.** **2. pal up with.** to become friends with. [Romany: brother]

palace ('pælɪs) *n.* **1.** the official residence of a king, queen, president, or archbishop. **2.** a large and richly furnished building resembling a royal palace. [Latin *Palātium* Palatine, the site of the palace of the emperors in Rome]

paladin ('pælədɪn) *n.* **1.** one of the legendary twelve peers of Charlemagne's court. **2.** (formerly) a knight who did battle for a king or queen. [Italian *paladino*]

Palaeocene *or U.S.* **Paleocene** ('pælɪəʊˌsiːn) *adj. Geol.* of the epoch of geological time about 65 million years ago. [Greek *palaeo-* ancient + *kainos* new]

palaeography *or U.S.* **paleography** (ˌpælɪ'ɒgrəfɪ) *n.* the study of ancient handwriting. [Greek *palaeo-*ancient + -*graphy*]

Palaeolithic *or U.S.* **Paleolithic** (ˌpælɪəʊˈlɪθɪk) *adj.* of the period from about 2.5 to 3 million years ago until about 12 000 B.C., during which primitive man emerged and unpolished chipped stone tools were made. [Greek *palaeo-* ancient + *lithos* stone]

palaeontology *or U.S.* **paleontology** (ˌpælɪɒn'tɒlədʒɪ) *n.* the study of past geological periods and fossils. [Greek *palaeo-* ancient + *ōn, ont-* being + -LOGY] —ˌpalaeon'tologist *or U.S.* ˌpaleon'tologist *n.*

Palaeozoic *or U.S.* **Paleozoic** (ˌpælɪəʊ-'zəʊɪk) *adj. Geol.* of an era of geological time that lasted from about 600 million years ago to 230 million years ago. [Greek *palaeo-* ancient + *zōion* animal]

palanquin *or* **palankeen** (ˌpælən'kiːn) *n.* (formerly, in the Orient) a covered bed in which someone could be carried on the shoulders of four men. [Portuguese *palanquim*]

palatable ('pælətəb°l) *adj.* **1.** (of food or drink) pleasant to taste. **2.** (of an experience or idea) acceptable or satisfactory.

palate ('pælɪt) *n.* **1.** the roof of the mouth. **2.** the sense of taste: *she had no palate for the wine.* [Latin *palātum*]

palatial (pə'leɪʃəl) *adj.* like a palace; sumptuous.

palatinate (pə'lætɪnɪt) *n.* a territory ruled by a palatine prince or noble or a count palatine.

palatine ('pæləˌtaɪn) *adj.* possessing royal prerogatives: *a count palatine.* [Latin *palātium* palace]

palaver (pə'lɑːvə) *n.* tedious or time-consuming business; fuss: *all the palaver of filling in forms.* [Portuguese *palavra* talk]

pale[1] (peɪl) *adj.* **1.** (of a colour) whitish: *pale blue.* **2.** (of a person or a person's complexion) having a whitish appearance, usually because of illness, shock, or fear. **3.** lacking brightness or colour: *pale morning light.* ~*vb.* **4.** to make or become pale or paler. [Latin *pallidus*] —**paleness** *n.*

pale[2] (peɪl) *n.* **1.** a wooden post or strip used in fences. **2.** an enclosing barrier, such as a fence made of pales. **3. beyond the pale.** outside the limits of social convention. [Latin *pālus* stake]

paleface ('peɪlˌfeɪs) n. a derogatory term for a White person, said to have been used by North American Indians.

Palestinian (ˌpælɪ'stɪnɪən) adj. **1.** of Palestine, a former country in the Middle East. ~n. **2.** a person from this area.

palette ('pælɪt) n. **1.** a flat piece of wood or plastic used by artists to mix paints. **2.** the range of colours characteristic of a particular artist or school of painting: a restricted palette. [French]

palette knife n. a spatula with a thin flexible blade used in painting or cookery.

palindrome ('pælɪnˌdrəʊm) n. a word or phrase that reads the same backwards or forwards, such as able was I ere I saw Elba. [Greek palindromos running back again]

paling ('peɪlɪŋ) n. **1.** a fence made of pales. **2.** pales collectively. **3.** a single pale.

palisade (ˌpælɪ'seɪd) n. **1.** a fence made of stakes driven into the ground. **2.** one of the stakes used in such a fence. [Latin pālus stake]

pall¹ (pɔːl) n. **1.** a cloth covering spread over a coffin. **2.** a coffin at a funeral ceremony. **3.** a dark heavy covering: the clouds formed a pall over the sky. **4.** a depressing atmosphere: her bereavement cast a pall on the party. [Latin pallium cloak]

pall² (pɔːl) vb. (foll. by on) to become boring to: history classes palled on me. [var. of appal]

palladium (pə'leɪdɪəm) n. Chem. a rare silvery-white element of the platinum metal group, used in jewellery. Symbol: Pd [after the asteroid Pallas]

pallbearer ('pɔːlˌbɛərə) n. a person who helps to carry or who escorts the coffin at a funeral.

pallet¹ ('pælɪt) n. a straw-filled mattress or bed. [Latin palea straw]

pallet² ('pælɪt) n. **1.** an instrument with a handle and a flat, sometimes flexible, blade used for shaping pottery. **2.** a portable platform for storing and moving goods. [Latin pala spade]

palliasse ('pælɪˌæs) n. a straw-filled mattress; pallet. [French paillasse]

palliate ('pælɪˌeɪt) vb. **1.** to lessen the severity of (pain or disease) without curing it. **2.** to cause (an offence) to seem less serious; excuse. [Latin pallium a cloak]

palliative ('pælɪətɪv) adj. **1.** relieving without curing. ~n. **2.** something that palliates something, such as a sedative drug.

pallid ('pælɪd) adj. lacking colour, brightness, or vigour: a pallid complexion; a pallid performance. [Latin pallidus]

pallor ('pælə) n. paleness of complexion, usually because of illness, shock, or fear. [Latin: whiteness]

pally ('pælɪ) adj. -lier, -liest. Informal. on friendly terms.

palm¹ (pɑːm) n. **1.** the inner part of the hand from the wrist to the base of the fingers. **2.** the part of a glove that covers the palm. **3. in the palm of one's hand.** at

one's mercy. ~vb. **4.** to hide (something) in the hand, for example in conjuring tricks. ~See also **palm off.** [Latin palma]

palm² or **palm tree** (pɑːm) n. any of several tropical or subtropical trees that have a straight unbranched trunk crowned with long pointed leaves. [Latin palma, from the likeness of its spreading fronds to a hand]

palmate ('pælmeɪt) adj. shaped like an open hand: palmate leaves.

palmetto (pæl'mɛtəʊ) n., pl. -tos. a small palm tree with fan-shaped leaves. [Spanish palmito a little palm]

palmistry ('pɑːmɪstrɪ) n. the process or art of predicting someone's future by examining the lines and bumps on his hand. —'palmist n.

palm off vb. **1.** to offer or sell fraudulently: to palm off a counterfeit coin. **2.** to divert (someone) in order to be rid of him: I palmed the unwelcome visitor off on John.

palm oil n. an oil obtained from the fruit of certain palm trees, used as an edible fat and in soap.

Palm Sunday n. the Sunday before Easter, commemorating Christ's entry into Jerusalem.

palmy ('pɑːmɪ) adj. palmier, palmiest. **1.** prosperous, flourishing, or luxurious: a palmy life. **2.** covered with palm trees: a palmy beach.

palomino (ˌpælə'miːnəʊ) n., pl. -nos. a golden or cream horse with a white mane and tail. [Spanish: dovelike]

palpable ('pælpəbᵊl) adj. **1.** easily perceived by the senses or the mind; obvious: a palpable lie. **2.** (of a feeling or an atmosphere) so intense as to seem capable of being touched. [Latin palpāre to touch] —'palpably adv.

palpate ('pælpeɪt) vb. Med. to examine (an area of the body) by touching. [Latin palpāre to stroke] —palpation (pæl-'peɪʃən) n.

palpitate ('pælpɪˌteɪt) vb. **1.** (of the heart) to beat rapidly. **2.** to flutter or tremble. [Latin palpitāre] —palpitation (ˌpælpɪ'teɪʃən) n.

palsy ('pɔːlzɪ) Pathol. ~n. **1.** paralysis of a specified type: cerebral palsy. ~vb. -sying, -sied. **2.** to paralyse (someone). [from paralysis]

paltry ('pɔːltrɪ) adj. -trier, -triest. insignificant, worthless, or petty. [Low Germanic palter, paltrig ragged]

pampas ('pæmpəs) n. (functioning as sing.) the extensive grassy plains of temperate South America. [American Indian bamba plain]

pampas grass n. a South American grass, widely cultivated for its large feathery silver-coloured flower branches.

pamper ('pæmpə) vb. to treat (someone) with excessive indulgence or care; spoil. [Germanic]

pamphlet ('pæmflɪt) n. a brief publication, usually with a paper cover and often on a subject of current interest. [Medieval Latin Pamphilus, title of a poem]

pamphleteer (ˌpæmflɪ'tɪə) n. a person who writes or issues pamphlets.

pan¹ (pæn) n. 1. a wide long-handled metal container used in cooking. 2. any of various similar containers used in industry, etc. 3. either of the two dishlike receptacles on a set of scales. 4. Brit. the bowl of a lavatory. 5. a natural or artificial hollow in the ground: a saltpan. ~vb. panning, panned. 6. to sift gold from (a river) in a shallow pan. 7. Informal. to criticize harshly: the critics panned his new play. ~See also **pan out**. [Old English panne]

pan² (pæn) vb. panning, panned. 1. to move (a film camera) or (of a film camera) to be moved so as to follow a moving object or obtain a panoramic effect. ~n. 2. the act of panning. [from panoramic]

pan- combining form. including or relating to all parts or members: Pan-American. [Greek]

panacea (ˌpænə'sɪə) n. a remedy for all diseases or problems. [Greek pan- all + akēs remedy]

panache (pə'næʃ) n. a dashing manner; swagger: he rides with panache. [Old Italian pennacchio feather]

panama hat or **panama** ('pænəˌmɑː) n. a straw hat with a rounded crown and a wide brim.

Pan-American adj. of North, South, and Central America collectively.

panatella (ˌpænə'tɛlə) n. a long slender cigar. [American Spanish: long thin biscuit]

pancake ('pænˌkeɪk) n. 1. a thin flat cake made from batter and fried on both sides. 2. Also called: **pancake landing**. an aircraft landing made by levelling out a few feet from the ground and then dropping onto it.

Pancake Day n. Shrove Tuesday, when people traditionally eat pancakes.

panchromatic (ˌpænkrəʊ'mætɪk) adj. Photog. (of an emulsion or film) sensitive to all colours.

pancreas ('pæŋkrɪəs) n. a large gland, situated behind the stomach, that secretes insulin and an alkaline juice containing digestive enzymes. [Greek pan- all + kreas flesh] —**pancreatic** (ˌpæŋkrɪ'ætɪk) adj.

panda ('pændə) n. 1. Also called: **giant panda**. a large black-and-white bearlike animal that inhabits the bamboo forests of China. 2. Also called: **lesser** or **red panda**. a raccoon-like animal of the mountain forests of S Asia, with a reddish-brown coat and ringed tail. [Nepalese]

panda car n. Brit. a police patrol car.

pandemic (pæn'dɛmɪk) adj. (of a disease) affecting people over a wide geographical area. [Greek pandēmos general]

pandemonium (ˌpændɪ'məʊnɪəm) n. wild confusion; uproar. [Greek pan- all + daimōn demon]

pander ('pændə) vb. 1. (foll. by to) to indulge (a person or his desires). ~n. 2. a person who procures a sexual partner for someone. [after Pandarus, in legend, the procurer of Cressida for Troilus]

pandit ('pændɪt) n. Hinduism. same as **pundit** (sense 2).

p & p Brit. postage and packing.

pane (peɪn) n. a sheet (of glass). [Latin pannus rag]

panegyric (ˌpænɪ'dʒɪrɪk) n. a formal speech or piece of writing that praises a person or event. [Greek panēguris public gathering]

panel ('pæn³l) n. 1. a flat section of a surface, such as a door or wall. 2. any distinct section of something formed from a sheet of material, such as part of a car body. 3. a piece of material inserted in a garment. 4. a. a group of people selected to act as a team in a quiz, to discuss a topic before an audience, etc. b. (as modifier): a panel game. 5. Law. a. a list of jurors. b. the people on a jury. 6. short for **instrument panel**. ~vb. **-elling**, **-elled** or U.S. **-eling**, **-eled**. 7. to furnish or decorate (something) with panels. [Old French: portion]

panelling or U.S. **paneling** ('pæn³lɪŋ) n. panels collectively, for example on a wall or ceiling.

panellist or U.S. **panelist** ('pæn³lɪst) n. a member of a panel, usually on radio or television.

panel van n. Austral. & N.Z. a small van.

pang (pæŋ) n. a sudden sharp feeling of loneliness, physical pain, or hunger. [Germanic]

pangolin (pæŋ'gəʊlɪn) n. an animal of tropical countries with a scaly body and a long snout for feeding on ants and termites. Also called: **scaly anteater**. [Malay penggōling]

panic ('pænɪk) n. 1. a sudden overwhelming feeling of terror or anxiety, sometimes affecting a whole group of people. 2. (modifier) of or resulting from such terror: panic measures. ~vb. **-icking**, **-icked**. 3. to feel or cause (someone) to feel panic. [Greek panikos emanating from Pan, god of the fields] —**panicky** adj.

panicle ('pænɪk³l) n. a loose, irregularly branched cluster of flowers, as in the oat. [Latin pānicula tuft]

panic-stricken adj. affected by panic.

panjandrum (pæn'dʒændrəm) n. a pompous self-important official. [after a character in a nonsense work]

pannier ('pænɪə) n. 1. one of a pair of bags slung either side of the back wheel of a bicycle or motorcycle. 2. one of a pair of large baskets slung over a beast of burden. [Old French panier]

panoply ('pænəplɪ) n. a complete or magnificent array: there was a full panoply of relatives at the wedding. [Greek pan- all + hopla armour]

panorama (ˌpænə'rɑːmə) n. 1. an extensive unbroken view in all directions. 2. a wide or comprehensive survey of a subject. 3. a picture of a scene unrolled before spectators a part at a time so as to appear continuous. [Greek pan- all + horāma view] —**panoramic** (ˌpænə'ræmɪk) adj.

pan out vb. 1. Informal. to work out; result: the meeting didn't pan out as ex-

pected. **2.** (of gravel) to yield gold by panning.

panpipes ('pæn,paɪps) *pl. n.* a musical wind instrument made of a number of tubes of graduated lengths bound together.

pansy ('pænzɪ) *n., pl.* **-sies. 1.** a garden plant having flowers with rounded white, yellow, or purple velvety petals. **2.** *Offensive slang.* an effeminate or homosexual man or boy. [Old French *pensée* thought]

pant (pænt) *vb.* **1.** to breathe with noisy gasps after exertion. **2.** to say (something) while breathing in this way. **3.** (foll. by *for*) to have a frantic desire for. ~*n.* **4.** the act of panting. [Greek *phantasioun* to have visions]

pantaloons (,pæntə'luːnz) *pl. n.* baggy trousers gathered at the ankles. [French *pantalon* trousers]

pantechnicon (pæn'tɛknɪkən) *n. Brit.* a large van used for furniture removals. [Greek *pant-* all + *tekhnē* art; orig. a London bazaar, later used as a furniture warehouse]

pantheism ('pænθɪ,ɪzəm) *n.* **1.** the belief that God is identical with the material universe or the forces of nature. **2.** readiness to worship all gods. —**pantheist** *n.* —**,panthe'istic** *adj.*

pantheon ('pænθɪən) *n.* **1.** (in ancient Greece or Rome) a temple erected to honour all the gods. **2.** a building commemorating a nation's dead heroes. [Greek *pan-* all + *theos* god]

panther ('pænθə) *n.* a leopard, usually a black one. [Greek]

panties ('pæntɪz) *pl. n.* women's or children's underpants.

pantihose ('pæntɪ,həʊz) *pl. n. Austral.* women's tights.

pantile ('pæn,taɪl) *n.* a roofing tile, with an S-shaped cross section. [PAN¹ + *tile*]

panto ('pæntəʊ) *n., pl.* **-tos.** *Brit. informal.* short for **pantomime** (sense 1).

pantograph ('pæntə,grɑːf) *n.* **1.** an instrument consisting of pivoted levers for copying drawings or maps to any scale. **2.** a similar instrument mounted on a train roof to convey current from an overhead wire. [Greek *pant-* all + *graphein* to write]

pantomime ('pæntə,maɪm) *n.* **1.** (in Britain) a play based on a fairy tale and usually performed at Christmas time. **2.** a theatrical entertainment in which words are replaced by gestures and bodily actions. **3.** *Informal, chiefly Brit.* a confused or farcical situation. [Greek *pantomīmos*]

pantry ('pæntrɪ) *n., pl.* **-tries.** a small room or large cupboard in which food is kept. [Latin *pānis* bread]

pants (pænts) *pl. n.* **1.** *Brit.* an undergarment with two leg holes, covering the body from the waist or hips to the thighs. **2.** *U.S. & Canad.* trousers. **3. bore** *or* **scare the pants off someone.** *Informal.* to bore or scare someone very much. [shortened from *pantaloons*]

panty hose ('pæntɪ) *pl. n. U.S.* women's tights.

pap¹ (pæp) *n.* **1.** a soft or semiliquid food for babies or invalids. **2.** worthless or oversimplified entertainment or information. **3.** *S. African.* maize porridge. [Latin *pappāre* to eat]

pap² (pæp) *n. Archaic or Scot. & N English dialect.* a nipple or teat. [Old Norse]

papa (pə'pɑː) *n. Old-fashioned, informal.* father. [French]

papacy ('peɪpəsɪ) *n., pl.* **-cies. 1.** the office or term of office of a pope. **2.** the system of government in the Roman Catholic Church that has the pope as its head. [Medieval Latin *pāpa* pope]

papal ('peɪp'l) *adj.* of the pope or the papacy.

paparazzo (,pæpə'rætsəʊ) *n., pl.* **-razzi** (-'rætsiː). a freelance photographer who specializes in candid-camera shots of famous people. [Italian]

papaya (pə'paɪə) *n.* a large green fruit with a sweet yellow flesh, that grows on a West Indian tree. [Spanish]

paper ('peɪpə) *n.* **1.** a flexible material made from wood pulp or other fibrous material and formed into flat thin sheets suitable for writing on, decorating walls, or wrapping parcels. **2.** (*pl.*) documents, such as a passport, for establishing the identity of the bearer. **3.** (*pl.*) the collected diaries, letters, etc., of a person's private or public life. **4.** short for **newspaper** or **wallpaper. 5.** a lecture or an essay on a specific subject. **6.** a set of examination questions. **7. on paper.** in theory, as opposed to fact: *the project looks impressive enough on paper.* ~*adj.* **8.** made of paper: *paper cups do not last long.* **9.** existing only as recorded on paper but not yet in practice: *paper expenditure.* ~*vb.* **10.** to cover (walls) with wallpaper. ~See also **paper over.** [Latin *papyrus*] —**'papery** *adj.*

paperback ('peɪpə,bæk) *n.* **1.** a book with covers made of flexible card. ~*adj.* **2.** of a paperback or publication of paperbacks.

paperboy ('peɪpə,bɔɪ) *or* **papergirl** *n.* a boy or girl employed to deliver newspapers to people's homes.

paper chase *n.* a cross-country run in which a runner lays a trail of paper for others to follow.

paperclip ('peɪpə,klɪp) *n.* a bent wire clip for holding sheets of paper together.

paperhanger ('peɪpə,hæŋə) *n.* a person who hangs wallpaper as an occupation.

paperknife ('peɪpə,naɪf) *n., pl.* **-knives.** a knife-shaped object with a blunt blade for opening sealed envelopes.

paper money *n.* banknotes, rather than coins.

paper over *vb.* to conceal (something unpleasant or difficult).

paperweight ('peɪpə,weɪt) *n.* a small heavy object placed on top of loose papers to prevent them from scattering.

paperwork ('peɪpə,wɜːk) *n.* clerical work, such as the writing of reports or letters.

papier-mâché (,pæpjeɪ'mæʃeɪ) *n.* **1.** a hard substance made of layers of paper mixed with paste and moulded when moist. ~*adj.* **2.** made of papier-mâché. [French, lit.: chewed paper]

papilla (pə'pɪlə) n., pl. **-lae** (-liː). Biol. a small projection of tissue at the base of a hair, tooth, or feather. [Latin: nipple] —**pa'pillary** adj.

papist ('peɪpɪst) n., adj. Usually offensive. same as **Roman Catholic**. [Church Latin pāpa pope]

papoose (pə'puːs) n. an American Indian baby. [American Indian papoos]

paprika ('pæprɪkə, pə'priː-) n. a mild powdered seasoning made from red peppers. [Hungarian]

Pap test or **smear** (pæp) n. Med. an examination of stained cells in a specimen taken from the neck or lining of the womb for detection of cancer. [after George Papanicolaou, anatomist]

papyrus (pə'paɪrəs) n., pl. **-ri** (-raɪ) or **-ruses**. 1. a tall water plant of S Europe and N and central Africa. 2. a kind of paper made from the stem of this plant, used by the ancient Egyptians, Greeks, and Romans. 3. an ancient document written on this paper. [Greek papūros reed]

par (pɑː) n. 1. the usual or average state or condition: I feel a bit below par today. 2. **on a par with.** equal or equivalent to: his latest film puts him on a par with the Hollywood greats. 3. Golf. a standard score for a hole or course that a good player should make: par for the course was 72. 4. Finance. the established value of the unit of one national currency in terms of the unit of another. 5. Commerce. short for **par value**. ~adj. 6. **par for the course.** to be expected; typical. [Latin: equal]

par. 1. paragraph. 2. parenthesis.

para ('pærə) n. Informal. 1. a paratrooper. 2. a paragraph.

para- or before a vowel **par-** prefix. 1. beside; near: parameter. 2. beyond: parapsychology. 3. resembling: paratyphoid fever. [Greek]

parable ('pærəb'l) n. a short story that uses familiar images to illustrate a religious or ethical point. [Greek parabolē analogy]

parabola (pə'ræbələ) n. Geom. an open plane curve formed by the intersection of a cone by a plane parallel to its side. [Greek parabolē a setting alongside] —**parabolic** (ˌpærə'bɒlɪk) adj.

paracetamol (ˌpærə'siːtəˌmɒl, -'sɛtə-) n. a mild pain-relieving drug. [from para-acetamidophenol]

parachute ('pærəˌʃuːt) n. 1. a device consisting of a large fabric canopy connected to a harness, used to slow down the descent of a person or package from an aircraft. ~vb. 2. to land or to drop (supplies or troops) by parachute from an aircraft. [French] —**'para,chutist** n.

parade (pə'reɪd) n. 1. an ordered march or procession, for example of troops being inspected. 2. a conspicuous display: to make a parade of one's grief. 3. a public promenade or street of shops. ~vb. 4. to walk or march, esp. in a procession. 5. to exhibit or flaunt: he was parading his medals. [French: a making ready]

parade ground n. a place where soldiers assemble regularly for inspection or display.

paradigm ('pærəˌdaɪm) n. a pattern, model, or example. [Greek paradeigma pattern]

paradise ('pærəˌdaɪs) n. 1. heaven; the abode of the righteous after death. 2. the Garden of Eden. 3. any place or condition that fulfils all one's desires. [Greek paradeisos garden]

paradise duck n. a New Zealand duck with bright plumage.

paradox ('pærəˌdɒks) n. 1. a seemingly absurd or self-contradictory statement that is or may be true: religious truths are often expressed in paradox. 2. a self-contradictory proposition, such as I always tell lies. 3. a person or thing that is made up of contradictory elements. [Greek paradoxos opposed to existing notions] —**para'doxical** adj. —**para'doxically** adv.

paraffin ('pærəfɪn) n. 1. a liquid mixture distilled from petroleum or shale and used as an aircraft fuel, in domestic heaters, and as a solvent. 2. Chem. any saturated hydrocarbon with the general formula C_nH_{2n+2} [Latin parum too little + affinis adjacent; so called from its chemical inertia]

paraffin wax n. a white waxlike substance distilled from petroleum and used in making candles and as a sealing agent.

paragon ('pærəgən) n. a model of excellence or perfection: a paragon of virtue. [Old Italian paragone comparison]

paragraph ('pærəˌgrɑːf) n. 1. a section of a piece of writing, usually devoted to one idea, which begins on a new line and is often indented. 2. Printing. the character ¶, used to indicate the beginning of a new paragraph. ~vb. 3. to form (a piece of writing) into paragraphs. [Greek paragraphos line drawing attention to part of a text]

parakeet ('pærəˌkiːt) n. a small colourful parrot with a long tail. [Spanish periquito & Old French paroquet parrot]

parallax ('pærəˌlæks) n. an apparent change in the position of an object resulting from a change in position of the observer. [Greek parallaxis change]

parallel ('pærəˌlɛl) adj. 1. separated by an equal distance at every point: parallel walls. 2. corresponding; similar: parallel situations. 3. Computers. operating on several items of information or instructions at the same time. ~n. 4. Maths. one of a set of parallel lines or planes. 5. something very similar or corresponding to something else. 6. a comparison; similarity between two things. 7. Also called: **parallel of latitude.** any of the imaginary lines around the earth parallel to the equator, marking degrees of latitude. 8. Printing. the character ‖, used as a reference mark. ~vb. 9. to be a parallel to; correspond to: your experience parallels mine. [Greek parallēlos alongside one another]

parallel bars pl. n. Gymnastics. a pair of

wooden bars on upright posts used for various exercises.

parallelepiped (ˌpærəˌlɛlɪˈpaɪpɛd) *n.* *Geom.* a solid shape whose six faces are parallelograms. [Greek *parallēlos* parallel + *epipedon* plane surface]

parallelism (ˈpærəˌlɛlɪzəm) *n.* **1.** the state of being parallel. **2.** a close likeness; similarity.

parallelogram (ˌpærəˈlɛləˌgræm) *n.* *Geom.* a plane figure whose opposite sides are parallel and equal in length. [Greek *parallēlos* parallel + *grammē* line]

paralyse *or U.S.* **-lyze** (ˈpærəˌlaɪz) *vb.* **1.** *Pathol.* to affect (someone) with paralysis. **2.** to make (someone) immobile: *paralysed with fright.* [French *paralyser*]

paralysis (pəˈrælɪsɪs) *n.* **1.** *Pathol.* impairment or loss of voluntary muscle function or sensation in all or part of the body. **2.** a state of inactivity: *paralysis of industry by strikes.* [Greek *paralusis,* from *para-* beyond + *lusis* a loosening]

paralytic (ˌpærəˈlɪtɪk) *adj.* **1.** of or relating to paralysis. **2.** *Brit. informal.* very drunk. ~*n.* **3.** a person who is paralysed.

paramecium (ˌpærəˈmiːsɪəm) *n., pl.* **-cia** (-sɪə). a unicellular animal which lives in ponds, puddles, and sewage filters and swims by means of cilia.

paramedic (ˌpærəˈmɛdɪk) *n.* a person, such as a laboratory technician, who supplements the work of the medical profession.

paramedical (ˌpærəˈmɛdɪkˀl) *adj.* supplementing the work of the medical profession.

parameter (pəˈræmɪtə) *n.* **1.** *Maths.* an arbitrary constant that determines the specific form of a mathematical expression, such as *a* and *b* in *y* = *ax²* + *b.* **2.** *Informal.* any constant or limiting factor: *a designer must work within the parameters of budget and practicality.* [Greek *para-* beside + *metron* measure]

paramilitary (ˌpærəˈmɪlɪtrɪ) *adj.* denoting a group of personnel with military structure working in support of military forces or as a guerilla or terrorist group.

paramount (ˈpærəˌmaunt) *adj.* of the greatest importance. [Old French *par* by + *-amont* above]

paramour (ˈpærəˌmuə) *n.* *Old-fashioned.* an adulterous lover. [Old French, lit.: through love]

paranoia (ˌpærəˈnɔɪə) *n.* **1.** a mental disorder characterized by delusions of grandeur or of persecution. **2.** *Informal.* intense fear or suspicion, usually when unfounded. [Greek *para-* beyond + *noos* mind] —ˈpara,noid *or* ˌparaˈnoiac *adj., n.*

paranormal (ˌpærəˈnɔːməl) *adj.* **1.** beyond normal scientific explanation. ~*n.* **2. the.** paranormal happenings or matters generally.

parapet (ˈpærəpɪt) *n.* **1.** a low wall or railing along the edge of a balcony or roof. **2.** *Mil.* a rampart or mound of sandbags in front of a trench to conceal and protect troops from fire. [Italian *parapetto*]

paraphernalia (ˌpærəfəˈneɪlɪə) *n.* miscella-neous articles or equipment. [Greek *para-* beyond + *phernē* dowry]

paraphrase (ˈpærəˌfreɪz) *n.* **1.** an expression of a statement or text in other words. ~*vb.* **2.** to put (a statement or text) into other words; restate. [Greek *paraphrazein* to recount]

paraplegia (ˌpærəˈpliːdʒə) *n.* *Pathol.* paralysis of the lower half of the body. [Greek: a blow on one side] —ˌparaˈplegic *adj., n.*

parapsychology (ˌpærəsaɪˈkɒlədʒɪ) *n.* the study of mental phenomena such as telepathy.

Paraquat (ˈpærəˌkwɒt) *n.* *Trademark.* an extremely poisonous weedkiller.

parasite (ˈpærəˌsaɪt) *n.* **1.** an animal or plant that lives in or on another from which it obtains nourishment. **2.** a person who habitually lives at the expense of others; sponger. [Greek *para-* beside + *sitos* grain] —**parasitic** (ˌpærəˈsɪtɪk) *adj.*

parasol (ˈpærəˌsɒl) *n.* an umbrella-like sunshade. [French]

paratrooper (ˈpærəˌtruːpə) *n.* a member of the paratroops.

paratroops (ˈpærəˌtruːps) *pl. n.* troops trained to be dropped by parachute into a battle area.

paratyphoid fever (ˌpærəˈtaɪfɔɪd) *n.* a disease resembling but less severe than typhoid fever.

parboil (ˈpɑːˌbɔɪl) *vb.* to boil (food) until partially cooked. [Late Latin *perbullīre* to boil thoroughly; modern meaning due to confusion of *par-* with *part*]

parcel (ˈpɑːsˀl) *n.* **1.** something wrapped up; a package. **2.** a quantity of some commodity offered for sale; lot. **3.** a distinct portion of land. ~*vb.* **-celling, -celled** *or U.S.* **-celing, -celed.** **4.** (foll. by *up*) to wrap (something) up into a parcel. **5.** (foll. by *out*) to divide (something) into portions. [Old French *parcelle*]

parch (pɑːtʃ) *vb.* **1.** to deprive (something) of water; dry up: *the sun parches the fields.* **2.** to make (someone) very thirsty: *I was parched after the run.* [origin unknown]

parchment (ˈpɑːtʃmənt) *n.* **1.** the skin of certain animals, such as sheep, treated to form a material for writing on. **2.** a manuscript made of this material. **3.** a stiff yellowish paper resembling parchment. [Greek *pergamēnē* from *Pergamēnos* of Pergamum (where parchment was made)]

pardon (ˈpɑːdˀn) *vb.* **1.** to forgive (a person) for (an offence or mistake): *to pardon someone; to pardon a fault.* ~*n.* **2.** forgiveness. **3.** official release from punishment for a crime. ~*interj.* **4.** *Also:* **pardon me, I beg your pardon.** **a.** sorry; excuse me. **b.** what did you say? [Medieval Latin *perdōnāre* to forgive freely] —ˈpar-donable *adj.*

pare (pɛə) *vb.* **1.** to peel (the outer layer) from (something): *to pare apples.* **2.** to cut the edges from (one's nails). **3.** to decrease bit by bit: *to pare down expenses.* [Latin *parāre* to make ready]

parent ('peərənt) n. 1. a father or mother. 2. a person acting as a father or mother; guardian. 3. a plant or animal that has produced one or more plants or animals. [Latin *parens* from *parere* to bring forth] —**parental** (pə'rɛntəl) adj. —'**parenthood** n.

parentage ('peərəntɪdʒ) n. ancestry; family.

parent company n. a company that owns a number of smaller companies.

parenthesis (pə'rɛnθɪsɪs) n., pl. **-ses** (-ˌsiːz). 1. a phrase inserted into a passage, often as an explanation, and marked off by brackets or dashes. 2. Also called: **bracket**. either of a pair of characters (), used to enclose such a phrase. [Greek: something placed in besides] —**parenthetical** (ˌpærən'θɛtɪkˀl) adj. —ˌparen'**thetically** adv.

parenting ('peərəntɪŋ) n. the activity of bringing up children.

parent-teacher association n. an organization consisting of the parents of children at a school and their teachers formed in order to promote better understanding between them.

par excellence (pɑːr ˌɛksə'lɒns) adv. beyond comparison: *she is a hostess par excellence.* [French]

parfait (pɑː'feɪ) n. a dessert consisting of layers of ice cream, fruit, and sauce, topped with whipped cream, and served in a tall glass. [French: perfect]

pariah (pə'raɪə) n. a social outcast. [Tamil *paraiyan*]

parietal (pə'raɪɪtˀl) adj. Anat., biol. of or forming the walls of a bodily cavity: *the parietal bones of the skull.* [Latin *pariēs* wall]

paring ('peərɪŋ) n. something that has been cut off something.

parish ('pærɪʃ) n. 1. an area that has its own church and clergyman. 2. the people who live in a parish. 3. (in England and, formerly, Wales) the smallest unit of local government. [Greek *paroikos* neighbour]

parish clerk n. a person who assists in various church duties.

parish council n. (in England and, formerly, Wales) the administrative body of a parish. See **parish** (sense 3).

parishioner (pə'rɪʃənə) n. a person who lives in a particular parish.

parish register n. a book in which the births, baptisms, marriages, and deaths in a parish are recorded.

parity ('pærɪtɪ) n. 1. equality, for example of rank or pay. 2. close or exact equivalence. 3. *Finance.* equivalence between the units of currency of two countries. [Latin *pār* equal]

park (pɑːk) n. 1. a large area of land preserved in a natural state for recreational use by the public. 2. a piece of open land in a town with public amenities. 3. a large area of land forming a private estate. 4. an area designed to accommodate a number of related enterprises: *a business park.* 5. *U.S. & Canad.* a playing field or sports stadium. 6. **the park**. *Brit. infor-*

mal. the pitch in soccer. ~vb. 7. to stop and leave (a vehicle) temporarily. 8. *Informal.* to leave or put (someone or something) somewhere: *park yourself in front of the fire.* [Germanic] —'**parking** n.

parka ('pɑːkə) n. a long jacket with a quilted lining and a fur-trimmed hood. [from Aleutian (language of Aleutian Islands, off Alaska): skin]

parkin ('pɑːkɪn) n. *Brit.* a moist spicy ginger cake containing oatmeal. [origin unknown]

parking meter ('pɑːkɪŋ) n. a coin-operated timing device beside a parking space that indicates how long a vehicle may be left parked.

parking ticket n. the notice of a fine served on a motorist for a parking offence.

Parkinson's disease ('pɑːkɪnsənz) or **Parkinsonism** n. a disorder of the central nervous system which causes tremor, rigidity, and impaired muscular coordination. [after James *Parkinson*, surgeon]

Parkinson's law n. the notion that work expands to fill the time available for its completion. [after C. N. *Parkinson*, economist]

parkland ('pɑːkˌlænd) n. grassland with scattered trees.

parky ('pɑːkɪ) adj. **parkier**, **parkiest**. *Brit. informal.* (of the weather) chilly. [origin unknown]

parlance ('pɑːləns) n. a particular manner of speaking: *political parlance.* [French *parler* to talk]

parley ('pɑːlɪ) n. 1. a discussion, for example between enemies to decide terms of surrender. ~vb. 2. to have a parley, usually with an enemy. [French *parler* to talk]

parliament ('pɑːləmənt) n. an assembly of the representatives of a political nation or people, usually the highest law-making authority. [Old French *parlement* from *parler* to speak]

Parliament ('pɑːləmənt) n. 1. the highest law-making authority in Britain, consisting of the House of Commons, the House of Lords, and the sovereign. 2. the equivalent law-making authority in another country.

parliamentarian (ˌpɑːləmən'tɛərɪən) n. an expert in parliamentary procedures.

parliamentary (ˌpɑːlə'mɛntrɪ) adj. 1. of or from a parliament: *a parliamentary decree.* 2. conforming to the procedures of a parliament: *parliamentary conduct.*

parlour or *U.S.* **parlor** ('pɑːlə) n. 1. Old-fashioned. a living room for receiving visitors in. 2. a room or shop equipped as a place of business: *an ice-cream parlour.* [Old French *parler* to speak]

parlous ('pɑːləs) adj. *Archaic or humorous.* dangerous: *the parlous state of the roof.* [var. of *perilous*]

Parmesan cheese or **Parmesan** ('pɑːmɪˌzæn) n. a hard strong-flavoured cheese used grated on pasta dishes and soups. [Italian *parmegiano* of Parma, Italy]

parochial (pəˈrəʊkɪəl) *adj.* **1.** narrow in outlook; provincial. **2.** of or relating to a parish. [see PARISH] —**paˈrochial,ism** *n.*

parody (ˈpærədɪ) *n., pl.* **-dies. 1.** a musical, literary, or other composition that mimics the style of another composer, author, etc., in a humorous way. **2.** something so badly done as to seem like an intentional mockery. ~*vb.* **3.** to make a parody of. [Greek *paroidiā* satirical poem] —**ˈparodist** *n.*

parole (pəˈrəʊl) *n.* **1.** the freeing of a prisoner before his sentence has expired, on condition that he behaves well. **2.** a promise given by a prisoner to behave well if granted liberty or partial liberty. **3. on parole.** conditionally released from prison. ~*vb.* **4.** to place (a person) on parole. [Old French *parole d'honneur* word of honour]

parotid gland (pəˈrɒtɪd) *n. Anat.* either of a pair of glands in front of and below the ears. [Greek *para-* near + *ous* ear]

paroxysm (ˈpærək,sɪzəm) *n.* **1.** an uncontrollable outburst of laughter, anger, or jealousy. **2.** *Pathol.* **a.** a sudden attack or recurrence of a disease. **b.** a fit or convulsion. [Greek *paroxunein* to goad] —,**parox'ysmal** *adj.*

parquet (ˈpɑːkeɪ) *n.* **1.** a floor covering made of pieces of parquetry. ~*vb.* **2.** to cover (a floor) with parquetry. [Old French: small enclosure]

parquetry (ˈpɑːkɪtrɪ) *n.* a geometric pattern of inlaid pieces of wood, used to cover floors.

parr (pɑː) *n.* a salmon up to two years of age. [origin unknown]

parricide (ˈpærɪˌsaɪd) *n.* **1.** a person who kills one of his parents. **2.** the act of killing either of one's parents. [Latin *parricīdium* murder of a parent or relative] —,**parri'cidal** *adj.*

parrot (ˈpærət) *n.* **1.** a tropical bird with a short hooked bill, bright plumage, and an ability to mimic human speech. **2.** a person who repeats or imitates someone else's words. ~*vb.* **3.** to repeat or imitate (someone else's words) without understanding them. [prob. from French *paroquet*]

parrot fever *n.* same as **psittacosis.**

parry (ˈpærɪ) *vb.* **-rying, -ried. 1.** to ward off (an attack) by blocking or deflecting, as in fencing. **2.** to avoid answering (questions) in a clever way. ~*n., pl.* **-ries. 3.** an instance of parrying. **4.** a skilful evasion of a question. [French *parer* to ward off]

parse (pɑːz) *vb.* to analyse (a sentence or the words in a sentence) grammatically. [Latin *pars* (*orātiōnis*) part (of speech)]

parsec (ˈpɑːˌsɛk) *n.* a unit of astronomical distance equivalent to 3.0857×10^{16} metres or 3.262 light years. [*parallax* + *second* (of time)]

parsimony (ˈpɑːsɪmənɪ) *n.* extreme caution in spending. [Latin *parcimōnia*] —**parsimonious** (,pɑːsɪˈməʊnɪəs) *adj.*

parsley (ˈpɑːslɪ) *n.* a herb with curled pleasant-smelling leaves, used for seasoning and decorating food. [Middle English *persely*]

parsnip (ˈpɑːsnɪp) *n.* a long tapering cream-coloured root vegetable. [Latin *pastināca*]

parson (ˈpɑːsᵊn) *n.* **1.** a parish priest in the Church of England. **2.** any clergyman. [Latin *persōna* personage]

parsonage (ˈpɑːsᵊnɪdʒ) *n.* the residence of a parson, provided by the parish.

parson's nose *n.* the rump of a fowl when cooked.

part (pɑːt) *n.* **1.** a piece or portion. **2.** one of several equal divisions: *mix two parts flour to one part water.* **3.** an actor's role in a play. **4.** a person's duty: *everyone must do his part.* **5.** (*pl.*) region; area: *he's well known in these parts.* **6.** *Anat.* an area of the body. **7.** a component that can be replaced in a vehicle or machine. **8.** *U.S. & Canad.* same as **parting** (sense 2). **9.** *Music.* a melodic line assigned to one or more instrumentalists or singers. **10. for my part.** as far as I am concerned. **11. for the most part.** generally. **12. in part.** to some degree; partly. **13. on the part of.** on behalf of. **14. part and parcel of.** an essential ingredient of. **15. play a part. a.** to pretend to be what one is not. **b.** (foll. by *in*) to have something to do with: *to play a part in the king's downfall.* **16. take part in.** to participate in. **17. take someone's part.** to support someone, for example in an argument. **18. take something in good part.** to respond to (teasing or criticism) with good humour. ~*vb.* **19.** to divide or separate from one another: *to part the curtains; the seams parted when I washed the dress.* **20.** to go away or cause (people) to go away from one another: *the couple parted amicably.* **21.** (foll. by *with*) to give up: *I wouldn't part with my Mini.* **22.** (foll. by *from*) to cause (someone) to give up: *he's not easily parted from his cash.* **23.** to split: *the path parts here.* **24.** to arrange (the hair) in such a way that a line of scalp is left showing. ~*adv.* **25.** to some extent; partly: *part woman, part child.* ~See also **parts.** [Latin *pars* a part]

partake (pɑːˈteɪk) *vb.* **-taking, -took, -taken. 1.** (foll. by *of*) to take (food or drink). **2.** (foll. by *in*) to participate in. [from earlier *part taker*]

parterre (pɑːˈtɛə) *n.* **1.** a formally patterned flower garden. **2.** the pit of a theatre. [French]

Parthian shot (ˈpɑːθɪən) *n.* a hostile remark or gesture delivered while departing. [from the custom of archers from Parthia, an ancient Asian empire, who shot their arrows backwards while retreating]

partial (ˈpɑːʃəl) *adj.* **1.** relating to only a part; not complete: *a partial eclipse.* **2.** biased: *a partial judge.* **3.** (foll. by *to*) having a particular liking for. [Latin *pars* part] —**partiality** (,pɑːʃɪˈælɪtɪ) *n.* —**ˈpartially** *adv.*

participate (pɑːˈtɪsɪˌpeɪt) *vb.* (foll. by *in*) to become actively involved in. [Latin *pars* part + *capere* to take] —**parˈticipant** *n.*

—**participation** (pɑː,tɪsɪ'peɪʃən) n. —**par'ticipatory** adj.

participle ('pɑːtɪsɪp'l) n. a form of a verb that is used in compound tenses or as an adjective. See also **present participle, past participle.** [Latin pars part + capere to take] —,**parti'cipial** adj.

particle ('pɑːtɪk'l) n. **1.** an extremely small piece or amount: food particles; it doesn't make a particle of difference. **2.** Grammar. an uninflected part of speech, such as an interjection or preposition. **3.** Physics. a minute piece of matter, such as an electron or proton. [Latin pars part]

parti-coloured or U.S. **particolored** ('pɑːtɪ,kʌləd) adj. having different colours in different parts. [from obs. party of more than one colour]

particular (pə'tɪkjʊlə) adj. **1.** of or belonging to a single or specific person, thing, or category: the particular demands of the job. **2.** exceptional or marked: a matter of particular importance. **3.** providing specific details or circumstances: a particular account. **4.** difficult to please; fussy. ~n. **5.** a separate distinct item that helps to form a generalization: moving from the general to the particular. **6.** an item of information; detail: complete in every particular. **7.** in particular. especially or exactly: there's one person in particular who may be able to help. [Latin particula a small part] —**par'ticularly** adv.

particularity (pə,tɪkjʊ'lærɪtɪ) n., pl. **-ties. 1.** great attentiveness to detail. **2.** the state or quality of being particular as opposed to general; individuality.

particularize or **-ise** (pə'tɪkjʊlə,raɪz) vb. to give details about (something). —**par,ticulari'zation** or **-i'sation** n.

parting ('pɑːtɪŋ) n. **1.** a departure or leave-taking. **2.** Brit. the line of scalp showing where sections of hair are combed in opposite directions. **3.** the act of dividing (something).

partisan (,pɑːtɪ'zæn, 'pɑːtɪ,zæn) n. **1.** a person who supports a particular cause or party. **2.** a member of an armed resistance group within occupied territory. ~adj. **3.** excessively devoted to a particular cause or party; one-sided. [Latin pars part] —,**parti'sanship** n.

partition (pɑː'tɪʃən) n. **1.** a large screen or thin wall that divides a room in two. **2.** the division of a country into two or more independent countries. ~vb. **3.** (foll. by off) to separate (a room) into sections. [Latin partire to divide]

partitive ('pɑːtɪtɪv) Grammar. ~adj. **1.** (of a noun) referring to part of something. The phrase some of the butter is a partitive construction. ~n. **2.** a partitive word, such as some or any. [Latin partire to divide]

partly ('pɑːtlɪ) adv. not completely.

partner ('pɑːtnə) n. **1.** either member of a couple in a relationship. **2.** a member of a business partnership. **3.** one of a pair of dancers or of players on the same side in a game: my bridge partner. **4.** an ally or companion: a partner in crime. ~vb. **5.** to

be the partner of (someone). [Middle English parcener joint inheritor]

partnership ('pɑːtnəʃɪp) n. **1.** a contractual relationship between two or more people or organizations in a joint business venture. **2.** the condition of being a partner.

part of speech n. Grammar. a class of words, such as a noun, verb, or adjective, sharing important syntactic or semantic features.

partook (pɑː'tʊk) vb. the past tense of **partake.**

partridge ('pɑːtrɪdʒ) n., pl. **-tridges** or **-tridge.** a game bird with an orange-brown head, greyish neck, and a short rust-coloured tail. [Latin perdix]

parts (pɑːts) pl. n. abilities or talents: a man of many parts.

part song n. a song composed in harmonized parts.

part-time adj. **1.** for less than the normal full working time: a part-time job. ~adv. **2.** on a part-time basis: he works part time. —**part-'timer** n.

parturient (pɑː'tjʊərɪənt) adj. giving birth. [Latin parturire to be in labour]

parturition (,pɑːtjʊ'rɪʃən) n. the process of giving birth. [Latin parturire to be in labour]

party ('pɑːtɪ) n., pl. **-ties. 1.** a social gathering for pleasure, often held as a celebration. **2.** a group of people associated in some activity: a rescue party. **3.** a group of people organized together to further a common political aim. **4.** the person or people taking part in legal proceedings: a party to the action. **5.** Informal, humorous. a person: he's an odd old party. ~vb. **-ties, -tying, -tied. 6.** Informal. to celebrate; revel. [Old French partie part]

party line n. **1.** the policies of a political party. **2.** a telephone line serving two or more subscribers.

party wall n. Property law. a wall separating two properties.

par value n. the value imprinted on the face of a share certificate or bond at the time of its issue.

parvenu or (fem.) **parvenue** ('pɑːvə,njuː) n. a person who, having risen socially or economically, is considered to be an upstart. [French]

pas (pɑː) n., pl. **pas.** a dance step. [French]

pascal ('pæsk'l) n. the derived SI unit of pressure; the pressure exerted on an area of 1 square metre by a force of 1 newton. [after B. Pascal, mathematician & scientist]

paschal ('pæsk'l) adj. **1.** of or relating to the Passover. **2.** of or relating to Easter. [Hebrew pesah Passover]

pas de deux (pɑː də 'dɜː) n., pl. **pas de deux.** Ballet. a dance for two people. [French: step for two]

pasha ('pɑːʃə) n. (formerly) a high official of the Ottoman Empire: placed after a name when used as a title. [Turkish paşa]

pas op ('pɑːs ,ɒp) interj. S. African. beware. [Afrikaans]

pasqueflower ('pɑːsk,flaʊə) n. a small

purple-flowered plant of Europe and Asia. [French *passefleur*, changed to *pasqueflower* Easter flower, because it blooms at Easter]

pass (paːs) *vb.* **1.** to go by or past (a person or thing). **2.** to run, extend, or lead (through, over, or across): *the route passes through the city.* **3.** to go through or cause (something) to go through (an obstacle or barrier): *to pass a needle through cloth.* **4.** to move onwards or over: *he passed his hand over her face.* **5.** to exceed: *this victory passes all expectations.* **6.** to gain or cause (someone) to gain an adequate mark or grade in (a test or examination). **7.** (of time) to elapse or to allow (time) to elapse: *we passed the time talking.* **8.** to take place: *what passed at the meeting?* **9.** to transfer or exchange or be transferred or exchanged: *the bomb passed from hand to hand.* **10.** to transfer or be transferred by inheritance: *the house passed to the younger son.* **11.** (of a law-making body) to agree to (a law or proposal): *the assembly passed 10 resolutions.* **12.** to pronounce (judgment): *the court passed sentence.* **13.** to go without comment: *the insult passed unnoticed.* **14.** to opt not to answer a question or not to make a bid or a play in card games. **15.** to discharge (waste matter or blood in the waste matter) from the body. **16.** to come to an end or disappear: *his anger soon passed.* **17.** (foll. by *for* or *as*) to be likely to be mistaken for (someone or something else): *you could easily pass for your sister.* **18.** *Sport.* to hit, kick, or throw (the ball) to another player. **19. pass away** or **on.** *Euphemistic.* to die. ~*n.* **20.** a route through a range of mountains where there is a gap between peaks. **21.** a permit, licence, or authorization to do something without restriction. **22.** *Mil.* a document authorizing leave of absence. **23.** *Brit.* the passing of a college or university examination to a satisfactory standard but not as high as honours. **24.** *Informal.* an attempt to invite sexual intimacy: *he made a pass at his secretary.* **25.** *Sport.* the transfer of a ball from one player to another. **26.** *Bridge, etc.* an instance of opting not to answer a question or not to make a bid or a play in card games. **27. a pretty pass.** a bad state of affairs. ~See also **pass off, pass out,** etc. [Latin *passūs* step]

pass. passive.

passable ('paːsəb'l) *adj.* **1.** adequate or acceptable: *a passable but not outstanding speech.* **2.** (of an obstacle) capable of being crossed. —'**passably** *adv.*

passage ('pæsɪdʒ) *n.* **1.** a channel or opening through or by which someone or something may pass. **2.** a hall or lobby. **3.** a section of a written work, speech, or piece of music. **4.** a journey by ship. **5.** the act or process of passing from one place or condition to another: *passage of a gas through a liquid.* **6.** the permission, right, or freedom to pass: *to be denied passage through a country.* **7.** the enactment of a law by a law-making body. [Old French *passer* to pass]

passageway ('pæsɪdʒ,weɪ) *n.* a long nar-

row space in a building or between buildings; passage.

passbook ('paːs,bʊk) *n.* **1.** a book issued by a building society for keeping a record of deposits and withdrawals. **2.** a book issued with some bank accounts for keeping a record of deposits and withdrawals. **3.** *S. African.* an official identity document.

passé ('pæseɪ) *adj.* out-of-date: *passé ideas.* [French]

passenger ('pæsɪndʒə) *n.* **1.** a person travelling in a vehicle driven by someone else. **2.** *Chiefly Brit.* a member of a team who is not participating fully in the work: *there's no room for passengers on this project.* [Old French *passager* passing]

passer-by (,paːsə'baɪ) *n., pl.* **passers-by.** a person who is walking past someone or something.

passerine ('pæsə,raɪn) *adj.* **1.** of or belonging to an order of perching birds that includes the larks, finches, and starlings. ~*n.* **2.** any bird of this order. [Latin *passer* sparrow]

passim ('pæsɪm) *adv.* throughout: used to indicate that what is referred to occurs frequently in a particular piece of writing. [Latin]

passing ('paːsɪŋ) *adj.* **1.** momentary: *a passing fancy.* **2.** casual: *a passing reference.* ~*n.* **3.** *Euphemistic.* death. **4.** the ending of something: *the passing of the silent film.* **5. in passing.** incidentally: *he mentioned your visit in passing.*

passion ('pæʃən) *n.* **1.** intense sexual love. **2.** a strong enthusiasm for something: *a passion for poetry.* **3.** any strongly felt emotion, such as love, hate, or envy. **4.** the object of an intense desire or enthusiasm: *jazz is his passion.* [Latin *patī* to suffer] —'**passionless** *adj.*

Passion ('pæʃən) *n.* the sufferings of Christ from the Last Supper to his death on the cross.

passionate ('pæʃənɪt) *adj.* **1.** showing intense sexual desire. **2.** capable of or revealing intense emotion: *a passionate plea.* —'**passionately** *adv.*

passionflower ('pæʃən,flaʊə) *n.* a tropical plant with red, yellow, greenish, or purple showy flowers. [parts of the flowers are said to resemble the instruments of the Crucifixion]

passion fruit *n.* the edible egg-shaped fruit of the passionflower.

Passion play *n.* a play about the Passion of Christ.

passive ('pæsɪv) *adj.* **1.** not active in an activity or organization. **2.** unresisting and receptive to outside forces; submissive. **3.** *Grammar.* denoting a form of verbs used to indicate that the subject is the recipient of the action, as *was broken* in *The glass was broken by a boy.* **4.** *Chem.* (of a substance) chemically unreactive. ~*n.* **5.** *Grammar.* the passive form of a verb. [Latin *passīvus* capable of suffering] —'**passively** *adv.* —**pas'sivity** *n.*

passive resistance *n.* resistance to a government, authority, or the law by nonviolent acts such as fasting, peaceful demonstrations, or refusing to cooperate.

passive smoking n. the inhaling of smoke from other people's cigarettes by a nonsmoker.

passkey ('pɑːsˌkiː) n. **1.** a private key; latchkey. **2.** same as **master key** or **skeleton key.**

pass law n. (in South Africa) a law restricting the movement of Black Africans.

pass off vb. **1.** to present (something or oneself) under false pretences: he passed the fake diamonds off as real. **2.** to come to a gradual end; disappear: eventually the pain passed off. **3.** to take place: the meeting passed off without disturbance.

pass out vb. **1.** Informal. to become unconscious; faint. **2.** Brit. (of an officer cadet) to qualify for a military commission.

pass over vb. **1.** to take no notice of; disregard: they passed me over in the last round of promotions. **2.** not to discuss: we shall pass over your former faults.

Passover ('pɑːsˌəʊvə) n. an eight-day Jewish festival commemorating the sparing of the Israelites in Egypt. [pass over, translation of Hebrew pesah]

passport ('pɑːspɔːt) n. **1.** an official document issued by a government, identifying an individual and granting him permission to travel abroad. **2.** a quality or asset that gains a person admission or acceptance: a good education is the passport to success. [French passer to pass + port port]

pass up vb. Informal. to let (something) go by; ignore: I won't pass up this opportunity.

password ('pɑːsˌwɜːd) n. a secret word or phrase that ensures admission by proving identity or membership.

past (pɑːst) adj. **1.** no longer in existence: past happiness. **2.** denoting the time that has elapsed at the present moment: the past history of the world. **3.** denoting a specific unit of time that immediately precedes the present one: the past month. **4.** denoting a person who has formerly held a position: a past president. **5.** Grammar. denoting a tense of verbs that is used in describing actions, events, or states that have been begun or completed at the time of utterance. ~n. **6. the past.** the period of time that has elapsed: forget the past. **7.** the history of a person or nation. **8.** an earlier disreputable period of a person's life: a man with a past. **9.** Grammar. **a.** the past tense. **b.** a verb in the past tense. ~adv. **10.** at a time before the present; ago: three years past. ~prep. **11.** beyond in time: it's past midnight. **12.** beyond in place or position: the library is past the church. **13.** beyond or above the reach, limit, or scope of: his foolishness is past comprehension. **14. not put it past someone.** to consider someone capable of (a particular action): I wouldn't put it past her to cheat. **15. past it.** Informal. unable to perform the tasks one could do when one was younger. [from past]

pasta ('pæstə) n. a type of food, such as spaghetti, that is made from a flour and water dough and formed into different shapes. [Italian]

paste (peɪst) n. **1.** a soft mixture, such as toothpaste. **2.** an adhesive made from water and flour or starch, used for joining pieces of paper. **3.** a preparation of fish or meat that has been pounded to a creamy mass, for spreading on bread: anchovy paste. **4.** dough for making pastry. **5.** a hard shiny glass used for making imitation gems. ~vb. **6.** to attach by or as if by using paste: he pasted posters onto the wall. **7.** Slang. to thrash or beat (someone); defeat. [Greek pasta barley porridge]

pasteboard ('peɪstˌbɔːd) n. a stiff board formed from layers of paper pasted together.

pastel ('pæstʲl) n. **1. a.** a crayon made of ground pigment bound with gum. **b.** a drawing done with such crayons. **2.** a pale delicate colour. ~adj. **3.** (of a colour) pale and delicate: pastel blue. [Latin pasta paste]

pastern ('pæstən) n. the part of a horse's foot between the fetlock and the hoof. [Old French pasture a tether]

paste-up n. Printing. a sheet of paper or board on which are pasted artwork and proofs for photographing prior to making a plate.

pasteurize or **-ise** ('pɑːstjəˌraɪz) vb. to destroy bacteria (in beverages, such as milk or beer, or solid foods, such as cheese or crab meat) by a special heating process. [after Louis Pasteur, chemist] —ˌpasteuri-'zation or-i'sation n.

pastiche (pæˈstiːʃ) n. a work of art that mixes styles or copies the style of another artist. [French]

pastille ('pæstɪl) n. a small fruit-flavoured and sometimes medicated sweet. [Latin pastillus small loaf]

pastime ('pɑːsˌtaɪm) n. an activity or entertainment which makes time pass pleasantly.

past master n. a person with a talent for or experience in a particular activity: a past master at chess.

pastor ('pɑːstə) n. a clergyman in charge of a congregation. [Latin: shepherd]

pastoral ('pɑːstərəl) adj. **1.** of or depicting rural life or scenery. **2.** (of land) used for pasture. **3.** of or relating to a clergyman or his duties. **4.** of or relating to shepherds or their work. ~n. **5.** a literary work, picture, or piece of music portraying rural life. **6.** a letter from a bishop to the clergy or people of his diocese. [Latin pastor shepherd]

pastorale (ˌpæstəˈrɑːl) n., pl. **-rales.** a musical composition that evokes rural life. [Italian]

pastoralism ('pɑːstərəlˌɪzəm) n. a system of agriculture in dry grassland regions based on raising stock such as cattle, sheep, or goats. —'pastoralist n.

pastorate ('pɑːstərɪt) n. **1.** the office or term of office of a pastor. **2.** a group of pastors.

past participle n. a form of verb that is used to form compound past tenses and passive forms of the verb and to modify nouns: *given* is the past participle of *give*.

pastrami (pə'strɑːmɪ) *n.* highly seasoned smoked beef. [Yiddish]

pastry ('peɪstrɪ) *n.* **1.** a dough of flour, water, and fat. **2.** baked foods, such as tarts, made with this dough. **3.** (*pl.* **-tries**) an individual cake or pie. [from *paste*]

pasturage ('pɑːstjərɪdʒ) *n.* **1.** the business of grazing cattle. **2.** same as **pasture**.

pasture ('pɑːstʃə) *n.* **1.** land covered with grass, suitable for grazing by farm animals. **2.** the grass growing on this land. [Latin *pascere* to feed]

pasty[1] ('peɪstɪ) *adj.* **pastier, pastiest.** (of the complexion) pale and unhealthy-looking.

pasty[2] ('pæstɪ) *n.*, *pl.* **pasties.** a round of pastry folded over a filling of meat and vegetables. [Old French *pastée*]

pat[1] (pæt) *vb.* **patting, patted. 1.** to hit (someone or something) lightly with the palm of one's hand. **2.** to shape or smooth (something) with a flat instrument or the palm of one's hand. **3. pat someone on the back.** *Informal.* to congratulate someone. ~*n.* **4.** a gentle tap or stroke. **5.** a small lump of something soft, such as butter. **6. pat on the back.** *Informal.* a gesture or word indicating approval. [prob. imit.]

pat[2] (pæt) *adv.* **1.** Also: **off pat.** exactly or fluently memorized: *he had the answers off pat.* **2. stand pat.** *Chiefly U.S. & Canad.* to stick firmly to a belief or decision. ~*adj.* **3.** exactly right; apt: *a pat reply.* **4.** too exactly fitting; glib: *a pat answer to a difficult problem.* [perhaps adv. use ("with a light stroke") of PAT[1]]

patch (pætʃ) *n.* **1.** a piece of material used to cover a hole in a garment or to make a sewn-on pocket. **2.** a small plot of land. **3.** *Med.* a protective covering for an injured eye. **4.** a small contrasting section: *a patch of cloud in the blue sky.* **5.** a scrap; remnant. **6.** the area patrolled by a particular policeman. **7. a bad patch.** a difficult time. **8. not a patch on.** not nearly as good as. ~*vb.* **9.** to mend (a garment) with a patch or patches. **10.** (foll. by *together*) to produce (something) by piecing parts together hurriedly or carelessly. **11.** (foll. by *up*) **a.** to mend (something) hurriedly or carelessly. **b.** to settle (a quarrel or differences). [perhaps from French *pieche* piece]

patchwork ('pætʃ,wɜːk) *n.* **1.** needlework done by sewing pieces of different materials together. **2.** something made up of various parts.

patchy ('pætʃɪ) *adj.* **patchier, patchiest. 1.** irregular in quality, occurrence or intensity: *a patchy essay.* **2.** having or forming patches.

pate (peɪt) *n.* Old-fashioned or humorous. the head or the crown of the head. [origin unknown]

pâté ('pæteɪ) *n.* a spread of finely minced meat, fish, or vegetables often served as a starter. [French]

pâté de foie gras (də fwɑː grɑː) *n.* a smooth rich paste made from the liver of specially fattened geese. [French: pâté de fat liver]

patella (pə'tɛlə) *n.*, *pl.* **-lae** (-liː). *Anat.* kneecap. [Latin] —**pa'tellar** *adj.*

paten ('pæt'n) *n.* a plate, usually made of silver or gold, used for the bread at Communion. [Latin *patina* pan]

patent ('peɪt'nt, 'pæt'nt) *n.* **1. a.** an official document granting an inventor or company the sole right to make, use, and sell an invention for a limited period. **b.** the right granted by such a document. **2.** an invention protected by a patent. ~*adj.* **3.** open or available for inspection: *letters patent.* **4.** ('peɪt'nt). obvious: *their scorn was patent to everyone.* **5.** concerning protection of or appointment by a patent. **6.** (of food, drugs, etc.) made or held under a patent. ~*vb.* **7.** to obtain a patent for (an invention). [Latin *patēre* to lie open]

patent leather ('peɪt'nt) *n.* leather processed with lacquer to give a hard glossy surface.

patently ('peɪt'ntlɪ) *adv.* obviously: *he was patently bored.*

patent medicine ('peɪt'nt) *n.* a medicine with a patent, available without a prescription.

Patent Office ('pæt'nt) *n.* a government department that issues patents.

pater ('peɪtə) *n.* Brit. slang. father. [Latin]

paternal (pə'tɜːn'l) *adj.* **1.** of or like a father; fatherly: *paternal love.* **2.** related through one's father: *his paternal grandfather.* [Latin *pater* father] —**pa'ternally** *adv.*

paternalism (pə'tɜːnə,lɪzəm) *n.* an attitude of a government or other authority that denies personal responsibility to the people for whom it is responsible. [Latin *pater* father] —**pa,ternal'istic** *adj.*

paternity (pə'tɜːnɪtɪ) *n.* **1.** the fact or state of being a father. **2.** descent or derivation from a father.

paternity suit *n.* legal proceedings, usually brought by an unmarried mother, in order to gain legal recognition that a particular man is the father of her child.

Paternoster (,pætə'nɒstə) *n.* R.C. Church. the Lord's Prayer. [Latin *pater noster* our father]

path (pɑːθ) *n.*, *pl.* **paths** (pɑːðz). **1.** a road or way, often a narrow trodden track. **2.** a surfaced walk, for example through a garden. **3.** the course or direction in which something moves: *the path of a whirlwind.* **4.** a course of conduct: *the path of virtue.* [Old English *pæth*]

pathetic (pə'θɛtɪk) *adj.* **1.** arousing pity or sympathy. **2.** distressingly inadequate or unsuccessful: *the old man sat huddled before a pathetic fire; a pathetic attempt.* [Greek *pathos* suffering] —**pa'thetically** *adv.*

pathetic fallacy *n.* (in literature) the presentation of inanimate objects in nature as possessing human feelings.

pathogen ('pæθə,dʒɛn) *n.* any agent, such as a bacterium, that can cause disease.

[Greek *pathos* suffering + *-gen* (suffix) producing] —**,patho'genic** *adj.*

pathological (,pæθə'lɒdʒɪk'l) *adj.* **1.** of or relating to pathology. **2.** *Informal.* compulsively motivated: *a pathological liar.*

pathology (pə'θɒlədʒɪ) *n.* the branch of medicine concerned with the cause, origin, and nature of disease. [Greek *pathos* suffering + -LOGY] —**pa'thologist** *n.*

pathos ('peɪθɒs) *n.* the quality or power, for example in literature or speech, of arousing feelings of pity or sorrow. [Greek: suffering]

pathway ('pɑːθ,weɪ) *n.* a path.

patience ('peɪʃəns) *n.* **1.** tolerant and even-tempered perseverance. **2.** the capacity for calmly enduring pain or difficult situations, etc. **3.** *Brit.* a card game for one player only. [Latin *pati* to suffer]

patient ('peɪʃənt) *adj.* **1.** enduring difficult situations with even temper. **2.** persevering or diligent: *a patient worker.* ~*n.* **3.** a person who is receiving medical care. —**'patiently** *adv.*

patina ('pætɪnə) *n.* **1.** a film formed on the surface of a metal, such as the green oxidation of bronze or copper. **2.** the sheen on a surface of something, such as an antique, caused by much handling. [Italian: coating]

patio ('pætɪ,əʊ) *n., pl.* **-tios. 1.** a paved area adjoining a house. **2.** an open inner courtyard in a Spanish or Spanish-American house. [Spanish: courtyard]

patisserie (pə'tiːsərɪ) *n.* **1.** a shop where fancy pastries are sold. **2.** such pastries. [French]

patois ('pætwɑː) *n., pl.* **patois** ('pætwɑːz). **1.** a regional dialect of a language, usually considered substandard. **2.** the jargon of a particular group. [Old French]

patrial ('peɪtrɪəl) *n.* (in Britain, formerly) a person with a right by statute to live in the United Kingdom, and so not subject to immigration control. [Latin *patria* native land]

patriarch ('peɪtrɪ,ɑːk) *n.* **1.** the male head of a tribe or family. **2.** *Bible.* any of the men regarded as the fathers of the human race or of the Hebrew people. **3. a.** *R.C. Church.* the pope. **b.** *Eastern Orthodox Church.* a highest-ranking bishop. **3.** a venerable old man. [Church Latin *patriarcha*] —**patri'archal** *adj.*

patriarchate ('peɪtrɪ,ɑːkɪt) *n.* the office, jurisdiction or residence of a patriarch.

patriarchy ('peɪtrɪ,ɑːkɪ) *n.* **1.** a form of social organization in which a male is the head of the family and descent, kinship, and title are traced through the male line. **2.** (*pl.* **-chies**) a society governed by such a system.

patrician (pə'trɪʃən) *n.* **1.** a member of the nobility of ancient Rome. **2.** an aristocrat. **3.** a person of refined conduct and tastes. ~*adj.* **4.** (in ancient Rome) of or relating to patricians. **5.** aristocratic. [Latin *patricius* noble]

patricide ('pætrɪ,saɪd) *n.* **1.** a person who kills his father. **2.** the act of killing one's

father. [Latin *pater* father + *caedere* to kill] —**,patri'cidal** *adj.*

patrimony ('pætrɪmənɪ) *n., pl.* **-nies.** an inheritance from one's father or other ancestor. [Latin *patrimonium* paternal inheritance]

patriot ('peɪtrɪət, 'pæt-) *n.* a person who vigorously supports his country and its way of life. [Greek *patris* native land] —**,patri'otic** *adj.* —**,patri'otically** *adv.* —**'patriot,ism** *n.*

patrol (pə'trəʊl) *n.* **1.** the action of going round an area or building at regular intervals for purposes of security or observation. **2.** a person or group that carries out such an action. **3.** a group of soldiers or ships involved in patrolling a particular area. **4.** a division of a troop of Scouts or Guides. ~*vb.* **-trolling, -trolled. 5.** to engage in a patrol of (a place). [French *patrouiller*]

patrol car *n.* a police car used for patrolling streets.

patron ('peɪtrən) *n.* **1.** a person who financially supports artists, writers, musicians, or charities; protector or benefactor. **2.** a regular customer of a shop, hotel, etc. [Latin *patrōnus* protector]

patronage ('pætrənɪdʒ) *n.* **1.** the support or custom given by a patron. **2.** (in politics) the practice of making appointments to office. **3.** a condescending manner.

patronize or **-ise** ('pætrə,naɪz) *vb.* **1.** to treat (someone) in a condescending way. **2.** to act as a patron by supporting (an artist, etc.) or bringing trade to (a shop, etc.). —**'patron,izing** or **-,ising** *adj.* —**'patron,izingly** or **-,isingly** *adv.*

patron saint *n.* a saint regarded as the particular guardian of a country or a group of people.

patronymic (,pætrə'nɪmɪk) *n.* a name derived from one's father's or a male ancestor's name. [Greek *patēr* father + *onoma* name]

patter¹ ('pætə) *vb.* **1.** to walk with quick soft steps. **2.** to make a quick succession of light tapping sounds. ~*n.* **3.** a quick succession of light tapping sounds, as of feet: *the patter of mice.* [from PAT¹]

patter² ('pætə) *n.* **1.** the glib rapid speech of comedians or salesmen. **2.** quick idle talk; chatter. **3.** the jargon of a particular group. ~*vb.* **4.** to speak glibly and rapidly. [Latin *pater* in *Pater Noster* Our Father]

pattern ('pæt'n) *n.* **1.** an arrangement of repeated or corresponding parts or decorative motifs. **2.** a plan or diagram used in making something: *a paper pattern for a dress.* **3.** a model worthy of imitation: *a pattern of kindness.* **4.** a representative sample. ~*vb.* **5.** (foll. by *after* or *on*) to model: *his behaviour is patterned on his father's.* [Medieval Latin *patrōnus* example]

patty ('pætɪ) *n., pl.* **-ties.** a small meat pie. [French *pâté*]

paua ('pɑʊə) *n.* an edible shellfish of New Zealand, which has an iridescent shell used for jewellery. [Maori]

paucity ('pɔːsɪtɪ) *n.* smallness of amount or number. [Latin *paucus* few]

paunch (pɔːntʃ) *n.* a protruding belly or abdomen. [Latin *panticēs* bowels] —'**paunchy** *adj.*

pauper ('pɔːpə) *n.* **1.** a person who is extremely poor. **2.** (formerly) a person supported by public charity. [Latin: poor]

pause (pɔːz) *vb.* **1.** to cease an action temporarily. **2.** to hesitate: *she replied without pausing.* ~*n.* **3.** a temporary stop or rest in speech or action. **4.** *Music.* a continuation of a note or rest beyond its normal length. **5. give someone pause.** to cause someone to hesitate. [Greek *pausis*]

pavane *or* **pavan** (pə'væn) *n.* **1.** a slow and stately dance of the 16th and 17th centuries. **2.** music for this dance. [Spanish *pavana*]

pave (peɪv) *vb.* **1.** to cover (a road or area of ground) with a firm surface suitable for travelling on, for example with paving stones or concrete. **2. pave the way for.** to prepare or make easier: *to pave the way for future development.* [Old French]

pavement ('peɪvmənt) *n.* **1.** a hard-surfaced path for pedestrians, alongside and a little higher than a road. **2.** the material used in paving. **3.** *U.S.* the surface of a road. [Latin *pavīmentum* hard floor]

pavilion (pə'vɪljən) *n.* **1.** *Brit.* a building at a sports ground, esp. a cricket pitch, in which players can wash and change. **2.** a summerhouse or other decorative shelter. **3.** an open building or temporary structure used for exhibitions. **4.** a large ornate tent. [Latin *pāpiliō* butterfly, tent]

paving ('peɪvɪŋ) *n.* **1.** a paved surface; pavement. **2.** material used for a pavement.

pavlova (pæv'ləʊvə) *n.* a meringue cake topped with whipped cream and fruit. [after Anna *Pavlova*, ballerina]

paw (pɔː) *n.* **1.** any of the feet of a four-legged mammal. **2.** *Informal.* a hand. ~*vb.* **3.** to scrape or hit with the paws. **4.** *Informal.* to touch or caress (someone) in a clumsy, rough, or overfamiliar manner. [Germanic]

pawl (pɔːl) *n.* a pivoted lever shaped to engage with a ratchet wheel to prevent motion in a particular direction. [Dutch *pal*]

pawn[1] (pɔːn) *vb.* **1.** to deposit (an article) as security for the repayment of a loan from a pawnbroker. **2.** to stake: *to pawn one's honour.* ~*n.* **3.** an article deposited as security. **4.** the condition of being so deposited: *in pawn.* [Old French *pan* security]

pawn[2] (pɔːn) *n.* **1.** a chess man of the lowest value. **2.** a person manipulated by another. [Anglo-Norman *poun,* from Medieval Latin *pedō* infantryman]

pawnbroker ('pɔːn,brəʊkə) *n.* a dealer licensed to lend money at interest on the security of personal property, which can be sold if the loan is not repaid within a specified period. —'**pawn,broking** *n.*

pawnshop ('pɔːn,ʃɒp) *n.* the premises of a pawnbroker.

pawpaw ('pɔː,pɔː) *n.* same as **papaya**.

pax (pæks) *n.* **1.** *Chiefly R.C. Church.* the kiss of peace. ~*interj.* **2.** *Brit. school slang.* a call signalling a desire to end hostilities. [Latin: peace]

pay (peɪ) *vb.* **paying, paid. 1.** to settle (a debt or obligation) by giving or doing something: *he paid his creditors.* **2.** to give (money) to (a person) in return for goods or services: *they pay their workers well.* **3.** to profit or benefit (a person): *it pays one to be honest.* **4.** to give (a compliment, regards, attention, etc.). **5.** to make (a visit or call). **6.** to give compensation or make amends: *she paid dearly for her mistake.* **7.** to yield a return of: *the shares pay 15 per cent.* **8. pay one's way. a.** to contribute one's share of expenses. **b.** to remain solvent without outside help. ~*n.* **9.** money given in return for work or services; a salary or wage. **10. in the pay of.** employed by. ~See also **pay back, pay for,** etc. [Latin *pācāre* to appease]

payable ('peɪəb'l) *adj.* **1.** (often foll. by *on*) to be paid: *payable on the third of each month.* **2.** that is capable of being paid.

pay back *vb.* **1.** to retaliate against: *to pay someone back for an insult.* **2.** to repay (a loan).

pay bed *n.* a bed in a hospital used by a patient who is paying for treatment.

PAYE (in Britain and New Zealand) pay as you earn; a system by which income tax is paid by employers directly to the government.

payee (peɪ'iː) *n.* the person to whom a cheque, money order, etc., is made out.

pay for *vb.* **1.** to make payment for. **2.** to suffer or be punished, as for a mistake.

paying guest *n. Euphemistic.* a lodger.

payload ('peɪ,ləʊd) *n.* **1.** that part of a cargo earning revenue. **2.** the passengers, cargo, or bombs carried by an aircraft. **3.** the explosive power of a warhead, bomb, etc., carried by a missile or aircraft.

paymaster ('peɪ,mɑːstə) *n.* an official responsible for the payment of wages and salaries.

payment ('peɪmənt) *n.* **1.** the act of paying. **2.** a sum of money paid. **3.** something given in return; punishment or reward.

pay off *vb.* **1.** to pay (a person) all that is due in wages and dismiss them from employment. **2.** to pay the complete amount of (a debt). **3.** to turn out to be effective: *the gamble paid off.* **4.** *Informal.* to give a bribe to. ~*n.* **payoff. 5.** the final settlement, esp. in retribution. **6.** *Informal.* the climax, consequence, or outcome of events, a story, etc. **7.** the final payment of a debt. **8.** *Informal.* a bribe.

payola (peɪ'əʊlə) *n. Informal.* a bribe given to secure special treatment, esp. to a disc jockey to promote a commercial product.

pay out *vb.* **1.** to spend (money) on a particular thing. **2.** to release (a rope) gradually, hand over hand.

payphone ('peɪ,fəʊn) *n.* a coin-operated telephone.

payroll ('peɪˌrəʊl) n. a list of employees, specifying the salary or wage of each.

payslip ('peɪˌslɪp) n. a note given to an employee each week or month stating how much money he has earned and how much tax, national insurance, etc., has been deducted.

pay up vb. to pay (money) promptly, in full, or on demand.

Pb Chem. lead. [New Latin plumbum]

pc 1. per cent. 2. postcard.

PC 1. (in Britain) Police Constable. 2. (in Britain) Privy Council(lor). 3. (in Canada) Progressive Conservative.

pd paid.

Pd Chem. palladium.

PDSA (in Britain) People's Dispensary for Sick Animals.

PDT (in the U.S. and Canada) Pacific Daylight Time.

PE physical education.

pea (piː) n. 1. an annual climbing plant with green pods containing green seeds. 2. the seed of this plant, eaten as a vegetable. [from pease (incorrectly assumed to be a pl.)]

peace (piːs) n. 1. the state existing during the absence of war. 2. a treaty marking the end of a war. 3. a state of harmony between people or groups. 4. law and order within a state: a breach of the peace. 5. absence of mental anxiety: peace of mind. 6. a state of stillness, silence, or serenity. 7. **at peace. a.** dead: the old lady is at peace now. **b.** in a state of harmony, friendship, or serenity. 8. **hold** or **keep one's peace.** to keep silent. 9. **keep the peace.** to maintain law and order. [Latin pāx]

peaceable ('piːsəb'l) adj. 1. inclined towards peace. 2. tranquil; calm.

peaceful ('piːsful) adj. 1. not in a state of war or disagreement. 2. calm; tranquil. —'**peacefully** adv.

peacemaker ('piːsˌmeɪkə) n. a person who establishes peace, esp. between others.

peace offering n. something given in order to maintain or bring about peace: I bought Mum some flowers as a peace offering.

peace pipe n. a long decorated pipe smoked by North American Indians, esp. as a token of peace.

peacetime ('piːsˌtaɪm) n. a period without war; time of peace.

peach (piːtʃ) n. 1. a soft juicy fruit with a downy reddish-yellow skin, yellowish-orange sweet flesh, and a single stone which grows on a small tree. 2. Informal. a person or thing that is especially pleasing: that was a peach of a shot! ~adj. 3. pinkish-yellow to orange. [Latin Persicum mālum Persian apple]

peach melba n. a dessert made of halved peaches, vanilla ice cream, and raspberries.

peachy ('piːtʃɪ) adj. **peachier, peachiest.** of or like a peach, esp. in colour or texture.

peacock ('piːˌkɒk) n., pl. **-cocks** or **-cock.**

1. a large bird of the pheasant family, the male of which has a crested head and a very large fanlike tail with blue and green eyelike spots. 2. a vain strutting person. [Latin pāvō peacock + cock] —'**pea,hen** fem. n.

pea-green adj. yellowish-green.

peak (piːk) n. 1. a pointed end, edge, or projection: the peak of a roof. 2. the pointed summit of a mountain. 3. a mountain with a pointed summit. 4. the point of greatest development, strength, etc.: the peak of his career. 5. a projecting piece on the front of some caps. ~vb. 6. to reach or cause to form or reach a peak. ~adj. 7. of or relating to a period of greatest use or demand: peak viewing hours. [perhaps from pike (the weapon)]

peaked (piːkt) adj. having a peak; pointed.

peak load n. the maximum load on an electrical power-supply system.

peaky ('piːkɪ) adj. **peakier, peakiest.** pale and sickly. [origin unknown]

peal (piːl) n. 1. a long loud echoing sound, as of bells, thunder, or laughter. ~vb. 2. to sound with a peal or peals. [Middle English pele]

peanut ('piːˌnʌt) n. a leguminous plant with edible nutlike seeds used for food and as a source of oil. See also **peanuts.**

peanut butter n. a brownish oily paste made from peanuts.

peanuts ('piːˌnʌts) n. Slang. a trifling amount of money.

pear (peə) n. a sweet juicy fruit with a narrow top and a rounded base that grows on a tree of the rose family. [Latin pirum]

pearl (pɜːl) n. 1. a hard smooth greyish-white rounded structure occurring on the inner surface of the shell of a clam or oyster; much valued as a gem. 2. See **mother-of-pearl.** 3. a person or thing that is like a pearl, esp. in beauty or value. ~adj. 4. of, made of, or set with pearl or mother-of-pearl. 5. having the shape or colour of a pearl. ~vb. 6. to set with or as if with pearls. 7. to shape into or assume a pearl-like form or colour. 8. to dive for pearls. [Latin perna sea mussel]

pearl barley n. barley ground into small round grains, used esp. in soups and stews.

pearly ('pɜːlɪ) adj. **pearlier, pearliest.** 1. resembling a pearl, esp. in lustre. 2. decorated with pearls or mother-of-pearl.

Pearly Gates pl. n. Informal. the entrance to heaven.

pearly king or (fem.) **pearly queen** n. the London costermonger whose ceremonial clothes display the most lavish collection of pearl buttons.

peasant ('pez²nt) n. 1. a member of a class of low social status that depends on agricultural labour as a means of subsistence. 2. Informal. an uncouth or uncultured person. [Old French païsant]

peasantry ('pez²ntrɪ) n. peasants as a class.

pease (piːz) n., pl. **pease.** Archaic or dialect. same as **pea.** [Old English peose]

pease pudding n. (esp. in Britain) a

dish of split peas that have been soaked and boiled.

peasouper (ˌpiːˈsuːpə) n. 1. Informal, chiefly Brit. dense dirty yellowish fog. 2. Canad. slang. a French Canadian.

peat (piːt) n. a compact brownish deposit of partially decomposed vegetable matter found in uplands and bogs and used as a fuel (when dried) and as a fertilizer. [perhaps Celtic]

pebble (ˈpebʰl) n. 1. a small smooth rounded stone, esp. one worn by the action of water. ~vb. 2. to cover with pebbles. [Old English papolstān pebble stone] —ˈpebbly adj.

pebble dash n. Brit. a finish for external walls consisting of small stones embedded in plaster.

pecan (pɪˈkæn, ˈpiːkən) n. a smooth oval nut with a sweet oily kernel that grows on hickory trees in the Southern U.S. [American Indian paccan]

peccadillo (ˌpekəˈdɪləʊ) n., pl. -los or -loes. a petty sin or fault. [Spanish, from Latin peccāre to sin]

peccary (ˈpekərɪ) n., pl. -ries or -ry. a piglike mammal of forests of southern North America, Central and South America. [Carib]

peck[1] (pek) n. 1. a unit of dry measure equal to 8 quarts or one quarter of a bushel. 2. a large quantity or number. [Anglo-Norman]

peck[2] (pek) vb. 1. to strike with the beak or with a pointed instrument. 2. to dig (a hole, etc.) by pecking. 3. (of birds) to pick up (corn, worms, etc.) by pecking. 4. Informal. to kiss (a person) quickly and lightly. 5. **peck at.** to eat slowly and reluctantly: peck at food. ~n. 6. a quick light blow, esp. a bird's beak. 7. a mark made by such a blow. 8. Informal. a quick light kiss. [origin unknown]

pecker (ˈpekə) n. **keep one's pecker up.** Brit. slang. to remain cheerful.

peckish (ˈpekɪʃ) adj. Informal, chiefly Brit. feeling slightly hungry.

pectin (ˈpektɪn) n. Biochem. a water-soluble carbohydrate that occurs in ripe fruit: used in the manufacture of jams because of its ability to gel. [Greek pēktos congealed]

pectoral (ˈpektərəl) adj. 1. of or relating to the chest, breast, or thorax: pectoral fins. 2. worn on the breast or chest: a pectoral medallion. ~n. 3. a pectoral organ or part, esp. a muscle or fin. [Latin pectus breast]

pectoral fin n. a fin, just behind the head in fishes, that helps to control the direction of movement.

peculate (ˈpekjʊˌleɪt) vb. to embezzle (public money). [Latin pecūlārī] —ˈpecuˈlation n.

peculiar (pɪˈkjuːlɪə) adj. 1. strange or unusual; odd: a peculiar idea. 2. distinct from others; special. 3. (foll. by to) belonging characteristically or exclusively (to): peculiar to North America. [Latin pecūliāris concerning private property]

peculiarity (pɪˌkjuːlɪˈærɪtɪ) n., pl. -ties. 1.

a strange or unusual habit or characteristic. 2. a distinguishing trait, etc., that is characteristic of a particular person; idiosyncrasy. 3. the state or quality of being peculiar.

pecuniary (pɪˈkjuːnɪərɪ) adj. 1. of or relating to money. 2. Law. (of an offence) involving a monetary penalty. [Latin pecūnia money]

pedagogue or U.S. (sometimes) **pedagog** (ˈpedəˌgɒg) n. a teacher, esp. a pedantic one. [Greek pais boy + agōgos leader] —ˌpedaˈgogic adj.

pedagogy (ˈpedəˌgɒdʒɪ) n. the principles, practice, or profession of teaching.

pedal[1] (ˈpedʰl) n. 1. any foot-operated lever, esp. one of the two levers that drive the chainwheel of a bicycle, the foot brake, clutch control, or accelerator of a car, or one of the levers on an organ or piano. ~vb. -alling, -alled or U.S. -aling, -aled. 2. to propel (a bicycle, etc.) by operating the pedals. 3. to operate the pedals of an organ, piano, etc. [Latin pedālis, from pes foot]

pedal[2] (ˈpiːdʰl) adj. of the foot or feet. [Latin pedālis, from pēs foot]

pedant (ˈpedʰnt) n. a person who relies too much on academic learning or who is concerned chiefly with insignificant detail. [Italian pedante teacher] —**pedantic** (pɪˈdæntɪk) adj. —peˈdantically adv.

pedantry (ˈpedʰntrɪ) n., pl. -ries. the habit or an instance of being a pedant, esp. in the minute observance of petty rules or details.

peddle (ˈpedʰl) vb. 1. to go from place to place selling (goods, esp. small articles). 2. to sell (illegal drugs, esp. narcotics). 3. to advocate (an idea or information) persistently: to peddle a new philosophy. [from pedlar]

pederasty or **paederasty** (ˈpedəˌræstɪ) n. homosexual relations between men and boys. [Greek pais boy + erastēs lover] —ˈpederˌast or ˈpaederˌast n.

pedestal (ˈpedɪstʰl) n. 1. a base that supports something, such as a statue. 2. **put someone on a pedestal.** to admire someone very much. [Old Italian piedestallo]

pedestrian (pɪˈdestrɪən) n. 1. a person travelling on foot; walker. ~adj. 2. dull; commonplace: a pedestrian style. [Latin pēs foot]

pedestrian crossing n. Brit. a path across a road marked as a crossing for pedestrians.

pedestrianize or **-ise** (pɪˈdestrɪəˌnaɪz) vb. to convert (a street or shopping area) into an area for the use of pedestrians only.

pedicure (ˈpedɪˌkjʊə) n. treatment of the feet, either by a medical expert or a beautician. [Latin pēs foot + curāre to care for]

pedigree (ˈpedɪˌgriː) n. 1. the line of descent of a purebred animal. 2. a document recording this. 3. a genealogical table, esp. one indicating pure ancestry. [Old French pie de grue crane's foot, allud-

ing to the spreading lines used in a genealogical chart]

pediment (ˈpɛdɪmənt) n. a low-pitched
gable, esp. one that is triangular as used in
classical architecture. [obs. *periment*, perhaps workman's corruption of *pyramid*]

pedlar or esp. U.S. **peddler** (ˈpɛdlə) n. a
person who peddles; hawker. [Middle English *ped* basket]

pedometer (pɪˈdɒmɪtə) n. a device that
records the number of steps taken in walking and hence the distance travelled. [Latin
pes foot + -METER]

peduncle (pɪˈdʌŋkˀl) n. 1. the stalk of a
plant bearing a flower cluster or solitary
flower. 2. *Anat., pathol.* any stalklike
structure. [Latin *pedūnculus* little foot]
—**peduncular** (pɪˈdʌŋkjʊlə) adj.

pee (piː) *Informal.* ~vb. **peeing, peed.** 1.
to urinate. ~n. 2. urine. 3. the act of
urinating. [euphemistic for *piss*]

peek (piːk) vb. 1. to glance quickly or
furtively. ~n. 2. such a glance. [Middle
English *pike*]

peel (piːl) vb. 1. to remove (the skin or
rind) of (a fruit or vegetable). 2. (of a
surface) to lose its outer covering of paint,
etc. 3. (of a person or part of the body) to
shed skin in flakes or (of skin) to be shed in
flakes, esp. as a result of sunburn. ~n. 4.
the skin or rind of a fruit, etc. [Latin
pilāre to make bald]

peeling (ˈpiːlɪŋ) n. a strip of skin, rind,
bark, etc., that has been peeled off: *a
potato peeling.*

peel off vb. 1. to remove or be removed
by peeling: *I peeled some moss off the
wood.* 2. *Slang.* to undress.

peen (piːn) n. the end of a hammer head
opposite the striking face, often rounded or
wedge-shaped. [origin unknown]

peep¹ (piːp) vb. 1. to look furtively or
secretly, as through a small opening or
from a hidden place. 2. to appear partially
or briefly: *the sun peeped through the
clouds.* ~n. 3. a quick or furtive look. 4.
the first appearance: *the peep of dawn.*
[var. of *peek*]

peep² (piːp) vb. 1. (esp. of young birds) to
utter shrill small noises. ~n. 2. a peeping
sound. [imit.]

Peeping Tom n. a man who furtively
observes women undressing. [after the
tailor who, according to legend, peeped at
Lady Godiva when she rode naked through
Coventry]

peepshow (ˈpiːpˌʃəʊ) n. a box containing a
series of pictures that can be seen through
a small hole.

peer¹ (pɪə) n. 1. a member of a nobility. 2.
a person who holds any of the five grades
of the British nobility: duke, marquess,
earl, viscount, and baron. 3. an equal in
social standing, rank, age, etc.: *to be tried
by one's peers.* [Latin *pār* equal]

peer² (pɪə) vb. 1. to look intently or as if
with difficulty: *to peer into the distance.*
2. to appear dimly: *the sun peered through
the fog.* [Flemish *pieren* to look with
narrowed eyes]

peerage (ˈpɪərɪdʒ) n. 1. the whole body of

peers; aristocracy. 2. the position, rank,
or title of a peer.

peeress (ˈpɪərɪs) n. 1. the wife or widow
of a peer. 2. a woman holding the rank of
a peer in her own right.

peer group n. a social group composed
of individuals of approximately the same
age.

peerless (ˈpɪəlɪs) adj. having no equals;
matchless.

peeve (piːv) *Informal.* ~vb. 1. to irritate; annoy. ~n. 2. something that irritates; vexation. [from *peevish*] —**peeved**
adj.

peevish (ˈpiːvɪʃ) adj. fretful or irritable.
[origin unknown] —**peevishly** adv.

peewit or **pewit** (ˈpiːwɪt) n. same as
lapwing. [imit. of its call]

peg (pɛg) n. 1. a small cylindrical pin or
bolt used to join two parts together. 2. a
pin driven into a surface: used to mark
scores, define limits, support coats, etc. 3.
Music. any of several pins on a stringed
instrument which can be turned so as to
tune strings wound around them. 4. Also
called: **clothes peg.** *Brit.* a split or hinged
pin for fastening wet clothes to a line to
dry. 5. *Brit.* a small drink of spirits. 6. an
opportunity or pretext for doing something: *a peg on which to hang a theory.* 7.
bring or **take (someone) down a peg.** to
lower the pride of (someone). 8. **off the
peg.** *Chiefly Brit.* (of clothes) ready-to-
wear, as opposed to tailor-made. ~vb.
pegging, pegged. 9. to insert a peg into.
10. to secure with pegs: *to peg a tent.* 11.
to mark (a score) with pegs, as in some
card games. 12. *Chiefly Brit.* to work
steadily: *he pegged away at his job for
years.* 13. to stabilize something, such as
the price of a commodity, at a fixed level.
[Low Germanic *pegge*]

pegboard (ˈpɛgˌbɔːd) n. 1. a board with
holes into which small pegs can be fitted,
used for playing certain games or keeping a
score. 2. hardboard with a row of holes in
which articles may be hung, as for display.

peg leg n. *Informal.* 1. an artificial leg.
2. a person with an artificial leg.

peg out vb. *Informal.* 1. to collapse or
die. 2. to mark or secure with pegs: *to peg
out one's claims to a piece of land.*

PEI Prince Edward Island.

peignoir (ˈpeɪnwɑː) n. a woman's dressing
gown. [French]

pejorative (pɪˈdʒɒrətɪv, ˈpiːdʒər-) adj. 1.
(of a word or expression) having an unpleasant or disparaging sense. ~n. 2. a
pejorative word or expression. [Late Latin
pējōrāre to make worse]

peke (piːk) n. *Informal.* a Pekingese dog.

Pekingese (ˌpiːkɪŋˈiːz) or **Pekinese**
(ˌpiːkəˈniːz) n. 1. (pl. **-ese**) a small dog
with a long straight coat, curled plumed
tail, and short wrinkled muzzle. 2. the
dialect of Mandarin Chinese spoken in
Peking. 3. (pl. **-ese**) a person from Peking,
in NE China. ~adj. 4. of Peking or its
people.

pelargonium (ˌpɛləˈgəʊnɪəm) n. a plant
with circular or lobed leaves and red, pink,

or white aromatic flowers: includes many cultivated geraniums. [Greek *pelargos* stork]

pelf (pelf) *n. Contemptuous.* money or wealth. [Old French *pelfre* booty]

pelican ('pɛlɪkən) *n.* a large water bird with a long straight flattened bill and a pouch for holding fish. [Greek *pelekān*]

pelican crossing *n.* a type of road crossing with a pedestrian-operated traffic-light system. [from *pe(destrian) li(ght) con(trolled) crossing,* with *-con* adapted to *-can* of *pelican*]

pelisse (pɛ'liːs) *n.* a usually fur-trimmed cloak or loose coat. [French, from Latin *pellis* skin]

pellagra (pə'leɪgrə, -'læ-) *n. Pathol.* a disease caused by a diet lacking a vitamin of the B complex, characterized by scaling of the skin, diarrhoea and mental disorder. [Italian, from *pelle* skin + Greek *agra* paroxysm]

pellet ('pɛlɪt) *n.* **1.** a small round ball, esp. of compressed matter. **2. a.** an imitation bullet used in toy guns. **b.** a piece of small shot. **3.** a small pill. [Latin *pila* ball]

pell-mell ('pɛl'mɛl) *adv.* **1.** in a confused headlong rush: *the hounds ran pell-mell into the yard.* **2.** in a disorderly manner: *the things were piled pell-mell in the room.* [Old French *pesle-mesle*]

pellucid (pɛ'luːsɪd) *adj.* **1.** transparent or translucent. **2.** extremely clear in style and meaning. [Latin *pellūcidus*]

pelmet ('pɛlmɪt) *n.* a board or piece of fabric fixed above a window to conceal the curtain rail. [prob. from French *palmette* palm-leaf decoration on cornice moulding]

pelota (pə'lɒtə) *n.* a game played by two players who use a basket strapped to their wrists or a wooden racket to propel a ball against a specially marked wall. [Spanish: ball]

pelt[1] (pɛlt) *vb.* **1.** to throw (missiles) at (someone or something). **2.** (foll. by *along,* etc.) to hurry. **3.** to rain heavily. ~*n.* **4.** a blow. **5.** *at full pelt.* very quickly: *she ran down the street at full pelt.* [origin unknown]

pelt[2] (pɛlt) *n.* **1.** the skin of a fur-bearing animal, esp. when it has been removed from the carcass. **2.** the hide of an animal, stripped of hair. [prob. from Latin *pellis* skin]

pelvis ('pɛlvɪs) *n.* **1.** the large funnel-shaped structure at the lower end of the trunk of most vertebrates. **2.** the bones that form this structure. [Latin: basin] —**pelvic** *adj.*

pen[1] (pɛn) *n.* **1.** an implement for writing or drawing using ink, with a metal nib attached to a holder. See also **ballpoint, fountain pen. 2. the pen.** writing as an occupation. ~*vb.* **penning, penned. 3.** to write or compose (a letter). [Latin *penna* feather]

pen[2] (pɛn) *n.* **1.** an enclosure in which domestic animals are kept. **2.** any place of confinement. ~*vb.* **penning, penned** or **pent. 3.** to enclose (animals) in a pen. [Old English *penn*]

pen[3] (pɛn) *n. U.S. & Canad. informal.* short for **penitentiary** (sense 1).

pen[4] (pɛn) *n.* a female swan. [origin unknown]

Pen. Peninsula.

penal ('piːn'l) *adj.* **1.** of or relating to punishment. **2.** used or designated as a place of punishment: *a penal institution.* [Latin *poena* penalty] —**penally** *adv.*

penal code *n.* the body of the laws that relate to crime and its punishment.

penalize or **-ise** ('piːnə,laɪz) *vb.* **1.** to impose a penalty on (someone), as for breaking a law or rule. **2.** to inflict a disadvantage on: *why should I be penalized just because I'm a woman?* —**penalization** or **-isation** *n.*

penalty ('pɛn'ltɪ) *n., pl.* **-ties. 1.** a legal punishment, such as a term of imprisonment or a fine. **2.** loss, suffering, or other unfortunate result of one's own action, error, etc: *I made a wrong decision and I had to pay the penalty.* **3.** *Sport, games, etc.* a handicap awarded against a player or team for illegal play, such as a free shot at goal by the opposing team. [Latin *poena*]

penalty box *n.* **1.** Also called: **penalty area.** *Soccer.* a rectangular area in front of the goal, within which a penalty is awarded for a foul by the defending team. **2.** *Ice hockey.* a bench for players serving time penalties.

penance ('pɛnəns) *n.* **1.** voluntary self-punishment to make amends for a sin. **2.** *R.C. Church.* a sacrament in which repentant sinners are absolved on condition of confession of their sins to a priest and of performing a penance. [Latin *paenitentia* repentancy]

pence (pɛns) *n.* a plural of **penny.**

penchant ('pɒŋʃɒn) *n.* strong inclination or liking; bent or taste. [French]

pencil ('pɛns'l) *n.* **1.** a thin cylindrical instrument used for writing or drawing, consisting of a rod of graphite encased in wood and sharpened. ~*vb.* **-cilling, -cilled** or *U.S.* **-ciling, -ciled. 2.** to draw, colour, write, or mark with a pencil. [Latin *pēnicillus* painter's brush]

pendant ('pɛndənt) *n.* **a.** an ornament that hangs from a piece of jewellery. **b.** a necklace with such an ornament. [Latin *pendēre* to hang down]

pendent ('pɛndənt) *adj.* **1.** dangling. **2.** jutting. [see PENDANT]

pending ('pɛndɪŋ) *prep.* **1.** while waiting for. ~*adj.* **2.** not yet decided, confirmed, or finished. **3.** imminent: *these developments have been pending for some time.*

pendulous ('pɛndjʊləs) *adj.* hanging downwards, esp. so as to swing from side to side. [Latin *pendēre* to hang down]

pendulum ('pɛndjʊləm) *n.* **1.** a body mounted so that it can swing freely under the influence of gravity. **2.** such a device used to regulate a clock mechanism.

penetrate ('pɛnɪ,treɪt) *vb.* **1.** to find or force a way into or through (something). **2.** to diffuse through (a substance, etc.); permeate. **3.** to see through: *their eyes* could not penetrate the fog. **4.** (of a man) to insert the penis into the vagina of (a woman). **5.** to grasp the meaning of (a principle, etc.). [Latin *penetrāre*] —'**penetrable** *adj.*

penetrating ('penɪˌtreɪtɪŋ) *adj.* tending to or able to penetrate: *a penetrating mind; a penetrating voice.*

penetration (ˌpenɪ'treɪʃən) *n.* **1.** the act or an instance of penetrating. **2.** the ability or power to penetrate. **3.** keen insight or perception.

pen friend *n.* a person with whom one exchanges letters, often a person in another country whom one has not met.

penguin ('peŋgwɪn) *n.* a flightless marine bird of cool southern, esp. Antarctic, regions with webbed feet and wings modified as flippers for swimming. [origin unknown]

penicillin (ˌpenɪ'sɪlɪn) *n.* an antibiotic used to treat diseases caused by bacteria. [Latin *pēncillus* tuft of hairs]

peninsula (pɪ'nɪnsjʊlə) *n.* a narrow strip of land projecting into a sea or lake from the mainland. [Latin, lit.: almost an island] —'**peninsular** *adj.*

penis ('piːnɪs) *n.*, *pl.* -**nises** *or* -**nes** (-niːz). the male organ of copulation in higher vertebrates, also used for urinating in many mammals. [Latin] —**penile** ('piːnaɪl) *adj.*

penitent ('penɪtənt) *adj.* **1.** feeling regret for one's sins; repentant. ~*n.* **2.** a person who is penitent. [Church Latin *paenitēns* regretting] —'**penitence** *n.*

penitential (ˌpenɪ'tenʃəl) *adj.* of, showing, or as a penance.

penitentiary (ˌpenɪ'tenʃərɪ) *n.*, *pl.* -**ries**. **1.** (in the U.S. and Canada) a state or federal prison. ~*adj.* **2.** of or for penance. **3.** used for punishment and reformation: *penitentiary measures.* [Latin *paenitēns* penitent]

penknife ('penˌnaɪf) *n.*, *pl.* -**knives**. a small knife with one or more blades that fold into the handle.

penmanship ('penmənʃɪp) *n.* style or technique of writing by hand.

pen name *n.* a name used by a writer instead of his real name; nom de plume.

pennant ('penənt) *n.* **1.** a long flag, esp. one flown from vessels as identification or for signalling. **2.** *Chiefly U.S., Canad., & Austral.* a flag serving as an emblem of championship in certain sports. [prob. a blend of *pendant & pennon*]

penniless ('penɪlɪs) *adj.* very poor; almost totally without money.

pennon ('penən) *n.* **1.** a long flag, often tapering and divided at the end, originally a knight's personal flag. **2.** a small tapering or triangular flag borne on a ship or boat. [Latin *penna* feather]

penny ('penɪ) *n.*, *pl.* **pennies** *or* **pence** (pens). **1.** *Brit.* **a.** a bronze coin worth one hundredth of a pound. **b.** (before 1971) a bronze or copper coin worth one twelfth of a shilling. **2.** (*pl.* **pennies**). *U.S. & Canad.* a cent. **3.** *Informal, chiefly Brit.* the least amount of money: *I don't have a penny.* **4.**

a pretty penny. *Informal.* a considerable sum of money. **5. spend a penny.** *Brit. informal.* to urinate. **6. the penny dropped.** *Informal, chiefly Brit.* the explanation of something was finally realized. [Old English *penig, pening*]

Penny Black *n.* the first adhesive postage stamp, issued in Britain in 1840.

penny-dreadful *n.*, *pl.* -**fuls**. *Brit. informal.* a cheap, often lurid book or magazine.

penny-farthing *n. Brit.* an early type of bicycle with a large front wheel and a small rear wheel.

penny-pinching *adj.* **1.** excessively careful with money; miserly. ~*n.* **2.** miserliness. —'**penny-ˌpincher** *n.*

pennyroyal (ˌpenɪ'rɔɪəl) *n.* a Eurasian plant with hairy leaves and small mauve flowers, yielding an aromatic oil used in medicine. [Old French *pouliol + real* royal]

penny-wise *adj.* **penny-wise and pound-foolish.** careful or thrifty in small matters but wasteful in large ventures.

pennywort ('penɪˌwɜːt) *n.* a Eurasian rock plant with whitish-green tubular flowers and rounded leaves.

pennyworth ('penɪˌwɜːθ) *n.* **1.** the amount that can be bought for a penny. **2.** a small amount: *he hasn't got a pennyworth of sense.*

penology (piː'nɒlədʒɪ) *n.* the study of the punishment of criminals and of prison management. [Greek *poinē* punishment]

pen pal *n.* same as **pen friend.**

penpusher ('penˌpʊʃə) *n.* a person whose work involves a lot of boring paperwork. —'**pen-ˌpushing** *adj.*, *n.*

pension[1] ('penʃən) *n.* **1.** a regular payment made by the state or a former employer to a person who has retired or to a widowed or disabled person. ~*vb.* **2.** to grant a pension to. [Latin *pēnsiō* a payment] —'**pensionable** *adj.* —'**pensioner** *n.*

pension[2] ('pɒnsjɒn) *n.* (in France and some other countries) a relatively cheap boarding house. [French: extended meaning of *pension* grant]

pension off *vb.* to cause (someone) to retire from a job and pay him pension.

pensive ('pensɪv) *adj.* deeply or seriously thoughtful, often with a tinge of sadness. [Latin *pensāre* to consider] —'**pensively** *adv.*

pent (pent) *vb.* past of **pen**[2].

penta- *combining form.* five: *pentagon; pentameter.* [Greek *pente*]

pentacle ('pentək'l) *n.* same as **pentagram.** [Italian *pentacolo* something having five corners]

pentagon ('pentəˌgɒn) *n.* a polygon having five sides. —**pentagonal** (pen'tægən'l) *adj.*

Pentagon ('pentəˌgɒn) *n.* a five-sided building that houses the headquarters of the U.S. Department of Defense.

pentagram ('pentəˌgræm) *n.* a star-shaped figure with five points.

pentameter (pɛn'tæmɪtə) n. a line of poetry consisting of five metrical feet.

Pentateuch ('pɛntə,tjuːk) n. the first five books of the Old Testament. [Greek *pente* five + *teukhos* scroll] —**,Penta'teuchal** adj.

pentathlon (pɛn'tæθlən) n. any of various athletic contests consisting of five different events. See also **modern pentathlon**. [Greek *pente* five + *athlon* contest]

pentatonic scale (,pɛntə'tɒnɪk) n. Music. any of several scales consisting of five notes.

Pentecost ('pɛntɪ,kɒst) n. a Christian festival occurring on Whit Sunday commemorating the descent of the Holy Ghost on the apostles. [Greek *pentēkostē* fiftieth (day after the Resurrection)]

Pentecostal (,pɛntɪ'kɒst'l) adj. of or relating to any of various Christian groups that emphasize the charismatic aspects of Christianity and adopt a fundamental attitude to the Bible.

penthouse ('pɛnt,haʊs) n. a luxurious flat or maisonette built onto the top floor or roof of a block of flats. [Middle English *pentis* (later *penthouse*), from Latin *appendere* to hang from]

pent-up adj. not released; repressed: *pent-up emotions.*

penultimate (pɪ'nʌltɪmɪt) adj. next to the last.

penumbra (pɪ'nʌmbrə) n., pl. **-brae** (-briː) or **-bras**. 1. a fringe region of half shadow resulting from the partial obstruction of light by an opaque object. 2. Astron. the lighter and outer region of a sunspot. [Latin *paene* almost + *umbra* shadow] —**pe'numbral** adj.

penurious (pɪ'njʊərɪəs) adj. 1. niggardly with money. 2. lacking money or means.

penury ('pɛnjʊrɪ) n. 1. extreme poverty. 2. extreme scarcity. [Latin *pēnūria*]

peon ('piːɒn) n. a Spanish-American farm labourer or unskilled worker. [Spanish]

peony ('piːənɪ) n., pl. **-nies**. a garden plant with large pink, red, white, or yellow flowers. [Greek *paiōnia*]

people ('piːp'l) n. (usually functioning as pl.) 1. persons collectively or in general. 2. a group of persons considered together: *blind people.* 3. (pl. **peoples**) the persons living in a particular country: *the French people.* 4. one's family: *he took her home to meet his people.* 5. **the people. a.** the mass of persons without special distinction or privileges. **b.** the body of persons in a country who are entitled to vote. ~vb. 6. to provide with or as if with people or inhabitants. [Latin *populus*]

pep (pɛp) n. 1. high spirits, energy, or vitality. 2. **pep up.** to stimulate; invigorate: *to pep up a party.* [short for *pepper*]

peplum ('pɛpləm) n., pl. **-lums** or **-la** (-lə). a flared ruffle attached to the waist of a garment. [Greek *peplos* shawl]

pepper ('pɛpə) n. 1. a sharp hot condiment obtained from the ground berry-like fruits of an East Indian climbing plant. 2. Also called: **capsicum**. a tropical fruit used as a vegetable and a condiment, which can have either a mild or a pungent taste. ~vb. 3. to season with pepper. 4. to sprinkle liberally; dot: *his prose was peppered with alliteration.* 5. to pelt with small missiles. [Greek *peperi*]

pepper-and-salt adj. 1. (of a fabric) marked with a fine mixture of black and white. 2. (of hair) streaked with grey.

peppercorn ('pɛpə,kɔːn) n. the small dried berry of the pepper plant.

peppercorn rent n. a rent that is very low or nominal.

pepper mill n. a small hand mill used to grind peppercorns.

peppermint ('pɛpə,mɪnt) n. 1. a mint plant with purple or white flowers and downy leaves, which yield a pungent oil, used as a flavouring. 2. a sweet flavoured with peppermint.

peppery ('pɛpərɪ) adj. 1. flavoured with or tasting of pepper. 2. quick-tempered; irritable.

pep pill n. Informal. a tablet containing a stimulant drug.

pepsin ('pɛpsɪn) n. an enzyme produced in the stomach, which, when activated by acid, breaks down proteins. [Greek *peptein* to digest]

pep talk n. Informal. an enthusiastic talk designed to increase confidence, production, cooperation, etc.

peptic ('pɛptɪk) adj. 1. of or aiding digestion. 2. of or caused by pepsin or the action of the digestive juices: *a peptic ulcer.* [Greek *peptein* to digest]

per (pɜː) det. 1. for every: *three pence per pound.* ~prep. 2. by; through. 3. **as per.** according to: *as per specifications.* 4. **as per usual** or **as per normal.** Informal. as usual. [Latin: by, for each]

peradventure (,pɜrəd'vɛntʃə, ,pɛr-) Archaic. ~adv. 1. by chance; perhaps. ~n. 2. chance or doubt. [Old French *par aventure* by chance]

perambulate (pə'ræmbjʊ,leɪt) vb. to walk about (a place). [Latin *per-* through + *ambulāre* to walk] —**per,ambu'lation** n.

perambulator (pə'ræmbjʊ,leɪtə) n. same as **pram**.

per annum (pər 'ænəm) adv. every year or by the year. [Latin]

percale (pə'keɪl, -'kɑːl) n. a close-textured woven cotton fabric, used esp. for sheets. [Persian *pargālah*]

per capita (pə 'kæpɪtə) adj., adv. of or for each person: *what is the average wage per capita?* [Latin, lit.: according to heads]

perceive (pə'siːv) vb. 1. to become aware of (something) through the senses; recognize or observe. 2. to come to comprehend; grasp. [Latin *percipere* to seize entirely] —**per'ceivable** adj.

per cent (pə 'sɛnt) adv. 1. in or for every hundred. ~n. also **percent.** 2. a percentage or proportion. [Medieval Latin *per centum* out of every hundred]

percentage (pə'sɛntɪdʒ) n. 1. proportion or rate per hundred parts. 2. any proportion in relation to the whole: *a small* *percentage of the population.* **3.** *Informal.* profit or advantage.

percentile (pə'sɛntaɪl) *n.* one of 99 actual or notional values of a variable dividing its distribution into 100 groups with equal frequencies.

perceptible (pə'sɛptəb'l) *adj.* able to be perceived; noticeable or recognizable. —**per₁cepti'bility** *n.*

perception (pə'sɛpʃən) *n.* **1.** the act or the effect of perceiving. **2.** insight or intuition gained by perceiving. **3.** the ability or capacity to perceive. **4.** way of perceiving; view: *advertising affects the customer's perception of a product.* [Latin *perceptiō* comprehension] —**perceptual** (pə'sɛp-tjʊəl) *adj.*

perceptive (pə'sɛptɪv) *adj.* **1.** quick at perceiving; observant. **2.** able to perceive. —**per'ceptively** *adv.* —**₁percep'tivity** *or* **per'ceptiveness** *n.*

perch[1] (pɜːtʃ) *n.* **1.** a pole, branch, or other resting place above ground on which a bird roosts. **2.** any raised resting place. **3.** same as **rod** (sense 5). ~*vb.* **4.** to alight, rest, or cause to rest on or as if on a perch: *the bird perched on the branch; the cap was perched on his head.* [Latin *pertica* long staff]

perch[2] (pɜːtʃ) *n., pl.* **perch** *or* **perches.** a spiny-finned freshwater food fish of Europe and North America. [Greek *perkē*]

perchance (pə'tʃɑːns) *adv. Archaic or poetic.* **1.** perhaps; possibly. **2.** by chance; accidentally. [Anglo-French *par chance*]

percipient (pə'sɪpɪənt) *adj.* quick at perceiving; observant. [Latin *percipiens* observing] —**per'cipience** *n.*

percolate ('pɜːkə₁leɪt) *vb.* **1.** to pass or ooze through (something) with very small holes in it: *rain percolated through the roof.* **2.** to spread gradually: *word percolated through to us.* **3.** to make (coffee) or (of coffee) to be made in a percolator. [Latin *per-* through + *cōlāre* to strain] —**₁perco'lation** *n.*

percolator ('pɜːkə₁leɪtə) *n.* a coffeepot in which boiling water is forced up through a tube and filters down through the coffee grounds into a container.

percussion (pə'kʌʃən) *n.* **1.** the striking of one body against another, as the hammer of a firearm against a percussion cap. **2.** *Music.* percussion instruments collectively. [Latin *percutere* to hit] —**per'cussive** *adj.*

percussion cap *n.* a detonator consisting of a paper or thin metal cap containing material that explodes when struck.

percussion instrument *n.* a musical instrument, such as the drums, that produces a sound when struck directly, as with a stick or mallet.

percussionist (pə'kʌʃənɪst) *n. Music.* a person who plays percussion instruments.

perdition (pə'dɪʃən) *n.* **1.** *Christianity.* final and irrevocable spiritual ruin; damnation. **2.** same as **hell.** [Late Latin *perditiō* ruin]

peregrinate ('pɛrɪgrɪ₁neɪt) *vb.* to travel or

wander about from place to place. [Latin *peregrīnārī* to travel] —**₁peregri'nation** *n.*

peregrine falcon *n.* a European falcon with dark plumage on the back and wings and lighter underparts. [Latin *peregrīnus* foreign]

peremptory (pə'rɛmptərɪ) *adj.* **1.** urgent or commanding: *a peremptory ring on the bell.* **2.** not able to be remitted or debated; decisive. **3.** dogmatic. [Latin *peremp-tōrius* decisive]

perennial (pə'rɛnɪəl) *adj.* **1.** lasting throughout the year or through many years. ~*n.* **2.** a plant that continues its growth for at least three years. [Latin *per-* through + *annus* year]

perestroika (₁pɛrə'strɔɪkə) *n.* the policy of restructuring the Soviet economy and institutions under Gorbachov. [Russian: reconstruction]

perfect *adj.* ('pɜːfɪkt). **1.** having all essential elements. **2.** unblemished; faultless: *a perfect gemstone.* **3.** correct or precise: *perfect timing.* **4.** utter or absolute: *a perfect stranger.* **5.** excellent in all respects: *a perfect day.* **6.** *Maths.* exactly divisible into equal integral or polynomial roots: *36 is a perfect square.* **7.** *Grammar.* denoting a tense of verbs used in describing an action that has been completed. ~*n.* ('pɜːfɪkt). **8.** *Grammar.* the perfect tense. ~*vb.* (pə'fɛkt). **9.** to improve to one's satisfaction: *he is in Paris to perfect his French.* **10.** to make fully accomplished. [Latin *perficere* to complete] —**'perfectly** *adv.*

perfectible (pə'fɛktəb'l) *adj.* capable of becoming or being made perfect. —**per₁fecti'bility** *n.*

perfection (pə'fɛkʃən) *n.* the act of perfecting or the state or quality of being perfect. [Latin *perfectiō* a completing]

perfectionism (pə'fɛkʃə₁nɪzəm) *n.* the demand for the highest standard of excellence. —**per'fectionist** *n., adj.*

perfect pitch *n.* same as **absolute pitch.**

perfidious (pə'fɪdɪəs) *adj.* treacherous or deceitful. [Latin *perfidus*] —**'perfidy** *n.*

perforate ('pɜːfə₁reɪt) *vb.* **1.** to make a hole or holes in (something). **2.** to punch rows of holes between (stamps) for ease of separation. [Latin *per-* through + *forāre* to pierce] —**perforable** ('pɜːfərəb'l) *adj.* —**'perfo₁rator** *n.*

perforation (₁pɜːfə'reɪʃən) *n.* **1.** a hole or holes made in something. **2.** any of a series of punched holes, as those between individual stamps.

perforce (pə'fɔːs) *adv.* by necessity; unavoidably. [Old French *par force*]

perform (pə'fɔːm) *vb.* **1.** to carry out (an action). **2.** to fulfil: *to perform someone's request.* **3.** to present (a play or concert): *the group performed Hamlet.* [Old French *parfournir*] —**per'formable** *adj.* —**per-'former** *n.*

performance (pə'fɔːməns) *n.* **1.** the act, process, or art of performing. **2.** artistic or dramatic production: *last night's performance was terrible.* **3.** manner or quality of functioning: *a machine's perfor-*

mance. **4.** *Informal.* mode of conduct or behaviour, esp. when distasteful: *what did you mean by that performance at the restaurant?*

perfume *n.* ('pɜːfjuːm). **1.** a liquid cosmetic prepared from a mixture of alcohol and essential oils extracted from flowers or made synthetically, and worn for its pleasant smell. **2.** a fragrant smell. ~*vb.* (pə'fjuːm). **3.** to impart a perfume to. [French *parfum*, from Latin *per* through + *fumare* to smoke] —**'perfumed** *adj.*

perfumer (pə'fjuːmə) *n.* a person who makes or sells perfume. —**per'fumery** *n.*

perfunctory (pə'fʌŋktərɪ) *adj.* done only as a matter of routine: *he gave his wife a perfunctory kiss.* [Late Latin *perfunctōrius* negligent] —**per'functorily** *adv.* —**per'functoriness** *n.*

pergola ('pɜːgələ) *n.* a horizontal trellis or framework, supported on posts, that carries climbing plants. [Italian]

perhaps (pə'hæps) *adv.* possibly; maybe. [earlier *perhappes*, from *per* by + *happes* chance]

perianth ('pɛrɪˌænθ) *n.* the outer part of a flower. [Greek *peri-* around + *anthos* flower]

pericardium (ˌpɛrɪ'kɑːdɪəm) *n., pl.* -**dia** (-dɪə). the membranous sac enclosing the heart. [Greek *peri-* around + *kardia* heart] —**peri'cardial** or **ˌperi'cardiˌac** *adj.*

pericarp ('pɛrɪˌkɑːp) *n.* the part of a fruit enclosing the seed that develops from the wall of the ovary. [Greek *peri-* around + *karpos* fruit]

perigee ('pɛrɪˌdʒiː) *n.* the point in its orbit when the moon or a satellite is nearest the earth. [Greek *peri-* near + *gea* earth]

perihelion (ˌpɛrɪ'hiːlɪən) *n., pl.* -**lia** (-lɪə). the point in its orbit when a planet or comet is nearest the sun. [Greek *peri-* near + *hēlios* sun]

peril ('pɛrɪl) *n.* exposure to risk or harm; danger or jeopardy. [Latin *perīculum*] —**'perilous** *adj.*

perimeter (pə'rɪmɪtə) *n.* **1.** *Maths.* **a.** the curve or line enclosing a plane area. **b.** the length of this curve or line. **2.** any boundary around something. [Latin *perimetros*]

perinatal (ˌpɛrɪ'neɪt'l) *adj.* of or occurring in the period from about three months before to one month after birth. [Greek *peri-* around + Latin *nātus* born]

perineum (ˌpɛrɪ'niːəm) *n., pl.* -**nea** (-'niːə). the region of the body between the anus and the genitals. [Greek *perinaion*] —**peri'neal** *adj.*

period ('pɪərɪəd) *n.* **1.** a portion of time of indefinable length: *he spent a period away from home.* **2.** a portion of time specified in some way: *Picasso's blue period.* **3.** an occurrence of menstruation. **4.** *Geol.* a unit of geological time during which a system of rocks is formed: *the Jurassic period.* **5.** a division of time at school, college, or university when a particular subject is taught. **6.** *Physics, maths.* the time taken to complete one cycle of a regularly recurring phenomenon. **7.** *Chem.* one of the horizontal rows of elements in

the periodic table. **8.** *Chiefly U.S. & Canad.* same as **full stop.** ~*adj.* **9.** dating from or in the style of an earlier time: *period costume.* [Greek *periodos* circuit]

periodic (ˌpɪərɪ'ɒdɪk) *adj.* happening or recurring at intervals or in cycles. —**peri'odically** *adv.* —**periodicity** (ˌpɪərɪə'dɪsɪtɪ) *n.*

periodical (ˌpɪərɪ'ɒdɪk'l) *n.* **1.** a publication issued at regular intervals, usually monthly or weekly. ~*adj.* **2.** of or relating to such publications. **3.** periodic or occasional.

periodic law *n.* the principle that the chemical properties of the elements are periodic functions of their atomic numbers.

periodic table *n.* a table of the elements, arranged in order of increasing atomic number, based on the periodic law.

peripatetic (ˌpɛrɪpə'tɛtɪk) *adj.* **1.** travelling from place to place. **2.** *Brit.* employed in two or more educational establishments and travelling from one to another: *a peripatetic football coach.* ~*n.* **3.** a peripatetic person. [Greek *peripatein* to pace to and fro]

peripheral (pə'rɪfərəl) *adj.* **1.** not relating to the most important part of something; incidental. **2.** of or relating to a periphery. ~*n.* **3.** *Computers.* any device, such as a disk drive, concerned with input/output or storage.

periphery (pə'rɪfərɪ) *n., pl.* -**eries**. **1.** the outermost boundary of an area. **2.** the outside surface of something. [Greek *peri-* around + *pherein* to bear]

periphrasis (pə'rɪfrəsɪs) *n., pl.* -**rases** (-rəˌsiːz). a roundabout way of expressing something; circumlocution. [Greek *peri-* around + *phrazein* to declare]

periscope ('pɛrɪˌskəʊp) *n.* an optical instrument that enables the user to view objects that are not in the direct line of vision, such as one in a submarine for looking above the surface of the water. They use a system of mirrors or prisms to reflect the light. [Greek *periskopein* to look around]

perish ('pɛrɪʃ) *vb.* **1.** to be destroyed or die. **2.** to cause to suffer: *we were perished with cold.* **3.** to rot or cause to rot: *leather perishes if exposed to bad weather.* [Latin *perīre* to pass away entirely]

perishable ('pɛrɪʃəb'l) *adj.* **1.** liable to rot. ~*n.* **2.** (*often pl.*) a perishable article, esp. food.

perishing ('pɛrɪʃɪŋ) *adj.* **1.** *Informal.* (of weather) extremely cold. **2.** *Slang.* confounded, blasted: *it's a perishing nuisance!*

peristalsis (ˌpɛrɪ'stælsɪs) *n., pl.* -**ses** (-siːz). *Physiol.* the wave-like involuntary muscular contractions of the walls of the digestive tract. [Greek *peri-* around + *stalsis* compression] —**peri'staltic** *adj.*

peritoneum (ˌpɛrɪtə'niːəm) *n., pl.* -**nea** (-'niːə) *or* -**neums.** a serous sac that lines the walls of the abdominal cavity and covers the abdominal organs. [Greek *peritonos* stretched around] —**peritoˈneal** *adj.*

peritonitis (ˌperɪtəˈnaɪtɪs) n. inflammation of the peritoneum.

periwig (ˈperɪˌwɪg) n. a wig formerly worn by men. [French *perruque*]

periwinkle[1] (ˈperɪˌwɪŋkᵊl) n. an edible marine gastropod with a spirally coiled shell. [origin unknown]

periwinkle[2] (ˈperɪˌwɪŋkᵊl) n. a Eurasian evergreen plant with trailing stems and blue flowers. [Old English *perwince*]

perjure (ˈpɜːdʒə) vb. *Criminal law.* to commit perjury. [Latin *perjūrāre*] —**ˈperjurer** n.

perjury (ˈpɜːdʒərɪ) n., pl. **-juries.** *Criminal law.* the deliberate giving of false evidence while under oath. [Latin *perjūrium* a false oath]

perk[1] (pɜːk) n. *Brit. informal.* short for **perquisite.**

perk[2] (pɜːk) vb. *Informal.* short for **percolate** (sense 3).

perk up vb. **1.** to make or become more cheerful, hopeful, or lively. **2.** to rise or cause to rise briskly: *the dog's ears perked up.* [origin unknown]

perky (ˈpɜːkɪ) adj. **perkier, perkiest. 1.** jaunty; lively. **2.** confident; spirited.

perm[1] (pɜːm) n. **1.** a hairstyle produced by treatment with chemicals which gives long-lasting waves or curls. ~vb. **2.** to give a perm to (hair).

perm[2] (pɜːm) n. *Informal.* short for **permutate, permutation** (sense 4).

permafrost (ˈpɜːməˌfrɒst) n. ground that is permanently frozen. [*perma(nent)* + *frost*]

permanent (ˈpɜːmənənt) adj. **1.** existing or intended to exist for an indefinite period: *a permanent structure.* **2.** not expected to change: *a permanent condition.* [Latin *permanens* continuing] —**ˈpermanence** n. —**ˈpermanently** adv.

permanent wave n. same as **perm**[1].

permanent way n. *Chiefly Brit.* the track of a railway, including the sleepers and rails.

permanganate (pɜːˈmæŋgəˌneɪt) n. a salt of an acid containing manganese, used as a disinfectant.

permeable (ˈpɜːmɪəbᵊl) adj. capable of being permeated, esp. by liquids. —**ˌpermeaˈbility** n.

permeate (ˈpɜːmɪˌeɪt) vb. **1.** to penetrate or pervade (a substance or area): *a lovely smell permeated the room.* **2.** to pass through or cause to pass through by osmosis or diffusion: *to permeate a membrane.* [Latin *permeāre*] —**ˌpermeˈation** n.

Permian (ˈpɜːmɪən) adj. *Geol.* of the period of geological time about 280 million years ago. [after *Perm*, Russian port]

permissible (pəˈmɪsəbᵊl) adj. permitted; allowable. —**perˌmissiˈbility** n.

permission (pəˈmɪʃən) n. authorization to do something.

permissive (pəˈmɪsɪv) adj. tolerant or lenient, esp. in sexual matters: *a permissive society.* —**perˈmissiveness** n.

permit vb. (pəˈmɪt), **-mitting, -mitted. 1.** to grant permission to do something: *you are permitted to smoke.* **2.** to consent to: *she will not permit him to come.* **3.** to allow the possibility (of): *his work permits him to relax nowadays.* ~n. (ˈpɜːmɪt). **4.** an official document granting authorization. [Latin *permittere*]

permutate (ˈpɜːmjuˌteɪt) vb. to alter the sequence or arrangement (of): *endlessly permutating three basic designs.*

permutation (ˌpɜːmjuˈteɪʃən) n. **1.** *Maths.* an ordered arrangement of the numbers or terms of a set into specified groups: *the permutations of a, b, and c, taken two at a time, are ab, ba, ac, ca, bc, cb.* **2.** a combination of items made by reordering. **3.** a transformation. **4.** a fixed combination for selections of results on football pools. [Latin *permūtāre* to change thoroughly]

pernicious (pəˈnɪʃəs) adj. **1.** wicked or malicious: *pernicious lies.* **2.** causing grave harm; deadly. [Latin *perniciēs* ruin]

pernicious anaemia n. a severe form of anaemia characterized by a reduction of the red blood cells, weakness, and a sore tongue.

pernickety (pəˈnɪkɪtɪ) adj. *Informal.* **1.** excessively precise; fussy. **2.** (of a task) requiring close attention. [origin unknown]

peroration (ˌperəˈreɪʃən) n. the concluding part of a speech in which points made previously are summed up. [Latin *perōrātiō*]

peroxide (pəˈrɒksaɪd) n. **1.** hydrogen peroxide as a hair bleach. **2.** any of a class of metallic oxides, such as sodium peroxide, Na$_2$O$_2$. **3.** (modifier) of, bleached with, or resembling peroxide: *a peroxide blonde.* ~vb. **4.** to bleach (the hair) with peroxide.

perpendicular (ˌpɜːpənˈdɪkjʊlə) adj. **1.** at right angles. **2.** denoting the style of English Gothic architecture characterized by vertical lines. **3.** upright; vertical. ~n. **4.** *Geom.* a line or plane perpendicular to another. [Latin *perpendiculum* a plumb line] —**perpendicularity** (ˌpɜːpənˌdɪkjuˈlærɪtɪ) n.

perpetrate (ˈpɜːpɪˌtreɪt) vb. to perform or be responsible for (a deception or crime). [Latin *perpetrāre*] —**perpeˈtration** n. —**ˈperpeˌtrator** n.

perpetual (pəˈpetjʊəl) adj. **1.** eternal; permanent. **2.** seemingly ceaseless because often repeated: *your perpetual complaints.* [Latin *perpetuālis*] —**perˈpetually** adv.

perpetual motion n. motion of a hypothetical mechanism that continues indefinitely without any external source of energy.

perpetuate (pəˈpetjuˌeɪt) vb. to cause to continue: *to perpetuate misconceptions.* [Latin *perpetuāre* to continue without interruption] —**perˌpetuˈation** n.

perpetuity (ˌpɜːpɪˈtjuːɪtɪ) n., pl. **-ties. 1.** eternity. **2.** the state of being perpetual. **3.** something perpetual, such as a pension that is payable indefinitely. **4. in perpetuity.** for ever. [Latin *perpetuitās* continuity]

perplex (pə'plɛks) vb. **1.** to puzzle; bewilder; confuse. **2.** to complicate: *to perplex an issue*. [Latin *perplexus* entangled] —**per'plexing** adj.

perplexity (pə'plɛksɪtɪ) n., pl. -**ties**. **1.** the state of being perplexed. **2.** something that perplexes.

perquisite ('pɜːkwɪzɪt) n. **1.** an incidental benefit gained from a certain type of employment, such as the use of a company car. **2.** a customary tip. **3.** something expected or regarded as an exclusive right. [Latin *perquirere* to seek earnestly for something]

perry ('pɛrɪ) n., pl. -**ries**. an alcoholic drink made from fermented pear juice. [Old French *peré*]

per se ('pɜː 'seɪ) adv. by or in itself; intrinsically. [Latin]

persecute ('pɜːsɪˌkjuːt) vb. **1.** to oppress, harass, or maltreat (someone), esp. because of race or religion. **2.** to bother (someone) persistently. [Latin *persequi* to take vengeance upon] —**perse'cution** n. —**'perse,cutor** n.

perseverance (ˌpɜːsɪ'vɪərəns) n. continued steady belief or efforts; persistence.

persevere (ˌpɜːsɪ'vɪə) vb. (often foll. by *in*) to show perseverance. [Latin *perseverus* very strict]

Persian ('pɜːʃən) adj. **1.** of ancient Persia or modern Iran, their inhabitants, or their languages. ~n. **2.** a person from Persia (now Iran). **3.** the language of Iran or Persia in any of its ancient or modern forms.

Persian cat n. a long-haired variety of domestic cat.

Persian lamb n. **1.** a black loosely curled fur from the karakul lamb. **2.** a karakul lamb.

persiflage ('pɜːsɪˌflɑːʒ) n. light frivolous conversation or writing. [French]

persimmon (pɜː'sɪmən) n. a sweet red tropical fruit, which is edible when completely ripe. [American Indian]

persist (pə'sɪst) vb. **1.** (often foll. by *in*) to continue obstinately despite opposition. **2.** to continue without interruption: *the rain persisted through the night*. [Latin *persistere*]

persistent (pə'sɪstənt) adj. **1.** showing persistence. **2.** unrelenting: *your persistent questioning*. —**per'sistence** n. —**per'sistently** adv.

person ('pɜːsən) n., pl. **persons**. **1.** an individual human being. **2.** the body of a human being: *guns hidden on his person*. **3.** a grammatical category into which pronouns and forms of verbs are subdivided depending on whether they refer to the speaker, the person addressed, or some other individual or thing. **4. in person.** actually present: *the author will be there in person*. [Latin *persōna* mask]

-person n. combining form. sometimes used instead of -man and -woman or -lady: *chairperson*.

persona (pɜː'səʊnə) n., pl. -**nae** (-niː). the personality that a person adopts and presents to other people. [Latin: mask]

personable ('pɜːsənəb'l) adj. pleasant in appearance and personality.

personage ('pɜːsənɪdʒ) n. **1.** an important or distinguished person. **2.** any person.

personal ('pɜːsən'l) adj. **1.** of the private aspects of a person's life: *personal letters*. **2.** of a person's body, its care, or its appearance: *personal hygiene*. **3.** undertaken by an individual: *a personal appearance by a celebrity*. **4.** referring to a person's individual personality or intimate affairs in an offensive way: *personal remarks*. **5.** having the attributes of an individual conscious being: *a personal God*. **6.** of grammatical person. **7.** *Law*. of movable property, such as money.

personal column n. a newspaper column containing personal messages and advertisements.

personal computer n. a small computer used for word processing or computer games.

personality (ˌpɜːsə'nælɪtɪ) n., pl. -**ties**. **1.** *Psychol*. distinctive characteristics by means of which an individual is recognized as being unique. **2.** the distinctive character of a person that makes him socially attractive: *a salesman needs a lot of personality*. **3.** a well-known person in a certain field, such as entertainment. **4.** a remarkable person: *the old fellow is a real personality*. **5.** (often pl.) a personal remark: *the discussion degenerated into personalities*.

personalize or -**ise** ('pɜːsənə,laɪz) vb. **1.** to base (an argument or discussion) around people's characters rather than on abstract arguments. **2.** to mark (stationery or clothing) with a person's initials or name. **3.** same as **personify**.

personally ('pɜːsənəlɪ) adv. **1.** without the help of others: *I'll attend to it personally*. **2.** in one's own opinion: *personally, I hate onions*. **3.** as if referring to oneself: *to take the insults personally*. **4.** as a person: *we like him personally, but professionally he's incompetent*.

personal pronoun n. a pronoun such as *I*, *you*, *he*, *she*, *we*, and *they* that represents a definite person or thing.

personal stereo n. a small audio cassette player worn attached to a belt and used with lightweight headphones.

persona non grata (pɜː'səʊnə nɒn 'grɑːtə) n., pl. **personae non gratae** (pɜː'səʊniː nɒn 'grɑːtiː). an unacceptable person. [Latin]

personate ('pɜːsə,neɪt) vb. *Criminal law*. to assume the identity of (another person) with intent to deceive. —**person'ation** n.

personify (pɜː'sɒnɪ,faɪ) vb. -**fying**, -**fied**. **1.** to attribute human characteristics to (a thing or abstraction). **2.** to represent (an abstract quality) in human or animal form. **3.** (of a person or thing) to represent (an abstract quality), as in art. **4.** to be the embodiment of: *she is meanness personified*. —**personification** (pɜːˌsɒnɪfɪ'keɪʃən) n.

personnel (ˌpɜːsə'nɛl) n. **1.** the people

employed in an organization or for a service. **2.** the department in an organization that appoints, or keeps records of employees. [French]

perspective (pə'spɛktɪv) *n.* **1.** a way of regarding situations or facts and judging their relative importance. **2.** the proper or accurate point of view or the ability to see it; objectivity: *try to get some perspective on your troubles.* **3.** the art of drawing on a flat surface to give the effect of solidity and relative distance and sizes. **4.** the appearance of objects or buildings relative to each other, as determined by their distance from the viewer. [Latin *perspicere* to inspect carefully]

Perspex ('pɜːspɛks) *n. Trademark.* any of various clear acrylic resins.

perspicacious (ˌpɜːspɪ'keɪʃəs) *adj.* acutely perceptive or discerning. [Latin *perspicax*] —**perspicacity** (ˌpɜːspɪ'kæsɪtɪ) *n.*

perspicuous (pə'spɪkjuəs) *adj.* (of speech or writing) easily understood; lucid. [Latin *perspicuus* transparent] —**perspicuity** (ˌpɜːspɪ'kjuːɪtɪ) *n.*

perspiration (ˌpɜːspə'reɪʃən) *n.* **1.** the salty fluid secreted by the sweat glands of the skin; sweat. **2.** the act of sweating.

perspire (pə'spaɪə) *vb.* to sweat. [Latin *per-* through + *spīrāre* to breathe]

persuade (pə'sweɪd) *vb.* **1.** to induce, urge, or prevail upon (someone) successfully: *he finally persuaded them to buy it.* **2.** to cause to believe; convince: *even with the evidence, the police were not persuaded.* [Latin *persuādēre*] —**per'suadable** *adj.*

persuasion (pə'sweɪʒən) *n.* **1.** the act of persuading or of trying to persuade. **2.** the power to persuade. **3.** a set of beliefs; creed: *the Roman Catholic persuasion; a young woman of radical persuasion.*

persuasive (pə'sweɪsɪv) *adj.* having the power or tending to persuade: *a persuasive salesman.* —**per'suasively** *adv.*

pert (pɜːt) *adj.* **1.** saucy, impudent, or forward. **2.** jaunty: *a pert little hat.* [Latin *apertus* open]

pertain (pə'teɪn) *vb.* (often foll. by *to*) **1.** to have reference or relevance: *the notes pertaining to the case.* **2.** to be appropriate. **3.** to belong (to) or be a part (of). [Latin *pertinēre*]

pertinacious (ˌpɜːtɪ'neɪʃəs) *adj.* doggedly resolute in purpose or belief. **2.** stubbornly persistent. [Latin *per-* (intensive) + *tenāx* clinging] —**pertinacity** (ˌpɜːtɪ'næsɪtɪ) *n.*

pertinent ('pɜːtɪnənt) *adj.* relating to the matter at hand; relevant. [Latin *pertinēns*] —**'pertinence** *or* **'pertinency** *n.*

perturb (pə'tɜːb) *vb.* **1.** to disturb the composure of; trouble. **2.** to throw into disorder. [Latin *perturbāre* to confuse]

perturbation (ˌpɜːtə'beɪʃən) *n.* **1.** the act of perturbing or the state of being perturbed. **2.** a cause of disturbance.

peruke (pə'ruːk) *n.* a wig for men in the 17th and 18th centuries. [French *perruque*]

peruse (pə'ruːz) *vb.* **1.** to read or examine with care. **2.** to browse or read in a leisurely way. [*per-* (intensive) + *use*] —**pe'rusal** *n.*

pervade (pɜː'veɪd) *vb.* to spread through or throughout. [Latin *per-* through + *vādere* to go] —**pervasion** (pɜː'veɪʒən) *n.* —**pervasive** (pɜː'veɪsɪv) *adj.*

perverse (pə'vɜːs) *adj.* **1.** deliberately deviating from what is regarded as normal, good, or proper. **2.** wayward or contrary; obstinate. [Latin *perversus* turned the wrong way] —**per'versely** *adv.* —**per'versity** *n.*

perversion (pə'vɜːʃən) *n.* **1.** any abnormal means of obtaining sexual satisfaction. **2.** the act of perverting or the state of being perverted.

pervert *vb.* (pə'vɜːt). **1.** to use wrongly or badly. **2.** to interpret wrongly or badly; distort. **3.** to lead (someone) into deviant or perverted beliefs or behaviour; corrupt. **4.** to debase. ~*n.* ('pɜːvɜːt). **5.** a person who practises sexual perversion. [Latin *pervertere* to turn the wrong way] —**per'verted** *adj.*

pervious ('pɜːvɪəs) *adj.* **1.** able to be penetrated; permeable: *pervious soil.* **2.** receptive to new ideas, etc.; open-minded. [Latin *per-* through + *via* a way]

peseta (pə'seɪtə) *n.* the standard monetary unit of Spain. [Spanish]

pesky ('pɛskɪ) *adj.* **peskier, peskiest.** *U.S. & Canad. informal.* troublesome. [prob. changed from *pesty*]

peso ('peɪsəʊ) *n., pl.* **-sos** (-səʊz). the standard monetary unit of Bolivia, Chile, Colombia, Cuba, the Dominican Republic, Mexico, the Philippines, and Uruguay. [Spanish: weight]

pessary ('pɛsərɪ) *n., pl.* **-ries.** *Med.* **1.** a device worn in the vagina, either as a support for the uterus or as a contraceptive. **2.** a vaginal suppository. [Greek *pessos* plug]

pessimism ('pɛsɪˌmɪzəm) *n.* **1.** the tendency to expect the worst in all things. **2.** the doctrine of the ultimate triumph of evil over good. [Latin *pessimus* worst] —**'pessimist** *n.* —ˌpessi'mistic *adj.* —ˌpessi'mistically *adv.*

pest (pɛst) *n.* **1.** an annoying person or thing; nuisance. **2.** any organism that damages crops, or injures or irritates livestock or man. [Latin *pestis* plague]

pester ('pɛstə) *vb.* to annoy or nag (someone) continually. [Old French *empestrer* to hobble (a horse)]

pesticide ('pɛstɪˌsaɪd) *n.* a chemical used for killing pests, esp. insects. [*pest* + Latin *caedere* to kill]

pestilence ('pɛstɪləns) *n.* any deadly infectious disease, such as the plague.

pestilent ('pɛstɪlənt) *adj.* **1.** annoying; irritating. **2.** highly destructive morally or physically. **3.** likely to cause infectious disease. [Latin *pestis* plague] —**pestilential** (ˌpɛstɪ'lɛnʃəl) *adj.*

pestle ('pɛsəl) *n.* a club-shaped instrument for grinding or pounding substances in a mortar. [Old French *pestel*]

pet[1] (pɛt) *n.* **1.** a tame animal kept for

companionship or pleasure. **2.** a person who is fondly indulged; favourite: *teacher's pet.* ~*adj.* **3.** kept as a pet: *a pet dog.* **4.** of or for pet animals: *pet food.* **5.** particularly cherished: *a pet hatred.* ~*vb.* **petting, petted. 6.** to treat (a person or animal) as a pet; pamper. **7.** to pat or stroke (a person or animal). **8.** *Informal.* (of two people) to caress each other in an erotic manner. [origin unknown]

pet² (pɛt) *n.* a fit of sulkiness. [origin unknown]

petal ('pɛt³l) *n.* any of the brightly-coloured leaflike parts which form the head of a flower. [Greek *petalon* leaf] —'**petalled** *adj.*

petard (pɪ'tɑːd) *n.* **1.** (formerly) a device containing explosives used to breach a wall or door. **2. hoist with one's own petard.** being the victim of one's own schemes. [French: firework]

peter out ('piːtə) *vb.* to gradually come to an end: *the cash petered out in three months.* [origin unknown]

Peter Pan *n.* a youthful or immature man. [after the main character in *Peter Pan,* a play]

pethidine ('pɛθɪˌdiːn) *n.* a white crystalline water-soluble drug used to relieve pain. [perhaps a blend of *piperidine* + *ethyl*]

petiole ('pɛtɪˌəʊl) *n.* the stalk which attaches a leaf to a plant. [Latin *petiolus* little foot]

petit bourgeois ('pɛtɪ 'bʊəʒwɑː) *n.,* pl. **petits bourgeois** ('bʊəʒwɑːz). the lower middle class. [French]

petite (pə'tiːt) *adj.* (of a woman) small, delicate, and dainty. [French]

petit four ('pɛtɪ 'fɔː) *n.,* pl. **petits fours** ('fɔːz). any of various very small fancy cakes and biscuits. [French, lit.: little oven]

petition (pɪ'tɪʃən) *n.* **1.** a written document signed by a large number of people demanding some form of action from a government or other authority. **2.** any formal request to a higher authority. **3.** *Law.* a formal application in writing made to a court asking for some specific judicial action: *a petition for divorce.* ~*vb.* **4.** to address or present a petition to (a government or to someone in authority): *to petition Parliament.* **5.** (foll. by *for*) to seek by petition: *to petition for a change in the law.* [Latin *petere* to seek] —**pe'titionary** *adj.*

petit mal ('pɛtɪ 'mæl) *n.* a mild form of epilepsy characterized by periods of loss of consciousness for up to 30 seconds. [French: little illness]

petit point ('pɛtɪ 'pɔɪnt) *n.* **1.** a small diagonal needlepoint stitch used for fine detail. **2.** work done with such stitches. [French: small point]

petrel ('pɛtrəl) *n.* a sea bird with a hooked bill and tubular nostrils, such as an albatross, storm petrel, or shearwater. [var. of earlier *pitteral*]

Petri dish ('piːtrɪ) *n.* a shallow dish used in laboratories, esp. for producing cultures

of bacteria. [after J.R. *Petri*, bacteriologist]

petrify ('pɛtrɪˌfaɪ) *vb.* **-fying, -fied. 1.** to stun or daze, as with fear. **2.** to convert (organic material) into stone. **3.** to make or become unable to change or develop: *a society petrified by convention.* [Greek *petra* stone] —**petrifi'cation** *n.*

petrochemical (ˌpɛtrəʊ'kɛmɪk³l) *n.* a substance, such as acetone, obtained from petroleum. —ˌ**petro'chemistry** *n.*

petrodollar ('pɛtrəʊˌdɒlə) *n.* money earned by a country by the exporting of petroleum.

petrol ('pɛtrəl) *n.* a volatile flammable liquid obtained from petroleum and used as a fuel for internal-combustion engines. [see PETROLEUM]

petrolatum (ˌpɛtrə'leɪtəm) *n.* a translucent jellylike substance obtained from petroleum; used as a lubricant and in medicine as an ointment base.

petrol bomb *n.* a simple grenade consisting of a bottle filled with petrol. A piece of cloth is put in the neck of the bottle and set alight just before the bomb is thrown.

petroleum (pə'trəʊlɪəm) *n.* a dark-coloured thick flammable crude oil occurring in sedimentary rocks, consisting mainly of hydrocarbons: the source of petrol and paraffin. [Latin *petra* stone + *oleum* oil]

petroleum jelly *n.* same as **petrolatum.**

petrol station *n.* *Brit.* same as **filling station.**

petticoat ('pɛtɪˌkəʊt) *n.* a woman's underskirt. [*petty* & *coat*]

pettifogger ('pɛtɪˌfɒgə) *n.* **1.** a lawyer who conducts unimportant cases, esp. one who resorts to trickery. **2.** any person who quibbles. [origin unknown] —'**pettiˌfogging** *adj.*

pettish ('pɛtɪʃ) *adj.* peevish; petulant. [from PET²] —'**pettishness** *n.*

petty ('pɛtɪ) *adj.* **-tier, -tiest. 1.** trivial; trifling: *petty details.* **2.** narrow-minded; mean: *petty spite.* **3.** minor or subordinate in rank: *petty officialdom.* [French *petit* little] —'**pettily** *adv.* —'**pettiness** *n.*

petty cash *n.* a small cash fund for minor incidental expenses.

petty officer *n.* a noncommissioned officer in the navy.

petulant ('pɛtjʊlənt) *adj.* irritable or upset in a peevish way. [Latin *petulāns* bold] —'**petulance** *n.* —'**petulantly** *adv.*

petunia (pɪ'tjuːnɪə) *n.* a tropical American plant with pink, white, or purple funnel-shaped flowers. [obs. French *petun* variety of tobacco]

pew (pjuː) *n.* **1.** (in a church) **a.** a long benchlike seat with a back, used by the congregation. **b.** an enclosed compartment reserved for the use of a family or group. **2.** *Brit. informal.* a seat: *take a pew.* [Greek *pous* foot]

pewter ('pjuːtə) *n.* **1.** an alloy containing tin, lead, sometimes copper and antimony. **2.** plate or kitchen utensils made from pewter. [Old French *peaultre*]

pfennig (ˈfɛnɪg) *n.* a German monetary unit worth one hundredth of a mark. [German]

PG a film certified for viewing by anyone, but which contains scenes that may be unsuitable for children, for whom parental guidance is necessary.

pH *n.* potential of hydrogen; a measure of the acidity or alkalinity of a solution.

phaeton (ˈfeɪtˈn) *n.* a light four-wheeled horse-drawn carriage with or without a top. [French]

phagocyte (ˈfægəˌsaɪt) *n.* a cell or protozoan that engulfs particles, such as microorganisms. [Greek *phagein* to eat + *kutos* vessel]

phalanger (fəˈlændʒə) *n.* an Australian marsupial with dense fur and a long tail. [Greek *phalaggion* spider's web, referring to its webbed hind toes]

phalanx (ˈfælæŋks) *n.*, *pl.* **phalanxes** or **phalanges** (fæˈlændʒiːz). **1.** any closely ranked unit or mass of people: *the police formed a phalanx to protect the embassy.* **2.** a number of people united for a common purpose. **3.** an ancient Greek battle formation of infantry in close ranks. [Greek]

phallic (ˈfælɪk) *adj.* of or resembling a phallus: *a phallic symbol.*

phallus (ˈfæləs) *n.*, *pl.* **-li** (-laɪ) or **-luses**. **1.** same as **penis**. **2.** an image of the penis as a symbol of reproductive power. [Greek *phallos*]

phantasm (ˈfæntæzəm) *n.* **1.** a phantom. **2.** an illusory perception of a person or thing. [Greek *phantasma*] —**phanˈtasmal** *adj.*

phantasmagoria (ˌfæntæzməˈɡɔːrɪə) *n.* *Psychol.* a shifting medley of real or imagined figures, as in a dream. [prob. from French] —**phantasmagoric** (ˌfæntæzməˈɡɒrɪk) *adj.*

phantasy (ˈfæntəsɪ) *n.*, *pl.* **-sies**. *Archaic.* same as **fantasy**.

phantom (ˈfæntəm) *n.* **1.** an apparition or spectre. **2.** the visible representation of something abstract, esp. as in a dream or hallucination: *the phantom of liberty.* ~*adj.* **3.** deceptive or unreal: *a phantom army marching through the sky.* [Italian *phantasma*]

Pharaoh (ˈfɛərəʊ) *n.* the title of the ancient Egyptian kings. [Egyptian *pr-ʹo* great house]

Pharisee (ˈfærɪˌsiː) *n.* **1.** a member of an ancient Jewish sect teaching strict observance of Jewish traditions. **2.** (*often not cap.*) a self-righteous or hypocritical person. [Hebrew *pārūsh* separated] —**Pharisaic** (ˌfærɪˈseɪɪk) *adj.*

pharmaceutical (ˌfɑːməˈsjuːtɪkˈl) *adj.* of or relating to drugs or pharmacy.

pharmaceutics (ˌfɑːməˈsjuːtɪks) *n.* (*functioning as sing.*) same as **pharmacy** (sense 1).

pharmacist (ˈfɑːməsɪst) *n.* a person qualified to prepare and dispense drugs.

pharmacology (ˌfɑːməˈkɒlədʒɪ) *n.* the science or study of drugs, including their characteristics, action, and uses. —**phar-**

macological (ˌfɑːməkəˈlɒdʒɪkˈl) *adj.* —**pharmaˈcologist** *n.*

pharmacopoeia (ˌfɑːməkəˈpiːə) *n.* an authoritative book containing a list of medicinal drugs with their uses, preparation and dosages. [Greek *pharmakopoiïa* art of preparing drugs]

pharmacy (ˈfɑːməsɪ) *n.*, *pl.* **-cies**. **1.** the preparing and dispensing of drugs. **2.** a dispensary. [Greek *pharmakon* drug]

pharyngitis (ˌfærɪnˈdʒaɪtɪs) *n.* inflammation of the pharynx; sore throat.

pharynx (ˈfærɪŋks) *n.*, *pl.* **pharynges** (fæˈrɪndʒiːz) or **pharynxes**. the part of the alimentary canal between the mouth and the oesophagus. [Greek *pharunx* throat] —**pharyngeal** (ˌfærɪnˈdʒiːəl) *adj.*

phase (feɪz) *n.* **1.** any distinct or characteristic period or stage in a sequence of events: *there were two phases to the revolution.* **2.** *Astron.* one of the recurring shapes of the portion of the moon, Mercury, or Venus illuminated by the sun. **3.** *Physics.* a particular stage in a periodic process or phenomenon. **4. in phase.** (of two waveforms) reaching corresponding phases at the same time. **5. out of phase.** (of two waveforms) not in phase. ~*vb.* **6.** to do, arrange, or introduce gradually or in stages: *the withdrawal was phased over several months.* [Greek *phasis* aspect]

phase in *vb.* to introduce in a gradual or cautious manner: *the legislation was phased in over two years.*

phase out *vb.* to discontinue or withdraw gradually.

PhD Doctor of Philosophy.

pheasant (ˈfɛzˈnt) *n.* a long-tailed bird with a brightly-coloured plumage in the male: native to Asia but introduced elsewhere. [Latin *phāsiānus*]

phenobarbitone (ˌfiːnəʊˈbɑːbɪˌtəʊn) or **phenobarbital** (ˌfiːnəʊˈbɑːbɪtˈl) *n.* a sedative used to treat insomnia and epilepsy.

phenol (ˈfiːnɒl) *n.* a white crystalline derivative of benzene, used as an antiseptic and disinfectant and in the manufacture of resins, explosives, and pharmaceuticals. [Greek *phaino-* shining; because orig. prepared from illuminating gas]

phenomena (fɪˈnɒmɪnə) *n.* a plural of **phenomenon**.

phenomenal (fɪˈnɒmɪnˈl) *adj.* **1.** of or relating to a phenomenon. **2.** extraordinary; outstanding: *a phenomenal achievement.* —**pheˈnomenally** *adv.*

phenomenalism (fɪˈnɒmɪnəˌlɪzəm) *n.* *Philosophy.* the doctrine that all knowledge comes from sense perception. —**pheˈnomenalist** *n.*, *adj.*

phenomenon (fɪˈnɒmɪnən) *n.*, *pl.* **-ena** (-ɪnə) or **-enons**. **1.** anything that can be perceived as an occurrence or fact by the senses. **2.** any remarkable occurrence or person. [Greek *phainomenon*, from *phainesthai* to appear]

phenyl (ˈfiːnaɪl) *n.* (*modifier*) of, containing, or consisting of the monovalent group C_6H_5, derived from benzene: *a phenyl group.*

phew (fjuː) *interj.* an exclamation of relief, surprise, disbelief or weariness.

phial (ˈfaɪəl) *n.* a small bottle for liquid medicine. [Greek *phialē* wide shallow vessel]

phil. 1. philharmonic. 2. philosophy.

philadelphus (ˌfɪləˈdɛlfəs) *n.* a shrub grown for its strongly scented showy flowers. [Greek *philadelphon*, lit.: loving one's brother]

philander (fɪˈlændə) *vb.* (of a man) to flirt with women. [Greek *philandros* fond of men, used as a name for a lover in literary works] —**phiˈlanderer** *n.*

philanthropy (fɪˈlænθrəpɪ) *n., pl.* **-pies.** 1. the practice of performing charitable or benevolent actions. 2. love of mankind in general. [Greek *philanthrōpia* love of mankind] —**philanthropic** (ˌfɪlənˈθrɒpɪk) *adj.* —**phiˈlanthropist** *n.*

philately (fɪˈlætəlɪ) *n.* the collection and study of postage stamps. [Greek *philos* loving + *ateleia* exemption from tax] —**phiˈlatelist** *n.*

philharmonic (ˌfɪlhɑːˈmɒnɪk) *adj.* 1. fond of music. ~*n.* 2. (*cap. when part of a name*) a specific philharmonic choir, orchestra, or society. [French *philharmonique*]

philippic (fɪˈlɪpɪk) *n.* a bitter verbal attack. [after the orations of Demosthenes against Philip of Macedon]

Philippine (ˈfɪlɪˌpiːn) *n., adj.* same as **Filipino.**

philistine (ˈfɪlɪˌstaɪn) *n.* 1. a person who is hostile towards culture and the arts. ~*adj.* 2. boorishly uncultured. —**philistinism** (ˈfɪlɪstɪˌnɪzəm) *n.*

Philistine (ˈfɪlɪˌstaɪn) *n.* a member of the non-semitic people who inhabited ancient Palestine.

philology (fɪˈlɒlədʒɪ) *n.* (no longer in scholarly use) comparative and historical linguistics. [Greek *philologia* love of language] —**philological** (ˌfɪləˈlɒdʒɪkˀl) *adj.* —**phiˈlologist** *n.*

philosopher (fɪˈlɒsəfə) *n.* 1. a student, teacher, or devotee of philosophy. 2. a person who is patient, wise, and stoical.

philosopher's stone *n.* a substance thought by alchemists to be capable of changing base metals into gold.

philosophize or **-phise** (fɪˈlɒsəˌfaɪz) *vb.* 1. to make philosophical pronouncements and speculations. 2. to explain philosophically. —**phiˈlosoˌphizer** or **-ˌphiser** *n.*

philosophy (fɪˈlɒsəfɪ) *n., pl.* **-phies.** 1. the academic discipline concerned with making explicit the nature and significance of beliefs and investigating the intelligibility of concepts by means of rational argument. 2. the particular doctrines of a specific individual or school relating to these issues: *the philosophy of Descartes.* 3. any system of beliefs, values, or tenets. 4. a personal outlook or viewpoint. 5. the ability to remain calm through upsets and difficulties. [Greek *philosophia* love of wisdom] —**philosophical** (ˌfɪləˈsɒfɪkˀl) *adj.*

philtre or *U.S.* **philter** (ˈfɪltə) *n.* a drink supposed to arouse desire. [Greek *philtron* love potion]

phlebitis (flɪˈbaɪtɪs) *n.* inflammation of a vein. [Greek *phleps* vein + *-itis* (suffix) inflammation] —**phlebitic** (flɪˈbɪtɪk) *adj.*

phlegm (flɛm) *n.* 1. the thick yellowish substance secreted by the walls of the respiratory tract. 2. apathy; stolidity; indifference. 3. calmness. [Greek *phlegma*] —**ˈphlegmy** *adj.*

phlegmatic (flɛɡˈmætɪk) *adj.* 1. having an unemotional disposition. 2. not easily excited.

phloem (ˈfləʊɛm) *n.* the plant tissue that acts as a path for the distribution of food substances to all parts of the plant. [Greek *phloos* bark]

phlox (flɒks) *n., pl.* **phlox** or **phloxes.** a plant with clusters of white, red, or purple flowers. [Greek, lit.: flame]

phobia (ˈfəʊbɪə) *n. Psychiatry.* an intense and irrational fear of a given situation or thing. [Greek *phobos* fear] —**ˈphobic** *adj., n.*

Phoenician (fəˈnɪʃɪən) *n.* 1. a person from Phoenicia. ~*adj.* 2. of Phoenicia, an ancient E Mediterranean maritime country or the Phoenicians.

phoenix (ˈfiːnɪks) *n.* a legendary Arabian bird said to set fire to itself and rise anew from the ashes every 500 years. [Greek *phoinix*]

phone (fəʊn) *n., vb.* short for **telephone.**

phonecard (ˈfəʊnˌkɑːd) *n.* 1. a public telephone that is operated by a special card instead of coins. 2. the card used.

phone-in *n.* a radio or television programme in which listeners' or viewers' questions or comments are telephoned to the studio and broadcast live as part of a discussion.

phoneme (ˈfəʊniːm) *n. Linguistics.* one of the set of speech sounds in any given language that serve to distinguish one word from another. [Greek *phōnēma* sound, speech] —**phonemic** (fəˈniːmɪk) *adj.*

phonemics (fəˈniːmɪks) *n.* (functioning as *sing.*) the classification and analysis of the phonemes of a language.

phonetic (fəˈnɛtɪk) *adj.* 1. of phonetics. 2. denoting any perceptible distinction between one speech sound and another. 3. conforming to pronunciation: *phonetic spelling.* [Greek *phōnein* to make sounds, speak] —**phoˈnetically** *adv.*

phonetics (fəˈnɛtɪks) *n.* (functioning as *sing.*) the study of speech processes, including the production, perception, and analysis of speech sounds.

phoney or *esp. U.S.* **phony** (ˈfəʊnɪ) *Informal.* ~*adj.* **-nier, -niest.** 1. not genuine; fake: *a phoney name; a phoney diamond.* 2. (of a person) insincere or pretentious. ~*n., pl.* **-neys** or *esp. U.S.* **-nies.** 3. an insincere or pretentious person. 4. something that is not genuine; a fake. [origin unknown]

phonograph (ˈfəʊnəˌɡrɑːf) *n.* 1. an early form of record player capable of recording and reproducing sound on wax cylinders.

2. *U.S. & Canad.* a record player. [Greek *phonē* sound + *graphein* to write]

phonology (fə'nɒlədʒɪ) *n., pl.* **-gies. 1.** the study of the sound system of a language or of languages in general. **2.** such a sound system. [Greek *phonē* sound, voice + -LOGY] **—phonological** (ˌfəunə'lɒdʒɪkʰl, ˌfɒn-) *adj.*

phooey ('fuːɪ) *interj. Informal.* an exclamation of scorn or contempt. [prob. var. of *phew*]

phosphate ('fɒsfeɪt) *n.* **1.** any salt or ester of any phosphoric acid. **2.** (*often pl.*) chemical fertilizer containing phosphorous compounds. **—phosphatic** (fɒs'fætɪk) *adj.*

phosphor ('fɒsfə) *n.* a substance capable of emitting light when irradiated with particles of electromagnetic radiation. [Greek *phōsphoros* phosphorus]

phosphoresce (ˌfɒsfə'rɛs) *vb.* to exhibit phosphorescence.

phosphorescence (ˌfɒsfə'rɛsəns) *n.* **1.** *Physics.* a fluorescence that persists after the bombarding radiation producing it has stopped. **2.** the light emitted in phosphorescence. **—ˌphospho'rescent** *adj.*

phosphoric (fɒs'fɒrɪk) *adj.* of or containing phosphorus in the pentavalent state.

phosphorous ('fɒsfərəs) *adj.* of or containing phosphorus in the trivalent state.

phosphorus ('fɒsfərəs) *n.* a toxic flammable nonmetallic element which appears luminous in the dark. It exists in two forms, white and red. Symbol: P [Greek *phōsphoros* light-bringing]

photo ('fəutəu) *n., pl.* **-tos.** short for **photograph.**

photo- *combining form.* **1.** of or produced by light: *photosynthesis.* **2.** indicating a photographic process: *photolithography.* [Greek *phōs, phōt-* light]

photocell ('fəutəuˌsɛl) *n.* a cell which produces a current or voltage when exposed to light or other electromagnetic radiation.

photocopier ('fəutəuˌkɒpɪə) *n.* a machine using light-sensitive photographic materials to reproduce written, printed, or graphic work.

photocopy ('fəutəuˌkɒpɪ) *n., pl.* **-copies. 1.** a photographic reproduction of written, printed, or graphic work. ~*vb.* **-copying, -copied. 2.** to reproduce (written, printed, or graphic work) on photographic material.

photoelectric (ˌfəutəuɪ'lɛktrɪk) *adj.* of or concerned with electric or electronic effects caused by light or other electromagnetic radiation. **—photoelectricity** (ˌfəutəuɪlek'trɪsɪtɪ) *n.*

photoengraving (ˌfəutəuɪn'greɪvɪŋ) *n.* **1.** a photomechanical process for producing letterpress printing plates. **2.** a print made from such a plate. **—ˌphotoen'grave** *vb.*

photo finish *n.* a finish of a race in which contestants are so close that a photograph is needed to decide the result.

photoflash ('fəutəuˌflæʃ) *n.* same as **flashbulb.**

photoflood ('fəutəuˌflʌd) *n.* a highly incandescent electric lamp used for indoor photography and television.

photogenic (ˌfəutə'dʒɛnɪk) *adj.* **1.** (esp. of a person) having a general facial appearance that looks attractive in photographs. **2.** *Biol.* producing or emitting light.

photograph ('fəutəˌgrɑːf) *n.* **1.** an image of an object, person or scene in the form of a print or slide recorded by a camera. ~*vb.* **2.** to take a photograph of (an object, person or scene).

photographic (ˌfəutə'græfɪk) *adj.* **1.** of or like photography or a photograph. **2.** (of a person's memory) able to retain facts or appearances in precise detail. **—photo'graphically** *adv.*

photography (fə'tɒgrəfɪ) *n.* **1.** the process of recording images on sensitized material by the action of light or other radiant energy. **2.** the art, practice, or occupation of taking photographs. **—pho'tographer** *n.*

photogravure (ˌfəutəugrə'vjuə) *n.* any of various methods in which an etched metal plate for printing is produced by the use of photography. [PHOTO- + French *gravure* engraving]

photolithography (ˌfəutəulɪ'θɒgrəfɪ) *n.* a lithographic printing process using photographically made plates. **—ˌphotoli'thographer** *n.*

photometer (fəu'tɒmɪtə) *n.* an instrument used to measure the intensity of light.

photometry (fəu'tɒmɪtrɪ) *n.* the branch of physics concerned with the measurement of the intensity of light. **—pho'tometrist** *n.*

photomontage (ˌfəutəumɒn'tɑːʒ) *n.* **1.** the combination of several photographs to produce a composite picture. **2.** a composite picture so produced.

photon ('fəutɒn) *n.* a quantum of electromagnetic radiation energy, such as light, having both particle and wave behaviour.

photosensitive (ˌfəutəu'sɛnsɪtɪv) *adj.* sensitive to electromagnetic radiation, esp. light.

Photostat ('fəutəuˌstæt) *n.* **1.** *Trademark.* a type of photocopying machine or process. **2.** any copy made by such a machine. ~*vb.* **-statting** *or* **-stating, -statted** *or* **-stated. 3.** to make a Photostat copy (of).

photosynthesis (ˌfəutəu'sɪnθɪsɪs) *n.* (in plants) the synthesis of organic compounds from carbon dioxide and water using light energy absorbed by chlorophyll. **—ˌphoto'synthesize** *or* **-sise** *vb.* **—photosynthetic** (ˌfəutəusɪn'θɛtɪk) *adj.*

phototropism (ˌfəutəu'trəupɪzəm) *n.* the growth of plants towards a source of light. [PHOTO- + Greek *tropos* turn] **—ˌphoto'tropic** *adj.*

phrasal verb *n.* a phrase that consists of a verb plus an adverb or preposition, esp. one the meaning of which cannot be deduced from its parts, such as *take in* meaning *deceive.*

phrase (freɪz) *n.* **1.** a group of words forming a unit of meaning in a sentence. **2.** an idiomatic or original expression. **3.** *Music.* a small group of notes forming a coherent unit of melody. ~*vb.* **4.** to express orally or in a phrase. **5.** *Music.* to divide (a melodic line or part) into musical phrases, esp. in performance. [Greek *phrasis* speech] —**'phrasal** *adj.*

phraseology (ˌfreɪzɪ'ɒlədʒɪ) *n., pl.* **-gies.** the manner in which words or phrases are used.

phrenology (frɪ'nɒlədʒɪ) *n.* (formerly) the study of the shape and size of the skull as a means of finding out a person's character and mental ability. [Greek *phrēn* mind + -LOGY] —**phrenological** (ˌfrenə'lɒdʒɪk⁸l) *adj.* —**phre'nologist** *n.*

phut (fʌt) *Informal.* ~*n.* **1.** a representation of a muffled explosive sound. ~*adv.* **2. go phut.** to break down or collapse. [imit.]

phylactery (fɪ'læktərɪ) *n., pl.* **-teries.** *Judaism.* either of the pair of square cases containing biblical passages, worn by Jewish men on the left arm and head during weekday morning prayers. [Greek *phulaktērion* safeguard]

phylum (ˈfaɪləm) *n., pl.* **-la.** a major taxonomic division of the animals and plants that contain one or more classes. [Greek *phulon* race]

physical (ˈfɪzɪk⁸l) *adj.* **1.** of the body, as distinguished from the mind or spirit. **2.** of material things or nature: *the physical universe.* **3.** of or concerned with matter and energy. **4.** of or relating to physics. —**'physically** *adv.*

physical education *n.* training and practice in sports and gymnastics.

physical geography *n.* the branch of geography that deals with the natural features of the earth's surface.

physical jerks *pl. n.* *Brit. informal.* repetitive keep-fit exercises.

physical science *n.* any of the sciences concerned with nonliving matter, such as physics, chemistry, astronomy, and geology.

physician (fɪ'zɪʃən) *n.* **1.** a medical doctor. **2.** *Archaic.* a healer. [Greek *phusis* nature]

physicist (ˈfɪzɪsɪst) *n.* a person versed in or studying physics.

physics (ˈfɪzɪks) *n.* (functioning as sing.) **1.** the branch of science concerned with the properties of matter and energy and the relationships between them. **2.** physical properties of behaviour: *the physics of the electron.* [translation of Greek *ta phusika* natural things]

physiognomy (ˌfɪzɪ'ɒnəmɪ) *n.* **1.** a person's features considered as an indication of personality. **2.** the outward appearance of something. [Greek *phusis* nature + *gnōmōn* judge]

physiography (ˌfɪzɪ'ɒɡrəfɪ) *n.* same as **physical geography.** [Greek *phusis* nature + -GRAPHY]

physiology (ˌfɪzɪ'ɒlədʒɪ) *n.* **1.** the branch of science concerned with the functioning of organisms. **2.** the processes and functions of all or part of an organism. [Greek *phusis* nature + -LOGY] —**ˌphysi'ologist** *n.* —**physiological** (ˌfɪzɪə'lɒdʒɪk⁸l) *adj.*

physiotherapy (ˌfɪzɪəʊ'θerəpɪ) *n.* the treatment of disease or injury by physical

means, such as massage or exercises, rather than by drugs. [*physio-* (prefix) physical + *therapy*] —**ˌphysio'therapist** *n.*

physique (fɪ'ziːk) *n.* the general appearance of the body with regard to size, shape, and muscular development. [French]

pi (paɪ) *n., pl.* **pis. 1.** the 16th letter in the Greek alphabet (Π, π). **2.** *Maths.* a number that is the ratio of the circumference of a circle to its diameter. Approximate value: 3.141 592... ; symbol: π

pia mater (ˈpaɪə 'meɪtə) *n.* the innermost of the three membranes that cover the brain and spinal cord. [Latin, lit.: pious mother]

pianissimo (pɪə'nɪsɪˌməʊ) *adj., adv. Music.* to be performed very quietly. Symbol: *pp* [Italian]

pianist (ˈpɪənɪst) *n.* a person who plays the piano.

piano[1] (pɪ'ænəʊ) *n., pl.* **-anos.** a musical stringed instrument played by depressing keys that cause hammers to strike the strings and produce audible vibrations. [short for *pianoforte*]

piano[2] (ˈpjɑːnəʊ) *adj., adv. Music.* to be performed softly. [Italian]

piano accordion (pɪ'ænəʊ) *n.* an accordion in which the right hand plays a pianolike keyboard. —**piano accordionist** *n.*

pianoforte (pɪˌænəʊ'fɔːtɪ) *n.* the full name for **piano**[1]. [Italian *piano e forte* soft & loud]

Pianola (pɪə'nəʊlə) *n. Trademark.* a type of mechanical piano, the music for which is encoded in perforations in a paper roll.

piazza (pɪ'ætsə) *n.* **1.** a large open square in an Italian town. **2.** *Chiefly Brit.* a covered passageway or gallery. [Italian: marketplace]

pibroch (ˈpiːbrɒx) *n.* a form of music for Scottish bagpipes, consisting of a theme and variations. [Gaelic *piobaireachd*]

pic (pɪk) *n., pl.* **pics** or **pix.** *Informal.* a photograph or illustration.

pica (ˈpaɪkə) *n.* **1.** a size of printer's type giving 6 lines to the inch. **2.** a typewriter type size having 10 characters to the inch. [Latin *pīca* magpie; sense connection obscure]

picador (ˈpɪkəˌdɔː) *n. Bullfighting.* a horseman who wounds the bull with a lance to weaken it. [Spanish]

picaresque (ˌpɪkə'rɛsk) *adj.* of or relating to a type of fiction in which the hero, a rogue, goes through a series of episodic adventures. [Spanish *pícaro* a rogue]

picayune (ˌpɪkə'juːn) *adj. U.S. & Canad. informal.* **1.** of small value or importance. **2.** mean; petty. ~*n.* **3.** any coin of little value, such as a five-cent piece. **4.** an unimportant person or thing. [French *picaillon* coin from Piedmont]

piccalilli (ˈpɪkəˌlɪlɪ) *n.* a pickle of mixed vegetables in a mustard sauce. [origin unknown]

piccanin (ˈpɪkəˌnɪn) *n. S. African informal.* a Black African child. [var. of *piccaninny*]

piccaninny *or esp. U.S.* **pickaninny**

(ˌpıkəˈnını) n., pl. **-nies**. Offensive. a small Black or Aboriginal child. [perhaps from Portuguese pequenino tiny one]

piccolo (ˈpıkəˌləʊ) n., pl. **-los**. a woodwind instrument an octave higher than the flute. [Italian: small]

pick[1] (pık) vb. **1.** to choose (someone or something) carefully; select. **2.** to gather (fruit, berries, or crops) from (a tree, bush, or field). **3.** to remove loose particles from (the teeth, nose, or nails). **4.** to pierce, dig, or break up (a hard surface) with a pick. **5.** (foll. by at) to nibble (at) without appetite. **6.** to separate (strands or fibres), as in weaving. **7.** to provoke (an argument or fight) deliberately. **8.** to steal (money or valuables) from (a person's pocket). **9.** to open (a lock) with an instrument other than a key. **10.** to make (one's way) carefully on foot: they picked their way through the rubble. **11. pick and choose.** to select fastidiously or fussily. ~n. **12.** freedom or right of selection: take your pick. **13.** a person or thing that is chosen first or preferred: the pick of the bunch. ~See also **pick off, pick on,** etc. [Middle English piken]

pick[2] (pık) n. **1.** a tool with a handle carrying a long steel head curved and tapering to a point at one or both ends, used for loosening soil or breaking rocks. **2.** any tool used for picking, such as an ice pick or toothpick. **3.** a plectrum. [perhaps a var. of PIKE[2]]

pickaback (ˈpıkəˌbæk) n., adv. same as **piggyback.**

pickaxe or U.S. **pickax** (ˈpıkˌæks) n. a large pick.

picket (ˈpıkıt) n. **1.** an individual or group standing outside an establishment to make a protest, or to dissuade strikebreakers from entering. **2.** a small detachment of troops positioned to give early warning of attack. **3.** a pointed stake that is driven into the ground to support a fence. ~vb. **4.** to post or act as pickets at (an establishment). **5.** to guard (a main body or place) by using or acting as a picket. [Old French piquer to prick]

picket fence n. a fence consisting of pickets driven into the ground.

picket line n. a line of people acting as pickets.

pickings (ˈpıkıŋz) pl. n. (sometimes sing.) money or profits acquired easily.

pickle (ˈpık°l) n. **1.** (often pl.) vegetables, such as onions and cucumbers, preserved in vinegar, brine, or a similar solution. **2.** any food preserved in this way. **3.** a liquid or marinade, such as spiced vinegar, for preserving vegetables, meat, or fish. **4.** Informal. an awkward or difficult situation: to be in a pickle. ~vb. **5.** to preserve or treat in a pickling liquid. [prob. Middle Dutch pekel]

pickled (ˈpık°ld) adj. **1.** (of food) preserved in a pickling liquid. **2.** Informal. intoxicated; drunk.

pick-me-up n. Informal. a tonic, esp. a special drink taken as a stimulant.

pick off vb. to aim at and shoot (people or things) one by one.

pick on vb. to select (someone) for something unpleasant, esp. in order to bully or blame.

pick out vb. **1.** to select for use or special consideration, as from a group. **2.** to distinguish (an object from its surroundings), as in painting: she picked out the woodwork in white. **3.** to recognize (a person or thing): we picked out his face among the crowd. **4.** to play (a tune) tentatively, as by ear.

pickpocket (ˈpıkˌpɒkıt) n. a person who steals from the pockets of others in public places.

pick-up n. **1.** a small truck with an open body used for light deliveries. **2.** Informal. a casual acquaintance, usually one made with sexual intentions. **3.** Informal. **a.** a stop to collect passengers or goods. **b.** the people or things collected. **4.** an electromagnetic transducer, such as that to which a record player stylus is attached, which converts vibrations into electrical signals. ~vb. **pick up. 5.** to gather up in the hand or hands. **6.** to raise (oneself) after a fall or setback. **7.** to obtain or purchase: she picked up nice shoes in the sales. **8.** to improve in health or condition: the market began to pick up. **9.** to learn gradually or as one goes along: I picked up dressmaking very quickly. **10.** to resume; return to. **11.** to accept the responsibility for paying (a bill). **12.** to collect or give a lift to (passengers or goods). **13.** Informal. to become acquainted with, esp. with a view to having sexual relations. **14.** Informal. to arrest. **15.** to receive (sounds or signals).

picky (ˈpıkı) adj. **pickier, pickiest.** Informal. fussy; finicky.

picnic (ˈpıknık) n. **1.** an excursion on which people bring food to be eaten in the open air. **2.** an informal meal eaten out-of-doors. **3.** Informal. an easy or agreeable task. ~vb. **-nicking, -nicked. 4.** to eat or take part in a picnic. [French piquenique] —ˈpicnicker n.

pico- prefix. denoting 10^{-12}: picofarad. [Spanish pico small quantity]

Pict (pıkt) n. a member of any of the peoples who lived in N Britain in the first to the fourth centuries A.D. [Late Latin Pictī painted men] —ˈPictish adj.

pictograph (ˈpıktəˌgrɑːf) n. **1.** a picture or symbol standing for a word or group of words, as in written Chinese. **2.** a chart on which symbols are used to represent values. [Latin pingere to paint] —ˌpictoˈgraphic adj.

pictorial (pıkˈtɔːrıəl) adj. **1.** relating to, consisting of, or expressed by pictures. ~n. **2.** a periodical containing many pictures. [Latin pingere to paint]

picture (ˈpıktʃə) n. **1.** a visual representation of a person, thing, or scene produced on a surface, as in a photograph or painting. **2.** a mental image: a clear picture of events. **3.** a situation considered as an observable scene: the political picture. **4.** a person or thing resembling another: he *was the picture of his father.* **5.** a person or scene typifying a particular state: *the picture of despair.* **6.** the image on a television screen. **7.** a motion picture. **8.** **the pictures.** *Chiefly Brit.* a cinema or film show. **9. in the picture.** informed about a situation. ~*vb.* **10.** to visualize or imagine. **11.** to describe or depict vividly. **12.** to put in a picture or make a picture of: *they were pictured sitting on the rocks.* [Latin *pingere* to paint]

picture moulding *or* **picture rail** *n.* the rail near the top of a wall from which pictures are hung.

picturesque (ˌpɪktʃəˈrɛsk) *adj.* **1.** visually pleasing, as in being striking or quaint: *a picturesque view.* **2.** (of language) graphic; vivid. [French *pittoresque*]

picture window *n.* a large window having a single pane of glass, usually facing a view.

piddle (ˈpɪdᵊl) *vb.* **1.** *Informal.* to urinate. **2.** (often foll. by *away*) to spend (one's time) aimlessly; fritter. [origin unknown]

piddling (ˈpɪdlɪŋ) *adj. Informal.* petty; trifling; trivial.

pidgin (ˈpɪdʒɪn) *n.* a language made up of elements of two or more other languages and used, often for trading purposes, between the speakers of other languages. [supposed Chinese pronunciation of *business*]

pidgin English *n.* a pidgin in which one of the languages involved is English.

pie (paɪ) *n.* **1.** a baked sweet or savoury filling in a pastry-lined dish, often covered with a pastry crust. **2. pie in the sky.** illusory hope or promise of some future good. [origin unknown]

piebald (ˈpaɪˌbɔːld) *adj.* **1.** marked in two colours, esp. black and white. ~*n.* **2.** a black-and-white horse. [dialect *pie* magpie + *bald*]

piece (piːs) *n.* **1.** an amount or portion forming a separate mass or structure; bit: *a piece of wood.* **2.** a small part, item, or amount broken off or separated from a whole: *a piece of bread.* **3.** an instance or occurrence: *a piece of luck.* **4.** an example or specimen of a style or type: *a beautiful piece of Dresden.* **5.** a literary, musical, or artistic composition. **6.** a coin: *a fifty-pence piece.* **7.** a firearm or cannon. **8.** a small object used in playing various games: *a chess piece.* **9. go to pieces.** (of a person) to lose control of oneself; have a breakdown. ~*vb.* **10.** (often foll. by *together*) to fit or assemble piece by piece. **11.** (often foll. by *up*) to patch or make up (a garment) by adding pieces. [Middle English *pece*]

pièce de résistance (ˌpjɛs də rɪˈziːstɒns) *n.* the principal or most outstanding item in a series. [French]

piece goods *pl. n.* goods, esp. fabrics, made in standard widths and lengths.

piecemeal (ˈpiːsˌmiːl) *adv.* **1.** bit by bit; gradually. ~*adj.* **2.** fragmentary or unsystematic: *a piecemeal approach.* [Middle English *pece* piece + *-mele* a measure]

piece of eight *n., pl.* **pieces of eight.** a former Spanish coin worth eight reals.

piecework (ˈpiːsˌwɜːk) *n.* work paid for according to the quantity produced.

pie chart *n.* a circular graph divided into sectors proportional to the sizes of the quantities represented.

pied (paɪd) *adj.* having markings of two or more colours. [dialect *pie* magpie]

pied-à-terre (ˌpjeɪtɑːˈtɛə) *n., pl.* **pieds-à-terre** (ˌpjeɪtɑːˈtɛə). a flat or other lodging for occasional use. [French, lit.: foot on (the) ground]

pie-eyed *adj. Slang.* drunk.

pier (pɪə) *n.* **1.** a structure with a deck that is built out over water, and used as a landing place or promenade. **2.** a pillar or support that bears heavy loads. **3.** the part of a wall between two adjacent openings. [Middle English *per*]

pierce (pɪəs) *vb.* **1.** to form or cut (a hole) in (something) as with a sharp instrument. **2.** to thrust into sharply: *the thorn pierced his heel.* **3.** to force (a way) through (something). **4.** (of light) to shine through (darkness). **5.** (of sounds or cries) to sound sharply through (the silence). **6.** to penetrate: *piercing cold.* [Old French *percer*] —**ˈpiercing** *adj.*

pier glass *n.* a tall narrow mirror, designed to hang on the wall between windows.

Pierrot (ˈpɪərəʊ) *n.* a male character from French pantomime with a whitened face, white costume, and pointed hat.

pietism (ˈpaɪɪˌtɪzəm) *n.* exaggerated piety.

piety (ˈpaɪɪtɪ) *n., pl.* **-ties. 1.** dutiful devotion to God and observance of religious principles. **2.** the quality of being pious. **3.** a pious action or saying. [Latin *pietās*]

piezoelectric effect (paɪˌiːzəʊɪˈlɛktrɪk) *or* **piezoelectricity** (paɪˌiːzəʊɪlɛkˈtrɪsɪtɪ) *n. Physics.* **a.** the production of electricity by applying a mechanical stress to certain crystals. **b.** the converse effect in which stress is produced in a crystal as a result of an applied voltage. [Greek *piezein* to press]

piffle (ˈpɪfᵊl) *n. Informal.* nonsense. [origin unknown]

piffling (ˈpɪflɪŋ) *adj. Informal.* worthless; trivial.

pig (pɪg) *n.* **1.** a wild or domesticated mammal typically having a long head with a movable snout and a thick bristle-covered skin. **2.** *Informal.* a dirty, greedy, or bad-mannered person. **3.** *Offensive slang.* a policeman. **4.** a mass of metal cast into a simple shape. **5.** *Brit. informal.* something that is difficult or unpleasant. **6. a pig in a poke.** something bought or received without prior sight or knowledge. **7. make a pig of oneself.** *Informal.* to overeat. ~*vb.* **pigging, pigged. 8.** (of a sow) to give birth. **9.** Also: **pig it.** *Informal.* to live in squalor. [Middle English *pigge*]

pigeon[1] (ˈpɪdʒɪn) *n.* **1.** a bird with a heavy body, small head, short legs, and long pointed wings. **2.** *Slang.* a victim or dupe. [Old French *pijon* young dove]

pigeon[2] ('pɪdʒɪn) *n. Brit. informal.* concern or responsibility: *that's your pigeon, John.* [from *pidgin*]

pigeonhole ('pɪdʒɪn,həʊl) *n.* **1.** a small compartment, as in a bureau, for filing papers. ~*vb.* **2.** to classify or categorize. **3.** to put aside or defer.

pigeon-toed *adj.* having the toes or feet turned inwards.

piggery ('pɪgərɪ) *n., pl.* **-geries.** a place where pigs are kept.

piggish ('pɪgɪʃ) *adj.* like a pig, esp. in appetite or manners. —**'piggishness** *n.*

piggy ('pɪgɪ) *n., pl.* **-gies.** **1.** a child's word for a **pig.** ~*adj.* **-gier, -giest.** **2.** same as **piggish.**

piggyback ('pɪgɪ,bæk) *or* **pickaback** *n.* **1.** a ride on the back and shoulders of another person. ~*adv., adj.* **2.** on the back and shoulders of another person.

piggy bank *n.* a child's coin bank shaped like a pig with a slot for coins.

pig-headed *adj.* stupidly stubborn.

pig iron *n.* crude iron produced in a blast furnace and poured into moulds.

Pig Islander *n. N.Z. informal.* a New Zealander.

piglet ('pɪglɪt) *n.* a young pig.

pigment ('pɪgmənt) *n.* **1.** any substance used to impart colour to paint or dye. **2.** a substance occurring in plant or animal tissue and producing a characteristic colour. [Latin *pigmentum*] —**'pigmentary** *adj.*

pigmentation (,pɪgmən'teɪʃən) *n.* coloration in plants, animals, or man caused by the presence of pigments.

Pigmy ('pɪgmɪ) *n., pl.* **-mies.** same as **Pygmy.**

pigskin ('pɪg,skɪn) *n.* **1.** the skin of the domestic pig. **2.** leather made of this skin. **3.** *U.S. & Canad. informal.* a football.

pigsty ('pɪg,staɪ) *or U.S. & Canad.* **pigpen** *n., pl.* **-sties.** **1.** a pen for pigs; sty. **2.** *Brit.* an untidy place.

pigswill ('pɪg,swɪl) *n.* waste food or other edible matter fed to pigs.

pigtail ('pɪg,teɪl) *n.* a plait of hair or one of two plaits on either side of the face.

pike[1] (paɪk) *n., pl.* **pike** *or* **pikes.** large predatory freshwater fish with a broad flat snout, strong teeth, and an elongated body covered with small scales. [Old English *pīc* point, from the shape of its jaw]

pike[2] (paɪk) *n.* a medieval weapon consisting of a metal spearhead joined to a long pole. [Old English *pīc* point] —**'pikeman** *n.*

pikestaff ('paɪk,stɑːf) *n.* the wooden handle of a pike.

pilaster (pɪ'læstə) *n.* a shallow rectangular column attached to the face of a wall. [Latin *pīla* pillar]

pilau (pɪ'laʊ) *or* **pilaf** ('pɪlæf) *n.* a dish originating from the East, consisting of rice flavoured with spices and cooked in stock, to which meat, poultry, or fish may be added. [Turkish *pilāw*]

pilchard ('pɪltʃəd) *n.* a European food fish of the herring family, with a rounded body

covered with large scales. [origin unknown]

pile[1] (paɪl) *n.* **1.** a collection of objects laid on top of one another. **2.** *Informal.* a large amount: *a pile of money; piles of work.* **3.** same as **pyre.** **4.** a large building or group of buildings. **5.** *Physics.* a nuclear reactor. ~*vb.* **6.** (often foll. by *up*) to collect or be collected into a pile: *snow piled up in the drive.* **7.** (foll. by *in, into, off, out,* etc.) to move in a group, often in a hurried manner: *to pile off the bus.* **8. pile it on.** *Informal.* to exaggerate. ~See also **pile up.** [Latin *pīla* stone pier]

pile[2] (paɪl) *n.* a long heavy beam driven into the ground as a foundation for a structure. [Latin *pīlum*]

pile[3] (paɪl) *n.* the yarns in a fabric that stand up or out from the weave, as in carpeting or velvet. [Latin *pilus* hair]

pile-driver *n.* a machine that drives piles into the ground.

piles (paɪlz) *pl. n.* haemorrhoids. [Latin *pilae* balls]

pile up *vb.* **1.** to gather or be gathered in a pile. ~*n.* **pile-up.** **2.** *Informal.* a multiple collision of vehicles.

pilfer ('pɪlfə) *vb.* to steal (minor items), esp. in small quantities. [Old French *pelfre* booty]

pilgrim ('pɪlgrɪm) *n.* **1.** a person who undertakes a journey to a sacred place. **2.** any wayfarer. [Latin *peregrinus* foreign]

pilgrimage ('pɪlgrɪmɪdʒ) *n.* **1.** a journey to a shrine or other sacred place. **2.** a journey or long search made for exalted or sentimental reasons.

Pilgrim Fathers *or* **Pilgrims** *pl. n.* **the.** the English Puritans who founded Plymouth Colony in SE Massachusetts (1620).

pill (pɪl) *n.* **1.** a small round or oval mass of a medicinal substance, intended to be swallowed whole. **2. the pill.** *Informal.* an oral contraceptive. **3.** something unpleasant that must be endured: *her reinstatement was a bitter pill to swallow.* [Latin *pilula* a little ball]

pillage ('pɪlɪdʒ) *vb.* **1.** to loot or plunder (a town). ~*n.* **2.** the act of pillaging; booty. [Old French *piller* to despoil]

pillar ('pɪlə) *n.* **1.** an upright structure of stone, brick or metal, used as a support; column. **2.** something resembling this: *a pillar of smoke.* **3.** a prominent supporter: *a pillar of the Church.* **4. from pillar to post.** from one place to another. [Latin *pīla*]

pillar box *n.* (in Britain) a red pillar-shaped public letter box situated on a pavement.

pillbox ('pɪl,bɒks) *n.* **1.** a box for pills. **2.** a small enclosed fortified emplacement, made of reinforced concrete. **3.** a small round hat.

pillion ('pɪljən) *n.* **1.** a seat or place behind the rider of a motorcycle or horse. ~*adv.* **2.** on a pillion: *to ride pillion.* [Gaelic]

pillory ('pɪlərɪ) *n., pl.* **-ries.** **1.** a wooden framework into which offenders were formerly locked by the neck and wrists and exposed to public abuse and ridicule. ~*vb.* **-rying, -ried.** 2. to expose to public scorn or ridicule. 3. to punish by putting in a pillory. [Old French *pilori*]

pillow ('pɪləʊ) *n.* 1. a cloth case stuffed with feathers or foam rubber used to support the head during sleep. ~*vb.* 2. to rest (one's head) on or as if on a pillow. [Old English *pylwe*]

pillowcase ('pɪləʊ,keɪs) *or* **pillowslip** ('pɪləʊ,slɪp) *n.* a removable washable cover of cotton or other fabric for a pillow.

pilot ('paɪlət) *n.* 1. a person who is qualified to operate an aircraft or spacecraft in flight. 2. a person employed to steer or guide a ship into or out of a port. 3. a person who acts as a guide. 4. (*modifier*) serving as a test or trial: *a pilot project.* 5. (*modifier*) serving as a guide: *a pilot beacon.* ~*vb.* 6. to act as pilot of. 7. to control the course of. 8. to guide or lead (a project or people). [French *pilote*, from Greek]

pilot light *n.* a small auxiliary flame that ignites the main burner of a gas appliance.

pilot officer *n.* the most junior commissioned rank in certain air forces.

pimento (pɪ'mentəʊ) *n., pl.* **-tos.** same as **allspice** or **pimiento.** [Spanish *pimiento* pepper plant]

pimiento (pɪ'mjentəʊ, -'mɛn-) *n., pl.* **-tos.** a Spanish pepper with a red fruit used as a vegetable. [var. of *pimento*]

pimp (pɪmp) *n.* 1. a man who obtains customers for a prostitute or brothel, in return for a share of the earnings. ~*vb.* 2. to act as a pimp. [origin unknown]

pimpernel ('pɪmpə,nel, -n²l) *n.* a plant, such as the scarlet pimpernel, typically having small star-shaped flowers. [Old French *pimpernelle*]

pimple ('pɪmp²l) *n.* a small round usually inflamed swelling of the skin. [Middle English] —'**pimpled** *adj.* —'**pimply** *adj.*

pin (pɪn) *n.* 1. a short stiff straight piece of wire with a pointed end and a rounded head: used mainly for fastening. 2. short for **cotter pin, hairpin, rolling pin,** or **safety pin.** 3. a peg or dowel. 4. a pin-shaped brooch. 5. (in various bowling games) a usually club-shaped wooden object set up in groups as a target. 6. a clip on a hand grenade that prevents its detonation until removed or released. 7. *Golf.* the flagpole marking the hole on a green. 8. (*usually pl.*) *Informal.* a leg. ~*vb.* **pinning, pinned.** 9. to attach, hold, or fasten with or as if with a pin or pins. 10. to transfix with a pin, spear, etc. 11. **pin (something) on someone.** *Informal.* to place the blame for (something) on someone: *he pinned the charge on his accomplice.* ~See also **pin down.** [Old English *pinn*]

pinafore ('pɪnə,fɔː) *n.* 1. *Chiefly Brit.* an apron with a bib. 2. a dress with a sleeveless bodice or bib top, worn over a jumper or blouse. [*pin* + *afore* in front]

pinball ('pɪn,bɔːl) *n.* a game in which the player shoots a small ball through several hazards on a table or electrically operated machine.

pince-nez ('pæns,neɪ) *n., pl.* **pince-nez.** glasses that are held in place only by means of a clip over the bridge of the nose. [French, lit.: pinch-nose]

pincers ('pɪnsəz) *pl. n.* 1. a gripping tool consisting of two hinged arms and curved jaws that close on the workpiece. 2. the jointed grasping arms of animals such as crabs. [Old French *pincier* to pinch]

pinch (pɪntʃ) *vb.* 1. to press (something, esp. flesh) tightly between a finger and thumb. 2. to squeeze or painfully press upon (a part of the body): *these shoes pinch.* 3. to cause stinging pain to: *the cold pinched his face.* 4. to make thin or drawn-looking, as from grief or lack of food. 5. (usually foll. by *off, out,* or *back*) to remove the tips of (a plant shoot) to correct or encourage growth. 6. *Informal.* to steal. 7. *Informal.* to arrest. ~*n.* 8. a squeeze or sustained nip. 9. the quantity of a substance, such as salt, that can be taken between a thumb and finger. 10. painful or extreme stress or need: *the pinch of poverty.* 11. **at a pinch.** if absolutely necessary. [prob. from Old French]

pinchbeck ('pɪntʃ,bek) *n.* 1. an alloy of copper and zinc, used as imitation gold. ~*adj.* 2. sham or cheap. [after C. *Pinchbeck,* watchmaker who invented the alloy]

pincushion ('pɪn,kʊʃən) *n.* a small cushion in which pins are stuck ready for use.

pin down *vb.* 1. to force (someone) to make a decision or carry out a promise. 2. to define clearly: *a suspicion that he couldn't quite pin down.*

pine[1] (paɪn) *n.* 1. an evergreen tree of the N hemisphere, with long needle-shaped leaves and brown cones. 2. the light-coloured wood of this tree. [Latin *pīnus*]

pine[2] (paɪn) *vb.* 1. (often foll. by *for*) to feel great longing or desire; yearn. 2. (often foll. by *away*) to become ill or thin through worry or longing. [Old English *pīnian* to torture]

pineal gland *or* **body** ('pɪnɪəl) *n.* a pea-sized organ situated at the base of the brain. [Latin *pinea* pine cone]

pineapple ('paɪn,æp²l) *n.* an oval yellow-fleshed fruit with a thick hard skin that grows on a tropical American plant. [Middle English *pinappel* pine cone]

pine cone *n.* the seed-producing structure of a pine tree.

pine marten *n.* a mammal of N European and Asian coniferous woods, with dark brown fur and a creamy-yellow patch on the throat.

ping (pɪŋ) *n.* 1. a short high-pitched sound, as of a bullet striking metal. ~*vb.* 2. to make such a noise. [imit.]

pinger ('pɪŋə) *n.* a device that makes a pinging sound, esp. one that can be preset to ring at a particular time.

Ping-Pong ('pɪŋ,pɒŋ) *n. Trademark.* same as **table tennis.**

pinhead ('pɪn,hed) *n.* 1. the head of a pin. 2. *Informal.* a stupid person. —'**pin-,headed** *adj.*

pinhole ('pɪn,həʊl) n. a small hole made with or as if with a pin.

pinion[1] ('pɪnjən) n. **1.** Chiefly poetic. a bird's wing. **2.** the outer part of a bird's wing including the flight feathers. ~vb. **3.** to hold or bind (the arms) of (a person) so as to immobilize him. **4.** to confine. [Latin pinna wing]

pinion[2] ('pɪnjən) n. a cogwheel that engages with a larger wheel or rack. [French pignon]

pink[1] (pɪŋk) n. **1.** a pale reddish colour. **2.** a plant, such as the garden pink, with pink, red, or white fragrant flowers. **3. in the pink.** in good health. ~adj. **4.** of the colour pink. **5.** Brit. informal. left-wing. ~vb. **6.** same as **knock** (sense 7). [origin unknown] —'**pinkish** or '**pinky** adj.

pink[2] (pɪŋk) vb. to cut with pinking shears. [perhaps from Low German]

pinkie or **pinky** ('pɪŋkɪ) n., pl. -**ies**. Scot., U.S., & Canad. the little finger. [Dutch pinkje]

pinking shears pl. n. scissors with a serrated edge on one or both blades, giving a wavy edge to material cut, thus preventing fraying.

pin money n. a small amount of extra money saved or earned for incidental expenses.

pinnace ('pɪnɪs) n. a ship's boat. [French pinace]

pinnacle ('pɪnək²l) n. **1.** the highest point of fame or success. **2.** a towering peak, as of a mountain. **3.** a slender spire on the top of a buttress, gable, or tower. [Latin pinna wing]

pinnate ('pɪneɪt) adj. (of compound leaves) having leaflets growing opposite each other in pairs. [Latin pinna feather]

pinny ('pɪnɪ) n., pl. -**nies**. a child's or informal name for **pinafore** (sense 1).

pinpoint ('pɪn,pɔɪnt) vb. **1.** to locate or identify exactly: we've pinpointed the fault. ~n. **2.** (modifier) exact: pinpoint accuracy.

pinprick ('pɪn,prɪk) n. a small irritation or annoyance.

pins and needles n. (functioning as sing.) Informal. a tingling sensation in a part of the body.

pinstripe ('pɪn,straɪp) n. (in textiles) a very narrow stripe in fabric or the fabric itself.

pint (paɪnt) n. **1.** a unit of liquid measure of capacity equal to one eighth of a gallon. 1 Brit. pint is equal to 0.568 litre, 1 U.S. pint to 0.473 litre. **2.** Brit. informal. a pint of beer. [Old French pinte]

pinta ('paɪntə) n. Informal. a pint of milk. [phonetic rendering of pint of]

pintail ('pɪn,teɪl) n., pl. -**tails** or -**tail**. a greyish-brown duck with a pointed tail.

pintle ('pɪnt²l) n. a pin or bolt forming the pivot of a hinge. [Old English pintel penis]

pinto ('pɪntəʊ) U.S. & Canad. ~adj. **1.** marked with patches of white; piebald. ~n., pl. -**tos**. **2.** a pinto horse. [American Spanish]

pint-size or **pint-sized** adj. Informal. very small.

pin tuck n. a narrow, ornamental fold, as used on shirt fronts and dress bodices.

pin-up n. **1.** Informal. a picture of a sexually attractive person, often when partially or totally undressed. **2.** Slang. a person who has appeared in such a picture. **3.** a photograph of a famous personality.

pinwheel ('pɪn,wiːl) n. same as **Catherine wheel.**

Pinyin ('pɪn'jɪn) n. a system of spelling used to transliterate Chinese characters into the Roman alphabet.

pion ('paɪɒn) or **pi meson** n. Physics. any of three subatomic particles which are classified as mesons.

pioneer (,paɪə'nɪə) n. **1.** an explorer or settler of a new land or region. **2.** an innovator or developer of something new. ~vb. **3.** to be a pioneer (in or of). **4.** to initiate or develop: to pioneer a medical programme. [Old French paonier infantryman]

pious ('paɪəs) adj. **1.** religious or devout. **2.** marked by false reverence; sanctimonious. [Latin pius] —'**piousness** n.

pip[1] (pɪp) n. the seed of a fleshy fruit, such as an apple or pear. [short for pippin]

pip[2] (pɪp) n. **1.** a short high-pitched sound, a sequence of which is used as a time signal on radio. **2.** any of the spots on a playing card, dice or domino. **3.** Informal. the emblem worn on the shoulder by junior officers in the British Army, indicating their rank. [imit.]

pip[3] (pɪp) n. **1.** a contagious disease of poultry. **2.** Facetious slang. a minor human ailment. **3.** Brit. slang. a bad temper or depression: she gives me the pip. [Middle Dutch pippe]

pip[4] (pɪp) vb. **pipping, pipped.** Brit. slang. **pip (someone) at the post.** to defeat (someone) whose success seems certain. [prob. from PIP[2]]

pipe (paɪp) n. **1.** a long tube used to convey water, oil or gas. **2. a.** a small bowl with an attached tubular stem, in which tobacco or other substances are smoked. **b.** the amount of tobacco that fills the bowl of a pipe. **3. put that in your pipe and smoke it.** Informal. accept that fact if you can. **4.** Zool., bot. any of various hollow organs, such as the respiratory passage of certain animals. **5. a.** any musical instrument whose sound production results from the vibration of an air column in a simple tube. **b.** any of the tubular devices on an organ. **6. the pipes.** See **bagpipes.** **7.** a boatswain's whistle. ~vb. **8.** to play (music) on a pipe. **9.** to summon or lead by a pipe: to pipe the dancers. **10.** to utter (something) shrilly. **11.** to convey (water, gas, etc.) by a pipe or pipes. **12.** to force cream or icing through a shaped nozzle to decorate food. ~See also **pipe down, pipe up.** [Old English]

pipeclay ('paɪp,kleɪ) n. a fine white pure clay, used in the manufacture of tobacco pipes and pottery and for whitening leather and similar materials.

pipe cleaner n. a short length of thin wires twisted so as to hold tiny tufts of yarn: used to clean the stem of a tobacco pipe.

piped music n. light music played through amplifiers as background music in a shop, restaurant or factory.

pipe down vb. Informal. to stop talking or making noise.

pipe dream n. a fanciful or impossible plan or hope. [alluding to dreams produced by smoking an opium pipe]

pipeline ('paɪp.laɪn) n. **1.** a long pipe used to transport oil or gas. **2.** a medium of communication, esp. a private one. **3. in the pipeline.** in the process of being completed, delivered, or produced

pipe organ n. same as **organ** (the musical instrument).

piper ('paɪpə) n. a person who plays a pipe or bagpipes.

pipette (pɪ'pɛt) n. a slender glass tube for transferring or measuring out known volumes of liquid. [French: little pipe]

pipe up vb. to speak up, esp. in a shrill voice.

pipi ('piːpiː) n., pl. **pipi** or **pipis**. **1.** an edible shellfish of New Zealand. **2.** an Australian mollusc of sandy beaches widely used as bait. [Maori]

piping ('paɪpɪŋ) n. **1.** pipes collectively, as in the plumbing of a house. **2.** a cord of icing or whipped cream often used to decorate desserts and cakes. **3.** a thin strip of covered cord or material, used to edge hems or cushions. **4.** a shrill voice or whistling sound. ~adj. **5.** making a shrill sound. **6. piping hot.** extremely hot.

pipistrelle (ˌpɪpɪ'strɛl) n. any of a genus of small brownish bats occuring in most parts of the world. [Italian pipistrello]

pipit ('pɪpɪt) n. a small songbird with a brownish speckled plumage and a long tail. [prob. imit.]

pippin ('pɪpɪn) n. any of several varieties of eating apple. [Old French pepin]

pipsqueak ('pɪpˌskwiːk) n. Informal. a person or thing that is insignificant or contemptible.

piquant ('piːkənt, -kɑːnt) adj. **1.** having a spicy taste. **2.** lively or stimulating to the mind. [French, lit.: prickling] —**'piquancy** n.

pique (piːk) n. **1.** a feeling of resentment or irritation, as from having one's pride wounded. ~vb. **piquing, piqued. 2.** to cause to feel resentment or irritation. **3.** to excite (curiosity or interest). [French piquer to prick]

piqué ('piːkeɪ) n. a close-textured fabric of cotton, silk, or spun rayon woven with lengthwise ribs. [French: pricked]

piquet (pɪ'kɛt, -'keɪ) n. a card game for two people played with a reduced pack. [French]

piracy ('paɪrəsɪ) n., pl. **-cies. 1.** Brit. robbery on the seas. **2.** a felony, such as robbery or hijacking, committed aboard a ship or aircraft. **3.** the unauthorized use

of patented or copyrighted material or ideas.

piranha (pɪ'rɑːnə) n. a small fierce freshwater fish of tropical America, with strong jaws and sharp teeth. [S. American Indian: fish with teeth]

pirate ('paɪrɪt) n. **1.** a person who commits piracy. **2.** a vessel used by pirates. **3.** a person who illicitly uses or appropriates someone else's literary, artistic, or other work. **4.** a person or group of people who broadcast illegally. ~vb. **5.** to use, appropriate, or reproduce (artistic work, ideas, etc.) illicitly. [Greek peira an attack] —**piratic** (paɪ'rætɪk) or **pi'ratical** adj.

pirouette (ˌpɪrʊ'ɛt) n. **1.** a body spin, esp. in dancing, on the toes or the ball of the foot. ~vb. **2.** to perform a pirouette. [French]

piscatorial (ˌpɪskə'tɔːrɪəl) adj. of or relating to fish, fishing, or fishermen. [Latin piscātōrius]

Pisces ('paɪsiːz, 'pɪ-) n. Astrol. the twelfth sign of the zodiac, the Fishes. [Latin: the fish (pl.)]

pisciculture ('pɪsɪˌkʌltʃə) n. the rearing and breeding of fish under controlled conditions. [Latin piscis fish]

piscine ('pɪsaɪn) adj. of or resembling a fish. [Latin piscis fish]

piss (pɪs) Taboo. ~vb. **1.** to urinate. **2.** to discharge as or in one's urine: to piss blood. ~n. **3.** an act of urinating. **4.** urine. [prob. imit.]

pissed (pɪst) adj. Brit. taboo slang. drunk.

piss off vb. Taboo slang. **1.** to annoy or disappoint. **2.** Chiefly Brit. to go away: often used to dismiss a person.

pistachio (pɪ'stɑːʃɪˌəʊ) n., pl. **-chios.** a Mediterranean nut with a hard shell and an edible green kernel. [Persian pistah]

piste (piːst) n. a slope or course for skiing. [French]

pistil ('pɪstɪl) n. the female reproductive part of a flower. [Latin pistillum pestle]

pistillate ('pɪstɪlɪt) adj. (of plants) having pistils.

pistol ('pɪst²l) n. a short-barrelled handgun. [Czech pišt'ala]

pistol-whip vb. **-whipping, -whipped.** U.S. to beat or strike with a pistol barrel.

piston ('pɪstən) n. a disc or cylindrical part that slides to and fro in a hollow cylinder. In an internal-combustion engine it is attached by a pivoted connecting rod to a crankshaft or flywheel, thus converting up-and-down motion into rotation. [Old Italian pistone]

pit¹ (pɪt) n. **1.** a large, usually deep opening in the ground. **2.** a mine or excavation, esp. for coal. **3.** a concealed danger or difficulty. **4. the pit.** hell. **5.** the area that is occupied by the orchestra in a theatre, located in front of the stage. **6.** an enclosure for fighting animals or birds. **7.** Anat. **a.** a small natural depression on the surface of a body, organ, or part. **b.** the floor of any natural bodily cavity: the pit of the stomach. **8.** Pathol. a pockmark. **9.** an area at the side of a motor-racing track for servicing or refuelling vehicles. **10.** the back of the ground floor of a theatre. **11.** same as **pitfall** (sense 2). ~vb. **pitting, pitted. 12.** (often foll. by *against*) to match in opposition, esp. as antagonists. **13.** to mark or become marked with pits. **14.** to place or bury in a pit. [Old English *pytt*]

pit² (pɪt) *Chiefly U.S. & Canad.* ~n. **1.** the stone of various fruits. ~vb. **pitting, pitted. 2.** to extract the stone from (a fruit). [Dutch: kernel]

pitapat ('pɪtə,pæt) *adv.* **1.** with quick light taps. ~n. **2.** such taps. [imit.]

pitch¹ (pɪtʃ) *vb.* **1.** to hurl or throw (something); fling. **2.** to set up: *pitch a tent.* **3.** to set the level, character, or slope of. **4.** to slope or fall forwards or downwards. **5.** (of a vessel) to dip and raise its bow and stern alternately. **6.** (foll. by *up*) *Cricket.* to bowl (a ball) so that it bounces near the batsman. **7.** *Music.* to sing or play (a note or interval) accurately. ~n. **8.** the degree of elevation or depression. **9.** the angle of descent of a downward slope. **10.** *Chiefly Brit.* (in many sports) the field of play. **11.** the distance between corresponding points or adjacent threads on a screw thread. **12.** the pitching motion of a ship. **13.** *Music.* the quality of the sound of a note that results from the frequency of the vibrations producing it: the higher the frequency, the higher the sound. **14.** the act or manner of pitching a ball, as in cricket, etc. **15.** *Chiefly Brit.* a vendor's station on a pavement. **16.** *Slang.* a persuasive sales talk, esp. one routinely repeated. ~See also **pitch in, pitch into.** [Middle English *picchen*]

pitch² (pɪtʃ) *n.* **1.** a thick sticky substance formed from coal tar and used for paving or waterproofing. **2.** any of various similar substances, such as asphalt, occurring as natural deposits. ~vb. **3.** to apply pitch to (something). [Old English *pic*]

pitch-black *adj.* extremely dark; unlit: *the room was pitch-black.*

pitchblende ('pɪtʃ,blɛnd) *n.* a blackish mineral which is the principal source of uranium and radium. [German *Pechblende*]

pitch-dark *adj.* extremely or completely dark.

pitched battle *n.* a fierce fight.

pitcher¹ ('pɪtʃə) *n.* a large jug, usually rounded with a narrow neck, used mainly for holding water. [Old French *pichier*]

pitcher² ('pɪtʃə) *n. Baseball.* the player on the fielding team who throws the ball to the batter.

pitcher plant *n.* a plant with leaves modified to form pitcher-like organs that attract and trap insects, which are then digested.

pitchfork ('pɪtʃ,fɔːk) *n.* **1.** a long-handled fork with two or three long curved prongs for tossing hay. ~vb. **2.** to use a pitchfork on (something).

pitch in *vb.* to cooperate or contribute.

pitch into *vb. Informal.* to attack (someone) physically or verbally.

pitch pine *n.* a pine tree of North America: a source of turpentine and pitch.

pitch pipe *n.* a small pipe that sounds a note. It is used for establishing the correct starting note for unaccompanied singing.

piteous ('pɪtɪəs) *adj.* exciting or deserving pity. —'**piteousness** *n.*

pitfall ('pɪt,fɔːl) *n.* **1.** an unsuspected difficulty or danger. **2.** a trap in the form of a concealed pit, designed to catch men or wild animals. [Old English *pytt* pit + *fealle* trap]

pith (pɪθ) *n.* **1.** the soft white lining inside the rind of fruits such as the orange. **2.** the essential part: *the pith of the matter was in those two phrases.* **3.** the soft spongy tissue in the centre of the stem of certain plants. [Old English *pitha*]

pithead ('pɪt,hɛd) *n.* the top of a mine shaft and the buildings and hoisting gear around it.

pith helmet *n.* a lightweight hat made of the pith of the sola, an E Indian swamp plant, that is worn for protection from the sun.

pithy ('pɪθɪ) *adj.* **pithier, pithiest. 1.** terse and full of meaning or substance. **2.** of, resembling, or full of pith. —'**pithiness** *n.*

pitiable ('pɪtɪəb'l) *adj.* exciting or deserving pity or contempt. —'**pitiableness** *n.*

pitiful ('pɪtɪfʊl) *adj.* **1.** arousing or deserving pity. **2.** arousing or deserving contempt. —'**pitifully** *adv.* —'**pitifulness** *n.*

pitiless ('pɪtɪlɪs) *adj.* having or showing little or no pity or mercy. —'**pitilessly** *adv.*

piton ('piːtɒn) *n. Mountaineering.* a metal spike that may be driven into a crevice and used to secure a rope. [French]

pits (pɪts) *pl. n. Slang.* the worst possible person, place, or thing. [perhaps from *armpits*]

pittance ('pɪt'ns) *n.* a very small amount of money. [Old French *pietance* ration]

pitter-patter ('pɪtə,pætə) *n.* **1.** the sound of light rapid taps or pats, as of raindrops. ~vb. **2.** to make such a sound.

pituitary (pɪ'tjuːɪtərɪ) or **pituitary gland** *n.* the master endocrine gland at the base of the brain. It secretes hormones affecting skeletal growth, development of the sex glands, and the functioning of the other endocrine glands. [Late Latin *pituītārius* slimy]

pity ('pɪtɪ) *n., pl.* **pities. 1.** sorrow felt for the sufferings of another. **2. have** (or **take**) **pity on.** to have sympathy or show mercy for. **3.** a cause of regret: *what a pity you can't come.* ~vb. **pitying, pitied. 4.** to feel pity for. [Latin *pietās* duty] —'**pitying** *adj.*

più (pju) *adv. Music.* more: *più allegro.* [Italian]

pivot ('pɪvət) *n.* **1.** a short shaft or pin supporting something that turns. **2.** a person or thing upon which progress or success depends. ~vb. **3.** to mount on or provide with a pivot or pivots. **4.** to turn on a pivot. [Old French]

pivotal ('pɪvət'l) adj. 1. of or acting as a pivot. 2. of crucial importance.

pix (pɪks) n. a plural of **pic**.

pixie or **pixy** ('pɪksɪ) n., pl. **pixies**. (in folklore) a fairy or elf.

pizza ('piːtsə) n. a dish of Italian origin consisting of a baked disc of dough covered with cheese, tomatoes, herbs, etc. [Italian]

pizzazz or **pizazz** (pə'zæz) n. Informal. an attractive combination of energy and style. [origin unknown]

pizzicato (ˌpɪtsɪ'kɑːtəʊ) Music. ~adj., adv. (in music for the violin family) to be plucked with the finger. [Italian: pinched]

Pl. (in street names) Place.

plaas (plɑːs) n. S. African. a farm. [Afrikaans]

placard ('plækɑːd) n. 1. a notice for public display; poster. ~vb. 2. to post placards on or in. [Old French plaquart]

placate (plə'keɪt) vb. to pacify or appease (someone). [Latin plācāre] —**pla'catory** adj.

place (pleɪs) n. 1. a particular point or part of space or of a surface, esp. that occupied by a person or thing. 2. a geographical point, such as a town or city. 3. a position or rank in a sequence or order. 4. an open square lined with houses in a city or town. 5. space or room. 6. a house or living quarters. 7. any building or area set aside for a specific purpose. 8. the point reached in reading or speaking: to lose one's place. 9. right or duty: it is your place to give a speech. 10. appointment, position, or job: a place at college. 11. position, condition, or state: if I were in your place. 12. a space or seat, as at a dining table. 13. Maths. the relative position of a digit in a number. 14. **all over the place**. in disorder or disarray. 15. **go places**. Informal. to become successful. 16. **in** (or **out of**) **place**. in (or out of) the proper or customary position. 17. **in place of**. **a**. instead of; in lieu of: go in place of my sister. **b**. in exchange for: he gave her it in place of her ring. 18. **know one's place**. to be aware of one's inferior position. 19. **put someone in his** (or **her**) **place**. to humble someone who is arrogant, conceited, etc. 20. **take place**. to happen or occur. 21. **take the place of**. to be a substitute for. ~vb. 22. to put in a particular or appropriate place. 23. to find or indicate the place of. 24. to identify or classify by linking with an appropriate context: to place a face. 25. to make (an order or bet). 26. to find a home or job for (someone). 27. (often foll. by with) to put under the care (of). 28. Brit. (of a racehorse, greyhound, athlete, etc.) to arrive in first, second, third, or sometimes fourth place. [Latin platēa courtyard]

placebo (plə'siːbəʊ) n., pl. **-bos** or **-boes**. Med. an inactive substance administered to a patient usually to compare its effects with those of a real drug but sometimes for the psychological benefit to the patient through his believing he is receiving treatment. [Latin: I shall please]

place kick n. Rugby, American football,

etc. a kick in which the ball is placed in position before it is kicked.

placement ('pleɪsmənt) n. 1. the act of placing or the state of being placed. 2. arrangement or position. 3. the process of finding employment.

placenta (plə'sentə) n., pl. **-tas** or **-tae** (-tiː). the organ formed in the womb of most mammals during pregnancy, providing oxygen and nutrients for the fetus. [Latin, from Greek plakoeis flat cake] —**pla'cental** adj.

place setting n. the cutlery, crockery, and glassware laid for one person at a dining table.

placid ('plæsɪd) adj. having a calm appearance or nature: placid waters; a placid disposition. [Latin placidus peaceful] —**placidity** (plə'sɪdɪtɪ) or **'placidness** n. —**'placidly** adv.

placket ('plækɪt) n. Dressmaking. an opening or slit at the waist of a dress or skirt for buttons or zips or for access to a pocket. [perhaps from Medieval Dutch plackaet breastplate]

plagiarize or **-ise** ('pleɪdʒəˌraɪz) vb. to steal (ideas or passages) from (another work or author). [Latin plagium kidnapping] —**'plagia,rism** n. —**'plagia,rizer** or **-iser** n.

plague (pleɪg) n. 1. any widespread and usually highly contagious disease with a high fatality rate. 2. an infectious disease of rodents transmitted to man by the bite of the rat flea. 3. something that afflicts or harasses. 4. Informal. a nuisance. ~vb. **plaguing**, **plagued**. 5. to afflict or harass. 6. Informal. to annoy. [Latin plāga a blow]

plaice (pleɪs) n., pl. **plaice** or **plaices**. a European flatfish with an oval brown body marked with red or orange spots and valued as a food fish. [Greek platus flat]

plaid (plæd, pleɪd) n. 1. a long piece of tartan cloth worn over the shoulder as part of Highland costume. 2. a crisscross weave or cloth. [Scot. Gaelic plaide]

Plaid Cymru (ˌplaɪd 'kʌmrɪ) n. the Welsh nationalist party. [Welsh]

plain (pleɪn) adj. 1. flat or smooth; level. 2. not complicated; clear: the plain truth. 3. honest or straightforward. 4. lowly, esp. in social rank or education. 5. without adornment: a plain coat. 6. (of fabric) without pattern or of simple untwilled weave. 7. not good-looking. 8. Knitting. of or done in plain. ~n. 9. a level or almost level tract of country. 10. a simple stitch in knitting made by passing the wool round the front of the needle. ~adv. 11. clearly or simply: just plain told. [Latin plānus level, clear] —**'plainly** adv. —**'plainness** n.

plainchant ('pleɪnˌtʃɑːnt) n. same as **plainsong**.

plain chocolate n. chocolate with a slightly bitter flavour and dark colour.

plain clothes pl. n. ordinary clothes, as distinguished from uniform, worn by a detective on duty.

plain flour *n.* flour to which no raising agent has been added.

plain sailing *n.* **1.** *Informal.* smooth or easy progress. **2.** *Naut.* sailing in a body of water that is unobstructed; clear sailing.

plainsong ('pleɪn,sɒŋ) *n.* the style of unison unaccompanied vocal music used in the medieval Church, esp. in Gregorian chant. [translation of Medieval Latin *cantus plānus*]

plain-spoken *adj.* candid; frank; blunt.

plaint (pleɪnt) *n.* **1.** *Archaic.* a complaint or lamentation. **2.** *Law.* a statement in writing of grounds of complaint made to a court of law. [Old French *plainte*]

plaintiff ('pleɪntɪf) *n.* a person who brings a civil action in a court of law. [Old French *plaintif* complaining]

plaintive ('pleɪntɪv) *adj.* expressing melancholy; mournful. [Old French *plaintif* grieving] —**plaintively** *adv.*

plait (plæt) *n.* **1.** a length of hair that has been plaited. ~*vb.* **2.** to intertwine (strands or strips) in a pattern. [Latin *plicāre* to fold]

plan (plæn) *n.* **1.** a scheme or method for doing or achieving something. **2.** a drawing to scale of a horizontal section through a building taken at a given level. **3.** an outline or sketch. ~*vb.* **planning, planned. 4.** to form a plan (for) or make plans (for). **5.** to make a plan of (a building). **6.** to intend. [Latin *plānus* flat]

planchette (plɑːn'ʃɛt) *n.* a device that writes messages under supposed spirit guidance. [French: little board]

plane¹ (pleɪn) *n.* **1.** *Maths.* a flat surface in which a straight line joining any two of its points lies entirely on that surface. **2.** a level surface. **3.** a level of existence or attainment. **4.** an aeroplane. ~*adj.* **5.** level or flat. **6.** *Maths.* lying entirely in one plane. ~*vb.* **7.** (of a boat) to skim over the water at high speed. [Latin *plānum* level surface]

plane² (pleɪn) *n.* **1.** a tool with a steel blade for smoothing timber. ~*vb.* **2.** to smooth (timber) using a plane. **3.** (often foll. by *off*) to remove using a plane. [Latin *plānāre* to level]

planet ('plænɪt) *n.* any of the nine celestial bodies, Mercury, Venus, earth, Mars, Jupiter, Saturn, Uranus, Neptune, or Pluto, that revolve around the sun in elliptical orbits. [Greek *planaein* to wander] —**planetary** *adj.*

planetarium (,plænɪ'tɛərɪəm) *n., pl.* **-iums** or **-ia** (-ɪə). **1.** an instrument for projecting images of the sun, moon, stars, and planets onto a domed ceiling. **2.** a building in which such an instrument is housed.

planetoid ('plænɪ,tɔɪd) *n.* See **asteroid.**

plane tree or **plane** (pleɪn) *n.* a tree with ball-shaped heads of fruit and leaves with pointed lobes. [Greek *platos* wide (because of its broad leaves)]

plank (plæŋk) *n.* **1.** a stout length of sawn timber. **2.** one of the policies in a political party's programme. **3. walk the plank.** to be forced by pirates to walk to one's death

off the end of a plank jutting out from the side of a ship. [Late Latin *planca*]

planking ('plæŋkɪŋ) *n.* a number of planks.

plankton ('plæŋktən) *n.* the organisms inhabiting the surface layer of a sea or lake, consisting of small drifting plants and animals. [Greek *planktos* wandering]

plant (plɑːnt) *n.* **1.** any living organism that typically synthesizes its food from inorganic substances, lacks specialized sense organs, and has no powers of locomotion. **2.** such an organism that is smaller than a shrub or tree. **3.** the land, building, and equipment used in an industry or business. **4.** a factory or workshop. **5.** mobile mechanical equipment for construction or road-making. **6.** *Informal.* a thing positioned secretly for discovery by another, often in order to incriminate an innocent person. ~*vb.* **7.** (often foll. by *out*) to set (seeds or crops) into (ground) to grow. **8.** to place firmly in position: *I planted my chair beside hers.* **9.** *Slang.* to deliver (a blow or kiss). **10.** *Informal.* to position or hide, often in order to deceive or observe. **11.** *Informal.* to hide or secrete, usually for some illegal purpose or in order to incriminate someone. [Old English]

plantain¹ ('plæntɪn) *n.* a plant with a rosette of broad leaves and a slender spike of small greenish flowers. [Latin *planta* sole of the foot]

plantain² ('plæntɪn) *n.* a large tropical plant with a green-skinned banana-like fruit which is eaten as a staple food in many tropical regions. [Spanish *platano*]

plantation (plæn'teɪʃən) *n.* **1.** an estate, esp. in tropical countries, where cash crops such as rubber or coffee are grown on a large scale. **2.** a group of cultivated trees or plants. **3.** (formerly) a colony or group of settlers.

planter ('plɑːntə) *n.* **1.** the owner or manager of a plantation. **2.** a decorative pot for house plants.

plantigrade ('plæntɪ,greɪd) *adj.* walking on the entire sole of the foot, as humans and bears do. [Latin *planta* sole of the foot + *gradus* a step]

plaque (plæk, plɑːk) *n.* **1.** an ornamental or commemorative inscribed tablet. **2.** Also called: **dental plaque.** a filmy deposit on teeth consisting of mucus, bacteria, food, etc. [French]

plasma ('plæzmə) *n.* **1.** the clear yellowish fluid portion of blood or lymph in which the corpuscles and cells are suspended. **2.** a sterilized preparation of such fluid, taken from the blood, for use in transfusions. **3.** a former name for **protoplasm. 4.** *Physics.* a hot ionized gas containing positive ions and free electrons. [Greek: something moulded]

plaster ('plɑːstə) *n.* **1.** a mixture of lime, sand, and water that is applied to a wall or ceiling as a soft paste that hardens when dry. **2.** *Brit.* an adhesive strip of material for dressing a cut or wound. **3.** short for **mustard plaster** or **plaster of Paris.** ~*vb.* **4.** to coat (a wall or ceiling) with plaster. **5.** to apply like plaster: *she plas-*

tered make-up on her face; the walls were plastered with posters. **6.** to cause to lie flat or to adhere: *his hair was plastered down to his eyebrows.* [Greek *emplastron* healing dressing] —'**plasterer** *n.*

plasterboard ('plɑːstə,bɔːd) *n.* a thin rigid board, made of plaster compressed between two layers of fibreboard, used to form or cover walls.

plastered ('plɑːstəd) *adj. Slang.* drunk.

plaster of Paris *n.* a white powder that sets to a hard solid when mixed with water, used for making sculptures and casts, as an additive for lime plasters, and for making casts for setting broken limbs.

plastic ('plæstɪk) *n.* **1.** any one of a large number of synthetic materials that can be moulded when soft and then set. ~*adj.* **2.** made of plastic. **3.** easily influenced. **4.** capable of being moulded or formed. **5.** of moulding or modelling: *the plastic arts.* **6.** *Slang.* superficially attractive yet unoriginal or artificial: *plastic food.* [Greek *plastikos* mouldable] —**plasticity** (plæ-'stɪsɪtɪ) *n.*

plastic bomb *n.* a bomb consisting of plastic explosive fitted around a detonator.

plastic bullet *n.* a solid PVC cylinder fired by the police in riot control.

plastic explosive *n.* an adhesive jelly-like explosive substance.

Plasticine ('plæstɪ,siːn) *n. Trademark.* a soft coloured material used, esp. by children, for modelling.

plasticize *or* **-cise** ('plæstɪ,saɪz) *vb.* to make or become plastic.

plasticizer *or* **-ciser** ('plæstɪ,saɪzə) *n.* a substance added to a plastic material to soften it and improve flexibility.

plastic surgery *n.* the branch of surgery concerned with the repair or re-formation of missing, injured, or malformed tissues or parts. —**plastic surgeon** *n.*

plate (pleɪt) *n.* **1.** a shallow dish made of porcelain, earthenware, glass, etc., on which food is served. **2.** Also called: **plateful.** the contents of a plate. **3.** a shallow dish for receiving a collection in church. **4.** flat metal of uniform thickness obtained by rolling. **5.** a thin coating of metal usually on another metal. **6.** dishes or cutlery made of gold or silver. **7.** a sheet of metal, plastic or rubber having a printing surface produced by a process such as stereotyping. **8.** a print taken from such a sheet or from a woodcut. **9.** a thin flat sheet of a substance, such as metal or glass. **10.** a small piece of metal or plastic designed to bear an inscription and to be fixed to another surface. **11.** *Photog.* a sheet of glass coated with photographic emulsion on which an image can be formed by exposure to light. **12.** *Informal.* same as **denture** (sense 1). **13.** *Anat.* any flat platelike structure. **14.** a cup awarded to the winner of a sporting contest, esp. a horse race. **15.** any of the rigid layers of the earth's crust. **16. on a plate.** acquired without trouble: *he was handed the job on a plate.* **17. on one's plate.** waiting to be done or dealt with: *she has a lot on her plate at the moment.* ~*vb.* **18.** to coat (a

surface, usually metal) with a thin layer of other metal, as by electrolysis. **19.** to cover with metal plates, as for protection. **20.** to form (metal) into plate, usually by rolling. [Old French: something flat]

plateau ('plætəʊ) *n., pl.* **-eaus** *or* **-eaux** (-əʊz). **1.** a wide mainly level area of elevated land. **2.** a relatively long period of stability; levelling off: *the rising prices reached a plateau.* [French]

plated ('pleɪtɪd) *adj.* coated with a layer of metal.

plate glass *n.* glass formed into a thin sheet by rolling, used for windows.

platelayer ('pleɪt,leɪə) *n. Brit.* a workman who lays and maintains railway track.

platelet ('pleɪtlɪt) *n.* a minute particle occurring in the blood of vertebrates and involved in the clotting of the blood.

platen ('plæt'n) *n.* **1.** a flat plate in a printing press that presses the paper against the type. **2.** the roller on a typewriter, against which the keys strike. [Old French *platine*]

platform ('plætfɔːm) *n.* **1.** a raised floor or other horizontal surface. **2.** a raised area at a railway station, from which passengers have access to the trains. **3.** See **drilling platform. 4.** the declared aims as of a political party. **5.** the thick raised sole of some shoes. [French *plat* flat + *forme* layout]

platform ticket *n.* a ticket for admission to railway platforms but not for travel.

plating ('pleɪtɪŋ) *n.* **1.** a coating or layer of material, esp. metal. **2.** a layer or covering of metal plates.

platinum ('plætɪnəm) *n.* a silvery-white metallic element, very resistant to heat and chemicals: used in jewellery, laboratory apparatus, electrical contacts, dentistry, electroplating, and as a catalyst. Symbol: Pt [Spanish *platina* silvery element]

platinum blonde *n.* a girl or woman with silvery blonde hair.

platitude ('plætɪ,tjuːd) *n.* a trite or unoriginal remark. [French: flatness] —,**plati'tudinous** *adj.*

Platonic (plə'tɒnɪk) *adj.* **1.** of Plato or his teachings. **2.** (*often not cap.*) free from physical desire: *Platonic love.*

Platonism ('pleɪtə,nɪzəm) *n.* the teachings of Plato (?427–?347 B.C.), Greek philosopher, and his followers. —'**Platonist** *n.*

platoon (plə'tuːn) *n. Mil.* a subunit of a company, usually comprising three sections of ten to twelve men. [French *peloton* little ball, group of men]

platteland ('platə,lant) *n.* **the.** (in South Africa) the area outside the cities and chief towns. [Afrikaans]

platter ('plætə) *n.* a large shallow usually oval dish or plate. [Anglo-Norman *plater*]

platypus ('plætɪpəs) *n., pl.* **-puses.** See **duck-billed platypus.** [Greek *platus* flat + *pous* foot]

plaudit ('plɔːdɪt) *n.* (*usually pl.*) **1.** an expression of enthusiastic approval. **2.** a round of applause. [Latin *plaudite* applaud]

plausible ('plɔːzɪb'l) *adj*. 1. apparently reasonable, valid or true: *a plausible excuse*. 2. apparently trustworthy or believable: *a plausible speaker*. [Latin *plausibilis* worthy of applause] —,**plausi'bility** *n*. —'**plausibly** *adv*.

play (pleɪ) *vb*. 1. to occupy oneself in (a sport or recreation). 2. to contend against (someone) in a sport or game: *Ed played Tony at chess*. 3. to fulfil or cause to fulfil (a particular role) in a team game: *he plays in the defence*. 4. (often foll. by *about* or *around*) to behave carelessly: *he plays about with her company*. 5. (often foll. by *at*) to act the part (of) in or as in a dramatic piece. 6. to perform (a dramatic piece). 7. to be able to perform on (a musical instrument): *she plays the harp*. 8. to reproduce (a piece of music or note) on an instrument. 9. to emit or cause to emit: *he played the hose onto the garden*. 10. to cause (a radio, etc.) to emit sound. 11. to move freely or quickly: *lights played on the scenery*. 12. *Stock Exchange*. to speculate for gain in (a market). 13. *Angling*. to tire (a hooked fish) by alternately letting out and reeling in the line. 14. to put (a card) into play. 15. to gamble. 16. **play fair** (*or* **false**). (often foll. by *with*) to act fairly (*or* unfairly). 17. **play for time**. to cause delay so as to gain time to one's own advantage. 18. **play into the hands of**. to act directly to the advantage of (an opponent). ~*n*. 19. a dramatic piece written for performance by actors. 20. the performance of a dramatic piece. 21. games or other activity undertaken for pleasure. 22. conduct: *fair play*. 23. the playing of a game or the time during which a game is in progress: *rain stopped play*. 24. gambling. 25. activity or operation: *the play of the imagination*. 26. freedom of movement: *too much play in the rope*. 27. free or rapidly shifting motion: *the play of light on the water*. 28. fun or sport: *I only did it in play*. 29. **in** (*or* **out of**) **play**. (of a ball in a game) in (or not in) a position for continuing play according to the rules. 30. **make a play for**. *Informal*. to make an obvious attempt to gain (something). ~See also **play along**, **playback**. [Old English *plega* (n.), *plegan* (vb.)] —'**playable** *adj*.

play along *vb*. to cooperate (with) temporarily: *I'll play along with them for the moment*.

playback ('pleɪ,bæk) *n*. 1. the playing of a recording on magnetic tape. ~*vb*. **play back**. 2. to play (a recording) on (a magnetic tape) by means of a tape recorder.

playbill ('pleɪ,bɪl) *n*. a poster or bill advertising a play.

playboy ('pleɪ,bɔɪ) *n*. a rich man who devotes himself to such pleasures as nightclubs and female company.

play down *vb*. to minimize the importance of: *she played down the problems of the company*.

player ('pleɪə) *n*. 1. a person who plays in or is skilled at some game or sport. 2. a

person who plays a musical instrument. 3. an actor.

player piano *n*. a mechanical piano; Pianola.

playful ('pleɪful) *adj*. 1. full of high spirits and fun: *a playful kitten*. 2. good-natured and humorous: *a playful remark*. —'**playfully** *adv*.

playgoer ('pleɪ,gəʊə) *n*. a person who goes often to the theatre.

playground ('pleɪ,graʊnd) *n*. an outdoor area for children's play, either with equipment such as swings and slides, or adjoining a school.

playgroup ('pleɪ,gruːp) *n*. a regular meeting of small children for supervised creative play.

playhouse ('pleɪ,haʊs) *n*. a theatre.

playing field *n*. *Chiefly Brit*. a field or open space used for sport.

playlist ('pleɪ,lɪst) *n*. a list of records chosen for playing, as on a radio station.

playmate ('pleɪ,meɪt) *n*. a companion in play or recreation.

play off *vb*. 1. (usually foll. by *against*) to manipulate: *to play one person off against another*. 2. to take part in a play-off. ~*n*. **play-off**. 3. *Sport*. an extra contest to decide the winner when there is a tie. 4. *Chiefly U.S. & Canad*. a contest or series of games to determine a championship.

play on *vb*. to exploit (the feelings or weakness of another): *he played on my sympathy*.

play on words *n*. same as **pun**.

playpen ('pleɪ,pɛn) *n*. a small portable enclosure in which a young child can safely be left to play.

playschool ('pleɪ,skuːl) *n*. an informal nursery group for preschool children.

plaything ('pleɪ,θɪŋ) *n*. 1. a toy. 2. a person regarded or treated as a toy.

playtime ('pleɪ,taɪm) *n*. a time for play or recreation, such as a school break.

play up *vb*. 1. to highlight: *to play up one's best features*. 2. *Brit. informal*. to behave irritatingly (towards). 3. to hurt; give (one) trouble: *my back's playing up again*. 4. **play up to**. **a**. to support (another actor) in a performance. **b**. to try to please by flattery.

playwright ('pleɪ,raɪt) *n*. a writer of plays.

plaza ('plɑːzə) *n*. 1. an open public square, usually in Spain. 2. *Chiefly U.S. & Canad*. a modern shopping complex. [Spanish]

PLC *or* **plc** Public Limited Company.

plea (pliː) *n*. 1. an earnest appeal. 2. *Law*. a statement by or on behalf of a defendant. 3. an excuse: *a plea of poverty*. [Anglo-Norman *plai*]

plead (pliːd) *vb*. **pleading**, **pleaded**, **plead** (plɛd), *or esp. Scot. & U.S.* **pled**. 1. (sometimes foll. by *with*) to appeal earnestly (to). 2. to give as an excuse: *to plead poverty*. 3. *Law*. to declare oneself to be (guilty or not guilty) to the charge. 4. *Law*. to present (a case) in a court of law. 5. to address a court as an advocate. [Latin *placēre* to please]

pleadings ('pliːdɪŋz) pl. n. Law. the formal written statements presented by the plaintiff and defendant in a lawsuit.

pleasant ('plɛz*n̩t) adj. **1.** pleasing; enjoyable. **2.** having pleasing manners or appearance. [Old French plaisant] —'**pleasantly** adv.

pleasantry ('plɛz*n̩trɪ) n., pl. **-ries**. **1.** (often pl.) a polite or jocular remark: they exchanged pleasantries. **2.** agreeable jocularity. [French plaisanterie]

please (pliːz) vb. **1.** to give pleasure or satisfaction to (a person). **2.** to be the will of: if it pleases you; the court pleases. **3. if you please**. if you wish, sometimes used in ironic exclamation. **4.** pleased with. happy because of. **5. please oneself**. to do as one likes. ~adv. **6.** used in making polite requests or pleading. **7. yes please**. a polite phrase used to accept an offer or invitation. [Latin placēre] —**pleased** adj.

pleasing ('pliːzɪŋ) adj. giving pleasure.

pleasurable ('plɛʒərəb*l̩) adj. enjoyable or agreeable. —'**pleasurably** adv.

pleasure ('plɛʒə) n. **1.** an enjoyable sensation or emotion: the pleasure of hearing good music. **2.** something that gives enjoyment: his garden was his only pleasure. **3.** amusement or enjoyment. **4.** Euphemistic. sexual gratification: he took his pleasure of her. **5.** a person's preference. [Old French plaisir]

pleat (pliːt) n. **1.** a fold formed by doubling back fabric and pressing or stitching into place. ~vb. **2.** to arrange (material) in pleats. [var. of plait]

pleb (plɛb) n. Brit. informal, often offensive. a common vulgar person.

plebeian (plə'biːən) adj. **1.** of the common people. **2.** unrefined; vulgar: plebeian tastes. ~n. **3.** one of the common people, usually of ancient Rome. **4.** a coarse or vulgar person. [Latin plēbs the common people of ancient Rome]

plebiscite ('plɛbɪˌsaɪt, -sɪt) n. a direct vote by all the electorate on an issue of national importance. [Latin plēbiscītum decree of the people]

plectrum ('plɛktrəm) n., pl. **-tra** (-trə) or **-trums**. an implement for plucking the strings of a guitar or similar instrument. [Greek plektron]

pled (plɛd) vb. U.S. or (esp. in legal usage) Scot. a past of **plead**.

pledge (plɛdʒ) n. **1.** a solemn promise or agreement. **2. a.** security for the payment of a debt or the performance of an obligation. **b.** the condition of being security: in pledge. **3.** a token: a pledge of good faith. **4.** an assurance of support or goodwill, given by drinking a toast: we drank a pledge to their success. **5. take** or **sign the pledge**. to vow not to drink alcohol. ~vb. **6.** to promise solemnly. **7.** to bind by or as if by a pledge: I was pledged to secrecy. **8.** to give or offer (one's word or property) as a guarantee. **9.** to drink a toast to (a person or cause). [Old French plege]

Pleiocene ('plaɪəˌsiːn) adj., n. same as **Pliocene**.

Pleistocene ('plaɪstəˌsiːn) adj. Geol. of the epoch of geological time about 600 000 years ago. [Greek pleistos most + kainos recent]

plenary ('pliːnərɪ, 'plɛn-) adj. **1.** full or complete: plenary powers. **2.** (of an assembly) attended by all the members. [Latin plēnus full]

plenipotentiary (ˌplɛnɪpə'tɛnʃərɪ) adj. **1.** (usually of a diplomat) invested with full authority. ~n., pl. **-aries**. **2.** a person, usually a diplomat invested with full authority to transact business. [Latin plēnus full + potentia power]

plenitude ('plɛnɪˌtjuːd) n. **1.** abundance. **2.** fullness; completeness. [Latin plēnus full]

plenteous ('plɛntɪəs) adj. **1.** ample; abundant: a plenteous supply. **2.** producing abundantly: a plenteous harvest.

plentiful ('plɛntɪfʊl) adj. **1.** ample; abundant. **2.** having or yielding an abundance: a plentiful year. —'**plentifully** adv.

plenty ('plɛntɪ) n., pl. **-ties**. **1.** (often foll. by of) a great number or amount; lots: plenty of time. **2.** ample supplies: an age of plenty. ~det. **3.** very many; ample: plenty of people hate spiders. ~adv. **4.** Informal. fully: the coat was plenty big enough. [Latin plēnus full]

pleonasm ('pliːəˌnæzəm) n. Rhetoric. **1.** the use of more words than necessary, such as a tiny little child. **2.** an unnecessary word or phrase. [Greek pleonasmos excess] —ˌpleo'**nastic** adj.

plethora ('plɛθərə) n. an excess; overabundance. [Greek plēthōrē fullness]

pleura ('plʊərə) n., pl. **pleurae** ('plʊəriː). the thin transparent membrane enveloping the lungs. [Greek: side, rib] —'**pleural** adj.

pleurisy ('plʊərɪsɪ) n. inflammation of the pleura, making breathing painful. —**pleuritic** (plʊ'rɪtɪk) adj., n.

plexus ('plɛksəs) n., pl. **-uses** or **-us**. a complex network of nerves or blood vessels. [Latin plectere to braid]

pliable ('plaɪəb*l̩) adj. easily bent, influenced, or altered. —ˌplia'**bility** n.

pliant ('plaɪənt) adj. **1.** easily bent; supple. **2.** adaptable; easily influenced. [Old French plier to fold] —'**pliancy** n.

pliers ('plaɪəz) pl. n. a gripping tool consisting of two hinged arms usually with serrated jaws. [from PLY[1]]

plight[1] (plaɪt) n. a condition of extreme hardship or danger. [Old French pleit fold]

plight[2] (plaɪt) vb. **1.** to promise formally. **2. plight one's troth**. to make a promise to marry. [Old English pliht peril]

Plimsoll line ('plɪmsəl) n. a line on the hull of a ship showing the level that the water should reach if the ship is properly loaded. [after Samuel Plimsoll, who advocated its adoption]

plimsolls ('plɪmsəlz) pl. n. Brit. light rubber-soled canvas sports shoes. [from the resemblance of the sole to a Plimsoll line]

plinth (plɪnθ) n. **1.** the rectangular block

that forms the base of a column, pedestal, or pier. **2.** a base on which a statue stands. [Greek *plinthos* brick]

Pliocene or **Pleiocene** ('plaɪəʊˌsiːn) *adj.* *Geol.* of the epoch of geological time about 10 million years ago. [Greek *pleiōn* more + *kainos* recent]

PLO Palestine Liberation Organization.

plod (plɒd) *vb.* **plodding, plodded.** **1.** to walk with heavy slow steps. **2.** to work slowly and perseveringly. ~*n.* **3.** the act of plodding. [imit.] —'**plodder** *n.*

plonk[1] (plɒŋk) *vb.* **1.** (often foll. by *down*) to drop or be dropped heavily: *he plonked the money on the table.* ~*n.* **2.** the act or sound of plonking. [var. of *plunk*]

plonk[2] (plɒŋk) *n. Informal.* inferior wine. [origin unknown]

plonker ('plɒŋkə) *n. Slang.* a stupid person. [origin unknown]

plop (plɒp) *n.* **1.** the sound made by an object dropping into water without a splash. ~*vb.* **plopping, plopped.** **2.** to fall or cause to fall with a plop: *the stone plopped into the water.* ~*adv.* **3.** with a plop: *to go plop.* [imit.]

plosive ('pləʊsɪv) *Phonetics.* ~*adj.* **1.** pronounced with a sudden release of breath. ~*n.* **2.** a plosive consonant. [French *explosif* explosive]

plot[1] (plɒt) *n.* **1.** a secret plan for an illegal purpose. **2.** the story of a play, novel, or film. ~*vb.* **plotting, plotted.** **3.** to plan secretly; conspire. **4.** to mark (a course) on a map. **5.** to make a plan or map of. **6.** **a.** to locate (points) on a graph by means of coordinates. **b.** to draw (a curve) through these points. **7.** to construct the plot of (a play, novel, or film). [from PLOT[2], infl. by obs. *complot* conspiracy] —'**plotter** *n.*

plot[2] (plɒt) *n.* a small piece of land: *a vegetable plot.* [Old English]

plough or *esp. U.S.* **plow** (plaʊ) *n.* **1.** an agricultural implement for cutting or turning over the earth. **2.** a similar implement, such as a device for clearing snow. ~*vb.* **3.** to till (the soil) with a plough. **4.** to make (furrows or grooves) in (something) with or as if with a plough. **5.** (sometimes foll. by *through*) to move (through something) in the manner of a plough. **6.** (foll. by *through*) to work at slowly or perseveringly. **7.** (foll. by *into* or *through*) (of a vehicle) to run uncontrollably into something. [Old English *plōg* plough land]

Plough (plaʊ) *n.* **the.** the group of the seven brightest stars in the constellation Ursa Major.

ploughman or *esp. U.S.* **plowman** ('plaʊmən) *n., pl.* **-men.** a man who ploughs.

ploughshare or *esp. U.S.* **plowshare** ('plaʊˌʃɛə) *n.* the cutting blade of a plough.

plover ('plʌvə) *n.* a shore bird with a round head, straight bill, and large pointed wings. [Old French *plovier* rainbird]

plow (plaʊ) *n., vb. U.S.* same as **plough**.

ploy (plɔɪ) *n.* a manoeuvre designed to gain advantage in a situation. [from obs. [1] sense of *employ* meaning an occupation]

pluck (plʌk) *vb.* **1.** to pull off (feathers or

fruit) from (a fowl or tree). **2.** (sometimes foll. by *at*) to pull or tug. **3.** (foll. by *off*, *away*, etc.) *Archaic.* to pull (something) forcibly or violently (from something or someone). **4.** to sound (the strings) of (a musical instrument) with the fingers or a plectrum. **5.** *Slang.* to swindle. ~*n.* **6.** courage. **7.** a pull or tug. **8.** the heart, liver, and lungs of an animal used for food. [Old English *pluccian*]

pluck up *vb.* to muster (courage).

plucky ('plʌkɪ) *adj.* **pluckier, pluckiest.** courageous. —'**pluckily** *adv.* —'**pluckiness** *n.*

plug (plʌg) *n.* **1.** a piece of solid material used to stop up holes or waste pipes. **2.** a device having one or more pins to which an electric cable is attached: used to make an electrical connection when inserted into a socket. **3.** See **spark plug.** **4.** a cake or piece of tobacco for chewing. **5.** *Informal.* a favourable mention of a product or show, as on television. ~*vb.* **plugging, plugged.** **6.** to stop up (a hole or gap) with or as if with a plug. **7.** *Informal.* to make favourable and frequent mentions of (a product or show). **8.** *Slang.* to shoot: *he plugged six rabbits.* **9.** *Slang.* to punch. **10.** (foll. by *along*, *away*, etc.) *Informal.* to work steadily. [Middle Dutch *plugge*]

plug in *vb.* to connect (an electrical appliance) with a power source by means of an electrical plug.

plum (plʌm) *n.* **1.** an edible oval purple, yellow, or green fruit with an oval stone, that grows on a small tree. **2.** a raisin, as used in a cake or pudding. **3.** *Informal.* something of a superior or desirable kind. ~*adj.* **4.** dark reddish-purple. [Old English *plūme*]

plumage ('pluːmɪdʒ) *n.* the feathers of a bird. [Old French *plume* feather]

plumb (plʌm) *n.* **1.** a lead weight suspended at the end of a line and used to determine water depth or whether a structure, such as a wall, is vertical. **2. out of plumb.** not vertical. ~*adv.* **3.** vertical or perpendicular. **4.** *Informal, chiefly U.S.* utterly: *plumb stupid.* **5.** *Informal.* exactly. ~*vb.* **6.** to test the alignment of or make vertical with a plumb line. **7.** to experience (the worst extremes of): *to plumb the depths of despair.* **8.** to understand (something obscure): *to plumb a mystery.* **9.** to connect (a device) to a water pipe or drainage system. [Latin *plumbum* lead]

plumber ('plʌmə) *n.* a person who fits and repairs pipes and fixtures for water, drainage, or gas. [Old French *plommier* worker in lead]

plumbing ('plʌmɪŋ) *n.* **1.** the trade or work of a plumber. **2.** the pipes and fixtures used in a water, drainage, or gas installation.

plumb line *n.* a string with a metal weight, or **plumb bob,** at one end, used to determine depth or whether a structure, such as a wall, is vertical.

plume (pluːm) *n.* **1.** a large or ornamental feather. **2.** a feather or feathers worn as a

badge or ornament in a headband or hat.
3. something like a plume: *a plume of
smoke*. ~*vb*. **4.** to adorn with plumes. **5.**
(of a bird) to preen (itself or its feathers).
6. (foll. by *on* or *upon*) to pride (oneself).
[Old French]

plummet ('plʌmɪt) *vb*. **1.** to drop down;
plunge. ~*n*. **2.** the weight on a plumb
line. **3.** a weight attached to a fishing-line.
[Old French *plommet* ball of lead]

plummy ('plʌmɪ) *adj*. **-mier, -miest.** **1.** of,
full of, or like plums. **2.** *Brit. informal.* (of
a voice) deep, rich, and usually affected.
3. *Brit. informal.* choice; desirable.

plump[1] (plʌmp) *adj*. **1.** full or rounded;
chubby: *a plump turkey*. ~*vb*. **2.** (often
foll. by *up* or *out*) to make or become
plump: *to plump up a pillow*. [Middle
Dutch *plomp* blunt] —**'plumpness** *n*.

plump[2] (plʌmp) *vb*. **1.** (often foll. by *down,
into, etc.*) to drop or fall suddenly and
heavily. **2.** **plump for.** to choose one out
of a number. ~*n*. **3.** a heavy abrupt fall
or the sound of this. ~*adv*. **4.** suddenly
or heavily. **5.** straight down; directly: *the
plane landed plump in the middle of the
field*. **6.** in a blunt, direct, or decisive
manner. [prob. imit.]

plum pudding *n*. *Brit.* a boiled or
steamed pudding made with flour, suet,
and dried fruit.

plumy ('pluːmɪ) *adj*. **plumier, plumiest.**
1. feathery. **2.** covered or adorned with
feathers.

plunder ('plʌndə) *vb*. **1.** to steal (valuables or goods) from (a place) by force,
usually in wartime; loot. **2.** to steal (choice
or desirable things) from (a place): *to
plunder an orchard*. ~*n*. **3.** anything
plundered; booty. **4.** ~*n*. a plundering; pillage.
[prob. from Dutch *plunderen*]

plunge (plʌndʒ) *vb*. **1.** (usually foll. by
into) to thrust or throw (something or
oneself): *they plunged into the sea*. **2.** to
throw or be thrown into a certain condition: *the room was plunged into darkness*.
3. (usually foll. by *into*) to involve or
become involved deeply (in). **4.** to move
swiftly or impetuously. **5.** to descend very
suddenly or steeply: *a plunging neckline*.
6. *Informal.* to gamble heavily. ~*n*. **7.** a
leap or dive. **8.** *Informal.* a swim; dip. **9.**
a pitching motion. **10.** **take the plunge.**
Informal. to decide to do something risky
which cannot be altered later. [Old French
plongier]

plunger ('plʌndʒə) *n*. **1.** a rubber suction
cup used to clear blocked drains. **2.** a
device with a plunging motion; piston.

plunk (plʌŋk) *vb*. **1.** to pluck (the strings)
of (an instrument) or (of an instrument) to
produce a twanging sound when played.
2. (often foll. by *down*) to drop or be
dropped heavily. ~*n*. **3.** the act or sound
of plunking. [imit.]

pluperfect (pluː'pɜːfɪkt) *Grammar.* ~*adj*.
1. denoting a tense of verbs used in relating
past events where the action had already
occurred at the time of the action of a main
verb that is itself in a past tense. In English
this is a compound tense formed with *had*
plus the past participle. ~*n*. **2.** the plu-

perfect tense. [Latin *plūs quam perfectum*
more than perfect]

plural ('pluərəl) *adj*. **1.** of or consisting of
more than one. **2.** denoting a word indicating more than one. ~*n*. **3.** *Grammar.* **a.**
the plural number. **b.** a plural form. [Latin
plūs more]

pluralism ('pluərə,lɪzəm) *n*. **1.** the holding
by a person of more than one office. **2.** the
existence in a society of groups with distinctive ethnic origin, cultures, or religions.
—**'pluralist** *n., adj*. —**,plural'istic** *adj*.

plurality (pluə'rælɪtɪ) *n., pl.* **-ties.** **1.** the
state of being plural. **2.** *Maths.* a number
greater than one. **3.** a large number. **4.** a
majority.

pluralize *or* **-ise** ('pluərə,laɪz) *vb*. to make
or become plural.

plus (plʌs) *prep*. **1.** increased by the addition of: *four plus two*. **2.** with the addition
of: *a good job, plus a new car*. ~*adj*. **3.**
indicating addition: *a plus sign*. **4.** *Maths.*
same as **positive** (sense 7). **5.** on the
positive part of a scale. **6.** indicating the
positive side of an electrical circuit. **7.**
involving advantage: *a plus factor*. **8.**
Informal. having a value above that stated:
she had charm plus. **9.** slightly above a
specified standard: *he received a B+ for
his essay*. ~*n*. **10.** the symbol +, indicating addition. **11.** a positive quantity. **12.**
Informal. something positive or to the
good. **13.** a gain, surplus, or advantage.
~Mathematical symbol: + [Latin: more]

plus fours *pl. n.* men's baggy knickerbockers reaching below the knee, now only
worn for hunting or golf. [because made
with four inches of material to hang over
at the knee]

plush (plʌʃ) *n*. **1.** a fabric with a long soft
pile. ~*adj*. **2.** Also: **plushy.** *Informal.*
luxurious; costly. [French *pluche*]

Pluto ('pluːtəʊ) *n*. **1.** *Greek myth.* the god
of the underworld; Hades. **2.** the second
smallest planet.

plutocracy (pluː'tɒkrəsɪ) *n., pl.* **-cies.** **1.**
government by the wealthy. **2.** a state
ruled by the wealthy. **3.** a group that
exercises power by virtue of its wealth.
[Greek *ploutos* wealth + *-kratia* rule]
—**plutocratic** (,pluːtə'krætɪk) *adj*.

plutocrat ('pluːtə,kræt) *n*. a member of a
plutocracy.

plutonic (pluː'tɒnɪk) *adj*. (of igneous
rocks) formed from molten rock that has
cooled and solidified below the earth's
surface. [after the Greek god *Pluto*]

plutonium (pluː'təʊnɪəm) *n*. a toxic radioactive metallic element. Symbol: Pu [after
Pluto because Pluto lies beyond Neptune
and plutonium was discovered soon after
neptunium]

pluvial ('pluːvɪəl) *adj*. of or due to the
action of rain; rainy. [Latin *pluvia* rain]

ply[1] (plaɪ) *vb*. **plying, plied.** **1.** to work at
(a job or trade). **2.** to use (a tool). **3.**
(usually foll. by *with*) to provide (with) or
subject (to) repeatedly or persistently: *he
plied us with drink; he plied me with
questions*. **4.** to work steadily. **5.** (of a
ship) to travel regularly along (a route): *to

ply the trade routes. [Middle English *plye*, short for *aplye* to apply]

ply[2] ('plaɪ) *n., pl.* **plies. 1.** a layer, fold, or thickness, as of yarn or wood. **2.** one of the strands twisted together to make rope or yarn. [Old French *pli* fold]

Plymouth Brethren ('plɪməθ) *pl. n.* a Puritanical religious sect with no organized ministry.

plywood ('plaɪˌwʊd) *n.* a board made of thin layers of wood glued together under pressure, with the grain of one layer at right angles to that of the next.

Pm *Chem.* promethium.

PM 1. Paymaster. **2.** Postmaster. **3.** Prime Minister.

p.m. 1. after noon. [Latin *post meridiem*] **2.** postmortem (examination).

PMG 1. Paymaster General. **2.** Postmaster General.

PMS premenstrual syndrome.

PMT premenstrual tension.

pneumatic (njʊ'mætɪk) *adj.* **1.** of or concerned with air, gases, or wind. **2.** operated by compressed air: *pneumatic drill.* **3.** containing compressed air: *a pneumatic tyre.* [Greek *pneuma* breath, wind]

pneumatics (njʊ'mætɪks) *n.* (*functioning as sing.*) the branch of physics concerned with the mechanical properties of air and other gases.

pneumonia (njuː'məʊnɪə) *n.* inflammation of one or both lungs. [Greek *pneumōn* lung]

po (pəʊ) *n., pl.* **pos.** *Brit. informal.* a chamber pot. [from *pot*[1]]

Po *Chem.* polonium.

PO 1. petty officer. **2.** Pilot Officer. **3.** Also: **p.o.** postal order. **4.** Post Office.

poach[1] (pəʊtʃ) *vb.* **1.** to catch (game or fish) illegally by trespassing on private property. **2.** to encroach on (another person's rights or duties) or steal (an idea, employee, or player). [Old French *pocher*] —'**poacher** *n.*

poach[2] (pəʊtʃ) *vb.* to simmer (food) very gently in liquid. [Old French *pochier* to enclose in a bag]

pock (pɒk) *n.* **1.** a pustule resulting from smallpox. **2.** a pockmark. [Old English *pocc*]

pocket ('pɒkɪt) *n.* **1.** a small pouch in a garment for carrying small articles. **2.** any pouch resembling this. **3.** a cavity in the earth, such as one containing ore. **4.** a small isolated area: *a pocket of resistance.* **5.** any of the six holes with pouches or nets at the corners and sides of a billiard table. **6. in one's pocket.** under one's control. **7. in** or **out of pocket.** having made a profit or loss. ~*adj.* **8.** small: *a pocket edition.* ~*vb.* **9.** to put into one's pocket. **10.** to take secretly or unlawfully; steal. **11.** (*usually passive*) to confine as if in a pocket. **12.** to receive (an insult) without retaliating. **13.** to conceal or suppress: *he pocketed his pride and asked for help.* **14.** *Billiards.* to drive (a ball) into a pocket. [Anglo-Norman *poket* a little bag]

pocketbook ('pɒkɪtˌbʊk) *n.* *Chiefly U.S.* a small case for money and papers.

pocket borough *n.* (before the Reform Act of 1832) an English borough constituency controlled by one person or family.

pocketful ('pɒkɪtfʊl) *n., pl.* **-fuls.** as much as a pocket will hold.

pocketknife ('pɒkɪtˌnaɪf) *n., pl.* **-knives.** a small knife with one or more blades that fold into the handle; penknife.

pocket money *n.* **1.** *Brit.* a small weekly sum of money given to children by parents. **2.** money for incidental expenses.

pockmark ('pɒkˌmɑːk) *n.* a pitted scar left on the skin after the healing of a smallpox or similar pustule. —'**pock,marked** *adj.*

poco ('pəʊkəʊ) *or* **un poco** *adj., adv. Music.* to a small degree: *poco rit.* [Italian]

pod (pɒd) *n.* **1. a.** the fruit of a leguminous plant, consisting of a long two-valved case that contains seeds. **b.** the seedcase as distinct from the seeds. ~*vb.* **podding, podded. 2.** to remove the pod from. [origin unknown]

podgy ('pɒdʒɪ) *adj.* **podgier, podgiest.** short and fat; chubby. [from *podge* a short plump person] —'**podginess** *n.*

podium ('pəʊdɪəm) *n., pl.* **-diums** *or* **-dia** (-dɪə). **1.** a small raised platform used by conductors or speakers. **2.** a plinth that supports a colonnade or wall. [Latin: platform]

poem ('pəʊɪm) *n.* **1.** a composition in verse, using such techniques as metre, rhyme, or alliteration. **2.** a literary composition that is not in verse but exhibits the intensity of imagination and language common to it: *a prose poem.* **3.** anything like a poem in beauty or effect. [Greek *poiēma* something created]

poesy ('pəʊɪzɪ) *n. Archaic.* poetry.

poet ('pəʊɪt) *n.* (*sometimes when fem.*) **poetess** *n.* **1.** a writer of poetry. **2.** a person with great imagination and creativity. [Greek *poiētēs* maker, poet]

poetaster (ˌpəʊɪ'tæstə, -'teɪ-) *n.* a writer of inferior verse.

poetic (pəʊ'ɛtɪk) *or* **poetical** *adj.* **1.** of poetry or poets. **2.** like poetry, as in being expressive or imaginative. **3.** recounted in verse.

poetic justice *n.* fitting retribution.

poetic licence *n.* justifiable departure from conventional rules of form or fact, as in poetry.

poet laureate *n., pl.* **poets laureate.** *Brit.* the poet appointed as court poet of Britain.

poetry ('pəʊɪtrɪ) *n.* **1.** poems collectively. **2.** the art or craft of writing poems. **3.** poetic qualities, spirit, or feeling. [Latin *poēta* poet]

po-faced *adj.* wearing a disapproving stern expression. [changed from *poor-faced*]

pogey *or* **pogy** ('pəʊgɪ) *n., pl.* **pogeys** *or* **pogies.** *Canad. slang.* **1.** financial or other relief given to the unemployed by the government; dole. **2.** unemployment insurance. **3.** the office distributing relief to the unemployed. [from earlier *pogie* work-house]

pogo stick ('pəʊgəʊ) *n.* a pole with steps for the feet and a spring at the bottom, so that the user can bounce up, down, and along on it. [origin unknown]

pogrom ('pɒgrəm) *n.* an organized persecution and massacre. [Russian: destruction]

poi (pɔɪ) *n.* N.Z. a ball of woven New Zealand flax swung rhythmically by Maori women while performing poi dances. [Maori]

poi dance *n.* N.Z. a women's formation dance that involves singing and manipulating a poi.

poignant ('pɔɪnjənt, -nənt) *adj.* 1. sharply painful to the feelings. 2. cutting: *poignant wit.* 3. pertinent in mental appeal: *a poignant subject.* [Latin *pungens* pricking] —'**poignancy** *n.*

poinsettia (pɔɪn'sɛtɪə) *n.* a shrub of Mexico and Central America, widely cultivated for its showy scarlet leaves. [after J. P. Poinsett, U.S. Minister to Mexico]

point (pɔɪnt) *n.* 1. a dot or tiny mark. 2. a location or position. 3. a dot used in writing or printing, such as a decimal point or a full stop. 4. the sharp tapered end of anything. 5. *Maths.* a geometric element having a position located by coordinates, but no magnitude. 6. a promontory. 7. a specific condition or degree: *freezing point.* 8. a moment: *at that point he left.* 9. a reason or aim: *what is the point of this exercise?* 10. an essential element in an argument: *I take your point.* 11. a detail or item. 12. a characteristic: *he has his good points.* 13. (*often pl.*) any of the extremities, such as the tail, ears, or feet, of a domestic animal. 14. (*often pl.*) *Ballet.* the tip of the toes. 15. a single unit for measuring something such as value, or of scoring in a game. 16. *Printing.* a unit of measurement equal to one twelfth of a pica. 17. *Navigation.* one of the 32 marks on the compass indicating direction. 18. *Cricket.* a fielding position at right angles to the batsman on the off side. 19. either of the two electrical contacts that make or break the circuit in the distributor of a motor vehicle. 20. *Brit.* (*often pl.*) a movable section of railway track used to direct a train from one line to another. 21. *Brit.* short for **power point.** 22. *Boxing.* a mark awarded for a scoring blow or knockdown. 23. **at** or **on the point of.** on the verge of: *on the point of leaving.* 24. **beside the point.** irrelevant. 25. **make a point of. a.** to make a habit of (something). **b.** to do (something) because one thinks it important. 26. **to the point.** relevant. 27. **up to a point.** not completely. ~*vb.* 28. (usually foll. by *at* or *to*) to indicate the location or direction of by extending (a finger or other pointed object) towards it. 29. (usually foll. by *at* or *to*) to indicate a specific person or thing among several: *all evidence pointed to Donald as the murderer.* 30. to direct or face in a specific direction: *point me in the right direction.* 31. (of gun dogs) to indicate the place where game is lying

by standing rigidly with the muzzle turned in its direction. 32. to finish or repair the joints of (brickwork) with mortar or cement. ~See also **point out.** [Latin *pungere* to pierce]

point-blank *adj.* 1. aimed or fired at a very close target; at nearly zero range. 2. plain or blunt: *a point-blank question.* ~*adv.* 3. directly or straight. 4. bluntly. [*point* + *blank* (centre spot of an archery target)]

point duty *n.* the stationing of a policeman at a road junction to control traffic.

pointed ('pɔɪntɪd) *adj.* 1. having a point. 2. cutting or incisive: *pointed wit.* 3. obviously directed at a particular person: *a pointed remark.* 4. emphasized or evident: *pointed ignorance.* —'**pointedly** *adv.*

pointer ('pɔɪntə) *n.* 1. an indicator on a measuring instrument. 2. a rod used to point to parts of a map or chart. 3. a breed of large smooth-coated gun dog. 4. a helpful hint.

pointillism ('pwæntɪ,lɪzəm) *n.* a technique of painting of some impressionists, in which dots of unmixed colour are juxtaposed so that from a distance they fuse in the viewer's eye. [French] —'**pointillist** *n., adj.*

pointing ('pɔɪntɪŋ) *n.* the act or process of repairing or finishing joints in brickwork with mortar.

pointless ('pɔɪntlɪs) *adj.* without meaning, purpose, or force.

point of no return *n.* a point at which an irreversible commitment must be made to an action.

point of order *n., pl.* **points of order.** a question in a meeting as to whether the rules of procedure are being broken.

point of view *n., pl.* **points of view.** 1. a position from which something is observed. 2. a mental viewpoint or attitude.

point out *vb.* to indicate or specify.

point-to-point *n.* Brit. a steeplechase organized by a hunt.

poise (pɔɪz) *n.* 1. composure or dignity. 2. physical balance. 3. stability. ~*vb.* 4. to be or cause to be balanced or suspended. 5. to hold in readiness: *to poise a lance.* [Old French *pois* weight]

poison ('pɔɪz'n) *n.* 1. a substance that causes death or injury when swallowed or absorbed. 2. something that destroys or corrupts. ~*vb.* 3. to give poison to. 4. to add poison to. 5. to taint or infect with poison. 6. (foll. by *against*) to turn (a person's mind) against: *he poisoned her mind against me.* [Latin *pōtiō* a drink, esp. a poisonous one] —'**poisoner** *n.*

poison ivy *n.* a North American climbing plant that causes an itching rash on contact.

poisonous ('pɔɪzənəs) *adj.* 1. having the effects or qualities of a poison. 2. corruptive or malicious.

poison-pen letter *n.* an abusive, usually anonymous, letter written in malice.

poke[1] (pəʊk) *vb.* 1. to jab or prod, as with the elbow or a stick. 2. to make (a hole) by poking. 3. (sometimes foll. by *at*) to thrust (at). **4.** (usually foll. by *in, through, etc.*) to stick out: *don't poke your tongue out at me.* **5.** to stir (a fire) by poking. **6.** (often foll. by *about* or *around*) to search or pry. **7. poke one's nose into.** to interfere with or meddle in. ~*n.* **8.** a jab or prod. [Low German & Middle Dutch *poken*]

poke² (pəʊk) *n.* **1.** *Dialect.* a pocket or bag. **2. a pig in a poke.** See **pig.** [Old French *poque*]

poker¹ ('pəʊkə) *n.* a metal rod with a handle for stirring a fire.

poker² ('pəʊkə) *n.* a card game of bluff and skill in which players bet on the hands dealt. [origin unknown]

poker face *n. Informal.* an expressionless face, as that of a poker player trying to hide the value of his cards. —**'poker-,faced** *adj.*

pokerwork ('pəʊkə,wɜːk) *n.* the art of producing pictures or designs on wood by charring it with a heated tool.

poky ('pəʊkɪ) *adj.* **pokier, pokiest.** (esp. of rooms) small and cramped. [from POKE¹ (in slang sense: to confine)] —**'pokiness** *n.*

pol. **1.** political. **2.** politics.

polar ('pəʊlə) *adj.* **1.** at, near, or of either of the earth's poles or the area inside the Arctic or Antarctic Circles. **2.** of or having a pole or poles. **3.** directly opposite in tendency or nature.

polar bear *n.* a white bear of coastal regions of the North Pole.

polar circle *n.* the Arctic or Antarctic Circle.

polarity (pəʊ'lærɪtɪ) *n., pl.* **-ties.** **1.** the condition of a body in which it has opposing physical properties, usually magnetic poles or electric charge. **2.** the particular state of a part that has polarity: *an electrode with positive polarity.* **3.** the state of having two directly opposite tendencies or opinions.

polarization *or* **-isation** (,pəʊləraɪ'zeɪʃən) *n.* **1.** the condition of acquiring or giving polarity. **2.** *Physics.* the condition in which waves of light or other radiation are restricted to certain directions of vibration.

polarize *or* **-ise** ('pəʊlə,raɪz) *vb.* **1.** to acquire or give polarity or polarization. **2.** to cause (people) to adopt directly opposite opinions: *to polarize opinion.*

Polaroid ('pəʊlə,rɔɪd) *n. Trademark.* **1.** a type of plastic sheet that can polarize light: used in sunglasses to eliminate glare. **Polaroid Camera.** a camera that produces a finished print by means of a developing and processing technique that occurs inside the camera and takes only a few seconds.

polder ('pəʊldə, 'pɒl-) *n.* a stretch of land reclaimed from the sea. [Middle Dutch *polre*]

pole¹ (pəʊl) *n.* **1.** a long slender rounded piece of wood, metal, or other material. **2.** same as **rod** (sense 5). **3. up the pole.** *Brit., Austral., & N.Z. informal.* **a.** slightly mad. **b.** in a predicament. ~*vb.* **4.** to punt (a boat). [Latin *pālus* a stake]

pole² (pəʊl) *n.* **1.** either end of the earth's

axis of rotation. See also **North Pole, South Pole.** **2.** *Physics.* **a.** either of the two regions at the ends of a magnet to which the lines of force converge. **b.** either of two points at which there are opposite electric charges. **3.** either of two directly opposite tendencies or opinions. **4. poles apart.** having widely divergent opinions or tastes. [Greek *polos* pivot]

Pole (pəʊl) *n.* a person from Poland.

poleaxe *or U.S.* **poleax** ('pəʊl,æks) *n.* **1.** an axe formerly used in battle or used by a butcher. ~*vb.* **2.** to hit or fell with or as if with a poleaxe. [Middle English *pollax* battle-axe]

polecat ('pəʊl,kæt) *n., pl.* **-cats** *or* **-cat.** **1.** a dark brown mammal like a weasel that gives off a foul smell. **2.** *U.S.* a skunk. [origin unknown]

polemic (pə'lɛmɪk) *adj. also* **polemical.** **1.** of or involving dispute or controversy. ~*n.* **2.** a dispute or controversy. [Greek *polemos* war] —**polemicist** (pə'lɛmɪsɪst) *n.*

polemics (pə'lɛmɪks) *n.* (*functioning as sing.*) the art or practice of dispute or argument.

pole position *n.* **1.** (in motor racing) the starting position on the inside of the front row, generally considered the best one. **2.** an advantageous starting position.

pole star *n.* a guiding principle or rule.

Pole Star *n.* **the.** the star closest to the N celestial pole.

pole vault *n.* **1. the.** a field event in which competitors try to clear a high bar with the aid of a very flexible long pole. ~*vb.* **pole-vault.** **2.** to perform or compete in the pole vault. —**'pole-,vaulter** *n.*

police (pə'liːs) *n.* **1.** (often preceded by *the*) the organized civil force of a state for keeping law and order. **2.** (*functioning as pl.*) the members of such a force collectively. **3.** an organized body with a similar function: *security police.* ~*vb.* **4.** to regulate or control by means of a police force or similar body. [French, from Latin *polītīa* administration]

police dog *n.* a dog trained to help the police.

policeman (pə'liːsmən) *or* (*fem.*) **policewoman** *n., pl.* **-men** *or* **-women.** a member of a police force.

police state *n.* a state in which a repressive government keeps control through the police.

police station *n.* the office of the police force of a district.

policy¹ ('pɒlɪsɪ) *n., pl.* **-cies.** **1.** a plan of action adopted by a person, group, or government. **2.** wisdom or prudence. [Old French *policie*, from Latin *polītīa* administration]

policy² ('pɒlɪsɪ) *n., pl.* **-cies.** a document containing an insurance contract. [Old French *police* certificate] —**'policy-,holder** *n.*

polio ('pəʊlɪəʊ) *n.* short for **poliomyelitis.**

poliomyelitis (,pəʊlɪəʊ,maɪə'laɪtɪs) *n.* an acute infectious viral disease, affecting the brain and spinal cord, causing paralysis.

[Greek *polios* grey + *muelos* marrow]

polish ('pɒlɪʃ) *vb.* **1.** to make or become smooth and shiny by rubbing. **2.** to perfect or complete. **3.** to make or become elegant or refined. ~*n.* **4.** a finish or gloss. **5.** a substance used to produce a shiny surface. **6.** elegance or refinement. [Latin *polire* to polish]

Polish ('pɒlɪʃ) *adj.* **1.** of Poland, its people, or their language. ~*n.* **2.** the official language of Poland.

polished ('pɒlɪʃt) *adj.* **1.** accomplished: *a polished actor.* **2.** impeccably or professionally done: *a polished performance.*

polish off *vb. Informal.* **1.** to finish completely. **2.** to dispose of or kill.

polish up *vb.* **1.** to make or become smooth and shiny by polishing. **2.** to improve (something) by working at it: *he's polishing up his German.*

Politburo ('pɒlɪt,bjʊərəʊ) *n.* the executive and policy-making committee of a Communist Party. [Russian]

polite (pə'laɪt) *adj.* **1.** having good manners; courteous. **2.** cultivated or refined: *polite society.* [Latin *polītus* polished] —**po'litely** *adv.* —**po'liteness** *n.*

politic ('pɒlɪtɪk) *adj.* **1.** artful or shrewd: *a politic manager.* **2.** crafty; cunning: *a politic old scoundrel.* **3.** wise or prudent: *a politic choice.* **4.** *Archaic.* political. ~See also **body politic.** [Old French *politique,* from Greek *polis* city]

political (pə'lɪtɪk'l) *adj.* **1.** of the state, government, or public administration. **2.** of or dealing with politics: *a political person.* **3.** of the parties and the partisan aspects of politics. —**po'litically** *adv.*

political prisoner *n.* a person imprisoned for holding particular political beliefs.

political science *n.* the study of the state, government, and politics. —**political scientist** *n.*

politician (,pɒlɪ'tɪʃən) *n.* a person actively engaged in politics, usually a full-time professional member of a deliberative assembly.

politicize *or* **-ise** (pə'lɪtɪ,saɪz) *vb.* **1.** to make political in character or awareness. **2.** to take part in political discussion or activity. —**po,litici'zation** *or* **-i'sation** *n.*

politics ('pɒlɪtɪks) *n.* **1.** (*functioning as sing.*) the art and science of government. **2.** (*functioning as pl.*) political activities or affairs: *party politics.* **3.** (*functioning as sing.*) the business or profession of politics. **4.** (*functioning as sing. or pl.*) any activity concerned with the acquisition of power: *company politics are often vicious.* **5.** (*functioning as pl.*) political opinions or sympathies: *his conservative politics.*

polity ('pɒlɪtɪ) *n., pl.* **-ties. 1.** a form of government of a state, church, or society. **2.** a politically organized state, church, or society. [Greek *politeia* citizenship, from *polis* city]

polka ('pɒlkə) *n.* **1.** a 19th-century dance in fast duple time. **2.** music for this dance. ~*vb.* **-kaing, -kaed. 3.** to dance a polka. [Czech *pulka* half-step]

polka dot *n.* one of a pattern of small circular regularly spaced spots on a fabric.

poll (pəʊl) *n.* **1.** the casting, recording, or counting of votes in an election; a voting. **2.** the result of such a voting: *a heavy poll.* **3.** Also called: **opinion poll.** a canvassing of a representative sample of people on some question in order to determine the general opinion. **4.** the head. ~*vb.* **5.** to receive (a certain number of votes). **6.** to receive, take, or record the votes of: *he polled the whole town.* **7.** to canvass (a person, group, or area) as part of a survey of opinion. **8.** to cast (a vote) in an election. **9.** to clip or shear. **10.** to remove or cut short the horns of (cattle). [Middle Low German *polle* hair, head, top of a tree]

pollack *or* **pollock** ('pɒlək) *n., pl.* **-lacks, -lack** *or* **-locks, -lock.** a food fish related to the cod, found in northern seas. [origin unknown]

pollard ('pɒləd) *n.* **1.** an animal that has shed its horns or has had them removed. **2.** a tree that has had its branches cut back to encourage a more bushy growth. ~*vb.* **3.** to make into a pollard. [see *poll*]

pollen ('pɒlən) *n.* a substance produced by the anthers of seed-bearing plants, consisting of numerous fine grains containing the male fertilizing cells. [Latin: powder]

pollen count *n.* a measure of the pollen present in the air over a 24-hour period, often published as a warning to hay fever sufferers.

pollinate ('pɒlɪ,neɪt) *vb.* to transfer pollen from the anthers to the stigma of (a flower). —**,polli'nation** *n.*

polling booth *n.* a semienclosed space in which a voter stands to mark a ballot paper during an election.

polling station *n.* a building designated as the place to which voters go during an election to cast their votes.

pollster ('pəʊlstə) *n.* a person who conducts opinion polls.

poll tax *n.* a tax levied per head of adult population, esp. (in Scotland from 1989 and England and Wales from 1990) a tax levied by a local authority to pay for council services, replacing domestic rates.

pollutant (pə'luːt'nt) *n.* a substance that pollutes, usually the chemical waste of an industrial process.

pollute (pə'luːt) *vb.* **1.** to contaminate with poisonous or harmful substances. **2.** to make morally corrupt. [Latin *polluere* to defile] —**pol'lution** *n.*

polo ('pəʊləʊ) *n.* **1.** a game like hockey played on horseback with long-handled mallets and a wooden ball. **2.** short for **water polo. 3.** Also called: **polo neck.** a collar on a garment, rolled over to fit closely round the neck. [Tibetan *pulu* ball]

polonaise (,pɒlə'neɪz) *n.* **1.** a stately Polish dance. **2.** music for this dance. [French *danse polonaise* Polish dance]

polonium (pə'ləʊnɪəm) *n.* a rare radioactive element found in trace amounts in uranium ores. Symbol: Po [Medieval Latin *Polōnia* Poland; in honour of the nationality of its discoverer, Marie Curie]

poltergeist ('pɒltə‚gaɪst) n. a spirit believed to manifest its presence by noises and acts of mischief, such as throwing objects about. [German *poltern* to be noisy + *Geist* ghost]

poltroon (pɒl'truːn) n. a complete coward. [Old Italian *poltrone* lazy good-for-nothing]

poly ('pɒlɪ) n., pl. **polys**. *Informal.* short for **polytechnic**.

poly- *combining form.* **1.** many or much: *polyhedron.* **2.** having an excessive number or amount: *polyphagia.* [Greek *polus*]

polyandry ('pɒlɪ‚ændrɪ) n. the practice or condition of having more than one husband at the same time. [Greek *polus* many + *anēr* man] —**poly'androus** adj.

polyanthus (‚pɒlɪ'ænθəs) n., pl. **-thuses.** a hybrid garden primrose with brightly coloured flowers. [Greek: having many flowers]

polychromatic (‚pɒlɪkrəʊ'mætɪk) adj. **1.** having various colours. **2.** (of radiation) containing more than one wavelength.

polyester (‚pɒlɪ'ɛstə) n. a synthetic polymer used to make plastics and textile fibres.

polyethylene (‚pɒlɪ'ɛθɪ‚liːn) n. same as **polythene**.

polygamy (pə'lɪgəmɪ) n. the practice of having more than one wife or husband at the same time. [Greek *polus* many + *gamos* marriage] —**po'lygamist** n. —**po'lygamous** adj.

polyglot ('pɒlɪ‚glɒt) adj. **1.** able to speak many languages. **2.** written in or using many languages. ~n. **3.** a person who can speak many languages. [Greek *poluglōttos* many-tongued]

polygon ('pɒlɪ‚gɒn) n. a closed plane figure with three or more sides and angles. [Greek *polugōnon* figure with many angles] —**polygonal** (pə'lɪgən³l) adj.

polygraph ('pɒlɪ‚grɑːf) n. an instrument for recording involuntary physiological activities such as pulse rate, often used as a lie detector. [Greek *polugraphos* writing copiously]

polygyny (pə'lɪdʒɪnɪ) n. the practice or condition of having more than one wife at the same time. [Greek *polus* many + *gunē* woman] —**po'lygynous** adj.

polyhedron (‚pɒlɪ'hiːdrən) n., pl. **-drons** or **-dra** (-drə). a solid figure consisting of four or more plane faces. [Greek *polus* many + *hedron* side] —**poly'hedral** adj.

polymath ('pɒlɪ‚mæθ) n. a person of great and varied learning. [Greek *polumathēs* having much knowledge]

polymer ('pɒlɪmə) n. a natural or synthetic compound that has large molecules made up of many relatively simple repeated units.

polymeric (‚pɒlɪ'mɛrɪk) adj. of or being a polymer: *a polymeric compound.* [Greek *polumerēs* having many parts]

polymerization or **-isation** (‚pɒlɪmərɑɪ-'zeɪʃən) n. the act or process of forming a polymer. —**'polymer‚ize** or **-‚ise** vb.

polymorphous (‚pɒlɪ'mɔːfəs) or **polymorphic** adj. having, taking, or passing through many different forms or stages. [Greek *polus* many + *morphē* form]

Polynesian (‚pɒlɪ'niːʒən, -ʒɪən) adj. **1.** of Polynesia, its people, or any of their languages. ~n. **2.** a person from Polynesia. **3.** any of the languages of Polynesia.

polynomial (‚pɒlɪ'nəʊmɪəl) adj. **1.** consisting of two or more terms. ~n. **2.** an algebraic expression consisting of the sum of a number of terms.

polyp ('pɒlɪp) n. **1.** *Zool.* a small sea creature that has a hollow cylindrical body with a ring of tentacles around the mouth. **2.** *Pathol.* a small growth on the surface of a mucous membrane. [Greek *polupous* having many feet]

polyphonic (‚pɒlɪ'fɒnɪk) adj. *Music.* composed of several different parts; contrapuntal.

polyphony (pə'lɪfənɪ) n., pl. **-nies.** polyphonic style of composition or a piece of music using it. [Greek *poluphōnia* diversity of tones]

polystyrene (‚pɒlɪ'staɪriːn) n. a plastic obtained by polymerizing styrene; used for insulating and packing.

polysyllable (‚pɒlɪ‚sɪləb³l) n. a word having more than two syllables. —**polysyllabic** (‚pɒlɪsɪ'læbɪk) adj.

polytechnic (‚pɒlɪ'tɛknɪk) n. **1.** *Brit.* a college offering advanced courses in many fields at and below degree standard. ~adj. **2.** of or relating to technical instruction. [Greek *polutekhnos* skilled in many arts]

polytheism ('pɒlɪθɪ‚ɪzəm, ‚pɒlɪ'θiːɪzəm) n. belief in more than one god. —**‚polythe'istic** adj. —**'poly‚theist** n.

polythene ('pɒlɪ‚θiːn) n. a light thermoplastic material made from ethylene.

polyunsaturated (‚pɒlɪʌn'sætʃə‚reɪtɪd) adj. of a class of animal and vegetable fats that do not contain cholesterol.

polyurethane (‚pɒlɪ'jʊərə‚θeɪn) n. a synthetic material mainly used as a foam for packing.

polyvinyl chloride n. See **PVC**.

pomace ('pʌmɪs) n. apple pulp left after pressing for juice. [Latin *pōmum* apple]

pomade (pə'mɑːd) n. a perfumed oil put on the hair. [French *pommade*]

pomander (pəʊ'mændə) n. **1.** a mixture of aromatic substances in a round container, used to perfume drawers or cupboards. **2.** a container for such a mixture. [Medieval Latin *pōmum ambrae* apple of amber]

pomegranate ('pɒmɪ‚grænɪt, 'pɒm‚grænɪt) n. the fruit of an Asian tree, which has tough reddish rind, juicy red pulp, and many seeds. [Latin *pōmum* apple + *grānātus* full of seeds]

pomelo ('pɒmɪ‚ləʊ) n., pl. **-los.** the edible yellow fruit, like a grapefruit, of a tropical tree. [Dutch *pompelmoes*]

Pomeranian (‚pɒmə'reɪnɪən) n. a breed of toy dog with a long straight silky coat. [after *Pomerania*, region of N central Europe]

pomfret ('pʌmfrɪt, 'pɒm-) or **pomfret-cake** n. a small black rounded liquorice sweet. [from *Pomfret,* earlier form of *Pontefract,* Yorks., where orig. made]

pommel ('pʌməl, 'pɒm-) *n.* **1.** the raised part on the front of a saddle. **2.** a knob at the top of a sword. ~*vb.* **-melling, -melled** *or U.S.* **-meling, -meled. 3.** same as **pummel.** [Old French *pomel* knob]

pommy ('pɒmɪ) *n., pl.* **-mies.** *(sometimes cap.) Slang.* a word used by Australians and New Zealanders for a British person. Sometimes shortened to **pom.** [origin unknown]

pomp (pɒmp) *n.* **1.** stately or splendid display. **2.** ostentatious display. [Greek *pompē* procession]

pom-pom ('pɒmpɒm) *n.* an automatic rapid-firing gun. [imit.]

pompon ('pɒmpɒn) *n.* **1.** a decorative ball of tufted silk or wool. **2.** the small round flower head of some dahlias and chrysanthemums. [French]

pompous ('pɒmpəs) *adj.* **1.** too consciously dignified or self-important. **2.** too consciously grand in style: *a pompous speech.* —**pomposity** (pɒm'pɒsɪtɪ) *n.* —'**pompously** *adv.*

ponce (pɒns) *Offensive slang, chiefly Brit.* ~*n.* **1.** an effeminate man. **2.** same as **pimp.** ~*vb.* **3.** (often foll. by *around* or *about*) to act like a ponce. [from Polari, an English slang derived from the Mediterranean ports]

poncho ('pɒntʃəʊ) *n., pl.* **-chos.** a cloak of a kind originally worn in South America, made of a piece of cloth with a hole in the middle for the head. [American Spanish]

pond (pɒnd) *n.* a pool of still water. [Middle English *ponde* enclosure]

ponder ('pɒndə) *vb.* (sometimes foll. by *on* or *over*) to consider thoroughly or deeply. [Latin *ponderāre* to weigh, consider] —'**ponderable** *adj.*

ponderous ('pɒndərəs) *adj.* **1.** heavy; huge. **2.** (of movement) lumbering or graceless. **3.** dull or laborious: *a ponderous speech.* [Latin *ponderōsus* of great weight]

pondok ('pɒndɒk) *or* **pondokie** *n.* (in southern Africa) a crudely made house or shack. [Malay *pondók* leaf house]

pondweed ('pɒnd,wiːd) *n.* a plant which grows in ponds and slow streams.

pong (pɒŋ) *Brit. informal.* ~*n.* **1.** a stink. ~*vb.* **2.** to stink. [origin unknown] —'**pongy** *adj.*

ponga ('pɒŋə) *n.* a tall New Zealand tree fern with large leathery leaves. [Maori]

poniard ('pɒnjəd) *n.* a small slender dagger. [Old French *poignard*]

pontiff ('pɒntɪf) *n.* a title now confined to the pope. [Latin *pontifex* high priest]

pontifical (pɒn'tɪfɪkᵊl) *adj.* **1.** of a pontiff. **2.** pompous or dogmatic in manner.

pontificate *vb.* (pɒn'tɪfɪˌkeɪt). **1.** to speak in a pompous or dogmatic manner. **2.** to officiate as a pontiff. ~*n.* (pɒn'tɪfɪkɪt). **3.** the office or term of office of a pope.

pontoon¹ (pɒn'tuːn) *n.* a floating platform used to support a bridge. [Latin *pontō* punt]

pontoon² (pɒn'tuːn) *n.* a card game in which players try to obtain sets of cards never worth more than 21 points. [prob. an alteration of French *vingt-et-un* twenty-one]

pony ('pəʊnɪ) *n., pl.* **-nies.** a breed of small horse. [Scot. *powney,* perhaps from Latin *pullus* young animal, foal]

ponytail ('pəʊnɪˌteɪl) *n.* a hairstyle in which the hair is gathered together by a band at the back of the head and hangs down like a tail.

pony trekking *n.* the pastime of riding ponies cross-country.

poodle ('puːdᵊl) *n.* a breed of dog with curly hair, which is usually clipped. [German *Pudel*]

poof (puf, puːf) *n. Brit. offensive slang.* a male homosexual. [French *pouffe* puff]

pooh (puː) *interj.* an exclamation of disdain, scorn, or disgust.

pooh-pooh ('puː'puː) *vb.* to express disdain or scorn for.

pool¹ (puːl) *n.* **1.** a small body of still water. **2.** a small body of spilt liquid: *a pool of blood.* **3.** a deep part of a stream or river. **4.** See **swimming pool.** [Old English *pōl*]

pool² (puːl) *n.* **1.** a communal combination of resources or funds: *a typing pool.* **2.** the combined stakes of the betters in many gambling games. **3.** *Commerce.* a group of producers who agree to maintain output levels and high prices. **4.** a billiard game in which the object is to pot all the balls with the cue ball. ~*vb.* **5.** to combine (resources or money) into a common fund. [French *poule,* lit.: hen used to signify stakes in a card game]

pools (puːlz) *pl. n.* **the.** *Brit.* an organized nationwide mainly postal gambling pool betting on the result of football matches.

poop (puːp) *n. Naut.* a raised structure or deck at the stern of a sailing ship. [Latin *puppis*]

pooped (puːpt) *adj. U.S. & Canad. slang.* exhausted; tired: *he was pooped after the race.* [Middle English *poupen* to blow]

poor (pʊə, pɔː) *adj.* **1.** not having enough money to live on. **2.** inadequate: *a poor salary.* **3.** (sometimes foll. by *in*) deficient in (something): *a region poor in wild flowers.* **4.** inferior: *poor quality.* **5.** disappointing or disagreeable: *a poor play.* **6.** deserving of pity; unlucky: *poor John is ill.* **7. poor man's (something).** a (cheaper) substitute for (something). [Latin *pauper*]

poorhouse ('pʊə,haʊs, 'pɔː-) *n.* same as **workhouse.**

poor law *n. English history.* a law providing for support of the poor from parish funds.

poorly ('pʊəlɪ, 'pɔː-) *adv.* **1.** badly. ~*adj.* **2.** *Informal.* rather ill.

poort (pʊət) *n.* (in South Africa) a steep narrow mountain pass. [Afrikaans]

poor White *n. Often offensive.* a poverty-stricken White person, usually in the southern U.S. and South Africa.

pop¹ (pɒp) *vb.* **popping, popped. 1.** to

make or cause to make a light sharp explosive sound. **2.** to burst with such a sound. **3.** (often foll. by *in, out, etc.*) *Informal.* to come (to) or go (from) briefly or suddenly. **4.** (of the eyes) to protrude. **5.** to place with a sudden movement: *she popped a pill into her mouth.* **6.** *Informal.* to pawn. **7. pop the question.** *Informal.* to propose marriage. ~*n.* **8.** a light sharp explosive sound. **9.** *Informal.* a fizzy drink. ~*adv.* **10.** with a pop. ~See also **pop off.** [imit.]

pop[2] (pɒp) *n.* **1.** music of general appeal, esp. among young people, that usually has a strong rhythm and uses electrical amplification. ~*adj.* **2.** of or playing pop music: *a pop group.* **3.** *Informal.* short for **popular.**

pop[3] (pɒp) *n. Informal.* **1.** father. **2.** an old man.

pop. **1.** popular(ly). **2.** population.

pop art *n.* a movement in modern art that uses the methods, styles, and themes of popular culture and mass media.

popcorn ('pɒp,kɔːn) *n.* maize kernels that puff up and burst when heated.

pope (pəʊp) *n.* (*often cap.*) the bishop of Rome as head of the Roman Catholic Church. [Greek *pappas* father]

popery ('pəʊpərɪ) *n. Offensive.* Roman Catholicism.

popeyed ('pɒp,aɪd) *adj.* **1.** having bulging eyes. **2.** staring in astonishment.

popgun ('pɒp,gʌn) *n.* a toy gun that fires a pellet or cork by means of compressed air.

popinjay ('pɒpɪn,dʒeɪ) *n.* a conceited or talkative person. [Arabic *babaghā* parrot]

popish ('pəʊpɪʃ) *adj. Offensive.* of or characteristic of Roman Catholicism.

poplar ('pɒplə) *n.* a tree with triangular leaves, catkins, and light soft wood. [Latin *pōpulus*]

poplin ('pɒplɪn) *n.* a strong plain-woven fabric, usually of cotton, with fine ribbing. [French *papeline*]

pop off *vb. Informal.* **1.** to depart suddenly. **2.** to die suddenly.

poppadom or **poppadum** ('pɒpədəm) *n.* a thin round crisp fried Indian bread. [Hindi]

popper ('pɒpə) *n. Brit. informal.* a press stud.

poppet ('pɒpɪt) *n.* a term of affection for a small child or sweetheart. [var. of *puppet*]

popping crease *n. Cricket.* a line in front of and parallel with the wicket at or behind which the batsman stands. [from obs. *pop* to hit]

poppy ('pɒpɪ) *n., pl.* -**pies.** **1.** a plant with showy red, orange, or white flowers and a milky sap. **2.** a drug, such as opium, obtained from these plants. **3.** an artificial red poppy worn to mark Remembrance Sunday. ~*adj.* **4.** reddish-orange. [Old English *popæg*]

poppycock ('pɒpɪ,kɒk) *n. Informal.* nonsense. [Dutch dialect *pappekak*, lit.: soft excrement]

Poppy Day *n. Informal.* Remembrance Sunday.

populace ('pɒpjʊləs) *n.* (*sometimes functioning as pl.*) the common people; masses. [Latin *populus*]

popular ('pɒpjʊlə) *adj.* **1.** widely liked or admired. **2.** liked by a person or group: *I'm not very popular with her.* **3.** prevailing among the general public: *popular discontent.* [Latin *populāris* of the people] —**popularity** (,pɒpjʊ'lærɪtɪ) *n.*

popular front *n.* (*often cap.*) a left-wing group or party opposed to fascism.

popularize or -**ise** ('pɒpjʊlə,raɪz) *vb.* **1.** to make popular. **2.** to make easily understandable. —,**populari'zation** or -**i'sation** *n.*

populate ('pɒpjʊ,leɪt) *vb.* **1.** (*often passive*) to live in; inhabit. **2.** to provide with inhabitants. [Latin *populus* people]

population (,pɒpjʊ'leɪʃən) *n.* **1.** (*sometimes functioning as pl.*) all the inhabitants of a place. **2.** the number of such inhabitants. **3.** (*sometimes functioning as pl.*) all the people of a particular class in a place: *the Chinese population of New York.* **4.** the act or process of providing a place with inhabitants.

populist ('pɒpjʊlɪst) *n.* a politician who claims to support the interests of the ordinary people.

populous ('pɒpjʊləs) *adj.* containing many inhabitants.

porangi ('pɔːræŋɪ) *N.Z. informal.* crazy; mad. [Maori]

porcelain ('pɔːslɪn) *n.* **1.** a translucent ceramic material. **2.** an object made of this or such objects collectively. [French *porcelaine,* from Italian *porcellana* cowrie shell]

porch (pɔːtʃ) *n.* a structure projecting from the doorway of a house and forming a covered entrance. [French *porche*]

porcine ('pɔːsaɪn) *adj.* of or like pigs. [Latin *porcus* a pig]

porcupine ('pɔːkjʊ,paɪn) *n.* a large rodent with a covering of protective quills. [Middle English *porc despyne* from Latin]

pore[1] (pɔː) *vb.* **1.** (foll. by *over*) to examine or study closely or intently: *he pored over his notes.* **2.** (foll. by *over, on,* or *upon*) to think deeply (about). [Middle English *pouren*]

pore[2] (pɔː) *n.* **1.** a small opening in the skin or outer surface of an animal or plant through which fluids may pass. **2.** any small hole, such as a space in a rock. [Greek *poros* passage, pore]

pork (pɔːk) *n.* the flesh of pigs used as food. [Latin *porcus* pig]

porker ('pɔːkə) *n.* a pig fattened for pork.

pork pie *n.* a pie filled with minced pork.

porky ('pɔːkɪ) *adj.* **porkier, porkiest.** **1.** of or like pork. **2.** *Informal.* fat; obese.

porn (pɔːn) or **porno** ('pɔːnəʊ) *n., adj. Informal.* short for **pornography** or **pornographic.**

pornography (pɔː'nɒgrəfɪ) *n.* writings, pictures, or films designed to be sexually exciting. [Greek *pornographos* writing of prostitutes] —**por'nographer** *n.* —**pornographic** (,pɔːnə'græfɪk) *adj.*

porous ('pɔːrəs) *adj.* **1.** able to absorb air or fluids. **2.** *Biol., geol.* having pores. [Late Latin *porus* passage, pore] —**porosity** (pɔː'rɒsɪtɪ) *n.*

porphyry ('pɔːfɪrɪ) *n., pl.* **-ries.** a reddish-purple rock consisting of large crystals of feldspar in a finer mass of minerals. [Greek *porphuros* purple] —**porphyritic** *adj.*

porpoise ('pɔːpəs) *n., pl.* **-poise** *or* **-poises.** a small mammal of the whale family with a blunt snout. [Latin *porcus* pig + *piscis* fish]

porridge ('pɒrɪdʒ) *n.* **1.** a dish made from oatmeal or other cereal, cooked in water or milk. **2.** *Slang.* imprisonment. [var. of *pottage*]

porringer ('pɒrɪndʒə) *n.* a small dish, often with a handle, for soup or porridge. [Middle English *potinger*]

port[1] (pɔːt) *n.* a town or place alongside navigable water where ships can load and unload. [Latin *portus*]

port[2] (pɔːt) *n.* **1.** the left side of an aircraft or ship when facing the bow. ~*vb.* **2.** to turn or be turned towards the port. [origin unknown]

port[3] (pɔːt) *n.* a sweet fortified wine. [after *Oporto*, Portugal, from where it came orig.]

port[4] (pɔːt) *n. Naut.* **a.** an opening with a watertight door in the side of a ship, for access to the holds. **b.** See **porthole.** [Latin *porta* gate]

portable ('pɔːtəb'l) *adj.* **1.** able to be easily carried or moved. ~*n.* **2.** an article designed to be easily carried or moved, such as a television or typewriter. [Latin *portāre* to carry] —**porta'bility** *n.*

portage ('pɔːtɪdʒ) *n.* **1.** the transporting of boats and supplies overland between navigable waterways. **2.** the route used for such transport. ~*vb.* **3.** to transport (boats and supplies) thus. [French]

portal ('pɔːt'l) *n.* an entrance, gateway, or doorway, usually a large and impressive one. [Latin *porta* gate]

portcullis (pɔːt'kʌlɪs) *n.* an iron grating suspended vertically in the gateway of a castle or town and able to be lowered so as to bar the entrance. [Old French *porte coleïce* sliding gate]

portend (pɔː'tend) *vb.* to be an omen of; foreshadow: *those clouds portend rain.* [Latin *portendere* to indicate]

portent ('pɔːtent) *n.* **1.** a sign of a future event; omen. **2.** great or ominous significance: *a cry of dire portent.* **3.** a marvel. [Latin *portentum* sign]

portentous (pɔː'tentəs) *adj.* **1.** of great or ominous significance. **2.** self-important or pompous: *portentous speechifying.*

porter[1] ('pɔːtə) *n.* a man employed to carry luggage at a railway station or hotel. [Latin *portāre* to carry] —**'porterage** *n.*

porter[2] ('pɔːtə) *n. Chiefly Brit.* a doorman or gatekeeper of a building. [Latin *porta* door]

porter[3] ('pɔːtə) *n. Brit.* a dark sweet ale brewed from black malt. [short for *porter's ale*]

porterhouse ('pɔːtə,haʊs) *n.* a thick choice beef steak. Also called: **porterhouse steak.** [formerly, a place that served porter, beer, and sometimes meals]

portfolio (pɔːt'fəʊlɪəʊ) *n., pl.* **-os.** **1.** a flat case for carrying maps, drawings, or papers. **2.** the contents of such a case, such as drawings or photographs, that show recent work. **3.** the responsibilities or role of the head of a government department: *the portfolio for foreign affairs.* **4. Minister without portfolio.** a cabinet minister who is not responsible for a government department. **5.** a list of investments held by an investor. [Italian *portafoglio*]

porthole ('pɔːt,həʊl) *n.* a small opening with a watertight cover in the side of a vessel, to admit light and air.

portico ('pɔːtɪkəʊ) *n., pl.* **-coes** *or* **-cos.** a porch or covered walkway consisting of a roof supported by columns. [Italian, from Latin *porticus*]

portion ('pɔːʃən) *n.* **1.** a part of a whole. **2.** a part allotted or belonging to a person or group. **3.** a helping of food served to one person. **4.** *Law.* a dowry. **5.** a person's lot or destiny. ~*vb.* **6.** to divide up; share out. **7.** to give a share to (a person). [Latin *portiō*]

portly ('pɔːtlɪ) *adj.* **-lier, -liest.** stout or rather fat. [from *port* (in the sense: deportment)]

portmanteau (pɔːt'mæntəʊ) *n., pl.* **-teaus** *or* **-teaux** (-təʊz). (formerly) a large travelling case made of stiff leather that opens out into two compartments. [French: cloak carrier]

portmanteau word *n.* a word made by joining together the beginning and end of two other words, such as *brunch.* Also called: **blend.**

portrait ('pɔːtrɪt, -treɪt) *n.* **1.** a painting, drawing, or photograph of a person, often only of the face. **2.** a description. [French] —**'portraitist** *n.*

portraiture ('pɔːtrɪtʃə) *n.* **1.** the making of portraits. **2. a.** a portrait. **b.** portraits collectively. **3.** a description.

portray (pɔː'treɪ) *vb.* **1.** to make a portrait of. **2.** to describe. **3.** to play the part of (a character) in a play or film. [Old French *portraire* to depict] —**por'trayal** *n.*

Portuguese (,pɔːtjʊ'giːz) *n.* **1.** the official language of Portugal and Brazil. **2.** (*pl.* **-guese**) a person from Portugal. ~*adj.* **3.** of Portugal, its people, or their language.

Portuguese man-of-war *n.* a large jellyfish with a sail-like float and long stinging tentacles.

pose (pəʊz) *vb.* **1.** to adopt or cause to adopt a physical attitude for an artist or photographer. **2.** (often foll. by *as*) to present oneself (as something one is not). **3.** to affect an attitude in order to impress others. **4.** to put forward or ask: *to pose a question.* ~*n.* **5.** a physical attitude adopted for an artist or photographer. **6.** behaviour adopted for effect. [Old French *poser* to set in place]

poser[1] ('pəʊzə) *n.* **1.** a person who poses.

2. *Informal.* a person who likes to be seen in trendy clothes in fashionable places.

poser² (ˈpəʊzə) n. a baffling question.

poseur (pɒˈzɜː) n. a person who affects an attitude in order to impress others. [French]

posh (pɒʃ) adj. *Informal, chiefly Brit.* **1.** smart or elegant. **2.** upper-class. [prob. from obs. slang *posh* (n.) a dandy]

posit (ˈpɒzɪt) vb. to assume or suggest as fact or the factual basis for an argument: *to posit a national scale of values.* [Latin *pōnere* to place]

position (pəˈzɪʃən) n. **1.** place or location: *he took up a position to the rear.* **2.** the proper or usual place. **3.** the way in which a person or thing is placed; arrangement. **4.** *Mil.* a place occupied for tactical reasons. **5.** point of view; stand: *what's your position on this issue?* **6.** social status, esp. high social standing. **7.** a post of employment; job. **8.** *Sport.* the part of a playing area where a player is placed. **9. in a position.** (foll. by an infinitive) able (to). ~vb. **10.** to put in the proper or usual place; locate. [Latin *pōnere* to place] —po'sitional adj.

positive (ˈpɒzɪtɪv) adj. **1.** expressing certainty or affirmation: *a positive answer.* **2.** possessing actual qualities; real: *a positive benefit.* **3.** tending to emphasize what is good; constructive: *positive criticism.* **4.** tending towards progress or improvement: *this is seen as a positive development.* **5.** *Philosophy.* constructive rather than sceptical. **6.** *Informal.* complete; downright: *a positive joy.* **7.** *Maths.* having a value greater than zero: *a positive number.* **8.** *Grammar.* denoting the unmodified form of an adjective as opposed to its comparative or superlative form. **9.** *Physics.* (of an electric charge) having an opposite charge to that of an electron. **10.** *Physics.* short for **electropositive.** **11.** *Med.* (of the result of an examination or test) indicating the presence of a suspected condition or organism. ~n. **12.** something positive. **13.** *Maths.* a quantity greater than zero. **14.** *Photog.* a print showing an image whose colours and tones correspond to those of the original subject. **15.** *Grammar.* the positive degree of an adjective or adverb. **16.** a positive object, such as a terminal in a cell. [Late Latin *positīvus*] —'positively adv. —'positiveness n.

positive discrimination n. the provision of special opportunities for a disadvantaged group.

positive vetting n. the checking of a person's background, political affiliation, and activities to assess his suitability for a position that may involve national security.

positivism (ˈpɒzɪtɪˌvɪzəm) n. a system of philosophy that accepts only observable phenomena and positive facts as sources of knowledge. —'positivist n., adj.

positron (ˈpɒzɪˌtrɒn) n. *Physics.* the antiparticle of the electron, having the same mass but an equal and opposite charge. [*posi(tive + elec)tron*]

poss. **1.** possession. **2.** possessive. **3.** possible. **4.** possibly.

posse (ˈpɒsɪ) n. **1.** *U.S.* a group of men in a district on whom the sheriff may call for assistance. **2.** (in W Canada), a troop of horses and riders who perform at rodeos. [Latin: to be able]

possess (pəˈzɛs) vb. **1.** to have as one's property; own. **2.** to have as a quality or attribute: *to possess courage.* **3.** to gain control over or dominate: *whatever possessed you to come?* [Latin *possidēre*] —pos'sessor n.

possessed (pəˈzɛst) adj. **1.** (foll. by *of*) owning or having: *possessed of talent.* **2.** under the influence of a powerful force, such as a spirit or strong emotion: *possessed by fury.*

possession (pəˈzɛʃən) n. **1.** a possessing or being possessed: *in possession of the crown.* **2.** anything that is possessed. **3.** (*pl.*) wealth or property. **4.** the state of being controlled by or as if by evil spirits. **5.** the occupancy of land or property: *to take possession of a house.* **6.** a territory subject to a foreign state. **7.** *Sport.* control of the ball by a player: *he got possession in his own half.*

possessive (pəˈzɛsɪv) adj. **1.** of possession. **2.** showing an excessive desire to possess or dominate: *a possessive husband.* **3.** *Grammar.* denoting a form of a noun or pronoun used to convey possession, as *my* or *Harry's.* ~n. **4.** *Grammar.* **a.** the possessive case. **b.** a word in the possessive case. —pos'sessiveness n.

possibility (ˌpɒsɪˈbɪlɪtɪ) n., pl. **-ties. 1.** the state of being possible. **2.** anything that is possible. **3.** a competitor or candidate with a chance of success. **4.** (*often pl.*) a future prospect or potential: *the idea has possibilities.*

possible (ˈpɒsɪbˈl) adj. **1.** capable of existing, happening, or proving true. **2.** capable of being done: *it is not possible to finish in three weeks.* **3.** having potential: *the idea is a possible money-spinner.* **4.** feasible but less than probable: *it is possible that man will live on Mars.* **5.** same as **possibility** (sense 3). [Latin *possibilis*]

possibly (ˈpɒsɪblɪ) adv. **1.** perhaps or maybe. **2.** by any means; at all: *he can't possibly come.*

possum (ˈpɒsəm) n. **1.** *Informal.* an opossum. **2.** *Austral. & N.Z.* a phalanger. **3. play possum.** to pretend to be dead, ignorant, or asleep in order to deceive an opponent.

post¹ (pəʊst) n. **1.** a length of wood, metal, or concrete fixed upright to serve as a support, marker, or point of attachment. **2.** *Horse racing.* **a.** either of two upright poles marking the beginning and end of a racecourse. **b.** the finish of a horse race. ~vb. **3.** (sometimes foll. by *up*) to put up (a notice) in a public place. **4.** to publish (a name) on a list. [Latin *postis*]

post² (pəʊst) n. **1.** a position to which a person is appointed; job. **2.** a position to which a soldier or guard is assigned for duty. **3.** a permanent military establishment. **4.** *Brit.* either of two military bugle calls (**first post** and **last post**) giving notice of the time to retire for the night. ~*vb.* **5.** to assign to or station at a particular place or position. **6.** *Chiefly Brit.* to transfer (someone) to a different unit or place on taking up a new appointment. [French *poste*, from Latin *pōnere* to place]

post³ (pəʊst) *n.* **1.** *Chiefly Brit.* letters or packages that are transported and delivered by the Post Office; mail. **2.** *Chiefly Brit.* a single collection or delivery of mail. **3.** *Brit.* an official system of mail delivery. **4.** *Brit.* a postbox or post office: *take this to the post.* ~*vb.* **5.** *Chiefly Brit.* to send by post. **6.** *Book-keeping.* **a.** to enter (an item) in a ledger. **b.** (often foll. by *up*) to enter all paper items in (a ledger). **7.** to inform of the latest news: *keep us posted.* [Latin *posita* something placed, from *pōnere* to put]

post- *prefix.* **1.** after in time; following: *postgraduate.* **2.** behind: *postorbital.* [Latin]

postage ('pəʊstɪdʒ) *n.* the charge for delivering a piece of mail.

postage stamp *n.* a printed paper label for attaching to mail as an official indication that the required postage has been paid.

postal ('pəʊst'l) *adj.* of a Post Office or the mail-delivery service.

postal order *n.* a money order obtainable and payable at a post office.

postbag ('pəʊst,bæg) *n.* **1.** *Chiefly Brit.* a mailbag. **2.** the mail received by a magazine, radio programme, or public figure.

postbox ('pəʊst,bɒks) *n.* same as **letterbox** (sense 2).

postcard ('pəʊst,kɑːd) *n.* a card, often with a picture on one side (**picture postcard**), for sending a message by post without an envelope.

post chaise *n.* a four-wheeled horse-drawn coach formerly used as a rapid means of carrying mail and passengers.

postcode ('pəʊst,kəʊd) *n.* a code of letters and digits used as part of a postal address.

postdate (pəʊst'deɪt) *vb.* **1.** to write a future date on (a cheque or document). **2.** to assign a date to (an event or period) that is later than its previously assigned date. **3.** to be or occur at a later date than.

poster ('pəʊstə) *n.* **1.** a placard posted in a public place as an advertisement. **2.** a large printed picture.

poste restante ('pəʊst rɪ'stænt) *n.* a post-office department where mail is kept until collected. [French, lit.: mail remaining]

posterior (pɒ'stɪərɪə) *adj.* **1.** at the back of or behind something. **2.** coming after in a series or time. ~*n.* **3.** the buttocks. [Latin: latter]

posterity (pɒ'stɛrɪtɪ) *n.* **1.** future generations. **2.** all of one's descendants. [Latin *posterus* coming after]

postern ('pɒstən) *n.* a back door or gate. [Old French]

post-free *adv., adj.* **1.** *Brit.* with the postage prepaid. **2.** free of postal charge.

postgraduate (pəʊst'grædjʊɪt) *n.* **1.** a person who is studying for a more advanced qualification after obtaining a university degree. **2.** (*modifier*) of or for postgraduates.

posthaste ('pəʊst'heɪst) *adv.* with great haste.

posthumous ('pɒstjʊməs) *adj.* **1.** happening after one's death. **2.** (of a book) published after the author's death. **3.** (of a child) born after the father's death. [Latin *postumus* the last] —'**posthumous**ly *adv.*

postilion or **postillion** (pɒ'stɪljən) *n.* a person who rides the near horse of a team drawing a coach. [French *postillon*]

postimpressionism (,pəʊstɪm'prɛʃə-,nɪzəm) *n.* a movement in painting in France at the end of the 19th century which rejected impressionism but adapted its use of pure colour to paint with greater subjective emotion. —,**postim'pression**ist *n., adj.*

postman ('pəʊstmən) or (*fem.*) **postwoman** *n., pl.* **-men** or **-women.** a person who delivers mail as a profession.

postmark ('pəʊst,mɑːk) *n.* **1.** a mark stamped on mail by postal officials, usually showing the date and place of posting. ~*vb.* **2.** to put such a mark on (mail).

postmaster ('pəʊst,mɑːstə) or (*fem.*) **postmistress** *n.* an official in charge of a local post office.

postmaster general *n., pl.* **postmasters general.** the executive head of the postal service.

postmeridian (,pəʊstmə'rɪdɪən) *adj.* of or in the afternoon. [Latin *postmerīdiānus*]

postmortem (pəʊst'mɔːtəm) *adj.* **1.** occurring after death. ~*n.* **2.** In full: **postmortem examination.** dissection and examination of a dead body to determine the cause of death. **3.** analysis of a recent event: *a postmortem on a game of chess.* [Latin, lit.: after death]

postnatal (pəʊst'neɪt'l) *adj.* occurring after childbirth: *postnatal depression.*

post office *n.* a building where stamps are sold and postal business is conducted.

Post Office *n.* a government department responsible for postal services.

postoperative (pəʊst'ɒpərətɪv) *adj.* of or occurring in the period after a surgical operation.

postpaid ('pəʊst'peɪd) *adv., adj.* with the postage prepaid.

postpone (pəʊst'pəʊn, pə'spəʊn) *vb.* to put off or delay until a future time. [Latin *postpōnere* to put after] —**post'pone**ment *n.*

postpositive (pəʊst'pɒzɪtɪv) *adj.* (of an adjective) placed after the word it modifies.

postprandial (pəʊst'prændɪəl) *adj.* after a meal. [Latin *post-* after + *prandium* midday meal]

postscript ('pəʊs,skrɪpt, 'pəʊst-) *n.* a message added at the end of a letter, after the signature. [Late Latin *postscribere* to write after]

postulant ('pɒstjʊlənt) n. an applicant, usually for admission to a religious order. [Latin postulāre to ask]

postulate vb. ('pɒstjʊ,leɪt). **1.** to assume to be true as the basis of an argument; take for granted. **2.** to ask, demand, or claim. ~n. ('pɒstjʊlɪt). **3.** something postulated. [Latin postulāre to ask for] —,postu'la-tion n.

posture ('pɒstʃə) n. **1.** a position or attitude of the body. **2.** a characteristic manner of bearing the body: good posture. **3.** a mental attitude: a cooperative posture. **4.** a state or condition. **5.** an affected attitude; pose. ~v. **6.** to assume or cause to assume a bodily attitude. **7.** to assume an affected attitude; pose. [Latin positūra] —'postural adj.

postviral (fatigue) syndrome (pəʊst-'vaɪrəl) n. a condition following a viral infection, characterized by fatigue, weakness, headaches, impaired balance, sight, and hearing, and an inability to concentrate.

postwar (pəʊst'wɔː) adj. occurring or existing after a war.

posy ('pəʊzɪ) n., pl. -sies. a small bunch of flowers. [var. of poesy]

pot¹ (pɒt) n. **1.** a round deep container, often having a handle and lid, used for cooking and other domestic purposes. **2.** the amount that a pot will hold; potful. **3.** the money in the pool in gambling games. **4.** a handmade piece of pottery. **5.** Billiards, etc. a shot by which a ball is pocketed. **6.** a chamber pot. **7.** (often pl.) Informal. a large sum of money. **8.** Informal. a cup or other trophy. **9.** short for **flowerpot, teapot. 10.** See **potbelly. 11.** **go to pot.** to go to ruin. ~vb. **potting, potted. 12.** to put or preserve (food) in a pot. **13.** to put (a plant) in soil in a flowerpot. **14.** to shoot (game) for food rather than for sport. **15.** to shoot casually or without careful aim. **16.** Billiards, etc. to pocket (a ball). **17.** Informal. to capture or win. [Old English pott]

pot² (pɒt) n. Slang. cannabis used as a drug. [perhaps from Mexican Indian potiguaya]

potable ('pəʊtəb'l) adj. drinkable. [Latin pōtāre to drink]

potage (pəʊ'tɑːʒ) n. thick soup. [French]

potash ('pɒt,æʃ) n. **1.** potassium carbonate, used as a fertilizer. **2.** a compound containing potassium: chloride of potash. [from pot ashes, because orig. obtained by evaporating the lye of wood ashes in pots]

potassium (pə'tæsɪəm) n. a light silvery element of the alkali metal group. Symbol: K [New Latin potassa potash]

potassium nitrate n. a crystalline compound used in gunpowders, fertilizers, and as a preservative for foods (E252).

potation (pəʊ'teɪʃən) n. **1.** the act of drinking. **2.** a drink, usually alcoholic. [Latin pōtāre to drink]

potato (pə'teɪtəʊ) n., pl. -toes. **a.** a plant widely cultivated for its edible tubers. **b.** the starchy tuber of this plant, cooked and eaten as a vegetable. [Spanish patata, from American Indian]

potato beetle n. same as **Colorado beetle.**

potato crisp n. same as **crisp** (sense 8).

potbelly ('pɒt,belɪ) n., pl. -lies. **1.** a bulging belly. **2.** a person with such a belly.

potboiler ('pɒt,bɔɪlə) n. Informal. an artistic work of little merit produced quickly to make money.

pot-bound adj. (of a pot plant) having roots too big for its pot, so that it can grow no further.

poteen ('pɒtiːn) or **poitín** (pɒ'tʃiːn) n. (in Ireland) illicit spirit. [Irish poitín little pot]

potent ('pəʊt'nt) adj. **1.** having great strength; powerful. **2.** (of arguments) persuasive or forceful. **3.** highly effective: a potent poison. **4.** (of a male) capable of having sexual intercourse. [Latin potēns able] —'potency n.

potentate ('pəʊt'n,teɪt) n. a ruler or monarch. [Latin potens powerful]

potential (pə'tenʃəl) adj. **1. a.** possible but not yet actual. **b.** capable of being or becoming; latent. ~n. **2.** latent but unrealized ability: Jones has great potential as a manager. **3.** In full: **electric potential.** the work required to transfer a unit positive electric charge from an infinite distance to a given point. [Latin potentia power] —po'tentially adv.

potential difference n. the difference in electric potential between two points in an electric field, measured in volts.

potentiality (pə,tenʃɪ'ælɪtɪ) n., pl. -ties. latent capacity for becoming or developing.

pother ('pɒðə) n. a commotion or fuss. [origin unknown]

potherb ('pɒt,hɜːb) n. a plant whose leaves, flowers, or stems are used in cooking.

pothole ('pɒt,həʊl) n. **1.** a deep hole in a limestone area. **2.** a hole produced in a road surface by wear or weathering.

potholing ('pɒt,həʊlɪŋ) n. Brit. the sport of exploring underground caves. —'pot,holer n.

pothook ('pɒt,hʊk) n. **1.** an S-shaped hook for suspending a pot over a fire. **2.** an S-shaped mark in handwriting.

pothunter ('pɒt,hʌntə) n. **1.** a hunter who shoots without regard to the rules of sport. **2.** Informal. a person who enters competitions solely to win prizes.

potion ('pəʊʃən) n. a drink of medicine, poison, or some supposedly magic liquid. [Latin pōtiō a drink, esp. a poisonous one]

potluck ('pɒt'lʌk) n. Informal. **1.** whatever food happens to be available. **2.** whatever is available: to take potluck.

potpourri (,pəʊ'pʊərɪ) n., pl. -ris. **1.** a fragrant mixture of dried flower petals. **2.** a miscellany or medley. [French, lit.: rotten pot]

pot roast n. meat cooked slowly in a covered pot with very little liquid.

potsherd ('pɒt,ʃɜːd) n. a broken piece of pottery. [pot + schoord piece of broken crockery]

pot shot n. **1.** a shot taken without

careful aim. **2.** a shot fired at quarry within easy range.

pottage ('pɒtɪdʒ) *n.* a thick soup. [Old French *potage* contents of a pot]

potted ('pɒtɪd) *adj.* **1.** grown in a pot. **2.** cooked or preserved in a pot: *potted shrimps.* **3.** *Informal.* abridged: *a potted history.*

potter[1] ('pɒtə) *n.* a person who makes pottery.

potter[2] ('pɒtə) *or esp. U.S. & Canad.* **putter** *vb.* **1.** (often foll. by *about* or *around*) to busy oneself in an aimless but pleasant manner. **2.** (often foll. by *along* or *about*) to move with little energy or direction: *to potter about town.* [Old English *potian* to thrust]

Potteries ('pɒtərɪz) *pl. n.* **the.** (*sometimes functioning as sing.*) a region of W central England, in Staffordshire, in which the china industries are concentrated.

potter's wheel *n.* a device with a horizontal rotating disc, on which clay is shaped by hand.

pottery ('pɒtərɪ) *n., pl.* **-teries. 1.** articles made from baked clay. **2.** a place where such articles are made. **3.** the craft or business of making such articles.

potting shed *n.* a building in which plants are put in flowerpots.

potty[1] ('pɒtɪ) *adj.* **-tier, -tiest.** *Brit. informal.* **1.** slightly crazy. **2.** trivial or insignificant. **3.** (foll. by *about*) very keen (on). [origin unknown] —**pottiness** *n.*

potty[2] ('pɒtɪ) *n., pl.* **-ties.** a child's chamber pot.

pouch (paʊtʃ) *n.* **1.** a small bag. **2.** a saclike structure in various animals, such as the cheek fold in rodents. ~*vb.* **3.** to place in or as if in a pouch. **4.** to make or be made into a pouch. [Old French *poche* bag]

pouf *or* **pouffe** (puːf) *n.* a large solid cushion used as a seat. [French]

poulterer ('pəʊltərə) *n.* a dealer in poultry.

poultice ('pəʊltɪs) *n. Med.* a moist and often heated dressing applied to inflamed skin. [Latin *puls* a thick porridge]

poultry ('pəʊltrɪ) *n.* domestic fowls collectively. [Old French *pouletrie*]

pounce (paʊns) *vb.* **1.** (often foll. by *on* or *upon*) to spring or swoop, as in capturing prey. ~*n.* **2.** a pouncing; a spring or swoop. [origin unknown]

pound[1] (paʊnd) *vb.* **1.** (sometimes foll. by *on* or *at*) to strike heavily and repeatedly. **2.** to beat to a pulp; pulverize. **3.** (foll. by *out*) to produce, as by typing heavily. **4.** to move with heavy steps. **5.** to throb heavily. [Old English *pūnian*]

pound[2] (paʊnd) *n.* **1.** an avoirdupois unit of weight divided into 16 ounces and equal to 0.453 592 kilograms. **2.** a troy unit of weight divided into 12 ounces and equal to 0.373 242 kilograms. **3.** the standard monetary unit of the United Kingdom, divided into 100 pence. Official name: **pound sterling. 4.** the standard monetary unit of various other countries, such as Ireland, Cyprus, and Malta. [Old English *pund*]

pound[3] (paʊnd) *n.* an enclosure for keeping officially removed vehicles or stray dogs. [Old English *pund-*]

poundage ('paʊndɪdʒ) *n.* **1.** a charge of so much per pound of weight. **2.** a charge of so much per pound sterling.

-pounder ('paʊndə) *n.* **1.** something weighing a specified number of pounds: *a 200-pounder.* **2.** something worth a specified number of pounds: *a ten-pounder.* **3.** a gun that discharges a shell weighing a specified number of pounds: *a two-pounder.*

pour (pɔː) *vb.* **1.** to flow or cause to flow in a stream. **2.** to emit profusely: *the words poured out of her.* **3.** to rain heavily. **4.** to move together in large numbers; swarm: *the fans poured onto the pitch.* [origin unknown]

pourboire ('puəbwɑː) *n.* a tip; gratuity. [French, lit.: for drinking]

pout (paʊt) *vb.* **1.** to thrust out (the lips), as when sullen, or (of the lips) to be thrust out. **2.** to swell out; protrude. ~*n.* **3.** a pouting. [origin unknown]

pouter ('paʊtə) *n.* a breed of domestic pigeon with a crop that can be greatly puffed out.

poverty ('pɒvətɪ) *n.* **1.** the condition of being without adequate food or money. **2.** scarcity: *a poverty of wit.* **3.** inferior quality or inadequacy: *the poverty of the soil.* [Old French *poverté*]

poverty-stricken *adj.* suffering from extreme poverty.

poverty trap *n.* the situation of being unable to raise one's living standard because of depending on state benefits which are reduced if one gains any extra income.

pow (paʊ) *interj.* an exclamation imitative of a collision or explosion.

POW prisoner of war.

powder ('paʊdə) *n.* **1.** a substance in the form of tiny loose particles. **2.** a preparation in this form, such as gunpowder or face powder. ~*vb.* **3.** to turn into powder; pulverize. **4.** to cover or sprinkle with or as if with powder. [Old French *poldre*, from Latin *pulvis* dust] —**'powdery** *adj.*

powder keg *n.* **1.** a small barrel to hold gunpowder. **2.** a potential source of violence or disaster.

powder puff *n.* a soft pad used to apply cosmetic powder to the skin.

powder room *n.* a ladies' cloakroom.

power ('paʊə) *n.* **1.** ability to do something. **2.** (*often pl.*) a specific ability or faculty. **3.** political, financial, or social force or influence. **4.** control or a position of control. **5.** a state with political, industrial, or military strength. **6.** a person or group that has control, influence, or authority. **7.** a prerogative or privilege: *the power of veto.* **8.** legal authority: *power of attorney.* **9.** *Maths.* the value of a number or quantity raised to some exponent. **10.** *Physics, engineering.* a measure of the rate of doing work expressed as the work done per unit time. **11.** the rate at which electrical energy is fed into or taken from a device or system, measured in watts. **12.** mechanical energy as opposed to manual labour. **13.** a particular form of energy: *nuclear power.* **14.** the magnifying capacity of a lens or optical system. **15.** *Informal.* a great deal: *a power of good.* **16. the powers that be.** established authority. ~*vb.* **17.** to supply with power. ~*adj.* **18.** producing or using mechanical or electrical energy: *a power tool.* [Anglo-Norman *poer*]

powerboat ('paʊə,bəʊt) *n.* a fast powerful motorboat.

power cut *n.* a temporary interruption in the supply of electrical power.

powerful ('paʊəfʊl) *adj.* **1.** having great power. **2.** extremely effective: *a powerful drug.* —**'powerfully** *adv.* —**'powerfulness** *n.*

powerhouse ('paʊə,haʊs) *n.* **1.** an electrical generating station. **2.** *Informal.* a forceful person or thing.

powerless ('paʊəlɪs) *adj.* without power or authority. —**'powerlessness** *n.*

power of attorney *n.* **1.** legal authority to act for another person. **2.** the document conferring such authority.

power point *n.* an electrical socket mounted on or recessed into a wall.

power station *n.* an electrical generating station.

power steering *n.* a form of steering on vehicles in which the turning of the steering wheel is assisted by power from the engine.

powwow ('paʊ,waʊ) *n.* **1.** a talk or meeting. **2.** a meeting of North American Indians. ~*vb.* **3.** to hold a powwow. [American Indian]

pox (pɒks) *n.* **1.** a disease accompanied by skin pustules. **2.** (usually preceded by *the*) *Informal.* syphilis. [changed from *pocks*, pl. of *pock*]

pp **1.** past participle. **2.** (in signing documents on behalf of someone else) by delegation to. [Latin *per procurationem*] **3.** *Music.* very quietly. [Italian *pianissimo*]

pp. pages.

PPS **1.** parliamentary private secretary. **2.** additional postscript. [Latin *post postscriptum*]

PQ **1.** (in Canada) Parti Québecois. **2.** Province of Quebec.

pr, *pl.* **prs.** pair.

Pr *Chem.* praseodymium.

PR **1.** proportional representation. **2.** public relations.

pr. **1.** price. **2.** pronoun.

practicable ('præktɪkəb^əl) *adj.* **1.** capable of being done; feasible. **2.** usable. [French *praticable*] —**,practica'bility** *n.*

practical ('præktɪk^əl) *adj.* **1.** involving or concerned with experience or actual use, rather than theory. **2.** concerned with ordinary affairs, work, and daily living: *a survivor must be practical.* **3.** adapted or adaptable for use: *penicillin became a practical antibiotic.* **4.** involving or trained by practice: *practical skills.* **5.** being such for all general purposes; virtual: *it's a practical certainty.* ~*n.* **6.** an examination or

lesson in a practical subject. [Greek *praktikos,* from *prassein* to experience] —**,practi'cality** *n.* —**'practically** *adv.*

practical joke *n.* a trick intended to make someone look foolish. —**practical joker** *n.*

practice ('præktɪs) *n.* **1.** a usual or customary action. **2.** repetition of an activity in order to gain skill: *piano practice.* **3.** the condition of being skilful in an activity through repetition: *in practice; out of practice.* **4.** the exercise of a profession: *he set up practice as a lawyer.* **5.** the act of doing something: *he put his plans into practice.* [Greek *praktikē* practical work]

practise or *U.S.* **practice** ('præktɪs) *vb.* **1.** to do repeatedly so as to gain skill. **2.** to do (something) regularly: *they practise torture.* **3.** to observe or pursue (something): *to practise Buddhism.* **4.** to work at (a profession): *he practises law.* [Greek *prattein* to do]

practitioner (præk'tɪʃənə) *n.* a person who practises a profession or art.

praetor ('priːtə, -tɔː) *n.* (in ancient Rome) a senior magistrate ranking just below the consuls. [Latin] —**prae'torian** *adj., n.*

pragmatic (præg'mætɪk) *adj.* **1.** advocating behaviour that is dictated by practical consequences rather than by theory. **2.** *Philosophy.* of pragmatism. [Greek *prāgmatikos*] —**prag,mati'cality** *n.*

pragmatism ('prægmə,tɪzəm) *n.* **1.** action or policy dictated by the practical consequences rather than by theory. **2.** *Philosophy.* the doctrine that the content of a concept consists only in its practical applicability. —**'pragmatist** *n., adj.*

prairie ('prɛərɪ) *n.* (*often pl.*) a treeless grassy plain of the central U.S. and S Canada. [French, from Latin *prātum* meadow]

prairie dog *n.* a rodent that lives in large complex burrows in the N American prairies.

praise (preɪz) *n.* **1.** the act of expressing admiration or approval. **2. sing someone's praises.** to praise someone highly. ~*vb.* **3.** to express admiration or approval for. **4.** to proclaim the glory of (a god) with homage and thanksgiving. [Latin *pretium* prize]

praiseworthy ('preɪz,wɜːðɪ) *adj.* deserving of praise; commendable.

praline ('prɑːliːn) *n.* a sweet made of nuts with caramelized sugar. [French]

pram (præm) *n. Brit.* a four-wheeled carriage for a baby. [altered from *perambulator*]

prance (prɑːns) *vb.* **1.** to swagger or strut. **2.** (of a horse) to move with high springing steps. ~*n.* **3.** a prancing. [origin unknown]

prang (præŋ) *Slang, chiefly Brit.* ~*n.* **1.** a crash in an aircraft or car. ~*vb.* **2.** to crash or damage (an aircraft or car). [perhaps imit.]

prank (præŋk) *n.* a mischievous trick. [origin unknown] —**'prankster** *n.*

praseodymium (,preɪzɪəʊ'dɪmɪəm) *n.* a

silvery-white element of the lanthanide series of metals. Symbol: Pr [New Latin]

prat (præt) *n. Slang.* an incompetent or ineffectual person. [prob. special use of earlier *prat* buttocks, origin unknown]

prate (preɪt) *vb.* **1.** to talk idly and at length; chatter. ~*n.* **2.** chatter. [Germanic]

prattle ('præt³l) *vb.* **1.** to talk or utter in a foolish or childish way. ~*n.* **2.** foolish or childish talk. [Middle Low German *pratelen* to chatter]

prawn (prɔːn) *n.* a small edible shellfish. [origin unknown]

praxis ('præksɪs) *n.* **1.** the practice of a profession or field of study, as opposed to the theory. **2.** accepted practice or custom. [Greek: deed, action]

pray (preɪ) *vb.* **1.** to utter prayers (to God or other object of worship). **2.** to beg or implore. ~*adv.* **3.** *Archaic.* I beg you; please: *pray, leave us alone.* [Latin *precārī* to implore]

prayer[1] ('preə) *n.* **1.** a thanksgiving or an appeal for something spoken to one's God. **2.** the practice of praying. **3.** (*often pl.*) a form of devotion spent mainly praying: *morning prayers.* **4.** a form of words used in praying: *the Lord's Prayer.* **5.** something prayed for. **6.** an earnest request or entreaty.

prayer[2] ('preɪə) *n.* a person who prays.

prayer book (preə) *n.* a book of prayers used in church or for private devotions.

prayer mat (preə) *n.* the small carpet on which a Muslim kneels while praying.

prayer wheel (preə) *n. Buddhism.* (in Tibet) a cylinder inscribed with prayers, each turning of which is counted as an uttered prayer.

praying mantis *n.* same as **mantis.**

pre- *prefix.* before in time or position: *predate; pre-eminent.* [Latin *prae*]

preach (priːtʃ) *vb.* **1.** to make known (religious truth) or give religious instruction in (sermons). **2.** to advocate (something) in a moralizing way. [Latin *praedicāre* to proclaim]

preacher ('priːtʃə) *n.* a person who preaches, usually a Protestant clergyman.

preamble (priː'æmb³l) *n.* a preliminary or introductory statement. [Latin *prae-* before + *ambulāre* to walk]

prearrange (ˌpriːə'reɪndʒ) *vb.* to arrange beforehand. —ˌprear'ranged *adj.* —ˌprear'rangement *n.*

prebend ('prɛbənd) *n.* **1.** the allowance paid by a cathedral or collegiate church to a canon or member of the chapter. **2.** the land or tithe from which this is paid. [Old French *prébende*] —**prebendal** (prɪ-'bɛnd³l) *adj.*

prebendary ('prɛbəndrɪ) *n., pl.* **-daries.** a canon or chapter member of a cathedral or collegiate church who holds a prebend.

Precambrian *or* **Pre-Cambrian** (priː-'kæmbrɪən) *adj. Geol.* of the earliest geological era, lasting from about 4500 million years ago to 600 million years ago.

precancerous (priː'kænsərəs) *adj.* of, re-

lating to, or denoting a growth that though not yet malignant will become so unless treated.

precarious (prɪ'kɛərɪəs) *adj.* (of a position or situation) dangerous or insecure. [Latin *precārius* obtained by begging]

precaution (prɪ'kɔːʃən) *n.* an action taken to avoid a dangerous or undesirable event. [Latin *prae* before + *cavēre* to beware] —pre'cautionary *adj.*

precede (prɪ'siːd) *vb.* to go or be before (someone or something) in time, place, or rank. [Latin *praecēdere*]

precedence ('prɛsɪdəns) *n.* **1.** the ceremonial order of priority to be observed on formal occasions: *the officers sat according to precedence.* **2.** a right to preferential treatment: *I take precedence over you.*

precedent *n.* ('prɛsɪdənt). **1.** *Law.* a judicial decision that serves as an authority for deciding a later case. **2.** an example used to justify later similar occurrences. ~*adj.* (prɪ'siːd³nt, 'prɛsɪdənt). **3.** preceding.

precentor (prɪ'sɛntə) *n.* a person who leads the singing in church services. [Latin *prae* before + *canere* to sing]

precept ('priːsɛpt) *n.* **1.** a rule of conduct. **2.** a rule for morals; maxim. **3.** *Law.* a writ or warrant. [Latin *praeceptum*] —pre'ceptive *adj.*

preceptor (prɪ'sɛptə) *n. Rare.* an instructor. —**preceptorial** (ˌpriːsɛp'tɔːrɪəl) *adj.*

precession (prɪ'sɛʃən) *n.* **1.** the act of preceding. **2.** the motion of a spinning body, in which the axis of rotation sweeps out a cone. [Latin *praecēdere* to precede]

precinct ('priːsɪŋkt) *n.* **1.** an enclosed area or building marked by a fixed boundary. **2.** an area in a town closed to traffic: *a shopping precinct.* **3.** *U.S.* a district of a city for administrative or police purposes. [Latin *praecingere* to surround]

precincts ('priːsɪŋkts) *pl. n.* the surrounding region or area.

preciosity (ˌprɛʃɪ'ɒsɪtɪ) *n., pl.* **-ties.** fastidiousness or affectation.

precious ('prɛʃəs) *adj.* **1.** beloved; dear; cherished. **2.** very costly or valuable. **3.** very fastidious or affected in speech, manners, or behaviour. **4.** *Informal.* worthless: *you and your precious ideas!* ~*adv.* **5.** *Informal.* very: *there's precious little left.* [Latin *pretiōsus* valuable]

precious metal *n.* gold, silver, or platinum.

precious stone *n.* a rare mineral, such as diamond, ruby, or opal that is highly valued as a gemstone.

precipice ('prɛsɪpɪs) *n.* the steep sheer face of a cliff or crag. [Latin *praecipitium* steep place]

precipitant (prɪ'sɪpɪtənt) *adj.* **1.** hasty or impulsive; rash. **2.** rushing or falling rapidly.

precipitate *vb.* (prɪ'sɪpɪˌteɪt). **1.** to cause to happen too soon. **2.** to throw as from a height. **3.** to cause (moisture) to condense and fall as snow or rain or (of moisture) to condense and fall thus. **4.** *Chem.* to undergo or cause to undergo a process in which a dissolved substance separates from solution as a suspension of solid particles. ~*adj.* (prɪˈsɪpɪtɪt). **5.** rushing ahead. **6.** done rashly or hastily. ~*n.* (prɪˈsɪpɪtɪt). **7.** *Chem.* a precipitated solid. [Latin *praecipitāre* to throw down headlong]

precipitation (prɪˌsɪpɪˈteɪʃən) *n.* **1.** *Meteorol.* **a.** rain, hail, snow, or sleet formed by condensation of water vapour in the atmosphere. **b.** the falling of these on the earth's surface. **2.** the formation of a chemical precipitate. **3.** a precipitating or being precipitated. **4.** rash haste.

precipitous (prɪˈsɪpɪtəs) *adj.* **1.** like a precipice; very steep. **2.** hasty or precipitate.

precis *or* **précis** (ˈpreɪsiː) *n.*, *pl.* **precis** *or* **précis** (ˈpreɪsiːz). **1.** a summary of a text. ~*vb.* **2.** to make a precis of. [French]

precise (prɪˈsaɪs) *adj.* **1.** strictly correct in amount or value: *a precise sum.* **2.** particular: *this precise moment.* **3.** operating with total accuracy: *precise instruments.* **4.** strict in observing rules or standards. [Latin *prae* before + *caedere* to cut] —**preˈcisely** *adv.*

precision (prɪˈsɪʒən) *n.* **1.** the quality of being precise; accuracy. **2.** (*modifier*) characterized by accuracy: *precision grinding.*

preclude (prɪˈkluːd) *vb.* to prevent or make impossible, usually beforehand. [Latin *prae* before + *claudere* to close]

precocious (prɪˈkəʊʃəs) *adj.* **1.** ahead in development of some faculty or characteristic. **2.** of or showing unusually early development: *a precocious feat.* [Latin *prae* early + *coquere* to ripen] —**precocity** (prɪˈkɒsɪtɪ)

precognition (ˌpriːkɒgˈnɪʃən) *n.* *Psychol.* the alleged ability to foresee future events. [Latin *praecognoscere* to foresee]

preconceive (ˌpriːkənˈsiːv) *vb.* to form an idea of beforehand. —**preconception** (ˌpriːkənˈsɛpʃən) *n.*

precondition (ˌpriːkənˈdɪʃən) *n.* a necessary or required condition; prerequisite.

precursor (prɪˈkɜːsə) *n.* **1.** a forerunner. **2.** a predecessor. [Latin *praecursor* one who runs in front]

pred. predicate.

predacious (prɪˈdeɪʃəs) *adj.* (of animals) habitually hunting and killing other animals for food. [Latin *praeda* plunder]

predate (priːˈdeɪt) *vb.* **1.** to write a date on (a document) that is earlier than the actual date. **2.** to be or occur at an earlier date than.

predator (ˈprɛdətə) *n.* a carnivorous animal.

predatory (ˈprɛdətrɪ) *adj.* **1.** (of animals) habitually hunting and killing other animals for food. **2.** of or given to plundering or robbing. [Latin *praedārī* to pillage]

predecease (ˌpriːdɪˈsiːs) *vb.* to die before (another person).

predecessor (ˈpriːdɪˌsɛsə) *n.* **1.** a person who precedes another, as in an office. **2.** something that precedes something else.

3. an ancestor. [Latin *prae* before + *dēcēdere* to go away]

predestination (priːˌdɛstɪˈneɪʃən) *n.* Christian *theol.* the act of God foreordaining everything.

predestine (priːˈdɛstɪn) *or* **predestinate** *vb.* **1.** to determine beforehand. **2.** Christian *theol.* (of God) to foreordain (any event). [Latin *praedestināre* to resolve beforehand]

predetermine (ˌpriːdɪˈtɜːmɪn) *vb.* **1.** to determine beforehand. **2.** to influence or bias.

predicable (ˈprɛdɪkəb'l) *adj.* capable of being predicated.

predicament (prɪˈdɪkəmənt) *n.* an embarrassing or difficult situation. [see PREDICATE]

predicant (ˈprɛdɪkənt) *adj.* **1.** of preaching. ~*n.* **2.** a member of a religious order founded for preaching, usually a Dominican. [Latin *praedicāns* preaching]

predicate *vb.* (ˈprɛdɪˌkeɪt). **1.** to declare or affirm. **2.** to imply or connote. **3.** Logic. to assert (something) about the subject of a proposition. ~*n.* (ˈprɛdɪkɪt). **4.** Grammar. the part of a sentence in which a statement is made about the subject of a sentence. **5.** Logic. something that is asserted about the subject of a proposition. [Latin *praedicāre* to assert publicly] —**prediˈcation** *n.* —**ˈpredicative** *adj.*

predict (prɪˈdɪkt) *vb.* to make a declaration about in advance; foretell. [Latin *praedīcere*] —**preˈdictable** *adj.* —**preˈdictably** *adv.* —**preˈdictor** *n.*

prediction (prɪˈdɪkʃən) *n.* **1.** the act of predicting. **2.** something predicted; a forecast.

predikant (ˌprɛdɪˈkænt) *n.* a minister in the Dutch Reformed Church in South Africa. [Dutch]

predilection (ˌpriːdɪˈlɛkʃən) *n.* a predisposition or preference. [French *prédilection*]

predispose (ˌpriːdɪˈspəʊz) *vb.* (often foll. by *to* or *towards*) to incline or make (someone) susceptible to something beforehand. —**ˌpredispoˈsition** *n.*

predominant (prɪˈdɒmɪnənt) *adj.* **1.** having power or influence over others. **2.** prevailing. —**preˈdominance** *n.* —**preˈdominantly** *adv.*

predominate (prɪˈdɒmɪˌneɪt) *vb.* **1.** (often foll. by *over*) to have power or influence. **2.** to prevail or preponderate. [Latin *prae* before + *dominārī* to bear rule]

pre-eminent (prɪˈɛmɪnənt) *adj.* extremely eminent; outstanding. —**pre-ˈeminence** *n.*

pre-empt (prɪˈɛmpt) *vb.* to get or do (something) in advance of or to the exclusion of others.

pre-emption (prɪˈɛmpʃən) *n.* Law. the purchase of or right to buy property in advance of others. [Medieval Latin *praeemere* to buy beforehand]

pre-emptive (prɪˈɛmptɪv) *adj.* Mil. designed to reduce or destroy an enemy's attacking strength before it can be used: *a pre-emptive strike.*

preen (priːn) *vb.* **1.** (of birds) to keep

(feathers) in good condition by arranging and cleaning with the bill. **2.** to smarten (oneself) carefully. **3.** (usually foll. by *on*) to pride or congratulate (oneself). [Middle English *preinen*]

pref. 1. preface. **2.** prefatory. **3.** preference. **4.** preferred. **5.** prefix.

prefab (ˈpriːˌfæb) *n.* a prefabricated building, usually a small house.

prefabricate (priːˈfæbrɪˌkeɪt) *vb.* to manufacture sections of (a building) so that they can be rapidly assembled.

preface (ˈprefɪs) *n.* **1.** a statement written as an introduction to a book, usually explaining its scope, intention, or method; foreword. **2.** anything introductory. ~*vb.* **3.** to provide with a preface, **4.** to act as a preface to. [Latin *praefārī* to say in advance]

prefatory (ˈprefətrɪ) *adj.* of or serving as a preface; introductory. [Latin *praefārī* to say in advance]

prefect (ˈpriːfekt) *n.* **1.** (in some countries) the chief administrative officer in a department. **2.** *Brit.* a senior pupil in a school given limited power to help maintain discipline. [Latin *praefectus* one put in charge]

prefecture (ˈpriːfekˌtjʊə) *n.* the office, position, or area of authority of a prefect.

prefer (prɪˈfɜː) *vb.* **-ferring, -ferred. 1.** to like better or value more highly: *I prefer to stand.* **2.** *Law.* to put (charges) before a court or magistrate for consideration and judgment. **3.** (*often passive*) to promote over another or others. [Latin *praeferre* to carry in front, prefer]

preferable (ˈprefərəbʲl) *adj.* preferred or more desirable. —**ˈpreferably** *adv.*

preference (ˈprefərəns, ˈprefrəns) *n.* **1.** a preferring. **2.** a person or thing preferred.

preference shares *pl. n. Brit.* shares issued by a company and giving their holders a prior right over ordinary shareholders to payment of dividend.

preferential (ˌprefəˈrenʃəl) *adj.* **1.** showing or resulting from preference. **2.** giving or receiving preference.

preferment (prɪˈfɜːmənt) *n.* promotion to a higher position or office.

prefigure (priːˈfɪɡə) *vb.* **1.** to represent or suggest in advance. **2.** to imagine beforehand.

prefix *n.* (ˈpriːfɪks). **1.** *Grammar.* a letter or group of letters that precedes the word to which it is attached, such as *un-* in *unhappy.* **2.** something coming or placed before. ~*vb.* (priːˈfɪks, ˈpriːfɪks). **3.** to put or place before. **4.** *Grammar.* to add (a letter or group of letters) as a prefix to the beginning of a word.

pregnant (ˈpreɡnənt) *adj.* **1.** carrying a fetus or fetuses within the womb. **2.** full of meaning or significance: *a pregnant pause.* [Latin *praegnāns*] —**ˈpregnancy** *n.*

prehensile (prɪˈhensaɪl) *adj.* adapted for grasping by wrapping around a support: *a prehensile tail.* [Latin *prehendere* to grasp]

prehistoric (ˌpriːhɪˈstɒrɪk) *adj.* of man's development before the appearance of the written word. —**preˈhistory** *n.*

preindustrial (ˌpriːɪnˈdʌstrɪəl) *adj.* of a time before the mechanization of industry.

prejudge (priːˈdʒʌdʒ) *vb.* to judge beforehand without sufficient evidence.

prejudice (ˈpredʒʊdɪs) *n.* **1.** an opinion formed beforehand. **2.** the act or condition of holding such opinions. **3.** intolerance of or dislike for people of a specific race, religion, or group. **4.** harm resulting from prejudice. **5. without prejudice.** *Law.* without detriment to an existing right or claim. ~*vb.* **6.** to cause to be prejudiced. **7.** to harm by prejudice. [Latin *prae* before + *jūdicium* sentence]

prejudicial (ˌpredʒʊˈdɪʃəl) *adj.* causing prejudice; damaging.

prelacy (ˈpreləsɪ) *n., pl.* **-cies. 1. a.** the office or status of a prelate. **b.** prelates collectively. **2.** *Often offensive.* government of the Church by prelates.

prelate (ˈprelɪt) *n.* a Church dignitary of high rank, such as a bishop. [Church Latin *praelātus,* from Latin *praeferre* to hold in special esteem]

preliminaries (prɪˈlɪmɪnərɪz) *pl. n.* same as **prelims.**

preliminary (prɪˈlɪmɪnərɪ) *adj.* **1.** occurring before or in preparation; introductory. ~*n., pl.* **-naries. 2.** a preliminary event. **3.** an eliminating contest held before a main competition. [Latin *prae* before + *limen* threshold]

prelims (ˈpriːlɪmz, prəˈlɪmz) *pl. n.* **1.** the pages of a book, such as the title page and contents, before the main text. **2.** the first public examinations in some universities. [a contraction of *preliminaries*]

prelude (ˈpreljuːd) *n.* **1. a.** the introductory section of a fugue or first movement of a suite. **b.** a short piece of music for piano or organ. **2.** an introduction or preceding event. ~*vb.* **3.** to act as a prelude to (something). **4.** to introduce by a prelude. [Latin *prae* before + *lūdere* to play]

premarital (priːˈmærɪtʲl) *adj.* occurring before marriage: *premarital sex.*

premature (ˌpreməˈtjʊə, ˈpreməˌtjʊə) *adj.* **1.** occurring or existing before the normal or expected time. **2.** impulsive or hasty: *a premature judgment.* **3.** (of an infant) born before the date when it was due to be born. [Latin *prae* in advance + *mātūrus* ripe]

premedication (ˌpriːmedɪˈkeɪʃən) *n. Surgery.* any drugs given to prepare a patient for a general anaesthetic.

premeditate (prɪˈmedɪˌteɪt) *vb.* to plan (something) beforehand. —**preˌmediˈtation** *n.*

premenstrual (priːˈmenstrʊəl) *adj.* of or occurring before a menstrual period.

premenstrual tension or **syndrome** *n.* symptoms, such as nervous tension, that may be experienced because of hormonal changes in the days before a menstrual period starts.

premier (ˈpremjə) *n.* **1.** a prime minister. **2.** a head of government of a Canadian province or Australian state. ~*adj.* **3.** first in importance or rank: *the premier competition.* **4.** first in occurrence; earliest. [Latin *primus* first]

premiere ('prɛmɪˌɛə, 'prɛmɪə) *n.* **1.** the first public performance of a film, play, or opera. ~*vb.* **2.** to give a premiere of: *the show was premiered on Broadway.* [French, fem. of *premier* first]

premise *or* **premiss** ('prɛmɪs) *n. Logic.* a statement that is assumed to be true and is used as a basis for an argument. [Medieval Latin *praemissa* sent on before]

premises ('prɛmɪsɪz) *pl. n.* **1.** a piece of land together with its buildings. **2.** *Law.* (in a deed) the matters referred to previously.

premium ('priːmɪəm) *n.* **1.** an amount paid in addition to a standard rate, price, or wage; bonus. **2.** the amount to be paid for an insurance policy. **3.** the amount above the usual value at which something sells. **4.** great value or regard: *to put a premium on honesty.* **5. at a premium. a.** in great demand, usually because of scarcity. **b.** at a higher price than usual. [Latin *praemium* prize]

Premium Savings Bonds *pl. n.* (in Britain) bonds issued by the Treasury, on which no interest is paid, but there is a monthly draw for cash prizes. Also called: **premium bonds.**

premolar (priː'məulə) *n.* a tooth between the canine and first molar in adult humans.

premonition (ˌprɛmə'nɪʃən) *n.* an intuition of a future occurrence; foreboding. [Latin *prae* before + *monēre* to warn] —**premonitory** (prɪ'mɒnɪtrɪ) *adj.*

prenatal (priː'neɪt°l) *adj.* before birth; during pregnancy.

preoccupy (priː'ɒkjʊˌpaɪ) *vb.* **-pying, -pied.** to engross the thoughts or mind of. [Latin *praeoccupāre* to capture in advance] —**preˌoccuˈpation** *n.*

preordain (ˌpriːɔː'deɪn) *vb.* to ordain or decree beforehand.

prep (prɛp) *n. Informal.* short for **preparation** (sense 4).

prep. 1. preparation. **2.** preparatory. **3.** preposition.

prepacked (priː'pækt) *adj.* (of goods) sold already wrapped or packed.

preparation (ˌprɛpə'reɪʃən) *n.* **1.** a preparing or being prepared. **2.** (*often pl.*) a measure done in order to prepare for something: *to make preparations for something.* **3.** something that is prepared, such as a medicine. **4. a.** homework. **b.** the period reserved for this.

preparatory (prɪ'pærətrɪ) *adj.* **1.** serving to prepare. **2.** introductory. **3. preparatory to.** before: *a drink preparatory to eating.*

preparatory school *n.* **1.** (in Britain) a private school for children between the ages of 6 and 13, generally preparing pupils for public school. **2.** (in the U.S.) a private secondary school preparing pupils for college.

prepare (prɪ'pɛə) *vb.* **1.** to make ready in advance for some use, event, or action: *to prepare a meal; to prepare to go.* **2.** to put together using parts or ingredients; construct. **3.** to equip or outfit, as for an expedition. **4. be prepared.** (*foll. by an infinitive*) to be willing and able: *I'm prepared to say.* [Latin *prae* before + *parāre* to make ready]

prepay (priː'peɪ) *vb.* **-paying, -paid.** to pay for in advance. —**preˈpayment** *n.*

preponderant (prɪ'pɒndərənt) *adj.* greater in amount, force, or influence. —**preˈponderance** *n.*

preponderate (prɪ'pɒndəˌreɪt) *vb.* (often foll. by *over*) to be more powerful, important, or numerous (than). [Late Latin *praeponderāre* to be of greater weight]

preposition (ˌprɛpə'zɪʃən) *n.* a word or group of words used before a noun or pronoun to relate it to another element of a sentence, for example *in* in *he is in the car.* [Latin *praepositiō* a putting before] —**ˌprepoˈsitional** *adj.*

prepossess (ˌpriːpə'zɛs) *vb.* **1.** to preoccupy or engross mentally. **2.** to make a favourable impression in advance. —**ˌprepos'session** *n.*

prepossessing (ˌpriːpə'zɛsɪŋ) *adj.* creating a good impression; attractive.

preposterous (prɪ'pɒstərəs) *adj.* contrary to nature or sense; absurd. [Latin *praeposterus* reversed]

prep school *n. Informal.* See **preparatory school.**

prepuce ('priːpjuːs) *n.* **1.** the retractable fold of skin covering the tip of the penis; foreskin. **2.** a similar fold of skin covering the tip of the clitoris. [Latin *praepūtium*]

Pre-Raphaelite (ˌpriː'ræfəlaɪt) *n.* **1.** a member of a society of painters founded in 1848 to revive the fidelity to nature and realistic colour considered typical of Italian painting before Raphael. ~*adj.* **2.** of or in the manner of Pre-Raphaelite painting and painters.

prerecord (ˌpriːrɪ'kɔːd) *vb.* to record (music or a programme) in advance so that it can be played or broadcast later. —**ˌprereˈcorded** *adj.*

prerequisite (priː'rɛkwɪzɪt) *adj.* **1.** required as a prior condition. ~*n.* **2.** something required as a prior condition.

prerogative (prɪ'rɒgətɪv) *n.* an exclusive privilege or right. [Latin *praerogātīva* privilege]

pres. 1. present (time). **2.** presidential.

Pres. President.

presage *n.* ('prɛsɪdʒ). **1.** a portent; omen. **2.** a foreboding. ~*vb.* ('prɛsɪdʒ, prɪ'seɪdʒ). **3.** to have a foreboding of. **4.** to give a forewarning of; portend: *what does it presage for the future?* [Latin *praesāgīre* to perceive beforehand]

presbyopia (ˌprɛzbɪ'əupɪə) *n.* a progressively diminishing ability of the eye to focus. [Greek *presbus* old man + *ōps* eye]

presbyter ('prɛzbɪtə) *n.* **1.** (in some episcopal Churches) an official with administrative and priestly duties. **2.** (in the Presbyterian Church) an elder. [Greek *presbuteros* an older man] —**ˌpresbyˈterial** *adj.*

presbyterian (ˌprezbɪˈtɪərɪən) *adj.* **1.** of or designating Church government by presbyters or elders. ~*n.* **2.** an upholder of this type of Church government. —ˌpresbyˈterianism *n.*

Presbyterian (ˌprezbɪˈtɪərɪən) *adj.* **1.** of any of various Protestant Churches governed by presbyters or elders. ~*n.* **2.** a member of a Presbyterian Church. —ˌPresbyˈterianism *n.*

presbytery (ˈprezbɪtərɪ) *n., pl.* -teries. **1.** *Presbyterian Church.* a local Church court. **2.** the part of a church east of the choir; a sanctuary. **3.** presbyters or elders collectively. **4.** *R.C. Church.* the residence of a parish priest. [see PRESBYTER]

preschool (priːˈskuːl) *adj.* of or provided for children before the age at which they must go to school: *a preschool playgroup.*

prescience (ˈpresɪəns) *n.* knowledge of events before they happen; foresight. [Latin *praescīre* to know beforehand] —**prescient** *adj.*

prescribe (prɪˈskraɪb) *vb.* **1.** to lay down as a rule. **2.** *Med.* to recommend the use of (a drug or other remedy). [Latin *praescrībere* to write previously]

prescript (ˈpriːskrɪpt) *n.* something laid down or prescribed.

prescription (prɪˈskrɪpʃən) *n.* **1. a.** written instructions from a doctor for the preparation and use of a medicine to be issued to a patient. **b.** the medicine prescribed. **2.** a prescribing. [legal Latin *praescriptiō* an order]

prescriptive (prɪˈskrɪptɪv) *adj.* **1.** making or giving directions or rules. **2.** based on long-standing custom.

presence (ˈprezəns) *n.* **1.** a being present. **2.** immediate proximity: *in his presence.* **3.** impressive personal appearance or bearing: *he had great physical presence.* **4.** an invisible spirit felt to be nearby: *I felt a presence in the room.* [Latin *praesentia* a being before]

presence of mind *n.* the ability to stay calm and act sensibly in a crisis.

present[1] (ˈprezənt) *adj.* **1.** existing at the time at which something is spoken or written. **2.** being in a specified place: *the murderer is present in this room.* **3.** now being dealt with or discussed: *the present author.* **4.** *Grammar.* denoting a tense of verbs used when the action or event described is happening at the time of utterance. ~*n.* **5.** *Grammar.* the present tense. **6. at present.** now. **7. for the present.** for now; temporarily. **8. the present.** the time being; now. ~See also **presents.** [Latin *praesens*]

present[2] *n.* (ˈprezənt). **1.** a gift. ~*vb.* (prɪˈzent). **2.** to introduce (a person) to another. **3.** to introduce to the public: *to present a play.* **4.** to introduce and compere (a radio or television show). **5.** to show; exhibit: *he presented a brave face to the world.* **6.** to bring or suggest to the mind: *to present a problem.* **7.** to put forward; submit: *to present a proposal.* **8.** to give or offer formally: *to present one's compliments; to present a prize.* **9.** to hand over for action or payment: *to present a bill.* **10.** to depict in a particular way: *the actor presented Hamlet as a very young man.* **11.** to aim (a weapon). **12. present arms.** to salute someone with one's weapon. [Latin *praesentāre* to exhibit]

presentable (prɪˈzentəb‹ə›l) *adj.* **1.** fit to be seen by or introduced to other people. **2.** fit to be shown or offered. —**preˌsentaˈbility** *n.*

presentation (ˌprezənˈteɪʃən) *n.* **1.** a presenting or being presented. **2.** the manner of presenting. **3.** a formal offering, as of a gift. **4.** a performance or representation, as of a play.

present-day *n.* (*modifier*) of the modern day; current: *I don't like present-day fashions.*

presenter (prɪˈzentə) *n. Radio, television.* a person who introduces and comperes a show and links the items in it.

presentiment (prɪˈzentɪmənt) *n.* a sense of something about to happen; premonition. [obs. French *pressentir* to sense beforehand]

presently (ˈprezəntlɪ) *adv.* **1.** soon. **2.** *Chiefly Scot., U.S., & Canad.* at the moment.

present participle (ˈprezˌnt) *n.* a participial form of verbs used adjectivally when the action it describes is happening at the same time as that of the main verb of a sentence.

present perfect (ˈprezˌnt) *adj., n. Grammar.* another term for **perfect** (senses 7, 8).

presents (ˈprezənts) *pl. n. Law.* used in a deed or document to refer to itself: *know all men by these presents.*

preservative (prɪˈzɜːvətɪv) *n.* **1.** something that preserves, usually a chemical added to foods. ~*adj.* **2.** that preserves.

preserve (prɪˈzɜːv) *vb.* **1.** to keep safe from danger or harm; protect. **2.** to protect from decay: *to preserve old buildings.* **3.** to maintain; keep up: *to preserve a façade of indifference.* **4.** to treat (something, such as food) in order to prevent it from decomposition or chemical change. **5.** to rear and protect (game) in restricted places for hunting or fishing. ~*n.* **6.** a special domain: *archaeology is the preserve of specialists.* **7.** (*usually pl.*) fruit preserved by cooking with sugar. **8.** an area where game is reared for private hunting or fishing. [Latin *prae* before + *servāre* to keep safe] —**preservation** (ˌprezəˈveɪʃən) *n.*

preset (priːˈset) *vb.* **1.** to set (the controls of a piece of equipment) before the time at which it is to work. ~*adj.* **2.** (of equipment) with the controls set in advance.

preside (prɪˈzaɪd) *vb.* **1.** to sit in or hold a position of authority, as over a meeting. **2.** to exercise authority; control. [Latin *praesidēre* to superintend]

presidency (ˈprezɪdənsɪ) *n., pl.* -cies. the office, dignity, or term of a president.

president (ˈprezɪdənt) *n.* **1.** (*often cap.*) the head of state of a republic, esp. of the U.S. **2.** (in the U.S.) the head of a company, corporation, or university. **3.** a person who presides over a meeting. **4.** the head of certain establishments of higher education. [Late Latin *praesidens* ruler] —**presidential** (ˌprezɪˈdenʃəl) *adj.*

presidium (prɪˈsɪdɪəm) *n.* (*often cap.*) (in Communist countries) a permanent administrative committee. [Russian *prezidium*]

press[1] (pres) *vb.* **1.** to apply weight, force, or steady pressure (to): *he pressed the button on the camera.* **2.** to squeeze or compress so as to alter in shape. **3.** to iron (clothing) so as to smooth out creases. **4.** to make (objects) from soft material by pressing with a mould. **5.** to squeeze; embrace: *she pressed his hand.* **6.** to extract or force out (juice) by pressure (from). **7.** to force or compel: *colonial powers could be pressed to carry out their mission.* **8.** to urge (someone) insistently: *they pressed for an answer.* **9.** to plead or put forward strongly: *to press a claim.* **10.** to be urgent: *time presses.* **11.** to have little of: *we're hard pressed for time.* **12.** (sometimes foll. by *on* or *forward*) to hasten or advance in a forceful manner: *they pressed on with their journey.* **13.** to crowd; push: *shoppers press along the pavements.* ~*n.* **14.** any machine that exerts pressure to form or cut materials or to extract liquids or compress solids. **15.** See **printing press.** **16.** the art or process of printing. **17. go to press.** to go to be printed: *when is this book going to press?* **18. the press.** news media collectively, esp. newspapers. **19.** the opinions and reviews in the newspapers: *the play received a poor press.* **20.** the act of pressing or state of being pressed. **21.** a crowd: *a press of people at the exit.* **22.** a cupboard for storing clothes or linen. [Old French *presser*]

press[2] (pres) *vb.* **1.** to recruit (men) by forcible measures for military service. **2.** to use for a purpose other than intended: *press into service.* [from *prest* to recruit soldiers]

press agent *n.* a person employed to obtain favourable publicity for an individual or organization.

press conference *n.* an interview for reporters given by a politician, film star, or someone in the news.

press gallery *n.* an area for newspaper reporters, esp. in a legislative assembly.

press gang *n.* **1.** (formerly) a group of men used to press civilians for service in the navy or army. ~*vb.* **press-gang.** **2.** to force (a person) to join the navy or army by a press gang. **3.** to induce (a person) to do something by forceful persuasion.

pressing (ˈpresɪŋ) *adj.* **1.** demanding immediate attention. ~*n.* **2.** a large number of gramophone records produced at one time.

press stud *n.* a fastening device in which one part with a projecting knob snaps into a hole on another part, used esp. on clothing.

press-up *n.* an exercise in which the body is raised from and lowered to the floor by the arms only, the trunk being kept straight.

pressure (ˈpreʃə) *n.* **1.** the state of pressing or being pressed. **2.** the exertion of force by one body on the surface of another. **3.** a moral force that compels: *to bring pressure to bear.* **4.** urgent claims or demands: *to work under pressure.* **5.** a burdensome condition that is hard to bear: *the pressure of grief.* **6.** the force applied to a unit area of a surface, measured in pascals, millibars, torrs, or atmospheres. ~*vb.* **7.** to constrain or compel, as by moral force. [Late Latin *pressūra* a pressing, from Latin *premere* to press]

pressure cooker *n.* an airtight pot in which food may be cooked quickly by steam under pressure. —**ˈpressureˌcook** *vb.*

pressure group *n.* a group of people who seek to influence legislators or public opinion.

pressurize *or* **-ise** (ˈpreʃəˌraɪz) *vb.* **1.** to make insistent demands of (someone); coerce. **2.** to increase the pressure in (an enclosure, such as an aircraft cabin) in order to maintain approximately atmospheric pressure when the external pressure is low. —ˌpressuriˈzation *or* -iˈsation *n.*

Prestel (ˈprestel) *n. Trademark.* (in Britain) the Post Office public viewdata service.

prestidigitation (ˌprestɪˌdɪdʒɪˈteɪʃən) *n.* same as **sleight of hand.** [French] —ˌprestiˈdigiˌtator *n.*

prestige (preˈstiːʒ) *n.* **1.** high status or reputation achieved through success, influence, or position. **2.** the power to impress. [Latin *praestigiae* tricks] —**prestigious** (preˈstɪdʒəs) *adj.*

presto (ˈprestəʊ) *Music.* ~*adv.* **1.** very fast. ~*n., pl.* **-tos. 2.** a passage to be played very quickly. [Italian]

prestressed concrete (ˌpriːˈstrest) *n.* concrete that contains stretched steel wires.

presumably (prɪˈzjuːməblɪ) *adv.* one supposes that: *presumably she'll arrive today.*

presume (prɪˈzjuːm) *vb.* **1.** to take (something) for granted; assume. **2.** to dare (to do something): *do you presume to copy my work?* **3.** (foll. by *on* or *upon*) to rely on or depend: *don't presume on his agreement.* **4.** (foll. by *on* or *upon*) to take advantage (of): *don't presume upon his good nature too far.* [Latin *praesūmere* to take in advance] —**presumedly** (prɪˈzjuːmɪdlɪ) *adv.* —**preˈsuming** *adj.*

presumption (prɪˈzʌmpʃən) *n.* **1.** the act of presuming. **2.** bold or insolent behaviour. **3.** a belief or assumption based on reasonable evidence. **4.** a basis on which to presume. —**preˈsumptive** *adj.*

presumptuous (prɪˈzʌmptjʊəs) *adj.* characterized by presumption; bold; forward.

presuppose (ˌpriːsəˈpəʊz) *vb.* **1.** to take for granted. **2.** to require as a necessary prior condition: *all arguments make use of logic and presuppose it.* —**presupposition** (ˌpriːsʌpəˈzɪʃən) *n.*

pretence or U.S. **pretense** (prɪ'tɛns) n.
1. the act of pretending. 2. a false display;
affectation. 3. a claim, esp. a false one, to
a right, title, or distinction. 4. make-
believe. 5. a pretext.

pretend (prɪ'tɛnd) vb. 1. to claim or
allege (something untrue): he pretended
that he was ill. 2. to make believe: you
pretend to be Ophelia. 3. (foll. by to) to
present a claim, esp. a dubious one: to
pretend to the throne. [Latin praetendere
to stretch forth, feign]

pretender (prɪ'tɛndə) n. a person who
mounts a claim, as to a throne or title.

pretension (prɪ'tɛnʃən) n. (often pl.) a
false claim to merit, worth, or importance.

pretentious (prɪ'tɛnʃəs) adj. 1. making
claim to distinction or importance, esp.
undeservedly. 2. ostentatious.

preterite or esp. U.S. **preterit** ('prɛtərɪt)
Grammar. ~n. 1. a tense of verbs used to
relate past action, as jumped, swam. 2. a
verb in this tense. ~adj. 3. denoting this
tense. [Late Latin praeteritum (tempus)
past (time)]

preternatural (ˌpriːtə'nætʃrəl) adj. 1. beyond what is ordinarily found in nature;
abnormal. 2. supernatural. [Latin praeter
natūram beyond the scope of nature]

pretext ('priːtɛkst) n. a fictitious reason
given in order to conceal the real one: he
put them off on one pretext or another.
[Latin praetextum disguise, from
praetexere to weave in front]

prettify ('prɪtɪˌfaɪ) vb. **-fying, -fied.** to
make pretty, esp. in a trivial fashion.

pretty ('prɪtɪ) adj. **-tier, -tiest.** 1. pleasing
or appealing in a delicate or graceful way.
2. dainty, neat, or charming. 3. Informal,
often ironical. excellent, grand, or fine:
here's a pretty mess! 4. **sitting pretty.**
Informal. in a favourable state. ~adv. 5.
Informal. fairly; somewhat: I'm pretty certain. [Old English prættig clever] —'**pretti-
ly** adv. —'**prettiness** n.

pretty-pretty adj. Informal. excessively
or ostentatiously pretty.

pretzel ('prɛtsəl) n. a brittle savoury biscuit in the form of a knot. [from German]

prevail (prɪ'veɪl) vb. 1. (often foll. by over
or against) to prove superior; gain mastery: skill will prevail. 2. to be the most
important feature; be prevalent: a mood of
sadness prevailed. 3. to exist widely; be in
force: the condition that now prevails. 4.
prevail on or **upon.** to succeed in persuading: she prevailed upon him to come to the
party. [Latin praevalēre to be superior in
strength]

prevailing (prɪ'veɪlɪŋ) adj. 1. generally
accepted; widespread: the prevailing opinion. 2. most frequent; predominant: the
prevailing wind is from the north.

prevalent ('prɛvələnt) adj. widespread or
current. —'**prevalence** n.

prevaricate (prɪ'værɪˌkeɪt) vb. to speak or
act falsely or evasively with intent to
deceive. [Latin praevāricārī to walk
crookedly] —pre,vari'cation n. —pre-
'vari,cator n.

prevent (prɪ'vɛnt) vb. 1. to keep from

happening; hinder. 2. (often foll. by from)
to keep (someone from doing something).
[Latin praevenire] —pre'ventable or
pre'ventible adj. —pre'vention n.

preventive (prɪ'vɛntɪv) adj. 1. tending or
intended to prevent or hinder. 2. Med.
tending to prevent disease. ~n. 3. something that serves to prevent. 4. Med. any
drug or agent that tends to prevent disease. Also: **preventative.** —pre'vention n.

preview ('priːˌvjuː) n. 1. an advance
showing before public presentation of a
film, art exhibition, or play. ~vb. 2. to
view in advance.

previous ('priːvɪəs) adj. 1. existing or
coming before something else. 2. Informal.
taking place or done too soon; premature:
your congratulations are a bit previous. 3.
previous to. before. [Latin praevius leading the way] —'**previously** adv.

prewar (ˌpriː'wɔː, 'priːˌwɔː) adj. of or occurring in the period before a war, esp.
before World War I or II.

prey (preɪ) n. 1. an animal hunted or
captured by another for food. 2. a person
or thing that becomes the victim of a
hostile person, influence, or emotion. 3.
bird or **beast of prey.** a bird or animal that
preys on others for food. ~vb. (often foll.
by on or upon) 4. to hunt food by killing
other animals. 5. to make a victim (of
others), as by profiting at their expense.
6. to exert a depressing or obsessive effect
(on the mind or spirits). [Old French preie]

price (praɪs) n. 1. the sum in money or
goods for which anything is or may be
bought or sold. 2. the cost at which
anything is obtained. 3. Gambling. odds.
4. **at any price.** whatever the price or cost.
5. **at a price.** at a high price. 6. **what
price (something)?** what are the chances
of (something) happening now? ~vb. 7.
to fix the price of. 8. to discover the price
of. [Latin pretium]

price-fixing n. the setting of prices by
agreement among producers and distributors.

priceless ('praɪslɪs) adj. 1. of inestimable
worth; invaluable. 2. Informal. extremely
amusing.

pricey ('praɪsɪ) adj. **pricier, priciest.** Informal. expensive.

prick (prɪk) vb. 1. to make (a small hole)
in (something) by piercing lightly with a
sharp point. 2. to cause or have a piercing
or stinging sensation. 3. to cause to feel a
sharp emotional pain: knowledge of such
poverty pricked his conscience. 4. to outline by dots or punctures. 5. (usually foll.
by up) to rise or raise erect: the dog
pricked his ears up. 6. **prick up one's
ears.** to start to listen attentively; become
interested. ~n. 7. the act of pricking or
the sensation of being pricked. 8. a mark
made by a sharp point; puncture. 9. a
sharp emotional pain: a prick of conscience. 10. Slang, taboo. a penis. 11.
Slang, offensive. a despicable man. [Old
English prica point, puncture]

prickle ('prɪkəl) n. 1. Bot. a pointed
thornlike growth on a stem or leaf. 2. a

pricking or stinging sensation. ~*vb.* **3.** to feel a stinging sensation. [Old English *pricel*]

prickly ('prɪklɪ) *adj.* **-lier, -liest. 1.** having or covered with prickles. **2.** stinging. **3.** irritable.

prickly heat *n.* a rash of small itchy spots on the skin that occurs in very hot weather.

prickly pear *n.* **1.** any of various tropical cactuses with edible oval fruit. **2.** the fruit of any of these plants.

pride (praɪd) *n.* **1.** a feeling of honour and self-respect; a sense of personal worth. **2.** excessive self-esteem; conceit. **3.** a source of pride: *his garden was his pride and joy.* **4.** satisfaction in one's own or another's success or achievements. **5.** the better or superior part of something; flower. **6.** a group (of lions). **7. pride of place.** the most important position. ~*vb.* **8.** (foll. by *on* or *upon*) to take pride in (oneself) for. [Old English *prȳda*]

prie-dieu (priː'djɜː) *n.* an upright frame with a ledge for kneeling upon, for use when praying. [French *prier* to pray + *Dieu* God]

priest (priːst) *n.* **1.** (in the Christian Church) a person ordained to administer the sacraments and preach. **2.** a minister of any religion. **3.** an official who offers sacrifice on behalf of the people and performs other religious ceremonies. [Old English *prēost*, apparently from *presbyter*] —**'priestess** *fem. n.* —**'priest,hood** *n.* —**'priestly** *adj.*

prig (prɪg) *n.* a person who is smugly self-righteous and narrow-minded. [origin unknown] —**'priggish** *adj.* —**'priggishness** *n.*

prim (prɪm) *adj.* **primmer, primmest.** affectedly proper, precise, or formal. [origin unknown] —**'primly** *adv.*

prima ballerina ('priːmə) *n.* a leading female ballet dancer. [Italian: first ballerina]

primacy ('praɪməsɪ) *n., pl.* **-cies. 1.** the state of being first in rank, grade, or order. **2.** *Christianity.* the office, rank, or jurisdiction of a primate.

prima donna ('priːmə 'dɒnə) *n., pl.* **prima donnas. 1.** a leading female operatic star. **2.** *Informal.* a temperamental person. [Italian: first lady]

prima facie ('praɪmə 'feɪʃɪ) *adv.* at first sight; as it seems at first. [Latin]

primal ('praɪməl) *adj.* **1.** first or original. **2.** chief or most important. [Latin *primus* first]

primarily ('praɪmərəlɪ) *adv.* **1.** principally; chiefly; mainly. **2.** at first; originally.

primary ('praɪmərɪ) *adj.* **1.** first in importance. **2.** first in position or time, as in a series. **3.** fundamental; basic. **4.** being the first stage; elementary. **5.** of or relating to the education of children up to the age of 11. **6.** (of the flight feathers of a bird's wing) outer and longest. **7.** being the part of an electric circuit in which a changing current induces a current in a neighbouring circuit: *a primary coil.* ~*n., pl.* **-ries. 8.** a

person or thing that is first in rank, occurrence, or importance. **9.** (in the U.S.) a preliminary election in which the voters of a state nominate a candidate for office. Full name: **primary election. 10.** short for **primary colour** or **primary school. 11.** any of the outer and longest flight feathers of a bird's wing. **12.** a primary coil, winding, inductance, or current in an electric circuit. [Latin *primārius* principal]

primary accent or **stress** *n.* *Linguistics.* the strongest accent in a word.

primary colour *n.* **1.** any of three colours (usually red, green, and blue) that can be mixed to match any other colour, excluding black. **2.** any one of the colours red, yellow, green, or blue. All other colours look like a mixture of two or more of these colours.

primary school *n.* **1.** (in England and Wales) a school for children below the age of 11. **2.** (in Scotland) a school for children below the age of 12. **3.** (in the U.S. and Canad.) a school equivalent to the first three or four grades of elementary school.

primate ('praɪmeɪt) *n.* **1.** an archbishop. **2.** any of an order of mammals including lemurs, apes, and man. [Latin *primās* principal]

prime (praɪm) *adj.* **1.** first in quality: *prime beef.* **2.** fundamental; original. **3.** first in importance; chief: *of prime importance.* ~*n.* **4.** the time when a thing is at its best. **5.** a period of power, vigour, and activity: *a man in the prime of life.* **6.** *Maths.* short for **prime number.** ~*vb.* **7.** to prepare (something). **8.** to apply a primer, such as paint or size, to (a surface). **9.** to fill (a pump) with its working fluid, in order to expel air from it before starting. **10.** to insert a primer into (a gun or mine) before detonating or firing. **11.** to provide with facts beforehand; brief. [Latin *primus* first]

prime meridian *n.* the 0° meridian from which the other meridians are calculated, usually taken to pass through Greenwich.

prime minister *n.* the head of a parliamentary government.

prime number *n.* an integer that cannot be divided into other integers but is only divisible by itself or 1, such as 2, 3, 7, and 11.

primer[1] ('praɪmə) *n.* an introductory text, such as a school textbook. [Medieval Latin *primārius (liber)* a first (book)]

primer[2] ('praɪmə) *n.* **1.** a device, such as a tube containing explosive, for detonating the main charge in a gun or mine. **2.** a substance, such as paint, applied to a surface as a base or sealer.

primeval (praɪ'miːvəl) *adj.* of or belonging to the first ages of the world. [Latin *primus* first + *aevum* age]

primitive ('prɪmɪtɪv) *adj.* **1.** of or belonging to the beginning; original. **2.** characteristic of an early state, esp. in being crude or uncivilized: *a primitive dwelling.* **3.** *Biol.* of, relating to, or resembling an early stage in development: *primitive amphibians.* ~*n.* **4.** a primitive person or thing. **5.** a painter of any era whose work appears childlike or untrained. **6.** a work by such an artist. [Latin *primitivus* earliest of its kind]

primogeniture (ˌpraɪməʊˈdʒɛnɪtʃə) n. **1.** the state of being a first-born. **2.** *Law.* the right of an eldest son to succeed to the estate of his ancestor. [Medieval Latin *prīmōgenitūra* birth of a first child]

primordial (praɪˈmɔːdɪəl) adj. existing at or from the beginning; primeval. [Late Latin *prīmōrdiālis* original]

primp (prɪmp) vb. to dress (oneself) carefully in fine clothes. [prob. from *prim*]

primrose (ˈprɪmˌrəʊz) n. **1.** a wild plant which has pale yellow flowers in spring. **2.** Also called: **primrose yellow.** a light yellow colour. ~adj. **3.** of or abounding in primroses. **4.** of the colour primrose. [Medieval Latin *prīma rosa* first rose]

primrose path n. (often preceded by *the*) a pleasurable way of life.

primula (ˈprɪmjʊlə) n. any of a genus of plants with white, yellow, pink, or purple funnel-shaped flowers with five spreading petals. [Medieval Latin *prīmula* (*vēris*) little first one (of the spring)]

Primus (ˈpraɪməs) n. *Trademark.* a portable paraffin cooking stove, used esp. by campers.

prince (prɪns) n. **1.** (in Britain) a son of the sovereign. **2.** a nonreigning male member of a sovereign family. **3.** the monarch of a small territory. **4.** any monarch. **5.** a nobleman in various countries. **6.** an outstanding member of a specified group: *a merchant prince*. [Latin *princeps* first man, ruler]

prince consort n. the husband of a female sovereign, who is himself a prince.

princely (ˈprɪnslɪ) adj. **-lier, -liest. 1.** generous or lavish. **2.** of or characteristic of a prince.

Prince of Wales (weɪlz) n. the eldest son and heir apparent of the British sovereign.

princess (prɪnˈsɛs) n. **1.** (in Britain) a daughter of the sovereign. **2.** a nonreigning female member of a sovereign family. **3.** the wife and consort of a prince.

princess royal n. the eldest daughter of a British sovereign.

principal (ˈprɪnsɪpˀl) adj. **1.** first in importance, rank, or value. ~n. **2.** a person who is first in importance. **3.** the head of a school or other educational institution. **4.** *Law.* **a.** a person who engages another to act as his agent. **b.** an active participant in a crime. **c.** the person primarily liable to fulfil an obligation. **5.** the leading performer in a play. **6.** *Finance.* **a.** capital or property, as contrasted with income. **b.** the original amount of a debt on which interest is calculated. [Latin *principālis* chief] —ˈ**principally** adv.

principal boy n. the leading male role in a pantomime, played by a woman.

principality (ˌprɪnsɪˈpælɪtɪ) n., pl. **-ties.** a territory ruled by a prince or from which a prince draws his title.

principal parts pl. n. *Grammar.* the main inflected forms of a verb, from which all other inflections may be deduced.

principle (ˈprɪnsɪpˀl) n. **1.** a standard or rule of personal conduct: *he'd stoop to anything - he has no principles*. **2.** a set of such moral rules: *a man of principle*. **3.** a fundamental or general truth: *the principle of equality*. **4.** the essence of something: *the male principle*. **5.** a source; origin: *principle of life*. **6.** a law concerning a natural phenomenon or the behaviour of a system: *the principle of the conservation of mass*. **7.** *Chem.* a constituent of a substance that gives the substance its characteristics. **8. in principle.** in theory. **9. on principle.** because of a principle. [Latin *principium* beginning, basic tenet]

prink (prɪŋk) vb. **1.** to dress (oneself) finely. **2.** to preen oneself. [prob. changed from *prank* to adorn]

print (prɪnt) vb. **1.** to reproduce (text or pictures) by applying ink to paper. **2.** to produce or reproduce (a manuscript) in print, as for publication. **3.** to write (words or letters) in the style of printed matter. **4.** to mark (a surface) by pressing (something) onto it. **5.** to produce a photographic print from (a negative). **6.** to fix in the mind or memory. ~n. **7.** printed matter, such as newsprint. **8.** a printed publication, such as a book. **9. in print. a.** in printed or published form. **b.** (of a book) offered for sale by the publisher. **10. out of print.** no longer available from a publisher. **11.** a design or picture printed from an engraved plate or wood block. **12.** printed text, esp. with regard to the typeface: *small print*. **13.** a positive photographic image produced from a negative image on film. **14.** a fabric with a printed design. **15.** a mark made by pressing something onto a surface. **16.** See **fingerprint.** ~See also **print out.** [Old French *preindre* to make an impression]

printed circuit n. an electronic circuit in which certain components and the connections between them are formed by etching a metallic coating on a thin insulating board.

printer (ˈprɪntə) n. **1.** a person or business engaged in printing. **2.** a machine that prints. **3.** *Computers.* an output device for printing results on paper.

printing (ˈprɪntɪŋ) n. **1.** the business or art of producing printed matter. **2.** printed text. **3.** all the copies of a book printed at one time. **4.** a form of writing in which letters resemble printed letters.

printing press n. any of various machines used for printing.

print out vb. **1.** (of a computer output device) to produce (printed information). ~n. **print-out. 2.** such printed information.

prior[1] (ˈpraɪə) adj. **1.** previous. **2. prior to.** before; until. [Latin: previous]

prior[2] (ˈpraɪə) n. **1.** the superior of a community in certain religious orders. **2.** the deputy head of a monastery or abbey. [Late Latin: head] —ˈ**prioress** fem. n.

priority (praɪˈɒrɪtɪ) n., pl. **-ties. 1.** the condition of being prior; precedence. **2.** the right of precedence. **3.** something given specified attention: *my first priority*.

priory ('praɪərɪ) *n., pl.* **-ories.** a religious house governed by a prior.

prise *or* **prize** (praɪz) *vb.* to force open or out by levering. [Old French *prise* a taking]

prism ('prɪzəm) *n.* **1.** a transparent polygonal solid, often having triangular ends and rectangular sides, for dispersing light into a spectrum. **2.** *Maths.* a polyhedron having parallel bases and sides that are parallelograms. [Greek *prisma*, something shaped by sawing]

prismatic (prɪz'mætɪk) *adj.* **1.** of or produced by a prism. **2.** exhibiting bright spectral colours: *prismatic light.*

prison ('prɪz'n) *n.* **1.** a public building used to house convicted criminals and accused persons awaiting trial. **2.** any place of confinement. [Old French *prisun*, from Latin *prēnsiō* a capturing]

prisoner ('prɪzənə) *n.* **1.** a person kept in custody as a punishment for a crime, while awaiting trial, or for some other reason. **2.** a person confined by any of various restraints: *we are all prisoners of time.* **3.** **take (someone) prisoner.** to capture and hold (someone) as a prisoner.

prisoner of war *n.* a serviceman captured by an enemy in time of war.

prissy ('prɪsɪ) *adj.* **-sier, -siest.** prim and prudish. [prob. from *prim* + *sissy*] —**'prissily** *adv.*

pristine ('prɪstaɪn, -tiːn) *adj.* **1.** of or involving the earliest period or state; original. **2.** completely new, clean, and pure. [Latin *pristinus* primitive]

privacy ('praɪvəsɪ, 'prɪvəsɪ) *n.* **1.** the condition of being private. **2.** secrecy.

private ('praɪvɪt) *adj.* **1.** not widely or publicly known: *they had private reasons for the decision.* **2.** confidential; secret: *a private conversation.* **3.** not for general or public use: *a private bathroom.* **4.** of or provided by a private individual or organization rather than by the state: *private medicine.* **5.** having no public office, rank, or position: *a private man.* **6.** (of a place) quiet and secluded: *the garden is completely private.* ~*n.* **7.** a soldier of the lowest rank in many armies and marine corps. **8.** **in private.** in secret. [Latin *prīvātus* belonging to one individual, withdrawn from public life] —**'privately** *adv.*

private bill *n.* a bill presented to Parliament on behalf of a private individual or corporation.

private company *n.* a limited company that does not issue shares for public subscription.

private detective *n.* an individual hired to do detective work on behalf of a client.

privateer (ˌpraɪvə'tɪə) *n.* **1.** an armed privately owned vessel commissioned for war service. **2.** a Commander of a privateer.

private eye *n. Informal.* a private detective.

private income *n.* income from sources other than employment, such as investment.

private member *n.* a member of a legislative assembly not having an appointment in the government.

private member's bill *n.* a parliamentary bill sponsored by a Member of Parliament who is not a government minister.

private parts *or* **privates** *pl. n. Euphemistic.* the genitals.

private school *n.* a school controlled by a private body, accepting mostly fee-paying pupils.

private sector *n.* the part of a country's economy that consists of privately owned enterprises.

privation (praɪ'veɪʃən) *n.* loss or lack of the necessities of life. [Latin *prīvātiō* deprivation]

privative ('prɪvətɪv) *adj.* **1.** causing privation. **2.** *Grammar.* expressing lack or absence, as for example *-less* and *un-.*

privatize *or* **-ise** ('praɪvɪˌtaɪz) *vb.* to take into, or return to, private ownership, a company or concern that has previously been owned by the state. —**privati-ˌzation** *or* **-iˌsation** *n.*

privet ('prɪvɪt) *n.* a bushy shrub with oval dark green leaves, used for hedges. [origin unknown]

privilege ('prɪvɪlɪdʒ) *n.* **1.** a benefit, immunity, or advantage granted under certain conditions to a person, group, or class. ~*vb.* **2.** to bestow a privilege upon. [Latin *prīvilēgium* law relevant to rights of an individual]

privileged ('prɪvɪlɪdʒd) *adj.* enjoying or granted as a privilege or privileges.

privy ('prɪvɪ) *adj.* **privier, priviest. 1. privy to.** participating in the knowledge of something secret. **2.** *Archaic.* secret; hidden. ~*n., pl.* **privies. 3.** a toilet, esp. an outside one. [Old French *privé* something private]

Privy Council *n.* **1.** the private council of the British sovereign. **2.** (in Canada) a ceremonial body of advisers of the governor general. —**Privy Councillor** *n.*

privy purse *n.* (*often cap.*) an allowance voted by Parliament for the private expenses of the monarch.

privy seal *n.* (*often cap.*) (in Britain) a seal affixed to certain documents issued by royal authority.

prize¹ (praɪz) *n.* **1.** something, such as a trophy, given to the winner of a contest or competition. **2.** something given to the winner of any game of chance, lottery, etc. **3.** something striven for. [Old French *prise* a capture]

prize² (praɪz) *vb.* to value highly. [Old French *preisier* to praise]

prizefight ('praɪzˌfaɪt) *n.* a boxing match for a prize or purse. —**'prizeˌfighter** *n.*

pro¹ (prəʊ) *adv.* **1.** in favour of a motion, issue, or course of action. ~*prep.* **2.** in favour of. ~*n., pl.* **pros. 3.** (*usually pl.*) an argument or vote in favour of a proposal or motion. See also **pros and cons.** [Latin *prō* in favour of]

pro² (prəʊ) *n., pl.* **pros.** *Informal.* **1.** short for **professional. 2.** a prostitute.

PRO public relations officer.

pro-[1] *prefix.* **1.** in favour of; supporting: *pro-Chinese.* **2.** acting as a substitute for: *proconsul; pronoun.* [Latin]

pro-[2] *prefix.* before in time or position; anterior; forward: *proboscis.* [Greek]

probability (ˌprɒbəˈbɪlɪtɪ) *n., pl.* **-ties. 1.** the condition of being probable. **2.** an event or other thing that is probable. **3.** *Statistics.* a measure of the degree of confidence one may have in the occurrence of an event.

probable (ˈprɒbəbʰl) *adj.* **1.** likely to be or to happen but not necessarily so. **2.** most likely: *the probable cause of the accident.* ~*n.* **3.** a person who is likely to be chosen for a team, event, etc. [Latin *probābilis* that may be proved]

probably (ˈprɒbəblɪ) *adv.* in all likelihood or probability: *I'll probably see you tomorrow.*

probate (ˈprəʊbɪt, -beɪt) *n.* **1.** the process of officially proving the validity of a will. **2.** the official certificate stating a will to be genuine. [Latin *probāre* to inspect]

probation (prəˈbeɪʃən) *n.* **1.** a system of dealing with offenders by placing them under the supervision of a probation officer. **2. on probation. a.** under the supervision of a probation officer. **b.** undergoing a test or trial period, as of a person's character or abilities. [Latin *probāre* to test] —**proˈbationary** *adj.*

probationer (prəˈbeɪʃənə) *n.* a person on probation.

probation officer *n.* an officer of a court who supervises offenders placed on probation.

probe (prəʊb) *vb.* **1.** to search into closely. **2.** to examine (something) with or as if with a probe. ~*n.* **3.** *Surgery.* a slender instrument for exploring a wound, etc. **4.** a thorough inquiry, such as one into corrupt practices. **5.** See **space probe.** [Latin *probāre* to test]

probity (ˈprəʊbɪtɪ) *n.* honesty; uprightness; integrity. [Latin *probitās* honesty]

problem (ˈprɒbləm) *n.* **1.** any thing, matter, or person that is difficult to deal with. **2.** a puzzle or question set for solution. **3.** *Maths.* a statement requiring a solution usually by means of several operations. **4.** (*modifier*) designating a literary work that deals with difficult moral questions: *a problem play.* [Greek *problēma* something put forward]

problematic (ˌprɒbləˈmætɪk) *or* **problematical** *adj.* difficult to solve or deal with; uncertain.

proboscis (prəʊˈbɒsɪs) *n.* **1.** a long flexible trunk or snout, as of an elephant. **2.** the elongated mouthpart of certain insects. [Greek *proboskis* trunk of an elephant]

procedure (prəˈsiːdʒə) *n.* **1.** a way of acting or progressing, esp. an established method. **2.** the established form of conducting the business of a legislature. —**proˈcedural** *adj.*

proceed (prəˈsiːd) *vb.* **1.** to advance or carry on, esp. after stopping. **2.** (often foll. by *with*) to continue: *he proceeded with his reading.* **3.** (often foll. by *against*) to institute or carry on a legal action. **4.** to originate; arise: *evil proceeds from the heart.* [Latin *prōcēdere* to advance]

proceeding (prəˈsiːdɪŋ) *n.* **1.** an act or course of action. **2.** (*pl.*) the events of an occasion: *millions watched the proceedings on television.* **3.** (*pl.*) the minutes of the meetings of a society. **4.** (*pl.*) legal action; litigation.

proceeds (ˈprəʊsiːdz) *pl. n.* the amount of money obtained from an event or activity.

process[1] (ˈprəʊsɛs) *n.* **1.** a series of actions which produce a change or development: *the process of digestion.* **2.** a method of doing or producing something. **3.** progress or course of time. **4. in the process of.** during or in the course of. **5. a.** a summons to appear in court. **b.** an action at law. **6.** a natural outgrowth or projection of a part or organism. ~*vb.* **7.** to subject to a routine procedure; handle. **8.** to treat or prepare by a special method, esp. to treat (food) in order to preserve it: *to process cheese.* **9.** *Computers.* to perform operations on (data) in order to obtain the required information. [Latin *prōcessus* an advancing]

process[2] (prəˈsɛs) *vb.* to proceed in a procession.

procession (prəˈsɛʃən) *n.* **1.** the act of proceeding in a regular formation. **2.** a group of people or vehicles moving forwards in an orderly, regular, or ceremonial manner. [Latin *prōcessiō* a marching forwards]

processional (prəˈsɛʃənəl) *adj.* **1.** of or suitable for a procession. ~*n.* **2.** *Christianity.* a hymn sung as the clergy enter church.

processor (ˈprəʊsɛsə) *n.* **1.** *Computers.* same as **central processing unit. 2.** a person or thing that carries out a process.

proclaim (prəˈkleɪm) *vb.* **1.** to announce publicly: *the Government proclaimed a state of emergency.* **2.** to indicate plainly: *the display proclaimed the designer's art.* [Latin *prōclāmāre* to shout aloud] —**proclamation** (ˌprɒkləˈmeɪʃən) *n.*

proclivity (prəˈklɪvɪtɪ) *n., pl.* **-ties.** a tendency or inclination. [Latin *prōclīvitās*]

procrastinate (prəʊˈkræstɪˌneɪt) *vb.* to put off (an action) until later; delay. [Latin *prōcrāstināre* to postpone until tomorrow] —**proˌcrastiˈnation** *n.* —**proˈcrastiˌnator** *n.*

procreate (ˈprəʊkrɪˌeɪt) *vb.* (of people or animals) to produce (offspring). [Latin *prōcreāre*] —**ˈprocreˌative** *adj.* —**ˌproˈcreˈation** *n.*

Procrustean (prəʊˈkrʌstɪən) *adj.* designed to produce conformity by ruthless methods. [after *Procrustes*, Greek robber who fitted travellers into his bed by stretching or lopping off their limbs]

proctor (ˈprɒktə) *n.* a member of the staff of certain universities having duties including the enforcement of discipline. [syncopated var. of *procurator*] —**proctorial** (prɒkˈtɔːrɪəl) *adj.*

procurator fiscal (ˈprɒkjʊˌreɪtə) *n.* (in

Scotland) a legal officer who performs the functions of public prosecutor and coroner.

procure (prəˈkjuə) vb. **1.** to obtain or acquire; secure. **2.** to obtain (women or girls) to act as prostitutes. [Latin *prōcūrāre* to look after] —pro'cure·ment n.

procurer (prəˈkjuərə) n. a person who procures, esp. one who procures women as prostitutes.

prod (prɒd) vb. **prodding, prodded. 1.** to poke with or as if with a pointed object. **2.** to rouse (someone) to action. ~n. **3.** the act or an instance of prodding. **4.** a reminder. [origin unknown]

prodigal (ˈprɒdɪgˀl) adj. **1.** recklessly wasteful or extravagant. **2.** lavish: *prodigal of compliments.* ~n. **3.** a person who spends lavishly or squanders money. [Latin *prōdigere* to squander] —,prodi'gality n.

prodigious (prəˈdɪdʒəs) adj. **1.** vast in size, extent, or power. **2.** wonderful or amazing. [Latin *prōdigiōsus* marvellous]

prodigy (ˈprɒdɪdʒɪ) n., pl. -gies. **1.** a person, esp. a child, of unusual or marvellous talents. **2.** anything that is a cause of wonder. [Latin *prōdigium* an unnatural happening]

produce vb. (prəˈdjuːs). **1.** to bring (something) into existence; yield. **2.** to make: *she produced a delicious dinner.* **3.** to give birth to. **4.** to present to view: *to produce evidence.* **5.** to bring before the public: *he produced a film last year.* **6.** to act as producer of. ~n. (ˈprɒdjuːs). **7.** anything produced; a product. **8.** agricultural products collectively: *farm produce.* [Latin *prōdūcere* to bring forward] —pro'ducible adj.

producer (prəˈdjuːsə) n. **1.** a person or thing that produces. **2.** *Brit.* a person responsible for the artistic direction of a play. **3.** *U.S. & Canad.* a person who organizes the stage production of a play, including the finance and management. **4.** the person who takes overall administrative responsibility for a film or television programme.

product (ˈprɒdʌkt) n. **1.** something produced by a natural, mechanical, or industrial process. **2.** a result or consequence: *their skill was the product of hours of training.* **3.** *Maths.* the result of the multiplication of two or more numbers or quantities.

production (prəˈdʌkʃən) n. **1.** the act of producing. **2.** anything that is produced; a product. **3.** the amount produced or the rate at which it is produced. **4.** *Econ.* the creation or manufacture of goods and services. **5.** any work created as a result of literary or artistic effort. **6.** the presentation of a play, opera, etc. **7.** *Brit.* the artistic direction of a play.

productive (prəˈdʌktɪv) adj. **1.** producing or having the power to produce; fertile. **2.** yielding favourable results. **3.** *Econ.* producing goods and services that have exchange value: *productive assets.* **4.** (foll. by *of*) resulting in: *productive of good results.* —productivity (,prɒdʌkˈtɪvɪtɪ) n.

proem (ˈprəuɛm) n. an introduction or preface. [Greek *pro-* before + *hoimē* song]

Prof. Professor.

profane (prəˈfeɪn) adj. **1.** having or indicating irreverence or disrespect for a divinity or something sacred. **2.** not designed for religious purposes; secular. **3.** coarse or blasphemous: *profane language.* ~vb. **4.** to treat (something sacred) with irreverence. **5.** to put to an unworthy use. [Latin *profānus* outside the temple] —profanation (,prɒfəˈneɪʃən) n.

profanity (prəˈfænɪtɪ) n., pl. -ties. **1.** the state or quality of being profane. **2.** vulgar or irreverent action or speech.

profess (prəˈfɛs) vb. **1.** to affirm or acknowledge: *to profess ignorance; to profess a belief in God.* **2.** to claim (something), often insincerely or falsely: *to profess to be a skilled driver.* **3.** to receive or be received into a religious order, as by taking vows. [Latin *profitērī* to confess openly] —pro'fessed adj.

profession (prəˈfɛʃən) n. **1.** an occupation that requires special training, such as law or medicine. **2.** the body of people in such an occupation. **3.** an avowal; declaration: *professions of concern.* **4.** a declaration of faith, esp. as made on entering a religious order. [Latin *professiō* public acknowledgment]

professional (prəˈfɛʃənˀl) adj. **1.** of, suitable for, or engaged in as a profession. **2.** engaging in an activity as a means of livelihood. **3.** extremely competent in a job. **4.** undertaken or performed by people who are paid. ~n. **5.** a professional person. —pro'fessiona,lism n. —pro'fessionally adv.

professor (prəˈfɛsə) n. **1.** the principal teacher holding a university chair. **2.** *Chiefly U.S. & Canad.* any teacher in a university or college. **3.** a person who professes his opinions or beliefs. [Latin: a public teacher] —professorial (,prɒfɪˈsɔːrɪəl) adj. —pro'fessorship n.

proffer (ˈprɒfə) vb. to offer for acceptance. [Old French *proffrir*]

proficient (prəˈfɪʃənt) adj. skilled; expert. [Latin *prōficere* to make progress] —pro'ficiency n.

profile (ˈprəufaɪl) n. **1.** a side view or outline, esp. of a human head. **2.** a short biographical sketch. [Italian *profilo*]

profit (ˈprɒfɪt) n. **1.** (*often pl.*) excess of revenues over outlays and expenses in a business enterprise. **2.** the monetary gain derived from a transaction. **3.** a gain, benefit, or advantage. ~vb. **4.** to gain profit. [Latin *prōficere* to make progress]

profitable (ˈprɒfɪtəbˀl) adj. making profit. —,profita'bility n.

profit and loss n. *Book-keeping.* an account showing the year's revenue and expense items and indicating gross and net profit or loss.

profiteer (,prɒfɪˈtɪə) n. **1.** a person who makes excessive profits by charging exorbitant prices for goods in short supply. ~vb. **2.** to make excessive profits.

profit-sharing n. a system in which a

portion of the net profit of a business is distributed to its employees.

profligate ('prɒflɪgɪt) adj. **1.** shamelessly immoral. **2.** wildly extravagant or wasteful. ~n. **3.** a profligate person. [Latin *prōflīgātus* corrupt] —**profligacy** ('prɒflɪgəsɪ) n.

pro forma ('prəʊ 'fɔːmə) adj. **1.** prescribing a set form or procedure. ~adv. **2.** performed in a set manner. [Latin: for form's sake]

profound (prə'faʊnd) adj. **1.** having, showing, or requiring great knowledge or understanding: *a profound treatise*. **2.** situated at or extending to a great depth. **3.** strongly felt; intense: *profound silence*. **4.** thoroughgoing; extensive: *profound changes*. [Latin *profundus* deep] —**pro-'foundly** adv. —**profundity** (prə'fʌndɪtɪ) n.

profuse (prə'fjuːs) adj. **1.** plentiful or abundant: *profuse compliments*. **2.** (often foll. by *in*) free or generous in the giving (of): *profuse in thanks*. [Latin *profundere* to pour lavishly] —**pro'fusely** adv. —**pro'fusion** n.

progenitor (prəʊ'dʒenɪtə) n. **1.** a direct ancestor. **2.** an originator or founder. [Latin: ancestor]

progeny ('prɒdʒɪnɪ) n., pl. **-nies.** **1.** offspring; descendants. **2.** a result or outcome. [Latin *prōgeniēs* lineage]

progesterone (prəʊ'dʒestəˌrəʊn) n. a steroid hormone, secreted in the ovary, that prepares and maintains the uterus for pregnancy. [PRO-¹ + *ge(station)* + *ster(ol)* + *-one*]

prognosis (prɒg'nəʊsɪs) n., pl. **-noses** (-'nəʊsiːz). **1.** *Med.* a prediction of the course or outcome of a disease. **2.** any prediction. [Greek: knowledge beforehand]

prognosticate (prɒg'nɒstɪˌkeɪt) vb. **1.** to foretell (future events). **2.** to indicate or suggest beforehand. [Medieval Latin *prognōsticāre* to predict] —**prog,nosti'cation** n. —**prog'nosti,cator** n.

program ('prəʊgræm) n. **1.** a sequence of coded instructions enabling a computer to perform specified logical and arithmetical operations on data. ~vb. **-gramming, -grammed. 2.** to arrange (data) so that it can be processed by a computer. **3.** to write a program. —**'programmer** n.

programmable or **programable** (prəʊ-'græməbəl) adj. capable of being programmed for computer processing.

programme or U.S. **program** ('prəʊgræm) n. **1.** a written or printed list of the events and performers in a public performance. **2.** a performance presented at a scheduled time on radio or television. **3.** a specially arranged selection of things to be done: *what's the programme for this afternoon?* **4.** a plan, schedule, or procedure: *the development of a nuclear power programme.* ~vb. **-gramming, -grammed** or U.S. **-graming, -gramed. 5.** to design or schedule (something) as a programme. [Greek *programma* written public notice] —**program'matic** adj.

programming language n. a language system by which instructions to a computer are coded, that is mutually comprehensible to user and computer.

progress n. ('prəʊgres). **1.** movement forwards, esp. towards a place or objective. **2.** satisfactory development or advance. **3.** advance towards completion or perfection. **4. in progress.** taking place. ~vb. (prə'gres). **5.** to move forwards or onwards. **6.** to move towards completion or perfection. [Latin *prōgressus*]

progression (prə'greʃən) n. **1.** the act of progressing; advancement. **2.** the act or an instance of moving from one thing in a sequence to the next. **3.** *Maths.* a sequence of numbers in which each term differs from the succeeding term by a constant relation.

progressive (prə'gresɪv) adj. **1.** of or relating to progress. **2.** progressing by steps or degrees. **3.** favouring or promoting political or social reform: *a progressive policy.* **4.** (esp. of a disease) advancing in severity, complexity, or extent. **5.** (of a dance, card game, etc.) involving a regular change of partners. ~n. **6.** a person who advocates political progress or reform. —**pro'gressively** adv.

prohibit (prə'hɪbɪt) vb. **1.** to forbid by law or other authority. **2.** to hinder or prevent. [Latin *prohibēre* to prevent] —**pro-'hibitor** n.

prohibition (ˌprəʊɪ'bɪʃən) n. **1.** the act of prohibiting or state of being prohibited. **2.** an order or decree that prohibits. **3.** a policy of legally forbidding the manufacture, sale, or consumption of alcoholic beverages. —**ˌprohi'bitionist** n.

Prohibition (ˌprəʊɪ'bɪʃən) n. the period (1920–33) when the manufacture, sale, and transportation of intoxicating liquors was banned in the U.S. —**ˌProhi'bitionist** n.

prohibitive (prə'hɪbɪtɪv) adj. **1.** prohibiting or tending to prohibit. **2.** (esp. of prices) tending or designed to discourage sale or purchase.

project n. ('prɒdʒekt). **1.** a proposal, scheme, or design. **2.** a detailed study of a particular subject. ~vb. (prə'dʒekt). **3.** to propose or plan. **4.** to throw forwards. **5.** to jut out. **6.** to make a prediction based on known data and observations. **7.** to transport in the imagination: *to project oneself into the future.* **8.** to cause (an image) to appear on a surface. **9.** to cause (one's voice) to be heard clearly at a distance. [Latin *prōicere* to throw down]

projectile (prə'dʒektaɪl) n. **1.** an object designed to be shot forward, such as a shell, rocket, or bullet. ~adj. **2.** designed to be hurled forwards. **3.** projecting forwards. [New Latin *prōjectilis* jutting forwards]

projection (prə'dʒekʃən) n. **1.** the act of projecting or the state of being projected. **2.** a part that juts out. **3.** the representation of a line, figure, or solid on a given plane as it would be seen from a particular direction or in accordance with an accepted set of rules. **4.** a prediction based on known evidence and observations. **5.** the process of showing film on a screen.

projectionist (prə'dʒɛkʃənɪst) *n.* a person responsible for the operation of film projection machines.

projector (prə'dʒɛktə) *n.* an apparatus for projecting photographic images, film, or slides onto a screen.

prolapse ('prəʊlæps, prəʊ'læps) *Pathol.* ~*n.* **1.** Also: **prolapsus** (prəʊ'læpsəs). the sinking or falling down of an organ or part. ~*vb.* **2.** (of an organ or part) to sink from its normal position. [Latin *prōlābi* to slide along]

prolate ('prəʊleɪt) *adj.* having a polar diameter of greater length than the equatorial diameter. [Latin *prōlātus* enlarged]

prole (prəʊl) *n., adj. Disparaging, slang, chiefly Brit.* short for **proletarian.**

proletariat (,prəʊlɪ'tɛərɪət) *n.* the lower or working class. [Latin *prōlētārius* one whose only contribution to the state was his offspring] —**prole'tarian** *adj., n.*

proliferate (prə'lɪfə,reɪt) *vb.* **1.** to grow or reproduce (new parts, such as cells) rapidly. **2.** to increase rapidly in numbers. [Latin *prōlēs* offspring + *ferre* to bear] —**pro,lifer'ation** *n.*

prolific (prə'lɪfɪk) *adj.* **1.** producing fruit or offspring in abundance. **2.** producing a constant creative output: *a prolific novelist.* **3.** (often foll. by *in* or *of*) rich or fruitful. [Latin *prōlēs* offspring] —**pro'lifically** *adv.*

prolix ('prəʊlɪks, prəʊ'lɪks) *adj.* (of a speech or book) so long as to be boring. [Latin *prōlixus* stretched out widely] —**pro'lixity** *n.*

prologue or *U.S.* (often) **prolog** ('prəʊlɒg) *n.* **1.** an introduction to a play or speech. **2.** a preliminary act or event. [Greek *pro-* before + *logos* discourse]

prolong (prə'lɒŋ) *vb.* to lengthen; extend. [Late Latin *prōlongāre*] —**prolongation** (,prəʊlɒŋ'geɪʃən) *n.*

prom (prɒm) *n.* **1.** *Brit.* short for **promenade** (sense 1) or **promenade concert.** **2.** *U.S. & Canad. informal.* a formal dance held at a high school or college.

PROM (prɒm) *Computers.* Programmable Read Only Memory.

promenade (,prɒmə'nɑːd) *n.* **1.** *Chiefly Brit.* a public walk, esp. at a seaside resort. **2.** a leisurely walk for pleasure or display. ~*vb.* **3.** to take a promenade in or through (a place). **4.** to display or exhibit (someone or oneself) on or as if on a promenade. [French]

promenade concert *n.* a concert at which some of the audience stand rather than sit.

promethium (prə'miːθɪəm) *n.* an artificial radioactive element of the lanthanide series. Symbol: Pm [from *Prometheus*, in Greek myth., the Titan who gave fire to mankind]

prominent ('prɒmɪnənt) *adj.* **1.** jutting or projecting outwards. **2.** standing out from its surroundings; noticeable. **3.** widely known; eminent. [Latin *prōminēre* to jut out] —**'prominence** *n.*

promiscuous (prə'mɪskjʊəs) *adj.* **1.** indulging in casual sexual relationships. **2.** consisting of different elements mingled indiscriminately. [Latin *prōmiscuus* indiscriminate] —**promiscuity** (,prɒmɪ'skjuːɪtɪ) *n.*

promise ('prɒmɪs) *vb.* **1.** to give an assurance of (something to someone): *I promise that I will come.* **2.** to undertake to give (something to someone): *he promised me a car for my birthday.* **3.** to cause people to expect that one is likely (to be or do something): *she promises to be a fine soprano.* **4.** to assure (someone) of the inevitability of something: *there'll be trouble, I promise you.* ~*n.* **5.** an assurance given by one person to another guaranteeing to do or not to do something. **6.** indication of forthcoming excellence: *a writer showing considerable promise.* [Latin *prōmissum* a promise]

Promised Land *n.* **1.** *Bible.* the land of Canaan. **2.** any longed-for place where one expects to find greater happiness.

promising ('prɒmɪsɪŋ) *adj.* showing promise of future success.

promissory note *n. Commerce.* a document containing a signed promise to pay a stated sum of money to a specified person.

promo ('prəʊməʊ) *n., pl.* **-mos.** *Informal.* something used to promote a product, such as a videotape film used to promote a pop record.

promontory ('prɒməntrɪ) *n., pl.* **-ries.** a high point of land that juts out into the sea. [Latin *prōmunturium* headland]

promote (prə'məʊt) *vb.* **1.** to encourage the progress of. **2.** to raise to a higher rank, status, or office. **3.** to work for: *to promote reform.* **4.** to encourage the sale of (a product) by advertising. [Latin *prōmovēre* to push onwards] —**pro'motion** *n.* —**pro'motional** *adj.*

promoter (prə'məʊtə) *n.* **1.** a person who helps to organize, develop, or finance an undertaking. **2.** a person who organizes and finances a sporting event, esp. a boxing match.

prompt (prɒmpt) *adj.* **1.** performed without delay. **2.** quick or ready to act or respond. ~*adv.* **3.** *Informal.* punctually: *at 9 o'clock prompt.* ~*vb.* **4.** to urge (someone to do something). **5.** to remind (an actor) of lines forgotten during a performance. **6.** to refresh the memory of. **7.** to give rise to by suggestion: *his affairs will prompt discussion.* ~*n.* **8.** anything that serves to remind. [Latin *promptus* evident] —**'promptly** *adv.* —**'promptness** *n.*

prompter ('prɒmptə) *n.* a person offstage who reminds the actors of forgotten lines.

promulgate ('prɒməl,geɪt) *vb.* **1.** to put into effect (a law or decree) by announcing it officially. **2.** to make widespread. [Latin *prōmulgāre*] —**,promul'gation** *n.* —**'promul,gator** *n.*

pron. 1. pronoun. **2.** pronunciation.

prone (prəʊn) *adj.* **1.** having a tendency to be affected by or do something: *prone to hay fever.* **2.** lying flat or face downwards; prostrate. [Latin *prōnus* bent forward]

prong (proŋ) n. a sharply pointed end of an instrument, such as on a fork. [origin unknown]

pronominal (prəʊ'nɒmɪn°l) adj. relating to or playing the part of a pronoun.

pronoun ('prəʊ,naʊn) n. one of a class of words that serves to replace a noun or noun phrase that has already been or is about to be mentioned. [Latin *prōnōmen*]

pronounce (prə'naʊns) vb. 1. to utter or speak (a sound or sounds). 2. to utter (words) in the correct way. 3. to proclaim officially: *I now pronounce you man and wife*. 4. to declare as one's judgment: *to pronounce the death sentence upon someone*. [Latin *prōnuntiāre* to announce] —**pro'nounceable** adj.

pronounced (prə'naʊnst) adj. strongly marked or indicated: *a pronounced change*.

pronouncement (prə'naʊnsmənt) n. a public or official announcement.

pronto ('prɒntəʊ) adv. *Informal*. at once. [Spanish: quick]

pronunciation (prə,nʌnsɪ'eɪʃən) n. 1. the act, instance, or manner of pronouncing sounds. 2. the supposedly correct manner of pronouncing sounds in a given language.

proof (pruːf) n. 1. any evidence that establishes or helps to establish the truth, validity, or quality of something. 2. *Law*. the whole body of evidence upon which the verdict of a court is based. 3. *Maths., logic*. a sequence of steps or statements that establishes the truth of a proposition. 4. the act of testing the truth of something. 5. a trial impression of printed matter for the correction of errors. 6. *Photog*. a trial print from a negative. 7. the alcoholic strength of proof spirit. ~adj. 8. (foll. by *against*) able to withstand; resistant (to): *the roof is proof against rain*. 9. having the alcoholic strength of proof spirit. ~vb. 10. to take a proof from (type matter). 11. to render (something) proof, esp. to waterproof. [Old French *preuve* a test]

proofread ('pruːf,riːd) vb. -reading, -read (-,red). to read (printer's proofs) and mark errors to be corrected. —**'proof-,reader** n.

proof spirit n. (in Britain) an alcoholic beverage that contains a standard percentage of alcohol.

prop[1] (prop) vb. **propping, propped.** (often foll. by *up*) 1. to support with a rigid object, such as a stick. 2. (often foll. by *against*) to place or lean. 3. to sustain or support. ~n. 4. something that gives rigid support, such as a stick. 5. a person or thing giving support, as of a moral nature. [perhaps from Middle Dutch *proppe*]

prop[2] (prop) n. short for **property** (sense 6).

prop[3] (prop) n. *Informal*. a propeller.

prop. 1. proper(ly). 2. property. 3. proposition. 4. proprietor.

propaganda (,prɒpə'gændə) n. 1. the organized promotion of certain information

or allegations, to assist or damage the cause of a government or movement. 2. such information or allegations. [Italian] —,**propa'gandist** n., adj.

propagate ('prɒpə,geɪt) vb. 1. *Biol*. to reproduce; breed. 2. *Horticulture*. to produce (plants) by layering, grafting, or cuttings. 3. to spread (information or ideas). 4. *Physics*. to transmit, esp. in the form of a wave: *to propagate sound*. [Latin *propāgāre* to increase (plants) by cuttings] —,**propa'gation** n. —'**propa,gator** n.

propane ('prəʊpeɪn) n. a flammable gaseous alkane found in petroleum and used as a fuel. [from *propionic* (*acid*)]

propel (prə'pel) vb. **-pelling, -pelled**. to impel, drive, or cause to move forwards. [Latin *prōpellere*] —**pro'pellant** n., adj.

propeller (prə'pelə) n. a device having blades radiating from a central hub that is rotated to produce thrust to propel a ship or aircraft.

propensity (prə'pensɪtɪ) n., pl. **-ties**. a natural tendency: *we recognize our own propensity to evil*. [Latin *prōpensus* inclined to]

proper ('prɒpə) adj. 1. appropriate or usual: *in its proper place*. 2. suited to a particular purpose: *use the proper knife to cut the bread*. 3. correct in behaviour: *proper young ladies*. 4. excessively moral: *a self-righteous sense of what is proper*. 5. real or genuine: *a proper job*. 6. *Brit. informal*. complete; utter: *I felt a proper fool*. [Latin *prōprius* special] —'**properly** adv.

proper fraction n. a fraction in which the numerator has a lower absolute value than the denominator, as ½.

proper noun or **name** n. the name of a person, place, or object, as for example *Iceland, Patrick,* or *Uranus*.

property ('prɒpətɪ) n., pl. **-ties**. 1. something owned, such as land. 2. *Law*. the right to possess, use, and dispose of anything. 3. possessions collectively. 4. land or real estate. 5. a quality or attribute, such as the density of a material. 6. any movable object used on the set of a stage play or film. [Latin *proprius* one's own]

prophecy ('prɒfɪsɪ) n., pl. **-cies**. 1. **a.** a message of divine truth revealing God's will. **b.** the act of uttering such a message. 2. a prediction or guess. 3. the function or activity of a prophet.

prophesy ('prɒfɪ,saɪ) vb. **-sying, -sied**. to foretell (something) by or as if by divine inspiration.

prophet ('prɒfɪt) n. 1. a person who supposedly speaks by divine inspiration. 2. a person who predicts the future: *a prophet of doom*. 3. a spokesman for some cause: *a prophet of socialism*. [Greek *prophētēs* one who declares the divine will] —'**prophetess** fem. n.

Prophet ('prɒfɪt) n. **the**. the principal designation of Mohammed as the founder of Islam.

prophetic (prə'fetɪk) adj. 1. of or relating to a prophet or prophecy. 2. of the nature of a prophecy. —**pro'phetically** adv.

prophylactic (ˌprɒfɪˈlæktɪk) *adj.* **1.** protecting from or preventing disease. ~*n.* **2.** a prophylactic drug or device. [Greek *prophulassein* to guard by taking advance measures]

propinquity (prəˈpɪŋkwɪtɪ) *n.* nearness in time, place, or relationship. [Latin *propinquus* near]

propitiate (prəˈpɪʃɪˌeɪt) *vb.* to appease (a god or person); make well disposed. [Latin *propitiāre*] —**pro'pitiable** *adj.* —**pro,pi-ti'ation** *n.* —**pro'piti,ator** *n.* —**pro'pitiatory** *adj.*

propitious (prəˈpɪʃəs) *adj.* **1.** favourable or auspicious: *a propitious time.* **2.** favourably inclined: *conditions are propitious for development.* [Latin *propitius* well disposed]

proponent (prəˈpəʊnənt) *n.* a person who argues in favour of something or puts forward a proposal. [Latin *prōpōnere* to propose]

proportion (prəˈpɔːʃən) *n.* **1.** relative magnitude or extent; ratio: *a large proportion of our revenue comes from advertisements.* **2.** correct relationship between parts; symmetry. **3.** a part considered with respect to the whole: *the proportion of women in the total workforce.* **4.** (*pl.*) dimensions or size: *a building of vast proportions.* **5.** *Maths.* a relationship between four numbers in which the ratio of the first pair equals the ratio of the second pair. ~*vb.* **6.** to adjust in relative amount or size. **7.** to cause to be harmonious in relationship of parts. [Latin *prō portiōne*, lit.: for (its, one's) portion]

proportional (prəˈpɔːʃən'l) *adj.* **1.** of, involving, or being in proportion. ~*n.* **2.** *Maths.* an unknown term in a proportion: in $a/b = c/x$, x is the fourth proportional. —**pro'portionally** *adv.*

proportional representation *n.* representation of parties in an elective body in proportion to the votes they win.

proportionate (prəˈpɔːʃənɪt) *adj.* being in proper proportion. —**pro'portionately** *adv.*

proposal (prəˈpəʊz'l) *n.* **1.** the act of proposing. **2.** something proposed, as a plan. **3.** an offer of marriage.

propose (prəˈpəʊz) *vb.* **1.** to put forward (a plan) for consideration. **2.** to nominate (someone), as for a position. **3.** to intend (to do something): *I propose to leave town now.* **4.** to announce the drinking of (a toast). **5.** (often foll. by *to*) to make an offer of marriage. [Old French *proposer*, from Latin *prōpōnere* to display]

proposition (ˌprɒpəˈzɪʃən) *n.* **1.** a proposal for consideration. **2.** *Logic.* a statement that affirms or denies something and is capable of being true or false. **3.** *Maths.* a statement or theorem, usually containing its proof. **4.** *Informal.* a person or matter to be dealt with: *he's a difficult proposition.* **5.** *Informal.* an invitation to engage in sexual intercourse. ~*vb.* **6.** to propose a plan to (someone), esp. to engage in sexual intercourse. [Latin *prōpositiō* a setting forth]

propound (prəˈpaʊnd) *vb.* to put forward for consideration. [Latin *prōpōnere* to set forth]

proprietary (prəˈpraɪətrɪ) *adj.* **1.** of or belonging to property or proprietors. **2.** privately owned and controlled. **3.** *Med.* denoting a drug manufactured and distributed under a trade name. [Late Latin *proprietārius* an owner]

proprietor (prəˈpraɪətə) *n.* an owner of a business establishment. —**proprietorial** (prəˌpraɪəˈtɔːrɪəl) *adj.* —**pro'prietress** *fem. n.*

propriety (prəˈpraɪətɪ) *n., pl.* **-ties. 1.** the quality or state of being appropriate or fitting. **2.** conformity to the prevailing standard of behaviour, speech, or morality. **3. the proprieties.** the standards of behaviour considered correct by polite society. [Old French *propriété*, from Latin *proprius* one's own]

propulsion (prəˈpʌlʃən) *n.* **1.** the act of propelling or the state of being propelled. **2.** a propelling force. [Latin *prōpellere* to propel] —**propulsive** (prəˈpʌlsɪv) *adj.*

pro rata (ˈprəʊ ˈrɑːtə) *adv., adj.* in proportion. [Medieval Latin]

prorogue (prəˈrəʊg) *vb.* to discontinue the meetings of (a legislative body) without dissolving it. [Latin *prorogāre*, lit.: to ask publicly] —**prorogation** (ˌprəʊrəˈgeɪʃən) *n.*

prosaic (prəʊˈzeɪɪk) *adj.* **1.** lacking imagination; dull. **2.** having the characteristics of prose. —**pro'saically** *adv.*

pros and cons *pl. n.* the various arguments for and against a motion or course of action. [Latin *prō* for + *con(tra)* against]

proscenium (prəˈsiːnɪəm) *n., pl.* **-nia** (-nɪə) or **-niums.** the arch separating the stage from the auditorium together with the area immediately in front of the arch. [Greek *pro-* before + *skēnē* scene]

proscribe (prəʊˈskraɪb) *vb.* **1.** to condemn or prohibit (something). **2.** to outlaw; banish; exile. [Latin *prōscrībere* to put up a public notice] —**proscription** (prəʊˈskrɪpʃən) *n.* —**pro'scriptive** *adj.*

prose (prəʊz) *n.* **1.** spoken or written language distinguished from poetry by its lack of a marked metrical structure. **2.** a passage set for translation into a foreign language. **3.** commonplace or dull talk. ~*vb.* **4.** to speak or write in a tedious style. [Latin *prōsa ōrātiō* straightforward speech]

prosecute (ˈprɒsɪˌkjuːt) *vb.* **1.** to bring a criminal action against (a person). **2. a.** to seek redress by legal proceedings. **b.** to institute or conduct a prosecution. **3.** to continue to do (a task, etc.). [Latin *prōsequī* to follow] —**'prose,cutor** *n.*

prosecution (ˌprɒsɪˈkjuːʃən) *n.* **1.** the act of prosecuting or the state of being prosecuted. **2.** the institution and conduct of legal proceedings against a person. **3.** the lawyers acting for the Crown to put the case against a person. **4.** the carrying on of something begun.

proselyte (ˈprɒsɪˌlaɪt) *n.* a person newly converted from one religion or belief to another. [Greek *prosēlutos* recent arrival, convert] —**proselytism** ('prɒsɪlɪˌtɪzəm) *n.*

proselytize *or* -**ise** ('prɒsɪlɪˌtaɪz) *vb.* to convert (someone) from one religion or belief to another.

prosody ('prɒsədɪ) *n.* **1.** the study of poetic metre and of the art of versification. **2.** the patterns of stress and intonation in a language. [Greek *prosōidia* song set to music] —**prosodic** (prə'sɒdɪk) *adj.* —'**prosodist** *n.*

prospect *n.* ('prɒspekt). **1.** (*sometimes pl.*) a probability of future success: *a job with prospects.* **2.** a view or scene. **3.** expectation, or what one expects: *she was excited at the prospect of living in London.* ~*vb.* (prə'spekt). **4.** (sometimes foll. by *for*) to explore (a region) for gold or other valuable minerals. [Latin *prōspectus* distant view]

prospective (prə'spektɪv) *adj.* **1.** future: *prospective customers.* **2.** expected or likely: *the prospective loss.* —**pro'spectively** *adv.*

prospector (prə'spektə) *n.* a person who searches for gold or other valuable minerals.

prospectus (prə'spektəs) *n., pl.* -**tuses.** **1.** a formal statement giving details of a forthcoming event, such as the issue of shares. **2.** a brochure giving details of courses, as at a school.

prosper ('prɒspə) *vb.* to thrive, do well, or be successful. [Latin *prosperāre* to succeed]

prosperity (prɒ'sperɪtɪ) *n.* the condition of prospering; success or wealth.

prosperous ('prɒspərəs) *adj.* **1.** flourishing; prospering. **2.** wealthy.

prostate ('prɒsteɪt) *n.* a gland in male mammals that surrounds the neck of the bladder. Also called: **prostate gland.** [Greek *prostatēs* something standing in front (of the bladder)]

prosthesis ('prɒsθɪsɪs) *n., pl.* -**ses** (-ˌsiːz). *Surgery.* **a.** the replacement of a missing bodily part with an artificial substitute. **b.** an artificial part such as a limb, eye, or tooth. [Greek: an addition] —**prosthetic** (prɒs'θetɪk) *adj.*

prostitute ('prɒstɪˌtjuːt) *n.* **1.** a woman who engages in sexual intercourse for money. **2.** a man who engages in such activity, esp. in homosexual practices. ~*vb.* **3.** to offer (oneself or another) in sexual intercourse for money. **4.** to offer (oneself or one's talent) for unworthy purposes. [Latin *prō-* in public + *statuere* to cause to stand] —ˌ**prosti'tution** *n.*

prostrate *adj.* ('prɒstreɪt). **1.** lying face downwards, as in submission. **2.** physically or emotionally exhausted. ~*vb.* (prɒ-'streɪt). **3.** to cast (oneself) down, as in submission. **4.** to make helpless or exhausted. [Latin *prōsternere* to throw to the ground] —**pros'tration** *n.*

prosy ('prəʊzɪ) *adj.* **prosier, prosiest.** dull, tedious, or long-winded. —'**prosily** *adv.*

Prot. **1.** Protectorate. **2.** Protestant.

protactinium (ˌprəʊtæk'tɪnɪəm) *n.* a toxic radioactive metallic element. Symbol: Pa

protagonist (prəʊ'tægənɪst) *n.* **1.** *Not universally accepted.* a supporter of a cause or party. **2.** the principal character in a play or story. [Greek *prōtos* first + *agōnistēs* actor]

protea ('prəʊtɪə) *n.* an African shrub having flowers with coloured bracts arranged in showy heads. [after *Proteus*, a sea god who could change shape, referring to the many forms of the plant]

protean (prəʊ'tiːən, 'prəʊtɪən) *adj.* readily taking on various shapes or forms; variable. [after *Proteus*; see PROTEA]

protect (prə'tekt) *vb.* **1.** to defend from trouble, harm, or loss. **2.** *Econ.* to assist (domestic industries) by tariffs on imports. [Latin *prōtegere* to cover before]

protection (prə'tekʃən) *n.* **1.** the act of protecting or the condition of being protected. **2.** something that protects. **3. a.** the imposition of duties on imports, for the protection of domestic industries. **b.** Also called: **protectionism.** the system or theory of such restrictions. **4.** *Informal.* Also called: **protection money.** money demanded by gangsters for freedom from attack. —**pro'tection**ˌ**ism** *n.* —**pro'tectionist** *n., adj.*

protective (prə'tektɪv) *adj.* giving, tending to, or capable of giving protection. —**pro'tectively** *adv.* —**pro'tectiveness** *n.*

protector (prə'tektə) *n.* **1.** a person or thing that protects. **2.** *History.* a person who exercised royal authority during the minority, absence, or incapacity of the monarch. —**pro'tectress** *fem. n.*

protectorate (prə'tektərɪt) *n.* **1.** a territory largely controlled by a stronger state. **2.** the office or period of office of a protector.

protégé *or* (*fem.*) **protégée** ('prəʊtɪˌʒeɪ) *n.* a person who is protected and aided by the patronage of another. [French *protéger* to protect]

protein ('prəʊtiːn) *n.* any of a large group of nitrogenous compounds that are essential constituents of all living organisms. [Greek *prōteios* primary]

pro tempore Latin. ('prəʊ 'tempərɪ) *adv., adj.* for the time being. Often shortened to **pro tem** (prəʊ 'tem).

protest *n.* ('prəʊtest). **1.** public, often organized, manifestation of dissent. **2.** a formal or solemn objection. **3.** a formal statement declaring that a debtor has dishonoured a bill. **4.** the act of protesting. ~*vb.* (prə'test). **5.** (sometimes foll. by *against, at, about,* etc.) to make a strong objection (to something, esp. a supposed injustice or offence). **6.** to disagree; object: *"I'm O.K." she protested.* **7.** to assert in a formal or solemn manner. **8.** *Chiefly U.S.* to object forcefully to: *leaflets protesting Dr King's murder.* [Latin *prōtestārī* to make a formal declaration] —**pro'testant** *adj., n.* —**pro'tester** *or* **pro'testor** *n.*

Protestant ('prɒtɪstənt) *n.* **1.** an adherent of the religious system or any of its churches that separated from the Roman Catholic Church in the sixteenth century.

~*adj.* **2.** of or relating to Protestants. —'**Protestant₁tism** *n.*

protestation (₁prəʊtɛs'teɪʃən) *n.* **1.** the act of protesting. **2.** a strong declaration.

protium ('prəʊtɪəm) *n.* the most common isotope of hydrogen, with a mass number of 1. [from Greek *prōtos* first]

proto- *or sometimes before a vowel* **prot-** *combining form.* **1.** first: *protomartyr.* **2.** original: *prototype.* [Greek *prōtos* first]

protocol ('prəʊtə₁kɒl) *n.* **1.** the formal etiquette and procedure for state and diplomatic ceremonies. **2.** a record of an agreement, esp. in international negotiations. [Late Greek *prōtokollon* sheet glued to the front of a manuscript]

proton ('prəʊtɒn) *n.* a stable, positively charged elementary particle, found in atomic nuclei in numbers equal to the atomic number of the element. [Greek *prōtos* first]

protoplasm ('prəʊtə₁plæzəm) *n.* Biol. the living contents of a cell: a complex translucent colourless substance. [Greek *prōtos* first + *plasma* form] —₁proto'plasmic *adj.*

prototype ('prəʊtə₁taɪp) *n.* **1.** one of the first units manufactured of a product, which is tested so that the design can be changed if necessary. **2.** a person or thing that serves as an example of a type.

protozoan (₁prəʊtə'zəʊən) *n., pl.* **-zoa** (-'zəʊə) a minute invertebrate, such as the amoeba. Also: **protozoon.** [Greek *prōtos* first + *zoion* animal]

protract (prə'trækt) *vb.* to lengthen or extend (a speech, occasion, or situation). [Latin *prōtrahere* to prolong] —**pro'tract-ed** *adj.* —**pro'traction** *n.*

protractor (prə'træktə) *n.* an instrument for measuring angles usually a semicircular transparent plastic sheet graduated in degrees.

protrude (prə'truːd) *vb.* **1.** to thrust forwards or outwards. **2.** to project. [PRO-² + Latin *trudere* to thrust] —**pro'trusion** *n.* —**pro'trusive** *adj.*

protuberant (prə'tjuːbərənt) *adj.* swelling out; bulging. [Late Latin *prōtūberāre* to swell] —**pro'tuberance** *n.*

proud (praʊd) *adj.* **1.** pleased or satisfied with oneself, one's possessions, or achievements, or another's achievements or qualities; *proud of one's family; very proud of her new car.* **2.** feeling honoured or gratified by some distinction. **3.** haughty; arrogant. **4.** characterized by or proceeding from a sense of pride: *a proud moment.* **5.** having a proper sense of self-respect: *too proud to accept charity.* **6.** (of a surface or edge) projecting or protruding. ~*adv.* **7.** **do** (**someone**) **proud.** to entertain (someone) on a grand scale: *they did us proud at the hotel.* [Old French *prud, prod* brave] —'**proudly** *adv.*

proud flesh *n.* a mass of tissue formed around a healing wound.

prove (pruːv) *vb.* **proving, proved;** **proved** *or* **proven.** **1.** to demonstrate the truth or validity of (something): *the autopsy proved that she had been drowned.* **2.**

to establish that (someone or something) has a particular quality: *his advice proved sound.* **3.** *Law.* to establish the genuineness of (a will). **4.** to show (oneself) able or courageous. **5.** to be found to be: *this has proved useless.* [Latin *probāre* to test] —'**provable** *adj.*

proven ('pruːvṇ, 'prəʊ-) *vb.* **1.** a past participle of **prove. 2.** See **not proven.** ~*adj.* **3.** tried; tested: *a proven method.*

provenance ('provinəns) *n.* a place of origin, as of a work of art. [French]

Provençal (₁provon'saːl) *adj.* **1.** of Provence, in SE France. ~*n.* **2.** a language of Provence. **3.** a person from Provence.

provender ('provɪndə) *n.* **1.** fodder for livestock. **2.** food in general. [Old French *provendre*]

proverb ('provɜːb) *n.* a short memorable saying that expresses a truth or gives a warning. An example is "*half a loaf is better than none*". [Latin *prōverbium*]

proverbial (prə'vɜːbɪəl) *adj.* **1.** well-known because commonly or traditionally referred to. **2.** of or resembling a proverb. —**pro'verbially** *adv.*

provide (prə'vaɪd) *vb.* **1.** to furnish or supply. **2.** to afford; yield: *this meeting provides an opportunity to talk.* **3.** (often foll. by *for* or *against*) to take careful precautions: *he provided against financial ruin by wise investment.* **4.** (foll. by *for*) to supply means of support (to): *he provides for his family.* **5.** (of a person, law, etc.) to state as a condition; stipulate. [Latin *prōvidēre* to provide for] —**pro'vid-er** *n.*

providence ('providəns) *n.* **1.** the foreseeing protection and care given by God or some other force. **2.** the foresight or care exercised by a person in the management of his affairs.

Providence ('providəns) *n.* Christianity. God, esp. as showing foreseeing care of his creatures.

provident ('providənt) *adj.* **1.** exercising foresight in the management of one's affairs. **2.** characterized by foresight. [Latin *prōvidens* foreseeing]

providential (₁provɪ'dɛnʃəl) *adj.* characteristic of or presumed to proceed from or as if from divine providence.

provident society *n.* same as **friendly society.**

providing (prə'vaɪdɪŋ) *or* **provided** *conj.* on the condition or understanding (that): *I'll play, providing you pay me.*

province ('provɪns) *n.* **1.** a territory governed as a unit of a country or empire. **2.** (*pl.*; usually preceded by *the*) those parts of a country lying outside the capital and regarded as outside the mainstream of sophisticated culture. **3.** an area of learning, activity, etc. **4.** the extent of a person's activities or office. [Latin *prōvincia* conquered territory]

provincewide ('provɪns₁waɪd) *Canad.* ~*adj.* **1.** covering or available to the whole of a province: *a provincewide referendum.* ~*adv.* **2.** throughout a province:

*an advertising campaign to go prov-
incewide.*

provincial (prəˈvɪnʃəl) *adj.* 1. of or connected with a province. 2. characteristic
of or connected with the provinces. 3.
having attitudes and opinions supposedly
common to people living in the provinces;
unsophisticated. 4. *N.Z.* denoting a football team representing a province. ~*n.* 5.
a person lacking the sophistications of city
life. 6. a person from a province or the
provinces. —**proˈvincia,lism** *n.*

provision (prəˈvɪʒən) *n.* 1. the act of
supplying something. 2. something supplied. 3. preparations: *she didn't make
any provision for her children.* 4. (*pl.*)
food and other necessities. 5. a stipulation
incorporated in a document. ~*vb.* 6. to
supply with provisions. [Latin *prōvīsiō* a
providing]

provisional (prəˈvɪʒənˀl) *adj.* subject to
later alteration; temporary or conditional:
a provisional decision. —**proˈvisional-
ly** *adv.*

Provisional (prəˈvɪʒənˀl) *n.* a member of
the Provisional IRA or Sinn Féin.

proviso (prəˈvaɪzəʊ) *n., pl.* **-sos** or **-soes.**
1. a conditional clause, as in a contract. 2.
a condition or stipulation. [Medieval Latin
prōvīsō quod it being provided that] —**pro-
ˈvisory** *adj.*

provocation (ˌprɒvəˈkeɪʃən) *n.* 1. the act
of provoking or inciting. 2. something that
causes indignation or anger.

provocative (prəˈvɒkətɪv) *adj.* serving or
intended to provoke or incite, esp. to anger
or sexual desire: *a provocative look; a
provocative remark.* —**proˈvocative-
ly** *adv.*

provoke (prəˈvəʊk) *vb.* 1. to anger or
infuriate. 2. to incite or stimulate. 3. to
promote (anger or indignation) in a person.
4. to bring about: *the accident provoked an
inquiry.* [Latin *prōvocāre* to call forth]
—**proˈvoking** *adj.*

provost (ˈprɒvəst) *n.* 1. the head of certain university colleges or schools. 2. (formerly) the principal magistrate of a Scottish burgh. [Old English *profost*]

provost marshal (prəˈvəʊ) *n.* the officer
in charge of military police in a camp or
city.

prow (praʊ) *n.* the bow of a vessel. [Greek
prōra]

prowess (ˈpraʊɪs) *n.* 1. outstanding or
superior skill or ability. 2. bravery or
fearlessness, esp. in battle. [Old French
proesce]

prowl (praʊl) *vb.* 1. (sometimes foll. by
around or *about*) to move stealthily around
(a place) as if in search of prey or plunder.
~*n.* 2. the act of prowling. 3. **on the
prowl.** moving around stealthily. [origin
unknown]

prox. proximo (next month).

proximate (ˈprɒksɪmɪt) *adj.* 1. next or
nearest in space or time. 2. very near;
close. 3. immediately preceding or following in a series. 4. approximate. [Latin
proximus next]

proximity (prɒkˈsɪmɪtɪ) *n.* 1. nearness in

space or time. 2. nearness or closeness in a
series. [Latin *proximitās* closeness]

proxy (ˈprɒksɪ) *n., pl.* **proxies.** 1. a person
authorized to act on behalf of someone
else; agent: *to vote by proxy.* 2. the
authority, esp. in the form of a document,
to act on behalf of someone else. [Latin
prōcūrātiō procuration]

prude (pruːd) *n.* a person who is excessively modest, prim, or proper, esp. regarding
sex. [Old French *prode femme* respectable
woman] —**ˈprudery** *n.* —**ˈprudish** *adj.*

prudent (ˈpruːdˀnt) *adj.* 1. discreet or
cautious in managing one's activities. 2.
practical and careful in providing for the
future. 3. exercising good judgment. [Lat-
in *prūdēns* far-sighted] —**ˈprudence** *n.*
—**ˈprudently** *adv.*

prudential (pruːˈdɛnʃəl) *adj.* showing prudence: *prudential reasons.* —**pruˈdential-
ly** *adv.*

prune[1] (pruːn) *n.* a purplish-black partially
dried plum. [Latin *prūnum* plum]

prune[2] (pruːn) *vb.* 1. to remove (dead or
superfluous twigs or branches) from (a
tree or shrub) by cutting off. 2. to remove
(anything undesirable or superfluous)
from (something, such as a book). [Old
French *proignier* to clip]

prurient (ˈprʊərɪənt) *adj.* 1. unusually interested in sexual thoughts or practices.
2. exciting lustfulness. [Latin *prūrīre* to
lust after, itch] —**ˈprurience** *n.*

Prussian (ˈprʌʃən) *adj.* 1. of, relating to,
or characteristic of Prussia, a former German state, esp. of its formal military tradition. ~*n.* 2. a German from Prussia.

prussic acid (ˈprʌsɪk) *n.* the extremely
poisonous solution of hydrogen cyanide.
[French *acide prussique* Prussian acid]

pry (praɪ) *vb.* **prying, pried.** (often foll. by
into) to make an impertinent or uninvited
inquiry (about a private matter). [origin
unknown]

PS 1. Also: **ps.** postscript. 2. private
secretary.

psalm (sɑːm) *n.* 1. (*often cap.*) any of the
sacred songs that constitute a book
(Psalms) of the Old Testament. 2. any
sacred song. [Greek *psalmos* song accompanied on the harp]

psalmist (ˈsɑːmɪst) *n.* a composer of
psalms.

psalmody (ˈsɑːmədɪ, ˈsæl-) *n., pl.* **-dies.** the
singing of psalms or hymns.

Psalter (ˈsɔːltə) *n.* 1. the Book of Psalms.
2. a book containing a version of Psalms.
[Greek *psaltērion* stringed instrument]

psaltery (ˈsɔːltərɪ) *n., pl.* **-teries.** an ancient stringed instrument played by plucking strings.

PSBR (in Britain) public sector borrowing
requirement; the money required by the
public sector of the economy for items not
financed from income.

psephology (sɛˈfɒlədʒɪ) *n.* the statistical
and sociological study of elections. [Greek
psephos pebble, vote + -LOGY] —**pse-
ˈphologist** *n.*

pseud (sjuːd) *n.* **1.** *Informal.* a false or pretentious person. ~*adj.* **2.** pseudo.

pseudo (ˈsjuːdəʊ) *adj. Informal.* not genuine.

pseudo- *or sometimes before a vowel* **pseud-** *combining form.* false, pretending, or unauthentic: *pseudo-intellectual.* [Greek *pseudēs* false]

pseudonym (ˈsjuːdəˌnɪm) *n.* a fictitious name adopted, esp. by an author. [Greek *pseudēs* false + *onoma* name] —ˌpseudoˈnymity *n.* —**pseudonymous** (sjuːˈdɒnɪməs) *adj.*

psittacosis (ˌsɪtəˈkəʊsɪs) *n.* a viral disease of parrots that can be transmitted to man. [Greek *psittakos* a parrot]

psoriasis (səˈraɪəsɪs) *n.* a skin disease characterized by reddish spots and patches covered with silvery scales. [Greek: itching disease]

psst (pst) *interj.* an exclamation of beckoning, esp. one made surreptitiously.

PST (in the U.S. and Canada) Pacific Standard Time.

PSV public service vehicle.

psyche (ˈsaɪkɪ) *n.* the human mind or soul. [Greek *psukhē* breath, soul]

psychedelic (ˌsaɪkɪˈdɛlɪk) *adj.* **1.** relating to or denoting altered perceptions, as through the use of hallucinogenic drugs. **2.** *Informal.* having the vivid colours and complex patterns popularly associated with the visual effects of psychedelic states. [Greek *psukhē* mind + *delos* visible]

psychiatry (saɪˈkaɪətrɪ) *n.* the branch of medicine concerned with the diagnosis and treatment of mental disorders. —**psychiatric** (ˌsaɪkɪˈætrɪk) *adj.* —**psyˈchiatrist** *n.*

psychic (ˈsaɪkɪk) *adj.* **1. a.** outside the possibilities defined by natural laws, as mental telepathy. **b.** (of a person) sensitive to forces not recognized by natural laws. ~*n.* **2.** a person who has psychic powers. —ˈ**psychical** *adj.*

psycho (ˈsaɪkəʊ) *n., pl.* **-chos,** *Informal.* same as **psychopath** or **psychopathic.**

psycho- *or sometimes before a vowel* **psych-** *combining form.* indicating the mind or psychological or mental processes: *psychology; psychosomatic.* [Greek *psukhē* spirit, breath]

psychoanalyse *or esp. U.S.* **-lyze** (ˌsaɪkəʊˈænəˌlaɪz) *vb.* to examine or treat (a person) by psychoanalysis.

psychoanalysis (ˌsaɪkəʊəˈnælɪsɪs) *n.* a method of treating mental and emotional disorders by revealing and investigating the role of the unconscious mind. —**psychoanalyst** (ˌsaɪkəʊˈænəlɪst) *n.* —**psychoanalytic** (ˌsaɪkəʊˌænəˈlɪtɪk) *or* ˌpsychoˌanaˈlytical *adj.*

psychogenic (ˌsaɪkəʊˈdʒɛnɪk) *adj. Psychol.* (esp. of disorders or symptoms) of mental, rather than organic, origin.

psychological (ˌsaɪkəˈlɒdʒɪkᵊl) *adj.* **1.** of or relating to psychology. **2.** of or relating to the mind or mental activity. **3.** affecting the mind. —ˌ**psychoˈlogically** *adv.*

psychological moment *n.* the most appropriate time for producing a desired effect.

psychological warfare *n.* the military application of psychology, esp. to influence morale in time of war.

psychology (saɪˈkɒlədʒɪ) *n., pl.* **-gies.** **1.** the scientific study of all forms of human and animal behaviour. **2.** *Informal.* the mental make-up of an individual. —**psyˈchologist** *n.*

psychopath (ˈsaɪkəʊˌpæθ) *n.* a person afflicted with a personality disorder characterized by a tendency to commit antisocial and sometimes violent acts. —ˌ**psychoˈpathic** *adj.*

psychopathology (ˌsaɪkəʊpəˈθɒlədʒɪ) *n.* the scientific study of mental disorders.

psychopathy (saɪˈkɒpəθɪ) *n.* any mental disorder or disease.

psychosis (saɪˈkəʊsɪs) *n., pl.* **-choses** (-ˈkəʊsiːz). any form of severe mental disorder in which the individual's contact with reality becomes highly distorted. —**psychotic** (saɪˈkɒtɪk) *adj.*

psychosomatic (ˌsaɪkəʊsəˈmætɪk) *adj.* of disorders, such as stomach ulcers, thought to be caused by psychological factors such as stress.

psychotherapy (ˌsaɪkəʊˈθɛrəpɪ) *n.* the treatment of nervous disorders by psychological methods. —ˌ**psychoˌtheraˈpeutic** *adj.* —ˌ**psychoˈtherapist** *n.*

psych up (saɪk) *vb.* to prepare (oneself or another) mentally for a contest, performance, or action.

pt **1.** part. **2.** point. **3.** port.

Pt *Chem.* platinum.

PT physical training.

pt. pint.

PTA Parent-Teacher Association.

Pte. *Mil.* private.

pterodactyl (ˌtɛrəˈdæktɪl) *n.* an extinct flying reptile with membranous wings. [Greek *pteron* wing + *daktulos* finger]

PTO *or* **pto** please turn over.

Ptolemaic (ˌtɒlɪˈmeɪɪk) *adj.* of or relating to Ptolemy, the 2nd-century A.D. Greek astronomer, or to his conception that the earth lay at the centre of the universe.

ptomaine *or* **ptomain** (ˈtəʊmeɪn) *n.* any of a group of alkaloid substances formed by decaying organic matter. [Greek *ptoma* corpse]

Pu *Chem.* plutonium.

pub (pʌb) *n.* **1.** *Chiefly Brit.* a building with a bar licensed for the sale and consumption of alcoholic drink. **2.** *Austral. & N.Z.* a hotel.

pub. **1.** public. **2.** publication. **3.** published. **4.** publisher. **5.** publishing.

pub-crawl *n. Informal, chiefly Brit.* a drinking tour of a number of pubs.

puberty (ˈpjuːbətɪ) *n.* the period at the beginning of adolescence when the sex glands become functional. [Latin *pūbertās* maturity] —ˈ**pubertal** *adj.*

pubes (ˈpjuːbiːz) *n., pl.* **pubes.** **1.** the region above the external genital organs.

2. pubic hair. 3. the plural of **pubis**. [Latin]

pubescent (pjuːˈbɛsˀnt) adj. 1. arriving or arrived at puberty. 2. covered with down, as some plants and animals. [Latin *pūbēscere* to reach manhood] —**puˈbescence** n.

pubic (ˈpjuːbɪk) adj. of or relating to the pubes or pubis: *pubic hair*.

pubis (ˈpjuːbɪs) n., pl. **-bes**. one of the three sections of the hipbone that forms part of the pelvis. [New Latin *os pūbis* bone of the pubes]

public (ˈpʌblɪk) adj. 1. of or concerning the people as a whole. 2. open to all: *public gardens*. 3. performed or made openly: *public proclamation*. 4. well-known: *a public figure*. 5. maintained at the expense of, serving, or for the use of a community: *a public library*. 6. open, acknowledged, or notorious: *a public scandal*. 7. **go public**. (of a private company) to offer shares for sale to the public. ~n. 8. the community or people in general. 9. a section of the community: *the racing public*. [Latin *pōplicus* of the people] —**ˈpublicly** adv.

public-address system n. a system of microphones, amplifiers, and loudspeakers for increasing the sound level at public gatherings.

publican (ˈpʌblɪkən) n. (in Britain) a person who keeps a public house.

publication (ˌpʌblɪˈkeɪʃən) n. 1. the publishing of a printed work. 2. any printed work offered for sale. 3. the act of making information known to the public.

public company n. a limited company whose shares may be purchased by the public.

public convenience n. a public lavatory.

public enemy n. a notorious person, such as a criminal, who is regarded as a menace to the public.

public house n. 1. Brit. a pub. 2. U.S. & Canad. an inn, tavern, or small hotel.

publicist (ˈpʌblɪsɪst) n. a person who publicizes something, such as a press agent or journalist.

publicity (pʌˈblɪsɪtɪ) n. 1. the technique or the information used to attract public attention to people or products. 2. public interest so aroused.

publicize or **-ise** (ˈpʌblɪˌsaɪz) vb. to bring to public notice; advertise.

public lending right n. the right of authors to receive payment when their books are borrowed from public libraries.

public prosecutor n. Law. an official in charge of prosecuting important cases.

public relations n. (functioning as sing. or pl.) the practice of creating, promoting, or maintaining goodwill and a favourable image among the public towards an institution, public body, or business.

public school n. 1. (in England and Wales) a private independent fee-paying secondary school. 2. in certain Canadian provinces, a public elementary school as distinguished from a separate school. 3.

any school that is part of a free local educational system.

public sector n. the part of an economy which consists of state-owned institutions, including nationalized industries and services provided by local authorities.

public servant n. 1. an elected or appointed holder of a public office. 2. Austral. & N.Z. a civil servant.

public service n. Austral. & N.Z. the civil service.

public-spirited adj. having or showing active interest in the good of the community.

public utility n. an enterprise that provides services, such as water or electricity, to the public.

publish (ˈpʌblɪʃ) vb. 1. to produce and issue (printed matter) for sale. 2. to have one's written work issued for publication. 3. to announce formally or in public. [Latin *pūblicāre* to make public]

publisher (ˈpʌblɪʃə) n. 1. a company or person engaged in publishing books, periodicals, music, etc. 2. U.S. & Canad. the proprietor of a newspaper.

puce (pjuːs) adj. purplish-brown. [French *couleur puce* flea colour]

puck[1] (pʌk) n. a small disc of hard rubber used in ice hockey. [origin unknown]

puck[2] (pʌk) n. a mischievous or evil spirit. [Old English *pūca*] —**ˈpuckish** adj.

pucker (ˈpʌkə) vb. 1. to gather (a soft surface, such as the skin) into wrinkles or (of such a surface) to be so gathered. ~n. 2. a wrinkle or crease. [origin unknown]

pudding (ˈpʊdɪŋ) n. 1. a sweetened, usually cooked dessert, made in many forms and containing various ingredients. 2. a savoury dish, usually consisting partially of pastry or batter: *steak-and-kidney pudding*. 3. the dessert course in a meal. 4. a sausage-like mass of meat: *black pudding*. [Middle English *poding*]

puddle (ˈpʌdˀl) n. 1. a small pool of water, esp. of rain. 2. a worked mixture of wet clay and sand that is impervious to water. ~vb. 3. to make (clay, etc.) into puddle. 4. to subject (iron) to puddling. [Middle English *podel*] —**ˈpuddly** adj.

pudendum (pjuːˈdɛndəm) n., pl. **-da** (-də). (often pl.) the human external genital organs collectively, esp. of a female. [Latin *pudenda* the shameful (parts)]

pudgy (ˈpʌdʒɪ) adj. **pudgier**, **pudgiest**. Chiefly U.S. podgy. [origin unknown] —**ˈpudginess** n.

puerile (ˈpjʊəraɪl) adj. 1. silly; immature. 2. childish. [Latin *puer* a boy] —**puerility** (pjʊəˈrɪlɪtɪ) n.

puerperal (pjuːˈɜːpərəl) adj. of or occurring during the period following childbirth. [Latin *puerperium* childbirth]

puerperal fever n. a serious, formerly widespread, form of blood poisoning caused by infection during childbirth.

puff (pʌf) n. 1. a short quick gust or emission, as of wind or smoke. 2. the amount of wind or smoke released in a puff. 3. the sound made by a puff. vb.

instance of inhaling and expelling the breath as in smoking. **5.** a light pastry usually filled with cream and jam. **6.** one's breath: *by the third flight of stairs she was out of puff.* ~*vb.* **7.** to blow or breathe in short quick draughts. **8.** (often foll. by *out*) to cause to be out of breath. **9.** to take draws at (a cigarette). **10.** to move with or by the emission of puffs: *the steam train puffed up the incline.* **11.** (often foll. by *up* or *out*) to swell, as with air, pride, or as a result of injury. [Old English *pyffan*] —'**puffy** *adj.*

puff adder *n.* a large venomous African viper that inflates its body when alarmed.

puffball ('pʌf₁bɔːl) *n.* a fungus with a round body that lets out a cloud of brown spores when mature.

puffin ('pʌfɪn) *n.* a northern diving bird with a black-and-white plumage and a brightly coloured vertically flattened bill. [origin unknown]

puff pastry *or U.S.* **puff paste** *n.* a dough used for making a rich flaky pastry.

pug (pʌg) *n.* a small compact breed of dog with a smooth coat, lightly curled tail, and a short wrinkled nose. [origin unknown]

pugilism ('pjuːdʒɪ₁lɪzəm) *n.* the art, practice, or profession of fighting with the fists; boxing. [Latin *pugil* a boxer] —'**pugilist** *n.* —₁pugi'listic *adj.*

pugnacious (pʌg'neɪʃəs) *adj.* ready and eager to fight; belligerent. [Latin *pugnāx*] —**pugnacity** (pʌg'næsɪtɪ) *n.*

pug nose *n.* a short stubby upturned nose. [from *pug* (the dog)] —'**pug₁nosed** *adj.*

puissance ('pjuːɪs'ns, 'pwiːsɑːns) *n.* a competition in showjumping that tests a horse's ability to jump large obstacles. [see PUISSANT]

puissant ('pjuːɪs'nt) *adj.* Archaic *or poetic.* powerful. [Old French, from Latin *potēns* mighty]

puke (pjuːk) *Slang.* ~*vb.* **1.** to vomit. ~*n.* **2.** the act of vomiting. **3.** the matter vomited. [prob. imit.]

pukeko ('pʊkəkəʊ) *n., pl.* -**kos.** a New Zealand wading bird with bright plumage. [Maori]

pukka *or* **pucka** ('pʌkə) *adj.* Anglo-Indian. proper; good; genuine. [Hindi *pakkā* firm]

pulchritude ('pʌlkrɪ₁tjuːd) *n.* Formal *or literary.* physical beauty. [Latin *pulchritūdō*] —₁pulchri'tudinous *adj.*

pule (pjuːl) *vb.* to cry plaintively; whimper. [imit.]

pull (pʊl) *vb.* **1.** to exert force on (an object) so as to draw it towards the source of the force. **2.** to remove; extract: *to pull a tooth.* **3.** to rend or tear. **4.** to strain (a muscle or tendon). **5.** (usually foll. by *off*) Informal. to bring about: *to pull off a million-pound deal.* **6.** (often foll. by *on*) Informal. to draw out (a weapon) for use: *he pulled a knife on his attacker.* **7.** Informal. to attract: *the pop group pulled a crowd.* **8.** (usually foll. by *on* or *at*) to drink or inhale deeply: *to pull at one's pipe.* **9.** to make (a grimace): *to pull a face.* **10.** (foll. by *away, out, over,* etc.) to move (a

vehicle) or (of a vehicle) to be moved in a specified manner. **11.** to possess or exercise the power to move: *this car doesn't pull well on hills.* **12.** Printing. to take (a proof) from type. **13.** Golf, baseball, etc. to hit (a ball) away from the direction in which the player intended to hit it. **14.** Cricket. to hit (a ball) to the leg side. **15.** to row (a boat) or take a stroke of (an oar) in rowing. **16. pull a fast one.** Slang. to play a sly trick. **17. pull apart** *or* **to pieces.** to criticize harshly. **18. pull (one's) punches.** to restrain the force of one's criticisms or blows. ~*n.* **19.** an act or an instance of pulling or being pulled. **20.** the force or effort used in pulling: *the pull of the moon affects the tides.* **21.** the act or an instance of taking in drink or smoke. **22.** Printing. a proof taken from type. **23.** something used for pulling, such as a handle. **24.** Informal. special advantage or influence: *his uncle is chairman of the company, so he has quite a lot of pull.* **25.** Informal. the power to attract attention or support. **26.** a single stroke of an oar in rowing. **27.** the act of pulling the ball in golf, cricket, etc. ~See also **pull down, pull in,** etc. [Old English *pullian*]

pull down *vb.* to destroy or demolish: *the old houses were pulled down.*

pullet ('pʊlɪt) *n.* a young hen of the domestic fowl, less than one year old. [Old French *poulet* chicken]

pulley ('pʊlɪ) *n.* a wheel with a grooved rim in which a belt, chain, or piece of rope runs in order to lift or lower heavy loads or change the direction of a pull. [Old French *polie*]

pull in *vb.* **1.** (often foll. by *to*) to reach a destination: *the train pulled in at the station.* **2.** Also: **pull over.** (of a motor vehicle) to draw in to the side of the road. **3.** to attract: *his appearance will pull in the crowds.* **4.** Brit. slang. to arrest. **5.** to earn or gain (money): *he pulls in twenty thousand a year.*

Pullman ('pʊlmən) *n., pl.* -**mans.** a luxurious railway coach. [after G. M. *Pullman,* its inventor]

pull off *vb.* to succeed in performing (a difficult feat).

pull out *vb.* **1.** to extract. **2.** to depart: *the train pulled out of the station.* **3.** Mil. to withdraw or be withdrawn: *the troops were pulled out of the ruined city.* **4.** (of a motor vehicle) **a.** to draw away from the side of the road. **b.** to draw out from behind another vehicle to overtake. **5.** to abandon a position or situation.

pullover ('pʊl₁əʊvə) *n.* a garment, esp. a sweater, that is pulled on over the head.

pull through *vb.* to survive or recover, esp. after a serious illness or crisis. Also: **pull round.**

pull together *vb.* **1.** to cooperate or work harmoniously. **2. pull oneself together.** Informal. to regain one's self-control or composure.

pull up *vb.* **1.** to remove by the roots. **2.** (often foll. by *with* or *on*) to move level (with) or ahead (of), esp. in a race. **3.** to stop: *the car pulled up suddenly.* **4.** to rebuke.

pulmonary (ˈpʌlmənərɪ, ˈpʊl-) *adj.* **1.** of or affecting the lungs. **2.** having lungs or lunglike organs. [Latin *pulmō* a lung]

pulp (pʌlp) *n.* **1.** soft or fleshy plant tissue, such as the succulent part of a fleshy fruit. **2.** a moist mixture of cellulose fibres, as obtained from wood, from which paper is made. **3.** a magazine or book containing trite or sensational material, and usually printed on cheap rough paper. ~*vb.* **4.** to reduce (a material) to pulp or (of a material) to be reduced to pulp. [Latin *pulpa*] —ˈ**pulpy** *adj.*

pulpit (ˈpʊlpɪt) *n.* **1.** a raised platform in churches as the appointed place for preaching. **2.** (usually preceded by *the*) preaching or the clergy. [Latin *pulpitum* a platform]

pulpwood (ˈpʌlp,wʊd) *n.* pine, spruce, or any other soft wood used to make paper.

pulsar (ˈpʌl,sɑː) *n.* any of a number of very small stars which emit regular pulses of polarized radiation. [from *puls(ating st)ar*]

pulsate (pʌlˈseɪt) *vb.* **1.** to expand and contract with a rhythmical beat; throb. **2.** *Physics.* to vary in intensity or magnitude. **3.** to quiver or vibrate. [Latin *pulsāre* to push] —pulˈsation *n.*

pulse[1] (pʌls) *n.* **1.** *Physiol.* **a.** the rhythmical contraction and expansion of an artery at each beat of the heart. **b.** a single such pulsation. **2.** *Physics, electronics.* a sudden change in a quantity, such as a voltage, that is normally constant in a system. **3.** a recurrent rhythmical series of beats or vibrations. **4.** bustle, vitality, or excitement: *the pulse of a city.* **5.** the feelings or thoughts of a group as they can be measured: *the pulse of the voters.* ~*vb.* **6.** to beat, throb, or vibrate. [Latin *pulsus* a beating]

pulse[2] (pʌls) *n.* the edible seeds of any of several leguminous plants, such as peas, beans, and lentils. [Latin *puls* pottage of pulse]

pulverize *or* **-ise** (ˈpʌlvə,raɪz) *vb.* **1.** to reduce (a substance) to fine particles, as by grinding, or (of a substance) to be so reduced. **2.** to destroy completely. [Latin *pulvis* dust] —ˌpulveriˈzation *or* -iˈsation *n.*

puma (ˈpjuːmə) *n.* a large American mammal of the cat family, with a plain greyish-brown coat and long tail. [S American Indian]

pumice (ˈpʌmɪs) *n.* a light porous volcanic rock used for scouring and, in powdered form, for polishing. Also called: **pumice stone.** [Old French *pomis*]

pummel (ˈpʌməl) *vb.* **-melling, -melled** *or* *U.S.* **-meling, -meled.** to strike repeatedly with or as if with the fists. [see POMMEL]

pump[1] (pʌmp) *n.* **1.** any device for compressing, driving, raising, or reducing the pressure of a fluid, esp. by means of a piston or set of rotating impellers. ~*vb.* **2.** (sometimes foll. by *from, out,* etc.) to raise or drive (air, liquid, etc., esp. into or

from something) with a pump. **3.** (usually foll. by *in* or *into*) to supply in large amounts: *to pump capital into a project.* **4.** to operate (something, esp. a handle) in the manner of a pump or (of something) to work in this way: *to pump the pedals of a bicycle.* **5.** to obtain (information) from (a person) by persistent questioning. [Middle Dutch *pumpe* pipe]

pump[2] (pʌmp) *n.* **1.** a low-cut low-heeled shoe, worn for dancing. **2.** a shoe with a rubber sole, used in games such as tennis; plimsoll. [origin unknown]

pumpernickel (ˈpʌmpə,nɪkⁿl) *n.* a slightly sour black bread made of coarse rye flour. [from German]

pumpkin (ˈpʌmpkɪn) *n.* **1.** a large round fruit with a thick orange rind, pulpy flesh, and numerous seeds. **2.** the creeping plant that bears this fruit. [Greek *pepōn* ripe]

pun (pʌn) *n.* **1.** the use of words to exploit double meanings for humorous effect. An example is "*my dog's a champion boxer*". ~*vb.* **punning, punned. 2.** to make puns. [origin unknown]

punch[1] (pʌntʃ) *vb.* **1.** to strike at with a clenched fist. ~*n.* **2.** a blow with the fist. **3.** *Informal.* point or vigour: *his arguments lacked punch.* [prob. var. of *pounce* to stamp]

punch[2] (pʌntʃ) *n.* **1.** a tool or machine for shaping, piercing, or engraving. **2.** *Computers.* a device for making holes in a card or paper tape. ~*vb.* **3.** to pierce, cut, stamp, shape, or drive with a punch. [Latin *pungere* to prick]

punch[3] (pʌntʃ) *n.* a mixed drink containing fruit juice and, usually, alcoholic liquor, generally hot and spiced. [origin unknown]

Punch (pʌntʃ) *n.* the main character in the children's puppet show **Punch and Judy.**

punchball (ˈpʌntʃ,bɔːl) *n.* a stuffed or inflated ball or bag, suspended or supported by a flexible rod, that is punched for exercise, esp. boxing training.

punchbowl (ˈpʌntʃ,bəʊl) *n.* a large bowl for serving punch.

punch-drunk *adj.* dazed; stupefied, as from repeated blows to the head.

punched card *or esp. U.S.* **punch card** *n. Computers.* a card on which data can be coded in the form of punched holes.

Punchinello (ˌpʌntʃɪˈnɛləʊ) *n., pl.* **-los** *or* **-loes.** a clown from Italian puppet shows, the prototype of Punch. [Italian *Polecenella*]

punch line *n.* the line of a joke or funny story that gives it its point.

punch-up *n. Brit. informal.* a fight or brawl.

punchy (ˈpʌntʃɪ) *adj. Informal.* incisive or forceful: *a punchy leaflet.*

punctilious (pʌŋkˈtɪlɪəs) *adj.* **1.** paying scrupulous attention to correctness in etiquette. **2.** attentive to detail. [Latin *punctum* a point] —puncˈtiliously *adv.*

punctual (ˈpʌŋktjʊəl) *adj.* **1.** arriving or taking place at an arranged time. **2.** (of a person) having the characteristic of always keeping to arranged times. [Medieval

Latin *punctuālis* concerning point]
—**ˌpunctuˈality** n. —**ˈpunctually** adv.

punctuate (ˈpʌŋktjʊˌeɪt) vb. **1.** to insert punctuation marks into (a written text). **2.** to interrupt at frequent intervals: *a meeting punctuated by heckling.* **3.** to emphasize. [Latin *pungere* to puncture]

punctuation (ˌpʌŋktjʊˈeɪʃən) n. **1.** the use of symbols not belonging to the alphabet to indicate intonation and meaning not otherwise conveyed in the written language. **2.** the symbols used for this purpose.

punctuation mark n. any of the signs used in punctuation, such as a comma.

puncture (ˈpʌŋktʃə) n. **1.** a small hole made by a sharp object. **2.** a perforation and loss of pressure in a pneumatic tyre. **3.** the act of puncturing or perforating. ~vb. **4.** to pierce a hole in (something) with a sharp object. **5.** to cause (something pressurized, esp. a tyre) to lose pressure by piercing, or (of a tyre) to collapse in this way. [Latin *pungere* to prick]

pundit (ˈpʌndɪt) n. **1.** a self-appointed expert. **2.** a Brahman learned in Hindu religion, philosophy, or law. [Hindi *pandit*]

pungent (ˈpʌndʒənt) adj. **1.** having an acrid smell or sharp bitter flavour. **2.** (of wit or satire) biting; caustic. [Latin *pungens* piercing] —**ˈpungency** n.

punish (ˈpʌnɪʃ) vb. **1.** to force (someone) to undergo a penalty for some crime or misdemeanour. **2.** to inflict punishment for (some crime or misdemeanour). **3.** to treat harshly, esp. as by overexertion: *to punish a horse.* [Latin *pūnīre*] —**ˈpunishing** adj.

punishment (ˈpʌnɪʃmənt) n. **1.** a penalty for a crime or offence. **2.** the act of punishing or state of being punished. **3.** *Informal.* rough treatment.

punitive (ˈpjuːnɪtɪv) adj. relating to, involving, or with the intention of inflicting punishment: *a punitive expedition.*

punk (pʌŋk) n. **1.** a worthless person. **2. a.** a youth movement of the late 1970s, characterized by anti-Establishment slogans and the wearing of worthless articles such as safety pins for decoration. **b.** (as modifier): *a punk record.* **3.** short for **punk rock.** ~adj. **4.** worthless; insignificant. [origin unknown]

punka or **punkah** (ˈpʌŋkə) n. a fan made of palm leaves. [Hindi *pankhā*]

punk rock n. rock music in a style of the late 1970s, characterized by energy and aggressive lyrics and performance. —**punk rocker** n.

punnet (ˈpʌnɪt) n. *Chiefly Brit.* a small basket for fruit. [origin unknown]

punster (ˈpʌnstə) n. a person who is fond of making puns.

punt¹ (pʌnt) n. **1.** an open flat-bottomed boat, propelled by a pole. ~vb. **2.** to propel (a punt) by pushing with a pole on the bottom of a river. [Latin *pontō*]

punt² (pʌnt) n. **1.** a kick in certain sports, such as rugby, in which the ball is released and kicked before it hits the ground. ~vb. **2.** to kick (a ball) using a punt. [origin unknown]

punt³ (pʌnt) *Chiefly Brit.* ~vb. **1.** to gamble; bet. ~n. **2.** a gamble or bet, esp. against the bank, as in roulette, or on horses. [French *ponter*]

punter (ˈpʌntə) n. **1.** a person who places a bet. **2.** *Informal.* any member of the public, esp. when a customer: *the punters flock into the sales.*

puny (ˈpjuːnɪ) adj. **-nier, -niest.** small and weakly. [Old French *puisné* born later]

pup (pʌp) n. **1. a.** a young dog; puppy. **b.** the young of various other animals, such as the seal. ~vb. **pupping, pupped. 2.** (of dogs, seals, etc.) to give birth to (young).

pupa (ˈpjuːpə) n., pl. **-pae** (-piː) or **-pas.** an insect at the immobile nonfeeding stage of development between larva and adult. [Latin: a doll] —**ˈpupal** adj.

pupil¹ (ˈpjuːp'l) n. a student who is taught by a teacher. [Latin *pūpus* a child]

pupil² (ˈpjuːp'l) n. the dark circular opening at the centre of the iris of the eye. [Latin *pūpilla*, diminutive of *pūpa* doll; from the tiny reflections in the eye]

puppet (ˈpʌpɪt) n. **1.** a small doll or figure moved by strings attached to its limbs or by the hand inserted in its cloth body. **2.** a person or state that appears independent but is controlled by another. [Latin *pūpa* doll]

puppeteer (ˌpʌpɪˈtɪə) n. a person who manipulates puppets.

puppy (ˈpʌpɪ) n., pl. **-pies. 1.** a young dog. **2.** *Informal, contemptuous.* a brash or conceited young man. [Old French *popée* doll] —**ˈpuppyish** adj.

puppy fat n. fatty tissue that develops in childhood or adolescence and usually disappears with maturity.

purblind (ˈpɜːˌblaɪnd) adj. **1.** partly or nearly blind. **2.** lacking in understanding; obtuse. [*pure* (that is, utterly) *blind*]

purchase (ˈpɜːtʃɪs) vb. **1.** to obtain (goods) by payment. **2.** to obtain by effort or sacrifice: *to purchase one's freedom.* ~n. **3.** something that is purchased. **4.** the act of buying. **5.** the mechanical advantage achieved by a lever. **6.** a firm foothold or grasp. [Old French *porchacier* to strive to obtain] —**ˈpurchaser** n.

purdah (ˈpɜːdə) n. the custom in some Muslim and Hindu communities of keeping women in seclusion, with clothing that conceals them completely when they go out. [Hindi *parda* veil]

pure (pjʊə) adj. **1.** not mixed with any materials or elements of other kinds or from other sources. **2.** free from tainting or polluting matter: *pure water.* **3.** free from moral taint or defilement: *pure love.* **4.** complete: *a pure coincidence.* **5.** (of a subject) studied in its theoretical aspects rather than for its practical applications: *pure mathematics.* **6.** of unmixed descent. [Latin *pūrus* unstained] —**ˈpurely** adv. —**ˈpureness** n.

purebred (ˈpjʊəˌbred) adj. denoting a pure strain obtained through many generations of controlled breeding.

purée (ˈpjʊəreɪ) n. **1.** a smooth thick pulp of sieved fruit, vegetables, meat, or fish.

~vb. **-reeing, -reed.** 2. to make (foods) into a purée. [French]

purgative ('pɜːɡətɪv) *Med.* ~n. 1. a medicine for purging the bowels. ~adj. 2. causing emptying of the bowels.

purgatory ('pɜːɡətrɪ) n. 1. *Chiefly R.C. Church.* a state or place in which the souls of those who have died undergo limited suffering for their sins on earth before they go to heaven. 2. a place or condition of temporary suffering or torment. [Latin *pūrgāre* to purify] —,purga'torial *adj.*

purge (pɜːdʒ) vb. 1. to rid (something) of (impure elements). 2. to rid (a state, organization, or political party) of (dissident people). 3. a. to empty (the bowels) by evacuation of faeces. b. to cause (a person) to evacuate his bowels. 4. a. to clear (a person) of a charge. b. to free (oneself) of guilt, as by atonement. 5. to be purified. ~n. 6. the act or process of purging. 7. the elimination of opponents or dissidents from a state, organization, or political party. 8. a purgative medicine. [Latin *pūrgāre* to purify]

purify ('pjʊərɪˌfaɪ) vb. **-fying, -fied.** 1. to free (something) of contaminating or debasing matter. 2. to free (a person) from sin or guilt. 3. to make clean, as in a ritual. [Latin *pūrus* pure + *facere* to make] —,purifi'cation n.

purism ('pjʊəˌrɪzəm) n. excessive insistence on the correctness of usage or style, as in grammar or art. —'purist *adj., n.* —pu'ristic *adj.*

puritan ('pjʊərɪt²n) n. 1. a person who adheres to strict moral or religious principles. ~adj. 2. characteristic of a puritan. [Late Latin *pūritās* purity] —'puritan,ism n.

Puritan ('pjʊərɪt²n) (in the late 16th and 17th centuries) ~n. 1. any of the extreme English Protestants who wished to purify the Church of England of most of its ceremony. ~adj. 2. of or relating to the Puritans. —'Puritan,ism n.

puritanical (ˌpjʊərɪˈtænɪk²l) adj. 1. *Usually disparaging.* strict in moral or religious outlook. 2. (*sometimes cap.*) of or relating to a puritan or the Puritans. —,puri'tanically adv.

purity ('pjʊərɪtɪ) n. the state or quality of being pure.

purl[1] (pɜːl) n. 1. a knitting stitch made by doing a plain stitch backwards. 2. a decorative border, as of lace. ~vb. 3. to knit in purl stitch. [dialect *pirl* to twist into a cord]

purl[2] (pɜːl) vb. (of a stream) to flow with a gentle swirling or rippling movement and a murmuring sound. [prob. imit.]

purlieu ('pɜːljuː) n. 1. *English history.* land on the edge of a royal forest. 2. (*usually pl.*) a neighbouring area; outskirts. 3. (*often pl.*) a place one frequents; haunt. [Anglo-French *puralé* a going through]

purlin *or* **purline** ('pɜːlɪn) n. a horizontal beam that supports the rafters of a roof. [origin unknown]

purloin (pɜːˈlɔɪn) vb. to steal. [Old French *porloigner* to put at a distance]

purple ('pɜːp²l) n. 1. a colour between red and blue. 2. cloth of this colour, often used to symbolize royalty or nobility. 3. the official robe of a cardinal. ~adj. 4. of the colour purple. 5. (of writing) excessively elaborate: *purple prose.* [Greek *porphura* the purple fish (murex)] —'purplish *adj.*

purple heart n. *Informal, chiefly Brit.* a heart-shaped purple tablet consisting mainly of amphetamine.

Purple Heart n. a decoration awarded to members of the U.S. Armed Forces for a wound received in action.

purport vb. (pɜːˈpɔːt) 1. to claim to be (true, official, etc.) by manner or appearance, esp. falsely. 2. (of speech or writing) to signify or imply. ~n. ('pɜːpɔːt) 3. meaning; significance. [Old French *porporter* to convey]

purpose ('pɜːpəs) n. 1. the reason for which anything is done, created, or exists. 2. a fixed design or idea that is the object of an action. 3. determination: *a man of purpose.* 4. practical advantage or use: *to work to good purpose.* 5. **on purpose.** intentionally. ~vb. 6. to intend or determine to do (something). [Old French *porposer* to plan]

purpose-built adj. made to serve a specific purpose.

purposeful ('pɜːpəsful) adj. with a fixed and definite purpose; determined. —'purposefully adv.

purposely ('pɜːpəslɪ) adv. on purpose.

purposive ('pɜːpəsɪv) adj. 1. having or indicating conscious intention. 2. useful.

purr (pɜː) vb. 1. (esp. of cats) to make a low vibrant sound, usually considered as expressing pleasure. 2. to express (pleasure) by this sound or by a sound suggestive of purring. ~n. 3. a purring sound. [imit.]

purse (pɜːs) n. 1. a small pouch for carrying money. 2. *U.S. & Canad.* a woman's handbag. 3. wealth; funds; resources. 4. a sum of money that is offered as a prize. ~vb. 5. to contract (the lips) into a small rounded shape. [Old English *purs*]

purser ('pɜːsə) n. an officer aboard a ship who keeps the accounts.

purse strings pl. n. **hold the purse strings.** to control the expenditure of a particular family, group, etc.

pursuance (pəˈsjuːəns) n. the carrying out of an action or plan.

pursue (pəˈsjuː) vb. **-suing, -sued.** 1. to follow (a person, vehicle, or animal) in order to capture or overtake. 2. to strive to attain (some desire or aim). 3. to follow the precepts of (a plan or policy). 4. to apply oneself to (studies or interests). 5. to follow persistently or seek to become acquainted with: *what a wonderful feeling to be loved and pursued!* 6. to continue to discuss or argue (a point or subject). [Old French *poursivre*] —pur'suer n.

pursuit (pəˈsjuːt) n. 1. the act of pursuing. 2. an occupation or pastime.

pursuivant (ˈpɜːsɪvənt) n. the lowest rank of heraldic officer. [Old French]

purulent (ˈpjʊərʊlənt) adj. of, relating to, or containing pus. [Latin *pūrulentus*] —**ˈpurulence** n.

purvey (pəˈveɪ) vb. to sell or provide (foodstuffs). [Old French *porveeir* to provide] —**purˈveyor** n.

purview (ˈpɜːvjuː) n. **1.** scope of operation. **2.** breadth or range of outlook. [Anglo-Norman *purveu*]

pus (pʌs) n. the yellowish fluid that comes from inflamed or infected tissue. [Latin]

push (pʊʃ) vb. **1.** (sometimes foll. by *off, away*, etc.) to apply steady force to in order to move. **2.** to thrust (one's way) through something, such as a crowd. **3.** (sometimes foll. by *for*) to be an advocate or promoter (of): *to push for acceptance of one's theories.* **4.** to spur or drive (oneself or another person) in order to achieve more effort or better results. **5.** *Informal.* to sell (narcotic drugs) illegally. ~n. **6.** the act of pushing; thrust. **7.** *Informal.* drive or determination. **8.** *Informal.* a special effort or attempt to get something done or finished. **9. the push.** *Informal, chiefly Brit.* dismissal from employment. ~See also **push about, push off,** etc. [Latin *pulsāre* to drive]

push about or **around** vb. *Informal.* to bully: *don't let them push you around.*

push-bike n. *Brit. informal.* a bicycle.

push button n. **1.** an electrical switch operated by pressing a button. ~*modifier.* **push-button. 2.** operated by a push button: *a push-button radio.*

pushchair (ˈpʊʃˌtʃɛə) n. *Brit.* a chair-shaped carriage for a small child.

pushed (pʊʃt) adj. (often foll. by *for*) *Informal.* short of: *pushed for time.*

pusher (ˈpʊʃə) n. *Informal.* a person who sells illegal drugs.

pushing (ˈpʊʃɪŋ) adv. **1.** almost or nearly (a certain age, speed, etc.): *pushing fifty.* ~adj. **2.** aggressively ambitious.

push off vb. *Informal.* to go away; leave.

pushover (ˈpʊʃˌəʊvə) n. *Informal.* **1.** something that is easily achieved. **2.** a person, team, etc., that is easily taken advantage of or defeated.

push-start vb. **1.** to start (a motor vehicle) by pushing it, thus turning the engine. ~n. **2.** this process.

push through vb. to compel to accept: *the bill was pushed through Parliament.*

pushy (ˈpʊʃɪ) adj. **pushier, pushiest.** *Informal.* offensively assertive or ambitious.

pusillanimous (ˌpjuːsɪˈlænɪməs) adj. timid and cowardly. [Latin *pusillus* weak + *animus* courage] —**pusillanimity** (ˌpjuːsɪləˈnɪmɪtɪ) n.

puss (pʊs) n. **1.** *Informal.* a cat. **2.** *Slang.* a girl or woman. [prob. Low German]

pussy[1] (ˈpʊsɪ) n., pl. **pussies. 1.** Also called: **pussycat.** *Informal.* a cat. **2.** *Taboo slang.* the female genitals. [from *puss*]

pussy[2] (ˈpʌsɪ) adj. **-sier, -siest.** containing or full of pus.

pussyfoot (ˈpʊsɪˌfʊt) vb. *Informal.* **1.** to

move about stealthily. **2.** to avoid committing oneself.

pussy willow (ˈpʊsɪ) n. a willow tree with silvery silky catkins.

pustulate (ˈpʌstjʊˌleɪt) vb. to form into pustules.

pustule (ˈpʌstjuːl) n. a small inflamed raised area of skin containing pus. [Latin *pustula* a blister] —**pustular** (ˈpʌstjʊlə) adj.

put (pʊt) vb. **putting, put. 1.** to cause to be (in a position or place): *to put a book on the table.* **2.** to cause to be (in a state, relation, or condition): *to put one's things in order.* **3.** to lay (blame, emphasis, trust, etc.) on a person or thing: *I put the blame on him.* **4.** to set or commit (to an action, task, or duty), esp. by force: *he put him to work.* **5.** (foll. by *at*) to estimate: *he put the distance at fifty miles.* **6.** (foll. by *to*) to utilize: *he put his knowledge to use.* **7.** to express: *to put it bluntly.* **8.** to make (an end or limit): *he put an end to the proceedings.* **9.** to present for consideration; propose: *he put the question to the committee.* **10.** to invest (money) in or expend (time or energy) on: *he put five thousand pounds into the project.* **11.** to throw or cast: *put the shot.* ~n. **12.** a throw, esp. in putting the shot. ~See also **put about, put across,** etc. [Middle English *puten* to push]

put about vb. **1.** to make widely known: *he put about the news of the air disaster.* **2.** *Naut.* to change course.

put across vb. to communicate comprehensively: *he couldn't put things across very well.*

put aside vb. **1.** to save: *to put money aside for a rainy day.* **2.** to disregard: *let us put aside our differences.*

putative (ˈpjuːtətɪv) adj. **1.** commonly regarded as being: *the putative father.* **2.** considered to exist or have existed; inferred: *a putative earlier form.* [Latin *putāre* to consider]

put away vb. **1.** to save: *to put away money for the future.* **2.** to lock up in a prison, mental institution, etc.: *they put him away for twenty years.* **3.** to eat or drink in large amounts.

put back vb. **1.** to return to its former place. **2.** to move to a later time: *the wedding was put back a fortnight.*

put down vb. **1.** to make a written record of. **2.** to repress: *to put down a rebellion.* **3.** to consider: *they put him down for an ignoramus.* **4.** to attribute: *the mistake was put down to inexperience.* **5.** to put (an animal) to death. **6.** *Slang.* to belittle or humiliate. ~n. **put-down. 7.** a cruelly crushing remark.

put forward vb. **1.** to propose; suggest. **2.** to offer the name of; nominate.

put in vb. **1.** to devote (time or effort): *he put in three hours overtime last night.* **2.** (often foll. by *for*) to apply (for a job). **3.** to submit: *he put in his claims form.* **4.** *Naut.* to bring a vessel into port.

put off vb. **1.** to postpone: *they have put off the dance until tomorrow.* **2.** to evade (a person) by postponement or delay: *they tried to put him off, but he came anyway.* **3.** to cause aversion: *he was put off by her appearance.* **4.** to cause to lose interest in: *the accident put him off driving.*

put on *vb.* **1.** to clothe oneself in. **2.** to adopt (an attitude or feeling) insincerely: *his misery was just put on.* **3.** to present (a play or show). **4.** to add: *she put on weight.* **5.** to cause (an electrical device) to function. **6.** to wager (money) on a horse race or game. **7.** to impose: *to put a tax on cars.*

put out *vb.* **1. a.** to annoy; anger. **b.** to disturb; confuse. **2.** to extinguish (something, such as a fire or light). **3.** to be a source of inconvenience to: *I hope I'm not putting you out.* **4.** to publish; broadcast: *the authorities put out a leaflet.* **5.** to dislocate: *he put out his shoulder in the accident.* **6.** *Cricket, etc.* to dismiss (a player or team).

put over *vb. Informal.* to communicate (facts or information).

putrefy ('pju:trɪˌfaɪ) *vb.* **-fying, -fied.** (of organic matter) to rot and produce an offensive smell. [Latin *putrefacere*] —**putrefaction** (ˌpju:trɪ'fækʃən) *n.*

putrescent (pju:'tres°nt) *adj.* becoming putrid; rotting. [Latin *putrescere* to become rotten] —**pu'trescence** *n.*

putrid ('pju:trɪd) *adj.* **1.** (of organic matter) in a state of decomposition: *putrid meat.* **2.** morally corrupt. **3.** sickening; foul: *a putrid smell.* **4.** *Informal.* deficient in quality or value: *a putrid film.* [Latin *putrēre* to be rotten] —**pu'tridity** *n.*

putsch (putʃ) *n.* a violent and sudden political revolt. [from German]

putt (pʌt) *Golf.* ~*n.* **1.** a stroke on the green with a putter to roll the ball into or near the hole. ~*vb.* **2.** to strike (the ball) in this way. [Scot.]

puttee ('pʌtɪ) *n.* (*often pl.*) a strip of cloth worn wound around the leg from the ankle to the knee. [Hindi *paṭṭī*]

putter ('pʌtə) *n. Golf.* a club with a short shaft for putting.

put through *vb.* **1.** to carry out to a conclusion: *he put through his plan.* **2.** to connect by telephone.

putting green ('pʌtɪŋ) *n.* (on a golf course) the area of closely mown grass where the hole is.

putty ('pʌtɪ) *n., pl.* **-ties.** **1.** a stiff paste made of whiting and linseed oil used to fix glass into frames and fill cracks in woodwork. ~*vb.* **-tying, -tied.** **2.** to fix or fill with putty. [French *potée* a potful]

put up *vb.* **1.** to build; erect: *to put up a statue.* **2.** to accommodate or be accommodated at: *can you put me up for tonight?* **3.** to increase (prices). **4.** to submit (a plan, case, etc.). **5.** to offer: *to put a house up for sale.* **6.** to give: *to put up a good fight.* **7.** to provide (money) for: *they put up five thousand for the new project.* **8.** to nominate or be nominated as a candidate: *he put up for president.* **9. put up to.** to incite to: *I wonder who put them up to it.* **10. put up with.** *Informal.* to endure;

tolerate. ~*adj.* **put-up. 11.** dishonestly or craftily prearranged: *a put-up job.*

put upon *vb.* to presume on (a person's generosity or good nature): *he's always being put upon.*

puzzle ('pʌz°l) *vb.* **1.** to perplex or be perplexed. **2. puzzle out.** to solve (a problem) by mental effort. **3. puzzle over.** to ponder about the cause of: *he puzzled over her absence.* ~*n.* **4.** a problem that cannot be easily solved. **5.** a toy, game, or question presenting a problem that requires skill or ingenuity for its solution. [origin unknown] —**'puzzlement** *n.* —**'puzzler** *n.* —**'puzzling** *adj.*

PVC polyvinyl chloride.

PW policewoman.

PWR pressurized-water reactor.

pyaemia or **pyemia** (paɪ'i:mɪə) *n.* blood poisoning characterized by pus-forming microorganisms in the blood. [Greek *puon* pus + *haima* blood]

pye-dog, pie-dog, or **pi-dog** ('paɪˌdɒg) *n.* an ownerless half-wild Asian dog. [Hindi *pāhī* outsider]

pygmy ('pɪgmɪ) *n., pl.* **-mies.** **1.** an abnormally undersized person. **2.** something that is a very small example of its type. **3.** a person of little importance or significance. **4.** (*modifier*) very small. [Greek *pugmaios* undersized]

Pygmy ('pɪgmɪ) *n., pl.* **-mies.** a member of one of the dwarf peoples of Equatorial Africa.

pyjamas or *U.S.* **pajamas** (pə'dʒɑːməz) *pl. n.* loose-fitting nightclothes comprising a jacket or top and trousers. [Persian *pai* leg + *jāma* garment]

pylon ('paɪlən) *n.* a large vertical steel tower-like structure supporting high-tension electrical cables. [Greek *pulōn* a gateway]

pyorrhoea or *esp. U.S.* **pyorrhea** (ˌpaɪə'rɪə) *n.* a discharge of pus, esp. in disease of the gums or tooth sockets. [Greek *puon* pus + *rhein* to flow]

pyramid ('pɪrəmɪd) *n.* **1.** a huge masonry construction that has a square base and, as in the ancient Egyptian royal tombs, four sloping triangular sides. **2.** *Maths.* a solid figure having a polygonal base and triangular sides that meet in a common vertex. [Greek *puramis*] —**pyramidal** (pɪ'ræmɪd°l) *adj.*

pyramid selling *n.* the practice of selling distributors batches of goods which they then subdivide and sell to other distributors. This process continues until the final distributors are left with a stock that is unsaleable except at a loss.

pyre ('paɪə) *n.* a pile of wood for cremating a corpse. [Greek *pur* fire]

pyrethrum (paɪ'ri:θrəm) *n.* **1.** a Eurasian chrysanthemum with white, pink, red, or purple flowers. **2.** an insecticide prepared from the dried flowers. [Greek *purethron*]

pyretic (paɪ'retɪk) *adj. Pathol.* of, relating to, or characterized by fever. [Greek *puretos* fever]

Pyrex ('paɪreks) *n. Trademark.* a variety

of heat-resistant glassware used in cookery and chemical apparatus.

pyrite ('paɪraɪt) *n.* a yellow mineral consisting of iron sulphide in cubic crystalline form. Formula: FeS_2 [Latin *pyrites* flint]

pyrites (paɪ'raɪtiːz; *in combination* 'paɪraɪts) *n., pl.* **-tes.** **1.** same as **pyrite.** **2.** any of a number of other disulphides of metals, esp. of copper and tin.

pyromania (ˌpaɪrəʊ'meɪnɪə) *n. Psychiatry.* the uncontrollable impulse and practice of setting things on fire. [Greek *pur* fire + *mania* madness] —ˌpyro'mani,ac *n., adj.*

pyrotechnics (ˌpaɪrəʊ'tɛknɪks) *n.* **1.** (*functioning as sing.*) the art of making fireworks. **2.** (*functioning as sing. or pl.*) a firework display. **3.** (*functioning as sing. or pl.*) brilliance of display, as in the performance of music. [Greek *pur* fire + *tekhnē* art] —ˌpyro'technic *adj.*

Pyrrhic victory ('pɪrɪk) *n.* a victory in which the victor's losses are as great as those of the defeated. [after *Pyrrhus*, who defeated the Romans in 279 B.C. but suffered heavy losses]

Pythagoras' theorem (paɪ'θægərəs) *n.* the theorem that in a right-angled triangle the square of the length of the hypotenuse equals the sum of the squares of the other two sides. [after *Pythagoras*, Greek philosopher and mathematician]

python ('paɪθən) *n.* a large nonvenomous snake of Africa, S Asia, and Australia. It kills its prey by constriction. [after *Python*, a dragon killed by Apollo]

pyx (pɪks) *n. Christianity.* any receptacle in which the Eucharistic Host is kept. [Latin *pyxis* small box]

Q

q *or* **Q** (kjuː) *n., pl.* **q's, Q's,** *or* **Qs.** the 17th letter of the English alphabet.

Q 1. *Chess.* queen. 2. question.

q. 1. quart. 2. quarter. 3. question. 4. quire.

Q. 1. Quebec. 2. Queen. 3. question.

QC Queen's Counsel.

QED which was to be shown or proved [Latin *quod erat demonstrandum*]

QM Quartermaster.

qr., *pl.* **qrs.** 1. quarter. 2. quire.

qt, *pl.* **qt** *or* **qts** quart.

q.t. on the q.t. *Informal.* secretly.

qua (kwɑː) *prep.* in the capacity of; by virtue of being. [Latin]

quack[1] (kwæk) *vb.* 1. (of a duck) to utter a harsh guttural sound. 2. to make a noise like a duck. ~*n.* 3. the sound made by a duck. [imit.]

quack[2] (kwæk) *n.* 1. an unqualified person who claims medical knowledge. 2. *Brit., Austral., & N.Z. informal.* a doctor. [short for *quacksalver*, from Dutch] —**'quackery** *n.*

quad[1] (kwɒd) *n.* short for **quadrangle** (sense 2).

quad[2] (kwɒd) *n. Informal.* a quadruplet.

quad[3] (kwɒd) *n.* 1. short for **quadraphonics.** ~*adj.* 2. short for **quadraphonic.**

Quadragesima (ˌkwɒdrəˈdʒɛsɪmə) *n.* the first Sunday in Lent. [Medieval Latin *quadragésima dies* the fortieth day]

quadrangle (ˈkwɒdˌræŋɡ'l) *n.* 1. *Geom.* a plane figure consisting of four points connected by four lines. 2. a rectangular courtyard with buildings on all four sides. [Late Latin *quadrangulum*] —**quadrangular** (kwɒˈdræŋɡjʊlə) *adj.*

quadrant (ˈkwɒdrənt) *n.* 1. *Geom.* **a.** a quarter of the circumference of a circle. **b.** the area enclosed by two perpendicular radii of a circle. 2. a piece of a mechanism in the form of a quarter circle. 3. an instrument formerly used in astronomy and navigation for measuring the altitudes of stars. [Latin *quadrāns* a quarter]

quadraphonic (ˌkwɒdrəˈfɒnɪk) *adj.* using four independent channels to reproduce or record sound. —**quadraˈphonics** *n.*

quadrate (ˈkwɒdreɪt) *n.* 1. a cube or square, or a square or cubelike object. ~*vb.* 2. to make square or rectangular. [Latin *quadrāre* to make square]

quadratic (kwɒˈdrætɪk) *Maths.* ~*n.* 1. Also called: **quadratic equation.** an equation in which the variable is raised to the power of two, but nowhere raised to a higher power: *solve the quadratic equation* $2x^2 - 3x - 6 = 3$. ~*adj.* 2. of or relating to the second power.

quadrennial (kwɒˈdrɛnɪəl) *adj.* 1. occurring every four years. 2. lasting four years.

quadri- *or before a vowel* **quadr-** *combining form:* four: *quadrilateral.* [Latin]

quadrilateral (ˌkwɒdrɪˈlætərəl) *adj.* 1. having four sides. ~*n.* 2. a polygon having four sides.

quadrille (kwəˈdrɪl) *n.* 1. a square dance for four couples. 2. music for this dance. [Spanish *cuadrilla*]

quadrillion (kwəˈdrɪljən) *n.* 1. (in Britain, France, and Germany) the number represented as one followed by 24 zeros (10^{24}). 2. (in the U.S. and Canada) the number represented as one followed by 15 zeros (10^{15}). [French *quadrillon*]

quadriplegia (ˌkwɒdrɪˈpliːdʒɪə) *n.* paralysis of all four limbs. [*quadri-* + Greek *plēssein* to strike] —**ˌquadriˈplegic** *adj., n.*

quadruped (ˈkwɒdrʊˌpɛd) *n.* an animal, esp. a mammal, that has all four limbs specialized for walking. [Latin *quadru-* four + *pēs* foot]

quadruple (ˈkwɒdrʊp'l, kwɒˈdruːp'l) *vb.* 1. to multiply by four. ~*adj.* 2. four times as much or as many. 3. consisting of four parts. 4. *Music.* having four beats in each bar. ~*n.* 5. a quantity or number four times as great as another. [Latin *quadru-* four + *-plus* -fold]

quadruplet (ˈkwɒdrʊplɪt, kwɒˈdruːplɪt) *n.* one of four offspring born at one birth.

quadruplicate *adj.* (kwɒˈdruːplɪkɪt). 1. fourfold or quadruple. ~*vb.* (kwɒˈdruːplɪˌkeɪt). 2. to multiply or be multiplied by four. [Latin *quadruplicāre* to increase fourfold]

quaff (kwɒf) *vb.* to drink heartily or in one draught. [perhaps imit.]

quagga (ˈkwæɡə) *n., pl.* **-gas** *or* **-ga.** a recently extinct zebra, striped only on the head and shoulders. [Hottentot *quagga*]

quagmire (ˈkwæɡˌmaɪə) *n.* a soft wet area of land that gives way under the feet; bog. [from *quag* bog + *mire*]

quail[1] (kweɪl) *n., pl.* **quails** *or* **quail.** a small game bird of the partridge family. [Old French *quaille*]

quail[2] (kweɪl) *vb.* to shrink back with fear; cower. [origin unknown]

quaint (kweɪnt) *adj.* attractively unusual, esp. in an old-fashioned style. [Old French *cointe*, from Latin *cognitus* known]

quake (kweɪk) *vb.* 1. to shake or tremble with or as with fear. 2. to convulse or quiver, as from instability. ~*n.* 3. a quaking. 4. *Informal.* an earthquake. [Old English *cwacian*]

Quaker (ˈkweɪkə) *n.* a member of a Christian sect, the Society of Friends. [orig. an offensive nickname] —**ˈQuakerism** *n.*

qualification (ˌkwɒlɪfɪˈkeɪʃən) *n.* 1. an ability, quality, or attribute, esp. one that fits a person to perform a particular job or task. 2. a condition that modifies or limits;

restriction. **3.** a qualifying or being qualified.

qualified ('kwɒlɪˌfaɪd) *adj.* **1.** having the abilities, qualities, or attributes necessary to perform a particular job or task. **2.** limited, modified, or restricted: *qualified praise.*

qualify ('kwɒlɪˌfaɪ) *vb.* **-fying, -fied. 1.** to provide or be provided with the abilities or attributes necessary for a task, office or duty: *his degree qualifies him for the job.* **2.** to moderate or restrict (something, esp. a statement). **3.** *Grammar.* to modify the sense of a word. See **modifier. 4.** to attribute a quality to; characterize: *the accident qualified as news.* **5.** to progress to the final stages of a competition, as by winning preliminary contests. [Latin *quālis* of what kind + *facere* to make] —'quali̱ˌfier *n.*

qualitative ('kwɒlɪtətɪv) *adj.* involving or relating to distinctions based on quality.

qualitative analysis *n. Chem.* analysis of a substance to determine its constituents.

quality ('kwɒlɪtɪ) *n., pl.* **-ties. 1.** a distinguishing characteristic or attribute. **2.** the basic character or nature of something. **3.** a feature of personality. **4.** degree or standard of excellence. **5.** (formerly) high social status. **6.** musical tone colour; timbre. **7.** (*modifier*) excellent or superior: *a quality product.* [Latin *quālis* of what sort]

quality control *n.* control of the relative quality of a manufactured product, usually by testing samples.

qualm (kwɑːm) *n.* **1.** a sudden feeling of sickness or nausea. **2.** a pang of conscience; scruple. **3.** a sudden sensation of misgiving. [Old English *cwealm* death or plague]

quandary ('kwɒndrɪ) *n., pl.* **-ries.** a difficult situation; predicament; dilemma. [origin unknown]

quango ('kwæŋgəʊ) *n., pl.* **-gos.** quasi-autonomous nongovernmental organization.

quantify ('kwɒntɪˌfaɪ) *vb.* **-fying, -fied.** to discover or express the quantity of. [Latin *quantus* how much + *facere* to make] —'quanti̱ˌfiable *adj.* —ˌquantifi'ca-tion *n.*

quantitative ('kwɒntɪtətɪv) *adj.* **1.** involving considerations of amount or size. **2.** capable of being measured.

quantitative analysis *n. Chem.* analysis of a substance to determine the proportions of its constituents.

quantity ('kwɒntɪtɪ) *n., pl.* **-ties. 1.** a specified or definite amount or number. **2.** the aspect of anything that can be measured, weighed, or counted. **3.** a large amount. **4.** *Maths.* an entity having a magnitude that may be denoted by a numerical expression. [Latin *quantus* how much]

quantity surveyor *n.* a person who estimates the cost of the materials and labour necessary for a construction job.

quantum ('kwɒntəm) *n., pl.* **-ta** (-tə). **1.**

Physics. the smallest quantity of some physical property that a system can possess. **2.** amount or quantity, esp. a specific amount. ~*adj.* **3.** of or designating a major breakthrough or sudden advance: *a quantum leap forward.* [Latin *quantus* how much]

quantum theory *n.* a theory concerning the behaviour of physical systems based on the idea that they can only possess certain properties, such as energy and angular momentum, in discrete amounts (quanta).

quarantine ('kwɒrənˌtiːn) *n.* **1.** a period of isolation, esp. of persons or animals arriving from abroad, to prevent the spread of disease. ~*vb.* **2.** to isolate in or as if in quarantine. [Italian *quarantina* period of forty days]

quark (kwɑːk) *n. Physics.* the hypothetical elementary particle postulated to be a fundamental unit of all baryons and mesons. [coined by James Joyce in the novel *Finnegans Wake*]

quarrel ('kwɒrəl) *n.* **1.** an angry disagreement; argument. **2.** a cause of dispute; grievance. ~*vb.* **-relling, -relled** or *U.S.* **-reling, -reled.** (often foll. by *with*) **3.** to engage in a disagreement or dispute; argue. **4.** to find fault; complain. [Latin *querēlla* complaint]

quarrelsome ('kwɒrəlsəm) *adj.* inclined to quarrel or disagree.

quarry[1] ('kwɒrɪ) *n., pl.* **-ries. 1.** a place where stone is dug from the surface of the earth. ~*vb.* **-rying, -ried. 2.** to extract (stone) from a quarry. [Old French *quarriere*]

quarry[2] ('kwɒrɪ) *n., pl.* **-ries. 1.** an animal that is being hunted; prey. **2.** anything pursued. [Middle English *quirre* entrails offered to the hounds]

quarry tile *n.* an unglazed floor tile.

quart (kwɔːt) *n.* a unit of liquid measure equal to a quarter of a gallon or two pints (1.136 litres). [Latin *quartus* fourth]

quarter ('kwɔːtə) *n.* **1.** one of four equal parts of something such as an object or quantity. **2.** the fraction equal to one divided by four (¼). **3.** *U.S. & Canad.* a 25-cent piece. **4.** a unit of weight equal to a quarter of a hundredweight. **5.** short for **quarter-hour. 6.** a fourth part of a year; three months. **7.** *Astron.* **a.** one fourth of the moon's period of revolution around the earth. **b.** either of two phases of the moon when half of the lighted surface is visible. **8.** *Informal.* a unit of weight equal to a quarter of a pound or 4 ounces. **9.** a region or district of a town or city: *the Spanish quarter.* **10.** a region, direction, or point of the compass. **11.** (*sometimes pl.*) an unspecified person or group of people: *the highest quarters.* **12.** mercy or pity, as shown to a defeated opponent: *he would give no quarter.* **13.** any of the four limbs of a quadruped. ~*vb.* **14.** to divide into four equal parts. **15.** (formerly) to dismember (a human body). **16.** to billet or be billeted in lodgings. **17.** *Heraldry.* to divide (a shield) into four separate bearings. ~*adj.* **18.** being or consisting of one of four equal parts. ~See also **quarters.** [Latin *quartus* fourth]

quarterback ('kwɔːtəˌbæk) *n.* a player in American football who directs attacking play.

quarter day *n.* any of four days in the year when certain payments become due.

quarterdeck ('kwɔːtəˌdɛk) *n. Naut.* the after part of the upper deck of a ship, traditionally for official or ceremonial use.

quarterfinal (ˌkwɔːtə'faɪn'l) *n.* the round before the semifinal in a competition.

quarter-hour *n.* **1.** a period of 15 minutes. **2.** either of the points of time 15 minutes before or after the hour.

quarterlight ('kwɔːtəˌlaɪt) *n. Brit.* a small pivoted window in the door of a car.

quarterly ('kwɔːtəlɪ) *adj.* **1.** occurring, done, due, or issued at intervals of three months. ~*n., pl.* **-lies. 2.** a periodical issued every three months. ~*adv.* **3.** once every three months.

quartermaster ('kwɔːtəˌmɑːstə) *n.* **1.** a military officer responsible for accommodation, food, and equipment. **2.** a naval officer responsible for navigation.

quarters ('kwɔːtəz) *pl. n.* **1.** accommodation, esp. as provided for military personnel. **2.** the stations assigned to crew members of a warship: *general quarters.*

quarter sessions *n. (functioning as sing. or pl.)* (formerly) a court with limited jurisdiction, held four times a year.

quarterstaff ('kwɔːtəˌstɑːf) *n., pl.* **-staves** (-ˌsteɪvz). a stout iron-tipped wooden staff about 6ft. long, formerly used as a weapon. [origin unknown]

quartet (kwɔː'tɛt) *n.* **1.** a group of four singers or instrumentalists or a piece of music composed for such a group. **2.** any group of four. [Italian *quarto* fourth]

quarto ('kwɔːtəʊ) *n., pl.* **-tos.** a book size resulting from folding a sheet of paper into four leaves or eight pages. [New Latin *quartō* in quarter]

quartz (kwɔːts) *n.* a hard glossy mineral consisting of crystalline silicon dioxide. [German *Quarz*]

quartz clock *or* **watch** *n.* a clock or watch that is operated by a vibrating quartz crystal.

quartz crystal *n.* a thin plate or rod cut from a piece of quartz and ground so that it vibrates at a particular frequency.

quasar ('kweɪzɑː, -sɑː) *n.* any of a class of extremely distant starlike objects that are powerful sources of radio waves and other forms of energy. [*quas(i-stell)ar (radio source)*]

quash (kwɒʃ) *vb.* **1.** to subdue forcefully and completely. **2.** to annul or make void (something, such as a law). **3.** to reject (something, for instance an indictment) as invalid. [Latin *quassāre* to shake]

quasi- *combining form.* **1.** almost but not really; seemingly: *a quasi-religious cult.* **2.** resembling but not actually being; so-called: *a quasi-scholar.* [Latin: as if]

quassia ('kwɒʃə) *n.* **1.** a tropical American tree with bitter bark and wood. **2.** the

wood of this tree or a bitter compound extracted from it, used in insecticides. [after Graman *Quassi*, who discovered its medicinal value]

quaternary (kwə'tɜːnərɪ) *adj.* consisting of fours or by fours. [Latin *quattuor* four]

Quaternary (kwə'tɜːnərɪ) *adj. Geol.* of the most recent period of geological time, which started about one million years ago.

quatrain ('kwɒtreɪn) *n.* a stanza or poem of four lines. [French, from Latin *quattuor* four]

quatrefoil ('kætrəˌfɔɪl) *n.* **1.** a leaf composed of four leaflets. **2.** *Archit.* a carved ornament of four arcs about a common centre. [Old French *quatre* four + *-foil* leaflet]

quattrocento (ˌkwætrəʊ'tʃɛntəʊ) *n.* the 15th century, esp. in reference to Renaissance Italian art. [Italian: four hundred (short for fourteen hundred)]

quaver ('kweɪvə) *vb.* **1.** (esp. of the voice) to quiver or tremble. **2.** to say or sing (something) with a trembling voice. ~*n.* **3.** *Music.* a note having the time value of an eighth of a semibreve. **4.** a tremulous sound or note. [Germanic] —'**quavering** *adj.*

quay (kiː) *n.* a wharf built parallel to the shoreline. [Old French *kai*]

Que. Quebec.

queasy ('kwiːzɪ) *adj.* **-sier, -siest. 1.** having the feeling that one is about to vomit; nauseous. **2.** feeling or causing uneasiness. [origin unknown] —'**queasily** *adv.* —'**queasiness** *n.*

queen (kwiːn) *n.* **1.** a female sovereign who is the official ruler or head of state. **2.** the wife of a king. **3.** a woman, thing, or place considered the best or most important of her or its kind: *the queen of ocean liners.* **4.** *Slang.* an effeminate male homosexual. **5.** the only fertile female in a colony of bees, wasps, or ants. **6.** a playing card bearing the picture of a queen. **7.** the most powerful chess piece, able to move in a straight line in any direction. ~*vb.* **8.** *Chess.* to promote (a pawn) to a queen when it reaches the eighth rank. **9. queen it.** (often foll. by *over*) *Informal.* to behave in an overbearing manner. [Old English *cwēn*] —'**queenly** *adj.*

Queen-Anne (ˌkwiːn'æn) *n.* an 18th-century style of furniture characterized by the use of curves.

queen consort *n.* the wife of a reigning king.

queen mother *n.* the widow of a former king who is also the mother of the reigning sovereign.

queen post *n.* one of a pair of vertical posts that connect the tie beam of a truss to the principal rafters.

Queen's Bench *n.* one of the divisions of the High Court of Justice.

Queensberry rules ('kwiːnzbərɪ) *pl. n.* the code of rules followed in modern boxing. [after the ninth Marquess of *Queensberry*, who originated the rules]

Queen's Counsel *n.* **1.** (in Britain) a barrister or advocate appointed Counsel to the Crown. **2.** (in Canada) an honorary title bestowed on lawyers with long experience.

Queen's English *n.* standard Southern British English.

queen's evidence *n. English law.* evidence given for the Crown against his former associates in crime by an accomplice.

Queen's Guide *or* **Scout** *n.* a Guide or Scout who has passed the highest tests of proficiency.

queen's highway *n.* **1.** (in Britain) any public road or right of way. **2.** (in Canada) a main road maintained by the provincial government.

queer (kwɪə) *adj.* **1.** not normal or usual; odd or strange. **2.** dubious; shady. **3.** faint, giddy, or queasy. **4.** *Informal, offensive.* homosexual. **5.** *Informal.* eccentric or slightly mad. ~*n.* **6.** *Informal, offensive.* a homosexual. ~*vb.* **7. queer someone's pitch.** *Informal.* to spoil or thwart someone's chances of something. [origin unknown]

queer street *n.* **in queer street.** *Informal.* in a difficult situation, such as debt or bankruptcy.

quell (kwɛl) *vb.* **1.** to suppress (rebellion or unrest); subdue. **2.** to overcome or allay. [Old English *cwellan* to kill]

quench (kwɛntʃ) *vb.* **1.** to satisfy (one's thirst); slake. **2.** to put out; extinguish. **3.** to suppress or subdue. **4.** to cool (hot metal) by plunging it into cold water. [Old English *ācwencan* to extinguish]

quern (kwɜːn) *n.* a stone hand mill for grinding corn. [Old English *cweorn*]

querulous (ˈkwɛrjʊləs) *adj.* complaining; whining or peevish. [Latin *querī* to complain] —**ˈquerulously** *adv.*

query (ˈkwɪərɪ) *n., pl.* **-ries.** **1.** a question, esp. one expressing doubt. **2.** a question mark. ~*vb.* **-rying, -ried.** **3.** to express uncertainty, doubt, or an objection concerning (something). **4.** to express as a query. [Latin *quaere* ask!]

quest (kwɛst) *n.* **1.** a looking for or seeking; search. **2.** the object of a search; a goal or target. ~*vb.* **3.** (foll. by *for* or *after*) to go in search of. **4.** to search for game. [Old French *queste*]

question (ˈkwɛstʃən) *n.* **1.** a form of words addressed to a person in order to obtain an answer; interrogative sentence. **2.** a point at issue: *it's only a question of time.* **3.** a difficulty or uncertainty. **4. a.** an act of asking. **b.** an investigation into some problem. **5.** a motion presented for debate. **6. beyond (all) question.** beyond (any) doubt. **7. call something into question. a.** to make something the subject of disagreement. **b.** to cast doubt upon the validity or truth of something. **8. in question.** under discussion: *this is the man in question.* **9. out of the question.** beyond consideration; impossible. ~*vb.* **10.** to put a question or questions to (a person); interrogate. **11.** to make (something) the subject of dispute. **12.** to express uncertainty; doubt. [Latin *quaestiō*]

questionable (ˈkwɛstʃənəbᵊl) *adj.* **1.** (esp. of a person's morality or honesty) dubious. **2.** of disputable value or authority. —**ˈquestionably** *adv.*

questioning (ˈkwɛstʃənɪŋ) *adj.* **1.** proceeding from or characterized by doubt or uncertainty. **2.** intellectually inquisitive: *a questioning mind.* ~*n.* **3.** interrogation.

question mark *n.* **1.** the punctuation mark ?, used at the end of questions. **2.** a doubt or uncertainty: *a question mark still hangs over their success.*

question master *n. Brit.* the chairman of a radio or television quiz or panel game.

questionnaire (ˌkwɛstʃəˈnɛə, ˌkɛs-) *n.* a set of questions on a form, used to collect statistical information or opinions from people.

question time *n.* (in parliamentary bodies of the British type) the time set aside each day for questions to government ministers.

queue (kjuː) *Chiefly Brit.* ~*n.* **1.** a line of people or vehicles waiting for something. ~*vb.* **queueing** *or* **queuing, queued.** **2.** (often foll. by *up*) to form or remain in a line while waiting. [Latin *cauda* tail]

quibble (ˈkwɪbᵊl) *vb.* **1.** to make trivial objections. ~*n.* **2.** a trivial objection or equivocation, esp. one used to avoid an issue. **3.** *Archaic.* a pun. [origin unknown]

quiche (kiːʃ) *n.* a savoury flan with an egg custard filling to which cheese, bacon, or vegetables are added. [French]

quick (kwɪk) *adj.* **1.** lasting or taking a short time. **2.** characterized by rapidity of movement or action; fast. **3.** immediate or prompt. **4.** eager or ready to perform (an action): *quick to criticize.* **5.** responsive to stimulation; alert; lively. **6.** easily excited or aroused. **7.** nimble in one's movements or actions; deft: *quick fingers.* ~*n.* **8.** any area of sensitive flesh, esp. that under a nail. **9. cut someone to the quick.** to hurt someone's feelings deeply. **10. the quick.** *Archaic.* living people. ~*adv.* **11.** *Informal.* in a rapid manner; swiftly. [Old English *cwicu* living] —**ˈquickly** *adv.*

quick-change artist *n.* an actor or entertainer who undertakes several rapid changes of costume during a performance.

quicken (ˈkwɪkən) *vb.* **1.** to make or become faster; accelerate. **2.** to impart to or receive vigour or enthusiasm: *science quickens the imagination.* **3. a.** (of a fetus) to begin to show signs of life. **b.** (of a pregnant woman) to reach the stage of pregnancy at which movements of the fetus can be felt.

quick-freeze *vb.* **-freezing, -froze, -frozen.** to preserve (food) by subjecting it to rapid refrigeration.

quickie (ˈkwɪkɪ) *n. Informal.* anything made or done rapidly.

quicklime (ˈkwɪkˌlaɪm) *n.* a white caustic solid, mainly composed of calcium oxide, used in the manufacture of glass and steel.

quicksand (ˈkwɪkˌsænd) *n.* a deep mass of loose wet sand that sucks anything on top of it inextricably into it.

quickset (ˈkwɪkˌsɛt) *Chiefly Brit.* ~*adj.*

1. (of plants or cuttings) set so as to form a hedge. ~*n.* **2.** a hedge composed of such plants.

quicksilver ('kwɪkˌsɪlvə) *n.* the metal mercury.

quickstep ('kwɪkˌstɛp) *n.* **1.** a modern ballroom dance in rapid quadruple time. **2.** music for this dance.

quick-tempered *adj.* easy to anger.

quick-witted *adj.* having a keenly alert mind. —ˌquick-ˈwittedness *n.*

quid[1] (kwɪd) *n., pl.* **quid.** *Brit. slang.* **1.** a pound (sterling). **2. be quids in.** to be in a very favourable or advantageous position. [origin unknown]

quid[2] (kwɪd) *n.* a piece of tobacco for chewing. [Old English *cwidu* chewing resin]

quiddity ('kwɪdɪtɪ) *n., pl.* **-ties.** **1.** the essential nature of something. **2.** a petty or trifling distinction. [Latin *quid* what]

quid pro quo ('kwɪd prəʊ 'kwəʊ) *n., pl.* **quid pro quos.** one thing, esp. an advantage or object, given in exchange for another. [Latin: something for something]

quiescent (kwɪ'ɛsˀnt) *adj.* quiet, inactive, or dormant. [Latin *quiescere* to rest] —quiˈescence *n.*

quiet ('kwaɪət) *adj.* **1.** characterized by an absence of noise. **2.** calm or tranquil: *the sea is quiet tonight.* **3.** untroubled: *a quiet life.* **4.** not busy: *business is quiet today.* **5.** private; secret: *a quiet word with someone.* **6.** free from anger, impatience, or other extreme emotion. **7.** not showy: *quiet colours; a quiet wedding.* **8.** modest or reserved: *quiet humour.* ~*n.* **9.** the state of being silent, peaceful, or untroubled. **10. on the quiet.** without other people knowing. ~*vb.* **11.** to make or become calm or silent. [Latin *quiēs* repose] —ˈquietly *adv.*

quieten ('kwaɪətˀn) *vb. Chiefly Brit.* **1.** (often foll. by *down*) to make or become calm or silent. **2.** to allay (fear or doubts).

quietism ('kwaɪəˌtɪzəm) *n.* passivity and calmness of mind towards external events. —ˈquietist *n., adj.*

quietude ('kwaɪəˌtjuːd) *n.* quietness, peace, or tranquillity.

quietus (kwaɪ'iːtəs, -'ɛɪtəs) *n., pl.* **-tuses.** **1.** a release from life; death. **2.** the discharge or settlement of debts or duties. [Latin *quiētus est,* lit.: he is at rest]

quiff (kwɪf) *n. Brit.* a tuft of hair brushed up above the forehead. [origin unknown]

quill (kwɪl) *n.* **1. a.** any of the large stiff feathers of the wing or tail of a bird. **b.** the hollow stem of a feather. **2.** Also called: **quill pen.** a feather made into a pen. **3.** any of the stiff hollow spines of a porcupine or hedgehog. [origin unknown]

quilt (kwɪlt) *n.* **1.** a cover for a bed, consisting of a soft filling sewn between two layers of material, usually with crisscross seams. **2.** a continental quilt; duvet. ~*vb.* **3.** to stitch together (two pieces of fabric) with (padding) between them. [Old French *coilte* mattress] —ˈquilted *adj.*

quin (kwɪn) *n.* a quintuplet.

quince (kwɪns) *n.* the acid-tasting pear-shaped fruit of an Asian tree, used in preserves. [Greek *kudōnion*]

quincentenary (ˌkwɪnsɛn'tiːnərɪ) *n., pl.* **-naries.** a 500th anniversary. [Latin *quinque* five + *centenary*] —quincentenial (ˌkwɪnsɛn'tɛnɪəl) *adj., n.*

quincunx ('kwɪnkʌŋks) *n.* a group of five objects arranged in the shape of a rectangle with one at each corner and the fifth in the centre. [Latin: five twelfths; in ancient Rome, this was a coin marked with five spots]

quinine (kwɪ'niːn; *U.S.* 'kwaɪnaɪn) *n.* a bitter drug extracted from cinchona bark, used as a tonic and formerly in malaria therapy. [Spanish *quina* cinchona bark]

Quinquagesima (ˌkwɪŋkwə'dʒɛsɪmə) *n.* the Sunday preceding Lent. [Latin *quinquāgēsima diēs* fiftieth day]

quinquennial (kwɪŋ'kwɛnɪəl) *adj.* occurring once every five years or over a period of five years.

quinquereme (ˌkwɪŋkwɪ'riːm) *n.* an ancient Roman galley with five banks of oars. [Latin *quinque*- five + *rēmus* oar]

quinsy ('kwɪnzɪ) *n.* inflammation of the tonsils and throat, with abscesses. [Greek *kuōn* dog + *ankhein* to strangle]

quint (kwɪnt) *n. U.S. & Canad.* a quintuplet.

quintal ('kwɪntˀl) *n.* **1.** a unit of weight equal to (esp. in Britain) 112 pounds or (esp. in U.S.) 100 pounds. **2.** a unit of weight equal to 100 kilograms. [Arabic *qintār*]

quintessence (kwɪn'tɛsəns) *n.* **1.** the most perfect representation of a quality or state. **2.** an extract of a substance containing its principle in its most concentrated form. [Medieval Latin *quinta essentia* the fifth essence] —quintessential (ˌkwɪntɪ'sɛnʃəl) *adj.*

quintet (kwɪn'tɛt) *n.* **1.** a group of five singers or instrumentalists or a piece of music composed for such a group. **2.** any group of five. [Italian *quintetto*]

quintillion (kwɪn'tɪljən) *n., pl.* **-lions** *or* **-lion.** **1.** (in Britain, France, and Germany) the number represented as one followed by 30 zeros (10^{30}). **2.** (in the U.S. and Canada) the number represented as one followed by 18 zeros (10^{18}). [Latin *quintus* fifth]

quintuple ('kwɪntjʊpˀl, kwɪn'tjuːpˀl) *vb.* **1.** to multiply by five. ~*adj.* **2.** five times as much or as many. **3.** consisting of five parts. ~*n.* **4.** a quantity or number five times as great as another. [Latin *quintus* fifth + -*plus* -fold]

quintuplet ('kwɪntjʊplɪt, kwɪn'tjuːplɪt) *n.* one of five offspring born at one birth.

quip (kwɪp) *n.* **1.** a witty saying. ~*vb.* **quipping, quipped.** **2.** to make a quip. [prob. from Latin *quippe* indeed, to be sure]

quire ('kwaɪə) *n.* a set of 24 or 25 sheets of paper. [Old French *quaier*]

quirk (kwɜːk) *n.* **1.** a peculiarity of character; mannerism or foible. **2.** an unexpected twist or turn: *a quirk of fate.* [origin unknown] —ˈquirky *adj.*

quisling ('kwɪzlɪŋ) *n.* a traitor who aids an

occupying enemy force; collaborator. [after Vidkun *Quisling*, Norwegian collaborator with the Nazis]

quit (kwɪt) *vb.* **quitting, quitted,** *or esp. U.S.* **quit.** **1.** to depart from; leave. **2.** to resign; give up (a job). **3.** (of a tenant) to move out of premises. **4.** *Chiefly U.S.* to desist or cease from (something or doing something). ~*adj.* **5.** (foll. by *of*) free from; released from. [Old French *quitter*] —'**quitter** *n.*

quitch *or* **quitch grass** (kwɪtʃ) *n.* same as **couch grass.**

quite (kwaɪt) *adv.* **1.** absolutely: *you're quite right.* **2.** (*not used with a negative*) somewhat: *she's quite pretty.* **3.** in actuality; truly. **4. quite a** *or* **an.** (*not used with a negative*) of an exceptional kind: *quite a girl.* **5. quite something.** a remarkable thing or person. **6.** an expression used to indicate agreement. [adverbial use of *quite* (adj.) quit]

quits (kwɪts) *adj. Informal.* **1.** on an equal footing. **2. call it quits.** to end a dispute or contest, agreeing that honours are even.

quittance ('kwɪt²ns) *n.* **1.** release from debt or other obligation. **2.** a document certifying this. [Old French *quitter* to release from obligation]

quiver[1] ('kwɪvə) *vb.* **1.** to shake with a tremulous movement; tremble. ~*n.* **2.** a shaking or trembling. [obs. *cwiver* quick, nimble] —'**quivering** *adj.*

quiver[2] ('kwɪvə) *n.* a case for arrows. [Old French *cuivre*]

quixotic (kwɪk'sɒtɪk) *adj.* unrealistically optimistic or chivalrous. [after Don *Quixote* in Cervantes' romance] —**quix'otically** *adv.*

quiz (kwɪz) *n., pl.* **quizzes.** **1.** an entertainment in which the knowledge of the players is tested by a series of questions. **2.** any set of quick questions designed to test knowledge. **3.** an investigation by close questioning. ~*vb.* **quizzing, quizzed.** **4.** to investigate by close questioning; interrogate. [origin unknown]

quizzical ('kwɪzɪk²l) *adj.* questioning and mocking or supercilious. —'**quizzically** *adv.*

quod (kwɒd) *n. Slang, chiefly Brit.* a jail. [origin unknown]

quoin (kwɔɪn, kɔɪn) *n.* **1.** an external corner of a wall. **2.** a cornerstone. **3.** a wedge. [var. of *coin* (in former sense of corner)]

quoit (kɔɪt) *n.* a large ring used in the game of quoits. [origin unknown]

quoits (kɔɪts) *pl. n.* (*usually functioning as sing.*) a game in which quoits are tossed at a stake in the ground in attempts to encircle it.

quondam ('kwɒndæm) *adj.* of an earlier time; former: *her quondam lover.* [Latin]

quorate ('kwɔːˌreɪt) *adj.* having or being a quorum: *the meeting is now quorate.*

quorum ('kwɔːrəm) *n.* the minimum number of members required to be present in a meeting or assembly before any business can be transacted. [Latin, lit.: of whom]

quota ('kwəʊtə) *n.* **1.** the share that is due from, due to, or allocated to a person or group. **2.** the prescribed number or quantity allowed, required, or admitted. [Latin *quotus* of what number]

quotation (kwəʊ'teɪʃən) *n.* **1.** a written or spoken passage repeated exactly in a later work, speech, or conversation, usually with an acknowledgment of its source. **2.** the act of quoting. **3.** an estimate of costs submitted by a contractor to a prospective client.

quotation mark *n.* either of the punctuation marks used to begin or end a quotation, respectively " and " or ' and '.

quote (kwəʊt) *vb.* **1.** to repeat words exactly from an earlier work, speech, or conversation, usually with an acknowledgment of their source. **2.** to put quotation marks round (words). **3.** to state a price for goods or a job of work. ~*n.* **4.** *Informal.* a quotation. **5.** (*often pl.*) *Informal.* a quotation mark. ~*interj.* **6.** an expression used to indicate that the words that follow are a quotation. [Medieval Latin *quotāre* to assign reference numbers to passages] —'**quotable** *adj.*

quoth (kwəʊθ) *vb. Archaic.* (used before *I, he,* or *she*) said. [Old English *cwæth*]

quotidian (kwəʊ'tɪdɪən) *adj.* **1.** daily. **2.** commonplace. **3.** (*esp. of fever*) recurring daily. [Latin *quotīdiānus*]

quotient ('kwəʊʃənt) *n.* the result of the division of one number or quantity by another. [Latin *quotiens* how often]

q.v. (denoting a cross-reference) which (word, item, etc.) see. [New Latin *quod vide*]

qwerty *or* **QWERTY keyboard** ('kwɜːtɪ) *n.* the standard English language typewriter keyboard with the characters q, w, e, r, t, and y at the top left of the keyboard.

R

r *or* **R** (ɑː) *n.*, *pl.* **r's, R's,** *or* **Rs. 1.** the 18th
letter of the English alphabet. **2.** See
three Rs, the.

R 1. *Chem.* radical. **2.** Registered Trademark. **3.** *Physics, electronics.* resistance.
4. *Chess.* rook.

r. 1. Also: **r** radius. **2.** *Cricket.* run(s).

R. 1. Regina. [Latin: Queen] **2.** Rex.
[Latin: King] **3.** Also: **r.** right. **4.** River.

Ra *Chem.* radium.

RA 1. rear admiral. **2.** (in Britain) Royal
Academician *or* Academy. **3.** (in Britain)
Royal Artillery.

rabbet (ˈræbɪt) *n.* **1.** a groove cut into a
piece of timber to receive a mating piece.
~*vb.* **2.** to cut a rabbet in (timber). **3.** to
join (pieces of timber) using a rabbet. [Old
French *rabattre* to beat down]

rabbi (ˈræbaɪ) *n.*, *pl.* **-bis. 1.** the spiritual
leader of a Jewish congregation. **2.** an
expert in or teacher of Jewish Law. [He-
brew: my master] —**rabbinical** (rə-
ˈbɪnɪkˀl) *adj.*

rabbit (ˈræbɪt) *n.*, *pl.* **-bits** *or* **-bit. 1.** a
common burrowing mammal with long ears
and a short fluffy tail. **2.** *Brit. informal.* a
poor performer at a game or sport. ~*vb.*
3. to hunt rabbits. **4.** (often foll. by *on* or
away) *Brit. informal.* to talk inconsequen-
tially; ramble. [origin unknown]

rabbit punch *n.* a short sharp blow to
the back of the neck.

rabble (ˈræbˀl) *n.* **1.** a disorderly crowd;
mob. **2. the rabble.** *Contemptuous.* the
common people. [origin unknown]

rabble-rouser *n.* a person who stirs up
the passions of the mob; demagogue.
—ˈ**rabble-ˌrousing** *adj., n.*

Rabelaisian (ˌræbəˈleɪzɪən) *adj.* of or like
the work of François Rabelais, French
writer, in broad, often bawdy humour and
sharp satire.

rabid (ˈræbɪd) *adj.* **1.** having rabies. **2.**
fanatical: *a rabid Tory.* [Latin *rabidus* fren-
zied] —**rabidity** (rəˈbɪdɪtɪ) *n.*

rabies (ˈreɪbɪːz) *n. Pathol.* a fatal infectious viral disease of the nervous system
transmitted by the saliva of infected animals, esp. dogs. [Latin: madness]

RAC 1. Royal Armoured Corps. **2.** Royal
Automobile Club.

raccoon *or* **racoon** (rəˈkuːn) *n.*, *pl.*
-coons *or* **-coon.** an American mammal
with a pointed muzzle, long tail, and
greyish-black fur with black bands around
the tail and across the face. [American
Indian]

race¹ (reɪs) *n.* **1.** a contest of speed, as in
running or driving. **2.** any competition or
rivalry: *the arms race.* **3.** a rapid current
of water. **4.** a channel of a stream: *a mill
race.* **5.** *Austral. & N.Z.* a narrow passage
through which sheep pass individually, as
to a sheep dip. ~*vb.* **6.** to engage in a
contest of speed with (another). **7.** to

enter (an animal or vehicle) in a race: *to
race pigeons.* **8.** to travel as fast as possible. **9.** to operate at a higher speed than
normal: *my heart raced; the engine began
to race.* ~See also **races.** [Old Norse *rās*
running]

race² (reɪs) *n.* **1.** a group of people of
common ancestry, distinguished from others by physical characteristics, such as
hair type, colour of skin, or stature. **2. the
human race.** human beings collectively.
3. a group of animals or plants having
common characteristics that distinguish
them from other members of the same
species. [Italian *razza*]

racecourse (ˈreɪsˌkɔːs) *n.* a long broad
track, over which horses are raced.

racehorse (ˈreɪsˌhɔːs) *n.* a horse specially
bred for racing.

raceme (rəˈsiːm) *n.* a cluster of flowers in
which the flowers are borne along the main
stem. [Latin *racēmus* bunch of grapes]

race meeting *n.* a prearranged fixture
for racing horses or greyhounds over a set
course.

race relations *n.* (*functioning as pl.*) the
relations between members of two or more
human races within a single community.

race riot *n.* a riot involving ill-feeling or
violence between people of different races.

races (ˈreɪsɪz) *pl. n.* **the races.** a series of
contests of speed between horses or greyhounds over a set course.

racetrack (ˈreɪsˌtræk) *n.* **1.** a circuit used
for races between cars, bicycles, or runners. **2.** *U.S. & Canad.* a racecourse.

racial (ˈreɪʃəl) *adj.* **1.** denoting or relating
to the division of the human species into
races. **2.** characteristic of any such group.
—ˈ**racially** *adv.*

racism (ˈreɪsɪˌɪzəm) *or* **racialism** (ˈreɪʃə-
ˌlɪzəm) *n.* **1.** discriminatory, oppressive,
abusive, or aggressive behaviour towards
people because they belong to a different
race. **2.** the belief that races have distinctive cultural characteristics determined by
hereditary factors and that this endows
some races with an intrinsic superiority.
—ˈ**racist** *or* ˈ**racialist** *n., adj.*

rack¹ (ræk) *n.* **1.** a framework for holding,
carrying, or displaying a specific load or
object. **2.** a toothed bar designed to engage
a pinion to form a mechanism that will
adjust the position of something. **3. the
rack.** an instrument of torture that
stretched the body of the victim. **4.** *U.S. &
Canad.* (in pool or snooker) the triangular
frame used to arrange the balls for the
opening shot. ~*vb.* **5.** to cause great
suffering to: *guilt racked his conscience.*
6. to torture on the rack. **7.** to place or
arrange in or on a rack. **8. rack one's
brains.** to try very hard to think of something. [prob. from Middle Dutch *rec* frame-
work]

rack² ('ræk) n. destruction (obs. except in **go to rack and ruin**). [var. of WRACK¹]

rack³ ('ræk) vb. to clear (wine or beer) by siphoning it off from the dregs.

rack-and-pinion n. a device for converting rotary into linear motion and vice versa, in which a gearwheel (the pinion) engages with a flat toothed bar (the rack).

racket¹ ('rækɪt) n. **1.** a noisy disturbance; clamour; din. **2.** an illegal enterprise carried on for profit; fraud. **3.** Slang. a business or occupation: what's your racket? ~vb. **4.** (often foll. by about) to make a commotion. [prob. imit.] —**'rackety** adj.

racket² or **racquet** ('rækɪt) n. a bat consisting of an open network of taut strings in an oval frame with a handle, used in games such as tennis, badminton, and squash. ~See also **rackets**. [French raquette]

racketeer (,rækɪ'tɪə) n. a person engaged in illegal enterprises for profit. —**,racket-'eering** n.

rackets ('rækɪts) n. (functioning as sing.) a game similar to squash.

rack railway n. a steep mountain railway with a middle rail fitted with a rack that engages a pinion on the locomotive to provide traction.

rack-rent n. an extortionate rent.

raconteur (,rækɒn'tɜː) n. a person skilled in telling stories. [French]

racoon (rə'kuːn) n., pl. **-coons** or **-coon**. same as **raccoon**.

racquet ('rækɪt) n. same as **racket²**.

racy ('reɪsɪ) adj. **racier, raciest**. **1.** lively and spirited in style. **2.** risqué; suggestive. —**'racily** adv. —**'raciness** n.

RADA ('rɑːdə) (in Britain) Royal Academy of Dramatic Art.

radar ('reɪdɑː) n. **1.** a method of detecting the position and velocity of a distant object by bouncing a narrow beam of extremely high-frequency radio pulses off it. **2.** the equipment used in such detection. [ra(dio) d(etecting) a(nd) r(anging)]

radar trap n. a device using radar to detect motorists who exceed the speed limit.

raddled ('ræd³ld) adj. (of a person) unkempt or run-down in appearance. [from rud red ochre]

radial ('reɪdɪəl) adj. **1.** (esp. of lines) emanating from a common central point; arranged like the radii of a circle. **2.** of a radius or ray. **3.** short for **radial-ply**. ~n. **4.** a radial-ply tyre. —**'radially** adv.

radial-ply adj. (of a tyre) having the fabric cords in the outer casing running radially to enable the sidewalls to be flexible.

radian ('reɪdɪən) n. an SI unit of plane angle; the angle between two radii of a circle that cut off on the circumference an arc equal in length to the radius. 1 radian is equivalent to 57.296 degrees.

radiant ('reɪdɪənt) adj. **1.** sending out rays of light; bright; shining. **2.** characterized by health and happiness: a radiant smile.

3. emitted as radiation: radiant heat. **4.** sending out heat by radiation: a radiant heater. ~n. **5.** a point or object that emits radiation. [Latin radiāre to shine] —**'radiance** n. —**'radiantly** adv.

radiant energy n. energy that is emitted or propagated in the form of particles or electromagnetic radiation.

radiate vb. ('reɪdɪ,eɪt). **1.** to emit (heat, light, or other forms of radiation) or (of heat, light, etc.) to be emitted as radiation. **2.** (esp. of lines) to spread out from a centre or be arranged in a radial pattern. **3.** (of a person) to show (an emotion such as happiness) to a great degree. ~adj. ('reɪdɪɪt). **4.** having rays or a radial structure. [Latin radiāre to emit rays]

radiation (,reɪdɪ'eɪʃən) n. **1.** Physics. **a.** the emission of energy as particles, electromagnetic waves or sound. **b.** the particles or waves emitted. **2.** the act or state of radiating or being radiated.

radiation sickness n. illness caused by overexposure of the body to radiation from radioactive material or x-rays.

radiator ('reɪdɪ,eɪtə) n. **1.** a device for heating a room or building, consisting of a series of pipes through which hot water passes. **2.** a device for cooling an internal-combustion engine, consisting of thin-walled tubes through which water passes.

radical ('rædɪk³l) adj. **1.** of the essential nature of a person or thing; fundamental: a radical fault. **2.** searching or thoroughgoing: radical thought. **3.** favouring or tending to produce fundamental changes in political, economic, or social conditions or institutions: a radical party. **4.** Maths. of or containing roots of numbers or quantities. ~n. **5.** a person who favours fundamental change in existing institutions or in political, social, or economic conditions. **6.** Maths. a root of a number or quantity, such as $\sqrt[3]{5}$, $\sqrt{x}$. **7.** Chem. an atom or group of atoms which belongs as a unit during chemical reactions. [Latin rādīx a root] —**'radica,lism** n. —**'radically** adv.

radical sign n. the symbol $\sqrt{}$ placed before a number or quantity to indicate the extraction of a root, esp. a square root. The value of a higher root is indicated by a raised digit in front of the symbol, as in $\sqrt[3]{}$.

radicle ('rædɪk³l) n. Bot. **a.** the part of the embryo of seed-bearing plants that develops into the main root. **b.** a very small root or rootlike part. [Latin rādīx root]

radii ('reɪdɪ,aɪ) n. a plural of **radius**.

radio ('reɪdɪəʊ) n., pl. **-dios**. **1.** the use of electromagnetic waves for broadcasting or two-way communication without the use of linking wires. **2.** an electronic device for converting radio signals into sounds. **3.** a communications device for sending and receiving messages using radio waves. **4.** sound broadcasting. ~adj. **5.** of, produced for, or using radio broadcasting or radio signals: radio drama; a radio station. **6.** of, using, or producing electromagnetic waves in the range used for radio signals: radio astronomy. ~vb. **7.** to transmit (a message) to (a person, place, or vehicle) by means of radio waves. [Latin radius ray]

radio- *combining form.* denoting: **1.** radio. **2.** radioactivity or radiation: *radiocarbon; radiochemistry.*

radioactive (ˌreɪdɪəʊˈæktɪv) *adj.* showing, using, or concerned with radioactivity.

radioactivity (ˌreɪdɪəʊækˈtɪvɪtɪ) *n.* the spontaneous emission of radiation from atomic nuclei. The radiation can consist of alpha or beta particles, or gamma rays.

radio astronomy *n.* astronomy using a radio telescope to analyse signals received from radio sources in space.

radiocarbon (ˌreɪdɪəʊˈkɑːbˀn) *n.* a radioactive isotope of carbon, esp. carbon-14.

radiocarbon dating *n.* same as **carbon dating**.

radiochemistry (ˌreɪdɪəʊˈkemɪstrɪ) *n.* the chemistry of radioactive substances.

radio-controlled *adj.* remote-controlled by means of radio signals.

radio frequency *n.* any electromagnetic frequency that lies in the range 10 kilohertz to 300 000 megahertz and can be used for broadcasting.

radiogram (ˈreɪdɪəʊˌɡræm) *n. Brit.* an old-fashioned unit comprising a radio and record player.

radiograph (ˈreɪdɪəʊˌɡrɑːf) *n.* an image produced on a special photographic film or plate by radiation, usually by x-rays.

radiography (ˌreɪdɪˈɒɡrəfɪ) *n.* the production of radiographs for use in medicine or industry. —**radiˈographer** *n.*

radioisotope (ˌreɪdɪəʊˈaɪsətəʊp) *n.* a radioactive isotope.

radiology (ˌreɪdɪˈɒlədʒɪ) *n.* the use of x-rays and radioactive substances in the diagnosis and treatment of disease. —**radiˈologist** *n.*

radiopaging (ˈreɪdɪəʊˌpeɪdʒɪŋ) *n.* a system whereby a person carrying a small radio receiver (**pager**) is alerted when it emits a signal in response to a call.

radioscopy (ˌreɪdɪˈɒskəpɪ) *n.* examination of a person or object by means of a fluorescent screen and an x-ray source.

radiosonde (ˈreɪdɪəʊˌsɒnd) *n.* an airborne instrument to send meteorological information back to earth by radio. [*radio-* + French *sonde* sounding line]

radiotelegraphy (ˌreɪdɪəʊtɪˈleɡrəfɪ) *n.* telegraphy in which messages are transmitted by radio waves.

radiotelephone (ˌreɪdɪəʊˈtelɪˌfəʊn) *n.* a telephone which sends and receives messages using radio waves rather than wires. —**radioteˈlephony** (ˌreɪdɪəʊtɪˈlefənɪ) *n.*

radio telescope *n.* an instrument used in radio astronomy to pick up and analyse radio waves from space.

radiotherapy (ˌreɪdɪəʊˈθerəpɪ) *n.* the treatment of disease, esp. of cancer, by means of radiation.

radish (ˈrædɪʃ) *n.* a small pungent red-skinned root vegetable which is eaten raw in salads. [Latin *rādīx* root]

radium (ˈreɪdɪəm) *n.* a highly radioactive luminescent metallic element, found in pitchblende. Symbol: Ra [Latin *radius* ray]

radius (ˈreɪdɪəs) *n., pl.* **-dii** *or* **-diuses. 1.** a straight line joining the centre of a circle or sphere to any point on the circumference. **2.** the length of this line. **3.** *Anat.* the outer, slightly shorter of the two bones of the forearm. **4.** a circular area of a size indicated by the length of its radius: *within a radius of four miles.* [Latin: ray, spoke]

radon (ˈreɪdɒn) *n.* a colourless radioactive element of the noble gas group. Symbol: Rn [from *radium*]

RAF (*Not standard* ræf) Royal Air Force.

Rafferty (ˈræfətɪ) *or* **Rafferty's rules** *n. Austral. & N.Z. slang.* no rules at all. [origin unknown]

raffia (ˈræfɪə) *n.* a fibre obtained from the leaves of a type of palm tree, and used for weaving. [Malagasy]

raffish (ˈræfɪʃ) *adj.* unconventional or slightly disreputable; rakish. [obs. *raff* rubbish]

raffle (ˈræfˀl) *n.* **1.** a lottery, often to raise money for charity, in which the prizes are goods rather than money. ~*vb.* **2.** to offer as a prize in a raffle. [Old French]

raft (rɑːft) *n.* a buoyant platform of logs, planks, or oil drums used as a vessel or moored platform. [Old Norse *raptr* rafter]

rafter (ˈrɑːftə) *n.* any of the parallel sloping beams that form the framework of a roof. [Old English]

rag¹ (ræɡ) *n.* **1.** a small piece of cloth, such as one torn from a discarded garment, or such pieces of cloth collectively. **2.** *Informal, contemptuous.* a newspaper. **3.** (*pl.*) old, torn, or worn-out clothing. [prob. formed from *ragged,* from Old English *raggig*]

rag² (ræɡ) *vb.* **ragging, ragged. 1.** to make teasing remarks about (a person). **2.** *Brit.* to play rough practical jokes on. ~*n.* **3.** *Brit.* a boisterous practical joke. **4.** (in British universities and colleges) a period in which various events are organized to raise money for charity. [origin unknown]

rag³ (ræɡ) *n.* a piece of ragtime music.

ragamuffin (ˈræɡəˌmʌfɪn) *n.* a ragged unkempt child. [prob. from RAG¹]

rag-and-bone man *n. Brit.* a man who buys and sells discarded items, such as old clothing or furniture.

ragbag (ˈræɡˌbæɡ) *n.* a confused assortment; jumble.

rage (reɪdʒ) *n.* **1.** intense anger; fury. **2.** a fashion or craze: *skateboards are all the rage again.* **3.** *Austral. & N.Z. informal.* a dance or party. ~*vb.* **4.** to feel or exhibit intense anger. **5.** (esp. of storms, fires, and battle) to move or surge with great violence. [Latin *rabiēs* madness]

ragged (ˈræɡɪd) *adj.* **1.** (of clothes) worn to rags; tattered. **2.** (of a person) dressed in tattered clothes. **3.** neglected; untidy: *ragged weeds.* **4.** having a rough or uneven surface or edge; jagged.

ragged robin *n.* a plant that has pink or white flowers with ragged petals.

raglan (ˈræɡlən) *adj.* **1.** (of a sleeve) joined to the garment by seams running diagonally from the collar to underneath the armpit. **2.** (of a garment) having this style of sleeve. [after Lord *Raglan*]

ragout (ræ'guː) n. a richly seasoned stew of meat and vegetables. [French]

ragtag ('ræg,tæg) n. **ragtag and bobtail.** the common people; rabble.

ragtime ('ræg,taɪm) n. a style of jazz piano music with a syncopated melody. [prob. *ragged time*]

rag trade n. *Informal.* the clothing business.

ragwort ('ræg,wɜːt) n. a plant with ragged leaves and yellow flowers.

raid (reɪd) n. **1.** a sudden surprise attack: *an air raid.* **2.** a surprise visit by police searching for criminals or illicit goods: *a fraud squad raid.* ~vb. **3.** to make a raid against (a person or thing). **4.** to sneak into (a place) in order to steal: *raiding the kitchen for a late-night snack.* [Old English *rād* military expedition] —'**raider** n.

rail[1] (reɪl) n. **1.** a horizontal bar supported by vertical posts, functioning as a fence or barrier. **2.** a horizontal bar on which to hang things: *a picture rail.* **3.** one of a pair of parallel bars that serve as a running surface for the wheels of a train. **4.** railway: *travel by rail.* **5. go off the rails.** to start behaving in a way considered improper or eccentric. ~vb. **6.** (usually foll. by *in* or *off*) to fence (an area) with rails. [Old French *raille* rod]

rail[2] (reɪl) vb. (foll. by *at* or *against*) to complain bitterly or vehemently. [Old French *railler* to mock]

rail[3] (reɪl) n. any of various small cranelike wading marsh birds. [Old French *raale*]

railcard ('reɪl,kɑːd) n. *Brit.* an identity card, which people such as pensioners or young people can buy, entitling the holder to reduced rail fares.

railhead ('reɪl,hɛd) n. **1.** a terminal of a railway. **2.** the farthest point reached by completed track on an unfinished railway.

railing ('reɪlɪŋ) n. (*often pl.*) a fence or balustrade that consists of rails.

raillery ('reɪlərɪ) n., pl. **-leries.** lighthearted ridicule. [French *railler* to tease]

railroad ('reɪl,rəʊd) n. **1.** *U.S.* a railway. ~vb. **2.** *Informal.* to force (a person) into (an action) with haste or by unfair means.

railway ('reɪl,weɪ) n. **1.** a track composed of a line of parallel metal rails fixed to sleepers, for trains to run on. **2.** any track for the wheels of a vehicle to run on: *a cable railway.* **3.** the rolling stock, buildings, and tracks used in such a transport system. **4.** the organization responsible for operating a railway network.

raiment ('reɪmənt) n. *Archaic or poetic.* clothing. [from *arrayment*]

rain (reɪn) n. **1. a.** water falling from the sky in drops formed by the condensation of water vapour in the atmosphere. **b.** a fall of rain; shower. **2.** a large quantity of anything falling rapidly: *a rain of bullets.* **3.** (**come**) **rain or** (**come**) **shine.** regardless of circumstances. **4. right as rain.** *Brit. informal.* perfectly all right. ~vb. **5.** (with *it* as subject) to be the case that rain is falling. **6.** to fall or cause to fall like rain: *to rain abuse on someone.* **7. rained off.** cancelled or postponed on account of

rain. *U.S. and Canad.* term: **rained out.** ~See also **rains.** [Old English *regn*] —'**rainy** adj.

rainbow ('reɪn,bəʊ) n. a bow-shaped display in the sky of the colours of the spectrum, caused by the refraction and reflection of the sun's rays through rain.

rainbow trout n. a freshwater fish of North American origin, with black spots and two longitudinal red stripes.

raincoat ('reɪn,kəʊt) n. a coat made of a waterproof material.

rainfall ('reɪn,fɔːl) n. the amount of rain, hail, or snow in a specified place and time.

rainforest ('reɪn,fɒrɪst) n. dense forest found in tropical areas of heavy rainfall.

rains (reɪnz) pl. n. **the rains.** the season of heavy rainfall, esp. in the tropics.

rainwater ('reɪn,wɔːtə) n. pure water from rain.

rainy day n. a future time of need, esp. financial.

raise (reɪz) vb. **1.** to elevate to a higher position or level; lift. **2.** to place in an upright position. **3.** to build: *to raise a barn.* **4.** to increase in amount, value, intensity, etc.: *we must raise our prices; to raise one's voice.* **5.** to advance in rank; promote. **6.** to arouse from sleep or death. **7.** to stir up: *to raise a mutiny.* **8. raise Cain. a.** to create a disturbance. **b.** to protest vehemently. **9.** to put forward for consideration: *to raise a question.* **10.** to collect or gather together: *raising money for charity; to raise an army.* **11.** to grow: *to raise a crop.* **12.** to bring up; rear: *to raise a family.* **13.** to cause to be expressed: *to raise a smile.* **14.** to bring to an end: *to raise a siege.* **15.** to cause (dough) to rise, as by the addition of yeast. **16.** to establish radio communications with: *we raised Moscow last night.* **17.** *Maths.* to multiply (a number) by itself a specified number of times: *8 is 2 raised to the power 3.* ~n. **18.** the act of raising. **19.** *Chiefly U.S. & Canad.* an increase in pay. [Old Norse *reisa*]

raised (reɪzd) adj. higher than the surrounding area: *a raised platform.*

raisin ('reɪz'n) n. a dried grape. [Old French: grape]

raison d'être ('reɪzon 'dɛtrə) n., pl. **raisons d'être** ('reɪzon 'dɛtrə). reason or justification for existence. [French]

raj (rɑːdʒ) n. **the Raj.** the British government in India before 1947. [Hindi]

rajah or **raja** ('rɑːdʒə) n. (in India, formerly) a ruler: sometimes used as a title preceding a name. [Hindi]

rake[1] (reɪk) n. **1.** a farm or garden tool consisting of a row of teeth set in a headpiece attached to a long shaft and used for gathering leaves or straw, or for smoothing loose earth. **2.** any of various implements similar in shape or function. ~vb. **3.** to scrape, gather, or remove (leaves, refuse, or hay) with a rake. **4.** to level or prepare (a surface) with a rake. **5.** (sometimes foll. by *out*) to clear (ashes) from (a fire). **6.** (foll. by *up* or *together*) to gather (items or people) with difficulty, as from a limited supply. **7.** (often foll. by *through* or *over*) to search or examine carefully. **8.** to scrape or graze: *the ship raked the side of the quay.* **9.** to direct (gunfire) along the length of (a target): *machine-guns raked the column.* ~See also **rake in, rake-off,** etc. [Old English *raca*]

rake[2] (reɪk) *n.* a dissolute man, esp. one in fashionable society. [short for *rakehell*]

rake[3] (reɪk) *vb.* **1.** to slope from the vertical, esp. (of a ship's mast) towards the stern. **2.** to construct with a backward slope. ~*n.* **3.** the degree to which an object slopes. [origin unknown]

rake in *vb. Informal.* to acquire (money) in large amounts.

rake-off *n. Slang.* a share of profits, esp. an illegal one.

rake up *vb.* to revive (something forgotten): *to rake up an old quarrel.*

rakish[1] (ˈreɪkɪʃ) *adj.* dissolute; profligate. [from RAKE[2]] —**ˈrakishly** *adv.*

rakish[2] (ˈreɪkɪʃ) *adj.* dashing; jaunty: *a hat set at a rakish angle.* [prob. from RAKE[3]]

rallentando (ˌrælɛnˈtændəʊ) *adj., adv. Music.* becoming slower. [Italian]

rally[1] (ˈrælɪ) *vb.* **-lying, -lied. 1.** to bring (a group) into order, as after dispersal, or (of such a group) to come to order. **2.** to come or bring together for a common cause. **3.** to summon up (one's strength or spirits). **4.** to recover (sometimes only temporarily) from an illness. **5.** *Stock Exchange.* to increase sharply after a decline. **6.** *Tennis, squash, etc.* to exchange a series of shots before one player wins the point. ~*n., pl.* **-lies. 7.** a large gathering of people for a common purpose. **8.** a marked recovery of strength, as during illness. **9.** *Stock Exchange.* a sharp increase in price or trading activity after a decline. **10.** *Tennis, squash, etc.* an exchange of several shots before one player wins the point. **11.** a type of motor competition over public roads. [Old French *rallier*] —**ˈrallier** *n.*

rally[2] (ˈrælɪ) *vb.* **-lying, -lied.** to mock or tease (someone) in a good-natured way. [Old French *railler* to tease]

rally round *vb.* to come to the aid of (someone); offer support.

ram (ræm) *n.* **1.** an uncastrated adult male sheep. **2.** a hydraulically or pneumatically driven piston. **3.** the falling weight of a pile driver. **4.** short for **battering ram.** ~*vb.* **ramming, rammed. 5.** (usually foll. by *into*) to force or drive, as by heavy blows: *to ram a post into the ground.* **6.** to crash violently. **7.** to stuff, cram, or thrust violently. **8.** **ram (something) down someone's throat.** to put forward or emphasize (an argument or idea) with excessive force. [Old English *ramm*]

RAM (ræm) *Computers.* random access memory: a temporary storage space which loses its contents when the computer is switched off.

Ramadan (ˌræməˈdɑːn) *n.* **1.** the ninth month of the Muslim year, 30 days long, during which strict fasting is observed from sunrise to sunset. **2.** the fast itself.

ramble (ˈræmbəl) *vb.* **1.** to walk for relaxation, sometimes with no particular direction. **2.** to grow or develop in a random fashion. **3.** to speak or write in a confused disconnected style. ~*n.* **4.** a walk, esp. in the countryside. [Middle English *romblen*] —**ˈrambling** *adj.*

rambler (ˈræmblə) *n.* **1.** a person who takes country walks. **2.** a vigorous climbing and spreading rose.

RAMC Royal Army Medical Corps.

ramekin (ˈræmɪkɪn) *n.* a small container for baking and serving one portion of food. [French *ramequin*]

ramification (ˌræmɪfɪˈkeɪʃən) *n.* **1.** a consequence or complication. **2.** a structure of branching parts. —**ˈramify** *vb.*

ramp (ræmp) *n.* **1.** a slope that joins two surfaces at different levels, such as one designed to be used instead of steps by someone pushing a pram. **2.** a place where the level of a road surface changes because of road works. **3.** a movable stairway by which passengers enter and leave an aircraft. ~*vb.* **4.** to act in a violent or threatening manner (esp. in **ramp and rage**). [Old French *ramper* to crawl or rear]

rampage *vb.* (ræmˈpeɪdʒ). **1.** to rush about in a violent disorderly fashion. ~*n.* (ˈræmpeɪdʒ). **2. on the rampage.** behaving violently or destructively. [Scot.]

rampant (ˈræmpənt) *adj.* **1.** unrestrained or violent in growth or spread. **2.** *Heraldry.* (of a beast) standing on the hind legs, the right foreleg raised above the left. [Old French *ramper* to crawl, rear]

rampart (ˈræmpɑːt) *n.* the surrounding embankment of a fort, often with a wall or parapets built on it. [Old French]

rampike (ˈræmˌpaɪk) *n. Canad.* a tall tree that has been burned bare of branches.

ramrod (ˈræmˌrɒd) *n.* a rod for cleaning the barrel of a gun or for ramming the charge of a muzzle-loading firearm into place.

ramshackle (ˈræmˌʃækəl) *adj.* (esp. of buildings) rickety, shaky, or derelict. [obs. *ransackle* to ransack]

ran (ræn) *vb.* the past tense of **run.**

ranch (rɑːntʃ) *n.* **1.** a large farm, esp. in North America, for rearing livestock, esp. cattle. **2.** *Chiefly U.S. & Canad.* any large farm for the rearing of a particular kind of livestock or crop: *a mink ranch.* ~*vb.* **3.** to run a ranch. [Mexican Spanish *rancho* small farm] —**ˈrancher** *n.*

rancherie (ˈrɑːntʃərɪ) *n.* (in British Columbia, Canada) a settlement of North American Indians. [Spanish *ranchería*]

rancid (ˈrænsɪd) *adj.* (of food, or a taste or smell) rank or sour; stale. [Latin *rancidus*] —**ˈrancidness** or **rancidity** (rænˈsɪdɪtɪ) *n.*

rancour or *U.S.* **rancor** (ˈræŋkə) *n.* bitter resentfulness or hostility. [Old French] —**ˈrancorous** *adj.*

rand (rænd, rɒnt) *n.* the standard monetary unit of the Republic of South Africa. [from *Witwatersrand,* S Transvaal, referring to the gold-mining there]

R & B rhythm and blues.

R & D research and development.

random ('rændəm) *adj.* **1.** lacking any definite plan or prearranged order; haphazard: *a random selection.* ~*n.* **2. at random.** not following any prearranged order. [Old French *randir* to gallop] —'**randomly** *adv.* —'**randomness** *n.*

random access *n.* a method of reading data from a computer file without having to read through the file from the beginning.

randy ('rændɪ) *adj.* **randier, randiest.** *Informal, chiefly Brit.* sexually eager or lustful. [prob. from *rand* to rant] —'**randily** *adv.* —'**randiness** *n.*

ranee ('rɑːnɪ) *n.* same as **rani**.

rang (ræŋ) *vb.* the past tense of **ring**[2].

rangatira (ˌrɑːŋəˈtɪərə) *n.* *N.Z.* a Maori chief of either sex. [Maori]

range (reɪndʒ) *n.* **1.** the limits within which a person or thing can function effectively: *the range of vision.* **2.** the limits within which something can lie: *a range of prices.* **3.** the total products of a manufacturer, designer, or stockist: *the new spring range.* **4. a.** the maximum effective distance of a projectile fired from a weapon. **b.** the distance between a target and a weapon. **5.** an area set aside for shooting practice or rocket testing. **6.** the total distance which a ship, aircraft, or land vehicle is capable of covering without taking on fresh fuel. **7.** the difference in pitch between the highest and lowest note of a voice or musical instrument. **8.** *Maths.* the set of values that a function or variable can take. **9.** *U.S. & Canad.* an extensive tract of open land on which livestock can graze. **10.** a rank, row, or series of items. **11.** a chain of mountains. **12.** a large cooking stove with one or more ovens, usually heated by solid fuel. ~*vb.* **13.** to establish or be situated in a line or series. **14.** (*often reflexive*, foll. by *with*) to put into a specific category; classify: *she ranged herself with the opposition.* **15.** to roam (over). **16.** to fluctuate within specific limits: *their ages range from 22 to 35.* **17.** to cover a specified period or specified things: *her book ranged as far back as the Middle Ages.* [Old French: row]

rangefinder ('reɪndʒˌfaɪndə) *n.* an instrument for determining how far away an object is, esp. in order to sight a gun or focus a camera.

ranger ('reɪndʒə) *n.* **1.** (*sometimes cap.*) an official in charge of a forest, park, or nature reserve. **2.** *U.S.* one of a body of armed troops employed to police a State or district: *a Texas ranger.*

Ranger *or* **Ranger Guide** ('reɪndʒə) *n.* *Brit.* a member of the senior branch of the Guides.

rangy ('reɪndʒɪ) *adj.* **rangier, rangiest.** having long slender limbs.

rani *or* **ranee** ('rɑːnɪ) *n.* the wife of a rajah. [Hindi]

rank[1] (ræŋk) *n.* **1.** a position within a social organization: *the rank of captain.* **2.** high social or other standing; status. **3.** a line or row of people or things. **4.** the position of an item in any ordering or sequence. **5.** *Brit.* a place where taxis wait to be hired. **6.** a line of people, esp. soldiers, positioned one beside the other. **7. close ranks.** to maintain solidarity. **8. pull rank.** to get one's own way by virtue of one's superior position. **9. rank and file.** the great mass of any group, as opposed to the leadership. ~*vb.* **10.** to arrange (people or things) in rows or lines. **11.** to give or hold a specific position in an organization or group. **12.** to arrange in sequence: *to rank students by their test scores.* **13.** to be important; rate: *money ranks low in her order of priorities.* [Old French *ranc*]

rank[2] (ræŋk) *adj.* **1.** showing vigorous and profuse growth: *rank weeds.* **2.** highly offensive or disagreeable, esp. in smell or taste. **3.** absolute; utter: *a rank outsider.* [Old English *ranc* straight, noble]

rankle ('ræŋk²l) *vb.* to cause severe and continuous irritation, anger, or bitterness. [Old French *draoncle* ulcer]

ransack ('rænsæk) *vb.* **1.** to search through every part of (a place or thing). **2.** to plunder; pillage. [Old Norse *rann* house + *saka* to search]

ransom ('rænsəm) *n.* **1.** the release of captured prisoners on payment of a stipulated price. **2.** the price demanded for such a release. **3. hold to ransom. a.** to keep (a prisoner) in confinement until payment is received. **b.** to attempt to force (a person) to comply with one's demands. ~*vb.* **4.** to pay a stipulated price and so obtain the release of (prisoners). **5.** to set free (prisoners) upon receiving the payment demanded. [Old French *ransoun*] —'**ransomer** *n.*

rant (rænt) *vb.* **1.** to utter (something) in loud, violent, or bombastic tones. ~*n.* **2.** loud, declamatory, or extravagant speech. [Dutch *ranten* to rave] —'**ranting** *adj., n.*

RAOC Royal Army Ordnance Corps.

rap[1] (ræp) *vb.* **rapping, rapped.** **1.** to strike (a fist, stick, etc.) against (something) with a sharp quick blow; knock. **2.** to knock loudly and sharply. **3.** to rebuke or criticize sharply. **4.** (foll. by *out*) to utter in sharp rapid speech: *to rap out orders.* **5.** *Slang.* to talk volubly. **6.** to perform a rhythmic monologue with musical backing. **7. rap over the knuckles.** to reprimand. ~*n.* **8.** a sharp quick blow or the sound produced by it. **9.** a sharp rebuke or criticism. **10.** a fast, rhythmic monologue over a musical backing. **11. take the rap.** *Slang.* to suffer the punishment for a crime, whether guilty or not. [prob. from Old Norse] —'**rapper** *n.*

rap[2] (ræp) *n.* (*used with a negative*) the least amount. [prob. from *ropaire* counterfeit coin formerly current in Ireland]

rapacious (rə'peɪʃəs) *adj.* **1.** greedy or grasping. **2.** (of animals, esp. birds) subsisting by catching living prey. [Latin *rapāx*] —**rapacity** (rə'pæsɪtɪ) *n.*

rape[1] (reɪp) *n.* **1.** the offence of forcing a person, esp. a woman, to submit to sexual intercourse against that person's will. **2.** any violation or abuse: *the rape of justice.* ~*vb.* **3.** to force (a person) to submit to sexual intercourse against that person's will. [Latin *rapere* to seize] —'**rapist** *n*.

rape² (reɪp) *n.* a yellow-flowered plant cultivated for its seeds, **rapeseed**, which yield a useful oil, **rape oil**, and as a fodder plant. [Latin *rāpum* turnip]

rapid ('ræpɪd) *adj.* **1.** (of an action) taking or lasting a short time; quick. **2.** acting or moving quickly; fast: *a rapid worker*. [Latin *rapere* to seize] —'**rapidly** *adv.* —**rapidity** (rə'pɪdɪtɪ) *or* '**rapidness** *n*.

rapids ('ræpɪdz) *pl. n.* part of a river where the water is very fast and turbulent.

rapier ('reɪpɪə) *n.* a long narrow two-edged sword used as a thrusting weapon. [Old French *espee rapiere* rasping sword]

rapine ('ræpaɪn) *n.* pillage or plundering. [Latin *rapīna*]

rapport (ræ'pɔt) *n.* (often foll. by *with*) a sympathetic relationship or understanding. [French]

rapprochement (rə'prɒʃmɒn) *n.* a resumption of friendly relations, esp. between two countries. [French]

rapscallion (ræp'skæljən) *n.* a rascal or rogue. [earlier *rascallion*]

rapt (ræpt) *adj.* **1.** totally engrossed; spellbound: *rapt with wonder*. **2.** characterized by or proceeding from rapture: *a rapt smile*. [Latin *raptus* carried away]

raptor ('ræptɔ) *n.* any bird of prey. [Latin: robber] —**rap'torial** *adj*.

rapture ('ræptʃə) *n.* **1.** extreme happiness or delight; joyous ecstasy. **2.** (often *pl.*) an expression of ecstatic joy. [Latin *raptus* carried away] —'**rapturous** *adj*.

rare¹ (rɛə) *adj.* **1.** uncommon or unusual: *a rare word*. **2.** (of a gas, esp. the atmosphere at high altitudes) having a low density; thin; rarefied. **3.** showing uncommon excellence: *rare skill*. [Latin *rārus* sparse]

rare² (rɛə) *adj.* (of meat) very lightly cooked. [Old English *hrēr*]

rarebit ('rɛəbɪt) *n.* same as **Welsh rabbit**.

rare earth *n.* **1.** any oxide of a lanthanide. **2.** Also called: **rare-earth element**. any element of the lanthanide series.

rarefied ('rɛərɪ,faɪd) *adj.* **1.** exalted in character; lofty: *a rarefied spiritual existence*. **2.** current within only a small group. **3.** thin: *air rarefied at altitude*.

rarefy ('rɛərɪ,faɪ) *vb.* **-fying, -fied.** to make or become less dense; thin out.

rarely ('rɛəlɪ) *adv.* **1.** hardly ever; seldom. **2.** to an unusual degree; exceptionally.

raring ('rɛərɪŋ) *adj.* ready; willing; enthusiastic (esp. in **raring to go**). [*rare*, var. of *rear*]

rarity ('rɛərɪtɪ) *n., pl.* **-ties. 1.** something valued because it is uncommon. **2.** the state of being rare.

rascal ('rɑːsk'l) *n.* **1.** a scoundrel or rogue. **2.** a mischievous child. [Old French *rascaille* rabble] —'**rascally** *adj*.

rase (reɪz) *vb.* same as **raze**.

rash¹ (ræʃ) *adj.* hasty, impetuous, or reckless. [Old High German *rasc* hurried, clever] —'**rashly** *adv.* —'**rashness** *n*.

rash² (ræʃ) *n.* an outbreak of spots, swellings, or reddening on the skin, caused by illness or allergy. [Old French *rasche*]

rasher ('ræʃə) *n.* a thin slice of bacon or ham. [origin unknown]

rasp (rɑːsp) *n.* **1.** a harsh grating noise. **2.** a coarse file with rows of raised teeth. ~*vb.* **3.** to scrape or rub (something) roughly, esp. with a rasp. **4.** to make a harsh grating noise. **5.** to irritate (one's nerves); grate (upon). [Old French *raspe*]

raspberry ('rɑːzbrɪ) *n., pl.* **-ries. 1.** the red fruits of a prickly shrub of Europe and North America. **2.** a spluttering noise made with the tongue and lips to express contempt: *she blew a loud raspberry*. [origin unknown]

Rastafarian (,ræstə'fɛərɪən) *n.* a believer in a religion of Jamaican origin that regards Ras Tafari, the former emperor of Ethiopia, Haile Selassie, as God. Often shortened to **Rasta**.

rat (ræt) *n.* **1.** a long-tailed rodent, similar to but larger than a mouse. **2.** *Informal.* someone who is disloyal or treacherous. **3. smell a rat.** to detect something suspicious. ~*vb.* **ratting, ratted. 4.** (usually foll. by *on*) to betray (a person) or go back on (an agreement). **5.** to hunt and kill rats. [Old English *ræt*]

ratable *or* **rateable** ('reɪtəb'l) *adj.* **1.** able to be rated or evaluated. **2.** *Brit.* (of property) liable to payment of rates.

ratable value *or* **rateable value** *n. Brit.* a fixed value assigned to a property, used to assess the rates due on it.

ratan (ræ'tæn) *n.* same as **rattan**.

ratatat-tat ('rætə,tæt'tæt) *or* **ratatat** ('rætə'tæt) *n.* the sound of knocking on a door.

ratatouille (,rætə'twiː) *n.* a vegetable casserole made of tomatoes, aubergines, etc., stewed slowly in oil. [French]

ratbag ('ræt,bæg) *n. Slang.* an eccentric or despicable person.

ratchet ('rætʃɪt) *n.* **1.** a device in which a toothed rack or wheel is engaged by a pivoted lever which permits motion in one direction only. **2.** the toothed rack or wheel in such a device. [French *rochet*]

rate¹ (reɪt) *n.* **1.** a quantity or amount considered in relation to or measured against another quantity or amount: *a rate of 70 miles an hour.* **2.** a price or charge with reference to a standard or scale: *rate of interest.* **3.** a charge made per unit for a commodity or service. **4.** See **rates. 5.** the speed of progress or change; pace: *the rate of production has doubled.* **6.** relative quality; class or grade: *first-rate ideas.* **7. at any rate.** in any case; anyway. ~*vb.* **8.** to assign a position on a scale of relative values; rank: *he is rated fifth in the world.* **9.** to estimate the value of: *we rate your services highly.* **10.** to be worthy of; deserve: *this hotel does not rate four stars.* **11.** to consider; regard: *I rate him among my friends.* **12.** *Brit.* to assess the value of (property) for the purpose of local taxation. [Medieval Latin *rata*]

rate² (reɪt) *vb.* to scold or criticize severely. [origin unknown]

rate-cap ('reɪt,kæp) *vb.* **-capping, -capped.** (in Britain) to impose on (a local authority) an upper limit on the rates it may levy. —**'rate-,capping** *n.*

ratepayer ('reɪt,peɪə) *n. Brit.* a person who pays local rates, esp. a householder.

rates (reɪts) *pl. n. Brit.* a tax on property levied by a local authority.

rather ('rɑːðə) *adv.* **1.** fairly; somewhat: *she's rather pretty; it's rather dull.* **2.** to a limited extent: *I rather thought that was the case.* **3.** more truly or appropriately: *it's no cause for congratulation, but rather for concern.* **4.** more willingly; sooner: *I would rather not see you tomorrow.* ~*interj.* ('rɑː'ðɜː). **5.** an expression of strong affirmation: *Is it worth seeing? Rather!* [Old English *hrathor*]

ratify ('rætɪ,faɪ) *vb.* **-fying, -fied.** to give formal consent to. [Latin *ratus* fixed + *facere* to make] —**ratifi'cation** *n.*

rating ('reɪtɪŋ) *n.* **1.** a classification according to order or grade; ranking. **2.** an ordinary seaman. **3.** the estimated financial or credit standing of a business enterprise or individual. **4.** *Radio & television.* the proportion of the total audience that tunes in to a specific programme.

ratio ('reɪʃɪəʊ) *n., pl.* **-tios.** **1.** a measure of the relative size of two classes expressible as a proportion: *the ratio of boys to girls is 2 to 1.* **2.** *Maths.* a quotient of two numbers or quantities. [Latin: a reckoning]

ration ('ræʃən) *n.* **1.** a fixed allowance of something that is scarce, such as food or petrol in wartime. **2.** (*usually pl.*) a fixed daily allowance of food, as in the armed forces. ~*vb.* **3.** (often foll. by *out*) to distribute (provisions), esp. to an army. **4.** to restrict the distribution of (a commodity): *the government has rationed sugar.* [Latin *ratio* reckoning] —**'rationing** *n.*

rational ('ræʃən²l) *adj.* **1.** using reason or logic in thinking out a problem. **2.** sensible; reasonable. **3.** of sound mind; sane: *the patient seemed quite rational.* **4.** able to reason: *man is a rational being.* **5.** *Maths.* expressible as a ratio of two integers: *a rational number.* [Latin *rationālis*] —**ratio'nality** *n.* —**'rationally** *adv.*

rationale (,ræʃə'nɑːl) *n.* the fundamental reasons on which an action, decision, or belief is based.

rationalism ('ræʃənə,lɪzəm) *n.* reliance on reason rather than intuition or experience as the basis for beliefs or actions. —**'rationalist** *n.* —**,rational'istic** *adj.*

rationalize *or* **-ise** ('ræʃənə,laɪz) *vb.* **1.** to justify (one's actions) with plausible reasons, esp. after the event. **2.** to apply logic or reason to (something). **3.** to get rid of unnecessary equipment or staff from (a workplace or industry), in order to make it more efficient. —**,rationali'zation** *or* **-i'sation** *n.*

rational number *n.* any real number of the form *a/b*, where *a* and *b* are integers and *b* is not zero, as 7 or 7/3.

rat race *n.* a continual routine of hectic competitive activity: *working in the City is a real rat race.*

ratsbane ('ræts,beɪn) *n.* rat poison.

rattan *or* **ratan** (ræ'tæn) *n.* a climbing palm with tough stems used for wicker-work and canes. [Malay *rōtan*]

ratter ('rætə) *n.* a dog or cat that catches and kills rats.

rattle ('ræt²l) *vb.* **1.** to make a rapid succession of short sharp sounds, as of loose pellets colliding when shaken in a container. **2.** to shake, producing such a sound. **3.** to send, move, or drive with such a sound: *the car rattled along the country road.* **4.** (foll. by *on* or *away*) to chatter idly: *he rattled on about his work.* **5.** (foll. by *off* or *out*) to recite perfunctorily or rapidly. **6.** *Informal.* to disconcert; make frightened or anxious. ~*n.* **7.** a rapid succession of short sharp sounds. **8.** a baby's toy filled with small pellets that rattle when shaken. [Middle Dutch *ratelen*] —**'rattly** *adj.*

rattlesnake ('ræt²l,sneɪk) *n.* a poisonous New World snake with a series of loose horny segments on the tail that are vibrated to produce a whirring sound.

rattletrap ('ræt²l,træp) *n. Informal.* a broken-down vehicle, esp. an old car.

rattling ('rætlɪŋ) *adv. Informal,* old-fashioned. very; exceptionally: *a rattling good lunch.*

ratty ('rætɪ) *adj.* **-tier, -tiest.** **1.** *Brit. & N.Z. informal.* irritable; annoyed. **2.** *Informal.* (of the hair) straggly and greasy. —**'rattily** *adv.* —**'rattiness** *n.*

raucous ('rɔːkəs) *adj.* harshly or hoarsely loud. [Latin *raucus*]

raunchy ('rɔːntʃɪ) *adj.* **-chier, -chiest.** *Slang.* openly sexual; earthy. [origin unknown]

ravage ('rævɪdʒ) *vb.* **1.** to cause extensive damage to. ~*n.* **2.** (often *pl.*) destructive action: *the ravages of time.* [Old French *ravir* to snatch away]

rave (reɪv) *vb.* **1.** to utter (something) in a wild or incoherent manner, as when delirious. **2.** (foll. by *over* or *about*) *Informal.* to write or speak (about) with great enthusiasm. ~*n.* **3.** *Informal.* an enthusiastically favourable review. **4.** Also called: **rave-up.** *Brit. slang.* a party. [prob. from Old French *resver* to wander]

ravel ('ræv²l) *vb.* **-elling, -elled** *or U.S.* **-eling, -eled.** **1.** to tangle or become entangled. **2.** (often foll. by *out*) to tease out (the fibres of a fabric) or (of a fabric) to fray out in loose ends; unravel. **3.** (usually foll. by *out*) to disentangle: *to ravel out a complicated story.* [Middle Dutch *ravelen*]

raven ('reɪv²n) *n.* **1.** a large bird of the crow family with a long wedge-shaped tail and shiny black feathers. **2.** a shiny black colour. [Old English *hræfn*]

ravening ('rævənɪŋ) *adj.* (of animals) hungrily searching for prey; predatory.

ravenous ('rævənəs) *adj.* **1.** famished; starving. **2.** rapacious; ravening. [Old French *ravineux*] —**'ravenously** *adv.*

raver ('reɪvə) *n. Brit. slang.* a person who leads a wild or uninhibited social life.

ravine (rə'viːn) *n.* a deep narrow steep-sided valley. [Old French: torrent]

raving ('reɪvɪŋ) *adj.* **1. a.** delirious; frenzied. **b.** (*as adv.*): *raving mad.* **2.** *Informal.* great or exceptional: *a raving beauty.* ~*n.* **3.** (*usually pl.*) frenzied or wildly extravagant talk or utterances.

ravioli (ˌrævɪ'əʊlɪ) *n.* small squares of pasta containing a savoury filling, such as meat or cheese. [Italian]

ravish ('rævɪʃ) *vb.* **1.** (*often passive*) to enrapture. **2.** to rape. [Latin *rapere* to seize] —'**ravishment** *n.*

ravishing ('rævɪʃɪŋ) *adj.* delightful; lovely; entrancing. —'**ravishingly** *adv.*

raw (rɔː) *adj.* **1.** (of food) not cooked. **2.** in an unfinished, natural, or unrefined state; not processed: *raw materials.* **3.** (of the skin or a wound) having the surface exposed or scraped away, esp. painfully. **4.** untrained, inexperienced, or immature: *a raw recruit.* **5.** not selected or modified: *raw statistics.* **6.** frank or realistic: *a raw picture of a marriage.* **7.** (of the weather) harshly cold and damp. **8.** *Informal.* unfair; unjust (esp. in **a raw deal**). ~*n.* **9. in the raw. a.** *Informal.* naked. **b.** in a natural state. **10. the raw.** *Brit. informal.* a sensitive point: *his criticism touched me on the raw.* [Old English *hreaw*]

rawboned ('rɔː'bəʊnd) *adj.* having a lean bony physique.

rawhide ('rɔːˌhaɪd) *n.* **1.** untanned hide. **2.** a whip or rope made of strips of this.

ray¹ (reɪ) *n.* **1.** a narrow beam of light. **2.** a slight indication: *a ray of solace.* **3.** *Maths.* a straight line extending from a point. **4.** a thin beam of electromagnetic radiation or particles. **5.** any of a set of lines emerging from a central point. **6.** any of the spines that support the fin of a fish. [Old French *rai*]

ray² (reɪ) *n.* a sea fish related to the sharks, with a flattened body and a long whiplike tail. [Old French *raie*]

ray³ (reɪ) *n. Music.* (in tonic sol-fa) the second degree of any major scale.

rayon ('reɪɒn) *n.* a textile fibre or fabric made from cellulose. [French]

raze *or* **rase** (reɪz) *vb.* to demolish (buildings, towns, etc.) completely. [Old French *raser*]

razoo (rɑː'zuː) *n., pl.* -**zoos.** *Austral. & N.Z. informal.* an imaginary coin: *not a brass razoo left.* [origin unknown]

razor ('reɪzə) *n.* an implement with a sharp blade, used esp. for shaving the face. [Old French *raseor*]

razorbill ('reɪzəˌbɪl) *n.* a common black-and-white auk with a deep narrow bill.

razor wire *n.* strong wire with pieces of sharp metal set across it at intervals.

razzle-dazzle ('ræz³l'dæz³l) *or* **razzmatazz** ('ræzmə'tæz) *n. Slang.* **1.** noisy or showy fuss or activity. **2.** a spree or frolic. [rhyming compound from *dazzle*]

Rb *Chem.* rubidium.

RC Roman Catholic.

Rd road.

re¹ (reɪ, riː) *n. Music.* same as **ray³**.

re² (riː) *prep.* with reference to: used esp. in the headings of business letters. [Latin *rēs* thing]

Re *Chem.* rhenium.

RE **1.** Religious Education. **2.** Royal Engineers.

re- *prefix.* used with many main words to mean: **1.** return to a previous condition: *rebuild; react.* **2.** repetition of an action: *remarry.* [Latin]

reach (riːtʃ) *vb.* **1.** to arrive at or get to (a place): *to reach the office.* **2.** to extend as far as (a point or place): *to reach the ceiling; can you reach?* **3.** to come to (a certain condition or situation): *to reach the point of starvation.* **4.** to arrive at or amount to (an amount or value): *temperatures in Greece reached 35° C yesterday.* **5.** *Informal.* to pass or give (something to a person) with the outstretched hand. **6.** (foll. by *out*, *for*, or *after*) to make a movement (towards), as if to grasp or touch. **7.** to make contact or communication with (someone): *we tried to reach him all day.* ~*n.* **8.** the extent or distance of reaching: *within reach.* **9.** the range of influence or power. **10.** an open stretch of water, esp. on a river. [Old English *rǣcan*] —'**reachable** *adj.*

reach-me-down *adj.* cheaply ready-made or second-hand: *reach-me-down finery.*

react (rɪ'ækt) *vb.* **1.** (of a person or thing) to act in response to another person, a stimulus, or a situation. **2.** (foll. by *against*) to act in an opposing or contrary manner. **3.** *Physics.* to exert an equal force in the opposite direction to an acting force. **4.** *Chem.* to undergo a chemical reaction. [Late Latin *reagere*]

reactance (rɪ'æktəns) *n.* the opposition to the flow of alternating current by the capacitance or inductance of an electrical circuit.

reactant (rɪ'æktənt) *n.* a substance that participates in a chemical reaction.

reaction (rɪ'ækʃən) *n.* **1.** a response to some foregoing action or stimulus. **2.** the reciprocal action of two things acting together. **3.** opposition to change, esp. political change. **4.** a response indicating a person's feelings. **5.** *Med.* any effect produced by a drug or by a substance (allergen) to which a person is allergic. **6.** *Chem.* a process that involves changes in the structure and energy content of atoms, molecules, or ions. **7.** the equal and opposite force that acts on a body whenever it exerts a force on another body.

reactionary (rɪ'ækʃənrɪ) *adj.* **1.** of or characterized by reaction, esp. against political or social change. ~*n., pl.* -**aries.** **2.** a person opposed to radical change.

reactivate (rɪ'æktɪˌveɪt) *vb.* to make (something) active again. —**re,acti'vation** *n.*

reactive (rɪ'æktɪv) *adj.* **1.** readily taking part in chemical reactions. **2.** of or having a reactance. **3.** responsive to stimulus. —**re'actively** *adv.* —**reactivity** (ˌriːæk'tɪvɪtɪ) *n.*

reactor (rɪ'æktə) *n.* short for **nuclear reactor.**

read (riːd) *vb.* **reading, read** (rɛd). **1.** to understand (something written or printed) by looking at and interpreting the written or printed characters. **2.** (often foll. by *out*) to speak aloud (something written or printed). **3.** to interpret the significance or meaning of: *to read a map.* **4.** to interpret (signs, characters, etc.) other than by visual means: *to read Braille.* **5.** to have sufficient knowledge of (a language) to understand the written word. **6.** to make out the true nature or mood of: *she could read his thoughts.* **7.** to interpret in a specified way: *it can be read as satire.* **8.** to have a certain wording: *the sentence reads as follows.* **9.** to undertake a course of study in (a subject): *to read history.* **10.** to gain knowledge by reading: *he read about the war; a well-read young woman.* **11.** to register or show: *the meter reads 100.* **12.** to put into a specified condition by reading: *I read my son to sleep.* **13.** to hear and understand, esp. when using a two-way radio: *we are reading you loud and clear.* **14.** *Computers.* to obtain (data) from a storage device, such as magnetic tape. ~*n.* **15.** matter suitable for reading: *this book is a very good read.* **16.** a spell of reading. ~See also **read into, read out,** etc. [Old English *rædan* to advise, explain]

readable ('riːdəbᵊl) *adj.* **1.** (of a style of writing) interesting or pleasant to read. **2.** (of handwriting or print) legible.

reader ('riːdə) *n.* **1.** a person who reads. **2.** *Chiefly Brit.* a member of staff below a professor but above a senior lecturer at a university. **3.** a book of texts for those learning a foreign language. **4.** a person who reads aloud in public. **5.** a person who reads and assesses the merit of manuscripts submitted to a publisher. **6.** a proofreader. **7.** short for **lay reader.**

readership ('riːdəʃɪp) *n.* all the readers collectively of a particular publication or author: *a readership of five million.*

reading ('riːdɪŋ) *n.* **1.** the act of a person who reads. **2.** ability to read: *her reading is good for a 6-year-old.* **3.** material for reading. **4.** a public recital of a literary work. **5.** the form of a particular word or passage in a given text, esp. where more than one version exists. **6.** an interpretation, as of a situation or something said. **7.** knowledge gained from books. **8.** a measurement indicated by a gauge or dial. **9.** *Parliamentary procedure.* one of the three stages in the passage of a bill through a legislative assembly. ~*adj.* **10.** of or for reading: *a reading lamp.*

read into (riːd) *vb.* to discern in or infer from a statement (meanings not intended by the speaker or writer).

read out (riːd) *vb.* **1.** to read (something) aloud. **2.** to retrieve information from a computer memory or storage device. ~*n.* **read-out.** **3. a.** the act of retrieving information from a computer. **b.** the information retrieved.

read up (riːd) *vb.* (often foll. by *on*) to

acquire information about (a subject) by reading intensively.

read-write head ('riːd'raɪt) *n.* *Computers.* an electromagnet that can both read and write information on a magnetic tape or disk.

ready ('rɛdɪ) *adj.* **readier, readiest. 1.** in a state of completion or preparedness, as for use or action. **2.** prompt or eager: *a ready response; ready with complaints.* **3.** quick; intelligent: *a ready wit.* **4.** (foll. by *to*) on the point (of) or liable (to): *ready to collapse.* **5.** easily available: *a ready market.* ~*n.* **6.** *Informal.* See **ready money. 7. at the ready.** poised for use: *with pen at the ready.* ~*vb.* **readying, readied. 8.** to put in a state of readiness; prepare. [Old English (*ge*)*ræde*] —'**readily** *adv.* —'**readiness** *n.*

ready-made *adj.* **1.** made for purchase and immediate use by any customer. **2.** extremely convenient or ideally suited: *a ready-made solution.*

ready money *n.* funds for immediate use; cash. Also: **the ready, the readies.**

reafforest (ˌriːə'fɒrɪst) *vb.* to replant (an area that was formerly forested). —ˌre-af,forest'ation *n.*

reagent (riː'eɪdʒənt) *n.* a substance for use in a chemical reaction.

real¹ (rɪəl) *adj.* **1.** existing or occurring in the physical world; not imaginary or theoretical. **2.** true; actual: *the real reason.* **3.** important or serious: *a real problem.* **4.** rightly so called: *a real friend.* **5.** not artificial: *real fur.* **6.** (of food or drink) made in a traditional way to ensure the best flavour. **7.** *Econ.* (of prices or incomes) considered in terms of purchasing power rather than nominal currency value. **8.** relating to immovable property such as land or buildings: *real estate.* **9.** *Maths.* involving or containing real numbers alone; having no imaginary part. **10. the real thing.** the genuine article, not a substitute. [Latin *rēs* thing]

real² (reɪ'ɑːl) *n.* a former small Spanish or Spanish-American silver coin. [Spanish, lit.: royal]

real estate *n.* *Chiefly U.S. & Canad.* immovable property, esp. land and houses.

realism ('rɪəˌlɪzəm) *n.* **1.** awareness or acceptance of things as they are, as opposed to the abstract or ideal. **2.** a style in art that seeks to represent the familiar or typical in real life. **3.** *Philosophy.* the theory that physical objects continue to exist whether they are perceived or not. —'**realist** *n.* —ˌrea'listic *adj.*

reality (rɪ'ælɪtɪ) *n., pl.* **-ties. 1.** the state of things as they are or appear to be, rather than as one might wish them to be. **2.** something that is real. **3.** the state of being real. **4. in reality.** actually; in fact.

realize *or* **-ise** ('rɪəˌlaɪz) *vb.* **1.** to become conscious or aware of (something). **2.**

readjust
readmission
readmit

readopt
reaffirmation
realign

realignment

(*often passive*) to bring (a plan or ambition) to fruition. **3.** (of goods or property) to sell for (a certain sum): *this table realized £800.* **4.** to convert (property or goods) into cash. **5.** to produce a complete work of art from an idea or draft. —**reali'zation** *or* **-i'sation** *n.*

really ('rɪəlɪ) *adv.* **1.** in reality: *it's really quite harmless.* **2.** truly; genuinely: *really beautiful.* ~*interj.* **3.** an exclamation of dismay, doubt, surprise, etc.

realm (rɛlm) *n.* **1.** a kingdom: *peer of the realm.* **2.** a field of interest or study: *the realm of the occult.* [Old French]

real number *n.* any rational or irrational number.

real tennis *n.* an ancient form of tennis played in a four-walled indoor court.

real-time *adj.* of a data-processing system in which a computer is on-line to a source of data and processes the data as it is generated.

realtor ('rɪəltə) *n. U.S. & Canad.* an estate agent.

realty ('rɪəltɪ) *n.* same as **real estate.**

ream (riːm) *n.* **1.** a number of sheets of paper, now equal to 500 or 516 sheets (20 quires). **2.** (*often pl.*) *Informal.* a large quantity, esp. of written matter: *he wrote reams.* [Arabic *rizmah* bale]

reap (riːp) *vb.* **1.** to cut or harvest (a crop) from (a field). **2.** to gain (something) as a reward for or result of some action. [Old English *riopan*]

reaper ('riːpə) *n.* **1.** a person who reaps or a machine for reaping. **2. the grim reaper.** death.

rear[1] (rɪə) *n.* **1.** the back part. **2.** the area or position that lies at the back: *a garden at the rear of the house.* **3.** *Informal.* the buttocks. **4. bring up the rear.** to be at the end; come last. **5.** (*modifier*) of or in the rear: *the rear side.* [Old French *rer*]

rear[2] (rɪə) *vb.* **1.** to care for and educate (children) until maturity; raise. **2.** to breed (animals) or grow (plants). **3.** to place or lift (something) upright. **4.** (often foll. by *up*) (esp. of horses) to lift the front legs in the air and stand nearly upright. **5.** (often foll. by *up* or *over*) (esp. of tall buildings) to rise high; tower. [Old English *rǣran*]

rear admiral *n.* a high-ranking naval officer.

rearguard ('rɪəˌɡɑːd) *n.* **1.** a body of troops who protect the rear of a military formation, esp. in retreat. **2. rearguard action.** an effort to prevent or postpone the inevitable.

rear light *or* **lamp** *n.* a red light, usually one of a pair, attached to the rear of a vehicle.

rearm (riːˈɑːm) *vb.* **1.** to arm again. **2.** to

equip with better weapons. —**re'armament** *n.*

rearmost ('rɪəˌməʊst) *adj.* nearest the back; coming last.

rear-view mirror *n.* a mirror on a motor vehicle enabling the driver to see traffic behind him.

rearward ('rɪəwəd) *adj., adv.* Also (for adv. only): **rearwards.** towards or in the rear.

reason ('riːz'n) *n.* **1.** a cause or motive, as for a belief or action. **2.** an argument in favour of or a justification for something. **3.** the faculty of rational argument, deduction, or judgment. **4.** sanity. **5. by reason of.** because of. **6. in** *or* **within reason.** within moderate or justifiable bounds. **7. it stands to reason.** it is logical or obvious. ~*vb.* **8.** to think logically or draw (logical conclusions) from facts or premises. **9.** (usually foll. by *with*) to seek to persuade by reasoning. **10.** (often foll. by *out*) to work out (a problem) by reasoning. [Latin *rērī* to think]

reasonable ('riːznəb'l) *adj.* **1.** showing reason or sound judgment. **2.** having modest expectations; not making unfair demands. **3.** moderate in price. **4.** fair; average: *reasonable weather.* —**'reasonably** *adv.* —**'reasonableness** *n.*

reasoning ('riːzənɪŋ) *n.* **1.** the process of drawing conclusions from facts or evidence. **2.** the conclusions reached.

reassure (ˌriːəˈʃʊə) *vb.* to relieve (someone) of anxieties; restore confidence to. —ˌreas'surance *n.* —ˌreas'suring *adj.*

rebate ('riːbeɪt) *n.* a refund of a fraction of the amount payable; discount. [Old French *rabattre* to beat down]

rebel *vb.* (rɪˈbɛl), **-belling, -belled.** (often foll. by *against*) **1.** to resist openly or fight against the established government. **2.** to reject an accepted moral code or convention of behaviour. ~*n.* ('rɛb'l). **3. a.** a person who rebels. **b.** (*as modifier*): *rebel troops.* **4.** a person who rejects some accepted moral code or convention of behaviour. [Latin *re-* again + *bellum* war]

rebellion (rɪˈbɛljən) *n.* **1.** organized opposition to a government or other authority. **2.** rejection of an accepted moral code or convention of behaviour. [Latin *rebelliō*]

rebellious (rɪˈbɛljəs) *adj.* rebelling or showing a tendency towards rebellion. —re'belliously *adv.*

rebirth (riːˈbɜːθ) *n.* a revival or renaissance: *the rebirth of learning.*

rebound *vb.* (rɪˈbaʊnd). **1.** to spring back, as from a sudden impact. **2.** (of a plan or action) to misfire so as to hurt the perpetrator. ~*n.* ('riːbaʊnd). **3.** the act of rebounding. **4. on the rebound.** *Informal.* while recovering from rejection: *he*

---

reallocate	reappraisal	reassemble
reappear	reappraise	reassert
reappearance	rearrange	reassess
reapply	rearrangement	reawaken
reappoint	rearrest	reborn

married her on the rebound from an unhappy love affair.

rebuff (rɪ'bʌf) *vb.* **1.** to snub and reject someone who offers help, advice, or sympathy or makes a suggestion or request. ~*n.* **2.** a blunt refusal; snub. [Old French *rebuffer*]

rebuke (rɪ'bjuːk) *vb.* **1.** to reprimand (someone). ~*n.* **2.** a reprimand. [Old French *rebuker*]

rebus ('riːbəs) *n., pl.* **-buses.** a puzzle consisting of pictures and symbols representing syllables and words; the word *hear* might be represented by H and a picture of an ear. [Latin *rēbus* by things]

rebut (rɪ'bʌt) *vb.* **-butting, -butted.** to disprove, esp. by offering a contrary argument. [Old French *reboter*] —**re'buttal** *n.*

recalcitrant (rɪ'kælsɪtrənt) *adj.* not willing to submit to, or cooperate with, authority. [Latin *re-* again + *calcitrāre* to kick] —**re'calcitrance** *n.*

recall (rɪ'kɔːl) *vb.* **1.** to bring back to mind; remember. **2.** to order to return. ~*n.* **3.** the act of recalling. **4.** the ability to remember things; recollection.

recant (rɪ'kænt) *vb.* to take back (a former belief or statement), esp. formally in public. [Latin *re-* again + *cantāre* to sing] —**recantation** (ˌriːkæn'teɪʃən) *n.*

recap *Informal.* ~*vb.* ('riː,kæp, riː'kæp), **-capping, -capped. 1.** to recapitulate. ~*n.* ('riː,kæp). **2.** a recapitulation.

recapitulate (ˌriːkə'pɪtjuˌleɪt) *vb.* to restate the main points of (an argument or speech). [Late Latin *recapitulāre*, lit.: put back under headings]

recapitulation (ˌriːkə,pɪtjuˈleɪʃən) *n.* **1.** the act of recapitulating. **2.** *Music.* the repeating of earlier themes, esp. in the final section of a movement.

recapture (riː'kæptʃə) *vb.* **1.** to relive vividly (a former experience or sensation): *recaptured images of the past.* **2.** to capture again. ~*n.* **3.** the act of recapturing.

recce ('rɛkɪ) *n., vb.* **-ceing, -ced** *or* **-ceed.** *Slang.* short for **reconnaissance** or **reconnoitre.**

recede (rɪ'siːd) *vb.* **1.** to withdraw from a point or limit; go back: *the tide receded.* **2.** to become more distant: *hopes of rescue receded.* **3.** to slope backwards: *apes have receding foreheads.* **4.** (of a man's hair) to cease to grow at the temples and above the forehead. [Latin *recēdere* to go back]

receipt (rɪ'siːt) *n.* **1.** a written acknowledgment by a receiver of money or goods that payment or delivery has been made. **2.** the act of receiving. **3.** (*usually pl.*) money taken in over a particular period, as by a shop. **4.** *Archaic.* a recipe. [Old French *receite*]

receive (rɪ'siːv) *vb.* **1.** to get (something offered or sent to one). **2.** to be informed of (news). **3.** to react to: *the book was well received.* **4.** to experience: *she received minor injuries.* **5.** to greet (guests). **6.** to have (an honour) bestowed: *he received*

the Order of the Garter. **7.** to admit (a person) to a society or condition: *he was received into the priesthood.* **8.** to support or sustain (the weight of something). **9.** to convert (incoming radio or television signals) into sounds or pictures. **10.** *Tennis, etc.* to play at the other end from the server. **11.** *Chiefly Brit.* to buy and sell stolen goods. [Latin *recipere*]

received (rɪ'siːvd) *adj.* generally accepted or believed: *received wisdom.*

Received Pronunciation *n.* the accent of standard Southern British English.

receiver (rɪ'siːvə) *n.* **1.** a person appointed by a court to manage property after the owner has been declared bankrupt. **2.** *Chiefly Brit.* a person who receives stolen goods knowing that they have been stolen. **3.** the equipment in a telephone, radio, or television that converts the incoming signals into sounds or pictures. **4.** the detachable part of a telephone that is held to the ear.

receivership (rɪ'siːvəʃɪp) *n. Law.* the condition of being administered by a receiver: *the company went into receivership.*

recent ('riːs°nt) *adj.* having appeared, happened, or been made not long ago. [Latin *recens* fresh] —**'recently** *adv.*

Recent ('riːs°nt) *adj. Geol.* of the current geological epoch, which began about 10 000 years ago.

receptacle (rɪ'sɛptək°l) *n.* **1.** an object that holds something; container. **2.** *Bot.* the enlarged or modified tip of the flower stalk that bears the flower. [Latin *receptāculum* store-place]

reception (rɪ'sɛpʃən) *n.* **1.** the act of receiving or state of being received. **2.** the manner in which something is received: *a hostile reception.* **3.** a formal party for guests, esp. after a wedding. **4.** an area in an office, hotel, etc., where visitors are received or reservations dealt with. **5.** *Radio & television.* the quality of a received broadcast: *the reception was poor.*

receptionist (rɪ'sɛpʃənɪst) *n.* a person employed in an office or surgery to receive clients and arrange appointments.

reception room *n.* (esp. in property advertisements) a room in a private house suitable for entertaining guests.

receptive (rɪ'sɛptɪv) *adj.* able and willing to consider and accept new ideas or suggestions. —**receptivity** (ˌriːsɛp'tɪvɪtɪ) *or* **re'ceptiveness** *n.*

recess *n.* (rɪ'sɛs, 'riːsɛs). **1.** a space, such as an alcove, set back in a wall. **2.** (*often pl.*) a secluded or secret place: *recesses of the mind.* **3.** a cessation of business, such as the closure of Parliament during a vacation. **4.** *U.S. & Canad.* a break between classes at a school. ~*vb.* (rɪ'sɛs). **5.** to set (something) in a recess. **6.** to build a recess in (something). [Latin *recessus* a retreat]

recession (rɪ'sɛʃən) *n.* **1.** a temporary

depression in economic activity or prosperity. **2.** the act of receding.

recessional (rɪˈsɛʃənˀl) *n.* a hymn sung as the clergy and choir withdraw after a church service.

recessive (rɪˈsɛsɪv) *adj.* **1.** tending to recede. **2.** *Genetics.* (in a pair of genes) designating a gene that has a characteristic which will only be passed on if the other gene has the same characteristic.

recherché (rəˈʃɛəʃeɪ) *adj.* **1.** known only to connoisseurs; choice or rare. **2.** studiedly refined or elegant. [French]

recidivism (rɪˈsɪdɪˌvɪzəm) *n.* habitual relapse into crime. [Latin *recidīvus* falling back] —**reˈcidivist** *n., adj.*

recipe (ˈrɛsɪpɪ) *n.* **1.** a list of ingredients and directions for making a particular dish. **2.** a method for achieving some desired objective: *a recipe for success.* [Latin, lit.: take (it)!]

recipient (rɪˈsɪpɪənt) *n.* a person who or thing that receives.

reciprocal (rɪˈsɪprəkˀl) *adj.* **1.** given, done, or felt by each of two people or groups about or to the other; mutual: *reciprocal trade.* **2.** given or done in return: *a reciprocal favour.* **3.** (of a pronoun) indicating that action is given and received by each subject; for example, *each other* in *they started to shout at each other.* ~*n.* **4.** Also called: **inverse.** *Maths.* a number or quantity that when multiplied by a given number or quantity gives a product of one: *the reciprocal of 2 is 0.5.* [Latin *reciprocus* alternating] —**reˈciprocally** *adv.*

reciprocate (rɪˈsɪprəˌkeɪt) *vb.* **1.** to give or feel in return: *his affection was not reciprocated.* **2.** (of a machine part) to move backwards and forwards. —**reˌciproˈcation** *n.*

reciprocity (ˌrɛsɪˈprɒsɪtɪ) *n.* **1.** reciprocal action or relation. **2.** a mutual exchange of commercial or other privileges.

recital (rɪˈsaɪtˀl) *n.* **1.** a musical performance by a soloist or soloists. **2.** the act of reciting something learned or prepared. **3.** a narration or description.

recitation (ˌrɛsɪˈteɪʃən) *n.* **1.** the act of reciting from memory, esp. before an audience. **2.** something recited.

recitative (ˌrɛsɪtəˈtiːv) *n.* a narrative passage in an opera or oratorio, reflecting the natural rhythms of speech. [Italian *recitativo*]

recite (rɪˈsaɪt) *vb.* **1.** to repeat (a poem or passage) aloud from memory before an audience. **2.** to give a detailed account of. [Latin *recitāre*]

reck (rɛk) *vb. Archaic* (*used mainly with a negative*) **1.** to mind or care about (something): *to reck nought.* **2.** to concern or interest (someone). [Old English *reccan*]

reckless (ˈrɛklɪs) *adj.* having or showing no regard for danger or consequences: *a reckless driver.* [Old English *recceleās*]

reckon (ˈrɛkən) *vb.* **1.** to calculate or compute. **2.** to include; count as part of a set or class. **3.** (*usually passive*) to consider: *he is reckoned clever.* **4.** *Informal.* to think; be of the opinion: *I reckon you don't know.* **5.** (foll. by *with* or *without*) to take into account or fail to take into account: *they reckoned without John.* **6.** (foll. by *on* or *upon*) to rely on or expect: *I reckon on your support.* [Old English *(ge)recenian* recount]

reckoning (ˈrɛkənɪŋ) *n.* **1.** counting or calculating: *by his reckoning, it had taken five hours.* **2.** settlement of an account or bill. **3.** retribution for one's actions: *the day of reckoning.*

reclaim (rɪˈkleɪm) *vb.* **1.** to regain possession of. **2.** to convert unusable or submerged land into land suitable for farming or building on. **3.** to recover (useful substances) from waste products. **4.** *Old-fashioned.* to convert (someone) from sin, folly, or vice. [Latin *reclāmāre* to cry out] —**reclamation** (ˌrɛkləˈmeɪʃən) *n.*

recline (rɪˈklaɪn) *vb.* to rest in a leaning position. [Latin *reclīnāre*]

reclining (rɪˈklaɪnɪŋ) *adj.* (of a seat) having a back that can be adjusted to slope at various angles.

recluse (rɪˈkluːs) *n.* a person who lives in seclusion; a hermit. [Late Latin *reclūdere* to shut away] —**reˈclusive** *adj.*

recognition (ˌrɛkəɡˈnɪʃən) *n.* **1.** the act of recognizing. **2.** acceptance or acknowledgment. **3.** formal acknowledgment of a government or of the independence of a country. **4. in recognition of.** as a token of thanks for.

recognizance *or* **recognisance** (rɪˈkɒɡnɪzəns) *n. Law.* **a.** an undertaking made before a court or magistrate by which a person promises to do something specified, such as to appear in court on a stated day. **b.** a sum of money pledged to the performance of such an act. [Old French *reconoissance*]

recognize *or* **-ise** (ˈrɛkəɡˌnaɪz) *vb.* **1.** to identify (a person or thing) as someone or something previously seen or known; know again. **2.** to accept or be aware of (a fact or problem): *to recognize necessity.* **3.** to give formal acknowledgment of the status or legality of (something or someone, esp. a government or a representative). **4.** to make formal acknowledgment of (a claim or duty). **5.** to show approval or appreciation of (something). [Latin *re-* again + *cognoscere* to know] —**ˈrecogˌnizable** *or* **-isable** *adj.*

recoil *vb.* (rɪˈkɔɪl). **1.** to jerk back, as from an impact or violent thrust. **2.** (often foll. by *from*) to draw back in fear, horror, or disgust. **3.** (foll. by *on* or *upon*) to go wrong, esp. so as to hurt the perpetrator. ~*n.* (rɪˈkɔɪl, ˈriːkɔɪl). **4.** the backward movement of a gun when fired. **5.** the act of recoiling. [Old French *reculer*]

recollect (ˌrekəˈlekt) *vb.* to remember. [Latin *recolligere*] —ˌrecolˈlection *n.*

recommend (ˌrekəˈmend) *vb.* **1.** to advise as the best course or choice. **2.** to praise or commend: *to recommend a new book.* **3.** to make attractive or advisable: *the trip has little to recommend it.* [Latin *re-* again + *commendāre* to commend] —**recommendation** (ˌrekəmenˈdeɪʃən) *n.*

recompense (ˈrekəmˌpens) *vb.* **1.** to pay or reward for service, work, or help. **2.** to compensate for loss or injury. ~*n.* **3.** compensation for loss or injury. **4.** reward, remuneration, or repayment. [Latin *re-* again + *compensāre* to balance]

reconcile (ˈrekənˌsaɪl) *vb.* **1.** (*often passive;* usually foll. by *to*) to make (oneself or another) no longer opposed; cause to accept something unpleasant: *she reconciled herself to poverty.* **2.** to re-establish friendly relations with (a person or people) or between (people). **3.** to settle (a quarrel). **4.** to make (two apparently conflicting things) compatible or consistent with each other. [Latin *reconciliāre*] —**reconciliation** (ˌrekənˌsɪliˈeɪʃən) *n.*

recondite (rɪˈkɒndaɪt, ˈrekənˌdaɪt) *adj.* **1.** requiring special knowledge; abstruse. **2.** dealing with abstruse or profound subjects. [Latin *reconditus* hidden away]

recondition (ˌriːkənˈdɪʃən) *vb.* to restore to good condition or working order: *a reconditioned engine.* —**reconditioned** *adj.*

reconnaissance (rɪˈkɒnɪsəns) *n.* **1.** the process of obtaining information about the position, strength, and movements of an enemy. **2.** a preliminary inspection. [French]

reconnoitre *or U.S.* **reconnoiter** (ˌrekəˈnɔɪtə) *vb.* to make a reconnaissance of. [obs. French *reconnoître*]

reconsider (ˌriːkənˈsɪdə) *vb.* to consider (something) again, with a view to changing one's policy or course of action. —**reconˌsiderˈation** *n.*

reconstitute (riːˈkɒnstɪˌtjuːt) *vb.* **1.** to restore (food) to its former state, as by adding water to a concentrate. **2.** to reconstruct (something), esp. in a slightly different form. —**reconstiˈtution** *n.*

reconstruct (ˌriːkənˈstrʌkt) *vb.* **1.** to form again; rebuild. **2.** to form a picture of (a past event, esp. a crime) by piecing together evidence. —**reconˈstruction** *n.*

record *n.* (ˈrekɔːd). **1.** an account in permanent form, esp. in writing, preserving knowledge or information. **2.** (*often pl.*) information or data on a subject collected over a long period: *weather records.* **3.** Also called: **disc.** a thin disc of a plastic material upon which sound has been recorded in a continuous spiral groove on each side. **4.** the best or most outstanding amount, rate, height, etc., ever attained, as in some field of sport: *a world record.* **5.** the sum of one's recognized achievements, career, or performance. **6.** a list of crimes

of which an accused person has previously been convicted. **7.** anything serving as evidence or as a memorial: *the First World War is a record of human folly.* **8.** *Computers.* a group of data or piece of information preserved as a unit in machine-readable form. **9. for the record.** for the sake of strict factual accuracy. **10. go on record.** to state one's views publicly. **11. have a record.** to have previous criminal convictions. **12. off the record.** confidential or confidentially. **13. on record. a.** stated in a public document. **b.** publicly known. ~*vb.* (rɪˈkɔːd). **14.** to set down in some permanent form so as to preserve the true facts of: *to record the minutes of a meeting.* **15.** to make a recording of (music or speech) for later reproduction or broadcasting. **16.** to show or register: *his face recorded his disappointment; this thermometer records how hot it is.* [Latin *recordārī* to remember]

recorded delivery *n.* a Post Office service by which an official record of posting and delivery is obtained for a letter or package.

recorder (rɪˈkɔːdə) *n.* **1.** a person or machine that records. **2.** short for **tape recorder.** **3.** *Music.* a wind instrument, blown through the end with finger-holes and a reedlike tone. **4.** (in England and Wales) a barrister or solicitor appointed to sit as a part-time judge in the crown court.

recording (rɪˈkɔːdɪŋ) *n.* **1.** the process of storing sounds or visual signals for later use. **2.** something that has been recorded, such as a radio programme.

record player *n.* a device for reproducing the sounds stored on a record. A stylus vibrates in accordance with the undulations of the walls of the groove in the rotating record, and its vibrations are converted into sound.

recount (rɪˈkaʊnt) *vb.* to tell the story or details of; narrate. [Old French *reconter*]

re-count *vb.* (riːˈkaʊnt). **1.** to count again. ~*n.* (ˈriːˌkaʊnt). **2.** a second or further count, esp. of votes in an election.

recoup (rɪˈkuːp) *vb.* **1.** to regain or make good (a financial or other loss). **2.** to reimburse or compensate (someone), as for a loss. [Old French *recouper* to cut back] —**reˈcoupment** *n.*

recourse (rɪˈkɔːs) *n.* **1. have recourse to.** to turn to a person, organization, or course of action (when in difficulty). **2.** a person, organization, or course of action that is turned to for help. [Latin *re-* back + *currere* to run]

recover (rɪˈkʌvə) *vb.* **1.** to find again or obtain the return of (something lost). **2.** (of a person) to regain health, spirits, or composure. **3.** to regain a former and better condition: *industry recovered after the war.* **4.** to get back or make good (expense or loss). **5.** *Law.* to gain (something) by the judgment of a court: *to recover damages.* **6.** to obtain (useful substances) from waste. [Latin *recuperāre*] —**re'coverable** *adj.*

recovery (rɪ'kʌvərɪ) *n., pl.* -**eries.** 1. the act or process of recovering, esp. from sickness, a shock, or a setback. 2. restoration to a former and better condition. 3. the regaining of something lost. 4. the extraction of useful substances from waste.

recreant ('rɛkrɪənt) *n. Archaic.* a disloyal or cowardly person. [Old French *recroire* to surrender]

re-create (,riːkrɪ'eɪt) *vb.* to create anew; reproduce. —,**re-cre'ation** *n.*

recreation (,rɛkrɪ'eɪʃən) *n.* 1. refreshment of health or spirits by relaxation and enjoyment. 2. an activity that promotes this. [Latin *recreāre* to refresh] —,**rec-re'ational** *adj.*

recrimination (rɪ,krɪmɪ'neɪʃən) *n. (often pl.)* accusations made by two people or groups about each other: *bitter recriminations; bouts of recrimination.* [Latin *re-* back + *crīminārī* to accuse] —**re'criminatory** *adj.*

recrudesce (,riːkruː'dɛs) *vb.* (of trouble or a disease) to break out or appear again after a period of quiet. [Latin *re-* again + *crūdus* bloody, raw] —,**recru'descence** *n.*

recruit (rɪ'kruːt) *vb.* 1. to enlist (people) for military service. 2. to enrol or obtain (members or support). ~*n.* 3. a newly joined member of a military service. 4. any new member or supporter. [French *recrute* new growth] —**re'cruitment** *n.*

rectal ('rɛktəl) *adj.* of the rectum.

rectangle ('rɛk,tæŋɡl) *n.* a shape with four straight sides and four right angles. [Latin *rectus* straight + *angulus* angle] —**rectangular** (rɛk'tæŋɡʊlə) *adj.*

rectify ('rɛktɪ,faɪ) *vb.* -**fying,** -**fied.** 1. to put right; correct. 2. to separate (a substance) from a mixture or refine (a substance) by distillation. 3. to convert (alternating current) into direct current. [Latin *rectus* straight + *facere* to make] —,**rectifi'cation** *n.* —**'recti,fier** *n.*

rectilinear (,rɛktɪ'lɪnɪə) *adj.* 1. in, moving in, or characterized by a straight line. 2. bounded by or formed of straight lines.

rectitude ('rɛktɪ,tjuːd) *n.* moral or religious correctness. [Latin *rectus* right]

recto ('rɛktəʊ) *n., pl.* -**tos.** 1. the front of a sheet of printed paper. 2. the right-hand pages of a book. [Latin: on the right]

rector ('rɛktə) *n.* 1. *Church of England.* a clergyman in charge of a parish in which he would, formerly, have received all the tithes. 2. *R.C. Church.* a cleric in charge of a college, religious house, or congregation. 3. *Chiefly Brit.* the head of certain schools, colleges, or universities. 4. (in Scotland) a high-ranking official in a university, elected by the students. [Latin: director] —**'rectorship** *n.*

rectory ('rɛktərɪ) *n., pl.* -**ries.** the house of a rector.

rectum ('rɛktəm) *n., pl.* -**tums** *or* -**ta.** the lower part of the alimentary canal, ending in the anus. [Latin: straight]

recumbent (rɪ'kʌmbənt) *adj.* lying down; reclining. [Latin *recumbere* to lie back]

recuperate (rɪ'kuːpə,reɪt) *vb.* to recover from illness or exhaustion. [Latin *recuperāre*] —**re,cuper'ation** *n.* —**re'cuperative** *adj.*

recur (rɪ'kɜː) *vb.* -**curring,** -**curred.** 1. to happen or occur again. 2. (of a thought or feeling) to come back to the mind. [Latin *re-* again + *currere* to run] —**recurrence** (rɪ'kʌrəns) *n.* —**re'current** *adj.* —**re'curring** *adj.*

recurring decimal *n.* a rational number that contains a pattern of digits repeated indefinitely after the decimal point: *1 divided by 11 gives the recurring decimal 0.09090909…*

recusant ('rɛkjʊzənt) *n.* 1. (in 16th to 18th century England) a Roman Catholic who did not attend the services of the Church of England. 2. any person who refuses to submit to authority. [Latin *recūsāns* refusing] —**'recusancy** *n.*

recycle (riː'saɪkl) *vb.* 1. to reprocess (something already used) for further use: *recycled paper.* 2. to pass (a substance) through a system again for further use.

red (rɛd) *n.* 1. any of a group of colours, such as that of a ripe tomato or fresh blood. 2. red cloth or clothing: *dressed in red.* 3. something that is red in colour, such as a red ball in snooker. 4. **in the red.** *Informal.* in debt. 5. **see red.** *Informal.* to become very angry. ~*adj.* **redder, reddest.** 6. of the colour red. 7. reddish in colour or having parts or marks that are reddish: *red hair; red deer.* 8. flushed in the face from anger or shame. 9. (of the eyes) bloodshot. 10. (of wine) made from black grapes and coloured by their skins. [Old English *rēad*] —**'reddish** *adj.* —**'redness** *n.*

Red (rɛd) *Informal.* ~*adj.* 1. revolutionary or socialist, esp. Communist. ~*n.* 2. a revolutionary or socialist, esp. a Communist.

red admiral *n.* a butterfly having black wings with red and white markings.

red blood cell *n.* same as **erythrocyte.**

red-blooded *adj. Informal.* vigorous; virile.

redbreast ('rɛd,brɛst) *n.* a bird with a red breast, esp. the Old World robin.

redbrick ('rɛd,brɪk) *n. (modifier)* of or relating to a British university founded in the late 19th or early 20th century.

red card *n. Soccer.* a piece of red pasteboard displayed by a referee to indicate that a player has been sent off.

red carpet *n.* very special treatment given to an important or honoured guest.

redcoat ('rɛd,kəʊt) *n.* 1. (formerly) a British soldier. 2. *Canad. informal.* a Mountie.

red corpuscle *n.* same as **erythrocyte.**

Red Crescent n. a national branch of the Red Cross Society in a Muslim country.

Red Cross n. an international organization (**Red Cross Society**) which helps victims of war or natural disaster.

redcurrant (ˌrɛdˈkʌrənt) n. the small edible rounded red berry of a widely-cultivated European shrub.

red deer n. a large deer of Europe and Asia, which has a reddish-brown coat and a short tail.

redden ('rɛd'n) vb. 1. to make or become red. 2. to blush, as with embarrassment.

redeem (rɪ'diːm) vb. 1. to recover possession of by payment of a price or service. 2. to convert (bonds or shares) into cash. 3. to pay off (a loan or debt). 4. to recover (something mortgaged or pawned). 5. to exchange (coupons) for goods. 6. to fulfil (a promise). 7. to reinstate in someone's good opinion: he redeemed himself by his altruistic action. 8. to make amends for. 9. to recover from captivity, esp. by a money payment. 10. Christianity. (of Christ as Saviour) to free (humanity) from sin by death on the Cross. [Latin re- back + emere to buy] —re'deemable adj. —re'deemer n.

Redeemer (rɪ'diːmə) n. the. Christianity. Jesus Christ.

redeeming (rɪ'diːmɪŋ) adj. serving to compensate for faults or deficiencies: he has no redeeming feature.

redemption (rɪ'dɛmpʃən) n. 1. the act of redeeming. 2. the state of being redeemed. 3. Christianity. deliverance from sin through the incarnation and death of Christ. —re'demptive adj.

Red Ensign n. the ensign of the British Merchant Navy. It has the Union Jack on a red background at the upper corner.

redeploy (ˌriːdɪ'plɔɪ) vb. to assign (people) to new positions or tasks. —ˌrede'ployment n.

redevelop (ˌriːdɪ'vɛləp) vb. to rebuild or renovate (an area or building). —ˌrede'veloper n. —ˌrede'velopment n.

redfish ('rɛd,fɪʃ) n., pl. -fish or -fishes. Canad. same as **kokanee**.

red flag n. 1. a symbol of revolution. 2. a warning of danger.

red-handed adj. in the act of committing a crime or doing something wrong: caught red-handed.

red hat n. the broad-brimmed crimson hat given to cardinals as the symbol of their rank.

redhead ('rɛd,hɛd) n. a person with reddish hair. —'red,headed adj.

red herring n. anything that diverts attention from a topic or line of inquiry.

red-hot adj. 1. (esp. of metal) heated to the temperature at which it glows red. 2. extremely hot. 3. keen, excited, or eager.

4. furious: red-hot anger. 5. very recent or topical: red-hot information.

red-hot poker n. a garden plant with spikes of red or yellow flowers.

Red Indian n., adj. Offensive. American Indian.

redistribution (ˌriːdɪstrɪ'bjuːʃən) n. 1. the act of distributing again. 2. a revision of the number of seats that each province has in the Canadian House of Commons, made every ten years.

red lead (lɛd) n. a bright-red poisonous insoluble oxide of lead.

red-letter day n. a memorably important or happy occasion. [from the red letters in ecclesiastical calendars to indicate saints' days]

red light n. 1. a signal to stop, esp. a red traffic signal. 2. a danger signal.

red-light district n. an area where many prostitutes work.

red meat n. any meat that is dark in colour, esp. beef and lamb.

redo (riː'duː) vb. -doing, -did, -done. 1. to do over again. 2. Informal. to redecorate: we redid the house last summer.

redolent ('rɛdəʊlənt) adj. 1. (foll. by of or with) smelling of: a room redolent of flowers. 2. (foll. by of or with) reminiscent or suggestive of: a picture redolent of the 18th century. [Latin redolens] —'redolence n.

redouble (rɪ'dʌb'l) vb. 1. to make or become much greater, esp. in intensity: to redouble one's efforts. 2. Bridge. to double (an opponent's double).

redoubt (rɪ'daʊt) n. 1. a small fort defending a hilltop or pass. 2. a stronghold. [French redoute]

redoubtable (rɪ'daʊtəb'l) adj. to be feared and respected; formidable. [Old French redouter to dread] —re'doubtably adv.

redound (rɪ'daʊnd) vb. 1. (foll. by to) to have an advantageous or disadvantageous effect on: brave deeds redound to your credit. 2. (foll. by on or upon) to recoil or rebound. [Latin redundāre to stream over]

redox ('riːdɒks) n. a chemical reaction between two substances, in which one is oxidized and the other reduced.

red pepper n. 1. the ripe red fruit of the sweet pepper. 2. cayenne pepper.

red rag n. a provocation; something that infuriates. [so called because red objects supposedly infuriate bulls]

redress (rɪ'drɛs) vb. 1. to put right (a wrong), esp. by compensation. 2. to correct or adjust (esp. in **redress the balance**). ~n. 3. the setting right of a wrong. 4. compensation or reparation. [Old French redrecier to set up again]

red salmon n. any salmon having reddish flesh.

redshank ('rɛd,ʃæŋk) n. a large common European sandpiper with red legs.

---

redecorate	redirect	redraft
redefine	rediscover	redraw
redesign	redistribute	

red shift n. a shift in the spectral lines of the spectrum of a star or galaxy towards the red end of the visible region relative to their position in the terrestrial spectrum. It is used to calculate the velocity of the object in relation to the earth.

redskin ('rɛd,skɪn) n. *Informal, offensive.* an American Indian. [so called because one now extinct tribe painted themselves with red ochre]

red squirrel n. a reddish-brown squirrel inhabiting woodlands of Europe and parts of Asia.

redstart ('rɛd,staːt) n. **1.** a European songbird of the thrush family: the male has an orange-brown tail and breast. **2.** a North American warbler. [Old English *rēad* red + *steort* tail]

red tape n. obstructive official routine or procedure; time-consuming bureaucracy. [from the red tape used to bind official government documents]

reduce (rɪ'djuːs) vb. **1.** to make or become smaller in size, number, or intensity. **2.** to bring into a certain condition: *to reduce a forest to ashes; he was reduced to tears.* **3.** to impoverish: *to be in reduced circumstances.* **4.** to bring into a state of submission; subjugate: *the whole country was reduced after three months.* **5.** to bring down the price of (a commodity). **6.** to lower the rank or status of; demote: *reduced to the ranks.* **7.** to set out systematically as an aid to understanding; simplify: *reducing the problem to three main issues.* **8.** *Maths.* to simplify the form of (an expression or equation), esp. by substitution of one term by another. **9.** *Chem.* **a.** to undergo a chemical reaction with hydrogen. **b.** to lose oxygen atoms. **c.** to increase the number of electrons. **10.** *Cookery.* to thicken (a sauce) by boiling away some of its liquid. [Latin *redūcere* to bring back] —**re'ducible** adj.

reduction (rɪ'dʌkʃən) n. **1.** the act of reducing. **2.** the amount by which something is reduced. **3.** a reduced form of an original, such as a copy of a document on a smaller scale. —**re'ductive** adj.

redundant (rɪ'dʌndənt) adj. **1.** deprived of one's job because it is no longer necessary or sufficiently profitable. **2.** surplus to requirements. [Latin *redundans* overflowing] —**re'dundancy** n.

reduplicate (rɪ'djuːplɪ,keɪt) vb. **1.** to make double; repeat. **2.** to repeat (a word or syllable) to form a new word, sometimes with changes, as in *chitchat*.

redwood ('rɛd,wʊd) n. a giant Californian conifer with reddish bark.

re-echo (riː'ɛkəʊ) vb. **-oing, -oed.** to echo a sound that is already an echo; resound.

reed (riːd) n. **1.** a tall grass that grows in swamps and shallow water and has jointed

hollow stalks. **2.** these stalks, esp. as used for thatching. **3.** *Music.* **a.** a thin piece of cane or metal in certain wind instruments, which vibrates producing a musical note when the instrument is blown. **b.** a wind instrument or organ pipe that sounds by means of a reed. [Old English *hrēod*]

reedy ('riːdɪ) adj. **reedier, reediest. 1.** (of a place) full of reeds. **2.** having a tone like a reed instrument; shrill or piping. —**'reedily** adv. —**'reediness** n.

reef[1] (riːf) n. **1.** a ridge of rock, sand, or coral, lying just beneath the surface of the sea. **2.** a vein of ore, esp. one of gold-bearing quartz. [Middle Dutch *ref*]

reef[2] (riːf) *Naut.* ~n. **1.** the part of a sail gathered in when sail area is reduced, as in a high wind. ~vb. **2.** to reduce the area of (sail) by taking in a reef. [Middle Dutch *rif*]

reefer ('riːfə) n. **1.** Also called: **reefer jacket, reefing jacket.** a man's short heavy double-breasted woollen jacket. **2.** *Slang.* a hand-rolled cigarette containing cannabis. [from the cigarette's resemblance to the rolled reef of a sail]

reef knot n. a knot consisting of two overhand knots turned opposite ways.

reek (riːk) vb. **1.** to give off a strong unpleasant smell; stink. **2.** (often foll. by *of*) to be permeated (by): *their lyrics reek of pretentiousness.* **3.** *Chiefly dialect.* to give off smoke or fumes. ~n. **4.** a strong offensive smell; stink. **5.** *Dialect.* smoke or steam. [Old English *rēocan*]

reel[1] (riːl, rɪəl) n. **1.** a cylindrical object or frame that turns on an axis and onto which film, tape, wire, thread, etc., may be wound. **2.** such a device attached to a fishing rod, used for casting and winding in the line. ~vb. **3.** (foll. by *in* or *out*) to wind or draw with a reel: *to reel in a fish.* [Old English *hrēol*]

reel[2] (riːl, rɪəl) vb. **1.** to sway, esp. under the shock of a blow or through dizziness or drunkenness. **2.** to whirl about or have the feeling of whirling about: *his brain reeled.* [prob. from REEL[1]]

reel[3] (riːl, rɪəl) n. any of various lively Scottish dances for a fixed number of couples who combine in square and circular formations. [from REEL[2]]

reel off vb. to recite or write fluently and without apparent effort.

re-entry (riː'ɛntrɪ) n., pl. **-tries. 1.** the act of coming back into a place, esp. a country. **2.** the return of a spacecraft into the earth's atmosphere.

reeve (riːv) n. **1.** *English history.* the local representative of the king in a shire until the early 11th century. **2.** (in medieval England) a steward who supervised the daily affairs of a manor. **3.** *Canad. gov-*

re-educate	re-employ	re-establish
re-elect	re-enact	re-examination
re-election	re-enactment	re-examine
re-emerge	re-enter	
re-emphasize	re-equip	

ernment. (in some provinces) a president of a local council. [Old English _gerēva_]

ref (rɛf) _n. Informal._ the referee in a sport.

refectory (rɪˈfɛktrɪ) _n., pl._ **-ries.** a dining hall in a religious or academic institution. [Latin _refectus_ refreshed]

refectory table _n._ a long narrow dining table supported by two trestles.

refer (rɪˈfɜː) _vb._ **-ferring, -ferred.** (often foll. by _to_). **1.** to make mention (of). **2.** to direct the attention of (someone) for information: _the reader is referred to the introduction._ **3.** to seek information (from): _he referred to his notes._ **4.** to be relevant or relate (to): _the question refers to the range of materials such devices can be made from._ **5.** to hand over for consideration or decision: _to refer a complaint to another department._ **6.** to direct (a patient or client) to another doctor or agency: _her GP referred her to a specialist._ [Latin _re-_ back + _ferre_ to carry] —**referable** (ˈrɛfərəb'l) _or_ **referrable** (rɪˈfɜːrəb'l) _adj._ —**reˈferral** _n._

referee (ˌrɛfəˈriː) _n._ **1.** the umpire in various sports, esp. football and boxing. **2.** a person who is willing to testify to the character or capabilities of someone. ~_vb._ **-eeing, -eed.** **3.** to act as a referee.

reference (ˈrɛfərəns, ˈrɛfrəns) _n._ **1.** the act of referring. **2.** direction to a passage elsewhere in a book or to another book. **3.** a book or passage referred to. **4.** a mention: _this book contains several references to the Civil War._ **5.** (_modifier_) containing information or facts: _a reference book._ **6.** a written testimonial regarding one's character or capabilities. **7.** a person referred to for such a testimonial. **8.** (foll. by _to_) relation or restriction, esp. to or by membership of a specific group: _without reference to sex or age._ **9. with reference to.** concerning. —**referential** (ˌrɛfəˈrɛnʃəl) _adj._

referendum (ˌrɛfəˈrɛndəm) _n., pl._ **-dums** _or_ **-da** (-də). submission of an issue of importance to the direct vote of the electorate. [Latin: something to be carried back]

refill _vb._ (riːˈfɪl). **1.** to fill (something) again. ~_n._ (ˈriːfɪl). **2.** a replacement supply of a substance in a permanent container. **3.** a second or subsequent filling. —**reˈfillable** _adj._

refine (rɪˈfaɪn) _vb._ **1.** to make free from impurities; purify. **2.** to separate (a mixture) into pure constituents, as in an oil refinery. **3.** to make elegant or subtly improved: _their theories are constantly being refined._

refined (rɪˈfaɪnd) _adj._ **1.** elegant, cultured, or polite. **2.** subtle; discriminating. **3.** freed from impurities; purified.

refinement (rɪˈfaɪnmənt) _n._ **1.** the act of refining. **2.** precision of thought, expression, or manners. **3.** an improvement to something, such as a piece of equipment. **4.** a subtle point or distinction.

refinery (rɪˈfaɪnərɪ) _n., pl._ **-eries.** a factory for purifying a raw material, such as sugar or oil.

refit _vb._ (riːˈfɪt), **-fitting, -fitted.** **1.** to make ready for use again by repairing or re-equipping. ~_n._ (ˈriːˌfɪt). **2.** a repair or re-equipping, as of a ship, for further use.

reflation (riːˈfleɪʃən) _n._ an increase in the supply of money and credit designed to encourage economic activity. [RE- + -flation, as in _inflation_] —**reˈflate** _vb._ —**reˈflationary** _adj._

reflect (rɪˈflɛkt) _vb._ **1.** (of a surface or object) to throw back (light, heat, or sound). **2.** (of a mirror) to form an image of (something) by reflection. **3.** to show: _his tactics reflect his desire for power._ **4.** to bring as a consequence: _their success reflected great credit on them._ **5.** (foll. by _on_ or _upon_) to cause to be regarded in a specified way: _her behaviour reflects on the whole group._ **6.** (usually foll. by _on_) to consider carefully; ponder. [Latin _re-_ back + _flectere_ to bend]

reflecting telescope _n._ a telescope in which the initial image is formed by a concave mirror.

reflection (rɪˈflɛkʃən) _n._ **1.** the act of reflecting. **2.** something reflected or the image so produced, as by a mirror. **3.** careful or long consideration. **4.** attribution of discredit or blame: _it's no reflection on you._ **5.** _Maths._ a transformation of a shape in which right and left, or top and bottom, are reversed.

reflective (rɪˈflɛktɪv) _adj._ **1.** characterized by quiet thought or contemplation. **2.** capable of reflecting: _a reflective surface._

reflector (rɪˈflɛktə) _n._ **1.** a piece of glass or plastic, as on the back of a bicycle, that glows when light shines on it. **2.** a reflecting telescope.

reflex (ˈriːflɛks) _n._ **1.** an immediate involuntary response, such as coughing, evoked by a given stimulus. **2.** a mechanical response to a particular situation, involving no conscious decision. **3.** an image produced by reflection. ~_adj._ **4.** of or caused by a reflex: _a reflex action._ **5.** _Maths._ (of an angle) between 180° and 360°. [Latin _reflexus_ bent back]

reflex camera _n._ a camera containing a mirror which directs the light from a lens to the viewfinder, so that the image seen closely resembles the image photographed.

reflexive (rɪˈflɛksɪv) _adj._ **1.** denoting a pronoun that refers back to the subject of a sentence or clause. Thus, in _that man thinks a great deal of himself,_ the pronoun _himself_ is reflexive. **2.** denoting a verb used with a reflexive pronoun as its direct object, as in _to dress oneself._ **3.** _Physiol._ of or relating to a reflex. ~_n._ **4.** a reflexive pronoun or verb.

reflexology (ˌriːflɛkˈsɒlədʒɪ) _n._ massage of the soles of the feet as a therapy in alternative medicine. —**ˌreflexˈologist** _n._

reform (rɪˈfɔːm) _vb._ **1.** to improve (an

existing institution or law) by correction of abuses. **2.** to give up or cause to give up a bad habit or way of life. ~n. **3.** correction of abuses or malpractices: *reform of the divorce laws; social reforms.* **4.** improvement of morals or behaviour. [Latin *reformāre* to form again] —**re'formative** *adj.* —**re'former** *n.*

reformation (ˌrɛfə'meɪʃən) *n.* **1.** the act of reforming or the state of being reformed. **2. the Reformation.** a religious movement in 16th-century Europe that began as an attempt to reform the Roman Catholic Church and resulted in the establishment of the Protestant Churches.

reformatory (rɪ'fɔːmətrɪ) *n., pl.* **-ries.** (formerly) a place where young offenders were sent for corrective training.

Reformed (rɪ'fɔːmd) *adj.* of or designating a Protestant Church, esp. the Calvinist.

refract (rɪ'frækt) *vb.* to cause light, heat, or sound to undergo refraction. [Latin *re-* back + *frangere* to break] —**re'fractive** *adj.* —**re'fractor** *n.*

refracting telescope *n.* a type of telescope in which the image is formed by a set of lenses. Also called: **refractor.**

refraction (rɪ'frækʃən) *n.* **1.** *Physics.* the change in direction of a wave, such as light or sound, in passing from one medium to another in which it has a different velocity. **2.** the amount by which a wave is refracted.

refractory (rɪ'fræktərɪ) *adj.* **1.** unmanageable or rebellious. **2.** *Med.* not responding to treatment. **3.** (of a material) able to withstand high temperatures without fusion or decomposition.

refrain[1] (rɪ'freɪn) *vb.* (usually foll. by *from*) to keep oneself from doing: *I carefully refrained from looking at him.* [Latin *refrēnāre* to check with a bridle]

refrain[2] (rɪ'freɪn) *n.* **1.** a regularly recurring melody, such as the chorus of a song. **2.** a much repeated saying or idea. [Latin *refringere* to break into pieces]

refrangible (rɪ'frændʒɪb'l) *adj.* refracted.

refresh (rɪ'frɛʃ) *vb.* **1.** to revive or reinvigorate, as through rest, drink, or food. **2.** to stimulate (the memory). **3.** to replenish or enliven with something new. [Old French *refreschir*] —**re'fresher** *n.* —**re'freshing** *adj.*

refreshment (rɪ'frɛʃmənt) *n.* **1.** the act of refreshing or the state of being refreshed. **2.** (*pl.*) snacks and drinks served as a light meal.

refrigerant (rɪ'frɪdʒərənt) *n.* **1.** a fluid capable of vaporizing at low temperatures: used as the working fluid of a refrigerator. ~*adj.* **2.** causing cooling or freezing.

refrigerate (rɪ'frɪdʒə,reɪt) *vb.* to chill or freeze, esp. in order to preserve. [Latin *refrīgerāre* to make cold] —**re,friger'ation** *n.*

refrigerator (rɪ'frɪdʒə,reɪtə) *n.* a cabinet or room for keeping food and drink cool. Informal name: **fridge.**

refuel (riː'fjuːəl) *vb.* **-elling, -elled** *or U.S.* **-eling, -eled.** to supply or be supplied with fresh fuel.

refuge ('rɛfjuːdʒ) *n.* **1.** shelter or protection, as from the weather or danger. **2.** a place, person, or thing that offers protection, help, or relief. [Latin *re-* back + *fugere* to escape]

refugee (ˌrɛfjʊ'dʒiː) *n.* a person who has fled from some danger, esp. war or political persecution.

refulgent (rɪ'fʌldʒənt) *adj. Literary.* shining, brilliant, or radiant. [Latin *refulgēre* to reflect] —**re'fulgence** *n.*

refund *vb.* (rɪ'fʌnd). **1.** to give back (money), as when an article purchased is unsatisfactory. **2.** to reimburse (a person). ~*n.* ('riː,fʌnd). **3.** return of money to a purchaser or the amount returned. [Latin *re-* back + *fundere* to pour] —**re'fundable** *adj.*

refurbish (riː'fɜːbɪʃ) *vb.* to renovate and brighten up. —**re'furbishment** *n.*

refusal (rɪ'fjuːz'l) *n.* **1.** the act of refusing. **2.** the opportunity to reject or accept; option: *he gave me first refusal.*

refuse[1] (rɪ'fjuːz) *vb.* **1.** to decline to accept (something offered): *to refuse promotion.* **2.** to decline to give or allow (something) to (someone). **3.** to be determined not (to do something): *he refuses to talk about it.* **4.** (of a horse) to be unwilling to take (a jump). [Latin *refundere* to pour back]

refuse[2] ('rɛfjuːs) *n.* anything thrown away; rubbish. [Old French *refuser* to refuse]

refusenik *or* **refusnik** (rɪ'fjuːznɪk) *n.* a Jew in the USSR who has been refused permission to emigrate.

refute (rɪ'fjuːt) *vb.* to prove (a statement, theory, or charge) to be false or incorrect. [Latin *refūtāre*] —**refu'tation** *n.*

regain (rɪ'geɪn) *vb.* **1.** to get back; recover. **2.** to reach again: *to regain the shore.*

regal ('riːg'l) *adj.* **1.** of or fit for a king or queen; royal. **2.** splendid and dignified; magnificent. [Latin *rēgālis*] —**re'gality** *n.* —**'regally** *adv.*

regale (rɪ'geɪl) *vb.* (usually foll. by *with*) **1.** to give delight or amusement to: *he regaled them with stories.* **2.** to provide with choice or abundant food or drink. [French *régaler*]

regalia (rɪ'geɪlɪə) *n.* (*pl.*, *sometimes functioning as sing.*) the ceremonial emblems or robes of royalty, high office, or a society. [Medieval Latin: royal privileges]

regard (rɪ'gɑːd) *vb.* **1.** to look closely or attentively at (something or someone). **2.** to look upon or think of in a specified way: *she regarded her brother as her responsibility; we regard your work very highly.* **3.** to take notice of: *he has never regarded the conventions.* **4. as regards.** in respect of; concerning. ~*n.* **5.** respect or affection. **6.** a gaze; look. **7.** attention; heed: *he spends without regard to his bank balance.*

8. reference or connection: *with regard to my complaint.* **9.** (*pl.*) good wishes or greetings; used at the close of a letter: *with kind regards, Bill.* [Old French *regarder* to look at, care about]

regardful (rɪˈgɑːdful) *adj.* (often foll. by *of*) heedful (of).

regarding (rɪˈgɑːdɪŋ) *prep.* in respect of; on the subject of.

regardless (rɪˈgɑːdlɪs) *adj.* **1.** (usually foll. by *of*) taking no notice; heedless: *regardless of what the law says.* ~*adv.* **2.** disregarding drawbacks or difficulties: *carried on regardless.*

regatta (rɪˈgætə) *n.* an organized series of races of boats, esp. yachts or rowing boats. [obs. Italian *rigatta* contest]

regency (ˈriːdʒənsɪ) *n., pl.* **-cies.** **1.** government by a regent. **2.** the office of a regent. **3.** a period when a regent is in power. [Latin *regere* to rule]

Regency (ˈriːdʒənsɪ) *adj.* of the regency (1811-20) of the Prince of Wales (later George IV) or the styles of architecture, furniture, etc. produced during it.

regenerate *vb.* (rɪˈdʒɛnəˌreɪt). **1.** to undergo moral, spiritual, or physical renewal. **2.** to come or bring into existence once again. **3.** to replace (lost or damaged tissues or organs) by new growth. ~*adj.* (rɪˈdʒɛnərɪt). **4.** morally, spiritually, or physically renewed or reborn. —reˌgenerˈation *n.* —reˈgenerative *adj.*

regent (ˈriːdʒənt) *n.* **1.** the ruler of a country during the childhood, absence, or incapacity of its monarch. **2.** *U.S. & Canad.* a member of the governing board of certain schools and colleges. ~*adj.* **3.** acting as a regent: *the Prince Regent.* [Latin *regere* to rule]

reggae (ˈrɛgeɪ) *n.* a type of popular music of Jamaican origin with four beats to the bar, the upbeat being strongly accented. [West Indian]

regicide (ˈrɛdʒɪˌsaɪd) *n.* **1.** the killing of a king. **2.** a person who kills a king. [Latin *rēx* king + *caedere* to kill]

regime (reɪˈʒiːm) *n.* **1.** a system of government or a particular administration: *a fascist regime.* **2.** a social system or order. **3.** *Med.* a regimen. [French]

regimen (ˈrɛdʒɪˌmɛn) *n. Med.* a systematic course of therapy, often including a recommended diet. [Latin: guidance]

regiment (ˈrɛdʒɪmənt) *n.* **1.** a military formation varying in size from a battalion to a number of battalions. **2.** a large number. [Late Latin *regimentum* government] —ˌregiˈmental *adj.*

regimentals (ˌrɛdʒɪˈmɛntʰlz) *pl. n.* **1.** the uniform and insignia of a regiment. **2.** military dress.

regimented (ˈrɛdʒɪˌmɛntɪd) *adj.* very strictly controlled: *the regimented lifestyle of the industrial world.* —ˌregimenˈtation *n.*

Regina (rɪˈdʒaɪnə) *n.* queen: now used chiefly in documents and inscriptions. [Latin]

region (ˈriːdʒən) *n.* **1.** any large continuous part of a surface or space. **2.** an area

considered as a unit for geographical, social, or cultural reasons. **3.** an administrative division of a country. **4.** a sphere of activity or interest. **5. in the region of.** approximately: *in the region of £150.* **6.** a part of the body: *the lumbar region.* [Latin *regiō*] —**regional** *adj.*

register (ˈrɛdʒɪstə) *n.* **1.** an official list recording names, events, or transactions. **2.** the book in which such a list is written. **3.** a device that records data, totals sums of money, etc.: *a cash register.* **4.** *Music.* **a.** the timbre characteristic of a certain manner of voice production. **b.** any of the stops on an organ in respect of its tonal quality: *the flute register.* **5.** a style of speaking or writing, such as slang, used in particular circumstances or social situations. ~*vb.* **6.** to enter (an event, person's name, ownership, etc.) in a register. **7.** to show on a scale or other measuring instrument: *the current didn't register on the meter.* **8.** to show in a person's face or bearing: *his face registered surprise.* **9.** *Informal.* to have an effect; make an impression: *the news of her uncle's death just did not register.* **10.** to have a letter or parcel insured against loss by the Post Office: *registered mail.* [Medieval Latin *registrum*] —**registration** (ˌrɛdʒɪˈstreɪʃən) *n.*

register office *n. Brit.* a government office where civil marriages are performed and births, marriages, and deaths are recorded.

registrar (ˌrɛdʒɪˈstrɑː) *n.* **1.** a person who keeps official records. **2.** an administrative official responsible for student records and enrolment in a college. **3.** *Brit. & N.Z.* a hospital doctor senior to a houseman but junior to a consultant.

registration document *n. Brit.* a document giving identification details of a vehicle, including its owner's name.

registration number *n.* a sequence of letters and numbers assigned to a motor vehicle when it is registered, displayed on numberplates at the front and rear.

registration plate *n. Austral. & N.Z.* the numberplate of a vehicle.

registry (ˈrɛdʒɪstrɪ) *n., pl.* **-tries.** **1.** a place where registers are kept. **2.** the registration of a ship's country of origin: *a ship of Liberian registry.*

registry office *n. Brit.* same as **register office.**

Regius professor (ˈriːdʒəs) *n. Brit.* a person appointed by the Crown to a university chair founded by a royal patron. [Latin *regius* royal]

regress *vb.* (rɪˈgrɛs). **1.** to revert to a former and worse condition. ~*n.* (ˈriːgrɛs). **2.** reversion to a former and worse condition. [Latin *regredī* to go back] —re**ˈgressive** *adj.*

regression (rɪˈgrɛʃən) *n.* **1.** *Psychol.* the adoption by an adult of behaviour more appropriate to a child. **2.** the act of regressing.

regret (rɪˈgrɛt) *vb.* **-gretting, -gretted. 1.** to feel sorry, repentant, or upset about. **2.** to express apology or distress: *we regret* *the inconvenience caused.* ~n. **3.** a sense of repentance, guilt, or sorrow. **4.** (pl.) a polite expression of refusal: *send my regrets.* [Old French *regreter*] —re'**gretful** adj. —re'**grettable** adj. —re'**grettably** adv.

regular ('rɛgjʊlə) adj. **1.** normal, customary, or usual. **2.** according to a uniform principle, arrangement, or order. **3.** occurring at fixed or prearranged intervals: *a regular call on a customer.* **4.** following a set rule or normal practice. **5.** symmetrical in appearance; even: *regular features.* **6.** officially qualified or recognized: *he's not a regular doctor.* **7.** complete; utter: *a regular fool.* **8.** *U.S. & Canad. informal.* likable: *a regular guy.* **9.** of or serving in the permanent military services: *a regular soldier.* **10.** *Grammar.* following the usual pattern of formation in a language: *regular verbs.* **11.** *Maths.* (of a polygon) having all its sides and angles the same. **12.** *Informal.* not constipated: *eating fresh vegetables helps keep you regular.* **13.** subject to the rule of an established religious community: *canons regular.* ~n. **14.** a professional long-term serviceman in a military unit. **15.** *Informal.* a frequent customer, visitor, or member of an audience. [Latin *rēgula* ruler, model] —**,regu'larity** n. —'**regular,ize** or -,**ise** vb. —'**regularly** adv.

regulate ('rɛgjʊ,leɪt) vb. **1.** to adjust (the amount of heat, sound, etc.) as required; control. **2.** to adjust (an instrument or appliance) so that it operates correctly. **3.** to bring into conformity with a rule, principle, or usage. [Late Latin *rēgulāre*] —'**regulatory** adj.

regulation (,rɛgjʊ'leɪʃən) n. **1.** the act of regulating. **2.** a rule that governs procedure or behaviour. **3.** (modifier) as required by official rules: *regulation uniform.* **4.** (modifier) conventional or customary: *the regulation wife and two kids.*

regulator ('rɛgjʊ,leɪtə) n. **1.** the mechanism by which the speed of a clock is regulated. **2.** a mechanism, such as a governor valve, for controlling fluid flow, pressure, temperature, etc.

regurgitate (rɪ'gɜːdʒɪ,teɪt) vb. **1.** to vomit up (partially digested food). **2.** (of some birds and animals) to bring back (partly digested food) to the mouth to feed the young. [Medieval Latin *re*- back + *gurgitāre* to flood] —re,gurgi'**tation** n.

rehabilitate (,riːə'bɪlɪ,teɪt) vb. **1.** to help (a disabled person or an ex-prisoner) to readapt to society or a new job, as by vocational guidance, retraining, or therapy. **2.** to restore to a former position or rank. **3.** to restore the good reputation of. [Medieval Latin *rehabilitāre* to restore] —,**reha,bili'tation** n.

rehash (riː'hæʃ) vb. **1.** to use (old or already used ideas or material) in a slightly

different form without real improvement. ~n. **2.** something consisting of rehashed material. [*re*- again + *hash* to chop into pieces]

rehearse (rɪ'hɜːs) vb. **1.** to practise (a play, concert, etc.), in preparation for public performance. **2.** to run through; recite: *he rehearsed the grievances of the committee.* **3.** to train (a person) for public performance. [Old French *rehercier* to harrow a second time] —re'**hearsal** n. —re'**hearser** n.

Reich (raɪx) n. the former German state, esp. the Nazi dictatorship in Germany from 1933–45 (**Third Reich**). [German: kingdom]

reign (reɪn) n. **1.** the period during which a monarch is the official ruler of a country. **2.** a period during which a person or thing is dominant: *a reign of terror.* ~vb. **3.** to hold the position of sovereign. **4.** to predominate; prevail: *darkness reigns.* **5.** (*usually present participle*) to be the most recent winner of a contest, etc.: *the reigning champion.* [Old French *reigne*]

reimburse (,riːɪm'bɜːs) vb. to repay (someone) for (expenses, losses, or damages). [Medieval Latin *imbursāre* to put in a moneybag] —,**reim'bursement** n.

rein (reɪn) n. **1.** (*often pl.*) one of a pair of long straps, one end of which is fastened to the bit, used to control a horse. **2.** (pl.) a similar device used to control a very young child. **3.** means of control: *to take up the reins of government.* **4.** **give (a) free rein.** to allow considerable freedom; remove restraints. **5.** **keep a tight rein on.** to control carefully: *we have to keep a tight rein on expenditure.* ~vb. **6.** to restrain or halt with or as if with reins. ~See also **rein in.** [Old French *resne*]

reincarnate (riː'ɪnkɑːneɪt) vb. (*often passive*) to be born again in a different body.

reincarnation (,riːɪnkɑː'neɪʃən) n. **1.** the belief that after death the soul is reborn in another body. **2.** embodiment again in a new form, as of a principle or idea.

reindeer ('reɪn,dɪə) n., pl. **-deer** or **-deers.** a deer with large branched antlers in both sexes that inhabits the arctic regions. [Old Norse *hreindȳri*]

reinforce (,riːɪn'fɔːs) vb. **1.** to give added strength or support to. **2.** to give added emphasis to; increase: *his rudeness reinforced my determination.* **3.** to give added support to (a military force) by providing more men or equipment. [French *renforcer*] —,**rein'forcement** n.

reinforced concrete n. concrete with steel bars or mesh embedded in it to strengthen it.

rein in vb. to stop (a horse) by pulling on the reins.

reinstate (,riːɪn'steɪt) vb. to restore to a

former rank or status. —,**rein'state-ment** n.

reiterate (riː'ɪtəˌreɪt) vb. to state again or repeatedly. [Latin *reiterāre*] —re,**iter'a-tion** n.

reject vb. (rɪ'dʒɛkt). **1.** to refuse to accept, use, believe, etc. **2.** to pass over or throw out as useless. **3.** to rebuff (a person). **4.** (of an organism) to fail to accept (a tissue graft or organ transplant). ~n. ('riːdʒɛkt). **5.** something rejected as imperfect, unsatisfactory, or useless. [Latin *rēicere* to throw back] —re'**jection** n.

rejig (riː'dʒɪg) vb. **-jigging, -jigged. 1.** to re-equip (a factory or plant). **2.** *Informal.* to manipulate in an unscrupulous way.

rejoice (rɪ'dʒɔɪs) vb. to feel or express great happiness. [Old French *resjoir*] —re'**joicing** n.

rejoin[1] (riː'dʒɔɪn) vb. to come together with (someone or something) again.

rejoin[2] (rɪ'dʒɔɪn) vb. to reply, esp. sharply or wittily. [Old French *rejoindre*]

rejoinder (rɪ'dʒɔɪndə) n. a reply, esp. a sharp or witty one.

rejuvenate (rɪ'dʒuːvɪˌneɪt) vb. to give new youth, restored vitality, or youthful ap-pearance to. [*re-* again + Latin *juvenis* young] —re,**juve'nation** n.

relapse (rɪ'læps) vb. **1.** to lapse back into a former state or condition, esp. an un-healthy or undesirable one. ~n. **2.** the act of relapsing. **3.** the return of ill health after an apparent or partial recovery. [Latin *re-* back + *labī* to slip]

relate (rɪ'leɪt) vb. **1.** to tell or narrate (a story). **2.** (often foll. by *to*) to form a connection (between two or more things) or (of something) to have reference (to something else). **3.** (often foll. by *to*) to form a sympathetic or significant relation-ship (with other people, things, etc.). [Latin *relātus* brought back]

related (rɪ'leɪtɪd) adj. **1.** connected; asso-ciated. **2.** linked by kinship or marriage.

relation (rɪ'leɪʃən) n. **1.** the state of being related or the manner in which things are related. **2.** connection by blood or mar-riage; kinship. **3.** a person who is connect-ed by blood or marriage; relative. **4. in or with relation to.** with reference to; in comparison with. **5.** the position or con-nection of one person or thing with regard to another. **6.** an account or narrative.

relations (rɪ'leɪʃənz) pl. n. **1.** social, politi-cal, or personal connections or dealings between or among individuals, groups, or nations. **2.** family or relatives. **3.** *Euphemistic.* sexual intercourse.

relationship (rɪ'leɪʃənʃɪp) n. **1.** the state of being related. **2.** association by blood or marriage; kinship. **3.** the mutual dealings, connections, or feelings that exist between two countries, people, or groups. **4.** an emotional or sexual affair.

relative ('rɛlətɪv) adj. **1.** having signifi-cance only in relation to something else: "hot" is a relative term. **2.** comparative:

relative comfort; relative density. **3.** re-spective: the relative qualities of speed and accuracy. **4.** (foll. by *to*) in proportion to: earnings relative to production. **5.** rel-evant: the facts relative to the enquiry. **6.** *Grammar.* of a clause (**relative clause**) that modifies a noun or pronoun occurring earlier in the sentence. **7.** *Grammar.* of or belonging to a class of words, such as *who*, *which*, or *that*, which function as conjunc-tions introducing relative clauses. ~n. **8.** a person who is related by blood or mar-riage; relation. —**'relatively** adv.

relative atomic mass n. same as **atomic weight.**

relativity (ˌrɛlə'tɪvɪtɪ) n. **1.** either of two theories developed by Albert Einstein, the **special theory of relativity**, which re-quires that the laws of physics shall be the same as seen by any two different observ-ers in uniform relative motion, and the **general theory of relativity**, which con-siders observers with relative acceleration and leads to a theory of gravitation. **2.** the state of being relative.

relax (rɪ'læks) vb. **1.** to make or become less tense, looser, or less rigid. **2.** to take rest, as from work or effort. **3.** to make (rules or discipline) less strict. **4.** (of a person) to become less formal. **5.** to lessen the intensity of: he relaxed his vigilance. [Latin *relaxāre* to loosen] —re'**laxed** adj.

relaxation (ˌriːlæk'seɪʃən) n. **1.** rest or refreshment, as after work or effort; rec-reation. **2.** a form of recreation: his re-laxation is cricket. **3.** the act of relaxing.

relay n. ('riːleɪ). **1.** a person or team of people relieving others, as on a shift. **2.** short for **relay race. 3.** an automatic device that controls a valve or switch, esp. one in which a small change in current or voltage controls the switching on or off of circuits. **4.** *Radio.* a combination of a receiver and transmitter designed to re-ceive radio signals and retransmit them. ~vb. (rɪ'leɪ). **5.** to receive (news or infor-mation) and pass it on to others. **6.** to retransmit (a signal) by means of a relay. **7.** *Brit.* to broadcast (a performance or event) as it happens. [Old French *relaier* to leave behind]

relay race n. a race between teams of contestants in which each contestant cov-ers a specified portion of the distance.

release (rɪ'liːs) vb. **1.** to free (a person or animal) from captivity or imprisonment. **2.** to free (someone) from obligation or duty. **3.** to free (something) from (one's grip); let fall. **4.** to issue (a record, film, or book) for sale. **5.** to make (news or infor-mation) known. **6.** to allow (something) to move freely, by undoing a catch or lock: she released the handbrake. **7.** to emit heat, energy, radiation, etc.: the accident released a cloud of poisonous gas. ~n. **8.** the act of freeing or state of being freed. **9.** the act of issuing for sale or publication. **10.** something issued for sale or public showing, esp. a film or a record: a new

---

rekindle relabel relearn

release from Bob Dylan. **11.** a news item made public: *a press release.* [Old French *relesser*]

relegate ('rɛlɪˌgeɪt) *vb.* **1.** to move to a position of less authority, importance, or status; demote. **2.** (*usually passive*) *Chiefly Brit.* to demote (a sports team) to a lower division. [Latin *re-* back + *lēgāre* to send] —ˌrele'gation *n.*

relent (rɪ'lɛnt) *vb.* **1.** to change one's mind about some decision, esp. a harsh one. **2.** to become milder or less severe. [Latin *re-* back + *lentāre* to bend]

relentless (rɪ'lɛntlɪs) *adj.* **1.** (of a person) harsh, pitiless, and unyielding. **2.** (of pace or intensity) sustained; unremitting.

relevant ('rɛlɪvənt) *adj.* having direct bearing on the matter in hand; pertinent. [Medieval Latin *relevans*] —'relevance *n.*

reliable (rɪ'laɪəb³l) *adj.* able to be trusted; dependable. —re,lia'bility *n.* —re'liably *adv.*

reliance (rɪ'laɪəns) *n.* dependence, confidence, or trust. —re'liant *adj.*

relic ('rɛlɪk) *n.* **1.** something that has survived from the past, such as an object or custom. **2.** something valued for its past associations. **3.** (*usually pl.*) a remaining part or fragment. **4.** *R.C. Church, Eastern Church.* part of the body of a saint or his belongings, venerated as holy. [Latin *reliquiae* remains]

relict ('rɛlɪkt) *n. Archaic.* **1.** a widow. **2.** a relic. [Latin *relictus* left behind]

relief (rɪ'liːf) *n.* **1.** a feeling of cheerfulness that follows the removal of anxiety, pain, or distress. **2.** deliverance from or alleviation of anxiety, pain, etc. **3.** money, food, or clothing given to people in special need: *famine relief.* **4.** a diversion from monotony. **5.** a person who replaces another at some task or duty. **6.** a bus, plane, etc., that carries additional passengers when a scheduled service is full. **7.** the act of freeing a besieged town or fortress: *the relief of Mafeking.* **8.** Also called: **relievo.** *Sculpture, archit.* the projection of figures from a flat surface, so that they are partly or wholly free of it. **9.** any vivid effect resulting from contrast: *comic relief.* **10.** variation in altitude in an area; difference between highest and lowest level. **11. on relief.** *U.S. & Canad.* (of people) in receipt of government aid because of personal need. [Old French *relever* to relieve]

relief map *n.* a map that shows the shape and height of the land surface, usually by means of contours.

relieve (rɪ'liːv) *vb.* **1.** to bring alleviation of (pain, distress, etc.) to (someone). **2.** to bring assistance to (someone in need). **3.** to take over the duties of (someone). **4.** to free (someone) from an obligation. **5.** (foll. by *of*) to take from: *the thief relieved him of his watch.* **6.** to make (something) less unpleasant, arduous, or monotonous. **7.** to set off by contrast: *black relieved with touches of white.* **8.** to bring a relieving force to (a besieged town, etc.). **9.** relieve

oneself. to urinate or defecate. [Latin *re-* again + *levāre* to lighten] —re'lieved *adj.*

religion (rɪ'lɪdʒən) *n.* **1.** belief in, worship of, or obedience to a supernatural power or powers considered to be divine or to have control of human destiny. **2.** any formal expression of such belief: *the Christian religion.* **3.** *Chiefly R.C. Church.* the way of life entered upon by monks and nuns: *to enter religion.* [Latin *religiō*]

religious (rɪ'lɪdʒəs) *adj.* **1.** of or concerned with religion. **2.** pious; devout; godly. **3.** scrupulous or conscientious. **4.** *Christianity.* of or relating to the way of life of monks and nuns. ~*n.* **5.** *Christianity.* a monk or nun. —re'ligiously *adv.*

relinquish (rɪ'lɪŋkwɪʃ) *vb.* **1.** to give up (a task or struggle); abandon. **2.** to renounce (a claim or right). **3.** to release one's hold on; let go. [Latin *relinquere*] —re'linquishment *n.*

reliquary ('rɛlɪkwərɪ) *n., pl.* **-quaries.** a container for relics of saints.

relish ('rɛlɪʃ) *vb.* **1.** to savour or enjoy (an experience) to the full. **2.** to anticipate eagerly. ~*n.* **3.** liking or enjoyment: *he accepted the challenge with relish.* **4.** pleasurable anticipation: *he didn't have much relish for the idea.* **5.** an appetizing or spicy food, such as a pickle, added to a main dish to enhance its flavour. **6.** a zestful touch: *there was a certain relish in all his writing.* [earlier *reles* aftertaste]

relive (riː'lɪv) *vb.* to experience (a sensation or event) again, esp. in the imagination.

relocate (ˌriːləʊ'keɪt) *vb.* (esp. of an employee or a business) to move or be moved to a new place or site. —ˌrelo'cation *n.*

reluctance (rɪ'lʌktəns) *n.* **1.** lack of eagerness; unwillingness. **2.** *Physics.* a measure of the resistance of a closed magnetic circuit to a magnetic flux. [Latin *reluctārī* to resist]

reluctant (rɪ'lʌktənt) *adj.* not eager; unwilling. —re'luctantly *adv.*

rely (rɪ'laɪ) *vb.* **-lying, -lied.** (foll. by *on* or *upon*) **1.** to be dependent (on): *he relies on his charm.* **2.** to have trust or confidence (in): *you can rely on us.* [Old French *relier* to fasten together]

remain (rɪ'meɪn) *vb.* **1.** to stay behind or in the same place: *to remain at home.* **2.** to continue to be: *to remain cheerful.* **3.** to be left, as after use or the passage of time. **4.** to be left to be done, said, etc.: *it remains to be pointed out.* [Latin *remanēre*]

remainder (rɪ'meɪndə) *n.* **1.** a part or portion that is left, as after use or the passage of time: *the remainder of the milk.* **2.** *Maths.* **a.** the amount left over when one quantity cannot be exactly divided by another: *for 10 ÷ 3, the remainder is 1.* **b.** the amount left over when one quantity is subtracted from another. **3.** a number of copies of a book left unsold when demand ceases, which are sold at a reduced price.

~*vb.* **4.** to sell (copies of a book) as a remainder.

remains (rɪˈmeɪnz) *pl. n.* **1.** any pieces that are left unused or still extant, as after use, consumption, or the passage of time: *archaeological remains.* **2.** a corpse.

remake (ˈriːˌmeɪk) *n.* something that is made again, esp. a new version of an old film.

remand (rɪˈmɑːnd) *vb.* **1.** *Law.* to send (a prisoner or accused person) back into custody to await trial. ~*n.* **2.** the sending of a prisoner or accused person back into custody to await trial. **3. on remand.** in custody or on bail awaiting trial. [Latin *re-* back + *mandāre* to command]

remand centre *n.* (in Britain) an institution where accused people are detained while awaiting trial.

remark (rɪˈmɑːk) *vb.* **1.** to pass a casual comment (about). **2.** to perceive; observe; notice. ~*n.* **3.** a brief casually expressed thought or opinion. **4.** notice, comment, or observation: *the event passed without remark.* [Old French *remarquer* to observe]

remarkable (rɪˈmɑːkəbʼl) *adj.* **1.** worthy of note or attention: *a remarkable achievement.* **2.** striking or extraordinary: *a remarkable sight.* —re**ˈmarkably** *adv.*

REME (ˈriːmɪ) Royal Electrical and Mechanical Engineers.

remedial (rɪˈmiːdɪəl) *adj.* **1.** providing or intended as a remedy; curative. **2.** of special teaching for slow learners: *remedial education.* —re**ˈmedially** *adv.*

remedy (ˈrɛmɪdɪ) *n., pl.* **-dies.** (usually foll. by *for* or *against*) **1.** any drug or agent that cures a disease or controls its symptoms. **2.** anything that serves to cure defects, improve conditions, etc.: *a remedy for industrial disputes.* ~*vb.* **3.** to relieve or cure (a disease). **4.** to correct (a fault, error, etc.). [Latin *remedium* a cure] —re**mediable** (rɪˈmiːdɪəbʼl) *adj.*

remember (rɪˈmɛmbə) *vb.* **1.** to become aware of (something forgotten) again. **2.** to keep (an idea, intention, etc.) in one's mind: *remember to do one's shopping.* **3.** to give money to (someone), as in a will or in tipping. **4.** (foll. by *to*) to mention (a person's name) to another person, as by way of greeting: *remember me to your mother.* **5.** to commemorate: *to remember the dead of the wars.* [Latin *re-* again + *memor* mindful]

remembrance (rɪˈmɛmbrəns) *n.* **1.** a remembering or being remembered. **2.** a memento or keepsake. **3.** the act of honouring some past event or person.

Remembrance Day *n.* **1.** (in Britain) Remembrance Sunday. **2.** (in Canada) a statutory holiday observed on November 11 in memory of the dead of both World Wars.

Remembrance Sunday *n.* (in Britain) the Sunday closest to November 11th, on which the dead of both World Wars are commemorated.

remind (rɪˈmaɪnd) *vb.* (usually foll. by *of*) to cause (a person) to remember (something or to do something); put (a person) in mind (of someone or something): *remind me to phone home; flowers remind me of holidays.* —re**ˈminder** *n.*

reminisce (ˌrɛmɪˈnɪs) *vb.* to talk or write about old times or past experiences.

reminiscence (ˌrɛmɪˈnɪsəns) *n.* **1.** the act of recalling or narrating past experiences. **2.** (*often pl.*) some past experience, event or feeling that is recalled.

reminiscent (ˌrɛmɪˈnɪsʼnt) *adj.* **1.** (foll. by *of*) stimulating memories (of) or comparisons (with). **2.** characterized by reminiscence. [Latin *reminisci* to call to mind]

remiss (rɪˈmɪs) *adj.* lacking in attention to duty; negligent. [Latin *remissus*]

remission (rɪˈmɪʃən) *n.* **1.** a reduction of the term of imprisonment, as for good conduct. **2.** forgiveness for sin. **3.** release from penalty or obligation. **4.** lessening of intensity, as in the symptoms of a disease.

remit *vb.* (rɪˈmɪt), **-mitting, -mitted. 1.** to send (payment), as for goods or service, esp. by post. **2.** *Law.* to send back (a case) to a lower court for further consideration. **3.** to refrain from exacting or cancel (a penalty or punishment). **4.** to slacken or ease off; abate. **5.** *Archaic.* to forgive (crime or sins). ~*n.* (ˈriːmɪt, rɪˈmɪt). **6.** area of authority (of a committee, inquiry, etc.). [Latin *re-* back + *mittere* to send]

remittance (rɪˈmɪtəns) *n.* money sent, esp. by post, as payment.

remittent (rɪˈmɪtʼnt) *adj.* (of a disease) periodically less severe.

remix *vb.* (riːˈmɪks). **1.** to change the relative volume and prominence of the individual performer's parts of (a recording). ~*n.* (ˈriːmɪks). **2.** a remixed version of a recording.

remnant (ˈrɛmnənt) *n.* **1.** (*often pl.*) a part left over. **2.** a surviving trace or vestige: *a remnant of imperialism.* **3.** a piece of material from the end of a roll. [Old French *remenant* remaining]

remonstrance (rɪˈmɒnstrəns) *n.* **1.** the act of remonstrating. **2.** a protest or reproof, esp. a petition protesting against something.

remonstrate (ˈrɛmənˌstreɪt) *vb.* to argue in protest or objection: *to remonstrate with the government.* [Latin *re-* again + *monstrāre* to show] —ˌre**monˈstration** *n.*

remorse (rɪˈmɔːs) *n.* **1.** a sense of deep regret and guilt for some misdeed. **2.** pity; compassion. [Medieval Latin *remorsus* a gnawing] —re**ˈmorseful** *adj.*

remote (rɪˈməʊt) *adj.* **1.** far away; distant. **2.** far from civilization. **3.** distant in time. **4.** operated from a distance; remote-controlled: *a remote monitor.* **5.** distantly related or connected: *a remote cousin.* **6.** slight or faint: *I haven't the remotest idea.* **7.** (of a person's manner) aloof or abstracted. [Latin *remōtus* far removed] —re**ˈmotely** *adv.*

remote control *n.* control of a system from a distance, as by radio or electrical signals. —**re'mote-con'trolled** *adj.*

remould *vb.* (ˌriːˈməʊld). **1.** to bond a new tread onto the casing of (a worn pneumatic tyre). ~*n.* (ˈriːˌməʊld). **2.** a tyre made by this process.

removal (rɪˈmuːvʲl) *n.* **1.** the act of removing or state of being removed. **2. a.** a change of residence. **b.** (*as modifier*): *a removal company.*

remove (rɪˈmuːv) *vb.* **1.** to take away and place elsewhere. **2.** to dismiss (someone) from office. **3.** to do away with; get rid of. **4.** *Formal.* to change the location of one's home or place of business. ~*n.* **5.** the act of removing, esp. (formal) a removal of one's residence or place of work. **6.** the degree of difference: *only one remove from madness.* **7.** *Brit.* (in certain schools) a class or form. [Old French *removoir*]

remunerate (rɪˈmjuːnəˌreɪt) *vb.* to reward or pay for work or service. [Latin *remūnerārī*] —**re,muner'ation** *n.* —**re'munerative** *adj.*

renaissance (rəˈneɪsəns; *U.S. & Canad. also* ˈrɛnəˌsɒns) *n.* a revival or rebirth, esp. of culture and learning. [French]

Renaissance (rəˈneɪsəns; *U.S. & Canad. also* ˈrɛnəˌsɒns) *n.* **1. the.** the great revival of art, literature, and learning in Europe in the 14th, 15th, and 16th centuries. ~*adj.* **2.** of or from the Renaissance.

renal (ˈriːnʲl) *adj.* of or near the kidney. [Latin *rēnēs* kidneys]

renascent (rɪˈnæsʲnt, -ˈneɪ-) *adj.* becoming active or vigorous again: *renascent nationalism.* [Latin *renascī* to be born again] —**re'nascence** *n.*

rend (rɛnd) *vb.* **rending, rent. 1.** to tear violently; rip. **2.** (of a noise or cry) to disturb (the silence) with a shrill or piercing tone. [Old English *rendan*]

render (ˈrɛndə) *vb.* **1.** to present or submit (something) for payment, approval, etc. **2.** to give or provide (aid, a service, etc.). **3.** to cause to become: *grief had rendered him simple-minded.* **4.** to portray (something), as in painting, music, or acting. **5.** to translate (something). **6.** to yield or give: *the tomb rendered up its secret.* **7.** to cover the surface of (brickwork, etc.) with a coat of plaster. **8.** (often foll. by *down*) to extract (fat) from (meat) by melting. [Old French *rendre*] —**'rendering** *n.*

rendezvous (ˈrɒndɪˌvuː) *n., pl.* **-vous** (-ˌvuːz). **1.** a meeting or an appointment to meet at a specified time and place. **2.** a place where people meet. ~*vb.* **3.** to meet at a specified time or place. [French]

rendition (rɛnˈdɪʃən) *n.* **1.** a performance of a musical composition, dramatic role, etc. **2.** a translation.

renegade (ˈrɛnɪˌgeɪd) *n.* a person who

deserts his cause or faith for another. [Spanish *renegado*]

renege (rɪˈniːg, -ˈneɪg) *vb.* **1.** (often foll. by *on*) to go back (on one's promise). ~*vb., n.* **2.** *Cards.* same as **revoke.** [Medieval Latin *renegāre* to renounce]

renew (rɪˈnjuː) *vb.* **1.** to take up again after a break. **2.** to begin (an activity) again; recommence. **3.** to restate or reaffirm (a promise). **4.** to make (a lease, guarantee, etc.) valid for a further period. **5.** to regain or recover (strength). **6.** to restore to a new or fresh condition. **7.** to replace (an old or worn-out part or piece). **8.** to replenish (a supply, etc.). —**re'newable** *adj.* —**re'newal** *n.*

rennet (ˈrɛnɪt) *n.* a substance prepared from the stomachs of calves and used for curdling milk to make cheese. [Old English *gerinnan* to curdle]

renounce (rɪˈnaʊns) *vb.* **1.** to give up formally (a claim or right): *to renounce a title.* **2.** to repudiate: *to renounce Christianity.* **3.** to give up (something) voluntarily: *to renounce one's old ways.* [Latin *renuntiāre*]

renovate (ˈrɛnəˌveɪt) *vb.* to restore (something) to good condition. [Latin *re-* again + *novāre* to make new] —**,reno'vation** *n.* —**'reno,vator** *n.*

renown (rɪˈnaʊn) *n.* widespread reputation, esp. of a good kind; fame. [Old French *renom*] —**re'nowned** *adj.*

rent[1] (rɛnt) *n.* **1.** a payment made periodically by a tenant to a landlord or owner for the occupation or use of land, buildings, equipment, etc. ~*vb.* **2.** to allow (a person) to use one's property in return for periodic payments. **3.** to occupy or use (property) in return for periodic payments. **4.** (often foll. by *at*) to be let or rented (for a specified amount). [Old French *rente* revenue]

rent[2] (rɛnt) *n.* **1.** a slit made by tearing. ~*vb.* **2.** the past of **rend.**

rental (ˈrɛntʲl) *n.* **1.** the amount paid or received as rent. ~*adj.* **2.** of or relating to rent.

rent boy *n.* a young male prostitute.

renunciation (rɪˌnʌnsɪˈeɪʃən) *n.* **1.** the act or an instance of renouncing. **2.** a formal declaration renouncing something.

rep[1] (rɛp) *n. Theatre.* short for **repertory company.**

rep[2] (rɛp) *n.* **1.** a sales representative. **2.** someone elected to represent a group of people: *the union rep.* **3.** *N.Z. informal.* a rugby player selected to represent his district.

repair[1] (rɪˈpɛə) *vb.* **1.** to restore (something damaged or broken) to good condition or working order. **2.** to heal (a breach or division) in (something): *to repair a broken marriage.* **3.** to make amends for (a mistake, injury, etc.). ~*n.* **4.** the act, task, or process of repairing. **5.** a part that has been repaired. **6.** state or condition: *in good repair.* [Latin *re-* again + *parāre* to make ready] —re'pairable *adj.*

repair² (rɪ'pɛə) *vb.* (usually foll. by *to*) to go (to a place). [Latin *re-* back + *patria* fatherland]

reparable ('rɛpərəbᵊl, 'rɛprə-) *adj.* able to be repaired or remedied.

reparation (ˌrɛpə'reɪʃən) *n.* **1.** the act or process of making amends. **2.** (*usually pl.*) compensation paid by a defeated nation after a war for the damage and injuries it caused. [Latin *reparāre* to repair]

repartee (ˌrɛpɑː'tiː) *n.* **1.** a sharp witty remark made as a reply. **2.** skill in making sharp witty replies. [French *repartie*]

repast (rɪ'pɑːst) *n.* a meal or the food provided at a meal. [Old French *repaistre* to feed]

repatriate *vb.* (riː'pætrɪ,eɪt). **1.** to send back (a person) to the country of his birth or citizenship. ~*n.* (riː'pætrɪɪt). **2.** a person who has been repatriated. [Latin *re-* back + *patria* fatherland] —re,patri'a-tion *n.*

repay (rɪ'peɪ) *vb.* -paying, -paid. **1.** to refund or reimburse. **2.** to make a return for (something): *to repay kindness.* —re-'payable *adj.* —re'payment *n.*

repeal (rɪ'piːl) *vb.* **1.** to cancel officially; revoke: *these laws were repealed.* ~*n.* **2.** annulment or withdrawal. [Old French *repeler*] —re'pealable *adj.*

repeat (rɪ'piːt) *vb.* **1.** to do or experience (something) again, esp. to say or write (something) again. **2.** to occur more than once: *the last figure repeats.* **3.** to say (the words or sounds) uttered by someone else; echo. **4.** to recite (a poem, etc.) from memory. **5.** (of food) to be tasted again after eating as the result of belching. **6.** to tell to another person (the secrets imparted to one by someone else). ~*n.* **7. a.** the act or an instance of repeating. **b.** (*as modifier*): *a repeat performance.* **8.** a word, action, pattern, etc., that is repeated. **9.** *Radio, television.* a broadcast of a programme which has been broadcast before. **10.** *Music.* a passage that is an exact restatement of the passage preceding it. [Latin *repetere*] —re'peated *adj.* —re-'peatedly *adv.*

repeater (rɪ'piːtə) *n.* **1.** a gun capable of firing several shots without reloading. **2.** a clock or watch which strikes the hour or quarter-hour just past, when a spring is pressed.

repel (rɪ'pɛl) *vb.* -pelling, -pelled. **1.** to force or drive back (someone or something). **2.** to cause (someone) to feel disgusted. **3.** to be effective in keeping away, controlling, or resisting: *a spray that repels flies.* **4.** to fail to mix with or absorb: *water and oil repel each other.* **5.** to reject or spurn (someone or something): *she re-pelled his advances.* [Latin *re-* back + *pellere* to push] —re'pellent *n., adj.*

repent (rɪ'pɛnt) *vb.* to feel remorse (for); show penitence (for). [Old French *repentir*] —re'pentance *n.* —re'pentant *adj.*

repercussion (ˌriːpə'kʌʃən) *n.* **1.** (*often pl.*) a result or consequence of an action or event: *the repercussions of the war are still felt.* **2.** an echo or reverberation. [Latin *repercutere* to strike back]

repertoire ('rɛpə,twɑː) *n.* **1.** all the works that a company or performer is competent to perform. **2.** the entire stock of skills or techniques that someone or something, such as a computer, is capable of. [French]

repertory ('rɛpətrɪ) *n., pl.* -ries. **1.** same as **repertoire** (sense 2). **2.** short for **repertory company.** [Late Latin *repertōrium* storehouse]

repertory company *n.* a theatrical company that performs plays from a repertoire.

repetition (ˌrɛpɪ'tɪʃən) *n.* **1.** the act or an instance of repeating; reiteration. **2.** a thing, word, action, etc., that is repeated. **3.** a replica or copy. —,repe'titious *adj.* —repetitive (rɪ'pɛtɪtɪv) *adj.*

repine (rɪ'paɪn) *vb.* to be fretful or discontented. [RE- + PINE²]

replace (rɪ'pleɪs) *vb.* **1.** to take the place of; supersede. **2.** to substitute a person or thing for (another); put in place of: *to replace an old pair of shoes.* **3.** to restore (something) to its rightful place.

replacement (rɪ'pleɪsmənt) *n.* **1.** the act or process of replacing. **2.** a person or thing that replaces another.

replay *n.* ('riː,pleɪ). **1.** a showing again of a sequence of action immediately after it happens. **2.** a second match between a pair or group of contestants, esp. one that takes place because the first match was drawn. ~*vb.* (riː'pleɪ). **3.** to play again (a record, sporting contest, etc.).

replenish (rɪ'plɛnɪʃ) *vb.* to make full or complete again by supplying what has been used up. [Old French *replenir*] —re'plen-ishment *n.*

replete (rɪ'pliːt) *adj.* **1.** (often foll. by *with*) well supplied (with); abounding (with). **2.** having one's appetite completely or excessively satisfied. [Latin *replētus*] —re'pletion *n.*

replica ('rɛplɪkə) *n.* an exact copy or reproduction, esp. on a smaller scale. [Italian, lit.: a reply]

reply (rɪ'plaɪ) *vb.* -plying, -plied. **1.** to make answer (to) in words or writing or by an action; respond. **2.** to say (something) in answer: *he replied that he didn't want to come.* ~*n., pl.* -plies. **3.** an answer; response. [Old French *replier* to fold again]

report (rɪ'pɔːt) *n.* **1.** an account prepared after investigation and published or broadcast. **2.** a statement made widely known; rumour: *according to report, he is not dead.* **3.** an account of the deliberations of a committee or other group of people: *a report of parliamentary proceedings.* **4.** *Brit.* a statement on the progress of each schoolchild. **5.** comment on a person's character or actions; reputation: *he is of good report here.* **6.** a sharp loud noise, esp. one made by a gun. ~*vb.* **7.** to give an account (of); describe. **8.** to give an account of the results of an investigation (into): *to report on housing conditions.* **9.** (of a committee or other group of people) to make a formal report on (a subject). **10.** to complain about (a person), esp. to a superior. **11.** to present (oneself) or be present at an appointed place or for a specific purpose: *report to the manager's office.* **12.** (foll. by *to*) to be responsible (to) and under the authority (of). **13.** to act as a reporter. [Latin *re*- back + *portāre* to carry] —**re'portedly** *adv.*

reported speech *n.* a report of what someone said that gives the content of the speech without repeating the exact words.

reporter (rɪ'pɔːtə) *n.* a person employed to gather news for a newspaper or broadcasting organization.

repose[1] (rɪ'pəʊz) *n.* **1.** a state of quiet restfulness; peace or tranquillity. **2.** calmness or composure. ~*vb.* **3.** to lie or lay down at rest. **4.** to lie when dead, as in the grave. [Old French *reposer*]

repose[2] (rɪ'pəʊz) *vb.* to put (trust) in a person or thing. [Latin *repōnere* to store up]

repository (rɪ'pɒzɪtrɪ) *n., pl.* **-ries.** **1.** a place or container in which things can be stored for safety. **2.** a person to whom a secret is entrusted; confidant. [Latin *repositōrium*]

repossess (ˌriːpə'zɛs) *vb.* to take back possession of (property), esp. when the buyer has not kept up payments. —**repossession** (ˌriːpə'zɛʃən) *n.*

reprehend (ˌrɛprɪ'hɛnd) *vb.* to find fault with; criticize. [Latin *reprehendere*]

reprehensible (ˌrɛprɪ'hɛnsɪb'l) *adj.* open to criticism; blameworthy.

represent (ˌrɛprɪ'zɛnt) *vb.* **1.** to stand as an equivalent of; correspond to. **2.** to act as a substitute (for). **3.** to act as or be the authorized delegate or agent for (a person, country, etc.): *an MP represents his constituency.* **4.** to be a means of expressing: *letters represent the sounds of speech.* **5.** to display the characteristics of; typify: *romanticism in music is represented by Liszt.* **6.** to present an image of through a picture or sculpture; portray. **7.** to bring clearly before the mind. **8.** to set forth in words; state or explain. **9.** to describe as having a specified character or quality: *he represented her as a saint.* **10.** to act out the part of on stage; portray. [Latin *repraesentāre* to exhibit]

representation (ˌrɛprɪzɛn'teɪʃən) *n.* **1.** the act or an instance of representing or the state of being represented. **2.** anything that represents, such as a pictorial por-

trait. **3.** a body of representatives. **4.** (*often pl.*) a statement of facts, true or alleged, esp. one seeking changes, or making a complaint. —ˌrepresen'tational *adj.*

representative (ˌrɛprɪ'zɛntətɪv) *n.* **1.** a person or thing that represents another. **2.** a person who represents and tries to sell the products or services of a firm. **3.** a typical example. **4.** a person representing a constituency in a legislative body. ~*adj.* **5.** serving to represent; symbolic. **6.** typical of a class or kind. **7.** including examples of all the interests, types, etc., in a group. **8.** acting as deputy for another. **9.** of or relating to the political representation of the people: *representative government.*

repress (rɪ'prɛs) *vb.* **1.** to keep (feelings) under control; restrain. **2.** to put into a state of subjugation: *to repress a people.* **3.** *Psychol.* to banish (unpleasant thoughts) from one's conscious mind. [Latin *reprimere* to press back] —**re'pression** *n.* —**re'pressive** *adj.*

reprieve (rɪ'priːv) *vb.* **1.** to postpone the punishment of (a person, esp. one condemned to death). **2.** to give temporary relief to (a person or thing). ~*n.* **3.** a postponement of punishment. **4.** a warrant granting a postponement. **5.** a temporary relief from pain or harm; respite. [Old French *repris* (something) taken back]

reprimand (ˈrɛprɪˌmɑːnd) *n.* **1.** a formal reproof or rebuke. ~*vb.* **2.** to admonish or rebuke, esp. formally. [French *réprimande*]

reprint *n.* (ˈriːˌprɪnt) **1.** a reissue of a printed work. ~*vb.* (riː'prɪnt) **2.** to print again.

reprisal (rɪ'praɪz'l) *n.* a taking of revenge; retaliation. [Old French *reprisaille*]

reproach (rɪ'prəʊtʃ) *vb.* **1.** to express disapproval of (someone's actions); rebuke. ~*n.* **2.** rebuke or censure; blame. **3.** disgrace or shame: *to bring reproach upon one's family.* **4.** beyond reproach. perfect; beyond criticism. [Old French *reprochier*] —**re'proachful** *adj.*

reprobate (ˈrɛprəʊˌbeɪt) *adj.* **1.** morally unprincipled; bad. ~*n.* **2.** an unprincipled bad person. [Late Latin *reprobātus* held in disfavour]

reprobation (ˌrɛprəʊ'beɪʃən) *n.* disapproval, blame, or censure.

reproduce (ˌriːprə'djuːs) *vb.* **1.** to make a copy or representation of; duplicate. **2.** *Biol.* to produce or cause to produce offspring. **3.** to bring back into existence; recreate. —ˌrepro'ducible *adj.*

reproduction (ˌriːprə'dʌkʃən) *n.* **1.** *Biol.* any process by which an animal or plant produces one or more individuals similar to itself. **2.** a copy of a work of art. **3.** (*modifier*) made in imitation of an earlier style: *reproduction furniture.* **4.** the quality of sound from an audio system. **5.** the

---

repot
reprocess

reprogram
reprogrammable

act or process of reproducing. —**repro-'ductive** adj.

reproof (rɪ'pruːf) n. a rebuke.

reprove (rɪ'pruːv) vb. to rebuke or scold. [Old French reprover] —**re'provingly** adv.

reptile ('reptaɪl) n. 1. any of the cold-blooded vertebrates covered by horny scales or plates, such as the tortoises, snakes, lizards, and crocodiles. 2. a grovelling insignificant person: you miserable little reptile! [Late Latin reptilis creeping] —**reptilian** (rep'tɪlɪən) n., adj.

republic (rɪ'pʌblɪk) n. 1. a form of government in which the people or their elected representatives possess the supreme power. 2. a country in which the head of state is an elected or nominated president. [Latin rēspublica, lit.: the public thing]

republican (rɪ'pʌblɪkən) adj. 1. of a republic. 2. supporting or advocating a republic. ~n. 3. a supporter or advocate of a republic. —**re'publican,ism** n.

Republican (rɪ'pʌblɪkən) adj. 1. belonging to a Republican Party. 2. belonging to the Irish Republican Army. ~n. 3. a member or supporter of a Republican Party. 4. a member or supporter of the Irish Republican Army. —**Re'publican,ism** n.

repudiate (rɪ'pjuːdɪˌeɪt) vb. 1. to reject the authority or validity of (something). 2. to refuse to acknowledge or pay (a debt). 3. to disown (a person). [Latin repudium divorce] —**re,pudi'ation** n.

repugnant (rɪ'pʌgnənt) adj. repellent to the senses; disgusting. [Latin repugnāns resisting] —**re'pugnance** n.

repulse (rɪ'pʌls) vb. 1. to drive back or ward off (an attacking force). 2. to reject with coldness or discourtesy: she repulsed his advances. ~n. 3. a driving back or warding off. 4. a cold discourteous rejection or refusal. [Latin repellere]

repulsion (rɪ'pʌlʃən) n. 1. a feeling of disgust or aversion. 2. Physics. a force separating two objects, such as the force between two like electric charges.

repulsive (rɪ'pʌlsɪv) adj. 1. disgusting or distasteful; loathsome. 2. Physics. of repulsion. —**re'pulsively** adv.

reputable ('repjʊtəbʰl) adj. of good reputation; trustworthy or respectable. —**'reputably** adv.

reputation (ˌrepjʊ'teɪʃən) n. 1. the estimation in which a person or thing is generally held; opinion. 2. a high opinion generally held about a person or thing; esteem. 3. notoriety or fame, esp. for some specified characteristic. [Latin reputātiō]

repute (rɪ'pjuːt) vb. 1. (usually passive) to consider (a person or thing) to be as specified: he is reputed to be rich. ~n. 2. public estimation: a writer of little repute. [Latin reputāre]

reputed (rɪ'pjuːtɪd) adj. supposed: reputed innocence. —**re'putedly** adv.

request (rɪ'kwest) vb. 1. to ask for or politely demand: to request a bottle of wine. ~n. 2. the act or an instance of asking for something. 3. something asked for. 4. **on request.** if asked for: application forms are available on request. [Old French requeste]

request stop n. a point on a route at which a bus stops only if signalled to do so.

Requiem ('rekwɪəm) n. 1. R.C. Church. a Mass celebrated for the dead. 2. a musical setting of this Mass. [Latin requiēs rest]

require (rɪ'kwaɪə) vb. 1. to need. 2. to be a necessary condition: this work requires precision. 3. to insist upon. 4. to order or command: to require someone to account for his actions. [Latin requīrere to seek to know]

requirement (rɪ'kwaɪəmənt) n. 1. something demanded or imposed as an obligation. 2. a thing desired or needed.

requisite ('rekwɪzɪt) adj. 1. absolutely essential; indispensable. ~n. 2. something indispensable; necessity. [Latin requisitus sought after]

requisition (ˌrekwɪ'zɪʃən) n. 1. an authoritative or formal request or demand. 2. an official form on which such a demand is made. 3. the act of taking something over, esp. temporarily for military or public use. ~vb. 4. to demand and take for use, esp. by military or public authority.

requite (rɪ'kwaɪt) vb. to make return to (a person for a kindness or injury); repay with a similar action. [re- back + obs. quite to repay] —**re'quital** n.

reredos ('rɪədɒs) n. a screen or wall decoration at the back of an altar. [Old French arere behind + dos back]

rerun vb. (riː'rʌn), **-running, -ran.** 1. to put on (a film or programme) again. 2. to run (a race) again. ~n. ('riːˌrʌn). 3. a repeat. 4. a race that is run again.

rescind (rɪ'sɪnd) vb. to annul or repeal. [Latin rēscindere to cut off]

rescission (rɪ'sɪʒən) n. a rescinding.

rescue ('reskjuː) vb. **-cuing, -cued.** 1. to bring (someone or something) out of danger or trouble; save. ~n. 2. the act or an instance of rescuing. [Old French rescourre] —**'rescuer** n.

research (rɪ'sɜːtʃ) n. 1. systematic investigation to establish facts or collect information on a subject. ~vb. 2. to carry out investigations into (a subject). [Old French recercher to search again] —**re'searcher** n.

resemble (rɪ'zembʰl) vb. to possess some similarity to; be like. [Old French resembler] —**re'semblance** n.

resent (rɪ'zent) vb. to feel bitter, indignant, or aggrieved at. [French ressentir] —**re'sentful** adj. —**re'sentment** n.

reservation (ˌrezə'veɪʃən) n. 1. something reserved, esp. a seat. 2. (often pl.) a qualification or uncertainty that prevents one's wholehearted acceptance or approval. **3.** an area of land set aside, esp. (in the U.S. and Canada) for American Indian peoples. **4.** *Brit.* the strip of land between the two carriageways of a dual carriageway.

reserve (rɪˈzɜːv) *vb.* **1.** to keep back or set aside, esp. for future use. **2.** to keep for oneself; retain: *I reserve the right to question these men later.* **3.** to obtain or secure by advance arrangement: *I have reserved two tickets.* **4.** to delay announcing (a legal judgment). ~*n.* **5.** something kept back or set aside for future use. **6.** the state or condition of being reserved: *I have plenty in reserve.* **7.** a tract of land set aside for a special purpose: *a nature reserve.* **8.** *Canad.* an Indian reservation. **9.** *Sport.* a substitute. **10.** that part of a nation's armed services not in active service. **11.** coolness or formality of manner; reticence. **12.** (*often pl.*) *Finance.* money or assets held by a bank or business to meet future expenses. [Latin *reservāre* to keep]

reserved (rɪˈzɜːvd) *adj.* **1.** set aside for use by a particular person. **2.** cool or formal in manner; reticent.

reserve price *n. Brit.* the minimum price acceptable to the owner of property being auctioned or sold.

reservist (rɪˈzɜːvɪst) *n.* a member of a nation's military reserve.

reservoir (ˈrezəˌvwɑː) *n.* **1.** a natural or artificial lake used for collecting and storing water for community use. **2.** a large supply of something: *a reservoir of talent.* [French *réservoir*]

reshuffle (riːˈʃʌfʳl) *n.* **1.** a reorganization of jobs in a government or cabinet. ~*vb.* **2.** to reorganize jobs or duties in a government.

reside (rɪˈzaɪd) *vb. Formal.* **1.** to live permanently (in a place); have one's home (in): *he resides in London.* **2.** (of things or qualities) to be inherently present (in); be vested (in): *political power resides in military strength.* [Latin *residēre* to sit back]

residence (ˈrezɪdəns) *n.* **1.** the place in which one resides; home. **2.** a large imposing house; mansion. **3.** the fact of residing in a place or a period of residing. **4. in residence. a.** actually resident: *the Queen is in residence.* **b.** designating a creative artist working for a set period at a college, gallery, etc.: *writer in residence.*

resident (ˈrezɪdənt) *n.* **1.** a person who resides in a place. **2.** a bird or animal that does not migrate. ~*adj.* **3.** living in a place; residing. **4.** living at a place in order to carry out a job or duty: *a resident caretaker.* **5.** (of birds and animals) not in the habit of migrating.

residential (ˌrezɪˈdenʃəl) *adj.* **1.** suitable for or used for residence: *a residential area.* **2.** relating to residence.

residential school *n.* a government boarding school in N Canada for Indian and Inuit students.

residual (rɪˈzɪdjʊəl) *adj.* **1.** of or being a remainder; leftover. ~*n.* **2.** something left over as a residue; remainder.

residue (ˈrezɪˌdjuː) *n.* **1.** matter remaining after something has been removed. **2.** *Law.* what is left of an estate after the discharge of debts and distribution of specific gifts. [Latin *residuus* remaining over]

residuum (rɪˈzɪdjʊəm) *n., pl.* **-ua** (-jʊə). same as **residue.**

resign (rɪˈzaɪn) *vb.* **1.** to give up (a job, office, etc.). **2.** to reconcile (oneself) to: *to resign oneself to death.* **3.** to give up (a right, claim, etc.); relinquish. [Latin *resignāre* to unseal, destroy]

resignation (ˌrezɪgˈneɪʃən) *n.* **1.** the act of resigning. **2.** a formal document stating one's intention to resign. **3.** passive endurance of difficulties.

resigned (rɪˈzaɪnd) *adj.* having or showing resignation; enduring passively. —**resignedly** (rɪˈzaɪmɪdlɪ) *adv.*

resilient (rɪˈzɪlɪənt) *adj.* **1.** (of an object) capable of regaining its original shape or position after bending, stretching, or compression; elastic. **2.** (of a person) recovering easily and quickly from illness or misfortune. [Latin *resilīre* to jump back] —**resilience** *n.*

resin (ˈrezɪn) *n.* **1.** a solid or semisolid substance exuded from certain plants: *pine resin.* **2.** a similar substance produced synthetically. ~*vb.* **3.** to treat or coat with resin. [Latin *rēsīna*] —**resinous** *adj.*

resist (rɪˈzɪst) *vb.* **1.** to stand firm against; not yield to: *he resisted the changes.* **2.** to be proof against: *to resist corrosion.* **3.** to refuse to comply with: *to resist arrest.* **4.** to refrain from, esp. in spite of temptation: *I cannot resist chocolate.* [Latin *resistere*] —**re'sistible** *adj.*

resistance (rɪˈzɪstəns) *n.* **1.** the act of resisting. **2.** the capacity to withstand something, esp. the body's natural capacity to withstand disease. **3.** the opposition to a flow of electric current through a circuit, component, or substance. **4.** any force that tends to retard or oppose motion: *wind resistance.* **5. line of least resistance.** the easiest, but not necessarily the best or most honourable, course of action. **6.** See **passive resistance.** —**re'sistant** *adj., n.*

Resistance (rɪˈzɪstəns) *n.* **the.** an illegal organization fighting for national liberty in a country under enemy occupation.

resistor (rɪˈzɪstə) *n.* an electrical component designed to introduce a known value of resistance into a circuit.

resit (riːˈsɪt) *vb.* **-sitting, -sat. 1.** to sit (an examination) again. ~*n.* **2.** an examination which one must sit again.

resoluble (rɪˈzɒljʊbʳl, ˈrezə-) *adj.* able to be resolved or analysed.

resolute (ˈrezəˌluːt) *adj.* firm in purpose or belief; steadfast; determined. [Latin *resolutus*] —**'reso_lutely** *adv.*

resolution (ˌrezəˈluːʃən) *n.* **1.** firmness or

determination. **2.** something resolved or determined; decision. **3.** a formal expression of opinion by a meeting. **4.** the act of separating something into its constituent elements. **5.** *Music.* the process in harmony whereby a dissonant note or chord is followed by a consonant one. **6.** the ability of a television to reproduce fine detail. **7.** *Physics.* Also called: **resolving power.** the ability of a telescope or microscope to produce separate images of closely placed objects.

resolve (rɪˈzɒlv) *vb.* **1.** to decide or determine firmly. **2.** to express (an opinion) formally, esp. by a vote. **3.** (usually foll. by *into*) to separate or cause to separate into (constituent parts). **4.** to find the answer or solution to. **5.** to explain away or dispel: *to resolve a doubt.* **6.** to bring to an end; conclude: *to resolve an argument.* **7.** *Music.* to follow (a dissonant note or chord) by one producing a consonance. **8.** *Physics.* to distinguish between (separate parts) of (an image) as in a microscope, telescope, or other optical instrument. ~*n.* **9.** something decided; resolution: *it was her resolve to work all day.* **10.** firmness of purpose; determination: *nothing can break his resolve.* [Latin *resolvere* to unfasten, reveal]

resolved (rɪˈzɒlvd) *adj.* fixed in purpose or intention; determined.

resonance (ˈrɛzənəns) *n.* **1.** the condition or quality of being resonant. **2.** sound produced by a body vibrating in sympathy with a neighbouring source of sound. [Latin *resonāre* to resound]

resonant (ˈrɛzənənt) *adj.* **1.** resounding or re-echoing. **2.** producing resonance: *resonant walls.* **3.** full of, or intensified by, resonance: *a resonant voice.*

resonate (ˈrɛzəˌneɪt) *vb.* to resound or cause to resound. —ˈreso,nator *n.*

resort (rɪˈzɔːt) *vb.* **1.** (usually foll. by *to*) to have recourse (to) for help, use, etc.: *to resort to violence.* **2.** to go, esp. often or habitually: *to resort to the beach.* ~*n.* **3.** a place to which many people go for recreation, etc.: *a holiday resort.* **4.** the use of something as a means or aid. **5. last resort.** the last possible course of action open to one. [Old French *resortir*]

resound (rɪˈzaʊnd) *vb.* **1.** to ring or echo with sound; reverberate. **2.** to make a prolonged echoing noise. **3.** (of sounds) to echo or ring. **4.** to be widely famous: *his fame resounded throughout India.* [Latin *resonāre* to sound again]

resounding (rɪˈzaʊndɪŋ) *adj.* **1.** clear and emphatic: *a resounding vote of confidence.* **2.** resonant; reverberating. —re'soundingly *adv.*

resource (rɪˈzɔːs, -ˈsɔːs) *n.* **1.** the ability to deal with problems; initiative or quick-wittedness: *a man of resource.* **2.** (often *pl.*) a source of economic wealth, esp. of a country or business enterprise: *natural resources.* **3.** something resorted to for aid or support: *resource centre.* **4.** a means of doing something; expedient: *flight was his only resource.* [Old French *resourdre* to spring up again]

resourceful (rɪˈzɔːsful, -ˈsɔːs-) *adj.* ingenious, capable, and full of initiative. —re'sourcefulness *n.*

respect (rɪˈspɛkt) *n.* **1.** an attitude of deference, admiration, or esteem. **2.** the state of being honoured or esteemed. **3.** a detail, point, or characteristic: *they differ in some respects.* **4. in respect of** or **with respect to.** in reference or relation to. **5.** consideration: *respect for people's feelings.* **6.** (*often pl.*) an expression of esteem or regard: *to pay one's respects.* ~*vb.* **7.** to have an attitude of esteem towards: *to respect one's elders.* **8.** to pay proper attention or consideration to: *to respect Swiss neutrality.* [Latin *respicere* to pay attention to] —re'specter *n.*

respectable (rɪˈspɛktəb'l) *adj.* **1.** having or deserving the respect of other people. **2.** having good social standing or reputation, esp. as regards morals: *a respectable woman.* **3.** relatively or fairly good: *a respectable salary.* **4.** fit to be seen by other people; presentable. —re,specta'bility *n.* —re'spectably *adv.*

respectful (rɪˈspɛktful) *adj.* full of, showing, or giving respect.

respecting (rɪˈspɛktɪŋ) *prep.* concerning; regarding.

respective (rɪˈspɛktɪv) *adj.* belonging or relating separately to each of several people or things: *we went our respective ways.*

respectively (rɪˈspɛktɪvlɪ) *adv.* (in listing things that refer to another list) separately in the order given: *he gave Janet and John a cake and a sweet respectively.*

respiration (ˌrɛspɪˈreɪʃən) *n.* **1.** the process in living organisms of taking in oxygen and giving out carbon dioxide. **2.** the breakdown of complex organic substances that takes place in the cells of animals and plants, producing energy and carbon dioxide. —**respiratory** (ˈrɛspɪrətrɪ) *adj.*

respirator (ˈrɛspɪˌreɪtə) *n.* **1.** an apparatus for providing artificial respiration. **2.** a device worn over the mouth and nose to prevent inhalation of noxious fumes.

respire (rɪˈspaɪə) *vb.* **1.** to inhale and exhale (air); breathe. **2.** to undergo respiration. [Latin *respīrāre* to exhale]

respite (ˈrɛspɪt, -paɪt) *n.* **1.** a pause from exertion; interval of rest. **2.** a temporary delay; reprieve. ~*vb.* **3.** to grant a respite to. [Old French *respit*]

resplendent (rɪˈsplɛndənt) *adj.* brilliant or splendid in appearance. [Latin *re-* again + *splendēre* to shine] —re'splendence *n.*

respond (rɪˈspɒnd) *vb.* **1.** to state or utter (something) in reply. **2.** to act in reply; react: *to respond by issuing an invitation.* **3.** (foll. by *to*) to react favourably: *this patient will respond to treatment.* [Old French *respondre*]

respondent (rɪˈspɒndənt) *n.* *Law.* a person against whom a petition is brought.

response (rɪˈspɒns) *n.* **1.** the act of responding; reply or reaction. **2.** (*usually pl.*) *Christianity.* a short sentence or phrase recited or sung in reply to the priest at a church service. **3.** a reaction to stimulation of the nervous system.

responsibility (rɪˌspɒnsɪˈbɪlɪtɪ) n., pl. **-ties.** 1. the state or position of being responsible. 2. a person or thing for which one is responsible.

responsible (rɪˈspɒnsɪbʔl) adj. 1. (usually foll. by for) having control or authority (over). 2. (foll. by to) being accountable for one's actions and decisions to: responsible to the manager. 3. (of a position, duty, etc.) involving decision and accountability. 4. (often foll. by for) being the agent or cause (of some action): responsible for a mistake. 5. rational and accountable for one's own actions. [Latin respondēre to respond] —reˈsponsibly adv.

responsive (rɪˈspɒnsɪv) adj. reacting or replying quickly or favourably, as to a suggestion or initiative. —reˈsponsiveness n.

rest[1] (rɛst) n. 1. relaxation from exertion or labour. 2. repose; sleep. 3. any relief or refreshment, as from worry. 4. calm; tranquillity. 5. death regarded as repose: eternal rest. 6. at rest. a. not moving. b. calm. c. dead. d. asleep. 7. a pause or interval. 8. a mark in a musical score indicating a pause of specific duration. 9. a thing or place on which to put something for support or to steady it. 10. lay to rest. to bury (a dead person). ~vb. 11. to become or make refreshed. 12. to position (oneself, etc.) for rest or relaxation. 13. to place for support or steadying: to rest one's elbows on the table. 14. to be at ease; be calm. 15. to cease or cause to cease from motion or exertion. 16. to remain without further attention or action: let the matter rest. 17. to direct (one's eyes) or (of one's eyes) to be directed: her eyes rested on the child. 18. to depend or cause to depend; rely: the whole argument rests on one crucial fact. 19. Law. to finish the introduction of evidence in (a case). 20. to put pastry in a cool place to allow the gluten to contract. [Old English ræst, reste]

rest[2] (rɛst) n. (usually preceded by the) 1. something left; remainder. 2. the others: the rest of the world. ~vb. 3. to continue to be (as specified); remain: rest assured. [Old French rester to remain]

rest area n. Austral. & N.Z. a motorist's stopping place, usually off a highway, equipped with tables and seats.

restaurant (ˈrɛstəˌrɒŋ, ˈrɛstrɒŋ) n. a place where meals are prepared and served to customers. [French]

restaurant car n. Brit. a railway coach in which meals are served.

restaurateur (ˌrɛstərəˈtɜː) n. a person who owns or runs a restaurant.

rest-cure n. a rest taken as part of a course of medical treatment.

restful (ˈrɛstfʊl) adj. relaxing or soothing.

restitution (ˌrɛstɪˈtjuːʃən) n. 1. the act of giving back something that has been lost or stolen. 2. Law. compensation for loss or injury. [Latin restituere to rebuild]

restive (ˈrɛstɪv) adj. 1. restless, nervous, or uneasy. 2. impatient of control or authority. [Old French restif balky]

restless (ˈrɛstlɪs) adj. 1. unable to stay still or quiet. 2. worried; anxious; uneasy. 3. not restful: a restless night.

restoration (ˌrɛstəˈreɪʃən) n. 1. the act of restoring to a former or original condition, place, etc. 2. the giving back of something lost or stolen. 3. something restored, replaced, or reconstructed. 4. a model or representation of a ruin or extinct animal. 5. the Restoration. Brit. history. the reestablishment of the monarchy in 1660 or the reign of Charles II (1660–85).

restorative (rɪˈstɒrətɪv) adj. 1. tending to renew health, spirits, etc. ~n. 2. anything that restores or revives.

restore (rɪˈstɔː) vb. 1. to return (something) to its original or former condition. 2. to bring back to health or good spirits. 3. to return (something lost or stolen) to its owner. 4. to reintroduce or re-enforce: to restore discipline. 5. to reconstruct (a ruin, extinct animal, etc.). [Latin restaurāre to rebuild] —reˈstorer n.

restrain (rɪˈstreɪn) vb. 1. to hold (someone) back from some action, esp. by force. 2. to deprive (someone) of liberty, as by imprisonment. 3. to limit or restrict. [Latin re- back + stringere to draw]

restrained (rɪˈstreɪnd) adj. not displaying emotion.

restraint (rɪˈstreɪnt) n. 1. the ability to control one's impulses or passions. 2. a restraining or being restrained. 3. a restriction.

restrict (rɪˈstrɪkt) vb. (often foll. by to) to confine or keep within certain, often specified, limits. [Latin restrictus bound up] —reˈstriction n. —reˈstrictive adj.

restrictive practice n. Brit. 1. a trading agreement against the public interest. 2. a practice of a union or other group tending to limit the freedom of other workers or employers.

rest room n. U.S. & Canad. a toilet in a public building.

result (rɪˈzʌlt) n. 1. the outcome or consequence of an action, policy, etc. 2. a number or value obtained by solving a mathematical problem. 3. (often pl.) the final score of a sporting contest. 4. (often pl.) the mark or grade obtained in an examination. ~vb. 5. (often foll. by from) to be the outcome or consequence (of). 6. (foll. by in) to end (in a specified way): to result in tragedy. [Latin resultāre to spring from]

resultant (rɪˈzʌltənt) adj. 1. that results; resulting. ~n. 2. Maths, physics. a single vector that is the vector sum of two or more other vectors, such as a force which results from two other forces acting on a single point.

resume (rɪ'zjuːm) vb. **1.** to begin again or go on with (something interrupted). **2.** to occupy again, take back, or recover: to resume one's seat. [Latin resūmere]

résumé ('rezjʊˌmeɪ) n. **1.** a short descriptive summary, as of events. **2.** U.S. & Canad. a curriculum vitae. [French]

resumption (rɪ'zʌmpʃən) n. the act of resuming or beginning again.

resurgent (rɪ'sɜːdʒənt) adj. rising again, as to new life or vigour: resurgent nationalism. [Latin resurgere to rise again] —re'surgence n.

resurrect (ˌrezə'rekt) vb. **1.** to bring or be brought back to life from death. **2.** to bring back into use or activity; revive.

resurrection (ˌrezə'rekʃən) n. **1.** a return to life by a dead person. **2.** revival or renewal. **3.** (usually cap.) Christian theol. the rising again of Christ from the tomb three days after his death. **4.** (usually cap.) the rising again from the dead of all people at the Last Judgment. [Latin resurgere to rise again]

resuscitate (rɪ'sʌsɪˌteɪt) vb. to restore to consciousness; revive. [Latin re- again + suscitāre to raise] —re,susci'tation n.

retail ('riːteɪl) n. **1.** the sale of goods individually or in small quantities to consumers. ~adj. **2.** of, relating to, or engaged in such selling: retail prices. ~adv. **3.** in small amounts or at a retail price. ~vb. **4.** to sell or be sold in small quantities to consumers. **5.** (rɪ'teɪl). to relate (gossip or scandal) in detail. [Old French re- again + taillier to cut] —'retailer n.

retain (rɪ'teɪn) vb. **1.** to keep in one's possession. **2.** to be able to hold or contain: soil that retains water. **3.** (of a person) to be able to remember (something) without difficulty. **4.** to hold in position. **5.** Law. to engage the services of (a barrister) by payment of a preliminary fee. [Latin retinēre to hold back]

retainer (rɪ'teɪnə) n. **1.** a fee paid in advance to secure first option on someone, esp. a barrister's services. **2.** a reduced rent paid for a flat, room, etc., to reserve it for future use. **3.** a servant who has been with a family for a long time.

retaining wall n. a wall constructed to hold back earth, loose rock, etc.

retake vb. (riː'teɪk), **-taking, -took, -taken. 1.** to take something, such as an examination or vote, again. **2.** to recapture: to retake a fortress. ~n. (ˈriːˌteɪk). **3.** Films. a rephotographed scene.

retaliate (rɪ'tælɪˌeɪt) vb. **1.** to repay some injury or wrong in kind. **2.** to cast (accusations) back upon a person. [Latin re- back + tālis of such kind] —re,tali'ation n. —retaliatory (rɪ'tælɪətrɪ) adj.

retard (rɪ'tɑːd) vb. to delay or slow down (the progress or speed) of (something). [Latin retardāre] —re'tardant n., adj. —ˌretar'dation n.

retarded (rɪ'tɑːdɪd) adj. underdeveloped, esp. mentally.

retch (retʃ, riːtʃ) vb. **1.** to undergo an involuntary spasm of ineffectual vomiting. ~n. **2.** an involuntary spasm of ineffectual vomiting. [Old English hræcan]

retention (rɪ'tenʃən) n. **1.** the act of retaining or state of being retained. **2.** the capacity to remember. **3.** Pathol. the abnormal holding of something within the body, esp. fluid. —re'tentive adj.

rethink vb. (riː'θɪŋk), **-thinking, -thought. 1.** to think about (something) again, esp. with a view to changing one's tactics or opinions. ~n. ('riːθɪŋk). **2.** the act or an instance of thinking again.

reticent ('retɪsənt) adj. not communicative; not saying all that one knows. [Latin reticēre to keep silent] —'reticence n.

reticulate adj. (rɪ'tɪkjʊlɪt) **1.** in the form of a network or having a network of parts: a reticulate leaf. ~vb. (rɪ'tɪkjʊˌleɪt). **2.** to form or be formed into a net. [Late Latin rēticulātus like a net] —re,ticu'lation n.

retina ('retɪnə) n., pl. **-nas** or **-nae** (-ˌniː). the light-sensitive inner lining of the back of the eyeball. [Medieval Latin] —'retinal adj.

retinue ('retɪˌnjuː) n. a body of aides and followers attending an important person. [Old French retenue]

retire (rɪ'taɪə) vb. **1.** to give up or to cause (a person) to give up work, esp. on reaching pensionable age. **2.** to go away, as into seclusion, esp. to rest. **3.** to go to bed. **4.** to withdraw from a sporting contest, esp. because of injury. **5.** to pull back (troops) from battle or (of troops) to fall back. [French retirer] —re'tired adj. —re'tirement n.

retirement pension n. Brit. a weekly payment made by the government to a retired man over 65 or a woman over 60.

retiring (rɪ'taɪərɪŋ) adj. shunning contact with others; shy; reserved.

retort[1] (rɪ'tɔːt) vb. **1.** to utter (something) quickly, wittily, or angrily, in response. **2.** to use (an argument) against its originator. ~n. **3.** a sharp, angry, or witty reply. **4.** an argument used against its originator. [Latin re- back + torquēre to twist, wrench]

retort[2] (rɪ'tɔːt) n. **1.** a glass vessel with a long tapering neck that is bent down, used for distillation. **2.** a vessel used for heating ores in the production of metals or heating coal to produce gas. [see RETORT[1]]

retouch (riː'tʌtʃ) vb. to restore, correct, or improve (a painting, photograph, make-up, etc.) with new touches.

retrace (rɪ'treɪs) vb. **1.** to go back over (one's steps, a route, etc.). **2.** to go over (a story, account, etc.) from the beginning.

retract (rɪ'trækt) vb. **1.** to draw in (a part or appendage): the plane's undercarriage had not yet retracted. **2.** to withdraw (a statement, opinion, charge, etc.) as invalid or unjustified. **3.** to go back on (a promise or agreement). [Latin retractāre to withdraw] —re'traction n.

retractile (rɪ'træktaɪl) *adj.* capable of being drawn in: *the retractile claws of a cat.*

retread *vb.* (riː'trɛd), **-treading**, **-treaded**. 1. to bond a new tread onto (a worn tyre). ~*n.* ('riː,trɛd). 2. a remoulded tyre.

retreat (rɪ'triːt) *vb.* 1. *Mil.* to withdraw or retire in the face of or from action with an enemy. 2. to retire or withdraw, as to seclusion or shelter. ~*n.* 3. the act of retreating or withdrawing. 4. *Mil.* **a.** a withdrawal or retirement in the face of the enemy. **b.** a bugle call signifying withdrawal or retirement. 5. a place to which one may retire, esp. for religious contemplation. 6. a period of seclusion, esp. for religious contemplation. [Old French *retret*]

retrench (rɪ'trɛntʃ) *vb.* to reduce (costs); economize. [Old French *re-* off + *trenchier* to cut] —**re'trenchment** *n.*

retribution (,rɛtrɪ'bjuːʃən) *n.* punishment or vengeance for wrongdoing, sin, or harm. [Latin *re-* back + *tribuere* to pay] —**retributive** (rɪ'trɪbjutɪv) *adj.*

retrieve (rɪ'triːv) *vb.* 1. to get or fetch back again; recover. 2. to bring back to a more satisfactory state; revive. 3. to rescue or save. 4. to recover or make newly available (stored information) from a computer system. 5. (of dogs) to find and fetch (shot birds and animals). 6. to recall; remember. ~*n.* 7. the chance of being retrieved: *beyond retrieve.* [Old French *retrover*] —**re'trievable** *adj.* —**re'trieval** *n.*

retriever (rɪ'triːvə) *n.* a dog trained to retrieve shot birds and animals.

retro ('rɛtrəʊ) *adj.* associated with or revived from the past: *retro fashion.*

retro- *prefix.* 1. back or backwards: *retroactive.* 2. located behind: *retrochoir.* [Latin]

retroactive (,rɛtrəʊ'æktɪv) *adj.* effective from a date in the past: *retroactive legislation.*

retrograde ('rɛtrəʊ,greɪd) *adj.* 1. moving or bending backwards. 2. (esp. of order) reverse or inverse. 3. tending towards an earlier worse condition; declining or deteriorating. ~*vb.* 4. to go backwards or deteriorate. [Latin *retro-* backwards + *gradi* to walk]

retrogress (,rɛtrəʊ'grɛs) *vb.* to go back to an earlier worse condition. [Latin *retrōgressus* having moved backwards] —**,retro'gression** *n.* —**,retro'gressive** *adj.*

retrorocket ('rɛtrəʊ,rɒkɪt) *n.* a small auxiliary rocket on a larger rocket or a spacecraft, that produces thrust in the opposite direction to the direction of flight in order to decelerate.

retrospect ('rɛtrəʊ,spɛkt) *n.* **in retrospect.** when looking back on the past. [Latin *retrōspicere* to look back]

retrospective (,rɛtrəʊ'spɛktɪv) *adj.* 1. looking backwards, esp. in time. 2. applying to the past; retroactive. ~*n.* 3. an exhibition of an artist's life's work.

retroussé (rə'truːseɪ) *adj.* (of a nose) turned up. [French]

retsina (rɛt'siːnə) *n.* a Greek wine flavoured with resin. [Modern Greek]

return (rɪ'tɜːn) *vb.* 1. to come back to a former place or state. 2. to replace or restore. 3. to repay with something of equivalent value: *return the compliment.* 4. to earn or yield (profit or interest). 5. to come back or revert in thought or speech: *I'll return to that later.* 6. to recur or reappear: *the symptoms have returned.* 7. to answer or reply. 8. to vote into office; elect. 9. *Law.* (of a jury) to deliver (a verdict). 10. *Ball games.* to hit, throw, or play (a ball) back. ~*n.* 11. the act or an instance of coming back. 12. something that is given or sent back, esp. unsatisfactory merchandise or a theatre ticket for resale. 13. replacement or restoration. 14. (*often pl.*) the yield or profit from an investment or venture. 15. **in return.** in exchange. 16. a recurrence or reappearance. 17. a statement of one's taxable income (a **tax return**). 18. (*often pl.*) a statement of the votes counted at an election. 19. an answer or reply. 20. *Brit.* short for **return ticket.** 21. *Ball games.* the act of playing or throwing a ball back. 22. (*modifier*) of, relating to, or characterized by a return: *a return visit.* 23. **by return (of post).** *Brit.* by the next post back to the sender. 24. **many happy returns (of the day).** a conventional birthday greeting. [Old French *retorner*] —**re'turnable** *adj.*

returned man *n. Austral. & Canad.* a soldier who has served abroad. Also (*Austral. & N.Z.*): **returned soldier.**

returning officer *n.* an official in charge of conducting an election in a constituency.

return ticket *n. Brit.* a ticket entitling a passenger to travel to his destination and back.

reunify (riː'juːnɪ,faɪ) *vb.* **-fying**, **-fied.** to bring together again something previously divided. —**,reunifi'cation** *n.*

reunion (riː'juːnjən) *n.* 1. the act of coming together again. 2. the state of having been brought together again. 3. a gathering of relatives, friends, or former associates.

rev (rɛv) *Informal.* ~*n.* 1. revolution per minute. ~*vb.* **revving**, **revved.** 2. (often foll. by *up*) to increase the speed of revolution of (an engine).

rev. 1. revise(d). 2. revision.

Rev. Reverend.

revamp (riː'væmp) *vb.* to patch up or renovate.

Revd. Reverend.

reveal (rɪ'viːl) *vb.* 1. to disclose or divulge

(a secret). **2.** to expose to view or show (something concealed). **3.** (of God) to disclose (divine truths). [Latin *revēlāre* to unveil]

reveille (rɪ'vælɪ) *n.* a signal given by a bugle or drum to awaken soldiers or sailors in the morning. [French *réveillez!* awake!]

revel ('rɛv'l) *vb.* **-elling, -elled** or *U.S.* **-eling, -eled. 1.** (foll. by *in*) to take pleasure or wallow: *to revel in success.* **2.** to take part in noisy festivities. ~*n.* **3.** (*often pl.*) an occasion of noisy merrymaking. [Old French *reveler*] —'**reveller** *n.*

revelation (ˌrɛvə'leɪʃən) *n.* **1.** the disclosure of a truth previously secret or obscure. **2.** a fact disclosed or revealed. **3.** *Christianity.* God's disclosure of his own nature and his purpose for mankind.

Revelation (ˌrɛvə'leɪʃən) *n.* (*popularly, often pl.*) the last book of the New Testament, containing visionary descriptions of heaven, and of the end of the world.

revelry ('rɛv'lrɪ) *n., pl.* **-ries.** noisy or unrestrained merrymaking.

revenge (rɪ'vɛndʒ) *n.* **1.** vengeance for wrongs or injury received. **2.** something done as a means of vengeance. ~*vb.* **3.** to inflict equivalent injury or damage for (injury received). **4.** to take vengeance for (oneself or another); avenge. [Old French *revenger*] —**re'vengeful** *adj.*

revenue ('rɛvɪˌnjuː) *n.* **1.** any income, esp. that obtained by a government from taxation. **2.** a government department responsible for collecting taxes. [Old French *revenir* to return]

reverberate (rɪ'vɜːbəˌreɪt) *vb.* **1.** to resound or re-echo. **2.** to reflect or be reflected many times. [Latin *re-* again + *verberāre* to beat] —**re,verber'ation** *n.*

revere (rɪ'vɪə) *vb.* to be in awe of and respect deeply. [Latin *reverērī*]

reverence ('rɛvərəns) *n.* profound respect, esp. towards the sacred or divine. —**reverential** (ˌrɛvə'rɛnʃəl) *adj.*

Reverence ('rɛvərəns) *n.* (preceded by *Your* or *His*) a title sometimes used for a Roman Catholic priest.

reverend ('rɛvərənd) *adj.* **1.** worthy of reverence. **2.** relating to or designating a clergyman. ~*n.* **3.** *Informal.* a clergyman.

Reverend ('rɛvərənd) *adj.* a title of respect for a clergyman.

reverent ('rɛvərənt, 'rɛvrənt) *adj.* feeling or expressing reverence.

reverie ('rɛvərɪ) *n.* absent-minded daydreaming. [Old French *resverie* wildness]

revers (rɪ'vɪə) *n., pl.* **-vers** (-'vɪəz). (*usually pl.*) the turned-back lining of part of a garment, esp. of a lapel or cuff. [French]

reverse (rɪ'vɜːs) *vb.* **1.** to turn or set in an opposite direction, order, or position. **2.** to change into something different or contrary: *reverse one's policy.* **3.** to move or cause to move backwards or in an opposite direction: *to reverse a car.* **4.** to run (machinery) in the opposite direction to normal. **5.** to turn inside out. **6.** *Law.* to revoke or set aside (a judgment or decree); annul. **7. reverse the charge(s).** to make a telephone call at the recipient's expense. ~*n.* **8.** the opposite or contrary of something. **9.** the back or rear side of something. **10.** a change to an opposite position, state, or direction. **11.** a change for the worse; setback or defeat. **12.** the mechanism or gears by which machinery or a vehicle can be made to go backwards. **13.** the side of a coin bearing a secondary design. **14. in reverse.** in an opposite or backward direction. **15. the reverse of.** emphatically not; not at all: *he was the reverse of polite.* ~*adj.* **16.** opposite or contrary in direction, position, order, nature, etc. **17.** operating or moving in a direction contrary to that which is usual. [Latin *reversus* turned back] —**re'versal** *n.*

reversible (rɪ'vɜːsɪb'l) *adj.* **1.** capable of being reversed: *a reversible decision.* **2.** (of a garment) made so that either side may be used as the outer side.

reversing light *n.* a light on the rear of a motor vehicle to provide illumination when the vehicle is being reversed.

reversion (rɪ'vɜːʃən) *n.* **1.** a return to an earlier condition, practice, or belief. **2.** *Biol.* the return of individuals or organs to a more primitive condition or type.

revert (rɪ'vɜːt) *vb.* (foll. by *to*). **1.** to go back to a former practice, condition, belief, or topic. **2.** *Biol.* (of individuals or organs) to return to a more primitive, earlier, or simpler condition or type. **3.** *Property law.* (of an estate) to return to its former owner or his heirs. [Latin *revertere*]

review (rɪ'vjuː) *vb.* **1.** to examine again: *to review a situation.* **2.** to look back upon (a period of time or sequence of events): *he reviewed his achievements with pride.* **3.** to inspect, esp. formally or officially: *the general reviewed his troops.* **4.** *Law.* to re-examine (a decision) judicially. **5.** to write a critical assessment of (a book, film, concert, etc.), esp. as a profession. ~*n.* **6.** the act or an instance of reviewing. **7.** a general survey or report: *a review of the political situation.* **8.** a critical assessment of a book, film, concert, etc., esp. in a newspaper. **9.** a publication containing such articles. **10.** a second consideration; re-examination. **11.** a retrospective survey. **12.** a formal or official inspection. **13.** *Law.* a re-examination of a case. [Latin *re-* again + *vidēre* to see] —**re'viewer** *n.*

revile (rɪ'vaɪl) *vb.* to use abusive or scornful language against (someone or something). [Old French *reviler*]

revise (rɪ'vaɪz) *vb.* **1.** to amend: *to revise one's opinion.* **2.** *Brit.* to reread (a subject or notes on it) so as to memorize it for an examination. **3.** to prepare a new edition of (a previously printed work). [Latin *re-* again + *vīsere* to inspect]

Revised Version *n.* a revision of the Authorized Version of the Bible published between 1881 and 1885.

revision (rɪ'vɪʒən) *n.* **1.** the act or process of revising. **2.** *Brit.* the process of rereading a subject or notes on it for an examination. **3.** a corrected or new version of a book, article, etc.

revisory (rɪ'vaɪzərɪ) *adj.* of or having the power of revision.

revitalize *or* **-lise** (riː'vaɪt³,laɪz) *vb.* to restore vitality or animation to.

revival (rɪ'vaɪv³l) *n.* **1.** a reviving or being revived. **2.** a renewed use or interest in (past customs or styles): *the Gothic revival.* **3.** a new production of a play that has not been recently performed. **4.** a reawakening of religious faith.

revivalism (rɪ'vaɪvə,lɪzəm) *n.* a movement that seeks to revive religious faith. —**re-'vivalist** *n., adj.*

revive (rɪ'vaɪv) *vb.* **1.** to bring or be brought back to life, consciousness, or strength: *revived by a drop of whisky.* **2.** to give or assume new vitality. **3.** to make or become operative or active again: *the youth movement was revived.* **4.** *Theatre.* to mount a new production of (an old play). [Latin *re-* again + *vīvere* to live]

revivify (rɪ'vɪvɪ,faɪ) *vb.* **-fying, -fied.** to give new life to. —**re,vivifi'cation** *n.*

revoke (rɪ'vəʊk) *vb.* **1.** to take back or cancel (an agreement, will, etc.). **2.** *Cards.* to break a rule by failing to follow suit when able to do so. ~*n.* **3.** *Cards.* the act of revoking. [Latin *revocāre* to call back] —**revocation** (,revə'keɪʃən) *n.*

revolt (rɪ'vəʊlt) *n.* **1.** a rebellion or uprising against authority. **2. in revolt.** in the state of rebelling. ~*vb.* **3.** to rise up in rebellion against authority. **4.** (*usually passive*) to feel or cause to feel revulsion, disgust, or abhorrence. [French *révolter*]

revolting (rɪ'vəʊltɪŋ) *adj.* nauseating, disgusting, or repulsive.

revolution (,revə'luːʃən) *n.* **1.** the overthrow of a regime or political system by the governed. **2.** (in Marxist theory) the transition from one system of production in a society to the next. **3.** a far-reaching and drastic change, esp. in ideas or methods. **4. a.** movement in or as if in a circle. **b.** one complete turn in a circle: *33 revolutions per minute.* **5.** a cycle of successive events. [Latin *revolvere* to revolve]

revolutionary (,revə'luːʃənərɪ) *n., pl.* **-aries. 1.** a person who advocates or engages in revolution. ~*adj.* **2.** of or like a revolution. **3.** advocating or engaged in revolution. **4.** radically new or different: *a revolutionary method of making plastics.*

revolutionize *or* **-ise** (,revə'luːʃə,naɪz) *vb.* to bring about a radical change in.

revolve (rɪ'vɒlv) *vb.* **1.** to move or cause to move around a centre; rotate. **2.** to occur periodically or in cycles. **3.** to consider or be considered. **4.** (foll. by *around* or *about*) to be centred or focused upon: *Juliet's thoughts revolved around Romeo.* [Latin *revolvere*] —**re'volvable** *adj.*

revolver (rɪ'vɒlvə) *n.* a pistol with a revolving cylinder that allows several shots to be fired without reloading.

revolving door *n.* a door that rotates about a vertical axis, esp. one with four leaves at right angles to each other.

revue (rɪ'vjuː) *n.* a light entertainment consisting of sketches, songs, etc. [French]

revulsion (rɪ'vʌlʃən) *n.* a sudden violent reaction in feeling, esp. one of extreme loathing. [Latin *revulsiō* a pulling away]

reward (rɪ'wɔːd) *n.* **1.** something given in return for a deed or service rendered. **2.** a sum of money offered, esp. for help in finding a criminal or missing property. **3.** something received in return for good or evil; deserts. ~*vb.* **4.** to give something to (someone), esp. in gratitude for a service rendered. [Old French *rewarder*]

rewarding (rɪ'wɔːdɪŋ) *adj.* giving personal satisfaction; gratifying.

rewarewa ('reɪwə'reɪwə) *n.* a tall New Zealand tree with reddish wood. [Maori]

rewind (riː'waɪnd) *vb.* **-winding, -wound.** to wind back, esp. a film or tape, to the beginning.

rewire (riː'waɪə) *vb.* to provide (a house, engine, etc.) with new wiring.

reword (riː'wɜːd) *vb.* to alter the wording of; express differently.

rewrite *vb.* (riː'raɪt), **-writing, -wrote, -written. 1.** to write (material) again, esp. changing the words or form. ~*n.* ('riː,raɪt). **2.** something rewritten.

Rex (reks) *n.* king: now used chiefly in documents and inscriptions. [Latin]

RFC 1. Royal Flying Corps. **2.** Rugby Football Club.

rh *or* **RH** right hand.

Rh 1. *Chem.* rhodium. **2.** See **Rh factor.**

rhapsodize *or* **-ise** ('ræpsə,daɪz) *vb.* to speak or write (something) with extravagant enthusiasm.

rhapsody ('ræpsədɪ) *n., pl.* **-dies. 1.** *Music.* a composition free in structure and highly emotional in character. **2.** an expression of ecstatic enthusiasm. [Greek *rhaptein* to sew together + *ōidē* song] —**rhapsodic** (ræp'sɒdɪk) *adj.*

rhea (rɪə) *n.* a large fast-running flightless bird of South America, similar to the ostrich. [after *Rhea*, mother of Zeus]

rhebuck ('riːbʌk) *n., pl.* **-bucks** *or* **-buck.** a southern African antelope with brownish-grey hair. [Afrikaans]

rhenium ('riːnɪəm) *n.* a silvery-white metallic element with a high melting point. Symbol: Re [Latin *Rhēnus* the Rhine]

rheostat ('rɪə,stæt) *n.* a variable resistor in an electrical circuit, such as one used to dim lights. [Greek *rheos* flow + *-statēs* stationary] —**,rheo'static** *adj.*

rhesus factor *n.* See **Rh factor.**

rhesus monkey *n.* a monkey of S Asia. [Greek *Rhesos*, mythical Thracian king]

rhetoric ('retərɪk) *n.* **1.** the art of using speech or writing to persuade or influence. **2.** speech that pretends to significance but lacks true meaning: *mere rhetoric.* [Greek *rhētorikē*] —**rhetorical** (rɪ'tɒrɪk³l) *adj.*

rhetorical question *n.* a question to which no answer is required: used for dramatic effect. An example is *Who knows?*

rheum (ruːm) *n.* a watery discharge from the eyes or nose. [Greek *rheuma* a flow] —**'rheumy** *adj.*

rheumatic (ruːˈmætɪk) *adj.* 1. of, caused by, or afflicted with rheumatism. ~*n.* 2. a person afflicted with rheumatism. —**rheuˈmatically** *adv.*

rheumatic fever *n.* a disease with inflammation and pain in the joints.

rheumatics (ruːˈmætɪks) *n.* (*functioning as sing.*) *Informal.* rheumatism.

rheumatism (ˈruːməˌtɪzəm) *n.* any painful disorder of joints, muscles, or connective tissue. [Greek *rheuma* a flow]

rheumatoid (ˈruːməˌtɔɪd) *adj.* (of symptoms) resembling rheumatism.

rheumatoid arthritis *n.* a chronic disease characterized by inflammation and swelling of the joints.

Rh factor *n.* an antigen commonly found in human blood: the terms **Rh positive** and **Rh negative** are used to indicate its presence or absence. [after the rhesus monkey, in which it was first discovered]

rhinestone (ˈraɪnˌstəʊn) *n.* an imitation diamond made of glass. [orig. made at Strasbourg, on the Rhine]

rhino (ˈraɪnəʊ) *n., pl.* **-nos** *or* **-no.** a rhinoceros.

rhinoceros (raɪˈnɒsərəs, -ˈnɒsrəs) *n., pl.* **-oses** *or* **-os.** a plant-eating mammal of SE Asia and Africa with one or two horns on the nose, a very thick skin, and a massive body. [Greek *rhis* nose + *keras* horn]

rhizome (ˈraɪzəʊm) *n.* a thick horizontal underground stem whose buds develop into new plants. [Greek *rhiza* a root]

rhodium (ˈrəʊdɪəm) *n.* a hard silvery-white metallic element, used to harden platinum and palladium. Symbol: Rh [Greek *rhodon* rose, from the pink colour of its compounds]

rhododendron (ˌrəʊdəˈdɛndrən) *n.* an evergreen shrub with clusters of showy red, purple, pink, or white flowers. [Greek *rhodon* rose + *dendron* tree]

rhombohedron (ˌrɒmbəʊˈhiːdrən) *n., pl.* **-drons** *or* **-dra** (-drə). a six-sided prism whose sides are parallelograms. [*rhombus* + Greek *-edron* -sided]

rhomboid (ˈrɒmbɔɪd) *n.* 1. a parallelogram having adjacent sides of unequal length. It resembles a rectangle but does not have 90° angles. ~*adj. also* **rhomˈboiˌdal.** 2. having such a shape. [Greek *rhomboeidēs* shaped like a rhombus]

rhombus (ˈrɒmbəs) *n., pl.* **-buses** *or* **-bi** (-baɪ). an oblique-angled parallelogram having four equal sides. [Greek *rhombos* something that spins] —**'rhombic** *adj.*

rhubarb (ˈruːbɑːb) *n.* 1. a large-leaved plant with long green and red acid-tasting edible leafstalks, eaten sweetened and cooked. 2. a related plant of central Asia, whose root can be dried and used as a laxative or astringent. ~*interj., n., vb.* 3. the noise made by actors to simulate conversation, esp. by repeating the word *rhubarb.* [Old French *reubarbe*]

rhyme (raɪm) *n.* 1. sameness of the final sounds in lines of verse or in words. 2. a word that is identical to another in its final sound: *"while" is a rhyme for "mile".* 3. a piece of poetry with corresponding sounds at the ends of the lines. 4. **rhyme or reason.** sense, logic, or meaning. ~*vb.* 5. to use (a word) or (of a word) to be used so as to form a rhyme. 6. to put (a subject) into rhyme. 7. to compose (verse) in a metrical structure. [Old French *rime*; spelling infl. by *rhythm*]

rhymester (ˈraɪmstə) *n.* a poet, esp. one considered to be mediocre.

rhyming slang *n.* slang in which a word is replaced by another word or phrase that rhymes with it; e.g. *apples and pears* meaning *stairs.*

rhythm (ˈrɪðəm) *n.* 1. any regular movement or beat: *the rhythm of her breathing.* 2. **a.** the arrangement of the durations of and accents on the notes of a melody, usually laid out into regular groups (**bars**) of beats. **b.** any specific arrangement of such groupings; time: *waltz rhythm.* 3. (in poetry) the arrangement of words into a sequence of stressed and unstressed or long and short syllables. [Greek *rhuthmos*] —**rhythmical** (ˈrɪðmɪk'l) *or* **'rhythmic** *adj.* —**'rhythmically** *adv.*

rhythm and blues *n.* (*functioning as sing.*) a kind of popular music of Black American origin, derived from and influenced by the blues.

rhythm method *n.* a method of contraception by restricting sexual intercourse to those days in a woman's menstrual cycle when conception is least likely to occur.

RI Rhode Island.

rialto (rɪˈæltəʊ) *n., pl.* **-tos.** a market or exchange. [after the *Rialto*, the business centre of medieval Venice]

rib¹ (rɪb) *n.* 1. any of the elastic arches of bone that together form the chest wall and are attached to the spinal column. 2. a cut of meat including one or more ribs. 3. a part or element similar in function to a rib, such as a structural member in an aeroplane wing. 4. one of a series of raised rows in knitted fabric. ~*vb.* **ribbing, ribbed.** 5. to provide or support with a rib or ribs. [Old English *ribb*] —**ribbed** *adj.*

rib² (rɪb) *vb.* **ribbing, ribbed.** *Informal.* to tease or ridicule. [short for *rib-tickle*] —**'ribbing** *n.*

RIBA Royal Institute of British Architects.

ribald (ˈrɪbᵊld) *adj.* coarse or obscene in a humorous or mocking way. [Old French *ribauld*] —**'ribaldry** *n.*

riband *or* **ribband** (ˈrɪbənd) *n.* a ribbon, esp. one awarded for some achievement.

ribbing (ˈrɪbɪŋ) *n.* 1. a framework or structure of ribs. 2. a pattern of ribs in knitted material.

ribbon (ˈrɪbᵊn) *n.* 1. a narrow strip of fine material used for trimming, tying, etc. 2. something resembling a ribbon; a long strip. 3. a long narrow strip of inked cloth or plastic used to produce print in a typewriter. 4. (*pl.*) ragged strips or shreds: *his clothes were torn to ribbons.* 5. a small strip of coloured cloth worn as a badge or as a symbol of an award. [Old French *riban*]

ribbon development *n. Brit.* the building of houses along a main road.

ribbonwood ('rɪbˌnˌwʊd) *n.* a small evergreen tree of New Zealand. Its wood is used in furniture making.

ribcage ('rɪbˌkeɪdʒ) *n.* the bony structure formed by the ribs that encloses the lungs.

riboflavin (ˌraɪbəʊ'fleɪvɪn) *n.* a vitamin of the B complex that occurs in green vegetables, milk, fish, egg yolk, liver, and kidney: used as a yellow or orange food colouring (**E 101**). Also called: **vitamin B₂**. [*ribose*, a sugar + Latin *flavus* yellow]

ribonucleic acid (ˌraɪbəʊnjuː'kliːɪk, -'kleɪɪk) *n.* the full name of **RNA**.

rice (raɪs) *n.* **1.** the edible grain of an erect grass that grows on wet ground in warm climates. ~*vb.* **2.** *U.S. & Canad.* to sieve (potatoes or other vegetables) to a coarse mashed consistency. [Greek *orūza*]

rice paper *n.* **1.** a thin edible paper made from rice straw. **2.** a thin Chinese paper made from the **rice-paper plant**, the pith of which is flattened into sheets.

rich (rɪtʃ) *adj.* **1.** owning a lot of money or property; wealthy. **2.** having an abundance of natural resources, minerals, etc.: *a land rich in metals.* **3.** producing abundantly; fertile: *rich soil.* **4.** well supplied (with desirable qualities); abundant (in): *a country rich with cultural interest.* **5.** luxuriant or prolific: *a rich growth of weeds.* **6.** (of food) having a large proportion of flavoursome or fatty ingredients. **7.** having a full-bodied flavour: *a rich ruby port.* **8.** (of colour) intense or vivid; deep: *a rich red.* **9.** (of sound or a voice) full, mellow, or resonant. **10.** (of a fuel-air mixture) containing a relatively high proportion of fuel. **11.** very amusing or ridiculous: *a rich joke.* [Old English *rīce*] —'**richness** *n.*

riches ('rɪtʃɪz) *pl. n.* wealth; an abundance of money or property.

richly ('rɪtʃlɪ) *adv.* **1.** in a rich or elaborate manner: *a richly decorated stairway.* **2.** fully and appropriately: *richly deserved contempt.*

Richter scale ('rɪxtə) *n.* a scale for expressing the magnitude of an earthquake, ranging from 0 to over 8. [after Charles *Richter*, seismologist]

rick¹ (rɪk) *n.* a large stack of hay, corn, etc. [Old English *hrēac*]

rick² (rɪk) *n.* **1.** a wrench or sprain, as of the neck. ~*vb.* **2.** to wrench or sprain (a joint, the neck, etc.). [var. of *wrick*]

rickets ('rɪkɪts) *n.* (functioning as *sing.* or *pl.*) a disease mainly of children, caused by a deficiency of vitamin D and characterized by softening of developing bone, and hence bow legs. [origin unknown]

rickety ('rɪkɪtɪ) *adj.* **1.** (of a structure or piece of furniture) likely to collapse or break. **2.** resembling or afflicted with rickets. —'**ricketiness** *n.*

rickrack or **ricrac** ('rɪkˌræk) *n.* a zigzag

braid used for trimming. [reduplication of RACK¹]

rickshaw ('rɪkʃɔː) or **ricksha** ('rɪkʃə) *n.* **1.** a small two-wheeled passenger vehicle drawn by one or two men, used in parts of Asia. **2.** a similar vehicle with three wheels, propelled by a man pedalling as on a tricycle. [Japanese *jinrikisha*]

ricochet ('rɪkəˌʃeɪ, 'rɪkəˌʃet) *vb.* -**cheting** (-ˌʃeɪɪŋ), -**cheted** (-ˌʃeɪd) or -**chetting** (-ˌʃetɪŋ), -**chetted** (-ˌʃetɪd). **1.** (esp. of a bullet) to rebound from a surface. ~*n.* **2.** the motion or sound of a rebounding object, esp. a bullet. [French]

rid (rɪd) *vb.* **ridding, rid** or **ridded. 1.** (foll. by *of*) to relieve (oneself) of something disagreeable or undesirable; make (a place) free of. **2. get rid of.** to relieve or free oneself of something unpleasant or undesirable. [Old Norse *rythja*]

riddance ('rɪdns) *n.* **good riddance.** relief at getting rid of someone or something.

ridden ('rɪdn) *vb.* **1.** the past participle of **ride.** ~*adj.* **2.** afflicted or dominated by something specified: *disease-ridden.*

riddle¹ ('rɪdl) *n.* **1.** a question, puzzle, or verse so phrased that ingenuity is required to find the answer or meaning. **2.** a puzzling person or thing. ~*vb.* **3.** to speak in riddles. [Old English *rǣdelle, rǣdelse*]

riddle² ('rɪdl) *vb.* **1.** (usually foll. by *with*) to pierce or perforate with numerous holes: *riddled with bullets.* **2.** to put through a sieve; sift. ~*n.* **3.** a coarse sieve. [Old English *hriddel* a sieve]

ride (raɪd) *vb.* **riding, rode, ridden. 1.** to sit on and control the movements of (a horse or other animal). **2.** to sit on and propel (a bicycle or similar vehicle). **3.** (often foll. by *on* or *in*) to travel on or in a vehicle: *she rides to work on the bus.* **4.** to travel over: *they rode the countryside in search of shelter.* **5.** to travel through or be carried across (sea, sky, etc.): *the small boat rode the waves; the moon was riding high.* **6.** *U.S. & Canad.* to cause to be carried: *to ride someone out of town.* **7.** (of a vessel) to lie at anchor. **8.** (usually passive) to tyrannize over or dominate: *ridden by fear.* **9.** *Informal.* to continue undisturbed: *let it ride.* **10. riding high.** confident, popular, and successful. ~*n.* **11.** a journey or outing on horseback or in a vehicle. **12.** a path for riding on horseback. **13.** transport in a vehicle; lift: *can you give me a ride to the station?* **14.** the type of movement experienced in a vehicle: *a bumpy ride.* **15. take for a ride.** *Informal.* to cheat, swindle, or deceive. [Old English *rīdan*]

ride out *vb.* to endure successfully; survive (a storm, crisis, etc.).

rider ('raɪdə) *n.* **1.** a person or thing that rides. **2.** an additional clause, amendment, or stipulation added to a document.

ride up *vb.* to work away from the proper position: *her new skirt rode up.*

ridge (rɪdʒ) *n.* **1.** a long narrow raised land formation with sloping sides. **2.** any long narrow raised strip, as on a fabric or in ploughed land. **3.** the top of a roof at the junction of two sloping sides. **4.** *Meteorol.*

an elongated area of high pressure. ~*vb.*
5. to form into a ridge or ridges. [Old
English *hrycg*] ~**ridgy** *adj.*

ridgepole ('rɪdʒ‚pəʊl) *n.* **1.** a timber along
the ridge of a roof, to which the rafters are
attached. **2.** the horizontal pole at the
apex of a tent.

ridicule ('rɪdɪ‚kjuːl) *n.* **1.** language or
behaviour intended to humiliate or mock.
~*vb.* **2.** to make fun of or mock. [Latin
rīdēre to laugh]

ridiculous (rɪ'dɪkjʊləs) *adj.* worthy of or
causing ridicule; absurd or laughable.

riding[1] ('raɪdɪŋ) *n.* the art or practice of
horsemanship.

riding[2] ('raɪdɪŋ) *n.* **1.** (*cap. when part of a
name*) any of the three former administra-
tive divisions of Yorkshire: **North Riding,
East Riding,** and **West Riding. 2.** *Canad.*
an electoral constituency. [Old English
thriding a third]

riding crop *n.* a short whip with a handle
at one end for opening gates.

riesling ('riːzlɪŋ, 'raɪz-) *n.* a medium-dry
white wine. [from German]

rife (raɪf) *adj.* **1.** widespread or common.
2. (foll. by *with*) abounding in: *a system
rife with errors.* [Old English]

riff (rɪf) *n. Jazz, rock.* a short repeated
melodic figure used as an introduction or
accompaniment. [prob. from REFRAIN[2]]

riffle ('rɪf³l) *vb.* **1.** (often foll. by *through*)
to flick rapidly through (pages of a book,
etc.). ~*n.* **2.** *U.S. & Canad.* **a.** a rapid in a
stream. **b.** a rocky shoal causing a rapid.
c. a ripple on water. **3.** a riffling. [prob.
from *ruffle*]

riffraff ('rɪf‚ræf) *n.* (*sometimes functioning
as pl.*) worthless people; rabble. [Old
French *rif et raf*]

rifle[1] ('raɪf³l) *n.* **1.** a firearm having a long
barrel with a spirally grooved interior,
which gives the bullet a spinning motion
and thus greater accuracy over a longer
range. **2.** (*pl.*) a unit of soldiers equipped
with rifles: *the King's Own Rifles.* ~*vb.*
3. to cut spiral grooves inside the barrel of
(a gun). [Old French *rifler* to scratch]

rifle[2] ('raɪf³l) *vb.* **1.** to search (a house or
safe) and steal from it; ransack. **2.** to steal
and carry off: *to rifle goods.* [Old French
rifler to plunder, scratch]

rift (rɪft) *n.* **1.** a gap or space made by
cleaving or splitting. **2.** a break in friendly
relations between people or groups of people. [Old Norse]

rift valley *n.* a long narrow valley resulting from the subsidence of land between
two faults.

rig (rɪg) *vb.* **rigging, rigged. 1.** *Naut.* to
equip (a vessel or mast) with (sails or
rigging). **2.** to set up or prepare (something) hastily ready for use. **3.** to manipulate in a fraudulent manner, for profit or
advantage: *to rig prices.* ~*n.* **4.** *Naut.* the
arrangement of the sails and masts of a
vessel. **5.** the installation used in drilling
for and exploiting natural gas and oil
deposits: *an oil rig.* **6.** apparatus or equipment. **7.** *U.S. & Canad.* an articulated

lorry. ~*See also* **rig out, rig up.** [Scandi-
navian]

-rigged *adj.* (of a sailing vessel) having a
rig of a certain kind: *schooner-rigged.*

rigging ('rɪgɪŋ) *n.* the ropes and cables
supporting the masts, sails, etc., of a vessel.

right (raɪt) *adj.* **1.** morally or legally acceptable or correct: *right conduct.* **2.** correct or true: *the right answer.* **3.** appropriate, suitable, or proper: *the right man for
the job.* **4.** most favourable or convenient:
the right time to act. **5.** in a satisfactory
condition: *things are right again now.* **6.**
accurate: *the clock is right.* **7.** correct in
opinion or judgment. **8.** sound in mind or
body. **9.** of or on the side of something or
someone that faces east when the front is
turned towards the north. **10.** (*sometimes
cap.*) conservative or reactionary: *the right
wing of the party.* **11.** *Geom.* formed by or
containing a line or plane perpendicular to
another line or plane: *a right angle.* **12.** of
or on the side of cloth worn or facing
outwards. **13. in one's right mind.** sane.
14. she'll be right. *Austral. & N.Z. informal.* that's all right; not to worry. **15. the
right side of. a.** in favour with: *you'd
better stay on the right side of him.* **b.**
younger than: *she's still on the right side of
fifty.* **16. too right.** *Austral. & N.Z. informal.* an exclamation of agreement. ~*adv.*
17. correctly: *to guess right.* **18.** in the
appropriate manner: *do it right next time!*
19. straight or directly: *right to the top.*
20. in the direction of the east from the
point of view of a person or thing facing
north. **21.** all the way: *the bus goes right
into town; she worked right through the
night.* **22.** without delay: *I'll be right over.*
23. exactly or precisely: *right here.* **24.**
fittingly: *it serves you right.* **25.** to good
or favourable advantage: *it all came out
right in the end.* ~*n.* **26.** a freedom or
power that is morally or legally due to a
person: *I know my rights.* **27.** anything
that accords with the principles of legal or
moral justice. **28. in the right.** the fact or
state of being in accordance with reason,
truth, or accepted standards. **29.** the right
side, direction, position, or part: *the right
of the army.* **30.** (*often cap.* and preceded
by *the*) the supporters or advocates of
conservatism or reaction. **31.** *Boxing.* a
punch with the right hand. **32.** (*often pl.*)
Finance. the privilege of a company's
shareholders to subscribe for new issues of
the company's shares on advantageous
terms. **33. by right** or **rights.** properly: *by
rights you should be in bed.* **34. in one's
own right.** having a claim or title oneself
rather than through marriage or other
connection. **35. to rights.** consistent with
justice or orderly arrangement: *he put the
matter to rights.* ~*vb.* **36.** to restore to or
attain a normal, esp. an upright, position:
the raft righted in a few seconds. **37.** to
make (something) accord with truth or
facts. **38.** to restore to an orderly state or
condition. **39.** to compensate for or redress: *to right a wrong.* ~*interj.* **40.** an
expression of agreement or compliance.
[Old English *riht, reoht*]

right angle n. **1.** an angle of 90° or π/2 radians. **2. at right angles.** perpendicular or perpendicularly. —**'right-,angled** adj.

right-angled triangle n. a triangle one angle of which is a right angle.

right away adv. without delay.

righteous ('raitʃəs) adj. **1.** moral, just, or virtuous: *a righteous man*. **2.** morally justifiable or right: *righteous indignation*. [Old English rihtwīs] —'**righteousness** n.

rightful ('raitful) adj. **1.** in accordance with what is right. **2.** having a legally or morally just claim: *the rightful owner*. **3.** held by virtue of a legal or just claim: *my rightful property*. —'**rightfully** adv.

right-hand adj. **1.** of, on, or towards the right: *a right-hand bend*. **2.** for use by the right hand. **3. right-hand man.** one's most valuable assistant.

right-handed adj. **1.** using the right hand with greater skill or ease than the left. **2.** made for or by the right hand. **3.** turning from left to right.

rightist ('raitist) adj. **1.** of the political right or its principles. ~n. **2.** a supporter of the political right. —'**rightism** n.

rightly ('raitli) adv. **1.** in accordance with the true facts. **2.** in accordance with justice or morality. **3.** with good reason: *he was rightly annoyed with her*.

right-minded adj. holding opinions or principles that accord with what is right or with the opinions of the speaker.

right of way n., pl. **rights of way.** **1.** the right of one vehicle or vessel to take precedence over another. **2. a.** the legal right of someone to pass over another's land. **b.** the path used by this right.

Right Reverend adj. (in Britain) a title of respect for a bishop.

rightward ('raitwəd) adj. **1.** situated on or directed towards the right. ~adv. **2.** Also: **rightwards.** on or towards the right.

right whale n. a large grey or black whalebone whale with a large head. [origin unknown]

right wing n. **1.** (*often cap.*) the conservative faction of a political body or party. **2.** *Sports.* **a.** the right-hand side of the field of play. **b.** a player positioned in this area in certain games. ~adj. **right-wing. 3.** of, belonging to, or relating to the right wing. —'**right-'winger** n.

rigid ('ridʒid) adj. **1.** physically inflexible or stiff: *a rigid piece of plastic*. **2.** rigorously strict: *rigid rules*. [Latin rigidus] —ri'**gidity** n.

rigmarole ('rigmə,rəʊl) n. **1.** any long complicated procedure. **2.** a set of incoherent or pointless statements. [earlier *ragman roll* a list]

rigor mortis ('rigə 'mɔːtis) n. the stiffness of joints and muscles of a dead body. [Latin: rigidity of death]

rigorous ('rigərəs) adj. **1.** harsh, strict, or severe: *rigorous discipline*. **2.** severely accurate: *rigorous book-keeping*. **3.** (esp. of weather) extreme or harsh.

rigour or U.S. **rigor** ('rigə) n. **1.** harsh but just treatment. **2.** a severe or cruel circum-

stance: *the rigours of famine*. **3.** strictness in judgment or conduct. [Latin rigor]

rig out vb. **1.** (often foll. by *with*) to equip (with): *his car is rigged out with gadgets*. **2.** to dress or be dressed: *rigged out smartly*. ~n. **rigout. 3.** *Informal.* a person's clothing or costume.

rig up vb. to erect or construct, esp. as a temporary measure: *cameras were rigged up to televise the event*.

rile (rail) vb. **1.** to annoy or anger. **2.** *U.S. & Canad.* to agitate (a liquid, such as water). [var. of roil to agitate]

rill (ril) n. a stream. [Low German rille]

rim (rim) n. **1.** the raised edge of an object, esp. of something circular such as a cup. **2.** the outer part of a wheel, to which the tyre is attached. [Old English rima]

rime[1] (raim) n. **1.** frost formed by the freezing of water droplets in fog onto solid objects. ~vb. **2.** to cover with rime or something resembling rime. [Old English hrīm] —'**rimy** adj.

rime[2] (raim) n., vb. *Archaic.* same as **rhyme.**

rind (raind) n. a hard outer layer or skin, as on bacon or cheese. [Old English rinde]

ring[1] (riŋ) n. **1.** a circular band of a precious metal worn upon the finger. **2.** any object or mark that is circular in shape. **3.** a circular path or course: *to run around in a ring*. **4.** a group of people or things standing or arranged so as to form a circle: *a ring of spectators*. **5.** a circular enclosure, esp. one where circus acts perform or livestock is sold at a market. **6.** a square raised platform, marked off by ropes, in which contestants box or wrestle. **7. the ring.** the sport of boxing. **8. throw one's hat in the ring.** to announce one's intention to be a candidate or contestant. **9.** a group of people, usually illegal, who cooperate to control the market in antiques, illicit drugs, etc. **10.** *Chem.* a closed loop of atoms in a molecule. **11.** one of the systems of circular bands orbiting the planets Saturn and Uranus. **12. run rings around.** *Informal.* to outclass completely. ~vb. **13.** to surround with, or as if with, or form a ring. **14.** to mark a bird with a ring or clip for subsequent identification. **15.** to fit a ring in the nose of (a bull, etc.) so that it can be led easily. **16.** to cut a ring of bark off a tree. [Old English hring] —**ringed** adj.

ring[2] (riŋ) vb. **ringing, rang, rung. 1.** to emit or cause to emit a resonant sound, like that of a bell. **2.** to cause (a bell) to emit a ringing sound or (of a bell) to emit such a sound. **3.** (of a building or place) to be filled with sound: *the church rang with singing*. **4.** (foll. by *for*) to call by means of a bell: *to ring for the butler*. **5.** Also: **ring up.** *Chiefly Brit.* to call (a person) by telephone. **6.** (of the ears) to have the sensation of humming or ringing. **7. ring a bell.** to bring something to the mind or memory: *that rings a bell*. **8. ring down the curtain. a.** to lower the curtain at the end of a theatrical performance. **b.** (foll. by *on*) to put an end (to). **9. ring true** (or **false**). to give the impression of being true (or false). ~*n.* **10.** the act of or a sound made by ringing. **11.** a sound produced by or suggestive of a bell. **12.** *Informal, chiefly Brit.* a telephone call. **13.** an inherent quality: *his explanation has the ring of sincerity.* ~See also **ring in, ring off,** etc. [Old English *hringan*]

ring binder *n.* a loose-leaf binder with metal rings that can be opened to insert perforated paper.

ringdove ('rɪŋ,dʌv) *n.* a wood pigeon.

ringer ('rɪŋə) *n.* a person or thing that is almost identical to another. Also called: **dead ringer.**

ring finger *n.* the third finger, esp. of the left hand, on which a wedding ring is worn.

ring in *vb.* to accompany the arrival of with bells: *ring in the New Year.*

ringleader ('rɪŋ,liːdə) *n.* a person who leads others in unlawful or mischievous activity.

ringlet ('rɪŋlɪt) *n.* a lock of hair hanging down in a spiral curl. —**'ringleted** *adj.*

ring main *n.* a domestic electrical supply in which outlet sockets are connected to the mains supply through a continuous closed circuit (**ring circuit**).

ringmaster ('rɪŋ,mɑːstə) *n.* the master of ceremonies in a circus.

ring off *vb. Chiefly Brit.* to end a telephone conversation by replacing the receiver; hang up.

ring out *vb.* **1.** to accompany the departure of with bells: *ring out the old year.* **2.** to send forth a loud resounding noise.

ring road *n.* a main road that bypasses a town or town centre.

ringside ('rɪŋ,saɪd) *n.* **1.** the row of seats nearest a boxing or wrestling ring. **2.** any place affording a close uninterrupted view.

ring up *vb.* **1.** *Chiefly Brit.* to make a telephone call to. **2.** to record on a cash register. **3. ring up the curtain. a.** to begin a theatrical performance. **b.** (often foll. by *on*) to make a start on.

ringworm ('rɪŋ,wɜːm) *n.* a fungal infection of the skin producing itching circular patches.

rink (rɪŋk) *n.* **1.** an expanse of ice for skating on, esp. one that is artificially prepared and under cover. **2.** an area for roller-skating on. **3.** a building or enclosure for ice-skating or roller-skating. **4.** (in bowls or curling) a strip of grass or ice on which a game is played. **5.** (in bowls or curling) the players on one side in a game. [Old French *renc* row]

rinkhals ('rɪŋk,hæls) *n., pl.* **-hals** *or* **-halses.** a venomous snake of southern Africa, which can spit venom from a distance. [Afrikaans]

rink rat *n. Canad. slang.* a youth who helps with odd chores at an ice-hockey rink in return for free admission to games.

rinse (rɪns) *vb.* **1.** to remove soap, detergent, or shampoo from (clothes, dishes, or hair) by washing it out with clean water. **2.** to wash lightly, esp. without using soap. **3.** to cleanse the mouth by swirling water or mouthwash in it and then spitting the

liquid out. **4.** to give a light tint to (hair). ~*n.* **5.** the act or an instance of rinsing. **6.** *Hairdressing.* a liquid preparation put on the hair when wet to give a tint to it: *a blue rinse.* [Old French *rincer*] —**'rinser** *n.*

riot ('raɪət) *n.* **1.** a disturbance made by an unruly mob or (in law) three or more persons. **2.** an occasion of boisterous merriment. **3.** *Slang.* a person who creates boisterous merriment. **4.** a dazzling display: *a riot of colour.* **5. read the riot act.** to reprimand severely. **6. run riot. a.** to behave without restraint. **b.** (of plants) to grow profusely. ~*vb.* **7.** to take part in a riot. [Old French *riote* dispute]

riotous ('raɪətəs) *adj.* **1.** like a riot or rioting. **2.** characterized by wanton revelry: *riotous living.* **3.** characterized by unrestrained merriment: *riotous laughter.*

riot shield *n.* a large shield used by police controlling crowds.

rip (rɪp) *vb.* **ripping, ripped. 1.** to tear or be torn violently or roughly. **2.** (foll. by *off* or *out*) to remove hastily or roughly. **3.** *Informal.* to move violently or hurriedly. **4. let rip.** to act or speak without restraint. ~*n.* **5.** a tear or split. ~See also **rip off.** [origin unknown]

RIP may he, she, *or* they rest in peace. [Latin: requiescat *or* requiescant in pace]

riparian (raɪ'pɛərɪən) *adj.* of or on the bank of a river. [Latin *rīpa* river bank]

ripcord ('rɪp,kɔːd) *n.* a cord that when pulled opens a parachute from its pack.

ripe (raɪp) *adj.* **1.** mature enough to be eaten or used: *ripe cheese; a ripe banana.* **2.** fully developed in mind or body. **3.** resembling ripe fruit, esp. in redness or fullness: *a ripe complexion.* **4.** (foll. by *for*) ready or eager (to undertake or undergo an action). **5.** (foll. by *for*) suitable: *the time is not yet ripe.* **6. ripe old age.** an elderly but healthy age. [Old English]

ripen ('raɪp°n) *vb.* to mature or become ripe.

rip off *Slang.* ~*vb.* **1.** to steal from or cheat (someone). **2.** to steal (something). ~*n.* **rip-off. 3.** a grossly overpriced article. **4.** the act of stealing or cheating.

riposte (rɪ'pɒst) *n.* **1.** a swift sharp reply. **2.** *Fencing.* a counterattack made immediately after a successful parry. ~*vb.* **3.** to make a riposte. [French]

ripple ('rɪp°l) *n.* **1.** a slight wave on the surface of water. **2.** a sound reminiscent of water flowing quietly in ripples: *a ripple of laughter.* ~*vb.* **3.** to form ripples or flow with a waving motion. **4.** (of sounds) to rise and fall gently. [origin unknown] —**'rippling** *or* **'ripply** *adj.*

rip-roaring *adj. Informal.* boisterous, noisy, and exciting.

ripsaw ('rɪp,sɔː) *n.* a handsaw for cutting along the grain of timber.

rise (raɪz) *vb.* **rising, rose, risen** ('rɪz°n). **1.** to get up from a lying, sitting, or kneeling position. **2.** to get out of bed, esp. to begin one's day: *he always rises early.* **3.** to move from a lower to a higher position or place. **4.** to ascend or appear above the horizon: *the sun is rising.* **5.** to increase in height or level: *the water rose.*

6. to increase in strength, degree, etc.: *the wind is rising.* **7.** to increase in amount or value: *house prices are always rising.* **8.** to swell up: *dough rises.* **9.** to become erect, or rigid: *the hairs on his neck rose in fear.* **10.** to revolt: *the people rose against their oppressors.* **11.** to slope upwards: *the ground rises beyond the lake.* **12.** to be resurrected. **13.** to originate: *that river rises in the mountains.* **14.** (of a session of a court, legislative assembly, etc.) to come to an end. **15.** *Angling.* (of fish) to come to the surface of the water. **16.** (often foll. by *to*) *Informal.* to respond (to teasing, etc.). ~*n.* **17.** the act or an instance of rising. **18.** an increase in height. **19.** an increase in rank, status, or position. **20.** an increase in amount, cost, or value. **21.** an increase in degree or intensity. **22.** *Brit.* an increase in salary or wages. **23.** the vertical height of a step or of a flight of stairs. **24.** a piece of rising ground; slope. **25. get** or **take a rise out of.** *Slang.* to provoke an angry or petulant reaction from. **26. give rise to.** to cause the development of. [Old English *rīsan*]

riser ('raɪzə) *n.* **1.** a person who rises from bed: *an early riser.* **2.** the vertical part of a stair.

risible ('rɪzɪb³l) *adj.* causing laughter; ridiculous. [Latin *rīdēre* to laugh]

rising ('raɪzɪŋ) *n.* **1.** a rebellion; revolt. ~*adj.* **2.** increasing in status or reputation: *a rising young politician.* **3.** growing up to adulthood: *the rising generation.*

rising damp *n.* seepage of moisture from the ground into the walls of buildings.

risk (rɪsk) *n.* **1.** the possibility of incurring misfortune or loss. **2.** a person or thing considered as a potential hazard: *that old heater must be a fire risk.* **3. at risk.** vulnerable. **4. take** or **run a risk.** to act without regard to the danger involved. ~*vb.* **5.** to expose to danger or loss. **6.** to act in spite of the possibility of (injury or loss): *to risk a fall in climbing.* [French *risque*] —'**risky** *adj.*

risotto (rɪ'zɒtəʊ) *n., pl.* -**tos.** a dish of rice cooked in stock with tomatoes, cheese, chicken, etc. [Italian]

risqué ('rɪskeɪ) *adj.* bordering on impropriety or indecency: *a risqué joke.* [French *risquer* to risk]

rissole ('rɪsəʊl) *n.* a mixture of minced cooked meat coated in egg and breadcrumbs and fried. [French]

ritardando (ˌrɪtɑː'dændəʊ) *adj., adv.* same as **rallentando.** [Italian]

rite (raɪt) *n.* **1.** a formal act which forms part of a religious ceremony: *the rite of baptism.* **2.** a particular body of such acts, esp. of a particular Christian Church: *the Latin rite.* [Latin *rītus*]

ritual ('rɪtjʊəl) *n.* **1.** the prescribed form of a religious or other ceremony. **2.** such prescribed forms in general or collectively. **3.** stereotyped activity or behaviour. **4.** any formal act, institution, or procedure that is followed consistently: *the ritual of the law.* ~*adj.* **5.** of or like religious, social, or other rituals. —'**ritually** *adv.*

ritualism ('rɪtjʊəˌlɪzəm) *n.* exaggerated emphasis on the importance of rites and ceremonies. —ˌritual'**istic** *adj.* —ˌritual-'**istically** *adv.*

ritzy ('rɪtsɪ) *adj.* **ritzier, ritziest.** *Slang.* luxurious or elegant. [after the hotels established by César Ritz]

rival ('raɪv³l) *n.* **1.** a person or group that competes with another for the same object or in the same field. **2.** a person or thing that is considered the equal of another: *she is without rival in the field of physics* ~*vb.* -**valling, -valled** or *U.S.* -**valing, -valed. 3.** to be the equal or near equal of: *an empire that rivalled Rome.* **4.** to try to equal or surpass. [Latin *rīvalis*, lit.: one who shares the same brook]

rivalry ('raɪvəlrɪ) *n., pl.* -**ries. 1.** the act of rivalling. **2.** the state of being a rival or rivals.

riven ('rɪv³n) *adj.* **1.** split asunder: *a tree riven by lightning.* **2.** torn apart: *riven to shreds.* [Old Norse *rifa*]

river ('rɪvə) *n.* **1.** a large natural stream of fresh water flowing along a definite course into the sea, a lake, or a larger river. **2.** any abundant stream or flow: *a river of blood.* [Old French *rivere*]

rivet ('rɪvɪt) *n.* **1.** a short metal pin for fastening two or more pieces together having a head at one end, the other end being hammered flat after being passed through holes in the pieces. ~*vb.* **2.** to join by riveting. **3.** (*often passive*) to cause to be riveted, as in fascinated attention or horror: *to be riveted to the spot.* [Old French *river* to fasten] —'**riveter** *n.* —'**riveting** *adj.*

rivulet ('rɪvjʊlɪt) *n.* a small stream. [Latin *rīvus* stream]

rm 1. ream. **2.** room.

RM 1. Royal Mail. **2.** Royal Marines. **3.** (in Canada) Rural Municipality.

Rn *Chem.* radon.

RN 1. (in Canada) Registered Nurse. **2.** Royal Navy.

RNA *n. Biochem.* ribonucleic acid; any of a group of nucleic acids, present in all living cells, that play an essential role in the synthesis of proteins.

RNLI Royal National Lifeboat Institution.

roach[1] (rəʊtʃ) *n., pl.* **roaches** or **roach.** a European freshwater food fish with a deep compressed body and reddish tail fins. [Old French *roche*]

roach[2] (rəʊtʃ) *n. Chiefly U.S. & Canad.* a cockroach.

road (rəʊd) *n.* **1. a.** an open way, usually surfaced, providing passage from one place to another. **b.** (*in combination*): *the roadside.* **2.** a street. **3.** a way, path, or course: *the road to fame.* **4.** (*often pl.*) *Naut.* a partly sheltered anchorage. **5. one for the road.** *Informal.* a last alcoholic drink before leaving. **6. on the road. a.** travelling about; on tour. **b.** leading a wandering life. [Old English *rād*]

roadblock ('rəʊdˌblɒk) *n.* a barrier set up across a road by the police or military, in order to stop and check vehicles.

road-fund licence *n. Brit.* a licence showing that the tax payable in respect of a motor vehicle has been paid.

road hog *n. Informal.* a selfish or aggressive driver.

roadholding ('rəud,həuldıŋ) *n.* the extent to which a vehicle is stable and does not skid, esp. on bends or wet roads.

roadhouse ('rəud,haus) *n.* a pub or restaurant at the side of a road.

roadie ('rəudı) *n. Informal.* a person who transports and sets up equipment for a band or group.

road metal *n.* crushed rock or broken stone used to construct a road.

road show *n.* **1.** *Radio.* a live programme transmitted from a radio van taking a particular show on the road. **2.** a group of entertainers on tour.

roadstead ('rəud,stɛd) *n. Naut.* same as **road.**

roadster ('rəudstə) *n. Old-fashioned.* an open car, esp. one seating only two.

road test *n.* **1.** a test of something, such as a vehicle in actual use. ~*vb.* **road-test. 2.** to test (a vehicle, etc.) in this way.

roadway ('rəud,weı) *n.* the part of a road that is used by vehicles.

road works *pl. n.* repairs to a road or cable under a road, esp. when forming a hazard or obstruction to traffic.

roadworthy ('rəud,wɜːðı) *adj.* (of a motor vehicle) mechanically sound; fit for use on the roads. —'**road,worthiness** *n.*

roam (rəum) *vb.* **1.** to walk about with no fixed purpose or direction. ~*n.* **2.** the act of roaming. [origin unknown]

roan (rəun) *adj.* **1.** (of a horse) having a brown or black coat sprinkled with white hairs. ~*n.* **2.** a horse having such a coat. [Spanish *roano*]

roar (rɔː) *vb.* **1.** (of lions and other animals) to make loud growling cries. **2.** (of people) to utter (something) with a loud deep cry, as in anger or triumph. **3.** to laugh in a loud hearty unrestrained manner. **4.** (of the wind, waves, etc.) to blow or break loudly and violently, as during a storm. **5.** (of a fire) to burn fiercely with a roaring sound. ~*n.* **6.** a loud deep cry, uttered by a person or crowd, esp. in anger or triumph. **7.** a prolonged loud cry of certain animals, esp. lions. **8.** any similar noise made by a fire, the wind, waves, an engine, etc. [Old English *rārian*]

roaring ('rɔːrıŋ) *adv.* **1.** noisily or boisterously: *roaring drunk.* ~*adj.* **2. a roaring trade.** a brisk and profitable business.

roast (rəust) *vb.* **1.** to cook (meat or other food) by dry heat, as in an oven or on a spit. **2.** to brown or dry (coffee or nuts) by exposure to heat. **3.** to be, become or make extremely hot. **4.** *Informal.* to criticize severely. ~*n.* **5.** something that has been roasted, esp. meat. ~*adj.* **6.** cooked by roasting: *roast parsnips.* [Old French *rostir*] —'**roaster** *n.*

roasting ('rəustıŋ) *Informal.* ~*adj.* **1.** extremely hot. ~*n.* **2.** severe criticism.

rob (rɒb) *vb.* **robbing, robbed. 1.** to take something from (a person or place) illegally, esp. by or with force. **2.** to deprive

unjustly: *to be robbed of an opportunity.* [Old French *rober*] —'**robber** *n.*

robbery ('rɒbərı) *n., pl.* -**beries. 1.** *Criminal law.* the stealing of property from a person by using or threatening to use force. **2.** the act or an instance of robbing.

robe (rəub) *n.* **1.** any loose flowing garment, esp. the official gown of a peer, judge, or academic. **2.** a dressing gown or bathrobe. ~*vb.* **3.** to put a robe on (oneself or someone else). [Old French]

robin ('rɒbın) *n.* **1.** Also called: **robin redbreast.** a small Old World songbird with a brown back and an orange-red breast and face. **2.** a North American thrush similar to but larger than the Old World robin. [arbitrary use of name *Robin*]

robot ('rəubɒt) *n.* **1.** a machine programmed to perform specific tasks in a human manner, esp., popularly, one with a human shape. **2.** a person who works or behaves like a machine. **3.** *S. African.* a set of traffic lights. [used in *R.U.R.*, a play by a Czech writer, from Czech *robota* work] —**ro'botic** *adj.*

robust (rəu'bʌst, 'rəubʌst) *adj.* **1.** strong in constitution. **2.** sturdily built: *a robust shelter.* **3.** requiring physical strength: *a robust sport.* [Latin *rōbur* an oak, strength]

roc (rɒk) *n.* (in Arabian legend) a bird of enormous size and power. [Persian *rukh*]

rock[1] (rɒk) *n.* **1.** *Geol.* the mass of mineral matter that makes up part of the earth's crust; stone. **2.** any hard mass of mineral matter, such as a boulder. **3.** *U.S., Canad., & Austral.* a stone. **4.** a person or thing suggesting a rock, esp. in being dependable, unchanging, or providing firm foundation. **5.** *Brit.* a hard sweet, typically a long brightly coloured peppermint-flavoured stick, sold esp. in holiday resorts. **6.** *Slang.* a jewel, esp. a diamond. **7. on the rocks. a.** (of a marriage) in trouble; about to end. **b.** (of drinks, esp. whisky) served with ice. [Old French *roche*]

rock[2] (rɒk) *vb.* **1.** to move or cause to move from side to side or backwards and forwards. **2.** to feel or cause to feel shock: *the scandal rocked the government.* **3.** to shake or move (something) violently. **4.** to dance to or play rock music. ~*n.* **5.** a rocking motion. **6.** Also called: **rock music.** rock and roll, or any of various styles of pop music with a heavy beat derived from it. [Old English *roccian*]

rockabilly ('rɒkə,bılı) *n.* a fast, spare style of White rock music which originated in the mid-1950s in the U.S. South. [*rock and roll* + *hillbilly*]

rock and roll *or* **rock'n'roll** *n.* a type of pop music originating in the 1950s as a blend of rhythm and blues and country and western.

rock bottom *n.* the lowest possible level.

rock-bound *adj.* hemmed in or encircled by rocks. Also (poetic): **rock-girt.**

rock cake *n.* a small cake containing dried fruit and spice, with a rough surface supposed to resemble a rock.

rock crystal *n.* a pure transparent colourless quartz.

rock dove *or* **pigeon** *n.* a common dove from which domestic and feral pigeons are descended.

rocker ('rɒkə) *n.* **1.** any of various devices that operate with or transmit a rocking motion. **2.** a rocking chair. **3.** either of two curved supports on the legs of a chair on which it may rock. **4.** a rock music performer, fan, or song. **5. off one's rocker.** *Slang.* crazy.

rockery ('rɒkərɪ) *n., pl.* **-eries.** a garden constructed with rocks, esp. one where alpine plants are grown.

rocket ('rɒkɪt) *n.* **1.** a self-propelling device, usually cylindrical, which produces thrust by expelling through a nozzle the gases produced by burning fuel, such as one used as a firework or distress signal. **2.** any vehicle propelled by a rocket engine, esp. one used to carry a spacecraft or as a missile. **3.** *Brit. & N.Z. informal.* a severe reprimand: *you'll get a rocket.* ~*vb.* **4.** to propel (a missile or spacecraft) by means of a rocket. **5.** to move rapidly: *she rocketed to the top.* [Italian *rochetto*]

rocketry ('rɒkɪtrɪ) *n.* the science and technology of the design and operation of rockets.

rock garden *n.* a garden featuring rocks or rockeries.

rocking chair *n.* a chair set on curving supports so that the sitter may rock backwards and forwards.

rocking horse *n.* a toy horse mounted on a pair of rocking supports on which a child can rock to and fro.

rock melon *n. U.S., Austral., & N.Z.* same as **cantaloupe**.

rock plant *n.* any plant that grows on rocks or in rocky ground.

rock rabbit *n. S. African.* a rodent-like mammal, the dassie or rock hyrax.

rock salmon *n. Brit.* a former term for dogfish when used as a food.

rock salt *n.* common salt as a naturally occurring solid mineral.

rock tripe *n. Canad.* any of various edible lichens that grow on rocks.

rocky[1] ('rɒkɪ) *adj.* **rockier, rockiest.** consisting of or abounding in rocks: *a rocky shore.* —**'rockiness** *n.*

rocky[2] ('rɒkɪ) *adj.* **rockier, rockiest.** weak, shaky, or unstable. —**'rockiness** *n.*

rococo (rə'kəʊkəʊ) *n. (often cap.)* **1.** an 18th-century style of architecture, decoration and music characterized by elaborate ornamentation. **2.** any florid or excessively ornamental style. ~*adj.* **3.** of or in the rococo style. **4.** florid or excessively elaborate. [French]

rod (rɒd) *n.* **1.** a slim cylinder of metal, wood, etc. **2.** a stick or cane used to beat people as a punishment. **3.** any of various staffs of insignia or office. **4.** short for fishing rod. **5.** a unit of length equal to 5½ yards. **6.** *U.S. slang.* a pistol. [Old English *rodd*] —**'rod,like** *adj.*

rode (rəʊd) *vb.* the past tense of **ride**.

rodent ('rəʊd²nt) *n.* any of the relatively small mammals with constantly growing incisor teeth specialized for gnawing. The group includes rats, mice and squirrels. [Latin *rōdere* to gnaw] —**'rodent-,like** *adj.*

rodeo ('rəʊdɪˌəʊ) *n., pl.* **-deos.** a display of the skills of cowboys, including bareback riding. [Spanish]

rodomontade (ˌrɒdəmɒn'teɪd, -'tɑːd) *n. Literary.* boastful words or behaviour. [French]

roe[1] (rəʊ) *n.* the ovary and eggs of a female fish. [Middle Dutch *roge*]

roe[2] (rəʊ) *or* **roe deer** *n.* a small graceful deer of woodlands of Europe and Asia, with small antlers. [Old English *rāha*]

Rogation Days *pl. n.* the three days before Ascension Day. [Latin *rogare* to ask]

roger ('rɒdʒə) *interj.* **1.** (used in signalling) message received and understood. **2.** an expression of agreement. [from the name *Roger*, representing *R* for received]

rogue (rəʊg) *n.* **1.** a dishonest or unprincipled person. **2.** a mischievous person, often a child. **3.** any inferior or defective specimen, esp. a defective crop plant. **4.** an animal of vicious character that leads a solitary life. [origin unknown] —**'roguish** *adj.*

roguery ('rəʊgərɪ) *n., pl.* **-gueries.** **1.** behaviour characteristic of a rogue. **2.** a roguish or mischievous act.

rogues' gallery *n.* a collection of portraits of known criminals kept by the police for identification purposes.

roister ('rɔɪstə) *vb.* to engage in noisy or unrestrained merrymaking. [Old French *rustre* lout] —**'roisterer** *n.*

role *or* **rôle** (rəʊl) *n.* **1.** a part in a play, film, etc. **2.** function: *what is his role in the organization?* [French]

roll (rəʊl) *vb.* **1.** to move or cause to move along by turning over and over. **2.** to move or cause to move along on wheels or rollers. **3.** to flow or cause to flow onwards in an undulating movement. **4.** (of animals) to turn onto the back and kick. **5.** to appear like a series of waves: *the hills roll down to the sea.* **6.** (foll. by *on, by,* etc.) to pass or elapse: *the years roll by.* **7.** to rotate or cause to rotate wholly or partially: *to roll one's eyes.* **8.** to curl, cause to curl, or make by curling into a ball, tube, or cylinder. **9.** (often foll. by *out*) to spread or cause to spread out flat or smooth as by a roller: *to roll pastry.* **10.** to make a deep prolonged reverberating sound: *the thunder rolled continuously.* **11.** to trill or cause to be trilled: *to roll one's r's.* **12.** (of a vessel, aircraft, or rocket) to turn from side to side around the longitudinal axis. **13.** to walk with a swaying gait, as when drunk. **14.** *Chiefly U.S.* to throw (dice). **15.** to operate or begin to operate: *the presses rolled.* ~*n.* **16.** the act or an instance of rolling. **17.** anything rolled up in a cylindrical form: *a roll of newspaper.* **18.** an official list or register, esp. of names: *an electoral roll.* **19.** a rounded mass: *rolls of flesh.* **20.** a small cake of bread for one person. **21.** a flat pastry or cake rolled up with a meat (**sausage roll**), jam (**jam roll**), or other filling. **22.** a swaying, rolling, or unsteady movement or gait. **23.** a deep prolonged reverberating sound: *a roll of thunder*. **24.** a trilling sound; trill. **25.** a very rapid beating of the sticks on a drum. **26.** a complete rotation about its longitudinal axis by an aircraft. **27. strike off the roll(s).** to expel from membership of a professional association. ~See also **roll in, roll on,** etc. [Old French *roler*]

roll call *n.* the reading aloud of an official list of names, those present responding when their names are read out.

rolled gold *n.* a metal, such as brass, coated with a thin layer of gold.

roller ('rəʊlə) *n.* **1.** a cylinder with an absorbent surface and a handle, used for spreading paint. **2.** Also called: **garden roller.** a heavy cast-iron cylinder on an axle to which a handle is attached; used for flattening lawns. **3.** a long heavy wave of the sea. **4.** a cylinder fitted on pivots, used to enable heavy objects to be easily moved. **5.** any of various rotating cylindrical devices, used for flattening, crushing, or spreading. **6.** a small cylinder onto which a woman's hair may be rolled to make it curl.

roller coaster *n.* (at a fair) a narrow railway with open carriages, sharp curves and steep inclines.

roller skate *n.* **1.** a device worn fastened to a shoe, with four small wheels that enable the wearer to glide swiftly over a floor. ~*vb.* **roller-skate. 2.** to move on roller skates. —**roller skater** *n.*

roller towel *n.* **1.** a towel with the two ends sewn together, hung on a roller. **2.** a towel wound inside a roller enabling a clean section to be pulled out when needed.

rollicking ('rɒlɪkɪŋ) *adj.* boisterously carefree. [origin unknown]

roll in *vb.* **1.** to arrive in large numbers. **2. be rolling in.** *Slang.* to have plenty of (wealth, money, etc.).

rolling ('rəʊlɪŋ) *adj.* **1.** having gentle rising and falling slopes: *rolling country.* **2.** progressing by stages or in succession: *a rolling strike.* **3.** subject to regular revision and updating: *a rolling plan for overseas development.*

rolling mill *n.* **1.** a factory where metal ingots are passed between rollers to produce sheets or bars of the required shape. **2.** a machine having rollers that may be used for this purpose.

rolling pin *n.* a cylinder with handles at both ends used for rolling pastry out flat.

rolling stock *n.* the wheeled vehicles of a railway, including the locomotives and coaches.

rolling stone *n.* a restless or wandering person.

rollmop ('rəʊl‚mɒp) *n.* a herring fillet rolled around onion slices and pickled. [German *rollen* to ROLL + *Mops* pug dog]

rollneck ('rəʊl‚nɛk) *adj.* (of a garment) having a high neck that may be rolled over.

roll on *vb.* **1.** *Brit.* used to express the wish that an eagerly anticipated event or date will come quickly: *roll on Saturday.* ~*adj.* **roll-on. 2.** (of a deodorant) applied by means of a revolving ball fitted into the neck of the container.

roll-on/roll-off *adj.* denoting a ship designed so that vehicles can be driven straight on and straight off.

roll-top desk *n.* a desk having a slatted wooden panel that can be pulled down over the writing surface when not in use.

roll up *vb.* **1.** to form or cause to form a cylindrical shape: *to roll up a map.* **2.** *Informal.* to arrive. ~*n.* **roll-up. 3.** *Brit. informal.* a cigarette made by hand from loose tobacco and cigarette papers.

roly-poly ('rəʊli'pəʊli) *adj.* **1.** plump or chubby. ~*n., pl.* **-lies. 2.** *Brit.* a strip of suet pastry spread with jam, rolled up, and baked or steamed. [prob. from *roll*]

ROM (rɒm) *Computers.* read only memory: a storage device that holds data permanently and cannot be altered by the programmer.

rom. *Printing.* roman (type).

roman ('rəʊmən) *adj.* **1.** in or relating to the vertical style of printing type used for most printed matter. ~*n.* **2.** roman type. [so called because the style of letters is that used in ancient Roman inscriptions]

Roman ('rəʊmən) *adj.* **1.** of Rome or its inhabitants in ancient or modern times. **2.** of Roman Catholicism or the Roman Catholic Church. ~*n.* **3.** a person from ancient or modern Rome.

Roman alphabet *n.* the alphabet evolved by the ancient Romans for writing Latin, used for writing most of the languages of W Europe, including English.

Roman candle *n.* a firework that produces a continuous shower of sparks punctuated by coloured balls of fire. [it originated in Italy]

Roman Catholic *adj.* **1.** of the Roman Catholic Church. ~*n.* **2.** a member of this Church. —**Roman Catholicism** *n.*

Roman Catholic Church *n.* the Christian Church over which the pope presides.

romance *n.* (rə'mæns, 'rəʊmæns). **1.** a love affair. **2.** love, esp. romantic love idealized for its purity or beauty. **3.** a spirit of or inclination for adventure or mystery. **4.** a mysterious, exciting, sentimental, or nostalgic quality. **5.** a story or film dealing with events and characters remote from ordinary life. **6.** a story or film dealing with love, usually in an idealized or sentimental way. **7.** an extravagant, absurd, or fantastic account. **8.** a medieval narrative dealing with adventures of chivalrous heroes. ~*vb.* (rə'mæns). **9.** to tell or write extravagant or romantic fictions. **10.** to tell extravagant or improbable lies. [Old French *romans*]

Romance (rə'mæns, 'rəʊmæns) *adj.* of or relating to the languages derived from Latin, including Italian, French, Spanish, Portuguese, and Romanian.

Romanesque (‚rəʊmə'nɛsk) *adj.* of or in

the style of architecture used in W and S Europe from the 9th to the 12th century, characterized by the rounded arch and massive-masonry wall construction.

Romanian (rəʊˈmeɪnɪən) n. **1.** the official language of Romania, in SE Europe. **2.** a person from Romania. ~*adj.* **3.** of Romania, its people, or their language.

Roman nose n. a nose with a high prominent bridge.

Roman numerals pl. n. the letters used as numerals by the Romans, used occasionally today: I (= 1), V (= 5), X (= 10), L (= 50), C (= 100), D (= 500), and M (= 1000). VI = 6 (V + I) but IV = 4 (V − I).

romantic (rəʊˈmæntɪk) adj. **1.** of, like, or characterized by romance. **2.** evoking or given to thoughts and feelings of love, esp. idealized or sentimental love: *a romantic setting.* **3.** impractical, visionary, or idealistic: *a romantic scheme.* **4.** (*often cap.*) of or relating to a movement in European art, music, and literature in the late 18th and early 19th centuries, characterized by an emphasis on feeling and content rather than order and form. ~n. **5.** a person who is romantic, as in being idealistic, amorous, or soulful. **6.** a person who likes or produces artistic works in the style of romanticism. —**ro'mantically** adv.

romanticism (rəʊˈmæntɪˌsɪzəm) n. **1.** (*often cap.*) the spirit and style of the romantic art, music, and literature of the late 18th and early 19th centuries. **2.** romantic attitudes, ideals, or qualities. —**ro'manticist** n.

romanticize or **-cise** (rəʊˈmæntɪˌsaɪz) vb. **1.** to make or become romantic. **2.** to describe or regard (something) in an unrealistic and idealized way: *her romanticized view of marriage.*

Romany (ˈrɒmənɪ, ˈrəʊ-) n. (*pl.* **-nies**) a Gypsy. **2.** the language of the Gypsies, belonging to the Indic branch of the Indo-European family. [Romany *romani* (adj.) Gypsy]

Romeo (ˈrəʊmɪəʊ) n., pl. **Romeos.** an ardent male lover. [after the hero of Shakespeare's *Romeo and Juliet*]

romp (rɒmp) vb. **1.** to play or run about wildly, boisterously, or joyfully. **2.** **romp home** (or **in**). to win a race or other competition easily. ~n. **3.** a noisy or boisterous game or prank. [prob. from Old French *ramper* to crawl, climb]

rompers (ˈrɒmpəz) pl. n. **1.** Also called: **romper suit.** a one-piece baby garment combining trousers and a top. **2.** *N.Z.* a type of costume worn by schoolgirls for games and gymnastics.

rondavel (ˌrɒnˈdɑːvəl) n. *S. African.* a circular building, often thatched. [origin unknown]

rondeau (ˈrɒndəʊ) n., pl. **-deaux** (-dəʊ, -dəʊz). a poem consisting of 13 or 10 lines with two rhymes and having the opening words of the first line used as an unrhymed refrain. [Old French]

rondo (ˈrɒndəʊ) n., pl. **-dos.** a piece of music in which a refrain is repeated between episodes: often forms the last movement of a sonata or concerto. [Italian]

roof (ruːf) n., pl. **roofs** (ruːfs, ruːvz). **1.** a structure that covers or forms the top of a building. **2.** the top covering of a vehicle, oven, or other structure: *the roof of a car.* **3.** *Anat.* any structure that covers an organ or part: *the roof of the mouth.* **4.** **hit** (or **go through**) **the roof.** *Informal.* to get extremely angry. **5.** **raise the roof.** *Informal.* to be very noisy. ~vb. **6.** to provide or cover with a roof or rooflike part. [Old English *hrōf*]

roof garden n. a garden on a flat roof of a building.

roofing (ˈruːfɪŋ) n. material used to construct a roof.

roof rack n. a rack attached to the roof of a motor vehicle for carrying luggage.

rooftree (ˈruːfˌtriː) n. same as **ridgepole.**

rooikat (ˈrɔɪˌkæt, ˈruːkæt) n. a South African lynx. [Afrikaans]

rooinek (ˈrɔɪˌnɛk, ˈruːnek) n. *S. African, facetious.* an Englishman. [Afrikaans]

rook[1] (rʊk) n. **1.** a large crowlike Eurasian bird, with a black plumage and a whitish base to its bill. ~vb. **2.** *Slang.* to overcharge, swindle, or cheat. [Old English *hrōc*]

rook[2] (rʊk) n. a chesspiece that may move any number of unoccupied squares in a straight line, horizontally or vertically; castle. [Arabic *rukhkh*]

rookery (ˈrʊkərɪ) n., pl. **-eries.** **1.** a group of nesting rooks. **2.** a colony of certain other birds or mammals, esp. penguins or seals.

rookie (ˈrʊkɪ) n. *Informal.* a newcomer, esp. a raw recruit in the army. [changed from *recruit*]

room (ruːm, rʊm) n. **1.** unoccupied or unobstructed space: *is there room to pass?* **2.** an area within a building enclosed by a floor, a ceiling, and walls. **3.** (*functioning as sing. or pl.*) the people present in a room: *the whole room was laughing.* **4.** (foll. by *for*) opportunity or scope: *room for manoeuvre.* **5.** (*pl.*) lodgings. ~vb. **6.** to occupy or share a room: *Jim and I used to room together.* [Old English *rūm*]

rooming house n. *U.S. & Canad.* a house having self-contained furnished rooms or flats for renting.

roommate (ˈruːmˌmeɪt, ˈrʊm-) n. a person with whom one shares a room.

room service n. service in a hotel providing food and drinks in guests' rooms.

roomy (ˈruːmɪ, ˈrʊmɪ) adj. **roomier, roomiest.** spacious. —**'roominess** n.

roost (ruːst) n. **1.** a place, such as a perch where birds, esp. domestic fowl, rest or sleep. ~vb. **2.** to rest or sleep on a roost. **3.** to settle down or stay. **4.** **come home to roost.** to have unfavourable repercussions. [Old English *hrōst*]

rooster (ˈruːstə) n. *Chiefly U.S. & Canad.* the male of the domestic fowl; a cock.

root[1] (ruːt) n. **1.** the part of a plant that anchors the rest of the plant in the ground and absorbs water and mineral salts from the soil. **2.** any plant part, such as a tuber, that resembles a root. **3.** the essential part or nature of something: *the root of the problem*. **4.** *Anat.* the embedded portion of a tooth, nail, hair, etc. **5.** origin or derivation. **6.** (*pl.*) a person's sense of belonging in a community or place, esp. the one in which he was born or brought up. **7.** *Linguistics.* the form of a word that remains after removal of all affixes. **8.** *Maths.* a quantity that when multiplied by itself a certain number of times equals a given quantity: *3 is a cube root of 27.* **9.** Also called: **solution.** *Maths.* a number that when substituted for the variable satisfies a given equation. **10.** *Austral. & N.Z. slang.* sexual intercourse. **11. root and branch.** entirely; utterly. ~*vb.* **12.** Also: **take root.** to establish a root and begin to grow. **13.** Also: **take root.** to become established, embedded, or effective. **14.** to embed with or as if with a root or roots. **15.** *Austral. & N.Z. slang.* to have sexual intercourse (with). ~See also **root out, roots.** [Old English *rōt*]

root² (ruːt) *vb.* **1.** (of a pig) to dig up the earth in search of food, using the snout. **2.** (foll. by *about, around,* etc.) *Informal.* to search vigorously but unsystematically. [Old English *wrōtan*]

root canal *n.* the passage in the root of a tooth through which its nerves and blood vessels enter.

root crop *n.* a crop, as of turnips or beets, cultivated for the food value of its roots.

root for *vb. Informal.* to give support to (a team or contestant), as by cheering. [origin unknown]

rootle (ˈruːtʲl) *vb. Brit.* same as **root²**.

rootless (ˈruːtlɪs) *adj.* having no roots, esp. (of a person) having no ties with a particular place.

root mean square *n.* the square root of the average of the squares of a set of numbers or quantities: *the root mean square of 1, 2, and 4 is* $\sqrt{[(1^2 + 2^2 + 4^2)/3]}$ $= \sqrt{7}$.

root out *vb.* to remove or eliminate completely: *we must root out inefficiency.*

roots (ruːts) *adj.* (of popular music) going back to the origins of a style, esp. in being unpretentious: *roots rock.*

rootstock (ˈruːtˌstɒk) *n.* same as **rhizome.**

rope (rəʊp) *n.* **1.** a fairly thick cord made of intertwined fibres or wire. **2.** a row of objects fastened to form a line: *a rope of pearls.* **3.** a filament or strand: *a rope of slime.* **4. know the ropes.** to have a thorough understanding of a particular activity. **5. the rope. a.** a rope noose used for hanging someone. **b.** death by hanging. ~*vb.* **6.** to bind, tie, or fasten with or as if with a rope. **7.** (usually foll. by *off*) to enclose or divide by means of a rope. [Old English *rāp*]

rope in *vb.* **1.** *Brit.* to persuade to take part in some activity. **2.** *U.S. & Canad.* to trick or entice into some activity.

ropy *or* **ropey** (ˈrəʊpɪ) *adj.* **ropier, ropiest.** *Brit. informal.* **1.** poor or unsatisfac-

tory in quality: *a ropy performance.* **2.** slightly unwell. —ˈ**ropiness** *n.*

Roquefort (ˈrɒkfɔː) *n.* a strong blue-veined cheese made from ewe's and goat's milk. [after *Roquefort*, village in S France]

ro-ro (ˈrəʊrəʊ) *adj.* (of a ferry) roll-on/roll-off.

rorqual (ˈrɔːkwəl) *n.* a whalebone whale with a dorsal fin. [Norwegian *rörhval*]

Rorschach test (ˈrɔːʃɑːk) *n. Psychol.* a personality test consisting of a number of unstructured inkblots for interpretation. [after H. *Rorschach*, psychiatrist]

rosaceous (rəʊˈzeɪʃəs) *adj.* of or belonging to a family of plants typically having five-petalled flowers, which includes the rose, strawberry, blackberry, and many fruit trees.

rosary (ˈrəʊzərɪ) *n.*, *pl.* **-saries.** *R.C. Church.* **a.** a series of prayers counted on a string of beads. **b.** a string of beads used to count these prayers as they are recited. [Latin *rosārium* rose garden]

rose¹ (rəʊz) *n.* **1.** a shrub or climbing plant with prickly stems and fragrant flowers. **2.** the flower of any of these plants. **3.** any of various similar plants, such as the Christmas rose. **4.** a purplish-pink colour. **5.** a rose as the national emblem of England. **6.** a perforated cap fitted to a watering can or hose, causing the water to issue in a spray. **7. bed of roses.** a situation of comfort or ease. [Latin *rosa*]

rose² (rəʊz) *vb.* the past tense of **rise.**

rosé (ˈrəʊzeɪ) *n.* a pink wine. [French]

roseate (ˈrəʊzɪˌeɪt) *adj.* **1.** of the colour rose or pink. **2.** excessively optimistic.

rosebay willowherb (ˈrəʊzˌbeɪ ˈwɪləʊˌhɜːb) *n.* a widespread perennial plant that has spikes of deep pink flowers.

rosebud (ˈrəʊzˌbʌd) *n.* the bud of a rose.

rose-coloured *adj.* **1.** excessively optimistic. **2. see through rose-coloured glasses** (*or* **spectacles**). to view in an excessively optimistic light.

rosehip (ˈrəʊzˌhɪp) *n.* the berry-like fruit of a rose plant.

rosemary (ˈrəʊzmərɪ) *n.*, *pl.* **-maries.** an aromatic European shrub widely cultivated for its grey-green evergreen leaves, which are used in cookery and perfumes. [Latin *rōs* dew + *marīnus* marine]

rose of Sharon (ˈʃærən) *n.* a creeping shrub with large yellow flowers.

rosette (rəʊˈzet) *n.* a decoration resembling a rose, esp. an arrangement of ribbons in a rose-shaped design worn as a badge or presented as a prize.

rose-water *n.* scented water made by the distillation of rose petals or by impregnation with oil of roses.

rose window *n.* a circular window with ornamental tracery radiating from the centre to form a symmetrical roselike pattern.

rosewood (ˈrəʊzˌwʊd) *n.* a hard dark wood with a roselike scent, used to make furniture.

rosin (ˈrɒzɪn) *n.* **1.** a translucent brittle substance produced in the distillation of crude turpentine and used for treating the bows of stringed instruments. ~*vb.* **2.** to treat or coat with rosin. [*var. of resin*]

ROSPA ('rɒspə) (in Britain) Royal Society for the Prevention of Accidents.

roster ('rɒstə) *n.* **1.** a list or register, esp. one showing the order of people enrolled for duty. ~*vb.* **2.** to place on a roster. [Dutch *rooster* grating or list]

rostrum ('rɒstrəm) *n., pl.* **-trums** *or* **-tra** (-trə). **1.** any platform on which public speakers stand. **2.** a platform in front of an orchestra on which the conductor stands. [Latin]

rosy ('rəʊzɪ) *adj.* **rosier, rosiest. 1.** of the colour rose or pink. **2.** having a healthy pink complexion: *rosy cheeks.* **3.** optimistic, esp. excessively so: *a rosy view of social improvements.* —'**rosiness** *n.*

rot (rɒt) *vb.* **rotting, rotted. 1.** to decay or cause to decay. **2.** to become weak or depressed, as through inertia or confinement: *rotting in prison.* ~*n.* **3.** the process of rotting or the state of being rotten. **4.** something decomposed. **5.** short for **dry rot. 6.** any of various plant or animal diseases which cause decay of the tissues. **7.** nonsense; rubbish. [Old English *rotian*]

rota ('rəʊtə) *n.* Chiefly Brit. a register of names showing the order in which people take their turn to perform certain duties. [Latin: a wheel]

rotary ('rəʊtərɪ) *adj.* **1.** operating by rotation. **2.** revolving. ~*n., pl.* **-ries. 3.** U.S. & Canad. a traffic roundabout.

Rotary Club *n.* any of the local clubs that form **Rotary International**, an international association of professional and business men founded in the U.S. in 1905 to promote community service. —**Rotarian** (rəʊ'tɛərɪən) *n., adj.*

rotate (rəʊ'teɪt) *vb.* **1.** to turn or cause to turn around an axis; spin. **2.** to follow or cause to follow a set sequence. **3.** to regularly change the type of crop grown on a piece of land in order to preserve the fertility of the soil. [Latin *rota* wheel] —**ro'tation** *n.*

rote (rəʊt) *n.* **1.** a habitual or mechanical routine or procedure. **2. by rote.** by repetition; by heart. [origin unknown]

rotgut ('rɒt,gʌt) *n. Facetious slang.* alcoholic drink, esp. spirits, of inferior quality.

rotisserie (rəʊ'tɪsərɪ) *n.* a rotating spit on which meat and poultry can be cooked. [French]

rotor ('rəʊtə) *n.* **1.** the rotating part of a machine or device, such as the revolving arm of the distributor of an internal-combustion engine. **2.** a rotating device with blades projecting from a hub which produces thrust to lift a helicopter.

Rotovator ('rəʊtə,veɪtə) *n. Trademark.* a mechanical cultivator with rotary blades.

rotten ('rɒt'n) *adj.* **1.** decomposing, decaying, or putrid. **2.** breaking up, esp. through age and hard use: *rotten ironwork.* **3.** morally corrupt. **4.** *Informal.* unpleasant: *rotten weather.* **5.** *Informal.* unsatisfactory: *rotten workmanship.* **6.** *Informal.* miserably unwell. **7.** *Informal.* distressed

and embarrassed: *I felt rotten breaking the news to him.* [Old Norse *rottin*]

rotter ('rɒtə) *n. Slang, chiefly Brit.* a worthless or despicable person.

rotund (rəʊ'tʌnd) *adj.* **1.** rounded or spherical in shape. **2.** plump. **3.** sonorous or grandiloquent. [Latin *rotundus*] —**ro'tundity** *n.* —**ro'tundly** *adv.*

rotunda (rəʊ'tʌndə) *n.* a circular building or room, esp. wih a dome. [Italian *rotonda*]

rouble *or* **ruble** ('ruːb'l) *n.* the standard monetary unit of the Soviet Union. [Russian *rubl*]

roué ('ruːeɪ) *n.* a man who gives himself over to a sensual immoral life. [French]

rouge (ruːʒ) *n.* **1.** a red cosmetic for adding redness to the cheeks. ~*vb.* **2.** to apply rouge to. [French: red]

rough (rʌf) *adj.* **1.** (of a surface) not smooth; uneven or irregular. **2.** (of ground) covered with scrub, boulders, etc. **3.** denoting or taking place on uncultivated ground: *rough grazing.* **4.** shaggy or hairy. **5.** turbulent: *a rough sea.* **6.** (of behaviour or character) rude, coarse, or violent. **7.** harsh or sharp: *rough words.* **8.** (of work, etc.) requiring physical rather than mental effort. **9.** *Informal.* ill: *he felt rough after an evening's drinking.* **10.** unfair: *rough luck.* **11.** harsh or grating to the ear. **12.** without refinement, luxury, etc. **13.** incomplete or rudimentary: *a rough draft.* **14.** (of a guess) approximate. ~*n.* **15.** rough ground. **16.** a sketch or preliminary piece of artwork. **17.** unfinished or crude state. **18. the rough.** *Golf.* the part of the course bordering the fairways where the grass is untrimmed. **19.** *Informal.* a violent person; thug. **20.** the unpleasant side of something: *to take the rough with the smooth.* ~*adv.* **21.** roughly. **22. sleep rough.** to spend the night in the open; be without shelter. ~*vb.* **23.** to make rough; roughen. **24.** (foll. by *out* or *in*) to prepare (a sketch, report, etc.) in preliminary form. **25. rough it.** *Informal.* to live without the usual comforts of life. ~See also **rough up.** [Old English *rūh*]

roughage ('rʌfɪdʒ) *n.* the coarse indigestible constituents of food, which provide bulk to the diet and aid digestion.

rough-and-ready *adj.* **1.** crude, unpolished, or hastily prepared, but sufficient for the purpose. **2.** (of a person) without formality or refinement.

rough-and-tumble *n.* **1.** a fight or scuffle without rules. ~*adj.* **2.** disorderly and without rules.

roughcast ('rʌf,kɑːst) *n.* **1.** a coarse plaster used to cover the surface of an external wall. ~*vb.* **-casting, -cast. 2.** to apply roughcast to (a wall).

rough diamond *n.* **1.** an unpolished diamond. **2.** an intrinsically trustworthy or good person with uncouth manners.

roughen ('rʌf'n) *vb.* to make or become rough.

rough-hew *vb.* **-hewing, -hewed; -hewed** *or* **-hewn.** to cut or shape roughly without finishing the surface.

roughhouse ('rʌf,haʊs) n. Slang. rough, disorderly, or noisy behaviour.

roughneck ('rʌf,nɛk) n. Slang. 1. a rough or violent person; thug. 2. a worker in an oil-drilling operation.

roughshod ('rʌf,ʃɒd) adj. 1. (of a horse) shod with rough-bottomed shoes to prevent sliding. ~adv. 2. **ride roughshod over.** to act with complete disregard for.

rough up vb. Informal. to beat up.

roulette (ruː'lɛt) n. a gambling game in which a ball is dropped onto a spinning horizontal wheel divided into numbered slots, with players betting on the slot into which the ball will fall. [French]

round (raʊnd) adj. 1. having a flat circular shape, as a hoop. 2. having the shape of a ball. 3. curved; not angular. 4. involving or using circular motion. 5. complete: a round dozen. 6. Maths. a. forming or expressed by a whole number, with no fraction. b. expressed to the nearest ten, hundred, or thousand: in round figures. 7. (of speech) candid: a round assertion. ~n. 8. a round shape or object. 9. **in the round. a.** in full detail. b. Theatre. with the audience all round the stage. 10. a session, as of a negotiation: a round of talks. 11. a series: a giddy round of parties. 12. **the daily round.** the usual activities of one's day. 13. a stage of a competition: he was eliminated in the first round. 14. (often pl.) a series of calls: a milkman's round. 15. a playing of all the holes on a golf course. 16. a single turn of play by each player, as in a card game. 17. one of a number of periods in a boxing, wrestling, or other match. 18. a single discharge by a gun. 19. a bullet or other charge of ammunition. 20. a number of drinks bought at one time for a group of people. 21. a. a single slice of bread. b. a serving of sandwiches made from two complete slices of bread. 22. a general outburst of applause. 23. movement in a circle. 24. Music. a part song in which the voices follow each other at equal intervals at the same pitch. 25. **go the rounds.** (of information, infection, etc.) to be passed around. ~prep. 26. surrounding, encircling, or enclosing: a band round her head. 27. on all or most sides of: to look round one. 28. on or outside the circumference or perimeter of. 29. from place to place in: driving round Ireland. 30. reached by making a partial circuit about: the shop round the corner. 31. revolving about (a centre or axis): the earth's motion round its axis. ~adv. 32. on all or most sides. 33. on or outside the circumference or perimeter: the racing track is two miles round. 34. to all members of a group: pass the food round. 35. in rotation or revolution: the wheels turn round. 36. by a circuitous route: the road to the farm goes round by the pond. 37. to a specific place: she came round to see me. 38. **all year round.** throughout the year. ~vb. 39. to make or become round. 40. to move or cause to move with turning motion: to round a bend. ~See also **round down, round off,** etc. [Old French ront]

roundabout ('raʊndə,baʊt) n. 1. Brit. a revolving circular platform, often with seats, on which people ride for amusement; merry-go-round. 2. a road junction in which traffic moves in one direction around a central island. ~adj. 3. indirect; devious: she found out by roundabout methods. ~adv., prep. **round about.** 4. approximately: at round about 5 o'clock.

round dance n. 1. a dance in which the dancers form a circle. 2. a ballroom dance, such as the waltz, in which couples revolve.

round down vb. to lower (a number) to the nearest whole number or ten, hundred, or thousand below it.

roundel ('raʊnd²l) n. 1. a circular identifying mark on military aircraft. 2. a small circular object, such as a window or medallion. [Old French rondel]

roundelay ('raʊndɪ,leɪ) n. a song in which a line or phrase is repeated as a refrain. [Old French rondelet]

rounders ('raʊndəz) n. (functioning as sing.) Brit. a bat and ball game in which players run between posts after hitting the ball, scoring a **rounder** if they run round all four posts before the ball is retrieved.

Roundhead ('raʊnd,hɛd) n. English history. a supporter of Parliament against Charles I during the Civil War. [referring to their short-cut hair]

roundhouse ('raʊnd,haʊs) n. U.S. & Canad. a circular building in which railway locomotives are serviced.

roundly ('raʊndlɪ) adv. bluntly or thoroughly: this policy has been roundly criticized.

round off vb. (often foll. by with) to complete, esp. agreeably: we rounded off the evening with a brandy.

round on vb. to attack or reply to (someone) with sudden irritation or anger.

round robin n. 1. a petition or protest with the signatures in a circle to disguise the order of signing. 2. a tournament in which each player plays against every other player.

round-shouldered adj. denoting a faulty posture with drooping shoulders and a slight forward bending of the back.

round table n. a meeting of parties or people on equal terms for discussion.

Round Table n. the. 1. (in Arthurian legend) the table of King Arthur, shaped so that his knights could sit around it without any having precedence. 2. one of an organization of clubs of young business and professional men who meet in order to further charitable work.

round-the-clock adj. (or as adv. **round the clock**) throughout the day and night.

round trip n. a trip to a place and back again, esp. returning by a different route.

round up vb. 1. to gather together: to round ponies up. 2. to raise (a number) to the nearest whole number or ten, hundred, or thousand above it. ~n. **roundup.** 3. the act of gathering together livestock, esp. cattle. 4. any similar act of bringing together: a roundup of today's news.

roundworm ('raʊnd,wɜːm) *n.* a worm that is a common intestinal parasite of man and pigs.

rouse (raʊz) *vb.* **1.** to wake up. **2.** to provoke: *to rouse someone's anger.* **3. rouse oneself.** to become energetic. [origin unknown]

rousing ('raʊzɪŋ) *adj.* tending to excite; lively or vigorous: *a rousing chorus.*

roustabout ('raʊstə,baʊt) *n.* an unskilled labourer on an oil rig.

rout[1] (raʊt) *n.* **1.** an overwhelming defeat. **2.** a disorderly retreat. **3.** a noisy rabble. **~*vb.* 4.** to defeat and cause to flee in confusion. [Anglo-Norman *rute*]

rout[2] (raʊt) *vb.* **1.** to dig up (something), esp. (of an animal) with the snout. **2.** (usually foll. by *out* or *up*) to find by searching. **3.** (usually foll. by *out*) to drive out: *they routed him out of bed at midnight.* **4.** to search, poke, or rummage. [var. of ROOT[2]]

route (ruːt) *n.* **1.** the choice of roads taken to get to a place. **2.** a regular journey travelled. **~*vb.* 3.** to send by a particular route. [Old French *rute*]

routemarch ('ruːt,mɑːtʃ) *n. Mil.* a long training march.

routine (ruː'tiːn) *n.* **1.** a usual or regular method of procedure, esp. one that is unvarying. **2.** *Computers.* a program or part of a program performing a specific function: *an input routine.* **3.** a set sequence of dance steps. **~*adj.* 4.** relating to or characteristic of routine. [Old French *route* a customary way]

roux (ruː) *n.* a cooked mixture of fat and flour used as a basis for sauces. [French: brownish]

rove (rəʊv) *vb.* **1.** to wander about (a place); roam. **2.** (of the eyes) to look around; wander. [Old Norse] **—'rover** *n.*

row[1] (rəʊ) *n.* **1.** an arrangement of people or things in a line: *a row of chairs.* **2.** *Chiefly Brit.* a street, esp. one lined with identical houses. **3.** a line of seats in a cinema or theatre. **4.** a horizontal line of numbers. **5. in a row.** in succession; one after the other: *he won two gold medals in a row.* [Old English *rāw, rēw*]

row[2] (rəʊ) *vb.* **1.** to propel (a boat) by using oars. **2.** to carry (people or goods) in a rowing boat. **3.** to take part in the racing of rowing boats as a sport. **~*n.* 4.** an act, period, or distance of rowing. **5.** an excursion in a rowing boat. [Old English *rōwan*]

row[3] (raʊ) *n.* **1.** a noisy quarrel. **2.** *Informal.* a controversy, esp. a political one: *a new row over NHS cuts.* **3.** a noisy disturbance: *we couldn't hear the music for the row next door.* **4.** a reprimand. **~*vb.* 5.** (often foll. by *with*) to quarrel noisily. [origin unknown]

rowan ('rəʊən, 'raʊ-) *n.* a European tree with white flowers and red berries; mountain ash. [Scandinavian]

rowdy ('raʊdɪ) *adj.* **-dier, -diest. 1.** rough, noisy, or disorderly: *a rowdy gang of football supporters.* **~*n., pl.* -dies. 2.** a person who behaves in such a fashion. [origin unknown] **—'rowdily** *adv.*

rowel ('raʊəl) *n.* a small spiked wheel at the end of a spur. [Old French *roel* a little wheel]

rowing boat ('rəʊɪŋ) *n. Chiefly Brit.* a small pleasure boat propelled by oars. Usual U.S. and Canad. word: **rowboat.**

rowlock ('rɒlək) *n.* a swivelling device attached to the top of the side of a boat that holds an oar in place.

royal ('rɔɪəl) *adj.* **1.** of or befitting a king or queen; regal. **2.** (*often cap.*) supported by or in the service of royalty: *the Royal Society of St George.* **3.** being a member of a royal family. **4.** better, bigger, or more impressive than usual. **~*n.* 5.** (*sometimes cap.*) a member of a royal family. [Old French *roial*] **—'royally** *adv.*

Royal Air Force *n.* the air force of Great Britain.

royal-blue *adj.* deep blue in colour.

royalist ('rɔɪəlɪst) *n.* **1.** a supporter of a monarch or monarchy. **~*adj.* 2.** of or relating to royalists. **—'royalism** *n.*

royal jelly *n.* a substance secreted by worker bees and fed to all larvae when very young and to larvae destined to become queens throughout their growth.

Royal Marines *pl. n. Brit.* a corps of soldiers specially trained in amphibious warfare.

Royal Navy *n.* the navy of Great Britain.

royalty ('rɔɪəltɪ) *n., pl.* **-ties. 1.** the rank, power, or position of a king or queen. **2.** royal persons individually or collectively. **3.** a percentage of the revenue from the sale of a book, performance of a work, use of a patented invention or of land, etc., paid to the author, inventor, or owner.

royal warrant *n.* an authorization to a tradesman to supply goods to a royal household.

RPI (in Britain) retail price index; a measure of the changes in the average level of retail prices of selected goods.

rpm revolutions per minute.

RR 1. Right Reverend. **2.** *Canad. & U.S.* rural route.

RSA 1. Republic of South Africa. **2.** (in New Zealand) Returned Services Association. **3.** Royal Scottish Academy. **4.** Royal Society of Arts.

RSFSR Russian Soviet Federative Socialist Republic.

RSI repetitive strain injury.

RSM regimental sergeant major.

RSPCA (in Britain) Royal Society for the Prevention of Cruelty to Animals.

RSVP please reply. [French *répondez s'il vous plaît*]

Rt Hon. Right Honourable: a title of respect for a Privy Councillor, certain peers, and the Lord Mayor or Lord Provost of certain cities.

Ru *Chem.* ruthenium.

rub (rʌb) *vb.* **rubbing, rubbed. 1.** to apply pressure and friction to (something) with a backward and forward motion. **2.** to move (something) with pressure along, over, or against (a surface). **3.** to chafe or fray. **4.** to bring into a certain condition by rubbing: *rub it clean.* **5.** to spread with pressure, so that it can be absorbed: *she rubbed ointment into his back.* **6.** to mix (fat) into flour with the fingertips, as in making pastry. **7.** (foll. by *off, out, away,* etc.) to remove or be removed by rubbing: *the mark would not rub off.* **8. rub it in.** to harp on something distasteful to a person. ~*n.* **9. rub up the wrong way.** to annoy. ~*n.* **10.** the act of rubbing. **11.** (preceded by *the*) an obstacle or difficulty: *there's the rub.* ~See also **rub along, rub down,** etc. [origin unknown]

rub along *vb. Brit.* **1.** to continue in spite of difficulties. **2.** to maintain an amicable relationship; not quarrel.

rubato (ruːˈbɑːtəʊ) *Music.* ~*n., pl.* **-tos. 1.** flexibility of tempo in performance. ~*adj., adv.* **2.** to be played with a flexible tempo. [Italian, lit.: robbed]

rubber[1] (ˈrʌbə) *n.* **1.** an elastic material obtained from the latex of certain plants, esp. the rubber tree. **2.** a similar substance produced synthetically. **3.** *Chiefly Brit.* a piece of rubber used for erasing something written; eraser. **4.** (*often pl.*) *Chiefly U.S. & Canad.* a rubber-coated waterproof overshoe. **5.** *Slang.* a condom. **6.** (*modifier*) made of or producing rubber: *a rubber ball; a rubber factory.* [the tree was so named because its product was used for rubbing out writing] —ˈ**rubbery** *adj.*

rubber[2] (ˈrʌbə) *n.* **1.** *Bridge, whist.* a match of three games. **2.** a series of matches or games in any of various sports. [origin unknown]

rubber band *n.* a continuous loop of thin rubber, used to hold papers, etc., together.

rubberize *or* **-ise** (ˈrʌbə͵raɪz) *vb.* to coat or impregnate with rubber.

rubberneck (ˈrʌbə͵nɛk) *Slang.* ~*n.* **1.** a person who stares or gapes inquisitively. **2.** a sightseer or tourist. ~*vb.* **3.** to stare in a naive or foolish manner.

rubber plant *n.* **1.** a large house plant with glossy leathery leaves. **2.** same as **rubber tree.**

rubber stamp *n.* **1.** a device used for imprinting dates, signatures, etc., on forms, invoices, etc. **2.** automatic authorization of a payment, proposal, etc. **3.** a person or body that gives official approval to decisions taken elsewhere but has no real power. ~*vb.* **rubber-stamp.** **4.** *Informal.* to approve automatically.

rubber tree *n.* a tropical tree cultivated for its latex, which is the major source of commercial rubber.

rubbing (ˈrʌbɪŋ) *n.* an impression taken of an incised or raised design by laying paper over it and rubbing with wax, graphite, etc.

rubbish (ˈrʌbɪʃ) *n.* **1.** anything worthless, useless, or unwanted. **2.** discarded or waste matter; refuse. **3.** foolish words or speech; nonsense. ~*vb.* **4.** *Informal.* to criticize; attack verbally. [origin unknown] —ˈ**rubbishy** *adj.*

rubble (ˈrʌbᵊl) *n.* **1.** pieces of broken stones or bricks. **2.** debris from ruined buildings. [origin unknown]

rub down *vb.* **1.** to dry or clean (a horse, oneself, etc.) vigorously, esp. after exercise. **2.** to make or become smooth by rubbing. **3.** to prepare (a surface) for painting by rubbing it with sandpaper.

rubella (ruːˈbɛlə) *n.* a mild contagious viral disease characterized by cough, sore throat, and skin rash. Also called: **German measles.** [Latin *rubellus* reddish]

Rubicon (ˈruːbɪkən) *n.* **1.** a stream in N Italy: in ancient times part of the Italian border. **2. cross** (*or* **pass**) **the Rubicon.** to commit oneself irrevocably to some course of action.

rubicund (ˈruːbɪkənd) *adj.* of a reddish colour; rosy. [Latin *rubicundus*]

rubidium (ruːˈbɪdɪəm) *n.* a soft highly reactive radioactive metallic element used in electronic valves, photocells, and special glass. Symbol: Rb [Latin *rubidus* red]

ruble (ˈruːbᵊl) *n.* same as **rouble.**

rub off *vb.* (often foll. by *on* or *onto*) to have an effect through close association: *her manners have rubbed off on you.*

rub out *vb.* **1.** to remove or be removed with a rubber. **2.** *U.S. slang.* to murder.

rubric (ˈruːbrɪk) *n.* **1.** a set of rules of conduct or procedure, esp. one for the conduct of Christian church services. **2.** a title, heading, or initial letter in a book, esp. one in red ink. [Latin *ruber* red]

ruby (ˈruːbɪ) *n., pl.* **-bies. 1.** a deep red transparent precious variety of corundum: used as a gemstone, in lasers, and in watchmaking. **2.** the deep-red colour of a ruby. **3.** (*modifier*) denoting a fortieth anniversary: *our ruby wedding.* [Latin *ruber* red]

RUC Royal Ulster Constabulary.

ruche (ruːʃ) *n.* a strip of pleated or frilled lace or ribbon used to decorate clothes. [French, lit.: beehive]

ruck[1] (rʌk) *n.* **1.** a large number or quantity of undistinguished people or things. **2.** *Rugby.* a loose scrum that forms around the ball when it is on the ground. [prob. Old Norse]

ruck[2] (rʌk) *n.* **1.** a wrinkle, crease, or fold. ~*vb.* **2.** (usually foll. by *up*) to wrinkle or crease. [Scandinavian]

rucksack (ˈrʌk͵sæk) *n.* a large bag, with two straps, carried on the back. [from German]

ruction (ˈrʌkʃən) *n. Informal.* **1.** an uproar; noisy or quarrelsome disturbance. **2.** (*pl.*) an unpleasant row; trouble. [origin unknown]

rudder (ˈrʌdə) *n.* **1.** *Naut.* a pivoted vertical vane that projects into the water at the stern: used to steer a vessel. **2.** a vertical control surface attached to the rear of the fin used to steer an aircraft. [Old English *rōther*] —ˈ**rudderless** *adj.*

ruddy (ˈrʌdɪ) *adj.* **-dier, -diest. 1.** (of the complexion) having a healthy reddish colour. **2.** red or pink: *a ruddy sky.* ~*adv., adj. Informal, chiefly Brit.* **3.** bloody; damned: *a ruddy fool.* [Old English *rudig*]

rude (ruːd) *adj.* **1.** insulting; discourteous; impolite. **2.** lacking refinement; uneducated. **3.** vulgar or obscene: *a rude joke.* **4.** roughly or crudely made: *we made a rude shelter on the island.* **5.** robust or sturdy: *in rude health.* **6.** unexpected and unpleasant: *a rude awakening.* [Latin *rudis*] —'**rudely** *adv.* —'**rudeness** *n.*

rudiment ('ru:dɪmənt) *n.* **1.** (*often pl.*) the first principles or elementary stages of a subject. **2.** (*often pl.*) a partially developed version of something. **3.** *Biol.* an organ or part that is incompletely developed or no longer functions. [Latin *rudīmentum*] —**rudimentary** (,ru:dɪ'mentrɪ) *adj.*

rue[1] (ru:) *vb.* **ruing, rued.** to feel sorrow, remorse, or regret for (one's wrongdoing, past events, etc.). [Old English *hrēowan*]

rue[2] (ru:) *n.* an aromatic shrub with bitter evergreen leaves formerly used in medicine. [Greek *rhutē*]

rueful ('ru:ful) *adj.* feeling or expressing sorrow or regret: *a rueful face.* —'**ruefully** *adv.*

ruff[1] (rʌf) *n.* **1.** a circular pleated or fluted cloth collar worn by men and women in the 16th and 17th centuries. **2.** a natural growth of long or coloured hair or feathers around the necks of certain animals or birds. **3.** a bird of the sandpiper family. [from *ruffle*]

ruff[2] (rʌf) *n., vb. Cards.* same as **trump**[1] (sense 1). [from French *roffle*]

ruffian ('rʌfɪən) *n.* a violent or lawless person.]Old French *rufien*]

ruffle ('rʌf³l) *vb.* **1.** to disturb the smoothness of: *a breeze ruffling the water.* **2.** to annoy, irritate, or be annoyed or irritated. **3.** (of a bird) to erect its feathers in anger, display, etc. **4.** to flick cards or pages rapidly. ~*n.* **5.** a strip of pleated material used as a trim. [Germanic]

rufous ('ru:fəs) *adj.* reddish-brown. [Latin *rūfus*]

rug (rʌg) *n.* **1.** a floor covering resembling a small carpet. **2.** *Chiefly Brit.* a blanket, esp. one used for travellers. **3. pull the rug out from under.** to betray, expose, or leave defenceless. [Scandinavian]

rugby *or* **rugby football** ('rʌgbɪ) *n.* a form of football played with an oval ball in which the handling and carrying of the ball is permitted. [after the public school at *Rugby*, where it was first played]

rugby league *n.* a form of rugby played between teams of 13 players, professionalism being allowed.

rugby union *n.* a form of rugby played only by amateurs, in teams of 15.

rugged ('rʌgɪd) *adj.* **1.** having an uneven or jagged surface. **2.** rocky or steep: *rugged scenery.* **3.** (of the face) strongfeatured or furrowed. **4.** rough, sturdy, or determined in character. **5.** (of equipment or machines) designed to withstand rough treatment or use in rough conditions. [Old Norse]

rugger ('rʌgə) *n. Informal, chiefly Brit.* rugby.

ruin ('ru:ɪn) *n.* **1.** a destroyed or decayed building or town. **2.** the state of being destroyed or decayed. **3.** loss of wealth,

status, or power, or something that causes such loss; downfall. **4.** something that is severely damaged: *his life was a ruin.* ~*vb.* **5.** to bring to ruin; destroy. **6.** to injure or spoil: *the town has been ruined with tower blocks.* [Latin *ruīna* a falling down]

ruination (,ru:ɪ'neɪʃən) *n.* **1.** the act of ruining or the state of being ruined. **2.** something that causes ruin.

ruinous ('ru:ɪnəs) *adj.* **1.** causing ruin or destruction. **2.** more expensive than can reasonably be afforded: *high interest rates are ruinous for industry.* —'**ruinously** *adv.*

rule (ru:l) *n.* **1.** a principle, regulation, or direction concerning method or procedure, as for a court of law, or sport: *judges' rules; play according to the rules.* **2.** the exercise of governmental authority or control: *the rule of Caesar.* **3.** the period of time in which a monarch or government has power: *his rule lasted 100 days.* **4.** a customary form or procedure: *he made a morning swim his rule.* **5.** (usually preceded by *the*) the common order of things: *violence was the rule.* **6.** a device with a straight edge for guiding or measuring; ruler: *a carpenter's rule.* **7.** *Printing.* a long thin line or dash. **8.** *Christianity.* a systematic body of laws and customs followed by members of a religious order. **9.** *Law.* an order by a court or judge. **10. as a rule.** ordinarily. ~*vb.* **11.** to govern (people or a political unit). **12.** to decide authoritatively; decree: *the chairman ruled against the proposal.* **13.** to mark with straight parallel lines or one straight line. **14.** to restrain or control. **15.** to be customary or prevalent: *chaos rules in this school.* **16.** to be pre-eminent or superior: *football rules in the field of sport.* **17. rule the roost.** to be pre-eminent; be in charge. [Old French *riule*]

rule of thumb *n.* a rough and practical approach, based on experience, rather than theory.

rule out *vb.* **1.** to dismiss from consideration. **2.** to make impossible; preclude.

ruler ('ru:lə) *n.* **1.** a person who rules or commands. **2.** a strip of wood, metal, or other material, having straight edges, used for measuring and drawing straight lines.

ruling ('ru:lɪŋ) *n.* **1.** a decision of someone in authority, such as a judge. ~*adj.* **2.** controlling or exercising authority. **3.** predominant.

rum[1] (rʌm) *n.* spirit made from sugar cane. [origin unknown]

rum[2] (rʌm) *adj.* **rummer, rummest.** *Brit. slang.* strange; odd. [origin unknown]

Rumanian (ru:'meɪnɪən) *n., adj.* same as **Romanian.**

rumba ('rʌmbə, 'rum-) *n.* **1.** a rhythmic and syncopated dance in duple time. **2.** music for this dance. [Spanish]

rumble ('rʌmb³l) *vb.* **1.** to make or cause to make a deep resonant sound: *thunder rumbled in the sky.* **2.** to move with such a sound: *the train rumbled along.* **3.** *Brit. slang.* to find out about (someone or something): *the police rumbled their plans.* ~*n.*

4. a deep resonant sound. **5.** *U.S. & N.Z. slang.* a gang fight. [prob. from Middle Dutch *rummelen*] —**'rumbling** *adj., n.*

rumbustious (rʌm'bʌstʃəs) *adj.* boisterous or unruly. [prob. var. of *robustious*]

ruminant ('ruːmɪnənt) *n.* **1.** any of a suborder of mammals which chew the cud and have a stomach of four compartments, including deer, antelopes, cattle, sheep, and goats. **2.** any other animal that chews the cud, such as a camel. ~*adj.* **3.** of such mammals. **4.** meditating or contemplating in a slow quiet way.

ruminate ('ruːmɪˌneɪt) *vb.* **1.** (of ruminants) to chew (the cud). **2.** (sometimes foll. by *upon* or *on*) to meditate or ponder (upon). [Latin *rūmināre* to chew the cud] —ˌrumi'nation. —'ruminative *adj.*

rummage ('rʌmɪdʒ) *vb.* **1.** (often foll. by *through*) to search untidily (through) while looking for something. ~*n.* **2.** an act of rummaging. [Old French *arrumage* to stow cargo]

rummage sale *n. U.S. & Canad.* a jumble sale.

rummy ('rʌmɪ) *n.* a card game based on collecting sets and sequences. [origin unknown]

rumour *or U.S.* **rumor** ('ruːmə) *n.* **1.** information, often a mixture of truth and untruth, passed around verbally. **2.** gossip or hearsay. ~*vb.* **3.** (*usually passive*) to pass around or circulate in the form of a rumour: *it is rumoured that the Queen is coming.* [Latin *rūmor*]

rump (rʌmp) *n.* **1.** the rear part of a mammal's or birds body. **2.** a person's buttocks. **3.** Also called: **rump steak.** a cut of beef from the rump. **4.** an inferior remnant. [Old Norse]

rumple ('rʌmp'l) *vb.* to make or become crumpled or dishevelled. [Middle Dutch *rompelen*]

rumpus ('rʌmpəs) *n., pl.* **-puses.** a noisy, confused, or disruptive commotion. [origin unknown]

run (rʌn) *vb.* **running, ran, run. 1.** to move on foot at a rapid pace, esp. (of a two-legged creature) so that both feet are off the ground for part of each stride. **2.** to pass over (a distance or route) in running: *to run a mile.* **3.** to run in or finish a race in a particular position or fashion: *John is running third.* **4.** to perform as by running: *to run an errand.* **5.** to flee. **6.** to track down or hunt (an animal): *to run a fox to earth.* **7.** (often foll. by *over, round,* or *up*) to make a short trip or brief visit: *I'll run over this afternoon.* **8.** to move quickly and easily on wheels by rolling, or in any of certain other ways: *a sledge running over snow.* **9.** to move with a specified result: *to run a ship aground; run into a tree.* **10.** (often foll. by *over*) to move or pass or cause to move or pass quickly: *to run one's eyes over a page.* **11.** to force, thrust, or drive: *she ran a needle into her finger.* **12.** to drive or maintain and operate (a vehicle). **13.** to give a lift to (someone) in a vehicle: *he ran her to the station.* **14.** to travel regularly between places on a route: *the bus runs from Piccadilly to* Golders Green. **15.** to function or cause to function: *the engine is running smoothly.* **16.** to manage: *to run a company.* **17.** to extend or continue in a particular direction, for a particular duration or distance, etc.: *the road runs north; the play ran for two years.* **18.** *Law.* to have legal force or effect: *the lease runs for two years.* **19.** to be subjected to, affected by, or incur: *to run a risk; run a temperature.* **20.** (often foll. by *to*) to tend or incline: *to run to fat.* **21.** to recur persistently or be inherent: *red hair runs in my family.* **22.** to cause or allow (liquids) to flow or (of liquids) to flow: *the well has run dry.* **23.** (of waves, tides, rivers, etc.) to rise high, surge, or be at a specified height: *a high sea was running.* **24.** to dissolve and spread: *the colours in my dress ran.* **25.** (of stitches) to unravel or (of a garment) to have stitches unravel. **26.** to spread or circulate quickly: *a rumour ran through the town.* **27.** to be stated or reported: *his story runs as follows.* **28.** to publish or be published in a newspaper or magazine: *they ran his story in the next issue.* **29.** (often foll. by *for*) *Chiefly U.S. & Canad.* to stand as a candidate for political or other office: *Jones is running for president.* **30.** to get past or through: *to run a blockade.* **31.** to smuggle (goods, esp. arms). **32.** (of fish) to migrate upstream from the sea, esp. in order to spawn. **33.** *Cricket.* to score (a run or number of runs) by hitting the ball and running between the wickets. ~*n.* **34.** an act, instance, or period of running. **35.** a gait, pace, or motion faster than a walk: *she went off at a run.* **36.** a distance covered by running or a period of running: *a run of ten miles.* **37.** a trip in a vehicle, esp. for pleasure: *to go for a run in the car.* **38.** free and unrestricted access: *we had the run of the house.* **39. a.** a period of time during which a machine or computer operates. **b.** the amount of work performed in such a period. **40.** a continuous or sustained period: *a run of good luck.* **41.** a continuous sequence of performances: *the play had a good run.* **42.** *Cards.* a sequence of winning cards in one suit: *a run of spades.* **43.** type, class, or category: *the usual run of graduates.* **44.** (usually foll. by *on*) a continuous and urgent demand: *a run on the dollar.* **45.** a series of unravelled stitches, esp. in tights; ladder. **46.** a steeply inclined course, esp. a snow-covered one used for skiing. **47.** an enclosure for domestic fowls or other animals: *a chicken run.* **48.** (esp. in Australia and New Zealand) a tract of land for grazing livestock. **49.** the migration of fish upstream in order to spawn. **50.** *Music.* a rapid scalelike passage of notes. **51.** *Cricket.* a score of one, normally achieved by both batsmen running from one end of the wicket to the other after one of them has hit the ball. **52.** *Baseball.* an instance of a batter touching all four bases safely, thereby scoring. **53. a run for one's money.** *Informal.* **a.** a close competition. **b.** pleasure or success from an activity. **54. in the long run.** as an eventual outcome. **55. on the run.** escaping from arrest; fugitive.

56. the runs. *Slang.* diarrhoea. ~See also **runabout**, **run across**, etc. [Old English *runnen*]

runabout ('rʌnə,baʊt) *n.* **1.** a small light vehicle, esp. a car. ~*vb.* **run about. 2.** to move busily from place to place.

run across *vb.* to meet unexpectedly by chance.

run along *vb.* to go away; leave.

run away *vb.* **1.** to take flight; escape. **2.** to go away; depart. **3.** (of a horse) to gallop away uncontrollably. **4. run away with. a.** to abscond or elope with: *he ran away with his boss's daughter.* **b.** to escape from the control of: *his enthusiasm ran away with him.* **c.** to win easily or be assured of victory in (a competition): *he ran away with the race.* ~*n.* **runaway. 5. a.** a person or animal that runs away. **b.** (*as modifier*): *a runaway horse.* **6.** (*modifier*) rising rapidly, as prices: *runaway inflation.* **7.** (*modifier*) (of a race or victory) easily won.

run down *vb.* **1.** (of a device such as a clock or battery) to lose power gradually and cease to function. **2.** to decline or reduce in number or size: *the firm ran down its sales force.* **3.** to criticize adversely. **4.** to hit and knock to the ground with a moving vehicle. **5.** to pursue and find or capture: *to run down a fugitive.* ~*adj.* **run-down. 6.** tired; exhausted. **7.** worn-out, shabby, or dilapidated. ~*n.* **rundown. 8.** a brief review, résumé, or summary. **9.** a reduction in number or size.

rune (ruːn) *n.* **1.** any of the characters of an ancient Germanic alphabet. **2.** any obscure piece of writing using mysterious symbols. [Old Norse *rūn* secret] —**'runic** *adj.*

rung[1] (rʌŋ) *n.* **1.** one of the bars forming the steps of a ladder. **2.** a crosspiece between the legs of a chair, etc. [Old English *hrung*]

rung[2] (rʌŋ) *vb.* the past participle of **ring**[2].

run in *vb.* **1.** to run (an engine) gently, usually when it is new. *Informal.* to arrest. ~*n.* **run-in. 3.** *Informal.* an argument or quarrel.

run into *vb.* **1.** to collide with or cause to collide with: *her car ran into a tree.* **2.** to encounter unexpectedly. **3.** to be beset by: *the project ran into difficulties.* **4.** to extend to: *debts running into thousands.*

runnel ('rʌnᵊl) *n. Literary.* a small stream. [Old English *rynele*]

runner ('rʌnə) *n.* **1.** a person who runs, esp. an athlete. **2.** a messenger for a firm. **3.** a person or vessel engaged in smuggling. **4. a.** either of the strips of metal or wood on which a sledge runs. **b.** the blade of an ice skate. **5.** a roller or guide for a sliding component. **6.** *Bot.* a slender horizontal stem, as of the strawberry, that grows along the surface of the soil and produces new roots and shoots. **7.** a long strip of cloth used to decorate a table or as a rug.

runner bean *n.* the edible pod and seeds of a type of climbing bean plant.

runner-up *n., pl.* **runners-up.** a contestant finishing a race or competition in second place.

running ('rʌnɪŋ) *adj.* **1.** maintained continuously; incessant: *running commentary.* **2.** without interruption; consecutive: *he lectured for two hours running.* **3.** operating: *the running time of a train; running machinery.* **4.** accomplished at a run: *a running jump.* **5.** moving or slipping easily, as a rope or a knot. **6.** discharging pus: *a running sore.* **7. a.** flowing: *running water.* **b.** supplied through a tap: *hot and cold running water.* ~*n.* **8.** management or organization: *the running of a company.* **9.** operation or maintenance: *the running of a machine.* **10. in** (or *out of*) **the running.** in (or out of) a competition or competitive situation. **11. make the running.** to set the pace in a competition or race.

running board *n.* a footboard along the side of a vehicle, esp. an early motorcar.

running head *or* **title** *n.* Printing. a heading printed at the top of every page of a book.

running repairs *pl. n.* repairs that do not, or do not greatly, interrupt operations.

runny ('rʌnɪ) *adj.* **-nier, -niest. 1.** tending to flow; liquid. **2.** (of the nose) exuding mucus.

run off *vb.* **1.** to depart in haste. **2.** to produce quickly, as copies on a duplicating machine. **3.** to drain (liquid) or (of liquid) to be drained. **4. run off with. a.** to steal. **b.** to elope with. ~*n.* **run-off. 5.** an extra race, contest, election, etc., to decide the winner after a tie. **6.** *N.Z.* grazing land for cattle.

run-of-the-mill *adj.* ordinary, average, or undistinguished.

run on *vb.* **1.** to continue without interruption. ~*n.* **run-on. 2.** a word added at the end of a dictionary entry whose meaning can be easily inferred from the definition of the headword.

run out *vb.* **1.** (often foll. by *of*) to use up (a supply of something) or (of a supply) to be used up. **2. run out on.** *Informal.* to desert or abandon. **3.** *Cricket.* to dismiss (a running batsman) by breaking the wicket with the ball while he is running between the wickets.

run over *vb.* **1.** to knock down (a person) with a moving vehicle. **2.** to overflow. **3.** to examine hastily.

runt (rʌnt) *n.* **1.** the smallest and weakest young animal in a litter. **2.** an undersized or inferior person. [origin unknown]

run through *vb.* **1.** to transfix with a sword or other weapon. **2.** to practise or rehearse: *let's run through the plan.* ~*n.* **run-through. 3.** a practice or rehearsal.

run to *vb.* to be sufficient for: *my income doesn't run to luxuries.*

run up *vb.* **1.** to amass; incur: *to run up debts.* **2.** to make by sewing together quickly. **3.** to hoist: *to run up a flag.* ~*n.* **run-up. 4.** a preliminary or preparatory period: *the run-up to the election.*

runway ('rʌn,weɪ) *n.* a hard level roadway where aircraft take off and land.

rupee (ruːˈpiː) *n.* the standard monetary

unit of India, Pakistan, Sri Lanka, the Maldive Islands, Mauritius, the Seychelles, and Nepal. [Hindi *rupaīyā*]

rupture ('rʌptʃə) *n.* **1.** the act of breaking or the state of being broken. **2.** a breach of peaceful or friendly relations. **3.** *Pathol.* a hernia. ~*vb.* **4.** to break or burst. **5.** to affect or be affected with a hernia. **6.** to undergo or cause to undergo a breach in relations or friendship. [Latin *rumpere* to burst forth]

rural ('ruǝrǝl) *adj.* in or of the countryside. [Latin *rūrālis*]

rural dean *n. Chiefly Brit.* a clergyman having authority over a group of parishes.

rural route *n. U.S. & Canad.* a mail service or route in a rural area.

rusbank ('rus,bæŋk) *n. S.African.* a wooden bench or settle without upholstery. [Afrikaans]

ruse (ruːz) *n.* an action intended to mislead, deceive, or trick. [Old French]

rush[1] (rʌʃ) *vb.* **1.** to hurry or cause to hurry. **2.** to make a sudden attack upon (a person or place). **3.** (often foll. by *at, in,* or *into*) to proceed or approach in a reckless manner. **4. rush one's fences.** to act too hurriedly. **5.** to come, flow, swell, etc., quickly or suddenly: *tears rushed to her eyes.* **6.** *U.S. & Canad.* to make a concerted effort to secure the agreement or participation of (a person). ~*n.* **7.** the act or condition of rushing. **8.** a sudden surge towards someone or something: *a gold rush.* **9.** a sudden surge of sensation, esp. from a drug. **10.** a sudden demand. **11.** (*usually pl.*) (in film-making) the initial prints of a scene before editing. ~*adj.* **12.** requiring speed or urgency: *a rush job.* [Old French *ruser* to put to flight]

rush[2] (rʌʃ) *n.* a plant which grows in wet places and has grasslike cylindrical leaves and small green or brown flowers. [Old English *risce, rysce*] —**'rushy** *adj.*

rush hour *n.* a period at the beginning and end of the day when large numbers of people are travelling to or from work.

rush light or **candle** *n.* a narrow candle, formerly in use, made of the pith of various types of rush dipped in tallow.

rusk (rʌsk) *n.* light bread baked twice until it is brown, hard, and crisp: often given to babies. [Spanish or Portuguese *rosca* screw, bread shaped in a twist]

russet ('rʌsɪt) *n.* **1.** any of various apples with rough brownish-red skins. ~*adj.* **2.** brown with a reddish tinge. [Latin *russus*]

Russian ('rʌʃǝn) *n.* **1.** the official language of the Soviet Union. **2.** a person from Russia or (loosely) the Soviet Union. ~*adj.* **3.** of Russia or the Soviet Union, its people, or their language.

Russian roulette *n.* an act of bravado in which a person spins the cylinder of a revolver loaded with only one cartridge and presses the trigger with the barrel against his own head.

Russo- ('rʌsǝʊ) *combining form.* Russia or Russian: *Russo-Japanese.*

rust (rʌst) *n.* **1.** a reddish-brown oxide coating formed on iron or steel by the action of oxygen and moisture. **2.** a strong brown colour, sometimes with a reddish or yellowish tinge. **3.** a fungal disease of plants which produces a reddish brown discolouration. **4.** any corrosive or weakening influence, esp. lack of use. ~*vb.* **5.** to become or cause to become coated with a layer of rust. **6.** to deteriorate as through lack of use: *he allowed his talent to rust over the years.* [Old English]

rustic ('rʌstɪk) *adj.* **1.** of or living in the country; rural. **2.** having qualities ascribed to country life or people; simple; unsophisticated: *rustic pleasures.* **3.** crude, awkward, or uncouth. **4.** made of untrimmed branches: *a rustic seat.* ~*n.* **5.** a person from the country. [Latin *rūsticus*] —**rusticity** (rʌ'stɪsɪtɪ) *n.*

rusticate ('rʌstɪ,keɪt) *vb.* **1.** to retire to the country. **2.** to make or become rustic. **3.** *Brit.* to send (a student) down from university for a specified time as a punishment. [Latin *rūs* the country]

rustle[1] ('rʌs²l) *vb.* **1.** to make or cause to make a low crisp whispering sound, as of dry leaves or paper. ~*n.* **2.** such a sound or sounds. [Old English *hrūxlian*]

rustle[2] ('rʌs²l) *vb. Chiefly U.S. & Canad.* to steal (livestock). [prob. from *rustle* in the sense: to move with a quiet sound] —**'rustler** *n.*

rustle up *vb. Informal.* to prepare (a meal) rapidly, esp. at short notice.

rusty ('rʌstɪ) *adj.* **rustier, rustiest.** **1.** affected by or consisting of rust: *a rusty machine.* **2.** of the colour of rust. **3.** discoloured by age: *a rusty coat.* **4.** out of practice in a skill or subject. —**'rustily** *adv.* —**'rustiness** *n.*

rut[1] (rʌt) *n.* **1.** a groove or furrow in a soft road, caused by wheels. **2.** dreary or unchanging routine: *in a rut.* [prob. from French *route* road]

rut[2] (rʌt) *n.* **1.** a recurrent period of sexual excitement in certain male ruminants. ~*vb.* **2.** (of male ruminants) to be in a period of sexual excitement. [Old French *rut* noise, roar]

ruthenium (ruː'θiːnɪǝm) *n.* a rare hard brittle white metallic element. Symbol: Ru [Medieval Latin *Ruthenia* Russia, where it was discovered]

ruthless ('ruːθlɪs) *adj.* feeling or showing no mercy; hardhearted. [*ruth* pity] —**'ruthlessly** *adv.* —**'ruthlessness** *n.*

rutted ('rʌtɪd) *adj.* (of a road) with many ruts; very uneven.

RV Revised Version (of the Bible).

rye (raɪ) *n.* **1.** a tall grasslike cereal grown for its light brown grain. **2.** the grain of this plant, used in making flour and whisky, and as a livestock food. **3.** Also called (esp. U.S.): **rye whiskey.** whisky distilled from rye. **4.** *U.S.* short for **rye bread.** [Old English *ryge*]

rye bread *n.* bread made entirely or partly from rye flour.

rye-grass *n.* any of various grasses with flattened flower spikes and hairless leaves, widely grown as animal fodder.

S

s or **S** (ɛs) *n.*, *pl.* **s's**, **S's**, or **Ss**. 1. the 19th letter of the English alphabet. 2. something shaped like an S.

s second (of time).

S 1. South. 2. *Chem.* sulphur.

-'s *suffix.* 1. forming the possessive singular of nouns and some pronouns: *man's; one's.* 2. forming the possessive plural of nouns whose plurals do not end in *-s: children's.* (The possessive plural of nouns ending in *s* is formed by the addition of an apostrophe after the final *s: girls'.*) 3. forming the plural of numbers, letters, or symbols: *20's.* 4. *Informal.* contraction of *is* or *has: it's gone.* 5. *Informal.* contraction of *us* with *let: let's.*

SA 1. Salvation Army. 2. South Africa. 3. South America. 4. South Australia.

Sabbath ('sæbəθ) *n.* 1. Saturday, observed by Jews as the day of worship and rest. 2. Sunday, observed by Christians as the day of worship and rest. [Hebrew *shābath* to rest]

SABC South African Broadcasting Corporation.

sabbatical (sə'bætɪk⁰l) *adj.* 1. denoting a period of leave granted at intervals to university teachers for rest, study, or travel: *a sabbatical year.* ~*n.* 2. a sabbatical period. [see SABBATH]

sable ('seɪb⁰l) *n.*, *pl.* **-bles** or **-ble.** 1. a marten of N Asia, N Europe, and America, with dark brown luxuriant fur. 2. the highly valued fur of this animal. ~*adj.* 3. dark brown-to-black. 4. *Heraldry.* black. [Slavic]

sable antelope *n.* a large black E African antelope with long backward-curving horns.

sabot ('sæbəʊ) *n.* a heavy wooden or wooden-soled shoe. [French]

sabotage ('sæbə,tɑːʒ) *n.* 1. the deliberate destruction or damage of equipment as by enemy agents or dissatisfied employees. 2. deliberate obstruction of or damage to a cause or effort. ~*vb.* 3. to destroy or disrupt by sabotage. [French]

saboteur (,sæbə'tɜː) *n.* a person who commits sabotage. [French]

sabre or *U.S.* **saber** ('seɪbə) *n.* 1. a stout single-edged cavalry sword with a curved blade. 2. a light sword used in fencing, with a narrow V-shaped blade. [German (dialect) *Sabel*]

sac (sæk) *n.* a pouch or pouchlike part in an animal or plant. [Latin *saccus*]

saccharin ('sækərɪn) *n.* a very sweet nonfattening sugar substitute. [Greek *sakkharon* sugar]

saccharine ('sækə,riːn) *adj.* 1. excessively sweet or sentimental: *a saccharine smile.* 2. like or containing sugar or saccharin.

sacerdotal (,sæsə'dəʊt⁰l) *adj.* of priests or priestly office. [Latin *sacerdōs* priest]

sachet ('sæʃeɪ) *n.* 1. a small sealed usually plastic envelope containing a small portion of a substance such as shampoo. 2. a small soft bag of perfumed powder, placed in drawers to scent clothing. [French]

sack¹ (sæk) *n.* 1. a large bag made of coarse cloth or thick paper and used as a container. 2. the amount contained in a sack. 3. **the sack.** *Informal.* dismissal from employment. 4. *Slang.* bed. 5. **hit the sack.** *Slang.* to go to bed. ~*vb.* 6. *Informal.* to dismiss from employment. 7. to put into a sack or sacks. [Greek *sakkos*] —**'sack,like** *adj.*

sack² (sæk) *n.* 1. the plundering of a captured town or city by an army or mob. ~*vb.* 2. to plunder and partially destroy (a town or city). [French *mettre à sac* to put (loot) in a sack]

sack³ (sæk) *n. Archaic except in trademarks.* a dry white wine from Spain or the Canary Islands. [French *vin sec* dry wine]

sackbut ('sæk,bʌt) *n.* a medieval form of trombone. [French *saqueboute*]

sackcloth ('sæk,klɒθ) *n.* 1. coarse cloth such as sacking. 2. garments made of such cloth, worn formerly to indicate mourning. 3. **sackcloth and ashes.** a public display of extreme grief.

sacking ('sækɪŋ) *n.* coarse cloth used for making sacks, woven from flax, hemp or jute.

sacrament ('sækrəmənt) *n.* 1. a symbolic religious ceremony in the Christian Church, such as baptism or communion. 2. (*often cap.*) Holy Communion. 3. something regarded as sacred. [Latin *sacrāre* to consecrate] —**sacramental** (,sækrə'mɛnt⁰l) *adj.*

sacred ('seɪkrɪd) *adj.* 1. exclusively devoted to a god or gods; holy. 2. regarded with reverence and respect, as if holy: *damage done in the sacred name of profit.* 3. connected with religion or intended for religious use: *sacred music.* 4. **sacred to.** dedicated to. [Latin *sacer* holy]

sacred cow *n. Informal.* a person, custom, belief, or institution regarded as being beyond criticism. [alluding to the Hindu belief that cattle are sacred]

sacrifice ('sækrɪ,faɪs) *n.* 1. a surrender of something of value in order to gain something more desirable or prevent some evil. 2. a ritual killing of a person or animal as an offering to a god. 3. a symbolic offering of something to a god. 4. the person, animal, or object killed or offered. ~*vb.* 5. to make a sacrifice (of). 6. *Chess.* to permit or force one's opponent to capture (a piece) as a tactical move. [Latin *sacer* holy + *facere* to make] —**sacrificial** (,sækrɪ'fɪʃəl) *adj.*

sacrifice paddock *n. N.Z.* a grassed field which is allowed to be grazed completely so that it can be cultivated and resown later.

sacrilege ('sækrɪlɪdʒ) *n.* 1. the desecration of anything regarded as sacred. **2.** the taking of anything sacred for secular use. [Latin *sacrilegus* temple robber] **—sacri'legious** *adj*.

sacristan ('sækrɪstən) *n.* **1.** a person in charge of the contents of a church. **2.** a sexton. [Latin *sacer* holy]

sacristy ('sækrɪstɪ) *n., pl.* **-ties.** a room attached to a church or chapel where the sacred objects and vestments are kept.

sacrosanct ('sækrəʊˌsæŋkt) *adj.* very sacred or holy; inviolable. [Latin *sacer* holy + *sanctus* hallowed] **—sacro'sanctity** *n*.

sacrum ('seɪkrəm) *n., pl.* **-cra** (-krə). the large wedge-shaped bone in the lower part of the back. [Latin *os sacrum* holy bone, because it was used in sacrifices]

sad (sæd) *adj.* **sadder, saddest. 1.** feeling sorrow; unhappy. **2.** causing, suggesting, or expressive of such feelings: *a sad story: a sad expression.* **3.** deplorably bad: *her clothes were in a sad state.* [Old English *sæd* weary] **—'sadly** *adv.* **—'sadness** *n*.

sadden ('sæd²n) *vb.* to make (someone) sad.

saddle ('sæd²l) *n.* **1.** a seat for a rider, usually made of leather, placed on a horse's back and secured under the belly. **2.** a similar seat on a bicycle, motorcycle, or tractor. **3.** a cut of meat, esp. mutton, consisting of both loins. **4. in the saddle.** in a position of control. *~vb.* **5.** (sometimes foll. by *up*) to put a saddle on (a horse). **6.** to burden: *I didn't ask to be saddled with this job.* [Old English *sadol, sædel*]

saddleback ('sæd²l,bæk) *n.* **1.** an animal with a marking resembling a saddle on its back. **2.** a hill with a concave upper outline. **—'saddle-,backed** *adj*.

saddlebag ('sæd²l,bæg) *n.* a pouch or small bag attached to the saddle of a horse, bicycle, or motorcycle.

saddle horse *n.* a horse trained for riding only.

saddler ('sædlə) *n.* a person who makes, deals in, or repairs saddles and other leather equipment for horses.

saddlery ('sædlərɪ) *n., pl.* **-dleries. 1.** saddles and harness for horses collectively. **2.** the work or place of work of a saddler.

saddle soap *n.* a soft soap used to preserve and clean leather.

saddletree ('sæd²l,triː) *n.* the frame of a saddle.

Sadducee ('sædjʊˌsiː) *n. Judaism.* a member of an ancient Jewish sect that denied the resurrection of the dead and accepted only the traditional written law.

sadhu ('sɑːduː) *n.* a Hindu wandering holy man. [Sanskrit]

sadism ('seɪdɪzəm) *n.* the gaining of pleasure, esp. sexual pleasure, from infliction of suffering on another person. [after the Marquis de *Sade*] **—'sadist** *n.* **—sadistic** (sə'dɪstɪk) *adj.* **—sadistically** (sə'dɪstɪkəlɪ) *adv*.

sadomasochism (ˌseɪdəʊ'mæsəˌkɪzəm) *n.* the combination of sadistic and masochistic elements in one person. **—ˌsado'masochist** *n.* **—ˌsadomaso'chistic** *adj*.

s.a.e. stamped addressed envelope.

safari (sə'fɑːrɪ) *n., pl.* **-ris.** an overland expedition for hunting or observing animals, esp. in Africa. [Swahili: journey]

safari park *n.* an enclosed park in which wild animals are kept uncaged in the open and can be viewed by the public from cars or buses.

safe (seɪf) *adj.* **1.** giving security or protection from harm: *a safe place.* **2.** free from danger: *you'll be safe here.* **3.** taking or involving no risks: *a safe investment.* **4.** worthy of trust: *a safe companion.* **5.** not dangerous: *water safe to drink.* **6. on the safe side.** as a precaution. *~n.* **7.** a strong metal container with a secure lock, for storing money or valuables. [Old French *salf*] **—'safely** *adv*.

safe-conduct *n.* **1.** a document giving official permission to travel through a dangerous region, esp. in time of war. **2.** the protection given by such a document.

safe-deposit *or* **safety-deposit** *n.* a place with facilities for the safe storage of money.

safeguard ('seɪf,gɑːd) *n.* **1.** a person or thing that ensures protection against danger or harm. *~vb.* **2.** to protect.

safekeeping ('seɪf'kiːpɪŋ) *n.* protection: *the painting was removed for safekeeping.*

safety ('seɪftɪ) *n., pl.* **-ties.** the quality or state of being free from danger.

safety belt *n.* same as **seat belt.**

safety curtain *n.* a fireproof curtain that can be lowered to separate the auditorium from the stage in a theatre to prevent the spread of a fire.

safety lamp *n.* a miner's oil lamp designed to prevent it from igniting combustible gas.

safety match *n.* a match that will light only when struck against a specially prepared surface.

safety net *n.* **1.** a large net under a trapeze or high wire to catch performers if they fall. **2.** something which can be relied on for help in the event of difficulties.

safety pin *n.* a pin bent back on itself so that it forms a spring, with the point shielded by a guard when closed.

safety razor *n.* a razor with a guard over the blade or blades to protect the skin from deep cuts.

safety valve *n.* **1.** a valve in a boiler or machine that allows fluid or gases to escape at excess pressure. **2.** a harmless outlet for emotion or energy.

safflower ('sæflaʊə) *n.* a thistle-like plant with orange-yellow flowers, which yields a dye and an oil used in paints, medicines, and cooking. [Old French *saffleur*]

saffron ('sæfrən) *n.* **1.** a species of crocus having purple or white flowers with orange stigmas. **2.** the dried stigmas of this plant, used for colouring or flavouring. *~adj.* **3.** orange to orange-yellow. [Arabic *za'farān*]

sag (sæg) *vb.* **sagging, sagged. 1.** to sink in the middle, as under weight or pressure: *the bed sags when I sit on it.* **2.** to fall in value: *prices sagged to a new low*. **3.** to hang unevenly. **4.** (of courage or spirits) to weaken. ~*n.* **5.** the act or state of sagging: *a sag in profits*. [Old Norse] —**'saggy** *adj.*

saga ('sɑːgə) *n.* **1.** a medieval Scandinavian prose narrative recounting the exploits of a hero or a family. **2.** *Informal.* a long story or series of events. [Old Norse]

sagacious (sə'geiʃəs) *adj.* having or showing insight or wisdom. [Latin *sagāx*] —**sa'gaciously** *adv.* —**sagacity** (sə'gæsiti) *n.*

sage[1] (seidʒ) *n.* **1.** a man regarded as being very wise. ~*adj.* **2.** very wise or prudent. [Latin *sapere* to be sensible]

sage[2] (seidʒ) *n.* **1.** a Mediterranean plant with grey-green leaves which are used in cooking for flavouring. **2.** short for **sagebrush.** [Latin *salvus* in good health (from its curative properties)]

sagebrush ('seidʒ,brʌʃ) *n.* an aromatic plant of W North America, with silver-green leaves and large clusters of small white flowers.

Sagittarius (,sædʒi'teəriəs) *n. Astrol.* the ninth sign of the zodiac; the Archer. [Latin]

sago ('seigəu) *n.* an edible starch obtained from the powdered pith of certain palm trees, used for puddings and as a thickening agent. [Malay *sāgū*]

sahib ('sɑːhib) *n.* an Indian term of address equivalent to *sir*, formerly used as a mark of respect to a European man. [Urdu]

said (sed) *adj.* **1.** (in documents) named or mentioned already. ~*vb.* **2.** past of **say.**

sail (seil) *n.* **1.** a sheet of canvas or other fabric, spread on rigging to catch the wind and propel a vessel over water. **2.** a voyage on such a vessel: *a sail down the river*. **3.** a vessel or vessels with sails. *to travel by sail*. **4.** one of the revolving arms of a windmill. **5. set sail.** to begin a voyage by water. **6. under sail. a.** with sail hoisted. **b.** under way. ~*vb.* **7.** to travel in a boat or ship: *we sailed to Le Havre*. **8.** to begin a voyage: *we sail at 5 o'clock*. **9.** (of a vessel) to move over the water. **10.** to navigate a vessel: *he sailed the schooner up the channel*. **11.** to sail over: *she sailed the Atlantic single-handed*. **12.** (often foll. by *through*) to progress quickly or effortlessly: *we sailed through the exams*. **13.** to move along smoothly; glide. **14.** (foll. by *in* or *into*) *Informal.* to make a violent attack on. [Old English *segl*]

sailboard ('seil,bɔːd) *n.* the craft used for windsurfing, consisting of a moulded board to which a mast bearing a single sail is attached.

sailcloth ('seil,klɒθ) *n.* **1.** any of various fabrics from which sails are made. **2.** a canvas-like cloth used for clothing.

sailfish ('seil,fiʃ) *n., pl.* **-fish** or **-fishes.** a large tropical game fish, with a long sail-like dorsal fin.

sailor ('seilə) *n.* **1.** any member of a ship's crew, esp. one below the rank of officer. **2.** a person considered as liable or not liable to seasickness: *a good sailor*.

sainfoin ('sænfɔin) *n.* a Eurasian plant

with pink flowers, widely grown as a fodder crop. [Medieval Latin *sānum faenum* wholesome hay]

saint (seint) *n.* **1.** a person who after death is formally recognized by a Christian Church as deserving special honour because of having lived a very holy life. **2.** a very holy or good person. [Latin *sanctus* holy] —**'sainthood** *n.* —**'saintlike** *adj.*

Saint Bernard ('bɜːnəd) *n.* a very large dog with a dense red-and-white coat, formerly used as a mountain rescue-dog.

sainted ('seintid) *adj.* **1.** canonized. **2.** like a saint. **3.** hallowed or holy.

Saint John's wort ('dʒɒnz) *n.* a plant with yellow flowers.

Saint Leger ('ledʒə) *n.* **the.** an annual horse race for three-year-olds, run at Doncaster.

saintly ('seintli) *adj.* like, relating to, or suitable for a saint. —**'saintliness** *n.*

Saint Vitus's dance ('vaitəsiz) *n. Pathol.* a nontechnical name for **chorea.**

saithe (seiθ) *n. Brit.* a dark-coloured food fish found in northern seas. [Old Norse]

sake[1] (seik) *n.* **1. for someone's** or **one's own sake.** for the benefit or interest of someone or oneself. **2. for the sake of something.** for the purpose of obtaining or achieving something. **3.** used in various exclamations of annoyance, impatience, or urgency: *for heaven's sake*. [Old English *sacu* lawsuit (hence, a cause)]

sake[2] or **saki** ('sɑːki) *n.* a Japanese alcoholic drink made from fermented rice. [Japanese]

salaam (sə'lɑːm) *n.* **1.** a Muslim greeting consisting of a deep bow with the right palm on the forehead. **2.** a greeting signifying peace. ~*vb.* **3.** to make a salaam (to). [Arabic *salām* peace]

salacious (sə'leiʃəs) *adj.* **1.** having an excessive interest in sex. **2.** (of books, films, or jokes) erotic or bawdy. [Latin *salax* fond of leaping] —**sa'laciousness** *n.*

salad ('sæləd) *n.* a dish of raw vegetables, often served with a dressing, eaten as a separate course or as part of a main course. [Old French *salade*]

salad days *pl. n.* a period of youth and inexperience.

salad dressing *n.* a sauce for salad, such as oil and vinegar or mayonnaise.

salamander ('sælə,mændə) *n.* **1.** a tailed amphibian which resembles a lizard. **2.** a mythical reptile supposed to live in fire. [Greek *salamandra*]

salami (sə'lɑːmi) *n.* a highly seasoned sausage, usually flavoured with garlic. [Italian]

salaried ('sælərid) *adj.* earning or providing a salary: *a salaried worker; salaried employment*.

salary ('sæləri) *n., pl.* **-ries.** a fixed regular payment made by an employer, usually monthly, for professional or office work. [Latin *salārium* the sum given to Roman soldiers to buy salt]

sale (seil) *n.* **1.** the exchange of goods or property for an agreed sum of money. **2.**

the amount sold. **3.** an event at which goods are sold at reduced prices. **4.** an auction. [Old English *sala*]

saleable *or U.S.* **salable** ('seɪləb'l) *adj.* fit for selling or capable of being sold. —,**salea'bility** *or U.S.* ,**sala'bility** *n.*

sale of work *n.* a sale of articles, often handmade, the proceeds of which go to a charity.

saleroom ('seɪl,ruːm) *n. Chiefly Brit.* a room where objects are displayed for sale by auction.

salesman ('seɪlzmən) *n., pl.* **-men. 1.** Also called: **saleswoman** (*fem.*), **salesgirl** (*fem.*), *or* **salesperson.** a person who sells goods in a shop. **2.** short for **travelling salesman.**

salesmanship ('seɪlzmənʃɪp) *n.* the technique of or skill in selling.

sales talk *or* **pitch** *n.* persuasive talk used in selling.

salicylic acid (,sælɪ'sɪlɪk) *n.* a white crystalline substance used to make aspirin and as a fungicide. [Latin *salix* willow]

salient ('seɪlɪənt) *adj.* **1.** conspicuous or striking: *a salient feature.* ~*n.* **2.** *Mil.* a projection of the forward line into enemy-held territory. [Latin *salīre* to leap]

saline ('seɪlaɪn) *adj.* **1.** of or containing salt: *a saline taste.* **2.** *Med.* of or relating to saline: *a saline drip.* ~*n.* **3.** *Med.* a solution of sodium chloride and water. [Latin *sal* salt] —**salinity** (sə'lɪnɪtɪ) *n.*

salinization *or* **-isation** (,sælɪnaɪ'zeɪʃən) *n.* the process by which salts accumulate in undrained land, adversely affecting its potential for plant growth.

saliva (sə'laɪvə) *n.* the watery fluid secreted by glands in the mouth, which aids digestion. [Latin] —**sa'livary** *adj.*

salivate ('sælɪ,veɪt) *vb.* to secrete saliva, esp. an excessive amount. —,**sali'vation** *n.*

sallow ('sæləʊ) *adj.* (of human skin) of an unhealthy pale or yellowish colour. [Old English *salu*] —'**sallowness** *n.*

sally ('sælɪ) *n., pl.* **-lies. 1.** a sudden brief attack by troops. **2.** an excursion. **3.** a jocular retort. ~*vb.* **-lying, -lied. 4.** to make a sudden violent attack. **5.** (often foll. by *forth*) to make an excursion. **6.** to come or set out in an energetic manner. [Latin *salīre* to leap]

salmon ('sæmən) *n., pl.* **-ons** *or* **-on.** a large pink-fleshed fish which is highly valued for food and sport: salmon live in the sea but return to fresh water to spawn. [Latin *salmō*]

salmonella (,sælmə'nelə) *n., pl.* **-lae** (-,liː). a bacterium which causes food poisoning. [after Daniel E. *Salmon*, veterinary surgeon]

salmon ladder *n.* a series of steps designed to enable salmon to move upstream to their breeding grounds.

salon ('sælɒn) *n.* **1.** a room in a large house in which guests are received. **2.** an informal gathering of major literary, artistic, and political figures in a fashionable household. **3.** a commercial establishment in which hairdressers or fashion designers carry on their business. **4.** an art exhibition. [French]

saloon (sə'luːn) *n.* **1.** *Brit.* a lounge bar. **2.** a large public room on a passenger ship. **3.** any large public room used for a purpose: *a billiard saloon.* **4.** *Chiefly U.S. & Canad.* a place where alcoholic drink is sold and consumed. **5.** a closed two-door or four-door car. [from *salon*]

salsa ('sælsə) *n.* a type of Puerto Rican big-band dance music. [Spanish, lit.: sauce]

salsify ('sælsɪfɪ) *n., pl.* **-fies.** a Mediterranean plant with a long white edible root. [Italian *sassefrica*]

salt (sɔːlt) *n.* **1.** sodium chloride, a white crystalline substance, used for seasoning and preserving food. **2.** (*modifier*) preserved in or tasting of salt: *salt pork.* **3.** *Chem.* a crystalline solid compound formed from an acid by replacing its hydrogen with a metal. **4.** liveliness or pungency: *his wit added salt to the discussion.* **5.** an experienced sailor. **6. rub salt into someone's wounds.** to make an unpleasant situation even worse for someone. **7. salt of the earth.** a person or people regarded as the finest of their kind. **8. take something with a pinch of salt.** to regard something sceptically. **9. worth one's salt.** worthy of one's pay. ~*vb.* **10.** to season or preserve with salt. **11.** to scatter salt over (an iced road or path) to melt the ice. ~*adj.* **12.** not sour, sweet, or bitter; salty. ~See also **salt away, salts.** [Old English *sealt*] —'**salted** *adj.*

SALT (sɔːlt) Strategic Arms Limitation Talks *or* Treaty.

salt away *vb.* to hoard or save (money or valuables).

saltcellar ('sɔːlt,selə) *n.* a small container for salt used at the table. [changed from *salt saler; saler* from Old French *saliere* container for salt]

salt lick *n.* **1.** a place where wild animals go to lick salt deposits. **2.** a block of salt given to domestic animals to lick.

saltpetre *or U.S.* **saltpeter** (,sɔːlt'piːtə) *n.* same as **potassium nitrate.** [Latin *sal petrae* salt of rock]

salts (sɔːlts) *pl. n.* **1.** *Med.* mineral salts used as a medicine. **2. like a dose of salts.** *Informal.* very quickly.

saltwater ('sɔːlt,wɔːtə) *adj.* of or inhabiting salt water, esp. the sea: *saltwater fishes.*

salty ('sɔːltɪ) *adj.* **saltier, saltiest. 1.** of, tasting of, or containing salt. **2.** (esp. of humour) sharp. —'**saltiness** *n.*

salubrious (sə'luːbrɪəs) *adj.* favourable to health. [Latin *salūs* health] —**sa'lubrity** *n.*

Saluki (sə'luːkɪ) *n.* a tall hound with a smooth coat and long fringes on the ears and tail. [Arabic]

salutary ('sæljʊtrɪ) *adj.* **1.** promoting some good purpose; beneficial: *a salutary warning.* **2.** promoting health. [Latin *salūtāris* wholesome]

salutation (,sæljʊ'teɪʃən) *n.* a phrase or gesture that serves as a greeting. [Latin *salūtāre* to greet]

salute (sə'luːt) *vb.* **1.** to greet with friendly words or gestures of respect, such as bowing. **2.** to acknowledge with praise: *we salute your gallantry.* **3.** *Mil.* to pay formal respect to (someone), as by raising the right hand to the forehead. ~*n.* **4.** the act of saluting. **5.** a formal military gesture of respect. [Latin *salūtāre* to greet]

salvage ('sælvɪdʒ) *n.* **1.** the rescue of a ship or its cargo from loss at sea. **2.** the saving of any goods or property from destruction or waste. **3.** the goods or property so saved. **4.** compensation paid for the salvage of a ship or its cargo. ~*vb.* **5.** to save (goods or property) from shipwreck, destruction, or waste. **6.** to gain (something beneficial) from a failure. [Latin *salvāre* to save] —'**salvageable** *adj.*

salvation (sæl'veɪʃən) *n.* **1.** a preserving from harm. **2.** a person or thing that preserves from harm. **3.** *Christianity.* spiritual deliverance from the consequences of sin. [Latin *salvātus* saved]

Salvation Army *n.* a Christian body organized on quasi-military lines for evangelism and social work among the poor.

salve (sælv, sɑːv) *n.* **1.** an ointment for wounds. **2.** anything that heals or soothes. ~*vb.* **3.** to soothe, comfort, or appease. [Old English *sealf*]

salver ('sælvə) *n.* a tray on which something is presented. [Spanish *salva* tray from which the king's taster sampled food]

salvia ('sælvɪə) *n.* any plant of the sage genus. [Latin]

salvo ('sælvəʊ) *n., pl.* **-vos** *or* **-voes. 1.** a unison firing of guns, in battle or on a ceremonial occasion. **2.** an outburst of applause or questions. [Italian *salva,* from Latin *salvē!* greetings!]

sal volatile (,sæl vɒ'lætɪlɪ) *n.* a solution of ammonium carbonate, used as smelling salts. [New Latin: volatile salt]

SAM (sæm) surface-to-air missile.

Samaritan (sə'mærɪt'n) *n.* **1.** short for **Good Samaritan. 2.** a member of a voluntary organization (**the Samaritans**) whose aim is to help people in distress or despair.

samarium (sə'meərɪəm) *n.* a silvery metallic element of the rare-earth series. Symbol: Sm [after Col. von *Samarski,* Russian inspector of mines]

samba ('sæmbə) *n., pl.* **-bas. 1.** a modern ballroom dance from Brazil in bouncy duple time. **2.** music for this dance. [Portuguese]

same (seɪm) *adj.* (usually preceded by *the*) **1.** being the very one: *she is wearing the same hat.* **2.** being the one previously referred to: *I didn't go for the same reason.* **3. a.** alike in kind or quantity: *two girls of the same age.* **b.** (as *n.*): *we'd like the same again.* **4.** unchanged in character or nature: *his attitude is the same as ever.* **5.** **all the same** *or* **just the same.** nevertheless; even so. **6. be all the same.** to be immaterial: *it's all the same to me.* ~*adv.* **7.** in the same way; similarly: *I feel the same about it.* [Old Norse *samr*] —'**sameness** *n.*

samizdat ('sæmɪz,dæt) *n.* (in the Soviet Union) a system of secret printing and distribution of banned literature. [Russian]

samosa (sə'məʊsə) *n.* (in Indian cookery) a small fried triangular spiced meat or vegetable pasty. Also (S. African): **samoosa** (sə'muːsə). [Hindi]

samovar ('sæmə,vɑː) *n.* a Russian metal tea urn in which the water is heated by an inner container. [Russian]

Samoyed ('sæmə,jed) *n.* a white or cream medium-sized dog with a dense coat and a tightly curled tail. [Russian]

sampan ('sæmpæn) *n.* a small flatbottomed boat with oars, widely used in the Orient. [Chinese]

samphire ('sæm,faɪə) *n.* a Eurasian coastal plant with fleshy leaves and clusters of small flowers. [French *herbe de Saint Pierre* Saint Peter's herb]

sample ('sɑːmp'l) *n.* **1.** a small part of anything, intended as being representative of the whole. ~*vb.* **2.** to take a sample or samples of. **3.** *Music.* **a.** to take a short extract from (one record) and mix it into a different backing track. **b.** to record (a sound) and feed it into a computerized synthesizer so that it can be reproduced at any pitch. [Latin: example] —'**sampling** *n.*

sampler ('sɑːmplə) *n.* a piece of embroidery done to show the embroiderer's skill in using many different stitches.

Samson ('sæmsən) *n.* a man of outstanding physical strength.

samurai ('sæmʊ,raɪ) *n., pl.* **-rai.** a member of the aristocratic warrior caste of feudal Japan. [Japanese]

sanatorium (,sænə'tɔːrɪəm) *or U.S.* **sanitarium** *n., pl.* **-riums** *or* **-ria** (-rɪə). **1.** an institution for the treatment of invalids or convalescents. **2.** *Brit.* a room in a boarding school where sick pupils may be treated. [Latin *sānāre* to heal]

sanctify ('sæŋktɪ,faɪ) *vb.* **-fying, -fied. 1.** to make holy. **2.** to free from sin. **3.** to sanction (an action or practice) as religiously binding: *to sanctify a marriage.* [Latin *sanctus* holy + *facere* to make] —,**sanctifi'cation** *n.*

sanctimonious (,sæŋktɪ'məʊnɪəs) *adj.* pretending to be very pious or holy. [Latin *sanctimonia* sanctity]

sanction ('sæŋkʃən) *n.* **1.** permission granted by authority. **2.** support or approval. **3.** something that gives binding force to a law, such as a penalty for breaking it or a reward for obeying it. **4.** a coercive measure, such as a boycott taken by one or more states against another guilty of violating international law. ~*vb.* **5.** to permit or give authority to. **6.** to confirm or ratify. [Latin *sancīre* to decree]

sanctity ('sæŋktɪtɪ) *n.* **1.** the condition of being sanctified; holiness. **2.** the condition of being inviolable: *the sanctity of human life.*

sanctuary ('sæŋktjʊərɪ) *n., pl.* **-aries. 1.** a holy place, such as a consecrated building or shrine. **2.** the holiest part of a sacred building, surrounding the main altar. **3.** a place of refuge or protection, esp., formerly, a church. **4.** refuge or safety: *he retreated to the sanctuary of his study.* **5.** a place, protected by law, where animals can live and breed without interference. [Latin *sanctus* holy]

sanctum ('sæŋktəm) *n., pl.* **-tums** *or* **-ta** (-tə). **1.** a sacred or holy place. **2.** a room or place of total privacy. [Latin]

sand (sænd) *n.* **1.** a powdery substance consisting of very small rock or mineral grains, found on the seashore and in deserts. **2.** (*pl.*) a large sandy area, esp. on the seashore or in a desert. ~*vb.* **3.** to smooth or polish the surface of (something) with sandpaper or a sander. **4.** to fill with sand: *the channel sanded up.* [Old English]

sandal ('sænd'l) *n.* a light shoe consisting of a sole held on the foot by thongs or straps. [Greek *sandalon*] —**'sandalled** *or U.S.* **'sandaled** *adj.*

sandalwood ('sænd'l,wʊd) *n.* **1.** the hard light-coloured heartwood of a S Asian or Australian tree, which is used for carving and for incense, and which yields an aromatic oil used in perfumery. **2.** a tree yielding this wood. [Sanskrit *candana*]

sandbag ('sænd,bæg) *n.* **1.** a sack filled with sand used to make a temporary defence against gunfire or floodwater, or as ballast. ~*vb.* **-bagging, -bagged. 2.** to protect or strengthen with sandbags.

sandbank ('sænd,bæŋk) *or* **sand bar** *n.* a bank of sand in a sea or river, that may be exposed at low tide.

sandblast ('sænd,blɑːst) *n.* **1.** a jet of sand blown from a nozzle under air or steam pressure. ~*vb.* **2.** to clean or decorate (a surface) with a sandblast. —**'sand,blaster** *n.*

sandboy ('sænd,bɔɪ) *n.* **happy as a sandboy.** very happy; high-spirited.

sand castle *n.* a mass of sand made into a castle-like shape by a child.

sander ('sændə) *n.* a power-driven tool for smoothing surfaces by rubbing with an abrasive disc.

sandman ('sænd,mæn) *n., pl.* **-men.** (in folklore) a magical person supposed to put children to sleep by sprinkling sand in their eyes.

sand martin *n.* a small brown European songbird which nests in tunnels bored in sand or river banks.

sandpaper ('sænd,peɪpə) *n.* **1.** a strong paper coated with sand or other abrasive material for smoothing or polishing a surface. ~*vb.* **2.** to smooth or polish (a surface) with sandpaper.

sandpiper ('sænd,paɪpə) *n.* a wading shore bird with a long bill and slender legs.

sandpit ('sænd,pɪt) *n.* a shallow pit or container holding sand for children to play in.

sandshoes ('sænd,ʃuːz) *pl. n.* light canvas shoes with rubber soles.

sandstone ('sænd,stəʊn) *n.* a sedimentary rock consisting mainly of sand grains, much used in building.

sandstorm ('sænd,stɔːm) *n.* a strong wind that whips up clouds of sand, esp. in a desert.

sandwich ('sænwɪdʒ) *n.* **1.** two or more slices of bread, usually buttered, with a layer of food between them. ~*vb.* **2.** to place between two other things. [after 4th Earl of *Sandwich,* who ate sandwiches rather than leave the gambling table for meals]

sandwich board *n.* one of two connected boards that are hung over the shoulders in front of and behind a person to display advertisements.

sandwich course *n.* an educational course consisting of alternate periods of study and industrial work.

sandy ('sændi) *adj.* **sandier, sandiest. 1.** resembling, containing, or covered with sand. **2.** (of hair) reddish-yellow. —**'sandiness** *n.*

sane (seɪn) *adj.* **1.** of sound mind; not mad. **2.** sensible or well-judged: *a sane policy.* [Latin *sānus* healthy]

sang (sæŋ) *vb.* the past tense of **sing.**

sang-froid (,sɒŋ'frwɑː) *n.* composure; self-possession. [French, lit.: cold blood]

sangoma (sæŋ'gəʊmə) *n.* S. African. a witch doctor. [Bantu]

sangria (sæŋ'griːə) *n.* a Spanish drink of red wine, sugar, and orange or lemon juice. [Spanish: a bleeding]

sanguinary ('sæŋgwɪnərɪ) *adj.* **1.** accompanied by much bloodshed. **2.** bloodthirsty. **3.** of or stained with blood. [Latin *sanguinārius*]

sanguine ('sæŋgwɪn) *adj.* **1.** cheerful and confident; optimistic. **2.** (of the complexion) ruddy. [Latin *sanguineus* bloody]

Sanhedrin ('sænɪdrɪn) *n. Judaism.* the highest court and supreme council of the ancient Jewish nation.

sanitary ('sænɪtrɪ) *adj.* **1.** promoting health by getting rid of dirt and germs. **2.** free from dirt or germs; hygienic. [Latin *sānitās* health]

sanitary towel *or esp. U.S.* **napkin** *n.* a pad worn externally by women during menstruation to absorb the flow of blood.

sanitation (,sænɪ'teɪʃən) *n.* **1.** the use of sanitary measures to maintain public health. **2.** drainage and disposal of sewage.

sanity ('sænɪtɪ) *n.* **1.** the state of being sane. **2.** good sense or soundness of judgment. [Latin *sānitās* health]

sank (sæŋk) *vb.* a past tense of **sink.**

sans-culotte (,sænzkjuː'lɒt) *n.* a revolutionary extremist. [French, lit.: without knee breeches, because during the French Revolution the revolutionaries wore trousers]

Sanskrit ('sænskrɪt) *n.* the classical literary language of India, used since ancient times for religious purposes. [Sanskrit *samskrta* perfected] —**San'skritic** *adj.*

sans serif (sæn 'serɪf) *n.* a style of printer's typeface in which the characters have no serifs.

Santa Claus ('sæntə ,klɔːz) *n.* the legendary patron saint of children, who brings presents to children on Christmas Eve, commonly identified with Saint Nicholas.

sap[1] ('sæp) n. **1.** a thin liquid that circulates in a plant, carrying food and water. **2.** energy; vigour. **3.** Slang. a gullible person. ~vb. **sapping, sapped. 4.** to drain of sap. [Old English]

sap[2] ('sæp) n. **1.** a deep and narrow trench used to approach or undermine an enemy position. ~vb. **sapping, sapped. 2.** to undermine (an enemy position) by digging saps. **3.** to weaken or exhaust. [Italian *zappa* spade]

sapient ('seɪpɪənt) adj. Often used ironically. wise or sagacious. [Latin *sapere* to taste, know] —'**sapience** n.

sapling ('sæplɪŋ) n. a young tree.

saponify (sə'pɒnɪˌfaɪ) vb. **-fying, -fied.** Chem. to convert (a fat) or (of a fat) to be converted into a soap by treatment with alkali. [Latin *sāpō* soap] —sa,**ponifi'cation** n.

sapper ('sæpə) n. **1.** a soldier who digs trenches. **2.** (in the British Army) a private of the Royal Engineers.

sapphire ('sæfaɪə) n. **1.** a transparent blue precious stone. ~adj. **2.** of the blue colour of sapphire. [Greek *sappheiros*]

sappy ('sæpɪ) adj. **-pier, -piest. 1.** (of plants) full of sap. **2.** full of energy or vitality.

saprophyte ('sæprəʊˌfaɪt) n. any plant, such as a fungus, that lives and feeds on dead organic matter. [Greek *sapros* rotten + *phuton* plant]

saraband or **sarabande** ('særəˌbænd) n. **1.** a stately slow Spanish dance in triple time. **2.** music for this dance. [Spanish *zarabanda*]

Saracen ('særəs'n) n. **1.** an Arab or Muslim who opposed the crusades. ~adj. **2.** of the Saracens. [Late Greek *Sarakēnos*]

sarcasm ('sɑːkæzəm) n. **1.** mocking or ironic language intended to convey scorn or insult. **2.** the use or tone of such language. [Greek *sarkazein* to rend the flesh]

sarcastic (sɑː'kæstɪk) adj. **1.** full of or showing sarcasm. **2.** given to the use of sarcasm. —sar'**castically** adv.

sarcoma (sɑː'kəʊmə) n., pl. **-mata** (-mətə) or **-mas.** Pathol. a malignant tumour beginning in connective tissue. [Greek *sarkōma* fleshy growth]

sarcophagus (sɑː'kɒfəgəs) n., pl. **-gi** (-ˌgaɪ) or **-guses.** a stone or marble coffin or tomb, esp. one bearing sculpture or inscriptions. [Greek *sarkophagos* flesh-devouring]

sardine (sɑː'diːn) n., pl. **-dine** or **-dines. 1.** a small food fish, often preserved in tightly packed tins. **2. like sardines.** very closely crowded together. [Latin *sardīna*]

sardonic (sɑː'dɒnɪk) adj. mocking or scornful. [Greek *sardonios*] —sar'**donically** adv.

sardonyx ('sɑːdənɪks) n. a variety of chalcedony with alternating reddish-brown and white parallel bands. [Greek *sardonux*]

sargassum (sɑː'gæsəm) n. a floating brown seaweed with ribbon-like fronds containing air sacs. [Portuguese *sargaço*]

sarge (sɑːdʒ) n. Informal. sergeant.

sari or **saree** ('sɑːrɪ) n., pl. **-ris** or **-rees.** the traditional dress of Hindi women, consisting of a very long piece of cloth swathed around the body with one end over the shoulder. [Hindi]

sarking ('sɑːkɪŋ) n. Scot., N English, & N.Z. flat planking supporting the roof cladding of a building. [Scot. *sark* shirt]

sarky ('sɑːkɪ) adj. **-kier, -kiest.** Brit. informal. sarcastic.

sarnie ('sɑːnɪ) n. Brit. informal. a sandwich.

sarong (sə'rɒŋ) n. a garment worn by Malaysian men and women, consisting of a long piece of cloth tucked around the waist or under the armpits. [Malay]

sarsaparilla (ˌsɑːsəpə'rɪlə) n. a nonalcoholic drink prepared from the roots of a tropical American climbing plant. [Spanish *zarzaparrilla*]

sartorial (sɑː'tɔːrɪəl) adj. of men's clothes or tailoring. [Latin *sartor* a patcher]

SAS Special Air Service.

sash[1] (sæʃ) n. a long piece of cloth worn around the waist or over one shoulder, as a symbol of rank. [Arabic *shāsh* muslin]

sash[2] (sæʃ) n. **1.** a frame that contains the panes of a window or door. **2.** a complete frame together with panes of glass. [French *châssis* a frame]

sash cord n. a strong cord connecting a weight to the sliding half of a sash window.

sashimi (sɑː'ʃiːmɪ) n. a Japanese dish of thin fillets of raw fish. [Japanese *sashi* piercing + *mi* fish]

sash window n. a window consisting of two sashes placed one above the other so that the window can be opened by sliding one frame over the front of the other.

Sask. Saskatchewan.

sassafras ('sæsəˌfræs) n. a tree of North America, whose aromatic dried root bark is used as a flavouring. [Spanish *sasafras*]

Sassenach ('sæsəˌnæx) n. Scot. & occasionally Irish. an English person or Lowland Scot. [Gaelic *Sassunach*]

sat (sæt) vb. past of **sit.**

Sat. Saturday.

Satan ('seɪt'n) n. the Devil, adversary of God, and tempter of mankind. [Hebrew: plotter]

satanic (sə'tænɪk) adj. **1.** of Satan. **2.** supremely evil or wicked.

Satanism ('seɪtəˌnɪzəm) n. the worship of Satan. —'**Satanist** n., adj.

satchel ('sætʃəl) n. a small bag, usually with a shoulder strap, used for carrying school books. [Old French *sachel*]

sate (seɪt) vb. **1.** to satisfy (a desire or appetite) fully. **2.** to satiate. [Old English *sadian*]

satellite ('sætəˌlaɪt) n. **1.** a heavenly body orbiting a planet or star: *the earth is a satellite of the sun.* **2.** a man-made device orbiting the earth or another planet, used in communications or to collect scientific information. **3.** a country controlled by or dependent on a more powerful one. **4.** (*modifier*) of, used in, or relating to the transmission of television signals from a satellite to the home: *a satellite dish aerial*. [Latin *satelles* an attendant]

satiable ('seɪʃɪəbᵊl) *adj.* capable of being satiated. —ˌsatia'bility *n.*

satiate ('seɪʃɪˌeɪt) *vb.* to provide with more than enough, so as to disgust or weary. [Latin *satiāre*] —ˌsati'ation *n.*

satiety (sə'taɪɪtɪ) *n.* the state of being satiated.

satin ('sætɪn) *n.* **1.** a fabric, usually of silk or rayon, closely woven to give a smooth glossy surface on one side. **2.** (*modifier*) like satin in texture: *a satin finish*. [Arabic *zaitūnī*] —'**satiny** *adj.*

satinwood ('sætɪnˌwʊd) *n.* **1.** a hard wood with a satiny texture, used in fine furniture. **2.** the East Indian tree yielding this wood.

satire ('sætaɪə) *n.* **1.** a work in which topical issues, folly, or evil are held up to scorn by means of ridicule. **2.** the use of ridicule or irony to create such an effect. [Latin *satira* a mixture] —**satirical** (sə'tɪrɪkᵊl) *adj.*

satirist ('sætərɪst) *n.* **1.** a writer of satire. **2.** a person who uses satire.

satirize *or* **-rise** ('sætəˌraɪz) *vb.* to ridicule (a person or thing) by means of satire. —ˌsatiri'zation *or* -ri'sation *n.*

satisfaction (ˌsætɪs'fækʃən) *n.* **1.** a satisfying or being satisfied. **2.** the pleasure obtained from the fulfilment of a desire. **3.** something that brings fulfilment. **4.** compensation for a wrong done.

satisfactory (ˌsætɪs'fæktrɪ) *adj.* **1.** adequate or suitable; acceptable. **2.** giving satisfaction. —ˌsatis'factorily *adv.*

satisfy ('sætɪsˌfaɪ) *vb.* **-fying, -fied. 1.** to fulfil the desires or needs of (a person). **2.** to provide amply for (a need or desire). **3.** to convince. **4.** to dispel (a doubt). **5.** to fulfil the requirements of; comply with: *you must satisfy the terms of your lease.* [Latin *satis* enough + *facere* to make] —'**satis,fiable** *adj.* —'**satis,fying** *adj.*

satrap ('sætrəp) *n.* **1.** (in ancient Persia) a provincial governor. **2.** a subordinate ruler. [Old Persian *khshathrapāvan,* lit.: protector of the land]

satsuma (sæt'suːmə) *n.* a small loose-skinned variety of orange with easily separable segments. [*Satsuma,* former province of Japan]

saturate ('sætʃəˌreɪt) *vb.* **1.** to soak completely. **2.** to fill so completely that no more can be added: *the police saturated the area with photographs of the wanted man.* **3.** *Chem.* to combine (a substance) or (of a substance) to be combined with the greatest possible amount of another substance. [Latin *saturāre*]

saturation (ˌsætʃə'reɪʃən) *n.* a saturating or being saturated.

saturation point *n.* **1.** the point at which the maximum amount of a substance has

been absorbed. **2.** the point at which some capacity is at its fullest; limit: *the market has reached saturation point.*

Saturday ('sætədɪ) *n.* the seventh and last day of the week. [Latin *Saturnī diēs* day of Saturn]

Saturn ('sætən) *n.* **1.** the Roman god of agriculture. **2.** the sixth planet from the sun, second largest in the solar system, around which revolve concentric rings.

Saturnalia (ˌsætə'neɪlɪə) *n., pl.* **-lia** *or* **-lias. 1.** the ancient Roman festival of Saturn, renowned for its unrestrained merry-making. **2.** (*sometimes not cap.*) a period of wild revelry. [Latin *Sāturnālis* relating to Saturn]

saturnine ('sætəˌnaɪn) *adj.* having a gloomy temperament or appearance. [Latin *Sāturnus* Saturn, from the gloomy influence attributed to the planet]

satyr ('sætə) *n.* **1.** *Greek myth.* a lecherous woodland god represented as having a man's body with the ears, horns, tail, and legs of a goat. **2.** a man who has strong sexual desires. [Greek *saturos*]

sauce (sɔːs) *n.* **1.** any liquid or semiliquid preparation eaten with food to enhance its flavour. **2.** anything that adds interest or zest. **3.** *Informal.* impudent language or behaviour. [Latin *salsus* salted]

sauce boat *n.* a boat-shaped container for serving sauce in.

saucepan ('sɔːspən) *n.* a metal pan with a long handle and often a lid, used for cooking food.

saucer ('sɔːsə) *n.* **1.** a small round dish on which a cup is set. **2.** something shaped like a saucer. [Old French *saussier*] —'**saucerful** *n.*

saucy ('sɔːsɪ) *adj.* **saucier, sauciest. 1.** impertinent. **2.** pert; jaunty: *a saucy hat.* —'**sauciness** *n.*

sauerkraut ('saʊəˌkraʊt) *n.* finely shredded cabbage which has been fermented in brine. [German *sauer* sour + *Kraut* cabbage]

sault (suː) *n. Canad.* a waterfall or rapids. [French *saut* a leap]

sauna ('sɔːnə) *n.* **1.** a Finnish-style hot steam bath, usually followed by a cold plunge. **2.** the place in which such a bath is taken. [Finnish]

saunter ('sɔːntə) *vb.* **1.** to walk in a casual manner; stroll. ~*n.* **2.** a leisurely pace or stroll. [origin unknown]

saurian ('sɔːrɪən) *adj.* of or resembling a lizard. [Greek *sauros*]

sausage ('sɒsɪdʒ) *n.* **1.** finely minced meat mixed with fat, cereal, and seasonings, and packed into a tube-shaped edible casing. **2.** an object shaped like a sausage. **3. not a sausage.** nothing at all. [Old French *saussiche*]

sausage roll *n. Brit.* a roll of sausage meat in pastry.

sauté ('səʊteɪ) *vb.* **-téing** *or* **-téeing, -téed. 1.** to fry (food) quickly in a little fat. ~*n.* **2.** a dish of sautéed food. ~*adj.* **3.** sautéed until lightly brown: *sauté potatoes.* [French: tossed]

savage ('sævɪdʒ) *adj.* **1.** wild; untamed: *savage beasts.* **2.** fierce or cruel: *a savage temper.* **3.** uncivilized; crude: *savage behaviour.* **4.** (of peoples) uncivilized or primitive: *a savage tribe.* **5.** (of terrain) wild and uncultivated. ~*n.* **6.** a member of an uncivilized or primitive society. **7.** a fierce or vicious person or animal. ~*vb.* **8.** to criticize violently. **9.** to attack ferociously and wound. [Latin *silvāticus* belonging to a wood] —'**savagely** *adv.*

savagery ('sævɪdʒrɪ) *n., pl.* -**ries.** viciousness and cruelty.

savanna *or* **savannah** (sə'vænə) *n.* open grasslands, usually with scattered bushes or trees, in or near the tropics. [Spanish *zavana*]

savant ('sævənt) *n.* a learned person; sage. [French] —'**savante** *fem. n.*

save[1] (seɪv) *vb.* **1.** to rescue or preserve (a person or thing) from danger or harm. **2.** to avoid the spending, waste, or loss of (something): *you save time, money, and fuel with a microwave oven.* **3.** to deliver from sin; redeem. **4.** (often foll. by *up*) to set aside or reserve (money or goods) for future use: *I'm saving up for a car.* **5.** to treat with care so as to preserve. **6.** to prevent the necessity for: *he resigned to save them the trouble of sacking him.* **7.** *Sport.* to prevent (a goal) by stopping (a ball or puck). ~*n.* **8.** *Sport.* the act of saving a goal. **9.** *Computers.* an instruction to write information from the memory onto a tape or disk. [Old French *salver*] —'**savable** *or* '**saveable** *adj.* —'**saver** *n.*

save[2] (seɪv) *Archaic.* ~*prep.* **1.** (often foll. by *for*) with the exception of. ~*conj.* **2.** but. [Middle English *sauf*]

save as you earn *n.* (in Britain) a savings scheme operated by the government, in which regular deposits are made into a savings account from a salary.

saveloy ('sævɪˌlɔɪ) *n.* a highly seasoned smoked sausage made from salted pork. [Italian *cervellato*]

saving ('seɪvɪŋ) *adj.* **1.** tending to rescue or preserve. **2. saving grace.** a redeeming or compensating quality. ~*n.* **3.** preservation or redemption. **4.** economy or avoidance of waste. **5.** anything saved. **6.** (*pl.*) money saved for future use. ~*prep.* **7.** with the exception of.

saviour *or U.S.* **savior** ('seɪvjə) *n.* a person who rescues another person or a thing from danger or harm. [Church Latin *Salvātor* the Saviour]

Saviour *or U.S.* **Savior** ('seɪvjə) *n. Christianity.* Jesus Christ, regarded as the saviour of men from sin.

savoir-faire ('sævwɑː'fɛə) *n.* the ability to say and do the right thing in any situation. [French]

savory ('seɪvərɪ) *n., pl.* -**vories.** an aromatic plant whose leaves are used in cooking. [Latin *saturēia*]

savour *or U.S.* **savor** ('seɪvə) *n.* **1.** the taste or smell of something. **2.** a slight but distinctive quality or trace. ~*vb.* **3.** (foll. by *of*) to possess the taste or smell of. **4.** (foll. by *of*) to have a suggestion of: *her*

actions savoured of melodrama. **5.** to relish or enjoy: *he savoured the word as he said it.* [Latin *sapor* taste]

savoury *or U.S.* **savory** ('seɪvərɪ) *adj.* **1.** attractive to the sense of taste or smell. **2.** salty or spicy: *a savoury dish.* **3.** pleasant or acceptable: *the less savoury episodes in her past.* ~*n., pl.* -**ries. 4.** *Chiefly Brit.* a savoury dish served as an hors d'oeuvre or dessert. —'**savouriness** *or U.S.* '**savoriness** *n.*

savoy (sə'vɔɪ) *n.* a cabbage with a compact head and wrinkled leaves. [after the *Savoy* region in France]

savvy ('sævɪ) *Slang.* ~*vb.* -**vying, -vied. 1.** to understand. ~*n.* **2.** understanding or common sense. [corruption of Spanish *sabe* (*usted*) (you) know]

saw[1] (sɔː) *n.* **1.** a cutting tool with a toothed metal blade or edge, either operated by hand or powered by electricity. ~*vb.* **sawing, sawed;** *or* **sawn.** **2.** to cut with or as if with a saw. **3.** to form by sawing. **4.** to move (an object) from side to side as if moving a saw. [Old English *sagu*]

saw[2] (sɔː) *vb.* the past tense of **see**[1].

saw[3] (sɔː) *n.* a wise saying, maxim, or proverb. [Old English *sagu* a saying]

sawdust ('sɔːˌdʌst) *n.* particles of wood formed by sawing.

sawfish ('sɔːˌfɪʃ) *n., pl.* -**fish** *or* -**fishes.** a sharklike ray with a long serrated snout resembling a saw.

sawmill ('sɔːˌmɪl) *n.* a factory where timber is sawn into planks.

sawn (sɔːn) *vb.* a past participle of **saw**[1].

sawn-off *or esp. U.S.* **sawed-off** *adj.* (of a shotgun) having the barrel cut short to make concealment of the weapon easier.

sawyer ('sɔːjə) *n.* a person who saws timber for a living.

sax (sæks) *n. Informal.* short for **saxophone.**

saxifrage ('sæksɪˌfreɪdʒ) *n.* a rock plant with small white, yellow, purple, or pink flowers. [Late Latin *saxifraga*, lit.: rock breaker]

Saxon ('sæksən) *n.* **1.** a member of a West Germanic people who raided and settled parts of Britain in the fifth and sixth centuries A.D. **2.** any of the West Germanic dialects spoken by the ancient Saxons. ~*adj.* **3.** of the ancient Saxons or their language. [Late Latin *Saxon-, Saxo*]

saxophone ('sæksəˌfəʊn) *n.* a keyed single-reed wind instrument with a usually curved metal body. [after Adolphe *Sax*, who invented it] —**saxophonist** (sæk-'sɒfənɪst) *n.*

say (seɪ) *vb.* **saying, said. 1.** to speak or utter. **2.** to express in words; tell: *I can't say what I feel.* **3.** to state (an opinion or fact) positively: *I say you are wrong.* **4.** to indicate or show: *the clock says ten to nine.* **5.** to recite: *to say grace.* **6.** to report or allege: *they say we shall have rain today.* **7.** to suppose: *let us say that he is lying.* **8.** to convey by means of artistic expression: *what does the artist have to say in this picture?* **9.** to make a case for: *there is* *much to be said for it.* **10. go without saying.** to be so obvious as to need no explanation. **11. to say the least.** at the very least. ~*adv.* **12.** approximately: *there were, say, 20 people present.* ~*n.* **13.** for example: *choose a number, say, four.* ~*n.* **14.** the right or chance to speak: *let him have his say.* **15.** authority, esp. to influence a decision: *he has a lot of say.* [Old English *secgan*]

SAYE (in Britain) save as you earn.

saying ('seɪɪŋ) *n.* a maxim, adage, or proverb.

Sb *Chem.* antimony. [New Latin *stibium*]

Sc *Chem.* scandium.

SC South Carolina.

scab (skæb) *n.* **1.** the dried crusty surface of a healing skin wound or sore. **2.** a contagious disease of sheep, caused by a mite. **3.** a fungal disease of plants. **4.** *Disparaging.* a person who refuses to support a trade union's actions, and continues to work during a strike. **5.** a despicable person. ~*vb.* **scabbing, scabbed.** **6.** to become covered with a scab. **7.** *Disparaging.* to work as a scab. [Old English *sceabb*]

scabbard ('skæbəd) *n.* a holder for a sword or dagger. [Middle English *scauberc*]

scabby ('skæbɪ) *adj.* **-bier, -biest.** **1.** *Pathol.* covered with scabs. **2.** *Informal.* despicable. —'**scabbiness** *n.*

scabies ('skeɪbɪz) *n.* a contagious skin infection caused by a mite, characterized by intense itching. [Latin *scabere* to scratch]

scabious ('skeɪbɪəs) *n.* a plant with showy blue, red, or whitish dome-shaped flower heads. [Medieval Latin *scabiōsa herba* the scabies plant]

scabrous ('skeɪbrəs) *adj.* **1.** rough and scaly. **2.** indecent or lewd: *scabrous humour.* [Latin *scaber* rough]

scaffold ('skæfəld) *n.* **1.** a temporary framework used to support workmen and materials during the construction or repair of a building. **2.** a raised wooden platform on which criminals are executed. [Old French *eschaffaut*]

scaffolding ('skæfəldɪŋ) *n.* **1.** a scaffold or scaffolds. **2.** the building materials used to make scaffolds.

scalar ('skeɪlə) *n.* **1.** a quantity, such as time or temperature, that has magnitude but not direction. ~*adj.* **2.** having magnitude but not direction. [Latin *scāla* ladder]

scalawag ('skælə,wæg) *n.* same as **scallywag**.

scald (skɔːld) *vb.* **1.** to burn with hot liquid or steam. **2.** to use boiling water on, so as to sterilize. **3.** to heat (a liquid) almost to boiling point. ~*n.* **4.** a burn caused by scalding. [Late Latin *excaldāre* to wash in warm water]

scale[1] (skeɪl) *n.* **1.** one of the thin flat horny plates covering the bodies of fishes and reptiles. **2.** a thin flat piece or flake. **3.** a coating which sometimes forms in kettles and hot-water pipes in areas where the water is hard. **4.** tartar formed on the

teeth. ~*vb.* **5.** to remove the scales or coating from. **6.** to peel off in flakes or scales. **7.** to cover or become covered with scales. [Old French *escale*] —'**scaly** *adj.*

scale[2] (skeɪl) *n.* **1.** (*often pl.*) a machine or device for weighing. **2.** one of the pans of a balance. **3. tip** or **turn the scales.** a. to have a decisive influence. **b.** (foll. by *at*) to amount in weight to. [Old Norse *skāl* bowl]

scale[3] (skeɪl) *n.* **1.** a sequence of marks at regular intervals, used as a reference in making measurements. **2.** a measuring instrument with such a scale. **3.** the ratio between the size of something real and that of a representation of it: *the map has a scale of one centimetre to a kilometre.* **4.** a series of degrees or graded system of things: *a wage scale for carpenters.* **5.** a relative degree or extent: *he entertained on a grand scale.* **6.** *Music.* a sequence of notes taken in ascending or descending order, esp. within the compass of one octave. **7.** *Maths.* the notation of a given number system: *the decimal scale.* ~*vb.* **8.** to climb to the top of (a height) by or as if by a ladder. **9.** (usually foll. by *up* or *down*) to increase or reduce proportionately in size. [Latin *scāla* ladder]

scalene ('skeɪliːn) *adj. Maths.* (of a triangle) having all sides of unequal length. [Greek *skalēnos*]

scallion ('skæljən) *n.* an onion, such as the spring onion, that has a small bulb and long leaves and is eaten in salads. [Anglo-French *scalun*]

scallop ('skɒləp, 'skæl-) *n.* **1.** an edible marine mollusc with two fluted fan-shaped shells. **2.** a single shell of this mollusc. **3.** one of a series of curves along an edge. ~*vb.* **4.** to decorate (an edge) with scallops. [Old French *escalope* shell] —'**scalloping** *n.*

scallywag ('skælɪ,wæg) *n. Informal.* a scamp; rascal. [origin unknown]

scalp (skælp) *n.* **1.** *Anat.* the skin and hair covering the top of the head. **2.** (among North American Indians) a part of this removed as a trophy from a slain enemy. ~*vb.* **3.** to cut the scalp from. **4.** *Informal, chiefly U.S.* to buy and resell so as to make a high or quick profit. [prob. from Old Norse]

scalpel ('skælp'l) *n.* a small surgical knife with a very sharp thin blade. [Latin *scalper* a knife]

scamp (skæmp) *n.* a mischievous person, esp. a child. [prob. from Middle Dutch *schampen* to decamp]

scamper ('skæmpə) *vb.* **1.** to run about hurriedly or quickly. ~*n.* **2.** the act of scampering. [see SCAMP]

scampi ('skæmpɪ) *n.* (*usually functioning as sing.*) large prawns, usually eaten fried in breadcrumbs. [Italian]

scan (skæn) *vb.* **scanning, scanned.** **1.** to scrutinize minutely. **2.** to glance at quickly. **3.** *Prosody.* to analyse (verse) by examining its rhythmical structure. **4.** *Prosody.* (of a line or verse) to be metrically correct. **5.** to examine or search (an area) by systematically moving a beam of light or electrons, or a radar or sonar beam over it. **6.** *Med.* to obtain an image of (a part of the body) by means of ultrasound or a scanner. ~*n.* **7.** an instance of scanning. [Latin *scandere* to climb]

scandal ('skænd'l) *n.* **1.** a disgraceful action or event: *his negligence was a scandal.* **2.** shame or outrage arising from a disgraceful action or event. **3.** malicious gossip. [Greek *skandalon* a trap] —'**scandalous** *adj.* —'**scandalously** *adv.*

scandalize *or* **-ise** ('skændə,laɪz) *vb.* to shock, as by improper behaviour.

scandalmonger ('skænd'l,mʌŋgə) *n.* a person who spreads or enjoys scandal or gossip.

Scandinavian (,skændɪ'neɪvɪən) *adj.* **1.** of Scandinavia (Norway, Sweden, Denmark, and Iceland), its inhabitants, or their languages. ~*n.* **2.** a person from Scandinavia. **3.** the group of Germanic languages spoken by the Scandinavians.

scandium ('skændɪəm) *n.* a rare silvery-white metallic element. Symbol: Sc [Latin *Scandia* Scandinavia, where discovered]

scanner ('skænə) *n.* **1.** an aerial or similar device designed to transmit or receive signals, esp. radar signals. **2.** a device used in medical diagnosis to obtain an image of an internal organ or part.

scansion ('skænʃən) *n.* the metrical scanning of verse.

scant (skænt) *adj.* scarcely sufficient; meagre: *he paid her scant attention.* [Old Norse *skamt*]

scanty ('skæntɪ) *adj.* **scantier, scantiest.** **1.** limited; barely enough. **2.** inadequate. —'**scantily** *adv.* —'**scantiness** *n.*

scapegoat ('skeɪp,gəʊt) *n.* a person made to bear the blame for others. [*escape* + *goat*, coined to translate Biblical Hebrew *azāzēl* (prob.) goat for Azazel, mistakenly thought to mean "goat that escapes"]

scapula ('skæpjʊlə) *n., pl.* **-lae** (-liː) *or* **-las.** the technical name for **shoulder blade.** [Late Latin: shoulder]

scapular ('skæpjʊlə) *adj.* **1.** *Anat.* of the scapula. ~*n.* **2.** a loose sleeveless garment worn by monks over their habits.

scar¹ (skɑː) *n.* **1.** a mark left on the skin following the healing of a wound. **2.** a permanent effect on a person's character resulting from emotional distress. **3.** a mark on a plant where a leaf was formerly attached. **4.** a mark of damage. ~*vb.* **scarring, scarred. 5.** to mark or become marked with a scar. [Greek *eskhara* scab]

scar² (skɑː) *n.* a bare craggy rock formation. [Old Norse *sker* low reef]

scarab ('skærəb) *n.* **1.** the black dung-beetle, regarded by the ancient Egyptians as divine. **2.** an image or carving of this beetle. [Latin *scarabaeus*]

scarce (skɛəs) *adj.* **1.** not common; rarely found. **2.** insufficient to meet the demand. **3. make oneself scarce.** *Informal.* to go away. ~*adv.* **4.** *Archaic or literary.* scarcely. [Old French *scars*]

scarcely ('skɛəslɪ) *adv.* **1.** hardly at all. **2.** Often used ironically. probably or definitely not: *that is scarcely justification for your actions.*

scarcity ('skɛəsɪtɪ) *n., pl.* **-ties.** inadequate supply.

scare (skɛə) *vb.* **1.** to fill or be filled with fear or alarm. **2.** (foll. by *away* or *off*) to drive away by frightening. ~*n.* **3.** a sudden attack of fear or alarm: *I had a terrible scare.* **4.** a period of general fear or alarm: *a rabies scare.* [Old Norse *skirra*]

scarecrow ('skɛə,krəʊ) *n.* **1.** an object, usually in the shape of a man, made out of sticks and old clothes to scare birds away from crops. **2.** *Informal.* a raggedly dressed person.

scaremonger ('skɛə,mʌŋgə) *n.* a person who starts or spreads rumours of disaster to frighten people. —'**scare,mongering** *n.*

scarf¹ (skɑːf) *n., pl.* **scarfs** *or* **scarves.** a square, triangular, or long narrow piece of cloth worn around the head, neck, or shoulders. [origin unknown]

scarf² (skɑːf) *n., pl.* **scarfs. 1.** a joint between two pieces of timber made by notching the ends and strapping or gluing the two pieces together. ~*vb.* **2.** to join (two pieces of timber) by means of a scarf. [prob. from Old Norse]

scarify ('skɛərɪ,faɪ) *vb.* **-fying, -fied. 1.** *Surgery.* to make slight incisions in (the skin). **2.** *Agriculture.* to break up and loosen (topsoil). **3.** to wound with harsh criticism. [Latin *scarifāre* to scratch open] —,**scarifi'cation** *n.*

scarlatina (,skɑːlə'tiːnə) *n.* the technical name for **scarlet fever.** [Italian *scarlatto* scarlet]

scarlet ('skɑːlɪt) *adj.* bright orange-red. [Old French *escarlate* fine cloth]

scarlet fever *n.* an acute contagious disease characterized by fever, a sore throat, and a red rash on the body.

scarp (skɑːp) *n.* **1.** a steep slope or ridge of rock. **2.** *Fortifications.* the side of a ditch cut nearest to a rampart. [Italian *scarpa*]

scarper ('skɑːpə) *vb. Brit. slang.* to run away or escape. [origin unknown]

scarves (skɑːvz) *n.* a plural of **scarf¹.**

scary ('skɛərɪ) *adj.* **scarier, scariest.** *Informal.* causing fear or alarm.

scat¹ (skæt) *vb.* **scatting, scatted.** (*usually imperative*) *Informal.* to go away in haste. [origin unknown]

scat² (skæt) *n.* **1.** a type of jazz singing characterized by improvised vocal sounds instead of words. ~*vb.* **scatting, scatted. 2.** to sing jazz in this way. [perhaps imit.]

scathing ('skeɪðɪŋ) *adj.* harshly critical; scornful. [Old Norse *skathi* harm] —'**scathingly** *adv.*

scatology (skæ'tɒlədʒɪ) *n.* preoccupation with obscenity, esp. with references to excrement. [Greek *skat-* excrement + -LOGY] —**scatological** (,skætə'lɒdʒɪk'l) *adj.*

scatter ('skætə) *vb.* **1.** to throw about in various directions: *his possessions were scattered all over the room.* **2.** to separate and move in various directions; disperse: *the crowd scattered when the alarm went off.* ~*n.* **3.** the act of scattering. **4.** a number of objects scattered about. [prob. var. of *shatter*]

scatterbrain ('skætə‚breɪn) *n*. a person who is incapable of serious thought or concentration. —'**scatter**‚**brained** *adj*.

scatty ('skætɪ) *adj*. **-tier, -tiest.** *Brit. informal.* empty-headed or thoughtless. [from *scatterbrained*] —'**scattiness** *n*.

scavenge ('skævɪndʒ) *vb*. to search for (anything usable) among discarded material.

scavenger ('skævɪndʒə) *n*. **1.** a person who collects things discarded by others. **2.** any animal that feeds on discarded or decaying matter. [Old French *escauwer* to scrutinize]

SCE (in Scotland) Scottish Certificate of Education.

scenario (sɪ'nɑːrɪ‚əʊ) *n., pl.* **-narios. 1.** a summary of the plot and characters of a play or film. **2.** an imagined sequence of future events. [Italian]

scene (siːn) *n*. **1.** the place where an action or event, real or imaginary, occurs. **2.** an incident or situation, real or imaginary, esp. as described or represented. **3.** a division of an act of a play, in which the setting is fixed and the action is continuous. **4.** *Films.* a shot or series of shots that constitutes a unit of the action. **5.** the backcloths or screens used to represent a location in a play or film set. **6.** the view of a place or landscape. **7.** a display of emotion: *don't make a scene in front of everyone*. **8.** *Informal.* a specific activity or interest: *the fashion scene*. **9. behind the scenes. a.** backstage. **b.** in secret or in private. [Greek *skēnē* tent, stage]

scenery ('siːnərɪ) *n., pl.* **-eries. 1.** the natural features of a landscape. **2.** *Theatre.* the painted backcloths or screens used to represent a location in a theatre or studio.

scenic ('siːnɪk) *adj*. **1.** of or having beautiful natural scenery: *a scenic drive*. **2.** of the stage or stage scenery: *scenic design*.

scent (sɛnt) *n*. **1.** a distinctive smell, esp. a pleasant one. **2.** a smell left in passing, by which a person or animal may be traced. **3.** a trail or series of clues by which something is followed: *on the scent of something big*. **4.** perfume. ~*vb*. **5.** to become aware of by smelling. **6.** to suspect: *I scent foul play*. **7.** to fill with odour or fragrance. [Old French *sentir* to sense] —'**scented** *adj*.

sceptic *or U.S.* **skeptic** ('skɛptɪk) *n*. **1.** a person who habitually doubts generally accepted beliefs. **2.** a person who mistrusts people or ideas in general. [Greek *skeptikos* one who reflects upon] —'**sceptical** *adj*. —'**sceptically** *adv*. —'**scepticism** *n*.

sceptre *or U.S.* **scepter** ('sɛptə) *n*. a ceremonial staff held by a monarch as the symbol of authority. [Greek *skeptron* staff] —'**sceptred** *or U.S.* '**sceptered** *adj*.

schedule ('ʃɛdjuːl; *also, esp. U.S.* 'skɛdʒuːl) *n*. **1.** a timed plan of procedure for a project. **2.** a list of details or items: *a*

schedule of fixed prices. **3.** a timetable. ~*vb*. **4.** to make a schedule of or place in a schedule. **5.** to plan to occur at a certain time. [Latin *scheda* sheet of paper]

schema ('skiːmə) *n., pl.* **-mata** (-mətə). a plan, diagram, or scheme. [Greek: form]

schematic (skɪ'mætɪk) *adj*. of or having the nature of a diagram or plan. —**sche-**'**matically** *adv*.

schematize *or* **-ise** ('skiːmə‚taɪz) *vb*. to form into or arrange in a scheme.

scheme (skiːm) *n*. **1.** a systematic plan for a course of action. **2.** a systematic arrangement of parts or features: *colour scheme*. **3.** a secret plot. **4.** a chart, diagram, or outline. **5.** *Chiefly Brit.* a plan formally adopted by a government or organization: *the state pension scheme*. ~*vb*. **6.** to plot (for) in an underhand manner. [Greek *skhēma* form] —'**schemer** *n*. —'**scheming** *adj., n*.

scherzo ('skɛətsəʊ) *n., pl.* **-zos** *or* **-zi** (-tsiː). a brisk lively piece of music, often the second or third movement in a sonata or symphony. [Italian: joke]

schilling ('ʃɪlɪŋ) *n*. the standard monetary unit of Austria. [from German]

schism ('sɪzəm, 'skɪz-) *n*. the division of a group, esp. a religious group, into opposing factions, due to differences in doctrine. [Greek *skhizein* to split] —**schis**'**matic** *adj*.

schist (ʃɪst) *n*. a metamorphic rock that can be split into thin layers. [Greek *skhizein* to split]

schizo ('skɪtsəʊ) *Informal.* ~*adj*. **1.** schizophrenic. ~*n., pl.* **-os. 2.** a schizophrenic person.

schizoid ('skɪtsɔɪd) *adj*. **1.** *Psychol.* having a personality disorder characterized by extreme shyness and oversensitivity. **2.** *Informal.* characterized by conflicting or contradictory ideas or attitudes. ~*n*. **3.** a person who has a schizoid personality.

schizophrenia (‚skɪtsəʊ'friːnɪə) *n*. **1.** a psychotic disorder characterized by withdrawal from reality, hallucinations, or emotional instability. **2.** *Informal.* behaviour that seems to be motivated by contradictory or conflicting principles. [Greek *skhizein* to split + *phrēn* mind] —**schizophrenic** (‚skɪtsəʊ'frɛnɪk) *adj., n*.

schmaltz (ʃmɔːlts) *n*. excessive sentimentality, esp. in music. [Yiddish: melted fat] —'**schmaltzy** *adj*.

schnapps (ʃnæps) *n*. (in Europe) any strong dry spirit, such as Dutch potato gin. [German *Schnaps*]

schnitzel ('ʃnɪtsəl) *n*. a thin slice of meat, esp. veal. [German: cutlet]

scholar ('skɒlə) *n*. **1.** a learned person. **2.** a person who studies; pupil. **3.** a student receiving a scholarship. [Latin *schola* SCHOOL] —'**scholarly** *adj*.

scholarship ('skɒləʃɪp) *n*. **1.** academic achievement; learning gained by serious study. **2.** financial aid provided for a scholar because of academic merit.

scholastic (skə'læstɪk) *adj*. **1.** of schools, scholars, or education. **2.** (*often cap.*) of or relating to scholasticism. ~*n*. **3.** a scholarly person. **4.** (*often cap.*) a disciple or adherent of scholasticism. [Greek *skholastikos* devoted to learning]

scholasticism (skə'læstɪ,sɪzəm) n. (*sometimes cap.*) the system of philosophy, theology, and teaching that dominated medieval Europe and was based on the writings of Aristotle.

school[1] (sku:l) n. **1.** an institution or building at which people, usually children and young people, are taught. **2.** a faculty or department specializing in a particular subject: *a law school.* **3.** the staff and pupils of a school. **4.** a regular session of instruction in a school: *he stayed after school to do extra work.* **5.** a place or sphere of activity that instructs: *the school of hard knocks.* **6.** a group of artists, writers, or thinkers, linked by the same style, teachers, or methods. **7.** *Informal.* a group assembled for a common purpose, such as gambling: *a card school.* ~vb. **8.** to educate in or as in a school. **9.** to discipline or control. [Greek *skholē* leisure spent in the pursuit of knowledge]

school[2] (sku:l) n. a group of fishes or other aquatic animals that swim together. [Old English *scolu*]

schoolboy ('sku:l,bɔɪ) or (*fem.*) **schoolgirl** n. a child attending school.

schoolhouse ('sku:l,haus) n. **1.** a building used as a school. **2.** a house attached to a school.

schooling ('sku:lɪŋ) n. education, esp. when received at school.

schoolmarm ('sku:l,mɑ:m) n. *Informal.* **1.** a woman schoolteacher. **2.** any woman considered to be prim or old-fashioned.

schoolmaster ('sku:l,mɑ:stə) or (*fem.*) **schoolmistress** n. a person who teaches in or runs a school.

schoolteacher ('sku:l,ti:tʃə) n. a person who teaches in a school.

school year n. **1.** a twelve-month period, usually of three terms, during which pupils remain in the same class. **2.** the time during this period when the school is open.

schooner ('sku:nə) n. **1.** a sailing vessel with at least two masts, rigged fore-and-aft. **2.** *Brit.* a large glass for sherry. **3.** *U.S., Canad., Austral., & N.Z.* a large glass for beer. [origin unknown]

schottische (ʃɒ'ti:ʃ) n. **1.** a 19th-century German dance resembling a slow polka. **2.** music for this dance. [German *der schottische Tanz* the Scottish dance]

schuss (ʃus) *Skiing.* ~n. **1.** a straight high-speed downhill run. ~vb. **2.** to perform a schuss. [from German]

schwa (ʃwɑ) n. **1.** the neutral vowel sound occurring in unstressed syllables in English, as in *around* and *sofa.* **2.** the symbol (ə) used to represent this sound. [Hebrew *shewā*]

sciatic (saɪ'ætɪk) adj. **1.** *Anat.* of the hip or the hipbone. **2.** of or afflicted with sciatica. [Greek *iskhia* hip joint]

sciatica (saɪ'ætɪkə) n. a form of neuralgia causing intense pain along the nerve run-

ning from the back of the thigh down to the calf of the leg.

science ('saɪəns) n. **1.** the systematic study of the nature and behaviour of the physical universe, based on observation, experiment, and measurement. **2.** the knowledge so obtained. **3.** any particular branch of this knowledge: *medical science.* **4.** any body of knowledge organized in a systematic manner. **5.** skill or technique. [Latin *scientia* knowledge]

science fiction n. a literary genre that makes imaginative use of scientific knowledge or theories.

science park n. an area where scientific research and commercial development are carried on in cooperation.

scientific (,saɪən'tɪfɪk) adj. **1.** of, derived from, or used in science: *scientific equipment.* **2.** conforming with the systematic methods used in science. —,**scien'tifically** adv.

scientist ('saɪəntɪst) n. a person who studies or practises a science.

sci-fi ('saɪ'faɪ) n. short for **science fiction.**

scilicet ('sɪlɪ,sɛt) adv. namely; that is to say: used esp. in explaining an obscure text or supplying a missing word. [Latin]

scimitar ('sɪmɪtə) n. a curved oriental sword. [prob. from Persian *shimshīr*]

scintilla (sɪn'tɪlə) n. a minute amount; hint or trace. [Latin: a spark]

scintillate ('sɪntɪ,leɪt) vb. **1.** to give off (sparks); sparkle. **2.** to talk or act with animation or brilliance. [Latin *scintilla* a spark] —'**scinti,lating** adj. —,scintil-'lation n.

scintillation counter n. an instrument for measuring the intensity of high-energy radiation, by counting the flashes of light produced when particles collide with a fluorescent material.

scion ('saɪən) n. **1.** a descendant or young member of a family. **2.** a shoot of a plant used to form a graft. [Old French *cion*]

scissors ('sɪzəz) pl. n. a cutting instrument held in one hand, with two crossed blades pivoted so that they close together on what is to be cut. [Old French *cisoires*]

sclera ('sklɪərə) n. the tough white fibrous membrane that forms the outer covering of the eyeball. [Greek *sklēros* hard]

sclerosis (sklɪə'rəusɪs) n., pl. **-ses** (-si:z). *Pathol.* an abnormal hardening or thickening of body tissues, esp. of the nervous system or the inner wall of arteries. [Greek *sklērōsis* a hardening]

sclerotic (sklɪə'rɒtɪk) adj. **1.** of or relating to the sclera. **2.** of, relating to, or having sclerosis.

scoff[1] (skɒf) vb. **1.** (often foll. by *at*) to speak contemptuously (about); mock. ~n. **2.** an expression of derision; jeer. [prob. from Old Norse] —'**scoffing** adj., n.

scoff[2] (skɒf) *Informal, chiefly Brit.* ~vb. **1.** to eat (food) fast and greedily. ~n. **2.** food. [var. of *scaff* food]

scold (skəuld) vb. **1.** to find fault with or reprimand (a person) harshly. **2.** to use harsh or abusive language. ~n. **3.** a person, esp. a woman, who constantly scolds. [from Old Norse] —**'scolding** n.

scollop ('skɒləp) n., vb. same as **scallop**.

sconce (skɒns) n. a bracket fixed to a wall for holding candles or lights. [Late Latin *absconsa* dark lantern]

scone (skɒn, skəʊn) n. a light doughy cake made from flour and fat, cooked in an oven or on a griddle. [Scot.]

scoop (skuːp) n. **1.** any of various spoon-like tools with a deep bowl, used for handling loose or soft materials such as flour or ice cream. **2.** the deep shovel of a mechanical digger. **3.** the quantity taken up by a scoop. **4.** the act of scooping or dredging. **5.** a news story reported in one newspaper before all the others. ~vb. **6.** (often foll. by *up*) to take up and remove (an object or substance) with or as if with a scoop. **7.** (often foll. by *out*) to hollow out with or as if with a scoop. **8.** to beat (rival newspapers) in uncovering a news item. [Germanic]

scoot (skuːt) vb. to go or leave quickly. [origin unknown]

scooter ('skuːtə) n. **1.** a child's toy vehicle consisting of a low footboard mounted between two small wheels with a raised handlebar for steering. **2.** same as **motor scooter**.

scope (skəʊp) n. **1.** opportunity for exercising the faculties or abilities: *there is no scope for originality in this job.* **2.** range of view or grasp: *these ideas are beyond my scope.* **3.** the area covered by an activity or topic: *the scope of his thesis was vast.* [Greek *skopos* target]

scorbutic (skɔːˈbjuːtɪk) adj. of or having scurvy. [Medieval Latin *scorbūtus*]

scorch (skɔːtʃ) vb. **1.** to burn or become burnt slightly on the surface. **2.** to wither or parch from exposure to heat. **3.** *Informal.* to criticize harshly. ~n. **4.** a slight burn. **5.** a mark caused by the application of too great a heat. [prob. from Old Norse *skorpna* to shrivel up] —**'scorching** adj.

scorcher ('skɔːtʃə) n. *Informal.* a very hot day.

score (skɔː) n. **1.** the total number of points made by a side or individual in a game. **2.** the act of scoring a point or points: *there was no score at the end of the first half.* **3. the score.** *Informal.* the actual situation: *you don't know the score.* **4.** a group or set of twenty: *three score years and ten.* **5.** (usually *pl.*; foll. by *of*) lots: *I have scores of things to do.* **6.** *Music.* the printed form of a piece of music in which the parts for each musician are printed one under the other on separate staves. **7. a.** the incidental music for a film or play. **b.** the songs and music for a stage or film musical. **8.** a mark or scratch. **9.** a record of amounts due. **10.** an amount recorded as due. **11.** a reason: *the book was rejected on the score of length.* **12.** a grievance: *I have a score to settle with you.* **13. over the score.** *Informal.* excessive; unfair. ~vb. **14.** to gain (a point or points) in a game or contest. **15.** to make a total score of. **16.** to keep a record of the score (of). **17.** to be worth (a certain

number of points) in a game: *red aces score twenty.* **18.** to make cuts or lines in or on. **19.** *Slang.* to obtain something desired, esp. to purchase an illegal drug. **20.** *Slang.* to be successful in seducing someone. **21.** to arrange (a piece of music) for specific instruments or voices. **22.** to write the music for (a film or play). **23.** to achieve (success or an advantage): *your idea scored with the boss.* [Old English *scora*] —**'scorer** n.

scoreboard ('skɔːˌbɔːd) n. *Sport.* a board for displaying the score of a game or match.

scorecard ('skɔːˌkɑːd) n. **1.** a card on which scores are recorded in games such as golf. **2.** a card identifying the players in a sports match, esp. cricket.

score off vb. to gain an advantage at someone else's expense.

scoria ('skɔːrɪə) n., pl. **-riae** (-rɪˌiː). **1.** a mass of solidified lava containing many cavities. **2.** refuse left after ore has been smelted. [Latin: dross]

scorn (skɔːn) n. **1.** open contempt for a person or thing. ~vb. **2.** to treat with contempt or derision. **3.** to reject with contempt. [Old French *escharnir*] —**'scornful** adj. —**'scornfully** adv.

Scorpio ('skɔːpɪˌəʊ) n. *Astrol.* the eighth sign of the zodiac; the Scorpion. [Latin]

scorpion ('skɔːpɪən) n. a creature of warm dry regions, which has an insect-like body with a long tail ending in a venomous sting. [Greek *skorpios*]

Scot (skɒt) n. a person from Scotland.

Scot. 1. Scotland. **2.** Scottish.

scotch (skɒtʃ) vb. **1.** to put an end to; crush: *bad weather scotched our plans.* **2.** to wound without killing. [origin unknown]

Scotch [1] (skɒtʃ) *Not universally accepted.* ~adj. **1.** same as **Scottish.** ~n. **2.** the. (*functioning as pl.*) the Scots or their language.

Scotch [2] (skɒtʃ) n. whisky distilled in Scotland from fermented malted barley.

Scotch broth n. *Brit.* a thick soup made from mutton or beef stock, vegetables, and pearl barley.

Scotch egg n. *Brit.* a hard-boiled egg enclosed in a layer of sausage meat, covered in egg and crumbs, and fried.

Scotch mist n. **1.** a heavy wet mist. **2.** drizzle.

Scotch terrier n. same as **Scottish terrier.**

scot-free adv., adj. without harm or punishment. [obs. *scot* a tax]

Scotland Yard ('skɒtlənd) n. the headquarters of the police force of metropolitan London.

Scots (skɒts) adj. **1.** of Scotland, its people or their language. ~n. **2.** any of the English dialects spoken or written in Scotland.

Scotsman ('skɒtsmən) or (*fem.*) **Scotswoman** n., pl. **-men** or **-women.** a person from Scotland.

Scots pine n. **1.** a hardy coniferous tree

of Europe and Asia, with blue-green needle-like leaves. **2.** the wood of this tree.

Scotticism ('skɒtɪ,sɪzəm) *n.* a Scottish expression or word.

Scottie ('skɒtɪ) *n., pl.* **-ties.** *Informal.* a Scottish terrier.

Scottish ('skɒtɪʃ) *adj.* of Scotland, its people, or their language.

Scottish terrier *n.* a small but sturdy long-haired terrier, usually with a black coat.

scoundrel ('skaʊndrəl) *n.* a worthless or villainous person. [origin unknown]

scour[1] ('skaʊə) *vb.* **1.** to clean or polish (a surface) by hard rubbing with something rough. **2.** to clear (a channel) by the force of water. ~*n.* **3.** the act of scouring. [Old French *escurer*] —'**scourer** *n.*

scour[2] ('skaʊə) *vb.* **1.** to make a thorough and energetic search of: *we have scoured the archives for information.* **2.** to move swiftly or energetically over (land), as in search or pursuit. [Old Norse *skūr*]

scourge (skɜːdʒ) *n.* **1.** a person who or thing which causes affliction or suffering. **2.** a whip used for inflicting punishment. ~*vb.* **3.** to whip. **4.** to afflict. [Latin *excoriāre* to whip]

Scouse (skaʊs) *Brit. informal.* ~*n.* **1.** a person from Liverpool. **2.** the Liverpool dialect. ~*adj.* **3.** of or from Liverpool. [from *lobscouse* a sailor's stew]

scout (skaʊt) *n.* **1.** *Mil.* a person or unit sent to reconnoitre the position of the enemy. **2.** same as **talent scout.** **3.** the act or an instance of scouting. ~*vb.* **4.** to examine or observe (something) in order to obtain information. **5.** (foll. by *about* or *around*) to go in search of. [Old French *ascouter* to listen to]

Scout *or* **scout** (skaʊt) *n.* a boy who is a member of the Scout Association, founded in 1908 by Lord Baden-Powell to promote outdoor activities and develop character. —'**Scouting** *n.*

scow (skaʊ) *n.* a flat-bottomed boat used for carrying freight. [Low German *schalde*]

scowl (skaʊl) *vb.* **1.** to draw one's brows together in an angry or bad-tempered expression. ~*n.* **2.** an angry or bad-tempered expression. [prob. from Old Norse]

scrabble ('skræb²l) *vb.* **1.** (foll. by *about* or *at*) to scrape at or grope for with hands, feet, or claws. **2.** (foll. by *for*) to struggle to gain possession of. ~*n.* **3.** a scrabbling. [Middle Dutch *schrabbelen*]

Scrabble ('skræb²l) *n. Trademark.* a board game in which words are formed by placing letter tiles in a pattern similar to a crossword puzzle.

scrag (skræg) *n.* **1.** a thin or scrawny person or animal. **2.** the thin end of a neck of veal or mutton. ~*vb.* **3.** **scragging,** **scragged.** **3.** *Informal.* to wring the neck of. [perhaps var. of *crag*]

scraggy ('skrægɪ) *adj.* **-gier, -giest.** thin or scrawny. —'**scragginess** *n.*

scram[1] (skræm) *vb.* **scramming,**

scrammed. (*often imperative*) *Informal.* to go away hastily. [from *scramble*]

scram[2] (skræm) *n.* **1.** an emergency shutdown of a nuclear reactor. ~*vb.* **scramming,** **scrammed.** **2.** (of a nuclear reactor) to shut down or be shut down in an emergency. [perhaps from SCRAM[1]]

scramble ('skræmb²l) *vb.* **1.** to climb or crawl hurriedly, esp. by using the hands to aid movement. **2.** to proceed hurriedly or in a disorderly fashion. **3.** (often foll. by *for*) to compete with others, often in a disordered manner. **4.** to jumble together in a haphazard manner. **5.** to cook (eggs that have been whisked up with milk) in a pan. **6.** *Mil.* (of a crew or aircraft) to take off quickly in an emergency. **7.** to make (speech) unintelligible during transmission by means of an electronic scrambler. ~*n.* **8.** the act of scrambling. **9.** a climb or trek over difficult ground. **10.** a disorderly struggle, as to gain possession of something. **11.** *Mil.* an immediate takeoff of crew or aircraft in an emergency. **12.** *Brit.* a motorcycle race across rough open ground. [blend of *scrabble* & *ramp*]

scrambler ('skræmblə) *n.* an electronic device that makes broadcast or telephone messages unintelligible without a special receiver.

scrap[1] (skræp) *n.* **1.** a small piece of something larger; fragment. **2.** waste material or used articles, often collected and reprocessed. **3.** (*pl.*) pieces of leftover food. ~*vb.* **scrapping, scrapped.** **4.** to discard as useless. [Old Norse *skrap*]

scrap[2] (skræp) *Informal.* ~*n.* **1.** a fight or argument. ~*vb.* **scrapping, scrapped.** **2.** to quarrel or fight. [perhaps from *scrape*]

scrapbook ('skræp,bʊk) *n.* a book of blank pages in which to mount newspaper cuttings or pictures.

scrape (skreɪp) *vb.* **1.** to move (a rough or sharp object) across (a surface), as to smooth or clean. **2.** (often foll. by *away* or *off*) to remove (a layer) by rubbing. **3.** to produce a grating sound by rubbing against (something else). **4.** to injure or damage by scraping: *to scrape one's knee.* **5.** to be very economical (esp. in **scrimp and scrape**). **6.** to draw the foot backwards in making a bow. ~*n.* **7.** the act of scraping. **8.** a scraped place. **9.** a harsh or grating sound. **10.** *Informal.* an awkward or embarrassing predicament. **11.** *Informal.* a conflict or struggle. [Old English *scrapian*] —'**scraper** *n.*

scrape through *vb.* to manage, succeed in, or survive with difficulty: *I just scraped through the exam.*

scrape together *or* **up** *vb.* to collect with difficulty: *to scrape together money for a new car.*

scrappy ('skræpɪ) *adj.* **-pier, -piest.** fragmentary; disjointed.

scratch (skrætʃ) *vb.* **1.** to mark or cut (the surface of something) with a rough or sharp instrument. **2.** (often foll. by *at, out,* or *off*) to tear or dig with the nails or claws. **3.** to scrape (the surface of the skin) with the nails to relieve itching. **4.** to chafe or irritate (the skin). **5.** to make or cause to make a grating sound. **6.** (sometimes foll. by *out*) to erase or cross out. **7.** to withdraw from a race or (U.S.) an election. ~*n.* **8.** the act of scratching. **9.** a slight injury. **10.** a mark made by scratching. **11.** a slight grating sound. **12.** (in a handicap sport) a competitor who has no allowance. **13. from scratch.** *Informal.* from the very beginning. **14. not up to scratch.** *Informal.* not up to standard. ~*adj.* **15.** put together hastily: *a scratch team.* **16.** (in a handicap sport) with no allowance. [Germanic] —'**scratchy** *adj.*

scratching ('skrætʃɪŋ) *n.* a percussive effect obtained by rotating a gramophone record manually.

scrawl (skrɔːl) *vb.* **1.** to write carelessly or hastily. ~*n.* **2.** careless or scribbled writing. [perhaps blend of SPRAWL & CRAWL] —'**scrawly** *adj.*

scrawny ('skrɔːnɪ) *adj.* **scrawnier, scrawniest.** very thin and bony. [dialect *scranny*] —'**scrawniness** *n.*

scream (skriːm) *vb.* **1.** to utter or emit (a sharp piercing cry or sound), as of fear or pain. **2.** to laugh wildly. **3.** to utter with or as if with a scream: *she stood there and screamed abuse at him.* **4.** to be unpleasantly conspicuous: *bad news screaming out from the headlines.* ~*n.* **5.** a sharp piercing cry or sound, esp. of fear or pain. **6.** *Informal.* a person or thing that causes great amusement. [Germanic]

scree (skriː) *n.* a pile of rock fragments at the foot of a cliff or hill, often forming a sloping heap. [Old English *scrīthan* to slip]

screech[1] (skriːtʃ) *n.* **1.** a shrill or high-pitched sound or cry. ~*vb.* **2.** to utter with or emit a screech. [earlier *scritch,* imit.] —'**screechy** *adj.*

screech[2] (skriːtʃ) *n. Canad. slang.* **1.** a dark rum. **2.** any strong cheap drink. [origin unknown]

screech owl *n.* **1.** *Brit.* same as **barn owl.** **2.** a small North American owl with a reddish-brown or grey plumage.

screed (skriːd) *n.* a long tiresome speech or piece of writing. [prob. Old English *scrēade* shred]

screen (skriːn) *n.* **1.** a light movable frame, panel, or partition serving to shelter, divide, or conceal. **2.** anything that shelters, protects, or conceals. **3.** a frame containing a mesh that is used to keep out insects. **4.** the blank surface of a television set or radar receiver, on which a visible image is formed. **5.** the white surface on which films or slides are projected. **6. the screen.** the film industry or films collectively. ~*vb.* **7.** (sometimes foll. by *off*) to shelter, protect, or conceal with or as if with a screen. **8.** to test or check (an individual or group) so as to determine suitability for a task or to detect the presence of a disease or weapons. **9.** to show (a film) in the cinema or show (a programme) on television. [Old French *escren*]

screenplay ('skriːn,pleɪ) *n.* the script for a film, including instructions for sets and camera work.

screen process *n.* a method of printing by forcing ink through a fine mesh of silk or nylon, some parts of which have been treated so as not to let the ink pass.

screw (skruː) *n.* **1.** a metal pin with a head threaded evenly with a spiral ridge, which is used to fasten materials together by being firmly twisted into them. **2.** a threaded cylindrical rod that engages with a similarly threaded cylindrical hole. **3.** a thread in a cylindrical hole corresponding with that on the screw with which it is designed to engage. **4.** anything resembling a screw in shape. **5.** *Slang.* a prison guard. **6.** *Taboo slang.* an act of or partner in sexual intercourse. **7. have a screw loose.** *Informal.* to be insane. **8. put the screws on.** *Slang.* to use force or compulsion on. ~*vb.* **9.** to rotate (a screw or bolt) so as to drive it into or draw it out of a material. **10.** to twist or turn in the manner of a screw. **11.** to attach or fasten with or as if with a screw or screws. **12.** *Informal.* to take advantage of; cheat. **13.** (often foll. by *up*) *Informal.* to distort or contort: *he screwed his face into a scowl.* **14.** (often foll. by *from* or *out of*) *Informal.* to force out of; extort. **15.** *Taboo slang.* to have sexual intercourse (with). **16. have one's head screwed on the right way.** *Informal.* to be sensible. ~See also **screw up.** [French *escroe*]

screwball ('skruː,bɔːl) *Slang, chiefly U.S. & Canad.* ~*n.* **1.** an odd or eccentric person. ~*adj.* **2.** odd; eccentric.

screwdriver ('skruː,draɪvə) *n.* **1.** a tool used for turning screws, consisting of a long thin metal rod with a flattened tip that fits into a slot in the head of the screw. **2.** a drink consisting of orange juice and vodka.

screw top *n.* **1.** a bottle top that screws onto the bottle, allowing the bottle to be resealed after use. **2.** a bottle with such a top. —'**screw-,top** *adj.*

screw up *vb.* **1.** to twist out of shape or distort. **2.** to summon up (courage). **3.** *Informal.* to mishandle or bungle.

screwy ('skruːɪ) *adj.* **screwier, screwiest.** *Informal.* odd, crazy, or eccentric.

scribble ('skrɪb'l) *vb.* **1.** to write hastily or illegibly. **2.** to make meaningless or illegible marks (on). ~*n.* **3.** hasty careless writing. **4.** meaningless or illegible marks. [Latin *scribere* to write] —'**scribbler** *n.* —'**scribbly** *adj.*

scribe (skraɪb) *n.* **1.** a person who made handwritten copies of manuscripts or documents before the invention of printing. **2.** *Bible.* a recognized scholar and teacher of the Jewish Law. [Latin *scrība* clerk]

scrim (skrɪm) *n.* a fine open-weave fabric, used in upholstery, lining, and bookbinding. [origin unknown]

scrimmage ('skrɪmɪdʒ) *n.* **1.** a rough or disorderly struggle. ~*vb.* **2.** to engage in a scrimmage. [earlier *skrimish*]

scrimp (skrɪmp) *vb.* (sometimes foll. by *on*) to be very sparing in the use (of): *I have to scrimp and save to get by.* [Scot.]

scrip (skrɪp) *n. Finance.* a certificate representing a claim to part of a share of stock. [short for *subscription receipt*]

script (skrɪpt) *n.* **1.** handwriting. **2.** a typeface which looks like a handwriting. **3.** an alphabet or system of writing: *Arabic script.* **4.** the text of a play or film for the use of performers. **5.** a candidate's answer paper in an examination. ~*vb.* **6.** to write a script for. [Latin *scriptum* something written]

scripture ('skrɪptʃə) *n.* the sacred writings of a religion. [Latin *scriptūra* written material] —'**scriptural** *adj.*

Scripture ('skrɪptʃə) *n. Christianity.* the Old and New Testaments.

scriptwriter ('skrɪpt,raɪtə) *n.* a person who prepares scripts, esp. for a film. —'**script,writing** *n.*

scrofula ('skrɒfjʊlə) *n.* (*no longer in technical use*) tuberculosis of the lymphatic glands. [Medieval Latin] —'**scrofulous** *adj.*

scroll (skrəʊl) *n.* **1.** a roll of parchment or paper usually inscribed with writing. **2.** an ancient book in the form of a roll of parchment, papyrus, or paper. **3.** a decorative carving or moulding resembling a scroll. ~*vb.* **4.** *Computers.* to move (text) on a screen in order to view a section that cannot be fitted into a single display. [Middle English *scrowle*]

Scrooge (skruːdʒ) *n.* a mean or miserly person. [after a character in Dickens' story *A Christmas Carol*]

scrotum ('skrəʊtəm) *n., pl.* **-ta** (-tə) *or* **-tums.** the pouch of skin containing the testicles in most male mammals. [Latin]

scrounge (skraʊndʒ) *vb. Informal.* to obtain or seek to obtain (something) by cadging or begging. [dialect *scrunge* to steal] —'**scrounger** *n.*

scrub[1] (skrʌb) *vb.* **scrubbing, scrubbed.** **1.** to rub (something) hard, with or as if with a brush, soap, and water, in order to clean it. **2.** to remove (dirt) by rubbing, esp. with a brush and water. **3.** (foll. by *up*) (of a surgeon) to wash the hands and arms thoroughly before operating. **4.** *Informal.* to delete or cancel. ~*n.* **5.** a scrubbing. [Middle Low German *schrubben* or Middle Dutch *schrobben*]

scrub[2] (skrʌb) *n.* **1.** vegetation consisting of stunted trees or bushes growing in a dry area. **2.** an area of dry land covered with such vegetation. **3.** a stunted or inferior person, animal, or thing. ~*adj.* **4.** stunted or inferior. [var. of *shrub*]

scrubber ('skrʌbə) *n.* **1.** *Offensive slang.* a promiscuous woman. **2.** an apparatus for purifying a gas.

scrubby ('skrʌbɪ) *adj.* **-bier, -biest.** **1.** covered with or consisting of scrub. **2.** stunted. **3.** *Brit. informal.* shabby.

scruff[1] (skrʌf) *n.* the nape of the neck: *he grabbed the boy by the scruff of the neck.* [perhaps from Old Norse *skoft* hair]

scruff[2] (skrʌf) *n. Informal.* an untidy scruffy person.

scruffy ('skrʌfɪ) *adj.* **scruffier, scruffiest.** unkempt or shabby.

scrum (skrʌm) *n.* **1.** *Rugby.* a formation in which players from each side form a tight pack and push against each other in an attempt to get the ball which is thrown on the ground between them. **2.** *Informal.* a disorderly struggle. ~*vb.* **scrumming, scrummed.** **3.** (usually foll. by *down*) *Rugby.* to form a scrum. [from *scrummage*]

scrum half *n. Rugby.* a player who puts in the ball at scrums and tries to get it away to his three-quarter backs.

scrummage ('skrʌmɪdʒ) *n., vb.* **1.** *Rugby.* same as **scrum.** **2.** same as **scrimmage.** [var. of *scrimmage*]

scrump (skrʌmp) *vb. Dialect.* to steal (apples) from an orchard or garden. [var. of *scrimp*]

scrumptious ('skrʌmpʃəs) *adj. Informal.* very pleasing; delicious. [prob. changed from *sumptuous*]

scrumpy ('skrʌmpɪ) *n.* a rough dry cider, brewed esp. in the West Country of England. [dialect *scrump* withered apples]

scrunch (skrʌntʃ) *vb.* **1.** to crumple or crunch or be crumpled or crunched. ~*n.* **2.** the act or sound of scrunching. [var. of *crunch*]

scruple ('skruːp'l) *n.* **1.** (*often pl.*) a doubt or hesitation as to what is morally right in a certain situation. ~*vb.* **2.** to have doubts (about), esp. on moral grounds. [Latin *scrūpulus* a small weight]

scrupulous ('skruːpjʊləs) *adj.* **1.** taking great care to do what is morally right. **2.** very careful or precise. [Latin *scrūpulōsus*] —'**scrupulously** *adv.*

scrutinize *or* **-nise** ('skruːtɪ,naɪz) *vb.* to examine carefully or in minute detail.

scrutiny ('skruːtɪnɪ) *n., pl.* **-nies.** **1.** close or minute examination. **2.** a searching look. [Late Latin *scrūtārī* to search]

scuba ('skjuːbə) *n.* an apparatus used in skin diving, consisting of cylinders containing compressed air attached to a breathing apparatus. [*s*elf-*c*ontained *u*nderwater *b*reathing *a*pparatus]

scud (skʌd) *vb.* **scudding, scudded.** **1.** (esp. of clouds) to move along swiftly. **2.** *Naut.* to run before a gale. ~*n.* **3.** the act of scudding. **4.** spray, rain, or clouds driven by the wind. [prob. Scandinavian]

scuff (skʌf) *vb.* **1.** to drag (one's feet) while walking. **2.** to scratch (a surface) or (of a surface) to become scratched. ~*n.* **3.** the act or sound of scuffing. **4.** a rubbed place caused by scuffing. [prob. imit.]

scuffle ('skʌf'l) *vb.* **1.** to fight in a disorderly manner. **2.** to move by shuffling. ~*n.* **3.** a disorderly struggle. **4.** the sound of scuffling. [Scandinavian]

scull (skʌl) *n.* **1.** a single oar moved from side to side over the stern of a boat to propel it. **2.** one of a pair of small oars, both of which are pulled by one oarsman. **3.** a racing boat propelled by a single oarsman pulling two oars. ~*vb.* **4.** to propel (a boat) with a scull. [origin unknown] —'**sculler** *n.*

scullery ('skʌlərɪ) *n., pl.* **-leries.** *Chiefly Brit.* a small room where washing-up and other kitchen work is done. [Anglo-Norman *squillerie*]

scullion ('skʌljən) *n. Archaic.* a servant employed to do the rough work in a kitchen. [Old French *escouillon* cleaning cloth]

sculpt (skʌlpt) *vb.* same as **sculpture**.

sculptor ('skʌlptə) *or (fem.)* **sculptress** *n.* a person who practises sculpture.

sculpture ('skʌlptʃə) *n.* **1.** the art of making figures or designs by carving wood, moulding plaster, chiselling stone, or casting metals. **2.** works or a work made in this way. *~vb.* **3.** to carve, cast, or fashion (a material) into figures or designs. **4.** to represent (a person or thing) by means of sculpture. **5.** to form in the manner of sculpture: *her delicately sculptured features.* **6.** to decorate with sculpture. [Latin *sculptūra* a carving] —'**sculptural** *adj.*

scum (skʌm) *n.* **1.** a layer of impure or waste matter that forms on the surface of a liquid: *there was green scum over the pond.* **2.** waste matter. **3.** a worthless person or people. *~vb.* **scumming, scummed.** **4.** to remove scum from. **5.** *Rare.* to form a layer of or become covered with scum. [Germanic] —'**scummy** *adj.*

scumbag ('skʌm,bæg) *n. Slang.* an offensive or despicable person. [perhaps from earlier U.S. sense: condom]

scungy ('skʌndʒɪ) *adj.* **scungier, scungiest.** *Austral. & N.Z. slang.* miserable; sordid. [origin unknown]

scunner ('skʌnə) *Dialect, chiefly Scot. ~vb.* **1.** to produce a feeling of dislike in. *~n.* **2.** a strong dislike (often in **take a scunner to**). **3.** an object of dislike. [Scot. *skunner*]

scupper[1] ('skʌpə) *n. Naut.* a drain or spout in a ship's side allowing water on the deck to flow overboard. [origin unknown]

scupper[2] ('skʌpə) *vb. Brit. slang.* **1.** to defeat or ruin: *our plans will be scuppered if he doesn't lend us the money.* **2.** to sink (one's ship) deliberately. [origin unknown]

scurf (skɜːf) *n.* **1.** same as **dandruff. 2.** any flaky or scaly matter sticking to or peeling off a surface. [Old English] —'**scurfy** *adj.*

scurrilous ('skʌrɪləs) *adj.* untrue or unfair, insulting, and designed to damage a person's reputation: *scurrilous rumours.* [Latin *scurra* buffoon] —**scurrility** (skə-'rɪlɪtɪ) *n.*

scurry ('skʌrɪ) *vb.* **-rying, -ried. 1.** to move about hurriedly. *~n., pl.* **-ries. 2.** the act or sound of scurrying. **3.** a flurry of rain or snow. [prob. from *hurry-scurry*]

scurvy ('skɜːvɪ) *n.* **1.** a disease caused by a lack of vitamin C, characterized by anaemia, spongy gums, and bleeding beneath the skin. *~adj.* **-vier, -viest. 2.** mean or despicable. [from *scurf*] —'**scurviness** *n.*

scut (skʌt) *n.* the short tail of animals such as the deer and rabbit. [prob. from Old Norse]

scuttle[1] ('skʌt³l) *n.* same as **coal scuttle.** [Latin *scutella* bowl]

scuttle[2] ('skʌt³l) *vb.* **1.** to run with short hasty steps. *~n.* **2.** a hurried pace or run. [prob. from *scud*]

scuttle[3] ('skʌt³l) *vb.* **1.** *Naut.* to cause (a vessel) to sink by making holes in the sides or bottom. **2.** to give up (hopes or plans). *~n.* **3.** *Naut.* a small hatch in a ship's deck or side. [Spanish *escotilla* a small opening]

Scylla ('sɪlə) *n.* **1.** *Gk myth.* a sea monster believed to drown sailors navigating the Straits of Messina. **2. between Scylla and Charybdis.** in a predicament in which avoidance of either of two dangers means exposure to the other.

scythe (saɪð) *n.* **1.** a long-handled tool for cutting grass or grain, with a curved sharpened blade that is swung parallel to the ground. *~vb.* **2.** to cut (grass or grain) with a scythe. [Old English *sigthe*]

SD *or* **S.Dak.** South Dakota.

SDI Strategic Defense Initiative.

Se *Chem.* selenium.

SE southeast(ern).

sea (siː) *n.* **1.** (usually preceded by *the*) the mass of salt water that covers three-quarters of the earth's surface. **2. a.** one of the smaller areas of this: *the Irish Sea.* **b.** a large inland area of water: *the Caspian Sea.* **3.** turbulence or swell: *heavy seas.* **4.** anything resembling the sea in size or apparent limitlessness: *a sea of faces.* **5. at sea. a.** on the ocean. **b.** in a state of confusion or bewilderment. **6. go to sea.** to become a sailor. **7. put out to sea.** to embark on a sea voyage. [Old English *sǣ*]

sea anchor *n. Naut.* a device, usually a canvas-covered frame, dragged in the water behind a vessel to slow it down or reduce drifting.

sea anemone *n.* a marine animal with a round body and rings of petal-like tentacles which trap food from the water.

sea bird *n.* a bird that lives on or near the sea.

seaboard ('siː,bɔːd) *n.* land bordering on the sea.

seaborne ('siː,bɔːn) *adj.* **1.** carried on or by the sea. **2.** transported by ship.

sea breeze *n.* a breeze blowing inland from the sea.

sea cow *n.* **1.** a dugong or manatee. **2.** *Archaic.* a walrus.

sea dog *n.* an experienced or old sailor.

seafarer ('siː,fɛərə) *n.* **1.** a traveller who goes by sea. **2.** a sailor.

seafaring ('siː,fɛərɪŋ) *adj.* **1.** travelling by sea. **2.** working as a sailor. *~n.* **3.** the act of travelling by sea. **4.** the work of a sailor.

seafood ('siː,fuːd) *n.* edible saltwater fish or shellfish.

seagoing ('siː,gəʊɪŋ) *adj.* built for travelling on the sea.

sea-green *adj.* bluish-green.

sea gull *n.* same as **gull** (the bird).

sea horse *n.* a small marine fish with a horselike head, which swims upright.

sea kale *n.* a European coastal plant with broad fleshy leaves and edible asparagus-like shoots.

seal[1] (siːl) *n.* **1.** a special design impressed

on a piece of wax, lead, or paper, and fixed to a letter or document as a mark of authentication. **2.** a stamp or signet ring engraved with a design to form such an impression. **3.** a substance, esp. wax, placed over an envelope or container, so that it cannot be opened without the seal being broken. **4.** any substance or device used to close or fasten tightly. **5.** anything that serves as a pledge or confirmation. **6.** a decorative adhesive stamp: *a Christmas seal.* **7. set one's seal on.** to endorse or approve. ~*vb.* **8.** to affix a seal to. **9.** to stamp with or as if with a seal. **10.** to approve or authorize. **11.** (sometimes foll. by *up*) to close or secure with or as if with a seal: *to seal one's lips.* **12.** (foll. by *off*) to enclose or isolate (a place) completely. **13.** to decide irrevocably: *your fate is sealed.* **14.** to close tightly so as to render airtight or watertight. **15.** to paint (a porous material) with a nonporous coating. [Latin *signum* a sign] —**'sealable** *adj.*

seal² (siːl) *n.* **1.** a fish-eating mammal with four flippers, which lives in the sea but comes ashore to breed. **2.** sealskin. ~*vb.* **3.** to hunt seals. [Old English *seolh*]

sealant ('siːlənt) *n.* any substance, such as wax, used for sealing, esp. to make airtight or watertight.

sea legs *pl. n. Informal.* the ability to maintain one's balance on board ship and to resist seasickness.

sea level *n.* the level of the surface of the sea with respect to the land, taken to be the mean level between high and low tide.

sealing wax *n.* a hard material made of shellac and turpentine, which softens when heated and which is used to make a seal.

sea lion *n.* a large eared seal, often used as a performing animal.

Sea Lord *n.* (in Britain) a naval officer on the admiralty board of the Ministry of Defence.

sealskin ('siːlˌskɪn) *n.* the skin or pre-pared fur of a seal, used to make garments.

seam (siːm) *n.* **1.** the line along which pieces of fabric are joined by stitching. **2.** a ridge or line made by joining two edges. **3.** a stratum of coal or ore. **4.** a mark or line like a seam, such as a wrinkle or scar. **5.** (*modifier*) *Cricket.* of a style of bowling in which the bowler uses the stitched seam round the ball in order to make it swing in flight and after touching the ground: *a seam bowler.* ~*vb.* **6.** to join together by or as if by a seam. **7.** to mark or become marked with or as if with a seam or wrinkle. [Old English] —**'seamless** *adj.*

seaman ('siːmən) *n., pl.* -**men.** **1.** a man ranking below an officer in a navy. **2.** a sailor.

seamanship ('siːmənʃɪp) *n.* skill in navigating and operating a vessel.

seamstress ('semstrɪs) *n.* a woman who sews, esp. professionally.

seamy ('siːmɪ) *adj.* **seamier, seamiest.** showing the least pleasant aspect; sordid. —**'seaminess** *n.*

seance *or* **séance** ('seɪɒns) *n.* a meeting at which spiritualists attempt to communicate with the spirits of the dead. [French]

seaplane ('siːˌpleɪn) *n.* an aircraft that is designed to land on and take off from water.

seaport ('siːˌpɔːt) *n.* a town or city with a harbour for seagoing vessels.

sear (sɪə) *vb.* **1.** to scorch or burn the surface of. **2.** to cause to wither. [Old English *sēarian* to become withered]

search (sɜːtʃ) *vb.* **1.** to look through (a place) thoroughly in order to find someone or something. **2.** to examine (a person) for concealed objects. **3.** to look at or examine (something) closely: *to search one's conscience.* **4.** (foll. by *out*) to find by searching. **5.** to make a search. **6. search me.** *Informal.* I don't know. ~*n.* **7.** a searching. [Old French *cerchier*]

searching ('sɜːtʃɪŋ) *adj.* keenly penetrating: *a searching look.* —**'searchingly** *adv.*

searchlight ('sɜːtʃˌlaɪt) *n.* **1.** a device which projects a powerful beam of light that can be shone in any direction. **2.** the beam of light produced by this device.

search warrant *n.* a legal order authorizing a constable to enter and search premises.

Sea Scout *n.* a member of the branch of the Scouts which gives training in seamanship.

seashell ('siːˌʃɛl) *n.* the empty shell of a marine mollusc.

seashore ('siːˌʃɔː) *n.* land bordering on the sea.

seasick ('siːˌsɪk) *adj.* suffering from nausea and dizziness caused by the motion of a ship at sea. —**'sea,sickness** *n.*

seaside ('siːˌsaɪd) *n.* an area bordering on the sea, esp. one regarded as a resort.

season ('siːzʰn) *n.* **1.** one of the four divisions of the year (spring, summer, autumn, and winter), each of which has characteristic weather conditions. **2.** a period of the year characterized by particular conditions or activities: *the rainy season; the holiday season.* **3.** the period during which any particular species of animal, bird, or fish is legally permitted to be caught or killed: *open season on red deer.* **4.** any definite or indefinite period: *the busy season.* **5.** fitting or proper time. **6. in season. a.** (of game) permitted to be killed. **b.** (of fresh food) readily available. **c.** (of animals) on heat. **d.** at the appropriate time. ~*vb.* **7.** to add herbs, salt, pepper, or spice to (food) in order to enhance the flavour. **8.** to add zest to. **9.** (in the preparation of timber) to dry and harden. **10.** to make experienced: *seasoned troops.* **11.** to moderate or temper. [Latin *satiō* a sowing] —**'seasoned** *adj.*

seasonable ('siːzənəbʰl) *adj.* **1.** suitable for the season: *a seasonable Christmas snow scene.* **2.** timely or opportune.

seasonal ('siːzənʰl) *adj.* of or depending on a certain season or seasons of the year: *seasonal labour.* —**'seasonally** *adv.*

seasoning ('siːzənɪŋ) *n.* something that is added to food to enhance the flavour.

season ticket *n.* a ticket for a series of events or number of journeys, usually obtained at a reduced rate.

seat (siːt) *n.* **1.** a piece of furniture designed for sitting on, such as a chair. **2.** the part of a chair or other piece of furniture on which one sits. **3.** a place to sit in a theatre, esp. one that requires a ticket: *I have two seats for the film tonight.* **4.** the buttocks. **5.** the part of a garment covering the buttocks. **6.** the part or surface on which an object rests. **7.** the place or centre in which something is based: *a seat of learning.* **8.** a country mansion. **9.** a membership or the right to membership of a legislative or administrative body: *a seat on the Board.* **10.** *Chiefly Brit.* a parliamentary constituency. **11.** the manner in which a rider sits on a horse. ~*vb.* **12.** to bring to or place on a seat. **13.** to provide seats for: *the bus seats fifty people.* **14.** to set firmly in place. **15.** to fix or install in a position of power. [Old English *gesete*]

seat belt *n.* a belt worn in a car or aircraft to prevent someone being thrown forward in the event of a collision.

sea urchin *n.* a small sea animal with a round body enclosed in a spiny shell.

seaward (ˈsiːwəd) *adv. also* **seawards. 1.** towards the sea. ~*adj.* **2.** directed or moving towards the sea.

seaweed (ˈsiːˌwiːd) *n.* any plant growing in the sea or on the seashore.

seaworthy (ˈsiːˌwɜːðɪ) *adj.* (of a ship) in a fit condition for a sea voyage. —**seaˌworthiness** *n.*

sebaceous (sɪˈbeɪʃəs) *adj.* of, like, or secreting fat. [Latin *sebum* tallow]

sebaceous glands *pl. n.* the small glands in the skin that secrete oil into hair follicles and onto most of the body surface.

sec[1] (sɛk) *adj.* (of wines) dry. [French]

sec[2] (sɛk) *n. Informal.* short for **second**[2]: *wait a sec.*

sec[3] (sɛk) secant.

sec. 1. second (of time). **2.** secondary. **3.** secretary.

secant (ˈsiːkənt) *n.* **1.** (in trigonometry) the ratio of the length of the hypotenuse to that of the adjacent side in a right-angled triangle; the reciprocal of cosine. **2.** a straight line that intersects a curve. [Latin *secāre* to cut]

secateurs (ˈsɛkətəz) *pl. n. Chiefly Brit.* a small pair of shears for pruning. [French]

secede (sɪˈsiːd) *vb.* (often foll. by *from*) to make a formal withdrawal of membership from a political alliance, federation, or group. [Latin *sē-* apart + *cēdere* to go]

secession (sɪˈsɛʃən) *n.* the act of seceding. —**seˈcessionˌism** *n.* —**seˈcessionist** *n., adj.*

seclude (sɪˈkluːd) *vb.* **1.** to remove from contact with others. **2.** to shut off or screen from view. [Latin *sēclūdere*]

secluded (sɪˈkluːdɪd) *adj.* **1.** kept apart from the company of others: *a secluded life.* **2.** private; sheltered: *a secluded garden.*

seclusion (sɪˈkluːʒən) *n.* **1.** a secluding or being secluded. **2.** a secluded place.

second[1] (ˈsɛkənd) *adj.* **1.** coming directly after the first in order; often written 2nd. **2.** graded or ranked between the first and third levels. **3.** alternate: *every second Thursday.* **4.** another of the same kind; additional: *a second opportunity.* **5.** resembling or comparable to a person or event from the past: *a second Wagner.* **6.** of subordinate importance or position; inferior. **7.** denoting the lowest but one gear in a motor vehicle. **8.** *Music.* denoting a musical part, voice, or instrument subordinate to or lower in pitch than another (the first): *the second tenors.* **9. at second hand.** by hearsay. ~*n.* **10.** a person or thing that is second. **11.** *Brit. education.* an honours degree of the second class. **12.** the lowest but one gear in a motor vehicle. **13.** (in boxing or duelling) an attendant who looks after a combatant. **14.** (*pl.*) goods of inferior quality. **15.** (*pl.*) *Informal.* a second helping of food. **16.** (*pl.*) the second course of a meal. ~*vb.* **17.** to give aid or backing to. **18.** (in boxing or duelling) to act as second to (a combatant). **19.** to express formal support for (a motion already proposed). ~*adv.* **20.** Also: **secondly.** in the second place. [Latin *secundus* next in order]

second[2] (ˈsɛkənd) *n.* **1.** $\frac{1}{60}$ of a minute of time. **2.** $\frac{1}{60}$ of a minute of angle. **3.** a very short period of time. [Latin *pars minūta secunda* the second small part (a minute being the first small part of an hour)]

second[3] (sɪˈkɒnd) *vb. Brit.* to transfer (a person) temporarily to another post, position, or job. [French *en second* in second rank] —**seˈcondment** *n.*

secondary (ˈsɛkəndrɪ) *adj.* **1.** coming next after the first. **2.** derived from or depending on what is primary or first: *a secondary source.* **3.** below the first in rank or importance. **4.** of or relating to the education of young people between the ages of 11 and 18: *secondary education.* ~*n., pl.* -aries. **5.** a person or thing that is secondary. **6.** a subordinate, deputy, or inferior.

secondary colour *n.* a colour formed by mixing two primary colours.

secondary picketing *n.* the picketing by striking workers of the premises of a firm that supplies or distributes goods to or from their employer.

second-best *adj.* **1.** next to the best. **2. come off second best.** *Informal.* to fail to win against someone. ~*n.* **second best. 3.** an inferior alternative.

second chamber *n.* the upper house of a two-chamber system of government.

second childhood *n.* dotage; senility: *the old dear is in her second childhood and doesn't know what she's saying.*

second class *n.* **1.** the class or grade next in value, rank, or quality to the first. ~*adj.* **second-class. 2.** of the class or grade next to the best in value, rank, or quality. **3.** shoddy or inferior. **4.** denoting the class of accommodation in a hotel or on a train, aircraft, or ship, lower in quality and price than first class. **5.** (of mail) sent by a cheaper type of postage and taking slightly longer to arrive than first-class mail. ~*adv.* **6.** by second-class mail, transport, etc.

Second Coming *n.* the prophesied return of Christ to earth at the Last Judgment.

second cousin *n.* the child of one's parent's first cousin.

second-degree burn *n. Pathol.* a burn in which blisters appear on the skin.

second fiddle *n. Informal.* a person who has a secondary status.

second floor *n. Brit.* the storey of a building immediately above the first and two floors up from the ground.

second hand *n.* a pointer on the face of a timepiece that indicates the seconds.

second-hand *adj.* **1.** previously owned or used. **2.** not from an original source or one's own experience: *a second-hand report.* **3.** dealing in or selling goods that are not new: *a second-hand car dealer.* ~*adv.* **4.** from a source of previously owned or used goods: *he prefers to buy second-hand.* **5.** not directly or from one's own experience: *he got the news second-hand.*

second lieutenant *n.* an officer holding the lowest commissioned rank in an army or navy.

secondly ('sɛkəndlı) *adv.* same as **second¹**.

second nature *n.* a habit or characteristic practised for so long that it seems to be part of one's character.

second person *n.* the form of a pronoun or verb used to refer to the person or people being addressed.

second-rate *adj.* **1.** not of the highest quality; mediocre. **2.** second in importance or rank: *a second-rate citizen.*

second sight *n.* the supposed ability to foresee the future or see actions taking place elsewhere.

second thoughts *pl. n.* a revised opinion or idea on a matter already considered.

second wind (wind) *n.* **1.** the return of normal breathing following strenuous exertion. **2.** renewed ability to continue in an effort.

secrecy ('si:krɪsı) *n., pl.* **-cies. 1.** the state of being secret. **2.** the ability or tendency to keep things secret.

secret ('si:krɪt) *adj.* **1.** kept hidden or separate from the knowledge of all or all but a few others. **2.** inclined to secrecy. **3.** operating without the knowledge of outsiders: *a secret society.* ~*n.* **4.** something kept or to be kept hidden. **5.** something unrevealed; a mystery: *the secrets of nature.* **6.** an underlying explanation or reason: *the secret of my success.* **7. in secret.** without the knowledge of others. [Latin *sēcrētus* concealed] —'**secretly** *adv.*

secret agent *n.* a person employed in spying, as for a government.

secretaire (ˌsɛkrɪ'tɛə) *n.* same as **escritoire**.

secretariat (ˌsɛkrɪ'tɛərɪət) *n.* **1. a.** an office responsible for the secretarial, clerical, and administrative affairs of a legislative body or international organization. **b.** the staff of such an office or department. **2.** the premises of a secretariat. [French]

secretary ('sɛkrətrı) *n., pl.* **-taries. 1.** a person who handles correspondence, keeps records, and does general clerical work for an individual or organization. **2.** the official manager of the day-to-day business of a society, club, or committee. **3.** (in Britain) a senior civil servant who assists a government minister. **4.** (in the U.S.) the head of a government administrative department. [Medieval Latin *sēcrētārius* someone entrusted with secrets] —**secretarial** (ˌsɛkrɪ'tɛərɪəl) *adj.*

secretary bird *n.* a large African long-legged bird of prey with a crest and a tail of long feathers.

secretary-general *n., pl.* **secretaries-general.** the chief administrative official of a legislative body or international organization.

secretary of state *n.* **1.** (in Britain) the head of a major government department. **2.** (in the U.S.) the head of the government department in charge of foreign affairs.

secrete¹ (sı'kri:t) *vb.* (of a cell, organ, or gland) to secrete and release (a secretion). —se'**cretory** *adj.*

secrete² (sı'kri:t) *vb.* to put in a hiding place. [var. of obs. *secret* to hide away]

secretion (sı'kri:ʃən) *n.* **1.** a substance that is released from a cell, organ, or gland. **2.** the process involved in producing and releasing such a substance. [Latin *sēcrētiō* a separation]

secretive ('si:krıtıv) *adj.* inclined to secrecy. —'**secretively** *adv.*

secret police *n.* a police force that operates secretly to suppress opposition to the government.

secret service *n.* a government agency or department that conducts intelligence or counterintelligence operations.

sect (sɛkt) *n.* **1.** a subdivision of a larger religious or political group, esp. one regarded as extreme in its beliefs or practices. **2.** a group of people with a common interest or philosophy. [Latin *secta* faction]

sectarian (sɛk'tɛərɪən) *adj.* **1.** of or belonging to a sect. **2.** narrow-minded as a result of adherence to a particular sect. ~*n.* **3.** a member of a sect. —**sec'tarian-ism** *n.*

section ('sɛkʃən) *n.* **1.** a part cut off or separated from the main body of something. **2.** a part or subdivision of a piece of writing or a book: *the sports section of the newspaper.* **3.** one of several separate parts. **4.** a distinct part of a country or community which make something up. **5.** the act or process of cutting or separating by cutting. **6.** *Geom.* a plane surface formed by cutting through a solid. ~*vb.* **7.** to cut or divide into sections. [Latin *secāre* to cut]

sectional ('sɛkʃən'l) *adj.* **1.** made of sections. **2.** of a section. **3.** concerned with a particular area or group within a country or community, esp. to the exclusion of others.

sector ('sɛktə) n. **1.** a part or subdivision, esp. of a society or an economy: *the private sector.* **2.** *Geom.* either portion of a circle bounded by two radii and the arc cut off by them. **3.** a portion into which an area is divided for military operations. [Latin: a cutter]

secular ('sɛkjʊlə) adj. **1.** relating to worldly as opposed to sacred things. **2.** not connected with religion or the church. **3.** (of clerics) not bound by religious vows to a monastic or other order. **4.** occurring once in an age or century. [Late Latin *saeculāris*]

secularism ('sɛkjʊlə,rɪzəm) n. the belief that religion should have no place in morality or education. —'**secularist** n., adj.

secularize or **-rise** ('sɛkjʊlə,raɪz) vb. to change (something, such as education) so that it is no longer connected with religion or the Church. —,**seculari'zation** or **-ri'sation** n.

secure (sɪ'kjʊə) adj. **1.** free from danger or damage. **2.** free from fear, doubt, or care. **3.** in safe custody. **4.** firmly held; stable. **5.** able to be relied on: *a secure investment.* ~vb. **6.** to obtain: *I will secure some good seats.* **7.** (often foll. by *against*) to make or become free from danger or fear. **8.** to make fast or firm. **9.** to guarantee (payment of a loan), as by giving security. [Latin *sēcūrus* free from care] —se'**curely** adv.

security (sɪ'kjʊərɪtɪ) n., pl. **-ties.** **1.** the state of being secure. **2.** assured freedom from poverty or want: *he needs the security of a permanent job.* **3.** precautions taken to ensure against theft, espionage, or other danger. **4.** (often pl.) a certificate of ownership, such as a share, stock, or bond. **5.** something given or pledged to secure the fulfilment of a promise or obligation.

security risk n. someone or something thought to be a threat to state security.

sedan (sɪ'dæn) n. *U.S., Canad., & N.Z.* a saloon car. [origin unknown]

sedan chair n. an enclosed chair for one passenger, carried on poles by two bearers, commonly used in the 17th and 18th centuries.

sedate[1] (sɪ'deɪt) adj. **1.** calm and composed in manner. **2.** sober or decorous. [Latin *sēdāre* to soothe] —se'**dately** adv.

sedate[2] (sɪ'deɪt) vb. to administer a sedative to.

sedation (sɪ'deɪʃən) n. **1.** a state of calm, esp. when brought about by sedatives. **2.** the administration of a sedative.

sedative ('sɛdətɪv) adj. **1.** having a soothing or calming effect. ~n. **2.** *Med.* a sedative drug or agent. [Latin *sēdātus*]

sedentary ('sɛdntrɪ) adj. **1.** characterized by much sitting and very little exercise: *sedentary work.* **2.** tending to sit about without taking much exercise. [Latin *sedēre* to sit]

sedge (sɛdʒ) n. a coarse grasslike plant

growing on wet ground. [Old English *secg*] —'**sedgy** adj.

sedge warbler n. a European songbird of swampy areas, having a streaked brownish plumage with white eye stripes.

sediment ('sɛdɪmənt) n. **1.** matter that settles to the bottom of a liquid. **2.** material that has been deposited by water, ice, or wind. [Latin *sedimentum* a settling] —**sedimentary** (,sɛdɪ'mɛntrɪ) adj.

sedition (sɪ'dɪʃən) n. speech, writing, or behaviour intended to encourage rebellion or resistance against the government. [Latin *sēditiō* discord] —se'**ditionary** n., adj. —se'**ditious** adj.

seduce (sɪ'djuːs) vb. **1.** to persuade to engage in sexual intercourse. **2.** to lead astray; tempt into wrongdoing. [Latin *sēdūcere* to lead apart] —**seduction** (sɪ'dʌkʃən) n.

seductive (sɪ'dʌktɪv) adj. tending to seduce or capable of seducing; enticing. —se'**ductively** adv. —se'**ductiveness** n.

sedulous ('sɛdjʊləs) adj. diligent; painstaking. [Latin *sēdulus*] —**sedulity** (sɪ'djuːlɪtɪ) n.

sedum ('siːdəm) n. a rock plant with thick fleshy leaves and clusters of white, yellow, or pink flowers. [Latin]

see[1] (siː) vb. **seeing, saw, seen.** **1.** to perceive with the eyes. **2.** to understand: *I explained the problem but he could not see it.* **3.** to perceive or be aware of: *I hate to see you so unhappy.* **4.** to view, watch, or attend: *I saw a good film last night.* **5.** to foresee: *I can see what will happen if you don't help.* **6.** to find out (a fact): *see who is at the door.* **7.** (sometimes foll. by *to*) to make sure (of something) or take care (of something): *see that he gets to bed early; don't worry, I'll see to it.* **8.** to consider, deliberate, or decide: *see if you can come next week.* **9.** to have experience of: *he had seen much unhappiness in his life.* **10.** to meet or pay a visit to: *to see one's solicitor.* **11.** to receive: *the Prime Minister will see the deputation now.* **12.** to frequent the company of: *she is seeing a married man.* **13.** to accompany: *I saw her to the door.* **14.** to refer to or look up: *for further information see the appendix.* **15.** (in gambling, esp. in poker) to match (another player's bet) or match the bet of (another player) by staking an equal sum. **16. see fit.** to consider it proper (to do something): *I don't see fit to allow her to come here.* **17. see you, see you later,** or **be seeing you.** an expression of farewell. ~See also **see about, see into,** etc. [Old English *sēon*]

see[2] (siː) n. the diocese of a bishop or the place within it where his cathedral is situated. [Latin *sēdēs* a seat]

see about vb. **1.** to take care of: *he couldn't see about the matter because he was ill.* **2.** to investigate: *to see about a new car.*

seed (siːd) n. **1.** *Bot.* the mature fertilized part of a plant, containing an embryo ready for germination. **2.** seeds used for growing. **3.** the source, beginning, or origin of anything: *the seeds of revolt.* **4.**

Chiefly Bible. descendants: *the seed of Abraham.* **5.** *Sport.* a seeded player. **6. go or run to seed. a.** (of plants) to produce and shed seeds after flowering. **b.** to lose vigour or usefulness. ~*vb.* **7.** to plant (seeds) in (soil). **8.** (of plants) to produce or shed seeds. **9.** to remove the seeds from (fruit or plants). **10.** to scatter certain substances, such as silver iodide, in (clouds) in order to cause rain. **11.** to arrange (the draw of a tournament) so that outstanding teams or players will not meet in the early rounds. [Old English *sǣd*] —**'seedless** *adj.*

seedbed ('siːd‚bed) *n.* **1.** an area of soil prepared for the growing of seedlings before they are transplanted. **2.** the place where something develops: *a seedbed of discontent.*

seedling ('siːdlɪŋ) *n.* a plant produced from a seed, esp. a very young plant.

seed pearl *n.* a tiny pearl, often imperfect.

seed pod *n.* a carpel or pistil enclosing the seeds of a plant, esp. a flowering plant.

seed vessel *n.* *Bot.* a dry hollow fruit containing seeds.

seedy ('siːdɪ) *adj.* **seedier, seediest. 1.** shabby in appearance: *seedy clothes.* **2.** (of a plant) at the stage of producing seeds. **3.** *Informal.* physically unwell. —**'seediness** *n.*

seeing ('siːɪŋ) *n.* **1.** the sense or faculty of sight. ~*conj.* **2.** (often foll. by *that*) in light of the fact (that).

see into *vb.* to discover the true nature of: *I can't see into your thoughts.*

seek (siːk) *vb.* **seeking, sought. 1.** (often foll. by *for* or *after*) to try to find by searching: *to seek a solution.* **2.** to try to obtain: *to seek happiness.* **3.** to try (to do something): *I'm only seeking to help.* [Old English *sēcan*]

seek out *vb.* to search hard for and find (a specific person or thing): *she sought out her friend from amongst the crowd.*

seem (siːm) *vb.* **1.** to appear to the mind or eye; give the impression of: *the car seems to be running well.* **2.** to appear to be: *there seems no need for all this nonsense.* **3.** to have the impression: *I seem to remember you were there too.* [Old Norse *sōma* to be suitable]

seeming ('siːmɪŋ) *adj.* apparent but not actual or genuine. —**'seemingly** *adv.*

seemly ('siːmlɪ) *adj.* **-lier, -liest.** proper or fitting.

seen (siːn) *vb.* the past participle of **see**[1].

see off *vb.* **1.** to be present at the departure of (a person making a journey). **2.** *Informal.* to cause to leave or depart, esp. by force.

seep (siːp) *vb.* to leak slowly as if through small openings. [Old English *sīpian*] —**'seepage** *n.*

seer (sɪə) *n.* **1.** a person who can supposedly see into the future. **2.** a person who sees.

seersucker ('sɪə‚sʌkə) *n.* a light cotton, linen, or other fabric with a crinkled surface. [Hindi *śīrśakar*]

seesaw ('siː‚sɔː) *n.* **1.** a plank balanced in the middle so that two people seated on the ends can ride up and down by pushing on the ground with their feet. **2.** an up-and-down or back-and-forth movement. ~*vb.* **3.** to move up and down or back and forth in such a manner. [reduplication of *saw*, alluding to the movement from side to side, as in sawing]

seethe (siːð) *vb.* **1.** to boil or to foam as if boiling. **2.** to be in a state of extreme agitation, esp. through anger. [Old English *sēothan*] —**'seething** *adj.*

see through *vb.* **1.** to help out in time of need or trouble. **2.** to remain with until the end or completion: *let's see the job through.* **3.** to perceive the true nature of: *I can see through your evasion.* ~*adj.* **see-through. 4.** (esp. of clothing) partly or wholly transparent.

segment *n.* ('segmənt). **1.** one of several parts or sections into which an object is divided. **2.** *Maths.* **a.** a part of a circle cut off by an intersecting line. **b.** a part of a sphere cut off by an intersecting plane or planes. ~*vb.* (seg'ment). **3.** to cut or divide into segments. [Latin *segmentum*] —**seg'mental** *adj.* —**‚segmen'tation** *n.*

segregate ('segrɪ‚geit) *vb.* **1.** to set apart from others or from the main group. **2.** to impose segregation on (a racial or minority group). [Latin *sē-* apart + *grex* a flock]

segregation (‚segrɪ'geiʃən) *n.* **1.** a segregating or being segregated. **2.** *Sociol.* the practice or policy of creating separate facilities within the same society for the use of a racial or minority group. —**‚segre-'gational** *adj.* —**‚segre'gationist** *n.*

seigneur (se'njɜː) *n.* a feudal lord, esp. in France. [Old French] —**sei'gneurial** *adj.*

seine (sem) *n.* **1.** a large fishing net that hangs vertically in the water by means of floats at the top and weights at the bottom. ~*vb.* **2.** to catch (fish) using this net. [Old English *segne*]

seismic ('saizmɪk) *adj.* relating to or caused by earthquakes. [Greek *seismos* earthquake]

seismograph ('saizmə‚grɑːf) *n.* an instrument that records the intensity and duration of earthquakes. [Greek *seismos* earthquake + *-graph*] —**seismographer** (saiz-'mografə) *n.* —**seis'mography** *n.*

seismology (saiz'molədʒɪ) *n.* the branch of geology concerned with the study of earthquakes. [Greek *seismos* earthquake + *-LOGY*] —**seis'mologist** *n.*

seismometer (saiz'momɪtə) *n.* same as **seismograph.**

seize (siːz) *vb.* **1.** to take hold of forcibly or quickly; grab. **2.** (sometimes foll. by *on* or *upon*) to understand quickly: *she immediately seized his idea.* **3.** to affect or fill the mind of suddenly: *alarm seized the crowd.* **4.** to take legal possession of. **5.** to take by force or capture: *the army seized the undefended town.* **6.** to take immediate advantage of: *to seize an opportunity.* **7.** (often foll. by *up*) (of mechanical parts) to become jammed, esp. because of overheating. [Old French *saisir*]

seizure (ˈsiːʒə) n. **1.** a seizing or being seized. **2.** *Pathol.* a sudden violent attack of an illness, such as an epileptic convulsion.

seldom (ˈsɛldəm) adv. rarely. [Old English seldon]

select (sɪˈlɛkt) vb. **1.** to choose (someone or something) in preference to another or others. ~adj. **2.** chosen in preference to others. **3.** limited as to membership or entry; exclusive: a select gathering. [Latin sēligere to sort] —se'**lector** n.

select committee n. (in Britain) a small committee of members of parliament, set up to investigate and report on a specified matter.

selection (sɪˈlɛkʃən) n. **1.** a selecting or being selected. **2.** a thing or number of things that have been selected. **3.** a range from which something may be selected: a good selection of clothes. **4.** Biol. the process by which certain organisms or individuals are reproduced and survive in preference to others.

selective (sɪˈlɛktɪv) adj. **1.** of or characterized by selection. **2.** tending to choose carefully or characterized by careful choice. —se'**lectively** adv. —se,lec'**tivity** n.

selenium (sɪˈliːnɪəm) n. a nonmetallic element used in photocells, solar cells, and in xerography. Symbol: Se [Greek selēnē moon]

self (sɛlf) n., pl. **selves. 1.** the distinct individuality or identity of a person or thing. **2.** a person's typical bodily make-up or personal characteristics: she's looking her old self again. **3.** one's own welfare or interests: he only thinks of self. **4.** an individual's consciousness of his own identity or being. ~pron. **5.** Not standard. myself, yourself, himself, or herself: seats for self and wife. [Old English seolf]

self- combining form. used with many main words to mean: **1.** of oneself or itself: self-defence. **2.** by, to, in, due to, for, or from the self: self-employed; self-respect. **3.** automatic or automatically: self-propelled.

self-abnegation n. the denial of one's own interests in favour of the interests of others.

self-absorption n. preoccupation with oneself to the exclusion of others. —,self-ab'**sorbed** adj.

self-abuse n. same as **masturbation.**

self-addressed adj. addressed for return to the sender.

self-aggrandizement n. the act of increasing one's own power, wealth, or importance.

self-appointed adj. having assumed authority without the agreement of others: a self-appointed critic.

self-assertion n. the act of putting forward one's own opinions or demanding one's own rights, esp. in an aggressive or confident manner. —,self-as'**sertive** adj.

self-assurance n. confidence in oneself, one's abilities, or one's judgment. —,self-as'**sured** adj.

self-catering adj. denoting accommodation in which the tenant provides and prepares his own food.

self-centred or U.S. **self-centered** adj. totally preoccupied with one's own concerns.

self-certification n. (in Britain) a formal assertion by a worker to his employer that absence from work for up to seven days was due to sickness.

self-coloured or U.S. **self-colored** adj. **1.** having only a single and uniform colour: a self-coloured dress. **2.** (of cloth or wool) having the natural or original colour.

self-confessed adj. according to one's own testimony or admission: a self-confessed liar.

self-confidence n. confidence in oneself, one's abilities, or one's judgment. —,self-'**confident** adj.

self-conscious adj. embarrassed or ill at ease through being unduly aware of oneself as the object of the attention of others. —,self-'**consciously** adv. —,self-'**consciousness** n.

self-contained adj. **1.** containing within itself all parts necessary for completeness. **2.** (of a flat) having its own kitchen, bathroom, and toilet not shared by others.

self-control n. the ability to control one's feelings, emotions, or reactions. —,self-con'**trolled** adj.

self-deception or **self-deceit** n. the act or an instance of deceiving oneself.

self-defence or U.S. **self-defense** n. **1.** the act or skill of defending oneself against physical attack. **2.** the act of defending one's actions, ideas, or rights.

self-denial n. the denial or sacrifice of one's own desires. —,self-de'**nying** adj.

self-determination n. **1.** the ability to make a decision for oneself without influence from outside. **2.** the right of a nation or people to determine its own form of government. —,self-de'**termined** adj.

self-discipline n. the act of controlling or power to control one's own feelings, desires, or behaviour. —,self-'**disciplined** adj.

self-drive adj. denoting or relating to a hired vehicle that is driven by the hirer.

self-educated adj. educated through one's own efforts without formal instruction.

self-effacement n. the act of making oneself or one's actions inconspicuous because of modesty or timidity. —**self-ef'facing** adj.

self-employed adj. earning one's living in one's own business, rather than as the employee of another.

self-esteem n. respect for or a favourable opinion of oneself.

self-evident adj. so obvious that no proof or explanation is needed. —**self-'evidently** adv.

self-explanatory adj. understandable without explanation; self-evident.

self-expression n. the expression of one's own personality or feelings, as in the creative arts. —**self-ex'pressive** adj.

self-government n. the government of a country, nation, or community by its own people. —**self-'governing** adj.

self-help n. the use of one's own abilities and resources to help oneself without relying on the assistance of others.

self-image n. one's own idea of oneself or sense of one's worth.

self-important adj. having an unduly high opinion of one's own importance. —**self-im'portance** n.

self-improvement n. the improvement of one's position, skills, or education by one's own efforts.

self-indulgent adj. tending to indulge one's own desires. —**self-in'dulgence** n.

self-interest n. 1. one's personal interest or advantage. 2. the pursuit of one's own interest. —**self-'interested** adj.

selfish ('sɛlfɪʃ) adj. 1. caring too much about oneself and not enough about others. 2. (of behaviour or attitude) motivated by self-interest. —**'selfishly** adv. —**'selfishness** n.

selfless ('sɛlflɪs) adj. having little concern for one's own interests. —**'selflessly** adv. —**'selflessness** n.

self-made adj. having achieved wealth or status by one's own efforts.

self-opinionated adj. adhering stubbornly to one's own opinions.

self-pity n. pity for oneself, esp. when greatly exaggerated. —**self-'pitying** adj.

self-possessed adj. having control of one's emotions or behaviour, esp. in difficult situations. —**self-pos'session** n.

self-preservation n. the instinctive behaviour that protects oneself from danger or injury.

self-propelled adj. (of a vehicle) provided with its own source of power rather than requiring an external means of propulsion. —**self-pro'pelling** adj.

self-raising adj. (of flour) having a raising agent, such as baking powder, already added.

self-realization n. the fulfilment of one's own potential or abilities.

self-regard n. 1. concern for one's own interest. 2. proper esteem for oneself.

self-reliance n. reliance on oneself or one's own abilities. —**self-re'liant** adj.

self-reproach n. the act of finding fault with or blaming oneself.

self-respect n. a proper sense of one's own dignity and integrity. —**self-re'specting** adj.

self-restraint n. restraint imposed by oneself on one's own feelings, desires, or actions.

self-righteous adj. thinking oneself more virtuous than others. —**self-'righteousness** n.

self-sacrifice n. the sacrifice of one's own interests for the wellbeing of others. —**self-'sacri,ficing** adj.

selfsame ('sɛlf,seɪm) adj. the very same.

self-satisfied adj. complacently satisfied with oneself or one's own actions. —**self-,satis'faction** n.

self-sealing adj. 1. (of an envelope) sealable by pressure alone. 2. (of a tyre) automatically sealing small punctures.

self-seeking n. 1. the act or an instance of seeking one's own profit or interest. ~adj. 2. having or showing an exclusive preoccupation with one's own profit or interest: a self-seeking attitude. —**self-'seeker** n.

self-service adj. 1. of or denoting a shop or restaurant where the customer serves himself and then pays a cashier. ~n. 2. the practice of serving oneself and then paying a cashier.

self-serving adj. habitually seeking one's own advantage, esp. at the expense of others.

self-starter n. 1. an electric motor used to start an internal-combustion engine. 2. a person who is strongly motivated and shows initiative at work.

self-styled adj. using a title or name that one has given oneself, esp. without right or justification: a self-styled expert.

self-sufficient adj. able to provide for or support oneself without the help of others. —**self-suf'ficiency** n.

self-supporting adj. 1. able to support or maintain oneself without the help of others. 2. able to stand up or hold firm without support, props, or attachments.

self-willed adj. stubbornly determined to have one's own way, esp. at the expense of others.

self-winding adj. (of a wristwatch) having a mechanism which winds itself automatically.

sell (sɛl) vb. **selling, sold.** 1. to exchange

self-examination	self-inflicted	self-promotion
self-focusing	self-perpetuating	self-regulating
self-fulfilling	self-pollination	self-taught
self-hypnosis	self-portrait	
self-imposed	self-proclaimed	

(something) for money. **2.** to deal in (objects or property): *he sells used cars.* **3.** to give up or surrender for a price or reward: *to sell one's honour.* **4.** to promote the sale of (objects or property): *publicity sells many products.* **5.** to gain acceptance of: *to sell an idea.* **6.** to be in demand on the market: *these dresses sell well.* **7. sell down the river.** *Informal.* to betray. **8. sell oneself. a.** to convince someone else of one's potential or worth. **b.** to give up one's moral standards for a price or reward. **9. sell someone short.** *Informal.* to belittle someone. ∼n. **10.** the act or an instance of selling: *a soft sell.* **11.** *Informal.* a hoax or deception. ∼See also **sell off, sell out, sell up.** [Old English *sellan* to lend, deliver] —**'seller** n.

sell off vb. to sell (remaining items) at reduced prices.

Sellotape ('sɛlə,teɪp) n. **1.** *Trademark.* a type of transparent adhesive tape. ∼vb. **2.** to seal or stick using adhesive tape.

sell out vb. **1.** to dispose of (something) completely by selling. **2.** *Informal.* to betray. ∼n. **sellout.** **3.** *Informal.* a performance of a play, film, or other form of entertainment for which all tickets are sold. **4.** a commercial success. **5.** *Informal.* a betrayal.

sell up vb. *Chiefly Brit.* to sell all one's goods or property.

salvage or **selvedge** ('sɛlvɪdʒ) n. a specially woven edge on a length of fabric to prevent it from unravelling. [*self* + *edge*] —**'selvaged** adj.

selves (sɛlvz) n. the plural of **self.**

semantic (sɪ'mæntɪk) adj. **1.** of or relating to the meanings of words. **2.** of or relating to semantics. [Greek *sēma* a sign]

semantics (sɪ'mæntɪks) n. (functioning as *sing.*) the branch of linguistics that deals with the study of meaning.

semaphore ('sɛmə,fɔː) n. **1.** a signalling device for conveying information by means of lights, flags, or movable arms. **2.** a system of signalling by holding a flag in each hand and moving the arms to designated positions for each letter of the alphabet. ∼vb. **3.** to signal (information) by means of semaphore. [Greek *sēma* a signal + *-phoros* carrying]

semblance ('sɛmbləns) n. outward or superficial appearance. [Old French *sembler* to seem]

semen ('siːmɛn) n. the thick whitish fluid containing spermatozoa that is secreted by the male reproductive organs and ejaculated from the penis. [Latin: seed]

semester (sɪ'mɛstə) n. *Chiefly U.S. & Canad.* either of two divisions of the academic year. [Latin *sēmestris* half-yearly]

semi ('sɛmɪ) n. *Brit. informal.* short for **semidetached** (house).

semi- prefix. used with many main words to mean: **1.** half: *semicircle.* **2.** partly or almost: *semiprofessional.* **3.** occurring

twice in a specified period: *semiweekly.* [Latin]

semiannual (,sɛmɪ'ænjʊəl) adj. **1.** occurring every half-year. **2.** lasting for half a year.

semiarid (,sɛmɪ'ærɪd) adj. denoting land that lies on the edges of a desert but has a slightly higher rainfall (above 300 mm) so that some farming is possible.

semiautomatic (,sɛmɪ,ɔːtə'mætɪk) adj. **1.** (of a firearm) self-loading but firing only one shot at each pull of the trigger. ∼n. **2.** a semiautomatic firearm.

semibreve ('sɛmɪ,briːv) n. *Music.* a note, now the longest in common use, having a time value that may be divided by any power of 2 to give all other notes.

semicircle ('sɛmɪ,sɜːk'l) n. **1.** one half of a circle. **2.** anything having the shape or form of half a circle. —**semicircular** (,sɛmɪ'sɜːkjʊlə) adj.

semicolon (,sɛmɪ'kəʊlən) n. the punctuation mark (;) used to separate clauses or items in a list, or to indicate a pause longer than that of a comma and shorter than that of a full stop.

semiconductor (,sɛmɪkən'dʌktə) n. a substance, such as silicon, which has an electrical conductivity that increases with temperature.

semiconscious (,sɛmɪ'kɒnʃəs) adj. not fully conscious. —**semi'consciousness** n.

semidetached (,sɛmɪdɪ'tætʃt) adj. **a.** (of a house) joined to another house on one side by a common wall. **b.** (as n.): *they live in a semidetached.*

semifinal (,sɛmɪ'faɪn'l) n. the round before the final in a competition. —**semi'finalist** n.

seminal ('sɛmɪn'l) adj. **1.** potentially capable of development. **2.** highly original and influential: *a seminal artist.* **3.** of semen: *seminal fluid.* **4.** *Biol.* of seed. [Latin *sēmen* seed]

seminar ('sɛmɪ,nɑː) n. **1.** a small group of students meeting regularly under the guidance of a tutor for study and discussion. **2.** one such meeting. [Latin *sēminārium* nursery garden]

seminary ('sɛmɪnərɪ) n., pl. **-naries.** an academy for the training of priests. [Latin *sēminārium* a nursery garden] —**seminarian** (,sɛmɪ'nɛərɪən) n.

semiotics (,sɛmɪ'ɒtɪks) n. (functioning as *sing.*) the study of human communication, esp. communication using signs and symbols. [Greek *sēmeion* a sign] —**semiotic** adj.

semipermeable (,sɛmɪ'pɜːmɪəb'l) adj. (of a cell membrane) allowing small molecules to pass through but not large ones.

semiprecious (,sɛmɪ'prɛʃəs) adj. (of certain stones) having less value than a precious stone.

semiprofessional (,sɛmɪprə'fɛʃən'l) adj. **1.** (of a person) engaged in an activity or sport part time for pay. **2.** (of an activity or sport) engaged in by semiprofessional people. ~n. **3.** a semiprofessional person.

semiquaver ('sɛmɪˌkweɪvə) n. Music. a note having the time value of one-sixteenth of a semibreve.

semiskilled (ˌsɛmɪˈskɪld) adj. partly skilled or trained but not sufficiently so to perform specialized work.

Semite ('siːmaɪt) n. a member of the group of peoples who speak a Semitic language, such as the Jews and Arabs. [New Latin *sēmīta* descendant of Shem, eldest of Noah's sons]

Semitic (sɪˈmɪtɪk) n. **1.** a group of languages that includes Arabic, Hebrew, and Aramaic. ~adj. **2.** belonging to this group of languages. **3.** of any of the peoples speaking a Semitic language, esp. the Jews or the Arabs. **4.** same as **Jewish.**

semitone ('sɛmɪˌtəʊn) n. the smallest interval between two notes in Western music represented on a piano by the difference in pitch between any two adjacent keys. —**semitonic** (ˌsɛmɪˈtɒnɪk) adj.

semitropical (ˌsɛmɪˈtrɒpɪkᵊl) adj. bordering on the tropics; nearly tropical. —ˌsemiˈtropics pl. n.

semivowel ('sɛmɪˌvaʊəl) n. Phonetics. a vowel-like sound that acts like a consonant, such as the sound of w in well.

semolina (ˌsɛməˈliːnə) n. the large hard grains of wheat left after flour has been milled, used for making puddings and pasta. [Italian *semolino*]

sempre ('sɛmprɪ) adv. Music. (of a tempo or volume) to be sustained throughout a piece or passage. [Italian]

SEN (in Britain) State Enrolled Nurse.

Sen. or **sen. 1.** senate. **2.** senator. **3.** senior.

Senate ('sɛnɪt) n. **1.** the upper chamber of the legislatures of the U.S., Canada, Australia, and many other countries. **2.** the main governing body at some universities. [Latin *senātus* council of the elders]

senator ('sɛnətə) n. a member of a Senate. —**senatorial** (ˌsɛnəˈtɔːrɪəl) adj.

send (sɛnd) vb. **sending, sent. 1.** to cause or order (a person or thing) to be taken, directed, or transmitted to another place: *to send a letter.* **2.** (foll. by *for*) to dispatch a request or command for (something): *he sent for a bottle of wine.* **3.** to cause to go to a place or point: *his blow sent the champion to the floor.* **4.** to bring to a state or condition: *this noise will send me mad.* **5.** to cause to happen or come: *misery sent by fate.* **6.** Slang. to move to excitement or rapture: *this music really sends me.* [Old English *sendan*] —**sender** n.

send down vb. **1.** Brit. to expel from a university. **2.** Informal. to send to prison.

sendoff ('sɛndˌɒf) n. **1.** Informal. a demonstration of good wishes to a person about to set off on a journey or start a new career. ~vb. **send off. 2.** to dispatch (something, such as a letter). **3.** Sport. (of

the referee) to dismiss (a player) from the field of play for some offence.

send up Brit. informal. ~vb. **1.** to make fun of by doing an imitation or parody. ~n. **send-up. 2.** a parody or imitation.

senescent (sɪˈnɛsᵊnt) adj. growing old. [Latin *senēscere* to grow old] —**seˈnescence** n.

seneschal ('sɛnɪʃəl) n. a steward of the household of a medieval prince or nobleman. [Old French]

senile ('siːnaɪl) adj. **1.** of old age. **2.** mentally or physically weak or infirm on account of old age. [Latin *senex* an old man] —**senility** (sɪˈnɪlɪtɪ) n.

senior ('siːnjə) adj. **1.** higher in rank or length of service. **2.** older in years: *senior citizens.* **3.** Education. of or designating more advanced or older pupils or students. ~n. **4.** a senior person. [Latin: older]

Senior ('siːnjə) adj. Chiefly U.S. being older than another of the same name: *Charles Parker, Senior.*

senior aircraftman n. an ordinary rank in the Royal Air Force.

senior citizen n. Euphemistic. an old age pensioner.

seniority (ˌsiːnɪˈɒrɪtɪ) n., pl. **-ties. 1.** the state of being senior. **2.** precedence in rank due to senior status.

senior service n. Brit. the Royal Navy.

senna ('sɛnə) n. **1.** a tropical plant with yellow flowers and long pods. **2.** the dried leaves and pods of this plant, used as a laxative. [Arabic *sanā*]

señor (sɛˈnjɔː) n., pl. **-ñors** or **-ñores** (-ˈnjɔːreɪ). a Spanish term of address equivalent to *sir* or *Mr*.

señora (sɛˈnjɔːrə) n. a Spanish term of address equivalent to *madam* or *Mrs.*

señorita (ˌsɛnjɔːˈriːtə) n. a Spanish term of address equivalent to *madam* or *Miss.*

sensation (sɛnˈseɪʃən) n. **1.** the power of feeling things physically: *I had lost all sensation in my legs.* **2.** a physical feeling: *a tingling sensation in my left arm.* **3.** a general feeling or awareness: *a sensation of fear.* **4.** a state of general excitement: *his announcement caused a sensation.* **5.** anything that causes such a state: *your speech was a sensation.* [Late Latin *sensātus* endowed with feelings]

sensational (sɛnˈseɪʃənᵊl) adj. **1.** causing or intended to cause intense feelings of shock, anger, or excitement: *sensational disclosures in the press.* **2.** Informal. extremely good: *a sensational skater.* **3.** of the senses or sensation. —**senˈsationally** adv.

sensationalism (sɛnˈseɪʃənᵊˌlɪzəm) n. the use of sensational language or subject matter to arouse intense feelings of shock, anger, or excitement. —**senˈsationalist** n.

sense (sɛns) n. **1.** any of the faculties (sight, hearing, touch, taste, and smell) by which the mind receives information about the external world or the state of the body. **2.** the ability to perceive. **3.** a feeling perceived through one of the senses: *a sense of warmth*. **4.** a mental perception or awareness: *a sense of happiness*. **5.** moral discernment: *a sense of right and wrong*. **6.** (*sometimes pl.*) sound practical judgment or intelligence: *take leave of one's senses*. **7.** reason or purpose: *what is the sense of going out?* **8.** general meaning: *he couldn't understand every word but he got the sense of what they were saying*. **9.** specific meaning; definition: *in what sense are you using the word?* **10. make sense.** to be understandable or practical. ~*vb.* **11.** to perceive through the senses. **12.** to perceive or detect without the evidence of the senses: *he sensed that he was being watched*. [Latin *sentīre* to feel]

senseless ('sɛnslɪs) *adj.* **1.** foolish: *a senseless plan*. **2.** unconscious. —'**senselessly** *adv.* —'**senselessness** *n.*

sense organ *n.* an organ or structure that receives stimuli and transmits them as sensations to the brain.

sensibility (ˌsɛnsɪ'bɪlɪtɪ) *n.*, *pl.* **-ties**. **1.** the ability to perceive or feel. **2.** (*often pl.*) the capacity for being affected emotionally. **3.** (*usually pl.*) tendency to be influenced or offended: *his sensibility to criticism*.

sensible ('sɛnsɪb°l) *adj.* **1.** having or showing good sense or judgment. **2.** (of clothing) serviceable; practical. **3.** capable of receiving sensation. **4.** capable of being perceived by the senses. **5.** perceptible to the mind. **6.** (sometimes foll. by *of*) aware: *sensible of your kindness*. [Latin *sentīre* to feel] —'**sensibly** *adv.*

sensitive ('sɛnsɪtɪv) *adj.* **1.** easily hurt; tender. **2.** responsive to external stimuli or impressions. **3.** easily offended or shocked. **4.** of the senses or sensation. **5.** (of an instrument) capable of registering small differences or changes in amounts. **6.** *Photog.* responding readily to light: *a sensitive emulsion*. **7.** *Chiefly U.S.* connected with matters affecting national security. **8.** (of a subject or issue) liable to arouse controversy or strong feelings. [Latin *sentīre* to feel] —'**sensitively** *adv.* —ˌsensi'**tivity** *n.*

sensitize *or* **-tise** ('sɛnsɪˌtaɪz) *vb.* to make sensitive. —ˌsensiti'**zation** *or* **-ti'sation** *n.*

sensor ('sɛnsə) *n.* a device that detects, measures, or records a physical property such as radiation.

sensory ('sɛnsərɪ) *adj.* of the senses or sensation.

sensual ('sɛnsjʊəl) *adj.* **1.** of the body and senses rather than the mind or soul. **2.** preoccupied with gratification of the senses. **3.** arousing the physical appetites, esp. the sexual appetite. [Latin *sēnsus* feeling] —'**sensualist** *n.*

sensuality (ˌsɛnsjʊ'ælɪtɪ) *n.* **1.** the quality or state of being sensual. **2.** excessive indulgence in sensual pleasures.

sensuous ('sɛnsjʊəs) *adj.* **1.** aesthetically pleasing to the senses. **2.** appreciative of qualities perceived by the senses. **3.** of or derived from the senses. —'**sensuously** *adv.*

sent (sɛnt) *vb.* past of **send**.

sentence ('sɛntəns) *n.* **1.** a sequence of words capable of standing alone to make an assertion, ask a question, or give a command, usually consisting of a subject and a predicate. **2. a.** the decision of a lawcourt, esp. as to what punishment is to be imposed. **b.** the punishment imposed. ~*vb.* **3.** to pronounce sentence on (a convicted person) in a lawcourt. [Latin *sententia* a way of thinking] —**sentential** (sɛn'tɛnʃəl) *adj.*

sententious (sɛn'tɛnʃəs) *adj.* **1.** full of or fond of using proverbs. **2.** given to pompous moralizing. [Latin *sententiōsus* full of meaning] —**sen'tentiousness** *n.*

sentient ('sɛntɪənt) *adj.* capable of perception and feeling. [Latin *sentiēns* feeling] —**sentience** ('sɛnʃəns) *n.*

sentiment ('sɛntɪmənt) *n.* **1.** susceptibility to tender or romantic emotion: *she has too much sentiment to be successful in business*. **2.** (*often pl.*) a thought, opinion, or attitude. **3.** exaggerated or mawkish emotion. **4.** a mental attitude based on a mixture of thoughts and feelings: *there is a strong revolutionary sentiment in this country*. **5.** a feeling conveyed or intended to be conveyed in words. [Latin *sentīre* to feel]

sentimental (ˌsɛntɪ'mɛnt°l) *adj.* **1.** tending to indulge the emotions excessively. **2.** making a direct appeal to the emotions, esp. to romantic feelings. —ˌsenti'**mentaˌlism** *n.* —ˌsenti'**mentalist** *n.* —sentimentality (ˌsɛntɪmɛn'tælɪtɪ) *n.* —ˌsenti'**mentally** *adv.*

sentimentalize *or* **-lise** (ˌsɛntɪ'mɛnt°ˌlaɪz) *vb.* to make sentimental or behave sentimentally.

sentimental value *n.* the value of an article to a particular person because of its sentimental associations.

sentinel ('sɛntɪn°l) *n.* a sentry. [Old French *sentinelle*]

sentry ('sɛntrɪ) *n.*, *pl.* **-tries.** a soldier who guards or prevents unauthorized access to a place. [perhaps from obs. *centrinel* sentinel]

sentry box *n.* a small shelter with an open front in which a sentry may stand during bad weather.

sepal ('sɛp°l) *n.* any of the separate parts of the calyx of a flower. [New Latin *sepalum*]

separable ('sɛpərəb°l) *adj.* able to be separated. —ˌsepara'**bility** *n.*

separate *vb.* ('sɛpəˌreɪt). **1.** to act as a barrier between: *a range of mountains separates the two countries*. **2.** to part or be parted from a mass or group. **3.** to discriminate between: *to separate the men from the boys*. **4.** to divide or be divided into component parts. **5.** to sever or be severed. **6.** (of a married couple) to stop living together. ~*adj.* ('sɛprɪt, 'sɛpərɪt). **7.** existing or considered independently: *a separate problem*. **8.** set apart from the main body or mass. **9.** distinct or individual. [Latin *sēparāre*] —'**separately** *adv.* —'**separateness** *n.* —'**sepaˌrator** *n.*

separates (ˈsɛprɪts, ˈsɛpərɪts) pl. n. garments, such as skirts, blouses, and trousers, that only cover part of the body and are designed to be worn together or separately.

separate school n. (in certain Canadian provinces) a school for a large religious minority financed by provincial grants in addition to the education tax.

separation (ˌsɛpəˈreɪʃən) n. 1. a separating or being separated. 2. the place or line where a separation is made. 3. a gap that separates. 4. *Family law.* an arrangement by which a husband and wife cease to live together.

separatist (ˈsɛpərətɪst) n. a person who advocates secession from an organization or country for his own political, religious, or racial group. —**ˈsepaˌtism** n.

sepia (ˈsiːpɪə) n. 1. a dark reddish-brown pigment obtained from the inky secretion of the cuttlefish. ~adj. 2. dark reddish-brown. [Latin: a cuttlefish]

sepoy (ˈsiːpɔɪ) n. (formerly) an Indian soldier in the service of the British. [Urdu *sipāhī*]

sepsis (ˈsɛpsɪs) n. poisoning caused by the presence of pus-forming bacteria in the body. [Greek: a rotting]

sept (sɛpt) n. a clan, esp. in Ireland or Scotland. [perhaps var. of *sect*]

Sept. September.

September (sɛpˈtɛmbə) n. the ninth month of the year. [Latin: the seventh (month)]

septennial (sɛpˈtɛnɪəl) adj. 1. occurring every seven years. 2. lasting seven years. [Latin *septem* + *annus* a year]

septet (sɛpˈtɛt) n. 1. *Music.* a group of seven performers or a piece of music composed for such a group. 2. a group of seven people or things. [Latin *septem* seven]

septic (ˈsɛptɪk) adj. of or caused by bacteria. —**septicity** (sɛpˈtɪsɪtɪ) n.

septicaemia or **septicemia** (ˌsɛptɪˈsiːmɪə) n. a disease caused by certain microorganisms and their poisonous products in the blood. [Greek *sēptos* decayed + *haima* blood] —**ˌseptiˈcaemic** or **ˌseptiˈcemic** adj.

septic tank n. a tank, usually below ground, in which sewage is decomposed by the action of bacteria.

septuagenarian (ˌsɛptjuədʒɪˈnɛərɪən) n. 1. a person who is from 70 to 79 years old. ~adj. 2. between 70 and 79 years old. [Latin *septuāgintā* seventy]

Septuagint (ˈsɛptjuəˌdʒɪnt) n. the ancient Greek version of the Old Testament, including the Apocrypha. [Latin *septuāgintā* seventy]

septum (ˈsɛptəm) n., pl. **-ta** (-tə). *Biol., anat.* a dividing partition between two tissues or cavities, as in the nose. [Latin *saeptum* wall]

septuple (ˈsɛptjupˈl) adj. 1. seven times as much or as many. 2. consisting of seven parts or members. ~vb. 3. to multiply by seven. [Latin *septem* seven]

sepulchral (sɪˈpʌlkrəl) adj. 1. suggestive of a tomb; gloomy. 2. of a sepulchre.

sepulchre or U.S. **sepulcher** (ˈsɛpəlkə) n. 1. a burial vault, tomb, or grave. ~vb. 2. to bury in a sepulchre. [Latin *sepulcrum*]

sepulture (ˈsɛpəltʃə) n. the act of placing in a sepulchre.

sequel (ˈsiːkwəl) n. 1. anything that follows from something else. 2. a consequence. 3. a novel, play, or film that continues a previously related story. [Latin *sequī* to follow]

sequence (ˈsiːkwəns) n. 1. an arrangement of two or more things in a successive order. 2. the successive order of two or more things: *chronological sequence.* 3. an action or event that follows another or others. 4. *Maths.* an ordered set of numbers or other quantities in one-to-one correspondence with the integers 1 to n. 5. a section of a film forming a single uninterrupted episode. [Latin *sequī* to follow]

sequential (sɪˈkwɛnʃəl) adj. characterized by or having a regular sequence.

sequester (sɪˈkwɛstə) vb. 1. to remove or separate. 2. to seclude. 3. *Law.* to confiscate (property) temporarily until creditors are satisfied or a court order is complied with. [Late Latin *sequestrāre* to surrender for safekeeping]

sequestrate (sɪˈkwɛstreɪt) vb. *Law.* same as **sequester** (sense 3). —**sequestration** (ˌsiːkwɛˈstreɪʃən) n. —**sequestrator** (ˈsiːkwɛsˌtreɪtə) n.

sequin (ˈsiːkwɪn) n. a small usually round piece of shiny metal foil, used to decorate garments. [Italian *zecchino*] —**ˈsequined** adj.

sequoia (sɪˈkwɔɪə) n. a giant Californian coniferous tree. [after *Sequoya*, American Indian scholar]

seraglio (sɛˈrɑːlɪˌəʊ) n., pl. **-raglios.** 1. the harem of a Muslim house or palace. 2. a Turkish sultan's palace. [Italian *serraglio* animal cage]

seraph (ˈsɛrəf) n., pl. **-aphs** or **-aphim** (-əfɪm). *Theol.* a member of the highest order of angels in the celestial hierarchy. [from Hebrew] —**seraphic** (sɪˈræfɪk) adj.

Serb (sɜːb) n., adj. same as **Serbian.**

Serbian (ˈsɜːbɪən) adj. 1. of Serbia, in Yugoslavia, its people, or their dialect of Serbo-Croatian. ~n. 2. the dialect of Serbo-Croatian spoken in Serbia. 3. a person from Serbia.

Serbo-Croatian (ˌsɜːbəʊkrəʊˈeɪʃən) or **Serbo-Croat** (ˌsɜːbəʊˈkrəʊæt) n. 1. the chief official language of Yugoslavia. ~adj. 2. of this language.

serenade (ˌsɛrɪˈneɪd) n. 1. a piece of music played outside a woman's window by a lover. 2. a piece of music suitable for this. 3. an orchestral suite for a small ensemble. ~vb. 4. to play a serenade (to). [French]

serendipity (ˌsɛrənˈdɪpɪtɪ) n. the natural talent for making fortunate discoveries by accident. [from the fairy tale *The Three Princes of Serendip,* in which the heroes possess this gift]

serene (sɪˈriːn) *adj.* **1.** peaceful or tranquil; calm. **2.** (of the sky) clear or bright. [Latin *serēnus*] —**seˈrenely** *adv.* —**serenity** (sɪˈrɛnɪtɪ) *n.*

serf (sɜːf) *n.* (esp. in medieval Europe) a labourer bound to the land on which he worked. [Latin *servus* a slave] —**serfdom** *n.*

serge (sɜːdʒ) *n.* a strong twill-weave fabric made of wool, cotton, silk, or rayon, used for clothing. [Old French *sarge*]

sergeant (ˈsɑːdʒənt) *n.* **1.** a noncommissioned officer in the armed forces. **2.** (in Britain) a police officer ranking between constable and inspector. [Old French *sergent*]

sergeant at arms *n.* an officer of a legislative body or court responsible for keeping order.

sergeant major *n.* a noncommissioned officer of the highest rank in a military headquarters.

serial (ˈsɪərɪəl) *n.* **1.** a story published or broadcast in instalments at regular intervals. **2.** a publication that is regularly issued and consecutively numbered. ~*adj.* **3.** of, in, or forming a series. **4.** published or presented as a serial. [Latin *seriēs* series]

serialize *or* **-lise** (ˈsɪərɪəˌlaɪz) *vb.* to publish or present in the form of a serial. —ˌseriali`ˈzation *or* -li`ˈsation *n.*

serial number *n.* any of the consecutive numbers assigned to objects in a series for identification.

series (ˈsɪərɪz) *n., pl.* **-ries. 1.** a group or succession of related things, usually arranged in order. **2.** a set of radio or television programmes dealing with the same subject, esp. one having the same characters but different stories. **3.** *Maths.* the sum of a finite or infinite sequence of numbers or quantities. **4.** *Electronics.* an arrangement of two or more components connected in a circuit so that the same current flows in turn through each of them: *a number of resistors in series.* **5.** a set of geological strata that represents the rocks formed during an epoch. [Latin: a row]

serif (ˈsɛrɪf) *n. Printing.* a small line projecting from a main stroke in a character. [origin unknown]

seriocomic (ˌsɪərɪəʊˈkɒmɪk) *adj.* mixing serious and comic elements.

serious (ˈsɪərɪəs) *adj.* **1.** grave in nature or disposition: *a serious person.* **2.** in earnest; sincere: *is he serious or joking?* **3.** concerned with important matters: *a serious conversation.* **4.** requiring concentration: *a serious book.* **5.** giving cause for concern: *a serious illness.* [Latin *sērius*] —**ˈseriously** *adv.* —**ˈseriousness** *n.*

serjeant (ˈsɑːdʒənt) *n.* same as **sergeant.**

sermon (ˈsɜːmən) *n.* **1.** a speech on a religious or moral subject given by a clergyman as part of a church service. **2.** a serious talk on behaviour, morals, or duty, esp. a long and tedious one. [Latin *sermō* discourse]

seropositive (ˌsɪərəʊˈpɒzɪtɪv) *adj.* (of a

person whose blood has been tested for a specific disease, such as AIDS) showing a significant level of serum antibodies, indicating the presence of the disease.

serous (ˈsɪərəs) *adj.* of, containing, or like serum.

serpent (ˈsɜːpənt) *n.* **1.** *Literary.* a snake. **2.** a sly or treacherous person. [Latin *serpēns* a creeping thing]

serpentine[1] (ˈsɜːpənˌtaɪn) *adj.* **1.** of or like a serpent. **2.** twisting; winding.

serpentine[2] (ˈsɜːpənˌtaɪn) *n.* a soft green or brownish-red mineral. [so named from its snakelike patterns]

serrate *adj.* (ˈsɛrɪt, -eɪt). **1.** having a notched or sawlike edge. ~*vb.* (sɛˈreɪt). **2.** to make serrate. [Latin *serrātus* sawshaped] —**serˈrated** *adj.* —**serˈration** *n.*

serried (ˈsɛrɪd) *adj.* in close or compact formation: *serried ranks of troops.* [Old French *serré* close-packed]

serum (ˈsɪərəm) *n.* **1.** the yellowish watery fluid left after the clotting factors have been removed from blood. **2.** antitoxin obtained from the blood serum of immunized animals. **3.** *Physiol., zool.* any clear watery animal fluid. [Latin: whey]

servant (ˈsɜːvənt) *n.* a person employed to work for another, esp. one who does household duties. [Old French: serving]

serve (sɜːv) *vb.* **1.** to work as a servant for (a person). **2.** to be of service to (a person, community, or cause); help. **3.** to perform an official duty or duties: *he served on the committee for three years.* **4.** to attend to (customers) in a shop. **5.** to provide (guests) with food or drink: *she served her guests with cocktails.* **6.** to provide (food or drink) for customers: *do you serve coffee?* **7.** to provide with something needed by the public: *the area served by London Transport.* **8.** to meet the needs of: *this will serve my purpose.* **9.** to perform a function: *this wood will serve to build a fire.* **10.** to go through (a due period of service, apprenticeship, or imprisonment). **11.** (of a male animal) to copulate with (a female animal). **12.** *Tennis, squash, etc.* to put (the ball) into play. **13.** to deliver (a legal document) to (a person). **14. serve someone right.** *Informal.* to be what someone deserves, esp. for doing something stupid or wrong. ~*n.* **15.** *Tennis, squash, etc.* short for **service.** [Latin *servus* a slave] —**ˈserver** *n.*

service (ˈsɜːvɪs) *n.* **1.** an act of help or assistance. **2.** an organization or system that provides something needed by the public: *telephone service.* **3.** the installation or maintenance of goods provided by a dealer after a sale. **4.** availability for use by the public: *the trams are no longer in service.* **5.** a periodic overhaul made on a machine or vehicle. **6.** the serving of guests or customers: *service is included in the price.* **7.** a department of public employment and its employees: *civil service.* **8.** one of the branches of the armed forces. **9.** the serving of food. **10.** a set of dishes, cups, and plates for use at table. **11.** a formal religious ceremony. **12.** *Tennis, squash, etc.* **a.** the act, manner, or right of serving a ball. **b.** the game in which a particular player serves: *he has lost his service.* **13.** (*modifier*) of or for the use of servants or employees: *service door.* **14.** (*modifier*) serving the public rather than producing goods: *service industry.* ~*vb.* **15.** to provide service or services to. **16.** to overhaul (a vehicle or machine). **17.** (of a male animal) to mate with (a female animal). ~See also **services.** [Latin *servitium* condition of a slave]

serviceable ('sɜːvɪsəb'l) *adj.* **1.** useful or ready for service. **2.** capable of giving good service. —,**servicea¹bility** *n.*

service area *n.* a place on a motorway providing garage services, restaurants, and toilet facilities.

service car *n.* N.Z. a bus operating on a long-distance route.

service charge *n.* a percentage added to a bill in a hotel or restaurant to pay for service.

service flat *n.* a flat where domestic services are provided by the management.

serviceman ('sɜːvɪsmən) *n., pl.* **-men.** **1.** a person in the armed services. **2.** a man employed to service and maintain equipment. —¹**service,woman** *fem. n.*

service road *n. Brit.* a narrow road running parallel to a main road that provides access to houses and shops situated along its length.

services ('sɜːvɪsɪz) *pl. n.* **1.** work performed in a job: *your services are no longer required.* **2.** (usually preceded by *the*) the armed forces. **3.** a system of providing the public with something it needs, such as gas or water.

service station *n.* **1.** a place that sells fuel and oil for motor vehicles and often carries out repairs and servicing. **2.** same as **service area.**

serviette (,sɜːvɪ'ɛt) *n. Chiefly Brit.* a table napkin. [Old French]

servile ('sɜːvaɪl) *adj.* **1.** obsequious or fawning in attitude or behaviour. **2.** of or suitable for a slave. [Latin *servus* slave] —**servility** (sɜː'vɪlɪtɪ) *n.*

serving ('sɜːvɪŋ) *n.* a portion of food.

servitor ('sɜːvɪtə) *n. Archaic.* a servant or attendant.

servitude ('sɜːvɪ,tjuːd) *n.* **1.** slavery or bondage. **2.** the state or condition of being completely dominated. [Latin *servus* a slave]

servomechanism ('sɜːvəʊ,mɛkə,nɪzəm) *n.* an automatic system in which feedback is used to compare output to input and any deviations in control are corrected.

sesame ('sɛsəmɪ) *n.* a plant of the East Indies, cultivated for its seeds and oil, which are used in cooking. [Greek]

sessile ('sɛsaɪl) *adj.* **1.** (of flowers or leaves) having no stalk. **2.** (of animals) fixed in one position. [Latin *sessilis* concerning sitting]

session ('sɛʃən) *n.* **1.** a meeting of a court, parliament, or council. **2.** a series or period of such meetings. **3.** a school or university term or year. **4.** any period devoted to

a particular activity. [Latin *sessiō* a sitting] —¹**sessional** *adj.*

sestet (sɛ'stɛt) *n.* **1.** *Prosody.* the last six lines of a sonnet. **2.** same as **sextet** (sense 1). [Italian *sesto* sixth]

set¹ (sɛt) *vb.* **setting, set. 1.** to put in a certain position or into a specified condition: *to set someone free.* **2.** (foll. by *to* or *on*) to bring (something) into contact with (something else): *he set fire to the house.* **3.** to put into order or readiness for use: *to set the table for dinner.* **4.** to form or be formed into a firm or rigid state: *the jelly set in three hours.* **5.** to put (a broken bone) or (of a broken bone) to be put into a normal position. **6.** to adjust (a clock or other instrument) to a particular position. **7.** to establish: *we have set the date for our wedding; set a bad example.* **8.** to prescribe or assign (a task or material for study): *the examiners have set "Paradise Lost".* **9.** to arrange in a decorative fashion: *she set her hair; a brooch set with rubies.* **10.** to provide music for (a poem or other text to be sung). **11.** *Printing.* **a.** to arrange (type) for printing. **b.** to put (text) into type. **12.** to arrange (a stage or television studio) with scenery and props. **13.** to represent (a scene or story) as happening at a certain time or place: *his novel is set in Russia.* **14.** (foll. by *on* or *by*) to value (something) at a specified price or worth: *he set a high price on his services.* **15.** (of the sun or moon) to disappear beneath the horizon. **16.** (of plants) to produce (fruits or seeds) or (of fruits or seeds) to develop. **17.** to place (a hen) on (eggs) for the purpose of incubation. **18.** (of a gun dog) to turn in the direction of game. ~*n.* **19.** a setting or being set. **20.** a condition of firmness or hardness. **21.** bearing, carriage, or posture: *the set of a gun dog when pointing.* **22.** the scenery and props used in a play or film. **23.** same as **sett.** ~*adj.* **24.** fixed or established by authority or agreement: *set hours of work.* **25.** rigid or inflexible: *she is set in her ways.* **26.** unmoving; fixed: *a set expression on his face.* **27.** conventional or stereotyped: *she made her apology in set phrases.* **28.** (foll. by *on* or *upon*) determined to (do or achieve something): *she is set upon marrying.* **29.** ready: *all set to go.* **30.** (of material for study) prescribed for students' preparation for an examination. ~See also **set about, set against,** etc. [Old English *settan*]

set² (sɛt) *n.* **1.** a number of objects or people grouped or belonging together: *a set of coins.* **2.** a group of people who associate with each other or have similar interests: *the tennis set.* **3.** *Maths.* a collection of numbers or objects that satisfy a given condition or share a property. **4.** a television or piece of radio equipment. **5.** *Tennis, squash, etc.* a group of games in a match, of which the winner must win a certain number. **6.** a series of songs or tunes performed by a musician or group on a given occasion: *the set included no new songs.* [Old French *sette*]

set about vb. **1.** to start or begin. **2.** to attack.

set against vb. **1.** to balance or compare. **2.** to cause to be unfriendly to.

set aside vb. **1.** to reserve for a special purpose. **2.** to discard or reject.

set back vb. **1.** to hinder; impede. **2.** Informal. to cost (a person) a specified amount. ~n. **setback. 3.** anything that hinders or impedes.

set down vb. **1.** to record in writing. **2.** to judge or regard: he set him down as an idiot. **3.** Brit. to allow (passengers) to alight from a bus, etc.

set forth vb. Formal or archaic. **1.** to state, express, or utter. **2.** to start out on a journey.

set in vb. **1.** to become established: the winter has set in. **2.** to insert.

set off vb. **1.** to embark on a journey. **2.** to cause (a person) to act or do something, such as laugh. **3.** to cause to explode. **4.** to act as a contrast to: that brooch sets your dress off well.

set on or **upon** vb. to attack or cause to attack: they set the dogs on him.

set out vb. **1.** to present, arrange, or display. **2.** to give a full account of: he set out the matter in full. **3.** to begin or embark on an undertaking, esp. a journey.

set piece n. **1.** a work of literature, music, or art, intended to create an impressive effect. **2.** a display of fireworks.

set square n. a thin flat piece of plastic or metal in the shape of a right-angled triangle, used in technical drawing.

sett or **set** (sɛt) n. **1.** a small rectangular paving block made of stone. **2.** a badger's burrow. [var. of SET¹ (n.)]

settee (sɛ'tiː) n. a seat, for two or more people, with a back and usually with arms. [from SETTLE²]

setter ('sɛtə) n. a large long-haired gun dog trained to point out game by standing rigid.

set theory n. Maths. the branch of mathematics concerned with the properties and interrelationships of sets.

setting ('sɛtɪŋ) n. **1.** the surroundings in which something is set. **2.** the scenery, properties, or background used to create the location for a stage play or film. **3.** Music. a composition consisting of a certain text and music arranged for it. **4.** the metal mounting in which a gem is set. **5.** the tableware and cutlery for a single place at table. **6.** one of the positions or levels to which the controls of a machine can be adjusted.

settle¹ ('sɛt'l) vb. **1.** to put in order: he settled his affairs before he died. **2.** to arrange or be arranged firmly or comfortably: he settled himself by the fire. **3.** to come down to rest: a bird settled on the hedge. **4.** to establish or become established as resident: the family settled in the country. **5.** to establish or become established in a way of life or job. **6.** to migrate to (a country) and form a community; colonize. **7.** to make or become quiet, calm, or stable. **8.** to cause (sediment) to sink to the bottom in a liquid or (of sediment) to

sink thus. **9.** to subside: the dust settled. **10.** (sometimes foll. by up) to pay off (a bill or debt). **11.** to decide or dispose of: to settle an argument. **12.** (often foll. by on or upon) to agree or fix: to settle upon a plan. **13.** (usually foll. by on or upon) to bestow (a title or property) on a person by gift or legal deed: he settled his property on his wife. **14.** to decide (a legal dispute) by agreement without court action: they settled out of court. [Old English setlan]

settle² ('sɛt'l) n. a long wooden bench with a high back and arms, sometimes having a storage space under the seat. [Old English setl]

settle down vb. **1.** to make or become quiet and orderly. **2.** (often foll. by to) to apply oneself diligently: please settle down to work. **3.** to adopt an orderly and routine way of life, esp. after marriage.

settle for vb. to accept or agree to in spite of dissatisfaction.

settlement ('sɛt'lmənt) n. **1.** a settling or being settled. **2.** a place newly settled; colony. **3.** subsidence of all or part of a building. **4.** an official agreement ending a dispute. **5.** Law. **a.** an arrangement by which property is transferred to a person's possession. **b.** the deed transferring such property.

settler ('sɛtlə) n. a person who settles in a new country or a colony.

set to vb. **1.** to begin working. **2.** to start fighting. ~n. **set-to. 3.** Informal. a brief disagreement or fight.

set up vb. **1.** to put into a position of power or wealth. **2.** to begin or enable (someone) to begin (a new venture). **3.** to build or construct: to set up a shed. **4.** to begin or produce: to set up a wail. **5.** to restore the health of: the sea air will set you up again. **6.** to establish: set up a theory. **7.** Informal. to cause (a person) to be blamed or accused. ~n. **setup. 8.** Informal. the way in which something is organized or arranged. **9.** Slang, chiefly U.S. & Canad. an event the result of which is prearranged.

seven ('sɛv'n) n. **1.** the cardinal number that is the sum of one and six. **2.** a numeral, 7, VII, representing this number. **3.** something representing or consisting of seven units. ~det. **4.** amounting to seven. [Old English seofon] —'**seventh** adj., n.

sevenfold ('sɛv'n,fəʊld) adj. **1.** having seven times as many. **2.** composed of seven parts. ~adv. **3.** by seven times as much.

seven seas pl. n. all the oceans of the world.

seventeen ('sɛv'n'tiːn) n. **1.** the cardinal number that is the sum of ten and seven. **2.** a numeral, 17, XVII, representing this number. **3.** something representing or consisting of seventeen units. ~det. **4.** amounting to seventeen. —'**seven'teenth** adj., n.

seventh heaven n. a state of supreme happiness.

seventy ('sɛv'ntɪ) n., pl. **-ties. 1.** the

cardinal number that is the product of ten and seven. **2.** a numeral, 70, LXX, representing this number. **3.** (*pl.*) the numbers 70–79, esp. the 70th to the 79th year of a person's life or of a century. **4.** something represented by or consisting of seventy units. ~*det.* **5.** amounting to seventy. —'**seventieth** *adj.*, *n.*

sever ('sɛvə) *vb.* **1.** to put or be put apart. **2.** to divide or be divided into parts. **3.** to break off or dissolve (a tie or relationship). [Latin *sēparāre* to separate] —'**severable** *adj.* —'**severance** *n.*

several ('sɛvrəl) *det.* **1.** more than a few: *several people objected.* ~*adj.* **2.** respective; separate: *the members with their several occupations.* **3.** distinct; different: *three several times.* [Medieval Latin *sēparālis*]

severance pay *n.* compensation paid by a firm to an employee for loss of employment.

severe (sɪ'vɪə) *adj.* **1.** strict or harsh in the treatment of others: *a severe parent.* **2.** serious in appearance or manner: *a severe expression; a severe hairstyle.* **3.** serious or dangerous: *a severe illness; a severe shortage.* **4.** causing discomfort by its harshness: *severe weather.* **5.** hard to perform or accomplish: *a severe test.* [Latin *sevērus*] —se'**verely** *adv.* —**severity** (sɪ'vɛrɪtɪ) *n.*

Seville orange (sə'vɪl) *n.* a bitter orange used to make marmalade. [after *Seville* in Spain]

Sèvres ('sɛvrə) *n.* a kind of fine French porcelain. [after *Sèvres*, near Paris]

sew (səʊ) *vb.* **sewing, sewed; sewn** *or* **sewed.** **1.** to join or decorate (pieces of fabric) by means of a thread repeatedly passed through with a needle. **2.** (often foll. by *on* or *up*) to attach, fasten, or close by sewing. ~See also **sew up.** [Old English *sēowan*]

sewage ('suːɪdʒ) *n.* waste matter that is carried away in sewers or drains.

sewage farm *n.* a place where sewage is treated so that it can be used as manure or disposed of safely.

sewer (suə) *n.* a drain or pipe, usually underground, used to carry away surface water or sewage. [Old French *essever* to drain]

sewerage ('suərɪdʒ) *n.* **1.** a system of sewers. **2.** the removal of surface water or sewage by means of sewers.

sewing ('səʊɪŋ) *n.* a piece of fabric or an article, that is sewn or to be sewn.

sewing machine *n.* a machine designed to sew material, with a needle driven by an electric motor, by a foot treadle, or by hand.

sewn (səʊn) *vb.* a past participle of **sew.**

sew up *vb.* **1.** to fasten or mend completely by sewing. **2.** *Informal.* to complete or negotiate successfully: *to sew up a deal.*

sex (sɛks) *n.* **1.** the characteristic of being either male or female. **2.** either of the two categories, male or female, into which organisms are placed. **3.** short for **sexual**

intercourse. **4.** feelings or behaviour connected with having sex or the desire to have sex. **5.** sexual matters in general. ~*modifier.* **6.** of sexual matters: *sex education.* **7.** based on or arising from the difference between the sexes: *sex discrimination.* ~*vb.* **8.** to ascertain the sex of. [Latin *sexus*]

sexagenarian (,sɛksədʒɪ'nɛərɪən) *n.* **1.** a person from 60 to 69 years old. ~*adj.* **2.** being from 60 to 69 years old. [Latin *sexāgintā* sixty]

sex appeal *n.* sexual attractiveness.

sex chromosome *n.* either of the chromosomes that determine the sex of an animal.

sexism ('sɛksɪzəm) *n.* discrimination on the basis of sex, esp. the oppression of women by men. —'**sexist** *n.*, *adj.*

sexless ('sɛkslɪs) *adj.* **1.** neither male nor female. **2.** having no sexual desires. **3.** sexually unattractive.

sex object *n.* someone, esp. a woman, regarded only in terms of physical attractiveness and not as a person.

sexology (sɛk'sɒlədʒɪ) *n.* the study of sexual behaviour in human beings. —**sex-'ologist** *n.*

sextant ('sɛkstənt) *n.* an instrument used in navigation for measuring angular distance, as between the sun and the horizon, to enable the position of a ship or aeroplane to be calculated. [Latin *sextāns* one sixth of a unit]

sextet (sɛks'tɛt) *n.* **1.** *Music.* a group of six performers or a piece of music composed for such a group. **2.** a group of six people or things. [var. of *sestet*]

sexton ('sɛkstən) *n.* a man employed to look after a church and its churchyard. [Medieval Latin *sacristānus* sacristan]

sextuple ('sɛkstjʊpʰl) *n.* **1.** a sixfold quantity or number. ~*adj.* **2.** six times as many. **3.** composed of six parts. [Latin *sextus* sixth]

sextuplet ('sɛkstjʊplɪt) *n.* one of six children born at one birth.

sexual ('sɛksjʊəl) *adj.* **1.** of or characterized by sex. **2.** (of reproduction) characterized by the union of male and female gametes. —**sexuality** (,sɛksjʊ'ælɪtɪ) *n.* —'**sexually** *adv.*

sexual harassment *n.* the persistent unwelcome directing of sexual remarks, looks, or advances, at a woman, esp. in the workplace.

sexual intercourse *n.* the sexual act in which the male's erect penis is inserted into the female's vagina, usually followed by the ejaculation of semen.

sexy ('sɛksɪ) *adj.* **sexier, sexiest.** *Informal.* **1.** provoking or intended to provoke sexual interest: *a sexy dress.* **2.** interesting, exciting, or trendy: *a sexy project; a sexy new car.* —'**sexiness** *n.*

sf *or* **sfz** *Music.* sforzando.

SF *or* **sf** science fiction.

SFA Scottish Football Association.

sforzando (sfɔː'tsændəʊ) *adv. Music.* to be played with sudden emphasis. [Italian]

Sgt. Sergeant.

sh (*spelling pron.* ʃ̃) *interj.* be quiet!

shabby ('ʃæbɪ) *adj.* **-bier, -biest. 1.** threadbare or dilapidated in appearance. **2.** wearing worn and dirty clothes. **3.** mean or unworthy: *shabby treatment*. [Old English *sceabb* scab] —'**shabbily** *adv.* —'**shabbiness** *n.*

shack (ʃæk) *n.* **1.** a roughly built hut. ~*vb.* **2.** See **shack up.** [perhaps from dialect *shackly* ramshackle]

shackle ('ʃæk³l) *n.* **1.** (*often pl.*) a metal ring or fastening, usually in pairs, used to secure a person's wrists or ankles. **2.** (*often pl.*) anything that confines or restricts freedom. **3.** a metal loop or link closed by a bolt, used for securing ropes or chains. ~*vb.* **4.** to confine or fasten with or as if with shackles. [Old English *sceacel*]

shack up *vb.* (foll. by *with*) *Slang.* to live with (a lover).

shad (ʃæd) *n., pl.* **shad** *or* **shads.** a herring-like food fish. [Old English *sceadd*]

shade (ʃeɪd) *n.* **1.** relative darkness produced by blocking out sunlight. **2.** a place made relatively darker or cooler than other areas by blocking out sunlight. **3.** a position of relative obscurity: *his present puts mine in the shade.* **4.** something used to provide a shield or protection from a direct source of light, such as a lampshade. **5.** a shaded area in a painting or drawing. **6.** a colour that varies slightly from a standard colour: *a darker shade of green.* **7.** a slight amount: *a shade of difference.* **8.** *Literary.* a ghost. ~*vb.* **9.** to screen or protect from heat or light. **10.** to make darker or dimmer. **11.** to represent (a darker area) in (a painting or drawing), by graded areas of tone, lines, or dots. **12.** to change slightly or by degrees. [Old English *sceadu*]

shades (ʃeɪdz) *pl. n.* **1.** gathering darkness at nightfall. **2.** *Slang.* sunglasses. **3.** (foll. by *of*) a reminder: *shades of Robin Hood!*

shading ('ʃeɪdɪŋ) *n.* the graded areas of tone, lines, or dots, indicating light and dark in a painting or drawing.

shadow ('ʃædəʊ) *n.* **1.** a dark image or shape cast on a surface when something stands between a light and the surface. **2.** an area of relative darkness. **3.** the dark portions of a picture. **4.** a hint or faint trace: *beyond a shadow of a doubt.* **5.** a weakened remnant: *a shadow of one's past self.* **6.** a threatening influence: *a shadow over one's happiness.* **7.** an inseparable companion. **8.** a person who trails another in secret, such as a detective. **9.** (*modifier*) *Brit.* designating a member or members of the main opposition party in Parliament who would hold ministerial office if their party were in power: *shadow cabinet.* ~*vb.* **10.** to cast a shade or shadow over. **11.** to make dark or gloomy. **12.** to follow or trail secretly. [Old English *sceadwe*]

shadow-box *vb. Boxing.* to box against an imaginary opponent for practice. —'**shadow-,boxing** *n.*

shadowy ('ʃædəʊɪ) *adj.* **1.** dark; shady. **2.** resembling a shadow in faintness: *a shadowy figure.* **3.** illusory or imaginary.

shady ('ʃeɪdɪ) *adj.* **shadier, shadiest. 1.** full of shade; shaded. **2.** giving or casting shade. **3.** *Informal.* questionable as to honesty or legality. —'**shadiness** *n.*

shaft (ʃɑːft) *n.* **1. a.** a spear or arrow. **b.** its long narrow stem. **2.** something directed at a person in the manner of a missile: *shafts of wit.* **3.** a ray or streak of light. **4.** the handle of a tool. **5.** a revolving rod in a machine that transmits motion or power. **6.** one of the two wooden poles by which an animal is harnessed to a vehicle. **7.** the middle part of a column or pier, between the base and the capital. **8.** a vertical passageway through a building, as for a lift. **9.** a vertical passageway into a mine. [Old English *sceaft*]

shag[1] (ʃæg) *n.* **1.** a matted tangle of hair or wool. **2.** a napped fabric, usually a rough wool. **3.** shredded coarse tobacco. [Old English *sceacga*]

shag[2] (ʃæg) *n.* same as **cormorant.** [special use of SHAG[1], with reference to its crest]

shaggy ('ʃægɪ) *adj.* **-gier, -giest. 1.** having or covered with rough unkempt fur, hair, or wool: *a shaggy dog.* **2.** rough or unkempt. —'**shagginess** *n.*

shagreen (ʃæ'griːn) *n.* **1.** the skin of a shark, used as an abrasive. **2.** a rough grainy leather made from certain animal hides. [French *chagrin*]

shah (ʃɑː) *n.* a ruler of certain Middle Eastern countries, esp. (formerly) Iran. [Persian: king]

shake (ʃeɪk) *vb.* **shaking, shook, shaken. 1.** to move up and down or back and forth with short quick movements. **2.** to sway or totter or cause to sway or totter. **3.** to clasp or grasp (the hand) of (a person) in greeting or agreement: *he shook John's hand.* **4. shake on it.** *Informal.* to shake hands in agreement or reconciliation. **5.** to wave or brandish: *he shook his sword.* **6.** (often foll. by *up*) to rouse or agitate. **7.** to shock, disturb, or upset: *he was shaken by the news.* **8.** to undermine or weaken: *the crisis shook his faith.* **9.** *U.S. & Canad. informal.* to get rid of. **10.** *Music.* to perform a trill on (a note). **11. shake one's head.** to indicate disagreement or disapproval by moving the head from side to side. ~*n.* **12.** the act or an instance of shaking. **13.** a tremor or vibration. **14. the shakes.** *Informal.* a state of uncontrollable trembling. **15.** *Informal.* a very short period of time: *in half a shake.* **16.** *Music.* same as **trill**[1] (sense 1). **17.** short for **milk shake.** ~See also **shake down, shake off, shake up.** [Old English *sceacan*]

shake down *vb.* **1.** to fall or settle or cause to fall or settle by shaking. **2.** to go to bed, esp. in a makeshift bed. ~*n.* **shakedown. 3.** a makeshift bed.

shake off *vb.* **1.** to remove or be removed with or as if with a quick movement: *she shook off her depression.* **2.** to escape from; elude: *they shook off the police.*

shaker ('ʃeɪkə) *n.* **1.** a container from which a powdered substance is shaken. **2.**

a container in which the ingredients of alcoholic drinks are shaken together.

Shakespearean or **Shakespearian** (ʃeik'spiəriən) adj. **1.** of William Shakespeare, English dramatist and poet, or his works. ~n. **2.** a student of or specialist in Shakespeare's works.

shake up vb. **1.** to shake in order to mix. **2.** to reorganize drastically. **3.** Informal. to shock mentally or physically. ~n. **shake-up. 4.** Informal. a radical reorganization, such as the reorganization of employees in a company.

shako ('ʃækəu) n., pl. **shakos** or **shakoes.** a tall cylindrical peaked military hat with a plume. [Hungarian csákó]

shaky ('ʃeiki) adj. **shakier, shakiest. 1.** tending to shake or tremble. **2.** unsound or infirm. **3.** uncertain or questionable: your arguments are very shaky. —'**shakily** adv.

shale (ʃeil) n. a soft fine-grained sedimentary rock formed by compression of successive layers of clay. [Old English scealu shell]

shall (ʃæl; unstressed ʃəl) vb. past **should.** used as an auxiliary: **1.** (esp. with I or we as subject) to make the future tense: we shall see you tomorrow. **2.** (with you, he, she, it, they, or a noun as subject) **a.** to indicate determination on the part of the speaker: you shall pay for this! **b.** to indicate compulsion or obligation, now esp. in official documents. **c.** to indicate certainty or inevitability: our day shall come. **3.** (with I or we as subject) in questions asking for advice or agreement: what shall we do now? shall I shut the door? [Old English sceal]

shallot (ʃə'lɒt) n. a small, onion-like plant with clusters of round bulbs which are used in cooking for flavouring. [Old French eschaloigne]

shallow ('ʃæləu) adj. **1.** having little depth. **2.** lacking depth of intellect or character; superficial. ~n. **3.** (often pl.) a shallow place in a body of water. [Middle English shalow] —'**shallowness** n.

sham (ʃæm) n. **1.** anything that is not genuine or is not what it appears to be. **2.** a person who pretends to be something other than he is. ~adj. **3.** counterfeit or false. ~vb. **shamming, shammed. 4.** to fake or feign (something); pretend: to sham illness. [origin unknown]

shaman ('ʃæmən) n. **1.** a priest of shamanism. **2.** a medicine man or witch doctor of a similar religion. [Russian]

shamanism ('ʃæmə,nizəm) n. a religion of northern Asia, based on a belief in good and evil spirits who can be influenced or controlled only by the shamans. —'**shamanist** n., adj.

shamble ('ʃæmbʲl) vb. **1.** to walk or move along in an awkward or unsteady way. ~n. **2.** an awkward or unsteady walk. [perhaps from shambles, referring to legs of a meat vendor's table] —'**shambling** adj., n.

shambles ('ʃæmbʲlz) n. (functioning as sing. or pl.) **1.** a place of great disorder: the room was a shambles after the party.

2. a slaughterhouse. **3.** any scene of great slaughter. [Middle English shamble table used by meat vendors]

shambolic (ʃæm'bɒlik) adj. Informal. completely disorganized; chaotic.

shame (ʃeim) n. **1.** a painful emotion resulting from an awareness of having done something dishonourable, unworthy, or foolish. **2.** capacity to feel such an emotion: have you no shame? **3.** ignominy or disgrace. **4.** a person or thing that causes this. **5.** a cause for regret or disappointment: it's a shame you can't come with us. **6. put to shame. a.** to disgrace. **b.** to surpass totally. ~vb. **7.** to cause to feel shame. **8.** to bring shame on. **9.** (often foll. by into) to compel through a sense of shame: I shamed him into apologizing. [Old English scamu]

shamefaced ('ʃeim,feist) adj. **1.** bashful or modest. **2.** showing shame. [earlier shamefast] —**shamefacedly** (ʃeim'feisid-li) adv.

shameful ('ʃeimful) adj. causing or deserving shame. —'**shamefully** adv.

shameless ('ʃeimlis) adj. **1.** having no sense of shame. **2.** without decency or modesty. —'**shamelessly** adv.

shammy ('ʃæmi) n., pl. **-mies.** Informal. same as **chamois** (sense 3). [var. of chamois]

shampoo (ʃæm'puː) n. **1.** a soapy liquid used to wash the hair. **2.** a similar liquid for washing carpets or upholstery. **3.** the process of shampooing. ~vb. **-pooing, -pooed. 4.** to wash (the hair, carpets, or upholstery) with shampoo. [Hindi]

shamrock ('ʃæm,rɒk) n. a small cloverlike plant with three round leaves on each stem: the national emblem of Ireland. [Irish Gaelic seamróg]

shandy ('ʃændi) n., pl. **-dies.** a drink made of beer and ginger beer or lemonade. [origin unknown]

shanghai ('ʃæŋhai, ʃæŋ'hai) Slang. ~vb. **-haiing, -haied. 1.** to kidnap (a man) for enforced service at sea. **2.** to force or trick (someone) into doing something. **3.** Austral. & N.Z. to shoot with a catapult. ~n. **4.** Austral. & N.Z. a catapult. [after the city of Shanghai]

shank (ʃæŋk) n. **1.** the part of the leg between the knee and the ankle. **2.** a cut of meat from the top part of an animal's shank. **3.** the long narrow part of a tool, key, spoon, or other object. [Old English scanca]

shanks's pony or U.S. **shanks's mare** ('ʃæŋksiz) n. Informal. one's own legs as a means of transportation.

shan't (ʃɑːnt) shall not.

shantung (,ʃæn'tʌŋ) n. a heavy silk fabric with a knobbly surface. [after province of NE China]

shanty¹ ('ʃænti) n., pl. **-ties.** a ramshackle hut; crude dwelling. [Canad. French chantier cabin built in a lumber camp]

shanty² ('ʃænti) or **chanty** n., pl. **-ties.** a rhythmical song originally sung by sailors as an accompaniment to work. [French chanter to sing]

shantytown ('ʃæntɪˌtaʊn) *n.* a town inhabited by poor people living in shanties.

shape (ʃeɪp) *n.* **1.** the outward form of an object, produced by its outline. **2.** the figure or outline of the body of a person. **3.** organized or definite form: *my plans are taking shape.* **4.** the specific form or guise that anything assumes. **5.** pattern; mould. **6.** condition or state of efficiency: *to be in good shape.* **7. take shape.** to assume a definite form. ~*vb.* **8.** (often foll. by *into* or *up*) to receive or cause to receive shape or form. **9.** to mould into a particular pattern or form. **10.** to plan, devise, or prepare: *to shape a plan of action.* ~See also **shape up.** [Old English *gesceap*]

shapeless ('ʃeɪplɪs) *adj.* **1.** having no definite shape or form: *a shapeless mass.* **2.** lacking a pleasing shape: *a shapeless figure.* —'**shapelessness** *n.*

shapely ('ʃeɪplɪ) *adj.* **-lier, -liest.** (esp. of a woman's body or legs) pleasing or attractive in shape. —'**shapeliness** *n.*

shape up *vb. Informal.* **1.** to proceed or develop satisfactorily. **2.** to develop a definite or proper form.

shard (ʃɑːd) *or* **sherd** *n.* a broken piece or fragment of pottery, glass, or metal. [Old English *sceard*]

share[1] (ʃɛə) *n.* **1.** a part or portion of something that belongs to or is contributed by a person or group. **2.** (*often pl.*) any of the equal parts into which the basic stock of a company is divided. ~*vb.* **3.** (often foll. by *out*) to divide and distribute. **4.** (often foll. by *in*) to receive or contribute a portion of: *we can share the cost of the petrol.* **5.** to join with another or others in the use of (something): *can I share your umbrella?* [Old English *scearu*]

share[2] (ʃɛə) *n.* short for **ploughshare.** [Old English *scear*]

shareholder ('ʃɛəˌhəʊldə) *n.* the owner of one or more shares in a company.

shark (ʃɑːk) *n.* **1.** a large, usually ferocious fish with a long body, two dorsal fins, and rows of sharp teeth. **2.** a person who swindles or extorts money from other people. [origin unknown]

sharkskin ('ʃɑːkˌskɪn) *n.* a smooth glossy fabric used for sportswear and petticoats.

sharp (ʃɑːp) *adj.* **1.** having a keen edge suitable for cutting. **2.** tapering to an edge or point. **3.** involving a sudden change in direction: *a sharp bend; a sharp rise in prices.* **4.** moving, acting, or reacting quickly: *sharp reflexes.* **5.** clearly defined: *a sharp contrast.* **6.** mentally acute; keen-witted; attentive. **7.** sly; clever in an underhand way: *sharp practice.* **8.** bitter or harsh: *sharp words.* **9.** shrill or penetrating: *a sharp cry.* **10.** having a bitter or sour taste. **11.** keen; biting: *a sharp wind.* **12.** *Music.* **a.** (of a note) raised in pitch by one semitone: *F sharp.* **b.** (of an instrument or voice) out of tune by being too high in pitch. **13.** *Informal.* stylish: *a sharp dresser.* ~*adv.* **14.** in a sharp manner. **15.** exactly: *six o'clock sharp.* **16.** *Music.* **a.** higher than a standard pitch. **b.** out of tune by being too high in pitch: *she sings sharp.* ~*n.* **17.** *Music.* **a.** an

accidental that raises the pitch of a note by one semitone. **b.** a note affected by this accidental. **18.** *Informal.* a cheat; sharper. [Old English *scearp*] —'**sharpish** *adj.* —'**sharply** *adv.* —'**sharpness** *n.*

sharpen ('ʃɑːpʰn) *vb.* to make or become sharp or sharper. —'**sharpener** *n.*

sharper ('ʃɑːpə) *n.* a person who cheats or swindles; fraud.

sharpshooter ('ʃɑːpˌʃuːtə) *n.* a skilled marksman.

sharp-tongued *adj.* bitter or critical in speech; sarcastic.

sharp-witted *adj.* having or showing a keen intelligence; perceptive.

shatter ('ʃætə) *vb.* **1.** to break suddenly into many small pieces. **2.** to impair or destroy: *his nerves were shattered by the torture.* **3.** to dumbfound or thoroughly upset: *she was shattered by the news.* **4.** *Informal.* to cause (someone) to be tired out or exhausted. [origin unknown] —'**shattered** *adj.* —'**shattering** *adj.*

shave (ʃeɪv) *vb.* **shaving, shaved;** **shaved** *or* **shaven** ('ʃeɪvʰn). **1.** to remove (the beard or hair) from (the face, head, or body) by using a razor or shaver. **2.** to remove thin slices from (wood or other material) with a sharp cutting tool. **3.** to touch (someone or something) lightly in passing. ~*n.* **4.** the act or an instance of shaving. **5.** a tool for cutting off thin slices. **6. close shave.** *Informal.* a narrow escape. [Old English *sceafan*]

shaver ('ʃeɪvə) *n.* **1.** an electrically powered razor. **2.** *Informal.* a young boy.

Shavian ('ʃeɪvɪən) *adj.* **1.** of or like George Bernard Shaw, Irish dramatist, or his works. ~*n.* **2.** an admirer of Shaw or his works.

shaving ('ʃeɪvɪŋ) *n.* **1.** a thin slice of something such as wood, which has been shaved off. ~*modifier.* **2.** used when shaving: *shaving cream.*

shawl (ʃɔːl) *n.* a piece of woollen cloth worn over the head or shoulders by a woman or wrapped around a baby. [Persian *shāl*]

she (ʃiː) *pron.* refers to: **1.** the female person or animal previously mentioned or in question: *she is an actress.* **2.** something regarded as female, such as a car, ship, or nation. ~*n.* **3.** a female person or animal. [Old English *sīe*]

sheaf (ʃiːf) *n., pl.* **sheaves. 1.** a bundle of reaped corn tied together. **2.** a bundle of objects tied together. ~*vb.* **3.** to bind or tie into a sheaf. [Old English *sceaf*]

shear (ʃɪə) *vb.* **shearing, sheared** *or* archaic, Austral., & N.Z. sometimes **shore; sheared** *or* **shorn. 1.** to remove (the fleece) of (a sheep) by cutting or clipping. **2.** to cut or cut through (something) with shears or a sharp instrument. **3.** *Engineering.* to cause (a part) to deform or fracture or (of a part) to deform or fracture through strain, fatigue, or twisting. **4.** (often foll. by *of*) to strip or divest: *to shear someone of his power.* ~*n.* **5.** deformation or fracture caused through strain, fatigue, or twisting. ~See also **shears.** [Old English *sceran*] —'**shearer** *n.*

shears (ʃɪəz) *pl. n.* **a.** large scissors. **b.** a large scissor-like cutting tool with flat blades, used for cutting hedges.

sheath (ʃiːθ) *n., pl.* **sheaths** (ʃiːðz). **1.** a case or covering for the blade of a knife or sword. **2.** *Biol.* an enclosing or protective structure. **3.** same as **condom. 4.** a close-fitting dress. [Old English *scēath*]

sheathe (ʃiːð) *vb.* **1.** to insert (a knife or sword) into a sheath. **2.** to enclose or encase in a sheath or sheathing.

sheathing (ˈʃiːðɪŋ) *n.* any material used as an outer layer.

sheave (ʃiːv) *vb.* to gather or bind into sheaves.

sheaves (ʃiːvz) *n.* the plural of **sheaf.**

shebeen *or* **shebean** (ʃəˈbiːn) *n. Irish, Scot., & S. African.* a place where alcoholic drink is sold illegally. [Irish Gaelic *sibín* beer of poor quality]

shed[1] (ʃɛd) *n.* **1.** a small, roughly made building used for storage or shelter. **2.** a large barnlike structure used for storage, repairing locomotives, or other purposes. [Old English *sced*]

shed[2] (ʃɛd) *vb.* **shedding, shed. 1.** to pour forth or cause to pour forth: *to shed tears.* **2. shed light on** *or* **upon.** to clarify (a problem or situation). **3.** to cast off or lose: *the snake shed its skin.* **4.** to cause to flow off: *this coat sheds water.* **5.** to separate or divide (a group of sheep). [Old English *sceadan*]

sheen (ʃiːn) *n.* a gleaming or glistening brightness; lustre. [Old English *sciene*]

sheep (ʃiːp) *n., pl.* **sheep. 1.** a cud-chewing mammal with a thick woolly coat, kept for its wool or meat. **2.** a meek or timid person. **3. separate the sheep from the goats.** to pick out the members of a group who are superior in some respects. [Old English *sceap*] —**ˈsheepˌlike** *adj.*

sheep-dip *n.* **1.** a liquid disinfectant and insecticide in which sheep are immersed. **2.** a deep trough containing such a liquid.

sheepdog (ˈʃiːpˌdɒg) *n.* **1.** a dog used for herding sheep. **2.** a breed of dog reared originally for herding sheep.

sheepfold (ˈʃiːpˌfəʊld) *n.* a pen or enclosure for sheep.

sheepish (ˈʃiːpɪʃ) *adj.* abashed or embarrassed, esp. through looking foolish. —**ˈsheepishly** *adv.*

sheepshank (ˈʃiːpˌʃæŋk) *n.* a knot made in a rope to shorten it temporarily.

sheepskin (ˈʃiːpˌskɪn) *n.* the skin of a sheep with the wool still attached, used to make clothing and rugs.

sheer[1] (ʃɪə) *adj.* **1.** perpendicular; very steep: *a sheer cliff.* **2.** (of textiles) so fine as to be transparent. **3.** absolute: *sheer folly.* ~*adv.* **4.** steeply. **5.** completely or absolutely. [Old English *scīr*]

sheer[2] (ʃɪə) *vb.* (foll. by *off* or *away* (*from*)). **1.** to change or cause to change course suddenly. **2.** to avoid an unpleasant person, thing, or topic. [origin unknown]

sheet[1] (ʃiːt) *n.* **1.** a large rectangular piece of cloth, generally one of a pair used as

inner bedclothes. **2.** a thin piece of material such as paper or glass, usually rectangular. **3.** a broad continuous surface or layer: *a sheet of water.* **4.** a newspaper. ~*vb.* **5.** to provide with, cover, or wrap in a sheet. [Old English *sciete*]

sheet[2] (ʃiːt) *n. Naut.* a line or rope for controlling the position of a sail. [Old English *scēata* corner of a sail]

sheet anchor *n. Naut.* a large strong anchor for use in an emergency.

sheeting (ˈʃiːtɪŋ) *n.* any material from which sheets are made.

sheet metal *n.* metal formed into a thin sheet by rolling or hammering.

sheet music *n.* music printed on unbound sheets of paper.

sheikh (ʃeɪk) *n.* (in Muslim countries) **a.** the head of an Arab tribe, village, or family. **b.** a religious leader. [Arabic *shaykh* old man] —**ˈsheikhdom** *n.*

sheila (ˈʃiːlə) *n. Austral. & N.Z. informal.* a girl or woman. [from the girl's name *Sheila*]

shekel (ˈʃɛkˀl) *n.* **1.** a former coin and unit of weight of the Near East. **2.** (*often pl.*) *Informal.* money. [Hebrew *sheqel*]

shelduck (ˈʃɛlˌdʌk) *or* (*masc.*) **sheldrake** (ˈʃɛlˌdreɪk) *n., pl.* **-ducks, -duck** *or* **-drakes, -drake.** a large brightly coloured wild duck of the Old World. [prob. from dialect *sheld* pied]

shelf (ʃɛlf) *n., pl.* **shelves. 1.** a thin flat plank of wood or other hard material, fixed horizontally against a wall or in a cupboard, for the purpose of holding objects. **2.** a projecting layer of ice or rock on land or in the sea. **3. on the shelf.** put aside or abandoned; used esp. of unmarried women considered to be past the age of marriage. [Old English *scylfe* ship's deck]

shelf life *n.* the length of time a packaged product will last without deteriorating.

shell (ʃɛl) *n.* **1.** the protective outer layer of an egg, fruit, or nut. **2.** the hard outer covering of an animal such as a crab or tortoise. **3.** any hard outer case. **4.** the external structure of a building, car, or ship, esp. one that is unfinished or gutted by fire. **5.** an explosive artillery projectile that can be fired from a large gun. **6.** a small-arms cartridge. **7.** *Rowing.* a very light narrow racing boat. **8. come** (*or* **bring**) **out of one's shell.** to become (*or* help to become) less shy and reserved. ~*vb.* **9.** to remove the shell or husk from. **10.** to bombard with artillery shells. ~See also **shell out.** [Old English *sciell*] —**ˈshell-ˌlike** *adj.*

she'll (ʃiːl; *unstressed* ʃɪl) she will *or* she shall.

shellac (ʃəˈlæk, ˈʃɛlæk) *n.* **1.** a yellowish resin used in varnishes and polishes. **2.** a varnish made by dissolving shellac in alcohol. ~*vb.* **-lacking, -lacked. 3.** to coat with shellac. [*shell* + *lac*]

shellfish (ˈʃɛlˌfɪʃ) *n., pl.* **-fish** *or* **-fishes.** an aquatic animal, esp. an edible one, having a shell or shell-like covering.

shell out *vb. Informal.* to pay out or hand over (money).

shell shock *n.* a neurotic condition characterized by anxiety, depression, and irritability, that occurs as a result of prolonged exposure to battle conditions. —**shell-shocked** *adj.*

Shelta ('ʃɛltə) *n.* a cant or jargon, based on Gaelic, used by some tinkers. [origin unknown]

shelter ('ʃɛltə) *n.* **1.** something that provides cover or protection, as from weather or danger. **2.** the protection afforded by such a cover. ~*vb.* **3.** to provide with shelter; protect. **4.** to take cover, as from rain. [origin unknown]

sheltered ('ʃɛltəd) *adj.* **1.** protected from wind and rain. **2.** protected from outside influences: *a sheltered upbringing*. **3.** specially designed to provide a safe environment for the elderly, handicapped, or disabled: *sheltered housing*.

shelve[1] (ʃɛlv) *vb.* **1.** to place (something, such as a book) on a shelf. **2.** to provide with shelves: *to shelve a cupboard*. **3.** to put aside or postpone from consideration: *to shelve a project*. **4.** to dismiss (someone) from active service.

shelve[2] (ʃɛlv) *vb.* to slope away gradually.

shelves (ʃɛlvz) *n.* the plural of **shelf**.

shelving ('ʃɛlvɪŋ) *n.* **1.** material for shelves. **2.** shelves collectively.

shenanigan (ʃɪ'nænɪɡən) *n. Informal.* **1.** (*usually pl.*) nonsense; mischief. **2.** trickery. [origin unknown]

shepherd ('ʃɛpəd) *n.* **1.** a person employed to tend sheep. **2.** a person, such as a clergyman, who watches over a group of people. ~*vb.* **3.** to guide or watch over in the manner of a shepherd. [*sheep* + *herd*] —**'shepherdess** *fem. n.*

shepherd's pie *n. Chiefly Brit.* a baked dish of minced meat covered with mashed potato.

Sheraton ('ʃɛrətən) *adj.* denoting furniture made by or in the style of Thomas Sheraton, English furniture maker, characterized by lightness and elegance.

sherbet ('ʃɜːbət) *n.* **1.** a fruit-flavoured slightly effervescent powder, eaten as a sweet or used to make a drink. **2.** *U.S. & Canad.* same as **sorbet**. [Turkish]

sherd (ʃɜːd) *n.* same as **shard**.

sheriff ('ʃɛrɪf) *n.* **1.** (in the U.S.) the chief elected law-enforcement officer in a county. **2.** (in Canada) a municipal officer who enforces court orders and escorts convicted criminals to prison. **3.** (in England and Wales) the chief executive officer of the Crown in a county, having chiefly ceremonial duties. **4.** (in Scotland) a judge in a sheriff court. [Old English *scīrgerēfa*]

sheriff court *n.* (in Scotland) a court having jurisdiction to try all but the most serious crimes and to deal with most civil actions.

Sherpa ('ʃɜːpə) *n., pl.* **-pas** *or* **-pa.** a member of a Tibetan people living in the southern slopes of the Himalayas.

sherry ('ʃɛrɪ) *n., pl.* **-ries.** a pale or dark brown fortified wine, originally from southern Spain. [Spanish *Xeres*, now *Jerez*, in Spain]

Shetland pony ('ʃɛtlənd) *n.* a very small sturdy breed of pony with a long shaggy mane and tail.

shibboleth ('ʃɪbə,lɛθ) *n.* **1.** a slogan or catch phrase, usually considered outworn, characteristic of a particular party or sect. **2.** a custom, phrase, or use of language that reliably distinguishes a member of one group or class from another. [word used in the Old Testament by the Gileadites as a test word for the Ephraimites, who could not pronounce *sh*]

shickered ('ʃɪkəd) *adj. Austral. & N.Z. slang.* drunk. [Yiddish]

shied (ʃaɪd) *vb.* past of **shy**.

shield (ʃiːld) *n.* **1.** a piece of defensive armour carried in the hand or on the arm to intercept blows or missiles. **2.** any person or thing that protects , hides, or defends. **3.** *Heraldry.* a representation of a shield used for displaying a coat of arms. **4.** anything that resembles a shield in shape, such as a trophy in a sports competition. ~*vb.* **5.** to protect, hide, or defend (someone or something) from danger or harm. [Old English *scield*]

shift (ʃɪft) *vb.* **1.** to move from one place or position to another. **2.** *U.S.* to change for another or others. **3.** to pass (blame or responsibility) onto someone else: *don't try to shift the blame onto me*. **4.** to change (gear) in a motor vehicle. **5.** to remove or be removed: *no detergent can shift these stains*. **6.** *Slang.* to move quickly. ~*n.* **7.** the act or an instance of shifting. **8. a.** a group of workers who work during a specific period. **b.** the period of time worked by such a group. **9.** an expedient, contrivance, or stratagem. **10.** a loose-fitting straight underskirt or dress. [Old English *sciftan*]

shiftless ('ʃɪftlɪs) *adj.* lacking in ambition or initiative.

shifty ('ʃɪftɪ) *adj.* **shiftier, shiftiest.** untrustworthy, furtive, or evasive. —**'shiftiness** *n.*

shillelagh *or* **shillala** (ʃə'leɪlə, -lɪ) *n.* (in Ireland) a stout club or cudgel. [Irish Gaelic *sail* cudgel + *éille* thong]

shilling ('ʃɪlɪŋ) *n.* **1.** a former British coin worth one twentieth of a pound, replaced by the 5p piece in 1971. **2.** the standard monetary unit in several E African countries. [Old English *scilling*]

shillyshally ('ʃɪlɪ,ʃælɪ) *vb. Informal.* **-lying, -lied.** to be indecisive; vacillate. [*shill I shall I*, reduplication of *shall I*]

shim (ʃɪm) *n.* **1.** a thin strip of wood, metal, or plastic, placed between two close surfaces to fill a gap. ~*vb.* **shimming, shimmed. 2.** to fit or fill up with a shim. [origin unknown]

shimmer ('ʃɪmə) *vb.* **1.** to shine with a faint unsteady light. ~*n.* **2.** a faint unsteady light. [Old English *scimerian*] —**'shimmering** *or* **'shimmery** *adj.*

shin (ʃɪn) *n.* **1.** the front part of the lower leg. **2.** *Chiefly Brit.* a cut of beef including the lower foreleg. ~*vb.* **shinning, shinned. 3.** (often foll. by *up*) to climb (something, such a rope or pole) by gripping with the hands or arms and the legs and hauling oneself up. [Old English *scinu*]

shinbone (ˈʃɪnˌbəʊn) *n.* the nontechnical name for **tibia**.

shindig (ˈʃɪnˌdɪg) or **shindy** (ˈʃɪndɪ) *n.*, *pl.* **-digs** or **-dies**. *Slang.* 1. a noisy party or dance. 2. a quarrel or commotion. [var. of *shinty*]

shine (ʃaɪn) *vb.* **shining, shone.** 1. to give off or reflect light. 2. to direct the light of (a lamp or torch): *he shone the torch in my eyes.* 3. (*p.t.* & *p.p.* **shined**) to cause to gleam by polishing: *to shine shoes.* 4. to excel: *she shines at tennis.* 5. to appear clearly. ~*n.* 6. the state or quality of shining; sheen; lustre. 7. **take a shine to someone.** *Informal.* to take a liking to someone. [Old English *scīnan*]

shiner (ˈʃaɪnə) *n. Informal.* a black eye.

shingle[1] (ˈʃɪŋgˀl) *n.* 1. a thin rectangular tile laid with others in overlapping rows to cover a roof or a wall. 2. a woman's short-cropped hairstyle. ~*vb.* 3. to cover (a roof or a wall) with shingles. 4. to cut (the hair) in a short-cropped style. [Latin *scindere* to split]

shingle[2] (ˈʃɪŋgˀl) *n.* coarse gravel found on beaches. [Scandinavian]

shingles (ˈʃɪŋgˀlz) *n.* (*functioning as sing.*) an acute viral disease characterized by painful blisters, often around the waist. [Medieval Latin *cingulum* girdle]

Shinto (ˈʃɪntəʊ) *n.* a Japanese religion emphasizing the worship of ancestors and nature spirits. [Japanese: the way of the gods] —ˈ**Shintoism** *n.* —ˈ**Shintoist** *n., adj.*

shinty (ˈʃɪntɪ) *n.* 1. a game like hockey but with taller goals. 2. (*pl.* **-ties**) the stick used in this game. [origin unknown]

shiny (ˈʃaɪnɪ) *adj.* **shinier, shiniest.** 1. glossy or polished; bright. 2. (of clothes or material) worn to a smooth and glossy state by continual rubbing.

ship (ʃɪp) *n.* 1. a large, seagoing vessel propelled by engines or sails. 2. short for **airship** or **spaceship**. 3. **when one's ship comes in.** when one has become successful. ~*vb.* **shipping, shipped.** 4. to send or transport by any carrier, esp. a ship. 5. *Naut.* to take in (water) over the side. 6. to bring or go aboard a vessel: *to ship oars.* 7. (often foll. by *off*) *Informal.* to send away: *they shipped the children off to boarding school.* 8. to be hired to serve aboard a ship: *I shipped aboard a Liverpool liner.* [Old English *scip*]

shipboard (ˈʃɪpˌbɔːd) *n.* (*modifier*) taking place or used aboard a ship: *a shipboard computer.*

shipbuilder (ˈʃɪpˌbɪldə) *n.* a person or company that builds ships. —ˈ**ship-ˌbuilding** *n.*

shipmate (ˈʃɪpˌmeɪt) *n.* a sailor who serves on the same ship as another.

shipment (ˈʃɪpmənt) *n.* 1. goods shipped together as part of the same lot: *a shipment of grain.* 2. the act of shipping cargo.

shipper (ˈʃɪpə) *n.* a person or company that ships.

shipping (ˈʃɪpɪŋ) *n.* 1. the business of

transporting freight, esp. by ship. 2. ships collectively: *there is a lot of shipping in the Channel.*

shipshape (ˈʃɪpˌʃeɪp) *adj.* 1. neat; orderly. ~*adv.* 2. in a neat and orderly manner.

shipwreck (ˈʃɪpˌrɛk) *n.* 1. the destruction of a ship at sea. 2. the remains of a wrecked ship. 3. ruin or destruction: *the shipwreck of all my hopes.* ~*vb.* 4. to wreck or destroy (a ship). 5. to bring to ruin or destruction.

shipwright (ˈʃɪpˌraɪt) *n.* someone, esp. a carpenter, who builds or repairs ships.

shipyard (ˈʃɪpˌjɑːd) *n.* a place where ships are built and repaired.

shire (ˈʃaɪə) *n.* 1. a county. 2. **the Shires.** the Midland counties of England. [Old English *scīr* office]

shire horse *n.* a large powerful cart-horse.

shirk (ʃɜːk) *vb.* to avoid doing (work or a duty). [prob. from German *Schurke* rogue] —ˈ**shirker** *n.*

shirt (ʃɜːt) *n.* 1. a garment worn on the upper part of the body, esp. by men, usually having a collar and sleeves and buttoning up the front. 2. **keep your shirt on.** *Informal.* keep your temper. 3. **put one's shirt on something.** *Informal.* to bet all one has on something. [Old English *scyrte*]

shirtsleeve (ˈʃɜːtˌsliːv) *n.* 1. the sleeve of a shirt. 2. **in one's shirtsleeves.** not wearing a jacket.

shirt-tail *n.* the part of a shirt that extends below the waist.

shirtwaister (ˈʃɜːtˌweɪstə) or *U.S.* **shirt-waist** *n.* a woman's dress with a tailored bodice resembling a shirt.

shirty (ˈʃɜːtɪ) *adj.* **shirtier, shirtiest.** *Slang, chiefly Brit.* bad-tempered or annoyed.

shish kebab (ˈʃiːʃ kəˈbæb) *n.* a dish consisting of small pieces of meat and vegetables threaded onto skewers and grilled. [Turkish *şiş kebab*]

shit (ʃɪt) *Taboo.* ~*vb.* **shitting; shitted** or **shit.** 1. to defecate. ~*n.* 2. faeces; excrement. 3. *Slang.* rubbish; nonsense. 4. *Slang.* an obnoxious or worthless person. ~*interj.* 5. *Slang.* an exclamation expressing anger or disgust. [Old English *scite*] —ˈ**shitty** *adj.*

shiver[1] (ˈʃɪvə) *vb.* 1. to tremble, as from cold or fear. ~*n.* 2. a shivering. 3. **the shivers.** a fit of shivering through fear or illness. [Middle English *chiveren*] —ˈ**shivering** *n., adj.* —ˈ**shivery** *adj.*

shiver[2] (ˈʃɪvə) *vb.* 1. to break into fragments. ~*n.* 2. a splintered piece. [Germanic]

shoal[1] (ʃəʊl) *n.* 1. a large group of fish swimming together. 2. a large group of people or things. ~*vb.* 3. to gather or move in such a group. [Old English *scolu*]

shoal[2] (ʃəʊl) *n.* 1. a stretch of shallow water. 2. a sandbank or rocky area, esp. one that is visible at low water. ~*vb.* 3. to make or become shallow. [Old English *sceald* shallow]

shock[1] (ʃɒk) vb. **1.** to cause (someone) to experience extreme horror, disgust, or astonishment: *the atrocities shocked us.* **2.** to cause a state of shock in (a person). ~n. **3.** a sudden and violent jarring blow or impact. **4. a.** sudden and violent emotional disturbance. **b.** something causing this. **5.** *Pathol.* a state of bodily collapse, as from severe injury, burns, or fright. **6.** pain and muscular spasm as the physical reaction through the passage of an electric current through a person's body. [Old French *choc*] —**'shocker** n.

shock[2] (ʃɒk) n. **1.** a number of grain sheaves set on end in a field to dry. ~vb. **2.** to set up (sheaves) in shocks. [prob. Germanic]

shock[3] (ʃɒk) n. a thick bushy mass of hair. [origin unknown]

shock absorber n. any device designed to absorb mechanical shock, esp. one fitted to a motor vehicle to reduce the effects of travelling over bumpy surfaces.

shocking ('ʃɒkɪŋ) adj. **1.** causing shock, horror, or disgust. **2.** shocking pink. of a garish shade of pink. **3.** *Informal.* very bad or terrible: *shocking weather.*

shockproof ('ʃɒk,pruːf) adj. capable of absorbing shock without damage.

shock therapy or **treatment** n. the treatment of certain psychotic conditions by injecting drugs or by passing an electric current through the brain.

shod (ʃɒd) vb. past of **shoe.**

shoddy ('ʃɒdɪ) adj. **-dier, -diest. 1.** imitating something of better quality. **2.** of poor quality; shabby: *shoddy treatment.* [origin unknown] —**'shoddily** adv. —**'shoddiness** n.

shoe (ʃuː) n. **1.** one of a matching pair of coverings shaped to fit the foot, made of leather or other strong material and usually ending below the ankle. **2.** anything resembling a shoe in shape, function, or position. **3.** short for **horse shoe. 4. be in a person's shoes.** *Informal.* to be in another's person's situation. ~vb. **shoeing, shod. 5.** to furnish with shoes. **6.** to fit (a horse) with horseshoes. [Old English *scōh*]

shoehorn ('ʃuː,hɔːn) n. a smooth curved implement inserted at the heel of a shoe to ease the foot into it.

shoelace ('ʃuː,leɪs) n. a cord or lace for fastening shoes.

shoemaker ('ʃuː,meɪkə) n. a person who makes or repairs shoes or boots. —**'shoe,making** n.

shoestring ('ʃuː,strɪŋ) n. **1.** same as **shoelace. 2.** *Informal.* a very small amount of money: *the film was made on a shoestring.*

shoetree ('ʃuː,triː) n. a long piece of metal, plastic, or wood, inserted into a shoe or boot to stretch it or preserve its shape.

shone (ʃɒn; *U.S.* ʃəʊn) vb. past of **shine.**

shoo (ʃuː) interj. **1.** go away!: used to drive away unwanted or annoying people or animals. ~vb. **shooing, shooed. 2.** to drive away by or as if by crying "shoo". [imit.]

shook (ʃʊk) vb. the past tense of **shake.**

shoot (ʃuːt) vb. **shooting, shot. 1.** to hit, wound, or kill with a missile discharged from a weapon. **2.** to discharge (a missile or missiles) from a weapon. **3.** to fire (a weapon). **4.** to send out or be sent out as if from a weapon: *he shot questions at her.* **5.** to move very rapidly. **6.** to slide or push into or out of a fastening: *to shoot a bolt.* **7.** to go or pass quickly over or through: *to shoot rapids.* **8.** to hunt game with a gun for sport. **9.** (of a plant) to put forth (a new growth or sprout). **10.** to photograph or film. **11.** to variegate or streak, as with colour: *his dark hair was shot with streaks of grey.* **12.** *Sport.* to take a shot at the goal. ~n. **13.** the act of shooting. **14.** a new growth or sprout of a plant. **15.** *Chiefly Brit.* a meeting or party organized for hunting game with guns. **16.** an area where game can be hunted with guns. **17.** a steep descent in a stream; rapid. [Old English *scēotan*] —**'shooter** n.

shooting star n. *Informal.* a meteor.

shooting stick n. a device that resembles a walking stick, having a spike at one end and a folding seat at the other.

shoot up vb. **a.** to grow or increase rapidly: *prices have shot up in the last year; your children have shot up since I last saw them.* **b.** to inject oneself with heroin or another strong drug.

shop (ʃɒp) n. **1.** a place for the retail sale of goods and services. **2.** a place where a specified type of work is done; workshop: *printing shop.* **3. all over the shop.** *Informal.* scattered everywhere: *his papers were all over the shop.* **4. shut up shop.** to close business at the end of the day or permanently. **5. talk shop.** *Informal.* to discuss one's business or work, esp. on a social occasion. ~vb. **shopping, shopped. 6.** (often foll. by *for*) to visit a shop or shops in order to buy (goods). **7.** *Slang, chiefly Brit.* to inform on (someone), esp. to the police. [Old English *sceoppa* stall] —**'shopper** n.

shop around vb. *Informal.* **1.** to visit a number of shops or stores to compare goods and prices. **2.** to consider a number of possibilities before making a choice.

shop assistant n. a person who serves in a shop.

shop floor n. **1.** the production area of a factory. **2.** workers, esp. factory workers, as opposed to management.

shopkeeper ('ʃɒp,kiːpə) n. a person who owns or manages a shop. —**'shop,keeping** n.

shoplifter ('ʃɒp,lɪftə) n. a customer who steals goods from a shop. —**'shop,lifting** n.

shopping ('ʃɒpɪŋ) n. **1.** the act of going to shops and buying things. **2.** things that have been bought in shops.

shopping centre n. **1.** the area of a town where most of the shops are situated. **2.** a complex of stores, restaurants, and sometimes banks, usually under the same roof.

shopping mall n. *Chiefly U.S., Canad., & Austral.* a large enclosed shopping centre.

shopping plaza n. Chiefly U.S. & Canad. a shopping centre, usually a small group of stores built as a strip.

shopsoiled ('ʃɒp,sɔɪld) adj. soiled or faded, from being displayed in a shop.

shop steward n. a trade-union official elected by his fellow workers to be their representative in dealing with their employer.

shoptalk ('ʃɒp,tɔːk) n. conversation concerning one's work, carried on outside working hours.

shopwalker ('ʃɒp,wɔːkə) n. Brit. a person employed by a department store to supervise sales personnel and assist customers.

shore[1] (ʃɔː) n. 1. the land along the edge of a sea, lake, or wide river. 2. land, as opposed to water: fifty yards from shore. 3. (pl.) a country: his native shores. [prob. from Middle Low German, Middle Dutch schöre]

shore[2] (ʃɔː) n. 1. a prop placed under or against something as a support. ~vb. 2. (foll. by up) to make (something) safe with or as if with a shore. [Middle Dutch schöre]

shoreline ('ʃɔː,laɪn) n. the edge of a sea, lake, or wide river.

shorn (ʃɔːn) vb. a past participle of **shear**.

short (ʃɔːt) adj. 1. of little length; not long. 2. of little height; not tall. 3. of limited duration. 4. deficient: the number of places laid at the table was short by four. 5. (foll. by of or on) lacking in: short of money; short on talent. 6. concise; succinct: the short answer is no. 7. (of drinks) consisting chiefly of a spirit, such as whisky. 8. (of someone's memory) lacking the ability to retain a lot of facts. 9. abrupt to the point of rudeness: the salesman was very short with me. 10. (of betting odds) almost even. 11. Finance. a. not possessing at the time of sale the stocks or commodities one sells. b. relating to such sales, which depend on falling prices for profit. 12. Phonetics. (of a vowel) of relatively brief duration. 13. (of pastry) crumbly in texture. 14. **in short supply.** scarce. 15. **short and sweet.** brief and to the point; pertinent. 16. **short for.** a shortened form of. ~adv. 17. abruptly: to stop short. 18. **be caught short.** to have a sudden need to go to the toilet. 19. **go short.** not to have enough. 20. **short of.** except: nothing short of a miracle can save him now. ~n. 21. a drink of spirits. 22. a short film shown before the main feature in a cinema. 23. same as **short circuit.** 24. **for short.** Informal. as a shortened form: he is called J.R. for short. 25. **in short.** briefly. ~vb. 26. to short-circuit. ~See also **shorts.** [Old English scort] —'**shortness** n.

shortage ('ʃɔːtɪdʒ) n. a deficiency of something needed.

shortbread ('ʃɔːt,brɛd) n. a rich crumbly biscuit made with a large proportion of butter.

shortcake ('ʃɔːt,keɪk) n. 1. shortbread. 2. a dessert made of layers of biscuit or cake filled with fruit and cream.

short-change vb. 1. to give (someone) less than the correct change. 2. Slang. to cheat or swindle (someone).

short circuit n. 1. a faulty or accidental connection between two points of different potential in an electric circuit, creating a path of low resistance through which the current is deflected, usually causing failure of the circuit. ~vb. **short-circuit.** 2. to develop a short circuit. 3. to bypass (a procedure). 4. to hinder or frustrate (a plan).

shortcoming ('ʃɔːt,kʌmɪŋ) n. a failing or defect.

shortcrust pastry ('ʃɔːt,krʌst) n. a type of pastry with a crisp but crumbly texture.

short cut n. 1. a route that is shorter than the usual one. 2. a means of saving time or effort.

shorten ('ʃɔːt²n) vb. to make or become short or shorter.

shortening ('ʃɔːt²nɪŋ) n. butter or other fat, used in pastry to make it crumbly.

shortfall ('ʃɔːt,fɔːl) n. 1. failure to meet a requirement. 2. the amount of such a failure.

shorthand ('ʃɔːt,hænd) n. a system of rapid writing using special strokes and other symbols to represent words or phrases.

shorthand typist n. Brit. a person skilled in the use of shorthand and in typing.

shorthorn ('ʃɔːt,hɔːn) n. a member of a breed of cattle with short horns.

short list Chiefly Brit. ~n. 1. Also called (Scot.): **short leet.** a list of suitable candidates for a job or prize, from which the successful candidate will be selected. ~vb. **short-list.** 2. to put (someone) on a short list.

short-lived adj. lasting only for a short time: his success was short-lived.

shortly ('ʃɔːtlɪ) adv. 1. in a short time; soon. 2. in a curt or rude manner.

shorts (ʃɔːts) pl. n. 1. trousers reaching the top of the thigh or partway to the knee. 2. Chiefly U.S. & Canad. men's underpants.

short shrift n. brief and unsympathetic treatment.

short-sighted adj. 1. unable to see faraway things clearly. 2. lacking foresight: a short-sighted plan. —,short-'sightedness n.

short-tempered adj. easily angered.

short-term adj. of, for, or lasting a short time.

short wave n. a radio wave with a wavelength in the range 10–100 metres.

short-winded adj. tending to run out of breath easily.

shot[1] (ʃɒt) n. 1. the act or an instance of firing a gun or rifle. 2. small round pellets of lead collectively, as used in shotguns. 3. a person who shoots, with regard to his ability: he is a good shot. 4. Informal. an attempt: I had a shot at changing the wheel. 5. Informal. a guess. 6. Sport. the act or an instance of hitting, kicking, or throwing the ball. 7. the launching of a rocket or spacecraft to a specified destination: *a moon shot.* **8. a.** a single photograph. **b.** an uninterrupted sequence of film taken by a single camera. **9.** *Informal.* an injection of a vaccine or narcotic drug. **10.** *Informal.* a drink of spirits. **11.** *Sport.* a heavy metal ball used in the shot put. **12. like a shot.** without hesitating. **13. shot in the arm.** *Informal.* something that brings back energy or confidence. **14. shot in the dark.** a wild guess. [Old English *scot*]

shot² (ʃɒt) *vb.* **1.** past of **shoot.** ~*adj.* **2.** (of textiles) woven to give a changing colour effect. **3.** streaked with colour.

shotgun (ˈʃɒtˌgʌn) *n.* a gun for firing a charge of shot at short range, used for hunting small game.

shot put *n.* an athletic event in which contestants hurl a heavy metal ball called a shot as far as possible. —'**shot-**ˌ**putter** *n.*

should (ʃʊd) *vb.* the past tense of **shall:** used to indicate that an action is considered by the speaker to be obligatory (*you should go*) or to form the subjunctive mood (*I should like to see you; if I should die; should I be late, start without me.*). [Old English *sceold*]

shoulder (ˈʃəʊldə) *n.* **1.** the part of the body where the arm, wing, or foreleg joins the trunk. **2.** a cut of meat including the upper part of the foreleg. **3.** the part of a garment that covers the shoulder. **4.** the strip of unpaved land that borders a road. **5. a shoulder to cry on.** a person one turns to for sympathy with one's troubles. **6. put one's shoulder to the wheel.** *Informal.* to work very hard. **7. rub shoulders with someone.** *Informal.* to mix with someone socially. **8. shoulder to shoulder. a.** side by side. **b.** working together. ~*vb.* **9.** to bear (a burden or responsibility). **10.** to push with one's shoulder: *he shouldered his way through the crowd.* **11.** to lift or carry on one's shoulders. **12. shoulder arms.** *Mil.* to bring one's rifle vertically close to one's right side with the muzzle uppermost. [Old English *sculdor*]

shoulder blade *n.* either of two large flat triangular bones one on each side of the back part of the shoulder.

shoulder strap *n.* a strap worn over the shoulder to hold up a garment or to support a bag.

shouldn't (ˈʃʊdᵊnt) should not.

shout (ʃaʊt) *n.* **1.** a loud cry, often to convey emotion or a command. **2.** *Informal.* one's turn to buy a round of drinks. ~*vb.* **3.** to cry out loudly. **4.** *Austral. & N.Z. informal.* to treat (someone) to (something, such as a round of drinks). [prob. from Old Norse *skúta* taunt]

shout down *vb.* to silence (someone) by talking loudly.

shove (ʃʌv) *vb.* **1.** to give a violent push to. **2.** to push (one's way) roughly. **3.** *Informal.* to put (something) somewhere quickly and carelessly: *shove it in the bin.* ~*n.* **4.** an instance of shoving. [Old English *scúfan*]

shovel (ˈʃʌvᵊl) *n.* **1.** a tool for lifting or moving loose material, consisting of a

broad blade attached to a large handle. **2.** a machine or part of a machine resembling a shovel in function. ~*vb.* **-elling, -elled** *or U.S.* **-eling, -eled. 3.** to lift or move (loose material) with a shovel. **4.** to put away large quantities of (something) in a hurried manner: *he shovelled food into his mouth.* [Old English *scofl*]

shove off *vb.* *Informal.* to go away; depart.

show (ʃəʊ) *vb.* **showing, showed; shown** *or* **showed. 1.** to make, be, or become visible or noticeable: *to show one's dislike; his anger showed.* **2.** to present for inspection: *he showed me a picture.* **3.** to demonstrate or prove: *to show that the earth moves round the sun.* **4.** to instruct by demonstration: *show me how to swim.* **5.** to indicate: *a barometer shows changes in the weather.* **6.** to grant or bestow: *to show favour to someone.* **7.** to exhibit or display (works of art): *three artists are showing at the gallery.* **8.** to present (a film or play) or (of a film or play) to be presented. **9.** to guide or escort: *please show me to my room.* **10.** *Informal.* to arrive. ~*n.* **11.** a display or exhibition. **12.** a public spectacle. **13.** pretence; mere display. **14.** a theatrical or other entertainment. **15.** *Slang, chiefly Brit.* a thing or affair: *a poor show.* ~See also **show off, show up.** [Old English *scéawian*]

show business *n.* the entertainment industry. Also (informal): **show biz.**

showcase (ˈʃəʊˌkeɪs) *n.* **1.** a glass case used to display objects in a museum or shop. **2.** a setting in which anything may be displayed to best advantage.

showdown (ˈʃəʊˌdaʊn) *n.* *Informal.* a confrontation that settles a dispute.

shower (ˈʃaʊə) *n.* **1.** a brief period of rain, hail, sleet, or snow. **2.** a sudden abundant fall of objects: *a shower of sparks.* **3. a. a** kind of bath in which a person stands upright and is sprayed with water from a nozzle. **b.** a device, room, or booth for such a bath. **4.** *Brit. slang.* a contemptible group of people. **5.** *U.S., Canad., Austral., & N.Z.* a party held to honour and present gifts to a prospective bride or prospective mother. ~*vb.* **6.** to sprinkle with or as if with a shower. **7.** to give (things) in abundance or present (a person) with things in abundance. **8.** to take a shower. [Old English *scúr*] —'**showery** *adj.*

showing (ˈʃəʊɪŋ) *n.* **1.** a presentation, exhibition, or display. **2.** manner of presentation.

showjumping (ˈʃəʊˌdʒʌmpɪŋ) *n.* the sport of riding horses in competitions to demonstrate skill in jumping. —'**show-**ˌ**jumper** *n.*

showman (ˈʃəʊmən) *n., pl.* **-men. 1.** a person who presents or produces a show. **2.** a person skilled at presenting anything in an effective manner. —'**showman-ship** *n.*

shown (ʃəʊn) *vb.* a past participle of **show.**

show off *vb.* **1.** to exhibit or display (something) so as to invite admiration. **2.** *Informal.* to behave flamboyantly in an attempt to attract attention. ~*n.* **show-**

off. 3. *Informal.* a person who behaves flamboyantly in an attempt to attract attention.

showpiece ('ʃəʊˌpiːs) *n.* **1.** anything displayed or exhibited. **2.** anything prized as a fine example of its type.

showplace ('ʃəʊˌpleɪs) *n.* a place visited for its beauty or interest.

showroom ('ʃəʊˌruːm) *n.* a room in which goods for sale are on display.

show up *vb.* **1.** to reveal or be revealed clearly. **2.** to expose the faults or defects of (someone or something) by comparison. **3.** *Informal.* to put (someone) to shame; embarrass. **4.** *Informal.* to arrive.

showy ('ʃəʊɪ) *adj.* **showier, showiest. 1.** gaudy or ostentatious. **2.** making an imposing display. —**'showily** *adv.* —**'showiness** *n.*

shrank (ʃræŋk) *vb.* a past tense of **shrink.**

shrapnel ('ʃræpn'l) *n.* **1.** an artillery shell containing a number of small pellets or bullets which it is designed to scatter on explosion. **2.** fragments from this type of shell. [after H. Shrapnel, who invented it]

shred (ʃred) *n.* **1.** a long narrow piece torn off something. **2.** a very small amount: *not a shred of evidence.* ~*vb.* **shredding, shredded** or **shred. 3.** to tear into shreds. [Old English *scread*] —**'shredder** *n.*

shrew (ʃruː) *n.* **1.** a small mouselike animal with a long snout. **2.** a bad-tempered woman. [Old English *scrēawa*] —**'shrewish** *adj.*

shrewd (ʃruːd) *adj.* clever and perceptive. [from *shrew* (obs. vb.) to curse, from *shrew*] —**'shrewdly** *adv.* —**'shrewdness** *n.*

shriek (ʃriːk) *n.* **1.** a shrill and piercing cry. ~*vb.* **2.** to utter (words or sounds) in a shrill piercing tone. [prob. from Old Norse *skrækja* to screech]

shrift (ʃrɪft) *n.* See **short shrift.** [Old English *scrift*]

shrike (ʃraɪk) *n.* a bird with a heavy hooked bill, which impales small animals on thorns. [Old English *scrīc* thrush]

shrill (ʃrɪl) *adj.* **1.** (of a sound) sharp and high-pitched. ~*vb.* **2.** to utter (words or sounds) in a shrill tone. [origin unknown] —**'shrillness** *n.* —**'shrilly** *adv.*

shrimp (ʃrɪmp) *n.* **1.** a small edible shellfish with a long tail and a pair of pincers. **2.** *Informal.* a small person. ~*vb.* **3.** to fish for shrimps. [prob. Germanic]

shrine (ʃraɪn) *n.* **1.** a place of worship associated with a sacred person or object. **2.** a container for sacred relics. **3.** the tomb of a saint or other holy person. **4.** a place that is visited and honoured because of its association with a famous person or event. [Latin *scrīnium* bookcase]

shrink (ʃrɪŋk) *vb.* **shrinking; shrank** or **shrunk; shrunk** or **shrunken. 1.** to become or cause to become smaller, sometimes because of wetness, heat, or cold. **2.** (foll. by *from*) **a.** to recoil or withdraw: *to shrink from the sight of blood.* **b.** to feel great reluctance (to perform a task or duty). ~*n.* **3.** *Slang.* a psychiatrist. [Old English *scrincan*]

shrinkage ('ʃrɪŋkɪdʒ) *n.* **1.** the fact of shrinking. **2.** the amount by which anything decreases in size, value, or weight.

shrink-wrap *vb.* **-wrapping, -wrapped.** to package (a product) in a flexible plastic wrapping which shrinks about its contours to seal it.

shrivel ('ʃrɪv'l) *vb.* **-elling, -elled** or *U.S.* **-eling, -eled.** to make or become shrunken and withered. [prob. Scandinavian]

shroud (ʃraʊd) *n.* **1.** a piece of cloth used to wrap a dead body in. **2.** anything that hides things: *a shroud of mist.* ~*vb.* **3.** to hide (something): *shrouded in mist; shrouded in secrecy.* [Old English *scrūd* garment]

Shrove Tuesday (ʃrəʊv) *n.* the day before Ash Wednesday. [from Old English *scrīfan* to confess one's sins]

shrub (ʃrʌb) *n.* a woody plant, smaller than a tree, with several stems instead of a trunk. [Old English *scrybb*] —**'shrubby** *adj.*

shrubbery ('ʃrʌbərɪ) *n., pl.* **-beries. 1.** an area planted with shrubs. **2.** shrubs collectively.

shrug (ʃrʌg) *vb.* **shrugging, shrugged. 1.** to draw up and drop (the shoulders) abruptly in a gesture expressing indifference or doubt. ~*n.* **2.** the gesture so made. [origin unknown]

shrug off *vb.* **1.** to dismiss (a matter) as unimportant. **2.** to get rid of (someone).

shrunk (ʃrʌŋk) *vb.* a past tense and past participle of **shrink.**

shrunken ('ʃrʌŋkən) *vb.* **1.** a past participle of **shrink.** ~*adj.* **2.** reduced in size.

shudder ('ʃʌdə) *vb.* **1.** to shake or tremble suddenly and violently, sometimes from horror or fear. ~*n.* **2.** a convulsive shaking or trembling. [Middle Low German *schōderen*]

shuffle ('ʃʌf'l) *vb.* **1.** to walk or move (the feet) with a slow dragging motion. **2.** to mix together in a jumbled mass: *he shuffled the papers nervously.* **3.** to mix up (playing cards) so as to change their order. ~*n.* **4.** an instance of shuffling. **5.** a rearrangement: *a Cabinet shuffle.* **6.** a dance with short dragging movements of the feet. [prob. from Low German *schüffeln*]

shufti ('ʃʌftɪ) *n. Brit. slang.* a look; peep. [Arabic]

shun (ʃʌn) *vb.* **shunning, shunned.** to avoid deliberately. [Old English *scunian*]

shunt (ʃʌnt) *vb.* **1.** to move (objects or people) to a different position. **2.** *Railways.* to transfer (engines or carriages) from track to track. **3.** to evade (work) by putting it off onto someone else. ~*n.* **4.** the act of shunting. **5.** a railway point. **6.** *Electronics.* a conductor connected in parallel across a part of a circuit to divert a known fraction of the current. [perhaps from Middle English *shunen* to shun]

shush (ʃʊʃ) *interj.* **1.** be quiet! hush! ~*vb.* **2.** to quiet (someone) by saying "shush". [imit.]

shut (ʃʌt) *vb.* **shutting, shut. 1.** to move (something) so as to cover an opening: *to* shut a door. **2.** to close (something) by bringing together the parts: *to shut a book*. **3.** (foll. by *up*) to close or lock the doors of: *to shut up a house*. **4.** (foll. by *in*) to confine or enclose. **5.** (foll. by *out*) to exclude. **6.** (of a shop or other establishment) to stop operating for the day: *the pubs shut at eleven*. ~*adj.* **7.** closed or fastened. ~See also **shutdown, shut off,** etc. [Old English *scyttan*]

shutdown ('ʃʌt,daʊn) *n.* **1.** the closing of a factory, shop, or other business. ~*vb.* **shut down. 2.** to cease or cause to cease operation.

shuteye ('ʃʌt,aɪ) *n. Slang.* sleep.

shut off *vb.* **1.** to cut off the flow or supply of. **2.** to isolate or separate.

shut out *vb.* **1.** to keep out or exclude. **2.** to conceal from sight: *we planted trees to shut out the view of the road*.

shutter ('ʃʌtə) *n.* **1.** a hinged doorlike cover, usually one of a pair, for closing of a window. **2. put up the shutters.** to close business at the end of the day or permanently. **3.** *Photog.* a device in a camera that opens to allow light through the lens so as to expose the film when a photograph is taken. ~*vb.* **4.** to close with a shutter or shutters. **5.** to equip with a shutter or shutters.

shuttle ('ʃʌt³l) *n.* **1.** a bobbin-like device used in weaving to pass the weft thread between the warp threads. **2.** a small bobbin-like device used to hold the thread in a sewing machine. **3.** a bus, train, or aircraft that makes frequent journeys between two places which are fairly near to each other. ~*vb.* **4.** to travel by shuttle. [Old English *scytel* bolt]

shuttlecock ('ʃʌt³l,kɒk) *n.* a rounded piece of cork or plastic having a flat end stuck with feathers, which is struck to and fro in badminton.

shut up *vb.* **1.** *Informal.* to stop talking or cause (someone) to stop talking: often used in commands. **2.** to confine or imprison (someone).

shy[1] (ʃaɪ) *adj.* **1.** not at ease in the company of others. **2.** easily frightened; timid. **3.** (foll. by *of*) cautious or wary of. **4.** showing disinclination: *workshy*. ~*vb.* **shying, shied. 5.** to move back or aside suddenly, as from fear: *the horse shied at the snake in the road*. **6.** (foll. by *away from*) to draw back from (doing something), through lack of confidence. ~*n., pl.* **shies. 7.** a sudden movement back or aside, as from fear. [Old English *sceoh*] —'**shyly** *adv.* —'**shyness** *n.*

shy[2] (ʃaɪ) *vb.* **shying, shied. 1.** to throw (something). ~*n., pl.* **shies. 2.** a quick throw. [Germanic]

Shylock ('ʃaɪ,lɒk) *n.* a heartless or demanding creditor. [after the heartless usurer in Shakespeare's *The Merchant of Venice*]

si (siː) *n. Music.* same as **te.**

Si *Chem.* silicon.

SI See **SI unit.**

Siamese (,saɪə'miːz) *n., pl.* **-mese. 1.**

same as **Siamese cat.** ~*adj., n., pl.* **-mese. 2.** same as **Thai.**

Siamese cat *n.* a short-haired cream-coloured cat with a tapering body, blue eyes, and dark ears, tail, and paws.

Siamese twins *pl. n.* twins born joined together at some point, such as at the hip.

sibilant ('sɪbɪlənt) *adj.* **1.** having a hissing sound. ~*n.* **2.** *Phonetics.* a consonant, such as *s* or *z*, that is pronounced with a hissing sound. [Latin *sibilāre* to hiss]

sibling ('sɪblɪŋ) *n.* a brother or sister. [Old English: a relative]

sibyl ('sɪbɪl) *n.* (in ancient Greece and Rome) a prophetess. [Greek *Sibulla*] —**sibylline** ('sɪbɪ,laɪn) *adj.*

sic[1] (sɪk) *adv.* thus: inserted in brackets in a text to indicate that an odd reading is in fact accurate. [Latin]

sic[2] (sɪk) *vb.* **sicking, sicked. 1.** to attack: used only in commands to a dog. **2.** to urge (a dog) to attack (someone). [dialect var. of *seek*]

sick (sɪk) *adj.* **1.** vomiting or likely to vomit. **2.** suffering from ill health. **3.** of or for ill people: *sick benefits*. **4.** deeply affected with mental or spiritual distress: *sick at heart*. **5.** mentally or spiritually disturbed. **6.** *Informal.* making fun of death, illness, or misfortune: *sick humour*. **7.** Also: **sick and tired.** (foll. by *of*) *Informal.* disgusted by or weary of: *I am sick of his everlasting laughter*. ~*n., vb.* **8.** *Informal.* same as **vomit.** [Old English *sēoc*]

sickbay ('sɪk,beɪ) *n.* a room for the treatment of sick people, for example on a ship.

sicken ('sɪkən) *vb.* **1.** to make (someone) feel nauseated or disgusted. **2.** (foll. by *for*) to show symptoms of (an illness).

sickening ('sɪkənɪŋ) *adj.* **1.** causing sickness or revulsion. **2.** *Informal.* extremely annoying. —'**sickeningly** *adv.*

sickie ('sɪkɪ) *n. Austral. & N.Z. informal.* a day of sick leave from work.

sickle ('sɪk³l) *n.* a tool for cutting grass and grain crops, with a curved blade and a short handle. [Old English *sicol*]

sick leave *n.* leave of absence from work through illness.

sickly ('sɪklɪ) *adj.* **-lier, -liest. 1.** not healthy; weak. **2.** suggesting sickness: *a sickly pallor*. **3.** (of a smell or taste) causing revulsion or nausea. **4.** insipid: *a sickly smile*. ~*adv.* **5.** suggesting sickness: *sickly pale*. —'**sickliness** *n.*

sickness ('sɪknɪs) *n.* **1.** an illness or disease. **2.** nausea or queasiness. **3.** vomiting.

side (saɪd) *n.* **1.** a line or surface that borders anything. **2.** *Geom.* a line forming part of the perimeter of a plane figure: *a hexagon has six sides*. **3.** either of two parts into which an object, surface, or area can be divided: *the right side and the left side*. **4.** either of the two surfaces of a flat object: *write on both sides of the page*. **5.** the sloping part of a hill or bank. **6.** either the left or the right half of the body, esp. the area around the waist: *I have a pain in my side*. **7.** the area immediately next to a person or thing: *he stood at her side*. **8.** a location within an area identified by reference to a central point: *the south side of the city*. **9.** the area at the edge of something, as opposed to the centre: *the side of the road*. **10.** aspect or part: *look on the bright side*. **11.** one of two or more contesting groups or teams. **12.** a position held in opposition to another in a dispute. **13.** line of descent: *he gets his brains from his mother's side*. **14.** *Informal.* a television channel. **15.** *Brit. slang.* insolence or pretentiousness: *to put on side*. **16. on one side.** apart from the rest. **17. on the side.** apart from or in addition to the main thing or part. **18. side by side. a.** close together. **b.** (foll. by *with*) beside or near to. **19. take sides.** to support one party in a dispute against another. ~*adj.* **20.** situated at the side: *the side door*. **21.** subordinate: *a side road*. ~*vb.* **22.** (foll. by *with*) to support (one party in a dispute). [Old English *side*]

sideboard ('said,bɔːd) *n.* a piece of furniture for a dining room, with drawers, cupboards, and shelves to hold tableware.

sideboards ('said,bɔːdz) *or esp. U.S. & Canad.* **sideburns** ('said,bɜːnz) *pl. n.* a man's whiskers grown down either side of the face in front of the ears.

sidecar ('said,kɑː) *n.* a small passenger car attached to the side of a motorcycle.

side effect *n.* **1.** a usually unwanted effect caused by a drug in addition to its intended one. **2.** any additional effect, usually an undesirable one.

sidekick ('said,kɪk) *n. Informal.* a close friend or associate.

sidelight ('said,laɪt) *n.* **1.** *Brit.* either of two small lights at the front of a motor vehicle. **2.** light coming from the side. **3.** either of the two navigational lights used by ships at night.

sideline ('said,laɪn) *n.* a subsidiary interest or source of income.

sidelines ('said,laɪnz) *pl. n.* **1.** *Sport.* **a.** the lines that mark the side boundaries of a playing area. **b.** the area just outside the playing area, where substitute players sit. **2. on the sidelines.** only passively involved.

sidelong ('said,lɒŋ) *adj.* **1.** directed to the side; oblique. ~*adv.* **2.** from the side; obliquely.

sidereal (saɪ'dɪərɪəl) *adj.* of or determined with reference to the stars: *the sidereal day*. [Latin *sīdus* a star]

side-saddle *n.* **1.** a riding saddle originally designed for women in skirts, allowing the rider to sit with both legs on the same side of the horse. ~*adv.* **2.** on or as if on a side-saddle.

sideshow ('said,ʃəʊ) *n.* **1.** a small show or entertainment offered along with the main show at a circus or fair. **2.** a subordinate event or incident.

side-splitting *adj.* causing a great deal of laughter.

sidestep ('said,stɛp) *vb.* **-stepping, -stepped.** **1.** to step out of the way of (something). **2.** to dodge (an issue). ~*n.*

side step. 3. a movement to one side, as in dancing or boxing.

sideswipe ('said,swaɪp) *n.* **1.** a glancing blow along or from the side. ~*vb.* **2.** to strike (someone) with such a blow.

sidetrack ('said,træk) *vb.* to distract (someone) from a main subject.

sidewalk ('said,wɔːk) *n. U.S. & Canad.* a pavement.

sideways ('said,weɪz) *adv.* **1.** moving, facing, or inclining towards one side. **2.** from one side; obliquely. **3.** with one side forward. ~*adj.* **4.** moving or directed to or from one side.

side whiskers *pl. n.* same as **sideboards.**

siding ('saidɪŋ) *n.* a short stretch of railway track connected to a main line, used for loading and unloading freight and storing engines and carriages.

sidle ('saidl) *vb.* to move in a furtive manner. [obs. *sideling* sideways]

SIDS sudden infant death syndrome; cot death.

siege (siːdʒ) *n.* **1.** a military operation carried out to capture a place by surrounding and blockading it. **2.** a similar operation carried out by police, for example to force people out of a place. **3. lay siege to.** to subject (a place) to a siege. [Old French *sege* a seat]

siemens ('siːmənz) *n., pl.* **siemens.** the SI unit of electrical conductance. [after E. W. von *Siemens*, Italian city]

sienna (sɪ'ɛnə) *n.* **1.** a natural earth used as a reddish-brown or yellowish-brown pigment. ~*adj.* **2. burnt sienna.** reddish-brown. **3. raw sienna.** yellowish-brown. [after *Siena*, Italian city]

sierra (sɪ'ɛərə) *n.* a range of mountains with jagged peaks in Spain or America. [Spanish, lit.: saw]

siesta (sɪ'ɛstə) *n.* an afternoon nap, taken in hot countries. [Spanish]

sieve (sɪv) *n.* **1.** a device for sifting or straining, consisting of a mesh container through which the material is shaken or poured. ~*vb.* **2.** to pass (material) through a sieve. [Old English *sife*]

sift (sɪft) *vb.* **1.** to sieve (a powdery substance) in order to remove the coarser particles. **2.** to separate (pieces of information) as if with a sieve. **3.** to examine minutely: *to sift evidence*. [Old English *siftan*]

sigh (saɪ) *vb.* **1.** to draw in and audibly let out a deep breath as an expression of sadness, weariness, longing, or relief. **2.** to make a sound resembling this. **3.** (foll. by *for*) to long for. **4.** to utter (something) with a sigh. ~*n.* **5.** the act or sound of sighing. [Old English *sīcan*]

sight (saɪt) *n.* **1.** the power or faculty of seeing; vision. **2.** an instance of seeing. **3.** the range of vision: *within sight of land*. **4.** point of view; judgment: *in his sight she could do no wrong*. **5.** anything that is seen. **6.** anything worth seeing: *the sights of London*. **7.** *Informal.* anything unpleasant to see: *his room was a sight!* **8.** a device used to assist the eye in aiming a gun or making an observation with an optical instrument. **9.** an aim or observation made with such a device. **10. a sight.** *Informal.* a great deal: *she's a sight too good for him.* **11. a sight for sore eyes.** a welcome sight. **12. catch sight of.** to glimpse. **13. know someone by sight.** to be able to recognize someone without having personal acquaintance with him. **14. lose sight of.** **a.** to be unable to see (something) any longer. **b.** to forget: *don't lose sight of your original intention.* **15. on sight.** as soon as someone or something is seen. **16. set one's sights on.** to have (a specified goal) in mind. **17. sight unseen.** without having seen the object at issue: *to buy a car sight unseen.* ~*vb.* **18.** to see, view, or glimpse. **19.** to aim (a firearm) using the sight. [Old English *sihth*]

sighted ('saitid) *adj.* not blind.

sightless ('saitlis) *adj.* blind.

sight-read ('sait,riːd) *vb.* **-reading, -read** (-,red). to sing or play (music in a printed form) without previous preparation. —**'sight-,reading** *n.*

sightscreen ('sait,skriːn) *n. Cricket.* a large white screen placed near the boundary behind the bowler, which helps the batsman see the ball.

sightseeing ('sait,siːiŋ) *n. Informal.* the act or practice of visiting the famous or interesting sights of a place. —**'sight-,seer** *n.*

sigma ('sigmə) *n.* **1.** the 18th letter in the Greek alphabet (Σ, σ). **2.** *Maths.* the symbol Σ, indicating summation.

sign (sain) *n.* **1.** something that indicates a fact or condition that is not immediately or outwardly observable: *a sign of weakness.* **2.** an action or gesture intended to convey an idea or information. **3.** a board or placard displayed in public and intended to advertise, inform, or warn. **4.** a conventional mark or symbol that has a specific meaning, for example £ for pounds. **5.** *Maths.* **a.** any symbol used to indicate an operation: *a plus sign.* **b.** a symbol used to indicate positivity or negativity of a number or expression. **6.** a visible indication: *the house showed no signs of being occupied.* **7.** an omen. **8.** *Med.* any objective evidence of the presence of a disease or disorder. **9.** *Astrol.* short for **sign of the zodiac.** ~*vb.* **10.** to write (one's name) on (a document or letter) to show its authenticity or one's agreement. **11.** to make a sign to someone so as to convey an idea or information. **12.** to engage or be engaged by signing a contract: *the team have signed a new player.* ~See also **sign away, sign in,** etc. [Latin *signum*]

signal ('signl) *n.* **1.** any sign, gesture, sound, or action used to communicate information. **2.** anything that causes immediate action: *the rise in prices was a signal for rebellion.* **3. a.** a variable voltage, current, or electromagnetic wave, by which information is conveyed through an electronic circuit. **b.** the information so conveyed. ~*adj.* **4.** remarkable or notable. ~*vb.* **-nalling, -nalled** or U.S. **-naling, -naled. 5.** to communicate (infor-

mation) by signal. [Latin *signum* sign] —**'signally** *adv.*

signal box *n.* a building from which railway signals are operated.

signalize or **-lise** ('signə,laiz) *vb.* to make noteworthy.

signalman ('signlmən) *n., pl.* **-men.** a railwayman in charge of the signals and points within a section.

signatory ('signətri) *n., pl.* **-ries. 1.** a person, organization, or state that has signed a document such as a treaty. ~*adj.* **2.** having signed a document or treaty.

signature ('signitʃə) *n.* **1.** a person's name written by himself, used in signing. **2.** a distinctive characteristic that identifies a person or animal. **3.** *Music.* a sign at the beginning of a piece to show key or time. **4.** *Printing.* a sheet of paper printed with several pages, which when folded becomes a section of a book. [Latin *signāre* to sign]

signature tune *n. Brit.* a melody used to introduce or identify a television or radio programme or performer.

sign away *vb.* to dispose of (something) by or as if by signing a document.

signboard ('sain,bɔːd) *n.* a board carrying a sign or notice, often to advertise a business or product.

signet ('signit) *n.* a small seal, used to stamp or authenticate documents. [Medieval Latin *signētum*]

signet ring *n.* a finger ring bearing a signet.

significance (sig'nifikəns) *n.* **1.** consequence or importance. **2.** meaning: *what is the significance of the name?*

significant (sig'nifikənt) *adj.* **1.** having or expressing a meaning. **2.** very important. —**sig'nificantly** *adv.*

significant figures *pl. n. Maths.* **1.** the figures of a number that express a magnitude to a specified degree of accuracy: *3.141 59 to four significant figures is 3.142.* **2.** the number of such figures: *3.142 has four significant figures.*

signify ('signi,fai) *vb.* **-fying, -fied. 1.** to indicate or suggest. **2.** to stand as a symbol or sign for. **3.** to be important. [Latin *signum* a mark + *facere* to make]

sign in *vb.* **1.** to sign a register on arrival at a place. **2.** to admit (a nonmember) to a club or institution as a guest by signing a register on his behalf.

sign language *n.* a system of communication by manual signs or gestures, such as one used by deaf people.

sign off *vb.* to announce the end of a radio or television programme.

sign of the zodiac *n. Astrol.* any of the 12 areas into which the zodiac is divided.

sign on *vb.* **1.** *Brit.* to register and report regularly at an unemployment-benefit office. **2.** to commit oneself to a job or activity by signing a form or contract.

signor ('siːnjɔː) *n., pl.* **signors** or **signori** (siː'njɔːriː). an Italian term of address equivalent to *sir* or *Mr.*

signora (siː'njɔːrə) *n., pl.* **-ras** or **-re** (-rei).

an Italian term of address equivalent to *madam* or Mrs.

signorina (ˌsiːnjɔːˈriːnə) *n.*, *pl.* **-nas** *or* **-ne** (-neɪ). an Italian term of address equivalent to *madam* or Miss.

sign out *vb.* to sign a register to indicate that one is leaving a place.

signpost ('saɪnˌpəʊst) *n.* 1. a post bearing a sign that shows the way. 2. a clue or indication. ~*vb.* 3. to mark (the way) with signposts.

sign up *vb.* to enlist for military service.

Sikh (siːk) *n.* 1. a member of an Indian religion that teaches that there is only one God. ~*adj.* 2. of the Sikhs or their religious beliefs or customs. [Hindi: disciple] —'**Sikh,ism** *n.*

silage ('saɪlɪdʒ) *n.* any crop harvested while green for fodder and kept succulent by partial fermentation in a silo.

silence ('saɪləns) *n.* 1. the state or quality of being silent. 2. the absence of sound. 3. refusal or failure to speak or communicate when expected: *his silence on their promotion was alarming.* ~*vb.* 4. to cause (someone or something) to become silent. 5. to put a stop to: *to silence all opposition.*

silencer ('saɪlənsə) *n.* any device designed to reduce noise, for example one fitted to the exhaust system of a motor vehicle or one fitted to the muzzle of a gun.

silent ('saɪlənt) *adj.* 1. characterized by an absence or near absence of sound: *a silent house.* 2. tending to speak very little. 3. failing to speak or communicate when expected: *the witness chose to remain silent.* 4. not spoken: *silent disapproval.* 5. (of a letter) used in the spelling of a word but not pronounced, such as the *k* in *know.* 6. denoting a film that has no soundtrack. [Latin *silēre* to be quiet] —'**silently** *adv.*

silhouette (ˌsɪluːˈɛt) *n.* 1. the outline of a dark figure seen against a light background. 2. an outline drawing, often a profile portrait, filled with black. ~*vb.* 3. to show (something) in silhouette. [after E. de *Silhouette*, politician]

silica ('sɪlɪkə) *n.* a hard glossy mineral, silicon dioxide, which occurs naturally as quartz and is used in the manufacture of glass. [Latin *silex* hard stone]

silicate ('sɪlɪkɪt) *n. Mineral.* a compound of silicon, oxygen, and a metal.

silicon ('sɪlɪkən) *n.* 1. a brittle nonmetallic element: used in transistors, solar cells, and alloys. Symbol: Si 2. (*modifier*) denoting an area of a country that contains much high-technology industry: *Silicon Valley.* [from *silica*]

silicon chip *n.* same as **chip** (sense 6).

silicone ('sɪlɪˌkəʊn) *n. Chem.* a tough synthetic material made from silicon and used in lubricants, paints, and resins.

silicosis (ˌsɪlɪˈkəʊsɪs) *n. Pathol.* a chronic lung disease caused by breathing in silica dust.

silk (sɪlk) *n.* 1. the fine soft fibre produced by a silkworm. 2. thread or fabric made from this fibre. 3. (*pl.*) garments made of this. 4. *Brit.* **a.** the gown worn by a

Queen's (or King's) Counsel. **b.** *Informal.* a Queen's (or King's) Counsel. **c. take silk.** to become a Queen's (or King's) Counsel. [Old English *sioluc*]

silken ('sɪlkən) *adj.* 1. made of silk. 2. resembling silk in smoothness or softness.

silk hat *n.* a top hat covered with silk.

silk-screen printing *n.* same as **screen process.**

silkworm ('sɪlkˌwɜːm) *n.* a caterpillar that spins a cocoon of silk.

silky ('sɪlkɪ) *adj.* **silkier, silkiest.** 1. resembling silk in texture; glossy. 2. made of silk. 3. (of a voice or manner) suave; smooth. —'**silkiness** *n.*

sill (sɪl) *n.* 1. a shelf at the bottom of a window, either inside or outside a room. 2. the lower horizontal part of a window or door frame. [Old English *syll*]

silly ('sɪlɪ) *adj.* **-lier, -liest.** 1. lacking in good sense; foolish. 2. dazed, as from a blow. 3. *Cricket.* (of a fielding position) near the batsman's wicket: *silly mid-on.* ~*n.*, *pl.* **-lies.** 4. *Informal.* a foolish person. [Old English *sǣlig* (unattested) happy] —'**silliness** *n.*

silo ('saɪləʊ) *n.*, *pl.* **-los.** 1. an airtight pit or tower in which silage is made and stored. 2. an underground structure in which missile systems are sited for protection. [Spanish]

silt (sɪlt) *n.* 1. a fine sediment of mud or clay deposited by moving water. ~*vb.* 2. (foll. by *up*) to fill or choke up with silt. [Old Norse]

Silurian (saɪˈlʊərɪən) *adj. Geol.* of a period of geological time about 425 million years ago, during which fishes first appeared. [after *Silures,* a Welsh tribe who opposed the Romans]

silvan ('sɪlvən) *adj.* same as **sylvan.**

silver ('sɪlvə) *n.* 1. a precious greyish-white metallic element: used in jewellery, tableware, and coins. Symbol: Ag 2. a coin or coins made of silver. 3. any household articles made of silver. 4. short for **silver medal.** ~*adj.* 5. greyish-white. 6. (of anniversaries) the 25th in a series: *Silver Jubilee; silver wedding.* ~*vb.* 7. to coat with silver or a silvery substance: *to silver a spoon.* 8. to cause (something) to become silvery in colour. [Old English *siolfor*]

silver beet *n.* a beet of Australia and New Zealand with edible spinach-like leaves.

silver birch *n.* a tree with silvery-white peeling bark.

silverfish ('sɪlvəˌfɪʃ) *n.*, *pl.* **-fish** *or* **-fishes.** 1. a silver-coloured fish. 2. a small wingless silver-coloured insect.

silver lining *n.* a hopeful aspect of an otherwise desperate or unhappy situation.

silver medal *n.* a medal of silver awarded to a competitor who comes second in a contest or race.

silver plate *n.* 1. a thin layer of silver deposited on a base metal. 2. articles, such as tableware, made of silver plate. —ˌsilver-'plate *vb.*

silver screen *n.* **the.** *Informal.* 1. films collectively or the film industry. 2. the screen onto which films are projected in a cinema.

silverside ('sɪlvə,saɪd) *n. Brit. & N.Z.* a cut of beef from below the rump and above the leg.

silversmith ('sɪlvə,smɪθ) *n.* a craftsman who makes or repairs articles of silver.

silver thaw *n. Canad.* **1.** a freezing rainstorm. **2.** same as **glitter** (sense 7).

silverware ('sɪlvə,wɛə) *n.* articles, such as tableware, made of or plated with silver.

silvery ('sɪlvərɪ) *adj.* **1.** having the appearance of silver: *the silvery moon.* **2.** having a clear ringing sound.

silviculture ('sɪlvɪ,kʌltʃə) *n.* the cultivation of forest trees. [Latin *silva* woodland + *culture*]

simian ('sɪmɪən) *adj.* **1.** of or resembling a monkey or ape. ~*n.* **2.** a monkey or ape. [Latin *sīmia* an ape]

similar ('sɪmɪlə) *adj.* **1.** showing resemblance in qualities, characteristics, or appearance. **2.** *Geom.* (of two or more figures) different in size or position, but with exactly the same shape. [Latin *similis*] —**similarity** (,sɪmɪ'lærɪtɪ) *n.* —**'similarly** *adv.*

simile ('sɪmɪlɪ) *n.* a figure of speech that likens one thing to another of a different category, usually introduced by *as* or *like.* [Latin: something similar]

similitude (sɪ'mɪlɪ,tjuːd) *n.* likeness; similarity.

simmer ('sɪmə) *vb.* **1.** to cook (food) gently at just below boiling point. **2.** to be in a state of suppressed rage. ~*n.* **3.** the state of simmering. [perhaps imit.]

simmer down *vb. Informal.* to grow calmer after intense rage.

simnel cake ('sɪmn³l) *n. Brit.* a fruit cake covered with a layer of marzipan, traditionally eaten during Lent or at Easter. [Latin *simila* fine flour]

simony ('saɪmənɪ) *n. Christianity.* the practice of buying or selling Church benefits such as pardons. [after *Simon Magus*, a biblical sorcerer who tried to buy magical powers]

simoom (sɪ'muːm) *n.* a hot suffocating sand-laden desert wind. [Arabic *samūm* poisonous]

simper ('sɪmpə) *vb.* **1.** to smile in a silly or affected way. **2.** to utter (something) with a simper. ~*n.* **3.** a simpering smile. [origin unknown] —**'simpering** *adj.*

simple ('sɪmp³l) *adj.* **1.** easy to understand or do: *a simple problem.* **2.** plain; unadorned: *a simple dress; the simple truth.* **3.** not combined or complex: *a simple mechanism.* **4.** unaffected or unpretentious: *although he became famous, he remained a simple man.* **5.** sincere; frank: *her simple explanation was readily accepted.* **6.** of humble condition or rank: *a simple peasant.* **7.** feeble-minded. **8.** straightforward: *a simple case of mumps.* **9.** *Music.* denoting a time where the number of beats per bar may be two, three, or four. [Latin *simplex* plain] —**simplicity** (sɪm'plɪsɪtɪ) *n.*

simple fraction *n. Maths.* a fraction in which the numerator and denominator are both whole numbers.

simple fracture *n.* a fracture in which the broken bone does not pierce the skin.

simple interest *n. Finance.* interest paid only on the original amount of a debt.

simple-minded *adj.* **1.** stupid; foolish. **2.** mentally defective. **3.** unsophisticated; artless. —**,simple-'mindedness** *n.*

simple sentence *n.* a sentence consisting of a single main clause.

simpleton ('sɪmp³ltən) *n.* a foolish or very unintelligent person.

simplify ('sɪmplɪ,faɪ) *vb.* **-fying, -fied.** **1.** to make (something) less complicated. **2.** *Maths.* to reduce (an equation or fraction) to its simplest form. [Latin *simplus* simple + *facere* to make] —**simplification** (,sɪmplɪfɪ'keɪʃən) *n.*

simplistic (sɪm'plɪstɪk) *adj.* oversimplified or oversimplifying.

simply ('sɪmplɪ) *adv.* **1.** in a simple manner. **2.** merely. **3.** absolutely; altogether: *a simply wonderful holiday.*

simulate ('sɪmjʊ,leɪt) *vb.* **1.** to make a pretence of: *to simulate anxiety.* **2.** to imitate the conditions of (a situation), as in carrying out an experiment: *to simulate weightlessness.* **3.** to have the appearance of: *simulated leather.* [Latin *simulāre* to copy] —**simulation** (,sɪmjʊ'leɪʃən) *n.*

simulator ('sɪmjʊ,leɪtə) *n.* a device that simulates specific conditions for the purposes of research or training: *a flight simulator.*

simultaneous (,sɪməl'teɪnɪəs) *adj.* occurring or existing at the same time. [Latin *simul* at the same time] —**simul'taneously** *adv.* —**simultaneity** (,sɪməltə'niːɪtɪ) *n.*

simultaneous equations *pl. n. Maths.* a set of equations that are all satisfied by the same values of the variables, the number of variables being equal to the number of equations.

sin¹ (sɪn) *n.* **1.** the breaking of a religious or moral law. **2.** any offence against a principle or standard. **3.** live in sin. *Old-fashioned, informal.* (of an unmarried couple) to live together. ~*vb.* **sinning, sinned.** **4.** to commit a sin. [Old English *synn*] —**'sinner** *n.*

sin² (saɪn) *Maths.* sine.

SIN (in Canada) Social Insurance Number.

sin bin *n. Slang.* the penalty box in ice hockey.

since (sɪns) *prep.* **1.** during the period of time after: *since May it has only rained once.* ~*conj.* **2.** (sometimes preceded by *ever*) continuously from the time given when: *I've been busy since we last spoke.* **3.** for the reason that; because. ~*adv.* **4.** from that time: *I haven't seen him since.* [Old English *siththan*]

sincere (sɪn'sɪə) *adj.* without pretence or deceit; genuine: *sincere regret.* [Latin *sincērus*] —**sin'cerely** *adv.* —**sincerity** (sɪn'sɛrɪtɪ) *n.*

sine (saɪn) *n.* (in trigonometry) the ratio of the length of the opposite side to that of the hypotenuse in a right-angled triangle. [Latin *sinus* a bend]

sinecure ('saɪnɪˌkjʊə) *n.* a paid job involving minimal duties. [Medieval Latin (*beneficium*) *sine cūrā* (benefice) without cure (of souls)]

sine die ('saɪnɪ 'daɪɪ) *adv.* without fixing a day for future action or meeting. [Latin, lit.: without a day]

sine qua non ('sɪnɪ kwɑː 'nɒn) *n.* an essential requirement. [Latin, lit.: without which not]

sinew ('sɪnjuː) *n.* **1.** *Anat.* same as **tendon. 2. a.** a source of strength or power. **b.** *Literary.* muscular strength. [Old English *sionu*]

sinewy ('sɪnjʊɪ) *adj.* lean and muscular.

sinful ('sɪnfʊl) *adj.* **1.** having committed or tending to commit sin: *a sinful person.* **2.** being a sin; wicked: *a sinful act.*

sing (sɪŋ) *vb.* **singing, sang, sung. 1.** to produce musical sounds with the voice. **2.** to perform (a song). **3.** (foll. by *of*) to tell a story in song about. **4.** (of certain birds and insects) to utter musical calls. **5.** to make a humming, ringing, or whistling sound: *the arrow sang past his ear.* **6.** (of one's ears) to be filled with a continuous ringing sound. **7.** to bring (someone) to a given state by singing: *to sing a child to sleep.* **8.** *Slang, chiefly U.S.* to act as an informer. ~See also **sing out.** [Old English *singan*] —'**singer** *n.* —'**singing** *adj., n.*

sing. singular.

singe (sɪndʒ) *vb.* **1.** to burn superficially; scorch: *to singe one's clothes.* ~*n.* **2.** a superficial burn. [Old English *sengan*]

Singhalese (ˌsɪŋəˈliːz) *n., pl.* **-leses -lese,** *adj.* same as **Sinhalese.**

singing telegram *n.* a service by which a person is employed to present greetings to someone by singing.

single ('sɪŋg'l) *adj.* **1.** existing alone; solitary: *at the top of the hill stood a single tower.* **2.** distinct from others of the same kind: *every single day.* **3.** designed for one user: *a single bed.* **4.** unmarried. **5.** involving two individuals: *single combat.* **6.** even one: *there wasn't a single person on the beach.* **7.** (of a flower) having only one circle of petals. ~*n.* **8.** a hotel bedroom for one person. **9.** a gramophone record with one short piece of music on each side. **10.** *Cricket.* a hit from which one run is scored. **11. a.** *Brit.* a pound note or coin. **b.** *U.S. & Canad.* a dollar bill. **12.** short for **single ticket.** ~*vb.* **13.** (foll. by *out*) to select from a group of people or things: *he singled him out for special mention.* ~See also **singles.** [Old French *sengle*]

single-breasted *adj.* (of a jacket or coat) having the fronts overlapping only slightly and with one row of fastenings.

single-decker *n. Brit. informal.* a bus with only one passenger deck.

single entry *n.* a book-keeping system in which all transactions are entered in one account only.

single file *n.* a line of people, one behind the other.

single-handed *adj., adv.* unaided or working alone: *a single-handed Atlantic crossing; he crossed the Atlantic single-handed.* —ˌsingle-'handedly *adv.*

single-minded *adj.* having one aim only; dedicated. —ˌsingle-'mindedly *adv.* —ˌsingle-'mindedness *n.*

single-parent family *n.* a family consisting of one parent and his or her child or children living together, the other parent being dead or permanently absent.

singles ('sɪŋg'lz) *pl. n. Sport.* a match played with one person on each side.

singles bar *n.* a bar that is a social meeting place for single people.

singlet ('sɪŋglɪt) *n. Chiefly Brit.* a man's sleeveless vest.

single ticket *n. Brit.* a ticket valid for a one-way journey only.

singleton ('sɪŋg'ltən) *n. Cards.* the only card of a particular suit held by a player.

singly ('sɪŋglɪ) *adv.* one at a time; one by one.

sing out *vb.* to call out loudly; shout.

singsong ('sɪŋˌsɒŋ) *n.* **1.** *Brit.* an informal group singing session. ~*adj.* **2.** having a monotonous rise and fall in tone: *a singsong accent.*

singular ('sɪŋgjʊlə) *adj.* **1.** *Grammar.* (of a word or form) denoting only one person or thing: *a singular noun.* **2.** remarkable; extraordinary: *a singular feat.* **3.** unusual; odd: *a singular character.* ~*n.* **4.** *Grammar.* the singular form of a word. [Latin *singulāris* single] —**singularity** (ˌsɪŋgjʊ-ˈlærɪtɪ) *n.* —'**singularly** *adv.*

Sinhalese (ˌsɪnhəˈliːz) *or* **Singhalese** *n.* **1.** (*pl.* **-leses** *or* **-lese**) a member of a people living mainly in Sri Lanka. **2.** the language of this people. ~*adj.* **3.** of this people or their language. ~See also **Sri Lankan.**

sinister ('sɪnɪstə) *adj.* **1.** threatening or suggesting evil or harm: *a sinister glance.* **2.** *Heraldry.* of, on, or starting from the bearer's left side. [Latin *sinister* on the left-hand side, considered by Roman augurers to be the unlucky one]

sink (sɪŋk) *vb.* **sinking, sank** *or* **sunk; sunk** *or* **sunken. 1.** to descend or cause to descend, esp. beneath the surface of a liquid. **2.** to appear to descend towards or below the horizon. **3.** (foll. by *into*) to pass into a specified lower state or condition: *to sink into apathy.* **4.** (of a voice) to become quieter. **5.** to make or become lower in amount or value. **6.** to become weaker in health. **7.** to seep or penetrate. **8.** to dig, drill, or excavate (a hole or shaft). **9.** to drive (a stake) into the ground. **10.** (foll. by *in* or *into*) to invest (money). **11.** *Golf, snooker.* to hit (the ball) into the hole or pocket: *he sank a 15-foot putt.* ~*n.* **12.** a fixed basin in a kitchen or bathroom, with a water supply and drainpipe. [Old English *sincan*]

sinker ('sɪŋkə) *n.* a weight attached to a fishing line or net to cause it to sink in water.

sink in *vb.* to penetrate the mind: *eventually the news sank in.*

sinking fund   *n.* a fund set aside to repay a long-term debt.

Sinn Féin (ˈʃɪn ˈfeɪn) *n.* an Irish Republican political movement linked to the revolutionary Irish Republican Army. [Irish Gaelic: we ourselves]

Sino- (ˈsaɪnəʊ) *combining form.* Chinese: *Sino-Tibetan; Sinology.* [Late Latin *Sīnae* the Chinese]

Sinology (saɪˈnɒlədʒɪ) *n.* the study of Chinese history, language, and culture. —**Siˈnologist** *n.*

sinuous (ˈsɪnjʊəs) *adj.* **1.** full of curves. **2.** having smooth twisting movements. [Latin *sinuōsus* winding] —**sinuosity** (ˌsɪnjʊˈɒsɪtɪ) *n.*

sinus (ˈsaɪnəs) *n. Anat.* a hollow space in bone, such as one in the skull opening into a nasal cavity. [Latin: a curve]

sinusitis (ˌsaɪnəˈsaɪtɪs) *n.* inflammation of the membrane lining a sinus.

sip (sɪp) *vb.* **sipping, sipped.** **1.** to drink (a liquid) in small mouthfuls. ~*n.* **2.** a quantity that is sipped. **3.** an instance of sipping. [prob. from Low German *sippen*]

siphon *or* **syphon** (ˈsaɪfʰn) *n.* **1.** a tube placed with one end at a certain level in a container of liquid and the other end outside the container below this level, so that atmospheric pressure forces the liquid through the tube and out of the container. **2.** same as **soda siphon.** ~*vb.* **3.** (foll. by *off*) to draw (liquid) off through a siphon. [Greek]

sir (sɜː) *n.* a polite term of address for a man. [var. of *sire*]

Sir (sɜː) *n.* a title placed before the name of a knight or baronet: *Sir Walter Raleigh.*

sire (ˈsaɪə) *n.* **1.** a male parent of a horse or other domestic animal. **2.** *Archaic.* a respectful term of address used to a king. ~*vb.* **3.** to father. [Old French]

siren (ˈsaɪərən) *n.* **1.** a device that gives out a loud wailing sound as a warning or signal. **2.** *Gk myth.* one of several sea nymphs whose singing lured sailors to destruction on the rocks. **3.** a dangerously alluring woman. [Greek *seirēn*]

sirloin (ˈsɜːˌlɔɪn) *n.* a prime cut of beef from the upper part of the loin. [Old French *surlonge*]

sirocco (sɪˈrɒkəʊ) *n., pl.* **-cos.** a hot oppressive wind blowing from N Africa into S Europe. [Italian]

sis (sɪs) *n. Informal.* short for **sister.**

sisal (ˈsaɪsʰl) *n.* a stiff fibre obtained from a Mexican plant and used for making rope. [after *Sisal,* a port in Mexico]

siskin (ˈsɪskɪn) *n.* a yellow-and-black finch. [Middle Dutch *sīseken*]

sissy *or* **cissy** (ˈsɪsɪ) *n., pl.* **-sies.** **1.** an effeminate, weak, or cowardly person. ~*adj.* **2.** effeminate, weak, or cowardly. [from *sis*]

sister (ˈsɪstə) *n.* **1.** a woman or girl having the same parents as another person. **2.** a female fellow member of a group, race, or profession. **3.** a female nurse in charge of a ward. **4.** *Chiefly R.C. Church.* a nun. **5.** (*modifier*) of the same class, origin, or design, as another: *a sister ship.* [Old English *sweostor*]

sisterhood (ˈsɪstəˌhʊd) *n.* **1.** the state of being sisters or like sisters. **2.** a religious group of sisters. **3.** a group of women united by common interests, aims, or beliefs.

sister-in-law *n., pl.* **sisters-in-law.** **1.** the sister of one's husband or wife. **2.** one's brother's wife.

sisterly (ˈsɪstəlɪ) *adj.* of or like a sister; affectionate.

sit (sɪt) *vb.* **sitting, sat.** **1.** to rest one's body on one's buttocks with one's torso upright: *to sit on a chair.* **2.** to cause (someone) to adopt such a posture. **3.** (of an animal) to rest with its hindquarters lowered to the ground. **4.** (of a bird) to perch or roost. **5.** (foll. by *on*) (of a bird) to cover its eggs so as to hatch them. **6.** to be located. **7.** to pose for a painting or photograph. **8.** to occupy a seat in some official capacity: *she sits on a number of committees.* **9.** (of an official body) to be in session. **10.** to remain unused: *his car sat in the garage.* **11.** (of a garment) to fit or hang as specified: *that dress sits well on you.* **12.** *Chiefly Brit.* to take (an examination): *he's sitting his bar finals.* **13.** (foll. by *for*) *Chiefly Brit.* to be a candidate for (a qualification): *he's sitting for a BA.* **14. sit tight.** *Informal.* **a.** to wait patiently. **b.** to maintain one's position firmly. ~See also **sit back, sit down,** etc. [Old English *sittan*]

sitar (sɪˈtɑː) *n.* an Indian stringed musical instrument with a long neck and a rounded body. [Hindi]

sit back *vb.* to relax or be passive when action should be taken: *many people just sit back and ignore the problems of today.*

sitcom (ˈsɪtˌkɒm) *n. Informal.* short for **situation comedy.**

sit down *vb.* **1.** to adopt or cause (someone) to adopt a sitting posture. **2.** (foll. by *under*) to suffer (insults or humiliations) without resistance. ~*n.* **sit-down.** **3.** a short rest sitting down. ~*adj.* **sit-down.** **4.** (of a meal) eaten while sitting down at a table.

sit-down strike *n.* a strike in which workers refuse to leave their place of employment until a settlement is reached.

site (saɪt) *n.* **1.** the piece of ground where something was, is, or is intended to be located: *a building site.* ~*vb.* **2.** to locate (something) on a specific site. [Latin *situs* position]

sit-in *n.* a protest in which the demonstrators occupy seats in a public place and refuse to move. ~*vb.* **sit in. 2.** (foll. by *for*) to deputize for. **3.** (foll. by *on*) to be present at (a meeting) as an observer.

sitkamer (ˈsɪtˌkɑːmə) *n. S. African.* a sitting room. [Afrikaans]

sitka spruce (ˈsɪtkə) *n.* a tall North American spruce tree, now often grown in Britain. [after *Sitka,* a town in Alaska]

sit on *vb. Informal.* **1.** to delay action on: *he's been sitting on that report for weeks.* **2.** to check or rebuke (someone).

sit out *vb.* **1.** to endure to the end: *although the play was terrible, I sat it out.* **2.** to take no part in (a dance or game).

sitter ('sɪtə) *n.* **1.** a person posing for his portrait or photograph. **2.** same as **baby-sitter.**

sitting ('sɪtɪŋ) *n.* **1.** a continuous period of being seated at some activity: *I read his novel at one sitting.* **2.** one of the times when a meal is served, when there is not enough space for everyone to eat at the same time: *dinner will be served in two sittings.* **3.** a period of posing for a painting or photograph. **4.** a meeting of an official body to conduct business. ~*adj.* **5.** current: *the sitting member for Hillhead.* **6.** seated: *in a sitting position.*

sitting duck *n. Informal.* a person or thing in a defenceless or vulnerable position.

sitting room *n.* a room in a house or flat where people sit and relax.

sitting tenant *n.* a tenant occupying a house or flat.

situate ('sɪtjʊ,eɪt) *vb.* to place. [Late Latin *situāre* to position]

situation (,sɪtjʊ'eɪʃən) *n.* **1.** location, with regard to the surroundings. **2. a.** state of affairs. **b.** a complex or critical state of affairs. **3.** social or financial circumstances. **4.** a position of employment.

situation comedy *n.* (on television or radio) a comedy series involving the same characters in various everyday situations.

sit up *vb.* **1.** to raise oneself from a lying position into a sitting one. **2.** to remain out of bed until a late hour. **3.** *Informal.* to become suddenly interested: *devaluation of the dollar made the money market sit up.* ~*n.* **sit-up. 4.** a physical exercise in which the body is brought into a sitting position from one of lying on the back.

SI unit *n.* any of the units (metre, kilogram, second, ampere, kelvin, candela, and mole) adopted for international use under the Système International d'Unités, now employed for all scientific and most technical purposes.

six (sɪks) *n.* **1.** the cardinal number that is the sum of one and five. **2.** a numeral, 6, VI, representing this number. **3.** something representing or consisting of six units. **4.** *Cricket.* a score of six runs, obtained by hitting the ball so that it crosses the boundary without bouncing. **5. at sixes and sevens.** in a state of confusion. **6. knock someone for six.** *Informal.* to upset or overwhelm someone completely. **7. six of one and half a dozen of the other.** a situation in which there is no real difference between the alternatives. ~*det.* **8.** amounting to six. [Old English *siex*] —**sixth** *adj., n.*

sixfold ('sɪks,fəʊld) *adj.* **1.** having six times as many. **2.** composed of six parts. ~*adv.* **3.** by six times as much.

sixpence ('sɪkspəns) *n.* (formerly) a small British coin worth six old pennies, or 2½ pence.

six-shooter *n. U.S. informal.* a revolver that fires six shots without reloading.

sixteen ('sɪks'tiːn) *n.* **1.** the cardinal number that is the sum of ten and six. **2.** a numeral, 16, XVI, representing this number. **3.** something representing or consisting of sixteen units. ~*det.* **4.** amounting to sixteen. —**'six'teenth** *adj., n.*

sixth form *n.* (in England and Wales) the most senior form in a secondary school, in which pupils over sixteen may take A levels or retake O levels. —**'sixth-,former** *n.*

sixth sense *n.* intuition or perception beyond the five senses of sight, hearing, touch, taste, and smell.

sixty ('sɪkstɪ) *n., pl.* **-ties. 1.** the cardinal number that is the product of ten and six. **2.** a numeral, 60, LX, representing this number. **3.** (*pl.*) the numbers 60-69, esp. the 60th to the 69th year of a person's life or of a century. **4.** something representing or consisting of sixty units. ~*det.* **5.** amounting to sixty. —**'sixtieth** *adj., n.*

sizable *or* **sizeable** ('saɪzəb'l) *adj.* quite large.

size[1] (saɪz) *n.* **1.** the dimensions, amount, or extent of something. **2.** large dimensions, amount, or extent. **3.** one of a series of graduated measurements for goods: *she takes size 4 shoes.* **4.** *Informal.* state of affairs as summarized: *he's bankrupt, that's about the size of it.* ~*vb.* **5.** to sort (things) according to size. [Old French *sise*]

size[2] (saɪz) *n.* **1.** a thin gluey substance that is used as a glaze or sealer on paper or plaster surfaces. ~*vb.* **2.** to treat (a surface) with size. [origin unknown]

sized (saɪzd) *adj.* of a specified size: *medium-sized.*

size up *vb. Informal.* to make an assessment of (a person or situation).

sizzle ('sɪz'l) *vb.* **1.** to make a hissing sound like the sound of frying fat. **2.** *Informal.* to be very hot. **3.** *Informal.* to be very angry. ~*n.* **4.** a hissing sound. [imit.] —**'sizzling** *adj.*

skate[1] (skeɪt) *n.* **1.** same as **ice skate** *or* **roller skate. 2. get one's skates on.** *Informal.* to hurry. ~*vb.* **3.** to glide swiftly on skates. **4. skate on thin ice.** to place oneself in a dangerous situation. [Old French *éschasse* stilt] —**'skater** *n.* —**'skating** *n.*

skate[2] (skeɪt) *n., pl.* **skate** *or* **skates.** a large fish with a broad flat body, a short spineless tail, and a pointed snout. [Old Norse *skata*]

skateboard ('skeɪt,bɔːd) *n.* **1.** a narrow board mounted on roller-skate wheels, usually ridden while standing up. ~*vb.* **2.** to ride on a skateboard. —**'skate-,boarding** *n.*

skate round *or* **over** *vb.* to avoid discussing or dealing with (a matter) fully.

skedaddle (skɪ'dæd'l) *vb. Informal.* to run off hastily. [origin unknown]

skein (skeɪn) *n.* a length of yarn or thread wound in a long coil. [Old French *escaigne*]

skeleton ('skɛlɪtən) *n.* **1.** the hard framework of bones that supports and protects the organs and muscles of the body. **2.**

Informal. an extremely thin person or animal. **3.** the essential framework of any structure. **4.** an outline consisting of bare essentials: *the skeleton of a novel.* **5.** *(modifier)* reduced to a minimum: *a skeleton staff.* **6. skeleton in the cupboard** *or* **closet.** a discreditable fact from one's past that one keeps secret. [Greek: something dried up]

skeleton key *n.* a key designed so that it can open many different locks.

skeptic ('skɛptɪk) *n. Archaic & U.S.* same as **sceptic.**

sketch (skɛtʃ) *n.* **1.** a quick rough drawing. **2.** a brief descriptive piece of writing. **3.** a short humorous piece of acting forming part of a show. **4.** any brief outline. ~*vb.* **5.** to make a quick rough drawing (of). **6.** (foll. by *out*) to make a brief description of. [Greek *skhedios* unprepared]

sketchbook ('skɛtʃ,bʊk) *n.* a book of blank pages for sketching on.

sketchy ('skɛtʃɪ) *adj.* **sketchier, sketchiest.** superficial or incomplete. —'**sketchily** *adv.*

skew (skjuː) *adj.* **1.** having a slanting position. ~*n.* **2.** a slanting position. ~*vb.* **3.** to take or cause to take an oblique or slanting position. **4.** to distort. [Old French *escuer* to shun]

skewbald ('skjuː,bɔːld) *adj.* **1.** marked or spotted in white and another colour. ~*n.* **2.** a horse with this marking. [origin unknown]

skewer (skjʊə) *n.* **1.** a long pin for holding meat together during cooking. ~*vb.* **2.** to fasten or pierce with or as if with a skewer. [prob. from dialect *skiver*]

skewwhiff ('skjuː'wɪf) *adj. Brit. informal.* not straight.

ski (skiː) *n., pl.* **skis** *or* **ski. 1.** one of a pair of wooden, metal, or plastic runners that are used, fastened to boots, for gliding over snow. ~*vb.* **2.** to travel on skis. [Norwegian] —'**skier** *n.* —'**skiing** *n.*

skid (skɪd) *vb.* **skidding, skidded. 1.** (of a vehicle or person) to slide sideways while in motion. ~*n.* **2.** an instance of skidding. [origin unknown]

skidoo (skɪ'duː) *Canad.* ~*n., pl.* **-doos. 1.** a snowmobile. ~*vb.* **-dooing, -dooed. 2.** to travel using a snowmobile. [*Ski-Doo,* orig. a trademark]

skid row (rəʊ) *n. Slang, chiefly U.S. & Canad.* a dilapidated section of a city, frequented by down-and-outs.

skiff (skɪf) *n.* a small boat propelled by oars, sail, or motor. [French *esquif*]

ski jump *n.* a steep snow-covered slope ending in a horizontal ramp from which skiers compete to make the longest jump.

skilful *or U.S.* **skillful** ('skɪlfʊl) *adj.* having or showing skill. —'**skilfully** *or U.S.* '**skillfully** *adv.*

ski lift *n.* any device, such as a chair lift, for carrying skiers up a slope.

skill (skɪl) *n.* **1.** special ability or expertise, often acquired by training. **2.** something, such as a trade, requiring special training

or expertise. [Old Norse *skil* distinction] —**skilled** *adj.*

skillet ('skɪlɪt) *n.* **1.** a small frying pan. **2.** *Chiefly Brit.* a long-handled cooking pot. [origin unknown]

skim (skɪm) *vb.* **skimming, skimmed. 1.** to remove floating material from the surface of (a liquid): *to skim milk.* **2.** to glide smoothly over (a surface). **3.** to throw (something) across a surface, so as to bounce it: *to skim stones over water.* **4.** (foll. by *through*) to read (a piece of writing) quickly and superficially. [Middle English *skimmen*]

skimmed *or* **skim milk** *n.* milk from which the cream has been removed.

skimp (skɪmp) *vb.* **1.** to be extremely sparing or supply (someone) sparingly. **2.** to do (something) carelessly or with inadequate materials. [perhaps a combination of *scant & scrimp*]

skimpy ('skɪmpɪ) *adj.* **skimpier, skimpiest.** meagre, insufficient, or scanty.

skin (skɪn) *n.* **1.** the tissue forming the outer covering of the body. **2.** a person's complexion: *a fair skin.* **3.** any outer layer or covering: *a banana skin.* **4.** a film on the surface of a liquid. **5.** the outer covering of a fur-bearing animal, removed and prepared for use. **6.** a container for liquids, made from animal skin. **7. by the skin of one's teeth.** by a narrow margin. **8. get under one's skin.** *Informal.* to annoy one. **9. no skin off one's nose.** *Informal.* not a matter that concerns one. **10. save one's skin.** to save one from death or harm. **11. skin and bone.** extremely thin. **12. thick** (*or* **thin**) **skin.** an insensitive (*or* sensitive) nature. ~*vb.* **skinning, skinned. 13.** to remove the outer covering from. **14.** to injure (a part of the body) by scraping some of the skin off: *he skinned his knee.* **15.** *Slang.* to swindle. [Old English *scinn*] —'**skinless** *adj.*

skin-deep *adj.* superficial; shallow.

skin diving *n.* the sport or activity of underwater swimming using only light breathing apparatus and without a special diving suit. —'**skin-,diver** *n.*

skin flick *n. Slang.* a pornographic film.

skinflint ('skɪn,flɪnt) *n.* a miserly person. [referring to a person so avaricious that he would skin (swindle) a flint]

skin graft *n.* a piece of skin removed from one part of the body and surgically grafted at the site of a severe burn or other injury.

skinhead ('skɪn,hɛd) *n. Brit.* a White boy who has closely cropped hair and wears heavy boots and braces.

skinny ('skɪnɪ) *adj.* **-nier, -niest.** extremely thin.

skint (skɪnt) *adj. Brit. slang.* without money. [var. of *skinned*]

skintight ('skɪn'taɪt) *adj.* (of garments) fitting tightly over the body; clinging.

skip[1] (skɪp) *vb.* **skipping, skipped. 1.** to spring or move lightly by hopping from one foot to the other. **2.** to jump over a skipping-rope. **3.** to cause (a stone) to skim over a surface or (of a stone) to move in this way. **4.** to omit (intervening matter): *he skipped a chapter of the book.* **5.** (foll. by *through*) *Informal.* to read or deal with (something) quickly or superficially. **6. skip it!** *Informal.* it doesn't matter! **7.** *Informal.* to miss deliberately: *to skip school.* **8.** *Informal, chiefly U.S. & Canad.* to leave (a place) in haste: *to skip town.* ~*n.* **9.** a skipping movement or action. [prob. from Old Norse]

skip² (skɪp) *n.* **1.** a large open container for transporting building materials or rubbish. **2.** a cage used as a lift in mines. [var. of *skep* a beehive]

ski pants *pl. n.* stretch trousers, worn for skiing or as a fashion garment, which are kept taut by straps under the feet.

skipper (ˈskɪpə) *n.* **1.** the captain of a ship or aircraft. **2.** the captain of a sporting team. ~*vb.* **3.** to be the captain of. [Middle Low German, Middle Dutch *schipper* shipper]

skipping (ˈskɪpɪŋ) *n.* the act of jumping over a rope held by the person jumping or by two other people, as a game or for exercise.

skipping-rope *n. Brit.* a rope, sometimes with handles, that is held in the hands and swung round and down so that the holder or others can jump over it.

skirl (skɜːl) *Scot. & N English dialect.* ~*vb.* **1.** (of bagpipes) to give out a shrill sound. ~*n.* **2.** the sound of bagpipes. [prob. from Old Norse]

skirmish (ˈskɜːmɪʃ) *n.* **1.** a minor short-lived battle. **2.** any brief or unimportant clash. ~*vb.* **3.** to engage in a skirmish. [Old French *eskirmir*]

skirt (skɜːt) *n.* **1.** a woman's or girl's garment hanging from the waist. **2.** the part of a dress or coat below the waist. **3.** a circular hanging flap, for example round the base of a hovercraft. **4.** *Brit.* a cut of beef from the flank. **5. bit of skirt.** *Offensive slang.* a girl or woman. ~*vb.* **6.** to lie along or form the edge of (something). **7.** (foll. by *around*) to go around the outer edge of (something). **8.** to avoid dealing with (an issue). [Old Norse *skyrta* shirt]

skirting board *n.* a moulding or board round the bottom of an interior wall where it joins the floor.

ski stick *or* **pole** *n.* one of a pair of sharp pointed sticks used by skiers to gain speed and maintain balance.

skit (skɪt) *n.* a brief satirical sketch. [prob. Scandinavian]

ski tow *n.* a device for pulling skiers uphill, usually a motor-driven rope grasped by the skier while riding on his skis.

skittish (ˈskɪtɪʃ) *adj.* **1.** playful or lively. **2.** (of a horse) excitable and easily frightened. [prob. from Old Norse]

skittle (ˈskɪt'l) *n.* **1.** (*pl.*; functioning as *sing.*) a bowling game in which players knock over as many wooden or plastic pins as possible by rolling a wooden ball at them. **2.** a pin used in this game. [origin unknown]

skive (skaɪv) *vb.* (often foll. by *off*) *Brit. informal.* to evade (work or responsibility). [origin unknown] —ˈ**skiver** *n.*

skivvy (ˈskɪvɪ) *Chiefly Brit., often disparaging.* ~*n., pl.* -**vies.** **1.** a female domestic servant; drudge. ~*vb.* -**vying, -vied.** **2.** to work as a skivvy. [origin unknown]

skookum (ˈskuːkəm) *adj. W Canad.* large. [American Indian]

skua (ˈskjuːə) *n.* a predatory aquatic gull-like bird having a dark plumage and long tail. [Faeroese *skúgvur*]

skulduggery *or U.S.* **skullduggery** (skʌlˈdʌgərɪ) *n. Informal.* underhand dealing; trickery. [origin unknown]

skulk (skʌlk) *vb.* **1.** to move stealthily, so as to avoid notice. **2.** to lie in hiding; lurk. [from Old Norse]

skull (skʌl) *n.* **1.** the bony framework of the head. **2.** *Informal.* the head or mind: *can't you get it into your thick skull?* [from Old Norse]

skull and crossbones *n.* a picture of the human skull above two crossed thighbones, formerly on the pirate flag, now used as a warning of danger or death.

skullcap (ˈskʌlˌkæp) *n.* a rounded brimless hat fitting the crown of the head.

skunk (skʌŋk) *n., pl.* **skunk** *or* **skunks.** **1.** a mammal with a black-and-white coat and bushy tail, which gives out a foul-smelling fluid when attacked. **2.** *Informal.* a despicable person. [American Indian]

sky (skaɪ) *n., pl.* **skies.** **1.** the upper atmosphere as seen from earth. **2.** to the skies. extravagantly. ~*vb.* **skying, skied.** **3.** *Informal.* to hit (a ball) high in the air. [Old Norse *skȳ*]

sky-blue *adj.* bright clear blue.

skydiving (ˈskaɪˌdaɪvɪŋ) *n.* the sport of jumping from an aircraft and performing manoeuvres before opening the parachute. —ˈ**sky**ˌ**diver** *n.*

Skye terrier (skaɪ) *n.* a short-legged terrier with long wiry hair and erect ears. [after *Skye,* Scot. island]

sky-high *adj., adv.* **1.** very high. **2. blow sky-high.** to destroy.

skyjack (ˈskaɪˌdʒæk) *vb.* to hijack (an aircraft). [*sky* + *hijack*]

skylark (ˈskaɪˌlɑːk) *n.* **1.** a lark that sings while hovering at a great height. ~*vb.* **2.** *Informal.* to romp or play jokes.

skylight (ˈskaɪˌlaɪt) *n.* a window placed in a roof or ceiling to admit daylight.

skyline (ˈskaɪˌlaɪn) *n.* **1.** the line at which the earth and sky appear to meet. **2.** the outline of buildings, trees, or hills, seen against the sky.

skyrocket (ˈskaɪˌrɒkɪt) *n.* **1.** same as **rocket** (sense 1). ~*vb.* **2.** *Informal.* to rise rapidly.

skyscraper (ˈskaɪˌskreɪpə) *n.* a very tall building.

skyward (ˈskaɪwəd) *adj.* **1.** towards the sky. ~*adv.* also **skywards.** **2.** towards the sky.

slab (slæb) *n.* a broad flat thick piece of wood, stone, or other material. [origin unknown]

slack[1] (slæk) *adj.* **1.** not tight, tense, or taut. **2.** negligent or careless. **3.** (esp. of water) moving slowly. **4.** (of trade) not busy. ~*n.* **5.** a part that is slack or hangs loose: *take in the slack*. **6.** a period of decreased activity. ~*vb.* **7.** to neglect (one's work or duty). **8.** (often foll. by *off*) to loosen or slacken. ~See also **slacks**. [Old English *slæc, sleac*] —**'slackness** *n.*

slack[2] (slæk) *n.* small pieces of coal with a high ash content. [prob. Middle Low German *slecke*]

slacken ('slækən) *vb.* (often foll. by *off*) **1.** to make or become looser. **2.** to make or become slower or less intense.

slacker ('slækə) *n.* a person who evades work or duty; shirker.

slacks (slæks) *pl. n.* informal trousers.

slag (slæg) *n.* **1.** the waste material left after metal has been smelted. ~*vb.* **slagging, slagged**. **2.** to form into slag. **3.** (sometimes foll. by *off*) *Slang.* to make disparaging comments about; slander. [Middle Low German *slagge*] —**'slagging** *n.* —**'slaggy** *adj.*

slag heap *n.* a pile of waste matter from metal smelting or coal mining.

slain (slein) *vb.* the past participle of **slay**.

slake (sleik) *vb.* **1.** *Literary.* to satisfy (thirst or desire). **2.** to add water to (lime) to produce calcium hydroxide. [Old English *slacian*]

slalom ('slɑːləm) *n. Skiing, canoeing.* a race over a winding course marked by artificial obstacles. [Norwegian]

slam[1] (slæm) *vb.* **slamming, slammed**. **1.** to close violently and noisily. **2.** to throw (something) down violently. **3.** *Slang.* to criticize harshly. **4.** to strike with violent force. ~*n.* **5.** the act or noise of slamming. [Scandinavian]

slam[2] (slæm) *n.* the winning of all (**grand slam**) or all but one (**little slam**) of the 13 tricks at bridge. [origin unknown]

slander ('slɑːndə) *n.* **1.** *Law.* the utterance of a false and damaging statement about a person. **2.** such a statement. ~*vb.* **3.** to utter or circulate slander (about). [Old French *escandle*] —**'slanderous** *adj.*

slang (slæŋ) *n.* **1.** informal words, expressions, and meanings avoided in formal speech or writing and often restricted to a particular social group or profession. ~*vb.* **2.** to use abusive language to (someone). [origin unknown] —**'slangy** *adj.*

slant (slɑːnt) *vb.* **1.** to slope or cause to slope at an oblique angle. **2.** to write or present (information) in a biased way. ~*n.* **3.** a sloping line or position. **4.** a point of view, esp. a biased one. **5. on a** (or **the**) **slant**. sloping. ~*adj.* **6.** oblique; sloping. [Scandinavian] —**'slanting** *adj.*

slap (slæp) *n.* **1.** a sharp blow or smack with something flat, such as the open hand. **2.** the sound made by or as if by such a blow. **3. slap and tickle**. *Brit. informal.* sexual play. **4. a slap in the face**. an insult or rebuff. **5. a slap on the back**. congratulations. ~*vb.* **slapping, slapped**. **6.** to strike sharply with something flat,

such as the open hand. **7.** to bring (something) down forcefully: *he slapped the papers on the table.* **8.** (usually foll. by *against*) to strike (something) with a slapping sound. **9.** *Informal, chiefly Brit.* to apply in large quantities, quickly or carelessly: *she slapped butter on the bread.* **10. slap on the back**. to congratulate. ~*adv. Informal.* **11.** exactly: *slap on time.* **12.** forcibly or abruptly: *to fall slap on the floor.* [Low German *slappe*]

slapdash ('slæp,dæʃ) *adv.* **1.** carelessly or hastily. ~*adj.* **2.** careless or hasty.

slaphappy ('slæp,hæpı) *adj.* **-pier, -piest**. *Informal.* cheerfully irresponsible or careless.

slapstick ('slæp,stɪk) *n.* comedy characterized by horseplay and boisterous action.

slap-up *adj. Brit. informal.* (esp. of meals) large and luxurious; lavish.

slash (slæʃ) *vb.* **1.** to cut (a person or thing) with sharp sweeping strokes. **2.** to make large gashes in: *to slash tyres.* **3.** to reduce drastically: *prices are being slashed.* **4.** to criticize harshly. ~*n.* **5.** a sharp sweeping stroke. **6.** a cut made by such a stroke. **7.** same as **solidus**. **8.** *Brit. slang.* the act of urinating. [origin unknown]

slasher ('slæʃə) *n. N.Z.* a tool used for cutting scrub or undergrowth in the bush.

slat (slæt) *n.* a narrow thin strip of wood or metal, as used in a Venetian blind. [Old French *esclat* splinter]

slate[1] (sleit) *n.* **1.** a fine-grained rock that can be easily split into thin layers and is used as a roofing material. **2.** a roofing tile of slate. **3.** (formerly) a writing tablet of slate. **4.** a dark grey colour. **5.** *Chiefly U.S. & Canad.* a list of candidates in an election. **6. clean slate**. a record without dishonour. **7. on the slate**. *Brit. informal.* on credit. ~*vb.* **8.** to cover (a roof) with slates. **9.** *Chiefly U.S.* to plan or schedule: *the visit is slated for October 16th.* ~*adj.* **10.** of the colour slate. [Old French *esclate*] —**'slaty** *adj.*

slate[2] (sleit) *vb. Informal, chiefly Brit.* to criticize harshly. [prob. from Old Norse] —**'slating** *n.*

slattern ('slætən) *n.* a slovenly woman or girl. [prob. from dialect *slatter* to slop] —**'slatternliness** *n.* —**'slatternly** *adj.*

slaughter ('slɔːtə) *n.* **1.** the killing of animals for food. **2.** the savage killing of a person. **3.** the indiscriminate or brutal killing of large numbers of people. ~*vb.* **4.** to kill (animals) for food. **5.** to kill in a brutal manner. **6.** to kill indiscriminately or in large numbers. [Old English *sleaht*]

slaughterhouse ('slɔːtə,haus) *n.* a place where animals are killed for food.

Slav (slɑːv) *n.* a member of any of the peoples of E Europe or Soviet Asia who speak a Slavonic language. [Medieval Latin *Sclāvus* a captive Slav]

slave (sleiv) *n.* **1.** a person legally owned by another for whom he has to work without freedom, pay, or rights. **2.** a person under the domination of another or of some habit or influence: *a slave to* *money*. **3.** a drudge. ~*vb.* **4.** (often foll. by *away*) to work like a slave. [Medieval Latin *Sclāvus* a Slav (the Slavonic races were frequently conquered in the Middle Ages)]

slave-driver *n.* **1.** (esp. formerly) a person forcing slaves to work. **2.** a person who makes people work very hard.

slaver[1] ('sleɪvə) *n.* **1.** a dealer in slaves. **2.** a ship used in the slave trade.

slaver[2] ('slævə) *vb.* **1.** to dribble saliva. **2.** (often foll. by *over*) to fawn or drool (over someone). ~*n.* **3.** saliva dribbling from the mouth. **4.** *Informal.* drivel. [prob. from Low German]

slavery ('sleɪvərɪ) *n.* **1.** the state or condition of being a slave. **2.** the practice or institution of owning slaves. **3.** toil or drudgery.

slave trade *n.* the buying and selling of slaves, esp. the transportation of Black Africans to America and the Caribbean from the 16th to the 19th centuries.

slavish ('sleɪvɪʃ) *adj.* **1.** of or like a slave. **2.** unoriginal; imitative. —**'slavishly** *adv.*

Slavonic (slə'vɒnɪk) *or esp. U.S.* **Slavic** *n.* **1.** a group of languages including Bulgarian, Russian, Polish, and Czech. ~*adj.* **2.** of this group of languages. **3.** of the people who speak these languages.

slay (sleɪ) *vb.* **slaying, slew, slain.** *Archaic or literary.* to kill, esp. violently. [Old English *slēan*] —**'slayer** *n.*

SLD Social and Liberal Democratic Party.

sleazy ('sliːzɪ) *adj.* **-zier, -ziest.** dirty, squalid, or disreputable: *a sleazy nightclub.* [origin unknown] —**'sleaziness** *n.*

sledge[1] (slɛdʒ) *or esp. U.S. & Canad.* **sled** (slɛd) *n.* **1.** a vehicle mounted on runners, drawn by horses or dogs, for transporting people or goods over snow. **2.** a light wooden frame used, esp. by children, for sliding over snow. ~*vb.* **3.** to convey or travel by sledge. [Middle Dutch *sleedse*]

sledge[2] (slɛdʒ) *n.* short for **sledgehammer.**

sledgehammer ('slɛdʒˌhæmə) *n.* **1.** a large heavy hammer with a long handle, used for breaking rocks and concrete. **2.** (*modifier*) crushingly powerful: *a sledgehammer blow.* [Old English *slecg* a large hammer]

sleek (sliːk) *adj.* **1.** smooth, shiny, and glossy: *sleek black hair.* **2.** (of a person) having a well-fed or well-groomed appearance. ~*vb.* **3.** to make sleek. [var. of *slick*]

sleep (sliːp) *n.* **1.** a periodic state of rest during which the eyes are closed, the muscles and nerves are relaxed, and the mind is unconscious. **2.** a period spent sleeping. **3.** a state of inactivity, like sleep. **4.** *Poetic.* death. ~*vb.* **sleeping, slept. 5.** to be in or as in the state of sleep. **6.** to be inactive or dormant. **7.** to have sleeping accommodation for (a certain number): *the boat sleeps six.* **8.** *Poetic.* to be dead. **9. sleep on it.** to delay making a decision about (something) until the next day, in order to think about it. ~See also

sleep around, sleep in, etc. [Old English *slǣpan*]

sleep around *vb. Informal.* to be sexually promiscuous.

sleeper ('sliːpə) *n.* **1.** a railway sleeping car or compartment. **2.** *Brit.* one of the blocks supporting the rails on a railway track. **3.** *Chiefly Brit.* a small plain gold ring worn in a pierced ear lobe to prevent the hole from closing up.

sleep in *vb. Brit.* to sleep longer than usual.

sleeping bag *n.* a large well-padded bag for sleeping in, esp. outdoors.

sleeping car *n.* a railway carriage with berths for people to sleep in.

sleeping partner *n.* a partner in a business who shares in the financing but does not play an active role.

sleeping pill *n.* a pill or tablet containing a sedative drug, used to induce sleep.

sleeping policeman *n.* a bump built across a road to deter motorists from speeding.

sleeping sickness *n.* an infectious, usually fatal, African disease transmitted by the bite of the tsetse fly, characterized by fever and sluggishness.

sleepless ('sliːplɪs) *adj.* **1.** without sleep or rest: *a sleepless journey.* **2.** unable to sleep. **3.** always alert. **4.** *Chiefly poetic.* always active. —**'sleeplessness** *n.*

sleep off *vb. Informal.* to get rid of by sleeping: *to sleep off a hangover.*

sleep out *vb.* to sleep in the open air.

sleepwalk ('sliːpˌwɔːk) *vb.* to walk while asleep. —**'sleepˌwalker** *n.* —**'sleepˌwalking** *n.*

sleep with *vb.* to have sexual intercourse and, usually, spend the night with.

sleepy ('sliːpɪ) *adj.* **sleepier, sleepiest. 1.** ready for sleep; about to fall asleep. **2.** inducing sleep. **3.** without activity or bustle: *a sleepy town.* —**'sleepily** *adv.*

sleet (sliːt) *n.* **1.** partly melted falling snow or hail or (esp. U.S.) partly frozen rain. ~*vb.* **2.** to fall as sleet. [Germanic]

sleeve (sliːv) *n.* **1.** the part of a garment covering the arm. **2.** a tubelike part which fits over or completely encloses another part. **3.** a flat cardboard container to protect a gramophone record. **4. up one's sleeve.** secretly ready: *he has a few tricks up his sleeve.* [Old English *slīf, slēf*] —**'sleeveless** *adj.*

sleigh (sleɪ) *n.* **1.** same as **sledge**[1] (sense 1). ~*vb.* **2.** to travel by sleigh. [Dutch *slee*]

sleight (slaɪt) *n. Archaic.* **1.** skill; dexterity. **2.** cunning. [Old Norse *slægth*]

sleight of hand *n.* **1.** manual dexterity used in performing conjuring tricks. **2.** the performance of such tricks.

slender ('slɛndə) *adj.* **1.** of small width relative to length or height. **2.** (esp. of a person's figure) slim and graceful. **3.** small or inadequate in amount or size: *slender resources.* [origin unknown]

slept (slɛpt) *vb.* past of **sleep.**

sleuth (sluːθ) *n. Informal.* a detective. [Old Norse *sloth* a trail]

slew[1] (sluː) *vb.* the past tense of **slay**.

slew[2] *or esp. U.S.* **slue** (sluː) *vb.* **1.** to twist or swing sideways, esp. awkwardly. ~*n.* **2.** the act of slewing. [origin unknown]

slice (slaɪs) *n.* **1.** a thin flat piece or wedge cut from something: *a slice of pork.* **2.** a share or portion: *a slice of the company's revenue.* **3.** a utensil having a broad flat blade. **4.** *Sport.* the hitting of a ball so that it travels obliquely. ~*vb.* **5.** to cut (something) into slices. **6.** (usually foll. by *through*) to cut through in a clean and effortless manner, with or as if with a knife. **7.** (usually foll. by *off, from, away*) to cut or be cut (from) a larger piece. **8.** to hit (a ball) with a slice. [Old French *esclice* a piece split off]

slick (slɪk) *adj.* **1.** persuasive and glib: *a slick salesman.* **2.** skilfully devised or executed: *a slick show.* **3.** *Informal, chiefly U.S. & Canad.* shrewd; sly. **4.** *Informal.* well-made and attractive, but superficial: *a slick publication.* **5.** *Chiefly U.S. & Canad.* slippery. ~*n.* **6.** a slippery area, esp. a patch of oil floating on water. ~*vb.* **7.** to make smooth or sleek. [prob. from Old Norse]

slide (slaɪd) *vb.* **sliding, slid** (slɪd), **slid. 1.** to move smoothly along a surface in continual contact with it: *doors that slide open.* **2.** to slip: *he slid on his back.* **3.** (usually foll. by *into, out of, away from*) to pass or move unobtrusively: *she slid into the room.* **4.** (usually foll. by *into*) to go (into a specified condition) by degrees: *he slid into loose living.* **5.** let slide. to allow to deteriorate by neglect: *to let things slide.* ~*n.* **6.** the act or an instance of sliding. **7.** a smooth surface, as of ice, for sliding on. **8.** a structure with a steep smooth slope for sliding down in playgrounds. **9.** a small glass plate on which specimens are mounted for study under a microscope. **10.** a photograph on a transparent base, mounted in a frame, that can be viewed by means of a projector. **11.** *Chiefly Brit.* an ornamental clip to hold hair in place. **12.** the sliding curved tube of a trombone that is moved in and out to allow different notes to be played. [Old English *slīdan*]

slide rule *n.* a calculating device consisting of two strips, one sliding along a central groove in the other, each strip graduated in two or more logarithmic scales of numbers.

sliding scale *n.* a variable scale according to which things such as wages or prices fluctuate in response to changes in other factors.

slight (slaɪt) *adj.* **1.** small in quantity or extent: *a slight accent.* **2.** of small importance. **3.** slim and delicate. **4.** lacking in strength or substance. ~*vb.* **5.** to show disregard for (someone); snub. ~*n.* **6.** an act of snubbing (someone). [Old Norse *slēttr* smooth] —'**slightly** *adv.*

slim (slɪm) *adj.* **slimmer, slimmest. 1.** small in width relative to height or length. **2.** poor; meagre: *slim chances of success.* ~*vb.* **3.** to make or become slim, esp. by diets and exercise. **4.** to reduce in size: *the workforce was slimmed.* [Dutch: crafty] —'**slimmer** *n.* —'**slimming** *n.*

Slim (slɪm) *n.* the E African name for **AIDS**. [from its wasting effects]

slime (slaɪm) *n.* **1.** soft runny mud or any sticky substance. esp. when disgusting or unpleasant. **2.** a thick, sticky substance produced by various fish, slugs, and fungi. [Old English *slīm*]

slimy ('slaɪmɪ) *adj.* **slimier, slimiest. 1.** of, like, or covered with slime. **2.** *Chiefly Brit.* offensively ingratiating.

sling[1] (slɪŋ) *n.* **1.** a rope or strap by which something may be lifted. **2.** *Med.* a wide piece of cloth suspended from the neck for supporting an injured hand or arm. **3.** a simple weapon consisting of a strap tied to cords, in which a stone is whirled and then released. ~*vb.* **slinging, slung. 4.** *Informal.* to throw. **5.** to carry or hang loosely from or as if from a sling: *to sling washing from the line.* **6.** to hurl with or as if with a sling. [prob. from Old Norse]

sling[2] (slɪŋ) *n.* a sweetened mixed drink with a spirit base: *gin sling.* [origin unknown]

slingback ('slɪŋ,bæk) *n.* a shoe with a strap instead of a complete covering for the heel.

sling off *vb.* (often foll. by *at*) *Austral. & N.Z. informal.* to mock; deride; jeer.

slink (slɪŋk) *vb.* **slinking, slunk.** to move or act in a furtive manner from or as if from fear or guilt. [Old English *slincan*]

slinky ('slɪŋkɪ) *adj.* **slinkier, slinkiest.** *Informal.* **1.** moving in a sinuously graceful or provocative way. **2.** (of clothes) figure-hugging.

slip[1] (slɪp) *vb.* **slipping, slipped. 1.** to move smoothly and easily: *the catch slips into place.* **2.** to place quickly or stealthily: *he slipped a coin into her hand.* **3.** to put on or take off easily or quickly: *to slip on a sweater.* **4.** to lose balance and slide unexpectedly: *he slipped on the ice.* **5.** to let loose or be let loose. **6.** to pass out of (the mind or memory). **7.** to move or pass swiftly or unperceived: *to slip quietly out of the room.* **8.** (sometimes foll. by *up*) to make a mistake. **9.** to become worse; weaken. **10.** to dislocate (a bone). **11.** to pass (a stitch) from one needle to another without knitting it. **12. let slip. a.** to allow to escape. **b.** to say unintentionally. ~*n.* **13.** a slipping. **14.** a mistake or oversight: *a slip of the pen.* **15.** a woman's sleeveless undergarment, worn under a dress. **16.** same as **slipway. 17.** *Cricket.* **a.** the fielder who stands a little behind and to the offside of the wicketkeeper. **b.** this position. **18. give someone the slip.** to escape from someone. ~See also **slip up.** [Middle Low German or Dutch *slippen*]

slip[2] (slɪp) *n.* **1.** a small piece of paper: *a receipt slip.* **2.** a cutting taken from a plant. **3.** a young slender person: *a slip of a child.* [prob. Middle Low German, Middle Dutch *slippe* to cut]

slip[3] (slɪp) *n.* clay mixed with water to a thin paste, used for decorating or patching a ceramic piece. [Old English *slyppe* slime]

slipe (slaɪp) *n. N.Z.* wool removed from the pelt of a slaughtered sheep by immersion in a chemical bath. [Middle English *slype* to skin]

slipknot ('slɪpˌnɒt) *n.* a nooselike knot tied so that it will slip along the rope round which it is made.

slip-on *adj.* **1.** (of a garment or shoe) made so as to be easily and quickly put on. ~*n.* **2.** a slip-on garment or shoe.

slipped disc *n. Pathol.* a painful condition in which one of the discs which connects the bones of the spine becomes displaced and presses on the adjacent nerves.

slipper ('slɪpə) *n.* a light soft shoe for indoor wear. —'**slippered** *adj.*

slippery ('slɪpərɪ, -prɪ) *adj.* **1.** liable or tending to cause objects to slip: *a slippery road.* **2.** liable to slip from one's grasp. **3.** not to be trusted: *a slippery character.* —'**slipperiness** *n.*

slippy ('slɪpɪ) *adj.* **-pier, -piest. 1.** *Informal or dialect.* same as **slippery** (senses 1, 2). **2.** *Brit. informal.* alert; quick: *look slippy!* —'**slippiness** *n.*

slip road *n. Brit.* a short road connecting a motorway to another road.

slipshod ('slɪpˌʃɒd) *adj.* **1.** (of an action) negligent; careless. **2.** (of a person's appearance) slovenly; down-at-heel.

slip-slop *n. S. African.* same as **flip-flop** (sense 5).

slipstream ('slɪpˌstriːm) *n.* the stream of air forced backwards by an aircraft propeller or other moving object.

slip up *Informal.* ~*vb.* **1.** to make a mistake. ~*n.* **slip-up. 2.** a mistake.

slipway ('slɪpˌweɪ) *n.* a large ramp that slopes down from the shore into the water, on which a ship is built or repaired and from which it is launched.

slit (slɪt) *vb.* **slitting, slit. 1.** to make a straight long incision in. **2.** to cut into strips lengthwise. ~*n.* **3.** a long narrow cut or opening. [Old English *slītan* to slice]

slither ('slɪðə) *vb.* **1.** to move or slide unsteadily, as on a slippery surface. ~*n.* **2.** a slithering motion. [Old English *slidrian*] —'**slithery** *adj.*

sliver ('slɪvə) *n.* **1.** a thin piece that is cut or broken off lengthwise. ~*vb.* **2.** to cut or break off in slivers. [obs. *sliven* to split]

Sloane Ranger (sləʊn) *n.* (in Britain) *Informal.* a young upper-class person having a home in London and in the country, characterized as wearing expensive informal clothes. [from *Sloane* Square, London + *Lone Ranger* cowboy hero]

slob (slɒb) *n. Informal.* a stupid or coarse person. [Irish Gaelic *slab* mud]

slobber ('slɒbə) *vb.* **1.** to dribble (liquid or saliva) from the mouth. **2.** to behave in a gushy or maudlin way. **3.** to smear with liquid dribbling from the mouth. ~*n.* **4.** liquid or saliva spilt from the mouth. [Middle Low German, Middle Dutch *slubberen*] —'**slobbery** *adj.*

slob ice *n. Canad.* sludgy masses of floating ice.

sloe (sləʊ) *n.* **1.** the small sour blue-black fruit of the blackthorn. **2.** same as **blackthorn.** [Old English *slāh*]

sloe-eyed *adj.* having dark almond-shaped eyes.

slog (slɒg) *vb.* **slogging, slogged. 1.** to hit hard. **2.** to work hard; toil. **3.** to make one's way with difficulty. ~*n.* **4.** a long and difficult walk. **5.** long exhausting work. **6.** a heavy blow. [origin unknown]

slogan ('sləʊgən) *n.* a catchword or phrase used in politics or advertising. [Gaelic *sluagh-ghairm* war cry]

sloop (sluːp) *n.* a single-masted sailing vessel, rigged fore-and-aft. [Dutch *sloep*]

sloot (sluːt) *n. S. African.* a ditch for irrigation or drainage. [Afrikaans]

slop (slɒp) *vb.* **slopping, slopped. 1.** (often foll. by *about*) to splash or spill (liquid) or (of liquid) to splash or spill. **2.** (foll. by *over*) *Informal,* chiefly *U.S. & Canad.* to be gushingly sentimental. ~*n.* **3.** a puddle of spilt liquid. **4.** (*pl.*) kitchen swill used to feed animals, esp. pigs. **5.** (*pl.*) waste food or liquid refuse. **6.** (*often pl.*) *Informal.* liquid food. [Old English *-sloppe*]

slope (sləʊp) *vb.* **1.** to slant or cause to slant. **2.** (esp. of natural features) to follow an inclined course: *many paths sloped down the hillside.* **3.** (foll. by *off* or *away*) *Informal.* to go furtively. **4.** *Mil.* **slope arms.** (formerly) to hold (a rifle) in a sloping position against the shoulder. ~*n.* **5.** an inclined portion of ground. **6.** (*pl.*) hills or foothills. **7.** any inclined surface. **8.** the degree of such inclination. [perhaps from Old English *āslūpan* to slip away]

slop out *vb.* (of prisoners) to empty chamber pots and collect water.

sloppy ('slɒpɪ) *adj.* **-pier, -piest. 1.** wet; slushy. **2.** *Informal.* careless; untidy. **3.** *Informal.* gushingly sentimental. —'**sloppily** *adv.* —'**sloppiness** *n.*

slosh (slɒʃ) *n.* **1.** slush. **2.** *Brit. slang.* a heavy blow. **3.** the sound of splashing liquid. ~*vb.* **4.** *Informal.* to throw or pour (liquid) carelessly. **5.** (often foll. by *about* or *around*) *Informal.* **a.** to shake or stir (something) in a liquid. **b.** (of a person) to splash (around) in water or mud. **6.** *Brit. slang.* to deal a heavy blow to. **7.** (usually foll. by *about* or *around*) *Informal.* to shake (a container of liquid) or (of liquid in a container) to be shaken. [var. of *slush*] —'**sloshy** *adj.*

sloshed (slɒʃt) *adj. Slang,* chiefly *Brit.* drunk.

slot (slɒt) *n.* **1.** a narrow opening or groove, such as one in a vending machine for inserting a coin. **2.** *Informal.* a place in a series or scheme. ~*vb.* **slotting, slotted. 3.** to provide with a slot or slots. **4.** (usually foll. by *in* or *into*) to fit or be fitted into a slot. [Old French *esclot* the depression of the breastbone]

sloth (sləʊθ) *n.* **1.** a slow-moving shaggy-coated animal of Central and South America, which hangs upside down in trees by its long arms and feeds on vegetation. **2.** laziness; indolence. [Old English *slǣwth*]

slothful ('sləʊθfʊl) *adj.* lazy; indolent.

slot machine *n.* a machine, esp. for gambling, worked by placing a coin in a slot.

slouch (slautʃ) *vb.* **1.** to sit, stand, or move with a drooping posture. ~*n.* **2.** a drooping posture. **3.** (*usually used in negative constructions*) *Informal.* an incompetent or slovenly person: *he's no slouch at football.* [origin unknown]

slouch hat *n.* a soft hat with a brim that can be pulled down over the ears.

slough[1] (slau) *n.* **1.** a swamp or marshy area. **2.** (sluː). *U.S. & Canad.* a large hole where water collects. **3.** despair or hopeless depression. [Old English *slōh*]

slough[2] (slʌf) *n.* **1.** any outer covering that is shed, such as the dead outer layer of the skin of a snake. ~*vb.* **2.** (*often foll. by off*) to shed (an outer covering) or (of an outer covering) to be shed. [Germanic]

slough off (slʌf) *vb.* to cast off (something unwanted or unneccessary).

sloven ('slʌv'n) *n.* a person who is habitually untidy, lazy, or careless in appearance or manner. [origin unknown]

slovenly ('slʌvənlɪ) *adj.* **1.** habitually unclean or untidy. **2.** negligent and careless: *slovenly manners.* ~*adv.* **3.** in a slovenly manner. —'**slovenliness** *n.*

slow (sləu) *adj.* **1.** taking a longer time than is usual or expected. **2.** characterized by lack of speed: *a slow walker.* **3.** adapted to or producing slow movement: *the slow lane of a motorway.* **4.** (of a clock or watch) indicating a time earlier than the correct time. **5.** not quick to understand: *a slow mind.* **6.** dull or uninteresting: *the play was very slow.* **7.** not easily aroused: *slow to anger.* **8.** (of business) unproductive; slack. **9.** (of a fire or oven) giving off low heat. **10.** *Photog.* requiring a relatively long time of exposure: *a slow film.* ~*adv.* **11.** in a slow manner. ~*vb.* **12.** (*often foll. by up or down*) to decrease or cause to decrease in speed or activity. [Old English *slāw* sluggish] —'**slowly** *adv.*

slowcoach ('sləu,kəutʃ) *n. Brit. informal.* a person who moves or works slowly.

slow motion *n.* **1.** *Films & television.* action that is made to appear slower than normal by filming at a faster rate or by replaying a video recording more slowly. ~*adj.* **slow-motion. 2.** of or relating to such action. **3.** moving at considerably less than usual speed.

slow virus *n.* a type of virus that is present in the body for a long time before it becomes active or infectious.

slowworm ('sləu,wɜːm) *n.* a legless lizard with a brownish-grey snakelike body.

sludge (slʌdʒ) *n.* **1.** soft mud or snow. **2.** any muddy or slushy sediment. **3.** sewage. [prob. rel. to *slush*] —'**sludgy** *adj.*

slug[1] (slʌg) *n.* a mollusc like a snail but without a shell. [prob. from Old Norse]

slug[2] (slʌg) *n.* **1.** a bullet. **2.** *Printing.* a line of type produced by a Linotype machine. **3.** a mouthful of alcoholic drink, esp. spirits. [prob. from SLUG[1], with allusion to the shape of the animal]

slug[3] (slʌg) *vb.* **slugging, slugged. 1.** *Chiefly U.S. & Canad.* to hit very hard. **2.** *U.S. & Canad.* a heavy blow. [prob. from SLUG[2] (bullet)]

sluggard ('slʌgəd) *n.* a person who is habitually lazy. [Middle English *slogarde*]

sluggish ('slʌgɪʃ) *adj.* **1.** lacking energy. **2.** functioning at below the normal rate.

sluice (sluːs) *n.* **1.** a channel that carries a rapid current of water, with a sluicegate to control the flow. **2.** the water controlled by a sluicegate. **3.** same as **sluicegate. 4.** *Mining.* a sloping trough for washing ore. ~*vb.* **5.** to draw off or drain by means of a sluice. **6.** to wash with a stream of water. **7.** (*often foll. by away or out*) (of water) to run or flow from or as if from a sluice. [Old French *escluse*]

sluicegate ('sluːs,geɪt) *n.* a valve or gate fitted to a sluice to control the rate of flow of water.

slum (slʌm) *n.* **1.** a squalid overcrowded house. **2.** (*often pl.*) a squalid overpopulated section of a city. ~*vb.* **slumming, slummed. 3.** to visit slums, esp. for curiosity. **4.** Also: **slum it.** to experience poorer than usual conditions. [origin unknown] —'**slummy** *adj.*

slumber ('slʌmbə) *vb.* **1.** to sleep. ~*n.* **2.** (*sometimes pl.*) sleep. [Old English *slūma*] —'**slumbering** *adj.*

slump (slʌmp) *vb.* **1.** (of commercial activity or prices) to decline suddenly. **2.** to sink or fall heavily and suddenly. ~*n.* **3.** a decline in commercial activity or prices; depression. **4.** a sudden or marked decline or failure. [prob. Scandinavian]

slung (slʌŋ) *vb.* past of **sling**[1].

slunk (slʌŋk) *vb.* past of **slink**.

slur (slɜː) *vb.* **slurring, slurred. 1.** to pronounce or utter (words) indistinctly. **2.** to speak disparagingly of. **3.** *Music.* to sing or play (successive notes) smoothly by moving from one to the other without a break. **4.** (*often foll. by over*) to treat superficially, hastily, or carelessly. ~*n.* **5.** a slighting remark intended to damage one's reputation. **6.** a slurring of words. **7.** *Music.* **a.** a slurring of successive notes. **b.** the curved line (⌢ or ⌣) indicating this. [prob. from Middle Low German]

slurp (slɜːp) *Informal.* ~*vb.* **1.** to eat or drink (something) noisily. ~*n.* **2.** a slurping sound. [Middle Dutch *slorpen* to sip]

slurry ('slʌrɪ) *n., pl.* -**ries.** a thin watery mixture of cement, mud, or other substance. [Middle English *slory*]

slush (slʌʃ) *n.* **1.** any watery muddy substance, esp. melting snow. **2.** *Informal.* sloppily sentimental language or writing. [origin unknown] —'**slushy** *adj.*

slush fund *n.* a fund for financing political or commercial corruption.

slut (slʌt) *n.* **1.** a dirty slovenly woman. **2.** a promiscuous woman. [origin unknown] —'**sluttish** *adj.*

sly (slaɪ) *adj.* **slyer, slyest** or **slier, sliest. 1.** crafty; artful: *a sly dodge.* **2.** secretive and cunning: *a sly manner.* **3.** roguish: *sly humour.* **4. on the sly.** secretively. [Old Norse *slǣgr* clever] —'**slyly** *adv.*

Sm *Chem.* samarium.

smack¹ (smæk) vb. **1.** to slap sharply. **2.** to strike loudly or to be struck loudly. **3.** to open and close (the lips) loudly to show pleasure or anticipation. ~n. **4.** a sharp resounding slap, or the sound of such a slap. **5.** a loud kiss. **6.** a sharp sound made by the lips in enjoyment. **7. smack in the eye.** Informal, chiefly Brit. a snub or rebuff. ~adv. Informal. **8.** directly; squarely: smack in the middle. **9.** sharply and unexpectedly: he drove smack into the back of our car. [prob. imit.]

smack² (smæk) n. **1.** a slight flavour, suggestion, or trace (of something): the smack of corruption. **2.** Slang. heroin. ~vb. (foll. by of) **3.** to have a slight smell or flavour (of something): to smack of the sea. **4.** to have a suggestion (of something): his speeches smacked of bigotry. [Old English smæc]

smack³ (smæk) n. a small single-masted fishing vessel. [Dutch smak]

smacker ('smækə) n. Slang. **1.** a loud kiss. **2.** a pound note or dollar bill.

small (smɔːl) adj. **1.** not large in size or amount. **2.** of little importance or on a minor scale: a small business. **3.** mean, ungenerous, or petty: a small mind. **4.** modest or humble: small beginnings. **5. feel small.** to be humiliated. **6.** (of a child or animal) young; not mature. **7.** unimportant; trivial: a small matter. **8.** (of a letter) written or printed in lower case rather than a capital. ~adv. **9.** into small pieces: cut it small. ~n. **10.** a small narrow part, esp. of the back. **11.** (pl.) Informal, chiefly Brit. underwear. [Old English smæl] —'smallish adj. —'smallness n.

small beer n. Informal, chiefly Brit. people or things of no importance.

small change n. coins of low value.

small fry pl. n. **1.** people regarded as unimportant. **2.** young children.

small goods pl. n. Austral. & N.Z. meats bought from a delicatessen, such as sausages.

smallholding ('smɔːl,həʊldɪŋ) n. a piece of agricultural land smaller than a farm. —'small,holder n.

small hours pl. n. the. the early hours of the morning, after midnight and before dawn.

small intestine n. the narrow, longer part of the alimentary canal, in which digestion is completed.

small-minded adj. narrow-minded; intolerant.

smallpox ('smɔːl,pɒks) n. a highly contagious viral disease causing fever, a rash, and blisters which usually leave permanent scars on the skin.

small print n. matter in a contract or document printed in small type, esp. when considered to be a trap for the unwary.

small-scale adj. of limited size or scope.

small talk n. light conversation for social occasions.

small-time adj. Informal. insignificant; minor: a small-time criminal.

smarm (smɑːm) vb. Brit. informal. **1.** (often foll. by down) to flatten (the hair) with grease. **2.** to ingratiate oneself (with). [origin unknown]

smarmy ('smɑːmɪ) adj. smarmier, smarmiest. obsequiously flattering or unpleasantly suave.

smart (smɑːt) adj. **1.** astute or shrewd. **2.** quick, witty, and often impertinent in speech: a smart talker. **3.** fashionable; chic: a smart hotel. **4.** well-kept; neat. **5.** causing a sharp stinging pain. **6.** vigorous or brisk: a smart pace. ~vb. **7.** to feel or cause a sharp stinging physical pain or keen mental distress: he smarted after their abuse. **8.** (often foll. by for) to suffer a harsh penalty. ~n. **9.** a stinging pain or feeling. ~adv. **10.** in a smart manner. ~See also **smarts.** [Old English smeortan] —'smartly adv. —'smartness n.

smart aleck ('ælɪk) n. Informal. a conceited know-all.

smarten ('smɑːt²n) vb. (usually foll. by up) to make or become smart.

smarts (smɑːts) pl. n. Slang, chiefly U.S. know-how, intelligence, or wits: street smarts.

smash (smæʃ) vb. **1.** to break into pieces violently and noisily. **2.** (often foll. by against, through or into) to throw or crash (against) vigorously, causing shattering: the sea smashed the boat against the rocks. **3.** to hit or collide forcefully and suddenly. **4.** Sport. to hit (the ball) fast and powerfully with an overhead stroke. **5.** to defeat or destroy: police smashed a drug ring. ~n. **6.** an act or sound of smashing. **7.** a violent collision, esp. of vehicles. **8.** a total failure or collapse, as of a business. **9.** Sport. a fast and powerful overhead stroke. **10.** Informal. a popular success. ~adv. **11.** with a smash. [prob. imit.]

smash-and-grab adj. Informal. of a robbery in which a shop window is broken and the contents removed.

smasher ('smæʃə) n. Informal, chiefly Brit. a person or thing that is very attractive or outstanding.

smashing ('smæʃɪŋ) adj. Informal, chiefly Brit. excellent or first-rate.

smash-up Informal. ~n. **1.** a bad collision, esp of cars. ~vb. **smash up.** **2.** to damage to the point of complete destruction: they smashed the place up.

smattering ('smætərɪŋ) n. a slight or superficial knowledge.

smear (smɪə) vb. **1.** to daub or cover with a greasy or sticky substance. **2.** to apply (a greasy or sticky substance) thickly. **3.** to rub so as to produce a smudge. **4.** to slander. ~n. **5.** a dirty mark or smudge. **6.** a slanderous attack. **7.** a small amount of a substance smeared onto a glass slide for examination under a microscope. [Old English smeoru] —'smeary adj.

smear test n. Med. same as **Pap test.**

smell (smel) vb. smelling, smelt or smelled. **1.** to perceive the scent of (a substance) by means of the nose. **2.** (foll. by an adj.) to have a specified smell: the curry smells spicy. **3.** (often foll. by of) to emit an odour (of): the park smells of *flowers.* **4.** (sometimes foll. by an adv.) to emit an unpleasant odour. **5.** (often foll. by *out*) to detect through shrewdness or instinct: *I smell danger.* **6.** to use the sense of smell; sniff. **7.** (foll. by *of*) to give indications of: *this action smells of treachery.* ~*n.* **8.** the sense by which scents or odours are perceived. **9.** an odour or scent. **10.** the act of smelling. [origin unknown]

smelling salts *pl. n.* a pungent preparation containing crystals of ammonium carbonate, sniffed to relieve faintness.

smelly ('smɛlɪ) *adj.* **smellier, smelliest.** having a nasty smell. —'**smelliness** *n.*

smelt[1] (smɛlt) *vb.* to extract (a metal) from (an ore) by heating. [Middle Low German, Middle Dutch *smelten*]

smelt[2] (smɛlt) *n., pl.* **smelt** or **smelts.** a small silvery food fish. [Old English *smylt*]

smelt[3] (smɛlt) *vb.* a past tense and past participle of **smell.**

smelter ('smɛltə) *n.* an industrial plant in which smelting is carried out.

smile (smaɪl) *n.* **1.** a facial expression in which the corners of the mouth are turned up, showing amusement or friendliness. ~*vb.* **2.** to wear or assume a smile. **3.** (foll. by *at*) **a.** to look at with a kindly expression. **b.** to look with amusement at. **4.** (foll. by *on* or *upon*) to regard favourably. **5.** to express by a smile: *she smiled a welcome.* [prob. from Old Norse]

smirch (smɜːtʃ) *vb.* **1.** to dirty; soil. ~*n.* **2.** a smirching or being smirched. **3.** a smear or stain. [origin unknown]

smirk (smɜːk) *n.* **1.** a smile expressing smugness rather than pleasure. ~*vb.* **2.** to give such a smile. [Old English *smearcian*]

smite (smaɪt) *vb.* **smiting, smote; smitten** or **smit** (smɪt). *Archaic.* **1.** to strike with a heavy blow. **2.** to affect severely: *smitten with flu.* **3.** to afflict in order to punish. **4.** (foll. by *on*) to strike forcibly or abruptly: *the sun smote down on him.* [Old English *smītan*]

smith (smɪθ) *n.* **1.** a person who works in metal: *silversmith.* **2.** See **blacksmith.** [Old English]

smithereens (ˌsmɪðəˈriːnz) *pl. n.* shattered fragments. [Irish Gaelic *smidirín*]

smithy ('smɪðɪ) *n., pl.* **smithies.** the workshop of a blacksmith; forge.

smitten ('smɪt'n) *vb.* **1.** a past participle of **smite.** ~*adj.* **2.** affected by love (for).

smock (smɒk) *n.* **1.** a loose outer garment, worn to protect the clothes. **2.** a loose blouselike garment worn by women. **3.** a loose protective overgarment decorated with smocking, worn formerly by farm workers. ~*vb.* **4.** to decorate with smocking. [Old English *smocc*]

smocking ('smɒkɪŋ) *n.* ornamental needlework used to gather material.

smog (smɒg) *n.* a mixture of smoke and fog. [*smoke* + *fog*] —'**smoggy** *adj.*

smoke (sməʊk) *n.* **1.** the visible vapour arising from something burning. **2.** the act of smoking tobacco. **3.** *Informal.* a cigarette or cigar. **4. go up in smoke. a.** to come to nothing. **b.** to burn up vigorously.

~*vb.* **5.** to give off smoke, sometimes excessively or in the wrong place. **6. a.** to draw the smoke of (burning tobacco) into the mouth and exhale it again. **b.** to do this habitually. **7.** to cure (meat or fish) by treating with smoke. [Old English *smoca*]

Smoke (sməʊk) *n.* **the.** *Brit. & Austral. slang.* a big city, esp. (in Britain) London.

smokeless ('sməʊklɪs) *adj.* having or producing little or no smoke: *smokeless fuel.*

smokeless zone *n.* an area where only smokeless fuels are permitted to be used.

smoke out *vb.* **1.** to drive out of hiding by means of smoke. **2.** to bring into the open: *they smoked out the plot.*

smoker ('sməʊkə) *n.* **1.** a person who habitually smokes tobacco. **2.** a train compartment where smoking is permitted.

smoke screen *n.* **1.** *Mil.* a cloud of smoke produced to obscure movements. **2.** something said or done to hide the truth.

smokestack ('sməʊkˌstæk) *n.* a tall chimney that carries smoke away from a factory.

smoko or **smokeho** ('sməʊkəʊ) *n., pl.* **-kos** or **-hos.** *Austral. & N.Z. n.formal.* **1.** a short break from work for tea or a cigarette. **2.** refreshment taken during this break.

smoky ('sməʊkɪ) *adj.* **smokier, smokiest. 1.** filled with or giving off smoke, sometimes excessively: *a smoky fire.* **2.** having the colour of smoke. **3.** having a smoky flavour. **4.** made dirty or hazy by smoke. —'**smokiness** *n.*

smolt (sməʊlt) *n.* a young salmon at the stage when it migrates from fresh water to the sea. [Scot.]

smooch (smuːtʃ) *Slang.* ~*vb.* **1.** (of two people) to kiss and cuddle. **2.** *Brit.* to dance very slowly and amorously with one's arms around another person or (of two people) to dance together in such a way. ~*n.* **3.** the act of smooching. [dialect *smouch*, imit.]

smoodge or **smooge** (smuːdʒ) *vb. Austral. & N.Z.* **1.** same as **smooch** (sense 1). **2.** to seek to ingratiate oneself.

smooth (smuːð) *adj.* **1.** having an even surface with no roughness, bumps, or holes. **2.** lacking obstructions or difficulties. **3.** charming or persuasive, often in an insincere way. **4.** without lumps: *smooth batter.* **5.** free from jolts: *smooth driving.* **6.** not harsh in taste: *a smooth wine.* ~*adv.* **7.** in a smooth manner. ~*vb.* **8.** (often foll. by *down*) to make or become even or without roughness. **9.** (often foll. by *out* or *away*) to remove in order to make smooth: *she smoothed out the creases in her dress.* **10.** to make calm; soothe. **11.** to make easier: *smooth his path.* ~*n.* **12.** the smooth part of something. **13.** the act of smoothing. [Old English *smōth*] —'**smoothly** *adv.*

smoothie or **smoothy** ('smuːðɪ) *n., adj.* **smoothies.** *Slang.* a man who is smooth or slick in speech, dress, or manner.

smooth over *vb.* to ease or gloss over: *to smooth over a difficulty.*

smooth-talking *or* **smooth-tongued** *adj.* speaking persuasively but not necessarily sincerely.

smorgasbord ('smɔːgəs,bɔːd) *n.* a variety of savoury dishes served as hors d'oeuvres or as a buffet meal. [Swedish]

smote (sməut) *vb.* the past tense of **smite**.

smother ('smʌðə) *vb.* **1.** to suffocate or stifle. **2.** to surround or overwhelm (with): *he smothered her with love.* **3.** to extinguish (a fire) by covering so as to cut it off from the air. **4.** to suppress or stifle: *smother a giggle.* **5.** to cover over thickly. [Old English *smorian* to suffocate]

smoulder *or U.S.* **smolder** ('sməuldə) *vb.* **1.** to burn slowly without flame, usually giving off smoke. **2.** (of anger or hatred) to exist in a suppressed state. ~*n.* **3.** a smouldering. [origin unknown]

smudge (smʌdʒ) *vb.* **1.** to make or become smeared or soiled. ~*n.* **2.** a smear or dirty mark. **3.** a blurred form or area: *that smudge in the distance is a quarry.* [origin unknown] —'**smudgy** *adj.*

smug (smʌg) *adj.* **smugger, smuggest.** excessively self-satisfied. [Germanic] —'**smugly** *adv.* —'**smugness** *n.*

smuggle ('smʌgʲl) *vb.* **1.** to import or export (prohibited or dutiable goods) secretly. **2.** (often foll. by *into* or *out*) to bring or take secretly. [Low German *smukkelen*] —'**smuggler** *n.* —'**smuggling** *n.*

smut (smʌt) *n.* **1.** a speck of soot or a dark mark left by soot. **2.** something obscene or indecent. **3.** a fungal disease of cereals, in which black sooty masses cover the affected parts. ~*vb.* **smutting, smutted. 4.** to mark or become marked with smuts. [Old English *smitte*] —'**smutty** *adj.*

Sn *Chem.* tin. [New Latin *stannum*]

snack (snæk) *n.* a light quick meal eaten between or in place of main meals. [prob. from Middle Dutch *snacken*]

snack bar *n.* a place where light meals or snacks are sold.

snaffle ('snæfʲl) *n.* **1.** a simple jointed bit for a horse. ~*vb.* **2.** *Brit. informal.* to steal or take. **3.** to equip or control (a horse) with a snaffle. [origin unknown]

snafu (snæ'fuː) *Slang, chiefly mil.* ~*n.* **1.** confusion or chaos regarded as the normal state. ~*adj.* **2.** confused or muddled up, as usual. [*s*(*ituation*) *n*(*ormal*): *a*(*ll*) *f*(*ucked*) *u*(*p*)]

snag (snæg) *n.* **1.** a difficulty or disadvantage: *the snag is that I have nothing to wear.* **2.** a sharp projecting point that may catch on things. **3.** a small hole in a fabric caused by a sharp object. **4.** a tree stump in a riverbed that is dangerous to navigation. ~*vb.* **snagging, snagged. 5.** to tear or catch on a snag. [Scandinavian]

snail (sneɪl) *n.* a slow-moving mollusc with a spirally coiled shell. [Old English *snægl*]

snail's pace *n.* a very slow speed.

snake (sneɪk) *n.* **1.** a reptile with a long scaly limbless body, lidless eyes, a tapering tail, and a jaw modified for swallowing large prey. **2.** Also: **snake in the grass.** a deceitful or treacherous person. ~*vb.* **3.** to glide or move in a winding course, like a snake. [Old English *snaca*]

snakebite ('sneɪk,baɪt) *n.* **1.** the bite of a snake. **2.** a drink of cider and lager.

snake charmer *n.* an entertainer who appears to hypnotize snakes by playing music.

snakes and ladders *n.* (*functioning as sing.*) a board game in which players move counters along a series of squares by means of dice, going up the ladders to squares nearer the finish and down the snakes to squares nearer the start.

snaky ('sneɪkɪ) *adj.* **snakier, snakiest. 1.** twisting; winding. **2.** treacherous.

snap (snæp) *vb.* **snapping, snapped. 1.** to break suddenly, esp. with a sharp sound. **2.** to make or cause to make a sudden sharp cracking sound: *snap one's fingers.* **3.** to give way or collapse suddenly under strain. **4.** to move or close with a sudden sharp sound. **5.** to move in a sudden or abrupt way. **6.** (often foll. by *at* or *up*) to seize suddenly or quickly. **7.** (often foll. by *at*) to bite at (something) suddenly. **8.** to speak (words) sharply or abruptly. **9.** to take a snapshot of (something). **10.** **snap one's fingers at.** *Informal.* **a.** to dismiss contemptuously. **b.** to defy. **11. snap out of it.** *Informal.* to recover quickly, esp. from depression or anger. ~*n.* **12.** the act of breaking suddenly or the sound of a sudden breakage. **13.** a sudden sharp sound. **14.** a catch, clasp, or fastener that closes with a snapping sound. **15.** a sudden grab or bite. **16.** a thin crisp biscuit: *ginger snaps.* **17.** *Informal.* same as **snapshot. 18.** a sudden brief spell of cold weather. **19.** *Brit.* a card game in which the word *snap* is called when two similar cards are turned up. **20.** (*modifier*) done on the spur of the moment: *a snap decision.* ~*adv.* **21.** with a snap. ~*interj.* **22. a.** *Cards.* the word called while playing snap. **b.** an exclamation used to draw attention to the similarity of two things. ~See also **snap up.** [Middle Dutch *snappen* to seize]

snapdragon ('snæp,drægən) *n.* a plant with spikes of colourful flowers that can open and shut like a mouth; antirrhinum.

snap fastener *n.* same as **press stud.**

snappy ('snæpɪ) *adj.* **-pier, -piest. 1.** Also: **snappish.** irritable or cross. **2.** brisk or lively: *a snappy pace.* **3.** chilly: *snappy weather.* **4.** smart and fashionable: *a snappy dresser.* **5. make it snappy.** *Slang.* hurry up! —'**snappiness** *n.*

snapshot ('snæp,ʃɒt) *n.* an informal photograph taken with a simple camera.

snap up *vb.* to take advantage of eagerly and quickly: *to snap up bargains.*

snare[1] (snɛə) *n.* **1.** a trap for birds or small animals, usually a flexible loop that is drawn tight around the prey. **2.** anything that entangles someone or something unawares. ~*vb.* **3.** to catch in or as if in a snare. [Old English *sneare*]

snare[2] (snɛə) *n.* *Music.* a set of strings fitted against the lower head of a snare drum, which produces a rattling sound when the drum is beaten. [Middle Dutch *snaer* or Middle Low German *snare* string]

snare drum *n. Music.* a small drum fitted with a snare.

snarl[1] (snɑːl) *vb.* **1.** (of an animal) to growl viciously, baring the teeth. **2.** to speak or say (something) viciously. ~*n.* **3.** a vicious growl or facial expression. **4.** the act of snarling. [Germanic]

snarl[2] (snɑːl) *n.* **1.** a tangled mass. **2.** a complicated or confused state. ~*vb.* **3.** (often foll. by *up*) to be, become, or make tangled or complicated. [from Old Norse]

snarl-up *n. Informal, chiefly Brit.* a confused, disorganized situation such as a traffic jam.

snatch (snætʃ) *vb.* **1.** to seize or grasp (something) suddenly: *he snatched the chocolate.* **2.** (usually foll. by *at*) to attempt to seize suddenly. **3.** to take hurriedly: *to snatch some sleep.* **4.** to remove suddenly: *she snatched her hand away.* ~*n.* **5.** an act of snatching. **6.** a fragment or incomplete part: *snatches of conversation.* **7.** a brief spell: *snatches of time off.* **8.** *Slang, chiefly U.S.* an act of kidnapping. **9.** *Brit. slang.* a robbery: *a diamond snatch.* [Middle English *snacchen*]

snazzy ('snæzɪ) *adj.* **-zier, -ziest.** *Informal.* (esp. of clothes) stylishly and often flashily attractive. [origin unknown]

sneak (sniːk) *vb.* **1.** to move furtively. **2.** to behave in a cowardly or underhand manner. **3.** to bring, take, or put stealthily. **4.** *Informal, chiefly Brit.* to tell tales (esp. in schools). ~*n.* **5.** a person who acts in an underhand or cowardly manner, esp. as an informer. ~*adj.* **6.** without warning: *a sneak attack.* [Old English *snīcan* to creep] —'**sneaky** *adj.*

sneakers ('sniːkəz) *pl. n. Chiefly U.S. & Canad.* canvas shoes with rubber soles.

sneaking ('sniːkɪŋ) *adj.* **1.** acting in a furtive or cowardly way. **2.** secret: *a sneaking desire to marry a millionaire.* **3.** slight but nagging: *a sneaking suspicion.*

sneak thief *n.* a burglar who sneaks into premises through open doors and windows.

sneer (snɪə) *n.* **1.** a facial expression of scorn or contempt, typically with the upper lip curled. **2.** a scornful or contemptuous remark. ~*vb.* **3.** to assume a facial expression of scorn or contempt. **4.** to say (something) in a scornful manner. [origin unknown] —'**sneering** *adj.*

sneeze (sniːz) *vb.* **1.** to expel air from the nose suddenly and involuntarily, esp. as the result of irritation in the nostrils. ~*n.* **2.** the act or sound of sneezing. [Old English *fnēosan* (unattested)]

sneeze at *vb.* (usually with a negative) *Informal.* to dismiss lightly: *his offer is not to be sneezed at.*

sneezewood ('sniːz,wʊd) *n.* **1.** a South African tree. **2.** its exceptionally hard wood, used for furniture, gateposts, and railway sleepers.

snick (snɪk) *n.* **1.** a small cut; notch. **2.** *Cricket.* a glancing blow off the edge of the bat. ~*vb.* **3.** to make a small cut or notch in (something). **4.** *Cricket.* to hit (the ball) with a snick. [prob. Scandinavian]

snicker ('snɪkə) *n., vb.* (esp. U.S. and Canad.) same as **snigger.** [prob. imit.]

snide (snaɪd) *adj.* maliciously derogatory: *snide comments.* [origin unknown]

sniff (snɪf) *vb.* **1.** to inhale through the nose in short audible breaths. **2.** (often foll. by *at*) to perceive or attempt to perceive (a smell) by sniffing. ~*n.* **3.** the act or sound of sniffing. [imit.] —'**sniffer** *n.*

sniff at *vb.* to express contempt or dislike for.

sniffle ('snɪfl) *vb.* **1.** to sniff repeatedly, as when the nasal passages are congested. ~*n.* **2.** the act or sound of sniffling.

sniffles ('snɪflz) *or* **snuffles** *pl. n.* **the.** *Informal.* a cold in the head.

sniff out *vb.* to detect through shrewdness or instinct.

sniffy ('snɪfɪ) *adj.* **-fier, -fiest.** *Informal.* contemptuous or disdainful.

snifter ('snɪftə) *n.* **1.** a pear-shaped brandy glass. **2.** *Informal.* a small quantity of alcoholic drink. [origin unknown]

snig (snɪg) *vb.* **snigging, snigged.** *N.Z.* to drag (a felled log) by a chain or cable. [English dialect]

snigger ('snɪgə) *n.* **1.** a sly or disrespectful laugh, esp. one partly stifled. ~*vb.* **2.** to utter such a laugh. [var. of *snicker*]

snip (snɪp) *vb.* **snipping, snipped. 1.** to cut with small quick strokes with scissors or shears. ~*n.* **2.** the act or sound of snipping. **3.** a small piece snipped off. **4.** a small cut made by snipping. **5.** *Informal, chiefly Brit.* a bargain. [Low German, Dutch *snippen*]

snipe (snaɪp) *n., pl.* **snipe** *or* **snipes. 1.** a wading bird with a long straight bill. ~*vb.* **2.** (often foll. by *at*) to shoot (a person or persons) from a place of hiding. **3.** (often foll. by *at*) to criticize a person or persons from a position of security. [Old Norse *snīpa*] —'**sniper** *n.*

snippet ('snɪpɪt) *n.* a small scrap or fragment: *snippets of information.*

snitch (snɪtʃ) *Slang.* ~*vb.* **1.** to steal or pilfer. **2.** to act as an informer. ~*n.* **3.** an informer. [origin unknown]

snitchy ('snɪtʃɪ) *adj.* **snitchier, snitchiest.** *N.Z. informal.* bad-tempered or irritable.

snivel ('snɪv'l) *vb.* **-elling, -elled** *or U.S.* **-eling, -eled. 1.** to cry and sniffle. **2.** to utter (something) tearfully; whine. **3.** to have a runny nose. ~*n.* **4.** the act of snivelling. [Middle English *snivelen*]

snob (snob) *n.* **1.** a person who tries to associate with those of higher social status and who despises those of a lower social status. **2.** a person who feels smugly superior with regard to his tastes or interests: *an intellectual snob.* [origin unknown] —'**snobbery** *n.* —'**snobbish** *adj.*

snoek (snʊk) *n.* a South African edible marine fish. [Afrikaans]

snog (snog) *Brit. slang.* ~*vb.* **snogging, snogged. 1.** to kiss and cuddle. ~*n.* **2.** the act of kissing and cuddling. [origin unknown]

snood (snuːd) *n.* a pouchlike hat, often of

net, loosely holding a woman's hair at the back. [Old English *snōd*]

snook (snuːk) *n. Brit.* **cock a snook at. a.** to make a rude gesture at by putting one thumb to the nose with the fingers of the hand outstretched. **b.** to show contempt for. [origin unknown]

snooker ('snuːkə) *n.* **1.** a game played on a billiard table with 15 red balls, six balls of other colours, and a white cue ball. **2.** a shot in which the cue ball is left in a position such that another ball blocks the target ball. ~*vb.* **3.** to leave (an opponent) in an unfavourable position by playing a snooker. **4.** (*often passive*) to thwart; defeat. [origin unknown]

snoop (snuːp) *Informal.* ~*vb.* **1.** (often foll. by *about* or *around*) to pry into the private business of others. ~*n.* **2.** the act of snooping. [Dutch *snoepen* to eat furtively] —'**snooper** *n.* —'**snoopy** *adj.*

snooty ('snuːtɪ) *adj.* **snootier, snootiest.** *Informal.* supercilious or snobbish. [from *snoot* nose]

snooze (snuːz) *Informal.* ~*vb.* **1.** to take a brief light sleep. ~*n.* **2.** a nap. [origin unknown]

snore (snɔː) *vb.* **1.** to breathe with snorting sounds while asleep. ~*n.* **2.** the act or sound of snoring. [imit.]

snorkel ('snɔːkəl) *n.* **1.** a tube allowing a swimmer to breathe while face down on the surface of the water. **2.** (on a submarine) a retractable device for air intake when submerged. ~*vb.* **-kelling, -kelled** *or U.S.* **-keling, -keled.** **3.** to swim with a snorkel. [German *Schnorchel*]

snort (snɔːt) *vb.* **1.** to exhale forcibly and noisily through the nostrils. **2.** to express contempt or annoyance by snorting. **3.** to utter with a snort. ~*n.* **4.** a forcible exhalation of air through the nostrils, esp. to express contempt or annoyance. [Middle English *snorten*]

snot (snɒt) *n.* (*usually considered vulgar*) **1.** nasal mucus or discharge. **2.** *Slang.* a contemptible person. [Old English *gesnot*]

snotty ('snɒtɪ) *adj.* **-tier, -tiest.** (*considered vulgar*) **1.** dirty with nasal discharge. **2.** *Slang.* contemptible; nasty. **3.** snobbish; conceited. —'**snottiness** *n.*

snout (snaʊt) *n.* **1.** the projecting nose and jaws of an animal. **2.** anything projecting like a snout. **3.** *Slang.* a person's nose. [Germanic]

snow (snəʊ) *n.* **1.** frozen vapour falling from the sky in flakes. **2.** a layer of snow on the ground. **3.** a falling of snow. **4.** *Slang.* cocaine. ~*vb.* **5.** (with *it* as subject) to be the case that snow is falling: *it's snowing outside.* **6.** (*usually passive*, foll. by *over, under, in,* or *up*) to cover or confine with a heavy fall of snow. **7.** to fall as or like snow. **8. be snowed under.** to be overwhelmed, esp. with paperwork. [Old English *snāw*] —'**snowy** *adj.*

snowball ('snəʊ,bɔːl) *n.* **1.** snow pressed into a ball for throwing. ~*vb.* **2.** to increase rapidly in size or importance. **3.** to throw snowballs.

snowberry ('snəʊbərɪ) *n., pl.* **-ries.** a shrub cultivated for its white berries.

snow-blind *adj.* temporarily blinded by the intense reflection of sunlight from snow. —**snow blindness** *n.*

snowbound ('snəʊ,baʊnd) *adj.* shut in or blocked off by snow.

snowcap ('snəʊ,kæp) *n.* a cap of snow, as on top of a mountain. —'**snow,capped** *adj.*

snowdrift ('snəʊ,drɪft) *n.* a bank of deep snow driven together by the wind.

snowdrop ('snəʊ,drɒp) *n.* a plant with small drooping white bell-shaped flowers.

snowfall ('snəʊ,fɔːl) *n.* **1.** a fall of snow. **2.** *Meteorol.* the amount of snow that falls in a specified place and time.

snowflake ('snəʊ,fleɪk) *n.* a single crystal of snow.

snow goose *n.* a North American goose having a white plumage with black wing tips.

snow lily *n. Canad.* same as **dogtooth violet.**

snow line *n.* (on a mountain) the altitude above which there is permanent snow.

snowman ('snəʊ,mæn) *n., pl.* **-men.** a figure like a man, made of packed snow.

snowmobile ('snəʊmə,biːl) *n.* a motor vehicle for travelling on snow, esp. one with caterpillar tracks and front skis.

snowplough *or esp. U.S.* **snowplow** ('snəʊ,plaʊ) *n.* a vehicle for clearing away snow.

snowshoe ('snəʊ,ʃuː) *n.* a racket-shaped frame with a network of thongs stretched across it, worn on the feet to facilitate walking on snow.

snowstorm ('snəʊ,stɔːm) *n.* a storm with heavy snow.

SNP Scottish National Party.

Snr *or* **snr** senior.

snub (snʌb) *vb.* **snubbing, snubbed. 1.** to insult (someone) deliberately. ~*n.* **2.** a deliberately insulting act or remark. ~*adj.* **3.** (of a nose) short and turned up. [Old Norse *snubba* to scold]

snub-nosed *adj.* having a short turned-up nose.

snuff[1] (snʌf) *vb.* **1.** to inhale through the nose. **2.** (esp. of an animal) to examine by sniffing. ~*n.* **3.** a sniff. [prob. Middle Dutch *snuffen* to snuffle]

snuff[2] (snʌf) *n.* **1.** finely powdered tobacco for sniffing up the nostrils. ~*vb.* **2.** to take snuff. [Dutch *snuf*]

snuff[3] (snʌf) *vb.* **1.** (often foll. by *out*) to put out (a candle). **2.** to cut off the charred part of (a candle wick). **3.** (usually foll. by *out*) *Informal.* to put an end to. **4. snuff it.** *Brit. informal.* to die. ~*n.* **5.** the burned portion of the wick of a candle. [origin unknown]

snuffbox ('snʌf,bɒks) *n.* a small container for holding snuff.

snuffle ('snʌfəl) *vb.* **1.** to breathe noisily or with difficulty. **2.** to say or speak in a nasal tone. **3.** to snivel. ~*n.* **4.** an act or the sound of snuffling. [Low German or Dutch *snuffelen*] —'**snuffly** *adj.*

snug (snʌg) *adj.* **snugger, snuggest. 1.** comfortably warm and well protected; cosy: *the children were snug in bed.* **2.** small but comfortable: *a snug cottage.* **3.** fitting closely and comfortably. ~*n.* **4.** (in Britain and Ireland) a small room in a pub. [origin unknown] —'**snugly** *adv.*

snuggery ('snʌgərɪ) *n., pl.* **-geries.** a cosy and comfortable place or room.

snuggle ('snʌg²l) *vb.* to nestle into or draw close to (somebody or something) for warmth or from affection. [from *snug*]

so[1] (səʊ) *adv.* **1.** to such an extent: *the river is so dirty that it smells.* **2.** (used with a negative; it replaces the first *as* in a comparison) to the same extent as: *she is not so old as you.* **3.** extremely: *it's so lovely.* **4.** in the state or manner expressed or implied: *they're happy and will remain so.* **5.** also: *I can speak Spanish and so can you.* **6.** thereupon: *and so we ended up in France.* **7.** and so on *or* forth. and continuing similarly. **8. or so.** approximately: *fifty or so people came to see me.* **9. so be it.** an expression of agreement or resignation. **10. so much. a.** a certain degree or amount (of). **b.** a lot (of): *it's just so much nonsense.* **11. so much for. a.** no more need be said about. **b.** used to express contempt for something that has failed: *so much for all our plans.* ~*conj.* (often foll. by *that*) **12.** in order (that): *to die so that you might live.* **13.** with the consequence (that): *he was late home, so that there was trouble.* **14. so as.** in order (to): *to diet so as to lose weight.* **15.** *Not universally accepted.* in consequence: *she wasn't needed, so she left.* **16. so what!** *Informal.* that is unimportant. ~*pron.* **17.** used to substitute for a clause or sentence, which may be understood: *you'll stop because I said so.* ~*adj.* **18.** true: *it can't be so.* ~*interj.* **19.** an exclamation of surprise, triumph, or realization. [Old English *swā*]

so[2] (səʊ) *n. Music.* same as **soh.**

soak (səʊk) *vb.* **1.** to make, become, or be thoroughly wet or saturated. **2.** (usually foll. by *in* or *into*) (of a liquid) to penetrate or permeate. **3.** (usually foll. by *in* or *up*) to take in; absorb: *the earth soaks up rainwater.* ~*n.* **4.** a soaking or being soaked. **5.** *Slang.* a person who drinks to excess. [Old English *sōcian* to cook] —'**soaking** *n., adj.*

so-and-so *n., pl.* **so-and-sos.** *Informal.* **1.** a person whose name is not specified. **2.** *Euphemistic.* a person or thing regarded as unpleasant: *which so-and-so broke my razor?*

soap (səʊp) *n.* **1.** a cleaning agent used with water to produce suds, made from an alkali and fats. **2.** *Informal.* short for **soap opera.** ~*vb.* **3.** to apply soap to. [Old English *sāpe*]

soapbox ('səʊp,bɒks) *n.* a crate used as a platform for speech-making.

soap opera *n.* a serialized radio or television drama, usually dealing with domestic themes. [so called because manufacturers of soap were typical sponsors]

soapstone ('səʊp,stəʊn) *n.* a compact soft variety of talc, used for making table tops, hearths, and ornaments.

soapsuds ('səʊp,sʌdz) *pl. n.* foam or lather made from soap.

soapy ('səʊpɪ) *adj.* **soapier, soapiest. 1.** containing or covered with soap: *soapy water.* **2.** like soap. **3.** *Slang.* flattering. —'**soapiness** *n.*

soar (sɔː) *vb.* **1.** to rise or fly upwards into the air. **2.** (of a bird or aircraft) to glide while maintaining altitude. **3.** to rise or increase suddenly above the usual level: *soaring prices.* [Old French *essorer*]

sob (sɒb) *vb.* **sobbing, sobbed. 1.** to weep with convulsive gasps. **2.** to utter with sobs. ~*n.* **3.** the act or sound of sobbing. [prob. from Low German]

sober ('səʊbə) *adj.* **1.** not drunk. **2.** temperate, esp. with regard to alcohol. **3.** serious and thoughtful: *a sober attitude to a problem.* **4.** (of colours) plain and dull or subdued. **5.** free from exaggeration: *he told us the sober truth.* ~*vb.* **6.** (usually foll. by *up*) to make or become less drunk. [Latin *sōbrius*] —'**sobering** *adj.*

sobriety (səʊ'braɪɪtɪ) *n.* the state or quality of being sober.

sobriquet *or* **soubriquet** ('səʊbrɪ,keɪ) *n.* a nickname. [French *soubriquet*]

sob story *n.* a tale of personal distress intended to arouse sympathy.

Soc. *or* **soc. 1.** socialist. **2.** society.

soca ('səʊkə) *n.* a mixture of soul and calypso music typical of the E Caribbean.

so-called *adj.* called or named thus, esp. (in the speaker's opinion) incorrectly: *a so-called genius.*

soccer ('sɒkə) *n.* a game in which two teams of eleven players try to kick or head a ball into their opponents' goal, only the goalkeeper on either side being allowed to touch the ball with his hands. [*Assoc(iation Football)*]

sociable ('səʊʃəb²l) *adj.* **1.** friendly or companionable. **2.** (of an occasion) providing the opportunity for friendliness and conviviality. —,**socia'bility** *n.* —'**sociably** *adv.*

social ('səʊʃəl) *adj.* **1.** living or preferring to live in a community rather than alone. **2.** of or relating to human society or organization. **3.** of the behaviour and interaction of persons living together in groups. **4.** of or for companionship or communal activities: *a social club.* **5.** of or engaged in social services: *a social worker.* **6.** relating to a certain class of society. **7.** (of certain species of insects) living together in organized colonies: *social bees.* ~*n.* **8.** an informal gathering, esp. of an organized group. [Latin *socius* a comrade] —'**socially** *adv.*

social contract *or* **compact** *n.* an agreement among individuals to cooperate for greater security, which entails the surrender of some personal liberties.

social democrat *n.* **1.** a socialist who believes in the gradual transformation of capitalism into democratic socialism. **2.** (*usually cap.*) a member of a Social Democratic Party. —**social democracy** *n.*

social fund n. (in Britain) a social security fund from which loans or payments may be made to people in cases of extreme need.

socialism ('səʊʃə₁lɪzəm) n. a political and economic theory or system in which the means of production, distribution, and exchange are owned by the community collectively, usually through the state. —'**socialist** n., adj.

socialite ('səʊʃə₁laɪt) n. a person who is prominent in fashionable society.

socialize or -**lise** ('səʊʃə₁laɪz) vb. 1. to behave in a sociable manner. 2. to prepare for life in society. 3. Chiefly U.S. to organize in accordance with socialist principles. —₁**sociali'zation** or -li'**sation** n.

social science n. the scientific study of society and of human relationships within society. —**social scientist** n.

social security n. public provision for the economic welfare of the aged, unemployed, or sick, through pensions and other financial aid.

social services pl. n. welfare activities organized by the state or a local authority.

social studies n. (functioning as sing.) the study of how people live and organize themselves in society.

social welfare n. 1. social services provided by a state for the benefit of its citizens. 2. (caps.) (in New Zealand) a government department concerned with pensions and benefits for the elderly, the sick, etc.

social work n. any of various social services designed to help the poor and aged and to increase the welfare of children. —**social worker** n.

society (sə'saɪətɪ) n., pl. -**ties.** 1. mankind, considered as a community. 2. a group of people forming a single community with its own distinctive cultural patterns and institutions. 3. the structure, cultural patterns, and institutions of such a group. 4. an organized group of people sharing a common aim or interest: a learned society. 5. the privileged class of people in a community, esp. as considered superior or fashionable. 6. companionship: I enjoy her society. [Latin societās]

Society of Friends n. the Quakers.

Society of Jesus n. the religious order of the Jesuits.

socioeconomic (₁səʊsɪəʊ₁iːkə'nɒmɪk, -₁ɛkə-) adj. of or involving economic and social factors.

sociology (₁səʊsɪ'ɒlədʒɪ) n. the study of the development, organization, functioning, and classification of human societies. —**sociological** (₁səʊsɪə'lɒdʒɪk²l) adj. —**soci'ologist** n.

sociopolitical (₁səʊsɪəʊpə'lɪtɪk²l) adj. of or involving political and social factors.

sock[1] (sɒk) n. 1. a cloth covering for the foot, reaching to between the ankle and knee and worn inside a shoe. 2. **pull one's socks up.** Brit. informal. to make a determined effort to improve. 3. **put a sock in it.** Brit. slang. be quiet! [Greek sukkhos]

sock[2] (sɒk) Slang. ~vb. 1. to hit with

force. ~n. 2. a forceful blow. [origin unknown]

socket ('sɒkɪt) n. 1. a device into which an electric plug can be inserted in order to make a connection in a circuit. 2. Anat. a bony hollow into which a part or structure fits: an eye socket. [Anglo-Norman soket a little ploughshare!]

Socratic (sɒ'krætɪk) adj. of the Greek philosopher Socrates, or his teachings.

Socratic method n. Philosophy. the method of instruction used by Socrates, in which a series of questions and answers lead to a logical conclusion.

sod[1] (sɒd) n. 1. a piece of grass-covered surface soil; turf. 2. Poetic. the ground. [Low German]

sod[2] (sɒd) Slang, chiefly Brit. ~n. 1. an obnoxious person. 2. Jocular. a person. 3. **sod all.** Slang. nothing. ~interj. 4. a strong exclamation of annoyance. [from sodomite] —'**sodding** adj.

soda ('səʊdə) n. 1. a simple inorganic compound of sodium, such as sodium carbonate or sodium bicarbonate. 2. same as **soda water.** 3. U.S. & Canad. a sweet fizzy drink. [perhaps from Arabic]

soda bread n. a type of bread leavened with sodium bicarbonate.

soda fountain n. U.S. & Canad. 1. a counter that serves soft drinks and snacks. 2. an apparatus dispensing soda water.

soda siphon n. a sealed bottle containing soda water under pressure, which is forced up a tube when a lever is pressed.

soda water n. a fizzy drink made by charging water with carbon dioxide under pressure.

sodden ('sɒd²n) adj. 1. completely saturated. 2. dulled, esp. by excessive drinking. [soden, obs. p.p. of seethe]

sodium ('səʊdɪəm) n. a very reactive soft silvery-white metallic element. Symbol: Na [from soda]

sodium bicarbonate n. a white crystalline soluble compound used in fizzy drinks, baking powder, and in medicine as an antacid.

sodium carbonate n. a colourless or white soluble crystalline compound used in the manufacture of glass, ceramics, soap, and paper, and as a cleansing agent.

sodium chlorate n. a colourless crystalline compound used as a bleaching agent, antiseptic, and weedkiller.

sodium chloride n. common table salt; a soluble colourless crystalline compound widely used as a seasoning and preservative for food and in the manufacture of chemicals, glass, and soap.

sodium hydroxide n. a white strongly alkaline solid used in making rayon, paper, and soap.

sodomite ('sɒdə₁maɪt) n. a person who practises sodomy.

sodomy ('sɒdəmɪ) n. anal intercourse committed by a man with another man or a woman. [Latin Sodoma Sodom]

Sod's Law (sɒdz) n. Informal. a jocular

maxim stating that if something can go wrong or turn out inconveniently it will.

sofa ('səʊfə) n. an upholstered seat with back and arms for two or more people. [Arabic *suffah*]

soft (sɒft) adj. **1.** easy to dent, shape, or cut: *soft material.* **2.** not hard; giving way easily under pressure: *a soft bed.* **3.** fine, smooth, or fluffy to the touch: *soft fur.* **4.** (of music or sounds) low and pleasing. **5.** (of light or colour) not excessively bright or harsh. **6.** (of a breeze or climate) temperate, mild, or pleasant. **7.** slightly blurred; not sharply outlined: *soft focus.* **8.** kind or lenient, often excessively so. **9.** easy to influence or impose upon. **10.** *Informal.* feeble or silly; simple: *soft in the head.* **11.** not strong or robust; unable to endure hardship. **12.** loving; tender: *soft words.* **13.** *Informal.* requiring little exertion; easy: *a soft job.* **14.** *Chem.* (of water) relatively free of mineral salts and therefore easily able to make soap lather. **15.** (of a drug) nonaddictive. **16.** *Phonetics.* denoting the consonants *c* and *g* when they are pronounced sibilantly, as in *cent* and *germ.* **17. soft on. a.** lenient towards. **b.** feeling infatuation for. ~*adv.* **18.** softly: *to speak soft.* ~*interj.* **19.** *Archaic.* quiet! [Old English *sōfte*] —**'softly** *adv.*

softball ('sɒft,bɔːl) n. a variation of baseball using a larger softer ball.

soft-boiled adj. (of an egg) boiled for a short time so that the yolk is still soft.

soft coal n. same as **bituminous coal**.

soft drink n. a nonalcoholic drink.

soften ('sɒf'n) vb. **1.** to make or become soft or softer. **2.** to make or become more gentle. —**'softener** n.

soft furnishings pl. n. Brit. curtains, hangings, rugs, and covers.

softhearted (,sɒft'hɑːtɪd) adj. easily moved to pity.

soft option n. in a number of choices, the one involving the least exertion.

soft palate n. the fleshy portion at the back of the roof of the mouth.

soft-pedal vb. **-alling, -alled** or U.S. **-aling, -aled. 1.** to deliberately avoid emphasizing (something). ~n. **soft pedal. 2.** a pedal on a piano that softens the tone.

soft sell n. a method of selling based on indirect suggestion or inducement.

soft-soap vb. Informal. to flatter (a person).

soft-spoken adj. speaking or said with a soft gentle voice.

soft touch n. Informal. a person easily imposed on, esp. to lend money.

software ('sɒft,wɛə) n. Computers. the programs used with a computer.

softwood ('sɒft,wʊd) n. the open-grained wood of coniferous trees.

softy or **softie** ('sɒftɪ) n., pl. **softies.** Informal. a person who is easily upset.

soggy ('sɒgɪ) adj. **-gier, -giest. 1.** soaked with liquid. **2.** moist and heavy: *a soggy cake.* [prob. from dialect *sog* marsh] —**'sogginess** n.

soh or **so** (səʊ) n. Music. the name used for the fifth note of a scale.

soigné or (fem.) **soignée** ('swɑːnjeɪ) adj. well-groomed; elegant. [French]

soil[1] (sɔɪl) n. **1.** the top layer of the land surface of the earth. **2.** a specific type of this material: *loamy soil.* **3.** land, country, or region: *one's native soil.* [Latin *solium* a seat, confused with *solum* the ground]

soil[2] (sɔɪl) vb. **1.** to make or become dirty or stained. **2.** to bring disgrace upon. ~n. **3.** a soiled spot. **4.** refuse, manure, or excrement. [Old French *soillier*]

soiree ('swɑːreɪ) n. an evening party or gathering. [French]

sojourn ('sɒdʒɜːn, 'sʌdʒ-) n. **1.** a temporary stay. ~vb. **2.** to stay or reside temporarily. [Old French *sojorner*]

sol[1] (sɒl) n. Music. same as **soh**.

sol[2] (sɒl) n. a liquid colloidal solution.

solace ('sɒlɪs) n. **1.** comfort in misery or disappointment. **2.** something that gives comfort or consolation. ~vb. **3.** to give comfort or cheer to (a person) in time of sorrow or distress. [Old French *solas*]

solan or **solan goose** ('səʊlən) n. Archaic. same as **gannet**. [from Old Norse]

solar ('səʊlə) adj. **1.** of the sun. **2.** operating by or using the energy of the sun: *solar cell.* [Latin *sōl* the sun]

solarium (səʊ'lɛərɪəm) n., pl. **-laria** (-'lɛərɪə) or **-lariums.** an establishment with beds equipped with ultraviolet lights used for acquiring an artificial suntan. [Latin: a terrace]

solar plexus n. **1.** Anat. a network of nerves behind the stomach. **2.** (not in technical usage) the vulnerable part of the stomach beneath the diaphragm.

solar system n. the system containing the sun and the planets, comets, and asteroids that go round it.

sold (səʊld) vb. **1.** past of **sell.** ~adj. **2. sold on.** Slang. uncritically attached to or enthusiastic about.

solder ('sɒldə; U.S. 'sɒdər) n. **1.** an alloy used for joining two metal surfaces by melting the alloy so that it forms a thin layer between the surfaces. ~vb. **2.** to join or mend or be joined or mended with solder. [Latin *solidāre* to strengthen]

soldering iron n. a hand tool with an iron or copper tip that is heated and used to melt and apply solder.

soldier ('səʊldʒə) n. **1. a.** a person who serves or has served in an army. **b.** a noncommissioned member of an army. ~vb. **2.** to serve as a soldier. [Old French *soudier*] —**'soldierly** adj.

soldier of fortune n. a man who seeks money or adventure as a soldier; mercenary.

soldier on vb. to persist in one's efforts in spite of difficulties or pressure.

sole[1] (səʊl) adj. **1.** being the only one; only. **2.** not shared; exclusive: *sole rights.* [Latin *sōlus* alone]

sole[2] (səʊl) n. **1.** the underside of the foot. **2.** the underside of a shoe. **3.** the lower surface of an object. ~vb. **4.** to provide (a shoe) with a sole. [Latin *solea* sandal]

sole³ (səʊl) n., pl. **sole** or **soles.** a flatfish highly valued as food. [Latin *solea* a sandal (from the fish's shape)]

solecism ('sɒlɪˌsɪzəm) n. **1.** a violation of the grammar or idiom of a language. **2.** a violation of good manners. [Greek *soloikos* speaking incorrectly] —ˌsole'cistic adj.

solely ('səʊllɪ) adv. **1.** only; completely. **2.** without others; singly.

solemn ('sɒləm) adj. **1.** serious; deeply sincere: *a solemn vow.* **2.** characterized by pomp, ceremony, or formality. **3.** serious or glum. **4.** inspiring awe: *a solemn occasion.* [Latin *sōllemnis* appointed]

solemnity (sə'lɛmnɪtɪ) n., pl. **-ties. 1.** the state or quality of being solemn. **2.** (*often pl.*) a solemn ceremony or ritual.

solemnize or **-ise** ('sɒləmˌnaɪz) vb. **1.** to celebrate or perform (a ceremony, esp. of marriage). **2.** to make solemn or serious. —ˌsolemniˈzation or -iˈsation n.

solenoid ('səʊlɪˌnɔɪd) n. a coil of wire, usually cylindrical, in which a magnetic field is set up by passing a current through it. [French *solénoïde*] —ˌsole'noidal adj.

sol-fa ('sɒl'fɑː) n. short for **tonic sol-fa.**

solicit (sə'lɪsɪt) vb. **1.** (foll. by *for*) to seek or request, esp. in a formal or persistent manner. **2.** to approach (a person) with an offer of sexual relations in return for money. [Latin *sollicitāre* to harass] —soˌliciˈtation n.

solicitor (sə'lɪsɪtə) n. (in Britain) a lawyer who advises clients on matters of law, draws up legal documents, and prepares cases for barristers.

Solicitor General n., pl. **Solicitors General.** (in Britain) the law officer of the Crown ranking next to the Attorney General (in Scotland to the Lord Advocate) and acting as his assistant.

solicitous (sə'lɪsɪtəs) adj. **1.** showing consideration, concern, or attention. **2.** keenly anxious or willing; eager. [Latin *sollicitus* anxious] —so'licitousness n.

solicitude (sə'lɪsɪˌtjuːd) n. **1.** the state or quality of being solicitous. **2.** anxiety or concern.

solid ('sɒlɪd) adj. **1.** (of a substance) in a physical state in which it resists changes in size and shape; not liquid or gaseous. **2.** consisting of matter all through; not hollow. **3.** of the same substance all through: *solid rock.* **4.** sound; proved or provable: *solid facts.* **5.** reliable or sensible; upstanding: *a solid citizen.* **6.** firm, strong, or substantial: *a solid table.* **7.** (of a meal or food) substantial. **8.** without interruption; continuous or unbroken: *solid bombardment.* **9.** financially sound: *a solid institution.* **10.** strongly united or consolidated: *a solid relationship.* **11.** *Geom.* having or relating to three dimensions. **12.** adequate; sound, but not brilliant: *a solid piece of work.* **13.** of a single uniform colour or tone. ~n. **14.** *Geom.* a three-dimensional shape. **15.** a solid substance. [Latin *solidus* firm] —**solidity** (sə'lɪdɪtɪ) n. —'solidly adv.

solidarity (ˌsɒlɪ'dærɪtɪ) n., pl. **-ties.** agreement in interests or sympathies among members of a group; total unity.

solid geometry n. the branch of geometry concerned with three-dimensional figures.

solidify (sə'lɪdɪˌfaɪ) vb. **-fying, -fied. 1.** to make or become solid or hard. **2.** to make or become strong, united, or determined. —soˌlidifi'cation n.

solid-state n. (*modifier*) (of an electronic device) using a semiconductor component, such as a transistor or silicon chip, in which current flow is through solid material, rather than a valve or mechanical part, in which current flow is through a vacuum.

solidus ('sɒlɪdəs) n., pl. **-di** (-ˌdaɪ). a short oblique stroke used in text to separate items, such as *and/or.*

soliloquize or **-ise** (sə'lɪləˌkwaɪz) vb. to utter a soliloquy.

soliloquy (sə'lɪləkwɪ) n., pl. **-quies. 1.** the act of speaking alone or to oneself, esp. as a theatrical device. **2.** a speech in a play that is spoken in soliloquy. [Latin *sōlus* alone + *loquī* to speak]

solipsism ('sɒlɪpˌsɪzəm) n. *Philosophy.* the denial of the possibility of any knowledge other than of one's own existence. [Latin *sōlus* alone + *ipse* self] —'solipsist n.

solitaire (ˌsɒlɪ'tɛə) n. **1.** a game played by one person, involving moving and taking pegs in a pegboard with the object of being left with only one. **2.** *U.S.* patience (the card game). **3.** a gem, esp. a diamond, set alone in a ring. [French]

solitary ('sɒlɪtrɪ) adj. **1.** following or enjoying a life of solitude: *a solitary disposition.* **2.** experienced or performed alone: *a solitary walk.* **3.** (of a place) unfrequented. **4.** single; sole: *a solitary cloud.* **5.** having few companions; lonely. ~n., pl. **-taries. 6.** a person who lives in seclusion; hermit. **7.** *Informal.* short for **solitary confinement:** *ten days in solitary.* [Latin *sōlitārius*] —'solitariness n.

solitary confinement n. isolation imposed on a prisoner by confinement in a special cell.

solitude ('sɒlɪˌtjuːd) n. the state of being solitary or secluded.

solo ('səʊləʊ) n., pl. **-los. 1.** a musical composition for one performer. **2. a.** any performance by an individual without assistance. **b.** (*as modifier*): *a solo flight.* **3.** Also: **solo whist.** a card game in which each person plays on his own. ~adv. **4.** by oneself; alone: *to fly solo.* [Latin *sōlus* alone] —soloist ('səʊləʊɪst) n.

Solomon ('sɒləmən) n. any person credited with great wisdom. [after 10th-cent. B.C. king of Israel]

Solomon's seal n. a plant with greenish flowers and long waxy leaves.

so long interj. **1.** *Informal.* farewell; goodbye. ~adv. **2.** *S. African slang.* for the time being; meanwhile.

solstice ('sɒlstɪs) n. either the shortest day of the year (**winter solstice**) or the longest day of the year (**summer solstice**).

[Latin *sōlstitium* the standing still of the sun]

soluble ('sɒljʊb'l) *adj.* **1.** (of a substance) capable of being dissolved. **2.** (of a mystery or problem) capable of being solved. —ˌsolu'bility *n.*

solute ('sɒljuːt) *n.* the substance in a solution that is dissolved. [Latin *solūtus* free]

solution (sə'luːʃən) *n.* **1.** a specific answer to or way of answering a problem. **2.** the act or process of solving a problem. **3.** a mixture of two or more substances in which the molecules or atoms of the substances are completely dispersed. **4.** the act or process of forming a solution. **5.** the state of being dissolved: *the sugar is held in solution.* [Latin *solūtiō* an unloosing]

solve (sɒlv) *vb.* to find the explanation for or solution to (a mystery or problem). [Latin *solvere* to loosen] —'solvable *adj.*

solvent ('sɒlvənt) *adj.* **1.** capable of meeting financial obligations. **2.** (of a liquid) capable of dissolving other substances. ~*n.* **3.** a liquid capable of dissolving other substances. [Latin *solvēns* releasing] —'solvency *n.*

solvent abuse *n.* the deliberate inhaling of intoxicating fumes given off by certain solvents.

Som. Somerset.

somatic (səʊ'mætɪk) *adj.* of or relating to the body as distinct from the mind: *a somatic disease.* [Greek *sōma* the body]

sombre *or U.S.* **somber** ('sɒmbə) *adj.* **1.** dismal; melancholy: *a sombre mood.* **2.** (of a place) dim, gloomy, or shadowy. **3.** (of colour or clothes) sober, dull, or dark. [Latin *sub* beneath + *umbra* shade] —'sombrely *or U.S.* 'somberly *adv.*

sombrero (sɒm'brɛərəʊ) *n.,* pl. **-ros.** a hat with a very wide brim, as worn in Mexico. [Spanish]

some (sʌm; *unstressed* səm) *det.* **1.** (a) certain unknown or unspecified: *some man called for you.* **2.** an unknown or unspecified quantity or number of: *there's some rice left.* **3. a.** a considerable number or amount of: *he lived some years afterwards.* **b.** *Informal.* show some respect. **4.** *Informal.* an impressive or remarkable: *that was some game!* ~*pron.* **5.** certain unknown or unspecified persons or things: *some can teach and others can't.* **6.** an unknown or unspecified quantity of something or number of persons or things: *I've got some at home.* ~*adv.* **7.** approximately: *some thirty pounds.* [Old English *sum*]

somebody ('sʌmbədɪ) *pron.* **1.** some person; someone. ~*n.,* pl. **-bodies. 2.** a person of great importance: *she was determined to be somebody.*

someday ('sʌmˌdeɪ) *adv.* at some unspecified time in the future.

somehow ('sʌmˌhaʊ) *adv.* **1.** in some unspecified way. **2.** for some unknown reason: *somehow it didn't seem to matter.*

someone ('sʌmˌwʌn, -wən) *pron.* some person; somebody.

someplace ('sʌmˌpleɪs) *adv. U.S. & Canad. informal.* same as **somewhere.**

somersault ('sʌməˌsɔːlt) *n.* **1.** a rolling

movement in which the head is placed on the ground and the trunk and legs are turned over it. **2.** such a rolling movement performed in midair, as in diving or gymnastics. ~*vb.* **3.** to perform a somersault. [Old French *soubresault*]

something ('sʌmθɪŋ) *pron.* **1.** an unspecified or unknown thing; some thing: *take something warm with you.* **2.** an unspecified or unknown amount: *something less than a hundred.* **3.** an impressive or important person, thing, or event: *isn't that something?* **4. something else.** *Slang, chiefly U.S.* a remarkable person or thing. ~*adv.* **5.** to some degree; somewhat: *he looks something like me.*

sometime ('sʌmˌtaɪm) *adv.* **1.** at some unspecified point of time. ~*adj.* **2.** former: *the sometime President.*

sometimes ('sʌmˌtaɪmz) *adv.* now and then; from time to time.

someway ('sʌmˌweɪ) *adv.* in some unspecified manner.

somewhat ('sʌmˌwɒt) *adv.* rather; a bit: *she found it somewhat odd.*

somewhere ('sʌmˌwɛə) *adv.* **1.** in, to, or at some unknown or unspecified place or point: *somewhere in England; somewhere between 3 and 4 o'clock.* **2. getting somewhere.** *Informal.* making progress.

somnambulism (sɒm'næmbjʊˌlɪzəm) *n.* walking while asleep or in a hypnotic trance. [Latin *somnus* sleep + *ambulāre* to walk] —som'nambulist *n.*

somnolent ('sɒmnələnt) *adj.* drowsy; sleepy. [Latin *somnus* sleep] —'somnolence *n.*

son (sʌn) *n.* **1.** a male offspring. **2.** a familiar term of address for a boy or man. **3.** a male who comes from a certain place or one closely connected with a certain environment, etc.: *a son of the circus.* [Old English *sunu*]

Son (sʌn) *n. Christianity.* the second person of the Trinity, Jesus Christ.

sonar ('sɒnɑː) *n.* a communication and position-finding device used in underwater navigation and target detection using sound waves. [*so*(und) *na*(vigation *and*) *r*(anging)]

sonata (sə'nɑːtə) *n.* an instrumental composition, usually in three or more movements, for piano or for another instrument with or without piano. [Italian]

son et lumière ('sɒn eɪ 'luːmɪˌɛə) *n.* an entertainment staged at night at a famous building or historical site, at which its history is presented by means of lighting effects, sound effects, and narration. [French, *lit.:* sound and light]

song (sɒŋ) *n.* **1.** a piece of music with words, composed for the voice. **2.** the tuneful call or sound made by certain birds or insects. **3.** the act or process of singing: *they raised their voices in song.* **4. for a song.** at a bargain price. **5. make a song and dance.** *Brit. informal.* to make an unnecessary fuss. [Old English *sang*]

songbird ('sɒŋˌbɜːd) *n.* any bird that has a musical call.

songololo (ˌsɒŋɡɒˈlɒlɒ) n., pl. **-los.** S. African. a kind of millipede. [Bantu]

songstress (ˈsɒŋstrɪs) n. a female singer, esp. of popular songs.

song thrush n. a common thrush noted for its song.

sonic (ˈsɒnɪk) adj. of, involving, or producing sound. [Latin sonus sound]

sonic barrier n. same as **sound barrier.**

sonic boom n. a loud explosive sound caused by the shock wave of an aircraft travelling at supersonic speed.

son-in-law n., pl. **sons-in-law.** the husband of one's daughter.

sonnet (ˈsɒnɪt) n. Prosody. a verse form consisting of 14 lines with a fixed rhyme scheme and rhythm pattern. [Old Provençal sonet a little poem]

sonny (ˈsʌnɪ) n. Often patronizing. a familiar term of address to a boy or man.

sonorous (səˈnɔːrəs, ˈsɒnərəs) adj. **1.** (of a sound) deep or resonant. **2.** (of speech) consciously grand; pompous. [Latin sonor a noise] —**sonority** (səˈnɒrɪtɪ) n.

soon (suːn) adv. **1.** in or after a short time; before long. **2. as soon as.** at the very moment that: as soon as she saw him. **3. as soon ... as.** used to indicate that the first alternative is slightly preferable to the second: I'd just as soon go by train as drive. [Old English sōna]

sooner (ˈsuːnə) adv. **1.** the comparative of **soon:** he came sooner than I thought. **2.** rather; in preference: I'd sooner die than give up. **3. no sooner ... than.** immediately after or when: no sooner had he got home than the rain stopped. **4. sooner or later.** eventually; inevitably.

soot (sʊt) n. a black powder deposited during the incomplete combustion of organic substances such as coal. [Old English sōt] —**sooty** adj.

sooth (suːθ) n. in **sooth.** Archaic or poetic. in truth. [Old English sōth]

soothe (suːð) vb. **1.** to make (someone) calm or tranquil. **2.** to relieve or assuage (pain, longing, etc.). [Old English sōthian to prove] —**soothing** adj.

soothsayer (ˈsuːθˌseɪə) n. a seer or prophet.

sop (sɒp) n. **1.** a concession or bribe given to placate or mollify someone: a sop to one's feelings. **2.** (pl.) food soaked in a liquid before being eaten. **3.** Informal. a stupid or weak person. ~vb. **sopping, sopped. 4.** (often foll. by up) to mop or absorb (liquid) as with a sponge. [Old English sopp]

sophism (ˈsɒfɪzəm) n. an argument that seems plausible though actually invalid and misleading. [Greek sophisma ingenious trick]

sophist (ˈsɒfɪst) n. a person who uses clever or quibbling but unsound arguments. [Greek sophistēs a wise man] —**sophistic** (səˈfɪstɪk) adj.

sophisticate vb. (səˈfɪstɪˌkeɪt). **1.** to make (someone) less natural or innocent, as by education. **2.** to make (a machine or method) more complex or refined. ~n.

(səˈfɪstɪˌkeɪt, -kɪt). **3.** a sophisticated person. [Latin sophisticus sophistic] —**soˌphistiˈcation** n.

sophisticated (səˈfɪstɪˌkeɪtɪd) adj. **1.** having refined or cultured tastes and habits. **2.** appealing to sophisticated people: a sophisticated restaurant. **3.** (of machines or methods) complex and refined.

sophistry (ˈsɒfɪstrɪ) n. **1.** the practice of using arguments which seem plausible though actually invalid and misleading. **2.** (pl. **-ries**) an instance of this.

sophomore (ˈsɒfəˌmɔː) n. Chiefly U.S. & Canad. a second-year student. [prob. from earlier sophum, var. of sophism]

soporific (ˌsɒpəˈrɪfɪk) adj. **1.** inducing sleep. ~n. **2.** a drug that induces sleep. [Latin sopor sleep]

sopping (ˈsɒpɪŋ) adj. completely soaked; wet through. Also: **sopping wet.**

soppy (ˈsɒpɪ) adj. **-pier, -piest.** Brit. informal. silly or sentimental. —**soppily** adv.

soprano (səˈprɑːnəʊ) n., pl. **-pranos. 1.** the highest adult female voice. **2.** the voice of a young boy before puberty. **3.** a singer with such a voice. **4.** the highest part of a piece of harmony. **5.** the highest or second highest instrument in a family of instruments. [Italian]

sorbet (ˈsɔːbeɪ) n. a water ice made from fruit juice, egg whites, etc. [French, from Arabic sharbah a drink]

sorcerer (ˈsɔːsərə) or (fem.) **sorceress** (ˈsɔːsərɪs) n. a person who uses magic powers; a wizard. [Old French sorcier]

sorcery (ˈsɔːsərɪ) n., pl. **-ceries.** the practice of magic, esp. black magic. [Old French sorcerie]

sordid (ˈsɔːdɪd) adj. **1.** dirty or squalid. **2.** degraded; vile; base. **3.** selfish and grasping; sordid avarice. [Latin sordidus]

sore (sɔː) adj. **1.** (of a wound, injury, etc.) painfully sensitive; tender. **2.** causing annoyance: a sore point. **3.** resentful; annoyed. **4.** urgent; pressing: in sore need. ~n. **5.** a painful or sensitive wound or injury. ~adv. **6. sore afraid.** Archaic. greatly frightened. [Old English sār]

sorely (ˈsɔːlɪ) adv. **1.** painfully or grievously: sorely wounded. **2.** pressingly or greatly: to be sorely tempted.

sorghum (ˈsɔːɡəm) n. a grass cultivated for grain, hay, and as a source of syrup. [Italian sorgo]

sorority (səˈrɒrɪtɪ) n., pl. **-ties.** Chiefly U.S. a society of female students. [Latin soror sister]

sorrel[1] (ˈsɒrəl) adj. **1.** light brown to brownish-orange. ~n. **2.** a horse of this colour. [Old French sorel]

sorrel[2] (ˈsɒrəl) n. a plant with acid-tasting leaves which are used in salads and sauces. [Old French surele]

sorrow (ˈsɒrəʊ) n. **1.** the feeling of sadness, grief, or regret associated with loss, bereavement, or sympathy for another's suffering. **2.** a particular cause of this. ~vb. **3.** to mourn or grieve. [Old English sorg] —**sorrowful** adj. —**sorrowfully** adv.

sorry ('sɒrɪ) adj. **-rier, -riest. 1.** (often foll. by for) feeling or expressing pity, sympathy, grief, or regret: I feel sorry for him. **2.** pitiful, wretched, or deplorable: a sorry sight. **3.** poor; paltry: a sorry excuse. ~interj. **4.** an exclamation expressing apology or requesting someone to repeat what he has said. [Old English sārig]

sort (sɔːt) n. **1.** a class, group, or kind, as distinguished by some common quality or characteristic. **2.** Informal. a type of character: he's a good sort. **3.** a more or less adequate example: it's a sort of review. **4. of sorts** or **of a sort. a.** of an inferior kind. **b.** of an indefinite kind. **5. out of sorts.** not in normal good health or temper. **6. sort of.** as it were; rather: I sort of fell; sort of frightening. ~vb. **7.** to arrange (things or people) according to class, type, etc. **8.** to put (something) into working order. **9.** to arrange (computer information) by machine in an order convenient to the user. [Latin sors fate]

sortie ('sɔːtɪ) n. **1.** a short trip to an unfamiliar place. **2.** (of troops) the act of attacking from a besieged position. **3.** an operational flight made by one aircraft. ~vb. **-tieing, -tied. 4.** to make a sortie. [French]

sort out vb. **1.** to find a solution to (a problem): to sort out the mess. **2.** to take or separate (things or people) from a larger group: to sort out the likely ones. **3.** to organize (things or people) into an orderly and disciplined group. **4.** Informal. to scold or punish (someone).

SOS n. **1.** an internationally recognized distress signal in which the letters SOS are repeatedly spelt out in Morse code. **2.** Informal. any call for help.

so-so Informal. ~adj. **1.** neither good nor bad. ~adv. **2.** in an average or indifferent manner.

sostenuto (ˌsɒstəˈnuːtəʊ) adv. Music. in a smooth sustained manner. [Italian]

sot (sɒt) n. a habitual drunkard. [Old English] —**ˈsottish** adj.

sotto voce ('sɒtəʊ 'vəʊtʃɪ) adv. in an undertone. [Italian]

sou (suː) n. **1.** a former French coin of low value. **2.** a very small amount of money: I haven't a sou. [French]

soubrette (suːˈbrɛt) n. a minor female role in comedy, often that of a pert lady's maid. [French]

soubriquet ('suːbrɪˌkeɪ) n. same as **sobriquet.**

soufflé ('suːfleɪ) n. a light fluffy dish made with beaten egg whites combined with other ingredients such as cheese or fish or chocolate and gelatin. [French]

sough (saʊ) vb. (of the wind) to make a sighing sound. [Old English swōgan]

sought (sɔːt) vb. past of **seek.**

souk (suːk) n. an open-air marketplace in Muslim countries. [Arabic]

soul (səʊl) n. **1.** the spirit or immaterial part of man, regarded as the centre of human personality, intellect, will, and emotions: believed by many to survive the body after death. **2.** the essential part or fundamental nature of anything: the soul of the American people. **3.** deep and sincere feelings: you've got no soul. **4.** Also called: **soul music.** a type of Black music resulting from the addition of jazz, gospel, and pop elements to blues. **5.** (modifier) of or relating to Black Americans and their culture: soul food. **6. the life and soul.** Informal. a person regarded as the main source of gaiety or merriment: the life and soul of the party. **7.** a person regarded as typifying some characteristic or quality: the soul of discretion. **8.** a person: a decent soul. [Old English sāwol]

soul-destroying adj. (of an occupation or situation) extremely monotonous.

soul food n. Informal. food, such as chitterlings and yams, which is traditionally eaten by U.S. Blacks.

soulful ('səʊlful) adj. expressing profound feelings.

soulless ('səʊllɪs) adj. **1.** lacking human qualities or influences; mechanical: soulless work. **2.** (of a person) lacking in sensitivity.

soul mate n. a person whom one finds instinctively compatible.

soul-searching n. deep examination of one's motives, actions, and beliefs.

sound[1] (saʊnd) n. **1.** Physics. mechanical vibrations that travel in waves through the air, water, etc. **2.** the sensation produced by such vibrations in the organs of hearing. **3.** anything that can be heard. **4.** impression or implication: I don't like the sound of that. **5.** (often pl.) Slang. music, esp. rock, jazz, or pop. ~vb. **6.** to cause (an instrument, etc.) to make a sound or (of an instrument, etc.) to emit a sound. **7.** to announce (something) by a sound: to sound the alarm. **8.** to resonate with a certain quality or intensity: to sound loud. **9.** to give the impression of being as specified: to sound reasonable. **10.** to pronounce (something) distinctly or audibly: to sound one's r's. [Latin sonus]

sound[2] (saʊnd) adj. **1.** free from damage, injury, or decay. **2.** firm; substantial: a sound basis. **3.** financially safe or stable: a sound investment. **4.** showing good judgment or reasoning; wise: sound advice. **5.** holding approved beliefs; ethically correct; honest. **6.** (of sleep) deep; peaceful; unbroken. **7.** thorough: a sound defeat. ~adv. **8. sound asleep.** in a deep sleep. [Old English sund] —**ˈsoundly** adv.

sound[3] (saʊnd) vb. **1.** to measure the depth of (a well, the sea, etc.). **2.** Med. to examine (a part of the body) by tapping or with a stethoscope. ~See also **sound out.** [Old French sonder]

sound[4] (saʊnd) n. a channel between two larger areas of sea or between an island and the mainland. [Old English sund]

sound barrier n. a sudden increase in the force of air against an aircraft flying at or above the speed of sound.

sound effects pl. n. sounds artificially produced, as from a recording, to create certain theatrical effects in a play or film.

sounding board *n.* a person or group used to test a new idea or policy.

soundings ('saʊndɪŋz) *pl. n.* measurements of the depth of a river, lake, etc.

sound out *vb.* to question (someone) in order to discover his opinion: *I intend to sound him out before the meeting.*

soundproof ('saʊnd,pruːf) *adj.* **1.** not penetrable by sound. ~*vb.* **2.** to make (a room) soundproof.

soundtrack ('saʊnd,træk) *n.* the recorded sound accompaniment to a film.

sound wave *n.* a wave that carries sound.

soup (suːp) *n.* **1.** a liquid food made by simmering meat, fish, or vegetables. **2. in the soup.** *Slang.* in trouble or difficulties. [Old French *soupe*] —**'soupy** *adj.*

soupçon ('suːpsɒn) *n.* a slight amount; dash. [French]

soup kitchen *n.* a place where food and drink is served to needy people.

soup up *vb. Slang.* to modify the engine of (a car or motorcycle) in order to increase its power.

sour ('saʊə) *adj.* **1.** having a sharp biting taste like the taste of lemon juice or vinegar. **2.** made acid or bad, as in the case of milk, by fermentation. **3.** (of a person's temperament) sullen or disagreeable. **4. go** *or* **turn sour.** to become unfavourable or inharmonious: *his marriage went sour.* ~*vb.* **5.** to make or become unfavourable or inharmonious. [Old English *sūr*] —**'sourly** *adv.*

source (sɔːs) *n.* **1.** the point, person, or place from which something originates. **2.** the area or spring where a river or stream begins. **3.** any person, book, or organization from which information or evidence is obtained. [Latin *surgere* to rise]

sour cream *n.* cream soured by bacteria for use in salad dressings, dips, etc.

sour grapes *n.* (*functioning as sing.*) the attitude of pretending to despise something because one cannot have it oneself.

sourpuss ('saʊə,pʊs) *n. Informal.* a person who is habitually gloomy or sullen.

souse (saʊs) *vb.* **1.** to plunge (something) into water or other liquid. **2.** to drench. **3.** to steep or cook (food) in a marinade. ~*n.* **4.** the liquid used in pickling. **5.** the act or process of sousing. [Old French *sous*]

soused (saʊst) *adj. Slang.* drunk.

soutane (suːˈtæn) *n. R.C. Church.* a priest's robe. [French]

south (saʊθ) *n.* **1.** one of the four cardinal points of the compass, at 180° from north and 90° clockwise from east and anticlockwise from west. **2.** the direction along a meridian towards the South Pole. **3. the south.** (*often cap.*) any area lying in or towards the south. ~*adj.* **4.** situated in, moving towards, or facing the south. **5.** (esp. of the wind) from the south. ~*adv.* **6.** in, to, or towards the south. [Old English *sūth*]

South (saʊθ) *n.* **the. 1.** the southern part of England. **2.** (in the U.S.) the Southern

states that formed the Confederacy during the Civil War. ~*adj.* **3.** of or denoting the southern part of a country, area, etc.

South African *adj.* **1.** of or relating to the Republic of South Africa. ~*n.* **2.** a person from the Republic of South Africa.

southeast (,saʊθˈiːst; *Naut.* ,saʊˈiːst) *n.* **1.** the direction midway between south and east. ~*adj. also* **southeastern. 2.** of or denoting that part of a country, area, etc. which lies in the southeast. **3.** situated in, moving towards, or facing the southeast. **4.** (esp. of the wind) from the southeast. ~*adv.* **5.** in, to, or towards the southeast. —,**south'easterly** *adj., adv., n.*

Southeast (,saʊθˈiːst) *n.* **the.** the southeast of Britain, esp. the London area.

southeaster (,saʊθˈiːstə; *Naut.* ,saʊˈiːstə) *n.* a strong wind or storm from the southeast.

southerly ('sʌðəlɪ) *adj.* **1.** of or in the south. ~*adv., adj.* **2.** towards the south. **3.** from the south: *a southerly wind.*

southern ('sʌðən) *adj.* **1.** situated in or towards the south. **2.** facing or moving towards the south. **3.** (*sometimes cap.*) of or characteristic of the south or South. —'**southern,most** *adj.*

Southerner ('sʌðənə) *n.* a person from the south of a country or area, esp. England or the U.S.

southern hemisphere *n.* that half of the globe lying south of the equator.

southern lights *pl. n.* same as **aurora australis.**

southpaw ('saʊθ,pɔː) *Informal.* ~*n.* **1.** any left-handed person, esp. a boxer. ~*adj.* **2.** left-handed.

South Pole *n.* the southernmost point on the earth's axis, at a latitude of 90°S.

South Seas *pl. n.* the seas south of the equator.

southward ('saʊθwəd; *Naut.* 'sʌðəd) *adv. also* **southwards. 1.** towards the south. ~*n.* **2.** the southward part, direction, etc.

southwest (,saʊθˈwɛst; *Naut.* ,saʊˈwɛst) *n.* **1.** the direction midway between west and south. ~*adj. also* **southwestern. 2.** of or denoting that part of a country, area, etc. which lies in the southwest. **3.** situated in, moving towards, or facing the southwest. **4.** (esp. of the wind) from the southwest. ~*adv.* **5.** in, to, or towards the southwest. —,**south'westerly** *adj., adv., n.*

Southwest (,saʊθˈwɛst) *n.* **the.** the southwestern part of Britain, esp. Cornwall, Devon, and Somerset.

southwester (,saʊθˈwɛstə; *Naut.* ,saʊˈwɛstə) *n.* a strong wind or storm from the southwest.

souvenir (,suːvəˈnɪə) *n.* an object that reminds one of a certain place, occasion, or person; memento. [French]

sou'wester (saʊˈwɛstə) *n.* a waterproof hat with a very broad rim at the back worn by seamen. [a contraction of *southwester*]

sovereign ('sɒvrɪn) *n.* **1.** a person who has supreme authority, esp. a monarch. **2.**

a former British gold coin worth one pound sterling. ~*adj.* **3.** independent of outside authority: *a sovereign state.* **4.** supreme in rank or authority: *a sovereign lord.* **5.** excellent or outstanding: *a sovereign remedy.* [Old French *soverain*]

sovereignty ('sɒvrənti) *n., pl.* **-ties. 1.** supreme and unrestricted power, as of a state. **2.** the position or authority of a sovereign.

soviet ('səʊviət, 'sɒv-) *n.* (in the Soviet Union) an elected government council at the local, regional, and national levels. [Russian *sovyet*]

Soviet ('səʊviət, 'sɒv-) *adj.* **1.** of or relating to the Soviet Union, its people, or its government. ~*n.* **2.** a person from the Soviet Union.

sow[1] (səʊ) *vb.* **sowing, sowed; sown** or **sowed. 1.** to scatter or place (seed) in or on (a piece of ground) so that it may grow: *to sow wheat; to sow a strip of land.* **2.** to implant or introduce: *to sow a doubt in someone's mind.* [Old English *sāwan*]

sow[2] (saʊ) *n.* a female adult pig. [Old English *sugu*]

soya bean ('sɔɪə) or *U.S. & Canad.* **soybean** ('sɔɪ,biːn) *n.* a bean which is used as food, forage, and as the source of an oil. [Japanese *shōyu*]

soy sauce (sɔɪ) *n.* a salty dark brown sauce made from fermented soya beans, used esp. in Chinese cookery.

sozzled ('sɒz'ld) *adj. Informal.* drunk. [origin unknown]

spa (spɑː) *n.* a mineral-water spring or a place where such a spring is found. [after *Spa*, a watering place in Belgium]

space (speɪs) *n.* **1.** the unlimited three-dimensional expanse in which all material objects are located. **2.** an interval of distance or time between two points, objects, or events. **3.** a blank portion or area. **4.** unoccupied area or room: *there is no space for a table.* **5.** the region beyond the earth's atmosphere containing other planets, stars, and galaxies; the universe. ~*vb.* **6.** to place or arrange (things) at intervals or with spaces between them. [Latin *spatium*]

space age *n.* **1.** the period in which the exploration of space has become possible. ~*adj.* **space-age. 2.** futuristic or ultramodern: *a space-age car.*

space-bar *n.* a bar on a typewriter that is pressed in order to. leave a space between words or letters.

space capsule *n.* a vehicle, sometimes carrying people or animals, designed to obtain scientific information from space and to be recovered on returning to earth.

spacecraft ('speɪs,krɑːft) *n.* a vehicle designed to orbit the earth or to travel to the Moon or to other planets.

Space Invaders *n. Trademark.* a video game in which players try to obliterate a series of symbols moving down the screen by operating levers or buttons.

spaceman ('speɪs,mæn) or (*fem.*) **spacewoman** *n., pl.* **-men** or (*fem.*) **-women.** a person who travels in space.

space probe *n.* a vehicle equipped to obtain scientific information, normally transmitted back to earth by radio, about a planet or conditions in space.

spaceship ('speɪs,ʃɪp) *n.* a manned spacecraft.

space shuttle *n.* a manned reusable spacecraft designed for making regular flights.

space station *n.* a large manned artificial satellite designed to orbit the earth during a long period of time thus providing a base for scientific research in space and for people travelling in space.

spacesuit ('speɪs,suːt) *n.* a sealed protective suit worn by astronauts.

space-time or **space-time continuum** *n. Physics.* the four-dimensional continuum having three space coordinates and one time coordinate that together completely specify the location of a particle or an event.

spacious ('speɪʃəs) *adj.* having a large capacity or area. —**'spaciousness** *n.*

spade[1] (speɪd) *n.* **1.** a tool for digging, with a flat steel blade and a long wooden handle. **2. call a spade a spade.** to speak plainly and frankly. [Old English *spadu*]

spade[2] (speɪd) *n.* **1. a.** (*pl.*) the suit of playing cards marked with a black symbol resembling a heart-shaped leaf with a stem. **b.** a card with one or more of these symbols on it. **2.** *Offensive.* a Black person. **3. in spades.** *Informal.* in the extreme; emphatically: *Hamburg's got nightlife, in spades.* [Italian *spada* sword, used as an emblem on playing cards]

spadework ('speɪd,wɜːk) *n.* dull or routine preparatory work.

spadix ('speɪdɪks) *n., pl.* **spadices** (speɪ-'daɪsiːz). a spike of small flowers on a fleshy stem. [Greek: torn-off frond]

spaghetti (spə'ɡɛtɪ) *n.* pasta in the form of long strings. [Italian]

spaghetti junction *n.* a junction between motorways with a large number of intersecting roads. [from the nickname of the Gravelly Hill Interchange, Birmingham]

spaghetti western *n.* a cowboy film made in Europe by an Italian director.

spake (speɪk) *vb. Archaic.* past of **speak.**

Spam (spæm) *n. Trademark.* tinned luncheon meat made largely from pork.

span (spæn) *n.* **1.** the interval, space, or distance between two points, such as the ends of a bridge. **2.** the complete extent: *the span of his life.* **3.** short for **wingspan. 4.** a unit of length based on the width of an expanded hand, usually taken as nine inches. ~*vb.* **spanning, spanned. 5.** to stretch or extend across, over, or around: *his career in Hollywood spanned three decades; three bridges span the East River.* [Old English *spann*]

spangle ('spæŋɡ'l) *n.* **1.** a small piece of metal or other shiny material used as a decoration, esp. on clothes; sequin. ~*vb.* **2.** to make (something) glitter as if with spangles. **3.** to cover (something) with spangles. [Middle English *spange* clasp]

Spaniard ('spænjəd) n. a person from Spain.

spaniel ('spænjəl) n. a dog with long drooping ears and a silky coat. [Old French *espaigneul* Spanish (dog)]

Spanish ('spænɪʃ) n. 1. the official language of Spain, Mexico, and most countries of South and Central America. 2. **the Spanish.** (*functioning as pl.*) the people of Spain. ~*adj.* 3. relating to Spain, Spaniards, or the Spanish language.

Spanish fly n. a beetle, the dried body of which is used medicinally.

Spanish Main n. 1. the N coast of South America. 2. the Caribbean Sea, the S part of which in colonial times was the haunt of pirates.

spank (spæŋk) vb. 1. to slap (someone) with the open hand, esp. on the buttocks. ~n. 2. such a slap. [prob. imit.]

spanking[1] ('spæŋkɪŋ) n. a series of spanks, usually as a punishment for children.

spanking[2] ('spæŋkɪŋ) adj. 1. *Informal.* outstandingly fine, smart, or large: *in spanking condition.* 2. quick and energetic: *a spanking pace.*

spanner ('spænə) n. 1. a steel tool with jaws or a hole, designed to grip a nut or bolt. 2. **throw a spanner in the works.** *Brit. informal.* to create an impediment or annoyance. [German *spannen* to stretch]

spanspek ('spæn,spɛk) n. *S. African.* a cantaloupe melon. [Afrikaans]

spar[1] (spɑː) n. a piece of nautical gear resembling a pole and used as a mast, boom, or gaff. [Old Norse *sperra* beam]

spar[2] (spɑː) vb. **sparring, sparred.** 1. *Boxing.* to box using light blows, as in training. 2. to argue with someone. [Old English]

spar[3] (spɑː) n. a light-coloured, crystalline, easily split mineral. [Middle Low German]

spare (spɛə) vb. 1. to refrain from killing, punishing, or injuring (someone). 2. to shield (someone) from (something unpleasant): *spare me the indignity.* 3. to be able to afford or give: *I can't spare the time.* 4. **not spare oneself.** to exert oneself to the full. 5. **to spare.** more than is required: *two minutes to spare.* ~*adj.* 6. in excess of what is needed; additional. 7. able to be used when needed: *a spare part.* 8. (of a person) thin. 9. (of a style) very plain or simple. 10. *Brit. slang.* upset, angry, or distracted: *Mum will go spare when she finds out.* ~n. 11. a duplicate kept as a replacement in case of damage or loss. [Old English *sparian*]

spareribs (,spɛə'rɪbz) pl. n. a cut of pork ribs with most of the meat trimmed off.

spare tyre n. 1. an additional tyre kept in a motor vehicle in case of puncture. 2. *Brit. slang.* a roll of fat just above the waist.

sparing ('spɛərɪŋ) adj. (sometimes foll. by *of*) economical or frugal (with).

spark (spɑːk) n. 1. a fiery particle thrown out or left by burning material or caused by the friction of two hard surfaces. 2. a momentary flash of light accompanied by a sharp crackling noise, produced by a sud-

den electrical discharge through the air. 3. a trace or hint: *a spark of interest.* 4. vivacity, enthusiasm, or humour: *there is no spark about him.* ~vb. 5. to give off sparks. 6. (often foll. by *off*) to initiate: *this discovery sparked off the investigation.* [Old English *spearca*]

sparkle ('spɑːk'l) vb. 1. to issue or reflect bright points of light. 2. (of wine or mineral water) to be slightly fizzy. 3. to be vivacious or witty. ~n. 4. a point of light, spark, or gleam. 5. vivacity or wit. [Middle English *sparklen*]

sparkler ('spɑːklə) n. 1. a type of handheld firework that throws out sparks. 2. *Informal.* a sparkling gem; esp. a diamond.

spark plug n. a device in an internal-combustion engine which ignites the explosive mixture by means of an electric spark. Also called: **sparking plug.**

sparring partner ('spɑːrɪŋ) n. 1. a person who practises with a boxer during training. 2. a person with whom one has friendly arguments.

sparrow ('spærəʊ) n. a very common small brown or grey bird which feeds on seeds and insects. [Old English *spearwa*]

sparrowhawk ('spærəʊ,hɔːk) n. a small hawk which preys on smaller birds.

sparse (spɑːs) adj. scattered or scanty. [Latin *sparsus*] —**sparsely** adv.

Spartan ('spɑːt'n) adj. 1. of or relating to the ancient Greek city of Sparta. 2. very strict or austere: *a Spartan upbringing.* ~n. 3. a citizen of Sparta. 4. a very strict or austere person.

spasm ('spæzəm) n. 1. an involuntary muscular contraction. 2. a sudden burst of activity or feeling: *to work in spasms; a spasm of anger.* [Greek *spasmos* a cramp]

spasmodic (spæz'mɒdɪk) adj. taking place in sudden brief spells. —**spasmodically** adv.

spastic ('spæstɪk) n. 1. a person who has cerebral palsy. ~adj. 2. affected by spasms: *a spastic colon.* 3. suffering from cerebral palsy. [Greek *spasmos* a cramp]

spat[1] (spæt) n. a slight quarrel. [prob. imit.]

spat[2] (spæt) vb. a past of **spit**[1].

spate (speɪt) n. 1. a fast flow, rush, or outpouring: *a spate of words.* 2. **in spate.** *Chiefly Brit.* (of a river) flooded. [origin unknown]

spathe (speɪð) n. a large bract that encloses a flower cluster. [Greek *spathē* a blade]

spatial ('speɪʃəl) adj. of or relating to space: *spatial distance.* —**spatially** adv.

spats (spæts) pl. n. cloth or leather coverings formerly worn by men over the ankle and instep. [obs. *spatterdash* a long gaiter]

spatter ('spætə) vb. 1. to scatter or splash (a substance, esp. a liquid) in scattered drops: *to spatter mud on the car.* 2. to sprinkle, cover, or spot (an object or a surface) with a liquid. ~n. 3. the sound of spattering. 4. something spattered, such as a spot or splash. [imit.]

spatula ('spætjʊlə) n. a utensil with a broad flat blade, used for lifting, spreading, or stirring foods or paint. [Latin: a broad piece]

spawn (spɔːn) n. **1.** the jelly-like mass of eggs laid by fish, amphibians, or molluscs. ~vb. **2.** (of fish, amphibians, or molluscs) to lay eggs. **3.** to cause (something) to be created: *the film spawned a successful TV series.* [Anglo-Norman *espaundre*]

spay (speɪ) vb. to remove the ovaries from (a female animal). [Old French *espeer* to cut with the sword]

speak (spiːk) vb. **speaking, spoke, spoken. 1.** to make verbal utterances; utter (words). **2.** to communicate or express (something) in words. **3.** to deliver a speech or lecture. **4.** to know how to talk in (a specified language): *he does not speak German.* **5. on speaking terms.** on good terms; friendly. **6. so to speak.** as it were. **7. speak one's mind.** to express one's opinions frankly and plainly. **8. to speak of.** of a significant or worthwhile nature: *no support to speak of.* [Old English *specan*]

speakeasy (ˈspiːkˌiːzɪ) n., pl. **-easies.** U.S. a place where alcoholic drink was sold illicitly during Prohibition.

speaker (ˈspiːkə) n. **1.** a person who speaks, esp. at a formal occasion. **2.** same as **loudspeaker.**

Speaker (ˈspiːkə) n. the presiding officer in any of numerous law-making bodies.

speak for vb. **1.** to speak as a representative of (other people). **2. speak for itself.** to be so evident that no further comment is necessary: *his talent speaks for itself.* **3. speak for yourself!** Informal. do not presume that other people agree with you!

speak up or **out** vb. **1.** to state one's beliefs bravely and firmly. **2.** to speak more loudly and clearly.

spear[1] (spɪə) n. **1.** a weapon consisting of a long shaft with a sharp point, which may be thrown or thrust. ~vb. **2.** to pierce (someone or something) with or as if with a spear. [Old English *spere*]

spear[2] (spɪə) n. a shoot, stalk, or blade, as of grass. [prob. var. of *spire*]

spearhead (ˈspɪəˌhɛd) vb. **1.** to lead or initiate (an attack or a campaign). ~n. **2.** the leading force in a military attack.

spearmint (ˈspɪəmɪnt) n. a minty flavouring used for sweets and toothpaste, which comes from a purple-flowered plant.

spec (spɛk) n. **on spec.** Informal. as a speculation or gamble: *all the tickets were sold so I went to the theatre on spec.*

special (ˈspɛʃəl) adj. **1.** distinguished from or better than others of its kind. **2.** designed or reserved for a particular purpose: *special boots for hill walking.* **3.** not usual or commonplace: *a special case.* **4.** particular or primary: *his special interest was music.* **5.** relating to the education of handicapped children: *a special school.* ~n. **6.** something that is special in some way, such as an extra edition of a newspaper. **7.** a dish or meal given prominence, usually at a lower price, in a café, pub, or

restaurant. **8.** short for **special constable.** [Latin *speciālis*] —**specially** adv.

Special Branch n. (in Britain) the department of the police force that is concerned with political security.

special constable n. a person recruited for occasional police duties, as in time of emergency.

special delivery n. the delivery of a piece of mail outside the time of a scheduled delivery, for an extra fee.

specialist (ˈspɛʃəlɪst) n. a person who specializes in a particular activity or field of knowledge.

speciality (ˌspɛʃɪˈælɪtɪ) or esp. U.S. & Canad. **specialty** n., pl. **-ties. 1.** a special interest or skill. **2.** a service or product specialized in.

specialize or **-ise** (ˈspɛʃəˌlaɪz) vb. **1.** to train in or devote oneself to a particular area of study, occupation, or activity: *she specializes in criminal law.* **2.** to modify (something) for a special use or purpose: *specialized television systems.* —**specialization** or **-isation** n.

special licence n. Brit. a licence permitting a marriage to take place without following all the usual legal procedures.

specialty (ˈspɛʃəltɪ) n., pl. **-ties.** Chiefly U.S. & Canad. same as **speciality.**

specie (ˈspiːʃiː) n. coin money, as distinguished from paper money. [Latin in *speciē* in kind]

species (ˈspiːʃiːz) n., pl. **-cies.** Biol. any of the groups into which a genus is divided, the members of which are able to interbreed. [Latin: appearance]

specific (spɪˈsɪfɪk) adj. **1.** explicit, particular, or definite. **2.** relating to a particular thing: *a specific treatment for arthritis.* ~n. **3.** (pl.) particular qualities or aspects of something: *let's get down to specifics.* **4.** Med. any drug used to treat a particular disease. [Latin *species* kind + *facere* to make] —**spe'cifically** adv.

specification (ˌspɛsɪfɪˈkeɪʃən) n. **1.** a detailed description of the required constituents, construction, or performance of a material or apparatus. **2.** an item or a detail specified. **3.** a specifying.

specific gravity n. Physics. the ratio of the density of a substance to the density of water.

specify (ˈspɛsɪˌfaɪ) vb. **-fying, -fied. 1.** to refer to or state (something) specifically. **2.** to state (something) as a condition. [Medieval Latin *specificāre* to describe]

specimen (ˈspɛsɪmɪn) n. **1.** an individual or part regarded as typical of its group or class. **2.** Med. a sample of tissue, blood, or urine taken for analysis. **3.** Informal. a person: *a fine healthy specimen.* [Latin: mark, proof]

specious (ˈspiːʃəs) adj. apparently correct or true, but actually wrong or false. [Latin *speciēs* outward appearance]

speck (spɛk) n. **1.** a very small mark or spot. **2.** a small or tiny piece of something: *a speck of dust.* [Old English *specca*]

speckle (ˈspɛkʔl) n. **1.** a small mark usually of a contrasting colour, as on the skin or on an egg. ~*vb.* **2.** to mark (something) with speckles. [Middle Dutch *spekkel*] —**'speckled** *adj.*

specs (spɛks) *pl. n. Informal.* **1.** short for **spectacles.** **2.** short for **specifications** (see **specification**).

spectacle ('spɛktəkʰl) *n.* **1.** a strange or interesting scene. **2.** an impressive, grand, or dramatic public show. **3. make a spectacle of oneself.** to draw attention to oneself by behaving outrageously. [Latin *spectāre* to watch]

spectacles ('spɛktəkˌlz) *pl. n.* a pair of glasses for correcting faulty vision.

spectacular (spɛk'tækjʊlə) *adj.* **1.** impressive, grand, or dramatic. ~*n.* **2.** a spectacular show. —**spec'tacularly** *adv.*

spectate (spɛk'teɪt) *vb.* to be a spectator; watch.

spectator (spɛk'teɪtə) *n.* a person viewing anything; onlooker; observer. [Latin *spectāre* to watch]

spectator ion *n. Chem.* an ion which is present in a mixture but plays no part in a reaction.

spectre *or U.S.* **specter** ('spɛktə) *n.* **1.** a ghost; phantom. **2.** an unpleasant or menacing mental image: *the spectre of redundancy.* [Latin *spectrum*] —**'spectral** *adj.*

spectrometer (spɛk'trɒmɪtə) *n. Physics.* an instrument for producing a spectrum, usually one in which wavelength, energy, or intensity can be measured.

spectroscope ('spɛktrəˌskəʊp) *n. Physics.* an instrument for forming or recording a spectrum by passing a light ray through a prism or grating.

spectrum ('spɛktrəm) *n., pl.* **-tra** (-trə). **1.** *Physics.* the distribution of colours produced when white light is dispersed by a prism or grating: violet, indigo, blue, green, yellow, orange, and red. **2.** *Physics.* the whole range of electromagnetic radiation with respect to its wavelength or frequency. **3.** a range or scale of anything such as opinions or emotions. [Latin *image*]

speculate ('spɛkjʊˌleɪt) *vb.* **1.** to conjecture about something without knowing all the facts. **2.** to buy securities or property in the hope of selling them at a profit. [Latin *speculārī* to spy out] —**'specu-ˌlation** *n.* —**'speculative** *adj.* —**'specu-ˌlator** *n.*

sped (spɛd) *vb.* a past of **speed.**

speech (spiːtʃ) *n.* **1.** the ability to speak: *he lost the power of speech.* **2.** that which is spoken; utterance: *in everyday speech.* **3.** a talk given to an audience: *the best man gives his speech.* **4.** a person's manner of speaking: *his speech was slurred.* **5.** a national or regional language or dialect: *cockney speech.* [Old English *spēc*]

speech day *n. Brit.* (in schools) an annual day on which prizes are presented and speeches are made by guest speakers.

speechify ('spiːtʃɪˌfaɪ) *vb.* **-fying, -fied.** to make a speech, usually one that is pompous and boring.

speechless ('spiːtʃlɪs) *adj.* **1.** temporarily unable to speak, owing to strong emo-

tion, amazement, or shock. **2.** unable to be expressed in words: *speechless fear.*

speed (spiːd) *n.* **1.** the quality of acting or moving fast; rapidity. **2.** the rate at which something moves, is done, or acts. **3.** a gear ratio in a motor vehicle or bicycle: *a three-speed gear.* **4.** *Photog.* a measure of the sensitivity to light of a particular type of film. **5.** *Slang.* amphetamine. **6. at speed.** quickly. ~*vb.* **speeding; sped** *or* **speeded.** **7.** to move or go somewhere quickly. **8.** to drive a motor vehicle faster than the legal limit. ~See also **speed up.** [Old English *spēd* (orig.: success)]

speedboat ('spiːdˌbəʊt) *n.* a high-speed motorboat.

speed limit *n.* the maximum speed at which a vehicle may legally travel on a particular road.

speedo ('spiːdəʊ) *n., pl.* **speedos.** *Informal.* a speedometer.

speedometer (spɪ'dɒmɪtə) *n.* a device in a vehicle which shows the speed of travel.

speed up *vb.* to increase or cause to increase in speed or rate; accelerate.

speedway ('spiːdˌweɪ) *n.* **1.** the sport of racing on light powerful motorcycles round cinder tracks. **2.** the track or stadium where such races are held.

speedwell ('spiːdˌwɛl) *n.* a small blue or pinkish-white flower.

speedy ('spiːdɪ) *adj.* **speedier, speediest. 1.** done without delay. **2.** (of a vehicle) able to travel fast. —**'speedily** *adv.*

spek (spɛk) *n. S. African.* bacon. [Afrikaans]

speleology *or* **spelaeology** (ˌspiːlɪ-'ɒlədʒɪ) *n.* the scientific study of caves. [Latin *spēlaeum* cave]

spell¹ (spɛl) *vb.* **spelling; spelt** *or* **spelled. 1.** to write or name in correct order the letters that make up (a word): *how do you spell 'coyote'?* **2.** (of letters) to make up (a word): *d-o-g spells dog.* **3.** to indicate or signify: *this flood spells ruin.* ~See also **spell out.** [Old French *espeller*]

spell² (spɛl) *n.* **1.** a verbal formula considered to have magical force. **2.** an irresistible influence; fascination. **3.** a state induced as by a spell; trance: *to break the spell.* **4. under someone's spell.** fascinated by someone. [Old English *spell* speech]

spell³ (spɛl) *n.* **1.** a period of time: *a spell of rain.* **2.** a period of duty after which one person or group relieves another. **3.** *Scot., Austral., & N.Z.* a period of rest. ~*vb.* **spelling, spelled.** **4.** to take over from (a person) for an interval of time. [Old English *spelian* to take the place of]

spellbinding ('spɛlˌbaɪndɪŋ) *adj.* entrancing or enthralling.

spellbound ('spɛlˌbaʊnd) *adj.* completely fascinated; as if in a trance.

spelling ('spɛlɪŋ) *n.* **1.** the way a word is spelt: *'center' is the U.S. spelling.* **2.** a person's ability to spell: *his spelling is atrocious.*

spell out *vb.* **1.** to make (something) clear or explicit: *let me spell out the problem.* **2.** to read with difficulty, working out each word letter by letter.

spelt (spelt) *vb.* the past of **spell**[1].

spend (spend) *vb.* **spending, spent.** **1.** to pay out (money). **2.** to pass (time) in a specific way or place: *we spent the night in London.* **3.** to concentrate (effort) on an activity. **4.** to use up completely: *the hurricane spent its force.* [Latin *expendere*] —'**spending** *n.*

spendthrift ('spend,θrift) *n.* **1.** a person who spends money extravagantly. ~*adj.* **2.** of or like a spendthrift: *his spendthrift ways.*

spent (spent) *vb.* **1.** past of **spend.** ~*adj.* **2.** used up or exhausted.

sperm (spɜːm) *n.* **1.** (*pl.* **sperm** *or* **sperms**) one of the male reproductive cells released in the semen during ejaculation. **2.** same as **semen.** [Greek *sperma*]

spermaceti (,spɜːmə'seti, -'siːti) *n.* a white waxy substance obtained from the sperm whale. [Medieval Latin *sperma cētī* whale's sperm]

spermatozoon (,spɜːmətəʊ'zəʊɒn) *n., pl.* **-zoa** (-'zəʊə). same as **sperm** (sense 1). [Greek *sperma* seed + *zōion* animal]

spermicide ('spɜːmɪ,saɪd) *n.* a substance that kills sperm. [*sperm* + Latin *caedere* to kill]

sperm oil *n.* an oil obtained from the head of the sperm whale, used as a lubricant.

sperm whale *n.* a large whale which is hunted for spermaceti and ambergris. [short for *spermaceti whale*]

spew (spjuː) *vb.* **1.** to vomit. **2.** (usually foll. by *out*) to send or be sent out in or as if in a stream: *flames spewed out.* [Old English *spīwan*]

sphagnum ('sfægnəm) *n.* a moss which is found in bogs and which decays to form peat. [Greek *sphagnos*]

sphere (sfɪə) *n.* **1.** *Geom.* a round solid figure in which every point on the surface is equally distant from the centre. **2.** an object having this shape, such as a planet. **3.** a particular field of activity. **4.** a social class. [Greek *sphaira*]

spherical ('sferɪk²l) *adj.* shaped like a sphere.

spheroid ('sfɪərɔɪd) *n.* *Geom.* a solid figure that is almost but not exactly a sphere.

sphincter ('sfɪŋktə) *n.* *Anat.* a ring of muscle surrounding the opening of a hollow organ and contracting to close it. [Greek *sphingein* to grip tightly]

sphinx (sfɪŋks) *n.* **1.** one of the huge statues built by the ancient Egyptians, having the body of a lion and the head of a man. **2.** a mysterious person.

Sphinx (sfɪŋks) *n.* **the. 1.** *Greek myth.* a monster with a woman's head and a lion's body, who set a riddle for travellers, killing them when they failed to answer it. Oedipus answered the riddle and the Sphinx then killed herself. **2.** the huge statue of a sphinx near the pyramids at El Gîza in Egypt. [Greek]

spice (spaɪs) *n.* **1. a.** an aromatic substance, such as ginger or cinnamon, used as flavouring. **b.** such substances collective-ly. **2.** something that adds zest or interest. ~*vb.* **3.** to flavour (food) with spices. **4.** to add zest or interest to (something): *his speech was spiced up with a few jokes.* [Old French *espice*]

spick-and-span *or* **spic-and-span** ('spɪkən'spæn) *adj.* very neat and clean. [obs. *spick* spike + *span*-new absolutely new, like a freshly cut spike]

spicy ('spaɪsɪ) *adj.* **spicier, spiciest. 1.** flavoured with spice. **2.** *Informal.* suggestive of scandal: *a spicy piece of gossip.*

spider ('spaɪdə) *n.* a small eight-legged creature, many species of which weave webs in which to trap insects for food. [Old English *spīthra*] —'**spidery** *adj.*

spider monkey *n.* a tree-living monkey with very long legs, a long prehensile tail, and a small head.

spiel (ʃpiːl) *n.* glib plausible talk, associated mainly with salesmen. [German *Spiel* play]

spigot ('spɪgət) *n.* **1.** a stopper for the vent hole of a cask. **2.** a wooden tap fitted to a cask. [prob. from Latin *spīca* a point]

spike[1] (spaɪk) *n.* **1.** a sharp point. **2.** a sharp-pointed metal object. **3.** a long metal nail. **4.** (*pl.*) sports shoes with metal spikes on the soles for greater grip. ~*vb.* **5.** to secure or supply (something) with spikes: *spiked shoes.* **6.** to impale on or injure with a spike or spikes. **7.** to add alcohol to (a drink). [Middle English *spyk*] —'**spiky** *adj.*

spike[2] (spaɪk) *n.* *Bot.* **1.** an arrangement of flowers attached at the base to a long stem. **2.** an ear of grain. [Latin *spīca* ear of corn]

spikenard ('spaɪknɑːd, 'spaɪkə,nɑːd) *n.* **1.** a fragrant Indian plant with rose-purple flowers. **2.** an ointment obtained from this plant. [Medieval Latin *spīca nardī*]

spill[1] (spɪl) *vb.* **spilling; spilt** *or* **spilled. 1.** to fall or cause to fall from or as from a container by accident. **2.** (of large numbers of people) to come out of a place: *the crowds spilled out on the street.* **3.** to shed (blood). **4. spill the beans.** *Informal.* to give away a secret. ~*n.* **5.** *Informal.* a fall or tumble. **6.** an amount of liquid spilt. [Old English *spillan* to destroy] —'**spillage** *n.*

spill[2] (spɪl) *n.* a splinter of wood or strip of paper for lighting pipes or fires. [Germanic]

spillikin ('spɪlɪkɪn) *n.* a strip of wood, cardboard, or plastic used in spillikins.

spillikins ('spɪlɪkɪnz) *n.* (*functioning as sing.*) *Brit.* a game in which players try to pick each spillikin from a heap without moving the others.

spin (spɪn) *vb.* **spinning, spun. 1.** to rotate or cause to rotate rapidly. **2.** to draw out and twist (natural fibres, such as silk or cotton) into a long continuous thread. **3.** (of a spider or silkworm) to form (a web or cocoon) from a silky fibre that comes out of the body. **4. spin a yarn.** to tell an improbable story. **5.** *Sport.* to throw, hit, or kick (a ball) so that it spins and changes direction or changes speed on bouncing. **6.** same as **spin-dry. 7.** to reel or grow dizzy: *my head is spinning.* ~*n.* **8.** a rapid rotating motion. **9.** a flight manoeuvre in which an aircraft performs a continuous spiral descent. **10.** *Sport.* a spinning motion given to a ball. **11.** *Informal.* a short car drive taken for pleasure. ~See also **spin out.** [Old English *spinnan*] —**'spinning** *n.*

spina bifida ('spaɪnə 'bɪfɪdə) *n.* a congenital condition in which part of the spinal cord protrudes through a gap in the backbone, sometimes causing paralysis. [New Latin: split spine]

spinach ('spɪnɪdʒ, -ɪtʃ) *n.* a dark green leafy vegetable. [Arabic *isfānākh*]

spinal column *n.* same as **spine** (sense 1).

spinal cord *n.* the thick cord of nerve tissue within the spine, which connects the brain to the nerves of the body.

spin bowler *n. Cricket.* same as **spinner** (sense 1b).

spindle ('spɪnd°l) *n.* **1.** a rod with a notch in the top for drawing out, twisting and winding the thread in spinning. **2.** a rotating rod that acts as an axle. [Old English *spinel*]

spindlelegs ('spɪnd°l,lɛgz) *or* **spindle-shanks** *n.* (*functioning as sing.*) a person with long thin legs.

spindly ('spɪndlɪ) *adj.* **-dlier, -dliest.** tall, slender, and frail.

spindrift ('spɪn,drɪft) *n.* spray blown up from the sea. [Scot. var. of *spoondrift*, from *spoon* to scud + *drift*]

spin-dry *vb.* **-drying, -dried.** to dry (clothes) in a spin-dryer.

spin-dryer *n.* a device that extracts water from clothes by spinning them in a perforated drum.

spine (spaɪn) *n.* **1.** the row of bony segments that surround and protect the spinal column. **2.** the back of a book, record sleeve, or video-tape box. **3.** a sharp point on the body of an animal or on a plant. [Latin *spīna*] —**'spinal** *adj.*

spine-chiller *n.* a film or story that arouses terror. —**'spine-,chilling** *adj.*

spineless ('spaɪnlɪs) *adj.* **1.** lacking character, willpower, or courage. **2.** having no spine.

spinet (spɪ'nɛt, 'spɪnɪt) *n.* a small harpsichord. [Italian *spinetta*]

spinnaker ('spɪnəkə; *Naut.* 'spæŋkə) *n.* a large triangular sail set from the foremast of a racing yacht. [prob. from *spin* but traditionally from *Sphinx*, the yacht that first used this type of sail]

spinner ('spɪnə) *n.* **1.** *Cricket.* **a.** a ball that is bowled with a spinning motion. **b.** a bowler who specializes in bowling such balls. **2.** a fishing lure that revolves in the water. **3.** a person or thing that spins.

spinneret ('spɪnə,rɛt) *n.* an organ through which silk threads come out of the body of a spider or insect.

spinney ('spɪnɪ) *n. Chiefly Brit.* a small wood. [Old French *espinei*]

spinning jenny *n.* an early type of spinning frame with several spindles.

spinning wheel *n.* a wheel-like machine

for spinning at home, having one hand- or foot-operated spindle.

spin-off *n.* **1.** a product or development derived incidentally as a result of activities designed to achieve something else. **2.** a television series derived from an earlier successful series.

spin out *vb.* **1.** to take longer than necessary to do (something). **2.** to make (money) last as long as possible.

spinster ('spɪnstə) *n.* an unmarried woman. [Middle English in the sense: a woman who spins] —**'spinsterish** *adj.*

spiny ('spaɪnɪ) *adj.* **spinier, spiniest.** (of animals or plants) covered with spines.

spiracle ('spaɪərək°l, 'spaɪrə-) *n. Zool.* a small blowhole for breathing through, such as that of a whale. [Latin *spīrāculum* vent]

spiraea *or esp. U.S.* **spirea** (spaɪ'rɪə) *n.* a plant with small white or pink flowers. [Greek *speiraia*]

spiral ('spaɪərəl) *n.* **1.** *Geom.* a plane curve formed by a point winding about a fixed point at an ever-increasing distance from it. **2.** something that follows a winding course or that has a twisting form. **3.** *Econ.* a continuous upward or downward movement in economic activity or prices. ~*adj.* **4.** having the shape of a spiral. ~*vb.* **-ralling, -ralled** *or U.S.* **-raling, -raled.** **5.** to follow a spiral course or be in the shape of a spiral. **6.** to increase or decrease with steady acceleration: *prices continue to spiral.* [Latin *spīra* a coil] —**'spirally** *adv.*

spire ('spaɪə) *n.* a tall structure that tapers upwards to a point, as on the roof of a church. [Old English *spīr* blade]

spirit[1] ('spɪrɪt) *n.* **1.** the force that gives life to the body of living things. **2.** temperament or disposition: *noble in spirit.* **3.** liveliness: *they set to it with spirit.* **4.** the fundamental, emotional, and activating principle of a person; will: *the experience broke his spirit.* **5.** the prevailing feeling: *a spirit of joy pervaded the atmosphere.* **6.** mood or attitude: *he did it in the wrong spirit.* **7.** (*pl.*) an emotional state: *in high spirits.* **8.** the deeper more significant meaning as opposed to a literal interpretation: *the spirit of the law.* **9.** the nonphysical aspect of a person: *I shall be with you in spirit.* **10.** a ghostly being, usually the soul of a dead person. ~*vb.* **11.** (foll. by *away* or *off*) to carry (someone or something) off mysteriously or secretly. [Latin *spīritus* breath, spirit]

spirit[2] ('spɪrɪt) *n.* **1.** distilled alcoholic liquor, such as whisky or gin. **2.** *Chem.* **a.** a solution of ethanol obtained by distillation. **b.** the essence of a substance, extracted as a liquid by distillation. **3.** *Pharmacol.* a solution of a volatile oil in alcohol. [special use of SPIRIT[1]]

spirited ('spɪrɪtɪd) *adj.* **1.** showing animation, vigour, or liveliness. **2.** characterized by mood or disposition as specified: *high-spirited; public-spirited.*

spirit gum *n.* a solution of gum in ether, used to stick on false hair.

spirit lamp *n.* a lamp that burns methylated or other spirits instead of oil.

spirit level *n.* a device for checking whether a surface is level, which consists of a block of wood or metal containing a tube partially filled with liquid set so that the air bubble in it rests between two marks on the tube when the block is level.

spiritual (ˈspɪrɪtjʊəl) *adj.* **1.** relating to the spirit or soul and not to physical things. **2.** relating to sacred things. ~*n.* **3.** Also called: **Negro spiritual.** a type of religious song originating among Black slaves in the American South. —**spirituality** (ˌspɪrɪtjʊˈælɪtɪ) *n.* —**ˈspiritually** *adv.*

spiritualism (ˈspɪrɪtjʊəˌlɪzəm) *n.* the belief that the spirits of the dead can communicate with the living. —**ˈspiritualist** *n.*

spirituous (ˈspɪrɪtjʊəs) *adj.* containing alcohol.

spirogyra (ˌspaɪrəˈdʒaɪrə) *n.* a multicellular green freshwater plant that floats on the surface of ponds and ditches. [Greek *speira* a coil + *guros* a circle]

spit[1] (spɪt) *vb.* **spitting, spat** *or* **spit. 1.** to force saliva out of one's mouth. **2.** *Informal.* to show scorn or hatred by spitting. **3.** (often foll. by *out*) to force (something) out of one's mouth: *he spat the food out.* **4.** (of a fire or hot fat) to throw out sparks or particles violently and explosively. **5.** to rain very lightly. **6.** (often foll. by *out*) to utter (short sharp words) in a violent manner. **7. spit it out!** *Brit. informal.* a command given to someone to say what is on his mind. ~*n.* **8.** same as **spittle. 9.** *Informal, chiefly Brit.* same as **spitting image.** [Old English *spittan*]

spit[2] (spɪt) *n.* **1.** a pointed rod on which meat is skewered and roasted over a fire or in an oven. **2.** a long strip of land projecting from a shore. [Old English *spitu*]

spit and polish *n. Informal.* strict attention to neatness and cleanliness, as in the armed forces.

spite (spaɪt) *n.* **1.** maliciousness; deliberate nastiness. **2. in spite of.** regardless of: *he went in spite of my warning.* ~*vb.* **3.** to annoy (someone) deliberately, out of spite: *she went out with Tom just to spite John.* [var. of *despite*] —**ˈspiteful** *adj.* —**ˈspitefully** *adv.*

spitfire (ˈspɪtˌfaɪə) *n.* a woman or girl who often has outbursts of spiteful temper.

spitting image *n. Informal.* a person who bears a strong physical resemblance to another. [from *spit* likeness]

spittle (ˈspɪtᵊl) *n.* the fluid that is produced in the mouth; saliva. [Old English *spætl* saliva]

spittoon (spɪˈtuːn) *n.* a bowl for spittle.

spitz (spɪts) *n.* a dog with a stocky build, a pointed face, erect ears, and a tightly curled tail. [from German]

spiv (spɪv) *n. Brit. slang.* a person who makes a living by underhand dealings; black marketeer. [dialect *spiving* smart]

splake (spleɪk) *n.* the hybrid offspring of a speckled trout and a lake trout. [*sp(eckled)* + *lake (trout)*]

splash (splæʃ) *vb.* **1.** to scatter (liquid) about in blobs; spatter. **2.** to cause (liquid) to fall or (of liquid) to fall upon (something) in scattered blobs. **3.** to print (a story or photograph) prominently in a newspaper. ~*n.* **4.** a splashing sound. **5.** an amount splashed. **6.** a mark created by or as if by splashing. **7. make a splash.** *Informal.* to attract a lot of attention. **8.** a small amount of liquid added to a drink. [alteration of *plash*]

splashdown (ˈsplæʃˌdaʊn) *n.* **1.** the landing of a spacecraft on water at the end of a flight. ~*vb.* **splash down. 2.** (of a spacecraft) to make a splashdown.

splatter (ˈsplætə) *vb.* **1.** to splash (something or someone) with small blobs. ~*n.* **2.** a splash of liquid.

splay (spleɪ) *vb.* to spread out; turn out or expand: *splayed fingers.* [short for *display*]

splayfooted (ˈspleɪˌfʊtɪd) *adj.* same as **flat-footed.**

spleen (spliːn) *n.* **1.** a spongy organ near the stomach, which filters bacteria from the blood. **2.** spitefulness or ill humour: *to vent one's spleen.* [Greek *splēn*]

spleenwort (ˈspliːnˌwɜːt) *n.* a kind of fern that grows on walls.

splendid (ˈsplɛndɪd) *adj.* **1.** very good: *a splendid idea.* **2.** brilliant or fine in appearance. [Latin *splendēre* to shine] —**ˈsplendidly** *adv.*

splendiferous (splɛnˈdɪfərəs) *adj. Facetious.* grand; splendid. [Latin *splendor* radiance + *ferre* to bring]

splendour *or U.S.* **splendor** (ˈsplɛndə) *n.* the state or quality of being splendid.

splenetic (splɪˈnɛtɪk) *adj.* spiteful or irritable. [from *spleen*]

splice (splaɪs) *vb.* **1.** to join up the trimmed ends of (two pieces of wire, film, or tape) with an adhesive material. **2.** to join (two ropes) by intertwining the strands. **3. get spliced.** *Informal.* to get married. [prob. from Middle Dutch *splissen*]

splint (splɪnt) *n.* a piece of wood used to support and restrict movement of a broken bone. [Middle Low German *splinte*]

splinter (ˈsplɪntə) *n.* **1.** a small thin sharp piece of wood or other material, broken off from something. ~*vb.* **2.** to break or be broken into small sharp fragments. [Middle Dutch *splinter*]

splinter group *n.* a number of members of an organization, who split from the main body and form an independent group of their own.

split (splɪt) *vb.* **splitting, split. 1.** to break or cause (something) to break into separate pieces. **2.** to separate (a piece) or (of a piece) to be separated from (something). **3.** to separate (a group) or (of a group) to be separated into smaller groups, through disagreement. **4.** (of a couple or group) to separate or to cause (a couple or group) to separate through disagreement. **5.** (often foll. by *up*) to divide (something) among two or more persons. **6.** *Slang.* to depart; leave. **7.** (foll. by *on*) *Slang.* to betray; inform: *he split on me to the cops.* **8. split one's sides.** to laugh heartily. ~*n.* **9.** a gap or rift caused by splitting. **10.** a division in a group or the smaller group resulting from such a division. **11.** a dessert of sliced fruit and ice cream, covered with whipped cream and nuts: *banana split.* ~*adj.* **12.** having a split or splits: *split ends.* ~See also **splits, split up.** [Middle Dutch *splitten*]

split infinitive *n.* (in English grammar) an infinitive used with another word between *to* and the verb, as in *to really finish it.* This practice is not universally accepted.

split-level *adj.* (of a house or room) having the floor level of one part about half a storey above that of the other.

split pea *n.* a pea dried and split and used in soups or as a vegetable.

split personality *n.* **1.** the tendency to change mood rapidly. **2.** a mental disorder in which a person's mind appears to have separated into two or more personalities.

splits (splɪts) *n.* (*functioning as sing.*) (in gymnastics and dancing) the act of sinking to the floor into a sitting position, with both legs straight, pointing in opposite directions, and at right angles to the body.

split second *n.* **1.** an extremely short period of time; instant. ~*adj.* **split-second.** **2.** made in an extremely short time: *a split-second decision.*

splitting (ˈsplɪtɪŋ) *adj.* (of a headache) extremely painful.

split up *vb.* **1.** to separate (something) into parts; divide. **2.** to become parted through disagreement. ~*n.* **split-up.** **3.** a separating.

splodge (splɒdʒ) *or U.S.* **splotch** (splɒtʃ) *n.* **1.** a large irregular spot. ~*vb.* **2.** to mark (something) with a splodge or splodges. [alteration of earlier *splotch*]

splurge (splɜːdʒ) *n.* **1.** a bout of extravagance. ~*vb.* **2.** (foll. by *on*) to spend (money) extravagantly: *he splurged his wages on a new suit.* [origin unknown]

splutter (ˈsplʌtə) *vb.* **1.** to spit out (something) from the mouth in an explosive manner, as through choking or laughing. **2.** to utter (words) with spitting sounds, as through rage or choking. **3.** to throw out or to be thrown out in an explosive manner: *sparks spluttered from the fire.* ~*n.* **4.** the act or noise of spluttering. [var. of *sputter*]

Spode (spəʊd) *n.* china or porcelain manufactured by the English potter Josiah Spode or his company.

spoil (spɔɪl) *vb.* **spoiling, spoilt** *or* **spoiled.** **1.** to damage (something), with regard to its value, beauty, or usefulness. **2.** to weaken the character of (a child) by giving it all it wants. **3.** (of perishable substances) to become unfit for consumption or use. **4. be spoiling for.** to have an aggressive desire for: *they are spoiling for a fight.* ~See also **spoils.** [Latin *spolium* booty]

spoilage (ˈspɔɪlɪdʒ) *n.* an amount of material that has been spoilt.

spoiler (ˈspɔɪlə) *n.* **1.** a device fitted to an aircraft wing to increase drag and reduce lift. **2.** a similar device fitted to a car.

spoils (spɔɪlz) *pl. n.* **1.** valuables seized by violence: *the spoils of war.* **2.** the rewards and benefits of public office.

spoilsport (ˈspɔɪlˌspɔːt) *n. Informal.* a person who spoils the pleasure of other people.

spoke[1] (spəʊk) *vb.* the past tense of **speak.**

spoke[2] (spəʊk) *n.* **1.** a bar joining the centre of a wheel to the rim. **2. put a spoke in someone's wheel.** *Brit.* to hinder someone's plans. [Old English *spaca*]

spoken (ˈspəʊkən) *vb.* **1.** the past participle of **speak.** ~*adj.* **2.** uttered in speech: *the spoken word.* **3.** having speech as specified: *soft-spoken.* **4. spoken for.** engaged or reserved.

spokesman (ˈspəʊksmən), **spokesperson** (ˈspəʊksˌpɜːsˀn), *or* **spokeswoman** (ˈspəʊksˌwʊmən) *n., pl.* **-men,** **-persons** *or* **-people,** *or* **-women.** a person authorized to speak on behalf of another person or group.

spoliation (ˌspəʊlɪˈeɪʃən) *n.* a plundering. [Latin *spoliāre* to plunder]

spondee (ˈspɒndiː) *n. Prosody.* a metrical foot consisting of two long syllables (ˉˉ). [Greek *spondē* ritual] —**spondaic** (spɒnˈdeɪɪk) *adj.*

sponge (spʌndʒ) *n.* **1.** a sea animal with a porous absorbent elastic skeleton. **2.** the skeleton of a sponge, or a piece of artificial sponge, used for bathing or cleaning. **3.** a soft absorbent material like a sponge. **4.** same as **sponge cake.** **5.** Also called: **sponge pudding.** *Brit.* a light steamed or baked spongy pudding. **6.** a rub with a wet sponge. **7. throw in the sponge.** See **throw in** (sense 3). ~*vb.* **8.** (often foll. by *down*) to clean (something) by rubbing it with a wet sponge. **9.** (usually foll. by *off, away,* or *out*) to remove (marks) by rubbing them with a wet sponge. **10.** to get (something) from someone by taking advantage of his generosity: *he sponges money off her; he sponges off his wife.* [Greek *spongia*] —**spongy** *adj.*

sponge bag *n.* a small waterproof bag for holding toilet articles when travelling.

sponge cake *n.* a light cake made of eggs, sugar, and flour.

sponger (ˈspʌndʒə) *n. Informal.* a person who lives off other people by continually taking advantage of their generosity.

sponsor (ˈspɒnsə) *n.* **1.** a person or group that promotes another person or group in an activity or the activity itself, either for profit or for charity. **2.** *Chiefly U.S. & Canad.* a person or firm that pays the costs of a radio or television programme in return for advertising time. **3.** a person who presents and supports a proposal or suggestion. **4.** a person who makes certain promises on behalf of a person being baptized and takes responsibility for his Christian upbringing. ~*vb.* **5.** to act as a sponsor for (someone or something). [Latin *spondēre* to promise solemnly] —**sponsored** *adj.* —**ˈsponsorˌship** *n.*

spontaneous (spɒnˈteɪnɪəs) *adj.* **1.** arising from a natural impulse; voluntary; unpremeditated: *spontaneous applause*. **2.** occurring or produced through natural processes without outside influence. [Latin *sponte* voluntarily] —**spon'taneously** *adv*. —**spontaneity** (ˌspɒntə'niːɪtɪ, -'neɪ-) *n*.

spontaneous combustion *n. Chem.* the bursting into flame of a substance as a result of internal oxidation processes, without heat from an outside source.

spoof (spuːf) *Informal*. ~*n*. **1.** a mildly satirical parody. **2.** a good-humoured deception or trick. ~*vb*. **3.** to indulge in a spoof of (a person or thing). [made-up word]

spook (spuːk) *Informal*. ~*n*. **1.** a ghost. **2.** a strange and frightening person. ~*vb*. *U.S. & Canad.* **3.** to frighten: *to spook a person*. [Dutch] —**spooky** *adj*.

spool (spuːl) *n*. a cylinder around which film, thread, tape, or wire can be wound. [Germanic]

spoon (spuːn) *n*. **1.** a small shallow bowl attached to a handle, used for eating, stirring, or serving food. **2. be born with a silver spoon in one's mouth.** to inherit wealth or social standing. ~*vb*. **3.** to scoop up (food or liquid) with or as if with a spoon. **4.** *Old-fashioned slang*. to kiss and cuddle. [Old English *spōn* splinter]

spoonbill ('spuːnˌbɪl) *n*. a wading bird with a long flat bill.

spoonerism ('spuːnəˌrɪzəm) *n*. the accidental changing over of the first sounds of a pair of words, often with an amusing result, such as *hush my brat* for *brush my hat*. [after W. A. *Spooner*, clergyman]

spoon-feed *vb*. **-feeding, -fed**. **1.** to feed (someone, usually a baby) using a spoon. **2.** to overindulge or spoil (someone).

spoor (spuə, spɔː) *n*. the trail of an animal. [Afrikaans]

sporadic (spə'rædɪk) *adj*. occurring at irregular points in time; intermittent: *sporadic firing*. [Greek *sporas* scattered] —**spo'radically** *adv*.

spore (spɔː) *n*. a reproductive body, produced by many plants, that develops into a new individual. [Greek *spora* a sowing]

sporran ('spɒrən) *n*. a large pouch worn hanging from a belt in front of the kilt in Scottish Highland dress. [Scot. Gaelic *sporan* purse]

sport (spɔːt) *n*. **1.** an individual or group activity pursued for exercise or pleasure, often having a competitive form: *football is my favourite sport*. **2.** such activities collectively: *do you like sport?* **3.** the pleasure derived from a pastime: *they hunt for sport rather than for food*. **4.** playful or good-humoured joking: *I only did it in sport*. **5. make sport of someone**. to mock someone. **6.** *Informal*. a person who reacts cheerfully even in trying circumstances; a good loser. **7.** an animal or plant that differs markedly from others of the same species, usually because of a mutation. **8.** *Austral. & N.Z. informal*. a term of address between males. ~*vb*. **9.** *Informal*. to

wear proudly: *she was sporting a new hat*. ~**See also sports**. [var. of Middle English *disporten* to disport]

sporting ('spɔːtɪŋ) *adj*. **1.** of sport. **2.** conforming to the ideas of sportsmanship; fair. **3. a sporting chance**. likelihood of a favourable outcome: *she's got a sporting chance of getting the job*.

sportive ('spɔːtɪv) *adj*. playful or joyous.

sports (spɔːts) *n*. **1.** (*modifier*) of or used in sports: *sports equipment*. **2.** Also called: **sports day**. *Brit*. a meeting held at a school or college for competitions in various athletic events.

sports car *n*. a fast car having a low body and usually seating only two persons.

sportscast ('spɔːtsˌkɑːst) *n. U.S.* a broadcast consisting of sports news. —**'sportsˌcaster** *n*.

sports jacket *n*. a man's informal jacket, usually made of tweed. Also called (*U.S., Austral., & N.Z.*): **sports coat**.

sportsman ('spɔːtsmən) *n., pl*. **-men**. **1.** a man who plays sports. **2.** a person who shows fairness, observance of the rules, and good humour when losing. —**'sportsman-ˌlike** *adj*. —**'sportsman-ˌship** *n*.

sportsperson ('spɔːtsˌpɜːs'n) *n*. a person who plays sports.

sportswear ('spɔːtsˌwɛə) *n*. clothes worn for sport or outdoor leisure wear.

sportswoman ('spɔːtsˌwumən) *n., pl*. **-women**. a woman who plays sports.

sporty ('spɔːtɪ) *adj*. **sportier, sportiest**. **1.** (of a person) interested in sport. **2.** (of cloths) suitable for sport. **3.** (of a car) small and fast.

spot (spɒt) *n*. **1.** a small mark on a surface, which has a different colour or texture from its surroundings: *this is the exact spot*. **2.** a location: *this is the exact spot*. **3.** a blemish or pimple on the skin. **4.** a flaw in a person's character. **5.** *Informal, chiefly Brit*. a small amount: *a spot of lunch*. **6.** *Informal*. an awkward situation: *I'm in a spot*. **7.** a short period between regular television or radio programmes that is used for advertising. **8.** a part of a show assigned to a specific performer. **9.** short for **spotlight** (sense 1). **10. high spot**. an outstanding event: *the high spot of the holiday*. **11. in a tight spot**. in a difficult situation. **12. knock spots off someone**. to be much better than someone. **13. on the spot. a.** immediately: *he died on the spot*. **b.** at the place in question: *the police were on the spot within minutes*. **c.** in an awkward predicament: *you've really put me on the spot*. **14. soft spot**. a special affection for someone: *I've always had a soft spot for Paul*. ~*vb*. **spotting, spotted**. **15.** to see (something or someone) suddenly. **16.** to put stains or spots on (something). **17.** (of some fabrics) to be susceptible to spotting by or as if by water: *silk spots easily*. **18.** to look out for and note (trains, planes, or talent). **19.** to rain lightly. [from German] —**'spotless** *adj*. —**'spotlessly** *adv*. —**'spotlessness** *n*.

spot check n. a quick random examination.

spotlight ('spɒt,laɪt) n. **1.** a powerful light focused so as to light up a small area. **2. the.** the centre of attention: *he's tired of being in the spotlight.* ~vb. **-lighting, -lit** or **-lighted. 3.** to direct a spotlight on (something). **4.** to focus attention on (something).

spot-on adj. Brit. informal. absolutely correct; very accurate: *her impression of the Prime Minister was spot-on.*

spotted ('spɒtɪd) adj. **1.** having a pattern of spots. **2.** stained or blemished.

spotted dick n. Brit. suet pudding containing dried fruit.

spotter ('spɒtə) n. a person whose hobby is watching for and noting numbers or types of trains or planes.

spotty ('spɒtɪ) adj. **-tier, -tiest. 1.** having spots or marks. **2.** not consistent; irregular or uneven. —**'spottiness** n.

spouse (spaʊs, spaʊz) n. a person's partner in marriage. [Latin *sponsus, sponsa* betrothed man or woman]

spout (spaʊt) vb. **1.** to discharge (a liquid) in a stream or jet or (of a liquid) to gush thus. **2.** Informal. to utter (a stream of words), often in a boring manner. ~n. **3.** a projecting tube or lip allowing the pouring of liquids. **4.** a stream or jet of liquid. **5. up the spout.** Slang. **a.** ruined or lost: *our plans are up the spout.* **b.** pregnant. [Middle English *spouten*]

spouting ('spaʊtɪŋ) n. N.Z. **a.** a rainwater downpipe on the outside of a building. **b.** such pipes collectively.

sprain (spreɪn) vb. **1.** to injure (a joint) by a sudden twist. ~n. **2.** this injury, which causes swelling and temporary disability. [origin unknown]

sprang (spræŋ) vb. a past tense of **spring.**

sprat (spræt) n. a small food fish of the herring family. [Old English *sprott*]

sprawl (sprɔːl) vb. **1.** to sit or lie in an ungainly manner with one's limbs spread out. **2.** to spread out in a straggling fashion: *his handwriting sprawled all over the paper.* ~n. **3.** a sprawling arrangement: *urban sprawl.* [Old English *spreawlian*] —**'sprawling** adj.

spray[1] (spreɪ) n. **1.** fine particles of a liquid. **2. a.** a liquid designed to be discharged from an aerosol or atomizer: *hair spray.* **b.** the aerosol or atomizer itself. **3.** a number of small objects flying through the air: *a spray of bullets.* ~vb. **4.** to scatter (liquid) in fine particles. **5.** to squirt (a liquid) from an aerosol or atomizer. **6.** to cover with a spray: *to spray the lawn.* [Middle Dutch *sprāien*]

spray[2] (spreɪ) n. **1.** a sprig or branch with buds, leaves, flowers, or berries. **2.** an ornament or design like this. [Germanic]

spray gun n. a device that sprays fine particles of a fluid such as paint.

spread (sprɛd) vb. **spreading, spread. 1.** to extend or unfold to the fullest width: *she spread the map.* **2.** to extend over a larger expanse: *the political unrest spread over several years.* **3.** to apply or be applied in a coating: *spread jam on the bread.* **4.** to be displayed to its fullest extent: *the landscape spread before us.* **5.** to send or be sent out in all directions; distribute or be distributed: *someone is spreading rumours; the disease spread quickly.* ~n. **6.** a spreading; distribution, dispersion, or expansion. **7.** Informal. the wingspan of an aircraft or bird. **8.** Informal, chiefly U.S. & Canad. a ranch or other large area of land. **9.** Informal. a large meal. **10.** a soft food which can be spread: *salmon spread.* **11.** two facing pages in a book or magazine. **12.** a widening of the hips and waist: *middle-age spread.* [Old English *sprǣdan*]

spread-eagled adj. with arms and legs outstretched.

spree (spriː) n. a bout of overindulgence, usually in drinking or in spending money. [Scot. *spreath* plundered cattle]

sprig (sprɪg) n. **1.** a shoot, twig, or sprout. **2.** an ornamental device like this. ~vb. **sprigging, sprigged. 3.** to ornament (fabric) with a design of sprigs. [Germanic]

sprightly ('spraɪtlɪ) adj. **-lier, -liest.** full of vitality; lively and brisk. [obs. *spright*, var. of *sprite*] —**'sprightliness** n.

spring (sprɪŋ) vb. **springing, sprang** or **sprung; sprung. 1.** to jump suddenly upwards or forwards. **2.** to release or be released from a forced position by elasticity: *the bolt sprang back.* **3.** to cause (something) to happen unexpectedly: *to spring a surprise.* **4.** (usually foll. by *from*) to originate; be descended: *the idea sprang from a chance meeting; he sprang from peasant stock.* **5.** (often foll. by *up*) to come into being or appear suddenly: *factories springing up.* **6.** to provide (something, such as a mattress) with springs. **7.** Informal. to arrange the escape of (someone) from prison. ~n. **8.** a leap or jump. **9.** the quality of resilience; elasticity. **10.** a natural pool forming the source of a stream. **11.** a coil which can be compressed, stretched, or bent and then return to its original shape when released. **12.** the season between winter and summer. [Old English *springan*] —**'spring-,like** adj.

spring balance or esp. U.S. **spring scale** n. a device that indicates the weight of an object by the extension of a spring to which the object is attached.

springboard ('sprɪŋ,bɔːd) n. **1.** a flexible board used to gain height or momentum in diving or gymnastics. **2.** anything that serves as a beginning or impetus.

springbok ('sprɪŋ,bɒk) n., pl. **-bok** or **-boks.** a S African antelope which moves in leaps. [Afrikaans]

spring chicken n. **1.** Chiefly U.S. a young chicken, which is tender for cooking. **2. he** or **she is no spring chicken.** Informal. he or she is no longer young.

spring-clean vb. **1.** to clean (a house) thoroughly, traditionally at the end of winter. ~n. **2.** an instance of this. —**,spring-'cleaning** n.

springer spaniel or **springer** ('sprɪŋə) n. a spaniel with a slightly domed head and ears of medium length.

spring onion *n.* an immature onion with a tiny bulb and long green leaves, eaten in salads.

spring tide *n.* either of the two tides at or just after new moon and full moon: the greatest rise and fall in tidal level.

springtime ('sprɪŋ,taɪm) *n.* the season of spring.

springy ('sprɪŋɪ) *adj.* **springier, springiest.** having resilience or elasticity. —'**springiness** *n.*

sprinkle ('sprɪŋk°l) *vb.* **1.** to scatter (liquid or powder) in tiny drops or particles over (something). **2.** to distribute over (something): *the field was sprinkled with flowers.* [prob. from Middle Dutch *sprenkelen*] —'**sprinkler** *n.*

sprinkling ('sprɪŋklɪŋ) *n.* a small quantity or amount: *a sprinkling of snow.*

sprint (sprɪnt) *n.* **1.** *Athletics.* **a.** a short race run at top speed. **b.** a fast run at the end of a longer race. **2.** any quick run. ~*vb.* **3.** to go at top speed, as in running or cycling. [Scandinavian] —'**sprinter** *n.*

sprit (sprɪt) *n. Naut.* a light spar crossing a sail diagonally from the mast to the peak. [Old English *spreot*]

sprite (spraɪt) *n.* (in folklore) an elf. [Latin *spiritus* spirit]

spritsail ('sprɪt,seɪl; *Naut.* 'sprɪtsəl) *n. Naut.* a sail mounted on a sprit.

spritzer ('sprɪtsə) *n.* a tall drink of wine and soda water. [German *spritzen* to splash]

sprocket ('sprɒkɪt) *n.* **1.** Also called: **sprocket wheel.** a wheel with teeth on the rim, that drives or is driven by a chain. **2.** a cylindrical wheel with teeth on one or both rims for pulling film through a camera or projector. [origin unknown]

sprout (spraʊt) *vb.* **1.** (of a plant or seed) to produce (new leaves or shoots). **2.** (often foll. by *up*) to begin to grow or develop. ~*n.* **3.** a new shoot or bud. **4.** same as **Brussels sprout.** [Old English *sprūtan*]

spruce[1] (spruːs) *n.* **1.** an evergreen pyramid-shaped tree with needle-like leaves and light-coloured wood. **2.** the wood of this tree. [obs. *Spruce* Prussia]

spruce[2] (spruːs) *adj.* neat and smart. [perhaps from *Spruce leather,* see SPRUCE[1]]

spruce up *vb.* to make neat and smart.

spruit (spreɪt) *n. S. African.* a small tributary stream or watercourse. [Afrikaans]

sprung (sprʌŋ) *vb.* a past tense and the past participle of **spring.**

spry (spraɪ) *adj.* **spryer, spryest** or **sprier, spriest.** active and brisk; nimble. [origin unknown]

spud (spʌd) *n. Informal.* a potato. [obs. *spudde* short knife]

spume (spjuːm) *n.* **1.** foam or froth. ~*vb.* **2.** to foam or froth. [Latin *spūma*]

spun (spʌn) *vb.* **1.** past of **spin.** ~*adj.* **2.** made by spinning: *spun gold; spun glass.*

spunk (spʌŋk) *n. Informal.* courage or spirit. [Scot. Gaelic *spong* tinder, sponge] —'**spunky** *adj.*

spur (spɜː) *n.* **1.** a sharp spiked wheel fixed to the heel of a rider's boot and used to urge his horse on. **2.** a stimulus or incentive. **3.** a sharp horny part sticking out from a cock's leg. **4.** a ridge sticking out from a mountain side. **5. on the spur of the moment.** on impulse. **6. win one's spurs.** to prove one's ability; gain distinction. ~*vb.* **spurring, spurred. 7.** (often foll. by *on*) to encourage (someone). [Old English *spura*]

spurge (spɜːdʒ) *n.* a plant with milky sap and small flowers. [Latin *expurgāre* to cleanse]

spurious ('spjʊərɪəs) *adj.* not genuine or real. [Latin *spurius* of illegitimate birth]

spurn (spɜːn) *vb.* to reject (a person or thing) with contempt. [Old English *spurnan*]

spurt (spɜːt) *vb.* **1.** to gush or cause (something) to gush out in a sudden stream or jet. **2.** to make a sudden effort. ~*n.* **3.** a short burst of activity, speed, or energy. **4.** a sudden stream or jet. [origin unknown]

sputnik ('spʊtnɪk) *n.* a Soviet artificial satellite. [Russian, lit.: fellow traveller]

sputter ('spʌtə) *vb., n.* same as **splutter.** [Dutch *sputteren,* imit.]

sputum ('spjuːtəm) *n., pl.* **-ta** (-tə). saliva, usually mixed with mucus. [Latin]

spy (spaɪ) *n., pl.* **spies. 1.** a person employed to obtain secret information about other countries or organizations. **2.** a person who secretly keeps watch on others. ~*vb.* **spying, spied. 3.** (foll. by *on*) to keep a secret watch on someone. **4.** to work as a spy. **5.** to catch sight of (someone or something). [Old French *espier*]

spyglass ('spaɪ,glɑːs) *n.* a small telescope.

spy out *vb.* to discover (something) secretly.

sq. square.

Sq. Square.

squab (skwɒb) *n., pl.* **squabs** or **squab.** a young unfledged bird. [prob. Germanic]

squabble ('skwɒb°l) *vb.* **1.** to quarrel over a small matter. ~*n.* **2.** a petty quarrel. [prob. Scandinavian]

squad (skwɒd) *n.* **1.** the smallest military formation, usually a dozen soldiers. **2.** any small group of people working together: *antiriot squads.* **3.** *Sport.* a number of players from which a team is to be selected. [Old French *esquade*]

squadron ('skwɒdrən) *n.* the basic unit of an air force. [Italian *squadrone* soldiers drawn up in square formation]

squadron leader *n.* a fairly senior commissioned officer in the air force.

squalid ('skwɒlɪd) *adj.* **1.** dirty and unattractive. **2.** morally sordid. [Latin *squālidus*]

squall[1] (skwɔːl) *n.* a sudden strong wind or brief violent storm. [perhaps a special use of SQUALL[2]]

squall[2] (skwɔːl) *vb.* **1.** to cry noisily; yell. ~*n.* **2.** a noisy cry or yell. [prob. Scandinavian]

squalor ('skwɒlə) *n.* the condition of being squalid; disgusting filth. [Latin]

squander ('skwɒndə) *vb.* to spend (money) wastefully. [origin unknown]

square (skwɛə) *n.* 1. a plane figure with four equal sides and four right angles. 2. anything of this shape. 3. an open area in a town, sometimes including the surrounding buildings, which may form a square. 4. *Maths.* the number produced when a number is multiplied by itself: *9 is the square of 3, written 3²*. 5. *Informal.* an old-fashioned person. 6. **go back to square one.** to return to the start because of failure or lack of progress. ~*adj.* 7. being a square in shape. 8. **a.** having the same area as that of a square with sides of a specified length: *a circle of four square feet.* **b.** denoting a square having a specified length on each side: *a board four feet square.* 9. fair and honest: *a square deal.* 10. *Informal.* old-fashioned. 11. having all debts or accounts settled: *if I give you 50 pence, then we'll be square.* 12. **all square.** on equal terms; even in score. 13. **square peg in a round hole.** *Informal.* a misfit. ~*vb.* 14. *Maths.* to multiply (a number or quantity) by itself. 15. to position so as to be straight or level: *to square the shoulders.* 16. to settle (a debt or account). 17. to level the score in (a game). 18. to agree or cause to agree: *your ideas don't square with mine.* ~*adv.* 19. *Informal.* same as **squarely.** ~See also **square off, square up.** [Old French *esquare*]

square-bashing *n. Brit. mil. slang.* drill on a barracks square.

square bracket *n.* either of a pair of characters [ ], used to separate a section of writing or printing from the main text.

square dance *n.* a formation dance in which the couples form squares.

square leg *n. Cricket.* a fielding position on the on the batsman's left.

squarely ('skwɛəlɪ) *adv.* 1. directly; straight: *he hit me squarely on the nose.* 2. in an honest, frank, and just manner: *he faced the problem squarely.*

square off *vb.* to assume a posture of opposition, as in boxing.

square-rigged *adj. Naut.* having sails set at right angles to the keel.

square root *n.* a number that when multiplied by itself gives a given number: *the square roots of 4 are 2 and −2.*

square up *vb.* 1. to settle bills or debts. 2. (foll. by *to*) to prepare to confront (a problem or a person).

squash¹ (skwɒʃ) *vb.* 1. to press or squeeze (something) so as to crush or flatten it. 2. to suppress or overcome (a person or thing). 3. to humiliate (someone) with a crushing retort. 4. (foll. by *in* or *into*) to push or force (oneself or a thing) into a confined space. ~*n.* 5. *Brit.* a drink made from fruit juice or fruit syrup diluted with water. 6. a crush, usually of people in a confined space. 7. Also called: **squash rackets.** a game for two players played in an enclosed court with a small rubber ball and long-handled rackets. [Old French *esquasser*]

squash² (skwɒʃ) *n., pl.* **squashes** or **squash.** *U.S. & Canad.* a marrow-like vegetable. [American Indian]

squashy ('skwɒʃɪ) *adj.* **squashier, squashiest.** easily squashed; pulpy.

squat (skwɒt) *vb.* **squatting, squatted.** 1. to crouch with the knees bent and the weight on the feet. 2. *Law.* to occupy an unused building to which one has no legal title. ~*adj.* 3. short and broad. ~*n.* 4. a building occupied by squatters. [Old French *esquater*]

squatter ('skwɒtə) *n.* a person who occupies an unused building to which he has no legal title.

squaw (skwɔ) *n. Offensive.* a North American Indian woman. [American Indian]

squawk (skwɔːk) *n.* 1. a loud harsh cry; screech. 2. *Informal.* a loud complaint. ~*vb.* 3. to make a squawk. [imit.]

squeak (skwiːk) *n.* 1. a short shrill cry or sound. 2. **a narrow squeak.** *Informal.* a narrow escape or success. ~*vb.* 3. to make a squeak. 4. (foll. by *through* or *by*) to pass (an examination) with only a narrow margin. [prob. Scandinavian] —'**squeaky** *adj.* —'**squeakiness** *n.*

squeal (skwiːl) *n.* 1. a high shrill yelp. ~*vb.* 2. to make a squeal. 3. *Slang.* to inform on someone to the police. 4. *Informal, chiefly Brit.* to complain loudly. [Middle English *squelen,* imit.] —'**squealer** *n.*

squeamish ('skwiːmɪʃ) *adj.* easily sickened, shocked, or frightened. [Anglo-French *escoymous*]

squeegee ('skwiːdʒiː) *n.* an implement with a rubber blade used for wiping away surplus water from a surface. [prob. imit.]

squeeze (skwiːz) *vb.* 1. to grip or press (something) firmly. 2. to crush or press (something) so as to extract (a liquid): *to squeeze an orange; freshly squeezed orange juice.* 3. to push or force (oneself or a thing) into a confined space. 4. to hug (someone) closely. 5. to put pressure on (someone) in order to obtain (something): *to squeeze money out of a victim by blackmail.* ~*n.* 6. a squeezing. 7. a hug. 8. a crush of people in a confined space. 9. *Chiefly Brit.* a restriction on borrowing imposed by a government to counteract price inflation. 10. an amount extracted by squeezing: *a squeeze of lemon juice.* 11. **put the squeeze on someone.** *Informal.* to out pressure on someone in order to obtain something. [Old English *cwȳsan*]

squelch (skwɛltʃ) *vb.* 1. to make a sucking noise, as by walking through mud. 2. *Informal.* to silence (someone) with a crushing retort. ~*n.* 3. a squelching sound. [imit.] —'**squelchy** *adj.*

squib (skwɪb) *n.* 1. a firework that burns with a hissing noise before exploding. 2. **damp squib.** something intended to impress but failing to do so. [prob. imit. of a light explosion]

squid (skwɪd) *n., pl.* **squid** or **squids.** a tenlimbed sea creature with a torpedo-shaped body. [origin unknown]

squiffy ('skwɪfɪ) adj. **-fier, -fiest.** Brit. informal. slightly drunk. [origin unknown]

squiggle ('skwɪg'l) n. a wavy line. [perhaps squirm + wiggle] —'**squiggly** adj.

squill (skwɪl) n. a Mediterranean plant of the lily family. [Greek skilla]

squint (skwɪnt) vb. **1.** to cross one's eyes partly. **2.** to have a squint. ~n. **3.** an eye disorder in which one or both eyes turn inwards or outwards from the nose. **4.** Informal. a quick look; glance: have a squint at this. ~adj. **5.** Informal. not straight; crooked. [short for asquint]

squire ('skwaɪə) n. **1.** a country gentleman in England, usually the main landowner in a country community. **2.** Informal, chiefly Brit. a term of address used by one man to another. ~vb. **3.** (of a man) to escort (a woman). [Old French esquier]

squirm (skwɜːm) vb. **1.** to wriggle. **2.** to feel deep discomfort, guilt, or embarrassment. ~n. **3.** a wriggling movement. [imit.]

squirrel ('skwɪrəl) n. a small bushy-tailed tree-living rodent which feeds on nuts. [Greek skiouros, from skia shadow + oura tail]

squirt (skwɜːt) vb. **1.** to force (a liquid) or (of a liquid) to be forced out of a narrow opening. **2.** to cover or spatter (a person or thing) with liquid in this manner. ~n. **3.** a jet of liquid. **4.** a squirting. **5.** Informal. an insignificant or contemptible short person. [imit.]

squish (skwɪʃ) vb. **1.** to crush (something) with a soft splashing noise. **2.** to make a splashing noise. ~n. **3.** a soft splashing sound. [imit.] —'**squishy** adj.

Sr 1. (after a name) senior. **2.** Señor. **3.** Chem. strontium.

Sri Lankan (srɪ 'læŋkən) adj. **1.** of Sri Lanka, a republic in S Asia, or its inhabitants. ~n. **2.** a person from Sri Lanka.

SRN (in Britain) State Registered Nurse.

SS 1. an organization in the Nazi party that provided Hitler's bodyguard, security forces, and concentration-camp guards. [German Schutzstaffel protection squad] **2.** steamship.

St 1. Saint. **2.** Street.

st. stone.

stab (stæb) vb. **stabbing, stabbed. 1.** to pierce (something) or injure (someone) with a sharp pointed instrument. **2.** (often foll. by at) to make a thrust (at); jab. **3. stab someone in the back.** to do harm to someone in a treacherous manner. ~n. **4.** a stabbing. **5.** a sudden, usually unpleasant, sensation: a stab of pity. **6.** Informal. an attempt: I'll have a stab at it. **7. stab in the back.** an action of betrayal that harms a person. [Middle English stabbe stab wound] —'**stabbing** n.

stability (stə'bɪlɪtɪ) n. the quality of being stable.

stabilize or **-ise** ('steɪbɪˌlaɪz) vb. to make or become stable or more stable. —,**stabili-** '**zation** or **-i**'**sation** n.

stabilizer or **-iser** ('steɪbɪˌlaɪzə) n. **1.** a device for stabilizing a child's bicycle, an aircraft, or a ship. **2.** a substance added to food to preserve its texture.

stable[1] ('steɪb'l) n. **1.** a building where horses are kept. **2.** an establishment that breeds and trains racehorses. **3.** Informal. a source of training: the two athletes were out of the same stable. ~vb. **4.** to put or keep (a horse) in a stable. [Latin stabulum shed]

stable[2] ('steɪb'l) adj. **1.** steady in position or balance; firm. **2.** lasting: a stable relationship. **3.** firm in character. **4.** (of an elementary particle) not subject to decay. **5.** (of a chemical compound) not easily decomposed. [Latin stabilis steady]

staccato (stə'kɑːtəʊ) adj. **1.** Music. (of notes) short and separate. **2.** consisting of short abrupt sounds: staccato cries. ~adv. **3.** in a staccato manner. [Italian]

stack (stæk) n. **1.** an ordered pile. **2.** a large orderly pile of hay or straw. **3.** (often pl.) a large amount. **4.** same as **chimney stack, smokestack. 5.** an area in a computer memory for temporary storage. ~vb. **6.** to place (things) in a stack. **7.** to load or fill (something) up with piles of objects: to stack a lorry with bricks. **8.** to control (a number of aircraft) waiting to land at an airport so that each flies at a different altitude. [Old Norse stakkr haystack]

stadium ('steɪdɪəm) n., pl. **-diums** or **-dia** (-dɪə). a sports arena with tiered seats for spectators. [Greek stadion]

staff (stɑːf) n., pl. **staffs** for senses 1 & 2; **staffs** or **staves** for senses 3 & 4. **1.** the people employed in a company, school, or organization. **2.** Mil. the officers appointed to assist a commander. **3.** a stick with some special use, such as a walking stick or an emblem of authority. **4.** Music. a set of five horizontal lines on which music is written and which, along with a clef, indicates pitch. ~vb. **5.** to provide (a company, school, or organization) with a staff. [Old English stæf]

staff nurse n. a qualified nurse ranking just below a sister or charge nurse.

Staffs. (stæfs) Staffordshire.

staff sergeant n. Mil. a noncommissioned officer in an army or in the U.S. Air Force or Marine Corps.

stag (stæg) n. **1.** the adult male of a deer. **2.** (modifier) (of a social gathering) attended by men only. [Old English stagga]

stag beetle n. a beetle with large branched jawbones.

stage (steɪdʒ) n. **1.** a distinct step or period of development, growth, or progress. **2.** the platform in a theatre where actors perform. **3. the.** the theatre as a profession. **4.** the scene of an event or action. **5.** a portion of a journey. **6.** short for **stagecoach. 7.** Brit. a division of a bus route for which there is a fixed fare. ~vb. **8.** to present (a dramatic production) on stage: to stage "Hamlet". **9.** to organize and carry out (an event). [Old French estage position]

stagecoach ('steɪdʒ,kəʊtʃ) n. a large four-wheeled horse-drawn vehicle formerly used to carry passengers and mail on a regular route.

stage direction n. an instruction to an actor, written into the script of a play.

stage door n. a door at a theatre leading backstage.

stage fright n. nervousness or panic felt by a person about to appear in front of an audience.

stagehand ('steɪdʒ,hænd) n. a person who sets the stage and moves props in a theatrical production.

stage-manage vb. to arrange (an event) from behind the scenes.

stage manager n. a person who supervises the stage arrangements of a theatrical production.

stage-struck adj. having an intense desire to act.

stage whisper n. 1. a loud whisper from an actor, intended to be heard by the audience. 2. any loud whisper that is intended to be overheard.

stagflation (stæg'fleɪʃən) n. inflation combined with stagnant or falling output and employment. [stagnation + inflation]

stagger ('stægə) vb. 1. to walk unsteadily. 2. to astound or overwhelm (someone), as with shock: I was staggered by his death. 3. to arrange in alternating or overlapping positions or periods: staggered holidays. ~n. 4. a staggering. [dialect stacker] —'staggering adj. —'staggeringly adv.

staggers ('stægəz) n. (functioning as sing. or pl.) a disease of horses and other domestic animals that causes staggering.

staging ('steɪdʒɪŋ) n. a temporary support used in building.

stagnant ('stægnənt) adj. 1. (of water or air) standing still; without flow or current; smelling foul from standing still. 2. stale or dull from inaction; not growing or developing. [Latin stagnāns]

stagnate (stæg'neɪt) vb. to be stagnant. —stag'nation n.

stag party n. a party for men only, held for a man who is about to get married.

stagy or U.S. **stagey** ('steɪdʒɪ) adj. **stagier**, **stagiest**. too theatrical or dramatic.

staid (steɪd) adj. sedate, steady, and rather dull. [obs. p.p. of stay]

stain (steɪn) vb. 1. to discolour (something) with marks that are not easily removed. 2. to dye (something) with a penetrating pigment. ~n. 3. a mark or discoloration that is not easily removed. 4. a moral blemish or slur: a stain on one's character. 5. a liquid used to penetrate the surface of a material, such as wood, and colour it without covering up the surface or grain. [Middle English steynen]

stained glass n. glass that has been coloured for artistic purposes.

stainless steel ('steɪnlɪs) n. a type of steel that does nor rust, as a result of the presence of large amounts of chromium.

stair (stɛə) n. 1. one step in a flight of

stairs. 2. a series of steps: a narrow stair. ~See also **stairs**. [Old English stæger]

staircase ('stɛə,keɪs) n. a flight of stairs, usually with a handrail or banisters.

stairs (stɛəz) pl. n. a flight of steps going from one level to another, usually indoors.

stairway ('stɛə,weɪ) n. a staircase.

stairwell ('stɛə,wɛl) n. a vertical shaft that contains a staircase.

stake[1] (steɪk) n. 1. a stick or metal bar driven into the ground as part of a fence or as a support or marker. 2. **be burned at the stake.** to be executed by being tied to a stake in the centre of a pile of wood that is then set on fire. ~vb. 3. to lay (a claim) to land or rights. 4. to support (something, such as a plant) with a stake. [Old English staca pin]

stake[2] (steɪk) n. 1. the money that a player must risk in order to take part in a gambling game or make a bet. 2. an interest, usually financial, held in something: a stake in the company's future. 3. (pl.) the money that a player has available for gambling. 4. (pl.) a prize in a race or contest. 5. (pl.) a horse race in which all owners of competing horses contribute to the prize. 6. **at stake.** at risk: lives are at stake. ~vb. 7. to risk (something, such as money) on a result. 8. to give financial support to (a business). [origin unknown]

stakeout ('steɪk,aʊt) n. 1. Slang, chiefly U.S. & Canad. a police surveillance of an area or house. ~vb. **stake out.** 2. Slang, chiefly U.S. & Canad. to keep an area or house under surveillance. 3. to surround (a piece of land) with stakes.

stalactite ('stælək,taɪt) n. a cylindrical mass of calcium carbonate hanging from the roof of a cave: formed by continually dripping water. [Greek stalaktos dripping]

stalagmite ('stæləg,maɪt) n. a cylindrical mass of calcium carbonate sticking up from the floor of a cave: formed by continually dripping water from a stalactite. [Greek stalagmos dripping]

stale (steɪl) adj. 1. (esp. of food) no longer fresh, having being kept too long. 2. (of air) stagnant; foul. 3. uninteresting from overuse: stale clichés. 4. no longer new: stale news. 5. lacking in energy or ideas through overwork or lack of variety. [prob. from Old French estale (unattested) motionless] —'staleness n.

stalemate ('steɪl,meɪt) n. 1. a chess position in which any of a player's moves would place his king in check: in this position the game ends in a draw. 2. a situation in which further action by two opposing forces is impossible or futile; deadlock. [obs. stale standing place + checkmate]

Stalinism ('stɑːlɪ,nɪzəm) n. the theory and form of government associated with Joseph Stalin (1879–1953), general secretary of the Communist Party of the Soviet Union 1922–53, which advocates only one political party and loyalty to the Soviet state. —'Stalinist n., adj.

stalk[1] (stɔːk) n. 1. the main stem of a plant. 2. a stem that joins a leaf or flower to the main stem of a plant. [prob. from Old English *stalu* upright piece of wood]

stalk² (stɔːk) *vb.* **1.** to follow or approach (an animal or person) stealthily. **2.** to spread over (a place) in a menacing way: *fever stalked the camp.* **3.** to walk in a haughty or stiff way. [Old English *bestealcian*]

stalking-horse *n.* something used as a means of concealing plans; pretext.

stall¹ (stɔːl) *n.* **1.** a compartment in a stable or shed for a single animal. **2.** a small stand or booth for the sale of goods. **3.** (*pl.*) (in a church) a row of seats, divided by armrests or a small screen, for the choir or clergy. **4.** any small room or compartment: *a shower stall.* **5.** (*pl.*) *Brit.* the seats on the ground floor of a theatre or cinema. ~*vb.* **6.** to stop (a motor vehicle or its engine) or (of a motor vehicle or its engine) to stop, by incorrect use of the clutch or incorrect adjustment of the fuel mixture. [Old English *steall* a place for standing]

stall² (stɔːl) *vb.* to employ delaying tactics towards (someone); to be evasive. [Anglo-French *estale* bird used as a decoy]

stallion (ˈstæljən) *n.* an uncastrated male horse, usually used for breeding. [Old French *estalon*]

stalwart (ˈstɔːlwət) *adj.* **1.** strong and sturdy. **2.** solid, dependable, and courageous. ~*n.* **3.** a stalwart supporter. [Old English *stælwirthe* serviceable]

stamen (ˈsteɪmen) *n.* the part of a flower that produces pollen. [Latin: the warp in an upright loom]

stamina (ˈstæmɪnə) *n.* enduring energy and strength. [Latin: the threads of life spun out by the Fates, hence energy, etc.]

stammer (ˈstæmə) *vb.* **1.** to speak or say (something) hesitantly, as a result of a speech disorder or through fear or other emotion. ~*n.* **2.** a speech disorder characterized by involuntary repetitions and hesitations. [Old English *stamerian*]

stamp (stæmp) *vb.* **1.** (often foll. by *on*) to bring (the foot) down heavily on (something, such as the ground). **2.** to walk with heavy or noisy footsteps. **3.** (foll. by *on*) to suppress: *he stamped on her enthusiasm.* **4.** to impress or mark (a pattern or sign) on (something). **5.** to mark (something) with an official seal or device. **6.** to impress permanently: *the date was stamped on her memory.* **7.** to stick a postage stamp on (an envelope). **8.** to characterize: *that behaviour stamps him as a cheat.* ~*n.* **9.** a stamping. **10.** same as **postage stamp.** **11.** a piece of gummed paper like a postage stamp, used for commercial or trading purposes. **12.** an instrument for stamping a design or device. **13.** a design, device, or mark that has been stamped. **14.** a characteristic feature: *the stamp of truth.* **15.** *Brit. informal.* a national insurance contribution, formerly recorded by a stamp on an official card. **16.** type or class: *men of his stamp.* [Old English *stampe*]

stampede (stæmˈpiːd) *n.* **1.** an impulsive headlong rush of startled cattle or horses.

2. headlong rush of a crowd. ~*vb.* **3.** to run away in a stampede. [Spanish *estampar* to stamp]

stamping ground *n.* a favourite meeting place.

stamp out *vb.* **1.** to suppress by force: *to stamp out a rebellion.* **2.** to put out by stamping: *to stamp out a fire.*

stance (stæns, stɑːns) *n.* **1.** the manner and position in which a person stands. **2.** *Sport.* the position taken when about to play the ball. **3.** a standpoint; attitude: *a leftist stance.* [Latin *stāre* to stand]

stanch (stɑːntʃ) *vb.* same as **staunch².** [Old French *estanchier*]

stanchion (ˈstɑːnʃən) *n.* a vertical pole or bar used as a support. [Old French *estanchon*]

stand (stænd) *vb.* **standing, stood. 1.** to be upright. **2.** to rise to an upright position. **3.** to place (something) upright. **4.** to have a specified height when standing: *to stand six feet tall.* **5.** to be situated: *the house stands in the square.* **6.** to be in a specified state or condition: *to stand in awe of someone.* **7.** to be in a specified position: *I stand to lose money in this venture.* **8.** to remain unchanged or valid: *my orders stand.* **9.** (foll. by *at*) (of a score or an account) to be in the specified position: *the score stands at 20 to 1.* **10.** (sometimes foll. by *for*) to tolerate or bear: *I won't stand for laziness; I can't stand spiders.* **11.** to survive: *to stand the test of time.* **12.** (often foll. by *for*) *Chiefly Brit.* to be a candidate: *stand for Parliament.* **13.** *Informal.* to buy: *to stand someone a drink.* **14. stand a chance,** to have a chance of succeeding. **15. stand one's ground,** to maintain a stance in the face of opposition. **16. stand trial,** to be tried in a lawcourt. ~*n.* **17.** a stall or counter from which goods may be sold: *a hamburger stand.* **18.** a structure at a sports ground where people can sit or stand. **19.** a standing. **20.** a firmly held opinion: *he took a stand on capital punishment.* **21.** *U.S.* a place in a lawcourt where a witness stands. **22.** a rack on which such articles as coats and hats may be hung. **23.** a small table or piece of furniture where articles may be placed or stored: *a music stand.* **24.** a halt to counter-attack, usually during a retreat and having some duration or success: *Custer's last stand.* **25.** *Cricket.* a long period at the wicket by two batsmen. **26.** See **one-night stand.** ~See also **stand by, stand down,** etc. [Old English *standan*]

standard (ˈstændəd) *n.* **1.** an accepted example of something against which others are judged or measured. **2.** a moral principle. **3.** a level of excellence or quality. **4.** a distinctive flag, as of a nation or cause. **5.** an upright pole or beam used as a support: *a lamp standard.* **6.** a song that has remained popular for many years. ~*adj.* **7.** of a usual, moderate, or accepted kind: *a standard size.* **8.** of recognized authority: *the standard work on Greece.* **9.** denoting pronunciations or grammar regarded as correct and acceptable by educated native speakers. [Old French *estandart*]

standard-bearer *n.* **1.** a person who carries a flag. **2.** a leader of a movement or party.

standard gauge *n.* **1.** a railway track with a distance of 56½ inches (1.435 m) between the lines; used on most railways. ~*adj.* **standard-gauge.** **2.** denoting a railway with a standard gauge.

standardize *or* **-ise** ('stændə‚daɪz) *vb.* to make (things) standard: *standardized tests.* —‚standardi'zation *or* -i'sation *n.*

standard lamp *n.* a lamp attached to an upright pole or beam on a base.

standard of living *n.* the level of comfort and wealth of a person or group.

standard time *n.* the official local time of a region or country determined by the distance from Greenwich of a line of longitude passing through the area.

stand by *vb.* **1.** to be available and ready to act if needed: *stand by with drinks for the runners.* **2.** to be present as an onlooker or without taking any action: *he stood by at the accident.* **3.** to be faithful to: *I'll stand by you.* ~*n.* **standby.** **4.** a person or thing that is ready for use or can be relied on in an emergency. **5.** **on stand-by.** ready for action or use. ~*adj.* **stand-by.** **6.** not booked in advance but subject to availability: *a stand-by ticket.*

stand down *vb.* to resign or withdraw, often in favour of another.

stand for *vb.* **1.** to represent: *UK stands for United Kingdom.* **2.** to support and symbolize (an idea or a belief): *I hate all that he stands for.* **3.** *Informal.* to tolerate or bear: *he won't stand for it.*

stand in *vb.* **1.** to act as a substitute: *she stood in for me while I was ill.* ~*n.* **stand-in.** **2.** a person who acts as a substitute for another.

standing ('stændɪŋ) *n.* **1.** social or financial status or reputation: *a man of some standing.* **2.** duration: *a friendship of some ten years' standing.* **3.** (*modifier*) used to stand in or on: *standing room.* ~*adj.* **4.** *Athletics.* (of a jump or the start of a race) begun from a standing position. **5.** permanent, fixed, or lasting: *a standing joke.*

standing order *n.* **1.** an instruction to a bank by a depositor to pay a stated sum to a person or organization at regular intervals. **2.** a rule or order governing the procedure of an organization.

standoff ('stænd‚ɒf) *n.* **1.** *U.S. & Canad.* the act or an instance of standing off or apart. **2.** a deadlock or stalemate. ~*vb.* **stand off.** **3.** to stay at a distance.

standoffish (‚stænd'ɒfɪʃ) *adj.* reserved or haughty.

stand out *vb.* **1.** to be distinctive or conspicuous. **2.** to refuse to agree or comply: *they stood out for a better price.*

standpipe ('stænd‚paɪp) *n.* a temporary freshwater outlet installed in a street when household water supplies are cut off.

standpoint ('stænd‚pɔɪnt) *n.* a mental position from which things are viewed.

standstill ('stænd‚stɪl) *n.* a complete stoppage or halt: *come to a standstill.*

stand to *vb.* **1.** *Mil.* to take up positions in order to resist attack. **2.** **stand to reason.** to be obvious or logical: *it stands to reason that he will be angry.*

stand up *vb.* **1.** to rise to one's feet. **2.** *Informal.* to fail to keep an appointment with (a boyfriend or girlfriend): *he stood her up.* **3.** to withstand examination: *his story won't stand up in court.* **4.** **stand up for.** to support or defend. **5.** **stand up to.** **a.** to confront or resist (someone) bravely. **b.** to withstand or endure (something, such as criticism). ~*adj.* **stand-up.** **6.** (of a comedian) telling jokes directly to an audience. **7.** being in an erect position: *a stand-up collar.* **8.** done while standing: *a stand-up meal.*

stank (stæŋk) *vb.* a past tense of **stink.**

stannary ('stænərɪ) *n.*, *pl.* **-ries.** a tin-mine. [Late Latin *stannum* tin]

stanza ('stænzə) *n.* *Prosody.* a verse of a poem. [Italian: halting place]

staple[1] ('steɪp[l]) *n.* **1.** a short length of wire bent into a square U-shape, used to fasten papers or secure things. ~*vb.* **2.** to secure (things) with staples. [Old English *stapol*] —**stapler** *n.*

staple[2] ('steɪp[l]) *adj.* **1.** of prime importance; principal: *staple foods.* ~*n.* **2.** something that forms a main part of the product, consumption, or trade of a region. **3.** a main constituent of anything. [Middle Dutch *stapel* warehouse]

star (stɑː) *n.* **1.** a planet or meteor visible in the clear night sky as a point of light. **2.** a hot gaseous mass, such as the sun, that radiates energy as heat and light, or in some cases as radio waves and x-rays. **3.** (*pl.*) same as **horoscope** (sense 1). **4.** an emblem with five or more radiating points, often used as a symbol of rank or an award. **5.** same as **asterisk.** **6.** a distinguished or glamorous celebrity, often from the entertainment world. **7.** **see stars.** to see flashes of light, as from a blow on the head. ~*vb.* **starring, starred.** **8.** to mark (something) with a star or stars. **9.** to feature (an actor or actress) or (of an actor or actress) to be featured as a star: *Olivier starred in "Hamlet".* [Old English *steorra*]

starboard ('stɑːbəd, -‚bɔːd) *n.* **1.** the right side of an aeroplane or ship when facing forwards. ~*adj.* **2.** of or on the starboard. [Old English *stēorbord*, lit.: steering side]

starch (stɑːtʃ) *n.* **1.** a fine white powder obtained from potatoes and some grain which, in solution with water, is used to stiffen fabric. **2.** food containing a large amount of starch, such as rice and potatoes. ~*vb.* **3.** to stiffen (cloth) with starch. [Old English *sterced* stiffened]

starchy ('stɑːtʃɪ) *adj.* **starchier, starchiest.** **1.** of or containing starch. **2.** very formal or stiff in manner.

star-crossed *adj.* (of lovers) destined to misfortune.

stardom ('stɑːdəm) n. the status of a star in the entertainment or sport world.

stare (steə) vb. 1. (often foll. by at) to look or gaze fixedly. 2. **stare one in the face**. to be glaringly obvious. ~n. 3. a staring. [Old English starian]

starfish ('stɑːˌfɪʃ) n., pl. **-fish** or **-fishes**. a star-shaped sea creature with a flat body and five arms.

star fruit n. same as **carambola**.

stargazer ('stɑːˌɡeɪzə) n. Informal. an astrologer. —'**star,gazing** n.

stark (stɑːk) adj. 1. grim; desolate: a stark landscape. 2. wihout elaboration; blunt: the stark facts. 3. utter; absolute: stark folly. ~adv. 4. completely: stark staring mad. [Old English stearc stiff] —'**starkly** adv. —'**starkness** n.

stark-naked adj. completely naked. Also (informal): **starkers**. [Middle English stert naket, lit.: tail naked]

starlet ('stɑːlɪt) n. a young actress who is presented as a potential star.

starlight ('stɑːˌlaɪt) n. the light that comes from the stars.

starling ('stɑːlɪŋ) n. a common songbird with shiny blackish feathers and a short tail. [Old English stærlinc]

starlit ('stɑːˌlɪt) adj. lit by starlight.

Star of David n. a symbol of Judaism, consisting of a star formed by two interlaced equilateral triangles.

starry ('stɑːrɪ) adj. **-rier, -riest**. 1. (of a sky or night) full of or lit by stars. 2. of or like a star or stars: a starry reception.

starry-eyed adj. full of naive optimism.

Stars and Stripes n. (functioning as sing.) **the**. the national flag of the United States of America.

Star-Spangled Banner n. **the**. 1. the national anthem of the United States of America. 2. same as **Stars and Stripes**.

star-studded adj. featuring many well-known performers: a star-studded cast.

start (stɑːt) vb. 1. to begin (something or to do something); come or cause (something) to come into being or operation: don't start a fight; work has started already. 2. (sometimes foll. by up) to set or be set in motion: he started up the machine. 3. to make a sudden involuntary movement, as from fright; jump. 4. to establish; set up: to start a business. 5. to support (someone) in the first part of a venture or career. 6. Brit. informal. to commence quarrelling or causing a disturbance: don't start with me. 7. **to start with**. in the first place. ~n. 8. the first part of something. 9. the place or time of starting, as of a race or performance. 10. a signal to begin, as in a race. 11. a lead or advantage, either in time or distance, in a competitive activity: he had an hour's start on me. 12. a slight involuntary movement, as from fright or surprise: she gave a start as I entered. 13. an opportunity to enter a career or undertake a project. 14. **for a start.** in the first place. ~See also **start off, start on**, etc. [Old English styrtan]

starter ('stɑːtə) n. 1. Chiefly Brit. the first course of a meal. 2. **for starters**. Slang. in the first place. 3. a device for starting an internal-combustion engine. 4. a person who signals the start of a race. 5. a competitor in a race or contest. 6. **under starter's orders**. (of competitors in a race) awaiting the signal to start.

startle ('stɑːt'l) vb. to slightly surprise or frighten someone. [Old English steartlian to stumble] —'**startling** adj.

start off vb. 1. to set out on a journey. 2. to be or make the first step in (an activity); initiate: he started the show off with a song. 3. to cause (a person) to do something, such as laugh.

start on vb. Brit. informal. to pick a quarrel with: don't start on me now.

start out vb. 1. to set out on a journey. 2. to take the first steps, for example in one's career or on a course of action: he started out as a salesman; they started out wanting a house, but finally got a flat.

start up vb. 1. to come or cause (something, such as a business) to come into being; originate. 2. to set (something) in motion: he started up the engine.

starve (stɑːv) vb. 1. to die from lack of food. 2. to deprive of food. 3. Informal. to be very hungry: I'm starving. 4. (foll. by of) to deprive (someone) of something that he needs: the child was starved of affection. 5. (foll. by into) to bring someone into a specified condition by starving: to starve someone into submission. [Old English steorfan to die] —**star'vation** n.

Star Wars n. (functioning as sing.) (in the U.S.) a proposed system of artificial satellites armed with lasers to destroy enemy missiles in space.

stash (stæʃ) vb. 1. (often foll. by away) Informal. to store (money or valuables) in a secret place for safekeeping. ~n. 2. Informal, chiefly U.S. & Canad. a secret store, usually of drugs, or the place where this is hidden. [origin unknown]

state (steɪt) n. 1. the condition of a person or thing. 2. ceremonious style, as befitting wealth or dignity: to live in state. 3. a sovereign political power or community. 4. the territory of such a community. 5. the sphere of power in such a community: affairs of state. 6. (often cap.) one of a number of areas or communities having their own governments and forming a federation under a sovereign government, as in the U.S. 7. (often cap.) the government, civil service, and armed forces. 8. **in a state**. Informal. in an emotional or agitated condition. 9. **lie in state**. (of a body) to be placed on public view before burial. 10. **state of affairs**. circumstances or condition: the current state of affairs. ~modifier. 11. controlled or financed by a state: state university. 12. of or concerning the State: State trial. 13. of a ceremonious occasion: state visit. ~vb. 14. to express (something) in words; utter. [Latin stāre to stand]

State Enrolled Nurse n. a nurse who has completed a two-year training course.

state house n. N.Z. a rented house built by the government.

stateless ('steɪtlɪs) *adj.* without nationality: *stateless persons*.

stately ('steɪtlɪ) *adj.* **-lier, -liest.** having a graceful, dignified, and imposing appearance or manner. —**'stateliness** *n.*

stately home *n. Brit.* a large mansion, usually one open to the public.

statement ('steɪtmənt) *n.* **1.** something stated, usually a formal prepared announcement or reply. **2.** the act of stating. **3.** an account containing a summary of bills or invoices and showing the total amount due. **4.** an account prepared by a bank for a client, usually at regular intervals, to show all credits and debits and the balance at the end of the period.

state of the art *n.* **1.** the current level of knowledge and development achieved in a technology, science, or art. ~*adj.* **state-of-the-art. 2.** the most recent and therefore considered the best; up-to-the-minute: *a state-of-the-art amplifier.*

State Registered Nurse *n.* a nurse who has completed an extensive three-year training course.

stateroom ('steɪtˌruːm) *n.* **1.** a private room on a ship. **2.** *Chiefly Brit.* a large room in a palace or other building for use on state occasions.

States (steɪts) *n.* (*functioning as sing. or pl.*) *Informal.* the United States of America.

state school *n.* a school maintained by the state, in which education is free.

statesman ('steɪtsmən) *n., pl.* **-men.** an experienced and respected political leader. —**'statesmanship** *n.*

static ('stætɪk) *adj.* **1.** not active or moving; stationary. **2.** *Physics.* (of a weight, force, or pressure) acting but causing no movement. **3.** *Physics.* of forces that do not produce movement. ~*n.* **4.** hissing or crackling or a speckled picture caused by interference in the reception of radio or television transmissions. **5.** electric sparks or crackling produced by friction. [Greek *statikos* causing to stand]

static electricity *n.* same as **static** (sense 5).

statics ('stætɪks) *n.* (*functioning as sing.*) the branch of mechanics concerned with the forces producing a state of equilibrium.

station ('steɪʃən) *n.* **1.** a place along a route or line at which a bus or train stops to pick up passengers or goods. **2.** the headquarters of an organization such as the police or fire service. **3.** a building with special equipment for some particular purpose: *power station; petrol station.* **4.** *Mil.* a place of duty. **5.** a television or radio channel. **6.** position in society: *he's getting ideas above his station.* **7.** *Austral. & N.Z.* a large sheep or cattle farm. **8.** the place or position where a person is assigned to stand: *don't leave your station before lunchtime.* ~*vb.* **9.** to assign (someone) to a station. [Latin *statiō* a standing still]

stationary ('steɪʃənərɪ) *adj.* **1.** not moving. **2.** unchanging: *the doctors said his condition was stationary.* [Latin *statiōnārius*]

stationer ('steɪʃənə) *n.* a person who sells

stationery or a shop where this is sold. [Medieval Latin *stationarius* a person having a regular station, hence a shopkeeper]

stationery ('steɪʃənərɪ) *n.* writing materials, such as paper, envelopes, and pens.

stationmaster ('steɪʃənˌmɑːstə) *n.* the senior official in charge of a railway station.

stations of the Cross *pl. n. R.C. Church.* **1.** a series of 14 crosses, often with pictures or carvings, arranged around the walls of a church, to commemorate 14 stages in Christ's journey to Calvary. **2.** a series of 14 prayers relating to each of these stages.

station wagon *n. U.S.* an estate car.

statistic (stə'tɪstɪk) *n.* a piece of numerical information which has been collected and classified systematically. —**sta'tistical** *adj.* —**sta'tistically** *adv.* —**statistician** (ˌstætɪ'stɪʃən) *n.*

statistics (stə'tɪstɪks) *n.* **1.** (*functioning as sing.*) the science dealing with the collection, classification, and interpretation of numerical information. **2.** (*functioning as pl.*) numerical information which has been collected, classified, and interpreted. [*orig.:* science dealing with facts of a state, from New Latin *statisticus* concerning state affairs]

statuary ('stætjʊərɪ) *n.* statues collectively.

statue ('stætjuː) *n.* a sculpture of a human or animal figure, usually life-size or larger. [Latin *statuere* to set up]

statuesque (ˌstætjʊ'ɛsk) *adj.* (of a woman) like a statue; tall and well-proportioned.

statuette (ˌstætjʊ'ɛt) *n.* a small statue.

stature ('stætʃə) *n.* **1.** height of a person. **2.** the degree of development of a person: *the stature of a champion.* **3.** intellectual or moral greatness: *a man of stature.* [Latin *stāre* to stand]

status ('steɪtəs) *n.* **1.** social position. **2.** a high position or standing. **3.** the legal standing or condition of a person: *the status of a minor.* **4.** degree of importance, as of a topic for discussion. [Latin: posture]

status quo (kwəʊ) *n.* **the.** the existing state of affairs. [*lit.:* the state in which]

status symbol *n.* a possession regarded as a mark of social position or wealth.

statute ('stætjuːt) *n.* **1.** a law made by a government and expressed in a formal document. **2.** a permanent rule made by a company or other institution. [Latin *statuere* to set up, decree]

statute law *n.* **1.** a law made by a government. **2.** such laws collectively.

statutory ('stætjʊtrɪ) *adj.* **1.** prescribed or authorized by statute. **2.** (of an offence) declared by statute to be punishable.

staunch[1] (stɔːntʃ) *adj.* loyal and firm: *a staunch ally.* [Old French *estanche*]

staunch[2] (stɔːntʃ) *or* **stanch** (stɑːntʃ) *vb.* to stop the flow of (blood) from someone's body.

stave (steɪv) *n.* **1.** one of the long strips of

wood joined together to form a barrel or bucket. **2.** a stick carried as a symbol of office. **3.** a verse of a poem. **4.** *Music.* same as **staff**. ~*vb.* **staving, staved** or **stove. 5.** (foll. by *in*) to burst a hole in something. [from *staves*, pl. of **staff**]

stave off *vb.* to avert (something) temporarily: *to stave off hunger.*

staves (stervz) *n.* a plural of **staff** or **stave.**

stay¹ (ster) *vb.* **1.** to continue or remain in a place, position, or condition: *to stay outside; to stay awake.* **2.** to reside temporarily: *to stay at a hotel.* **3.** *Scot. & S. African.* to reside permanently or habitually; live. **4.** to endure (something testing or difficult): *to stay the course.* ~*n.* **5.** the period during which one stays in a place. **6.** the suspension of a judicial proceeding: *stay of execution.* [Old French *ester*]

stay² (ster) *n.* something that supports or steadies something, such as a prop or buttress. [Old French *estaye*]

stay³ (ster) *n.* a rope, cable, or chain, used for supporting uprights, such as masts or funnels. [Old English *stæg*]

stay-at-home *adj.* **1.** (of a person) enjoying a quiet, settled, and unadventurous life. ~*n.* **2.** a stay-at-home person.

staying power *n.* endurance; stamina.

stays (sterz) *pl. n.* old-fashioned corsets with bones in them.

staysail ('ster,serl; *Naut.* 'sters²l) *n.* a sail fastened on a stay.

STD 1. sexually transmitted disease. **2.** subscriber trunk dialling.

STD code *n. Brit.* a code preceding a local telephone number, which enables a caller to dial direct, without the operator's help. [*s(ubscriber)* *t(runk)* *d(ialling)*]

stead (sted) *n.* **1. stand someone in good stead.** to be useful to someone in the future. **2.** *Rare.* the function or position that should be taken by another: *to come in someone's stead.* [Old English *stede*]

steadfast ('stedfəst, -,faːst) *adj.* firm or determined. —'**steadfastly** *adv.* —'**steadfastness** *n.*

steady ('stedı) *adj.* **steadier, steadiest. 1.** not shaky. **2.** without much change or variation: *a steady pace.* **3.** not easily excited; sober. **4.** regular; habitual: *a steady drinker.* **5.** continuous: *a steady flow.* ~*vb.* **steadying, steadied. 6.** to make or become steady. ~*adv.* **7.** in a steady manner. **8. go steady.** *Informal.* to date one person regularly. ~*n., pl.* **steadies. 9.** *Informal.* one's regular boyfriend or girlfriend. ~*interj.* **10.** a warning to keep calm or be careful. [from *stead*] —'**steadily** *adv.* —'**steadiness** *n.*

steady state *n. Physics.* the condition of a system when all or most changes or disturbances have been eliminated from it.

steak (sterk) *n.* **1.** a lean piece of beef for grilling or frying. **2.** a cut of beef for braising or stewing. **3.** a thick slice of pork, veal, or fish. [Old Norse *steik* roast]

steakhouse ('sterk,haʊs) *n.* a restaurant that specializes in steaks.

steal (stiːl) *vb.* **stealing, stole, stolen. 1.**

to take (something) from someone without permission or unlawfully. **2.** to obtain (something) surreptitiously: *to steal a kiss.* **3.** to use (someone else's ideas or work) without acknowledgment. **4.** to move stealthily: *they stole along the corridor.* ~*n.* **5.** *U.S. & Canad. informal.* something acquired easily or at little cost. [Old English *stelan*]

stealth (stɛlθ) *n.* **1.** moving with great care and quietness, so as to avoid detection. **2.** cunning or underhand behaviour. [Old English *stelan* to steal] —'**stealthy** *adj.* —'**stealthily** *adv.*

steam (stiːm) *n.* **1.** the gas or vapour into which water changes when boiled. **2.** the mist formed when such gas or vapour condenses in the atmosphere. **3.** *Informal.* power, energy, or speed. **4. let off steam.** *Informal.* to release pent-up energy or feelings. **5.** (*modifier*) operated, heated, or powered by steam: *a steam radiator.* ~*vb.* **6.** to give out steam. **7.** (of a vehicle) to move by steam power. **8.** *Informal.* to proceed quickly and often forcefully. **9.** to cook (food) in steam. **10.** to treat (something) with steam or apply steam to (something), as in cleaning or pressing clothes. ~See also **steam up.** [Old English]

steam engine *n.* an engine that uses steam to produce mechanical work.

steamer ('stiːmə) *n.* **1.** a boat or ship driven by steam engines. **2.** a container with holes in the bottom, used to cook food by steam.

steam iron *n.* an electric iron that uses steam produced from water put into the iron to take creases out of clothes.

steamroller ('stiːm,rəʊlə) *n.* **1.** a steam-powered vehicle with heavy rollers used for flattening road surfaces during road-making. ~*vb.* **2.** to make (someone) do what one wants by overpowering force.

steamship ('stiːm,ʃɪp) *n.* a ship powered by steam engines.

steam up *vb.* **1.** to cover (windows or glasses) or (of windows or glasses) to become covered with steam. **2. steamed up.** *Slang.* excited or angry.

steamy ('stiːmı) *adj.* **steamier, steamiest. 1.** full of steam. **2.** *Informal.* lustful or erotic: *a steamy play.*

steatite ('stɪə,taɪt) *n.* same as **soapstone.** [Greek *stear* fat]

steed (stiːd) *n. Archaic or literary.* a horse. [Old English *stēda* stallion]

steel (stiːl) *n.* **1.** an alloy of iron and carbon, often with small quantities of other elements. **2.** a steel rod used for sharpening knives. **3.** the quality of hardness, with regard to a person's character or attitude. ~*vb.* **4.** to make hard and unfeeling: *he steeled his heart against her sorrow; he steeled himself for the blow.* [Old English *stēli*] —'**steely** *adj.*

steel band *n. Music.* a band, popular in the Caribbean Islands, consisting of percussion instruments made from oil drums, hammered or embossed to produce notes.

steel-blue *adj.* dark bluish-grey.

steel wool *n.* a mass of fine steel fibres, used for cleaning metal surfaces.

steelworks (ˈstiːlˌwɜːks) *n.* (*functioning as sing. or pl.*) a factory where steel is made. —**'steel,worker** *n.*

steep[1] (stiːp) *adj.* **1.** having a sharp slope. **2.** *Informal.* (of a fee, price, or demand) unduly high; unreasonable. [Old English *steap*] —**'steeply** *adv.* —**'steepness** *n.*

steep[2] (stiːp) *vb.* **1.** to soak or be soaked in a liquid in order to soften or cleanse. **2. steeped in.** filled with: *steeped in history.* [Old English *stēpan*]

steepen (ˈstiːpᵊn) *vb.* to become or cause (something) to become steep or steeper.

steeple (ˈstiːpᵊl) *n.* a tall ornamental tower on a church roof. [Old English *stēpel*]

steeplechase (ˈstiːpᵊlˌtʃeɪs) *n.* **1.** a horse race over a course with obstacles to be jumped. **2.** a track race in which the runners have to leap hurdles and a water jump. ~*vb.* **3.** to race in a steeplechase.

steeplejack (ˈstiːpᵊlˌdʒæk) *n.* a person who repairs steeples and chimneys.

steer[1] (stɪə) *vb.* **1.** to direct the course of (a vehicle or vessel) with a steering wheel or rudder. **2.** to direct the movements or course of (a person or conversation). **3.** to pursue (a specified course). **4. steer clear of.** to avoid. [Old English *stieran*]

steer[2] (stɪə) *n.* a castrated male ox or bull. [Old English *stēor*]

steerage (ˈstɪərɪdʒ) *n.* **1.** the cheapest accommodation on a passenger ship. **2.** a steering.

steering committee *n.* a committee set up to prepare and arrange topics to be discussed, and the order of business, for a government or other group.

steering wheel *n.* a wheel turned by the driver of a vehicle in order to change direction.

steersman (ˈstɪəzmən) *n., pl.* **-men.** the person who steers a vessel.

stein (staɪn) *n.* an earthenware beer mug. [German *Stein*, lit.: stone]

stele (ˈstiːlɪ, stiːl) *or* **stela** (ˈstiːlə) *n., pl.* **stelae** (ˈstiːliː) *or* **steles.** an upright stone slab or column decorated with figures or inscriptions, common in prehistoric times. [Greek]

stellar (ˈstɛlə) *adj.* of or like a star or stars. [Latin *stella* star]

stem[1] (stɛm) *n.* **1.** the long thin central part of a plant. **2.** a stalk that bears a flower, fruit, or leaf. **3.** the long slender part of anything, such as a goblet. **4.** *Linguistics.* the form of a word that remains after removal of all inflectional endings. ~*vb.* **stemming, stemmed. 5.** (foll. by *from*) to be derived; originate. [Old English *stemn*]

stem[2] (stɛm) *vb.* **stemming, stemmed.** to stop (the flow of something): *to stem the flow of illegal drugs.* [Old Norse *stemma*]

stemmed (stɛmd) *adj.* having a stem: *a long-stemmed glass.*

stench (stɛntʃ) *n.* a strong and very unpleasant odour. [Old English *stenc*]

stencil (ˈstɛnsᵊl) *n.* **1.** a device for marking a design or letters on a surface, consisting of a thin sheet of plastic, metal, or paper, in which the design or letters have been cut so that ink or paint can be applied through the cuts onto the surface. **2.** a design or letters made in this way. ~*vb.* **-cilling, -cilled** *or U.S.* **-ciling, -ciled. 3.** to make (a design or letters) with a stencil. [Old French *estenceler* to decorate brightly]

Sten gun (stɛn) *n.* a light sub-machine-gun. [*S & T* (initials of the inventors) + *-en*, as in *Bren gun*]

stenographer (stəˈnɒɡrəfə) *n. U.S. & Canad.* a shorthand typist. [Greek *stenos* narrow + *graphein* to write]

stentorian (stɛnˈtɔːrɪən) *adj.* (of the voice) very loud: *stentorian tones.* [after *Stentor*, a herald in Greek myth.]

step (stɛp) *n.* **1.** the act of moving and setting down one's foot, as when walking. **2.** the distance covered by such a movement. **3.** the sound made by such a movement. **4.** manner of walking; gait. **5.** one of a sequence of foot movements that make up a dance. **6.** one of a sequence of stages in the progression towards a goal. **7.** a rank or grade in a series or scale. **8.** a surface that offers support for the foot when ascending or descending. **9.** (*pl.*) a flight of stairs, usually out of doors. **10.** (*pl.*) same as **stepladder. 11.** a short easily walked distance: *it is only a step.* **12. break step.** to stop marching in step. **13. in step. a.** marching or dancing at a specified pace or at exactly the same time as other people. **b.** *Informal.* in agreement or harmony: *in step with public opinion.* **14. out of step. a.** not marching or dancing at a specified pace or at exactly the same time as other people. **b.** *Informal.* not in agreement; out of harmony. **15. step by step.** gradually. **16. take steps.** to do what is necessary to achieve something). **17. watch one's step. a.** *Informal.* to behave with caution. **b.** to walk carefully. ~*vb.* **stepping, stepped. 18.** to move by executing a step, as in walking. **19.** to walk a short distance: *step this way.* **20.** (foll. by *into*) to enter (a situation) apparently with ease: *she stepped into a life of luxury.* ~See also **step down, step in,** etc. [Old English *stepe, stæpe*]

stepbrother (ˈstɛpˌbrʌðə) *n.* a son of one's stepmother or stepfather.

stepchild (ˈstɛpˌtʃaɪld) *n., pl.* **-children.** a stepson or stepdaughter.

stepdaughter (ˈstɛpˌdɔːtə) *n.* a daughter of one's husband or wife by an earlier relationship.

step down *vb. Informal.* to resign from a position.

stepfather (ˈstɛpˌfɑːðə) *n.* a man who has married one's mother after the death or divorce of one's father.

stephanotis (ˌstɛfəˈnəʊtɪs) *n.* a tropical climbing shrub with sweet-smelling white flowers. [Greek: fit for a crown]

step in *vb. Informal.* to intervene (in a quarrel or difficult situation).

stepladder (ˈstɛpˌlædə) *n.* a folding portable ladder made of broad flat steps fixed to a self-supporting frame.

stepmother ('stɛp,mʌðə) n. a woman who has married one's father after the death or divorce of one's mother.

step on vb. **1.** to place or press the foot on (something): *step on the accelerator.* **2.** *Informal.* to behave harshly or contemptuously towards (someone). **3. step on it.** *Informal.* to go more quickly; hurry up.

step out vb. **1.** to leave a room briefly. **2.** to walk quickly, taking long strides.

step-parent ('stɛp,pɛərənt) n. a stepfather or stepmother.

steppe (stɛp) n. (*often pl.*) a wide grassy plain without trees. [Old Russian *step* lowland]

stepping stone n. **1.** one of a series of stones acting as footrests for crossing a stream. **2.** something that helps progress towards some goal.

stepsister ('stɛp,sɪstə) n. a daughter of one's stepmother or stepfather.

stepson ('stɛp,sʌn) n. a son of one's husband or wife by an earlier relationship.

step up vb. *Informal.* to increase (something) by stages; accelerate.

stereo ('stɛrɪəʊ, 'stɪər-) adj. **1.** short for **stereophonic.** ~n., pl. **stereos.** **2.** a stereophonic record player. **3.** stereophonic sound: *to broadcast in stereo.*

stereophonic (,stɛrɪə'fɒnɪk, ,stɪər-) adj. (of a sound system) using two or more separate microphones to feed two or more loudspeakers through separate channels. [Greek *stereos* solid + *phōnē* sound]

stereotype ('stɛrɪə,taɪp, 'stɪər-) n. **1.** a standardized image or idea of a type of person. **2.** an idea that has grown stale through fixed usage. ~vb. **3.** to form a standard image or idea of (a type of person). [Greek *stereos* solid + *type*]

sterile ('stɛraɪl) adj. **1.** free from germs. **2.** unable to produce offspring. **3.** (of plants) not producing or bearing seeds. **4.** lacking inspiration or vitality. [Latin *sterilis*] —**sterility** (stɪ'rɪlɪtɪ) n.

sterilize or **-ise** ('stɛrɪ,laɪz) vb. to make sterile. —,sterili'zation or -i'sation n.

sterling ('stɜːlɪŋ) n. **1.** British money: *pound sterling.* ~adj. **2.** genuine and reliable; first-class: *sterling quality.* [prob. Old English *steorra* star, referring to a small star on early Norman pennies]

sterling silver n. **1.** an alloy containing at least 92.5 per cent of silver. **2.** articles made of sterling silver.

stern[1] (stɜːn) adj. **1.** strict. **2.** difficult and, often, unpleasant: *the stern demands of parenthood.* **3.** severe in appearance. [Old English *styrne*] —**'sternly** adv.

stern[2] (stɜːn) n. the rear part of a vessel. [Old Norse *stjórn* steering]

sternum ('stɜːnəm) n., pl. **-na** (-nə) or **-nums.** a long flat bone in the front of the body, to which the collarbone and most of the ribs are attached. [Greek *sternon*]

steroid ('stɪərɔɪd) n. *Biochem.* an organic compound containing a carbon ring system, such as sterols and many hormones.

sterol ('stɛrɒl) n. *Biochem.* a natural insoluble alcohol such as cholesterol and ergos-

terol. [shortened from *cholesterol, ergosterol,* etc.]

stertorous ('stɜːtərəs) adj. (of breathing) laboured and noisy. [Latin *stertere* to snore]

stet (stɛt) vb. **setting, stetted. 1.** used as an instruction to indicate to a printer that certain deleted matter is to be retained. **2.** to mark (matter) in this way. [Latin, lit.: let it stand]

stethoscope ('stɛθə,skəʊp) n. *Med.* an instrument for listening to the sounds made inside the body, consisting of a hollow disc that transmits the sound through hollow tubes to earpieces. [Greek *stēthos* breast + *skopein* to look at]

stetson ('stɛts'n) n. a felt hat with a broad brim and high crown, worn mainly by cowboys. [after John *Stetson,* American hat maker]

stevedore ('stiːvɪ,dɔː) n. a person employed to load or unload ships. [Spanish *estibador* a packer]

stew (stjuː) n. **1.** a dish of meat, fish, or other food, cooked by stewing. **2. in a stew.** *Informal.* in a troubled or worried state. ~vb. **3.** to cook by long slow simmering. **4.** *Informal.* (of a person) to be too hot. **5.** to cause (tea) to become bitter or (of tea) to become bitter through infusing for too long. **6. stew in one's own juice.** to suffer unaided the consequences of one's actions. [*stuen* to take a very hot bath]

steward (stjʊəd) n. **1.** a person who looks after passengers and serves meals on a ship or aircraft. **2.** an official who helps to supervise a public event, such as a race. **3.** a person who administers someone else's property. **4.** a person who manages the eating arrangements, staff, or service at a club or hotel. **5.** See **shop steward.** ~vb. **6.** to act as a steward (of). [Old English *stigweard* hall keeper]

stewardess ('stjʊədɪs, ,stjʊə'dɛs) n. a female steward on an aircraft or ship.

stewed (stjuːd) adj. **1.** (of food) cooked by stewing. **2.** *Brit.* (of tea) bitter through having been left to infuse for too long. **3.** *Slang.* drunk.

stick[1] (stɪk) n. **1.** a small thin branch of a tree. **2. a.** a long thin piece of wood. **b.** such a piece of wood shaped for a special purpose: *a walking stick; a hockey stick.* **3.** a piece of something shaped like a stick: *a stick of celery.* **4.** *Slang.* verbal abuse, criticism: *I got some stick for my mistake.* **5.** (pl.) pieces of furniture: *these few sticks are all I have.* **6.** (pl.) *Informal.* a country area considered remote or backward: *I live out in the sticks.* **7.** *Informal.* a person: *not a bad old stick.* **8. get hold of the wrong end of the stick.** to misunderstand a situation or an explanation completely. [Old English *sticca*]

stick[2] (stɪk) vb. **sticking, stuck. 1.** to push (a pointed object) or (of a pointed object) to be pushed into another object. **2.** to fasten (something) in position by or as if by pins or nails: *to stick a picture on the wall.* **3.** (foll. by *out, up, through,* etc.) to protrude or cause to protrude: *to stick* one's hand up. **4.** *Informal.* to place (something) in a specified position: *stick your coat on this chair.* **5.** to fasten or be fastened by or as if by an adhesive substance. **6.** to come or be brought to a standstill: *stuck in a traffic jam; the wheels stuck.* **7.** to remain for a long time: *the memory sticks in my mind.* **8.** *Slang, chiefly Brit.* to tolerate; abide: *I can't stick him.* **9. be stuck.** *Informal.* to be at a loss; be baffled or puzzled: *I was totally stuck for an answer.* **10.** *Slang.* to impose something unpleasant. ~See also **stick around, stick by,** etc. [Old English *stician*]

stick around *vb. Informal.* to remain in a place, often when waiting for something.

stick by *vb.* to remain faithful to: *she stuck by him through thick and thin.*

sticker ('stɪkə) *n.* **1.** an adhesive label or paper. **2.** a persevering or industrious person.

sticking plaster *n.* a piece of adhesive material used for covering slight wounds.

stick insect *n.* a tropical insect with a long thin body and legs, which resembles a twig.

stick-in-the-mud *n. Informal.* a conservative person who lacks initiative or imagination.

stickleback ('stɪkᵊl,bæk) *n.* a small fish with a series of spines along its back. [Old English *stickel* prick, sting]

stickler ('stɪklə) *n.* a person who makes insistent demands: *a stickler for accuracy.*

stick out *vb.* **1.** to project or cause (something) to project: *the child stuck his tongue out.* **2.** *Informal.* to endure (something disagreeable): *I hate my job but I'll stick it out till May.* **3. stick out a mile** or **like a sore thumb.** *Informal.* to be very obvious. **4. stick out for.** to insist on (a demand), refusing to yield until it is met.

stick to *vb.* **1.** to adhere or cause (something) to adhere to: *toffee sticks to your teeth.* **2.** to remain faithful to (a person, promise, or rule). **3.** not to move away from: *stick to the subject.*

stick-up *n. Slang, chiefly U.S.* a robbery at gunpoint; hold-up.

stick up for *vb. Informal.* to support or defend (oneself, another person, or a principle).

sticky ('stɪkɪ) *adj.* **stickier, stickiest. 1.** covered with an adhesive substance: *sticky hands.* **2.** intended to stick to a surface: *sticky tape.* **3.** (of weather) warm and humid. **4.** *Informal.* difficult or painful: *a sticky situation.* —'**stickiness** *n.*

sticky wicket *n.* **on a sticky wicket.** *Informal.* in a difficult situation.

stiff (stɪf) *adj.* **1.** not easily bent; inflexible. **2.** not moving easily: *a stiff handle.* **3.** difficult to accept in its severity: *a stiff punishment.* **4.** moving with pain or difficulty: *a stiff neck.* **5.** difficult: *a stiff exam.* **6.** unrelaxed or awkward; formal. **7.** fairly firm in consistency; thick. **8.** powerful; strong: *a stiff breeze; a stiff drink.* ~*n.* **9.** *Slang.* a corpse. ~*adv.* **10.** completely or utterly: *bored stiff.* [Old

English *stīf*] —'**stiffly** *adv.* —'**stiffness** *n.*

stiffen ('stɪfᵊn) *vb.* to make or become stiff or stiffer.

stiff-necked *adj.* haughtily stubborn.

stifle ('staɪfᵊl) *vb.* **1.** to smother or suppress (something): *stifle a cough.* **2.** to feel discomfort and difficulty in breathing. **3.** to kill (someone) by preventing him from breathing. [prob. from Old French *estouffer* to smother]

stigma ('stɪgmə) *n., pl.* **stigmas** or **stigmata** ('stɪgmətə, stɪg'mɑːtə). **1.** a mark of social disgrace: *the stigma of having been in prison.* **2.** *Bot.* the part of a flower that receives pollen. **3.** (*pl.*) *Christianity.* marks resembling the wounds of the crucified Christ, believed to appear on the bodies of certain individuals. [Greek: brand]

stigmatize or **-ise** ('stɪgmə,taɪz) *vb.* to mark (something) out as being shameful.

stile (staɪl) *n.* a set of steps in a wall or fence to allow people, but not animals, to pass over. [Old English *stigel*]

stiletto (stɪ'letəʊ) *n., pl.* **-tos. 1.** Also called: **spike heel, stiletto heel.** a high narrow heel on a woman's shoe or a shoe with such a heel. **2.** a small dagger with a slender tapered blade. [Italian]

still¹ (stɪl) *adj.* **1.** motionless; stationary. **2.** undisturbed; silent and calm. **3.** (of a soft drink) not fizzy. **4.** gentle or quiet; subdued. ~*adv.* **5.** continuing now or in the future as in the past: *do you still love me?* **6.** up to this or that time; yet: *I still can't hear you.* **7.** even or yet: *still more insults.* **8.** even then; nevertheless: *the baby has been fed and still cries.* **9.** quietly or without movement: *sit still.* ~*n.* **10.** *Poetic.* silence or tranquillity: *the still of the night.* **11.** a still photograph from a film. ~*vb.* **12.** to make or become still, quiet, or calm. **13.** to relieve or end: *her fears were stilled.* [Old English *stille*] —'**stillness** *n.*

still² (stɪl) *n.* an apparatus for distilling spirits. [Latin *stilla* a drip]

stillborn ('stɪl,bɔːn) *adj.* **1.** (of a baby) dead at birth. **2.** (of an idea or plan) completely unsuccessful. —'**still,birth** *n.*

still life *n., pl.* **still lifes. 1.** a painting or drawing of objects such as fruit or flowers. **2.** this kind of painting or drawing.

still room *n. Brit.* **1.** a room in which distilling is carried out. **2.** a pantry or storeroom in a large house.

stilt (stɪlt) *n.* **1.** either of a pair of long poles with footrests on which a person stands and walks, as used by circus clowns. **2.** a long post or column used with others to support a building above ground level. [Middle English *stilte*]

stilted ('stɪltɪd) *adj.* (of speech, writing, or behaviour) formal or pompous; not flowing continuously or naturally.

Stilton ('stɪltᵊn) *n. Trademark.* a strong-flavoured blue-veined cheese. [named after *Stilton,* Cambridgeshire]

stimulant ('stɪmjʊlənt) *n.* **1.** a drug, food, or drink that increases the heart rate or other physical or mental activity. **2.** any stimulating thing. ~*adj.* **3.** stimulating.

stimulate ('stɪmjʊˌleɪt) *vb.* **1.** to arouse the senses of (a person). **2.** *Physiol.* to excite (a nerve or organ) with a stimulus. [Latin *stimulāre*] —'stimuˌlating *adj.* —ˌstimu'lation *n.*

stimulus ('stɪmjʊləs) *n.,* *pl.* **-li** (-ˌlaɪ, -ˌliː). **1.** something that stimulates or acts as an incentive to (someone). **2.** something, such as a drug or electrical impulse, that is capable of causing a response in a person or an animal. [Latin: a cattle goad]

sting (stɪŋ) *vb.* **stinging, stung. 1.** (of certain animals and plants) to inflict a wound on (someone) by the injection of poison. **2.** to feel or cause (someone) to feel a sharp mental or physical pain. **3.** to goad or incite: *they were stung into action.* **4.** *Informal.* to cheat (someone) by overcharging. ~*n.* **5.** a skin wound caused by stinging. **6.** pain caused by or as if by a sting. **7.** a mental pain: *a sting of conscience.* **8.** the sharp pointed organ of certain animals or plants by which poison can be injected. **9.** *Slang.* a deceptive trick. [Old English *stingan*] —'stinging *adj.*

stinging nettle *n.* same as **nettle** (sense 1).

stingray ('stɪŋˌreɪ) *n.* a flat fish with a jagged whiplike tail which can inflict painful wounds.

stingy ('stɪndʒɪ) *adj.* **-gier, -giest.** mean or miserly. [perhaps from *stinge*, dialect var. of *sting*] —'stinginess *n.*

stink (stɪŋk) *n.* **1.** a strong unpleasant smell. **2. make, create,** *or* **kick up a stink.** *Slang.* to make a fuss. ~*vb.* **stinking, stank** *or* **stunk; stunk. 3.** to give off a strong unpleasant smell. **4.** *Slang.* to be thoroughly unpleasant: *this town stinks.* [Old English *stincan*]

stink bomb *n.* a small glass globe used by practical jokers: it releases a liquid with a strong unpleasant smell when broken.

stinker ('stɪŋkə) *n. Slang.* a difficult or very unpleasant person or thing.

stinking ('stɪŋkɪŋ) *adj.* **1.** having a strong unpleasant smell. **2.** *Informal.* unpleasant or disgusting. ~*adv.* **3. stinking rich.** *Informal.* very wealthy.

stink out *vb.* **1.** to drive (people) away by a foul smell. **2.** *Brit.* to cause (a place) to stink: *his cigars stink out the room.*

stint (stɪnt) *vb.* **1.** to be miserly with (something): *don't stint on the potatoes.* ~*n.* **2.** an allotted amount of work. [Old English *styntan* to blunt]

stipend ('staɪpɛnd) *n.* a regular amount of money paid as a salary or allowance, as to a clergyman. [Latin *stīpendium* tax]

stipendiary (staɪ'pɛndɪərɪ) *adj.* **1.** receiving a stipend. ~*n.,* *pl.* **-aries. 2.** a person who receives a stipend. [Latin *stīpendiārius* concerning tribute]

stipple ('stɪpʰl) *vb.* to draw, engrave, or paint (something) using dots or flecks. [Dutch *stippelen*]

stipulate ('stɪpjʊˌleɪt) *vb.* to specify (something) as a condition of an agreement. [Latin *stipulārī*] —ˌstipu'lation *n.*

stir¹ (stɜː) *vb.* **stirring, stirred. 1.** to move an implement such as a spoon around in (a liquid) so as to mix it up. **2.** to change or cause to change position. **3.** (foll. by *from*) to depart (from one's usual or preferred place). **4.** to get up after sleeping. **5.** to excite or stimulate (someone) emotionally. **6.** to move (oneself) briskly or vigorously; exert (oneself). **7.** to awaken: *to stir someone from sleep.* ~*n.* **8.** a stirring. **9.** a strong reaction, usually of excitement: *his publication caused a stir.* ~See also **stir up.** [Old English *styrian*]

stir² (stɜː) *n. Slang.* prison: *in stir.*

stir-crazy *adj. Slang, chiefly U.S. & Canad.* mentally disturbed as a result of being in prison. [origin unknown]

stir-fry *vb.* **-frying, -fried. 1.** to cook (food) rapidly by stirring it in a wok or frying pan over a high heat. ~*n.,* *pl.* **-fries. 2.** a dish cooked in this way.

stirrer ('stɜːrə) *n. Informal.* a person who deliberately causes trouble.

stirring ('stɜːrɪŋ) *adj.* exciting the emotions; stimulating.

stirrup ('stɪrəp) *n.* a metal loop attached to a saddle, with a flat footpiece through which a rider puts his foot for support. [Old English *stīg* step + *rāp* rope]

stirrup cup *n.* a cup containing an alcoholic drink offered to a horseman ready to ride away.

stirrup pump *n.* a hand-operated pump, the base of which is placed in a bucket of water: used in fighting fires.

stir up *vb.* to set (something) in motion; instigate: *he stirred up trouble.*

stitch (stɪtʃ) *n.* **1.** a link made by drawing a thread through material with a needle. **2.** a loop of yarn formed around a needle or hook in knitting or crocheting. **3.** a particular kind of stitch. **4.** *Informal.* a suture. **5.** a sharp pain in the side caused by running or exercising. **6. in stitches.** *Informal.* laughing uncontrollably. **7. not a stitch.** *Informal.* no clothes at all. ~*vb.* **8.** to sew or fasten (something) with stitches. **9.** to be engaged in sewing. [Old English *stice* sting] —'stitching *n.*

stoat (stəʊt) *n.* a small brown N European mammal related to the weasels: in winter it has a white coat and is then known as an ermine. [origin unknown]

stock (stɒk) *n.* **1.** the total amount of goods kept on the premises of a shop or business. **2.** a supply of something stored for future use. **3.** *Finance.* **a.** the money raised by a company through selling shares entitling their holders to dividends, partial ownership, and usually voting rights. **b.** the proportion of this money held by an individual shareholder. **c.** the shares of a specified company or industry. **4.** standing or status. **5.** farm animals bred and kept for their meat, skins, etc. **6.** the original type from which a particular race, family, or group is derived. **7.** the part of a rifle or air gun into which the barrel is set: held by the firer against the shoulder. **8.** a liquid or broth in which meat, fish, bones, or vegetables have been simmered for a long time. **9.** a kind of plant cultivated for its brightly coloured flowers. **10.** See **laughing stock. 11. in stock.** stored on the premises or available for sale or use. **12. out of stock.** not immediately available for sale or use. **13. take stock.** to make a general appraisal of a situation or resources. ~*adj.* **14.** staple; standard: *stock sizes in clothes.* **15.** being a cliché; hackneyed: *a stock phrase.* ~*vb.* **16.** to keep (goods) for sale. **17.** (usually foll. by *up* or *up on*) to obtain a store of (something) for future use or sale: *to stock up on beer.* **18.** to supply (a farm) with animals or (a lake or stream) with fish. ~See also **stocks.** [Old English *stocc*]

stockade (stɒˈkeɪd) *n.* an enclosure or barrier of stakes. [Spanish *estacada*]

stockbreeder (ˈstɒkˌbriːdə) *n.* a person who breeds or rears livestock.

stockbroker (ˈstɒkˌbrəʊkə) *n.* a person who buys and sells stocks and shares on a commission basis for customers. —**ˈstockˌbroking** *n.*

stock car *n.* a car that has been strengthened and modified for a form of racing in which the cars often collide.

stock exchange *n.* **1. a.** a highly organized market for the purchase and sale of stocks and shares, operated by professional stockbrokers and market makers according to fixed rules. **b.** a place where stocks and shares are traded. **2.** the prices or trading activity of a stock exchange: *the stock exchange fell heavily today.*

stockholder (ˈstɒkˌhəʊldə) *n.* an owner of some of a company's stock.

stockinet (ˌstɒkɪˈnɛt) *n.* a machine-knitted elastic fabric. [perhaps from *stocking-net*]

stocking (ˈstɒkɪŋ) *n.* a close-fitting garment of nylon or knitted yarn to cover the foot and part or all of the leg. [dialect *stock* stocking]

stockinged (ˈstɒkɪŋd) *adj.* **in one's stockinged feet.** wearing stockings, tights, or socks but no shoes.

stock in trade *n.* anything constantly used by someone as a part of his profession or trade: *friendliness is the salesman's stock in trade.*

stockist (ˈstɒkɪst) *n. Commerce, Brit.* a dealer who stocks a particular product.

stock market *n.* same as **stock exchange.**

stockpile (ˈstɒkˌpaɪl) *vb.* **1.** to store a large quantity of (something) for future use. ~*n.* **2.** a large store accumulated for future use.

stockpot (ˈstɒkˌpɒt) *n. Chiefly Brit.* a pot in which stock for soup is made.

stockroom (ˈstɒkˌruːm) *n.* a room in which a stock of goods is kept, as in a shop or factory.

stock route *n. Austral. & N.Z.* a route designated for droving farm animals, so as to avoid traffic.

stocks (stɒks) *pl. n. History.* an instrument of punishment consisting of a heavy wooden frame with holes in which the feet, hands, or head of an offender were locked.

stock-still *adv.* absolutely still; motionless.

stocktaking (ˈstɒkˌteɪkɪŋ) *n.* **1.** the examination, counting, and valuing of goods in a shop or business. **2.** a reassessment of one's current situation and prospects.

stocky (ˈstɒkɪ) *adj.* **stockier, stockiest.** (of a person) broad and sturdy. —**ˈstockily** *adv.* —**ˈstockiness** *n.*

stockyard (ˈstɒkˌjɑːd) *n.* a large yard with pens or covered buildings where farm animals are sold.

stodge (stɒdʒ) *n. Informal.* heavy filling starchy food. [perhaps blend of *stuff* + *podge*]

stodgy (ˈstɒdʒɪ) *adj.* **stodgier, stodgiest. 1.** (of food) heavy or uninteresting. **2.** (of a person) excessively formal and conventional. [from STODGE] —**ˈstodginess** *n.*

stoep (stuːp) *n.* (in South Africa) a veranda. [Afrikaans]

stoic (ˈstəʊɪk) *n.* **1.** a person who has stoical qualities. ~*adj.* **2.** same as **stoical.**

Stoic (ˈstəʊɪk) *n.* **1.** a member of the ancient Greek school of philosophy which believed that virtue and happiness could be achieved only by submission to destiny and the natural law. ~*adj.* **2.** of or relating to the Stoics. [Greek *stoa* porch] —**Stoicism** (ˈstəʊɪˌsɪzəm) *n.*

stoical (ˈstəʊɪkᵊl) *adj.* suffering great difficulties without showing one's feelings. —**ˈstoically** *adv.* —**stoicism** (ˈstəʊɪˌsɪzəm) *n.*

stoke (stəʊk) *vb.* **1.** to feed, stir, and tend (a fire or furnace). **2.** to arouse or encourage (a strong emotion) in oneself or someone else. ~Also **stoke up.** [from *stoker*]

stokehold (ˈstəʊkˌhəʊld) *n. Naut.* the hold for a ship's boilers; fire room.

stokehole (ˈstəʊkˌhəʊl) *n.* a hole in a furnace through which it is stoked.

stoker (ˈstəʊkə) *n.* a person employed to tend a furnace, as on a steamship. [Dutch *stoken* to stoke]

stole¹ (stəʊl) *vb.* the past tense of **steal.**

stole² (stəʊl) *n.* a long scarf or shawl, worn by women. [Greek *stolē* clothing]

stolen (ˈstəʊlən) *vb.* the past participle of **steal.**

stolid (ˈstɒlɪd) *adj.* showing little or no emotion or interest. [Latin *stolidus* dull] —**stoˈlidity** *n.* —**ˈstolidly** *adv.*

stoma (ˈstəʊmə) *n., pl.* **stomata** (ˈstəʊmətə, stəʊˈmɑːtə) **1.** *Bot.* a pore in a plant leaf that controls the passage of gases into and out of the plant. **2.** *Zool.* a mouth or mouthlike part. [Greek: mouth]

stomach (ˈstʌmək) *n.* **1.** an organ inside the body in which food is stored until it has been partially digested. **2.** the abdominal region. **3.** desire, appetite, or inclination: *I have no stomach for arguments.* ~*vb.* **4.** to tolerate; bear: *I can't stomach his bragging.* [Greek *stoma* mouth]

stomachache (ˈstʌmɪkˌeɪk) *n.* pain in the stomach, as from indigestion. Also called: **stomach upset, upset stomach.**

stomacher (ˈstʌməkə) *n. Hist.* a decorative V-shaped panel of stiff material worn over the chest and stomach mainly by women.

stomach pump *n. Med.* a suction device for removing stomach contents through a tube inserted down the throat.

stomp (stɒmp) *vb.* to tread or stamp heavily. [var. of *stamp*]

stone (stəʊn) *n.* **1.** the hard nonmetallic material of which rocks are made. **2.** a small lump of rock; pebble. **3.** Also called: **gemstone.** a precious or semiprecious stone that has been cut and polished. **4.** a piece of rock used for some particular purpose: *gravestone; millstone.* **5.** something that resembles a stone: *hailstone.* **6.** the hard central part of such fruits as the peach or date. **7.** (*pl.* **stone**) *Brit.* a unit of weight equal to 14 pounds or 6.350 kilograms. **8.** *Pathol.* a stonelike mineral growth found in organs of the body. **9.** (*modifier*) made of stoneware: *a stone jar.* **10. heart of stone.** a hard or unemotional nature. **11. leave no stone unturned.** to do everything possible to achieve something. ~*vb.* **12.** to throw stones at (someone), esp. to kill him. **13.** to remove the stones from (a fruit). [Old English *stān*]

Stone Age *n.* a period in human culture identified by the use of stone implements.

stonechat (ˈstəʊnˌtʃæt) *n.* a songbird that has a black plumage with a reddish-brown breast. [from its cry, which sounds like clattering pebbles]

stone-cold *adj.* **1.** completely cold. ~*adv.* **2. stone-cold sober.** completely sober.

stoned (stəʊnd) *adj. Slang.* under the influence of drugs or alcohol.

stone-deaf *adj.* completely deaf.

stone fruit *n.* same as **drupe.**

stonemason (ˈstəʊnˌmeɪsˈn) *n.* a person who is skilled in preparing stone for building.

stone's throw *n.* a short distance.

stonewall (ˌstəʊnˈwɔːl) *vb.* **1.** to obstruct or hinder discussion. **2.** *Cricket.* (of a batsman) to play defensively.

stoneware (ˈstəʊnˌwɛə) *n.* a hard opaque pottery, fired at a very high temperature.

stonewashed (ˈstəʊnˌwɒʃt) *adj.* (of clothes or fabric) given a worn faded look by being washed with many small pieces of stone.

stonework (ˈstəʊnˌwɜːk) *n.* any structure or part of a building made of stone.

stony *or* **stoney** (ˈstəʊnɪ) *adj.* **stonier, stoniest.** **1.** covered with stones: *a stony beach.* **2.** (of a face, voice, or attitude) unfeeling or hard. —**stonily** *adv.*

stony-broke *adj. Brit. slang.* completely without money; penniless.

stood (stʊd) *vb.* past of **stand.**

stooge (stuːdʒ) *n.* **1.** an actor who feeds lines to a comedian or acts as the butt of his jokes. **2.** *Slang.* someone who is taken advantage of by someone in a superior position. [origin unknown]

stool (stuːl) *n.* **1.** a seat with legs but no

back. **2.** waste matter from the bowels. [Old English *stōl*]

stool pigeon *n.* an informer for the police.

stoop¹ (stuːp) *vb.* **1.** to bend (the body) forward and downward. **2.** to carry oneself with head and shoulders habitually bent forward. **3.** (foll. by *to*) to degrade oneself: *I wouldn't stoop to his level.* ~*n.* **4.** the act, position, or habit of stooping. [Old English *stūpan*] —**stooping** *adj.*

stoop² (stuːp) *n. U.S.* an open porch or small platform with steps leading up to it at the entrance to a building. [Dutch *stoep*]

stop (stɒp) *vb.* **stopping, stopped.** **1.** to cease from doing (something); discontinue. **2.** to cause (something moving) to halt or (of something moving) to come to a halt. **3.** to prevent the continuance or completion of (something). **4.** (often foll. by *from*) to prevent or restrain: *he stopped George from fighting.* **5.** to keep back: *to stop supplies.* **6.** (foll. by *up*) to block or plug: *to stop up a pipe.* **7.** to instruct a bank not to honour (a cheque). **8.** to deduct (money) from pay. **9.** *Informal.* to receive (a blow or hit). **10.** to stay or rest: *we stopped at the Robinsons'.* **11.** *Music.* to alter the vibrating length of (a string on a violin, guitar, etc.) by pressing down on it at some point with the finger. **12. stop at nothing.** to be prepared to do anything; be unscrupulous or ruthless. ~*n.* **13.** prevention of movement or progress: *to put a stop to something.* **14.** the act of stopping or the state of being stopped: *to come to a stop.* **15.** a place where something halts or pauses: *a bus stop.* **16.** the act or an instance of blocking or obstructing. **17.** a device that prevents, limits, or ends the motion of a mechanism or moving part. **18.** *Brit.* a full stop. **19.** *Music.* a knob on an organ that is operated to allow sets of pipes to sound. **20. pull out all the stops.** to make a great effort. [Old English *stoppian* (unattested)]

stopbank (ˈstɒpˌbæŋk) *n. N.Z.* an embankment to prevent flooding.

stopcock (ˈstɒpˌkɒk) *n.* a valve used to control or stop the flow of a fluid in a pipe.

stopgap (ˈstɒpˌgæp) *n.* a temporary substitute.

stop off *vb.* (often foll. by *at*) to halt and call somewhere on the way to another place.

stopover (ˈstɒpˌəʊvə) *n.* **1.** a break in a journey. ~*vb.* **stop over.** **2.** to make a stopover.

stoppage (ˈstɒpɪdʒ) *n.* **1.** the act of stopping something or the state of being stopped. **2.** a deduction of money, as from pay. **3.** an organized stopping of work, as during a strike.

stopper (ˈstɒpə) *n.* a plug or bung for closing a bottle, pipe, etc.

stop press *n. Brit.* news items inserted into a newspaper after the printing has been started.

stopwatch (ˈstɒpˌwɒtʃ) *n.* a watch used for timing sporting events accurately, hav-

ing a device for stopping the hands instantly.

storage ('stɔːrɪdʒ) n. **1.** the act of storing
or the state of being stored. **2.** space for
storing. **3.** *Computers.* the process of storing information in a computer.

storage device n. a piece of computer
equipment, such as a magnetic tape or a
disk in or on which information can be
stored.

storage heater n. an electric device
capable of accumulating and radiating heat
generated by off-peak electricity.

store (stɔː) vb. **1.** to keep, set aside, or
accumulate (things) for future use. **2.** to
place furniture or other possessions in a
warehouse for safekeeping. **3.** to supply
or stock (certain goods). **4.** *Computers.* to
enter or retain (information) in a storage
device. ~n. **5.** a shop (in Britain usually
a large one). **6.** a large supply or stock
kept for future use. **7.** short for **department store. 8.** a storage place, such as a
warehouse. **9.** *Computers, chiefly Brit.*
same as **memory** (sense 7). **10. in store.**
forthcoming or imminent: *I wonder what's
in store for us today.* **11. set great store
by something.** to value something or regard something as important. ~See also
stores. [Old French *estor*]

storehouse ('stɔːˌhaʊs) n. a place where
things are stored.

storeroom ('stɔːˌruːm) n. a room in which
things are stored.

stores (stɔːz) pl. n. supply or stock of food
and other essentials for a journey.

storey or esp. U.S. **story** ('stɔːrɪ) n., pl.
-reys or **-ries.** a floor or level of a building.
[Anglo-Latin *historia* picture, prob. from
the pictures on medieval windows]

stork (stɔːk) n. a large wading bird with
very long legs, a long bill, and a white-and-
black plumage. [Old English *storc*]

storm (stɔːm) n. **1.** a violent weather
condition of strong winds, rain, hail, thunder, lightning, etc. **2.** a violent disturbance
or quarrel. **3.** a heavy discharge of bullets
or missiles. **4. take a place by storm. a.** to
capture or overrun a place by a violent
assault. **b.** to overwhelm and enthral a
place or the people in it. ~vb. **5.** to
attack or capture (a place) suddenly and
violently. **6.** to shout angrily. **7.** to move
or rush violently or angrily: *he stormed out
of the meeting.* [Old English]

storm centre n. **1.** the centre of a
storm, where pressure is lowest. **2.** the
centre of any disturbance or trouble.

storm door n. an additional door outside
an ordinary door, providing extra protection against wind, cold, and rain.

storm trooper n. a member of the Nazi
terrorist militia.

stormy ('stɔːmɪ) adj. **stormier, stormiest.**
1. characterized by storms: *stormy weather.* **2.** involving violent disturbance or
emotional outbursts: *a stormy relationship.*

stormy or **storm petrel** n. **1.** a small
petrel with dark plumage and paler underparts. **2.** a person who brings trouble.

story[1] ('stɔːrɪ) n., pl. **-ries. 1.** a description

of a chain of events told or written in prose
or verse. **2.** Also called: **short story.** a
piece of fiction, briefer and usually less
detailed than a novel. **3.** Also called: **story
line.** the plot of a book or film. **4.** a
newspaper report. **5.** the event or material
for such a report. **6.** *Informal.* a lie.
[Latin *historia* inquiry]

story[2] ('stɔːrɪ) n., pl. **-ries.** Chiefly. U.S.
same as **storey.**

storybook ('stɔːrɪˌbʊk) n. **1.** a book containing stories for children. ~adj. **2.**
unreal or fantastic: *a storybook world.*

stoup or **stoop** (stuːp) n. a small basin for
holy water. [from Old Norse]

stoush (staʊʃ) Austral. & N.Z. slang. ~vb.
1. to hit or punch (someone). ~n. **2.**
fighting or violence. [origin unknown]

stout (staʊt) adj. **1.** solidly built or fat. **2.**
resolute or brave: *stout fellow.* **3.** strong
and robust. ~n. **4.** strong dark beer.
[Old French *estout* bold] —'**stoutly** adv.

stouthearted (ˌstaʊt'hɑːtɪd) adj. resolute
or brave.

stove[1] (stəʊv) n. **1.** same as **cooker** (sense
1). **2.** any heating apparatus, such as a
kiln. [Old English *stofa* bathroom]

stove[2] (stəʊv) vb. a past tense and past
participle of **stave.**

stovepipe ('stəʊvˌpaɪp) n. a pipe that
serves as a flue to a stove.

stow (stəʊ) vb. (often foll. by *away*) to
pack or store (something). [Old English
stōwian to keep]

stowage ('stəʊɪdʒ) n. **1.** space, room, or a
charge for stowing goods. **2.** a stowing.

stowaway ('stəʊəˌweɪ) n. **1.** a person who
hides aboard a vehicle, ship, or aircraft in
order to travel free. ~vb. **stow away. 2.**
to travel in such a way.

strabismus (strə'bɪzməs) n. Pathol. same
as **squint** (sense 3). [Greek *strabismos*]

straddle ('stræd³l) vb. **1.** to have one leg
or part on each side of (something). **2.**
U.S. & Canad. informal. to be in favour of
both sides of (an issue). [from *stride*]

Stradivarius (ˌstrædɪ'vɛərɪəs) n. a violin
manufactured in Italy by Antonio
Stradivari (?1644–1737) or his family.

strafe (strɑːf) vb. to machine-gun (troops)
from the air. [German *strafen* to punish]

straggle ('stræg³l) vb. **1.** to go or spread
in a rambling or irregular way. **2.** to linger
behind or wander from a main line or
part. [origin unknown] —'**straggler** n.
—'**straggly** adj.

straight (streɪt) adj. **1.** not curved or
crooked; continuing in the same direction
without bending. **2.** straightforward, outright, or candid: *a straight rejection.* **3.**
even, level, or upright. **4.** in keeping with
the facts; accurate. **5.** honest, respectable,
or reliable. **6.** continuous; uninterrupted:
in straight succession. **7.** (of an alcoholic
drink) undiluted; neat. **8.** not wavy or
curly: *straight hair.* **9.** correctly arranged;
orderly. **10.** (of a play or acting style)
straightforward or serious. **11.** Slang.
heterosexual. **12.** Informal. no longer owing or being owed something: *if you buy
the next round we'll be straight.* **13.** Slang.

conventional in views, customs, or appearance. ~*adv.* **14.** in a straight line or direct course. **15.** immediately; at once: *he came straight back.* **16.** in an even, level, or upright position: *stand up straight.* **17.** continuously; uninterruptedly. **18.** (often foll. by *out*) frankly; candidly: *he told me straight out.* **19. go straight.** *Informal.* to reform after having been a criminal. ~*n.* **20.** a straight line, form, part, or position. **21.** *Brit.* a straight part of a racetrack. [Old English *streccan* to stretch]

straightaway (ˌstreɪtəˈweɪ) *or* **straight away** *adv.* at once.

straighten ('streɪt²n) *vb.* (sometimes foll. by *up* or *out*) **1.** to make or become straight. **2.** to make (something) neat or tidy.

straighten out *vb.* to make (something) less complicated or confused.

straight face *n.* a serious facial expression which conceals a desire to laugh. —ˌstraight-ˈfaced *adj.*

straight fight *n.* a contest between two candidates only.

straightforward (ˌstreɪtˈfɔːwəd) *adj.* **1.** (of a person) honest, frank, or simple. **2.** *Chiefly Brit.* (of a task) simple; easy.

straight man *n.* an actor who acts as stooge to a comedian.

strain¹ (streɪn) *vb.* **1.** to draw (something) taut or be drawn taut. **2.** to exert or use (resources) to the utmost extent. **3.** to injure or damage (oneself or a part of one's body) by overexertion: *he strained himself.* **4.** to make intense or violent efforts: *he is straining to keep up with the other runners.* **5.** to subject (someone) to mental tension or stress. **6.** to pour (a substance) through a sieve or filter. **7.** (foll. by *at*) to push, pull, or work with violent exertion (on something). ~*n.* **8.** the damage resulting from excessive physical exertion. **9.** an intense physical or mental effort. **10.** (*pl.*) *Music.* a theme, melody, or tune. **11.** a great demand on the emotions, resources, etc. **12.** a way of speaking; tone of voice: *don't go on in that strain.* **13.** tension or tiredness resulting from overwork or worry. **14.** *Physics.* the change in dimension of a body caused by outside forces. [Latin *stringere* to bind tightly]

strain² (streɪn) *n.* **1.** a group of animals or plants within a species or variety, distinguished by one or more minor characteristics. **2.** a streak; trace. [Old English *strēon*]

strained (streɪnd) *adj.* **1.** (of an action, expression, etc.) not natural or spontaneous. **2.** (of an atmosphere, relationship, etc.) not relaxed; tense.

strainer ('streɪnə) *n.* a sieve used for straining sauces, vegetables, or tea.

strait (streɪt) *n.* **1.** (*often pl.*) a narrow channel of the sea linking two larger areas of sea. **2.** (*pl.*) a position of acute difficulty: *in dire straits.* [Old French: narrow]

straitened ('streɪt²nd) *adj.* **in straitened circumstances.** not having much money.

straitjacket ('streɪtˌdʒækɪt) *n.* **1.** a strong canvas jacket with long sleeves for binding the arms of violent prisoners or mental patients. **2.** a restriction or limitation.

strait-laced *or* **straight-laced** *adj.* prudish or puritanical.

strand¹ (strænd) *vb.* **1.** to leave or drive (ships or fish) ashore. **2.** to leave (someone) helpless, for example without transport or money. ~*n.* **3.** *Chiefly poetic.* a shore or beach. [Old English]

strand² (strænd) *n.* **1.** one of the individual fibres or threads of string, wire, etc., that form a rope, cord, etc. **2.** a single length of string, hair, wool, wire, etc. **3.** a string of pearls or beads. **4.** a constituent element of something. [origin unknown]

strange (streɪndʒ) *adj.* **1.** odd, unusual, or peculiar. **2.** not known, seen, or experienced before; unfamiliar. **3.** (foll. by *to*) inexperienced (in) or unaccustomed (to): *strange to a task.* [Latin *extrāneus* foreign] —ˈstrangely *adv.* —ˈstrangeness *n.*

stranger ('streɪndʒə) *n.* **1.** any person whom one does not know. **2.** a person who is new to a particular locality or who comes from another region or town. **3.** (foll. by *to*) a person who is unfamiliar with or new to something: *he is no stranger to computers.*

strangle ('stræŋg²l) *vb.* **1.** to kill (someone) by pressing his windpipe; throttle. **2.** to prevent the growth or development of: *to strangle originality.* **3.** to suppress (an utterance) by or as if by swallowing suddenly: *a strangled cry.* [Greek *strangalē* a halter] —ˈstrangler *n.*

stranglehold ('stræŋg²lˌhəʊld) *n.* **1.** a wrestling hold in which a wrestler's arms are pressed against his opponent's windpipe. **2.** complete power or control over a person or situation.

strangulate ('stræŋgjʊˌleɪt) *vb.* **1.** *Pathol.* to constrict (a hollow organ or vessel) so as to stop the flow of air or blood through it: *a strangulated hernia.* **2.** same as **strangle.** —ˌstranguˈlation *n.*

strap (stræp) *n.* **1.** a strip of leather or similar material used for carrying, lifting, fastening, or holding things in place. **2.** a loop of leather or rubber, hanging from the roof in a bus or train for standing passengers to hold on to. **3.** short for **shoulder strap. 4. the strap.** a beating with a strap as a punishment. ~*vb.* **strapping,** **strapped. 5.** to tie or bind (something) with a strap. [var. of *strop*]

straphanger ('stræpˌhæŋə) *n. Informal.* a passenger in a bus or train who has to travel standing and holding on to a strap.

strapping ('stræpɪŋ) *adj.* tall and sturdy: *a strapping young man.* [from *strap* (in the archaic sense: to work vigorously)]

strata ('strɑːtə) *n.* a plural of **stratum.**

stratagem ('strætɪdʒəm) *n.* a clever plan to deceive an enemy. [Greek *stratēgos* general]

strategic (strəˈtiːdʒɪk) *adj.* **1.** of or characteristic of strategy. **2.** (of weapons, esp. missiles) directed against an enemy's homeland rather than used on a battlefield. —straˈtegically *adv.*

strategy ('strætɪdʒɪ) *n., pl.* **-gies. 1.** the

art of the planning and conduct of a war. **2.** a long-term plan for success, as in politics or business. [Greek *stratēgia* function of a general] —**'strategist** *n.*

strath (stræθ) *n. Scot.* a flat river valley. [Scot. & Irish Gaelic *srath*]

strathspey (ˌstræθ'speɪ) *n.* **1.** a Scottish dance with gliding steps, slower than a reel. **2.** music for this dance. [after *Strathspey*, valley of the River Spey]‖

stratified ('strætɪˌfaɪd) *adj.* ‖**1.** (of rocks) formed in layers or strata. **2.** *Sociol.* (of a society) divided into status groups. [New Latin *stratificāre*] —**ˌstratifi'cation** *n.*

stratocumulus (ˌstrætəʊ'kjuːmjʊləs) *n., pl.* **-li** (-ˌlaɪ). *Meteorol.* a uniform stretch of cloud containing dark grey masses.

stratosphere ('strætəˌsfɪə) *n.* the atmospheric layer between about 15 and 50 km above the earth.

stratum ('strɑːtəm) *n., pl.* **-ta** or **-tums. 1.** any of the distinct layers into which certain rocks are divided. **2.** a layer of ocean or atmosphere marked off either naturally or arbitrarily. **3.** a social class. [Latin: something strewn]

stratus ('streɪtəs) *n., pl.* **-ti** (-taɪ). a grey layer cloud. [Latin: strewn]

straw (strɔː) *n.* **1. a.** stalks of threshed grain, such as wheat or barley, used for plaiting or as fodder. **b.** (*as modifier*): *a straw hat.* **2.** a single stalk of straw. **3.** a long thin hollow paper or plastic tube, used for sucking up liquids into the mouth. **4. clutch at straws.** to turn in desperation to measures with little chance of success. **5. draw the short straw.** to be the person chosen to perform an unpleasant task. ~*adj.* **6.** pale yellow. [Old English *strēaw*]

strawberry ('strɔːbərɪ) *n., pl.* **-ries.** a sweet fleshy red fruit with small seedlike parts on the outside. [Old English *strēaberige*]

strawberry blonde *adj.* **1.** (of hair) reddish blonde. ~*n.* **2.** a woman with such hair.

strawberry mark *n.* a red birthmark.

straw poll or **vote** *n.* an unofficial poll or vote taken to determine the opinion of a group or the public on some issue.

stray (streɪ) *vb.* **1.** to wander away from the correct path or from a given area. **2.** to move away from the point or lose concentration. **3.** to deviate from certain moral standards: *he promised his wife that he would never stray again.* ~*n.* **4. a.** a domestic animal that has wandered away from its place of keeping and is lost. **b.** (*as modifier*): *stray dogs.* **5.** a lost or homeless person, esp. a child: *waifs and strays.* ~*adj.* **6.** scattered, random, or haphazard: *a stray bullet.* [Old French *estraier*]

streak (striːk) *n.* **1.** a long thin stripe or trace of some contrasting colour. **2.** (of lightning) a sudden flash. **3.** a quality or characteristic: *a jealous streak.* **4.** a short stretch of good or bad luck: *a winning streak.* **5.** *Informal.* an instance of running naked through a public place. ~*vb.* **6.** to mark (something) with a streak or streaks:

her face was streaked with tears. **7.** to move rapidly in a straight line. **8.** *Informal.* to run naked through a public place. [Old English *strica*] —**streaked** or **'streaky** *adj.* —**'streaker** *n.*

stream (striːm) *n.* **1.** a small river. **2.** any steady flow of water or other fluid. **3.** something that resembles a stream in moving continuously in a line or particular direction: *a steady stream of customers.* **4.** a rapid or unbroken flow of speech: *a stream of abuse.* **5.** *Brit.* a class of schoolchildren grouped together because of similar ability. ~*vb.* **6.** to pour in a continuous flow: *his nose streamed blood.* **7.** (of a crowd of people or vehicles) to move in unbroken succession. **8.** to float freely or with a waving motion: *bunting streamed in the wind.* **9.** *Brit.* to group (schoolchildren) in streams. [Old English] —**'streaming** *n.* —**'streamlet** *n.*

streamer ('striːmə) *n.* **1.** a long coiled ribbon of coloured paper that unrolls when tossed. **2.** a long narrow flag.

streamline ('striːmˌlaɪn) *vb.* to make (something) streamlined.

streamlined ('striːmˌlaɪnd) *adj.* **1.** offering or designed to offer the minimum resistance to the flow of a gas or liquid. **2.** made more efficient, esp. by simplifying.

street (striːt) *n.* **1.** a public road that is usually lined with buildings, esp. in a town: *Oxford Street.* **2.** the part of the road between the pavements, used by vehicles. **3.** the people living in a particular street. **4. on the streets.** homeless. **5. right up one's street.** *Informal.* just what one knows or likes best. **6. streets ahead of.** *Informal.* superior to or more advanced than. [Old English *strēt*]

streetcar ('striːtˌkɑː) *n. U.S. & Canad.* a tram.

streetwalker ('striːtˌwɔːkə) *n.* a prostitute who tries to find customers in the streets.

streetwise ('striːtˌwaɪz) *adj.* knowing how to survive or succeed in poor and often criminal sections of big cities.

strength (strɛŋθ) *n.* **1.** the state or quality of being physically or mentally strong. **2.** the ability to withstand great force, stress, or pressure. **3.** something regarded as beneficial or a source of power: *their chief strength is technology.* **4.** potency, as of a drink or drug. **5.** power to convince: *the strength of an argument.* **6.** degree of intensity or concentration of colour, light, sound, or flavour. **7.** the total number of people in a group: *at full strength; below strength.* **8. go from strength to strength.** to have ever-increasing success. **9. on the strength of.** on the basis of or relying upon. [Old English *strengthu*]

strengthen ('strɛŋθən) *vb.* to make (something) stronger or become stronger.

strenuous ('strɛnjʊəs) *adj.* requiring or involving the use of great energy or effort. [Latin *strēnuus* brisk] —**'strenuously** *adv.*

streptococcus (ˌstrɛptəʊ'kɒkəs) *n., pl.* **-cocci** (-'kɒkaɪ). a bacterium occurring in chains and including many disease-causing species. [Greek *streptos* crooked + *kokkos* berry]

streptomycin (ˌstreptəʊˈmaɪsɪn) *n.* an antibiotic used in the treatment of tuberculosis and other bacterial infections. [Greek *streptos* crooked + *mukēs* fungus]

stress (stres) *n.* **1.** special emphasis or significance. **2.** mental, emotional, or physical strain or tension. **3.** emphasis placed upon a syllable by pronouncing it more loudly than those that surround it. **4.** *Physics.* force producing a change in shape or volume. ~*vb.* **5.** to give emphasis to (a point or subject): *she stressed the need for improved facilities for the disabled.* **6.** to pronounce (a word or syllable) more loudly than those surrounding it. **7.** to subject (someone or something) to stress. [shortened from *distress*] —ˈ**stressful** *adj.*

stretch (stretʃ) *vb.* **1.** to draw out or extend (something) or to be drawn out or extended in length or area. **2.** to distort or lengthen (something) or to be distorted or lengthened permanently. **3.** to extend (the limbs or body), for example when one has just woken up. **4.** to reach or suspend (a rope, etc.) from one place to another. **5.** to draw (something) tight; tighten. **6.** (often foll. by *out, forward,* etc.) to reach or hold out (a part of one's body). **7.** (usually foll. by *over*) to extend in time: *the course stretched over three months.* **8.** (foll. by *for, over,* etc.) (of a region) to extend in length or area. **9.** to put a great strain upon (one's money or resources). **10.** to make do with (limited resources): *to stretch one's budget.* **11.** to extend (someone) to the limit of his abilities. **12. stretch a point.** to make a concession or exception not usually made. ~*n.* **13.** the act of stretching. **14.** a large or continuous expanse or distance: *a stretch of water.* **15.** extent in time. **16. a.** ability to be stretched, as in some garments. **b.** (*as modifier*): *stretch pants.* **17.** *Slang.* a term of imprisonment. **18. at a stretch.** *Chiefly Brit.* **a.** with some difficulty; by making a special effort. **b.** at one time: *he sometimes read for hours at a stretch.* [Old English *streccan*] —ˈ**stretchy** *adj.*

stretcher (ˈstretʃə) *n.* a device for transporting an ill or injured person consisting of a frame covered by canvas or other material.

stretcher-bearer *n.* a person who helps to carry a stretcher.

strew (struː) *vb.* **strewing, strewed; strewn.** to spread or scatter (things) or to be spread or scattered over a surface or area. [Old English *streowian*]

strewth (struːθ) *interj.* an expression of surprise or dismay. [alteration of *God's truth*]

stria (ˈstraɪə) *n., pl.* **striae** (ˈstraɪiː). *Geol.* a scratch or groove on the surface of a rock crystal. [Latin: a groove]

striation (straɪˈeɪʃən) *n.* **1.** an arrangement or pattern of striae. **2.** same as **stria**. —**striated** (straɪˈeɪtɪd) *adj.*

stricken (ˈstrɪkən) *adj.* badly affected by

disease, pain, grief, etc.: *grief-stricken.* [p.p. of *strike*]

strict (strɪkt) *adj.* **1.** adhering closely to specified rules. **2.** (of a rule or law) enforced stringently; rigorous: *a strict code of conduct.* **3.** severely correct in attention to conduct or morality: *a strict teacher.* **4.** (of a punishment, etc.) harsh; severe. **5.** complete; absolute: *strict secrecy.* [Latin *strictus*] —ˈ**strictly** *adv.* —ˈ**strictness** *n.*

stricture (ˈstrɪktʃə) *n.* a severe criticism. [Latin *strictūra* contraction]

stride (straɪd) *n.* **1.** a long step or pace. **2.** the space measured by such a step. **3.** a striding walk. **4.** progress or development: *we have made rapid strides in computer technology.* **5.** a regular pace or rate of progress: *it put me off my stride.* **6. take something in one's stride.** to do something without difficulty or effort. ~*vb.* **striding, strode, stridden** (ˈstrɪdən). **7.** to walk with long steps or paces, as in haste. **8.** (foll. by *over* or *across*) to cross (over a space or an obstacle) with a stride. [Old English *strīdan*]

strident (ˈstraɪdənt) *adj.* **1.** (of a voice or sound) loud or harsh. **2.** loudly persistent or forceful: *strident demands.* [Latin *strīdēns*] —ˈ**stridency** *n.*

strife (straɪf) *n.* angry or violent struggle; conflict. [Old French *estrif*]

strike (straɪk) *vb.* **striking, struck. 1.** (of workers) to cease work collectively as a protest against working conditions, low pay, etc. **2.** to hit (someone). **3.** to cause (something) to come into sudden or violent contact with something. **4.** (foll. by *at*) to attack (someone or something). **5.** to cause (a match) to light by friction. **6.** to sound (a specific note) on a musical instrument. **7.** (of a clock) to indicate (a specific time) by the sound of a bell. **8.** (of a poisonous snake) to cause injury by biting. **9.** to affect (someone) deeply in a particular way: *her appearance struck him as strange.* **10.** to enter the mind of: *it struck me that he had become very quiet.* **11.** (*past participle* **struck** or **stricken**) to render: *struck dumb.* **12.** to be noticed by; catch: *the glint of metal struck his eye.* **13.** to arrive at (something) suddenly or unexpectedly: *to strike on a solution.* **14.** to afflict (someone) with a disease: *he was struck with polio.* **15.** to discover or come upon a source of (gold, oil, etc.). **16.** to take apart or pack up: *to strike camp.* **17.** to form or impress (a coin or metal) by or as if by stamping it. **18.** to take up (an attitude or a posture). **19.** to reach (something) by agreement: *to strike a bargain.* **20. strike home.** to achieve the intended effect. **21. strike it rich.** *Informal.* to have an unexpected financial success. ~*n.* **22.** a stopping of work, as a protest against working conditions, low pay, etc.: *on strike.* **23.** an act or instance of striking. **24.** a military attack, esp. an air attack on a surface target: *an air strike.* **25.** *Baseball.* a pitched ball swung at and missed by the batter. **26.** *Tenpin bowling.* the knocking down of all the pins with one bowl. **27.** the discovery of a source of gold, oil, etc. ~See also **strike off, strike out, strike up**. [Old English *strīcan*]

strikebreaker ('straɪk,breɪkə) *n*. a person who tries to make a strike fail by working or by taking the place of those on strike.

strike off *vb*. to remove the name of (a doctor or lawyer who has done something wrong) from an official register, preventing him from practising again.

strike out *vb*. **1.** to score out (something written). **2.** to start out or begin: *to strike out on one's own*.

strike pay *n*. money paid to strikers by a trade union.

striker ('straɪkə) *n*. **1.** a person who is on strike. **2.** *Soccer*. an attacking player.

strike up *vb*. **1.** (of a band or an orchestra) to begin to play. **2.** to bring about; start: *to strike up a friendship*.

striking ('straɪkɪŋ) *adj*. **1.** attracting attention; fine; impressive: *a striking beauty*. **2.** conspicuous; noticeable: *a striking difference*. —'**strikingly** *adv*.

Strine (straɪn) *n*. a humorous transliteration of Australian pronunciation, as in *Gloria Soame* for *glorious home*. [a jocular rendering of the Australian pronunciation of *Australian*]

string (strɪŋ) *n*. **1.** thin cord or twine used for tying, hanging, or binding things: *a ball of string*. **2.** a group of objects threaded on a single strand: *a string of beads*. **3.** a series of things or events: *a string of girlfriends*. **4.** a tightly stretched wire or cord by means of which stringed instruments, such as the violin, guitar, and piano, are played. **5.** *Music*. (*pl*.; usually preceded by *the*) **a.** violins, violas, cellos, and double basses collectively. **b.** the section of an orchestra consisting of such instruments. **6.** a group of characters that can be treated as a unit by a computer program. **7.** (*pl*.) complications or conditions: *no strings attached*. **8.** (*modifier*) composed of stringlike strands woven in a large mesh: *a string vest*. **9. pull strings**. *Informal*. to exert power or influence, esp. secretly or unofficially. ~*vb*. **stringing, strung**. **10.** to provide (something) with a string or strings. **11.** to hang or stretch (something) from one point to another. **12.** to thread (beads) on a string. **13.** to extend in a line or series: *signposts strung out along the road*. [Old English *streng*] —'**string,like** *adj*.

string along *vb*. *Informal*. **1.** (foll. by *with*) to accompany: *I'll string along with you*. **2.** to deceive (someone) over a period of time: *she's just stringing him along till something better turns up*.

string course *n*. *Archit*. an ornamental projecting band along a wall.

stringed (strɪŋd) *adj*. (of musical instruments) having strings.

stringent ('strɪndʒənt) *adj*. requiring strict attention to rules or detail. [Latin *stringere* to bind] —'**stringency** *n*.

stringer ('strɪŋə) *n*. **1.** *Archit*. a long horizontal timber beam that connects upright posts. **2.** a journalist employed by a

newspaper on a part-time basis to cover a particular town or area.

string quartet *n*. *Music*. **1.** a group of musicians consisting of two violins, one viola, and one cello. **2.** a piece of music composed for such a group.

string up *vb*. *Informal*. to kill (a person) by hanging.

stringy ('strɪŋɪ) *adj*. **stringier, stringiest**. **1.** resembling strings: *stringy hair*. **2.** (of meat or other food) fibrous.

strip¹ (strɪp) *vb*. **stripping, stripped**. **1.** to take (the covering or clothes) off (oneself, another person, or thing). **2. a.** to undress completely. **b.** to perform a striptease. **3.** to empty (a building) of all furniture. **4.** to take something away from (someone): *stripped of possessions*. **5.** to remove (paint) from (a surface or furniture): *stripped pine*. **6.** to dismantle (an engine or a mechanism). ~*n*. **7.** the act or an instance of undressing or of performing a striptease. [Old English *bestrēpian* to plunder]

strip² (strɪp) *n*. **1.** a long narrow piece of something. **2.** short for **airstrip**. **3.** the clothes worn by the members of a football team. [Middle Dutch *stripe* stripe]

strip cartoon *n*. a sequence of drawings in a newspaper or magazine, telling a humorous story or an adventure.

strip club *n*. a club in which striptease performances take place.

stripe¹ (straɪp) *n*. **1.** a long band of colour that differs from the surrounding material. **2.** a strip, band, or chevron worn on a uniform to indicate rank. ~*vb*. **3.** to mark (something) with stripes. [prob. from Middle Dutch *stripe*] —**striped** or '**stripy** *adj*.

stripe² (straɪp) *n*. a stroke from a whip, rod or cane. [from Middle Low German]

strip lighting *n*. electric lighting by means of long glass tubes that are fluorescent lamps.

stripling ('strɪplɪŋ) *n*. a lad.

stripper ('strɪpə) *n*. **1.** a striptease artiste. **2.** a device or substance for removing paint or varnish.

strip-searching *n*. the practice by police or customs officials of stripping a prisoner or suspect naked and searching him or her for drugs or smuggled goods.

striptease ('strɪp,tiːz) *n*. a form of erotic entertainment in which a person gradually undresses to music.

strive (straɪv) *vb*. **striving, strove, striven** ('strɪvⁿn). to make a great effort: *to strive for freedom*. [Old French *estriver*]

strobe (strəʊb) *n*. short for **strobe lighting** or **stroboscope**.

strobe lighting *n*. a flashing beam of very bright light produced by a perforated disc rotating in front of a light source.

stroboscope ('strəʊbə,skəʊp) *n*. an instrument producing a very bright flashing light which makes moving people appear stationary. [Greek *strobos* a whirling + *skopein* to look at]

strode (strəʊd) *vb.* the past tense of **stride.**

stroganoff ('strɒgəˌnɒf) *n.* a dish of sliced beef cooked with onions and mushrooms, served in a sour-cream sauce. Also called: **beef stroganoff.** [after Count *Stroganoff,* Russian diplomat]

stroke (strəʊk) *n.* **1.** *Pathol.* rupture of a blood vessel in the brain resulting in loss of consciousness, often followed by paralysis. **2.** a blow, knock, or hit. **3.** an action, movement, or occurrence of the kind specified: *a stroke of luck; a stroke of genius.* **a.** the striking of a clock. **b.** the hour registered by this: *on the stroke of three.* **5.** a mark made by a pen or paintbrush. **6.** same as **solidus**: used esp. when dictating or reading aloud. **7.** a light touch or caress with the fingers. **8.** the swinging at and hitting of the ball in sports such as golf or cricket. **9.** any one of the repeated movements used by a swimmer. **10.** a particular style of swimming, such as the crawl. **11.** a single pull on an oar or oars in rowing. **12. at a stroke.** with one action. **13. not a stroke (of work).** no work at all. ~*vb.* **14.** to touch or brush (someone or something) lightly or gently. [Old English *strācian*]

stroll (strəʊl) *vb.* **1.** to walk about in a leisurely manner. ~*n.* **2.** a leisurely walk. [prob. from dialect German *strollen*]

strong (strɒŋ) *adj.* **stronger** ('strɒŋɡə), **strongest** ('strɒŋɡɪst). **1.** possessing strength. **2.** solid or robust; not easily broken or injured. **3.** resolute or morally firm: *strong views.* **4.** intense in quality; not faint or feeble: *a strong voice; a strong smell.* **5.** easily defensible: *strong arguments.* **6.** concentrated; not weak or diluted. **7.** containing or having a specified number: *a navy 40 000 strong.* **8.** having a powerful taste or smell: *strong cheese.* **9.** having an extreme or drastic effect: *strong discipline.* **10.** emphatic or immoderate: *strong language.* **11.** (of a colour) having a high degree of purity; very intense. **12.** (of a wind, current, or earthquake) moving fast. **13.** (of a currency, an industry, etc.) characterized by firm or increasing prices. ~*adv.* **14. come on strong.** to make a forceful or exaggerated impression. **15. going strong.** *Informal.* thriving. [Old English *strang*] —'**strongly** *adv.*

strong-arm *n. (modifier) Informal.* involving physical force or violence: *strong-arm tactics.*

strongbox ('strɒŋˌbɒks) *n.* a box in which valuables are locked for safety.

strong drink *n.* alcoholic drink.

stronghold ('strɒŋˌhəʊld) *n.* **1.** a defensible place; fortress. **2.** an area of predominance of a particular belief: *a Tory stronghold.*

strong-minded *adj.* firm, resolute, and determined.

strong point *n.* something at which one excels: *maths was never my strong point.*

strongroom ('strɒŋˌruːm) *n.* a specially designed room in which valuables are locked for safety.

strontium ('strɒntɪəm) *n. Chem.* a soft silvery-white metallic element. The radioactive isotope **strontium-90** is used in nuclear power sources and is a hazardous nuclear fallout product. Symbol: Sr [from *Strontian,* in Scotland, where discovered]

strop (strɒp) *n.* a leather strap or an abrasive strip for sharpening razors. [Greek *strophos* cord]

stroppy ('strɒpɪ) *adj.* **-pier, -piest.** *Brit. informal.* angry or awkward. [from *obstreperous*]

strove (strəʊv) *vb.* the past tense of **strive.**

struck (strʌk) *vb.* past of **strike.**

structural ('strʌktʃərəl) *adj.* **1.** of or having structure or a structure. **2.** of or forming part of the structure of a building. **3.** *Chem.* of or involving the arrangement of atoms in molecules: *a structural formula.* —'**structurally** *adv.*

structuralism ('strʌktʃərəˌlɪzəm) *n.* an approach to social sciences and to literature in terms of oppositions, contrasts, and structures, esp. as they might reflect universal mental characteristics or organizing principles. —'**structuralist** *n., adj.*

structure ('strʌktʃə) *n.* **1.** a complex construction. **2.** the arrangement and interrelationship of parts in a construction. **3.** the manner of construction or organization. **4.** *Chem.* the arrangement of atoms in a molecule of a chemical compound. **5.** *Geol.* the way in which a rock is made up of its component parts. ~*vb.* **6.** to give a structure to (something). [Latin *structūra*]

strudel ('struːdəl) *n.* a thin sheet of filled dough rolled up and baked: *apple strudel.* [from German]

struggle ('strʌg'l) *vb.* **1.** to work or strive: *they struggled for independence; we struggled to finish the work on time.* **2.** to move about strenuously so as to escape from something confining. **3.** to fight with someone, often for possession of something. **4.** to go or progress with difficulty. ~*n.* **5.** a laboured or strenuous exertion or effort. **6.** a fight or battle. [origin unknown] —'**struggling** *adj.*

strum (strʌm) *vb.* **strumming, strummed. 1.** to play (a stringed instrument) with a downward or upward sweep of the thumb or of a plectrum. **2.** to play (a tune) in this way. [prob. imit.]

strumpet ('strʌmpɪt) *n. Archaic.* a prostitute or promiscuous woman. [origin unknown]

strung (strʌŋ) *vb.* past of **string.**

strung up *adj. Informal.* tense or nervous: *I was too strung up to eat anything.*

strut (strʌt) *vb.* **strutting, strutted. 1.** to walk in a pompous manner; swagger. ~*n.* **2.** a piece of wood or metal that forms part of the framework of a structure. [Old English *strūtian* to stand stiffly]

strychnine ('strɪkniːn) *n.* a very poisonous drug used in small quantities as a stimulant. [Greek *strukhnos* nightshade]

Stuart ('stjʊət) *adj.* of or relating to the royal house that ruled Scotland from 1371 to 1714 and England from 1603 to 1714.

stub (stʌb) *n.* **1.** a short piece remaining

after something has been used: *a cigar stub.* **2.** the section of a ticket or cheque which the purchaser keeps as a receipt. ~*vb.* **stubbing, stubbed. 3.** to strike (one's toe or foot) painfully against a hard surface. **4.** (foll. by *out*) to put out (a cigarette or cigar) by pressing the end against a surface. [Old English *stubb*]

stubble ('stʌb'l) *n.* **1.** the short stalks left in a field where a crop has been harvested. **2.** the short bristly hair on the chin of a man who has not shaved for a while. [Old French *estuble*] —'**stubbly** *adj.*

stubble-jumper *n. Canad. slang.* a prairie grain farmer.

stubborn ('stʌb'n) *adj.* **1.** refusing to agree or give in. **2.** persistent and determined. **3.** difficult to handle, treat, or overcome: *a stubborn stain.* [origin unknown] —'**stubbornness** *n.*

stubby ('stʌbɪ) *adj.* **-bier, -biest.** short and broad.

stucco ('stʌkəʊ) *n.* **1.** any of various types of cement or plaster used for coating or decorating outside walls. ~*vb.* **-coing, -coed. 2.** to apply stucco to (a building). [Italian]

stuck (stʌk) *vb.* **1.** past of **stick²**. ~*adj.* **2.** *Informal.* baffled. **3.** (foll. by *on*) *Slang.* infatuated (with). **4. get stuck in.** *Informal.* to perform a task with determination.

stuck-up *adj. Informal.* conceited, arrogant, or snobbish.

stud¹ (stʌd) *n.* **1.** a small piece of metal protruding from a surface, usually as decoration. **2.** a fastener consisting of two discs at either end of a short bar, usually used with clothes. **3.** one of a number of rounded objects attached to the sole of a football boot to give better grip. ~*vb.* **studding, studded. 4.** to decorate or cover (something) with or as if with studs: *the park was studded with daisies.* [Old English *studu*]

stud² (stʌd) *n.* **1.** a male animal, esp. a stallion, kept principally for breeding purposes. **2.** Also: **stud farm.** a place where animals are bred. **3.** the state of being kept for breeding purposes. **4.** *Slang.* a virile or sexually active man. [Old English *stōd*]

student ('stjuːd'nt) *n.* **1.** a person following a course of study in a school, college, or university. **2.** a person who makes a thorough study of a subject: *a student of human nature.* [Latin *studēns* diligent]

studied ('stʌdɪd) *adj.* carefully practised or planned: *with studied indifference.*

studio ('stjuːdɪəʊ) *n., pl.* **-dios. 1.** a room in which an artist, photographer, or musician works. **2.** a room used to record television or radio programmes or to make films or records. **3.** (*pl.*) the premises of a radio, television, record, or film company. [Italian]

studio couch *n.* a backless couch that can be converted into a double bed.

studio flat *n.* a flat with one main room and, usually, a small kitchen and bathroom.

studious ('stjuːdɪəs) *adj.* **1.** of a serious, thoughtful, and hard-working character. **2.** precise, careful, or deliberate. [Latin *studiōsus* devoted to] —'**studiously** *adv.*

study ('stʌdɪ) *vb.* **studying, studied. 1.** to apply the mind to the learning or understanding of (a subject), esp. by reading. **2.** to investigate or examine (something), as by observation and research. **3.** to look at (something or someone) closely; scrutinize. ~*n., pl.* **studies. 4.** the act or process of studying. **5.** a room used for studying, reading, or writing. **6.** (*often pl.*) work relating to a particular area of learning: *environmental studies.* **7.** an investigation and analysis of a particular subject. **8.** a product of studying, such as a written paper or book. **9.** a drawing, sculpture, etc., done for practice or in preparation for another work. **10.** a musical composition intended to develop one aspect of performing technique. [Latin *studium* zeal]

stuff (stʌf) *vb.* **1.** to pack or fill (something) completely; cram. **2.** to force, shove, or squeeze (something somewhere): *to stuff money into a pocket.* **3.** to fill (food such as poultry or tomatoes) with a stuffing. **4.** to fill (a dead animal's skin) with material so as to restore the shape of the live animal. **5.** *Taboo slang.* to have sexual intercourse with (a woman). **6. get stuffed!** *Brit. taboo slang.* an exclamation of contemptuous anger or annoyance with someone. **7. stuff oneself** *or* **one's face.** to eat large quantities. ~*n.* **8.** any general or unspecified substance or accumulation of objects. **9.** the raw material of something. **10.** subject matter, skill, etc.: *he knows his stuff.* **11.** woollen fabric. **12. do one's stuff.** *Informal.* to do what is expected of one. [Old French *estoffe*]

stuffed shirt *n. Informal.* a pompous person.

stuffed-up *adj.* having the passages of one's nose blocked with mucus.

stuffing ('stʌfɪŋ) *n.* **1.** the material with which something is stuffed. **2.** a mixture of ingredients with which poultry or meat is stuffed before cooking.

stuffy ('stʌfɪ) *adj.* **-ier, -iest. 1.** lacking fresh air. **2.** excessively dull, staid, or conventional. —'**stuffiness** *n.*

stultify ('stʌltɪˌfaɪ) *vb.* **-fying, -fied.** to dull (the brain) by boring routine. [Latin *stultus* stupid + *facere* to make] —'**stulti,fying** *adj.*

stumble ('stʌmb'l) *vb.* **1.** to trip or fall while walking or running. **2.** to walk in an awkward, unsteady, or unsure way. **3.** to make mistakes or hesitate in speech or actions. **4.** (foll. by *across, on,* or *upon*) to come across (someone or something) by accident. ~*n.* **5.** a false step, trip, or blunder. [Middle English *stomble*]

stumbling block *n.* any impediment or obstacle.

stump (stʌmp) *n.* **1.** the base of a tree trunk left standing after the tree has been cut down or has fallen. **2.** the part of something, such as a tooth, limb, or blade, that remains after a larger part has been removed. **3.** *Cricket.* any of three upright wooden sticks that, with two bails laid across them, form a wicket. ~*vb.* **4.** to stop or confuse (someone). **5.** to plod or trudge heavily. **6.** *Cricket.* to dismiss (a batsman) by breaking his wicket with the ball. **7.** *Chiefly U.S. & Canad.* to campaign or canvass (an area), by political speech-making. [Middle Low German]

stump up *vb. Brit. informal.* to give (the money required).

stumpy ('stʌmpɪ) *adj.* **stumpier, stumpiest.** short and thick like a stump; stubby.

stun (stʌn) *vb.* **stunning, stunned. 1.** (of a heavy blow or fall) to make (someone) unconscious. **2.** to shock or overwhelm (someone). [Old French *estoner* to daze]

stung (stʌŋ) *vb.* past of **sting**.

stunk (stʌŋk) *vb.* a past of **stink**.

stunner ('stʌnə) *n. Informal.* a person or thing of great beauty.

stunning ('stʌnɪŋ) *adj. Informal.* very attractive or impressive. —**'stunningly** *adv.*

stunt[1] (stʌnt) *vb.* to prevent or impede (the growth or development) of a plant, animal, or person. [Old English: foolish] —**'stunted** *adj.*

stunt[2] (stʌnt) *n.* **1. a.** an acrobatic or dangerous piece of action in a film or television programme. **b.** (*as modifier*): *a stunt man.* **2.** anything spectacular or unusual done for attention: *a publicity stunt.* [origin unknown]

stupefaction (ˌstjuːpɪˈfækʃən) *n.* the state of being stupefied.

stupefy ('stjuːpɪˌfaɪ) *vb.* **-fying, -fied. 1.** to make (someone) feel insensitive or lethargic. **2.** to confuse or astound (someone). [Old French *stupefier*] —**'stupeˌfying** *adj.*

stupendous (stjuːˈpɛndəs) *adj.* astounding, wonderful, or huge. [Latin *stupēre* to be amazed] —**stuˈpendously** *adv.*

stupid ('stjuːpɪd) *adj.* **1.** lacking in common sense, perception, or intelligence. **2.** dazed or stupefied: *stupid from lack of sleep.* **3.** trivial or silly. [Latin *stupidus*] —**stuˈpidity** *n.* —**'stupidly** *adv.*

stupor ('stjuːpə) *n.* **1.** a state of unconsciousness. **2.** mental dullness. [Latin]

sturdy ('stɜːdɪ) *adj.* **-dier, -diest. 1.** (of a person) healthy, strong, and vigorous. **2.** (of a piece of furniture, shoes, etc.) strongly built or made. [Old French *estordi* dazed] —**'sturdily** *adv.*

sturgeon ('stɜːdʒən) *n.* a bony fish of the N hemisphere, from which caviar is obtained. [Old French *estourgeon*]

stutter ('stʌtə) *vb.* **1.** to speak (a word or phrase) with recurring repetition of initial consonants. ~*n.* **2.** the act or habit of stuttering. [Middle English *stutten*] —**'stuttering** *n.*

sty[1] (staɪ) *n., pl.* **sties.** a pen in which pigs are kept. [Old English *stig*]

sty[2] or **stye** (staɪ) *n., pl.* **sties** or **styes.** inflammation of a gland at the base of an eyelash. [Old English *stigend* swelling + *ye* eye]

Stygian ('stɪdʒɪən) *adj. Chiefly literary.* dark or gloomy. [after the *Styx*, a river in Hades]

style (staɪl) *n.* **1.** a form of appearance, design, or production; type or make. **2.** the way in which something is done: *the modern style of education.* **3.** a distinctive, formal, or characteristic manner of expression in words, music, painting, etc. **4.** elegance or refinement of manners, dress, etc.: *he's got lots of style.* **5.** prevailing fashion in dress, looks, etc.: *that look has gone out of style.* **6.** a fashionable or showy way of life: *to live in style.* **7.** the particular kind of spelling, punctuation, design, etc., followed in a book, journal, or publishing house. **8.** *Bot.* the stemlike part of a flower that bears the stigma. ~*vb.* **9.** to design, shape, or tailor: *to style hair.* **10.** to name or call: *to style a man a fool.* [Latin *stylus*]

styling mousse *n.* a light foamy substance applied to the hair before styling in order to hold the style.

stylish ('staɪlɪʃ) *adj.* smart; fashionable. —**'stylishly** *adv.*

stylist ('staɪlɪst) *n.* **1.** a hairdresser who styles hair. **2.** a person who performs, writes, or acts with attention to style.

stylistic (staɪˈlɪstɪk) *adj.* of artistic or literary style. —**styˈlistically** *adv.*

stylized or **-ised** ('staɪlaɪzd) *adj.* conforming to an established stylistic form.

stylus ('staɪləs) *n.* a needle-like device in the pick-up arm of a record player that rests in the groove in the record and picks up the sound signals. [Latin *stilus* writing implement]

stymie ('staɪmɪ) *vb.* **-mieing, -mied. 1.** to hinder or thwart (someone). ~*n., pl.* **-mies. 2.** *Golf.* (formerly) a situation in which an opponent's ball is blocking the line between the hole and the ball about to be played. [origin unknown]

styptic ('stɪptɪk) *adj.* **1.** used to stop bleeding: *a styptic pencil.* ~*n.* **2.** a styptic drug. [Greek *stuphein* to contract]

suave (swɑːv) *adj.* (esp. of a man) smooth and sophisticated in manner. [Latin *suāvis* sweet] —**'suavely** *adv.*

sub (sʌb) *n.* **1.** short for **subeditor, submarine, subscription,** or **substitute. 2.** *Brit. informal.* an advance payment of wages or salary. Formal term: **subsistence allowance.** ~*vb.* **subbing, subbed. 3.** to act as a substitute.

sub- or before *r* **sur-** *prefix.* used with many main words to mean: **1.** situated under or beneath: *subterranean.* **2.** secondary in rank; subordinate: *sublieutenant; surrogate.* **3.** falling short of; less than or imperfectly: *subarctic; subhuman.* **4.** forming a subdivision or subordinate part: *subcommittee.* [Latin]

subaltern ('sʌbltən) *n.* any commissioned army officer below the rank of captain. [Latin *sub-* under + *alter* another]

subaqua (ˌsʌbˈækwə) *adj.* of or relating to underwater sport: *subaqua swimming.*

subatomic (ˌsʌbəˈtɒmɪk) *adj. Physics.* of, relating to, or being one of the particles making up an atom.

subcommittee ('sʌbkəˌmɪtɪ) *n.* a small committee which consists of members of a larger committee and which is set up to look into a particular matter.

subconscious (sʌbˈkɒnʃəs) adj. **1.** acting or existing without one's awareness. ~n. **2.** Psychol. the part of the mind that contains memories and motives of which one is not aware but which can influence one's behaviour. —**sub'consciously** adv.

subcontinent (sʌbˈkɒntɪnənt) n. a large land mass that is a distinct part of a continent, such as India is of Asia.

subcontract n. (sʌbˈkɒntrækt). **1.** a subordinate contract under which the supply of materials, labour, etc., is let out to someone other than a party to the main contract. ~vb. (ˌsʌbkənˈtrækt). **2.** to let out (work) on a subcontract. —**subcon'tractor** n.

subculture (ˈsʌbˌkʌltʃə) n. a subdivision of a national culture with a distinct pattern of behaviour, beliefs, and attitudes.

subcutaneous (ˌsʌbkjuːˈteɪnɪəs) adj. Med. beneath the skin.

subdivide (ˌsʌbdɪˈvaɪd, ˈsʌbdɪˌvaɪd) vb. to divide (a part of something) into smaller parts. —**subdivision** (ˈsʌbdɪˌvɪʒən) n.

subdue (səbˈdjuː) vb. **-duing, -dued. 1.** to overcome and bring (a person or people) under control by persuasion or force. **2.** to make (feelings, colour, or lighting) less intense. [Latin subdūcere to remove]

subeditor (sʌbˈedɪtə) n. a person who checks and edits text for a newspaper or other publication.

subgroup (ˈsʌbˌɡruːp) n. a small group that is part of a larger group.

subheading (ˈsʌbˌhedɪŋ) n. the heading of a subdivision of a piece of writing.

subhuman (sʌbˈhjuːmən) adj. less than human.

subject n. (ˈsʌbdʒɪkt). **1.** the main theme or topic, as of a book or discussion. **2.** any branch of learning considered as a course of study. **3.** Grammar. a word or phrase that represents the person or thing performing the action of the verb in a sentence; for example, the cat in the sentence The cat catches mice. **4.** a person or thing that undergoes an experiment or treatment. **5.** a person under the rule of a monarch or government: British subjects. **6.** a figure, scene, etc., as portrayed by an artist or photographer. ~adj. (ˈsʌbdʒɪkt). **7.** being under the rule or a monarch or government: subject peoples. **8.** subject to. **a.** showing a tendency towards: a child subject to indiscipline. **b.** exposed or vulnerable to: subject to ribaldry. **c.** conditional upon: the results are subject to correction. ~adv. (ˈsʌbdʒɪkt). **9.** subject to. under the condition that something takes place: we accept, subject to her agreement. ~vb. (səbˈdʒekt). **10.** (foll. by to) to cause (someone) to experience (something unpleasant): they subjected him to torture. **11.** (foll. by to) to bring under the control or authority (of): to subject a soldier to discipline. [Latin subjectus brought under] —**sub'jection** n.

subjective (səbˈdʒektɪv) adj. **1.** of or based on a person's emotions or prejudices.

2. Grammar. denoting a case of nouns and pronouns that identifies the subject of a verb. ~n. **3.** Grammar. the subjective case. —**sub'jectively** adv.

sub judice (ˈdʒuːdɪsɪ) adj. before a court of law: we cannot comment on this matter publicly because it is sub judice. [Latin]

subjugate (ˈsʌbdʒʊˌɡeɪt) vb. **1.** to bring (a group of people) under one's control. **2.** to make (someone) subservient or submissive. [Latin sub- under + jugum yoke] —ˌsubju'gation n.

subjunctive (səbˈdʒʌŋktɪv) Grammar. ~adj. **1.** denoting a mood of verbs used when the content of the clause is being doubted, supposed, or feared true, for example were in the sentence: I'd think seriously about it if I were you. ~n. **2.** the subjunctive mood. [Latin subjungere to add to]

sublet (sʌbˈlet) vb. **-letting, -let.** to rent out property which one is renting from somebody else.

sublieutenant (ˌsʌbləˈtenənt) n. a junior officer in a navy.

sublimate (ˈsʌblɪˌmeɪt) vb. Psychol. to direct the energy of (a primitive impulse) into activities that are socially more acceptable. [Latin sublīmāre to elevate] —ˌsubli'mation n.

sublime (səˈblaɪm) adj. **1.** of high moral, intellectual, or spiritual value; noble. **2.** unparalleled; supreme. ~n. **3.** the sublime. something that is sublime. ~vb. **4.** Chem., physics. to change directly from a solid to a vapour without first melting. [Latin sublīmis lofty] —**sub'limely** adv.

subliminal (sʌbˈlɪmɪnˈl) adj. resulting from or relating to mental processes of which the individual is not aware: subliminal advertising. [Latin sub- below + līmen threshold]

sub-machine-gun n. a portable automatic or semiautomatic light gun.

submarine (ˈsʌbməˌriːn, ˌsʌbməˈriːn) n. **1.** a vessel, esp. a warship, capable of operating below the surface of the sea. ~adj. **2.** existing or located below the surface of the sea: a submarine cable. —**submariner** (sʌbˈmærɪnə) n.

submerge (səbˈmɜːdʒ) vb. **1.** to plunge, sink, or dive or cause (something) to plunge, sink, or dive below the surface of water or other liquid. **2.** to overwhelm (someone), as with work. [Latin submergere] —**sub'mersion** n.

submersible (səbˈmɜːsɪbˈl) adj. **1.** capable of operating under water. ~n. **2.** a vessel designed to operate under water.

submission (səbˈmɪʃən) n. **1.** an act or instance of submitting. **2.** something submitted, such as a proposal. **3.** the quality or condition of being submissive.

submissive (səbˈmɪsɪv) adj. showing quiet obedience, humility, or servility. —**sub'missively** adv. —**sub'missiveness** n.

submit (səbˈmɪt) vb. **-mitting, -mitted. 1.** to yield to the will of another person or a superior force. **2.** to be voluntarily subjected (to analysis or treatment). **3.** to refer (something) to someone for judgment or consideration. [Latin *submittere* to place under]

subnormal (sʌbˈnɔːməl) *adj.* **1.** less than the normal. **2.** having a low intelligence. ~*n.* **3.** a subnormal person.

subordinate *adj.* (səˈbɔːdɪnɪt). **1.** of lesser rank or importance. ~*n.* (səˈbɔːdɪnɪt). **2.** a person or thing that is subordinate. ~*vb.* (səˈbɔːdɪˌneɪt) **3.** (usually foll. by *to*) to regard (something) as less important than another. [Latin *sub-* lower + *ordō* rank] —**subˌordiˈnation** *n.*

subordinate clause *n. Grammar.* a clause that functions as an adjective, an adverb, or a noun rather than one that functions as a sentence in its own right.

suborn (səˈbɔːn) *vb.* to bribe or incite (a person) to commit a wrongful act. [Latin *subornāre*]

subplot (ˈsʌbˌplɒt) *n.* a secondary plot in a novel, play, film, etc.

subpoena (səbˈpiːnə) *n.* **1.** a legal document issued by a court of law requiring a person to appear before the court at a specified time. ~*vb.* **-naing, -naed. 2.** to serve (someone) with a subpoena. [Latin: under penalty]

sub-post office *n.* (in Britain) a post office which is run by a sub-postmaster or sub-postmistress as a self-employed agent for the Post Office.

sub rosa (ˈrəʊzə) *adv.* in secret. [Latin, lit.: under the rose]

subroutine (ˈsʌbruːˌtiːn) *n.* a section of a computer program that is stored only once but can be used at several different points in the program.

subscribe (səbˈskraɪb) *vb.* **1.** (usually foll. by *to*) to pay (money) as a contribution (to a fund, for a magazine, etc.), esp. at regular intervals. **2.** (foll. by *to*) to give support or approval: *to subscribe to the theory of reincarnation.* [Latin *subscrībere* to write underneath] —**subˈscriber** *n.*

subscriber trunk dialling *n. Brit.* a system by which telephone users can obtain trunk calls by dialling direct without the help of an operator.

subscript (ˈsʌbskrɪpt) *Printing.* ~*adj.* **1.** (of a character) written or printed below the line. ~*n.* **2.** a subscript character.

subscription (səbˈskrɪpʃən) *n.* **1.** a payment for consecutive issues of a publication over a specified period of time. **2.** money paid or promised, as to a charity, or the fund raised in this way. **3.** *Chiefly Brit.* the membership fees paid to a society. **4.** an advance order for a new product.

subsection (ˈsʌbˌsɛkʃən) *n.* any of the smaller parts into which a section may be divided.

subsequent (ˈsʌbsɪkwənt) *adj.* occurring after; succeeding. [Latin *subsequēns*] —**ˈsubsequently** *adv.*

subservient (səbˈsɜːvɪənt) *adj.* overeager to comply with someone else's wishes. [Latin *subserviēns*] —**subˈservience** *n.*

subset (ˈsʌbˌsɛt) *n.* a mathematical set contained within a larger set.

subside (səbˈsaɪd) *vb.* **1.** to become less

loud, excited, or violent; abate. **2.** to sink to a lower level. **3.** (of the surface of the earth) to cave in; collapse. [Latin *subsīdere*] —**subsidence** (səbˈsaɪdˈns, ˈsʌbsɪdˈns) *n.*

subsidiary (səbˈsɪdɪərɪ) *adj.* **1.** of lesser importance; subordinate. ~*n., pl.* **-aries. 2.** a subsidiary person or thing. **3.** Also called: **subsidiary company.** a company which is at least half owned by another company. [Latin *subsidiārius* supporting]

subsidize *or* **-ise** (ˈsʌbsɪˌdaɪz) *vb.* to aid or support (an industry, a person, a public service, or a venture) with a subsidy.

subsidy (ˈsʌbsɪdɪ) *n., pl.* **-dies. 1.** financial aid supplied by a government, for example to industry, or for public welfare. **2.** any financial aid, grant, or contribution. [Latin *subsidium* assistance]

subsist (səbˈsɪst) *vb.* (foll. by *on*) to be sustained; manage to live: *to subsist on milk.* [Latin *subsistere* to stand firm] —**subˈsistence** *n.*

subsistence farming *n.* a type of farming in which most of the produce is consumed by the farmer and his family.

subsoil (ˈsʌbˌsɔɪl) *n.* the layer of soil beneath the surface soil.

subsonic (sʌbˈsɒnɪk) *adj.* being or moving at a speed below that of sound.

substance (ˈsʌbstəns) *n.* **1.** the basic matter of which a thing consists. **2.** a specific type of matter with definite or fairly definite chemical composition: *an oily substance.* **3.** the essential meaning of a speech, thought, or written article. **4.** solid or meaningful quality: *an education of substance.* **5.** material possessions or wealth: *a man of substance.* **6. in substance.** with regard to the most important points. [Latin *substantia*]

substandard (sʌbˈstændəd) *adj.* below an established or required standard.

substantial (səbˈstænʃəl) *adj.* **1.** of a considerable size or value: *substantial funds; a substantial reform.* **2.** (of food or a meal) sufficient and nourishing. **3.** solid or strong: *a substantial door.* **4.** real; actual; true: *substantial evidence.* **5.** of or relating to the basic material substance or aspects of a thing. —**subˈstantially** *adv.*

substantiate (səbˈstænʃɪˌeɪt) *vb.* to establish (a story) as genuine. —**subˌstantiˈation** *n.*

substantive (ˈsʌbstəntɪv) *n.* **1.** *Grammar.* a noun or pronoun used in place of a noun. ~*adj.* **2.** of, relating to, containing, or being the essential element of a thing. [Latin *substāre* to stand beneath]

substitute (ˈsʌbstɪˌtjuːt) *vb.* **1.** (often foll. by *for*) to take the place of or put (someone or something) in place of another person or thing. **2.** *Chem.* to replace (an atom or group in a molecule) with (another atom or group). ~*n.* **3.** a person or thing that takes the place of another, such as a player who takes the place of a team-mate. [Latin *substituere*] —**ˌsubstiˈtution** *n.*

substitution reaction *n. Chem.* the replacing of an atom or group in a molecule by another atom or group.

substructure (ˈsʌbˌstrʌktʃə) n. 1. a structure that forms the basis of anything. 2. a structure that forms a foundation or framework for a building.

subsume (səbˈsjuːm) vb. to incorporate (an idea, case, etc.) under a comprehensive or inclusive classification. [Latin sub- under + sumere to take]

subtenant (sʌbˈtɛnənt) n. a person who rents property from a tenant. —**subˈtenancy** n.

subtend (səbˈtɛnd) vb. Geom. to be opposite (an angle or side). [Latin subtendere to extend beneath]

subterfuge (ˈsʌbtəˌfjuːdʒ) n. a trick used to conceal something, avoid an argument, etc. [Latin subterfugere to escape by stealth]

subterranean (ˌsʌbtəˈreɪnɪən) adj. 1. found or operating below the surface of the earth. 2. existing or operating in concealment. [Latin sub beneath + terra earth]

subtitle (ˈsʌbˌtaɪtᵊl) n. 1. (pl.) Films. a written translation at the bottom of the picture in a film with foreign dialogue. 2. a secondary title given to a book or play. ~vb. 3. to provide a subtitle for (a book or play) or subtitles for (a film).

subtle (ˈsʌtᵊl) adj. 1. not immediately obvious. 2. delicate or highly refined: a subtle scent. 3. marked by or requiring mental ingenuity; discriminating. [Latin subtilis finely woven] —**ˈsubtly** adv.

subtlety (ˈsʌtᵊltɪ) n. 1. (pl. -ties) a fine distinction. 2. the state or quality of being subtle; delicacy.

subtract (səbˈtrækt) vb. 1. Maths. to take (one number or quantity) away from another. 2. to remove (a part of something) from the whole. [Latin subtrahere to draw away from beneath] —**subtraction** (səbˈtrækʃən) n.

subtropical (sʌbˈtrɒpɪkᵊl) adj. of the region lying between the tropics and temperate lands.

suburb (ˈsʌbɜːb) n. a residential district on the outskirts of a city or town. [Latin suburbium, from sub- close to + urbs a city]

suburban (səˈbɜːbᵊn) adj. 1. of, in, or inhabiting a suburb. 2. Mildly disparaging. narrow or unadventurous in outlook.

suburbanite (səˈbɜːbəˌnaɪt) n. a person who lives in a suburb.

suburbia (səˈbɜːbɪə) n. suburbs or the people living in them considered as an identifiable community or class in society.

subvention (səbˈvɛnʃən) n. a grant or subsidy, for example one from a government. [Late Latin subventiō assistance]

subversion (səbˈvɜːʃən) n. the act or an instance of attempting to weaken or overthrow a government or an institution.

subversive (səbˈvɜːsɪv) adj. 1. intended or intending to weaken or overthrow a government or an institution. ~n. 2. a person engaged in subversive activities.

subvert (səbˈvɜːt) vb. to bring about the downfall or ruin of (something existing by a system of law, such as a government). [Latin subvertere to overturn]

subway (ˈsʌbˌweɪ) n. 1. Brit. an underground tunnel enabling pedestrians to cross a road or railway. 2. an underground railway.

subzero (sʌbˈzɪərəʊ) adj. lower than zero: subzero temperatures.

succeed (səkˈsiːd) vb. 1. to accomplish an aim. 2. to happen in the manner desired: the plan succeeded. 3. to do well in a specified field: one must be ruthless to succeed in business. 4. to come next in order after (someone or something): three weeks of frantic activity were succeeded by a week of calm. 5. (often foll. by to) to take over (a position) from (someone): to succeed to the throne; Bush succeeded Reagan as President. [Latin succēdere to follow after] —**sucˈceeding** adj.

success (səkˈsɛs) n. 1. the favourable outcome of something attempted. 2. the attainment of wealth, fame, or position. 3. a person or thing that is successful: her last novel was a huge success. [Latin successus an outcome]

successful (səkˈsɛsfʊl) adj. 1. having a favourable outcome. 2. having attained fame, wealth, or position. —**sucˈcessfully** adv.

succession (səkˈsɛʃən) n. 1. a number of people or things following one another in order. 2. the act, process, or right by which one person succeeds to the position of another. 3. in succession. one after another: three years in succession.

successive (səkˈsɛsɪv) adj. following another or others without interruption: six successive months. —**sucˈcessively** adv.

successor (səkˈsɛsə) n. a person or thing that follows another, esp. a person who takes over another's job or position.

succinct (səkˈsɪŋkt) adj. brief and clear: a succinct account of the events. [Latin succinctus] —**sucˈcinctly** adv.

succour or U.S. **succor** (ˈsʌkə) n. 1. help in time of difficulty. ~vb. 2. to give aid to (someone in time of difficulty). [Latin succurrere to hurry to help]

succubus (ˈsʌkjʊbəs) n., pl. -bi (-ˌbaɪ). a female demon fabled to have sexual intercourse with sleeping men. [Latin succubāre to lie beneath]

succulent (ˈsʌkjʊlənt) adj. 1. juicy. 2. (of plants) having thick fleshy leaves or stems. ~n. 3. a plant that can exist in very dry conditions by using water stored in its fleshy tissues. [Latin sūcus juice] —**ˈsucculence** n.

succumb (səˈkʌm) vb. (foll. by to) 1. to give way to the force of or desire for (something). 2. to die of (a disease). [Latin succumbere]

such (sʌtʃ) det. 1. of the sort specified or understood: such books; such is life; robbers, rapists, and such. 2. so great; so much: such a help. 3. as such. in itself or themselves: intelligence as such can't guarantee success. 4. such and such. specific, but not known or named: at such and such a time. 5. such as. for example: animals, such as tigers. ~adv. 6. extremely: such a nice person. [Old English swilc]

suck (sʌk) vb. **1.** to draw (a liquid) into the mouth throught pursed lips. **2.** to extract liquid from (a solid food): *to suck a lemon.* **3.** to draw in (fluid) as if by sucking: *plants suck moisture from the soil.* **4.** to drink milk from (a mother's breast); suckle. **5.** to take (something) into the mouth and moisten, dissolve, or roll it around with the tongue: *to suck one's thumb.* **6.** (often foll. by *down, in,* etc.) to draw (a thing or person somewhere) by using irresistible force. ~n. **7.** a sucking. [Old English *sūcan*]

sucker ('sʌkə) n. **1.** *Slang.* a person who is easily deceived or swindled. **2.** *Slang.* a person who cannot resist something: *he's a sucker for blondes.* **3.** *Zool.* a part of the body of certain animals that is used for sucking or adhering. **4.** a cup-shaped device, generally made of rubber, that may be attached to articles allowing them to adhere to a surface by suction. **5.** *Bot.* a strong shoot that arises in a mature plant from a root or the base of the main stem.

suck into vb. to draw (someone) into (a situation) by using strong inducement or force: *he was sucked into a life of crime.*

suckle ('sʌk'l) vb. to give (a baby or young animal) milk from the breast or udder or (of a baby or young animal) to suck milk from its mother's breast or udder.

suckling ('sʌklɪŋ) n. a baby or young animal that is still sucking milk from its mother's breast or udder.

suck up vb. *Informal.* to flatter (someone) for one's own profit.

sucrose ('suːkrəuz, -krəus) n. *Chem.* sugar. [French *sucre* sugar]

suction ('sʌkʃən) n. **1.** the act or process of sucking. **2.** the force produced by drawing air out of a space to make a vacuum that will suck in a substance from another space. [Latin *sūgere* to suck]

Sudanese (ˌsuːd'nˈiːz) adj. **1.** of or relating to the Sudan, in NE Africa. ~n., pl. -nese. **2.** a person from the Sudan.

sudden ('sʌd'n) adj. **1.** occurring or performed quickly and without warning. ~n. **2. all of a sudden.** without warning; unexpectedly. [Latin *subitus* unexpected] —'**suddenly** adv. —'**suddenness** n.

sudden death n. *Sport.* an extra period of play to decide the winner of a tied competition: the first player or team to go into the lead is the winner.

sudden infant death syndrome n. same as **cot death.**

sudorific (ˌsjuːdə'rɪfɪk) adj. **1.** causing sweating. ~n. **2.** a drug that causes sweating. [Latin *sudor* sweat + *facere* to make]

suds (sʌdz) pl. n. the bubbles on the surface of water in which soap or detergent has been dissolved; lather. [prob. from Middle Dutch *sudse* marsh]

sue (suː) vb. **suing, sued.** to start legal proceedings (against): *they sued the surgeon for negligence; she's going to sue for divorce.* [Latin *sequī* to follow]

suede (sweɪd) n. a leather with a fine velvet-like surface on one side. [French *gants de Suède,* lit.: gloves from Sweden]

suet ('suːɪt) n. a hard fat obtained from sheep and cattle and used for making pastry and puddings. [Old French *seu*]

suffer ('sʌfə) vb. **1.** to undergo or be subjected to (pain). **2.** to be set at a disadvantage: *this author suffers in translation.* **3.** to tolerate: *he does not suffer fools gladly.* **4. suffer from.** to be afflicted with: *he suffers from bronchitis.* [Latin *sufferre*] —'**sufferer** n. —'**suffering** n.

sufferance ('sʌfərəns, 'sʌfrəns) n. **on sufferance.** tolerated with reluctance: *she knew she was there on sufferance.*

suffice (sə'faɪs) vb. **1.** to be adequate or satisfactory for a purpose. **2. suffice it to say...** it is enough to say...: *suffice it to say that I missed the bus.* [Latin *sufficere*]

sufficiency (sə'fɪʃənsɪ) n., pl. -cies. an adequate amount.

sufficient (sə'fɪʃənt) adj. enough to meet a need or purpose; adequate. [Latin *sufficiens*] —**suf'ficiently** adv.

suffix ('sʌfɪks) *Grammar.* ~n. **1.** a letter or letters added to the end of a word to form another word, such as -s and -ness in *dogs* and *softness.* ~vb. **2.** to add (a letter or letters) to the end of a word to form another word. [Latin *suffixus* fastened below]

suffocate ('sʌfə,keɪt) vb. **1.** to kill or die through lack of oxygen, as by blockage of the air passage. **2.** to feel discomfort from heat and lack of air. [Latin *suffocāre*] —'**suffo,cating** adj. —,suffo'cation n.

suffragan ('sʌfrəgən) n. a bishop subordinate to and assisting his superior archbishop. [Medieval Latin *suffrāgium* assistance]

suffrage ('sʌfrɪdʒ) n. the right to vote in public elections. [Latin *suffrāgium*]

suffragette (ˌsʌfrə'dʒɛt) n. (in Britain at the beginning of the 20th century) a woman who campaigned militantly for women to be given the right to vote in public elections.

suffragist ('sʌfrədʒɪst) n. (in Britain at the beginning of the 20th century) a person who campaigned for women to be given the right to vote in public elections.

suffuse (sə'fjuːz) vb. to spread through or over (something): *a room suffused with light.* [Latin *suffūsus* overspread with] —**suffusion** (sə'fjuːʒən) n.

sugar ('ʃʊgə) n. **1.** a sweet-tasting carbohydrate, usually in the form of white or brown crystals, which is found in many plants and is used to sweeten food and drinks. **2.** *Informal, chiefly U.S. & Canad.* a term of affection. ~vb. **3.** to add sugar to (food or drink) to make it sweet. **4.** to cover with sugar: *sugared almonds.* **5. sugar the pill.** to make something unpleasant more agreeable by adding something pleasant. [Old French *çucre,* from Sanskrit *śarkarā*] —'**sugared** adj.

sugar beet n. a beet cultivated for its white roots from which sugar is obtained.

sugar cane n. a tropical grass cultivated

for its tall stout canes from which sugar is obtained.

sugaring off *n. Canad.* the boiling down of maple sap to produce sugar, traditionally a social event in early spring.

sugar loaf *n.* a large cone-shaped mass of hard refined sugar.

sugar maple *n.* a North American maple tree, grown as a source of sugar, which is extracted from the sap.

sugary ('ʃʊgərɪ) *adj.* **1.** of, like, or containing sugar. **2.** deceptively pleasant; insincere: *a sugary smile.* —'**sugariness** *n.*

suggest (sə'dʒɛst) *vb.* **1.** to put forward (a plan or an idea) for consideration: *I suggest that we wait for Mother.* **2.** to bring (a person or thing) to the mind by the association of ideas: *that painting suggests home to me.* **3.** to give an indirect hint of: *his face always suggests his peace of mind.* [Latin *suggerere* to bring up]

suggestible (sə'dʒɛstɪb'l) *adj.* easily influenced by ideas provided by other persons.

suggestion (sə'dʒɛstʃən) *n.* **1.** something that is suggested. **2.** a hint or indication: *a suggestion of the odour of violets.* **3.** *Psychol.* the process whereby the presentation of an idea to a receptive individual leads to the acceptance of that idea.

suggestive (sə'dʒɛstɪv) *adj.* **1.** improper or indecent: *suggestive remarks.* **2. suggestive of.** conveying a hint of.

suicidal (ˌsuːɪˈsaɪd'l) *adj.* **1.** tending towards suicide. **2.** liable to result in suicide: *a suicidal attempt.* **3.** liable to destroy one's own interests or prospects; dangerously rash.

suicide ('suːɪˌsaɪd) *n.* **1.** the act or an instance of killing oneself intentionally: *she committed suicide.* **2.** a person who killed himself intentionally. **3.** the self-inflicted ruin of one's own prospects or interests: *a merger would be financial suicide.* [Latin *sui* of oneself + *caedere* to kill]

suit (suːt) *n.* **1.** a set of clothes of the same material designed to be worn together, usually a jacket with matching trousers or skirt. **2.** an outfit worn for a specific purpose: *a bathing suit.* **3.** any of the four types of card in a pack of playing cards: spades, hearts, diamonds, or clubs. **4.** a civil proceeding; lawsuit. **5. follow suit.** to act in the same way as someone else. ~*vb.* **6.** to be fit or appropriate for: *that dress suits your figure.* **7.** to be agreeable or acceptable to (someone). **8. suit oneself.** to do what one wants without considering other people. [Old French *sieute*] —'**suited** *adj.*

suitable ('suːtəb'l) *adj.* appropriate; proper; fit. —ˌsuita'**bility** *n.* —'**suitably** *adv.*

suitcase ('suːtˌkeɪs) *n.* a portable travelling case for clothing.

suite (swiːt) *n.* **1.** a set of connected rooms in a hotel. **2.** a matching set of furniture, for example two armchairs and a settee. **3.** a group of attendants or followers. **4.** *Music.* an instrumental composition consisting of several movements in the same key. [French]

suitor ('suːtə) *n.* **1.** *Old-fashioned.* a man

who wants to marry a woman; wooer. **2.** *Law.* a person who starts legal proceedings against someone; plaintiff. [Latin *secūtor* follower]

sulk (sʌlk) *vb.* **1.** to be silent and resentful because of a wrong done to one: *the child sulked after being slapped.* ~*n.* **2.** (often *pl.*) a resentful or sullen mood: *he's in a sulk; he's got the sulks.*

sulky ('sʌlkɪ) *adj.* **sulkier, sulkiest.** moody or withdrawn through or as if through resentment. [perhaps from obs. *sulke* sluggish] —'**sulkily** *adv.* —'**sulkiness** *n.*

sullen ('sʌlən) *adj.* unwilling to talk or be sociable; sulky; morose. [Latin *sōlus* alone] —'**sullenly** *adv.* —'**sullenness** *n.*

sully ('sʌlɪ) *vb.* **-lying, -lied.** to ruin (someone's reputation). [prob. from French *souiller* to soil]

sulpha *or U.S.* **sulfa drug** ('sʌlfə) *n. Pharmacol.* any of a group of sulphonamides that prevent the growth of bacteria: used to treat bacterial infections.

sulphate *or U.S.* **sulfate** ('sʌlfeɪt) *n. Chem.* a salt or ester of sulphuric acid.

sulphide *or U.S.* **sulfide** ('sʌlfaɪd) *n. Chem.* a compound of sulphur with another element.

sulphite *or U.S.* **sulfite** ('sʌlfaɪt) *n.* any salt or ester of sulphurous acid.

sulphonamide *or U.S.* **sulfonamide** (sʌl'fɒnəˌmaɪd) *n. Pharmacol.* any of a class of organic compounds that prevent the growth of bacteria. An important class of sulphonamides are the sulpha drugs.

sulphur *or U.S.* **sulfur** ('sʌlfə) *n. Chem.* a light yellow, highly inflammable, nonmetallic element used in the production of sulphuric acid, in the vulcanization of rubber, and in medicine. Symbol: S [Latin *sulfur*] —**sulphuric** *or U.S.* **sulfuric** (sʌl-'fjʊərɪk) *adj.*

sulphur dioxide *n. Chem.* a strong-smelling colourless soluble gas, used in the manufacture of sulphuric acid and in the preservation of foodstuffs.

sulphureous *or U.S.* **sulfureous** (sʌl-'fjʊərɪəs) *adj.* same as **sulphurous** (sense 1).

sulphuric acid *n. Chem.* a colourless dense oily corrosive liquid used in the manufacture of fertilizers and explosives.

sulphurize, -ise, *or U.S.* **sulfurize** ('sʌlfjuˌraɪz) *vb. Chem.* to combine with or treat (something) with sulphur or a sulphur compound.

sulphurous *or U.S.* **sulfurous** ('sʌlfərəs) *adj. Chem.* **1.** of or resembling sulphur: *a sulphurous colour.* **2.** containing sulphur, esp. with a valence of four.

sultan ('sʌltən) *n.* the sovereign of a Muslim country. [Arabic]

sultana (sʌl'tɑːnə) *n.* **1.** the dried fruit of a small white seedless grape. **2.** a wife, concubine, or female relative of a sultan. [Italian]

sultanate ('sʌltəˌneɪt) *n.* **1.** the territory ruled by a sultan. **2.** the office or rank of a sultan.

sultry ('sʌltrɪ) *adj.* **-trier, -triest.** **1.** (of

weather or climate) very hot and humid. **2.** displaying or suggesting passion; sensual: *sultry eyes*. [obs. *sulter* to swelter]

sum (SAM) *n.* **1.** the result of the addition of numbers or quantities. **2.** one or more columns or rows of numbers to be added, subtracted, multiplied, or divided. **3.** a quantity of money: *he borrows enormous sums*. **4.** the essence or gist of a matter: *in sum*. **5.** (*modifier*) complete or final: *the sum total*. ~*vb.* **summing, summed**. See **sum up**. [Latin *summa* the top, sum]

summarize *or* **-ise** ('sAmə,raız) *vb.* to make a summary of (something).

summary ('sAmərı) *n., pl.* **-maries**. **1.** a brief account giving the main points of something. ~*adj.* **2.** performed quickly, without formality or attention to details: *a summary execution*. [Latin *summārium*] —'**summarily** *adv.*

summation (sA'meɪʃən) *n.* **1.** the process of working out a sum; addition. **2.** the result of such a process. **3.** a summary.

summer ('sAmə) *n.* **1.** the warmest season of the year, between spring and autumn. **2.** a time of blossoming or of greatest happiness. [Old English *sumor*] —'**summery** *adj.*

summerhouse ('sAmə,haʊs) *n.* a small building in a garden, used for shade in the summer.

summer school *n.* an academic course held during the summer.

summer solstice *n.* the time, about June 21, at which the sun is at its northernmost point in the sky.

summertime ('sAmə,taɪm) *n.* the period or season of summer.

summing-up *n.* **1.** a review or summary of the main points of an argument, speech, or piece of writing. **2.** concluding statements made by a judge to the jury before they retire to consider their verdict.

summit ('sAmɪt) *n.* **1.** the highest point or part of a mountain or hill. **2.** the highest possible degree or state; peak or climax: *the summit of ambition*. **3.** a meeting of chiefs of governments or other high officials. [Old French *somet*]

summon ('sAmən) *vb.* **1.** to order (someone) to come; send for (someone), esp. to attend court, by issuing a summons. **2.** to order or instruct (someone) to do something or call (someone) to something: *the bell summoned them to their work*. **3.** to convene (a meeting). **4.** (often foll. by *up*) to gather (one's strength, courage, or other quality). [Latin *summonēre* to give a discreet reminder]

summons ('sAmənz) *n., pl.* **-monses**. **1.** a call or an order to attend a specified place at a specified time. **2.** an official order requiring a person to attend court, either to answer a charge or to give evidence. ~*vb.* **3.** to take out a summons against (a person).

sumo ('suːməʊ) *n.* the national style of wrestling of Japan, in which two contestants of great height and weight attempt to force each other out of the ring. [Japanese]

sump (sAmp) *n.* **1.** a receptacle in an internal-combustion engine into which oil can drain. **2.** same as **cesspool**. **3.** *Mining.* a hollow at the bottom of a shaft where water collects. [Middle Dutch *somp* marsh]

sumptuary ('sAmptjʊərı) *adj.* controlling expenditure or extravagance. [Latin *sumptuārius* concerning expense]

sumptuous ('sAmptjʊəs) *adj.* expensive or extravagant; splendid: *sumptuous costumes*. [Latin *sumptuōsus* costly]

sum up *vb.* **1.** to summarize (the main points of an argument, speech, or piece of writing). **2.** to form a quick opinion of: *I summed him up in five minutes*.

sun (sAn) *n.* **1.** the star that is the source of heat and light for the planets in the solar system. **2.** any star around which a system of planets revolves. **3.** the heat and light received from the sun; sunshine. **4. catch the sun**. to become slightly suntanned. **5. under the sun**. on earth; at all: *nobody under the sun eats more than you*. ~*vb.* **sunning, sunned**. **6.** to expose (oneself) to the sunshine. [Old English *sunne*] —'**sunless** *adj.*

Sun. Sunday.

sunbathe ('sAn,beɪð) *vb.* to lie or sit in the sunshine, in order to get a suntan. —'**sun-,bather** *n.* —'**sun,bathing** *n.*

sunbeam ('sAn,biːm) *n.* a ray of sunlight.

sunburn ('sAn,bɜːn) *n.* painful reddening of the skin caused by overexposure to the sun. —'**sun,burnt** *or* '**sun,burned** *adj.*

sundae ('sAndı, -deɪ) *n.* ice cream topped with a sweet sauce, nuts, whipped cream, and fruit. [origin unknown]

Sunday ('sAndı) *n.* the first day of the week and the Christian day of worship. [Old English *sunnandæg* day of the sun]

Sunday best *n.* one's best clothes, sometimes regarded as those most suitable for churchgoing.

Sunday school *n.* a school for the religious instruction of children on Sundays, usually held in a church.

sundial ('sAn,daɪəl) *n.* a device indicating the time during the hours of sunlight by means of a pointer that casts a shadow onto a surface marked in hours.

sundown ('sAn,daʊn) *n.* same as **sunset**.

sundry ('sAndrı) *det.* **1.** several or various; miscellaneous. ~*pron.* **2. all and sundry**. everybody. ~*n., pl.* **-dries**. **3.** (*pl.*) miscellaneous unspecified items. [Old English *syndrig* separate]

sunfish ('sAn,fɪʃ) *n., pl.* **-fish** *or* **-fishes**. a large sea fish with a rounded body.

sunflower ('sAn,flaʊə) *n.* **1.** a very tall plant which has large flower heads with yellow rays. **2. sunflower seed oil**. the oil extracted from sunflower seeds, used as a salad oil and in margarine.

sung (sAŋ) *vb.* the past participle of **sing**.

sunglasses ('sAn,glɑːsɪz) *pl. n.* glasses with darkened lenses that protect the eyes from the sun's glare.

sun-god *n.* the sun considered as a god.

sunk (sAŋk) *vb.* a past tense and past participle of **sink**.

sunken ('sʌŋkən) *vb.* **1.** a past participle of **sink.** ~*adj.* **2.** unhealthily hollow: *sunken cheeks.* **3.** situated at a lower level than the surrounding or usual one: *a sunken bath.* **4.** situated under water; submerged: *sunken treasure.*

sun lamp *n.* a lamp that gives off ultraviolet rays, used for obtaining an artificial suntan or for muscular therapy.

sunlight ('sʌnlaɪt) *n.* the light that comes from the sun. —**'sunlit** *adj.*

sun lounge *or U.S.* **sun parlor** *n.* a room with large windows designed to receive as much sunlight as possible.

sunny ('sʌnɪ) *adj.* **-nier, -niest. 1.** full of or exposed to sunlight. **2.** full of good humour: *a sunny disposition.*

sunroof ('sʌnˌruːf) *n.* a panel in the roof of a car that may be opened to allow air or sunshine into the car.

sunrise ('sʌnˌraɪz) *n.* **1.** the daily appearance of the sun above the horizon. **2.** the time at which the sun rises.

sunrise industry *n.* any of the fast-developing high-technology industries, such as electronics.

sunset ('sʌnˌsɛt) *n.* **1.** the daily disappearance of the sun below the horizon. **2.** the time at which the sun sets.

sunshade ('sʌnˌʃeɪd) *n.* a device, such as a parasol or awning, used to shade people from the sun.

sunshine ('sʌnˌʃaɪn) *n.* **1.** the light and warmth from the sun. **2.** a light-hearted or ironic term of address.

sunspot ('sʌnˌspɒt) *n.* **1.** *Informal.* a sunny holiday resort. **2.** a dark cool patch on the surface of the sun.

sunstroke ('sʌnˌstrəʊk) *n.* a condition resulting from prolonged exposure to intensely hot sunlight and causing high fever and sometimes loss of consciousness.

suntan ('sʌnˌtæn) *n.* a brownish colouring of the skin caused by exposure to the sun or a sun lamp. —**'sunˌtanned** *adj.*

sup¹ (sʌp) *vb.* **supping, supped. 1.** to consume (liquid) by swallowing a little at a time. ~*n.* **2.** a sip. [Old English *sūpan*]

sup² (sʌp) *vb.* **supping, supped.** *Archaic.* to have supper. [Old French *soper*]

super ('suːpə) *Informal.* **1.** ~*adj.* outstanding; exceptional. ~*n.* **2.** *Austral. & N.Z. informal.* superannuation. **3.** *Austral. & N.Z. informal.* superphosphate. [Latin: above]

super- *prefix.* used with many main words to mean: **1.** above or over: *superscript.* **2.** outstanding: *superstar.* **3.** of greater size, extent, or quality: *supermarket.* [Latin]

superabundant (ˌsuːpərə'bʌndənt) *adj.* existing in very large numbers or amount. —ˌsupera'bundance *n.*

superannuated (ˌsuːpər'ænjuˌeɪtɪd) *adj.* **1.** discharged with a pension, owing to age or illness. **2.** too old to be useful; obsolete. [Medieval Latin *superannātus* aged more than one year]

superannuation (ˌsuːpərˌænjuˈeɪʃən) *n.* **a.** the amount deducted regularly from employees' incomes in a contributory pension scheme. **b.** the pension finally paid.

superb (suˈpɜːb) *adj.* **1.** extremely good. **2.** majestic or imposing. [Latin *superbus* distinguished] —**su'perbly** *adv.*

Super Bowl *n. American football.* the championship game held annually between the best team of the American Football Conference and that of the National Football Conference.

supercharge ('suːpəˌtʃɑːdʒ) *vb.* **1.** to increase the power of (an internal-combustion engine) with a supercharger. **2.** to charge (the atmosphere, a remark, etc.) with an excess amount of (tension, emotion, etc.). **3.** to apply pressure to (a fluid); pressurize.

supercharger ('suːpəˌtʃɑːdʒə) *n.* a device that increases the power of an internal-combustion engine by forcing extra air into it.

supercilious (ˌsuːpə'sɪlɪəs) *adj.* showing arrogant pride or scorn. [Latin *supercilium* eyebrow] —ˌsuper'ciliously *adv.* —ˌsuper'ciliousness *n.*

superconductivity (ˌsuːpəˌkɒndʌk'tɪvɪtɪ) *n. Physics.* the ability of certain substances to conduct electric current with almost no resistance at very low temperatures. —ˌsupercon'ductive *adj.* —ˌsupercon'ductor *n.*

superego (ˌsuːpər'iːgəʊ, -'ɛgəʊ) *n., pl.* **-gos.** *Psychoanal.* that part of the unconscious mind that acts as a conscience.

supererogation (ˌsuːpərˌɛrə'geɪʃən) *n.* the act of doing more work than is required. [Latin *supererogāre* to spend over and above]

superficial (ˌsuːpə'fɪʃəl) *adj.* **1.** of, near, or forming the surface: *superficial bruising.* **2.** without thoroughness or care: *a superficial inspection.* **3.** only outwardly apparent rather than genuine or actual: *the similarity was merely superficial.* **4.** (of a person) having no depth of character or feeling. [Late Latin *superficiālis*] —**superficiality** (ˌsuːpəˌfɪʃɪ'ælɪtɪ) *n.* —ˌsuper'ficially *adv.*

superfluous (suˈpɜːfluəs) *adj.* more than is sufficient or required. [Latin *superfluus* overflowing] —ˌsuper'fluity *n.*

superglue ('suːpəˌgluː) *n.* an extremely strong and quick-drying glue.

superhuman (ˌsuːpə'hjuːmən) *adj.* beyond normal human ability or experience: *a superhuman strength.*

superimpose (ˌsuːpərɪm'pəʊz) *vb.* to set or place (something) on or over something else.

superintend (ˌsuːpərɪn'tɛnd) *vb.* to supervise (a person or an activity). [Latin *super-* above + *intendere* to give attention to]

superintendent (ˌsuːpərɪn'tɛndənt) *n.* **1.** a senior police officer. **2.** a person who directs and manages an organization or office.

superior (suːˈpɪərɪə) *adj.* **1.** greater in quality, usefulness, quantity, etc. **2.** of high or extraordinary worth or merit. **3.** higher in rank or status. **4.** believing oneself to be better than others. **5.** placed higher up. **6.** *Printing.* (of a character) written or printed above the line. ~*n.* **7.** a person of greater rank or status. **8.** See **mother superior.** [Latin *superus* placed above] —**superiority** (suːˌpɪərɪ'ɒrɪtɪ) *n.*

superlative (suː'pɜːlətɪv) *adj.* **1.** of outstanding quality; supreme. **2.** *Grammar.* denoting the form of an adjective or adverb that expresses the highest degree of quality. ~*n.* **3.** the highest quality. **4.** *Grammar.* the superlative form of an adjective or adverb. [Old French *superlatif*]

superman ('suːpəˌmæn) *n., pl.* **-men.** any man of apparently superhuman powers.

supermarket ('suːpəˌmɑːkɪt) *n.* a large self-service store selling food and household goods.

supernatural (ˌsuːpə'nætʃərəl) *adj.* **1.** of or relating to things that cannot be explained according to natural laws. ~*n.* **2.** **the supernatural.** supernatural forces, occurrences, and beings collectively.

supernova (ˌsuːpə'nəuvə) *n., pl.* **-vae** (-viː) *or* **-vas.** a star that explodes, and for a few days, becomes one hundred million times brighter than the sun.

supernumerary (ˌsuːpə'njuːmərərɪ) *adj.* **1.** exceeding a regular or proper number; extra. **2.** employed as a substitute or assistant. ~*n., pl.* **-aries. 3.** a person or thing that exceeds the required or regular number. **4.** a substitute or assistant. **5.** an actor who has no lines. [Latin *super-* above + *numerus* number]

superphosphate (ˌsuːpə'fɒsfeɪt) *n.* a chemical fertilizer, esp. one made by treating rock phosphate with sulphuric acid.

superpower ('suːpəˌpauə) *n.* an extremely powerful state, such as the U.S.

superscript ('suːpəˌskrɪpt) *Printing.* ~*adj.* **1.** (of a character) written or printed above the line. ~*n.* **2.** a superscript character.

supersede (ˌsuːpə'siːd) *vb.* **1.** to take the place of (something old-fashioned or less appropriate); supplant. **2.** to replace (someone) in function or office. [Latin *supersedēre* to sit above]

supersonic (ˌsuːpə'sɒnɪk) *adj.* being, having, or capable of a speed greater than the speed of sound.

superstar ('suːpəˌstɑː) *n.* an extremely popular and famous entertainer or sportsperson.

superstition (ˌsuːpə'stɪʃən) *n.* **1.** irrational belief in the significance of particular omens, charms, etc. **2.** a notion, act, or ritual that derives from such belief. [Latin *superstitiō*] —ˌsuper'stitious *adj.*

superstore ('suːpəˌstɔː) *n.* a large supermarket.

superstructure ('suːpəˌstrʌktʃə) *n.* **1.** any structure or concept erected on something else. **2.** *Naut.* any structure above the main deck of a ship.

supertanker ('suːpəˌtæŋkə) *n.* a very large fast tanker.

supertax ('suːpəˌtæks) *n.* an extra tax on incomes above a certain level.

supervene (ˌsuːpə'viːn) *vb.* to occur as an unexpected development. [Latin *supervenīre* to come upon] —**supervention** (ˌsuːpə'venʃən) *n.*

supervise ('suːpəˌvaɪz) *vb.* **1.** to direct or oversee the performance or operation of (an activity or a process). **2.** to watch over (people) so as to maintain order. [Latin *super-* over + *vidēre* to see] —**supervision** (ˌsuːpə'vɪʒən) *n.* —'super,visor *n.* —'super,visory *adj.*

supine ('suːpaɪn) *adj.* lying on one's back. [Latin *supīnus*]

supper ('sʌpə) *n.* a light evening meal. [Old French *soper*]

supplant (sə'plɑːnt) *vb.* to take the place of (someone or something). [Latin *supplantāre* to trip up]

supple ('sʌp'l) *adj.* **1.** (of a person) capable of or showing easy or graceful movement. **2.** bending easily without damage. [Latin *supplex* bowed] —'**suppleness** *n.*

supplement *n.* ('sʌplɪmənt). **1.** an addition designed to complete something or make up for a lack. **2.** a magazine that is inserted into a weekly newspaper. **3.** a section added to a publication to supply further information or correct errors. ~*vb.* ('sʌplɪˌment). **4.** to provide a supplement to (something), esp. in order to make up for a lack. [Latin *supplēmentum*] —ˌsupple'mentary *adj.*

supplementary benefit *n.* (in Britain) an earlier form of income support.

supplicant ('sʌplɪkənt) *n.* a person who makes a supplication. [Latin *supplicāns* beseeching]

supplication (ˌsʌplɪ'keɪʃən) *n.* a humble request for help. [Latin *supplicāre* to beg on one's knees]

supply (sə'plaɪ) *vb.* **-plying, -plied. 1.** to provide (a person or an institution) with something required: *can you supply me with the appropriate forms?* **2.** to make available or provide (something desired or lacking): *to supply books to the library.* ~*n., pl.* **-plies. 3.** the act of providing something. **4.** an amount available for use; stock: *food supply.* **5.** (*pl.*) food and equipment needed for a campaign or trip. **6.** *Econ.* the amount of a commodity that producers are willing and able to offer for sale at a specified price: *supply and demand.* **7. a.** a person who acts as a temporary substitute. **b.** (*as modifier*): *a supply teacher.* [Latin *supplēre* to complete] —**sup'plier** *n.*

support (sə'pɔːt) *vb.* **1.** to carry the weight of (a thing or person). **2.** to provide the necessities of life for (a family or person). **3.** to tend to establish (a theory or statement) by providing new facts. **4.** to speak in favour of (a motion). **5.** to give practical or emotional help to (someone). **6.** to give approval to (a cause or principle). **7.** to take an active interest in and be loyal to (a particular football or other sport team). **8.** (in a concert) to perform earlier than (the main attraction). **9.** *Films, theatre.* to play a subordinate role to (the leading actor or actress). ~*n.* **10.** the act of supporting or the condition of being supported. **11.** a thing that bears the weight of a construction. **12.** a person who gives someone practical or emotional help. **13.** the means of maintenance of a family or person. **14.** a band or entertainer not topping the bill. [Latin *supportāre* to bring] —**sup'portive** *adj.*

supporter (sə'pɔːtə) *n.* a person who supports a sports team, politician, etc.

suppose (sə'pəʊz) *vb.* **1.** to presume (something) to be true without certain knowledge: *I suppose he meant to kill her.* **2.** to consider (something) as a possible suggestion for the sake of discussion: *suppose that he wins.* **3.** (of a theory) to depend on the truth or existence of: *your policy supposes full employment.* [Latin *suppōnere* to substitute]

supposed (sə'pəʊzd, -'pəʊzɪd) *adj.* **1.** supposed to. expected or obliged to: *I'm supposed to be there.* **2.** presumed to be true without certain knowledge; doubtful: *the supposed advantages.* —**supposedly** (sə'pəʊzɪdlɪ) *adv.*

supposition (ˌsʌpə'zɪʃən) *n.* **1.** an idea or a statement that is supposed. **2.** the act of supposing: *that statement is based on supposition.*

supposititious (ˌsʌpɒzɪ'tɪʃəs) *or* **supposititious** (sə'pɒzɪ'tɪʃəs) *adj.* **1.** deduced from supposition; hypothetical. **2.** substituted with intent to mislead or deceive.

suppository (sə'pɒzɪtrɪ) *n.*, *pl.* -**ries.** *Med.* a solid medication for insertion into the vagina or rectum. [Latin *suppositus* placed beneath]

suppress (sə'pres) *vb.* **1.** to put an end to (something). **2.** to hold (an emotion or a response) in check; restrain: *I was obliged to suppress a smile.* **3.** to prevent circulation or publication of: *to suppress seditious pamphlets.* **4.** *Electronics.* to reduce or eliminate (interference) in a circuit. [Latin *suppressus* held down] —**suppression** (sə'preʃən) *n.*

suppurate ('sʌpjʊˌreɪt) *vb. Pathol.* (of a wound or sore) to produce or leak pus. [Latin *suppūrāre*]

supremacy (sʊ'preməsɪ) *n.* **1.** supreme power; authority. **2.** the quality or condition of being supreme.

supreme (sʊ'priːm) *adj.* **1.** of highest status or power: *the Supreme Court.* **2.** of highest quality, importance, etc.: *supreme artistry.* **3.** greatest in degree; extreme: *supreme folly.* [Latin *suprēmus* highest] —**su'premely** *adv.*

supremo (sʊ'priːməʊ) *n.*, *pl.* -**mos.** *Brit. informal.* a person in overall authority.

sur-[1] *prefix.* over; above; beyond: *surcharge; surrealism.* [Old French]

sur-[2] *prefix.* See **sub-**.

surcharge *n.* ('sɜːˌtʃɑːdʒ). **1.** a charge in addition to the usual payment or tax. **2.** an excessive sum charged, often unlawfully. ~*vb.* (sɜː'tʃɑːdʒ, 'sɜːˌtʃɑːdʒ). **3.** to charge (someone) an additional sum or tax. **4.** to overcharge (someone) for something.

surd (sɜːd) *Maths.* ~*n.* **1.** an irrational number. ~*adj.* **2.** of or relating to a surd. [Latin *surdus* muffled]

sure (ʃʊə, ʃɔː) *adj.* **1.** free from hesitancy or uncertainty (in regard to a belief or conviction): *we are sure of the accuracy of the data; I am sure that he is lying.* **2.** (foll. by *of*) having no doubt, as of the occurrence of a future state or event: *sure of success.* **3.** reliable in indication or accuracy: *a sure sign.* **4.** not open to doubt: *sure proof.* **5.** bound to be or occur; inevitable: *victory is sure.* **6.** bound inevitably (to be or do something); certain: *she is sure to be there.* **7.** physically secure: *a sure footing.* **8. be sure.** to be careful or certain: *be sure to shut the door.* **9. for sure.** without a doubt. **10. make sure.** to make certain; ensure: *make sure the gas is turned off.* **11. sure enough.** *Informal.* in fact: *I thought I might see him and sure enough, there he was.* **12. to be sure.** it has to be acknowledged; admittedly. ~*adv.* **13.** *U.S. & Canad. informal.* without question; certainly: *it sure is hot.* ~*interj.* **14.** *U.S. & Canad. informal.* willingly; yes. [Old French *seur*] —**'sureness** *n.*

sure-fire *adj. Informal.* certain to succeed; assured: *a sure-fire scheme.*

sure-footed *adj.* **1.** unlikely to fall, slip, or stumble. **2.** unlikely to make a mistake.

surely ('ʃʊəlɪ, 'ʃɔː-) *adv.* **1.** am I not right in thinking that?; I am sure that: *surely you don't mean it?* **2.** without doubt; assuredly. **3. slowly but surely.** gradually but noticeably. ~*interj.* **4.** *Chiefly U.S. & Canad.* willingly; yes.

surety ('ʃʊətɪ, 'ʃʊərɪtɪ) *n.*, *pl.* -**ties.** **1.** a person who takes legal responsibility for the fulfilment of another's debt or obligation. **2.** security given as a guarantee that an obligation will be met. [Latin *sēcūritās* security]

surf (sɜːf) *n.* **1.** foam caused by waves breaking on the shore or on a reef. ~*vb.* **2.** to take part in surfing. [prob. var. of *sough*] —**'surfer** *n.*

surface ('sɜːfɪs) *n.* **1.** the outside or top of an object. **2.** the size of such an area. **3.** material covering the surface of an object. **4.** the superficial appearance as opposed to the real nature of something. **5.** *Geom.* **a.** the complete boundary of a solid figure. **b.** something that has length and breadth but no thickness. **6.** the uppermost level of the land or sea. **7. come to the surface.** to become apparent. ~*vb.* **8.** to rise to the surface of water. **9.** to give (something) a particular kind of surface. **10.** to become apparent. **11.** *Informal.* to get up out of bed. [French]

surface tension *n. Physics.* a property of liquids, caused by molecular forces, that leads to the apparent presence of a surface film and to rising and falling in contact with solids.

surfboard ('sɜːfˌbɔːd) *n.* a long narrow board used in surfing.

surfeit ('sɜːfɪt) *n.* **1.** an excessive amount. **2.** overindulgence in eating or drinking. **3.** disgust or nausea caused by such overindulgence. [French *sourfait*]

surfing ('sɜːfɪŋ) *n.* the sport of riding towards shore on the crest of a wave by standing or lying on a surfboard.

surge (sɜːdʒ) *n.* **1.** a sudden increase: *a*

surge of anger. **2.** a strong rolling movement of the sea. **3.** a heavy rolling motion or sound: *the surge of the crowd.* ~*vb.* **4.** (of the sea) to rise or roll with a heavy swelling motion. **5.** to move forward strongly and suddenly. [Latin *surgere* to rise]

surgeon ('sɜːdʒən) *n.* a medical doctor who specializes in surgery.

surgery ('sɜːdʒərɪ) *n., pl.* -geries. **1.** medical treatment in which a person's body is cut open by a surgeon in order to treat or remove the problem part. **2.** *Brit.* a place where, or time when, a doctor or dentist can be consulted. **3.** *Brit.* a time when an MP can be consulted. [Greek *kheir* hand + *ergon* work]

surgical ('sɜːdʒɪkˀl) *adj.* involving or used in surgery. —**'surgically** *adv.*

surgical spirit *n.* methylated spirit used medically for cleaning wounds and sterilizing equipment.

surly ('sɜːlɪ) *adj.* -lier, -liest. ill-tempered and rude. [from obs. *sirly* haughty]

surmise (sɜː'maɪz) *vb.* **1.** to guess (something) from incomplete or uncertain evidence. ~*n.* **2.** a conclusion reached on the basis of incomplete or uncertain evidence. [Old French *surmettre* to accuse]

surmount (sɜː'maʊnt) *vb.* **1.** to overcome (a problem). **2.** to lie on top of (something): *a steeple surmounted by a cross.* [Old French *surmonter*] —**sur'mountable** *adj.*

surname ('sɜːˌneɪm) *n.* a family name as opposed to a Christian name. [Old French *sur-* over + *nom* name]

surpass (sɜː'pɑːs) *vb.* **1.** to be greater than (something or someone) in degree or extent. **2.** to be superior to (someone or something) in achievement or excellence. [French *surpasser*]

surplice ('sɜːplɪs) *n.* a loose wide-sleeved knee-length garment, worn by clergymen and choristers. [Old French *sourpelis*]

surplus ('sɜːpləs) *n.* **1.** a quantity or amount in excess of what is required. **2.** *Accounting.* an excess of income over spending. ~*adj.* **3.** being in excess; extra: *surplus to our requirements.* [Old French]

surprise (sə'praɪz) *vb.* **1.** to cause (someone) to feel amazement or wonder. **2.** to encounter or discover (someone) unexpectedly or suddenly. **3.** to capture or attack (someone) suddenly and without warning. **4.** (foll. by *into*) to provoke (someone) to unintended action by a trick, etc. ~*n.* **5.** the act of taking someone unawares: *an element of surprise.* **6.** a sudden or unexpected event, gift, etc.: *what a pleasant surprise.* **7.** the feeling of being surprised; astonishment: *much to my surprise.* **8.** (*modifier*) causing surprise: *a surprise move.* **9. take someone by surprise.** to capture someone unexpectedly or catch someone unprepared. [Old French *surprendre* to overtake] —**sur'prised** *adj.* —**sur'prising** *adj.* —**sur'prisingly** *adv.*

surrealism (sə'rɪəˌlɪzəm) *n.* (*sometimes cap.*) a movement in art and literature in the 1920s, involving the combination of images that would not normally be found together, such as in a dream. [French *surréalisme*] —**sur'real** *adj.* —**sur'realist** *n., adj.* —**ˌsur,real'istic** *adj.*

surrender (sə'rɛndə) *vb.* **1.** to give (something) up to another, under pressure or on demand: *to surrender a city.* **2.** to give (something) up voluntarily to another: *he surrendered his place to a lady.* **3.** to give oneself up physically to an enemy. **4.** to allow oneself to yield to a temptation or an influence. ~*n.* **5.** the act or instance of surrendering. [Old French *surrendre*]

surreptitious (ˌsʌrəp'tɪʃəs) *adj.* done in secret or by improper means: *a surreptitious glance at the clock.* [Latin *surrepticius* furtive] —**ˌsurrep'titiously** *adv.*

surrogate ('sʌrəgɪt) *n.* **a.** a person or thing acting as a substitute. **b.** (*as modifier*): *a surrogate uncle.* [Latin *surrogāre* to substitute]

surrogate mother *n.* a woman who gives birth to a child on behalf of a couple who cannot have a baby themselves, usually by artificial insemination. —**surrogate motherhood** *or* **surrogacy** ('sʌrəgəsɪ) *n.*

surround (sə'raʊnd) *vb.* **1.** to encircle or enclose (something or someone). **2.** to exist around (someone or something): *the people who surround her.* ~*n.* **3.** *Chiefly Brit.* a border, such as the area of uncovered floor between the walls of a room and the carpet. [Old French *suronder*] —**sur'rounding** *adj.*

surroundings (sə'raʊndɪŋz) *pl. n.* the conditions, scenery, etc., around a person, place, or thing.

surtax ('sɜːˌtæks) *n.* an extra tax on incomes above a certain level.

surveillance (sɜː'veɪləns) *n.* close observation of a person in custody or under suspicion. [French]

survey *vb.* (sɜː'veɪ, 'sɜːveɪ). **1.** to view or consider (something) in a comprehensive or general way: *she surveyed his handiwork.* **2.** to make a detailed map of (an area of land) by measuring or calculating distances and height. **3.** *Brit.* to inspect (a building) to assess its condition and value. **4.** to run a statistical survey on the incomes, opinions, etc. (of a group of people). ~*n.* ('sɜːveɪ). **5.** a detailed investigation of the incomes, opinions, etc., of a group of people. **6.** the act of making a detailed map of an area of land by measuring or calculating distance and height. **7.** *Brit.* an inspection of a building to assess its condition and value. [French *surveoir*] —**sur'veying** *n.* —**sur'veyor** *n.*

survival (sə'vaɪvˀl) *n.* **1. a.** the condition of having survived something. **b.** (*as modifier*): *survival kit.* **2.** a person or thing that survives, such as a custom.

survive (sə'vaɪv) *vb.* **1.** to live after the death of (another). **2.** to continue in existence or use after (a passage of time or a difficult or dangerous experience). [Old French *sourvivre*] —**sur'vivor** *n.*

susceptibility (səˌsɛptə'bɪlɪtɪ) *n., pl.* -ties. **1.** the quality or condition of being susceptible to something. **2.** (*pl.*) emotional feelings.

susceptible (sə'sɛptəb'l) *adj.* **1. susceptible to. a.** yielding readily to: *susceptible to control.* **b.** liable to be afflicted by: *susceptible to colds.* **2.** easily impressed emotionally. [Late Latin *susceptibilis*]

sushi ('su:ʃɪ) *n.* a Japanese dish consisting of small cakes of cold rice with a topping, esp. of raw fish. [Japanese]

suspect *vb.* (sə'spɛkt). **1.** to believe (someone) guilty of a specified offence without proof. **2.** to think (something) false or questionable: *she suspected his sincerity.* **3.** to believe (something) to be the case; think probable: *I suspect they are planning a surprise party; the police suspect fraud.* ~*n.* ('sʌspɛkt). **4.** a person who is believed guilty of a specified offence. ~*adj.* ('sʌspɛkt). **5.** causing suspicion. [Latin *suspicere* to mistrust]

suspend (sə'spɛnd) *vb.* **1.** to hang (something) from a high place. **2.** to cause (something) to remain floating or hanging: *a cloud of smoke was suspended over the town.* **3.** to cause (something) to cease temporarily: *to suspend hostilities.* **4.** to remove (someone) temporarily from a job or position, usually as a punishment. [Latin *sub-* over + *pendere* to hang]

suspended animation *n.* a temporary stoppage of the vital functions, as by freezing an animal.

suspended sentence *n.* a sentence of imprisonment that is not served by an offender unless he commits a further offence during a specified time.

suspender belt *n.* a belt with suspenders hanging from it for holding up women's stockings.

suspenders (sə'spɛndəz) *pl. n.* **1.** *Brit.* **a.** elastic straps attached to a belt or corset, with fasteners for holding up women's stockings. **b.** similar fasteners attached to garters for holding up men's socks. **2.** *U.S. & Canad.* braces.

suspense (sə'spɛns) *n.* **1.** mental uncertainty; anxiety: *their father's illness kept them in a state of suspense.* **2.** excitement felt at the approach of the climax of a book, film, or play: *a play of terrifying suspense.* [Medieval Latin *suspensum* delay] —**sus'penseful** *adj.*

suspension (sə'spɛnʃən) *n.* **1.** an interruption or temporary cancellation: *the suspension of a law.* **2.** temporary removal from a job or position, usually as a punishment. **3.** the act of suspending or the state of being suspended. **4.** a system of springs and shock absorbers that supports the body of a vehicle. **5.** a device or structure, usually a wire or spring, that suspends or supports something, such as the pendulum of a clock. **6.** *Chem.* a mixture in which fine solid or liquid particles are suspended in a fluid.

suspension bridge *n.* a bridge suspended from cables or chains that hang between two towers and are anchored at both ends.

suspicion (sə'spɪʃən) *n.* **1.** the act or an instance of suspecting; belief without sure proof that something is wrong. **2.** a feeling

of mistrust. **3.** a slight trace: *the least suspicion of danger.* **4. above suspicion.** not suspected of any wrongdoing, through having an unblemished reputation. **5. under suspicion.** suspected of wrongdoing. [Latin *suspīciō* distrust]

suspicious (sə'spɪʃəs) *adj.* **1.** arousing suspicion; questionable: *suspicious circumstances.* **2.** suspecting or inclined to suspect something wrong: *a suspicious person.* —**sus'piciously** *adv.*

suss out (sʌs) *vb. Brit. & N.Z. slang.* to work out (a situation or a person's character), using one's intuition. [from *suspect*]

sustain (sə'steɪn) *vb.* **1.** to suffer (an injury or loss): *to sustain a broken arm.* **2.** to maintain or prolong: *to sustain a discussion.* **3.** to support (something) physically from below. **4.** to keep up the vitality or courage of (someone): *a cup of coffee to sustain you; her faith sustains her.* **5.** to affirm the justice or validity of: *to sustain a decision.* [Latin *sustinēre* to hold up] —**sus'tained** *adj.*

sustenance ('sʌstɪnəns) *n.* means of maintaining health or life; nourishment.

suture ('su:tʃə) *n. Surgery.* a stitch made with catgut or silk thread, to join the edges of a wound together. [Latin *suere* to sew]

suzerain ('su:zəˌreɪn) *n.* **1.** a state or sovereign that has some degree of control over a dependent state. **2.** (formerly) a person who had power over many people. [French] —**suzerainty** ('su:zərəntɪ) *n.*

svelte (svɛlt, sfɛlt) *adj.* attractively or gracefully slim; slender. [French]

SW 1. southwest(ern). **2.** short wave.

swab (swɒb) *n.* **1.** *Med.* a small piece of cotton wool used for applying medication or cleansing a wound. ~*vb.* **swabbing, swabbed.** **2.** to clean or medicate (a wound) with a swab. **3.** to clean (the deck of a ship) with a mop. [prob. from Middle Dutch *swabbe* mop]

swaddle ('swɒd'l) *vb.* to wrap (a baby) in swaddling clothes. [Old English *swæthel* swaddling clothes]

swaddling clothes *pl. n.* long strips of cloth formerly wrapped round a newborn baby.

swag (swæg) *n.* **1.** *Slang.* stolen property. **2.** *Austral. & N.Z. informal.* a swagman's pack containing personal belongings. [prob. Scandinavian]

swagger ('swægə) *vb.* **1.** to walk or behave in an arrogant manner. ~*n.* **2.** an arrogant walk or manner. [prob. from *swag*]

swagger stick *n.* a short cane carried by army officers.

swagman ('swægˌmæn, -mən) *n., pl.* **-men.** *Austral. & N.Z. informal.* a tramp who carries his possessions on his back.

Swahili (swɑː'hiːlɪ) *n.* a language of E Africa that is an official language of Kenya and Tanzania. [Arabic *sawāhil* coasts]

swain (sweɪn) *n. Archaic or poetic.* **1.** a male lover or admirer. **2.** a country youth. [Old English *swān* swineherd]

swallow[1] ('swɒləʊ) *vb.* **1.** to pass (food, drink, etc.) through the mouth and gullet to the stomach. **2.** *Informal.* to believe (something) trustingly: *he will never swallow such an excuse.* **3.** not to show: *to swallow one's disappointment.* **4.** to put up with (an insult) without retaliation. **5.** to make a gulping movement in the throat, as when nervous. **6. be swallowed up.** to be taken into and made a part of something: *he was swallowed up by the crowd.* ~*n.* **7.** the act of swallowing. **8.** the amount swallowed at any single time; mouthful. [Old English *swelgan*]

swallow² ('swɒləʊ) *n.* a songbird with long pointed wings and a forked tail. [Old English *swealwe*]

swallow dive *n.* a dive in which the diver keeps his legs straight and his arms outstretched while in the air, finally entering the water headfirst.

swallowtail ('swɒləʊˌteɪl) *n.* **1.** a butterfly with a long tail-like part on each hind wing. **2.** the forked tail of a swallow or similar bird.

swam (swæm) *vb.* the past tense of **swim.**

swami ('swɑːmɪ) *n., pl.* **-mies** or **-mis.** a Hindu religious teacher. [Hindi *svāmī*]

swamp (swɒmp) *n.* **1.** an area of permanently waterlogged ground. ~*vb.* **2.** *Naut.* to cause (a boat) to sink or fill with water. **3.** to overburden or overwhelm (a person or place), for example with excess work or great numbers of people. [prob. from Middle Dutch *somp*] —'**swampy** *adj.*

swan (swɒn) *n.* **1.** a large, usually white, water bird with a long neck. ~*vb.* **swanning, swanned. 2.** (foll. by *around* or *about*) *Informal.* to wander about idly. [Old English]

swank (swæŋk) *Informal.* ~*vb.* **1.** to show off or boast. ~*n.* **2.** showing off or boasting. [origin unknown] —'**swanky** *adj.*

swan song *n.* the last performance, publication, etc., of a person before retirement or death.

swap *or* **swop** (swɒp) *vb.* **swapping, swapped** *or* **swopping, swopped. 1.** to exchange (something) for something else. ~*n.* **2.** an exchange. [orig., to shake hands on a bargain, strike: prob. imit.]

SWAPO *or* **Swapo** ('swɑːpəʊ) South-West Africa People's Organization.

sward (swɔːd) *n.* a stretch of turf or grass. [Old English *sweard* skin]

swarm¹ (swɔːm) *n.* **1.** a group of bees, led by a queen, that has left the hive to make a new home. **2.** a large mass of insects or other small animals. **3.** a moving mass of people. ~*vb.* **4.** to move in a swarm. **5.** to be overrun: *swarming with rats.* [Old English *swearm*]

swarm² (swɔːm) *vb.* (foll. by *up*) to climb (a ladder or rope) by gripping it with the hands and feet: *the boys swarmed up the rigging.* [origin unknown]

swarthy ('swɔːðɪ) *adj.* **swarthier, swarthiest.** dark-complexioned. [obs. *swarty*]

swash (swɒʃ) *n.* the rush of water up a beach following each break of the waves. [probably imit.]

swashbuckler ('swɒʃˌbʌklə) *n.* a daredevil adventurer, esp. in period films. [obs. *swash* to make the noise of a sword striking a shield + *buckler*] —'**swash-,buckling** *adj.*

swastika ('swɒstɪkə) *n.* **1.** a primitive religious symbol in the shape of a Greek cross with the ends of the arms bent at right angles. **2.** this symbol with clockwise arms as the emblem of Nazi Germany. [Sanskrit *svastika*]

swat (swɒt) *vb.* **swatting, swatted. 1.** to hit sharply: *to swat a fly.* ~*n.* **2.** a sharp blow. [dialect var. of *squat*]

swatch (swɒtʃ) *n.* **1.** a sample of cloth. **2.** a collection of such samples. [origin unknown]

swath (swɔːθ) *or* **swathe** (sweɪð) *n., pl.* **swaths** (swɔːðz) *or* **swathes. 1.** the width of one sweep of a scythe or of the blade of a mowing machine. **2.** the strip cut in one such sweep. **3.** the quantity of cut crops left in one such sweep. **4.** a long narrow strip of land. [Old English *swæth*]

swathe (sweɪð) *vb.* **1.** to wrap a bandage, garment, or piece of cloth around (a person or part of the body). ~*n.* **2.** a bandage or wrapping. **3.** same as **swath.** [Old English *swathian*]

sway (sweɪ) *vb.* **1.** to swing to and fro: *the door swayed in the wind.* **2.** to lean to one side and then the other: *sway in time to the music.* **3.** waver between two or more opinions. **4.** to influence (someone) in his opinion or judgment. ~*n.* **5.** power or influence. **6.** a swinging or leaning movement. **7. hold sway.** to have power or influence. [prob. from Old Norse *sveigja* to bend]

swear (swɛə) *vb.* **swearing, swore, sworn. 1.** to blaspheme or use swearwords. **2.** to promise solemnly on oath; vow: *he swore he would never be unfaithful again.* **3.** (foll. by *by*) to have complete confidence in (something). **4.** to state (something) with great earnestness: *I swear I saw a mouse.* **5.** to give evidence on oath in a lawcourt. [Old English *swerian*]

swear in *vb.* to make (someone) take an oath when taking up an official position or entering the witness box to give evidence in court: *to be sworn in as president.*

swear off *vb.* to promise to give up: *to swear off drink.*

swearword ('swɛəˌwɜːd) *n.* a word considered obscene or blasphemous.

sweat (swɛt) *n.* **1.** the salty liquid that comes out of the pores of one's skin during strenuous activity in excessive heat or when nervous or afraid. **2.** the state or condition of sweating: *he broke into a sweat.* **3.** *Slang.* drudgery or hard labour: *mowing lawns is a real sweat!* **4. in a sweat.** *Informal.* in a state of worry. **5. no sweat.** *Slang.* no problem. ~*vb.* **sweating; sweat** *or* **sweated. 6.** to have sweat come through the pores of one's skin, as a result of strenuous activity, excessive heat, nervousness, or fear. **7.** *Informal.* to suffer anxiety or distress. **8. sweat blood.** *Informal.* **a.** to work very hard. **b.** to be filled with anxiety. ~See also **sweats.** [Old English *swætan*] —'**sweaty** *adj.*

sweatband ('swɛt,bænd) n. a piece of cloth tied around the forehead or around the wrist to absorb sweat, for example in sports.

sweater ('swɛtə) n. a warm knitted garment covering the upper part of the body.

sweat off vb. Informal. to get rid of (weight) by strenuous exercise.

sweat out vb. **sweat it out.** Informal. to endure hardships for a time.

sweats (swɛts) pl. n. sweat shirts and sweat-suit trousers collectively.

sweat shirt n. a long-sleeved casual top made of knitted cotton or cotton mixture, brushed on the reverse side.

sweatshop ('swɛt,ʃɒp) n. a workshop where employees work long hours in poor conditions for low pay.

sweat suit n. a suit worn by athletes for training, comprising a sweat shirt and trousers made of the same material.

swede (swiːd) n. a round root vegetable with a purplish-brown skin and yellow flesh. [introduced from Sweden in the 18th century]

Swede (swiːd) n. a person from Sweden.

Swedish ('swiːdɪʃ) adj. 1. relating to Sweden, its people, or their language. ~n. 2. the official language of Sweden.

sweep (swiːp) vb. **sweeping, swept.** 1. to clean (a floor or chimney) with a brush. 2. (often foll. by up) to remove or collect (dirt or rubbish) with a brush. 3. to move smoothly and quickly: cars swept along the road. 4. to move in a proud or dignified fashion: she swept past. 5. to spread rapidly across or through (a place): the news swept through the town. 6. to direct (one's gaze, line of fire, etc.) over (a place). 7. (foll. by away or off) to overwhelm (someone) emotionally: she was swept away by his charm. 8. to brush or lightly touch (a surface): the dress swept along the ground. 9. (often foll. by away) to convey, clear, or abolish (something), esp. with strong or continuous movements: the sea swept the sandcastle away; secondary modern schools were swept away. 10. to stretch out gracefully or majestically, esp. in a wide circle: the plains sweep down to the sea. 11. to win overwhelmingly in an election: Labour swept the country. 12. **sweep the board.** to win every event or prize in a contest. ~n. 13. the act or an instance of sweeping. 14. a swift or steady movement: with a sweep of the hand. 15. a wide expanse: the sweep of the plains. 16. any curving line or contour, such as a driveway. 17. short for **sweepstake.** 18. Chiefly Brit. same as **chimney sweep.** 19. **make a clean sweep.** to win an overwhelming victory. [Middle English swepen]

sweeper ('swiːpə) n. 1. a device for sweeping carpets. 2. Informal, soccer. a defensive player usually positioned in front of the goalkeeper.

sweeping ('swiːpɪŋ) adj. 1. comprehensive and wide-ranging: sweeping reforms. 2. indiscriminate or without reservations: sweeping statements. 3. decisive or overwhelming: a sweeping victory. 4. taking in a wide area: a sweeping glance.

sweepstake ('swiːp,steɪk) or esp. U.S. **sweepstakes** n. 1. a lottery in which the stakes of the participants make up the prize. 2. a horse race involving such a lottery. [orig. referring to someone who sweeps or takes all the stakes in a game]

sweet (swiːt) adj. 1. having a taste like that of sugar. 2. agreeable to the senses or the mind: sweet music. 3. having pleasant manners; kind and gentle: a sweet child. 4. (of wine) having a high sugar content; not dry. 5. fresh, clear, and clean: sweet water; sweet air. 6. **sweet on someone.** fond of or infatuated with someone. ~n. 7. Brit. any of numerous kinds of confectionery consisting wholly or partly of sugar. 8. Brit. a dessert. [Old English swēte] —**sweetly** adv. —**sweetness** n.

sweet-and-sour adj. (of food) cooked in a sauce made from sugar and vinegar and other ingredients.

sweetbread ('swiːt,brɛd) n. the pancreas of an animal, used for food.

sweetbrier ('swiːt,braɪə) n. a wild rose with sweet-smelling leaves and pink flowers.

sweet corn n. 1. a kind of maize whose kernels are rich in sugar and eaten as a vegetable when young. 2. the sweet kernels removed from the maize cob, cooked as a vegetable.

sweeten ('swiːtᵊn) vb. 1. to make (food or drink) sweet or sweeter. 2. to be nice to (someone) in order to ensure cooperation. 3. to make (an offer or a proposal) more agreeable.

sweetener ('swiːtᵊnə) n. 1. a sweetening agent that does not contain sugar. 2. Slang. a bribe.

sweetheart ('swiːt,hɑːt) n. 1. one's boyfriend or girlfriend. 2. Informal. a lovable, generous, or obliging person: your father is an old sweetheart. 3. a term of endearment.

sweetie ('swiːtɪ) n. Informal. 1. a term of endearment. 2. Brit. same as **sweet** (sense 7). 3. Chiefly Brit. a lovable, generous, or obliging person.

sweetmeat ('swiːt,miːt) n. a sweetened delicacy, such as a sweet, cake, or pastry.

sweet pea n. a climbing plant widely cultivated for its sweet-smelling pastel-coloured flowers.

sweet pepper n. the large bell-shaped fruits of the pepper plant, which is eaten unripe (**green pepper**) or ripe (**red pepper**) as a vegetable.

sweet potato n. a root vegetable, grown in the tropics, with pinkish-brown skin and yellow flesh.

sweet-talk Informal. ~vb. 1. to coax (someone) by flattery: he sweet-talked me into making dinner. ~n. **sweet talk.** 2. flattery; coaxing.

sweet tooth n. a strong liking for sweet foods.

sweet william ('wɪljəm) n. a garden plant with clusters of white, pink, red, or purple flowers.

swell (swɛl) *vb.* **swelling, swelled; swollen** *or* **swelled.** **1.** to grow or cause (something) to grow in size, as a result of injury or infection or by being filled with air or liquid: *her finger swelled up; rice swells when it is boiled.* **2.** to grow or cause (something) to grow in numbers, amount, intensity, or degree: *the party is swelling with new recruits.* **3.** to puff or be puffed up with pride or another emotion. **4.** (of the seas) to rise in waves. **5.** (of a sound) to become gradually louder and then die away. ~*n.* **6.** the waving movement of the surface of the open sea. **7.** an increase in size, numbers, amount, or degree. **8.** a bulge. **9.** *Informal.* a person who is very fashionably dressed or of high social standing. **10.** *Music.* an increase in sound followed by an immediate dying away. ~*adj.* **11.** *Slang, chiefly U.S.* excellent; first-class. [Old English *swellan*]

swelling ('swɛlɪŋ) *n.* an enlargement of a part of the body as the result of injury or infection.

swelter ('swɛltə) *vb.* **1.** to suffer under extreme heat. ~*n.* **2.** a sweltering condition: *I'm in a swelter.* [Old English *sweltan* to die]

sweltering ('swɛltərɪŋ) *adj.* uncomfortably hot: *a sweltering day.*

swept (swɛpt) *vb.* past of **sweep.**

swerve (swɜːv) *vb.* **1.** to turn aside from a course sharply or suddenly. ~*n.* **2.** the act of swerving. [Old English *sweorfan* to scour]

swift (swɪft) *adj.* **1.** moving or able to move quickly; fast. **2.** occurring or performed quickly or suddenly: *a swift exit.* **3. swift to.** prompt to (do something): *swift to take revenge.* ~*n.* **4.** a small fast-flying insect-eating bird with long wings. [Old English] —'**swiftly** *adv.* —'**swiftness** *n.*

swig (swɪg) *Informal.* ~*n.* **1.** a large swallow or deep drink, esp. from a bottle. ~*vb.* **swigging, swigged.** **2.** to drink (some liquid) in large swallows, esp. from a bottle. [origin unknown]

swill (swɪl) *vb.* **1.** to drink large quantities of (an alcoholic drink). **2.** (often foll. by *out*) *Chiefly Brit.* to rinse (something) in large amounts of water. ~*n.* **3.** wet food for pigs, consisting of kitchen waste, skim milk, etc. **4.** a deep drink, esp. of beer. [Old English *swilian* to wash out]

swim (swɪm) *vb.* **swimming, swam, swum.** **1.** to move along in water by means of movements of the arms and legs, or (in the case of fish) tail and fins. **2.** to cover (a distance or stretch of water) in this way: *the youngest person to swim the Channel.* **3.** to float on a liquid: *flies swimming on the milk.* **4.** to reel or seem to reel: *my head swam; the room swam around me.* **5.** (often foll. by *in* or *with*) to be covered or flooded with water or other liquid. ~*n.* **6.** the act, an instance, or a period of swimming. **7. in the swim.** *Informal.* fashionable or active in social or political activities. [Old English *swimman*] —'**swimmer** *n.* —'**swimming** *n.*

swimming bath *n.* an indoor swimming pool.

swimming costume *or* **bathing costume** *n. Chiefly Brit.* same as **swimsuit.**

swimmingly ('swɪmɪŋlɪ) *adv.* successfully, effortlessly, or well: *the party went swimmingly.*

swimming pool *n.* an artificial pool for swimming in.

swimsuit ('swɪm,suːt) *n.* a woman's swimming garment that leaves the arms and legs bare.

swindle ('swɪnd'l) *vb.* **1.** to cheat (someone) out of money. **2.** to obtain (money) from someone by fraud. ~*n.* **3.** an instance of cheating someone out of money. [German *schwindeln*] —'**swindler** *n.*

swine (swaɪn) *n.* **1.** a contemptible person. **2.** (*pl.* **swine**) same as **pig.** [Old English *swin*] —'**swinish** *adj.*

swing (swɪŋ) *vb.* **swinging, swung.** **1.** to move rhythmically to and fro; sway. **2.** to walk with a relaxed and swaying motion. **3.** to pivot or cause (something) to pivot, as on a hinge. **4.** to move in a curve: *the car swung around the bend.* **5.** to hang so as to be able to turn freely. **6.** *Slang.* to be hanged: *he'll swing for it.* **7.** to alter one's opinion, attitude, etc., in a sudden or extreme way. **8.** *Informal.* to manipulate successfully: *I hope he can swing the deal.* **9.** (often foll. by *at*) to hit out with a sweeping motion. **10.** to play (music) in the style of swing. **11.** *Slang.* to be lively and modern. ~*n.* **12.** the act of swinging. **13.** a sweeping stroke or punch. **14.** a suspended seat on which a person may swing back and forth. **15.** popular dance music played by big bands in the 1930s. **16.** *Informal.* the normal round or pace: *it's hard to get back into the swing of things after a holiday.* **17.** a sudden or extreme change, for example in some business activity or voting pattern. **18. go with a swing.** to go well; be successful: *the party went with a swing.* **19. in full swing.** at the height of activity. [Old English *swingan*]

swingboat ('swɪŋ,bəʊt) *n.* a boat-shaped carriage for swinging in at a fairground.

swing bridge *n.* a bridge that can be swung open to let ships pass through.

swingeing ('swɪndʒɪŋ) *adj. Chiefly Brit.* punishing; severe: *a swingeing rent increase.*

swipe (swaɪp) *vb.* **1.** (usually foll. by *at*) *Informal.* to try to hit (someone or something) with a sweeping blow. **2.** *Slang.* to steal (something). ~*n.* **3.** *Informal.* a hard blow. [origin unknown]

swirl (swɜːl) *vb.* **1.** to turn in a twisting spinning fashion. ~*n.* **2.** a whirling or spinning motion. **3.** a twisting shape. [prob. from Dutch *zwirrelen*] —'**swirling** *adj.*

swish (swɪʃ) *vb.* **1.** to move with or cause (something) to make a whistling or hissing sound. ~*n.* **2.** a hissing or rustling sound or movement. ~*adj.* **3.** *Informal, chiefly Brit.* fashionable; smart. [imit.]

Swiss (swɪs) *adj.* **1.** relating to Switzerland or its people. ~*n.*, *pl.* **Swiss.** 2. a person from Switzerland.

swiss roll *n.* a sponge cake spread with jam or cream and rolled up.

switch ('swɪtʃ) *n.* 1. a mechanical, electrical, or electronic device for opening or closing a circuit. 2. a sudden swift change. 3. an exchange or swap. 4. a flexible rod or twig, used for punishment. 5. *U.S. & Canad.* a pair of movable rails for diverting moving trains from one track to another. ~*vb.* 6. to change swiftly and suddenly. 7. to exchange (places); replace (something by something else). 8. *Chiefly U.S. & Canad.* to transfer (rolling stock) from one railway track to another. 9. See **switch off, switch on.** [prob. from Middle Dutch *swijch* twig]

switchback ('swɪtʃˌbæk) *n.* a steep mountain road, railway, or track with very sharp bends.

switchboard ('swɪtʃˌbɔːd) *n.* an installation in a telephone exchange or office building where telephone calls are connected.

switch off *vb.* 1. to cause (a device) to stop operating by moving a switch, knob, or lever: *he switched the lamp off.* 2. *Informal.* to become bored and stop paying attention: *when the conversation turned to football I switched off.*

switch on *vb.* 1. to cause (a device) to operate by moving a switch, knob, or lever. 2. *Informal.* to produce (charm, tears, or a smile) suddenly or automatically.

swither ('swɪðə) *Scot.* ~*vb.* 1. to hesitate; be perplexed. ~*n.* 2. hesitation; perplexity; agitation. [origin unknown]

swivel ('swɪv'l) *n.* 1. a coupling device which allows an attached object to turn freely. ~*vb.* **-elling, -elled** or *U.S.* **-eling, -eled.** 2. to turn or swing as if on a pivot. [Old English *swīfan* to turn]

swivel chair *n.* a chair, whose seat is joined to the legs by a swivel, enabling it to be spun round.

swizz (swɪz) *n. Brit. informal.* a swindle or disappointment. [origin unknown]

swizzle stick ('swɪz'l) *n.* a small stick used to stir cocktails.

swollen ('swəʊlən) *vb.* 1. a past participle of **swell.** ~*adj.* 2. enlarged by swelling.

swoon (swuːn) *vb.* 1. *Literary.* to faint. 2. to become ecstatic: *all the girls were swooning over the new history teacher.* ~*n.* 3. *Literary.* a faint. [Old English *geswōgen* insensible] —**'swooning** *adj.*

swoop (swuːp) *vb.* 1. (usually foll. by *down, on,* or *upon*) to sweep or pounce suddenly. ~*n.* 2. the act of swooping. [Old English *swāpan* to sweep]

swoosh (swuʃ) *vb.* 1. to make a swirling or rustling sound when moving or pouring out. ~*n.* 2. a swirling or rustling sound or movement. [imit.]

swop (swɒp) *vb.* **swopping, swopped,** *n.* same as **swap.**

sword (sɔːd) *n.* 1. a weapon with a long blade. 2. **the sword. a.** military power. **b.** death; destruction: *to be put to the sword.* [Old English *sweord*]

sword dance *n.* a dance in which the performer dances over swords on the ground.

swordfish ('sɔːdˌfɪʃ) *n., pl.* **-fish** or **-fishes.** a large fish with a very long upper jaw.

Sword of Damocles ('dæməˌkliːz) *n.* a disaster that is about to take place. [after a flattering courtier forced by Dionysius, tyrant of ancient Syracuse, to sit under a sword suspended by a hair]

swordplay ('sɔːdˌpleɪ) *n.* the action or art of fighting with a sword.

swordsman ('sɔːdzmən) *n., pl.* **-men.** a person who is skilled in the use of a sword. —**'swordsmanship** *n.*

swordstick ('sɔːdˌstɪk) *n.* a hollow walking stick that contains a sword.

swore (swɔː) *vb.* the past tense of **swear.**

sworn (swɔːn) *vb.* 1. the past participle of **swear.** ~*adj.* 2. bound or pledged by or as if by an oath: *sworn enemies.*

swot[1] (swɒt) *Brit. informal.* ~*vb.* **swotting, swotted.** 1. (often foll. by *up*) to study (a subject) very hard, as for an examination; cram. ~*n.* 2. a person who works or studies hard. [var. of *sweat*]

swot[2] (swɒt) *vb.* **swotting, swotted,** *n.* same as **swat.**

swum (swʌm) *vb.* the past participle of **swim.**

swung (swʌŋ) *vb.* past of **swing.**

sybarite ('sɪbəˌraɪt) *n.* 1. a person devoted to luxury and pleasure. ~*adj.* 2. luxurious; sensuous. [after *Sybaris,* an ancient Greek colony in S Italy, famed for its luxury] —**sybaritic** (ˌsɪbə'rɪtɪk) *adj.*

sycamore ('sɪkəˌmɔː) *n.* 1. a tree with five-pointed leaves and two-winged fruits. 2. *U.S. & Canad.* an American plane tree. [Latin *sȳcomorus*]

sycophant ('sɪkəfənt) *n.* a person who uses flattery to win favour from people with power or influence. [Greek *sukophantēs*] —**'sycophancy** *n.* —**sycophantic** (ˌsɪkə'fæntɪk) *adj.*

syllabic (sɪ'læbɪk) *adj.* of or relating to syllables.

syllabify (sɪ'læbɪˌfaɪ) *vb.* **-fying, -fied.** to divide (a word) into syllables. —**syl,labifi-¹cation** *n.*

syllable ('sɪləb'l) *n.* 1. a part of a word which is pronounced as a unit, and which contains a single vowel sound, and which may or may not contain consonants: for example, "paper" has two syllables. 2. the least mention: *don't breathe a syllable of it.* 3. **in words of one syllable.** simply; bluntly. [Greek *sullabē*]

syllabub ('sɪləˌbʌb) *n. Brit.* a dessert made from milk or cream beaten with sugar, wine, and lemon juice. [origin unknown]

syllabus ('sɪləbəs) *n., pl.* **-buses** or **-bi** (-ˌbaɪ). *Brit.* **a.** the subjects studied for a particular course. **b.** a list of these subjects. [Late Latin]

syllogism ('sɪləˌdʒɪzəm) *n.* a form of reasoning consisting of two premises and a conclusion, for example *some temples are in ruins; all ruins are fascinating; so some* *temples are fascinating.* [Greek *sullogismos*] —**syllo'gistic** *adj.*

sylph (sɪlf) *n.* **1.** a slender graceful girl or young woman. **2.** an imaginary being supposed to inhabit the air. [New Latin *sylphus*] —**'sylph,like** *adj.*

sylvan *or* **silvan** ('sɪlvən) *adj. Chiefly poetic.* of or consisting of woods or forests. [Latin *silva* forest]

symbiosis (,sɪmbɪ'əʊsɪs) *n.* **1.** *Biol.* a close association of two animals or plants of different species. **2.** a similar relationship between persons or groups. [Greek: a living together] —**symbiotic** (,sɪmbɪ'ɒtɪk) *adj.*

symbol ('sɪmb²l) *n.* **1.** something that represents or stands for something else, usually a material object used to represent something abstract. **2.** a letter, figure, or sign used in mathematics, music, etc., to represent a quantity, operation, function, etc. [Greek *sumbolon* sign]

symbolic (sɪm'bɒlɪk) *adj.* **1.** of or relating to a symbol or symbols. **2.** being a symbol of something. —**sym'bolically** *adv.*

symbolism ('sɪmbə,lɪzəm) *n.* **1.** the representation of something by the use of symbols. **2.** an art movement involving the use of symbols to express mystical or abstract ideas.

symbolize *or* **-ise** ('sɪmbə,laɪz) *vb.* to be a symbol of (something). —**,symboli'zation** *or* **-i'sation** *n.*

symmetry ('sɪmɪtrɪ) *n., pl.* **-tries. 1.** the state of having two halves that are mirror images of each other. **2.** beauty resulting from a proportionate arrangement of parts. [Greek *summetria* proportion] —**symmetrical** (sɪ'mɛtrɪk²l) *adj.* —**sym'metrically** *adv.*

sympathetic (,sɪmpə'θɛtɪk) *adj.* **1.** feeling or showing sympathy; understanding. **2.** likeable; appealing: *a sympathetic character.* **3. sympathetic to.** showing agreement or favour towards: *sympathetic to the cause.* —**,sympa'thetically** *adv.*

sympathize *or* **-ise** ('sɪmpə,θaɪz) *vb.* (foll. by *with*) **1.** to feel or express sympathy for: *he sympathized with my troubles.* **2.** to agree with or support: *she sympathized with the miners' strike.* —**'sympa,thizer** *or* **-iser** *n.*

sympathy ('sɪmpəθɪ) *n., pl.* **-thies. 1.** the sharing of someone's sorrow or anguish; compassion. **2.** agreement with someone's feelings or interests: *I found myself in sympathy with the hero's wife.* **3.** mutual affection or understanding arising from a sympathetic relationship. **4.** feelings of loyalty or support for an idea or a cause: *his sympathies lay with the Confederates.* [Greek *sympatheia*]

symphony ('sɪmfənɪ) *n., pl.* **-nies. 1.** a large-scale orchestral composition with several movements. **2.** an orchestral movement in a vocal work such as an oratorio. **3.** short for **symphony orchestra. 4.** anything that has a pleasing arrangement of colours or shapes: *she was a symphony in black and gold.* [Greek *sun-* together + *phōnē* sound] —**symphonic** (sɪm'fɒnɪk) *adj.*

symphony orchestra *n. Music.* a large orchestra that performs symphonies.

symposium (sɪm'pəʊzɪəm) *n., pl.* **-siums** *or* **-sia** (-zɪə). **1.** a conference for the discussion of an academic topic or social problem. **2.** a collection of essays on a particular subject. [Greek *symposion*]

symptom ('sɪmptəm) *n.* **1.** *Med.* an indication of a disease noticed by a patient. **2.** anything that is taken as an indication that something is wrong: *a symptom of a decline in moral standards.* [Greek *sumptōma* chance] —**,sympto'matic** *adj.*

synagogue ('sɪnə,gɒg) *n.* a building for Jewish religious services and religious instruction. [Greek *sunagōgē* a gathering]

sync *or* **synch** (sɪŋk) *Films, television, computers, informal.* ~*vb.* **1.** to synchronize. ~*n.* **2.** synchronization: *the film is out of sync.*

synchromesh ('sɪŋkrəʊ,mɛʃ) *adj.* **1.** (of a gearbox) having a system of clutches that synchronizes the speeds of the gearwheels before engagement. ~*n.* **2.** a gear system having these features. [*synchronized mesh*]

synchronism ('sɪŋkrə,nɪzəm) *n.* the quality or condition of being synchronous.

synchronize *or* **-ise** ('sɪŋkrə,naɪz) *vb.* **1.** (of two or more people) to perform (an action) at the same time: *synchronized swimming.* **2.** to cause (two or more clocks or watches) to indicate the same time. **3.** *Films.* to match (the soundtrack and the action of a film) precisely. —**,synchroni'zation** *or* **-i'sation** *n.*

synchronous ('sɪŋkrənəs) *adj.* occurring at the same time and rate. [Greek *sun-* together + *khronos* time]

syncline ('sɪŋklaɪn) *n. Geol.* a downward fold of rock in which the strata slope towards a vertical axis.

syncopate ('sɪŋkə,peɪt) *vb. Music.* to stress the weak beats in (a rhythm or a piece of music) instead of the strong beats. [Medieval Latin *syncopāre* to omit a letter or syllable] —**,synco'pation** *n.*

syncope ('sɪŋkəpɪ) *n.* **1.** *Med.* a faint. **2.** *Linguistics.* the omission of sounds or letters from the middle of a word, as in *ne'er* for *never.* [Greek *sunkopē* a cutting off]

syndic ('sɪndɪk) *n. Brit.* a business agent of some universities or other bodies. [Greek *sundikos* defendant's advocate]

syndicalism ('sɪndɪkə,lɪzəm) *n.* a movement advocating seizure of the means of production and distribution by workers' unions. —**'syndicalist** *n.*

syndicate *n.* ('sɪndɪkɪt). **1.** an association of business enterprises or individuals organized to undertake a joint project. **2.** an association of individuals who control organized crime. **3.** a news agency that sells articles, photographs, etc., to a number of newspapers for simultaneous publication. ~*vb.* ('sɪndɪ,keɪt). **4.** to sell (articles, photographs, etc.) to several newspapers for simultaneous publication. **5.** to form a syndicate of (people). [Old French *syndicat*] —**,syndi'cation** *n.*

syndrome ('sɪndrəʊm) *n.* **1.** *Med.* a combination of signs and symptoms that indicate a particular disease. **2.** a set of symptoms or characteristics indicating the existence of a particular condition or problem. [Greek *sundromē*, lit.: a running together]

synecdoche (sɪnˈɛkdəkɪ) *n.* a figure of speech in which a part is substituted for a whole or a whole for a part, as in *50 head of cattle* for *50 cows*. [Greek *sunekdokhē*]

synod ('sɪnəd, 'sɪnɒd) *n.* a special church council, formally convened to discuss church affairs. [Greek *sunodos*]

synonym ('sɪnənɪm) *n.* a word that means the same as another word, such as *bucket* and *pail*. [Greek *sun-* together + *onoma* name]

synonymous (sɪˈnɒnɪməs) *adj.* (foll. by *with*) **1.** having the same meaning. **2.** closely associated (with): *his name was synonymous with greed.*

synopsis (sɪˈnɒpsɪs) *n., pl.* **-ses** (-siːz). a brief review of a subject; summary. [Greek *sunopsis*]

synoptic (sɪˈnɒptɪk) *adj.* **1.** of or relating to a synopsis. **2.** *Bible.* of or relating to (the Gospels of Matthew, Mark, and Luke). —**syn'optically** *adv.*

synovia (saɪˈnəʊvɪə, sɪ-) *n.* a clear thick fluid that lubricates the body joints. [New Latin] —**syn'ovial** *adj.*

syntax ('sɪntæks) *n.* the grammatical arrangement of words in a language. [Greek *suntassein* to put in order] —**syn'tactic** *or* **syn'tactical** *adj.*

synthesis ('sɪnθɪsɪs) *n., pl.* **-ses** (-ˌsiːz). **1.** the process of combining objects or ideas into a complex whole. **2.** the combination produced by such a process. **3.** the process of producing a compound by one or more chemical reactions, usually from simpler starting materials. [Greek *sunthesis*]

synthesize *or* **-sise** ('sɪnθɪˌsaɪz) *vb.* **1.** to combine (objects or ideas) into a complex whole. **2.** to produce (a compound) by synthesis.

synthesizer ('sɪnθɪˌsaɪzə) *n.* a keyboard instrument in which speech, music, or other sounds are produced electronically.

synthetic (sɪnˈθɛtɪk) *adj.* **1.** (of a substance or material) made artificially by chemical reaction. **2.** not genuine; insincere: *synthetic compassion.* ~*n.* **3.** a synthetic substance or material. [Greek *sunthetikos* expert in putting together] —**syn'thetically** *adv.*

syphilis ('sɪfɪlɪs) *n.* a sexually transmitted disease that causes sores on the genitals and eventually on other parts of the body. [*Syphillis* hero of a Latin poem (1530)] —**syphilitic** (ˌsɪfɪˈlɪtɪk) *adj.*

syphon ('saɪfⁿn) *n., vb.* same as **siphon**.

Syrian ('sɪrɪən) *adj.* **1.** of or relating to Syria, a republic in W Asia, its people, or their dialect of Arabic. ~*n.* **2.** a person from Syria.

syringa (sɪˈrɪŋɡə) *n.* same as **mock orange** (sense 1) or **lilac**. [Greek *surinx* tube (its hollow stems were used for pipes)]

syringe ('sɪrɪndʒ, sɪˈrɪndʒ) *n.* **1.** *Med.* a device consisting of a hollow cylinder of glass or plastic, a tightly fitting piston, and a hollow needle, used for withdrawing or injecting fluids, cleaning wounds, etc. ~*vb.* **2.** to cleanse, inject, or spray with a syringe: *I'm going to have my ears syringed.* [Greek *surinx* tube]

syrup ('sɪrəp) *n.* **1.** a solution of sugar dissolved in water and often flavoured with fruit juice: used for sweetening fruit, etc. **2.** a thick sweet liquid prepared for cooking or table use from molasses, sugars, etc.: *maple syrup.* **3.** *Informal.* excessive sentimentality. **4.** a liquid medicine containing a sugar solution: *syrup of figs.* [Arabic *sharāb* a drink] —**'syrupy** *adj.*

system ('sɪstəm) *n.* **1.** a method or set of methods: *he has a perfect system at roulette.* **2.** orderliness; an ordered manner. **3. the system.** society or the government regarded as exploiting, restricting, and repressing individuals. **4.** any scheme of classification or arrangement. **5.** a network of communications, transportation, or distribution. **6** *Biol.* an animal considered as a whole. **7.** *Biol.* any of various bodily parts or structures that together perform some function: *the digestive system.* **8.** one's physiological or psychological constitution: *get it out of your system.* **9.** an assembly of electronic or mechanical parts forming a self-contained unit: *a brake system.* [Greek *sustēma*]

systematic (ˌsɪstɪˈmætɪk) *adj.* using or showing order and planning; methodical: *a systematic administrator.* —ˌ**system'atically** *adv.*

systematize *or* **-tise** ('sɪstɪməˌtaɪz) *vb.* to arrange (information) in a system. —ˌ**systemati'zation** *or* **-i'sation** *n.*

systemic (sɪˈstɛmɪk, -ˈstiː-) *adj.* *Biol.* (of a poison, disease, etc.) affecting the entire animal or body. —**sys'temically** *adv.*

systems analysis *n.* the analysis of the requirements of a task and the expression of these in a form that enables a computer to perform the task. —**systems analyst** *n.*

systole ('sɪstəlɪ) *n.* *Physiol.* contraction of the heart, during which blood is pumped into the arteries. [Greek *sustolē*] —**systolic** (sɪˈstɒlɪk) *adj.*

T

t *or* **T** (tiː) *n., pl.* **t's, T's,** *or* **Ts.** **1.** the 20th letter of the English alphabet. **2.** something shaped like a T. **3. to a T.** in every detail; perfectly.

t **1.** tonne(s). **2.** troy (weight).

T *Chem.* tritium.

t. **1.** temperature. **2.** ton(s).

ta (tɑː) *interj. Brit. informal.* thank you. [imit. of baby talk]

Ta *Chem.* tantalum.

TA (in Britain) Territorial Army (now superseded by **TAVR**).

tab¹ (tæb) *n.* **1.** a small flap of material, esp. one on a garment for decoration or for fastening to a button. **2.** any similar flap, such as a piece of paper attached to a file for identification. **3.** *Chiefly U.S. & Canad.* a bill, esp. for a meal or drinks. **4. keep tabs on.** *Informal.* to keep a watchful eye on. *~vb.* **tabbing, tabbed. 5.** to supply (something) with a tab or tabs. [origin unknown]

tab² (tæb) *n.* short for **tabulator.**

tabard (ˈtæbəd) *n.* **1.** a sleeveless jacket, esp. (in the Middle Ages) one worn by a knight over his armour. **2.** a short coat bearing the coat of arms of the sovereign, worn by a herald. [Old French *tabart*]

Tabasco (təˈbæskəʊ) *n. Trademark.* a very hot red sauce made from peppers.

tabby (ˈtæbɪ) *adj.* **1.** (esp. of cats) having dark stripes or wavy markings on a lighter background. *~n., pl.* **-bies. 2.** a tabby cat. [from the girl's name *Tabitha,* influenced by *tabby,* old kind of striped silk]

tabernacle (ˈtæbəˌnækʲl) *n.* **1.** (*often cap.*) *Bible.* the portable sanctuary in which the ancient Israelites carried the Ark of the Covenant. **2.** any place of worship that is not called a church. **3.** *R.C. Church.* a receptacle in which the Blessed Sacrament is kept. [Latin *tabernāculum* a tent]

tabla (ˈtæblə) *n., pl.* **-bla** *or* **-blas.** one of a pair of drums used in Indian music, played with the hands. [Hindi, from Arabic: drum]

table (ˈteɪbʲl) *n.* **1.** a flat horizontal slab or board supported by one or more legs. **2.** an arrangement of words, numbers, or signs, in parallel columns. **3.** any flat or level area, such as a plateau. **4.** a tablet on which laws were inscribed by the ancient Romans, Hebrews, and others. **5. turn the tables.** to cause a complete reversal of circumstances. *~vb.* **6.** *Brit.* to submit (a bill) for consideration by a legislative body. **7.** *U.S.* to suspend discussion of (a proposal) indefinitely. [Latin *tabula* a writing tablet]

tableau (ˈtæbləʊ) *n., pl.* **-leaux** (-ləʊ, -ləʊz) *or* **-leaus.** a group of people arranged motionlessly on a stage to represent a scene from history, legend, or literature. [French]

tablecloth (ˈteɪbʲlˌklɒθ) *n.* a cloth for covering the top of a table, esp. during meals.

table d'hôte (ˈtɑːbʲl ˈdəʊt) *adj.* **1.** (of a meal) consisting of a set number of courses with a limited choice of dishes offered at a fixed price. *~n., pl.* **tables d'hôte** (ˈtɑːbʲlz ˈdəʊt). **2.** a table d'hôte meal or menu. [French: the host's table]

tableland (ˈteɪbʲlˌlænd) *n.* a flat area of high ground.

table licence *n.* a licence authorizing the sale of alcoholic drinks with meals only.

tablespoon (ˈteɪbʲlˌspuːn) *n.* **1.** a spoon, larger than a dessertspoon, used for serving food. **2.** Also called: **tablespoonful.** the amount contained in such a spoon. **3.** a unit of capacity used in cooking, equal to half a fluid ounce.

tablet (ˈtæblɪt) *n.* **1.** a pill consisting of a compressed medicinal substance. **2.** a flattish cake of some substance, such as soap. **3.** a slab of stone, wood, etc., used for inscriptions. **4.** a pad of writing paper. [Latin *tabula* a board]

table tennis *n.* a miniature form of tennis played on a table with bats and a small light ball.

tabloid (ˈtæblɔɪd) *n.* a small-sized newspaper, usually with many photographs and a concise and often sensational style. [from *tablet*]

taboo *or* **tabu** (təˈbuː) *adj.* **1.** forbidden or disapproved of: *taboo words. ~n., pl.* **-boos** *or* **-bus. 2.** a restriction or prohibition resulting from social or other conventions. **3.** ritual prohibition, esp. of something that is considered holy or unclean. [Tongan *tabu*]

tabor (ˈteɪbə) *n.* a small drum used esp. in the Middle Ages, struck with one hand while the other held a pipe. [Old French *tabour*]

tabular (ˈtæbjʊlə) *adj.* arranged in parallel columns so as to form a table. [Latin *tabula* a board]

tabulate (ˈtæbjʊˌleɪt) *vb.* to arrange (information) in tabular form. —**ˌtabuˈlation** *n.*

tabulator (ˈtæbjʊˌleɪtə) *n.* a key on a typewriter or word processor that sets stops so that data can be arranged in columns.

tachograph (ˈtækəˌɡrɑːf) *n.* a tachometer that produces a record (**tachogram**) of its readings, esp. a device for recording the speed of a vehicle and the distance that it covers. [Greek *takhos* speed + -GRAPH]

tachometer (tæˈkɒmɪtə) *n.* any device for measuring speed, esp. the rate of revolution of a shaft. [Greek *takhos* speed + -METER]

tacit (ˈtæsɪt) *adj.* implied or inferred without direct expression; understood: *a tacit agreement.* [Latin *tacitus* silent]

taciturn (ˈtæsɪˌtɜːn) *adj.* habitually silent, reserved, or uncommunicative. [Latin *tacēre* to be silent] —**ˌtaciˈturnity** *n.*

tack[1] (tæk) n. **1.** a short sharp-pointed nail with a large flat head. **2.** Brit. a long loose temporary stitch used in dressmaking. **3.** a temporary fastening. ~vb. **4.** to secure (something) by a tack or tacks. **5.** Brit. to sew (something) with long loose temporary stitches. **6.** to attach or append: tack this letter onto the other pages. [Middle English tak fastening, nail]

tack[2] (tæk) n. **1.** Naut. the heading of a vessel that is sailing to windward, stated in terms of the side of the sail against which the wind is pressing: on the port tack. **2.** a course of action or a policy: they didn't seem convinced, so I tried another tack. ~vb. **3.** Naut. to steer a sailing vessel on a zigzag course, so as to make progress against the wind. **4.** Naut. to change the heading of a sailing vessel to the opposite tack. [from tack rope used to secure a sail]

tack[3] (tæk) n. riding harness for horses, including saddles and bridles. [from tackle]

tackies ('tækɪz) pl. n., sing. **tacky.** S. African informal. tennis shoes or plimsolls. [prob. from tacky sticky]

tackle ('tæk'l) n. **1.** an arrangement of ropes and pulleys designed to lift heavy weights. **2.** the equipment required for a particular sport or occupation: fishing tackle. **3.** Sport. an attempt to get the ball away from an opposing player. **4.** Naut. the halyards and other running rigging aboard a vessel. ~vb. **5.** to undertake (a task). **6.** to confront (esp. an opponent) with a difficult proposition. **7.** Sport. to attempt to get the ball away from (an opposing player). [Middle English]

tacky[1] ('tækɪ) adj. **tackier, tackiest.** slightly sticky. [earlier tack stickiness] —'**tackiness** n.

tacky[2] ('tækɪ) adj. **tackier, tackiest.** Informal. **1.** shabby or shoddy: a row of tacky shops. **2.** ostentatious and vulgar: tacky jewellery. [origin unknown] —'**tackiness** n.

tact (tækt) n. **1.** a sense of what is fitting and considerate in dealing with others, so as to avoid giving offence. **2.** skill in handling difficult situations; diplomacy. [Latin tactus a touching] —'**tactful** adj. —'**tactfully** adv. —'**tactless** adj. —'**tactlessly** adv. —'**tactlessness** n.

tactic ('tæktɪk) n. a tactical move. See also **tactics.**

tactical ('tæktɪk'l) adj. **1.** of or employing tactics: a tactical error. **2.** (of missiles, bombing, etc.) for use in limited military operations. —'**tactically** adv.

tactics ('tæktɪks) pl. n. **1.** (functioning as sing.) Mil. the science of the detailed direction of forces in battle to achieve an aim or task. **2.** the manoeuvres used to achieve an aim or task. **3.** plans followed to achieve a particular short-term aim. [Greek tassein to arrange] —**tactician** (tæk'tɪʃən) n.

tactile ('tæktaɪl) adj. of or having a sense of touch: a tactile organ. [Latin tactilis]

tadpole ('tæd,pəʊl) n. the aquatic larva of frogs and toads, which develops from a limbless tailed form with external gills into a form with internal gills, limbs, and a reduced tail. [Middle English tadde toad + pol head]

taffeta ('tæfɪtə) n. a thin plain-weave fabric of silk or rayon used esp. for women's clothes. [Persian tāftah spun]

taffrail ('tæf,reɪl) n. Naut. a rail at the stern of a vessel. [Dutch tafereel panel]

Taffy ('tæfɪ) n., pl. **-fies.** Slang. a Welshman. [the supposed Welsh pronunciation of the name Davy]

tag[1] (tæg) n. **1.** a piece of paper, leather, etc., for attaching to something as a mark or label: a price tag. **2.** a point of metal or plastic at the end of a cord or lace. **3.** a verbal appendage such as the refrain of a song or the moral of a fable. **4.** a brief quotation. **5.** an electronic device worn by a prisoner under house arrest so that his movements can be monitored. ~vb. **tagging, tagged. 6.** to mark with a tag. **7. tag along.** to accompany someone, esp. when uninvited: would you mind if I just tagged along? [origin unknown]

tag[2] (tæg) n. **1.** a children's game in which one player chases the others in an attempt to catch one of them, who will then become the chaser. ~vb. **tagging, tagged. 2.** to catch (another child) in the game of tag. ~Also called: **tig.** [origin unknown]

Tagalog (tə'ɡɑːlɒg) n. **1.** (pl. **-logs** or **-log**) a member of a people of the Philippines. **2.** the language of this people. ~adj. **3.** of this people or their language.

tag end n. **1.** Chiefly U.S. & Canad. the last part of something. **2.** a loose end of cloth, thread, etc.

tagetes (tæ'dʒiːtiːz) n., pl. **-tes.** any of a genus of plants with yellow or orange flowers, including the French and African marigolds. [Latin Tages, an Etruscan god]

tagliatelle (,tæljə'tɛlɪ) n. a form of pasta made in narrow strips. [Italian]

tail[1] (teɪl) n. **1.** the rear part of an animal's body, usually forming a flexible appendage to the trunk. **2.** anything resembling such an appendage: the tail of a shirt. **3.** the last part or parts: the tail of the storm. **4.** the rear part of an aircraft. **5.** Astron. the luminous stream of gas and dust particles driven from the head of a comet when it is close to the sun. **6.** Informal. a person employed to follow and spy upon another. **7.** (modifier) coming from or situated in the rear: a tail wind. **8. turn tail.** to run away; escape. **9. with one's tail between one's legs.** completely defeated and demoralized. ~vb. **10.** Informal. to follow (someone) stealthily. ~See also **tail off, tails.** [Old English tægel] —'**tailless** adj.

tail[2] (teɪl) n. Law. the limitation of an estate or interest to a person and his descendants. [Old French taille a division] —'**tailless** adj.

tailback ('teɪl,bæk) n. a queue of traffic stretching back from an obstruction.

tailboard ('teɪl,bɔːd) n. a board at the rear of a lorry, etc., that can be removed or let down.

tail coat n. a man's black coat having a

horizontal cut over the hips and a tapering tail with a vertical slit up to the waist.

tailgate ('teɪlˌgeɪt) n. **1.** same as **tailboard**. **2.** a door at the rear of a hatchback vehicle.

tail-light ('teɪlˌlaɪt) or **tail-lamp** n. U.S. & Canad. same as **rear light**.

tail off or **away** vb. to decrease gradually: her interest in stamp collecting tailed off over the years.

tailor ('teɪlə) n. **1.** a person who makes, repairs, or alters outer garments, esp. menswear. ~vb. **2.** to cut or style (material) to satisfy certain requirements. **3.** to adapt so as to make suitable: he tailored his speech to suit a younger audience. [Old French taillier to cut] —'**tailored** adj.

tailorbird ('teɪləˌbɜːd) n. any of several tropical Asian warblers that build nests by sewing together large leaves using plant fibres.

tailor-made adj. **1.** (of clothing) made by a tailor to fit exactly. **2.** perfect for a particular purpose: a girl tailor-made for him. ~n. **3.** a tailor-made garment.

tailpiece ('teɪlˌpiːs) n. **1.** an appendage. **2.** a decorative design at the end of a chapter.

tailpipe ('teɪlˌpaɪp) n. a pipe from which exhaust gases are discharged, esp. the pipe at the end of the exhaust system of a motor vehicle.

tailplane ('teɪlˌpleɪn) n. a small horizontal wing at the tail of an aircraft to provide longitudinal stability.

tails (teɪlz) pl. n. **1.** Informal. same as **tail coat**. ~interj., adv. **2.** with the side of a coin uppermost that does not have a portrait of a head on it.

tailspin ('teɪlˌspɪn) n. **1.** Aeronautics. same as **spin** (sense 9). **2.** Informal. a state of confusion or panic.

tailwind ('teɪlˌwɪnd) n. a wind blowing in the same direction as the course of an aircraft or vehicle.

taint (teɪnt) vb. **1.** to affect by pollution or contamination. **2.** to tarnish (someone's reputation, etc.). ~n. **3.** a defect or flaw. **4.** a trace of contamination or infection. [Old French teindre to dye]

take (teɪk) vb. **taking**, **took**, **taken**. **1.** to remove from a place, usually by grasping with the hand: he took a book from the shelf. **2.** to accompany, escort, or convey: we took the children to Spain. **3.** to use as a means of transport: I shall take the bus. **4.** to conduct or lead: this road takes you to the station. **5.** to obtain possession of (something), often dishonestly: someone has taken my watch. **6.** to win or capture (a trick, piece, etc.). **7.** to put an end to: she took her own life. **8.** to require (time, resources, or ability): the job took two days. **9.** to use as a particular case: take hotels for example. **10.** to proceed to occupy: to take a seat. **11.** to assume the obligations of: to take office. **12.** to receive in a specified way: she took the news very well. **13.** to receive and make use of: to take advice; take an opportunity. **14.** to receive into the body; swallow: to take a

pill. **15.** to perform (an action, esp. one that brings some benefit to the person who does it): to take a look; take a deep breath; take a chance; take a bath. **16.** to put into effect: to take steps to ascertain the answer. **17.** to make (a photograph). **18.** to write down or copy: to take notes. **19.** to work at or study: to take economics at college. **20.** to begin to experience or feel: to take an interest; take offence. **21.** to consider or regard: I take him to be honest. **22.** to accept (responsibility, etc.): to take the blame for an accident. **23.** to accept as valid: I take your point. **24.** to stand up to or endure: I can't take his arrogance. **25.** to adopt as one's own: to take someone's part in a quarrel. **26.** to ascertain by measuring: to take a pulse. **27.** to subtract or deduct. **28.** to aim or direct: he took a swipe at Jim. **29.** to have or produce the intended effect: her vaccination took. **30.** (of seedlings) to start growing successfully. **31. take account of** or **take into account.** to consider and make plans or allowances for: to take account of two years of overspending. **32. take advantage of.** to make use of (someone or something) for one's own benefit, esp. unfairly. **33. take care.** to watch out or look after oneself. **34. take care of.** to look after; tend. **35. take it.** to assume or believe: I take it you'll be back later. **36. take part.** to participate or join in. **37. take place.** to happen. **38. take upon oneself.** to assume the right or duty (to do something). **take your time.** use as much time as you need. ~n. **40.** Films, music. one of a series of recordings from which the best will be selected. ~See also **take after**, **take apart**, etc. [Old English tacan] —'**taker** n.

take after vb. to resemble in appearance, character, or behaviour.

take apart vb. **1.** to separate (something) into component parts. **2.** to criticize severely.

take away vb. **1.** to subtract: take away four from nine to leave five. ~prep. **2.** minus: nine take away four is five. ~adj. **takeaway**. **3.** Brit., Austral., & N.Z. sold for consumption away from the premises: a takeaway meal. ~n. **takeaway**. Brit., Austral., & N.Z. **4.** a shop or restaurant that sells such food. **5.** a meal sold for consumption away from the premises.

take back vb. **1.** to retract or withdraw (something said or promised). **2.** to regain possession of. **3.** to return for exchange: to take back an unsatisfactory garment. **4.** to accept (someone) back (into one's home, affections, etc.). **5.** to remind one of the past: that tune takes me back.

take down vb. **1.** to record in writing. **2.** to dismantle or remove. **3.** to reduce (someone) in power, arrogance, etc.: we'll take him down a peg or two.

take for vb. Informal. to consider or suppose to be, esp. mistakenly: the fake coins were taken for genuine; what do you take me for?

take-home pay n. the remainder of

one's pay after income tax and other compulsory deductions have been made.

take in vb. **1.** to understand. **2.** to include: *her thesis takes in that point.* **3.** to receive into one's house: *to take in lodgers.* **4.** to make (clothing) smaller by altering seams. **5.** *Informal.* to cheat or deceive. **6.** *U.S.* to go to: *let's take in a movie tonight.*

taken ('teɪkən) vb. **1.** the past participle of **take.** ~adj. **2.** (foll. by *with*) enthusiastically impressed by.

take off vb. **1.** to remove (a garment). **2.** (of an aircraft) to become airborne. **3.** *Informal.* to set out or cause to set out on a journey: *they took off for Spain.* **4.** *Informal.* to become successful or popular. **5.** to deduct: *the shop took off ten per cent.* **6.** *Informal.* to mimic (someone). ~n. **take-off. 7.** the act or process of making an aircraft airborne. **8.** *Informal.* an act of mimicry.

take on vb. **1.** to employ or hire. **2.** to assume or acquire: *his voice took on a plaintive note.* **3.** to agree to do; undertake. **4.** to compete against; fight.

take out vb. **1.** to extract or remove. **2.** to obtain or secure: *I want to take out an insurance policy.* **3.** to go out with; escort. **4.** **take it** or **a lot out of.** *Informal.* to sap the energy or vitality of. **5. take it out on.** *Informal.* to vent (anger) on: *just because she let you down you don't have to take it out on me.* ~adj., n. **takeout. 6.** *U.S. & Canad.* See **takeaway** (senses 3, 4, 5).

take over vb. **1.** to obtain control or management of. ~n. **takeover. 2.** the act of obtaining control of something, esp. of another company by buying its shares.

take to vb. **1.** to form a liking for. **2.** to have recourse to: *to take to the bottle.*

take up vb. **1.** to occupy or fill (space or time). **2.** to adopt the study, practice, or activity of: *to take up gardening.* **3.** to shorten (a garment). **4.** to accept (an offer). **5. take up on. a.** to discuss (something) further with (someone): *can I take you up on two points in your talk?* **b.** to accept what is offered by (someone): *let me take you up on your invitation.* **6. take up with. a.** to discuss (an issue) with (someone). **b.** to begin to keep company or associate with.

taking ('teɪkɪŋ) adj. charming, fascinating, or intriguing.

takings ('teɪkɪŋz) pl. n. receipts; earnings.

talc (tælk) n. also **talcum. 1.** See **talcum powder. 2.** a soft mineral, consisting of magnesium silicate, used in the manufacture of ceramics, paints, and talcum powder. [Persian *talk*]

talcum powder ('tælkəm) n. a powder made of purified talc, usually scented, used for perfuming the body.

tale (teɪl) n. **1.** a report, narrative, or story. **2. a.** a malicious piece of gossip. **b.** a false statement. **3. tell tales. a.** to tell fanciful lies. **b.** to report malicious stories or trivial complaints, esp. to someone in authority. **4. tell a tale.** to reveal some-

thing important. **5. tell its own tale.** to be self-evident. [Old English *talu* list]

talent ('tælənt) n. **1.** innate ability, aptitude, or faculty: *a talent for cooking; a child with talent.* **2.** a person or persons with such ability. **3.** any of various units of weight and money used by the ancient Babylonians, Greeks, Romans, and others. **4.** *Informal.* members of the opposite sex collectively: *the local talent.* [Greek *talanton* unit of money] —**'talented** adj.

talent scout n. a person whose occupation is the search for talented people, such as sportsmen or performers, for engagements as professionals.

talisman ('tælɪzmən) n., pl. -**mans.** a stone or other small object, usually inscribed or carved, believed to protect the wearer from evil influences. [Medieval Greek *telesma* ritual] —**talismanic** (,tælɪz-'mænɪk) adj.

talk (tɔːk) vb. **1.** (often foll. by *to* or *with*) to express one's thoughts, feelings, or desires by means of words. **2.** (usually foll. by *about*) to exchange ideas or opinions about (a subject). **3.** to give voice to; utter: *to talk rubbish.* **4.** to discuss: *to talk business.* **5.** to reveal information: *the prisoner talked after torture.* **6.** to know how to communicate in (a language or idiom): *he talks English.* **7.** to spread rumours or gossip. **8.** to be effective or persuasive: *money talks.* **9. now you're talking.** *Informal.* at last you're saying something agreeable. **10. you can** or **can't talk.** *Informal.* you are in no position to comment or criticize. ~n. **11.** a speech or lecture. **12.** an exchange of ideas or thoughts. **13.** idle chatter, gossip, or rumour. **14.** (often pl.) a conference, discussion, or negotiation. ~See also **talk back, talk down,** etc. [Middle English *talkien*] —**'talker** n.

talkative ('tɔːkətɪv) adj. given to talking a great deal.

talk back vb. **1.** to answer (someone) boldly or impudently. ~n. **talkback. 2.** *Television, radio.* a system of telephone links enabling spoken directions to be given during the production of a programme.

talk down vb. **1.** (foll. by *to*) to speak to someone in a patronizing manner. **2.** to give instructions to (an aircraft) by radio to enable it to land.

talkie ('tɔːkɪ) n. *Informal.* an early film with a soundtrack.

talking book n. a recording of a book, designed to be used by the blind.

talking-to n. *Informal.* a session of criticism: *I got a severe talking-to when I got home.*

talk into vb. to persuade (someone) to do something by talking to him: *I talked her into buying the house.*

talk out vb. **1.** to resolve (a problem) by talking. **2.** *Brit.* to block (a bill) in a legislative body by lengthy discussion. **3. talk out of.** to dissuade (someone) from doing something by talking to him.

talk round vb. **1.** to persuade (someone) to agree with one's opinion or suggestion.

2. to discuss (a subject), esp. without coming to a conclusion.

tall (tɔːl) *adj.* **1.** of more than average height. **2.** having a specified height: *five feet tall*. [Middle English]

tallboy ('tɔːlˌbɔɪ) *n.* a high chest of drawers made in two sections placed one on top of the other.

tall order *n. Informal.* a difficult or unreasonable request.

tallow ('tæləʊ) *n.* a fatty substance extracted from the suet of sheep and cattle: used for making soap, candles, and food. [Old English *tælg* a dye]

tall story *n. Informal.* an exaggerated or unlikely account of something.

tally ('tælɪ) *vb.* **-lying, -lied. 1.** to correspond one with the other: *the two stories don't tally.* **2.** to keep score. **~*n.*, *pl.* -lies. 3.** any record of debit, credit, the score in a game, etc. **4.** an identifying label or mark. **5.** a stick used (esp. formerly) as a record of the amount of a debt according to the notches cut in it. [Latin *tālea* a stick]

tally clerk *n. Austral. & N.Z.* a person, esp. on a wharf, who checks the count of goods being loaded or unloaded.

tally-ho (ˌtælɪˈhəʊ) *interj.* the cry of a participant at a hunt when the quarry is sighted.

Talmud ('tælmʊd) *n. Judaism.* the primary source of Jewish religious law. [Hebrew *talmūdh* instruction] —**Tal'mudic** *adj.* —**'Talmudist** *n.*

talon ('tælən) *n.* a sharply hooked claw, esp. of a bird of prey. [Latin *tālus* ankle]

tamarind ('tæmərɪnd) *n.* a tropical evergreen tree with fruit whose acid pulp is used as a food and to make beverages and medicines. [Arabic *tamr hindī* Indian date]

tamarisk ('tæmərɪsk) *n.* a tree or shrub of the Mediterranean region and S Asia, with scalelike leaves, slender branches, and feathery flower clusters. [Latin *tamarix*]

tambour ('tæmbʊə) *n.* **1.** a small embroidery frame, consisting of two hoops over which the fabric is stretched while being worked. **2.** a drum. [French]

tambourine (ˌtæmbəˈriːn) *n. Music.* a percussion instrument consisting of a single piece of skin stretched over a circular wooden frame, which is hung with pairs of metal discs that jingle when it is struck or shaken. [from Old French]

tame (teɪm) *adj.* **1.** changed by man from a wild state into a domesticated state. **2.** (of animals) not fearful of human contact. **3.** meek or submissive: *a tame personality.* **4.** flat, insipid, or uninspiring: *a tame ending to a book.* **~*vb.* 5.** to make (an animal) tame; domesticate. **6.** to break the spirit of, subdue. [Old English *tam*]

Tamil ('tæmɪl) *n.* **1.** (*pl.* **-ils** or **-il**) a member of a people of S India and Sri Lanka. **2.** the language of this people. **~*adj.* 3.** of this people or their language.

tam-o'-shanter (ˌtæməˈʃæntə) *n.* a Scottish brimless wool or cloth cap with a bobble in the centre. [after the hero of Burns's poem *Tam o' Shanter*]

tamp (tæmp) *vb.* to force or pack down firmly by repeated blows: *to tamp down concrete.* [prob. from obs. *tampin* plug for gun's muzzle]

tamper ('tæmpə) *vb.* (foll. by *with*) **1.** to interfere. **2.** to attempt to influence someone, esp. by bribery. [alteration of *temper* (*vb.*)]

tampon ('tæmpon) *n.* a plug of lint, cotton wool, etc., inserted into a wound or body cavity to stop the flow of blood or absorb secretions. [French]

tan¹ (tæn) *n.* **1.** the brown colour produced on the skin after exposure to ultraviolet rays, esp. those of the sun. **~*vb.* tanning, tanned. 2.** to go brown after exposure to ultraviolet rays. **3.** to convert (a skin or hide) into leather by treating it with a tanning agent. **4.** *Slang.* to beat or flog. **~*adj.* 5.** yellowish-brown. [Medieval Latin *tannāre*] —**'tanner** *n.*

tan² (tæn) *Maths.* tangent.

tandem ('tændəm) *n.* **1.** a bicycle with two sets of pedals and two saddles, arranged one behind the other for two riders. **2.** a two-wheeled carriage drawn by two horses harnessed one behind the other. **~*adv.* 3.** one behind the other. [Latin *tandem* at length]

tandoori (tænˈdʊərɪ) *n.* an Indian method of cooking spiced meat or vegetables on a spit in a clay oven. [Urdu, from *tandoor* clay oven]

tang (tæŋ) *n.* **1.** a strong taste or smell. **2.** a trace or hint of something. **3.** the pointed end of a tool, such as a chisel, which is fitted into a handle or shaft. [Old Norse *tangi* point] —**'tangy** *adj.*

tangent ('tændʒənt) *n.* **1.** a geometric line, curve, or plane that touches another curve or surface at one point but does not intersect it. **2.** a trigonometric function that in a right-angled triangle is the ratio of the length of the opposite side to that of the adjacent side. **3. at a tangent.** on a completely different or divergent course, esp. of thought. **~*adj.* 4.** of or involving a tangent. **5.** touching at a single point. [Latin *līnea tangēns* the touching line]

tangential (tænˈdʒɛnʃəl) *adj.* **1.** of or in the direction of a tangent. **2.** of superficial relevance only; digressive. —**tan'gentially** *adv.*

tangerine (ˌtændʒəˈriːn) *n.* **1.** an Asian citrus tree cultivated for its small orange-like fruits which have a sweet juicy flesh. **~*adj.* 2.** reddish-orange. [*Tangier*, a port in Morocco]

tangi ('tæŋɪ) *n. N.Z.* **1.** a Maori funeral ceremony. **2.** *Informal.* a lamentation.

tangible ('tændʒɪb²l) *adj.* **1.** capable of being touched or felt. **2.** capable of being clearly grasped by the mind. **3.** having a physical existence: *tangible property.* [Latin *tangere* to touch] —ˌtangi'bility *n.* —**'tangibly** *adv.*

tangle ('tæŋg²l) *n.* **1.** a confused or complicated mass of things, such as hair or fibres, knotted or coiled together. **2.** a complicated problem or situation. **~*vb.* 3.** to twist (things, such as hair or fibres) together in a confused mass. **4.** (often foll. by *with*) to come into conflict: *to tangle with the police*. **5.** to ensnare or trap, as in a net. [Middle English *tangilen*] —**'tangled** *adj.*

tango ('tæŋgəʊ) *n., pl.* **-gos. 1.** a Latin-American dance characterized by long gliding steps and sudden pauses. **2.** music for this dance. ~*vb.* **-going, -goed. 3.** to perform this dance. [American Spanish]

tank (tæŋk) *n.* **1.** a large container for the mass storage of liquids or gases. **2.** an armoured combat vehicle moving on tracks and armed with guns. **3.** Also called: **tankful.** the quantity contained in a tank. [Gujarati (a language of W India) *tānkh* artificial lake]

tankard ('tæŋkəd) *n.* a large one-handled drinking vessel sometimes fitted with a hinged lid. [Middle English]

tanked up *adj. Slang, chiefly Brit.* very drunk.

tanker ('tæŋkə) *n.* a ship or lorry designed to carry liquid in bulk, such as oil.

tank farming *n.* same as **hydroponics.** —**tank farmer** *n.*

tannery ('tænərɪ) *n., pl.* **-neries.** a place or building where skins and hides are tanned.

tannic ('tænɪk) *adj.* of, containing, or produced from tan, tannin, or tannic acid.

tannin ('tænɪn) *n.* a yellowish compound found in many plants and used as a tanning agent, mordant, medical astringent, etc. Also called: **tannic acid.**

Tannoy ('tænɔɪ) *n. Trademark.* a type of public-address system.

tansy ('tænzɪ) *n., pl.* **-sies.** a plant with yellow flowers in flat-topped clusters. [Greek *athanasia* immortality]

tantalize or **-lise** ('tæntə,laɪz) *vb.* to tease or make frustrated, for example by tormenting (someone) with the sight of something that he wants but cannot have. [after *Tantalus*, a mythological king condemned to stand in water that receded when he tried to drink it and under fruit that moved away when he reached for it] —**'tanta,lizing** or **-,lising** *adj.* —**'tanta,lizingly** or **-,lisingly** *adv.*

tantalum ('tæntələm) *n.* a hard greyish-white metallic element that resists corrosion. Symbol: Ta [after *Tantalus* (see TANTALIZE), from the metal's incapacity to absorb acids]

tantalus ('tæntələs) *n. Brit.* a case in which bottles may be locked with their contents tantalizingly visible.

tantamount ('tæntə,maʊnt) *adj.* (foll. by *to*) as good as; equivalent in effect to. [Anglo-French *tant amunter*]

tantrum ('tæntrəm) *n.* (often *pl.*) an outburst of bad temper. [origin unknown]

Taoism ('taʊɪzəm) *n.* a system of religion and philosophy advocating a simple honest life and noninterference with the course of natural events. —**'Taoist** *n., adj.*

tap¹ (tæp) *vb.* **tapping, tapped. 1.** to strike (something) lightly and usually repeatedly. **2.** to strike lightly with (something): *to tap one's finger on the desk.* ~*n.* **3.** a light blow or knock, or the sound made by it. **4.** the metal piece attached to the toe or heel

of a shoe used for tap-dancing. ~See also **taps.** [Middle English *tappen*]

tap² (tæp) *n.* **1.** *Chiefly Brit.* a valve by which the flow of a liquid or gas from a pipe can be controlled. Usual U.S. word: **faucet.** **2.** a stopper to plug a cask or barrel. **3.** *Med.* the withdrawal of fluid from a bodily cavity. **4.** *Electronics, chiefly U.S. & Canad.* a connection made at some point between the terminals of an inductor, resistor, etc. Usual Brit. word: **tapping.** **5.** a concealed listening or recording device connected to a telephone. **6. on tap. a.** *Informal.* ready for use. **b.** (of drinks) on draught. ~*vb.* **tapping, tapped. 7.** to connect a tap to (a telephone). **8.** to make a connection to (a pipe, drain, etc.). **9.** to draw off with or as if with a tap. **10.** to cut into (a tree) and draw off sap from it. **11.** *Brit. informal.* to ask (someone) for money: *he tapped me for a fiver.* [Old English *tæppa*]

tap dance *n.* a dance in which the performer wears shoes with taps that make a rhythmic sound on the stage as he dances. —**'tap-,dancer** *n.* —**'tap-,dancing** *n.*

tape (teɪp) *n.* **1.** a long thin strip of cotton or linen used for binding or fastening. **2.** a long narrow strip of paper, metal, etc. **3.** a string stretched across the track at the end of a race course. **4.** See **magnetic tape, ticker tape, tape recording.** ~*vb.* **5.** to bind or fasten with tape. **6. have (a person** or **situation) taped.** *Brit. informal.* to have full understanding and control of (a person or situation). **7.** Also: **tape-record.** to record (speech, music, etc.) on magnetic tape. [Old English *tæppe*]

tape deck *n.* the platform supporting the spools, cassettes, or cartridges of a tape recorder, incorporating the motor and the playback, recording, and erasing heads.

tape measure *n.* a tape or length of metal marked off in centimetres or inches, used for measuring.

taper ('teɪpə) *vb.* **1.** to become narrower towards one end. **2. taper off.** to become gradually less. ~*n.* **3.** a thin candle. **4.** a thin wooden or waxed strip for transferring a flame; spill. **5.** a narrowing. [Old English *tapor*]

tape recorder *n.* an electrical device used for recording and reproducing sounds on magnetic tape.

tape recording *n.* **1.** the act of recording sounds on magnetic tape. **2.** the magnetic tape used for this. **3.** the sounds so recorded.

tapestry ('tæpɪstrɪ) *n., pl.* **-tries. 1.** a heavy woven fabric, often in the form of a picture, used for wall hangings or furnishings. **2.** same as **needlepoint** (sense 1). [Old French *tapisserie* carpeting] —**'tapestried** *adj.*

tapeworm ('teɪp,wɜːm) *n.* a long flat parasitic worm that inhabits the intestines of vertebrates, including man.

tapioca (,tæpɪ'əʊkə) *n.* a beadlike starch obtained from cassava root, used in puddings. [S American Indian *tipioca* pressed-out juice]

tapir ('teɪpə) n., pl. **-pirs** or **-pir.** a piglike mammal of South and Central America and SE Asia, having a long snout, three-toed hind legs, and four-toed forelegs. [S American Indian *tapira*]

tappet ('tæpɪt) n. a short steel rod in an engine which moves up and down transferring movement from one part of the machine to another. [from TAP¹]

taproom ('tæp,ruːm) n. Old-fashioned. the public bar in a hotel or pub.

taproot ('tæp,ruːt) n. the main root of plants such as the dandelion, which grows vertically downwards and bears smaller lateral roots.

taps (tæps) n. (functioning as sing.) (in the Guide movement) a closing song sung at an evening camp fire or at the end of a meeting.

tapster ('tæpstə) n. **1.** Old-fashioned. a barman. **2.** (in W Africa) a man who taps palm trees for their sap.

tar¹ (tɑː) n. **1.** a dark sticky substance obtained by distillation of organic matter such as coal, wood, or peat. **2.** same as **coal tar.** ~vb. **tarring, tarred. 3.** to coat with tar. **4. tar and feather.** to cover (someone) with tar and feathers as a punishment. **5. tarred with the same brush.** having the same faults. [Old English *teoru*]

tar² (tɑː) n. Informal. a seaman. [short for *tarpaulin*]

tarakihi ('tɑrə,kiːhiː) or **terakihi** ('terə,kiːhiː) n., pl. **-kihis.** a common edible sea fish of New Zealand waters. [Maori]

taramasalata (,tærəmæsə'lɑːtə) n. a creamy pale pink pâté, made from the eggs of fish, esp. smoked cod, and served as an hors d'oeuvre. [Modern Greek]

tarantella (,tærən'tɛlə) n. **1.** a peasant dance from S Italy. **2.** a piece of music for this dance. [Italian]

tarantula (tə'ræntjʊlə) n., pl. **-las** or **-lae** (-,liː). any of various large hairy spiders of tropical America with a poisonous bite. [Medieval Latin]

tarboosh (tɑː'buːʃ) n. a felt or cloth brimless cap, usually red and often with a silk tassel, formerly worn by Muslim men. [Arabic *tarbūsh*]

tardy ('tɑːdɪ) adj. **-dier, -diest. 1.** occurring later than expected. **2.** slow in progress, growth, etc. [Latin *tardus* slow] —'**tardily** adv. —'**tardiness** n.

tare¹ (tɛə) n. **1.** any of various vetch plants of Eurasia and N Africa. **2.** Bible. a weed, thought to be the darnel. [origin unknown]

tare² (tɛə) n. **1.** the weight of the wrapping or container in which goods are packed. **2.** the weight of an unladen vehicle. [Arabic *tarhah* something discarded]

target ('tɑːgɪt) n. **1.** an object at which an archer or marksman aims, usually a round flat surface marked with circles. **2.** any point or area aimed at. **3.** a fixed goal or objective. **4.** a person or thing at which criticism or ridicule is directed. ~vb. **5.** to direct or aim: to target benefits at those most in need. [Old French *targette* a little shield]

tariff ('tærɪf) n. **1. a.** a tax levied by a government on imports or occasionally exports. **b.** a list of such taxes. **2.** a list of fixed prices: a hotel tariff. **3.** Chiefly Brit. a method of charging for services such as gas and electricity by setting a price per unit. [Arabic *ta'rifa* to inform]

tarlatan ('tɑːlətən) n. an open-weave cotton fabric, used for stiffening garments. [French *tarlatane*]

Tarmac ('tɑːmæk) n. **1.** Trademark. (often not cap.) a paving material made of crushed stone bound with a mixture of tar and bitumen, used for a road or airport runway. ~vb. **-macking, -macked. 2.** (usually not cap.) to apply Tarmac to (a surface). [TAR + MAC(ADAM)]

tarn (tɑːn) n. a small mountain lake. [from Old Norse]

tarnish ('tɑːnɪʃ) vb. **1.** (of a metal) to lose its shine, esp. by exposure to air or moisture. **2.** to damage; taint: a fraud that tarnished his reputation. ~n. **3.** a tarnished condition, surface, or film on a surface. [Old French *ternir* to make dull]

taro ('tɑːrəʊ) n., pl. **-ros.** an Asian plant with a large edible rootstock. [Tahitian & Maori]

tarot ('tærəʊ) n. **1.** one of a special pack of cards, now used mainly for fortune-telling. **2.** a card in a tarot pack with distinctive symbolic design. [French]

tarpaulin (tɑː'pɔːlɪn) n. **1.** a heavy waterproof fabric made of canvas or similar material coated with tar, wax, or paint. **2.** a sheet of this fabric. [prob. from TAR¹ + PALL¹]

tarragon ('tærəgən) n. a European herb with narrow leaves, which are used as seasoning in cooking. [Old French *targon*]

tarry ('tærɪ) vb. **-rying, -ried.** Old-fashioned. **1.** to delay; linger. **2.** to stay briefly. [origin unknown]

tarsal ('tɑːs'l) adj. **1.** of the tarsus or tarsi. ~n. **2.** a tarsal bone.

tarseal ('tɑː,siːl) n. N.Z. **1.** the bitumen surface of a road. **2. the tarseal.** the main highway.

tarsus ('tɑːsəs) n., pl. **-si** (-saɪ). **1.** the bones of the ankle and heel collectively. **2.** the corresponding part in other mammals and in amphibians and reptiles. [Greek *tarsos* flat surface, instep]

tart¹ (tɑːt) n. **1.** Chiefly Brit. a pastry case, often having no top crust, with a sweet filling, such as jam or custard. **2.** Chiefly U.S. a small open pie with a fruit filling. [Old French *tarte*]

tart² (tɑːt) adj. **1.** (of a flavour) sour; acid. **2.** cutting; sharp: a tart remark. [Old English *teart* rough] —'**tartly** adv. —'**tartness** n.

tart³ (tɑːt) n. Informal. a sexually provocative or promiscuous woman. [from *sweetheart*]

tartan ('tɑːt'n) n. **1.** a design of straight lines, crossing at right angles to give a chequered appearance, esp. one of the distinctive designs each of which is associated with a Scottish clan. **2.** a fabric or garment with this design. [origin unknown]

tartar[1] ('tɑːtə) n. **1.** a hard deposit on the teeth. **2.** a brownish-red substance deposited in a cask during the fermentation of wine. [Medieval Greek *tartaron*]

tartar[2] ('tɑːtə) n. a fearsome or formidable person. [from *Tatar*]

Tartar ('tɑːtə) n., adj. same as **Tatar**.

tartaric (tɑː'tærɪk) adj. of or derived from tartar or tartaric acid.

tartaric acid n. a colourless crystalline acid which is found in many fruits.

tartar sauce n. a mayonnaise sauce mixed with hard-boiled egg yolks, chopped herbs, and capers.

tartrazine ('tɑːtrə,ziːn) n. a dye that produces a yellow colour: used as a food additive, in drugs, and to dye textiles.

tart up vb. Brit. informal. **1.** to dress and make (oneself) up in a sexually provocative way. **2.** to decorate in a cheap and flashy way: *to tart up a bar.*

Tarzan ('tɑːzən) n. (*sometimes not cap.*) Informal, often ironical. a man with great physical strength, agility, and virility. [after the hero of stories by E. R. Burroughs]

task (tɑːsk) n. **1.** a specific piece of work required to be done. **2.** an unpleasant or difficult job or duty. **3. take to task.** to criticize or rebuke. ~vb. **4.** to subject to severe strain; tax. [Old French *tasche*]

task force n. **1.** a temporary grouping of military units formed to undertake a specific mission. **2.** any organization set up to carry out a continuing task.

taskmaster ('tɑːsk,mɑːstə) n. a person who enforces hard or continuous work. —'task,mistress fem. n.

Tasmanian devil (tæz'meɪnɪən) n. a small ferocious flesh-eating marsupial of Tasmania.

Tass (tæs) n. the principal news agency of the Soviet Union.

tassel ('tæsʲl) n. a tuft of loose threads secured by a knot or knob, used to decorate something, such as a lampshade or piece of clothing. [Old French]

taste (teɪst) n. **1.** the sense by which the flavour of a substance is distinguished by the taste buds. **2.** the sensation experienced by means of the taste buds. **3.** a small amount eaten, sipped, or tried on the tongue. **4.** a brief experience of something: *a taste of the whip.* **5.** a liking for something: *to have a taste for danger.* **6.** the ability to appreciate what is beautiful and excellent. ~vb. **7.** to distinguish the taste of (a substance) by means of the taste buds. **8.** to take a small amount of (a food or liquid) into the mouth, esp. in order to test the flavour. **9.** (often foll. by *of*) to have a specific flavour or taste: *the tea tastes of soap.* **10.** to have an experience of (something): *to taste success.* [Old French *taster*]

taste bud n. any of the cells on the surface of the tongue, by means of which the sensation of taste is experienced.

tasteful ('teɪstful) adj. having or showing good taste: *a tasteful design.* —'**tastefully** adv.

tasteless ('teɪstlɪs) adj. **1.** lacking in flavour; insipid. **2.** lacking social or aesthetic taste. —'**tastelessly** adv. —'**tastelessness** n.

taster ('teɪstə) n. a person who tastes, esp. one employed to test the quality of food or drink by tasting it.

tasty ('teɪstɪ) adj. **tastier, tastiest.** having a pleasant flavour.

tat[1] (tæt) vb. **tatting, tatted.** to make (lace) by looping a thread of cotton or linen with a hand shuttle. [origin unknown]

tat[2] (tæt) n. tatty or tasteless articles.

ta-ta (tæ'tɑː) interj. Brit. informal. goodbye. [origin unknown]

Tatar or **Tartar** ('tɑːtə) n. **1.** a member of a Mongoloid people who established a powerful state in central Asia in the 13th century. They are now scattered throughout the Soviet Union. ~adj. **2.** of the Tatars. [Persian *Tātār*]

tater ('teɪtə) n. Dialect. a potato.

tattered ('tætəd) adj. **1.** ragged or torn: *a tattered coat.* **2.** wearing ragged or torn clothing: *a tattered old man.*

tatters ('tætəz) pl. n. **1.** torn ragged clothing. **2. in tatters. a.** (of clothing) torn in several places. **b.** (of an argument, plan, etc.) completely destroyed.

tatting ('tætɪŋ) n. **1.** an intricate type of lace made by looping a thread of cotton or linen with a hand shuttle. **2.** the work of producing this. [origin unknown]

tattle ('tætʲl) vb. **1.** to gossip about someone else's personal matters or secrets. **2.** to talk idly; chat. ~n. **3.** the act or an instance of tattling. [Middle Dutch *tatelen*] —'**tattler** n.

tattletale ('tætʲl,teɪl) n. Chiefly U.S. & Canad. a scandalmonger or gossip.

tattoo[1] (tæ'tuː) n., pl. **-toos. 1.** (formerly) a signal by drum or bugle ordering soldiers to return to their quarters. **2.** a military display or pageant. **3.** any drumming or tapping. [Dutch *taptoe*]

tattoo[2] (tæ'tuː) vb. **-tooing, -tooed. 1.** to make (pictures or designs) on (a person's skin) by pricking and staining it with indelible colours. ~n., pl. **-toos. 2.** a design made by this process. [Tahitian *tatau*] —**tat'tooer** or **tat'tooist** n.

tatty ('tætɪ) adj. **-tier, -tiest.** Chiefly Brit. worn out, shabby, or unkempt. [Scot.]

taught (tɔːt) vb. past of **teach.**

taunt (tɔːnt) vb. **1.** to tease or provoke (someone) with jeering remarks. ~n. **2.** a jeering remark. [French *tant pour tant* like for like] —'**taunting** adj.

taupe (təup) adj. brownish-grey. [French: mole]

Taurus ('tɔːrəs) n. the second sign of the zodiac; the bull. [Latin: bull]

taut (tɔːt) adj. **1.** tightly stretched: *a taut rope.* **2.** showing nervous strain. **3.** Naut. in good order; neat. [Middle English *tought*]

tauten ('tɔːtʲn) vb. to make or become taut.

tautology (tɔː'tɒlədʒɪ) n., pl. **-gies.** the use

of words that merely repeat elements of the meaning already conveyed, as in "adequate enough". [Greek *tautologia*] —**tautological** (ˌtɔːtə'lɒdʒɪk'l) *or* **tautologous** (tɔː'tɒləgəs) *adj.*

tavern ('tævən) *n.* **1.** a pub. **2.** *U.S., Canad., & N.Z.* a place licensed for the sale and consumption of alcoholic drink. [Latin *taberna* hut]

tawdry ('tɔːdrɪ) *adj.* **-drier, -driest.** cheap, showy, and of poor quality: *tawdry jewellery*. [Middle English *seynt Audries lace*, finery sold at the fair of St *Audrey*]

tawny ('tɔːnɪ) *adj.* brown to brownish-orange. [Old French *tané*]

tawny owl *n.* a European owl having a reddish-brown plumage and a round head.

tawse *or* **taws** (tɔːz) *n. Scot.* a leather strap having one end cut into thongs, formerly used as an instrument of punishment by schoolteachers. [prob. pl. of obs. *taw* strip of leather]

tax (tæks) *n.* **1.** a compulsory financial contribution imposed by a government to raise revenue, levied on income, property, or goods and services. **2.** a heavy demand on something; strain: *a tax on our resources*. ~*vb.* **3.** to levy a tax on (persons, companies, etc.). **4.** to make heavy demands on; strain. **5.** to accuse: *he was taxed with the crime*. [Latin *taxāre* to appraise] —**'taxable** *adj.*

taxation (tæk'seɪʃən) *n.* the act or principle of levying taxes or the condition of being taxed.

tax avoidance *n.* reduction of tax liability by lawful methods.

tax-deductible *adj.* legally deductible from income or wealth before tax assessment.

tax evasion *n.* reduction of tax liability by illegal methods.

tax haven *n.* a country or state having a lower rate of taxation than elsewhere.

taxi ('tæksɪ) *n., pl.* **taxis** *or* **taxies. 1.** Also called: **cab, taxicab**, a car, usually fitted with a taximeter, that may be hired to carry passengers to any specified destination. ~*vb.* **taxiing, taxied. 2.** (of an aircraft) to move along the ground, esp. before takeoff and after landing. **3.** to travel in a taxi. [*taximeter cab*]

taxidermy ('tæksɪˌdɜːmɪ) *n.* the art or process of preparing, stuffing, and mounting animal skins so that they have a lifelike appearance. [Greek *taxis* arrangement + *derma* skin] —**'taxi,dermist** *n.*

taximeter ('tæksɪˌmiːtə) *n.* a meter fitted to a taxi to register the fare, based on the length of the journey.

taxi rank *n.* a place where taxis wait to be hired.

taxonomy (tæk'sɒnəmɪ) *n.* **1.** the branch of biology concerned with the classification of plants and animals into groups based on their similarities and differences. **2.** the science or practice of classification. [Greek *taxis* order + *nomia* law] —**taxonomic** (ˌtæksə'nɒmɪk) *adj.* —**tax'onomist** *n.*

taxpayer ('tæks,peɪə) *n.* a person or organization that pays taxes.

tax return *n.* a declaration of personal income used as a basis for assessing an individual's liability for taxation.

Tb *Chem.* terbium.

TB tuberculosis.

T-bone steak *n.* a large choice steak cut from the sirloin of beef, containing a T-shaped bone.

tbs. *or* **tbsp.** tablespoon(ful).

Tc *Chem.* technetium.

te *or* **ti** (tiː) *n. Music.* (in tonic sol-fa) the syllable used for the seventh note or subtonic of any scale.

Te *Chem.* tellurium.

tea (tiː) *n.* **1.** an evergreen shrub of tropical and subtropical Asia with white fragrant flowers. **2. a.** the dried and shredded leaves of this shrub, used to make a drink by infusion in boiling water. **b.** such a drink, served hot or iced. **3.** *Chiefly Brit.* a light meal eaten in midafternoon, usually consisting of tea and cakes, sometimes with sandwiches. **4.** *Brit., Austral., & N.Z.* the main evening meal. [Ancient Chinese *d'a*]

tea bag *n.* a small bag containing tea leaves, infused in boiling water to make tea.

tea ball *n. Chiefly U.S.* a perforated metal ball filled with tea leaves, used to make tea.

teacake ('tiːˌkeɪk) *n. Brit.* a flat bun, usually eaten toasted and buttered.

teach (tiːtʃ) *vb.* **teaching, taught. 1.** to help to learn; tell or show (someone) how to do something. **2.** to give instruction or lessons in (a subject) to (students). **3.** to cause to learn or understand: *experience taught him that he could not be a journalist*. [Old English *tǣcan*] —**'teachable** *adj.*

teacher ('tiːtʃə) *n.* a person whose occupation is teaching others, esp. children.

tea chest *n.* a large light wooden box used for exporting tea or storing things in.

teaching ('tiːtʃɪŋ) *n.* **1.** the art or profession of a teacher. **2.** (*sometimes pl.*) something taught; precept.

tea cloth *n.* same as **tea towel.**

tea cosy *n.* a covering for a teapot to keep the contents hot.

teacup ('tiːˌkʌp) *n.* **1.** a cup out of which tea may be drunk. **2.** Also called: **teacupful.** the amount a teacup will hold.

teahouse ('tiːˌhaʊs) *n.* a restaurant, esp. in Japan or China, where tea and light refreshments are served.

teak (tiːk) *n.* the hard yellowish-brown wood of an East Indian tree, used for furniture making. [Malayalam (a language of S India) *tēkka*]

teal (tiːl) *n., pl.* **teals** *or* **teal.** a small freshwater duck related to the mallard. [Middle English *tele*]

tea leaves *pl. n., sing.* **tea leaf.** the dried and shredded leaves of the tea shrub, esp. those left behind in a cup or teapot after tea has been made and drunk.

team (tiːm) *n.* (*sometimes functioning as*

pl.) **1.** a group of players forming one of the sides in a sporting contest. **2.** a group of people organized to work together. **3.** two or more animals working together. ~*vb.* **4.** (often foll. by *up with*) to make or join a team. [Old English: offspring]

team-mate *n.* a fellow member of a team.

team spirit *n.* willingness to cooperate as part of a team.

teamster ('tiːmstə) *n.* **1.** (formerly) a driver of a team of horses. **2.** *U.S. & Canad.* a truck driver.

teamwork ('tiːm,wɜːk) *n.* the cooperative work done by a team.

teapot ('tiː,pɒt) *n.* a container with a lid, spout, and handle, in which tea is made and from which it is served.

tear[1] (tɪə) *n.* **1.** Also called: **teardrop.** a drop of salty fluid appearing in and falling from the eye. **2. in tears.** weeping. [Old English *tēar*]

tear[2] (tɛə) *vb.* **tearing, tore, torn. 1.** to come apart or cause to come apart; rip. **2.** to make (a hole or split) in (something). **3.** (often foll. by *along*) to hurry or rush. **4.** (usually foll. by *away* or *from*) to remove or take by force: *the boat was torn from its moorings by the storm.* **5.** (foll. by *at*) to cause distress or anguish to: *it tore at her heartstrings to see the starving children.* ~*n.* **6.** a hole, cut, or split. **7.** the act of tearing. ~See also **tear away, tear down, tear into.** [Old English *teran*]

tear away (tɛə) *vb.* **1.** to persuade (oneself or someone else) to leave: *I couldn't tear myself away from the television.* ~*n.* **tearaway. 2.** *Brit.* a reckless, impetuous, or unruly person.

tear down (tɛə) *vb.* to destroy or demolish: *to tear down an argument.*

tear duct (tɪə) *n.* a short tube in the inner corner of the eyelid, through which tears drain into the nose.

tearful ('tɪəful) *adj.* crying or about to cry. —'**tearfully** *adv.*

tear gas (tɪə) *n.* a gas that makes the eyes sore and causes temporary blindness; used in warfare and to control riots.

tearing ('tɛərɪŋ) *adj.* violent or furious: *I'm in a tearing hurry this morning.*

tear into (tɛə) *vb. Informal.* to attack vigorously and damagingly.

tear-jerker ('tɪə,dʒɜːkə) *n. Informal.* an excessively sentimental film or book.

tearoom ('tiː,ruːm) *n. Brit.* a restaurant where tea and light refreshments are served.

tease (tiːz) *vb.* **1.** to make fun of (someone) in a provocative and often playful manner. **2.** to comb (flax, wool, or hair) so as to get the tangles out. **3.** to raise the nap of (a fabric) with a teasel. ~*n.* **4.** a person or thing that teases. **5.** the act of teasing. [Old English *tǣsan*] —'**teaser** *n.* —'**teasing** *adj.*

teasel, teazel, *or* **teazle** ('tiːzəl) *n.* **1.** a plant of Eurasia and N Africa, with prickly heads of yellow or purple flowers. **2.** the dried flower head of a teasel, used for teasing. [Old English *tǣsel*]

teaspoon ('tiː,spuːn) *n.* **1.** a small spoon used for stirring tea or coffee. **2.** Also called: **teaspoonful.** the amount contained in such a spoon.

teat (tiːt) *n.* **1.** the nipple of a breast or udder. **2.** something resembling a teat such as the rubber mouthpiece of a feeding bottle. [Old French *tete*]

tea towel *or* **tea cloth** *n.* a towel for drying dishes.

tech (tɛk) *n. Informal.* a technical college.

tech. **1.** technical. **2.** technology.

technetium (tɛk'niːʃɪəm) *n.* a silvery-grey metallic element, produced artificially, esp. by the fission of uranium. Symbol: Tc [Greek *tekhnētos* man-made]

technical ('tɛknɪkˀl) *adj.* **1.** of or specializing in industrial, practical, or mechanical arts and applied sciences: *a technical institute.* **2.** skilled in practical activities rather than abstract thinking. **3.** relating to a particular field of activity: *the technical jargon of linguistics.* **4.** existing by virtue of a strict application of rules or a strict interpretation of wording: *a technical loophole in the law.* **5.** showing technique: *technical brilliance.* —'**technically** *adv.*

technical college *n. Brit.* an institution for further education that provides courses in art and technical subjects.

technical drawing *n.* drawing done by a draughtsman with compasses, T-squares, etc.

technicality (,tɛknɪ'kælɪtɪ) *n., pl.* **-ties. 1.** a petty formal point arising from a strict interpretation of the law or a set of rules. **2.** the state or quality of being technical.

technical knockout *n. Boxing.* a judgment of a knockout given when a boxer is, in the referee's opinion, too badly beaten to continue without risk of serious injury.

technician (tɛk'nɪʃən) *n.* a person skilled in a particular technical field: *a laboratory technician.*

Technicolor ('tɛknɪ,kʌlə) *n. Trademark.* a process of producing colour film by superimposing synchronized films of the same scene, each having a different colour filter.

technique (tɛk'niːk) *n.* **1.** a practical method, skill, or art applied to a particular task. **2.** proficiency in a practical or mechanical skill. **3.** special facility; knack. [Greek *tekhnē* skill]

technocracy (tɛk'nɒkrəsɪ) *n., pl.* **-cies.** government by scientists, engineers, and other experts. [Greek *tekhnē* skill + *kratos* power] —**technocrat** ('tɛknə,kræt) *n.* —,**techno'cratic** *adj.*

technology (tɛk'nɒlədʒɪ) *n., pl.* **-gies. 1.** the application of practical or mechanical sciences to industry or commerce. **2.** the methods governing such application. [Greek *tekhnologia* systematic treatment] —**technological** (,tɛknə'lɒdʒɪkˀl) *adj.* —**tech'nologist** *n.*

tectonics (tɛk'tɒnɪks) *n.* (functioning as *sing.*) *Geol.* the study of the earth's crust and the forces that produce changes in it. [Greek *tektōn* a builder]

ted[1] (tɛd) *vb.* **tedding, tedded.** to shake out (hay), so as to dry it. [Old Norse *tethja*]

ted² (tɛd) *n. Informal.* short for **teddy boy.**

teddy¹ ('tɛdɪ) *n., pl.* **-dies.** short for **teddy bear.**

teddy² ('tɛdɪ) *n., pl.* **-dies.** a woman's one-piece undergarment incorporating a cami-sole top and French knickers. [origin unknown]

teddy bear *n.* a stuffed toy bear. [after *Teddy* (Theodore) Roosevelt, U.S. president]

teddy boy *n.* (in Britain, esp. in the mid-1950s) a youth who wore mock Edwardian fashions. [*Teddy*, from *Edward*]

Te Deum (ˌtiː 'dɪəm) *n. Christianity.* an ancient Latin hymn beginning Te Deum Laudamus (we praise thee, O God).

tedious ('tiːdɪəs) *adj.* causing fatigue or tedium; monotonous. —'**tediously** *adv.* —'**tediousness** *n.*

tedium ('tiːdɪəm) *n.* the state of being bored or the quality of being boring; monotony. [Latin *taedium*]

tee¹ (tiː) *n.* a pipe fitting in the form of a letter *T*, used to join three pipes.

tee² (tiː) *n.* **1.** a support for a golf ball, usually a small wooden or plastic peg, used when teeing off. **2.** an area on a golf course from which the first stroke of a hole is made. **3.** a mark used as a target in certain games such as curling and quoits. ~See also **tee off.** [origin unknown]

tee-hee *or* **te-hee** ('tiː'hiː) *interj.* an exclamation of mocking laughter. [imit.]

teem¹ (tiːm) *vb.* (usually foll. by *with*) to be abundant (in): *the town was teeming with sightseers.* [Old English *tēman* to produce offspring]

teem² (tiːm) *vb.* (of rain) to pour down in torrents. [Old Norse *tœma*]

teen (tiːn) *adj. Informal.* same as **teenage.**

teenage ('tiːnˌeɪdʒ) *adj.* of the time in a person's life between the ages of 13 and 19.

teenager ('tiːnˌeɪdʒə) *n.* a person between the ages of 13 and 19.

teens (tiːnz) *pl. n.* **1.** the years of a person's life between the ages of 13 and 19. **2.** all the numbers that end in -teen.

teeny ('tiːnɪ) *adj.* **-nier, -niest.** extremely small; tiny. [var. of *tiny*]

teenybopper ('tiːnɪˌbɒpə) *n. Old-fashioned slang.* a young teenager, usually a girl, who avidly follows fashions in clothes and pop music. [*teeny* teenage + *-bopper* someone who bops]

tee off *vb. Golf.* to strike (the ball) from a tee, as when starting a hole.

teepee ('tiːpiː) *n.* same as **tepee.**

teeter ('tiːtə) *vb.* to move or cause to move unsteadily; wobble. [Middle English *titeren*]

teeth (tiːθ) *n.* **1.** the plural of **tooth. 2.** the power to produce a desired effect: *a law with no teeth.* **3. armed to the teeth.** very heavily armed. **4. get one's teeth into.** to become engrossed in. **5. in the teeth of.** in direct opposition to; against.

teethe (tiːð) *vb.* to cut one's baby (deciduous) teeth.

teething ring *n.* a hard ring on which babies may bite while teething.

teething troubles *pl. n.* problems arising during the early stages of a project.

teetotal (tiː'təʊt²l) *adj.* practising · total abstinence from alcoholic drink. [reduplication of *t* + *total*] —**tee'totaller** *n.*

te-hee ('tiː'hiː) *interj.* same as **tee-hee.**

tel. telephone.

tele- *combining form.* **1.** at or over a distance: *telescope.* **2.** television: *telecast.* **3.** via telephone or television: *teleshopping.* [Greek *tele* far]

telecast ('tɛlɪˌkɑːst) *vb.* **-casting, -cast** *or* **-casted. 1.** to broadcast by television. ~*n.* **2.** a television broadcast. —'**tele-ˌcaster** *n.*

telecommunications (ˌtɛlɪkəˌmjuːnɪ'keɪʃənz) *n. (functioning as sing.)* communications using electronic equipment, such as telephony, radio, and television.

telegram ('tɛlɪˌgræm) *n.* (formerly) a communication transmitted by telegraph.

telegraph ('tɛlɪˌgrɑːf) *n.* **1.** (formerly) a system by which information could be transmitted over a distance, using electrical signals sent along a transmission line. ~*vb.* **2.** (formerly) to send (a message) to (a person or place) by telegraph. **3.** *Canad. informal.* to cast (a vote) illegally by impersonating a registered voter. —**telegrapher** (tɪ'lɛgrəfə) *or* **te'legraphist** *n.* —ˌtele'**graphic** *adj.*

telegraphy (tɪ'lɛgrəfɪ) *n.* (formerly) a system of telecommunications providing reproduction at a distance of written, printed, or pictorial matter.

telekinesis (ˌtɛlɪkɪ'niːsɪs) *n.* movement of a body by thought or willpower, without the application of a physical force. —**tele-kinetic** (ˌtɛlɪkɪ'nɛtɪk) *adj.*

telemeter (tɪ'lɛmɪtə) *n.* any device for recording or measuring a distant event and transmitting the data to a receiver. —**telemetric** (ˌtɛlɪ'mɛtrɪk) *adj.*

teleology (ˌtiːlɪ'ɒlədʒɪ) *n.* **1.** *Philosophy.* the doctrine that there is evidence of purpose or design in the universe. **2.** *Biol.* the belief that natural phenomena have a predetermined purpose and are not determined by mechanical laws. [Greek *telos* end + -LOGY] —**teleological** (ˌtiːlɪə-'lɒdʒɪk²l) *adj.* —ˌtele'**ologist** *n.*

telepathy (tɪ'lɛpəθɪ) *n.* the communication between people of thoughts and feelings involving mechanisms that cannot be understood in terms of known scientific laws. [Greek *tele* far + *pathos* suffering] —**telepathic** (ˌtɛlɪ'pæθɪk) *adj.* —**te'lepathist** *n.*

telephone ('tɛlɪˌfəʊn) *n.* **1.** an electrical device for transmitting speech, consisting of a microphone and receiver mounted on a handset and connected to a telecommunications network. ~*vb.* **2.** to call or talk to (a person) by telephone. [Greek *tele* far + *phōnē* voice] —**telephonic** (ˌtɛlɪ'fɒnɪk) *adj.*

telephone box *n.* a soundproof enclosure from which a paid telephone call can be made.

telephone directory *n.* a book listing the names, addresses, and telephone numbers of subscribers in a particular area.

telephonist (tɪ'lɛfənɪst) *n. Brit.* a person who operates a telephone switchboard.

telephony (tɪ'lɛfənɪ) *n.* a system of tele-communications for the transmission of speech or other sounds.

telephotography (ˌtɛlɪfə'tɒɡrəfɪ) *n.* the process or technique of photographing distant objects using a telephoto lens.

telephoto lens ('tɛlɪˌfəʊtəʊ) *n.* a lens fitted to a camera to produce a magnified image of a distant object.

teleprinter ('tɛlɪˌprɪntə) *n.* an apparatus, similar to a typewriter, by which typed messages are sent and received by wire.

Teleprompter ('tɛlɪˌprɒmptə) *n. Trademark.* a device for displaying a script under a television camera, so that a speaker can read it while appearing to look at the camera.

telesales ('tɛlɪˌseɪlz) *pl. n.* the selling of a commodity or service by telephone.

telescope ('tɛlɪˌskəʊp) *n.* **1.** an optical instrument for making distant objects appear closer by use of a combination of lenses. **2.** See **radio telescope.** ~*vb.* **3.** to fit together as a set of cylinders that slide into one another, thus allowing extension and shortening. **4.** to crush so as to foreshorten: *the car was telescoped by the impact.* [New Latin *telescopium* far-seeing instrument] —**telescopic** (ˌtɛlɪ'skɒpɪk) *adj.*

telescopic sight *n.* a sight on a rifle, etc., consisting of a telescope, used for aiming at distant objects.

teletext ('tɛlɪˌtɛkst) *n.* a videotext service in which the consumer is not able to interact with the computer. Cf. **viewdata.**

Teletype ('tɛlɪˌtaɪp) *n. Trademark.* a type of teleprinter.

televangelist (ˌtɛlɪ'vændʒəlɪst) *n. U.S.* an evangelical preacher who appears regularly on television, preaching the gospel and appealing for donations from viewers. [*tele(vision)* + *(e)vangelist*]

televise ('tɛlɪˌvaɪz) *vb.* to transmit (a programme) by television.

television ('tɛlɪˌvɪʒən) *n.* **1.** the system or process of producing on a distant screen a moving image with accompanying sound. **2.** Also called: **television set.** a device designed to receive and convert incoming electrical signals into a series of visible images on a screen together with accompanying sound. **3.** the content of television programmes. **4.** (*modifier*) of or used in television: *a television transmitter.* ~Abbrev.: **TV** —**televisual** (ˌtɛlɪ'vɪʒʊəl) *adj.*

telex ('tɛlɛks) *n.* **1.** an international text-transmission service in which teleprinters are rented out to subscribers. **2.** a teleprinter used in such a service. **3.** a message transmitted or received by telex. ~*vb.* **4.** to transmit (a message) by telex. [*tel(eprinter) ex(change)*]

Telidon ('tɛlɪˌdɒn) *n. Trademark.* a Canadian interactive viewdata service.

tell (tɛl) *vb.* **telling, told. 1.** to say to (someone); assure or notify: *he told me he*

would go. **2.** to order or instruct (someone to do something): *I told her to send the letter airmail.* **3.** (usually foll. by *of*) to give an account of (an event or situation). **4.** to communicate by words: *to tell the truth.* **5.** (used with *can* or *could*) to discover, distinguish, or discern: *I can tell what is wrong; he couldn't tell chalk from cheese.* **6.** to have or produce an impact or effect: *every step told on his bruised feet.* **7.** *Informal.* to reveal secrets or gossip. **8. tell the time.** to read the time from a clock. **9. you're telling me.** *Slang.* I know that very well. ~See also **tell apart, tell off.** [Old English *tellan*]

tell apart *vb.* to distinguish between: *can you tell the twins apart?*

teller ('tɛlə) *n.* **1.** a bank cashier. **2.** a person appointed to count votes.

telling ('tɛlɪŋ) *adj.* having a marked effect or impact: *a telling blow.*

tell off *vb. Informal.* to reprimand (someone).

telltale ('tɛlˌteɪl) *n.* **1.** a person who tells tales about others. **2.** (*modifier*) indicating something concealed: *telltale signs of movement.*

tellurian (tɛ'lʊərɪən) *adj.* of the earth. [Latin *tellūs* the earth]

tellurium (tɛ'lʊərɪəm) *n.* a brittle silvery-white nonmetallic element. Symbol: Te [Latin *tellūs* the earth]

telly ('tɛlɪ) *n., pl.* **-lies.** *Informal, chiefly Brit.* short for **television.**

temerity (tɪ'mɛrɪtɪ) *n.* rashness or boldness. [Latin *temere* at random]

temp (tɛmp) *Informal.* ~*n.* **1.** a person, esp. a typist or other office worker, employed on a temporary basis. ~*vb.* **2.** to work as a temp.

temp. 1. temperature. **2.** temporary.

temper ('tɛmpə) *n.* **1.** a sudden outburst of anger: *to get into a temper.* **2.** a tendency to have sudden outbursts of anger: *she has a nasty temper.* **3.** a mental condition of moderation and calm: *he lost his temper; keep your temper.* **4.** a person's frame of mind; mood or humour: *what sort of temper is he in?* ~*vb.* **5.** to modify so as to make less extreme or more acceptable: *he tempered his criticism with sympathy.* **6.** to strengthen or toughen (a metal) by heating and quenching. **7.** *Music.* to adjust the frequency differences between the notes of a scale on (a keyboard instrument). [Latin *temperāre* to mix]

tempera ('tɛmpərə) *n.* a painting medium for powdered pigments, consisting usually of egg yolk and water. [Italian *temperare* to mingle]

temperament ('tɛmpərəmənt) *n.* a person's character or disposition. [Latin *temperāmentum* a mixing]

temperamental (ˌtɛmpərə'mɛntəl) *adj.* **1.** tending to be moody and have sudden outbursts of anger. **2.** of or caused by temperament. **3.** *Informal.* working erratically and inconsistently; unreliable: *a temperamental sewing machine.* —,**tempera-'mentally** *adv.*

temperance ('tɛmpərəns) *n.* **1.** restraint

or moderation, esp. in yielding to one's appetites or desires. **2.** abstinence from alcoholic drink. [Latin *temperāre* to regulate]

temperate ('tɛmpərɪt) *adj.* **1.** having a climate intermediate between tropical and polar. **2.** mild in quality or character; exhibiting temperance. [Latin *temperātus*]

Temperate Zone *n.* those parts of the earth's surface lying between the Arctic Circle and the tropic of Cancer and between the Antarctic Circle and the tropic of Capricorn.

temperature ('tɛmprɪtʃə) *n.* **1.** the degree of hotness of a body, substance, or medium, esp. as measured on a scale that has one or more fixed reference points. **2.** *Informal.* a body temperature in excess of the normal. [Latin *temperātūra* proportion]

tempest ('tɛmpɪst) *n. Literary.* a violent wind or storm. [Latin *tempestās*]

tempestuous (tɛm'pɛstjʊəs) *adj.* **1.** of or relating to a tempest. **2.** violent or stormy. —**tem'pestuously** *adv.*

template ('tɛmplɪt) *n.* a wood or metal pattern, used to help cut out shapes accurately. [from *temple* a part in a loom that keeps the cloth stretched]

temple[1] ('tɛmp'l) *n.* a building or place dedicated to the worship of a deity or deities. [Latin *templum*]

temple[2] ('tɛmp'l) *n.* the region on each side of the head in front of the ear and above the cheek bone. [Latin *tempus*, pl. *tempora*]

tempo ('tɛmpəʊ) *n., pl.* **-pos** *or* **-pi** (-piː). **1.** the speed at which a piece of music is played or meant to be played. **2.** rate or pace. [Italian]

temporal[1] ('tɛmpərəl) *adj.* **1.** of or relating to time. **2.** of secular as opposed to spiritual or religious affairs. **3.** lasting for a relatively short time. [Latin *tempus* time]

temporal[2] ('tɛmpərəl) *adj. Anat.* of or near the temple or temples.

temporal bone *n.* either of two compound bones forming the sides of the skull.

temporary ('tɛmpərərɪ) *adj.* not permanent; lasting only a short time: *temporary accommodation; temporary relief from pain.* [Latin *temporārius*] —**'temporarily** *adv.*

temporize *or* **-ise** ('tɛmpə,raɪz) *vb.* **1.** to delay, act evasively, or protract a negotiation in order to gain time or effect a compromise. **2.** to adapt oneself to circumstances, as by temporary or apparent agreement. [Latin *tempus* time]

tempt (tɛmpt) *vb.* **1.** to entice (someone) to do something, esp. something morally wrong or unwise. **2.** to allure or attract. **3.** to risk provoking: *she was tempting fate.* [Latin *temptāre* to test] —**'tempter** *n.* —**'temptress** *fem. n.*

temptation (tɛmp'teɪʃən) *n.* **1.** the act of tempting or the state of being tempted. **2.** a person or thing that tempts.

tempting ('tɛmptɪŋ) *adj.* attractive or inviting: *a tempting meal.* —**'tempting-ly** *adv.*

ten (tɛn) *n.* **1.** the cardinal number that is the sum of nine and one. **2.** a numeral, 10, X, representing this number. **3.** something representing or consisting of ten units. ~*det.* **4.** amounting to ten. [Old English] —**tenth** *adj., n.*

ten. *Music.* **1.** tenor. **2.** tenuto.

tenable ('tɛnəb'l) *adj.* able to be upheld, believed, maintained, or defended: *a tenable proposition.* [Latin *tenēre* to hold] —,**tena'bility** *n.* —**'tenably** *adv.*

tenacious (tɪ'neɪʃəs) *adj.* **1.** holding firmly: *a tenacious grip.* **2.** exceptionally good at remembering: *a tenacious memory.* **3.** stubborn or persistent: *a tenacious character.* [Latin *tenēre* to hold] —**te'naciously** *adv.* —**tenacity** (tɪ'næsɪtɪ) *n.*

tenancy ('tɛnənsɪ) *n., pl.* **-cies.** **1.** the temporary possession by a tenant of lands or property owned by another. **2.** the period of holding or occupying such property.

tenant ('tɛnənt) *n.* **1.** a person who pays rent for the use of land or property. **2.** any holder or occupant. [Old French: one who is holding]

tenant farmer *n.* a person who farms land rented from another.

tenantry ('tɛnəntrɪ) *n. Old-fashioned.* tenants collectively.

tench (tɛntʃ) *n.* a European freshwater game fish of the carp family. [Old French *tenche*]

Ten Commandments *pl. n.* **the.** *Bible.* the commandments given by God to Moses on Mount Sinai, summarizing the basic obligations of man towards God and his fellow men.

tend[1] (tɛnd) *vb.* (usually foll. by *to* or *towards*) **1.** to have a general disposition to take a particular kind of action or to be in a particular condition; be inclined: *children tend to prefer sweets to meat.* **2.** to go or move (in a particular direction): *to tend to the south.* [Latin *tendere* to stretch]

tend[2] (tɛnd) *vb.* **1.** to care for; look after: *to tend a sick mother.* **2.** (foll. by *to*) to attend to: *to tend to someone's wishes.* **3.** to handle or control: *to tend a fire.* [var. of *attend*]

tendency ('tɛndənsɪ) *n., pl.* **-cies.** **1.** (often foll. by *to*) an inclination to act in a particular way. **2.** the general course, purport, or drift of something, esp. a written work. [Latin *tendere* to stretch]

tendentious (tɛn'dɛnʃəs) *adj.* having or showing a particular tendency or bias, esp. a controversial one. —**ten'dentiously** *adv.*

tender[1] ('tɛndə) *adj.* **1.** having or expressing gentle and sympathetic feelings: *a tender smile; a tender heart.* **2.** easily damaged; vulnerable or sensitive: *at a tender age.* **3.** easily hurt when touched: *a tender spot on one's hand.* [Old French *tendre*] —**'tenderly** *adv.* —**'tenderness** *n.*

tender[2] ('tɛndə) *vb.* **1.** to present or offer: *to tender one's resignation.* **2.** (foll. by *for*) to make a formal offer or estimate (for a job or contract). ~*n*. **3.** a formal offer to supply specified goods or services at a stated cost or rate. [Latin *tendere* to extend] —'**tenderer** *n*.

tender³ ('tɛndə) *n.* **1.** a small boat that brings supplies to larger vessels in a port. **2.** a vehicle drawn behind a steam locomotive to carry the fuel and water. [var. of *attender*]

tenderfoot ('tɛndə,fut) *n., pl.* -**foots** or -**feet**. **1.** a newcomer, esp. to the mines or ranches of the southwestern U.S. **2.** (formerly) a beginner in the Scouts or Guides.

tenderize or -**ise** ('tɛndə,raɪz) *vb.* to make (meat) tender, as by pounding it or adding a substance to break down the fibres. —'**tender,izer** or -'**iser** *n*.

tenderloin ('tɛndə,lɔɪn) *n.* a tender cut of pork or other meat from between the sirloin and ribs.

tendon ('tɛndən) *n.* a band of tough tissue that attaches a muscle to a bone or some other part. [Medieval Latin *tendō*]

tendril ('tɛndrɪl) *n.* a threadlike leaf or stem of a climbing plant that attaches itself to a support by twining. [prob. from Old French *tendron*]

tenement ('tɛnəmənt) *n.* a large building divided into several different apartments or flats. [Latin *tenēre* to hold]

tenet ('tɛnɪt, 'tiːnɪt) *n.* a belief, opinion, or dogma. [Latin, lit.: he (it) holds]

tenfold ('tɛn,fəʊld) *adj.* **1.** having ten times as many or as much. **2.** composed of ten parts. ~*adv.* ten times as many or as much.

ten-gallon hat *n.* (in the U.S.) a cowboy's broad-brimmed felt hat with a very high crown.

Tenn. Tennessee.

tenner ('tɛnə) *n. Informal.* **1.** *Brit.* a ten-pound note. **2.** *U.S.* a ten-dollar bill.

tennis ('tɛnɪs) *n.* a game played between two players or pairs of players who use a racket to hit a ball to and fro over a net on a rectangular court. See also **lawn tennis**, **real tennis**, **table tennis**. [prob. from Anglo-French *tenetz* hold (imperative)]

tennis elbow *n.* inflammation of the elbow, typically caused by exertion in playing tennis.

tenon ('tɛnən) *n.* a projecting end of a piece of timber, formed to fit into a corresponding slot in another piece. [Old French]

tenor ('tɛnə) *n.* **1.** *Music.* **a.** the male voice between alto and baritone. **b.** a singer with such a voice. **c.** a saxophone, horn, or other musical instrument between the alto and baritone or bass. **2.** general drift of thought; purpose. **3.** a settled course of progress. [Old French *tenour*]

tenpin bowling ('tɛn,pɪn) *n.* a bowling game in which bowls are rolled down a lane to knock over the ten target pins.

tense¹ (tɛns) *adj.* **1.** characterized by, causing, or suffering from mental or emotional strain: *a very tense person; a tense atmosphere*. **2.** stretched or stressed tightly; taut or rigid. ~*vb.* **3.** (often foll. by

up) to make or become tense. [Latin *tensus* taut] —'**tensely** *adv.* —'**tenseness** *n*.

tense² (tɛns) *n. Grammar.* a category of the verb or verbal inflections, typically present, past, and future, that expresses the temporal relations between what is reported in a sentence and the time of its utterance. [Old French *tens* time]

tensile ('tɛnsaɪl) *adj.* of or relating to tension or being stretched: *the tensile strength of steel*.

tensile strength *n.* a measure of the ability of a material to withstand lengthwise stress, expressed as the greatest stress that the material can stand without breaking.

tension ('tɛnʃən) *n.* **1.** a force that stretches or the state or degree of being stretched tight. **2.** mental or emotional strain; stress. **3.** a situation or condition of hostility, suspense, or uneasiness. **4.** *Physics.* a force that tends to produce an elongation of a body or structure. **5.** *Physics.* voltage, electromotive force, or potential difference. [Latin *tensiō*]

tent (tɛnt) *n.* **1.** a portable shelter made of canvas or other fabric supported on poles, stretched out, and fastened to the ground by pegs and ropes. **2.** something resembling this in function or shape. [Old French *tente*]

tentacle ('tɛntək'l) *n.* any of various flexible organs that grow near the mouth in many invertebrates and are used for feeding, grasping, etc. [Latin *tentāre* to feel] —'**tentacled** *adj.*

tentative ('tɛntətɪv) *adj.* **1.** provisional or experimental: *a tentative plan*. **2.** hesitant, uncertain, or cautious: *a tentative smile*. [Latin *tentāre* to test] —'**tentatively** *adv.* —'**tentativeness** *n*.

tenter ('tɛntə) *n.* a frame on which cloth is stretched in order that it may retain its shape while drying. [Latin *tentus* stretched]

tenterhook ('tɛntə,hʊk) *n.* **1.** one of a series of hooks used to hold cloth on a tenter. **2. on tenterhooks.** in a state of tension or suspense.

tenth (tɛnθ) *adj., n.* See **ten.**

tenuous ('tɛnjʊəs) *adj.* **1.** insignificant or flimsy: *a tenuous argument*. **2.** slim, fine, or delicate: *a tenuous thread*. [Latin *tenuis*] —'**tenuously** *adv.*

tenure ('tɛnjʊə, 'tɛnjə) *n.* **1.** the possession or holding of an office or position. **2.** the length of time an office or position lasts. **3.** the holding of a teaching position on a permanent basis. **4.** the legal right to live in a place or to use land or buildings for a period of time. [Latin *tenēre* to hold]

tenuto (tɪ'njuːtəʊ) *adj., adv. Music.* (of a note) to be held for or beyond its full time value. [Italian]

tepee or **teepee** ('tiːpiː) *n.* a cone-shaped tent of animal skins, formerly used by American Indians. [Siouan *tīpī*]

tepid ('tɛpɪd) *adj.* **1.** slightly warm; lukewarm. **2.** relatively unenthusiastic or apathetic: *the play had a tepid reception*.

[Latin *tepidus*] **—te'pidity** *n.* **—'tepidly** *adv.*

tequila (tɪ'kiːlə) *n.* a Mexican spirit that is distilled from the agave plant. [after *Tequila*, district in Mexico]

ter. **1.** terrace. **2.** territory.

tera- ('tɛrə) *prefix.* one million million. [Greek *teras* monster]

terbium ('tɜːbɪəm) *n.* a soft silvery-grey element of the lanthanide series of metals. Symbol: Tb [after *Ytterby*, Sweden, where discovered]

tercel ('tɜːs'l) *n.* a male falcon or hawk. [from Old French]

tercentenary (,tɜːsɛn'tiːnərɪ) *or* **tercentennial** *adj.* **1.** of a 300th anniversary. **~***n.*, *pl.* **-tenaries** *or* **-tennials.** **2.** an anniversary of 300 years. [Latin *ter* three times + *centenary*]

tercet ('tɜːsɪt, tɜː'sɛt) *n.* a group of three lines of verse that rhyme with adjacent groups of three lines. [French]

teredo (tɛ'riːdəʊ) *n.*, *pl.* **-dos** *or* **-dines** (-dɪ-,niːz). a marine mollusc that bores into and destroys submerged timber. [Greek *terēdōn* wood-boring worm]

tergiversate ('tɜːdʒɪvə,seɪt) *vb.* **1.** to change sides or loyalties. **2.** to be evasive or ambiguous. [Latin *tergiversārī* to turn one's back] **—,tergiver'sation** *n.* **—'tergiver,sator** *n.*

term (tɜːm) *n.* **1.** a word or expression used for some particular thing, esp. in a specialized field of knowledge: *a medical term.* **2.** any word or expression. **3.** a limited period of time: *a prison term.* **4.** the end of a specific period of time: *the project had reached full term.* **5.** the period of pregnancy when childbirth is imminent. **6.** a division of the academic year during which a school, college, or university is in session. **7.** one of the periods of time during which sessions of courts of law are held. **8.** *Maths.* any distinct quantity making up a fraction or proportion, or contained in a sequence, series, etc. **9.** *Logic.* any of the three subjects or predicates occurring in a syllogism. **~***vb.* **10.** to designate; call: *a breakthrough in what is termed "birth technology".* **~**See also **terms.** [Latin *terminus* end]

termagant ('tɜːməgənt) *n. Literary.* an unpleasant shrewish woman; scold. [earlier *Tervagaunt*, after an arrogant character in medieval mystery plays]

terminable ('tɜːmɪnəb'l) *adj.* capable of being terminated: *a terminable annuity.* **—,termina'bility** *n.*

terminal ('tɜːmɪn'l) *adj.* **1.** (of an illness) terminating in death. **2.** situated at an end, terminus, or boundary: *a terminal bud.* **~***n.* **3.** a terminating point, part, or place. **4.** a point at which current enters or leaves an electrical device. **5.** *Computers.* a device, usually a keyboard and a visual display unit, having input/output links with a computer. **6.** a place where vehicles, passengers, or goods begin or end a journey: *a bus terminal; an oil terminal.* [Latin *terminus* end] **—'terminally** *adv.*

terminal velocity *n. Physics.* the maximum velocity reached by a body falling under gravity through a fluid, esp. the atmosphere.

terminate ('tɜːmɪ,neɪt) *vb.* to come to an end or put an end to; conclude. [Latin *termināre* to set boundaries]

termination (,tɜːmɪ'neɪʃən) *n.* **1.** the act of terminating or the state of being terminated. **2.** something that terminates. **3.** a final result.

terminology (,tɜːmɪ'nɒlədʒɪ) *n.*, *pl.* **-gies.** the body of specialized words and expressions relating to a particular subject. **—terminological** (,tɜːmɪnə'lɒdʒɪk'l) *adj.* **—,termin'ologist** *n.*

terminus ('tɜːmɪnəs) *n.*, *pl.* **-ni** (-naɪ) *or* **-nuses.** **1.** the final point. **2.** either end of a railway, bus route, etc. **3.** a station or town at such a point. [Latin: end]

termite ('tɜːmaɪt) *n.* a whitish antlike insect of warm and tropical regions. [New Latin *termītēs* white ants]

terms (tɜːmz) *pl. n.* **1.** the actual language or mode of presentation used: *he described the project in loose terms.* **2.** the conditions of an agreement. **3.** (usually preceded by *on*) mutual relationship or standing: *they are on affectionate terms.* **4. come to terms.** to reach acceptance or agreement. **5. in terms of.** as expressed by; regarding: *in terms of money he was no better off.*

tern (tɜːn) *n.* a sea bird with a forked tail, long narrow wings, and a typically black-and-white plumage. [Old Norse *therna*]

ternary ('tɜːnərɪ) *adj.* **1.** consisting of three items or groups of three items. **2.** *Maths.* (of a number system) to the base three. [Latin *ternārius*]

Terpsichore (tɜːp'sɪkərɪ) *n. Greek myth.* the Muse of the dance and of choral song.

Terpsichorean (,tɜːpsɪkə'riːən, -'kɔːrɪən) *adj. Often used facetiously.* of or relating to dancing.

terrace ('tɛrəs) *n.* **1.** a row of houses, usually identical and joined together by common dividing walls, or the street onto which they face. **2.** a paved area alongside a building. **3.** a horizontal flat area of ground, often one of a series in a slope. **4.** (usually *pl.*) unroofed tiers around a football pitch on which the spectators stand. **~***vb.* **5.** to make into terraces. [Latin *terra* earth]

terraced house *n. Brit.* a house that is part of a terrace.

terracotta (,tɛrə'kɒtə) *n.* **1.** a hard unglazed brownish-red earthenware used for pottery, sculpture, etc. **~***adj.* **2.** made of terracotta. **3.** brownish-orange. [Italian, lit.: baked earth]

terra firma ('fɜːmə) *n.* the solid earth; firm ground. [Latin]

terrain (tə'reɪn) *n.* a piece of ground, esp. with reference to its physical character: *a rocky terrain.* [Latin *terra* earth]

terra incognita ('tɛrə ɪn'kɒgnɪtə) *n.* an unexplored region. [Latin]

terrapin ('tɛrəpɪn) *n.* a web-footed reptile of N America that lives in fresh water and on land and feeds on small aquatic animals. [American Indian]

terrarium (tɛ'rɛərɪəm) n., pl. **-riums** or **-ria** (-rɪə). **1.** an enclosure for small land animals. **2.** a glass container, often a globe, in which plants are grown. [Latin *terra* earth]

terrazzo (tɛ'rætsəʊ) n., pl. **-zos.** a floor made by setting marble chips into a layer of mortar and polishing the surface. [Italian]

terrestrial (tə'rɛstrɪəl) adj. **1.** of the planet earth. **2.** of the land as opposed to the sea or air. **3.** (of animals and plants) living or growing on the land. **4.** earthly, worldly, or mundane. [Latin *terra* earth]

terrible ('tɛrəb⁰l) adj. **1.** very serious or extreme: *a terrible cough.* **2.** *Informal.* of poor quality; unpleasant or bad: *a terrible play.* **3.** causing terror. [Latin *terribilis*] —**'terribly** adv.

terrier ('tɛrɪə) n. any of several small active breeds of dog, originally trained to hunt animals living underground. [Old French *chien terrier* earth dog]

terrific (tə'rɪfɪk) adj. **1.** very great or intense: *a terrific noise.* **2.** *Informal.* very good; excellent: *a terrific singer.* **3.** very frightening. [Latin *terrēre* to frighten] —**ter'rifically** adv.

terrify ('tɛrɪˌfaɪ) vb. **-fying, -fied.** to inspire fear or dread in; frighten greatly. [Latin *terrificāre*] —**'terriˌfying** adj. —**'terriˌfyingly** adv.

terrine (tɛ'riːn) n. **1.** an oval earthenware cooking dish with a tightly fitting lid. **2.** the food cooked or served in such a dish, esp. pâté. [earlier form of *tureen*]

territorial (ˌtɛrɪ'tɔːrɪəl) adj. **1.** of or relating to a territory or territories. **2.** restricted to or owned by a particular territory. **3.** local or regional. **4.** pertaining to a territorial army, providing a reserve of trained men for use in emergency. —**ˌterri'torially** adv. —**territoriality** (ˌtɛrɪˌtɔːrɪ'ælɪtɪ) n.

Territorial (ˌtɛrɪ'tɔːrɪəl) n. a member of a Territorial Army.

Territorial Army n. (in Britain) a standing reserve army.

territorial waters pl. n. the waters over which a nation exercises jurisdiction and control.

territory ('tɛrɪtrɪ) n., pl. **-ries. 1.** any tract of land; district. **2.** the geographical domain under the jurisdiction of a political unit, esp. a sovereign state. **3.** the district for which a travelling salesman is responsible. **4.** an area inhabited and defended by a particular animal or pair of animals. **5.** an area of knowledge. **6.** (*often cap.*) a region of a country, esp. of a federal state, that enjoys less autonomy and a lower status than most constituent parts of the state. [Latin *territōrium* land surrounding a town]

terror ('tɛrə) n. **1.** great fear, panic, or dread. **2.** a person or thing that inspires great dread. **3.** *Informal.* a troublesome person, esp. a child. [Latin]

terrorism ('tɛrəˌrɪzəm) n. the systematic use of violence and intimidation to achieve political ends. —**'terrorist** n., adj.

terrorize or **-ise** ('tɛrəˌraɪz) vb. **1.** to coerce or control by violence, fear, threats, etc. **2.** to inspire with dread; terrify. —ˌterrori'zation or -i'sation n. —**'terrorˌizer** or -ˌiser n.

terry ('tɛrɪ) n., pl. **-ries. 1.** an uncut loop in the pile of towelling or a similar fabric. **2.** a fabric with such a pile. [origin unknown]

terse (tɜːs) adj. **1.** neatly brief and concise. **2.** curt; abrupt. [Latin *tersus* precise] —**'tersely** adv. —**'terseness** n.

tertiary ('tɜːʃərɪ) adj. third in degree, order, etc. [Latin *tertius*]

Tertiary ('tɜːʃərɪ) adj. *Geol.* of the period of geological time lasting from about 65 million years ago to 600 000 years ago.

Terylene ('tɛrɪˌliːn) n. *Trademark.* a synthetic polyester fibre or fabric.

tessellated ('tɛsɪˌleɪtɪd) adj. paved or inlaid with a mosaic of small tiles. [Latin *tessellātus* checked]

tessera ('tɛsərə) n., pl. **-serae** (-səˌriː). a small square tile of stone, glass, etc., used in mosaics. [Latin]

test¹ (tɛst) n. **1.** to ascertain (the worth, capability, or endurance) of (a person or thing) by trying it out. **2.** (often foll. by *for*) to carry out an examination on (a substance, material, or system) in order to discover whether a particular substance, component, or feature is present: *to test food for arsenic.* ~n. **3.** a method, practice, or examination designed to test a person or thing. **4.** a series of questions or problems designed to test a specific skill or knowledge. **5.** a standard of judgment; criterion. **6.** a chemical reaction or physical procedure for testing the composition or other qualities of a substance. **7.** *Sport.* See **test match.** [Latin *testum* earthen vessel] —**'testable** adj. —**'testing** adj.

test² (tɛst) n. the hard outer covering of certain invertebrates. [Latin *testa* shell]

testa ('tɛstə) n., pl. **-tae** (-tiː). the hard outer layer of a seed. [Latin: shell]

testaceous (tɛ'steɪʃəs) adj. *Biol.* of or possessing a hard continuous shell. [Latin *testācens*, from TESTA]

testament ('tɛstəmənt) n. **1.** *Law.* a will: *last will and testament.* **2.** a proof or tribute: *his success was a testament to his skills.* [Latin *testis* a witness] —ˌtesta'mentary adj.

Testament ('tɛstəmənt) n. either of the two main parts of the Bible: the Old Testament or the New Testament.

testate ('tɛsteɪt, 'tɛstɪt) *Law.* ~adj. **1.** having left a legally valid will at death. ~n. **2.** a person who dies testate. [Latin *testārī* to make a will] —**testacy** ('tɛstəsɪ) n.

testator (tɛ'steɪtə) or (fem.) **testatrix** (tɛ'steɪtrɪks) n. *Law.* a person who has made a will, esp. one who has died testate.

test case n. a legal action that serves as a precedent in deciding similar succeeding cases.

testicle ('tɛstɪk⁰l) n. either of the two male

reproductive glands, in most mammals enclosed within the scrotum, that produce spermatozoa. [Latin *testis* a witness (to masculinity)]

testify ('tɛstɪˌfaɪ) *vb.* **-fying, -fied. 1.** *Law.* to declare or give (evidence) under oath, esp. in court. **2.** (often foll. by *to*) to be evidence of; serve as witness to: *the money testified to his good faith.* [Latin *testis* witness]

testimonial (ˌtɛstɪˈməʊnɪəl) *n.* **1.** a recommendation of the character, ability, etc., of a person or of the quality of a product or service. **2.** a tribute given for services or achievements. ~*adj.* **3.** of a testimony or testimonial.

testimony ('tɛstɪmənɪ) *n., pl.* **-nies. 1.** a declaration of truth or fact. **2.** *Law.* evidence given by a witness, esp. in court under oath. **3.** evidence testifying to something: *her success was a testimony to her good luck.* [Latin *testimōnium*]

testis ('tɛstɪs) *n., pl.* **-tes.** same as **testicle.**

test match *n.* (in various sports, esp. cricket) any of a series of international matches.

testosterone (tɛˈstɒstəˌrəʊn) *n.* a steroid male sex hormone secreted by the testes.

test paper *n.* **1.** the question sheet of a test. **2.** *Chem.* paper impregnated with an indicator for use in chemical tests.

test pilot *n.* a pilot who flies aircraft of new design to test their performance in the air.

test tube *n.* a cylindrical round-bottomed glass tube open at one end: used in scientific experiments.

test-tube baby *n.* **1.** a fetus that has developed from an ovum fertilized in an artificial womb. **2.** a baby conceived by artificial insemination.

testy ('tɛstɪ) *adj.* **-tier, -tiest.** irritable or touchy. [Anglo-Norman *testif* headstrong] —'**testily** *adv.* —'**testiness** *n.*

tetanus ('tɛtənəs) *n.* an acute infectious disease in which sustained muscular spasm, contraction, and convulsion are caused by the release of toxins from a bacterium; lockjaw. [Greek *tetanos*]

tetchy ('tɛtʃɪ) *adj.* **tetchier, tetchiest.** cross, irritable, or touchy. [prob. from obs. *tetch* defect] —'**tetchily** *adv.* —'**tetchiness** *n.*

tête-à-tête (ˌteɪtɑːˈteɪt) *n., pl.* **-têtes** *or* **-tête. 1.** a private conversation between two people. ~*adv.* **2.** intimately; in private. [French, lit.: head to head]

tether ('tɛðə) *n.* **1.** a rope or chain by which an animal is tied to a particular spot. **2. at the end of one's tether.** at the limit of one's patience or endurance. ~*vb.* **3.** to tie with or as if with a tether. [Old Norse *tjothr*]

tetra- *combining form.* four: tetrahedron.

tetrad ('tɛtræd) *n.* a group or series of four. [Greek *tetras*]

tetraethyl lead (ˌtɛtrəˈiːθaɪl lɛd) *n.* a colourless oily insoluble liquid used in petrol to prevent knocking.

tetragon ('tɛtrəˌgɒn) *n.* same as **quadrilateral** (sense 2). [Greek *tetragōnon*]

tetrahedron (ˌtɛtrəˈhiːdrən) *n., pl.* **-drons** *or* **-dra** (-drə). a solid figure having four plane faces. [Late Greek *tetraedron*] —ˌ**tetra'hedral** *adj.*

tetralogy (tɛˈtrælədʒɪ) *n., pl.* **-gies.** a series of four related works, as in drama or opera. [Greek *tetralogia*]

tetrameter (tɛˈtræmɪtə) *n. Prosody.* a line of verse consisting of four metrical feet. [Greek *tetras* four + *meter*]

Teut. Teuton(ic).

Teuton ('tjuːtən) *n.* **1.** a member of an ancient Germanic people of N Europe. **2.** a member of any people speaking a Germanic language, esp. a German. ~*adj.* **3.** Teutonic. [Latin *Teutonī* the Teutons]

Teutonic (tjuːˈtɒnɪk) *adj.* **1.** characteristic of or relating to the German people. **2.** of the ancient Teutons.

Tex. Texas.

Tex-Mex ('tɛksˌmɛks) *adj.* **1.** combining elements of Texan and Mexican culture. ~*n.* **2.** Tex-Mex music or cooking.

text (tɛkst) *n.* **1.** the main body of a printed or written work as distinct from items such as notes or illustrations. **2.** words displayed on a visual display unit. **3.** a short passage of the Bible used as a starting point for a sermon. **4.** a novel or play prescribed as part of a course of study. [Latin *texere* to compose]

textbook ('tɛkstˌbʊk) *n.* **1.** a book used as a standard source of information on a particular subject. ~*adj.* **2.** perfect; exemplary: *she made a textbook landing.*

textile ('tɛkstaɪl) *n.* **1.** any fabric or cloth, esp. woven. **2.** raw material suitable to be made into cloth. ~*adj.* **3.** of or relating to fabrics. [Latin *textilis* woven]

textual ('tɛkstjʊəl) *adj.* of, based on, or relating to, a text or texts. —'**textually** *adv.*

texture ('tɛkstʃə) *n.* **1.** the surface of a material, esp. as perceived by the sense of touch. **2.** the structure, appearance, and feel of a woven fabric. ~*vb.* **3.** to give a distinctive texture to (something). [Latin *texere* to weave] —'**textural** *adj.*

Th *Chem.* thorium.

Thai (taɪ) *adj.* **1.** of Thailand, its people, or their language. ~*n.* **2.** (*pl.* **Thais** *or* **Thai**) a person from Thailand. **3.** the language of Thailand.

thalidomide (θəˈlɪdəˌmaɪd) *n.* a drug formerly used as a sedative and hypnotic but withdrawn from use when found to cause abnormalities in developing fetuses. [*thali-* (*mi*)*do*(*glutari*)*mide*]

thallium ('θælɪəm) *n.* a soft highly toxic white metallic element. Symbol: Tl [Greek *thallos* a green shoot; from the green line in its spectrum]

than (ðæn; *unstressed* ðən) *conj., prep.* **1.** used to introduce the second element of a comparison, the first element of which expresses difference: *shorter than you.* **2.** used after the adverbs *rather* and *sooner* to introduce a rejected alternative: *rather* *than be imprisoned, I shall die.* [Old English *thanne*]

thane *or* **thegn** (θeɪn) *n.* **1.** (in Anglo-Saxon England) a noble retainer who held land from the king or from a superior nobleman in return for certain services. **2.** (in medieval Scotland) a person of rank holding land from the king. [Old English *thegn*]

thank (θæŋk) *vb.* **1.** to convey feelings of gratitude to. **2.** to hold responsible: *he has his creditors to thank for his bankruptcy.* **3. thank you** *or* **thanks.** a polite response or expression of gratitude. **4. thank goodness, thank heavens,** *or* **thank God.** an exclamation of relief. [Old English *thancian*]

thankful ('θæŋkfʊl) *adj.* grateful and appreciative. —'**thankfully** *adv.*

thankless ('θæŋklɪs) *adj.* **1.** receiving no thanks or appreciation. **2.** ungrateful. —'**thanklessly** *adv.* —'**thanklessness** *n.*

thanks (θæŋks) *pl. n.* **1.** an expression of appreciation or gratitude. **2. thanks to.** because of: *thanks to him we lost the match.* ~*interj.* **3.** *Informal.* an exclamation expressing gratitude.

thanksgiving (,θæŋks'gɪvɪŋ) *n.* a formal public expression of thanks to God.

Thanksgiving Day *n.* (in North America) an annual day of holiday celebrated on the fourth Thursday of November in the United States and on the second Monday of October in Canada.

that *det.* (ðæt). **1.** used preceding a noun that has been mentioned or is already familiar: *that idea of yours.* **2.** used preceding a noun that denotes something more remote: *that building over there.* **3. and (all) that.** *Informal.* and everything connected with the subject mentioned: *he knows a lot about building and that.* **4. at that.** additionally, all things considered, or nevertheless: *I might decide to go at that.* **5. that is. a.** to be precise. **b.** in other words. **6. that's that.** there is no more to be said or done. ~*pron.* (ðæt). **7.** used to denote something already mentioned or understood: *don't eat that.* **8.** used to denote a more remote person or thing: *that is John and this is his wife.* **9.** used to introduce a restrictive relative clause: *the book that we want.* ~*conj.* (ðæt; unstressed ðət). **10.** used to introduce a noun clause: *I believe that you'll come.* **11.** used, usually after *so,* to introduce a clause of purpose: *they fought so that others might have peace.* **12.** used to introduce a clause of result: *he laughed so hard that he cried.* **13.** *Literary.* used to introduce a clause expressing desire, indignation, or amazement: *oh, that I had never lived!* ~*adv.* (ðæt). **14.** Also: **all that.** *Informal.* (used for emphasis): *he wasn't that upset.* [Old English]

thatch (θætʃ) *n.* **1.** Also called: **thatching.** a roofing material that consists of straw or reeds. **2.** a roof made of such a material. **3.** anything resembling this, such as the hair of the head. ~*vb.* **4.** to cover with thatch. [Old English *theccan* to cover] —'**thatcher** *n.*

thaw (θɔː) *vb.* **1.** to melt or cause to melt: *the snow thawed.* **2.** (of frozen food) to become or cause to become unfrozen; defrost. **3.** to be the case that the ice or snow is melting: *it's thawing fast.* **4.** to become more relaxed or friendly. ~*n.* **5.** the act or process of thawing. **6.** a spell of relatively warm weather, causing snow or ice to melt. [Old English *thawian*]

the¹ (*stressed or emphatic* ðiː; *unstressed before a consonant* ðə; *unstressed before a vowel* ðɪ) *det.* (*article*) **1.** used preceding a noun that has been previously specified or is a matter of common knowledge: *the pain should disappear soon.* **2.** used to indicate a particular person or object: *ask the man standing outside.* **3.** used preceding certain nouns associated with one's culture, society, or community: *to go to the doctor; to listen to the news.* **4.** used preceding an adjective that is functioning as a collective noun: *the deaf and the blind.* **5.** used preceding titles and certain proper nouns: *the United States; the Chairman.* **6.** used preceding a qualifying adjective or noun in certain names or titles: *Edward the First.* **7.** used preceding a noun to make it refer to its class generically: *the white seal is hunted for its fur.* **8.** used instead of *my, your, her,* etc., with parts of the body: *take me by the hand.* **9.** (*stressed*) used as the best or most remarkable: *Harry's is the club in this town.* [Old English *thē*]

the² (ðə, ðɪ) *adv.* used correlatively before each of two comparative adjectives or adverbs to indicate equality: *the sooner you come, the better; the more I see you, the more I love you.* [Old English *thī, thȳ*]

theatre *or* U.S. **theater** ('θɪətə) *n.* **1.** a building designed for the performance of plays, operas, etc. **2.** a large room or hall with tiered seats for an audience. **3.** a room in a hospital equipped for surgical operations. **4. the theatre.** the world of actors and theatrical companies. **5.** U.S., Austral., & N.Z. same as **cinema** (sense 1). [Greek *theatron*]

theatrical (θɪ'ætrɪk²l) *adj.* **1.** of or relating to the theatre or dramatic performances. **2.** exaggerated and affected in manner or behaviour. —the,atri'cality *n.* —the'atrically *adv.*

theatricals (θɪ'ætrɪk²lz) *pl. n.* dramatic performances, esp. as given by amateurs.

thee (ðiː) *sing. pron.* Archaic. the objective form of **thou**¹.

theft (θeft) *n.* the act or an instance of stealing. [Old English *thēofth*]

thegn (θeɪn) *n.* same as **thane** (sense 1).

their (ðeə) *det.* of or associated with them: *their own clothes; she tried to combat their mocking her.* [Old Norse *theira*]

theirs (ðeəz) *pron.* **1.** something or someone belonging to or associated with them: *ours is easy, theirs is difficult.* **2.** of theirs. belonging to them.

theism ('θiːɪzəm) *n.* **1.** belief in one God as the creator of everything in the universe. **2.** belief in the existence of a God or gods. [Greek *theos* god] —'**theist** *n., adj.* —the'istic *or* the'istical *adj.*

them (ðɛm; *unstressed* ðəm, əm) *pl. pron.* (*objective*) refers to things or people other than the speaker or people addressed. [Old English]

theme (θiːm) *n.* **1.** the main idea or topic in a discussion or lecture. **2.** (in literature, music, or art) an idea, image, or motif, repeated or developed throughout a work. **3.** *Music.* a group of notes forming a recognizable melodic unit, used as the basis of part or all of a composition. **4.** a short essay, esp. one set as an exercise for a student. [Greek *thema*] —**thematic** (θɪˈmætɪk) *adj.* —**theˈmatically** *adv.*

theme park *n.* an area planned as a leisure attraction in which all the displays and activities are based on a particular theme, story, or idea.

themselves (ðəmˈsɛlvz) *pron.* **1. a.** the reflexive form of *they* or *them*: *they introduced themselves.* **b.** (used for emphasis): *the team themselves voted in favour of the proposal.* **2.** their normal or usual selves: *they don't seem themselves any more.*

then (ðɛn) *adv.* **1.** at that time; over that period of time: *there were no cars then; space travel will be commonplace then.* **2.** in that case; that being so: *then why don't you ask her?* go on then, take it. **3.** after that: *then John left the room.* **4. then and there.** immediately and in that place: *he signed the requisition then and there.* ~*pron.* **5.** that time: *from then on.* ~*adj.* **6.** existing or functioning at that time: *the then prime minister.* [Old English *thenne*]

thence (ðɛns) *adv. Formal.* **1.** from that place. **2.** from that time; thereafter. **3.** therefore. [Middle English *thannes*]

thenceforth (ˌðɛnsˈfɔːθ) *or* **thenceforward** (ðɛnsˈfɔːwəd) *adv. Formal.* from that time on.

theocracy (θɪˈɒkrəsɪ) *n., pl.* **-cies.** **1.** government by a deity or by a priesthood. **2.** a community under such government. [Greek *theos* god + *kratos* power] —**ˈtheoˌcrat** *n.* —**theoˈcratic** *adj.* —**ˌtheoˈcratically** *adv.*

theodolite (θɪˈɒdəˌlaɪt) *n.* an instrument used in surveying for measuring horizontal and vertical angles. [origin unknown]

theol. 1. theological. **2.** theology.

theologian (ˌθɪəˈləʊdʒɪən) *n.* a person versed in the study of theology.

theology (θɪˈɒlədʒɪ) *n., pl.* **-gies.** **1.** the systematic study of religions and religious beliefs. **2.** a specific system, form, or branch of this study. [Greek *theos* god + *-logy*] —**theological** (ˌθɪəˈlɒdʒɪkˀl) *adj.* —**ˌtheoˈlogically** *adv.*

theorem (ˈθɪərəm) *n.* a statement that can be deduced from the axioms of a formal system by means of its rules of inference. [Greek *theōrein* to view]

theoretical (ˌθɪəˈrɛtɪkˀl) *or* **theoretic** *adj.* **1.** of or based on theory. **2.** lacking practical application or actual existence; hypothetical. **3.** using or dealing in theory; impractical. —**ˌtheoˈretically** *adv.*

theoretician (ˌθɪərɪˈtɪʃən) *n.* a student or user of the theory of a subject rather than its practical aspects.

theorize *or* **-ise** (ˈθɪəˌraɪz) *vb.* to produce or use theories; speculate. —**ˈtheorist** *n.*

theory (ˈθɪərɪ) *n., pl.* **-ries.** **1.** a set of hypotheses related by logical arguments to explain a wide variety of connected phenomena in general terms: *the theory of relativity.* **2.** abstract knowledge or reasoning. **3.** a conjectural view or idea: *I have a theory about that.* **4.** an ideal or hypothetical situation: *in theory all British subjects are eligible.* [Greek *theōria* a sight]

theosophy (θɪˈɒsəfɪ) *n.* a religious or philosophical system claiming to be based on an intuitive insight into the divine nature. [Greek *theos* god + *sophia* wisdom] —**theosophical** (ˌθɪəˈsɒfɪkˀl) *or* **ˌtheoˈsophic** *adj.* —**theˈosophist** *n.*

therapeutic (ˌθɛrəˈpjuːtɪk) *adj.* of or relating to the treatment and cure of disease. [Greek *therapeuein* to minister to] —**ˌtheraˈpeutically** *adv.*

therapeutics (ˌθɛrəˈpjuːtɪks) *n.* (*functioning as sing.*) the branch of medicine concerned with the treatment of disease.

therapy (ˈθɛrəpɪ) *n., pl.* **-pies.** the treatment of physical, mental, or social disorders or disease. [Greek *therapeia* attendance] —**ˈtherapist** *n.*

there (ðɛə) *adv.* **1.** in, at, or to that place or position: *we never go there.* **2.** in that respect: *I agree with you there.* ~*adj.* **3. not all there.** *Informal.* mentally defective or silly. ~*pron.* **4.** that place: *near there.* **5.** used as a grammatical subject when the true subject follows the verb, esp. the verb "to be": *there is a girl in that office.* **6. so there.** an exclamation that usually follows a declaration of refusal or defiance: *you can't have any more, so there.* **7. there you are. a.** an expression used when handing a person something requested or desired. **b.** an exclamation of satisfaction or vindication: *there you are, I knew that would happen.* ~*interj.* **8.** an expression of sympathy, as in consoling a child: *there, there, dear.* [Old English *thær*]

thereabouts (ˈðɛərəˌbaʊts) *or U.S.* **thereabout** *adv.* near that place, time, amount, etc.: *meet at three o'clock or thereabouts.*

thereafter (ˌðɛərˈɑːftə) *adv. Formal.* from that time onwards.

thereby (ˌðɛəˈbaɪ, ˈðɛəˌbaɪ) *adv. Formal.* by that means.

therefore (ˈðɛəˌfɔː) *adv.* thus; hence; consequently: *those people have their umbrellas up, therefore it must be raining.*

therein (ˌðɛərˈɪn) *adv. Formal.* in or into that place or thing.

thereof (ˌðɛərˈɒv) *adv. Formal.* **1.** of or concerning that or it. **2.** from or because of that.

thereto (ˌðɛəˈtuː) *adv. Formal.* **1.** to that or it. **2.** Also: **thereunto.** in addition to that.

thereupon (ˌðɛərəˈpɒn) *adv.* **1.** immediately after that; at that point. **2.** *Formal.* concerning that subject.

therm (θɜːm) *n. Brit.* a unit of heat equal to 100 000 British thermal units. One therm is equal to $1.055\ 056 \times 10^8$ joules. [Greek *thermē* heat]

thermal ('θɜːməl) *adj.* **1.** of, caused by, or generating heat. **2.** hot or warm: *thermal baths.* **3.** (of garments) specially made so as to have exceptional heat-retaining qualities: *thermal underwear.* **4.** See **British thermal unit.** ~*n.* **5.** a column of rising air caused by uneven heating of the land surface, and used by gliders and birds to gain height.

thermionic valve *or esp. U.S. & Canad.* **thermionic tube** *n.* an electronic valve in which electrons are emitted from a heated heater through a cold cathode.

thermocouple ('θɜːməʊˌkʌpᵊl) *n.* a device for measuring temperature, consisting of a pair of wires of different metals joined at both ends.

thermodynamics (ˌθɜːməʊdaɪˈnæmɪks) *n.* (*functioning as sing.*) the branch of physical science concerned with the relationship between heat and other forms of energy.

thermoelectric (ˌθɜːməʊˈlɛktrɪk) *or* **thermoelectrical** *adj.* of, relating to, or operated by the conversion of heat energy to electrical energy.

thermometer (θəˈmɒmɪtə) *n.* an instrument used to measure temperature, esp. one in which a thin column of liquid, such as mercury, expands and contracts within a graduated sealed tube.

thermonuclear (ˌθɜːməʊˈnjuːklɪə) *adj.* **1.** involving nuclear fusion. **2.** involving thermonuclear weapons.

thermoplastic (ˌθɜːməʊˈplæstɪk) *adj.* **1.** (of a material, esp. a synthetic plastic) becoming soft when heated and rehardening on cooling. ~*n.* **2.** a synthetic plastic or resin, such as polystyrene.

Thermos *or* **Thermos flask** ('θɜːməs) *n.* *Trademark.* a type of stoppered vacuum flask used to preserve the temperature of its contents.

thermosetting (ˌθɜːməʊˈsɛtɪŋ) *adj.* (of a material, esp. a synthetic plastic) hardening permanently after one application of heat and pressure.

thermostat ('θɜːməˌstæt) *n.* a device that is sensitive to temperature and that can operate a switch automatically when a certain temperature is reached. —ˌ**thermoˈstatic** *adj.* —ˌ**thermoˈstatically** *adv.*

thesaurus (θɪˈsɔːrəs) *n.*, *pl.* **-ri** (-raɪ) *or* **-ruses.** a book containing systematized lists of synonyms and related words. [Greek *thēsaurus* a treasury]

these (ðiːz) *det.* the form of **this** used before a plural noun: *these men.*

thesis ('θiːsɪs) *n.*, *pl.* **-ses** (-siːz). **1.** a written work resulting from original research, esp. one submitted for a higher degree in a university. **2.** a doctrine maintained in argument. **3.** *Logic.* an unproved statement put forward as a premise in an argument. [Greek: a placing]

Thespian ('θɛspɪən) *adj.* **1.** of or relating to drama and the theatre; dramatic. ~*n.* **2.** *Often facetious.* an actor or actress. [after *Thespis,* a Greek poet]

theta ('θiːtə) *n.* the eighth letter in the

Greek alphabet (θ, Θ), used as a symbol in logic, linguistics, and the phonetic alphabet.

they (ðeɪ) *pl. pron.* (*subjective*) refers to: **1.** people or things other than the speaker or people addressed: *they fight among themselves.* **2.** people in general: *in Australia they have Christmas in the summer.* [Old Norse *their*]

they'd (ðeɪd) they would *or* they had.

they'll (ðeɪl) they will *or* they shall.

they're (ðɛə, 'ðeɪə) they are.

they've (ðeɪv) they have.

thiamine ('θaɪəˌmiːn) *or* **thiamin** ('θaɪəmɪn) *n.* vitamin B$_1$, a white crystalline compound that occurs in the outer coat of rice and other grains: deficiency of this vitamin leads to nervous disorders and to beriberi. [Greek *theion* sulphur + *vitamin*]

thick (θɪk) *adj.* **1.** of relatively great extent from one surface to the other: *a thick slice of bread.* **2.** of specific extent from one surface to the other: *ten centimetres thick.* **3.** having a dense consistency: *thick soup; a thick fog.* **4.** abundantly covered: *the furniture was thick with dust.* **5.** *Informal.* stupid, slow, or insensitive. **6.** throaty and badly articulated: *a voice thick with emotion.* **7.** (of an accent) pronounced: *a thick Irish accent.* **8.** *a bit thick. Brit.* unfair or unreasonable: *only two pounds an hour, that's a bit thick!* **9.** *thick as thieves. Informal.* very friendly. ~*adv.* **10.** in order to produce something thick: *to slice bread thick.* **11.** profusely; in quick succession: *the replies came in thick and fast.* **12.** *lay it on thick. Informal.* **a.** to exaggerate a story. **b.** to flatter someone excessively. ~*n.* **13.** *the thick.* the most intense or active part: *in the thick of the battle.* **14.** *through thick and thin.* in good times and bad. [Old English *thicce*] —ˈ**thickish** *adj.*

thicken ('θɪkən) *vb.* **1.** to make or become thick or thicker. **2.** to become more involved: *the plot thickened.* —ˈ**thickener** *n.*

thickening ('θɪkənɪŋ) *n.* **1.** something added to a liquid to thicken it. **2.** a thickened part or piece.

thicket ('θɪkɪt) *n.* a dense growth of small trees, shrubs, and similar plants. [Old English *thiccet*]

thickhead ('θɪkˌhɛd) *n.* *Slang.* a stupid or ignorant person; fool. —ˌ**thickˈheaded** *adj.*

thickness ('θɪknɪs) *n.* **1.** the state or quality of being thick. **2.** the dimension through an object, as opposed to length or width. **3.** a layer: *three thicknesses of cloth.*

thickset (ˌθɪkˈsɛt) *adj.* **1.** stocky in build; sturdy. **2.** densely planted or placed.

thick-skinned *adj.* insensitive to criticism or hints; not easily upset.

thief (θiːf) *n.*, *pl.* **thieves** (θiːvz). a person who steals something from another. [Old English *thēof*] —ˈ**thievish** *adj.*

thieve (θiːv) *vb.* to steal other people's possessions. [Old English *thēofian*] —ˈ**thieving** *adj.*

thigh (θaɪ) *n.* the part of the leg between

the hip and the knee in man. [Old English *thēh*]

thighbone ('θaɪˌbəʊn) *n.* same as **femur.**

thimble ('θɪmbᵊl) *n.* a small metal or plastic cap used to protect the end of the finger from the needle when sewing. [Old English *thȳmel* thumbstall]

thin (θɪn) *adj.* **thinner, thinnest. 1.** of relatively small extent from one side to the other. **2.** (of a person or animal) slim or lean. **3.** sparsely placed; meagre: *thin hair.* **4.** of low density: *a thin liquid.* **5.** weak; poor: *a thin disguise.* ~*adv.* **6.** in order to produce something thin: *to cut bread thin.* ~*vb.* **thinning, thinned. 7.** to make or become thin or sparse. [Old English *thynne*] —'**thinness** *n.*

thine (ðaɪn) *Archaic.* ~*det.* **1.** (*preceding a vowel*) of or associated with you (thou): *thine eyes.* ~*pron.* **2.** something belonging to you (thou): *thine is the greatest burden.* [Old English *thīn*]

thing (θɪŋ) *n.* **1.** an object, fact, circumstance, or concept considered as being a separate entity. **2.** any inanimate physical object. **3.** an object or entity that cannot or need not be precisely named. **4.** *Informal.* a person or animal: *you poor thing.* **5.** (*often pl.*) a possession, article of clothing, etc. **6.** *Informal.* a preoccupation or obsession: *she has a thing about dogs.* **7. do one's (own) thing.** to engage in an activity or mode of behaviour satisfying to one's personality. **8. make a thing of.** to exaggerate the importance of. **9. the thing.** the latest fashion. [Old English: assembly]

thingumabob *or* **thingamabob** ('θɪŋ-əməˌbɒb) *n.* *Informal.* a person or thing the name of which is unknown, temporarily forgotten, or deliberately overlooked. Also: **thingumajig, thingamajig,** *or* **thingummy.**

think (θɪŋk) *vb.* **thinking, thought. 1.** to consider, judge, or believe: *he thinks my ideas are impractical.* **2.** (often foll. by *about*) to exercise the mind, for example in order to make a decision. **3.** to engage in conscious thought: *man is the only animal that thinks.* **4.** (usually foll. by *of*) to remember; recollect: *I can't think of his name.* **5.** (foll. by *of*) to make the mental choice (of): *think of a number.* **6.** to be considerate enough or remember to do something: *he did not think to thank them.* **7. think twice.** to consider something carefully before making a decision. ~*n.* **8.** *Informal.* a careful, open-minded assessment: *let's have a fresh think about this.* ~See also **think over, think up.** [Old English *thencan*] —'**thinker** *n.*

thinking ('θɪŋkɪŋ) *n.* **1.** opinion or judgment. **2.** the process of thought. ~*adj.* **3.** using intelligent thought: *thinking people.*

think over *vb.* to ponder or consider.

think-tank *n.* *Informal.* a group of specialists commissioned to undertake intensive study and research into specified problems.

think up *vb.* to invent or devise.

thinner ('θɪnə) *n.* (often *pl.*, functioning as

sing.) a solvent, such as turpentine, added to paint or varnish to dilute it.

thin-skinned *adj.* sensitive to criticism or hints; easily upset.

third (θɜːd) *adj.* **1.** coming after the second in order. **2.** rated, graded, or ranked below the second level. **3.** denoting the third from lowest forward ratio of a gearbox in a motor vehicle. ~*n.* **4.** one of three equal parts of an object or quantity. **5.** the fraction equal to one divided by three (⅓). **6.** the forward ratio above second of a gearbox in a motor vehicle. **7.** *Music.* the interval between one note and another three notes away from it counting inclusively along the diatonic scale. **8.** *Brit.* an honours degree of the third and usually the lowest class. ~*adv.* **9.** Also: **thirdly.** in the third place. [Old English *thirda*]

third class *n.* **1.** the class or grade next in value, quality, etc., to the second. ~*adj.* **2.** of the class or grade next in value, quality, etc., to the second.

third degree *n.* *Informal.* torture or bullying, esp. as used to extort confessions or information.

third-degree burn *n.* *Pathol.* the most severe type of burn, involving the destruction of both epidermis and dermis.

third dimension *n.* the dimension of depth, by which a solid object may be distinguished from a two-dimensional drawing or picture of it.

third man *n.* *Cricket.* a fielding position on the off side, near the boundary behind the batsman's wicket.

third party *n.* **1.** a person who is involved by chance or only incidentally in an event, legal proceeding, agreement, or other transaction. ~*adj.* **2.** *Insurance.* providing protection against liability caused by accidental injury or death of other persons.

third person *n.* a grammatical category of pronouns and verbs used when referring to objects or individuals other than the speaker or his addressee or addressees.

third-rate *adj.* mediocre or inferior.

Third World *n.* the countries of Africa, Asia, and Latin America collectively, esp. when viewed as underdeveloped.

thirst (θɜːst) *n.* **1.** a craving to drink, accompanied by a feeling of dryness in the mouth and throat. **2.** an eager longing, craving, or yearning. ~*vb.* **3.** to feel a thirst. [Old English *thyrstan*]

thirsty ('θɜːstɪ) *adj.* **thirstier, thirstiest. 1.** feeling a desire to drink. **2.** (foll. by *for*) feeling an eager desire for. **3.** causing thirst: *thirsty work.* —'**thirstily** *adv.*

thirteen ('θɜːˈtiːn) *n.* **1.** the cardinal number that is the sum of ten and three. **2.** a numeral, 13, XIII, representing this number. **3.** something representing or consisting of thirteen units. ~*det.* **4.** amounting to thirteen. —'**thir'teenth** *adj., n.*

thirty ('θɜːtɪ) *n., pl.* **-ties. 1.** the cardinal number that is the product of ten and three. **2.** a numeral, 30, XXX, representing this number. **3.** something representing or consisting of thirty units. ~*det.* **4.** amounting to thirty. —'**thirtieth** *adj., n.*

Thirty-nine Articles *pl. n.* a set of formulas defining the doctrinal position of the Church of England.

this (ðɪs) *det.* **1.** used preceding a noun referring to something or someone that is closer: *look at this picture.* **2.** used preceding a noun that has just been mentioned or is understood: *this plan of yours won't work.* **3.** used to refer to something about to be mentioned: *consider this argument.* **4.** used to refer to the present time or occasion: *this time you'll know better.* **5.** *Informal.* an emphatic form of **a** or **the**[1]: *I saw this big brown bear.* **6. this and that.** various unspecified and trivial events or facts. ~*pron.* **7.** used to denote a person or thing that is relatively close: *take this.* **8.** used to denote something already mentioned or understood: *I first saw this on Sunday.* **9.** used to denote something about to be mentioned: *listen to this.* **10.** the present time or occasion: *before this, I was mistaken.* [Old English *thēs*]

thistle ('θɪs'l) *n.* a plant with prickly-edged leaves, dense flower heads, and feathery hairs on the seeds. [Old English *thistel*] —'**thistly** *adj.*

thistledown ('θɪs'l,daʊn) *n.* the mass of feathery plumed seeds produced by a thistle.

thither ('ðɪðə) *adv. Formal.* to or towards that place; in that direction. [Old English *thider*]

tho or **tho'** (ðəʊ) *conj., adv. U.S.* or *poetic.* same as **though.**

thole (θəʊl) or **tholepin** ('θəʊl,pɪn) *n.* one of a pair of wooden pins set upright in the gunwale on either side of a rowing boat to serve as a fulcrum in rowing. [Old English *tholl*]

thong (θɒŋ) *n.* **1.** a thin strip of leather or other material. **2.** *U.S., Canad., Austral., & N.Z.* same as **flip-flop** (sense 5). [Old English *thwang*]

thorax ('θɔːræks) *n., pl.* **thoraxes** or **thoraces** ('θɔːrə,siːz, θɔː'reɪsiːz). **1.** the part of the human body enclosed by the ribs. **2.** the part of an insect's body between the head and abdomen. [Greek: breastplate, chest] —**thoracic** (θɔː'ræsɪk) *adj.*

thorium ('θɔːrɪəm) *n.* a silvery-white radioactive metallic element. It is used in electronic equipment and as a nuclear power source. Symbol: Th [after *Thor*, Norse god of thunder]

thorn (θɔːn) *n.* **1.** a sharp pointed woody extension of a stem or leaf. **2.** any of various trees or shrubs having thorns, esp. the hawthorn. **3. a thorn in one's side** or **flesh.** a source of irritation: *she has been a thorn in the flesh since she arrived.* [Old English] —'**thornless** *adj.*

thorny ('θɔːnɪ) *adj.* **thornier, thorniest. 1.** bearing or covered with thorns. **2.** difficult or unpleasant: *a thorny problem.*

thorough ('θʌrə) *adj.* **1.** carried out completely and carefully. **2.** utter: *a thorough bore.* **3.** painstakingly careful. [Old English *thurh*] —'**thoroughly** *adv.* —'**thoroughness** *n.*

thoroughbred ('θʌrə,bred) *adj.* **1.** obtained through successive generations of selective breeding: *a thoroughbred stallion.* ~*n.* **2.** a pedigree animal, esp. a horse.

thoroughfare ('θʌrə,fɛə) *n.* a way through from one place to another: *no thoroughfare.*

thoroughgoing ('θʌrə,gəʊɪŋ) *adj.* **1.** extremely thorough. **2.** absolute; complete: *thoroughgoing incompetence.*

those (ðəʊz) *det.* the form of **that** used before a plural noun. [Old English *thās*]

thou[1] (ðaʊ) *sing. pron. (subjective) Archaic.* refers to the person addressed: used mainly in familiar address. [Old English *thū*]

thou[2] (θaʊ) *n., pl.* **thou.** *Informal.* **1.** one thousandth of an inch. **2.** a thousand.

though (ðəʊ) *conj.* **1.** (sometimes preceded by *even*) despite the fact that: *even though it was a hot day, she was wearing a fur coat.* ~*adv.* **2.** nevertheless; however: *he can't dance — he sings well, though.* [Old English *theah*]

thought (θɔːt) *vb.* **1.** past of **think.** ~*n.* **2.** the act or process of thinking. **3.** a concept or idea. **4.** ideas typical of a particular time or place: *German thought in the 19th century.* **5.** application of mental attention; consideration: *I will give some thought to the problem.* **6.** purpose or intention: *I have no thought of giving up.* **7.** expectation: *no thought of reward.* [Old English *thōht*]

thoughtful ('θɔːtful) *adj.* **1.** considerate in the treatment of other people. **2.** showing careful thought: *a thoughtful essay.* **3.** pensive; reflective. —'**thoughtfully** *adv.* —'**thoughtfulness** *n.*

thoughtless ('θɔːtlɪs) *adj.* inconsiderate; having no regard for the feelings of other people —'**thoughtlessly** *adv.* —'**thoughtlessness** *n.*

thousand ('θaʊzənd) *n.* **1.** the cardinal number that is the product of one hundred tens. **2.** a numeral, 1000, 10^3, representing this number. **3.** (*often pl.*) a very large but unspecified number, amount, or quantity. **4.** something representing or consisting of 1000 units. ~*det.* **5.** amounting to a thousand. [Old English *thūsend*] —'**thousandth** *adj., n*

thrall (θrɔːl) *n.* **1.** Also: **thraldom** or *U.S.* **thralldom** ('θrɔːldəm). the state or condition of being in the power of another person. **2.** a person who is in such a state. [Old English *thrǣl* slave]

thrash (θræʃ) *vb.* **1.** to beat (someone) with a whip or stick. **2.** to defeat totally: *the home team thrashed the visiting team.* **3.** to move about in a wild manner: *the boy was thrashing around, trying to get free.* **4.** same as **thresh.** ~*n.* **5.** the act of thrashing; beating. **6.** *Informal.* a party. ~See also **thrash out.** [Old English *threscan*]

thrashing ('θræʃɪŋ) *n.* a physical assault; flogging.

thrash out *vb.* to discuss (a problem or

difficulty) fully in order to come to an agreement or decision about it.

thread (θrεd) *n.* **1.** a fine strand, filament, or fibre of some material. **2.** a fine cord of twisted yarns, esp. of cotton, used in sewing or weaving. **3.** the spiral ridge on a screw, bolt, or nut. **4.** a very thin seam of coal or vein of ore. **5.** something acting as the continuous link or theme of a whole: *the thread of the story.* ~*vb.* **6.** to pass (thread) through the (eye of a needle) before sewing with it. **7.** to string together: *she threaded the beads onto a piece of string to make a necklace.* **8.** to make (one's way) through or over (a crowd of people or group of objects). [Old English *thrǣd*] —**'thread,like** *adj.*

threadbare ('θrεd,bεə) *adj.* **1.** (of cloth, clothing, or carpet) having the nap worn off so that the threads are exposed; worn out. **2.** hackneyed: *a threadbare argument.* **3.** wearing threadbare clothes; shabby.

threadworm ('θrεd,wɜːm) *n.* a small threadlike worm, esp. the pinworm.

threat (θrεt) *n.* **1.** a declaration of an intention to inflict harm. **2.** an indication of imminent harm, danger, or pain. **3.** a person or thing that is regarded as dangerous and likely to inflict harm. [Old English]

threaten ('θrεt'n) *vb.* **1.** to express a threat to (a person or people). **2.** to be a threat to. **3.** to be a menacing indication of (something): *dark clouds threatened rain.* —**'threatening** *adj.* —**'threateningly** *adv.*

three (θriː) *n.* **1.** the cardinal number that is the sum of two and one. **2.** a numeral, 3, III, representing this number. **3.** something representing or consisting of three units. ~*det.* **4.** amounting to three. [Old English *thrēo*]

three-decker *n.* **1.** anything having three levels, layers, or tiers. **2.** a warship with guns on three decks.

three-dimensional *adj.* **1.** having three dimensions. **2.** lifelike: *the characters in the novel are three-dimensional.*

threefold ('θriː,fəʊld) *adj.* **1.** having three times as many or as much; triple. **2.** composed of three parts. ~*adv.* **3.** three times as many or as much.

three-legged race *n.* a race in which pairs of competitors run with their adjacent legs tied together.

three-ply *adj.* (of wool, wood, etc.) having three layers or strands.

three-point turn *n.* a complete turn of a motor vehicle using forward and reverse gears alternately, and completed after only three movements.

three-quarter *adj.* **1.** being three quarters of something. **2.** being three quarters of the normal length: *a three-quarter-length coat.* ~*n.* **3.** *Rugby.* one of the four players between the fullback and the scrum half, whose role is mainly to run with the ball when it is passed to them.

three Rs *pl. n.* **the.** reading, writing, and arithmetic regarded as the three funda-

mental skills to be taught in primary schools. [humorous spelling of *reading, 'riting, and 'rithmetic*]

threescore ('θriː'skɔː) *det. Archaic.* sixty.

threesome ('θriːsəm) *n.* a group of three people.

threnody ('θrεnədı) *n., pl.* **threnodies.** an ode, song, or speech of lamentation, esp. for the dead. [Greek *thrēnōidia*] —**threnodic** (θrı'nɒdık) *adj.* —**'threnodist** *n.*

thresh (θrεʃ) *vb.* **1.** to beat stalks of ripe corn, rice, etc., either with a hand implement or a machine to separate the grain from the husks and straw. **2.** to beat or strike. **3.** (often foll. by *about*) to toss and turn; thrash. [Old English *threscan*]

thresher ('θrεʃə) *n.* any of a genus of large sharks occurring in tropical and temperate seas. They have a very long whiplike tail.

threshold ('θrεʃ,həʊld) *n.* **1.** the sill of an entrance or doorway, esp. one made of stone or hardwood. **2.** any doorway or entrance. **3.** the starting point of an experience, event, or venture. **4.** the strength at which a stimulus is just strong enough to produce a response: *the threshold of consciousness.* [Old English *therscold*]

threw (θruː) *vb.* the past tense of **throw.**

thrice (θraıs) *adv.* **1.** three times. **2.** threefold. **3.** *Archaic.* greatly. [Old English *thrīwa, thrīga*]

thrift (θrıft) *n.* **1.** wisdom and caution in the management of money. **2.** a low-growing plant of Europe, W Asia, and North America, with narrow leaves and round heads of pink or white flowers. [Old Norse: success] —**'thriftless** *adj.*

thrifty ('θrıftı) *adj.* **thriftier, thriftiest.** showing thrift; economical or frugal. —**'thriftily** *adv.* —**'thriftiness** *n.*

thrill (θrıl) *n.* **1.** a sudden sensation of excitement and pleasure. **2.** a situation producing such a sensation. **3.** a sudden trembling sensation caused by fear or emotional shock. ~*vb.* **4.** to feel or cause to feel a thrill. **5.** to tremble or cause to tremble; vibrate or quiver. [Old English *thȳrlian* to pierce] —**'thrilling** *adj.*

thriller ('θrılə) *n.* a book, film, or play depicting crime, mystery, or espionage in an atmosphere of excitement and suspense.

thrips (θrıps) *n., pl.* **thrips.** a small slender-bodied insect with piercing mouthparts which feeds on plant sap. [Greek: woodworm]

thrive (θraıv) *vb.* **thriving; thrived** or **throve; thrived** or **thriven** ('θrıv'n). **1.** to do well; prosper. **2.** to grow strongly and vigorously. [Old Norse *thrífask* to grasp for oneself]

thro' or **thro** (θruː) *prep., adv. Informal.* same as **through.**

throat (θrəʊt) *n.* **1.** the top part of the alimentary and respiratory tract, running from the mouth and nose down towards the stomach and lungs. **2.** the front part of the neck. **3.** something resembling a throat, esp. in shape or function: *the throat of a chimney.* **4. cut someone's throat.** to kill someone. **5. cut one's (own) throat.** to bring about one's own ruin. **6. ram** or **force (something) down someone's throat.** to insist that someone listen to or accept (something). [Old English *throtu*]

throaty ('θrəʊtɪ) *adj.* **throatier, throatiest. 1.** indicating a sore throat; hoarse: *a throaty cough.* **2.** deep, husky, or guttural.

throb (θrɒb) *vb.* **throbbing, throbbed. 1.** to pulsate or beat repeatedly, esp. with abnormally strong force: *her head was throbbing.* **2.** (of engines, drums, etc.) to have a strong rhythmic vibration or beat. ~*n.* **3.** a throbbing, esp. a rapid pulsation as of the heart: *a throb of pleasure.* [imit.]

throes (θrəʊz) *pl. n.* **1.** a condition of violent pangs, pain, or convulsions: *death throes.* **2. in the throes of.** struggling with great effort with: *a country in the throes of revolution.* [Old English *thrāwu* threat]

thrombosis (θrɒm'bəʊsɪs) *n., pl.* **-ses** (-siːz). coagulation of the blood in the heart or in a blood vessel, forming a blood clot. [Greek: curdling]

throne (θrəʊn) *n.* **1.** the ceremonial seat occupied by a monarch or bishop on occasions of state. **2.** the office or rank of a royal person. [Greek *thronos*]

throng (θrɒŋ) *n.* **1.** a great number of people or things crowded together. ~*vb.* **2.** to gather in or fill (a place) in large numbers; crowd. [Old English *gethrang*]

throstle ('θrɒsəl) *n. Poetic.* a song thrush. [Old English]

throttle ('θrɒtəl) *n.* **1.** a device that controls the fuel-and-air mixture entering an engine. ~*vb.* **2.** to kill or injure (someone) by squeezing his throat. **3.** to suppress or censor. **4.** to control or restrict (a flow of fluid) by means of a throttle valve. [Middle English *throtel* throat]

through (θruː) *prep.* **1.** going in at one side and coming out at the other side of: *a path through the wood.* **2.** occupying or visiting several points scattered around in (an area). **3.** as a result of: *the thieves were captured through his vigilance.* **4.** Chiefly U.S. up to and including: *Monday through Friday.* **5.** during: *through the night.* ~*adj.* **6.** at an end: *his days of acting were through.* **7.** having successfully completed some specified activity. **8.** (on a telephone line) connected. **9.** no longer able to function successfully in some specified capacity: *as a journalist, you're through.* **10.** continuous or unbroken: *a through train.* ~*adv.* **11.** through some specified thing, place, or period of time: *all year through.* **12. through and through.** completely: *the boards are rotten through and through.* [Old English *thurh*]

throughout (θruː'aʊt) *prep.* **1.** through the whole of (a place or a period of time): *throughout the day.* ~*adv.* **2.** throughout some specified period or area: *the children sat quietly throughout.*

throughput ('θruː,pʊt) *n.* the amount of material processed in a given period, esp. by a computer.

throve (θrəʊv) *vb.* a past tense of **thrive.**

throw (θrəʊ) *vb.* **throwing, threw, thrown. 1.** to hurl (something) through the air, esp. with a rapid motion of the arm. **2.** (foll. by *in, on, onto,* etc.) to put or move suddenly, carelessly, or violently. **3.** to bring to or cause to be in a specified state or condition, esp. suddenly: *the news threw them into a panic.* **4.** to direct or cast (a shadow, light, etc.): *she threw him a nervous glance; the lamp threw a shadow on the ceiling.* **5.** to project (the voice) so as to make it appear to come from some other source. **6.** to give or hold (a party). **7.** to cause to fall or be upset: *the horse threw his rider.* **8. a.** to tip (dice) out onto a flat surface. **b.** to obtain (a specified number) in this way: *to throw two sixes.* **9.** to shape (a pot or vessel) on a potter's wheel. **10.** to move (a switch or lever) so as to engage or disengage a mechanism. **11.** *Informal.* to confuse: *the question threw me.* **12.** *Informal.* to lose (a contest) deliberately. **13. throw oneself at.** to strive very hard to attract the attention or win the affection of. **14. throw oneself into.** to involve oneself enthusiastically in. **15. throw oneself on.** to rely entirely upon (someone's goodwill, etc.): *he threw himself on her mercy.* ~*n.* **16.** the act or an instance of throwing. **17.** *Chiefly U.S. & Canad.* a decorative blanket or cover. ~See also **throwaway, throwback,** etc. [Old English *thrāwan* to turn, torment]

throwaway ('θrəʊə,weɪ) *adj.* **1.** *Chiefly Brit.* said or done incidentally; casual: *a throwaway remark.* **2.** designed to be discarded after use: *a throwaway carton.* ~*n.* **3.** *Chiefly U.S. & Canad.* a handbill. ~*vb.* **throw away. 4.** to get rid of; discard. **5.** to fail to make good use of; waste.

throwback ('θrəʊ,bæk) *n.* **1.** a person, animal, or plant that has the characteristics of an earlier type. ~*vb.* **throw back. 2.** to revert to an earlier type. **3.** (foll. by *on*) to force to depend (on): *the crisis threw her back on her faith in God.*

throw in *vb.* **1.** to add at no additional cost: *the hotel throws in a cooked breakfast.* **2.** to contribute (a remark) in a discussion. **3. throw in the towel** or **sponge.** *Informal.* to give in; accept defeat. ~ *n.* **throw-in. 4.** *Soccer.* the method of putting the ball into play after it has gone out of play, by throwing it towards a teammate.

throw off *vb.* **1.** to free oneself of; discard: *to throw off the yoke of the oppressor.* **2.** to utter in a casual manner: *to throw off a witty remark.*

throw out *vb.* **1.** to discard or reject. **2.** to expel or dismiss, esp. forcibly. **3.** to utter in a casual or indirect manner: *to throw out a hint.*

throw over *vb.* to forsake or abandon; jilt.

throw together *vb.* **1.** to assemble (something) hurriedly. **2.** to cause to become casually acquainted.

throw up *vb.* **1.** *Informal.* to vomit. **2.** to give up; abandon: *he threw up his job.* **3.** to construct (a building or structure) hastily. **4.** to produce: *every generation throws up its own leaders.*

thru (θruː) *prep., adv., adj. Chiefly U.S.* same as **through**.

thrum[1] (θrʌm) *vb.* **thrumming, thrummed. 1.** to strum rhythmically but without expression on (a musical instrument). **2.** to drum incessantly: *rain thrummed on the roof.* ~*n.* **3.** a repetitive strumming. [imit.]

thrum[2] (θrʌm) *n.* **1.** any of the unwoven ends of warp thread remaining on the loom when the web has been removed. **2.** such ends of thread collectively. [Old English]

thrush[1] (θrʌʃ) *n.* any of a large group of songbirds, esp. one having a brown plumage with a spotted breast, such as the mistle thrush and song thrush. [Old English *thrýsce*]

thrush[2] (θrʌʃ) *n.* **1.** a fungal disease, esp. of infants, in which whitish spots form on the mouth, throat, and lips. **2.** a vaginal infection caused by the same fungus. [origin unknown]

thrust (θrʌst) *vb.* **thrusting, thrust. 1.** to push (someone or something) with force. **2.** to force upon (someone) or into (some condition or situation): *they thrust responsibilities upon her; they thrust her into a position of responsibility.* **3.** (foll. by *through*) to pierce; stab. **4.** to make a stab or lunge at. ~*n.* **5.** a forceful drive, push, stab, or lunge. **6.** a force, esp. one that produces motion. **7.** a propulsive force produced by the fluid pressure in a jet engine or rocket engine. **8.** *Physics.* a continuous pressure exerted by one part of an object against another. **9.** *Informal.* intellectual or emotional drive; forcefulness: *a man with thrust and energy.* **10.** the essential or most forceful part: *the thrust of the argument.* [Old Norse *thrysta*]

thud (θʌd) *n.* **1.** a dull heavy sound. **2.** a blow or fall that causes such a sound. ~*vb.* **thudding, thudded. 3.** to make or cause to make such a sound. [Old English *thyddan* to strike]

thug (θʌg) *n.* **1.** a tough and violent man, esp. a criminal. **2.** (*sometimes cap.*) (formerly) a member of an organization of robbers and assassins in India. [Hindi *thag* thief] —**'thuggery** *n.* —**'thuggish** *adj.*

thulium (ˈθjuːlɪəm) *n.* a silvery-grey element of the lanthanide series. Symbol: Tm [after *Thule* a region thought, by ancient geographers, to be northernmost in the world]

thumb (θʌm) *n.* **1.** the first and usually shortest and thickest finger of the hand. **2.** the part of a glove shaped to fit the thumb. **3. all thumbs.** very clumsy. **4. thumbs down.** an indication of refusal or disapproval. **5. thumbs up.** an indication of encouragement or approval. **6. under someone's thumb.** completely under someone else's control. ~*vb.* **7.** to touch, mark, or move with the thumb. **8.** (often foll. by *through*) to flip the pages of (a book or magazine) in order to glance at the contents. **9.** to attempt to obtain (a lift in a motor vehicle) by signalling with the

thumb. **10. thumb one's nose at.** to deride or flout. [Old English *thūma*]

thumb index *n.* a series of notches cut into the fore-edge of a book to facilitate quick reference.

thumbnail (ˈθʌmˌneɪl) *n.* **1.** the nail of the thumb. **2.** (*modifier*) concise and brief: *a thumbnail sketch.*

thumbscrew (ˈθʌmˌskruː) *n.* (formerly) an instrument of torture that pinches or crushes the thumbs.

thump (θʌmp) *n.* **1.** the sound of something heavy hitting a comparatively soft surface. **2.** a heavy blow with the hand. ~*vb.* **3.** to strike or beat heavily; pound. **4.** to throb, beat, or pound violently: *my heart was thumping.* [imit.]

thumping (ˈθʌmpɪŋ) *adj. Slang.* huge or excessive: *a thumping loss.*

thunder (ˈθʌndə) *n.* **1.** a loud cracking or deep rumbling noise caused by the rapid expansion of atmospheric gases that are suddenly heated by lightning. **2.** any loud booming sound. **3. steal someone's thunder.** to lessen the effect of someone's idea or action by anticipating it. ~*vb.* **4.** to make (a loud sound) or utter (words) in a manner suggesting thunder. **5.** to be the case that thunder is being heard: *it is thundering.* **6.** to move fast, heavily, and noisily: *the bus thundered downhill.* [Old English *thunor*] —**'thundery** *adj.*

thunderbolt (ˈθʌndəˌbəʊlt) *n.* **1.** a flash of lightning accompanying thunder. **2.** the imagined agency of destruction produced by a flash of lightning.

thunderclap (ˈθʌndəˌklæp) *n.* **1.** a loud outburst of thunder. **2.** something as violent or unexpected as a clap of thunder.

thundercloud (ˈθʌndəˌklaʊd) *n.* a towering electrically charged cloud associated with thunderstorms.

thundering (ˈθʌndərɪŋ) *adj. Slang.* very great or excessive: *a thundering idiot.*

thunderous (ˈθʌndərəs) *adj.* **1.** threatening; angry. **2.** resembling thunder in loudness.

thunderstorm (ˈθʌndəˌstɔːm) *n.* a storm with thunder and lightning and usually heavy rain or hail.

thunderstruck (ˈθʌndəˌstrʌk) *or* **thunderstricken** (ˈθʌndəˌstrɪkən) *adj.* amazed or shocked.

thurible (ˈθjʊərɪbˈl) *n.* same as **censer**. [Latin *tūribulum* incense]

Thurs. Thursday.

Thursday (ˈθɜːzdɪ) *n.* the fifth day of the week; fourth day of the working week. [Old English *Thursdæg* Thor's day]

thus (ðʌs) *adv.* **1.** in this manner: *do it thus.* **2.** to such a degree: *thus far and no further.* **3.** therefore: *We have failed. Thus we have to take the consequences.* [Old English]

thwack (θwæk) *vb.* **1.** to beat with something flat. ~*n.* **2. a.** a blow with something flat. **b.** the sound made by it. [imit.]

thwart (θwɔːt) *vb.* **1.** to prevent; frustrate: *they thwarted his plan.* ~*n.* **2.** an oarsman's seat lying across a boat. [Old Norse *thvert*]

thy (ðaɪ) *det. Archaic.* belonging to or associated in some way with you (thou): *thy goodness and mercy.* [var. of *thine*]

thyme (taɪm) *n.* a small shrub with white, pink, or red flowers and scented leaves used for seasoning. [Greek *thumon*]

thymol ('θaɪmɒl) *n.* a white crystalline substance obtained from thyme, used as a fungicide, antiseptic, etc.

thymus ('θaɪməs) *n., pl.* **-muses** or **-mi** (-maɪ). a glandular organ situated near the base of the neck. [Greek *thumos* sweetbread]

thyroid ('θaɪrɔɪd) *Anat.* ~*adj.* **1.** of or relating to the thyroid gland. **2.** of or relating to the largest cartilage of the larynx. ~*n.* **3.** the thyroid gland. [Greek *thureos* oblong]

thyroid gland *n. Anat.* an endocrine gland that secretes hormones that control metabolism and body growth.

thyself (ðaɪ'sɛlf) *pron. Archaic.* the reflexive form of **thou**[1].

ti (tiː) *n. Music.* same as **te**.

Ti *Chem.* titanium.

tiara (tɪ'ɑːrə) *n.* **1.** a semicircular jewelled headdress worn by women of high social rank for formal occasions. **2.** a headdress worn by the pope, consisting of a beehive-shaped diadem surrounded by three coronets. [Greek]

tibia ('tɪbɪə) *n., pl.* **tibiae** ('tɪbɪˌiː) *or* **tibias**. the inner and thicker of the two bones of the human leg below the knee; shinbone. [Latin: leg, pipe] —**'tibial** *adj.*

tic (tɪk) *n.* spasmodic twitching of a particular group of muscles. [French]

tick[1] (tɪk) *n.* **1.** a mark (√) used to check off or indicate the correctness of something. **2.** a recurrent metallic tapping or clicking sound, such as that made by a clock. **3.** *Brit. informal.* a moment or instant: *I'll be back in a tick.* ~*vb.* **4.** (often foll. by *off*) to mark or check with a tick. **5.** to produce a recurrent tapping sound or indicate by such a sound: *the clock ticked the minutes away.* **6. what makes someone tick.** *Informal.* the basic motivation of a person. ~See also **tick off, tick over.** [Low German *tikk* touch]

tick[2] (tɪk) *n.* a small parasitic creature typically living on the skin of warm-blooded animals and feeding on the blood and tissues of their hosts. [Old English *ticca*]

tick[3] (tɪk) *n.* **1.** the strong covering of a pillow or mattress. **2.** *Informal.* short for **ticking.** [prob. from Middle Dutch *tike*]

tick[4] (tɪk) *n. Brit. informal.* account or credit: *we bought the furniture on tick.* [from *ticket*]

ticker ('tɪkə) *n. Slang.* the heart.

ticker tape *n.* (formerly) a continuous paper tape on which current stock quotations were printed by machine.

ticket ('tɪkɪt) *n.* **1.** a printed piece of paper or cardboard showing that the holder is entitled to certain rights, such as

travel on a train or bus or entry to a place of public entertainment. **2.** a label or tag attached to an article showing information such as its price and size. **3.** an official notification of a parking or traffic offence. **4.** *Chiefly U.S.* the declared policy of a political party. **5. that's (just) the ticket.** *Informal.* that's the right or appropriate thing. ~*vb.* **6.** to issue or attach a ticket or tickets to. [Old French *etiquet*]

ticking ('tɪkɪŋ) *n.* a strong cotton fabric, often striped, used esp. for mattress and pillow covers. [from TICK[3]]

tickle ('tɪkl̩) *vb.* **1.** to touch or stroke (someone), so as to produce laughter or a twitching sensation. **2.** to delight or entertain: *to tickle someone's fancy.* **3.** to itch or tingle. **4. tickled pink** or **to death.** *Informal.* greatly pleased. ~*n.* **5.** a sensation of light stroking or itching. **6.** the act of tickling. **7.** *Canad.* (in the Atlantic Provinces) a narrow strait. [Middle English *tikelen*]

tickler ('tɪklə) *n. Informal, chiefly Brit.* a difficult problem.

ticklish ('tɪklɪʃ) *adj.* **1.** sensitive to being tickled. **2.** delicate or difficult: *a ticklish situation.* **3.** easily upset or offended.

tick off *vb.* **1.** to mark with a tick. **2.** *Informal, chiefly Brit.* to reprimand (someone).

tick over *vb.* **1.** *Brit.* (of an engine) to run at low speed with the transmission disengaged. **2.** to run smoothly without any major changes: *the business is ticking over nicely.*

ticktack ('tɪkˌtæk) *n. Brit.* a system of sign language, mainly using the hands, by which bookmakers transmit their odds to each other at race courses.

ticktock ('tɪkˌtɒk) *n.* a ticking sound as made by a clock.

tidal ('taɪdl̩) *adj.* **1.** relating to, characterized by, or affected by tides. **2.** dependent on the tide: *a tidal ferry.*

tidal wave *n.* **1.** a name (not in technical use) for **tsunami.** **2.** an unusually large incoming wave, often caused by high winds and spring tides. **3.** a forceful and widespread movement in public opinion, action, etc.

tiddler ('tɪdlə) *n. Brit. informal.* **1.** a very small fish, esp. a stickleback. **2.** a small child. [perhaps from TIDDLY[1]]

tiddly[1] ('tɪdlɪ) *adj.* **-dlier, -dliest.** *Brit.* small; tiny. [childish var. of *little*]

tiddly[2] ('tɪdlɪ) *adj. Slang, chiefly Brit.* slightly drunk. [origin unknown]

tiddlywinks ('tɪdlɪˌwɪŋks) *n.* (functioning as *sing.*) a game in which players try to flick discs of plastic into a cup by pressing them with other larger discs. [origin unknown]

tide (taɪd) *n.* **1.** the alternate rise and fall of sea level caused by the gravitational pull of the sun and moon. **2.** the current, ebb, or flow of water at a specified place resulting from these changes in level: *the tide is coming in.* **3.** a widespread tendency or movement: *the tide of resentment against the government.* **4.** *Archaic except* *in combination.* a season or time: *Christmastide.* ~*vb.* **5.** to be carried with or as if with the tide. **6.** to ebb and flow like the tide. [Old English *tīd* time]

tidemark ('taɪd,mɑːk) *n.* **1.** a mark left by the highest or lowest point of a tide. **2.** *Chiefly Brit.* a mark showing a level reached by a liquid: *a tidemark on the bath.* **3.** *Informal, chiefly Brit.* a dirty mark on the skin, indicating the extent to which someone has washed.

tide over *vb.* to help (someone) to get through (a period of difficulty or distress): *this will tide you over until you get paid.*

tidings ('taɪdɪŋz) *pl. n.* information or news. [Old English *tīdung*]

tidy ('taɪdɪ) *adj.* **-dier, -diest. 1.** characterized by neatness and order. **2.** *Informal.* considerable: *a tidy sum of money.* ~*vb.* **-dying, -died. 3.** (usually foll. by *up*) to put (things) in order; neaten. ~*n.*, *pl.* **-dies. 4.** a small container for odds and ends. [(orig.: timely, excellent) from *tide*] —'**tidily** *adv.* —'**tidiness** *n.*

tie (taɪ) *vb.* **tying, tied. 1.** (often foll. by *up*) to fasten or be fastened with string, rope, etc. **2.** to make (a knot or bow) in (something). **3.** to restrict or limit: *her family commitments have always tied her down.* **4.** to equal (the score) of a competitor or fellow candidate. ~*n.* **5.** a bond, link, or fastening. **6.** a restriction or restraint. **7.** a string, wire, etc., with which something is tied. **8.** a long narrow piece of material worn, esp. by men, under the collar of a shirt, tied in a knot close to the throat with the ends hanging down the front. **9. a.** an equality in score or attainment in a contest. **b.** the match or competition in which the scores or results are equal. **10.** a structural member such as a tie beam. **11.** *Sport, Brit.* a match in a knockout competition: *a cup tie.* **12.** *U.S. & Canad.* a sleeper on a railway track. **13.** *Music.* a curved line connecting two notes of the same pitch indicating that the sound is to be prolonged for their joint time value. ~*See also* **tie in, tie up.** [Old English *tīgan*]

tie beam *n.* a horizontal beam that holds two parts of a structure together, such as one that connects two corresponding rafters in a roof.

tiebreaker ('taɪ,breɪkə) *n.* an extra game or question that decides the result of a contest that has ended in a draw.

tied (taɪd) *adj. Brit.* **1.** (of a public house) obliged to sell only the beer of a particular brewery. **2.** (of a house) rented out to the tenant for as long as he is employed by the owner.

tie-dyeing, tie-dye, *or* **tie and dye** *n.* a method of dyeing textiles to produce patterns by tying sections of the cloth together so that they will not absorb the dye. —'**tie-,dyed** *adj.*

tie in *vb.* **1.** to come or bring into a certain relationship; coordinate. ~*n.* **tie-in. 2.** a link, relationship, or coordination.

tiepin ('taɪ,pɪn) *n.* an ornamental pin used to pin the two ends of a tie to a shirt.

tier (tɪə) *n.* one of a set of rows placed one

above and behind the other, such as theatre seats. [Old French *tire*]

tiercel ('tɪəs'l) *n.* same as **tercel.**

tie up *vb.* **1.** to bind (someone or something) securely with string or rope. **2.** to moor (a vessel). **3.** to commit (funds, etc.) and so make unavailable for other uses. ~*n.* **tie-up. 4.** a link or connection.

tiff (tɪf) *n.* a petty quarrel. [origin unknown]

tiffin ('tɪfɪn) *n.* (in India) a light meal, esp. at midday. [prob. from obs. *tiff* to sip]

tiger ('taɪgə) *n.* **1.** a large Asian mammal of the cat family having a tawny yellow coat with black stripes. **2.** a dynamic, forceful, or cruel person. [Greek *tigris*] —'**tigerish** *or* '**tigrish** *adj.*

tiger lily *n.* a lily of China and Japan with black-spotted orange flowers.

tiger moth *n.* a moth with conspicuously striped and spotted wings.

tight (taɪt) *adj.* **1.** stretched or drawn so as not to be loose; taut: *a tight cord.* **2.** fitting in a close manner. **3.** held, made, fixed, or closed firmly and securely: *a tight knot.* **4.** constructed so as to prevent the passage of water, air, etc. **5.** unyielding or stringent: *to keep a tight hold on resources.* **6.** cramped or constricted: *a tight fit.* **7.** mean or miserly. **8.** difficult and problematic: *a tight situation.* **9.** (of a match or game) very close or even: *a tight race.* **10.** *Informal.* drunk. ~*adv.* **11.** in a close, firm, or secure way. [Old Norse *thēttr* close] —'**tightly** *adv.* —'**tightness** *n.*

tighten ('taɪt'n) *vb.* to make (something) tight or tighter or become tight or tighter.

tightfisted (,taɪt'fɪstɪd) *adj.* mean; miserly.

tightknit (,taɪt'nɪt) *adj.* closely integrated: *a tightknit community.*

tight-lipped *adj.* **1.** unwilling to divulge information. **2.** with the lips pressed tightly together, as through anger.

tightrope ('taɪt,rəʊp) *n.* a rope stretched taut on which acrobats perform.

tights (taɪts) *pl. n.* a one-piece clinging garment covering the body from the waist to the feet, worn by women and also by acrobats, dancers, etc.

tigress ('taɪgrɪs) *n.* **1.** a female tiger. **2.** a fierce, cruel, or passionate woman.

tike (taɪk) *n.* same as **tyke.**

tiki ('tiːkiː) *n.* a Maori greenstone neck ornament in the form of a fetus. [Maori]

tilde ('tɪldə) *n.* a mark (˜) placed over a letter to indicate a nasal sound, as in Spanish *señor.* [Spanish]

tile (taɪl) *n.* **1.** a flat thin slab of fired clay, linoleum, etc., used with others to cover a surface, such as a floor or wall. **2.** a short pipe used with others to form a drain. **3.** a rectangular block used as a playing piece in mahjong and other games. **4. on the tiles.** *Informal.* on a spree, esp. of drinking. ~*vb.* **5.** to cover (a surface) with tiles. [Latin *tēgula*] —'**tiler** *n.*

tiling ('taɪlɪŋ) *n.* **1.** tiles collectively. **2.** something made of or surfaced with tiles.

till[1] (tıl) *conj., prep.* short for **until**. [Old English *til*]

till[2] (tıl) *vb.* to cultivate and work (land) for the raising of crops. [Old English *tilian* to try, obtain] —**'tillable** *adj.* —**'tiller** *n.*

till[3] (tıl) *n.* a box or drawer into which money taken from customers is put, now usually part of a cash register. [origin unknown]

tillage ('tılıdʒ) *n.* **1.** the act, process, or art of tilling. **2.** tilled land.

tiller ('tılə) *n. Naut.* a handle used to turn the rudder when steering a boat. [Anglo-French *teiler* beam of a loom]

tilt (tılt) *vb.* **1.** to incline at an angle. **2.** to attack or overthrow (a person) in a tilt or joust. **3.** (often foll. by *at*) to aim or thrust: *to tilt a lance.* ~*n.* **4.** a slope or angle: *at a tilt.* **5.** the act of tilting. **6.** (esp. in medieval Europe) **a.** a jousting contest. **b.** a thrust with a lance delivered during a tournament. **7.** any dispute or contest. **8. (at) full tilt.** at full speed or force. [Old English *tealtian*]

tilth (tılθ) *n.* **1.** the tilling of land. **2.** the condition of land that has been tilled.

timber ('tımbə) *n.* **1.** wood, esp. when regarded as building material. **2.** trees collectively. **3.** a piece of wood used in a structure. **4.** *Naut.* a frame in a wooden vessel. [Old English] —**'timbered** *adj.* —**'timbering** *n.*

timber limit *n. Canad.* **1.** the area to which rights of cutting timber, granted by a government licence, are limited. **2.** same as **timber line**.

timber line *n.* the geographical limit beyond which trees will not grow.

timbre ('tımbə, 'tæmbə) *n.* the distinctive quality of a sound produced by a particular voice or musical instrument. [French]

timbrel ('tımbrəl) *n. Chiefly biblical.* a tambourine. [Old French]

Timbuktu (ˌtımbʌk'tuː) *n.* any distant or outlandish place: *from here to Timbuktu.* [after *Timbuktu*, town in Africa]

time (taım) *n.* **1.** the continuous passage of existence in which events pass from a state of potentiality in the future, through the present, to a state of finality in the past. **2.** *Physics.* a quantity measuring duration, with reference to the rotation of the earth or from the vibrations of certain atoms. **3.** a specific point in time expressed in hours and minutes: *the time is four o'clock.* **4.** a system of reckoning for expressing time: *Greenwich Mean Time.* **5.** an unspecified interval; a while: *I was there for a time.* **6.** (*often pl.*) a period or point marked by specific attributes or events: *the Victorian times.* **7.** a sufficient interval or period: *have you got time to help me?* **8.** an instance or occasion: *I called you three times.* **9.** an occasion or period of specified quality: *have a good time.* **10.** a suitable moment: *it's time I told you.* **11.** (*pl.*) indicating an amount calculated by multiplication with the number specified: *ten times three is thirty.* **12.** *Brit.* the time at which licensed premises are legally obliged to stop selling alcoholic drinks. **13. a.** a customary or full period of work. **b.** the rate of pay for this period. **14. a.** the system of combining beats in music into successive groupings by which the rhythm of the music is established. **b.** a specific system having a specific number of beats in each grouping or bar: *duple time.* **15. against time.** in an effort to complete something in a limited period. **16. ahead of time.** before the deadline. **17. at one time. a.** once; formerly. **b.** simultaneously. **18. at the same time. a.** simultaneously. **b.** nevertheless; however. **19. at times.** sometimes. **20. beat time.** to indicate the tempo of a piece of music by waving a baton, hand, etc. **21. do time.** to serve a term in jail. **22. for the time being.** for the moment; temporarily. **23. from time to time.** at intervals; occasionally. **24. have no time for.** to have no patience with; not tolerate. **25. in no time.** very quickly. **26. in one's own time. a.** outside paid working hours. **b.** at one's own rate. **27. in time. a.** early or at the appointed time. **b.** eventually: *in time he'll see sense.* **c.** *Music.* at a correct metrical or rhythmical pulse. **28. make time.** to find an opportunity. **29. on time.** at the expected or scheduled time. **30. pass the time of day.** to exchange casual greetings (with an acquaintance). **31. time and again.** frequently. **32. time of one's life.** a memorably enjoyable time. **33. time out of mind.** from time immemorial. **34.** (*modifier*) operating automatically at or for a set time: *time lock; time switch.* ~*vb.* **35.** to measure the duration or speed of: *to time a race.* **36.** to set a time for. ~*interj.* **37.** the word called out by a publican signalling that it is closing time. [Old English *tīma*]

time and a half *n.* a rate of pay one and a half times the normal rate, often offered for overtime work.

time and motion study *n.* the analysis of work procedures to determine the most efficient methods of operation.

time bomb *n.* a bomb containing a timing mechanism that determines when it will explode.

time capsule *n.* a container holding articles representative of the current age, buried for discovery in the future.

time clock *n.* a clock with a device for recording the time of arrival or departure of an employee.

time exposure *n.* a photograph produced by exposing film for a relatively long period, usually a few seconds.

time-honoured *adj.* having been observed for a long time and sanctioned by custom.

timekeeper ('taımˌkiːpə) *n.* **1.** a person or thing that keeps or records time. **2.** an employee who maintains a record of the hours worked by the other employees. **3.** an employee whose record of punctuality is of a specified nature: *a bad timekeeper.* —**'time,keeping** *n.*

timeless ('taımlıs) *adj.* **1.** unaffected or unchanged by time; ageless. **2.** eternal. —**'timelessness** *n.*

timely ('taɪmlɪ) adj. **-lier, -liest,** adv. at the right or an appropriate time.

time-out n. **1.** Sport, chiefly U.S. & Canad. an interruption in play during which players rest, discuss tactics, etc. **2. take time out.** to take a break from a job or activity.

timepiece ('taɪm,piːs) n. a device, such as a clock or watch which measures and indicates time.

timer ('taɪmə) n. a device for measuring time, esp. a switch or regulator that causes a mechanism to operate at a specific time.

timeserver ('taɪm,sɜːvə) n. a person who compromises and changes his opinions to gain support or favour.

time sharing n. **1.** a system of part ownership of a property for use as a holiday home whereby each participant owns the property for a particular period every year. **2.** a system by which users at different terminals of a computer can communicate with it at the same time.

time signature n. Music. a sign usually consisting of two figures placed after the key signature, that indicates the tempo.

timetable ('taɪm,teɪbʰl) n. **1.** a list of departure and arrival times of trains or buses. **2.** a chart of the period allotted to different subjects at a school or college. **3.** a plan of the times when a job or activity should be done.

time value n. Music. the duration of a note relative to other notes in a composition and considered in relation to the basic tempo.

timeworn ('taɪm,wɔːn) adj. **1.** showing the adverse effects of overlong use or of old age. **2.** hackneyed; trite.

time zone n. a region throughout which the same standard time is used.

timid ('tɪmɪd) adj. **1.** easily frightened or upset; shy. **2.** indicating shyness or fear. [Latin timēre to fear] —**ti'midity** or **'timidness** n. —**'timidly** adv.

timing ('taɪmɪŋ) n. the regulation of actions or remarks in relation to others to produce the best effect, as in music or in the theatre.

timorous ('tɪmərəs) adj. **1.** fearful or timid. **2.** indicating fear or timidity. [Latin timor fear] —**'timorously** adv.

timpani or **tympani** ('tɪmpənɪ) pl. n. (sometimes functioning as sing.) a set of kettledrums. [Italian] —**'timpanist** or **'tympanist** n.

tin (tɪn) n. **1.** a soft silvery-white metallic element. Symbol: Sn **2.** an airtight metal container used for preserving and storing food or drink. **3.** any container made of metallic tin. **4.** Also called: **tinful.** the contents of a tin. **5.** Brit., Austral., & N.Z. galvanized iron: a tin roof. ~vb. **tinning, tinned. 6.** to put (food) into a tin or tins. [Old English]

tin can n. a metal food container, esp. when empty.

tincture ('tɪŋktʃə) n. **1.** a medicinal extract in a solution of alcohol. **2.** a tint or tinge. **3.** a slight trace. ~vb. **4.** to tint or colour. [Latin tinctūra a dyeing]

tinder ('tɪndə) n. dry wood or other easily combustible material used for lighting a fire. [Old English tynder] —**'tindery** adj.

tinderbox ('tɪndə,bɒks) n. a small box for tinder, esp. one fitted with a flint and steel.

tine (taɪn) n. a slender prong of a fork or a deer's antler. [Old English tind] —**tined** adj.

tinfoil ('tɪn,fɔɪl) n. a paper-thin sheet of metal, used for wrapping foodstuffs.

ting (tɪŋ) n. a high metallic sound such as that made by a small bell. [imit.]

ting-a-ling ('tɪŋə'lɪŋ) n. the sound of a small bell.

tinge (tɪndʒ) n. **1.** a slight tint or colouring. **2.** a very small amount; hint. ~vb. **tingeing** or **tinging, tinged. 3.** to colour or tint faintly. **4.** to give a slight trace to: her thoughts were tinged with nostalgia. [Latin tingere to colour]

tingle ('tɪŋgʰl) vb. **1.** to feel or cause to feel a prickling or stinging sensation of the flesh, as from cold or excitement. ~n. **2.** a feeling of tingling. [prob. a var. of tinkle] —**'tingling** adj. —**'tingly** adj.

tin god n. a self-important person.

tinker ('tɪŋkə) n. **1.** (esp. formerly) a travelling mender of pots and pans. **2.** Scot. & Irish. a Gypsy. **3.** a mischievous person, esp. a child. ~vb. **4.** (foll. by with) to meddle with something, such as a car engine, esp. while undertaking repairs. **5.** to mend (pots and pans) as a tinker. [origin unknown]

tinker's damn or **cuss** n. Slang. the slightest heed: I don't give a tinker's damn what she says, I'm going anyway.

tinkle ('tɪŋkʰl) vb. **1.** to ring with a high tinny sound like a small bell. **2.** to cause to tinkle. ~n. **3.** a high clear ringing sound. **4.** Brit. informal. a telephone call. [imit.] —**'tinkly** adj.

tinny ('tɪnɪ) adj. **-nier, -niest. 1.** of or resembling tin. **2.** cheap or shoddy. **3.** (of a sound) high, thin, and metallic.

tin-opener n. a small tool for opening tins.

tin plate n. thin steel sheet coated with a layer of tin to protect it from corrosion.

tinpot ('tɪn,pɒt) adj. Brit. informal. **1.** inferior, cheap, or worthless. **2.** petty; unimportant: a tinpot little dictatorship.

tinsel ('tɪnsəl) n. **1.** a decoration consisting of a piece of metallic thread with thin strips of metal foil attached along its length. **2.** anything cheap, showy, and gaudy. ~adj. **3.** made of or decorated with tinsel. **4.** showily but cheaply attractive; gaudy. [Latin scintilla a spark] —**'tinselly** adj.

tinsmith ('tɪn,smɪθ) n. a person who works with tin or tin plate.

tint (tɪnt) n. **1.** a shade of a colour, esp. a pale one. **2.** a colour that is softened by the addition of white. **3.** a dye for the hair. **4.** a trace or hint. ~vb. **5.** to give a tint to (something, such as hair). [Latin tingere to colour]

tintinnabulation (,tɪntɪ,næbjʊ'leɪʃən) n.

the ringing or pealing of bells. [Latin *tintinnāre* to tinkle]

tiny (ˈtaɪnɪ) *adj.* **tinier, tiniest.** very small. [origin unknown]

tip¹ (tɪp) *n.* **1.** a narrow or pointed end of something. **2.** the top or summit. **3.** a small piece forming an end: *a metal tip on a cane.* ~*vb.* **tipping, tipped. 4.** to adorn or mark the tip of. [Old Norse *typpa*]

tip² (tɪp) *vb.* **tipping, tipped. 1.** to tilt. **2. tip over.** to tilt so as to overturn or fall. **3.** *Brit.* to dump (rubbish). ~*n.* **4.** a tipping or being tipped. **5.** *Brit.* a dump for rubbish. [origin unknown]

tip³ (tɪp) *n.* **1.** an amount of money given to someone, such as a waiter, in return for service. **2.** a helpful hint or warning. **3.** a piece of inside information, esp. in betting or investing. ~*vb.* **tipping, tipped. 4.** to give a tip to. [origin unknown]

tip⁴ (tɪp) *vb.* **tipping, tipped. 1.** to hit or strike lightly. ~*n.* **2.** a light blow. [origin unknown]

tip-off *n.* **1.** a warning or hint, esp. given confidentially and based on inside information. ~*vb.* **tip off. 2.** to give a hint or warning to.

tippet (ˈtɪpɪt) *n.* a scarflike piece of fur, often made from the whole skin of a dead animal, worn around a woman's shoulders. [prob. from TIP¹]

tipple (ˈtɪpʰl) *vb.* **1.** to make a habit of taking (alcoholic drink), esp. in small quantities. ~*n.* **2.** alcoholic drink. [origin unknown] —ˈ**tippler** *n.*

tipstaff (ˈtɪpˌstɑːf) *n.* **1.** a court official. **2.** a metal-tipped staff formerly used as a symbol of office.

tipster (ˈtɪpstə) *n.* a person who sells tips as to people betting on horse races or speculating on the stock market.

tipsy (ˈtɪpsɪ) *adj.* **-sier, -siest.** slightly drunk. [from TIP²] —ˈ**tipsiness** *n.*

tiptoe (ˈtɪpˌtəʊ) *vb.* **-toeing, -toed. 1.** to walk quietly with the heels off the ground. ~*n.* **2. on tiptoe.** on the tips of the toes or on the ball of the foot and the toes. ~*adv.* **3.** on tiptoe.

tiptop (ˈtɪpˈtɒp) *adj., adv.* **1.** at the highest point of health, excellence, etc. ~*n.* **2.** the best in quality.

tip-up *adj.* able to be turned upwards around a hinge or pivot: *a tip-up seat.*

TIR International Road Transport. [French *Transports Internationaux Routiers*]

tirade (taɪˈreɪd) *n.* a long angry speech or denunciation. [French]

tire¹ (ˈtaɪə) *vb.* **1.** to reduce the energy of, as by exertion; weary. **2.** to become wearied or bored; flag. [Old English *tēorian*] —ˈ**tiring** *adj.*

tire² (ˈtaɪə) *n., vb. U.S.* same as **tyre.**

tired (ˈtaɪəd) *adj.* **1.** weary; fatigued. **2.** no longer fresh; hackneyed: *the same tired old jokes.*

tireless (ˈtaɪəlɪs) *adj.* unable to be tired. —ˈ**tirelessly** *adv.*

tiresome (ˈtaɪəsəm) *adj.* boring and irritating.

tiro (ˈtaɪrəʊ) *n., pl.* **-ros.** same as **tyro.**

'tis (tɪz) *Poetic or dialect.* it is.

tissue (ˈtɪsjuː, ˈtɪʃuː) *n.* **1.** a group of cells in an animal or plant having a similar structure and function. **2.** a thin piece of soft absorbent paper used as a disposable handkerchief, towel, etc. **3.** See **tissue paper. 4.** an interwoven series: *a tissue of lies.* **5.** a woven cloth, esp. of a light gauzy nature. [Old French *tissu* woven cloth]

tissue paper *n.* very thin soft delicate paper used esp. to wrap breakable goods.

tit¹ (tɪt) *n.* any of various small European songbirds, such as the bluetit, that feed on insects and seeds. [Middle English *tite* little]

tit² (tɪt) *n.* **1.** *Slang.* a female breast. **2.** a teat or nipple. [Old English *titt*]

titan (ˈtaɪtʰn) *n.* a person of great strength or size. [after *Titans*, a family of gods in Greek myth.]

titanic (taɪˈtænɪk) *adj.* possessing or requiring colossal strength: *a titanic battle.*

titanium (taɪˈteɪnɪəm) *n.* a strong white metallic element used in the manufacture of strong lightweight alloys, esp. aircraft parts. Symbol: Ti [from *titan*]

titbit (ˈtɪtˌbɪt) *or esp. U.S.* **tidbit** *n.* **1.** a tasty small piece of food. **2.** a pleasing scrap of scandal. [origin unknown]

titfer (ˈtɪtfə) *n. Brit. slang.* a hat. [rhyming slang *tit for tat*]

tit for tat *n.* an equivalent given in return or retaliation; blow for blow. [earlier *tip for tap*]

tithe (taɪð) *n.* **1.** (*often pl.*) a tenth part of the annual produce of one's land or of one's annual income paid to support the church or clergy. **2.** a tenth or very small part of anything. ~*vb.* **3.** to exact or demand a tithe from. **4.** to pay a tithe or tithes. [Old English *teogoth*] —ˈ**tithable** *adj.*

tithe barn *n.* a large barn where, formerly, the agricultural tithe of a parish was stored.

Titian (ˈtɪʃən) *adj.* reddish-yellow. [from *Titian* Italian painter, because he often used this hair colour in his paintings]

titillate (ˈtɪtɪˌleɪt) *vb.* **1.** to arouse or excite pleasurably. **2.** to tickle. [Latin *titillāre*] —ˈ**titilˌlating** *adj.* —ˌtitilˈlation** *n.*

titivate (ˈtɪtɪˌveɪt) *vb.* to smarten up; spruce up. [perhaps from *tidy* & *cultivate*] —ˌtitiˈvation** *n.*

title (ˈtaɪtʰl) *n.* **1.** the distinctive name of a work of art, musical, or literary composition, etc. **2.** a descriptive name or heading of a section of a book, speech, etc. **3.** See **title page. 4.** a name or epithet signifying rank, office, or function. **5.** a formal designation, such as *Mr.* **6.** *Sport.* a championship. **7.** *Law.* the legal right to possession of property. [Latin *titulus*]

title deed *n.* a document containing evidence of a person's legal right or title to property, esp. a house or land.

titleholder (ˈtaɪtʰlˌhəʊldə) *n.* a person who holds a title, esp. a sporting championship.

title page *n.* the page in a book that gives the title, author, publisher, etc.

title role *n.* the role of the character after whom a play or film is named.

titmouse ('tɪt,maʊs) *n., pl.* **-mice.** same as **tit**[1]. [Middle English *tite* little + *mouse*]

titrate ('taɪtreɪt) *vb. Chem.* to measure the volume or concentration of (a solution) by titration. [French *titrer*]

titration (taɪ'treɪʃən) *n. Chem.* an operation in which a measured amount of one solution is added to a known quantity of another solution until the reaction between the two is complete. If the concentration of one solution is known, that of the other can be calculated.

titter ('tɪtə) *vb.* **1.** to snigger, esp. derisively or in a suppressed way. ~*n.* **2.** a suppressed laugh or snigger. [imit.]

tittle ('tɪt'l) *n.* a jot; particle. [Latin *titulus* title]

tittle-tattle *n.* **1.** idle chat or gossip. ~*vb.* **2.** to chatter or gossip.

tittup ('tɪtəp) *vb.* **-tupping, -tupped** or *U.S.* **-tuping, -tuped.** **1.** to prance or frolic. ~*n.* **2.** a caper. [prob. imit.]

titular ('tɪtjʊlə) *adj.* **1.** of a title. **2.** in name only: *a titular leader.* **3.** bearing a title.

tizzy ('tɪzɪ) *n., pl.* **-zies.** *Informal.* a state of confusion or excitement. [origin unknown]

T-junction *n.* a road junction in which one road joins another at right angles but does not cross it.

Tl *Chem.* thallium.

Tm *Chem.* thulium.

TN Tennessee.

TNT *n.* 2,4,6-trinitrotoluene; a yellow solid: used chiefly as a high explosive.

to (tuː; *unstressed* tʊ, tə) *prep.* **1.** used to indicate the destination of the subject or object of an action: *he climbed to the top.* **2.** used to mark the indirect object of a verb: *telling stories to children.* **3.** used to mark the infinitive of a verb: *he wanted to go.* **4.** as far as; until: *working from Monday to Friday.* **5.** used to indicate equality: *16 ounces to the pound.* **6.** against; upon; onto: *put your ear to the wall.* **7.** before the hour of: *five to four.* **8.** accompanied by: *dancing to loud music.* **9.** as compared with, as against: *the score was eight to three.* **10.** used to indicate a resulting condition: *they starved to death.* ~*adv.* **11.** towards a fixed position, esp. (of a door) closed. [Old English *tō*]

toad (təʊd) *n.* **1.** a tailless amphibian with a dry warty skin, that lives on moist land. **2.** a loathsome person. [Old English *tādige*]

toadflax ('təʊd,flæks) *n.* a perennial plant with yellow-orange flowers.

toad-in-the-hole *n. Brit.* a dish made of sausages baked in a batter.

toadstool ('təʊd,stuːl) *n.* a fungus with a caplike top that is poisonous. Cf. **mushroom.**

toady ('təʊdɪ) *n., pl.* **toadies. 1.** a person who flatters and ingratiates himself in a fawning way. ~*vb.* **toadying, toadied. 2.** to fawn on and flatter (someone). [shortened from *toadeater*, orig. a quack's assis-

tant who pretended to eat toads, hence a flatterer] —'**toadyism** *n.*

to and fro *adv., adj. also* **to-and-fro. 1.** back and forth. **2.** here and there. —**toing and froing** *n.*

toast[1] (təʊst) *n.* **1.** sliced bread browned by exposure to heat. ~*vb.* **2.** to brown (bread) under a grill or over a fire. **3.** to warm or be warmed: *to toast one's hands by the fire.* [Latin *tōstus* parched]

toast[2] (təʊst) *n.* **1.** a proposal of health or success given to a person or thing and marked by people raising glasses and drinking together. **2.** a person or thing so honoured. ~*vb.* **3.** to propose or drink a toast to (a person or thing). [from the spiced toast formerly put in wine]

toaster ('təʊstə) *n.* an electrical device for toasting bread.

toastmaster ('təʊst,mɑːstə) *n.* a person who introduces speakers and proposes toasts at public dinners. —'**toast,mistress** *fem. n.*

tobacco (tə'bækəʊ) *n., pl.* **-cos** or **-coes.** an American plant with large leaves which are dried and prepared for snuff, chewing, or smoking. [Spanish *tabaco*]

tobacconist (tə'bækənɪst) *n. Chiefly Brit.* a person or shop that sells tobacco, cigarettes, pipes, etc.

-to-be *adj.* about to be; future: *a mother-to-be; the bride-to-be.*

toboggan (tə'bɒgən) *n.* **1.** a long narrow sledge used for sliding over snow and ice. ~*vb.* **2.** to ride on a toboggan. [American Indian]

toby ('təʊbɪ) *n., pl.* **-bies.** *N.Z.* a water stopcock at the boundary of a street and house section. [origin unknown]

toby jug *n.* a beer mug or jug in the form of a stout seated man wearing a three-cornered hat and smoking a pipe. [from the name *Tobias*]

toccata (tə'kɑːtə) *n.* a composition for the organ, harpsichord, or piano, usually in a rhythmically free style. [Italian]

Toc H ('tɒk 'eɪtʃ) *n.* a society formed after World War I to encourage Christian comradeship. [from initials of *Talbot House,* Poperinge, Belgium, its original headquarters]

tocsin ('tɒksɪn) *n.* **1.** a warning signal. **2.** an alarm bell. [French]

tod (tɒd) *n.* **on one's tod.** *Brit. slang.* alone. [rhyming slang *Tod Sloan/alone*]

today (tə'deɪ) *n.* **1.** this day, as distinct from yesterday or tomorrow. **2.** the present age: *women of today.* ~*adv.* **3.** during or on this day. **4.** nowadays. [Old English *tō dæge,* lit.: on this day]

toddle ('tɒd'l) *vb.* **1.** to walk with short unsteady steps, as a child. **2.** (foll. by *off*) *Jocular.* to depart: *I'll toddle off now.* ~*n.* **3.** a toddling. [origin unknown]

toddler ('tɒdlə) *n.* a young child, usually between the ages of one and two and a half.

toddy ('tɒdɪ) *n., pl.* **-dies.** a drink made from spirits, esp. whisky, hot water, sugar, and usually lemon juice. [Hindi *tārī* juice of the palmyra palm]

to-do (tə'duː) *n., pl.* **-dos.** a commotion, fuss, or quarrel.

toe (təʊ) *n.* **1.** any one of the digits of the foot. **2.** the part of a shoe or sock covering the toes. **3. on one's toes.** alert. **4. tread on someone's toes.** to offend a person, esp. by trespassing on his field of responsibility. ~*vb.* **toeing, toed. 5.** to touch or kick with the toe. **6. toe the line.** to conform to expected attitudes or standards. [Old English *tā*]

toecap ('təʊˌkæp) *n.* a reinforced covering for the toe of a boot or shoe.

toehold ('təʊˌhəʊld) *n.* **1.** a small space on a rock, mountain, etc., for supporting the toe of the foot in climbing. **2.** any means of gaining access, support, etc.

toff (tɒf) *n. Brit. slang.* a well-dressed or upper-class person. [perhaps from *tuft*, nickname for a commoner at Oxford University]

toffee ('tɒfɪ) *n.* **1.** a sweet made from sugar or treacle boiled with butter, nuts, etc. **2. for toffee.** (preceded by *can't*) *Informal.* to be incompetent at: *he can't sing for toffee.* [earlier *taffy*]

toffee-apple *n.* an apple fixed on a stick and coated with a thin layer of toffee.

toffee-nosed *adj. Slang, chiefly Brit.* pretentious or supercilious; used esp. of snobbish people.

tofu ('təʊˌfuː) *n.* unfermented soya-bean curd: a food with a soft cheeselike consistency. [Japanese]

tog (tɒg) *Informal.* ~*vb.* **togging, togged. 1.** (often foll. by *up* or *out*) to dress oneself, esp. in smart clothes. ~*n.* **2.** (*pl.*) clothes. [prob. from *toga*]

toga ('təʊgə) *n.* a garment worn by citizens of ancient Rome, consisting of a piece of cloth draped around the body. [Latin] —'**togaed** *adj.*

together (tə'gɛðə) *adv.* **1.** with cooperation between members, etc.: *we worked together.* **2.** in or into contact with each other: *to stick papers together.* **3.** in or into one place; with each other: *the people are gathered together.* **4.** at the same time: *we left school together.* **5.** considered collectively: *all our wages put together couldn't buy that car.* **6.** continuously: *working for eight hours together.* **7.** *Informal.* organized: *to get things together.* **8. together with.** in addition to. ~*adj.* **9.** *Slang.* self-possessed, competent, and well-organized. [Old English *tōgædre*]

togetherness (tə'gɛðənɪs) *n.* a feeling of closeness or affection from being united with other people.

toggle ('tɒg'l) *n.* **1.** a peg or rod at the end of a rope or chain for fastening by insertion through an eye in another rope or chain. **2.** a bar-shaped button inserted through a loop for fastening. [origin unknown]

toggle joint *n.* a device consisting of two arms pivoted at a common joint and at their outer ends and used to apply pressure by straightening the angle between the two arms.

toggle switch *n.* **1.** an electric switch with a projecting lever that is moved in a particular way to open or close a circuit. **2.** a computer device used to turn a feature on or off.

toheroa (ˌtəʊə'rəʊə) *n.* a large edible bivalve mollusc of New Zealand with a distinctive flavour. [Maori]

tohunga ('təʊhʊŋə) *n. N.Z.* a Maori priest. [Maori]

toil (tɔɪl) *n.* **1.** hard or exhausting work. ~*vb.* **2.** to work hard; labour. **3.** to progress with slow painful movements. [Anglo-French *toiler* to struggle]

toilet ('tɔɪlɪt) *n.* **1. a.** a bowl fitted with a water-flushing device and connected to a drain, for receiving and disposing of urine and faeces. **b.** a room with such a fitment. **2.** the act of dressing and preparing oneself. [French *toilette* dress]

toilet paper *n.* thin absorbent paper used for cleaning oneself after defecation or urination.

toiletry ('tɔɪlɪtrɪ) *n., pl.* **-ries.** an object or cosmetic used in making up, dressing, etc.

toilette (twɑː'lɛt) *n.* same as **toilet** (sense 2). [French]

toilet water *n.* a form of liquid perfume lighter than cologne.

toilsome ('tɔɪlsəm) *adj.* requiring hard work; laborious.

token ('təʊkən) *n.* **1.** a symbol, sign, or indication of something: *as a token of affection.* **2.** a memento. **3.** a gift voucher that can be used as payment for goods of a specified value. **4.** a metal or plastic disc, such as a substitute for currency for use in a slot machine. **5.** (*modifier*) as a matter of form only; nominal: *a token increase in salary.* [Old English *tācen*]

tokenism ('təʊkəˌnɪzəm) *n.* the practice of making only a token effort or doing no more than the minimum, esp. in order to comply with a law. —'**tokenist** *adj.*

token strike *n.* a brief stoppage of work intended to convey strength of feeling on a disputed issue.

told (təʊld) *vb.* past of **tell**[1].

tolerable ('tɒlərəb'l) *adj.* **1.** able to be tolerated; endurable. **2.** *Informal.* fairly good. —'**tolerably** *adv.*

tolerance ('tɒlərəns) *n.* **1.** the quality of accepting other people's rights to their own opinions, beliefs, or actions. **2.** capacity to endure something, esp. pain or hardship. **3.** the permitted variation in some characteristic of an object or workpiece. **4.** *Med.* the capacity to endure the effects of a continued or increasing dose of a drug, poison, etc.

tolerant ('tɒlərənt) *adj.* **1.** able to tolerate the beliefs, actions, etc., of others. **2.** able to withstand extreme amounts of heat and cold.

tolerate ('tɒləˌreɪt) *vb.* **1.** to treat (someone) with generous respect. **2.** to permit (something) to happen. **3.** to put up with (someone or something). [Latin *tolerāre* to sustain]

toleration (ˌtɒləˈreɪʃən) n. 1. the act or practice of tolerating. 2. freedom to hold religious opinions that differ from the established religion of a country.

toll¹ (təʊl) vb. 1. to ring (a bell) slowly and recurrently. 2. to announce by tolling: *the bells tolled the Queen's death.* ~n. 3. the act or sound of tolling. [origin unknown]

toll² (təʊl, tɒl) n. 1. a charge for the use of certain roads and bridges. 2. loss or damage incurred through a disaster: *the war took its toll of the inhabitants.* [Old English *toln*]

tollgate (ˈtəʊlˌgeɪt, ˈtɒl-) n. a gate across a toll road or bridge at which travellers must pay.

tollie (ˈtɒlɪ) n. S. African. a castrated calf. [Xhosa]

tolu (tɒˈluː) n. an aromatic balsam obtained from a South American tree, used in medicine and perfume. [after *Santiago de Tolu*, Colombia]

toluene (ˈtɒljʊˌiːn) n. a flammable liquid obtained from petroleum and coal tar and used as a solvent and in the manufacture of dyes, explosives, etc. [previously obtained from tolu]

tom (tɒm) n. the male of various animals, esp. the cat. [from *Thomas*]

tomahawk (ˈtɒməˌhɔːk) n. a fighting axe used by the North American Indians. [American Indian]

tomato (təˈmɑːtəʊ) n., pl. -toes. a soft fruit that grows on a South American plant, eaten in salads, as a vegetable, etc. [S American Indian *tomatl*]

tomb (tuːm) n. 1. a place for the burial of a corpse. 2. a monument to the dead. 3. **the tomb.** Poetic. death. [Greek *tumbos*]

tombola (tɒmˈbəʊlə) n. Brit. a type of lottery, in which tickets are drawn from a revolving drum. [Italian]

tomboy (ˈtɒmˌbɔɪ) n. a girl who behaves or plays like a boy.

tombstone (ˈtuːmˌstəʊn) n. a gravestone.

tome (təʊm) n. a large heavy book. [Greek *tomos* a slice]

tomfoolery (ˌtɒmˈfuːlərɪ) n. foolish behaviour.

Tommy (ˈtɒmɪ) n., pl. -mies. Brit. informal. a private in the British Army. [orig. *Thomas Atkins*, name used in specimen copies of official forms]

Tommy gun n. a type of .45-calibre submachine-gun. [in full *Thompson submachine-gun*, from the name of the manufacturer]

tommyrot (ˈtɒmɪˌrɒt) n. utter nonsense.

tomorrow (təˈmɒrəʊ) n. 1. the day after today. 2. the future. ~adv. 3. on the day after today. 4. at some time in the future. [Old English *tō morgenne*]

Tom Thumb n. a dwarf; midget. [after *Tom Thumb*, the tiny hero of folk tales]

tomtit (ˈtɒmˌtɪt) n. Brit. a small European bird that eats insects and seeds.

tom-tom n. a drum usually beaten with the hands as a signalling instrument. [Hindi *tamtam*]

ton¹ (tʌn) n. 1. Brit. a unit of weight equal to 2240 pounds or 1016.046 909 kilograms. 2. U.S. & Canad. a unit of weight equal to 2000 pounds or 907.184 kilograms. 3. See **metric ton.** ~adv. 4. tons. much: *the new flat is tons better than the old one.* [var. of *tun*]

ton² (tʌn) n. Slang, chiefly Brit. a hundred miles per hour, as on a motorcycle. [special use of TON¹]

tonal (ˈtəʊnʲl) adj. of or relating to tone or tonality.

tonality (təʊˈnælɪtɪ) n., pl. -ties. 1. Music. the presence of a musical key in a composition. 2. the overall scheme of colours and tones in a painting.

tone (təʊn) n. 1. sound with reference to quality, pitch, or volume. 2. U.S. & Canad. same as **note** (sense 9). 3. Music. an interval of a major second; whole tone. 4. the quality or character of a sound: *a nervous tone of voice.* 5. general aspect, quality, or style: *I didn't like the tone of her speech.* 6. high quality or style: *to lower the tone of a place.* 7. the quality of a given colour, as modified by mixture with white or black; shade; tint. 8. Physiol. the natural firmness of the tissues and normal functioning of bodily organs in health. ~vb. 9. (often foll. by *with*) to be of a matching or similar tone (to). 10. to give a tone to or correct the tone of. [Greek *tonos*] —'**toneless** adj. —'**tonelessly** adv.

tone-deaf adj. unable to distinguish subtle differences in musical pitch.

tone down vb. to moderate or become moderated in tone: *to tone down an argument.*

tone poem n. Music. an extended orchestral composition based on nonmusical material, such as a work of literature or a fairy tale.

tone up vb. to make or become more vigorous, healthy, etc.: *exercise tones up the muscles.*

tong (tɒŋ) n. (formerly) a secret society of Chinese Americans. [Chinese (Cantonese) *t'ong* meeting place]

tongs (tɒŋz) pl. n. a tool for grasping or lifting, consisting of a hinged or pivoted pair of arms. [pl. of Old English *tange*]

tongue (tʌŋ) n. 1. a movable mass of muscular tissue attached to the floor of the mouth. It is used in tasting, eating, and (in man) speaking. 2. the tongue of certain animals used as food. 3. a language, dialect, or idiom: *the English tongue.* 4. the ability to speak: *to lose one's tongue.* 5. a manner of speaking: *a glib tongue.* 6. a narrow strip of land that extends into a body of water. 7. a flap of leather on a shoe. 8. the clapper of a bell. 9. a projecting strip along an edge of a board that is made to fit a groove in another board. 10. **hold one's tongue.** to keep quiet. 11. **on the tip of one's tongue.** about to come to mind. 12. **with (one's) tongue in (one's) cheek.** with insincere or ironical intent. [Old English *tunge*]

tongue-tie n. a congenital condition in which movement of the tongue is limited as the result of an abnormally short fold of skin under the tongue.

tongue-tied *adj.* speechless, esp. with embarrassment or shyness.

tongue twister *n.* a sentence or phrase that is difficult to say clearly and quickly, such as *Peter Piper picked a peck of pickled pepper.*

tonguing (ˈtʌŋɪŋ) *n.* a technique of playing a wind instrument by obstructing and uncovering the air passage through the lips with the tongue.

tonic (ˈtɒnɪk) *n.* **1.** a medicine that improves the functioning of the body or increases the feeling of wellbeing. **2.** anything that enlivens or strengthens. **3.** Also called: **tonic water.** a carbonated beverage containing quinine and often mixed with alcoholic drinks. **4.** *Music.* the first degree of a major or minor scale and the tonal centre of a piece composed in a particular key. ~*adj.* **5.** serving to enliven and invigorate: *a tonic wine.* **6.** *Music.* of the first degree of a major or minor scale. [Greek *tonikos* concerning tone]

tonic sol-fa *n.* a method of teaching music, by which syllables are used as names for the notes of the major scale in any key.

tonight (təˈnaɪt) *n.* **1.** the night or evening of this present day. ~*adv.* **2.** in or during the night or evening of this day. [Old English *tōniht*]

tonnage (ˈtʌnɪdʒ) *n.* **1.** the capacity of a merchant ship expressed in tons. **2.** the weight of the cargo of a merchant ship. **3.** the total amount of shipping of a port or nation.

tonne (tʌn) *n.* a unit of mass equal to 1000 kg or 2204.6 pounds. [French]

tonsil (ˈtɒnsəl) *n.* either of two small oval lumps of spongy tissue situated one on each side of the back of the mouth. [Latin *tōnsillae* (pl.) tonsils] —**ˈtonsillar** *adj.*

tonsillectomy (ˌtɒnsɪˈlɛktəmɪ) *n., pl.* **-mies.** surgical removal of the tonsils. [*tonsil* + Greek *-tomia* a cutting]

tonsillitis (ˌtɒnsɪˈlaɪtɪs) *n.* inflammation of the tonsils.

tonsorial (tɒnˈsɔːrɪəl) *adj. Often facetious.* of a barber or his trade. [Latin *tondēre* to shave]

tonsure (ˈtɒnʃə) *n.* **1.** (in certain religions and monastic orders) **a.** the shaving of the head or the crown of the head only. **b.** the part of the head left bare by shaving. ~*vb.* **2.** to shave the head of. [Latin *tōnsūra* a clipping] —**ˈtonsured** *adj.*

ton-up *adj. Brit. informal.* **1.** (esp. of a motorcycle) capable of speeds of a hundred miles per hour. **2.** liking to travel at such speeds: *a ton-up boy.*

too (tuː) *adv.* **1.** as well; also: *can I come too?* **2.** in or to an excessive degree: *I have too many things to do.* **3.** extremely: *you're too kind.* **4.** *U.S. & Canad. informal.* used to reinforce a command: *you will too do it!* [Old English *tō*]

took (tʊk) *vb.* the past tense of **take.**

tool (tuːl) *n.* **1. a.** an implement, such as a hammer, saw, or spade, that is used by hand. **b.** a power-driven instrument; machine tool. **2.** the cutting part of such an instrument. **3.** a person used to perform dishonourable or unpleasant tasks for another. **4.** a necessary medium for one's profession: *numbers are the tools of the mathematician's trade.* ~*vb.* **5.** to work, cut, or form (something) with a tool. **6.** (often foll. by *up*) to furnish with tools. [Old English *tōl*]

tool-maker *n.* a person who specializes in the production or reconditioning of machine tools. —**ˈtool-ˌmaking** *n.*

toot (tuːt) *vb.* **1.** to give or cause to give (a short blast, hoot, or whistle). ~*n.* **2.** the sound made by or as if by a horn, whistle, etc. **3.** *U.S. & Canad. slang.* a drinking spree. [imit.]

tooth (tuːθ) *n., pl.* **teeth** (tiːθ). **1.** any of various bonelike structures set in the jaws of most vertebrates and used for biting, tearing, or chewing. **2.** anything resembling a tooth in shape, prominence, or function: *the tooth of a comb.* **3.** taste or appetite: *a sweet tooth.* **4. long in the tooth.** old or ageing. **5. tooth and nail.** with ferocity and force: *we fought tooth and nail.* [Old English *tōth*] —**ˈtoothless** *adj.*

toothache (ˈtuːθˌeɪk) *n.* a pain in or about a tooth.

toothbrush (ˈtuːθˌbrʌʃ) *n.* a small brush with a long handle, for cleaning the teeth.

toothpaste (ˈtuːθˌpeɪst) *n.* a paste used for cleaning the teeth, applied with a toothbrush.

toothpick (ˈtuːθˌpɪk) *n.* a small wooden or plastic stick used for extracting pieces of food from between the teeth.

tooth powder *n.* a powder used for cleaning the teeth, applied with a toothbrush.

toothsome (ˈtuːθsəm) *adj.* of delicious or appetizing appearance, flavour, or smell.

toothy (ˈtuːθɪ) *adj.* **toothier, toothiest.** having or showing numerous, large, or projecting teeth: *a toothy grin.*

tootle (ˈtuːtᵊl) *vb.* **1.** to hoot softly or repeatedly. ~*n.* **2.** a soft hoot or series of hoots.

top[1] (tɒp) *n.* **1.** the highest point or part of anything: *the top of a hill.* **2.** the most important or successful position: *the top of the class.* **3.** a lid, cap, or other device that covers the uppermost part of anything. **4.** the highest degree or point: *at the top of his career.* **5.** the most important person: *he's the top of this organization.* **6.** the loudest or highest pitch: *she was shouting at the top of her voice.* **7.** a garment, esp. for a woman, that extends from the shoulders to the waist or hips. **8.** the part of a plant that is above ground: *carrot tops.* **9.** same as **top gear. 10. off the top of one's head.** without previous preparation or careful thought: *I'll give you the estimate off the top of my head.* **11. on top of. a.** in addition to: *on top of his accident, he lost his job.* **b.** *Informal.* in complete control of: *I'm on top of the problem now.* **12. over the top. a.** over the edge of a trench. **b.** lacking restraint or a sense of proportion. ~*adj.* **13.** of, relating to, serving as,

or situated on the top. ~*vb.* **topping,
topped. 14.** to form a top on (something):
to top a cake with cream. **15.** to reach or
pass the top of. **16.** to be at the top of: *he
tops the team.* **17.** to exceed or surpass:
the fund topped five hundred pounds.
~See also **top off, top out,** etc. [Old
English *topp*]

top[2] (tɒp) *n.* **1.** a toy that is spun on its
pointed base. **2. sleep like a top.** to sleep
very soundly. [Old English]

topaz ('təupæz) *n.* a hard glassy yellow,
pink, or colourless mineral used in making
jewellery. [Greek *topazos*]

top brass *n.* (*functioning as pl.*) the most
important or high-ranking officials or leaders.

topcoat ('tɒp,kəut) *n.* **1.** an overcoat. **2.**
a final coat of paint applied to a surface.

top dog *n. Informal.* the leader or chief
of a group.

top drawer *n.* people of the highest social
standing.

top dressing *n.* a layer of fertilizer or
manure spread on the surface of land.
—'**top-,dress** *vb.*

tope[1] (təup) *vb.* to drink (alcohol) usually
in large quantities. [perhaps from French
toper to take a bet] —'**toper** *n.*

tope[2] (təup) *n.* a small grey shark of European coastal waters. [origin unknown]

topee *or* **topi** ('təupiː, -pɪ) *n., pl.* **-pees** *or*
-pis. same as **pith helmet.** [Hindi *topī*
hat]

top-flight *adj.* of superior or excellent
quality.

topgallant (,tɒp'gælənt; *Naut.* tə'gælənt)
n. **1.** a mast or sail above a topmast. **2.**
(*modifier*) of or relating to a topgallant.

top gear *n.* the highest forward ratio of a
gearbox in a motor vehicle.

top hat *n.* a man's hat with a tall cylindrical crown and narrow brim, now worn for
some formal occasions.

top-heavy *adj.* unstable through being
overloaded at the top.

topiary ('təupɪərɪ) *adj.* **1.** of or relating to
the trimming of trees or bushes into artificial decorative shapes. ~*n.* **2.** topiary
work. the art of topiary. [Latin *topia*
decorative garden work] —'**topiarist** *n.*

topic ('tɒpɪk) *n.* a subject of a speech,
book, conversation, etc. [Greek *topos*
place]

topical ('tɒpɪk[ə]l) *adj.* of or relating to
current affairs. —**topicality** (,tɒpɪ'kælɪtɪ)
n. —'**topically** *adv.*

topknot ('tɒp,nɒt) *n.* a crest, tuft, decorative bow, chignon, etc., on the top of the
head.

topless ('tɒplɪs) *adj.* **1.** having no top. **2.**
denoting or wearing a costume which has
no covering for the breasts.

top-level *n.* (*modifier*) of, involving, or
by those on the highest level of influence
or authority: *top-level talks.*

topmast ('tɒp,mɑːst; *Naut.* 'tɒpməst) *n.*
the mast next above a lower mast on a
sailing vessel.

topmost ('tɒp,məust) *adj.* at or nearest the
top.

topnotch ('tɒp'nɒtʃ) *adj. Informal.* excellent; superb: *a topnotch actress.*

top off *vb.* to finish or complete, esp. with
some decisive action.

topography (tə'pɒɡrəfɪ) *n., pl.* **-phies. 1.**
the study or description of the surface
features of a region, such as its hills,
valleys, or rivers. **2.** the representation of
these features on a map. **3.** the surveying
of a region's surface features. [Greek *topos* a place + -GRAPHY] —to'**pographer** *n.*
—**topographical** (,tɒpə'ɡræfɪk[ə]l) *adj.*

topology (tə'pɒlədʒɪ) *n.* a branch of geometry describing the properties of a figure
that are unaffected by continuous distortion. [Greek *topos* a place + -LOGY]
—**topological** (,tɒpə'lɒdʒɪk[ə]l) *adj.*

top out *vb.* to place the highest stone on (a
building).

topper ('tɒpə) *n. Informal.* a top hat.

topping ('tɒpɪŋ) *n.* **1.** a sauce or garnish
for food. ~*adj.* **2.** *Brit. slang.* excellent;
splendid.

topple ('tɒp[ə]l) *vb.* **1.** to tip over or cause
(something) to tip over, esp. from a height.
2. to overthrow; oust: *to topple a government.* [from TOP[1] (*vb.*)]

tops (tɒps) *Slang.* ~*n.* **1. the tops.** a
person or thing of top quality. ~*adj.* **2.**
excellent.

topsail ('tɒp,seɪl; *Naut.* 'tɒpsəl) *n.* a square
sail carried on a yard set on a topmast.

top-secret *adj.* (of military or government information) classified as needing the
highest level of secrecy and security.

topside ('tɒp,saɪd) *n.* **1.** *Brit. & N.Z.* a
lean cut of beef from the thigh containing
no bone. **2.** (*often pl.*) the part of a ship's
sides above the water line.

topsoil ('tɒp,sɔɪl) *n.* the surface layer of
soil.

topsy-turvy ('tɒpsɪ'tɜːvɪ) *adj.* **1.** upside
down. **2.** in a state of confusion. ~*adv.*
3. in a topsy-turvy manner. [prob. *top* +
obs. *tervy* to turn upside down]

top up *vb. Brit.* **1.** to refill (a container),
usually to the brim: *he topped up the petrol
tank before he left.* **2.** to provide extra
money, provisions, etc. to make (the total
amount) sufficient: *to top up students'
grants with loans.*

toque (təuk) *n.* **1.** a woman's small round
brimless hat. **2.** *Canad.* a knitted cap with
a round tassel on top. [French]

tor (tɔː) *n.* a high hill, esp. a bare rocky one.
[Old English *torr*]

Torah ('təurə) *n.* the whole body of traditional Jewish teaching, including the Oral
Law. [Hebrew: precept]

torch (tɔːtʃ) *n.* **1.** a small portable electric
lamp powered by batteries. **2.** a wooden
shaft dipped in wax or tallow and set
alight. **3.** anything regarded as a source of
enlightenment, guidance, etc.: *the torch of
learning.* **4. carry a torch for.** to be in
love with someone, esp. unrequitedly. [Old
French *torche* handful of twisted straw]

tore (tɔː) *vb.* the past tense of **tear**[2].

toreador ('tɒrɪəˌdɔː) n. a bullfighter, esp. on horseback. [Spanish]

torero (tɒ'rɛərəʊ) n., pl. **-ros.** a bullfighter, esp. on foot. [Spanish]

torment vb. (tɔː'mɛnt). **1.** to cause (someone) great pain, suffering, or anguish; torture. **2.** to tease or pester (a person or animal) in an annoying or cruel way: *don't torment the dog.* ~n. ('tɔːmɛnt). **3.** physical or mental pain. **4.** a source of pain, worry, or annoyance. [Latin *tormentum*] —**tor'mentor** n.

tormentil ('tɔːməntɪl) n. a perennial plant with yellow flowers. [Old French *tormentille*]

torn (tɔːn) vb. **1.** the past participle of **tear**[2]. ~adj. **2.** split or cut. **3.** divided or undecided, in preference: *torn between staying and leaving.*

tornado (tɔː'neɪdəʊ) n., pl. **-does** or **-dos.** a rapidly whirling column of air, usually characterized by a dark funnel-shaped cloud causing damage along its path. [Spanish *tronada* thunderstorm]

torpedo (tɔː'piːdəʊ) n., pl. **-does.** **1.** a cylindrical self-propelled weapon carrying explosives that is launched from aircraft, ships, or submarines and follows an underwater path to hit its target. ~vb. **-doing, -doed. 2.** to attack or hit (a ship) with one or a number of torpedoes. **3.** to destroy or wreck: *to torpedo the administration's plan.* [Latin: crampfish (whose electric discharges can cause numbness)]

torpedo boat n. (formerly) a small high-speed warship for torpedo attacks.

torpid ('tɔːpɪd) adj. **1.** sluggish or dull: a *torpid mind.* **2.** (of a hibernating animal) dormant. **3.** unable to move or feel. [Latin *torpēre* to be numb] —**tor'pidity** n.

torpor ('tɔːpə) n. drowsiness and apathy.

torque (tɔːk) n. **1.** a force that causes rotation around a central point such as an axle. **2.** an ancient Celtic necklace or armband made of twisted metal. [Latin *torquēs* necklace & *torquēre* to twist]

torr (tɔː) n., pl. **torr.** a unit of pressure equal to one millimetre of mercury. [after E. *Torricelli*, physicist]

torrent ('tɒrənt) n. **1.** a fast or violent stream, esp. of water. **2.** a rapid flow of questions, abuse, etc. [Latin *torrēns*] —**torrential** (tɒ'rɛnʃəl) adj.

torrid ('tɒrɪd) adj. **1.** so hot and dry as to parch or scorch. **2.** arid or parched. **3.** highly charged emotionally: a *torrid love scene.* [Latin *torrēre* to scorch]

torsion ('tɔːʃən) n. the twisting of a part by equal forces being applied at both ends but in opposite directions. [Latin *torquēre* to twist] —**torsional** adj.

torso ('tɔːsəʊ) n., pl. **-sos.** **1.** the trunk of the human body. **2.** a statue of a nude human trunk, esp. without the head or limbs. [Italian: stalk, stump]

tort (tɔːt) n. Law. a civil wrong or injury, independent of any contract, for which an action for damages may be brought. [Latin *torquēre* to twist]

tortilla (tɔː'tiːə) n. Mexican cookery. a kind of thin pancake made from corn meal. [Spanish]

tortoise ('tɔːtəs) n. a toothless land reptile with a heavy dome-shaped shell and clawed limbs. [Medieval Latin *tortūca*]

tortoiseshell ('tɔːtəsˌʃɛl) n. **1.** the horny yellow-and-brown mottled shell of a sea turtle: used for making ornaments and jewellery. **2.** a domestic cat with black, cream, and brownish markings. **3.** a butterfly which has orange-brown wings with black markings. **4.** (modifier) made of tortoiseshell.

tortuous ('tɔːtjʊəs) adj. **1.** twisted or winding: a *tortuous road.* **2.** devious or cunning: a *tortuous argument.*

torture ('tɔːtʃə) vb. **1.** to cause (someone) extreme physical pain, esp. to extract information, etc.: *to torture prisoners.* **2.** to cause (someone) mental anguish. ~n. **3.** physical or mental anguish. **4.** the practice of torturing a person. **5.** a cause of mental agony. [Latin *torquēre* to twist] —**'torturer** n. —**'torturous** adj.

Tory ('tɔːrɪ) n., pl. **-ries.** **1.** a member of the Conservative Party in Great Britain or Canada. **2.** History. a member of the English political party that supported the Church and Crown and traditional political structures and opposed the Whigs. ~adj. **3.** of or relating to Tories. **4.** (sometimes *not cap.*) ultraconservative or reactionary. [Irish *tōraidhe* outlaw] —**'Toryism** n.

toss (tɒs) vb. **1.** to throw (something) lightly. **2.** to fling or be flung about, esp. in an violent way: a *ship tosses in a storm.* **3.** to coat (food) with a dressing by gentle stirring or mixing: *to toss the salad.* **4.** (of a horse) to throw (its rider). **5.** (of an animal) to butt with the head or the horns and throw into the air. **6.** to move (one's head) suddenly backwards, as in impatience. **7.** to toss up a coin with (someone) in order to decide something. ~n. **8.** the act or an instance of tossing. **9.** the act of tossing up a coin. See **toss up. 10.** a fall from a horse. [Scandinavian]

toss off vb. **1.** to perform, write, etc., quickly and easily: *she tossed off a letter to Jim.* **2.** to finish (a drink) in one swallow.

toss up vb. **1.** to spin (a coin) in the air in order to decide between alternatives by guessing which side will fall uppermost. ~n. **toss-up. 2.** an instance of tossing up a coin. **3.** Informal. an even chance or risk: *it was a toss-up who would get there first.*

tot[1] (tɒt) n. **1.** a young child; toddler. **2.** a small measure of spirits. [origin unknown]

tot[2] (tɒt) vb. **totting, totted.** (usually foll. by *up*) Chiefly Brit. to add (numbers) together. [from *total*]

total ('təʊt'l) n. **1.** the whole, esp. regarded as the sum of a number of parts. ~adj. **2.** complete: a *total failure.* **3.** being or related to a total: *the total number of passengers.* ~vb. **-talling, -talled** or U.S. **-taling, -taled. 4.** to amount to: *to total six pounds.* **5.** to add up: *to total a list of prices.* [Latin *tōtus* all] —**'totally** adv.

totalitarian (təʊˌtælɪ'tɛərɪən) adj. of a dictatorial one-party government. —**to,tali'tarianism** n.

totality (təʊˈtælɪtɪ) n., pl. **-ties**. **1.** the whole amount. **2.** the state of being total.

totalizator (ˈtəʊtˈlaɪˌzeɪtə), **totalizer** or **totalisator**, **totaliser** n. a machine to operate a system of betting on a racecourse in which money is paid out to the winners in proportion to their stakes.

tote¹ (təʊt) vb. Informal. **1.** to carry or wear (a gun). **2.** to carry, convey, or drag. [origin unknown]

tote² (təʊt) n. (usually preceded by the) Informal. short for **totalizator.**

tote bag n. a large handbag or shopping bag.

totem (ˈtəʊtəm) n. **1.** (esp. among North American Indians) an object or animal symbolizing a clan or family. **2.** a representation of such an object. [American Indian] —**totemic** (təʊˈtɛmɪk) adj. —ˈto-tem₁ism n.

totem pole n. a pole carved or painted with totemic figures set up by certain North American Indians as a tribal symbol.

totter (ˈtɒtə) vb. **1.** to move in an unsteady manner. **2.** to sway or shake as if about to fall. **3.** to be failing, unstable, or precarious: the wartime Liberal Government was tottering. ~n. **4.** the act or an instance of tottering. [origin unknown]

toucan (ˈtuːkən) n. a tropical American fruit-eating bird with a large brightly coloured bill. [Portuguese tucano]

touch (tʌtʃ) n. **1.** the sense by which the texture and other qualities of objects can be experienced when they come in contact with a part of the body surface, esp. the tips of the fingers. **2.** the quality of an object as perceived by this sense; feel. **3.** the act or an instance of something coming into contact with the body. **4.** a gentle push, tap, or caress. **5.** a small amount; hint: a touch of sarcasm. **6.** any slight stroke or mark. **7.** characteristic style: the artist had a distinctive touch. **8.** a detail of some work: she added a few finishing touches to the book. **9.** a slight attack: a touch of the flu. **10. in touch.** aware of a situation or in contact with someone. **11.** the technique of fingering a keyboard instrument. **12.** Slang. **a.** the act of asking for money. **b.** a person asked for money: she was an easy touch. ~vb. **13.** to cause or permit a part of the body to come into contact with (someone or something). **14.** to tap, feel, or strike (someone or something). **15.** to come or cause (something) to come into contact with (something else). **16.** to be in contact with (someone). **17.** to move or disturb by handling: someone's touched my desk. **18.** to have an effect on: the war scarcely touched our town. **19.** to produce an emotional response in: she was touched by his sad story. **20.** to eat or drink: she doesn't touch alcohol. **21.** (foll. by on) to allude to briefly or in passing: the speech touched on several subjects. **22.** to compare to in quality or attainment; equal or match: there's no-one to touch her. **23.** Slang. to ask (someone) for a loan or gift of money. ~See also **touchdown, touch off, touch up.** [Old French tochier]

touch and go adj. risky or critical: it was touch and go whether we would be in time; a touch-and-go situation.

touchdown (ˈtʌtʃˌdaʊn) n. **1.** the moment at which a landing aircraft or spacecraft comes into contact with the landing surface. ~vb. **touch down. 2.** (of an aircraft or spacecraft) to land.

touché (tuːˈʃeɪ) interj. **1.** an acknowledgment of a scoring hit in fencing. **2.** an acknowledgment of the striking home of a remark or witty reply. [French, lit.: touched]

touched (tʌtʃt) adj. **1.** moved to sympathy or emotion: I was touched by their generosity. **2.** showing slight insanity: she's a bit touched.

touching (ˈtʌtʃɪŋ) adj. **1.** arousing tender feelings. ~prep. **2.** on the subject of; relating to.

touch judge n. one of the two linesmen in rugby.

touchline (ˈtʌtʃˌlaɪn) n. either of the lines marking the side of the playing area in certain games, such as rugby.

touch off vb. **1.** to cause to explode, as by touching with a match. **2.** to cause (a disturbance, violence, etc.) to begin.

touchpaper (ˈtʌtʃˌpeɪpə) n. paper soaked in saltpetre for firing gunpowder.

touchstone (ˈtʌtʃˌstəʊn) n. **1.** a standard by which judgment is made. **2.** a hard dark stone that is used to test gold and silver from the streak they produce on it.

touch-type vb. to type without looking at the keyboard. —ˈtouch-ˌtypist n.

touch up vb. to enhance, renovate, or falsify by putting extra touches to: touch up a photograph.

touchwood (ˈtʌtʃˌwʊd) n. something, esp. dry wood or fungus material, used as tinder. [touch in the sense: to kindle]

touchy (ˈtʌtʃɪ) adj. **touchier, touchiest. 1.** easily upset or irritated. **2.** requiring careful and tactful handling: a touchy subject. —ˈtouchiness n.

tough (tʌf) adj. **1.** strong or resilient; durable: a tough material. **2.** not tender: a tough steak. **3.** hardy and fit. **4.** rough or pugnacious: a tough gangster. **5.** resolute or intractable: a tough employer. **6.** difficult or troublesome to do or deal with: a tough problem. **7.** Informal. unfortunate or unlucky: it's tough on him. ~n. **8.** a rough, vicious, or pugnacious person. [Old English tōh] —ˈtoughness n.

toughen (ˈtʌfən) vb. to make or become tough or toughen.

toupee (ˈtuːpeɪ) n. a hairpiece worn by men to cover a bald place. [French toupet forelock]

tour (tʊə) n. **1.** an extended journey visiting places of interest along the route. **2.** Mil. a period of service, esp. in one place. **3.** a trip, as by a theatre company, to perform in several places. **4.** an overseas trip made by a cricket team, rugby team, etc., to play in several places. ~vb. **5.** to make a tour of (a place). [Old French: turn]

tour de force (ˌtʊə də ˈfɔːs) n., pl. **tours de force.** a masterly or brilliant stroke, creation, effect, or accomplishment. [French, lit.: feat of skill or strength]

tourism ('tʊərɪzəm) *n.* tourist travel, esp. when regarded as an industry.

tourist ('tʊərɪst) *n.* **1.** a person who travels for pleasure, usually sightseeing and staying in hotels. **2.** a person on an excursion or sightseeing tour. **3.** the lowest class of accommodation on a passenger ship. ~*adj.* **4.** of the lowest class of accommodation on a passenger ship.

touristy ('tʊərɪstɪ) *adj. Informal, often disparaging.* full of tourists or tourist attractions.

tourmaline ('tʊəmə,liːn) *n.* a hard crystalline mineral used in jewellery and electrical equipment. [German *Turmalin*]

tournament ('tʊənəmənt) *n.* **1.** a sporting competition in which contestants play a series of games to determine an overall winner. **2.** *Medieval history.* Also: **tourney.** a contest in which mounted knights fought for a prize. [Old French *torneiement*]

tournedos ('tʊənə,dəʊ) *n., pl.* **-dos** (-,dəʊz). a thick round steak of beef. [French]

tourniquet ('tʊənɪ,keɪ) *n. Med.* any device for constricting an artery of the arm or leg to control bleeding. [French]

tousle ('taʊzªl) *vb.* to tangle, ruffle, or disarrange (hair or clothes). [Low German *tūsen* to shake]

tout (taʊt) *vb.* **1.** to solicit (business, customers, etc.) or try to sell (goods), esp. in a persistent manner. **2.** to spy on racehorses being trained in order to obtain information for betting purposes. ~*n.* **3.** a person who sells tickets for a heavily booked event at inflated prices. [Old English *tȳtan* to peep]

tow¹ (təʊ) *vb.* **1.** to pull or drag (a vehicle), esp. by means of a rope or cable. ~*n.* **2.** the act or an instance of towing. **3. in tow. a.** (of a vehicle) being towed. **b.** in one's charge or under one's influence: *he arrived with his children in tow.* **4. on tow.** (of a vehicle) being towed. [Old English *togian*]

tow² (təʊ) *n.* the coarse and broken fibres of hemp, flax, jute, etc., prepared for spinning. [Old English *tōw*] —**'towy** *adj.*

towards (tə'wɔːdz, tɔːdz) *prep.* **1.** in the direction of: *towards London.* **2.** with regard to: *her feelings towards me.* **3.** as a contribution to: *money towards a new car.* **4.** just before: *towards noon.* ~Also: **toward.**

towbar ('təʊ,bɑː) *n.* a rigid metal bar or frame used for towing vehicles.

towel ('taʊəl) *n.* **1.** a piece of absorbent cloth or paper used for drying things. **2. throw in the towel.** See **throw in** (sense 3). ~*vb.* **-elling, -elled** or *U.S.* **-eling, -eled. 3.** to dry or wipe with a towel. [Old French *toaille*]

towelling or *U.S.* **toweling** ('taʊəlɪŋ) *n.* an absorbent fabric used esp. for making towels.

tower ('taʊə) *n.* **1.** a tall, usually square or circular structure, sometimes part of a larger building and usually built for a

specific purpose. **2.** a place of defence or retreat. **3. tower of strength.** a person who supports or comforts someone else at a time of difficulty. ~*vb.* **4.** to be or rise like a tower; loom. [Latin *turris*]

towering ('taʊərɪŋ) *adj.* **1.** very tall; lofty. **2.** very intense: *a towering rage.*

towhead ('təʊ,hɛd) *n.* **1.** a person with blond or yellowish hair. **2.** a head of such hair. [*tow* flax] —,**tow'headed** *adj.*

town (taʊn) *n.* **1.** a densely populated urban area, typically smaller than a city and larger than a village. **2.** a city, borough, or other urban area. **3.** the nearest town or commercial district. **4.** London or the chief city of an area. **5.** the people of a town. **6. go to town.** to make a supreme or unrestricted effort. **7. on the town.** seeking out entertainments and amusements. [Old English *tūn* village]

town clerk *n.* (in Britain until 1974) the chief administrative officer of a town.

town crier *n.* (formerly) a person employed to make public announcements in the streets.

townee (taʊ'niː) or **townie** ('taʊnɪ) *n. Informal, often disparaging.* a resident in a town, esp. as distinct from country dwellers.

town gas *n.* coal gas manufactured for domestic and industrial use.

town hall *n.* a large building in a town often containing the council offices and a hall for public meetings.

town house *n.* **1.** a terraced house in an urban area, esp. a fashionable one. **2.** a person's town residence as distinct from his country residence.

town planning *n.* the comprehensive planning of the physical and social development of a town.

township ('taʊnʃɪp) *n.* **1.** a small town. **2.** (in the U.S. and Canada) a territorial area, esp. a subdivision of a county: often organized as a unit of local government. **3.** (in Canada) a land-survey area, usually 36 square miles (93 square kilometres). **4.** (in South Africa) a planned urban settlement of Black Africans or Coloureds. **5.** *English history.* any of the local districts of a large parish.

townsman ('taʊnzmən) *n., pl.* **-men.** an inhabitant of a town. —'**towns,woman** *fem. n.*

townspeople ('taʊnz,piːpªl) or **townsfolk** ('taʊnz,fəʊk) *pl. n.* the people of a town; citizens.

towpath ('təʊ,pɑːθ) *n.* a path beside a canal or river, used by people or animals towing boats.

towrope ('təʊ,rəʊp) *n.* a rope or cable used for towing a vehicle or vessel.

toxaemia or *U.S.* **toxemia** (tɒk'siːmɪə) *n.* **1.** a condition characterized by the presence of bacterial toxins in the blood. **2.** a condition in pregnant women characterized by high blood pressure. [Greek *toxikon* poison + *haima* blood] —**tox'aemic** or *U.S.* **tox'emic** *adj.*

toxic ('tɒksɪk) *adj.* **1.** of or caused by a toxin or poison. **2.** harmful or deadly.

[Greek *toxikon* (*pharmakon*) (poison) used on arrows] —**toxicity** (tɒkˈsɪsɪtɪ) *n.*

toxicology (ˌtɒksɪˈkɒlədʒɪ) *n.* the branch of science concerned with poisons, their effects, antidotes, etc. —**toxicological** (ˌtɒksɪkəˈlɒdʒɪkᵊl) *adj.* —**toxiˈcologist** *n.*

toxin (ˈtɒksɪn) *n.* **1.** any of various poisonous substances produced by microorganisms and causing certain diseases. **2.** any other poisonous substance of plant or animal origin.

toy (tɔɪ) *n.* **1.** an object designed to be played with, esp. by children. **2.** any small thing of little value; trifle. **3.** a miniature variety of a breed of dog. ~*vb.* **4.** (usually foll. by *with*) to play, fiddle, or flirt. [origin unknown]

toy boy *n.* the much younger male lover of an older woman.

trace[1] (treɪs) *n.* **1.** a mark, footprint, or other sign that a person, animal, or thing has been in a place. **2.** a scarcely detectable amount or characteristic: *a trace of humour.* **3.** any line drawn by a recording instrument or a record consisting of a number of such lines. **4.** something drawn, such as a tracing. ~*vb.* **5.** to follow, discover, or ascertain the course or development of (something). **6.** to track down and find, as by following a trail. **7.** to copy (a design, map, etc.) by drawing over the lines visible through a superimposed sheet of transparent paper. **8.** to outline or sketch (an idea, etc.). **9.** (usually foll. by *back*) to date back: *his ancestors trace back to the 16th century.* [French *tracier*] —**ˈtraceable** *adj.*

trace[2] (treɪs) *n.* **1.** either of the two side straps that connect a horse's harness to the vehicle being pulled. **2. kick over the traces.** to escape or defy control. [Old French *trait*]

trace element *n.* a chemical element that occurs in very small amounts in soil, water, etc., and is essential for healthy growth.

tracer (ˈtreɪsə) *n.* **1.** a projectile that can be observed when in flight by the burning of chemical substances in its base. **2.** *Med.* an element or other substance introduced into the body to study metabolic processes.

tracer bullet *n.* a round of small arms ammunition containing a tracer.

tracery (ˈtreɪsərɪ) *n., pl.* **-eries.** **1.** a pattern of interlacing lines, esp. as used in a stained glass window. **2.** any fine lacy pattern resembling this.

trachea (trəˈkiːə) *n., pl.* **-cheae** (-ˈkiːiː). *Anat., zool.* the tube that carries inhaled air from the throat to the lungs; windpipe. [Greek]

tracheotomy (ˌtrækɪˈɒtəmɪ) *n., pl.* **-mies.** surgical incision into the trachea, as performed when the air passage has been blocked. [*trachea* + Greek *-tomia* a cutting]

trachoma (trəˈkəʊmə) *n.* a chronic contagious disease of the eye characterized by inflammation of the inner surface of the lids and the formation of scar tissue. [Greek *trakhōma* roughness]

tracing (ˈtreɪsɪŋ) *n.* **1.** a copy of something, such as a map, made by tracing. **2.** a line traced by a recording instrument.

track (træk) *n.* **1.** the mark or trail left by something that has passed by. **2.** any road or path, esp. a rough one. **3.** a rail or pair of parallel rails on which a vehicle, such as a train, runs. **4.** a course of action, thought, etc.: *don't start on that track again!* **5.** an endless band on the wheels of a tank to enable it to move across rough ground. **6.** a course for running or racing. **7.** any of a number of separate sections on either side of a gramophone record. **8. keep** (*or* **lose**) **track of.** to follow (*or* fail to follow) the course or progress of someone or something. **9. off the track.** away from what is correct or true. ~*vb.* **10.** to follow the trail of (a person or animal). **11.** to follow the flight path of (a satellite, etc.) by picking up signals transmitted or reflected by it. **12.** *Film.* to follow (a moving object) while filming. [Old French *trac*] —**ˈtracker** *n.*

track down *vb.* to find (someone or something) by tracking or pursuing.

tracker dog *n.* a dog specially trained to search for missing people.

track event *n.* a competition in athletics, such as sprinting, that takes place on a running track.

track record *n. Informal.* the past record of the accomplishments and failures of a person or organization.

tracks (træks) *pl. n.* **1.** (*sometimes sing.*) a mark, such as footprint, left by someone or something that has passed. **2. in one's tracks.** on the very spot where one is standing: *the screams stopped him dead in his tracks.* **3. make tracks.** to leave or depart: *it's late, I'd better make tracks.*

track shoe *n.* a light running shoe fitted with steel spikes for better grip.

tracksuit (ˈtrækˌsuːt) *n.* a warm suit worn by athletes, etc., esp. during training.

tract[1] (trækt) *n.* **1.** an extended area, as of land. **2.** *Anat.* a system of organs or glands that has a particular function: *the digestive tract.* [Latin *tractus* a stretching out]

tract[2] (trækt) *n.* a pamphlet, esp. a religious one. [Latin *tractātus*]

tractable (ˈtræktəbᵊl) *adj.* easily controlled, managed, or dealt with: *a tractable child; tractable materials.* [Latin *tractāre* to manage] —**ˌtractaˈbility** *n.*

traction (ˈtrækʃən) *n.* **1.** the act of pulling, esp. by engine power. **2.** *Med.* the application of a steady pull on a limb using a system of weights and pulleys or splints. **3.** adhesive friction, as between a wheel of a motor vehicle and the road. [Latin *tractus* dragged]

traction engine *n.* a steam-powered locomotive used, esp. formerly, for drawing heavy loads along roads or over rough ground.

tractor (ˈtræktə) *n.* a motor vehicle with large rear wheels, used to pull heavy loads, esp. farm machinery. [Late Latin: one who pulls]

trade (treɪd) n. 1. the buying and selling of goods and services. 2. a personal occupation, esp. a craft requiring skill. 3. the people and practices of an industry, craft, or business. 4. exchange of one thing for something else. 5. the regular customers of a firm: *open for the breakfast trade.* 6. amount of custom or commercial dealings; business: *brisk trade.* 7. a specified market or business: *the tailoring trade.* ~vb. 8. to buy and sell (merchandise). 9. to exchange (one thing) for another. 10. to engage in trade. 11. to deal or do business (with). [Low German: track, hence, a regular business] —'tradable *or* 'tradeable *adj.*

trade-in n. 1. a used article given in part payment for the purchase of a new article. ~vb. **trade in.** 2. to give (a used article) as part payment for a new article.

trademark ('treɪd,mɑːk) n. 1. **a.** the name or other symbol used by a manufacturer to distinguish his products from those of competitors. **b. Registered Trademark.** one that is officially registered and legally protected. 2. any distinctive sign or mark of a person or thing.

trade name n. 1. the name used by a trade to refer to a product or range of products. 2. the name under which a commercial enterprise operates in business.

trade-off n. an exchange, esp. as a compromise.

trade on vb. to exploit or take advantage of: *he traded on her endless patience.*

trader ('treɪdə) n. 1. a person engaged in trade. 2. a ship regularly employed in trade.

tradescantia (,trædes'kænʃɪə) n. a widely cultivated plant with striped variegated leaves. [after John *Tradescant*, botanist]

trade secret n. a secret formula, technique, or process known and used to advantage by only one manufacturer.

tradesman ('treɪdzmən) n., pl. **-men.** a man engaged in trade, esp. a shopkeeper. —'trades,woman fem. n.

Trades Union Congress n. the major association of British trade unions, which includes all the larger unions.

trade union *or* **trades union** n. an association of employees formed to improve their incomes and working conditions by collective bargaining. —**trade unionist** *or* **trades unionist** n.

trade wind (wɪnd) n. a wind blowing steadily towards the equator either from the northeast in the N hemisphere or the southeast in the S hemisphere.

trading estate n. *Chiefly Brit.* a large area in which a number of commercial or industrial firms are situated.

tradition (trə'dɪʃən) n. 1. the handing down from generation to generation of customs, beliefs, etc. 2. the body of customs, thought, etc., belonging to a particular country, people, family, or institution over a long period. [Latin *trāditiō* a handing down]

traditional (trə'dɪʃənʰl) adj. of, relating to, or being a tradition. —tra'ditionally adv.

traduce (trə'djuːs) vb. to speak badly of (someone). [Latin *trādūcere* to lead over, disgrace] —tra'ducement n. —tra'ducer n.

traffic ('træfɪk) n. 1. the vehicles coming and going on roads. 2. the movement of vehicles or people in a particular place or for a particular purpose: *sea traffic.* 3. (usually foll. by *with*) dealings or business. 4. trade, esp. of an illicit kind: *drug traffic.* ~vb. -ficking, -ficked. 5. (often foll. by *in*) to carry on trade or business, esp. of an illicit kind. 6. (usually foll. by *with*) to have dealings. [Old French *trafique*] —'trafficker n.

traffic island n. a raised area in the middle of a road designed as a guide for traffic flow and to provide a stopping place for pedestrians crossing.

traffic light n. one of a set of coloured lights placed at a junction to control the flow of traffic.

traffic warden n. *Brit.* a person employed to supervise road traffic and report traffic offences.

tragedian (trə'dʒiːdɪən) *or* (fem.) **tragedienne** (trə,dʒiːdɪ'en) n. 1. an actor who specializes in tragic roles. 2. a writer of tragedy.

tragedy ('trædʒɪdɪ) n., pl. **-dies.** 1. a shocking or sad event; disaster. 2. a serious play, film, or opera in which the main character falls to disaster through the combination of a personal failing and adverse circumstances. [Greek *tragoedia*]

tragic ('trædʒɪk) adj. 1. of, relating to, or characteristic of tragedy. 2. mournful or pitiable: *a tragic face.* —'tragically adv.

tragicomedy (,trædʒɪ'kɒmɪdɪ) n., pl. **-dies.** play or other written work having both comic and tragic aspects. —,tragi'comic adj.

trail (treɪl) vb. 1. to drag, stream, or permit (something) to drag or stream along a surface, esp. the ground. 2. to follow or hunt (an animal or person) by following marks or tracks. 3. to lag behind (a person or thing). 4. (esp. of plants) to extend or droop over or along a surface. 5. to be falling behind in a race. 6. to move wearily or slowly: *we trailed through the city.* ~n. 7. a print, mark, or scent made by a person, animal, or object. 8. a path, track, or road. 9. something that trails behind. 10. a sequence of results from an event: *a trail of disasters.* [Old French *trailler* to tow]

trail away *or* **off** vb. to become fainter, quieter, or weaker: *his voice trailed away.*

trailblazer ('treɪl,bleɪzə) n. 1. a pioneer in a particular field. 2. a person who blazes a trail. —'trail,blazing adj., n.

trailer ('treɪlə) n. 1. a road vehicle, usually two-wheeled, towed by a motor vehicle: used for transporting boats, etc. 2. the rear section of an articulated lorry. 3. a series of short extracts from a film, used to advertise it in a cinema or on television. 4. *U.S. & Canad.* same as **caravan** (sense 1).

train (trein) *vb.* **1.** to teach someone (to do something), as by subjecting to various exercises or experiences. **2.** to discipline (an animal) to perform tricks or obey commands. **3.** to control or guide towards a specific goal: *to train a plant up a wall.* **4.** to do exercises and prepare for a specific purpose: *the athlete trained for the Olympics.* **5.** to focus or bring to bear (on something): *to train a telescope on the moon.* ~*n.* **6.** a line of coaches or trucks coupled together and drawn by a railway engine. **7.** a sequence or series: *a train of thought.* **8.** the long back section of a dress that trails along the floor. **9.** a group of followers or attendants; retinue. [Old French *trahiner*]

trainbearer ('trein,beərə) *n.* an attendant who holds up the train of a dignitary's robe or bride's gown.

trainee (trei'ni:) *n.* a person undergoing training.

trainer ('treinə) *n.* **1.** a person who coaches athletes. **2.** a person who trains racehorses. **3.** a piece of equipment employed in training, such as a simulated aircraft cockpit. **4.** a running shoe.

training ('treinin) *n.* the process of bringing a person to an agreed standard of proficiency by practice and instruction.

train spotter *n.* a person who collects the numbers of railway locomotives.

traipse (treips) *Informal.* ~*vb.* **1.** to walk heavily or tiredly. ~*n.* **2.** a long or tiring walk. [origin unknown]

trait (treit, trei) *n.* a characteristic feature or quality distinguishing a particular person or thing. [French]

traitor ('treitə) *n.* a person who is guilty of treason or treachery, in betraying friends, country, a cause, etc. [Latin *trādere* to hand over] —'**traitorous** *adj.* —'**traitress** *fem. n.*

trajectory (trə'dʒɛktəri) *n., pl.* **-ries.** the path described by an object moving in air or space, esp. the curved path of a projectile. [Latin *trājectus* cast over]

tram (træm) *n.* **1.** an electrically driven public transport vehicle that runs on rails laid into the road. **2.** a small vehicle on rails for carrying loads in a mine. [prob. from Low German *traam* beam]

tramline ('træm,lain) *n.* **1.** (*often pl.*) the tracks on which a tram runs. **2.** (*often pl.*) the outer markings along the sides of a tennis or badminton court.

trammel ('træməl) *n.* **1.** (*often pl.*) something that impedes free action or movement. **2.** a fishing net in three sections, the two outer nets having a large mesh and the middle one a fine mesh. ~*vb.* **-elling, -elled** *or U.S.* **-eling, -eled.** **3.** to hinder or restrain. **4.** to catch or ensnare. [Old French *tramail* three-mesh net]

tramp (træmp) *vb.* **1.** to walk long and far; hike. **2.** to walk heavily or firmly across or through (a place). **3.** to wander about as a tramp. **4.** to make (a journey) on foot, esp. laboriously or wearily. **5.** to tread or trample. ~*n.* **6.** a person who travels about on foot, living by begging or doing

casual work. **7.** a long hard walk; hike. **8.** the sound of heavy treading. **9.** a merchant ship that does not run on a regular schedule. **10.** *Slang, chiefly U.S. & Canad.* a promiscuous woman. [prob. from Middle Low German *trampen*]

tramping ('træmpiŋ) *n. N.Z.* the leisure activity of walking in the bush. —'**tramper** *n.*

trample ('træmp'l) *vb.* (sometimes foll. by *on, upon,* or *over*) **1.** to stamp or walk roughly (on). **2.** to treat (someone) inconsiderately so as to hurt: *to trample on someone's feelings.* ~*n.* **3.** the action or sound of trampling. [from *tramp*]

trampoline ('træmpəlin, -,li:n) *n.* **1.** a tough canvas sheet suspended by springs or cords from a frame, used by acrobats, gymnasts, etc. ~*vb.* **2.** to exercise on a trampoline. [Italian *trampolino*]

trance (trɑ:ns) *n.* **1.** a hypnotic state resembling sleep in which a person is unable to move or act of his own will. **2.** a dazed or stunned state. **3.** a state of ecstasy or mystic absorption so intense as to cause a temporary loss of consciousness at the earthly level. [Latin *trānsīre* to go over]

trannie *or* **tranny** ('træni) *n., pl.* **-nies.** *Informal, chiefly Brit.* a transistor radio.

tranquil ('træŋkwil) *adj.* calm, peaceful, or quiet. [Latin *tranquillus*] —'**tranquilly** *adv.*

tranquillity *or U.S.* (*sometimes*) **tranquility** (træŋ'kwiliti) *n.* a state of calmness or peacefulness.

tranquillize, -ise, *or U.S.* **tranquilize** ('træŋkwi,laiz) *vb.* to make or become calm or calmer. —,**tranquilli'zation, -i'sation,** *or U.S.* ,**tranquili'zation** *n.*

tranquillizer, -iser *or U.S.* **tranquilizer** ('træŋkwi,laizə) *n.* a drug that calms someone suffering from anxiety, tension, etc.

trans. **1.** transaction. **2.** transitive. **3.** translated. **4.** transport(ation).

trans- *prefix.* **1.** across, beyond, crossing, on the other side: *transatlantic.* **2.** changing thoroughly: *transliterate.* [Latin]

transact (træn'zækt) *vb.* to do, conduct, or negotiate (a business deal). [Latin *trānsigere* to drive through]

transaction (træn'zækʃən) *n.* **1.** something that is transacted, esp. a business deal. **2.** (*pl.*) the records of the proceedings of a society, etc.

transalpine (trænz'ælpain) *adj.* situated in or relating to places beyond the Alps, esp. from Italy.

transatlantic (,trænzət'læntik) *adj.* **1.** on or from the other side of the Atlantic. **2.** crossing the Atlantic.

transceiver (træn'si:və) *n.* a combined radio transmitter and receiver. [*trans*(*mitter*) + (*re*)*ceiver*]

transcend (træn'sɛnd) *vb.* **1.** to go above or beyond (a limit, expectation, etc.), as in degree or excellence. **2.** to be superior to. [Latin *trānscendere* to climb over]

transcendent (træn'sɛndənt) *adj.* **1.** exceeding or surpassing in degree or excellence. **2.** *Theol.* (of God) having existence outside the created world. **—tran'scendence** or **tran'scendency** n.

transcendental (ˌtrænsɛnˈdɛntᵊl) adj. **1.** superior or surpassing. **2.** Philosophy. based on intuition or innate belief rather than experience. **3.** supernatural or mystical. **—ˌtranscenˈdentally** adv.

transcendentalism (ˌtrænsɛnˈdɛntəˌlɪzəm) n. any system of philosophy that seeks to discover the nature of reality by examining the processes of thought rather than the things thought about, or that emphasizes intuition as a means to knowledge. **—ˌtranscenˈdentalist** n., adj.

transcendental meditation n. a technique, based on Hindu traditions, for relaxing and refreshing the mind and body through the silent repetition of a special formula of words.

transcribe (trænˈskraɪb) vb. **1.** to write, type, or print out (a text) fully from a speech or notes. **2.** to make an electrical recording of (a programme or speech) for a later broadcast. **3.** Music. to rewrite (a piece of music) for an instrument other than that originally intended; arrange. [Latin transcrībere] **—tranˈscriber** n.

transcript (ˈtrænskrɪpt) n. **1.** a written, typed, or printed copy made by transcribing. **2.** Chiefly U.S. & Canad. an official record of a student's school progress.

transcription (trænˈskrɪpʃən) n. **1.** the act of transcribing. **2.** something transcribed.

transducer (trænzˈdjuːsə) n. any device, such as a microphone or electric motor, that converts one form of energy into another. [Latin transducere to lead across]

transept (ˈtrænsɛpt) n. either of the two wings of a cross-shaped church at right angles to the nave. [Latin trāns- across + saeptum enclosure]

transfer vb. (trænsˈfɜː), **-ferring**, **-ferred**. **1.** to change or move from one thing, person, point, etc., to another: they transferred from the Park Hotel to the Imperial; she transferred her affections to her dog. **2.** Law. to make over (property) to another; convey. **3.** to move (a drawing or design) from one surface to another. ~n. (ˈtrænsfɜː). **4.** the act, process, or system of transferring, or the state of being transferred. **5.** a person or thing that transfers or is transferred. **6.** a design or drawing that is transferred from one surface to another. **7.** Law. the passing of title to property or other right from one person to another; conveyance. **8.** any document effecting a transfer. [Latin trāns- across + ferre to carry] **—transˈferable** or **transˈferrable** adj.

transfiguration (ˌtrænsfɪɡjʊˈreɪʃən) n. a transfiguring or being transfigured.

Transfiguration (ˌtrænsfɪɡjʊˈreɪʃən) n. **1.** New Testament. the change in the appearance of Christ on the mountain. **2.** the Church festival held in commemoration of this on Aug. 6.

transfigure (trænsˈfɪɡə) vb. **1.** to change or cause to change in appearance. **2.** to become or cause to become more exalted. [Latin trāns- beyond + figūra appearance]

transfix (trænsˈfɪks) vb. **-fixing**, **-fixed** or **-fixt**. **1.** to make (someone) motionless, esp. with horror or shock. **2.** to pierce through (a person or animal) with a sharp weapon or other device. [Latin trānsfīgere to pierce through]

transform (trænsˈfɔːm) vb. **1.** to alter or be altered in form, function, etc. **2.** to convert (one form of energy) to another. **3.** Maths. to change the form of (an equation, expression, etc.) without changing its value. **4.** to change (an alternating current or voltage) using a transformer. [Latin trānsformāre] **—transforˈmation** n.

transformer (trænsˈfɔːmə) n. a device that transfers an alternating current from one circuit to one or more other circuits, usually with a change of voltage.

transfuse (trænsˈfjuːz) vb. **1.** to permeate or infuse. **2.** to inject (blood or other fluid) into a blood vessel. [Latin trānsfundere to pour out]

transfusion (trænsˈfjuːʒən) n. **1.** a transfusing. **2.** the injection of blood, blood plasma, etc., into the blood vessels of a patient.

transgress (trænzˈɡrɛs) vb. **1.** to break (a law, etc.). **2.** to overstep (a limit). [Latin trāns beyond + gradī to step] **—transˈgression** n. **—transˈgressor** n.

transient (ˈtrænzɪənt) adj. **1.** for a short time only; temporary. ~n. **2.** a transient person or thing. [Latin trānsiēns going over] **—ˈtransience** n.

transistor (trænˈzɪstə) n. **1.** a semiconductor device used to amplify electric currents. **2.** Informal. a small portable radio containing transistors. [transfer + resistor]

transistorize or **-ise** (trænˈzɪstəˌraɪz) vb. to equip (a device) with transistors.

transit (ˈtrænsɪt, ˈtrænz-) n. **1.** the passage or conveyance of goods or people. **2.** a route. **3.** Astron. the apparent passage of a celestial body across the meridian. **4. in transit.** while travelling or being taken from one place to another: the parcel has been lost in transit. [Latin trānsitus a going over]

transit camp n. a camp in which refugees, soldiers, etc., live temporarily.

transition (trænˈzɪʃən) n. **1.** change or passage from one state or stage to another. **2.** the period of time during which something changes. **3.** Music. a movement from one key to another. **4.** a gradual change in the style of architecture, in Britain, from Norman to Early English. [Latin transitio a going over] **—tranˈsitional** adj.

transitive (ˈtrænsɪtɪv) adj. Grammar. denoting a verb that requires a direct object.

transitory (ˈtrænsɪtrɪ) adj. lasting only for a short time.

translate (trænsˈleɪt, trænz-) vb. **1.** to express or be capable of being expressed in another language. **2.** to act as translator. **3.** to express or explain (something) in simple or less technical language. **4.** to interpret the significance of (a gesture, action, etc.). **5.** to transform or convert: to translate hope into reality. **6.** to transfer from one place or position to another. [Latin *trānslātus* carried over] —**trans'latable** *adj.* —**trans'lator** *n.*

translation (trænz'leɪʃən, trænz-) *n.* **1.** a piece of writing or speech that is or has been translated into another language. **2.** a translating or being translated. **3.** *Maths.* a transformation in which the origin of a coordinate system is moved to another position so that each axis retains the same direction. —**trans'lational** *adj.*

transliterate (trænz'lɪtə,reɪt) *vb.* to write or spell (a word, etc.) into corresponding letters of another alphabet. [Latin *trāns-* across + *lĭttera* letter] —,**transliter'ation** *n.* —**trans'liter,ator** *n.*

translucent (trænz'luːs'nt) *adj.* allowing light to pass through; semitransparent. [Latin *trānslūcēre* to shine through] —**trans'lucence** *or* **trans'lucency** *n.*

transmigrate (,trænzmaɪ'greɪt) *vb.* (of souls) to pass from one body into another at death. —,**transmi'gration** *n.*

transmission (trænz'mɪʃən) *n.* **1.** the act of transmitting. **2.** something that is transmitted, esp. a radio or television broadcast. **3.** a system of shafts and gears that transmits power from the engine to the driving wheels of a motor vehicle.

transmit (trænz'mɪt) *vb.* **-mitting, -mitted.** **1.** to pass (something, such as a message or disease) from one place or person to another. **2.** to allow the passage of (particles, energy, etc.): *radio waves are transmitted through the atmosphere.* **3. a.** to send out (signals) by means of radio waves. **b.** to broadcast (a radio or television programme). **4.** to transfer (a force, motion, etc.) from one part of a mechanical system to another. [Latin *trānsmittere* to send across] —**trans'mittable** *adj.*

transmitter (trænz'mɪtə) *n.* **1.** a person or thing that transmits. **2.** a piece of equipment used for broadcasting radio or television programmes.

transmogrify (trænz'mɒgrɪ,faɪ) *vb.* **-fying, -fied.** *Jocular.* to change or transform (someone or something) into a different shape or appearance, esp. a grotesque or bizarre one. [origin unknown] —**trans,mogrifi'cation** *n.*

transmute (trænz'mjuːt) *vb.* to change the form, character, or substance of. [Latin *trānsmūtāre* to shift] —,**transmu'tation** *n.*

transom ('trænsəm) *n.* **1.** a horizontal bar across a window. **2.** a horizontal bar that separates a door from a window over it. [Old French *traversin*]

transparency (træns'pærənsɪ) *n., pl.* **-cies.** **1.** the state of being transparent. **2.** a positive photograph on a transparent base, usually mounted in a frame or between glass plates. It can be viewed by means of a slide projector.

transparent (træns'pærənt) *adj.* **1.** permitting the uninterrupted passage of light; clear. **2.** easy to see through, understand, or recognize; obvious: *a transparent lie.* **3.** candid, open, or frank. [Latin *trāns-* through + *pārēre* to appear] —**trans'parently** *adv.*

transpire (træn'spaɪə) *vb.* **1.** to come to light; be known. **2.** *Not universally accepted.* to happen or occur. **3.** *Physiol.* to give off (water or vapour) through the pores of the skin, etc. [Latin *trāns-* through + *spīrāre* to breathe] —**transpiration** (,trænspə'reɪʃən) *n.*

transplant *vb.* (træns'plɑːnt). **1.** *Surgery.* to transfer (an organ or tissue) from one part of the body or from one person to another. **2.** to remove or transfer (esp. a plant) from one place to another. ~*n.* ('træns,plɑːnt). **3.** *Surgery.* **a.** the procedure involved in transferring an organ or tissue. **b.** the organ or tissue transplanted. —,**transplan'tation** *n.*

transponder (træn'spɒndə) *n.* a type of radio or radar transmitter-receiver that transmits signals automatically when it receives predetermined signals. [*transmitter* + *responder*]

transport *vb.* (træns'pɔːt). **1.** to carry or move (people or goods) from one place to another, esp. over some distance. **2.** to exile (a criminal) to a penal colony. **3.** to have a strong emotional effect on: *transported with joy.* ~*n.* ('træns,pɔːt). **4.** the business or system of transporting goods or people. **5.** *Brit.* freight vehicles generally. **6.** a vehicle used to transport goods or people, esp. troops. **7.** a transporting or being transported. **8.** ecstasy, rapture, or any powerful emotion. [Latin *trāns-* across + *portāre* to carry] —**trans'portable** *adj.* —**trans'porter** *n.*

transportation (,trænspɔː'teɪʃən) *n.* **1.** a means or system of transporting. **2.** the act of transporting or the state of being transported. **3.** (esp. formerly) deportation to a penal colony.

transport café ('træns,pɔːt) *n. Brit.* an inexpensive eating place on a main route, used mainly by long-distance lorry drivers.

transpose (træns'pəʊz) *vb.* **1.** to alter the positions of; interchange, as words in a sentence. **2.** *Music.* to play (notes, music, etc.) in a different key. **3.** *Maths.* to move (a term) from one side of an equation to the other with a corresponding reversal in sign. [Old French *transposer*] —**transposition** (,trænspə'zɪʃən) *n.*

transsexual (trænz'sɛksjʊəl) *n.* **1.** a person who is completely identified with the opposite sex. **2.** a person who has had medical treatment to alter sexual characteristics to those of the opposite sex.

transship (træns'ʃɪp) *vb.* **-shipping, -shipped.** to transfer or be transferred from one ship or vehicle to another. —**trans'shipment** *n.*

transubstantiation (,trænsəb,stænʃɪ'eɪʃən) *n.* (esp. in Roman Catholic theology) the doctrine that the whole substance of the bread and wine changes into the substance of the body and blood of Christ when consecrated in the Eucharist. [Latin *trāns-* over + *substantia* substance]

transuranic (,trænzjʊ'rænɪk) *adj.* (of an element) having an atomic number greater than that of uranium.

transverse (trænz'vɜːs) *adj.* crossing from side to side; crossways. [Latin *trāns-*

vertere to turn across]

transvestite (trænz'vestaɪt) *n.* a person, esp. a man, who seeks sexual pleasure from wearing clothes of the opposite sex. [Latin *trāns-* over + *vestītus* clothed] —**trans'vestism** *n.*

trap[1] (træp) *n.* **1.** a device or hole in which something, esp. an animal, is caught. **2.** a plan for tricking a person into being caught unawares. **3.** a bend in a pipe that contains standing water to prevent the passage of gases. **4.** a device that hurls clay pigeons into the air to be fired at. **5.** a boxlike stall in which greyhounds are enclosed before the start of a race. **6.** See **trap door. 7.** a light two-wheeled carriage. **8.** *Slang.* the mouth. ~*vb.* **trapping, trapped. 9.** to catch (an animal) in a trap. **10.** to trick (someone). **11.** to set traps in (a place), esp. for animals. [Old English *træppe*]

trap[2] (træp) *vb.* **trapping, trapped.** (foll. by *out*) to dress or adorn. [Old French *drap* cloth]

trap[3] (træp) *n.* any fine-grained dark igneous rock, esp. basalt, used in road making. [Swedish *trappa* stair (from its steplike formation)]

trap door *n.* a hinged door in a ceiling, floor, or stage.

trapeze (trə'piːz) *n.* a free-swinging bar attached to two ropes, used by circus acrobats. [French]

trapezium (trə'piːzɪəm) *n., pl.* **-ziums** or **-zia** (-zɪə). **1.** *Chiefly Brit.* a quadrilateral having two parallel sides of unequal length. **2.** *Chiefly U.S. & Canad.* a quadrilateral having neither pair of sides parallel. [Greek *trapeza* table] —**tra'pezial** *adj.*

trapezoid ('træpɪˌzɔɪd) *n.* **1.** a quadrilateral having neither pair of sides parallel. **2.** *U.S. & Canad.* same as **trapezium** (sense 1). [Greek *trapeza* table]

trapper ('træpə) *n.* a person who traps animals, esp. for their furs or skins.

trappings ('træpɪŋz) *pl. n.* **1.** the accessories that symbolize a condition, office, etc.: *the trappings of success.* **2.** ceremonial harness for a horse or other animal. [from TRAP[2]]

Trappist ('træpɪst) *n.* a member of a branch of the Cistercian order of Christian monks, noted for their rule of silence.

trash (træʃ) *n.* **1.** foolish ideas or talk; nonsense. **2.** *Chiefly U.S. & Canad.* unwanted objects; rubbish. **3.** *Chiefly U.S. & Canad.* a worthless person or group of people. [origin unknown] —**'trashy** *adj.*

trattoria (ˌtrætɔ'riːə) *n.* an Italian restaurant. [Italian]

trauma ('trɔːmə) *n.* **1.** *Psychol.* an emotional shock that may have long-lasting effects. **2.** *Pathol.* any bodily injury or wound. [Greek: a wound] —**traumatic** (trɔː'mætɪk) *adj.* —**trau'matically** *adv.* —**'trauma,tize** or **-ise** *vb.*

travail ('træveɪl) *Literary.* ~*n.* **1.** painful or excessive work. **2.** the pangs of childbirth; labour. ~*vb.* **3.** to suffer or labour painfully, esp. in childbirth. [Old French *travaillier*]

travel ('træv'l) *vb.* **-elling, -elled** or *U.S.* **-eling, -eled. 1.** to go, move, or journey from one place to another. **2.** to go, move, or journey through or across (an area, region, etc.). **3.** to go, move, or cover a distance. **4.** to go from place to place as a salesman. **5.** (esp. of perishable goods) to withstand a journey. **6.** (of a machine or part) to move in a fixed path. **7.** *Informal.* to move rapidly: *that car certainly travels.* ~*n.* **8.** the act of travelling. **9.** (*usually pl.*) a tour or journey: *Mary told us all about her travels.* **10.** the distance moved by a mechanical part, such as the stroke of a piston. [Old French *travaillier* to travail]

travel agency *n.* an agency that arranges flights, hotel accommodation, etc., for travellers. —**travel agent** *n.*

traveller ('trævələ, 'trævlə) *n.* **1.** a person who travels, esp. habitually. **2.** a travelling salesman.

traveller's cheque *n.* a cheque sold by a bank, travel agency, etc., to the bearer, who signs it on purchase and can cash it abroad by signing it again.

travelling salesman *n.* a salesman who travels within an assigned territory in order to sell goods or get orders from the commercial enterprise he represents.

travelogue ('trævəˌlɒg) *n.* a film, lecture, or brochure on travels and travelling.

traverse ('trævɜːs, trə'vɜːs) *vb.* **1.** to pass or go over or back and forth over (something); cross. **2.** to move sideways or crosswise. **3.** to extend or reach across. **4.** to look over or examine carefully. ~*n.* **5.** something being or lying across, such as a crossbar. **6.** the act or an instance of traversing or crossing. **7.** a path or road across. ~*adj.* **8.** being or lying across; transverse. [Latin *trānsversus*] —**tra'versal** *n.*

travesty ('trævɪstɪ) *n., pl.* **-ties. 1.** a grotesque imitation; mockery. ~*vb.* **-tying, -tied. 2.** to make or be a travesty of. [French *travesti* disguised]

travois (trə'vɔɪ) *n., pl.* **-vois** (-'vɔɪz). *Canad.* a sled used for dragging logs. [Canadian French]

trawl (trɔːl) *n.* **1.** a large net, usually in the shape of a sock or bag, drawn at deep levels behind special boats (trawlers). ~*vb.* **2.** to catch (fish) with a trawl net. [Middle Dutch *traghelen* to drag]

trawler ('trɔːlə) *n.* a ship used for trawling.

tray (treɪ) *n.* **1.** a thin flat piece of wood, plastic, or metal, usually with a raised edge on which things, such as food or drink, can be carried. **2.** a shallow receptacle for papers, sometimes forming a drawer in a cabinet or box. [Old English *trieg*]

treacherous ('tretʃərəs) *adj.* **1.** betraying or likely to betray faith or confidence. **2.** unstable, unreliable, or dangerous: *treacherous conditions.*

treachery ('tretʃərɪ) *n., pl.* **-eries.** the act or an instance of wilful betrayal. [Old French *trecherie*]

treacle ('triːk'l) *n. Brit.* a thick dark syrup obtained during the refining of sugar. [Latin *thēriaca* antidote to poison] —'**treacly** *adj.*

tread (tred) *vb.* **treading, trod, trodden** or **trod. 1.** to walk or trample in, on, over, or across (something). **2.** (sometimes foll. by *on*) to crush or squash by or as if by treading: *to tread grapes; to tread on a spider.* **3.** to do by walking or dancing: *to tread a measure.* **4.** (of a male bird) to copulate with (a female bird). **5. tread lightly.** to proceed in a delicate or tactful manner. **6. tread water.** to stay afloat in an upright position by moving the legs in a walking motion. ~*n.* **7.** a style of walking or dancing: *a light tread.* **8.** the act of treading. **9.** the top surface of a step in a staircase. **10.** the outer part of a tyre or wheel that touches the road. **11.** the part of a rail that wheels touch. **12.** the part of a shoe that is generally in contact with the ground. [Old English *tredan*]

treadle ('tred°l) *n.* a lever operated by the foot to drive a sewing machine, spinning, wheel, etc. [Old English *tredan* to tread]

treadmill ('tred,mɪl) *n.* **1.** (formerly) an apparatus turned by the weight of men or animals climbing steps on a revolving cylinder or wheel. **2.** a dreary routine. **3.** an exercise machine that consists of a continuous moving belt on which to walk or jog.

treason ('triːz°n) *n.* **1.** betrayal of one's sovereign or country, esp. by attempting to overthrow the government. **2.** any treachery or betrayal. [Latin *trāditiō* a handing over] —'**treasonable** *adj.*

treasure ('trɛʒə) *n.* **1.** wealth and riches, usually hoarded, esp. in the form of money, precious metals, or gems. **2.** a thing or person that is highly prized or valued: *my cleaning lady's a little treasure.* ~*vb.* **3.** to cherish (someone or something). **4.** to store up and save (money, etc.); hoard. [Greek *thēsauros*]

treasure hunt *n.* a game in which players act upon successive clues to find a hidden prize.

treasurer ('trɛʒərə) *n.* a person appointed to look after the funds of a society or other organization.

treasure-trove *n. Law.* any articles, such as coins or valuable objects found hidden and of unknown ownership. [Anglo-French *tresor trové* treasure found]

treasury ('trɛʒərɪ) *n., pl.* **-uries. 1.** a storage place for treasure. **2.** the revenues or funds of a government or organization.

Treasury ('trɛʒərɪ) *n.* (in various countries) the government department in charge of finance.

Treasury Bench *n.* (in Britain) the row of seats to the right of the Speaker in the House of Commons, traditionally reserved for members of the Government.

treat (triːt) *n.* **1.** a celebration, entertainment, gift, or meal given for or to someone and paid for by someone else. **2.** any delightful surprise or specially pleasant occasion. ~*vb.* **3.** to deal with or regard in a certain manner: *she treats school as a joke.* **4.** to apply treatment to (an illness, injury, or disease). **5.** to subject to a

process or to the application of a substance: *to treat photographic film with developer.* **6.** (often foll. by *to*) to provide (someone) with as a treat. **7.** (usually foll. by *of*) to deal with, as in writing or speaking. [Old French *tretier*] —'**treatable** *adj.*

treatise ('triːtɪz) *n.* a formal piece of writing that deals systematically with a particular subject. [Anglo-French *tretiz*]

treatment ('triːtmənt) *n.* **1.** the medical or surgical care given to a patient. **2.** the manner or practice of handling a person or thing, as in a literary or artistic work.

treaty ('triːtɪ) *n., pl.* **-ties. 1.** a formal written agreement between two or more states, such as an alliance or trade arrangement. **2.** an agreement between two parties concerning the purchase of property. [Old French *traité*]

treble ('treb°l) *adj.* **1.** threefold; triple. **2.** of or denoting a soprano voice or part or a high-pitched instrument. ~*n.* **3.** treble the amount, size, etc. **4.** a soprano voice or part or a high-pitched instrument. ~*vb.* **5.** to make or become three times as much: *the population has nearly trebled in thirty years.* [Latin *triplus* threefold] —'**trebly** *adv., adj.*

treble chance *n.* a method of betting in football pools in which the chances of winning are related to the number of draws and the number of home and away wins forecast by the competitor.

treble clef *n. Music.* the clef that establishes G a fifth above middle C as being on the second line of the staff.

tree (triː) *n.* **1.** any large woody perennial plant with a distinct trunk and usually having leaves and branches. **2.** See **family tree, shoetree, saddletree. 3. at the top of the tree.** in the highest position of a profession. **4. up a tree.** *U.S. & Canad. informal.* in a difficult situation. ~*vb.* **treeing, treed. 5.** to chase (an animal or person) up a tree. [Old English *treo*] —'**treeless** *adj.*

tree creeper *n.* a small songbird of the N hemisphere that creeps up trees to feed on insects.

tree fern *n.* any of numerous large tropical ferns with a trunklike stem.

tree line *n.* same as **timber line.**

tree surgery *n.* the treatment of damaged trees by filling cavities, applying braces, etc. —**tree surgeon** *n.*

trefoil ('trefɔɪl) *n.* **1.** a plant, such as clover, with leaves divided into three smaller leaves. **2.** *Archit.* a carved ornament like this. [Latin *trifolium* three-leaved herb] —'**trefoiled** *adj.*

trek (trɛk) *n.* **1.** a long and often difficult journey. **2.** *S. African.* a journey or stage of a journey, esp. a migration by ox wagon. ~*vb.* **trekking, trekked. 3.** to make a trek. [Afrikaans]

trellis ('trɛlɪs) *n.* a frame made of vertical and horizontal strips of wood, esp. one used to support climbing plants. [Old French *treliz*] —'**trellis,work** *n.*

tremble ('tremb°l) *vb.* **1.** to shake with

short slight movements: *she was trembling with fear.* **2.** to experience fear or anxiety: *we trembled for him.* ~*n.* **3.** the act or an instance of trembling. [Latin *tremere*] —**'trembling** *adj.*

tremendous (trɪ'mɛndəs) *adj.* **1.** vast; huge: *tremendous pillars.* **2.** *Informal.* very exciting or unusual: *a tremendous play.* **3.** *Informal.* great: *a tremendous help.* [Latin *tremendus* terrible] —**tre'mendously** *adv.*

tremolo ('trɛmə,ləʊ) *n., pl.* -**los.** *Music.* **1.** (in playing the violin or other stringed instrument) the rapid repetition of a note or notes to produce a trembling effect. **2.** (in singing) a fluctuation in pitch. [Italian]

tremor ('trɛmə) *n.* **1.** an involuntary shudder or vibration: *she spoke with a tremor in her voice.* **2.** a trembling movement: *an earth tremor.* [Latin]

tremulous ('trɛmjʊləs) *adj.* trembling, as from fear, anxiety, or excitement. [Latin *tremere* to shake] —**'tremulously** *adv.*

trench (trɛntʃ) *n.* **1.** a long narrow ditch in the ground, esp. one used by soldiers as a defensive position. ~*vb.* **2.** to make a trench in (a place). **3.** to fortify with a trench. [Old French *trenche* something cut]

trenchant ('trɛntʃənt) *adj.* **1.** keen or incisive: *trenchant criticism.* **2.** vigorous and effective: *a trenchant foreign policy.* [Old French: cutting] —**'trenchancy** *n.*

trench coat *n.* a belted raincoat similar in style to a military officer's coat.

trencher ('trɛntʃə) *n.* (esp. formerly) a wooden board on which food was served or cut. [Old French *trencheoir*]

trencherman ('trɛntʃəmən) *n., pl.* -**men.** a person who enjoys food; hearty eater.

trench warfare *n.* a type of warfare in which opposing armies face each other in entrenched positions.

trend (trɛnd) *n.* **1.** general tendency or direction. **2.** fashion; mode. ~*vb.* **3.** to take a certain trend. [Old English *trendan* to turn]

trendsetter ('trɛnd,sɛtə) *n.* a person or thing that creates, or may create, a new fashion. —**'trend,setting** *adj.*

trendy ('trɛndɪ) *Brit. informal.* ~*adj.* **trendier, trendiest. 1.** consciously fashionable. ~*n., pl.* **trendies. 2.** a trendy person. —**'trendily** *adv.*

trepidation (,trɛpɪ'deɪʃən) *n.* a state of fear or anxiety. [Latin *trepidātiō*]

trespass ('trɛspəs) *vb.* **1.** (often foll. by *on* or *upon*) to go or intrude (on the property, privacy, or preserves of another) with no right or permission. **2.** *Law.* to commit a trespass. ~*n.* **3.** an intrusion on another's privacy, property, or rights. [Old French *trespas* a passage] —**'trespasser** *n.*

tress (trɛs) *n.* (often *pl.*) a lock of hair, esp. a long lock of woman's hair. [Old French *trece*]

trestle ('trɛs²l) *n.* a framework of a horizontal beam supported at each end by a pair of spreading legs, used to form a table top, etc. [Old French *trestel*]

trews (truːz) *pl. n. Chiefly Brit.* close-fitting trousers of tartan cloth. [Scot. Gaelic *triubhas*]

tri- *prefix.* **1.** three or thrice: *trisect.* **2.** occurring every three: *trimonthly.* [Latin *trēs*]

triad ('traɪæd) *n.* **1.** a group of three; trio. **2.** *Music.* a three-note chord consisting of a note and the third and fifth above it. [Greek *trias*] —**tri'adic** *adj.*

Triad ('traɪæd) *n.* any of several Chinese secret societies, esp. one involved in criminal activities, such as drug trafficking.

trial ('traɪəl, traɪl) *n.* **1.** the act or an instance of trying or proving; test or experiment. **2.** *Law.* judicial examination to decide whether a person is innocent or guilty of a crime by questioning them and considering the evidence. **3.** an annoying or frustrating person or thing. **4.** (often *pl.*) a competition for individuals: *sheepdog trials.* **5. on trial. a.** undergoing trial, esp. before a court of law. **b.** being tested, as before a commitment to purchase: *I only have the car out on trial.* [Anglo-French *trier* to try]

trial and error *n.* a method of discovery based on practical experiment and experience rather than on theory: *he learnt to cook by trial and error.*

trial balance *n. Book-keeping.* a statement of all the debit and credit balances in the double-entry ledger.

triangle ('traɪ,æŋg²l) *n.* **1.** *Geom.* a plane figure with three sides and three angles. **2.** any object shaped like a triangle. **3.** any situation involving three people or points of view. **4.** *Music.* a percussion instrument that consists of a metal bar bent into a triangular shape, beaten with a metal stick. [TRI- + Latin *angulus* corner] —**tri'angular** *adj.*

triangulate (traɪ'æŋgjʊ,leɪt) *vb.* to survey (an area) by dividing it into triangles.

triangulation (traɪ,æŋgjʊ'leɪʃən) *n.* a method of surveying in which an area is divided into triangles, one side (the base line) and all angles of which are measured and the lengths of the other lines calculated by trigonometry.

Triassic (traɪ'æsɪk) *adj. Geol.* of the period of geological time about 230 million years ago. [Latin *trias* triad]

triathlon (traɪ'æθlɒn) *n.* an athletic contest in which each athlete competes in three different events: swimming, cycling, and horse riding. [TRI- + Greek *athlon* contest]

tribalism ('traɪbə,lɪzəm) *n.* loyalty to a tribe, esp. as opposed to a modern political entity such as a state.

tribe (traɪb) *n.* a group of families or clans believed to have a common ancestor. [Latin *tribus*] —**'tribal** *adj.*

tribesman ('traɪbzmən) *n., pl.* -**men.** a member of a tribe.

tribulation (,trɪbjʊ'leɪʃən) *n.* great distress. [Latin *trībulāre* to afflict]

tribunal (traɪ'bjuːn²l, trɪ-) *n.* **1.** a court of justice. **2.** (in Britain) a special court, convened by the government to inquire into a specific matter. **3.** the seat of a judge. [Latin *tribūnus* TRIBUNE]

tribune ('trɪbjuːn) *n.* **1.** a person who upholds public rights. **2.** (in ancient Rome) an officer elected by the plebs to protect their interests. [Latin *tribunus*]

tributary ('trɪbjʊtərɪ) *n., pl.* **-taries. 1.** a stream or river that flows into a larger one. **2.** a person, nation, or people that pays tribute. ~*adj.* **3.** (of a stream or river) flowing into a larger stream. **4.** given or owed as a tribute. **5.** paying tribute.

tribute ('trɪbjuːt) *n.* **1.** something given, done, or said as a mark of respect or admiration. **2.** a payment by one ruler or state to another, usually as an acknowledgment of submission. [Latin *tribūtum*]

trice (traɪs) *n.* **in a trice.** in a moment: *I'll be back in a trice.* [orig., at one tug, from *trice* to haul up]

triceps ('traɪsɛps) *n.* any muscle having three heads, esp. the one at the back of the upper arm. [Latin]

trichology (trɪ'kɒlədʒɪ) *n.* the branch of medicine concerned with the hair and its diseases. [Greek *thrix* hair] —**tri'chologist** *n.*

trichromatic (ˌtraɪkrəʊ'mætɪk) *adj.* **1.** having or involving three colours. **2.** of or having normal colour vision. —**tri'chroma,tism** *n.*

trick (trɪk) *n.* **1.** a deceitful or cunning action or plan. **2.** a mischievous, malicious, or humorous action or plan; joke: *she's up to her tricks again.* **3.** an illusory or magical feat or device: *a conjuring trick.* **4.** a simple feat learned by an animal or person. **5.** an adroit or ingenious device; knack: *a trick of the trade.* **6.** a habit or mannerism: *she had a trick of saying "oh dear".* **7.** *Cards.* a batch of cards played in turn and won by the person playing the highest card. **8. do the trick.** *Informal.* to produce the desired result. **9. how's tricks?** *Slang.* how are you? ~*vb.* **10.** to defraud, deceive, or cheat (someone). [Old French *trique*] —**'trickery** *n.*

trickle ('trɪk²l) *vb.* **1.** to flow or cause to flow in a thin stream or drops: *the tears were trickling down her cheeks.* **2.** to move gradually: *the crowd trickled away.* ~*n.* **3.** a thin, irregular, or slow flow of something. [prob. imit.]

trick out *or* **up** *vb.* to dress up; deck out: *tricked out in frilly dresses.*

trickster ('trɪkstə) *n.* a person who deceives or plays tricks.

tricky ('trɪkɪ) *adj.* **trickier, trickiest. 1.** involving snags or difficulties: *a tricky job.* **2.** needing careful handling: *a tricky situation.* **3.** sly; wily: *a tricky dealer.* —**'trickily** *adv.* —**'trickiness** *n.*

tricolour *or U.S.* **tricolor** ('trɪkələ) *n.* a flag with three equal stripes in different colours, esp. the French or Irish national flags.

tricot ('trɪkəʊ, 'triː-) *n.* **1.** a thin rayon or nylon fabric knitted or resembling knitting, used for dresses, etc. **2.** a type of ribbed dress fabric. [French *tricoter* to knit]

tricycle ('traɪsɪk²l) *n.* a three-wheeled cycle, esp. driven by pedals. —**'tricyclist** *n.*

trident ('traɪd²nt) *n.* a three-pronged spear. [Latin *tridēns* three-pronged]

Tridentine (traɪ'dɛntaɪn) *adj.* in accord with Tridentine doctrine: *Tridentine mass.* [Medieval Latin *Tridentum* Trent]

tried (traɪd) *vb.* past of **try.**

triennial (traɪ'ɛnɪəl) *adj.* occurring every three years. [TRI- + Latin *annus* year] —**tri'ennially** *adv.*

trier ('traɪə) *n.* a person or thing that tries.

trifle ('traɪf²l) *n.* **1.** a thing of little or no value or significance. **2.** a small amount; bit: *a trifle more enthusiasm.* **3.** *Brit.* a cold dessert made of sponge cake spread with jam or fruit, soaked in sherry, covered with custard and cream. ~*vb.* **4.** (usually foll. by *with*) to deal with as if worthless; dally: *to trifle with a person's affections.* [Old French *trufle* mockery]

trifling ('traɪflɪŋ) *adj.* insignificant, petty, or frivolous: *a trifling matter.*

trig. 1. trigonometrical. **2.** trigonometry.

trigger ('trɪgə) *n.* **1.** a small lever that releases a catch on a gun or machine. **2.** any event that sets a course of action in motion. ~*vb.* **3.** (usually foll. by *off*) to set (an action or process) in motion. [Dutch *trekker*]

trigger-happy *adj. Informal.* quick to resort to the use of guns or violence.

trigonometry (ˌtrɪgə'nɒmɪtrɪ) *n.* the branch of mathematics concerned with the relations of sides and angles of triangles used in surveying, navigation, etc. [Greek *trigōnon* triangle] —**trigonometric** (ˌtrɪgənə'mɛtrɪk *or* ˌtrigono'metrical *adj.*

trig point *n.* a point on a hilltop, etc., used for triangulation by a surveyor.

trike (traɪk) *n. Informal.* a tricycle.

trilateral (traɪ'lætərəl) *adj.* having three sides.

trilby ('trɪlbɪ) *n., pl.* **-bies.** a man's soft felt hat with an indented crown. [after *Trilby*, the heroine of a novel by George Du Maurier]

trill (trɪl) *n.* **1.** *Music.* a rapid alternation between a principal note and the note above it. **2.** a shrill warbling sound made by some birds. **3.** the articulation of an (r) sound produced by the rapid vibration of the tongue. ~*vb.* **4.** to sound, sing, or play (a trill or with a trill). [Italian *trillo*]

trillion ('trɪljən) *n.* **1.** (in Britain, France, and Germany) the number represented as one followed by eighteen zeros (10^{18}); a million million million. **2.** (in the U.S. and Canada) the number represented as one followed by twelve zeros (10^{12}); a million million. ~*adj.* **3.** amounting to a trillion. [French] —**'trillionth** *n., adj.*

trillium ('trɪljəm) *n.* a plant of Asia and North America, having three leaves at the top of the stem with a single white, pink, or purple three-petalled flower. [New Latin]

trilobite ('traɪlə,baɪt) *n.* an extinct marine arthropod, found as a fossil. [Greek *trilobos* having three lobes]

trilogy ('trɪlədʒɪ) *n., pl.* **-gies.** a series of

three plays, novels, operas, etc., which form a related group but are each complete works in themselves. [Greek *trilogia*]

trim (trɪm) *adj.* **trimmer, trimmest.** **1.** neat and spruce in appearance. **2.** slim; slender. **3.** in good condition. ~*vb.* **trimming, trimmed.** **4.** to put (something, such as a hedge) in good order, esp. by cutting or pruning. **5.** to adorn or decorate (something, such as a garment) with lace, ribbons, etc. **6.** (sometimes foll. by *off* or *away*) to cut so as to remove: *to trim off a branch.* **7. a.** to adjust the balance of (a ship or aircraft) by shifting cargo, etc. **b.** to adjust (a ship's sails) to take advantage of the wind. **8.** *Informal.* to thrash or beat. **9.** *Informal.* to rebuke. ~*n.* **10.** a decoration or adornment. **11.** the upholstery and decorative facings of a car's interior. **12.** proper order or fitness; good shape. **13.** a haircut that neatens but does not alter the existing hairstyle. [Old English *trymman* to strengthen]

trimaran (ˈtraɪməˌræn) *n.* a boat usually with two hulls flanking the main hull. [*tri-* + (*cata*)*maran*]

trimming (ˈtrɪmɪŋ) *n.* **1.** an extra piece added to a garment for decoration. **2.** (*pl.*) usual or traditional accompaniments: *roast turkey with all the trimmings.*

Trinitarian (ˌtrɪnɪˈtɛərɪən) *n.* **1.** a person who believes in the doctrine of the Trinity. ~*adj.* **2.** of or relating to the Trinity. —ˌTriniˈtarianˌism *n.*

trinitrotoluene (traɪˌnaɪtrəʊˈtɒljuˌiːn) *or* **trinitrotoluol** *n.* the full name for TNT.

trinity (ˈtrɪnɪtɪ) *n.*, *pl.* **-ties.** a group of three people or things. [Latin *trīnus* triple]

Trinity (ˈtrɪnɪtɪ) *n. Christian theol.* the union of three persons, the Father, Son, and Holy Spirit, in one Godhead.

Trinity Sunday *n.* the Sunday after Whit Sunday.

trinket (ˈtrɪŋkɪt) *n.* a small or worthless ornament or piece of jewellery. [origin unknown]

trio (ˈtriːəʊ) *n.*, *pl.* **trios.** **1.** a group of three people or things. **2.** *Music.* a group of three singers or musicians or a piece of music composed for such a group. [Italian]

trip (trɪp) *n.* **1.** an outward and return journey, often for a specific purpose. **2.** a false step; stumble. **3.** a light step or tread. **4.** a catch on a mechanism that acts as a switch. **5.** *Informal.* a hallucinogenic drug experience. ~*vb.* **tripping, tripped.** **6.** (often foll. by *up, on,* or *over*) to stumble or cause (someone) to stumble. **7.** (often foll. by *up*) to trap or catch (someone) in a mistake. **8.** to go on a short journey. **9.** to move or tread lightly. **10.** *Informal.* to experience the effects of a hallucinogenic drug. [Old French *triper* to tread]

tripartite (traɪˈpɑːtaɪt) *adj.* involving or composed of three people or parts. —triˈpartism *n.*

tripe (traɪp) *n.* **1.** the stomach lining of an ox, cow, or pig prepared for cooking. **2.** *Informal.* nonsense; rubbish. [Old French]

triple (ˈtrɪpᵊl) *adj.* **1.** consisting of three parts; threefold. **2.** (of musical time or

rhythm) having three beats in each bar. **3.** three times as great or as much. ~*n.* **4.** a threefold amount. **5.** a group of three. ~*vb.* **6.** to increase threefold; treble. [Latin *triplus*] —ˈtriply *adv.*

triple jump *n.* an athletic event in which the competitor has to perform a hop, a step, and a jump in a continuous movement.

triple point *n. Chem.* the temperature and pressure at which the three phases of a substance are in equilibrium.

triplet (ˈtrɪplɪt) *n.* **1.** one of three offspring born at one birth. **2.** a group or set of three similar things. **3.** a group of three musical notes.

triplicate *adj.* (ˈtrɪplɪkɪt). **1.** triple. ~*vb.* (ˈtrɪplɪˌkeɪt). **2.** to multiply or be multiplied by three. ~*n.* (ˈtrɪplɪkɪt). **3.** a group of three things. **4. in triplicate.** written out three times. [Latin *triplicāre* to triple] —ˌtripliˈcation *n.*

tripod (ˈtraɪpɒd) *n.* **1.** a three-legged stand to which a camera, etc., can be attached to hold it steady. **2.** a three-legged stool, table, etc. [TRI- + Greek *pous* a foot]

tripos (ˈtraɪpɒs) *n. Brit.* the final honours degree examinations at Cambridge University. [Latin *tripūs* tripod]

tripper (ˈtrɪpə) *n. Chiefly Brit.* a tourist.

triptych (ˈtrɪptɪk) *n.* a set of three pictures or panels, usually hinged together: often used as an altarpiece. [TRI- + Greek *ptux* plate]

trireme (ˈtraɪriːm) *n.* an ancient Greek warship with three banks of oars on each side. [TRI- + Latin *rēmus* oar]

trisect (traɪˈsɛkt) *vb.* to divide into three parts, esp. three equal parts. [TRI- + Latin *secāre* to cut] —**trisection** (traɪˈsɛkʃən) *n.*

trismus (ˈtrɪzməs) *n. Pathol.* the state of being unable to open the mouth because of sustained contractions of the jaw muscles, caused by tetanus. Nontechnical name: **lockjaw.** [Greek *trismos* a grinding]

triste (triːst) *adj. Archaic.* sad. [French]

trite (traɪt) *adj.* hackneyed; dull: *a trite comment.* [Latin *trītus* worn down]

tritium (ˈtrɪtɪəm) *n.* a radioactive isotope of hydrogen. Symbol: T or ^{3}H [Greek *tritos* third]

triumph (ˈtraɪəmf) *n.* **1.** the feeling of great happiness resulting from a victory or major achievement. **2.** the act or condition of being victorious; victory. **3.** (in ancient Rome) a procession held in honour of a victorious general. ~*vb.* **4.** (often foll. by *over*) to win a victory or control: *to triumph over one's weaknesses.* **5.** to rejoice over a victory. **6.** to celebrate a Roman triumph. [Latin *triumphus*] —**triumphal** (traɪˈamfəl) *adj.*

triumphant (traɪˈamfənt) *adj.* **1.** experiencing or displaying triumph. **2.** exultant through triumph. —**triˈumphantly** *adv.*

triumvir (traɪˈamvə) *n.* (esp. in ancient Rome) a member of a triumvirate. [Latin]

triumvirate (traɪˈamvɪrɪt) *n.* **1.** joint rule by three men. **2.** (in ancient Rome) a board of three officials jointly responsible for some task.

trivalent (traɪ'veɪlənt, 'trɪvələnt) adj. Chem. **1.** having a valency of three. **2.** having three valencies. —**tri'valency** n.

trivet ('trɪvɪt) n. **1.** a three-legged stand for holding a pot, kettle, etc., over a fire. **2.** a short metal stand on which hot dishes are placed on a table. [Old English trefet]

trivia ('trɪvɪə) n. (functioning as sing. or pl.) petty details or considerations.

trivial ('trɪvɪəl) adj. **1.** of little importance; petty or frivolous: trivial complaints. **2.** ordinary or commonplace; trite: trivial conversation. [Latin trivium junction of three roads] —**trivi'ality** n. —**'trivially** adv.

trod (trɒd) vb. the past tense and a past participle of **tread.**

trodden ('trɒd'n) vb. a past participle of **tread.**

troglodyte ('trɒglə‚daɪt) n. a cave dweller, esp. of prehistoric times. [Greek trōglodutēs one who enters caves]

troika ('trɔɪkə) n. **1.** a Russian vehicle drawn by three horses abreast. **2.** three horses harnessed abreast. **3.** a group of three people in authority. [Russian]

Trojan ('trəʊdʒən) n. **1.** a person from ancient Troy. **2.** a hard-working person. ~adj. **3.** of ancient Troy or its people.

Trojan Horse n. **1.** Greek myth. the huge wooden hollow figure of a horse used by the Greeks to enter Troy. **2.** a trap intended to undermine an enemy.

troll¹ (trəʊl) vb. Angling. **a.** to draw (a baited line, etc.) through the water. **b.** to fish (a stretch of water) by trolling. **c.** to fish (for) by trolling. [Old French troller to run about]

troll² (trəʊl) n. (in Scandinavian folklore) any of certain supernatural creatures that dwell in caves or mountains and are depicted either as dwarfs or as giants. [Old Norse: demon]

trolley ('trɒlɪ) n. **1.** Brit. a small table on casters used for carrying food or drink. **2.** Brit. a wheeled cart or stand used for moving heavy items, such as shopping in a supermarket or luggage at a railway station. **3.** Brit. See **trolley bus. 4.** U.S. & Canad. See **trolley car. 5.** a device, such as a wheel that collects the current from an overhead wire, to drive the motor of an electric vehicle. **6.** Chiefly Brit. a low truck running on rails, used in factories, mines, etc. [prob. from TROLL¹]

trolley bus n. an electrically driven public-transport vehicle that does not run on rails but takes its power from an overhead wire.

trolley car n. U.S. & Canad. same as **tram¹** (sense 1).

trollop ('trɒləp) n. a promiscuous or untidy woman. [origin unknown]

trombone (trɒm'bəʊn) n. a brass musical instrument with a sliding tube. [Italian] —**trom'bonist** n.

trompe l'oeil (‚trɒmp 'lɜːɪ) n., pl. **trompe l'oeils.** **1.** a painting, etc., giving a convincing illusion that the objects represented are real. **2.** an effect of this kind. [French, lit.: deception of the eye]

tronk (trɒŋk) n. S. African slang. a prison. [Afrikaans]

troop (truːp) n. **1.** a large group or assembly. **2.** a subdivision of a cavalry or armoured regiment. **3.** (pl.) armed forces; soldiers. **4.** a large group of Scouts patrols. ~vb. **5.** to gather, move, or march in or as if in a crowd. **6.** Mil., chiefly Brit. to parade (the colour or flag) ceremonially: the trooping of the colour. [French troupe]

trooper ('truːpə) n. **1.** a soldier in a cavalry regiment. **2.** U.S. & Austral. a mounted policeman. **3.** U.S. a state policeman. **4.** a cavalry horse. **5.** Informal, chiefly Brit. a troopship.

troopship ('truːp‚ʃɪp) n. a ship used to transport military personnel.

trope (trəʊp) n. a word or expression used in a figurative sense. [Greek tropos style, turn]

trophy ('trəʊfɪ) n., pl. **-phies.** **1.** an object such as a silver cup that is symbolic of victory in a contest, esp. a sporting contest; prize. **2.** a memento of success, esp. one taken in war or hunting. **3.** (in ancient Greece and Rome) captured arms displayed as a memorial of victory. **4.** an ornamental carving that represents a group of weapons, etc. [Greek tropaion]

tropic ('trɒpɪk) n. **1.** (sometimes cap.) either of the parallel lines of latitude at about 23½°N (**tropic of Cancer**) and 23½°S (**tropic of Capricorn**) of the equator. **2.** **the tropics.** (often cap.) that part of the earth's surface between the tropics of Cancer and Capricorn. ~adj. **3.** tropical. [Greek tropos a turn; from the belief that the sun turned back at the solstices]

tropical ('trɒpɪk'l) adj. situated in, used in, characteristic of, or relating to the tropics. —**'tropically** adv.

tropism ('trəʊpɪzəm) n. the tendency of a plant or animal to turn or curve in response to an external stimulus. [Greek tropos a turn]

troposphere ('trɒpə‚sfɪə) n. the lowest atmospheric layer, about 18 kilometres (11 miles) thick at the equator to about 6 km (4 miles) at the Poles. [Greek tropos a turn + sphere]

trot (trɒt) vb. **trotting, trotted. 1.** to move or cause (a person or animal) to move at a trot. ~n. **2.** a gait of a horse in which diagonally opposite legs come down together. **3.** a steady brisk pace. **4. on the trot.** Informal. **a.** one after the other: to read two books on the trot. **b.** busy, esp. on one's feet: I've been on the trot all day. **5. the trots.** Informal. diarrhoea. [Old French]

Trot (trɒt) n. Informal. a follower of Trotsky; Trotskyite.

troth (trəʊθ) n. Archaic. **1.** a pledge of fidelity, esp. a betrothal. **2. in troth.** truely. **3.** loyalty; fidelity. [Old English trēowth]

trot out vb. Informal. to bring forward (old information or ideas), as for approval or admiration, esp. repeatedly.

Trotskyite ('trɒtskɪ‚aɪt) or **Trotskyist** ('trɒtskɪɪst) adj. **1.** of the theories or Leon

Trotsky (1879-1940), Russian revolutionary and writer. ~*n.* **2.** a supporter of Trotsky. —'**Trotsky,ism** *n.*

trotter ('trɒtə) *n.* **1.** a horse that is specially trained to trot fast. **2.** (*usually pl.*) the foot of certain animals, esp. of pigs.

troubadour ('truːbə,dʊə) *n.* any of a class of lyric poets in S France and N Italy from the 11th to the 13th century who wrote chiefly on courtly love. [French]

trouble ('trʌbªl) *n.* **1.** a state of mental distress or anxiety. **2.** a state of disorder or unrest: *industrial trouble.* **3.** a condition of disease, pain, or malfunctioning: *liver trouble.* **4.** a cause of distress, disturbance, or pain: *what's the trouble?* **5.** effort or exertion taken to do something. **6.** a personal weakness or cause of annoyance: *his trouble is he's too soft.* **7. in trouble. a.** likely to suffer punishment: *he's in trouble with the police.* **b.** pregnant when not married. ~*vb.* **8.** to cause trouble to. **9.** (foll. by *about*) to put oneself to inconvenience; be concerned: *don't trouble about me.* **10.** to take pains; exert oneself. **11.** to cause inconvenience or discomfort to: *does this noise trouble you?* [Old French *troubler*]

troublemaker ('trʌbªl,meikə) *n.* a person who makes trouble, esp. between people. —'**trouble,making** *adj., n.*

troubleshooter ('trʌbªl,ʃuːtə) *n.* a person employed to locate and correct faults in machinery or problems in a company. —'**trouble,shooting** *n., adj.*

troublesome ('trʌbªlsəm) *adj.* causing trouble.

troublous ('trʌbləs) *adj. Archaic or literary.* unsettled; agitated.

trough (trɒf) *n.* **1.** a narrow open container, esp. one in which food or water for animals is put. **2.** a narrow channel, gutter, or gulley. **3.** *Meteorol.* an elongated area of low pressure. [Old English *trōh*]

trounce (traʊns) *vb.* to beat or defeat (someone) utterly. [origin unknown]

troupe (truːp) *n.* a company of actors or other performers, esp. one that travels. [French]

trouper ('truːpə) *n.* **1.** a member of a troupe. **2.** an experienced person.

trouser ('traʊzə) *n.* (*modifier*) of or relating to trousers: *trouser buttons.*

trousers ('traʊzəz) *pl. n.* a garment that covers the body from the waist to the ankles or knees with separate tube-shaped sections for both legs. [Scot. Gaelic *triubhas* trews]

trousseau ('truːsəʊ) *n., pl.* **-seaux** or **-seaus** (-səʊz). the clothes, linen, and other possessions collected by a bride for her marriage. [Old French]

trout (traʊt) *n., pl.* **trout** or **trouts.** any of various game fishes related to the salmon and found chiefly in fresh water in northern regions. [Old English *trūht*]

trove (trəʊv) *n.* See **treasure-trove.**

trow (trəʊ) *vb. Archaic.* to think, believe, or trust. [Old English *treow*]

trowel ('traʊəl) *n.* **1.** any of various small hand tools having a flat metal blade, used for spreading plaster or similar materials. **2.** a similar tool with a curved blade used by gardeners for lifting plants, etc. [Latin *trulla* a scoop]

troy weight *or* **troy** (trɔɪ) *n.* a system of weights used for precious metals and gemstones in which one pound equals twelve ounces. [after the city of *Troyes,* France, where first used]

truant ('truːənt) *n.* **1.** a person who is absent without leave, esp. from school. **2. play truant.** to stay away, esp. from school, without permission. ~*adj.* **3.** being or relating to a truant. [Old French: vagabond] —'**truancy** *n.*

truce (truːs) *n.* **1.** an agreement to stop fighting, esp. temporarily. **2.** a temporary halt of something unpleasant. [pl. of Old English *treow* trow]

truck[1] (trʌk) *n.* **1.** *Brit.* a vehicle for carrying freight on a railway; wagon. **2.** *Chiefly U.S. & Canad.* a lorry. **3.** a frame carrying two or more pairs of wheels attached under an end of a railway coach, etc. **4.** any wheeled vehicle used to move goods. [perhaps from *truckle* a small wheel]

truck[2] (trʌk) *n.* **1.** commercial exchange. **2.** payment of wages in kind. **3. have no truck with someone.** to have no dealings with someone. ~*vb.* **4.** to exchange (goods); barter. [Old French *troquer* (unattested) to barter]

truckle ('trʌkªl) *vb.* (usually foll. by *to*) to yield weakly; give in: *I'm sick of having to truckle to you!* [from obs. *truckle* to sleep in a truckle bed]

truckle bed *n.* a low bed on wheels, stored under a larger bed.

truculent ('trʌkjʊlənt) *adj.* defiantly aggressive or bad-tempered. [Latin *trux* fierce] —'**truculence** *n.*

trudge (trʌdʒ) *vb.* **1.** to walk or plod (somewhere) heavily or wearily. **2.** to pass over (something) by trudging. ~*n.* **3.** a long tiring walk. [origin unknown]

true (truː) *adj.* **truer, truest. 1.** not false, fictional, or illusory; factual. **2.** real; not synthetic: *true leather.* **3.** faithful and loyal. **4.** conforming to a required standard, law, or pattern: *a true aim.* **5.** (of a compass bearing) according to the earth's geographical rather than magnetic poles: *true north.* **6. in** (*or* **out of**) **true.** in (or not in) correct alignment. ~*adv.* **7.** truthfully; rightly. **8.** precisely or unswervingly: *he shot true.* [Old English *triewe*]

true-blue *adj.* **1.** staunchly loyal. ~*n.* **true blue. 2.** *Chiefly Brit.* a staunch royalist or Conservative.

true-life *adj.* directly comparable to reality: *a true-life story.*

truelove ('truː,lʌv) *n.* someone truly loved; sweetheart.

true north *n.* the direction from any point along a meridian towards the North Pole.

truffle ('trʌfªl) *n.* **1.** a round mushroom-like fungus regarded as a delicacy. **2.** Also called: **rum truffle.** *Chiefly Brit.* a sweet flavoured with chocolate or rum. [French *truffe*]

trug (trʌg) n. a long shallow basket for carrying garden tools, flowers, etc. [perhaps var. of *trough*]

truism ('truːɪzəm) n. a statement that is clearly true and well known.

truly ('truːlɪ) adv. 1. in a true, just, or faithful manner. 2. really: *a truly great man*.

trump¹ (trʌmp) n. 1. Also called: **trump card. a.** any card from the suit that ranks higher than any other suit in one particular game. **b.** this suit itself. 2. a decisive or advantageous move, resource, etc., held in reserve. 3. *Informal.* a fine or reliable person. ~vb. 4. to play a trump card on (a card of a suit that is not trumps). 5. to outdo or surpass. ~See also **trumps**. [var. of *triumph*]

trump² (trʌmp) n. Archaic or literary. 1. a trumpet or the sound produced by one. 2. **the last trump.** the final trumpet call on the Day of Judgment. [Old French *trompe*]

trumped up adj. (of charges, excuses, etc.) made up in order to deceive.

trumpery ('trʌmpərɪ) n., pl. -eries. 1. foolish talk or actions. 2. a useless or worthless article. ~adj. 3. useless or worthless. [Old French *tromperie* deceit]

trumpet ('trʌmpɪt) n. 1. a valved brass musical instrument consisting of a narrow tube ending in a flare. 2. a loud sound such as that of a trumpet. 3. short for **ear trumpet.** 4. **blow one's own trumpet.** to boast about one's own skills or good qualities. ~vb. 5. to proclaim or sound loudly. [Old French *trompette*] —'**trumpeter** n.

trumps (trʌmps) pl. n. 1. (*sometimes sing.*) Cards. any one of the four suits that outranks all the other suits for the duration of a deal or game. 2. **turn up trumps.** (of a person) to bring about a happy or successful conclusion, esp. unexpectedly.

truncate (trʌŋ'keɪt) vb. to shorten by cutting. [Latin *truncāre*] —**trun'cation** n.

truncated (trʌŋ'keɪtɪd) adj. shortened by or as if by cutting off.

truncheon ('trʌntʃən) n. 1. Chiefly Brit. a short thick stick carried by a policeman. 2. a staff or baton carried as a symbol of authority. [Old French *tronchon* stump]

trundle ('trʌndᵊl) vb. to move heavily on or as if on wheels: *the bus trundled by.* [Old English *tryndel*]

trundler ('trʌndlə) n. N.Z. 1. a golf or shopping trolley. 2. a child's pushchair.

trunk (trʌŋk) n. 1. the main stem of a tree. 2. a large strong case or box used to contain clothes when travelling and for storage. 3. the body excluding the head, neck, and limbs; torso. 4. the long nasal part of an elephant. 5. U.S. same as **boot¹** (sense 2). ~See also **trunks**. [Latin *truncus* cut short]

trunk call n. Chiefly Brit. a long-distance telephone call.

trunk line n. 1. a direct link between two distant telephone exchanges or switchboards. 2. the main route or routes on a railway.

trunk road n. Brit. a main road, esp. one that is suitable for heavy vehicles.

trunks (trʌŋks) pl. n. a man's garment worn for swimming, boxing, etc., extending from the waist to the thigh.

truss (trʌs) vb. 1. to tie or bind (someone) up. 2. to bind the wings and legs of (a fowl) before cooking. 3. to support or stiffen (a roof, bridge, etc.) with a structural framework. ~n. 4. a structural framework of wood or metal used to support a roof, bridge, etc. 5. Med. a device for holding a hernia in place. 6. a cluster of flowers or fruit growing at the end of a single stalk. 7. a bundle or pack. [Old French *trousse*]

trust (trʌst) n. 1. reliance on and confidence in the truth, worth, reliability, etc., of a person or thing; faith. 2. the obligation of someone in a responsible position: *a position of trust.* 3. custody, charge, or care: *a child placed in my trust.* 4. **a.** an arrangement between two people whereby property is kept, used, or administered by one person for the benefit of the other. **b.** property that is the subject of such an arrangement. 5. Chiefly U.S. & Canad. a group of companies joined together to control the market for any commodity. 6. (*modifier*) of or relating to a trust or trusts. ~vb. 7. to expect, hope, or suppose: *I trust that you are well.* 8. to place confidence in (someone to do something); rely (upon). 9. to consign for care: *the child was trusted to my care.* 10. to allow (someone to do something) with confidence in his or her good sense or honesty. [Old Norse *traust*]

trustee (trʌ'stiː) n. 1. a person to whom the legal title to property is entrusted. 2. a member of a board that manages the affairs of an institution or organization.

trustful ('trʌstfʊl) or **trusting** adj. characterized by a readiness to trust others. —'**trustfully** or '**trustingly** adv.

trust fund n. money, securities, etc., held in trust.

trustworthy ('trʌst,wɜːðɪ) adj. (of a person) honest, reliable, or dependable.

trusty ('trʌstɪ) adj. **trustier, trustiest.** 1. faithful or reliable: *a trusty old dog.* ~n., pl. **trusties.** 2. a trustworthy convict to whom special privileges are granted.

truth (truːθ) n. 1. the quality of being true, genuine, actual, or factual. 2. something that is true. 3. a proven or verified fact, principle, etc.: *the truths of astronomy.* [Old English *triewth*]

truthful ('truːθfʊl) adj. 1. telling the truth; honest. 2. realistic: *a truthful portrayal of the king.* —'**truthfully** adv. —'**truthfulness** n.

try (traɪ) vb. **trying, tried.** 1. to make an effort or attempt: *I don't know if I can, but I'll try; he tried to climb a cliff.* 2. to sample, test, or give experimental use to (something). 3. to put strain or stress on: *he tries my patience.* 4. to give pain, affliction, or vexation to: *I have been sorely tried by those children.* 5. **a.** to examine and determine the issues involved in (a cause) in a court of law. **b.** to hear evidence in order to determine the guilt or innocence of (a person). ~n., pl. **tries. 6.** an attempt or effort. **7.** Rugby. a score made by placing the ball down behind the opposing team's goal line. [Old French trier to sort]

trying ('traɪɪŋ) adj. upsetting, difficult, or annoying.

try on vb. **1.** to put on (a garment) to find out whether it fits. **2. try it on.** Informal. to attempt to deceive or fool someone. ~n. **try-on. 3.** Brit. informal. something done to test out a person's tolerance, etc.

try out vb. **1.** to test (something) or put (something) to experimental use. ~n. **try-out. 2.** Chiefly U.S. & Canad. a trial or test, as of an athlete or actor.

trysail ('traɪˌseɪl; Naut. 'traɪs²l) n. a small fore-and-aft sail set on a sailing vessel to help keep her head to the wind in a storm.

tryst (trɪst, traɪst) n. Archaic or literary. **1.** an appointment to meet, esp. secretly. **2.** the place of such a meeting or the meeting itself. [Old French triste lookout post]

tsar or **czar** (zɑː) n. (until 1917) the emperor of Russia. [Russian: Caesar] —**'tsardom** or **'czardom** n.

tsarevitch or **czarevitch** ('zɑːrəvɪtʃ) n. the eldest son of a Russian tsar.

tsarina or **czarina** (zɑː'riːnə) n. the wife of a Russian tsar; Russian empress.

tsetse fly or **tzetze fly** ('tsɛtsɪ) n. a bloodsucking African fly which transmits disease, esp. sleeping sickness. [from a S African language]

T-shirt or **tee-shirt** n. a lightweight, usually short-sleeved, casual garment for the upper body. [T-shape formed when laid flat]

tsp. teaspoon.

T-square n. a T-shaped ruler used for drawing horizontal lines and to support set squares when drawing vertical and inclined lines.

tsunami (tsʊ'nɑːmɪ) n., pl. **-mis** or **-mi.** a large, often destructive, sea wave, usually caused by an earthquake under the sea. [Japanese]

TT 1. teetotal. **2.** teetotaller. **3.** tuberculin-tested.

TU trade union.

Tu. Tuesday.

tub (tʌb) n. **1.** a low wide, usually round container. **2.** a small plastic or cardboard container for ice cream, etc. **3.** Chiefly U.S. same as **bath** (sense 1). **4.** Also called: **tubful.** the amount a tub will hold. **5.** a slow and uncomfortable boat or ship. [Middle Dutch tubbe]

tuba ('tjuːbə) n. a valved brass musical instrument of low pitch. [Latin]

tubby ('tʌbɪ) adj. **-bier, -biest.** (of a person) fat and short. —**'tubbiness** n.

tube (tjuːb) n. **1.** a long hollow cylindrical object, used for the passage of fluids or as a container. **2.** a pliable cylindrical container of soft metal or plastic closed with a cap, used to hold semiliquids or pastes: a

tube of toothpaste. **3.** Anat. any hollow cylindrical structure. **4.** (sometimes cap.) Brit. **the tube.** an underground railway system, esp. that in London. **5.** Electronics. **a.** same as **valve** (sense 3). **b.** See **electron tube, cathode-ray tube. 6.** Slang, chiefly U.S. a television set. [Latin tubus] —**'tubeless** adj.

tuber ('tjuːbə) n. a fleshy underground root of a plant, such as a potato plant. [Latin: hump]

tubercle ('tjuːbək²l) n. **1.** a small rounded lump, esp. on the skin, on a bone, or on a plant. **2.** any abnormal hard swelling, esp. one characteristic of tuberculosis. [Latin tūberculum a little swelling]

tubercular (tjʊ'bɜːkjʊlə) or **tuberculous** adj. **1.** of or symptomatic of tuberculosis. **2.** of or relating to a tubercle.

tuberculin (tjʊ'bɜːkjʊlɪn) n. a sterile liquid prepared from cultures of the tubercle bacillus and used in the diagnosis of tuberculosis.

tuberculin-tested adj. (of milk) produced by cows that have been certified as free of tuberculosis.

tuberculosis (tjʊˌbɜːkjʊ'ləʊsɪs) n. an infectious disease characterized by the formation of tubercles, esp. in the lungs.

tuberous ('tjuːbərəs) adj. (of plants) forming, bearing, or resembling a tuber or tubers.

tubing ('tjuːbɪŋ) n. **1.** a length of tube. **2.** a system of tubes.

tubular ('tjuːbjʊlə) adj. **1.** having the shape of a tube or tubes. **2.** of or relating to a tube or tubing.

tubule ('tjuːbjuːl) n. any small tubular structure in an animal or plant.

TUC (in Britain) Trades Union Congress.

tuck (tʌk) vb. **1.** to push or fold into a small confined space or concealed place or between two surfaces: to tuck a letter into an envelope. **2.** to thrust the loose ends or sides of (something) into a confining space, so as to make neat and secure. **3.** to make a tuck or tucks in (a garment). ~n. **4.** a tucked object or part. **5.** a pleat or fold in a part of a garment, usually stitched down. **6.** Brit. informal. food, esp. cakes and sweets. [Old English tūcian to torment]

tuck away vb. Informal. **1.** to eat (a large amount of food). **2.** to store (something), esp. in a place difficult to find.

tucker¹ ('tʌkə) n. a detachable yoke of lace, linen, etc., formerly worn over the breast of a low-cut dress.

tucker² ('tʌkə) vb. (usually foll. by out) Informal, chiefly U.S. & Canad. to weary or tire.

tuck in vb. **1.** Also: **tuck into.** to put (someone) to bed and make snug. **2.** to thrust the loose ends or sides of (something) into a confining space: tuck the blankets in. **3.** Also: **tuck into.** Informal. to eat, esp. heartily. ~n. **tuck-in. 4.** Brit. informal. a meal, esp. a large one.

tuck shop n. Chiefly Brit. a shop in or near a school, where cakes and sweets are sold.

Tudor ('tjuːdə) adj. **1.** of or relating to the

English royal house ruling from 1485 to 1603. **2.** denoting a style of architecture characterized by half-timbered houses.

Tues. Tuesday.

Tuesday ('tjuːzdɪ) *n.* the third day of the week; second day of the working week. [Old English *tīwesdæg*]

tufa ('tjuːfə) *n.* a porous rock formed of calcium carbonate deposited from springs. [Italian *tufo*]

tuff (tʌf) *n.* a porous rock formed from volcanic dust or ash. [Old French *tuf*]

tuffet ('tʌfɪt) *n.* a small mound or low seat. [from *tuft*]

tuft (tʌft) *n.* a bunch of feathers, grass, hair, threads, etc., held together at the base. [prob. from Old French *tufe*] —'**tufted** *adj.* —'**tufty** *adj.*

tug (tʌg) *vb.* **tugging, tugged. 1.** to pull or drag with sharp or powerful movements: *the boy tugged at the door handle.* **2.** to tow (a vessel) by means of a tug. ~*n.* **3.** a strong pull or jerk. **4.** Also called: **tugboat.** a boat with a powerful engine, used for towing barges, ships, etc. [Middle English *tuggen*]

tug of war *n.* **1.** a contest in which two people or teams pull opposite ends of a rope in an attempt to drag the opposition over a central line. **2.** any hard struggle between two people or two groups.

tuition (tjuːˈɪʃən) *n.* **1.** instruction, esp. that received individually or in a small group. **2.** the payment for instruction, esp. in colleges or universities. [Latin *tuērī* to watch over]

tulip ('tjuːlɪp) *n.* **1.** a spring-blooming bulb plant with single showy bell-shaped flowers. **2.** the flower or bulb. [Turkish *tülbend* turban]

tulip tree *n.* a North American tree with tulip-shaped greenish-yellow flowers and long conelike fruits.

tulle (tjuːl) *n.* a fine net fabric of silk, rayon, etc. [French]

tumble ('tʌmbəl) *vb.* **1.** to fall, esp. awkwardly or violently: *I tumbled down the stairs.* **2.** to decrease in value suddenly: *share prices tumbled.* **3.** (usually foll. by *about*) to roll or twist, esp. in playing: *the kittens tumbled about on the floor.* **4.** to perform leaps or somersaults. **5.** to move in a heedless or hasty way: *they came tumbling into the room.* **6.** to disturb, rumple, or toss around: *to tumble the bed clothes.* ~*n.* **7.** a tumbling. **8.** a fall or toss. **9.** an acrobatic feat, esp. a somersault. **10.** a confused or untidy state. [Old English *tumbian*]

tumbledown ('tʌmbəl,daʊn) *adj.* (of a building) falling to pieces; dilapidated.

tumble dryer *n.* an electrically-operated machine that dries wet laundry by rotating it in warmed air inside a metal drum.

tumbler ('tʌmblə) *n.* **1. a.** a flat-bottomed drinking glass with no handle or stem. **b.** the amount a tumbler will hold. **2.** a person who performs somersaults and other acrobatic feats. **3.** same as **tumble dryer. 4.** a part of the mechanism of a lock.

tumble to *vb.* to understand; become aware of: *she quickly tumbled to his plan.*

tumbrel *or* **tumbril** ('tʌmbrəl) *n.* a farm cart, esp. one that tilts backwards to empty its load. A cart of this type was used to take condemned prisoners to the guillotine during the French Revolution. [Old French *tumberel*]

tumescent (tjuːˈmɛsʰnt) *adj.* swollen or becoming swollen.

tumid ('tjuːmɪd) *adj.* **1.** (of an organ or part) enlarged or swollen. **2.** pompous or fulsome in style: *tumid prose.* [Latin *tumēre* to swell] —**tu'midity** *n.*

tummy ('tʌmɪ) *n., pl.* **-mies.** an informal or childish word for **stomach.**

tumour *or U.S.* **tumor** ('tjuːmə) *n.* Pathol. **a.** any abnormal swelling. **b.** a mass of tissue formed by a new growth of cells. [Latin *tumēre* to swell] —'**tumorous** *adj.*

tumult ('tjuːmʌlt) *n.* **1.** a loud confused noise, as of a crowd; commotion. **2.** violent agitation or disturbance. **3.** great emotional disturbance. [Latin *tumultus*]

tumultuous (tjuːˈmʌltjʊəs) *adj.* **1.** exciting, confused, or turbulent: *tumultuous feelings; a tumultuous decade.* **2.** unruly, noisy, or excited: *a tumultuous welcome.*

tumulus ('tjuːmjʊləs) *n., pl.* **-li** (-laɪ). Archaeol. (no longer in technical usage) same as **barrow²**. [Latin: a hillock]

tun (tʌn) *n.* **1.** a large beer cask. **2.** a measure of capacity, usually equal to 252 wine gallons. [Old English *tunne*]

tuna ('tjuːnə) *n., pl.* **-na** *or* **-nas. 1.** a large marine spiny-finned fish. **2.** the flesh of this fish, often tinned for food. [American Spanish]

tundra ('tʌndrə) *n.* a vast treeless Arctic region with permanently frozen subsoil. [Russian]

tune (tjuːn) *n.* **1.** a melody, esp. one for which harmony is not essential. **2.** the correct musical pitch: *this piano's out of tune.* **3. call the tune.** to be in control of the proceedings. **4. change one's tune.** to alter one's attitude or tone of speech. **5. in** (*or* **out of**) **tune with.** in (*or* not in) agreement with. **6. to the tune of.** *Informal.* to the amount or extent of. ~*vb.* **7.** to adjust (a musical instrument) to a certain pitch. **8.** (often foll. by *up*) to make fine adjustments to (an engine, machine, etc.) to obtain the proper or desired performance. [var. of *tone*] —'**tuner** *n.*

tuneful ('tjuːnfʊl) *adj.* having a pleasant tune; melodious. —'**tunefully** *adv.*

tune in *vb.* **1.** (often foll. by *to*) to adjust (a radio or television) to receive (a station or programme). **2. tuned in to.** *Slang.* aware of or knowledgeable about: *tuned in to what computers can do.*

tuneless ('tjuːnlɪs) *adj.* having no melody or tune.

tune up *vb.* **1.** to adjust (a musical instrument) to a particular pitch. **2.** to adjust (an engine) in (a car, etc.) to improve performance.

tungsten ('tʌŋstən) *n.* a hard greyish-white element. Symbol: W [Swedish *tung* heavy + *sten* stone]

tunic ('tjuːnɪk) n. any of various hip-length or knee-length garments, such as the loose sleeveless garb worn in ancient Greece or Rome, the jacket of some soldiers, or a woman's hip-length garment, worn with a skirt or trousers. [Latin *tunica*]

tuning fork n. a two-pronged metal fork that when struck produces a pure note of constant specified pitch.

tunnel ('tʌnʲl) n. **1.** an underground passageway, esp. one for trains or cars. **2.** any passage or channel through or under something. ~vb. **-nelling, -nelled** or U.S. **-neling, -neled. 3.** to make or force (a way) through or under (something). **4.** (foll. by *through, under,* etc.) to make or force a way (through or under something). [Old French *tonel* cask]

tunnel vision n. **1.** a condition in which a person is unable to see things that are not straight in front of them. **2.** narrowness of viewpoint resulting from concentration on a single idea, opinion, etc.

tunny ('tʌnɪ) n., pl. **-nies** or **-ny.** same as **tuna.** [Latin *thunnus*]

tup (tʌp) n. Chiefly Brit. a male sheep; ram. [origin unknown]

tupik ('tuːpək) n. a tent of seal or caribou skin used for shelter by the Inuit in summer. [Eskimo]

tuppence ('tʌpəns) n. Brit. same as **twopence.** —'**tuppenny** adj.

tuque (tuːk) n. (in Canada) a knitted cap with a long tapering end. [Canad. French]

turban ('tɜːbʲn) n. **1.** a head-covering worn esp. by Muslims, Hindus, and Sikhs. **2.** any head-covering resembling this. [Turkish *tülbend*] —'**turbaned** adj.

turbid ('tɜːbɪd) adj. **1.** muddy or clouded, as from having the sediment stirred up. **2.** dense, thick, or cloudy: *turbid fog.* [Latin *turbāre* to agitate] —**tur'bidity** n.

turbine ('tɜːbɪn, -baɪn) n. a machine in which power is produced by a stream of water, air, etc., that pushes the blades of a wheel and causes it to rotate. [Latin *turbō* whirlwind]

turbofan (ˌtɜːbəʊ'fæn) n. a type of engine in which a large fan driven by a turbine forces air rearwards to increase the propulsive thrust.

turbojet (ˌtɜːbəʊ'dʒɛt) n. **1.** a gas turbine in which the exhaust gases provide the propulsive thrust to drive an aircraft. **2.** an aircraft powered by turbojet engines.

turboprop (ˌtɜːbəʊ'prɒp) n. a gas turbine for driving an aircraft propeller.

turbot ('tɜːbət) n., pl. **-bot** or **-bots.** a European flatfish, highly valued as a food fish. [Old French *tourbot*]

turbulence ('tɜːbjʊləns) n. **1.** a state or condition of confusion, movement, or agitation. **2.** Meteorol. instability in the atmosphere causing gusty air currents.

turbulent ('tɜːbjʊlənt) adj. **1.** being in a state of turbulence. **2.** wild or disobedient; unruly. [Latin *turba* confusion]

turd (tɜːd) n. Taboo. **1.** a piece of excrement. **2.** Slang. a contemptible person. [Old English *tord*]

tureen (təˈriːn) n. a large deep dish with a cover, used for serving soups. [French *terrine* earthenware vessel]

turf (tɜːf) n., pl. **turfs** or **turves. 1.** a surface layer of earth containing a dense growth of grasses with their roots; sod. **2.** a piece cut from this layer. **3. the turf. a.** a track where horse races are run. **b.** horse racing as a sport or industry. **4.** same as **peat.** ~vb. **5.** to cover (an area of ground) with pieces of turf. [Old English]

turf accountant n. Brit. same as **bookmaker.**

turf out vb. Brit. informal. to throw (someone or something) out.

turgescent (tɜː'dʒɛsʲnt) adj. becoming or being swollen. —**tur'gescence** n.

turgid ('tɜːdʒɪd) adj. **1.** swollen and distended. **2.** (of language) pompous; bombastic. [Latin *turgēre* to swell] —**tur'gidity** n.

Turk (tɜːk) n. **1.** a person from Turkey. **2.** a native speaker of any Turkic language.

Turk. **1.** Turkey. **2.** Turkish.

turkey ('tɜːkɪ) n., pl. **-keys** or **-key. 1.** a large bird of North America bred for its flesh. **2.** U.S. & Canad. informal. something, esp. a theatrical production, that fails. **3. cold turkey.** Slang. a method of curing drug addiction by abrupt withdrawal of all doses. **4. talk turkey.** Informal, chiefly U.S. & Canad. to discuss, esp. business, frankly and practically. [used at first of the African guinea fowl (because it was brought through Turkish territory), later applied by mistake to the American bird]

turkey cock n. **1.** a male turkey. **2.** an arrogant person.

Turkic ('tɜːkɪk) n. a family of Asian languages including Turkish and Tatar.

Turkish ('tɜːkɪʃ) adj. **1.** of Turkey, its people, or their language. ~n. **2.** the official language of Turkey.

Turkish bath n. **1.** a type of bath in which the bather sweats freely in a steam room, is then washed, often massaged, and has a cold plunge or shower. **2.** (sometimes pl.) an establishment for such baths.

Turkish coffee n. very strong black coffee.

Turkish delight n. a jelly-like sweet flavoured with flower essences, usually cut into cubes and covered in icing sugar.

Turkish towel n. a rough loose-piled towel.

turmeric ('tɜːmərɪk) n. **1.** a tropical Asian plant with yellow flowers and an aromatic underground stem. **2.** the powdered stem of this plant, used as a flavouring and as a yellow dye. [Old French *terre merite* meritorious earth]

turmoil ('tɜːmɔɪl) n. a violent or confused state; agitation. [origin unknown]

turn (tɜːn) vb. **1.** to move around an axis: *to turn a knob.* **2.** to change or cause to change position by moving: *he turned the chair to face the light.* **3.** to change or cause to change in course, direction, etc.:

turn right at the end of the road. **4.** to go round (a corner, etc.). **5.** to assume or cause to assume a curved or folded form: *the road turns here.* **6.** to reverse or cause to reverse position: *turn the page.* **7.** to perform or do by a rotating movement: *to turn a somersault.* **8.** to shape (wood, metal, etc.) on a lathe. **9.** (foll. by *into* or *to*) to change or convert or be changed or converted: *to turn base metals into gold.* **10.** (foll. by *into*) to change or cause to change in nature, character, etc.: *the frog turned into a prince.* **11.** to change so as to become: *he turned nasty.* **12.** to cause (foliage, etc.) to change colour or (of foliage, etc.) to change colour. **13.** to cause (milk) to become sour or (of milk) to become sour. **14.** to change or cause to change in subject, trend, etc.: *the conversation turned to fishing.* **15.** to direct or apply or be directed or applied: *he turned his attention to the problem.* **16.** (foll. by *to*) to appeal or apply to for help, advice, etc. **17.** to reach, pass, or progress beyond in age, time, etc.: *she has just turned twenty.* **18.** to cause or allow to go: *to turn an animal loose.* **19.** to affect or be affected with nausea or giddiness: *it made my stomach turn.* **20.** to translate into another language. **21.** (usually foll. by *against* or *from*) to transfer or reverse (one's loyalties, affections, etc.). **22. turn someone's head.** to affect someone mentally or emotionally. ~*n.* **23.** a turning or being turned. **24.** a movement of complete or partial rotation. **25.** a change of direction or position. **26.** direction or drift: *his thoughts took a new turn.* **27.** same as **turning** (sense 1). **28.** the right or opportunity to do something in an agreed order or succession: *now it's George's turn.* **29.** a change in nature, condition, etc.: *a turn for the worse.* **30.** a period of action, work, etc. **31.** a short walk, ride, or excursion. **32.** natural inclination: *a speculative turn of mind.* **33.** distinctive form or style: *a neat turn of phrase.* **34.** a deed that helps or hinders someone: *a good turn.* **35.** a twist, bend, or distortion in shape. **36.** *Music.* a melodic ornament that makes a turn around a note, beginning with the note above, in a variety of sequences. **37.** a short theatrical act: *a comedy turn.* **38.** *Informal.* a shock or surprise: *the news gave her quite a turn.* **39. turn and turn about.** one after another; alternately. **40. to a turn.** to the proper amount; perfectly: *cooked to a turn.* ~See also **turn down, turn in,** etc. [Old English *tyrnian*] —'**turner** *n.*

turnabout ('tɜːnəˌbaʊt) *n.* **1.** the act of turning so as to face a different direction. **2.** a reversal of opinion, attitude, etc.

turnbuckle ('tɜːnˌbʌk²l) *n.* an open mechanical sleeve usually having a swivel at one end and a thread at the other to enable a threaded wire or rope to be tightened.

turncoat ('tɜːnˌkəʊt) *n.* a person who deserts one cause or party to join an opposing one.

turn down *vb.* **1.** to reduce (the volume or brightness) of (something). **2.** to reject

or refuse: *I turned down his invitation.* **3.** to fold down (sheets, etc.).

turn in *vb. Informal.* **1.** to go to bed for the night. **2.** to hand in: *to turn in an essay.* **3.** to give up: *we turned in the game when it started to rain.*

turning ('tɜːnɪŋ) *n.* **1.** a road, river, or path that turns off the main way. **2.** the point where such a way turns off. **3.** the process of turning objects on a lathe. **4.** (*pl.*) the waste produced in turning on a lathe.

turning circle *n.* the smallest circle in which a vehicle can turn.

turning point *n.* a moment when a decisive change occurs.

turnip ('tɜːnɪp) *n.* a vegetable with a large yellow or white edible root. [Latin *nāpus*]

turnkey ('tɜːnˌkiː) *n. Archaic.* a jailer.

turn off *vb.* **1.** to leave (a road or path). **2.** (of a road or path) to deviate from (another road or path). **3.** to cause (something) to stop operating by turning a knob, pushing a button, etc. **4.** *Informal.* to cause (a person) to feel dislike for (something): *this music turns me off.* ~*n.* **turnoff.** **5.** a road or other way branching off from the main thoroughfare. **6.** *Informal.* a person or thing that causes dislike.

turn on *vb.* **1.** to cause (something) to operate by turning a knob, etc. **2.** to become hostile to; retaliate against: *the dog turned on the children.* **3.** *Informal.* to produce suddenly or automatically: *turn on the charm.* **4.** *Slang.* to arouse emotionally or sexually. **5.** to depend or hinge on: *the success of the party turns on you.* ~*n.* **turn-on.** **6.** *Slang.* a person or thing that causes emotional or sexual arousal.

turn out *vb.* **1.** to cause (something, esp. a light) to stop operating by or as if by turning a knob, etc. **2.** to produce by an effort or process: *she turned out fifty units per hour.* **3.** to dismiss or expel: *he was turned out of his new home.* **4.** to empty the contents of (something). **5.** to end up; result: *it all turned out well.* **6.** to fit as with clothes: *that woman turns her children out well.* **7.** to assemble or gather: *the crowd turned out for the fair.* **8.** (of a soldier) to parade or to call (a soldier) to parade. ~*n.* **turnout.** **9.** the body of people appearing together at a gathering. **10.** the quantity or amount produced. **11.** an array of clothing or equipment.

turn over *vb.* **1.** to change or cause (something) to change position, esp. so as to reverse top and bottom. **2.** to start (an engine), esp. with a starting handle, or (of an engine) to start or function correctly. **3.** to shift or cause to shift position, as by rolling from side to side. **4.** to consider carefully: *he turned over the problem for hours.* **5.** *Slang.* to rob: *this shop has been turned over.* ~*n.* **turnover.** **6. a.** the amount of business transacted by a company during a specified period. **b.** the rate at which stock in trade is sold and replenished. **7.** a small pastry case filled with fruit or jam. **8.** the number of workers employed by a firm in a given period to replace those who have left.

turnpike ('tɜːnˌpaɪk) n. 1. Hist. a barrier across a road to prevent vehicles or pedestrian passing until a charge (toll) had been paid. 2. U.S. a motorway for use of which a toll is charged. [turn + pike a spike]

turnstile ('tɜːnˌstaɪl) n. a mechanical barrier with metal arms that are turned to admit one person at a time.

turntable ('tɜːnˌteɪb'l) n. 1. the circular platform that rotates a gramophone record while it is being played. 2. a circular platform used for turning locomotives and cars.

turn to vb. to set about a task.

turn up vb. 1. to arrive or appear: she turned up late. 2. to find or be found, esp. by accident: the letter turned up in the drawer. 3. to increase the flow, volume, etc., of: turn up the radio. ~n. **turn-up**. 4. (often pl.) Brit. the turned-up fold at the bottom of some trouser legs. 5. **a turn-up for the book**. Informal. an unexpected happening.

turpentine ('tɜːp'nˌtaɪn) n. 1. a semisolid mixture of resin and oil obtained from various coniferous trees and used as the main source of commercial turpentine. 2. a colourless volatile oil distilled from turpentine resin. It is used as a solvent for paints and in medicine. 3. (not in technical usage) any one of a number of thinners for paints and varnishes, consisting of fractions of petroleum. [Latin terebinthina]

turpitude ('tɜːpɪˌtjuːd) n. depravity; wickedness. [Latin turpitūdō ugliness]

turps (tɜːps) n. (functioning as sing.) Brit. short for **turpentine** (sense 2).

turquoise ('tɜːkwɔːz, -kwɑːz) n. 1. a greenish-blue gemstone. ~adj. 2. greenish-blue. [Old French turqueise Turkish (stone)]

turret ('tʌrɪt) n. 1. a small tower that projects from the wall of a building, esp. a castle. 2. (on a tank or warship) a rotating structure on which weapons are mounted. 3. (on a machine tool) a turret-like steel structure with tools projecting radially that can be pivoted to bring each tool to bear on the work. [Latin turris tower] —'**turreted** adj.

turtle ('tɜːt'l) n. 1. an aquatic reptile with a flattened shell enclosing the body and flipper-like limbs adapted for swimming. 2. **turn turtle**. (of a boat) to capsize. [French tortue tortoise]

turtledove ('tɜːt'lˌdʌv) n. an Old World dove noted for its soft cooing and devotion to its mate. [Old English turtla]

turtleneck ('tɜːt'lˌnɛk) n. a round high close-fitting neck on a sweater or the sweater itself.

tusk (tʌsk) n. a long pointed usually paired tooth in the elephant, walrus, and certain other mammals. [Old English tūsc] —**tusked** adj.

tussle ('tʌs'l) vb. 1. to fight or wrestle in a vigorous way. ~n. 2. a vigorous fight; scuffle. [Middle English tusen to pull]

tussock ('tʌsək) n. a dense tuft of vegetation, esp. of grass. [origin unknown] —'**tussocky** adj.

tut (tʌt) interj., n., vb. **tutting, tutted**. short for **tut-tut**.

tutelage ('tjuːtɪlɪdʒ) n. 1. the act or office of a guardian or tutor. 2. instruction or guidance, esp. by a tutor. 3. the condition of being supervised by a guardian or tutor. [Latin tuērī to watch over]

tutelary ('tjuːtɪlərɪ) adj. 1. invested with the role of guardian or protector. 2. of a guardian.

tutor ('tjuːtə) n. 1. a teacher, usually instructing individual pupils. 2. (at a college or university) a member of staff responsible for the teaching and supervision of a certain number of students. ~vb. 3. to act as a tutor to (someone). [Latin: a watcher] —'**tutorship** n.

tutorial (tjuːˈtɔːrɪəl) n. 1. a period of intensive tuition given by a tutor to an individual student or to a small group of students. ~adj. 2. of or relating to a tutor.

tutti ('tʊtɪ) adj., adv. Music. to be performed by the whole orchestra, choir, etc. [Italian]

tutti-frutti ('tʊtɪˈfruːtɪ) n., pl. -**fruttis**. an ice cream or other sweet food containing small pieces of candied or fresh fruits. [Italian, lit.: all the fruits]

tut-tut ('tʌtˈtʌt) interj. 1. an exclamation of mild reprimand, disapproval, or surprise. ~vb. -**tutting, -tutted**. 2. to express disapproval by the exclamation of "tut-tut". ~n. 3. the act of tut-tutting.

tutu ('tuːtuː) n. a very short skirt worn by ballerinas, made of projecting layers of stiffened material. [French]

tu-whit tu-whoo (təˈwɪt təˈwuː) interj. an imitation of the sound made by an owl.

tuxedo (tʌkˈsiːdəʊ) n., pl. -**dos**. U.S. & Canad. a dinner jacket. [after a country club in Tuxedo Park, New York]

TV television.

TVEI technical and vocational educational initiative: a national educational scheme in which pupils gain practical experience in technology and industry, often through work placement.

twaddle ('twɒd'l) n. 1. silly, trivial, or pretentious talk or writing. ~vb. 2. to talk or write in a silly or pretentious way. [earlier twattle]

twain (tweɪn) det., n. Archaic. two. [Old English twēgen]

twang (twæŋ) n. 1. a sharp ringing sound produced by or as if by the plucking of a taut string. 2. the act of plucking a string to produce such a sound. 3. a strongly nasal quality in a person's speech. ~vb. 4. to make or cause to make a twang: to twang a guitar. [imit.] —'**twangy** adj.

twat (twæt, twɒt) n. Taboo slang. 1. the female genitals. 2. a foolish person. [origin unknown]

tweak (twiːk) vb. 1. to twist or pinch with a sharp or sudden movement: to tweak someone's nose. ~n. 2. a tweaking. [Old English twiccian]

twee (twiː) adj. Brit. informal. excessively

sentimental, sweet, or pretty. [from *tweet,* affected pronunciation of *sweet*]

tweed (twiːd) *n.* **1.** a thick woollen cloth produced originally in Scotland. **2.** (*pl.*) clothes made of this. [prob. from *tweel,* Scot. var. of *twill*]

tweedy ('twiːdɪ) *adj.* **tweedier, tweediest. 1.** of, made of, or resembling tweed. **2.** showing a fondness for a hearty outdoor life, usually associated with wearers of tweeds.

tweet (twiːt) *interj.* **1.** an imitation of the thin chirping sound made by small birds. ~*vb.* **2.** to make this sound. [imit.]

tweeter ('twiːtə) *n.* a loudspeaker used in high-fidelity systems for the reproduction of high audio frequencies.

tweezers ('twiːzəz) *pl. n.* a small pincer-like instrument used for such tasks as handling small objects or plucking out hairs. [obs. *tweeze* case of instruments]

Twelfth Day *n.* Jan. 6, the twelfth day after Christmas and the feast of the Epiphany.

twelfth man *n.* a reserve player in a cricket team.

Twelfth Night *n.* **a.** the evening of Jan 5, the eve of the Twelfth Day. **b.** the evening of Twelfth Day itself.

twelve (twelv) *n.* **1.** the cardinal number that is the sum of ten and two. **2.** a numeral, 12, XII, representing this number. **3.** something representing or consisting of twelve units. ~*det.* **4.** amounting to twelve. [Old English *twelf*] —**twelfth** *adj., n.*

twelvemonth ('twelv,mʌnθ) *n. Archaic, chiefly Brit.* a year.

twelve-tone *adj.* of or denoting the type of serial music which uses as musical material a tone row formed by the 12 semitones of the chromatic scale.

twenty ('twentɪ) *n., pl.* **-ties. 1.** the cardinal number that is the product of ten and two. **2.** a numeral, 20, XX, representing this number. **3.** something representing or consisting of twenty units. ~*det.* **4.** amounting to twenty. —**'twentieth** *adj., n.*

twerp *or* **twirp** (twɜːp) *n. Informal.* a silly, weak-minded, or contemptible person. [origin unknown]

twice (twaɪs) *adv.* **1.** two times; on two occasions or in two cases. **2.** double in degree or quantity: *twice as long.* [Old English *twiwa*]

twiddle ('twɪd'l) *vb.* **1.** to turn, twirl, or fiddle (with), often in an idle way: *she twiddled with a pencil.* **2. twiddle one's thumbs.** to rotate one's thumbs around one another, when inactive, waiting, or bored. ~*n.* **3.** an act or instance of twiddling. [prob. *twirl* + *fiddle*]

twig[1] (twɪg) *n.* a small branch or shoot of a tree. [Old English *twigge*] —**'twiggy** *adj.*

twig[2] (twɪg) *vb.* **twigging, twigged.** *Brit. informal.* to realize or understand (something): *he hasn't twigged yet.* [origin unknown]

twilight ('twaɪ,laɪt) *n.* **1.** the soft dim light that occurs when the sun is just below the horizon, esp. following sunset. **2.** the period in which this light occurs. **3.** any faint light. **4.** a period in which strength, importance, etc., is gradually declining. **5.** (*modifier*) of or relating to twilight; dim. [Old English *twi*- half + *light*] —**twilit** ('twaɪ,lɪt) *adj.*

twilight zone *n.* **1.** an inner-city area where houses have become dilapidated. **2.** any indefinite condition or area.

twill (twɪl) *adj.* **1.** (in textiles) of a weave in which the yarns are worked to produce an effect of parallel diagonal lines or ribs. ~*n.* **2.** any fabric so woven. [Old English *twilic* having a double thread]

twin (twɪn) *n.* **1.** either of two persons or animals conceived at the same time. **2.** either of two persons or things that are identical or very similar. ~*vb.* **twinning, twinned. 3.** to pair or be paired together. **4.** to bear twins. [Old English *twinn*]

twin bed *n.* one of a pair of matching single beds.

twine (twaɪn) *n.* **1.** string made by twisting fibres of hemp, cotton, etc., together. **2.** a twist or coil. ~*vb.* **3.** to twist together; interweave: *she twined the wicker to make a basket.* **4.** to form by or as if by twining: *to twine a garland.* **5.** (often foll. by *around*) to wind or cause to wind, esp. in spirals: *the creeper twines around the tree.* [Old English *twīn*]

twin-engined *adj.* (of an aeroplane) having two engines.

twinge (twɪndʒ) *n.* **1.** a sudden brief darting or stabbing pain. **2.** a sharp emotional pang: *a twinge of guilt.* [Old English *twengan* to pinch]

twinkle ('twɪŋk'l) *vb.* **1.** to shine brightly and intermittently; sparkle. **2.** (of the eyes) to sparkle, esp. with amusement or delight. ~*n.* **3.** a flickering brightness; sparkle. **4.** an instant. [Old English *twinclian*]

twinkling ('twɪŋklɪŋ) *n.* **in the twinkling of an eye.** in a very short time; moment.

twinset ('twɪn,set) *n. Brit.* a matching jumper and cardigan.

twirl (twɜːl) *vb.* **1.** to move around rapidly and repeatedly in a circle. **2.** to twist, wind, or twiddle, often idly: *she twirled her hair around her finger.* ~*n.* **3.** a whirl or twist. **4.** a written flourish. [origin unknown]

twist (twɪst) *vb.* **1.** to cause (one end or part) to turn or (of one end or part) to turn in the opposite direction from another. **2.** to distort or be distorted: *a twisted smile.* **3.** to wind or twine: *to twist flowers into a wreath.* **4.** to force or be forced out of the natural form or position: *to twist one's ankle.* **5.** to change the meaning of; pervert: *she twisted the statement.* **6.** to revolve; rotate. **7.** to wrench with a turning action: *to twist the top off a bottle.* **8.** to follow a winding course. **9.** to dance the twist. **10. twist someone's arm.** to persuade or coerce someone. ~*n.* **11.** a twisting. **12.** something formed by or as if by twisting. **13.** a decisive change of direction, aim, meaning, or character. **14.** (in a story, play, or film) an unexpected event, revelation, etc. **15.** a bend: *a twist in the road.* **16.** a distortion of the original shape or form. **17.** a jerky pull, wrench, or turn. **18. the twist.** a dance popular in the 1960s, in which dancers vigorously twist the hips. **19. round the twist.** *Brit. slang.* mad; eccentric. [Old English]

twister ('twɪstə) *n. Brit.* a swindling or dishonest person.

twit¹ (twɪt) *vb.* **twitting, twitted.** to tease, taunt, or reproach (someone) often in jest. [Old English *ætwītan*]

twit² (twɪt) *n. Informal, chiefly Brit.* a foolish or stupid person; idiot. [from TWIT¹]

twitch (twɪtʃ) *vb.* **1.** (of a person or part of a person's body) to move in a jerky spasmodic way. **2.** to pull (something) with a quick jerky movement. ~*n.* **3.** a sharp jerking movement, esp. one caused by a nervous condition. [Old English *twiccian* to pluck]

twitter ('twɪtə) *vb.* **1.** (esp. of a bird) to utter a succession of chirping sounds. **2.** to talk rapidly and tremulously. **3.** to utter in a chirping way. ~*n.* **4.** the act or sound of twittering. **5. in a twitter.** in a state of nervous excitement. [imit.] —'**twittery** *adj.*

two (tuː) *n.* **1.** the cardinal number that is the sum of one and one. **2.** a numeral, 2, II, representing this number. **3.** something representing or consisting of two units. **4. in two.** in or into two parts. **5. put two and two together.** to reach an obvious conclusion by considering the evidence available. **6. that makes two of us.** the same applies to me. ~*det.* **7.** amounting to two. [Old English *twā*]

two-edged *adj.* **1.** (of a knife, saw, etc.) having two cutting edges. **2.** (esp. of a remark) having two interpretations, such as *she looks nice when she smiles.*

two-faced *adj.* deceitful; hypocritical.

twofold ('tuː,fəʊld) *adj.* **1.** equal to twice as many or twice as much. **2.** composed of two parts. ~*adv.* **3.** doubly.

two-handed *adj.* **1.** requiring the use of both hands. **2.** requiring the participation of two people.

twopence *or* **tuppence** ('tʌpəns) *n. Brit.* **1.** the sum of two pennies. **2.** something of little value: *not care twopence.*

twopenny *or* **tuppenny** ('tʌpənɪ) *adj. Chiefly Brit.* **1.** cheap or tawdry. **2.** worth or costing two pence. **3. not care a twopenny damn.** to not care at all.

two-piece *adj.* **1.** consisting of two separate parts, usually matching, as of a garment. ~*n.* **2.** such an outfit.

two-ply *adj.* **1.** made of two thicknesses, layers, or strands. ~*n., pl.* **-plies.** **2.** a two-ply wood, knitting yarn, etc.

two-sided *adj.* **1.** having two sides or aspects. **2.** controversial; debatable: *a two-sided argument.*

twosome ('tuːsəm) *n.* two together, esp. two people.

two-step *n.* **1.** an old-time dance in duple time. **2.** a piece of music for this dance.

two-stroke *adj.* of an internal-combustion engine whose piston makes two strokes for every explosion.

two-time *vb. Informal.* to deceive (someone, esp. a lover) by carrying on a relationship with someone else. —,**two-'timer** *n.*

two-way *adj.* **1.** moving, permitting movement, or operating in either of two opposite directions: *two-way traffic.* **2.** involving reciprocal obligation or mutual action: *a two-way cultural exchange.* **3.** (of a radio, telephone, etc.) allowing communications in two directions using both transmitting and receiving equipment.

TX Texas.

tycoon (taɪ'kuːn) *n.* a businessman of great wealth and power. [Japanese *taikun* great ruler]

tyke *or* **tike** (taɪk) *n.* **1.** *Informal.* a small or cheeky child. **2.** *Brit. dialect.* a rough ill-mannered person. [Old Norse *tīk* bitch]

tympani ('tɪmpənɪ) *pl. n.* same as **timpani**.

tympanic membrane *n.* same as **eardrum.**

tympanum ('tɪmpənəm) *n., pl.* **-nums** *or* **-na** (-nə). **1. a.** the cavity of the middle ear. **b.** same as **tympanic membrane. 2.** *Archit.* **a.** the recessed, esp. triangular, space bounded by the cornices of a pediment. **b.** the recessed space bounded by an arch and the lintel of a doorway or window below it. **3.** *Music.* a drum or drumhead. [Greek *tumpanon* drum] —**tympanic** (tɪm-'pænɪk) *adj.*

Tynwald ('tɪnwəld, 'taɪn-) *n.* **the.** the Parliament of the Isle of Man. [Old Norse *thing* assembly + *vollr* field]

type (taɪp) *n.* **1.** a kind, class, or category, the constituents of which share similar characteristics. **2.** a subdivision of a particular class; sort: *what type of shampoo do you use?* **3.** the general form, plan, or design distinguishing a particular group. **4.** *Informal.* a person, esp. of a specified kind: *he's a strange type.* **5.** a small metal or sometimes wooden block, bearing a letter or character on its upper surface for use in printing. **6.** characters printed from type; print. ~*vb.* **7.** to write (copy) using a typewriter or word processor. **8.** to be a symbol of; typify. **9.** to decide the type of. [Greek *tupos* image]

typecast ('taɪp,kɑːst) *vb.* **-casting, -cast.** to cast (an actor or actress) in the same kind of role continually.

typeface ('taɪp,feɪs) *n.* same as **face** (sense 10).

typescript ('taɪp,skrɪpt) *n.* any typewritten document.

typeset ('taɪp,sɛt) *vb.* **-setting, -set.** *Printing.* to set (textual matter) in type.

typesetter ('taɪp,sɛtə) *n.* a person who sets type; compositor.

typewriter ('taɪp,raɪtə) *n.* a keyboard machine for writing mechanically in characters resembling print.

typhoid ('taɪfɔɪd) *Pathol.* ~*adj.* **1.** resembling typhus. ~*n.* **2.** short for **typhoid fever.**

typhoid fever *n.* an acute infectious

disease characterized by high fever, spots, abdominal pain, etc. It is spread by contaminated food or water.

typhoon ('taɪ'fuːn) n. a violent tropical storm, esp. in the China Seas and W Pacific. [Chinese *tai fung* great wind]

typhus ('taɪfəs) n. an acute infectious disease transmitted by lice or mites and characterized by high fever, skin rash, and severe headache. [Greek *tuphos* fever]

typical ('tɪpɪkʰl) adj. **1.** being or serving as a representative example of a particular type; characteristic. **2.** considered to be an example of some undesirable trait: *that is typical of you!* **3.** of or relating to a representative specimen or type. [Greek *tupos* image] —**typically** adv.

typify ('tɪpɪˌfaɪ) vb. **-fying, -fied. 1.** to be typical of; characterize. **2.** to symbolize or represent completely, by or as if by a type.

typist ('taɪpɪst) n. a person who types, esp. for a living.

typo ('taɪpəʊ) n., pl. **-pos.** Informal. a typographical error.

typography (taɪ'pɒgrəfɪ) n. **1.** the art, craft, or process of composing type and printing from it. **2.** the planning, selection, and setting of type for a printed work. —**typographical** (ˌtaɪpəˈgræfɪkʰl) adj. —ˌtypoˈgraphically adv.

tyrannical (tɪ'rænɪkʰl) adj. characteristic of a tyrant; oppressive.

tyrannize or **-ise** ('tɪrəˌnaɪz) vb. to rule or exercise power (over) in a cruel or oppressive manner.

tyrannosaur (tɪ'rænəˌsɔː) n. a large two-footed dinosaur common in North America in Cretaceous times. [Greek *turannos* tyrant + *sauros* lizard]

tyranny ('tɪrənɪ) n., pl. **-nies. 1. a.** government by a tyrant. **b.** oppressive and unjust government by more than one person. **2.** arbitrary or unreasonable behaviour or use of authority. **3.** a tyrannical act. —**tyrannous** adj.

tyrant ('taɪrənt) n. **1.** a person who governs oppressively, unjustly, and arbitrarily. **2.** any person who exercises authority in a tyrannical manner. [Greek *turannos*]

tyre or U.S. **tire** ('taɪə) n. a usually inflated rubber ring placed over the rim of a wheel of a road vehicle to grip the road. [earlier *tire*, prob. archaic var. of *attire*]

Tyrian ('tɪrɪən) n. **1.** a person from ancient Tyre, a port in S Lebanon and centre of ancient Phoenician culture. ~adj. **2.** of or relating to ancient Tyre.

tyro or **tiro** ('taɪrəʊ) n., pl. **-ros.** a novice or beginner. [Latin *tīrō* recruit]

tzar (zɑː) n. same as **tsar.**

tzetze fly ('tsetsɪ) n. same as **tsetse fly.**

U

u *or* **U** (juː) *n., pl.* **u's, U's,** *or* **Us.** **1.** the 21st letter of the English alphabet. **2.** something shaped like a U.

U 1. united. **2.** unionist. **3.** university. **4.** (in Britain) universal (used to describe a film certified as suitable for viewing by anyone). **5.** *Chem.* uranium. ~*adj.* **6.** *Brit. informal.* (of language or behaviour) characteristic of the upper class.

UB40 *n.* (in Britain) **1.** a registration card issued to an unemployed person. **2.** *Informal.* a person registered as unemployed.

ubiquitous (juːˈbɪkwɪtəs) *adj.* being or seeming to be everywhere at once. [Latin *ubīque* everywhere]

U-boat *n.* a German submarine. [German *Unterseeboot* undersea boat]

u.c. *Printing.* upper case.

UCCA (ˈʌkə) (in Britain) Universities Central Council on Admissions.

udder (ˈʌdə) *n.* the large baglike milk-producing gland of cows, sheep, or goats, with two or more teats. [Old English *ūder*]

UDI Unilateral Declaration of Independence.

UEFA (juːˈeɪfə, ˈjuːfə) Union of European Football Associations.

UFO (ˌjuː ɛf ˈəʊ, ˈjuːfəʊ) unidentified flying object.

ugh (ʊx, ʊh, ʌx) *interj.* an exclamation of disgust, annoyance, or dislike.

ugli (ˈʌglɪ) *n., pl.* **-lis** *or* **-lies.** a yellow citrus fruit: a cross between a tangerine, grapefruit, and orange. [prob. an alteration of *ugly,* from its wrinkled skin]

ugly (ˈʌglɪ) *adj.* **uglier, ugliest. 1.** of unpleasant appearance. **2.** repulsive or displeasing: *war is ugly.* **3.** ominous or menacing: *an ugly situation.* **4.** bad-tempered or sullen: *an ugly mood.* [Old Norse *uggligr* dreadful] —**ˈugliness** *n.*

ugly duckling *n.* a person or thing, initially ugly or unpromising, that becomes beautiful or admirable. [from *The Ugly Duckling* by Hans Christian Andersen]

UHF *Radio.* ultrahigh frequency.

UHT ultra-heat-treated (milk or cream).

UK United Kingdom.

ukase (juːˈkeɪz) *n.* **1.** (in imperial Russia) an edict of the tsar. **2.** *Rare.* an edict. [Russian *ukaz*]

Ukrainian (juːˈkreɪnɪən) *adj.* **1.** of the Ukraine, its people, or their language. ~*n.* **2.** the official language of the Ukrainian SSR. **3.** a person from the Ukraine.

ukulele (ˌjuːkəˈleɪlɪ) *n.* a small four-stringed guitar. [Hawaiian, lit.: jumping flea]

ulcer (ˈʌlsə) *n.* an open sore on the surface of the skin or a mucous membrane. [Latin *ulcus*]

ulcerate (ˈʌlsəˌreɪt) *vb.* to make or become ulcerous. —ˌulceˈration *n.*

ulcerous (ˈʌlsərəs) *adj.* of, like, or characterized by ulcers.

ulna (ˈʌlnə) *n., pl.* **-nae** (-niː) *or* **-nas.** the inner and longer of the two bones of the human forearm or of the forelimb in other vertebrates. [Latin: elbow] —**ˈulnar** *adj.*

ulster (ˈʌlstə) *n.* a man's heavy double-breasted overcoat. [*Ulster,* the northernmost province of Ireland]

Ulsterman (ˈʌlstəmən) *n., pl.* **-men.** a person from Ulster. —**ˈUlster,woman** *fem. n.*

ult. 1. ultimate(ly). **2.** ultimo.

ulterior (ʌlˈtɪərɪə) *adj.* lying beyond what is revealed or seen: *ulterior motives.* [Latin: further]

ultimate (ˈʌltɪmɪt) *adj.* **1.** final in a series or process: *ultimate success.* **2.** the highest or most significant: *the ultimate goal.* **3.** fundamental or essential. ~*n.* **4.** the highest or most significant thing. [Latin *ultimus* last, distant] —**ˈultimately** *adv.*

ultimatum (ˌʌltɪˈmeɪtəm) *n., pl.* **-tums** *or* **-ta** (-tə). a final communication by a party setting forth conditions on which it insists, as during negotiations.

ultimo (ˈʌltɪˌməʊ) *adv. Now rare except when abbreviated to ult. in formal correspondence.* in or during the previous month: *a letter of the 7th ultimo.* [Latin *ultimō* on the last]

ultra (ˈʌltrə) *adj.* extreme or immoderate in beliefs or opinions. [Latin: beyond]

ultra- *prefix.* **1.** beyond a specified extent, range, or limit: *ultrasonic.* **2.** extremely: *ultramodern.* [Latin]

ultraconservative (ˌʌltrəkənˈsɜːvətɪv) *adj.* **1.** highly reactionary. ~*n.* **2.** a reactionary person.

ultrahigh frequency (ˈʌltrəˌhaɪ) *n.* a radio frequency between 3000 and 300 megahertz.

ultramarine (ˌʌltrəməˈriːn) *n.* **1.** a blue pigment originally made from lapis lazuli. ~*adj.* **2.** vivid blue. [Latin *ultrā* beyond + *mare* sea; because the lapis lazuli from which the pigment was made was imported from Asia]

ultramodern (ˌʌltrəˈmɒdən) *adj.* extremely modern.

ultramontane (ˌʌltrəmɒnˈteɪn) *adj.* **1.** on the other side of the mountains, usually the Alps, from the speaker or writer. **2.** of a movement in the Roman Catholic Church which favours supreme papal authority. ~*n.* **3.** a person from beyond the Alps. **4.** a member of the ultramontane party of the Roman Catholic Church.

ultrasonic (ˌʌltrəˈsɒnɪk) *adj.* of or producing sound waves with higher frequencies than humans can hear. —ˌultraˈsonically *adv.*

ultrasonics (ˌʌltrəˈsɒnɪks) *n.* (*functioning as sing.*) the branch of physics concerned with ultrasonic waves.

ultrasound (ˌʌltrəˈsaʊnd) *n.* ultrasonic waves, used in echo sounding, medical diagnosis, and therapy.

ultrasound scan *n.* an examination of an internal bodily structure by the use of ultrasonic waves, esp. for diagnosing abnormality in a fetus.

ultraviolet (ˌʌltrəˈvaɪəlɪt) *n.* **1.** the part of the electromagnetic spectrum with wavelengths shorter than light but longer than x-rays. ~*adj.* **2.** of or consisting of radiation lying in the ultraviolet: *ultraviolet radiation.*

ululate (ˈjuːljʊˌleɪt) *vb.* to howl or wail. [Latin *ululāre*] —**ululation** *n.*

umbel (ˈʌmbªl) *n.* a type of compound flower in which the flowers arise from the same point in the main stem and have stalks of the same length, to give a cluster with the youngest flowers at the centre. [Latin *umbella* a sunshade] —**umbellate** (ˈʌmbɪlɪt, -ˌleɪt) *adj.*

umbelliferous (ˌʌmbɪˈlɪfərəs) *adj.* of or denoting a plant with flowers in umbels, such as fennel, parsley, carrot, or parsnip. [Latin *umbella* a sunshade + *ferre* to bear]

umber (ˈʌmbə) *n.* **1.** a natural brown earth containing ferric oxide together with lime and oxides of aluminium, manganese, and silicon. **2.** a dark brown to greenish-brown colour produced by this pigment. ~*adj.* **3.** of or stained with umber. [French (*terre d'*)*ombre* or Italian (*terra di*) *ombra* shadow (earth)]

umbilical (ʌmˈbɪlɪkªl, ˌʌmbɪˈlaɪkªl) *adj.* of or like the umbilicus or the umbilical cord.

umbilical cord *n.* the long flexible cord-like structure that connects a fetus with the placenta.

umbilicus (ʌmˈbɪlɪkəs, ˌʌmbɪˈlaɪkəs) *n. Anat.* the navel. [Latin: navel, centre]

umbra (ˈʌmbrə) *n., pl.* -**brae** (-briː) *or* -**bras.** a shadow, usually the shadow cast by the moon onto the earth during a solar eclipse. [Latin: shade]

umbrage (ˈʌmbrɪdʒ) *n.* displeasure or resentment; offence (in **give** *or* **take umbrage**). [Latin *umbra* shade]

umbrella (ʌmˈbrelə) *n.* **1.** a portable device used for protection against rain, consisting of a light canopy supported on a collapsible metal frame mounted on a central rod. **2.** a protective shield or screen. **3.** anything that has the effect of a protective screen, general cover, or organizing agency: *under the umbrella of the UK air defence.* [Italian *ombrella*, from *ombra* shade] —**umˈbrella-like** *adj.*

umfazi (ˌʊmˈfaːzɪ) *n. S. African.* a Black married woman. [Bantu]

umiak, oomiak, *or* **oomiac** (ˈuːmɪˌæk) *n.*

a large open boat made of stretched skins, used by Eskimos. [Eskimo]

umlaut (ˈʊmlaʊt) *n.* **1.** the mark (¨) placed over a vowel, esp. in German, indicating change in its sound. **2.** (esp. in Germanic languages) the change of a vowel brought about by the influence of a vowel in the next syllable. [German, from *um* around + *Laut* sound]

umlungu (ˌʊmˈlʊŋgʊ) *n. S. African.* a White man: used esp. as a term of address. [Bantu]

umpire (ˈʌmpaɪə) *n.* **1.** an official who rules on the playing of a game, as in cricket. ~*vb.* **2.** to act as umpire in (a game). [Old French *nomper* not one of a pair]

umpteen (ˈʌmpˈtiːn) *det. Informal.* very many: *umpteen things to do.* [*umpty* a great deal + *-teen* ten] —**ˈumpˈteenth** *n., adj.*

UN United Nations.

un-[1] *prefix.* (*freely used with adjectives, participles, and their derivative adverbs and nouns: less frequently used with certain other nouns*) not; contrary to; opposite of: *uncertain; untidiness; unbelief; untruth.* [Old English *on-, un-*]

un-[2] *prefix forming verbs.* **1.** denoting reversal of an action or state: *uncover; untie.* **2.** denoting removal from, release, or deprivation: *unharness; unthrone.* **3.** (*intensifier*): *unloose.* [Old English *un-, on-*]

unable (ʌnˈeɪbªl) *adj.* (foll. by *to*) lacking the necessary power, ability, or authority to (do something); not able.

unaccountable (ˌʌnəˈkaʊntəbªl) *adj.* **1.** that cannot be explained. **2.** extraordinary: *an unaccountable fear of heights.* **3.** (foll. by *to*) not answerable to. —**ˌunacˈcountably** *adv.*

unaccustomed (ˌʌnəˈkʌstəmd) *adj.* **1.** (foll. by *to*) not used to: *unaccustomed to pain.* **2.** not familiar: *his unaccustomed leisure.*

unadopted (ˌʌnəˈdɒptɪd) *adj. Brit.* (of a road) not maintained by a local authority.

unadvised (ˌʌnədˈvaɪzd) *adj.* **1.** rash or unwise. **2.** not having received advice. —**unadvisedly** (ˌʌnədˈvaɪzɪdlɪ) *adv.*

unaffected[1] (ˌʌnəˈfɛktɪd) *adj.* unpretentious, natural, or sincere.

unaffected[2] (ˌʌnəˈfɛktɪd) *adj.* not affected.

unalienable (ʌnˈeɪljənəbªl) *adj. Law.* same as **inalienable.**

un-American *adj.* **1.** not in accordance with the aims, ideals, or customs of the U.S. **2.** against the interests of the U.S. —**ˌun-Aˈmericanism** *n.*

unanimous (juːˈnænɪməs) *adj.* **1.** in com-

---

plete agreement. **2.** characterized by complete agreement: *a unanimous decision.* [Latin *ūnus* one + *animus* mind] —**unanimity** (ˌjuːnəˈnɪmɪtɪ) *n.*

unapproachable (ˌʌnəˈprəʊtʃəbᵊl) *adj.* discouraging friendliness; aloof.

unarmed (ʌnˈɑːmd) *adj.* without weapons.

unassailable (ˌʌnəˈseɪləbᵊl) *adj.* **1.** not able to be attacked. **2.** undeniable.

unassuming (ˌʌnəˈsjuːmɪŋ) *adj.* modest or unpretentious.

unattached (ˌʌnəˈtætʃt) *adj.* **1.** not connected with any specific body or group. **2.** not engaged or married.

unavailing (ˌʌnəˈveɪlɪŋ) *adj.* useless or futile.

unaware (ˌʌnəˈwɛə) *adj.* not aware or conscious: *unaware of the time.* ~*adv.* **2.** *Not universally accepted.* same as **unawares.**

unawares (ˌʌnəˈwɛəz) *adv.* **1.** by surprise: *she caught him unawares.* **2.** without knowing: *he lost it unawares.*

unbalanced (ʌnˈbælənst) *adj.* **1.** lacking balance. **2.** mentally deranged. **3.** biased; one-sided: *unbalanced reporting.*

unbearable (ʌnˈbɛərəbᵊl) *adj.* not able to be endured. —**unˈbearably** *adv.*

unbecoming (ˌʌnbɪˈkʌmɪŋ) *adj.* **1.** unattractive or unsuitable: *an unbecoming hat.* **2.** not proper or appropriate to a person or position: *conduct unbecoming to an officer.*

unbeknown (ˌʌnbɪˈnəʊn) *adv.* (foll. by *to*) without the knowledge of (a person): *unbeknown to him she had left the country.* Also (esp. Brit.): **unbeknownst.** [archaic *beknown* known]

unbelievable (ˌʌnbɪˈliːvəbᵊl) *adj.* unable to be believed. —**unbeˈlievably** *adv.*

unbeliever (ˌʌnbɪˈliːvə) *n.* a person who does not believe in a religion.

unbend (ʌnˈbend) *vb.* **-bending, -bent. 1.** to release or be released from the restraints of formality and ceremony: *he did his best to unbend and get to know her relatives.* **2.** *Informal.* to relax (the mind) or (of the mind) to become relaxed. **3.** to straighten out from a bent shape.

unbending (ʌnˈbendɪŋ) *adj.* rigid or inflexible: *an unbending rule.*

unbidden (ʌnˈbɪdᵊn) *adj.* not ordered or asked; voluntary or spontaneous: *her tears came unbidden.*

unbind (ʌnˈbaɪnd) *vb.* **-binding, -bound. 1.** to set free from bonds or chains. **2.** to unfasten or untie.

unblushing (ʌnˈblʌʃɪŋ) *adj.* immodest or shameless.

unbolt (ʌnˈbəʊlt) *vb.* to unfasten a bolt of (a door).

unborn (ʌnˈbɔːn) *adj.* **1.** not yet born. **2.** still to come; future: *the unborn world.*

unbosom (ʌnˈbʊzəm) *vb.* to relieve (oneself) of (secrets or feelings) by telling someone. [UN-² + *bosom* (in the sense: centre of the emotions)]

unbounded (ʌnˈbaʊndɪd) *adj.* having no boundaries or limits.

unbowed (ʌnˈbaʊd) *adj.* **1.** not bowed or bent. **2.** unsubdued: *bloody but unbowed.*

unbridled (ʌnˈbraɪdᵊld) *adj.* unrestrained: *unbridled greed.*

unbroken (ʌnˈbrəʊkən) *adj.* **1.** complete or whole. **2.** continuous: *unbroken sunshine.* **3.** (of animals, esp. horses) not tamed. **4.** not disturbed or upset: *unbroken silence.* **5.** (of a record) not improved upon.

unburden (ʌnˈbɜːdᵊn) *vb.* **1.** to remove a burden from. **2.** to relieve (one's mind or oneself) of a worry or trouble by telling someone about it.

uncalled-for (ˌʌnˈkɔːldfɔː) *adj.* unnecessary or unwarranted: *an uncalled-for remark.*

uncanny (ʌnˈkænɪ) *adj.* **1.** weird; mysterious: *an uncanny silence.* **2.** beyond what is normal: *uncanny accuracy.* —**unˈcannily** *adv.* —**unˈcanniness** *n.*

uncared-for (ˌʌnˈkɛədfɔː) *adj.* not cared for; neglected.

unceremonious (ˌʌnserɪˈməʊnɪəs) *adj.* without ceremony; abrupt, rude, or undignified. —**ˌuncereˈmoniously** *adv.*

uncertain (ʌnˈsɜːtᵊn) *adj.* **1.** not able to be accurately known or predicted: *the outcome is uncertain.* **2.** not definitely decided: *uncertain plans.* **3.** not to be depended upon: *an uncertain vote.* **4.** changeable: *the weather is uncertain.* —**unˈcertainty** *n.*

unchristian (ʌnˈkrɪstʃən) *adj.* not in accordance with Christian principles.

uncial (ˈʌnsɪəl) *adj.* **1.** of or written in letters that resemble modern capitals, as used in Greek and Latin manuscripts of the third to ninth centuries. ~*n.* **2.** an uncial letter or manuscript. [Late Latin *unciāles litterae* letters an inch long]

uncircumcised (ʌnˈsɜːkəmˌsaɪzd) *adj.* **1.** not circumcised. **2.** not Jewish; gentile.

uncivil (ʌnˈsɪvᵊl) *adj.* lacking civility or good manners. —**unˈcivilly** *adv.*

uncivilized *or* **-ised** (ʌnˈsɪvɪˌlaɪzd) *adj.*
1. (of a tribe or people) not yet civilized.
2. lacking culture or sophistication.

unclasp (ʌnˈklɑːsp) *vb.* **1.** to unfasten the
clasp of (something). **2.** to release one's
grip on (an object).

uncle (ˈʌŋkʰl) *n.* **1.** a brother of one's
father or mother. **2.** the husband of one's
aunt. **3.** a child's term of address for a
male friend of its parents. **4.** *Slang.* a
pawnbroker. [Latin *avunculus*]

unclean (ʌnˈkliːn) *adj.* lacking moral, spiritual, or physical cleanliness.

Uncle Sam (sæm) *n.* a personification of
the government of the United States. [ap-
parently a humorous interpretation of the
letters stamped on army supply boxes
during the War of 1812: *U.S.*]

Uncle Tom (tɒm) *n. Informal, offensive.* a
Black person whose behaviour towards
White people is regarded as servile. [from
Uncle Tom's Cabin by H. B. Stowe]

unclose (ʌnˈkləʊz) *vb.* **1.** to open or cause
to open. **2.** to come or bring to light.

unclothe (ʌnˈkləʊð) *vb.* **-clothing, -clothed**
or **-clad.** **1.** to take off garments from;
strip. **2.** to uncover or lay bare.

uncoil (ʌnˈkɔɪl) *vb.* to unwind or become
unwound; untwist.

uncomfortable (ʌnˈkʌmftəbʰl) *adj.* **1.** not
comfortable. **2.** feeling or causing discomfort. **—unˈcomfortably** *adv.*

uncommitted (ˌʌnkəˈmɪtɪd) *adj.* not
bound to a specific opinion, course of
action, or cause.

uncommon (ʌnˈkɒmən) *adj.* **1.** beyond
normal experience. **2.** in excess of what is
normal: *an uncommon liking for honey.*

uncommonly (ʌnˈkɒmənlɪ) *adv.* **1.** in an
unusual manner or degree. **2.** extremely:
you're uncommonly friendly.

uncommunicative (ˌʌnkəˈmjuːnɪkətɪv)
adj. disinclined to talk or give information.

uncompromising (ʌnˈkɒmprəˌmaɪzɪŋ)
adj. not prepared to compromise; inflexible.

unconcern (ˌʌnkənˈsɜːn) *n.* apathy or indifference.

unconcerned (ˌʌnkənˈsɜːnd) *adj.* **1.** lacking in concern or involvement. **2.** unwor-
ried. **—unconcernedly** (ˌʌnkənˈsɜːnɪdlɪ)
adv.

unconditional (ˌʌnkənˈdɪʃənʰl) *adj.* without conditions or limitations: *unconditional
surrender.*

unconscionable (ʌnˈkɒnʃənəbʰl) *adj.* **1.**
unscrupulous or unprincipled: *an unconscionable liar.* **2.** immoderate or excessive:
unconscionable demands.

unconscious (ʌnˈkɒnʃəs) *adj.* **1.** lacking
normal awareness through the senses; insensible. **2.** not aware of one's actions or
behaviour: *unconscious of his mistake.* **3.**
not realized or intended: *an unconscious
blunder.* **4.** coming from or produced by
the unconscious: *unconscious resentment.*
~n. **5.** *Psychoanal.* the part of the mind
containing instincts, impulses, and ideas
that are not available for direct examination. **—unˈconsciously** *adv.*

unconstitutional (ˌʌnkɒnstɪˈtjuːʃənʰl) *adj.*
at variance with or not permitted by
a constitution. **—unconstitutionality**
(ˌʌnkɒnstɪˌtjuːʃəˈnælɪtɪ) *n.*

unconventional (ˌʌnkənˈvɛnʃənʰl) *adj.* not
conforming to accepted rules or standards.
—unconventionality (ˌʌnkənˌvɛnʃəˈnæl-
ɪtɪ) *n.*

uncork (ʌnˈkɔːk) *vb.* **1.** to draw the cork
from (a bottle). **2.** to release (emotions).

uncouple (ʌnˈkʌpʰl) *vb.* to disconnect or
become disconnected.

uncouth (ʌnˈkuːθ) *adj.* lacking in good
manners, refinement, or grace. [Old English *un-* not + *cūth* familiar]

uncover (ʌnˈkʌvə) *vb.* **1.** to remove the
cover or top from. **2.** to reveal or disclose:
to uncover a plot. **3.** to take off (one's hat
or cap) as a mark of respect.

uncrowned (ʌnˈkraʊnd) *adj.* **1.** with powers of or like royalty, but without the title.
2. not yet crowned.

unction (ˈʌŋkʃən) *n.* **1.** *Chiefly R.C. &
Eastern Churches.* the act of anointing
with oil in sacramental ceremonies. **2.** oily
charm. **3.** an ointment or unguent. **4.**
anything soothing. [Latin *unguere* to
anoint]

unctuous (ˈʌŋktjʊəs) *adj.* **1.** affecting an
oily charm. **2.** slippery or greasy. [Latin
unctum ointment]

undaunted (ʌnˈdɔːntɪd) *adj.* not put off,
discouraged, or beaten.

undeceive (ˌʌndɪˈsiːv) *vb.* to reveal the
truth to (someone previously misled or
deceived).

undecided (ˌʌndɪˈsaɪdɪd) *adj.* **1.** not having made up one's mind. **2.** (of an issue or
problem) not agreed or decided upon.

undeniable (ˌʌndɪˈnaɪəbʰl) *adj.* **1.** unques-

unclaimed	uncontaminated	uncurl
unclassified	uncontrollable	uncut
unclear	uncontroversial	undamaged
uncluttered	unconvinced	undated
uncomplaining	unconvincing	undeclared
uncomplicated	uncooked	undefeated
uncomplimentary	uncooperative	undefended
uncomprehending	uncoordinated	undefiled
unconcealed	uncorroborated	undemanding
unconfirmed	uncountable	undemocratic
unconnected	uncritical	undemonstrative
unconquered	uncultured	

tionably true. **2.** of unquestionable excellence: *a man of undeniable character.* —**unde'niably** *adv.*

under ('ʌndə) *prep.* **1.** directly below; on, to, or beneath the underside or base of: *under one's feet.* **2.** less than: *under forty years.* **3.** lower in rank than: *under a corporal.* **4.** subject to the supervision, control, or influence of: *under the last Government.* **5.** subject to (conditions); in (certain circumstances): *under stress.* **6.** in (a specified category): *a book under theology.* **7.** known by: *under an assumed name.* **8.** planted with: *a field under corn.* **9.** powered by: *under sail.* ~*adv.* **10.** below; to a position underneath. [Old English]

under- *prefix.* **1.** below or beneath: *underarm; underground.* **2.** of lesser importance or lower rank: *undersecretary.* **3.** insufficient or insufficiently: *underemployed.* **4.** indicating secrecy or deception: *underhand.*

underachieve (ˌʌndərə'tʃiːv) *vb.* to fail to achieve a performance appropriate to one's age or talents. —**undera'chiever** *n.*

underage (ˌʌndər'eɪdʒ) *adj.* below the required or standard age, usually below the legal age for voting or drinking.

underarm ('ʌndərˌɑːm) *adj.* **1.** *Sport.* denoting a style of throwing, bowling, or serving in which the hand is swung below shoulder level. **2.** below the arm. ~*adv.* **3.** in an underarm style.

underbelly ('ʌndəˌbɛlɪ) *n., pl.* **-lies. 1.** the part of an animal's belly nearest the ground. **2.** a vulnerable or unprotected part, aspect, or region.

underbid (ˌʌndə'bɪd) *vb.* **-bidding, -bid. 1.** to make a bid lower than that of (others): *I underbid the other dealers.* **2.** *Bridge.* to bid (one's hand) at a lower level than the strength of the hand warrants.

undercarriage ('ʌndəˌkærɪdʒ) *n.* **1.** the assembly of wheels, shock absorbers, and struts that supports an aircraft on the ground and enables it to take off and land. **2.** the framework supporting the body of a vehicle.

undercharge (ˌʌndə'tʃɑːdʒ) *vb.* **1.** to charge too little for something. **2.** to load (a gun or electric circuit) with an inadequate charge.

underclothes ('ʌndəˌkləʊðz) *pl. n.* same as **underwear.** Also called: **underclothing.**

undercoat ('ʌndəˌkəʊt) *n.* **1.** a coat of paint applied before the top coat. **2.** *Zool.* a layer of soft fur beneath the outer fur of animals such as the otter. ~*vb.* **3.** to apply an undercoat to (a surface).

undercover (ˌʌndə'kʌvə) *adj.* done or acting in secret: *undercover operations.*

undercurrent ('ʌndəˌkʌrənt) *n.* **1.** a current that is not apparent at the surface. **2.** an underlying opinion or emotion.

undercut *vb.* (ˌʌndə'kʌt), **-cutting, -cut. 1.** to charge less than (a competitor) in order to obtain trade. **2.** to cut away the

under part of (something). **3.** *Sport.* to hit (a ball) in such a way as to impart backspin. ~*n.* ('ʌndəˌkʌt). **4.** a tenderloin of beef.

underdeveloped (ˌʌndədɪ'vɛləpt) *adj.* **1.** immature or undersized. **2.** relating to societies lacking the finance, industries, and organization necessary to advance.

underdog ('ʌndəˌdɒg) *n.* **1.** the losing competitor in a fight or contest. **2.** a person in adversity or a position of inferiority.

underdone (ˌʌndə'dʌn) *adj.* insufficiently or lightly cooked.

underemployed (ˌʌndərɪm'plɔɪd) *adj.* not fully or adequately employed.

underestimate *vb.* (ˌʌndər'ɛstɪˌmeɪt). **1.** to make too low an estimate of: *he underestimated the cost.* **2.** to think insufficiently highly of: *to underestimate a person.* ~*n.* (ˌʌndər'ɛstɪmɪt). **3.** too low an estimate. —**under,esti'mation** *n.*

underexpose (ˌʌndərɪk'spəʊz) *vb.* *Photog.* to expose (a film, plate, or paper) for too short a period or with insufficient light. —**underex'posure** *n.*

underfelt ('ʌndəˌfɛlt) *n.* thick felt laid under a carpet to increase insulation.

underfoot (ˌʌndə'fʊt) *adv.* **1.** underneath the feet; on the ground. **2.** in a position of subjugation. **3.** in the way.

undergarment ('ʌndəˌgɑːmənt) *n.* a garment worn under the outer clothes.

undergo (ˌʌndə'gəʊ) *vb.* **-going, -went, -gone.** to experience, endure, or sustain: *to undergo a change of feelings.* [Old English]

undergraduate (ˌʌndə'grædjʊɪt) *n.* a person studying in a university for a first degree.

underground *adj.* ('ʌndəˌgraʊnd), *adv.* (ˌʌndə'graʊnd). **1.** occurring, situated, used, or going below ground level. **2.** secret; hidden: *underground activities.* ~*n.* ('ʌndəˌgraʊnd). **3.** a movement dedicated to overthrowing a government or occupation forces. **4.** (often preceded by *the*) an electric passenger railway operated in underground tunnels. **5.** (usually preceded by *the*) any avant-garde, experimental, or subversive movement in popular art, films, or music.

undergrowth ('ʌndəˌgrəʊθ) *n.* small shrubs and bushes growing beneath taller trees in a wood or forest.

underhand ('ʌndəˌhænd) *adj. also* **underhanded. 1.** sly, deceitful, and secretive. **2.** *Sport.* underarm. ~*adv.* **3.** in an underhand manner or style.

underlay *vb.* (ˌʌndə'leɪ), **-laying, -laid. 1.** to place (something) underneath in order to support or raise. ~*n.* ('ʌndəˌleɪ). **2.** a lining or support laid underneath something. **3.** felt or rubber laid under a carpet to increase insulation and resilience.

underlie (ˌʌndə'laɪ) *vb.* **-lying, -lay, -lain. 1.** to lie or be placed under. **2.** to be the foundation, cause, or basis of: *careful planning underlies all our decisions.*

---

underline (ˌʌndəˈlaɪn) vb. **1.** to put a line under. **2.** to emphasize.

underling (ˈʌndəlɪŋ) n. a subordinate.

underlying (ˌʌndəˈlaɪɪŋ) adj. **1.** concealed but detectable: *underlying guilt.* **2.** fundamental; basic: *the underlying principle.* **3.** lying under: *the underlying soil.*

undermentioned (ˈʌndəˌmenʃənd) adj. mentioned below or later.

undermine (ˌʌndəˈmaɪn) vb. **1.** to weaken gradually or insidiously: *he undermined her confidence.* **2.** (of the sea or wind) to wear away the base of (cliffs).

underneath (ˌʌndəˈniːθ) prep., adv. **1.** under; beneath. ~adj. **2.** lower. ~n. **3.** a lower part or surface. [Old English *underneothan*]

undernourished (ˌʌndəˈnʌrɪʃt) adj. lacking the food needed for health and growth. —ˌunderˈnourishment n.

underpants (ˈʌndəˌpænts) pl. n. a man's undergarment covering the body from the waist or hips to the thighs.

underpass (ˈʌndəˌpɑːs) n. **1.** a section of a road that passes under another road or a railway line. **2.** a subway.

underpay (ˌʌndəˈpeɪ) vb. **-paying, -paid.** to pay (someone) insufficiently. —ˌunderˈpayment n.

underpin (ˌʌndəˈpɪn) vb. **-pinning, -pinned.** **1.** to support from beneath by a prop: *to underpin a wall.* **2.** to give strength or support to: *informal relationships that underpin any community.*

underplay (ˌʌndəˈpleɪ) vb. **1.** to achieve (an effect) by deliberate lack of emphasis. **2.** *Cards.* to play a lower card deliberately when holding a higher one.

underprivileged (ˌʌndəˈprɪvɪlɪdʒd) adj. lacking the rights and advantages of other members of society; deprived.

underproduction (ˌʌndəprəˈdʌkʃən) n. *Commerce.* production below full capacity or below demand.

underrate (ˌʌndəˈreɪt) vb. to underestimate. —ˌunderˈrated adj.

undersea (ˈʌndəˌsiː) adj., adv. below the surface of the sea.

underseal (ˈʌndəˌsiːl) *Brit.* ~n. **1.** a special coating applied to the underside of a motor vehicle to prevent corrosion. ~vb. **2.** to apply such a coating to (a motor vehicle).

undersecretary (ˌʌndəˈsekrətrɪ) n., pl. **-taries.** a senior civil servant or junior minister in a government department.

undersell (ˌʌndəˈsel) vb. **-selling, -sold.** to sell at a price lower than that of (another seller).

undersexed (ˌʌndəˈsekst) adj. having weaker than normal sexual urges.

undershirt (ˈʌndəˌʃɜːt) n. *U.S. & Canad.* a vest.

undershoot (ˌʌndəˈʃuːt) vb. **-shooting, -shot.** to land (an aircraft) short of (a runway) or (of an aircraft) to land in this way.

underside (ˈʌndəˌsaɪd) n. the bottom or lower surface.

undersigned (ˈʌndəˌsaɪnd) n. **1. the.** the person or persons who have signed at the foot of a document, statement, or letter. ~adj. **2.** having signed at the foot of a document, statement, or letter.

undersized (ˌʌndəˈsaɪzd) adj. of less than usual size.

underskirt (ˈʌndəˌskɜːt) n. a skirtlike garment worn under a skirt or dress; petticoat.

understand (ˌʌndəˈstænd) vb. **-standing, -stood.** **1.** to know and comprehend the nature or meaning of: *I understand you.* **2.** to realize or grasp (something): *he understands your position.* **3.** to assume, infer, or believe: *I understand you are thinking of marrying.* **4.** to know how to translate or read: *can you understand Spanish?* **5.** to be sympathetic to or compatible with: *we understand each other.* [Old English *understandan*] —ˌunderˈstandable adj. —ˌunderˈstandably adv.

understanding (ˌʌndəˈstændɪŋ) n. **1.** the ability to learn, judge, or make decisions. **2.** personal opinion or interpretation of a subject: *my understanding of your position.* **3.** a mutual agreement, usually an informal or private one. ~adj. **4.** sympathetic, tolerant, or wise towards people.

understate (ˌʌndəˈsteɪt) vb. **1.** to state (something) in restrained terms, often to obtain an ironic effect. **2.** to state that (something, such as a number) is less than it is. —ˌunderˈstatement n.

understood (ˌʌndəˈstʊd) vb. **1.** past of **understand.** ~adj. **2.** implied or inferred. **3.** taken for granted.

understudy (ˈʌndəˌstʌdɪ) vb. **-studying, -studied.** **1.** to study (a role) so as to be able to replace the usual actor if necessary. **2.** to act as understudy to (an actor). ~n., pl. **-studies.** **3.** an actor who studies a part so as to be able to replace the usual actor if necessary. **4.** anyone who is trained to take the place of another if necessary.

undertake (ˌʌndəˈteɪk) vb. **-taking, -took, -taken.** **1.** to agree to or commit oneself to (something) or (to do something): *to undertake a job.* **2.** to promise.

undertaker (ˈʌndəˌteɪkə) n. a person whose profession is the preparation of the dead and the management of funerals.

undertaking (ˈʌndəˌteɪkɪŋ) n. **1.** a task or enterprise. **2.** an agreement to do something. **3.** the business of an undertaker.

undertone (ˈʌndəˌtəʊn) n. **1.** a quiet tone of voice. **2.** an underlying quality or feeling: *undertones of dishonesty.*

undertow (ˈʌndəˌtəʊ) n. **1.** the seaward undercurrent following the breaking of a wave on the beach. **2.** any strong undercurrent flowing in a different direction from the surface current.

---

undermanned   underpopulated   underused
underpaid   understaffed

undervalue (ˌʌndəˈvæljuː) vb. **-valuing, -valued.** to value (a person or thing) at less than the true worth or importance.

underwater (ˈʌndəˈwɔːtə) adj. **1.** situated, occurring, or for use under the surface of the water. ~adv. **2.** beneath the surface of the water.

under way adj. **1.** in progress; in operation: *the show was under way.* **2.** *Naut.* in motion in the direction headed.

underwear (ˈʌndəˌwɛə) n. clothing worn under the outer garments, usually next to the skin.

underweight (ˌʌndəˈweɪt) adj. weighing less than is average, expected, or healthy.

underwent (ˌʌndəˈwɛnt) vb. the past tense of **undergo.**

underworld (ˈʌndəˌwɜːld) n. **1.** criminals and their associates. **2.** *Greek & Roman myth.* the regions below the earth's surface regarded as the abode of the dead.

underwrite (ˈʌndəˌraɪt, ˌʌndəˈraɪt) vb. **-writing, -wrote, -written. 1.** to accept financial responsibility for (a commercial project or enterprise). **2.** to sign and issue (an insurance policy) thus accepting liability. **3.** to support. —'**under,writer** n.

undesirable (ˌʌndɪˈzaɪərəbˀl) adj. **1.** not desirable or pleasant; objectionable. ~n. **2.** a person considered undesirable.

undies (ˈʌndɪz) pl. n. *Informal.* women's underwear.

undine (ˈʌndiːn) n. a female water spirit. [Latin *unda* a wave]

undo (ʌnˈduː) vb. **-doing, -did, -done. 1.** to untie, unwrap, or open or become untied, unwrapped, or opened. **2.** to reverse the effects of: *all our patient work has been undone.* **3.** to cause the downfall of.

undoing (ʌnˈduːɪŋ) n. **1.** ruin; downfall. **2.** the cause of someone's downfall: *drink was his undoing.*

undone[1] (ʌnˈdʌn) adj. not done or completed; unfinished.

undone[2] (ʌnˈdʌn) adj. **1.** ruined; destroyed. **2.** unfastened; untied.

undoubted (ʌnˈdaʊtɪd) adj. beyond doubt; certain or indisputable. —un'**doubtedly** adv.

undreamed (ʌnˈdriːmd) or **undreamt** (ʌnˈdrɛmt) adj. (often foll. by *of*) not thought of or imagined.

undress (ʌnˈdrɛs) vb. **1.** to take off clothes from (oneself or another). ~n. **2.** partial or complete nakedness. **3.** informal or ordinary working clothes or uniform. —un'**dressed** adj.

undue (ʌnˈdjuː) adj. excessive or unwarranted: *undue pressure.*

undulate (ˈʌndjʊˌleɪt) vb. **1.** to move or cause to move in waves. **2.** to have or provide with a wavy form or appearance. [Latin *unda* a wave] —,undu'**lation** n.

unduly (ʌnˈdjuːlɪ) adv. excessively.

undying (ʌnˈdaɪɪŋ) adj. unending; eternal.

unearned (ʌnˈɜːnd) adj. **1.** not deserved. **2.** not yet earned.

unearned income n. income from property or investments rather than work.

unearth (ʌnˈɜːθ) vb. **1.** to dig up out of the earth. **2.** to discover by searching.

unearthly (ʌnˈɜːθlɪ) adj. **1.** ghostly; eerie: *unearthly screams.* **2.** heavenly; sublime: *unearthly music.* **3.** ridiculous or unreasonable: *an unearthly hour.* —un'**earthliness** n.

uneasy (ʌnˈiːzɪ) adj. **1.** (of a person) anxious; apprehensive. **2.** (of a condition) precarious: *an uneasy truce.* **3.** (of a thought or feeling) disquieting. —un'**ease** n. —un'**easily** adv. —un'**easiness** n.

uneatable (ʌnˈiːtəbˀl) adj. (of food) so rotten or unattractive as to be unfit to eat.

uneconomic (ˌʌniːkəˈnɒmɪk, ˌʌnɛkə-) adj. not economic; not profitable.

unemployed (ˌʌnɪmˈplɔɪd) adj. **1. a.** without paid employment; out of work. **b.** (as collective n.; preceded by *the*): *the unemployed.* **2.** not being used; idle.

unemployment (ˌʌnɪmˈplɔɪmənt) n. **1.** the condition of being unemployed. **2.** the number of unemployed workers.

unemployment benefit n. (in the British National Insurance scheme) a regular payment to an unemployed person.

unequal (ʌnˈiːkwəl) adj. **1.** not equal in quantity, size, rank, or value. **2.** (foll. by *to*) inadequate for: *unequal to the task.* **3.** not evenly balanced. **4.** of varying quality; inconsistent. **5.** (of a contest) having competitors of different ability. —un'**equally** adv.

unequalled or *U.S.* **unequaled** (ʌnˈiːkwəld) adj. not equalled; supreme.

unequivocal (ˌʌnɪˈkwɪvəkˀl) adj. not ambiguous; plain. —,une'**quivocally** adv.

unerring (ʌnˈɜːrɪŋ) adj. never mistaken; consistently accurate.

UNESCO (juːˈnɛskəʊ) United Nations Educational, Scientific, and Cultural Organization.

uneven (ʌnˈiːvən) adj. **1.** (of a surface) not level or flat. **2.** not uniform; variable: *an uneven performance.* **3.** not parallel,

undeserved	undisguised	unemotional
undetected	undismayed	unencumbered
undeterred	undisputed	unending
undeveloped	undistinguished	unendurable
undignified	undisturbed	unenlightened
undiluted	undivided	unenthusiastic
undiminished	uneaten	unenviable
undiplomatic	uneconomical	unescorted
undisciplined	uneducated	unethical
undiscovered	unelectable	

straight, or horizontal. **4.** not fairly matched: *an uneven race.*

uneventful (ˌʌnɪˈvɛntfʊl) *adj.* ordinary, routine, or quiet. —**unˈeventfully** *adv.*

unexampled (ˌʌnɪgˈzɑːmpəld) *adj.* without precedent.

unexceptionable (ˌʌnɪkˈsɛpʃənəbəl) *adj.* beyond criticism or objection.

unexceptional (ˌʌnɪkˈsɛpʃənəl) *adj.* **1.** usual, ordinary, or normal. **2.** subject to or allowing no exceptions.

unexpected (ˌʌnɪkˈspɛktɪd) *adj.* surprising or unforeseen. —ˌunexˈpectedly *adv.*

unfailing (ʌnˈfeɪlɪŋ) *adj.* continuous; reliable: *unfailing support.* —**unˈfailingly** *adv.*

unfair (ʌnˈfɛə) *adj.* **1.** unequal or unjust. **2.** dishonest or unethical. —**unˈfairly** *adv.* —**unˈfairness** *n.*

unfaithful (ʌnˈfeɪθfʊl) *adj.* **1.** not true to a promise or vow. **2.** guilty of adultery. —**unˈfaithfulness** *n.*

unfamiliar (ˌʌnfəˈmɪljə) *adj.* **1.** not known; strange: *unfamilar surroundings.* **2.** (foll. by *with*) not acquainted: *I am unfamiliar with the procedure.* —**unfamiliarity** (ˌʌnfəˌmɪlɪˈærɪtɪ) *n.*

unfasten (ʌnˈfɑːsən) *vb.* to undo, untie, or open or become undone, untied, or opened.

unfathomable (ʌnˈfæðəməbəl) *adj.* incomprehensible.

unfavourable *or U.S.* **unfavorable** (ʌnˈfeɪvərəbəl) *adj.* not favourable; adverse or inauspicious. —**unˈfavourably** *or U.S.* **unˈfavorably** *adv.*

unfeeling (ʌnˈfiːlɪŋ) *adj.* without sympathy; callous.

unfettered (ʌnˈfɛtəd) *adj.* not limited or controlled: *unfettered monopolies.*

unfinished (ʌnˈfɪnɪʃt) *adj.* **1.** incomplete or imperfect. **2.** (of paint) without an applied finish.

unfit (ʌnˈfɪt) *adj.* **1.** (foll. by *for*) unqualified or incapable of: *unfit for military service.* **2.** (often foll. by *for*) unsuitable: *the ground was unfit for football.* **3.** in poor physical condition. ~*vb.* **-fitting,** **-fitted.** **4.** *Rare.* to make unfit.

unflappable (ʌnˈflæpəbəl) *adj. Informal.* hard to upset; calm; composed. —**unˌflappaˈbility** *n.*

unfledged (ʌnˈflɛdʒd) *adj.* **1.** (of a young bird) not having developed adult feathers. **2.** immature and inexperienced.

unflinching (ʌnˈflɪntʃɪŋ) *adj.* not shrinking from danger or difficulty.

unfold (ʌnˈfəʊld) *vb.* **1.** to open or spread out or be opened or spread out from a folded state. **2.** to reveal or be revealed: *the truth unfolds.* **3.** to develop or be developed: *the story unfolded.*

unforthcoming (ˌʌnfɔːθˈkʌmɪŋ) *adj.* not inclined to speak, explain, or communicate.

unfortunate (ʌnˈfɔːtʃənɪt) *adj.* **1.** causing or attended by misfortune: *an unfortunate accident.* **2.** unlucky: *an unfortunate man.* **3.** regrettable or unsuitable: *an unfortunate comment.* ~*n.* **4.** an unlucky person. —**unˈfortunately** *adv.*

unfounded (ʌnˈfaʊndɪd) *adj.* (of ideas, fears, or allegations) without good reason; groundless.

unfreeze (ʌnˈfriːz) *vb.* **-freezing, -froze, -frozen.** **1.** to thaw or cause to thaw. **2.** to relax governmental restrictions on (wages, prices, or credit).

unfriendly (ʌnˈfrɛndlɪ) *adj.* **-lier, -liest.** not friendly; hostile.

unfrock (ʌnˈfrɒk) *vb.* to deprive (a person in holy orders) of ecclesiastical status.

unfurl (ʌnˈfɜːl) *vb.* to unroll or spread out (an umbrella, flag, or sail) or (of an umbrella, flag, or sail) to be unrolled or spread out.

ungainly (ʌnˈgeɪnlɪ) *adj.* **-lier, -liest.** lacking grace when moving. [dialect *gainly* graceful] —**unˈgainliness** *n.*

ungodly (ʌnˈgɒdlɪ) *adj.* **-lier, -liest.** **1.** wicked; sinful. **2.** *Informal.* unreasonable; outrageous: *an ungodly hour.* —**unˈgodliness** *n.*

ungovernable (ʌnˈgʌvənəbəl) *adj.* not able to be disciplined or restrained: *an ungovernable temper.*

unguarded (ʌnˈgɑːdɪd) *adj.* **1.** unprotected. **2.** open; frank: *unguarded conversation.* **3.** incautious or careless: *an unguarded movement.*

unguent (ˈʌŋgwənt) *n.* an ointment. [Latin *unguere* to anoint]

ungulate (ˈʌŋgjʊlɪt, -ˌleɪt) *n.* a hoofed mammal. [Latin *ungula* hoof]

unhallowed (ʌnˈhæləʊd) *adj.* **1.** not consecrated or holy: *unhallowed ground.* **2.** sinful.

unhand (ʌnˈhænd) *vb. Archaic or literary.* to release from one's grasp.

unhappy (ʌnˈhæpɪ) *adj.* **-pier, -piest.** **1.** sad or depressed. **2.** unfortunate or wretched. —**unˈhappily** *adv.* —**unˈhappiness** *n.*

unhealthy (ʌnˈhɛlθɪ) *adj.* **-healthier, -healthiest.** **1.** characterized by ill health; sick. **2.** of, causing, or due to ill health: *an unhealthy pallor.* **3.** morbid or unwholesome: *an unhealthy interest in death.* **4.** *Informal.* dangerous; risky. —**unˈhealthiness** *n.*

unheard-of (ʌnˈhɜːdɒv) *adj.* **1.** without precedent: *an unheard-of treatment.* **2.** highly offensive: *unheard-of behaviour.*

---

unexciting	unforgiving	unharmed
unexplained	unformed	unheard
unexpurgated	unfulfilled	unheeded
unfashionable	unfurnished	unhelpful
unforeseen	ungracious	unheralded
unforgettable	ungrammatical	unhindered
unforgivable	ungrateful	

unhinge (ʌnˈhɪndʒ) vb. to derange or unbalance (a person or his mind).

unholy (ʌnˈhəʊlɪ) adj. **-lier, -liest. 1.** immoral or wicked. **2.** Informal. outrageous or unnatural: an unholy alliance. —**unˈholiness** n.

unhook (ʌnˈhʊk) vb. **1.** to remove (something) from a hook. **2.** to unfasten the hooks of (a garment).

unhorse (ʌnˈhɔːs) vb. to knock or throw from a horse.

uni (ˈjuːnɪ) n. Informal. short for **university.**

uni- combining form. of, consisting of, or having only one: unilateral. [Latin ūnus one]

unicameral (ˌjuːnɪˈkæmərəl) adj. of or with a single legislative chamber.

UNICEF (ˈjuːnɪˌsɛf) United Nations Children's Fund.

unicellular (ˌjuːnɪˈsɛljʊlə) adj. (of organisms) consisting of a single cell.

unicorn (ˈjuːnɪˌkɔːn) n. an imaginary creature usually depicted as a white horse with one horn growing from its forehead. [Latin ūnus one + cornu a horn]

unicycle (ˈjuːnɪˌsaɪkˀl) n. a one-wheeled vehicle driven by pedals, used in a circus. —**ˈuniˌcyclist** n.

uniform (ˈjuːnɪˌfɔːm) n. **1.** a special identifying set of clothes for the members of an organization, such as soldiers. ~adj. **2.** unvarying: a uniform surface. **3.** alike or like: a line of uniform toys. [Latin ūnus one + forma shape] —ˌuniˈformity n. —ˈuniˌformly adv.

unify (ˈjuːnɪˌfaɪ) vb. **-fying, -fied.** to make or become one; unite. [Latin ūnus one + facere to make] —ˌunifiˈcation n.

unilateral (ˌjuːnɪˈlætərəl) adj. **1.** of, affecting, or occurring on only one side. **2.** involving or done by only one side: unilateral disarmament. —ˌuniˈlateralism n.

unimpeachable (ˌʌnɪmˈpiːtʃəbˀl) adj. of unquestionable honesty and truth.

uninterested (ʌnˈɪntrɪstɪd) adj. indifferent.

union (ˈjuːnjən) n. **1.** a uniting or being united. **2.** an association or confederation of individuals or groups for a common purpose, usually political. **3.** agreement or harmony. **4.** short for **trade union. 5.** marriage or sexual intercourse. **6.** (often cap.) **a.** an association of students at a university or college formed to look after the students' interests. **b.** the buildings of such an organization. **7.** Maths. a set containing all members of two given sets. **8.** (in 19th-century England) a workhouse maintained by a number of parishes. **9.**

(modifier) of a trade union. [Latin ūnus one]

unionism (ˈjuːnjəˌnɪzəm) n. **1.** the principles of trade unions. **2.** adherence to the principles of trade unions. —**ˈunionist** n., adj.

Unionist (ˈjuːnjənɪst) n. a supporter of union between Britain and Northern Ireland.

unionize or **-nise** (ˈjuːnjəˌnaɪz) vb. **1.** to organize (workers) into a trade union. **2.** to subject to the rules of a trade union. —ˌunioniˈzation or **-niˈsation** n.

Union Jack n. the national flag of the United Kingdom, combining the crosses of Saint George, Saint Andrew, and Saint Patrick.

union shop n. an establishment where nonunion labour is employed only on the condition that such labour joins the union within a specified time period.

unique (juːˈniːk) adj. **1.** being the only one of a particular type. **2.** without equal or like. **3.** Informal. remarkable. [Latin ūnicus unparalleled] —**uˈniquely** adv.

unisex (ˈjuːnɪˌsɛks) adj. (of clothing, a hairstyle, or hairdressers) for both sexes.

unisexual (ˌjuːnɪˈsɛksjʊəl) adj. **1.** of one sex only. **2.** (of an organism) having either male or female reproductive organs but not both.

unison (ˈjuːnɪsˀn) n. **1.** Music. identical pitch. **2.** complete agreement: they acted in unison throughout. [Latin ūnus one + sonus sound]

unit (ˈjuːnɪt) n. **1.** a single undivided entity or whole. **2.** a group or individual regarded as a basic element of a larger whole. **3.** a mechanical part that performs a specific function: a filter unit. **4.** a complete system or establishment that performs a specific function: a production unit. **5.** a subdivision of a military formation. **6.** a standard amount of a physical quantity, such as length or energy, used to express magnitudes of that quantity: the second is a unit of time. **7.** the digit or position immediately to the left of the decimal point. **8.** a piece of furniture designed to be fitted with other similar pieces: kitchen units. **9.** Austral. & N.Z. short for **home unit.** [from unity]

Unitarian (ˌjuːnɪˈtɛərɪən) n. **1.** a person who believes that God is one being and rejects the Trinity. ~adj. **2.** of Unitarians or Unitarianism. —**ˌUniˈtariˌanism** n.

unitary (ˈjuːnɪtrɪ) adj. **1.** of a unit or units. **2.** based on or marked by unity.

unit cost n. the actual cost of producing one article.

---

unhurried	unimportant	unintelligent
unhurt	unimpressed	unintelligible
unhygienic	uninformed	unintended
unidentified	uninhabited	unintentional
unimaginable	uninhibited	uninteresting
unimaginative	uninspired	uninterrupted
unimpeded	uninspiring	uninvited

unite (juːˈnaɪt) *vb.* **1.** to make or become an integrated whole. **2.** to unify or be unified in purpose, action, or beliefs. **3.** to enter or cause to enter into an association or alliance. [Latin *ūnus* one]

united (juːˈnaɪtɪd) *adj.* **1.** produced by two or more persons or things in combination: *a united effort.* **2.** in agreement. **3.** in association or alliance.

United Kingdom *n.* a kingdom of NW Europe, consisting of the island of Great Britain together with Northern Ireland.

United Nations *n.* (*functioning as sing. or pl.*) an international organization of independent states, formed to promote peace and international security.

unit price *n.* the price charged per unit.

unit trust *n. Brit.* an investment trust that issues units for public sale and invests the money in many different businesses.

unity (ˈjuːnɪtɪ) *n., pl.* **-ties. 1.** a being one; oneness. **2.** something complete that is composed of separate parts. **3.** mutual agreement; harmony: *unity of purpose.* **4.** *Maths.* the number or numeral one. [Latin *ūnus* one]

Univ. University.

univalent (ˌjuːnɪˈveɪlənt, juːˈnɪvələnt) *adj. Chem.* same as **monovalent.**

universal (ˌjuːnɪˈvɜːsəl) *adj.* **1.** of or typical of the whole of mankind or of nature. **2.** common to all in a particular group. **3.** applicable to or affecting many individuals, conditions, or cases. **4.** existing everywhere. —**universality** (ˌjuːnɪvɜːˈsælɪtɪ) *n.* —**uniˈversally** *adv.*

universal joint *or* **coupling** *n.* a form of coupling between two rotating shafts allowing freedom of movement in all directions.

universe (ˈjuːnɪˌvɜːs) *n.* **1.** the whole of all existing matter, energy, and space. **2.** the world. [Latin *ūniversum* the whole world]

university (ˌjuːnɪˈvɜːsɪtɪ) *n., pl.* **-ties. 1.** an institution of higher education having authority to award degrees. **2.** the buildings, members, staff, or campus of a university. [Medieval Latin *universitās* group of scholars]

unjust (ʌnˈdʒʌst) *adj.* not fair or just.

unkempt (ʌnˈkempt) *adj.* **1.** (of the hair) uncombed; dishevelled. **2.** ungroomed; slovenly: *unkempt appearance.* [Old English *uncembed,* from *cemban* to comb]

unkind (ʌnˈkaɪnd) *adj.* lacking kindness; unsympathetic or cruel. —**unˈkindly** *adv.* —**unˈkindness** *n.*

unknown (ʌnˈnəʊn) *adj.* **1.** not known, understood, or recognized. **2.** not famous: *an unknown artist.* **3. unknown quantity.** a person or thing whose action or effect is unknown or unpredictable. ~*n.* **4.** an unknown person, quantity, or thing. ~*adv.* **5. unknown to someone.** without someone being aware: *unknown to them he was nearby.*

unleaded (ʌnˈledɪd) *adj.* (of petrol) containing less tetraethyl lead, in order to reduce environmental pollution.

unlearn (ʌnˈlɜːn) *vb.* **-learning, -learnt** *or* **-learned** (-ˈlɜːnd). to try to forget (something learnt) or to discard (accumulated knowledge).

unlearned (ʌnˈlɜːnɪd) *adj.* ignorant or uneducated.

unlearnt (ʌnˈlɜːnt) *or* **unlearned** (ʌnˈlɜːnd) *adj.* **1.** denoting knowledge or skills innately present rather than learnt. **2.** not learnt or taken notice of: *unlearnt lessons.*

unleash (ʌnˈliːʃ) *vb.* to release from or as if from a leash.

unleavened (ʌnˈlevənd) *adj.* (of bread) made without yeast or leavening.

unless (ʌnˈles) *conj.* except under the circumstances that; except on the condition that: *I'll sell it unless you want it.*

unlettered (ʌnˈletəd) *adj.* uneducated; illiterate.

unlike (ʌnˈlaɪk) *adj.* **1.** dissimilar; different. ~*prep.* **2.** not like; not typical of: *unlike his father he is tall.* —**unˈlikeness** *n.*

unlikely (ʌnˈlaɪklɪ) *adj.* not likely; improbable. —**unˈlikeliness** *n.*

unlimited (ʌnˈlɪmɪtɪd) *adj.* **1.** very large in size or amount: *unlimited supplies.* **2.** not restricted or limited: *unlimited power.*

unlisted (ʌnˈlɪstɪd) *adj.* **1.** not entered on a list. **2.** (of securities) not quoted on a stock exchange.

unload (ʌnˈləʊd) *vb.* **1.** to remove (cargo) from (a ship, lorry, or plane). **2.** to give vent to (anxiety or troubles). **3.** to get rid of or dispose of. **4.** to remove the ammunition from (a firearm).

unlock (ʌnˈlɒk) *vb.* **1.** to unfasten (a lock or door). **2.** to release or let loose.

unlooked-for (ˌʌnˈlʊktfɔː) *adj.* unexpected; unforeseen.

unloose (ʌnˈluːs) *or* **unloosen** *vb.* to set free; release.

unlovely (ʌnˈlʌvlɪ) *adj.* unpleasant in appearance or character.

unlucky (ʌnˈlʌkɪ) *adj.* **1.** characterized by misfortune: *an unlucky chance.* **2.** ill-omened; inauspicious: *an unlucky date.* —**unˈluckily** *adv.*

unmade (ʌnˈmeɪd) *adj.* **1.** (of a bed) with the bedclothes not smoothed and tidied. **2.** (of a road) not surfaced with tarmac. **3.** not yet made.

unmake (ʌnˈmeɪk) *vb.* **-making, -made. 1.** to undo or destroy. **2.** to depose from office or authority.

unman (ʌnˈmæn) *vb.* **-manning, -manned. 1.** to cause to lose courage or nerve. **2.** to make effeminate.

unmanly (ʌnˈmænlɪ) *adj.* **1.** not masculine or virile. **2.** cowardly or dishonourable.

unmanned (ʌnˈmænd) *adj.* **1.** lacking personnel or crew: *an unmanned ship.* **2.** (of an aircraft or spacecraft) operated by automatic or remote control.

unmannerly (ʌnˈmænəlɪ) *adj.* lacking manners; discourteous. —**unˈmannerliness** *n.*

unmask (ʌnˈmɑːsk) *vb.* **1.** to remove the mask or disguise from. **2.** to appear or cause to appear in true character.

unmeaning (ʌnˈmiːnɪŋ) *adj.* **1.** having no meaning. **2.** showing no intelligence.

unmentionable (ʌnˈmɛnʃənəbᵊl) *adj.* unsuitable as a topic of conversation.

unmerciful (ʌnˈmɜːsɪful) *adj.* **1.** showing no mercy; relentless. **2.** extreme or excessive. —**unˈmercifully** *adv.*

unmistakable *or* **unmistakeable** (ˌʌnmɪsˈteɪkəbᵊl) *adj.* not mistakable; clear or unambiguous. —ˌunmisˈtakably *or* ˌunmisˈtakeably *adv.*

unmitigated (ʌnˈmɪtɪˌɡeɪtɪd) *adj.* **1.** not diminished in intensity. **2.** total; complete: *an unmitigated disaster.*

unmoral (ʌnˈmɒrəl) *adj.* outside morality; amoral. —**unmorality** (ˌʌnmɒˈrælɪtɪ) *n.*

unmuzzle (ʌnˈmʌzᵊl) *vb.* **1.** to take the muzzle off (a dog). **2.** to free from control or censorship.

unnatural (ʌnˈnætʃərəl) *adj.* **1.** contrary to nature; abnormal. **2.** not in accordance with accepted standards of behaviour: *unnatural love.* **3.** affected or forced: *an unnatural manner.* **4.** inhuman; monstrous: *an unnatural crime.* —**unˈnaturally** *adv.*

unnecessary (ʌnˈnɛsɪsərɪ) *adj.* not essential. —**unˈnecessarily** *adv.*

unnerve (ʌnˈnɜːv) *vb.* to cause to lose courage, confidence, or self-control.

unnumbered (ʌnˈnʌmbəd) *adj.* **1.** countless; innumerable. **2.** not counted or given a number.

UNO United Nations Organization.

unoccupied (ʌnˈɒkjʊˌpaɪd) *adj.* **1.** (of a building) without occupants. **2.** unemployed or idle. **3.** (of an area or country) not overrun by foreign troops.

unorganized *or* **-nised** (ʌnˈɔːɡəˌnaɪzd) *adj.* **1.** not arranged into an organized system. **2.** (of workers) not unionized.

unpack (ʌnˈpæk) *vb.* **1.** to remove the packed contents of (a case). **2.** to take (something) out of a packed container.

unparalleled (ʌnˈpærəˌlɛld) *adj.* not equalled; supreme.

unparliamentary (ˌʌnpɑːlɪəˈmɛntrɪ) *adj.* not consistent with parliamentary procedure or practice.

unperson (ˈʌnpɜːsᵊn) *n.* a person whose existence is officially denied or ignored.

unpick (ʌnˈpɪk) *vb.* to undo (the stitches) of (a piece of sewing).

unpin (ʌnˈpɪn) *vb.* **-pinning, -pinned.** **1.** to remove a pin or pins from. **2.** to unfasten by removing pins.

unpleasant (ʌnˈplɛzᵊnt) *adj.* not pleasant or agreeable. —**unˈpleasantly** *adv.* —**unˈpleasantness** *n.*

unplumbed (ʌnˈplʌmd) *adj.* **1.** not measured. **2.** not understood in depth.

unpopular (ʌnˈpɒpjʊlə) *adj.* not popular with a person or group. —**unpopularity** (ˌʌnpɒpjʊˈlærɪtɪ) *n.*

unpractised *or U.S.* **unpracticed** (ʌnˈpræktɪst) *adj.* without skill or experience.

unprecedented (ʌnˈprɛsɪˌdɛntɪd) *adj.* having no precedent; unparalleled.

unprincipled (ʌnˈprɪnsɪpᵊld) *adj.* lacking moral principles; unscrupulous.

unprintable (ʌnˈprɪntəbᵊl) *adj.* unsuitable for printing for reasons of obscenity, libel, or indecency.

unprofessional (ˌʌnprəˈfɛʃᵊnᵊl) *adj.* **1.** contrary to the accepted code of a profession. **2.** not belonging to a profession.

unputdownable (ˌʌnpʊtˈdaʊnəbᵊl) *adj.* (of a book, usually a novel) so gripping as to be read at one sitting.

unqualified (ʌnˈkwɒlɪˌfaɪd) *adj.* **1.** lacking the necessary qualifications. **2.** not modified: *an unqualified criticism.* **3.** total or complete: *an unqualified success.*

unquestionable (ʌnˈkwɛstʃənəbᵊl) *adj.* not to be doubted; indisputable.

unquiet (ʌnˈkwaɪət) *adj. Chiefly literary.* anxious; uneasy.

unquote (ʌnˈkwəʊt) *interj.* an expression used parenthetically to indicate that the preceding quotation is finished.

unravel (ʌnˈrævᵊl) *vb.* **-elling, -elled** *or U.S.* **-eling, -eled.** **1.** to reduce (something knitted or woven) to separate strands. **2.** to explain or solve: *the mystery was unravelled.* **3.** to become unravelled.

unread (ʌnˈrɛd) *adj.* **1.** (of a book or article) not yet read. **2.** (of a person) having read little.

unreadable (ʌnˈriːdəbᵊl) *adj.* **1.** illegible. **2.** too difficult or dull to read.

unready (ʌnˈrɛdɪ) *adj.* **1.** not ready or prepared. **2.** slow to act.

unreal (ʌnˈrɪəl) *adj.* **1.** imaginary or seemingly so: *an unreal situation.* **2.** insincere or artificial. —**unreality** (ˌʌnrɪˈælɪtɪ) *n.*

unmarked	unpaid	unproductive
unmarried	unpalatable	unprofitable
unmoved	unpardonable	unpromising
unnamed	unplanned	unprompted
unnoticed	unplug	unpronounceable
unobserved	unpolluted	unprotected
unobtainable	unpredictable	unprovoked
unobtrusive	unprejudiced	unpublished
unofficial	unprepared	unpunished
unopened	unprepossessing	unquestioning
unorthodox	unpretentious	unrealistic

unreasonable (ʌnˈriːznəbᵊl) adj. **1.** immoderate: *unreasonable demands*. **2.** refusing to listen to reason. —**unˈreasonably** adv.

unreasoning (ʌnˈriːzənɪŋ) adj. not controlled by reason; irrational.

unregenerate (ˌʌnrɪˈdʒɛnərɪt) adj. **1.** unrepentant; unreformed. **2.** obstinately adhering to one's own views.

unrelenting (ˌʌnrɪˈlɛntɪŋ) adj. **1.** refusing to relent or take pity. **2.** not diminishing in determination, effort, or force.

unremitting (ˌʌnrɪˈmɪtɪŋ) adj. never slackening or stopping; constant.

unreserved (ˌʌnrɪˈzɜːvd) adj. **1.** without reserve; open in manner. **2.** without reservation. **3.** not booked or bookable. —**unreservedly** (ˌʌnrɪˈzɜːvɪdlɪ) adv.

unrest (ʌnˈrɛst) n. **1.** a rebellious state of discontent. **2.** an uneasy or troubled state.

unrighteous (ʌnˈraɪtʃəs) adj. **1.** sinful; wicked. **2.** unfair; unjust.

unripe (ʌnˈraɪp) adj. not fully matured.

unrivalled or U.S. **unrivaled** (ʌnˈraɪvᵊld) adj. having no equal; matchless.

unroll (ʌnˈrəʊl) vb. **1.** to open out or unwind (something rolled or coiled) or (of something rolled or coiled) to become opened out or unwound. **2.** to make or become visible or apparent.

unruffled (ʌnˈrʌfᵊld) adj. **1.** unmoved; calm. **2.** still: *the unruffled seas*.

unruly (ʌnˈruːlɪ) adj. **-lier, -liest.** given to disobedience or indiscipline. —**unˈruliness** n.

unsaddle (ʌnˈsædᵊl) vb. **1.** to remove the saddle from (a horse). **2.** to unhorse.

unsaid (ʌnˈsɛd) adj. not said or expressed.

unsaturated (ʌnˈsætʃəˌreɪtɪd) adj. **1.** not saturated. **2.** *Chem.* (of an organic compound) capable of undergoing addition reactions.

unsavoury or U.S. **unsavory** (ʌnˈseɪvərɪ) adj. objectionable or distasteful.

unsay (ʌnˈseɪ) vb. **-saying, -said.** to retract or withdraw (something said).

unscathed (ʌnˈskeɪðd) adj. not harmed or injured.

unscramble (ʌnˈskræmbᵊl) vb. **1.** to resolve from confusion or disorderliness. **2.** to restore (a scrambled message) to an intelligible form. —**unˈscrambler** n.

unscrew (ʌnˈskruː) vb. **1.** to remove a screw from (an object). **2.** to loosen (a screw or lid) by rotating.

unscrupulous (ʌnˈskruːpjʊləs) adj. without scruples; unprincipled.

unseasonable (ʌnˈsiːzənəbᵊl) adj. **1.** (esp. of the weather) inappropriate for the season. **2.** untimely; inopportune.

unseat (ʌnˈsiːt) vb. **1.** to throw or displace from a seat or saddle. **2.** to depose from office or position.

unseeded (ʌnˈsiːdɪd) adj. (of a player in a sport) not given a top player's position in the opening rounds of a tournament.

unseemly (ʌnˈsiːmlɪ) adj. not in good style or taste. —**unˈseemliness** n.

unselfish (ʌnˈsɛlfɪʃ) adj. not selfish; generous. —**unˈselfishly** adv. —**unˈselfishness** n.

unsettle (ʌnˈsɛtᵊl) vb. **1.** to change or become changed from a fixed or settled condition. **2.** to confuse or agitate (a person or the mind).

unsettled (ʌnˈsɛtᵊld) adj. **1.** lacking order or stability: *an unsettled era*. **2.** disturbed and restless: *feeling unsettled*. **3.** constantly changing or moving from place to place: *an unsettled life*. **4.** (of controversy) not resolved. **5.** (of debts or law cases) not disposed of.

unshakable or **unshakeable** (ʌnˈʃeɪkəbᵊl) adj. (of beliefs) utterly firm and unwavering.

unshaken (ʌnˈʃeɪkən) adj. (of faith or feelings) not having been weakened.

unsheathe (ʌnˈʃiːð) vb. to pull out (a weapon) from a sheath.

unsightly (ʌnˈsaɪtlɪ) adj. unpleasant to look at; ugly. —**unˈsightliness** n.

unskilful or U.S. **unskillful** (ʌnˈskɪlful) adj. lacking dexterity or proficiency. —**unˈskilfully** or U.S. **unˈskillfully** adv.

unskilled (ʌnˈskɪld) adj. not having or requiring any special skill or training.

unsociable (ʌnˈsəʊʃəbᵊl) adj. (of a person) disinclined to associate with others.

unsocial (ʌnˈsəʊʃəl) adj. **1.** antisocial. **2.** (of the hours of work of a job) falling outside the normal working day.

unsophisticated (ˌʌnsəˈfɪstɪˌkeɪtɪd) adj. **1.** lacking experience or worldly wisdom. **2.** lacking refinement or complexity: *an unsophisticated machine*.

unsound (ʌnˈsaʊnd) adj. **1.** unhealthy or unstable: *of unsound mind*. **2.** based on faulty ideas: *unsound advice*. **3.** not firm: *unsound foundations*. **4.** not financially reliable: *an unsound enterprise*.

unsparing (ʌnˈspɛərɪŋ) adj. **1.** not frugal; lavish. **2.** harsh or severe. —**unˈsparingly** adv.

unspeakable (ʌnˈspiːkəbᵊl) adj. **1.** incapable of expression in words: *unspeakable ecstasy*. **2.** indescribably bad or evil. **3.** not to be uttered: *unspeakable thoughts.* —**un'speakably** *adv.*

unstable (ʌn'steɪbᵊl) *adj.* **1.** lacking stability or firmness. **2.** having abrupt changes of mood or behaviour. **3.** *Chem., physics.* readily decomposing.

unsteady (ʌn'stedɪ) *adj.* **1.** not securely fixed: *an unsteady foothold.* **2.** (of a manner of walking, standing, or holding) shaky or staggering. —**un'steadily** *adv.* —**un'steadiness** *n.*

unstring (ʌn'strɪŋ) *vb.* **-stringing, -strung. 1.** to remove the strings of. **2.** to remove (beads) from a string.

unstructured (ʌn'strʌktʃəd) *adj.* without formal or systematic organization.

unstrung (ʌn'strʌŋ) *adj.* **1.** emotionally distressed; unnerved. **2.** (of a stringed instrument) with the strings detached.

unstuck (ʌn'stʌk) *adj.* **1.** freed from being stuck, glued, or fastened. **2. come unstuck.** to suffer failure or disaster.

unstudied (ʌn'stʌdɪd) *adj.* natural; spontaneous: *unstudied grace.*

unsubstantial (ˌʌnsəb'stænʃəl) *adj.* **1.** lacking weight or firmness. **2.** having no material existence.

unsung (ʌn'sʌŋ) *adj.* not acclaimed or honoured: *unsung deeds.*

unsuspected (ˌʌnsə'spektɪd) *adj.* **1.** not under suspicion. **2.** not known to exist: *unsuspected difficulties.*

unswerving (ʌn'swɜːvɪŋ) *adj.* not turning aside; constant.

untangle (ʌn'tæŋgᵊl) *vb.* to free from tangles or confusion.

untaught (ʌn'tɔːt) *adj.* **1.** without training or education. **2.** acquired without instruction.

unthinkable (ʌn'θɪŋkəbᵊl) *adj.* **1.** not to be contemplated; out of the question. **2.** unimaginable; inconceivable.

unthinking (ʌn'θɪŋkɪŋ) *adj.* **1.** thoughtless; inconsiderate. **2.** heedless; inadvertent: *it was done in an unthinking moment.* —**un'thinkingly** *adv.*

unthrone (ʌn'θrəʊn) *vb.* to dethrone.

untidy (ʌn'taɪdɪ) *adj.* **-dier, -diest.** not neat; slovenly. —**un'tidily** *adv.* —**un'tidiness** *n.*

untie (ʌn'taɪ) *vb.* **-tying, -tied. 1.** to unfasten or free (something that is tied). **2.** to free from constraint.

until (ʌn'tɪl) *conj.* **1.** up to a time that: *I laughed until I cried.* **2.** (used with a negative) before (a time or event): *until we change, we can't leave.* ~*prep.* **3.** (often preceded by *up*) in or throughout the period before: *wait until six.* **4.** (used with a negative) before: *he won't come until Friday.* [earlier *untill*]

untimely (ʌn'taɪmlɪ) *adj.* **1.** occurring before the expected or normal time: *an untimely death.* **2.** inappropriate to the occasion or time: *his joking at the funeral was most untimely.* —**un'timeliness** *n.*

unto ('ʌntuː) *prep. Archaic.* to. [Old Norse]

untold (ʌn'təʊld) *adj.* **1.** incapable of description: *untold suffering.* **2.** incalculably great in number or quantity: *untold thousands.* **3.** not told.

untouchable (ʌn'tʌtʃəbᵊl) *adj.* **1.** above reproach or suspicion. **2.** unable to be touched. ~*n.* **3.** a member of the lowest class in India, whose touch was formerly regarded as defiling to the four main castes.

untoward (ˌʌntə'wɔːd) *adj.* **1.** causing misfortune or annoyance. **2.** unfavourable: *untoward circumstances.* **3.** out of the ordinary; out of the way: *nothing untoward happened.*

untrue (ʌn'truː) *adj.* **1.** incorrect or false. **2.** disloyal. **3.** diverging from a rule or standard; inaccurate.

untruthful (ʌn'truːθfʊl) *adj.* **1.** (of a person) given to lying. **2.** diverging from the truth. —**un'truthfully** *adv.*

untutored (ʌn'tjuːtəd) *adj.* **1.** without formal education. **2.** lacking sophistication or refinement.

unused *adj.* **1.** (ʌn'juːzd). not being or never having been used. **2.** (ʌn'juːst). (foll. by *to*) not accustomed to.

unusual (ʌn'juːʒʊəl) *adj.* uncommon; extraordinary. —**un'usually** *adv.*

unutterable (ʌn'ʌtərəbᵊl) *adj.* incapable of being expressed in words. —**un'utterably** *adv.*

unvarnished (ʌn'vɑːnɪʃt) *adj.* not elaborated upon; plain: *the unvarnished truth.*

unveil (ʌn'veɪl) *vb.* **1.** to remove the cover from in the ceremonial unveiling of a monument. **2.** to remove the veil from (one's own or another person's face). **3.** to make (something concealed) known or public.

unveiling (ʌn'veɪlɪŋ) *n.* **1.** a ceremony involving the removal of a veil covering a statue. **2.** the presentation of something for the first time.

unvoiced (ʌn'vɔɪst) *adj.* **1.** not expressed or spoken. **2.** *Phonetics.* voiceless.

unwaged (ʌn'weɪdʒd) *adj.* (of a person) not having a paid job.

unspoiled	unsurpassed	untrained
unspoken	unsurprising	untreated
unsporting	unsuspecting	untried
unstinting	unsweetened	untroubled
unstoppable	unsympathetic	untrustworthy
unsubstantiated	untamed	unusable
unsuccessful	untaxed	unwanted
unsuitable	untenable	unwarranted
unsure	untested	

unwary (ʌnˈwɛərɪ) *adj.* lacking caution or prudence. —**unˈwarily** *adv.* —**unˈwariness** *n.*

unwell (ʌnˈwɛl) *adj.* not well; ill.

unwept (ʌnˈwɛpt) *adj.* not wept for or lamented.

unwholesome (ʌnˈhəʊlsəm) *adj.* **1.** harmful to the body or mind: *an unwholesome climate.* **2.** morally harmful: *unwholesome practices.* **3.** unhealthy-looking. **4.** (of food) of inferior quality.

unwieldy (ʌnˈwiːldɪ) *adj.* too heavy, large, or awkward to be easily handled.

unwilling (ʌnˈwɪlɪŋ) *adj.* **1.** reluctant. **2.** done or said with reluctance. —**unˈwillingly** *adv.* —**unˈwillingness** *n.*

unwind (ʌnˈwaɪnd) *vb.* -**winding**, -**wound**. **1.** to slacken, undo, or unravel or cause to slacken, undo, or unravel. **2.** to make or become relaxed: *he finds it hard to unwind.*

unwise (ʌnˈwaɪz) *adj.* lacking wisdom or prudence. —**unˈwisely** *adv.*

unwitting (ʌnˈwɪtɪŋ) *adj.* **1.** not knowing or conscious. **2.** not intentional; inadvertent. [Old English *witting*, present participle of *witan* to know] —**unˈwittingly** *adv.*

unwonted (ʌnˈwəʊntɪd) *adj.* out of the ordinary; unusual.

unworldly (ʌnˈwɜːldlɪ) *adj.* **1.** not concerned with material values or pursuits. **2.** lacking sophistication; naive.

unworthy (ʌnˈwɜːðɪ) *adj.* **1.** (often foll. by *of*) not deserving: *unworthy of the honour.* **2.** (often foll. by *of*) beneath the level considered befitting (to): *an unworthy thought.* **3.** lacking merit or value. **4.** undeserved. —**unˈworthiness** *n.*

unwrap (ʌnˈræp) *vb.* -**wrapping**, -**wrapped**. to remove the wrapping from (something) or (of something wrapped) to have the covering removed.

unwritten (ʌnˈrɪtˀn) *adj.* **1.** not printed or in writing. **2.** operating only through custom: *an unwritten law.*

unzip (ʌnˈzɪp) *vb.* -**zipping**, -**zipped**. to unfasten the zip of (a garment) or (of a zip or a garment with a zip) to become unfastened: *her skirt unzipped as she sat down.*

up (ʌp) *prep.* **1.** indicating movement to a higher position: *go up the stairs.* **2.** at a higher or further level or position in or on: *a shop up the road.* ~*adv.* **3.** to an upward, higher, or erect position, usually indicating readiness for an activity: *up and about.* **4.** indicating intensity or completion of an action: *he tore up the cheque.* **5.** to the place referred to or where the speaker is: *a man came up to me.* **6. a.** to a more important place: *up to London.* **b.** to a more northerly place: *up to Scotland.* **c.** to or at university. **7.** above the horizon: *the sun is up.* **8.** appearing for trial: *up before the judge.* **9.** having gained: *ten pounds up on the deal.* **10.** higher in price: *tea is up again.* **11. all up with someone.** *Informal.* over for or hopeless for someone.

12. something's up. *Informal.* something strange is happening. **13. up against. a.** touching. **b.** having to cope with: *look what we're up against now.* **14. up for.** being a candidate or applicant for: *he's up for the job.* **15. up to. a.** occupied with; scheming: *she's up to no good.* **b.** dependent upon: *the decision is up to you.* **c.** equal to or capable of (something or doing something): *are you up to playing in the final?* **d.** as far as: *up to his neck in mud.* **e.** as many as: *up to two years' credit.* **f.** comparable with: *not up to my usual standard.* **16. what's up?** *Informal.* **a.** what is the matter? **b.** what is happening? ~*adj.* **17.** of a high or higher position. **18.** out of bed: *aren't you up yet?* **19.** of or relating to a train going to a more important place: *the up platform.* ~*vb.* -**upping**, -**upped**. **20.** to increase or raise. **21.** (foll. by and with a verb) *Informal.* to do something suddenly: *she upped and married someone else.* ~*n.* **22.** a high point: *we have our ups and downs.* **23. on the up and up. a.** trustworthy or honest. ~*adv.* **b.** *Brit.* on an upward trend: *our firm's on the up and up.* [Old English *upp*]

up-and-coming *adj.* promising future success; enterprising.

upbeat (ˈʌpˌbiːt) *n.* **1.** *Music.* **a.** an unaccented beat. **b.** the upward gesture of a conductor's baton indicating this. ~*adj.* **2.** *Informal.* cheerful; optimistic.

upbraid (ʌpˈbreɪd) *vb.* to reproach; censure. [Old English *upbregdan*]

upbringing (ˈʌpˌbrɪŋɪŋ) *n.* the education of a person during his formative years.

upcountry (ʌpˈkʌntrɪ) *adj.* **1.** of or from the interior of a country. **2.** towards or in the interior of a country.

update (ʌpˈdeɪt) *vb.* to bring up to date.

upend (ʌpˈɛnd) *vb.* to turn or set or become turned or set on end.

upfront (ˈʌpˈfrʌnt) *adj.* **1.** open and frank. ~*adv., adj.* **2.** (of money) paid out at the beginning of a business arrangement.

upgrade (ʌpˈgreɪd) *vb.* **1.** to promote (a person or job) to a higher rank. **2.** to raise in value, importance, or esteem.

upheaval (ʌpˈhiːvˀl) *n.* a strong, sudden, or violent disturbance.

uphill (ˈʌpˈhɪl) *adj.* **1.** sloping or leading upwards. **2.** requiring a great deal of effort: *an uphill task.* ~*adv.* **3.** up a slope.

uphold (ʌpˈhəʊld) *vb.* -**holding**, -**held**. **1.** to maintain or defend against opposition. **2.** to give moral support to. —**upˈholder** *n.*

upholster (ʌpˈhəʊlstə) *vb.* to fit (chairs or sofas) with padding, springs, and covering. —**upˈholsterer** *n.* —**upˈholstery** *n.*

upkeep (ˈʌpˌkiːp) *n.* **1.** the act or process of keeping something in good repair. **2.** the cost of maintenance.

upland (ˈʌplənd) *n.* **1.** an area of high or relatively high ground. ~*adj.* **2.** of or in an upland.

uplift vb. (ʌpˈlɪft). **1.** to raise; lift up. **2.** to raise morally or spiritually. ~n. (ˈʌpˌlɪft). **3.** the act, process, or result of lifting up. **4.** the act or process of bettering moral, social, or cultural conditions. **5.** (modifier) denoting a bra for lifting and supporting the breasts. —**upˈlifting** adj.

up-market adj. expensive and of superior quality.

upmost (ˈʌpˌməʊst) adj. same as **uppermost**.

upon (əˈpɒn) prep. **1.** on. **2.** up and on: climb upon my knee. [up + on]

upper (ˈʌpə) adj. **1.** higher or highest in physical position, wealth, rank, or status. **2.** Geol. denoting the late part or division of a period or system: Upper Palaeolithic. ~n. **3.** the part of a shoe above the sole. **4. on one's uppers.** destitute.

upper-case adj. denoting capital letters as used in printed or typed matter.

upper class n. **1.** the highest social class; aristocracy. ~adj. **upper-class. 2.** of the upper class.

upper crust n. Informal. the upper class.

uppercut (ˈʌpəˌkʌt) n. a short swinging upward punch delivered to the chin.

upper hand n. **the.** the position of control: he has the upper hand.

Upper House n. one of the two houses of a two-chamber legislature.

uppermost (ˈʌpəˌməʊst) adj. also **upmost. 1.** highest in position, power, or importance. ~adv. **2.** in or into the highest place or position.

uppish (ˈʌpɪʃ) adj. Brit. informal. uppity.

uppity (ˈʌpɪtɪ) adj. Informal. snobbish, arrogant, or presumptuous. [up + fanciful ending]

upright (ˈʌpˌraɪt) adj. **1.** vertical or erect. **2.** honest or just. ~adv. **3.** vertically. ~n. **4.** a vertical support, such as a post. **5.** short for **upright piano. 6.** the state of being vertical. —**upˈrightness** n.

upright piano n. a piano which has a rectangular vertical case.

uprising (ˈʌpˌraɪzɪŋ, ʌpˈraɪzɪŋ) n. a revolt or rebellion.

uproar (ˈʌpˌrɔː) n. a commotion or disturbance characterized by loud noise and confusion.

uproarious (ʌpˈrɔːrɪəs) adj. **1.** very funny. **2.** (of laughter) loud and boisterous.

uproot (ʌpˈruːt) vb. **1.** to pull up by or as if by the roots. **2.** to displace (a person or people) from native or usual surroundings. **3.** to remove or destroy utterly.

ups and downs pl. n. alternating periods of good and bad luck or high and low spirits.

upset vb. (ʌpˈsɛt), -**setting**, -**set. 1.** to tip or be tipped over; overturn or spill. **2.** to disturb the normal state or stability of: to upset the balance of nature. **3.** to disturb mentally or emotionally. **4.** to make physically ill: alcohol upsets my stomach. ~n. (ˈʌpˌsɛt). **5.** an unexpected defeat or reversal, as in a contest or plans. **6.** a disturbance or disorder of the emotions, mind, or body. ~adj. (ʌpˈsɛt). **7.** over-

turned. **8.** emotionally or physically disturbed or distressed. —**upˈsetting** adj.

upset price n. Chiefly Scot., U.S., & Canad. the lowest price acceptable for something that is for sale, usually a house.

upshot (ˈʌpˌʃɒt) n. the final result; conclusion; outcome. [up + shot]

upside down (ˌʌpsaɪd ˈdaʊn) adj. **1.** turned over completely; inverted. **2.** Informal. confused; topsy-turvy. ~adv. **3.** in an inverted fashion. **4.** in a chaotic manner. [by folk etymology, from upsodown]

upsides (ˌʌpˈsaɪdz) adv. Informal, chiefly Brit. (foll. by with) equal or level with, as through revenge.

upstage (ˈʌpˈsteɪdʒ) adv. **1.** on, at, or to the rear of the stage. ~adj. **2.** of the back half of the stage. **3.** Informal. haughty. ~vb. **4.** to move upstage of (another actor), forcing him to turn away from the audience. **5.** Informal. to draw attention to oneself from (someone else).

upstairs (ˈʌpˈstɛəz) adv. **1.** up the stairs; to or on an upper floor. **2.** Informal. to or into a higher rank or office. ~n. (functioning as sing. or pl.) **3.** an upper floor. ~adj. **4.** situated on an upper floor: an upstairs room.

upstanding (ʌpˈstændɪŋ) adj. **1.** of good character. **2.** upright and vigorous in build.

upstart (ˈʌpˌstɑːt) n. a person who has risen suddenly to a position of power and behaves arrogantly.

upstream (ˈʌpˈstriːm) adv., adj. in or towards the higher part of a stream; against the current.

upsurge (ˈʌpˌsɜːdʒ) n. a rapid rise or swell.

upswing (ˈʌpˌswɪŋ) n. **1.** Econ. a recovery period in the trade cycle. **2.** any increase or improvement.

upsy-daisy (ˈʌpsɪˈdeɪzɪ) or **upsadaisy** interj. an expression of reassurance, when a child stumbles or is being lifted up. [orig. up-a-daisy]

uptake (ˈʌpˌteɪk) n. **quick** (or **slow**) **on the uptake.** Informal. quick (or slow) to understand or learn.

upthrust (ˈʌpˌθrʌst) n. **1.** an upward push. **2.** Geol. a violent upheaval of the earth's surface.

uptight (ʌpˈtaɪt) adj. Informal. **1.** nervously tense, irritable, or angry. **2.** unable to express one's feelings.

up-to-date adj. modern or fashionable: an up-to-date magazine.

upturn n. (ˈʌpˌtɜːn). **1.** an upward trend or improvement. ~vb. (ʌpˈtɜːn). **2.** to turn or cause to turn over or upside down. **3.** an upheaval.

upward (ˈʌpwəd) adj. **1.** directed or moving towards a higher place or level. ~adv. also **upwards. 2.** from a lower to a higher place, level, or condition.

upward mobility n. movement from a lower to a higher economic and social status.

upwind (ˈʌpˈwɪnd) adv. **1.** into or against the wind. **2.** towards or on the side where the wind is blowing. ~*adj.* **3.** going against the wind. **4.** on the windward side.

uranium (juˈreɪnɪəm) *n. Chem.* a radioactive silvery-white metallic element of the actinide series. It is used chiefly as a source of nuclear energy by fission of the radioisotope **uranium-235**. Symbol: U [*Uranus* from the fact that the element was discovered soon after the planet]

Uranus (juˈreɪnəs, ˈjʊərənəs) *n.* **1.** *Greek myth.* a god; the personification of the sky. **2.** the seventh planet from the sun. [Greek *Ouranos* heaven]

urban (ˈɜːbªn) *adj.* of or living in a city or town. [Latin *urbs* city]

urban district *n.* formerly, an urban division of an administrative county with an elected council.

urbane (ɜːˈbeɪn) *adj.* characterized by courtesy, elegance, and sophistication. [Latin *urbānus* of the town]

urban guerrilla *n.* a guerrilla who operates in a town or city, engaging in terrorism and kidnapping.

urbanity (ɜːˈbænɪtɪ) *n.* the quality of being urbane.

urbanize *or* **-nise** (ˈɜːbə‚naɪz) *vb.* (*usually passive*) to make (a rural area) more industrialized and urban. —‚urbaniˈzation *or* -niˈsation *n.*

urban renewal *n.* the process of redeveloping dilapidated or neglected urban areas.

urchin (ˈɜːtʃɪn) *n.* **1.** a mischievous child. **2.** See **sea urchin**. [Latin *ēricius* hedgehog]

Urdu (ˈʊəduː, ˈɜː-) *n.* an Indic language of the Indo-European family which is an official language of Pakistan and is also spoken in India. It is closely related to Hindi but the script is primarily Persian. [Hindustani (*zabāni*) *urdū* (language of the) camp]

urea (ˈjʊərɪə) *n.* a white soluble crystalline compound found in urine. [Greek *ouron* urine]

ureter (juˈriːtə) *n.* the tube that carries urine from the kidney to the bladder. [Greek *ourein* to urinate]

urethra (juˈriːθrə) *n., pl.* **-thrae** (-θriː) *or* **-thras.** the canal that in most mammals carries urine from the bladder out of the body. [Greek *ourein* to urinate]

urethritis (‚jʊərɪˈθraɪtɪs) *n.* inflammation of the urethra.

urge (ɜːdʒ) *n.* **1.** a strong impulse, inner drive, or yearning. ~*vb.* **2.** to plead with or press (someone to do something): *we urged him to go.* **3.** to advocate earnestly and persistently: *to urge the need for safety.* **4.** to force, drive, or hasten onwards: *he urged the horses on.* [Latin *urgēre*]

urgent (ˈɜːdʒənt) *adj.* **1.** requiring speedy action or attention: *the matter is urgent.* **2.** earnest and persistent. [Latin *urgēre* to urge] —ˈurgency *n.* —ˈurgently *adv.*

uric (ˈjʊərɪk) *adj.* of or derived from urine.

uric acid *n.* a white odourless crystalline acid present in the blood and urine.

urinal (juˈraɪnªl, ˈjʊərɪ-) *n.* **1.** a sanitary fitting, used by men for urination. **2.** a room containing urinals.

urinary (ˈjʊərɪnərɪ) *adj. Anat.* of urine or the organs that secrete and pass urine.

urinary bladder *n.* a membranous sac that can expand in which urine excreted from the kidneys is stored.

urinate (ˈjʊərɪ‚neɪt) *vb.* to excrete urine. —‚uriˈnation *n.*

urine (ˈjʊərɪn) *n.* the pale yellow fluid excreted by the kidneys, containing waste products from the blood. It is stored in the bladder and discharged through the urethra. [Latin *ūrīna*]

urinogenital (‚jʊərɪnəʊˈdʒɛnɪtªl) *adj.* same as **urogenital.**

urn (ɜːn) *n.* **1.** a vaselike container, usually with a foot and a rounded body. **2.** a vase used as a container for the ashes of the dead. **3.** a large metal container, with a tap, used for making and holding tea or coffee. [Latin *ūrna*]

urogenital (‚jʊərəʊˈdʒɛnɪtªl) *or* **urinogenital** *adj.* of the urinary and genital organs and their functions. Also: **genitourinary.**

urology (juˈrɒlədʒɪ) *n.* the branch of medicine concerned with the urogenital tract and its diseases.

ursine (ˈɜːsaɪn) *adj.* of or like a bear. [Latin *ursus* a bear]

us (ʌs) *pl. pron.* (*objective*) **1.** refers to the speaker or writer and another person or other people: *don't hurt us.* **2.** refers to all people or people in general: *this table shows us the tides.* **3.** *Informal.* me: *give us a kiss!* **4.** a formal word for **me**, used by monarchs. [Old English *ūs*]

U.S. *or* **US** United States.

USA United States Army.

U.S.A. *or* **USA** United States of America.

usable (ˈjuːzəbªl) *adj.* able to be used. —‚usaˈbility *n.*

usage (ˈjuːsɪdʒ, -zɪdʒ) *n.* **1.** the act or a manner of using; use. **2.** constant use, custom, or habit. **3.** what is actually said in a language. [Latin *ūsus* USE (n.)]

use *vb.* (juːz). **1.** to put into service or action; employ for a given purpose: *use a spoon to stir with.* **2.** to make a practice of employing: *he uses his brain.* **3.** to behave towards in a particular way, usually selfishly: *he uses people.* **4.** to consume or expend: *the engine uses very little oil.* ~*n.* (juːs). **5.** a using or being used: *worn out through constant use.* **6.** the ability or permission to use. **7.** need or opportunity to use: *I have no use for this paper.* **8.** an instance or manner of using. **9.** usefulness; advantage: *it is of no use to complain.* **10.** custom; habit: *long use has inured him to it.* **11.** the purpose for which something is used. **12. have no use for.** a. to have no need of. **b.** to have a contemptuous dislike for. **13. make use of.** **a.** to employ; use. **b.** to exploit (a person). ~See also **use up.** [Latin *ūsus* having used] —ˈuser *n.*

used (juːzd) *adj.* second-hand: *used cars.*

used to (juːst) *adj.* **1.** accustomed to: *I am used to the cold.* ~*vb.* **2.** (*takes an infinitive or implied infinitive*) used as an auxiliary to express habitual or accustomed actions or states taking place in the past but no longer doing so: *I used to be rich.*

useful ('juːsful) *adj.* **1.** able to be used advantageously or for several purposes. **2.** *Informal.* commendable or capable: *a useful day's work.* —**'usefully** *adv.*

useless ('juːslɪs) *adj.* **1.** having no practical use. **2.** *Informal.* ineffectual, weak, or stupid: *he's useless at history.* —**'uselessly** *adv.* —**'uselessness** *n.*

user-friendly *adj.* easy to familiarize oneself with, understand, and use.

use up *vb.* to finish (a supply); consume completely.

usher ('ʌʃə) *n.* **1.** an official who shows people to their seats, as in a church. **2.** a person who acts as doorkeeper in a court of law. **3.** an officer who precedes persons of rank in a procession. **4.** to conduct or escort. **5.** (foll. by *in*) to be a precursor or herald of. [Old French *huissier* doorkeeper]

usherette (ˌʌʃəˈrɛt) *n.* a woman assistant in a cinema, who shows people to their seats.

USSR Union of Soviet Socialist Republics.

usual ('juːʒʊəl) *adj.* **1.** of the most normal, frequent, or regular type: *it's the usual thing to do.* ~*n.* **2.** ordinary or commonplace events: *nothing out of the usual.* **3.** **as usual.** as happens normally. **4.** **the usual.** *Informal.* the habitual or usual drink. [Latin *ūsus* use] —**'usually** *adv.*

usurp (juːˈzɜːp) *vb.* to seize (a position or power) without authority. [Latin *ūsūrpāre* to take into use] —ˌusur'pation *n.* —u'surper *n.*

usury ('juːʒərɪ) *n., pl.* **-ries.** **1.** the practice of loaning money at an exorbitant rate of interest. **2.** an unlawfully high rate of interest. [Latin *ūsūra* usage] —**'usurer** *n.*

UT Utah.

utensil (juːˈtɛnsəl) *n.* a tool or container for practical use: *writing utensils.* [Latin *ūtēnsilia* necessaries]

uterine ('juːtəˌraɪn) *adj.* of or affecting the uterus.

uterus ('juːtərəs) *n., pl.* **uteri** ('juːtəˌraɪ). *Anat.* a hollow muscular organ lying within the pelvic cavity of female mammals, which houses the developing fetus; womb. [Latin]

utilidor (juːˈtɪlədə; *Canad.* -ˌdɔr) *n.* *Canad.* above-ground insulated casing for pipes carrying water in permafrost regions. [*utility* + *-dor*, from Greek *dōron* gift]

utilitarian (ˌjuːtɪlɪˈtɛərɪən) *adj.* **1.** of utilitarianism. **2.** designed for use rather than beauty. ~*n.* **3.** an advocate of utilitarianism.

utilitarianism (ˌjuːtɪlɪˈtɛərɪəˌnɪzəm) *n.* *Ethics.* the doctrine that right action is that which brings about the greatest good for the greatest number.

utility (juːˈtɪlɪtɪ) *n., pl.* **-ties.** **1.** usefulness. **2.** something useful. **3.** a public service, such as water or electricity. ~*adj.* **4.** designed for use rather than beauty: *utility goods.* [Latin *ūtilitās* usefulness, from *ūtī* to use]

utility room *n.* a room used for large domestic appliances and equipment.

utility truck *n.* *Austral.* & *N.Z.* a small truck with an open body and low sides.

utilize *or* **-lise** ('juːtɪˌlaɪz) *vb.* to make practical or worthwhile use of. —ˌutili'zation *or* -li'sation *n.*

utmost ('ʌtˌməʊst) *adj.* **1.** of the greatest possible degree or amount: *the utmost degree.* **2.** at the furthest limit: *the utmost town on the peninsula.* ~*n.* **3.** the greatest possible degree or amount: *he tried his utmost.* [Old English *ūtemest*]

Utopia (juːˈtəʊpɪə) *n.* (*sometimes not cap.*) any real or imaginary society, place, or state considered to be perfect or ideal. [(coined by Sir Thomas More in 1516 as the title of his book that described an imaginary island representing the perfect society) lit.: no place, from Greek *ou* not + *topos* a place] —U'topian *adj.*

utricle ('juːtrɪkꞏl) *n.* **1.** *Anat.* the larger of the two parts of the internal ear. **2.** *Bot.* the bladder-like fruit of certain plants. [Latin *ūtriculus* a little bag]

utter¹ ('ʌtə) *vb.* **1.** to express (something) audibly: *to utter a growl.* **2.** *Criminal law.* to put (counterfeit money or forged cheques) into circulation. [Middle Dutch *ūteren*]

utter² ('ʌtə) *adj.* total; absolute: *an utter fool.* [Old English *utera* outer] —**'utterly** *adv.*

utterance ('ʌtərəns) *n.* **1.** something uttered. **2.** the act or power of uttering.

uttermost ('ʌtəˌməʊst) *adj., n.* same as **utmost.**

U-turn *n.* **1.** a turn, made by a vehicle, in the shape of a U, resulting in a reversal of direction. **2.** a complete change in policy.

UV ultraviolet.

uvula ('juːvjʊlə) *n., pl.* **-las** *or* **-lae** (-ˌliː). the small fleshy part of the soft palate that hangs in the back of the throat. [Medieval Latin, lit.: a little grape] —**'uvular** *adj.*

uxorious (ʌkˈsɔːrɪəs) *adj.* excessively fond of or dependent on one's wife. [Latin *uxor* wife]

V

v or **V** (viː) *n.*, *pl.* **v's**, **V's**, or **Vs**. 1. the 22nd letter of the English alphabet. 2. something shaped like a V.

V 1. *Chem.* vanadium. 2. volt. 3. the Roman numeral for five.

v. 1. verb. 2. verse. 3. versus. 4. very. 5. see. [Latin *vide*] 6. volume.

VA or **Va.** Virginia.

vac (væk) *n. Brit. informal.* short for **vacation**.

vacancy ('veɪkənsɪ) *n.*, *pl.* **-cies**. 1. the state of being vacant; emptiness. 2. an unoccupied job or position: *we have a vacancy in the accounts department.* 3. an unoccupied room in a hotel or guesthouse: *put up the "No Vacancies" sign.*

vacant ('veɪkənt) *adj.* 1. without any contents; empty. 2. having no job holder: *a vacant post.* 3. having no tenant or occupant: *a vacant house.* 4. suggesting lack of thought or intelligent awareness: *a vacant expression.* 5. (of time) not allocated to any activity: *a vacant hour in one's day.* [Latin *vacāre* to be empty] —'**vacantly** *adv.*

vacate (və'keɪt) *vb.* 1. to cause (something) to be empty by departing from it: *to vacate a room.* 2. to give up (a job or position).

vacation (və'keɪʃən) *n.* 1. *Chiefly Brit.* a period of the year when the lawcourts or universities are closed. 2. *U.S. & Canad.* same as **holiday** (sense 1). *~vb.* 3. *U.S. & Canad.* to take a holiday. [Latin *vacātiō* freedom]

vaccinate ('væksɪ‚neɪt) *vb.* to inoculate (a person) with vaccine so as to produce immunity against a specific disease. —**vaccination** (‚væksɪ'neɪʃən) *n.*

vaccine ('væksiːn) *n. Med.* 1. a suspension of dead or weakened microorganisms for inoculation to produce immunity to a disease. 2. a preparation of the virus of cowpox inoculated in humans to produce immunity to smallpox. [Latin *vacca* a cow]

vacillate ('væsɪ‚leɪt) *vb.* to waver in one's opinions; be indecisive. [Latin *vacillāre* to sway] —**vacillation** (‚væsɪ'leɪʃən) *n.*

vacuity (və'kjuːɪtɪ) *n.* 1. the state or quality of being vacuous. 2. (*pl.* **-ties**) an empty space or void. 3. lack of normal intelligence or awareness.

vacuous ('vækjʊəs) *adj.* 1. empty. 2. lacking in ideas or intelligence. 3. suggesting vacancy of mind: *a vacuous gaze.* 4. indulging in no useful mental or physical activity. [Latin *vacuus* empty]

vacuum ('vækjʊəm) *n.*, *pl.* **vacuums** or **vacua** ('vækjʊə). 1. a region containing no free matter: in technical contexts now often called **free space**. 2. the degree of exhaustion of gas within an enclosed space: *a perfect vacuum.* 3. a feeling of emptiness: *his death left a vacuum in her life.* 4. short for **vacuum cleaner**. *~vb.*

5. to clean (something) with a vacuum cleaner. [Latin *vacuus* empty]

vacuum cleaner *n.* an electrical household appliance used for cleaning carpets, furniture, etc., by suction. —**vacuum cleaning** *n.*

vacuum flask *n.* an insulating flask that has double walls with an evacuated space between them. It is used for keeping drinks at high or low temperatures.

vacuum-packed *adj.* packed in an airtight container in order to maintain freshness.

vacuum tube or **valve** *n.* same as **valve** (sense 3).

vade mecum ('vɑːdɪ 'meɪkʊm) *n.* a handbook carried for immediate use when needed. [Latin, lit.: go with me]

vagabond ('vægə‚bɒnd) *n.* 1. a person with no fixed home. 2. an idle wandering beggar or thief. [Latin *vagārī* to roam]

vagary ('veɪgərɪ, və'gɛərɪ) *n.*, *pl.* **-garies**. an erratic notion or action. [prob. Latin *vagārī* to roam]

vagina (və'dʒaɪnə) *n.*, *pl.* **-nas** or **-nae** (-niː). the passage in most female mammals that extends from the neck of the womb to an external opening in the vulva. [Latin: sheath] —**va'ginal** *adj.*

vagrant ('veɪgrənt) *n.* 1. a person of no settled home, income, or job; tramp. *~adj.* 2. wandering about. [prob. Old French *waucrant*] —**vagrancy** *n.*

vague (veɪg) *adj.* 1. (of statements, meaning, etc.) imprecise: *vague promises.* 2. not clearly perceptible or discernible: *a vague idea.* 3. not clearly established or known: *a vague rumour.* 4. (of a person or his expression) absent-minded. [Latin *vagus* wandering] —**vaguely** *adv.*

vain (veɪn) *adj.* 1. excessively proud of one's appearance, possessions, or achievements. 2. senseless or futile: *a vain attempt.* *~n.* 3. **in vain**. without success. [Latin *vānus*] —**vainly** *adv.*

vainglory (‚veɪn'glɔːrɪ) *n.* boastfulness or vanity. —**vainglorious** *adj.*

valance ('væləns) *n.* a short piece of drapery hung round the edge of a bed or above a window. [possibly after *Valence* in SE France]

vale (veɪl) *n. Literary.* a valley. [Latin *vallis* valley]

valediction (‚vælɪ'dɪkʃən) *n.* 1. the act or an instance of saying goodbye. 2. any farewell statement or speech. [Latin *valē* farewell + *dīcere* to say] —**valedictory** *adj.*

valence ('veɪləns) *n. Chem.* the phenomenon of forming chemical bonds.

valency ('veɪlənsɪ) or esp. *U.S. & Canad.* **valence** *n.*, *pl.* **-cies** or **-ces**. *Chem.* the number of atoms of hydrogen that an atom or group could combine with or displace in forming compounds. [Latin *valēre* to be strong]

valentine ('vælən,taɪn) *n.* **1.** a card or gift expressing love, sent, often anonymously, on Saint Valentine's Day. **2.** the person to whom one sends such a greeting. [after Saint *Valentine*]

valerian (və'lɪərɪən) *n.* a plant with small white or pinkish flowers and a medicinal root. [Medieval Latin *valeriana* (*herba*) (herb) of *Valerius*]

valet ('vælɪt, 'væleɪ) *n.* a manservant who acts as personal attendant to his employer, looking after his clothing and serving his meals. [Old French *vaslet* page]

valetudinarian (,vælɪ,tjuːdɪ'nɛərɪən) *n.* **1.** a person who is chronically sick. **2.** a hypochondriac. ~*adj.* **3.** relating to or resulting from poor health. **4.** being a valetudinarian. [Latin *valētūdō* state of health] —,vale,tudi'narian,ism *n.*

Valhalla (væl'hælə) *n. Norse myth.* the great hall of Odin where warriors who die as heroes in battle dwell eternally. [Old Norse *valr* slain warriors + *höll* HALL]

valiant ('væljənt) *adj.* courageous or brave: *a valiant deed.* [Latin *valēre* to be strong] —'valiantly *adv.*

valid ('vælɪd) *adj.* **1.** having some foundation; based on truth. **2.** legally acceptable: *a valid licence.* **3.** effective or convincing: *a valid point in a debate.* [Latin *validus* robust] —**validity** (və'lɪdɪtɪ) *n.*

validate ('vælɪ,deɪt) *vb.* **1.** to confirm or corroborate. **2.** to give legal force or official confirmation to. —,vali'dation *n.*

valise (və'liːz) *n.* a small overnight travelling case. [Italian *valigia*]

Valium ('vælɪəm) *n. Trademark.* a drug used as a tranquillizer.

Valkyrie ('vælkɪrɪ) *n. Norse myth.* any of the beautiful maidens who take the dead heroes to Valhalla. [Old Norse *valr* slain warriors + *köri* to choose]

valley ('vælɪ) *n.* a long area of low land between hills, usually containing a river. [Latin *vallis*]

valour *or U.S.* **valor** ('vælə) *n.* courage or bravery, esp. in battle. [Latin *valēre* to be strong] —'valorous *adj.*

valuable ('væljuəb'l) *adj.* **1.** having considerable monetary worth. **2.** of considerable importance or quality: *valuable information.* ~*n.* **3.** (*pl.*) valuable articles of personal property, such as jewellery.

valuation (,vælju'eɪʃən) *n.* **1.** the act of making a formal assessment of the worth of something, such as a house. **2.** the price arrived at by the process of valuing.

value ('væljuː) *n.* **1.** the desirability of a thing, often in terms of its usefulness or exchangeability. **2.** an amount of money or goods considered to be a fair exchange for a thing: *the value of the picture is £10 000.* **3.** satisfaction: *value for money.* **4.** (*pl.*) the moral principles or accepted standards of a person or group. **5.** *Maths.* a particular number or quantity represented by a figure or symbol. **6.** *Music.* short for **time value**. ~*vb.* **-uing, -ued. 7.** to assess the worth, merit, or desirability of

(someone or something). **8.** to have a high regard for (someone or something) in respect of worth, usefulness, or merit. **9.** to fix the financial or material worth of (something, such as a unit of currency or a work of art). [Latin *valēre* to be worth] —'valued *adj.* —'valueless *adj.* —'valuer *n.*

value-added tax *n.* See **VAT**.

value judgment *n.* a subjective assessment based on one's own values.

valve (vælv) *n.* **1.** any device that shuts off, starts, regulates, or controls the flow of a fluid. **2.** *Anat.* a flaplike structure in a hollow organ, such as the heart, that controls the one-way passage of fluid through that organ. **3.** an evacuated electron tube containing a cathode, anode, and, usually, one or more additional control electrodes. When a positive potential is applied to the anode, it produces a one-way flow of current. **4.** *Zool.* one of the hinged shells of an oyster or clam. **5.** *Music.* a device on some brass instruments by which the effective length of the tube may be varied. [Latin *valva* a folding door]

valvular ('vælvjulə) *adj.* **1.** of, operated by, or having a valve or valves. **2.** having the shape or function of a valve.

vamoose (və'muːs) *vb. Slang, chiefly U.S.* to leave a place hurriedly. [Spanish *vamos* let's go]

vamp[1] (væmp) *Informal.* ~*n.* **1.** a seductive woman who exploits men by use of her sexual charms. ~*vb.* **2.** (of a woman) to seduce (a man). [short for *vampire*]

vamp[2] (væmp) *n.* **1.** the front part of the upper of a shoe. ~*vb.* **2.** (foll. by *up*) to make (something) seem new. **3.** to improvise an accompaniment to (a tune). [Old French *avantpié* the front part of a shoe]

vampire ('væmpaɪə) *n.* **1.** (in European folklore) a corpse that rises nightly from its grave to drink the blood of living people. **2.** a person who preys mercilessly upon others. [Magyar]

vampire bat *n.* a bat of tropical regions of Central and South America that feeds on the blood of birds and mammals.

van[1] (væn) *n.* **1.** a motor vehicle for transporting goods by road. **2.** *Brit.* a closed railway wagon in which the guard travels, for transporting goods. [shortened from *caravan*]

van[2] (væn) *n.* short for **vanguard**.

vanadium (və'neɪdɪəm) *n. Chem.* a silvery-white metallic element used in steel alloys. Symbol: V [Old Norse *Vanadis*, epithet of the goddess Freya]

Van Allen belt (væn 'ælən) *n.* either of two regions of charged particles several thousand kilometres above the earth. [after J. A. *Van Allen*, physicist]

vandal ('vænd'l) *n.* a person who deliberately causes damage to personal or public property. [from the name of a Germanic tribe of the 3rd and 4th centuries A.D.] —'vandal,ism *n.*

vandalize *or* **-lise** ('vændə,laɪz) *vb.* to cause damage to (personal or public property) deliberately

Vandyke beard ('vændaɪk) n. a short pointed beard. [after Sir Anthony *Van Dyck*, Flemish painter]

vane (veɪn) n. 1. a flat blade of metal mounted on a vertical axis in an exposed position to indicate wind direction. 2. any one of the flat blades forming part of the wheel of a windmill. 3. any flat or shaped plate used to direct fluid flow, for example in a turbine. [Old English *fana*]

vanguard ('væn‚gɑːd) n. 1. the leading division or units of a military force. 2. the leading position in any movement or field of activity or the people who occupy this position. [Old French *avant-garde* advance guard]

vanilla (və'nɪlə) n. 1. the pod or bean of a tropical climbing orchid, used to flavour food. 2. a flavouring extract prepared from vanilla beans and used in cooking. ~*adj.* 3. flavoured with vanilla: *vanilla ice cream.* [Latin *vāgīna* sheath]

vanish ('vænɪʃ) vb. 1. to disappear suddenly or mysteriously. 2. to cease to exist. [Latin *ēvānēscere* to evaporate]

vanishing cream n. a cosmetic cream that is colourless once applied.

vanishing point n. the point in the distance at which parallel lines appear to meet.

vanity ('vænɪtɪ) n. 1. the state or quality of being vain. 2. (pl. **-ties**) something about which one is vain. [Latin *vānitās* emptiness]

vanity unit n. a hand basin built into a surface, usually with a cupboard below it.

vanquish ('væŋkwɪʃ) vb. 1. to defeat or overcome (someone) in a battle, contest, or argument. 2. to conquer (an emotion). [Latin *vincere*]

vantage ('vɑːntɪdʒ) n. 1. a state, position, or opportunity offering advantage. 2. *Tennis.* an advantage. [Old French *avantage* advantage]

vantage point n. a position that gives one an overall view of a scene or situation.

vapid ('væpɪd) adj. 1. weak, colourless, or flavourless. 2. boring or dull: *vapid talk.* [Latin *vapidus*] —**va'pidity** n.

vapor ('veɪpə) n. U.S. same as **vapour**.

vaporize or U.S. **-rise** ('veɪpə‚raɪz) vb. to change into vapour. —‚vapori'zation or -ri'sation n.

vaporous ('veɪpərəs) adj. resembling or full of vapour.

vapour or U.S. **vapor** ('veɪpə) n. 1. particles of moisture suspended in air and visible as clouds, smoke, or mist. 2. the gaseous form of a substance that is usually a liquid or a solid. 3. **the vapours.** *Archaic.* a depressed mental condition. [Latin *vapor*]

var. variant.

variable ('veərɪəb'l) adj. 1. liable to or capable of change: *variable weather.* 2. (of behaviour or emotions) lacking constancy. 3. *Maths.* having a range of possible values. ~n. 4. something that is subject to variation. 5. *Maths.* an expression that can be assigned any of a set of values. [Latin *variāre* to diversify] —‚varia'bility n. —'variably adv.

variance ('veərɪəns) n. 1. a disagreement. 2. **at variance.** not in agreement.

variant ('veərɪənt) adj. 1. displaying variation. 2. differing from a standard or type: *a variant spelling.* ~n. 3. something that differs from a standard or type.

variation (‚veərɪ'eɪʃən) n. 1. the act, process, condition, or result of changing or varying. 2. an instance of varying or the amount, rate, or degree of such change. 3. something that differs from a standard or convention. 4. *Music.* a repetition of a musical theme in which the rhythm, harmony, or melody is altered or embellished.

varicoloured or U.S. **varicolored** ('veərɪ‚kʌləd) adj. having many colours.

varicose ('værɪ‚kəʊs) adj. of or resulting from varicose veins: *a varicose ulcer.* [Latin *varix* a swollen vein]

varicose veins pl. n. veins, usually in the legs, which have become knotted, swollen, and sometimes painful.

varied ('veərɪd) adj. displaying variety; diverse.

variegated ('veərɪ‚geɪtɪd) adj. 1. displaying different-coloured spots or streaks. 2. (of foliage) having pale patches. —**variegation** (‚veərɪ'geɪʃən) n.

variety (və'raɪɪtɪ) n., pl. **-ties**. 1. the quality or condition of being diversified or various. 2. a collection of unlike things of the same general group. 3. a different form or kind within a general category: *varieties of behaviour.* 4. *Taxonomy.* a race whose distinct characters do not justify classification as a separate species. 5. a type of entertainment consisting of a series of short unrelated acts, such as comedy turns, songs, and dances. [Latin *varietās*]

various ('veərɪəs) adj. 1. several different: *he is an authority on various subjects.* 2. of different kinds: *his disguises are many and various.* [Latin *varius* changing] —'variously adv.

varlet ('vɑːlɪt) n. *Archaic.* 1. a menial servant. 2. a rascal. [Old French *vaslet*]

varmint ('vɑːmɪnt) n. *Informal.* an irritating or obnoxious person or animal. [dialect var. of *varmin* vermin]

varnish ('vɑːnɪʃ) n. 1. a preparation consisting of a solvent, oil, and resin or rubber, which gives a hard glossy transparent coating to a surface. 2. a similar preparation consisting of shellac dissolved in alcohol. 3. a smooth surface, coated with or as if with varnish. 4. an artificial, superficial, or deceptively pleasing manner, covering, or appearance. 5. *Chiefly Brit.* same as **nail polish**. ~vb. 6. to cover with varnish. 7. to impart a more attractive appearance to. [Old French *vernis*]

varsity ('vɑːsɪtɪ) n., pl. **-ties**. *Brit. & N.Z. informal.* short for **university**.

vary ('veərɪ) vb. **varying, varied**. 1. to undergo or cause to undergo change or modification in appearance, character, or form. 2. to be different or cause to be different; be subject to change. 3. to give variety to. 4. to change in accordance with another variable: *her mood varies with the weather.* [Latin *varius* changing] —'**varying** *adj.*

vas (væs) *n., pl.* **vasa** ('veisə). *Anat., zool.* a vessel or tube that carries a fluid. [Latin: vessel]

vascular ('væskjulə) *adj. Biol., anat.* of or relating to the vessels that conduct and circulate body fluids such as blood or sap: *a vascular bundle.* [Latin *vās* vessel]

vas deferens ('defə,renz) *n., pl.* **vasa deferentia** (,defə'renʃiə). *Anat.* the duct within each testicle that conveys sperm to the penis. [Latin *vās* vessel + *deferēns* carrying away]

vase (vɑːz) *n.* a glass or pottery jar used as an ornament or for holding cut flowers. [Latin *vās* vessel]

vasectomy (və'sɛktəmɪ) *n., pl.* **-mies.** surgical removal of all or part of the vas deferens as a method of contraception.

Vaseline ('væsɪ,liːn) *n. Trademark.* petroleum jelly.

vassal ('væs'l) *n.* **1.** (in feudal society) a man who gave military service to a lord in return for protection and often land. **2.** a person, nation, or state in a subordinate position to another. [Latin *vassus* servant] —'**vassalage** *n.*

vast (vɑːst) *adj.* unusually large in size, degree, or number. [Latin *vastus* deserted] —'**vastly** *adv.* —'**vastness** *n.*

vat (væt) *n.* a large container for holding or storing liquids. [Old English *fæt*]

VAT (,viː eɪ 'tiː, væt) (in Britain) value-added tax: a tax levied on the difference between the cost of materials and the selling price of a commodity or service.

Vatican ('vætɪkən) *n.* **the. 1.** the palace of the Pope, in Rome. **2.** the authority of the Pope. [Latin *Vātīcānus mons* Vatican hill]

vaudeville ('vəudəvɪl, 'vɔː-) *n.* variety entertainment consisting of short acts such as song-and-dance routines and comic turns. [French]

vault¹ (vɔːlt) *n.* **1.** an arched structure that forms a roof or ceiling. **2.** an underground burial chamber. **3.** a strongroom for the storage of valuables. **4.** a cellar for the storage of wine. **5.** the sky. ~*vb.* **6.** to furnish with or as if with an arched roof. **7.** to construct in the shape of a vault. [Old French *voute, voulte*]

vault² (vɔːlt) *vb.* **1.** to spring over (an object), with the aid of a long pole or with one's hands resting on the object. ~*n.* **2.** the act of vaulting. [Italian *voltare*] —'**vaulter** *n.*

vaulting¹ ('vɔːltɪŋ) *n.* one or more vaults in a building or such structures considered collectively.

vaulting² ('vɔːltɪŋ) *adj.* excessively confident: *vaulting arrogance.*

vaunt (vɔːnt) *vb.* **1.** to describe, praise, or display (one's success or possessions) boastfully. ~*n.* **2.** a boast. [Latin *vānus* vain] —'**vaunted** *adj.*

VC 1. Vice Chancellor. **2.** Victoria Cross. **3.** Vietcong: the Communist-led guerrilla force of South Vietnam.

VCR video cassette recorder.

VD venereal disease.

VDU visual display unit.

veal (viːl) *n.* the flesh of a calf, used as food. [Latin *vitulus* calf]

vector ('vɛktə) *n.* **1.** *Maths.* a variable quantity, such as force, that has magnitude and direction. **2.** *Pathol.* an animal, usually an insect, that carries a disease-producing microorganism from person to person. [Latin: carrier]

Veda ('veɪdə) *n.* any or all of the most ancient sacred writings of Hinduism. [Sanskrit: knowledge] —'**Vedic** *adj.*

veer (vɪə) *vb.* **1.** to change direction. **2.** to change from one position or opinion to another. ~*n.* **3.** a change of course or direction. [Old French *virer*]

veg (vɛdʒ) *n. Informal.* a vegetable or vegetables.

vegan ('viːgən) *n.* a person who uses no animal products.

vegetable ('vɛdʒtəb'l) *n.* **1.** a plant with parts that are used as food, such as peas, potatoes, cauliflowers, and onions. **2.** *Informal.* a person who is unable to move or think, as a result of brain damage. **3.** (*modifier*) derived from, or consisting of plants or plant material: *the vegetable kingdom.* [Late Latin *vegetābilis*]

vegetable marrow *n.* an oblong green striped vegetable which can be cooked and eaten.

vegetable oil *n.* any of a group of oils that are obtained from plants.

vegetal ('vɛdʒɪt'l) *adj.* of or relating to plant life.

vegetarian (,vɛdʒɪ'tɛərɪən) *n.* **1.** a person who does not eat meat or fish. ~*adj.* **2.** excluding meat and fish: *a vegetarian diet.* —,**vege'tarianism** *n.*

vegetate ('vɛdʒɪ,teɪt) *vb.* to lead a life characterized by monotony, passivity, or mental inactivity.

vegetation (,vɛdʒɪ'teɪʃən) *n.* plant life as a whole.

vegetative ('vɛdʒɪtətɪv) *adj.* **1.** of or concerned with plant life or plant growth. **2.** (of reproduction) characterized by asexual processes.

vehement ('viːɪmənt) *adj.* **1.** expressing intensity of feeling or conviction. **2.** (of actions or gestures) performed with great energy, vigour, or force. [Latin *vehemēns* ardent] —'**vehemence** *n.* —'**vehemently** *adv.*

vehicle ('viːɪk'l) *n.* **1.** any conveyance in or by which people or objects are transported. **2.** a medium for the expression or communication of ideas. **3.** *Pharmacol.* an inactive substance mixed with the active ingredient in a medicine. **4.** a painting medium, such as oil, in which pigments are suspended. [Latin *vehere* to carry] —ve**hicular** (vɪ'hɪkjulə) *adj.*

veil (veɪl) *n.* **1.** a piece of more or less transparent material, usually attached to a hat or headdress, used to conceal a woman's face. **2.** the part of a nun's headdress that falls round her face onto her shoulders. **3.** something that covers, conceals, or separates: *a veil of reticence.* **4. take the veil.** to become a nun. ~*vb.* **5.** to cover, conceal, or separate with or as if with a veil. [Latin *vēlum* a covering]

veiled (veild) *adj.* disguised: *a veiled insult.*

vein (vein) *n.* **1.** any of the tubes that convey blood to the heart. **2.** any of the ribs that form the supporting framework of an insect's wing or a leaf. **3.** a clearly defined mass of ore or mineral in rock. **4.** an irregular streak of colour in marble, wood, or cheese. **5.** a distinctive trait or quality in speech, writing, or character: *a vein of humour.* **6.** a temporary mood: *the debate entered a frivolous vein.* [Latin *vēna*] —**veined** *or* **veiny** *adj.*

Velcro ('vɛlkrəʊ) *n. Trademark.* a fastening consisting of two strips of nylon fabric, one having tiny hooked threads and the other a coarse surface, that form a strong bond when pressed together.

veld *or* **veldt** (fɛlt, vɛlt) *n.* high open grassland in Southern Africa. [Afrikaans]

veleta (vəˈliːtə) *n.* a ballroom dance in triple time. [Spanish: weather vane]

vellum ('vɛləm) *n.* **1.** a fine parchment prepared from the skin of a calf, kid, or lamb. **2.** a work printed or written on vellum. **3.** a heavy paper resembling vellum. [Old French *velin* of a calf]

velocipede (vɪˈlɒsɪˌpiːd) *n.* an early form of bicycle. [Latin *vēlōx* swift + *pēs* foot]

velocity (vɪˈlɒsɪtɪ) *n., pl.* **-ties.** speed of motion; swiftness. [Latin *vēlōx* swift]

velours *or* **velour** (vəˈlʊə) *n.* a fabric with a velvet-like finish. [Latin *villus* shaggy hair]

velvet ('vɛlvɪt) *n.* **1.** a fabric of silk, cotton, or nylon, with a thick close soft pile. **2.** the furry covering of the newly formed antlers of a deer. **3. on velvet.** *Slang.* in a condition of ease, advantage, or wealth. ~*adj.* **4.** made of velvet. **5.** soft or smooth like velvet. **6. an iron hand in a velvet glove.** determination concealed by gentleness. [Old French, from Latin *villus* shaggy hair] —**velvety** *adj.*

velveteen (ˌvɛlvɪˈtiːn) *n.* a cotton fabric resembling velvet with a short thick pile.

Ven. Venerable.

venal ('viːnᵊl) *adj.* **1.** easily bribed or corrupted: *a venal magistrate.* **2.** associated with corruption or bribery. [Latin *vēnum sale*] —**venality** (viːˈnælɪtɪ) *n.* —**venally** *adv.*

vend (vɛnd) *vb.* to sell (goods). [Latin *vendere* to sell]

vendetta (vɛnˈdɛtə) *n.* **1.** a private feud, in which the relatives of a murdered person seek revenge by killing the murderer or some member of his family. **2.** any prolonged feud. [Italian]

vending machine *n.* a machine that automatically dispenses food, drinks, or cigarettes when money is inserted.

vendor ('vɛndə) *n.* **1.** a person who sells goods such as newspapers or hamburgers from a stall, tray, or cart: *street vendors.* **2.** *Chiefly law.* a person who sells property.

veneer (vɪˈnɪə) *n.* **1.** a thin layer of fine wood, plastic, etc., that is bonded to the surface of a less expensive material. **2.** a superficial appearance: *a veneer of gentility.* ~*vb.* **3.** to cover (a surface) with a veneer. **4.** to conceal (something) under a superficially pleasant surface. [Old French *fournir* to furnish]

venerable ('vɛnərəbᵊl) *adj.* **1.** (of a person) worthy of reverence on account of great age, religious associations, or character. **2.** (of inanimate objects) revered on account of age or historical or religious association. **3.** *R.C. Church.* a title given to a dead person who is going to be declared a saint. **4.** *Church of England.* a title given to an archdeacon. [Latin *venerārī* to venerate]

venerate ('vɛnəˌreɪt) *vb.* to hold (someone) in deep respect. [Latin *venerārī*] —**venerˌator** *n.*

veneration (ˌvɛnəˈreɪʃən) *n.* **1.** a feeling or expression of awe or reverence. **2.** the act of venerating or the state of being venerated.

venereal (vɪˈnɪərɪəl) *adj.* **1.** for the treatment of venereal diseases: *a venereal clinic.* **2.** transmitted by sexual intercourse: *a venereal infection.* **3.** of the genitals: *venereal warts.* [Latin *venus* sexual love]

venereal disease *n.* any of various diseases, such as syphilis or gonorrhoea, transmitted by sexual intercourse.

Venetian (vɪˈniːʃən) *adj.* **1.** of or relating to Venice, a port in NE Italy, or its inhabitants. ~*n.* **2.** a person from Venice.

Venetian blind *n.* a window blind consisting of a number of horizontal slats.

vengeance ('vɛndʒəns) *n.* **1.** the act of or desire for taking revenge. **2. with a vengeance.** to an excessive degree: *he's a coward with a vengeance.* [Old French, from Latin *vindicāre* to punish]

vengeful ('vɛndʒfʊl) *adj.* **1.** desiring revenge. **2.** taking revenge: *a vengeful act.*

venial ('viːnɪəl) *adj.* easily excused or forgiven: *a venial sin.* [Latin *venia* forgiveness] —**veniality** (ˌviːnɪˈælɪtɪ) *n.* —**venially** *adv.*

venison ('vɛnɪsᵊn) *n.* the flesh of a deer, used as food. [Old French, from Latin *vēnārī* to hunt]

Venn diagram (vɛn) *n. Maths.* a diagram in which mathematical sets are represented by overlapping circles. [after John Venn, logician]

venom ('vɛnəm) *n.* **1.** a poisonous fluid produced by certain snakes and scorpions when they bite or sting. **2.** malice; spite. [Latin *venēnum* poison, love potion] —**venomous** *adj.* —**venomously** *adv.*

venous ('viːnəs) *adj.* of or relating to veins. [Latin *vēna* vein]

vent[1] (vɛnt) *n.* **1.** a small opening for the escape of fumes, liquids, etc. **2.** the shaft of a volcano through which lava and gases erupt. **3.** the excretory opening of lower vertebrates. **4. give vent to.** to release (an emotion) in an outburst. ~*vb.* **5.** to release or express freely (an emotion): *he* vents his anger on his wife. **6.** to make vents in. [Old French *esventer* to blow out]

vent² (vent) *n.* a vertical slit in the lower hem of a jacket, either in the middle of the back, or one of a pair at either side of the back. [Latin *findere* to cleave]

ventilate ('vɛntɪˌleɪt) *vb.* **1.** to let fresh air into (a room or building). **2.** to expose (a question, grievance, etc.) to public discussion. [Latin *ventilāre* to fan] —**ventilation** (ˌvɛntɪˈleɪʃən) *n.*

ventilator ('vɛntɪˌleɪtə) *n.* an opening or device, such as a fan, used to let fresh air into a room or building.

ventral ('vɛntrəl) *adj.* relating to the front part of the body. [Latin *venter* abdomen] —**'ventrally** *adv.*

ventricle ('vɛntrɪkəl) *n. Anat.* **1.** a chamber of the heart that pumps blood to the arteries. **2.** any one of the four main cavities of the brain. [Latin *ventriculus*] —**ven'tricular** *adj.*

ventriloquism (vɛnˈtrɪləˌkwɪzəm) *n.* the art of producing vocal sounds that appear to come from another source. [Latin *venter* belly + *loquī* to speak] —**ven'triloquist** *n.*

venture ('vɛntʃə) *n.* **1.** an undertaking that is risky or of uncertain outcome. **2.** a commercial undertaking in which there is the risk of loss as well as the opportunity for profit. ~*vb.* **3.** to expose to danger: *he ventured his life.* **4.** to brave the dangers of (something): *I'll venture the seas.* **5.** to dare (to do something): *does he venture to object?* **6.** to express in spite of possible criticism: *if I may venture an opinion; I venture that he is not that honest.* **7.** (foll. by *out* or *forth*) to embark on a possibly hazardous journey or undertaking: *to venture forth upon the high seas.* [var. of *adventure*] —**'venturer** *n.*

Venture Scout or **Venturer** *n. Brit.* a member of the senior branch of the Scouts.

venturesome ('vɛntʃəsəm) *adj.* willing to take risks; daring.

venue ('vɛnjuː) *n.* **1.** any place where an organized gathering, such as a concert or a sporting event, is held. **2.** *Law.* **a.** the place fixed for a trial. **b.** the locality from which the jurors must be summoned. [Latin *venīre*]

Venus ('viːnəs) *n.* **1.** the Roman goddess of love. **2.** the planet second nearest to the sun.

Venus's-flytrap or **Venus flytrap** *n.* a plant with hinged two-lobed leaves which snap closed, trapping insects which it then digests.

veracious (vəˈreɪʃəs) *adj.* habitually truthful. [Latin *vērus* true]

veracity (vəˈræsɪtɪ) *n.* **1.** habitual truthfulness. **2.** accuracy.

veranda or **verandah** (vəˈrændə) *n.* **1.** a porch, sometimes partly enclosed, along the outside of a building. **2.** *N.Z.* a continuous overhead canopy that gives shelter to pedestrians. [Portuguese *varanda* railing]

verb (vɜːb) *n.* any of a large class of words that serve to indicate the occurrence or performance of an action or the existence of a state. Such words as *run, make,* and *do* are verbs. [Latin *verbum* word]

verbal ('vɜːbəl) *adj.* **1.** of, relating to, or using words: *merely verbal concessions.* **2.** spoken rather than written: *a verbal agreement.* **3.** *Grammar.* of or relating to a verb. —**'verbally** *adv.*

verbalism ('vɜːbəˌlɪzəm) *n.* an exaggerated emphasis on the importance of words.

verbalize or **-lise** ('vɜːbəˌlaɪz) *vb.* **1.** to express (an idea or feeling) in words. **2.** to be long-winded.

verbal noun *n.* a noun derived from a verb, such as *smoking* in the sentence *smoking is bad for you.*

verbatim (vɜːˈbeɪtɪm) *adv., adj.* using exactly the same words; word for word. [Medieval Latin: word by word]

verbena (vɜːˈbiːnə) *n.* a plant with red, white, or purple sweet-smelling flowers. [Latin: sacred bough used by the priest in religious acts]

verbiage ('vɜːbɪɪdʒ) *n.* the excessive and often meaningless use of words. [Latin *verbum* word]

verbose (vɜːˈbəʊs) *adj.* using an excess of words, so as to be annoying or boring. —**verbosity** (vɜːˈbɒsɪtɪ) *n.*

verdant ('vɜːdənt) *adj.* covered with green vegetation. [Old French, from Latin *viridis* green]

verdict ('vɜːdɪkt) *n.* **1.** the findings of a jury on the issues of fact submitted to it for examination and trial. **2.** any decision or conclusion. [Latin *vērē dictum* truly spoken]

verdigris ('vɜːdɪˌgrɪs) *n.* a green or bluish coating which forms on copper, brass, or bronze that has been exposed to damp. [Old French *vert de Grice* green of Greece]

verdure ('vɜːdʒə) *n.* flourishing green vegetation or its colour. [from Latin *viridis* green]

verge¹ (vɜːdʒ) *n.* **1.** an edge or rim; margin. **2.** a limit beyond which something occurs: *on the verge of ecstasy.* **3.** *Brit.* a grass border along a road. ~*vb.* **4.** (foll. by *on*) **a.** to be near to: *to verge on chaos.* **b.** to serve as the edge of (something). [Latin *virga* rod]

verge² (vɜːdʒ) *vb.* (foll. by *to* or *towards*) to move in a specified direction. [Latin *vergere*]

verger ('vɜːdʒə) *n. Chiefly Church of England.* **1.** a church official who acts as caretaker and attendant. **2.** an official who carries the rod of office before a bishop or dean in ceremonies and processions. [Latin *virga* rod, twig]

verify ('vɛrɪˌfaɪ) *vb.* **-fying, -fied. 1.** to prove (something) to be true; confirm. **2.** to check the truth of (something) by investigation. [Latin *vērus* true + *facere* to make] —**'veri,fiable** *adj.* —**,verifi'cation** *n.*

verily ('vɛrɪlɪ) *adv. Archaic.* in truth; truly: *verily, thou art a man of God.* [from *very*]

verisimilitude (ˌvɛrɪsɪˈmɪlɪˌtjuːd) *n.* the appearance of truth or reality. [Latin *vērus* true + *similitūdō* similitude]

veritable ('vɛrɪtəbᵊl) *adj.* rightly called; real: *he's a veritable swine!* —'**veritably** *adv.*

verity ('vɛrɪtɪ) *n., pl.* **-ties.** a true statement, idea, or principle. [Latin *vērus* true]

vermicelli (ˌvɜːmɪ'tʃɛlɪ) *n.* **1.** very fine strands of pasta. **2.** tiny chocolate strands used as a topping for cakes or ice cream. [Italian: little worms]

vermicide ('vɜːmɪˌsaɪd) *n.* a substance used to kill worms. [Latin *vermis* worm + *caedere* to kill]

vermiform ('vɜːmɪˌfɔːm) *adj.* resembling a worm.

vermiform appendix *n. Anat.* same as **appendix.**

vermilion (və'mɪljən) *adj.* **1.** orange-red. ~*n.* **2.** mercuric sulphide, used as an orange-red pigment; cinnabar. [Latin *vermiculus*]

vermin ('vɜːmɪn) *n. (functioning as pl.)* **1.** small animals collectively, such as insects and rodents, that spread disease and damage crops. **2.** unpleasant people. [Latin *vermis* worm] —'**verminous** *adj.*

vermouth ('vɜːməθ) *n.* wine flavoured with herbs. [German *Wermut* wormwood]

vernacular (və'nækjʊlə) *n.* **1. the.** the commonly spoken language or dialect of a particular people or place. ~*adj.* **2.** relating to or in the vernacular. [Latin *vernāculus* belonging to a household slave]

vernal ('vɜːnᵊl) *adj.* of or occurring in spring. [Latin *vēr* spring] —'**vernally** *adv.*

vernier ('vɜːnɪə) *n.* a small movable scale in certain measuring instruments such as theodolites, used to obtain a fractional reading of one of the divisions on the main scale. [after Paul *Vernier*, mathematician]

veronica (və'rɒnɪkə) *n.* a plant with small blue, pink, or white flowers. [perhaps from the name *Veronica*]

verruca (və'ruːkə) *n., pl.* **-cae** (-siː) *or* **-cas.** *Pathol.* a wart, usually on the sole of the foot. [Latin: wart]

versatile ('vɜːsəˌtaɪl) *adj.* capable of many different uses or skills; able to change or be changed quickly; flexible. [Latin *versāre* to turn] —**versatility** (ˌvɜːsə'tɪlɪtɪ) *n.*

verse (vɜːs) *n.* **1.** a division of a poem or song. **2.** poetry as distinct from prose. **3.** one of the short sections into which chapters of the books of the Bible are divided. **4.** a poem. [Latin *versus* furrow, lit.: a turning (of the plough)]

versed (vɜːst) *adj.* **versed in.** knowledgeable about, acquainted with, or skilled in.

versify ('vɜːsɪˌfaɪ) *vb.* **-fying, -fied. 1.** to put (something) into verse. **2.** to write in verse. [Latin *versus* verse + *facere* to make] —ˌ**versifi'cation** *n.* —'**versiˌfier** *n.*

version ('vɜːʃən) *n.* **1.** an account of an incident from a certain point of view: *his version of the accident is different from the policeman's.* **2.** a translation from one language into another. **3.** a variant form of something. **4.** an adaptation, for example of a book or play into a film. [Latin *vertere* to turn]

verso ('vɜːsəʊ) *n., pl.* **-sos. 1.** the back of a sheet of printed paper. **2.** any of the left-hand pages of a book, bearing the even numbers. [New Latin *versō foliō* the leaf having been turned]

versus ('vɜːsəs) *prep.* **1.** (in a sporting competition or lawsuit) against. **2.** in contrast with. [Latin: turned (in the direction of), opposite]

vertebra ('vɜːtɪbrə) *n., pl.* **-brae** (-briː) *or* **-bras.** one of the bony segments of the spinal column. [Latin] —'**vertebral** *adj.*

vertebrate ('vɜːtɪbrɪt) *n.* **1.** any animal with a backbone, such as a fish, amphibian, reptile, bird, or mammal. ~*adj.* **2.** having a backbone.

vertex ('vɜːtɛks) *n., pl.* **-texes** *or* **-tices** (-tɪˌsiːz). **1.** the highest point. **2.** *Maths.* **a.** the point opposite the base of a figure. **b.** the point of intersection of two sides of a plane figure or angle. [Latin: whirlpool]

vertical ('vɜːtɪkᵊl) *adj.* **1.** at right angles to the horizon; upright: *a vertical wall.* **2.** straight up and down: *vertical stripes.* **3.** *Econ.* of or relating to associated or consecutive, though not identical, stages of industrial activity: *vertical integration.* **4.** of or relating to the vertex. ~*n.* **5.** a vertical plane, position, or line. [from Latin *vertex* top, pole of the sky] —'**vertically** *adv.*

vertiginous (vɜː'tɪdʒɪnəs) *adj.* producing dizziness.

vertigo ('vɜːtɪˌgəʊ) *n. Pathol.* a sensation of dizziness resulting from a disorder of the sense of balance. [Latin: a whirling round]

vervain ('vɜːveɪn) *n.* a plant with long slender spikes of purple, blue, or white flowers. [Latin *verbēna* sacred bough]

verve (vɜːv) *n.* great vitality and liveliness. [Latin *verba* words, chatter]

very ('vɛrɪ) *adv.* **1.** used to add emphasis to adjectives that are able to be graded: *very good; very tall.* ~*adj.* **2.** used with nouns to give emphasis to the significance or relevance of a noun in a particular context, or to give exaggerated intensity to certain nouns: *the very man I want to see; the very back of the room.* [Old French *verai* true]

very high frequency *n.* a radio-frequency band lying between 300 and 30 megahertz.

Very light ('vɛrɪ) *n.* a coloured flare for signalling at night. [after Edward W. *Very,* naval ordnance officer]

vesicle ('vɛsɪkᵊl) *n. Biol.* **a.** any small sac or cavity, esp. one filled with fluid. **b.** a blister. [Latin *vesica* bladder, sac]

vespers ('vɛspəz) *n. (functioning as sing.)* an evening service in some Christian churches. [Latin *vesper* the evening star]

vessel ('vɛsᵊl) *n.* **1.** an object used as a container for liquid. **2.** a ship or large boat. **3.** a tubular structure that transports fluids such as blood in humans and water in plants. [Latin *vās* vase]

vest (vɛst) *n.* **1.** an undergarment covering the top half of the body. **2.** *U.S., Canad., &*

Austral. a waistcoat. ~*vb.* **3.** (foll. by *in*) to place or settle (power, rights, or property) on: *power was vested in the committee.* **4.** (foll. by *with*) to bestow on: *the company was vested with authority.* [Latin *vestis* clothing]

vestal ('vɛstᵊl) *adj.* **1.** chaste or pure. ~*n.* **2.** a chaste woman. [Latin *Vestālis* virgin priestess of the goddess Vesta]

vestal virgin *n.* (in ancient Rome) one of the virgin priestesses dedicated to the goddess Vesta and to maintaining the sacred fire in her temple.

vested ('vɛstɪd) *adj. Property law.* having an existing right to the immediate or future possession of property.

vested interest *n.* **1.** *Property law.* an existing right to the immediate or future possession of property. **2.** a strong personal concern in something, usually resulting in personal gain.

vestibule ('vɛstɪˌbjuːl) *n.* a small entrance hall. [Latin *vestibulum*]

vestige ('vɛstɪdʒ) *n.* **1.** a small trace; hint: *a vestige of truth.* **2.** *Biol.* an organ or part that is a small nonfunctioning remnant of a functional organ in an ancestor. [Latin *vestīgium* track] —**ves′tigial** *adj.*

vestments ('vɛstmənts) *pl. n.* **1.** robes denoting office, authority, or rank. **2.** ceremonial garments worn by the clergy at religious services. [Latin *vestīre* to clothe]

vestry ('vɛstrɪ) *n., pl.* **-tries.** a room in or attached to a church, in which vestments and sacred vessels are kept. [prob. Old French *vestiarie* wardrobe]

vet[1] (vɛt) *n.* **1.** short for **veterinary surgeon.** ~*vb.* **vetting, vetted.** **2.** *Chiefly Brit.* to make a careful check of (a person, document, etc.) for suitability: *the candidates were well vetted.*

vet[2] (vɛt) *n. U.S. & Canad.* short for **veteran.**

vetch (vɛtʃ) *n.* **1.** a climbing plant with blue or purple flowers. **2.** the beanlike fruit of the vetch, used as fodder. [Latin *vicia*]

veteran ('vɛtərən) *n.* **1.** a person who has given long service in some capacity. **2.** a soldier who has seen a lot of active service. **3.** *U.S. & Canad.* a person who has served in the military forces. [Latin *vetus* old]

veteran car *n. Brit.* a car constructed before 1919, esp. before 1905.

veterinarian (ˌvɛtrɪˈnɛərɪən) *n. U.S. & Canad.* a veterinary surgeon.

veterinary ('vɛtrɪnərɪ) *adj.* of or relating to veterinary science. [Latin *veterīnae* draught animals]

veterinary science *or* **medicine** *n.* the branch of medicine concerned with the treatment of animals.

veterinary surgeon *n. Brit.* a person qualified to practise veterinary science.

veto ('viːtəʊ) *n., pl.* **-toes.** **1.** the power to prevent legislation or action proposed by others: *the presidential veto.* **2.** the exercise of this power. ~*vb.* **-toing, -toed.** **3.** to refuse consent to (a proposal, such as a government bill). **4.** to prohibit or forbid:

her parents vetoed her trip. [Latin: I forbid]

vex (vɛks) *vb.* to anger or annoy. [Latin *vexāre* to jolt (in carrying)] —**′vexing** *adj.*

vexation (vɛkˈseɪʃən) *n.* **1.** a vexing or being vexed. **2.** something that vexes.

vexatious (vɛkˈseɪʃəs) *adj.* vexing or tending to vex.

vexed (vɛkst) *adj.* **1.** annoyed, confused, or agitated. **2.** much debated: *a vexed question.*

VHF *or* **vhf** *Radio.* very high frequency.

VHS Video Home System: a video cassette recorder system using ½in. magnetic tape.

via ('vaɪə) *prep.* by way of; by means of: *to London via Paris.* [Latin *via* way]

viable ('vaɪəbᵊl) *adj.* **1.** practicable: *a viable proposition.* **2.** (of seeds or eggs) capable of growth. **3.** (of a fetus) sufficiently developed to survive outside the uterus. [Latin *vīta*] —,**via′bility** *n.*

viaduct ('vaɪəˌdʌkt) *n.* a bridge for carrying a road or railway across a valley. [Latin *via* way + *dūcere* to bring]

vial ('vaɪəl) *n.* same as **phial.** [Greek *phialē* a bowl]

viand ('vaɪənd) *n.* **1.** a type of food. **2.** (*pl.*) provisions. [Latin *vīvenda* things to be lived on]

viaticum (vaɪˈætɪkəm) *n., pl.* **-ca** (-kə) *or* **-cums.** *Christianity.* Holy Communion given to a person dying or in danger of death. [Latin *viāticus* belonging to a journey]

vibes (vaɪbz) *pl. n.* **1.** *Informal.* short for **vibraphone.** **2.** *Slang.* **a.** the emotional reactions between people. **b.** the atmosphere of a place.

vibrant ('vaɪbrənt) *adj.* **1.** characterized by or exhibiting vibration. **2.** full of life, energy, and enthusiasm: *a vibrant image.* **3.** resonant: *vibrant tones.* [Latin *vibrāre* to agitate] —**′vibrancy** *n.*

vibraphone ('vaɪbrəˌfəʊn) *n.* a percussion instrument consisting of metal bars over tubular metal resonators, which are made to vibrate electronically.

vibrate (vaɪˈbreɪt) *vb.* **1.** to move or cause to move back and forth rapidly. **2.** to resonate or cause to resonate. **3.** *Physics.* to undergo or cause to undergo vibration. [Latin *vibrāre*] —**vibratory** ('vaɪbrətərɪ) *adj.*

vibration (vaɪˈbreɪʃən) *n.* **1.** a vibrating. **2.** *Physics.* **a.** a periodic motion about an equilibrium position, such as in the production of sound. **b.** a single cycle of such a motion.

vibrato (vɪˈbrɑːtəʊ) *n., pl.* **-tos.** *Music.* a slight rapid fluctuation in the pitch of a note.

vibrator (vaɪˈbreɪtə) *n.* a device for producing a vibratory motion, as in massage.

vicar ('vɪkə) *n.* **1.** *Church of England.* (in Britain) a clergyman appointed to act as priest of a parish from which, formerly, he did not receive tithes but a stipend. **2.** *R.C. Church.* a church officer acting as deputy to a bishop. [Latin *vicārius* a deputy] —**vicarial** (vɪˈkɛərɪəl) *adj.*

vicarage ('vɪkərɪdʒ) n. the residence or benefice of a vicar.

vicar apostolic n. R.C. Church. a titular bishop having jurisdiction in missionary countries.

vicar general n., pl. **vicars general**. an official appointed to assist the bishop in his administrative duties.

vicarious (vɪ'kɛərɪəs, vaɪ-) adj. **1.** undergone at second hand as if by taking part in another's experiences. **2.** undergone or done as the substitute for another: *vicarious punishment.* **3.** delegated: *vicarious authority.* [Latin *vicārius* substituted]

Vicar of Christ n. R.C. Church. the Pope as Christ's earthly representative.

vice[1] (vaɪs) n. **1.** an immoral or evil habit, action, or trait. **2.** frequent indulgence in immoral practices. **3.** a specific form of immoral conduct, such as sexual perversion. **4.** an imperfection in character or conduct: *smoking is his only vice.* [Latin *vitium* a defect]

vice[2] or U.S. (often) **vise** (vaɪs) n. an appliance with a pair of jaws for holding an object while work is done on it. [Latin *vītis* vine, plant with spiralling tendrils]

vice[3] (vaɪs) adj. serving in the place of. [Latin *vicis* interchange]

vice[4] ('vaɪsɪ) prep. instead of; as a substitute for. [Latin *vicis* change]

vice admiral n. a senior commissioned officer in certain navies.

vice chancellor n. the chief executive or administrator at some British universities.

vicegerent (,vaɪs'dʒɛrənt) n. a person appointed to exercise all or some of the authority of another. [VICE[3] + Latin *gerere* to manage]

vice president n. an officer ranking immediately below a president and serving as his deputy.

viceregal (,vaɪs'riːgʰl) adj. **1.** of a viceroy. **2.** Chiefly Austral. & N.Z. of a governor or governor general.

viceroy ('vaɪsrɔɪ) n. a governor of a colony, country, or province who acts for and rules in the name of his sovereign or government. [VICE[3] + French *roi* king] —**viceroyship** or **,vice'royalty** n.

vice squad n. a police division responsible for the enforcement of gaming and prostitution laws.

vice versa ('vaɪsɪ 'vɜːsə) adv. the other way around. [Latin: relations being reversed]

Vichy water ('viːʃiː) n. a natural mineral water from springs at Vichy in France.

vicinity (vɪ'sɪnɪtɪ) n., pl. **-ties**. **1.** a surrounding area; neighbourhood. **2.** a being close. [Latin *vīcīnus* neighbouring]

vicious ('vɪʃəs) adj. **1.** wicked or cruel: *a vicious thug.* **2.** characterized by violence or ferocity: *a vicious blow.* **3.** unpleasantly severe; harsh: *a vicious wind.* **4.** malicious: *vicious lies.* **5.** (of animals) ferocious or hostile. **6.** invalidated by defects; unsound: *a vicious inference.* [Latin *vitiōsus* full of faults] —**'viciously** adv. —**'viciousness** n.

vicious circle n. **1.** a situation in which an attempt to resolve one problem creates new problems that recreate the original one. **2.** Logic. a form of reasoning in which a conclusion is inferred from premises the truth of which cannot be established independently of that conclusion.

vicissitude (vɪ'sɪsɪˌtjuːd) n. a variation in circumstance or fortune. [Latin *vicis* change]

victim ('vɪktɪm) n. **1.** a person or thing that suffers harm or death: *victims of tyranny.* **2.** a person who is tricked or swindled. **3.** a living person or animal sacrificed in a religious rite. [Latin *victima*]

victimize or **-mise** ('vɪktɪˌmaɪz) vb. **1.** to punish or discriminate against selectively or unfairly. **2.** to make a victim of. —**,victimi'zation** or **-mi'sation** n.

victor ('vɪktə) n. **1.** a person or nation that has defeated an adversary in war. **2.** the winner of any contest, conflict, or struggle. [Latin, from *vincere* to conquer]

victoria (vɪk'tɔːrɪə) n. **1.** a light four-wheeled horse-drawn carriage with a folding hood. **2.** Also called: **victoria plum.** Brit. a large sweet variety of plum, red and yellow in colour. [after Queen *Victoria*]

Victoria Cross n. the highest decoration for gallantry in battle awarded to the British and Commonwealth armed forces.

Victorian (vɪk'tɔːrɪən) adj. **1.** of or characteristic of Queen Victoria or her reign (1837–1901). **2.** exhibiting the characteristics popularly attributed to the Victorians, esp. prudery, bigotry, or hypocrisy. ~n. **3.** a person who lived during the reign of Queen Victoria.

Victoriana (vɪkˌtɔːrɪ'ɑːnə) n. objects of the Victorian period.

victorious (vɪk'tɔːrɪəs) adj. **1.** having defeated an adversary: *the victorious nations.* **2.** of, indicating, or characterized by victory: *a victorious conclusion.*

victory ('vɪktrɪ) n., pl. **-ries**. **1.** final superiority in a war or battle. **2.** success attained in any contest or struggle. [Latin *victōria*]

victual ('vɪtʰl) vb. **-ualling, -ualled** or U.S. **-ualing, -ualed**. to supply with or obtain victuals. [Latin *victus* sustenance] —**'victualler** or U.S. **-ualer** n.

victuals ('vɪtʰlz) pl. n. food provisions.

vicuña (vɪ'kjuːnə) n. **1.** a tawny Andean mammal like the llama. **2.** the fine wool obtained from this animal. [Spanish]

vide ('vaɪdɪ) (used to direct a reader to a specified place in a text or another book) refer to, see. [Latin]

videlicet (vɪ'diːlɪˌsɛt) adv. namely: used to specify items. [Latin]

video ('vɪdɪəʊ) adj. **1.** of or used in the transmission or reception of a televised image. ~n., pl. **-os**. **2.** the visual elements of a television broadcast. **3.** a film recorded on a video cassette. **4.** short for **video cassette** or **video cassette recorder**. ~vb. **videoing, videoed**. **5.** to record (a television programme or an event) on a video cassette recorder. [Latin *vidēre* to see]

video cassette *n.* a cassette containing video tape.

video cassette recorder *n.* a tape recorder for vision and sound signals using magnetic tape in closed plastic cassettes: used for recording and playing back television programmes and films.

video frequency *n.* the frequency of a signal conveying the image and synchronizing pulses in a television broadcasting system.

video nasty *n.* a film, usually specially made for video, that is explicitly horrific and pornographic.

videophone ('vɪdɪəʊ,fəʊn) *n.* a telephonic device in which there is both verbal and visual communication between parties.

video recorder *n.* short for **video cassette recorder.**

video tape *n.* **1.** magnetic tape used mainly for recording the video-frequency signals of a television programme or film for subsequent transmission. ~*vb.* **videotape. 2.** to record (a film or programme) on video tape.

video tape recorder *n.* a tape recorder for visual signals, using magnetic tape on open spools: used in television broadcasting.

videotex ('vɪdɪəʊ,tɛks) *n.* same as **viewdata.**

videotext ('vɪdɪəʊ,tɛkst) *n.* a means of providing a written or graphical representation of computerized information on a television screen.

vie (vaɪ) *vb.* **vying, vied.** (foll. by *with* or *for*) to attempt to do or have (something) before or better than (another person). [prob. Old French *envier* to challenge] —'**vying** *adj., n.*

vies (fɪs) *adj.* S. African slang. angry. [Afrikaans, from Dutch: nasty]

Vietnamese (,vjɛtnə'miːz) *adj.* **1.** of Vietnam, in SE Asia, its people, or their language. ~*n.* **2.** (*pl.* -**ese**) a person from Vietnam. **3.** the language of Vietnam.

view (vjuː) *n.* **1.** the act of seeing or observing. **2.** vision or sight, esp. range of vision: *the church is out of view.* **3.** everything that can be seen from a particular place or in a particular direction: *the view from the top was superb.* **4.** a pictorial representation of a scene, such as a photograph. **5.** (*sometimes pl.*) opinion: *my own view on the matter differs from yours.* **6.** (foll. by *to*) an intention: *he has a view to securing further qualifications.* **7. in view of.** taking into consideration. **8. on view.** exhibited to the public gaze. **9. take a dim** *or* **poor view of.** to regard (something) with disfavour. ~*vb.* **10.** to look at. **11.** to consider in a specified manner: *they view the growth of Communism with horror.* **12.** to examine or inspect carefully: *to view the accounts.* **13.** to watch (television). [Latin *vidēre* to see]

viewdata ('vjuː,deɪtə) *n.* an interactive videotext service in which the consumer is linked to a computer by telephone and is thus able to select the information required.

viewer ('vjuːə) *n.* **1.** a person who views something, esp. television. **2.** any optical device used for viewing something, esp. one for viewing photographic transparencies.

viewfinder ('vjuː,faɪndə) *n.* a device on a camera that lets the user see what will be included in the photograph.

viewpoint ('vjuː,pɔɪnt) *n.* the mental attitude that determines a person's judgments.

vigil ('vɪdʒɪl) *n.* **1.** a purposeful watch maintained, esp. at night, to guard, observe, or pray. **2.** *R.C. Church, Church of England.* the eve of certain major festivals. [Latin *vigil* alert]

vigilance ('vɪdʒɪləns) *n.* the fact, quality, or condition of being vigilant.

vigilance committee *n.* (in the U.S.) a self-appointed body of citizens organized to maintain order.

vigilant ('vɪdʒɪlənt) *adj.* keenly alert to or on the watch for trouble or danger. [Latin *vigilāre* to be watchful]

vigilante (,vɪdʒɪ'læntɪ) *n.* a self-appointed protector of public order. [Spanish, from Latin *vigilāre* to keep watch]

vignette (vɪ'njɛt) *n.* **1.** a small illustration at the beginning or end of a book or chapter. **2.** a short graceful literary sketch. **3.** a photograph or drawing with edges that are shaded off. [French, lit.: little vine (frequently used to embellish a text)]

vigorous ('vɪgərəs) *adj.* **1.** having, bodily or mental strength or vitality. **2.** having, displaying, or performed with vigour: *vigorous growth.* —'**vigorously** *adv.*

vigour *or U.S.* **vigor** ('vɪgə) *n.* **1.** exuberant and resilient strength of body or mind. **2.** forcefulness: *I was surprised by the vigour of her complaints.* **3.** strong healthy growth. [Latin *vigor*]

Viking ('vaɪkɪŋ) *n.* any of the Scandinavians who raided by sea most of N and W Europe from the 8th to the 11th centuries. [Old Norse *vīkingr*]

vile (vaɪl) *adj.* **1.** morally wicked; evil: *vile accusations.* **2.** disgusting; foul: *a vile smell.* **3.** tending to humiliate or degrade: *only slaves would perform such vile tasks.* **4.** unpleasant or bad: *vile weather.* [Latin *vīlis* cheap] —'**vilely** *adv.*

vilify ('vɪlɪ,faɪ) *vb.* -**fying, -fied.** to speak very badly of (someone); malign. [Latin *vīlis* worthless + *facere* to make] —**vilification** (,vɪlɪfɪ'keɪʃən) *n.*

villa ('vɪlə) *n.* **1.** a large country residence. **2.** *Brit.* a detached or semidetached suburban house. **3.** a house rented to holidaymakers. [Latin: a farmhouse]

village ('vɪlɪdʒ) *n.* **1.** a small group of houses in the country, larger than a hamlet. **2.** the inhabitants of such a community. [Latin *villa* a farmhouse] —'**villager** *n.*

villain ('vɪlən) *n.* **1.** a wicked or evil person. **2.** (in a novel or play) the main evil character. [Late Latin *vīllānus* worker on a country estate]

villainous ('vɪlənəs) adj. of, like, or appropriate to a villain.

villainy ('vɪlənɪ) n., pl. **-lainies.** evil or vicious behaviour or action.

villein ('vɪlən) n. (in medieval Europe) a peasant personally bound to his lord, to whom he paid dues and services in return for his land. [from VILLAIN] —**'villeinage** n.

vim (vɪm) n. Slang. exuberant vigour and energy. [Latin vīs force]

vinaigrette (ˌvɪneɪ'grɛt) n. salad dressing made from oil and vinegar with seasonings. [French]

vindicate ('vɪndɪˌkeɪt) vb. **1.** to clear from guilt, blame, or suspicion. **2.** to provide justification for: his promotion vindicated his unconventional attitude. [Latin vindex claimant] —**'vindiˌcator** n. —**'vindiˌcatory** adj.

vindication (ˌvɪndɪ'keɪʃən) n. **1.** the act of vindicating or the condition of being vindicated. **2.** a fact or piece of evidence that serves to vindicate.

vindictive (vɪn'dɪktɪv) adj. **1.** disposed to seek vengeance. **2.** characterized by spite or rancour. [Latin vindicāre to avenge] —**vin'dictively** adv. —**vin'dictiveness** n.

vine (vaɪn) n. **1.** any of various plants, esp. the grapevine, with long flexible stems that climb by clinging to a support. **2.** the stem of such a plant. [Latin vīnea vineyard] —**'viny** adj.

vinegar ('vɪnɪgə) n. **1.** a sour-tasting liquid made by fermentation of beer, wine, or cider: used as a condiment or preservative. **2.** sourness or peevishness of temper, speech, or character. [French vin wine + aigre sour] —**'vinegary** adj.

vineyard ('vɪnjəd) n. a plantation of grapevines, esp. where wine grapes are produced. [Old English wīngeard]

vingt-et-un (ˌvænteɪ'æn) n. same as **pontoon²**. [French, lit.: twenty-one]

viniculture ('vɪnɪˌkʌltʃə) n. the process or business of growing grapes and making wine. [Latin vinum wine + culture] —**ˌvini'culturist** n.

vino ('viːnəʊ) n., pl. **-nos.** Informal. wine. [Spanish or Italian: wine]

vinous ('vaɪnəs) adj. of or characteristic of wine. [Latin vīnum wine]

vintage ('vɪntɪdʒ) n. **1.** the wine obtained from a particular harvest of grapes. **2.** the harvest from which such a wine is obtained. **3.** a time of origin: a car of Edwardian vintage. ~adj. **4.** (of wine) of an outstandingly good year. **5.** representative of the best and most typical: vintage Shakespeare. [Latin vindēmia]

vintage car n. Chiefly Brit. an old car, esp. one constructed between 1919 and 1930.

vintner ('vɪntnə) n. a wine merchant. [Latin vīnētum vineyard]

vinyl ('vaɪnɪl) n. **1.** (modifier) of or containing the monovalent group of atoms CH₂CH—: vinyl chloride. **2.** any of various strong plastics made by the polymerization of vinyl compounds, such as PVC. **3.**

(modifier) of or made of vinyl: a vinyl raincoat. **4.** conventional records made of vinyl as opposed to compact discs. [Latin vinum wine]

viol ('vaɪəl) n. any of a family of stringed musical instruments that preceded the violin, consisting of a fretted fingerboard, a body with a flat back, and six strings. [Old Provençal viola]

viola¹ (vɪ'əʊlə) n. a bowed stringed instrument of the violin family, slightly larger and lower in pitch than the violin. [Italian]

viola² ('vaɪələ, vaɪ'əʊ-) n. any of various plants, the flowers of which have showy irregular petals, white, yellow, blue, or mauve in colour. [Latin: violet]

viola da gamba (vɪ'əʊlə də 'gæmbə) n. the second largest and lowest member of the viol family. [Italian, lit.: viol for the leg]

violate ('vaɪəˌleɪt) vb. **1.** to break, disregard, or infringe (a law, agreement, or treaty). **2.** to rape. **3.** to disturb rudely or improperly: no-one violated his privacy. **4.** to treat disrespectfully: he violated a sanctuary. [Latin violāre to do violence to] —ˌvio'lation n. —'vioˌlator n.

violence ('vaɪələns) n. **1.** the exercise or an instance of physical force, usually intended to cause injuries or destruction. **2.** great force or strength as in actions, feeling, or expression. **3.** an unjust or unlawful display of force. **4. do violence to. a.** to inflict harm upon: they did violence to the prisoners. **b.** to distort the meaning of: the reporters did violence to my speech. [Latin violentus violent]

violent ('vaɪələnt) adj. **1.** marked or caused by great physical force or violence: a violent stab. **2.** marked by intensity of any kind: a violent clash of colours; I took a violent dislike to her. **3.** characterized by an undue use of force. —'violently adv.

violet ('vaɪəlɪt) n. **1.** any of a genus of plants, such as the **sweet** (or **garden**) **violet**, having mauve or bluish flowers with irregular showy petals. **2.** a purplishblue colour. **3.** a dye or pigment of or producing this colour. ~adj. **4.** purplishblue. [Latin viola violet]

violin (ˌvaɪə'lɪn) n. a musical instrument, the highest member of the violin family, with four strings played with a bow. [Italian violino a little viola]

violinist (ˌvaɪə'lɪnɪst) n. a person who plays the violin.

violist (vɪ'əʊlɪst) n. a person who plays the viola.

violoncello (ˌvaɪələn'tʃɛləʊ) n., pl. **-los.** same as **cello**. [Italian]

VIP very important person.

viper ('vaɪpə) n. **1.** any of a family of venomous snakes. **2.** a malicious or treacherous person. [Latin]

virago (vɪ'rɑːgəʊ) n., pl. **-goes** or **-gos.** a loud, violent, and ill-tempered woman. [Latin: a manlike maiden]

viral ('vaɪrəl) adj. of or caused by a virus.

virgin ('vɜːdʒɪn) n. **1.** a person, esp. a woman, who has never had sexual intercourse. ~adj. **2.** of or like a virgin or virgins. **3.** pure and natural, uncorrupted or untouched: *virgin purity.* **4.** not yet cultivated, explored, or exploited by man: *the virgin forests.* [Latin *virgō*]

Virgin ('vɜːdʒɪn) *n.* **1. the.** same as **Virgin Mary. 2.** a statue or picture of the Virgin Mary.

virginal[1] ('vɜːdʒɪn'l) *adj.* **1.** of or characterized by virginity; chaste. **2.** extremely pure or fresh.

virginal[2] ('vɜːdʒɪn'l) *n.* (*often pl.*) an early keyboard instrument, like a small harpsichord, but oblong in shape. [prob. Latin *virginālis* virginal, perhaps because it was played largely by young ladies]

Virgin Birth *n. Christianity.* the doctrine that Jesus Christ was conceived solely by the direct intervention of the Holy Spirit so that Mary remained miraculously a virgin.

Virginia creeper (və'dʒɪnɪə) *n.* a climbing plant of North America, with leaves that turn red in autumn.

virginity (və'dʒɪnɪtɪ) *n.* the condition or fact of being a virgin.

Virgin Mary *n.* **the.** *Christianity.* Mary, the mother of Christ.

Virgo ('vɜːgəʊ) *n.* the sixth sign of the zodiac; the virgin. [Latin]

virgule ('vɜːgjuːl) *n. Printing.* same as **solidus.** [Latin *virga* rod]

virile ('vɪraɪl) *adj.* **1.** of or characteristic of an adult male. **2.** (of a male) having a high sexual drive and capacity for sexual intercourse. **3.** strong, forceful, or vigorous. [Latin *virīlis* manly] —**virility** (vɪ'rɪlɪtɪ) *n.*

virology (vaɪ'rɒlədʒɪ) *n.* the branch of medicine concerned with the study of viruses. —**virological** (ˌvaɪrə'lɒdʒɪk'l) *adj.*

virtual ('vɜːtʃʊəl) *adj.* **1.** having the essence or effect but not the appearance or form of: *a virtual revolution.* **2.** *Computers.* designed so as to extend the potential of a finite system beyond its immediate limits. **Virtual memory** increases the potential of a computer by transferring programs or parts of programs between core and store. [Latin *virtūs* virtue]

virtually ('vɜːtʃʊəlɪ) *adv.* in effect though not in fact; practically; nearly.

virtue ('vɜːtjuː) *n.* **1.** moral excellence or righteousness. **2.** a particular moral excellence: *the virtue of tolerance.* **3.** any admirable quality or trait. **4.** chastity, esp. in women. **5. by** or **in virtue of.** by reason of. [Latin *virtūs* manliness, courage]

virtuoso (ˌvɜːtjʊ'əʊzəʊ, -səʊ) *n., pl.* -**sos** or -**si** (-siː). **1.** a skilled master of musical technique and artistry. **2.** a person who has a masterly or dazzling skill in any field of activity. **3.** (*modifier*) showing masterly skill or brilliance: *a virtuoso performance.* [Italian: skilled] —**virtuosity** (ˌvɜːtjʊ'ɒsɪtɪ) *n.*

virtuous ('vɜːtjʊəs) *adj.* **1.** characterized by or possessing virtue. **2.** (of a woman) chaste. —**virtuously** *adv.*

virulent ('vɪrʊlənt) *adj.* **1. a.** (of a microorganism) extremely infective. **b.** (of a disease) having a violent effect. **2.** extremely poisonous or injurious: *a virulent poison.* **3.** extremely bitter or hostile: *virulent criticism.* [Latin *virulentus* full of poison] —**virulence** *n.*

virus ('vaɪrəs) *n.* **1.** any of a group of very simple organisms that are smaller than bacteria and can cause disease in animals and plants. **2.** *Informal.* a disease caused by a virus. **3.** any corrupting influence. **4.** *Computers.* a short program inserted without authorization into a computer's main program, which, when activated, interferes with the operation of the computer and other computers with which it is linked. [Latin: slime, poisonous liquid]

visa ('viːzə) *n.* an endorsement in a passport permitting its bearer to travel into or through the country of the government issuing it. [Latin: things seen]

visage ('vɪzɪdʒ) *n. Chiefly literary.* **1.** face or countenance. **2.** appearance. [Latin *vīsus* appearance]

vis-à-vis (ˌviːzɑː'viː) *prep.* **1.** in relation to. **2.** face to face with. —*adv., adj.* **3.** face to face; opposite. —*n., pl.* **vis-à-vis. 4.** a person or thing that is opposite another. [French: face-to-face]

viscera ('vɪsərə) *pl. n., sing.* **viscus** ('vɪskəs). *Anat.* the large internal organs of the body collectively. [Latin: entrails]

visceral ('vɪsərəl) *adj.* **1.** of or affecting the viscera. **2.** characterized by instinct rather than intellect.

viscid ('vɪsɪd) *adj.* sticky. [Latin *viscum* mistletoe, birdlime]

viscose ('vɪskəʊs) *n.* **1.** a sticky solution obtained by dissolving cellulose: used in the manufacture of rayon and cellophane. **2.** rayon made from this material. [Latin *viscum* birdlime]

viscosity (vɪs'kɒsɪtɪ) *n., pl.* -**ties. 1.** the state or property of being viscous. **2.** *Physics.* the extent to which a fluid resists a tendency to flow.

viscount ('vaɪkaʊnt) *n.* (in the British Isles) a nobleman ranking below an earl and above a baron. [Old French] —**'viscountcy** *n.* —**'viscountess** *fem. n.*

viscous ('vɪskəs) *adj.* (of liquids) thick and sticky; not flowing easily.

vise (vaɪs) *n. U.S.* same as **vice**[2].

visibility (ˌvɪzɪ'bɪlɪtɪ) *n.* **1.** the condition or fact of being visible. **2.** the relative possibility of seeing. **3.** the range of vision: *visibility is 500 yards.*

visible ('vɪzɪb'l) *adj.* **1.** capable of being perceived by the eye. **2.** capable of being perceived by the mind: *no visible dangers.* [Latin *vīsibilis*] —**visibly** *adv.*

vision ('vɪʒən) *n.* **1.** the act of perceiving or the ability to perceive with the eye; sight. **2.** the image on a television screen. **3.** great perception, esp. of future developments: *a man of vision.* **4.** a hallucination, esp. one resulting from a mystical or religious experience: *the vision of St John of the Cross.* **5.** (*sometimes pl.*) a vivid mental image produced by the imagination: *he had visions of becoming famous.* **6.** a person or thing of extraordinary beauty. [Latin *vīsiō* sight, from *vidēre* to see]

visionary ('vɪʒənərɪ) adj. 1. marked by vision or foresight: a visionary leader. 2. idealistic but impractical. 3. given to having visions. 4. of, like, or seen in visions. ~n., pl. -aries. 5. a visionary person.

visit ('vɪzɪt) vb. 1. to go or come to see (a person or place). 2. to stay with (someone) as a guest. 3. (of a disease or disaster) to afflict. 4. (foll. by upon or on) to inflict (punishment). 5. (foll. by with) U.S. & Canad. informal. to chat with (someone). ~n. 6. the act or an instance of visiting. 7. a stay as a guest. 8. a professional or official call. [Latin visitāre to go to see]

visitant ('vɪzɪtənt) n. 1. a ghost; apparition. 2. a migratory bird temporarily resting in a particular region.

visitation (,vɪzɪ'teɪʃən) n. 1. an official visit for the purpose of inspecting an institution. 2. a visiting of punishment or reward from heaven. 3. any disaster or catastrophe: a visitation of the plague.

Visitation (,vɪzɪ'teɪʃən) n. a. the visit made by the Virgin Mary to her cousin Elizabeth (Luke 1: 39–56). b. the Church festival commemorating this, held on July 2.

visitor ('vɪzɪtə) n. a person who pays a visit; caller, guest, or tourist.

visor ('vaɪzə) n. 1. a transparent flap on a helmet that can be pulled down to protect the face. 2. a small movable screen used as protection against glare from the sun, esp. one attached above the windscreen of a motor vehicle. [Old French vis face]

vista ('vɪstə) n. 1. a view, esp. through a long narrow avenue of trees or buildings. 2. a comprehensive mental view of a series of future events. [Italian]

visual ('vɪʒuəl) adj. 1. of, done by, or used in seeing. 2. capable of being seen; visible. [Latin visus sight] —**'visually** adv.

visual aids pl. n. devices, such as films or models, that display in visual form material to be understood or remembered.

visual display unit n. Computers. a device that displays characters or diagrams representing data in a computer memory.

visualize or **-lise** ('vɪʒuə,laɪz) vb. to form a mental image of (something not at that moment visible). —**,visuali'zation** or **-li'sation** n.

vital ('vaɪt'l) adj. 1. essential to maintain life: the lungs perform a vital function. 2. forceful, energetic, or lively: a vital person. 3. of or having life: a vital organism. 4. indispensable or essential: books vital to this study. 5. of great importance: a vital game. ~n. 6. (pl.) the bodily organs, such as the brain, liver, heart, and lungs, that are necessary to maintain life. [Latin vita life] —**'vitally** adv.

vitality (vaɪ'tælɪtɪ) n., pl. -ties. 1. physical or mental energy. 2. the power to continue in existence, live, or grow: the vitality of a movement.

vitalize or **-lise** ('vaɪtə,laɪz) vb. to make vital or alive. —**,vitali'zation** or **-li'sation** n.

vital statistics pl. n. 1. population statistics, such as the numbers of births, marriages, and deaths. 2. Informal. the measurements of a woman's bust, waist, and hips.

vitamin ('vɪtəmɪn, 'vaɪ-) n. any of a group of substances that occur naturally in certain foods and are essential for the normal functioning of metabolism in the body. [from Latin vita life + -amin from amine]

vitamin A n. a vitamin occurring in green and yellow vegetables, butter, egg yolk, and fish-liver oil. It prevents night blindness.

vitamin B n., pl. B vitamins. any of the vitamins in the vitamin B complex.

vitamin B complex n. a large group of vitamins occurring esp. in liver and yeast: includes thiamine (vitamin B_1), riboflavin (vitamin B_2), vitamin B_6, and vitamin B_{12}.

vitamin C n. a vitamin occurring in citrus fruits, tomatoes, and green vegetables. It prevents and cures scurvy.

vitamin D n., pl. D vitamins. any of the vitamins occurring in fish-liver oils, milk, butter, and eggs, and used in the treatment of rickets.

vitamin E n. a vitamin occuring in wheatgerm oil, lettuce, egg yolk, and milk. It is thought to be necessary for some aspects of reproduction.

vitamin K n., pl. K vitamins. any of the vitamins, occurring in green leafy vegetables, fish meal, egg yolks, and tomatoes, which are essential for the normal clotting of blood.

vitamin P n., pl. P vitamins. any of a group of crystalline substances occurring mainly in citrus fruits, blackcurrants, and rosehips: they regulate the strength of the blood capillaries.

vitiate ('vɪʃɪ,eɪt) vb. 1. to spoil or weaken the effectiveness of (something). 2. to destroy the legal effect of (a contract). [Latin vitiāre to injure] —,**viti'ation** n.

viticulture ('vɪtɪ,kʌltʃə) n. the cultivation of grapevines. [Latin vitis vine]

vitreous ('vɪtrɪəs) adj. 1. of or like glass. 2. of or relating to the vitreous humour. [Latin vitrum glass]

vitreous humour or **body** n. a transparent gelatinous substance that fills the eyeball between the lens and the retina.

vitrify ('vɪtrɪ,faɪ) vb. **-fying, -fied.** to convert or be converted into glass or a glassy substance. —**vitrification** (,vɪtrɪfɪ'keɪʃən) n.

vitriol ('vɪtrɪɒl) n. 1. sulphuric acid. 2. speech or criticism displaying hatred or bitterness. [Latin vitrum glass, referring to the glossy appearance of the sulphates]

vitriolic (,vɪtrɪ'ɒlɪk) adj. (of speech or criticism) severely bitter or caustic.

vituperate (vɪ'tjuːpə,reɪt) vb. to speak (against) abusively; revile. [Latin vituperāre to blame] —**vi,tuper'ation** n. —**vi'tuperative** adj.

viva[1] ('viːvə) interj. long live; up with (a specified person or thing). [Italian, lit.: may (he) live!]

viva[2] ('vaɪvə) Brit. ~n. 1. an oral examination. ~*vb.* **-vaing, -vaed. 2.** to examine orally. [from VIVA VOCE]

vivace (vɪˈvɑːtʃɪ) *adv. Music.* to be performed in a lively manner. [Italian]

vivacious (vɪˈveɪʃəs) *adj.* full of high spirits and animation. [Latin *vīvax* lively]

vivacity (vɪˈvæsɪtɪ) *n.* the quality or condition of being vivacious.

vivarium (vaɪˈveərɪəm) *n., pl.* **-iums** or **-ia** (-ɪə). a place where live animals are kept under natural conditions. [Latin *vīvus* alive]

viva voce (ˈvaɪvə ˈvəʊtʃɪ) *adv., adj.* **1.** by word of mouth. ~*n., vb.* **2.** same as **viva²**. [Medieval Latin, lit.: with living voice]

vivid (ˈvɪvɪd) *adj.* **1.** (of a colour) very bright; intense. **2.** conveying striking realism, freshness, or trueness to life: *a vivid account.* **3.** (of a memory) remaining distinct. **4.** (of the imagination) easily forming lifelike images. [Latin *vīvidus* animated] —**ˈvividly** *adv.* —**ˈvividness** *n.*

vivify (ˈvɪvɪˌfaɪ) *vb.* **-fying, -fied. 1.** to bring to life; animate. **2.** to make more vivid or striking. [Latin *vīvus* alive + *facere* to make]

viviparous (vɪˈvɪpərəs) *adj.* (of most mammals) giving birth to living offspring. [Latin *vīvus* alive + *parere* to bring forth]

vivisect (ˈvɪvɪˌsɛkt, ˌvɪvɪˈsɛkt) *vb.* to subject (an animal) to vivisection. —**ˈviviˌsector** *n.*

vivisection (ˌvɪvɪˈsɛkʃən) *n.* the performing of experiments on living animals, involving cutting into or dissecting the body. [Latin *vivus* living + *section*, as in *dissection*] —ˌvivi**ˈsectionist** *n.*

vixen (ˈvɪksən) *n.* **1.** a female fox. **2.** a quarrelsome or spiteful woman. [related to Old English *fyxe*, fem. of *fox*]

viz (vɪz) *adv.* namely: used to specify items. [abbreviated from Latin *vidēlicet* namely]

vizier (vɪˈzɪə) *n.* a high official in certain Muslim countries. [Turkish *vezīr*]

vizor (ˈvaɪzə) *n.* same as **visor**.

VL Vulgar Latin.

V neck *n.* **a.** a neck on a garment that comes down to a point, like the letter V. **b.** a sweater with such a neck. —**ˈV-ˌneck** or **ˈV-ˌnecked** *adj.*

voc. or **vocat.** vocative.

vocab (ˈvəʊkæb) *n.* short for **vocabulary**.

vocable (ˈvəʊkəbəl) *n.* any word regarded simply as a sequence of letters or spoken sounds. [Latin *vocāre* to call]

vocabulary (vəˈkæbjʊlərɪ) *n., pl.* **-laries. 1.** a listing containing the words and phrases of a language, with meanings or translations into another language. **2.** all the words used by a particular person, class, or profession. **3.** all the words contained in a language. **4.** a range of symbols or techniques as used in any of the arts or crafts: *a wide vocabulary of textures and colours.* [Latin *vocābulum* vocable]

vocal (ˈvəʊkəl) *adj.* **1.** of, for, or produced by the voice: *vocal music.* **2.** connected with the production of the voice: *vocal organs.* **3.** inclined to express opinions or criticisms strongly and clearly in speech: *a vocal minority.* ~*n.* **4.** a piece of jazz or pop music that is sung. [Latin *vōx* voice] —**ˈvocally** *adv.*

vocal cords *pl. n.* either of two pairs of membranous folds in the larynx. The lower pair can be made to vibrate and produce sound by forcing air from the lungs over them.

vocalist (ˈvəʊkəlɪst) *n.* a singer with a pop group.

vocalize or **-ise** (ˈvəʊkəˌlaɪz) *vb.* **1.** to express with or use the voice. **2.** to make vocal or articulate. **3.** *Phonetics.* to articulate (a speech sound) with voice. **4.** to sing a melody on a vowel. —ˌvocaliˈzation or -iˈsation *n.*

vocation (vəʊˈkeɪʃən) *n.* **1.** a specified profession or trade. **2. a.** a special urge to a particular calling or career, esp. a religious one. **b.** such a calling or career. [Latin *vocāre* to call] —**voˈcational** *adj.*

vocative (ˈvɒkətɪv) *Grammar.* ~*adj.* **1.** denoting a case of nouns, in some inflected languages, used when addressing a person or thing. ~*n.* **2.** the vocative case. [Latin *vocāre* to call]

vociferate (vəʊˈsɪfəˌreɪt) *vb.* to exclaim or cry out about (something) noisily or vehemently. [Latin *vōx* voice + *ferre* to bear] —voˌciferˈation *n.*

vociferous (vəʊˈsɪfərəs) *adj.* noisy or vehement: *vociferous protests.*

vodka (ˈvɒdkə) *n.* a clear alcoholic spirit originating in Russia, made from grain. [Russian]

vogue (vəʊg) *n.* **1.** the popular style at a given time: *miniskirts are in vogue.* **2.** a period of general popularity: *the vogue for such dances is over.* ~*adj.* **3.** fashionable: *a vogue word.* [French] —**ˈvoguish** *adj.*

voice (vɔɪs) *n.* **1.** the sound made by the vibration of the vocal cords, esp. when modified by the tongue and mouth. **2.** distinctive tone of the speech sounds characteristic of a particular person. **3.** the condition or quality of such sounds: *a hysterical voice.* **4.** the musical sound of a singing voice: *she has a lovely voice.* **5.** the ability to speak or sing: *he has lost his voice.* **6.** written or spoken expression of feeling or opinion: *she gave voice to her fears.* **7.** a stated choice, wish, or opinion: *I had no voice in the decision.* **8.** an agency through which is communicated another's purpose or policy: *such groups are the voice of our enemies.* **9.** *Phonetics.* the sound characterizing the articulation of several speech sounds, that is produced when the vocal cords are vibrated by the breath. **10.** *Grammar.* a category of the verb that expresses whether it is active or passive. **11. in voice.** in a condition to sing or speak well. **12. with one voice.** unanimously. ~*vb.* **13.** to express: *to voice a complaint.* **14.** to articulate (a speech sound) with voice. [Latin *vōx*]

voiced (vɔɪst) *adj.* **1.** expressed by the voice. **2.** *Phonetics.* articulated with accompanying vibration of the vocal cords: *in English* (b) *is a voiced consonant.*

voiceless (ˈvɔɪslɪs) adj. **1.** without a voice. **2.** Phonetics. articulated without accompanying vibration of the vocal cords: in English (p) is a voiceless consonant.

voice-over n. the voice of an unseen commentator heard during a film.

void (vɔɪd) adj. **1.** without contents. **2.** not legally binding: null and void. **3.** (foll. by of) destitute or devoid: void of hope. **4.** useless: all his efforts were rendered void. ~n. **5.** an empty space or area. **6.** a feeling or condition of loneliness or deprivation. ~vb. **7.** to make ineffective or invalid. **8.** to empty (contents) or make empty of contents. **9.** to discharge the contents of (the bowels or bladder). [Latin vacāre to be empty]

voile (vɔɪl) n. a light semitransparent dress fabric of silk, rayon, or cotton. [French]

vol. **1.** volcano. **2.** volume. **3.** volunteer.

volatile (ˈvɒləˌtaɪl) adj. **1.** (of a substance) changing readily from a solid or liquid form to a vapour. **2.** (of persons) liable to sudden and unexpected changes of mood and behaviour. **3.** (of circumstances) liable to sudden change. [Latin volāre to fly] —**volatility** (ˌvɒləˈtɪlɪtɪ) n.

volatilize or **-lise** (vɒˈlætɪˌlaɪz) vb. to change or cause to change from a solid or liquid to a vapour. —**voˌlatiliˈzation** or **-liˈsation** n.

vol-au-vent (ˈvɒləʊˌvɒŋ) n. a very light puff pastry case filled with a savoury mixture. [French, lit.: flight in the wind]

volcanic (vɒlˈkænɪk) adj. **1.** of, produced by, or characterized by volcanoes: a volcanic region. **2.** suggestive of or like an erupting volcano: a volcanic temper.

volcano (vɒlˈkeɪnəʊ) n., pl. **-noes** or **-nos. 1.** an opening in the earth's crust from which molten lava, ashes, dust, and gases are ejected from below the earth's surface. **2.** a mountain formed from volcanic material ejected from a vent. [Italian, from Volcānus Vulcan, Roman god of fire]

vole (vəʊl) n. a small rodent with a stocky body, short tail, and inconspicuous ears. [short for volemouse, from Old Norse vollr field + mus mouse]

volition (vəˈlɪʃən) n. the act or faculty of using the will: of one's own volition. [Latin volō I will] —**voˈlitional** adj.

volley (ˈvɒlɪ) n. **1.** the simultaneous discharge of several weapons. **2.** the missiles so discharged. **3.** a burst of words occurring simultaneously or in rapid succession. **4.** Sport. a stroke, shot, or kick at a moving ball before it hits the ground. ~vb. **5.** to discharge (weapons) in or as if in a volley or (of weapons) to be discharged. **6.** Sport. to strike or kick (a moving ball) before it hits the ground. [French volée a flight]

volleyball (ˈvɒlɪˌbɔːl) n. a game in which two teams hit a large ball back and forth over a high net with their hands.

volt (vəʊlt) n. the derived SI unit of electric potential; the potential difference between two points on a conductor carrying a current of 1 ampere, when the power dissipated between these points is 1 watt. [after Count Alessandro Volta, physicist]

voltage (ˈvəʊltɪdʒ) n. an electromotive force or potential difference expressed in volts.

voltaic (vɒlˈteɪɪk) adj. same as **galvanic** (sense 1).

volte-face (ˈvɒltˈfɑːs) n., pl. **volte-face.** a reversal, as in opinion. [Italian volta turn + faccia face]

voltmeter (ˈvəʊltˌmiːtə) n. an instrument for measuring voltage.

voluble (ˈvɒljʊbˀl) adj. talking easily and at length. [Latin volūbilis turning readily] —**voluˈbility** n. —**ˈvolubly** adv.

volume (ˈvɒljuːm) n. **1.** the magnitude of the three-dimensional space enclosed within or occupied by something. **2.** a large mass or quantity: the volume of protest. **3.** an amount or total: the volume of exports. **4.** fullness of sound. **5.** the control on a radio, television, or record player, for adjusting the intensity of sound. **6.** a bound collection of printed or written pages; book. **7.** any of several books forming part of a series. **8.** a set of issues of a periodical over a specified period. [Latin volūmen a roll]

volumetric (ˌvɒljʊˈmetrɪk) adj. of or using measurement by volume: volumetric analysis.

voluminous (vəˈluːmɪnəs) adj. **1.** (of clothes) large and roomy. **2.** (of writing) consisting of or sufficient to fill volumes.

voluntary (ˈvɒləntrɪ) adj. **1.** done or undertaken by free choice: a voluntary donation. **2.** (of persons) serving without pay: a voluntary social worker. **3.** done by or composed of volunteers: a voluntary association. **4.** exercising or having the faculty of willing: a voluntary agent. **5.** (of muscles) having their action controlled by the will. **6.** maintained by the voluntary actions or contributions of individuals and not by the state: voluntary schools. ~n., pl. **-taries. 7.** Music. a composition, usually for organ, played at the beginning or end of a church service. [Latin voluntārius] —**ˈvoluntarily** adv.

volunteer (ˌvɒlənˈtɪə) n. **1.** a person who performs or offers to perform voluntary service. **2.** a person who freely undertakes military service. ~vb. **3.** to offer (oneself or one's services) by choice and without being forced. **4.** to do, give, or communicate voluntarily: to volunteer help. **5.** to enlist voluntarily for military service.

voluptuary (vəˈlʌptjʊərɪ) n., pl. **-aries.** a person devoted to luxury and sensual pleasures. [Latin voluptās pleasure]

voluptuous (vəˈlʌptjʊəs) adj. **1.** of, characterized by, or consisting of sensual pleasures. **2.** (of a woman) sexually alluring through shapeliness or fullness of body. —**voˈluptuously** adv. —**voˈluptuousness** n.

volute (ˈvɒljuːt, vəˈluːt) n. **1.** a spiral or twisting turn, form, or object. **2.** a carved spiral scroll, esp. on an Ionic capital. **3.** any of the whorls of a snail's spiral shell. [Latin volvere to roll up]

vomit (ˈvɒmɪt) vb. **1.** to eject (the contents of the stomach) through the mouth. **2.** to eject or be ejected forcefully. ~*n.* **3.** the matter ejected in vomiting. [Latin *vomitāre* to vomit repeatedly]

voodoo ('vuːduː) *n.* **1.** Also called: **voodooism.** a religious cult involving witchcraft, common among Blacks in the West Indies. ~*adj.* **2.** relating to or associated with voodoo. ~*vb.* **-dooing,** **-dooed. 3.** to affect by or as if by voodoo. [West African] —'**voodooist** *n.*

voorkamer ('fuə,kɑːmə) *n. S. African.* the front room of a house. [Afrikaans]

voracious (vɒ'reɪʃəs) *adj.* **1.** devouring or craving food in great quantities. **2.** very eager or insatiable in some activity: *voracious reading.* [Latin *vorāre* to devour] —**voracity** (vɒ'ræsɪtɪ) *n.*

vortex ('vɔːtɛks) *n., pl.* **-texes** *or* **-tices** (-tɪ,siːz). **1.** a whirling mass or motion, such as a whirlpool. **2.** any situation viewed as irresistibly engulfing. [Latin: a whirlpool] —**vortical** ('vɔːtɪkˀl) *adj.*

votary ('vəʊtərɪ) *n., pl.* **-ries. 1.** *R.C. Church, Eastern Churches.* a person, such as a monk, who has dedicated himself to religion by taking vows. **2.** a person devoted to a cause. ~Also: **votarist.** [Latin *vōtum* a vow] —'**votaress** *fem. n.*

vote (vəʊt) *n.* **1.** an indication of choice, opinion, or will on a question, such as the choosing of a candidate: *10 votes for Jones.* **2.** the opinion of a group of people as determined by voting: *it was put to the vote.* **3.** a body of votes or voters collectively: *the Jewish vote.* **4.** the total number of votes cast. **5.** the right to vote. **6.** a means of voting, such as a ballot. ~*vb.* **7.** to express (one's preference or will) (for or against a question): *to vote by ballot.* **8.** to declare oneself as being (something or in favour of something) by voting: *to vote socialist.* **9.** to authorize or allow by voting: *vote us a rise.* **10.** *Informal.* to declare by common opinion: *the party was voted a failure.* [Latin *vōtum* a solemn promise]

vote down *vb.* to decide against or defeat in a vote: *the bill was voted down.*

voter ('vəʊtə) *n.* a person who can or does vote.

votive ('vəʊtɪv) *adj.* given, done, or dedicated in fulfilment of a vow. [Latin *vōtīvus* promised by a vow]

vouch (vaʊtʃ) *vb.* **1.** (foll. by *for*) to give personal assurance of: *I'll vouch for his safety.* **2.** (foll. by *for*) to give supporting evidence for or be proof of. [Latin *vocāre* to call]

voucher ('vaʊtʃə) *n.* **1.** a document serving as evidence for a transaction, such as having received or spent money. **2.** *Brit.* a ticket or card serving as a substitute for cash: *a gift voucher.* [Old French *voucher* to summon]

vouchsafe (,vaʊtʃ'seɪf) *vb.* **1.** to give or grant: *she vouchsafed no reply.* **2.** to condescend to agree, promise, or permit: *he vouchsafed to come yesterday.* [*vouch* + *safe*]

vow (vaʊ) *n.* **1.** a solemn and binding promise made esp. to a deity or saint. **2.** **take vows.** to enter a religious order and

commit oneself to its rule of life by the vows of poverty, chastity, and obedience. ~*vb.* **3.** to pledge, promise, or undertake solemnly: *he vowed to return.* **4.** to assert or swear emphatically. [Latin *vōtum* a vow]

vowel ('vaʊəl) *n.* **1.** *Phonetics.* a voiced speech sound made with the mouth open and the stream of breath unobstructed by the tongue, teeth, or lips. **2.** a letter or character representing a vowel. [Latin *vocalis (littera)*, from *vox* voice]

vox pop (vɒks) *n.* interviews with members of the public on a radio or television programme.

vox populi (vɒks 'pɒpjʊ,laɪ) *n.* the voice of the people; public opinion. [Latin]

voyage ('vɔɪdʒ) *n.* **1.** a long journey, esp. one to a distant land or by sea or in space. ~*vb.* **2.** to travel: *we will voyage to Africa.* [Latin *viāticum* provision for travelling] —'**voyager** *n.*

voyageur (,vɔɪə'dʒɜː) *n.* (in Canada) a woodsman, guide, trapper, boatman, or explorer, esp. in the North. [French: voyager]

voyeur (vwɑː'jɜː) *n.* a person who obtains sexual pleasure from watching people undressing or having sexual intercourse. [French, lit.: one who sees] —**vo'yeurism** *n.* —,**voyeur'istic** *adj.*

vrou (frəʊ) *n. S. African.* an Afrikaner woman, esp. a married woman. [Afrikaans]

vs versus.

V-sign *n.* **1.** (in Britain) an offensive gesture made by sticking up the index and middle fingers with the palm of the hand inwards. **2.** a similar gesture with the palm outwards meaning victory or peace.

VSO (in Britain) Voluntary Service Overseas.

VSOP very special (*or* superior) old pale: used of brandy or port.

VT *or* **Vt.** Vermont.

VTOL ('viːtɒl) vertical takeoff and landing.

VTR video tape recorder.

vulcanite ('vʌlkə,naɪt) *n.* a hard black rubber produced by vulcanizing natural rubber with sulphur. It is used for electrical insulators.

vulcanize *or* **-nise** ('vʌlkə,naɪz) *vb.* to treat (rubber) with sulphur under heat and pressure to improve elasticity and strength. [Latin *Vulcan* Roman god of fire] —,**vulcani'zation** *or* **-ni'sation** *n.*

Vulg. Vulgate.

vulgar ('vʌlgə) *adj.* **1.** marked by lack of taste, culture, delicacy, or manners: *vulgar language.* **2.** (*often cap.*) denoting a form of a language, esp. of Latin, current among common people. [Latin *vulgus* the common people] —'**vulgarly** *adv.*

vulgar fraction *n.* same as **simple fraction.**

vulgarian (vʌl'gɛərɪən) *n.* a vulgar person, usually one who is rich.

vulgarism ('vʌlgə,rɪzəm) *n.* a coarse, crude, or obscene expression.

vulgarity (vʌl'gærɪtɪ) *n., pl.* **-ties. 1.** the

condition of being vulgar; lack of good manners. **2.** a vulgar action or phrase.

vulgarize *or* **-rise** ('vʌlgə,raɪz) *vb.* **1.** to make vulgar. **2.** to make (something little known or difficult to understand) popular. —,vulgari'zation *or* -ri'sation *n.*

Vulgar Latin *n.* any of the dialects of Latin spoken in the Roman Empire other than classical Latin.

Vulgate ('vʌlgeɪt, -gɪt) *n.* the fourth-century Latin version of the Bible.

vulnerable ('vʌlnərəbᵊl) *adj.* **1.** able to be physically or emotionally hurt. **2.** open to temptation or censure. **3.** *Mil.* exposed to attack. **4.** *Bridge.* (of a side who have won one game towards rubber) subject to increased bonuses or penalties. [Latin *vulnus* a wound] —,vulnera'bility *n.*

vulpine ('vʌlpaɪn) *adj.* **1.** of or like a fox. **2.** clever and cunning. [Latin *vulpēs* fox]

vulture ('vʌltʃə) *n.* **1.** a very large bird of prey that feeds on carrion. **2.** a person or thing that preys greedily and ruthlessly on others. [Latin *vultur*]

vulva ('vʌlvə) *n.* the external genitals of human females. [Latin: covering, womb, matrix]

vv vice versa.

W

w *or* **W** (ˈdʌbˌljuː) *n., pl.* **w's, W's,** *or* **Ws.** the 23rd letter of the English alphabet.

W **1.** *Chem.* tungsten. [German *Wolfram*] **2.** watt. **3.** West. **4.** *Physics.* work.

w. **1.** week. **2.** weight. **3.** *Cricket.* wicket. **4.** wide. **5.** wife. **6.** with.

WA **1.** Washington (state). **2.** Western Australia.

wacky (ˈwækɪ) *adj.* **wackier, wackiest.** *Slang.* eccentric, funny, or exciting: *a wacky new comedy.* [dialect: a fool]

wad (wɒd) *n.* **1.** a small mass or ball of soft material, such as cotton wool, used for packing or stuffing. **2.** a roll or bundle of something, esp. of banknotes. ~*vb.* **wadding, wadded.** **3.** to make (something) into a wad. **4.** to pack or stuff (something) with wadding. [Late Latin *wadda*]

wadding (ˈwɒdɪŋ) *n.* a soft material used for padding or stuffing.

waddle (ˈwɒdˀl) *vb.* **1.** to walk with short steps, rocking slightly from side to side. ~*n.* **2.** a swaying gait or motion. [from *wade*]

wade (weɪd) *vb.* **1.** to walk slowly and with difficulty through something such as water or mud. **2. wade through.** to proceed with difficulty: *to wade through a book.* **3. wade in** *or* **into.** to begin doing something in an energetic way. ~*n.* **4.** the act or an instance of wading. [Old English *wadan*]

wader (ˈweɪdə) *n.* a long-legged bird, such as the heron or stork, that lives near water and feeds on fish. Also called: **wading bird.**

waders (ˈweɪdəz) *pl. n.* long waterproof boots worn by anglers.

wadi *or* **wady** (ˈwɒdɪ) *n., pl.* **-dies.** a watercourse in N Africa and Arabia, which is dry except in the rainy season. [Arabic]

wafer (ˈweɪfə) *n.* **1.** a thin crisp sweetened biscuit, often served with ice cream. **2.** *Christianity.* a thin disc of unleavened bread used at Communion. **3.** *Electronics.* a small thin slice of semiconductor material, such as silicon, that is separated into numerous individual components or circuits. **4.** a small disc of sticky paper used as a seal on letters or documents. [Old French *waufre*]

waffle¹ (ˈwɒfˀl) *Informal, chiefly Brit.* ~*vb.* **1.** (often foll. by *on*) to speak or write in a vague and wordy manner. ~*n.* **2.** vague and wordy speech or writing. [origin unknown]

waffle² (ˈwɒfˀl) *n.* a square crisp pancake with deep hollows on both sides, forming a grid-like pattern. [Dutch *wafel*]

waft (wɑːft, wɒft) *vb.* **1.** to carry or be carried gently on or as if on the air or water: *the smell of her perfume wafted across the room.* ~*n.* **2.** something, such as a scent, carried on the air. [Middle Dutch *wachter* guard]

wag¹ (wæg) *vb.* **wagging, wagged.** **1.** to move rapidly and repeatedly from side to side or up and down. ~*n.* **2.** the act or an instance of wagging. [Old English *wagian*]

wag² (wæg) *n.* a humorous or jocular person; wit. [origin unknown]

wage (weɪdʒ) *n.* **1.** (*often pl.*) the money paid in return for a person's work, esp. when paid weekly or daily rather than as a monthly salary: *I get my wages on Thursday; less than the legal minimum wage.* **2.** (*pl., sometimes functioning as sing.*) recompense or return: *the wages of sin is death.* ~*vb.* **3.** to engage in (an activity). [Old French *wagier* to pledge]

wager (ˈweɪdʒə) *n.* **1.** a bet on the outcome of an event or activity. ~*vb.* **2.** to bet (something, esp. money) on the outcome of an event or activity. [Old French *wagier* to pledge]

waggle (ˈwægˀl) *vb.* to move with a rapid shaking or wobbling motion. [from WAG¹] —ˈwaggly *adj.*

Wagnerian (vɑːɡˈnɪərɪən) *adj.* of or suggestive of the operas of Richard Wagner, German composer.

wagon *or* **waggon** (ˈwægən) *n.* **1.** a four-wheeled vehicle used for carrying heavy loads, esp. a trailer drawn by a horse or tractor. **2.** *Brit.* an open railway freight truck. **3. on** (*or* **off**) **the wagon.** *Informal.* abstaining (*or* no longer abstaining) from alcoholic drinks. [Dutch *wagen*] —ˈwagoner *or* ˈwaggoner *n.*

wagtail (ˈwægˌteɪl) *n.* a small songbird of Eurasia and Africa with a very long tail that wags up and down when the bird walks.

wahine (wɑːˈhiːnɪ) *n.* *N.Z.* a Maori woman. [Maori]

waif (weɪf) *n.* **1.** a person, esp. a child, who is homeless, friendless, or neglected. **2.** anything found and apparently without an owner. [Anglo-Norman] —ˈwaifˌlike *adj.*

wail (weɪl) *vb.* **1.** to utter a prolonged high-pitched cry, as of grief or misery. **2.** to make a sound resembling such a cry: *the wind wailed in the trees.* ~*n.* **3.** a prolonged high-pitched mournful cry or sound. [from Old Norse]

wain (weɪn) *n.* *Chiefly poetic.* a farm cart. [Old English *wægn*]

wainscot (ˈweɪnskət) *n.* a wooden covering on the lower half of the walls of a room. Also called: **wainscoting** *or* **wainscotting.** [Middle Low German *wagenschot*]

waist (weɪst) *n.* **1.** *Anat.* the part of the body between the ribs and hips. **2.** the part of a garment covering the waist. **3.** the middle part of something, such as a violin, that resembles the waist in narrowness or position. [origin unknown]

waistband (ˈweɪstˌbænd) *n.* a band of

material sewn on to the waist of a garment to strengthen it.

waistcoat ('weɪs,kəʊt) n. a sleeveless waistlength garment which buttons up the front and is usually worn by men over a shirt and under a jacket.

waistline ('weɪst,laɪn) n. 1. an imaginary line around the body at the narrowest part of the waist. 2. the place where the upper and lower part of a garment are joined together.

wait (weɪt) vb. 1. (often foll. by for, until, or to) to stay in one place or remain inactive in expectation (of something). 2. to delay temporarily or be temporarily delayed: that work can wait. 3. (usually foll. by for) (of things) to be ready; be in store (for a person): supper was waiting for them when they got home. 4. to act as a waiter or waitress. ~n. 5. the act or a period of waiting. 6. **lie in wait.** to prepare an ambush (for someone). ~See also **wait on, wait up.** [Old French waitier]

waiter ('weɪtə) n. a man who serves people with food and drink in a restaurant.

waiting game n. the postponement of action or decision in order to gain the advantage.

waiting list n. a list of people waiting for something that is not immediately available.

waiting room n. a room in which people may wait, as at a railway station or doctor's surgery.

wait on vb. 1. to serve at the table of. 2. to act as an attendant to. ~interj. 3. N.Z. stop! hold on! ~Also (for senses 1, 2): **wait upon.**

waitress ('weɪtrɪs) n. a woman who serves people with food and drink in a restaurant.

wait up vb. to delay going to bed in order to await some event.

waive (weɪv) vb. 1. to give up; relinquish: to waive one's right to something. 2. to refrain from enforcing or applying (a law or penalty). [Old French weyver]

waiver ('weɪvə) n. the voluntary giving up of some claim or right.

wake[1] (weɪk) vb. **waking, woke, woken.** 1. (often foll. by up) to rouse or become roused from sleep. 2. (often foll. by up) to rouse or become roused from inactivity. 3. (often foll. by to or up to) to become conscious or aware: at last he woke up to the situation. 4. **waking hours.** the time when a person is awake: she spends most of her waking hours working. ~n. 5. a watch or vigil held over the body of a dead person during the night before burial. 6. **Wakes.** an annual holiday in various towns in Northern England. [Old English wacian]

wake[2] (weɪk) n. 1. the track left by a ship moving through water. 2. **in the wake of.** following close behind: wrecked houses in the wake of the hurricane. [Scandinavian]

wakeful ('weɪkfʊl) adj. 1. unable or unwilling to sleep. 2. sleepless. 3. alert. —**wakefully** adv. —**wakefulness** n.

waken ('weɪkən) vb. to rouse or be roused from sleep or some other inactive state.

wale (weɪl) n. 1. same as **weal**[1]. 2. the weave or texture of a fabric, such as the ribs in corduroy. 3. Naut. a ridge of planking along the rail of a ship. [Old English walu]

walk (wɔːk) vb. 1. to move on foot at a moderate rate with at least one foot always on the ground. 2. to pass through, on, or over on foot. 3. to escort or accompany (a person or animal) by walking: to walk someone home; I must walk the dog. 4. to follow a certain course or way of life: to walk in misery. 5. to bring into a certain condition by walking: I walked my shoes to shreds. 6. to disappear or be stolen: where's my pencil?, it seems to have walked. 7. **walk it.** to win easily. 8. **walk on air.** to be delighted or exhilarated. 9. **walk the streets.** to wander about, esp. when looking for work or when homeless. ~n. 10. the act or an instance of walking. 11. the distance walked. 12. a manner of walking; gait. 13. a place or route for walking. 14. social position or profession: the committee come from many different walks of life. ~See also **walk into, walk out,** etc. [Old English wealcan] —'**walkable** adj.

walkabout ('wɔːkə,baʊt) n. an occasion when celebrities, royalty, or politicians walk among and meet the public.

walker ('wɔːkə) n. 1. a person who walks. 2. Also called: **baby walker.** a tubular frame on wheels or casters to support a baby learning to walk. 3. a similar support used by disabled or infirm people for walking.

walkie-talkie (,wɔːkɪ'tɔːkɪ) n., pl. **-talkies.** a small combined radio transmitter and receiver that can be carried around by one person.

walking stick n. a stick or cane carried in the hand to assist walking.

walk into vb. to meet with unwittingly: he had walked into their trap.

Walkman ('wɔːkmən) n., pl. **-mans.** Trademark. a small portable cassette player with headphones.

walk-on n. a small part in a play or film, esp. one without any lines.

walk out vb. 1. to leave without explanation, esp. in anger. 2. (of workers) to go on strike. 3. **walk out on.** Informal. to abandon or desert someone. ~n. **walkout.** 4. a strike by workers. 5. the act of leaving a meeting as a protest.

walkover ('wɔːk,əʊvə) n. 1. Informal. an easy or unopposed victory. ~vb. **walk over.** 2. to win easily or without being opposed.

walkway ('wɔːk,weɪ) n. 1. a path designed for pedestrian use. 2. a passage or pathway between two buildings.

wall (wɔːl) n. 1. a vertical structure made of stone, brick, or wood with a length and height much greater than its thickness, used to enclose, divide, or support. 2. (often pl.) a fortification built around a position or place for defensive purposes. 3. anything that suggests a wall in function or effect: a wall of fire. 4. Anat. any lining or membrane that encloses a bodily cavity or structure: abdominal wall. 5. **go to the**

wall. *Informal.* to be ruined, esp. financially. **6. go** (*or* **drive**) **up the wall.** *Slang.* to become (*or* cause to become) crazy or furious. **7. have one's back to the wall.** to be in a very difficult situation. ~*vb.* **8.** to protect, provide, or confine with or as if with a wall. **9.** (often foll. by *up*) to block (an opening) with a wall. **10.** (often foll. by *in* or *up*) to seal by or within a wall or walls. [Old English *weall*] —**walled** *adj.*

wallaby ('wɒləbɪ) *n., pl.* -**bies** *or* -**by.** a plant-eating marsupial of Australia and New Guinea, similar to but smaller than a kangaroo. [Aboriginal]

wallah ('wɒlə) *n. Informal.* a person involved with or in charge of a (specified thing): *the book wallah.* [Hindi -*wālā*]

wall bars *pl. n.* a series of horizontal bars attached to a wall and used in gymnastics.

wallet ('wɒlɪt) *n.* a small folding case, usually of leather, for holding paper money or other things, such as credit cards. [Germanic]

walleyed ('wɔːl,aɪd) *adj.* having eyes with an abnormal amount of white showing because of a divergent squint. [Old Norse *vagleygr*]

wallflower ('wɔːl,flaʊə) *n.* **1.** a plant grown for its clusters of yellow, orange, brown, red, or purple fragrant flowers. **2.** *Informal.* a woman who stays on the fringes of a dance or party because she is shy or does not have a partner.

Walloon (wɒ'luːn) *n.* **1.** a member of a French-speaking people living chiefly in S Belgium and adjacent parts of France. **2.** the French dialect of Belgium. ~*adj.* **3.** of the Walloons or their dialect. [Germanic]

wallop ('wɒləp) *Informal.* ~*vb.* **1.** to hit (someone or something) hard. **2.** to defeat (a person or team) utterly. ~*n.* **3.** a hard blow. [Old French *waloper* to gallop]

walloping ('wɒləpɪŋ) *Informal.* ~*n.* **1.** a thrashing. ~*adj.* **2.** large or great: *a walloping drop in sales.*

wallow ('wɒləʊ) *vb.* **1.** to indulge oneself in some emotion: *to wallow in self-pity.* **2.** (esp. of certain animals) to roll about in mud or water for pleasure. **3.** (of a ship) to roll from side to side and move forward with difficulty. ~*n.* **4.** the act or an instance of wallowing. **5.** a muddy place where animals wallow. [Old English *wealwian*]

wallpaper ('wɔːl,peɪpə) *n.* **1.** a printed or embossed paper for covering walls and ceilings. ~*vb.* **2.** to cover (a surface) with wallpaper.

Wall Street *n.* a street in lower Manhattan, New York, where the Stock Exchange and major banks are situated: regarded as the place where the most important financial business is conducted.

wall-to-wall *adj.* (esp. of carpeting) completely covering a floor.

wally ('wɒlɪ) *n., pl.* -**lies.** *Slang.* a stupid person. [from the name *Walter*]

walnut ('wɔːl,nʌt) *n.* **1.** a two-lobed edible nut with a hard wrinkled shell. **2.** any of various trees on which this nut grows. **3.** the yellowish-brown wood of any of these

trees, used for making furniture. [Old English *walh-hnutu* foreign nut]

walrus ('wɔːlrəs, 'wɒl-) *n., pl.* -**ruses** *or* -**rus.** a mammal of northern seas, having two tusks that project from the upper jaw, tough thick skin, and coarse whiskers. [Dutch: whale horse]

waltz (wɔːls) *n.* **1.** a ballroom dance in triple time in which couples spin around as they progress round the room. **2.** music for this dance. ~*vb.* **3.** to dance a waltz. **4.** to move in a relaxed and confident way. **5.** *Informal.* to succeed easily. [German *Walzer*]

wampum ('wɒmpəm) *n.* (formerly) money used by North American Indians, made of shells strung or woven together. [American Indian]

wan (wɒn) *adj.* **wanner, wannest.** unnaturally pale as a result of sickness, grief, or unhappiness. [Old English *wann* dark] —**'wanly** *adv.*

wand (wɒnd) *n.* **1.** a rod used by a magician when performing a trick or by a fairy when casting a spell. **2.** a thin rod carried as a symbol of authority. **3.** a conductor's baton. [Old Norse *vöndr*]

wander ('wɒndə) *vb.* **1.** to move or travel about, in, or through (a place) without any definite purpose or destination. **2.** to proceed in an irregular course; meander. **3.** to go astray, as from a path or course. **4.** (of the mind) to lose concentration. ~*n.* **5.** the act or an instance of wandering. [Old English *wandrian*] —**'wanderer** *n.* —**'wandering** *adj., n.*

wandering Jew *n.* any of several creeping or trailing houseplants.

wanderlust ('wɒndə,lʌst) *n.* a great desire to travel.

wane (weɪn) *vb.* **1.** to decrease gradually in size, strength, or power. **2.** (of the moon) to show a gradually decreasing portion of illuminated surface, between full moon and new moon. ~*n.* **3.** a decrease, as in size, strength, or power. **4.** the period during which the moon wanes. **5. on the wane.** in a state of decline. [Old English *wanian*] —**'waney** *or* **'wany** *adj.*

wangle ('wæŋg'l) *vb. Informal.* to use devious methods to get or achieve (something): *he wangled himself a salary increase.* [origin unknown]

wanigan ('wɒnɪgən) *n. Canad.* **1.** a lumberjack's chest or box. **2.** a cabin or houseboat. [American Indian]

wank (wæŋk) *Taboo slang.* ~*vb.* **1.** (of a man) to masturbate. ~*n.* **2.** an act of masturbating. [origin unknown]

want (wɒnt) *vb.* **1.** to feel a need or longing for: *I want a new hat.* **2.** to wish, need, or desire (something or to do something): *he wants to go home.* **3.** (often foll. by *for*) to be lacking or deficient (in something necessary or desirable): *the child wants for nothing.* **4.** *Chiefly Brit.* to have need of or require (doing or being something): *your shoes want cleaning.* **5.** to be destitute. **6.** to request the presence of: *you're wanted upstairs.* **7.** *Informal.* should or ought (to do something): *you* *don't want to go out so late.* ~*n.* **8.** the act or an instance of wanting. **9.** anything that is needed, desired, or lacked: *to supply someone's wants.* **10.** a lack, shortage, or absence: *for want of common sense.* **11.** the state of being in need: *the state should help those in want.* [Old Norse *vanta* to be deficient]

wanting ('wɒntɪŋ) *adj.* **1.** lacking or absent. **2.** not meeting requirements or expectations: *you have been found wanting.*

wanton ('wɒntən) *adj.* **1.** licentious or immoral. **2.** without motive, provocation, or justification: *wanton destruction.* **3.** maliciously and unnecessarily cruel. **4.** unrestrained: *wanton spending.* **5.** *Archaic or poetic.* playful or capricious. ~*n.* **6.** a licentious person, esp. a woman. ~*vb.* **7.** to behave in a wanton manner. [Middle English *wantowen* unruly]

wapiti ('wɒpɪtɪ) *n.*, *pl.* **-tis.** a large North American deer, now also found in New Zealand. [American Indian]

war (wɔː) *n.* **1.** open armed conflict between two or more parties, nations, or states. **2.** a particular armed conflict: *the Vietnam war.* **3.** the techniques of armed conflict as a study, science, or profession. **4.** any conflict or contest: *the war against crime.* **5.** (*modifier*) of, like, or caused by war: *war damage; a war story.* **6.** **have been in the wars.** *Informal.* to look as if one has been in a fight. ~*vb.* **warring, warred.** **7.** to conduct a war. [Old Northern French *werre*]

War. Warwickshire.

warble ('wɔːb'l) *vb.* **1.** to sing (words or songs) in a high-pitched voice, often with trills and vibrations. ~*n.* **2.** the act or an instance of warbling. [Old French *werbler*]

warbler ('wɔːblə) *n.* any of various small songbirds.

war crime *n.* a crime committed in wartime in violation of the accepted customs, such as ill-treatment of prisoners. —**war criminal** *n.*

war cry *n.* **1.** a rallying cry used by combatants in battle. **2.** a cry or slogan used to rally support for a cause.

ward (wɔːd) *n.* **1.** a room in a hospital for patients requiring similar kinds of care: *a maternity ward.* **2.** one of the districts into which a town, parish, or other area is divided for administration or elections. **3.** *Law.* Also called: **ward of court.** a person, esp. a child or one legally incapable of managing his own affairs, placed under the control or protection of a guardian or of a court. **4.** an internal ridge or notch in a lock that prevents an incorrectly cut key from turning. ~See also **ward off.** [Old English *weard* protector] —'**wardship** *n.*

-ward *suffix.* **1.** (*forming adjectives*) indicating direction towards: *a backward step.* **2.** (*forming adverbs*) a variant and the usual U.S. and Canad. form of **-wards.** [Old English *-weard*]

warden ('wɔːd'n) *n.* **1.** a person who is in charge of a building and its occupants: *a youth hostel warden.* **2.** a public official, esp. one responsible for the enforcement of certain regulations: *a traffic warden.* **3.**

Chiefly U.S. & Canad. the chief officer in charge of a prison. [Old French *wardein*]

warder ('wɔːdə) or (*fem.*) **wardress** *n. Chiefly Brit.* a prison officer. [Old French *warder* to guard]

ward off *vb.* to avert (something, such as danger or illness): *to ward off a punch; to ward off evil.*

wardrobe ('wɔːdrəʊb) *n.* **1.** a tall cupboard, with a rail or hooks on which to hang clothes. **2.** the total collection of articles of clothing belonging to one person. **3.** the collection of costumes belonging to a theatre or theatrical company. [Old French *warder* to guard + *robe* robe]

wardroom ('wɔːd,ruːm, -,rʊm) *n.* the quarters assigned to the officers (except the captain) of a warship.

-wards or **-ward** *suffix forming adverbs.* indicating direction towards: *a step backwards.* [Old English *-weardes*]

ware (wɛə) *n.* articles of the same kind or material: *silverware.* See also **wares.** [Old English *waru*]

warehouse *n.* ('wɛə,haʊs). **1.** a place where goods are stored prior to their sale or distribution. **2.** *Chiefly Brit.* a large commercial, esp. wholesale, establishment. ~*vb.* ('wɛə,haʊz, -,haʊs). **3.** to store or place in a warehouse.

wares (wɛəz) *pl. n.* **1.** articles of manufacture considered as being for sale. **2.** any talent or asset regarded as a saleable commodity.

warfare ('wɔː,fɛə) *n.* **1.** the act of waging war. **2.** a violent conflict of any kind.

war game *n.* **1.** a notional tactical exercise for training military commanders, in which no military units are actually deployed. **2.** a game in which model soldiers are used to create battles, esp. past battles, in order to study tactics.

warhead ('wɔː,hɛd) *n.* the front section of a missile or projectile that contains explosives.

warhorse ('wɔː,hɔːs) *n.* **1.** a horse used in battle. **2.** *Informal.* a veteran soldier or politician.

warlike ('wɔː,laɪk) *adj.* **1.** of, relating to, or used in war. **2.** hostile or belligerent.

warlock ('wɔː,lɒk) *n.* a man who practises black magic. [Old English *wǣrloga* oath breaker]

warm (wɔːm) *adj.* **1.** characterized by or having a moderate degree of heat. **2.** maintaining or imparting heat: *a warm coat.* **3.** kindly or affectionate: *a warm personality.* **4.** lively or passionate: *a warm debate.* **5.** cordial or enthusiastic: *warm support.* **6.** (of colours) predominantly red or yellow in tone. **7.** (of a scent trail) recently made. **8.** near to finding a hidden object or guessing facts, as in children's games. **9.** *Informal.* uncomfortable or disagreeable: *I'll make things warm for her.* ~*vb.* **10.** (sometimes foll. by *up*) to make or become warm or warmer. **11.** (often foll. by *to*) to make or become excited or passionate (about): *he warmed to the idea of buying a new car.* **12.** (often foll. by *to*) to feel affection or kindness (for

someone): *I warmed to her from the start.*
~*n. Informal.* **13.** a warm place or area:
come into the warm. **14.** the act or an
instance of warming or being warmed.
~See also **warm up.** [Old English *wearm*]
—**'warmly** *adv.* —**'warmness** *n.*

warm-blooded *adj.* **1.** ardent, impetuous, or passionate. **2.** *Zool.* (of mammals
and birds) having a constant body temperature, usually higher than the surrounding temperature. —**,warm-'bloodedness** *n.*

war memorial *n.* a monument to those
who die in a war, esp. those from a
particular locality.

warm front *n. Meteorol.* the boundary
between a warm air mass and the cold air
it is replacing.

warm-hearted *adj.* kind, affectionate, or
sympathetic. —**,warm-'heartedly** *adv.*
—**,warm-'heartedness** *n.*

warming pan *n.* a long-handled pan,
filled with hot coals and formerly drawn
over the sheets to warm a bed.

warmonger ('wɔː,mʌŋgə) *n.* a person who
fosters warlike ideas or advocates war.
—**'war,mongering** *n.*

warmth (wɔːmθ) *n.* **1.** the state, quality, or
sensation of being warm. **2.** intensity of
emotion: *he denied the accusation with
some warmth.* **3.** affection or cordiality.

warm up *vb.* **1.** to make or become warm
or warmer. **2.** to prepare for a race,
sporting contest, or exercise routine by
doing gentle exercises immediately beforehand. **3.** to run (an engine or machine) until
the working temperature is reached or (of
an engine or machine) to undergo this
process. **4.** to make or become more lively:
the party warmed up when Tom came. **5.**
to reheat (already cooked food) or (of such
food) to be reheated. ~*n.* **warm-up.** **6.**
the act or an instance of warming up. **7.** a
preparatory exercise routine.

warn (wɔːn) *vb.* **1.** to notify or make
(someone) aware of danger or harm. **2.** to
advise or caution (someone) about his behaviour: *I'm warning you, don't do that
again.* **3.** to inform (someone) in advance:
he warned them that he would arrive late.
4. (usually foll. by *away* or *off*) to tell to go
away or be off. [Old English *wearnian*]

warning ('wɔːnɪŋ) *n.* **1.** a hint, threat, or
advance notice of harm or danger. **2.**
advice not to do something. ~*adj.* **3.**
intended or serving to warn: *a warning
look.*

warp (wɔːp) *vb.* **1.** to twist out of shape,
as from heat or damp. **2.** to turn from a
true, correct, or proper course. **3.** *Naut.* to
move (a vessel) by hauling on a rope fixed
to a stationary object ashore or (of a
vessel) to be moved thus. ~*n.* **4.** the state
of being twisted out of shape. **5.** a twist,
distortion, or bias. **6.** a mental or moral
deviation. **7.** the yarns arranged lengthways on a loom through which the weft
yarns are woven. **8.** *Naut.* a rope used for
warping a vessel. [Old English *wearp* a
throw] —**warped** *adj.*

war paint *n.* **1.** paint applied to the face
and body by certain North American In-

dians before battle. **2.** *Informal.* cosmetics.

warpath ('wɔː,pɑːθ) *n.* **on the warpath. a.**
preparing to engage in battle. **b.** *Informal.*
in a state of anger.

warrant ('wɒrənt) *n.* **1.** an official
authorization. **2.** a document that certifies
or guarantees, such as a receipt or licence.
3. *Law.* an official document issued by a
magistrate that grants the police permission to search premises or arrest someone.
4. (in certain armed services) the official
authority for the appointment of warrant
officers. ~*vb.* **5.** to guarantee the quality
or condition of (something). **6.** to give
authority or power to. **7.** to attest to the
character or worthiness of. **8.** to guarantee (a purchaser of merchandise) against
loss of, damage to, or misrepresentation
concerning the merchandise. **9.** to declare
confidently. [Old French *guarant*] —**'war-
rantable** *adj.*

warrant officer *n.* an officer in certain
armed services with a rank between those
of commissioned and noncommissioned officers.

Warrant of Fitness *n. N.Z.* a six-monthly
certificate required for a motor vehicle
certifying that it is mechanically sound.

warrantor ('wɒrən,tɔː) *n.* an individual or
company that provides a warrant.

warranty ('wɒrəntɪ) *n., pl.* **-ties.** a guarantee or assurance that goods meet a specified standard or that the facts in a legal
document are as stated. [Anglo-French
warantie]

warren ('wɒrən) *n.* **1.** a series of interconnected underground tunnels in which rabbits live. **2.** an overcrowded building or
area of a city. [Anglo-French *warenne*]

warrior ('wɒrɪə) *n.* a person engaged in,
experienced in, or devoted to war. [Old
French *werreieor*]

warship ('wɔː,ʃɪp) *n.* a ship designed for
naval warfare.

wart (wɔːt) *n.* **1.** *Pathol.* a firm abnormal
growth on the skin caused by a virus. **2.**
Bot. a small rounded outgrowth. **3. warts
and all.** with all blemishes evident. [Old
English *weart(e)*] —**'warty** *adj.*

wart hog *n.* a wild African pig with
heavy tusks, wartlike-lumps on the face,
and a mane of coarse hair.

wartime ('wɔː,taɪm) *n.* a time of war.

wary ('wεərɪ) *adj.* **warier, wariest. 1.**
watchful or cautious. **2.** characterized by
caution or watchfulness. [Old English *wær*
to beware] —**'warily** *adv.* —**'wariness** *n.*

was (wɒz; *unstressed* wəz) *vb.* (used with *I,
he, she, it,* and with singular nouns) the
past tense of **be.** [Old English *wæs*]

wash (wɒʃ) *vb.* **1.** to apply water, usually
with soap, to (oneself, a person, or a thing)
in order to cleanse. **2.** (often foll. by *away,
from, off,* etc.) to remove by the application of water and usually soap: *she washed
the dirt from her clothes.* **3.** (of dye or a
fabric) to be capable of being washed
without damage or loss of colour. **4.** (of an
animal such as a cat) to cleanse (itself or
another animal) by licking. **5.** to make

pure. **6.** to make wet or moist. **7.** (often foll. by *away*) to move or be moved by water: *the flood washed away the bridge.* **8.** (esp. of waves) to flow or sweep against or over (a surface or object), often with a lapping sound. **9.** to form by erosion or be eroded: *the stream washed a ravine in the hill.* **10.** to apply a thin coating of paint or metal to (a surface). **11.** to separate (ore) from (gravel or earth) by immersion in water. **12.** *Informal, chiefly Brit.* to be believable or acceptable when tested or scrutinized: *your excuses won't wash with me.* ~*n.* **13.** the act or process of washing. **14.** a quantity of articles washed together. **15.** a preparation or liquid used as a coating or in washing: *a thin wash of paint.* **16.** land that is habitually washed by tidal or river waters. **17.** the disturbance in the air or water produced at the rear of an aircraft, boat, or other moving object. **18.** liquid refuse fed to pigs. **19. come out in the wash.** *Informal.* to become known or apparent in the course of time. ~See also **wash down, wash out, wash up.** [Old English *wæscan, waxan*] —**'washable** *adj.*

washbasin ('wɒʃ,beɪs'n) *n.* **1.** a basin or bowl for washing the face and hands. **2.** Also called: **wash-hand basin.** a bathroom fixture with taps, used for washing the face and hands.

wash down *vb.* **1.** to wash from top to bottom. **2.** to take drink with or after (food or another drink).

washed out *adj.* **1.** faded or colourless. **2.** pale through exhaustion.

washed up *adj. Informal, chiefly U.S., Canad., & N.Z.* no longer hopeful; finished: *our hopes for the new deal are all washed up.*

washer ('wɒʃə) *n.* a flat ring of rubber, felt, or metal used to provide a seal under a nut or bolt or in a tap or valve.

washerwoman ('wɒʃə,wumən) *n., pl.* **-women.** a woman who washes clothes for a living.

washing ('wɒʃɪŋ) *n.* articles that have been or are to be washed together on a single occasion.

washing machine *n.* a machine, usually powered by electricity, for washing clothes or linen.

washing soda *n.* crystalline sodium carbonate, esp. when used as a cleansing agent.

washing-up *n. Brit.* **1.** the washing of dishes and cutlery after a meal. **2.** dishes and cutlery waiting to be washed up.

wash out *vb.* **1.** to wash (the inside of something) so as to remove (dirt). **2.** Also: **wash off.** to remove or be removed by washing: *grass stains don't wash out easily.* ~*n.* **washout. 3.** *Informal.* a total failure or disaster.

washroom ('wɒʃ,ruːm, -,rum) *n. U.S. & Canad.* a toilet.

washstand ('wɒʃ,stænd) *n.* a piece of furniture designed to hold a basin for washing the face and hands.

wash up *vb.* **1.** *Chiefly Brit.* to wash (dishes and cutlery) after a meal. **2.** *U.S. & Canad.* to wash one's face and hands.

washy ('wɒʃɪ) *adj.* **washier, washiest. 1.** over-diluted or weak. **2.** lacking intensity or strength.

wasn't ('wɒz'nt) was not.

wasp (wɒsp) *n.* a common stinging insect with a smooth slender black-and-yellow body. [Old English]

Wasp or **WASP** (wɒsp) *n. U.S. & Canad., usually offensive.* a White Anglo-Saxon Protestant.

waspish ('wɒspɪʃ) *adj.* easily annoyed or angered.

wasp waist *n.* a very slender waist. —**'wasp-,waisted** *adj.*

wassail ('wɒseɪl) *n.* **1.** (formerly) a toast made to a person at festivities. **2.** a festivity when much drinking takes place. ~*vb.* **3.** to drink the health of (a person) at a wassail. [Old Norse *ves heill* be in good health]

wastage ('weɪstɪdʒ) *n.* **1.** anything lost by wear or waste. **2.** the process of wasting. **3. natural wastage.** reduction in size of a workforce by not filling vacancies.

waste (weɪst) *vb.* **1.** to use, consume, or expend thoughtlessly, carelessly, or to no avail. **2.** to fail to take advantage of: *to waste an opportunity.* **3.** (often foll. by *away*) to lose or cause to lose bodily strength or health. **4.** to exhaust or become exhausted. ~*n.* **5.** the act of wasting or state of being wasted. **6.** a failure to take advantage of something. **7.** anything unused or not used to full advantage. **8.** anything or anyone rejected as useless, worthless, or in excess of what is required. **9.** garbage, rubbish, or trash. **10.** (*pl.*) a land or region that is wild or uncultivated. **11.** *Physiol.* matter excreted from the body, as faeces or urine. ~*adj.* **12.** rejected as useless, unwanted, or worthless. **13.** produced in excess of what is required. **14.** not cultivated, inhabited, or productive: *waste land.* **15.** *Physiol.* excreted from the body as faeces or urine. **16. lay waste.** to devastate or destroy. [Latin *vastāre* to lay waste]

wasteful ('weɪstfʊl) *adj.* tending to waste or squander. —**'wastefully** *adv.*

wasteland ('weɪst,lænd) *n.* **1.** a barren or desolate area of land. **2.** a place or time that is considered spiritually, intellectually, or aesthetically barren.

wastepaper ('weɪst,peɪpə) *n.* paper discarded after use.

waster ('weɪstə) *n.* a ne'er-do-well or wastrel.

wasting ('weɪstɪŋ) *adj.* reducing the vitality and strength of the body: *a wasting disease.*

wastrel ('weɪstrəl) *n.* **1.** a wasteful person; spendthrift; prodigal. **2.** an idler or vagabond.

watap (wæ'tɑːp, wɑː-) *n.* a stringy thread made by North American Indians from the roots of conifers. [American Indian]

watch (wɒtʃ) *vb.* **1.** to look at or observe closely or attentively. **2.** (foll. by *for*) to wait attentively. **3.** to guard or tend (something) closely or carefully. **4.** to keep vigil. **5.** to maintain an interest in: *to watch the progress of a child at school.* **6. watch it!** be careful! ~*n.* **7.** a small portable timepiece, usually worn strapped to the wrist (a **wristwatch**) or in a waistcoat pocket. **8.** a watching. **9.** a period of vigil, esp. during the night. **10.** *Naut.* **a.** any of the periods, usually of four hours, during which part of a ship's crew are on duty. **b.** those officers and crew on duty during a specified watch. **11. on the watch.** on the lookout. ~See also **watch out.** [Old English *wæccan*] —'**watcher** *n.*

watchdog ('wɒtʃ,dɒg) *n.* **1.** a dog kept to guard property. **2.** a person or group that acts as a guard against inefficiency or illegality.

watchful ('wɒtʃful) *adj.* vigilant or alert. —'**watchfully** *adv.* —'**watchfulness** *n.*

watchmaker ('wɒtʃ,meɪkə) *n.* a person who makes or mends watches and clocks. —'**watch,making** *n.*

watchman ('wɒtʃmən) *n., pl.* **-men.** a person employed to guard buildings or property.

watch-night service *n.* (in Protestant churches) a service held on the night of December 31, to mark the passing of the old year.

watch out *vb.* to be careful or on one's guard.

watchstrap ('wɒtʃ,stræp) *n.* a strap attached to a watch for fastening it around the wrist. Also called (U.S. and Canad.): **watchband.**

watchtower ('wɒtʃ,taʊə) *n.* a tower on which a sentry keeps watch.

watchword ('wɒtʃ,wɜːd) *n.* **1.** a password. **2.** a rallying cry or slogan.

water ('wɔːtə) *n.* **1.** a clear colourless tasteless liquid that is essential for plant and animal life that falls as rain and forms oceans, rivers, and lakes. **2. a.** any body or area of this liquid, such as a sea, lake, river, etc. **b.** (*as modifier*): *water sports; a water plant.* **3.** the surface of such a body or area: *fish swam below the water.* **4.** any form of this liquid, such as rain. **5.** the level of the tide: *high water.* **6.** a solution of a chemical substance in water: *ammonia water.* **7.** *Physiol.* **a.** any fluid secreted from the body, such as sweat, urine, or tears. **b.** (*usually pl.*) the fluid surrounding a fetus in the womb. **8.** *Archaic.* the degree of brilliance in a diamond. **9. hold water.** to prove credible, logical, or consistent: *his alibi did not hold water.* **10. make** *or* **pass water.** to urinate. **11. of the first water.** of the highest quality or the most extreme degree: *she's a fool of the first water.* **12. water under the bridge.** events that are past and done with. ~*vb.* **13.** to sprinkle, moisten, or soak with water. **14.** (often foll. by *down*) to dilute. **15.** (of the eyes) to fill with tears. **16.** (of the mouth) to fill with saliva in anticipation of food. **17.** to irrigate or provide with water: *to water the land.* **18.** (of an animal) to drink water. ~See also **water down.** [Old English] —'**waterless** *adj.*

water bed *n.* a waterproof mattress filled with water.

water biscuit *n.* a thin crisp unsweetened biscuit, usually served with butter or cheese.

water buffalo *n.* an ox-like draught animal of swampy regions of S Asia, with widely spreading back-curving horns.

water cannon *n.* a machine that pumps a jet of water through a nozzle at high pressure, used to disperse crowds.

water chestnut *n.* the edible tuber of a Chinese plant, used in Oriental cookery.

water closet *n.* **1.** a toilet flushed by water. **2.** a small room that has a toilet. ~Usually abbreviated to **WC.**

watercolour *or U.S.* **watercolor** ('wɔːtə,kʌlə) *n.* **1.** paint or pigment thinned with water rather than oil. **2.** a painting done in watercolours.

water-cooled *adj.* (of an engine) kept from overheating by a flow of water circulating in an enclosed jacket.

watercourse ('wɔːtə,kɔːs) *n.* the channel, bed, or route of a stream, river, or canal.

watercress ('wɔːtə,krɛs) *n.* a plant that grows in clear ponds and streams, with pungent leaves that are used in salads and as a garnish.

water diviner *n. Brit.* a person able to locate the presence of water, esp. underground, with a divining rod.

water down *vb.* **1.** to dilute or weaken with water. **2.** to modify, esp. so as to omit anything unpleasant or offensive: *to water down the truth.* —,**watered-'down** *adj.*

waterfall ('wɔːtə,fɔːl) *n.* a cascade of falling water where there is a vertical or almost vertical step in a river.

waterfowl ('wɔːtə,faʊl) *n.* **1.** a bird that lives on or near the water, esp. one that swims, such as a duck or swan. **2.** such birds collectively.

waterfront ('wɔːtə,frʌnt) *n.* the area of a town or city alongside a body of water, such as a harbour or dockyard.

water gate *n.* a gate in a canal that can be opened or closed to control the flow of water.

Watergate ('wɔːtə,geɪt) *n.* any public scandal involving politicians or a possible cover-up. [a scandal over a break-in at the Democratic Party headquarters in the Watergate building, Washington, DC, during the 1972 U.S. presidential elections]

water glass *n.* a syrupy solution of sodium silicate in water: used as a protective coating for cement and a preservative, esp. for eggs.

water hole *n.* a pond or pool in a desert or other dry area, used by animals as a drinking place.

water ice *n.* an ice cream made from a frozen sugar syrup flavoured with fruit juice or purée.

watering can *n.* a container with a handle and a spout with a perforated nozzle, used to sprinkle water over plants.

watering hole *n.* **1.** a place where animals drink; water hole. **2.** *Facetious slang.* a pub.

watering place *n.* **1.** a place where drinking water for people or animals may be obtained. **2.** *Brit.* a spa or seaside resort.

water jump *n.* a ditch or brook over which athletes or horses must jump in a steeplechase or similar contest.

water level *n.* **1.** the level reached by the surface of a body of water. **2.** same as **water line.**

water lily *n.* a aquatic plant with large leaves and showy flowers that float on the surface of the water.

water line *n.* the level to which a ship's hull will be immersed when afloat.

waterlogged ('wɔːtə,lɒgd) *adj.* **1.** saturated with water. **2.** (of a boat still afloat) having taken in so much water as to be unmanageable.

water main *n.* a principal supply pipe in an arrangement of pipes for distributing water.

watermark ('wɔːtə,mɑːk) *n.* **1.** a mark impressed on paper during manufacture, visible when the paper is held up to the light. **2.** a line marking the level reached by a body of water. ~*vb.* **3.** to mark (paper) with a watermark.

water meadow *n.* a meadow that remains fertile by being periodically flooded by a stream.

watermelon ('wɔːtə,melən) *n.* an African melon with a hard green rind and sweet watery reddish flesh.

water pistol *n.* a toy pistol that squirts a stream of water.

water polo *n.* a game played in water by two teams of seven swimmers in which each side tries to throw or propel an inflated ball into the opponents' goal.

water power *n.* the power of flowing or falling water to drive machinery, esp. for generating electricity.

waterproof ('wɔːtə,pruːf) *adj.* **1.** not allowing water to pass through. ~*n.* **2.** *Chiefly Brit.* a waterproof garment, esp. a raincoat. ~*vb.* **3.** to make (a fabric or garment) waterproof.

water rat *n.* same as **water vole.**

water rate *n.* a charge made for the public supply of water.

water-resistant *adj.* (of fabrics or garments) having a finish that resists the absorption of water.

watershed ('wɔːtə,ʃed) *n.* **1.** the dividing line between two adjacent river systems, such as a ridge. **2.** an important period or factor that serves as a dividing line.

waterside ('wɔːtə,saɪd) *n.* the area of land beside a body of water.

water-ski *n.* **1.** a type of ski used for gliding over water. ~*vb.* **-skiing, -skied** or **-ski'd. 2.** to ride over water on waterskis while holding a rope towed by a speedboat. —'**water-,skier** *n.* —'**water-,skiing** *n.*

water softener *n.* a device or substance

which removes the minerals that make water hard.

waterspout ('wɔːtə,spaut) *n.* a tornado occurring over water that forms a column of water and mist.

water table *n.* the level below which the ground is saturated with water.

watertight ('wɔːtə,taɪt) *adj.* **1.** not permitting the passage of water either in or out: *a watertight boat.* **2.** without loopholes: *a watertight argument.*

water tower *n.* a storage tank mounted on a tower so that water can be distributed at a uniform pressure.

water vapour *n.* water in the gaseous state, esp. when due to evaporation at a temperature below the boiling point.

water vole *n.* a small rat-like animal that can swim and lives on the banks of streams and ponds.

waterway ('wɔːtə,wei) *n.* a river, canal, or other navigable channel used as a means of travel or transport.

water wheel *n.* a large wheel with vanes set across its rim, which is turned by flowing water to drive machinery.

water wings *pl. n.* an inflatable rubber device shaped like a pair of wings, which is placed under the arms of a person learning to swim.

waterworks ('wɔːtə,wɜːks) *n.* **1.** (*functioning as sing.*) an establishment for storing, purifying, and distributing water for community supply. **2.** (*functioning as pl.*) *Brit. informal, euphemistic.* the urinary system. **3. turn on the waterworks.** *Informal.* to begin to cry deliberately in order to attract attention or gain sympathy.

watery ('wɔːtəri) *adj.* **1.** of, like, or containing water. **2.** (of eyes) filled with tears. **3.** insipid, thin, or weak: *watery sunshine.*

watt (wɒt) *n.* the SI unit of power, equal to 1 joule per second. [after J. *Watt*, engineer]

wattage ('wɒtɪdʒ) *n.* the amount of electrical power, expressed in watts, that an appliance uses or generates.

wattle ('wɒt'l) *n.* **1.** a frame of rods or stakes interwoven with twigs or branches used to make fences. **2.** a loose fold of skin, often brightly coloured, hanging from the neck or throat of certain birds and lizards. **3.** any of various Australian acacia trees with spikes of small brightly coloured flowers and flexible branches. ~*adj.* **4.** made of, formed by, or covered with wattle. [Old English *watol*] —'**wattled** *adj.*

wattle and daub *n.* a method of building walls using interwoven twigs plastered with a mixture of clay and water.

wave (weɪv) *vb.* **1.** to move the hand to and fro as a greeting. **2.** to hold (something) up and move it from side to side, for example to attract attention. **3.** to direct (someone) to move in a particular direction by waving. **4.** to move freely to and fro: *the banner waved in the wind.* ~*n.* **5.** one of a sequence of ridges or undulations that moves across the surface of a body of water, esp. the sea. **6.** a curve or series of curves in the hair. **7.** a sudden rise in the frequency of something: *a crime wave.* **8.** a widespread movement that advances in a body: *a wave of settlers.* **9.** the act or an instance of waving. **10.** *Physics.* an energy-carrying disturbance travelling through a medium or space by a series of vibrations without any overall movement of matter. **11.** a prolonged spell of some particular type of weather: *a heat wave.* **12. make waves.** to cause trouble; disturb the status quo. [Old English *wafian*] —'**waveless** *adj.*

waveband ('weiv,bænd) *n.* a range of wavelengths or frequencies used for a particular type of radio transmission.

wave down *vb.* to signal to (the driver of a vehicle) to stop.

wavelength ('weiv,leŋθ) *n.* **1.** the distance between two points of the same phase in consecutive cycles of a wave. **2.** the wavelength of the carrier wave used by a particular broadcasting station. **3. on someone's** *or* **the same wavelength.** *Informal.* having similar views, feelings, or thoughts (as someone else).

waver ('weivə) *vb.* **1.** to hesitate between possibilities; be indecisive. **2.** to become unsteady. **3.** to tremble: *her voice wavered.* **4.** to move back and forth or one way and another. **5.** (of light) to flicker or flash. [Old Norse *vafra* to flicker]

wavey ('weivi) *n. Canad.* a snow goose or other wild goose. [American Indian]

wavy ('weivi) *adj.* **wavier, waviest. 1.** forming or full of waves. **2.** (of hair) set in or having waves.

wax[1] (wæks) *n.* **1.** any of various viscous or solid materials which are typically slightly shiny, insoluble in water, and soften when heated. **2.** short for **beeswax** or **sealing wax. 3.** *Physiol.* a brownish-yellow waxy substance secreted by glands in the ear. *~vb.* **4.** to coat or polish with wax. [Old English *weax*] —'**waxy** *adj.*

wax[2] (wæks) *vb.* **1.** to become larger, more powerful, or more intense. **2.** (of the moon) to show a gradually increasing portion of illuminated surface, between new moon and full moon. **3.** to become: *to wax eloquent.* [Old English *weaxan*]

waxen ('wæksən) *adj.* **1.** made of, treated with, or covered with wax. **2.** resembling wax in colour or texture.

waxeye ('wæks,ai) *n.* a small New Zealand bird with a white circle around its eye.

wax paper *n.* paper treated or coated with wax or paraffin to make it waterproof.

waxwing ('wæks,wiŋ) *n.* a songbird with red wing tips, a yellow tip to its tail, and a crested head.

waxwork ('wæks,wɜːk) *n.* **1.** a life-size lifelike wax figure of a famous person. **2.** (*pl.; functioning as sing. or pl.*) a museum or exhibition of wax figures.

way (wei) *n.* **1.** a manner, method, or means: *a way of life; two ways of looking at the problem.* **2.** a route or direction: *the way home.* **3.** a means or line of passage,

such as a path or track. **4.** space or room for movement or activity: *you're in the way; get out of my way!* **5.** distance: *you've come a long way.* **6.** a passage or journey: *on the way.* **7.** characteristic style or manner: *I did it my way.* **8.** (*often pl.*) habit: *he has some offensive ways.* **9.** an aspect of something; particular: *in many ways he was right.* **10.** a street or road: *Icknield Way.* **11.** something wished for: *that child always gets his own way.* **12.** *Informal.* a state or condition, usually financial or concerning health: *she's in a bad way.* **13.** *Informal.* the area or direction of one's home: *drop in if you're ever over my way.* **14. a.** a choice or option, as in a vote: *the vote could go either way.* **b.** a group supporting a particular viewpoint: *a three-way spilt.* **15. by the way.** incidentally. **16. by way of. a.** via. **b.** serving as: *by way of introduction.* **17. come one's way.** to be encountered in one's everyday life. **18. give way. a.** to collapse or break down. **b.** to yield. **19. give way to. a.** to step aside or stop for. **b.** to give full rein to (emotions). **20. go out of one's way.** to take considerable trouble or inconvenience oneself. **21. have it both ways.** to enjoy two things that would normally be mutually exclusive. **22. in a way.** in some respects. **23. in no way.** not at all. **24. lead the way. a.** to go first. **b.** to set an example. **25. make one's way. a.** to proceed or advance. **b.** to achieve success in life. **26. on the way out.** *Informal.* becoming unfashionable. **27. out of the way. a.** removed or dealt with so as to be no longer a hindrance. **b.** remote. **28. see one's way (clear).** to find it possible and be willing (to do something). **29. under way.** having started moving or making progress. *~adv.* **30.** *Informal.* very far: *way over yonder; they're way up the mountain.* [Old English *weg*]

waybill ('wei,bil) *n.* a document stating the nature, origin, and destination of goods in transit.

wayfarer ('wei,fɛərə) *n.* a person who goes on a journey. —'**way,faring** *n., adj.*

waylay (wei'lei) *vb.* **-laying, -laid. 1.** to lie in wait for and attack. **2.** to intercept (someone) unexpectedly. —**way'layer** *n.*

wayleave ('wei,liːv) *n.* access to property granted by a landowner for payment, for example to allow a contractor access to a building site.

way-out *adj. Informal.* extremely unconventional or experimental.

ways and means *pl. n.* **1.** the methods and resources for accomplishing something. **2.** the money and the methods of raising the money needed for the functioning of a political unit.

wayside ('wei,said) *n.* **1.** (*modifier*) situated by the side of a road: *a wayside inn.* **2. fall by the wayside.** to cease or fail to continue doing something: *of the nine starters, three fell by the wayside.*

wayward ('weiwəd) *adj.* erratic, selfish, or stubborn. [AWAY + -WARD]

Wb *Physics.* weber.

WC *or* **wc** *n.* a toilet.

we (wiː) *pl. pron.* (*used as the subject of a verb*) **1.** the speaker or writer and another person or other people: *we should go now.* **2.** all people or people in general: *the planet on which we live.* **3.** a formal word for **I** used by editors or other writers, and formerly by monarchs. **4.** *Informal.* used instead of *you* with a tone of condescension or sarcasm: *how are we today?* [Old English *wē*]

WEA (in Britain) Workers' Educational Association.

weak (wiːk) *adj.* **1.** lacking in physical or mental strength. **2.** liable to give way: *a weak link in a chain.* **3.** lacking in resolution or firmness of character. **4.** lacking strength or power: *a weak voice.* **5. a.** not functioning as well as is normal: *weak eyes.* **b.** easily upset: *a weak stomach.* **6.** lacking in conviction or persuasiveness: *a weak argument.* **7.** lacking in political or strategic strength: *a weak administration.* **8.** lacking the usual, full, or desirable strength of flavour: *weak tea.* **9.** (of a currency or shares) falling in price or characterized by falling prices. [Old English *wāc* soft] —**'weakish** *adj.*

weaken (ˈwiːkən) *vb.* to become or make weak or weaker.

weak-kneed *adj. Informal.* lacking strength, courage, or resolution.

weakling (ˈwiːklɪŋ) *n.* a person or animal that is lacking in strength or weak in constitution or character.

weakly (ˈwiːklɪ) *adj.* **-lier, -liest. 1.** sickly; feeble. ~*adv.* **2.** in a weak or feeble manner.

weak-minded *adj.* **1.** lacking resolution or willpower. **2.** of very low intelligence; foolish.

weakness (ˈwiːknɪs) *n.* **1.** a being weak. **2.** a failing, as in a person's character. **3.** a self-indulgent liking: *a weakness for chocolates.*

weal[1] (wiːl) *n.* a raised mark on the skin produced by a blow. [var. of *wale*]

weal[2] (wiːl) *n. Archaic.* prosperity or well-being: *the common weal.* [Old English *wela*]

wealth (wɛlθ) *n.* **1.** a large amount of money and valuable material possessions. **2.** the state of being rich. **3.** a great amount; abundance: *a wealth of gifts.* [Middle English *welthe*]

wealthy (ˈwɛlθɪ) *adj.* **wealthier, wealthiest. 1.** possessing wealth; rich. **2.** of or relating to wealth. **3.** abounding: *wealthy in friends.* —**'wealthiness** *n.*

wean[1] (wiːn) *vb.* **1.** to accustom (a child or young mammal) to take food other than its mother's milk. **2.** (usually foll. by *from*) to cause (someone) to give up former habits. [Old English *wenian* to accustom]

wean[2] (wein) *n. Scot. & N English dialect.* a child. [prob. from *wee ane* wee one]

weapon (ˈwɛpən) *n.* **1.** an object, such as a knife or gun, used in fighting. **2.** anything that serves to get the better of an opponent: *his power of speech was his best weapon.* [Old English *wǣpen*]

weaponry (ˈwɛpənrɪ) *n.* weapons regarded collectively.

wear (wɛə) *vb.* **wearing, wore, worn. 1.** to carry or have (a garment or jewellery) on one's person as clothing or ornament. **2.** to have or display in one's expression: *to wear a smile.* **3.** to deteriorate or cause to deteriorate by constant use or action. **4.** to react to constant use or action in a specified way: *his suit wears well.* **5.** to harass or weaken. **6.** (often foll. by *on*) (of time) to pass or be passed slowly. **7.** *Brit. informal.* to accept: *Larry won't wear that argument.* **8. wear thin.** to become weaker or less acceptable through overuse or repetition: *my patience is wearing thin; her excuses were starting to wear thin.* ~*n.* **9.** the act of wearing or state of being worn. **10.** anything designed to be worn: *leisure wear.* **11.** deterioration from constant or normal use. **12.** the quality of resisting the effects of constant use. ~See also **wear down, wear off, wear out.** [Old English *werian*]

wear and tear *n.* damage, depreciation, or loss resulting from ordinary use.

wear down *vb.* **1.** to impair or be impaired by long or constant wearing or rubbing: *to wear down the heels on shoes.* **2.** to overcome or be overcome gradually by persistent effort: *to wear down the management.*

wearing (ˈwɛərɪŋ) *adj.* causing fatigue or exhaustion; tiring.

wearisome (ˈwɪərɪsəm) *adj.* causing fatigue or annoyance; tedious.

wear off *vb.* to gradually decrease in intensity: *the pain will wear off soon.*

wear out *vb.* **1.** to make or become unfit or useless through wear. **2.** to exhaust or tire.

weary (ˈwɪərɪ) *adj.* **-rier, -riest. 1.** tired or exhausted. **2.** causing fatigue or exhaustion. **3.** caused by or suggestive of weariness: *a weary laugh.* **4.** (often foll. by *of* or *with*) discontented or bored. ~*vb.* **-rying, -ried. 5.** to make or become weary. **6.** to make or become discontented or impatient. [Old English *wērig*] —**'wearily** *adv.* —**'weariness** *n.* —**'wearying** *adj.*

weasel (ˈwiːz²l) *n., pl.* **-sel** or **-sels.** a small flesh-eating mammal with reddish-brown fur, a long body and neck, and short legs. [Old English *wesle*]

weather (ˈwɛðə) *n.* **1.** the day-to-day atmospheric conditions such as temperature, cloudiness, and rainfall, affecting a specific place. **2. make heavy weather of.** *Informal.* to carry out a task with great difficulty or needless effort. **3. under the weather.** *Informal.* not in good health. ~*adj.* **4.** on or at the side or part towards the wind: *the weather anchor.* ~*vb.* **5.** to expose or be exposed to the action of the weather. **6.** to undergo or cause to undergo changes, such as discoloration, due to the action of the weather. **7.** to come safely through (a storm, problem, or difficulty). **8.** to sail to the windward of (a place or thing): *to weather a point.* [Old English *weder*]

weather-beaten *adj.* **1.** worn or damaged as a result of exposure to the weather. **2.** tanned by exposure to the weather: *a weather-beaten face.*

weatherboard ('wɛðə,bɔːd) *n.* a timber board that is fixed with others in overlapping horizontal rows to form an exterior cladding on a wall or roof. —'**weather-,boarding** *n.*

weathercock ('wɛðə,kɒk) *n.* **1.** a weather vane in the shape of a cock. **2.** a person who is fickle or changeable.

weather eye *n.* **keep one's weather eye open.** to stay on the alert.

weathering ('wɛðərɪŋ) *n.* the breakdown of rocks by the action of the weather.

weatherman ('wɛðə,mæn) *n.*, *pl.* -**men.** *Informal.* a person who forecasts the weather on radio or television.

weatherproof ('wɛðə,pruːf) *adj.* designed or able to withstand exposure to weather without deterioration.

weather vane *n.* a vane designed to indicate the direction in which the wind is blowing.

weave (wiːv) *vb.* **weaving, wove** *or* **weaved; woven** *or* **weaved. 1.** to form (a fabric) by interlacing (yarn) on a loom. **2.** to make by such a process: *to weave a shawl.* **3.** to construct by interlacing (cane or twigs). **4.** to compose (a story or plan) by combining separate elements into a whole. **6.** (often foll. by *in, into,* or *through*) to introduce: *to weave factual details into a fiction.* **7.** to move from side to side while going forwards: *to weave through a crowd.* **8. get weaving.** *Informal.* to hurry. ~*n.* **9.** the structure or pattern of a woven fabric: *an open weave.* [Old English *wefan*] —'**weaver** *n.*

web (wɛb) *n.* **1.** a mesh of fine tough threads built by a spider to trap insects. **2.** anything formed by or as if by weaving or interweaving. **3.** a membrane connecting the toes of some aquatic birds or the digits of such aquatic mammals as the otter. **4.** a continuous strip of paper fed from a reel into some printing presses. **5.** anything that is intricately formed or complex: *a web of intrigue.* [Old English *webb*] —**webbed** *adj.*

webbing ('wɛbɪŋ) *n.* a strong fabric of hemp, cotton, or jute woven in strips and used under springs in upholstery or for straps.

weber ('veɪbə) *n.* the SI unit of magnetic flux. [after W. E. *Weber,* physicist]

web-footed *or* **web-toed** *adj.* (of certain animals or birds) having webbed feet that aid swimming.

wed (wɛd) *vb.* **wedding, wedded** *or* **wed. 1.** to take (a person) as a husband or wife; marry. **2.** to join (two people) in marriage. **3.** to unite closely. [Old English *weddian*] —'**wedded** *adj.*

Wed. Wednesday.

wedding ('wɛdɪŋ) *n.* **1.** the act of marrying or a marriage ceremony. **2.** the anniversary of a marriage (in such combinations as **silver wedding** or **diamond wedding**).

wedding breakfast *n.* the meal usually served after a wedding ceremony or just before the bride and bridegroom leave for their honeymoon.

wedding cake *n.* a rich iced fruit cake, with one, two, or more tiers, which is served at a wedding reception.

wedding ring *n.* a ring, typically of precious metal, worn to indicate that one is married.

wedge (wɛdʒ) *n.* **1.** a block of solid material, esp. wood or metal, that is shaped like a narrow V in cross section and can be pushed or driven between two objects or parts of an object in order to split or secure them. **2.** anything in the shape of a wedge: *a wedge of cheese.* **3.** something, such as an idea or action, that tends to cause division. **4.** *Golf.* a club with a wedge-shaped face, used for bunker or pitch shots. **5. the thin end of the wedge.** anything unimportant in itself that implies the start of something much larger. ~*vb.* **6.** to secure with or as if with a wedge. **7.** to squeeze or be squeezed like a wedge into a narrow space. **8.** to force apart or divide with or as if with a wedge. [Old English *wecg*]

Wedgwood ('wɛdʒwud) *n. Trademark.* a type of fine pottery with applied decoration in white on a coloured ground. [after Josiah *Wedgwood,* potter]

wedlock ('wɛdlɒk) *n.* **1.** the state of being married. **2. born out of wedlock.** born when one's parents are not legally married. [Old English *wedlāc*]

Wednesday ('wɛnzdɪ) *n.* the fourth day of the week. [Old English *Wōdnes dæg* Woden's day]

wee[1] (wiː) *adj.* small in size, amount, or extent. [Old English *wǣg* weight]

wee[2] (wiː) *Informal, chiefly Brit.* ~*n.* **1. a.** an instance of urinating. **b.** urine. ~*vb.* **2.** to urinate. ~*Also:* **wee-wee.** [origin unknown]

weed (wiːd) *n.* **1.** any plant that grows wild and profusely, esp. one that grows among cultivated plants. **2.** *Slang.* **a. the weed.** tobacco. **b.** marijuana. **3.** *Informal.* a thin scraggy ineffectual person. ~*vb.* **4.** to remove (useless or troublesome plants) from (a garden). [Old English *weod*]

weedkiller ('wiːd,kɪlə) *n.* a substance, usually a chemical or hormone, used for killing weeds.

weed out *vb.* to separate out, remove, or eliminate (anything unwanted): *to weed out troublesome students.*

weeds (wiːdz) *pl. n.* a widow's black mourning clothes. [Old English *wǣd* a band worn in mourning]

weedy ('wiːdɪ) *adj.* **weedier, weediest. 1.** full of weeds: *weedy land.* **2.** (of a plant) resembling a weed in straggling growth. **3.** *Informal.* thin or weakly in appearance.

week (wiːk) *n.* **1.** a period of seven consecutive days, esp. one beginning with Sunday. **2.** a period of seven consecutive days from a specified day: *a week from Wednesday.* **3.** the period of time within a week devoted to work. ~*adv.* **4.** *Chiefly*

Brit. seven days before or after a specified day: *I'll visit you Wednesday week.* [Old English *wice, wicu*]

weekday ('wi:k,deɪ) *n.* any day of the week other than Saturday or Sunday.

weekend (,wi:k'ɛnd) *n.* the period from Friday night until the end of Sunday.

weekly ('wi:klɪ) *adj.* **1.** happening once a week or every week. **2.** determined or calculated by the week: *weekly sales figures.* ~*adv.* **3.** once a week or every week. ~*n., pl.* **-lies.** **4.** a newspaper or magazine issued every week.

weeny ('wi:nɪ) *adj.* **-nier, -niest.** *Informal.* very small; tiny. [from WEE¹]

weep (wi:p) *vb.* **weeping, wept.** **1.** to shed tears. **2.** (foll. by *for*) to lament (for something). **3.** to ooze liquid: *a weeping sore.* ~*n.* **4.** a spell of weeping. [Old English *wēpan*]

weeping willow *n.* a willow tree with graceful drooping branches.

weepy ('wi:pɪ) *Informal.* ~*adj.* **weepier, weepiest.** **1.** liable or tending to weep. ~*n., pl.* **weepies.** **2.** a sentimental film or book.

weevil ('wi:vɪl) *n.* a beetle with a long snout that feeds on plants and plant products. [Old English *wifel*]

wee-wee *n., vb.* same as **wee²**.

weft (wɛft) *n.* the yarn woven across the width of the fabric through the lengthways warp yarn. [Old English]

weigh (weɪ) *vb.* **1.** to measure the weight of. **2.** to have weight: *she weighs more than her sister.* **3.** (often foll. by *out*) to measure out by weight. **4.** to consider carefully: *to weigh the facts of a case.* **5.** to be influential: *his words weighed little with the jury.* **6.** (often foll. by *on*) to be oppressive or burdensome to. **7. weigh anchor.** to raise a vessel's anchor or (of a vessel) to have its anchor raised. ~See also **weigh down, weigh in,** etc. [Old English *wegan*]

weighbridge ('weɪ,brɪdʒ) *n.* a machine for weighing vehicles by means of a metal plate set into a road.

weigh down *vb.* to press (a person) down by or as if by weight: *weighed down by troubles.*

weigh in *vb.* **1.** (of a boxer, wrestler, or jockey) to be weighed to check that one is of the declared weight. **2.** *Informal.* to contribute to a discussion or conversation: *he weighed in with a few sharp comments.* ~*n.* **weigh-in.** **3.** *Sport.* the act of checking a competitor's weight.

weight (weɪt) *n.* **1.** the heaviness of an object; the amount anything weighs. **2.** *Physics.* the vertical force experienced by a mass as a result of gravitation. **3.** a system of units used to express weight: *troy weight.* **4.** a unit used to measure weight: *the kilogram is the weight used in SI units.* **5.** any mass or object used for its heaviness: *a paperweight.* **6.** an oppressive force: *the weight of cares.* **7.** any heavy load: *the bag was such a weight.* **8.** the main force; preponderance: *the weight of evidence.* **9.** importance; influence: *his*

opinion carries weight. **10. pull one's weight.** *Informal.* to do one's full share of a task. **11. throw one's weight about** or **around.** *Informal.* to act in an aggressive overauthoritarian manner. ~*vb.* **12.** to add weight to. **13.** to burden or oppress. **14.** to increase the value of (an item or group of items in a list or average), so as to reflect their relative importance. [Old English *wiht*]

weighting ('weɪtɪŋ) *n.* an allowance paid to compensate for higher living costs: *a London weighting.*

weightless ('weɪtlɪs) *adj.* **1.** seeming to have very little weight or no weight at all. **2.** seeming not to be affected by gravity, as in the case of astronauts in an orbiting spacecraft. —'**weightlessness** *n.*

weightlifting ('weɪt,lɪftɪŋ) *n.* the sport of lifting barbells of specified weights in a prescribed manner. —'**weight,lifter** *n.*

weight training *n.* physical exercise using light or heavy weights as a way of improving muscle performance.

weighty ('weɪtɪ) *adj.* **weightier, weightiest.** **1.** having great weight. **2.** important: *weighty problems.* **3.** causing worry: *weighty responsibilities.* —'**weightiness** *n.*

weigh up *vb.* to make an assessment of (a person or situation); judge.

weir (wɪə) *n.* **1.** a low dam that is built across a river to raise the water level, divert the water, or control its flow. **2.** a fence-like trap built across a stream to catch fish. [Old English *wer*]

weird (wɪəd) *adj.* **1.** suggestive of the supernatural; eerie. **2.** strange or bizarre. [Old English *(ge)wyrd* destiny] —'**weirdly** *adv.* —'**weirdness** *n.*

weirdo ('wɪədəʊ) *n., pl.* **-dos.** *Informal.* a person who behaves in a bizarre or eccentric manner.

welch (wɛlʃ) *vb.* same as **welsh.**

welcome ('wɛlkəm) *adj.* **1.** gladly received or admitted: *a welcome guest.* **2.** bringing pleasure: *a welcome gift.* **3.** freely permitted or invited: *you are welcome to call.* **4. you're welcome.** an expression used to acknowledge someone's thanks. ~*n.* **5.** the act of greeting or receiving a person or thing; reception: *the new theory had a cool welcome.* **6. overstay one's welcome.** to come more often or stay longer than is pleasing. ~*vb.* **7.** to greet the arrival of (guests) cordially. **8.** to receive or accept, esp. gladly. [Old English *wilcume*] —'**welcoming** *adj.*

weld (wɛld) *vb.* **1.** to join (pieces of metal or plastic), as by softening with heat and hammering or by fusion. **2.** to unite closely: *the tragedy welded the family together.* ~*n.* **3.** a joint formed by welding. [obs. *well* to melt, weld] —'**welder** *n.*

welfare ('wɛl,fɛə) *n.* **1.** health, happiness, prosperity, and wellbeing in general. **2.** financial and other assistance given to people in need. **3. on welfare.** *Chiefly U.S. & Canad.* receiving financial aid from a government agency or other source. [see WELL¹, FARE]

welfare state *n.* a system in which the government undertakes responsibility for the wellbeing of its population, usually through unemployment insurance, old age pensions, and other social-security measures.

well[1] (wɛl) *adv.* **better, best. 1.** satisfactorily: *the party went very well; well-proportioned.* **2.** skilfully: *she plays the violin well; a well-chosen example.* **3.** carefully: *listen well to my words.* **4.** prosperously: *to live well.* **5.** suitably; fittingly: *you can't very well say that.* **6.** intimately: *I knew him well.* **7.** in a kind or favourable manner: *she speaks well of you.* **8.** fully: *to be well informed.* **9.** by a considerable margin: *let me know well in advance; well over fifty.* **10.** (preceded by *could, might,* or *may*) indeed: *you may well have to do it yourself.* **11. all very well.** used ironically to express discontent or dissent. **12. as well. a.** in addition; too. **b.** (preceded by *may* or *might*) with equal effect: *you might as well come.* **13. as well as.** in addition to. **14. (just) as well.** preferable or advisable: *it would be just as well if you paid me now.* **15. leave well (enough) alone.** to refrain from interfering with something that is satisfactory. **16. well and good.** used to indicate calm acceptance, as of a decision. ~*adj.* **17.** in good health: *I'm very well, thank you; he's not a well man.* **18.** satisfactory or pleasing. **19.** prudent; advisable: *it would be well to make no comment.* ~*interj.* **20. a.** an expression of surprise, indignation, or reproof. **b.** an expression of anticipation in waiting for an answer or remark. [Old English *wel*]

well[2] (wɛl) *n.* **1.** a hole or shaft bored into the earth to tap a supply of water, oil, or gas. **2.** a natural pool where water comes to the surface. **3.** a cavity, space, or container for holding a liquid, such as an inkwell. **4.** an open shaft through the floors of a building, such as one used for a staircase. **5.** a deep enclosed space in a building or between buildings that is open to the sky. **6.** (in England) the open space in the centre of a law court. **7.** an abundant source: *he is a well of knowledge.* ~*vb.* **8.** to flow or cause to flow upwards or outwards: *tears welled from her eyes.* [Old English *wella*]

we'll (wiːl) we will *or* we shall.

well-advised *adj.* prudent or sensible: *you'd be well-advised to forget about him.*

well-appointed *adj.* (of a room or building) well equipped or furnished to a high standard.

well-balanced *adj.* sane or sensible.

well-behaved *adj.* **1.** having good manners; not causing trouble or mischief. **2.** (of an animal) properly trained.

wellbeing ('wɛl'biːɪŋ) *n.* the condition of being contented or healthy.

well-bred *adj.* **1.** Also: **well-born.** of respected or noble ancestry. **2.** indicating good breeding: *well-bred manners.* **3.** of good thoroughbred stock: *a well-bred spaniel.*

well-built *adj.* strong and well-proportioned.

well-connected *adj.* having influential or important relatives or friends.

well-disposed *adj.* inclined to be sympathetic, kindly, or friendly.

well-done *adj.* **1.** (of food, esp. meat) cooked thoroughly. **2.** made or accomplished satisfactorily.

well-founded *adj.* having good grounds: *well-founded rumours.*

well-groomed *adj.* having a tidy pleasing appearance.

well-grounded *adj.* well instructed in the basic elements of a subject.

wellhead ('wɛl,hɛd) *n.* **1.** the source of a well or stream. **2.** a source, fountainhead, or origin.

well-heeled *adj. Informal.* rich; prosperous; wealthy.

wellies ('wɛlɪz) *pl. n. Brit. informal.* Wellington boots.

well-informed *adj.* **1.** having knowledge about a great variety of subjects: *he seems to be a well-informed person.* **2.** possessing reliable information on a particular subject.

Wellington boots ('wɛlɪŋtən) *or* **wellingtons** *pl. n. Brit.* knee-length or calf-length rubber boots, worn in wet or muddy conditions. [after the 1st Duke of *Wellington,* soldier & statesman]

well-intentioned *adj.* having good or kindly intentions, usually with unfortunate results.

well-known *adj.* **1.** widely known; famous. **2.** known fully or clearly.

well-meaning *adj.* having or indicating good intentions, usually with unfortunate results.

well-nigh *adv. Archaic or poetic.* nearly; almost: *it's well-nigh three o'clock.*

well-off *adj.* **1.** financially well provided for; moderately rich. **2.** in a comfortable or favourable position or state.

well-preserved *adj.* **1.** kept in a good condition. **2.** continuing to appear youthful: *a well-preserved old lady.*

well-read ('wɛl'rɛd) *adj.* having read widely and intelligently.

well-rounded *adj.* **1.** rounded in shape or well developed: *a well-rounded figure.* **2.** full, varied, and satisfying: *a well-rounded life.*

well-spoken *adj.* **1.** having a clear, articulate, and socially acceptable accent and way of speaking. **2.** spoken satisfactorily or pleasingly.

wellspring ('wɛl,sprɪŋ) *n.* **1.** the source of a spring or stream. **2.** a source of abundant supply.

well-thought-of *adj.* respected.

well-to-do *adj.* moderately wealthy.

well-wisher *n.* a person who shows benevolence or sympathy towards a person or cause. —'**well-**,**wishing** *adj., n.*

well-worn *adj.* **1.** so much used as to be affected by wear: *a well-worn coat.* **2.** hackneyed: *a well-worn phrase.*

welsh *or* **welch** (wɛlʃ) *vb.* (often foll. by *on*) to fail to pay a debt or fulfil an obligation. [origin unknown]

Welsh (wɛlʃ) *adj.* **1.** of or relating to Wales, its people, their language, or their dialect of English. ~*n.* **2.** a Celtic language of Wales. **3. the Welsh.** (*functioning as pl.*) the people of Wales. [Old English *Wēlisc, Wælisc*]

Welshman ('wɛlʃmən) *or* (*fem.*) **Welshwoman** *n., pl.* -**men** *or* -**women.** a person from Wales.

Welsh rabbit *n.* melted cheese sometimes mixed with milk or seasonings, served on hot toast. Also called: **Welsh rarebit, rarebit.**

welt (wɛlt) *n.* **1.** a raised or strengthened seam in a garment. **2.** a raised mark on the skin produced by a blow. **3.** (in shoemaking) a strip of leather between the outer sole and the inner sole and upper. ~*vb.* **4.** to put a welt in (a garment or shoe). **5.** to beat soundly. [origin unknown]

welter ('wɛltə) *vb.* **1.** to roll about, writhe, or wallow. **2.** to lie drenched in blood. ~*n.* **3.** a confused mass; jumble. [Middle Low German, Middle Dutch *weltern*]

welterweight ('wɛltə,weɪt) *n.* **1.** a professional boxer weighing up to 147 pounds or an amateur boxer weighing up to 148 pounds. **2.** a professional wrestler weighing up to 75 kg or an amateur wrestler weighing up to 74 kg.

wen (wɛn) *n. Pathol.* a harmless cyst on the scalp. [Old English *wenn*]

wench (wɛntʃ) *n.* **1.** a girl or young woman: now used facetiously. **2.** *Archaic.* a prostitute or female servant. [Old English *wencel* child]

wend (wɛnd) *vb.* to direct (one's course or way); travel. [Old English *wendan*]

wensleydale ('wɛnzlɪ,deɪl) *n.* a type of white cheese with a flaky texture. [after *Wensleydale,* North Yorkshire]

went (wɛnt) *vb.* the past tense of **go.**

wept (wɛpt) *vb.* the past of **weep.**

were (wɜː; *unstressed* wə) *vb.* the form of the past tense of **be** used after *we, you, they,* or a plural noun. It is also used as a subjunctive, esp. in conditional sentences. [Old English *wērun, wæron*]

we're (wɪə) we are.

weren't (wɜːnt) were not.

werewolf ('wɪə,wulf, 'wɛə-) *n., pl.* -**wolves.** (in folklore) a person who has been changed or is able to change into a wolf. [Old English *wer* man + *wulf* wolf]

Wesleyan ('wɛzlɪən) *adj.* **1.** of or characterizing Methodism. ~*n.* **2.** a member of the Methodist Church. [John *Wesley,* preacher who founded Methodism] —'**Wesleyan,ism** *n.*

west (wɛst) *n.* **1.** the direction along a parallel towards the sunset, at 270° clockwise from north. **2. the west.** (*often cap.*) any area lying in or towards the west. ~*adj.* **3.** situated in, moving towards, or facing the west. **4.** (of the wind) from the

west. ~*adv.* **5.** in, to, or towards the west. **6. go west.** *Informal.* **a.** to be lost or destroyed. **b.** to die. [Old English]

West (wɛst) *n.* **the. 1.** the western part of the world contrasted historically and culturally with the East or Orient. **2.** the non-Communist countries of Europe and America contrasted with the Communist states of the East. ~*adj.* **3.** of or denoting the western part of a specified country or area.

westbound ('wɛst,baʊnd) *adj.* going or leading towards the west.

West Country *n.* **the.** the southwest of England, esp. Cornwall, Devon, and Somerset.

West End *n.* **the.** a part of W central London containing the main shopping and entertainment areas.

westerly ('wɛstəlɪ) *adj.* **1.** of or situated in the west. ~*adv., adj.* **2.** towards the west. **3.** (of the wind) from the west. ~*n., pl.* -**lies. 4.** a wind blowing from the west.

western ('wɛstən) *adj.* **1.** in, towards, or facing the west. **2.** (of a wind) coming from the west. —'**western,most** *adj.*

Western ('wɛstən) *adj.* **1.** of or characteristic of the Americas and the parts of Europe not under Communist rule. **2.** of or characteristic of the West as opposed to the Orient. ~*n.* **3.** (*often not cap.*) a film or book about cowboys in the western states of the U.S. in the 19th century.

westerner ('wɛstənə) *n.* a person from the west of any specific region.

Western Hemisphere *n.* that half of the globe containing the Americas.

westernize *or* -**ise** ('wɛstə,naɪz) *vb.* to influence or make familiar with the customs or practices of the West. —,**westerni'zation** *or* -**i'sation** *n.*

Westminster ('wɛst,mɪnstə) *n.* the British Houses of Parliament.

westward ('wɛstwəd) *adj., adv.* also **westwards. 1.** towards the west. ~*n.* **2.** the westward part or direction. —'**westwardly** *adj., adv.*

wet (wɛt) *adj.* **wetter, wettest. 1.** moistened, covered, or soaked with water or some other liquid. **2.** not yet dry or solid: *wet varnish.* **3.** rainy: *wet weather.* **4.** *Brit. informal.* feeble or foolish. **5. wet behind the ears.** *Informal.* immature or inexperienced. ~*n.* **6.** wetness or moisture. **7.** rainy weather. **8.** *Brit. informal.* a feeble or foolish person. **9.** (*often cap.*) *Brit. informal.* a Conservative politician who supports moderate policies. ~*vb.* **wetting, wet** *or* **wetted. 10.** to make or become wet. **11.** to urinate on (something). [Old English *wæt*] —'**wetly** *adv.* —'**wetness** *n.*

wet blanket *n. Informal.* a person whose low spirits or lack of enthusiasm have a depressing effect on others.

wet dream *n.* an erotic dream accompanied by an emission of semen.

wether ('wɛðə) *n.* a male sheep, esp. a castrated one. [Old English *hwæther*]

wetland ('wɛtlənd) *n.* (*sometimes pl.*) an area of marshy land.

wet nurse n. (esp. formerly) a woman hired to breast-feed the child of another.

wet suit n. a close-fitting rubber suit used by skin-divers or yachtsmen to retain body heat.

W. Glam. West Glamorgan.

whack (wæk) vb. **1.** to strike with a sharp resounding blow. ~n. **2.** a sharp resounding blow or the noise made by such a blow. **3.** Informal. a share or portion. **4. have a whack at.** to attempt. [imit.]

whacked (wækt) adj. Brit. informal. completely exhausted.

whacking ('wækɪŋ) Informal, chiefly Brit. ~adj. **1.** enormous. ~adv. **2.** very: a whacking big lie.

whale (weɪl) n., pl. **whales** or **whale. 1.** any of various large marine mammals which have flippers and a horizontally flattened tail and breathe through a blowhole on the top of the head. **2. a whale of a.** Informal. an exceptionally large or fine example of a (person or thing): I had a whale of a time. [Old English hwæl]

whalebone ('weɪl,bəʊn) n. **1.** a horny elastic material that hangs from the upper jaw in the toothless (whalebone) whales and strains plankton from water entering the mouth. **2.** a thin strip of this substance, used, esp. formerly, for stiffening corsets and bodices.

whalebone whale n. any whale with a double blowhole and strips of whalebone between the jaws instead of teeth, including the right whale and the blue whale.

whaler ('weɪlə) n. **1.** a person employed in whaling. **2.** a vessel engaged in whaling.

whaling ('weɪlɪŋ) n. the hunting and killing of whales for food or oil.

wham (wæm) n. **1.** a forceful blow or impact or the sound produced by it. ~vb. **whamming, whammed. 2.** to strike with great force. [imit.]

wharepuni ('fɔːrɛ,pʊnɪ) n. N.Z. in a Maori community, a lofty carved building used as a guesthouse. [Maori]

wharf (wɔːf) n., pl. **wharves** (wɔːvz) or **wharfs.** a platform along the side of a waterfront for docking, loading, and unloading ships. [Old English hwearf heap]

wharfage ('wɔːfɪdʒ) n. **1.** accommodation for ships at wharves. **2.** a charge for use of a wharf.

wharfie ('wɔːfɪ) n. Austral. & N.Z. a dock labourer.

what (wɒt) det. **1. a.** used with a noun in requesting further information about the identity or categorization of something: what job does he do?; tell me what she said. **b.** (as pron.): what is her address? **2.** the person, thing, people, or things that: we photographed what animals we could see; bring me what you've written. **3.** used in exclamations to add emphasis: what a good book! ~adv. **4.** in what respect? to what degree?: what do you care? **5. what about.** what do you think or know concerning? **6. what for?** why? **7. what have you.** someone or something unspecified: cars, motorcycles, or what have you. **8.**

what's what. Informal. the true state of affairs. [Old English hwæt]

whatever (wɒt'ɛvə) pron. **1.** everything or anything that: do whatever he asks you to. **2.** no matter what: whatever he does, he is forgiven. **3.** Informal. an unspecified thing: take a hammer, chisel, or whatever. **4.** an intensive form of what, used in questions: whatever can he have said to upset her so much? ~det. **5.** an intensive form of what: use whatever tools you can get hold of. ~adj. **6.** at all: I saw no point whatever in continuing.

whatnot ('wɒt,nɒt) n. Informal. unspecified similar things: we had eggs, bacon, and whatnot.

whatsoever (,wɒtsəʊ'ɛvə) adj. at all: used for emphasis after a noun phrase that uses words such as none or any: no doubt whatsoever; is there any evidence whatsoever?

wheat (wiːt) n. the light brown grain of any of a variety of grasses, used in making flour and pasta. [Old English hwǣte]

wheatear ('wiːt,ɪə) n. a small northern songbird with a conspicuous white rump. [from white + arse]

wheaten ('wiːtʾn) adj. made of the grain or flour of wheat.

wheat germ n. the vitamin-rich embryo of the wheat kernel.

wheatmeal ('wiːt,miːl) n. a brown flour intermediate between white flour and wholemeal flour.

wheedle ('wiːdʾl) vb. **1.** to persuade or try to persuade (someone) by coaxing or flattery. **2.** to obtain thus: she wheedled some money out of her father. [origin unknown] —'wheedling adj.

wheel (wiːl) n. **1.** a solid disc or circular rim joined to a hub by spokes, that is mounted on a shaft about which it can turn, as in vehicles. **2.** anything like a wheel in shape or function: a steering wheel; a water wheel. **3.** a pivoting movement. **4. at the wheel. a.** driving or steering a vehicle. **b.** in charge. **5. big wheel.** Informal, chiefly U.S. & Canad. an important or influential person. ~vb. **6.** to push or pull (a vehicle or object with wheels). **7.** to turn on or as if on an axis. **8.** (often foll. by round) to change direction or turn round suddenly. **9. wheel and deal.** to operate shrewdly and sometimes unscrupulously in order to advance one's own interests. ~See also **wheels.** [Old English hweol, hweowol]

wheelbarrow ('wiːl,bærəʊ) n. a shallow open box for carrying small loads, with a wheel at the front and two shafts for pushing or pulling it.

wheelbase ('wiːl,beɪs) n. the distance between the front and back axles of a motor vehicle.

wheelchair ('wiːl,tʃɛə) n. a special chair on large wheels, for use by people for whom walking is impossible or inadvisable.

wheel clamp n. a device fixed onto one wheel of an illegally parked car to prevent the car being driven off. The driver has to pay to have the clamp removed.

wheeler-dealer (ˈwiːləˈdiːlə) n. a person who wheels and deals.

wheelhouse (ˈwiːlˌhaus) n. an enclosed structure on the bridge of a ship from which it is steered.

wheelie (ˈwiːlɪ) n. a manoeuvre on a bicycle or motorbike in which the front wheel is raised off the ground.

wheels (wiːlz) pl. n. **1.** the main force and mechanism of an organization: *the wheels of government.* **2.** *Informal.* a car. **3. wheels within wheels.** a series of intricately connected events or plots.

wheelwright (ˈwiːlˌrait) n. a person who makes or mends wheels as a trade.

wheeze (wiːz) vb. **1.** to breathe with a rasping or whistling sound. ~n. **2.** a wheezing breath. **3.** *Brit. old-fashioned slang.* a trick or plan. [prob. from Old Norse *hvēsa* to hiss] —**ˈwheezy** adj. —**ˈwheeziness** n.

whelk (wɛlk) n. an edible mollusc of coastal waters, with a strong snail-like shell. [Old English *weoloc*]

whelp (wɛlp) n. **1.** a young offspring of a wolf or dog. **2.** *Disparaging.* a youth. ~vb. **3.** (of an animal) to give birth to (young). [Old English *hwelp(a)*]

when (wɛn) adv. **1.** at what time? over what period?: *when is he due?; when was the act in force?* **2. say when.** to state when an action is to be stopped, as when someone is pouring a drink. ~conj. **3.** at a time at which; just as; after: *I found it easy when I tried.* **4.** although: *he drives when he might walk.* **5.** considering the fact that: *how did you pass the exam when you hadn't worked for it?* ~pron. **6.** at which time: *an age when men were men.* [Old English *hwanne, hwænne*]

whence (wɛns) *Archaic or formal.* ~adv. **1.** from what place, cause, or origin? ~conj. **2.** to the place which: *return whence you came.* [Middle English *whannes*]

whenever (wɛnˈɛvə) conj. **1.** at every or any time that; when: *I laugh whenever I see that.* ~adv. **2.** no matter when: *it'll be here, whenever you decide to come for it.* **3.** *Informal.* at an unknown or unspecified time: *I'll take it if it comes today, tomorrow, or whenever.* **4.** an intensive form of *when*, used in questions: *whenever did he escape?*

where (wɛə) adv. **1.** in, at, or to what place, point, or position?: *where are you going?; I don't know where they are.* ~pron. **2.** in, at, or to which place: *the hotel where we spent our honeymoon.* ~conj. **3.** in the place at which: *where we live it's always raining.* [Old English *hwǣr*]

whereabouts (ˈwɛərəˌbauts) adv. **1.** at what approximate place; where: *whereabouts are you?* ~n. **2.** (functioning as *sing. or pl.*) the place, esp. the approximate place, where a person or thing is.

whereas (wɛərˈæz) conj. **1.** but on the other hand: *I like to go swimming whereas Sheila likes to sail.* **2.** (in formal documents) it being the case that; since.

whereby (wɛəˈbaɪ) pron. by or because of which: *the means whereby he took his life.*

wherefore (ˈwɛəˌfɔː) n. **1. the whys and wherefores.** the reasons or explanation. ~conj. **2.** *Archaic or formal.* for which reason: used in legal preambles.

wherein (wɛərˈɪn) *Archaic or formal.* ~adv. **1.** in what place or respect? ~pron. **2.** in which place or thing: *the room wherein she lay.*

whereof (wɛərˈɒv) *Archaic or formal.* ~adv. **1.** of what or which person or thing? ~pron. **2.** of which person or thing: *the man whereof I speak is no longer alive.*

whereupon (ˌwɛərəˈpɒn) conj. at which point; upon which.

wherever (wɛərˈɛvə) pron. **1.** at, in, or to every place or point which; where: *wherever she went, he would be there.* ~conj. **2.** in, to, or at whatever place: *wherever we go the weather is always bad.* ~adv. **3.** no matter where: *I'll find you, wherever you are.* **4.** *Informal.* at, in, or to an unknown or unspecified place: *I'll go anywhere to escape: London, Paris, or wherever.* **5.** an intensive form of *where*, used in questions: *wherever can they be?*

wherewithal (ˈwɛəwɪˌðɔːl) n. **the wherewithal.** necessary funds, resources, or equipment: *these people lack the wherewithal for a decent existence.*

wherry (ˈwɛrɪ) n., pl. **-ries. 1.** a light rowing boat. **2.** a large light barge. [origin unknown] —**ˈwherryman** n.

whet (wɛt) vb. **whetting, whetted. 1.** to increase (appetite or desire). **2.** *Old-fashioned.* to sharpen. [Old English *hwettan*]

whether (ˈwɛðə) conj. **1.** used to introduce an indirect question or a clause expressing doubt or choice: *he doesn't know whether she's in Britain or France; anyone, whether liberal or conservative, would agree with me; you'll eat it whether you like it or whether you don't.* **2. whether or no.** in any case: *he will be here tomorrow, whether or no.* [Old English *hwæther*]

whetstone (ˈwɛtˌstəʊn) n. a stone used for sharpening edged tools or knives.

whew (hwjuː) interj. an exclamation expressing relief, surprise, or delight.

whey (weɪ) n. the watery liquid that separates from the curd when milk is clotted, as in making cheese. [Old English *hwǣg*]

which (wɪtʃ) det. **1. a.** used with a noun in requesting that the particular thing being referred to is further identified or distinguished: *which house did you want to buy?; I don't know which route is quickest.* **b.** (as pron.): *which did you find?* **2. a.** whichever: *bring which car you want.* **b.** (as pron.): *choose which of the cars suits you.* ~pron. **3.** used in relative clauses referring to an inanimate noun: *the house, which is old, is in poor repair.* **4.** as; and that: *he died of cancer, which is what I predicted.* [Old English *hwelc*]

whichever (wɪtʃˈɛvə) det. **1. a.** any out of several: *take whichever car you like.* **b.** (as pron.): *choose whichever appeals to* *you.* **2. a.** no matter which one or ones: *whichever card you pick you'll still be making a mistake.* **b.** (as pron.): *it won't make any difference, whichever comes first.*

whiff (wɪf) *n.* **1.** a passing odour. **2.** a brief gentle gust of air or smoke. **3.** a trace or hint: *a whiff of scandal.* [imit.]

Whig (wɪg) *n.* **1.** a member of an English, and later British, political party that supported a limited monarchy, later represented the desires of industrialists and Dissenters for political and social reform, and provided the core of the Liberal Party. ~*adj.* **2.** of or relating to Whigs. [prob. from *whiggamore*, one of a group of 17th-century Scottish rebels] —**'Whiggery** or **'Whiggism** *n.* —**'Whiggish** *adj.*

while (waɪl) *conj. also* **whilst. 1.** at the same time that: *please light the fire while I'm cooking.* **2.** all the time that: *I stay inside while it's raining.* **3.** in spite of the fact that: *while I agree about his brilliance I still think he's rude.* **4.** whereas; and in contrast: *houses are expensive, while flats are cheap.* ~*n.* **5.** a period of time: *once in a long while.* **6. worth one's while.** worthy of time or effort. [Old English *hwīl*]

while away *vb.* to pass (time) idly and usually pleasantly.

whilst (waɪlst) *conj. Chiefly Brit.* same as **while.**

whim (wɪm) *n.* a sudden, passing, and often fanciful idea. [origin unknown]

whimper (ˈwɪmpə) *vb.* **1.** to cry, complain, or say (something) in a whining plaintive way. ~*n.* **2.** a soft plaintive whine. [imit.]

whimsical (ˈwɪmzɪkˀl) *adj.* **1.** fanciful or playful. **2.** (of a person) given to whims; capricious. **3.** unusual in a quaint or fantastic way. —**whimsicality** (ˌwɪmzɪˈkælɪtɪ) *n.* —**'whimsically** *adv.*

whimsy or **whimsey** (ˈwɪmzɪ) *n., pl.* **-sies** or **-seys. 1.** a capricious idea. **2.** light or fanciful humour. [from *whim*]

whin (wɪn) *n.* same as **gorse.** [from Old Norse]

whine (waɪn) *n.* **1.** a long high-pitched plaintive cry or moan. **2.** a peevish complaint, esp. one repeated. ~*vb.* **3.** to whine or utter in a whine. [Old English *hwīnan*] —**'whining** *n., adj.*

whinge (wɪndʒ) *vb.* **1.** to complain in a moaning manner. ~*n.* **2.** a complaint. [Old English *hwinsian* to whine]

whinny (ˈwɪnɪ) *vb.* **-nying, -nied. 1.** (of a horse) to neigh softly or gently. ~*n., pl.* **-nies. 2.** a gentle or low-pitched neigh. [imit.]

whip (wɪp) *vb.* **whipping, whipped. 1.** to strike (a person or thing) with several strokes of a strap or cane. **2.** (foll. by *out* or *away*) to pull or remove (something) with sudden rapid motion: *to whip out a gun.* **3.** (foll. by *down, into, out of,* etc.) *Informal.* to move in a rapid sudden manner: *they whipped into the bar for a drink.* **4.** to strike as if by whipping: *the cold wind whipped her face.* **5.** to bring (someone)

into a particular condition: *whipped into a frenzy.* **6.** (often foll. by *on, out,* or *off*) to drive or urge by or as if by whipping. **7.** *Informal.* to steal (something). **8.** to wind (cord) round (a rope or cable) to prevent fraying. **9.** to beat (eggs or cream) with a whisk or similar utensil to incorporate air. ~*n.* **10.** a device consisting of a lash or flexible rod attached at one end to a stiff handle and used for driving animals or beating people. **11.** (in a legislative body) **a.** a member of a party chosen to organize and discipline the people in his party. **b.** a call issued to members of a party, insisting with varying degrees of urgency upon their presence or loyal voting behaviour. In the British Parliament this is done in writing, with each item of the week's schedule underlined to indicate its importance: three lines means that the item is very important. **12.** a dessert made from egg whites or cream beaten stiff. ~See also **whip-round, whip up.** [perhaps from Middle Dutch *wippen* to swing] —**'whipping** *n.*

whipcord (ˈwɪpˌkɔːd) *n.* a strong worsted or cotton fabric with a diagonally ribbed surface.

whip hand *n.* **the whip hand.** an advantage or dominating position.

whiplash (ˈwɪpˌlæʃ) *n.* a quick lash or stroke of a whip or like that of a whip.

whiplash injury *n.* any injury to the neck resulting from a sudden thrusting forwards and snapping back of the head, as in a car crash.

whipper-in *n., pl.* **whippers-in.** a huntsman's assistant who manages the hounds.

whippersnapper (ˈwɪpəˌsnæpə) *n.* an insignificant but pretentious person.

whippet (ˈwɪpɪt) *n.* a small slender breed of dog similar to a greyhound. [perhaps based on *whip it!* move quickly!]

whipping boy *n.* a scapegoat.

whippoorwill (ˈwɪpʊˌwɪl) *n.* an American nightjar. [imit. of its cry]

whip-round *n. Informal, chiefly Brit.* an impromptu collection of money.

whipstock (ˈwɪpˌstɒk) *n.* a whip handle.

whip up *vb.* **1.** to excite; arouse: *to whip up a mob; to whip up discontent.* **2.** *Informal.* to prepare quickly: *to whip up a meal.*

whirl (wɜːl) *vb.* **1.** to spin, turn, or revolve. **2.** to seem to spin from dizziness or confusion: *my head's whirling.* **3.** to move or drive or be moved or driven at high speed. ~*n.* **4.** the act or an instance of whirling. **5.** a confused or giddy condition: *her accident left me in a whirl.* **6.** a round of intense activity: *the social whirl.* **7. give (something) a whirl.** *Informal.* to attempt or try (something). [Old Norse *hvirfla* to turn about]

whirligig (ˈwɜːlɪˌgɪg) *n.* **1.** a spinning toy, such as a top. **2.** same as **merry-go-round. 3.** anything that whirls.

whirlpool (ˈwɜːlˌpuːl) *n.* a powerful circular current or vortex of water, into which objects floating nearby are drawn.

whirlwind (ˈwɜːlˌwɪnd) *n.* **1.** a column of air whirling violently upwards in a spiral.

~*adj.* **2.** done or happening much more quickly than normal: *a whirlwind romance.*

whirlybird (ˈwɜːlɪˌbɜːd) *n. Informal.* a helicopter.

whirr *or* **whir** (wɜː) *n.* **1.** a prolonged soft whiz or buzz. ~*vb.* **whirring, whirred. 2.** to make or cause to make a whir. [prob. from Old Norse]

whisk (wɪsk) *vb.* **1.** to brush or sweep away lightly. **2.** to move or carry with a rapid sweeping motion: *the taxi whisked us to the airport.* **3.** to whip (eggs or cream) to a froth. ~*n.* **4.** the act of whisking. **5.** a light rapid sweeping movement. **6.** a utensil for whipping eggs or cream. **7.** a small brush or broom. [Old Norse *visk* wisp]

whisker (ˈwɪskə) *n.* **1.** any of the long stiff hairs growing on the face of a cat or other mammal. **2.** any of the hairs growing on a man's face, esp. on the cheeks or chin. **3.** (*pl.*) a beard or that part of it growing on the sides of the face. **4. by a whisker.** by a very small distance or amount: *he escaped death by a whisker.* [Old Norse *visk* wisp]

whiskey (ˈwɪskɪ) *n. Irish & U.S.* same as **whisky.**

whisky (ˈwɪskɪ) *n., pl.* **-kies.** a spirit made by distilling fermented cereals. [Scot. Gaelic *uisge beatha* water of life]

whisky-jack *n. Canad.* same as **Canada jay.**

whisper (ˈwɪspə) *vb.* **1.** to speak or utter (something) very softly, using the breath instead of the vocal cords. **2.** to speak or utter (something) secretly or privately. **3.** to make a low soft rustling sound. ~*n.* **4.** a low soft voice: *to speak in a whisper.* **5.** something uttered in a whisper. **6.** a low soft rustling sound. **7.** *Informal.* a rumour. [Old English *hwisprian*]

whist (wɪst) *n.* a card game for two pairs of players. [perhaps from *whisk*, referring to the whisking up of the tricks]

whist drive *n.* a social gathering where whist is played.

whistle (ˈwɪsᵊl) *vb.* **1.** to produce (a shrill sound) by forcing breath between the pursed lips. **2.** to signal or command by whistling or blowing a whistle: *the referee whistled the end of the game.* **3.** (of a kettle or train) to produce (a shrill sound) caused by the forcing of steam through a small opening. **4.** to move with a whistling sound. **5.** (of animals, esp. birds) to give a shrill cry. **6. whistle in the dark.** to try to keep up one's confidence in spite of fear. ~*n.* **7.** an instrument for making a shrill sound by means of air or steam under pressure. **8.** the act or sound of whistling. **9. blow the whistle.** (usually foll. by *on*) *Informal.* to inform (on). **10. wet one's whistle.** *Informal.* to take a drink. [Old English *hwistlian*]

whistle for *vb. Informal.* to seek or expect in vain.

whistle stop *n.* **1.** *U.S. & Canad.* a small town at which trains stop only if signalled. **2.** a brief appearance in a town, esp. by a political candidate.

whit (wɪt) *n.* (*usually used with a negative*) the smallest particle; iota; jot: *he has changed not a whit.* [prob. var. of obs. *wight* a person]

Whit (wɪt) *n.* **1.** See **Whitsuntide.** ~*adj.* **2.** of Whitsuntide.

white (waɪt) *adj.* **1.** having no hue, owing to the reflection of all or almost all light. **2.** of light or pale colour. **3.** (of an animal) albino. **4.** pale, as from pain, emotion, illness, or fear. **5.** (of hair) having lost its colour, usually from age. **6.** (of coffee or tea) with milk or cream. **7.** (of wine) made from pale grapes or from black grapes separated from their skins. **8.** denoting flour, or bread made from flour, that has had part of the grain removed. **9. bleed white.** to deprive slowly of resources. ~*n.* **10.** a white colour. **11.** the clear fluid that surrounds the yolk of a bird's egg; albumen. **12.** *Anat.* the white part of the eyeball. **13.** *Chess, draughts.* **a.** a white or light-coloured piece or square. **b.** the player playing with such pieces. **14.** anything white, such as a white paint or white clothing. **15.** *Archery.* the outer ring of the target, having the lowest score. ~See also **whites.** [Old English *hwīt*] —**ˈwhiteness** *n.* —**ˈwhitish** *adj.*

White (waɪt) *n.* **1.** a member of the Caucasoid race. **2.** a person of European ancestry. ~*adj.* **3.** of or denoting a White or Whites.

white ant *n.* same as **termite.**

whitebait (ˈwaɪtˌbeɪt) *n.* the young of herrings, sprats, or pilchards cooked and eaten whole as a delicacy.

white blood cell *n.* a nontechnical name for **leucocyte.**

whitecap (ˈwaɪtˌkæp) *n.* a wave with a white broken crest.

white-collar *adj.* of or designating nonmanual workers employed in professional and clerical occupations.

white dwarf *n.* a small, faint, very dense star.

white elephant *n.* a possession that is unwanted by its owner.

white feather *n.* **1.** a symbol of cowardice. **2. show the white feather.** to act in a cowardly manner.

white fish *n.* any of various sea fishes with white flesh used as food, such as cod or haddock.

white flag *n.* a signal of surrender or to request a truce.

whitefly (ˈwaɪtˌflaɪ) *n., pl.* **-flies.** a tiny whitish insect harmful to greenhouse crops.

white friar *n.* a Carmelite friar, so called from the white cloak worn by these friars.

white gold *n.* a white lustrous hard-wearing alloy containing gold together with platinum or other metals, used in jewellery.

white goods *pl. n.* large household appliances, such as refrigerators or cookers.

Whitehall (ˌwaɪtˈhɔːl) *n.* **1.** a street in London which is the site of the main government offices. **2.** the British Government.

white heat *n.* **1.** intense heat characterized by emission of white light. **2.** *Informal.* a state of intense excitement or activity.

white hope *n. Informal.* a person who is expected to accomplish much.

white horse *n.* (*usually pl.*) a wave with a white broken crest.

white-hot *adj.* **1.** at such a high temperature that white light is emitted. **2.** *Informal.* in a state of intense emotion.

White House *n.* **the. 1.** the official Washington residence of the president of the U.S. **2.** the executive branch of the U.S. government.

white lead (led) *n.* a white powder, usually a mixture of lead carbonate and lead hydroxide, used as a pigment and in making putty and ointments.

white lie *n.* a small lie, usually told to avoid hurting someone's feelings.

white light *n.* light that contains all the wavelengths of the visible spectrum, such as sunlight.

White man's burden *n.* the supposed duty of the White race to bring education and Western culture to the non-White inhabitants of their colonies.

white matter *n.* the whitish tissue of the brain and spinal cord, consisting mainly of nerve fibres.

white meat *n.* any meat that is light in colour, such as veal or the breast of turkey.

whiten ('waɪt³n) *vb.* to make or become white or whiter. —'**whitening** *n.*

white noise *n.* noise that has a wide range of frequencies of uniform intensity.

whiteout ('waɪtaʊt) *n.* an atmospheric condition in which blizzards or low clouds make it very difficult to see.

white paper *n.* (*often caps.*) an official government report which sets out the government's policy on a specific matter.

white pepper *n.* a condiment made from the husked seeds of the pepper plant.

White Russian *adj.* **1.** of Byelorussia, an administrative division of the W Soviet Union. **2.** of Byelorussia, its people, or their language. ~*n.* **3.** the official language of Byelorussia. **4.** a person from Byelorussia.

whites (waɪts) *pl. n.* **1.** household linen or cotton goods, such as sheets. **2.** white clothing, such as that worn for playing cricket.

white sauce *n.* a thick sauce made from flour, butter, seasonings, and milk or stock.

white slave *n.* a girl or woman forced or sold into prostitution.

white spirit *n.* a colourless liquid obtained from petroleum and used as a substitute for turpentine.

white tie *n.* **1.** a white bow tie worn as part of a man's formal evening dress. **2.** formal evening dress for men.

whitewash ('waɪt.wɒʃ) *n.* **1.** a suspension of lime or whiting in water for whitening walls and other surfaces. **2.** *Informal.* an

attempt to conceal defects or gloss over failings. ~*vb.* **3.** to cover with whitewash. **4.** *Informal.* to conceal the defects or gloss over the failings of.

white whale *n.* a small white toothed whale of northern waters.

whitewood ('waɪt.wʊd) *n.* **1.** a light-coloured wood. **2.** a tree yielding such wood.

whither ('wɪðə) *Archaic or poetic.* ~*adv.* **1.** to what place? **2.** to what end or purpose? ~*conj.* **3.** to whatever place or purpose. [Old English *hwider, hwæder*]

whiting[1] ('waɪtɪŋ) *n.* an important white-fleshed food fish of European seas.

whiting[2] ('waɪtɪŋ) *n.* white powdered chalk, used in making whitewash and metal polish.

whitlow ('wɪtləʊ) *n.* an inflamed sore on the end of a finger or toe. [orig. *white + flaw*]

Whitsun ('wɪts³n) *n.* **1.** short for **Whitsuntide.** ~*adj.* **2.** of Whit Sunday or Whitsuntide.

Whit Sunday *n.* the seventh Sunday after Easter. [Old English *hwīta sunnandæg* white Sunday]

Whitsuntide ('wɪts³n.taɪd) *n.* the week that begins with Whit Sunday.

whittle ('wɪt³l) *vb.* **1.** to cut or shave strips or pieces from (wood) with a knife. **2.** to make or shape in this way. **3.** (often foll. by *away* or *down*) to reduce, destroy, or wear away gradually. [Old English *thwītan* to cut]

whizz *or* **whiz** (wɪz) *vb.* **whizzing, whizzed. 1.** to make or cause to make a loud humming or buzzing sound. **2.** to move or cause to move with such a sound. **3.** *Informal.* to move or go rapidly. ~*n., pl.* **whizzes. 4.** a whizzing sound. **5.** *Informal.* a person who is extremely good at something. [imit.]

whizz kid *or* **whiz kid** *n. Informal.* a person who is outstandingly able and successful for his or her age.

who (huː) *pron.* **1.** which person? what person? used in direct and indirect questions: *he can't remember who did it; who met you?* **2.** used at the beginning of a relative clause referring to a person or persons already mentioned: *the people who lived here have left.* **3.** the one or ones who; whoever: *bring who you want.* [Old English *hwā*]

WHO World Health Organization.

whoa (wəʊ) *interj.* a command used esp. to horses to stop or slow down.

whodunit *or* **whodunnit** (huː'dʌnɪt) *n. Informal.* a novel, play, or film concerned with the solving of a crime, esp. murder.

whoever (huː'ɛvə) *pron.* **1.** any person who: *whoever wants it can have it.* **2.** no matter who: *I'll come round tomorrow, whoever may be here.* **3.** an intensive form of *who,* used in questions: *whoever could have thought that?* **4.** *Informal.* an unspecified person: *give those to Cathy or whoever.*

whole (həʊl) *adj.* **1.** containing all the component parts; complete: *a whole apple.*

2. constituting the full quantity or extent: *the whole day.* **3.** uninjured or undamaged. **4.** healthy. **5.** having no fractional or decimal part; integral: *10 is a whole number.* ~*adv.* **6.** in an undivided or unbroken piece: *to swallow a plum whole.* ~*n.* **7.** all there is of a thing; totality. **8.** an assemblage of parts viewed together as a unit. **9.** a thing complete in itself. **10. as a whole.** considered altogether; completely. **11. on the whole. a.** taking all things into consideration. **b.** in general. [Old English *hāl, hǣl*] —**'wholeness** *n.*

wholefood ('həʊl,fuːd) *n.* (*sometimes pl.*) food that has been refined or processed as little as possible.

wholehearted (,həʊl'hɑːtɪd) *adj.* done with total sincerity, enthusiasm, or commitment. —**,whole'heartedly** *adv.*

wholemeal ('həʊl,miːl) *adj. Brit.* **a.** (of flour) made from the entire wheat kernel. **b.** made from wholemeal flour: *wholemeal bread.*

whole note *n. U.S. & Canad.* same as **semibreve.**

whole number *n.* **1.** an integer. **2.** a natural number.

wholesale ('həʊl,seɪl) *n.* **1.** the business of selling goods in large quantities to retailers for resale. ~*adj., adv.* **2.** of or by such business. **3.** on a large scale or indiscriminately. ~*vb.* **4.** to sell (goods) at wholesale. —**'whole,saler** *n.*

wholesome ('həʊlsəm) *adj.* **1.** promoting health or wellbeing. **2.** promoting moral wellbeing. [from *whole* (healthy)]

whole-wheat *adj. U.S. & Canad.* same as **wholemeal.**

wholly ('həʊllɪ) *adv.* completely.

whom (huːm) *pron.* the objective form of *who: whom did you say you had seen? he can't remember whom he saw.* [Old English *hwām*]

whomever (huːm'ɛvə) *pron.* the objective form of *whoever: I'll hire whomever I can find.*

whoop (wuːp) *vb.* **1.** to utter (speech) with loud cries, esp. of excitement or joy. **2.** (huːp). *Med.* to cough convulsively with a crowing sound. **3.** (wʊp, wuːp). **whoop it up.** *Informal.* to indulge in a noisy celebration. ~*n.* **4.** a loud cry, esp. of excitement or joy. **5.** (huːp). *Med.* the convulsive crowing sound made during whooping cough. [imit.]

whoopee *Informal.* ~*interj.* (wʊ'piː). **1.** an exclamation of joy or excitement. ~*n.* ('wʊpiː). **2. make whoopee. a.** to engage in noisy merrymaking. **b.** to make love.

whooping cough ('huːpɪŋ) *n.* an acute infectious disease characterized by coughing spasms that end with a shrill crowing sound on breathing in.

whoops (wʊps) *interj.* an exclamation of surprise or of apology.

whop (wɒp) *Informal.* ~*vb.* **whopping, whopped.** **1.** to strike, beat, or thrash. **2.** to defeat utterly. ~*n.* **3.** a heavy blow or the sound of it. [origin unknown]

whopper ('wɒpə) *n. Informal.* **1.** an

usually large example of its kind. **2.** a big lie.

whopping ('wɒpɪŋ) *adj. Informal.* unusually large.

whore (hɔː) *n.* **1.** a prostitute or promiscuous woman: often a term of abuse. ~*vb.* **2.** to be or act as a prostitute. **3.** (of a man) to have promiscuous sexual relations, esp. with prostitutes. [Old English *hōre*]

whorehouse ('hɔː,haʊs) *n.* a brothel.

whorl (wɜːl) *n.* **1.** *Bot.* a circular arrangement of parts around a stem. **2.** *Zool.* a single turn in a spiral shell. **3.** anything shaped like a coil. [prob. var. of *whirl*]

whortleberry ('wɜːtl,bɛrɪ) *n., pl.* **-ries.** **1.** a small Eurasian shrub with edible sweet blackish berries. **2.** the fruit of this shrub. [dialect var. of *hurtleberry*]

who's (huːz) who is *or* who has.

whose (huːz) *det.* **1.** of who? belonging to who? used in direct and indirect questions: *I told him whose fault it was; whose car is this?* **2.** of who; of which: used as a relative pronoun: *a man whose reputation has suffered.* [Old English *hwæs,* genitive of *hwā* who & *hwæt* what]

whosoever (,huːsəʊ'ɛvə) *pron. Archaic or formal.* same as **whoever.**

who's who *n.* a book or list containing the names and short biographies of famous people.

why (waɪ) *adv.* **1. a.** for what reason?: *why are you here?* **b.** (*used in indirect questions*): *tell me why you're here.* ~*pron.* **2.** for or because of which: *there is no reason why he shouldn't come.* ~*n., pl.* **whys.** **3.** (*usually pl.*) the cause of something: *I want to know the whys and wherefores.* ~*interj.* **4.** an exclamation of surprise, indignation, or impatience: *why, don't be silly!* [Old English *hwī*]

WI **1.** West Indies. **2.** Wisconsin. **3.** (in Britain) Women's Institute.

wick (wɪk) *n.* **1.** a cord or tape in a candle or lamp through which the fuel reaches the flame. **2. get on (someone's) wick.** *Brit. slang.* to annoy (someone). [Old English *weoce*]

wicked ('wɪkɪd) *adj.* **1.** morally bad. **2.** playfully mischievous or roguish: *a wicked grin.* **3.** troublesome or unpleasant. **4.** *Slang.* very good. [Old English *wicca* sorcerer, *wicce* witch] —**'wickedly** *adv.* —**'wickedness** *n.*

wicker ('wɪkə) *n.* **1.** a slender flexible twig, esp. of willow. ~*adj.* **2.** made of wicker. [from Old Norse]

wickerwork ('wɪkə,wɜːk) *n.* a material consisting of woven wicker.

wicket ('wɪkɪt) *n.* **1.** *Cricket.* **a.** either of two sets of three stumps stuck in the ground with two wooden bails resting on top, at which the batsman stands. **b.** the playing space between these. **c.** the act or instance of a batsman being got out: *the bowler took six wickets.* **2.** a small door or gate, esp. one that is near to or part of a larger one. [Old French *wiket*]

wicketkeeper ('wɪkɪt,kiːpə) *n. Cricket.* the fielder positioned directly behind the wicket.

widdershins ('wɪdə,ʃɪnz) adv. Chiefly Scot. same as **withershins**.

wide (waɪd) adj. **1.** having a great extent from side to side. **2.** spacious or extensive. **3. a.** having a specified extent from side to side: two yards wide. **b.** (in combination): extending throughout: nationwide. **4.** remote from the desired point or mark: your guess is wide of the mark. **5.** (of eyes) opened fully. **6.** exhibiting a considerable spread: a wide variation. **7.** Brit. slang. unscrupulous and shrewd: a wide boy. ~adv. **8.** over an extensive area: to travel far and wide. **9.** to a large or full extent: he opened the door wide. **10.** far from the desired point or mark. ~n. **11.** (in cricket) a ball bowled outside the batsman's reach, which scores a run for the batting side. [Old English wid] —'widely adv.

wide-angle lens n. a lens on a camera which can cover a wider angle of view than an ordinary lens.

wide-awake adj. **1.** fully awake. **2.** keen, alert, or observant.

wide-eyed adj. innocent or naive.

widen ('waɪd'n) vb. to make or become wide or wider.

wide-open adj. **1.** open to the full extent. **2.** exposed to attack; vulnerable.

widespread ('waɪd,sprɛd) adj. **1.** extending over a wide area. **2.** accepted by or occurring among many people.

widgeon ('wɪdʒən) n. same as **wigeon**.

widow ('wɪdəʊ) n. **1.** a woman who has lost her husband by death and has not remarried. **2.** (with a modifier) Informal. a woman whose husband frequently leaves her alone while he indulges in a specified hobby or sport: a golf widow. ~vb. (usually passive) **3.** to cause to become a widow. [Old English widuwe] —'widowhood n.

widower ('wɪdəʊə) n. a man who has lost his wife by death and has not remarried.

width (wɪdθ) n. **1.** the extent or measurement of something from side to side. **2.** the state or fact of being wide. **3.** a piece of something of a particular width: a width of cloth. **4.** the distance across a rectangular swimming bath, as opposed to its length.

wield (wiːld) vb. **1.** to handle or use (a weapon or tool). **2.** to exert or maintain (power or authority). [Old English wieldan, wealdan]

wife (waɪf) n., pl. **wives. 1.** a man's partner in marriage; a married woman. **2.** Archaic or dialect. a woman. [Old English wif] —'wifely adj.

wig (wɪg) n. an artificial head of hair. [from periwig] —'wigged adj.

wigeon or **widgeon** ('wɪdʒən) n. a wild duck of marshland. [origin unknown]

wigging ('wɪgɪŋ) n. Brit. slang. a reprimand. [origin unknown]

wiggle ('wɪg'l) vb. **1.** to move or cause to move with jerky movements from side to side. ~n. **2.** the act of wiggling. [Middle Low German, Middle Dutch wiggelen] —'wiggly adj.

wight (waɪt) n. Archaic. a human being. [Old English]

wigwam ('wɪg,wæm) n. a dwelling of the North American Indians, made of bark, rushes, or skins spread over a set of arched poles lashed together. [American Indian]

wilco ('wɪlkəʊ) interj. an expression in signalling and telecommunications, indicating that a message just received will be complied with. [abbrev. for I will comply]

wild (waɪld) adj. **1.** (of animals) living independently of man; not domesticated or tame. **2.** (of plants) growing in a natural state; not cultivated. **3.** uninhabited; desolate: a wild stretch of land. **4.** living in a savage or uncivilized way: wild tribes. **5.** lacking restraint or control: wild merriment. **6.** of great violence: a wild storm. **7.** dishevelled; untidy: wild hair. **8.** in a state of extreme emotional intensity: wild with grief. **9.** random: a wild guess. **10.** (foll. by about) Informal. very enthusiastic: I'm wild about my new boyfriend. **11.** Informal. very angry: Dad will be wild when he hears this. ~adv. **12.** in a wild manner. **13. run wild. a.** to grow without cultivation: the garden has run wild. **b.** to behave without restraint: his children run wild. ~n. **14.** (often pl.) a desolate or uninhabited region. **15. the wild.** a free natural state of living. [Old English wilde] —'wildly adv.

wildcat ('waɪld,kæt) n., pl. **-cats** or **-cat. 1.** a wild European cat that resembles the domestic tabby but is larger and has a bushy tail. **2.** Informal. a savage or aggressive person. **3.** Chiefly U.S. & Canad. an exploratory drilling for petroleum or natural gas. **4.** (modifier) Chiefly U.S. risky, esp. financially unsound: a wildcat project.

wildcat strike n. a strike begun by workers spontaneously or without union approval.

wildebeest ('wɪldɪ,biːst, 'vɪl-) n., pl. **-beests** or **-beest.** same as **gnu.** [Afrikaans]

wilderness ('wɪldənɪs) n. **1.** a wild uninhabited uncultivated region. **2.** a confused mass or tangle. **3. a voice (crying) in the wilderness.** a person or group making a suggestion or plea that is ignored. [Old English wildēor wild beast]

wildfire ('waɪld,faɪə) n. **1.** a highly flammable material formerly used in warfare. **2. spread like wildfire.** to spread very quickly or uncontrollably.

wild flower n. any flowering plant that grows in an uncultivated state.

wildfowl ('waɪld,faʊl) n. **1.** any game bird. **2.** such birds collectively. —'wild,fowling adj., n.

wild-goose chase n. an absurd or hopeless search or undertaking.

wildlife ('waɪld,laɪf) n. wild animals and plants collectively.

wild rice n. an aquatic North American grass with dark-coloured edible grain.

Wild West n. the western U.S. during its settlement, esp. with reference to its lawlessness.

wile (waɪl) *n.* **1.** (*usually pl.*) an artful or seductive trick or ploy. ~*vb.* **2.** to lure or beguile. [Old Norse *vel* craft]

wilful *or U.S.* **willful** ('wɪlful) *adj.* **1.** intent on having one's own way; headstrong or obstinate. **2.** intentional: *wilful murder.* —'**wilfully** *adv.*

will[1] (wɪl) *vb. past* **would.** used as an auxiliary: **1.** (esp. with *you, he, she, it, they,* or a noun as subject) to make the future tense. **2.** to express resolution on the part of the speaker: *I will buy that radio if it's the last thing I do.* **3.** to indicate willingness: *will you help me with this problem?* **4.** to express commands: *you will report your findings to me.* **5.** to express ability: *this rope will support a load.* **6.** to express probability or expectation: *that will be Jim telephoning.* **7.** to express customary practice: *boys will be boys.* **8.** to express desire: *stay if you will.* [Old English *willan*]

will[2] (wɪl) *n.* **1.** the faculty of conscious and deliberate choice of action. **2.** the act or an instance of asserting a choice. **3. a.** the declaration of a person's wishes regarding the disposal of his property after his death. **b.** the document containing this. **4.** desire; wish. **5.** determined intention: *where there's a will there's a way.* **6.** attitude towards others: *he bears you no ill will.* **7. at will.** at one's own desire or choice. **8. with a will.** heartily; energetically. ~*vb.* **9.** to exercise the will in an attempt to accomplish (something): *he willed himself to recover.* **10.** to bequeath (property) by a will: *he willed his art collection to the nation.* **11.** to wish or desire: *wander where you will.* [Old English *willa*]

willie *or* **willy** ('wɪlɪ) *n. Brit. informal.* a childish or jocular name for **penis.**

willies ('wɪlɪz) *pl. n.* **the.** *Slang.* nervousness, jitters, or fright: *spiders give me the willies.* [origin unknown]

willing ('wɪlɪŋ) *adj.* **1.** favourably disposed or inclined; ready: *are you willing to agree?* **2.** cheerfully compliant: *a willing worker.* **3.** done or given freely or voluntarily. —'**willingly** *adv.* —'**willingness** *n.*

will-o'-the-wisp (ˌwɪləðə'wɪsp) *n.* **1.** a pale light sometimes seen over marshy ground at night. **2.** a person or thing that is elusive or allures and misleads. [*Will,* short for *William* + *wisp,* twist of hay burning as a torch]

willow ('wɪləʊ) *n.* a tree or shrub with pliant wood used in weaving baskets and making cricket bats. [Old English *welig*]

willowherb ('wɪləʊˌhɜːb) *n.* a plant with narrow leaves and purplish flowers.

willow pattern *n.* a pattern incorporating a willow tree, river, bridge, and figures, usually in blue on a white ground, used on china.

willowy ('wɪləʊɪ) *adj.* **1.** slender and graceful. **2.** shaded with willows.

willpower ('wɪlˌpaʊə) *n.* the ability to control oneself and determine one's actions.

willy-nilly ('wɪlɪ'nɪlɪ) *adv.* whether desired or not. [Old English *wile hē, nyle hē,* will he or will he not]

wilt[1] (wɪlt) *vb.* **1.** to become or cause to become limp or drooping: *insufficient water makes plants wilt.* **2.** to lose or cause to lose courage or strength. ~*n.* **3.** a plant disease characterized by wilting. [perhaps from obs. *wilk* to wither]

wilt[2] (wɪlt) *vb. Archaic or dialect.* (used with the pronoun *thou*) a singular form of the present tense of **will**[1].

Wilts. (wɪlts) Wiltshire.

wily ('waɪlɪ) *adj.* **wilier, wiliest.** sly or crafty. —'**wiliness** *n.*

wimp (wɪmp) *n. Informal.* a feeble ineffective person. [origin unknown] —'**wimpish** *or* '**wimpy** *adj.*

wimple ('wɪmp'l) *n.* a piece of cloth draped around the head to frame the face, worn by women in the Middle Ages and now by some nuns. [Old English *wimpel*]

Wimpy ('wɪmpɪ) *n., pl.* **-pies.** *Trademark.* a hamburger served in a soft bread roll.

win (wɪn) *vb.* **winning, won.** **1.** to achieve first place in a competition. **2.** to gain (a prize or first place) in a competition. **3.** to succeed in or gain (something) with an effort: *we won recognition.* **4.** to gain victory or triumph in (a battle, argument, or struggle). **5.** to gain (the sympathy, favour, or support) of someone. **6. you can't win.** *Informal.* there is no way to succeed. ~*n.* **7.** *Informal.* a success, victory, or triumph. **8.** profit; winnings. ~See also **win over.** [Old English *winnan*] —'**winnable** *adj.*

wince (wɪns) *vb.* **1.** to draw back slightly, as with sudden pain; flinch. ~*n.* **2.** the act of wincing. [Old French *wencier, guenchir* to avoid]

winceyette (ˌwɪnsɪ'ɛt) *n. Brit.* a soft cotton fabric with slightly raised nap. [Scot. *wincey,* prob. from *woolsey* in *linsey-woolsey,* a fabric made of linen & wool]

winch (wɪntʃ) *n.* **1.** a lifting or hauling device consisting of a rope or chain wound round a barrel or drum. **2.** a hand- or power-operated crank by which a machine is driven. ~*vb.* **3.** (often foll. by *up* or *in*) to haul or lift using a winch. [Old English *wince* pulley]

Winchester rifle ('wɪntʃɪstə) *n. Trademark.* a slide-action repeating rifle. [after O. F. *Winchester,* U.S. manufacturer]

wind[1] (wɪnd) *n.* **1.** a current of air moving across the earth's surface. **2.** air artificially moved, as by a fan. **3.** a trend, tendency, or force: *the winds of revolution.* **4.** *Informal.* a hint; suggestion: *we got wind that you were coming.* **5.** foolish or empty talk: *that's a lot of wind.* **6.** breath, as used in respiration or talk: *you're just wasting wind.* **7.** (often used in sports) the power to breathe normally: *his wind is weak.* **8.** *Music.* a wind instrument or wind instruments collectively. **9.** gas in the stomach or intestines; flatulence. **10.** the air on which the scent of an animal is carried to hounds or on which the scent of a hunter is carried to his quarry. **11.**

break wind. to release intestinal gas through the anus. **12. get** *or* **have the wind up.** *Informal.* to become frightened. **13. in the wind.** about to happen. **14. put the wind up.** *Informal.* to frighten or alarm. **15. sail close to the wind.** to come near the limits of honesty or decency. **16. take the wind out of someone's sails.** to disconcert or deflate someone. **17. which way the wind blows.** what appears probable. ~*vb.* **18.** to cause (someone) to be short of breath: *the blow winded him.* **19.** to detect the scent of. **20.** to cause (a baby) to bring up wind after feeding. [Old English] —'**windless** *adj.*

wind² (waɪnd) *vb.* **winding, wound. 1.** to coil (something flexible) around some object or (of something flexible) to be coiled around some object: *he wound a scarf around his head.* **2.** (often foll. by *up*) to tighten the spring of (a clockwork mechanism). **3.** to move in a twisting, spiral, or circular course: *the river winds through the hills.* ~*n.* **4.** a winding or being wound. **5.** a single turn or bend: *a wind in the river.* ~See also **wind down, wind up.** [Old English *windan*] —'**winding** *n., adj.*

windbag ('wɪnd,bæg) *n. Slang.* a person who talks a lot but says little of interest.

windblown ('wɪnd,bləʊn) *adj.* **1.** blown by the wind. **2.** (of trees or shrubs) growing in a shape determined by the prevailing winds.

wind-borne ('wɪnd-) *adj.* (esp. of plant seeds or pollen) carried by wind.

windbreak ('wɪnd,breɪk) *n.* a fence or line of trees serving as a protection from the wind by breaking its force.

windcheater ('wɪnd,tʃiːtə) *n.* a warm jacket, usually with a close-fitting knitted neck, cuffs, and waistband.

wind-chill ('wɪnd-) *n.* the serious chilling effect of wind and low temperature.

wind cone (wɪnd) *n.* same as **windsock.**

wind down (waɪnd) *vb.* **1.** to lower or move down by cranking. **2.** (of a clockwork mechanism) to slow down before stopping completely. **3.** to diminish gradually in force or power; relax.

winded ('wɪndɪd) *adj.* temporarily out of breath from strenuous exercise or a blow to the stomach.

windfall ('wɪnd,fɔːl) *n.* **1.** a piece of unexpected good fortune, esp. financial gain. **2.** a fruit blown down by the wind.

wind gauge (wɪnd) *n.* same as **anemometer.**

winding sheet *n.* a sheet in which a corpse is wrapped for burial; shroud.

wind instrument (wɪnd) *n.* a musical instrument sounded by blowing air through it, such as a flute.

windjammer ('wɪnd,dʒæmə) *n.* a large merchant sailing ship.

windlass ('wɪndləs) *n.* **1.** a machine for lifting objects by winding a rope or chain around a barrel or drum driven by a crank or motor. ~*vb.* **2.** to lift (an object) by means of a windlass. [Old Norse *vindáss*]

windmill ('wɪnd,mɪl) *n.* **1.** a machine for grinding or pumping driven by sails that

are turned by the wind. **2.** *Brit.* a toy consisting of a stick with plastic vanes attached, which revolve in the wind. **3. tilt at windmills.** to fight an imaginary opponent or evil.

window ('wɪndəʊ) *n.* **1.** an opening in a wall that is provided to let in light or air or to see through. **2.** a framework that contains a glass pane or panes and is placed in an opening in a wall. **3.** short for **windowpane. 4.** the display area behind a glass window in a shop. **5.** a window-like opening or structure. [Old Norse *vindauga* wind eye]

window box *n.* a long narrow box, placed on a windowsill, in which plants are grown.

window-dressing *n.* **1.** the art of arranging goods in shop windows to attract customers. **2.** an attempt to make something seem better than it is by stressing only its attractive features.

windowpane ('wɪndəʊ,peɪn) *n.* a sheet of glass in a window.

window seat *n.* **1.** a seat below a window. **2.** a seat beside a window in a bus, train, or aeroplane.

window-shopping *n.* looking at goods in shop windows without intending to buy. —'**window-,shop** *vb.*

windowsill ('wɪndəʊ,sɪl) *n.* a sill below a window.

windpipe ('wɪnd,paɪp) *n.* a nontechnical name for **trachea.**

windscreen ('wɪnd,skriːn) *n. Brit.* the sheet of glass that forms the front window of a motor vehicle.

windscreen wiper *n. Brit.* an electrically operated blade with a rubber edge that wipes a windscreen clear of rain.

windshield ('wɪnd,ʃiːld) *n. U.S. & Canad.* same as **windscreen.**

windsock ('wɪnd,sɒk) *n.* a cloth cone mounted on a mast, used, esp. at airports, to indicate wind direction.

Windsor chair ('wɪnzə) *n.* a style of wooden chair with a shaped seat and a back made up of turned spokes.

Windsor knot *n.* a wide triangular knot, produced by making extra turns in tying a tie.

windsurfing ('wɪnd,sɜːfɪŋ) *n.* the sport of riding on water using a surfboard steered and propelled by an attached sail.

windswept ('wɪnd,swept) *adj.* exposed to or swept by the wind.

wind tunnel (wɪnd) *n.* a chamber through which a stream of air is forced to test the effects of wind on aircraft.

wind up (waɪnd) *vb.* **1.** to bring to or reach a conclusion: *he wound up the proceedings.* **2.** to tighten the spring of (a clockwork mechanism). **3.** (*usually passive*) *Informal.* to make nervous or tense: *he was all wound up before the big fight.* **4.** to roll (something flexible) into a ball. **5.** *Informal.* same as **liquidate** (sense 2). **6.** *Informal.* to end up (in a specified state): *you'll wind up dead.* **7.** *Brit. slang.* to tease (someone). ~*n.* **wind-up. 8.** the act of concluding. **9.** the end.

windward ('wɪndwəd) *Chiefly naut.* ~*adj.* **1.** of or in the direction from which the wind blows. ~*n.* **2.** the windward direction. ~*adv.* **3.** towards the wind.

windy ('wɪndɪ) *adj.* **windier**, **windiest**. **1.** of or characterized by wind; stormy. **2.** swept by or exposed to winds. **3.** long-winded or pompous: *windy orations*. **4.** *Informal.* flatulent. **5.** *Slang.* frightened. —'**windiness** *n.*

wine (waɪn) *n.* **1. a.** an alcoholic drink produced by the fermenting of grapes with water and sugar. **b.** an alcoholic drink produced in this way from other fruits or flowers: *elderberry wine.* **2.** a dark red colour with a purplish tinge. ~*vb.* **3. wine and dine.** to entertain or be entertained with wine and fine food. [Latin *vīnum*]

wine bar *n.* a bar in a restaurant, or an establishment that specializes in serving wine and usually food.

winebibber ('waɪn,bɪbə) *n.* a person who drinks a great deal of wine.

wine cellar *n.* **1.** a cellar where wine is stored. **2.** the stock of wines stored there.

wineglass ('waɪn,glɑːs) *n.* a glass for wine, usually having a small bowl on a stem, with a flared base.

winepress ('waɪn,prɛs) *n.* a machine used to squeeze the juice from grapes in order to make wine.

wineskin ('waɪn,skɪn) *n.* the skin of a sheep or goat sewn up and used to hold wine.

wing (wɪŋ) *n.* **1.** one of the limbs or organs of a bird, bat, or insect that are specialized for flight. **2.** one of the two winglike supporting parts of an aircraft. **3.** a means or cause of flight or rapid motion: *fear gave wings to his feet.* **4.** *Brit.* the part of a car body surrounding the wheels. **5.** *Sport.* **a.** either of the two sides of the pitch near the touchline. **b.** a player stationed in such a position; winger. **6.** a faction or group within a political party or other organization. **7.** a projecting part of a building. **8.** (*pl.*) the space offstage to the right or left of the acting area in a theatre. **9. in the wings.** ready to step in when needed. **10.** a tactical formation in some air forces, consisting of two or more squadrons. **11. on the wing. a.** flying. **b.** travelling. **12. spread one's wings.** to make full use of one's abilities. **13. take wing.** to lift off or fly away. **14. under one's wing.** in one's care. ~*vb.* **15.** to make (one's way) swiftly on or as if on wings. **16.** to shoot or wound superficially in the wing or arm. **17.** to cause to fly or move swiftly: *to wing an arrow.* **18.** to provide with wings. [from Old Norse] —**winged** *adj.* —'**wingless** *adj.*

wing chair *n.* an easy chair with side pieces extending forward from a high back.

wing commander *n.* a middle-ranking commissioned Air Force officer.

winger ('wɪŋə) *n. Sport.* a player stationed on the wing.

wing nut *n.* a threaded nut with two flat projections which allow it to be turned by the thumb and forefinger.

wingspan ('wɪŋ,spæn) *or* **wingspread** ('wɪŋ,sprɛd) *n.* the distance between the wing tips of an aircraft, bird, insect, or bat.

wink (wɪŋk) *vb.* **1.** to close and open one eye quickly as a signal. **2.** to close and open (an eye or the eyes) momentarily. **3.** (of a light) to twinkle. ~*n.* **4.** a winking, esp. as a signal. **5.** a twinkling of light. **6.** a brief moment of sleep: *I didn't sleep a wink.* **7.** *Informal.* the smallest amount of sleep: *I didn't sleep a wink.* **8. tip the wink.** *Brit. informal.* to give a hint. [Old English *wincian*]

wink at *vb.* to pretend not to notice: *the authorities winked at corruption.*

winker ('wɪŋkə) *n.* a flashing light on a motor vehicle that indicates turning.

winkle ('wɪŋk⁺l) *n.* **1.** same as **periwinkle**[1]. ~*vb.* **2.** (usually foll. by *out*) *Informal, chiefly Brit.* to extract or prise out.

winkle-pickers *pl. n.* shoes with very pointed narrow toes.

winner ('wɪnə) *n.* **1.** a person or thing that wins. **2.** *Informal.* a person or thing that seems sure to win or succeed.

winning ('wɪnɪŋ) *adj.* **1.** charming, engaging, or attractive: *a winning smile.* **2.** gaining victory: *the winning goal.* ~*n.* **3.** (*pl.*) something won, esp. in gambling.

winnow ('wɪnəʊ) *vb.* **1.** to separate (grain) from (chaff) by a current of air. **2.** to examine in order to select the desirable elements. [Old English *windwian*]

wino ('waɪnəʊ) *n., pl.* **winos.** *Informal.* a down-and-out who habitually drinks cheap wine.

win over *vb.* to gain the support or consent of (someone).

winsome ('wɪnsəm) *adj.* charming; winning; engaging: *a winsome smile.* [Old English *wynsum*]

winter ('wɪntə) *n.* **1.** (*sometimes cap.*) the coldest season of the year, between autumn and spring. ~*vb.* **2.** to spend the winter in a specified place. [Old English]

wintergreen ('wɪntə,griːn) *n.* **1.** an evergreen shrub from which a sweet smelling oil is obtained. **2. oil of wintergreen.** an aromatic compound, formerly made from this plant but now synthesized: used medicinally and for flavouring.

winter solstice *n.* the time in the northern hemisphere, about December 22, at which the sun is at its southernmost point in the sky.

winter sports *pl. n.* open-air sports held on snow or ice.

wintertime ('wɪntə,taɪm) *n.* the winter season.

wintry ('wɪntrɪ) *adj.* **-trier, -triest. 1.** (esp. of weather) of or characteristic of winter. **2.** lacking cheer or warmth; bleak: *a wintry stare.* —'**wintriness** *n.*

winy ('waɪnɪ) *adj.* **winier, winiest.** having the taste of wine; heady.

wipe (waɪp) *vb.* **1.** to rub (a surface or object) lightly, esp. with a cloth or the hand, to remove dirt or liquid from it. **2.** (usually foll. by *off, away, from* or *up*) to remove by or as if by wiping: *he wiped the dirt from his hands.* **3.** to erase (a recording) from (a tape). **4.** to apply (a substance) by wiping. **5.** to **wipe the floor with (someone).** *Informal.* to defeat (someone) decisively. ~*n.* **6.** the act or an instance of wiping. [Old English *wīpian*]

wipe out *vb.* **1.** to destroy completely. **2.** *Informal.* to kill.

wiper ('waɪpə) *n.* **1.** a piece of cloth used for wiping. **2.** same as **windscreen wiper.**

wire ('waɪə) *n.* **1.** a slender flexible strand of metal. **2.** a length of this used to carry electric current in a circuit. **3.** anything made of wire, such as wire netting. **4.** a long continuous wire or cable connecting points in a telephone or telegraph system. **5.** *Informal.* a telegram or telegraph. **6. get one's wires crossed.** *Informal.* to misunderstand. ~*vb.* **7.** to send a telegram to (a person or place). **8.** to send (something) by telegraph: *he wired her the money to fly home.* **9.** to equip (an electrical system, circuit, or component) with wires. **10.** to fasten with wire. [Old English *wīr*]

wire-haired *adj.* (of an animal) having a rough wiry coat.

wireless ('waɪəlɪs) *n. Chiefly Brit.* same as **radio.**

wire netting *n.* a net made of wire, used for fencing.

wirepuller ('waɪə,pʊlə) *n. Chiefly U.S. & Canad.* a person who uses private or secret influence for his own ends.

wire service *n. Chiefly U.S. & Canad.* an agency supplying news by telegraph to subscribing newspapers, radio, and television stations.

wiretap ('waɪə,tæp) *vb.* **-tapping, -tapped.** **1.** to make a connection to a telegraph or telephone wire in order to obtain information secretly. **2.** to tap (a telephone) or the telephone of (a person).

wire wool *n.* a mass of fine wire, used esp. to clean kitchen articles.

wireworm ('waɪə,wɜːm) *n.* a destructive wormlike beetle larva.

wiring ('waɪərɪŋ) *n.* the network of wires used in an electrical system, device, or circuit.

wiry ('waɪərɪ) *adj.* **wirier, wiriest. 1.** (of people or animals) slender but strong. **2.** resembling wire, esp. in stiffness: *wiry hair.* —**'wiriness** *n.*

wisdom ('wɪzdəm) *n.* **1.** the ability to use one's experience and knowledge to make sensible decisions or judgments. **2.** accumulated knowledge or learning. **3.** *Archaic.* a wise saying or sayings. [Old English]

wisdom tooth *n.* any of the four molar teeth, one at the back of each side of the jaw, that are the last of the permanent teeth to come through.

wise¹ (waɪz) *adj.* **1.** possessing or showing wisdom. **2.** prudent; sensible: *a wise plan.* **3.** learned; erudite. **4. none the wiser.** knowing no more than before. **5. be** *or* **get wise.** (often foll. by *to*) *Informal.* to be or become aware or informed (of something). **6. put wise.** (often foll. by *to*) *Slang.* to

inform or warn (of). [Old English *wīs*] —**'wisely** *adv.*

wise² (waɪz) *n. Archaic.* way, manner, or respect: *in any wise; in no wise.* [Old English *wīse* manner]

-wise *adv. combining form.* **1.** indicating direction or manner: *clockwise; likewise.* **2.** with reference to: *businesswise.* [Old English *-wīsan*]

wiseacre ('waɪz,eɪkə) *n.* a person who wishes to seem wise. [Middle Dutch *wijsseggher* soothsayer]

wisecrack ('waɪz,kræk) *Informal.* ~*n.* **1.** a flippant or sardonic remark. ~*vb.* **2.** to make a wisecrack.

wise guy *n. Informal.* a person who is given to making conceited, sardonic, or insolent comments.

wise up *vb. Slang, chiefly U.S. & Canad.* (often foll. by *to*) to become or cause to become aware or informed (of).

wish (wɪʃ) *vb.* **1.** to want or desire (something, often that which cannot be or is not the case): *I wish I lived in Italy.* **2.** to feel or express a hope concerning the welfare, health or success of (a person): *I wish you well.* **3.** to desire or prefer to be as specified: *I wish to leave now.* **4.** to greet as specified: *he wished us good afternoon.* ~*n.* **5.** the expression of some desire: *to make a wish.* **6.** something desired or wished for: *he got his wish.* **7.** (usually *pl.*) expressed hopes for someone's welfare, health, or success: *give your mother our best wishes.* [Old English *wȳscan*]

wishbone ('wɪʃ,bəʊn) *n.* the V-shaped bone above the breastbone in most birds.

wishful ('wɪʃfʊl) *adj.* desirous or longing. —**'wishfulness** *n.*

wishful thinking *n.* an interpretation of the facts as one would like them to be, rather than as they are.

wish on *vb.* to hope that (someone or something) should be imposed (on someone): *I wouldn't wish my cold on anyone.*

wishy-washy ('wɪʃɪ,wɒʃɪ) *adj. Informal.* **1.** lacking in character, force, or colour. **2.** watery; thin.

wisp (wɪsp) *n.* **1.** a thin, delicate, or filmy piece or strand: *a wisp of smoke.* **2.** a small bundle or tuft: *a wisp of hay.* **3.** anything slender and delicate: *a wisp of a girl.* [origin unknown] —**'wispy** *adj.*

wisteria (wɪ'stɪərɪə) *n.* a twining woody climbing plant with blue, purple, or white flowers in large drooping clusters. [after Caspar *Wistar*, anatomist]

wistful ('wɪstfʊl) *adj.* sadly wishing for something lost or unobtainable. —**'wistfully** *adv.* —**'wistfulness** *n.*

wit¹ (wɪt) *n.* **1.** the ability to use words or ideas in a clever, amusing, and imaginative way. **2.** speech or writing showing this ability. **3.** a person possessing, or noted for such an ability. **4.** practical intelligence: *nobody had the wit to bring a tin-opener.* ~See also **wits.** [Old English *witt*]

wit² (wɪt) *vb.* **to wit.** that is to say; namely (used to introduce statements, as in legal documents). [Old English *witan*]

witblits ('vɪt,blɪts) *n. S. African.* alcoholic drink illegally distilled. [Afrikaans]

witch (wɪtʃ) *n.* **1.** a person, usually female, who practises magic or sorcery, esp. black magic. **2.** an ugly or wicked old woman. **3.** a fascinating or enchanting woman. [Old English *wicca*]

witchcraft ('wɪtʃ,krɑːft) *n.* **1.** the use of magic; sorcery. **2.** bewitching influence or charm.

witch doctor *n.* a man in certain tribal societies, who appears to possess magical powers, used to cure sickness but also to harm people.

witch-elm *n.* same as **wych-elm.**

witchery ('wɪtʃərɪ) *n., pl.* **-eries. 1.** the practice of witchcraft. **2.** bewitching influence or charm.

witch hazel *or* **wych-hazel** *n.* **1.** a shrub of North America, with ornamental yellow flowers. **2.** an astringent medicinal solution made from the bark and leaves of this shrub, applied to treat bruises and inflammation.

witch-hunt *n.* a rigorous campaign to expose and discredit people considered to hold unorthodox views on the pretext of safeguarding the public welfare.

with (wɪð, wɪθ) *prep.* **1.** using; by means of: *he killed her with an axe.* **2.** accompanying; in the company of: *the lady you were with.* **3.** possessing; having: *a man with a red moustache.* **4.** concerning or regarding: *be patient with her.* **5.** in a manner characterized by: *writing with abandon.* **6.** as a result of: *shaking with rage.* **7.** having the same opinions as; supporting. **8.** following the line of thought of (a person). **9. with it.** *Informal.* **a.** fashionable; in style. **b.** alert and understanding what is going on. [Old English]

withal (wɪ'ðɔːl) *adv.* **1.** *Literary.* as well. **2.** *Archaic.* with that.

withdraw (wɪð'drɔː) *vb.* **-drawing, -drew, -drawn. 1.** to take or draw back or away; remove. **2.** to remove (money) from a bank account or savings account. **3.** to retract or recall (something said). **4.** to retire or retreat: *the troops withdrew.* **5.** (often foll. by *from*) to depart (from): *he withdrew from public life.* **6.** to detach oneself socially, emotionally, or mentally. [*with* in the sense: away from]

withdrawal (wɪð'drɔːəl) *n.* **1.** an act or process of withdrawing. **2.** the period a drug addict goes through after ceasing to use narcotics, usually characterized by physical and mental symptoms (**withdrawal symptoms**).

withdrawn (wɪð'drɔːn) *vb.* **1.** the past participle of **withdraw.** ~*adj.* **2.** unusually reserved or shy.

withe (wɪθ, wɪð, waɪð) *n.* a strong flexible twig, esp. of willow, used for binding things together. [Old English *withthe*]

wither ('wɪðə) *vb.* **1.** to make or become dried up or shrivelled. **2.** (often foll. by *away*) to fade or waste: *all hope withered away.* **3.** to humiliate (someone) with a scornful look or remark. [prob. var. of *weather* (vb.)] —'**withering** *adj.*

withers ('wɪðəz) *pl. n.* the highest part of the back of a horse, between the shoulders. [earlier *widersones*, from obs. *wider* with + *-sones*, perhaps sinews]

withershins ('wɪðə,ʃɪnz) *adv. Chiefly Scot.* in the direction opposite to the apparent course of the sun; anticlockwise. [Middle Low German *weddersinnes*]

withhold (wɪð'həʊld) *vb.* **-holding, -held. 1.** to keep back: *he withheld his permission.* **2.** to hold back; restrain.

within (wɪ'ðɪn) *prep.* **1.** in; inside; enclosed by. **2.** before (a period of time) has passed: *within a week.* **3.** not beyond: *live within your means; within reach.* ~*adv.* **4.** *Formal.* inside; internally.

without (wɪ'ðaʊt) *prep.* **1.** not having: *a traveller without much money.* **2.** not accompanied by: *he came without his wife.* **3.** not making use of: *to undo screws without a screwdriver.* **4.** (foll. by a present participle) while not or after not: *she can sing for two minutes without drawing breath.* **5.** *Archaic.* outside: *without the city walls.* ~*adv.* **6.** *Formal.* outside.

withstand (wɪð'stænd) *vb.* **-standing, -stood.** to resist, oppose, or endure successfully.

witless ('wɪtlɪs) *adj.* lacking wit, intelligence, or sense. —'**witlessness** *n.*

witness ('wɪtnɪs) *n.* **1.** a person who has seen or can give first-hand evidence of some event. **2.** evidence; testimony: *his smile was a witness to his happiness.* **3.** a person who testifies in court. **4.** a person who attests to the genuineness of a document or signature by adding his own signature. **5. bear witness to. a.** to give testimony to. **b.** to be evidence or proof of. ~*vb.* **6.** to see, be present at, or know at first hand. **7.** to give evidence of. **8.** to be the scene or setting of: *this field has witnessed a battle.* **9.** to testify in court. **10.** to attest to the genuineness of (a document or signature) by adding one's own signature. [Old English *witnes*]

witness box *or esp. U.S.* **witness stand** *n.* the place in a court of law in which witnesses stand to give evidence.

wits (wɪts) *pl. n.* **1.** (sometimes *sing.*) the ability to reason and act, esp. quickly: *have one's wits about one.* **2.** (sometimes *sing.*) right mind, sanity: *out of one's wits.* **3. at one's wits' end.** at a loss to know what to do. **4. live by one's wits.** to gain a livelihood by craftiness rather than by hard work.

witter ('wɪtə) *vb.* (often foll. by *on*) *Informal.* to chatter or babble pointlessly or at unnecessary length. [origin unknown]

witticism ('wɪtɪ,sɪzəm) *n.* a clever or witty remark.

witty ('wɪtɪ) *adj.* **-tier, -tiest.** characterized by clever humour or wit. —'**wittily** *adv.* —'**wittiness** *n.*

wives (waɪvz) *n.* **1.** the plural of **wife. 2. old wives' tale.** a superstitious tradition.

wizard ('wɪzəd) *n.* **1.** a magician or sorcerer. **2.** a person who is outstandingly gifted in some specified field. ~*adj.* **3.** *Infor-*

mal, chiefly Brit. superb; outstanding. [from *wise*]

wizardry ('wɪzədrɪ) *n.* magic; sorcery.

wizened ('wɪz'nd) *adj.* shrivelled, wrinkled, or dried up, esp. with age.

woad (wəʊd) *n.* **1.** a European plant with leaves which yield a blue dye. **2.** this dye, used esp. by the ancient Britons as a body dye. [Old English *wād*]

wobble ('wɒb'l) *vb.* **1.** to move or sway unsteadily. **2.** to shake: *her voice wobbled with emotion.* **3.** to waver with indecision. **4.** to cause to wobble. ~*n.* **5.** a wobbling movement or sound. [Low German *wabbeln*] —**'wobbly** *adj.*

wodge (wɒdʒ) *n. Brit. informal.* a thick lump or chunk of something. [from *wedge*]

woe (wəʊ) *n.* **1.** *Literary.* intense grief. **2.** (*often pl.*) affliction or misfortune. **woe betide (someone):** misfortune will befall (someone): *woe betide you if you arrive late.* ~*interj.* Also: **woe is me.** *Archaic.* alas. [Old English *wā, wǣ*]

woebegone ('wəʊbɪˌgɒn) *adj.* sorrowful or sad in appearance. [*woe* + obs. *bego* to surround]

woeful ('wəʊfʊl) *adj.* **1.** sad; mournful. **2.** bringing or causing woe. **3.** pitiful; deplorable: *a woeful standard of work.* —**'woefully** *adv.* —**'woefulness** *n.*

wog (wɒg) *n. Brit. slang, offensive.* a person who is not White. [prob. from *golliwog*]

wok (wɒk) *n.* a large bowl-shaped metal Chinese cooking pot: used esp. for stir-frying. [Chinese (Cantonese)]

woke (wəʊk) *vb.* the past tense of **wake**[1].

woken ('wəʊkən) *vb.* the past participle of **wake**[1].

wold (wəʊld) *n.* a tract of high open rolling country. [Old English *weald* bush]

wolf (wʊlf) *n., pl.* **wolves.** **1.** a predatory canine mammal which hunts in packs. **2.** *Informal.* a man who habitually tries to seduce women. **3. cry wolf.** to give a false alarm. **4. keep the wolf from the door.** to keep away poverty or hunger. **5. lone wolf.** a person or animal who prefers to be alone. **6. wolf in sheep's clothing.** a malicious person in a harmless or benevolent disguise. ~*vb.* **7.** (often foll. by *down*) to gulp (down). [Old English *wulf*]

wolfhound ('wʊlfˌhaʊnd) *n.* a large dog, used formerly to hunt wolves.

wolfram ('wʊlfrəm) *n.* same as **tungsten.** [from German]

wolfsbane ('wʊlfsˌbeɪn) *n.* a poisonous plant with hoodlike flowers.

wolf whistle *n.* a whistle made by a man to express admiration of a woman's appearance.

wolverine ('wʊlvəˌriːn) *n.* a large carnivorous mammal of Eurasia and North America with dark very thick fur. [earlier *wolvering,* from *wolf*]

wolves (wʊlvz) *n.* the plural of **wolf.**

woman ('wʊmən) *n., pl.* **women.** **1.** an adult female human being. **2.** (*modifier*) female: *a woman politician.* **3.** women collectively. **4.** (usually preceded by *the*)

feminine nature or feelings: *babies bring out the woman in him.* **5.** a female servant or domestic help. **6.** *Informal.* a wife or girlfriend. [Old English *wīfmann, wimman*]

womanhood ('wʊmənˌhʊd) *n.* **1.** the state or quality of being a woman or being womanly. **2.** women collectively.

womanish ('wʊmənɪʃ) *adj.* **1.** unmanly; effeminate. **2.** characteristic of or suitable for a woman.

womanize *or* **-ise** ('wʊməˌnaɪz) *vb.* (of a man) to indulge in casual affairs with women. —**'woman,izer** *or* -,**iser** *n.*

womanly ('wʊmənlɪ) *adj.* possessing qualities generally regarded as typical of, or appropriate to, a woman.

womb (wuːm) *n.* the nontechnical name for **uterus.** [Old English *wamb*]

wombat ('wɒmbæt) *n.* a heavily-built burrowing herbivorous Australian marsupial. [Aboriginal]

women ('wɪmɪn) *n.* the plural of **woman.**

womenfolk ('wɪmɪnˌfəʊk) *pl. n.* **1.** women collectively. **2.** a group of women, esp. the female members of one's family.

Women's Institute *n.* (in Britain and Commonwealth countries) a society for women interested in engaging in craft and cultural activities.

Women's Liberation *n.* a movement for the removal of inequalities based upon the assumption that men are superior to women. Also called: **women's lib.**

won (wʌn) *vb.* the past of **win.**

wonder ('wʌndə) *n.* **1.** the feeling of surprise, amazement, and sometimes awe, caused by something strange. **2.** something that causes such a feeling. **3.** (*modifier*) causing wonder by virtue of spectacular results achieved: *a wonder drug; a wonder boy.* **4. do** *or* **work wonders.** to achieve spectacularly good results. **5. no wonder.** (I am) not surprised at all (that): *no wonder he couldn't come.* **6. small wonder.** (I am) hardly surprised (that): *small wonder he couldn't make it tonight.* ~*vb.* **7.** (often foll. by *about*) to have curiosity or doubt about: *I wondered about what she said.* **8.** (often foll. by *at*) to be amazed (at something): *I wonder at your impudence.* [Old English *wundor*] —**'wonderment** *n.*

wonderful ('wʌndəfʊl) *adj.* **1.** causing a feeling of wonder. **2.** extremely fine; excellent. —**'wonderfully** *adv.*

wonderland ('wʌndəˌlænd) *n.* **1.** an imaginary land of marvels or wonders. **2.** an actual place of great or strange beauty.

wondrous ('wʌndrəs) *Archaic or literary.* ~*adj.* **1.** causing wonder; marvellous. ~*adv.* **2.** extremely: *wondrous cold.*

wonky ('wɒŋkɪ) *adj.* **-kier, -kiest.** *Brit. slang.* **1.** unsteady. **2.** crooked. **3.** liable to break down. [dialect *wanky*]

wont (wəʊnt) *adj.* **1.** accustomed (to doing something): *he was wont to get up early.* ~*n.* **2.** usual practice: *I got up early, as is my wont.* [Old English *gewunod*]

won't (wəʊnt) will not.

wonted ('wəʊntɪd) *adj.* accustomed; usual: *she is in her wonted place.*

woo (wuː) *vb.* **wooing, wooed. 1.** to court (a woman) with a view to marriage. **2.** to seek zealously: *to woo fame.* **3.** to coax or urge (someone). [Old English *wōgian*]

wood (wʊd) *n.* **1.** the hard fibrous substance that occurs beneath the bark in trees and shrubs. **2.** this substance cut and prepared for use in building or carpentry; timber. **3.** a thick growth of trees, usually smaller than a forest: *an oak wood.* **4.** fuel; firewood. **5.** *Golf.* a long-shafted club with a wooden head. **6.** one of the biased wooden bowls used in the game of bowls. **7. not out of the wood** *or* **woods.** still in a difficult or dangerous situation. **8. cannot see the wood for the trees.** to be so involved in the details of something that one loses sight of the main issue. **9.** (*modifier*) made of, employing, or for use with wood: *a wood fire.* ∼See also **woods.** [Old English *widu, wudu*]

wood alcohol *n.* same as **methanol.**

wood anemone *n.* a woodland anemone with white flowers.

woodbine ('wʊdˌbaɪn) *n.* a wild honeysuckle with fragrant yellow flowers.

woodcarving ('wʊdˌkɑːvɪŋ) *n.* **1.** the act or craft of carving wood. **2.** a work of art produced by carving wood.

woodchuck ('wʊdˌtʃʌk) *n.* a North American marmot with coarse reddish-brown fur. [by folk etymology from American Indian *otcheck* marten]

woodcock ('wʊdˌkɒk) *n.* a game bird like a large snipe.

woodcraft ('wʊdˌkrɑːft) *n. Chiefly U.S. & Canad.* **1.** ability and experience in matters relating to the woods such as hunting or camping. **2.** ability or skill at woodwork or carving.

woodcut ('wʊdˌkʌt) *n.* **1.** a block of wood with a design from which prints are made. **2.** a print from a woodcut.

woodcutter ('wʊdˌkʌtə) *n.* a person who fells trees or chops wood.

wooded ('wʊdɪd) *adj.* covered with woods or trees.

wooden ('wʊdᵊn) *adj.* **1.** made from or consisting of wood. **2.** awkward or clumsy. **3.** lacking spirit or animation: *a wooden expression.*

wood engraving *n.* **1.** the art of engraving pictures or designs on wood by cutting across the grain. **2.** a block of wood so engraved or a print taken from it.

wooden spoon *n.* a booby prize, esp. in sporting contests.

woodland ('wʊdlənd) *n.* land that is mostly covered with woods or trees.

woodlouse ('wʊdˌlaʊs) *n., pl.* **-lice** (-ˌlaɪs). a very small land creature with a grey plated body and many legs that lives in damp places.

woodpecker ('wʊdˌpekə) *n.* a bird with a strong bill with which it bores into trees for insects.

wood pigeon *n.* a large pigeon with white patches on the wings and neck.

woodpile ('wʊdˌpaɪl) *n.* a pile of firewood.

wood pulp *n.* pulp made from wood fibre, used in the manufacture of paper.

woodruff ('wʊdrʌf) *n.* a plant with small sweet-scented white flowers and fragrant leaves. [Old English *wudurofe*]

woods (wʊdz) *pl. n.* closely packed trees forming a forest or wood.

woodshed ('wʊdˌʃed) *n.* a small shed for storing firewood.

woodsman ('wʊdzmən) *n., pl.* **-men.** a person who lives in a wood or who is skilled in woodcraft.

woodwind ('wʊdˌwɪnd) *Music.* ∼*adj.* **1.** of or denoting a type of wind instrument, such as the oboe. ∼*n.* **2.** (*functioning as pl.*) the woodwind instruments of an orchestra.

woodwork ('wʊdˌwɜːk) *n.* **1.** the art or craft of making things in wood. **2.** things made of wood, such as doors.

woodworm ('wʊdˌwɜːm) *n.* **1.** a beetle larva that bores into wooden furniture or beams. **2.** the condition caused in wood by these larvae.

woody ('wʊdɪ) *adj.* **woodier, woodiest. 1.** covered with forest or woods. **2.** consisting of or containing wood: *woody tissue; woody stems.*

woody nightshade *n.* a woody plant with purple flowers and poisonous red berry-like fruits.

woof[1] (wuːf) *n.* same as **weft.** [Old English *ōwef*]

woof[2] (wʊf) *interj.* **1.** the bark or growl of a dog. ∼*vb.* **2.** (of dogs) to bark.

woofer ('wuːfə) *n.* a loudspeaker used in high-fidelity systems for the reproduction of low audio frequencies.

wool (wʊl) *n.* **1.** the soft, curly hair of sheep and other animals. **2.** yarn spun from this, used in weaving and knitting. **3.** cloth or a garment made from this yarn. **4.** something that looks like wool: *steel wool.* **5. pull the wool over someone's eyes.** to deceive someone. [Old English *wull*]

woolgathering ('wʊlˌgæðərɪŋ) *n.* idle or absent-minded daydreaming.

woolgrower ('wʊlˌgrəʊə) *n.* a person who keeps sheep for their wool.

woollen *or U.S.* **woolen** ('wʊlən) *adj.* **1.** relating to or consisting partly or wholly of wool. ∼*n.* **2.** (*often pl.*) a woollen garment, esp. a knitted one.

woolly *or U.S.* (*often*) **wooly** ('wʊlɪ) *adj.* **-lier, -liest. 1.** consisting of or like wool. **2.** covered in wool. **3.** confused or indistinct: *woolly thinking.* ∼*n., pl.* **-lies. 4.** (*often pl.*) a woollen garment, such as a sweater. —'**woolliness** *n.*

woolpack ('wʊlˌpæk) *n.* **1.** the cloth wrapping used to pack a bale of wool. **2.** a bale of wool.

woolsack ('wʊlˌsæk) *n.* (in Britain) the seat of the Lord Chancellor in the House of Lords, formerly made of a large square sack of wool.

woolshed ('wʊlˌʃed) *n. Austral. & N.Z.* a large building in which sheepshearing takes place.

woozy (ˈwuːzɪ) *adj.* **woozier, wooziest.** *Informal.* **1.** dazed or confused. **2.** experiencing slight dizziness or nausea. [origin unknown] —ˈ**wooziness** *n.*

wop (wɒp) *n. Slang, offensive.* a member of a Latin race, esp. an Italian. [prob. from Italian dialect *guappo* dandy]

Worcester sauce (ˈwʊstə) *n.* a piquant sauce, made from soy sauce, vinegar, and spices.

Worcs. Worcestershire.

word (wɜːd) *n.* **1.** the smallest single meaningful unit of speech or writing. **2.** a chat, talk, or discussion: *to have a word with someone.* **3.** an utterance, esp. a brief one: *a word of greeting.* **4.** news or information: *he sent word that he would be late.* **5.** a verbal signal for action; command: *when I give the word, fire!* **6.** a promise: *he kept his word.* **7.** an order: *his word must be obeyed.* **8.** a watchword or slogan: *the word now is "freedom".* **9.** *Computers.* a set of bits used to store, transmit, or operate upon an item of information in a computer. **10. as good as one's word.** doing what one has promised to do. **11. by word of mouth.** orally rather than by written means. **12. in a word.** briefly or in short. **13. take someone at his or her word.** to assume that someone means what he or she says: *when he told her to go, she took him at his word and left.* **14. take someone's word for it.** to accept or believe what someone says. **15. the last word. a.** the closing remark of a conversation or argument, esp. that supposedly settles an issue. **b.** the latest or most fashionable design: *the last word in bikinis.* **c.** the finest example: *the last word in luxury.* **16. (upon) my word!** an exclamation of surprise or annoyance. **17. word for word.** using exactly the same words; verbatim: *he has copied my report word for word.* **18. word of honour.** a promise; oath. ~*vb.* **19.** to state in words; phrase. ~See also **words.** [Old English]

Word (wɜːd) *n.* **the.** the message and teachings contained in the Bible. Also: **the Word of God.**

word blindness *n.* the nontechnical name for **dyslexia.** —ˈ**word-ˌblind** *adj.*

word game *n.* any game involving the discovery, formation, or alteration of a word or words.

wording (ˈwɜːdɪŋ) *n.* **1.** the way in which words are used to express something. **2.** the words themselves.

word order *n.* the order of words in a phrase, clause, or sentence.

word-perfect *or U.S.* **letter-perfect** *adj.* able to repeat from memory the exact words of a text one has learned.

word processing *n.* the storage and organization of text by electronic means, esp. for business purposes.

word processor *n.* an electronic machine for word processing, typically consisting of a keyboard, a VDU incorporating a microprocessor, and a printer.

words (wɜːdz) *pl. n.* **1.** the text of an actor's part. **2.** the text of a song, as opposed to the music. **3.** a quarrel: *we had words about his behaviour.* **4. eat one's words.** to retract a statement. **5. in other words.** expressing the same idea but differently. **6. in so many words.** explicitly or bluntly: *she called him a liar, in so many words.* **7. of many** (*or* **few**) **words.** (not) talkative. **8. put into words.** to express in speech or writing.

wordy (ˈwɜːdɪ) *adj.* **wordier, wordiest.** using or containing too many words: *a wordy document.* —ˈ**wordiness** *n.*

wore (wɔː) *vb.* the past tense of **wear.**

work (wɜːk) *n.* **1.** physical or mental effort directed to doing or making something. **2.** paid employment at a job, trade, or profession. **3.** a duty or task: *there's lots of work to be done.* **4.** something done or made as a result of effort: *a work of art.* **5.** the place where a person is employed. **6.** decoration, esp. of a specified kind: *needlework.* **7.** *Physics.* the transfer of energy occuring when a force is applied to move a body. **8.** a fortification. **9. at work.** in action; working. **10. make short work of.** *Informal.* to finish (something) quickly. **11.** (*modifier*) of or for work: *work clothes; a work permit.* ~*vb.* **12.** to do work; labour; toil. **13.** to be employed. **14.** to cause to labour or toil: *he works his men hard.* **15.** to operate or cause to operate, esp. effectively: *to work a lathe; that clock doesn't work.* **16.** to cultivate (land). **17.** to knead or manipulate: *to work dough.* **18.** to shape or process: *to work copper.* **19.** to reach or cause to reach a specific condition gradually: *the rope worked loose.* **20.** to move in agitation: *his face worked with anger.* **21.** (often foll. by *up*) to provoke or arouse: *to work someone into a frenzy.* **22.** to effect or accomplish: *to work wonders.* **23.** to make (one's way) with effort: *he worked his way through the crowd.* **24.** to sew or embroider: *she was working a sampler.* **25.** *Informal.* to manipulate to one's own advantage. ~See also **work in, work off, works,** etc. [Old English *weorc*]

workable (ˈwɜːkəbʰl) *adj.* **1.** practicable or feasible. **2.** able to be worked. —ˌ**work-aˈbility** *n.*

workaday (ˈwɜːkəˌdeɪ) *adj.* **1.** commonplace; ordinary. **2.** suitable for working days; practical: *workaday clothes.*

workaholic (ˌwɜːkəˈhɒlɪk) *n.* a person obsessively addicted to work.

workbench (ˈwɜːkˌbentʃ) *n.* a heavy table at which a craftsman or mechanic works.

worker (ˈwɜːkə) *n.* **1.** a person that works, usually at a specific job: *a research worker.* **2.** an employee, as opposed to an employer. **3.** a manual labourer in a manufacturing industry. **4.** a sterile female bee, ant, or wasp that works for the colony.

work ethic *n.* a belief in the moral value of work.

workforce (ˈwɜːkˌfɔːs) *n.* **1.** the total number of workers employed by a company. **2.** the total number of people available for work: *the country's workforce is growing.*

workhouse (ˈwɜːkˌhaʊs) *n.* (formerly in

England) a public institution where the very poor did work in return for food and accommodation.

work in vb. **1.** to insert, merge, or blend: *work the fat into the flour with your fingers.* **2.** to find space for; fit in: *I'll work this job in during the day.* ~n. **work-in. 3.** a form of industrial action in which a factory that is to be closed down is occupied and run by its workers.

working ('wɜːkɪŋ) n. **1.** the operation or mode of operation of something. **2.** (*often pl.*) a part of a mine or quarry that is being or has been worked. **3.** a record of the steps by which the solution of a problem or calculation is obtained: *all working is to be submitted to the examiners.* ~adj. **4.** (of a person or thing) that works: *a working man.* **5.** concerned with, used in, or suitable for work: *working clothes.* **6.** capable of being operated or used: *a working model; in working order.* **7.** adequate for normal purposes: *a working majority; a working knowledge of German.* **8.** providing a temporary basis, allowing action or progress: *a working title.*

working class n. **1.** the social stratum that consists of those who earn wages, esp. as manual workers. ~adj. **working-class. 2.** of or characteristic of the working class.

working day or esp. U.S. & Canad. **workday** n. **1.** a day on which work is done: *working days lost as a result of backache.* **2.** the part of the day allocated to work: *the unions demand a shorter working day.*

working party n. a committee established to investigate a problem.

workload ('wɜːkˌləʊd) n. the amount of work to be done, esp. in a specified period.

workman ('wɜːkmən) n., pl. **-men. 1.** a man who is employed in manual labour or who works an industrial machine. **2.** a craftsman of skill as specified: *a bad workman.*

workmanlike ('wɜːkmənˌlaɪk) adj. characteristic of a good workman.

workmanship ('wɜːkmənˌʃɪp) n. **1.** the art or skill of a workman; craftsmanship. **2.** the degree of art or skill exhibited in the finished product.

workmate ('wɜːkˌmeɪt) n. a person who works with another; fellow worker.

work of art n. **1.** a piece of fine art, such as a painting or sculpture. **2.** something that may be likened to a piece of fine art, in beauty or intricacy: *this car is a work of art.*

work off vb. to get rid of, as by effort: *he worked off some of his energy by digging the garden.*

work on vb. to persuade or influence or try to persuade or influence someone.

work out vb. **1.** to accomplish by effort. **2.** to solve or find out by reasoning or calculation: *to work out an answer; to work out a sum.* **3.** to devise or formulate: *to work out a plan.* **4.** to prove satisfactory: *did your plan work out?* **5.** to happen as specified: *it all worked out well.* **6.** to take part in physical exercise. **7.** (often foll. by *to* or *at*) to reach a total: *your bill*

works out at a pound. ~n. **workout. 8.** a session of physical exercise for training or to keep fit.

work over vb. Slang. to beat (someone) up severely.

works (wɜːks) pl. n. **1.** (*often functioning as sing.*) a place where something is manufactured. **2.** the sum total of a writer's or artist's achievements, esp. when considered together: *the works of Shakespeare.* **3.** the deeds of a person: *works of charity.* **4.** the interior parts of the mechanism of a machine: *the works of a clock.* **5. the works.** Slang. **a.** full treatment; the whole lot: *he bought her dinner, champagne, flowers — the works.* **b.** a very violent physical beating: *to give someone the works.*

workshop ('wɜːkˌʃɒp) n. **1.** a room or building in which manufacturing or other manual work is carried on. **2.** a group of people engaged in intensive study or work in a creative or practical field: *a music workshop.*

workshy ('wɜːkˌʃaɪ) adj. not inclined to work.

work station n. an area in an office or seat at a computer terminal where one person works.

worktable ('wɜːkˌteɪbˀl) n. a table at which writing, sewing, or other work may be done.

worktop ('wɜːkˌtɒp) n. a surface in a kitchen, often of heat-resistant plastic, used for food preparation.

work-to-rule n. a form of industrial action in which employees keep strictly to all the working rules laid down by their employers with the deliberate intention of reducing the work rate.

work up vb. **1.** to arouse the feelings of; excite. **2.** to cause to grow or develop: *to work up an appetite.* **3.** to gain skill at (a subject). **4.** (foll. by *to*) to develop gradually towards: *working up to a climax.*

world (wɜːld) n. **1.** the earth as a planet. **2.** mankind; the human race. **3.** people generally; the public: *in the eyes of the world.* **4.** social or public life: *to go out into the world.* **5.** any planet or moon, esp. one that might be inhabited. **6.** (*often cap.*) a particular group of countries or period of history, or its inhabitants: *the Ancient World; the Third World.* **7.** an area, sphere, or realm considered as a complete environment: *the animal world; the world of television.* **8.** a state of existence: *the next world.* **9.** the total circumstances and experience of an individual that make up his life: *his narrow little world.* **10.** a great deal: *worlds apart; a world of difference.* **11.** worldly or secular life, ways, or people. **12. bring into the world.** to deliver or give birth to (a baby). **13. come into the world.** to be born. **14. for all the world.** in every way; exactly. **15. not for the world.** not for any inducement, however great. **16. in the world.** used to emphasize a statement: *no-one in the world can help; what in the world do you mean?; all the time in the world.* **17. man** (or **woman**) **of the world.**

a man (or woman) experienced in social or public life. **18. on top of the world.** *Informal.* elated or very happy. **19. out of this world.** *Informal.* wonderful; excellent. **20. think the world of.** to be extremely fond of or think very highly of. **21.** (*modifier*) of or concerning the entire world; worldwide: *world politics; a world record.* **22.** (*in combination*) throughout the world: *world-famous.* [Old English *w(e)orold*]

World Bank *n.* an international cooperative organization established to assist developing nations by loans.

world-beater *n.* a person or thing that surpasses all others; champion.

World Cup *n.* an international football championship competition held every four years between national teams.

worldly ('wɜːldlɪ) *adj.* **-lier, -liest. 1.** not spiritual; earthly or temporal. **2.** absorbed in or concerned with material things. **3.** wise in the ways of the world; sophisticated. —**'worldliness** *n.*

world music *n.* popular music of various ethnic origins and styles.

world-shaking *adj.* of enormous significance; momentous.

World War I *n.* the war (1914–18) between the Allies (principally France, Russia, Britain, and Italy, and the U.S.) and the Central Powers (principally Germany, Austria-Hungary, and Turkey). Also: **First World War.**

World War II *n.* the war (1939–45) between the Allies (Britain and France, the U.S., and the Soviet Union) and the Axis (Germany, Italy, and Japan). Also: **Second World War.**

world-weary *adj.* no longer finding pleasure in living.

worldwide ('wɜːld'waɪd) *adj.* applying or extending throughout the world.

worm (wɜːm) *n.* **1.** an invertebrate with a long slender body and no limbs. **2.** an insect larva resembling a worm. **3.** a wretched or spineless person. **4.** a shaft on which a spiral thread has been cut, as in a gear arrangement in which such a shaft drives a toothed wheel. ~*vb.* **5.** to move or act with the slow sinuous movement of a worm. **6.** (foll. by *in, into, out of*) to make (one's) way slowly and stealthily; insinuate (oneself). **7.** (often foll. by *out of* or *from*) to extract (information) from someone by persistent questioning. **8.** to purge of worms. ~See also **worms.** [Old English *wyrm*]

WORM (wɜːm) *n. Computers.* write once read many times: an optical disk which enables users to store their own data.

wormcast ('wɜːm,kɑːst) *n.* a coil of earth or sand that has been excreted by a burrowing worm.

worm-eaten *adj.* eaten into by worms: *a worm-eaten chair.*

worm gear *n.* **1.** a device consisting of a threaded shaft that drives a toothed gearwheel. **2.** a gear-wheel driven by a threaded shaft or worm.

wormhole ('wɜːm,həʊl) *n.* a hole made by a worm in timber, plants, or fruit.

worms (wɜːmz) *n.* (*functioning as sing.*) a disease caused by parasitic worms living in the intestines.

wormwood ('wɜːm,wʊd) *n.* **1.** a plant yielding a bitter oil used in making absinthe. **2.** an unpleasant experience that causes bitterness. [Old English *wormōd, wermōd*]

wormy ('wɜːmɪ) *adj.* **wormier, wormiest.** worm-infested or worm-eaten.

worn (wɔːn) *vb.* **1.** the past participle of **wear.** ~*adj.* **2.** showing signs of long use or wear: *a worn suit.* **3.** haggard; drawn: *looking tired and worn.*

worn-out *adj.* **1.** worn or used until threadbare, valueless, or useless. **2.** exhausted; very weary.

worrisome ('wʌrɪsəm) *adj.* causing worry; vexing.

worry ('wʌrɪ) *vb.* **-rying, -ried. 1.** to be or cause to be anxious or uneasy. **2.** to annoy; bother: *don't worry me with trivialities.* **3.** (often foll. by *away*) to struggle or work: *to worry away at a problem.* **4.** (of a dog) to bite or tear (at) repeatedly with the teeth: *your dog has been worrying sheep.* ~*n., pl.* **-ries. 5.** a state or feeling of anxiety. **6.** a person or thing that causes anxiety. [Old English *wyrgan*] —**'worried** *adj.* —**'worriedly** *adv.* —**'worrying** *adj., n.*

worry beads *pl. n.* a string of beads that when fingered or played with supposedly relieves nervous tension.

worse (wɜːs) *adj.* **1.** the comparative of **bad. 2. none the worse for.** not harmed by (adverse events or circumstances). **3. the worse for wear.** shabby or worn. **4. worse luck!** *Informal.* unhappily; unfortunately. **5. worse off.** in a worse, esp. a worse financial, condition. ~*n.* **6.** something that is worse. **7. for the worse.** into a worse condition: *a change for the worse.* ~*adv.* **8.** more severely or unpleasantly: *his nose bled worse than before.* **9.** less effectively or successfully: *you write even worse than I do.* [Old English *wiersa*]

worsen ('wɜːs°n) *vb.* to grow or cause to grow worse.

worship ('wɜːʃɪp) *vb.* **-shipping, -shipped** or *U.S.* **-shiping, -shiped. 1.** to show profound religious devotion to; adore or venerate (a deity). **2.** to have intense love and admiration for. **3.** to attend services for worship. ~*n.* **4.** religious adoration or devotion. **5.** rites, prayers, or other formal expression of religious adoration. **6.** admiring love or devotion. [Old English *weorthscipe*] —**'worshipper** *n.*

Worship ('wɜːʃɪp) *n. Chiefly Brit.* (preceded by *Your, His,* or *Her*) a title for a mayor or magistrate.

worshipful ('wɜːʃɪpfʊl) *adj.* **1.** feeling or showing reverence or adoration. **2.** (*often cap.*) *Chiefly Brit.* (in titles for various people or bodies of distinguished rank) honourable, respected.

worst (wɜːst) *adj.* **1.** the superlative of **bad.** ~*adv.* **2.** most extremely or badly:

the worst affected areas. ~n. **3. the worst.** the least good person, thing, or part. **4.** (often preceded by *at*) the worst quality or condition: *television is at its worst these days.* **5.** the greatest amount of damage or wickedness possible: *the invaders came and did their worst.* **6. at worst.** in the worst possible situation. **7. get the worst of it.** to be defeated. **8. if the worst comes to the worst.** if the situation develops in the worst possible way. ~vb. **9.** to defeat or beat. [Old English *wierrest*]

worsted ('wʊstɪd) *n.* **1.** a closely twisted woollen yarn or thread. **2.** a hard smooth close-textured fabric made from this. [after *Worstead*, a district in Norfolk]

wort (wɜːt) *n.* **1.** (*in combination*) a plant, esp. one formerly used to cure diseases: *liverwort.* **2.** an infusion of ground malt, fermented to make a malt liquor. [Old English *wyrt* root]

worth (wɜːθ) *adj.* **1.** worthy of; meriting or justifying: *it's not worth discussing.* **2.** having a value of: *the book is worth £30.* **3. for all one is worth.** to the utmost. **4. worth one's weight in gold.** extremely useful, helpful, or kind. ~n. **5.** high quality; excellence. **6.** value; price. **7.** the amount of something that can be bought for a specified price: *five pounds' worth of petrol.* [Old English *weorth*]

worthless ('wɜːθlɪs) *adj.* **1.** without value or usefulness. **2.** without merit.

worthwhile ('wɜːθ'waɪl) *adj.* sufficiently important, rewarding, or valuable to justify time or effort spent.

worthy ('wɜːðɪ) *adj.* **-thier, -thiest. 1.** having sufficient merit or value (for a specified person or thing); deserving: *not worthy of the honour.* **2.** having worth, value, or merit. ~n., *pl.* **-thies. 3.** *Often facetious.* an important person. —'worthi·ly *adv.* —'worthiness *n.*

would (wʊd; *unstressed* wəd) *vb.* used as an auxiliary: **1.** to form the past tense or subjunctive mood of will[1]: *you said you would come.* **2.** (with *you, he, she, it, they,* or a noun as subject) to express a polite request: *would you help me, please?* **3.** to describe a habitual past action: *every day we would go for walks.* **4.** I wish: *would that he were here.*

would-be *adj.* *Usually disparaging.* wanting or pretending to be: *a would-be politician.*

wouldn't ('wʊdˀnt) would not.

wound[1] (wuːnd) *n.* **1.** an injury done to living tissue as the result of violence. **2.** an injury to the feelings or reputation. ~vb. **3.** to inflict a wound or wounds upon. [Old English *wund*] —'wounding *adj.*

wound[2] (waʊnd) *vb.* the past of **wind**[2].

wove (wəʊv) *vb.* a past tense of **weave**.

woven ('wəʊvˀn) *vb.* a past participle of **weave**.

wow (waʊ) *interj.* **1.** an exclamation of admiration or amazement. ~n. **2.** *Slang.* a person or thing that is amazingly success-

ful. ~vb. **3.** *Slang.* to be a great success with. [Scot.]

wowser ('waʊzə) *n.* *Austral. & N.Z. slang.* **1.** a fanatically puritanical person. **2.** a teetotaller. [dialect *wow* to complain]

wp word processor.

WPC (in Britain) woman police constable.

wpm words per minute.

WRAC (in Britain) Women's Royal Army Corps.

wrack[1] *or* **rack** (ræk) *n.* collapse or destruction: *wrack and ruin.* [Old English *wræc* persecution]

wrack[2] (ræk) *n.* seaweed that is floating in the sea or has been cast ashore. [prob. from Middle Dutch *wrak* wreckage]

WRAF (in Britain) Women's Royal Air Force.

wraith (reɪθ) *n.* **1.** the apparition of a living person, supposed to appear just before his death. **2.** a ghost. [Scot.]

wrangle ('ræŋgˀl) *vb.* **1.** to argue noisily or angrily. ~n. **2.** a noisy or angry argument. [Low German *wrangeln*]

wrap (ræp) *vb.* **wrapping, wrapped. 1.** to fold or wind (something) around (a person or thing) so as to cover. **2.** (often foll. by *up*) to fold a covering around and fasten securely. **3.** to enclose, immerse, or absorb: *wrapped in sorrow.* **4.** (often foll. by *about, around, round*) to fold, wind, or coil: *he wrapped his arms around her.* ~n. **5.** a garment worn wrapped around the body, esp. the shoulders. **6.** *Chiefly U.S.* wrapping or a wrapper. **7. keep under wraps.** to keep secret. **8. take the wraps off.** to reveal. [origin unknown]

wrapper ('ræpə) *n.* **1.** the cover, usually of paper or cellophane, in which something is wrapped. **2.** a dust jacket of a book. **3.** a loose negligee or dressing gown.

wrapping ('ræpɪŋ) *n.* the material used to wrap something.

wrapround ('ræp,raʊnd) *or* **wraparound** *adj.* **1.** made so as to be wrapped round something: *a wraparound skirt.* **2.** extending in a curve from the front around to the sides.

wrap up *vb.* **1.** to fold paper around. **2.** to put warm clothes on. **3.** (*usually imperative*) *Slang.* to be silent. **4.** *Informal.* to finish or settle (a matter).

wrasse (ræs) *n.* a brightly-coloured marine fish. [Cornish *wrach*]

wrath (rɒθ) *n.* intense anger. [Old English *wrǣththu*] —'wrathful *adj.*

wreak (riːk) *vb.* **1.** to inflict (vengeance) or to cause (chaos): *to wreak havoc on the enemy.* **2.** to express or gratify (anger or hatred). [Old English *wrecan*]

wreath (riːθ) *n.*, *pl.* **wreaths** (riːðz, riːθs). **1.** a twisted band or ring of flowers or leaves, placed on a grave as a memorial or worn on the head as a garland or a mark of honour. **2.** anything circular or spiral: *wreaths of smoke.* [Old English *wrǣth*]

wreathe (riːð) *vb.* **1.** to form into or take the form of a wreath by intertwining or twisting together. **2.** to encircle or adorn with or as if with a wreath: *his face was* *wreathed in smiles.* **3.** to move or cause to move in a twisting way: *smoke wreathed up to the ceiling.*

wreck (rɛk) *vb.* **1.** to break, spoil, or destroy completely. **2.** to cause the wreck of (a ship). ~*n.* **3. a.** the accidental destruction of a ship at sea. **b.** the ship so destroyed. **4.** a person in a poor mental or physical state. **5.** the remains of something destroyed. [from Old Norse]

wreckage ('rɛkɪdʒ) *n.* **1.** the act of wrecking or the state of being wrecked. **2.** the remains of something destroyed.

wrecker ('rɛkə) *n.* **1.** *Chiefly U.S. & Canad.* a person whose job is to demolish buildings or dismantle cars. **2.** (formerly) a person who lures ships to destruction to plunder the wreckage. **3.** *U.S. & Canad.* a breakdown van.

wren (rɛn) *n.* a small brown songbird with a stubby, erect tail. [Old English *wrenna*]

Wren (rɛn) *n. Informal.* a member of the Women's Royal Naval Service. [from abbrev. *WRNS*]

wrench (rɛntʃ) *vb.* **1.** to give (something) a forceful twist or pull, esp. so as to remove it from that to which it is attached: *to wrench a door off its hinges.* **2.** to injure (a limb or joint) by a sudden twist. ~*n.* **3.** a forceful twist or pull. **4.** an injury to a limb or joint, caused by twisting. **5.** a parting that is difficult or painful to make. **6.** a spanner with adjustable jaws. [Old English *wrencan*]

wrest (rɛst) *vb.* **1.** to take or force away by violent pulling or twisting. **2.** to seize forcibly by violent or unlawful means. [Old English *wrǣstan*]

wrestle ('rɛsᵊl) *vb.* **1.** to fight (another person) by grappling and trying to throw or pin him to the ground. **2.** to participate in wrestling. **3.** (foll. by *with* or *against*) to struggle hard with (a person, problem, or thing): *wrestle with one's conscience.* ~*n.* **4.** the act of wrestling. **5.** a struggle or tussle. [Old English *wrǣstlian*] —'**wrestler** *n.*

wrestling ('rɛslɪŋ) *n.* a sport in which each contestant tries to overcome the other either by throwing or pinning him to the ground or by causing him to submit.

wretch (rɛtʃ) *n.* **1.** a despicable person. **2.** a person pitied for his misfortune. [Old English *wrecca*]

wretched ('rɛtʃɪd) *adj.* **1.** in poor or pitiful circumstances. **2.** feeling misery; very unhappy. **3.** poor or inferior. **4.** undesirable or displeasing: *a wretched nuisance.* —'**wretchedly** *adv.*

wrick (rɪk) *n.* **1.** a sprain or strain. ~*vb.* **2.** to sprain or strain.

wriggle ('rɪgᵊl) *vb.* **1.** to make or cause to make twisting movements. **2.** to move along by twisting and turning. **3.** (foll. by *into* or *out of*) to manoeuvre oneself by clever or devious means: *wriggle out of an embarrassing situation.* ~*n.* **4.** a wriggling movement or action. [Middle Low German *wriggeln*] —'**wriggly** *adj.*

wright (raɪt) *n.* (*now chiefly in combination*) a person who creates or builds some-

thing specified: *a playwright; a shipwright.* [Old English *wryhta*]

wring (rɪŋ) *vb.* **wringing, wrung.** **1.** (often foll. by *out*) to twist and compress to squeeze (a liquid) from (cloth). **2.** to twist forcibly: *wring its neck.* **3.** to clasp and twist (one's hands), esp. in anguish. **4.** to distress: *wring one's heart.* **5.** to grip (someone's hand) vigorously in greeting. **6.** to obtain by forceful means: *wring information out of.* **7. wringing wet.** soaking; drenched. ~*n.* **8.** an act or the process of wringing. [Old English *wringan*]

wringer ('rɪŋə) *n.* same as **mangle²** (sense 1).

wrinkle¹ ('rɪŋkᵊl) *n.* **1.** a slight ridge in the smoothness of a surface, such as a crease in the skin as a result of age. ~*vb.* **2.** to make or become wrinkled. [Old English *wrinclian* to wind around] —'**wrinkly** *adj.*

wrinkle² ('rɪŋkᵊl) *n. Informal.* a useful hint or dodge. [Old English *wrenc* trick]

wrist (rɪst) *n.* **1.** *Anat.* the joint between the forearm and the hand. **2.** the part of a sleeve that covers the wrist. [Old English]

wristwatch ('rɪst‚wɒtʃ) *n.* a watch worn strapped around the wrist.

writ (rɪt) *n.* a formal legal document ordering a person to do or refrain from doing some specified act. [Old English]

write (raɪt) *vb.* **writing, wrote, written.** **1.** to draw or mark (symbols, letters, or words) on a surface, usually paper, with a pen, pencil, or other instrument. **2.** to describe or record (something) in writing. **3.** to write (a letter) to or correspond regularly with (a person or organization). **4.** to say or communicate by letter: *he wrote that he was on his way.* **5.** *Informal, chiefly U.S. & Canad.* to send a letter to (a person or organization). **6.** to be the author or composer of (literature or music). **7.** to fill in the details for (a document, form, or cheque). **8.** to produce by writing: *he wrote ten pages.* **9.** to show clearly: *envy was written all over his face.* **10.** to produce writing of a specified kind: *write neatly.* **11.** *Computers.* to record (data) in a storage device. [Old English]

write down *vb.* **1.** to set down in writing. **2.** to disparage or belittle (a person) in writing. **3.** (foll. by *to* or *for*) to write in a simplified way (for a supposedly less cultured readership).

write off *vb.* **1.** *Accounting.* to cancel (a bad debt) from the accounts. **2.** to acknowledge as a complete loss. **3.** to dismiss from consideration: *he wrote her off as a hysterical woman.* **4.** to send a written order (for something): *she wrote off for a brochure.* **5.** *Informal.* to damage (something, esp. a car) beyond repair. ~*n.* **write-off. 6.** *Informal.* something damaged beyond repair, esp. a car.

write out *vb.* to put into writing or reproduce in full form in writing.

writer ('raɪtə) *n.* **1.** a person who writes as an occupation; author. **2.** the person who has written something specified.

write up *vb.* **1.** to describe fully, complete, or bring up to date in writing: *write* *up a diary.* **2.** to praise or bring to public notice in writing. ~*n.* **write-up. 3.** a published account of something, such as a review in a newspaper or magazine.

writhe (raɪð) *vb.* **1.** to twist or squirm in or as if in pain. **2.** to suffer acute emotional discomfort: *writhe in embarrassment.* [Old English *wrīthan*]

writing (ˈraɪtɪŋ) *n.* **1.** anything which is written. **2.** short for **handwriting. 3.** literary composition. **4.** the work of a writer. **5.** literary style, art, or practice. **6.** written form: *give it to me in writing.* **7. writing on the wall.** a sign or signs of approaching disaster. [sense 7: allusion to Daniel 5:5]

writing desk *n.* a piece of furniture with a writing surface and compartments for papers and writing materials.

writing paper *n.* paper for writing letters.

written (ˈrɪtᵊn) *vb.* **1.** the past participle of **write.** ~*adj.* **2.** taken down in writing: *written evidence; the written word.*

WRNS Women's Royal Naval Service.

wrong (rɒŋ) *adj.* **1.** not correct or truthful: *the wrong answer.* **2.** acting or judging in error: *you are wrong to think that.* **3.** immoral; bad: *it is wrong to cheat.* **4.** not in accordance with correct or conventional rules or standards. **5.** not intended or appropriate: *the wrong road.* **6.** not working properly; amiss: *something is wrong with the engine.* **7.** (of a side of a fabric or knitting) intended to face the inside so as not to be seen. **8. get on the wrong side of.** *Informal.* to come into disfavour with. ~*adv.* **9.** in the wrong direction or manner. **10. get (someone or something) wrong. a.** to fail to understand (someone or something) properly. **b.** to fail to provide the correct answer to. **11. go wrong. a.** to turn out other than intended: *my plans have gone wrong.* **b.** to make a mistake. **c.** (of a machine) to cease to function properly. **d.** to go astray morally. ~*n.* **12.** something bad, immoral, or unjust. **13.** *Law.* an infringement of another person's

rights or a violation of public rights and duties. **14. in the wrong.** mistaken or guilty. ~*vb.* **15.** to treat unjustly. **16.** to discredit, malign, or misrepresent. [Old English *wrang* injustice] —ˈ**wrongly** *adv.*

wrongdoer (ˈrɒŋˌduːə) *n.* a person who acts immorally or illegally. —ˈ**wrongˌdoing** *n.*

wrongful (ˈrɒŋful) *adj.* unjust or illegal. —ˈ**wrongfully** *adv.*

wrong-headed *adj.* **1.** constantly wrong in judgment. **2.** foolishly stubborn; obstinate.

wrote (rəʊt) *vb.* the past tense of **write.**

wroth (rəʊθ, rɒθ) *adj. Archaic or literary.* angry; wrathful. [Old English *wrāth*]

wrought (rɔːt) *vb.* **1.** *Archaic.* a past of **work.** ~*adj.* **2.** *Metallurgy.* shaped by hammering or beating.

wrought iron *n.* a pure form of iron with a low carbon content: often used for decorative work.

wrought-up *adj.* agitated or excited.

wrung (rʌŋ) *vb.* the past of **wring.**

WRVS Women's Royal Voluntary Service.

wry (raɪ) *adj.* **wrier, wriest** or **wryer, wryiest. 1.** dryly humorous; sardonic. **2.** (of a facial expression) produced by contorting the features. **3.** twisted, contorted, or askew. [Old English *wrīgian* to turn] —ˈ**wryly** *adv.*

wrybill (ˈraɪˌbɪl) *n.* a New Zealand plover whose bill is bent to one side enabling it to search for food beneath stones.

wryneck (ˈraɪˌnɛk) *n.* an Old World woodpecker which has a habit of twisting its neck round.

wt. weight.

wych-elm or **witch-elm** (ˈwɪtʃˌɛlm) *n.* a Eurasian elm tree with longish pointed leaves, clusters of small flowers, and winged fruits. [Old English *wice*]

WYSIWYG (ˈwɪzɪˌwɪg) *n., adj. Computers.* what you see is what you get: referring to what is displayed on the screen being the same as what will be printed out.

X

x or **X** (ɛks) n., pl. **x's, X's,** or **Xs.** the 24th letter of the English alphabet.

x Maths. **1.** (along with y and z) an unknown quantity. **2.** the multiplication symbol.

X 1. (formerly) indicating a film that may not be publicly shown to anyone under 18. Since 1982 replaced by symbol 18. **2.** denoting an unknown, unspecified, or variable factor, number, person, or thing. **3.** (on letters or greetings cards) denoting a kiss. **4.** (on ballot papers) indicating choice. **5.** (on examination papers) indicating error. **6.** the Roman numeral for ten.

Xanthippe (zænˈθɪpɪ) or **Xantippe** (zænˈtɪpɪ) n. a nagging, peevish, or irritable woman. [after Socrates' wife]

X-chromosome n. the sex chromosome that occurs in pairs in the females of many animals, including humans, and as one of a pair with the Y-chromosome in males.

Xe Chem. xenon.

xenon (ˈzɛnɒn) n. Chem. a colourless odourless gaseous element occurring in minute quantities in the air. Symbol: Xe [Greek: something strange]

xenophobia (ˌzɛnəˈfəʊbɪə) n. hatred or fear of foreigners or strangers. [Greek xenos foreign + phobos fear] —**xenoˈphobic** adj.

xerography (zɪəˈrɒɡrəfɪ) n. a photocopying process in which an image of the written or printed material is electrically charged on a surface and attracts oppositely charged dry ink particles which are then fixed by heating. [Greek xēros dry + -GRAPHY] —**xerographic** (ˌzɪərəˈɡræfɪk) adj.

Xerox (ˈzɪərɒks) n. **1.** Trademark. **a.** a machine for copying printed material. **b.** a copy made by such a machine. ~vb. **2.** to produce a copy of (a document) using such a machine.

Xhosa (ˈkɔːsə) n. **1.** (pl. **-sa** or **-sas**) a member of a Negroid people living chiefly in Cape Province in the Republic of South Africa. **2.** the language of this people, which has several clicks in its sound system. —**ˈXhosan** adj.

Xmas (ˈɛksməs, ˈkrɪsməs) n. Informal. short for **Christmas.** [from the Greek letter khi (X), first letter of Khristos Christ]

x-ray or **X-ray** n. **1.** a stream of electromagnetic radiation of short wavelength that can pass through some solid materials. **2.** a picture produced by exposing photographic film to x-rays: used in medicine as a diagnostic aid, since parts of the body, such as bones, absorb x-rays and so appear as opaque areas on the picture. ~vb. **3.** to photograph, treat, or examine (a person or part of his body) using x-rays.

x-ray diffraction n. Physics. the scattering of x-rays on contact with matter, resulting in changes in radiation intensity, which is used for studying atomic structure.

xylem (ˈzaɪləm) n. Bot. a plant tissue that conducts water and mineral salts from the roots to all other parts. [Greek xulon wood]

xylene (ˈzaɪliːn) n. Chem. a hydrocarbon existing in three isomeric forms, all three being colourless flammable volatile liquids used as solvents and in the manufacture of synthetic resins, dyes, and insecticides. [Greek xulon wood]

xylophone (ˈzaɪləˌfəʊn) n. Music. a percussion instrument consisting of a set of wooden bars of graduated length. It is played with hard-headed hammers. [Greek xulon wood] —**xylophonist** (zaɪˈlɒfənɪst) n.

Y

y *or* **Y** (waɪ) *n., pl.* **y's, Y's,** *or* **Ys.** the 25th letter of the English alphabet.

y *Maths.* (along with *x* and *z*) an unknown quantity.

Y **1.** an unknown, unspecified, or variable factor, number, person, or thing. **2.** *Chem.* yttrium.

yacht (jɒt) *n.* **1.** a large boat propelled by sail or power, used for pleasure cruising or racing. ~*vb.* **2.** to sail or cruise in a yacht. [obs. Dutch *jaghte*] —'**yachting** *n., adj.*

yachtsman ('jɒtsmən) *or* (*fem.*) **yachts-woman** *n., pl.* **-men** *or* **-women.** a person who sails a yacht.

yack (jæk) *n., vb.* same as **yak²**.

yah (jɑː) *interj.* **1.** *Informal.* same as **yes.** **2.** an exclamation of derision or disgust.

yahoo (jə'huː) *n., pl.* **-hoos.** a crude, brutish, or obscenely coarse person. [after the brutish creatures in *Gulliver's Travels*]

Yahweh ('jɑːweɪ) *or* **Yahveh** ('jɑːveɪ) *n. Bible.* a personal name of God. [Hebrew YHVH, with conjectural vowels]

yak¹ (jæk) *n.* an ox of Tibet with long shaggy hair. [Tibetan *gyag*]

yak² (jæk) *Slang.* ~*n.* **1.** noisy, continuous, and trivial talk. ~*vb.* **yakking, yakked.** **2.** to chatter or talk in this way. [imit.]

Yale lock (jeɪl) *n. Trademark.* a type of cylinder lock using a flat serrated key. [after L. *Yale,* inventor]

yam (jæm) *n.* **1.** any of various twining plants of tropical and subtropical regions, cultivated for their starchy roots which are eaten as a vegetable. **2.** *Southern U.S.* the sweet potato. [Portuguese *inhame*]

yammer ('jæmə) *Informal.* ~*vb.* **1.** to whine in a complaining manner. ~*n.* **2.** a yammering sound. **3.** nonsense; jabber. [Old English *geōmrian* to grumble]

Yang (jæŋ) *n.* See **Yin and Yang.**

yank (jæŋk) *vb.* **1.** to pull (someone or something) with a sharp movement; tug. ~*n.* **2.** a jerk. [origin unknown]

Yank (jæŋk) *n. Slang.* a person from the U.S.; American.

Yankee ('jæŋkɪ) *n.* **1.** *Slang.* same as **Yank.** **2.** a person from New England or from a Northern state of the U.S. ~*adj.* **3.** of or characteristic of Yankees. [perhaps from Dutch *Jan Kees* John Cheese, nickname for English colonists]

yap (jæp) *vb.* **yapping, yapped.** **1.** (of a dog) to bark in quick sharp bursts; yelp. **2.** *Informal.* to talk at length in an annoying or stupid way; jabber. ~*n.* **3.** a high-pitched bark; yelp. **4.** *Slang.* annoying or stupid speech; jabber. [imit.] —'**yappy** *adj.*

yarborough ('jɑːbərə) *n. Bridge, whist.* a hand in which no card is higher than nine. [supposedly after the second Earl of Yar-

borough, said to have bet a thousand to one against its occurrence]

yard¹ (jɑːd) *n.* **1.** a unit of length equal to 3 feet, or 0.9144 metre. **2.** *Naut.* a spar slung from a mast of a ship and used for suspending a sail. [Old English *gierd* rod, twig]

yard² (jɑːd) *n.* **1.** a piece of enclosed ground, often adjoining or surrounded by a building or buildings. **2.** an enclosed or open area where a particular type of work is done: *a builder's yard.* **3.** *U.S. & Canad.* same as **garden** (sense 1). **4.** *U.S. & Canad.* the winter pasture of deer, moose, and similar animals. [Old English *geard*]

Yard (jɑːd) *n. the. Brit. informal.* short for **Scotland Yard.**

yardarm ('jɑːd,ɑːm) *n. Naut.* the outer end of a yard.

Yardie ('jɑːdɪ) *n.* a member of a Black criminal syndicate originally based in Jamaica. [origin unknown]

yardstick ('jɑːd,stɪk) *n.* **1.** a measure or standard used for comparison: *she is my yardstick for success.* **2.** a graduated measuring stick one yard long.

yarmulke ('jɑːmɔlkə) *n. Judaism.* a skullcap worn during prayer by Jewish men and at all times by Orthodox Jewish men. [Yiddish]

yarn (jɑːn) *n.* **1.** a continuous twisted strand of natural or synthetic fibres, used in weaving or knitting. **2.** *Informal.* a long and often involved story, usually of incredible or fantastic events. **3. spin a yarn.** *Informal.* to tell such a story. [Old English *gearn*]

yarrow ('jærəʊ) *n.* a plant with finely divided leaves and flat clusters of white flower heads. [Old English *gearwe*]

yashmak ('jæʃmæk) *n.* a veil worn by Muslim women in public, to cover their faces, apart from their eyes. [Arabic]

yaw (jɔː) *vb.* **1.** (of an aircraft) to turn about its vertical axis. **2.** (of a ship) to turn aside temporarily from a straight course. ~*n.* **3.** the movement of an aircraft about its vertical axis. **4.** (of a ship) the act of turning aside from a straight course. [origin unknown]

yawl (jɔːl) *n.* **1.** a two-masted sailing boat. **2.** a ship's small boat. [Dutch *jol* or Middle Low German *jolle*]

yawn (jɔːn) *vb.* **1.** to open one's mouth wide and take in air deeply, often when sleepy or bored. **2.** to be open wide as if threatening to engulf someone or something: *the mine shaft yawned below.* ~*n.* **3.** the act or an instance of yawning. [Old English *gionian*] —'**yawning** *adj.*

yaws (jɔːz) *n.* (*usually functioning as sing.*) an infectious disease of tropical climates characterized by red skin eruptions. [Carib]

Yb *Chem.* ytterbium.

Y-chromosome *n.* the sex chromosome

that occurs as one of a pair with the X-chromosome in the males of many animals, including humans.

yd *or* **yd.** yard (measure).

YDT (in Canada) Yukon Daylight Time.

ye¹ (jiː, *unstressed* jɪ) *pron. Archaic or dialect.* refers to more than one person including the person addressed. [Old English *gē*]

ye² (ðiː, *spelling pron.* jiː) *det.* a form of **the**¹, used as a supposed archaism: *ye olde oake.* [a misinterpretation of *the* written with the old letter thorn (þ), representing *th*]

yea (jeɪ) *interj.* **1.** same as **aye** (yes). ~*adv.* **2.** *Archaic or literary.* indeed; truly: *yea, though they spurn me, I shall prevail.* [Old English *gēa*]

yeah (jɛə) *interj. Informal.* same as **yes.**

year (jɪə) *n.* **1.** the period of time, the **calendar year,** containing 365 days or in a **leap year** 366 days. It is divided into 12 months, and reckoned from January 1 to December 31. **2.** a period of twelve months from any specified date. **3.** a specific period of time, usually occupying a definite part or parts of a twelve-month period, used for some particular activity: *a school year.* **4.** the period of time during which the earth makes one revolution around the sun, approximately 365 days. **5.** the period of time taken by a specified planet to complete one revolution around the sun. **6.** (*pl.*) a long time: *it's years since I've been there.* **7.** (*pl.*) age, usually old age: *a man of his years should be more careful.* **8.** (*pl.*) time: *in years to come.* **9.** a group of pupils or students who have started a course in the same academic year. **10. year in, year out.** regularly or monotonously, over a long period. [Old English *gear*]

yearbook ('jɪəˌbʊk) *n.* a reference book published once a year that contains details of events of the British monarch.

yearling ('jɪəlɪŋ) *n.* **1.** an animal that is between one and two years old. ~*adj.* **2.** being a year old.

yearly ('jɪəlɪ) *adj.* **1.** occurring, done, or appearing once a year or every year; annual. **2.** lasting or valid for a year; annual: *a yearly subscription.* ~*adv.* **3.** once a year; annually.

yearn (jɜːn) *vb.* **1.** to have an intense desire or longing: *we yearned for home.* **2.** to feel tenderness or affection: *her heart yearned for the starving child.* [Old English *giernan*] —**'yearning** *n., adj.*

yeast (jiːst) *n.* a yellowish fungus an extract of which is used in fermenting alcoholic drinks, such as beer or whisky, and in raising dough for bread. [Old English *giest*]

yeasty ('jiːstɪ) *adj.* **yeastier, yeastiest.** **1.** of, resembling, or containing yeast. **2.** fermenting or causing fermentation. **3.** (of talk) frivolous. **4.** covered with or containing froth or foam.

yell (jɛl) *vb.* **1.** to shout, scream, cheer, or utter in a loud or piercing way. ~*n.* **2.** a

loud piercing inarticulate cry of pain, anger, or fear. [Old English *giellan*]

yellow ('jɛləʊ) *n.* **1.** any of a group of colours such as that of a lemon or an egg yolk, which vary in strength but have the same hue. **2.** a yellow pigment or dye. **3.** yellow cloth or clothing: *dressed in yellow.* ~*adj.* **4.** of the colour yellow. **5.** yellowish in colour or having parts or marks that are yellowish. **6.** having a yellowish skin; Mongoloid. **7.** *Informal.* cowardly or afraid. ~*vb.* **8.** to make or become yellow. [Old English *geolu*] —**'yellowish** *adj.* —**'yellowness** *n.*

yellow-belly *n., pl.* **-lies.** *Slang.* a coward. —**'yellow-,bellied** *adj.*

yellow card *n. Soccer.* a card of a yellow colour raised by a referee to indicate that a player has been booked for a serious violation of the rules.

yellow fever *n.* an acute infectious tropical disease which causes fever, haemorrhages, vomiting, and jaundice: caused by a virus transmitted to man by the bite of a certain mosquito.

yellowhammer ('jɛləʊˌhæmə) *n.* a European songbird with a yellowish head and body and brown-streaked wings and tail. [origin unknown]

yellow pages *pl. n.* a telephone directory or section of a directory that lists people and companies under the headings of the type of business or service they provide.

yellow streak *n. Informal.* a cowardly or weak trait.

yelp (jɛlp) *vb.* **1.** (of an animal or a person) to utter a sharp or high-pitched cry, often indicating pain. ~*n.* **2.** a sharp or high-pitched cry. [Old English *gielpan* to boast]

yen¹ (jɛn) *n., pl.* **yen.** the standard monetary unit of Japan. [Japanese *en*]

yen² (jɛn) *Informal.* ~*n.* **1.** a longing or desire. ~*vb.* **yenning, yenned.** **2.** to have a longing. [perhaps from Chinese *yan* a craving]

yeoman ('jəʊmən) *n., pl.* **-men.** *History.* a member of a class of small freeholders who cultivated their own land. [perhaps from *yongman* young man]

yeoman of the guard *n.* a member of the ceremonial bodyguard (**Yeomen of the Guard**) of the British monarch.

yeomanry ('jəʊmənrɪ) *n.* **1.** yeomen collectively. **2.** (in Britain) a volunteer cavalry force, organized in 1761 for home defence: merged into the Territorial Army in 1907.

yep (jɛp) *interj. Informal.* same as **yes.**

yes (jɛs) *interj.* **1.** used to express affirmation, consent, agreement, or approval, or to answer when one is addressed. **2.** used to signal someone to speak or keep speaking, enter a room, or do something. ~*n.* **3.** an answer or vote of yes. **4.** a person who votes in the affirmative. [Old English *gēse*]

yes man *n.* a person who agrees with every suggestion or opinion offered by his employer in order to gain favour.

yesterday ('jɛstədɪ) *n.* **1.** the day before

today. **2.** the recent past. ~*adv.* **3.** on or during the day before today. **4.** in the recent past.

yesteryear (ˈjestəˌjɪə) *Formal or literary.* ~*n.* **1.** last year or the past in general. ~*adv.* **2.** during last year or the past in general.

yet (jet) *conj.* **1.** nevertheless; still: *I want to, yet I haven't the courage.* ~*adv.* **2.** so far; up until then or now: *they're not home yet; is it teatime yet?* **3.** now (as contrasted with later): *we can't stop yet.* **4.** even; still: *yet more potatoes for sale.* **5.** eventually in spite of everything: *we'll convince him yet.* **6. as yet.** so far; up until then or now. [Old English *gēta*]

yeti (ˈjetɪ) *n.* same as **abominable snowman.** [Tibetan]

yew (juː) *n.* an evergreen tree with flat-tened needle-like leaves, red berry-like fruits, and fine-grained elastic wood. [Old English *īw*]

Y-fronts *pl. n. Trademark.* boys' or men's underpants having a front opening within an inverted Y shape.

YHA (in Britain) Youth Hostels Associa-tion.

yid (jɪd) *n. Slang, offensive.* a Jew. [prob. from *Yiddish*]

Yiddish (ˈjɪdɪʃ) *n.* **1.** a language derived from High German, spoken by Jews in Europe and elsewhere by Jewish emi-grants, and usually written in the Hebrew alphabet. ~*adj.* **2.** in or relating to this language. [German *jüdisch* Jewish]

yield (jiːld) *vb.* **1.** to give forth or supply (a product or result), for example by culti-vation or labour; produce or bear. **2.** to furnish as a return: *the shares yielded three per cent.* **3.** (foll. by *up*) to give up; surrender. **4.** to give way, submit, or surrender, through force or persuasion: *she yielded to his superior knowledge.* **5.** (foll. by *to*) to agree to; comply with: *he eventually yielded to their request for money.* **6.** to grant or allow; concede: *to yield right of way.* ~*n.* **7.** the result, product, or amount yielded. [Old English *gieldan*]

yielding (ˈjiːldɪŋ) *adj.* **1.** compliant, sub-missive, or flexible. **2.** pliable or soft: *a yielding material.*

Yin and Yang (jɪn) *n.* two complementary principles of Chinese philosophy: Yin is negative, dark, and feminine, Yang is posi-tive, bright, and masculine. [Chinese *yin* dark + *yang* bright]

yippee (jɪˈpiː) *interj.* an exclamation of joy, pleasure, or anticipation.

YMCA Young Men's Christian Association.

yob (jɒb) *or* **yobbo** (ˈjɒbəʊ) *n., pl.* **yobs** *or* **yobbos.** *Brit. slang.* a bad-mannered ag-gressive youth. [possibly back slang for *boy*] —ˈ**yobbish** *adj.*

yodel (ˈjəʊdˀl) *vb.* **-delling, -delled** *or U.S.* **-deling, -deled.** **1.** to sing (a song) with abrupt changes back and forth between the normal chest voice and falsetto, as in folk songs of the Swiss Alps. ~*n.* **2.** the act or sound of yodelling. [German *jodeln,* imit.] —ˈ**yodeller** *or U.S.* ˈ**yodeler** *n.*

yoga (ˈjəʊgə) *n.* **1.** a Hindu system of philosophy aiming at spiritual, mental, and physical wellbeing by means of deep medi-tation, prescribed postures, and controlled breathing. **2.** a system of exercising in-volving such meditation, postures, and breathing. [Sanskrit: a yoking]

yoghurt, yogurt, *or* **yoghourt** (ˈjɒgət, ˈjɒg-) *n.* a slightly sour, thick, custard-like food prepared from milk curdled by bacte-ria, often sweetened and flavoured with fruit. [Turkish]

yogi (ˈjəʊgɪ) *n.* a person who practises or is a master of yoga.

yo-heave-ho (ˌjəʊhiːvˈhəʊ) *interj.* a cry formerly used by sailors while pulling or lifting together in rhythm.

yoicks (haɪk, jɔɪk) *interj.* a cry used by fox-hunters to urge on the hounds.

yoke (jəʊk) *n., pl.* **yokes** *or* **yoke.** **1.** a wooden frame with a bar for attaching to the necks of a pair of animals, such as oxen, so that they can be worked as a team. **2.** a pair of animals joined by a yoke. **3.** something resembling a yoke, such as a frame fitting over a person's shoulders for carrying buckets. **4.** an oppressive force or burden: *the yoke of a tyrant.* **5.** a fitted part of a garment, for example around the neck, shoulders, and chest or around the hips, to which a gathered, pleated, flared, or unfitted part is attached. ~*vb.* **6.** to harness (two animals) to a plough by means of a yoke. **7.** to join or be joined by means of a yoke; couple, unite, or link. [Old English *geoc*]

yokel (ˈjəʊkˀl) *n. Disparaging.* a person who lives in the country, usually one who is simple and old-fashioned. [perhaps from dialect *yokel* green woodpecker]

yolk (jəʊk) *n.* the yellow part in the middle of an egg that nourishes the developing embryo. [Old English *geoloca*]

Yom Kippur (jɒm ˈkɪpə; kɪˈpʊə) *n.* an annual Jewish holiday celebrated as a day of fasting, with prayers of penitence. [He-brew *yōm* day + *kippūr* atonement]

yon (jɒn) *det.* **1.** *Chiefly Scot. & N English.* an archaic or dialect word for **that:** *yon man.* **2.** same as **yonder.** ~*pron.* **3.** yonder person or thing: *yon's a fool.* [Old English *geon*]

yonder (ˈjɒndə) *adv.* **1.** at, in, or to that relatively distant place; over there. ~*det.* **2.** being at a distance, either within view or as if within view: *yonder valleys.* [Old English *geond*]

yonks (jɒŋks) *pl. n. Informal.* a very long time; ages: *I haven't seen him in yonks.* [origin unknown]

yoo-hoo (ˈjuːˌhuː) *interj.* a call to attract a person's attention.

yore (jɔː) *n.* **of yore.** a long time ago: *in days of yore.* [Old English *geāra*]

yorker (ˈjɔːkə) *n. Cricket.* a ball bowled so as to pitch just under or just beyond the bat. [prob. after the *Yorkshire* County Cricket Club]

Yorkist (ˈjɔːkɪst) *English history.* ~*n.* **1.** a supporter of the royal House of York, esp. during the Wars of the Roses. ~*adj.*

2. of or relating to the supporters or members of the House of York.

Yorks. (jɔːks) Yorkshire.

Yorkshire pudding (ˈjɔːkʃɪə) *n. Chiefly Brit.* a baked pudding made from a batter of flour, eggs, and milk, often served with roast beef.

Yorkshire terrier *n.* a very small terrier with a long straight steel-blue and tan coat.

you (juː; *unstressed* jʊ) *pron.* (*sing. or pl., subjective or objective*) refers to: **1.** the person or persons addressed: *you know better; the culprit is among you.* **2.** an unspecified person or people in general: *you can't tell the boys from the girls.* ~*n.* **3.** *Informal.* the personality of the person being addressed: *that hat isn't really you.* [Old English *ēow*]

you'd (juːd; *unstressed* jʊd) you had *or* you would.

you'll (juːl; *unstressed* jʊl) you will *or* you shall.

young (jʌŋ) *adj.* **younger** (ˈjʌŋɡə), **youngest** (ˈjʌŋɡɪst). **1.** having lived or existed for a relatively short time: *a young man; a young movement.* **2.** having qualities associated with youth; vigorous or lively: *she has a very young outlook.* **3.** of or relating to youth: *in my young days.* **4.** of or relating to a group representing the younger members of a larger organization: *Young Socialists.* ~*n.* **5.** (*functioning as pl.*) offspring, esp. young animals: *a rabbit with her young.* [Old English *geong*] —**youngish** (ˈjʌŋɡɪʃ) *adj.*

youngster (ˈjʌŋstə) *n.* a young person; child or youth.

your (jɔː, jʊə; *unstressed* jə) *det.* **1.** of, belonging to, or associated with you: *your nose.* **2.** of, belonging to, or associated with an unspecified person or people in general: *the path is on your left heading north.* **3.** *Informal.* used to indicate all things or people of a certain type: *your part-time worker is a problem.* [Old English *eower*]

you're (jɔː; *unstressed* jə) you are.

yours (jɔːz, jʊəz) *pron.* **1.** something belonging to you: *yours is the first name on the list; I prefer yours.* **2.** your family: *greetings to you and yours.* **3.** used in closing phrases at the end of a letter: *yours sincerely; yours faithfully.* **4.** of yours. belonging to you.

yourself (jɔːˈsɛlf, jʊə-) *pron., pl.* **-selves. 1. a.** the reflexive form of *you.* **b.** (used for emphasis): *you yourself control your destiny.* **2.** your normal self: *you're not yourself.*

yours truly *pron. Informal.* I *or* me. [from the closing phrase of letters]

youth (juːθ) *n.* **1.** the quality or condition of being young, immature, or inexperienced: *his youth told against him in the contest.* **2.** the period between childhood and maturity. **3.** the freshness, vigour, or

vitality associated with being young. **4.** (*pl.* **youths** (juːðz)) a young man or boy. **5.** young people collectively: *the youth of today.* [Old English *geogoth*]

youth club *n.* a club that provides leisure activities for young people.

youthful (ˈjuːθfʊl) *adj.* **1.** of, relating to, possessing, or associated with youth: *youthful enthusiasm.* **2.** vigorous or active: *he's surprisingly youthful for his age.* —ˈ**youthfully** *adv.* —ˈ**youthfulness** *n.*

youth hostel *n.* an inexpensive lodging place for young people travelling cheaply.

you've (juːv; *unstressed* jʊv) you have.

yowl (jaʊl) *vb.* **1.** to produce a loud mournful wail or cry; howl. ~*n.* **2.** a wail or howl. [Old Norse *gaula*]

yo-yo (ˈjəʊjəʊ) *n., pl.* **-yos. 1.** a toy consisting of a spool attached to a string, the end of which is held while it is repeatedly spun out and reeled in. ~*vb.* **yo-yoing, yo-yoed. 2.** to change repeatedly from one position to another. [orig. a trademark for this type of toy]

yrs 1. years. **2.** yours.

YST (in Canada) Yukon Standard Time.

YT Yukon Territory.

YTS (in Britain) Youth Training Scheme.

ytterbium (ɪˈtɜːbɪəm) *n. Chem.* a soft silvery element that is used to improve the mechanical properties of steel. Symbol: Yb [after *Ytterby*, Swedish quarry where discovered]

yttrium (ˈɪtrɪəm) *n. Chem.* a silvery metallic element used in various alloys and in lasers. Symbol: Y [see YTTERBIUM]

yuan (ˈjuːˈæn) *n., pl.* **-an.** the standard monetary unit of the People's Republic of China. [Chinese *yüan* round object]

yucca (ˈjʌkə) *n.* a tropical plant with spikes of white flowers. [American Indian]

yucky *or* **yukky** (ˈjʌkɪ) *adj.* **yuckier, yuckiest** *or* **yukkier, yukkiest.** *Slang.* disgusting; nasty. [from *yuck,* exclamation of disgust]

Yugoslav (ˈjuːɡəʊˌslɑːv) *n.* **1.** a person from Yugoslavia. ~*adj.* **2.** of, relating to, or characteristic of Yugoslavia or its people.

Yule (juːl) *n. Literary, archaic, or dialect.* Christmas or the Christmas season: *Yuletide.* [Old English *geōla,* orig. a pagan feast lasting 12 days]

yummy (ˈjʌmɪ) *Slang.* ~*interj.* **1.** Also: **yum-yum.** an exclamation indicating pleasure or delight, as in anticipation of delicious food. ~*adj.* **-mier, -miest. 2.** delicious, delightful, or attractive: *yummy ice cream.* [*yum-yum,* imit.]

Yuppie (ˈjʌpɪ) *n.* **1.** a young urban (*or* upwardly mobile) professional. ~*adj.* **2.** designed for or appealing to Yuppies.

YWCA Young Women's Christian Association.

Z

z *or* **Z** (zɛd; *U.S.* ziː) *n., pl.* **z's, Z's,** *or* **Zs.** the 26th and last letter of the English alphabet.

z *Maths.* (along with *x* and *y*) an unknown quantity.

Z *Chem.* atomic number.

zabaglione (ˌzæbəˈljəʊnɪ) *n.* a dessert made of egg yolks, sugar, and wine, whipped together. [Italian]

zambuck (ˈzæmbʌk) *n. Austral. & N.Z. informal.* a first-aid attendant at a sports event. [from trade name of an ointment]

zany (ˈzeɪnɪ) *adj.* **zanier, zaniest.** comical in an endearing way. [Italian dialect *Zanni,* nickname for *Giovanni* John; traditional name for a clown]

zap (zæp) *Slang.* ~*vb.* **zapping, zapped.** 1. to kill (someone), esp. by shooting him. 2. to move quickly. 3. to change television channels rapidly by remote control. ~*n.* 4. energy or vigour. [imit.]

zeal (ziːl) *n.* fervent or enthusiastic devotion, for example to a religious movement. [Greek *zēlos*]

zealot (ˈzɛlət) *n.* an extremely zealous adherent to a cause; fanatic. —**ˈzealotry** *n.*

zealous (ˈzɛləs) *adj.* extremely eager or enthusiastic; fervent. —**ˈzealously** *adv.*

zebra (ˈziːbrə, ˈzɛbrə) *n., pl.* **-ras** *or* **-ra.** an African animal of the horse family, with a distinctive black-and-white striped hide. [African]

zebra crossing *n. Brit.* a pedestrian crossing marked by broad alternate black and white stripes. Once on the crossing the pedestrian has right of way.

zebu (ˈziːbuː) *n.* a domesticated ox of Africa and Asia, with a humped back and long horns. [French]

zed (zɛd) *n.* the British spoken form of the letter *z.*

zee (ziː) *n.* the U.S. spoken form of the letter *z.*

Zeitgeist (ˈtsaɪtˌgaɪst) *n.* the spirit or general outlook of a specific time or period. [German, lit.: time spirit]

Zen (zɛn) *n.* a Japanese school of Buddhism teaching that contemplation of one's essential nature to the exclusion of all else is the only way of achieving pure enlightenment.

Zend-Avesta (ˌzɛndəˈvɛstə) *n.* the Zoroastrian scriptures (the **Avesta**), together with the traditional interpretive commentary known as the **Zend.**

zenith (ˈzɛnɪθ) *n.* 1. the point in the sky directly above an observer. 2. the highest point; peak: *the zenith of someone's achievements.* [Arabic *samt arrās* path over one's head] —**ˈzenithal** *adj.*

zephyr (ˈzɛfə) *n.* a soft gentle breeze. [Greek *zephuros* the west wind]

Zeppelin (ˈzɛpəlɪn) *n.* a large cylindrical rigid German airship of the early 20th century. [after Count von *Zeppelin,* its designer]

zero (ˈzɪərəʊ) *n., pl.* **-ros** *or* **-roes.** 1. the ordinal number between +1 and −1. 2. the symbol, 0, representing this number. 3. nothing; nil. 4. the lowest point or degree: *his prospects were put at zero.* 5. the line or point on a scale of measurement from which the graduations commence. 6. the temperature, pressure, etc., that registers a reading of zero on a scale. ~*adj.* 7. having no measurable quantity or magnitude. 8. *Meteorol.* (of visibility) limited to a very short distance. ~*vb.* **-roing, -roed.** 9. to adjust (an instrument or scale) so as to read zero. [Arabic *sifr* empty]

zero gravity *n.* the state of weightlessness.

zero hour *n.* 1. *Mil.* the time set for the start of an operation. 2. *Informal.* a critical time, usually at the beginning of an action.

zero in on *vb.* 1. to aim a weapon at (a target). 2. to concentrate one's attention on (something). 3. *Informal.* to converge upon: *the police zeroed in on the criminals' hideout.*

zero-rated *adj.* denoting goods on which the buyer pays no value-added tax.

zest (zɛst) *n.* 1. invigorating or keen excitement or enjoyment: *a zest for living.* 2. added interest, flavour, or charm: *her presence gave zest to the occasion.* 3. the peel of an orange or lemon, used as flavouring. [French *zeste*] —**ˈzestful** *adj.*

ziggurat (ˈzɪɡʊˌræt) *n.* (in ancient Mesopotamia) a temple in the shape of a pyramidal tower. [Assyrian *ziqquratu* summit]

zigzag (ˈzɪɡˌzæɡ) *n.* 1. a line or course having sharp turns in alternating directions. 2. one of a series of such turns. 3. something having the form of a zigzag. ~*adj.* 4. formed in or proceeding in a zigzag. ~*adv.* 5. in a zigzag manner. ~*vb.* **-zagging, -zagged.** 6. to move in a zigzag. [German *zickzack*]

zilch (zɪltʃ) *n. Slang, chiefly U.S. & Canad.* nothing. [origin unknown]

zillion (ˈzɪljən) *n., pl.* **-lions** *or* **-lion.** (*often pl.*) *Informal.* an extremely large but unspecified number: *zillions of flies in this camp.* [after *million*]

Zimmer (ˈzɪmə) *n. Trademark.* a tubular frame with rubber feet, used as a support to help disabled or infirm people walk. Also: **Zimmer aid.**

zinc (zɪŋk) *n. Chem.* a brittle bluish-white metallic element that is used in alloys such as brass, to form a protective coating on metals, and in battery electrodes. Symbol: Zn [German *Zink*]

zinc ointment *n.* a medicinal ointment consisting of zinc oxide, petroleum jelly, and paraffin.

zinc oxide *n. Chem., pharmacol.* a white

insoluble powder used as a pigment and in making zinc ointment.

zing (zɪŋ) *Informal.* ~*n.* **1.** a short high-pitched buzzing sound, like the sound of a bullet or vibrating string. **2.** vitality; zest. ~*vb.* **3.** to make or move with or as if with a high-pitched buzzing sound. [imit.]

zinnia (ˈzɪnɪə) *n.* a plant of tropical and subtropical America, with solitary heads of brightly coloured flowers. [after J. G. Zinn, botanist]

Zion (ˈzaɪən) *n.* **1.** the hill on which the city of Jerusalem stands. **2. a.** the modern Jewish nation. **b.** Israel as the national home of the Jewish people. **3.** *Christianity.* heaven.

Zionism (ˈzaɪəˌnɪzəm) *n.* a political movement for the establishment and support of a national homeland for Jews in what is now Israel. —**ˈZionist** *n., adj.*

zip (zɪp) *n.* **1.** Also called: **zip fastener.** a fastener with two parallel rows of metal or plastic teeth on either side of a closure, which are interlocked by a sliding tab. **2.** a short sharp whizzing sound, like the sound of a passing bullet. **3.** *Informal.* energy; vigour; vitality. ~*vb.* **zipping, zipped.** **4.** (often foll. by *up*) to fasten (clothing or a bag) with a zip. **5.** to move with a zip: *the bullet zipped past.* **6.** (often foll. by *along* or *through*) to hurry; rush. [imit.]

zip code *n.* the U.S. equivalent of **postcode.** [z(one) i(mprovement) p(lan)]

zipper (ˈzɪpə) *n.* *U.S. & Canad.* same as **zip** (sense 1).

zippy (ˈzɪpɪ) *adj.* **-pier, -piest.** *Informal.* full of energy; lively.

zircon (ˈzɜːkən) *n.* *Mineral.* a reddish-brown, grey, green, blue, or colourless hard mineral consisting of zirconium silicate, which is used as a gemstone. [German *Zirkon*]

zirconium (zɜːˈkəʊnɪəm) *n.* *Chem.* a greyish-white metallic element, occurring chiefly in zircon, that is exceptionally corrosion-resistant. Symbol: Zr

zither (ˈzɪðə) *n.* a plucked musical instrument consisting of numerous strings stretched over a box, a few of which may be stopped on a fretted fingerboard. [Greek *kithara*] —**ˈzitherist** *n.*

zloty (ˈzlɒtɪ) *n., pl.* **-tys** or **-ty.** the standard monetary unit of Poland. [Polish]

Zn *Chem.* zinc.

zodiac (ˈzəʊdɪˌæk) *n.* **1.** an imaginary belt in the sky within which the sun, moon, and planets appear to move. It is divided into 12 equal areas called **signs of the zodiac,** each named after the constellation which once lay in it. **2.** *Astrol.* a diagram, usually circular, representing this belt. [Greek *zōidion* animal sign, from *zōion* animal] —**zodiacal** (zəʊˈdaɪəkˀl) *adj.*

zombie or **zombi** (ˈzɒmbɪ) *n., pl.* **-bies** or **-bis.** **1.** a person who appears to be lifeless, apathetic, or totally lacking in independent judgment. **2.** a corpse brought to life supernaturally. [W African *zumbi* good-luck fetish]

zone (zəʊn) *n.* **1.** a region, area, or section characterized by some distinctive feature

or quality: *a demilitarized zone; the erogenous zones.* **2.** *Geog.* one of the latitudinal divisions of the earth's surface according to temperature. **3.** *Archaic or literary.* a girdle or belt. **4.** *N.Z.* a section on a transport route; fare stage. **5.** *N.Z.* a catchment area for a specific school. **6.** to divide (a place) into zones for different uses or activities. **7.** to designate (a place) as a zone. [Greek *zōnē* girdle] —**ˈzonal** *adj.* —**ˈzoning** *n.*

zonked (zɒŋkt) *adj.* *Slang.* **1.** highly intoxicated with drugs or alcohol. **2.** exhausted. [imit.]

zoo (zuː) *n., pl.* **zoos.** a place where live animals are kept, studied, bred, and exhibited to the public. [from *zoological garden*]

zooid (ˈzəʊɔɪd) *n.* **1.** any independent animal body, such as an individual of a coral colony. **2.** a cell or body, produced by an organism and capable of independent motion, such as a gamete. [Greek *zōion* animal]

zool. 1. zoological. **2.** zoology.

zoological garden *n.* the formal term for **zoo.**

zoology (zəʊˈɒlədʒɪ, zuː-) *n.* the study of animals, including their classification, structure, physiology, and history. [Greek *zōion* animal + -LOGY] —**zoological** (ˌzəʊəˈlɒdʒɪkˀl, ˌzuːə-) *adj.* —**zoˈologist** *n.*

zoom (zuːm) *vb.* **1.** to move very rapidly; rush: *we zoomed through town.* **2.** to make or move with a continuous buzzing or humming sound. **3.** (of prices) to rise rapidly. ~*n.* **4.** the sound or act of zooming. **5.** a zoom lens. [imit.]

zoom in or **out** *vb. Photog., films, television.* to increase or decrease rapidly the magnification of the image of a distant object by means of a zoom lens.

zoom lens *n.* a lens system that allows the focal length of a camera lens to be varied continuously without altering the sharpness of the image.

zoophyte (ˈzəʊəˌfaɪt) *n.* any animal resembling a plant, such as a sea anemone. [Greek *zōion* animal + *phuton* plant]

Zoroastrianism (ˌzɒrəʊˈæstrɪənˌɪzəm) or **Zoroastrism** *n.* the dualistic religion founded by the ancient Persian prophet Zoroaster, based on the concept of a continuous struggle between the god of creation, light, and goodness, and the spirit of evil and darkness. —**ˌZoroˈastrian** *adj., n.*

Zouave (zuːˈɑːv, zwɑːv) *n.* (formerly) a member of a body of French infantry composed of Algerian recruits, noted for their dash, hardiness, and colourful uniforms. [*Zwāwa*, tribal name in Algeria]

zounds (zaʊndz) *interj. Archaic.* a mild oath indicating surprise or indignation. [euphemistic shortening of *God's wounds*]

Zr *Chem.* zirconium.

zucchetto (tsuːˈkɛtəʊ, suː-, zuː-) *n., pl.* **-tos.** *R.C. Church.* a small round skullcap worn by clergymen and varying in colour according to the rank of the wearer. [Italian]

zucchini (zuːˈkiːnɪ) *n., pl.* **-ni** or **-nis.** *Chief-*

ly *U.S., Canad., & Austral.* a courgette. [Italian]

Zulu ('zuːlʊ, -luː) *n.* **1.** (*pl.* **-lus** *or* **-lu**) a member of a tall Negroid people of SE Africa. **2.** the language of this people.

zygote ('zaɪɡəʊt, 'zɪɡ-) *n.* the cell resulting from the union of an ovum and a spermatozoon; fertilized egg cell. [Greek *zugōtos* yoked]

zymotic (zaɪ'mɒtɪk) *adj.* **1.** of or causing fermentation. **2.** of or caused by infection or infectious disease. [Greek *zumē* leaven] —**zy'motically** *adv.*

zymurgy ('zaɪmɜːdʒɪ) *n.* the branch of chemistry concerned with fermentation processes in brewing.

PUNCTUATION MARKS AND OTHER SYMBOLS

,	comma		*** ***	*** .. .. .. —** or **- - - -** ellipsis to indicate a break in a narrative, or an omission
;	semicolon			
:	colon		***⁎***	or **⁎⁎⁎** asterism, used to call attention to a particular passage
.	full stop			
—	dash		**. . .**	**. .** or **- - - -** leaders, to direct the eye to a certain point
!	exclamation mark			
?	interrogation or doubt		**¶**	paragraph
-	hyphen, as in *knick-knack*		*****	star, asterisk (1) a reference mark (2) used in philology to denote forms assumed to have existed though not recorded
'	apostrophe, as in *Queen's English*			
( )	parentheses			
[ ]	brackets		**†**	dagger, obelisk (1) a reference mark (2) obsolete or dead
}	brace, to enclose two or more lines			
			‡	double dagger, a reference mark
´	acute accent, as in *blasé*		**²**	superior figure, used (1) as a reference mark (2) to indicate a homonym
`	grave accent ⎫ as in			
^	circumflex ⎭ *tête-à-tête*			
˜	tilde, used over *n* in certain Spanish words to denote the sound of *ny*, as in *señor*		**ª**	superior letter
			§	section mark
			‖	parallel mark
¸	cedilla, to denote that *c* is pronounced soft, as in *façade*		**☛**	index, hand, fist
			#	number; space
" "	quotation marks		**„**	ditto
' '	quotation marks, when used within a quotation, as in *"He said, 'I will go at once' and jumped into the car."*		**&**	ampersand, and
			&c	et cetera
			@	at
			℞	per
—	macron, to mark length of sound, as in *cōbra*		**%**	per cent; per hundred
			©	copyright
˘	breve, marking a short sound, as in *līnen*		**®**	registered; registered trademark
¨	diaeresis, as in *daïs*		**♂**	male
¨	in German, used to denote modification of the vowel sound, as in *Köln* (Cologne)		**♀**	female.
⋏	caret, marking a word or letter to be inserted in the line			

MATHEMATICAL SYMBOLS

$+$	1. plus, addition sign 2. positive	$\bigcirc$	circle; circumference
$-$	1. minus, subtraction sign 2. negative	$\frown$	arc of a circle
$\times$	multiplied by	$\triangle$	triangle
$\div$	divided by; also indicated by oblique stroke (8/2) or horizontal line $\dfrac{8}{2}$	$\square$	square
		$\square$	rectangle
		$\square$	parallelogram
$=$	equals; is equal to	$\sqrt{}$	radical sign (ie square root sign)
$\neq$	is not equal to	$\sum$	sum
$\equiv$	is identical with; is congruent to	$\int$	integral
$\sim$	difference between; is equivalent to	$\cup$	union
$\simeq, \approx$	is approximately equal to	$\cap$	intersection
$>$	is greater than	$\in$	is a member of; is an element of; belongs to
$<$	is less than	$\subseteq$	is contained as subclass within
$\not>$	is not greater than	$\supseteq$	contains as subclass
$\not<$	is not less than	$\{\ \}$	set braces
$\leqslant$	less than or equal to	ϕ	the empty set
$\geqslant$	greater than or equal to	$|\ |$	absolute value of; modulus of
$\cong$	is isomorphic to	$\triangleleft$	is a normal subgroup of
$:$	is to; ratio sign	μ	mean (population)
$::$	as : used between ratios	σ	standard deviation (population)
∞	infinity	$\bar{x}$	mean (sample)
$\propto$	varies as, proportional to	s	standard deviation (sample)
$\therefore$	therefore	π	ratio of circumference of any circle to its diameter
$\because$	since, because	e	base of natural logarithms
$\angle$	angle	$^\circ$	degrees of arc or temperature
$\llcorner$	right angle	$'$	minutes of arc or time; feet
$\perp$	is perpendicular to	$''$	seconds of arc or time; inches
$\parallel$	is parallel to		

NAMES AND SYMBOLS OF METRIC UNITS

Quantity	Name of Unit	Value	Symbol
LENGTH	metre	base unit	m
	centimetre	0.01 m	cm
	millimetre	0.001 m	mm
	micrometre	0.000 001 m	μm (or um)
	kilometre	1 000 m	km
	international nautical mile (for navigation)	1 852 m	n mile
MASS (weight)	kilogram	base unit	kg
	milligram	0.000 001 kg	mg
	gram	0.001 kg	g
	tonne	1 000 kg	t
TIME	second	base unit	s
	minute	60 s	min
	hour	60 min	h
	day	24 h	d
AREA	square metre	SI unit	m^2
	square millimetre	0.000 001 m^2	mm^2
	square centimetre	0.000 1 m^2	cm^2
	hectare	10 000 m^2	ha
	square kilometre	1 000 000 m^2	km^2
VOLUME	cubic metre	SI unit	m^3
	cubic centimetre	0.000 001 m^3	cm^3
VOLUME (for fluids)	litre	0.001 m^3	l
	millilitre	0.001 l	ml
	kilolitre	1 000 l (1 m^3)	kl
VELOCITY	metre per second	SI unit	m/s
	kilometre per hour	0.27 m/s	km/h
	knot	1 n mile/h or o.514 m/s	kn
FORCE	newton	SI unit	N
	kilonewton	1 000 N	kN
	meganewton	1 000 000 N	MN
ENERGY	joule	SI unit	J
	kilojoule	1 000 J	kJ
	megajoule	1 000 000 J	MJ

NAMES AND SYMBOLS OF METRIC UNITS

Quantity	Name of Unit	Value	Symbol
POWER	watt	SI unit	W
	kilowatt	1 000 W	kW
	megawatt	1 000 000 W	MW
DENSITY	kilogram per cubic metre	SI unit	kg/m³
	tonne per cubic metre	1 000 kg/m³	t/m³
	gram per cubic metre	0.001 kg/m³	g/m³
DENSITY (for fluids)	kilogram per litre	1 000 kg/m³	kg/l
PRESSURE	pascal	SI unit (N/m²)	Pa
	kilopascal	1 000 Pa	kPa
	megapascal	1 000 000 Pa	MPa
PRESSURE (for meteorology)	millibar	100 Pa	mb
ELECTRIC CURRENT	ampere	base unit	A
	milliampere	0.001 A	mA
POTENTIAL DIFFERENCE	volt	SI unit	V
	microvolt	0.000 001 V	μV
	millivolt	0.001 V	mV
	kilovolt	1 000 V	kV
	megavolt	1 000 000 V	MV
ELECTRICAL RESISTANCE	ohm	SI unit	Ω
	microhm	0.000 001Ω	$\mu\Omega$
	megohm	1 000 000Ω	MΩ
FREQUENCY	hertz	SI unit	Hz
	kilohertz	1 000 Hz	kHz
	megahertz	1 000 000 Hz	MHz
	gigahertz	1 000 000 000 Hz	GHz
TEMPERATURE	kelvin	SI unit	K
	degree Celsius	K-273.15	°C

CHEMICAL SYMBOLS

Each element is placed in alphabetical order of its symbol and is followed by its atomic number.

Ac actinium, 89	**Ge** germanium, 32	**Po** polonium, 84
Ag silver, 47	**H** hydrogen, 1	**Pr** praseodymium, 59
Al aluminium, 13	**Ha** hahnium, 105	**Pt** platinum, 78
Am americium, 95	**He** helium, 2	**Pu** plutonium, 94
Ar argon, 18	**Hf** hafnium, 72	**Ra** radium, 88
As arsenic, 33	**Hg** mercury, 80	**Rb** rubidium, 37
At astatine, 85	**Ho** holmium, 67	**Re** rhenium, 75
Au gold, 79	**I** iodine, 53	**Rf** rutherfordium, 104
B boron, 5	**In** indium, 49	**Rh** rhodium, 45
Ba barium, 56	**Ir** iridium, 77	**Rn** radon, 86
Be beryllium, 4	**K** potassium, 19	**Ru** ruthenium, 44
Bi bismuth, 83	**Kr** krypton, 36	**S** sulphur, 16
Bk berkelium, 97	**La** lanthanum, 57	**Sb** antimony, 51
Br bromine, 35	**Li** lithium, 3	**Sc** scandium, 21
C carbon, 6	**Lr** lawrencium, 103	**Se** selenium, 34
Ca calcium, 20	**Lu** lutetium, 71	**Si** silicon, 14
Cd cadmium, 48	**Md** mendelevium, 101	**Sm** samarium, 62
Ce cerium, 58	**Mg** magnesium, 12	**Sn** tin, 50
Cf californium, 98	**Mn** manganese, 25	**Sr** strontium, 38
Cl chlorine, 17	**Mo** molybdenum, 42	**Ta** tantalum, 73
Cm curium, 96	**N** nitrogen, 7	**Tb** terbium, 65
Co cobalt, 27	**Na** sodium, 11	**Tc** technetium, 43
Cr chromium, 24	**Nb** niobium, 41	**Te** tellurium, 52
Cs caesium, 55	**Nd** neodymium, 60	**Th** thorium, 90
Cu copper, 29	**Ne** neon, 10	**Ti** titanium, 22
Dy dysprosium, 66	**Ni** nickel, 28	**Tl** thallium, 81
Er erbium, 68	**No** nobelium, 102	**Tm** thulium, 69
Es einsteinium, 99	**Np** neptunium, 93	**U** uranium, 92
Eu europium, 63	**O** oxygen, 8	**V** vanadium, 23
F fluorine, 9	**Os** osmium, 76	**W** tungsten, 74
Fe iron, 26	**P** phosphorus, 15	**Xe** xenon, 54
Fm fermium, 100	**Pa** protactinium, 91	**Y** yttrium, 39
Fr francium, 87	**Pb** lead, 82	**Yb** ytterbium, 70
Ga gallium, 31	**Pd** palladium, 46	**Zn** zinc, 30
Gd gadolinium, 64	**Pm** promethium, 61	**Zr** zirconium, 40